Y TERMIADUR

English – Welsh

ISBN 1-86112-588-7 £15

9 781861 125880

Y TERMIADUR

Standardized Welsh terminology

English – Welsh

Welsh – English

Yn ddiáu, o ddydd i ddydd – y mae'r hen
Iaith Gymraeg ar gynnydd;
Cadarnhau holl dermau'r dydd
A wna'r Termiadur newydd.

Iolo Wyn Williams

Compiled by

Delyth Prys J P M Jones Owain Davies Gruffudd Prys

University of Wales, Bangor

accac

Sponsored by Welsh Assembly Government

2006

Published by the
Qualifications, Curriculum and Assessment Authority for Wales

A catalogue record for this book is available from the British Library

ISBN 1 86112 588 7
ACCAC ref: AC/OM/0609

Designed and typeset in Wales by MAGMA ✆ 01248 810833
Printed by Clays Ltd

Preface

In 1998, the Qualifications, Curriculum and Assessment Authority for Wales (ACCAC) published *Y Termiadur Ysgol*. The main purpose of this volume was to standardize the Welsh-medium terms used in the teaching of National Curriculum subjects up to the standard of the General Certificate of Secondary Education. It ensured consistency in the language used in examinations and in the tests and tasks held to assess pupils aged 7, 11 and 14.

There have been changes both in the nature of the curriculum and methods of assessment in recent years and since that volume was produced. There are no longer statutory assessments for pupils aged 7, 11 or 14 and the scope of the curriculum has been extended. More vocational subjects are taught in schools as well as in colleges and the Advanced Level subject areas taught through the medium of Welsh are also being extended.

In consequence, there has been a need to standardize terms now used in these vocational and Advanced Level subjects alike. These terms are presented in this volume together with the original ones. This publication has also provided an opportunity to correct or update some records in the original *Y Termiadur Ysgol* and these changes are clearly noted ▶ in the text.

Once again, the work has been located at the University of Wales, Bangor with Delyth Prys as the chief editor. The original work was based at the Terminology Centre at the School of Education, which has since become part of Canolfan Bedwyr at the University. Other members of the editorial team were Owain Davies and Gruffudd Prys; while Owain Gwilym and Sioned Roberts also participated in the project. The computing work was done by Dewi Bryn Jones, and Dr J Prys Morgan Jones took on the role of consultant for the project.

Since *Y Termiadur Ysgol* was first published, a CD-ROM containing all the terms together with some updates was produced. This disk could be purchased separately. This time, a CD-ROM is included with the paper version so that all the terms can be loaded into a computer's memory to enable their easy access.

Again, as we present this new volume to the pupils, teachers, students and lecturers of Wales, we wish them well and hope that education through the medium of Welsh continues to flourish.

Guidelines

1 How to look up a term

The Welsh alphabetical order is used to list Welsh terms and the English alphabetical order to list English ones. An individual entry is available for every term so that terms which contain more than one word are listed under the first word in the term, e.g. 'law of gravitation' comes after 'law' and not as a sub-entry under 'gravitation'.

Where a word has more than one meaning, there is a separate entry for each meaning, followed by the disambiguator in brackets. The disambiguator is a short definition in brackets which follows the English terms in order to differentiate between words which look the same but which have different meanings. Terms containing one word followed by its disambiguator are listed first, and terms containing more than one word are listed afterwards. For example, 'centre (brain)', 'centre (= middle point)', 'centre (of attention etc'), 'centre (person)', 'centre (= place in centre)', 'centre (= place or group of buildings)', come before 'centre back', 'centre dotting', 'centre drill', 'centre for policy studies', 'centre front', 'centre half' and so on.

2 How parts of speech are shown

This dictionary shows parts of speech for Welsh terms when they are nouns, verbs or adjectives, as that information aids the user with grammatical mutations. Other words and phrases are usually left with no part of speech, but noun phrases are labelled as nouns since the entire phrase may cause a mutation, e.g. in 'sbectol haul' (sunglasses) 'sbectol' is a feminine noun and 'haul' is a masculine noun, but the entire phrase is labelled as feminine since it causes following adjectives to mutate, i.e. 'sbectol haul dywyll' not 'sbectol haul tywyll' (showing that it is the glasses that are dark, not the sun).

Parts of speech are only shown in English when there is a need to differentiate between a verb, noun and adjective, and they therefore act as disambiguators in a similar way to the definitions in brackets which follow some terms. For example, 'call' in English can be a noun or a verb ('a call' and 'to call').

The two entries are shown in *Y Termiadur* as:

call *n* galwad *eb* galwadau
call *v* galw *be*

3 Grammatical gender and plural form of nouns

Some nouns in Welsh may be either masculine or feminine in grammatical gender, usually varying according to dialect. These have been noted as *eg/b*, leaving it up to individuals to use the forms which sounds right to them. Where an *eg/b* noun forms part of a term containing more than one word, however, a decision was made to show only one form in order to avoid repeating forms which mutate, e.g. 'diweddeb' can be either a masculine or a feminine noun. When it is treated as a masculine noun the form is 'diweddeb perffaith' and when it is feminine, 'diweddeb berffaith'. The noun 'diweddeb' has been treated as a feminine noun in *Y Termiadur* and so it causes soft mutation in composite nouns. However the alternative masculine form should also be accepted as correct, and so on in other terms containing more than one word, where the noun can be either masculine or feminine.

It should be remembered also that a very small number of Welsh nouns have a different meaning according to whether they are masculine or feminine in gender. For example, in *Y Termiadur* 'y de' (masculine noun) gives us 'the south' in English, and 'y dde' (feminine noun) gives us 'the right [side]' in English.

Sometimes there are different meanings to plural forms of nouns, although the singular forms may look the same, e.g. llwyth (= tribe) plural: llwythau; llwyth (= load) plural: llwythi.

4 Correspondence of verbs and nouns in English and Welsh

Verbs and verb-nouns are often used in Welsh where English tends to use nouns. For the phrase 'do a headstand' in English, for example, the corresponding Welsh phrase would be 'sefwch ar eich pen' (stand on your head). Some contemporary Welsh dictionaries give a verb-noun to translate an English noun, in order to remind the user not to follow the English construction in Welsh. There are times, however, when a noun is needed in Welsh to correspond to a noun in English, especially with numbers. Therefore, if you have a list of gymnastic movements noting how many times a pupil must perform a specific movement, e.g. '10 headstands', a new noun such as 'pensafiad' has to be coined. *Y Termiadur* endeavours to keep the correspondence of parts of speech as far as is possible, but urges translators to bear in mind that, in many contexts, using a verb-noun rather than a noun often makes for a more naturally Welsh construction.

5 Criteria for standardization of terms

Objective criteria were followed in the compilation of *Y Termiadur*. These were based on the standards of the International Standards Organization, including ISO 704 on Standardization of Terms and ISO 860 on Harmonization of Concepts and Terms. These note, among other points, the following:

- A term should be linguistically correct.
- It should reflect, as far as possible, the characteristics of the concept which it represents.

- It should be concise.
- It should be able to generate to other forms.
- There should only be one term for a single concept.

6 Standard orthography

We have followed as far as possible the orthography of *Geiriadur Prifysgol Cymru* (University of Wales Press 1950–2001) which, in turn, follows the guidelines of *Orgraff yr Iaith Gymraeg* Rhan II, Geirfa 1987 (University of Wales Press, 1987). Sometimes there is a choice of possible spellings, with both forms being regarded as correct. One example of this is the forms *project* and *prosiect*. In such cases, choosing one over the other is a matter of consistency and house style, and does not make the alternative spelling incorrect.

With regard to the spelling of international words Welsh orthographical conventions were followed; thus 'cilo' and 'sinc' appear as the Welsh words in *Y Termiadur* rather than 'kilo' and 'zinc'. The international symbols, such as 'k' for 'kilo' and the symbols for the chemical elements, of course, remain unchanged. The only exceptions are to be found in proper nouns and religious terms, which keep their original spelling, or the internationally recognised transliteration into the Latin script if they have been transliterated from another script (see below, section 11).

7 Understanding the meaning of terms

It is important to understand the conceptual meaning of the terms which are used. Mistranslation can occur when a dictionary is consulted and a term is found which appears to be a translation, but which in reality translates an entirely different concept. A word such as 'grain' in English, for example, can have a number of meanings, such as 'a grain of sand' (gronyn), 'the grain of the wood' (graen), and 'grain grown for food' (grawn). Choosing the wrong meaning can sometimes lead to serious errors, such as in misunderstanding the meaning of the word 'seal' in the phrase 'the seal of Edward I', and translating it as 'morlo Edward I' (morlo = a type of sea mammal), rather than as 'sêl Edward I' (as on a document). The most important point to remember when translating terms is that it is never possible to translate word for word without understanding the concept being conveyed, i.e.

not English term = Welsh term

but rather English term = concept = Welsh term.

The disambiguators used in *Y Termiadur* are meant to help choose the correct concept where there is a possibility of confusion. However, some words may have additional meanings not covered in *Y Termiadur*, and readers should use their common sense if the translation suggested in *Y Termiadur* does not seem suitable in a particular context. A good monolingual English dictionary can provide guidance as to various possible meanings and concepts, thereby helping to ensure a correct Welsh translation.

8 Synonyms and different language registers

It is sometimes difficult to choose between two or more terms because their meanings are similar. In everyday language a variety of words can be used as synonyms. However, in technical contexts specialist concepts need accurate terms. The technical name for this language register is 'language for special purposes'. The more technical the context, the more the care needed to ensure that standardized terms are used. *Y Termiadur* now covers a wide range of school subjects from primary school to Advanced Level, and users will need to employ careful discretion in deciding when it is appropriate to use technical terms and when there is no need to do so. For example, the word 'munud' (minute) technically means an interval of a particular length (namely 60 seconds). In informal speech, however, it is possible to say 'aros funud' (wait a minute) without meaning 'wait for exactly 60 seconds'. Phrases such as 'aros ychydig' (wait a while), 'aros foment' (wait a moment), or 'aros eiliad' (wait a second) can be used instead without changing the meaning. It is important to understand that technical terms need not be used outside the domain of language for special purposes, and that within non-technical and informal contexts there is a degree of flexibility.

It may be difficult in a school situation to decide how technical a particular context is, and therefore how technical the vocabulary should be, especially at the primary and lower secondary levels. As a general rule, if there is no need to teach the technical concept, then there is no need for the technical vocabulary. Thus when discussing 'cyflymder' and 'buanedd' ('velocity' and 'speed') there is no need to differentiate between them except in a technical scientific or mathematical context. 'Cyflymder' does not have to be changed to 'buanedd' in more general, non-technical contexts.

9 Dialectal variations

The only exception to the practice of offering only one term in Welsh for the English term is when there is a clear split between usage in north and south Wales, e.g. 'gwahadden' is used in south Wales and 'twrch daear' in north Wales for the animal 'mole'. In such cases, it was not thought fair to give precedence to one form over the other, and both terms have been included. It is recommended that both terms be used together in assessment materials, but that teachers and pupils use the term with which they are more familiar in their classroom environment. This is not a dictionary of dialects however and, where it was judged that one form was acceptable as the standard form, other dialectical words and forms have not been included.

10 Place names in geography

Place names and proper names pose special problems within the school curriculum. Geography teachers have argued for years that the best answer was to adopt the preferred indigenous form of place names when referring to places outside Wales, using *Yr Atlas Cymraeg Newydd* (WJEC, 1999) as the standard. Where the native forms are written in non-Latin scripts, the Atlas employs the international transliteration into Latin script for such names. It is recommended that this practice be continued when teaching geography as a subject.

However in general contexts outside the confines of technical usage traditional Welsh usage may be followed. For example, the Italian form 'Roma' is used for the capital city of Italy in *Yr Atlas Cymraeg Newydd*, and in a technical geographical context this form should be used. However, when the city is mentioned in a general context, for example in history or music, it is still acceptable to call the city 'Rhufain'.

11 Terms in religious education

A particular problem exists with terms used in religions other than Christianity where the original language uses a script other than the Latin script. Some of these scripts have many more characters than the Latin script, and need more than one character in the Latin alphabet to transliterate them. For example, the Gurumukhi holy script of the Sikhs has forty characters, with one character transliterated as 'kh', another as 'k', another as 'c' and another as 'ch'. The Welsh alphabet does not contain the characters 'k', 'q', 'v' and 'x', but it does follow the international method for the Latinization of other scripts (for example ISO 233 on the transliteration of Arabic characters into Roman characters). This can be compared to the way Welsh accepts proper names including these characters, for example, Keller, Quentin and Vivian. It would be misleading to use the letter 'c' in Welsh for 'k' when referring for example to the five sacred 'k's of the Sikhs. These terms which are borrowed from other languages should not be perceived as English terms but rather as quotations from their original languages transliterated into Latin script. In 1994 the *Religious Education: Glossary of Terms* was published by the School Curriculum and Assessment Authority (SCAA) and approved by the different faith communities and contains the accepted Latin transliteration of vocabulary which belong to the different religions.

However, as with place names in geography, in general contexts, outside the confines of technical usage, traditional Welsh usage may be followed. For example, in religious education, the founder of Islam should be referred to as 'Muhammed', but in a general context, the traditional Welsh use of the form 'Mohamed' may be used.

12 Use of foreign terms

Foreign terms in subject areas other than religious education may also be used in Welsh without translation. For example it is common in music to use Italian terms such as 'appoggiatura' or German ones such as 'Lied'. These terms have traditionally been italicized in the Welsh text to show that they are not Welsh terms. However, italic fonts may not always be available for this purpose, either because the work is handwritten or because the italic font has already been used by the publishers for some other purpose, e.g. the titles of publications. Italics have not been used to denote foreign terms in *Y Termiadur*.

13 Acronyms

Acronyms are problematic in Welsh, in education as in so many other areas. They cause confusion because of their unfamiliarity, the need for mutations and also because of a preponderance of the letters 'C and 'G' and a lack of vowels in many acronyms. Acronyms should therefore not be translated into Welsh, with the exception of a few examples such as CBAC (Cyd-Bwyllgor Addysg Cymru) for WJEC (Joint Welsh Education Committee) where the acronym has long since become established, and the still fewer examples (such as ACCAC) where the

Welsh acronym (Awdurdod Cymwysterau, Cwricwlwm ac Asesu Cymru) is used in both English and Welsh. The accepted practice in Welsh is to give the name of the organization in full the first time it is used in speech or in a document, and thereafter to refer to it as the 'Authority', 'Society' etc. if it is clear which organization, society etc. is meant.

A

a cappella a cappella *adf*
A level Safon Uwch *eb*
A line skirt sgert linell A *eb* sgertiau llinell A
A major A fwyaf *eb*
A minor A leiaf *eb*
a posteriori a posteriori
a priori a priori
a priori method dull a priori *eg*
Aaronic Blessing Bendith Aaron *eb*
AB design cynllun AB *eg*
AB produced AB wedi ei estyn *eg*
AB styrene styren AB *eg*
ABA or ABAB ABA neu ABAB
abacus abacws *eg* abaci
abandon gadael *be*
abandoned meander ystumllyn *eg* ystumllynnoedd
abasement darostyngiad *eg*
abaxial allechelinol *ans*
abbacy abadaeth *eb* abadaethau
abbess abades *eb* abadesau
abbey abaty *eg* abatai
abbot abad *eg* abadau
abbreviate talfyrru *be*
abbreviation (=abbreviated form) talfyriad *eg* talfyriadau
abbreviation (in typography) byrfodd *eg* byrfoddau
abc behaviour ymddygiad abc *eg*
abc procedure dull gweithredu abc *eg*
abdicate (the crown) ildio'r goron *be*
abdication ymddiorseddiad *eg*
abdication crisis argyfwng yr ymddiorseddiad *eg*
abdomen abdomen *eg* abdomenau
abdominal abdomenol *ans*
abdominal cavity ceudod abdomenol *eg*
abdominal exercise ymarfer abdomen *eg* ymarferion abdomen
abducent nerve nerf abdwcent *eg*
Abelian group grŵp Abel *eg*
Abendlied Abendlied *eg* Abendlieder
aberrant gwyrol *ans*
aberrant species rhywogaeth wyrol *eb* rhywogaethau gwyrol
aberration egwyriant *eg* egwyriannau
abhorrer ffieiddiwr *eg* ffieiddwyr
ability gallu *eg* galluoedd
ability group grŵp gallu *eg* grwpiau gallu
ability grouping grwpio yn ôl gallu *be*
ability range ystod gallu *eb*
ability test prawf gallu *eg* profion gallu
abiotic anfiotig *ans*
abjuration ymwadiad ar lw *eg*
Abjuration Oath Llw Ymwadiad *eg*
abjure ymwadu ar lw *be*
ablate abladu *be*
ablation abladiad *eg* abladiadau
ablation till til abladu *eg*
able galluog *ans*
ablution golchiad *eg* golchiadau
abnormal annormal *ans*
abnormal data data annormal *ell*
abnormality annormaledd *eg*
abolish dileu *be*
abolition dilead *eg* dileadau
abolition of slavery dileu caethwasiaeth *be*
Abolition of Slavery Act Deddf Dileu Caethwasiaeth *eb*
abomasum abomaswm *eg*
aboriginal cynfrodorol *ans*
aboriginal art celfyddyd gynfrodorol *eb*
aborigine cynfrodor *eg* cynfrodorion
abort (a fetus) erthylu *be*
abort (action) atal *be*
abortifacient cyffur erthylu *eg* cyffuriau erthylu
abortion erthyliad *eg* erthyliadau
abozzo (sketch) abozzo *eg*
Abra file ffeil Abra *eb* ffeiliau Abra
Abra frame ffrâm Abra *eb* fframiau Abra
abrade sgrafellu *be*
abraded sgrafellog *ans*
abrasion (on land) sgrafelliad *eg* sgrafelliadau
abrasion (on metal etc) sgraffiniad *eg* sgraffiniadau
abrasion (on skin) crafiad *eg* crafiadau
abrasive *adj* sgraffiniol *ans*
abrasive *n* sgraffinydd *eg* sgraffinyddion
abrasive action arwaith sgraffinio *eg*
abrasive faults beiau sgraffinio *ell*
abrasive grades graddau sgraffinio *ell*
abrasive paper papur sgraffinio *eg* papurau sgraffinio
abrasive sheet dalen sgraffinio *eb* dalennau sgraffinio
abrogate diddymu *be*
abrupt cadence diweddeb swta *eb* diweddebau swta
abscess crawniad *eg* crawniadau
abscisic acid asid absgisig *eg*
abscissa absgisa *eg*

abscission absgisedd *eg*
abscission layer haenen absgisaidd *eb* haenau absgisaidd
abseil *n* abseil *eg* abseiliau
abseil *v* abseilio *be*
absence absenoldeb *eg*
absence of light diffyg golau *eg*
absent *adj* absennol *ans*
absentee *n* absenolwr *eg* absenolwyr
absenteeism absenoliaeth *eb*
absolute absoliwt *ans*
absolute address cyfeiriad absoliwt *eg* cyfeiriadau absoliwt
absolute advantage mantais lwyr *eb*
absolute alcohol alcohol pur *eg*
absolute humidity lleithder absoliwt *eg*
absolute monarchy brenhiniaeth absoliwt *eb*
absolute music cerddoriaeth absoliwt *eb*
absolute Oneness of God Undod absoliwt Duw *eg*
absolute pitch traw cynhenid *eg*
absolute reference cyfeirnod absoliwt *eg* cyfeirnodau absoliwt
absolute ruler rheolwr absoliwt *eg* rheolwyr absoliwt
absolute scale of temperature graddfa tymheredd absoliwt *eb*
absolute spectrum sbectrwm absoliwt *eg*
absolute threshold trothwy absoliwt *eg*
absolute value gwerth absoliwt *eg* gwerthoedd absoliwt
absolution maddeuant *eg*
absolutism absoliwtiaeth *eb*
absolved soul enaid rhydd *eg* eneidiau rhydd
absorb amsugno *be*
absorbance amsugnedd *eg*
absorbed stain staen wedi'i amsugno *eg* staeniau wedi'u hamsugno
absorbency amsugnedd *eg*
absorbent *adj* amsugnol *ans*
absorbent *n* amsugnydd *eg* amsugnyddion
absorbent fabric ffabrig amsugnol *eg* ffabrigau amsugnol
absorbent material defnydd amsugnol *eg* defnyddiau amsugnol
absorbent pad pad amsugnol *eg* padiau amsugnol
absorbent paper papur amsugnol *eg* papurau amsugnol
absorber amsugnydd *eg* amsugnyddion
absorption amsugniad *eg* amsugniadau
absorption band band amsugno *eg*
absorption coefficient cyfernod amsugno *eg* cyfernodau amsugno
absorption costing costio amsugno *be*
absorption spectrum sbectrwm amsugno *eg*
absorptive cell cell amsugno *eb* celloedd amsugno
abstinence ymataliad *eg*
abstract *adj* haniaethol *ans*
abstract (=consider abstractly) *v* haniaethu *be*
abstract (=intangible thing) *n* haniaeth *eb* haniaethau
abstract (=summarize) *v* crynhoi *be*
abstract (=summary) *n* crynodeb *eg/b* crynodebau
abstract (=take from) *v* alldynnu *be*
abstract art celfyddyd haniaethol *eb*
abstract concept cysyniad haniaethol *eg* cysyniadau haniaethol
abstract design (of drawing) dyluniad haniaethol *eg* dyluniadau haniaethol
abstract design (of plan) cynllun haniaethol *eg* cynlluniau haniaethol
abstract expressionism mynegiadaeth haniaethol *eb*
abstract music cerddoriaeth haniaethol *eb*
abstract painting (of picture) paentiad haniaethol *eg* paentiadau haniaethol
abstract painting (of process or art) peintio haniaethol *be*
abstract pattern patrwm haniaethol *eg* patrymau haniaethol
abstract thought meddwl haniaethol *eg*
abstraction haniaeth *eb* haniaethau
absurd afresymol *ans*
abundance (=plenty) digonedd *eg*
abundance (percentage or fraction) cyflenwad *eg*
abuse (=ill-treat) *v* cam-drin *be*
abuse (=ill-treatment) *n* camdriniaeth *eb*
abuse (=misuse) *n* camddefnydd *eg*
abuse (=misuse) *v* camddefnyddio *be*
abut (in general) ymylu ar *be*
abut (of lands, premises) ffinio â *be*
abutment (architectural) ategwaith *eg* ategweithiau
abutment (in general) ateg *eb* ategion
abysmal affwysol *ans*
abyss affwys *eg* affwysau
abyssal deposits (of the ocean) dyddodion affwys *ell*
a.c. generator generadur cerrynt eiledol *eg* generaduron cerrynt eiledol
academic *adj* academaidd *ans*
academic counselling cynghori academaidd *be*
academic dress gwisg academaidd *eb*
academic historian hanesydd academaidd *eg* haneswyr academaidd
academic infrastructure isadeiledd academaidd *eg*
academic registrar cofrestrydd academaidd *eg* cofrestryddion academaidd
academic standard safon academaidd *eb* safonau academaidd
academic success llwyddiant academaidd *eg* llwyddiannau academaidd
academic year blwyddyn academaidd *eb* blynyddoedd academaidd
academician academydd *eg* academyddion
academicism academiaeth *eb*
academy academi *eb* academïau
academy board bwrdd academi *eg* byrddau academi
academy figure ffigur academi *eg* ffigurau academi
acanthus carving cerfiad acanthws *eg* cerfiadau acanthws

ACCAC: Qualifications, Curriculum and Assessment Authority for Wales ACCAC: Awdurdod Cymwysterau, Cwricwlwm ac Asesu Cymru *eg*
accelerate cyflymu *be*
accelerated cyflymedig *ans*
accelerated course cwrs carlam *eg* cyrsiau carlam
accelerated freeze dried *adj* sychrewedig cyflym *ans*
accelerated freeze drying *v* sychrewi cyflym *be*
accelerated programme rhaglen garlam *eb* rhaglenni carlam
accelerating cavity ceudod cyflymu *eg* ceudodau cyflymu
accelerating field maes cyflymu *eg*
accelerating potential difference gwahaniaeth potensial cyflymu *eg*
acceleration cyflymiad *eg* cyflymiadau
acceleration /time diagram diagram cyflymiad /amser *eg* diagramau cyflymiad /amser
acceleration due to gravity cyflymiad disgyrchiant *eg*
acceleration graph graff cyflymiad *eg* graffiau cyflymiad
accelerator cyflymydd *eg* cyflymyddion
accelerator nerve nerf cyflymu *eg*
accelerator theory damcaniaeth cyflymu *eb*
accent *n* acen *eb* acenion
accent *v* acennu *be*
accented acennog *ans*
accented passing note nodyn camu acennog *eg* nodau camu acennog
accept derbyn *be*
acceptable use policy polisi defnydd derbyniol *eg*
acceptance derbyniad *eg*
acceptance testing profi derbyniad *be*
acceptor derbynnydd *eg* derbynyddion
acceptor atom atom derbyn *eg* atomau derbyn
acceptor circuit cylched dderbyn *eb* cylchedau derbyn
access (=a way of approaching) *n* mynediad *eg* mynediadau
access (=get to) *v* cael at *be*
access (=the action of gaining access to a file, data etc) *n* cyrchiad *eg* cyrchiadau
access (=the right to reach or see) *n* hawl gweld *eg*
access (a file, data etc) *v* cyrchu *be*
access control rheoli cyrchu *be*
access course cwrs mynediad *eg* cyrsiau mynediad
Access database cronfa ddata Access *eb* cronfeydd data Access
access information cyrchu'r wybodaeth *be*
access privilege cyrchfraint *eg* cyrchfreintiau
access road ffordd fynediad *eb* ffyrdd mynediad
access staircase grisiau mynediad *ell*
access time (in computing) amser cyrchu *eg* amserau cyrchu

Access to Justice Act Deddf Mynediad i Gyfiawnder *eb*
accessibility hygyrchedd *eg*
accessibility index mynegai hygyrchedd *eg* mynegeion hygyrchedd
accessibility of task hygyrchedd tasg *eg*
accessible hygyrch *ans*
accessory *adj* ategol *ans*
accessory (of dress) *n* cyfwisg *eb* cyfwisgoedd
accessory (of tools etc) *n* ategolyn *eg* ategolion
accessory bone asgwrn atodol *eg* esgyrn atodol
accessory bud blaguryn atodol *eg* blagur atodol
accessory course cwrs atodol *eg* cyrsiau atodol
accessory nerve nerf atodol *eg* nerfau atodol
acciaccatura acciaccatura *eg* acciaccature
accident damwain *eb* damweiniau
accident and emergency damwain ac argyfwng
accident and emergency department adran ddamweiniau ac achosion brys *eb* adrannau damweiniau ac achosion brys
accidental (=musical sign) hapnod *eg* hapnodau
accidents (in theology) anhanfodion *ell*
acclimatization ymaddasiad *eg* ymaddasiadau
acclimatize ymaddasu *be*
accommodate (=adapt) *v.intrans* ymgymhwyso *be*
accommodate (=adapt) *v.trans* cymhwyso *be*
accommodate (=provide lodging for) *v* lletya *be*
accommodation (=adaptation) cymhwysiad *eg* cymwysiadau
accommodation (=place to live) llety *eg* lletyau
accommodation (of lens, of oneself) ymgymhwysiad *eg* ymgymwysiadau
accompanied canon canon â chyfeiliant *eb* canonau â chyfeiliant
accompanied fugue ffiwg â chyfeiliant *eb* ffiwgiau â chyfeiliant
accompaniment (to food) cyfwyd *eg* cyfwydydd
accompaniment (with music) cyfeiliant *eg* cyfeiliannau
accompanist (with music) cyfeilydd *eg* cyfeilyddion
accompany (=go with) mynd gyda *be*
accompany (with music) cyfeilio *be*
accompanying (of file etc) cysylltiedig *ans*
accomplishment (=fulfilment of task) cyflawniad *eg* cyflawniadau
accomplishment (=thing done) llwyddiant *eg* llwyddiannau
accordance of summit levels cyfuchedd copaon *eg*
accordant cyfuwch *ans*
according to (=as stated by) yn ôl
according to (=in a manner corresponding to) yn unol â
according to weighting yn ôl y pwysoli
accordingly (=as required) yn unol â hynny
accordingly (=therefore) felly *adf*
accordion acordion *eg* acordiynau
accordion pleating pletio acordion *be*
account (=description) *n* disgrifiad *eg* disgrifiadau

account (=report) *n* adroddiad *eg* adroddiadau
account (in bank etc) *n* cyfrif *eg* cyfrifon
account for *v* rhoi cyfrif am *be*
account name enw'r cyfrif *eg*
accountability atebolrwydd *eg*
accountable (to) atebol *ans*
accountancy cyfrifeg *eb*
accountant cyfrifydd *eg* cyfrifwyr
accounting cost cost gyfrifyddol *eb* costau cyfrifyddol
accounting system system gyfrifydda *eb*
accounts clerk clerc cyfrifon *eg* clercod cyfrifon
accredit *v* achredu *be*
accreditation achrediad *eg* achrediadau
accreditation of prior learning achredu dysgu blaenorol *be*
accreditation procedure trefn achredu *eb* trefnau achredu
Accredited Training Organization (ATO) Cyfundrefn Hyfforddi Gydnabyddedig *eb*
accretion croniant *eg* croniannau
accrued interest llog cronedig *eg*
acculturation goddiwylliannu *be*
accumulate cronni *be*
Accumulated Information Field (AIF) Maes Gwybodaeth Gronedig *eg*
accumulated temperature tymheredd cronedig *eg* tymereddau cronedig
accumulation croniad *eg* croniadau
accumulative cronnol *ans*
accumulator croniadur *eg* croniaduron
accuracy (=correctness) cywirdeb *eg*
accuracy (=exact precision) manwl gywirdeb *eg*
accuracy of the performance cywirdeb y perfformiad *eg*
accurate (=correct) cywir *ans*
accurate (=exactly precise) manwl gywir *ans*
accurate record cofnod cywir *eg* cofnodion cywir
accurate shape siâp cywir *eg* siapiau cywir
accurate size maint cywir *eg* meintiau cywir
acellular anghellog *ans*
acetabular asetabwlaidd *ans*
acetabulum asetabwlwm *eg*
acetal asetal *eg* asetalau
acetal resin resin asetal *eg*
acetate asetad *eg* asetadau
acetate cellulose cellwlos asetad *eg*
acetate sheet asetyn *eg* asetynnau
acetic asetig *ans*
acetic acid asid asetig *eg* asidau asetig
acetone aseton *eg*
acetyl asetyl *eg*
acetyl CoA asetyl CoA *eg*
acetylation asetyleiddio *be*
acetylcholine asetylcolin *eg*
acetylcholinesterase asetylcolinesteras *eg*
acetylene asetylen *eg*
acetylene welding weldio asetylen *be*
achene achen *eg* achenau
achieve (=accomplish or carry out) cyflawni *be*
achieve (=be successful) llwyddo *be*
achieve (=reach or attain by effort) ennill *be*
achieve an objective cyflawni amcan *be*
achievement (=exploit) camp *eb* campau
achievement (in National Curriculum) cyflawniad *eg* cyflawniadau
achievement (of objective) cyflawni *be*
achievement age oed cyrhaeddiad *eg*
achievement test prawf cyrhaeddiad *eg*
achiral anghirol *ans*
achromatic acromatig *ans*
achromatic vision golwg acromatig *eg*
achromatopsia acromatopsia *eg*
acid asid *eg* asidau
acid base balance cydbwysedd asid bas *eg*
acid bath baddon asid *eg* baddonau asid
acid Bessemer process proses asid Bessemer *eb*
acid dissociation constant cysonyn daduniad asid *eg*
acid dye llifyn asid *eg* llifynnau asid
acid mordant (etching) mordant asid *eg*
acid open hearth process proses asid tân agored *eb*
acid pickle picl asid *eg*
acid rain glaw asid *eg*
acid resisting gwrthasid *ans*
acid resisting varnish farnais gwrthasid *eg* farneisiau gwrthasid
acid strength cryfder asid *eg*
acid test prawf asid *eg*
acid test ratio cymhareb prawf asid *eb*
acid-base asid-bas *ans*
acid-base titration titradu asid-bas *be*
acidic asidig *ans*
acidified asidiedig *ans*
acidify asidio *be*
acidity asidedd *eg*
acidosis asidosis *eg*
acidulated asidiedig *ans*
acknowledge cydnabod *be*
acme acme *eg*
acme thread edau acme *eb* edafedd acme
acolyte acolit *eg* acolitiaid
acoustic acwstig *ans*
acoustic bass bas acwstig *eg*
acoustic board bwrdd acwstig *eg* byrddau acwstig
acoustic coupler cyplydd acwstig *eg* cyplyddion acwstig
acoustic guitar gitâr acwstig *eb* gitarau acwstig
acoustic plaster plastr acwstig *eg*
acoustics acwsteg *eb*
acquire caffael *be*
acquired caffaeledig *ans*
acquired dyslexia dyslecsia caffaeledig *eg*
acquired feature nodwedd gaffaeledig *eb* nodweddion caffaeledig

Acquired Immune Deficiency Syndrome (AIDS) Syndrom Diffyg Imiwnedd Caffaeledig *eg*
acquired immunity imiwnedd caffaeledig *eg*
acquired language iaith gaffaeledig *eb* ieithoedd caffaeledig
acquired word blindness dallineb geiriau caffaeledig *eg*
acquiring authority awdurdod caffaelol *eg*
acquisition (of language, skills) caffaeliad *eg*
acquisition number rhif derbyn *eg* rhifau derbyn
acquisitive society cymdeithas feddiangar *eb* cymdeithasau meddiangar
acquittal rhyddfarn *eb* rhyddfarnau
acre erw *eb* erwau
Acrilan Acrilan *eg*
acrobat acrobat *eg* acrobatiaid
acrocentric acrosentrig *ans*
acronym acronym *eg* acronymau
acrosome acrosom *eg*
across the grain ar draws y graen
acrostic acrostig *ans*
acrylic *adj* acrylig *ans*
acrylic *n* acrylig *eg* acryligion
acrylic canvas cynfas acrylig *eg* cynfasau acrylig
acrylic colour lliw acrylig *eg* lliwiau acrylig
acrylic medium cyfrwng acrylig *eg*
acrylic paint paent acrylig *eg* paentiau acrylig
acrylic resin resin acrylig *eg* resinau acrylig
acryloid acryloid *eg*
act *v* gweithredu *be*
act (=deed, action) *n* gweithred *eb* gweithredoedd
act (=law) *n* deddf *eb* deddfau
Act Against Pluralities yn Erbyn Amlblwyfiaeth *eb*
Act for the Propagation of the Gospel Deddf Taenu'r Efengyl *eb*
Act in Absolute Restraint of Annates i Lwyr Atal Anodau *eb*
Act in Conditional Restraint of Annates Deddf Amodol Atal Anodau *eb*
Act of Annates Deddf Anodau *eb*
Act of Appeals Deddf Apeliadau *eb*
Act of Attainder Deddf Adendro *eb*
Act of Dispensations Deddf Trwyddedau *eb*
act of God gweithred Duw *eb*
act of parliament deddf seneddol *eb* deddfau seneddol
Act of Revocation Deddf Dirymiad *eb*
Act of Settlement Deddf Ardrefnu *eb*
Act of Six Articles Deddf y Chwe Erthygl *eb*
Act of Submission of the Clergy Deddf Ymostyngiad y Clerigwyr *eb*
Act of Supremacy Deddf Goruchafiaeth *eb*
Act of Treasons Deddf Brad *eb*
Act of Uniformity Deddf Unffurfiaeth *eb*
Act of Union Deddf Uno *eb* Deddfau Uno
act tune entr'acte *eg* entr'actes
act utilitarianism iwtilitariaeth gweithredoedd *eb*

actinium (Ac) actiniwm *eg*
actinoid actinoid *ans*
actinomorphic actinomorffig *ans*
action (=effect) effaith *eg/b* effeithiau
action (=exertion of energy or influence) arwaith *eg* arweithiau
action (=thing done) gweithred *eb* gweithredoedd
action (in dance) symudiad *eg* symudiadau
action (in opera) drama *eb*
action and reaction arwaith ac adwaith
action of acid on copper effaith asid ar gopr *eb*
action painting (of painted picture) paentiad gweithredol *eg* paentiadau gweithredol
action painting (of process or art) peintio gweithredol *be*
action plan cynllun gweithredu *eg* cynlluniau gweithredu
action point pwynt gweithredu *eg* pwyntiau gweithredu
action potential potensial gweithredu *eg*
▸ **action research** ymchwil gweithredol *eg*
action song cân actol *eb* caneuon actol
action spectrum sbectrwm gweithredu *eg* sbectra gweithredu
actionable per se cyfreithadwy per se *ans*
actions on the floor gweithrediadau ar y llawr *ell*
action-space gofod gweithredu *eg*
activate (in chemistry) actifadu *be*
activate (in general) ysgogi *be*
activated (in chemistry) actifedig *ans*
activation actifiant *eg* actifiannau
activation energy egni actifadu *eg*
activational effect effaith ysgogi *eb*
activator actifadydd *eg* actifadyddion
active (=lively) bywiog *ans*
active (=operative) gweithredol *ans*
active (in science) actif *ans*
active (of mind) effro *ans*
active (of person, life) gweithgar *ans*
active audience cynulleidfa weithredol *eb*
active centre canolfan actif *eb*
active character set set nodau gweithredol *eb* setiau nodau gweithredol
active flux fflwcs gweithredol *eg* fflycsau gweithredol
active immunity imiwnedd gweithredol *eg*
active lifestyle dull o fyw bywiog *eg*
active listening gwrando gweithredol *be*
active planning cynllunio gweithredol *be*
active population poblogaeth o oed gwaith *eb*
active reading darllen gweithredol *be*
active transport (in biology) cludiant actif *eg*
active window ffenestr weithredol *eb* ffenestri gweithredol
activity (in general sense) gweithgaredd *eg* gweithgareddau
activity (of chemical function) actifedd *eg* actifeddau
activity coefficient cyfernod actifedd *eg* cyfernod actifedd

eg/b enw gwrywaidd/benywaidd, *masculine/feminine noun* ***ell*** enw lluosog, *plural noun* ***v*** berf, *verb* ***n*** enw, *noun* ▸ wedi newid, *changed*

activity flow llif gweithgaredd *eg*
activity learning dysgu drwy weithgaredd *be*
activity method dull dysgu drwy weithgaredd *eg* dulliau dysgu drwy weithgaredd
activity specific gweithgaredd benodol *ans*
activity teaching addysgu drwy weithgaredd *be*
actor-observer effect effaith actor-gwyliwr *eb*
actual cost cost wirioneddol *eb* costau gwirioneddol
actual instruction (that blows) cyfarwyddyd gwirioneddol *eg* cyfarwyddiadau gwirioneddol
actual investment (cord, rope etc) buddsoddiad cyflawnedig *eg* buddsoddiadau cyflawnedig
actual parameter paramedr gwirioneddol *eg* paramedrau gwirioneddol
actual sin pechod gweithredol *eg*
actual size maint iawn *eg*
actuality digwyddiadau ar y pryd *ell*
actuate ysgogi *be*
actuating plate plât ysgogi *eg* platiau ysgogi
acuity craffter *eg*
acupuncture aciwbigo *be*
acute (with feminine and nouns) llem *ans*
acute (with masculine and plural nouns) llym *ans*
acute angle ongl lem *eb* onglau llym
acute angled triangle triongl ongl lem *eg* trionglau onglau llym
acute confusional state cyflwr dryslyd llym *eg*
acute illness afiechyd llym *eg*
acute pain poen llym *eg*
acyl asyl *ans*
acyl halide asyl halid *eg* asyl halidau
acylate asyleiddio *be*
acylation asyleiddiad *eg*
AD (Anno Domini) OC *eg*
ad hoc ad hoc *ans*
ad lib *n* ad lib *eg*
ad lib *v* ad libio *be*
ad valorem subsidy cymhorthdal ad valorem *eg*
ad valorem tax treth ad valorem *eb*
Adam Adda *eg*
Adam of Usk Adda o Frynbuga *eg*
adapt *v.intrans* ymaddasu *be*
adapt *v.trans* addasu *be*
adapt to a specialized environment ymaddasu i amgylchfyd arbennig *be*
adaptability hyblygrwydd *eg*
adaptable (in general addasadwy *ans*
adaptable (of person) hyblyg *ans*
adaptation (in general) addasiad *eg* addasiadau
adaptation (of self) ymaddasiad *eg* ymaddasiadau
adaptation of pattern addasiad patrwm *eg* addasiadau patrwm
adaptive (in general) addasol *ans*
adaptive (of self) ymaddasol *ans*
adaptive behaviour ymddygiad ymaddasol *eg*
adaptive development datblygiad ymaddasol *eg*
adaptive education addysg ymaddasol *eb*
adaptive programme rhaglen ymaddasol *eb* rhaglenni ymaddasol
adaptive response ymateb ymaddasol *eg* ymatebion ymaddasol
adaptive significance arwyddocâd addasu *eg*
adaptor addasydd *eg* addasyddion
adaxial adechelinol *ans*
add (numbers) adio *be*
add (to something else) ychwanegu *be*
add current page ychwanegu'r dudalen gyfredol *be*
added (in music) atodol *ans*
added note nodyn atodol *eg* nodau atodol
added sixth chweched atodol *eg* chwechedau atodol
added sixth chord cord y chweched atodol *eg*
added value (of musical note) hyd atodol *eg*
added value note nodyn hyd atodol *eg* nodau hyd atodol
addend adend *eg* adendau
addendum adendwm *eg* adenda
adder (related to addition) adydd *eg* adyddion
addict adict *eg* adictiaid
addicted (to drugs etc) caeth *ans*
addiction caethiwed *eg*
addictive caethiwus *ans*
adding machine peiriant adio *eg* peiriannau adio
addition (=thing added) ychwanegiad *eg* ychwanegiadau
addition (in counting numbers) adiad *eg* adiadau
addition law deddf adio *eb*
addition polymerization polymeriad adio *eg*
addition reaction adwaith adio *eg*
additional ychwanegol *ans*
additional accompaniment cyfeiliant ychwanegol *eg*
additional capital cyfalaf ychwanegol *eg*
additional component cydran ychwanegol *eb* cydrannau ychwanegol
additional force grym ychwanegol *eg*
additional guidance canllaw pellach *eg* canllawiau pellach
additional income incwm ychwanegol *eg*
additional piece darn ychwanegol *eg* darnau ychwanegol
additive *adj* adiol *ans*
additive (of numbers) *n* adiolyn *eg* adiolion
additive (of substance) *n* ychwanegyn *eg* ychwanegion
additive bilingualism dwyieithrwydd cynyddol *eg*
additive printing argraffu ychwanegol *be*
Addled Parliament (1614) Senedd Glwc *eb*
add-on ychwanegyn *eg* ychwanegion
address (=speech) *n* anerchiad *eg* anerchiadau
address (a ball in sport) *v* cyfarch *be*
address (a letter) *v* cyfeirio *be*
address (a meeting) *v* annerch *be*
address (an issue) *v* mynd i'r afael *be*
address (on a letter etc) *n* cyfeiriad *eg* cyfeiriadau

address a memory cyfeirio cof *eg*
address area adran cyfeiriadau *eb* adrannau cyfeiriadau
address generation cynhyrchu cyfeiriad *be*
address modification addasu cyfeiriad *be*
address register cofrestr cyfeiriadau *eb* cofrestri cyfeiriadau
addressing mode modd cyfeirio *eg*
adenine adenin *eg*
adenosine adenosin *eg*
adenosine diphosphate (ADP) adenosin deuffosffad *eg*
adenosine monophosphate (AMP) adenosin monoffosffad *eg*
adenosine triphosphate (ATP) adenosin triffosffad *eg*
adenyl cyclase adenyl cyclas *eg*
adequate digonol *ans*
adequate control rheolaeth ddigonol *eb*
adequate movement symudiad digonol *eg* symudiadau digonol
adequate size maint digonol *eg* meintiau digonol
adhere (=keep to rules etc) cadw at *be*
adhere (in general) glynu *be*
adhere (of person) ymlynu *be*
adhere (of substance) adlynu *be*
adherence (of person) ymlyniad *eg* ymlyniadau
adherence (of substance) adlyniad *eg* adlyniadau
adherent ymlynwr *eg* ymlynwyr
adhesion (of person) ymlyniad *eg*
adhesion (of substance) adlyniad *eg* adlyniadau
adhesive *adj* adlynol *ans*
adhesive (=glue) *n* gludydd *eg* gludyddion
adhesive (in technical usage) *n* adlyn *eg* adlynion
adhesive cell cell adlynol *eb* celloedd adlynol
adhesive dressing gorchudd adlynol *eg* gorchuddion adlynol
adhesive power nerth adlynol *eg*
adhesive putty pwti adlynol *eg*
adhesive strapping stribedyn adlynol *eg* stribedi adlynol
adhesive tape tâp adlynol *eg* tapiau adlynol
Adi Granth Adi Granth *eg*
adiabatic adiabatig *ans*
adipose blonegog *ans*
adipose tissue meinwe bloneg *eb* meinweoedd bloneg
adiposity blonegrwydd *eg*
adjacency principle egwyddor cyfagosrwydd *eb*
adjacent cyfagos *ans*
adjacent angle ongl gyfagos *eb* onglau cyfagos
adjacent face wyneb cyfagos *eg* wynebau cyfagos
adjacent part darn cyfagos *eg* darnau cyfagos
adjacent side ochr gyfagos *eb* ochrau cyfagos
adjoined cydiedig *ans*
adjoint atgyd *eg* atgydion
adjourn gohirio *be*
adjournment gohiriad *eg* gohiriadau
adjudication beirniadaeth *eb* beirniadaethau
adjudicator beirniad *eg* beirniaid
adjugate atgydiol *ans*
adjust (=make suitable) addasu *be*
adjust (=regulate) cymhwyso *be*
adjust intensity addasu dwysedd *be*
adjust the budget addasu'r gyllideb *be*
adjust the spectrometer cymhwyso'r sbectromedr *be*
adjustable cymwysadwy *ans*
adjustable arm braich gymwysadwy *eb* breichiau cymwysadwy
adjustable attachment atodyn cymwysadwy *eg* atodion cymwysadwy
adjustable bevel befel cymwysadwy *eg* befelau cymwysadwy
adjustable fence ffens gymwysadwy *eb* ffensys cymwysadwy
adjustable frame ffrâm gymwysadwy *eb* fframiau cymwysadwy
adjustable reamer agorell gymwysadwy *eb* agorellau cymwysadwy
adjustable shelf silff gymwysadwy *eb* silffoedd cymwysadwy
adjustable shelf support cynheiliad silffoedd cymwysadwy *eg* cynheiliaid silffoedd cymwysadwy
adjustable spanner sbaner cymwysadwy *eg* sbaneri cymwysadwy
adjustable table bwrdd cymwysadwy *eg* byrddau cymwysadwy
adjustable wrench tyndro cymwysadwy *eg* tyndroeon cymwysadwy
adjusted (with feminine nouns) wedi'i chymhwyso *ans* wedi'u cymhwyso
adjusted (with masculine nouns) wedi'i gymhwyso *ans* wedi'u cymhwyso
adjuster cymhwysydd *eg* cymwysyddion
adjusting device dyfais gymhwyso *eb* dyfeisiau cymhwyso
adjusting mechanism peirianwaith cymhwyso *eg* peirianweithiau cymhwyso
adjusting nut nyten gymhwyso *eb* nytiau cymhwyso
adjusting rod rhoden gymhwyso *eb* rhodenni cymhwyso
adjusting screw sgriw gymhwyso *eb* sgriwiau cymhwyso
adjusting setting cymhwyso gosodiad *be*
adjusting strap strap gymhwyso *eb* strapiau cymhwyso
adjustment cymhwysiad *eg* cymwysiadau
administer (=manage) gweinyddu *be*
administer (=provide a remedy) gweini *be*
administrating system system weinyddu *eb* systemau gweinyddu
administration (=application of remedies) gweiniad *eg*
administration (=body or management) gweinyddiaeth *eb* gweinyddiaethau
administration (act of) gweinyddiad *eg*

administration department adran weinyddu *eb* adrannau gweinyddu
administration system (in IT) system weinyddu *eb* systemau gweinyddu
administrative gweinyddol *ans*
administrative authority awdurdod gweinyddol *eg* awdurdodau gweinyddol
administrative headquarters pencadlys gweinyddol *eg* pencadlysoedd gweinyddol
administrative history hanes gweinyddol *eg*
administrative procedure trefn weinyddol *eb*
administrative region rhanbarth gweinyddol *eg* rhanbarthau gweinyddol
administrative tribunal tribiwnlys gweinyddol *eg*
administrative unit uned weinyddol *eb* unedau gweinyddol
administrator gweinyddwr *eg* gweinyddwyr
admiral llyngesydd *eg* llyngesyddion
Admiralty Morlys *eg*
Admiralty brass pres Morlys *eg*
admiralty court llys morlys *eg*
Admiralty gunmetal gwnfetel Morlys *eg*
admiration edmygedd *eg*
admire edmygu *be*
admissible derbyniadwy *ans*
admission (=acknowledgement) cyfaddefiad *eg* cyfaddefiadau
admission (=person admitted) derbyniad *eg* derbyniadau
admissions criteria meini prawf derbyn *ell*
admissions policy polisi derbyn *eg* polisïau derbyn
admissions procedure trefn dderbyn *eb*
admittance (=process or right of entering) mynediad *eg*
admixture cymysgiad *eg* cymysgiadau
admonish (clergy) siarsio *be*
admonition (to clergy) siars *eb* siarsiau
Admonition to the Parliament Cerydd i'r Senedd *eg*
adolescence llencyndod *eg*
adolescent *adj* llencynnaidd *ans*
adolescent *n* person ifanc *eg* pobl ifanc
adopt (a measure) derbyn *be*
adopt (in general) mabwysiadu *be*
adopted mabwysiedig *ans*
adoption mabwysiad *eg* mabwysiadau
Adoption Act Deddf Mabwysiadu *eb*
adoption agency asiantaeth fabwysiadu *eb* asiantaethau mabwysiadu
adoptionism mabwysiadaeth *eb*
adoptive parent rhiant mabwysiadol *eg* rhieni mabwysiadol
adoration (in technical usage) addoliad *eg*
adorn adorn *be*
adornment addurn *eg* addurniadau
adrenal cortex cortecs y chwarren adrenal *eg*
adrenal cortex stimulating hormone (HSCA) hormon symbylu'r cortecs adrenal (HSCA) *eg*
adrenal gland chwarren adrenal *eb* chwarennau adrenal
adrenal medulla medwla y chwarren adrenal *eg*
adrenalin adrenalin *eg*
adrenocorticotrophic hormone hormon adrenocorticotroffig *eg* hormonau adrenocorticotroffig
adret (=sonnenseite) llygad haul *eg*
adsorb arsugno *be*
adsorbate arsugnyn *eg* arsugnynnau
adsorbency arsugnedd *eg*
adsorbent arsugnydd *eg* arsugnyddion
adsorption arsugniad *eg*
aduki beans ffa adwci *ell*
Adullamites Adulamiaid *ell*
adult oedolyn *eg* oedolion
adult education addysg oedolion *eb*
adult expectations disgwyliadau oedolion *ell*
adult form of the parasite oedolyn y parasit *eg*
adult life bywyd oedolyn *eg*
adult literacy and basic skills unit uned llythrennedd a sgiliau sylfaenol i oedolion *eb* unedau llythrennedd a sgiliau sylfaenol i oedolion
adult stage ffurf oedolyn *eb* ffurfiau oedolyn
adult training centre canolfan hyfforddi oedolion *eb* canolfannau hyfforddi oedolion
adulterate difwyno *be*
adulteration difwyniad *eg*
adultery godineb *eg*
advance (=move forward) *v* symud ymlaen *be*
advance (in fencing) *v* blaenu *be*
advance (in general) cynnydd *eg*
advance (of ice-sheet etc) *n* estyniad *eg* estyniadau
advance (of ice-sheet etc) *v* estyn *be*
advance (of money) *n* blaenswm *eg* blaensymiau
advance and retreat (of ice-sheet etc) estyn ac encilio
advance factory ffatri barod *eb* ffatrïoedd parod
advanced (=developed) datblygedig *ans*
advanced (=higher) uwch *ans*
advanced (of ideas, opinions) blaengar *ans*
advanced disk filing system (ADFS) system ddisg-ffeilio uwch *eb*
advanced engineering peirianneg uwch *eb*
advanced feature nodwedd uwch *eb* nodweddion uwch
advanced further education addysg bellach uwch *eb*
advanced gas-cooler reactor adweithydd nwy-oeredig uwch *eg* adweithyddion nwy-oeredig uwch
advanced learner dysgwr uwch *eg* dysgwyr uwch
advanced search chwiliad uwch *eg* chwiliadau uwch
advancement (=movement forward) symudiad ymlaen *eg* symudiadau ymlaen
advantage mantais *eb* manteision
advantage law rheol fantais *eb*
advantageous promise addewid manteisiol *eg*
advection llorfudiant *eg*
advection fog niwl llorfudol *eg*

advenae estroniaid *ell*
Advent Adfent *eg*
adventitious root adwreiddyn *eg* adwreiddiau
adventive cone côn parasitig *eg* conau parasitig
adventure activity gweithgaredd antur *eg* gweithgareddau antur
adventure learning dysgu antur *be*
adventure play chwarae antur *eg*
▶ **adventure playground** maes chwarae antur *eg* meysydd chwarae antur
adventure training hyfforddiant antur *eg*
adventurous activity gweithgaredd antur *eg* gweithgareddau antur
adversarial system system wrthwynebol *eb*
adversely er gwaeth *adf*
advertise hysbysebu *be*
advertisement hysbyseb *eb* hysbysebion
advertising agency asiantaeth hysbysebu *eb*
advertising agent asiant hysbysebu *eg* asiantiaid hysbysebu
advertising campaign ymgyrch hysbysebu *eb* ymgyrchoedd hysbysebu
advertising media cyfryngau hysbysebu *ell*
advertising slogan slogan hysbysebu *eg*
Advertising Standards Authority Awdurdod Safonau Hysbysebu *eg*
advice cyngor *eg* cynghorion
advice and information service gwasanaeth cyngor a gwybodaeth *eg* gwasanaethau cyngor a gwybodaeth
advice slip slip hysbysu *eg* slipiau hysbysu
adviser ymgynghorydd *eg* ymgynghorwyr
advisory ymgynghorol *ans*
advisory and peripatetic teacher (female) athrawes ymgynghorol a chylchynol *eg* athrawesau ymgynghorol a chylchynol
advisory and peripatetic teacher (male) athro ymgynghorol a chylchynol *eg* athrawon ymgynghorol a chylchynol
advisory committee pwyllgor ymgynghorol *eg* pwyllgorau ymgynghorol
Advisory Committee for Wales Pwyllgor Ymgynghorol Cymru *eg*
advisory committee on education pwyllgor addysg ymgynghorol *eg*
advisory committee on legal education and conduct pwyllgor ymgynghorol ar addysg ac ymddygiad cyfreithiol *eg*
Advisory, Conciliation and Arbitration Service (ACAS) Gwasanaeth Cymodi ACAS *eg*
advisory council cyngor ymgynghorol *eg* cynghorau ymgynghorol
advisory function swyddogaeth ymgynghorol *eb* swyddogaethau ymgynghorol
advisory officer swyddog cynghori *eg* swyddogion cynghori
advisory service gwasanaeth cynghori *eg* gwasanaethau cynghori
advocacy eiriolaeth *eb* eiriolaethau
advocate (=barrister in Scotland) adfocad *eg* adfocadau
advocate (=person who pleads for another) eiriolwr *eg* eiriolwyr
advowry adfowri *eg* adfowrïau
advowson adfowswn *eg* adfowsynau
adze neddyf *eb* neddyfau
aeolian aeolaidd *ans*
aeolian harp telyn awelon *eb* telynau awelon
Aeolian mode modd Aeolaidd *eg*
aeon aeon *eg*
aerate awyru *be*
aerated awyrog *ans*
aeration awyriad *eg*
aeration stream llif awyru *eg*
aerator pump pwmp awyru *eg* pympiau awyru
aerial *adj* awyrol *ans*
aerial *n* erial *eb* erialau
aerial photograph awyrlun *eg* awyrluniau
aerial ropeway rhaffordd awyr *eb* rhaffyrdd awyr
aerobic aerobig *ans*
aerobic exercise ymarfer aerobig *eg* ymarferion aerobig
aerobic respiration resbiradaeth aerobig *eb*
aerobic running rhedeg aerobig *be*
aerobics aerobeg *eb*
aerodynamics aerodynameg *eb*
aerography aerograffiaeth *eb*
aerology aeroleg *eb*
aeronautics awyrennaeth *eb*
aeronautics industry diwydiant awyrennau *eg*
aerosol aerosol *eg* aerosolau
aerosol fixative sefydlyn aerosol *eg* sefydlynnau aerosol
aerosol inhaler anadlydd aerosol *eg* anadlyddion aerosol
aerosol spray chwistrell aerosol *eb* chwistrelli aerosol
aerospace awyrofod *eg*
aerospace industry diwydiant awyrofod *eg*
aesthetic esthetig *ans*
aesthetic quality priodoledd esthetig *eg* priodoleddau esthetig
aestheticism esthetigaeth *eb*
aesthetics estheteg *eb*
aetiological achosegol *ans*
aetiological legend chwedl achosegol *eb* chwedlau achosegol
aetiology achoseg *eb*
AF (across the flats of hexagonal nut) AFF
affair (=noteworthy thing) achos *eg* achosion
affair (=notorious happening) helynt *eg* helyntion
affair (=public matter) mater *eg* materion
affect *n* affaith *eg* affeithiau
affect *v* affeithio *be*
affection (=fondness) serch *eg* serchiadau
affection (=tenderness) anwyldeb *eg*
affective affeithiol *ans*

affective disorder anhwylder affeithiol *eg* anhwylderau affeithiol
affective domain maes affeithiol *eg* meysydd affeithiol
affective psychosis seicosis affeithiol *eg*
affectivity affeithiolrwydd *eg*
afferent afferol *ans*
afferent neuron niwron afferol *eg*
affiliate cysylltu *be*
affiliated cyswllt *ans*
affiliated member aelod cyswllt *eg* aelodau cyswllt
affine affin *eg*
affinity (=relationship through marriage other than blood relationship) cysylltiad drwy briodas *eg* cysylltiadau drwy briodas
affinity (in biochemistry) affinedd *eg* affineddau
affirmation cadarnhad *eg*
affix sicrhau *be*
afflation anadliad *eg* anadliadau
affluent (=tributary stream) llednant *eb* llednentydd
affluent society cymdeithas gefnog *eb* cymdeithasau cefnog
afforestation coedwigo *be*
African drumming music cerddoriaeth ddrymio Affricanaidd *eb*
African empire ymerodraeth Affrica *eb*
afterbirth brych *eg*
after-care ôl-ofal *eg*
after-effect ôl-effaith *eb* ôl-effeithiau
afterglow ôl-dywyn *eg* ôl-dywynnau
after-image ôl-ddelwedd *eb*
aftermath canlyniad *eg*
after-sales service gwasanaeth ôl-werthu *eg* gwasanaethau ôl-werthu
after-school club clwb ar ôl ysgol *eg* clybiau ar ôl ysgol
after-school lesson gwers ar ôl ysgol *eb* gwersi ar ôl ysgol
aftershock ôl-gryniad *eg* ôl-gryniadau
against the grain yn erbyn y graen *adf*
agape (=Christian fellowship) agape *eg*
agate agat *eg* agatau
agate ware crochenwaith agat *eg*
age (=period) oes *eb* oesoedd
age (of person) oed *eg*
Age Concern Cyngor yr Henoed *eg*
age equivalent cyfatebiaeth oed *eb*
age group grŵp oedran *eg* grwpiau oedran
age hardening oed galedu *be*
age norm norm oed *eg*
Age of Austerity Oes y Llymder *eb*
Age of Enlightenment Oes y Goleuo *eb*
Age of Faith Oes Ffydd *eb*
Age of Improvement Oes Cynnydd *eb*
Age of Reason Oes Rheswm *eb*
Age of the Saints Oes y Saint *eb*
age phase lefel *eg/b* lefelau
age phase thesaurus thesawrws lefel *eg*
age range ystod oedran *eb*
age regression adlithro oed *be*
age structure adeiledd oedran *eg* adeileddau oedran
aged (of person) oedrannus *ans*
ageing heneiddio *be*
ageing population poblogaeth sy'n heneiddio *eb* poblogaethau sy'n heneiddio
ageism rhagfarn oed *eb*
agency asiantaeth *eb* asiantaethau
agenda agenda *eg* agendâu
agent (of force or effect) cyfrwng *eg* cyfryngau
agent (of person) asiant *eg* asiantiaid
agglomerate (in geology) *n* llosg-garnedd *eb* llosg-garneddau
agglomerate (in geology) *v* athyrru *be*
agglomeration cydgrynhoad *eg*
agglutinate cyfludo *be*
agglutinated cyfludedig *ans*
agglutination cyfludiad *eg* cyfludiadau
aggradation adraddiant *eg*
aggrade adraddu *be*
aggregate (=collect together) cydgasglu *be*
aggregate (=combine into mass) *v* agregu *be*
aggregate (in mathematics) *adj* cyfanredol *ans*
aggregate (in mathematics) *n* cyfanred *eg* cyfanredau
aggregate (of stone) *n* agreg *eg* agregau
aggregate analysis dadansoddiad cyfanredol *eg* dadansoddiadau cyfanredol
aggregate demand galw cyfanredol *eg*
aggregate results canlyniadau cyfanredol *ell*
aggregate schools budget cyllideb gyfanredol ysgolion *eb* cyllidebau cyfanredol ysgolion
aggregate supply cyflenwad cyfanredol *eg* cyflenwadau cyfanredol
aggression (=attack) ymosodiad *eg* ymosodiadau
aggression (in psychology) ymosodedd *eg*
aggression (of behaviour) ymddygiad ymosodol *eg*
aggressive ymosodol *ans*
aggressor ymosodwr *eg* ymosodwyr
agile ystwyth *ans*
agility ystwythder *eg*
agitate cynhyrfu *be*
agitation cynnwrf *eg*
agitator cynhyrfwr *eg* cynhyrfwyr
agnate agnawd *ans*
agnosia agnosia *eg*
agnostic agnostig *ans*
agnosticism agnosticiaeth *eb*
agonist (of muscles) gweithydd *eg* gweithyddion
agony ing *eg* ingoedd
agoraphobia agoraffobia *eg*
agrammatism agramadegiaeth *eb*
agranulocyte agranwlocyt *eg* agranwlocytau
agrarian amaethyddol *ans*
agrarian history hanes amaethyddiaeth *eg*
agrarian reform diwygio amaethyddol *be*

agreeableness hynawsedd *eg*
agreed cytûn *ans*
agreed policy polisi cytûn *eg* polisïau cytûn
agreed syllabus maes llafur cytûn *eg* meysydd llafur cytûn
agreement cytundeb *eg* cytundebau
Agreement of the People Cydsyniad y Bobl *eg*
agreement trial treial cytuno *eg* treialon cytuno
Agricultural Adjustments Act Deddf Cymhwyso Amaethyddiaeth *eb*
agricultural area ardal amaethyddol *eb* ardaloedd amaethyddol
agricultural deficiency area ardal o dangynhyrchu amaethyddol *eb* ardaloedd o dangynhyrchu amaethyddol
Agricultural Revolution Chwyldro Amaethyddol *eg*
agricultural surplus area ardal o orgynhyrchu amaethyddol *eb* ardaloedd o orgynhyrchu amaethyddol
agriculture amaethyddiaeth *eb*
agrostis maeswellt *eg*
ague clefyd crynu *eg*
aid *v* cynorthwyo *be*
aid (in general) *n* cymorth *eg* cymhorthion
aid (tax) cymhorthdreth *eb* cymorthdrethi
aid and trade cymorth a masnach
aide (e.g. teacher's aide) cymhorthiad *eg* cymhorthiaid
► **AIDS** AIDS *eg*
aiguille nodwydd *eb* nodwyddau
ailment anhwylder *eg* anhwylderau
aim (in education) *n* nod *eg* nodau
aim (in sport) *n* aneliad *eg* aneliadau
aim (towards a target) *v* anelu *be*
aim a stroke anelu ergyd *be*
aim for the hurdle anelu at y glwyd *be*
aim the ball anelu'r bêl *be*
aim the volley *v* anelu'r foli *be*
aiming error gwall anelu *eg*
aims and objectives nodau ac amcanion
air (as a place) awyr *eg*
air (as a substance) aer *eg*
air (clothes) *v* crasu *be*; caledu *be*
air (in penillion singing) cainc *eb* ceinciau
air bladder chwysigen aer *eb* chwysigod aer
air brush brwsh aer *eg* brwshys aer
air column colofn aer *eb* colofnau aer
air cool awyr-oeri *be*
air cored solenoid solenoid craidd aer *eg* solenoidau craidd aer
air corridor coridor awyr *eg* coridorau awyr
air current cerrynt aer *eg* ceryntau aer
air extraction duct dwythell echdynnu aer *eb* dwythellau echdynnu aer
air filter hidlydd aer *eg* hidlyddion aer
air force llu awyr *eg* lluoedd awyr
air grinder llifanydd aer *eg* llifanyddion aer
air hardening aergaledu *be*
air lock aerglo *eg* aergloeau
air passage pibell aer *eb*
air piracy awyr-ladrad *eg*
air power grym awyrennol *eg*
air pressure gwasgedd aer *eg*
air raid cyrch awyr *eg* cyrchoedd awyr
air resistance gwrthiant aer *eg*
air route llwybr awyr *eg* llwybrau awyr
air sac coden aer *eb* codennau aer
air survey arolwg awyr *eg* arolygon awyr
air with variations alaw ag amrywiadau *eb* alawon ag amrywiadau
air-borne troops awyrfilwyr *ell*
air-condition aerdymheru *be*
air-conditioned aerdymherus *ans*
air-conditioner aerdymherydd *eg* aerdymherwyr
air-cored coil coil craidd aer *eg*
aircraft carrier llong awyrennau *eb* llongau awyrennau
aircraft industry diwydiant awyrennau *eg*
air-cushion clustog aer *eb* clustogau aer
airfield maes glanio *eg* meysydd glanio
airing cupboard cwpwrdd crasu dillad *eg* cypyrddau crasu dillad; cwpwrdd caledu *eg* cypyrddau crasu dillad
airing rack rhesel grasu dillad *eb* rheseli crasu dillad; rhesel galedu
airlift awyrgludiad *eg* awyrgludiadau
airline cwmni hedfan *eg* cwmnïau hedfan
air-mass aergorff *eg* aergyrff
airport maes awyr *eg* meysydd awyr
air-raid shelter lloches cyrch awyr *eb* llochesau cyrch awyr
airscrew aersgriw *eb* aersgriwiau
airtight aerglos *ans*
air-track trac aer *eg* traciau aer
airway llwybr anadlu *eg*
aisle eil *eb* eiliau
aisled eiliog *ans*
akirah akirah *ell*
alabaster alabastr *eg*
alalia alalia *eg*
alanine alanin *eg*
alarm larwm *eg* larymau
alb alb *eb*
albatross albatros *eg* albatrosiaid
albedo albedo *eg*
Alberti bass bas Alberti *eg*
Albigensian *adj* Albigensaidd *ans*
Albigensian *n* Albigensiad *eg* Albigensiaid
Albigensian Crusade Croesgad yn erbyn yr Albigensiaid *eb*
albinism albinedd *eg*
albino *adj* albinaidd *ans*
albino *n* albino *eg* albinoaid
alborada alborada *eg* alboradas
album albwm *eg* albymau
Albumblatt Albumblatt *eg* Albumblätter

albumen albwmen *eg*
alchemist alcemydd *eg* alcemyddion
alchemy alcemeg *eb*
alclad alclad *eg*
alcohol alcohol *eg* alcoholau
alcoholic *adj* alcoholig *ans*
alcoholic *n* alcoholig *eg* alcoholigion
alcoholic drink diod feddwol *eb* diodydd meddwol
alcoholism alcoholiaeth *eb*
alcove alcof *eb* alcofau
aldehyde aldehyd *eg* aldehydau
alder gwernen *eb* gwern
alderman henadur *eg* henaduriaid
Aldine Press Gwasg Aldus Manutius *eb*
aleatory aleatoraidd *ans*
alellopathy alelopathi *eg*
alert rhybudd *eg* rhybuddion
aleurone alewron *eg*
aleurone layer haenen alewron *eb* haenau alewron
Alexander the Great Alecsander Fawr *eg*
Alexandrine Alecsandraidd *ans*
alfalfa maglys *eg*
Alfred the Great Alffred Fawr *eg*
alga alga *eg* algâu
algebra algebra *eg/b*
algebraic expression mynegiad algebraidd *eg* mynegiadau algebraidd
algebraic number rhif algebraidd *eg* rhifau algebraidd
algebraic skill sgìl algebraidd *eg* sgiliau algebraidd
ALGOL ALGOL
algorithm algorithm *eg* algorithmau
algorithmic algorithmig *ans*
alias enw arall *eg* enwau eraill
alicyclic aligylchol *ans*
alidade alidad *eg* alidadau
alien *adj* estron *ans*
alien *n* estron *eg* estroniaid
alien priory allbriordy *eg* allbriordai
alienate (a person) gelyniaethu *be*
alienate (property) arallu *be*
alienation (=cause to become hostile) gelyniaethiad *eg*
alienation (of property etc) aralliad *eg*
alienation office swyddfa arallu *eb* swyddfeydd arallu
Aliens Act Deddf Estroniaid *eb*
align alinio *be*
align bottom alinio'r gwaelod *be*
align centre alinio'r canol *be*
align centre horizontally alinio'r canol yn llorweddol *be*
align centre vertically alinio'r canol yn fertigol *be*
align data source alinio ffynhonnell y data *be*
align dots down alinio dotiau i lawr *be*
align left alinio i'r chwith *be*
align middle alinio i'r canol *be*
align right alinio i'r dde *be*
align to bottom alinio i'r gwaelod *be*
align to grid alinio i'r grid *be*
align to top alinio i'r brig *be*
align vertical centre alinio i'r canol fertigol *be*
aligned aliniedig *ans*
alignment aliniad *eg* aliniadau
alimentary canal llwybr ymborth *eg*
alimentation (of snow) croniad eira *eg*
aliphatic aliffatig *ans*
aliquot *adj* cydrifol *ans*
aliquot (in chemistry) *n* alicwot *eg*
aliquot (in mathematics) *n* cyfnifer *eg* cyfniferoedd
alizarin brown brown alisarin *eg*
alizarin crimson rhuddgoch alisarin *eg*
alizarin dye llifyn alisarin *eg* llifynnau alisarin
alizarin green gwyrdd alisarin *eg*
alizarin purple lake llif porffor alisarin *eg*
alizarin violet fioled alisarin *eg*
alizarin yellow melyn alisarin *eg*
alkali alcali *eg* alcalïau
alkali metal metel alcalïaidd *eg* metelau alcalïaidd
alkaline alcalïaidd *ans*
alkaline earth metal metel mwynol alcalïaidd *eg*
alkaline glaze gwydredd alcalïaidd *eg*
alkaline hydrolysis hydrolysis alcalïaidd *eg*
alkalinity alcalinedd *eg*
alkane alcan *eg* alcanau
alkanoic acid (generic name) asid alcanöig *eg* asidau alcanöig
alkaptonuria alcaptonwria *eg*
alkene alcen *eg* alcenau
alkybenzene alcybensen *eg* alcybensenau
alkyl alcyl *eg* alcylau
alkylate alcyleiddio *be*
alkylation alcyleiddiad *eg*
alkylmagnesium halide alcylmagnesiwm halid *eg* alcylmagnesiwm halidau
alkyne alcyn *eg* alcynau
all (on menu) popeth *eg*
all axes pob echel
all axis grids pob grid echel
all caps priflythrennau'n unig
all certificates pob tystysgrif
all charts pob siart
all documents pob dogfen
all fields pob maes
all files pob ffeil
all folders pob ffolder
all groups pob grŵp
▸ **all important** hollbwysig *ans*
all indexes pob mynegai
all languages pob iaith
all levels pob lefel
all messages pob neges
all properties pob priodwedd
all slides pob sleid

all square sgwâr *eg*
all squared i gyd wedi'u sgwario
all styles pob arddull
all titles pob teitl
all values pob gwerth
All Wales Strategy (AWS) Strategaeth Cymru Gyfan *eb*
alla cappella alla cappella *adf*
Allah Allah *eg*
allantois alantois *eg*
allegation honiad *eg* honiadau
allege honni *be*
allegiance teyrngarwch *eg*
allegiance homage gwrogaeth teyrngarwch *eb*
allegorical alegorïaidd *ans*
allegory alegori *eg* alegorïau
allele alel *eg* alelau
allele frequency amlder alel *eg*
allelomorph alelomorff *eg* alelomorffau
allemande allemande *eb* allemandes
Allen key allwedd Allen *eb* allweddi Allen
Allen screw sgriw Allen *eb* sgriwiau Allen
allergic alergaidd *ans*
allergic reaction adwaith alergaidd *eg* adweithiau alergaidd
allergy alergedd *eg* alergeddau
allesthesia alesthesia *eg*
all-hard blade llafn cwbl-galed *eg* llafnau cwbl-galed
all-hard hacksaw blade llafn haclif cwbl-galed *eg* llafnau haclif cwbl-galed
alliance cynghrair *eg/b* cynghreiriau
Alliance Control Commission Comisiwn Rheoli'r Gynghrair *eb*
Alliance for Progress Cynghrair er Cynnydd *eb*
allied (=related) perthynol *ans*
allied (in war) cynghreiriol *ans*
allied landing glaniad y cynghreiriaid *eg*
alligator jaw safn aligator *eb* safnau aligator
all-interval series cyfres pob cyfwng *eb* cyfresi pob cyfwng
alliteration cyflythreniad
allocate (resources etc) dyrannu *be*
allocate (students) dosbarthu *be*
allocation (of resources etc) dyraniad *eg* dyraniadau
allocation (of students) dosbarthiad *eg* dosbarthiadau
allocative efficiency effeithlonrwydd dyrannol *eg*
allogenic alogenig *ans*
allometric growth twf alometrig *eg*
allomorph alomorff *eg* alomorffau
allophone aloffon *eg* aloffonau
allopolyploid alopolyploid *ans*
allopolyploidy alopolyploidi *eg*
allot pennu *be*
allotetraploid alotetraploid *ans*
allotment rhandir *eg* rhandiroedd
allotrope alotrop *eg* alotropau
allotropic alotropig *ans*
allotropy alotropaeth *eb*
all-over pattern patrwm trosodd *eg*
allow caniatáu *be*
allow additions caniatáu ychwanegiadau *be*
allow background save caniatáu cadw cefndir *be*
allow blank caniatáu lle gwag *be*
allow effects caniatáu effeithiau *be*
allow fast save caniatáu cadw cyflym *be*
allow interaction caniatáu rhyngweithio *be*
allow modifications caniatáu newidiadau *be*
allow quick editing caniatáu golygu cyflym *be*
allowance lwfans *eg* lwfansau
alloy aloi *eg* aloion
alloy steel dur aloi *eg*
alloying elements elfennau aloi *ell*
all-rounder chwaraewr amryddawn *eg* chwaraewyr amryddawn
allspice pupur Jamaica *eg*
all-through primary school ysgol gynradd ddilyniannol *eb* ysgolion cynradd dilyniannol
alluvial llifwaddodol *ans*
alluvial deposit llifwaddod *eg* llifwaddodion
alluvial fan bwa llifwaddod *eg* bwâu llifwaddod
alluvial plain gwastatir llifwaddod *eg* gwastatiroedd llifwaddod
alluvium llifwaddod *eg* llifwaddodion
ally cynghreiriad *eg* cynghreiriaid
allylics alylicion *ell*
almighty hollalluog *ans*
almond cneuen almon *eb* cnau almon
almond essence rhinflas almon *eg*
almoner elusennwr *eg* elusenwyr
almonry elusenfa *eb* elusenfeydd
alms elusen *eb* elusennau
almshouse elusendy *eg* elusendai
alocryl alocryl *eg*
alocryl medium cyfrwng alocryl *eg*
along the grain ar hyd y graen
alp alp *eg* alpau
alpenhorn alpgorn *eg* alpgyrn
alpha alffa *eg*
alpha activity gweithgarwch alffa *eg*
alpha level lefel alffa *eb*
alpha particle gronyn alffa *eg* gronynnau alffa
alphabet gwyddor *eb* gwyddorau
alphabet agencies adrannau'r wyddor *ell*
alphabetic method dull a, b, c *eg*
alphabetical order trefn y wyddor *ans*
alphameric alffamerig *ans*
alphanumeric alffaniwmerig *ans*
alpine alpaidd *ans*
alpine butterfly cwlwm canolwr *eg*
Alps Alpau *ell*
al-Qad'r al-Qad'r *eg*
altar allor *eb* allorau
altar piece allorlun *eg* allorluniau

altarage allordal *eg* allordaliadau
altars once so privileged allorau mawr eu braint *ell*
alter sensitivity newid sensitifrwydd *be*
alteration newid *eg* newidiadau
alteration line llinell newid *eb* llinellau newid
alternate *v* aryneilio *be*
alternate (in general) *adj* bob yn ail *ans*
alternate (in technical usage) *adj* eiledol *ans*
alternate angle ongl eiledol *eb* onglau eiledol
alternate bud blaguryn eiledol *eg* blagur eiledol
alternate grasp gafael bob yn ail *be*
alternate layers haenau eiledol *ell*
alternating eiledol *ans*
alternating current (A.C.) cerrynt eiledol *eg*
alternation of generations eiledEdd cenedlaethau *eg*
alternative *n* dewis *eg* dewisiadau
alternative (=other) *adj* arall *ans*
alternative (=preferable) *adj* amgen *ans*
alternative forms of care mathau eraill o ofal *ell*
alternative hypothesis rhagdybiaeth arall *eb*
alternative medicine meddygaeth amgen *eb*
alternative narrative naratif arall *eg* naratifau eraill
alternative society cymdeithas amgen *eb*
alternative technology technoleg amgen *eb*
alternative worship addoliad amgen *eg* addoliadau amgen
alternativo alternativo *eg* alternativi
alternator eiliadur *eg* eiliaduron
altimeter altimedr *eg* altimedrau
altiplanation uwchwastadiant *eg*
altitude uchder *eg* uchderau
altmode eilfodd *eg*
alto alto *eg/b* altos
alto clarinet clarinét alto *eg* clarinetau alto
alto flute ffliwt alto *eb* ffliwtiau alto
altocumulus altocumulus *eg*
alto-relievo cerfwedd uchel *eb* cerfweddau uchel
altostratus altostratus *eg*
altruism allgaredd *eg*
alum alwm *eg*
alumina alwmina *eg*
aluminate ion ïon alwminad *eg* ïonau alwminad
aluminium (Al) alwminiwm *eg*
aluminium alloy aloi alwminiwm *eg* aloion alwminiwm
aluminium ammonium sulfate(III)-12-water alwminiwm amoniwm sylffad(III)-12-dŵr *eg*
aluminium ammonium sulfate(V)-12-water alwminiwm amoniwm sylffad(V)-12-dŵr *eg*
aluminium bromide alwminiwm bromid *eg*
aluminium bronze efydd alwminiwm *eg*
aluminium chloride alwminiwm clorid *eg*
aluminium foil ffoil alwminiwm *eg*
aluminium hydroxide alwminiwm hydrocsid *eg*
aluminium ion ïon alwminiwm *eg* ïonau alwminiwm
aluminium nitrate(V) alwminiwm nitrad(V) *eg*
aluminium oxide alwminiwm ocsid *eg*
aluminium oxide (corundum) alwminiwm ocsid (corundwm) *eg*
aluminium oxide paper papur alwminiwm ocsid *eg*
aluminium phosphate(V) alwminiwm ffosffad(V) *eg*
aluminium potassium sulfate(VI)-12-water alwminiwm potasiwm sylffad(VI)-12-dŵr *eg*
aluminium screw sgriw alwminiwm *eb* sgriwiau alwminiwm
aluminium sulfate(VI) alwminiwm sylffad(VI) *eg*
aluminium track trac alwminiwm *eg* traciau alwminiwm
aluminium(III) bromide alwminiwm(III) bromid *eg*
alveolar (of gums) gorfannol *ans*
alveolar (of lungs) alfeolaidd *ans*
alveolar bone asgwrn y gorfant *eg*
alveolar ridge trum gorfant *eg* trumiau gorfant
alveolus alfeolws *eg* alfeoli
always bob tro *adf*
always execute gweithredu bob tro *be*
always on connection cysylltiad parhaol *ans*
always replace newid bob tro *be*
Alzheimer's disease clefyd Alzheimer *eg*
amalgam amalgam *eg* amalgamau
amalgamate cyfuno *be*
amalgamation cyfuniad *eg* cyfuniadau
amanuensis ysgrifennydd *eg* ysgrifenyddion
amateur amatur *eg* amaturiaid
amateurism amaturiaeth *eb*
ambassador llysgennad *eg* llysgenhadon
amber (=fossilized resin) ambr *eg*
amber (enamelling colour) melyngoch *eg*
amber brown (enamelling colour) melynfrown *eg*
ambient light golau'r amgylchedd *eg*
ambiguous amwys *ans*
Ambrose Emrys *eg*
Ambrosian chant siant Ambrosaidd *eb* siantiau Ambrosaidd
ambulance ambiwlans *eg* ambiwlansys
ambulance driver gyrrwr ambiwlans *eg* gyrwyr ambiwlans
ambulant yn gallu cerdded
ambulatory cerddedfa *eb* cerddedfeydd
ambush rhagod *eg* rhagodau
amen amen *eg* ameniau
amen cadence diweddeb amen *eb* diweddebau amen
amend diwygio *be*
amended template templed diwygiedig *eg* templedi diwygiedig
amendment (to a resolution) gwelliant *eg* gwelliannau
amendment (to a text) newid *eg* newidiadau
amenity mwynder *eg* mwynderau
amerce amersu *be*
amercement amersiad *eg* amersiadau
American organ organ Americanaidd *eb* organau Americanaidd

American Revolution Chwyldro Americanaidd *eg*
American sign language iaith arwyddion America *eb*
americium (Am) americiwm *eg*
amicable grant grant gwirfoddol *eg* grantiau gwirfoddol
amicable loan benthyciad cyfeillgar *eg* benthyciadau cyfeillgar
amice amis *eg*
amide amid *eg*
amination amineiddiad *eg*
amine amin *eg* aminau
amino acid asid amino *eg* asidau amino
amino plastics aminoblastigion *ell*
amino resins resinau amino *ell*
2-aminobenzenecarboxylic acid asid 2-aminobensencarbocsylig *eg*
4-aminobenzenecarboxylic acid asid 4-aminobensencarbocsylig *eg*
4-aminobenzenesulfonamide 4-aminobensensylffonamid *eg*
4-aminobenzenesulfonic acid asid 4-aminobensensylffonig *eg*
aminobutanedioic acid asid aminobwtandeuöig *eg*
aminoethanoic acid asid aminoethanöig *eg*
2-aminoethanol 2-aminoethanol *eg*
2-aminopentanedioic acid asid 2-aminopentandeuöig *eg*
2-aminophenol 2-aminoffenol *eg*
4-aminophenylammonium chloride 4-aminoffenylamoniwm clorid *eg*
2-aminopropanoic acid asid 2-aminopropanöig *eg*
aminosulfonic acid asid aminosylffonig *eg*
amitosis amitosis *eg*
ammeter amedr *eg* amedrau
ammonia amonia *eg*
ammoniac amoniac *ans*
ammoniacal copper(I) chloride copr(I) clorid amoniaidd *eg*
ammoniacal silver nitrate(V) arian nitrad(V) amoniaidd *eg*
ammoniacal silver(I) nitrate(V) arian(I) nitrad(V) amoniaidd *eg*
ammonification amoneiddio *be*
ammonium benzenecarboxylate (or benzoate) amoniwm bensencarbocsylad (neu bensoad) *eg*
ammonium cerium(IV) sulfate(VI) amoniwm ceriwm(IV) sylffad(VI) *eg*
ammonium chloride amoniwm clorid *eg*
ammonium copper(II) sulfate(VI)-6-water amoniwm copr(II) sylffad(VI)-6-dŵr *eg*
ammonium dichromate amoniwm deucromad *eg*
ammonium dichromate(VI) amoniwm deucromad(VI) *eg*
ammonium dihydrogenphosphate(V) amoniwm deuhydrogenffosffad(V) *eg*
ammonium ethanedioate amoniwm ethandeuoad *eg*
ammonium ethanoate amoniwm ethanoad *eg*
ammonium hydrogencarbonate amoniwm hydrogencarbonad *eg*
ammonium hydrogenphosphate(V) amoniwm hydrogenffosffad(V) *eg*
ammonium hydrogensulfate(VI) amoniwm hydrogensylffad(VI) *eg*
ammonium ion ïon amoniwm *eg* ïonau amoniwm
ammonium iron(II) sulfate(VI)-6-water amoniwm haearn(II) sylffad(VI)-6-dŵr *eg*
ammonium iron(III) sulfate(VI)-12-water amoniwm haearn(III) sylffad(VI)-12-dŵr *eg*
ammonium methanoate amoniwm methanoad *eg*
ammonium nickel(II) sulfate(VI)-6-water amoniwm nicel(II) sylffad(VI)-6-dŵr *eg*
ammonium nitrate(V) amoniwm nitrad(V) *eg*
ammonium peroxodisulfate(VI) amoniwm perocsodeusylffad(VI) *eg*
ammonium phosphate(V) amoniwm ffosffad(V) *eg*
ammonium polytrioxovanadate(V) amoniwm polytriocsofanadad(V) *eg*
ammonium sodium hydrogenphosphate(V) amoniwm sodiwm hydrogenffosffad(V) *eg*
ammonium sulfate(VI) amoniwm sylffad(VI) *eg*
ammonium sulphide amoniwm sylffid *eg*
ammonium thiocyanate amoniwm thiocyanad *eg*
ammonolysis amonolysis *eg*
amnesia amnesia *eg*
amnesty amnest *eg* amnestau
Amnesty International Amnest Rhyngwladol *eg*
amnion amnion *eg*
amniotic fluid hylif amniotig *eg*
▸ **amniotic sac** cwd amniotig *eg*
amoeboid amoebaidd *ans*
amorphous amorffaidd *ans*
amorphous peat mawn amorffaidd *eg*
amount (=quantity) swm *eg* symiau
amount (=total) cyfanswm *eg* cyfansymiau
amount of substance (in chemistry) swm y sylwedd *eg*
amount owing swm sy'n ddyledus *eg*
ampere amper *eg* amperau
ampersand (&) ampersand *eg*
amphibian amffibiad *eg* amffibiaid
amphibious amffibiaidd *ans*
amphibrach corfan amgyrch *eg* corfannau amgyrch
amphictyony amffictyoni *eg*
amphipathic amffipathig *ans*
amphiprostyle amffiprostyl *eg* amffiprostylau
amphitheatre amffitheatr *eg* amffitheatrau
amphoteric amffoterig *ans*
amphoteric character nodwedd amffoterig *eb* nodweddion amffoterig
amplification mwyhad *eg*
amplifier mwyhadur *eg* mwyhaduron
amplify mwyhau *be*
amplitude (in mathematics) arg *eg* argiau
amplitude (in physics) osgled *eg* osgledau

amplitude envelope chwydd-amlen *eb* chwydd-amlenni
amplitude modulated carrier wave ton gario wedi'i modylu'n osgledol *eb*
amplitude modulation modyliad osgled *eg* modyliadau osgled
amplitude swing (electronics) osgiliad *eg* osgiliadau
ampoule ampwl *eg* ampylau
amputate trychu *be*
amputation trychiad *eg* trychiadau
Amrit-dhari Amrit-dhari *eg*
Amrit-sanskar Amrit-sanskar *eg*
amygdala amygdala *eg*
amyl acetate amyl asetad *eg*
amylase amylas *eg*
amyloplast amyloplast *eg* amyloplastau
Anabaptist Ailfedyddiwr *eg* Ailfedyddwyr
anabatic anabatig *ans*
anabolic anabolig *ans*
anabolism anabolaeth *eb*
anacrusis anacrwsis *eg* anacrwses
anacrustic anacrwstig *ans*
anaemia anaemia *eg*
anaerobic *adj* anaerobig *ans*
anaerobic respiration resbiradaeth anaerobig *eb*
anaerobic running rhedeg anaerobig *be*
anaesthetic anaesthetig *eg* anaesthetigion
anaesthetics anaestheteg *eb*
anaesthetist anaesthetegydd *eg* anaesthetegyddion
anal rhefrol *ans*
anal stage cyfnod yr anws *eg*
analgesic *adj* poenleddfol *ans*
analgesic *n* poenleddfwr *eg* poenleddfwyr
analogical cydweddiadol *ans*
analogous (=partially similar) cydweddol *ans*
analogous (of computer or electronic process) analogaidd *ans*
analogue *adj* analog *ans*
analogue *n* analog *eg* analogau
analogue computer (ADC) cyfrifiadur analog *eg* cyfrifiaduron analog
analogue format fformat analog *eg* fformatau analog
analogue signal signal analog *eg*
analogue to digital converter trawsnewidydd analog-digidol *eg* trawsnewidyddion analog-digidol
analogy cydweddiad *eg* cydweddiadau
analyse dadansoddi *be*
analyser dadansoddydd *eg* dadansoddyddion
analysis dadansoddiad *eg* dadansoddiadau
analysis of cost-threat dadansoddiad cost-bygythiad *eg*
analysis of variance dadansoddiad amrywiant *eg*
analysis system system ddadansoddi *eb* systemau dadansoddi
analyst dadansoddwr *eg* dadansoddwyr
analytical dadansoddol *ans*
analytical chemistry cemeg ddadansoddol *eb*
analytical continuation parhad dadansoddol *eg*
analytical notes nodiadau dadansoddol *ell*
analytical orientation gogwydd dadansoddol *eg*
analytical study astudiaeth ddadansoddol *eb*
anapaest corfan cyrch dyrchafedig *eg* corfannau cyrch dyrchafedig
anaphase anaffas *eg*
anaphylactic shock sioc anaffylactig *eb*
anarchism anarchiaeth *eb*
anarchist *adj* anarchaidd *ans*
anarchist *n* anarchydd *eg* anarchwyr
Anarchist Party Plaid Anarchaidd *eb*
anarchy anarchiaeth *eb*
anastomosis anastomosis *eg* anastomoses
anatman (=anatta) anatman *eg*
anatomical anatomegol *ans*
anatomical coding codio anatomegol *be*
anatomical direction cyfeiriad anatomegol *eg*
anatomy (=body) anatomi *eg*
anatomy (as science) anatomeg *eb*
anatta (=anatman) anatta *eg*
ancestor hynafiad *eg* hynafiaid
ancestor worship addoli cyndadau *be*
ancestral hynafiadol *ans*
ancestral traits nodweddion hynafiadol *ell*
ancestry llinach *eb* llinachau
anchor angor *eg/b* angorau
anchor bracket braced angor *eb* bracedi angor
anchor to character angori i'r nod *be*
anchor to frame angori i'r ffrâm *be*
anchor to page angori i'r dudalen *be*
anchor to paragraph angori i'r paragraff *be*
anchorage angorfa *eb* angorfâu
anchorite ancr *eg* ancriaid
anchovy brwyniad *eg* brwyniaid
anchovy essence rhinflas brwyniaid *eg*
ancient hynafol *ans*
Ancient Britons Hen Frythoniaid *ell*
Ancient Egypt Hen Aifft *eb*
Ancient Greece Hen Roeg *eb*
ancient history hanes yr hen fyd *eg*
ancient monument heneb *eb* henebion
Ancient of Days Hen Ddihenydd *eg*
ancillary ategol *ans*
ancillary industry diwydiant ategol *eg* diwydiannau ategol
ancillary staff staff ategol *ell*
ancillary support cefnogaeth ategol *eb*
AND (logic) AC
AND circuit cylched AC *eb* cylchedau AC
AND element elfen AC *eb* elfennau AC
AND gate adwy AC *eb* adwyon AC
AND operation gweithrediad AC *eg* gweithrediadau AC
androecium androeciwm *eg*
androgen androgen *eg* androgenau

adf, adv adferf, *adverb* ***ans, adj*** ansoddair, *adjective* ***be*** berf, *verb* ***eb*** enw benywaidd, *feminine noun* ***eg*** enw gwrywaidd, *masculine noun*

androgen insensitivity ansensitifrwydd i androgenau *eg*
androgyny androgynedd *eg*
anecdotal art celfyddyd storïol *eb*
anemometer anemomedr *eg* anemomedrau
anemophily anemoffiledd *eg*
aneroid *adj* aneroid *ans*
aneroid *n* aneroid *eg* aneroidau
aneroid barometer baromedr aneroid *eg* baromedrau aneroid
aneuploid anewploid *eg* anewploidau
aneurine anewrin *eg*
angel angel *eg* angylion
angelica angelica *eg*
anger management rheolaeth dicter *eb*
Angevin Angefin *eg* Angefiniaid
angiosperm angiosberm *eg* angiosbermau
angle *n* ongl *eb* onglau
angle *v* ongli *be*
angle bead glain ongl *eg* gleiniau ongl
angle bracket braced ongl *eb* bracedi ongl
angle bridle bagl ongl *eb* baglau ongl
angle dovetail joint uniad cynffonnog onglog *eg* uniadau cynffonnog onglog
angle halving haneru ongl *be*
angle halving joint uniad haneru ongl *eg* uniadau haneru ongl
angle headstand pensafiad plyg *eg* pensafiadau plyg
angle iron haearn ongl *eg* heyrn ongl
angle of contact ongl gyswllt *eb* onglau cyswllt
angle of cutting tool ongl erfyn torri *eb* onglau offer torri
angle of depression ongl ostwng *eb* onglau gostwng
angle of deviation ongl wyriad *eb* onglau gwyriad
angle of elevation ongl godiad *eb* onglau codiad
angle of friction ongl ffrithiant *eb* onglau ffrithiant
angle of grazing incidence ongl prin drawiad *eb* onglau prin drawiad
angle of incidence ongl drawiad *eb* onglau trawiad
angle of inclination ongl oledd *eb* onglau goledd
angle of intersection ongl groestoriad *eb* onglau croestoriad
angle of obliquity ongl letrawsedd *eb* onglau lletrawsedd
angle of projection ongl dafluniad *eb* onglau tafluniad
angle of reflection ongl adlewyrchiad *eb* onglau adlewyrchiad
angle of refraction ongl blygiant *eb* onglau plygiant
angle of rotation ongl gylchdro *eb* onglau cylchdro
angle of turning tool ongl erfyn turnio *eb* onglau offer turnio
angle plate plât ongl *eg* platiau ongl
angle projection tafluniad ongl *eg* tafluniadau ongl
angle shot ergyd onglog *eb* ergydion onglog
angled connector line llinell gyswllt onglog *eb* llinellau cyswllt onglog
angled line llinell onglog *eb* llinellau onglog
angled return dychweliad lletraws *eg* dychweliadau lletraws
angled text testun onglog *eg* testunau onglog
angler fish cythraul môr *eg* cythreuliaid môr
Anglican *adj* Anglicanaidd *ans*
Anglican *n* Anglican *eg* Anglicaniaid
Anglican chant siant Anglicanaidd *eb* siantiau Anglicanaidd
Anglicanism Anglicaniaeth *eb*
Anglicization (of language, society) Seisnigo *be*
Anglicized Seisnigaidd *ans*
Anglo-Irish Treaty Cytundeb Eingl-Wyddelig *eg*
Anglo-Norman *adj* Eingl-Normanaidd *ans*
Anglo-Norman *n* Eingl-Norman *eg* Eingl-Normaniaid
Anglo-Norman Law Cyfraith Eingl-Normanaidd *eb*
Anglo-Saxon *adj* Eingl-Sacsonaidd *ans*
Anglo-Saxon (language) Eingl-Sacsoneg *eb*
Anglo-Saxon Chronicles Croniclau'r Eingl-Sacsoniaid *ell*
Anglo-Saxon Law Cyfraith Eingl-Sacsonaidd *eb*
angora angora *eg*
angular (having angles) onglog *ans*
angular (of velocity etc) onglaidd *ans*
angular deformation anffurfiad onglog *eg* anffurfiadau onglog
angular face wyneb onglog *eg* wynebau onglog
angular frequency amledd cylchdro *eg*
angular magnification chwyddhad onglog *eg* chwyddadau onglog
angular momentum momentwm onglaidd *eg* momenta onglaidd
angular period cyfnod cylchdro *eg*
angular perspective persbectif onglog *eg* persbectifau onglog
angular spread ymlediad onglog *eg*
angular thread edau onglog *eb* edafedd onglog
angular velocity cyflymder onglaidd *eg* cyflymderau onglaidd
angularity onglogrwydd *eg*
anharmonic *adj* anharmonig *ans*
anharmonic *n* anharmonig *eg* anharmonigau
anhedonia anhedonia *eg*
anhydrate anhydrad *eg* anhydradau
anhydride anhydrid *eg* anhydridau
anhydrous anhydrus *ans*
anicca (=anitya) anicca *eg*
aniline anilin *eg*
aniline colours lliwiau anilin *ell*
aniline dyes llifion anilin *ell*
animal *adj* anifeilaidd *ans*
animal *n* anifail *eg* anifeiliaid
animal fat braster anifail *eg*
animal fibre ffibr anifail *eg* ffibrau anifail
animal form ffurf anifeiliaid *eb*
animal glue glud anifail *eg*
animal marionette marionét anifail *eg* marionetau anifeiliaid

animal suffering dioddefaint anifeiliaid *eg*
animate animeiddio *be*
animated graphic graffigyn wedi'i animeiddio *eg* graffigau wedi'u hanimeiddio
animation *count noun* animeiddiad *eg* animeiddiadau
animation *mass noun* animeiddio *be*
animation effect effaith animeiddio *eb* effeithiau animeiddio
animation group grŵp animeiddio *eg* grwpiau animeiddio
animation order trefn animeiddio *eb*
animation parameter paramedr animeiddio *eg* paramedrau animeiddio
animator animeiddydd *eg* animeiddwyr
animism animistiaeth *eb*
animist animistiad *eg/b* animistiaid
animistic animistaidd *ans*
anion anion *eg* anionau
anionic anionig *ans*
anitya (=anicca) anitya *eg*
ankle ffêr *eb* fferau; pigwrn *eg* pigyrnau
anklewarmers socasau *ell*
annal blwyddnod *eg* blwyddnodau
annates (=first fruits) anodau *ell*
anneal anelio *be*
annelid anelid *eg* anelidau
annex *v* cyfeddiannu *be*
annexation cyfeddiant *eg*
annexe (to building) *n* rhandy *eg* rhandai
annexe (to document) *n* atodiad *eg* atodiadau
annihilate (in literal sense) difodi *be*
annihilate (in metaphorical sense) chwalu'n llwyr *be*
anniversary pen-blwydd *eg* penblwyddi
Anno Domini (AD) Oed Crist
annotate anodi *be*
annotated drawing lluniad anodedig *eg*
annotated map map anodedig *eg* mapiau anodedig
annotated sketch braslun anodedig *eg* brasluniau anodedig
annotated sketch map llinfap wedi'i labelu â nodiadau *eg*
annotated visual records cofnodion gweledol gyda nodiadau *ell*
annotation anodiad *eg* anodiadau
annual (=lasting for one year) *adj* unflwydd *ans*
annual (=occurring every year) *adj* blynyddol *ans*
annual (flower) *n* blodyn unflwydd *eg* blodau unflwydd
annual premium premiwm blynyddol *eg* premiymau blynyddol
annual rainfall glawiad blynyddol *eg*
annual ring cylch blynyddol *eg* cylchoedd blynyddol
annual thickening tewychu unflwydd *be*
annual wage cyflog blynyddol *eg*
annuity blwydd-dal *eg* blwydd-daliadau
annul dirymu *be*
annular (=ring-shaped) modrwyol *ans*
annular (in physics) anwlar *ans*
annular lignification ligneiddiad modrwyol *eg*
annulate modrwywedd *ans*
annulment dirymiad *eg* dirymiadau
annulus (in biology) modrwy *eb* modrwyau
annulus (in physics) anwlws *eg* anwli
annunciation cyfarchiad *eg* cyfarchiadau
anode anod *eg* anodau
anodic anodig *ans*
anodic oxidation ocsidiad anodig *eg*
anodize anodeiddio *be*
anoint eneinio *be*
anointed eneiniog *ans*
anointing eneiniad *eg*
anomalous (in astronomy) anomalus *ans*
anomalous (in biology etc) anrheolaidd *ans*
anomalous (in general) afreolaidd *ans*
anomaly (in astronomy) anomaledd *eg*
anomaly (in biology etc) achos anrheolaidd *eg* achosion anrheolaidd
anomaly (in general) anghysondeb *eg* anghysondebau
anonymity anhysbysrwydd *eg*
anonymous FTP FTP anhysbys *eg*
anonymous posting postio dienw *be*
anorexia nervosa anorecsia nerfosa *eg*
anorexic anorecsig *ans*
anoxia anocsia *eg*
Ansoff Matrix Matrics Ansoff *eg*
answer *n* ateb *eg* atebion
answer *v* ateb *be*
antacid gwrthasid *eg*
antagonist (of muscles) gwrthweithydd *eg* gwrthweithyddion
antagonistic (of muscles) gwrthweithiol *ans*
antagonistic muscle pairs parau gwrthweithiol o gyhyrau *ell*
Antarctic Antartig *eg*
antecedent (e.g. drainage) *adj* rhagosod *ans*
antecedent (in canon) *n* rhagalaw *eb* rhagalawon
antecedent (in general) *n* rhagflaenydd *eg* rhagflaenwyr
antechamber rhagsiambr *eb* rhagsiambrau
antenatal cyn-geni *ans*
antenatal care gofal cyn-geni *eg*
antenatal clinic clinig cyn-geni *eg* clinigau cyn-geni
antenatal parents rhieni sy'n disgwyl *ell*
antenna (=aerial) antena *eg* antenau
antenna (of anthropod) teimlydd *eg* teimlyddion
antennule antennyn *eg* antenynnau
anterior *adj* blaen *ans*
anterior *n* pen blaen *eg*
anterior root (of nerve) nerfwreiddyn blaen *eg* nerfwreiddiau blaen
anterograde amnesia amnesia anterograd *eg*
anthem anthem *eb* anthemau
anther anther *eg* antheri

anthocyanin anthocyanin *eg* anthocyaninau
anthoxanthin anthocsanthin *eg* anthocsanthinau
anthracene anthrasen *eg*
anthracene-9,10-dione anthrasen-9,10-deuon *eg*
anthracite glo carreg *eg*
anthranilic acid asid anthranilig *eg*
anthropic principle egwyddor anthropig *eb*
anthropogenic anthropogenig *ans*
anthropoid anthropoid *eg* anthropoidau
anthropology anthropoleg *eb*
anthropometric anthropometrig *ans*
anthropometrics anthropometreg *eb*
anthropomorphic anthropomorffaidd *ans*
anthropomorphism anthropomorffaeth *eb*
anti bonding (of orbitals) gwrthfondio *ans*
anti-anxiety drug cyffur lleihau gorbryder *eg* cyffuriau lleihau gorbryder
anti-bacterial (of finish) gwrthfacteria *ans*
antibiotic *adj* gwrthfiotig *ans*
antibiotic *n* gwrthfiotig *eg* gwrthfiotigau
antibody gwrthgorff *eg* gwrthgyrff
anti-caking agent cyfrwng gwrthdalpio *eg* cyfryngau gwrthdalpio
anti-capillary groove rhigol wrthgapilari *eb* rhigolau gwrthgapilari
anti-catholic gwrth-Babyddol *ans*
Antichrist Anghrist *eg*
anticipate (in general) rhagweld *be*
anticipate (in music) rhagdaro *be*
anticipate response rhagweld ymateb *be*
anticipation (of musical note) rhagdrawiad *eg* rhagdrawiadau
anticipatory anxiety gorbryder rhagweledol *eg*
anticlerical gwrthglerigol *ans*
anti-clericalism gwrthglerigaeth *eb*
anticlinal anticlinol *ans*
anticline anticlin *eg* anticlinau
anticlinorium anticlinoriwm *eg* anticlinoria
anticlockwise gwrthglocwedd *ans*
anticlockwise direction cyfeiriad gwrthglocwedd *eg*
anti-coagulant cyffur gwrthgeulo *eg* cyffuriau gwrthgeulo
anticodon gwrthgodon *eg*
anti-colonialist gwrthdrefedigaethol *ans*
anti-Comintern pact pact gwrth-Gomintern *eg*
Anti-Corn Law League Cynghrair er Diddymu'r Deddfau Ŷd *eb*
anti-corrosion agent cyfrwng gwrthgyrydu *eg*
anticyclone antiseiclon *eg* antiseiclonau
anticyclonic antiseiclonig *ans*
antidepressant (drug) gwrthiselydd *eg* gwrthiselyddion
antidepressant drug cyffur gwrthiselder *eg* cyffuriau gwrthiselder
anti-discrimination gwrthwahaniaethol *be*
antidiuretic gwrthddiwretig *ans*
antidiuretic hormone hormon gwrthddiwretig *eg*
antidote gwrthwenwyn *eg*
anti-dust chalk sialc di-lwch *eg*
antiemetic (drug) gwrthgyfogydd *eg* gwrthgyfogyddion
antiepileptic (drug) cyffur atal epilepsi *eg* cyffuriau atal epilepsi
anti-European gwrth-Ewropeaidd *ans*
anti-fascist gwrth-ffasgaidd *ans*
anti-flame gwrth-fflam *ans*
anti-friction gwrth-ffrithiant *ans*
anti-friction grease saim gwrth-ffrithiant *eg* seimiau gwrth-ffrithiant
anti-friction metal metel gwrth-ffrithiant *eg* metelau gwrth-ffrithiant
antigen antigen *eg* antigenau
antihypertensive (of drug) gwrthorbwysol *ans*
antihypotensive (of drug) gwrthisbwysol *ans*
anti-inflammatory (of drug) gwrthlidiol *ans*
anti-inflationary gwrthchwyddiannol *ans*
antilogarithm gwrthlogarithm *eg* gwrthlogarithmau
anti-manic drug cyffur gwrthfania *eg* cyffuriau gwrthfania
Anti-Marcionite Prologues Prologau Gwrth-Farcionaidd *ell*
antimonate(III) ion ïon antimonad(III) *eg* ïonau antimonad(III)
antimonate(V) ion ïon antimonad(V) *eg* ïonau antimonad(V)
antimony (Sb) antimoni *eg*
antimony(III) chloride antimoni(III) clorid *eg*
antimony(III) chloride oxide antimoni(III) clorid ocsid *eg*
antimony(III) oxide antimoni(III) ocsid *eg*
antimony(III) potassium antimoni(III) potasiwm *eg*
antimony(V) oxide antimoni(V) ocsid *eg*
anti-moth gwrthwyfyn *ans*
anti-natalist (policies etc) gwrth-eni *ans*
antinodal antinodol *ans*
antinode antinod *eg* antinodau
antinomian *adj* antinomaidd *ans*
antinomian *n* antinomiad *eg* antinomiaid
antinomianism antinomiaeth *eb*
Antiochene Antiochaidd *ans*
antioxidant gwrthocsidydd *eg* gwrthocsidyddion
antipapal gwrth-Babaidd *ans*
antiparallel gwrthbaralel *ans*
antiphase (out of phase) gwrthwedd *ans*
antiphon antiffon *eb* antiffonau
antipope gwrthbab *eg* gwrthbabau
antiproton antiproton *eg* antiprotonau
antipsychotic drug cyffur gwrthseicotig *eg* cyffuriau gwrthseicotig
antiquarian hynafiaethol *ans*
antiquary hynafiaethydd *eg* hynafiaethwyr
antique *adj* hynafol *ans*
antique *n* hynafolyn *eg* hynafolion
antique cymbals symbalau Groeg *ell*
antique paper papur bras *eg*
antique shop siop hen bethau *eb* siopau hen bethau

antiquity (=ancient times) hen fyd *eg*
antiquity (of objects or customs) hynafiaeth *eb* hynafiaethau
anti-racism gwrth-hiliaeth *eb*
anti-racist education addysg wrth-hiliol *eb*
anti-Semitism gwrth-Semitiaeth *eb*
antiseptic *adj* antiseptig *ans*
antiseptic *n* antiseptig *eg*
anti-slavery movement mudiad gwrthgaethwasiaeth *eg*
anti-slip gwrth-lithr *ans*
anti-snake bar braich sadio *eb* breichiau sadio
antisocial behaviour ymddygiad gwrthgymdeithasol *eg*
antisocial personality disorder anhwylder personoliaeth anghymdeithasol *eg*
antistatic gwrthstatig *ans*
antisymmetric gwrthgymesur *ans*
antisymmetry gwrthgymesuredd *eg* gwrthgymesureddau
anti-terrorism gwrthderfysgaeth *eb*
anti-terrorist gwrthderfysgwr *eg* gwrthderfysgwyr
anti-terrorist device dyfais wrthderfysgol *eb* dyfeisiau gwrthderfysgol
antithesis antithesis *eg*
anti-trades gwrthwyntoedd cyson *ell*
anti-virus measure mesur gwrthfirysau *eg* mesurau gwrthfirysau
anti-virus software meddalwedd gwrthfirysau *eg*
antivivisection gwrthfywddyraniad *eg*
anuria anwria *eg*
anus anws *eg*
anvil eingion *eb* eingionau
anvil horn scrolls heyrn sgrôl *ell*
anxiety (non-technical usage) pryder *eg* pryderon
anxiety (technical usage) gorbryder *eg*
anxiety disorder anhwylder gorbryder *eg*
any record unrhyw gofnod
aorta aorta *eg*
aortic arch bwa aortig *eg* bwâu aortig
aortic body corffyn aortig *eg* corffynnau aortig
APA format fformat APA *eg*
apart ar wahân *ans*
apartheid apartheid *eg*
apartment fflat *eb* fflatiau
apathy apathi *eg*
aperient carthydd *eg* carthyddion
aperiodic digyfnod *ans*
aperture agorfa *eb* agorfeydd
► **apetalous** dibetal *ans*
apex apig *eb* apigau
apgar score chart siart sgôr apgar *eg* siartiau sgôr apgar
aphasia affasia *eg*
aphelion affelion *eg*
aphid pryf glas *eg* pryfed gleision
apical apigol *ans*
apical bud blaguryn apigol *eg* blagur apigol
apical dominance trechedd apigol *eg*
apical meristem meristem apigol *eg*
► **apnoea** apnoea *eg*
apocalypse datguddiad *eg* datguddiadau
apocalyptic *adj* apocalyptaidd *ans*
apocalyptic *n* apocalypteg *eb*
apocalyptic literature llenyddiaeth apocalyptaidd *eb*
apocarpous apocarpog *ans*
apocrypha apocryffa *eg*
apocryphal new testament testament newydd apocryffaidd *eg*
apogean tide llanw apogeaidd *eg*
apogee apoge *eg*
apologetic (of reasoned defence) diffyniadol *ans*
apologetics diffyniadaeth *eb*
apologetist diffynnydd *eg* diffynwyr
apology (=defence) diffyniad *eg* diffyniadau
apology (=regret) ymddiheuriad *eg* ymddiheuriadau
apology of the Commons cyfiawnhad y Senedd *eg*
apophthegm doethair *eg* doetheiriau
apoplast apoplast *eg*
aposematic rhybuddiol *ans*
apostasy gwrthgiliad *eg* gwrthgiliadau
apostate *adj* gwrthgiliol *ans*
apostate *n* gwrthgiliwr *eg* gwrthgilwyr
apostle apostol *eg* apostolion
apostleship apostoliaeth *eb*
apostolic apostolaidd *ans*
Apostolic Constitutions, the Gosodiadau Apostolaidd, y *ell*
Apostolic Fathers Tadau Apostolaidd *ell*
Apostolic Succession Olyniaeth Apostolaidd *eb*
apostolicity apostoligrwydd *eg*
apostrophe collnod *eg* collnodau
apoyando apoyando *eg*
apparatus cyfarpar *eg*
apparent (=obvious) amlwg *ans*
apparent (=seeming) ymddangosiadol *ans*
apparent (in physics) ymddangosol *ans*
apparent motion of the moon mudiant ymddangosol y lleuad *eg*
apparent movement symudiad ymddangosol *eg* symudiadau ymddangosol
apparent time amser haul *eg*
appeal *n* apêl *eb* apeliadau
appeal *v* apelio *be*
appeal court llys apêl *eg* llysoedd apêl
appear ymddangos *be*
appearance ymddangosiad *eg* ymddangosiadau
appease dyhuddo *be*
appeasement dyhuddiad *eg* dyhuddiadau
appeasement gesture ystum cymodi *eg* ystumiau cymodi
appeasement policy polisi dyhuddo *eg* polisïau dyhuddo
Appelate Jurisdiction Act Deddf Awdurdod Apeliadol *eb*
appellant apelydd *eg* apelyddion

Appellant Lords Arglwyddi Apelyddol *ell*
append atodi *be*
append libraries atodi llyfrgelloedd *be*
append sheet atodi dalen *be*
append space atodi gofod *be*
appendicitis llid y pendics *eg*
appendicular skeleton sgerbwd atodol *eg* sgerbydau atodol
appendix (of anatomy) pendics *eg*
appendix (to a document) atodiad *eg* atodiadau
apperception cyfarganfod *be*
apperceptive agnosia agnosia cyfarganfod *eg*
appetite archwaeth *eb*
appetite centre canolfannyn ymborthi *eg* canolfanynnau ymborthi
appetizer blasyn *eg* blasynnau
appetizing blasus *ans*
apple Charlotte Charlotte afal *eg*
apple core craidd afal *eg* creiddiau afalau
apple corer digreiddiwr afal *eg* digreiddwyr afalau
apple dumpling twmplen afal *eb* twmplenni afal
apple sauce saws afal *eg*
applet rhaglennig *eb* rhaglenigau
appliance offeryn *eg* offer
applicability cymhwysedd *eg*
applicable cymwys *ans*
application (=diligence) dyfalbarhad *eg*
application (=formal request) cais *eg* ceisiadau
application (=piece of software) rhaglen *eb* rhaglenni
application (=the use to which something can be put) cymhwysiad *eg* cymwysiadau
application (to work) ymroddiad *eg*
application form ffurflen gais *eb* ffurflenni cais
application of science cymhwysiad o wyddoniaeth *eg*
▶ **application package** pecyn rhaglen *eg* pecynnau rhaglen
application window ffenestr y rhaglen *eb* ffenestri'r rhaglen
applications programmer rhaglennydd rhaglenni *eg* rhaglenwyr rhaglenni
applications software meddalwedd rhaglenni *eb*
applied (=put on) gosod *ans*
applied (as a subject of study) cymhwysol *ans*
applied art celfyddyd gymhwysol *eb* celfyddydau cymhwysol
applied behaviour analysis dadansoddi ymddygiad cymhwysol *be*
applied braid brêd gosod *eg* brediau gosod
applied ethics moeseg gymhwysol *eb*
applied facing wynebyn gosod *eg* wynebynnau gosod
applied flounce fflowns osod *eb* fflownsiau gosod
applied force grym gosod *eg*
applied forms ffurfiau gosod *ell*
applied geography daearyddiaeth gymhwysol *eb*
applied lipping ymyl osod *eb* ymylon gosod
applied mathematics mathemateg gymhwysol *eb*
applied moulding mowldin gosod *eg*
applied ornament addurn gosod *eg* addurniadau gosod
applied research ymchwil cymhwysol *eg*
applied resist gwrthydd gosod *eg*
appliqué appliqué *eg*
apply (=devote oneself) ymroi *be*
apply (=make a formal request) gwneud cais *be*
apply (=make use of as relevant or suitable) cymhwyso *be*
apply (=put into operation) gweithredu *be*
apply (=set, put) rhoi *be*
apply attributes gweithredu priodoleddau *be*
apply autoformat options gweithredu dewisiadau awtofformat *be*
apply border gweithredu border *be*
apply cell style gweithredu arddull cell *be*
apply columns gweithredu colofnau *be*
apply field format gweithredu fformat maes *be*
apply filter gweithredu hidlydd *be*
apply frame style gweithredu arddull ffrâm *be*
apply names gweithredu enwau *be*
apply page style gweithredu arddull tudalen *be*
apply paint peintio *be*
apply polish llathru *be*
apply presentation layout gweithredu gosodiad cyflwyniad *be*
apply replacement table gweithredu tabl newid *be*
apply ruler gweithredu mesurydd *be*
apply style gweithredu arddull *be*
apply table attributes gweithredu priodoleddau tabl *be*
apply theme gweithredu thema *be*
apply user data gweithredu data defnyddiwr *be*
appoggiatura appoggiatura *eg* appoggiature
appointment (to a post) penodiad *eg* penodiadau
appointment (to see someone) apwyntiad *eg* apwyntiadau
app-on-tap rhaglen ar alwad *eb* rhaglenni ar alwad
appraisal gwerthusiad *eg* gwerthusiadau
appraisal procedures trefn werthuso *eb*
appraisal scheme cynllun gwerthuso *eg* cynlluniau gwerthuso
appraisal system system werthuso *eb* systemau gwerthuso
appraise gwerthuso *be*
appreciate gwerthfawrogi *be*
appreciation (=favourable recognition) gwerthfawrogiad *eg* gwerthfawrogiadau
appreciation (in value) arbrisiant *eg* arbrisiannau
apprehend (=arrest) restio *be*
apprehend (=understand) dirnad *be*
apprehension (=anxiety) pryder *eg*
apprehension (=understanding) dirnadaeth *eb*
apprehensive subject role rôl cyfrannwr pryderus *eb*
apprentice prentis *eg* prentisiaid

apprenticeship prentisiaeth *eb*
appresorium apresoriwm *eg*
approach (=come near) *v* agosáu *be*
approach (=way of dealing with person or thing) *n* dull *eg* dulliau
approach (a matter) *v* ymdrin â *be*
approach (a person) *v* mynd at *be*
approach (to a house etc) *n* dyfodfa *eb* dyfodfeydd
approach run *n* atrediad *eg* atrediadau
approach run *v* atredeg *be*
approach to history ymagwedd at hanes *eb*
appropriate (=fit for purpose) *adj* pwrpasol *ans*
appropriate (=suitable) *adj* addas *ans*
appropriate (in performance criteria) *adj* priodol *ans*
appropriate (money, property etc) *v* adfeddu *be*
appropriate accuracy manwl gywirdeb priodol *eg*
appropriate activity gweithgaredd priodol *eg* gweithgareddau priodol
appropriate behaviour ymddygiad addas *eg*
appropriate decision penderfyniad priodol *eg* penderfyniadau priodol
appropriate direction cyfeiriad priodol *eg* cyfeiriadau priodol
appropriate dress gwisg briodol *eb* gwisgoedd priodol
appropriate evidence tystiolaeth briodol *eb*
appropriate illustration (=drawing) darluniad pwrpasol *eg* darluniadau pwrpasol
appropriate illustration (=explanation) eglureb bwrpasol *eb* eglurebau pwrpasol
appropriate method dull priodol *eg* dulliau priodol
appropriate position safle priodol *eg* safleoedd priodol
appropriate response ymateb priodol *eg* ymatebion priodol
appropriate setting cyd-destun priodol *eb* cyd-destunau priodol
appropriate source ffynhonnell briodol *eb* ffynonellau priodol
appropriate use of the body defnyddio'r corff yn briodol *be*
appropriate vocabulary geirfa briodol *eb*
appropriated tithe degwm adfedd *eg* degymau adfedd
appropriately pitched priodol o ran anhawster *ans*
appropriation adfeddiad *eg* adfeddiadau
approval label label cymeradwyaeth *eg* labeli cymeradwyaeth
approver trwyddedwr *eg* trwyddedwyr
approximate *adj* bras *ans*
approximate *v* brasamcanu *be*
approximate answer (=rough answer) ateb bras *eg* atebion bras
approximately tua *adf*
approximation brasamcan *eg* brasamcanion
apraxia apracsia *eg*
apricot bricyllen *eb* bricyll
apron ffedog *eb* ffedogau
apron stage llwyfan ffedog *eg* llwyfannau ffedog
apse cromfan *eb* cromfannau
apsidal cromfannol *ans*
apsidal tower tŵr cromfannol *eg* tyrau cromfannol
aptitude tueddfryd *eg*
aptitude test prawf tueddfryd *eg* profion tueddfryd
aquaculture acwafeithrin *be*
aquarium acwariwm *eg* acwaria
aquatic dyfrol *ans*
aquatic feeders bwytawyr dyfrol *ell*
aquatint acwatint *eg*
aqueduct traphont ddŵr *eb* traphontydd dŵr
aqueous dyfrllyd *ans*
aqueous ammonia amonia dyfrllyd *eg*
aqueous calcium hydroxide calsiwm hydrocsid dyfrllyd *eg*
aqueous humour hylif dyfrllyd *eg*
aqueous silver nitrate arian nitrad dyfrllyd *eg*
aqueous sodium hydroxide sodiwm hydrocsid dyfrllyd *eg*
aqueous solution hydoddiant dyfrllyd *eg*
► **aquifer** dyfrhaen *eb* dyfrhaenau
Arab League Cynghrair Arabaidd *eb*
arab spring sbring arab *eg* sbringiau arab
arabesque arabésg *eg* arabesgau
Arabic gum gwm Arabig *eg*
arable âr *ans*
arable land tir âr *eg*
Aramaic Arameaidd *ans*
Aramaic (of language) Aramaeg *eb*
Aramaism Aramaegeb *eb* Aramaegebau
arbitrariness mympwy *eg*
arbitrary mympwyol *ans*
arbitrary constant cysonyn mympwyol *eg* cysonion mympwyol
arbitrary unit uned fympwyol *eb* unedau mympwyol
arbitrate cyflafareddu *be*
arbitration cyflafareddiad *eg* cyflafareddiadau
arbitrator cyflafareddwr *eg* cyflafareddwyr
arbor arbor *eg* arborau
arbor chuck crafanc arbor *eb* crafangau arbor
arbor hole twll arbor *eg* tyllau arbor
arboriculture coedyddiaeth *eb*
arbuscule arbwsciwl *eg*
arc arc *eb* arcau
arc cutting torri arc *be*
arc of contact arc gyffwrdd *eb* arcau cyffwrdd
arc welding arc-weldio *be*
arcade arcêd *eb* arcedau
arch *v* pontio *be*
arch (in dancing) *n* pont *eb* pontydd
arch (in general) *n* bwa *eg* bwâu
arch form ffurf bwa *eb* ffurfiau bwa
arch in situ bwa rhededog *eg* bwâu rhededog
Arch of Covenant, the Arch y Cyfamod *eb*
archaeology archaeoleg *eb*
archaic hynafol *ans*
archaism (in general) hynafiaeth *eb* hynafiaethau

archaism (in religion) hynafoliad *eg*
archangel archangel *eg* archangylion
archbishop archesgob *eg* archesgobion
archduchess archdduges *eb* archddugesau
archduchy archddugiaeth *eb* archddugiaethau
archegonium archegoniwm *eg*
archer saethwr *eg* saethwyr
archery saethyddiaeth *eb*
archetype archdeip *eg* archdeipiau
Archimedean drill dril Archimedes *eg* driliau Archimedes
Archimedean spiral sbiral Archimedes *eb* sbiralau Archimedes
architect pensaer *eg* penseiri
architectural pensaernïol *ans*
architectural art celfyddyd bensaernïol *eb*
architectural style arddull pensaernïol *eg* arddulliau pensaernïol
architecture pensaernïaeth *eb*
architecture saernïaeth *eb*
architrave architraf *eg* architrafau
architrave moulding mowldin architraf *eg* mowldinau architraf
archive *n* archif *eg* archifau
archive *v* archifo *be*
archive file ffeil archif *eb* ffeiliau archif
archive record cofnod archifol *eg* cofnodion archifol
archive tape tâp archifol *eg* tapiau archifol
archiving system system archifo *eb* systemau archifo
archivist archifydd *eg* archifyddion
archivolt moltas *eg* molteisi
arctangent gwrthdangiad *eg* gwrthdangiadau
Arctic Arctig *eg*
arctic air aer arctig *eg*
arctic alpine arctig alpinaidd *eg*
arcuate bwaog *ans*
are (unit of area) âr *eg* arau
area (=district in general) ardal *eb* ardaloedd
area (=extent or measure of a surface) arwynebedd *eg* arwynebeddau
area (=region or tract) rhanbarth *eg* rhanbarthau
area (=scope or range of activity) maes *eg* meysydd
area (=section or part) adran *eb* adrannau
area network rhwydwaith ardal *eg*
area of great environmental value ardal o werth amgylcheddol mawr *eb* ardaloedd o werth amgylcheddol mawr
area of scenic attraction ardal hynod o hardd *eb* ardaloedd hynod o hardd
area of scenic beauty ardal â golygfeydd prydferth *eb* ardaloedd â golygfeydd prydferth
area of the sector arwynebedd y sector *eg*
area of triangle arwynebedd triongl *eg*
area sample samplu ardal *be*
area school ysgol ardal *eb* ysgolion ardal
areal differentiation gwahaniaethiad arwynebedd *eg*
arena arena *eb* arenau
arenaceous tywodlyd *ans*
arene aren *eg* arenau
areolar tissue meinwe areolaidd *eb*
arête crib *eg/b* cribau
Argand diagram diagram Argand *eg*
argenine argenin *eg*
Argentine *adj* Archentaidd *ans*
Argentine *n* Archentwr *eg* Archentwyr
argillaceous cleiog *ans*
arginine arginin *eg*
arginine side-chain ochr-gadwyn arginin *eb*
argon (Ar) argon *eg*
argument (=amplitude) arg *eg* argiau
argument (=debate) dadl *eb* dadleuon
argument (=reasoning) ymresymiad *eg* ymresymiadau
arhant/arahant arhant/arahant
arhat arhat
arhythmic arhythmig *ans*
aria aria *eb* ariâu
arid cras *ans*
arioso arioso *eg* ariosi
aristocracy pendefigaeth *eb*
aristocrat pendefig *eg* pendefigion
arithmetic rhifyddeg *eb*
arithmetic base rhifyddeg bôn *eb*
arithmetic mean cymedr rhifyddol *eg*
arithmetic overflow gorlif rhifyddol *eg*
arithmetic shift syfliad rhifyddol *eg* syfliadau rhifyddol
arithmetical rhifyddol *ans*
arithmetical progression dilyniant rhifyddol *eg*
arithmetician rhifyddwr *eg* rhifyddwyr
arithmetic-logic unit (ALU) uned rifyddeg-resymeg *eb* unedau rhifyddeg-resymeg
arithmogon rhifogon *eg* rhifogonau
Arkansas oilstone carreg hogi Arkansas *eb*
arm *n* braich *eb* breichiau
arm (in dancing) *v* breichio *be*
arm (with weapons) *v* arfogi *be*
arm jump naid braich *eb* neidiau braich
arm jumping braich-neidio *be*
arm ladder ysgol fraich *eb* ysgolion braich
arm palette palet braich *eg*
arm walking braich-gerdded *be*
armada armada *eb* armadau
armament industry diwydiant arfau *eg* diwydiannau arfau
armaments arfau *ell*
armature armatwr *eg* armatyrau
armchair cadair freichiau *eb* cadeiriau breichiau
armed neutrality niwtraliaeth arfog *eb*
armhole twll llawes *eg* tyllau llewys
armhole facing wynebyn twll llawes *eg* wynebynnau twll llawes
Arminian *adj* Arminaidd *ans*

Arminian *n* Arminiad *eg* Arminiaid
Arminianism Arminiaeth *eb*
armistice cadoediad *eg* cadoediadau
armonica armonica *eg* armonicau
armour arfogaeth *eb*
armour bright arfloyw *ans*
armoured division adran arfog *eb* adrannau arfog
armoured hose arfbib *eb* arfbibau
armoured ply pren haengaled *eg*
armoury ystordy arfau *eg* ystordai arfau
armpit cesail *eb* ceseiliau
arms bend breichiau'n blyg
arms race ras arfau *eb*
arms sideways breichiau ar led
arms swinging swingio'r breichiau *be*
arms upwards breichiau i fyny
army byddin *eb* byddinoedd
army division adran o'r fyddin *eb* adrannau'r fyddin
Army High Command Pen Reolaeth y Fyddin *eb*
army officer swyddog o'r fyddin *eg* swyddogion y fyddin
Arnulph Arnwlff *eg*
aroma arogl *eg* aroglau
aromatic (in chemistry) aromatig *ans*
aromatic (in general) persawrus *ans*
around o amgylch *adf*
arpeggio arpeggio *eg* arpeggi
arpeggio 6/4 chord cord 6/4 arpeggio *eg* cordiau 6/4 arpeggio
arraign cyhuddo *be*
arrange trefnu *be*
arrange horizontally trefnu'n llorweddol *be*
arrange icons trefnu eiconau *be*
arrange object trefnu gwrthrych *be*
arrange order gosod trefn *be*
arrange vertically trefnu'n fertigol *be*
arrange windows trefnu ffenestri *be*
arrange windows horizontal trefnu ffenestri'n llorweddol *be*
arrange windows vertical trefnu ffenestri'n fertigol *be*
arrangement (=preparation) trefniad *eg* trefniadau
arrangement (in music, building etc) trefniant *eg* trefniannau
arranger trefnydd *eg* trefnyddion
arras brithlen *eb* brithlenni
array arae *eb* araeau
arrearage ôl-ddylediaeth *eb*
arrears ôl-ddyled *eb* ôl-ddyledion
arrears of rent ôl-ddyledion rhent *ell*
arrest *n* arestiad *eg* arestiadau
arrest *v* arestio *be*
arris ymyl fain *eb* ymylon main
arrival (of person) dyfodiad *eg* dyfodiaid
arrival and departure cyrraedd a gadael
arrive cyrraedd *be*
arrow saeth *eb* saethau
arrow concave saeth geugrom *eb* saethau ceugrwm
arrow diagram diagram saeth *eg* diagramau saeth
arrow key bysell saeth *eb* bysellau saeth
arrow style arddull saeth *eg* arddulliau saeth
arrowhead pen saeth *eg* pennau saethau
arrowhead tack tac pen saeth *eg* taciau pen saeth
arrowloop agen saethu *eb* agennau saethu
arrowroot arorwt *eg*
arsenal (=weapons store) arfdy *eg* arfdai
arsenal (in geography) arsenal *eg* arsenalau
arsenate(III) ion ïon arsenad(III) *eg* ïonau arsenad(III)
arsenate(V) ion ïon arsenad(V) *eg* ïonau arsenad(V)
arsenic (As) arsenig *eg*
arsenic trichloride arsenig triclorid *eg*
arsenic(III) oxide arsenig(III) ocsid *eg*
arsenic(V) oxide arsenig(V) ocsid *eg*
arsine arsin *eg*
arson llosgi bwriadol *be*
art (in full) celfyddyd *eb* celfyddydau
art (short form) celf *eb*
art board bwrdd arlunio *eg* byrddau arlunio
art form ffurf gelf *eb* ffurfiau celf
art materials defnyddiau celf *ell*
Art Nouveau Art Nouveau *eb*
art package pecyn arlunio *eg* pecynnau arlunio
art therapist therapydd celf *eg* therapyddion celf
art vocabulary geirfa gelf *eb*
artefact arteffact *eg* arteffactau
arterial rhydwelïol *ans*
arterial line llinell rhydweli *eb* llinellau rhydwelïau
arterial road ffordd brifwythiennol *eb* ffyrdd prifwythiennol
arteriole rhydwelïyn *eg* rhydwelïau
arteriosclerosis arteriosglerosis *eg*
artery (in anatomy) rhydweli *eb* rhydwelïau
artery (of communication) prif wythïen *eb* prif wythiennau
artesian well ffynnon artesaidd *eb* ffynhonnau artesaidd
arthritis arthritis *eg*
arthropod arthropod *eg* arthropodau
Arthurian legend chwedl Arthuraidd *eb* chwedlau Arthuraidd
artic skua sgiwen y gogledd *eb* sgiwennod y gogledd
artichoke artisiog *eg* artisiogau
article erthygl *eb* erthyglau
articles of association erthyglau cymdeithasiad *ell*
articles of the treaty of Rome erthyglau cytundeb Rhufain *ell*
articulate (=jointed) *adj* cymalog *ans*
articulate (of bones) *v* ymgymalu *be*
articulate (of instrument) *v* canu'n lân *be*
articulate (of speech) *adj* croyw *ans*
articulate (of voice) *v* ynganu *be*
articulate performer (of gymnast) perfformiwr cymalog *eg* perfformwyr cymalog
articulated (of skeleton, vehicle) cymalog *ans*

articulation (of instrument) canu glân *be*
articulation (of voice) ynganiad *eg*
articulatory loop cylch ynganu *eg*
artificial (=fake) ffug *ans*
artificial (=imitating the natural) artiffisial *ans*
artificial (of fabricated objects) gwneud *ans*
artificial (of teeth, limbs) gosod *ans*
artificial harmonics cyseiniau gwneud *ell*
artificial insemination semenu artiffisial *be*
artificial intelligence deallusrwydd artiffisial *eg*
artificial kidney aren artiffisial *eb* arennau artiffisial
artificial light golau artiffisial *eg*
▶ **artificial limb** aelod artiffisial *eg* aelodau artiffisial
artificial manure gwrtaith artiffisial *eg* gwrteithiau artiffisial
artificial marble marmor artiffisial *eg*
artificial respiration resbiradaeth artiffisial *eb*
artificial seasoning sychu mewn odyn *be*
artificial silk sidan gwneud *eg*
artificial stone carreg ffug *eb* cerrig ffug
artificial stonework gwaith cerrig ffug *eg*
artificial ventilation awyru artiffisial *be*
artificial whetstone carreg hogi wneud *eb* cerrig hogi gwneud
artillery magnelaeth *eb*
artillery range (=firing range) maes tanio *eg* meysydd tanio
artilleryman magnelwr *eg* magnelwyr
artisan crefftwr *eg* crefftwyr
artisan painter arlunydd gwlad *eg* arlunwyr gwlad
Artisans' Dwelling Act Deddf Anheddau'r Gweithwyr *eb*
artist (=painter) arlunydd *eg* arlunwyr
artist (=practitioner of any art) artist *eg* artistiaid
artistic (of natural skill) celfydd *ans*
artistic (relating to art) artistig *ans*
artistic intention bwriad artistig *eg* bwriadau artistig
artist's canvas cynfas arlunio *eg* cynfasau arlunio
artist's materials defnyddiau arlunio *ell*
artist's reconstruction adluniad arlunydd *eg* adluniadau arlunydd
arts and entertainment celfyddydau ac adloniant
Aryan *adj* Ariaidd *ans*
Aryan *n* Ariad *eg* Ariaid
Aryan Race Hil Ariaidd *eb*
aryl aryl *eg*
as and when necessary yn ôl yr angen
as described yn ôl y disgrifiad
as high as cyfuwch â *ans*
as indicated by fel y dangosir gan
as is (of condition) fel y mae
AS level Safon Uwch Atodol *eb*
asbestos asbestos *eg*
asbestos glove maneg asbestos *eb* menig asbestos
asbestos mat mat asbestos *eg* matiau asbestos
asbestos pad pad asbestos *eg* padiau asbestos
ascend esgyn *be*
ascendancy goruchafiaeth *eb*
ascender (in general) esgynnwr *eg* esgynwyr
ascender (in typography) esgynnydd *eg* esgynyddion
ascending esgynnol *ans*
ascending colon colon esgynnol *eg*
ascending order trefn esgynnol *eb*
ascending powers pwerau esgynnol *ell*
ascending scale graddfa esgyn *eb* graddfeydd esgyn
ascending sort trefniad esgynnol *eg* trefniadau esgynnol
ascension esgyniad *eg* esgyniadau
Ascension Thursday Dydd Iau Dyrchafael *eg*
ascent esgyniad *eg* esgyniadau
ascetic asgetig *ans*
Ascetic Theology Diwinyddiaeth Asgetig *eb*
asceticism asgetigiaeth *eb*
ASCII code cod ASCII *eg*
ascites asgites *eg*
ascorbic acid asid asgorbig *eg*
ascribe glory to God gogoneddu Duw *be*
ascription (of glory) gogoneddiad *eg*
ascus asgws *eg* asgi
asepsis asepsis *eg*
aseptic aseptig *ans*
aseptic technique techneg aseptig *eb* technegau aseptig
asexual anrhywiol *ans*
asexual reproduction atgynhyrchu anrhywiol *be*
ash *n* lludw *eg*
ash *v* llwyrlosgi *be*
ash content cynnwys lludw *eg*
ash tray blwch llwch *eg* blychau llwch
ash tree onnen *eb* ynn
Ash Wednesday Dydd Mercher Lludw *eg*
Asharite Asharitiad *eg* Asharitiaid
ashlar (of masonry work) gwaith cerrig nadd *eg*
ashlar (of stone) carreg nadd *eb* cerrig nadd
ashlar finish gorffeniad cerrig nadd *eg*
ashlaring (of boarding) estyll croglofft *ell*
ashrama / aśrama ashrama / aśrama *ell*
asiento asiento *eg*
askew (in carpentry) ar letraws *ans*
asparagine asparagin *eg*
asparagus asbaragws *eg*
aspartase asbartas *eg*
aspartic acid asid asbartig *eg*
aspect agwedd *eb* agweddau
aspects of dance agweddau ar ddawnsiau *ell*
Asperger's syndrome syndrom Asperger *eg*
aspersion (liturgical) taenelliad *eg*
asphalt asffalt *eg*
asphyxia myctod *eg*
asphyxiate mygu *be*
aspic asbig *eg*
aspirate sugno *be*
aspiration (=desire) dyhead *eg* dyheadau

eg/b enw gwrywaidd/benywaidd, *masculine/feminine noun* ***ell*** enw lluosog, *plural noun* ***v*** berf, *verb* ***n*** enw, *noun* ▶ wedi newid, *changed*

aspiration (=drawing of breath) sugniad *eg* sugniadau
assart asart *eg* asartau
assassin asasin *eg* asasiniaid
assassination llofruddiaeth *eb*
assault *n* ymosodiad *eg* ymosodiadau
assault *v* ymosod *be*
assault and battery ymosod a churo
assay mark nod prawf *eg* nodau prawf
assayable solder sodr prawf arian *eg* sodrau prawf arian
assemblage casgliad *eg* casgliadau
assemble (=fit together) cydosod *be*
assembler cydosodydd *eg* cydosodyddion
assembly (in school) gwasanaeth *eg* gwasanaethau
assembly (of parts) cydosodiad *eg* cydosodiadau
assembly (political) cynulliad *eg* cynulliadau
assembly (religious) cymanfa *eb* cymanfaoedd
assembly drawing (of act) lluniadu cydosod *be*
assembly drawing (of object) lluniad cydosod *eg* lluniadau cydosod
assembly language iaith gydosod *eb* ieithoedd cydosod
assembly line llinell gydosod *eb* llinellau cydosod
assembly of notables cymanfa'r hynodion *eb*
assembly plant gwaith cydosod *eg* gweithfeydd cydosod
assembly-line production cynhyrchu llinell gydosod *be*
assertive pendant *ans*
assertiveness pendantrwydd *eg*
assertiveness training hyfforddiant pendantrwydd *eg*
assess asesu *be*
assessment asesiad *eg* asesiadau
assessment arrangements trefniadau asesu *ell*
assessment centre canolfan asesu *eb* canolfannau asesu
assessment criterion maen prawf asesu *eg* meini prawf asesu
assessment grid grid asesu *eg* gridiau asesu
assessment guide canllaw asesu *eg* canllawiau asesu
assessment mode modd asesu *eg* moddau asesu
assessment objective amcan asesu *eg* amcanion asesu
assessment of mobility asesu symudedd *be*
assessment plan cynllun asesu *eg* cynlluniau asesu
assessment tool dull asesu *eg* dulliau asesu
assessor aseswr *eg* aseswyr
asset ased *eg* asedau
asset turnover trosiant asedau *eg*
assign neilltuo *be*
assign particle to cell neilltuo gronyn i gell *be*
assignment (=statement that allocates a value to a variable) neilltuad *eg* neilltuadau
assignment (=task allotted to a person) aseiniad *eg* aseiniadau
assimilate *v* cymathu *be*
assimilation (in general) cymathiad *eg*
assimilation (in Piaget's child development model) cydweddiad *eg*
► **assimilative** cymathol *ans*
► **assimilative hyphae** hyffae cymathol *ell*
assimilator *n* cymathyn *eg* cymathion
Assisi embroidery brodwaith Assisi *eg*
assist cynorthwyo *be*
assistance cymorth *eg* cymhorthion
assistance exercise ymarfer cynorthwyo *eg* ymarferion cynorthwyo
assistant cynorthwyydd *eg* cynorthwywyr
assistantship swydd cynorthwyydd *eb* swyddi cynorthwywyr
assisted area ardal gynorthwyedig *eb* ardaloedd cynorthwyedig
assisted transport cludiant cynorthwyedig *eg*
assize brawdlys *eg* brawdlysoedd
assize of arms aséis arfau *eg*
associate member aelod cysylltiol *eg* aelodau cysylltiol
associate nurse nyrs gysylltiol *eb* nyrsys cysylltiol
associated cysylltiol *ans*
associated norm norm cysylltiol *eg*
association (=society) cymdeithas *eb* cymdeithasau
association (ecological) cydgymuned *eb* cydgymunedau
association centre canolfan gydgysylltiol *eb* canolfannau cydgysylltiol
association of ideas cymdeithasiad syniadau *eg*
associative cysylltiadol *ans*
associative agnosia agnosia cysylltiadol *eg*
associative law deddf gysylltiadol *eb* deddfau cysylltiadol
associative memory cof cysylltiadol *eg*
associative play chwarae cysylltiadol *eg*
associative store stôr gysylltiadol *eb* storau cysylltiadol
associator (=connector neurone) niwron cysylltiol *eg* niwronau cysylltiol
assort dosrannu *be*
assorted amrywiol *ans*
assorted colours lliwiau amrywiol *ell*
assortment amrywiaeth *eb* amrywiaethau
assortment of materials amrywiaeth defnyddiau *eb*
assume tybio *be*
assume flesh ymgnawdoli *be*
assumption tybiaeth *eb* tybiaethau
assumption of flesh ymgnawdoliad *eg*
assurance (=certainty) sicrwydd *eg*
assurance (=insurance) yswiriant *eg* yswiriannau
astable multivibrator amlddirgrynydd gwrthsefydlog *eg* amlddirgrynwyr gwrthsefydlog
astatine (At) astatin *eg*
asterisk seren *eb* sêr
asteroid asteroid *eg* asteroidau
asthma asthma *eg*

astigmatism astigmatedd *eg*
astragal astragal *eg* astragalau
astragal moulding mowldin astragal *eg* mowldinau astragal
astral serol *ans*
astride (position) traed ar led
astride jump naid ar led *eb* neidiau ar led
astride vault llofnaid ar led *eb* llofneidiau ar led
astrolabe astrolab *eg*
astrolatry sêr-addoliaeth *eb*
astrological sêr-ddewiniol *ans*
astrology sêr-ddewiniaeth *eb*
astro-mythology sêr-fytholeg *eb*
astronomy seryddiaeth *eb*
astrophysics astroffiseg *eb*
asymmetric anghymesur *ans*
asymmetric digital subscriber line llinell danysgrifio ddigidol anghymesur *eb* llinellau tanysgrifio digidol anghymesur
asymmetric fold plyg anghymesur *eg* plygion anghymesur
asymmetrical anghymesurol *ans*
asymmetry anghymesuredd *eg* anghymesureddau
asymptote asymptot *eg* asymptotau
asymptotic asymptotig *ans*
asynchronous anghydamseredig *ans*
asystole ataliad y galon *eg*
at a discount ar ddisgownt
at a premium ar bremiwm
at an angle ar ongl
at an angle of 35° ar ongl 35°
at home gartref
at par ar lawn werth
at random ar hap
at risk mewn perygl
at the rate of yn ôl y gyfradd o
atactic atactig *ans*
ataxia atacsia *eg*
atheism anffyddiaeth *eb*
atheist anffyddiwr *eg* anffyddwyr
athematic athematig *ans*
atherosclerosis atherosglerosis *eg*
athlete athletwr *eg* athletwyr
athlete in training athletwr sy'n ymarfer *eg* athletwyr sy'n ymarfer
athletic athletaidd *ans*
athletic activity gweithgaredd athletaidd *eg* gweithgareddau athletaidd
athletic performance perfformiad athletaidd *eg*
athletics athletau *ell*
athletics club clwb athletau *eg* clybiau athletau
Atlantic Charter Siarter yr Iwerydd *eg*
Atlantic coast arfordir yr Iwerydd *eg*
Atlantic Revolution, The Chwyldro Môr Iwerydd *eg*
Atlantic roller gwaneg Iwerydd *eb* gwanegau Iwerydd
atlas atlas *eg* atlasau
atman atman *eg*
atmosphere (=mood) awyrgylch *eg/b*
atmosphere (of gases, pressure) atmosffer *eg* atmosfferau
atmospheric atmosfferig *ans*
atmospheric circulation cylchrediad atmosfferig *eg*
atmospheric conditions amodau atmosfferig *ell*
atmospheric pollution llygredd atmosfferig *eg*
atmospheric pressure gwasgedd atmosfferig *eg*
atmospheric process proses atmosfferig *eb* prosesau atmosfferig
atoll atol *eb* atolau
atom atom *eg/b* atomau
atomic atomig *ans*
atomic mass màs atomig *eg*
atomic mass number rhif màs atomig *eg*
atomic number rhif atomig *eg* rhifau atomig
atomic spacing gwahaniad atomig *eg*
atomic structure adeiledd yr atom *eg*
atomicity atomedd *eg*
atomization atomeiddiad *eg*
atomize atomeiddio *be*
atomizer atomadur *eg* atomaduron
atonal digywair *ans*
atonalist digyweirydd *eg* digyweirwyr
atonality digyweiredd *eg*
atone gwneud iawn *be*
atonement iawn *eg*
Atonement, The Iawn, Yr *eg*
atrial atrïaidd *ans*
atrio-ventricular node (AVN) nod atrio-fentriglaidd (NAF) *eg*
atrium atriwm *eg*
atrocity erchyllter *eg* erchyllterau
atrophy *n* crebachiad *eg*
atrophy *v* crebachu *be*
at-symbol (@) symbol at *eg*
attach (=arrest) arestio *be*
attach (=fasten) cydio *be*
attach (a document) atodi *be*
attach data atodi data *be*
attach file atodi ffeil *be*
attached ynghlwm *ans*
attached dune twyn cysylltiedig *eg* twyni cysylltiedig
attachment (=accessory) atodyn *eg* atodion
attachment (=link) cydfan *eg* cydfannau
attachment (=stage in child development) ymlyniad *eg*
attachment (to an e-mail) atodiad *eg* atodiadau
attachment site cyfanbwynt *eg* cyfanbwyntiau
attack *n* ymosodiad *eg* ymosodiadau
attack *v* ymosod *be*
attack on the blade ymosod ar y llafn *be*
attack with edge ymosod â'r min *be*
attacker ymosodwr *eg* ymosodwyr
attacking position safle ymosodol *eg* safleoedd ymosodol

attacking stroke ergyd ymosodol *eb* ergydion ymosodol
attain its bounds cyrraedd ei arffiniau *be*
attainder adendriad *eg*
attainment cyrhaeddiad *eg* cyraeddiadau
attainment keys allweddi cyrhaeddiad *ell*
attainment level lefel cyrhaeddiad *eb* lefelau cyrhaeddiad
attainment of objectives cyflawni amcanion *be*
attainment target targed cyrhaeddiad *eg* targedau cyrhaeddiad
attainment test prawf cyrhaeddiad *eg* profion cyrhaeddiad
attaint adendro *be*
attend (=pay attention) rhoi sylw *be*
attend (school) mynychu *be*
attendance presenoldeb *eg*
attendance allowance lwfans gweini *eg* lwfansau gweini
attendance centre canolfan fynychu *eb* canolfannau mynychu
attendance record cofnod mynychu *eg* cofnodion mynychu
attendant keys cyweiriau perthynol *ell*
attention sylw *eg*
attention deficit disorder
attention deficit hyperactivity disorder anhwylder diffyg canolbwyntio a gorfywiogrwydd *eg*
attention span cyfnod canolbwyntio *eg* cyfnodau canolbwyntio
attentional bias tuedd sylwol *eb*
attentiveness gallu i dalu sylw *eg*
attenuate gwanhau *be*
attenuation gwanhad *eg*
attenuator gwanhadur *eg* gwanaduron
attitude (of aeroplane, rocks) osgo *eg*
attitude (of mind) agwedd *eb* agweddau
attojoule atojoule *eg* atojouleau
attorney twrnai *eg* twrneiod
Attorney-General Twrnai Cyffredinol *eg* Twrneiod Cyffredinol
attract atynnu *be*
attraction atyniad *eg* atyniadau
attractive atyniadol *ans*
attractive (=charming) deniadol *ans*
attractive (of force) atynnol *ans*
attractive force grym atynnol *eg* grymoedd atynnol
attribute priodoledd *eg* priodoleddau
attributes and variates priodoleddau ac amryweddau
attribution priodoliad *eg* priodoliadau
attribution bias tuedd priodoli *eb*
attribution theory damcaniaeth priodoli *eb*
attrition athreuliad *eg*
au gratin au gratin *ans*
aubade aubade *eg* aubades
aubergine planhigyn wy *eg* planhigion wy
auction sale arwerthiant *eg* arwerthiannau
auctioneer arwerthwr *eg* arwerthwyr
audibility clywadwyedd *eg*
audible clywadwy *ans*
audible range amrediad clywadwy *eg*
audience cynulleidfa *eb* cynulleidfaoedd
Audience Court Cwrt Gwrandawiad *eg*
audience engagement ymrwymiad cynulleidfa *eg*
audience expectations disgwyliadau cynulleidfa *ell*
audience reception derbyniad cynulleidfa *eg*
audience survey arolwg cynulleidfa *eg* arolygon cynulleidfa
audio clywedol *ans*
audio book llyfr llafar *eg* llyfrau llafar
audio file ffeil sain *eb* ffeiliau sain
audio frequency amledd awdio *eg*
audio visual aids adnoddau clyweled *ell*
audiogram awdiogram *eg* awdiogramau
audiolingual clywieithol *ans*
audiology clinic clinig clyw *eg* clinigau clyw
audiometer awdiomedr *eg* awdiomedrau
audiometry awdiometreg *eb*
audiotyping clywdeipio *be*
audio-visual scratchpad cof clyweled tymor byr *eg*
audit *n* archwiliad *eg* archwiliadau
audit *v* archwilio *be*
audit agency asiantaeth archwilio *eb* asiantaethau archwilio
audit moderator cymedrolwr archwilio *eg* cymedrolwyr archwilio
audit trail trywydd archwilio *eg* trywyddau archwilio
auditor archwiliwr *eg* archwilwyr
auditor of accounts archwiliwr cyfrifon *eg* archwilwyr cyfrifon
auditory clybodol *ans*
auditory canal tiwb y glust *eg*
auditory capsule cwpan y glust *eg*
auditory discrimination gwahaniaethu sŵn *be*
auditory hair cell cell blewyn y clyw *eb* celloedd blew y clyw
auditory meatus cyntedd y glust *eg*
auditory memory cof clywedol *eg*
auditory nerve nerf y clyw *eg*
auditory perception canfod sŵn *be*
auditory training hyfforddiant gwrando *eg*
augend awgend *eg* awgendau
auger taradr *eg* terydr
auger bit ebill taradr *eg* ebillion taradr
augment (=add to) ychwanegu *be*
augment (in music) estyn *be*
augmentation (=addition) ychwanegiad *eg* ychwanegiadau
augmentation (in music) estyniad *eg* estyniadau
Augmentations Court Cwrt yr Ychwanegiadau *eg*
augmented (in music) estynedig *ans*
augmented chord cord estynedig *eg* cordiau estynedig
augmented interval cyfwng estynedig *eg* cyfyngau estynedig

augmented seventh chord cord y seithfed estynedig *eg* cordiau'r seithfed estynedig
augmented sixth chord cord y chweched estynedig *eg* cordiau'r chweched estynedig
augmenter ychwanegydd *eg* ychwanegyddion
augury darogan *eg* daroganau
Augustinian *adj* Awstinaidd *ans*
Augustinian *n* Awstiniad *eg* Awstiniaid
Augustinian Canons Canoniaid Awstinaidd *ell*
Augustinian Friars Brodyr Sant Awstin *ell*
Augustinian Order Urdd Sant Awstin *eb*
Augustinian theodicy theodiciaeth Awstin *eb*
Augustinianism Awstiniaeth *eb*
Auld Alliance Hen Gynghrair *eb*
aulos awlos *eg* awloi
aura awra *eb*
aural clywedol *ans*
aural aids cymhorthion clywedol *ell*
aural perception canfyddiad clywedol *eg*
aural stimulation cyffroad clywedol *eg*
aural stimulus ysgogiad clywadwy *eg* ysgogiadau clywadwy
aural work sain glust *eb*
aureole lleugylch *eg* lleugylchoedd
auricle awrigl *eg* awriglau
auricular confession cyffes gudd *eb* cyffesion cudd
aurora awrora *eg* awrorau
Aurora Australis Goleuni'r De *eg*
Aurora Borealis Goleuni'r Gogledd *eg*
auroral awroraidd *ans*
austenite awstenit *eg* awstenitiau
austerity llymder *eg*
Austria Awstria *eb*
Austro-Prussian war rhyfel Awstria a Phrwsia *eg*
Austro-Piedmontese war rhyfel Awstria a Piedmont *eg*
autarchy awtarchiaeth *eb*
autecology awtecoleg *eb*
auteur auteur *eg* auteurs
authentic dilys *ans*
authentic mode modd sylfaenol *eg* moddau sylfaenol
authenticate dilysu *be*
authenticating body corff dilysu *eg* cyrff dilysu
authentication dilysiad *eg*
authentication dilysu *be*
authenticity dilysrwydd *eg*
authigenic awthigenig *ans*
author awdur *eg* awduron
authoring awduro *be*
authoring package pecyn awduro *eg* pecynnau awduro
authoritarian awdurdodaidd *ans*
authoritarian parenting magu gorawdurdodol *be*
authoritarianism awdurdodaeth *eb*
authoritative awdurdodol *ans*
authoritative parenting magu awdurdodol *be*
authority awdurdod *eg* awdurdodau
authorization awdurdodiad *eg* awdurdodiadau
authorize awdurdodi *be*
authorized awdurdodedig *ans*
authorized version fersiwn awdurdodedig *eg*
autism awtistiaeth *eb*
autistic awtistig *ans*
autistic child plentyn awtistig *eg* plant awtistig
autistic disorder anhwylder awtistig *eg*
autistic syndrome disorder anhwylder syndrom awtistiaeth *eg*
auto awto *ans*
auto arrange awtodrefnu *be*
auto closing awto-gau *be*
auto detect awtoganfod *be*
auto line length hyd llinell awtomatig *eg*
auto update awtoddiweddaru *be*
autoabstract to presentation awtogrynhoi ar gyfer cyflwyniad *be*
autoalign awto-alinio *be*
auto-analyser dadansoddydd awtomatig *eg* dadansoddyddion awtomatig
autoarrange awtodrefnu *be*
autobiographical memory cof hunangofiannol *eg*
autocatalysis awtocatalysis *ans*
autochthonous brodorol *ans*
autoclave ffwrn aerglos *eb* ffyrnau aerglos
autocorrect awtogywiro *be*
autocorrect configuration ffurfweddiad awtogywiro *eg* ffurfweddiadau awtogywiro
autocorrelation hunangydberthynas *eb* hunangydberthnasau
autocracy unbennaeth *eb*
autocrat unben *eg* unbeniaid
autocratic unbenaethol *ans*
autocratic empire ymerodraeth unbenaethol *eb*
autocratic leader arweinydd unbenaethol *eg*
autocratic rule rheolaeth unbenaethol *eb*
autofill awtolanw *be*
autofilter awtohidlydd *eg* awtohidlyddion
autofit awtoffitio *be*
autofit frame height uchder ffrâm awtoffitio *eg*
autofit frame width lled ffrâm awtoffitio *eg*
autofit height uchder awtoffitio *eg*
autofit width lled awtoffitio *eg*
autoformat awtofformat *eg* awtofformatau
autoformat chart siart awtofformat *eg* siartiau awtofformat
autoformat configuration ffurfweddiad awtofformat *eg* ffurfweddiadau awtofformat
autoformat table tabl awtofformat *eg* tablau awtofformat
autogenic hunangenedledig *ans*
autograph llofnod *eg* llofnodion
autoharp telyn ddodi *eb* telynau dodi
autoheight awto-uchder *eg*
autohorizontal awtolorweddol *ans*
► **autohyphenate** awtogysylltnodi *be*

autoimmunity awtoimiwnedd *eg*
autoinclude awtogynnwys *be*
autoincrement awtogynyddiad *eg* awtogynyddiadau
autoinput awtofewnbwn *eg* awtofewnbynnau
autoload awtolwytho *be*
automail awtobost *eg*
automate awtomeiddio *be*
automated system system wedi'i hawtomeiddio *eb*
automatic awtomatig *ans*
automatic centre punch pwnsh canoli awtomatig *eg* pynsiau canoli awtomatig
automatic checking gwirio awtomatig *be*
automatic cut-off torbwynt awtomatig *eg* torbwyntiau awtomatig
automatic feed porthiant awtomatig *eg* porthiannau awtomatig
automatic gearbox gerbocs awtomatig *eg* gerbocsys awtomatig
automatic hyphenation cysylltnodi awtomatig *be*
automatic machine peiriant awtomatig *eg* peiriannau awtomatig
automatic processing prosesu awtomatig *be*
automatic reciprocation cilyddu awtomatig *be*
automatic row break toriad rhes awtomatig *eg* toriadau rhes awtomatig
automatic sort trefnu awtomatig *be*
automatic stabilizer sefydlogydd awtomatig *eg* sefydlogyddion awtomatig
automatic thoughts meddyliau awtomatig *ell*
automatic word completion cwblhau geiriau awtomatig *be*
automatic wrap-around amlap awtomatig *eg* amlapiau awtomatig
automation awtomatiaeth *eb*
automation equipment offer awtomatiaeth *ell*
automation process proses awtomatiaeth *eb* prosesau awtomatiaeth
automatism awtomatedd *eb*
automobile modur *eg* moduron
automobile component cydran modur *eb* cydrannau moduron
automorphic awtomorffig *ans*
autonomic awtonomig *ans*
autonomic nervous system cyfundrefn nerfol awtonomig *eb*
autonomous ymreolaethol *ans*
autonomous reader darllenydd annibynnol *eg* darllenwyr annibynnol
autonomous user defnyddiwr annibynnol *eg* defnyddwyr annibynnol
autonomy ymreolaeth *eb*
autonumbering awtorifo *be*
autooutline *n* awtoamlinelliad *eg* awtoamlinelliadau
autopilot awtobeilot *eg*
autopilot agenda agenda awtobeilot *eg* agendâu awtobeilot
autopilot fax ffacs awtobeilot *eg* ffacsys awtobeilot
autopilot form ffurflen awtobeilot *eb* ffurflenni awtobeilot
autopilot group element elfen grŵp awtobeilot *eb* elfennau grŵp awtobeilot
autopilot internet setup gosodiad rhyngrwyd awtobeilot *eg* gosodiadau rhyngrwyd awtobeilot
autopilot letter llythyr awtobeilot *eg* llythyrau awtobeilot
autopilot memo memo awtobeilot *eg* memos awtobeilot
autopilot table tabl awtobeilot *eg* tablau awtobeilot
autopilot table element elfen tabl awtobeilot *eb* elfennau tabl awtobeilot
autopilot web page tudalen we awtobeilot *eb* tudalennau gwe awtobeilot
autopolyploid awtopolyploid *eg*
autopolyploidy awtopolyploidi *eg*
autopsy awtopsi *eg*
autorefresh awtoadnewyddu *be*
autoregression ymatchweliad *eg* ymatchweliadau
autoregressive ymatchwelaidd *ans*
autoreload awtoail-lwytho *be*
autorepeat awtoailadrodd *be*
autosave awtogadw *be*
autosize text awtosiapio testun *be*
autosomal awtosomaidd *ans*
autosome awtosom *eg* awtosomau
autospellcheck awtowirio sillafu *be*
autostart awtogychwyn *be*
autoswitch awtonewid *be*
autotext awtodestun *eg* awtodestunau
autotext directory cyfeiriadur awtodestun *eg* cyfeiriaduron awtodestun
autotopagnosia awtotopagnosia *eg*
autotroph hunanborthwr *eg* hunanborthwyr
autotype recognition adnabod awtodeip *be*
autoupdate awtoddiweddaru *be*
autovalue awto-werth *eg* awtowerthoedd
autovertical awtofertigol *ans*
autowidth awtoled *eg*
autumn equinox cyhydnos yr hydref *eb*
auxiliary (=assistant) cynorthwyol *ans*
auxiliary (in general) ategol *ans*
auxiliary (of musical note, chord) tonnog *ans*
auxiliary 6/4 chord cord 6/4 tonnog *eg* cordiau 6/4 tonnog
auxiliary circle cylch ategol *eb* cylchoedd ategol
auxiliary circle method dull cylch ategol *eg*
auxiliary elevation golwg ategol *eg* golygon ategol
auxiliary equation hafaliad ategol *eg* hafaliadau ategol
auxiliary front elevation blaenolwg ategol *eg* blaenolygon ategol
auxiliary industry diwydiant cynorthwyol *eg* diwydiannau cynorthwyol
auxiliary plan (of view) uwcholwg ategol *eg* uwcholygon ategol
auxiliary projection tafluniad ategol *eg* tafluniadau ategol
auxiliary teacher (female) athrawes gynorthwyol *eb* athrawesau cynorthwyol

auxiliary teacher (male) athro cynorthwyol *eg* athrawon cynorthwyol
auxiliary view golwg ategol *eg* golygon ategol
auxin awcsin *eg* awcsinau
availability argaeledd *eg*
availability heuristic hewristig argaeledd *eg*
available ar gael *ans*
available disk space lle ar gael ar ddisg *eg*
available field maes ar gael *eg* meysydd ar gael
available relief tirwedd leol *eb* tirweddau lleol
avalanche eirlithrad *eg* eirlithradau
avant-garde avant-garde *eg/b*
avarice cybydd-dod *eg*
avaricious cybyddlyd *ans*
avatar /avatara avatar /avatara *eg*
aventurine afentwrin *eg*
avenue rhodfa *eb* rhodfeydd
average *n* cyfartaledd *eg* cyfartaleddau
average (=ordinary standard) *adj* canolig *ans*
average (worked out mathematically) *adj* cyfartalog *ans*
average ability gallu canolig *eg*
average attainment cyrhaeddiad ar gyfartaledd *eg*
average capital cyfalaf cyfartalog *eg*
average child plentyn cyffredin *eg* plant cyffredin
average cost cost gyfartalog *eb* costau cyfartalog
AVERAGE function ffwythiant AVERAGE *eg* fwythiannau AVERAGE
average income incwm cyfartalog *eg* incymau cyfartalog
average price pris cyfartalog *eg* prisiau cyfartalog
average product cynnyrch cyfartalog *eg*
average propensity to consume tuedd gyfartalog i ddefnyddio *eb*
average propensity to save tuedd gyfartalog i gynilo *eb*
average rainfall glawiad cyfartalog *eg* glawiadau cyfartalog
average rate cyfradd gyfartalog *eb* cyfraddau cyfartalog
average rate of return cyfradd adenillion gyfartalog *eb*
average rep time amser cyfartalog ail-wneud *eg*
average revenue refeniw cyfartalog *eg*
average scale factor ffactor graddfa gyfartalog *eb*
average stock stoc gyfartalog *eb*
average temperature tymheredd cyfartalog *eg* tymereddau cyfartalog
aversion therapy therapi anghymell *eg*
aversive stimulus ysgogiad anghymhellol *eg* ysgogiadau atgas
Avery label label Avery *eb* labelau Avery
aviation hedfan *be*
aviation industry diwydiant awyrennau *eg*
Avignon Papacy Pabaeth Avignon *eb*
avocado pear afocado *eg* afocados
avoid osgoi *be*
avoidance behaviour ymddygiad osgoi *eg*
avoidance response ymateb osgoi *eg* ymatebion osgoi
avoidant attachment ymlyniad osgoi *eg* ymlyniadau osgoi
avoided cadence diweddeb annisgwyl *eb* diweddebau annisgwyl
award (=give prize) *v* gwobrwyo *be*
award (=judgement) *n* dyfarniad *eg* dyfarniadau
award (=prize) *n* gwobr *eb* gwobrau
award (by referee's decision) *v* dyfarnu *be*
award damages dyfarnu iawndal *be*
awarding body corff dyfarnu *eg* cyrff dyfarnu
awareness ymwybyddiaeth *eb*
awareness of space ymwybyddiaeth o ofod *eb*
awareness of the dangers ymwybyddiaeth o beryglon *eb*
awayswinger gwyriad allan *eg* gwyriadau allan
awkward lletchwith *ans*
awl mynawyd *eg* mynawydau
awn col *eg* colion
axe bwyell *eb* bwyeill
axe head pen bwyell *eg* pennau bwyeill
axes of reference echelinau lleoli *ell*
axial echelinol *ans*
axial plane plân echelinol *eg* planau echelinol
axial skeleton sgerbwd echelinol *eg* sgerbydau echelinol
axial trajectory taflwybr echelinol *eg* taflwybrau echelinol
axil cesail *eb* ceseiliau
axillary ceseilaidd *ans*
axillary bud blaguryn ceseilaidd *eg* blagur ceseilaidd
axiom gwireb *eb* gwirebau
axiomatic gwirebol *ans*
axis (of bone; in psychology) acsis *eg*
axis (of line) echelin *eb* echelinau
axis of fold echelin plyg *eb* echelinau plyg
axis of symmetry echelin cymesuredd *eb*
Axis Powers Pwerau'r Axis *ell*
axle echel *eb* echelau
axle pulley echel bwli *eb* echelau pwli
axon acson *eg* acsonau
axon hillock bryncyn acson *eg*
ayah ayah *eg* ayat
ayre ayre *eb* ayres
azeotrope aseotrop *eg* aseotropau
azide ion ïon asaid *eg* ïonau asaid
azimuth asimwth *eg* asimwthau
azimuthal projection tafluniad asimwthol *eg* tafluniadau asimwthol
azo dye llifyn aso *eg* llifynnau aso
azomethane asomethan *eg*
azonal anaeddfed *ans*
Azores high gwasgedd uchel Azores *eg*
Aztec *adj* Astecaidd *ans*
Aztec *n* Astec *eg* Asteciaid
azygotic asygotig *ans*

B

B lymphocyte lymffocyt B *eg* lymffocytau B
B major B fwyaf *eb*
B minor B leiaf *eb*
babbitt metal metel babbitt *eg*
babble baldordd *eg*
babbling (in development of children's speech) clebran baban *be*
baby buggy coets baban *eb* coetsys babanod
baby lotion trwyth baban *eg*
baby massage tylino baban *be*
baby signing arwyddo baban *be*
babygro dilledyn babygro *eg* dillad babygro
babyhood babandod *eg*
babysit gwarchod *be*
babysitter gwarchodwr *eg* gwarchodwyr
baby-walker cerddwr *eg* cerddwyr
baccalaureate bagloriaeth *eb*
back (command button) nôl *adf*
back (in general) *n* cefn *eg* cefnau
back (in needlework) *v* rhoi cefnyn *be*
back (of person) *n* olwr *eg* olwyr
back arrow saeth yn ôl *eb*
back bench mainc gefn *eb* meinciau cefn
back board cefnfwrdd *eg* cefnfyrddau
back bodice bodis cefn *eg* bodisiau cefn
back button (on computer screen) botwm yn ôl *eg* botymau yn ôl
back drop cefnlen *eb* cefnlenni
back electromotive force ôl-rym electromotif *eg*
back facing wynebyn cefn *eg* wynebynnau cefn
back fill ôl-lenwi *be*
back iron haearn cefn *eg* heyrn cefn
back mutation ôl-fwtaniad *eg* ôl-fwtaniadau
back opening agoriad cefn *eg* agoriadau cefn
back pay ôl-dâl *eg*
back roller rholer ôl *eg* rholeri ôl
back row rheng ôl *eb* rhengoedd ôl
back screen sgrin gefn *eb* sgriniau cefn
back sight ôl-olwg *eg*
back spring sbring cefn *eg* sbringiau cefn
back stick (spinning) ffon wasgu *eb* ffyn gwasgu
back sticks (in hockey) cefn ffyn *ell*
back stitch pwyth ôl *eg* pwythau ôl
back stop stop cefn *eg* stopiau cefn
back to back (do-si-do) cefn wrth gefn *adf*
back to back (of houses) cefngefn *ans*
back to back houses tai cefngefn *ell*
back to main menu nôl i'r brif ddewislen
back vault llofnaid gefn *eb* llofneidiau cefn
back view cefnlun *eg* cefnluniau
back wall mur cefn *eg* muriau cefn
back wall out of court line ffin gefn *eb* ffiniau cefn
backbearing ôl-gyfeiriad *eg* ôl-gyfeiriadau
backboard bwrdd cefn *eg* byrddau cefn
backbone asgwrn cefn *eg* esgyrn cefn
backcloth cefnlen *eb* cefnlenni
backcrawl nofio ar y cefn *be*
backcross ôl-groesiad *eg* ôl-groesiadau
backdoor drws cefn *eg* drysau cefn
backend processor ôl-brosesydd *eg* ôl-brosesyddion
backfire tanio'n ôl *be*
backflap hinge colfach llydan *eg* colfachau llydan
backflow ôl-lifiad *eg* ôl-lifiadau
background cefndir *eg* cefndiroedd
background colour lliw cefndir *eg* lliwiau cefndir
background count cyfrif cefndir *eg*
background count rate cyfradd cyfrif cefndir *eb*
background design dyluniad cefndir *eg* dyluniadau cefndir
background enamel enamel cefndir *eg*
background heat gwres cefndir *eg*
background music cerddoriaeth gefndir *eb*
background process proses gefndir *eb* prosesau cefndir
background processing prosesu cefndir *be*
background punch pwnsh cefndir *eg* pynsiau cefndir
background study astudiaeth gefndir *eb* astudiaethau cefndir
backhand gwrthlaw *eb*
backhand side ochr wrthlaw *eb* ochrau gwrthlaw
backhand stroke ergyd wrthlaw *eb* ergydion gwrthlaw
back-heel *v* ôl-sodli *be*
backing (=musical accompaniment) cyfeiliant *eg*
backing (=support) cefnogaeth *eb*
backing (material) cefnyn *eg* cefnynnau
backing (of wind) gwrthwyro *be*
backing (tambour door) cymorth cefn *eg* cymhorthion cefn
backing board bwrdd cefnu *eg* byrddau cefnu
backing hammer morthwyl cefnu *eg* morthwylion cefnu
backing off cefnu *be*
backing sheet dalen gefnu *eb* dalennau cefnu
backing store storfa gynorthwyol *eb* storfeydd cynorthwyol

backland (=hinterland) cefnwlad *eb* cefnwledydd
backlash adlach *eb* adlachau
back-payment ôl-daliad *eg* ôl-daliadau
backplate cefnblat *eg* cefnblatiau
backrest cefnell *eb* cefnellau
backsaw llif gefn *eb* llifiau cefn
backshore cefndraeth *eg* cefndraethau
▶ **backslash** ôl-slaes *eg* ôl-slaesau
backslope cefnlethr *eg* cefnlethrau
backspace olio *be*
▶ **BACKSPACE key** bysell BACKSPACE *eb* bysellau BACKSPACE
backspin troelli o dan y bêl *be*
backstitch ôl-bwyth *eg* ôl-bwythau
backstroke nofio ar y cefn *be*
back-up *adj* wrth gefn *ans*
back-up (=support) *n* cefnogaeth *eb*
back-up (of copy) *n* copi wrth gefn *eg* copïau wrth gefn
back-up copy copi wrth gefn *eg* copïau wrth gefn
back-up power supply cyflenwad pŵer wrth gefn *eg* cyflenwadau pŵer wrth gefn
back-up storage storfa wrth gefn *eb* storfeydd wrth gefn
back-up support ategiad *eg* ategiadau
Backus-Naur form ffurf Backus-Naur *eb*
backwall cefnfur *eg* cefnfuriau
backward (=primitive) annatblygedig *ans*
backward (=slow) araf *ans*
backward (of movement) yn ôl
backward area ardal arafgynnydd *eb* ardaloedd arafgynnydd
backward chaining cadwyno'n ôl *be*
backward child plentyn araf *eg* plant araf
backward hanging hongian ôl *be*
backward masking masgio am yn ôl *be*
backward point ôl-bwynt *eg* ôl-bwyntiau
backward reaction ôl-adwaith *eg*
backward roll rhôl yn ôl *eb* rholiau yn ôl
backward spring naid yn ôl *eb* neidiau yn ôl
backward tilt gogwyddo'n ôl *be*
backwardness arafwch *eg*
backwards (=with the back foremost) wysg y cefn *adf*
backwash tynddwr *eg*
backwasting ôl-ddarfodiant *eg*
backwater merddwr *eg* merddyfroedd
backwoods gwylltgoed *ell*
bacon cig moch *eg*
bacon rind crofen *eb* crofennau
baconer mochyn bacwn *eg* moch bacwn
bacterial bacteriol *ans*
bactericidal bacterioleiddiol *ans*
bacteriologist bacteriolegydd *eg* bacteriolegwyr
bacteriology bacterioleg *eb*
bacteriophage bacterioffag *eg* bacterioffagau
bacteriostat bacteriostat *eg*
bacteriostatic bacteriostatig *ans*
bacteriostatic (finish) gwrthfacteria *ans*
bacterium bacteriwm *eg* bacteria
bad practice arfer gwael *eg* arferion gwael
badge bathodyn *eg* bathodynnau
badge reader darllenydd bathodynnau *eg* darllenyddion bathodynnau
badland *adj* garwdirol *ans*
badlands *n* garwdiroedd *ell*
badminton badminton *eg*
bag bag *eg* bagiau
bagatelle bagatelle *eg* bagatelles
baghouse (for filtering dust) tŷ hidlo *eg* tai hidlo
bagpipe bacbib *eb* bacbibau
bail mechnïaeth *eb*
bail (of cricket stumps) caten *eb* catiau
bailey beili *eg* beilïau
bain-marie bain-marie *eg* bains-marie
Baisakhi /Vaisakhi Baisakhi /Vaisakhi
baize beias *eg*
bake pobi *be*
bake blind pobi'n wag *be*
baked apple afal pob *eg* afalau pob
baked beans ffa pob *ell*
baked enamel enamel cras *eg*
Bakelite Bakelite *eg*
baker pobydd *eg* pobyddion
Baker's fluid hylif Baker *eg*
bakestone maen *eg* meini; gradell *eb* gredyll
Bakewell tart tarten Bakewell *eb* tartenni Bakewell
baking powder powdr codi *eg*
baking tin tun pobi *eg* tuniau pobi
balalaika balalaica *eg* balalaicau
balance (=create equilibrium) *v.trans* cydbwyso *be*
balance (=equilibrium) *n* cydbwysedd *eg* cydbwyseddau
balance (=keep equilibrium) *v.intrans* cadw cydbwysedd *be*
balance (=measure mass) *v* cloriannu *be*
balance (financial transactions) *v.trans* mantoli *be*
balance (for weighing) *n* clorian *eb* cloriannau; tafol *eb* tafolau
balance (of money) *n* gweddill *eg* gweddillion
balance an equation cydbwyso hafaliad *be*
balance due balans dyledus *eg*
balance flue simnai gytbwys *eb* simneiau cytbwys
balance line llinell gydbwysedd *eb* llinellau cydbwysedd
balance marks marciau cydbwysedd *ell*
balance of community cydbwysedd cymuned *eg*
balance of nature cydbwysedd natur *eg*
balance of payments mantol daliadau *eb*
balance of power cydbwysedd grym *eg*
balance of trade mantol fasnach *eb*
balance point pwynt cydbwysedd *eg* pwyntiau cydbwysedd
balance sheet mantolen *eb* mantolenni

balance support (in athletics) ymgynnal cytbwys *be*
balance the accounts mantoli'r cyfrifon *be*
balance wheel (of machine part) olwyn cydbwysedd *eb* olwynion cydbwysedd
balanced cytbwys *ans*
balanced bilingual cytbwys ddwyieithog *ans*
balanced budget cyllideb fantoledig *eb* cyllidebau mantoledig
balanced diet deiet cytbwys *eg*
balanced economy economi cytbwys *eg* economïau cytbwys
balanced flue ffliw gytbwys *eb* ffliwiau cytbwys
balanced forces grymoedd cytbwys *ell*
balanced intake derbyn nifer cytbwys *be*
balanced judgement barn gytbwys *eb*
balanced Latin square sgwâr Lladin cytbwys *eg*
balanced shape ffurf gytbwys *eb* ffurfiau cytbwys
balanced step gris cytbwys *eg* grisiau cytbwys
balanced swell pedal chwyddbedal cytbwys *eg* chwyddbedalau cytbwys
balancer veneer argaen cydbwyso *eg*
balancing cydbwysol *ans*
balancing mechanism mecanwaith cydbwysol *eg*
balancing skill sgìl cydbwyso *eg* sgiliau cydbwyso
balcony balconi *eg* balconïau
bale bwrn *eg* byrnau
bale loader codwr byrnau *eg* codwyr byrnau
baler byrnwr *eg* byrnwyr
Balkan countries gwledydd y Balcan *eg*
▸ **Balkans** Balcanau, y *ell*
ball (of wool etc) pellen *eb* pellenni
ball (single delivery of) pelen *eb* pelenni
ball (to play with) pêl *eb* peli
ball and claw foot troed pelen a chrafanc *eb* traed pelen a chrafanc
ball and socket joint cymal pelen a chrau *eg* cymalau pelen a chrau
ball boy bachgen y bêl *eg* bechgyn y bêl
ball castor castor pêl *eg* castorau pêl
ball catch clicied bêl *eb* cliciedau pêl
ball clay clai pêl *eg*
ball foot troed bêl *eb* traed peli
ball girl merch y bêl *eb* merched y bêl
ball mill melin bêl *eb* melinau pêl
ball of the foot pelen y droed *eb*
ball peen wyneb crwn *eg*
ball peen hammer morthwyl wyneb crwn *eg* morthwylion wyneb crwn
ball pointed bodkin botgin pengrwn *eg* botginau pengrwn
ball valve pêl-falf *eb* pêl-falfiau
ballad baled *eb* baledi
ballad opera opera faled *eb* operâu baled
ballade ballade *eg* ballades
ball-bearing pelferyn *eg* pelferynnau
ball-bearing runner rhedwr pelferyn *eg* rhedwyr pelferyn
ballet bale *eg* dawnsiau bale
ballet chorus dawnsgor bale *eb* dawnsgorau bale
ballet dancer dawnsiwr bale *eg* dawnswyr bale
ballet mistress meistres y bale *eb* meistresi'r bale
ballet music cerddoriaeth fale *eb*
ballett (song) balet *eb* baletau
ball-head stake bonyn pengrwn *eg* bonion pengrwn
ballistic balistig *ans*
ballistic missile taflegryn balistig *eg* taflegrau balistig
ballistics balisteg *eb*
balloon balŵn *eg/b* balwnau
balloon framing ffrâm falŵn *eb* fframiau balŵn
ball-point needle nodwydd belenbwynt *eb* nodwyddau pelenbwynt
ballroom dance dawns neuadd *eb* dawnsiau neuadd
ball-winner enillydd y bêl *eg* enillwyr y bêl
balsa balsa *eg*
balsa cement sment balsa *eg*
balsa wood pren balsa *eg*
baluster balwster *eg* balwsterau
balustrade balwstrad *eg* balwstradau
bamboo bambŵ *eg*
bamboo cane cansen fambŵ *eb* cansenni bambŵ
banana banana *eb* bananas
band *n* band *eg* bandiau
band (in computing) *v* corlannu *be*
band nipper niper bandio *eg* niperi bandio
band spectrum sbectrwm band *eg* sbectra band
band stitch pwyth band *eg* pwythau band
bandage *n* rhwymyn *eg* rhwymynnau
bandage *v* rhwymo *be*
banded bandog *ans*
banding bandin *eg* bandinau
banding menu dewislen gorlannu *eb* dewislenni corlannu
banding wheel olwyn fandio *eb* olwynion bandio
bandsaw cylchlif *eb* cylchlifiau
bandwidth lled band *eg*
banister canllaw grisiau *eg* canllawiau grisiau
banister brush brwsh canllaw grisiau *eg* brwshys canllaw grisiau
banjo banjo *eg* banjos
bank (for money) banc *eg* banciau
bank (of earth) clawdd *eg* cloddiau
bank (of river) glan *eb* glannau
bank account cyfrif banc *eg* cyfrifon banc
bank balance balans yn y banc *eg*
bank branch cangen banc *eb* canghennau banc
bank charges treuliau banc *ell*
Bank Charter Act Deddf Siarter y Banc *eb*
bank loan benthyciad banc *eg* benthyciadau banc
bank manager rheolwr banc *eg* rheolwyr banciau
bank of drawers banc o ddroriau *eg* banciau o ddroriau
Bank of England Banc Lloegr *eg*
Bank of Scotland Banc yr Alban *eg*
bank rate cyfradd banc *eb* cyfraddau banc

adf, adv adferf, *adverb* ***ans, adj*** ansoddair, *adjective* ***be*** berf, *verb* ***eb*** enw benywaidd, *feminine noun* ***eg*** enw gwrywaidd, *masculine noun*

bank reserve cronfa banc *eb* cronfeydd banciau
bank statement cyfriflen *eb* cyfriflenni
banker's order archeb banc *eb* archebion banc
bankful cyforlan *eb* cyforlannau
banking bancio *be*
banking centre canolfan fancio *eb* canolfannau bancio
banking industry diwydiant bancio *eg*
banking system cyfundrefn fancio *eb* cyfundrefnau bancio
banking up (fire) anhuddo *be*
banknotes arian papur *ell*
bankrupt (person) methdalwr *eg* methdalwyr
bankruptcy methdaliad *eg* methdaliadau
bankruptcy court llys methdaliad *eg*
banner (=flag) baner *eb* baneri
banner (headline) pennawd bras *eg* penawdau bras
banner advert hysbyseb fras *eb*
bantam weight pwysau bantam *ell*
baptism bedydd *eg*
baptismal font bedyddfaen *eb* bedyddfeini
Baptist Bedyddiwr *eg* Bedyddwyr
baptistry bedyddfa *eb* bedyddfeydd
bar bar *eg* barrau
bar chart siart bar *eg* siartiau bar
▶**bar code** cod bar *eg* codau bar
▶**bar code reader** darllenydd codau bar *eg* darllenwyr codau bar
bar feed (mechanism) porthiant bar *eg*
bar graph graff bar *eg* graffiau bar
bar height uchder y bar *eg*
bar magnet barfagnet *eg* barfagnetau
bar tack tac cynnal *eg* taciau cynnal
bar vocational course cwrs galwedigaethol y bar *eg*
barathea barathea *eg*
barb adfach *eg* adfachau
barbiturate barbitwrad *eg* barbitwradau
barbola barbola *eg*
barbola paste past barbola *eg*
barbola varnish farnais barbola *eg*
barbola work gwaith barbola *eg*
barbule adfachyn *eg* adfachau
barcarolle barcaról *eg* barcarolau
barchan barchan *eg* barchanau
▶ **bar-coded label** label cod bar *eg* labeli cod bar
bare noeth *ans*
bare wire gwifren noeth *eb* gwifrau noeth
barefaced mortise and tenon mortais a thyno unysgwyddog
barefaced tenon tyno unysgwyddog *eg* tynoau unysgwyddog
barefoot troednoeth *ans*
barette barette *eb* barettes
bargain bargen *eb* bargeinion
barge (=type of boat) *n* ysgraff *eb* ysgraffau
barge (in sport) *n* hyrddiad *eg* hyrddiadau
barge (in sport) *v* hyrddio *be*
barge-board astell dywydd *eb* estyll tywydd
baritone bariton *eg* baritonwyr
baritone-clef allwedd y bariton *eb* allweddi'r bariton
barium (Ba) bariwm *eg*
barium ion ïon bariwm *eg* ïonau bariwm
barium peroxide bariwm perocsid *eg*
bark (of tree) rhisgl *eg* rhisglau
barley haidd *eg*
barley bread bara haidd *eg*
barley seeds hadau haidd *ell*
barley water dŵr haidd *eg*
bar line (in music) llinell bar *eb* llinellau bar
barline graph graff barlinell *eg* graffiau barlinell
barnacle cragen long *eb* cregyn llong
barnacle gŵydd fôr *eb* gwyddau môr
Barnum effect effaith Barnum *eb*
barogram barogram *eg* barogramau
barograph barograff *eg* barograffau
barometer baromedr *eg* baromedrau
▶ **barometric** barometrig *ans*
▶ **barometric gradient** graddiant barometrig *eg*
▶ **barometric tendency** tueddiad barometrig *eg* tueddiadau barometrig
baron barwn *eg* barwniaid
baronetcy barwnigaeth *eb* barwnigaethau
baronial barwnol *ans*
barony barwni *eb* barwnïau
baroque baróc *ans*
baroque art celfyddyd faróc *eb*
barrack block rhes o farics *eb* rhesi o farics
barrack building adeilad barics *eg* adeiladau barics
barracks barics *ell*
barrage bared *eg* baredau
barre barre *eg* barres
barred door drws barrog *eg* drysau barrog
barrel (=cask) casgen *eb* casgenni
barrel (=cylindrical tube) baril *eb* barilau
barrel bolt barilfollt *eb* barilfolltau
barrel cam cam baril *eg* camau baril
barrel ceiling nenfwd baril *eg* nenfydau baril
barrel organ organ gelwrn *eb* organau celwrn
barrel printer argraffydd celwrn *eg* argraffyddion celwrn
barrel spring sbring baril *eg* sbringiau baril
barrel vault pont faril *eb* pontydd baril
barren diffrwyth *ans*
barricade baricêd *eg* baricedau
barrier (=obstacle) rhwystr *eg* rhwystrau
barrier beach bardraeth *eg* bardraethau
barrier cream eli rhwystrol *eg*
barrier lake barlyn *eg* barlynnoedd
barrier method dull rhwystrol *eg* dulliau rhwystrol
barrier nursing nyrsio rhwystrol *be*
barrier reef barriff *eg* barriffiau
barrier to entry rhwystr mynediad *eg*
barrier to participation rhwystr sy'n atal pobl rhag cymryd rhan *eg*

barriers to communication rhwystrau i gyfathrebu *ell*
barrister bargyfreithiwr *eg* bargyfreithwyr
barrow (=burial mound) crug *eg* crugiau
barrow (=wheelbarrow) berfa *eb* berfâu
Barrowist dilynwr Barrow *eg* dilynwyr Barrow
barter ffeirio *be*
Bartholomew Bartholomeus *eg*
barysphere barysffer *eg* barysfferau
barytite x-ray plaster plastr gwrthymbelydrol *eg*
baryton baryton *eg* barytonau
basal gwaelodol *ans*
basal body corffyn gwaelodol *eg* corffynnau gwaelodol
basal ganglia ganglia gwaelodol *ell*
Basal Metabolic Rate (BMR) Cyfradd Metabolaeth Waelodol *eb*
basal metabolism metabolaeth waelodol *eb*
basal sapping gwaelod-danseilio *be*
basalt basalt *eg*
basalt ware crochenwaith basalt *eg*
base (=bottom) gwaelod *eg* gwaelodion
base (=headquarters) canolfan *eg/b* canolfannau
base (in arithmetic, also of hedge, tree) bôn *eg* bonion
base (in chemistry, also in baseball) bas *eg* basau
base (of pyramid) sylfaen *eg/b* sylfeini
base (of triangle) sail *eb* seiliau
base angle ongl sail *eb* onglau sail
base coat haen sail *eb* haenau sail
base current cerrynt y sail *eg*
base level gwaelodfa *eb* gwaelodfeydd
base map map sylfaen *eg* mapiau sylfaen
base moulding addurn gwaelod *eg* addurniadau gwaelod
base of scrum bôn y sgrym *eg*
base period cyfnod sail *eg*
base sequence dilyniant bas *eg*
base strength cryfder bas *eg*
base-acid bas-asid *eg*
based on seiliedig ar *adf*
based on geometrical shapes seiliedig ar ffurfiau geometrig *ans*
based on texture seiliedig ar wead *ans*
baseline (=starting point) man cychwyn *eg* mannau cychwyn
baseline (clinical usage etc) gwaelodlin *eb* gwaelodliniau
baseline (in tennis) llinell gefn *eb* llinellau cefn
baseline assessment asesiad gwaelodlin *eg* asesiadau gwaelodlin
▸ **baseline data** data gwaelodlin *ell*
baseline testing (in psychology) profi gwaelodlin *be*
baseline testing (in education) asesu sylfaen *be*
baseman baswr *eg* baswyr
basement islawr *eg* isloriau
basement membrane pilen waelodol *eb* pilenni gwaelodol
base-rate fallacy twyllresymeg cyfradd sylfaenol *eb*
BASIC BASIC *eb*
basic sylfaenol *ans*
basic (in chemistry, geology and metals) basig *ans*
basic action gweithrediad sylfaenol *eg* gweithrediadau sylfaenol
basic aluminium ethanoate alwminiwm ethanoad basig *eg*
basic beryllium ethanoate beryliwm ethanoad basig *eg*
basic Bessemer process proses fasig Bessemer *eb*
basic calculator cyfrifiannell sylfaenol *eb* cyfrifianellau sylfaenol
basic colour lliw sylfaenol *eg* lliwiau sylfaenol
basic competence cymhwysedd sylfaenol *eg* cymwyseddau sylfaenol
basic constituent cyfansoddyn sylfaenol *ell* cyfansoddion sylfaenol
basic construction adeiladwaith sylfaenol *eg*
basic curriculum cwricwlwm sylfaenol *eg*
basic difference gwahaniaeth sylfaenol *eg* gwahaniaethau sylfaenol
basic family teulu sylfaenol *eg* teuluoedd sylfaenol
basic feasible solution (bfs) datrysiad dichonadwy sylfaenol *eg*
basic form ffurf sylfaenol *eb* ffurfiau sylfaenol
basic function swyddogaeth sylfaenol *eb* swyddogaethau sylfaenol
basic ground plan cynllun llawr sylfaenol *eg* cynlluniau llawr sylfaenol
basic human need angen dynol sylfaenol *eg* anghenion dynol sylfaenol
basic industry diwydiant sylfaen *eg* diwydiannau sylfaen
basic lower body exercise ymarfer sylfaenol i'r corff isaf *eg* ymarferion sylfaenol i'r corff isaf
basic material defnydd sylfaenol *eg* defnyddiau sylfaenol
basic movement symudiad sylfaenol *eg* symudiadau sylfaenol
basic on-line system system ar-lein sylfaenol *eb* systemau ar-lein sylfaenol
basic open hearth process proses fasig tân agored *eb*
basic orientation cyfeiriadaeth sylfaenol *eb*
basic pattern patrwm sylfaenol *eg* patrymau sylfaenol
basic rate cyfradd sylfaenol *eb* cyfraddau sylfaenol
basic recipe rysáit sylfaenol *eb* ryseitiau sylfaenol
basic research ymchwil sylfaenol *eg*
basic rest-activity cycle cylch ymlacio-gweithredu sylfaenol *be*
basic rock craig fasig *eb* creigiau basig
basic salary cyflog sylfaenol *eg* cyflogau sylfaenol
basic sight vocabulary geirfa weledol sylfaenol *eb*
basic size maint sylfaenol *eg* meintiau sylfaenol
basic skill sgil sylfaenol *eg* sgiliau sylfaenol
basic slag slag basig *eg*
basic subject pwnc sylfaen *eg* pynciau sylfaen

basic surveying calculations cyfrifiadau syrfeo sylfaenol *ell*
basic unit of charge uned sylfaenol gwefr *eb*
basic upper body exercise ymarfer sylfaenol i'r corff uchaf *eg* ymarferion sylfaenol i'r corff uchaf
basic vocabulary geirfa sylfaenol *eb*
basic wage cyflog sylfaenol *eg* cyflogau sylfaenol
basicity basigedd *eg*
basic-level concept cysyniad lefel sylfaenol *eg*
basidiomycete basidiomycet *eg* basidiomycetau
basidiospore basidiosbor *eg* basidiosborau
basidium basidiwm *eg* basidia
basil basil *eg*
basilar membrane pilen waelodol *eb* pilenni gwaelodol
basilica basilica *eg* basilicâu
basin basn *eg* basnau
basin and range country tir basn a chadwyn *eg* tiroedd basn a chadwyn
basin of reception basn derbyn *eg* basnau derbyn
basipetal basipetalaidd *ans*
basis sail *eb* seiliau
basket basged *eb* basgedi
basket frame ffrâm fasged *eb* fframiau basged
basket handle dolen fasged *eb* dolennau basged
basket maker gwneuthurwr basgedi *eg* gwneuthurwyr basgedi
basket weave gwead basged *eg*
basket work basgedwaith *eg*
basketball pêl-fasged *eb*
basketry gwaith basged *eg*
basophil basoffil *eg* basoffiliau
basophilic basoffilig *ans*
bas-relief cerfwedd isel *eb* cerfweddau isel
bass (of voice, instrument) bas *eg* basau
bass (sea perch) draenogiad y môr *eg* draenogiaid y môr
bass boost atgyfnerthiad bas *eg*
bass clarinet clarinét bas *eg* clarinetau bas
bass clarinettist bas-glarinetydd *eg* bas-glarinetwyr
bass clef cleff bas *eg* cleffiau bas
bass cut toriad bas *eg*
bass drum drwm bas *eg* drymiau bas
bass flute ffliwt fas *eb* ffliwtiau bas
bass horn corn bas *eg* cyrn bas
bass horn player canwr corn bas *eg* canwyr corn bas
bass trombonist bas-drombonydd *eg* bas-drombonwyr
bass trumpet utgorn bas *eg* utgyrn bas
bass viol feiol fas *eb* feiolau bas
bass-bar (=piece of wood inside belly of violin) basfar *eg* basfarrau
basset horn corn baset *eg* cyrn baset
basset horn clarinet clarinét tenor *eg* clarinetau tenor
basset horn player canwr corn baset *eg* canwyr corn baset
basso ostinato basso ostinato *eg*
bassoon baswn *eg* baswnau
bassoonist baswnydd *eg* baswnwyr
bast bast *eg*
bastard cut toriad bastard *eg* toriadau bastard
bastard cut file ffeil fastard *eb* ffeiliau bastard
bastard feudalism ffug ffiwdaliaeth *eb*
bastard file ffeil fastard *eb* ffeiliau bastard
baste (in cooking) brasteru *be*
baste (in needlework) brasbwytho *be*
bastide bastid *eg* bastidau
basting stitch brasbwyth *eg* brasbwythau
bat *n* bat *eg* batiau
bat *v* batio *be*
batch swp *eg* sypiau
batch baking pobiad *eg* pobiadau
batch culture swp-feithrin *be*
batch culture fermenter eplesydd swp-feithrin *eg*
batch processing swp-brosesu *be*
batch production swp-gynhyrchu *be*
batch reactor swp-adweithydd *eg* swp-adweithyddion
batch service swp-wasanaeth *eg* swp-wasanaethau
Batesian mimicry dynwarediad Batesaidd *eg* dynwarediadau Batesaidd
bath *n* baddon *eg* baddonau
bath *v* bathio *be*
bath building baddondy *eg* baddondai
bathe *v.intrans* ymolch *be*
bathe *v.trans* golchi *be*
bathing costume gwisg nofio *eb* gwisgoedd nofio
batholith batholith *eg* batholithau
batholithic batholithig *ans*
bathroom ystafell ymolch *eb* ystafelloedd ymolch
bathroom cabinet cabinet ystafell ymolch *eg* cabinetau ystafell ymolch
bathroom suite unedau ystafell ymolch *ell*
bathyal zone cylchfa fathyal *eb* cylchfaoedd bathyal
bathygraph bathygraff *eg* bathygraffau
bathymetric bathymetrig *ans*
bathymetry bathymetreg *eb*
bathysphere bathysffer *eg*
batik batic *eg*
batik dyeing llifo batic *be*
batik wax cwyr batic *eg*
baton batwn *eg* batynau
batsman batiwr *eg* batwyr
battalion bataliwn *eg* bataliynau
battels bateloedd *ell*
batten *n* astell *eb* estyll
batten *v* estyllu *be*
batten board astell stribed *eb* estyll stribed
batter (for coating food) cytew *eg*
batter (of slope of wall, hedge) ôl-ogwydd *eg*
batter rails rheiliau goleddf *ell*
battered baby baban wedi'i guro *eg* babanod wedi'u curo

battered wife gwraig gleisiog *eb* gwragedd cleisiog
battery batri *eg* batrïau
battery egg wy batri *eg* wyau batri
battery hen iâr fatri *eb* ieir batri
batting crease cris batio *eg* crisiau batio
batting glove maneg fatio *eb* menig batio
batting technique techneg batio *eb* technegau batio
battle brwydr *eb* brwydrau
battle axe cadfwyell *eb* cadfwyeill
battle cry rhyfelgri *eb*
Battle of Britain Brwydr Prydain *eb*
battle of Lepanto brwydr Lepanto *eb*
battle of the gauges brwydr lled y cledrau *eb*
Battle of the Somme Brwydr y Somme *eb*
battle order trefn y gad *eb*
battlefield maes brwydr *eg* meysydd brwydr
battlements (=crenellations) murfylchau *ell*
battlements (=parapet) bylchfuriau *ell*
battleship llong ryfel *eb* llongau rhyfel
batwing sleeve llawes ystlum *eb* llewys ystlum
baud baud *eg*
baud rate cyfradd baud *eb* cyfraddau baud
Bauhaus designer dylunydd Bauhaus *eg* dylunwyr Bauhaus
baulk trawst bras *eg* trawstiau bras
bauxite bocsit *eg*
bauxite brick bricsen focsit *eb* brics bocsit
Bavarian *adj* Bafaraidd *ans*
Bavarian *n* Bafariad *eg* Bafariaid
bay bae *eg* baeau
bay bar bar bae *eg* barrau baeau
bay window ffenestr grom *eb* ffenestri crwm
Bayeux Tapestry Tapestri Bayeux *eg*
bay-head beach cildraeth *eg* cildraethau
bayleaf deilen llawryf *eb* dail llawryf
bayonet bidog *eb* bidogau
bazaar basar *eg* basarau
BC (Before Christ) CC
beach traeth *eg* traethau
beach material defnyddiau traeth *ell*
beachhead blaenlaniad *eg* blaenlaniadau
beachwear dillad traeth *ell*
beacon (=high place) ban *eg* bannau
beacon (=tower) tŵr *eg* tyrau
beacon (=warning or guiding light) goleufa *eg* goleufâu
bead *n* glain *eg* gleiniau
bead *v* gleinio *be*
bead and butt panel panel glain ac ymyl *eg* paneli glain ac ymyl
bead and reel glain a rîl
bead moulding mowldin glain *eg*
bead trimming addurn glain *eg* addurniadau glain
beaded esker esgair gnapiog *eb* esgeiriau cnapiog
beadhouse betws *eg* betysau
beading gleinwaith *eg*
beading needle nodwydd gleinwaith *eb* nodwyddau gleinwaith
beadle bedel *eg* bedeliaid
beadsman paderwr *eg* paderwyr
beadwork gleinwaith *eg*
beak pig *eg/b* pigau
beaker bicer *eg* biceri
beaker folk bicerwyr *ell*
beam (of light) paladr *eg* pelydr
beam (of wood, metal etc) trawst *eg* trawstiau
beam balance clorian drawst *eb* cloriannau trawst
beam engine peiriant trawst *eg* peiriannau trawst
beam in situ trawst sefydlog *eg*
beam saddle cyfrwy trawst *eg* cyfrwyau trawst
bean ffeuen *eb* ffa
bean bag (for sitting on) sach eistedd *eb* sachau eistedd
bean bag (for throwing) bag ffa *eg* bagiau ffa
bean sprouts egin ffa *ell*
beard barf *eb* barfau
bearer (drawer) cynhalydd *eg* cynalyddion
bearer rail rheilen gynnal *eb* rheiliau cynnal
bearing (mechanical) beryn *eg* berynnau
bearing line cyfeirlin *eb* cyfeirlinau
bearing rest gorffwysfan beryn *eg* gorffwysfannau beryn
bearing shell cragen feryn *eb* cregyn beryn
bearings (=position, orientation) cyfeiriad *eg* cyfeiriadau
beast of burden anifail pwn *eg* anifeiliaid pwn
beat *n* curiad *eg* curiadau
beat *v* curo *be*
beat frequency amledd curiad *eg* amleddau curiad
beat frequency oscillator osgiliadur amledd curiad *eg* osgiliaduron amledd curiad
beaten metalwork gwaith morthwyl *eg*
beater curwr *eg* curwyr
beating time curo amser *be*
Beaufort Scale Graddfa Beaufort *eb*
beaumontage beaumontage *eg*
beauty harddwch *eg*
Bebung Bebung *eg*
BECA Network Band Eang Cymru Ar-lein *eg*
bechamel sauce saws bechamel *eg*
bed *v* gwelyo *be*
bed (=stratum) *n* haen *eb* haenau
bed (in general) *n* gwely *eg* gwelyau
bed chamber siambr wely *eb* siambrau gwely
bed jacket siaced wely *eb* siacedi gwely
bed linen dillad gwely *ell*
bedding (=bedclothes) *n* dillad gwely *ell*
bedding (of strata) *adj* haenol *ans*
bedding (of strata) *n* haenau *ell*
bedding plane plân haenu *eg* planau haenu
Bede, the Venerable Beda Ddoeth *eg*
Bedivere Bedwyr *eg*
Bedouin Bedwin *eg* Bedwiniaid

bedpan padell wely *eb* pedyll gwely
bedrest gorffwys gwely *eg*
bedridden gorweddog *ans*
► **bedrock** creigwely *eg* creigwelyau
bedroom ystafell wely *eb* ystafelloedd gwely
bedsitter fflat un ystafell *eg* fflatiau un ystafell
bedsock hosan wely *eb* sanau gwely
bedsore briw gorwedd *eg* briwiau gorwedd
bedspread cwrlid *eg* cwrlidau
bedways (lathe) cledrau *ell*
bed-wetting gwlychu gwely *be*
beech ffawydden *eb* ffawydd
beech mallet gordd ffawydd *eb* gyrdd ffawydd
beech tree ffawydden *eb* ffawydd
beech wood pren ffawydd *eg*
beech wood mallet gordd bren ffawydd *eb* gyrdd pren ffawydd
beef cig eidion *eg*
beef extract rhin cig eidion *eb*
beef olives olifau cig eidion *ell*
beef tea te cig eidion *eg*
beefburger eidionyn *eg* eidionod
beer cwrw *eg*
beeswax cwyr gwenyn *eg*
beeswax polish llathrydd cwyr gwenyn *eg*
beet sugar siwgr betys *eg*
beetle chwilen *eb* chwilod
beetroot betysen *eg* betys
before o flaen
Before Christ (BC) Cyn Crist
Before Present (BP) Cyn y Presennol
before tax cyn tynnu treth
beggar cardotyn *eg* cardotwyr
begin dechrau *be*
beginner dechreuwr *eg* dechreuwyr
beginning dechrau *eg* dechreuadau
Beguine Lleian Le Begue *eb* Lleianod Le Begue
behaviour ymddygiad *eg* ymddygiadau
behaviour difficulties anawsterau ymddygiad *ell*
behaviour genetics geneteg ymddygiad *eb*
behaviour management rheoli ymddygiad *be*
behaviour modification addasu ymddygiad *be*
behaviour objectives amcanion ymddygiad *ell*
behaviour policy polisi ymddygiad *eg* polisïau ymddygiad
behaviour therapy therapi ymddygiad *eg*
behavioural ymddygiadol *ans*
behavioural evidence tystiolaeth ymddygiadol *eb*
behavioural inhibition system system atal ymddygiad *eb*
behavioural problems problemau ymddygiad *ell*
behavioural psychology seicoleg ymddygiad *eb*
behavioural theory damcaniaeth ymddygiad *eb*
behavioural unit uned ymddygiad *eb* unedau ymddygiad
behaviourism ymddygiadaeth *eb*
beheaded stream ffrwd bengoll *eb* ffrydiau pengoll
being bod *eg* bodau
being cared for o dan ofal
bel bel *eg* belau
belay belai *eg* belaiau
belfry clochdy *eg* clochdai
Belgium Gwlad Belg *eb*
belief credo *eb* credoau
belief in a just world cred mewn byd cyfiawn *eb*
belief system system cred *eb* systemau cred
believe credu *be*
believer's baptism bedydd cred *eg*
bell cloch *eb* clychau
bell chuck crafanc gloch *eb* crafangau clychau
bell harp telyn glychsain *eb* telynau clychsain
bell metal metel cloch *eg*
bell pit pwll cloch *eg* pyllau cloch
bell punch pwnsh cloch *eg* pynsiau cloch
bell sleeve llawes gloch *eb* llewys cloch
bell tower clochdy *eg* clochdai
bell-jar clochen *eb* clochenni
bellows megin *eb* meginau
belly (of instrument) bol *eg* bolïau
belly pork porc bol *eg*
belly-dancer boladdawnswraig *eb* boladdawnswragedd
below the belt dan y belt *adf*
belt (=area) ardal *eb* ardaloedd
belt (=region) rhanbarth *eg* rhanbarthau
belt (=strip of land) llain *eb* lleiniau
belt (for wearing, also of encircling land) gwregys *eg* gwregysau
belt (on machine) belt *eb* beltiau
belt carrier dolen belt *eb* dolennau belt
belt coupling cyplydd belt *eg* cyplyddion belt
belt dressing dresin belt *eg*
belt pouch pwrs gwregys *eg* pyrsiau gwregys
belt pulley pwli belt *eg* pwlïau belt
belt rivet rhybed belt *eg* rhybedion belt
belt sander sandiwr belt *eg* sandwyr belt
belt screw sgriw belt *eb* sgriwiau belt
belt shifter symudydd belt *eg* symudwyr belt
belt stretcher estynnwr belt *eg* estynwyr belt
belt tightener tynhawr belt *eg* tynhawyr belt
bench mainc *eb* meinciau
bench drill dril mainc *eg* driliau mainc
bench drilling machine peiriant drilio mainc *eg* peiriannau drilio mainc
bench end ystlys mainc *eb* ystlysau mainc
bench end vice feis ben mainc *eb* feisiau pen mainc
bench grinder llifanydd mainc *eg* llifanwyr mainc
bench holdfast dalbren mainc *eg* dalbrennau mainc
bench hook bachyn mainc *eg* bachau mainc
bench jump naid fainc *eb* neidiau mainc
bench plane plaen mainc *eg* plaeniau mainc
bench rib asen y fainc *eb* asennau'r fainc
bench shears gwellaif mainc *eg* gwelleifiau mainc
bench stop rhagod *eg* rhagodion

Bench, the Fainc, y *eb*
bench tools offer mainc *ell*
bench vice feis fainc *eb* feisiau mainc
bench well cafn mainc *eg* cafnau mainc
bench work gwaith mainc *eg*
bencher meinciwr *eg* meincwyr
benchmark meincnod *eg* meincnodau
benchmarking meincnodi *be*
bend *n* plyg *eg* plygion
bend *v* plygu *be*
bend backwards plygu'n ôl *be*
bend down plygu i lawr *be*
bend line llinell blygu *eb* llinellau plygu
bendability plygiannedd *eg*
bending (angular/radius) plygu *be*
bending bar bar plygu *eg* barrau plygu
bending equipment offer plygu *ell*
bending jig jig plygu *eg* jigiau plygu
bending moment moment plygu *eg*
Benedict reagent adweithydd Benedict *eg*
Benedictine *adj* San Bened *ans*
Benedictine *n* Benedictiad *eg* Benedictiaid
benediction bendith *eb* bendithion
benefice bywoliaeth *eb* bywoliaethau
beneficed mewn bywoliaeth *ans*
benefit (=advantage) budd *eg* buddion
benefit (=insurance or social security payment) budd-dal *eg* budd-daliadau
benefit (legal) braint *eb* breintiau
benefit of clergy braint clerigwyr *eb*
benevolence (=forced loan) benthyciad gorfodol *eg* benthyciadau gorfodol
benevolent cyfeillgar *ans*
benevolent despot unben goleuedig *eg* unbeniaid goleuedig
benevolent despotism unbennaeth oleuedig *eb*
benevolent neutrality niwtraliaeth gyfeillgar *eb*
bent backward hanging hongian ôl plyg *be*
bent bodkin botgin cam *eg* botginau cam
bent bond bond cam *eg*
bent flat bodkin botgin fflat cam *eg* botginau fflat cam
bent frame ffrâm blyg *eb* fframiau plyg
bent gouge gaing gau blyg *eb* geingiau cau plyg
bent grass (=agrostis) maeswellt *eg*
bent locking plate plât cloi plyg *eg* platiau cloi plyg
bent nose pliers gefelen drwyn cam *eb* gefeiliau trwyn cam
bent wire (decorative process) gwifren blyg *eb* gwifrau plyg
benthic benthig *ans*
benthos benthos *eg*
bent-tail carrier cariwr cynffon plyg *eg* carwyr cynffon plyg
bentwood chair cadair bren plyg *eb* cadeiriau pren plyg
bentwood furniture dodrefn pren plyg *ell*
benzene bensen *eg*
benzenecarbaldehyde bensencarbaldehyd *eg*
benzenecarbaldehyde oxime bensencarbaldehyd ocsim *eg*
benzenecarbonitrile bensencarbonitril *eg*
benzenecarbonyl chloride bensencarbonyl clorid *eg*
benzenecarboxamide bensencarbocsamid *eg*
benzenecarboxylic acid asid bensencarbocsylig *eg*
benzene-1,4-diamine bensen-1,4-deuamin *eg*
benzene-1,4-diammonium chloride bensen-1,4-deuamoniwm clorid *eg*
benzenediazonium ion ïon bensendeuasoniwm *eg* ïonau bensendeuasoniwm
benzene-1,2-dicarboximide bensen-1,2-deucarbocsimid *eg*
benzene-1,2-dicarboxylic acid asid bensen-1,2-deucarbocsylig *eg*
benzene-1,3-dicarboxylic acid asid bensen-1,3-deucarbocsylig *eg*
benzene-1,4-dicarboxylic acid asid bensen-1,4-deucarbocsylig *eg*
benzene-1,2-dicarboxylic anhydride bensen-1,2-deucarbocsylig anhydrid *eg*
benzene-1,2-diol bensen-1,2-deuol *eg*
benzene-1,3-diol bensen-1,3-deuol *eg*
benzene-1,4-diol bensen-1,4-deuol *eg*
benzeneperoxocarboxylic acid asid bensenperocsocarbocsylig *eg*
benzenesulfonic acid asid bensensylffonig *eg*
benzene-1,2,3-triol bensen-1,2,3-triol *eg*
benzene-1,3,5-triol bensen-1,3,5-triol *eg*
benzodiazepine bensodiasepin *eg*
benzoic acid asid bensöig *eg*
bequeath cymynroddi *be*
bequest cymynrodd *eb* cymynroddion
berceuse berceuse *eb* berceuses
bereavement profedigaeth *eb* profedigaethau
beret beret *eg* berets
bergamask bergamasca *eg* bergamasce
bergwind bergwynt *eg* bergwyntoedd
berkelium (Bk) berceliwm *eg*
Berlin airlift awyrgludiad Berlin *eg*
Berlin Congress Cyngres Berlin *eb*
berry aeronen *eb* aeron
berth *n* docfa *eb* docfâu
berth *v* docio *be*
besiege gosod gwarchae ar *be*
beryllium (Be) beryliwm *eg*
Bessemer converter trawsnewidydd Bessemer *eg*
Bessemer converter furnace ffwrnais drawsnewidydd Bessemer *eb*
best before ar ei orau cyn
best face wyneb gorau *eg*
best fit ffit orau *eb*
best position safle gorau *eg* safleoedd gorau
best time amser gorau *eg* amserau gorau
beta activity gweithgarwch beta *eg*
beta particle gronyn beta *eg* gronynnau beta

beta software meddalwedd beta *eb*
betaine betain *eg*
betrothal dyweddïad *eb* dyweddiadau
between centres (on a lathe) rhwng canolau *adf*
between groups variance amrywiant rhwng grwpiau *eg*
between needle nodwydden *eb* nodwyddennau
between-groups design cynllun rhyng-grwpiau *eg* cynlluniau rhyng-grwpiau
between-subjects design cynllun rhyng-gyfranwyr *eg* cynlluniau rhyng-gyfranwyr
bevel *n* befel *eg* befelau
bevel *v* befelu *be*
bevel chisel cŷn befel *eg* cynion befel; gaing befel *eb* geingiau befel
bevel gears gerau befel *ell*
bevel panel panel befel *eg* paneli befel
bevel wheels olwynion befel *ell*
bevelled edge ymyl befel *eb* ymylon befel
bevelled panel panel befel *eg* paneli befel
beverage diod *eb* diodydd
bezel gwefl *eb* gweflau
bezelled gweflog *ans*
Bezier curve cromlin Bezier *eb*
Bhagavad Gita Bhagavad Gita *eg*
bhakti bhakti *eg*
bias (=inclination) *n* gogwydd *eg* gogwyddiadau
bias (in physics and of fabric) *n* bias *eg* biasau
bias (in physics and of fabric) *v* biasu *be*
bias (in statistics) *n* tuedd *eb* tueddiadau
bias binding rhwymyn bias *eg* rhwymynnau bias
bias extension estyniad bias *eg* estyniadau bias
bias facing wynebyn bias *eg* wynebynnau bias
biased tueddol *ans*
biased estimate (in statistics) amcangyfrif â thuedd *eg*
bib bib *eg* bibiau
Bible Beibl *eg* Beiblau
Biblical Beiblaidd *ans*
bibliography llyfryddiaeth *eb*
bicarbonate of soda soda pobi *eg*
bicellular deugellog *ans*
biceps cyhyryn deuben *eg* cyhyrynnau deuben
bicimal *adj* deuol *ans*
bicimal *n* deuolyn *eg* deuolion
bicimal point pwynt deuol *eg*
bick iron bonyn pig *eg* bonion pig
bicollateral bundle sypyn deugyfraidd *eg* sypynnau deugyfraidd
biconcave deugeugrwm *ans*
biconcave lens lens deugeugrwm *eg* lensiau deugeugrwm
biconvex deuamgrwm *ans*
bicultural deuddiwylliannol *ans*
bicuspid valve falf ddwylen *eb* falfiau dwylen
bidirectional bus bws deugyfeiriadol *eg* bysiau deugyfeiriadol
bid-rent curve cromlin rhent cynnig *eb* cromliniau rhent cynnig
biennial *adj* eilflwydd *ans*
biennial *n* eilflwyddiad *eg* eilflwyddiadau
biennial flower blodyn eilflwydd *eg* blodau eilflwydd
bifilar suspension croglin ddwbl *eb* crogliniau dwbl
bifocal deuffocal *ans*
bifurcated deufforchiog *ans*
bifurcated rivet rhybed deufforchog *eg* rhybedion deufforchog
bifurcation deufforchiad *eg* deufforchiadau
bifurcation ratio cymhareb ddeufforchio *eb* cymarebau deufforchio
big end bearing beryn y pen mawr *eg* berynnau y pen mawr
bigger than mwy na
bight geneufor *eg* geneuforoedd
bijective mapping mapio deusaethol *be*
bikini bicini *eg* bicinis
bilateral dwyochrol *ans*
bilateral cleavage ymraniad cyfartal *eg* ymraniadau cyfartal
bilateral monopoly monopoli dwyffordd *eg* monopolïau dwyffordd
bilateral symmetry cymesuredd dwyochrol *eg*
bilaterally symmetrical dwyochrol gymesur *ans*
bilberries llus *ell*
bile *adj* bustlog *ans*
bile acids asidau bustlog *ell*
bile duct dwythell y bustl *eb*
bile pigment pigment y bustl *eg* pigmentau'r bustl
bile salts halwynau'r bustl *ell*
bilge keel cilbren sadio *eg* cilbrennau sadio
bilinear deulinol *ans*
bilingual *adj* dwyieithog *ans*
bilingual *n* person dwyieithog *eg* pobl ddwyieithog
bilingual education addysg ddwyieithog *eb*
bilingualism dwyieithrwydd *eg*
bilious *n* bustl *eg*
bilirubin bilirwbin *eg*
biliverdin biliferdin *eg*
bill (=statement of charges) bil *eg* biliau
bill (before parliament) mesur seneddol *eg*
bill of exchange bil cyfnewid *eg* biliau cyfnewid
bill of indictment bil ditio *eg* biliau ditio
bill of loading bil llwytho *eg* biliau llwytho
bill of quantities bil priodweddau *eg* biliau priodweddau
Bill of Rights Mesur Iawnderau *eg*
bill of sale bil gwerthiant *eg* biliau gwerthiant
billet lletya milwyr *be*
billet moulding mowldin bilet *eg*
billhook bilwg *eg* bilygau
billion biliwn *eg* biliynau
bimetallic deufetel *ans*
bimetallic strip stribed deufetel *eg* stribedi deufetel
bimodal deufodd *ans*
bimolecular deufoleciwlaidd *ans*

bin bin *eg* biniau
binary deuaidd *ans*
binary arithmetic rhifyddeg ddeuaidd *eb*
binary arithmetic operation gweithrediad rhifyddeg ddeuaidd *eg* gweithrediadau rhifyddeg ddeuaidd
binary bit did deuaidd *eg* didau deuaidd
binary cell cell ddeuaidd *eb* celloedd deuaidd
binary code cod deuaidd *eg* codau deuaidd
binary coded character nod cod deuaidd *eg* nodau cod deuaidd
binary coded decimal degolyn cod deuaidd *eg* degolion cod deuaidd
binary coded decimal notation nodiant degolion cod deuaidd *eg*
binary coded digit digid cod deuaidd *eg* digidau cod deuaidd
binary counter rhifydd deuaidd *eg* rhifyddion deuaidd
binary digit *v* digid deuaidd *eg* digidau deuaidd
binary dump *n* dymp deuaidd *eg* dympiau deuaidd
binary dump *v* dympio deuaidd *be*
binary fission ymholltiad deuaidd *eg* ymholltiadau deuaidd
binary form ffurf ddeuaidd *eb* ffurfiau deuaidd
► **binary half-adder** hanner-adydd deuaidd *eg* hanner-adyddion deuaidd
binary image delwedd ddeuaidd *eb* delweddau deuaidd
binary notation nodiant deuaidd *eg*
binary number rhif deuaidd *eg* rhifau deuaidd
binary numeral rhifolyn deuaidd *eg* rhifolion deuaidd
binary operation gweithrediad deuaidd *eg* gweithrediadau deuaidd
binary opposition cyferbynnu deuaidd *be*
binary point pwynt deuaidd *eg* pwyntiau deuaidd
binary search chwiliad deuaidd *eg* chwiliadau deuaidd
binary star seren ddwbl *eb* sêr dwbl
binary time amser dwyran *eg*
binary to decimal conversion trawsnewidiad deuaidd i ddegol *eg* trawsnewidiadau deuaidd i ddegol
binary tree coeden ddeuaidd *eb* coed deuaidd
binary variable newidyn deuaidd *eg* newidynnau deuaidd
binaural deuglust *ans*
bind (books etc; with bandages etc) rhwymo *be*
bind (with rope etc; in physics) clymu *be*
binder (of person) rhwymwr *eg* rhwymwyr
binder (machine attachments) rhwymell *eb* rhwymellau
binding (=something that binds) rhwymyn *eg* rhwymynnau
binding (of book) rhwymiad *eg* rhwymiadau
binding energy egni clymu *eg* egnïon clymu
binding margin ymyl rhwymo *eb* ymylon rhwymo
binding medium cyfrwng rhwymo *eg* cyfryngau rhwymo
binding precedent cynsail rwymol *eb*
binding wire gwifren rwymo *eb* gwifrau rhwymo
Binet-Simon scale graddfa Binet-Simon *eb*
binocular deulygad *ans*
binocular vision golwg deulygad *eg* golygon deulygad
binoculars ysbienddrych *eg* ysbienddrychau
binomial *adj* binomaidd *ans*
binomial *n* binomial *eg* binomialau
binomial distribution gwasgariad binomial *eg*
binomial distribution dosraniad binomaidd *eg*
binomial nomenclature dull enwi binomaidd *eg*
binomial theorem theorem binomial *eb*
bioaccumulation biogynyddiad *eg*
bioavailability bioargaeledd *eg*
biochemical biocemegyn *eg* biocemegion
biochemist biocemegydd *eg* biocemegwyr
biochemistry biocemeg *eb*
biochore bïocor *eg* biocorau
bioclimatology biohinsoddeg *eb*
biodegradable bioddiraddadwy *ans*
biofeedback bioadborth *eg*
biogenesis biogenesis *eg*
biogeochemical bioddaeargemegol *ans*
biogeography bioddaearyddiaeth *eb*
biological biolegol *ans*
biological control rheoli biolegol *be*
biological detergent glanedydd biolegol *eg* glanedyddion biolegol
biological evolution esblygiad biolegol *eg*
biological half life hanner oes biolegol *eg*
biological reductionism lleihadaeth fiolegol *eb*
biological value gwerth biolegol *eg*
biology (of winter) bioleg *eb*
bioluminescence bioymoleuedd *eb*
biomass biomas *eg*
biome bïom *eg* bïomau
biomechanics biomecaneg *eb*
biomedical model model biofeddygol *eg*
biopsychosocial model model bioseicogymdeithasol *eg*
biosensor biosynhwyrydd *eg* biosynwyryddion
biosome biosom *eg*
biosphere biosffer *eg*
biosynthesize biosynthesu *be*
biotechnology biotechnoleg *eb*
biotic biotig *ans*
biotransformation biotrawsffurfiant *eg* biotrawsffurfiannau
bipartite deurannol *ans*
bipedalism symudedd dwy-droed *eg*
biphenyl-4,4'-diamine biffenyl-4,4'-deuamin *eg*
bipolar deubegwn *ans*
bipolar cell (unfair) cell ddeubegwn *eb* celloedd deubegwn
bipolar disorder anhwylder deubegwn *eg*
birch bedwen *eb* bedw

birch plywood pren haenog bedw *eg*
bird's eye (maple) llygad aderyn *ans*
bird's eye view golygfa trem aderyn *eb*
bird's foot delta delta crafanc *eg* deltâu crafanc
birdsmouth ceg aderyn *eb*
birth genedigaeth *eb* genedigaethau
birth and death statistics ystadegau geni a marw *ell*
birth certificate tystysgrif geni *eb* tystysgrifau geni
birth control rheoli cenhedlu *be*
birth defect nam geni *eg* namau geni
birth rate cyfradd genedigaethau *eb*
birth weight pwysau geni *ell*
birthmark man geni *eg* mannau geni
birthright genedigaeth-fraint *eb*
1,2-bis[bis(carboxymethyl)amino]ethane 1,2-bis[bis(carbocsimethyl)amino]ethan *eg*
bis(butanedione dioximato)nickel(II) bis(bwtandeuon deuocsimato)nicel(II) *eg*
biscuit bisged *eb* bisgedi
biscuit firing tanio bisged *be*
bisect (=divide in two) dwyrannu *be*
bisect (=halve) haneru *be*
bisector hanerydd *eg* haneryddion
bisexual deurywiol *ans*
bishop esgob *eg* esgobion
Bishop of Bangor's jig dawns Esgob Bangor *eb*
bishop sleeve llawes esgob *eb* llewys esgob
Bishop William Morgan Esgob William Morgan *eg*
bishopland tir esgob *eg* tiroedd esgob
bishopric esgobaeth *eb* esgobaethau
bishop's commissary comisari'r esgob *eg*
bishop's palace palas esgob *eg* palasau esgobion
Bishops' Wars, the Rhyfel yr Esgobion *eg*
Bismarckian system cyfundrefn Fismarcaidd *eb*
bismuth (Bi) bismwth *eg*
bismuthate(V) ion ïon bismwthad(V) *eg* ïonau bismwthad(V)
bismuth(III) chloride bismwth(III) clorid *eg*
bismuth(III) chloride oxide bismwth(III) clorid ocsid *eg*
bismuth(III) ion ïon bismwth(III) *eg* ïonau bismwth(III)
bistable deusad *eg* deusadau
bit (for soldering) haearn sodro *eg* heyrn sodro
bit (in computing) did *eg* didau
bit (in music) crwcddarn *eg* crwcddarnau
bit (of drill etc) ebill *eg* ebillion
bit density dwysedd didol *eg* dwyseddau didol
bit location lleoliad did *eg* lleoliadau did
bit map map didau *eg* mapiau didau
bit pattern patrwm didol *eg* patrymau didol
bit position safle didol *eg* safleoedd didol
bit rate cyfradd ddidol *eb* cyfraddau didol
bit string llinyn didau *eg* llinynnau didau
bite (=small piece) tamaid *eg* tameidiau
bite (describing texture) cnoad *eg*
bitmap didfap *eg* didfapiau
bitonal deugywair *ans*
bitonality deugyweiredd *eg*
bits per second didau yr eiliad
bitter chwerw *ans*
bitter lake llyn chwerw *eg* llynnoedd chwerw
bitterness chwerwedd *eg*
bitumen bitwmen *eg*
bituminous coal glo rhwym *eg*
bituminous paint paent bitwmen *eg*
bitwise modd did *eg*
biuret biwret *eg*
bivalent deufalent *ans*
bivalve *adj* dwygragennog *ans*
black (enamelling colour) du *eg*
Black Acts Deddfau Duon *ell*
black bar bar du *eg* barrau du
black beans ffa du *ell*
black body radiator pelydrydd cyflawn *eg* pelydryddion cyflawn
black bonding bondin du *eg*
Black Book of the Household Llyfr Du Cyfrifon y Llys *eg*
black check banding bandin siec du *eg*
Black Code (Code Noir) Cod y Caethion Du *eg*
Black Country Gwlad Ddu *eb*
Black Death Pla Du *eg*
black economy economi du *eg*
Black Friar Brawd Du *eg* Brodyr Duon
Black Friday Dydd Gwener Du *eg*
black frost rhew du *eg*
Black Hand Llaw Ddu *eb*
black heat gwres du *eg*
black ice iâ du *eg*; rhew du *eg*
black market marchnad ddu *eb*
black mild steel (B.M.S.) dur meddal du *eg*
black powder powdr du *eg* powdrau du
Black Power Pŵer Du *eg*
Black Prince Tywysog Du *eg*
black pudding pwdin gwaed *eg* pwdinau gwaed
black rubric cyfeireb ddu *eb* cyfeirebau du
blackberries mwyar *ell*
blackboard bwrdd du *eg* byrddau du
blackcurrants cyrens duon *ell*
black-eyed beans ffa llygatddu *ell*
blackheart cast iron haearn bwrw hydrin *eg*
blacking (decorative process) duo *be*
blackjack (blende) blacjac *eg*
blackleg blacleg *eg* blaclegwyr
blacks and whites duon a gwynion
blackshirts crysau duon *eg*
blacksmith gof *eg* gofaint
blacksmith's forge gefail gof *eg* gefeiliau gof
blacksmith's hearth tân gof *eg* tanau gof
bladder (of animals) pledren *eb* pledrennau
bladder (of plants) chwysigen *eb* chwysigod
blade (of knife, bat) llafn *eg/b* llafnau
blade of grass gwelltyn *eg* gwellt

blanch blansio *be*
blank *adj* gwag *ans*
blank (=blank space) *n* bwlch *eg* bylchau
blank cheque siec wag *eb* sieciau gwag
blank column colofn wag *eb* colofnau gwag
blank disk disg gwag *eg* disgiau gwag
blank document dogfen wag *eb* dogfennau gwag
blank grey area lle llwyd gwag *eg* llefydd llwyd gwag
blank line rhes wag *eb* rhesi gwag
blank page tudalen wag *eb* tudalennau gwag
blanket blanced *eb* blancedi
blanket bath ymolch yn y gwely *be*
blanket bog gorgors *eb* gorgorsydd
blanket stitch pwyth blanced *eg* pwythau blanced
Blanketeers Blancedwyr *ell*
▶ **blank-fill** *n* gwag-lenwad *eg* gwag-lenwadau
▶ **blank-fill** *v* gwag-lenwi *be*
blasphemy cabledd *eg* cableddau
blast *adj* chwyth *ans*
blast (=blow air on) *v* chwythellu *be*
blast (=explosion) *n* ffrwydrad *eg* ffrwydradau
blast (=strong gust) *n* chwythiad *eg* chwythiadau
blast furnace ffwrnais chwyth *eb* ffwrneisi chwyth
blast hole chwythdwll *eg* chwythdyllau
blastocoel blastocoel *eg* blastocoelau
blastocyte blastocyt *eg* blastocytau
blastoderm blastoderm *eg* blastodermau
blastomere blastomer *eg* blastomerau
blastophore blastoffor *eg* blastofforau
blastula blastwla *eg* blastwlâu
bleach *n* cannydd *eg* canyddion
bleach *v* cannu *be*
bleach solution hydoddiant cannu *eg*
bleached can *ans*
bleached area rhan wedi'i channu *eb*
bleached calico calico can *eg*
bleached cane gwialen gan *eb* gwialennau can
bleached white calico calico gwyn can *eg*
bleaching agent cannydd *eg* canyddion
bleaching powder powdr cannu *eg* powdrau cannu
bleeding gwaedu *be*
bleeding of dye llifyn yn rhedeg
bleep test prawf blip *eg*
bleeper blipiwr *eg* blipwyr
blend (in biology) *v* cymhlitho *be*
blend (in cooking) *n* cymysgedd *eg* cymysgeddau
blend (in cooking) *v* cymysgu *be*
blend (voices) *v* asio *be*
blende (zinc) blend *eg*
blended fabric ffabrig cymysg *eg*
blended fibre ffibr cymysg *eg*
blended inheritance etifeddiaeth gymhlith *eb*
blended material defnydd cymysg *eg*
blended-hair brush brwsh blew cymysg *eg* brwshys blew cymysg
blender cymysgydd *eg* cymysgyddion
Blessed Gwynfydedig *ans*
blessed sacrament cymun bendigaid *eg*
Blessed Virgin Mary Morwyn Fair Fendigaid *eb*
blessing bendith *eb* bendithion
blight (of planning) malltod *eg*
blind (=unable to see) *adj* dall *ans*
blind (on window) *n* cysgodlen *eb* cysgodlenni
blind alley (figurative sense) llwybr diffrwyth *eg* llwybrau diffrwyth
blind carbon copy copi carbon dall *eg* copïau carbon dall
blind child plentyn dall *eg* plant dall
blind experiment arbrawf dall *eg* arbrofion dall
blind hem hem gudd *eb* hemiau cudd
blind hole twll dall *eg* tyllau dall
blind mortise mortais dall *eg* morteisiau dall
blind nailing hoelio dall *be*
blind pupil disgybl dall *eg* disgyblion dall
blind side ochr dywyll *eb* ochrau tywyll
blind side wing forward blaenasgell dywyll *eb*
blind spot dallbwynt *eg* dallbwyntiau
blind-ending pengaead *ans*
blindness dallineb *eg*
blindsight dallolwg *eb*
blister pothell *eb* pothelli
blister copper copr pothell *eg*
blister steel dur pothell *eg*
blistering pothellu *be*
Blitz, The Blitz, Y *eg*
blizzard storm eira *eb* stormydd eira
bloating ymchwyddo *be*
blob smotyn *eg* smotiau
block *n* bloc *eg* blociau
block (=obstruct) *v* rhwystro *be*
block (=to use a block) *v* blocio *be*
block capital letter priflythyren *eb* priflythrennau
block chart siart bloc *eg* siartiau bloc
block clamp clamp bloc *eg* clampiau bloc
block colour lliw bloc *eg* lliwiau bloc
block cutter blocdorrwr *eg* blocdorwyr
block cutting tool erfyn ysgythru *eg* offer ysgythru
block design test prawf trefnu patrymau *eg* profion trefnu patrymau
block diagram diagram bloc *eg* diagramau bloc
block field (felsenmeer) cludair *eg* cludeiriau
block form ffurf bloc *eb* ffurfiau bloc
block graph graff bloc *eg* graffiau bloc
block image from loading rhwystro delwedd rhag llwytho *be*
block lava bloc lafa *eg* blociau lafa
block length hyd bloc *eg* hydoedd bloc
block lettering prif lythrennu *be*
block letters prif lythrennau *ell*
block mountain blocfynydd *eg* blocfynyddoedd
block move symudiad bloc *eg* symudiadau bloc
block paragraph paragraff ochr *eg* paragraffau ochr
block pattern patrwm bloc *eg* patrymau bloc

block placement lleoliad mewn bloc *eg* lleoliadau mewn bloc
block plane plaen bach *eg* plaeniau bach
block printing printio bloc *be*
block randomization blociau hap *ell*
block scree sgri bloc *eg* sgrïau bloc
block structure strwythur bloc *eg* strwythurau bloc
block structured language iaith strwythur bloc *eb*
block tackle tacl floc *eb* taclau bloc
block wall wal flociau *eb* waliau blociau
block work gwaith blociau *eg*
blockade gwarchae *eg* gwarchaeon
blockboard blocfwrdd *eg* blocfyrddau
blocked account cyfrif gwaharddedig *eg* cyfrifon gwaharddedig
blocking anticyclone antiseiclon rhwystrol *eg* antiseiclonau rhwystrol
blocking factor ffactor flocio *eb* ffactorau blocio
blocking hammer morthwyl blocio *eg* morthwylion blocio
blocking software meddalwedd rhwystro *eb*
blocks and clamps blociau a chlampiau
blockwork gwaith bloc /blociau *eg*
blog *n* blog *eg* blogiau
blog *v* blogio *be*
blogger blogiwr *eg* blogwyr
blood gwaed *eg*
blood and iron gwaed a haearn
blood bank banc gwaed *eg* banciau gwaed
Blood Bath of Stockholm Galanas Stockholm *eb*
blood circulation cylchrediad y gwaed *eg*
blood clot tolchen *eb* tolchennau
blood clotting ceulo'r gwaed *be*
blood corpuscle corffilyn y gwaed *eg* corffilod y gwaed
blood count cyfrif gwaed *eg*
blood donor rhoddwr gwaed *eg* rhoddwyr gwaed
blood feud (in general) cynnen waed *eb*
blood feud (in old Welsh law) galanas *eb*
blood glucose glwcos gwaed *eg*
blood glucose level lefel glwcos yn y gwaed *eb*
blood group grŵp gwaed *eg* grwpiau gwaed
blood pressure pwysau gwaed *ell*
blood relationship perthynas drwy waed *eb*
blood space gwagle gwaed *eg* gwagleoedd gwaed
blood stream llif y gwaed *eg*
blood sugar siwgr gwaed *eg*
blood test prawf gwaed *eg* profion gwaed
blood transfusion trallwysiad gwaed *eg*
blood-brain barrier gwahanfur gwaed-ymennydd *eg*
blood clot tolchen *eb* tolchenni
bloodless revolution chwyldro di-drais *eg*
blood-vessel pibell waed *eb* pibellau gwaed
Bloody Assizes Brawdlys Gwaedlyd *eg*
Bloody Mary Mari Waedlyd *eb*
bloody question cwestiwn marwol *eg*
Bloody Sunday Sul y Gwaed *eg*

bloom (industrial) blwm *eg* blymau
blotting paper papur sugno *eg*
blouse blows *eb* blowsys
blouson blowson *eb* blowsonau
blow *n* ergyd *eg/b* ergydion
blow *v* chwythu *be*
blow an EPROM chwythu EPROM *be*
blow holes (casting) chwythdyllau *ell*
blow moulding chwythfowldio *be*
blower chwythwr *eg* chwythwyr
blow-hole mordwll *eg* mordyllau
blowlamp chwythlamp *eb* chwythlampau
blown sand tywod chwyth *eg*
blowpipe chwythbib *eb* chwythbibau
blue (colour) glas *eg*
blue (for brightening clothes) bliw *eg*
blue baby baban glas *eg* babanod glas
blue flag award gwobr y faner las *eb*
blue litmus solution hydoddiant litmws glas *eg*
'blue' notes nodau 'blue' *ell*
blue precipitate gwaddod glas *eg*
blue red (crimson) coch glas *eg*
blue-collar worker gweithiwr coler las *eg* gweithwyr coler las
blueprint glasbrint *eg* glasbrintiau
blues (=song) blues *ell*
blues and violets gleision a fioledau
blues singing canu'r felan *be*
bluff blwff *eg* blyffiau
bluing (decorative process) glasu *be*
blunger peiriant cymysgu clai *eg* peiriannau cymysgu clai
blunging cymysgu clai *be*
blunt *adj* pŵl *ans*
blunt *v* pylu *be*
bluntness pylni *eg*
blur *n* brycheuyn *eg* brychau
blur *v* pylu *be*
Boadicea Buddug *eb*
board (=plank) astell *eb* estyll
board (in general) bwrdd *eg* byrddau
board and easel bwrdd ac îsl
board based bwrdd seiliedig *ans*
board loom gwŷdd bwrdd *eg* gwyddau bwrdd
Board of Admiralty Bwrdd y Morlys *eg*
Board of Education Bwrdd Addysg *eg*
Board of Guardians Bwrdd Gwarcheidwaid *eg*
Board of Health Bwrdd Iechyd *eg*
Board School Ysgol Bwrdd *eb* Ysgolion Bwrdd
boarded astellog *ans*
boarding school ysgol breswyl *eb* ysgolion preswyl
boat neck gwddf bad *eg*
bob bob *eg* bobiau
bob line llinyn plwm *eg*
bobbin bobin *eg* bobiniau
bobbin case cas bobin *eg* casys bobiniau
bobbin lace les bobin *eg*

bobbin winder gwas dirwyn *eg* gweision dirwyn
Bodhisattva Bodhisattva *eg*
bodice bodis *eg* bodisiau
bodice block bloc bodis *eg* blociau bodis
bodice facing wynebyn bodis *eg* wynebynnau bodis
bodily activity gweithgarwch corfforol *eg*
bodkin botgin *eg* botginau
Bodleian Library Llyfrgell Bodley *eb*
body (in general) corff *eg* cyrff
body (object) gwrthrych *eg* gwrthrychau
body awareness ymwybyddiaeth gorfforol *eb*
body building foods bwydydd cryfhau'r corff *ell*
body cavity ceudod y corff *eg*
body cell corffgell *eb* corffgelloedd
body clearance (drill) cliriad y dril *eg*
body colour lliw di-draidd *eg* lliwiau di-draidd
body control rheolaeth gorfforol *eb*
body fluids hylifau'r corff *ell*
body image delwedd y corff *eb*
body language iaith y corff *eb*
body management rheolaeth dros y corff *eb*
body mass index indecs màs y corff *eg*
body percussion taro'r corff *be*
body politic cenedl wleidyddol *eb*
body rhythm rhythm corff *eg* rhythmau corff
body stain staen di-draidd *eg* staeniau di-draidd
body temperature tymheredd y corff *eg*
body tension tyndra'r corff *eg*
body text corff y testun *eg*
body type math o gorff *eg* mathau o gyrff
body weight pwysau'r corff *ell*
body-centred cubic lattice dellten giwbig gorff-ganolog *eb* delltiau ciwbig corff-ganolog
body-centred cubic metal metel ciwbig corff-ganolog *eg* metelau ciwbig corff-ganolog
bodying-in llenwi'r mân dyllau *be*
bodyless digorff *ans*
bodyless puppet pyped digorff *eg* pypedau digorff
Boer Boer *eg* Boeriaid
Boer War Rhyfel y Boer *eg*
bog cors *eb* corsydd
bog moss migwyn *eg*
Bohemian Brethren Brodyr Bohemia *ell*
boil *n* cornwyd *eg* cornwydydd
boil *v* berwi *be*
boiled egg wy wedi'i ferwi *eg* wyau wedi'u berwi
boiled linseed oil olew had llin wedi'i ferwi *eg*
boiled oil olew wedi'i ferwi *eg*
boiled water dŵr wedi'i ferwi *eg*
boiler boeler *eg* boeleri
boiling berw *ans*
boiling fowl iâr i'w berwi *eb* ieir i'w berwi
boiling point berwbwynt *eg*
boiling tube tiwb berwi *eg* tiwbiau berwi
boiling water dŵr berw *eg*
Bokhara couching cowtsio Bokhara *be*
bold (of type) trwm *ans*
bole (of tree) boncyff *eg* boncyffion
bolero bolero *eg* boleros
Bolshevik *adj* Bolsiefigaidd *ans*
Bolshevik *n* Bolsiefig *eg* Bolsiefigiaid
bolson bolson *eg* bolsonau
bolster bolster *eg* bolsteri
bolt *n* bollt *eb* bolltau
bolt *v* bolltio *be*
bolt catch clicied follt *eb* cliciedau bollt
bolt cutter torrwr bollt *eg* torwyr bollt
bolt tongs gefel follt *eb* gefeiliau bollt
bolted bolltiog *ans*
bolted joint uniad bolltiog *eg* uniadau bolltiog
bolus bolws *eg* bolysau
bolus ground grwnd bolws *eg*
bomb calorimeter calorimedr bom *eg*
bombard peledu *be*
bombarding peledol *ans*
bombardon bombardon *eg* bombardonau
bombed site safle wedi'i fomio *eg* safleoedd wedi'u bomio
Bonapartism Bonapartiaeth *eb*
bond *v* bondio *be*
bond (financial and physics) *n* bond *eg* bondiau
bond (of relationship) *n* cwlwm agosrwydd *eg*
bond dissociation energy egni daduno bond *eg*
bond energy term term egni bond *eg*
bond failure gwrthod gafael *be*
Bond of Association Cwlwm Cydweithred *eg*
bond polarity polaredd bond *eg*
bond service taeogwasanaeth *eg*
bond strength cryfder bond *eg*
bondage taeogaeth *eb*
bonded (finish) bondiog *ans*
bonded fabric ffabrig bondiog *eg* ffabrigau bondiog
bonded floor llawr wedi'i fondio *eg* lloriau wedi'u bondio
bonded surface arwyneb bondiog *eg* arwynebau bondiog
bonded warehouse warws ecseis *eg* warysau ecseis
bonding (building material) bondin *eg*
bonding (of relationship) sefydlu cwlwm agosrwydd *be*
bonding adhesive adlyn bondio *eg*
bonding agent cyfrwng bondio *eg* cyfryngau bondio
bondsman taeog *eg* taeogion
bone asgwrn *eg* esgyrn
bone and hide glue glud asgwrn a chroen *eg*
bone awl mynawyd asgwrn *eg*
bone china tsieni asgwrn *eg*
bone conduction dargludo drwy'r asgwrn *be*
bone folder plygell asgwrn *eb* plygellau asgwrn
bone marrow mêr *eg*
bone scraper crafwr asgwrn *eg* crafwyr asgwrn
bongo bongo *eg* bongos
boning (in cooking) tynnu esgyrn *be*
boning rod rhoden asgwrn *eb* rhodenni asgwrn

adf, adv adferf, *adverb* ***ans, adj*** ansoddair, *adjective* ***be*** berf, *verb* ***eb*** enw benywaidd, *feminine noun* ***eg*** enw gwrywaidd, *masculine noun*

bonnet boned *eb* bonedau
bonus bonws *eg*
bonus payment tâl bonws *eg* taliadau bonws
bony fish pysgodyn esgyrnog *eg*
boogie-woogie bwgi-wgi *eg*
book *n* llyfr *eg* llyfrau
book (=make a reservation) *v* archebu *be*
book binder rhwymwr llyfrau *eg* rhwymwyr llyfrau
book binding rhwymo llyfrau *be*
book craft crefft llyfrau *eb*
book jacket siaced lwch *eb* siacedi llwch
book leather lledr llyfr *eg*
Book of Advertisements Llyfr yr Hysbysebion *eg*
Book of Discipline Llyfr Disgyblaeth *eg*
Book of Hours Llyfr Oriau *eg*
Book of Martyrs Llyfr Merthyron *eg*
Book of Orders Llyfr Gorchmynion *eg*
Book of Sports Llyfr Chwaraeon *eg*
book trough cafn llyfrau *eg* cafnau llyfrau
bookbinder's bench mainc rhwymo llyfrau *eb* meinciau rhwymo llyfrau
bookbinder's press gwasg rhwymwr llyfrau *eb* gweisg rhwymwr llyfrau
bookbinding cloth lliain rhwymo llyfrau *eg*
bookcase cwpwrdd llyfrau *eg* cypyrddau llyfrau
bookcloth lliain llyfrau *eg*
book-end bwtres llyfrau *eg* bwtresi llyfrau
booking bwciad *eg* bwciadau
booking checklist rhestr wirio bwcio *eb*
booking form ffurflen bwcio *eb*
booklet llyfryn *eg* llyfrynnau
bookmark nod tudalen *eg* nodau tudalen
bookmark this link rhoi nod tudalen i'r cyswllt hwn *be*
bookmark this page rhoi nod tudalen yma *be*
book-plate plât llyfr *eg* platiau llyfr
bookrack rhesel lyfrau *eb* rheseli llyfrau
bookshelf silff lyfrau *eb* silffoedd llyfrau
Boolean Boole *ans*
Boolean algebra algebra Boole *eg*
Boolean expression mynegiad Boole *eg* mynegiadau Boole
Boolean logic rhesymeg Boole *eb*
Boolean operation gweithrediad Boole *eg* gweithrediadau Boole
Boolean operator gweithredydd Boole *eg* gweithredyddion Boole
Boolean search chwiliad Boole *eg* chwiliadau Boole
Boolean type math Boole *eg* mathau Boole
Boolean value gwerth Boole *eg* gwerthoedd Boole
Boolean variable newidyn Boole *eg* newidynnau Boole
boom (at harbour mouth) trawst *eg* trawstiau
boom (in industry, economy) ffyniant *eg*
boom (on boat) bŵm *eg* bwmau
boombams bwmbamau *ell*
booming ffyniannus *ans*
booster atgyfnerthol *ans*
booster (for electrical power) cyfnerthydd *eg* cyfnerthyddion
booster dose dos atgyfnerthol *eg* dosau atgyfnerthol
booster injection pigiad atgyfnerthol *eg* pigiadau atgyfnerthol
boot (=kick) *v* cicio *be*
boot (=start computer) *v* cychwyn *be*
boot (for rugby, soccer etc) *n* esgid *eb* esgidiau
booth bwth *eg* bythod
bootstrap loader ymlwythwr *eg* ymlwythwyr
bootstrapping ymlwytho *be*
boracic glaze gwydredd borasig *eg*
borate ion ïon borad *eg* ïonau borad
borax boracs *eg*
borax cone côn boracs *eg* conau boracs
borax palette palet boracs *eg* paletau boracs
border (of area, country) goror *eg* gororau
border (on paper, materials) border *eg* borderi
border colour lliw border *eg* lliwiau border
border design dyluniad border *eg* dyluniadau borderi
border style arddull border *eg* arddulliau border
bordered pits mân-bantiau gweflog *ell*
borderer (=tenant) bordar *eg* bordariaid
borderline *adj* ffiniol *ans*
borderline *n* ffin *eb* ffiniau
borderline candidate ymgeisydd ffiniol *eg* ymgeiswyr ffiniol
borderline case achos ffiniol *eg* achosion ffiniol
borderline reviewing adolygu'r achosion ffiniol *be*
bore (=diameter) *n* tyllfedd *eg* tyllfeddau
bore (=make a hole) *v* tyllu *be*
bore (of tidal wave) *n* eger *eg* egerau
bore box blwch tyllu *eg* blychau tyllu
bored (=fed up) diflas *ans*
boredom diflastod *eg*
bore-hole twll turio *eg* tyllau turio
borer tyllwr *eg* tyllwyr
boric acid asid borig *eg*
boring (=uninteresting) diflas *ans*
boring bar bar tyllu *eg* barrau tyllu
boring tool erfyn tyllu *eg* offer tyllu
boron (B) boron *eg*
boron trifluoride boron triffworid *eg*
boron(III) oxide boron(III) ocsid *eg*
borough bwrdeistref *eb* bwrdeistrefi
borough corporation corfforaeth y fwrdeistref *eb* corfforaethau'r bwrdeistrefi
borough franchise etholfraint fwrdeistrefol *eb*
borough history hanes bwrdeistrefol *eg*
borrow benthyca *be*
borrowed light golau benthyg *eg*
borrower benthyciwr *eg* benthycwyr
boss dwrn addurnedig *eg* dyrnau addurnedig
boss (=protuberance) cnap *eg* cnapiau
boss (of shield) bogail *eg* bogeiliau
bossing mallet gordd ben wy *eb* gyrdd pen wy
bote budd *eg* buddion

bottle potel *eb* poteli
bottle feeding bwydo o'r botel *be*
bottle warmer gwresogydd potel *eg* gwresogyddion poteli
bottleneck tagfa *eb* tagfeydd
bottom gwaelod *eg* gwaelodion
bottom drawer rail rheilen waelod drôr *eb* rheiliau gwaelod drôr
bottom edge ymyl waelod *eb* ymylon gwaelod
bottom frame ffrâm waelod *eb* fframiau gwaelod
▸ **bottom fuller** pannydd isaf *eg* panwyr isaf
bottom gear gêr isaf *eg*
bottom margin ymyl waelod *eb* ymylon gwaelod
bottom of baseline godre'r gwaelodlin *eg*
bottom of character gwaelod y nod *eg*
bottom of line gwaelod y llinell *eg*
bottom part darn gwaelod *eg* darnau gwaelod
bottom rail rheilen isaf *eb* rheiliau isaf
bottom rake gwyredd gwaelod *eg*
bottom set bed gwely is-haen *eg* gwelyau is-haen
bottom swage darfath isaf *eg*
bottom to top o'r gwaelod i'r brig
bottoming stake bonyn gwaelodi *eg* bonion gwaelodi
bottoming tap tap gwaelodi *eg* tapiau gwaelodi
bottom-up processing prosesu o'r gwaelod i fyny *be*
bottom-up programming rhaglennu adeiladol *be*
botulism botwliaeth *eb*
bouclé bouclé *eg*
bouclé yarn edafedd bouclé *ell*
bough cangen *eb* canghennau
boulder clogfaen *eg* clogfeini
boulder choke tagfa glogfeini *eb* tagfeydd clogfeini
boulder clay clog-glai *eg*
bounce *n* sbonc *eb* sbonciau
bounce *v* sboncio *be*
bounce back *n* adlam *eg* adlamiadau
bounce back *v* adlamu *be*
bounce of the ball sbonc y bêl *eb*
bounce on the ground *v* sboncio ar y ddaear *be*
bounce pass pàs sboncio *eb* pasiau sboncio
bound (=jump) *n* llam *eg* llamau
bound (=jump) *v* llamu *be*
bound (=limitation) *n* arffin *eb* arffiniau
bound (of electron) *adj* rhwym *ans*
bound buttonhole twll botwm wedi'i rwymo *eg* tyllau botymau wedi'u rhwymo
bound by contract rhwym dan gontract *ans*
bound column colofn arffin *eb* colofnau arffin
bound opening agoriad rhwymog *eg* agoriadau rhwymog
bound slot pocket poced agen *eb* pocedi agen
boundary ffin *eb* ffiniau
boundary (fence) terfyn *eg* terfynau
boundary conditions amodau ffin *ell*
boundary layer haen ffin *eb* haenau ffin
bounded ffinedig *ans*
bounded variation amrywiad ffinedig *eg* amrywiadau ffinedig
bounding plane plân terfyn *eg* planau terfyn
bouquet garni bouquet garni *eg* bouquets garnis
Bourbon restoration adferiad y Bourboniaid *eg*
Bourbons Bourboniaid *ell*
bourgeois bourgeois *ans*
bourgeoisie bourgeoisie *eg*
bourn nant hafesb *eb* nentydd hafesb
bourrée bourrée *eg* bourrées
bout bowt *eg* bowtiau
bovate bufedd *eb* bufeddi
bow (=bend) *v* crymu *be*
bow (=inclination of the head or trunk) *n* ymgrymiad *eg* ymgrymiadau
bow (=incline the head or trunk) *v* ymgrymu *be*
bow (for archery) *n* bwa *eg* bwâu
bow (in needlework) *n* dolen *eb* dolennau
bow (with stringed instrument) *v* tynnu bwa *be*
bow case cas bwa *eg* casys bwa
bow down bwa i lawr
bow knot cwlwm dolen *eg* clymau dolen
bow knot pattern patrwm cwlwm dolen *eg* patrymau cwlwm dolen
bow side (in rowing) ochr dde *eb*
Bow Street Runner Ceidwad Bow Street *eg* Ceidwaid Bow Street
bow tie tei bô *eg*
bow up bwa i fyny
bow window ffenestr fwa *eb* ffenestri bwa
bowed harp telyn fwa *eb* telynau bwa
bowel perfedd *eg* perfeddion
bow-fronted blaengrwm *ans*
bowing (in a score) bwa-nodi *be*
bowl *n* powlen *eb* powlenni
bowl *v* bowlio *be*
bowl (=action of bowling) *n* bowliad *eg* bowliadau
bowl out bowlio allan *be*
bowl over the wicket bowlio dros y wiced *be*
bowl overarm bowlio dros ysgwydd *be*
bowl round the wicket bowlio rownd y wiced *be*
bowl underarm bowlio dan ysgwydd *be*
bowled ball pelen *eb* pelenni
bowler bowliwr *eg* bowlwyr
bowlful powlaid *eb*
bowline bowlin *eb* bowliniau
bowling crease cris bowlio *eg* crisiau bowlio
bowling method dull o fowlio *eg* dulliau o fowlio
bowling speed cyflymder y bowlio *eg*
Bowman's capsule cwpan Bowman *eg*
Bow's notation nodiant Bow *eg*
bow-saw llif fwa *eb* llifiau bwa
bowstring llinyn bwa *eg* llinynnau bwa
bow-stringed truss cwpl bwaog *eg* cyplau bwaog
box *v* bocsio *be*
box (gymnastic apparatus) *n* bocs *eg* bocsys
box (in general) *n* blwch *eg* blychau

box angle plate plât ongl blwch *eg* platiau ongl blwch
box construction adeiladwaith blwch *eg*
box crosswise bocs ar groes *eg*
box drawing lluniad blwch *eg* lluniadau blwch
box frame ffrâm bocs *eg* fframiau bocs
box joint uniad blwch *eg* uniadau blwch
box lengthwise bocs ar hyd *eg*
box lock clo blwch *eg* cloeon blychau
box pleat plet bocs *eb* pletiau bocs
box pleat opening agoriad plet bocs *eg* agoriadau pletiau bocs
box spanner sbaner blwch *eg* sbaneri blwch
box square sgwâr blwch *eg* sgwariau blwch
box tongs gefel flwch *eb* gefeiliau blwch
box wood pren bocs *eg*
Boxer Rising Gwrthryfel y Bocswyr *eg*
box-trap magl-flwch *eb* magl-flychau
boxwood mallet gordd pren bocs *eb* gyrdd pren bocs
boxwood ruler riwl pren bocs *eb* riwliau pren bocs
boy bachgen *eg* bechgyn
Boyar Boiar *eg* Boiariaid
boycott boicotio *be*
brace (=cleat) *n* cledd *eg* cleddau
brace (=cleat) *v* cleddu *be*
brace (=device for clamping) *n* carntro *eg* carntroeon
brace (=mark in printing, music) *n* cyplysydd *eg* cyplyswyr
brace (for teeth) *n* ffrâm ddannedd *eb* fframiau dannedd
brace (the bow) *v* tynhau *be*
brace and bit carntro ac ebill
braced cleddog *ans*
braced door drws cleddog *eg* drysau cleddog
braced truss cwpl cleddog *eg* cyplau cleddog
bracer breichydd *eg* breichwyr
brachial breichiol *ans*
bracket (=printing mark) cromfach *eg* cromfachau
bracket (for shelving) braced *eg/b* bracedi
bracket foot troed fraced *eb* traed bracedi
bracketing bracedu *be*
brackish water dŵr lled hallt *eg* dyfroedd lled hallt
bract bract *eg* bractau
bract scales cen bract *eg* cennau bract
bracteole bractolyn *eg* bractolynnau
brad (cut nail) hoelen fain *eb* hoelion main
bradawl mynawyd *eg* mynawydau
bradycardia bradycardia *eg*
Brahman Brahman *eg*
Brahmin Brahmin *eg*
braid brêd *eg* brediau
braid loom gwŷdd brêd *eg* gwyddiau brêd
braided river afon blethog *eb* afonydd plethog
braiding plethu *be*
brain ymennydd *eg* ymenyddiau
brain damage niwed i'r ymennydd *eg*
brain dead ymennydd yn farw
brain death marwolaeth yr ymennydd *eg*
brain scanning sganio'r ymennydd *be*
brain stem coesyn yr ymennydd *eg* coesynnau'r ymennydd
brain storming ystyried syniadau *be*
braise brwysio *be*
brake brêc *eg* breciau
brake block bloc brêc *eg* blociau brêc
brake cylinder silindr brêc *eg* silindrau brêc
brake drum drwm brêc *eg* drymiau brêc
brake fluid hylif brêc *eg*
brake handle dolen frêc *eb* dolennau brêc
brake horse power marchnerth brêc *eg*
brake lever lifer brêc *eg* liferi brêc
brake resistance gwrthedd brêc *eg* gwrtheddau brêc
brake shoe esgid brêc *eb* esgidiau brêc
brake wheel olwyn frêc *eb* olwynion brêc
braking distance pellter brecio *eg* pellterau brecio
bran bran *eg*
branch *n* cangen *eb* canghennau
branch *v* ymganghennu *be*
branch *v* canghennu *be*
branch (factory) ffatri gangen *eb* ffatrïoedd cangen
branch circumference cylchedd cangen *eg*
branch development datblygiad cangen *eg*
branch instruction cyfarwyddyd canghennu *eg* cyfarwyddiadau canghennu
branch line lein gangen *eb* leiniau cangen
branch pipe pibell gangen *eb* pibellau cangen
branch pipe junction cydiad pibell gangen *eg* cydiadau pibellau cangen
branch prism prism cangen *eg* prismau cangen
branch shop siop gangen *eb* siopau cangen
branched canghennog *ans*
branched terminals of the axon terfyniadau canghennog yr acson *ell*
branchia (=gill) tagell *eb* tagellau
branchial tagellog *ans*
branching database cronfa ddata ganghennog *eb* cronfeydd data canghennog
branching programme rhaglen ganghennog *eb* rhaglenni canghennog
brand (=assign a brand name to) brandio *be*
brand (=make of goods) *n* brand *eg* brandiau
brand (=mark with disgrace) *v* gwarthnodi *be*
brand image delwedd brand *eb* delweddau brand
brand name enw brand *eg* enwau brand
branded goods nwyddau brand *ell*
brandering brandro *be*
brandy brandi *eg*
brandy butter menyn brandi *eg*
brandy snap crimpen frandi *eb* crimp brandi
brash malurion *ell*
brass pres *eg*
brass backed cefn pres *eg* cefnau pres
brass bush bwsh pres *eg* bwshys pres
brass drawing pin pin bawd pres *eg* pinnau bawd pres
brass eyelet llygaden bres *eb* llygadennau pres

brass filings efyddlifion *ell*
brass handle dolen bres *eb* dolennau pres
brass head nail hoelen ben pres *eb* hoelion pen pres
brass instrument offeryn pres *eg* offerynnau pres
brass nail hoelen bres *eb* hoelion pres
brass rubbing rhwbiad pres *eg* rhwbiadau pres
brass screw sgriw bres *eb* sgriwiau pres
brass section adran bres *eb* adrannau pres
brass solo unawd pres *eb* unawdau pres
brass wire gwifren bres *eb* gwifrau pres
brassback saw llif gefn bres *eb* llifiau cefn pres
brassica crop cnwd bresych *eg* cnydau bresych
Brave West Winds Gwyntoedd Grymus y Gorllewin *ell*
bravura brafwra *eg*
brawn cosyn pen *eg* cosynnau pen
brayer (roller) rholer *eg* rholeri
braze presyddu *be*
brazed joint uniad wedi'i bresyddu *eg* uniadau wedi'u presyddu
brazing clamp clamp presyddu *eg* clampiau presyddu
brazing hearth aelwyd bresyddu *eb* aelwydydd presyddu
brazing process proses bresyddu *eb* prosesau presyddu
brazing spelter sbelter presyddu *eg* sbelterau presyddu
brazing torch tortsh bresyddu *eb* tortshys presyddu
brazing wire gwifren bresyddu *eb* gwifrau presyddu
breach (=break through) *v* bylchu *be*
breach (=gap) *n* bwlch *eg* bylchau
breach (of whales etc) llamu *be*
breach of contract tor-contract *eg*
breach of duty tor-dyletswydd *eb*
breach of peace tor-heddwch *eg*
breached bylchog *ans*
bread bara *eg*
bread and butter bara menyn *eg*
bread and butter pudding pwdin bara menyn *eg* pwdinau bara menyn
bread crumbs briwsion bara *ell*
bread roll rholyn bara *eg* rholiau bara
breadboard bwrdd bara *eg* byrddau bara
breadth lled *eg* lledau
break *n* toriad *eg* toriadau
break *v* torri *be*
break crop cnwd saib *eg* cnydau saib
break even adennill costau *be*
break even chart siart adennill costau *eg* siartiau adennill costau
break frequency amledd torri *eg*
break ground torri tir *be*
break joint uniad toriad *eg* uniadau toriad
BREAK key bysell BREAK *eb* bysellau BREAK
break line llinell doriad *eb* llinellau toriad
break loan torfenthyciad *eg* torfenthyciadau
break the wicket torri'r wiced *be*
break with Rome torri oddi wrth Rufain *be*
breakage toriad *eg* toriadau
breakdown (=disintegration) ymddatodiad *eg* ymddatodiadau
breakdown (=failure) methiant *eg* methiannau
breakdown (of machinery) torri i lawr *be*
breaker (of wave) moryn *eg* morynnau
breakfast brecwast *eg* brecwastau
breakfast cereal grawnfwyd brecwast *eg* grawnfwydydd brecwast
breaking news newyddion sy'n torri *ell*
breaking of voice llais yn torri
breakpoint torbwynt *eg* torbwyntiau
breakwater morglawdd *eg* morgloddiau
bream gwrachen ddu *eb* gwrachod du
breast (in general) brest *eb* brestiau
breast (of woman) bron *eb* bronnau
breast cancer canser y fron *eg*
breast drill dril brest *eg* driliau brest
breast feeding bwydo o'r fron *be*
breast self-examination hunan archwiliad o'r fron *eg*
breast shot wheel rhod ffrwd ganol *eb* rhodau ffrwd ganol
breaststroke nofio broga *be*
breath anadl *eg/b* anadliadau
breath mark marc anadlu *eg* marciau anadlu
breathe anadlu *be*
breathed sound sain anadl *eb* seiniau anadl
breathing exercise ymarfer anadlu *eg* ymarferion anadlu
breathing movement symudiad anadlu *eg* symudiadau anadlu
breathing rate cyfradd anadlu *eb*
breathless (with feminine nouns) byr ei hanadl *ans* byr eu hanadl
breathless (with masculine nouns) byr ei anadl *ans* byr eu hanadl
breech birth esgoriad ffolennol *eg* esgoriadau ffolennol
breeches clos pen-glin *eg*
breed *n* brid *eg* bridiau
breed *v* bridio *be*
breeder reactor adweithydd bridiol *eg* adweithyddion bridiol
breeding cycle cylchred fridio *eb* cylchredau bridio
breeze (=light wind) awel *eb* awelon
breeze (blues) chwa *eb* chwaon
breeze block bloc bris *eg* blociau bris
breeze slab slab bris *eg* slabiau bris
Brethren of the Common Life Brodyr y Bywyd Cyffredin *ell*
breve brif *eg* brifiau
brevet dogfen braint filwrol *eb* dogfennau braint filwrol
breviary llyfr gwasanaeth *eg* llyfrau gwasanaeth
brew (alcohol) *v.trans* bragu *be*
brew (of tea) *v.intrans* bwrw ffrwyth *be*

bribe *n* llwgrwobr *eb* llwgrwobrwyon
bribe *v* llwgrwobrwyo *be*
bribery and corruption llwgrwobrwyo a llygru
brick bricsen *eb* brics
brick clay bric-glai *eg*
brick cutting torri briciau *be*
brick dust llwch brics *eg*
brick earth bric-bridd *eg*
brickwork bricwaith *eg*
bricolage bricolage *eg*
bride-price cowyll *eg* cowyllion
bridge *n* pont *eb* pontydd
bridge *v* pontio *be*
bridge circuit cylched bont *eb* cylchedau pont
bridge passage pont *eb* pontydd
bridge point man pontio *eg* mannau pontio
bridge tone traws-dôn *eb* trawsdonau
bridgehead (in architecture) talbont *eb* talbontydd
bridgehead (military) blaenlaniad *eg* blaenlaniadau
bridging course cwrs pontio *eg* cyrsiau pontio
bridging joist (flooring) trawst pontio *eg* trawstiau pontio
bridging loan benthyciad dros dro *eg* benthyciadau dros dro
bridle *n* ffrwyn *eb* ffrwynau
bridle *v* ffrwyno *be*
bridle bit genfa ffrwyn *eb* genfeydd ffrwyn
bridle joint uniad bagl *eg* uniadau bagl
brief *n* briff *eg* briffiau
brief *v* rhagbaratoi *be*
brief (=concise) cryno *ans*
brief (in general) *adj* byr *ans*
brief outline amlinelliad byr *eg* amlinelliadau byr
brief title teitl cryno *eg* teitlau cryno
brigade brigâd *eb* brigadau
Brigadier Brigadydd *eg* Brigadyddion
brigand gwylliad *eg* gwylliaid
bright llachar *ans*
bright colour lliw llachar *eg* lliwiau llachar
bright dip dip gloywi *eg* dipiau gloywi
bright drawn bars barrau gloyw *ell*
bright drawn mild steel (B.D.M.S.) dur meddal gloyw wedi'i dynnu *eg*
bright mild steel (B.M.S.) dur meddal gloyw *eg*
bright orange (enamelling colour) oren llachar *eg*
bright red heat (cherry red) gwres cochias *eg*
bright yellow heat gwres eirias *eg*
brightness disgleirdeb *eg*
brightness constancy cysondeb disgleirdeb *eg*
brightness contrast cyferbyniad disgleirdeb *eg*
brightness control rheolydd disgleirdeb *eg* rheolyddion disgleirdeb
brill bril *eg*
brilliance disgleirdeb *eg*
brilliance of colour disgleirdeb lliw *eg*
brilliant llachar *ans*
brilliant blue glas llachar *eg*
brilliant colour lliw llachar *eg* lliwiau llachar
brilliant green gwyrdd llachar *eg*
brine heli *eg*
brine test prawf heli *eg*
bring to front dwyn i'r blaen *be*
bring-and-buy moes a phryn
brinkmanship hwylio yn agos i'r gwynt *be*
brioche brioche *eb* brioches
brisket brisged *eb*
brisling corbennog *eg* corbenogiaid
bristle (of animal) gwrychyn *eg* gwrych
bristle (of brush) blewyn *eg* blew
bristle brush brwsh blew *eg* brwshys blew
Bristol board bwrdd Bryste *eg*
Britannia metal metel Britannia *eg*
British Crime Survey Arolwg Trosedd Prydain *eg*
British Electrical Approvals Board (BEAB) Bwrdd Cymeradwyo Trydan Prydain *eg*
British film industry diwydiant ffilm Prydain *eg*
British Savings Bonds Bondiau Cynilo Prydeinig *ell*
British School Ysgol Brydeinig *eb* Ysgolion Prydeinig
British sign language iaith arwyddion Prydain *eb*
British Standard Safon Brydeinig *eb* Safonau Prydeinig
British Standard specification manyleb Safonau Prydeinig *eb* manylebau Safonau Prydeinig
British Standards Institution Sefydliad Safonau Prydeinig *eg*
Briton (Ancient) Brython *eg* Brythoniaid
Briton (Modern) Prydeiniwr *eg* Prydeinwyr
brittle brau *ans*
brittleness breuder *eg*
broach (=bit for boring) cŷn main *eg* cynion main
broad llydan *ans*
broad beans ffa *ell*
broad pen pen llydan *eg* pennau llydan
broad pen lettering llythrennu pen llydan *be*
broad trend tuedd gyffredinol *eb*
broadband band llydan *eg*
broadband fixed wireless access mynediad diwifr sefydlog band llydan *eg*
Broadband Marketing (name of programme) Marchnata Band Eang *be*
Broadband Wales (name of programme) Band Eang Cymru *eb*
Broadband Wales programme rhaglen Band Eang Cymru *eb*
Broadband Wales Taskforce Representative Cynrychiolydd Tasglu Band Eang Cymru *eg*
Broadband Wales Unit Uned Band Eang Cymru *eg*
broadcast *n* darllediad *eg* darllediadau
broadcast *v* darlledu *be*
broadcast quality ansawdd darlledu *eg*
Broadcasting Standards Commission Comisiwn Safonau Darlledu *eg*
broaden lledu *be*
broadleaved llydanddail *ans*

broadleaved tree coeden lydanddail *eb* coed llydanddail
Broadmann's area rhan Broadmann *eb* rhannau Broadmann
broadsheet papur safonol *eg* papurau safonol
brocade brocêd *eg*
Broca's area rhan Broca *eb*
broccoli brocoli *ell*
brochure llyfryn *eg* llyfrynnau
broderie anglaise broderie anglaise *eb*
broiler cyw brwylio *eg* cywion brwylio
broken cadence diweddeb annisgwyl *eb* diweddebau annisgwyl
broken chord cord gwasgar *eg* cordiau gwasgar
broken colour rhaniadliw *eg*
broken consort consort cymysg *eg*
broken line llinell doredig *eb* llinellau toredig
broker brocer *eg* broceriaid
brokerage broceriaeth *eb*
bromate(I) ion ïon bromad(I) *eg* ïonau bromad(I)
bromate(V) ion ïon bromad(V) *eg* ïonau bromad(V)
bromic(I) acid asid bromig(I) *eg*
bromic(V) acid asid bromig(V) *eg*
brominate bromineiddio *be*
bromination bromineiddiad *eg*
bromine (Br) bromin *eg*
bromine trifluoride bromin trifflworid *eg*
bromine water dŵr bromin *eg*
bromobenzene bromobensen *eg*
bromoethane bromoethan *eg*
bronchiole bronciolyn *eg* bronciolynnau
bronchitis broncitis *eg*
bronchus broncws *eg* bronci
bronze efydd *eg* **Bronze Age** Oes Efydd *eb*
bronze alloy aloi efydd *eg*
bronze green (enamelling colour) gwyrdd efydd *eg*
bronze hoard celc efydd *eg* celciau efydd
brooch tlws *eg* tlysau
brooch back cefn tlws *eg* cefnau tlysau
brooch pin tlysbin *eg* tlysbinau
broom ysgubell *eb* ysgubellau
broomstick coes ysgubell *eb* coesau ysgubell
broth potes *eg*
Brother Preacher Brawd-Bregethwr *eg* Brawd-Bregethwyr
brotherhood brawdoliaeth *eb* brawdoliaethau
brow ael *eb* aeliau
brown *n* brown *eg* browniau
brown *v* brownio *be*
brown bread bara brown *eg*
brown coal glo brown *eg*
brown earth pridd brown *eg* priddoedd brown
brown earth soil pridd brown *eg* priddoedd brown
brown field site safle tir llwyd *eg* safleoedd tir llwyd
brown paper papur llwyd *eg* papurau llwyd
brown paper tape tâp papur llwyd *eg*
brown sugar (demerara) siwgr coch *eg*
brown sugar (soft) siwgr meddal *eg*
Brownian movement (motion) symudiad Brown *eg*
brownish brownaidd *ans*
brownshirts crysau brown *ell*
browse pori *be*
browser porwr *eg* porwyr
browser options dewisiadau porwr *ell*
bruise *n* clais *eg* cleisiau
bruise *v* cleisio *be*
brush *n* brwsh *eg* brwshys
brush *v* brwsio *be*
brush care gofal brwsh *eg*
brush handle coes brwsh *eb* coesau brwsh
brush polish llathrydd brwsh *eg* llathryddion brwsh
brush stand stand brwshys *eg* standiau brwshys
brush stroke strôc brwsh *eb* strociau brwsh
brushed (finish) gwlanog *ans*
brushed cotton cotwm gwlanog *eg*
brushed nylon neilon gwlanog *eg*
brushwood prysgwydd *ell*
brushwork brwshwaith *eg*
Brussels sprouts ysgewyll *ell*
bryophyte bryoffyt *eg* bryoffytau
Brythonic Brythonaidd *ans*
B.S. recommendation argymhelliad B.S. *eg*
bubble *n* swigen *eb* swigod
bubble *v.intrans* byrlymu *be*
bubble *v.trans* gyrru swigod drwy *be*
buccal cavity ceudod bochaidd *eg* ceudodau bochaidd
buccaneer bycanîr *eg* bycaniriaid
buck (in gymnastics) ebol *eg* ebolion
buck crosswise ebol ar groes *eg* ebolion ar groes
bucket bwced *eg* bwcedi
buckle crychu *be*
buckle *n* bwcl *eg* byclau
buckle *v* bwclo *be*
buckler bwcler *eg* bwcleri
buckram bwcram *eg*
buckwheat gwenith yr hydd *eg*
bud *n* blaguryn *eg* blagur
bud *v* blaguro *be*
bud scale cen blaguro *eg* cennau blaguro
Buddha Bwdha *eg*
Buddhahood Bwdhadod *eg*
Buddhism Bwdhaeth *eb*
Buddhist *adj* Bwdhaidd *ans*
Buddhist *n* Bwdhydd *eg* Bwdhyddion
budding ymflagurol *ans*
budgerigar green (enamelling colour) gwyrdd bwdgerigar *eg*
budget *n* cyllideb *eb* cyllidebau
budget *v* cyllidebu *be*
budget account cyfrif cyllido *eg* cyfrifon cyllido
budget deficit diffyg cyllidol *eg* diffygion cyllidol
budget share cyfran o'r gyllideb *eb* cyfrannau o'r gyllideb

budgetary cyllidol *ans*
budgetary arrangement trefniant cyllidol *eg* trefniadau cyllidol
budgetary control rheolaeth gyllidol *eb* rheolaethau cyllidol
buff *n* bwff *eg* bwffiau
buff *v* bwffio *be*
buff mop mop bwffio *eg* mopiau bwffio
buff wheel olwyn fwffio *eb* olwynion bwffio
buffer *n* byffer *eg* byfferau
buffer *v* byffro *be*
buffer beam trawst byffer *eg* trawstiau byffer
buffer solution hydoddiant byffer *eg*
buffer spring sbring byffer *eg* sbringiau byffer
buffer state gwladwriaeth glustog *eb* gwladwriaethau clustog
buffered input mewnbwn byfferog *eg* mewnbynnau byfferog
buffered output allbwn byfferog *eg* allbynnau byfferog
buffet bwffe *eg* bwffes
bug byg *eg* bygiau
bug (=fault) nam *eg* namau
bugle biwgl *eg* biwglau
build adeiladu *be*
build in ymgorffori *be*
building adeilad *eg* adeiladau
building insurance yswiriant adeiladau *eg*
building regulation rheoliad adeiladu *eg* rheoliadau adeiladu
building society cymdeithas adeiladu *eb* cymdeithasau adeiladu
building survey arolwg adeiladu *eg* arolygon adeiladu
building surveyor syrfëwr adeiladu *eg* syrfewyr adeiladu
building technology technoleg adeiladu *eb*
building use survey arolwg defnyddio adeiladau *eg* arolygon defnyddio adeiladau
buildings and structures adeiladau ac adeileddau
built environment sector sector amgylchedd adeiledig *eg*
built-in cupboard cwpwrdd gosod *eg*
built-up area ardal adeiledig *eb* ardaloedd adeiledig
built-up stain staen adeiledig *eg* staeniau adeiledig
bulb bwlb *eg* bylbiau
bulb holder gafaelydd bwlb *eg* gafaelyddion bylbiau
bulbous oddfog *ans*
bulbous leg coes oddfog *eb* coesau oddfog
bulbous turnery turnwriaeth oddfog *eb*
bulge *n* gwrym *eg* gwrymiau
bulge *v* bolio *be*
bulimia bwlimia *eg*
bulk swmp *eg* sympau
bulk buying swmp brynu *be*
bulk carrier swmp gludydd *eg* swmp gludyddion
bulk materials defnyddiau swmp *ell*
bulk of the goods rhan fwyaf o'r nwyddau *eb*
bulk storage storfa swmp *eb* storfeydd swmp
bulk supplies cyflenwadau sylweddol *ell*
bulk tank swmp-danc *eg* swmpdanciau
bulk transport swmpgludo *be*
bulked yarn edafedd wedi'u swmpuso *ell*
bulkflow swmplif *eg*
bulking action gweithred swmpuso *eb*
bulky swmpus *ans*
bulky goods nwyddau swmpus *ell*
bull (papal) bwla *eg* bwlaon
bull wheel (shaper) olwyn strôc *eb* olwynion strôc
bullet bwled *eg* bwledi
bullet point pwynt bwled *eg* pwyntiau bwled
bulleted list rhestr o bwyntiau bwled *eb* rhestri o bwyntiau bwled
bulletin bwletin *eg* bwletinau
bulletin board hysbysfwrdd *eg* hysbysfyrddau
bullion bwliwn *eg*
bull-nosed plane plaen trwyn byr *eg* plaeniau trwyn byr
bully (in hockey) *n* bwli *eg* bwlïau
bully off *v* bwlïo *be*
bumper bymper *eg* bymperi
bun bynen *eb* byns
bunch grass (tussock) sypwellt *eg*
bund bwnd *eg* byndiau
bundle sypyn *eg* sypynnau
bundle sheath gwain sypyn *eb*
bung topyn *eg* topynnau
bungaloid growth twf byngaloaidd *eg*
bungalow byngalo *eg* byngalos
bunny jump naid cwningen *eb* neidiau cwningen
Bunsen burner llosgydd Bunsen *eg* llosgyddion Bunsen
bunt hit bwnt *eg*
buoy bwi *eg* bwiau
buoyancy hynofedd *eg*
buoyancy bag bag hynofedd *eg* bagiau hynofedd
buoyancy tank tanc hynofedd *eg* tanciau hynofedd
buoyant hynawf *ans*
bur (of plant) masgl pigog *eg* masglau pigog
buran bwrán *eg*
burden baich *eg* beichiau
bureau biwro *eg* biwroau
bureau fall clawr biwro *eg* cloriau biwro
bureaucracy biwrocratiaeth *eb*
bureaucrat biwrocrat *eg* biwrocratiaid
bureaucratic biwrocrataidd *ans*
burette bwred *eb* bwredau
burgage tir bwrdais *eg*
burgage borough bwrdeistref fwrgais *eb*
burgage tenure daliadaeth fwrgeisiol *eb*
burgher bwrdais *eg* bwrdeisiaid
burghol bwrdeisiol *ans*
Burgundian *adj* Bwrgwynaidd *ans*
Burgundian *n* Bwrgwyniad *eg* Bwrgwyniaid
burial claddedigaeth *eb* claddedigaethau

burial chamber siambr gladdu *eb* siambrau claddu
burial ground man claddu *eg* mannau claddu
burial mound tomen gladdu *eb* tomenni claddu
burin (graver) ysgythrydd *eg* ysgythryddion
burlap bwrlap *eg*
burlesque bwrlesg *eg*
burn *n* llosg *eg* llosgiadau
burn *v* llosgi *be*
burn out llwyrlosgi *be*
burnable llosgadwy *ans*
burner llosgydd *eg* llosgyddion
burnish *n* bwrnais *eg* bwrneisiau
burnish *v* bwrneisio *be*
burnisher bwrneisydd *eg* bwrneisyddion
burn-out chwythu plwc *be*
burns unit uned losgiadau *eb* unedau llosgiadau
burnt llosg *ans*
burnt offering poethoffrwm *eg* poethoffrymau
burnt sienna sienna llosg *eg*
burnt umber wmber llosg *eg*
burpee naid wasg *eb* neidiau gwasg
burr (in timber) bwr *eg*
burr (of scraper) min *eg*
burr (on metal or paper) ymyl arw *eb* ymylon garw
burrow (of fox) daear *eb* daeërydd
burrow (of rabbits) twll *eb* tyllau
burrowing tyrchu *be*
burrows (of sand) twyni *ell*
bursar bwrsar *eg* bwrsariaid
bursary bwrsari *eg* bwrsarïau
burst ebychiad *eg* ebychiadau
burst of monsoon toriad y monsŵn *eg*
burster ffrwydriad *eg* ffrwydriaid
bus bws *eg* bysiau
bus speed cyflymder bws *eg*
bus type math bws *eg*
bush (=shrub) llwyn *eg* llwyni
bush (=metal lining) bwsh *eg* bwshys
bushel bwysel *eg* bwyseli
bushmen pobl y prysglwyni *eb*
bushveld ffeld prysglwyni *eg* ffeldiau prysglwyni
bushy trwchus *ans*
business busnes *eg* busnesau
business account cyfrif busnes *eg* cyfrifon busnes
business activity gweithgaredd busnes *eg* gweithgareddau busnes
business data data busnes *ell*
business development datblygu busnes *be*
business document dogfen busnes *eb* dogfennau busnes
business environment amgylchedd busnes *eg*
business ethics moeseg busnes *eb*
business function swyddogaeth fusnes *eb* swyddogaethau busnes
business letter llythyr busnes *eg* llythyrau busnes
business objective amcan busnes *eg*
business plan cynllun busnes *eg*
business rates trethi busnes *ell*
business system system fusnes *eb* systemau busnes
business user defnyddiwr busnes *eg* defnyddwyr busnes
bust (=human chest) mynwes *eb* mynwesau
bust (in sculpture) penddelw *eg* penddelwau
bustline llinell fynwes *eb* llinellau mynwes
busy prysur *ans*
buta-1,3-diene bwta-1,3-deuen *eg*
butan-2-al bwtan-2-al *eg*
butanal bwtanal *eg*
butane bwtan *eg*
butanedial bwtandeual *eg*
butanedioic acid asid bwtandeuöig *eg*
butanedioic anhydride bwtandeuöig anhydrid *eg*
butanedione bwtandeuon *eg*
butanedione dioxime bwtandeuon deuocsim *eg*
butanoic acid asid bwtanöig *eg*
butan-1-ol bwtan-1-ol *eg*
butan-2-ol bwtan-2-ol *eg*
butanone bwtanon *eg*
butan-2-yl bwtan-2-yl *eg*
butcher cigydd *eg* cigyddion
but-1-ene bwt-1-en *eg*
but-2-ene bwt-2-en *eg*
butt *n* bôn *eg* bonau
butt *v* bytio *be*
butt brazed (lathe toll forms) presyddiad bôn *eg* presyddiadau bôn
butt end rammer hyrddwr pen ôl *eg* hyrddwyr pen ôl
butt hinge colfach ymyl *eg* colfachau ymyl
butt joint uniad bôn *eg* uniadau bôn
butt measurement mesuriad bôn *eg* mesuriadau bôn
butt mitred and keyed joint uniad bôn meitrog cudd *eg* uniadau bôn meitrog cudd
butt mitred joint uniad bôn meitrog *eg* uniadau bôn meitrog
butt weld weldiad bôn *eg* weldiadau bôn
butter menyn *eg*
butter beans ffa menyn *ell*
butterfat braster menyn *eg*
butterfish llyfrothen *eb* llyfrothod
butterfly glöyn byw *eg* glöynnod byw
butterfly hinge colfach glöyn byw *eg* colfachau glöyn byw
butterfly stroke nofio pilipala *be*
buttermilk llaeth enwyn *eg*
butter-nut pattern patrwm cnau menyn *eg* patrymau cnau menyn
butterscotch cyflaith menyn *eg*
buttock ffolen *eb* ffolennau
button *n* botwm *eg* botymau
button *v* botymu *be*
button mortise mortais botwm *eg* morteisiau botwm
button mould mowld botwm *eg* mowldiau botwm
button polish llathr botwm *eg*
button slot slot botwm *eg* slotiau botwm

button type math o fotwm *eg*
buttonhole twll botwm *eg* tyllau botwm
buttonhole loop dolen botwm *eb* dolennau botwm
buttonhole scissors siswrn twll botwm *eg* sisyrnau twll botwm
buttonhole stitch pwyth twll botwm *eg* pwythau twll botwm
buttonhole thread edau gyfrodedd *eb* edafedd cyfrodedd
buttonholer botymell *eb* botymellau
buttress (in needlework) bwtres *eg/b* bwtresi
buttress (on mountain) gwanas *eg/b* gwanasau
buttress thread edau fwtres *eb* edafedd bwtres
butyl- bwtyl-
butylate bwtyleiddio *be*
butyrate bwtyrad *eg*
butyric acid asid bwtyrig *eg*
buy prynu *be*
buyer prynwr *eg* prynwyr
buying price pris prynu *eg* prisiau prynu
buzzer swnyn *eg* swnwyr
by instalment fesul rhandal
bye heibiad *eg* heibiadau
by-election isetholiad *eg* isetholiadau
bye-stakes cil fonynnau *ell*
by-law (=local law) deddf leol *eb* deddfau lleol
by-law (=subsidiary law) is-ddeddf *eg* is-ddeddfau
by-movement symudiad sgil *eg* symudiadau sgil
bypass around a settlement ffordd osgoi aneddiadau *eb* ffyrdd osgoi aneddiadau
by-product sgil gynnyrch *eg* sgil gynhyrchion
bystander intervention ymyrraeth gwyliedydd *eb*
byte beit *eg* beitiau
byway cilffordd *eb* cilffyrdd
byway open to all traffic cilffordd yn agored i bob trafnidiaeth *eb* cilffyrdd yn agored i bob trafnidiaeth
Byzantine Bysantaidd *ans*
Byzantine chant siant Fysantaidd *eb* siantiau Bysantaidd
Byzantine music cerddoriaeth Fysantaidd *eb*

C

'C' /'S' scroll sgrôl 'C' /'S' *eb*
C clef cleff C *eg*
C major C fwyaf *eb*
C minor C leiaf *eb*
cabbage bresychen *eb* bresych
cabin hook bach caban *eg* bachau caban
cabin lift caban codi *eg* cabanau codi
cabinet cabinet *eg* cabinetau
cabinet file ffeil gabinet *eb* ffeiliau cabinet
cabinet fittings ffitiadau cabinet *ell*
cabinet maker saer dodrefn *eg* seiri dodrefn
cabinet organ organ gist *eb* organau cist
cabinet rasp rhathell gabinet *eb* rhathellau cabinet
cabinet scraper sgrafell gabinet *eb* sgrafelli cabinet
cabinet screwdriver tyrnsgriw cabinet *eg* tyrnsgriwiau cabinet
cabinet work gwaith dodrefn *eg*
cable cebl *eg* ceblau
cable modem modem cebl *eg* modemau cebl
cable smocking smocwaith rhaff *eg*
cable stitch pwyth rhaff *eg* pwythau rhaff
cable system system gebl *eb* systemau cebl
cable yarn edafedd rhaffog *ell*
cabriole leg coes gabriol *eb* coesau cabriol
cache storfa *eb* storfeydd
cache memory cof dros dro *eg*
cache store storfa dros dro *eb* storfeydd dros dro
cacophonous cacoffonig *ans*
cacophony cacoffoni *eg*
cactus cactws *eg* cacti
cadaver celain *eb* celanedd
cadence diweddeb *eg/b* diweddebau
cadence chord cord diweddeb *eg* cordiau diweddeb
cadential diweddebol *ans*
cadential 6/4 diweddeb 6/4 *eb* diweddebau 6/4
cadential 6/4 chord cord 6/4 diweddebol *eg* cordiau 6/4 diweddebol
cadenza cadenza *eg* cadenze
cadmium (Cd) cadmiwm *eg*
cadmium ion ïon cadmiwm *eg* ïonau cadmiwm
cadmium orange oren cadmiwm *eg*
cadmium red coch cadmiwm *eg*
cadmium scarlet sgarlad cadmiwm *eg*
cadmium yellow melyn cadmiwm *eg*
caducous (=fleeting, transitory) byrhoedlog *ans*
caducous (in botany) cwympol *ans*
caecum caecwm *eg*
Caerffili cheese caws Caerffili *eg*
Caesar Cesar *eg*
Caesarean birth genedigaeth Gesaraidd *eb* genedigaethau Cesaraidd
Caesarean section toriad Cesaraidd *eg* toriadau Cesaraidd
caesium (Cs) cesiwm *eg*
caesium chloride cesiwm clorid *eg*
caesium ion ïon caesiwm *eg* ïonau caesiwm
caesium surface arwyneb cesiwm *eg*
café caffi *eg*
caffeine caffein *eg*
cage cawell *eg* cewyll
CAI: computer aided instruction CAI: hyfforddiant drwy gymorth cyfrifiadur *eg*
cairn carnedd *eb* carneddau
cake teisen *eb* teisennau; cacen *eb* cacennau
cake glue glud slab *eg*
calamine calamin *eg*
calcareous calchaidd *ans*
calcification calcheiddiad *eg*
calcified matrix matrics calcheiddiedig *eg*
calcifuge calchgas *ans*
calcify calcheiddio *be*
calcinate calchynnu *be*
calcination calchyniad *eg* calchyniadau
calciphile calchgar *ans*
calciphobe calchgas *ans*
calcite calchit *eg*
calcitonin calsitonin *eg*
calcium (Ca) calsiwm *eg*
calcium carbide calsiwm carbid *eg*
calcium carbonate calsiwm carbonad *eg*
calcium cyanamide calsiwm cyanamid *eg*
calcium dicarbide calsiwm deucarbid *eg*
calcium diethynediide calsiwm deuethyndeuid *eg*
calcium ethynediide calsiwm ethyndeuid *eg*
calcium hydroxide calsiwm hydrocsid *eg*
calcium ion ïon calsiwm *eg* ïonau calsiwm
calcium magnesium biscarbonate (dolomite) calsiwm magnesiwm biscarbonad (dolomit) *eg*
calcium octadecanoate calsiwm octadecanoad *eg*
calcium oxide calsiwm ocsid *eg*
calcium silicate calsiwm silicad *eg*
calcium sulfate(VI) (anhydrite) calsiwm sylffad(VI) (anhydrit) *eg*
calcium sulfate(VI)-Ω-water calsiwm sylffad(VI)-Ω-dŵr *eg*
calcium sulfate(VI)-2-water (gypsum) calsiwm sylffad(VI)-2-dŵr (gypswm) *eg*

calculate cyfrifo *be*
calculate selection cyfrifo'r dewis *be*
calculate table cyfrifo'r tabl *be*
calculating machine peiriant cyfrifo *eg* peiriannau cyfrifo
calculating method dull cyfrifo *eg* dulliau cyfrifo
calculation cyfrifiad *eg* cyfrifiadau
calculator cyfrifiannell *eg* cyfrifianellau
calculator display dangosydd cyfrifiannell *eg* dangosyddion cyfrifiannell
calculus calcwlws *eg*
calculus of variation calcwlws amrywiad *eg*
caldera callor *eg* callorau
Caledonian Caledonaidd *ans*
calendar calendr *eg* calendrau
calf (of leg) croth y goes *eb*; poten y goes *eb*
calf muscle cyhyr croth y goes *eg* cyhyrau croth y goes
calgon calgon *eg*
calibrate graddnodi *be*
calibrated (with feminine nouns) wedi'i graddnodi *ans* wedi'u graddnodi
calibrated (with masculine nouns) wedi'i raddnodi *ans* wedi'u graddnodi
calibration graddnodiad *eg* graddnodiad
calibration constant cysonyn graddnodiad *eg*
calibration mark graddnod *eg* graddnodau
calico calico *eg* calicoau
calico buff bwff calico *eg* bwffiau calico
calico mop mop calico *eg* mopiau calico
calico patch clwt calico *eg* clytiau calico
californium (Cf) califforniwm *eg*
calkin (horse shoe) cawc *eg* cawciau
call *n* galwad *eb* galwadau
call *v* galw *be*
call by name galw wrth enw *be*
call by value galw wrth werth *be*
calligraphic caligraffig *ans*
calligraphic hand llaw galigraffig *eb*
calligraphist caligraffydd *eg* caligraffwyr
calligraphy caligraffeg *eb*
calling sequence dilyniant galw *eg* dilyniannau galw
calliper caliper *eg* caliperau
calliper gauge medrydd caliper *eg* medryddion caliper
callosal syndrome syndrom y caloswm *eg*
callus caleden *eb* caledennau
calm gosteg *eg* gostegau
calorie calori *eg* caloriau
calorific caloriffig *ans*
calorific value gwerth caloriffig *eg* gwerthoedd caloriffig
calorifier caloriffydd *eg* caloriffyddion
calorimeter calorimedr *eg* calorimedrau
calorimetric technique techneg galorimetrig *eb* technegau calorimetrig
calorimetry calorimedreg *eb*
calorizing caloreiddio *be*
Calvin Calfin *eg*
Calvin cycle cylchred Calvin *eb*
calving (in geomorphology) ymrannu *be*
Calvinism Calfiniaeth *eb*
Calvinistic Methodism Methodistiaeth Galfinaidd *eb*
calypso cân galypso *eb* caneuon calypso
calyx calycs *eg*
calyx eye needle nodwydd llygad agored *eb* nodwyddau llygad agored
cam cam *eg* camau
cam follower dilynwr cam *eg* dilynwyr cam
cam profile proffil cam *eg* proffiliau cam
camber *n* cambr *eg* cambrau
camber *v* cambro *be*
camber arch bwa cambr *eg* bwâu cambr
cambiata cambiata *eg* cambiatâu
cambium cambiwm *eg*
cambium layer haen gambiwm *eb* haenau cambiwm
Cambrian Cambriaidd *ans*
cambric cambrig *eg* cambrigau
camcorder video clip clip fideo camcordor *eg* clipiau fideo camcordor
camel hair brush brwsh blew camel *eg* brwshys blew camel
cameo cameo *eg* cameos
camera camera *eg* camerâu
camera still images delweddau camera llonydd *ell*
camiknickers nicers cami *eg*
camisole camisol *eg* camisolau
camomile camil *eb*
camouflage *n* cuddliw *eg* cuddliwiau
camouflage *v* cuddliwio *be*
camp gwersyll *eg* gwersylloedd
camp stool stôl blygu *eb* stolion plygu
campaign *n* ymgyrch *eb* ymgyrchoedd
campaign *v* ymgyrchu *be*
campanology campanoleg *eb*
camphor camffor *eg*
campus campws *eg* campysau
camshaft camsiafft *eg* camsiafftiau
can tun *eg* tuniau
Canadian Shield Tariandir Canada *eg*
canal camlas *eb* camlesi
canal, lock and towpath camlas, lloc a llwybr tynnu
canalicular camlesynnaidd *ans*
canalicus camlesyn *eg* camlesynnau
canapés canapés *ell*
cancel (in general) canslo *be*
cancel (in music) diddymu *be*
cancel autopilot canslo awtobeilot *be*
CANCEL key bysell CANSLO *eg* bysellau CANSLO
cancel mark nod canslo *eg* nodau canslo
cancellation (in general) canslad *eg* cansladau
cancellation (in music) diddymiad *eg* diddymiadau
cancer canser *eg* canserau
cancer of the bowel canser y coluddyn *eg*
cancrizans cancrizans *ell*

candid didwyll *ans*
candidate ymgeisydd *eg* ymgeiswyr
candied peel candi pîl *eg*
candle cannwyll *eb* canhwyllau
candle grease gwêr cannwyll *eg*
Candlemas Gŵyl Fair y Canhwyllau *eb*
candle-power canhwyllnerth *eg*
candlestick canhwyllbren *eg* canwyllbrennau
candlewick pabwyrgotwm *eg*
cane gwialen *eb* gwialennau
cane sugar siwgr cansen *eg*
canework gwaith gwiail *eg*
▶ **caneworker's bodkin** botgin gweithiwr gwiail *eg* botginau gweithwyr gwiail
caneworker's hammer morthwyl gweithiwr gwiail *eg* morthwylion gweithwyr gwiail
caneworker's pliers gefelen gweithiwr gwiail *eb* gefeiliau gweithwyr gwiail
canine tooth dant llygad *eg* dannedd llygad
canker cancr *eg*
canned food bwyd tun *eg* bwydydd tun
cannel coal glo cannwyll *eg*
cannery canerdy *eg* canerdai
canning canio *be*
canning industry diwydiant canio *eg*
cannon magnel *eb* magnelau
cannon ball pêl fagnel *eb* peli magnel
cannon ball service serfiad canon *eg* serfiadau canon
cannula caniwla *eg*
canoe canŵ *eg* canŵod
canon (in music) canon *eg/b* canonau
canon (of law) canon *eg* canonau
canon (of person) canon *eg* canoniaid
canon at the fifth canon yn y pumed *eb* canonau yn y pumed
canon at the octave canon yn yr wythfed *eb* canonau yn yr wythfed
canon at the unison canon unsain *eb* canonau unsain
canon by augmentation canon drwy estyniad *eb* canonau drwy estyniad
canon by diminution canon drwy gywasgiad *eb* canonau drwy gywasgiad
canon by inversion canon drwy wrthdro *eb* canonau drwy wrthdro
canon law (in general) cyfraith eglwysig *eb*
Canon Law (Roman Catholic) Cyfraith Ganonaidd *eb*
canon per arsin et thesin canon per arsin et thesin *eb* canonau per arsin et thesin
canon recte et retro canon recte et retro *eb* canonau recte et retro
canon rectus et inversus canon rectus et inversus *eb* canonau rectus et inversus

canonic imitation dynwarediad canonaidd *eg* dynwarediadau canonaidd
canonical canonaidd *ans*
canonical form ffurf ganonaidd *eb* ffurfiau canonaidd
canonical penalty penyd canonaidd *eg* penydiau canonaidd
canonize canoneiddio *be*
canonry canoniaeth *eb* canoniaethau
canonry magnelaeth *eb*
canopy canopi *eg* canopïau
cant goleddu *be*
can't open directory methu agor cyfeiriadur *be*
can't open file methu agor ffeil *be*
can't redo methu ailwneud *be*
can't restore methu adfer *be*
can't revoke methu dirymu *be*
can't undo methu dadwneud *be*
cantata cantata *eg* cantatau
canteen ffreutur *eg* ffreuturau
canteen staff staff ffreutur *ell*
canticle cantigl *eg/b* cantiglau
cantilena cantilena *eg* cantilenâu
cantilever cantilifer *eg* cantilifrau
cantilevered beam trawst cantilifer *eg* trawstiau cantilifer
canting saw llif oleddu *eb* llifiau goleddu
canting table bwrdd goleddu *eg* byrddau goleddu
canton canton *eg* cantonau
cantor cantor *eg* cantoriaid
cantoris cantoris *eg*
cantus fermus cantus fermus *eg*
canvas *n* cynfas *eg* cynfasau
canvas backing cefn cynfas *eg* cefnau cynfas
canvas board bwrdd cynfas *eg* byrddau cynfas
canvas boot esgid gynfas *eb* esgidiau cynfas
canvas embroidery brodwaith cynfas *eg*
canvas grain graen cynfas *eg*
canvas pin pin cynfas *eg* pinnau cynfas
canvas stitch pwyth cynfas *eg* pwythau cynfas
canvas straining tynhau cynfas *be*
canvas stretcher estynnwr cynfas *eg* estynwyr cynfas
canvass canfasio *be*
canyon canion *eg* canionau
canzona canzona *eg* canzone
canzonet canzonetta *eg* canzonette
cap (machine screws) cap *eg* capiau
cap cell cell gapan *eb* celloedd capan
cap iron haearn cefn *eg*
cap rock capgraig *eb* capgreigiau
cap sleeve llawes gap *eb* llewys cap
capability gallu *eg* galluoedd
capable galluog *ans*
capacitance cynhwysiant *eg* cynwysiannau
capacitive cynhwysaidd *ans*

capacitor (=condenser) cynhwysydd *eg* cynwysyddion
capacitor-load cynhwysydd-llwyth *eg*
capacity cynhwysedd *eg* cynwyseddau
cape (=cloak) clogyn *eg* clogynnau
cape (=headland) penrhyn *eg* penrhynau
Cape Horn Horn, Yr *eg*
Cape of Good Hope Penrhyn Gobaith Da *eg*
caper (for cooking) capryn *eg* caprau
Capetian Capetaidd *ans*
caphead screw sgriw ben cap *eb* sgriwiau pen cap
capillarity capiaredd *eg* capilareddau
capillary capilari *eg* capilarïau
capillary bed gwely capilarïau *eg* gwelyau capilarïau
capillary network rhwyllen capilarïau *eb* rhwyllenni capilarïau
capillary rise codiad capilari *eg* codiadau capilari
capillary sphincter sffincter capilari *eg*
capillary tube tiwb capilari *eg* tiwbiau capilari
capillary web gwe capilarïau *eb* gweoedd capilarïau
capital (=capital letter) priflythyren *eb* priflythrennau
capital (city) prifddinas *eb* prifddinasoedd
capital (finance) cyfalaf *eg*
capital (of Gothic harp) galeri *eg* galerïau
capital (of harp) pen *eg* pennau
capital account cyfrif cyfalaf *eg* cyfrifon cyfalaf
capital accumulation cronnedd cyfalaf *eg*
capital allowance lwfans cyfalaf *eg* lwfansau cyfalaf
capital depreciation dibrisiad cyfalaf *eg*
capital expenditure gwariant cyfalaf *eg*
capital gain enillion cyfalaf *ell*
capital gains tax treth enillion cyfalaf *eb*
capital goods nwyddau cyfalaf *ell*
capital growth twf cyfalaf *eg*
capital input mewnbwn cyfalaf *eg*
capital intensive cyfalaf-ddwys *ans*
capital letter priflythyren *eb* priflythrennau
capital offence trosedd farwol *eb* troseddau marwol
capital punishment cosb eithaf *eb*
capital sum swm cyfalaf *eg*
Capital Transfer Tax Treth Trosglwyddo Cyfalaf *eb*
capitalism cyfalafiaeth *eb*
capitalist *adj* cyfalafol *ans*
capitalist *n* cyfalafwr *eg* cyfalafwyr
capitalist agriculture amaethyddiaeth gyfalafol *eb*
capitalization error gwall priflythrennu *eg*
capitate flower fflurben *eg* fflurbennau
capitation allowance lwfans y pen *eg* lwfansau'r pen
capitation grant grant y pen *eg* grantiau'r pen
capitation tax treth y pen *eb* trethi y pen
capitular cabidylwr *eg* cabidylwyr
capitulate ildio *be*
capon caprwn *eg* capryniaid
capotasto branell *eb* branellau
cappella cappella *eg*
capriccio capriccio *eg* capricci
CAPS lock (computer key) clo CAPS *eg*
capsize dymchwel *be*
capsize drill dril dymchwel *eg* driliau dymchwel
capstone maen capan *eg* meini capan
capsular capsiwlaidd *ans*
capsule (in botany) capsiwl *eg* capsiwlau
capsule (in physiology) cwpan *eg* cwpanau
captain capten *eg* capteiniaid
captaincy capteniaeth *eb*
caption pennawd *eg* penawdau
caption character nod egluryn *eg* nodau egluryn
caption text testun pennawd *eg* testunau pennawd
capture (a particle) dal *be*
capture (in computing) cipio *be*
Capuchin Friar Brawd Cycyllog *eg* Brodyr Cycyllog
Capuchin Order Urdd y Brodyr Cycyllog *eb*
caput capwt *eg*
car hire llogi car *be*
car industry diwydiant ceir *eg* diwydiannau ceir
Caractacus Caradog *eg*
caramel caramel *eg*
caramelization carameleiddio *be*
carapace argragen *eb*
caravel carafel *eg* carafelau
caraway seed hedyn carwe *eg* hadau carwe
carbamate ion ïon carbamad *eg* ïonau carbamad
carbamic acid asid carbamig *eg*
carbamide carbamid *eg*
carbanion carbanion *eg*
carbide ion ïon carbid *eg* ïonau carbid
carbide tipped blaen carbid *ans*
carbohydrate carbohydrad *eg* carbohydradau
carbon (C) carbon *eg* carbonau
carbon (**animal charcoal**) carbon (golosg anifail) *eg*
carbon (**charcoal**) carbon (golosg) *eg*
carbon copy copi carbon *eg* copïau carbon
carbon cycle cylchred garbon *eb*
carbon dating dyddio carbon *be*
carbon (**diamond**) carbon (deiamwnt) *eg*
carbon dioxide carbon deuocsid *eg*
carbon disulfide carbon deusylffid *eg*
carbon fullerene carbon fulleren *eg*
carbon (**graphite**) carbon (graffit) *eg*
carbon monoxide carbon monocsid *eg*
carbon paper papur carbon *eg* papurau carbon
carbon racket raced carbon *eg* racedi carbon
carbon steel dur carbon *eg*
carbon tetrachloride carbon tetraclorid *eg*
carbon (**wood charcoal**) carbon (golosg pren) *eg*
Carbonari Carbonariaid *ell*
carbonate carbonad *eg* carbonadau
carbonate ion ïon carbonad *eg* ïonau carbonad
carbonated carbonedig *ans*
carbonation carbonadu *be*
carbonic acid asid carbonig *eg*
carbonic anhydrase carbonig anhydras *ans*
carboniferous carbonifferaidd *ans*

carboniferous limestone calchfaen carbonifferaidd *eg*
carbonization carboneiddiad *eg*
carbonize carboneiddio *be*
carbonyl dichloride carbonyl deuclorid *eg*
carborundum carborwndwm *eb*
carborundum stone carreg hogi *eg* cerrig hogi
carboxyhaemoglobin carbocsihaemoglobin *eg*
carboxylation carbocsyleiddiad *eg*
carboxylic carbocsylig *ans*
carboxylic acid asid carbocsylig *eg* asidau carbocsylig
(carboxymethyl)ammonium chloride (carbocsimethyl)amoniwm clorid *eg*
carboxymethyl-cellulose (CMC) carbocsimethyl-cellwlos *eg*
carburettor carbwradur *eg* carbwraduron
carburize carbwreiddio *be*
carcass sgerbwd *eg* sgerbydau
carcass construction adeiladwaith sgerbwd *eg*
carcinogen carsinogen *eg* carsinogenau
carcinogenic carsinogenaidd *ans*
card *n* cerdyn *eg* cardiau
card *v* cribo *be*
card code cod cerdyn *eg* codau cerdyn
card column colofn gerdyn *eb* colofnau cerdyn
card cutter torrwr cerdyn *eg* torwyr cerdyn
card feed porthydd cardiau *eg* porthyddion cardiau
card field maes cerdyn *eg* meysydd cerdyn
card format fformat cerdyn *eg* fformatau cerdyn
card hopper hopran gardiau *eb* hopranau cardiau
card image delwedd cerdyn *eb* delweddau cerdyn
card index mynegai cardiau *eg* mynegeion cardiau
card jam tagfa gardiau *eb* tagfeydd cardiau
card knife cyllell torri cerdyn *eb* cyllyll torri cerdyn
card loom gwŷdd cerdyn *eg* gwyddiau cerdyn
card punch tyllwr cardiau *eg* tyllwyr cardiau
card puppet pyped cerdyn *eg* pypedau cerdyn
card reader darllenydd cardiau *eg* darllenyddion cardiau
card reproducer dyblygydd cardiau *eg* dyblygyddion cardiau
card stacker pentyrrwr cardiau *eg* pentyrwyr cardiau
card stacking pentyrru cardiau *be*
card template patrymlun cerdyn *eg* patrymluniau cerdyn
card verifier gwiriwr cardiau *eg* gwirwyr cardiau
card wreck drylliad cardiau *eg* drylliadau cardiau
cardboard cardbord *eg*
cardboard model model cardbord *eg* modelau cardbord
cardboard tube tiwb cardbord *eg* tiwbiau cardbord
carder cribwr *eg* cribwyr
cardiac cardiaidd *ans*
cardiac arrest ataliad y galon *eg* ataliadau'r galon
cardiac cycle cylchred gardiaidd *eb*
cardiac disease afiechyd y galon *eg*
cardiac output allbwn y galon *eg*
cardigan cardigan *eb* cardiganau
cardinal cardinal *eg* cardinaliaid
cardinal number rhif prifol *eg* rhifau prifol
cardinal point pwynt prifol *eg* pwyntiau prifol
carding brush brwsh ffeil *eg* brwshys ffeil
cardioid cardioid *eg* cardioidau
cardiologist cardiolegydd *eg* cardiolegyddion
cardiology cardioleg *eb*
cardiopulmonary resuscitation adfywio'r galon a'r ysgyfaint *be*
cardiovascular centre canolfannyn cardiofasgwlar *eg*
cardiovascular disorder anhwylder cardiofasgwlar *eg* anhwylderau cardiofasgwlar
▶ **cardiovascular health** iechyd cardiofasgwlar *eg*
▶ **cardiovascular system** system gardiofasgwlar *eb*
care gofal *eg* gofalon
care and after-care gofal ac ôl-ofal
care centre canolfan gofal *eb* canolfannau gofal
Care Council for Wales Cyngor Gofal Cymru *eg*
care home cartref gofal *eg* cartrefi gofal
care label label gofal *eg* labeli gofal
care management rheoli gofal *be*
care management process proses reoli gofal *eb*
care manager rheolwr gofal *eg* rheolwyr gofal
care needs anghenion gofal *ell*
care of the elderly gofal yr henoed *eg*
care of the environment gofal am yr amgylchedd *eg*
care order gorchymyn gofal *eg* gorchmynion gofal
care plan cynllun gofalu *eg* cynlluniau gofalu
care practice arferion gofal *ell*
care staff staff gofal *ell*
care unit uned gofal *eb* unedau gofal
care value gwerthoedd gofal *ell*
care value base sylfaen gwerthoedd gofal *eb*
care value component cydran gwerth gofal *eb* cydrannau gwerth gofal
care worker gweithiwr gofal *eg* gweithwyr gofal
career gyrfa *eb* gyrfaoedd
career choice dewis gyrfa *eg* dewisiadau gyrfa
career guidance arweiniad ar yrfa *eg*
career objective amcan gyrfaol *eg* amcanion gyrfaol
career opportunity cyfle gyrfaol *eg* cyfleoedd gyrfaol
career planning cynllunio ar gyfer gyrfa *be*
career prospects rhagolygon am yrfa *ell*
career service gwasanaeth gyrfaoedd *eg* gwasanaethau gyrfaoedd
careers education addysg gyrfaoedd *eb*
careers teacher (female) athrawes yrfaoedd *eg* athrawesau gyrfaoedd
careers teacher (male) athro gyrfaoedd *eg* athrawon gyrfaoedd
caregiver gofalydd *eg* gofalwyr
carer gofalwr *eg* gofalwyr
caret lleolnod *eg* lleolnodau
caretaker gofalwr *eg* gofalwyr

caretaker government llywodraeth ofalu *eb* llywodraethau gofalu
caricature gwawdlun *eg* gwawdluniau
caricaturist gwawdlunydd *eg* gwawdlunwyr
caries pydredd dannedd *eg*
carillon (=bells) clychau *ell*
carillon (=instrument) carilon *eg/b* carilonau
carillon (=tune) tôn glychau *eb* tonau clychau
caring services gwasanaethau gofal *ell*
Carlsbad decrees archddyfarniadau Carlsbad *ell*
Carmelite Friar Brawd Carmelaidd *eg* Brodyr Carmelaidd
Carmelite Order Urdd y Carmeliaid *eb*
carmine carmin *eg*
carnauba wax cwyr carnawba *eg*
carnivore cigysydd *eg* cigysyddion
carnivorous cigysol *ans*
carob carob *eg*
carol carol *eb* carolau
Carolingian Carolingaidd *ans*
Carolingian art celfyddyd Garolingaidd *eb*
carotene caroten *eg*
carotenoid carotenyn *eg* carotenau
carotid artery rhydweli garotid *eb* rhydwelïau carotid
carotid body corffyn carotid *eg* corffynnau carotid
carp carp *eg* carpiaid
carpal carpal *eg* carpalau
carpel carpel *eg* carpelau
carpenter saer coed *eg* seiri coed
carpenter's pencil pensil saer *eg* pensiliau saer
carpentry gwaith saer *eg*
carpentry and joinery gwaith saer ac asiedydd
carpet carped *eg* carpedi
carpet sweeper ysgubwr carpedi *eg* ysgubwyr carpedi
carpet underlay isgarped *eg* isgarpedi
carpogonium carpogoniwm *eg* carpogonia
carr ffen *eg* ffeniau
carrack carac *eg* caracau
Carragheen moss mwsogl Carragheen *eg*
carriage (=lathe part) cludydd *eg* cludyddion
carriage (=transport) cludiant *eg*
carriage bolt bollt wagen *eb* bolltau wagen
carriage return dychwelydd *eg* dychwelyddion
carriageway ffordd gerbydau *eb* ffyrdd cerbydau
carrier (in general) cludydd *eg* cludyddion
carrier (lathe dog) cariwr *eg* carwyr
carrier language iaith gyfarwyddyd *eb* ieithoedd cyfarwyddyd
carrier molecule moleciwl cludo *eg* moleciwlau cludo
carrier pulse train curiadau'r don gario *ell*
carrier wave ton gario *eb* tonnau cario
carrot moronen *eb* moron
carry *n* car-rif *eg* car-rifau
carry *v* cario *be*
carry bit did cario *eg* didau cario
carry flag lluman cario *eg* llumanau cario
carry out (an experiment) cynnal *be*
carry out a fair test cynnal prawf teg *be*
carry prediction circuit cylched ragfynegi car-rif *eb* cylchedau rhagfynegi car-rif
carry the baton cario'r batwn *be*
carrycot caricot *eg* caricotau
carrycot stand stand caricot *eg* standiau caricot
carrying capacity cynhwysedd cludo *eg*
carrying figure ffigur i'w gario *eg* ffigurau i'w cario
carrying service gwasanaeth cludo *eg* gwasanaethau cludo
carryover effect effaith cario drosodd *eb* effeithiau cario drosodd
cartel cartel *eg* cartelau
cartelize carteleiddio *be*
Cartesian Cartesaidd *ans*
Cartesian coordinates cyfesurynnau Cartesaidd *ell*
Cartesian dualism deuoliaeth Gartesaidd *eb*
Cartesian equation hafaliad Cartesaidd *eg*
Carthusian Carthwsiad *eg* Carthwsiaid
Carthusian Order Urdd y Carthwsiaid *eb*
cartilage cartilag *eg*
cartilaginous cartilagaidd *ans*
cartilaginous fish pysgodyn cartilagaidd *eg* pysgod cartilagaidd
cartographic cartograffig *ans*
cartographic information gwybodaeth gartograffig *eb*
cartographic material deunydd cartograffig *eg*
cartography cartograffeg *eb*
carton carton *eg* cartonau
cartoon cartŵn *eg* cartwnau
cartridge cetrisen *eb* cetris
cartridge brass pres cetris *eg*
cartridge disk disg cetrisen *eg* disgiau cetris
cartridge paper papur cetris *eg*
cartulary cartwlari *eg* cartwlarïau
cartwheel *v* olwyndroi *be*
cartwheel (in athletics) *n* olwyn dro *eb* olwynion tro
carucate carwgad *eg* carwgadau
caruncle carwngl *eg* carynglau
carve cerfio *be*
carved cerfiedig *ans*
carved head pen cerfiedig *eg* pennau cerfiedig
carver (=carving knife) cyllell gerfio *eb* cyllyll cerfio
carver (of person) cerfiwr *eg* cerfwyr
carving cerfiad *eg* cerfiadau
carving chisel cŷn cerfio *eg* cynion cerfio; gaing gerfio *eb* geingiau cerfio
carving mallet gordd gerfio *eb* gyrdd cerfio
caryatid caryatid *eg* caryatidau
cascade *n* rhaeadr *eb* rhaeadrau
cascade *v* rhaeadru *be*
cascaded rhaeadrol *ans*
cascading style sheet dalen diwyg raeadrol *eb* dalennau diwyg rhaeadrol
case (for carrying) cas *eg* casys

case (in general) achos *eg* achosion
case conference cynhadledd achos *eb* cynadleddau achos
case hardened wedi'i grofennu *ans* wedi'u crofennu
case hardening crofennu *be*
case history hanes achos *eg*
case law cyfraith achosion *eb*
case load baich achosion *eb* beichiau achosion
case record cofnod achos *eg* cofnodion achos
case study astudiaeth achos *eb* astudiaethau achos
casein casein *eg*
casein colour lliw casein *eg* lliwiau casein
casein glue glud casein *eg*
caseinogen caseinogen *eg*
casement fastener ffasnydd ffenestr adeiniog *eg* ffasnyddion ffenestr adeiniog
casement window ffenestr adeiniog *eb* ffenestri adeiniog
cash arian parod *eg*
cash allocation dyraniad arian *eg* dyraniadau arian
cash and carry shop siop talu a chludo *eb* siopau talu a chludo
cash book dyddlyfr arian *eg* dyddlyfrau arian
cash dispenser peiriant arian *eg* peiriannau arian
cash flow llif arian *eg*
cash flow forecast rhagolwg llif arian *eg*
cash limit cyfyngiad arian *eg* cyfyngiadau arian
cash limited budget cyllideb arian cyfyngedig *eb* cyllidebau arian cyfyngedig
cash machine peiriant arian parod *eg* peiriannau arian parod
cash payment taliad arian parod *eg* taliadau arian parod
cash value gwerth ariannol *eg*
cashless society cymdeithas heb arian parod *eb*
casing casin *eg* casinau
casket (for jewellery) blwch gemau *eg*
blychau gemau
Casket Letters Llythyrau'r Blwch *ell*
Casparian strip stribed Caspari *eg*
cassava casafa *eg*
casserole caserol *eg* caserolau
cassette casét *eg* casetiau
cassette player chwaraeydd casét *eg* chwaraewyr casét
cassette recorder recordydd casét *eg* recordwyr casét
cassiterite casiterit *eg*
cassock casog *eb* casogau
cast bwrw *be*
cast (out of shape) camdroi *be*
cast iron haearn bwrw *eg*
cast iron vice feis haearn bwrw *eb* feisiau haearn bwrw
cast off (in knitting) cau pwythau *be*
cast on (in knitting) ystofi pwythau *be*
cast out troi allan *be*
cast steel dur bwrw *eg*

castanet castanét *eg* castanetau
caste cast *eg* castiau
caste system cyfundrefn gast *eb*
castellan castellydd *eg* castellwyr
castellated (=castle-like) castellaidd *ans*
castellated (=having battlements) castellog *ans*
castellated prop ateg gastellaidd *eb* ategion castellaidd
castellation castelliad *eg* castelliadau
caster sugar siwgr mân *eg*
Castilian *adj* Castilaidd *ans*
Castilian *n* Castiliad *eg* Castiliaid
casting *n* castin *eg* castinau
casting *v* castio *be*
casting apparatus cyfarpar castio *eg*
casting down castio i lawr *be*
casting plaster castin plastr *eg*
casting up castio i fyny *be*
casting vote pleidlais fwrw *eb*
castle castell *eg* cestyll
castle nut nyten gastell *eb* nytiau castell
castleguard gwarchodaeth castell *eb*
castor castor *eg* castorau
casual employment gwaith ysbeidiol *eg*
casual labour llafur ysbeidiol *eg*
casual unemployment diweithdra ysbeidiol *eg*
casual water dŵr achlysurol *eg*
casuals dillad segura *ell*
casualty (=accident) damwain *eb* damweiniau
casualty (=injured person) anafedig *eg* anafedigion
casuistry twyllresymeg *eb*
catabatic catabatig *ans*
catabolic catabolig *ans*
catabolism catabolaeth *eb*
catabolite catabolyn *eg* catabolynnau
catalase catalas *eg*
catalogue *n* catalog *eg* catalogau
catalogue *v* catalogio *be*
catalogue number rhif yn y catalog *eg*
catalyse catalyddu *be*
catalysis catalysis *eg*
catalyst catalydd *eg* catalyddion
catalytic catalytig *ans*
catalytic hydrogenation hydrogeniad catalytig *eg*
cataplexy cataplecsi *eg*
cataract cataract *eg* cataractau
catastrophic misinterpretation camddehongliad catastroffig *eg* camddeongliadau catastroffig
catastrophism trychinebedd *eg*
catastrophizing trychinebu *be*
catatonic schizophrenia sgitsoffrenia catatonig *eg*
catch *v* dal *be*
catch (of ball etc) *n* daliad *eg* daliadau
catch (of door) *n* clicied *eb* cliciedau
catch a crab cranca *be*
catch crop byrgnwd *eg* byrgnydau

catch plate plât cydio *eg* platiau cydio
catch stitch pwyth cydio *eg* pwythau cydio
catch stitched hem hem pwyth cudd *eb* hemiau pwyth cudd
catch weights pwysau agored *ell*
catcher daliwr *eg* dalwyr
catchment dalgylch *eg* dalgylchoedd
catchment area dalgylch *eg* dalgylchoedd
catchy gafaelgar *ans*
CATE: Committee for the Accreditation of Teachers Education Pwyllgor Achredu Addysg Athrawon *eg*
catechism (in general) catecism *eg* catecismau
catechism (in Welsh Nonconformity) holwyddoreg *eb* holwyddoregau
catecholamine catecolamin *eg*
categorize categoreiddio *be*
category categori *eg* categorïau
catena catena *eb* catenâu
catenary catena *eb* catenâu
catenate cadwyno *be*
catenation cadwynedd *eg* cadwyneddau
catenoid catenoid *eg* catenoidau
cater (=provide) darparu *be*
cater (food) arlwyo *be*
caterer arlwywr *eg* arlwywyr
catering arlwyo *be*
catering and hotel trade masnach arlwyo a gwestya *eb*
caterpillar lindysyn *eg* lindys
catgut coludd *eg* coluddion
Cathar Cathariad *eg* Cathariaid
catharsis catharsis *eg*
cathartic *n* carthydd *eg* carthyddion
Cathay Company Cwmni Cathay *eg*
cathedral eglwys gadeiriol *eb* eglwysi cadeiriol
cathedral close clos eglwys gadeiriol *eg* closydd eglwysi cadeiriol
Catherine Catrin *eb*
Catherine the Great Catrin Fawr *eb*
catheter cathetr *eg* cathetrau
cathode catod *eg* catodau
cathode ray pelydryn catod *eg* pelydrau catod
cathode ray tube tiwb pelydrau catod *eg* tiwbiau pelydrau catod
cathodic catodig *ans*
catholic (=universal) *adj* catholig *ans*
Catholic (of Roman Catholic) *n* Pabydd *eg* Pabyddion
catholic (of Roman Catholic Church) *adj* pabyddol *ans*
Catholic association cymdeithas Gatholig *eb* cymdeithasau Catholig
Catholic church eglwys Gatholig *eb* eglwysi Catholig
Catholic Emancipation Rhyddfreinio'r Pabyddion *be*
Catholic Emancipation Act Deddf Rhyddfreinio'r Pabyddion *eb*
Catholic leadership arweinwyr Catholig *ell*
Catholic Majesties Eu Mawrhydi Catholig *ell*
Catholic Martyrs Merthyron Pabyddol *ell*
catholic mass offeren Babyddol *eb*
Catholicism Pabyddiaeth *eb*
cation catïon *eg* catïonau
cation exchange column colofn cyfnewid catïonau *eb* colofnau cyfnewid catïonau
cationic cationig *ans*
catkin (hazel) cynffon oen bach *eg* cynffonnau ŵyn bach
cat-o'-nine-tails fflangell *eb* fflangellau
CATS: Consortium for Assessment and Testing in Schools CAPY: Consortiwm Asesu a Phrofi mewn Ysgolion *eg*
CATS: Credit Accumulation and Transfer Scheme Cynllun Casglu a Throsglwyddo Credydau *eg*
catspring naid cath *eb* neidiau cath
cattle cake cêc gwartheg *eg*
cattle range maestir gwartheg *eg* maestiroedd gwartheg
caudal cynffonnol *ans*
caudal vertebra fertebra cynffonnol *eg* fertebrâu cynffonnol
caught out (in cricket) allan drwy ddal
caul gwasgblat *eg* gwasgblatiau
caul veneering argaenu gwasgblat *be*
cauldron pair *eg* peiriau
cauliflower blodfresychen *eb* blodfresych
cauliflower cheese blodfresych caws *ell*
caulk calcio *be*
caulking strip stribed calcio *eg* stribedi calcio
caulking tool erfyn calcio *eg* offer calcio
causal achosol *ans*
causal event or determinant digwyddiad achosol *eg* digwyddiadau achosol
causal phase cyfnod achosol *eg* cyfnodau achosol
causal relationship perthynas achosol *eb*
causalgia llosgwayw *eg*
causality achosiaeth *eb*
causation (=causality) achosiaeth *eb*
causation (action of causing something) achosiad *eg*
causative factor ffactor achosol *eb* ffactorau achosol
cause *v* achosi *be*
cause of pollution achos llygredd *eg* achosion llygredd
causes of ill health achosion afiechyd *ell*
causeway sarn *eg* sarnau
causeway camp gwersyll sarnau *eg*
caustic curve cromlin gawstig *eb* cromliniau cawstig
caustic soda soda brwd *eg*
caution (=care) gofal *eg*
caution (=warning) rhybudd *eg* rhybuddion
cavalier *adj* cafaliraidd *ans*
cavalier *n* cafalîr *eg* cafaliriaid
cavalry gwŷr meirch *ell*
cavalry twill cafalri caerog *eg*

cavatina cafatina *eg* cafatinâu
cave ogof *eb* ogofâu
cave dwelling ogof-annedd *eb* ogof-anheddau
cave painting paentiad ogof *eg* paentiadau ogof
cavern ceudwll *eg* ceudyllau
cavernous ceudyllog *ans*
cavetto moulding mowldin cafeto *eg* mowldinau cafeto
cavetto panel panel cafeto *eg* paneli cafeto
caviare cafiar *eg*
cavity ceudod *eg* ceudodau
cavity wall wal geudod *eb* waliau ceudod
cay cai *eg* caion
cayenne cayenne *eg*
CD ROM drive gyriant CD ROM *eg* gyriannau CD ROM
cedar cedrwydden *eb* cedrwydd
cedar oil olew cedrwydden *eg*
cedarwood pencil pensil pren cedrwydd *eg* pensiliau pren cedrwydd
cede ildio *be*
ceiling nenfwd *eg* nenfydau
ceiling effect effaith nenfwd *eb*
ceiling joist trawst nenfwd *eg* trawstiau nenfwd
ceiling rack rhesel nenfwd *eb* rheseli nenfwd
cejuela cejuela *eg* cejuelas
celadon (green colour) seladon *eg*
celebrate dathlu *be*
celebration dathliad *eg* dathliadau
celery seleri *eg*
celesta selesta *eg* selestâu
celestial wybrennol *ans*
celestial equator cyhydedd wybrennol *eg*
celestial sphere sffêr wybrennol *eg*
celibacy ymgadw'n ddibriod *be*
cell cell *eb* celloedd
cell attribute priodoledd celloedd *eg* priodoleddau celloedd
cell body cellgorff *eg* cellgyrff
cell contents cynnwys celloedd *eg*
cell division cellraniad *eg* cellraniadau
cell grid grid cell *eg* gridiau cell
cell membrane cellbilen *eb* cellbilenni
cell plate cellblat *eg* cellblatiau
cell pore celldwll *eg* celldyllau
cell production cynhyrchu celloedd *be*
cell reference cyfeirnod cell *eg* cyfeirnodau cell
cell sap cellnodd *eg*
cell surface arwyneb y gell *eg*
cell wall cellfur *eg* cellfuriau
cellarer selerwr *eg* selerwyr
cellarium seler *eb* seleri
cell-free di-gell *ans*
cellist sielydd *eg* sielyddion
cello sielo *eg* sieloau
cellophane seloffan *eg*
cellular cellog *ans*
cellular adhesive gludydd cellog *eg* gludyddion cellog
cellular network rhwydwaith cellog *eg*
cellular respiration resbiradaeth gellog *eb*
cellular structure adeiledd cellog *eg* adeileddau cellog
celluloid cellwloid *eg*
cellulose cellwlos *eg*
cellulose finish gorffeniad cellwlos *eg*
cellulose lacquer lacr cellwlos *eg* lacrau cellwlos
cellulose paste past cellwlos *eg*
cellulose paste powder powdr past cellwlos *eg*
cellulosics cellwlosigion *ell*
Celsius Celsius *ans*
Celtic *adj* Celtaidd *ans*
Celtic (language) *n* Celteg *eb*
Celtic art celfyddyd Geltaidd *eb*
Celtic cross croes Geltaidd *eb* croesau Celtaidd
Celtic form ffurf Geltaidd *eb* ffurfiau Celtaidd
Celtic harp telyn Geltaidd *eb* telynau Celtaidd
Celtic society cymdeithas Geltaidd *eb* cymdeithasau Celtaidd
cembalo cembalo *eg* cembali
cement *n* sment *eg* smentiau
cement *v* smentio *be*
cementation smentiad *eg*
cementation of sediments smentiad gwaddodion *eg*
cemented carbide sment carbid *eg*
cementite smentit *eg*
censer (in church) thuser *eb* thuserau
censor sensor *eg* sensoriaid
censorship sensoriaeth *eb*
censure cerydd *eg* ceryddon
census cyfrifiad *eg* cyfrifiadau
census data data cyfrifiad *ell*
census return ffurflen gyfrifiad *eb* ffurflenni cyfrifiad
centenary canmlwyddiant *eg*
centigrade canradd *ans*
centile canradd *eg* canraddau
centile chart siart canraddau *eg* siartiau canraddau
centile rank safle canrannol *eg* safleoedd canrannol
centilitre centilitr *eg* centilitrau
centimetre (cm) centimetr *eg* centimetrau
central agitator cynhyrfydd canolog *eg* cynhyrfwyr canolog
central bank banc canolog *eg* banciau canolog
central business district (C.B.D.) canol busnes y dref *eg*
central canal tiwb canolog *eg* tiwbiau canolog
central care area ardal gofalon canolog *eb* ardaloedd gofalon canolog
central column colofn ganolog *eb* colofnau canolog
central core craidd canolog *eg* creiddiau canolog
Central Criminal Court Llys Troseddol Canolog *eg*
central executive goruchwyliwr canolog *eg* goruchwylwyr canolog
central government llywodraeth ganolog *eb*

central heating gwres canolog *eg*
central nervous system prif system nerfol *eb*
Central Office of Information Swyddfa Hysbysrwydd Ganolog *eb*
central perspective persbectif canolog *eg* persbectifau canolog
Central Place Theory Damcaniaeth Man Canol *eb*
central processing unit (CPU) uned brosesu ganolog *eb* unedau prosesu canolog
central processor prosesydd canolog *eg* prosesyddion canolog
central route llwybr canolog *eg*
central server gweinydd canolog *eg* gweinyddion canolog
central tendency canolduedd *eb*
central trait prif nodwedd *eb* prif nodweddion
central venous pressure pwysau gwythiennol canolog *eg*
Central Welsh Board Bwrdd Canol Cymreig *eg*
centrality canolrwydd *eg*
centralization canoli *be*
centralize canoli *be*
centralized canoledig *ans*
centre *v* canoli *be*
centre (=middle point) *n* canol *eg* canolau
centre (=place or group of buildings) *n* canolfan *eg/b* canolfannau
centre (brain) *n* canolfannyn *eg* canolfanynnau
centre (of attention etc) *n* canolbwynt *eg* canolbwyntiau
centre (person in sport) *n* canolwr *eg* canolwyr
centre arrowend canoli diwedd saeth *be*
centre arrowhead canoli pensaeth *be*
centre back canol cefn *eg*
centre bar (lettering) bar canol *eg* barrau canol
centre bit ebill canoli *eg* ebillion canoli
centre bit ebill canolog *eg* ebillion canolog
centre cane gwialen ganol *eb* gwialennau canol
centre circle cylch canol *eg* cylchoedd canol
centre coordinator cydlynydd canolfan *eg* cydlynwyr canolfannau
centre dots canoli dotiau *be*
centre dotting canolfarcio *be*
centre drill (slocombe) dril canoli *eg* driliau canoli
Centre for Policy Studies Canolfan Astudiaethau Polisi *eb*
centre front canol blaen *eg*
centre hinge colfach canol *eg* colfachau canol
centre horizontal canoli'r llorweddol *be*
centre lathe turn canol *eg* turniau canol
centre line llinell ganol *eb* llinellau canol
centre of balance ffwlcrwm *eg* ffwlcrymau
centre of baseline canol y waelodlin *eg*
centre of character canol y nod *eg*
centre of curvature craidd crymedd *eg* creiddiau crymedd
centre of excellence canolfan rhagoriaeth *eb* canolfannau rhagoriaeth
centre of gravity craidd disgyrchiant *eg* creiddiau disgyrchiant
centre of mass craidd màs *eg* creiddiau màs
centre of percussion craidd taro *eg* creiddiau taro
centre of pressure canolbwynt gwasgedd *eg* canolbwyntiau gwasgedd
centre of rotation canol cylchdro *eg* canolau cylchdro
centre of similitude pwynt cyfluniant *eg* pwyntiau cyfluniant
centre of symmetry canol cymesuredd *eg*
centre of the court canol y cwrt *eg*
centre outfielder maeswr canol *eg* maeswyr canol
centre pass pàs gyntaf *eb* pasiau cyntaf
centre point canolbwynt *eg* canolbwyntiau
centre popping canolbopio *be*
centre punch pwnsh canoli *eg* pynsiau canoli
centre punching canolbwnsio *be*
centre serving line llinell serfio ganol *eb* llinellau serfio canol
centre spot marc canol *eg* marciau canol
centre square sgwâr canoli *eg* sgwariau canoli
centre the ball canoli'r bêl *be*
centreboard bwrdd canol *eg* byrddau canol
centred canolog *ans*
centre-face atom atom canol-yr-wyneb *eg* atomau canol-yr-wyneb
centre-half canolwr *eg* canolwyr
centrifugal allgyrchol *ans*
centrifugal casting castio allgyrchol *be*
centrifugal force grym allgyrchol *eg* grymoedd allgyrchol
centrifuge *n* allgyrchydd *eg* allgyrchion
centrifuge *v* allgyrchu *be*
centring canoli *be*
centriole centriol *eg* centriolau
centripetal mewngyrchol *ans*
centripetal force grym mewngyrchol *eg* grymoedd mewngyrchol
centroid craidd *eg* creiddiau
centromere centromer *eg* centromerau
Centronics interface rhyngwyneb Centronics *eg* rhyngwynebau Centronics
centrosome centrosom *eg* centrosomau
century canrif *eb* canrifoedd
century (=unit of soldiers) centuria *eb*
cephalic ceffalig *ans*
cephalic index indecs ceffalig *eg*
cephalisation ceffaleiddiad *eg*
cephalo- ceffalo-
ceramic ceramig *ans*
ceramic stilts stiltiau ceramig *ell*
ceramic tile teilsen geramig *eb* teils ceramig
ceramics cerameg *eb*
cerate(IV) ion ïon cerad(IV) *eg* ïonau cerad(IV)
cerdd dant cerdd dant *eg*
cerdd dant arrangement trefniant cerdd dant *eg*
cereal grawnfwyd *eg* grawnfwydydd

cerebellum ymennydd bach *eg*
cerebellum cerebelwm *eg*
cerebral ymenyddol *ans*
cerebral cerebrol *ans*
cerebral cortex cortecs cerebrol *eg*
cerebral haemorrhage gwaedlif ar yr ymennydd *eg*
cerebral hemisphere hemisffer cerebrol *eg*
cerebral palsy parlys yr ymennydd *eg*
cerebrospinal cerebrosbinol *ans*
cerebrospinal fluid hylif yr ymennydd *eg*
cerebrovascular accident damwain gerebrofasgwlar *eb*
cerebrum cerebrwm *eg* cerebra
ceremony seremoni *eb* seremonïau
cerise ceirios *eg*
cerium (Ce) ceriwm *eg*
cerium(III) ion ïon ceriwm(III) *eg* ïonau ceriwm(III)
cerium(IV) ion ïon ceriwm(IV) *eg* ïonau ceriwm(IV)
certain sicr *ans*
certificate tystysgrif *eb* tystysgrifau
Certificate of Education (CoE) Tystysgrif Addysg *eb*
Certificate of Extended Education (CEE) Tystysgrif Addysg Estynedig *eb*
Certificate of Pre-Vocational Education (CPVE) Tystysgrif Addysg Gyn-Alwedigaethol *eb*
certification (in general) ardystio *be*
certification (of film) rhoi tystysgrif *be*
certified seed had ardyst *eg*
certify ardystio *be*
cerulean blue glas y nen *eg*
cervical cerfigol *ans*
cervical cancer canser gwddf y groth *eg*
cervical smear prawf gwddf y groth *eg* profion gwddf y groth
cervical vertebra fertebra gyddfol *eg* fertebrâu gyddfol
cervix (=neck of womb) gwddf y groth *eg*
CESIL CESIL *eb*
cesspool carthbwll *eg* carthbyllau
CFCs CFCau *ell*
chaconne chaconne *eg* chaconnes
chaetae caetae *ell*
chafe rhathu *be*
chafing rhathiad *eg*
chain *n* cadwyn *eb* cadwynau
chain *v* cadwyno *be*
chain drilling drilio cadwynol *be*
chain drive gyriant cadwyn *eg*
chain line llinell gadwyn *eb* llinellau cadwyn
chain link dolen gadwyn *eb* dolennau cadwyn
chain mechanism mecanwaith cyswllt *eg*
chain molecules moleciwlau cadwynol *ell*
chain of command cadwyn awdurdod *eb*
chain of production cadwyn gynhyrchu *eb*
chain printer argraffydd cadwyn *eg* argraffyddion cadwyn
chain reaction adwaith cadwynol *eg* adweithiau cadwynol
chain reflex atgyrch cadwynol *eg*
chain riveting rhybedu cadwynol *be*
chain rule rheol cadwyn *eb*
chain stitch pwyth cadwyn *eg* pwythau cadwyn
chain store siop gadwyn *eb* siopau cadwyn
chain survey tirfesur cadwyn *be*
chain wrench tyndro cadwyn *eg* tyndroeon cadwyn
chained cadwynog *ans*
chained feather stitch pwyth plu cadwynog *eg* pwythau plu cadwynog
chair *n* cadair *eb* cadeiriau
chair *v* cadeirio *be*
chair back gorchudd cefn cadair *eg* gorchuddion cefn cadair
chair lift cadair godi *eb* cadeiriau codi
chairbound pupil disgybl sy'n gaeth i'w gadair *eg* disgyblion sy'n gaeth i'w cadair
chairman designate darpar gadeirydd *eg* darpar gadeiryddion
chalaza calasa *eg*
chalcopyrite calcopyrit *eg*
chalet chalet *eg* chalets
chalice caregl *eg* careglau
chalk *n* sialc *eg* sialciau
chalk *v* sialcio *be*
chalk drawing llun sialc *eg* lluniau sialc
challenge *n* her *eb*
challenge *v* herio *be*
challenger heriwr *eg* herwyr
challenging behaviour ymddygiad heriol *eg*
chalumeau chalumeau *eg* chalumeaux
chamber (in general) siambr *eb* siambrau
chamber (in quarry) agor *eg* agorydd
chamber music cerddoriaeth siambr *eb*
chamber of trade cymdeithas fasnach *eb* cymdeithasau masnach
chamber tomb beddrod siambr *eg* beddrodau siambr
chamberlain siambrlen *eg* siambrleniaid
Chambers of Reunion Siambrau Ailuniad *ell*
chamfer *n* siamffer *eg* siamfferi
chamfer *v* siamffro *be*
chamfered siamffrog *ans*
chamfered neck gwddf siamffrog *eg*
chamois siami *eg*
chamois glove maneg siami *eb* menig siami
chamois leather lledr siami *eg*
champion (female) pencampwraig *eb* pencampwragedd
champion (male and general) pencampwr *eg* pencampwyr
champion land tir agored *eg*
championship pencampwriaeth *eb* pencampwriaethau
champlevé champlevé *eg*
chance siawns *eb* siawnsiau
chancel cangell *eb* canghellau

chancel arch bwa cangell *eg* bwâu cangell
chancellor canghellor *eg* cangellorion
Chancellor of the Exchequer Canghellor y Trysorlys *eg*
Chancery Siawnsri *eg*
chandelier canhwyllyr *eg* canwyllyriau
chandler siandler *eg* siandleriaid
change newid *eg* newidiadau
change anchor newid angor *be*
change database newid cronfa ddata *be*
change database range newid ystod cronfa ddata *be*
change direction newid cyfeiriad *be*
change font newid ffont *be*
change mode newid modd *be*
change name newid enw *be*
change of engagement newid cyweddiad *be*
change of pace newid cyflymdra *be*
change one factor newid un ffactor *be*
change page number newid rhif tudalen *be*
change password newid cyfrinair *be*
change password protection newid diogelwch cyfrinair *be*
change position newid safle *be*
change scale newid graddfa *be*
change slides manually newid sleidiau â llaw *be*
change to a document newid i ddogfen *eg* newidiadau i ddogfen
change wheel olwyn newid *eb* olwynion newid
changing face of the family wyneb newidiol y teulu *eg*
changing notes nodau cyfnewid *ell*
changing voice llais yn newid *eg*
channel *n* sianel *eb* sianelau
channel *v* sianelu *be*
► **channel efficiency** effeithlonrwydd sianel *eg*
chanson chanson *eb* chansons
chant (=spoken singsong phrase) *n* siant *eb* siantiau
chant (formally) *v* llafarganu *be*
chant (informally) *v* siantio *be*
chant (of canticle) *n* côr-gân *eb* corganau
chant (of psalm) *n* salm-dôn *eb* salmdonau
chanting rhythmically llafarganu'n rhythmig *be*
chantry siantri *eg* siantrïau
chantry priest offeiriad siantri *eg* offeiriaid siantri
chaos anhrefn *eg/b*
chaotic sky awyr afluniaidd *eb*
chaparral mangoed *eg*
chapel capel *eg* capeli
chapel of ease capel anwes *eg* capeli anwes
chapel without tower or spire capel heb dŵr na meindwr *eg*
chapelry capeliaeth *eb* capeliaethau
chaplain caplan *eg* caplaniaid
chaplaincy caplaniaeth *eb*
chaplet coronbleth *eb* coronblethau
chapter (=canons of a cathedral) cabidwl *eg* cabidylau
chapter (=division of a book) pennod *eb* penodau
chapterhouse cabidyldy *eg* cabidyldai
char torgoch *eg* torgochiaid
character (=symbol) nod *eg* nodau
character (of biological species etc) nodwedd *eb* nodweddion
character (of person) cymeriad *eg* cymeriadau
character code cod nodau *eg* codau nodau
character coding codio nod *be*
character font ffont nodau *eg* ffontiau nodau
character motivation and action cymhelliad a gweithred cymeriad
character of a puppet cymeriad pyped *eg* cymeriadau pyped
character of vegetation nodwedd llystyfiant *eb* nodweddion llystyfiant
character printer argraffydd nodau *eg* argraffyddion nodau
character reader darllenydd nodau *eg* darllenwyr nodau
character recognition adnabod nodau *be*
character reference geirda cymeriad *eg*
character set set nodau *eb* setiau nodau
character string llinyn nodau *eg* llinynnau nodau
characteristic *adj* nodweddiadol *ans*
characteristic (in general) *n* nodwedd *eb* nodweddion
characteristic (logarithms) *n* nodweddrif *eg* nodweddrifau
characteristic curve cromlin nodweddiadol *eb* cromliniau nodweddiadol
characteristic feature arwedd nodweddiadol *eb* arweddion nodweddiadol
characteristic note nodyn nodweddiadol *eg* nodau nodweddiadol
characterization cymeriadaeth *eb*
characters per second (cps) nodau yr eiliad *ell*
charcoal siarcol *eg*
charcoal drawing llun siarcol *eg* lluniau siarcol
charcoal pencil pensil siarcol *eg* pensiliau siarcol
charge (electrical) *n* gwefr *eb* gwefrau
charge (electrical) *v* gwefru *be*
charge (furnace or crucible) *v* llwytho *be*
charge (in sport) *n* hyrddiad *eg* hyrddiadau
charge (in sport) *v* hyrddio *be*
charge (money) *n* cost *eb* costau
charge (money) *v* codi tâl *be*
charge density meter mesurydd dwysedd gwefr *eg*
charge nurse (=male sister) prif weinydd nyrsio *eg* prif weinyddion nyrsio
charge nurse (female) prif weinyddes nyrsio *eb* prif weinyddesau nyrsio
charged (electrical, with feminine nouns) wedi'i gwefru *ans* wedi'u gwefru
charged (electrical, with masculine nouns) wedi'i wefru *ans* wedi'u gwefru
charged condenser cynhwysydd wedi'i wefru *eg* cynwysyddion wedi'u gwefru

charged particle gronyn wedi'i wefru *eg* gronynnau wedi'u gwefru
charging policy polisi codi tâl *eg* polisïau codi tâl
chariot cerbyd rhyfel *eg* cerbydau rhyfel
chariot wheel pattern patrwm olwyn cerbyd *eg* patrymau olwyn cerbyd
charismatic carismataidd *ans*
charity elusen *eb* elusennau
charity education addysg elusennol *eb*
charity school ysgol elusennol *eb* ysgolion elusennol
Charlemagne Siarlymaen *eg*
Charles the Bald Siarl Foel *eg*
Charles the Bold Siarl Ddewr *eg*
Charles the Good Siarl Dda *eg*
Charles the Great Siarl Fawr *eg*
chart siart *eg* siartiau
chart bar bar siart *eg* barrau siart
chart colour lliw siart *eg* lliwiau siart
chart data data siart *ell*
chart floor llawr siart *eg* lloriau siart
chart mode modd siart *eg*
chart object gwrthrych siart *eg* gwrthrychau siart
chart options dewisiadau siart *ell*
chart title teitl siart *eg* teitlau siart
chart type math o siart *eg* mathau o siart
charter siarter *eg/b* siarterau
charter of enfranchisement siarter rhyddfreinio *eg* siarterau rhyddfreinio
Charter Roll Rhôl Siarter *eb*
chartism siartaeth *eb*
chartist siartydd *eg* siartwyr
Chartist movement mudiad y Siartwyr *eg*
chase *n* helfa *eb* helfeydd
chase *v* ymlid *be*
chaser siaswr *eg* siaswyr
chasing *n* siasin *eg* siasinau
chasing *v* siasio *be*
chasing hammer morthwyl siasio *eg*
chasm agendor *eb* agendorau
chassis siasi *eg* siasïau
chassis frame ffrâm siasi *eb* fframiau siasi
chastity diweirdeb *eg*
chasuble casul *eg* casuliau
chat room ystafell sgwrsio *eb* ystafelloedd sgwrsio
chatter *n* sgrytiad *eg* sgrytiadau
chatter *v* sgrytian *be*
chattermark rhewgraith *eb* rhewgreithiau
chaudfroid chaudfroid *ans*
chauvinism siofiniaeth *eb*
check (=a tick) *n* tic *eg* ticiau
check (=split/defect in wood) *n* hollt *eg/b* holltau
check (=test) *n* prawf *eg* profion
check (=test) *v* profi *be*
check (=tick a box) *v* ticio *be*
check (=verification) *n* gwiriad *eg* gwiriadau
check (=verify) *v* gwirio *be*
check (of pattern) *adj* siec *ans*
check all gwirio oll *be*
check box blwch ticio *eg* blychau ticio
check digit gwirio digid *eg*
check nut (lock nut) nyten gloi *eb* nytiau cloi
check pattern patrwm siec *eg* patrymau siec
check pointer pwyntydd stac *eg* pwyntyddion stac
check selection gwirio dewisiad *be*
checked item (=ticked item) eitem wedi'i thicio *eb* eitemau wedi'u ticio
checked material defnydd siec *eg* defnyddiau siec
checkered sgwariog *ans*
checkered diagonal croesgornel sgwariog *ans*
checklist (for reference) rhestr gyfeirio *eb* rhestri cyfeirio
▶ **checklist** (for verification) rhestr wirio *eb* rhestri gwirio
checkout desg talu *eb* desgiau talu
checksum prawfswm *eg* prawfsymiau
check-up (medical) archwiliad *eg* archwiliadau
Cheddar cheese caws Cheddar *eg*
cheek boch *eb* bochau
cheese caws *eg* cawsiau
cheese curd ceuled caws *eg*
cheese straws rhimynnau caws *ell*
cheeseboard bwrdd caws *eg* byrddau caws
▶ **cheeseburger** eidionyn caws *eg* eidionod caws
cheesecake cacen gaws *eb* cacennau caws
cheesecloth lliain caws *eg* llieiniau caws
cheese-head bolt bollt bencosyn *eb* bolltau pencosyn
cheese-head rivet rhybed pencosyn *eg* rhybedion pencosyn
cheese-head screw sgriw bencosyn *eb* sgriwiau pencosyn
chef-d'oeuvre (masterpiece) campwaith *eg* campweithiau
chelate celadu *be*
chelated celedig *ans*
chelation celadiad *eg*
Chelsea bun bynen Chelsea *eb* byns Chelsea
chemical *adj* cemegol *ans*
▶ **chemical** *n* cemegyn *eg* cemegion
chemical action effaith gemegol *eb* effeithiau cemegol
chemical behaviour ymddygiad cemegol *eg*
▶ **chemical industry** diwydiant cemegion *eg* diwydiannau cemegion
chemical kinetics cineteg gemegol *eb*
chemical reaction adwaith cemegol *eg* adweithiau cemegol
chemical shift symudiad cemegol *eg*
chemical stain staen cemegol *eg* staeniau cemegol
chemical structure adeiledd cemegol *eg*
chemical symbol symbol cemegol *eg* symbolau cemegol
chemical weed killer chwynladdwr cemegol *eg* chwynladdwyr cemegol
chemisorption cemsugniad *eg*

chemist (=expert in chemistry) cemegydd *eg* cemegwyr
chemist (=pharmacist) fferyllydd *eg* fferyllwyr
chemistry cemeg *eg/b*
chemistry of food cemeg bwyd *eb*
chemoreceptor cemodderbynnydd *eg* cemodderbynyddion
chemosense cemosynnwyr *eg*
chemosensory cemosynhwyraidd *ans*
chemosynthesis cemosynthesis *eg*
chemotaxis cemotacsis *eg*
chemotherapy cemotherapi *eg*
chemotropism cemotropedd *eg*
chenille needle nodwydd chenille *eb* nodwyddau chenille
cheque siec *eb* sieciau
chequer plate plât siecer *eg* platiau siecer
chequered chain stitch pwyth cadwyn amryliw *eg* pwythau cadwyn amryliw
cherry ceiriosen *eb* ceirios
chert cornfaen *eg* cornfeini
Cheshire cheese caws Caer *eg*
chessmen gwerin gwyddbwyll *ell*
chest (for storing things) cist *eb* cistiau
chest (of human) brest *eb* brestiau
chest compression cywasgu'r frest *be*
chest freezer rhewgist *eb* rhewgistiau
chest medicine meddygaeth y frest *eb*
chest of drawers cist o ddroriau *eb* cistiau o ddroriau
chest of viols cist o feiolau *eb* cistiau o feiolau
chest pass pàs o'r frest *eb* pasiau o'r frest
chest register llais y frest *eg*
chestnut cneuen gastan *eb* cnau castan
chestnut brown (enamelling colour) gwinau *eg*
chestnut brown (of soil) cochddu *ans*
chevron (architecture) cwplws *eg* cyplysau
chevron banding bandin ceibr *eg* bandinau ceibr
chevron stitch pwyth ceibr *eg* pwythau ceibr
chi (χ) square chi (χ) sgwâr *eg*
chiaroscuro chiaroscuro *eg*
chiasma ciasma *eg* ciasmata
chicanery twyll *eg*
chicken cyw iâr *eg* cywion ieir
chicken-pox brech yr ieir *eb*
chicory sicori *eg*
chief education officer prif swyddog addysg *eg* prif swyddogion addysg
chief executive officer prif weithredwr *eg* prif weithredwyr
Chief Justice Prif Ustus *eg* Prif Ustusiaid
chief superintendent prif arolygydd *eg* prif arolygwyr
chief-rent rhent arglwydd *eg*
chieftain pennaeth *eg* penaethiaid
chiffon shiffon *eg*
child plentyn *eg* plant
child abuse cam-drin plant *be*
child abuse register cofrestr plant a gamdriniwyd *eb* cofrestri plant a gamdriniwyd
child allowance budd-dal plant *eg*
child assessment order gorchymyn asesu plentyn *eg* gorchmynion asesu plant
child at risk plentyn mewn perygl *eg* plant mewn perygl
child care gofal plant *eg*
Child Care Act Deddf Gofal Plant *eb*
child care assistant cynorthwyydd gofal plant *eg* cynorthwywyr gofal plant
child care officer swyddog gofal plant *eg* swyddogion gofal plant
child care worker gweithiwr gofal plant *eg* gweithwyr gofal plant
child development datblygiad plant *eg*
child guidance cyfarwyddo plant *be*
child guidance centre canolfan cyfarwyddo plant *eb* canolfannau cyfarwyddo plant
child guidance clinic clinig cyfarwyddo plant *eg* clinigau cyfarwyddo plant
child having special educational needs plentyn ag anghenion addysgol arbennig *eg* plant ag anghenion addysgol arbennig
child in need plentyn mewn angen *eg* plant mewn angen
child minder gwarchodwr plant *eg* gwarchodwyr plant
child protection diogelu plant *be*
child protection register cofrestr amddiffyn plant *eb* cofrestri amddiffyn plant
child psychiatrist seiciatrydd plant *eg* seiciatryddion plant
child psychiatry seiciatreg plant *eb*
child psychology seicoleg plant *eb*
child welfare lles plant *eg*
child welfare clinic clinig lles plant *eg* clinigau lles plant
childbirth genedigaeth *eb* genedigaethau
child-centred approach dull plentyn ganolog *eg* dulliau plentyn ganolog
child-centred education addysg plant ganolog *eb*
child-centred teaching addysgu plant ganolog *be*
child-directed speech cyfathrebu addas i'r plentyn *be*
childhood plentyndod *eg*
childish plentynnaidd *ans*
Children's Charter, The Siarter y Plant *eg*
Children's Crusade Croesgad y Plant *eb*
children's home cartref plant *eg* cartrefi plant
children's literature llenyddiaeth plant *eb*
chill oeri *be*
chill bar bar rhynnu *eg* barrau rhynnu
chilli chilli *eg*
chilling compartment adran oeri *eb* adrannau oeri
chime clychsain *eb* clychseiniau
chime bar bar cloch *eg* barrau clych
chimney simnai *eb* simneiau

chin gên *eb* genau
chin rest gên-bwys *eg* genbwysau
china tsieni *eg*
china cabinet cabinet llestri *eg* cabinetau llestri
china clay caolin *eg*
china palette palet tsieni *eg* paletau tsieni
china ware llestri tsieni *ell*
Chinese block bloc Tsieineaidd *eg* blociau Tsieineaidd
Chinese white gwyn Tsieina *eg*
chintz chintz *eg*
chip (in football) *n* tsip *eg* tsipiau
chip (in football) *v* tsipio *be*
chip (in general) *n* sglodyn *eg* sglodion
chip (in general) *v* sglodi *be*
chip breaker torrwr sglodion *eg* torwyr sglodion
chip the ball tsipio'r bêl *be*
chipboard bwrdd sglodion *eg* byrddau sglodion
chipped (of surface) tolciog *ans*
chipped grain graen sglodion *eg*
chipped potatoes sglodion *ell*
chipping block bloc sglodi *eg* blociau sglodi
chipping chisel cŷn sglodi *eg* cynion sglodi; gaing sglodi *eb* geingiau glodi
chipping face wyneb sglodi *eg* wynebau sglodi
chipping hammer morthwyl sglodi *eg* morthwylion sglodi
chipping resistance gwrthiant sglodi *eg*
chiral cirol *ans*
chirality ciroledd *eg*
chiropodist ciropodydd *eg* ciropodyddion
chiropody trin traed *be*
chisel *n* cŷn *eg* cynion; gaing *eb* geingiau
chisel *v* naddu *be*
chisel blade llafn cŷn *eg* llafnau cŷn; llafn gaing *eg* llafnau gaing
chisel edge ymyl cŷn *eb* ymylon cŷn; ymyl gaing *eb* ymylon gaing
chisel parts rhannau cŷn *ell*; rhannau gaing *ell*
chisel shaped arrowhead pen saeth ffurf cŷn *eg* pennau saeth ffurf cŷn
chitin citin *eg*
chivalry sifalri *eg*
chivalry order urdd sifalri *eb* urddau sifalri
chives cennin syfi *ell*
chlamydospore clamydosbor *eg*
chloramine cloramin *eg*
chlorate(I) ion ïon clorad(I) *eg* ïonau clorad(I)
chlorate(III) ion ïon clorad (III) *eg* ïonau clorad (III)
chlorate(V) ion ïon clorad(V) *eg* ïonau clorad(V)
chlorate(VII) ion ïon clorad(VII) *eg* ïonau clorad(VII)
chloric(I) acid asid clorig(I) *eg*
chloric(III) acid asid clorig(III) *eg*
chloric(V) acid asid clorig(V) *eg*
chloric(VII) acid asid clorig(VII) *eg*
chloride clorid *eg*
chloride ion ïon clorid *eg* ïonau clorid
chloride shift symudiad clorid *eg*
chlorinate clorineiddio *be*
chlorinated clorinedig *ans*
chlorine (Cl) clorin *eg*
chlorine dioxide clorin deuocsid *eg*
2-chlorobuta-1,3-diene 2-clorobwta-1,3-deuen *eg*
chloroethane cloroethan *eg*
chloroethanoic acid asid cloroethanöig *eg*
2-chloroethanol 2-cloroethanol *eg*
chloroethene cloroethen *eg*
chloroform clorofform *eg*
chloromethane cloromethan *eg*
1-chloro-2-methylbenzene 1-cloro-2-methylbensen *eg*
(chloromethyl)benzene (cloromethyl)bensen *eg*
chlorophyll cloroffyl *eg*
chloroplast cloroplast *eg* cloroplastau
chloropropane cloropropan *eg*
3-chloroprop-1-ene 3-cloroprop-1-en *eg*
chlorosis (in botany) clorosis *eg*
chlorosis (medical) gwyrddwst *eg*
chlorosulfonic acid asid clorosylffonig *eg*
chockstone tagen *eb* tagenni
chocolate siocled *eg*
choice dewis *eg* dewisiadau
choice chamber siambr ddewis *eb*
choir côr *eg* corau
choir boy bachgen côr *eg* bechgyn côr
choir organ organ gôr *eb* organau côr
choir stall sedd gôr *eb* seddau côr
choir-monk côr-fynach *eg* côr-fynaich
choke *n* tagydd *eg* tagyddion
choke *v* tagu *be*
cholecalciferol colecalchifferol *eg*
cholecystokinin colesystocinin *eg*
cholera colera *eg*
cholera epidemic epidemig colera *eg* epidemigau colera
cholesterol colesterol *eg*
cholic acid asid colig *eg*
cholinergic colinergig *ans*
cholinesterase colinesteras *eg*
cholosterolaemia colosterolaemia *eg*
chondral condrol *ans*
chondroid condroid *ans*
chondroitin condroitin *eg*
chop (in tennis) *n* cildoriad *eg* cildoriadau
chop (in tennis) *v* cildorri *be*
chop (mortise) *v* torri *be*
chop (of meat) *n* golwyth *eg* golwython
chopper (meat) bwyell gig *eb* bwyeill cig
chopper grip gafael bwyell *eb* gafaelion bwyeill
chopping board bwrdd torri *eg* byrddau torri
chorale corâl *eg* coralau
chorale prelude preliwd corâl *eg* preliwdiau corâl
chord *n* cord *eg* cordiau
chord *v* cordio *be*

chord figuring rhifoli cord *be*
chord in first inversion cord gwrthdro cyntaf *eg* cordiau gwrthdro cyntaf
chord in root position cord safle gwreiddiol *eg* cordiau safle gwreiddiol
chord in second inversion cord ail wrthdro *eg* cordiau ail wrthdro
chord in third inversion cord trydydd gwrthdro *eg* cordiau trydydd gwrthdro
chord indication dynodi cord *be*
chord of the seventh cord seithfed *eg* cordiau seithfed
chord progression dilyniad cordiau *eg* dilyniadau cordiau
chord sequence dilyniant o gordiau *eg* dilyniannau o gordiau
chordal block bloc cordiau *eg* blociau cordiau
chordal structure adeiledd cordiol *eg* adeileddau cordiol
chordate cordat *eg* cordatau
choreographer coreograffydd *eg* coreograffwyr
choreography coreograffi *eg*
chorion corion *eb*
chorister aelod o gôr *eg* aelodau o gôr
choroid coroid *ans*
choroid layer haenen goroid *eb* haenau coroid
choroid plexus plecsws coroid *eg*
choropleth coropleth *eg*
chorus (=group of singers) côr *eg* corau
chorus (=piece of music) cytgan *eg/b* cytganau
chorus (in opera and secular music) corws *eg* corysau
chorus girl côr-ferch *eb* côr-ferched
chorus master côr-feistr *eg* côr-feistri
chosen physical activity gweithgaredd corfforol dewisol *eg* gweithgareddau corfforol dewisol
chrismation eneinio *be*
Christ Crist *eg*
Christendom Gwledydd Cred *ell*
christening robe gŵn bedydd *eg* gynau bedydd
Christian *adj* Cristnogol *ans*
Christian *n* Cristion *eg* Cristnogion
Christian belief cred Gristnogol *eb*
Christian church eglwys Gristnogol *eb* eglwysi Cristnogol
Christian Church Eglwys Gristnogol, yr *eb*
Christian Court Cwrt Eglwysig *eg*
Christian Democrat Party Plaid Ddemocrataidd Gristnogol *eb*
Christian faith ffydd Gristnogol *eb*
Christian family teulu Cristnogol *eg* teuluoedd Cristnogol
Christian heritage etifeddiaeth Gristnogol *eb*
Christian teaching dysgeidiaeth Gristnogol *eb*
Christianity Cristnogaeth *eb*
Christmas Nadolig *eg*
chromate(III) ion ïon cromad(III) *eg* ïonau cromad(III)
chromate(VI) ion ïon cromad(VI) *eg* ïonau cromad(VI)
chromatic cromatig *ans*
chromatic chord cord cromatig *eg* cordiau cromatig
chromatic harp telyn gromatig *eb* telynau cromatig
chromatic scale graddfa gromatig *eb* graddfeydd cromatig
chromatic semitone hanner tôn cromatig *eg* hanner tonau cromatig
chromaticism cromatyddiaeth *eb*
chromatid cromatid *eg* cromatidau
chromatin cromatin *eg*
chromatographic cromatograffig *ans*
chromatography cromatograffaeth *eb*
chrome crôm *eg*
chrome green gwyrdd crôm *eg*
chrome orange oren crôm *eg*
chromic(VI) acid asid cromig(VI) *eg*
chromising cromeiddio *be*
chromium (Cr) cromiwm *eg*
chromium screw sgriw gromiwm *eb* sgriwiau cromiwm
chromium(II) ionïon cromiwm(II) *eg* ïonau cromiwm(II)
chromium(III) ion ïon cromiwm(III) *eg* ïonau cromiwm(III)
chromium(III) oxide cromiwm(III) ocsid *eg*
chromium(III) potassium sulfate(VI)-12-water cromiwm(III) potasiwm sylffad(VI)-12-dŵr *eg*
chromium(VI) dichloride dioxide cromiwm(VI) deuclorid deuocsid *eg*
chromium(VI) oxide cromiwm(VI) ocsid *eg*
chromomer cromomer *eg* cromomerau
chromophore cromoffor *eg*
chromosomal cromosomaidd *ans*
chromosomal aberration gwyriad yn y cromosom *eg* gwyriadau yn y cromosomau
chromosome cromosom *eg* cromosomau
chromosome map (in biology) map cromosomau *eg* mapiau cromosomau
chromosome number rhif cromosom *eg* rhifau cromosomau
chromosphere cromosffer *eg* cromosfferau
chronic cronig *ans*
chronic confusional state cyflwr dryslyd cronig *eg*
▶ **chronic illness** gwaeledd cronig *eg*
chronic pain poen cronig *eg*
chronological cronolegol *ans*
chronological age oed cronolegol *eg*
chronological order trefn gronolegol *eb*
chronological understanding dealltwriaeth gronolegol *eb*
chronological writing ysgrifennu cronolegol *be*
chronology cronoleg *eb*
chronometer coronomedr *eg* cronomedrau
chrysalis chwiler *eg* chwilerod
chuck crafanc *eb* crafangau
chuck key allwedd grafanc *eb* allweddi crafanc

chuck steak stêc balfais *eb* steciau palfais
chucking crafangu *be*
chucking piece darn crafangu *eg* darnau crafangu
chunking talpio *be*
church eglwys *eb* eglwysi
church cadence diweddeb amen *eb* diweddebau amen
church committee pwyllgor eglwys *eg* pwyllgorau eglwys
church embroidery brodwaith eglwysig *eg*
church governor llywodraethwr eglwysig *eg* llywodraethwyr eglwysig
Church in Wales Eglwys yng Nghymru, yr *eb*
church mode modd eglwysig *eg* moddau eglwysig
Church of England Eglwys Loegr *eb*
church order trefn eglwys *eb*
church with tower eglwys gyda thŵr *eb*
churchwarden warden eglwys *eg* wardeiniaid eglwys
churchyard mynwent eglwys *eb* mynwentydd eglwysi
churn *v* corddi *be*
churn (=can to hold milk) *n* can llaeth *eg* caniau llaeth
churn (to make butter) *n* buddai *eb* buddeiau
chutney siytni *eg*
chyle caul *eg*
chylomicron ceulomicron *eg* ceulomicronau
chyme treulfwyd *eg*
chymosin cymosin *eg*
chymotrypsin cymotrypsin *eg*
cichlid ciclid *eg* ciclidiaid
cider seidr *eg* seidrau
ciliary ciliaraidd *ans*
ciliary body corffyn ciliaraidd *eg* corffynnau ciliaraidd
ciliary feeding ymborthi ciliaraidd *be*
ciliary muscle cyhyr ciliaraidd *eg* cyhyrau ciliaraidd
ciliated epithelium epitheliwm ciliedig *eg*
cilium ciliwm *eg* cilia
cimbalom simbalom *eg* simbalomau
cinder cone côn lludw *eg* conau lludw
cinema auteur auteur sinema *eg* auteurs sinema
cingulotomy cingwlotomi *eg*
cinnamon sinamon *eg*
Cinque Ports Pum Porthladd *eg*
cipher seiffr *eg* seiffrau
circadian rhythm rhythm circadaidd *eg*
circle *n* cylch *eg* cylchoedd
circle *v* cylchu *be*
circle chart siart cylch *eg* siartiau cylch
circle formation trefniant cylch *eg*
circle of fifths cylch pumedau *eg* cylchoedd pumedau
circle sector sector cylch *eg* sectorau cylch
circle segment segment cylch *eg* segmentau cylch
circling (of foot, arms) cylchu *be*
circlip cylchglip *eg* cylchglipiau
circuit (=running track) cylch rhedeg *eg* cylchoedd rhedeg
circuit (in electronics) cylched *eb* cylchedau
circuit (of judge, preacher) cylchdaith *eb* cylchdeithiau
circuit breaker torrwr cylched *eg* torwyr cylchedau
circuit diagram diagram cylched *eg* diagramau cylched
circuit judge barnwr cylchdaith *eg* barnwyr cylchdaith
circuit response ymateb cylched *eg*
circuit training hyfforddiant cylchol *eg*
circuit tuning cyweirio cylched *be*
circuit wave-forms tonffurfiau cylched *ell*
circular (=round) *adj* crwn *ans*
circular (letter) *n* cylchlythyr *eg* cylchlythyrau
circular (turning in circle) *adj* cylchol *ans*
circular arch bwa crwn *eg* bwâu crwn
circular base gwaelod crwn *eg* gwaelodion crwn
circular buffer byffer cylchol *eg* byfferau cylchol
circular cylinder silindr cylch *eg* silindrau cylch
circular dance dawns gylch *eb* dawnsiau cylch
circular die dei crwn *eg* deiau crwn
circular end pen crwn *eg* pennau crwn
circular flow of income llif cylchol incwm *eg*
circular land (of reamer) glan gylchol *eb* glannau cylchol
circular lap seam sêm lap gylchol *eb* semau lap cylchol
circular list rhestr gylchol *eb* rhestri cylchol
circular motion mudiant mewn cylch *eg*
circular motion stitching pwytho cylchdro *be*
circular muscle cyhyryn crwn *eg* cyhyrynnau crwn
circular parry pario cylchol *be*
circular overfolded seam sêm orlap gylchol *eb* semau gorlap cylchol
circular prism prism crwn *eg* prismau crwn
circular pyramid pyramid crwn *eg* pyramidiau crwn
circular saw llif gron *eb* llifiau crwn
circular shift syfliad cylchol *eg* syfliadau cylchol
circular skirt sgert gylch *eb* sgertiau cylch
circular split die dei crwn hollt *eg* deiau crwn hollt
circulate cylchredeg *be*
circulating cylchredol *ans*
circulating capital cyfalaf cylchredol *eg*
circulating school ysgol gylchynol *eb* ysgolion cylchynol
circulating waters dyfroedd cylchredol *ell*
circulation cylchrediad *eg* cylchrediadau
circulatory system system cylchrediad gwaed *eb*
circumcentre amganol *eg* amganolau
circumcircle amgylch *eg* amgylchoedd
circumcision enwaediad *eg*
circumduction cylchddwytho *be*
circumference (line) cylchyn *eg* cylchynnau
circumference (measurement) cylchedd *eg* cylcheddau
circumflex acen grom *eb* acenion crwm
circumnavigate cylchfordeithio *be*
circumnavigation cylchfordaith *eb* cylchfordeithiau

circumnavigator cylchforwr *eg* cylchforwyr
circumpolar constellation cytser ambegynol *eg* cytserau ambegynol
circumpolar star seren ambegynol *eb* sêr ambegynol
circumscribe amgylchu *be*
circumscribed amgylchol *ans*
circumscribed circle amgylch *eg* amgylchoedd
circumscribed polygon polygon amgylchol *eg* polygonau amgylchol
circus syrcas *eg* syrcasau
cire perdue cwyr coll *eg*
cirque cwm *eg* cymoedd
cirrocumulus cirrocumulus *eg*
cirrostratus cirrostratus *eg*
cirrus cirrus *eg*
cis cis *eg*
Cisalpine Republic Gweriniaeth Isalpaidd *eb*
cissoid cisoid *eg* cisoidau
cist cistfaen *eb* cistfeini
Cistercian *adj* Sistersaidd *ans*
Cistercian *n* Sistersiad *eg* Sistersiaid
cistern seston *eb* sestonau
cistern tower tŵr dyfrgist *eg* tyrau dyfrgist
cis-trans effect effaith trans-cis *eb*
cistron cistron *eg* cistronau
citadel caer ddinesig *eb* caerau dinesig
citizen dinesydd *eg* dinasyddion
Citizens Advice Bureau Canolfan Gynghori *eb* Canolfannau Cynghori
citizenship dinasyddiaeth *eb*
citric acid asid citrig *eg*
citrulline citrwlin *eg*
citrus citrws *eg*
citrus fruit ffrwyth citrws *eg* ffrwythau citrws
cittern sitern *eg* siternau
city dinas *eb* dinasoedd
city blues melan y ddinas *eb*
city centre canol y ddinas *eg*
city region rhanbarth dinas *eg* rhanbarthau dinasoedd
city state gwladwriaeth ddinas *eb* gwladwriaethau dinas
City Technology College (CTC) Coleg Technegol Dinas *eg*
civic dinesig *ans*
civic mathematics mathemateg ddinesig *eb*
civic sense synnwyr dinesig *eg*
civil (=polite) moesgar *ans*
civil (of citizens) sifil *ans*
Civil Code Cod Sifil *eg*
civil constitution cyfansoddiad sifil *eg*
civil jurisdiction awdurdodaeth sifil *eb*
civil defence amddiffyn sifil *eg*
civil disobedience anufudd-dod sifil *eg*
civil engineering peirianneg sifil *eb*
Civil Law Cyfraith Sifil *eb*
civil list rhestr sifil *eb* rhestri sifil
civil proceedings achos sifil *eg*
civil rights iawnderau sifil *ell*
civil service gwasanaeth sifil *eg*
civil settlement anheddiad sifil *eb* aneddiadau sifil
civil war rhyfel cartref *eg* rhyfeloedd cartref
civilian sifiliad *eg* sifiliaid
civility gwarineb *eg*
civilization gwareiddiad *eg* gwareiddiadau
civilized society cymdeithas wâr *eb* cymdeithasau gwâr
cladding cladin *eg* cladinau
claim *n* hawl *eg/b* hawliau
claim *v* hawlio *be*
clamp *n* clamp *eg* clampiau
clamp *v* clampio *be*
clamping device dyfais glampio *eb* dyfeisiau clampio
clamping screw sgriw glampio *eb* sgriwiau clampio
clan clan *eg* claniau
clang association cysylltiad sain *eg*
clap *n* clap *eg* clapiau
clap *v* clapio *be*
clap a steady beat clapio curiad cyson *be*
clap hands curo dwylo *be*
clap partner's hands curo dwylo partner *be*
clapper box blwch clepian *eg* blychau clepian
clarified fat saim gloyw *eg*
clarify (in cooking) gloywi *be*
clarinet clarinét *eg* clarinetau
clarinettist clarinetydd *eg* clarinetwyr
clarity eglurder *eg*
clarity of body shape eglurder siâp y corff *eg*
clarity of the notation eglurder y nodiant *eg*
clarsach clarsach *eg* clarsachau
clash gwrthdaro *be*
clasp clesbyn *eg* clasbiau
clasp nail hoelen lorio *eb* hoelion llorio
clasper clasper *eg* clasperi
class dosbarth *eg* dosbarthiadau
class distinction gwahaniaeth dosbarth *eg* gwahaniaethau dosbarth
class interval cyfwng dosbarth *eg* cyfyngau dosbarth
class management rheolaeth dosbarth *eb*
class mark marc dosbarth *eg* marciau dosbarth
class separation gwahaniad dosbarth *eg*
class structure fframwaith dosbarth *eg*
class struggle rhyfel dosbarth *eg*
classes of food mathau o fwyd *ell*
classic pass pàs glasurol *eb* pasiau clasurol
classic profile proffil clasurol *eg* proffiliau clasurol
classic style arddull clasurol *eg*
classical clasurol *ans*
classical conditioning cyflyru clasurol *be*
classical curriculum cwricwlwm clasurol *eg*
classical music cerddoriaeth glasurol *eb*
classical studies astudiaethau clasurol *ell*
classicism clasuriaeth *eb*
classicist clasurwr *eg* clasurwyr

classics clasuron *ell*
classification *n* dosbarthiad *eg* dosbarthiadau
classification system *n* trefn ddosbarthu *eb*
classify dosbarthu *be*
classify information dosbarthu gwybodaeth *be*
classroom ystafell ddosbarth *eb* ystafelloedd dosbarth
classroom behaviour ymddygiad yn yr ystafell ddosbarth *eg*
classroom climate naws yr ystafell ddosbarth *eb*
classroom ensemble ensemble dosbarth *eg* ensembles dosbarth
classroom environment amgylchedd yr ystafell ddosbarth *eg*
classroom feedback adborth o'r ystafell ddosbarth *eg*
classroom observation arsylwi yn yr ystafell ddosbarth *be*
classroom-based activities gweithgareddau ystafell ddosbarth *ell*
classroom-based task tasg ystafell ddosbarth *eb* tasgau ystafell ddosbarth
clastic clastig *ans*
clathrate *adj* cawellog *ans*
clathrate *n* clathrad *eg* clathradau
clause cymal *eg* cymalau
claustral clwystrol *ans*
clausula diweddeb *eg/b* diweddebau
clavecin clafesin *eg*
claveciniste chwaraewr clafesin *eg* chwaraewyr clafesin
claves clafiau *ell*
clavichord claficord *eg* claficordiau
clavicle pont yr ysgwydd *eb*
clavicymbal clafisymbal *eg* clafisymbalau
clavier (instrument) offeryn llawfwrdd *eg* offerynnau llawfwrdd
clavier (keyboard) llawfwrdd *eg* llawfyrddau
claw crafanc *eb* crafangau
claw clutch cydiwr crafanc *eg* cydwyr crafanc
claw foot troed crafanc *eb* traed crafanc
claw hammer morthwyl crafanc *eg* morthwylion crafanc
claw wrench tyndro crafanc *eg* tyndroeon crafanc
clay clai *eg* cleiau
clay bin bin clai *eg* biniau clai
clay cutter torrell glai *eb* torellau clai
clay modelling modelu â chlai *be*
clay modelling tool erfyn modelu clai *eg* offer modelu clai
clay relief cerfwedd glai *eb* cerfweddau clai
clay tools offer clai *ell*
clay vale dyffryndir clai *eg* dyffryndiroedd clai
clay with flints clai â challestr *eg*
clean glân *ans*
clean cut toriad glân *eg* toriadau glân
clean hole twll glân *eg* tyllau glân
clean mould mowld glân *eg* mowldiau glân
clean thread edau lân *eb* edafedd glân
cleaner (female) glanhawraig *eb* glanhawragedd
cleaner (male and general) glanhawr *eg* glanhawyr
cleaner (of material) defnydd glanhau *eg* defnyddiau glanhau
cleaning appliance dyfais lanhau *eb* dyfeisiau glanhau
cleaning fluid hylif glanhau *eg* hylifau glanhau
cleanliness glendid *eg*
cleanse glanhau *be*
cleanser glanweithydd *eg* glanweithyddion
cleansing department adran lanweithio *eb* adrannau glanweithio
cleansing lotion trwyth glanhau *eg*
clear *v* clirio *be*
clear (=distinct) *adj* pendant *ans*
clear (=not confused) *adj* eglur *ans*
clear (=transparent and most other senses) *adj* clir *ans*
clear beginning dechrau pendant *eg*
clear cache clirio'r storfa *be*
clear disk cache clirio storfa'r disg *be*
clear end diwedd pendant *eg*
clear finish gorffeniad clir *eg* gorffeniadau clir
clear flute ffliwt glir *eb* ffliwtiau clir
clear glaze gwydredd gloyw *eg*
clear lacquer lacr clir *eg*
clear lamp lamp glir *eb* lampau clir
clear memory cache clirio storfa'r cof *be*
clear middle canol pendant *eg*
clear plastic plastig clir *eg*
clear polish llathrydd clir *eg* llathryddion clir
clear print range (command) clirio'r ystod argraffu *be*
clear query (command) clirio'r ymholiad *be*
clear set of values set eglur o werthoedd *eb*
clear sketch braslun eglur *eg* brasluniau eglur
clear varnish farnais clir *eg* farneisiau clir
clearance cliriad *eg* cliriadau
clearance angle ongl gliriad *eb* onglau cliriad
clearance drill dril cliriad *eg* driliau cliriad
clearance hole twll cliriad *eg* tyllau cliriad
clearing llannerch *eb* llennyrch
clearing (in histology) gloywi *be*
clearing agent gloywydd *eg* gloywyddion
clearing bank banc clirio *eg* banciau clirio
clearway clirffordd *eb* clirffyrdd
cleat *n* cledd *eg* cleddau
cleat *v* cleddu *be*
cleavage (in biology) ymraniad *eg* ymraniadau
cleavage (in chemistry) holltiad *eg* holltiadau
cleavage plane plân hollti *eg* planau hollti
clef cleff *eg* cleffiau
cleft hollt *eg/b* holltau
clench (a nail, a rivet) clensio *be*
clerestory llofft olau *eb* llofftydd golau
clergyman clerigwr *eg* clerigwyr

cleric clerigwr *eg* clerigwyr
clerical clerigol *ans*
clericalism clerigiaeth *eb*
clerk clerc *eg* clercod
clerk of the course clerc y maes *eg* clercod y maes
clerks regular clerigwyr rheolaidd *ell*
clevis pin pìn clefis *eg* pinnau clefis
click *n* clic *eg* cliciau
click *v* clicio *be*
clickable image map map delweddau cliciadwy *be* mapiau delweddau cliciadwy
client cleient *eg* cleientiaid
client confidentiality cyfrinachedd cleient *eg*
client dignity urddas y cleient *eg*
client diversity amrywiaeth o gleientiaid *eb*
client group grŵp o gleientiaid *eg*
client state gwladwriaeth ddibynnol *eb* gwladwriaethau dibynnol
clientage cleientaeth *eb*
client-based filter hidlydd cleient *eg* hidlyddion cleient
client-centred cleient ganolog *ans*
client-centred therapy therapi cleient ganolog *eg*
client-directed approach dull wedi'i gyfeirio at y cleient *eg*
cliff clogwyn *eg* clogwyni
cliff collapse clogwyn yn syrthio *eg*
cliff line llinell glogwyn *eb* llinellau clogwyn
cliff recession enciliad clogwyn *eg* enciliadau clogwyn
climate hinsawdd *eb* hinsoddau
climate barrier gwahanfur rhag yr hinsawdd *eg*
climatic conditions hinsawdd *eb*
climatic extremes eithafion hinsawdd *ell*
climatic feature nodwedd hinsoddol *eb* nodweddion hinsoddol
climatic region rhanbarth hinsoddol *eg* rhanbarthau hinsoddol
climatology hinsoddeg *eb*
climax uchafbwynt *eg* uchafbwyntiau
climax vegetation uchafbwynt llystyfiant *eg* uchafbwyntiau llystyfiant
climb dringo *be*
climb high dringo'n uchel *be*
climb milling (down cut) melino dringol *eg*
climbing feed porthiant dringol *eg*
climbing frame ffrâm ddringo *eb* fframiau dringo
climbing plant planhigyn dringo *eg* planhigion dringo
climbing rope rhaff ddringo *eb* rhaffau dringo
climbing wall wal ddringo *eb* waliau dringo
clinch a deal taro bargen *be*
cling film haenen lynu *eb* haenau glynu
clinic clinig *eg* clinigau
clinical clinigol *ans*
clinical assessment asesiad clinigol *eg* asesiadau clinigol
clinical audit archwiliad clinigol *eg* archwiliadau clinigol
clinical decision-making gwneud penderfyniadau clinigol *be*
clinical judgement barn glinigol *eb*
clinical neuropsychology niwroseicoleg glinigol *eb*
clinical psychologist seicolegydd clinigol *eg* seicolegwyr clinigol
clinical psychology seicoleg glinigol *eb*
clinical study astudiaeth glinigol *eb* astudiaethau clinigol
clinical thermometer thermomedr clinigol *eg* thermomedrau clinigol
clinical training hyfforddiant clinigol *eg*
clinically clean clinigol lân *ans*
clinker clincer *eg* clinceri
clinker eight clincer wyth *eg*
clinker four clincer pedwar *eg*
clinker nailed boots esgidiau hoelion clincer *ell*
clinometer clinomedr *eg* clinomedrau
clint clint *eg* clintiau
clip *n* clip *eg* clipiau
clip *v* clipio *be*
clip art cliplun *eg* clipluniau
clip art library llyfrgell glipluniau *eb* llyfrgelloedd clipluniau
clipboard clipfwrdd *eg* clipfyrddau
clipping distortion afluniad clipio *eg*
clitellum clitelwm *eg*
cloaca cloaca *eg*
cloak clogyn *eg* clogynnau
clock cloc *eg* clociau
clock arithmetic rhifyddeg cloc *eb*
clock glass gwydryn cloc *eg* gwydrynnau cloc
clock pulse curiad cloc *eg* curiadau cloc
clock pulse generator generadur curiadau cloc *eg* generaduron curiadau cloc
clock rate cyfradd cloc *eb* cyfraddau cloc
clock signal signal cloc *eg* signalau cloc
clockwise clocwedd *ans*
clockwise consecutive revolutions cylchdroeon clocwedd olynol *ell*
clockwise direction cyfeiriad clocwedd *eg*
clockwise moment moment clocwedd *eg*
clog (=choke) *v* tagu *be*
clog (=wooden shoe) *n* clocsen *eb* clocsiau
clog dance dawns y glocsen *eb* dawnsiau'r glocsen
clog rattle rhuglen glocsen *eb* rhuglenni clocsiau
clogged surface arwyneb wedi tagu *eg* arwynebau wedi tagu
cloisonné enamel enamel cloisonné *eg*
cloister clwysty *eg* clwystai
cloistered clwystredig *ans*
clone *n* clôn *eg* clonau
clone *v* clonio *be*
close *adj* agos *ans*
close *v* cau *be*
close (in music) *n* diweddeb *eg/b* diweddebau
close active window cau'r ffenestr weithredol *be*
close all cau popeth *be*

close all files cau pob ffeil *be*
close all windows cau pob ffenestr *be*
close application (command) cau'r rhaglen *be*
close combat gornest glòs *eb* gornestau clòs
close dialog (command) cau'r ddeialog *be*
close document (command) cau'r ddogfen *be*
close grain graen clòs *eg*
close harmony harmoni clòs *eg*
close horizontally cau'n llorweddol *be*
close mail (command) cau'r e-bost *be*
close object (command) cau'r gwrthrych *be*
close packing pacio'n dynn *be*
close polygon (command) cau'r polygon *be*
Close Roll Rhôl Clos *eb*
close task cau'r dasg *be*
close the key (of a switch) cau'r agoriad *be*
close the switch cau'r switsh *be*
close the tap cau'r tap *be*
close vertically cau'n fertigol *be*
close window (command) cau'r ffenestr *be*
close woven fabric ffabrig gwead clos *eg* ffabrigau gwead clos
closed caeedig *ans*
closed (shop sign etc) ar gau *ans*
closed circuit cylched gaeedig *eb* cylchedau caeedig
closed circuit television (CCTV) teledu cylch-caeedig *eg*
closed circulation cylchrediad caeedig *eg*
closed eaves bondo caeedig *eg* bondoeau caeedig
closed fracture torasgwrn caeedig *eg* toresgyrn caeedig
closed interval cyfwng caeedig *eg* cyfyngau caeedig
closed loop dolen gaeedig *eb* dolennau caeedig
closed pack pecyn caeedig *eg* pecynnau caeedig
closed pipe pibell gaeedig *eb* pibellau caeedig
closed question cwestiwn caeedig *eg* cwestiynau caeedig
closed shop siop gaeedig *eb* siopau caeedig
closed stance safiad caeedig *eg*
closed system cyfundrefn gaeedig *eb* cyfundrefnau caeedig
close-mouth tongs gefel gegdyn *eb* gefeiliau cegdyn
close-packing pacio tyn
closest approach nesâd agosaf *eg*
close-up (diagram) agoslun *eg* agosluniau
closing balance balans terfynol *eg* balansau terfynol
closing stile cledren gau *eb* cledrau cau
closing stock stoc derfynol *eb*
closure caefa *eb* caefeydd
Closure Rule Rheol Gaefa *eb*
clot *n* tolchen *eb* tolchennau
clot *v* ceulo *be*
cloth (for wiping etc) clwt *eg* clytiau
cloth (of heavy material) brethyn *eg* brethynnau
cloth (of light material) lliain *eg* llieiniau
cloth body corff lliain *eg* cyrff lliain
cloth patch clwt brethyn *eg* clytiau brethyn
cloth trade masnach frethyn *eb*
clothes dillad *ell*
clothes basket basged ddillad *eb* basgedi dillad
clothes hanger cambren dillad *eg* cambrenni dillad
clothes horse hors ddillad *eb* horsys dillad
clothes line lein ddillad *eb* leiniau dillad
clothes peg peg dillad *eg* pegiau dillad
clothes rack rhesel ddillad *eb* rheseli dillad
clothier brethynnwr *eg* brethynwyr
clotted cream hufen tolch *eg*
cloud cwmwl *eg* cymylau
cloud base gwaelod cwmwl *eg* gwaelodion cwmwl
cloud chamber llestr niwl *eg* llestri niwl
cloud cover gorchudd cwmwl *eg* gorchuddion cwmwl
cloudburst torgwmwl *eg* torgymylau
cloudiness cymyledd *eg*
cloudlet cymylyn *eg* cymylynnau
clout nail hoelen benfawr *eb* hoelion penfawr
clove clof *eg* clofau
clove hitch cwlwm glyn *eg* clymau glyn
clover meillionen *eb* meillion
clover leaf junction cyffordd dail meillion *eb* cyffyrdd dail meillion
clown clown *eg* clowniaid
cloze exercise ymarfer llenwi bylchau *eg* ymarferion llenwi bylchau
cloze procedure dull cyfannu *eg* dulliau cyfannu
club clwb *eg* clybiau
club foot troed glwb *eb* traed clwb
clubhouse tŷ clwb *eg* tai clwb
club-moss clwbfwsogl *eg* clwbfwsoglau
clumsiness lletchwithdod *eg*
clumsy child syndrome syndrom plentyn afrosgo *eg*
Cluniac Order Urdd Cluny *eb*
cluster *n* clwstwr *eg* clystyrau
cluster *v* clystyru *be*
cluster analysis dadansoddi clwstwr *be*
clutch *n* cydiwr *eg* cydwyr
clutch *v* gafael *be*
clutch lever lifer cydiwr *eg* liferi cydiwr
clutch plate plât cydio *eg* platiau cydio
CNAA Cyngor Dyfarniadau Academaidd Cenedlaethol *eg*
coacervate coaserfad *eg* coaserfadau
coacervation coaserfadiad *eg*
coach *v* hyfforddi *be*
coach (=bus) *n* bws moethus *eg* bysiau moethus
coach (=trainer, female) *n* hyfforddwraig *eb* hyfforddwragedd
coach (=trainer, male and general) *n* hyfforddwr *eg* hyfforddwyr
coach bolt bollt goets *eb* bolltau coets
coach horn corn cerbyd *eg* cyrn cerbyd
coach screw sgriw goets *eb* sgriwiau coets
coaching hyfforddiant *eg*
coagulate (in chemistry) clystyru *be*

adf, adv adferf, *adverb* ***ans, adj*** ansoddair, *adjective* ***be*** berf, *verb* ***eb*** enw benywaidd, *feminine noun* ***eg*** enw gwrywaidd, *masculine noun*

coagulate (in general) ceulo *be*
coagulate (of blood) tolchennu *be*
coagulated ceuledig *ans*
coagulation (in general) ceulad *eg*
coagulation (of blood) tolcheniad *eg*
coal glo *eg*
coal industry diwydiant glo *eg*
coal measures cystradau glo *ell*
coal tar *n* col-tar *eg*
coal tar *v* coltario *be*
coal tar dye llifyn col-tar *eg* llifynnau col-tar
coal-bearing rocks creigiau â glo *ell*
coalesce cyfuno *be*
coalescence cyfuniad *eg* cyfuniadau
coalfield maes glo *eg* meysydd glo
coalfish chwitlyn glas *eg* chwitlyniaid glas
coalition clymblaid *eb* clymbleidiau
coaming ymyled *eg*
coarse (=large grained) bras *ans*
coarse (=rough textured) garw *ans*
coarse adjustment cymhwysiad bras *eg* cymwysiadau bras
coarse control rheolydd bras *eg* rheolyddion bras
coarse feed porthiant garw *eg* porthiannau garw
coarse grain graen bras *eg*
coarse grit grit bras *eg*
coarse knurl nwrl bras *eg* nwrliau bras
coarse oilstone carreg hogi gradd arw *eg* cerrig hogi gradd arw
coarse pitch pitsh bras *eg*
coarse surface arwyneb bras *eg* arwynebau bras
coarse texture gwead bras *eg*
coarse thread edau fras *eb* edafedd bras
coarseness garwedd *eg*
coast arfordir *eg* arfordiroedd
coast of emergence arfordir cyfodol *eg* arfordiroedd cyfodol
coastal arfordirol *ans*
coastal current cerrynt arfordirol *eg* ceryntau arfordirol
coastal feature arwedd arfordirol *eb* arweddion arfordirol
coastal flooding llifogydd arfordirol *ell*
coastal landform tirffurf arfordirol *eb* tirffurfiau arfordirol
coastal marsh morfa *eg/b* morfeydd
coastal plain gwastadedd arfordirol *eg* gwastadeddau arfordirol
coastguard gwyliwr y glannau *eg* gwylwyr y glannau
coasting cowstio *be*
coastline morlin *eg* morlinau
coat (in cooking) *n* caen *eg* caenau
coat (in cooking) *v* caenu *be*
coat (in metalwork, plastics) *n* araen *eb* araenau
coat (in metalwork, plastics) *v* araenu *be*
coat (of clothing, paint) *n* cot *eb* cotiau
coat of arms arfbais *eb* arfbeisiau
coat weight pwysau cot *ell*
coat-dress cot ffrog *eb* cotiau ffrog
coating batter cytew caenu *eg*
coaxial cyfechelog *ans*
coaxial cable cebl cyfechelog *eg* ceblau cyfechelog
coaxial circles cylchoedd cyfechelin *ell*
cobalt (Co) cobalt *eg*
cobalt green gwyrdd cobalt *eg*
cobalt violet fioled cobalt *eg*
cobalt(II) dicobalt(III) oxide cobalt(II) deucobalt(III) ocsid *eg*
cobalt(II) ion ïon cobalt(II) *eg* ïonau cobalt(II)
cobalt(III) ion ïon cobalt(III) *eg* ïonau cobalt(III)
cobble cobl *eg* coblau
COBOL COBOL *eb*
cobra bit ebill cobra *eg* ebillion cobra
cobweb site *n* gwefan lychlyd *eb* gwefannau llychlyd
coccidiosis cocsidiosis *eg*
coccus cocws *eg* coci
coccyx asgwrn cynffon *eg* esgyrn cynffon
cochlea cochlea *eg*
cochlear canal tiwb y cochlea *eg*
cockfeather pluen geiliog *eb* plu ceiliog
cockle cocosen *eb* cocos
cockpit talwrn *eg* talyrnau
cocktail coctel *eg* coctels
cocktail stick pren coctel *eg* prennau coctel
cocktail-party phenomenon ffenomen parti coctels *eb*
cocoa coco *eg*
coconut cneuen goco *eb* cnau coco
cocoon cocŵn *eg* cocynau
cocotte cocotte *eb* cocottes
cod penfras *eg* penfreision
cod steak stecen benfras *eb* steciau penfras
coda coda *eg* codâu
CODASYL CODASYL *eb*
code *n* cod *eg* codau
code *v* codio *be*
code figure rhif cod *eg* rhifau cod
code generation cynhyrchu cod *be*
code of behaviour cod ymddygiad *eg*
code of conduct cod ymddygiad *eg* codau ymddygiad
code of good practice cod ymarfer da *eg* codau ymarfer da
code of practice cod ymarfer *eg* codau ymarfer
code walkthrough (in computer programming) archwiliad cod *eg*
co-dependency cyd-ddibyniaeth *eb*
coder codydd *eg* codyddion
codetta codeta *eg* codetâu
codex codecs *eg* codecsau
codification codeiddiad *eg*
codifier codeiddiwr *eg* codeiddwyr
codify codeiddio *be*
coding codio *be*
coding sheet taflen godio *eb* taflenni codio

co-dominance cyd-drechedd *eg*
▶ **co-dominant** *adj* cyd-drechol *ans*
co-dominant *n* cyd-drechydd *eg* cyd-drechyddion
co-education cydaddysg *eb*
co-educational scheme cynllun cydaddysgol *eg* cynlluniau cydaddysgol
co-educational school ysgol gydaddysgol *eb* ysgolion cydaddysgol
coefficient cyfernod *eg* cyfernodau
coefficient of expansion cyfernod ehangiad *eg* cyfernodau ehangiad
coefficient of friction cyfernod ffrithiant *eg* cyfernodau ffrithiant
coefficient of linear expansion cyfernod ehangiad llinol *eg* cyfernodau ehangiad llinol
coefficient of regression cyfernod atchwel *eg* cyfernodau atchwel
coefficient of resistance cyfernod gwrthiant *eg* cyfernodau gwrthiant
coefficient of restitution cyfernod adfer *eg* cyfernodau adfer
coefficient of variation cyfernod amrywiad *eg* cyfernodau amrywiad
coeliac coeliag *ans*
coelom coelom *eg* coelomau
coenobites coenobia *eg* coenobiaid
co-enzyme cydensym *eg* cydensymau
coerce gorfodi *be*
coercion gorfodaeth *eb*
Coercion Act Deddf Gorfodaeth *eb*
coffee coffi *eg*
coffee beans ffa coffi *ell*
coffee break amser paned *eg*
coffee maker peiriant coffi *eg* peiriannau coffi
coffee table bwrdd coffi *eg* byrddau coffi
coffer coffr *eg* coffrau
cog cocsen *eb* cocs
cogged danheddog *ans*
cogged joint uniad cocsen *eg* uniadau cocsen
cogging (using fullers) cogyddio *be*
cognition gwybyddiaeth *eb*
cognitive gwybyddol *ans*
cognitive ability gallu gwybyddol *eg* galluoedd gwybyddol
cognitive analytic therapy therapi dadansoddiad gwybyddol *eg*
cognitive appraisal gwerthusiad gwybyddol *eg* gwerthusiadau gwybyddol
cognitive behaviour therapy therapi ymddygiad gwybyddol *eg*
cognitive competence cymhwysedd gwybyddol *eg*
cognitive deficit diffyg gwybyddol *eg* diffygion gwybyddol
cognitive development datblygiad gwybyddol *eg*
cognitive disorder anhwylder gwybyddol *eg* anhwylderau gwybyddol
cognitive dissonance theory damcaniaeth anghyseinedd gwybyddol *eb*
cognitive disturbance tarfiad gwybyddol *eg* tarfiadau gwybyddol
cognitive domain maes gwybyddol *eg*
cognitive interview cyfweliad gwybyddol *eg* cyfweliadau gwybyddol
cognitive learning dysgu gwybyddol *be*
cognitive meaning ystyr gwybyddol *eg* ystyron gwybyddol
cognitive neuroscience niwrowyddoniaeth wybyddol *eb*
cognitive objective amcan gwybyddol *eg* amcanion gwybyddol
cognitive overload gorlwytho gwybyddol *be*
cognitive process proses wybyddol *eb* prosesau gwybyddol
cognitive psychology seicoleg wybyddol *eb*
cognitive reappraisal ailystyried gwybyddol *be*
cognitive rehabilitation adferiad gwybyddol *eg*
cognitive restructuring ailstrwythuro gwybyddol *be*
cognitive science gwyddor gwybyddiaeth *eb*
cognitive structure strwythur gwybyddol *eg* strwythurau gwybyddol
cognitive test prawf gwybyddol *eg* profion gwybyddol
cognitive therapy therapi gwybyddol *eg*
cognitive triad triawd gwybyddol *eg*
cognizance of pleas hawl pledio *eg*
cogwheel olwyn gocos *eb* olwynion cocos
coherence cydlyniad *eg*
coherent (of argument etc) rhesymegol *ans*
coherent (of language) dealladwy *ans*
coherent (of person) trefnus *ans*
coherent (of whole, of parts) cydlynol *ans*
cohesion cydlyniad *eg* cydlyniadau
cohesive cydlynol *ans*
cohesiveness cydlynrwydd *eg*
cohort (=people treated as a group) carfan *eb* carfanau
cohort (Roman military usage) mintai *eb* minteioedd
coil (in electronics) coil *eg* coiliau
coil (of rope, hair, clay) torch *eg* torchau
coil ignition taniad coil *eg* taniadau coil
coil spring sbring coil *eg* sbringiau coil
coiled torchog *ans*
coiling (pottery) torchi *be*
coin darn arian *eg* darnau arian
coin hoard celc arian bath *eg* celciau arian bath
coinage arian bath *eg*
coincide cyd-daro *be*
coincident cyd-drawol *ans*
co-ionic coïonig *ans*
coke golosg *eg*
coke fuel tanwydd golosg *eg*
coke oven batteries cyfres ffyrnau golosg *eb* cyfresi ffyrnau golosg
coking coal glo golosg *eg*
col col *eg* colau
col legno col legno *adf*

colander colandr *eg* colandrau
co-latitude cyfledred *eg* cyfledredion
cold *adj* oer *ans*
cold *n* oerni
cold (=common cold) *n* annwyd *eg* anwydau
cold chisel cŷn caled *eg* cynion caled; gaing galed *eb* geingiau caled
cold colour lliw oer *eg* lliwiau oer
cold drawn (with feminine nouns) wedi'i thynnu'n oer *ans* wedi'u tynnu'n oer
cold drawn (with masculine nouns) wedi'i dynnu'n oer *ans* wedi'u tynnu'n oer
cold front ffrynt oer *eg* ffryntiau oer
cold glue glud oer *eg*
cold restart ailgychwyniad oer *eg* ailgychwyniadau oer
cold riveting rhybedu oer *be*
cold set set oer *eb* setiau oer
cold shortness oer freuder *eg*
cold soldering sodro oer *be*
cold strip mill melin strip oer *eb* melinau strip oer
cold sweet pwdin oer *eg*
cold war rhyfel oer *eg* rhyfeloedd oer
cold water dye llifyn dŵr oer *eg* llifynnau dŵr oer
cold water glue glud dŵr oer *eg*
cold water paste past dŵr oer *eg*
cold water starch startsh dŵr oer *eg*
cold welding weldio oer *be*
cold wind rhewynt *eg* rhewyntoedd
cold working of materials gweithio defnyddiau'n oer *be*
cold-forming ffurfio'n oer *be*
coleoptile coleoptil *eg* coleoptilau
coleorhiza coleorhisa *eg* coleorhisâu
coleslaw coleslaw *eg*
coley celog *eg* celogiaid
colic colig *eg*
co-linear cydlinol *ans*
colitic colitig *ans*
collaborator cydweithredwr *eg* cydweithredwyr
collage collage *eg*
collagen colagen *eg*
collapse *n* cwymp *eg* cwympiadau
collapse *v* cwympo *be*
collapse the scrum cwympo'r sgrym *be*
collar coler *eg/b* coleri
collar hammer morthwyl coleru *eg* morthwylion coleru
collar with band coler â band *eg* coleri â band
collarbone pont yr ysgwydd *eb*
collared urn wrn colerog *eg* yrnau colerog
collaring coleru *be*
collate coladu *be*
collateral bundle sypyn cyfraidd *eg* sypynnau cyfraidd
collation coladiad *eg* coladiadau
collator coladydd *eg* coladwyr
collect casglu *be*
collect information casglu gwybodaeth *be*
collect the ball casglu'r bêl *be*
collection casgliad *eg* casgliadau
collective bargaining cydfargeinio *be*
collective farm fferm gyfunol *eb* ffermydd cyfunol
collective unconscious anymwybod cyffredinol *eg*
collective worship addoli ar y cyd *be*
collectivism cyfunoliaeth *eb*
collectivization cyfunoliad *eg*
collector current cerrynt y casglydd *eg*
college coleg *eg* colegau
college board bwrdd coleg *eg* byrddau coleg
college of education coleg addysg *eg* colegau addysg
college of further education coleg addysg bellach *eg* colegau addysg bellach
college of higher education coleg addysg uwch *eg* colegau addysg uwch
collegiate church eglwys golegaidd *eb* eglwysi colegaidd
collegiate university prifysgol golegol *eb* prifysgolion colegol
collenchyma colencyma *eg*
collet colet *eg* coletau
collet chuck crafanc colet *eb* crafangau colet
collet hammer morthwyl colet *eg* morthwylion colet
collide gwrthdaro *be*
collider gwrthdrawydd *eg* gwrthdrawyddion
colliery pwll glo *eg* pyllau glo
colligate cydglymu *be*
colligative property priodwedd gydglymu *eb* priodweddau cydglymu
collimator cyflinydd *eg* cyflinyddion
collinear unllin *ans*
collinearity unllinedd *eg* unllineddau
collineation unlliniad *eg* unlliniadau
collision gwrthdrawiad *eg* gwrthdrawiadau
collisionless model model anwrthdrawol *eg* modelau anwrthdrawol
colloid coloid *eg* coloidau
colloidal coloidaidd *ans*
colloidal solution hydoddiant coloidaidd *eg* hydoddiannau coloidaidd
colloquy cynulliad *eg* cynulliadau
collusion cydgynllwynio *be*
colluvial casglifol *ans*
colluvium casglifiad *eg*
cologarithm cyflogarithm *eg* cyflogarithmau
colon colon *eg* colonau
colon cancer canser y colon *eg*
colonel cyrnol *eg* cyrnolau
colonial trefedigaethol *ans*
colonial history hanes y trefedigaethau *eg*
colonial preference blaenoriaeth i'r trefedigaethau *eb*
Colonial Secretary Ysgrifennydd y Trefedigaethau *eg*
colonization gwladychiad *eg* gwladychiadau

colonize (in biology) cytrefu *be*
colonize (in history) trefedigaethu *be*
colony (in biology) cytref *eb* cytrefi
colony (in history) trefedigaeth *eb* trefedigaethau
coloratura coloratwra *ans*
coloratura soprano soprano goloratwra *eb* sopranos coloratwra
colorimeter colorimedr *eg* colorimedrau
colostomy colostomi *eg* colostomïau
colostrum colostrwm *eg*
colour *n* lliw *eg* lliwiau
colour *v* lliwio *be*
colour additive ychwanegyn lliw *eg* ychwanegion lliw
colour bar (in apartheid) gwaharddiad lliw *eg*
colour bar (in computing) bar lliwiau *eg* barrau lliwiau
colour blind dall i liwiau *ans*
colour blindness dallineb lliw *eg*
colour block bloc lliw *eg* blociau lliw
colour box blwch lliw *eg* blychau lliw
colour cake teisen liw *eb* teisennau lliw
colour chart siart lliwiau *eg* siartiau lliwiau
colour coding cod lliwiau *eg*
colour combinations cyfuniadau o liwiau *ell*
colour depth dyfnder lliw *eg*
colour filter hidlydd lliw *eg* hidlyddion lliw
colour format fformat lliw *eg* fformatau lliw
colour image delwedd lliw *eb* delweddau lliw
colour medium cyfrwng lliw *eg*
colour mixing cymysgu lliwiau *be*
colour palette palet lliw *eg* paletau lliw
colour pencil pensil lliw *eg* pensiliau lliw
colour perspective persbectif lliw *eg*
colour preview rhagolwg lliw *eg* rhagolygon lliw
colour print print lliw *eg* printiadau lliw
colour quality ansawdd lliw *eg* ansoddau lliw
colour range amrediad lliw *eg*
colour rendering rendro lliw *be*
colour resolution cydraniad lliw *eg* cydraniadau lliw
colour sample sampl lliw *eb* samplau lliw
colour scheme cynllun lliw *eg* cynlluniau lliw
colour selection dewis lliw *be*
colour stick ffon lliw *eb* ffyn lliw
colour tooling leaf dalen offeru lliw *eb* dalennau offeru lliw
colour vision golwg lliw *eg*
colourant lliwydd *eg* lliwyddion
colouration lliwiad *eg* lliwiadau
coloured bead glain lliw *eg* gleiniau lliw
coloured card cerdyn lliw *eg* cardiau lliw
coloured cardboard cardbord lliw *eg*
coloured cartridge paper papur cetris lliw *eg*
coloured cellophane seloffan lliw *eg*
coloured cement sment lliw *eg*
coloured chalk sialc lliw *eg* sialciau lliw
coloured drawing ink inc lluniadu lliw *eg* inciau lluniadu lliw
coloured eyelet llygaden liw *eb* llygadennau lliw
coloured felt ffelt lliw *eg*
coloured glass gwydr lliw *eg*
coloured glassware llestri gwydr lliw *ell*
coloured lace carrai liw *eb* careiau lliw
coloured paper papur lliw *eg*
coloured perspex persbecs lliw *eg*
coloured plasticine plastisin lliw *eg*
coloured starch startsh lliw *eg*
coloured tab control rheolydd tabiau lliw *eg* rheolyddion tabiau lliw
coloured tissue paper papur sidan lliw *eg*
colourfast dye llifyn anniflan *eg* llifynnau anniflan
colouring (in finishing metal) lliwio *be*
colouring agent cyfrwng lliwio *eg* cyfryngau lliwio
colourless di-liw *ans*
column colofn *eb* colofnau
column break toriad colofn *eg* toriadau colofn
column chart siart colofnau *eg* siartiau colofnau
column configuration ffurfweddiad colofn *eg* ffurfweddiadau colofnau
column graph graff colofn *eg* graffiau colofn
column header pennyn colofn *eg* penynnau colofnau
column matrix matrics colofn *eg* matricsau colofn
column name enw colofn *eg* enwau colofnau
column not found heb ganfod colofn
column of threes (Llanofer) colofn drioedd *eb*
column property priodwedd colofn *eb* priodweddau colofnau
column spacing bylchiad colofnau *eg* bylchiadau colofnau
column vector fector colofn *eg* fectorau colofn
column width lled colofn *eg*
columnar epithelium epitheliwm colofnog *eg*
comb *n* crib *eg/b* cribau
comb *v* cribo *be*
comb joint uniad crib *eg* uniadau crib
comb of harp crib telyn *eb* cribau telynau
combat gornest *eb* gornestau
combination *adj* cyfunol *ans*
combination *n* cyfuniad *eg* cyfuniadau
Combination Act Deddf Cyfuno *eb*
combination callipers caliperau cyfunol *ell*
combination chuck crafanc gyfunol *eb* crafangau cyfunol
combination drill dril canoli cyfunol *eg* driliau canoli cyfunol
combination easel îsl cyfunol *eg* islau cyfunol
combination hinge colfach cyfunol *eg* colfachau cyfunol
combination of the two cyfuniad o'r ddau *eg*
combination of units cyfuniad o unedau *eg*
combination oilstone carreg hogi ddwbl *eb* cerrig hogi dwbl
combination pedal pedal cyfuno *eg* pedalau cyfuno

combination piston piston cyfuno *eg* pistonau cyfuno
combination plane plaen amlddefnydd *eg* plaeniau amlddefnydd
combination pliers gefelen gyfunol *eb* gefeiliau cyfunol
combination punches cyfuniad dyrnodau *eg*
combination set set gyfunol *eb* setiau cyfunol
combination square sgwâr cyfunol *eg* sgwariau cyfunol
combination stop stop cyfuno *eg* stopiau cyfuno
combination tone cyfunsain *eg* cyfunseiniau
combinatorial cyfuniadol *ans*
combine cyfuno *be*
combine harvester dyrnwr medi *eg* dyrnwyr medi
combine paragraphs cyfuno paragraffau *be*
combined cyfunol *ans*
combined carbon carbon cyfunol *eg*
combined gate knife and heart trowel cyllell gât a thrywel calon cyfunol
combined rivet set and snap set a snap rhybed cyfunol
combined subject syllabus maes llafur pwnc cyfun *eg* meysydd llafur pynciau cyfun
combined vaults llofneidiau cysylltiol *ell*
combining data cyfuno data *be*
combining text cyfuno testun *be*
combustible hylosg *ans*
combustion (in chemistry) hylosgiad *eg* hylosgiadau
combustion (in general) taniad *eg* taniadau
come to rest dod i aros *be*
comet comed *eb* comedau
comfort *n* cysur *eg* cysuron
comfort *v* cysuro *be*
comfort conditions amodau cysur *ell*
comfort survey arolwg cyfforddusrwydd *eg* arolygon cyfforddusrwydd
comfortable cyffyrddus *ans*
comic atmosphere awyrgylch comig *eg*
comic character cymeriad comig *eg* cymeriadau comig
comic opera opera gomig *eb* operâu comig
Cominform Cominfform *eg*
comma coma *eg* comas
command *n* gorchymyn *eg* gorchmynion
command *v* gorchymyn *be*
command button botwm gorchymyn *eg* botymau gorchymyn
command code cod gorchymyn *eg* codau gorchymyn
command line interface rhyngwyneb llinell orchymyn *eg* rhyngwynebau llinell orchymyn
command word gair gorchymyn *eg* geiriau gorchymyn
commander (military) cadlywydd *eg* cadlywyddion
commander (naval) comander *eg* comanderiaid
commander-in-chief cadbennaeth *eg* cadbenaethiaid
commandery pencadlys *eg* pencadlysoedd
command-response method dull gorchymyn ac ymateb *eg*
commencement date dyddiad cychwyn *eg* dyddiadau cychwyn
commendation cymeradwyaeth *eb*
commensal cydfwytaol *ans*
commensalism cydfwytäedd *eg*
commensurable cyfesur *ans*
comment sylw *eg* sylwadau
comment bank cronfa sylwadau *eb* cronfeydd sylwadau
commentary (=descriptive spoken account) sylwebaeth *eb* sylwebaethau
commentary (=explanatory notes) esboniad *eg* esboniadau
commentator (on bible) esboniwr *eg* esbonwyr
commentator (on game etc) sylwebydd *eg* sylwebwyr
commerce masnach *eb* masnachau
commercial masnachol *ans*
commercial application cymhwysiad masnachol *eg* cymwysiadau masnachol
commercial arithmetic rhifyddeg masnach *eb*
commercial art celfyddyd fasnachol *eb*
commercial baby foods bwydydd masnachol i fabanod *ell*
commercial bank banc masnachol *eg* banciau masnachol
commercial capitalism cyfalafiaeth fasnach *eb*
Commercial Code Cod Masnach *eg*
commercial court llys masnach *eg*
commercial data processing prosesu data masnachol *be*
commercial education addysg fasnachol *eb*
commercial function swyddogaeth fasnachol *eb* swyddogaethau masnachol
commercial laundry golchdy masnachol *eg* golchdai masnachol
commercial law cyfraith fasnachol *eb*
commercial pattern patrwm parod *eg* patrymau parod
commercial privilege braint fasnachol *eb* breintiau masnachol
commercial rivalry cystadleuaeth fasnachol *eb*
commercial software meddalwedd fasnachol *eb*
commercial traveller trafaeliwr *eg* trafaelwyr
commercial viability dichonoldeb masnachol *eg*
comminution pyloriant *eg*
commissar comisar *eg* comisariaid
commissary general dirprwy cyffredinol *eg* dirprwyaid cyffredinol
commission *n* comisiwn *eg* comisiynau
commission *v* comisiynu *be*
commission of array comisiwn aráe *eg*
commission of oyer and terminer comisiwn oyer a terminer *eg*

commissioner comisiynydd *eg* comisiynwyr
Commissions for Sequestration Comisiynwyr yr Atafaeliad *ell*
commit (for trial) traddodi *be*
commit suicide cyflawni hunanladdiad *be*
commitment ymrwymiad *eg* ymrwymiadau
commitments to expenditure ymrwymiadau gwario *ell*
committed ymrwymedig *ans*
committee pwyllgor *eg* pwyllgorau
Committee for Plundered Ministers Pwyllgor y Gweinidogion Ysbeiliedig *eg*
Committee for the Propagation of the Gospel Pwyllgor er Taenu'r Efengyl *eg*
Committee of Accounts Pwyllgor Cyfrifon *eg*
Committee of Delinquency Pwyllgor Troseddau *eg*
Committee of Public Safety Pwyllgor Diogelwch y Cyhoedd *eg*
commode comôd *eg* comodau
commodity nwydd *eg* nwyddau
commodore comodor *eg* comodoriaid
common cyffredin *ans*
common agricultural policy (CAP) polisi amaethyddol cyffredin *eg*
common ancestor cyd-hynafiad *eg* cyd-hynafiaid
common assault ymosod cyffredin *be*
common chord cord cyffredin *eg* cordiau cyffredin
common cold annwyd *eg* anwydau
common component cydran gyffredin *eb* cydrannau cyffredin
common curriculum cwricwlwm cyffredin *eg*
common data data cyffredin *ell*
common difference gwahaniaeth cyffredin *eg*
common ethos ethos cyffredin *eg*
common file ffeil gyffredin *eb* ffeiliau cyffredin
common fraction ffracsiwn cyffredin *eg* ffracsiynau cyffredin
common joint uniad cyffredin *eg* uniadau cyffredin
common land tir comin *eg* tiroedd comin
common law cyfraith gwlad *eb*
common logarithm logarithm cyffredin *eg* logarithmau cyffredin
common metre mesur cyffredin *eg*
common mode modd-cyffredin *ans*
common mode rejection ratio cymhareb wrthod modd-cyffredin *eb*
common of pasture cytawl pori *eb*
common of turbary hawl torri mawn *eg*
common penny treth y geiniog *eb*
common practice course cwrs ymarfer cyffredinol *eg* cyrsiau ymarfer cyffredinol
common professional examination arholiad cyffredinol proffesiynol *eg* arholiadau cyffredinol proffesiynol
common ratio cymhareb gyffredin *eb* cymarebau cyffredin
common room ystafell gyffredin *eb* ystafelloedd cyffredin
common salt halen *eg*
common sense synnwyr cyffredin *eg*
common speech iaith gyffredin *eb*
common standard unit uned safonol gyffredin *eb* unedau safonol cyffredin
common standards safonau cyffredin *ell*
common syllabus maes llafur cyffredin *eg* meysydd llafur cyffredin
common thread edau gyffredin *eb* edafedd cyffredin
common time amser cyffredin *eg*
common values gwerthoedd cyffredin *ell*
Common Weal Lles Cyffredin *eg*
commonalty pobl gyffredin *eb*
commoner gwrêng *eg* gwrengod
Commonwealth Games Gemau'r Gymanwlad *ell*
Commonwealth of Independent States Cymanwlad y Gwladwriaethau Annibynnol *eb*
Commonwealth, the (modern British) Cymanwlad: y Gymanwlad *eb*
Commonwealth, the (17th century) Gwerinlywodraeth: y Werinlywodraeth*eb*
commote cwmwd *eg* cymydau
communal cymunedol *ans*
commune comiwn *eg* comiwnau
communicate *v.intrans* cyfathrebu *be*
communicate *v.trans* cyfleu *be*
communicate ideas cyfleu syniadau *be*
communicate information cyfleu gwybodaeth *be*
communicate meaning cyfleu ystyr *be*
communication cyfathrebiad *eg* cyfathrebiadau
communication channel sianel gyfathrebu *eb* sianelau cyfathrebu
communication difficulty anhawster cyfathrebu *eg* anawsterau cyfathrebu
communication line lein gyfathrebu *eb* leiniau cyfathrebu
communication link cyswllt cyfathrebu *eg* cysylltau cyfathrebu
communication network rhwydwaith cyfathrebu *eg* rhwydweithiau cyfathrebu
communication service gwasanaeth cyfathrebu *eg* gwasanaethau cyfathrebu
communication skill sgìl cyfathrebu *eg* sgiliau cyfathrebu
communication system system gyfathrebu *eb* systemau cyfathrebu
communicational cyfathrebol *ans*
communications processing prosesu cyfathrebiadau *be*
communion cymundeb *eg*
communion table bwrdd y cymun *eg*
communism comiwnyddiaeth *eb*
communist *adj* comiwnyddol *ans*
communist *n* comiwnydd *eg* comiwnyddion
Communist Party Plaid Gomiwnyddol *eb*
community cymuned *eb* cymunedau
community care gofal yn y gymuned *eg*
community care plan cynllun gofal yn y gymuned *eg*

community care worker gweithiwr gofal yn y gymuned *eg* gweithwyr gofal yn y gymuned
community centre canolfan gymunedol *eb* canolfannau cymunedol
community college coleg cymunedol *eg* colegau cymunedol
community development datblygiad cymunedol *eg* datblygiadau cymunedol
community education addysg gymunedol *eb*
Community Health Council Cyngor Iechyd Cymdeithas *eg* Cynghorau Iechyd Cymdeithas
community home cartref cymuned *eg* cartrefi cymuned
community hospital ysbyty cymuned *eg* ysbytai cymuned
community links cysylltiadau gyda'r gymuned *ell*
community living service gwasanaeth byw yn y gymuned *eg* gwasanaethau byw yn y gymuned
community mental health team tîm cymuned iechyd meddwl *eg* timau cymuned iechyd meddwl
community nurse nyrs cymuned *eb* nyrsys cymuned
community nurse, mental health nyrs cymuned, iechyd meddwl *eb* nyrsys cymuned, iechyd meddwl
community physician meddyg cymuned *eg* meddygon cymuned
community psychiatric nurse nyrs seiciatrig cymuned *eb* nyrsys seiciatrig cymuned
community school ysgol gymunedol *eb* ysgolion cymunedol
community spirit ysbryd cymunedol *eg*
community support service gwasanaeth cynnal yn y gymuned *eg* gwasanaethau cynnal yn y gymuned
community unit uned gymunedol *eb* unedau cymunedol
commutation cymudiad *eg*
commutative cymudol *ans*
commutative group grŵp cymudol *eg* grwpiau cymudol
commutative law deddf gymudol *eb* deddfau cymudol
commutator cymudadur *eg* cymudaduron
commute cymudo *be*
commuter cymudwr *eg* cymudwyr
commuting pattern patrwm cymudo *eg* patrymau cymudo
compact *adj* cryno *ans*
compact *v* cywasgu *be*
compact disk cryno ddisg *eg* cryno ddisgiau
compact disk read only memory cof darllen yn unig cryno ddisg *eg*
compaction cywasgiad *eg*
compactness crynoder *eg*
compactor crynodiadur *eg* crynodiaduron
companion cell cymargell *eb* cymargelloedd
companion teaching addysgu cefnogol *be*
companionate love cariad cymar *eg*
company cwmni *eg* cwmnïau
company finance arian cwmni *eg*
company limited by guarantee cwmni cyfyngedig trwy warant *eg* cwmnïau cyfyngedig trwy warant
company logo logo'r cwmni *eg*
company secretary ysgrifennydd y cwmni *eg* ysgrifenyddion cwmnïau
company union undeb y cwmni *eg* undebau cwmnïau
company unionism undebaeth cwmni *eb*
company website gwefan cwmni *eb* gwefannau cwmnïau
comparability cymaroldeb *eg*
comparable (in economics) cymaradwy *ans*
comparative cymharol *ans*
comparative advantage mantais gymharol *eb* manteision cymharol
comparative cost cost gymharol *eb* costau cymharol
comparative linguistics ieithyddiaeth gymharol *eb*
comparative psychology seicoleg gymharol *eb*
comparative reading darllen cymharol *eg*
comparative scale graddfa gymharol *eb* graddfeydd cymharol
comparative study astudiaeth gymharol *eb* astudiaethau cymharol
comparator cymharydd *eg* cymaryddion
compare cymharu *be*
compare results cymharu canlyniadau *be*
comparison cymhariaeth *eb* cymariaethau
comparison goods nwyddau cymhariaeth *ell*
compartment adran *eb* adrannau
compass (=extent, range of tone) cwmpas *eg* cwmpasau
compass (to find direction) cwmpawd *eg* cwmpawdau
compass callipers caliperau cwmpas *ell*
compass housing amgaead cwmpawd *eg* amgaeadau cwmpawdau
compass north gogledd cwmpawd *eg*
compass plane plaen amgrwm *eg* plaeniau amgrwm
compass saw llif gwmpas *eb* llifiau cwmpas
compass walk taith gwmpawd *eb* teithiau cwmpawd
compassion tosturi *eg*
compatibility (in general) cydnawsedd *eg*
compatibility (of computer parts) cydweddiad *eg*
compatible (in general) cydnaws *ans*
compatible (of computer parts) cydwedd *ans*
compensate (=make amends) gwneud iawn *be*
compensate (=recompense) digolledu *be*
compensation iawndal *eg* iawndaliadau
compensation agreement cytundeb iawndal *eg* cytundebau iawndal
compensatory changes newidiadau cydadferol *ell*
compensatory education addysg gydadferol *eb*
compensatory exercise ymarfer cydadfer *eg* ymarferion cydadfer
compensatory programme rhaglen gydadferol *eb* rhaglenni cydadferol
compete cystadlu *be*
compete for the ball cystadlu am y bêl *be*

competence (in education) cymhwysedd *eg* cymwyseddau
competence (of river) cymhwyster *eg*
competent cymwys *ans*
competition cystadleuaeth *eb* cystadlaethau
Competition Commission Comisiwn Cystadleuaeth *eg*
competition for resources cystadlu am adnoddau *be*
competition pricing prisio ar sail cystadleuaeth *be*
competition rule rheol cystadlu *eb* rheolau cystadlu
competitive cystadleuol *ans*
competitive exclusion gwaharddiad cystadleuol *eg*
competitive game gêm gystadleuol *eb* gemau cystadleuol
competitive play chwarae cystadleuol *eg*
competitive release rhyddhad cystadleuol *eg*
competitive task tasg gystadleuol *eb* tasgau cystadleuol
competitive team games gemau tîm cystadleuol *ell*
competitiveness awydd i gystadlu *eg*
competitor cystadleuydd *eg* cystadleuwyr
compilation crynhoad *eg* crynoadau
compilation process proses grynhoad *eb*
compile crynhoi *be*
compile error gwall crynhoi *eg* gwallau crynhoi
compiled language iaith grynoadol *eb* ieithoedd crynoadol
compiler crynhoydd *eg* crynoyddion
compiling program rhaglen grynhoi *eb* rhaglenni crynhoi
complain cwyno *be*
complaint (=grievance) cwyn *eb* cwynion
complaint (physical /medical) anhwylder *eg* anhwylderau
complaints procedure dull gweithredu cwynion *eg*
complement *n* cyflenwad *eg* cyflenwadau
complement *v* cyflenwi *be*
complementarity cyfatebolrwydd *eg*
complementary cyflenwol *ans*
complementary addition method dull adio cyflenwol *eg*
complementary angle ongl gyflenwol *eb* onglau cyflenwol
complementary base pair pâr cyflenwol o fasau *eg*
complementary colour lliw cyflenwol *eg* lliwiau cyflenwol
complementary medicine meddygaeth gyflenwol *eb*
complementary therapy therapi cyflenwol *eg*
complements (of goods) cyfun-nwyddau *ell*
complete *adj* cyflawn *ans*
complete *v* cwblhau *be*
complete cadence diweddeb berffaith *eb* diweddebau perffaith
complete circuit cylched gyflawn *eb* cylchedau cyflawn
complete primitive datrysiad cyflawn *eg* datrysiadau cyflawn
complete radiation pelydriad cyflawn *eg*
complete revolution cylchdro cyflawn *eg* cylchdroeon cyflawn
complete section trychiad cyflawn *eg* trychiadau cyflawn
complete sectional elevation golwg trychiadol cyflawn *eg* golygon trychiadol cyflawn
complete the square cwblhau'r sgwâr *be*
complete turn tro cyflawn *eg* troeon cyflawn
complete view golwg cyflawn *eg* golygon cyflawn
completely yn llwyr *adf*
completeness cyflawnrwydd *eg*
complex (=complicated) *adj* cymhleth *ans*
complex (consisting of related parts; composite) *adj* cymhlyg *ans*
complex (in chemistry) *n* cymhlygyn *eg* cymhlygion
complex (of chemicals) *v* cymhlygu *be*
complex conjugate cyfiau cymhlyg *eg* cyfieuau cymhlyg
complex event digwyddiad cymhleth *eg* digwyddiadau cymhleth
complex function ffwythiant cymhlyg *eg* ffwythiannau cymhlyg
complex instruction set set cyfarwyddiadau cymhleth *eb* setiau cyfarwyddiadau cymhleth
complex number rhif cymhlyg *eg* rhifau cymhlyg
complex roots gwreiddiau cymhlyg *ell*
complex sequence of movements dilyniant cymhleth o symudiadau *eg* dilyniannau cymhleth o symudiadau
complex skills sgiliau cymhleth *ell*
complex variable newidyn cymhlyg *eg* newidynnau cymhlyg
complexity cymhlethdod *eg* cymhlethdodau
compliance (=active obedience) ufudd-dod *eg*
compliance (in general) cydymffurfiad *eg*
complicated fracture torasgwrn cymhleth *eg* toresgyrn cymhleth
complication cymhlethdod *eg* cymhlethdodau
compline cwmplin *eg*
compoboard cywasgfwrdd *eg* cywasgfyrddau
component cydran *eb* cydrannau
component drawing lluniad cydrannau *eg* lluniadau cydrannau
component molecule moleciwl cydrannol *eg* moleciwlau cydrannol
component of a force cydran grym *eb* cydrannau grym
component of velocity cydran cyflymder *eb* cydrannau cyflymder
component part darn cydrannol *eg* darnau cydrannol
componential intelligence dealltwriaeth gydrannol *eb*
compose cyfansoddi *be*
compose sequences cyfansoddi dilyniannau *be*
composer cyfansoddwr *eg* cyfansoddwyr
composite cyfansawdd *ans*
composite demand galw cyfansawdd *eg*

composite end view ochrolwg cyfansawdd *eg* ochrolygon cyfansawdd
composite materials defnyddiau cyfansawdd *ell*
composite stitch pwyth cyfansawdd *eg* pwythau cyfansawdd
composite view golwg cyfansawdd *eg* golygon cyfansawdd
composition (=essay) traethawd *eg* traethodau
composition (in general) cyfansoddiad *eg* cyfansoddiadau
composition of blood cyfansoddiad gwaed *eg*
composition pedal pedal cyfuno *eg* pedalau cyfuno
composition piston piston cyfuno *eg* pistonau cyfuno
compositional cyfansoddiadol *ans*
compositional weight pwyslais cyfansoddiadol *eg*
compote compot *eg* compotau
compound *adj* cyfansawdd *ans*
compound *n* cyfansoddyn *eg* cyfansoddion
compound (a problem etc) *v* cymhlethu *be*
compound attack ymosod cyfun *eg*
compound binary form ffurf ddwyran gyfansawdd *eb* ffurfiau dwyran cyfansawdd
compound curve cromlin gyfansawdd *eb* cromliniau cyfansawdd
compound drive gyriad cyfansawdd *eg* gyriadau cyfansawdd
compound eye llygad cyfansawdd *eg* llygaid cyfansawdd
compound fracture torasgwrn agored *eg* toresgyrn agored
compound gear train trên gêr cyfansawdd *eg* trenau gêr cyfansawdd
compound inflorescence fflurgainc gyfansawdd *eb* fflurgeinciau cyfansawdd
compound interest adlog *eg* adlogau
compound interval cyfwng cyfansawdd *eg* cyfyngau cyfansawdd
compound key allwedd gyfansawdd *eb* allweddi cyfansawdd
compound leaf deilen gyfansawdd *eb* dail cyfansawdd
compound line graph graff llinell gyfansawdd *eg* graffiau llinellau cyfansawdd
compound matrix matrics cyfansawdd *eg* matricsau cyfansawdd
compound pendulum pendil cyfansawdd *eg* pendiliau cyfansawdd
compound riposte riposte cyfun *eg* ripostes cyfun
compound shape siâp cyfansawdd *eg* siapiau cyfansawdd
compound shoreline traethlin cyfansawdd *eg* traethlinau cyfansawdd
compound slide llithryn cyfansawdd *eg* llithrynnau cyfansawdd
compound stain staen cyfansawdd *eg* staeniau cyfansawdd
compound train trên cyfansawdd *eg* trenau cyfansawdd
compound wound dirwyniad cyfansawdd *eg* dirwyniadau cyfansawdd
compounding vectors cyfuno fectorau *be*
comprehensibility eglurder *eg*
comprehension dealltwriaeth *eb*
comprehension test prawf darllen a deall *eg* profion darllen a deall
comprehensive (=all-inclusive) cynhwysfawr *ans*
comprehensive (of education system) cyfun *ans*
comprehensive education addysg gyfun *eb*
comprehensive insurance yswiriant cyfun *eg*
comprehensive school ysgol gyfun *eb* ysgolion cyfun
comprehensive training programme rhaglen hyfforddi gynhwysfawr *eb* rhaglenni hyfforddi cynhwysfawr
compress cywasgu *be*
compressed cywasgedig *ans*
compressed air aer cywasgedig *eg*
compressibility cywasgadwyedd *eg*
compressible cywasgadwy *ans*
compression (=reduction in volume) cywasgedd *eg* cywasgeddau
compression (action of) cywasgiad *eg* cywasgiadau
compression moulding mowldin cywasgedd *eg* mowldinau cywasgedd
compression spring sbring cywasgu *eg* sbringiau cywasgu
compressive cywasgol *eg*
compressive force grym cywasgol *eg* grymoedd cywasgol
compressor cywasgydd *eg* cywasgyddion
compromise cyfaddawd *eg* cyfaddawdau
compromise of Avranches cyfaddawd Avranches *eg*
comptroller distain *eg* disteiniaid
compulsion gorfodaeth *eb* gorfodaethau
compulsory gorfodol *ans*
compulsory count cownt gorfod *eg*
compulsory education addysg orfodol *eb*
compulsory purchase order gorchymyn prynu gorfodol *eg* gorchmynion prynu gorfodol
compulsory subject pwnc gorfodol *eg* pynciau gorfodol
computation cyfrifiant *eg* cyfrifiannau
computational method dull cyfrifiannu *eg* dulliau cyfrifiannu
compute cyfrifiannu *be*
computer *adj* cyfrifiadurol *ans*
computer *n* cyfrifiadur *eg* cyfrifiaduron
computer aided design (CAD) cynllunio drwy gymorth cyfrifiadur *be*
computer aided education (CAE) addysg drwy gymorth cyfrifiadur *eb*
computer aided instruction (CAI) hyfforddiant drwy gymorth cyfrifiadur *eg*
computer aided learning (CAL) dysgu drwy gymorth cyfrifiadur *be*

computer aided manufacture (CAM)
gweithgynhyrchu drwy gymorth cyfrifiadur *be*
computer aided production management (CAPM)
rheoli cynhyrchu drwy gymorth cyfrifiadur *be*
computer application rhaglen gyfrifiadurol *eb*
rhaglenni cyfrifiadurol
computer architecture saernïaeth gyfrifiadurol *eb*
computer assisted learning
dysgu drwy gymorth cyfrifiadur *be*
computer based method dull cyfrifiadurol *eg*
dulliau cyfrifiadurol
computer based training
hyfforddiant yn seiliedig ar gyfrifiadur *eg*
computer breakdown methiant cyfrifiadurol *eg*
methiannau cyfrifiadurol
computer control rheolaeth gyfrifiadurol *eb*
computer game gêm cyfrifiadur *eb* gemau cyfrifiadur
computer graphics graffigwaith cyfrifiadurol *eg*
Computer Integrated Manufacture
Gweithgynhyrchu drwy Integreiddio Cyfrifiaduron *be*
computer interface rhyngwyneb cyfrifiadurol *eg*
rhyngwynebau cyfrifiadurol
computer knowledge gwybodaeth gyfrifiadurol *eb*
computer literacy llythrennedd cyfrifiadurol *eg*
computer managed learning (CML)
dysgu dan arweiniad cyfrifiadur *be*
computer model model cyfrifiadurol *eg*
modelau cyfrifiadurol
computer modelling modelu cyfrifiadurol *be*
computer music cerddoriaeth gyfrifiadur *eb*
computer network rhwydwaith cyfrifiadurol *eg*
rhwydweithiau cyfrifiadurol
computer operator cyfrifiadurwr *eg* cyfrifiadurwyr
computer output to microfilm (COM)
microffilm o gyfrifiadur *eg*
computer performance perfformiad cyfrifiadur *eg*
computer personnel personél cyfrifiadur *ell*
computer printout allbrint cyfrifiadurol *eg*
allbrintiau cyfrifiadurol
computer programmer rhaglennydd *eg* rhaglenwyr
computer readable darllenadwy i gyfrifiadur *ans*
computer related matter mater perthnasol i gyfrifiaduron *eg* materion perthnasol i gyfrifiaduron
computer science cyfrifiadureg *eb*
computer scientist cyfrifiadurwr *eg* cyfrifiadurwyr
computer simulation efelychiad cyfrifiadurol *eg*
efelychiadau cyfrifiadurol
computer solution ateb cyfrifiadurol *eg*
atebion cyfrifiadurol
computer spreadsheet taenlen gyfrifiadurol *eb*
taenlenni cyfrifiadurol
computer staff staff cyfrifiadurol *eg*
computer studies astudiaethau cyfrifiadur *ell*
computer system system gyfrifiadurol *eb*
systemau cyfrifiadurol
computer user defnyddiwr cyfrifiadur *eg*
defnyddwyr cyfrifiadur
computer workstation gweithfan cyfrifiadur *eb*
computer-controlled a reolir gan gyfrifiadur *ans*
computerize cyfrifiaduro *be*
computerized cyfrifiadurol *ans*
computerized booking system
system archebu gyfrifiadurol *eb*
computerized food ordering
system archebu bwyd gyfrifiadurol *eb*
computerized literature search
chwiliad cyfrifiadurol o lenyddiaeth *eg*
chwiliadau cyfrifiadurol o lenyddiaeth
computer-literate cyfrifiadurol lythrennog *ans*
computerized tomography
tomograffeg gyfrifiadurol *eb*
computer-marked assignment (CMA)
aseiniad a fercir â chyfrifiadur *eg*
aseiniadau a fercir â chyfrifiadur
computing cyfrifiadura *be*
comrade cymrawd *eg* cymrodyr
con sordino con sordino *eg* con sordini
conation ymdrechiad *eg* ymdrechiadau
conative ymdrechol *ans*
concatenate cydgadwyno *be*
concatenation cydgadwynedd *eg*
concave ceugrwm *ans*
concave curvature ceugrymedd *eg* ceugrymeddau
concave curve cromlin geugrwm *eb*
cromliniau ceugrwm
concave lens lens ceugrwm *eg* lensiau ceugrwm
concave milling cutter melinwr ceugrwm *eg*
melinwyr ceugrwm
concave slope llethr ceugrwm *eg* llethrau ceugrwm
concave surface arwyneb ceugrwm *eg*
arwynebau ceugrwm
concavity ceugrymedd *eg* ceugrymeddau
conceal cuddio *be*
concealed cudd *ans*
concealed coalfield maes glo cudd *eg*
meysydd glo cudd
concealed lighting golau cudd *eg*
concealed opening agoriad cudd *eg* agoriadau cudd
conceive (=become pregnant) *v.intrans* beichiogi *be*
conceive (a child) *v.trans* cenhedlu *be*
concentrate (in chemistry) crynodi *be*
concentrate (mind) canolbwyntio *be*
concentrate (sauce) dwysáu *be*
concentrated (in chemistry) crynodedig *ans*
concentrated acid asid crynodedig *eg*
asidau crynodedig
concentration (in chemistry) crynodiad *eg*
crynodiadau
concentration camp gwersyll crynhoi *eg*
gwersylloedd crynhoi
concentration gradient graddiant crynodiad *eg*
graddiannau crynodiad
concentric cydganol *ans*
concentric circles cylchoedd cydganol *ell*
concept cysyniad *eg* cysyniadau
concept keyboard cyffyrddell *eb* cyffyrddellau
concept of capacitance cysyniad cynhwysiant *eg*
concept of god cysyniad o dduw *eg*

concept sorting test prawf cysyniadau *eg* profion cysyniadau
conceptacle conseptagl *eg* conseptaglau
conception (of a child) cenhedliad *eg*
concepts of leisure cysyniadau hamdden *ell*
conceptual cysyniadol *ans*
conceptual development datblygiad cysyniadol *eg* datblygiadau cysyniadol
conceptual framework fframwaith cysyniadol *eg* fframweithiau cysyniadol
conceptual replication atgynhyrchu cysyniad *be*
conceptual understanding dealltwriaeth gysyniadol *eb*
concert cyngerdd *eg/b* cyngherddau
concert harp telyn gyngerdd *eb* telynau cyngerdd
Concert of Europe Cytgord Ewrop *eg*
concert overture agorawd cyngerdd *eb* agorawdau cyngerdd
concert pitch traw cyngerdd *eg*
concertante concertante *eg* concertanti
concertina consertina *eg* consertinâu
concertino concertino *eg* concertini
concerto concerto *eg* concerti
concerto grosso concerto grosso *eg* concerti grossi
concession consesiwn *eg* consesiynau
conchoid concoid *eg* concoidau
conchoidal concoidaidd *ans*
conciliar cynghoraidd *ans*
Conciliar Movement Mudiad y Cynghorau *eg*
conciliation cymodi *be*
concise cryno *ans*
conclave cymanfa *eb* cymanfaoedd
conclave of cardinals cymanfa'r cardinaliaid *eb*
conclusion casgliad *eg* casgliadau
concomitant cydredol *ans*
concord (=harmony) cytgord *eg* cytgordiau
concord (=treaty) cytundeb *eg* cytundebau
concordant cydgordiol *ans*
concordat concordat *eg* concordatiau
concrete *adj* diriaethol *ans*
concrete *n* concrit *eg*
concrete aggregates agregau concrit *ell*
concrete art celfyddyd ddiriaethol *eb*
concrete foundation sylfaen goncrit *eb* sylfeini concrit
concrete music cerddoriaeth ddiriaethol *eb*
concrete operational stage stad weithredu ddiriaethol *eb*
concrete operational thought meddwl gweithredu diriaethol *eg*
concrete pad pad concrit *eg* padiau concrit
concretion concretiad *eg*
concretization diriaetholi *be*
concubinage gordderchaeth *eb*
concubine gordderch *eb* gordderchadon
concur (in mathematics) cydgroesi *be*
concurrent cydamserol *ans*
concurrent (lines etc) cytgroes *ans*
concurrent (processes) cyfamserol *ans*
concyclic cydgylchol *ans*
condensation (in science) cyddwysiad *eg*
condensation centre canolfan cyddwysiad *eb*
condensation polymer polymer cyddwyso *eg*
condensation reaction adwaith cyddwyso *eg*
condense cyddwyso *be*
condensed cyddwysedig *ans*
condensed milk llaeth cyddwysedig *eg*
condenser (=capacitor) cynhwysydd *eg* cynwysyddion
condenser (distilling in chemistry) cyddwysydd *eg* cyddwysyddion
condenser lens lens cyddwyso *eg* lensys cyddwyso
condiments pupur a halen
condition (=state) cyflwr *eg* cyflyrau
condition (=stipulation etc) amod *eg* amodau
condition code cod cyflwr *eg* codau cyflwr
condition of sale amod gwerthu *eg* amodau gwerthu
condition of service amod gwasanaeth *eg* amodau gwasanaeth
condition of worth amod gwerth *eg* amodau gwerth
condition survey arolwg cyflwr *eg* arolygon cyflwr
conditional amodol *ans*
conditional branch instruction cyfarwyddyd canghennu amodol *eg* cyfarwyddiadau canghennu amodol
conditional fee ffi amodol *eb* ffioedd amodol
conditional fee arrangements trefniadau ffioedd amodol *ell*
conditional jump naid amodol *eb* neidiau amodol
conditional probability tebygolrwydd amodol *eg* tebygolrwyddau amodol
conditional response ymateb cyflyrol *eg*
conditional stimulus ysgogiad cyflyrol *eg*
conditional transfer trosglwyddiad amodol *eg* trosglwyddiadau amodol
conditioned (as of reflex) cyflyredig *ans*
conditioned emotional response ymateb emosiynol cyflyrol *eg*
conditioned flavour-aversion learning cyflyru dysgu osgoi-blas *be*
conditioned punisher cosbydd cyflyrol *eg* cosbyddion cyflyrol
conditioned reflex atgyrch cyflyredig *eg*
conditioned reinforcer atgyfnerthydd cyflyrol *eg* atgyfnerthwyr cyflyrol
conditioned stimulus pre-exposure effect effaith cyn-amlygiad ysgogiad wedi'i gyflyru *eb*
conditioner cyflyrydd *eg* cyflyrwyr
conditioning cyflyru *be*
conditions of trading amodau masnach *ell*
condom condom *eg* condomau
condominium (joint control of a State's affairs by other States) cydlywodraeth *eb* cydlywodraethau
condominium (of building) condominiwm *eg* condominia
conduct (=behaviour) *n* ymddygiad *eg*
conduct (=lead) *v* arwain *be*

conduct (=transmit by conduction) *v* dargludo *be*
conduct (an experiment) *v* cynnal *be*
conduct disorder anhwylder ymddygiad *eg* anhwylderau ymddygiad
conductance dargludiant *eg* dargludiannau
conducting dargludol *ans*
conduction dargludiad *eg* dargludiadau
conductive hearing loss colli clyw yn y glust ganol
conductivity dargludedd *eg* dargludeddau
conductor (of electricity) dargludydd *eg* dargludyddion
conductor (of orchestra) arweinydd *eg* arweinyddion
conductor of heat dargludydd gwres *eg* dargludyddion gwres
conduit cwndid *eg* cwndidau
condyle condyl *eg* condylau
cone côn *eg* conau
cone (of the eye) pigwrn *eg* pigyrnau
cone centre canol côn *eg* canolau côn
cone pat pat côn *eg* patiau côn
cone pulley pwli côn *eg* pwlïau côn
cone stand ateg gôn *eb* ategion côn
confectionery melysion *ell*
Confederacy (US) taleithiau Cydffederal *ell*
▸ **confederate state** (US) talaith gydffederal *eb* taleithiau cydffederal
confederation cydffederasiwn *eg* cydffederasiynau
Confederation of the Rhine Cydffederasiwn y Rhein *eg*
confer ymgynghori *be*
conference cynhadledd *eb* cynadleddau
conference proceedings trafodion cynhadledd *ell*
conference report adroddiad cynhadledd *eg* adroddiadau cynhadledd
confess cyffesu *be*
confession (=admission of guilt) cyfaddefiad *eg* cyfaddefiadau
confession (in general) cyffes *eb* cyffesion
Confession of Augsburgh Cyffes Augsburg *eb*
confession of faith cyffes ffydd *eb*
confessional cyffesgell *eb* cyffesgelloedd
confessor cyffeswr *eg* cyffeswyr
confidence hyder *eg*
confidence in water hyder mewn dŵr *eg*
confidence interval cyfwng hyder *eg* cyfyngau hyder
confidence level lefel hyder *eb*
confidence limit ffin hyder *eb* ffiniau hyder
confidential cyfrinachol *ans*
confidential information gwybodaeth gyfrinachol *eb*
confidential record cofnod cyfrinachol *eg* cofnodion cyfrinachol
confidentiality cyfrinachedd *eg*
confidentiality level lefel cyfrinachedd *eb* lefelau cyfrinachedd
configuration ffurfweddiad *eg* ffurfweddiadau
configuration file ffeil ffurfweddu *eb* ffeiliau ffurfweddu
configuration menu dewislen ffurfweddu *eb* dewislenni ffurfweddu
configure ffurfweddu *be*
confinement cyfnod geni *eg*
confirm cadarnhau *be*
confirm delete cadarnhau dileu *be*
confirm password cadarnhau cyfrinair *be*
confirm receipt cadarnhau derbyn *be*
confirmation (=establish more fully) cadarnhad *eg*
confirmation (in church) bedydd esgob *eg*
confirmation bias tuedd i gytuno *eb*
conflict gwrthdaro *be*
conflicting demands gofynion sy'n gwrthdaro *ell*
confluence cydlifiad *eg* cydlifiadau
confocal cydffocal *ans*
conformable cydffurfiadwy *ans*
conformable beds haenau cydffurfiadwy *ell*
conformal cydffurf *ans*
conformal mapping mapio cydffurfiol *be*
conformation cydffurfiad *eg* cydffurfiadau
conformational cydffurfiol *ans*
conformational analysis dadansoddiad cydffurfiol *eg* dadansoddiadau cydffurfiol
conforming bandage rhwymyn cydffurfiol *eg* rhwymynnau cydymffurfiol
conforming shape function ffwythiant siâp cydffurfiol *eg* ffwythiannau siâp cydffurfiol
conformity cydymffurfiad *eg*
confound *n* elfen ddryslyd *eb* elfennau dryslyd
confound *v* drysu *be*
confounding variable newidyn dryslyd *eg* newidynnau dryslyd
Confraternity of Christian Doctrine Brawdoliaeth Dysgeidiaeth Gristnogol *eb*
confrontation gwrthdaro *be*
Confucian *adj* Conffiwsaidd *ans*
Confucian *n* Conffiwsiad *eg/b* Conffiwsiaid
confuse *v.intrans* drysu *be*
confuse *v.trans* cymysgu *be*
confused drainage draeniad dryslyd *eg* draeniadau dryslyd
conga conga *eg* congâu
congeliturbate rhewdyrfiad *eg* rhewdyrfiadau
congeliturbation rhewdyrfiad *eg* rhewdyrfiadau
congenital malformation camffurfiad cynhenid *eg* camffurfiadau cynhenid
conger eel congren *eb* congrod
congest gordyrru *be*
congested gordyrrog *ans*
Congested Local Board Bwrdd Lleol Gorboblogaeth *eg*
congestion (of blood, mucus etc) gorlenwad *eg*
congestion (of traffic) tagfa *eb* tagfeydd
conglomerate *v* cyd-dyrru *be*
conglomerate (in geology) *n* clymfaen *eg* clymfeini
conglomerate (of company, organization) uwchgwmni *eg* uwchgwmnïau

conglomeration (in commerce) cyd-dyriad *eg* cyd-dyriadau
conglomeration (in geology) crugiad *eg* crugiadau
congregation cynulleidfa *eb* cynulleidfaoedd
Congregationalist *adj* Annibynnol *ans*
Congregationalist *n* Annibynnwr *eg* Annibynwyr
Congregations of Christ Cynulleidfaoedd Crist *ell*
Congregations of Congress Cyfarfodydd Cyngres *ell*
congress cyngres *eb* cyngresau
Congress of Berlin Cyngres Berlin *eb*
Congress Party Plaid y Gyngres *eb*
Congress System Cyfundrefn Gyngresol *eb*
congressional cyngresol *ans*
congruence cyfathiant *eg* cyfathiannau
congruent cyfath *ans*
congruent triangles trionglau cyfath *ell*
conic conig *ans*
conic section trychiad conig *eg* trychiadau conig
conical conigol *ans*
conical flask fflasg gonigol *eb* fflasgiau conigol
conical head rivet rhybed pen côn *eg* rhybedion pen côn
conical projection tafluniad conigol *eg* tafluniadau conigol
conicoid conicoid *eg* conicoidau
conifer conwydden *eb* conwydd
coniferous forest coedwig gonwydd *eb* coedwigoedd conwydd
coniferous tree conwydden *eb* conwydd
conjecture dyfaliad *eg* dyfaliadau
conjugate *adj* cyfieuol *ans*
conjugate *n* cyfiau *eg* cyfieuau
conjugate *v* cyfuno *be*
conjugate acid asid cyfieuol *eg* asidau cyfieuol
conjugate base bas cyfieuol *eg* basau cyfieuol
conjugate movement symudiad cyfiau *eg* symudiadau cyfiau
conjugate pair pâr cyfiau *eg*
conjugate point pwynt cyfiau *eg* pwyntiau cyfiau
conjugated cyfunedig *ans*
conjugation (in grammar) rhediad *eg* rhediadau
conjugation (in science) cyfunedd *eg*
conjunct motion symud gam a cham *be*
conjunctiva (of eye) cyfbilen *eb* cyfbilennau
conjunctivitis llid y gyfbilen *eg*
connect cysylltu *be*
connect time amser cysylltu *eg*
connected cysylltiedig *ans*
connecting device dyfais gysylltu *eb* dyfeisiau cysylltu
connecting rod rhoden gyswllt *eb* rhodenni cyswllt
connection cysylltiad *eg* cysylltiadau
connective *adj* cyswllt *ans*
connective *n* cysylltyn *eg* cysylltion
► **connective tissue** meinwe gyswllt *eb*
connectivity cysylltedd *eg*
connector cysylltydd *eg* cysylltyddion
connotation arwyddocâd *eg*
conoid conoid *eg* conoidau
conqueror gorchfygwr *eg* gorchfygwyr
conquest concwest *eg/b* concwestau
conscience cydwybod *eb*
conscientiousness cydwybodolrwydd *eg*
consciousness ymwybyddiaeth *eb*
consciousness-raising codi ymwybyddiaeth *be*
conscription consgripsiwn *eg*
consecrate cysegru *be*
consecrated cysegredig *ans*
consecrated wafer afrlladen *eb* afrlladau
consecration cysegriad *eg*
consecutive dilynol *ans*
consecutive fifths and octaves pumedau ac wythfedau dilynol *ell*
consecutive revolutions cylchdroeon dilynol *ell*
consecutives dilynolion *ell*
consensual behaviour ymddygiad cydsyniol *eg*
consensus consensws *eg*
consent cydsyniad *eg*
consent form ffurflen gydsynio *eb* ffurflenni cydsynio
consequence canlyniad *eg* canlyniadau
consequent *adj* canlynol *ans*
consequent (in canon) *n* canlyniad *eg* canlyniadau
consequent (stream) *n* cydlif *eg* cydlifau
consequent stream ffrwd gydlif *eb* ffrydiau cydlif
consequentialism canlyniadaeth *eb*
conservation (of mass, energy, momentum) cadwraeth *eb* cadwraethau
conservation area ardal gadwraeth *eb* ardaloedd cadwraeth
conservation of charge cadwraeth gwefr *eb*
conservation of energy cadwraeth egni *eb*
conservation of momentum cadwraeth momentwm *eb*
conservation of number cadwraeth rhif *eb*
conservation officer (of person) swyddog cadwraeth *eg* swyddogion cadwraeth
conservatism ceidwadaeth *eb*
conservative *n* ceidwadwr *eg* ceidwadwyr
conservative (in scientific usage) *adj* cadwrol *ans*
conservative (in social and political usage) *adj* ceidwadol *ans*
conservative field of force maes cadwrol grym *eg*
Conservative Party Plaid Geidwadol *eb*
conservative replication dyblygiad cadwrol *eg*
conservative treatment triniaeth geidwadol *eb* triniaethau ceidwadol
conservatoire conservatoire *eg* conservatoires
conserve (=fruit preserve) *n* cyffrwyth meddal *eg*
conserve (=keep from damage) *v* gwarchod *be*
conserve (=not waste) *v* cynilo *be*
consider ystyried *be*
consideration ystyriaeth *eb* ystyriaethau
consignment llwyth *eg* llwythi
consistency (=degree of density) ansawdd *eg*
consistency (=state of being constant) cysondeb *eg*

consistent cyson *ans*
consistent performance perfformio cyson *be*
consistorial consistoraidd *ans*
consistory consistori *eg* consistorïau
console consol *eg* consolau
console light lamp gonsol *eb* lampau consol
console log log consol *eg* logiau consol
console switch switsh consol *eg* switshis consol
console typewriter teipiadur consol *eg* teipiaduron consol
consolidate cyfnerthu *be*
consolidate skills cyfnerthu medrau *be*
consolidated cyfnerthedig *ans*
consolidated fund prif gronfa wladol *eb* prif gronfeydd gwladol
consolidation cyfnerthu *be*
consommé consommé *eg*
consonance cyseinedd *eg*
consonant interval cyfwng cyseiniol *eg* cyfyngau cyseiniol
consort (=wife or husband, especially of royalty) cydweddog *eg/b* cydweddogion
consort (in music) consort *eg* consortiau
consort of viols consort feiolau *eg* consortiau feiolau
consortium consortiwm *eg* consortia
conspiracy cynllwyn *eg* cynllwynion
Conspiracy & Protection of Property Act Deddf Cynllwyn a Diogelu Eiddo *eb*
Conspiracy of Equals Cynllwyn y Cydraddolion *eg*
conspire cynllwynio *be*
constable cwnstabl *eg* cwnstabliaid
constancy sefydlogrwydd *eg*
constancy of colour unffurfiaeth lliw *eb*
constancy of shape unffurfiaeth siâp *eb*
constant *adj* cyson *ans*
constant *n* cysonyn *eg* cysonion
constant acceleration cyflymiad cyson *eg*
constant boiling mixture cymysgedd pwynt berwi cyson *eb*
constant of proportionality cysonyn cyfrannol *eg*
constant pressure gwasgedd cyson *eg*
constant ratio curve cromlin cymhareb gyson *eb*
constant slope llethr cyson *eg* llethrau cyson
constant temperature tymheredd cyson *eg*
constant velocity cyflymder cyson *eg*
Constantine the Great Cystennin Fawr *eg*
constellation (=group of persons, ideas etc) clwstwr *eg* clystyrau
constellation (of stars) cytser *eg* cytserau
constellation of towns clwstwr o drefi *eg* clystyrau o drefi
constipated rhwym *ans*
constipation rhwymedd *eg*
constituent (chemical) ansoddyn *eg* ansoddau
constituent (of nucleus) cyfansoddyn *eg* cyfansoddion
constituent assembly cynulliad cyfansoddol *eg*
constituent element elfen ansoddol *eb* elfennau ansoddol
constituent group grŵp cyfansoddol *eg* grwpiau cyfansoddol
constitution cyfansoddiad *eg* cyfansoddiadau
constitutional cyfansoddiadol *ans*
constitutional history hanes cyfansoddiadol *eg*
constitutionalism cyfansoddiaeth *eb*
constrain (=bring about by compulsion) gorfodi *be*
constrained motion mudiant cyfyngedig *eg*
constrained to move horizontally (with feminine nouns) wedi'i gorfodi i symud yn llorweddol *ans* wedi'u gorfodi i symud yn llorweddol
constrained to move horizontally (with masculine nouns) wedi'i orfodi i symud yn llorweddol *ans* wedi'u gorfodi i symud yn llorweddol
constrained to move vertically (with feminine nouns) wedi'i gorfodi i symud yn fertigol *ans* wedi'u gorfodi i symud yn fertigol
constrained to move vertically (with masculine nouns) wedi'i orfodi i symud yn fertigol *ans* wedi'u gorfodi i symud yn fertigol
constraint (in economics) cyfyngiad *eg* cyfyngiadau
constraint (in physics) cyfyngydd *eg* cyfyngyddion
constrict darwasgu *be*
constricted darwasgedig *ans*
constriction darwasgiad *eg* darwasgiadau
construct (=form, create) *v* llunio *be*
construct (of the mind etc) *n* lluniad *eg* lluniadau
construct shapes llunio siapiau *be*
construct validity dilysrwydd lluniad *eg*
constructed estuary moryd wneud *eb* morydau gwneud
constructing an ellipse llunio elips *be*
construction (of abstract/geometrical) lluniad *eg* lluniadau
construction (of frame/building) adeiladwaith *eg* adeiladweithiau
construction craft crefft adeiladu *eb*
construction drawing lluniad adeiladu *eg* lluniadau adeiladu
construction line llinell lunio *eb* llinellau llunio
construction paper papur adeiladwaith *eg*
construction technology technoleg adeiladu *eb*
constructional toy tegan adeiladu *eg* teganau adeiladu
constructive adeiladol *ans*
constructive interference ymyriant adeiladol *eg*
constructive plate margins ymylon platiau adeiladol *ell*
constructive wave ton adeiladol *eb* tonnau adeiladol
constructivism (in mathematics, art) adeileddiaeth *eb*
constructivism (in psychology) lluniadaeth *eb*
constructivist (in mathematics, art) *adj* adeileddol *ans*
constructivist (in mathematics, art) *n* adeileddwr *eg* adeileddwyr
consubstantiation cydsylweddiad *eg*

consul conswl *eg* conswliaid
consulate (in ancient Rome) conswliaeth *eb*
consulate (modern) swyddfa is-gennad *eb* swyddfeydd is-genhadon
consultancy ymgynghoriaeth *eb* ymgyngoriaethau
consultant *adj* ymgynghorol *ans*
consultant *n* ymgynghorydd *eg* ymgynghorwyr
consumables defnyddiau traul *ell*
consumer (=fire, bacteria, predator etc that consume) ysydd *eg* ysyddion
consumer (=person who uses a product) defnyddiwr *eg* defnyddwyr
Consumer Advice Service Gwasanaeth Cynghori Defnyddwyr *eg*
consumer boom ffyniant defnyddwyr *eg*
consumer conglomerate cyd-dyriad defnyddwyr *eg*
Consumer Credit Act Deddf Credyd Defnyddwyr *eb*
consumer education addysg defnyddwyr *eb*
consumer expenditure gwariant defnyddwyr *eg*
consumer goods nwyddau traul *ell*
consumer industry diwydiant nwyddau traul *eg* diwydiannau nwyddau traul
consumer market marchnad defnyddwyr *eb*
Consumer Protection Act 1987 Deddf Gwarchod Defnyddwyr 1987 *eb*
Consumer Protection Department Adran Gwarchod Defnyddwyr *eb*
Consumer Protection Department Act Deddf Adran Gwarchod Defnyddwyr *eb*
consumer psychology seicoleg defnyddwyr *eb*
consumer rights hawliau defnyddwyr *ell*
consumer sovereignty sofraniaeth defnyddwyr *eb*
consumer spending gwariant defnyddwyr *eg*
consumer surplus gwarged defnyddwyr *eb*
consumption (medical condition) darfodedigaeth *eb*
consumption (of food) cymeriant *eg*
consumption (of goods) treuliant *eg*
contact *v* cysylltu *be*
contact (=communication or meeting) *n* cyswllt *eg* cysylltau
contact (=physical touch) *n* cyffyrddiad *eg* cyffyrddiadau
contact adhesive gludydd cyswllt *eg* gludyddion cyswllt
contact bounce adlam y cysylltau *eg* adlamau y cysylltau
▶ **contact breaker** cyswllt-dorrwr *eg* cyswllt-dorwyr
contact force grym cyffwrdd *eg*
contact glue glud cyswllt *eg*
contact grill gridyll cyswllt *eg* gridyllau cyswllt
contact hours oriau cyswllt *ell*
contact hypothesis rhagdybiaeth cyswllt *eb*
contact line llinell gyswllt *eb* llinellau cyswllt
contact mike meic cyswllt *eg* meiciau cyswllt
contact process proses gyffwrdd *eb* prosesau cyffwrdd
contact push gwthiad cyffwrdd *eg*
contact sounds seiniau cyffwrdd *ell*
contact time amser cyswllt *eg* amserau cyswllt
contact zone cylchfa gyswllt *eb* cylchfaoedd cyswllt
contagious cyffwrdd-ymledol *ans*
contagious disease clefyd cyffwrdd-ymledol *eg* clefydau cyffwrdd-ymledol
contain cynnwys *be*
container cynhwysydd *eg* cynwysyddion
container depot depo amlwytho *eg* depos amlwytho
containerization amlwythiant *eg*
containment cyfyngiant *eg*
contaminate halogi *be*
contamination halogiad *eg*
contemporary *adj* cyfoes *ans*
contemporary *n* cyfoeswr *eg* cyfoeswyr
contemporary art celfyddyd gyfoes *eb*
contemporary design (as a genre) cynllunio cyfoes *be*
contemporary design (of specific examples) cynllun cyfoes *eg* cynlluniau cyfoes
contemporary society cymdeithas gyfoes *eb*
contemporary style arddull cyfoes *eg* arddulliau cyfoes
contempt of court dirmyg llys *eg*
contender cystadleuydd *eg* cystadleuwyr
content *adj* bodlon *ans*
content *n* cynnwys *eg* cynhwysion
content addressable file store (CAFS) storfa ffeiliau gynnwys-gyfeiriedig *eb* storfeydd ffeiliau cynnwys-gyfeiriedig
content analysis dadansoddi cynnwys *be*
content of science cynnwys gwyddoniaeth *eg*
content word gair cynnwys *eg* geiriau cynnwys
content-free penagored *ans*
contention ymryson *eg* ymrysonau
contentious cynhennus *ans*
contents of paint cynhwysion paent *ell*
contest cystadleuaeth *eb* cystadlaethau
contest (boxing etc) gornest *eb* gornestau
context cyd-destun *eg* cyd-destunau
contextual intelligence dealltwriaeth gyd-destunol *eb*
contextual issue mater cyd-destunol *eg* materion cyd-destunol
contextual study astudiaeth gyd-destunol *eg* astudiaethau cyd-destunol
contiguity cyfagosrwydd *eg*
continent cyfandir *eg* cyfandiroedd
continental drift drifft cyfandirol *eg*
continental Europe cyfandir Ewrop *eg*
continental powers pwerau cyfandirol *ell*
continental shelf sgafell gyfandirol *eb* sgafelli cyfandirol
Continental System (1806-12) System Gyfandirol *eb*
continentality cyfandiroledd *eg*
contingency (in psychology etc) amodoldeb *eb*
contingency plan cynllun wrth gefn *eg* cynlluniau wrth gefn
contingency table tabl newidynnau *eg* tablau newidynnau

continuation parhad *eg*
continuation notice hysbysiad parhad *eg* hysbysiadau parhad
continuation page tudalen parhad *eb* tudalennau parhad
continuation page number rhif tudalen parhad *eg* rhifau tudalennau parhad
continue parhau *be*
continue search backwards parhau i chwilio nôl *be*
continue search forward parhau i chwilio ymlaen *be*
continuing education addysg barhaus *eb*
continuity parhad *eg*
continuity of care dilyniant mewn gofal
continuo continuo *eg* continui
continuous (=unbroken) di-dor *ans*
continuous assessment asesu parhaus *be*
continuous creation creu parhaus *be*
continuous curve cromlin ddi-dor *eb* cromliniau di-dor
continuous data data di-dor *ell*
continuous distribution dosraniad di-dor *eg* dosraniadau di-dor
continuous fibre ffibr di-dor *eg* ffibrau di-dor
continuous free curve cromlin rydd ddi-dor *eb* cromliniau rhydd di-dor
continuous guidance arweiniad parhaus *eg*
continuous infusion (of action) arllwysiad parhaus *eg* arllwysiadau parhaus
continuous infusion (of liquid) trwyth parhaus *eg* trwythau parhaus
continuous lap agoriad di-dor *eg* agoriadau di-dor
continuous line llinell ddi-dor *eb* llinellau di-dor
continuous random variable hapnewidyn di-dor *eg* hapnewidynnau di-dor
continuous smooth curve cromlin lefn ddi-dor *eb* cromliniau llyfn di-dor
continuous spectrum sbectrwm di-dor *eg* sbectra di-dor
continuous stationery papur di-dor *eg*
continuous stream ffrwd ddi-dor *eb* ffrydiau di-dor
continuous strip mill melin strip ddi-dor *eb* melinau strip di-dor
continuous variable newidyn di-dor *eg* newidynnau di-dor
continuous yarn edafedd di-dor *ell*
continuum continwwm *eg* continwa
contour (=outline) amlinell *eb* amlinellau
contour (in geography) cyfuchlinedd *eg* cyfuchlineddau
contour (in mathematics) amlin *eb* amliniau
contour dialog deialog amlinell *eb* deialogau amlinell
contour editor golygydd amlinell *eg* golygyddion amlinell
contour interval cyfwng cyfuchlinol *eg* cyfyngau cyfuchlinol
contour line cyfuchlin *eg* cyfuchlinau
contour map map cyfuchlinol *eg* mapiau cyfuchlinol
contour mode modd amlinell *eg*
contour plan cynllun cyfuchlin *eg*
contra bass bas dwbl *eg* basau dwbl
contra bass player canwr bas dwbl *eg* canwyr bas dwbl
contra bassoon baswn dwbl *eg* baswnau dwbl
contra bassoonist canwr baswn dwbl *eg* canwyr baswn dwbl
contraception atal cenhedlu *be*
contraceptive device cyfarpar atal cenhedlu *eg*
contraceptive method dull atal cenhedlu *eg* dulliau atal cenhedlu
contract (=agreement) *n* contract *eg* contractau
contract (=become smaller) *v* cyfangu *be*
contract (=draw together) *v* crebachu *be*
contract costing costio contractau *be*
contracted out (with feminine nouns) wedi'i chontractio allan *ans* wedi'u contractio allan
contracted out (with masculine nouns) wedi'i gontractio allan *ans* wedi'u contractio allan
contractile cyfangol *eg*
contractile root gwreiddyn cyfangol *eg* gwreiddiau cyfangol
contractile vacuole gwagolyn cyfangol *eg* gwagolynnau cyfangol
contracting industry diwydiant enciliol *eg* diwydiannau enciliol
contraction cyfangiad *eg* cyfangiadau
contraction pattern patrwm cyfangiad *eg* patrymau cyfangiad
contraction rule riwl gyfangiad *eb* riwliau cyfangiad
contractor contractwr *eg* contractwyr
contracts of adhesion contractau ymlyniad *ell*
contradiction gwrthddywediad *eg* gwrthddywediadau
contra-indication gwrthrybudd *eg*
contralateral cydgyferbyniol *ans*
contralto contralto *eb* contraltos
contrapuntal gwrthbwyntiol *ans*
contrapuntalist gwrthbwyntydd *eg* gwrthbwyntwyr
contrary cyferbyn *ans*
contrary motion gwrthsymudiad *eg* gwrthsymudiadau
contrast *n* cyferbyniad *eg* cyferbyniadau
contrast *v* cyferbynnu *be*
contrast (on computer screen) cyferbynnedd *eg* cyferbyneddau
contrast of continuity cyferbyniad parhad *eg*
contrast of level cyferbyniad lefel *eg*
contrast of shape cyferbyniad siâp *eg*
contrast of size cyferbyniad maint *eg*
contrast of tension cyferbyniad tyndra *eg*
contrasted characteristics nodweddion cyferbyniol *ell*
contrasting cyferbyniol *ans*
contrasting colour lliw cyferbyniol *eg* lliwiau cyferbyniol
contrasting locality ardal gyferbyniol *eb* ardaloedd cyferbyniol
contrasting stimuli ysgogiadau cyferbyniol *ell*
contrasting wood pren cyferbyniol *eg*

contravening croes *ans*
contribute cyfrannu *be*
contribution cyfraniad *eg* cyfraniadau
contributor cyfrannwr *eg* cyfranwyr
contributory pension pensiwn cyfrannol *eg* pensiynau cyfrannol
control (=manage) *v* rheoli *be*
control (=management) *n* rheolaeth *eb* rheolaethau
control (a class etc) *v* cadw trefn *be*
control (in control experiment) *n* rheolydd *eg* rheolyddion
control bar bar rheoli *eg* barrau rheoli
control card cerdyn rheoli *eg* cardiau rheoli
control character nod rheoli *eg* nodau rheoli
control code cod rheoli *eg* codau rheoli
control condition cyflwr rheolydd *eg*
control description disgrifiad o'r rheolfan *eg* disgrifiadau o'r rheolfan
control device dyfais reoli *eb* dyfeisiau rheoli
control experiment arbrawf cymharu *eg*
control floods rheoli llifogydd *be*
control group grŵp rheolydd *eg* grwpiau rheolydd
control injection pigiad rheoledig *eg* pigiadau rheoledig
control key bysell reoli *eb* bysellau rheoli
control marker marciwr rheoli *eg* marcwyr rheoli
control measure mesur rheoli *eg* mesuriadau rheoli
control measurement mesuriad rheoli *eg*
control memory cof rheoli *eg* cofion rheoli
control of equipment rheoli offer *be*
control of fullness rheoli llawnder *be*
Control of Substances Hazardous to Health Rheoli Sylweddau sy'n Beryglus i Iechyd *be*
control panel panel rheoli *eg* paneli rheoli
control point rheolfan *eg/b* rheolfannau
control program rhaglen reoli *eb* rhaglenni rheoli
control rod rhoden reoli *eb* rhodenni rheoli
control setting rheolydd *eg* rheolyddion
control shoot cyffyn cymharu *eg*
control switch switsh rheoli *eg* switshis rheoli
control system system reoli *eb* systemau rheoli
control technique techneg reoli *eb* technegau rheoli
control technology technoleg reoli *eb* technolegau rheoli
control the ball rheoli'r bêl *be*
control theory damcaniaeth reoli *eb*
control unit uned reoli *eb* unedau rheoli
control variable newidyn rheolydd *eg* newidynnau rheolydd
controlled drug cyffur rheoledig *eg* cyffuriau rheoledig
controlled grazing pori rheoledig *be*
controlled reading darllen dan oruchwyliaeth *eg*
controlled test prawf dan oruchwyliaeth *eg* profion dan oruchwyliaeth
controller (=regulator) rheolydd *eg* rheolyddion
conurbation cytref *eb* cytrefi
conus arteriosus conws arteriosws *eg*
convalesce gwella *be*
convalescence cyfnod gwella *eg*
▶ **convalescent diet** deiet gwella *eg*
convection darfudiad *eg* darfudiadau
convectional darfudol *ans*
convectional rain glaw darfudol *eg*
convector drier sychydd darfudol *eg* sychwyr darfudol
convector heater gwresogydd darfudol *eg* gwresogyddion darfudol
convener cynullydd *eg* cynullyddion
convenience food bwyd cyfleus *eg* bwydydd cyfleus
convenience goods nwyddau cyfleus *ell*
convenient cyfleus *ans*
convent lleiandy *eg* lleiandai
conventicle confentigl *eb* confentiglau
Conventigles Act Deddf y Confentiglau *eb*
convention (=assembly) cynulliad *eg* cynulliadau
convention (=customary practice) confensiwn *eg* confensiynau
conventional confensiynol *ans*
conventional art celfyddyd gonfensiynol *eb*
conventional feed porthiant confensiynol *eg*
▶ **conventional isometric projection** tafluniad isometrig confensiynol *eg* tafluniadau isometrig confensiyno
conventional joint uniad confensiynol *eg* uniadau confensiynol
conventional level lefel gonfensiynol *eb*
conventional mathematical notation nodiant mathemategol confensiynol *eg*
conventional method dull confensiynol *eg* dulliau confensiynol
conventional milling (up-cut) melino confensiynol *be*
conventional notation nodiant confensiynol *eg*
conventional sign arwydd confensiynol *eg* arwyddion confensiynol
conventional symbol symbol confensiynol *eg* symbolau confensiynol
conventions of fair play confensiynau chwarae teg *ell*
conventual *adj* cwfeiniol *ans*
conventual *n* cwfeiniad *eg* cwfeiniaid
converge cydgyfeirio *be*
convergence cydgyfeiriant *eg* cydgyfeiriannau
convergence in distribution cydgyfeiriant o ran dosraniad *eg*
convergence in probability cydgyfeiriant o ran tebygolrwydd *eg*
convergence in quadratic mean cydgyfeiriant o ran cymedr cwadratig *eg*
convergence limit terfan cydgyfeiriant *eb*
convergent cydgyfeiriol *ans*
convergent question cwestiwn cydgyfeiriol *eg* cwestiynau cydgyfeiriol
convergent series cyfres gydgyfeiriol *eb* cyfresi cydgyfeiriol

converging electron lens lens electron cydgyfeiriol *eg* lensiau electron cydgyfeiriol
converging lens lens cydgyfeiriol *eg* lensiau cydgyfeiriol
converging operations gweithgareddau cydgyfeiriol *ell*
converging point pwynt cydgyfeiriol *eg* pwyntiau cydgyfeiriol
conversation sgwrs *eb* sgyrsiau
conversation piece (of painting) darlun ymddiddan *eg* darluniau ymddiddan
conversational system system sgyrsiol *eb* systemau sgyrsiol
converse cyfdro *eg* cyfdroeon
converse theorem theorem gyfdro *eb*
conversi brodyr lleyg *ell*
conversion (in religion) tröedigaeth *eb* tröedigaethau
conversion (in science) trawsnewidiad *eg* trawsnewidiadau
conversion (timber) trosiad *eg* trosiadau
conversion disorder anhwylder trosi *eg*
conversion graph graff trawsnewid *eg* graffiau trawsnewid
conversion of energy trawsnewidiad ynni *eg*
conversion process proses drosi *eb* prosesau trosi
conversion table tabl trawsnewid *eg* tablau trawsnewid
convert (a try) trosi *be*
convert (in science) trawsnewid *be*
converted try trosgais *eg*
converter (e.g. Bessemer) trawsnewidydd *eg* trawsnewidyddion
convex amgrwm *ans*
convex curvature amgrymedd *eg* amgrymeddau
convex curve cromlin amgrwm *eb* cromliniau amgrwm
convex face wyneb amgrwm *eg* wynebau amgrwm
convex hull hwl amgrwm *eg* hyliau amgrwm
convex lens lens amgrwm *eg* lensiau amgrwm
convex slope llethr amgrwm *eg* llethrau amgrwm
convexity amgrymedd *eg* amgrymeddau
convey (=carry) cludo *be*
convey (=transfer legal title) trosglwyddo *be*
conveyance (=transport) cludiant *eg* cludiannau
conveyance (of legal title) trosglwyddiad *eg*
conveyance deed trawsgludiad *eg*
conveyancer trawsgludwr *eg* trawsgludwyr
conveyancing trawsgludo *be*
conveyor cludydd *eg* cludyddion
conveyor belt cludfelt *eg* cludfeltiau
convocation confocasiwn *eg* confocasiynau
convolution (=faltung) ffaltwng *eg* ffaltyngau
convoy cymdaith *eg* cymdeithiau
convulsion (in earthquake) dirgryniad *eg* dirgryniadau
convulsion (medical) confylsiwn *eg* confylsiynau
Conway Races Campau Conwy *ell*
cook coginio *be*
cooker popty *eg* poptai
cooker hood lwfer popty *eg* lwfrau popty
cooker range popty estynedig *eg* poptai estynedig
cooker ring alch *eb* eilch
cookie cwci *eg* cwcis
cooking apple afal coginio *eg* afalau coginio
cool (=cold) *adj* oer *ans*
cool (in general) *v* oeri *be*
cool (of iron setting, weather) *adj* claear *ans*
cool (of weather) claearu *be*
cool colour lliw oeraidd *eg* lliwiau oeraidd
cool iron haearn claear *eg*
cool temperate tymherus claear *ans*
cool temperate zone cylchfa dymherus glaear *eb*
coolant oerydd *eg* oeryddion
cooling fan gwyntyll oeri *eb* gwyntyllau oeri
cooling media cyfryngau oeri *ell*
cooling system system oeri *eb* systemau oeri
cooling tank tanc oeri *eg* tanciau oeri
coombe rock cwmgraig *eb* cwmgreigiau
cooper cowper *eg* cowperiaid
cooper jointing uniadu cylchwr *be*
cooperate cydweithredu *be*
cooperation cydweithrediad *eg* cydweithrediadau
cooperative cydweithredol *ans*
cooperative bank banc cydweithredol *eg* banciau cydweithredol
cooperative business busnes cydweithredol *eg* busnesau cydweithredol
cooperative play chwarae cydweithredol *eg*
cooperative shop siop gydweithredol *eb* siopau cydweithredol
cooperative society cymdeithas gydweithredol *eb* cymdeithasau cydweithredol
cooperative teaching addysgu cydweithredol *be*
co-opt cyfethol *be*
co-opted member aelod cyfetholedig *eg* aelodau cyfetholedig
coordinate (fashion items) *n* cydweddyn *eg* cydweddion
coordinate (fashion items) *v* cydweddu *be*
coordinate (in administration) *v* cydgysylltu *be*
coordinate (in order to fix a position) *n* cyfesuryn *eg* cyfesurynnau
coordinate (of covalent bond) *adj* cyd-drefnol *ans*
coordinate (of covalent bond) *v* cyd-drefnu *be*
coordinate axes echelinau cyfesurynnol *ell*
coordinate bond bond cyd-drefnol *eg*
coordinate geometry geometreg gyfesurynnol *eb*
coordinate system system gyfesurynnol *eb* systemau cyfesurynnol
coordinated provision cyd-ddarpariaeth *eb*
coordinated separates amrywion cydwedd *ell*
coordinating power gallu cyd-drefnu *eg*
coordination (in administration) cydgysylltu *be*
coordination (of covalent bond) cyd-drefniant *eg*
coordination (of movements) cydsymud *be*

coordination number rhif cyd-drefnol *eg* rhifau cyd-drefnol
coordinator cydgysylltwr *eg* cydgysylltwyr
copal varnish farnais copal *eg*
cope *v* ymdopi *be*
cope (in metalwork) *n* copa *eg* copâu
cope and drag copa a drag
copier copïwr *eg* copïwyr
coping (of wall) copin *eg* copinau
coping saw llif fwa fach *eb* llifiau bwa bach
coping skills sgiliau ymdopi *ell*
coping stone carreg gopa *eb* cerrig copa
coping strategy strategaeth ymdopi *eb*
coplanar cymhlan *ans*
coplanar forces grymoedd cymhlan *ell*
copper (Cu) copr *eg*
copper atom atom copr *eg* atomau copr
copper blank blanc copr *eg*
copper brown brown copr eg
copper filings naddion copr *ell*
copper hammer morthwyl copr *eg* morthwylion copr
copper money arian cochion *ell*
copper nail hoelen gopr *eb* hoelion copr
copper ore mwyn copr *eg*
copper screw sgriw gopr *eb* sgriwiau copr
copper stud styden gopr *eb* stydiau copr
copper sulphate copr sylffad *eg*
copper washer wasier gopr *eb* wasieri copr
copper wire gwifren gopr *eb* gwifrau copr
coppered screw sgriw goprog *eb* sgriwiau coprog
coppered wire gwifren goprog *eb* gwifrau coprog
copper(I) chloride copr(I) clorid *eg*
copper(I) ion ïon copr(I) *eg* ïonau copr(I)
copper(II) carbonate dihydroxide (malachite) copr(II) carbonad deuhydrocsid (malachit) *eg*
copper(II) ion ïon copr(II) *eg* ïonau copr(II)
copper(II) iron(II) disulfide (chalcopyrite) copr(II) haearn(II) deusylffid (calcopyrit) *eg*
copper(II) sulfate(VI) copr(II) sylffad(VI) *eg*
coppice *n* coedlan *eb* coedlannau
coppice *v* prysgoedio *be*
coprophage carthysydd *eg* carthysyddion
coprosterol coprosterol *eg*
copulate ymgydio *be*
copulation ymgydiad *eg* ymgydiadau
copunctual cydbwyntiol *ans*
copy *n* copi *eg* copïau
copy *v* copïo *be*
copy and paste copïo a gludo
copy, cut and paste copïo, torri a gludo
copy formatting copïo fformatio *be*
copy image location copïo lleoliad y ddelwedd *be*
copy key bysell gopïo *eb* bysellau copïo
copy link location copïo lleoliad y cyswllt *be*
copy menu dewislen gopïo *eb* dewislenni copïo
copy ruler *n* mesurydd copïo *eg* mesuryddion copïo
copy ruler *v* copïo mesurydd *be*
copy-cat crime trosedd efelychu *eb* troseddau efelychu
copycat theory damcaniaeth efelychu *eb* damcaniaethau efelychu
copyholder copiddeiliad *eg* copiddeiliaid
copyleft haelfraint *eb*
copyright hawlfraint *eb*
cor anglais cor anglais *eg* cors anglais
coral cwrel *eg* cwrelau
coral stitch pwyth cwrel *eg* pwythau cwrel
coralline cwrelaidd *ans*
corbel corbel *eg* corbelau
corbelled arch bwa corbelaidd *eg* bwâu corbelaidd
cord *n* cortyn *eg* cortynnau
corded weave gwehyddiad cordynnog *eg*
cordial cordial *eg*
cordillera cadwyn *eb* cadwynau
cordless diwifr *ans*
corduroy melfaréd *eg*
core craidd *eg* creiddiau
core and foundation subjects pynciau craidd a sylfaen *ell*
core area maes craidd *eg* meysydd craidd
core box blwch craidd *eg* blychau craidd
core culture diwylliant craidd *eg* diwylliannau craidd
core curriculum cwricwlwm craidd *eg*
core diameter diamedr craidd *eg* diamedrau craidd
core impression argraff craidd *eb*
core lipped and veneered door drws craidd wedi'i ymylu a'i argaenu *eg* drysau craidd wedi'u hymylu a'u hargaenu
core memory cof craidd *eg* cofion craidd
core pattern patrwm craidd *eg* patrymau craidd
core print argraffiad craidd *eg* argraffiadau craidd
core store storfa graidd *eb* storfeydd craidd
core subject pwnc craidd *eg* pynciau craidd
core syllabus maes llafur craidd *eg* meysydd llafur craidd
core vocabulary geirfa graidd *eb* geirfâu craidd
core yarn edafedd craidd *ell*
co-reactive cydadweithiol *ans*
coreboard craiddfwrdd *eg* craiddfyrddau
cored pattern patrwm creiddig *eg* patrymau creiddig
cored solder sodr craidd *eg* sodrau craidd
core-domain-sphere craidd-parth-cylch *eg*
corer digreiddiwr *eg* digreiddwyr
co-respondent cydatebydd *eg* cydatebyddion
coriander coriander *eg*
Coriolis force grym Coriolis *eg*
cork *adj* corc *ans*
cork *n* corcyn *eg* cyrc
cork block bloc corc *eg* blociau corc
cork bung topyn corc *eg* topynnau corc
cork oak derwen gorc *eb* derw corc
cork ring cylch corc *eg*
cork rubber rwber corc *eg* rwberi corc

cork slab tafell gorc *eb* tafelli corc
cork tile teilsen gorc *eb* teils corc
corky corcaidd *ans*
corm corm *eg* cormau
cormoid cormaidd *ans*
corn (=maize) corn *eg*
corn (wheat, oats etc) ŷd *eg*
corn cob tywysen corn *eb* tywysennau corn
Corn Hog Belt Ardal Corn a Moch *eb*
Corn Law Deddf Ŷd *eb* Deddfau Ŷd
corn oil olew corn *eg*
corn-beef cornbiff *eg*
cornea cornbilen *eg* cornbilennau
corneal cornbilennol *ans*
corner *n* cornel *eg/b* corneli
corner *v* cornelu *be*
corner arc arc y gornel *eb*
corner block bloc cornel *eg* blociau cornel
corner bridle joint uniad bagl cornel *eg* uniadau bagl cornel
corner flag lluman cornel *eg* llumanau cornel
corner halving haneru cornel *be*
corner halving joint uniad haneru cornel *eg* uniadau haneru cornel
corner hit ergyd gornel *eb* ergydion cornel
corner joint uniad cornel *eg* uniadau cornel
corner kick cic gornel *eb* ciciau cornel
corner tear darn craith rhwyg cornel *eb* creithiau rhwyg cornel
corner unit uned gornel *eb* unedau cornel
corneto cornet *eg* cornetau
cornett cornetto *eg* cornetti
cornetist canwr cornett *eg* canwyr cornett
cornflakes creision ŷd *ell*
cornflour blawd corn *eg*
cornflour mould mowld blawd corn *eg* mowldiau blawd corn
cornice cornis *eg* cornisiau
cornice (of ice, snow, rock) gordo *eg* gordoeau
cornice moulding mowldin cornis *eg* mowldinau cornis
Cornish pasty pastai Gernyw *eb* pasteiod Cernyw
cornopean cornopean *eg* cornopeanau
coro coro *eg* cori
corolla corola *eg* corolae
corollary canlyneb *eb* canlynebau
corona corona *eg* coronâu
coronary coronaidd *ans*
coronary artery rhydweli goronaidd *eb* rhydwelïau coronaidd
coronary heart disease clefyd coronaidd y galon *eg*
coronary thrombosis thrombosis coronaidd *eg*
coroner crwner *eg* crwneriaid
coroner's inquest cwest crwner *eg*
corporal corporal *eg* corporaliaid
corporal punishment cosb gorfforol *eb* cosbau corfforol
corporate corfforaethol *ans*
corporate act of worship cydaddoliad *eg*
corporate culture diwylliant corfforaethol *eg*
corporate identity hunaniaeth gorfforaethol *eb*
corporate image delwedd gorfforaethol *eb*
corporate state gwladwriaeth gorfforaethol *eb* gwladwriaethau corfforaethol
corporate worship cydaddoli *be*
corporation corfforaeth *eb* corfforaethau
Corporation Act Deddf Corfforaeth *eb*
corporation tax treth gorfforaeth *eb*
Corporations & Municipalities Act Deddf Trefi a Chorfforaethau *eb*
corpus corpws *eg*
corpus callosum corpws caloswm *eg*
corpus cavernosum corpws cafernoswm *eg*
corpus luteum corpws lwtewm *eg*
corpus spongiosum corpws spongioswm *eg*
corpus striatum corpws striatwm *eg*
corpuscle corffilyn *eg* corffilod
corral corlan *eb* corlannau
corrasion cyrathiad *eg*
correct *adj* cywir *ans*
correct *v* cywiro *be*
correct angle ongl gywir *eb* onglau cywir
correct position safle cywir *eg* safleoedd cywir
correct proportion cyfrannedd cywir *eg* cyfraneddau cywir
correct sequence trefn gywir *eb*
correction cywiriad *eg* cywiriadau
correction procedure trefn gywiro *eb* trefnau cywiro
correctional mechanism mecanwaith cywiro *eg* mecanweithiau cywiro
corrective reading darllen a chywiro
correlate *adj* cydberthynol *ans*
correlate *n* cydberthyniad *eg*
correlate *v* cydberthyn *be*
correlation cydberthyniad *eg* cydberthyniadau
correlation coefficient cyfernod cydberthyniad *eg* cyfernodau cydberthyniad
correlation matrix matrics cydberthyniad *eg* matricsau cydberthyniad
correlational research ymchwil cydberthynol *eg*
correspond cyfateb *be*
correspond by email ehebu *be*
correspondence (=letters) gohebiaeth *eb* gohebiaethau
correspondence (=similarity) cyfatebiaeth *eb* cyfatebiaethau
correspondence course cwrs drwy'r post *eg* cyrsiau drwy'r post
correspondence education addysg drwy'r post *eb*
corresponding cyfatebol *ans*
corresponding angles onglau cyfatebol *ell*
corresponding sides ochrau cyfatebol *ell*
corresponding society cymdeithas ohebu *eb* cymdeithasau gohebu
corridor coridor *eg* coridorau
corridor kitchen cegin hirgul *eb* ceginau hirgul

corrie peiran *eg* peirannau
corrode cyrydu *be*
corrosion cyrydiad *eg* cyrydiadau
corrosion inhibitor atalydd rhwd *eg* atalyddion rhwd
corrosion of iron cyrydu haearn *be*
corrosion resistant gwrthgyrydiad *ans*
corrosive cyrydol *ans*
corrugated rhychiog *ans*
corrugated card cerdyn rhychiog *eg* cardiau rhychiog
corrugated fastener hoelen rychiog *eb* hoelion rhychiog
corrugated fastener (wiggle nail) ffasnydd rhychiog *eg* ffasnyddion rhychiog
corrugated iron haearn rhychiog *eg*
corrugated paper papur rhychiog *eg* papurau rhychiog
corrupt llygru *be*
corrupt *adj* llwgr *ans*
Corrupt Practices Act Deddf Gweithrediadau Llwgr *eb*
corruption llygredd *eg*
corruption of electronic information llygru gwybodaeth electronig *be*
corset staes *eb* staesys
cortex cortecs *eg*
corticosterone corticosteron *eg*
corticotrophin corticotroffin *eg*
cosecant (cosec) cosecant *eg* cosecannau
cosech cosech *eg* cosechau
cosh cosh *eg* coshau
cosine (cos) cosin *eg* cosinau
cosmetics cosmetigau *ell*
cosmic cosmig *ans*
cosmological cosmolegol *ans*
cosmological argument dadl gosmolegol *eb*
cosmology cosmoleg *eb*
cosmopolitan amlgenhedlig *ans*
Cossack Cosac *eg* Cosaciaid
cost cost *eb* costau
cost analysis dadansoddiad costau *eg* dadansoddiadau costau
cost centre canolfan gost *eb* canolfannau cost
cost classification sheet taflen dosbarthu costau *eb* taflenni dosbarthu costau
cost effectiveness effeithiolrwydd cost *eg*
cost management rheoli costau *be*
cost of living index mynegai costau byw *eg*
cost plus pricing prisio cost plws *be*
cost price pris cost *eg*
cost push inflation chwyddiant cynnydd cost *eg*
costal asennol *ans*
cost-benefit analysis dadansoddiad cost a budd *eg* dadansoddiadau cost a budd
cost-effective cost effeithiol *ans*
costing costiad *eg* costiadau
costs line llinell y costau *eb*
costume gwisg *eb* gwisgoedd
cot crud *eg* crudiau
cot death marwolaeth yn y crud *eb* marwolaethau yn y crud
cotangent (cot) cotangiad *eg* cotangiadau
coterminal cyd-derfynol *ans*
coth coth *eg* cothau
co-tidal line llinell gyflanw *eb* llinellau cyflanw
cottage cheese caws colfran *eg*
cottage industry diwydiant cartref *eg* diwydiannau cartref
cottage loom gwŷdd bwthyn *eg* gwyddau bwthyn
► **cottage pie** pastai'r bwthyn *eb* pasteiod bwthyn
cottar cotywr *eg* cotywyr
cotter coter *eg* coteri
cotter pìn pin hollt *eg* pinnau hollt
cotton cotwm *eg*
cotton apron ffedog gotwm *eb* ffedogau cotwm
cotton ball pellen gotwm *eb* pellenni cotwm
cotton bandage rhwymyn cotwm *eg* rhwymynnau cotwm
cotton belt ardal gotwm *eb* ardaloedd cotwm
cotton linters linteri cotwm *ell*
cotton tape tâp cotwm *eg* tapiau cotwm
cotton thread edau gotwm *eb* edafedd cotwm
cotton twine cortyn cotwm *eg* cortynnau cotwm
cotton waste gwastraff cotwm *eg*
cotton wool gwlân cotwm *eg*
cottonbud ffon gotwm *eb* ffyn cotwm
cotyledon cotyledon *eb* cotyledonau
couch grass marchwellt *ell*
couching *n* pwyth gorwedd *eg* pwythau gorwedd
couching *v* cowtsio *be*
cough *n* peswch *eg*
cough *v* pesychu *be*
coulomb coulomb *eg* coulombau
coulombmeter coulombmedr *eg*
coulter cwlltwr *eg* cylltyrau
council cyngor *eg* cynghorau
council estate stad cyngor *eb* stadau cyngor
Council for Educational Technology Cyngor Addysg a Thechnoleg *eg*
council house estate stad dai cyngor *eb* stadau tai cyngor
Council of Blood Cyngor Gwaedlyd *eg*
Council of Regency Cyngor y Rhaglywiaeth *eg*
Council of the North Cyngor y Gogledd *eg*
council on tribunals cyngor ar dribiwnlysoedd *eg*
councillor cynghorydd *eg* cynghorwyr
counsel *v* cynghori *be*
Counsel Learned in the Law Cwnsler Dysgedig yn y Gyfraith *eg*
counselling service gwasanaeth cynghori *eg* gwasanaethau cynghori
counselling technique techneg gynghori *eb* technegau cynghori
counsellor cynghorwr *eg* cynghorwyr
counsellor training hyfforddi cynghorwyr *be*
count *n* cyfrif *eg* cyfrifon

count *v* cyfrif *be*
count out cyfrif allan *be*
Count Palatine Cownt Palatin *eg*
count rate cyfradd cyfrif *eb*
countability rhifadwyedd *eg*
countable rhifadwy *ans*
countably infinite yn rhifadwy anfeidraidd *adf*
counted thread stitch pwyth cyfrif edau *eg* pwythau cyfrif edau
counter (house) *n* masnachdy *eg* masnachdai
counter (in computing) *n* rhifydd *eg* rhifyddion
counter (in sport) *n* gwrthiad *eg* gwrthiadau
counter (in sport) *v* gwrthio *be*
counter enamel enamel cefndir *eg*
counter exposition gwrthddangosiad *eg* gwrthddangosiadau
counter revolution gwrthchwyldro *eg* gwrthchwyldroadau
counter riposte riposte gwrthol *eg* ripostes gwrthol
counter spit gwrthdafod *eg* gwrthdafodau
counter veneer gwrthargaen *eg* gwrthargaenau
counteract gwrthweithio *be*
counter-attack *n* gwrthymosodiad *eg* gwrthymosodiadau
counterbalance *v* gwrthbwyso *be*
counterbalance (ice snout) *n* gwrthgytbwys *eg* gwrthgytbwysau
counterbalanced gwrthgytbwys *ans*
counterbore gwrthdyllu *be*
counterbored hole twll gwrthfor *eg* tyllau gwrthfor
counterchange *n* gwrthgyfnewidiad *eg* gwrthgyfnewidiadau
counterchange *v* gwrthgyfnewid *be*
counterchange design cynllun gwrthgyfnewid *eg* cynlluniau gwrthgyfnewid
counterchange pattern patrwm gwrthgyfnewid *eg* patrymau gwrthgyfnewid
► **counter-current** gwrthgerrynt *eg* gwrthgerhyntau
counter-current flow llif gwrthgerrynt *eg*
counter-example gwrthenghraifft *eb* gwrthenghreifftiau
counterfactor gwrthffactor *eg* gwrthffactorau
counterflow gwrthlif *eg*
counterfoil bonyn *eg* bonion
countermelody cyfalaw *eb* cyfalawon
counterpart gwrthran *eb* gwrthrannau
counterpoint gwrthbwynt *eg* gwrthbwyntiau
counterproof gwrthbrawf *eg* gwrthbrofion
counter-reformation gwrthddiwygiad *eg*
Counter-Remonstrants Gwrth-Haerwyr *ell*
counter-revolutionary gwrthchwyldroadol *ans*
countershading gwrthliwio *be*
countersink *n* gwrthsoddydd *eg* gwrthsoddyddion
countersink *v* gwrthsoddi *be*
countersink bit ebill gwrthsoddi *eg* ebillion gwrthsoddi
countersink drill dril gwrthsoddi *eg* driliau gwrthsoddi
countersunk gwrthsodd *ans*
countersunk (machine screws) pengwrthsodd *ans*
countersunk head bolt bollt ben gwrthsodd *eb* bolltau pen gwrthsodd
countersunk head rivet rhybed pen gwrthsodd *eg* rhybedion pen gwrthsodd
countersunk hole twll gwrthsodd *eg* tyllau gwrthsodd
countersunk rivet rhybed gwrthsodd *eg* rhybedion gwrthsodd
countersunk screw sgriw wrthsodd *eb* sgriwiau gwrthsodd
countertenor uwchdenor *eg* uwchdenoriaid
countertransference trawsdrosglwyddiad *eg*
counter-urbanisation gwrthdrefoli *be*
counterweight gwrthbwysyn *eg* gwrthbwysynnau
countess iarlles *eb* iarllesau
counting song cân gyfrif *eb* caneuon cyfrif
country *adj* gwledig *ans*
country *n* gwlad *eb* gwledydd
country and western canu gwlad *eg*
Country Code, The Rheolau Cefn Gwlad *ell*
country dance dawns wledig *eb* dawnsiau gwledig
country house plasty yn y wlad *eg* plastai yn y wlad
country rock craig gysefin *eb* creigiau cysefin
country seat plas *eg* plasau
country town tref wledig *eb* trefi gwledig
countryside cefn gwlad *eg*
countryside area ardal wledig *eb* ardaloedd gwledig
countryside recreation adloniant cefn gwlad *eg*
county sir *eb* siroedd
county committee pwyllgor sirol *eg* pwyllgorau sirol
county community cymuned sirol *eb* cymunedau sirol
county councillor cynghorydd sir *eg* cynghorwyr sir
county court llys sirol *eg* llysoedd sirol
county court claim form ffurflen hawlio'r llys sirol *eb* ffurflenni hawlio'r llys sirol
county palatine iarllaeth balatin *eb* iarllaethau palatin
county record office archifdy'r sir *eg* archifdai'r siroedd
couple *n* cwpl *eg* cyplau
couple *v* cyplu *be*
couple family teulu cwpl *eg* teuluoedd cwpl
coupled cypledig *ans*
coupler cyplydd *eg* cyplyddion
coupler stop stop cyplu *eg* stopiau cyplu
couplet (in rondeau) cwpled *eg* cwpledi
coupling cyplydd *eg* cyplyddion
coupling flange fflans gyplydd *eb* fflansiau cyplydd
coupling of valves cyplysu falfiau *be*
coupon cwpon *eg* cwponau
Coupon Election Etholiad y Cwpon *eg*
courante courante *eg* courantes
courgettes courgettes *ell*
course cwrs *eg* cyrsiau

course team tîm y cwrs *eg*
courseware meddalwedd cyrsiau *eb*
coursework gwaith cwrs *eg*
court (in sport and historical) cwrt *eg* cyrtiau
court (modern legal) llys *eg* llysoedd
court and country llys a gwlad
court leet cwrt lit *eg*
Court of Admiralty Llys y Morlys *eg*
Court of Appeal Llys Apêl *eg*
Court of Arches Cwrt y Bwâu *eg*
Court of Chancery Cwrt Siawnsri *eg*
Court of Common Pleas Cwrt Pledion Cyffredin *eg*
court of competent jurisdiction llys ag awdurdod digonol *eg*
Court of Criminal Appeal Llys Apêl Troseddol *eg*
Court of Exchequer Cwrt y Siecr *eg*
Court of First Fruits and Tenths Cwrt Anodau a Degawdau *eg*
Court of General Surveyors Cwrt Archwilwyr Cyffredinol *eg*
Court of Great Sessions Llys y Sesiwn Fawr *eb*
Court of High Commission Cwrt yr Uchel Gomisiwn *eg*
Court of King's Bench Cwrt Mainc y Brenin *eg*
Court of Petty Sessions Llys Bach *eg*
court of protection llys gwarchod *eg*
Court of Quarter Sessions Llys Chwarter *eg*
Court of Requests Cwrt y Deisyfion *eg*
court of special jurisdiction llys awdurdod arbennig *eg*
Court of Star Chamber Llys Siambr y Seren *eg*
Court of Wards & Liveries Cwrt Gward a Lifrai *eg*
court poet bardd llys *eg* beirdd llys
court-baron cwrt barwn *eg*
courtelle courtelle *eg*
courtier gŵr llys *eg* gwŷr llys
Courts and Legal Services Act Deddf Llysoedd a Gwasanaethau Cyfreithiol *eb*
Courts of Assize Brawdlys *eg*
courtyard iard *eb* iardiau
covalency cofalens *eg* cofalensau
covalent cofalent *ans*
covalent bond bond cofalent *eg* bondiau cofalent
covariance cydamrywiad *eg* cydamrywiadau
covariate cyd-newidyn *eg* cyd-newidynnau
cove cildraeth *eg* cildraethau
covenant cyfamod *eg* cyfamodau
cover (a topic) *v* ymdrin â *be*
cover (in cricket) *v* cyfro *be*
cover (in general) *n* gorchudd *eg* gorchuddion
cover (in general) *v* gorchuddio *be*
cover (of book etc) *n* clawr *eg* cloriau
cover board bwrdd clawr *eg* byrddau clawr
cover crop cnwd gorchudd *eg* cnydau gorchudd
cover drive dreif gyfar *eb* dreifiau cyfar
cover note nodyn diogelu *eg*
cover paper papur clawr *eg*
cover point cyfar *eg*
coverage (in media) sylw *eg*
covered button botwm gorchudd *eg* botymau gorchudd
cover-land tir gorchudd *eg* tiroedd gorchudd
coverlet cwrlid *eg*
coversine cyfersin *eg* cyfersinau
coverslip arwydryn *eg* arwydrau
covert sensitization sensiteiddio cudd *be*
cow horn corn gwartheg *eg* cyrn gwartheg
cowbells clychau gwartheg *ell*
cowl cwfl *eg* cyflau
cowl collar coler cwfl *eg* coleri cwfl
cowl neck gwddf cwfl *eg*
Cowper's gland chwarren Cowper *eb*
cow's tongue stake bonyn tafod buwch *eg* bonion tafod buwch
cox *n* cocs *eg* cocsys
cox *v* cocsio *be*
coxed four pedwar a chocs
coxed pair pâr a chocs
coxless four pedwar *eg* pedwarau
coxless pair pâr *eg* parau
crab cranc *eg* crancod
crack *n* crac *eg* craciau
crack *v* cracio *be*
cracked enamel enamel cracellu *eg*
cracker cracydd *eg* cracyddion
crackle cracellu *be*
cradle *n* crud *eg* crudiau
cradle (in metalwork) *v* crudo *be*
cradle song hwiangerdd *eb* hwiangerddi
cradlecap crudgen *eg*
cradle V crud V *eg*
cradling crudiad *eg* crudiadau
cradling piece (hearth) darn crudiad *eg*
craft crefft *eb* crefftau
craft (boat) bad *eg* badau
Craft Design Technology (CDT) Crefft Dylunio a Thechnoleg
craft dye llifyn crefft *eg* llifynnau crefft
craft guild gild crefft *eg* gildiau crefft
craft knife cyllell grefft *eb* cyllyll crefft
craft paint paent crefft *eg*
craft process proses grefft *eb*
craft skill sgìl crefft *eg* sgiliau crefft
craftsman crefftwr *eg* crefftwyr
craftsmanship crefftwriaeth *eb*
craftworker crefftwr *eg* crefftwyr
crag clegyr *eg* clegyrau
crag and tail clegyr a chynffon
craggy clegyrog *ans*
cramp *n* cramp *eg* crampiau
cramp *v* crampio *be*
cramping action arwaith crampio *eg*
cramping blocks blociau crampio *ell*
crampon crampon *eg* cramponau
cranberries llugaeron *ell*

crane craen *eg* craeniau
cranial *adj* creuanol *ans*
cranial nerve nerf creuanol *eg* nerfau creuanol
cranium *n* creuan *eb* creuanau
crank cranc *eg* cranciau
crank pin crancbin *eg* crancbinnau
crank pivot crancgolyn *eg* crancgolynnau
crank spanner sbaner cranc *eg* sbaneri cranc
cranked cam *ans*
cranked centre hinge colfach canol camdro *eg* colfachau canol camdro
cranked handle dolen gamdro *eb* dolennau camdro
cranked palette knife cyllell balet gam *eb* cyllyll palet cam
crankshaft crancsiafft *eg* crancsiafftiau
crash cwymp *eg* cwympiadau
crash *n* chwalfa *eb* chwalfeydd
crash *v* chwalu *be*
crash course cwrs carlam *eg* cyrsiau carlam
crate cawell *eb* cewyll
crater crater *eg* craterau
crating *n* cawell *eg* cewyll
crating *v* cawellu *be*
craton tarian *eb* tariannau
craving chwant *eg*
crawfish cimwch coch *eg* cimychiaid coch
crawl (of baby) cropian *be*
crawl enamel enamel llusg *eg*
crawl enamelling enamlo llusg *be*
crawler ymlusgwr *eg* ymlusgwyr
crawling (glazing fault) ymlusgo *be*
crayfish (freshwater) cimwch yr afon *eg* cimychiaid yr afon
crayon creon *eg* creonau
crayon engraving ysgythriad creon *eg* ysgythriadau creon
crayon pencil pensil creon *eg* pensiliau creon
crazing cracellu *be*
C.R.C.A. sheet siten ddur meddal gloyw wedi'i rholio'n oer a'i hanelio'n oer *eb*
sitiau dur meddal gloyw wedi'u rholio'n oer a'u hanelio'n oer
cream *n* hufen *eg*
cream *v* hufennu *be*
cream cracker bisged gracer *eb* bisgedi cracer
cream horn corn hufen *eg* cyrn hufen
cream of tartar powdr tartar *eg*
cream slice tafell hufen *eb* tafelli hufen
creaming method dull hufennu *eg*
creamy hufennog *ans*
creamy consistency ansawdd hufennog *eg*
crease *n* crych *eg* crychau
crease *v* crychu *be*
crease (in cricket) *n* cris *eg* crisiau
crease recovery datgrychu *be*
crease-resistant gwrthgrych *ans*
creasing hammer morthwyl crychu *eg* morthwylion crychu
creasing stake bonyn crychu *eg* bonion crychu
creasing tool erfyn crychu *eg* offer crychu
create creu *be*
create autoabstract creu awtogrynodeb *be*
create back-up creu copi wrth gefn *be*
create characters creu cymeriadau *be*
create control creu rheolydd *be*
create datapilot table creu tabl databeilot *be*
create directory creu cyfeiriadur *be*
create document creu dogfen *be*
create extrusion object creu gwrthrych allwthiad *be*
create form creu ffurflen *be*
create from file creu o ffeil *be*
create group creu grŵp *be*
create link creu cyswllt *be*
create master document creu meistrddogfen *be*
create mode modd creu *eg*
create new folder creu ffolder newydd *be*
create new section creu adran newydd *be*
create new template creu templed newydd *be*
create primary key creu allwedd gynradd *be*
create rotation object creu gwrthrych troi *be*
create style creu arddull *be*
create summary creu crynodeb *be*
create table creu tabl *be*
create target directory creu cyfeiriadur targed *be*
create template creu templed *be*
create title page creu tudalen deitl *be*
creation creadigaeth *eb* creadigaethau
creation date dyddiad creu *eg* dyddiadau creu
creative creadigol *ans*
creative ability test prawf gallu creadigol *eg* profion gallu creadigol
creative approach agwedd greadigol *eb* agweddau creadigol
creative arts celfyddydau creadigol *ell*
creative craftwork crefftwaith creadigol *eg*
creative design cynllun creadigol *eg* cynlluniau creadigol
creative expression mynegiant creadigol *eg*
creative play chwarae creadigol *eg*
creative response ymateb creadigol *eg*
creative thinking meddwl creadigol *be*
creative work gwaith creadigol *eg*
creative writing ysgrifennu creadigol *be*
creativity creadigrwydd *eg*
creativity test prawf creadigrwydd *eg* profion creadigrwydd
creator creawdwr *eg* creawdwyr
crèche meithrinfa *eb* meithrinfeydd
credibility hygrededd *eg*
credit *n* credyd *eg* credydau
credit *v* cyfrif yn gredyd *be*
credit accumulation casglu credydau *be*
credit agreement cytundeb credyd *eg* cytundebau credyd
credit buying prynu ar gredyd *be*

credit card cerdyn credyd *eg* cardiau credyd
credit control rheolaeth credyd *eb*
credit control system system rheoli credyd *eb* systemau rheoli credyd
credit controller rheolwr credyd *eg* rheolwyr credyd
credit creation creu credyd *be*
credit exemption esgusodi rhag credyd *be*
credit note nodyn credyd *eg* nodion credyd
credit sale gwerthiant credyd *eg*
credit scheme cynllun credydau *eg* cynlluniau credydau
credit terms telerau credyd *ell*
credit transfer trosglwyddiad credyd *eg*
creditor credydwr *eg* credydwyr
credits (of names of people) clodrestr *eb*
creed credo *eg* credoau
creek (=inlet, bay) cilfach *eb* cilfachau
creek (in USA) nant *eb* nentydd
creel (spool rack) rhesel sbwliau *eb* rheseli sbwliau
creep (of soil) ymgripiad *eg*
creep feeding didol borthi *be*
creep feeding of lambs didol borthi ŵyn bach
creep feeding of suckling pigs didol borthi moch bach
cremation amlosgiad *eg* amlosgiadau
Creole (of language) iaith Creol *eb* ieithoedd Creol
Creole (of person) Creol *eg* Creoliaid
creosote oil olew creosot *eg*
crêpe (=pancake) crempog *eb* crempogau
crêpe (of paper) crêp *eg*
crêpe bandage rhwymyn crêp *eg* rhwymynnau crêp
crêpe de chine crêpe de chine *eg*
crêpe paper papur crêp *eg*
crepitation rhugliad *eg* rhugliadau
crescent cilgant *eg* cilgantau
crescent moon lleuad gilgant *eb*
crescentic cilgantaidd *ans*
cress berwr *eg*
crest (of bird) crib *eg/b* cribau
crest (of hill etc) brig *eg* brigau
crested chain stitch pwyth cadwyn cribog *eg* pwythau cadwyn cribog
cresting arwydd *eg/b* arwyddion
cretaceous cretasig *ans*
Crete Creta *eb*
cretinism cretinedd *eg*
crevasse crefas *eg* crefasau
crevice tool (vacuum tools) teclyn corneli *eg* taclau corneli
crewel needle nodwydd frodio *eb* nodwyddau brodio
cricket criced *eg*
cricket club clwb criced *eg* clybiau criced
cricket field maes criced *eg* meysydd criced
cricket shoe esgid griced *eb* esgidiau criced
cricketer cricedwr *eg* cricedwyr
cri-du-chat syndrome syndrom cri-du-chat *eg*
crime trosedd *eg/b* troseddau
crime scene analysis dadansoddiad safle trosedd *eg* dadansoddiadau safle trosedd
Crimean War Rhyfel y Crimea *eg*
criminal *adj* troseddol *ans*
criminal *n* troseddwr *eg* troseddwyr
Criminal Code Cod Troseddol *eg*
criminal consistency hypothesis damcaniaeth cysondeb troseddau *eb*
criminal justice cyfiawnder troseddol *eg*
criminal law cyfraith trosedd *eb*
Criminal Law Act Deddf Cyfraith Trosedd *eb*
Criminal Law Amendment Act Deddf Newid y Gyfraith Trosedd *eb*
criminal law and justice cyfraith troseddau a chyfiawnder
criminal psychology seicoleg troseddu *eb*
criminology troseddeg *eb*
crimp crimpio *be*
Crimplene Crimplene *eg*
crimson (enamelling colour) rhuddgoch *eg*
crimson lake llif rhuddgoch *eg*
crinkle crychu *be*
crinkled paper papur crych *eg*
crisis argyfwng *eg* argyfyngau
crisp claps clapio clir *be*
crispbread tafell gras *eb* tafelli cras
crisps creision tatws *ell*
criss-cross croesymgroes *eg*
crista crista *eg* cristâu
criteria instrument offeryn meini prawf *eg* offer meini prawf
criteria referencing cyfeirio at feini prawf *be*
criterion maen prawf *eg* meini prawf
criterion-referenced maen prawf gyfeiriol *ans*
criterion-referenced assessment asesiad maen prawf gyfeiriol *eg* asesiadau maen prawf gyfeiriol
criterion-referenced test prawf maen prawf gyfeiriol *eg* profion maen prawf gyfeiriol
criterion-referenced testing profi maen prawf gyfeiriol *be*
critic beirniad *eg* beirniaid
critic (=reviewer) adolygydd *eg* adolygwyr
critical (=decisive, crucial) allweddol *ans*
critical (in mathematics and physics) critigol *ans*
critical (of faculty) beirniadol *ans*
critical (of or at a crisis) argyfyngus *ans*
critical and contextual studies astudiaethau beirniadol a chyd-destunol *ell*
critical angle ongl critigol *eb*
critical autonomy annibyniaeth feirniadol *eb*
critical evaluation gwerthusiad beirniadol *eg*
critical incident digwyddiad critigol *eg* digwyddiadau critigol
critical learning period cyfnod dysgu allweddol *eg* cyfnodau dysgu allweddol
critical path analysis dadansoddiad llwybr critigol *eg*
critical path method (CPM) dull llwybr critigol *eg*

critical period cyfnod allweddol *eg* cyfnodau allweddol
critical point pwynt critigol *eg* pwyntiau critigol
critical range amrediad critigol *eg* amrediadau critigol
critical ratio cymhareb gritigol *eb* cymarebau critigol
critical region rhanbarth critigol *eg*
critical size maint critigol *eg*
critical temperature tymheredd critigol *eg* tymereddau critigol
critical thinker meddyliwr beirniadol *eg* meddylwyr beirniadol
criticism beirniadaeth *eb* beirniadaethau
crochet *n* gwaith crosio *eg*
crochet *v* crosio *be*
crochet hook bach crosio *eg* bachau crosio
crocheted lace les wedi'i grosio *eg*
crockery llestri *ell*
crocus saffrwm *eg*
crocus powder powdr crocws *eg*
croft crofft *eg* crofftau
crofter crofftwr *eg* crofftwyr
crofting system cyfundrefn grofftio *eb*
crook bagl *eb* baglau
crooked grain graen cam *eg*
crop *n* cnwd *eg* cnydau
crop (in photography) *v* tocio *be*
crop rotation cylchdro cnydau *eg* cylchdroeon cnydau
croquette croquette *eb* croquettes
crosier bagl *eb* baglau
cross *v* croesi *be*
cross (=act of crossing) *n* croesiad *eg* croesiadau
cross (in general) *n* croes *eb* croesau
cross banded plinth plinth bandin croes *eg* plinthiau bandin croes
cross banding bandin croes *eg* bandinau croes
cross beam trawst *eg* trawstiau
cross country traws gwlad *ans*
cross country event cystadleuaeth draws gwlad *eb* cystadlaethau traws gwlad
cross country race ras draws gwlad *eb* rasys traws gwlad
cross cut *n* trawstoriad *eg*
cross cut *v* trawstorri *be*
cross elasticity trawselastigedd
cross elasticity of demand trawselastigedd y galw *eg*
cross feed trawsborthiant *eg*
cross grain graen croes *eg*
cross halving haneru croes *be*
cross halving joint uniad croes haneru *eg* uniadau croes haneru
cross hey hai croes *eg*
cross infection traws-heintiad *eg* traws-heintiadau
cross kick cic groes *eb* ciciau croes
cross member trawsaelod *eg* trawsaelodau
cross multiply trawsluosi *be*
cross over trawsgroesiad *eg* trawsgroesiadau
cross peen wyneb croes *eg* wynebau croes
cross peen hammer morthwyl wyneb croes *eg* morthwylion wyneb croes
cross piece darn croes *eg* darnau croes
cross pollination trawsbeilliad *eg*
cross profile trawsbroffil *eg* trawsbroffilau
cross rail rheilen groes *eb* rheiliau croes
cross slide trawslithryn *eg* trawslithrynnau
cross stitch pwyth croes *eg* pwythau croes
cross stretcher estynnwr croes *eg* estynwyr croes
cross striated croesresog *ans*
cross the goal line croesi'r llinell gôl *be*
cross the line croesi'r llinell *be*
cross tongue tafod croes *eg* tafodau croes
cross wall croesfur *eg* croesfuriau
cross wires croeswifrau *ell*
cross-accent croesacen *eb* croesacenion
crossbar croesfar *eg* croesfarrau
cross-bedded trawshaenog *ans*
cross-bedding trawshaenu *be*
crossbow bwa croes *eg* bwâu croes
cross-breeding croesfridio *be*
cross-channel boat cwch sianel *eg* cychod sianel
cross-compiler traws-grynhoydd *eg* traws-grynoyddion
cross-contamination traws-halogiad *eg*
cross-cultural psychology seicoleg drawsddiwylliannol *eb*
cross-culture study astudiaeth drawsddiwylliannol *eb* astudiaethau trawsddiwylliannol
cross-curricular trawsgwricwlaidd *ans*
cross-curricular issue mater trawsgwricwlaidd *eg* materion trawsgwricwlaidd
cross-curricular theme thema drawsgwricwlaidd *eb* themâu trawsgwricwlaidd
cross-curricularity trawsgwricwledd *eg*
cross-cut chisel cŷn trawstor *eg* cynion trawstor; gaing drawstor *eb* geingiau trawstor
cross-cut darn craith trawstoriad *eb* creithiau trawstoriad
cross-cut saw trawslif *eb* trawslifiau
crossed cheque siec wedi'i chroesi *eb* sieciau wedi'u croesi
cross-fade croesbylu *be*
cross-fade attributes priodoleddau croesbylu *ell*
cross-fade effect effaith croesbylu *eb*
cross-fade from bottom croesbylu o'r gwaelod *be*
cross-fade from left croesbylu o'r chwith *be*
cross-fade from right croesbylu o'r dde *be*
cross-fade from top croesbylu o'r brig *be*
cross-feed lever lifer trawsborthiant *eg* liferi trawsborthiant
cross-filing croesffeilio *be*
cross-fertilization trawsffrwythloni *be*
cross-hair croeslin *eb* croeslinau
cross-hair cursor cyrchwr traws *eg* cyrchwyr traws

► **cross-hatching** croeslinellu *be*
crossing croesfan *eb* croesfannau
cross-lagged panel correlation cydberthyniad panel dros amser *eg*
► **cross-laterality** trawsochredd *eg*
cross-legged (sitting) coesgroes *ans*
cross-linguistic trawsieithyddol *ans*
cross-link trawsgysylltiad *eg*
cross-linkage trawsgyswllt *eg*
cross-linking trawsgysylltu *be*
cross-post trawsbostio *be*
cross-ratio cymhareb draws *eb* cymarebau traws
cross-rhythm trawsrythm *eg* trawsrythmau
cross-section trawstoriad *eg* trawstoriadau
cross-sectional study astudiaeth drawstoriadol *eb* astudiaethau trawstoriadol
cross-sequential design cynllun trawsddilynol *eg* cynlluniau trawsddilynol
cross-striated croesresog *ans*
crossway facing wynebyn croes *eg* wynebynnau croes
crossway fold plyg croesraen *eg* plygion croesraen
crossway strip stribed croesraen *eg* stribedi croesraen
crotales crotalau *ell*
crotch seam sêm fforch *eb* semau fforch
crotchet crosiet *eg* crosietau
crouch *v* cyrcydu *be*
crouch (position) *n* cwrcwd *eg*
crouch jump naid gwrcwd *eb* neidiau cwrcwd
crouched burial claddu cwrcwd *be*
► **crouch-running** rhedeg gwargam *be*
croute crwst *eg*
crouton crouton *eg* croutons
crowbar trosol *eg* trosolion
crowd (musical instrument) crwth *eg* crythau
crown (of the head) corun *eg* corunau
crown (worn by monarch) coron *eb* coronau
Crown Court Llys y Goron *eg*
crown fitting line llinell ffitio pen *eb*
crown glass gwydr crwm *eg*
crown guard gard uchaf *eg* gardiau uchaf
crown land tir y goron *eg* tiroedd y goron
crown of sleeve pen llawes *eg*
crown plate plât gwarchod *eg* platiau gwarchod
crown prosecution erlynydd y goron *eg*
Crown Prosecution Service Gwasanaeth Erlyn y Goron *eg*
crown rail rheilen warchod *eb*
crucible crwsibl *eg* crwsiblau
crucible furnace ffwrnais grwsibl *eb* ffwrneisi crwsibl
crucible steel dur crwsibl *eg*
crucible tongs gefel grwsibl *eb* gefeiliau crwsibl
crucifix croes *eb* croesau
crucifixion croeshoeliad *eg*
cruciform croesffurf *ans*
cruck nenfforch *eb* nenffyrch
cruck framed house tŷ ffrâm nenfforch *eg* tai ffrâm nenfforch
crucked nenffyrchog *ans*
crude (=natural or raw state) crai *ans*
crude (=not adjusted or corrected) amrwd *ans*
crude birth/death rate cyfradd geni/marw syml *eb*
crude oil olew crai *eg*
cruiser llong ryfel gyflym *eb* llongau rhyfel cyflym
crum horn crwmgorn *eg* crwmgyrn
crumb briwsionyn *eg* briwsion
crumble briwsioni *be*
crumble cap (fungus) cap inc clystyrog *eg*
crumbly briwsionllyd *ans*
crumpet cramwythen *eb* cramwyth
crumple crychu *be*
crumple zone cywasgran *eb* cywasgrannau
crunchy creisionllyd *ans*
crunode crwnod *eg* crwnodau
crusade croesgad *eb* croesgadau
crush malu'n fân *be*
crush injury anaf mathru *eg* anafiadau mathru
crushed enamel enamel mâl *eg*
crusher malwr *eg* malwyr
crust cramen *eb* cramennau
crustacean cramennog *eg* cramenogion
crustaceous cramennog *ans*
crustal cramennol *ans*
crustal plate plât cramennol *eg* platiau cramennol
crutch bagl *eb* baglau
Crutched Friar Brawd y Groes *eg* Brodyr y Groes
crwth crwth *eg* crythau
crwth player crythor *eg* crythorion
cryogenics cryogeneg *eb*
cryolite cryolit *eg*
cryopedology rhewbriddeg *eb*
cryophil cryoffil *eg*
cryophilic cryoffilig *ans*
cryoplanation rhew-wastadiant *eg*
cryoscopy cryosgopi *eg*
cryptic cryptig *ans*
cryptic coloration cêl-liwiad *eg*
cryptophyte cryptoffyt *eg* cryptoffytau
crypts of Lieberkuhn cryptau Lieberkuhn *ell*
crystabolite cristabolit *eg*
crystal grisial *eg* grisialau
crystalline grisialog *ans*
crystalline glaze gwydredd grisialog *eg*
crystalline lens lens grisialog *eg* lensiau grisialog
crystalline pigment pigment grisialog *eg*
crystalline structure ffurfiad grisialog *eg* ffurfiadau grisialog
crystallization grisialiad *eg* grisialiadau
crystallize grisialu *be*
crystallized fruit ffrwythau grisialog *ell*
crystallography grisialograffaeth *eb*
CTRL key bysell CTRL *eb* bysellau CTRL

cub cenau *eg* cenawon
cube *n* ciwb *eg* ciwbiau
cube *v* torri'n giwbiau *be*
cube root trydydd israddd *eg* trydydd israddau
cube roots of unity trydydd israddau un *ell*
cubic ciwbig *ans*
cubic close-packing pacio tyn ciwbig
cubic equation hafaliad ciwbig *eg* hafaliadau ciwbig
cubic metre metr ciwbig *eg* metrau ciwbig
cubical ciwbigol *ans*
cubism ciwbiaeth *eb*
Cubist Ciwbaidd *ans*
Cubist Ciwbydd *eg* Ciwbwyr
cubit cufydd *eg* cufyddau
cuboid ciwboid *eg* ciwboidau
cuboid epithelium epitheliwm ciwboid *eg*
cucumber ciwcymer *eg* ciwcymerau
cuddle anwesu *be*
cuddly toy tegan anwes *eg* teganau anwes
cue (pool, snooker) ciw *eg* ciwiau
cuff cyffen *eb* cyffiau
cufflink dolen lawes *eb* dolennau llawes
cultic myth myth cyltig *eg*
cultivate (land) trin *be*
cultivated crop cnwd trin *eg* cnydau trin
cultivation triniad *eg*
cultural diwylliannol *ans*
cultural aspect agwedd ddiwylliannol *eb* agweddau diwylliannol
cultural context cyd-destun diwylliannol *eg* cyd-destunau diwylliannol
cultural deprivation amddifadiad diwylliannol *eg*
cultural development datblygiad diwylliannol *eg*
cultural diversity amrywiaeth ddiwylliannol *eb*
cultural evolution esblygiad diwylliannol *eg*
cultural heritage etifeddiaeth ddiwylliannol *eb*
cultural imperialism imperialaeth ddiwylliannol *eb*
cultural landscape tirlun diwylliannol *eg*
cultural overlay troshaen ddiwylliannol *eb*
cultural psychology seicoleg ddiwylliannol *eb*
culturalization diwylliannu *be*
culturally disadvantaged dan anfantais ddiwylliannol
culture (=customs etc) *n* diwylliant *eg* diwylliannau
culture (bacteria etc) *v* meithrin *be*
culture (of bacteria etc) *n* meithriniad *eg* meithriniadau
culture cells celloedd meithrin *ell*
culture element elfen ddiwylliannol *eb* elfennau diwylliannol
culture medium cyfrwng meithrin *eg* cyfryngau meithrin
culture solution hydoddiant meithrin *eg* hydoddiannau meithrin
culture tissues meinweoedd meithrin *ell*
culture-bound syndrome syndrom diwylliannol-glwm *eg*
cultured (of person) diwylliedig *ans*
cummerbund cummerbund *eg*
cumulative cronnus *ans*
cumulative achievement record cofnod cyrhaeddiad cronnus *eg* cofnodion cyrhaeddiad cronnus
cumulative causation achosiaeth gronnus *eb*
cumulative distribution function ffwythiant dosraniad cronnus *eg*
cumulative frequency amlder cronnus *eg* amlderau cronnus
cumulative frequency curve cromlin amlder cronnus *eb* cromliniau amlder cronnus
cumulative frequency diagram diagram amlder cronnus *eg* diagramau amlder cronnus
cumulative frequency distribution dosraniad amlder cronnus *eg*
cumulative frequency graph graff amlder cronnus *eg* graffiau amlder cronnus
cumulative frequency polygon polygon amlder cronnus *eg* polygonau amlder cronnus
cumulative hey hai cynnydd *eg*
cumulative record cofnod cronnus *eg* cofnodion cronnus
cumulative recorder recordydd cynyddol *eg* recordwyr cynyddol
cumulative song cân gronnus *eb* caneuon cronnus
cumulative spelling sillafu cronnus *be*
cumulative total cyfanswm cronnus *eg* cyfansymiau cronnus
cumulonimbus cwmwlonimbws *eg*
cumulus cwmwlws *eg*
cuneiform cynffurf *ans*
cunning man dyn hysbys *eg* dynion hysbys
cup chuck crafanc gwpan *eb* crafangau cwpan
cup final gornest derfynol *eb* gornestau terfynol
cup handle dolen gwpan *eb* dolennau cwpan
cup shake hollt cwpan *eg* holltau cwpan
cupboard cwpwrdd *eg* cypyrddau
cupboard bolt bollt gwpwrdd *eb* bolltau cwpwrdd
cupboard lock clo cwpwrdd *eg* cloeon cwpwrdd
cupful cwpanaid *eg/b* cwpaneidiau
cupola cwpola *eg* cwpolau
cupola furnace ffwrnais gwpola *eb* ffwrneisi cwpola
cupping cwpanu *be*
cupro-nickel nicel coprog *eg*
cup-tie gornest gwpan *eb* gornestau cwpan
cupula cwpwla *eg*
curd ceuled *eg*
curdle cawsio *be*
curds and whey ceuled a maidd
cure *n* iachâd *eg*
cure (glue) *v* caledu *be*
cure (of a curate) *n* gofalaeth *eb* gofalaethau
curfew (bell) hwyrgloch *eb* hwyrglychau
Curia (papal) Llys y Pab *eg*
Curia Regis Roll Rhôl Llys y Brenin *eb*
curing (fish) cochi *be*
curing (leather) cyweirio *be*

curing (pork) halltu *be*
curium (Cm) curiwm *eg*
curl *n* cwrl *eg* cyrlau
curl *v* cyrlio *be*
curly brackets { } bachau cyrliog *ell*
currant cyrensen *eb* cyrens
currant bread bara brith *eg*
currency arian cyfred *eg*
currency symbol symbol arian *eg* symbolau arian
current *adj* cyfredol *ans*
current *n* cerrynt *eg* ceryntau
current account cyfrif cyfredol *eg* cyfrifon cyfredol
current assets asedau cyfredol *ell*
current balance (in physics) clorian gerrynt *eb* cloriannau cerrynt
current band corlan gyfredol *eb* corlannau cyfredol
current bedding llifhaenau *ell*
current database cronfa ddata gyfredol *eb* cronfeydd data cyfredol
current date dyddiad cyfredol *eg* dyddiadau cyfredol
current enquiry ymholiad cyfredol *eg* ymholiadau cyfredol
current font ffont cyfredol *eg* ffontiau cyfredol
current index mynegai cyfredol *eg* mynegeion cyfredol
current standard safon gyfredol *eg* safonau cyfredol
current liability rhwymedigaeth gyfredol *eb* rhwymedigaethau cyfredol
current library llyfrgell gyfredol *eb* llyfrgelloedd cyfredol
current money arian treigl *eg*
current nib pin cyfredol *eg* pinnau cyfredol
current operation gweithred gyfredol *eb* gweithredoedd cyfredol
current price pris cyfredol *eg* prisiau cyfredol
current rate cyfradd gyfredol *eb* cyfraddau cyfredol
current section adran gyfredol *eb* adrannau cyfredol
current setting gosodiad cyfredol *eg* gosodiadau cyfredol
▶ **current sprite** corlun cyfredol *eg* corluniau cyfredol
current variable newidyn cyfredol *eg* newidynnau cyfredol
current window ffenestr gyfredol *eb* ffenestri cyfredol
curricular cwricwlaidd *ans*
curricular experiences profiadau yn y cwricwlwm *ell*
curriculum cwricwlwm *eg* cwricwla
curriculum leader arweinydd cwricwlwm *eg* arweinwyr cwricwlwm
curriculum panel panel cwricwlwm *eg* panelau cwricwlwm
curriculum planning cynllunio'r cwricwlwm *be*
curriculum studies astudiaethau'r cwricwlwm *ell*
curriculum time amser y cwricwlwm *eg*
curriculum vitae curriculum vitae *eg*
curry cyri *eg*
cursive rhedol *ans*
cursive writing ysgrifennu sownd *be*
cursor cyrchwr *eg* cyrchwyr
cursor address cyfeiriad cyrchwr *eg*
cursor home position cartref y cyrchwr *eg*
cursor key bysell y cyrchwr *eb* bysellau'r cyrchwr
cursor position safle cyrchwr *eg*
curtain llen *eg/b* llenni
curtain ring dolen llenni *eb* dolennau llenni
curtain wall murlen *eg* murlenni
curtsy *n* cyrtsi *eg* cyrtsïau
curvature crymedd *eg* crymeddau
curve *v* crymu *be*
curve (=bend) *n* tro *eg* troeon
curve (=curved line) *n* cromlin *eb* cromliniau
curve of intersection cromlin groestoriad *eb* cromliniau croestoriad
curved (with feminine nouns) crom *ans*
curved (with masculine nouns) crwm *ans*
curved area arwynebedd crwm *eg* arwynebeddau crwm
curved bodkin botgin crwm *eg* botginau crwm
curved edge ymyl grom *eb* ymylon crwm
curved line llinell grom *eb* llinellau crwm
curved open seam sêm agored grom *eb* semau agored crwm
curved rail rheilen grom *eb* rheiliau crwm
curved scraper sgrafell grom *eb* sgrafelli crwm
curved snips snipiwr crwm *eg* snipwyr crwm
curved spit tafod crwm *eg* tafodau crwm
curved stretcher estynnwr crwm *eg* estynwyr crwm
curved surface arwyneb crwm *eg* arwynebau crwm
curved tinsnips snipiwr tun crwm *eg* snipwyr tun crwm
curvilinear cromlinog *ans*
curvilinear decoration addurn cromlinog *eg* addurniadau cromlinog
curvilinear trajectory taflwybr cromlinog *eg* taflwybrau cromlinog
cushion clustog *eb* clustogau
cushion cover gorchudd clustog *eg* gorchuddion clustogau
cusp cwsb *eg* cysbau
custard cwstard *eg*
custodian ceidwad *eg* ceidwaid
custom arfer *eg/b* arferion
custom house tollty *eg* tolltai
custom keyword allweddair addasu *eg* allweddeiriau addasu
custom of the manor arfer y faenor *eb*
custom style arddull wedi'i addasu *eg*
Customary Law Cyfraith Defod *eb*
customer cwsmer *eg* cwsmeriaid
customer feedback adborth cwsmeriaid *eg*
customer service gwasanaeth i gwsmeriaid *eg* gwasanaethau i gwsmeriaid
customer service skill sgil gwasanaeth i gwsmeriaid *eg* sgiliau gwasanaeth i gwsmeriaid
customize addasu *be*

customize buttons addasu'r botymau *be*
customize toolbars addasu'r barrau offer *be*
customs tollau *ell*
customs and excise tollau tramor a chartref *ell*
customs and excise officer swyddog tollau *eg* swyddogion tollau
customs duty tolldal *eg* tolldaliadau
cut *v* torri *be*
cut (=engraved block for printing) *n* torlun *eg* torluniau
cut (=wound) *n* archoll *eg* archollion
cut (in general) *n* toriad *eg* toriadau
cut and paste torri a gludo
cut and thrust trychu a gwanu
cut at cheek trychu at foch *be*
cut at chest trychu at fynwes *be*
cut at flank trychu at ystlys *be*
cut at head trychu at ben *be*
cut clasp nail hoelen lorio *eb* hoelion llorio
cut door-lock torglo drws *eg* torgloeon drysau
cut glassware llestri gwydr cerfiedig *ell*
cut nail torhoelen *eb* torhoelion
cut off *v* torri i ffwrdd *be*
cut on the thread torri ar yr edau *be*
cut out torri allan *be*
cut out on the bias torri ar y bias *be*
cut out on the cross torri ar y groes *be*
cut over trostorri *be*
cut paper papur wedi'i dorri *eg*
cut shoot cyffyn a dorrwyd o blanhigyn *eg* cyffion a dorrwyd o blanhigion
cut shot trawsergyd *eg/b* trawsergydion
cut stem coesyn a dorrwyd o blanhigyn *eg* coesynnau a dorrwyd o blanhigion
cut surface arwyneb y toriad *eg*
cut tack hoelen fer *eb* hoelion byr
cut through torri trwodd *be*
cutaneous croenol *ans*
cuticle cwtigl *eg* cwtiglau
cutlery cyllyll a ffyrc
cut-off *n* torbwynt *eg* torbwyntiau
cut-off bay cilfae *eg* cilfaeau
cuts gostyngiadau *ell*
cutter torrwr *eg* torwyr
cutter bar bar torri *eg* barrau torri
cutter block bloc torri *eg* blociau torri
cutting (in botany) toriad *eg* toriadau
cutting action arwaith torri *eg* arweithiau torri
cutting angle ongl dorri *eb* onglau torri
cutting blade llafn torri *eg* llafnau torri
cutting board bwrdd torri *eg* byrddau torri
cutting clearance cliriad torri *eg* cliriadau torri
cutting edge ymyl dorri *eb* ymylon torri
cutting fluid hylif torri *eg* hylifau torri
cutting gauge medrydd torri *eg* medryddion torri
cutting iron llafn torri *eg* llafnau torri
cutting knife cyllell dorri *eb* cyllyll torri
cutting line llinell dorri *eb* llinellau torri
cutting list rhestr dorri *eb* rhestri torri
cutting out paper papur torri allan *eg*
cutting plane plân torri *eg* planau torri
cutting plate plât torri *eg* platiau torri
cutting pliers gefelen dorri *eb* gefeiliau torri
cutting press gwasg dorri *eb* gweisg torri
cutting stroke strôc dorri *eb* strociau torri
cutting tools offer torri *ell*
cutting wire gwifren dorri *eb* gwifrau torri
cutting-out scissors (for fabric) siswrn torri defnydd *eg* sisyrnau torri defnydd
cuttlefish casting castio môr-gyllell *be*
cutwork torwaith *eg*
cwm (in Wales) cwm *eg* cymoedd
cyanate ion ïon cyanad *eg* ïonau cyanad
cyanide cyanid *eg*
cyanide ion ïon cyanid *eg* ïonau cyanid
cyanidin cyanidin *eg*
cyanogen cyanogen *eg*
cyanosis dulasedd *eg*
cybercafé caffi'r we *eg* caffis y we
cybernetic seibernetaidd *ans*
cybernetics seiberneteg *eb*
cyberspace seiberofod *eg*
cybersquatter seibersgwatiwr *eg* seibersgwatwyr
cyberzone seiberbarth *eg* seiberbarthau
cycle (in physics etc) cylchred *eg/b* cylchredau
cycle (of songs, poems) cylch *eg* cylchoedd
cycle of disadvantage cylch anfantais *eb*
cycle of erosion cylchred erydu *eb* cylchredau erydu
cycle of fifths cylch pumedau *eg* cylchoedd pumedau
cyclic (in biology) seiclig *ans*
cyclic (in chemistry, music) cylchol *ans*
cyclic AMP AMP cylchol *eg*
cyclic group grŵp cylchol *eg* grwpiau cylchol
cyclic mass offeren gylch *eb* offerennau cylch
cyclic quadrilateral pedrochr cylchol *eg* pedrochrau cylchol
cyclical cylchol *ans*
cyclical unemployment diweithdra cylchol *eg*
cycling cylchynu *be*
cyclohexadiene-1,4-dione cylchohecsadeuen-1,4-deuon *eg*
cyclohexane cylchohecsan *eg*
cyclohexanol cylchohecsanol *eg*
cycloid cylchoid *eg* cylchoidau
cycloidal curves cromliniau cylchoidol *ell*
cycloidal gear tooth dant gêr cylchoidol *eg* dannedd gêr cylchoidol
cyclomatic number rhif seiclomatig *eg* rhifau seiclomatig
cyclone seiclon *eg* seiclonau
cyclorama seiclorama *eg* seicloramau
cyclostome seiclostom *eg*
cyclosymmetry cylchgymesuredd *eg* cylchgymesureddau

cyclotherm cylchtherm *ans*
cyclothymic disorder anhwylder cylchthymig *eg*
► **cyclotron** cylchotron *eg* cylchotronau
cylchoalkane cylchoalcan *eg* cylchoalcanau
cylchoalkene cylchoalcen *eg* cylchoalcenau
cylinder silindr *eg* silindrau
cylinder (vacuum cleaner) sugnwr llwch silindr *eg* sugnwyr llwch silindr
cylindrical silindrog *ans*
cylindrical core craidd silindrog *eg* creiddiau silindrog
cylindrical cuffs cyffiau silindrog *ell*
cylindrical development datblygiad silindrog *eg* datblygiadau silindrog
cylindrical former ffurfydd silindrog *eg* ffurfyddion silindrog
cylindrical projection tafluniad silindrog *eg* tafluniadau silindrog
cylindroid silindroid *eg* silindroidau
cymatogenic symatogenig *ans*
cymbal symbal *eg* symbalau
Cymru Ar-lein Division Is-adran Cymru Ar-lein *eb*
Cyrillic alphabet gwyddor Gyrilig *eb*
cyst coden *eb* codennau
cysteine cystein *eg*
cystic cystig *ans*
cystic (medical) pledrennol *ans*
cystic fibrosis ffibrosis y bledren *eg*
cystine cystin *eg*
cystitis llid y bledren *eg*
cytokinesis cytocinesis *eg*
cytokinin cytocinin *eg* cytocininau
cytology cytoleg *eb*
cytoplasm cytoplasm *eg*
cytoskeleton cytosgerbwd *eg*
cytosol cytosol *eg*
cytosome cytosom *eg*
cytotoxic drug cyffur cytotocsig *eg* cyffuriau cytotocsig
Czech crisis argyfwng Tsiecoslofacia *eg*

D

D major D fwyaf *eb*
D minor D leiaf *eb*
dab *n* dab *eg* dabiau
dab *v* dabio *be*
dabbed resist gwrthydd dabio *eg* gwrthyddion dabio
Dada Dada *eg*
Dadaism Dadaiaeth *eb*
dado dado *eg*
dado joint uniad dado *eg* uniadau dado
dagger dagr *eg* dagerau
daily change newid beunyddiol *eg* newidiadau beunyddiol
daily cleaning glanhau dyddiol *be*
daily collective worship cydaddoliad dyddiol *eg*
daily living activities gweithgareddau byw bob dydd *ell*
daily office gwasanaeth beunyddiol *eg*
daily task tasg ddyddiol *eb* tasgau dyddiol
Dainty Davy dance Dawns Dafydd Gain *eb*
dairy llaethdy *eg* llaethdai
dairy farm fferm laeth *eb* ffermydd llaeth
dairy industry diwydiant llaethdy *eg*
dairy products cynnyrch llaeth *eg*
dais esgynlawr *eg* esgynloriau
daisy-wheel olwyn argraffu *eb* olwynion argraffu
daisy-wheel printer argraffydd olwyn *eb* argraffyddion olwyn
Dalai Lama Dalai Lama *eg*
Dalit Dalit *eg*
dam *n* argae *eg* argaeau
dam *v* cronni *be*
damage *n* difrod *eg*
damage *v* difrodi *be*
damage to the ozone layer difrod i'r haen oson *eg*
damages (=compensation) iawndal *eg*
damascene *n* damasgin *eg*
damascene *v* damasgu *be*
damask damasg *eg*
dame school ysgol hen ferch *eb* ysgolion hen ferched
dammed lake cronlyn *eg* cronlynnoedd
damp *adj* llaith *ans*
damp *n* lleithder *eg*
damp (a sound) *v* gwanychu *be*
damp storage storfa laith *eb* storfeydd llaith
damped (of sound) gwanychol *ans*
damped oscillation osgiliad gwanychol *eg* osgiliadau gwanychol
damped vibration dirgryniad gwanychol *eg* dirgryniadau gwanychol
dampen lleithio *be*
damper (=shock absorber) damper *eg* damperau
damping (of sound) gwanychiad *eg* gwanychiadau
dampness lleithder *eg*
damp-proof course (D.P.C.) cwrs gwrthleithder *eg*
damsons eirin duon *ell*
dana dana *eg*
dance *v* dawnsio *be*
dance (form or motion) *n* dawns *eb* dawnsiau
dance (occasion) *n* dawns *eb* dawnsfeydd
dance composition cyfansoddiad dawns *eg* cyfansoddiadau dawns
dance figure ffigur dawns *eg* ffigurau dawns
dance form ffurf dawns *eb* ffurfiau dawns
dance freely dawnsio'n rhydd *be*
dance movement symudiad dawns *eg* symudiadau dawns
dance on the spot dawnsio yn yr unfan *be*
dance routine dawnsdrefn *eb* dawnsdrefnau
dance-band band dawns *eg* bandiau dawns
dandruff cen ar y pen *eg*
Dane Daniad *eg* Daniaid
Danegeld Treth y Daniaid *eb*
Danelaw Rhanbarth y Daniaid *eg*
danger area (on playing field) llain waharddedig *eb* lleiniau gwaharddedig
dangerous play chwarae peryglus *eg*
dangling hongian yn rhydd *be*
Danish *adj* Danaidd *ans*
Danish (language) *n* Daneg *eb*
dariole mould mowld dariol *eg* mowldiau dariol
dark tywyll *ans*
dark adaption addasu i'r tywyllwch *be*
Dark Ages Oesoedd Tywyll *ell*
dark brown (enamelling colour) brown tywyll *eg*
dark colour lliw tywyll *eg*
dark figure ffigur tywyll *eg* ffigurau tywyll
dark green (enamelling colour) gwyrdd tywyll *eg*
dark purple (tempering colour) porffor tywyll *eg*
dark ruby (enamelling colour) rhuddliw tywyll *eg*
dark straw (tempering colour) melyn tywyll *eg*
dark tone (of colour) tôn tywyll *eg* tonau tywyll
darkness tywyllwch *eg*
darn *n* craith *eb* creithiau
darn *v* trwsio *be*
darning hoop cylch creithio *eg* cylchoedd creithio
darning needle nodwydd greithio *eb* nodwyddau creithio
dart *n* dart *eg* dartiau

dart *v* gwibio *be*
dart perforation twll dart *eg* tyllau dart
dart slash toriad dart *eg* toriadau dart
Darwin finch pinc Darwin *eg* pincod Darwin
Darwinism Darwiniaeth *eb*
dash (in computing) llinell doriad *eb* llinellau toriad
dashed line llinell doredig *eb* llinellau toredig
dashes and dots toriadau a dotiau
data data *ell*
data array arae data *eb* araeau data
data bank banc data *eg* banciau data
data capture cipio data *be*
data cartridge cetrisen data *eb* cetris data
data channel sianel ddata *eb* sianeli data
data collection (=group of data) casgliad data *eg* casgliadau data
data collection (act of) casglu data *be*
data communication cyfathrebiad data *eg* cyfathrebiadau data
data compression cywasgu data *be*
data controller rheolydd data *eg* rheolyddion data
data density dwysedd data *eg* dwyseddau data
data dictionary geiriadur data *eg* geiriaduron data
data encryption amgryptio data *be*
data entering cofnodi data *be*
data entering mewnbynnu data *be*
data entry cofnod data *eg* cofnodion data
data file ffeil ddata *eb* ffeiliau data
data flow diagram diagram llif data *eg* diagramau llif data
data format fformat data *eg* fformatau data
data independence annibyniaeth data *eb*
data item eitem o ddata *eb* eitemau o ddata
data logging logio data *be*
data manipulation language (DML) iaith trin data *eb*
data mining cloddio data *be*
data model model data *eg* modelau data
data portability cludadwyedd data *eg*
data preparation paratoi data *be*
data preparation operator gweithredwr paratoi data *eg* gweithredwyr paratoi data
data processing prosesu data *be*
data processing cycle cylchred prosesu data *eb* cylchredau prosesu data
data processing department adran brosesu data *eb* adrannau prosesu data
data processing manager goruchwyliwr prosesu data *eg* goruchwylwyr prosesu data
data processing supervisor goruchwyliwr prosesu data *eg* goruchwylwyr prosesu data
data projector taflunydd data *eg* taflunyddion data
data protection gwarchod data *be*
Data Protection Act Deddf Gwarchod Data *eb*
data protection commissioner comisiynydd gwarchod data *eg* comisiynwyr gwarchod data
data protection legislation deddfwriaeth gwarchod data *eb* deddfwriaethau gwarchod data
data range ystod data *eb* ystodau data
data representation cynrychioliad data *eg* cynrychioliadau data
data retrieval adalw data *be*
data set set ddata *eb* setiau data
data sheet dalen ddata *eb* dalennau data
data source ffynhonnell data *eb* ffynonellau data
data storage (act of) storio data *be*
data storage (of place) storfa ddata *eb* storfeydd data
data structure strwythur data *eg* strwythurau data
data traffic traffig data *eg*
data transfer trosglwyddo data *be*
data transfer rate cyfradd trosglwyddo data *eb* cyfraddau trosglwyddo data
data transmission (act of) trawsyrru data *be*
data transmission (countable event) trawsyriad data *eg* trawsyriadau data
data type math data *eg* mathau data
data validation (act of) dilysu data *be*
data validation (countable event) dilysiad data *eg* dilysiadau data
data verification gwireddu data *be*
database cronfa ddata *eb* cronfeydd data
database bar bar cronfa ddata *eg* barrau cronfa ddata
database column colofn cronfa ddata *eb* colofnau cronfa ddata
database content cynnwys cronfa ddata *eg*
database converter troswr cronfa ddata *eg* troswyr cronfa ddata
database field maes cronfa ddata *eg* meysydd cronfa ddata
database file ffeil cronfa ddata *eb* ffeiliau cronfa ddata
database front end pen blaen cronfa ddata *eg* pennau blaen cronfa ddata
database management rheolaeth cronfeydd data *eb*
database management system system rheoli cronfeydd data *eb*
database name enw cronfa ddata *eg* enwau cronfeydd data
database password cyfrinair cronfa ddata *eg* cyfrineiriau cronfeydd data
database query ymholiad cronfa ddata *eg* ymholiadau cronfa ddata
database table tabl cronfa ddata *eg* tablau cronfa ddata
data-handling package pecyn trin data *eg* pecynnau trin data
datapilot databeilot *eg* databeilotiaid
datapilot category categori databeilot *eg* categorïau databeilot
datapilot corner cornel databeilot *eb* corneli databeilot
datapilot field maes databeilot *eg* meysydd databeilot
datapilot pop-up menu naidlen databeilot *eb* naidlenni databeilot
datapilot result canlyniad databeilot *eg* canlyniadau databeilot
datapilot table tabl databeilot *eg* tablau databeilot

datapilot title teitl databeilot *eg* teitlau databeilot
datapilot value gwerth databeilot *eg* gwerthoedd databeilot
data-response task tasg ymateb i ddata *eb* tasgau ymateb i ddata
date (=type of fruit) datysen *eb* datys
date (on calendar) dyddiad *eg* dyddiadau
date and time dyddiad ac amser
date field maes dyddiad *eg* meysydd dyddiad
date format fformat dyddiad *eg* fformatau dyddiad
dated (=containing the date) dyddiedig *ans*
dated (=old-fashioned) wedi dyddio *ans*
datum datwm *eg* data
datum edge ymyl ddatwm *eb* ymylon datwm
datum face wyneb datwm *eg* wynebau datwm
datum line llinell ddatwm *eb* llinellau datwm
datum side ochr ddatwm *eb* ochrau datwm
daughter cell epilgell *eb* epilgelloedd
daughter centriole epilgentriol *eg* epilgentriolau
daughter house (of nunnery) cangen *eb* canghennau
daughter isotope epilisotop *eg* epilisotopau
daughter nucleus epilgnewyllyn *eg* epilgnewyll
daughter nuclide epilniwclid *eg*
▸ **daughter product** epilgynnyrch *eg* epilgynhyrchion
day (=period of 24 hours) diwrnod *eg* diwrnodau
day (with named days and as opposed to night) dydd *eg* dyddiau
day and night dydd a nos
day book dyddlyfr *eg* dyddlyfrau
day care gofal dydd *eg*
day centre canolfan ddydd *eb* canolfannau dydd
day hospital ysbyty dydd *eg* ysbytai dydd
day nursery meithrinfa ddydd *eb* meithrinfeydd dydd
Day of Atonement Dydd y Cymod *eg*
Day of Barricades Dydd y Baricedau *eg*
Day of Dupes Dydd y Twyllo *eg*
day of the March dydd Mers *eg*
day room ystafell ddydd *eb* ystafelloedd dydd
day shift shifft dydd *eg* shiftiau dydd
day visitor ymwelydd undydd *eg* ymwelwyr undydd
daylight golau dydd *eg*
daylight factor ffactor golau dydd *eb*
day-neutral dydd-niwtral *ans*
Days of Gladness Dyddiau Llawenydd *ell*
days of notification diwrnodau o rybudd *ell*
day-work gwaith dydd *eg*
D-Day landings glaniadau D-Day *ell*
de Moivre's theorem theorem de Moivre *eb*
deacon diacon *eg* diaconiaid
deaconess diacones *eb* diaconesau
dead ball pêl farw *eb*
dead ball line llinell gwsg *eb* llinellau cwsg
dead cell cell farw *eb* celloedd marw
dead centre canol llonydd *eg* canolau llonydd
dead heat ras gyfartal *eb* rasys cyfartal
dead knot cainc farw *eb* ceinciau marw
dead record cofnod marw *eg* cofnodion marw
dead shore ateg unionsyth *eb* ategion unionsyth
dead size union faint *eg*
dead smooth file ffeil orlefn *eb* ffeiliau gorlyfn
dead space (in windpipes) gwagle diddefnydd *eg*
dead wood pren marw *eg* prennau marw
deadbeat (of mechanism) curiad stond *eg* curiadau stond
deadline terfyn amser *eg* terfynau amser
deadlock (=impasse) sefyllfa ddiddatrys *eb* sefyllfaoedd diddatrys
deadlock (=type of lock) llwyrglo *eg* llwyrgloeon
deadweight tonnage tunelledd llwyth *eg*
deaf byddar *ans*
deaf child plentyn byddar *eg* plant byddar
deafness byddardod *eg*
de-airing datawyru *be*
deal *n* bargen *eb* bargeinion
deal *v* delio *be*
dealing with customers delio â chwsmeriaid *be*
deaminase dadaminas *eg*
deaminate dadamineiddio *be*
deamination dadamineiddiad *eg*
dean deon *eg* deoniaid
deanery deondy *eg* deondai
dearcuate delta delta bwaog *eg* deltâu bwaog
death marwolaeth *eb* marwolaethau
death certificate tystysgrif marwolaeth *eb* tystysgrifau marwolaeth
death duty toll farwolaeth *eb* tollau marwolaeth
death grant grant marwolaeth *eg* grantiau marwolaeth
death penalty cosb eithaf *eb*
death rate cyfradd marwolaethau *eb* cyfraddau marwolaethau
death warrant gwarant dienyddio *eb* gwarantau dienyddio
deathwatch beetle ticbryf *eg* ticbryfed
debasement (of coinage) llygriad *eg*
debate dadl *eb* dadleuon
debility llesgedd *eg*
debit *n* debyd *eg* debydau
▸ **debit** *v* debydu *be*
debit account cyfrif debyd *eg* cyfrifon debyd
debit interest llog ar ddebyd *eg*
deblocking dadflocio *be*
debouncing dadadlamu *be*
debridement digramennu *be*
debriefing adrodd yn ôl *be*
debris (=detritus) malurion *ell*
debris (=man-made rubble etc) rwbel *eg*
debt dyled *eb* dyledion
debt crisis argyfwng dyledion *eg*
debtor dyledwr *eg* dyledwyr
Debtor's Prison Carchar Dyledwyr *eg*
debug dadfygio *be*

debugger dadfygiwr *eg* dadfygwyr
debugging dadfygio *be*
début début *eg* débuts
decade degawd *eg/b* degawdau
decadence (in art etc) dirywiaeth *eb*
decagon decagon *eg* decagonau
decalcification datgalchiad *eg*
decalcify datgalchu *be*
decalescent point pwynt caledu *eg* pwyntiau caledu
decanedioic acid asid decandeuöig *eg*
decanedioyl dichloride decandeuoyl deuclorid *eg*
decani decani *eg*
decant ardywallt *be*
decarbonize datgarboneiddio *be*
decarboxylate datgarbocsyleiddio *be*
decay (in biology) *n* pydredd *eg*
decay (in biology) *v* pydru *be*
decay (in chemistry and radioactive) *n* dadfeiliad *eg* dadfeiliadau
decay (in chemistry and radioactive) *v* dadfeilio *eg*
decay chain cadwyn bydredd *eb*
decay constant cysonyn dadfeilio *eg*
decay series cyfres ddadfeiliad *eb*
decayed tooth dant wedi pydru *eg* dannedd wedi pydru
deceive twyllo *be*
decelerate arafu *be*
deceleration arafiad *eg* arafiadau
Decembrists' Revolt Gwrthryfel y Rhagfyrwyr *eg*
decentralization datganoliad *eg*
decentralize datganoli *be*
deception twyll *eg*
deceptive cadence diweddeb annisgwyl *eb* diweddebau annisgwyl
decibel desibel *eg* desibelau
decide penderfynu *be*
deciduous collddail *ans*
deciduous tooth dant cyntaf *eg* dannedd cyntaf
deciduous tree coeden gollddail *eb* coed collddail
deciduous woodland coetir collddail *eg* coetiroedd collddail
decile degradd *eg* degraddau
decile point pwynt degradd *eg* pwyntiau degradd
decilitre decilitr *eg* decilitrau
decimal *adj* degol *ans*
decimal *n* degolyn *eg* degolion
decimal coinage arian degol *ell*
decimal fraction ffracsiwn degol *eg* ffracsiynau degol
decimal notation nodiant degol *eg*
decimal place lle degol *eg* lleoedd degol
decimal point pwynt degol *eg* pwyntiau degol
decimal system system ddegol *eb* systemau degol
decimal tab tab degol *eg* tabiau degol
decimalize degoli *be*
decimation (=destruction) dinistrio *be*
decimation (=exaction of tithes) degymu *be*
decimetre decimetr *eg* decimetrau
decision penderfyniad *eg* penderfyniadau
decision box blwch penderfyniad *eg* blychau penderfyniad
decision making penderfynu *be*
decision making process proses benderfynu *eb* prosesau penderfynu
decision table tabl penderfyniad *eg* tablau penderfyniad
decision tree coeden benderfyniadau *eb*
deck dec *eg* deciau
declaim traethu *be*
declaration datganiad *eg* datganiadau
Declaration of Independence Datganiad Annibyniaeth *eg*
Declaration of Indulgence Datganiad Pardwn *eg*
Declaration of Rights Datganiad Iawnderau *eg*
declaration of war cyhoeddi rhyfel *be*
Declaratory Act Deddf Datganiad *eb*
declare datgan *be*
declare an interest cyhoeddi diddordeb *be*
declare the innings closed cau'r batiad *be*
declination gogwyddiad *eg* gogwyddiadau
decline (=decrease in price etc) gostyngiad *eg*
decline (=deterioration) dirywiad *eg*
declining industry diwydiant sy'n dirywio *eg* diwydiannau sy'n dirywio
declivity goriwaered *eg*
decode dadgodio *be*
decoder datgodiwr *eg* datgodwyr
decollator decoladydd *eg* decoladwyr
decolonize dad-drefedigaethu *be*
decolourize dadliwio *be*
decompile dadgrynhoi *be*
decompose dadelfennu *be*
decomposer dadelfennydd *eg* dadelfenyddion
decomposition dadelfeniad *eg* dadelfeniadau
decomposition method dull dadelfennu *eg*
decomposition of azomethane dadelfeniad asomethan *eg*
decompress datgywasgu *be*
decompression datgywasgiad *eg*
deconstruct dadadeiladu *be*
decontaminate dadlygru *be*
decontrol dadreoli *be*
décor décor *eg*
decorate addurno *be*
decorated addurnedig *ans*
decorating punch pwnsh addurno *eg* pynsiau addurno
decoration addurn *eg* addurniadau
decorative addurnol *ans*
decorative art celfyddyd addurnol *eb*
decorative chamfer siamffer addurnol *eg* siamffrau addurnol
decorative container cynhwysydd addurnol *eg* cynwysyddion addurnol
decorative details manylion addurnol *ell*

decorative finish gorffeniad addurnol *eg* gorffeniadau addurnol
decorative hem hem addurnol *eb* hemiau addurnol
decorative panel panel addurnol *eg* paneli addurnol
decorative process proses addurnol *eb* prosesau addurnol
decorative relief cerfwedd addurnol *eb* cerfweddau addurnol
decorative seam sêm addurnol *eb* semau addurnol
decorative stitch pwyth addurnol *eg* pwythau addurnol
decorative technique techneg addurnol *eb* technegau addurnol
decorative through dovetail joint uniad cynffonnog trwodd addurnol *eg* uniadau cynffonnog trwodd addurnol
decorative unit uned addurnol *eb* unedau addurnol
decorative veneer argaen addurnol *eg* argaenau addurnol
decouple dadgyplu *be*
decrease *n* lleihad *eg* lleihadau
decrease *v* lleihau *be*
decrease (in knitting) *v* gostwng pwythau *be*
decrease indent lleihau mewnoliad *be*
decrease spacing lleihau bylchu *be*
decrease through back of stitch cyfyngu drwy gefn y pwyth *be*
decreasing (in economics) gostyngol *ans*
decreasing (in general) lleihaol *ans*
decreasing cost cost ostyngol *eb* costau gostyngol
decree (=official order) *n* ordinhad *eg* ordinhadau
decree (=order) *v* ordeinio *be*
decree (in courts of law) *n* archddyfarniad *eg* archddyfarniadau
decree (in courts of law) *v* archddyfarnu *be*
decree absolute archddyfarniad absoliwt *eg*
decree nisi archddyfarniad amodol *eg*
decrement (=decrease) lleihad *eg* lleihadau
decrement (=ratio or amount lost) gostyngiad *eg* gostyngiadau
decrement (act of decreasing) gostwng *be*
decrepitate clindarddach *be*
decretal decretal *eg*
decryption dadgryptio *be*
decumbent gorweddol *ans*
decurion dengwriad *eg* dengwriaid
decurrent llorestynnol *ans*
decussate croesedig *ans*
dedendum circle cylch dedendwm *eg* cylchoedd dedendwm
dedicate (a book, music etc) cyflwyno *be*
dedicate (a church) cysegru *be*
dedicated computer cyfrifiadur un pwrpas *eg* cyfrifiaduron un pwrpas
dedicated line llinell wedi'i neilltuo *eb* llinellau wedi'u neilltuo
dedicated register cofrestr un pwrpas *eb* cofrestri un pwrpas
dedicated word processor prosesydd geiriau un pwrpas *eg* prosesyddion geiriau un pwrpas
dedication (of book, music etc) cyflwyniad *eg* cyflwyniadau
dedication (of church) cysegriad *eg* cysegriadau
deduce (technical usage) diddwytho *be*
deduce that (imperative) diddwythwch
deduct (in arithmetic) didynnu *be*
deduction (=infer, draw conclusions) tynnu casgliadau *be*
deduction (=inference, conclusion drawn) casgliad *eg* casgliadau
deduction (in arithmetic) didyniad *eg* didyniadau
deduction (of money) tynnu *be*
deduction (theory) diddwythiad *eg* diddwythiadau
deductive proof prawf diddwythol *eg*
deductive reasoning rhesymu diddwythol *be*
deed gweithred *eb* gweithredoedd
deed of partnership gweithred partneriaeth *eb*
deep dwfn *ans*
deep chrome yellow melyn crôm dwfn *eg*
deep dyslexia dyslecsia dwfn *eg*
deep end of the bath pen dwfn y baddon *eg*
deep fat frying ffrio dwfn *be*
deep freeze cabinet cwpwrdd rhew *eg* cypyrddau rhew
deep freeze chest rhewgist *eb* rhewgistiau
deep lemon yellow melyn lemwn dwfn *eg*
deep litter (for hens) gwasarn *eg*
deep mid wicket canolwr wiced bell *eg* canolwyr wiced bell
deep Naples yellow melyn dwfn Naploli *eg*
deep processing prosesu dwfn *be*
deep saw llif dwfn *be* llifio dwfn
deep sea fishing pysgota'r cefnfor *be*
Deep South (US) De Eithaf *eg*
deep square leg coeswr pell sgwâr *eg* coeswyr pell sgwâr
deep sunken wedi'i suddo'n ddwfn *ans* wedi'u suddo'n ddwfn
deep throat G cramp cramp G dyfnwddf *eg* crampiau G dyfnwddf
deepen dyfnhau *be*
defamation difenwad *eg*
default *adj* rhagosodedig *ans*
default *n* rhagosodiad *eg* rhagosodiadau
default *v* diofynnu *be*
default button botwm rhagosodedig *eg* botymau rhagosodedig
default colours lliwiau rhagosodedig *ell*
default control rheolaeth ragosodedig *eb*
default filter hidlydd rhagosodedig *eg* hidlyddion rhagosodedig
default font ffont rhagosodedig *eg* ffontiau rhagosodedig
default language iaith ragosodedig *eb* ieithoedd rhagosodedig
default orientation gogwydd rhagosodedig *eg*

default printer argraffydd rhagosodedig *eg* argraffyddion rhagosodedig
default protocol protocol rhagosodedig *eg* protocolau rhagosodedig
default response ymateb rhagosodedig *eg* ymatebion rhagosodedig
default setting rhagosodiad *eg* rhagosodiadau
default status statws rhagosodedig *eg*
default template templed rhagosodedig *eg* templedi rhagosodedig
default value gwerth rhagosodedig *eg* gwerthoedd rhagosodedig
defaulter methdalwr *eg* methdalwyr
defeat trechu *be*
defeatist *adj* gwangalon *ans*
defeatist (of person) *n* gwangalonnwr *eg* gwangalonwyr
defecate ymgarthu *be*
defecation ymgarthiad *eg*
defect *v* gwrthgilio *be*
defect (=imperfection) *n* diffyg *eg* diffygion
defect (physical) *n* nam *eg* namau
defective (=faulty) gwallus *ans*
defective (=imperfect) diffygiol *ans*
defector gwrthgiliwr *eg* gwrthgilwyr
defence (=fortifications) amddiffynfa *eb* amddiffynfeydd
defence (=justification in response to accusation) amddiffyniad *eg* amddiffyniadau
defence (in sport) amddiffyn *eg*
Defence Bonds Bondiau Amddiffyn *ell*
defence mechanism mecanwaith amddiffyn *eg* mecanweithiau amddiffyn
defend amddiffyn *be*
defend off the front leg amddiffyn oddi ar y droed flaen *be*
defend the goal amddiffyn y gôl *be*
defend the wicket amddiffyn y wiced *be*
defendant diffynnydd *eg* diffynyddion
defender (in soccer, rugby) cefnwr *eg* cefnwyr
Defender of the Faith Amddiffynnydd y Ffydd *eg*
defensible space gwagle amddiffynnol *eg*
defensive amddiffynnol *ans*
defensive bowling bowlio amddiffynnol *be*
defensive shot ergyd amddiffynnol *eb* ergydion amddiffynnol
defensive stroke ergyd amddiffynnol *eb* ergydion amddiffynnol
deference parch *eg*
deferred confluence cydlifiad gohiriedig *eg* cydlifiadau gohiriedig
deferred imitation oedi dynwared *be*
deferred imitation paradigm paradeim oedi dynwared *eg*
deferred payment tâl gohiriedig *eg* taliadau gohiriedig
deficiency (=lack, deficit) diffyg *eg* diffygion
deficiency characteristic nodwedd diffyg *eb*
deficiency disease clefyd diffyg *eg* clefydau diffyg
deficiency payment tâl diffyg *eg* taliadau diffyg
deficiency symptom symptom diffyg *eg* symptomau diffyg
deficient diffygiol *ans*
deficit diffyg *eg* diffygion
deficit model model diffyg *eg* modelau diffyg
defile (=narrow passage) *n* cyfyng *eg* cyfyngoedd
define diffinio *be*
define bibliography entry diffinio cofnod llyfryddiaeth *be*
define database range diffinio ystod cronfa ddata *be*
define label range diffinio ystod labeli *be*
define print range diffinio ystod argraffu *be*
define range diffinio ystod *be*
define range names diffinio ystod enwau *be*
define text attributes diffinio priodoleddau testun *be*
definite pendant *ans*
definite integral integryn pendant *eg* integrynnau pendant
definiteness pendantrwydd *eg*
definition diffiniad *eg* diffiniadau
deflagrating spoon llwy ffaglu *eb* llwyau ffaglu
deflate (a tyre etc) gollwng aer allan *be*
deflate (in economics) dadchwyddo *be*
deflate (in physics) dadchwythu *be*
deflated dadchwythedig *ans*
deflation (in economics) dadchwyddiant *eg*
deflation (in physics /geology) dadchwythiad *eg* dadchwythiadau
deflect (in physics) allwyro *be*
deflect the ball gwyro'r bêl *be*
deflecting allwyriadol *ans*
deflecting field maes allwyriadol *eg*
deflection allwyriad *eg* allwyriadau
deflocculate datglystyru *be*
deflocculation datglystyriad *eg*
defoaming diewynnu *be*
defoliate diddeilio *be*
deforestate datgoedwigo *be*
deform anffurfio *be*
deformation anffurfiad *eg* anffurfiadau
deformity anffurfiad *eg* anffurfiadau
defragment dad-ddarnio *be*
defraud twyllo *be*
defrost dadrewi *be*
defuzzification dadniwlo *be*
degassing dinwyo *be*
degassing plunger plymiwr dinwyo *eg* plymwyr dinwyo
degassing tablet tabled ddinwyo *eb* tabledi dinwyo
degeneracy dirywiad *eg* dirywiadau
degenerate *adj* dirywiedig *ans*
degenerate *v* dirywio *be*
degenerating dirywiol *ans*
degenerative disease clefyd dirywiol *eg* clefydau dirywiol
deglaciation dadrewlifiant *eg* dadrewlifiannau

deglutition llyncu *be*
degradation diraddiad *eg* diraddiadau
degrade diraddio *be*
degraded diraddedig *ans*
degreasant datseimydd *eg* datseimyddion
degrease datseimio *be*
degree gradd *eb* graddau
degree exercise cyfansoddiad gradd *eg* cyfansoddiadau gradd
degree of dissociation gradd ddaduno *eb*
degree of freedom gradd o ryddid *eb* graddau o ryddid
degree of pitch serthiant *eg*
degrees of freedom graddau rhyddid *ell*
degrees of the scale graddau'r raddfa *ell*
dehisce ymagor *be*
dehiscent ymagorol *ans*
dehorning digornio *be*
dehumanize dad-ddyneiddio *be*
dehydrate dadhydradu *be*
dehydrated dadhydredig *ans*
dehydration (of food) dadhydradiad *eg*
dehydration (of person) diffyg hylif *eg*
dehydration agent dadhydradydd *eg* dadhydradyddion
dehydrogenase dadhydrogenas *eg*
dehydrogenase activity gweithgaredd dadhydrogenas *eg*
dehydrogenate dadhydrogenu *be*
dehydrogenation dadhydrogeniad *eg*
deindividuation dadunigoleiddio *be*
deism dëistiaeth *eb*
delamination dadlaminadu *be*
delay *n* oediad *eg* oediadau
delay *v* oedi *be*
delay line llinell oedi *eb* llinellau oedi
delayed riposte riposte oediog *eg* ripostes oediog
delayed speech hwyr yn siarad *ans*
delayer (in order to simplify) dihaenu *be*
delegate *n* cynrychiolydd *eg* cynrychiolwyr
delegate *v* dirprwyo *be*
delegate the management of dirprwyo rheolaeth *be*
delegated budget cyllideb ddirprwyedig *eb* cyllidebau dirprwyedig
delegated expenditure gwariant dirprwyedig *eg*
delegated item eitem ddirprwyedig *eb* eitemau dirprwyedig
delegated legislation deddfwriaeth ddirprwyedig *eb*
delegated power pŵer dirprwyedig *eg* pwerau dirprwyedig
Delegates Court Llys Anfonogion *eg*
delegation dirprwyaeth *eb* dirprwyaethau
delegation of budgets dirprwyo cyllidebau *be*
delegation of requirements dirprwyo gofynion *be*
delete dileu *be*
delete all dileu popeth *be*
delete all files dileu pob ffeil *be*
delete autoformat dileu awtofformat *be*
delete bookmark dileu nod tudalen *be*
delete colour dileu lliw *be*
delete column dileu colofn *be*
delete column break dileu toriad colofn *be*
delete contents dileu cynnwys *be*
delete data dileu data *be*
delete data source dileu ffynhonnell data *be*
delete datapilot table dileu tabl databeilot *be*
delete directories dileu cyfeiriaduron *be*
delete drawing objects dileu gwrthrychau lluniadu *be*
delete entry dileu cofnod *be*
delete file dileu ffeil *be*
delete frame dileu ffrâm *be*
delete gradient dileu graddiant *be*
delete graphics dileu graffigau *be*
delete group dileu grŵp *be*
delete hatching dileu croeslinellu *be*
delete history dileu hanes *be*
delete icon dileu eicon *be*
delete image dileu delwedd *be*
delete index dileu mynegai *be*
delete join dileu uniad *be*
delete key dilëwr *eg* dilewyr
delete line end dileu diwedd llinell *be*
delete line style dileu arddull llinell *be*
delete local settings dileu gosodiadau lleol *be*
delete manual break dileu toriad llaw *be*
delete message dileu neges *be*
delete numbering dileu rhifo *be*
delete object dileu gwrthrych *be*
delete options dileu dewisiadau *be*
delete page dileu tudalen *be*
delete page breaks dileu toriadau tudalen *be*
delete record dileu cofnod *be*
delete row dileu rhes *eb*
delete row break dileu toriad rhes *be*
delete section dileu adran *be*
delete selected design dileu cynllun ddewiswyd *be*
delete sheet dileu dalen *be*
delete sheet window dileu ffenestr dalen *be*
delete slide dileu sleid *be*
delete snap line dileu llinell snap *be*
delete snap point dileu pwynt snap *be*
delete user dileu defnyddiwr *be*
deleted items folder ffolder eitemau wedi'u dileu *eb* ffolderi eitemau wedi'u dileu
deletion dilead *eg* dileadau
Delft ware crochenwaith Delft *eg*
delicate (=finely beautiful) cain *ans*
delicate (=frail) eiddil *ans*
delicate (fabric) main *ans*
delicate (of touch) ysgafn *ans*
delimit amffinio *be*
delimiter amffinydd *eg* amffinyddion
delinquency tramgwyddaeth *eb*
delinquent *adj* tramgwyddus *ans*

delinquent *n* tramgwyddwr *eg* tramgwyddwyr
delinquent behaviour ymddygiad tramgwyddus *eg*
deliquescence gwlybyredd *eg*
deliquescent gwlybyrol *ans*
delirium deliriwm *eg*
delivery (of a baby) genedigaeth *eb* genedigaethau
► **delivery date** dyddiad trosglwyddo *eg* dyddiadau trosglwyddo
delivery note nodyn trosglwyddo *eg*
delivery tube tiwb cludo *eg* tiwbiau cludo
delocalization dadleoliad *eg*
delocalize dadleoli *be*
delocalized dadleoledig *ans*
delta delta *eg* deltâu
delta activity gweithgarwch delta *eg*
deltaic deltaidd *ans*
deltoid ridge crib ddeltoid *eb* cribau deltoid
delurk dadlercian *be*
delusion rhithdyb *eb* rhithdybiau
delusions of control rhithdybiau rheolaeth *ell*
delusions of grandeur rhithdybiau mawredd *ell*
delusions of persecution rhithdybiau erledigaeth *ell*
delustre diloywi *be*
dem dem *eg* demau
demagnetize dadfagneteiddio *be*
demagogue demagog *eg* demagogiaid
demand *n* galw *eg* galwadau
demand (in economics) *v* galw *bedescant*
demand (in general) *v* hawlio *be*
demand characteristic nodwedd awgrymu ymateb *eb* nodweddion awgrymu ymateb
demand curve cromlin galw *eb* cromliniau galw
demand feeding bwydo ar alw *be*
demand pull inflation chwyddiant cynnydd galw *eg*
demanded quantity (in economics) maint y galw *eg*
dematerialize difateroli *be*
► **dementia** dementia *eg*
dementia of the Alzheimer type dementia math Alzheimer *eg*
demerit (of goods) dirinwedd *ans*
demerit goods nwyddau dirinwedd *ell*
demersal fishing pysgota'r gwaelod *be*
demesne demen *eg* demenau
demi semiquaver chwarter cwafer *eg* chwarteri cwafer
demi-cadence diweddeb amherffaith *eb* diweddebau amherffaith
demilitarize dadfilwrio *be*
► **demilitarized zone** ardal ddadfilwroledig *eb* ardaloedd dadfilwroledig
demise by will cymynaeth *eb* cymynaethau
demo software meddalwedd arddangos *eb*
democracy democratiaeth *eb*
democrat democrat *eg* democratiaid
democratic democrataidd *ans*
democratic leader arweinydd democrataidd *eg* arweinwyr democrataidd
Democratic Party Plaid Ddemocrataidd *eb*
demodulate dadfodiwliad *eg* dadfodiwliadau
demodulator dadfodylydd *eg* dadfodylyddion
demographic demograffig *ans*
demographic change newid demograffig *eg*
demographic characteristic nodwedd ddemograffig *eb* nodweddion demograffig
demographic revolution chwyldro demograffig *eg*
demographic structure strwythur demograffig *eg*
demographic transition trawsnewid demograffig *eg*
demographic trend tuedd ddemograffig *eb*
demographics demograffeg *eb*
demography demograffeg *eb*
demolish chwalu *be*
demolition order gorchymyn chwalu *eg* gorchmynion chwalu
demon cythraul *eg* cythreuliaid
demonstrate (=protest) gwrthdystio *be*
demonstrate (=show) arddangos *be*
demonstration (=protest) gwrthdystiad *eg* gwrthdystiadau
demonstration (=show) arddangosiad *eg* arddangosiadau
demonstration lesson gwers enghreifftiol *eb* gwersi enghreifftiol
demonstration program rhaglen arddangos *eb* rhaglenni arddangos
demutualization datgilyddu *be*
denary degaidd *ans*
denary number rhif degaidd *eg* rhifau degaidd
denationalize dadwladoli *be*
denaturation dadnatureiddiad *eg*
denature dadnatureiddio *be*
denatzification dadnatsieiddio *be*
dendrite dendrid *eg* dendridau
dendritic canghennog *ans*
dendrochronology dendrocronoleg *eb*
denervate dadnerfogi *be*
denial gwadu *be*
denier denier *eg*
denim denim *eg*
denitrification dadnitreiddiad *eg*
denitrify dadnitreiddio *be*
denitrifying bacteria bacteria dadnitreiddio *ell*
denizenship dinasyddiaeth *eb*
denomination (of religion) enwad *eg* enwadau
denominational religious education addysg grefyddol enwadol *eb*
denominational school ysgol enwadol *eb* ysgolion enwadol
denotation dynodiad *eg*
denote dynodi *be*
dense (of bush etc) trwchus *ans*
dense (of sound quality, in physics etc) dwys *ans*
dense growth tyfiant trwchus *eg* tyfiannau trwchus
density dwysedd *eg* dwyseddau

density gradient centrifugation allgyrchu graddiant dwysedd *be*
density independent factor ffactor dwysedd annibynnol *eg*
dent *n* tolc *eg* tolciau
dent *v* tolcio *be*
dentage (of heddle) dentiad *eg*
dental deintiol *ans*
dental brace ffrâm ddannedd *eb* fframiau dannedd
dental decay pydredd dannedd *eg*
dental floss edau ddeintiol *eb* edafedd deintiol
dental formula patrwm dannedd *eg*
dental plaque plac deintiol *eg*
denticle deintigl *eg* deintiglau
dentine dentin *eg*
denting dentio *be*
dentist deintydd *eg* deintyddion
dentistry deintyddiaeth *eb*
dentures dannedd gosod *ell*; dannedd dodi *ell*
denudation treuliant *eg*
denudation chronology cronoleg treuliant *eb*
deny gwadu *be*
deodorant diaroglydd *eg* diaroglyddion
deodorize diarogli *be*
deontological deontolegol *ans*
deoxygenated deocsigenedig *ans*
deoxyribonucleic acid asid deocsiriboniwcleig *eg*
deoxyribose deocsiribos *eg*
depart gadael *be*
department adran *eb* adrannau
Department for Education and Employment Adran Addysg a Chyflogaeth *eb*
Department of Trade and Industry Adran Diwydiant a Masnach *eb*
department store siop adrannol *eb* siopau adrannol
departmental adrannol *ans*
departure ymadawiad *eg* ymadawiadau
dependant dibynnydd *eg* dibynyddion
dependence (=being unable to do without) caethiwed *eb*
dependence (=reliance) dibyniaeth *eb*
dependency (in general) dibyniaeth *eb*
dependency (of country) tiriogaeth ddibynnol *eb* tiriogaethau dibynnol
dependent (=depending on) dibynnol *ans*
dependent behaviour ymddygiad dibynnol *eg*
dependent child plentyn dibynnol *eg* plant dibynnol
dependent population poblogaeth ddibynnol *eb* poblogaethau dibynnol
dependent variable newidyn dibynnol *eg* newidynnau dibynnol
depersonalization dadbersonoli *be*
depigmentation dadbigmentiad *eg*
depilate diflewio *be*
deplete (in biology) darwagio *be*
depleted (of uranium) diffygiol *ans*
depleted uranium wraniwm diffygiol *eg*
depleted uranium tip treiddiwr wraniwm diffygiol *eg*
depletion (in general) disbyddiad *eg* disbyddiadau
depletion layer haen ddisbydd *eb* haenau disbydd
deploy (troops) trefnu (milwyr) *be*
depolarization dadbolariad *eg* dadbolariadau
depolarize dadbolaru *be*
depolarizer dadbolarydd *eg* dadbolaryddion
depopulate diboblogi *be*
depopulated area ardal wedi'i diboblogi *eb* ardaloedd wedi'u diboblogi
depopulation diboblogaeth *eb*
deport alltudio *be*
deportation alltudiaeth *eb*
depose (=dethrone) diorseddu *be*
depose (other than king / queen) diswyddo *be*
deposit (=first payment) *n* blaendal *eg* blaendaliadau
deposit (=money given as pledge) *n* ernes *eb* ernesau
deposit (chemical, silt etc) *n* dyddodyn *eg* dyddodion
deposit (chemical, silt etc) *v* dyddodi *be*
deposit (of assets) *n* adnau *eg* adneuon
deposit account cyfrif cadw *eg* cyfrifon cadw
deposition (=dethronement) diorseddiad *eg* diorseddiadau
deposition (=sworn evidence) deponiad *eg* deponiadau
deposition (of official) diswyddiad *eg* diswyddiadau
deposition (of sediment) dyddodiad *eg* dyddodiadau
depositional dyddodol *ans*
depositor adneuwr *eg* adneuwyr
depreciate dibrisio *be*
depreciation (act of) dibrisiad *eg*
depreciation (of currency) dibrisiant *eg*
depress (=lower) gostwng *be*
depress (push down) gwasgu *be*
depressed area ardal ddirwasgedig *eb* ardaloedd dirwasgedig
▸ **depression** (=low spirits) iselder ysbryd *eg*
depression (=lowering) gostyngiad *eg* gostyngiadau
depression (in economics) dirwasgiad *eg* dirwasgiadau
depression (in land) pant *eg* pantiau
▸ **depression** (of weather) diwasgedd *eg* diwasgeddau
depression of freezing point gostyngiad *eg*
depressor gostyngydd *eg* gostyngwyr
depressor nerve nerf gostyngol *eg* nerfau gostyngol
deprivation amddifadedd *eg*
deprive (=depose clergyman from office) difydio *be*
deprive (in general) amddifadu *be*
deprived (of area) difreintiedig *ans*
deprived (of child) amddifadus *ans*
deprived area ardal ddifreintiedig *eb* ardaloedd difreintiedig
deprived child plentyn amddifadus *eg* plant amddifadus
depth dyfnder *eg* dyfnderau
depth charge ffrwydryn tanddwr *eg* ffrwydrynnau tanddwr

depth dimension dimensiwn dyfnder *eg*
depth gauge medrydd dyfnder *eg* medryddion dyfnder
depth line llinell ddyfnder *eb* llinellau dyfnder
depth of field dyfnder ffocws *eg*
depth perception canfyddiad o ddyfnder *eg*
depth stop stop dyfnder *eg* stopiau dyfnder
deputation dirprwyaeth *eb* dirprwyaethau
deputy dirprwy *eg* dirprwyon
deputy head (of school) dirprwy bennaeth *eg* dirprwy benaethiaid
deputy headmistress dirprwy brifathrawes *eb* dirprwy brifathrawesau
deputy lieutenant dirprwy raglaw *eg* dirprwy raglawiaid
▸ **deregulate** dadreoleiddio *be*
derelict diffaith *ans*
dereliction diffeithdra *eg*
dereliction order gorchymyn dirywiad llwyr *eg*
derivation deilliant *eg* deilliannau
derivative *adj* deilliadol *ans*
derivative *n* deilliad *eg* deilliadau
derivative art celfyddyd ddeilliadol *eb*
derive deillio *be*
derive an expression deillio mynegiad *be*
derived deilliadol *ans*
derived function ffwythiant deilliadol *eg* ffwythiannau deilliadol
derived scale graddfa ddeilliadol *eb* graddfeydd deilliadol
dermal croenol *ans*
dermal plexus plethwaith (plecsws) dermaidd *eg*
dermatitis dermatitis *eg*
dermatologist dermatolegydd *eg* dermatolegwyr
dermatology dermatoleg *eb*
derrick deric *eg* dericiau
desalination dihalwyno *be*
descale digennu *be*
descant desgant *eg* desgantau
descant recorder recorder desgant *eg* recorderau desgant
descant viol feiol ddesgant *eb* feiolau desgant
descend disgyn *be*
descendant disgynnydd *eg* disgynyddion
descending disgynnol *ans*
descending colon colon disgynnol *eg*
descending order trefn ddisgynnol *eb*
descending scale graddfa ddisgyn *eb* graddfeydd disgyn
descending sort trefniad disgynnol *eg* trefniadau disgynnol
descent disgyniad *eg*
describe disgrifio *be*
description disgrifiad *eg* disgrifiadau
description of type disgrifiad o fath *eg*
descriptive disgrifiadol *ans*
descriptive language iaith ddisgrifiadol *eb*
descriptive music cerddoriaeth ddisgrifiadol *eb*
descriptive observation arsylwi disgrifiadol *be*
descriptive statistics ystadegau disgrifiadol *ell*
descriptor disgrifydd *eg* disgfrifwyr
desegregation dadwahanu *be*
deselect dad-ddewis *be*
desert diffeithdir *eg* diffeithdiroedd
desert place diffeithle *eg* diffeithleoedd
desert varnish farnais y diffeithdir *eg*
deserted village pentref anghyfannedd *eg* pentrefi anghyfannedd
deserter enciliwr *eg* encilwyr
desertification diffeithdiro *be*
desiccate (non-technical usage) sychu *be*
desiccate (technical usage) dysychu *be*
desiccated dysychedig *ans*
desiccated coconut coconyt mân *eg*
desiccation dysychiad *eg*
desiccator sychiadur *eg* sychiaduron
design (=draw a plan) *v* dylunio *be*
design (=plan) *n* cynllun *eg* cynlluniau
design (=plan) *v* cynllunio *be*
design (=sketch or plan drawn) *n* dyluniad *eg* dyluniadau
design a system cynllunio system *be*
design and technology dylunio a thechnoleg
design brief briff dylunio *eg* briffiau dylunio
design criteria meini prawf dylunio *ell*
design development datblygiad cynllun *eg* datblygiadau cynllun
design evaluation gwerthuso cynllun *be*
design folio ffolio dylunio *eg* ffolios dylunio
design framework fframwaith dylunio *eg*
design label label cynllun *eg* labeli cynllun
design loop dolen ddylunio *eb* dolennau dylunio
design of a batik dyluniad batik *eg* dyluniadau batik
design process proses ddylunio *eb* prosesau dylunio
design refinements gorffeniadau yn y cynllun *ell*
design thinking ystyried dylunio *be*
design view golwg dylunio *eg*
designate *adj* darpar *ans*
designate *v* dynodi *be*
designated dynodedig *ans*
designated area maes dynodedig *eg* meysydd dynodedig
designated school ysgol ddynodedig *eb* ysgolion dynodedig
designer dylunydd *eg* dylunyddion
designing of programme cynllunio rhaglen *be*
desk desg *eb* desgiau
desk check gwiriad desg *eg* gwiriadau desg
desktop bwrdd gwaith *eg* byrddau gwaith
desktop case cas bwrdd gwaith *eg* casys bwrdd gwaith
desktop environment amgylchedd bwrdd gwaith *eg* amgylcheddau bwrdd gwaith
desktop integration integreiddio bwrdd gwaith *be*
desktop machine peiriant bwrdd gwaith *eg* peiriannau bwrdd gwaith

desktop publishing cyhoeddi bwrdd gwaith *be*
desktop publishing software meddalwedd cyhoeddi bwrdd gwaith *eb*
desloughing dadgennu *be*
desmomome desmomom *eg* desmomomau
desolate diffaith *ans*
despot unben *eg* unbeniaid
despotism unbennaeth *eb*
dessert pwdin *eg* pwdinau
dessert apple afal bwyta *eg* afalau bwyta
dessertspoon llwy bwdin *eb* llwyau pwdin
dessertspoonful llond llwy bwdin *eg* llond llwyau pwdin
de-Stalinization dadstalineiddio *be*
destarch dadstartsio *be*
destination cyrchfan *eg/b* cyrchfannau
destination disk cyrchddisg *eg* cyrchddisgiau
destination feature nodwedd cyrchfan *eb* nodweddion cyrchfan
destination file ffeil gyrchfan *eb* ffeiliau cyrchfan
destination folder ffolder cyrchfan *eb* ffolderi cyrchfan
destroy dinistrio *be*
destroyer (ship) llong ryfel fechan *eb* llongau rhyfel bychain
destructive distrywiol *ans*
destructive interference ymyriant distrywiol *eg*
destructive readout allddarlleniad distrywiol *eg* allddarlleniadau distrywiol
detach datgysylltu *be*
detachable datgysylltiol *ans*
detachable collar coler rhydd *eg* coleri rhydd
detached datgysylltiedig *ans*
detached chain stitch pwyth cadwyn unigol *eg* pwythau cadwyn unigol
detached house tŷ sengl *eg* tai sengl
detail *n* manylyn *eg* manylion
detail *v* manylu *be*
detail drawing lluniad manylion *eg* lluniadau manylion
detail paper papur manylion *eg*
detail scenery set fanwl *eb* setiau manwl
detailed manwl *ans*
detailed drawing lluniad manwl *eg* lluniadau manwl
details manylion *ell*
detect canfod *be*
detector canfodydd *eg* canfodyddion
detector valve falf ganfod *eb* falfiau canfod
detention centre canolfan gadw *eb* canolfannau cadw
detergency glanedwaith *eg*
detergent glanedydd *eg* glanedyddion
deteriorate dirywio *be*
deterioration dirywiad *eg* dirywiadau
determinant (in immunology) penderfynyn *eg* penderfynynnau
determinant (in mathematics) determinant *eg* determinannau
determinate penderfynedig *ans*
determinate key cywair penodol *eg* cyweiriau penodol
determination (of size) mesuriad *eg* mesuriadau
determine darganfod *be*
determine (in economics) pennu *be*
determine (movement) penderfynu *be*
determined coefficient cyfernod pendant *eg* cyfernodau pendant
determinism penderfyniaeth *eb*
determinist *adj* penderfyniadol *ans*
determinist *n* penderfyniedydd *eg* penderfyniedwyr
deterministic penderfynedig *ans*
deterrent *adj* ataliol *ans*
deterrent *n* arf ataliol *eg* arfau ataliol
detour dargyfeiriad *eb* dargyfeiriadau
detour index mynegrif dargyfeirio *eg* mynegrifau dargyfeirio
detoxicate dadwenwyno *be*
detoxication dadwenwyniad *eg*
detritivore detritysydd *eg* detritysyddion
detritus (=debris) malurion *ell*
detritus (in biology) detritws *eg*
deuce diws *eg*
deuteranopia diwteranopia *eg*
deuteron diwteron *eg* diwteronau
devaluation dibrisiad *eg* dibrisiadau
devaluation of the pound dibrisio'r bunt *be*
devastating dinistriol *ans*
develop datblygu *be*
develop control meithrin rheolaeth *be*
develop hypotheses datblygu rhagdybiaethau *be*
develop knowledge datblygu gwybodaeth *be*
develop performance datblygu perfformiad *be*
develop rule datblygu rheol *be*
develop skills meithrin sgiliau *be*
developed country gwlad ddatblygedig *eb* gwledydd datblygedig
developing country gwlad sy'n datblygu *eb* gwledydd sy'n datblygu
developing embryo embryo datblygol *eg* embryonau datblygol
development datblygiad *eg* datblygiadau
development agency asiantaeth ddatblygu *eb* asiantaethau datblygu
development area ardal ddatblygu *eb* ardaloedd datblygu
development chart siart datblygiad *eg* siartiau datblygiad
development company cwmni datblygu *eg* cwmnïau datblygu
development grant grant datblygu *eg* grantiau datblygu
development land tax treth tir datblygu *eb* trethi tir datblygu
development process proses ddatblygu *eb* prosesau datblygu
development site safle datblygu *eg* safleoedd datblygu

development sketch braslun datblygiad *eg* brasluniau datblygiad
developmental datblygiadol *ans*
developmental age oed datblygiad *eg*
developmental curriculum cwricwlwm datblygiadol *eg*
► **developmental delay** oediad datblygiad *be*
developmental dyslexia dyslecsia datblygiad *eg*
developmental guidance arweiniad ar ddatblygiad *eg*
developmental maturity aeddfedrwydd datblygiad *eg*
developmental process proses ddatblygiadol *eb* prosesau datblygiadol
developmental psychology seicoleg datblygiad *eb*
developmental quotient cyniferydd datblygiad *eg*
developmental reading darllen datblygiadol *eg*
developmental stage cam datblygiadol *eg* camau datblygiadol
developmental subquotient isgyniferydd datblygiad *eg*
developmentally appropriate addas o ran datblygiad *ans*
deviance amplification ymhelaethiad o wyriant *eg*
deviant gwyrdröedig *ans*
deviant behaviour ymddygiad gwyrdröedig *eg*
deviant-case analysis dadansoddi achos-gwyredig *be*
deviate gwyro *be*
deviation gwyriad *eg* gwyriadau
deviation IQ IQ gwyriad *eg*
device dyfais *eb* dyfeisiau
device driver gyriant dyfais *eg* gyriannau dyfais
devilled poeth *ans*
devise dyfeisio *be*
devitrification diwydriad *eg*
devolution datganoli *be*
devoted ymroddedig *ans*
devotion ymroddiad *eg* ymroddiadau
dew gwlith *eg* gwlithoedd
dew point gwlithbwynt *eg* gwlithbwyntiau
de-waxing digwyro *be*
Dewey Decimal System System Ddegol Dewey *eb*
dewpond gwlithbwll *eg* gwlithbyllau
dexterity deheurwydd *eg*
dextrose decstros *eg*
(+)-(D)-glucose (+)-(D)-glwcos *eg*
dhamma (=dharma) dhamma *eg*
dharma (=dhamma) dharma *eg*
Dhootie cloth brethyn Dhootie *eg*
diabase diabas *eg* diabasau
► **diabetes** diabetes *eg*
diabetic *adj* diabetig *ans*
diabetic child plentyn diabetig *eg* plant diabetig
diaeresis didolnod *eg* didolnodau
diagnose gwneud diagnosis *be*
diagnosis diagnosis *eg* diagnosau
diagnosis related groups grwpiau diagnosis perthynol *ell*
diagnostic diagnostig *ans*
Diagnostic and Statistical Manual Llawlyfr DSM *eg*
diagnostic assessment asesiad diagnostig *eg* asesiadau diagnostig
diagnostic program rhaglen ddiagnostig *eb* rhaglenni diagnostig
diagnostic routine rheolwaith diagnostig *eg* rheolweithiau diagnostig
diagnostic test prawf diagnostig *eg* profion diagnostig
diagnostic testing profi diagnostig *be*
diagnostics diagnosteg *eb*
diagonal *n* croeslin *eg* croesliniau
diagonal (=from one corner to another) *adj* croesgornel *ans*
diagonal (=slanted) *adj* lletraws *ans*
diagonal (on a straight sided figure) *adj* croeslinol *ans*
diagonal bracing cleddu croeslinol *be*
diagonal cutting pliers gefelen dorri croeslin *eb* gefeiliau torri croeslin
diagonal dominance trechedd croeslinol *eg*
diagonal hip pocket poced glun letraws *eb* pocedi clun lletraws
diagonal kick cic letraws *eb* ciciau lletraws
diagonal pass pàs letraws *eb* pasiau lletraws
diagonal rail rheilen groeslinol *eb* rheiliau croeslinol
diagonal scale graddfa groeslinol *eb* graddfeydd croeslinol
diagonal stretcher estynnwr croeslinol *eg* estynwyr croeslinol
diagonal stripe rhes groeslinol *eb* rhesi croeslinol
diagonal stroke (lettering) strôc groeslinol *eg* strociau croeslinol
diagonal test prawf croeslinol *eg* profion croeslinol
diagonal testing profi croeslinol *be*
diagonal wedging lletemu croeslinol *be*
diagonal-cutting nipper niper torri croeslinol *eg* niperi torri croeslinol
diagonally (=to opposite corner) yn groesgornel *adf*
diagonally (in general) yn groeslinol *adf*
diagram diagram *eg* diagramau
diagrammatic approach dull diagramatig *eg* dulliau diagramatig
diagrammatic notation nodiant arluniol *eg*
diagrammatic representation cynrychioliad diagramatig *eg* cynrychioliadau diagramatig
diagrammatic technique techneg ddiagramatig *eb*
diakinesis diacinesis *eg*
dial deial *eg* deialau
dial gauge medrydd deial *eg* medryddion deial
dial test indicator (D.T.I.) prawf-ddangosydd deial *eg* prawf-ddangosyddion deial
dialect tafodiaith *eb* tafodieithoedd
dialectal tafodieithol *ans*
dialectic dilechdid *eg*

dialectical materialism materoliaeth ddilechdidol *eb*
dialer deialwr *eg* deialwyr
dialog deialog *eb* deialogau
dialog box blwch deialog *eg* blychau deialog
dialog centre canolfan ddeialog *eb* canolfannau deialog
dialogue deialog *eb* deialogau
dial-up account cyfrif deialu *eg* cyfrifon deialu
dial-up modem modem deialu *eg* modemau deialu
dialysate dialysad *eg*
dialysis dialysis *eg*
diamagnetism diamagnetedd *eg*
diameter diamedr *eg* diamedrau
diametral diamedrol *ans*
diametral pitch pitsh diamedrol *eg*
diamminecopper(I) chloride deuamincopr(I) clorid *eg*
diamond diemwnt *eg* diemyntau
diamond banding bandin diemwnt *eg* bandinau diemwnt
diamond knurl nwrl diemwnt *eg* nwrliau diemwnt
diamond point pwynt diemwnt *eg* pwyntiau diemwnt
diamond point chisel cŷn trwyn diemwnt *eg* cynion trwyn diemwnt; gaing drwyn diemwnt *eb* geingiau trwyn diemwnt
diamond tipped blaen diemwnt *ans*
diamond tool erfyn diemwnt *eg* offer diemwnt
diamond wheel olwyn ddiemwnt *eb* olwynion diemwnt
diapason diapason *eg* diapasonau
diaper diaper *eg*
diaphragm (=muscular partition in mammals) llengig *eg* llengigoedd
diaphragm (in plants and animals other than mammals) diaffram *eg* diafframau
diarrhoea dolur rhydd *eg*
diary dyddiadur *eg* dyddiaduron
diary method dull dyddiadur *eg*
diastase diastas *eg*
diastole diastole *eg*
diastolic diastolig *ans*
diastrophism diastroffedd *eg*
diathesis diathesis *eg*
diathesis model model diathesis *eg*
diathesis stress model model straen diathesis *eg*
diatom (alga) diatom *eg* diatomau
diatomic (yn cynnwys dau atom) deuatomig *ans*
diatonic diatonig *ans*
diatonic semitone hanner tôn diatonig *eg* hanner tonau diatonig
diatonicism diatonyddiaeth *eb*
di(benzenecarbonyl) peroxide deu(bensencarbonyl) perocsid *eg*
1,1-dibromoethane 1,1-deubromoethan *eg*
1,2-dibromoethane 1,2-deubromoethan *eg*
dice *n* dis *eg* disiau
dice *v* deisio *be*
dicentric deusentrig *ans*
dichlorine oxide deuclorin ocsid *eg*
Dichloro Diphenyl Trichloroethane (DDT) Deucloro Deuffenyl Tricloroethan (DDT) *eg*
4-dichlorobenzene 4-deuclorobensen *eg*
1,4-dichlorobenzene 1,4-deuclorobensen *eg*
1,2-dichloroethene 1,2-deucloroethen *eg*
(dichloromethyl)benzene (deucloromethyl)bensen *eg*
2,4-dichlorophenoxyacetic acid asid 2,4-dicloroffenocsiasetig *eg*
dichotic listening gwrando deugotig *be*
dichromate(VI) ion ïon deucromad(VI) *eg* ïonau deucromad(VI)
dichromium(III) copper(II) oxide deucromiwm(III) copr(II) ocsid *eg*
dicopper(I) ethynediide deucopr(I) ethyndeuid *eg*
dicotyledon deugotyledon *eg*
dicotyledonous deugotyledonaidd *ans*
dictator unben *eg* unbeniaid
dictatorial unbenaethol *ans*
dictatorship unbennaeth *eb*
dictatorship of the proletariat unbennaeth y proletariat *eb*
diction ynganiad *eg* ynganiadau
dictionary geiriadur *eg* geiriaduron
dictionary error gwall geiriadur *eg* gwallau geiriadur
didactic apparatus cyfarpar didactig *eg*
didactic model model didactig *eg*
di(dodecanoyl) peroxide deu(dodecanoyl) perocsid *eg*
die dei *eg* deiau
die nut nyten ddei *eb* nytiau dei
die-casting deigastio *be*
diegetic sound sain gynefin *eb*
dielectric *adj* deuelectrig *ans*
dielectric *n* deuelectryn *eg* deuelectrynnau
dielectric constant cysonyn deuelectrig *eg* cysonion deuelectrig
▶ **diet** deiet *eg* deietau
Diet of Worms Diet Worms *eg*
▶ **dietary** deietegol *ans*
▶ **dietary deficiencies** diffygion deiet *ell*
▶ **dietary fibre** ffibr deietegol *eg*
dietary value sheet taflen gwerth deietegol *eb* taflenni gwerth deietegol
dietetics deieteg *eb*
1,1-diethoxyethane 1,1-deuethocsiethan *eg*
diethylamine deuethylamin *eg*
▶ **dietitian** deietegydd *eg* deietegwyr
difference gwahaniaeth *eg* gwahaniaethau
difference amplifier mwyhadur gwahaniaeth *eg* mwyhaduron gwahaniaeth
difference of means gwahaniaeth cymedrau *eg*
difference of two squares gwahaniaeth rhwng dau sgwâr
difference threshold trothwy gwahaniaeth *eg*
different gwahanol *ans*
differentiability differadwyedd *eg*

differentiable differadwy *ans*
differential *n* differyn *eg* differynnau
differential (in general) *adj* gwahaniaethol *ans*
differential (in mathematics and physics) *adj* differol *ans*
differential assembly cydosodiad differyn *eg* cydosodiadau differyn
differential axis echelin ddifferyn *eb* echelinau differyn
differential calculus calcwlws differol *eg*
differential coefficient cyfernod differol *eg* cyfernodau differol
differential equation hafaliad differol *eg* hafaliadau differol
differential erosion erydiad gwahaniaethol *eg*
differential permeability athreiddedd gwahaniaethol *eg*
differential pulley pwli differol *eg* pwlïau differol
differential tone rhyng-dôn *eg* rhyngdonau
differentially permeable differol athraidd
differentiate (in general) gwahaniaethu *be*
differentiate (in mathematics) differu *be*
differentiated gwahaniaethol *ans*
differentiated curriculum cwricwlwm gwahaniaethol *eg*
differentiated examination arholiad gwahaniaethol *eg* arholiadau gwahaniaethol
differentiated paper papur gwahaniaethol *eg* papurau gwahaniaethol
differentiation (in general) gwahaniaethiad *eg*
differentiation (in mathematics and physics) differiad *eg* differiadau
differentiation by outcome gwahaniaethu yn ôl y canlyniad *be*
difficult anodd *ans*
difficulty anhawster *eg* anawsterau
diffract diffreithio *be*
diffraction diffreithiant *eg* diffreithiannau
diffraction grating gratin diffreithiant *eg*
diffraction patterns patrymau diffreithiant *ell*
diffuse *adj* tryledol *ans*
diffuse (=spread out) *v* ymledu *be*
diffuse (in meteorology) *v* cymysgu *be*
diffuse (in physics and chemistry) *v* tryledu *be*
diffuse porous mandyllog tryledol *ans*
diffused lighting golau tryledol *eg*
diffuser tryledwr *eg* tryledwyr
diffuser spray tryledwr chwistrell *eg* tryledwyr chwistrell
diffusion lledaenu *be*
diffusion (=spreading out) ymlediad *eg* ymlediadau
diffusion (in physics and chemistry) trylediad *be* trylediadau
diffusion cloud chamber llestr niwl trylediad *eg*
diffusion of responsibility gwasgariad cyfrifoldeb *eg*
diffusivity trylededd *eg* trylededdau
dig *v* cloddio *be*
dig (archaeological) *n* cloddfa *eb* cloddfeydd

digest treulio *be*
digestibility treuliadwyedd *eg*
digestibility coefficient cyfernod treuliadwyedd *eg* cyfernodau treuliadwyedd
digestible treuliadwy *ans*
digestion treuliad *eg* treuliadau
digestive biscuit bisged ddigestif *eb* bisgedi digestif
digestive enzyme ensym treulio *eg* ensymau treulio
digestive juice sudd treulio *eg* suddion treulio
digestive system system dreulio *eb* systemau treulio
Diggers Cloddwyr *ell*
digit digid *eg* digidau
digit repetition test prawf ailadrodd rhifau *eg* profion ailadrodd rhifau
digital digidol *ans*
digital camera camera digidol *eg* camerâu digidol
digital computer cyfrifiadur digidol *eg* cyfrifiaduron digidol
digital dice dis digidol *eg* disiau digidol
digital form ffurf ddigidol *eb* ffurfiau digidol
digital meter mesurydd digidol *eg* mesuryddion digidol
digital plotter plotydd digidol *eg* plotyddion digidol
digital root isradd digidol *eg* israddau digidol
digital signal signal digidol *eg* signalau digidol
Digital Versatile Disk Disg Amlbwrpas Digidol *eg* Disgiau Amlbwrpas Digidol
digital-analogue converter (DAC) trawsnewidydd digidol-analog *eg* trawsnewidyddion digidol-analog
digitation (in botany and zoology) byseddiad *eg* byseddiadau
► **digitation** (in computing) digideiddiad *eg* digideiddiadau
digitize digido *be*
digitizer digidydd *eg* digidyddion
dignity urddas *eg*
digraph deugraff *eg* deugraffau
dihedral deuhedrol *ans*
dihedral angle ongl ddeuhedrol *eb* onglau deuhedrol
dihybrid deuhybrid *eg*
dihydrogenphosphate(V) ion ïon deuhydrogenffosffad(V) *eg* ïonau deuhydrogenffosffad(V)
2,3-dihydroxybutanedioate oxide 2,3-deuhydrocsibwtandeuoad ocsid *eg*
(-)-2,3-dihydroxybutanedioic acid asid (-)-2,3-deuhydrocsibwtandeuöig *eg*
(±)-2,3-dihydroxybutanedioic acid asid (±)-2,3-deuhydrocsibwtandeuöig *eg*
diiodine hexachloride deuïodin hecsaclorid *eg*
2,4-diisocyanato-1-methylbenzene 2,4-deuisocyanato-1-methylbensen *eg*
dilate (of blood-vessel etc) ymagor *be*
dilate (of pupils, cervix) ymledu *be*
dilation ymlediad *eg* ymlediadau
dilead(II) lead(IV) oxide deuplwm(II) plwm(IV) ocsid *eg*
dilemma cyfyng-gyngor *eg*
diluent gwanedydd *eg* gwanedyddion

dilute *adj* gwanedig *ans*
dilute *v* gwanedu *be*
dilute acid asid gwanedig *eg*
dilute sulphuric acid asid sylffwrig gwanedig *eg*
dilution gwanediad *eg* gwanediadau
dilution (of skilled workers) teneuo *be*
dim *adj* pŵl *ans*
dim *v* pylu *be*
dimension *n* dimensiwn *eg* dimensiynau
dimension *v* dimensiynu *be*
dimension line llinell dimensiwn *eb* llinellau dimensiwn
dimension line overhang bargod llinell dimensiwn *eg* bargodion llinell dimensiwn
dimension line space bwlch llinell dimensiwn *eg* bylchau llinell dimensiwn
dimension value format fformat gwerth dimensiwn *eg* fformatau gwerth dimensiwn
dimensional dimensiynol *ans*
dimensional control rheolaeth ddimensiynol *eb*
dimensional sketch braslun dimensiynol *eg* brasluniau dimensiynol
dimensioned drawing lluniad dimensiynol *eg* lluniadau dimensiynol
dimer deumer *eg* deumerau
dimercury(I) ion ïon deumercwri(I) *eg* ïonau deumercwri(I)
dimethyl benzene-1,2-dicarboxylate deumethyl bensen-1,2-deucarbocsylad *eg*
1,2-dimethylbenzene 1,2-deumethylbensen *eg*
3,3-dimethylbiphenyl-4,4'-diamine 3,3-deumethylbiffenyl-4,4'-deuamin *eg*
2,2-dimethylbutane 2,2-deumethylbwtan *eg*
2,3-dimethylbutane-2,3-diol 2,3-deumethylbwtan-2,3-deuol *eg*
3,3-dimethylbutanone 3,3-deumethylbwtanon *eg*
dimethylethanedioate deumethylethandeuoad *eg*
2,2-dimethylpropan-1-ol 2,2-deumethylpropan-1-ol *eg*
dimetric projection tafluniad deufetrig *eg* tafluniadau deufetrig
diminish (in general) lleihau *be*
diminish (in music) cywasgu *be*
diminished (in general) llai *ans*
diminished (in music) cywasg *ans*
diminished chord cord cywasg *eg* cordiau cywasg
diminished image delwedd lai *eb* delweddau llai
diminished interval cyfwng cywasg *eg* cyfyngau cywasg
diminished seventh chord cord seithfed cywasg *eg* cordiau seithfed cywasg
diminishing returns enillion lleihaol *ell*
diminution (in general) lleihad *eg* lleihadau
diminution (in music) cywasgiad *eg* cywasgiadau
dimmer pylydd *eg* pylyddion
dimmer board bwrdd pylu *eg* byrddau pylu
dimmer-switch switsh pylu *eg* switshis pylu
dining chair cadair ystafell fwyta *eb* cadeiriau ystafell fwyta
dining table bwrdd bwyd *eg* byrddau bwyd
dining room ystafell fwyta *eb* ystafelloedd bwyta
1,3-dinitrobenzene 1,3-deunitrobensen *eg*
dinitrogen oxide deunitrogen ocsid *eg*
dinner lady cynorthwyydd cinio *eg* cynorthwywyr cinio
dinosaur dinosor *eg* dinosoriaid
dinucleotide deuniwcliotid *eg* deuniwcliotidau
diocesan esgobaethol *ans*
diocese esgobaeth *eb* esgobaethau
diode deuod *eg* deuodau
dioecious deuoecaidd *ans*
diol (generic name) deuol *eg* deuolau
diorama diorama *eg* dioramau
diorite diorit *eg*
dioxide deuocsid *eg*
dioxouranium(VI) zinc ethanoate deuocsowraniwm(VI) sinc ethanoad *eg*
dioxygenated deuocsigenedig *ans*
dip gogwyddiad *eg* gogwyddiadau
dip *n* dip *eg* dipiau
dip *v* dipio *be*
dip (for sheep) trochdrwyth *eg*
dip (of strata) *n* goledd *eg*
dip (of strata) *v* goleddu *be*
dip coating trocharaenu *be*
dip slope golethr *eg* golethrau
1,2-diphenylethanedione 1,2-deuffenylethandeuon *eg*
1,2-diphenylethene 1,2-deuffenylethen *eg*
diphenylmethanone deuffenylmethanon *eg*
diphosphane deuffosffan *eg*
diphtheria difftheria *eg*
diploid diploid *ans*
diploid nucleus niwclews diploid *eg*
diploidy diploidi *eg*
diploma diploma *eg* diplomâu
diplomacy diplomyddiaeth *eb*
diplomat diplomydd *eg* diplomyddion
diplomatic diplomyddol *ans*
diplomatic history hanes diplomyddiaeth *eg*
diplomatics diplomateg *eb*
dipole deupol *eg* deupolau
dipole moment moment deupol *eg*
dipper trochydd *eg* trochyddion
dipper (oil painting) dipell *eb* dipelli
dipping trochi *be*
dipstick trochbren *eb* trochbrennau
direct uniongyrchol *ans*
direct (sign) cyfeirydd *eg* cyfeiryddion
direct access *n* mynediad uniongyrchol *eg*
direct access *v* cyrchu uniongyrchol *be*
direct addressing cyfeirio uniongyrchol *be*
direct advertising hysbysebu uniongyrchol *be*
direct application (of paint etc) rhoi *be*

direct care gofal uniongyrchol *eg*
direct column break toriad colofn uniongyrchol *eg* toriadau colofn uniongyrchol
direct contact cyswllt uniongyrchol *eg*
direct current (D.C.) cerrynt union *eg*
direct current motor modur cerrynt union *eg*
direct cursor cyrchwr uniongyrchol *eg* cyrchwyr uniongyrchol
direct data entry cofnodi data uniongyrchol *be*
► **direct dye** llifyn uniongyrchol *eg* llifynnau uniongyrchol
direct experience profiad uniongyrchol *eg* profiadau uniongyrchol
direct free kick cic rydd uniongyrchol *eb* ciciau rhydd uniongyrchol
direct instruction dysgu uniongyrchol *be*
direct lighting golau uniongyrchol *eg*
direct line break toriad llinell uniongyrchol *eg* toriadau llinell uniongyrchol
direct marketing marchnata uniongyrchol *eg*
direct method dull uniongyrchol *eg* dulliau uniongyrchol
direct moulding clay clai modelu uniongyrchol *eg*
direct page break toriad tudalen uniongyrchol *eg* toriadau tudalen uniongyrchol
direct painting peintio uniongyrchol *be*
direct parry pario union *be*
direct proportion cyfrannedd union *eg* cyfraneddau union
direct ratio cymhareb union *eb* cymarebau union
direct replication atgynhyrchu uniongyrchol *be*
direct riposte riposte union *eg* ripostes union
direct taxes trethi uniongyrchol *ell*
direct thrust gwaniad union *eg* gwaniadau union
direct variation amrywiad union *eg* amrywiadau union
direct vision spectroscope sbectrosgop golwg union *eg* sbectrosgopau golwg union
directed number rhif cyfeiriol *eg* rhifau cyfeiriol
directed work gwaith gosod *eg*
direction cyfeiriad *eg* cyfeiriadau
direction of arrow A cyfeiriad saeth A *eg*
direction of cut cyfeiriad y toriad *eg*
direction of feed cyfeiriad porthiant *eg*
direction of grain cyfeiriad y graen *eg*
direction of movement cyfeiriad symudiad *eg*
direction of rotation (D.O.R.) cyfeiriad y cylchdro *eg*
direction of the ball cyfeiriad y bêl *eg*
direction of throw cyfeiriad y tafliad *eg*
directional cyfeiriadol *ans*
directional selection detholiad cyfeiriadol *eg*
directions test prawf dilyn cyfarwyddiadau *eg* profion dilyn cyfarwyddiadau
directive (in computing etc) cyfarwyddeb *eb* cyfarwyddebau
directive (in general) cyfarwyddyd *eg* cyfarwyddiadau
director cyfarwyddwr *eg* cyfarwyddwyr
director circle cyfeirgylch *eg* cyfeirgylchoedd
director of education cyfarwyddwr addysg *eg* cyfarwyddwyr addysg
director of nursing services cyfarwyddwr gwasanaethau nyrsio *eg* cyfarwyddwyr gwasanaethau nyrsio
Director of Public Prosecutions Cyfarwyddwr Erlyniadau Cyhoeddus *eg*
directory cyfeiriadur *eg* cyfeiriaduron
Directory Directoire *eg*
directory contents cynnwys cyfeiriadur *eg*
directory path llwybr cyfeiriadur *eg* llwybrau cyfeiriadur
directory structure strwythur y cyfeiriadur *eg*
directory tree coeden cyfeiriaduron *eb* coed cyfeiriaduron
directrix cyfeirlin *eb* cyfeirlinau
disability anabledd *eg* anableddau
disable analluogi *be*
disable cookies analluogi cwcis *be*
disable interruptions analluogi ymyriadau *be*
disabled anabl *ans*
disabled people pobl anabl *eb*
disabled relief rhyddhad anabledd *eg*
disablement anabledd *eg*
disablement allowance lwfans yr anabl *eg* lwfansau'r anabl
disablement pension pensiwn yr anabl *eg*
disablement resettlement officer swyddog ailsefydlu'r anabl *eg* swyddogion ailsefydlu'r anabl
disaccharide deusacarid *eg* deusacaridau
disadvantaged dan anfantais *ans*
disadvantaged group grŵp sydd dan anfantais *eg* grwpiau sydd dan anfantais
disadvantaged socially dan anfantais gymdeithasol
disaffection annheyrngarwch *eg*
disaggregate dadagregu *be*
disapplication datgymhwysiad *eg* datgymwysiadau
disapply datgymhwyso *be*
disarm diarfogi *be*
Disarmament Commission Comisiwn Diarfogi *eg*
disassemble dadgydosod *be*
disassembler dadgydosodydd *eg* dadgydosodyddion
disc disg *eg/b* disgiau
disc sander sandiwr disg *eg* sandwyr disg
discard gwaredu *be*
discharge (=release) *v* rhyddhau *be*
discharge (electrical) *n* dadwefriad *eg* dadwefriadau
discharge (electricity) *v* dadwefru *be*
discharge (of pus, liquid etc) *n* rhedlif *eg* rhedlifau
discharge (water) *n* arllwysiad *eg* arllwysiadau
discharge (water) *v* arllwys *be*
discharge emission allyriad *eg* allyriadau
discharge planning cynllunio rhyddhau *be*
discharge tube tiwb dadwefru *eg* tiwbiau dadwefru
discharger dadwefrydd *eg* dadwefryddion
disciplinarian disgyblwr *eg* disgyblwyr
disciplinary action camau i ddisgyblu *ell*

discipline disgyblaeth *eb* disgyblaethau
disciplined disgybledig *ans*
disclaimer ymwrthodiad *eg* ymwrthodiadau
disclose (information etc) datgelu *be*
disclosure datgeliad *eg* datgeliadau
disco disgo *eg* disgos
discography disgyddiaeth *eb* disgyddiaethau
discolour afliwio *be*
discolouration afliwiad *eg* afliwiadau
disconnect datgysylltu *be*
discontent anniddigrwydd *eg*
discontinuity diffyg parhad *eg*
discontinuous (=intermittent) toredig *ans*
discontinuous (of variation) amharhaol *ans*
discord anghytgord *eg* anghytgordiau
discordant (of colours) anghydnaws *ans*
discordant (of music) anghytgordiol *ans*
discordant (of opinions) anghytûn *ans*
discount disgownt *eg* disgowntiau
discount store siop ddisgownt *eb* siopau disgownt
discounted cash flow llif arian disgowntiedig *eg*
discourse analysis dadansoddi disgwrs *be*
discovery darganfyddiad *eg* darganfyddiadau
discrete (=independent) annibynnol
discrete (separate and distinct) arwahanol *ans*
discrete area of activity maes gweithgaredd annibynnol *eg* meysydd gweithgaredd annibynnol
discrete data data arwahanol *ell*
discrete programme of study rhaglen astudio annibynnol *eb* rhaglenni astudio annibynnol
discrete random variable hapnewidyn arwahanol *eg* hapnewidynnau arwahanol
discrete variable newidyn arwahanol *eg* newidynnau arwahanol
discretion disgresiwn *eg*
discretionary dewisol *ans*
discretionary exception eithriad dewisol *eg* eithriadau dewisol
discretionary grant grant dewisol *eg* grantiau dewisol
discriminant gwahanolyn *eg* gwahanolion
discriminate gwahaniaethu *be*
discrimination (=good taste) dirnadaeth *eb* dirnadaethau
discrimination (against) gwahaniaethu *be*
discrimination (in exam questions) didoli *be*
discrimination index cyfeirnod didoli *eg* cyfeirnodau didoli
discriminative stimulus ysgogiad gwahaniaethol *eb* ysgogiadau gwahaniaethol
discriminatory behaviour ymddygiad gwahaniaethol *eg*
discriminatory practice arfer gwahaniaethol *eg* arferion gwahaniaethol
discus disgen *eb* disgiau
discuss trafod *be*
discussion trafodaeth *eb* trafodaethau
discussion board bwrdd trafod *eg* byrddau trafod
discussion group (formal) grŵp trafod *eg* grwpiau trafod
discussion group (informal) cylch trafod *eg* cylchoedd trafod
disease clefyd *eg* clefydau
diseased afiach *ans*
diseconomies of scale annarbodion maint *ell*
disembark glanio *be*
disendow dadwaddoli *be*
disendowment dadwaddoliad *eg*
disenfranchise dadryddfreinio *be*
disengage datgyweddu *be*
disengagement datgyweddiad *eg* datgyweddiadau
disequilibrium diffyg cydbwysedd *eg*
disequilibrium unemployment diweithdra heb gydbwysedd *eg*
disestablish datgysylltu *be*
disestablishment datgysylltiad *eg*
disfigurement anffurfiad *eg* anffurfiadau
disguise (=conceal) cuddio *be*
dish dysgl *eb* dysglau
dished base gwaelod dysglog *eg* gwaelodion dysglog
dished blank blanc dysglog *eg* blanciau dysglog
dished shape siâp dysglog *eg* siapiau dysglog
dishing (=make concave) pantio *be*
dishing (=make convex) bolio *be*
dishwasher peiriant golchi llestri *eg* peiriannau golchi llestri
disillusion dadrithio *be*
disilver(I) ethynediide deuarian(I) ethyndeuid *eg*
disincentive anghymhelliad *eg* anghymelliadau
disinfect diheintio *be*
disinfectant diheintydd *eg* diheintyddion
disinfected diheintiedig *ans*
disinfection diheintiad *eg*
disintegrate (in physics) ymddatod *be*
disintegrate (of rock) chwalu *be*
disintegrated chwilfriw *ans*
disintegration (in physics) ymddatodiad *eg*
disintegration (of rock) chwilfriwiant *eg*
disjoint sets setiau digyswllt *ell*
disk disg *eg/b* disgiau
disk cache storfa disg *eb* storfeydd disg
disk controller rheolydd disgiau *eg* rheolyddion disgiau
disk crash chwalfa disg *eb*
disk drive disgyrrwr *eg* disgyrwyr
disk filing system (DFS) system ddisg-ffeilio *eb*
disk format fformat disg *eg* fformatau disg
disk head pen disg *eg* pennau disg
disk operating system (DOS) system weithredu disg *eb*
disk pack pecyn disgiau *eg* pecynnau disgiau
dislocate afleoli *be*
dislocation afleoliad *eg* afleoliadau
dismantle datgysylltu *be*

dismembered drainage draeniad datgymalog *eg*
dismount dadlwytho *be*
disobedience anufudd-dod *eg*
disobedient anufudd *ans*
disodium tetraborate(III)-10-water deusodiwm tetraborad(III)-10-dŵr *eg*
disorder (=lack of order) anhrefn *eg/b*
disorder (medical) anhwylder *eg* anhwylderau
disorderly pupil disgybl anystywallt *eg* disgyblion anystywallt
disorganised schizophrenia sgitsoffrenia anhrefnus *eg*
dispensary dosbarthfa *eb* dosbarthfeydd
dispersal gwasgariad *eg*
dispersal of spores gwasgariad sborau *eg*
disperse gwasgaru *be*
disperse medium cyfrwng gwasgaru *eg* cyfryngau gwasgaru
disperse phase gwasgarwedd *eb* gwasgarweddau
dispersed gwasgarog *ans*
dispersion gwasgariad *eg* gwasgariadau
dispersive gwasgarol *ans*
dispersive power nerth gwasgaru *eg* nerthoedd gwasgaru
displace dadleoli *be*
displacement (of gases) dadleoliad *eg*
displacement /time diagram diagram dadleoliad / amser *eg* diagramau dadleoliad /amser
displacement angle ongl ddadleoliad *eb* onglau dadleoliad
displacement diagram diagram dadleoliad *eg* diagramau dadleoliad
displacement reaction adwaith dadleoli *eg*
displacement tonnage tunelledd dadleoliad *eg*
display *v* arddangos *be*
display (=small exhibition) *n* arddangosfa *eb* arddangosfeydd
display (screen) *n* dangosydd *eg* dangosyddion
display (act of) *n* arddangosiad *eg* arddangosiadau
display additional information dangos gwybodaeth ychwanegol *be*
display all dangos popeth *be*
display area lle dangos *eg* llefydd dangos
display board bwrdd arddangos *eg* byrddau arddangos
display bullets dangos bwledi *be*
display colours dangos lliwiau *be*
display documents dangos dogfennau *be*
display drop caps dangos priflythrennau bach *be*
display field dangos maes *be*
display grayscale dangos graddlwyd *be*
display grid dangos grid *be*
display inactive records dangos cofnodion anweithredol *be*
display of dancing arddangosfa ddawnsio *eb* arddangosfeydd dawnsio
display panel panel arddangos *eg* paneli arddangos
display plug-ins dangos ategion *be*
display properties dangos priodweddau *be*
display rule rheol arddangos *eb* rheolau arddangos
display screen sgrin arddangos *eb* sgriniau arddangos
display setting gosodiad y dangosydd *eg* gosodiadau'r dangosydd
display stand stand arddangos *eg* standiau arddangos
display unit uned arddangos *eb* unedau arddangos
display warning dangos rhybudd *be*
displayed formula fformiwla graffig *eb* fformiwlâu graffig
disposable tafladwy *ans*
disposable income incwm gwario *eg*
disposable nappy cewyn parod *eg* cewynnau parod; clwt parod *eg* clytiau parod
disposable palette palet hepgor *eg* paletau hepgor
disposal gwarediad *eg*
dispose gwaredu *be*
dispose of fullness ad-drefnu llawnder *be*
disproportionation dadgyfraniad *eg* dadgyfraniadau
disputant dadleuwr *eg* dadleuwyr
disputation dadl *eb* dadleuon
dispute anghydfod *eg*
dispute resolution process proses datrys anghydfod *eb* prosesau datrys anghydfod
disqualification diarddeliad *eg* diarddeliadau
disqualify diarddel *be*
disqualify from the race diarddel o'r ras *be*
disrupt aflonyddu *be*
disruption aflonyddwch *eg*
disruptive aflonyddgar *ans*
disruptive behaviour ymddygiad aflonyddgar *eg*
disruptive pupil disgybl aflonyddgar *eg* disgyblion aflonyddgar
disruptive selection detholiad rhwygol *eg*
disruptiveness aflonyddwch *eg*
dissect dyrannu *be*
dissected plateau llwyfandir dyranedig *eg* llwyfandiroedd dyranedig
dissected rat llygoden fawr ddyranedig *be* llygod mawr dyranedig
dissection dyraniad *eg* dyraniadau
disseminate lledaenu *be*
dissemination of good practice lledaenu ymarfer da *be*
dissent anghydffurfiaeth *eb*
dissenter anghydffurfiwr *eg* anghydffurfwyr
dissenting anghydffurfiol *ans*
dissipate afradloni *be*
dissipation afradlonedd *eg* afradloneddau
dissociate daduno *be*
dissociation daduniad *eg*
dissociation constant cysonyn daduniad *eg*
dissociation curve cromlin ddaduniad *eb*
dissociative disorder anhwylder datgysylltiol *eg* anhwylderau datgysylltiol
dissociative identity disorder anhwylder hunaniaeth datgysylltiol *eg*

dissolution diddymiad *eg* diddymiadau
dissolution of the monasteries diddymu'r mynachlogydd *be*
dissolve (=dismiss or annul) diddymu *be*
dissolve (e.g. solid in a liquid) hydoddi *be*
dissolve (in film editing and non-technical usage) toddi *be*
dissonance anghyseinedd *eg*
dissonant anghyseiniol *ans*
dissonant interval cyfwng anghyseiniol *eg* cyfyngau anghyseiniol
distaff cogail *eg* cogeiliau
distal distal *ans*
distal convoluted tubule tiwbyn troellog pen pellaf *eg*
distal end pen pellaf *eg* pennau pellaf
distal tubule pen pella'r tiwbyn *eg* pennau pella'r tiwbynnau
distance pellter *eg* pellterau
distance education addysg o bell *eb*
distance learning dysgu o bell *be*
distance piece darn pellter *eg* darnau pellter
distance swimming nofio pellter *be*
distance teaching addysgu o bell *be*
distance-decay gwanhad-pellter *eg*
distemper distemper *eg*
distemper paint paent distemper *eg*
distended chwyddedig *ans*
distention chwyddiant *eg*
distil distyllu *be*
distillate distyllad *eg* distylladau
distillation distyllu *be*
distilled water dŵr distyll *eg*
distinct amlwg *ans*
distinctive nodedig *ans*
distinctive feature nodwedd nodedig *eb* nodweddion nodedig
distinctiveness gwahanolrwydd *eg*
distinguish gwahaniaethu *be*
distinguishable gwahaniaethadwy *ans*
distinguishing note (sol-fa) nodyn dangos *eg* nodau dangos
distort (facts) ystumio *be*
distort (image) aflunio *be*
► **distort sprite** aflunio corlun *be*
distortion (of facts) ystumiad *eg* ystumiadau
distortion (of image) afluniad *eg* afluniadau
distract gwrthdynnu *be*
distraction gwrthdyniad *eg* gwrthdyniadau
distractor (in objective questions) gwrthdynnwr *eg* gwrthdynwyr
distrain atafaelu *be*
distraint atafaeliad *eg* atafaeliadau
distress cyfyngder *eg*
distress signal arwydd cyfyngder *eg* arwyddion cyfyngder
distress warrant gwarant atafaelu *eg* gwarantau atafaelu
distributary allafon *eb* allafonydd
distributary channel allsianel *eb* allsianelau
distribute (=share out) dosbarthu *be*
distribute (in statistics) dosrannu *be*
distributed computer system system gyfrifiadurol wasgaredig *eb*
distributed loading llwyth dosbarthedig *eg* llwythi dosbarthedig
distribution (=division into parts, classification) dosraniad *eg*
distribution (=sharing out or dispersal) dosbarthiad *eg*
distribution channel sianel dosbarthu *eb* sianeli dosbarthu
distribution coefficient cyfernod dosraniad *eg* cyfernodau dosraniad
distribution curve cromlin ddosraniad *eb*
distribution list rhestr ddosbarthu *eb* rhestri dosbarthu
distribution of wealth dosbarthiad cyfoeth *eg*
distribution pattern patrwm dosbarthiad *eg* patrymau dosbarthiad
distributional dosraniadol *ans*
distributive dosbarthol *ans*
distributive law deddf ddosbarthol *eb*
distributive trade masnach ddosbarthu *eb*
distributor dosbarthydd *eg* dosbarthwyr
district (=area with common characteristics) ardal *eb* ardaloedd
district (=division of county electing its own councillors) dosbarth *eg* dosbarthiadau
district council cyngor dosbarth *eg* cynghorau dosbarth
district education officer swyddog addysg rhanbarthol *eg* swyddogion addysg rhanbarthol
district general hospital ysbyty cyffredinol dosbarth *eg* ysbytai cyffredinol dosbarth
District Health Authority (DHA) Awdurdod Iechyd Dosbarth *eg*
district nurse nyrs ardal *eb* nyrsys ardal
district valuer prisiwr rhanbarth *eg* priswyr rhanbarth
disturb tarfu ar *be*
disturbance (=agitation) cynnwrf *eg* cynhyrfau
disturbance (=unrest) aflonyddwch *eg*
disturbed (=agitated) aflonydd *ans*
disturbed (of psychological condition) cythryblus *ans*
disturbed pupil disgybl cythryblus *eg* disgyblion cythryblus
disulfate(IV) ion ïon deusylffad(IV) *eg* ïonau deusylffad(IV)
disulfur dichloride deusylffwr deuclorid *eg*
disunite tynnu'n rhydd *be*
dital harp telyn fysell *eb* telynau bysell
dither mwydro *be*
dithionate ion ïon deuthionad *eg* ïonau deuthionad
ditty canig *eb* canigau
diuresis troethlif *eg*

diuretic *adj* diwretig *ans*
diuretic *n* diwretig *eg* diwretigion
diurnal dyddiol *ans*
dive *n* deif *eb* deifiau
dive *v* deifio *be*
dive at a striker's feet
deifio wrth draed ymosodwr *be*
dive for the ball deifio am y bêl *be*
dive forward roll deifrol ymlaen *eb* deifroliau ymlaen
diverge dargyfeirio *be*
divergence dargyfeiriad *eg* dargyfeiriadau
divergent dargyfeiriol *ans*
divergent question cwestiwn dargyfeiriol *eg*
cwestiynau dargyfeiriol
divergent series cyfres ddargyfeiriol *eb*
cyfresi dargyfeiriol
divergent thinking meddwl dargyfeiriol *eg*
diverging lens lens dargyfeirio *eg* lensiau dargyfeirio
diversify amrywiaethu *be*
diversion dargyfeiriad *eg* dargyfeiriadau
diversity amrywiaeth *eb*
divertimento divertimento *eg* divertimenti
divide *n* gwahanfa ddŵr *eb* gwahanfeydd dŵr
divide *v* rhannu *be*
divide by a number rhannu â rhif *be*
divided rhanedig *ans*
divided attention sylw rhanedig *eg*
dividend (=number to be divided) rhannyn *eg*
rhanynnau
dividend (=sum of money) buddran *eb* buddrannau
divider rhannwr *eg* rhanwyr
dividers cwmpas mesur *eg* cwmpasau mesur
dividing a line rhannu llinell *be*
dividing areas rhannu arwynebedd *be*
dividing head pen rhannu *eg* pennau rhannu
dividing lines in perspective
rhannu llinellau mewn persbectif *be*
Divine Right of Kings Dwyfol Hawl Brenhinoedd *eb*
divisibility rhanadwyedd *eg*
divisible rhanadwy *ans*
division (=part) rhaniad *eg* rhaniadau
division (COBOL) adran *eb* adrannau
division (of football league etc) adran *eb* adrannau
division (of scale) gradden *eb* graddennau
division by factors rhannu â ffactorau *be*
division of labour rhaniad llafur *eg*
divisional court llys adrannol *eg* llysoedd adrannol
Divisional Court of the QBD
Llys Adrannol Mainc y Frenhines *eg*
Divisionist Rhaniadwr *eg* Rhaniadwyr
divisions (=variations) amrywiadau *ell*
divisor rhannydd *eg* rhanyddion
divorce *n* ysgariad *eg* ysgariadau
divorce *v* ysgaru *be*
Diwali Diwali *eg*
dizygotic (DZ) deusygotig (DS) *ans*
dizygotic twin gefell deusygotig *eg*
gefeilliaid deusygotig

dizziness pendro *eb*
do nothing instruction cyfarwyddyd gwneud dim *eg*
cyfarwyddiadau gwneud dim
doatiness llwydni mewn pren *eg*
docking station gorsaf ddocio *eb* gorsafoedd docio
doctor meddyg *eg* meddygon
doctorate doethuriaeth *eb*
doctor-centred style arddull meddyg-ganolog *eg*
doctrine athrawiaeth *eb* athrawiaethau
doctrine of apperception
athrawiaeth cyfarganfod *eb*
doctrine of association of ideas
athrawiaeth cysylltu syniadau *eb*
Doctrine of Atonement Athrawiaeth yr Iawn *eb*
Doctrine of Non-recognition
Athrawiaeth Gwrthod Cydnabod *eb*
Doctrine of Papal Infallibility
Athrawiaeth Anffaeledigrwydd y Pab *eb*
doctrine of specific nerve energies
athrawiaeth egnïon nerfau arbennig *eb*
document *n* dogfen *eb* dogfennau
document *v* dogfennu *be*
document a system dogfennu system *be*
document as e-mail dogfen fel e-bost
document close button botwm cau dogfen *eg*
botymau cau dogfen
document contents cynnwys dogfen *eg*
document count cyfrif dogfennau *be*
document from abstract dogfen o grynodeb *eb*
document holder daliwr dogfen *eg* dalwyr dogfen
document language iaith dogfen *eb*
document manager rheolwr dogfennau *eg*
rheolwyr dogfennau
document mode modd dogfen *eg*
document number rhif dogfen *eg* rhifau dogfen
document properties priodweddau dogfen *ell*
document reader darllenydd dogfennau *eg*
darllenyddion dogfennau
document selection dewis dogfen *be*
document title teitl dogfen *eg* teitlau dogfennau
document view golwg dogfen *eg*
document window ffenestr dogfen *eb*
ffenestri dogfen
documentation dogfennaeth *eb*
docusoap sebon dogfennol *eg*
dodecagon dodecagon *eg* dodecagonau
dodecahedron dodecahedron *eg* dodecahedronau
dodecanal dodecanal *eg*
dodecan-1-ol dodecan-1-ol *eg*
dodecaphonic dodecaffonig *ans*
dodecaphonic scale graddfa ddodecaffonig *eb*
dodecaphony dodecaffoni *eg*
dodge *v* osgoi *be*
dog paddle nofio ci *be*
dogfish morgi *eg* morgwn
doily doili *eg* doilis
doldrums doldrymau *ell*
dolerite dolerit *eg* doleritau

dolina dolin *eg* dolinau
doll choice dewis doliau *eg*
dollar doler *eb* doleri
dollar key bysell doler *eb* bysellau doler
dolly doli *eb* doliau
dolly peg peg doli *eg* pegiau doli
dolly riveting (bolster) rhybedu doli *be*
dolman sleeve llawes ddolman *eb* llewys dolman
dolmen dolmen *eb* dolmenni
dolomite dolomit *eg* dolomitiau
dolphin dolffin *eg* dolffiniaid
dolphin kick cic dolffin *eb* ciciau dolffin
domain parth *eg* parthau
domain name enw parth *eg* enwau parth
domain name resolution cydrannu enw parth *be*
domain name system system enw parth *eb* systemau enw parth
domain user defnyddiwr parth *eg* defnyddwyr parth
dome *n* cromen *eb* cromenni
dome *v* cromennu *be*
dome castor castor cromen *eg* castorau cromen
domed cromennog *ans*
domed blank blanc crymdo *eg* blanciau crymdo
domed button botwm cromen *eg* botymau cromen
Domesday Book Llyfr Domesday *eg*
domestic (in general) domestig *ans*
domestic (not foreign) mewnol *ans*
domestic affair mater mewnol *eg* materion mewnol
domestic demand galw mewnol *eg*
domestic fuel tanwydd domestig *eg*
domestic history hanes teuluol *eg*
domestic industry diwydiant aelwyd *eg* diwydiannau aelwyd
domestic iron haearn smwddio *eg* heyrn smwddio
domestic mains supply prif gyflenwad domestig *eg*
► **domestic policy** polisi cartref *eg* polisïau cartref
domestic science gwyddor cartref *eb*
domestic staff staff domestig *ell*
domestic studies astudiaethau cartref *ell*
domestic system trefn aelwyd *eb*
domestic tourist (in Britain) ymwelydd o Brydain *eg* ymwelwyr o Brydain
domestic violence trais yn y cartref *eg*
domesticate dofi *be*
domiciliary cartref *ans*
domiciliary service gwasanaeth cartref *eg* gwasanaethau cartref
domiciliary visit ymweliad cartref *eg* ymweliadau cartref
dominance goruchafiaeth *eb*
dominant (in general) *adj* trechol *ans*
dominant (in music) *n* llywydd *eg*
dominant allele alel trechol *eg* alelau trechol
dominant attribute priodwedd drechol *eb* priodweddau trechol
dominant cadence diweddeb amherffaith *eb* diweddebau amherffaith
dominant colour lliw trechol *eg* lliwiau trechol
dominant factor ffactor drechol *eb* ffactorau trechol
dominant feature nodwedd drechol *eb* nodweddion trechol
dominant seventh chord cord seithfed y llywydd *eg*
dominant wind gwynt cryfaf *eg*
dominate (in the natural environment) goruchafu *be*
dominate (of people) tra-arglwyddiaethu *be*
domination tra-arglwyddiaeth *eb*
doming hammer morthwyl cromennu *eg* morthwylion cromennu
Dominican *adj* Dominicaidd *ans*
Dominican *n* Dominiciad *eg* Dominiciaid
Dominican Order Urdd Sant Dominic *eb*
dominion (=control) awdurdod *eg*
dominion (=territory) dominiwn *eg* dominiynau
domino domino *eg* dominos
domino banding bandin domino *eg* bandinau domino
Donation of Constantine Rhodd Cystennin *eb*
done (screen message) wedi gorffen
donkey (easel) seddisl *eb* seddislau
donor rhoddwr *eg* rhoddwyr
donor molecule moleciwl cyfrannol *eg* moleciwlau cyfrannol
doodling dwdlan *be*
door drws *eg* drysau
door fitting gosod drws *be*
door frame ffrâm ddrws *eb* fframiau drws
door furniture celfi drws *ell*
door latch clicied drws *eb* cliciedau drws
door lock clo drws *eg* cloeon drws
door panel panel drws *eg* paneli drws
door-to-door salesman gwerthwr o ddrws i ddrws *eg* gwerthwyr o ddrws i ddrws
dopamine dopamin *eg*
dopamine hypothesis rhagdybiaeth dopamin *eb*
doping amhureddu *be*
Dorian mode modd Doriaidd *eg*
dormancy cysgiad *eg*
dormant cwsg *ans*
dormant bud blaguryn cwsg *eg* blagur cwsg
dormant volcano llosgfynydd cwsg *eg* llosgfynyddoedd cwsg
dormer roof to dormer *eg* toeon dormer
dormer window ffenestr do *eb* ffenestri to
dormitory dortur *eg* dorturiau
dormitory town tref noswylio *eb* trefi noswylio
dormitory village pentref noswylio *eg* pentrefi noswylio
dorsal dorsal *ans*
dorsal exercise ymarfer uwchgefn *eg* ymarferion uwchgefn
dorsal fin asgell ddorsal *eb* esgyll dorsal
dorsal spine pigyn dorsal *eg* pigynnau dorsal
dorsiflexion cefnblygiad *eg*
dorsiventral cefndorrol *ans*
dorter dortur *eg* dorturiau

dose dos *eg* dosiau
do-se-do do-si-do *eg*
dot *n* dot *eg* dotiau
dot *v* dotio *be*
dot dash dot llinell doriad *eg* dotiau llinell doriad
dot matrix printer argraffydd matrics *eg* argraffyddion matrics
dot pitch pitsh dotiau *eg*
dot punch pwnsh dotio *eg* pynsiau dotio
dot punching dotbwnsio *be*
dots to top dotiau i'r brig *ell*
dots vertically dotiau'n fertigol *ell*
dotted dotiog *ans*
dotted line llinell doredig *eb* llinellau toredig
dotted note nodyn dot *eg* nodau dot
dotted rest tawnod dot *eg* tawnodau dot
dotted underline tanlinellu dotiog *be*
double *adj* dwbl *ans*
double *n* dwbl *eg* dyblau
double *v* dyblu *be*
double action harp telyn arwaith dwbl *eb* telynau arwaith dwbl
double arch (in dance) dwy law i ffurfio pont
double arrow saeth ddwbl *eb* saethau dwbl
double arrow left saeth ddwbl i'r chwith *eg* saethau dwbl i'r chwith
double arrow right saeth ddwbl i'r dde *eb*
double aspect theory damcaniaeth agwedd ddwbl *eb*
double award dyfarniad dwbl *eg* dyfarniadau dwbl
double back stitch pwyth ôl dwbl *eg* pwythau ôl dwbl
double bar bar dwbl *eg* barau dwbl
double bar line llinell bar dwbl *eb* llinellau bar dwbl
double bass bas dwbl *eg* basau dwbl
double bass player canwr bas dwbl *eg* canwyr bas dwbl
double bassoon baswn dwbl *eg* baswnau dwbl
double bassoonist canwr baswn dwbl *eg* canwyr baswnau dwbl
double blast foot bellows megin droed chwyth dwbl *eb* meginau troed chwyth dwbl
double bond bond dwbl *eg* bondiau dwbl
double buffering byffro dwbl *be*
double chain stitch pwyth cadwyn ddwbl *eg* pwythau cadwyn ddwbl
double chorus côr dwbl *eg* corau dwbl
double circulation cylchrediad dwbl *eg*
double click *n* clic dwbl *eg* cliciau dwbl
double click *v* dwbl-glicio *be*
double concerto concerto dwbl *eg* concerti dwbl
double counterpoint gwrthbwynt dwbl *eg*
double cream hufen dwbl *eg*
double cropping cnydio dwbl *be*
double decomposition dadelfeniad dwbl *eg*
double density dwysedd dwbl *eg*
double diapason diapason dwbl *eg*
double dipper dipell ddwbl *eb* dipelli dwbl
double dot dot dwbl *eg* dotiau dwbl
double dotted note nodyn deuddot *eg* nodau deuddot
double dribble dribl dwbl *eg*
double ended dart dart deubwynt *eg* dartiau deubwynt
double engagement cyweddiad dwbl *eg*
double entry llyfrifo dwbl *be*
double exposition dangosiad dwbl *eg* dangosiadau dwbl
double faced hammer morthwyl dau wyneb crwn *eg* morthwylion dau wyneb crwn
double faggot stitch pwyth ffagod dwbl *eg* pwythau ffagod dwbl
double fault ffawt ddwbl *eb* ffawtiau dwbl
double flat meddalnod dwbl *eg* meddalnodau dwbl
double folded seam sêm ddeublyg *eb* semau deublyg
double fugue ffiwg ddwbl *eb* ffiwgiau dwbl
double glazing gwydro dwbl *be*
double haunched dwbl hansiedig *ans*
double helix helics dwbl *eg*
double hem hem ddwbl *eb* hemiau dwbl
double hollow-bit tongs gefel gegron ddwbl *eb* gefeiliau cegrwn dwbl
double incontinence anymataliaeth ddwbl *eb*
double integral integryn dwbl *eg* integrynnau dwbl
double knot stitch pwyth cwlwm dwbl *eg* pwythau cwlwm dwbl
double lapped dovetail joint goruniad cynffonnog dwbl *eg* goruniadau cynffonnog dwbl
double length hyd dwbl *eg*
double length arithmetic rhifyddeg hyd dwbl *eb*
double lesson gwers ddwbl *eb* gwersi dwbl
double line llinell ddwbl *eb* llinellau dwbl
double machine stitched seam sêm ffel ddwbl *eb* semau ffel dwbl
double mortise and tenon joint uniad mortais a thyno dwbl *eg* uniadau mortais a thyno dwbl
double open diapason diapason agored dwbl *eg*
double patch pocket poced glwt ddwbl *eb* pocedi clwt dwbl
double pointed dart dart deubwynt *eg* dartiau deubwynt
double precision trachywiredd dwbl *eg*
double precision arithmetic rhifyddeg trachywiredd dwbl *eb*
double quote dyfynnod dwbl *eg* dyfynodau dwbl
double reed brwynen ddwbl *eb* brwyn dwbl
double roof to trawslath *eg* toeon trawslath
double scull sgwl dwbl *eg* sgyliau dwbl
double sharp llonnod dwbl *eg* llonnodau dwbl
double sheet cynfas ddwbl *eb* cynfasau dwbl
double somersault trosben dwbl *eg* trosbennau dwbl
double spacing bylchiad dwbl *eg* bylchiadau dwbl
double spacing bylchu dwbl *be*
double square brackets bachau petryal dwbl *ell*

double stopping gwasgiad dwbl *eg* gwasgiadau dwbl
double strike trawiad dwbl *eg* trawiadau dwbl
double strikethrough *n* dwy linell drwodd *eb*
double suspension (in music) gohiriant dwbl *eg* gohiriannau dwbl
double take-off esgyniad deudroed *eg*
double tenon tyno dwbl *eg* tynoau dwbl
double thickness trwch dwbl *eg*
double thread edau ddwbl *eb* edafedd dwbl
double tide dau lanw *eg*
double tonguing tafodi dwbl *be*
double turning troad dwbl *eg* troadau dwbl
double underline tanlinellu dwbl *be*
double virginal firdsinal ddwbl *eb* firdsinalau dwbl
double wave ton ddwbl *eb* tonnau dwbl
double-acting coupler cyplydd dwyffordd *eg* cyplyddion dwyffordd
double-acting cylinder silindr gweithrediad-dwbl *eg* silindrau gweithrediad-dwbl
double-angled line llinell wedi'i hongli *eb* llinellau wedi'u hongli
double-blind experiment arbrawf dwbl-ddall *eg* arbrofion dwbl-ddall
double-blind study astudiaeth ddwbl-ddall *eb* astudiaethau dwbl-ddall
double-boarded floor llawr estyll dwbl *eg* lloriau estyll dwbl
double-breasted (coat) â chaead dwbl *ans*
double-ended bolt bollt ddeuben *eb* bolltau deuben
double-coil lamp lamp coil dwbl *eb* lampau coil dwbl
double-ended bolt bollt ddeuben *eb* bolltau deuben
double-ended spanner sbaner deuben *eg* sbaneri deuben
double-glazed door drws dwbl-wydrog *eg* drysau dwbl-wydrog
double-glazed window ffenestr gwydr dwbl *eb* ffenestri gwydr dwbl
double-headed screw sgriw edau ddeuben *eb* sgriwiau edau deuben
double-lap tile teilsen lap dwbl *eb* teils lap dwbl
double-line spacing bylchiad llinellau dwbl *eg* bylchiadau llinellau dwbl
doubles parau *ell*
doubles game gêm i barau *eb* gemau i barau
doublet dwbled *eb* dwbledi
dove grey (enamelling colour) llwydlas *eg*
dovetail angle ongl gynffonnog *eb* onglau cynffonnog
dovetail bridle bagl gynffonnog *eb* baglau cynffonnog
dovetail bridle joint uniad bagl cynffonnog *eg* uniadau bagl cynffonnog
dovetail cleat cledd cynffonnog *eg* cleddau cynffonnog
dovetail halving haneru cynffonnog *be*
dovetail halving joint uniad haneru cynffonnog *eg* uniadau haneru cynffonnog
dovetail housing joint uniad rhigol gynffonnog *eg* uniadau rhigol gynffonnog
dovetail joint uniad cynffonnog *eg* uniadau cynffonnog
dovetail key clo cynffonnog *eg* cloeon cynffonnog
dovetail nailing hoelio cynffonnog *be*
dovetail pin pìn cynffonnog *eg* pinnau cynffonnog
dovetail saw llif dyno fach *eb* llifiau tyno bach
dovetail slope goledd cynffonnog *eg* goleddau cynffonnog
dovetail tapered housing joint uniad rhigol gynffonnog daprog *eg* uniadau rhigol gynffonnog daprog
dovetail template patrymlun cynffonnog *eg* patrymluniau cynffonnog
dovetailed key allwedd gynffonnog *eb* allweddi cynffonnog
dovetailing tryfalu *be*
dovetailing machine peiriant uniadau cynffonnog *eg* peiriannau uniadau cynffonnog
dowager gweddw *eb* gweddwon
dowel hoelbren *eb* hoelbrennau
dowel bit ebill hoelbren *eg* ebillion hoelbren
dowel construction adeiladwaith hoelbren *eg*
dowel groove rhigol hoelbren *eb* rhigolau hoelbren
dowel guide cyfeirydd hoelbren *eg* cyfeiryddion hoelbren
dowel jig jig hoelbrennau *eg* jigiau hoelbrennau
dowel joint uniad hoelbren *eg* uniadau hoelbren
dowel peg peg hoelbren *eg* pegiau hoelbren
dowel plate plât hoelbrennau *eg* platiau hoelbrennau
dowel rod rhoden hoelbren *eb* rhodenni hoelbren
down i lawr *adf*
down arrow saeth i lawr *eb*
down beat music cerddoriaeth curiad cryf *eb*
down cutting (=vertical corrasion) tyrchu *be*
down payment blaendal *eg* blaendaliadau
down time amser di-fynd *eg* amserau di-fynd
downbeat curiad i lawr *eg* curiadau i lawr
down-count cyfrif i lawr *eg*
downdate dad-ddiweddaru *be*
down-field (of magnetic field) i lawr y maes
downfold plyg i lawr *eg* plygion i lawr
downhill side ochr waered *eb* ochrau gwaered
downhill transition trawsnewid gwaeredol *eg*
downland twyndir *eg* twyndiroedd
download llwytho i lawr *be*
download an image llwytho delwedd i lawr *be*
download more llwytho rhagor i lawr *be*
download presentation llwytho cyflwyniad i lawr *be*
downloaded file ffeil wedi'i llwytho i lawr *eb* ffeiliau wedi'u llwytho i lawr
downpour cawod drom *eg* cawodydd trwm
Down's syndrome syndrom Down *eg*
downstream i lawr yr afon
down-stroke ôl-strôc *eb*
downthrow side ochr syrthiedig *eb* ochrau syrthiedig
downtown canol tref *eg*
downward i lawr *adf*
downward pressure gwasgedd tuag i lawr *eg*

downward sloping curve cromlin ddisgynnol *eb* cromliniau disgynnol
downward vertical fertigol i lawr *ans*
downward-sideways i lawr ac i'r ochr
downwarp crychiad i lawr *eg* crychiadau i lawr
dowried gwaddoledig *ans*
dowry gwaddol *eg* gwaddolion
draft *n* drafft *eg* drafftiau
draft *v* drafftio *be*
draft a pattern drafftio patrwm *be*
draft document dogfen ddrafft *eb* dogfennau drafft
drafted pattern patrwm drafft *eg* patrymau drafft
drafting paper papur drafftio *eg*
drafting process proses ddrafftio *eb*
drag *n* llusgiad *eg* llusgiadau
drag *v* llusgo *be*
drag and drop llusgo a gollwng
drag bar (command) llusgo bar *be*
dragonnade erledigaeth filwrol *eb*
dragoon dragŵn *eg* dragwniaid
drain *n* draen *eg* draeniau
drain *v* draenio *be*
drainage (in general) draeniad *eg*
drainage (of sewage) carthffosiaeth *eb*
drainage bag bag draenio *eg* bagiau draenio
drainage basin dalgylch afon *eg* dalgylchoedd afonydd
drainage pattern patrwm draeniad *eg* patrymau draeniad
drainage runs dyfnder draeniau *eg*
draining board astell ddiferu *eb* estyll diferu
draining paper papur diferu *eg*
drama drama *eb* dramâu
drama in education drama mewn addysg *eb*
dramatic dramatig *ans*
dramatic form ffurf ddramatig *eb*
dramatic skill sgil dramatig *eg*
dramatic structure strwythur dramatig *eg*
dramatic theory theori drama *eb*
dramatize dramateiddio *be*
drape gorchuddio *be*
draped backcloth cefnliain gorchuddio *eg* cefnlieiniau gorchuddio
draper dilledydd *eg* dilledyddion
drapery dilladaeth *eb*
draping qualities gorweddiad *eg*
draught drafft *eg* drafftiau
draught (of ship) tynfa *eb* tynfeydd
draught animal anifail gwedd *eg* anifeiliaid gwedd
draughtsman drafftsmon *eg* drafftsmyn
draughtsmanship drafftsmonaeth *eb*
draw (a drawing in the technical sense) lluniadu *be*
draw /paint computer system system luniadu /peintio ar gyfrifiadur *eb* systemau lluniadu /peintio ar gyfrifiadur
draw a cross-section llunio trawstoriad *be*
draw a line tynnu llinell *be*
draw a picture tynnu llun *be*
draw a tangent tynnu tangiad *be*
draw a thread tynnu edau *be*
draw attention (to) tynnu sylw *be*
draw conclusions tynnu casgliadau *be*
draw down tynnu lawr *be*
draw function swyddogaeth luniadu *eb* swyddogaethau lluniadu
draw leaf table bwrdd dalen estynedig *eg* byrddau dalenni estynedig
draw object gwrthrych lluniadu *eg* gwrthrychau lluniadu
draw object text testun gwrthrych lluniadu *eg* testunau gwrthrych lluniadu
draw off tapio *be*
draw plate plât tynnu *eg* platiau tynnu
draw spike sbigyn tynnu *eg* sbigynnau tynnu
draw text testun lluniadu *eg* testunau lluniadu
draw to scale lluniadu wrth raddfa *be*
draw tongs gefel dynnu *eb* gefeiliau tynnu
draw toolbox blwch offer lluniadu *eg* blychau offer lluniadu
draw-a-man test prawf tynnu llun person *eg* profion tynnu llun person
drawbolt tynfollt *eg* tynfolltau
drawboring darforio *be*
drawbridge pont godi *eb* pontydd codi
drawer drôr *eg* droriau
drawer and cupboard pulls dolennau droriau a chypyrddau *ell*
drawer base gwaelod drôr *eg* gwaelodion droriau
drawer bearer cynhalydd drôr *eg* cynalyddion drôr
drawer bottom gwaelod drôr *eg* gwaelodion droriau
drawer construction adeiladwaith drôr *eg*
drawer guide rhedwr drôr *eg* rhedwyr drôr
drawer joint uniad drôr *eg* uniadau drôr
drawer lock clo drôr *eg* cloeon drôr
drawer lock chisel cŷn clo drôr *eg* cynion clo drôr; gaing glo drôr *eb* geingiau clo drôr
drawer opening agoriad drôr *eg* agoriadau drôr
drawer rail rheilen ddrôr *eb* rheiliau drôr
drawer runner rhedwr drôr *eg* rhedwyr drôr
drawer side ochr ddrôr *eb* ochrau drôr
drawer slip drôr-gryfhawr *eg* drôr-gryfhawyr
drawfiling darffeilio *be*
drawing (in general) llun *eg* lluniau
drawing (in technical sense) lluniad *eg* lluniadau
drawing convention confensiwn lluniadu *eg*
drawing down (forging process) tynnu lawr *be*
drawing ink inc lluniadu *eg* inciau lluniadu
drawing instruments offer lluniadu *ell*
drawing mode modd lluniadu *eg*
drawing object bar bar gwrthrych lluniadu *eg* barrau gwrthrych lluniadu
drawing options dewisiadau lluniadu *ell*
drawing pencil pensil lluniadu *eg* pensiliau lluniadu
drawing program rhaglen luniadu *eb* rhaglenni lluniadu

drawing technique techneg luniadu *eb* technegau lluniadu
drawing view golwg lluniadu *eb*
drawing-board bwrdd lluniadu *eg* byrddau lluniadu
drawing-board clamp clamp bwrdd lluniadu *eg* clampiau bwrdd lluniadu
drawing-board clip clip bwrdd lluniadu *eg* clipiau bwrdd lluniadu
drawing-paper papur lluniadu *eg*
drawing-pin pìn bawd *eg* pinnau bawd
drawknife cyllell ddeugarn *eb* cyllyll deugarn
drawn fabric embroidery brodwaith ffabrig *eg*
drawn game gêm gyfartal *eb* gemau cyfartal
drawn line llinelliad *eg* llinelliadau
drawn thread embroidery brodwaith tynnu edau *eg*
drawsheet cynfas dynnu *eb* cynfasau tynnu
drawstring llinyn tynnu *eg* llinynnau tynnu
dredge carthu *be*
dredger (=dredging ship) llong garthu *eb* llongau carthu
dredger (for sprinkling) sgeintydd *eg* sgeintyddion
Dreikaiserbund Cynghrair y Tri Brenin *eb*
dress *v* gwisgo *be*
dress (=clothing) *n* gwisg *eb* gwisgoedd
dress (=frock) *n* ffrog *eb* ffrogiau
dress (in cooking) *v* trin *be*
dress placket opening agoriad placed ffrog *eg*
dress sense chwaeth gwisgo *eb*
dress shield pad chwys *eg* padiau chwys
dress the set gwisgo'r set *be*
dress the stage gwisgo'r llwyfan *be*
dress weight pwysau ffrog *ell*
dresser (furniture) dreser *eb* dreserau
dressing (for salad) dresin *eg* dresins
dressing (on wound) gorchudd *eg* gorchuddion
dressing gown gŵn tŷ *eg* gynau tŷ
dressing table bwrdd gwisgo *eg* byrddau gwisgo
dressing up gwisgo *be*
dressmaker gwniyddes *eb* gwniyddesau
dressmaker's dummy model gwniyddes *eg* modelau gwniyddes
dressmaker's pin pìn bach *eg* pinnau bach
Dreyfus affair helynt Dreyfus *eg*
dribble (in sport) *n* dribl *eg*
dribble (in sport) *v* driblo *be*
dribble (saliva) *v* glafoerio *be*
dribbler driblwr *eg* driblwyr
dried fruits ffrwythau sych *ell*
dried milk llaeth powdr *eg*
drier sychydd *eg* sychyddion
drift (fishing) *v* drifftio *be*
drift (longshore) *n* drifft *eg* drifftiau
drift (of snow etc) lluwch *eg* lluwchfeydd
drift net rhwyd ddrifft *eb* rhwydi drifft
drift velocity cyflymder drifft *eg*
drifter (ship) driffter *eb* driffterau
drifting (forging process) drifftio *be*
drifting (of holes) gwneud tyllau *be*
driftwood broc *eg*
drill *n* dril *eg* driliau
drill *v* drilio *be*
drill bit ebill dril *eg* ebillion dril
drill chuck crafanc dril *eb* crafangau dril
drill part rhan dril *eg* rhannau dril
drill size maint dril *eg* meintiau driliau
drill socket soced dril *eg* socedi dril
drill table bwrdd drilio *eg* byrddau drilio
driller driliwr *eg* drilwyr
drilling capacity maint drilio *be*
drilling jig jig drilio *eg* jigiau drilio
drilling machine peiriant drilio *eg* peiriannau drilio
drinking chocolate siocled yfed *eg*
drip rings modrwyau *ell*
drip tray (for drip-dry and synthetics) hambwrdd diferu *eg* hambyrddau diferu
drip-dry *adj* dripsych *ans*
drip-dry *v* dripsychu *be*
dripping toddion *ell*
dripstone bargodfaen *eg* bargodfeini
drive (a nail) *v* curo *be*
drive (act of) *n* gyriad *eg* gyriadau
drive (in general) *v* gyrru *be*
drive (in sport) *n* dreif *eb* dreifiau
drive (of car, computer etc) *n* gyriant *eg* gyriannau
drive (urge) *n* ysfa *eb*
drive reduction hypothesis rhagdybiaeth lleihau ysfa *eb*
drive the ball dreifio'r bêl *be*
driver gyrrwr *eg* gyrwyr
driver and driven gyrru a gyredig
driver cell cell yrru *eb* celloedd gyrru
driver circuit cylched yrru *eb* cylchedau gyrru
driver settings gosodiadau gyrrwr *ell*
driving belt belt yrru *eb* beltiau gyrru
driving disk disg gyrru *eg* disgiau gyrru
driving dog cariwr *eg* carwyr
driving fit ffit orwasg *eb* ffitiau gorwasg
driving plate plât troi *eg* platiau troi
drizzle glaw mân *eg*
drone drôn *eg*
drone accompaniment cyfeiliant drôn *eg*
drone bass bas drôn *eg* basau drôn
drop (=fall) *n* cwymp *eg*
drop (a ball) *v* gollwng *be*
drop (of liquid) *n* diferyn *eg* diferion
drop (of liquid) *v* diferu *be*
drop caps priflythrennau bach *ell*
drop forging delw ofannu *be*
drop goal gôl adlam *eb* goliau adlam
drop in gollwng *be*
drop kick cic adlam *eb* ciciau adlam
drop out (of ball) *v* adlamu allan *be*
drop pattern patrwm disgyn *eg* patrymau disgyn
drop shot ergyd gwta *eb* ergydion cwta

drop-down door drws gostwng *eg* drysau gostwng
drop-down menu cwymplen *eb* cwymplenni
drop-leaf table bwrdd dalen blyg *eg* byrddau dalenni plyg
droplet defnyn *eg* defnynnau
droplet infection heintiad defnynnau *eg*
dropped ball pêl gwymp *eb* peli cwymp
dropped shoulder ysgwydd isel *eb* ysgwyddau isel
dropper diferydd *eg* diferyddion
dropping funnel twndis diferu *eg* twndisau diferu; twmffat diferu *eg* twmffedi diferu
dropping the atomic bomb gollwng y bom atomig *be*
drops of blood dafnau gwaed *ell*
drops of moisture dafnau hylif *ell*
dross amhuredd *eg*
drought sychder *eg* sychderau
drover porthmon *eg* porthmyn
drowned valley dyffryn boddedig *eg* dyffrynnoedd boddedig
drowsy swrth *ans*
drug cyffur *eg* cyffuriau
drug abuse camddefnyddio cyffuriau *be*
drug addiction caethiwed i gyffuriau *eb*
drug administration gweini cyffuriau *be*
drug dependency dibyniaeth ar gyffuriau *eb*
drug levels lefelau cyffuriau *ell*
drug resistance ymwrthiant cyffuriau *eg*
drugs and alcohol cyffuriau ac alcohol
druid derwydd *eg* derwyddon
druidism derwyddiaeth *eb*
drum drwm *eg* drymiau
drum and sticks drwm a ffyn
drum kit offer drymiau *ell*
drum printer argraffydd drwm *eg* argraffyddion drwm
drum roll bwrlwm drwm *eg* bwrlwm drymiau
drumlin drymlin *eb* drymlinau
drummer drymiwr *eg* drymwyr
drunk *adj* meddw *ans*
drunk *n* meddwyn *eg* meddwon
drunken saw llif chwil *eb* llifiau chwil
drunken screw sgriw chwil *eb* sgriwiau chwil
drunken thread edau chwil *eb* edafedd chwil
drupe drŵp *eg* drwpiau
druxiness marc gwyn mewn pren *eg* marciau gwyn mewn pren
dry *adj* sych *ans*
dry *v* sychu *be*
dry brush brwsh sych *eg* brwshys sych
dry cleaned sychlan *ans*
dry cleaners sychlanhawyr *ell*
dry cleaning sychlanhau *be*
dry colourant lliwydd sych *eg* lliwyddion sych
dry frying ffrio sych *be*
dry point engraving ysgythriad sychbwynt *eg* ysgythriadau sychbwynt
dry point site safle sych *eg* safleoedd sych
dry rot pydredd sych *eg*
dry run rhediad ffug *eg* rhediadau ffug
dry transfer lettering llythrennu troslun sych *be*
dry valley dyffryn sych *eg* dyffrynnoedd sych
dry weight pwysau sych *ell*
dry-bright polish llathr disgleirsych *eg*
drying agent cyfrwng sychu *eg*
drying cabinet cwpwrdd sychu *eg* cypyrddau sychu
drying process proses sychu *eb* prosesau sychu
drying rack rhesel sychu *eb* rheseli sychu
drying time amser sychu *eg* amserau sychu
drypoint etching ysgythru sychbwynt *be*
dual deuol *ans*
dual alliance cynghrair ddeublyg *eb* cynghreiriau deublyg
dual carriageway ffordd ddeuol *eb* ffyrdd deuol
dual inline memory module modiwl cof mewnlin deuol *eg* modiwlau cof mewnlin deuol
Dual Monarchy Brenhiniaeth Ddeuol *eb*
dual ownership perchenogaeth ddeublyg *eb* perchenogaethau deublyg
dual purpose pwrpas deublyg *eg*
dual sensory impairment nam ar ddau synnwyr *eg*
dual-action antidepressant gwrthiselydd deuweithredol *eg* gwrthiselyddion deuweithredol
dualism deuoliaeth *eb*
dual-route model of reading model darllen deulwybr *eg*
dual-task methodology methodoleg ddwy-dasg *eb*
dubbing (of sound) tros-seinio *be*
dubbing (of speech translation) trosleisio *be*
ducal dugol *ans*
Duchenne smile gwên Duchenne *eb*
duchess duges *eb* dugesau
duchesse set matiau duchesse *ell*
duchy dugaeth *eb* dugaethau
duck hwyaden *eb* hwyaid
duck dive deif hwyaden *eb* deifiau hwyaden
duck-board bwrdd cerdded *eg* byrddau cerdded
ducking dowcio *be*
ducking stool stôl drochi *eb* stolion trochi
duct dwythell *eb* dwythellau
ductile hydwyth *ans*
ductility hydwythedd *eg*
ductless diddwythell *ans*
ductless gland chwarren ddiddwythell *eb* chwarennau diddwythell
duel gornest *eb* gornestau
duet deuawd *eb* deuawdau
dugout twll ymochel *eg* tyllau ymochel
duke dug *eg* dugiaid
Duke of Lancaster Dug Lancaster *eg*
Duke of York Dug Efrog *eg*
dukedom dugaeth *eb*
dukha (=dukka) dukha *eg*
dukka (=dukha) dukka *eg*
dulciana dulciana *eg*

dulcimer dwlsimer *eg* dwlsimerau
dulcitone dylsiton *eg* dylsitonau
duly (=as is right) yn briodol *adf*
duma dwma *eg*
dumb child plentyn mud *eg* plant mud
dumb terminal terfynell fud *eb* terfynellau mud
dummy *v* ffugio *be*
dummy (=false pass) *n* ffugiad *eg* ffugiadau
dummy (for sucking) *n* dymi *eg* dymïau
dummy (in rugby) *n* ffug-bàs *eg/b* ffugbasiau
dummy pipe (on organ) pibell fud *eb* pibellau mud
dump *n* tomen *eb* tomennydd
dump *n* dymp *eg* dympiau
dump *v* dympio *be*
dumpling twmplen *eb* twmplenni
Dundee cake teisen Dundee *eb* teisennau Dundee; cacen Dundee *eb* cacen Dundee
dune twyn *eg* twyni
dune community cymuned dwyni *eb* cymunedau twyni
dune slack llac twyni *eg* llaciau twyni
dungarees dyngarîs *eg*
dungeon dwnsiwn *eg* dwnsiynau
duodecimal deuddegol *ans*
duodenum dwodenwm *eg*
duple dyblyg *ans*
duple minor set set ddeubar *eb* setiau deubar
duple time amser dau *eg*
duplet dwbled *eg* dwbledau
duplex dwplecs *eg* dwplecsau
duplicate *adj* dyblyg *ans*
duplicate *n* copi dyblyg *eg* copïau dyblyg
duplicate *n* dyblygeb *eb* dyblygebau
duplicate *v* dyblygu *be*
duplicate slide sleid ddyblyg *eb* sleidiau dyblyg
duplication dyblygiad *eg* dyblygiadau
durability gwydnwch *eg*
durable gwydn *ans*
durable colour lliw sy'n para *eg* lliwiau sy'n para
durable goods nwyddau sy'n para *ell*
duralumin dwralwmin *eg*
duramen dwramen *eg*
duration parhad *eg*
duration (of heart beat) amser parhad *eg*
duration of pause hyd yr oedi *eg*
Durga Durga *eb*
Durga Puja Durga Puja *eb*
duricrust cramen galed *eb* cramennau caled
dust *n* llwch *eg*
dust *v* tynnu llwch *be*
dust board (drawer) bwrdd llwch *eg* byrddau llwch
dust bowl powlen lwch *eb* powlenni llwch
dust devil cythraul llwch *eg* cythreuliaid llwch
dust free atmosphere atmosffer di-lwch *eg*
dust particle gronyn llwch *eg* gronynnau llwch
dustbin bin sbwriel *eg* biniau sbwriel
dust-free di-lwch *ans*
dustpan padell lwch *eb* pedyll llwch
dust-proof rhydd o lwch *ans*
dusty llychlyd *ans*
Dutch *adj* Iseldiraidd *ans*
Dutch (language) *n* Iseldireg *eb*
Dutch elm disease clefyd llwyfen yr Iseldiroedd *eg*
Dutch metal aloi'r Iseldiroedd *eg*
Dutchman Iseldirwr *eg* Iseldirwyr
duty (=tax) toll *eb* tollau
duty of care dyletswydd gofal *eb*
duty officer swyddog dyletswydd *eg* swyddogion dyletswydd
duumvir deuwriad *eg* deuwriaid
duumvirate deuwraeth *eb*
duvet duvet *eg*
duxelles duxelles *ell*
dwarf pea corbysen *eb* corbys
dwarf plant corblanhigyn *eg* corblanhigion
dwarf shrub corwrych *eg* corwrychoedd
dwarf star seren gorrach *eb* sêr corrach
dwarf willow corhelygen *eb* corhelyg
dwarfism corachedd *eg*
dwell angle ongl breswyl *eb* onglau preswyl
dwelling annedd *eg/b* anheddau
dyad deuad *eg* deuadau
dye *n* llifyn *eg* llifynnau
dye *v* llifo *be*
dye fix sefydlyn llifyn *eg* sefydlynnau llifyn
dye loss colli llifyn *be*
dye pick-up codi llifyn *be*
dyebath baddon llifo *eg* baddonau llifo
dyed llifedig *ans*
▸ **dyed cane** gwialen liw *eb* gwialennau lliw
dyed hessian hesian llifedig *eg*
dyed seagrass morwellt llifedig *ell*
dyed string llinyn llifedig *eg* llinynnau llifedig
dyestuff defnydd llifo *eg*
dyke (=ditch) ffos *eb* ffosydd
dyke (=sea wall) morglawdd *eg* morgloddiau
dyke (=wall) clawdd *eg* cloddiau
dyke (in geology) deic *eg* deiciau
dyke swarm clwstwr deiciau *eg* clystyrau deiciau
dynamic *adj* dynamig *ans*
dynamic allocation dyrannu dynamig *be*
dynamic data structure strwythur data dynamig *eg*
dynamic equilibrium ecwilibriwm dynamig *eg*
dynamic memory cof dynamig *eg* cofion dynamig
dynamic random access memory (DRAM) cof hapgyrch dynamig *eg*
dynamic screen sgrin ddynamig *eb* sgriniau dynamig
dynamic store storfa ddynamig *eb* storfeydd dynamig
dynamical dynamegol *ans*
dynamically updateable web page tudalen we y gellir ei diweddaru'n ddynamig *eb* tudalennau gwe y gellir eu diweddaru'n ddynamig

dynamically updated web page tudalen we wedi'i diweddaru'n ddynamig *eb* tudalennau gwe wedi'u diweddaru'n ddynamig

dynamics dynameg *eb*

dynamite dynameit *eg*

dynamo dynamo *eg* dynamoau

dynamometer dynamometr *eg* dynamometrau

dynastic llinachyddol *ans*

dynasticism llinachyddiaeth *eb*

dynasty llinach *eb*

dynatron dynatron *eg* dynatronau

dysarthria parlys lleferydd *eg*

dysentery dysentri *eg*

dysfluency diffyg rhuglder *eg*

dysfunction camweithrediad *eg* camweithrediadau

dyslexia dyslecsia *eg*

dyslexic dyslecsig *ans*

dyspepsia diffyg traul *eg*

dyspeptic dyspeptig *ans*

dysphasia dysffasia *eg*

dyspnoea dyspnoea *eg*

dysprosium (Dy) dysprosiwm *eg*

dysthymic disorder anhwylder dysthymig *eg*

dystrophic camfaethol *ans*

dystrophy (in physiology) nychdod *eg*

E

'E' alloy aloi 'E' *eg*
E major E fwyaf *eb*
E minor E leiaf *eb*
eager awyddus *ans*
ear clust *eg/b* clustiau
ear discharge rhedlif clust *eg*
ear drum tympan y glust *eg*
ear flick plwc clust *eg*
ear, nose and throat clust, trwyn a gwddf
ear ossicle esgyrnyn y glust *eg* esgyrnynnau'r glust
earache clust dost *eb* clustiau tost; pigyn clust
eardrum pilen y glust *eb* pilennau'r clustiau
earl iarll *eg* ieirll
Earl Marshall Iarll Farsial *eg*
earldom iarllaeth *eb* iarllaethau
early adolescence llencyndod cynnar *eg*
early adopter mabwysiadwr cynnar *eg* mabwysiadwyr cynnar
Early Bronze Age Oes Efydd Gynnar *eb*
early childhood plentyndod cynnar *eg*
Early Christian art Celfyddyd Cristnogaeth Gynnar *eb*
early history hanes cynnar *eg*
early modern history hanes modern cynnar *eg*
early modern period cyfnod modern cynnar *eg*
early modern world byd modern cynnar *eg*
early peoples pobloedd cynnar *ell*
early years blynyddoedd cynnar *ell*
early years education service gwasanaeth addysg blynyddoedd cynnar *eg* gwasanaethau addysg blynyddoedd cynnar
early years learning dysgu blynyddoedd cynnar *be*
early years worker gweithiwr blynyddoedd cynnar *eg* gweithwyr blynyddoedd cynnar
earmark clustnodi *be*
earmarked funding cyllid a glustnodwyd *eg*
earned income incwm gwaith *eg*
earnings enillion *ell*
earphone ffôn clust *eg* ffonau clust
earring clustdlws *eg* clustdlysau
earth *v* daearu *be*
earth (=soil) *n* pridd *eg* priddoedd
earth (of land) *n* daear *eb* daearoedd
Earth (of planet) *n* Daear *eb*
earth flow tirlif *eg* tirlifiau
earth movement symudiad daear *eg* symudiadau daear
earth tremor daeargryd *eg* daeargrydiau
earth wire gwifren ddaearu *eb* gwifrau daearu
earthenware llestri pridd *ell*
earthing daearu *be*
earthquake daeargryn *eg* daeargrynfeydd
earthquake hazard perygl o ddaeargryn *eg*
earthshine llewyrch daear *eg*
earthwork gwrthglawdd *eg* gwrthgloddiau
ease *n* esmwythder *eg*
ease *v* lleddfu *be*
ease (easing of fullness) *v* esmwytho *be*
ease of flow rhwyddineb llifo *eg*
ease of formation rhwyddineb ffurfiant *eg*
easel îsl *eg* islau
easel tray hambwrdd îsl *eg* hambyrddau îsl
east dwyrain *eg*
East India Company Cwmni India'r Dwyrain *eg*
Easter Pasg *eg*
Easter day Sul y Pasg *eg*
Eastern Europe Dwyrain Ewrop *eb*
Eastern grip gafael y flaen-llaw *eb*
eastern margins glandiroedd dwyreiniol *ell*
Eastern Question Cwestiwn y Dwyrain *eg*
Eastern religions crefyddau'r Dwyrain *ell*
easting dwyreiniad *eg* dwyreiniaid
easy hawdd *ans*
easy solder sodr rhwydd *eg* sodrau rhwydd
easy-flo solder sodr llifrwydd *eg* sodrau llifrwydd
eaves bondo *eg* bondoeau
ebb trai *eg* treiau
EBCDIC code cod EBCDIC *eg*
ebonizing eboneiddio *be*
ebony eboni *eg*
ebony stain staen eboni *eg* staeniau eboni
EBP: Education Business Partnership PAB: Partneriaeth Addysg Busnes *eb*
ebullioscopic ebwliosgopig *ans*
ebullioscopy ebwliosgopaeth *eg*
ebullition byrlymu *be*
eccentric (of geometrical figures, ellipses) echreiddig *ans*
eccentric centre allganol *eg* allganolau
eccentric circle allgylch *eg* allgylchoedd
eccentric disc disg echreiddig *eg* disgiau echreiddig
eccentricity echreiddiad *eg* echreiddiadau
ecclesiastical eglwysig *ans*
ecclesiastical canon canon eglwysig *eg* canonau eglwysig
ecclesiastical embroidery brodwaith eglwysig *eg*

ecclesiastical history hanes eglwysig *eg*
ecclesiastical mode modd eglwysig *eg* moddau eglwysig
Ecclesiastical Ordinances Ordinhadau Eglwysig *ell*
ecclesiasticism eglwysyddiaeth *eb*
ecdysis ecdysis *eg*
echelon echelon *eg*
echelon form ffurf echelon *eb* ffurfiau echelon
echinoderm echinoderm *eg* echinodermau
echo *n* atsain *eb* atseiniau
echo *v* atseinio *be*
echo chorus côr atsain *eg* corau atsain
echo game gêm atsain *eb* gemau atsain
echo organ organ atsain *eb* organau atsain
echoic memory cof adleisiol *eg*
echolalia ecolalia *eg*
echolalic speech lleferydd ecolalig *eg*
echolocation lleoliad adlais *eg*
eclair eclair *eb* eclairs
eclectic eclectig *ans*
eclectic approach dull eclectig *eg*
eclipse (of sun, moon) diffyg *eg*
eclipsed conformation cydffurfiad gorchuddiedig *eg* cydffurfiadau gorchuddiedig
ecliptic ecliptig *ans*
ecliptic plane plân ecliptig *eg* planau ecliptig
eclogue bugeilgerdd *eb* bugeilgerddi
ecocline ecoclin *eg*
ecological ecolegol *ans*
ecological pattern patrwm ecolegol *eg* patrymau ecolegol
ecological validity dilysrwydd ecolegol *eg*
ecology ecoleg *eb*
e-commerce e-fasnach *eb*
econometrics econometreg *eb*
economic economaidd *ans*
Economic & Social Council Cyngor Economaidd a Chymdeithasol *eg*
economic activity gweithgaredd economaidd *eg* gweithgareddau economaidd
economic and industrial understanding dealltwriaeth economaidd a diwydiannol *eb*
economic cost cost economaidd *eg*
economic development datblygu economaidd *be*
economic factor ffactor economaidd *eb* ffactorau economaidd
economic goods nwyddau economaidd *ell*
economic growth twf economaidd *eg*
economic history hanes economaidd *eg*
economic prosperity ffyniant economaidd *eg*
economic recovery adferiad economaidd *eg*
economic rent rhent economaidd *eg*
economical (=frugal) darbodus *ans*
economically developing country gwlad sy'n datblygu'n economaidd *eb* gwledydd sy'n datblygu'n economaidd
economics economeg *eb*
economics of education economeg addysgu *eb*
economies of scale darbodion maint *ell*
economist economegydd *eg* economegwyr
economize gwneud arbedion *be*
economy economi *eg/b* economïau
ecospecies ecorywogaeth *eb*
ecosystem ecosystem *eb* ecosystemau
ecotone cyffindir *eg* cyffindiroedd
ecotone ecotôn *eg* ecotonau
ecotype ecoteip *eg* ecoteipiau
ectoderm ectoderm *eg*
ectoparasite ectoparasit *eg* ectoparasitiaid
ectoplasm ectoplasm *eg*
ecumene byd cyfannedd, y *eg*
ecumenical eciwmenaidd *ans*
ecumenical movement mudiad eciwmenaidd *eg* mudiadau eciwmenaidd
ecumenism eciwmeniaeth *eb*
eczema ecsema *eg*
edaphic edaffig *ans*
eddy *n* trolif *eg* trolifau
eddy *v* trolifo *be*
eddy current cerrynt trolif *eg* ceryntau trolif
edge *v* ymylu *be*
edge (=rim, side) *n* ymyl *eg/b* ymylon
edge (=sharpness) *n* min *eg* minion
edge detection canfod ymyl *be*
edge guide ffin-ganllaw *eg* ffin-ganllawiau
edge joint uniad ymyl *eg* uniadau ymyl
edge jointing ymyluno *be*
edge mark marc ymyl *eg* marciau ymyl
edge stitch ymylbwytho *be*
edge to edge ymyl wrth ymyl
edge treatment triniaeth ymyl *eb*
edged tools offer miniog *ell*
edging ymylwaith *eg*
edict cyhoeddeb *eb* cyhoeddebau
Edict of Emancipation Cyhoeddeb Rhyddfreiniad *eb*
Edict of Fraternity Cyhoeddeb Brawdgarwch *eb*
Edict of Restitution (1629) Cyhoeddeb Adferiad *eb*
edit golygu *be*
edit all axes golygu pob echel *be*
edit all titles golygu pob teitl *be*
edit applet golygu rhaglennig *be*
edit autocorrect golygu awtogywiro *be*
edit autotext golygu awtodestun *be*
edit axis golygu echel *be*
edit bibliography entry golygu cofnod llyfryddiaeth *be*
edit cell style golygu arddull cell *be*
edit changes golygu newidiadau *be*
edit chart data golygu data siart *be*
edit chart floor golygu llawr siart *be*
edit chart type golygu math o siart *be*
edit chart wall golygu mur siart *be*
edit column description golygu disgrifiad colofn *be*
edit comment golygu sylw *be*
edit concordance file golygu ffeil mynegeiriau *be*

edit contour golygu amlinell *be*
edit custom dictionary golygu geiriadur addasu *be*
edit data golygu data *be*
edit data point golygu pwynt data *be*
edit data series golygu cyfres data *be*
edit datapilot table golygu tabl databeilot *be*
edit field golygu maes *be*
edit file golygu ffeil *be*
edit filter settings golygu gosodiadau hidlydd *be*
edit folder bookmarks golygu nodau tudalen ffolder *be*
edit footnote golygu troednodyn *be*
edit forms golygu ffurflenni *be*
edit frame golygu ffrâm *be*
edit frameset golygu fframset *be*
edit graphics golygu graffigau *be*
edit grid golygu grid *be*
edit hyperlink golygu hypergyswllt *be*
edit index golygu mynegai *be*
edit index entry golygu cofnod mynegai *be*
edit labels golygu labeli *be*
edit legend golygu allwedd *be*
edit links golygu cysylltiadau *be*
edit macros golygu macros *be*
edit number format golygu fformat rhif *be*
edit object golygu gwrthrych *be*
edit page style golygu arddull tudalen *be*
edit print range golygu ystod argraffu *be*
edit script golygu sgript *be*
edit sections golygu adrannau *be*
edit snap line golygu llinell osod *be*
edit snap point golygu pwynt gosod *be*
edit style golygu arddull *be*
edit subtitle golygu isdeitl *be*
edit symbols golygu symbolau *be*
edit table golygu tabl *be*
edit template golygu templed *be*
edit title golygu teitl *be*
edit variable golygu newidyn *be*
editing tool offeryn golygu *eg* offer golygu
edition argraffiad *eg* argraffiadau
editor golygydd *eg* golygyddion
educability addysgedd *eg*
educable addysgadwy *ans*
education addysg *eb*
Education Act Deddf Addysg *eb*
education authority awdurdod addysg *eg* awdurdodau addysg
education committee pwyllgor addysg *eg* pwyllgorau addysg
education officer swyddog addysg *eg* swyddogion addysg
education priority area ardal o flaenoriaeth addysgol *eb* ardaloedd o flaenoriaeth addysgol
Education Reform Act Deddf Diwygio Addysg *eb*
Education Secretary Ysgrifennydd Addysg *eg*
education welfare officer swyddog lles addysg *eg* swyddogion lles addysg
educational addysgol *ans*
educational advantage mantais addysgol *eb* manteision addysgol
► **educational approach** dull addysgol *eg* dulliau addysgol
educational development datblygiad addysgol *eg* datblygiadau addysgol
educational facilities cyfleusterau addysgol *ell*
educational guidance cyfarwyddyd addysgol *eg*
educational gymnastics gymnasteg addysgol *eb*
educational needs anghenion addysgol *ell*
educational program rhaglen addysgol *eb* rhaglenni addysgol
educational psychologist seicolegydd addysg *eg* seicolegwyr addysg
educational psychology seicoleg addysg *eb*
educational quotient cyniferydd addysgol *eg* cyniferyddion addysgol
educational support grant grant cynnal addysg *eg* grantiau cynnal addysg
educational toy tegan addysgol *eg* teganau addysgol
educationalist addysgwr *eg* addysgwyr
educative addysgiadol *ans*
educe edwytho *be*
eduction edwythiad *eg*
Edward the Confessor Edward Gyffeswr *eg*
Edward the Elder Edward yr Hynaf *eg*
Edwardian Edwardaidd *ans*
Edwardian Conquest Goresgyniad Edward *eg*
Edwardian era oes Edwardaidd *eb*
Edwardian Settlement Ardrefniant Edward *eg*
eel llysywen *eb* llyswennod
eelpout gweflogyn *eg* gweflogynion
e-enable e-alluogi *be*
effect effaith *eg/b* effeithiau
effect of frequency effaith amledd *eb*
effect of pollution effaith llygredd *eb* effeithiau llygredd
effective effeithiol *ans*
effective movement symudiad effeithiol *eg* symudiadau effeithiol
effective performance perfformiad effeithiol *eg* perfformiadau effeithiol
effective rainfall glawiad effeithiol *eg*
effective response ymateb effeithiol *eg* ymatebion effeithiol
effectiveness effeithiolrwydd *eg*
effector effeithydd *eg* effeithyddion
efferent echddygol *ans*
efferent nerve nerf echddygol *eg* nerfau echddygol
efferent neuron niwron echddygol *eg* niwronau echddygol
effervesce eferwi *be*
effervescence eferwad *eg*
effervescing eferwol *ans*
efficacy effeithiolrwydd *eg*
efficiency (in general) effeithlonrwydd *eg*

efficiency (of machines, in technical usage) effeithlonedd *eg*
► **efficiency and effectiveness** effeithlonrwydd ac effeithiolrwydd
efficiency savings arbedion effeithlonrwydd *ell*
efficient effeithlon *ans*
efficient cause achos effeithlon *eg*
effigy arddelw *eb* arddelwau
efflorescence ewlychiad *eg* ewlychiadau
efflorescent ewlychol *ans*
effluence elifiant *eg* elifiannau
effluent *adj* elifol *ans*
effluent (in general) *n* elifyn *eg* elifion
effluent (of sewage) *n* carthffrwd *eb* carthffrydiau
effort ymdrech *eg/b* ymdrechion
effortful processing prosesu ymdrechol *be*
egalitarian *adj* egalitaraidd *ans*
egalitarian *n* egalitariad *eg* egalitariaid
egalitarianism egalitariaeth *eb*
egest carthu *be*
egestion (amoeba) allfwrw *be*
egestion (digestive tract) carthiad *eg*
egg wy *eg* wyau
egg and dart treatment addurn wy a saethell *eg*
egg cup cwpan wy *eg* cwpanau wy
egg custard cwstard wy *eg*
egg custard sauce saws cwstard wy *eg*
egg custard tart tarten gwstard wy *eb* tartenni cwstard wy
egg formation ffurfiant wy *eg*
egg membrane pilen wy *eb* pilenni wy
egg nucleus cnewyllyn wy *eg*
egg shape ar ffurf wy *ans*
egg tempera tempera wy *eg*
egg yolk melynwy *eg*
egg-shaped head pen ffurf wy *eg* pennau ffurf wy
eggshell plisgyn wy *eg* plisg wy
eggshell finish gorffeniad plisgyn wy *eg*
eggshell paint paent plisgyn wy *eg*
eggshell porcelain porslen plisgyn wy *eg*
ego ego *eg*
egocentric myfïol *ans*
egocentricity myfïaeth *eb*
ego-ideal hunanddelfryd *eg*
e-government e-lywodraeth *eb*
Egyptian hieroglyphics hieroglyffigau'r Eifftwyr *ell*
Egyptology Eifftoleg *eb*
eiderdown cwrlid plu *eg* cwrlidau plu
eigen function ffwythiant eigen *eg* ffwythiannau eigen
eigen value gwerth eigen *eg* gwerthoedd eigen
eigen vector fector eigen *eg* fectorau eigen
eight wyth *eg/b* wythau
eight (of person) wythwr *eg* wythwyr
eight bit buffer byffer wyth did *eg*
eight points of the compass wyth pwynt y cwmpawd *eg*
Eightfold Path (in Buddhism) Llwybr Wythblyg *eg*
eighth (interval) wythfed *eg* wythfedau
eighth-note (quaver) nodyn wyth *eg* nodau wyth
einsteinium (Es) einsteiniwm *eg*
Einstellung Einstellung *eg*
eisteddfod eisteddfod *eb* eisteddfodau
either way offence trosedd neillfordd *eb* troseddau neillfordd
ejaculate alldaflu *be*
ejaculation (in physiology) alldafliad *eg* alldafliadau
ejaculatory alldaflol *ans*
eject bwrw allan *be*
ejection allfwriad *eg* allfwriadau
Ejection of Scandalous Ministers Act Deddf Diarddel Gweinidogion Gwarthus *eb*
ejector drift drifft llacio *eg*
e-journal e-gyfnodolyn *eg* e-gyfnodolion
ekistics anheddeg *eb*
El Niño El Niño *eg*
elaborate (=detail) *v* manylu *be*
elaborate (=detailed) *adj* manwl *ans*
elaborate (a work of art) *v* coethi *be*
elaborate (of work of art) *adj* coeth *ans*
elaboration likelihood model model manylder tebygolrwydd *eg*
elaborative rehearsal ymarfer manwl *eg*
elapsed seconds (of document done) ers eiliad
elapsed time amser a aeth heibio *eg*
elastic *adj* elastig *ans*
elastic *n* elastig *eg*
elastic band band elastig *eg* bandiau elastig
elastic energy egni elastig *eg*
elastic fibre ffibr elastig *eg* ffibrau elastig
elastic limit terfan elastig *eb* terfannau elastig
elastic potential energy egni potensial elastig *eg*
elastic recoil adlamiad elastig *eg*
elastic scattering gwasgariad elastig *eg*
elasticity (of material, in economics) elastigedd *eg* elastigeddau
elasticity of demand elastigedd y galw *eg*
elastine elastin *eg*
elastomeric elastomerig *ans*
elastomers elastomerau *ell*
elation (in physics) ymlediad *eg* ymlediadau
elbow penelin *eg/b* penelinoedd
elbow angle ongl benelin *eb* onglau penelin
elbow joint cymal penelin *eg* cymalau penelin
elbow of capture elin ladrad *eb* elin ladradau
elder henuriad *eg* henaduriaid
elder statesman gwladweinydd hŷn *eg* gwladweinwyr hŷn
elderly *adj* oedrannus *ans*
elderly *n* henoed *ell*
elderly visitor ymwelydd oedrannus *eg* ymwelwyr oedrannus
e-learning e-ddysgu *be*
elect *adj* etholedig *ans*

elect *n* etholedig rai *ell*
elect *v* ethol *be*
election etholiad *eg* etholiadau
elective monarchy brenhiniaeth etholedig *eb*
elective mutism dewis peidio â siarad *be*
elector etholwr *eg* etholwyr
Elector (Germany) Etholydd *eg* Etholyddion
Elector Archbishop Etholydd Archesgob *eg*
Elector Palatine Etholydd Palatin *eg*
electoral etholiadol *ans*
electoral machinery peirianwaith etholiadol *eg*
electoral reform diwygio etholiadol *be*
electoral representation cynrychiolaeth etholiadol *eb*
electoral system trefn etholiadol *eb*
electorate etholwyr *ell*
Electra complex cymhleth Electra *eg*
electric *adj* trydanol *ans*
electric *n* trydan *eg*
electric arc furnace ffwrnais arc drydan *eb* ffwrneisi arc trydan
electric arc welding weldio arc drydan *be*
electric blanket blanced drydan *eb* blancedi trydan
electric blue (enamelling colour) glas trydan *eg*
electric circuit cylched drydanol *eb* cylchedau trydanol
electric current cerrynt trydan *eg* ceryntau trydan
electric drill dril trydan *eg* driliau trydan
electric element elfen drydan *eb* elfennau trydan
electric field line llinell faes drydanol *eb* llinellau maes trydanol
electric field meter mesurydd maes trydanol *eg* mesuryddion maes trydanol
electric finishing stove stof orffennu drydan *eb* stofiau gorffennu trydan
electric flex fflecs drydan *eb* fflecsys trydan
electric force of attraction grym atyniad trydanol *eg*
electric force of repulsion grym gwrthyriad trydanol *eg*
electric fuse ffiws trydan *eg* ffiwsys trydan
electric guitar gitâr drydan *eb* gitarau trydan
electric iron haearn trydan *eg*
electric kiln odyn drydan *eb* odynnau trydan
electric motor modur trydan *eg* moduron trydan
electric musical instrument offeryn cerdd trydan *eg* offerynnau cerdd trydan
electric organ organ drydan *eb* organau trydan
electric plane plaen trydan *eg* plaeniau trydan
electric plug plwg trydan *eg* plygiau trydan
electric potential difference gwahaniaeth potensial trydanol *eg*
electric power pŵer trydanol *eg*
electric power point pwynt trydan *eg* pwyntiau trydan
electric shock sioc drydan *eb* siociau trydan
electric socket soced trydan *eg* socedi trydan
electric spot welding sbotweldio trydan *be*
electric storage heater gwresogydd stôr trydan *eg* gwresogyddion stôr trydan
electric terminal terfynell drydan *eb* terfynellau trydan
electrical trydanol *ans*
electrical appliance dyfais drydanol *eb* dyfeisiau trydanol
electrical component cydran drydanol *eb* cydrannau trydanol
electrical generator generadur trydan *eg* generaduron trydan
electrical insulator ynysydd trydanol *eg* ynysyddion trydanol
electrical resistance gwrthiant trydanol *eg*
electrician trydanwr *eg* trydanwyr
electrician's insulated pliers gefelen ynysedig trydanwr *eb* gefeiliau ynysedig trydanwr
electrician's screwdriver tyrnsgriw trydanwr *eg* tyrnsgriwiau trydanwr
electricity trydan *eg*
electricity supply cyflenwad trydan *eg*
electricity transmission line lein trawsyrru trydan *eb*
electrify trydanu *be*
electroacoustic equipment cyfarpar electroacwstig *eg*
electrocardiogram electrocardiogram *eg* electrocardiogramau
electrochemical *adj* electrocemegol *ans*
electrochemical *n* electrocemegyn *eg* electrocemegau
electrochemical equivalent cywerth electrocemegol *eg* cywerthoedd electrocemegol
electroconvulsive therapy (ECT) therapi electrogynhyrfol *eg*
electrode electrod *eg* electrodau
electroencephalogram electroenceffalogram *eg* electroenceffalogramau
electrolyse electroleiddio *be*
electrolysis electrolysis *eg*
electrolyte electrolyt *eg* electrolytau
electrolytic electrolytig *ans*
electrolytic capacitor cynhwysydd electrolytig *eg* cynwysyddion electrolytig
electrolytic reaction adwaith electrolytig *eg* adweithiau electrolytig
electromagnetic electromagnetig *ans*
electromagnetic induction anwythiad electromagnetig *eg*
electromagnetic radiation pelydriad electromagnetig *eg*
electromagnetic spectrum sbectrwm electromagnetig *eg*
electromagnetism (phenomenon) electromagnetedd *eg/b*
electromagnetism (study of) electromagneteg *eb*
electrometer electromedr *eg* electromedrau
electromotive force (emf) grym electromotif *eg*
electromyogram electromyogram *eg* electromyogramau

electron electron *eg* electronau
electron acceptor derbynnydd electronau *eg* derbynyddion electronau
electron affinity affinedd electronol *eg*
electron carrier cludydd electronau *eg* cludyddion electronau
electron cloud cwmwl electronau *eg* cymylau electronau
electron cloud overlap gorgyffyrddiad cymylau electronau *eg*
electron configuration ffurfwedd electronau *eb* ffurfweddau electronau
electron delocalization dadleoliad electronau *eg*
electron density distribution dosbarthiad dwysedd electronau *eg*
electron diffraction diffreithiant electronau *eg*
electron donor cyfrannydd electronau *eg* cyfranwyr electronau
electron flow llif electronau *eg*
electron in bound state electron mewn cyflwr rhwym *eg* electronau mewn cyflwr rhwym
electron lens lens electronau *eg*
electron microscope electronmicrosgop *eg* electronmicrosgopau
electron pair repulsion theory damcaniaeth gwrthyriad parau electron *eb*
electron shell plisgyn electronau *eg* plisg electronau
electron stream llif electronau *eg* llifoedd electronau
electron-deficient electron-ddiffygiol *ans*
electronegative electronegatif *ans*
electronegativity electronegatifedd *eg*
electronic electronig *ans*
electronic area ardal electronig *eb* ardaloedd electronig
electronic chip sglodyn electronig *eg* sglodion electronig
electronic circuit cylched electronig *eb* cylchedau electronig
electronic communicator cyfathrebwr electronig *eg* cyfathrebwyr electronig
electronic component cydran electronig *eb* cydrannau electronig
electronic computer cyfrifiadur electronig *eg* cyfrifiaduron electronig
electronic conduction dargludiad electronig *eg*
electronic configuration ffurfwedd electronig *eb*
electronic container cynhwysydd electronig *eg* cynwysyddion electronig
electronic data interchange ymgyfnewid data electronig *be*
electronic data interchange (EDI) link cyswllt ymgyfnewid data electronig (EDI) *eg*
electronic data processing (EDP) prosesu data electronig *be*
electronic equipment offer electronig *ell*
electronic file ffeil electronig *eb* ffeiliau electronig
electronic form (of document) ffurflen electronig *eb* ffurflenni electronig
electronic form (of medium) ffurf electronig *eb* ffurfiau electronig
electronic funds transfer trosglwyddo cyfalaf electronig *be*
electronic information gwybodaeth electronig *eb*
electronic information system system gwybodaeth electronig *eb* systemau gwybodaeth electronig
electronic keyboard allweddell electronig *eb* allweddellau electronig
electronic machine peiriant electronig *eg* peiriannau electronig
electronic mail (correspondence) ehebiaeth *eb*
electronic mail (e-mail) post electronig *eg*
electronic mall marchnad electronig *eb* marchnadoedd electronig
electronic news gathering casglu newyddion yn electronig
electronic organ organ electronig *eb* organau electronig
electronic reverse auction arwerthiant electronig dwyffordd *eg*
electronic sound sain electronig *eb* seiniau electronig
electronic storefront blaen siop electronig *eg*
electronic structure adeiledd electronig *eg* adeileddau electronig
electronics electroneg *eb*
electronmicrograph electronmicrograff *eg* electronmicrograffau
electro-oculogram electro-ocwlogram *eg* electro-ocwlogramau
electrophile electroffil *eg* electroffiliau
electrophilic addition adiad electroffilig *eg*
electrophoresis electrofforesis *eg*
electrophorus electrofforws *eg* electroffori
electroplate *n* electroplat *eg* electroplatiau
electroplate *v* electroplatio *be*
electropositive electropositif *ans*
electropositivity electropositifedd *eg*
electroreceptor electrondderbynydd *eg* electrodderbynyddion
electroscope electrosgop *eg* electrosgopau
electrostatic electrostatig *ans*
electrostatic attraction atyniad electrostatig *eg*
electrostatic charge gwefr electrostatig *eb* gwefrau electrostatig
electrostatic induction anwythiad electrostatig *eg*
electrostatic phenomenon ffenomen electrostatig *eb* ffenomenau electrostatig
electrostatic potential potensial electrostatig *eg*
electrostatics electrostateg *eb*
electrovalent electrofalent *ans*
electro-weak force grym electro-gwan *eg*
elegy galargan *eb* galarganeuon
element elfen *eb* elfennau
element of competence elfen cymhwysedd *eb* elfennau cymhwysedd
elemental elfennaidd *ans*
elementary elfennol *ans*
elementary education addysg elfennol *eb*

elementary entity unffurfedd elfennol *eg*
elementary particle gronyn elfennol *eg* gronynnau elfennol
elementary school ysgol elfennol *eb* ysgolion elfennol
elements of painting elfennau peintio *ell*
elevation (of boiling point) codiad *eg*
elevation (of drawing) golwg *eg/b* golygon
elevation view golwg anghyflawn *eg* golygon anghyflawn
elevator (=lift) lifft *eg* lifftiau
elevator (for grain) codwr *eg* codwyr
eleven a side game gêm un ar ddeg bob ochr *eb* gemau un ar ddeg bob ochr
Eleven Years Tyranny Gormes yr Un Mlwydd ar Ddeg *eb*
eleventh (interval) unfed ar ddeg *eg* unfedau ar ddeg
elfinwood ellyllbren *eg*
elicit ennyn *be*
eligible cymwys *ans*
eliminant dileÿdd *eg* dileÿddion
eliminate dileu *be*
elimination (from the body) gwaredu *be*
elimination (in biology) bwrw allan *be*
elimination (in chemistry) dilead *eg* dileadau
elimination by substitution dileu drwy amnewid *be*
elimination print dileubrint *eg* dileubrintiau
elimination printing dileubrintio *be*
elimination reaction (in chemistry) adwaith dileu *eg* adweithiau dileu
elite *adj* elitaidd *ans*
elite *n* elit *eg* elitau
elitism elitaeth *eb*
elitist elitydd *eg* elitwyr
Elizabeth I Elizabeth I *eb*
Elizabethan Elisabethaidd *ans*
Elizabethan Church Settlement Ardrefniant Eglwysig Elizabeth *eg*
Elizabethan history hanes oes Elizabeth *eg*
ellipse elips *eg* elipsau
ellipsis coll geiriau *eg*
ellipsoid elipsoid *eg* elipsoidau
ellipsoidal elipsoidol *ans*
elliptic eliptig *ans*
elliptical eliptigol *ans*
elliptical arch bwa eliptigol *eg* bwâu eliptigol
elliptical flange fflans eliptigol *eb* fflansiau eliptigol
Elohim Elohim
elongate hwyhau *be*
elongated hirgul *ans*
elongation hwyhad *eg* hwyhadau
eluent echludydd *eg*
elute echludo *be*
elution echludiad *eg* echludiadau
eluvial echlifol *ans*
eluviation echlifiant *eg*
e-mail (=correspond by email) *v* e-hebu *be*
e-mail (=send an e-mail) *v* e-bostio *be*
e-mail (of mail sent or received) *n* e-hebiaeth *eb*
e-mail (of medium) *n* e-bost *eg*
e-mail attachment atodiad e-bost *eg* atodiadau e-bost
emancipate rhyddfreinio *be*
emancipation rhyddfreiniad *eg*
Emancipation Act Deddf Rhyddfreinio *eb*
emancipation of the serfs rhyddfreinio'r taeogion *be*
embargo gwaharddiad *eg* gwaharddiadau
embark byrddio *be*
embassy llysgenhadaeth *eb* llysgenadaethau
embayment amfae *eg* amfaeau
► **embed** mewnblannu *be*
embedded character nod wedi'i fewnblannu *eg* nodau wedi'u mewnblannu
embellishment addurniad *eg* addurniadau
emblem arwyddlun *eg* arwyddluniau
emboss boglynnu *be*
embossed boglynnog *ans*
embossed wallpaper papur boglynnog *eg*
embossing boglynwaith *eg* boglynweithiau
embracery rhaithymyrraeth *eb*
embroider brodio *be*
embroidered collage collage brodwaith *eg*
embroidered lace les wedi'i frodio *eg*
embroidered textiles tecstilau wedi'u brodio *ell*
embroidery brodwaith *eg*
embroidery cotton edau frodwaith *eb* edafedd brodwaith
embroidery frame ffrâm frodio *eb* fframiau brodio
embroidery needle nodwydd frodio *eb* nodwyddau brodio
embroidery scissors siswrn brodio *eg* sisyrnau brodio
embroidery thread edau frodio *eb* edafedd brodio
embroidery wool gwlân brodio *eg*
embryo embryo *eg* embryonau
embryo dune egin-dwyn *eg* egin-dwyni
embryo sac coden embryo *eb* codennau embryo
embryo stage cyfnod embryo *eg*
emerald emrallt *eg*
emerge dod allan *be*
emerged cyfodol *ans*
emergency *adj* brys *ans*
emergency *n* argyfwng *eg* argyfyngau
emergency protection order gorchymyn amddiffyn brys *eg* gorchmynion amddiffyn brys
emergency stop stop brys *eg* stopiau brys
emergent allddodol *ans*
emergent beam paladr allddodol *eg* pelydr allddodol
emergent nation cenedl ddatblygol *eb* cenhedloedd datblygol
emergent tree coeden ymwthiol *eb* coed ymwthiol
emery emeri *eg*
emery cloth clwt emeri *eg* clytiau emeri
emery paste past emeri *eg*
emery powder powdr emeri *eg* powdrau emeri

emery wheel olwyn emeri *eb* olwynion emeri
emetic cyfoglyn *eg* cyfoglynnau
emigrant ymfudwr *eg* ymfudwyr
emigrate ymfudo *be*
e-Minister e-Weinidog *eg* e-Weinidogion
emission allyriad *eg* allyriadau
emission spectroscopy sbectrosgopeg allyriant *eb*
emission spectrum sbectrwm allyrru *eg*
emissivity allyrredd *ans*
emit allyrru *be*
emitter allyrrydd *eg* allyrwyr
Emmanuel the Fortunate Emaniwel Ffodus *eg*
emoticon gwenoglun *eg* gwenogluniau
emotion emosiwn *eg* emosiynau
emotionable stability sefydlogrwydd emosiynol *eg*
emotional emosiynol *ans*
emotional abuse camdriniaeth emosiynol *eb*
emotional and behavioural difficulties anawsterau ymddygiad ac emosiwn *ell*
emotional and social development datblygiad emosiynol a chymdeithasol *eg*
emotional deprivation amddifadiad emosiynol *eg*
emotional development datblygiad emosiynol *eg*
emotional disturbance cythrwfl emosiynol *eg*
emotional stability sefydlogrwydd emosiynol *eg*
emotion-focused coping ymdopi drwy ganolbwyntio ar emosiwn *be*
empathy empathi *eg*
emperor ymerawdwr *eg* ymerawdwyr
emphasis pwyslais *eg* pwysleisiau
emphasise pwysleisio *be*
emphasized pwysleisiol *ans*
emphysema emffysema *eg*
empire ymerodraeth *eb* ymerodraethau
empirical empirig *ans*
empirical formula fformiwla empirig *eb* fformiwlâu empirig
empirical investigation ymchwiliad empirig *eg* ymchwiliadau empirig
empirical method dull empirig *eg* dulliau empirig
► **empiricism** empiriaeth *eb*
empiricist empirydd *eg* empirwyr
employ cyflogi *be*
employability cyflogadwyedd *eg*
employable cyflogadwy *ans*
employed cyflogedig *ans*
employee (=paid worker) gweithiwr cyflogedig *eg* gweithwyr cyflogedig
employee (=worker, staff member) gweithiwr *eg* gweithwyr
employee organisation cymdeithas i weithwyr *eb* cymdeithasau i weithwyr
employer cyflogwr *eg* cyflogwyr
employer employee relations cysylltiadau rhwng y cyflogwr a'r gweithwyr *ell*
Employers' and Workmen's Act Deddf Cyflogwyr a Gweithwyr *eb*
employment cyflogaeth *eb*
employment appeal tribunal tribiwnlys apêl cyflogaeth *eg*
employment contract contract cyflogaeth *eg* contractau cyflogaeth
employment exchange swyddfa gyflogi *eb* swyddfeydd cyflogi
empower (=authorize) awdurdodi *be*
empower (clients) rhoi grym *be*
empowerment model model rhoi grym *eg*
empress ymerodres *eb* ymerodresau
emulate efelychu *be*
emulator efelychydd *eg* efelychwyr
emulsification emwlseiddio *be*
emulsifier emwlsydd *eg* emwlsyddion
emulsify emwlsio *be*
emulsion paint paent emwlsiwn *eg*
emulsion polish llathr emwlsiwn *eg*
enable galluogi *be*
enable cookies galluogi cwcis *be*
enable features galluogi nodweddion *be*
enable interrupts galluogi ymyriadau *be*
enabler galluogwr *eg* galluogwyr
enabling act deddf alluogi *eb* deddfau galluogi
enabling signal signal galluogi *eg* signalau galluogi
enactive thinking meddwl enactif *be*
enamel *n* enamel *eg* enamelau
enamel *v* enamlo *be*
enamel chips sglodion enamel *ell*
enamel paint paent enamel *eg*
enamel thread edau enamel *eb* edafedd enamel
enamelled enamlog *ans*
enamelling colour lliw enamlo *eg* lliwiau enamlo
enamelling kiln odyn enamlo *eb* odynnau enamlo
enantiomer enantiomer *eg* enantiomerau
enantiomorph enantiomorff *eg* enantiomorffau
encampment gwersyllfan *eg* gwersyllfannau
encapsulation mewngapsiwleiddio *be*
encaustic llosgliw *ans*
encaustic tile teilsen losgliw *eb* teils llosgliw
encephalitis enceffalitis *eg*
encephalization cynnydd ymenyddol *eg*
encircle amgylchynu *be*
encirclement amgylchyniad *eg* amgylchyniadau
enclave clofan *eg* clofannau
enclose (in letter) amgáu *be*
enclose (land etc) cau *be*
enclosed amgaeedig *ans*
enclosed choir organ organ gôr gaeedig *eb* organau côr caeedig
enclosed land tir caeedig *eg* tiroedd caeedig
enclosed solo organ organ solo gaeedig *eb* organau solo caeedig
enclosure (=enclosed land) tir caeedig *eg* tiroedd caeedig
enclosure (archaeological) lloc *eg* llociau
Enclosure Acts Deddfau Cau Tiroedd *ell*
enclosure movement mudiad cau tiroedd *eg*

Enclosure of Common Land Act
Deddf Cau Tir Comin *eb*
encode amgodio *be*
encoding specificity amgodio penodol *be*
▶ **encompass** cwmpasu *be*
encourage annog *be*
encroach (upon rights) llechfeddiannu *be*
encroachment (of rights) llechfeddiant *eg*
encrypt amgryptio *be*
encryption amgryptiad *eg* amgryptiadau
encyclical (papal) cylchlythyr y pab *eg*
cylchlythyrau'r pab
encyclopaedia gwyddoniadur *eg* gwyddoniaduron
encyclopaedist gwyddoniadurwr *eg*
gwyddoniadurwyr
encysted cystiedig *ans*
end elevation ochrolwg *eg* ochrolygon
end face wyneb pen *eg* wynebau pen
end grain graen pen *eg*
end milling cutter melinwr ochr *eg* melinwyr ochr
end moraine marian terfynol *eg* marianau terfynol
end of dance diwedd dawns *eg*
end of data diwedd y data *eg*
end of field diwedd maes *eg*
end of file diwedd ffeil *eg*
end of job diwedd gorchwyl *eg*
end of record diwedd cofnod *eg*
end of run diwedd rhediad *eg*
end of table talcen bwrdd *eg* talcenni byrddau
end of tape diwedd tâp *eg*
end of the race diwedd y ras *eg*
end organ terfynolyn *eg* terfynolynnau
end paper papur terfyn *eg* papurau terfyn
end play llacrwydd y pen *eg*
end point pwynt terfyn *eg* pwyntiau terfyn
end point (titration) diweddbwynt *eg*
diwedd bwyntiau
end product cynnyrch terfynol *eg*
end product inhibition
ataliad gan gynnyrch terfynol *eg*
end view ochrolwg *eg* ochrolygon
end-cutting nipper niper torri blaen *eg*
niperi torri blaen
endemic endemig *ans*
endergonic endergonig *ans*
endive endif *eg*
endnote ôl-nodyn *eg* ôl-nodion
endnote anchor angor ôl-nodyn *eg*
angorau ôl-nodyn
endnote area rhan ôl-nodyn *eb* rhannau ôl-nodyn
endocarp endocarp *eg*
endocrine endocrinaidd *ans*
endocrine gland chwarren endocrin *eb*
chwarennau endocrin
endocrine system system endocrin *eb*
endocrinology endocrinoleg *eb*
endocycle endoseicl *eg*
endocyst endocyst *eg*
endodermal endodermaidd *ans*
end-of-module test prawf diwedd modiwl *eg*
profion diwedd modiwl
endogenesis mewndarddiad *eg*
endogenous mewndarddol *ans*
endolymph endolymff *eg*
endometrium endometriwm *eg*
endomorphic endomorffig *ans*
endoplasmic reticulum reticwlwm endoplasmig *eg*
endorphin endorffin *eg* endorffinau
endorse (=confirm) cadarnhau *be*
endorse (=support) cefnogi *be*
endorse (=write on the back of a cheque etc)
arnodi *be*
endorsed arnodedig *ans*
endorsement (=confirmation) cadarnhad *eg*
endorsement (=support) cefnogaeth *eb*
endorsement (=writing on back of cheque etc)
arnodiad *eg* arnodiadau
endoscope endosgop *eg* endosgopau
endoskeleton sgerbwd mewnol *eg*
sgerbydau mewnol
endosperm endosberm *eg*
endothelium endotheliwm *eg*
endothermic endothermig *ans*
endow gwaddoli *be*
endowed gwaddoledig *ans*
endowed school ysgol waddoledig *eb*
ysgolion gwaddoledig
endowment gwaddol *eg* gwaddolion
endowment assurance aswiriant gwaddol *eg*
endowment mortgage morgais gwaddol *eg*
morgeisi gwaddol
endowment policy polisi gwaddol *eg*
polisïau gwaddol
end-point diweddbwynt *eg* diweddbwyntiau
endrumpf lledwastad terfynol *eg*
lledwastadau terfynol
endurance dygnwch *eg*
enema enema *eg* enemâu
enemy gelyn *eg* gelynion
enemy action ymgyrch y gelyn *eb*
enemy lines llinellau'r gelyn *ell*
energetic egnïol *ans*
energetic activity gweithgaredd egnïol *eg*
gweithgareddau egnïol
energetics egnïeg *eb*
energize egnioli *be*
energized egnioledig *ans*
energy egni *eg* egnïon
energy balance cydbwysedd egni *eg*
energy barrier rhwystr egni *eg*
energy content cynnwys egni *eg*
energy demands gofynion egni *ell*
▶ **energy efficiency** effeithlonrwydd egni *eg*
energy expenditure traul egni *eb*
energy flow llif egni *eg*
energy harnessing harnesu egni *be*

energy issues materion egni *ell*
energy level lefel egni *eb* lefelau egni
energy sink suddfan egni *eg* suddfannau egni
energy source ffynhonnell egni *eb* ffynonellau egni
energy system system egni *eb* systemau egni
energy transfer trosglwyddo egni *be*
energy value gwerth egni *eg*
energy value of food cyfwerth egni bwyd *eg*
energy yield cynnyrch egni *eg*
energy-rich bond bond egnioledig *eg* bondiau egnioledig
enfeoff enffeodu *be*
enfold ymblygu *eg*
enfranchise rhyddfreinio *be*
engage (the blade) cyweddu *be*
engage with gweithio'n agos gyda *be*
engaged column colofn gyswllt *eb* colofnau cyswllt
engaged tone tôn brysur *eb*
engagement (commitment) ymrwymiad *eg* ymrwymiadau
engagement (in fencing) cyweddiad *eg* cyweddiadau
engagement (in war) cyrch milwrol *eg*
engagement (to get married) dyweddïad *eg* dyweddiadau
engine (in general) peiriant *eg* peiriannau
engine (of steam train) injan *eb* injans
engine cylinder silindr peiriant *eg* silindrau peiriant
engine friction ffrithiant peiriant *eg* ffrithiannau peiriant
engine house (historically, in quarries etc) tŷ injan *eg* tai injan
engine house (technical usage) peiriandy *eg* peiriandai
engineer peiriannydd *eg* peirianwyr
engineering peirianneg *eb*
engineering activities gweithgareddau peirianyddol *ell*
engineering brick bricsen beirianneg *eb* brics peirianneg
engineering drawing (of activity) lluniadu peirianegol *be*
engineering drawing (of produce) lluniad peirianegol *eg* lluniadau peirianegol
engineering function swyddogaeth peirianneg *eb*
engineering industry diwydiant peirianneg *eg*
engineering system system beirianegol *eb* systemau peirianegol
engineer's hammer morthwyl peiriannydd *eg* morthwylion peiriannydd
engineer's marking blue hylif marcio glas *eg*
engineer's square sgwâr peiriannydd *eg* sgwariau peiriannydd
engineer's vice feis peiriannydd *eb* feisiau peiriannydd
englacial mewnrewlifol *ans*
englacial moraine marian perfedd *eg* marianau perfedd
England regions rhanbarthau Lloegr *ell*
English bond bondin Seisnig *eg*
English Common Law Cyfraith Gwlad Lloegr *eb*
English garden wall bonding bondin seisnig wal gardd *eg*
English horn cor anglais *eg* cors anglais
English Law Cyfraith Loegr *eb*
English quilting cwiltio Seisnig *be*
English suite cyfres Seisnig *eb* cyfresi Seisnig
englishry saesonaeth *eb*
engrain engreinio *be*
engrave ysgythru *be*
engraved glassware llestri gwydr ysgythredig *ell*
engraving ysgythriad *eg* ysgythriadau
engraving block bloc ysgythru *eg* blociau ysgythru
engraving line llin-ysgythriad *eg* llin-ysgythriadau
engraving tool erfyn ysgythru *eg* offer ysgythru
engross (=produce a fair copy) brasgopïo *be*
engross (=reproduce in larger letters) braslythrennu *be*
engrossment (=fair copy) brasgopi *eg* brasgopïau
engrossment (=large writing) braslythreniad *eg*
engulf (amoeba etc) amlyncu *be*
enhance gwella *be*
enhanced gwell *ans*
enharmonic enharmonig *ans*
enharmonic change newid enharmonig *eg* newidiadau enharmonig
enharmonic interval cyfwng enharmonig *eg* cyfyngau enharmonig
enharmonic note nodyn enharmonig *eg* nodau enharmonig
enigma enigma *eg*
enjoy mwynhau *be*
enjoyment mwynhad *eg*
enlarge helaethu *be*
enlarge a pattern helaethu patrwm *be*
enlarged image delwedd fwy *eb* delweddau mwy
enlargement helaethiad *eg* helaethiadau
enlargement and reduction helaethu a lleihau
enlightened goleuedig *ans*
enlightened absolutism absoliwtiaeth oleuedig *eb*
Enlightenment Goleuo *be*
enlist ymrestru *be*
enmeshed family teulu rhwydol *eg* teuluoedd rhwydol
enquiry ymholiad *eg* ymholiadau
enquiry frame ffrâm holi *eb* fframiau holi
enquiry question cwestiwn ymholi *eg* cwestiynau ymholi
enrichment cyfoethogi *be*
enrol cofrestru *be*
enrolled nurse nyrs restredig *eb* nyrsys rhestredig
enrolment cofrestriad *eg* cofrestriadau
ensemble ensemble *eg* ensembles
ensign (=flag) lluman *eg/b* llumanau
ensign (of person) llumanwr *eg* llumanwyr
ensure sicrhau *be*
entail *n* entael *eg* enteiliau
entail *v* enteilio *be*

entail fee ffi entael *eb* ffioedd entael
entemophilous entemoffilaidd *ans*
entente entente *eb*
enter rhoi *be*
enter (=go in) mynd i mewn *be*
enter (=penetrate) treiddio *be*
enter (for an exam) cofrestru *be*
enteral tube feeding bwydo gyda thiwb *be*
enteritis enteritis *eg*
enterokinase enterocinas *eg*
enterprise menter *eb* mentrau
enterprise zone ardal fenter *eb* ardaloedd menter
entertainment adloniant *eg* adloniannau
enthalpy enthalpi *eg* enthalpïau
enthalpy change newid enthalpi *eg*
enthalpy change of atomization newid enthalpi atomeiddiad *be*
enthalpy change of combustion newid enthalpi hylosgiad *be*
enthalpy change of formation newid enthalpi ffurfiant *be*
enthalpy change of hydration newid enthalpi hydradiad *be*
enthalpy change of neutralization newid enthalpi niwtraliad *be*
enthalpy change of solution newid enthalpi toddiant *be*
enthalpy change of sublimation newid enthalpi sychdarthiad *be*
enthalpy changes of formation newidiadau enthalpi ffurfiant *ell*
enthalpy of vaporization enthalpi anweddiad *eg*
entire cyfan *ans*
entirety cyfanrwydd *eg*
entitlement hawl *eg/b* hawliau
entity endid *eg* endidau
entity FAULT endid DIFFYG *eg*
entity-relationship diagram diagram perthynas endidau *eg* diagramau perthynas endidau
entomology entomoleg *eb*
entr'acte entr'acte *eg* entr'actes
entrance (=opening) agoriad *eg* agoriadau
entrance (=way in) mynedfa *eb* mynedfeydd
entrée dish (of container) llestr entrée *eg* llestri entrée
entrée dish (of food) saig entrée *eb* seigiau entrée
entrenched meander ystum culrych *eg* ystumiau culrych
entrepreneur entrepreneur *eg* entrepreneuriaid
entropy entropi *eg*
entry (=act or instance of going in) mynediad *eg* mynediadau
entry (=doorway) mynedfa *eb* mynedfeydd
entry (=record) cofnod *eg* cofnodion
entry (in composition) caniad *eg* caniadau
entry (in ensemble) cydiad *eg* cydiadau
entry (in fugue) datganiad *eg* datganiadau
entry point (in discussion etc) man cyflwyno *eg* mannau cyflwyno
enumerable rhifadwy *ans*
enumerate rhifo *be*
enumeration rhifiad *eg* rhifiadau
enuresis enwresis *eg*
envelope amlen *eb* amlenni
envelope of straight lines amlen llinellau syth *eb* amlenni llinellau syth
environment amgylchedd *eg* amgylcheddau
environment committee pwyllgor amgylchedd *eg* pwyllgorau amgylchedd
environmental amgylcheddol *ans*
environmental challenge her yr amgylchedd *eg*
environmental conservation and protection gwarchod ac amddiffyn yr amgylchedd
environmental education addysg amgylcheddol *eb*
environmental factor ffactor amgylcheddol *eb* ffactorau amgylcheddol
environmental hazard perygl amgylchedd *eg* peryglon amgylchedd
environmental health iechyd yr amgylchedd *eg*
Environmental Health Department Adran Iechyd yr Amgylchedd *eb*
environmental impact effaith amgylcheddol *eb* effeithiau amgylcheddol
environmental pollution llygredd amgylcheddol *eg*
environmental protection amddiffyn yr amgylchedd *be*
Environmental Protection Act Deddf Amddiffyn yr Amgylchedd *eb*
environmental studies astudiaethau'r amgylchedd *ell*
envoy cennad *eg* cenhadon
enzyme ensym *eg* ensymau
enzyme activator actifadydd ensym *eg* actifadyddion ensym
enzyme activity actifedd ensymig *eg*
enzyme detergent glanedydd ensym *eg* glanedyddion ensym
enzyme inhibition ataliad ensym *eg*
enzyme prosthetic group grŵp prosthetig ensym *eg*
enzyme specificity penodolrwydd ensym *eg*
Eocene Ëosen *eb*
eosin eosin *eg*
eosinophil eosinoffil *eg* eosinoffilau
epaulette epaulette *eg* epaulettes
epée epée *eg* epées
epeiric sea môr epeirig *eg* moroedd epeirig
epeirogenetic epeirogenetig *ans*
ephemera effemera *eg*
ephermeris effermeris *eg*
epic *adj* arwrol *ans*
epic *n* arwrgerdd *eg* arwrgerddi
epicentre uwchganolbwynt *eg* uwchganolbwyntiau
epicotyl epicotyl *eg*
epicyclic episeiclig *ans*
epicycloid episeicloid *eg* episeicloidau
epidemic epidemig *eg* epidemigau
epidemiological data data epidemiolegol *ell*

epidemiology epidemioleg *eb*
epidermal epidermaidd *ans*
epidural epidwral *ans*
epidural analgesic poenleddfwr epidwral *eg* poenleddfwyr epidwral
epigeal epigeal *ans*
epiglottis epiglotis *eg*
epigynous epigynol *ans*
epilepsy epilepsi *eg*
epileptic epileptig *ans*
epileptic child plentyn epileptig *eg* plant epileptig
epimerism epimeredd *eg*
epimerization epimeru *be*
epimorphic epimorffig *ans*
epipetalous epipetalog *ans*
Epiphany Ystwyll *eg*
epiphysis epiffysis *eg*
epiphyte epiffyt *eg*
epiphytic epiffytig *ans*
episcopacy esgobaeth *eb*
episcopal esgobol *ans*
Episcopal authority awdurdod Esgobaethol *eg* awdurdodau Esgobaethol
episcopalian *adj* esgobaethol *ans*
episcopalian *n* esgobwr *eg* esgobwyr
episcopalianism esgobwriaeth *eb*
episcopate esgobaeth *eb* esgobaethau
episiotomy episiotomi *eg* episiotomïau
episode (in book) pennod *eb* penodau
episode (in music) atgan *eb* atganau
episodic memory cof cyfnodol *eg*
episodical atganol *ans*
epistemology epistemoleg *be*
epistle epistol *eg* epistolau
epitaph beddargraff *eg* beddargraffiadau
epithelial epithelaidd *ans*
epithelium epitheliwm *eg* epithelia
epitrochoid epitrocoid *eg* epitrocoidau
epoch cyfnod *eg* cyfnodau
epoxy epocsi *eg* epocsiau
epoxy resin resin epocsi *eg* resinau epocsi
epoxy resin glue glud resin epocsi *eg*
epoxyethane epocsiethan *eg*
epoxypropane epocsipropan *eg*
e-publishing e-gyhoeddi *be*
equable (=not varying) cyson *ans*
equable (of climate) cymedrol *ans*
equal (in general) cyfartal *ans*
equal (in mathematics) hafal *ans*
equal (magnitude) unfaint *ans*
equal addition method dull adio cyfartal *eg*
equal and opposite hafal a dirgroes
equal area arwynebedd cyfartal *eg* arwynebeddau cyfartal
equal constituencies etholaethau cyfartal *ell*
equal divisions rhannau unfaint *ell*
equal interval cyfwng hafal *eg* cyfyngau hafal
equal opportunities policy polisi cyfle cyfartal *eg* polisïau cyfle cyfartal
equal opportunity cyfle cyfartal *eg* cyfleoedd cyfartal
equal partition dosrannu cyfartal *be*
equal pay cyflog cydradd *eg*
equal rights hawliau cyfartal *ell*
equal sign (=) hafalnod *eg* hafalnodau
equal stretching ymestyn cyfartal *be*
equal temperament ardymer cyfartal *eg*
equality (in general) cydraddoldeb *eg*
equality (mathematical) hafaledd *eg* hafaleddau
equalize (in general) cyfartalu *be*
equalize (in mathematics) hafalu *be*
equally likely yr un mor debygol
equally likely principle egwyddor tebygolrwydd hafal *eb*
equally spaced cytbell *ans*
equate hafalu *be*
equation hafaliad *eg* hafaliadau
equator cyhydedd *eg* cyhydeddau
equatorial cyhydeddol *ans*
equatorial projection tafluniad cyhydeddol *eg* tafluniadau cyhydeddol
equiangular hafalonglog *ans*
equi-area projection tafluniad arwynebedd hafal *eg* tafluniadau arwynebedd hafal
equidistant cytbell *ans*
equidistant projection tafluniad cytbell *eg* tafluniadau cytbell
equilateral hafalochrog *eg*
equilateral arch bwa hafalochrog *eg* bwâu hafalochrog
equilateral triangle triongl hafalochrog *eg* trionglau hafalochrog
equilibrate ecwilibreiddio *be*
equilibrium ecwilibriwm *eg*
equilibrium concentration crynodiad ecwilibriwm *eg*
equilibrium constant cysonyn ecwilibriwm *eg*
equilibrium expression mynegiad ecwilibriwm *eg*
equilibrium position safle ecwilibriwm *eg*
equilibrium potential potensial ecwilibriwm *eg*
equilibrium price pris ecwilibriwm *eg*
equilibrium unemployment diweithdra ecwilibriwm *eg*
equinox cyhydnos *eb* cyhydnosau
equi-partition hafal-ymraniad *eg* hafal-ymraniadau
equipluve glawlin cymarebol *eg* glawlinau cymarebol
equipment (for kitchen, camping) offer *ell*
equipment (in general) cyfarpar *eg*
equipotential unbotensial *ans*
equispaced â lle gwag cyfartal
equitable redemption adbryniad ecwitïol *eg*
equity (jurisdiction) ecwiti *eg*
Equity Court Cwrt Ecwiti *eg*
Equity Law Cyfraith Ecwiti *eb*
equivalence cywerthedd *eg*

equivalence relation perthynas cywerthedd *eb*
equivalent *adj* cywerth *ans*
equivalent *n* cywerthydd *eg* cywerthyddion
equivalent area arwynebedd cywerth *eg* arwynebeddau cywerth
equivalent circuit cylched gywerth *eb* cylchedau cywerth
equivalent fractions ffracsiynau cywerth *ell*
equivalent lens lens cywerth *eg* lensiau cywerth
equivalent sets setiau cywerth *ell*
equivalent systems systemau cywerth *ell*
equivalent weight pwysau cywerth *ell*
era oes *eb* oesau
erase dileu *be*
eraser dilëwr *eg* dilewyr
Erasmianism Erasmiaeth *eb*
Erastianism Erastiaeth *eb*
erasure dilead *eg* dileadau
erbium (Er) erbiwm *eg*
erect *adj* unionsyth *ans*
erect *v* codi *be*
erect image delwedd unionsyth *eb* delweddau unionsyth
erectile tissue meinwe sythu *eg*
erection (in physiology) codiad *eg* codiadau
erector muscle cyhyryn sythu *eg* cyhyrynnau syth
eremite ermid *eg* ermidion
eremitical meudwyaidd *ans*
Erfurt union undeb Erfurt *eg*
ergodic ergodig *ans*
ergonomic aids cymhorthion ergonomig *ell*
ergonomics ergonomeg *eb*
ergot mallryg *eg*
ermine carlwm *eg* carlymiaid
erode erydu *be*
eroded surface arwyneb erydog *eg* arwynebau erydog
erosion erydiad *eg*
erosion platform llwyfan erydu *eg* llwyfannau erydu
erosion surface arwyneb erydiad *eg* arwynebau erydiad
erosive erydol *ans*
erosive agent erydydd *eg* erydyddion
error (=amount of inaccuracy) cyfeiliornad *eg* cyfeiliornadau
error (=mistake) gwall *eg* gwallau
error alert rhybudd gwall *eg* rhybuddion gwall
error analysis dadansoddi gwallau *be*
error category categori gwallau *eg* categorïau gwallau
error character gwallnod *eg* gwallnodau
error checking code cod archwilio gwallau *eg* codau archwilio gwallau
error code cod gwallau *eg* codau gwallau
error correcting code cod cywiro gwallau *eg* codau cywiro gwallau
error creating object gwall creu gwrthrych *eg*
error description disgrifiad o'r gwall *eg* disgrifiadau o'r gwallau
error detecting code cod darganfod gwallau *eg* codau darganfod gwallau
error diagnostics diagnosteg gwallau *eb*
error handling trin gwallau *be*
error indicator dangosydd gwall *eg* dangosyddion gwall
error interrupt ymyriad gwall *eg* ymyriadau gwallau
error list rhestr gwallau *eb* rhestri gwallau
► **error message** neges gwall *eb* negesau gwall
error of commission gwall trwy gamwaith *eg* gwallau trwy gamwaith
error of failure gwall methiant *eg* gwallau methiant
error of order gwall trefn *eg* gwallau trefn
error of timing gwall amseru *eg* gwallau amseru
error range amrediad gwallau *eg* amrediadau gwallau
error routine rheolwaith gwallau *eg* rheolweithiau gwallau
error trap magl gwallau *eb* maglau gwallau
error trapping maglu gwallau *be*
error while printing gwall wrth argraffu *eg* gwallau wrth argraffu
error while renaming gwall wrth ailenwi *eg* gwallau wrth ailenwi
erupt echdorri *be*
eruption echdoriad *eg*
eruv eruv *eg*
erythrocyte (=corpuscle) corffilyn coch y gwaed *eg* corffilod coch y gwaed
escalate (of conflict) dwysáu *be*
escalate (of prices) codi *be*
escalope escalope *eb* escalopes
ESCAPE key bysell ESCAPE *eb* bysellau ESCAPE
escape response ymateb ffoi *eg*
escape velocity cyflymder dianc *eg*
escapement (plane) cilfa *eb* cilfâu
escarpment sgarp *eg* sgarpiau
eschatological myth myth eschatolegol *eg*
eschatology eschatoleg *eb*
escheat *n* siêd *eg* siedau
escheat *v* siedu *be*
escheator siedwr *eg* siedwyr
escribed circle allgylch *eg* allgylchoedd
escutcheon esgytsiwn *eg* esgytsiynau
escutcheon pin pìn esgytsiwn *eg* pinnau esgytsiwn
escutcheon plate plât esgytsiwn *eg* platiau esgytsiwn
esker esgair *eb* esgeiriau
Espagnole sauce saws Espagnole *eg*
esparto esparto *eg*
espionage ysbïo *be*
esquire yswain *eg* ysweiniaid
essay traethawd *eg* traethodau
essence rhinflas *eg* rhinflasau
essential hanfodol *ans*
essential boundary conditions amodau ffin hanfodol *ell*

essential dimensions dimensiynau hanfodol *ell*
essential note nodyn anhepgor *eg* nodau anhepgor
essential traffic trafnidiaeth hanfodol *eb*
essentials hanfodion *ell*
establish sefydlu *be*
established conservation area ardal gadwraeth sefydledig *eb* ardaloedd cadwraeth sefydledig
established routine trefn sefydledig *eb*
establishing shot llun lleoli *eg* lluniau lleoli
establishment sefydliad *eg* sefydliadau
estate stad *eb* stadau
estate agent gwerthwr eiddo *eg* gwerthwyr eiddo
estate agent details manylion y gwerthwr eiddo *ell*
estate duty treth stad *eb*
estate ownership perchenogaeth stad *eb*
Estates General Stadau Cyffredinol *ell*
estates of the realm stadau'r deyrnas *eb*
ester ester *eg* esterau
esterification esteriad *eg*
esterify esteru *be*
estimate *n* amcangyfrif *eg* amcangyfrifon
estimate *v* amcangyfrif *be*
estimated perspective persbectif amcangyfrifol *eg*
estimated uncertainty ansicrwydd amcangyfrifol *eg*
estimation (=opinion) barn *eb*
estimation (=rough calculation) *n* amcangyfrif *eg* amcangyfrifon
estimation of error amcangyfrif cyfeiliornad *eg*
estimator amcangyfrifyn *eg* amcangyfrifynnau
estreat ystrêd *eg* ystredau
estuary moryd *eb* morydau
etch ysgythru *be*
etch plain gwastadedd ysgythru *eg* gwastadeddau ysgythru
etched glassware llestri gwydr ysgythrog *ell*
etcher ysgythrwr *eg* ysgythrwyr
etching ysgythriad *eg* ysgythriadau
etching ground grwnd ysgythru *eg* grwndiau ysgythru
etching needle nodwydd ysgythru *eb* nodwyddau ysgythru
etching press gwasg ysgythru *eb* gweisg ysgythru
ethanal ethanal *eg*
ethanal oxime ethanal ocsim *eg*
ethanal tetramer ethanal tetramer *eg*
ethanal trimer ethanal trimer *eg*
ethanamide ethanamid *eg*
ethane ethan *eg*
ethanedial ethandeual *eg*
ethanediamide ethandeuamid *eg*
ethane-1,2-diamine ethan-1,2-deuamin *eg*
ethanedioic acid asid ethandeuöig *eg*
ethane-1,2-diol ethan-1,2-deuol *eg*
ethanenitrile ethanenitril *eg*
ethanenitrile dimethyl ether ethanenitril deumethyl ether *eg*
ethanethiol ethanthiol *eg*
ethanoate ethanoad *eg* ethanoadau
► **ethanoic** ethanöig *ans*
ethanoic acid asid ethanöig *eg*
ethanoic anhydride ethanöig anhydrid *eg*
ethanoic methanoic anhydride ethanöig methanöig anhydrid *eg*
ethanol ethanol *ans*
ethanolic sodium hydroxide sodiwm hydrocsid ethanolig *eg*
ethanolic solution of iodomethane hydoddiant iodomethan ethanolig *eg*
ethanoyl chloride ethanoyl clorid *eg*
2-ethanoyloxybenzenecarboxylic acid asid 2-ethanoylocsibensencarbocsylig *eg*
Ethelred the Unready Ethelred y Digyngor *eg*
ethene ethen *eg*
ethene ozonide ethen osonid *eg*
ethenone ethenon *eg*
ethenyl- ethenyl-
ethenyl ethanoate ethenyl ethanoad *eg*
ether ether *eg*
ethernet ether-rwyd *eb*
etheryser etherydd *eg*
ethical moesegol *ans*
ethical issue mater moesegol *eg* materion moesegol
ethical monotheism undduwiaeth foesegol *eb*
ethical teaching addysgu am foeseg *be*
ethical theory damcaniaeth moesegol *eb* damcaniaethau moesegol
ethics moeseg *eb*
ethics group grŵp moeseg *eg* grwpiau moeseg
ethnic ethnig *ans*
ethnic group grŵp ethnig *eg* grwpiau ethnig
ethnic minority group grŵp lleiafrifol ethnig *eg* grwpiau lleiafrifol ethnig
ethnic origin tarddiad ethnig *eg*
ethnicity ethnigedd *eg*
ethnocentric ethnoganolog *ans*
ethnographic area ardal ethnograffig *eb* ardaloedd ethnograffig
ethnography ethnograffeg *eb*
ethnological legend chwedl ethnolegol *eb*
ethnology ethnoleg *eb*
ethnomusicology ethnogerddoleg *eb*
ethogram ethogram *eg* ethogramau
ethology etholeg *eb*
ethos ethos *eg*
ethoxybenzene ethocsibensen *eg*
ethoxyethane ethocsiethan *eg*
ethyl alcohol ethyl alcohol *eg*
ethyl benzenecarboxylate ethyl bensencarbocsylad *eg*
ethyl benzoate ethyl bensoad *eg*
ethyl ethanoate ethyl ethanoad *eg*
ethyl 3-oxobutanoate ethyl 3-ocsobwtanoad *eg*
ethylamine ethylamin *eg*
ethylammonium chloride ethylamoniwm clorid *eg*
ethylbenzene ethylbensen *eg*

ethyl-lithium ethyl-lithiwm *eg*
ethylmagnesium bromide ethylmagnesiwm bromid *eg*
ethyne ethyn *eg*
ethynediide ethyndeuid *eg*
etiolated heglog *ans*
etiolate ymheglu *be*
etiolation hegledd *eg*
Etruscan art celfyddyd Etrwsgaidd *eb*
étude étude *eb* études
Eucharist Ewcharist *eg*
Euclidean Ewclidaidd *ans*
Euclid's algorithm algorithm Ewclid *eg*
eukaryote ewcaryot *eg* ewcaryotau
eukaryotic ewcaryotig *ans*
euphonious persain *ans*
euphony perseinedd *eg*
euro ewro *eg* ewros
European classical tradition traddodiad clasurol Ewropeaidd *eg*
European Coal & Steel Community Cymuned Glo a Dur Ewrop *eb*
European Computer Driving Licence Trwydded Yrru Gyfrifiadurol Ewropeaidd *eb*
European context cyd-destun Ewropeaidd *eg*
European Convention on Human Rights Confensiwn Ewropeaidd ar Hawliau Dynol *eg*
European dimension dimensiwn Ewropeaidd *eg*
European exploration fforio Ewropeaidd *be*
European Free Trade Area Ardal Fasnach Rydd Ewropeaidd *eb*
European law cyfraith Ewrop *eb*
European Law Convention on Human Rights Cytundeb Iawnderau Dynol Ewrop *eg*
European Union Undeb Ewropeaidd *eg*
Europeanization Ewropeiddio *be*
europium (Eu) ewropiwm *eg*
Eurosize (cartons) Ewrofaint *ans*
Eurozone Ewrodir *eg*
Eustachian tube tiwb Eustachio *eg* tiwbiau Eustachio
eustatic ewstatig *ans*
eutectic mixture cymysgedd ewtectig *eb*
eutectic point pwynt ewtectig *eg* pwyntiau ewtectig
eutectics ewtecteg *eb*
euthanasia ewthanasia *eg*
eutherian ewtheraidd *ans*
eutrophic ewtroffig *ans*
eutrophication ewtroffigedd *eg*
evacuate gwagio *be*
evacuation ymgiliad *eg*
evacuation procedures trefn ymgilio *eb*
evacuee faciwî *eg/b* faciwîs
evaded cadence diweddeb annisgwyl *eb* diweddebau annisgwyl
evagination allweiniad *eg*
evaluate (in appraisal process) gwerthuso *be*
evaluate (in general) cloriannu *be*
evaluate (in mathematics) enrhifo *be*
evaluate evidence gwerthuso tystiolaeth *be*
evaluate expressions enrhifo mynegiadau *be*
evaluation (in appraisal process) gwerthusiad *eg* gwerthusiadau
evaluation (in mathematics) enrhifiad *eg* enrhifiadau
evaluation criterion maen prawf gwerthuso *eg* meini prawf gwerthuso
evangelical efengylaidd *ans*
evangelist efengylwr *eg* efengylwyr
Evans' Jig Dawns Ifan *eb*
evaporate anweddu *be*
evaporating basin dysgl anweddu *eb* dysglau anweddu
evaporation anweddiad *eg* anweddiadau
evapotranspiration anwedd-drydarthiad *eg*
even llyfn *ans*
even chance siawns deg *eb* siawnsiau teg
even crestline briglin cyson *eg* briglinau cyson
even down llyfnhau *be*
even function eil-ffwythiant *eg* eil-ffwythiannau
even grain graen llyfn *eg*
even number eilrif *eg* eilrifau
even parity eilbaredd *eg* eilbareddau
even parity check gwiriad eilbaredd *eg* gwiriadau eilbaredd
even pitch pitsh llyfn *eg*
even plaid plad cyson *eg*
even pressure gwasgedd llyfn *eg*
even texture gwead llyfn *eg* gweadau llyfn
even weave gwehyddiad llyfn *eg*
evening class dosbarth nos *eg* dosbarthiadau nos
evening dress ffrog fin nos *eb* ffrogiau fin nos
evening meal pryd o fwyd gyda'r hwyr *eg* prydau o fwyd gyda'r hwyr
evens siawns deg *eb*
evensong gosber *eg* gosberau
event (=competition) cystadleuaeth *eb* cystadlaethau
event (=happening) digwyddiad *eg* digwyddiadau
event handling trin digwyddiadau *be*
event-related potential potensial digwyddiad-berthynol *eg*
everglaze (finish) sglein parhaol *eg*
evergreen *adj* bythwyrdd *ans*
evergreen *n* coeden fythwyrdd *eb* coed bythwyrdd
eversion echdroad *eg*
evict troi allan *be*
evidence tystiolaeth *eb* tystiolaethau
evidential tystoliaethol *ans*
evil drygioni *eg*
evil and suffering drygioni a dioddefaint
evolute efoliwt *eg* efoliwtiau
evolution esblygiad *eg* esblygiadau
evolutionary esblygiadol *ans*
evolutionary preparedness parodrwydd esblygol *eg*
evolutionary psychology seicoleg esblygol *eb*
evolve (=develop) datblygu *be*

evolve (in biology) esblygu *be*
evolve (of gases) cynhyrchu *be*
evolve a design datblygu cynllun *be*
evolved gases nwyon cynyrchiedig *ell*
ex post facto ex post facto
exacerbation gwaethygiad *eg*
exact union *ans*
exact length hyd cywir *eg* hydoedd cywir
exact money arian cywir *eg*
exact sampling distribution dosraniad samplu union *eg*
exact size maint cywir *eg* meintiau cywir
exactly yn union *adf*
exactness manwl gywirdeb *eg*
exaggerate gorliwio *be*
exaggeration gorliwiad *eg* gorliwiadau
examination (formal test) arholiad *eg* arholiadau
examination (of patient etc) archwiliad *eg* archwiliadau
examination component cydran arholiad *eb* cydrannau arholiad
examination paper papur arholiad *eg* papurau arholiad
examination under anaesthetic archwiliad dan anaesthetig *eg* archwiliadau dan anaesthetig
examinations board bwrdd arholi *eg* byrddau arholi
examine (=look closely at) archwilio *be*
examine (=test in an examination) arholi *be*
examining magistrate ynad archwiliol *eg* ynadon archwiliol
example enghraifft *eb* enghreifftiau
excavate cloddio *be*
excavation cloddiad *eg* cloddiadau
exceed bod yn fwy na *be*
excentric (in biology) allganol *ans*
except *v* eithrio *be*
exception eithriad *eg* eithriadau
exception word gair eithriad *eg* geiriau eithriad
exceptional child plentyn eithriadol *eg* plant eithriadol
excess gormodedd *eg* gormodeddau
excess demand goralw *eg*
excess energy gormodedd egni *eg*
excess pressure gormodedd gwasgedd *eg*
excessive gormodol *ans*
excessive end play llacrwydd gormodol ar y pen *eg*
excessive slackness llacrwydd gormodol *eg*
exchange *n* cyfnewidfa *eb* cyfnewidfeydd
exchange *v* cyfnewid *be*
exchange background page cyfnewid tudalen gefndir *be*
exchange characters cyfnewid nodau *be*
exchange database cyfnewid cronfa ddata *be*
exchange rate cyfradd gyfnewid *eb* cyfraddau cyfnewid
exchange reaction adwaith cyfnewid *eg*
exchange scheme cynllun cyfnewid *eg* cynlluniau cyfnewid
exchange source cyfnewid ffynhonnell *be*
exchangeable cyfnewidiadwy *ans*
exchangeable disk disg cyfnewidiadwy *eg* disgiau cyfnewidiadwy
exchangeable disk store (EDS) storfa ddisg gyfnewidiadwy *eb* storfeydd disg cyfnewidiadwy
exchequer trysorlys *eg*
Exchequer Court Llys y Siecr *eg*
excircle allgylch *eg* allgylchoedd
excise ecseis *eg*
exciseman ecseismon *eg* ecseismyn
excision toriad *eg* toriadau
excitable cyffroadwy *ans*
excitation cyffroad *eg*
excitation waves tonnau cyffroad *ell*
excitatory centre canolfannyn cyffroadol *eg*
excitatory post-synaptic potential (**EPSP**) potensial ôl-synaptig cyffroadol *eg*
excite cynhyrfu *be*
excited state cyflwr cynhyrfol *eg* cyflyrau cynhyrfol
excitement cynnwrf *eg*
exciting cynhyrfus *ans*
exclamation mark ebychnod *eg* ebychnodau
exclave allglofan *eg* allglofannau
exclosure gwaharddle *eg* gwaharddleoedd
exclude (=prohibit) gwahardd *be*
exclude (=shut out) cau allan *be*
excluded child plentyn wedi'i wahardd *eg* plant wedi'u gwahardd
Exclusion Act Deddf Gwahardd *eb*
exclusion clause cymal eithrio *eg* cymalau eithrio
Exclusion Crisis Argyfwng y Gwahardd *eg*
exclusion principle egwyddor wahardd *eb*
exclusive anghynhwysol *ans*
exclusive OR NEU anghynhwysol *eg*
excommunicant ysgymunwr *eg* ysgymunwyr
excommunicate ysgymuno *be*
excommunication ysgymuniad *eg* ysgymuniadau
excrete ysgarthu *be*
excretion ysgarthiad *eg* ysgarthiadau
excretory ysgarthol *ans*
excretory ysgarthle *eg*
excretory cavity ceudod ysgarthiol *eg*
excretory organ organ ysgarthu *eg*
excretory substance sylwedd ysgarthiol *eg* sylweddau ysgarthiol
executable gweithredadwy *ans*
execute (=act) gweithredu *be*
execute (=carry into effect) cyflawni *be*
execute (=kill) dienyddio *be*
execute cycle cylchred weithredu *eb* cylchredau gweithredu
EXECUTE key bysell EXECUTE *eg* bysellau EXECUTE
execute macro (command) gweithredu macro *be*
execute phase gwedd weithredu *eb* gweddau gweithredu
execute program gweithredu'r rhaglen *be*

execute query immediately
gweithredu ymholiad yn syth *be*
execute SQL statement
gweithredu datganiad SQL *be*
execution time amser gweithredu *eg*
amserau gweithredu
executive *adj* gweithredol *ans*
executive *n* gweithredwr *eg* gweithredwyr
executive (department) *n* adran weithredol *eb*
adrannau gweithredol
executive (officer) *n* swyddog gweithredol *eg*
swyddogion gweithredol
executive body corff gweithredol *eg*
cyrff gweithredol
executive committee (in general)
pwyllgor gwaith *eg* pwyllgorau gwaith
executive committee (with emphasis on action)
pwyllgor gweithredu *eg* pwyllgorau gweithredu
executive program rhaglen oruchwylio *eb*
rhaglenni goruchwylio
executor ysgutor *eg* ysgutorion
exemplar enghraifft batrymol *eb*
enghreifftiau patrymol
exempt (with feminine nouns) wedi'i hesgusodi *ans*
wedi'u hesgusodi
exempt (with masculine nouns) wedi'i esgusodi *ans*
wedi'u hesgusodi
exemption (from income tax) rhyddhad *eg*
rhyddhadau
exemption (in general) esgusodiad *eg* esgusodiadau
exemption clause cymal eithrio *eg* cymalau eithrio
exercise *n* ymarfer *eg* ymarferion
exercise *v* ymarfer *be*
exercise activity (physical activity)
gweithgaredd ymarfer corff *eg*
exercise adherence (physical activity)
ymlyniad at ymarfer corff *eg*
► **exercise plan** (physical activity)
cynllun ymarfer corff *eg* cynlluniau ymarfer corff
exercise programme (physical activity)
rhaglen ymarfer corff *eb* rhaglenni ymarfer corff
exergonic ecsergonig *ans*
exert a force rhoi grym *be*
Exeter pattern hammer morthwyl patrwm Exeter *eg*
morthwylion patrwm Exeter
exhalant siphon siffon allanadlu *eg*
siffonau allanadlu
exhale allanadlu *be*
exhaled gases nwyon allanadledig *ell*
exhaust (=use up) disbyddu *be*
exhaust (evacuate) gwacáu *be*
exhaust air aer gwacáu *eg*
exhaust gas nwy gwacáu *eg* nwyon gwacáu
exhaust manifold maniffold gwacáu *eg*
maniffoldau gwacáu
exhaust pipe pibell wacáu *eb* pibellau gwacáu
exhaust port porth gwacáu *eg* pyrth gwacáu
exhaust pump pwmp gwacáu *eg* pympiau gwacáu
exhausted (of seams of coal) disbyddedig *ans*
exhaustible disbyddadwy *ans*
exhaustion gorludded *eg*
exhibit arddangos *be*
exhibition (act of) arddangosiad *eg*
exhibition (display of art etc) arddangosfa *eb*
arddangosfeydd
exhibitionism arddangosiaeth *eb*
exhibitor arddangoswr *eg* arddangoswyr
exhorter cymhellwr *eg* cymhellwyr
exhumed (of landform) datgladdedig *ans*
exile *v* alltudio *be*
exile (in general) *n* alltud *eg* alltudion
Exile (of Jews in Old Testament) *n* Caethglud *eb*
existence bodolaeth *eb* bodolaethau
existence of God bodolaeth Duw *eb*
existence theorem theorem bodolaeth *eb*
theoremau bodolaeth
existing (=present in program) presennol *ans*
existing column colofn bresennol *eb*
colofnau presennol
existing design cynllun presennol *eg*
cynlluniau presennol
existing field maes presennol *eg* meysydd presennol
existing use defnydd presennol *eg*
existing version fersiwn presennol *eg*
fersiynau presennol
exit (=way out) *n* allanfa *eb* allanfeydd
exit (in menu choice) *v* gadael *be*
exit all groups gadael pob grŵp *be*
exit direction cyfeiriad gadael *eg*
exit direction bottom cyfeiriad gadael i'r gwaelod *eg*
exit direction left cyfeiriad gadael i'r chwith *eg*
exit direction right cyfeiriad gadael i'r dde *eg*
exit direction top cyfeiriad gadael i'r brig
exit fill mode gadael modd llanw *be*
exit group gadael grŵp *be*
exit presentation gadael y cyflwyniad *be*
exit recording gadael y recordiad *be*
exocrine ecsocrin *eg*
exocrine gland chwarren ecsocrin *eb*
chwarennau ecsocrin
Exodus (book in the Bible) Exodus
exogenesis alldarddiad *eg*
exogenic alldarddol *ans*
exogenous alldarddol *ans*
exorcise bwrw allan *be*
exoskeleton sgerbwd allanol *eg* sgerbydau allanol
exothermic ecsothermig *ans*
exothermic heat gwres ecsothermig *eg*
exotic (of plants) *adj* egsotig *ans*
exotic (of river) *n* alldardd *eg*
expand *v.intrans* ymledu *be*
expand *v.trans* ehangu *be*
expand formatting ehangu fformatio *be*
expand single word ehangu gair unigol *be*
expand slide ehangu sleid *be*
expanded ehangedig *ans*
expanded metal metel ehangedig *eg*
metelau ehangedig

expanding industry diwydiant ehangol *eg* diwydiannau ehangol
expanding reamer agorell gymwysadwy *eb* agorellau cymwysadwy
expansion ehangiad *eg* ehangiadau
expansion allowance lwfans ehangu *eg* lwfansau ehangu
expansion bolt bollt ymestyn *eb* bolltau ymestyn
expansion cloud chamber llestr niwl ehangiad *eg*
expansion slot slot ehangu *eg* slotiau ehangu
expansion slot agen ehangu *eb* agennau ehangu
expansive bit ebill ymledu *eg* ebillion ymledu
expansivity eangolrwydd *eg*
expectancy disgwyliad *eg*
expectant mother mam feichiog *eb* mamau beichiog
expected (of value) disgwyliedig *ans*
expected value gwerth disgwyliedig *eg* gwerthoedd disgwyliedig
expectorant poergarthydd *eg* poergarthyddion
expediency buddioldeb *eb*
expedition (military) ymgyrch *eb* ymgyrchoedd
expedition (outdoor pursuit) alldaith *eb* alldeithiau
expel (from country) alltudio *be*
expel (from institution, movement) diarddel *be*
expenditure gwariant *eg*
expenditure retained gwariant a gedwir yn ôl *eg*
expense traul *eb* treuliau
experience profiad *eg* profiadau
experience of nirvana profiad o nirfana *eg*
experiential exercise ymarfer drwy brofiadau *eg*
experiential intelligence deallusrwydd drwy brofiadau *eg*
experiential learning dysgu drwy brofiadau *be*
experiment *n* arbrawf *eg* arbrofion
experiment *v* arbrofi *be*
experimental arbrofol *ans*
experimental brain lesion niwed arbrofol i'r ymennydd *eg*
experimental control rheolydd arbrawf *eb*
experimental data data arbrofion *ell*
experimental design cynllun arbrawf *eg* cynlluniau arbrofion
► **experimental error** cyfeiliornad mewn arbrawf *eg* cyfeiliornadau mewn arbrawf
experimental evidence tystiolaeth arbrofol *eb*
experimental film ffilm arbrofol *eb* ffilmiau arbrofol
experimental group grŵp arbrofol *eg* grwpiau arbrofol
experimental method dull arbrofol *eg* dulliau arbrofol
experimental paradigm paradeim arbrawf *eg* paradeimau arbrawf
experimental procedure dull o weithredu arbrawf *eg* dulliau o weithredu arbrawf
experimental technique techneg arbrofi *eb* technegau arbrofi
experimental work gwaith arbrofi *eg*
expert arbenigwr *eg* arbenigwyr
expert system system arbenigo *eb* systemau arbenigo
expertise arbenigedd *eg* arbenigeddau
expiration (=breathing out) allanadliad *eg*
expire (=breath out) allanadlu *be*
expire (=come to an end) dod i ben *be*
explain egluro *be*
explanation esboniad *eg* esboniadau
explanatory diagram diagram eglurhaol *eg* diagramau eglurhaol
explicit (in computing) penodol *ans*
explicit (in mathematics) echblyg *ans*
explicit function (in mathematics) ffwythiant echblyg *eg*
explicit memory atgof echblyg *eg* atgofion echblyg
explode ffrwydro *be*
exploded (of drawing etc) taenedig *ans*
exploded drawing lluniad taenedig *eg* lluniadau taenedig
exploded isometric isomedrig taenedig *eg*
exploded isometric view golwg isomedrig taenedig *eg* golygon isomedrig taenedig
exploded sketch braslun taenedig *eg* brasluniau taenedig
exploded view golwg taenedig *eg* golygon taenedig
exploit (=develop) datblygu *be*
► **exploit** (=use unfairly) ecsbloetio *be*
exploitation ecsbloetiaeth *eb*
exploitation of resources datblygu adnoddau *be*
exploration (of ideas) archwiliad *eg* archwiliadau
exploration (of land) fforiad *eg* fforiadau
exploration method dull archwilio *eg* dulliau archwilio
exploratory archwiliadol *ans*
exploratory behaviour gweithgaredd chwilio *eg* gweithgareddau chwilio
exploratory play chwarae archwiliadol *be*
explore (ideas) archwilio *be*
explore (land) fforio *be*
explorer fforiwr *eg* fforwyr
explosion ffrwydrad *eg* ffrwydradau
explosive *adj* ffrwydrol *ans*
explosive *n* ffrwydryn *eg* ffrwydron
exponent (in mathematics) esbonydd *eg* esbonyddion
exponential esbonyddol *ans*
exponential definition diffiniad esbonyddol *eg*
exponential functions ffwythiannau esbonyddol *ell*
exponential phase gwedd esbonyddol *eb*
export *n* allforyn *eg* allforion
export *v* allforio *be*
export duty toll allforio *eb* tollau allforio
export setting gosodiad allforio *eg* gosodiadau allforio
exporter allforiwr *eg* allforwyr
expose (facts etc) datgelu *be*
expose (in photography) dinoethi *be*

expose to light rhoi yn y golau *be*
exposed (in music) noeth *ans*
exposed (to the weather) agored *ans*
exposed eighth wythfed noeth *eg* wythfedau noeth
exposed fifth pumed noeth *eg* pumedau noeth
exposed octave wythfed noeth *eg* wythfedau noeth
exposition dangosiad *eg* dangosiadau
exposure (=being exposed to the elements) oerfel *eg*
exposure (in photography) dinoethiad *eg* dinoethiadau
exposure (to air, light etc) datguddiad *eg*
express mynegi *be*
expressed emotion mynegiad emosiwn *eg*
expression (=phrase) ymadrodd *eg* ymadroddion
expression (in mathematics, act of expressing) mynegiad *eg* mynegiadau
expression (of ideas etc) mynegiant *eg* mynegiannau
expression mark marc mynegiant *eg* marciau mynegiant
expressionism mynegiadaeth *eb*
expressionist *adj* mynegiadol *ans*
expressionist *n* mynegiadwr *eg* mynegiadwyr
expressive llawn mynegiant *ans*
expressive arts celfyddydau mynegiannol *ell*
expressive language disorder diffyg mynegiant llafar *eg*
expressive movement symudiad mynegiannol *eg* symudiadau mynegiannol
expressiveness mynegolrwydd *eg*
expressway ffordd gyflym *eb* ffyrdd cyflym
expropriate difeddiannu *be*
expulsion (from country) alltudiad *eg* alltudiadau
expulsion (from movement) diarddeliad *eg* diarddeliadau
expulsion (in childbirth) ymwthiad *eg* ymwthiadau
extempore byrfyfyr *adv*
extemporization (performance) datganiad ar y pryd *eg* datganiadau ar y pryd
extemporization passage darn byrfyfyr *eg* darnau byrfyfyr
extemporize (in singing) datganu ar y pryd *be*
extend *v.intrans* ymestyn *be*
extend *v.trans* estyn *be*
extended estynedig *be*
extended day diwrnod estynedig *eg* diwrnodau estynedig
extended family teulu estynedig *eg* teuluoedd estynedig
extended help cymorth estynedig *eg*
extended language iaith estynedig *eb*
extended line llinell estynedig *eb* llinellau estynedig
extended modulator cyweiriadur mawr *eg* cyweiriaduron mawr
extended prose rhyddiaith estynedig *eb*
extended reading darllen estynedig *eg*
extended search chwiliad estynedig *eg* chwiliadau estynedig
extender estynnydd *eg* estynyddion
extensible estynadwy *ans*
extension estyniad *eg* estyniadau
extension (of muscles) ymestyniad *eg*
extension activity gweithgaredd estyn *eg* gweithgareddau estyn
extension booklet llyfryn ymestyn *eg* llyfrynnau ymestyn
extension hinge colfach estyn *eg* colfachau estyn
extension organ organ estyn *eb* organau estyn
extension paper papur estynedig *eg* papurau estynedig
extension study astudiaeth estyn *eb* astudiaethau estyn
extensive eang *ans*
extensive listening gwrando eang *be*
extensive reading darllen eang *be*
extensor muscle cyhyryn estyn *eg* cyhyrynnau estyn
extent (=size) maint *eg*
extent (land) stent *eg* stentau
extent of reaction (in chemistry) lledaeniad yr adwaith *eg*
exterior *adj* allanol *ans*
exterior *n* tu allan *eg*
exterior angle ongl allanol *eb* onglau allanol
exterior plywood pren haenog allanol *eg*
exterminate difodi *be*
extermination camp gwersyll difodi *eg* gwersylloedd difodi
external allanol *ans*
external amplifier mwyhadur allanol *eg* mwyhaduron allanol
external assessment asesu allanol *be*
external assessor aseswr allanol *eg* aseswyr allanol
external benefit budd allanol *eg* buddion allanol
external bisector hanerydd allanol *eg* hanerwyr allanol
external chest compression cywasgiad allanol ar y frest *eg* cywasgiadau allanol ar y frest
external circlip cylchglip allanol *eg* cylchglipiau allanol
external communication cyfathrebu allanol *be*
external cost cost allanol *eb* costau allanol
external degree gradd allanol *eb* graddau allanol
external examiner arholwr allanol *eg* arholwyr allanol
external growth twf allanol *eg*
external hard disk disg caled allanol *eg* disgiau caled allanol
external locus of control locws rheolaeth allanol *eg*
external memory cof allanol *eg*
external part rhan allanol *eb* rhannau allanol
external point pwynt allanol *eg* pwyntiau allanol
external pressure gwasgedd allanol *eg*
external recruitment recriwtio allanol *be*
external respiration resbiradaeth allanol *eb*
external validator dilysydd allanol *eg* dilyswyr allanol

external validity dilysrwydd allanol *eg*
externality effect effaith allanoldeb *eb* effeithiau allanoldeb
extinct diflanedig *ans*
extinct volcano llosgfynydd marw *eg* llosgfynyddoedd marw
extinction difodiant *eg*
extinguisher stake bonyn hirbig *eg* bonion hirbig
extort cribddeilio *be*
extorter cribddeiliwr *eg* cribddeilwyr
extortion cribddeiliaeth *eb*
extortionate gormodol *ans*
extra contractual referral (ECR) achos all-gontract *eg* achosion all-gontract
extra embryonic allembryonig *eg*
extra fine mân iawn *ans*
extra galactic echalaethog *ans*
extra high tension (e.h.t) tensiwn arbennig o uchel (t.a.u) *eg*
extracellular allgellog *ans*
extract *v* echdynnu *be*
extract (=part of something) *n* detholiad *eg* detholiadau
extract (=something extracted) *n* echdynnyn *eg* echdynion
extract (of map) *n* rhanfap *eg* rhanfapiau
extract (of meat) *n* rhin *eb* rhiniau
extract a resource echdynnu adnodd *be*
extract water echdynnu dŵr *be*
extraction echdyniad *eg* echdyniadau
extraction rate of flour cyfradd echdynnol blawd *eb*
extractive echdynnol *ans*
extractive industry diwydiant echdynnol *eg* diwydiannau echdynnol
extractor echdynnwr *eg* echdynwyr
extractor fan gwyntyll echdynnu *eb* gwyntyllau echdynnu
extra-curricular activity gweithgaredd allgyrsiol *eg* gweithgareddau allgyrsiol
extradition estraddodi *be*
extrados of an arch cromlin allanol bwa *eb* cromliniau allanol bwa
extra-evidential alldystiolaethol *ans*
extra-musical stimulus ysgogiad allgerddorol *eg* ysgogiadau allgerddorol
extraneous (=foreign) estron *ans*
extraneous (=outside) allanol *ans*
extranet allrwyd *eb* allrwydi
extra-nuclear allniwclear *ans*
extrapolate allosod *be*
extrapolation allosodiad *eg* allosodiadau
extra-sensory perception canfyddiad allsynhwyraidd *eg*
extraterritorial alldiriogaethol *ans*
extreme eithaf *ans*
extreme pressure oil (E.P.) olew gwasgedd eithaf *eg*
extreme unction eneiniad olaf *eg*
extreme value gwerth eithaf *eg* gwerthoedd eithaf
extreme west gorllewin eithaf *eg*
extremely thankful hynod ddiolchgar *adf*
extremes eithafion *ell*
extremes of weather eithafion tywydd *ell*
extremist *adj* eithafol *ans*
extremist *n* eithafwr *eg* eithafwyr
extremities eithafoedd *ell*
extrinsic anghynhenid
extroversion allblygedd *eg*
extrovert allblyg *ans*
extrude allwthio *be*
extrusion allwthiad *eg* allwthiadau
extrusion object gwrthrych allwthiad *eg* gwrthrychau allwthiad
extrusive allwthiol *ans*
extrusive rock craig allwthiol *eb* creigiau allwthiol
exudate archwys *eg*
exudation archwysiad *eg* archwysiadau
exude archwysu *be*
eye (=hole in needle etc) crau *eg* creuau
eye (=organ of sight) llygad *eg/b* llygaid
eye bolt bollt ddolen *eb* bolltau dolen
eye contact cyswllt llygaid *eg*
eye lens lens y llygad *eg* lensiau'r llygad
eye movement symudiad llygad *eg* symudiadau llygaid
eye muscle cyhyr llygad *eg* cyhyrau llygad
eye of hammer crau morthwyl *eg* creuau morthwylion
eye of needle crau nodwydd *eg* creuau nodwyddau
eye ring cylch llygad *eg* cylchoedd llygaid
eye tooth dant llygad *eg* dannedd llygad
eyeball pelen y llygad *eb* pelenni'r llygaid
eyebrow ael *eb* aeliau
eyelash blewyn amrant *eg* blew amrant
eyelet llygaden *eb* llygadennau
eyelet hole twll llygaden *eg* tyllau llygaden
eyelet pliers gefelen llygaden *eb* gefeiliau llygaden
eyelet punch tyllwr llygadennau *eg* tyllwyr llygadennau
eyelet tools offer llygadennu *ell*
eye-level llinell orwel *eb* llinellau gorwel
eye-level grill gridyll uchel *eg* gridyllau uchel
eyepiece (microscope) sylladur *eg* sylladuron
eyepiece graticule sylladur graticwl *eg*
eyewitness testimony tystiolaeth llygad-dyst *eb*
eyot ynysig *eb* ynysigau
eyre (of justices) cylchdaith *eb* cylchdeithiau
Eysenck personality inventory rhestren bersonoliaeth Eysenck *eb*
e-zine e-grawn *eg* e-gronau

F

F attachment (trombone) ymlyniad F *eg*
F clef cleff F *eg*
'F' hole seindwll *eg* seindyllau
F major F fwyaf *eb*
F minor F leiaf *eb*
F ratio cymhareb F *eb*
Fabian Society Cymdeithas y Ffabiaid *eb*
Fabianism Ffabiaeth *eb*
Fablon Fablon *eg*
fabric ffabrig *eg* ffabrigau
fabric colour lliw ffabrig *eg* lliwiau ffabrig
fabric conditioner cyflyrydd ffabrig *eg* cyflyryddion ffabrig
fabric craft crefft ffabrig *eb* crefftau ffabrig
fabric dressing gorchudd ffabrig *eg* gorchuddion ffabrig
fabric dye llifyn ffabrig *eg* llifynnau ffabrig
fabric medium cyfrwng ffabrig *eg* cyfryngau ffabrig
fabric printing printio ffabrig *be*
fabric printing mallet gordd brintio ffabrig *eb* gyrdd printio ffabrig
fabric softener cyflyrydd ffabrig *eg* cyflyryddion ffabrig
fabricate ffabrigo *be*
fabricated ffabrigedig *ans*
facade ffasâd *eg* ffasadau
face *n* wyneb *eg* wynebau
face *v* wynebu *be*
face downwards wyneb i waered *adf*
face edge ymyl wyneb *eg/b* ymylon wyneb
face edge mark marc ymyl wyneb *eg* marciau ymyl wyneb
face plate plât wyneb *eg* platiau wyneb
face side ochr wyneb *eb* ochrau wyneb
face the direction of the throw wynebu cyfeiriad y tafliad *be*
face the net wynebu'r rhwyd *be*
face to face wyneb yn wyneb
face value wynebwerth *eg* wynebwerthoedd
face vault llofnaid wyneb *eb* llofneidiau wyneb
face veneer argaen wyneb *eg* argaenau wyneb
face-centred cubic ciwbig wyneb-ganolog *ans*
face-centred cubic lattice dellten giwbig wyneb-ganolog *eb* delltiau ciwbig wyneb-ganolog
faced hem hem wedi'i hwynebu *eb* hemiau wedi'u hwynebu
faced opening agoriad wedi'i wynebu *eg* agoriadau wedi'u wynebu
faced plywood pren haenog wedi'i wynebu *eg*
faced scalloping sgolop wedi'i wynebu *eg* sgolopiau wedi'u hwynebu
faceplate turning turnio ar wynebplat *be*
facet ffased *eg* ffasedau
faceted spur sbardun ffasedaidd *eg* sbardunau ffasedaidd
facial wynebol *ans*
facial feedback hypothesis rhagdybiaeth adborth yr wyneb *eb*
facial nerve nerf wynebol *eg* nerfau wynebol
facial plane plân wynebol *eg* planau wynebol
facies gwedd *eb* gweddau
facilitate hwyluso *be*
facilitated transport cludiant cynorthwyedig *eg*
facilitator hwyluswr *eg* hwyluswyr
facilities cyfleusterau *ell*
facilities and amenities cyfleusterau a mwynderau
facility (=aptitude) dawn *eb* doniau
facility (=ease, fluency) rhwyddineb *eg*
facility (=specific feature) cyfleuster *eg* cyfleusterau
facing *n* wynebyn *eg* wynebynnau
facing fillet ffiled wynebu *eb* ffiledau wynebu
facing left (of lathe tools) wynebu'r chwith *be*
facing right (of lathe tools) wynebu'r dde *be*
facing tool erfyn wynebu *eg* offer wynebu
facsimile ffacsimili *eg* ffacsimilïau
facsimile message neges ffacs *eb* negeseuon ffacs
facsimile number rhif ffacs *eg* rhifau ffacs
fact ffaith *eb* ffeithiau
faction carfan *eb* carfanau
factionalism carfanyddiaeth *eb*
factor ffactor *eg/b* ffactorau
factor analysis dadansoddi ffactorau *be*
factorial *adj* ffactoraidd *ans*
factorial *n* ffactorial *eg* ffactorialau
factorial design cynllun ffactoraidd *eg* cynlluniau ffactoraidd
factorial ecology ecoleg ffactoraidd *eb*
▶ **factorizable** ffactoriadwy *ans*
factorization ffactoriad *eg* ffactoriadau
factorize ffactorio *be*
factorize completely ffactorio yn llwyr *be*
factorizing ffactoriaeth *eb*
factors of production ffactorau cynhyrchu *ell*
factory ffatri *eb* ffatrïoedd
Factory Acts Deddfau Ffatri *ell*
factory farming ffermio gorddwys *be*
factory legislation deddfwriaeth ffatri *eb*
factory shop siop ffatri *eb* siopau ffatri

factory system trefn ffatri *eb*
facultative (in biology) amryddawn *ans*
faculty (=aptitude or inherent power) cynneddf *eb* cyneddfau
faculty (group of subject departments) cyfadran *eb* cyfadrannau
fad chwiw *eb* chwiwiau
fade (of colour) colli lliw *be*
fade (of image on screen) pylu *be*
fade clockwise pylu clocwedd *be*
fade counter-clockwise pylu gwrthglocwedd *be*
fade from centre pylu o'r canol *be*
fade horizontally pylu'n llorweddol *be*
fade object pylu gwrthrych *be*
fade out pylu allan *be*
fade to centre pylu i'r canol *be*
fade vertically pylu'n fertigol *be*
faeces ymgarthion *ell*
faggot ffagotsen *eb* ffagots
faggot stitch pwyth ffagod *eg* pwythau ffagod
faggot weld weldiad ffagod *eg* weldiadau ffagod
faggotting ffagodwaith *eg*
fagotto fagotto *eg* fagotti
faience (=pottery) faience *eg*
failure methiant *eg* methiannau
failure to thrive diffyg cynnydd *eg*
faint *n* llewyg *eg*
faint *v* llewygu *be*
faint relief (of landscape) tirwedd anamlwg *eb* tirweddau anamlwg
fair teg *ans*
fair catch daliad glân *eg* daliadau glân
fair ground tir teg *eg*
fair play chwarae teg *eg*
fair test prawf teg *eg* profion teg
fair testing profi teg *be*
fair trading masnachu teg *be*
Fair Trading Office Act Deddf Swyddfa Masnachu Teg *eb*
fairway (for shipping) sianel fordwyo *eb* sianeli mordwyo
fairy tale stori tylwyth teg *eb* straeon tylwyth teg
faith ffydd *eb*
faithful subject role rôl cyfrannwr ffyddlon *eb*
fake *adj* ffug *ans*
fake *n* ffugwaith *eg* ffugweithiau
fake *v* ffugio *be*
falconer hebogydd *eg* hebogwyr
fall cwymp *eg* cwympiadau
fall line llinell gwymp *eb* llinellau cwymp
fallen angel angel syrthiedig *eg* angylion syrthiedig
falling rolls gostyngiad mewn nifer *eg*
Fallopian tube tiwb Fallopio *eg* tiwbiau Fallopio
fallout (radioactive) llwch ymbelydrol *eg*
fallow (land) *n* braenar *eg*
fallow (land) *v* braenaru *be*
false (in general) ffug *ans*
false (of prophets etc) gau *ans*
false attack ffug ymosod *be*
false bedding ffug haenau *ell*
false close diweddeb annisgwyl *eb* diweddebau annisgwyl
false consensus consensws ffug *eg*
false entry camgydiad *eg* camgydiadau
false front (of drawer) ffrynt ffug *eg* ffryntiau ffug
false fruit ffug ffrwythyn *eg* ffug ffrwythau
false hem hem ffug *eb* hemiau ffug
false relation gau berthynas *eb* gau berthnasau
false root gwreiddyn ffug *eg* gwreiddiau ffug
false tooth dant gosod *eg* dannedd gosod
falsifiability view agwedd natur ffugiadwy *eb*
faltung ffaltwng *eg* ffaltyngau
familial teuluol *ans*
familiar context cyd-destun cyfarwydd *eg*
familiar technology technoleg gyfarwydd *eb*
familiarisation trip taith ymgyfarwyddo *eb* teithiau ymgyfarwyddo
familiarize oneself with ymgyfarwyddo â *be*
family teulu *eg* teuluoedd
family allowance lwfans teulu *eg*
family credit credyd teulu *eg*
family doctor meddyg teulu *eg* meddygon teulu
Family Expenditure Survey Arolwg Gwariant Teulu *eg*
family group grŵp teulu *eg* grwpiau teulu
family grouping grwpio teuluol *be*
Family Health Services Authority (FHSA) Awdurdod Gwasanaethau Iechyd Teulu *eg*
Family Income Supplement Atodiad Incwm Teulu *eg*
family life bywyd teuluol *eg*
family planning cynllunio teulu *be*
family planning clinic clinig cynllunio teulu *eg*
family practitioner meddyg teulu *eg* meddygon teulu
family psychotherapy seicotherapi teuluol *eg*
family therapy therapi teulu *eg*
family tree cart achau *eg* cartiau achau
famine newyn *eg* newynau
fan (=fan shaped object) bwa *eg* bwâu
fan (=keen follower) ffan *eg* ffaniau
fan (of device) gwyntyll *eb* gwyntyllau
fan heater tân chwythu *eg* tanau chwythu
fan vaulting ffanfowt *eg* ffanfowtiau
fancy (of needlework etc) ffansi *ans*
fanfare ffanfer *eg* ffanferau
fan-fold paper papur igam ogam *eg*
fanglomerate bwa malurion *eg* bwâu malurion
fantasia ffantasia *eb* ffantasïau
fantasy ffantasi *eb* ffantasïau
fantasy figure ffigur ffantasi *eg* ffigurau ffantasi
fantasy play chwarae ffantasi *eg*
fanzine ffansîn *eg*
far pell *ans*
Far East Dwyrain Pell *eg*

far side ochr bellaf *eb* ochrau pellaf
farad ffarad *eg* ffaradau
farce (=forcemeat) stwffin *eg*
farm *n* fferm *eb* ffermydd
farm *v* ffermio *be*
farm implements offer fferm *ell*
farmer ffermwr *eg* ffermwyr
farming community cymuned amaethyddol *eb* cymunedau amaethyddol
farthingale cylchbais *eb* cylchbeisiau
fascia ffasgau *ell*
fascia board astell dywydd *eb* estyll tywydd
fasciated ffasgol *ans*
fasciation ffasgedd *eg*
fascicle ffasgell *eb* ffasgellau
fascicular ffasgellol *ans*
fascism ffasgaeth *eb*
fascist *adj* ffasgaidd *ans*
fascist *n* ffasgydd *eg* ffasgwyr
fascist dictator unben ffasgaidd *eg* unbeniaid ffasgaidd
Fascist Italy Yr Eidal Ffasgaidd *eb*
fashion ffasiwn *eg/b* ffasiynau
fashion trend gogwydd ffasiwn *eg*
Fashoda crisis argyfwng Fashoda *eg*
fast *adj* cyflym *ans*
fast *n* ympryd *eg* ymprydiau
fast *v* ymprydio *be*
fast (of colour) anniflan *ans*
fast access storage storfa fuangyrch *eb* storfeydd buangyrch
fast ball pêl gyflym *eb* peli cyflym
fast bowler bowliwr cyflym *eg* bowlwyr cyflym
fast bowling bowlio cyflym *be*
fast colour (enamelling colour) lliw anniflan *eg* lliwiau anniflan
fast dye llifyn anniflan *eg* llifynnau anniflan
fast food bwyd cyflym *eg*
fast mapping mapio sydyn *be*
fast reaction adwaith cyflym *eg* adweithiau cyflym
fast starter cychwynnwr cyflym *eg* cychwynwyr cyflym
fasten (with hook) bachu *be*
fasten (with nails) hoelio *be*
fasten (with rope) clymu *be*
fastener ffasnydd *eg* ffasnyddion
fastening device dyfais sicrhau *eb* dyfeisiau sicrhau
fastening screw sgriw sicrhau *eb* sgriwiau sicrhau
fastenings dull cau *eg* dulliau cau
fastness (of colour) anniflanedd *eg*
fat braster *eg* brasterau
fat depot storfa fraster *eb* storfeydd braster
fat globule globwl braster *eg* globylau braster
fat pigment pigment bras *eg* pigmentau bras
fat soluble vitamin fitamin braster-hydawdd *eg* fitaminau braster-hydawdd
fatal dose dos angheuol *eg* dosau angheuol
fatal error gwall angheuol *eg* gwallau angheuol
father tape mam-dâp *eg* mam-dapiau
fathom gwryd *eg* gwrhydau
fatigue (of muscle, metal) lludded *eg*
fatty brasterog *ans*
fatty acid asid brasterog *eg* asidau brasterog
fatty marrow mêr brasterog *eg*
fatty meat cig gwyn *eg*
fault (=blame) *n* bai *eg* beiau
fault (=defect) *n* diffyg *eg* diffygion
fault (in geology and tennis) *n* ffawt *eg/b* ffawtiau
fault (in geology and tennis) *v* ffawtio *be*
fault line ffawtlin *eg* ffawtlinau
fault processing system system prosesu diffygion *eb* systemau prosesu diffygion
fault rate cyfradd diffygion *eb* cyfraddau diffygion
fault status statws diffyg *eg*
fault zone cylchfa ffawtio *eb* cylchfaoedd ffawtio
faulted strata haenau ffawtiedig *ell*
faulty diffygiol *ans*
faulty bully bwli cam *eg* bwlïau cam
faulty goods nwyddau diffygiol *ell*
fauna ffawna *ell*
faux bourdon faux bourdon *eg* faux bourdons
favour ffafrio *be*
favourite ffefryn *eg* ffefrynnau
fax *n* ffacs *eg* ffacsys
fax *v* ffacsio *be*
fax gateway porth ffacs *eg* pyrth ffacs
fax header template patrymlun pennawd ffacs *eg* patrymluniau pennawd ffacs
fax modem modem ffacs *eg* modemau ffacs
fax template templed ffacs *eg* templedi ffacs
fealty llw ffyddlondeb *eg*
fealty homage gwrogaeth llw ffyddlondeb *eb*
feasibility study astudiaeth dichonoldeb *eb* astudiaethau dichonoldeb
feasible dichonadwy *ans*
feasible region rhanbarth dichonadwy *eg* rhanbarthau dichonadwy
feasible solution datrysiad dichonadwy *eg* datrysiadau dichonadwy
feast gŵyl *eb* gwyliau
feast day dydd gŵyl *eg* dyddiau gŵyl
Feast of Andrew the Apostle Gŵyl Sant Andreas *eb*
Feast of Edward, the Confessor Gŵyl Edward Frenin *eb*
Feast of James the Apostle Gŵyl Iago'r Apostol *eb*
Feast of John the Apostle Gŵyl Ioan yr Apostol *eb*
Feast of John the Baptist Gŵyl Ifan *eb*
Feast of Lucy Gŵyl Lleuan Wyryf *eb*
Feast of Matthew the Apostle Gŵyl Fathew yr Apostol *eb*
Feast of Peter and Paul Gŵyl Bedr a Phawl *eb*
Feast of Pope Calixtus Gŵyl y Pab Calixtus *eb*
Feast of St Benedict Gŵyl Sant Benedict *eb*
Feast of St Cecilia Gŵyl Cecilia Wyryf *eb*

Feast of St David Gŵyl Ddewi *eb*
Feast of St Denis Gŵyl Sant Denis *eb*
Feast of St Hilary Gŵyl Sant Hyllar *eb*
Feast of St Luke the Evangelist Gŵyl Luc Efengylwr *eb*
Feast of St Martin Gŵyl Sant Martin *eb*
Feast of St Mary, August Gŵyl Fair yn Awst *eb*
Feast of St Mary, Nativity Gŵyl Eni'r Arglwyddes Fair *eb*
Feast of St Mary, September Gŵyl Fair ym Medi *eb*
Feast of St Michael Gŵyl Sant Mihangel *eb*
Feast of St Patrick Gŵyl Badrig *eb*
Feast of St Paul Gŵyl Bawl *eb*
Feast of Stephen the Martyr Gŵyl San Steffan *eb*
Feast of Thomas the Apostle Gŵyl Tomos yr Apostol *eb*
feather *n* pluen *eb* plu
feather *v* pluo *be*
feather key allwedd bluen *eb* allweddi pluen
feather smocking smocwaith pluen *eg*
feather stitch pwyth pluen *eg* pwythau pluen
feather weight pwysau plu *ell*
feathering (pottery decoration) pluo *be*
feature (=feature article) erthygl nodwedd *eb* erthyglau nodwedd
feature (in general) nodwedd *eb* nodweddion
feature (on surface) arwedd *eb* arweddion
feature film prif ffilm *eb*
feature length film prif ffilm *eb*
feature variants amrywiolion nodwedd *ell*
features (of face) wynepryd *eg*
febrile twymynol *ans*
fecundity ffrwythlonedd *eg*
federal ffederal *ans*
federal republic gweriniaeth ffederal *eb* gweriniaethau ffederal
federalism ffederaliaeth *eb*
federate ffederaleiddio *be*
federation ffederasiwn *eg*
fee ffi *eb* ffioedd
feed *n* porthiant *eg* porthiannau
feed (in general) *v* bwydo *be*
feed (livestock) *v* porthi *be*
feed dog (on machine) dannedd *ell*
feed hole twll porthi *eg* tyllau porthi
feed shaft siafft borthi *eb* siafftau porthi
feedback *n* adborth *eg* adborthion
feedback *v* adborthi *be*
feedback control loop dolen adborth a rheoli *eb*
feedback loop dolen adborth *eb* dolennau adborth
feedback sheet dalen adborth *eb* dalennau adborth
feeder (of animal) ymborthwr *eg* ymborthwyr
feeder (of stream, road etc) cyflenwydd *eg* cyflenwyddion
feeding habits arferion bwyta *ell*
feeding relationship perthynas bwydo *eb*
feeding-bottle potel fwydo *eb* poteli bwydo
feeding-time amser bwydo *eg*
feel *v* teimlo *be*
feel (=atmosphere) *n* naws *eg*
feel (=touch) *n* teimlad *eg*
feeler gauge medrydd teimlo *eg* medryddion teimlo
feeling teimlad *eg* teimladau
Fehlings solution hydoddiant Fehling *eg*
feigned relic crair ffug *eg* creiriau ffug
feint ffugio *be*
feint of disengagement datgyweddiad ffug *eg* datgyweddiadau ffug
feldspar ffelsbar *eg*
feldspathic ffelspathig *ans*
felling (timber) cwympo coed *be*
felloe camog *eg* camogau
fellow (in university) cymrawd *eg* cymrodorion
fellowship (in university) cymrodoriaeth *eb* cymrodoriaethau
felon ffelon *eg* ffeloniaid
felonious ffelonaidd *ans*
felony ffeloniaeth *eb* ffeloniaethau
felsenmeer ffelsenmer *eg*
felt ffelt *eg*
felt buff bwff ffelt *eg* bwffiau ffelt
felt marker marciwr ffelt *eg* marcwyr ffelt
felt mop mop ffelt *eg* mopiau ffelt
felt nail hoelen benfawr *eb* hoelion penfawr
felt pad pad ffelt *eg* padiau ffelt
felt pen pen ffelt *eg* pennau ffelt
felt pen drawing llun pen ffelt *eg* lluniau pen ffelt
felt ring cylch ffelt *eg* cylchoedd ffelt
felt work gwaith ffelt *eg*
felted carpet carped ffeltiog *eg* carpedi ffeltiog
felting ffeltin *eg*
felt-tip pen pen blaen ffelt *eg* pennau blaen ffelt
female *adj* benywol *ans*
female *n* benyw *eb* benywod
female gamete gamet benyw *eg* gametau benyw
female screw sgriw fenyw *eb* sgriwiau benyw
female sexual dysfunction camweithredu rhywiol mewn merched *eg*
female thread edau fenyw *eb* edafedd benyw
feminine benywaidd *ans*
feminism ffeministiaeth *eb*
feminist *adj* ffeministaidd *ans*
feminist *n* ffeminist *eg* ffeministiaid
feminist model model ffeministaidd *eg*
feminist theology diwinyddiaeth ffeministaidd *eb*
femoral morddwydol *ans*
femur asgwrn y forddwyd *eg*
fen ffen *eg* ffeniau
fence *n* ffens *eb* ffensys
fence *v* ffensio *be*
fence saw llif ffens *eb* llifiau ffens
fencer ffensiwr *eg* ffenswyr
fenestra ovalis ffenestr hirgron *eb* ffenestri hirgrwn
Fenian Ffeniad *eg* Ffeniaid

Fenian Brotherhood Brawdoliaeth y Ffeniaid *eb*
Fenian Movement Mudiad y Ffeniaid *eg*
fenlands ffendiroedd *ell*
fennel ffenigl *eg*
fenstra rotunda ffenestr gron *eb* ffenestri crwn
feodary ffeodariad *eg* ffeodariaid
feoffee ffeodai *eg* ffeodeion
feoffees for impropriation ffeodeion amfeddiad *ell*
feoffment ffeodiad *eg* ffeodiadau
feoffor ffeodwr *eg* ffeodwyr
Ferdinand Fferdinand *eg*
fermata daliant *eg* daliannau
ferment *n* eples *eg*
ferment *v* eplesu *be*
fermentation eplesiad *eg* eplesiadau
fermentation science epleseg *eb*
fermentative eplesol *ans*
fermenter eplesydd *eg*
fermium (Fm) ffermiwm *eg*
fern rhedynen *eb* rhedyn
ferric fferrig *ans*
ferric chloride fferrig clorid *eg*
ferrite fferrit *eg*
ferrite core craidd fferrit *eg* creiddiau fferrit
ferro-concrete fferoconcrit *eg*
ferromagnetism fferomagnetedd *eg*
ferrous fferrus *ans*
ferrous core craidd fferrus *eg*
ferrous metal metel fferrus *eg* metelau fferrus
ferrule amgarn *eg/b* amgarnau
ferrule slot slot amgarn *eg* slotiau amgarn
ferry fferi *eb* fferïau
▸ **ferry glide** llithriad fferi *eg* llithriadau fferi
fertile ffrwythlon *ans*
Fertile Crescent Cilgant Ffrwythlon *eg*
fertilised ffrwythlonedig *ans*
fertility ffrwythlondeb *eg*
fertility rate cyfradd ffrwythlondeb *eb*
fertilization ffrwythloniad *eg*
fertilize (in agriculture) gwrteithio *be*
fertilize (in biology) ffrwythloni *be*
fertilizer gwrtaith *eg* gwrteithiau
fescue peiswellt *eg*
festival gŵyl *eb* gwyliau
festival theatre theatr gŵyl *eb* theatrau gŵyl
fetal alcohol syndrome syndrom alcohol y ffetws *eg*
fetal learning dysgu tra'n ffetws *be*
fetal stage cyfnod ffetws *eg*
fetch *n* cyrch *eg* cyrchoedd
fetch *v* cyrchu *be*
fetch (computer command) *v* cywain *be*
fetch /execute cycle
cylchred cywain /gweithredu *eb*
cylchredau cywain /gweithredu
▸ **fetish** ffetish *eg* ffetisiau
fetishism ffetisiaeth *eb*
fettle ffetlo *be*
fetus ffetws *eg* ffetysau
feud cynnen *eb* cynhennau
feudal ffiwdal *ans*
feudal aid cymhorthdreth ffiwdal *eb*
feudal court llys ffiwdal *eg* llysoedd ffiwdal
feudal incident hawl ffiwdal *eg* hawliau ffiwdal
▸ **feudal overlord** uwcharglwydd ffiwdal *eg*
uwcharglwyddi ffiwdal
feudal overlordship uwcharglwyddiaeth ffiwdal *eb*
uwcharglwyddiaethau ffiwdal
feudal system trefn ffiwdal *eb*
feudalism ffiwdaliaeth *eb*
feudalize ffiwdaleiddio *be*
fever twymyn *eb* twymynau
fibre ffibr *eg* ffibrau
fibre content cynnwys ffibr *eg*
fibre mat mat ffibr *eg* matiau ffibr
fibre optics opteg ffibr *eb*
fibre pen pen ffibr *eg* pennau ffibr
fibre plug plwg ffibr *eg* plygiau ffibr
fibre track trac ffibr *eg* traciau ffibr
fibre washer wasier ffibr *eb* wasieri ffibr
fibreboard bwrdd ffibr *eg* byrddau ffibr
fibreglass gwydr ffibr *eg*
fibreglass bar bar o wydr ffibr *eg* barrau o wydr ffibr
fibreglass racket raced ffibr gwydr *eg*
racedi ffibr gwydr
fibre-tip pen pen blaen ffibr *eg* pennau blaen ffibr
fibril ffibrolyn *eg* ffibrolion
fibrillation ffibriliad *eg* ffibriliadau
fibrin ffibrin *eg*
fibrinogen ffibrinogen *eg*
fibroblast ffibroblast *eg*
fibrocyte ffibrocyt *eg* ffibrocytau
fibrous ffibrog *ans*
fibrous coat cot ffibrog *eb* cotiau ffibrog
fibrous peat mawn ffibrog *eg*
fibrous root gwreiddyn ffibrog *eg* gwreiddiau ffibrog
fibula ffibwla *eg* ffibwlâu
fictitious dychmygol *ans*
fictitious statute statud ffug *eg* statudau ffug
fiddle ffidil *eb* ffidlau
fiddle back cefn crwth *ans*
fiddle back chair cadair gefn crwth *eb*
cadeiriau cefn crwth
fiddler ffidlwr *eg* ffidlwyr
fief ffiff *eg* ffiffiau
field *v* maesu *be*
field (in a database) maes *eg* meysydd
field (in agriculture) *n* cae *eg* caeau
field (of study etc) *n* maes *eg* meysydd
field centre canolfan maes *eb* canolfannau maes
field coil coil maes *eg*
field data data maes *ell*
field dependence dibyniaeth maes *eb*
field event cystadleuaeth faes *eb* cystadlaethau maes
field experiment arbrawf maes *eg* arbrofion maes

field ion microscope microsgop maes ïonau *eg*
field length hyd maes *eg* hydoedd maes
field line llinell faes *eb*
field mapping mapio maes *be*
field marshal maeslywydd *eg* maeslywyddion
field notes nodiadau maes *ell*
field of force maes grym *eg*
Field of the Cloth of Gold Maes y Brethyn Euraid *eg*
field of view maes gweld *eg* meysydd gweld
field on the boundary *v* maesu ar y ffin *be*
field research ymchwil maes *eg*
field sketch braslun maes *eg* brasluniau maes
field strength cryfder maes *eg*
field test prawf maes *eg* profion maes
field worker gweithiwr maes *eg* gweithwyr maes
fielder maeswr *eg* maeswyr
fields of pasture tir pori *eg*
▶ **field-upgradeable** maes-uwchriaddadwy *ans*
fieldwork gwaith maes *eg*
fieldwork investigation ymchwiliad gwaith maes *eg* ymchwiliadau gwaith maes
fieldwork report adroddiad gwaith maes *eg* adroddiadau gwaith maes
fifth (musical interval) pumed *eg* pumedau
fifth column pumed golofn *eb*
Fifth Monarchist Pumed Frenhinwr *eg* Pumed Frenhinwyr
Fifth Monarchy Pumed Frenhiniaeth *eb*
Fifth Republic Pumed Weriniaeth *eb*
fig ffigysen *eb* ffigys
fight or flight ymladd neu ffoi
fight or flight response ymateb ymladd neu ffoi *eg*
fighting arm braich ymladd *eb* breichiau ymladd
figment of imagination creadigaeth y dychymyg *eb* creadigaethau'r dychymyg
figurative ffigurol *ans*
figurative painting (of painted picture) paentiad ffigurol *eg* paentiadau ffigurol
figurative painting (of process or art) peintio ffigurol *be*
figure ffigur *eg/b* ffigurau
figure eight ffigur wyth *eg* ffigurau wyth
figured rhifoledig *ans*
figured bass bas rhifoledig *eg*
figure-ground ffigur-grwnd *eg*
figurine ffiguryn *eg* ffigurynnau
figuring rhifoli *be*
figuring of chords rhifoli cordiau *be*
filament ffilament *eg* ffilamentau
filament yarn edau ffilament *eb* edafedd ffilament
filamentous ffilamentog *ans*
filbert shape brush brwsh siâp cneuen *eg* brwshys siâp cneuen
file *n* ffeil *eb* ffeiliau
file *v* ffeilio *be*
file access cyrchu o ffeil *be*
file backup ffeil wrth gefn *eb* ffeiliau wrth gefn
file compression cywasgu ffeiliau *be*
file creation creu ffeil *be*
file extension estyniad ffeil *eg* estyniadau ffeil
file extent maint ffeil *eg* meintiau ffeil
file handling trin ffeiliau *be*
file librarian llyfrgellydd ffeiliau *eg* llyfrgellwyr ffeiliau
file maintenance cynnal ffeiliau *be*
file name enw ffeil *eg* enwau ffeiliau
file organization trefnu ffeiliau *be*
file parts rhannau ffeil *ell*
file pricker priciwr ffeil *eg* pricwyr ffeiliau
file processing prosesu ffeil *be*
file protection diogelu ffeil *be*
file protection code cod diogelu ffeil *eg* codau diogelu ffeiliau
file recovery adfer ffeil *be*
file server gweinydd ffeiliau *eg* gweinyddion ffeiliau
file sharing rhannu ffeiliau *be*
file store storfa ffeiliau *eb* storfeydd ffeiliau
file structure strwythur ffeiliau *eg*
file to convert ffeil i'w throsi *eb* ffeiliau i'w trosi
file transfer protocol protocol trosi ffeiliau *eg* protocolau trosi ffeiliau
file type math o ffeil *eg* mathau o ffeil
filename extension estyniad enw ffeil *eg* estyniadau enw ffeil
filial mabol *ans*
filiform edeuffurf *ans*
filigree ffiligri *eg*
filing menu dewislen ffeilio *eb* dewislenni ffeilio
filings naddion *ell*
fill *v* llenwi *be*
fill (e.g. in volcano vent) *n* llenwad *eg* llenwadau
fill down llanw i lawr *be*
fill entire page llanw'r dudalen gyfan *be*
fill left llanw i'r chwith *be*
fill mode modd llanw *eg*
fill parameter paramedr llanw *eg* paramedrau llanw
fill right llanw i'r dde *be*
fill row llanw rhes *be*
fill series llanw cyfres *be*
fill sheet llanw dalen *be*
fill up llanw i fyny *be*
filled (3rds, 4ths, etc) llanw *ans*
filled tooth dant â llenwad *eg*
filler llenwad *eg* llenwyddion
fillet *n* ffiled *eb* ffiledau
fillet *v* ffiledu *be*
fillet gauge medrydd ffiled *eg* medryddion ffiled
fillet moulding mowldin ffiled *eg* mowldinau ffiled
fillet weld lleinweldiad *eg* lleinweldiadau
filling llenwad *eg* llenwadau
filling rod rhoden lenwi *eb* rhodenni llenwi
filling station gorsaf betrol *eb* gorsafoedd petrol
filling stitch pwyth llenwi *eg* pwythau llenwi
fillister plane plaen ffilistr *eg* plaeniau ffilistr
film ffilm *eb* ffilmiau
film consumption gwylio ffilmiau *be*

film culture diwylliant ffilmiau *eg*
film form ffurf ffilm *eb*
film former ffurfiwr ffilm *eg* ffurfwyr ffilm
film journalism newyddiaduraeth ffilm *eb*
film language iaith ffilm *eb*
film library llyfrgell ffilmiau *eb* llyfrgelloedd ffilmiau
film movement mudiad ffilmiau *eg*
film strip stribed ffilm *eg* stribedi ffilm
film synopsis crynodeb (o) ffilm *eg*
film trailer rhaglun ffilm *eg*
filter *v* hidlo *be*
filter (of light, sound) *n* hidlydd *eg* hidlyddion
filter (of solid particles) *n* hidlen *eb* hidlenni
filter accumulation cronedd hidlo *eb*
filter bar bar hidlo *eg* barrau hidlo
filter bed haen hidlo *eb* haenau hidlo
filter by selection hidlo drwy ddewis *be*
filter funnel twndis hidlo *eg* twndisau hidlo; twmffat hidlo *eg* twmffedi hidlo
filter options dewisiadau hidlo *ell*
filter paper papur hidlo *eg* papurau hidlo
filter proposal cynnig hidlo *eg* cynigion hidlo
filter pump pwmp hidlo *eg* pympiau hidlo
filter setting gosodiad hidlo *eg* gosodiadau hidlo
filter unit uned hidlo *eb* unedau hidlo
filterable virus firws hidladwy *eg*
filtered coffee coffi wedi'i hidlo *eg*
filtering software meddalwedd hidlo *eb*
filtrate hidlif *eg* hidlifau
filtration hidliad *eg*
fin asgell *eb* esgyll
final terfynol *ans*
final cause achos terfynol *eg*
final concord cytundeb terfynol *eg* cytundebau terfynol
final domestic demand galw mewnol terfynol *eg*
final drive gyriad terfynol *eg* gyriadau terfynol
final outcome gwrthrych terfynol *eg*
final report adroddiad terfynol *eg* adroddiadau terfynol
Final Solution Ateb Terfynol *eg*
final treatment triniaeth derfynol *eb*
final velocity cyflymder terfynol *eg*
finale finale *eg* finales
finals arholiadau terfynol *ell*
finance *n* cyllid *eg*
finance *v* ariannu *be*
finance the activities ariannu'r gweithgareddau *be*
financial ariannol *ans*
financial aims and objectives nodau ac amcanion ariannol
financial boom ffyniant ariannol *eg*
financial document dogfen ariannol *eb* dogfennau ariannol
financial information gwybodaeth ariannol *eb*
financial performance perfformiad ariannol *eg*
financial ratio cymhareb ariannol *eb*
financial regulations rheoliadau ariannol *ell*
financial service gwasanaeth ariannol *eg* gwasanaethau ariannol
financial transaction trafod ariannol *eg* trafodion ariannol
financial year blwyddyn ariannol *eb*
financial year basis sail blwyddyn ariannol *eb*
financier ariannwr *eg* arianwyr
finch pinc *eg* pincod
finch population poblogaeth y pincod *eb*
find *n* darganfyddiad *eg* darganfyddiadau
find *v* (computing etc) canfod *be*
find *v* (in general) *v* darganfod *be*
find address canfod cyfeiriad *be*
find and replace canfod a newid *be*
find file canfod ffeil *be*
find function swyddogaeth canfod *eb*
find graphics canfod graffigau *be*
find original canfod y gwreiddiol *be*
find parentheses canfod cromfachau *be*
find record canfod cofnod *be*
find solutions darganfod atebion *be*
findings (in report etc) casgliadau *ell*
fine *v* dirwyo *be*
fine (=payment) *n* tâl *eg* taliadau
fine (=penalty) *n* dirwy *eb* dirwyon
fine (=worked in slender thread) *adj* manwl *ans*
fine (of cloth) *adj* main *ans*
fine (of small particles, print) *adj* mân *ans*
fine adjustment cymhwysiad manwl *eg* cymwysiadau manwl
fine art celfyddyd gain *eb* celfyddydau cain
fine beam paladr main *eg*
fine brass wire gwifren bres fain *eb* gwifrau pres main
fine control rheolaeth fanwl *eb* rheolaethau manwl
fine control (dial switch) rheolydd manwl *eg* rheolyddion manwl
fine dashed line llinell doredig fân *eb* llinellau toredig mân
fine dust llwch mân *eg*
fine grain graen mân *eg*
fine grit grit mân *eg*
fine knurl nwrl mân *eg*
fine leg coeswr cul *eg* coeswyr cul
fine manipulative skills sgiliau llawdrin manwl *ell*
fine mesh rhwyll fain *eb* rhwyllau main
fine motor skills sgiliau echddygol manwl *ell*
fine orifice agorfa fach *eb* agorfeydd bach
fine point pwynt main *eg* pwyntiau main
Fine Roll Rhôl Tâl am Fraint *eb*
fine structure mân-adeiledd *eb* mân-adeileddau
fine surface arwyneb llyfn *eg* arwynebau llyfn
fine teeth dannedd mân *ell*
fine texture gwead main *eg*
fine-motor movement symudiad echddygol manwl *eg* symudiadau echddygol manwl

fineness (of fabric) meinder *eg*
fineness (of sand, fragments) manedd *eg*
fines herbes sawrlysiau cymysg *ell*
finger *n* bys *eg* bysedd
finger *v* byseddu *be*
finger cymbals symbalau bys *ell*
finger gauge medrydd bys *eg* medryddion bys
finger holds gafaelion bysedd *ell*
finger hole twll bys *eg* tyllau bysedd
finger joint (box) uniad bys *eg* uniadau bys
finger lake llyn hirgul *eg* llynnoedd hirgul
finger paint paent bys *eg*
finger painting (of painted picture) paentiad bys *eg* paentiadau bys
finger painting (of process or art) peintio bys *be*
finger plate plât bys *eg* platiau bys
finger puppet pyped bys *eg* pypedau bys
fingered bysedig *ans*
fingering byseddu *be*
fingerprint ôl bys *eg* ôl bysedd
finish *n* diwedd *eg*
finish *n* gorffeniad *eg* gorffeniadau
finish *v* gorffen *be*
finished gorffenedig *ans*
finished appearance gwedd orffenedig *eb*
finished dimensions dimensiynau gorffenedig *ell*
finished drawing lluniad gorffenedig *eg* lluniadau gorffenedig
finished goods nwyddau gorffenedig *ell*
finished product cynnyrch gorffenedig *eg* cynhyrchion gorffenedig
finished size maint gorffenedig *eg* meintiau gorffenedig
finished surface arwyneb gorffenedig *eg* arwynebau gorffenedig
finishing gorffennu *be*
finishing cuts toriadau gorffennu *ell*
finishing press gwasg orffennu *eb* gweisg gorffennu
finishing process proses orffennu *eb* prosesau gorffennu
finishing stove stof orffennu *eb* stofiau gorffennu
finishing technique techneg orffennu *eb* technegau gorffennu
finishing tools offer gorffennu *ell*
finite meidraidd *ans*
finite canon canon gyfanedig *eb* canonau cyfanedig
finitely generated generadol feidraidd *ans*
fiord ffiord *eg* ffiordau
fire *n* tân *eg* tanau
fire *v* tanio *be*
fire (enamel) *v* ffwrndanio *be*
fire blanket blanced dân *eb* blancedi tân
fire bote hawl cynuta *eg* hawliau cynuta
fire damp nwy pwll glo *eg*
fire extinguisher diffoddwr tân *eg* diffoddwyr tân
fire protection diogelwch rhag tân *eg*
fire weld tân weldio *be*
firebrick bricsen dân *eb* brics tân
fireclay clai tân *eg*
firedamp explosion tanchwa *eb* tanchwaoedd
fireguard gard tân *eg* gardiau tân
fireplace lle tân *eg* lleoedd tân
fireproof gwrthdan *ans*
fireproof material defnydd gwrthdan *eg* defnyddiau gwrthdan
fireside chat sgwrs aelwyd *eb* sgyrsiau aelwyd
firewall (for computer systems) mur gwarchod *eg* muriau gwarchod
firewall (in general) wal dân *eb* waliau tân
firing (kiln) tanio *be*
firing chamber siambr danio *eb* siambrau tanio
firing fork fforch danio *eb* ffyrch tanio
firm *adj* cadarn *ans*
firm *n* cwmni *eg* cwmnïau
firm joint calliper caliper cymal cadarn *eg* caliperau cymal cadarn
firm wrist arddwrn cadarn *eg* arddyrnau cadarn
firmer chisel cŷn ffyrf *eg* cynion ffyrf gaing fferf *eb* geingiau ffyrf
firmer gouge gaing gau gefn *eb* geingiau gau cefn
firming piece darn lletemu *eg* darnau lletemu
firmware cadarnwedd *ell*
firn ffirn *eg* ffirniau
first aid cymorth cyntaf *eg*
first angle projection tafluniad ongl gyntaf *eg* tafluniadau ongl gyntaf
first cause achos cyntaf *eg*
first degree equation hafaliad unradd *eg* hafaliadau unradd
first floor llawr cyntaf *eg* lloriau cyntaf
first fold plyg cyntaf *eg* plygion cyntaf
first fruits blaenffrwyth *eg*
First Fruits and Tenths Act Deddf Blaenffrwyth a Degadau *eb*
first generation cenhedlaeth gyntaf *eb*
first generation network rhwydwaith cenhedlaeth gyntaf *eg*
first in – first out (FIFO) cyntaf i mewn – cyntaf allan *ans*
First International (Working-Men's Association) Cymdeithas Ryngwladol Gyntaf *eb*
first inversion gwrthdro cyntaf *eg* gwrthdroeon cyntaf
first language pupil disgybl iaith gyntaf *eg* disgyblion iaith gyntaf
first law of thermodynamics deddf gyntaf thermodynameg *eb*
first movement form (in music) ffurf symudiad cyntaf *eb*
first order trefn un *eb*
first order differential equation hafaliad differol trefn un *eg* hafaliadau differol trefn un
first order reaction adwaith gradd un *eg*
first order stream ffrwd gradd un *eb* ffrydiau gradd un
first point pwynt cyntaf *eg* pwyntiau cyntaf

first reported assessment asesiad cyntaf sy'n destun adroddiad *eg*
First Republic Gweriniaeth Gyntaf *eb*
first serve serf gyntaf *eb* serfiau cyntaf
first sharp remove gwyriad y llonnod cyntaf *eg*
first slip slip cyntaf *eg*
first unreported assessment asesiad cyntaf nad yw'n destun adroddiad *eg*
First World War Rhyfel Byd Cyntaf *eg*
first-line indent mewnoliad llinell gyntaf *eg* mewnoliadau llinell gyntaf
fiscal cyllidol *ans*
fiscal drag llusgiad cyllidol *eg*
fiscal policy polisi cyllidol *eg*
fish pysgodyn *eg* pysgod
fish bowl exercise ymarfer powlen bysgod *eg*
fish eating bird aderyn pysgysol *eg* adar pysgysol
fish finger bys pysgodyn *eg* bysedd pysgod
fish liver oil olew iau pysgod *eg*; olew afu pysgod
fish meal blawd pysgod *eg*
fish slice sleis bysgod *eb* sleisiau pysgod
fishbone stitch pwyth asgwrn pysgodyn *eg* pwythau asgwrn pysgodyn
fishcake cacen bysgod *eb* cacennau pysgod
Fisher Exact Probability Test Prawf Tebygolrwydd Union Fisher *eg*
fisherman pysgotwr *eg* pysgotwyr
fisherman's joining knot cwlwm pysgotwr *eg* clymau pysgotwr
fishing pysgota *be*
fishing ground pysgodfa *eb* pysgodfeydd
fishing village pentref pysgota *eg* pentrefi pysgota
fishmonger gwerthwr pysgod *eg* gwerthwyr pysgod
fish-tail scroll sgrôl cynffon pysgodyn *eb* sgroliau cynffon pysgodyn
fissile ymholltog *ans*
fission ymholltiad *eg* ymholltiadau
fission product cynnyrch ymhollti *eg* cynhyrchion ymhollti
fission reaction adwaith ymholltiad *eg*
fissure agen *eb* agennau
fist dwrn *eg* dyrnau
fit *adj* ffit *ans*
fit *n* ffit *eb* ffitiau
fit *v* ffitio *be*
fitch hog brush brwsh blew ffwlbart *eg* brwshys blew ffwlbart
fitment dodrefnyn sefydlog *eg* dodrefn sefydlog
fitness (physical) ffitrwydd *eg*
fitness component elfen ffitrwydd *eb* elfennau ffitrwydd
fitness test prawf ffitrwydd *eg* profion ffitrwydd
fits and limits ffitiau a therfynau
fitted sheet cynfas ffitiedig *eb* cynfasau ffitiedig
fitted sleeve llawes hirgul *eb* llewys hirgul
fitter ffitiwr *eg* ffitwyr
fitting device dyfais ffitio *eb* dyfeisiau ffitio
fitting line llinell ffitio *eb* llinellau ffitio
fitting point pwynt ffitio *eg* pwyntiau ffitio
fittings mân daclau *ell*
fit-up stage llwyfan cludadwy *eg* llwyfannau cludadwy
five pump *eg* pumoedd
five bearded rockling brithyll Mair pumbarf *eg* brithyllod Mair pumbarf
Five Books, the Pum Llyfr, y
Five Classics (in Confucianism) Pum Clasur *eg*
five factor model model pum ffactor *eg*
Five Mile Act Deddf Pum Milltir *eb*
Five Pillars of Islam Pum Piler Islam *eg*
Five Pillars, the Pum Piler, y
five ply plywood pren haenog pum haen *eg*
five steps pum cam *eg*
Five Ways Pum Ffordd
five yard line llinell bumllath *eb*
five year plan cynllun pum mlynedd *eg* cynlluniau pum mlynedd
five-minute gun ergyd pum munud *eb*
five-ply wood pren pum haen *eg*
fix (=install) gosod *be*
fix (in economics) pennu *be*
fix (in photography and biology) sefydlogi *be*
fixation (=obsession) obsesiwn *eg*
fixation (of biological process) sefydlogiad *eg*
fixation point pwynt sefydlogi *eg* pwyntiau sefydlogi
fixative sefydlyn *eg* sefydlynnau
fixative spray chwistrell sefydlogi *eg* chwistrellau sefydlogi
fixator sefydlogydd *eg* sefydlogyddion
fixed (=given) gosodedig *ans*
fixed (=specified) penodol *ans*
fixed (=unchangeable) sefydlog *ans*
fixed asset ased sefydlog *eg* asedau sefydlog
fixed capital cyfalaf sefydlog *eg*
fixed composition cyfansoddiad sefydlog *eg*
fixed cost cost sefydlog *eb* costau sefydlog
fixed costs figure ffigwr costau sefydlog *eg*
fixed dune twyn sefydlog *eg* twyni sefydlog
fixed exchange rate cyfradd gyfnewid osodedig *eb*
fixed field maes sefydlog *eg* meysydd sefydlog
fixed fret cribell osod *eb* cribellau gosod
fixed grill gridyll sefydlog *eg* gridyllau sefydlog
fixed guide tywysydd sefydlog *eg* tywyswyr sefydlog
fixed interest llog penodol *eg*
fixed interval schedule amserlen ysbeidiau sefydlog *eb*
fixed jaw safn sefydlog *eb* safnau sefydlog
fixed knife (veneer cutting) cyllell sefydlog *eb* cyllyll sefydlog
fixed length hyd penodol *eg* hydoedd penodol
fixed length record cofnod hyd penodol *eg* cofnodion hyd penodol
fixed mass màs penodol *eg* masau penodol
fixed mass of gas màs penodol o nwy *eg*
fixed pin roloc sefydlog *eg* rolocs sefydlog
fixed point pwynt sefydlog *eg* pwyntiau sefydlog

fixed point arithmetic rhifyddeg pwynt sefydlog *eb*
fixed position safle sefydlog *eg* safleoedd sefydlog
fixed powder colour powdrliw sefydlog *eg* powdrliwiau sefydlog
fixed price pris penodol *eg* prisiau penodol
fixed ratio schedule amserlen cymarebau sefydlog *eb*
fixed seat sedd sefydlog *eb* seddi sefydlog
fixed shelf silff sefydlog *eb* silffoedd sefydlog
fixed size reamer agorell maint sefydlog *eb* agorellau maint sefydlog
fixed steady sadydd disymud *eg* sadyddion disymud
fixed table bwrdd sefydlog *eg* byrddau sefydlog
fixed tub twb sefydlog *eg* tybiau sefydlog
fixed word length hyd gair penodol *eg*
fixer sefydlyn *eg* sefydlynnau
fixing pin pìn sefydlu *eg* pinnau sefydlu
fixity of tenure sicrwydd daliadaeth *eg*
fixture gosodyn *eg* gosodion
fjard ffiard *eg* ffiardau
flaccid llipa *ans*
flag *v* llumanu *be*
flag (in general) *n* baner *eb* banerau
flag (in sport) *n* lluman *eg/b* llumanau
flagellum fflagelwm *eg* fflagela
flageolet beans ffa flageolet *ell*
flagship llong y llyngesydd *eb* llongau'r llyngeswyr
flagstone carreg lorio *eb* cerrig llorio
flake fflaw *eg* fflawiau
flake culture diwylliant fflawiau *eg*
flake test (jam) prawf haenu *eg*
flake white gwyn plwm *eg*
flaked fflawiog *ans*
flaky pastry crwst haenog *eg*
flambé flambé *ans*
flame *n* fflam *eg* fflamau
flame *v* fflamio *be*
flame cell cell fflam *eb* celloedd fflam
flame cutter fflamdorrwr *eg* fflamdorwyr
flame probe chwiliedydd fflam *eg* chwiliedyddion fflam
flame proof gwrth-fflam *ans*
flame test prawf fflam *eg* profion fflam
flame war rhyfel fflamio *eg* rhyfeloedd fflamio
flame-failure device dyfais ailgynnau fflam *eb* dyfeisiau ailgynnau fflam
flammability fflamadwyedd *eg*
flammable fflamadwy *ans*
flan fflan *eb* fflaniau
flan ring cylch fflan *eg* cylchoedd fflan
flange *n* fflans *eg/b* fflansiau
flange *v* fflansio *be*
flange disc disg fflans *eg* disgiau fflans
flanged rail rheilen fflans *eb* rheiliau fflans
flanged seam sêm fflans *eb* semau fflans
flanged spigot sbigot fflans *eg* sbigotau fflans
flank ystlys *eb* ystlysau
flanking transmission trawsyriant ochrol *eg*
flannel gwlanen *eb* gwlanenni
flannel patch clwt gwlanen *eg* clytiau gwlanen
flannel seam sêm wlanen *eb* semau gwlanen
flannelette fflaneléd *eg*
flap fflap *eg* fflapiau
flap pocket poced fflap *eb* pocedi fflap
flapjacks fflapjacs *ell*
flapping chwifio *be*
flare *n* fflêr *eb* fflerau
flare *v* fflerio *be*
flared skirt sgert fflêr *eb* sgertiau fflêr
flash fflach *eb* fflachiau
flash card cerdyn fflachio *eg* cardiau fflachio
flash converter trawsnewidydd fflach *eg* trawsnewidyddion fflach
flash flood fflachlif *eg* fflachlifau
flash point fflachbwynt *eg* fflachbwyntiau
flashback ôl-fflach *eb* ôl-fflachiau
flashbulb memory cof fflachfwlb *eg*
flashed fflachedig *ans*
flashing (over door, window) plygiad plwm *eg* plygiadau plwm
flashing cursor cyrchwr fflachiog *eg* cyrchwyr fflachiog
flashover fflachiad *eg* fflachiadau
flask fflasg *eb* fflasgiau
flat (=level, smooth) *adj* gwastad *ans*
flat (=of little depth) *adj* fflat *ans*
flat (=set of rooms, geographical feature) *n* fflat *eg* fflatiau
flat (musical note) meddalnod *eg* meddalnodau
flat bit ebill gwastad *eg* ebillion gwastad
flat drawer slip drôr-gryfhawr fflat *eg* drôr-gryfhawyr fflat
flat key (in old Welsh music) lleddf gywair *eg*
flat locking plate plât cloi fflat *eg* platiau cloi fflat
flat metal axe bwyell fetel fflat *eb* bwyeill metel fflat
flat organisational structure strwythur trefniadaeth gwastad *eg*
flatfish lleden *eb* lledod
flatiron haearn smwddio *eg* heyrn smwddio
flatness gwastadrwydd *eg*
flatpack furniture dodrefn fflatpac *ell*
flatplan cynllun fflat *eg* cynlluniau fflat
flat-rate increase cynnydd unradd *eg*
flatten (musical pitch) gostwng traw *be*
flattened gwastad *ans*
flatter fflatiwr *eg* fflatwyr
flatting (of forging process) fflatio *be*
flatulence gwynt *eg*
flatus fflatws *eg*
flautist ffliwtydd *eg* ffliwtwyr
flavonoid fflafonoid *eg* fflafonoidau
flavour blas *eg*
flavouring cyflasyn *eg* cyflasynnau
flaw diffyg *eg* diffygion

flax llin *eg*
flax cord (sash window) cortyn llin *eg* cortynnau llin
flax fibre ffibr llin *eg* ffibrau llin
flea chwannen *eg* chwain
fleck *n* brychni *eg*
fleck *v* brychu *be*
flecnode fflecnod *eg* fflecnodau
fleece cnu *eg* cnuoedd
fleecy cnufiog *ans*
Flemish bond bondin Ffleminaidd *eg*
Flemish garden wal bonding bondin Ffleminaidd wal gardd *eg*
fleshy cnodiog *ans*
flexibility hyblygrwydd *eg*
flexibility regime rhaglen hyblygrwydd *eb* rhaglenni hyblygrwydd
flexible (=able to bend without breaking) hyblyg *ans*
flexible (=supple) ystwyth *ans*
flexible cold glue glud oer ystwyth *eg*
flexible coupling cyplydd hyblyg *eg* cyplyddion hyblyg
flexible hours scheme cynllun oriau hyblyg *eg* cynlluniau oriau hyblyg
flexible joint cymal hyblyg *eg* cymalau hyblyg
flexible workforce gweithlu hyblyg *eg*
flexure plygiant *eg* plygiannau
flexure strength nerth plygiant *eg*
flick *n* fflic *eg* ffliciau
flick *v* fflicio *be*
flick-flack fflic-fflac *eg*
flight feather pluen hedfan *eb* plu hedfan
flip chart siart troi *eg* siartiau troi
float *v* arnofio *be*
float (=swimming aid) *n* fflôt *eg* fflotiau
floating exchange rate cyfradd cyfnewid arnawf *eb*
floating leaf deilen arnawf *eb* dail arnawf
floating point pwynt arnawf *eg* pwyntiau arnawf
floating point arithmetic rhifyddeg pwynt arnawf *eb*
floating point overflow gorlif pwynt arnawf *eg*
flock praidd *eg* preiddiau
flock print print ffloc *eg* printiau ffloc
flocked carpet carped ffloc *eg* carpedi ffloc
flood llifogydd *ell*
flood hydrograph hydrograff llifogydd *eg* hydrograffau llifogydd
flood plain gorlifdir *eg*
flooding (in psychotherapy) llwyrfoddi *be*
floor effect effaith waelodi *eb*
floor joist trawst llawr *eg* trawstiau llawr
floor level lefel llawr *eb* lefelau llawr
floor turtle crwban llawr *eg* crwbanod llawr
floorboard astell *eb* estyll
flooring saw llif lorio *eb* llifiau llorio
floorwork gwaith ar y llawr *eg*
floppy disk disg hyblyg *eg* disgiau hyblyg
floppy disk drive gyriant disg hyblyg *eg* gyriannau disg hyblyg
flora fflora *ell*
floral (in biology) fflurol *ans*
floral (in general) blodeuog *ans*
floral diagram diagram fflurol *eg* diagramau fflurol
floral formula fformiwla fflurol *eb* fformiwlâu fflurol
Florentine art celfyddyd Fflorens *eb*
floret blodigyn *eg* blodigion
florid blodeuog *ans*
florigen fflorigen *eg*
florist's wire gwifren gwerthwr blodau *eb* gwifrau gwerthwr blodau
flotation arnofiad *eg* arnofiadau
flotilla llynges fach *eb* llyngesau bach
flounce fflowns *eb* fflownsiau
flounder lleden *eb* lledod
flour blawd *eg* blodiau
flour improvers cemegion aeddfedu blawd *ell*
flour paper papur blawd *eg*
flour paste past blawd *eg*
flourish (=decorative passage) *n* rhan flodeuog *eb* rhannau blodeuog
flourish (=fanfare) *n* ffanffer *eg* ffanfferau
flourish (of person) *v* blodeuo *be*
floury blodiog *ans*
flow *n* llif *eg* llifoedd
flow *v* llifo *be*
flow diagram diagram llif *eg* diagramau llif
flow function llif-ffwythiant *eg*
flow indicator dangosydd llif *eg*
flow line llifin *eb* llifiniau
flow of charge llif gwefr *eg*
flow pattern (of waves) patrwm llif *eg* patrymau llif
flow production llif-gynhyrchu *be*
flow rate cyfradd llifiant *eb*
flow sheet llifddalen *eb* llifddalenni
flowchart siart llif *eg* siartiau llif
flower blodyn *eg* blodau
flower head fflurben *eg* fflurbennau
flower-inducing period cyfnod peri-blodeuo *eg*
flowering plant planhigyn blodeuol *eg* planhigion blodeuol
flowers of sulphur blawd sylffwr *eg*
flowery blodeuog *ans*
flowing garment dilledyn llac *eg* dillad llac
flowing water dŵr rhedegog *eg*
flowline llinell rhediad *eb* llinellau rhediad
flowstone carreg ddylif *eb* cerrig dylif
fluctuate (in general) anwadalu *be*
fluctuate (of electric current) tonni *be*
fluctuating anwadal *ans*
fluctuating harmony harmoni anwadal *eg* harmonïau anwadal
fluctuation anwadaliad *eg* anwadaliadau
fluctuative tonnog *ans*
flue (in chimney, organ) ffliw *eb* ffliwiau
fluency (in calculation) rhwyddineb *eg*
fluff fflwff *eg*

fluff filter hidlen fflwff *eb* hidlenni fflwff
fluffing fflwffio *be*
fluid (=liquid) *n* hylif *eg* hylifau
fluid (in general) *adj* hylifol *ans*
fluid (of gas or liquid) *adj* llifyddol *ans*
fluid (of gas or liquid) *n* llifydd *eg* llifyddion
fluid (of style) *adj* llyfn *ans*
fluid flow llif hylifau *eg*
fluid mosaic mosaig hylifol *eg*
fluid mosaic model model mosaig hylifol *eg*
fluidity (of gas or liquid) llifedd *eg* llifeddau
fluidization hylifo *be*
fluidized bed gwely llifol *eg* gwelyau llifol
fluidizer hylifydd *eg* hylifyddion
fluke llabed *eg/eb* llabedau
flume (=channel) cafn *eg* cafnau
flume (=ravine) ceunant *eg* ceunentydd
fluoresce fflwroleuo *be*
fluorescein fflworesin *eg*
fluorescence fflwroleuedd *eg*
fluorescent fflwroleuol *ans*
fluorescent colour lliw fflwroleuol *eg* lliwiau fflwroleuol
fluorescent dye llifyn fflwroleuol *eg* llifynnau fflwroleuol
fluorescent lighting fflwrolau *eg* fflwroleuadau
fluorescent whitener gwynnydd fflwroleuol *eg*
fluorescer fflworesydd *eg* fflworesyddion
fluoridation fflworeiddiad *eg*
fluoride fflworid *eg*
fluoride ion ïon fflworid *eg* ïonau fflworid
fluorimeter fflworimedr *eg* fflworimedrau
fluorine (F) fflworin *eg*
fluoroplastics fflworoblastigion *ell*
fluorosis fflworosis *eg*
flush *adj* cyfwyneb *ans*
flush *v* gwacáu *be*
flush (=blush) *n* gwrid *eg*
flush (of water) *n* rhuthr dŵr *eg*
flush bolt bollt gyfwyneb *eb* bolltau cyfwyneb
flush door drws cyfwyneb *eg* drysau cyfwyneb
flush drawer slip drôr-gryfhawr cyfwyneb *eg* drôr-gryfhawyr cyfwyneb
flush eave bondo cyfwyneb *eg* bondoeau cyfwyneb
flush joint uniad cyfwyneb *eg*
flush moulding mowldin cyfwyneb *eg* mowldinau cyfwyneb
flush panel panel cyfwyneb *eg* paneli cyfwyneb
flush rails rheilen gyfwyneb *eb*
flush surface arwyneb cyfwyneb *eg* arwynebau cyfwyneb
flush-beaded panel panel gleinio cyfwyneb *eg* paneli gleinio cyfwyneb
flute *n* ffliwt *eb* ffliwtiau
flute *v* rhychu *be*
flute player ffliwtydd *eg* ffliwtwyr
fluted rhychiog *ans*
fluted cutter torrell rychiog *eb* torellau rhychiog
fluted edge ymyl rychiog *eb* ymylon rhychiog
fluted flan ring cylch fflan rhychiog *eg* cylchoedd fflan rhychiog
fluted hardboard caledfwrdd rhychiog *eg* caledfyrddau rhychiog
fluted lace les rhychiog *eg*
fluted reamer agorell rychiog *eb* agorellau rhychiog
fluted screwdriver tyrnsgriw rhychiog *eg* tyrnsgriwiau rhychiog
fluting rhychwaith *eg*
flutter tonguing cryndafodi *be*
fluttering hwyfo *be*
fluvial afonol *ans*
fluvioglacial material defnyddiau ffrwdrewlifol *ell*
flux fflwcs *eg* fflycsau
flux density dwysedd fflwcs *eg*
flux linkage cysylltedd fflwcs *eg*
fluxing agent cyfrwng fflycsio *eg*
fluxion fflycsiwn *eg* fflycsiynau
fluxocarbon fflwcsocarbon *eg*
flux-turns interlinkage cydgysylltedd troadau fflwcs *eg*
fly cutter cŷn hedegog *eg* cynion hedegog; gaing hedegog *eb* geingiau hedegog
fly kick cic wib *eb* ciciau gwib
fly milling cutter melinwr hedegog *ans* melinwyr hedegog
fly on the wall documentary rhaglen ddogfen 'pry ar y wal' *eb* rhaglenni dogfen 'pry ar y wal'
fly opening copis *eg* copisau; balog *eg* balogau
fly press gwasg hedegog *eb* gweisg hedegog
fly spring naid ddeudroed *eb* neidiau deudroed
fly stitch pwyth pryf *eg* pwythau pryf
fly weight pwysau pryf *ell*
flying picket picedwr gwib *eg* picedwyr gwib
flying shore ateg fwa *eb* ategion bwa
flying shuttle gwennol hedegog *eb* gwenoliaid hedegog
flying tackle tacl wib *eb* taclau gwib
fly-leaf dalen frig *eb* dalennau brig
flyover trosffordd *eb* trosffyrdd
flyspring sbring deudroed *eg* sbringiau deudroed
flywheel chwylrod *eb* chwylrodau
foam (mass of bubbles) *n* ewyn *eg* ewynnau
foam *v* ewynnu *be*
foam (filling) sbwng *eg*
foam rubber rwber sbwng *eg*
foam stabilizer sefydlogydd trochion *eg* sefydlogyddion trochion
foambacked cefnsbwng *ans*
focal ffocal *ans*
focal length hyd ffocal *eg* hydoedd ffocal
focal point (in optics etc) pwynt ffocal *eg* pwyntiau ffocal
focal point (of concentration etc) canolbwynt *eg* canolbwyntiau
focus (=concentrate) *v* canolbwyntio *be*

focus (in optics etc) *n* ffocws *eg* ffocysau
focus (in optics etc) *v* ffocysu *be*
focus (of concentration, earthquake etc) *n* canolbwynt *eg*
focus area ardal ffocws *eb* ardaloedd ffocws
focus film ffilm ffocws *eb* ffilmiau ffocws
focus group grŵp ffocws *eg* grwpiau ffocws
focused canolbwyntiedig *ans*
fodder porthiant *eg*
fodder crop cnwd porthiant *eg* cnydau porthiant
foetal alcohol syndrome syndrom alcohol y ffoetws *eg*
foetal membrane pilen y ffoetws *eb* pilenni ffoetysau
foetus ffoetws *eg* ffoetysau
fog *n* niwl *eg* niwloedd
fog *v* niwlo *be*
foggara ffogara *eg* ffogarau
fogging niwl *eg*
foil (=thin metal) ffoil *eg* ffoiliau
foil (in fencing) ffwyl *eg* ffwyliau
foilist ffwyliwr *eg* ffwylwyr
folar deiliog *ans*
fold *n* plyg *eg* plygion
fold *v* plygu *be*
fold in (in cooking) cyfuno *be*
fold line llinell blygu *eb* llinellau plygu
fold-away grill gridyll plygu *eg* gridyllau plygu
fold-down screen sgrin blygu *eb* sgriniau plygu
folded plyg *ans*
folded beds (strata) haenau plyg *ell*
folded metal back saw llif gefn fetel plyg *eb* llifiau cefn metel plyg
folded seam sêm blyg *eb* semau plyg
folded wall of the intestine mur plyg y coluddyn *eg* muriau plyg y coluddion
▶ **folder** ffolder *eb* ffolderi
folding bars barrau plygu *ell*
folding keel cilbren plygu *eg* cilbrennau plygu
folding rule riwl blygu *eb* riwliau plygu
folding wedge lletem gyflin *eb* lletemau cyflin
folding work gwaith plygu *eg*
foliage deiliant *eg* deiliannau
foliage sculpture cerflunwaith deiliant *eg*
foliated deiliog *ans*
foliation deiliogrwydd *eg*
folio ffolio *eg* ffolios
folium ffoliwm *eg* ffolia
folk dance dawns werin *eb* dawnsiau gwerin
folk dance (occasion) twmpath dawns *eg* twmpathau dawns
folk dance caller geilwad *eg* geilwaid
folk dancing dawnsio gwerin *be*
folk dancing skills sgiliau dawnsio gwerin *ell*
folk school ysgol werin *eb* ysgolion gwerin
folk song cân werin *eb* caneuon gwerin
folklore llên gwerin *eb*
follicle ffoligl *eg* ffoliglau
follicle-stimlating hormone hormon symbylu ffoliglau *eg*
follicular ffoliglaidd *ans*
follow dilyn *be*
follow on *v* dilyn ymlaen *be*
follow through *v* dilyn drwodd *be*
follower dilynwr *eg* dilynwyr
following routes dilyn llwybrau *be*
follow-up *adj* dilynol *ans*
follow-up *n* dilyniant *eg* dilyniannau
follow-up visit ymweliad dilynol *eg* ymweliadau dilynol
fondant ffondant *eg*
font (=set of type) ffont *eg* ffontiau
font (for baptism) bedyddfaen *eg* bedyddfeini
font setting gosodiad ffont *eg* gosodiadau ffont
font size maint ffont *eg* meintiau ffont
fontanelle ffontanél *eg* ffontanelau
food bwyd *eg* bwydydd
Food & Agriculture Organization (FAO) Cyfundrefn Fwyd ac Amaeth *eb*
food additive ychwanegyn bwyd *eg* ychwanegion bwyd
Food and Drugs Act Deddf Bwyd a Chyffuriau *eb*
food chain cadwyn fwyd *eb* cadwynau bwydydd
food components cydrannau bwyd *ell*
food composition cyfansoddiad bwyd *eg*
food content cynnwys bwyd *eg*
food cycle cylchred fwyd *eb* cylchredau bwydydd
food digestion treulio bwyd *be*
food group grŵp bwyd *eg* grwpiau bwyd
food hygiene hylendid bwyd *eg*
food intolerance anoddefgarwch bwyd *eg*
food materials defnyddiau bwyd *ell*
food mixer cymysgydd bwyd *eg* cymysgyddion bwyd
food outlet allfa fwyd *eb* allfeydd bwyd
food poisoning gwenwyn bwyd *eg*
food preparation area lle paratoi bwyd *eg* lleoedd paratoi bwyd
food preservation cyffeithio bwyd *be*
food preservative cyffeithydd bwyd *eg* cyffeithyddion bwyd
food processor prosesydd bwyd *eg* prosesyddion bwyd
food product cynnyrch bwyd *eg*
food product designer dylunydd cynhyrchion bwyd *eg* dylunwyr cynhyrchion bwyd
food pyramid pyramid bwydydd *eg* pyramidiau bwydydd
food rationing dogni bwyd *be*
food spoilage dirywiad bwyd *eg*
food supplies cyflenwad bwyd *eg* cyflenwadau bwyd
food table tabl bwyd *eg*
food vessel bwydlestr *eg* bwydlestri
food web gwe fwydydd *eb* gweoedd bwydydd
food wrap defnydd lapio bwyd *eg* defnyddiau lapio bwyd

food-related custom arfer bwyd *eg* arferion bwyd
foodstuff bwyd *eg* bwydydd
foolscap ffwlsgap *eg* ffwlsgapau
foot (=measurement) troedfedd *eb* troedfeddi
foot (of body part) troed *eg/b* traed
foot and mouth crisis argyfwng clwy'r traed a'r genau *eg*
foot bellows megin droed *eb* meginau troed
foot control (of machine part) rheolydd troed *eg* rheolwyr troed
foot fault ffawt troed *eb* ffawtiau traed
foot glacier troed-rewlif *eg* troed-rewlifau
foot music cerddoriaeth traed *eb*
foot of perpendicular troed y perpendicwlar *eb*
foot run (of timber) troedfedd o hyd *eb*
foot super troedfedd sgwâr o bren *eb* troedfeddi sgwâr o bren
footage darn o ffilm *eg*
football pêl-droed *eg* peli troed
football field maes pêl-droed *eg* meysydd pêl-droed
football pitch cae pêl-droed *eg* caeau pêl-droed
football stadium stadiwm pêl-droed *eg* stadia pêl-droed
footballer pêl-droediwr *eg* pêl-droedwyr
footbath baddon traed *eg* baddonau traed
footbridge pompren *eb* pomprennau
footer troedyn *eg* troedynnau
foothills godrefryniau *ell*
foothold gafael troed *eb* gafaelion traed
footlights golau'r godre *eg*
► **foot-loose industry** diwydiant rhyddsymudol *eg* diwydiannau rhyddsymudol
footnote troednodyn *eg* troednodiadau
footpath llwybr troed *eg* llwybrau troed
footpower loom gwŷdd troedlath *eg* gwyddau troedlath
footprint (in computing) maint troed *eg* maint traed
footprint (in general) ôl troed *eg* olion traed
footrest stôl droed *eb* stoliau troed
foot-rush cwrs traed *eg* cyrsiau traed
footstool stôl droed *eb* stoliau troed
footwear esgidiau *ell*
footwork troedwaith *eg*
forage porthiant *eg*
foraging chwilota *be*
foramen fforamen *eg* fforamina
force *v* gorfodi *be*
force (=army) *n* byddin *eb* byddinoedd
force (=compulsion) *n* gorfodaeth *eb*
force (in science) *n* grym *eg* grymoedd
force constant cysonyn grym *eg*
force exerted grym a roir
force fit ffit orwasg *eb* ffitiau gorwasg
force of gravity grym disgyrchiant *eg* grymoedd disgyrchiant
force pump pwmp grym *eg* pympiau grym
force ratio cymhareb grym *eb* cymarebau grym
force the follow on gorfodi'r dilyn ymlaen *be*
force 10 wind gwynt grym 10 *eg*
forced choice test prawf dewis gorfodol *eg* profion dewis gorfodol
forced economy economi gorfodol *eg*
forced labour llafur gorfodol *eg*
forced loan benthyciad gorfodol *eg* benthyciadau gorfodol
forced oscillation osgiliad gorfod *eg* osgiliadau gorfod
forced vibration dirgryniad gorfod *eg* dirgryniadau gorfod
forcemeat stwffin *eg*
forcemeter mesurydd grym *eg* mesuryddion grym
forceps gefel *eb* gefeiliau
ford rhyd *eb* rhydau
fore blaen *ans*
forearm elin *eb* elinau
forearm deflection eliniad *eg*
forearm shield elinwisg *eb* elinwisgoedd
fore-brain blaen-ymennydd *eg*
forecast *n* rhagolwg *eg* rhagolygon
forecast *v* rhagweld *be*
foreclose blaen-gau *be*
foredeep blaenddwfn *eg* blaenddyfnion
foredune cyn-dwyn *eg* cyn-dwyni
fore-edge painting peintio ymylodol *be*
forefinger mynegfys *eg* mynegfysedd
foreground blaendir *eg* blaendiroedd
foreground processing blaenbrosesu *be*
forehand blaenllaw *eg*
forehand side ochr flaenllaw *eb*
forehand stroke ergyd flaenllaw *eb* ergydion blaenllaw
foreign (=alien) estron *ans*
foreign (=overseas) tramor *ans*
foreign affair mater tramor *eg* materion tramor
foreign body corffyn estron *eg* corffynnau estron
foreign exchange cyfnewidfa dramor *eb* cyfnewidfeydd tramor
foreign key allwedd estron *eb*
foreign policy polisi tramor *eg*
foreign trade masnach dramor *eb*
foreigner tramorwr *eg* tramorwyr
foreknowledge rhagwybodaeth *eb*
foreland (=headland) penrhyn *eg* penrhynau
foreland (=land in front of something) rhagdir *eg* rhagdiroedd
fore-limb coes flaen *eb* coesau blaen
foremast hwylbren blaen *eg* hwylbrennau blaen
forensic clinical psychology seicoleg glinigol fforensig *eb*
forensic hypnosis hypnosis fforensig *eg*
forensic psychology seicoleg fforensig *eb*
fore-rib asen flaen *eb* asennau blaen
foresail (jib) hwyl flaen *eb* hwyliau blaen
foreset bed gwely blaen-haen *eg* gwelyau blaen-haen
foresheet rhaff flaen *eb* rhaffau blaen
foreshore blaendraeth *eg* blaendraethau

eg/b enw gwrywaidd/benywaidd, *masculine/feminine noun* ***ell*** enw lluosog, *plural noun* ***v*** berf, *verb* ***n*** enw, *noun* ► wedi newid, *changed*

foreshorten rhagfyrhau *be*
foreshortening *n* rhagfyriad *eg* rhagfyriadau
foreskin blaengroen *eg* blaengrwyn
forest coedwig *eb* coedwigoedd
forest law cyfraith fforest *eb*
forest school ysgol goedwig *eb* ysgolion coedwig
forest soils fforestbriddoedd *ell*
forester coedwigwr *eg* coedwigwyr
forestry coedwigaeth *eb*
Forestry Commission Comisiwn Coedwigaeth *eg*
forfeiture fforffediad *eg* fforffediadau
forge *n* gefail *eb* gefeiliau
forge *v* gofannu *be*
forge parts rhannau gefail *ell*
forgery ffugiad *eg* ffugiadau
forgework gwaith gof *eg*
forging gofaniad *eg* gofaniadau
forging hammer morthwyl gofannu *eg*
forging process proses ofannu *eb* prosesau gofannu
forging tongs gefel ofannu *eb* gefeiliau gofannu
forgive maddau *be*
forgiveness maddeuant *eg*
fork (for digging or lifting, a divergence of anything) fforch *eb* ffyrch
fork (for eating or cooking) fforc *eb* ffyrc
fork centre canol fforch *eg* canolau ffyrch
fork chuck crafanc fforch *eb* crafangau fforch
forked fforchog *ans*
forked tenon tyno fforchog *eg* tynoau fforchog
form *v* ffurfio *be*
form (=document) *n* ffurflen *eb* ffurflenni
form (=shape) *n* ffurf *eb* ffurfiau
form a line-out leinio *be*
form a star ffurfio seren *be*
form and content ffurf a chynnwys
form constancy cysondeb ffurf *eg*
form footer troedyn ffurflen *eg* troedynnau ffurflen
form header pennyn ffurflen *eg* penynnau ffurflen
form letter llythyr parod *eg* llythyrau parod
form room ystafell ddosbarth *eb* ystafelloedd dosbarth
form sequences ffurfio dilyniannau *be*
form support cefnogaeth i ffurflenni *eb*
form teacher (female) athrawes ddosbarth *eb* athrawesau dosbarth
form teacher (male) athro dosbarth *eg* athrawon dosbarth
form tools offer ffurfio *ell*
form tutor tiwtor dosbarth *eg* tiwtoriaid dosbarth
formal ffurfiol *ans*
formal algebra algebra ffurfiol *eg*
formal carer gofalydd ffurfiol *eg* gofalwyr ffurfiol
formal channel of communication sianel cyfathrebu ffurfiol *eb* sianelai cyfathrebu ffurfiol
formal concept cysyniad ffurfiol *eg* cysyniadau ffurfiol
formal drawing lluniad ffurfiol *eg* lluniadau ffurfiol
formal group grŵp ffurfiol *eg* grwpiau ffurfiol
formal gymnastics gymnasteg ffurfiol *eb*
formal logic rhesymeg ffurfiol *eb*
formal operational stage stad weithredu ffurfiol *eb*
formal operational thought meddwl gweithredu ffurfiol *eg*
formal parameter paramedr ffurfiol *eg* paramedrau ffurfiol
formal pattern patrwm ffurfiol *eg* patrymau ffurfiol
formal proof prawf ffurfiol *eg* profion ffurfiol
formal science education addysg wyddonol ffurfiol *eb*
formaldehyde fformaldehyd *eg*
formalism ffurfiolaeth *eb*
formant fformant *eg* fformantau
format *n* fformat *eg* fformatau
format *v* fformatio *be*
formation (=arrangement) trefniant *eg* trefniannau
formation (in general) ffurfiant *eg* ffurfiannau
formative ffurfiannol *ans*
formative assessment asesiad ffurfiannol *eg* asesiadau ffurfiannol
formative evaluation gwerthusiad ffurfiannol *eg* gwerthusiadau ffurfiannol
formative recording cofnodi ffurfiannol *be*
format-mode modd fformat *eg*
formatter fformatydd *eg* fformatyddion
formatting toolbar bar offer fformatio *eg* barrau offer fformatio
formed follower dilynwr ffurfiedig *eg* dilynwyr ffurfiedig
former ffurfydd *eg* ffurfwyr
former lake cynlyn *eg* cynlynnoedd
form-feed *n* dalen-borthiad *eg* dalen-borthiadau
form-feed *v* dalen-borthi *be*
form-feed character nod dalen-borthi *eg* nodau dalen-borthi
formic acid asid fformig *eg*
formica fformica *eg*
forming tool erfyn ffurfio *eg* offer ffurfio
form-line ffurflin *eg* ffurflinau
forms of equation of the circle ffurfiau hafaliad y cylch *ell*
formula fformiwla *eb* fformiwlâu
formula area rhan fformiwla *eb* rhannau fformiwla
formula cell cell fformiwla *eb* celloedd fformiwla
formulary fformiwlari *eg*
formwork ffurfwaith *eg* ffurfweithiau
Forstner bit ebill Forstner *eg* ebillion Forstner
fort caer *eb* caerau
fortepiano fortepiano *eg* fortepianos
fortification caer *eb* caerau
fortified manor house maenordy ag amddiffynfeydd *eg* maenordai ag amddiffynfeydd
fortify atgyfnerthu *be*
fortress caer *eb* caerau
Forty Two Articles Dwy Erthygl a Deugain *eb*

forty-shilling freeholder rhydd-ddeiliad deugain swllt *eg* rhydd-ddeiliaid deugain swllt
forum fforwm *eg* fforymau
forward *adv* ymlaen *adf*
forward *n* blaen *eg*
forward (female) *n* blaenwraig *eb* blaenwragedd
forward (male) *n* blaenwr *eg* blaenwyr
forward and back a double (in dancing) llanw a thrai
forward and backward ymlaen ac yn ôl
forward and downward ymlaen ac i lawr
forward and sideways ymlaen ac i'r ochr
forward and upward ymlaen ac i fyny
forward arc arc flaen *eb* arcau blaen
forward arrow saeth ymlaen *eb* saethau ymlaen
forward chaining cadwyno ymlaen *be*
forward paddling stroke strôc badlo ymlaen *eb* strociau padlo ymlaen
forward pass pàs ymlaen *eb* pasiau ymlaen
forward pivot colyn blaen *eg* colynnau blaen
forward policy (of imperialist advance) polisi ymwthiol *eg* polisïau ymwthiol
forward reaction blaenadwaith *eg*
forward roll rhôl ymlaen *eb* rholiau ymlaen
forward rush cwrs blaenwyr *eg* cyrsiau blaenwyr
forward slash blaenslaes *eg* blaenslaesau
forward thrust gwthiad ymlaen *eg*
fossil *adj* ffosilaidd *ans*
fossil *n* ffosil *eg* ffosiliau
fossil fuels tanwydd ffosil *eg* tanwyddau ffosil
fossil record cofnod ffosil *eg*
fossilation ffosileiddiad *eg*
fossiliferous ffosilifferaidd *ans*
fossilize ffosileiddio *be*
foster maethu *be*
foster care gofal maeth *eg*
foster carer gofalwr maeth *eg* gofalwyr maeth
foster child plentyn maeth *eg* plant maeth
foster home cartref maeth *eg* cartrefi maeth
foster mother mam faeth *eb* mamau maeth
foster parent rhiant maeth *eg* rhieni maeth
fosterage cyfundrefn faeth *eb*
foul *n* trosedd *eg/b* troseddau
foul play chwarae brwnt *eg*
foul shot cam ergyd *eb* cam ergydion
foul throw camdaflu *be*
foulard foulard *eg*
fouling ffowlio *be*
found (establish) sefydlu *be*
found material defnydd hapgael *eg* defnyddiau hapgael
found object gwrthrych hapgael *eg* gwrthrychau hapgael
foundation *adj* sylfaen *ans*
foundation (=base) *n* sylfaen *eg/b* sylfeini
foundation (=establishment) *n* sefydliad *eg* sefydliadau
foundation bolt bollt sylfaen *eb* bolltau sylfaen
foundation colour lliw sylfaen *eg* lliwiau sylfaen
foundation course cwrs sylfaen *eg* cyrsiau sylfaen
foundation garment dilledyn sail *eg* dillad sail
foundation school (under British law) ysgol sefydledig *eb* ysgolion sefydledig
foundation stage curriculum cwricwlwm cyfnod sylfaenol *eg*
foundation stop stop sylfaen *eg* stopiau sylfaen
foundation subject pwnc sylfaen *eg* pynciau sylfaen
founder sylfaenydd *eg* sylfaenwyr
founding (e.g. iron) bwrw haearn *be*
foundry ffowndri *eb* ffowndrïau
foundry ladle lletwad ffowndri *eb* lletwadau ffowndri
foundry mould mowld ffowndri *eg* mowldiau ffowndri
foundry sand tywod ffowndri *eg*
four pedwar *eg* pedwarau
four ball pedair pêl *eb*
four figure table tabl pedwar ffigur *eg* tablau pedwar ffigur
Four Freedoms Pedwar Rhyddid *eg*
four hundred metres pedwar can metr *eg*
four in one canon canon bedwar yn un *eb* canonau pedwar yn un
four lane highway ffordd fawr pedair lôn *eb* ffyrdd mawr pedair lôn
four points of contact pedwar pwynt cyswllt *eg*
Four Sights, The Pedair Golygfa, Y *eb*
four-centred arch bwa pedwar canolbwynt *eg* bwâu pedwar canolbwynt
four-division saucer soser bedair rhan *eb* soseri pedair rhan
four-figure grid grid pedwar ffigur *eg* gridiau pedwar ffigur
four-jaw chuck crafanc pedair safn *eb* crafangau pedair safn
four-shaft loom gwŷdd pedair siafft *eg* gwyddau pedair siafft
foursided stitch pwyth petryal *eg* pwythau petryal
foursome pedwarawd *eg* pedwarawdau
four-stroke pedair strôc *ans*
four-stroke cycle cylchred pedair strôc *eb* cylchredau pedair strôc
four-stroke engine peiriant pedair strôc *eg* peiriannau pedair strôc
fourth (interval) pedwerydd *eg* pedweryddau
four-way tool post post pedwar erfyn *eg* pyst pedwar erfyn
fovea ffofea *eg*
fowl cyw iâr *eg* cywion ieir
fox wedging lletemu cudd *be*
foxiness (in wood) staeniau brown *ell*
foxtrot ffocstrot *eg* dawnsiau ffocstrot
fox-wedged (with feminine nouns) wedi'i lletemu'n gudd *ans* wedi'u lletemu'n gudd
fox-wedged (with masculine nouns) wedi'i letemu'n gudd *ans* wedi'u lletemu'n gudd
fox-wedged tenon tyno wedi'i letemu'n gudd *eg* tynoau wedi'u lletemu'n gudd

fractal ffractal *eg* ffractalau
fraction ffracsiwn *eg* ffracsiynau
fractional ffracsiynol *ans*
fractional crystallization grisialu ffracsiynol *be*
fractional distillation distyllu ffracsiynol *be*
fractionating column colofn ffracsiynu *eb* colofnau ffracsiynu
fractions of a complete turn ffracsiynau o dro cyflawn *ell*
fracture *n* toriad *eg* toriadau
fracture *v* torri *be*
fragile brau *ans*
fragile X X fregus *eg*
fragment darn *eg* darnau
fragmentary darniog *ans*
fragmentation darniad *eg* darniadau
fragmentation of holdings darnio ffermydd *be*
fragmented tameidiog *ans*
frail bregus *ans*
frame *n* ffrâm *eb* fframiau
frame *v* fframio *be*
frame connector cysylltydd ffrâm *eg* cysylltwyr ffrâm
frame construction adeiladwaith ffrâm *eg*
frame grabber fframgipiwr *eg* fframgipwyr
frame of reference ffrâm gyfeirio *eb* fframiau cyfeirio
frame saw llif ffrâm *eb* llifiau ffrâm
framed construction adeiladwaith ffrâm *eg*
framed door drws fframiog *eg* drysau fframiog
framed roof to fframiog *eg* toeon fframiog
frame-weaving worker gweithiwr ffrâm wehyddu *eg* gweithwyr ffrâm wehyddu
framework fframwaith *eg* fframweithiau
framework member aelod o fframwaith *eg* aelodau o fframwaith
framework of care fframwaith gofal *eg*
franchise (in commerce) masnachfraint *eb* masnachfreintiau
franchise (land) tir breiniol *eg* tiroedd breiniol
franchise (voting right) etholfraint *eb* etholfreintiau
franchised course cwrs breiniol *eg* cyrsiau breiniol
franchised pupil disgybl breiniol *eg* disgyblion breiniol
franchisee deiliad braint *eg* deiliaid braint
franchisor breiniwr *eg* breinwyr
Francis Ffransis *eg*
Franciscan *adj* Ffransisgaidd *ans*
Franciscan *n* Ffransisiad *eg* Ffransisiaid
Franciscan Order Urdd Sant Ffransis *eb*
francium (Fr) ffranciwm *eg*
Franco-Prussian War Rhyfel Ffrainc a Phrwsia *eg*
frankalmoign elusendir *eg*
Frankish Ffrancaidd *ans*
franklin rhydd-ddeiliad *eg* rhydd-ddeiliaid
frankpledge tangwystl *eg*
Franks Ffranciaid *ell*
frater ffreutur *eg* ffreuturiau
fraternal twins (non-identical) gefeilliaid annhebyg *ell*
fraternity (=brotherliness) brawdgarwch *eg*
fraternity (=group of men) brawdoliaeth *eb* brawdoliaethau
fratricide brawd-laddiad *eg*
fraud twyll *eg*
fray *n* rhaflad *eg* rhafladau
fray *v* rhaflo *be*
frayed carpet carped treuliedig *eg* carpedi treuliedig
fraying rhaflog *ans*
frazil ffrasil *eg* ffrasilau
Frederick Ffredric *eg*
Frederick the Great Ffredric Fawr *eg*
free *adj* rhydd *ans*
free *v* rhyddhau *be*
free arm (of machine part) braich rydd *eb* breichiau rhydd
free association rhyddgysylltu *be*
free bargaining bargeinio rhydd *be*
free blending rhyddgymysgu *be*
free canon rhyddganon *eg/b* rhyddganonau
free carbon carbon rhydd *eg*
free church eglwys rydd *eb* eglwysi rhyddion
free company cwmni hur *eg* cwmnïau hur
free counterpoint gwrthbwynt rhydd *eg* gwrthbwyntiau rhydd
free curve cromlin rydd *eb* cromliniau rhydd
free cutting rhydd-dorri *be*
free dancing dawnsio rhydd *be*
free electron electron rhydd *eg* electronau rhydd
free embroidery brodwaith rhydd *eg*
free energy egni parod *eg* egnïon parod
free enterprise rhyddfenter *eb*
free face wyneb rhydd *eg* wynebau rhydd
free fantasia ffantasia rydd *eb* ffantasïau rhydd
free flow play chwarae llif rhydd *eg*
free flowing rhyddlifo *be*
free formation trefniant rhydd *eg*
Free French Ffrancwyr Rhydd *ell*
free goods nwyddau di-gost *ell*
free group grŵp rhydd *eg* grwpiau rhydd
free hit ergyd rydd *eb* ergydion rhydd
free kick cic rydd *eb* ciciau rhydd
free machine embroidery brodwaith rhydd â pheiriant *eg*
free market marchnad rydd *eb* marchnadoedd rhydd
free market economy economi marchnad rydd *eg*
free metre mesur rhydd *eg* mesurau rhydd
free movement symudiad rhydd *eg* symudiadau rhydd
free nerve ending terfyn nerf rhydd *eg* terfynau nerfau rhydd
free painting (of painted picture) paentiad rhydd *eg* paentiadau rhydd
free painting (of process or act) peintio rhydd *be*
free period gwers rydd *eb* gwersi rhydd
free port porthladd rhydd *eg* porthladdoedd rhydd

free practice ymarfer rhydd *eg* ymarferion rhydd
free radical radical rhydd *eg*
free recall atgofio rhydd *be*
free sale gwerthiant rhydd *eg*
free school ysgol rad *eb* ysgolion rhad
free slope llethr rhydd *eg* llethrau rhydd
free software rhyddwedd *eg/b*
free space gofod gwag *eg*
free stroke symudiad rhydd *eg* symudiadau rhydd
free style dull rhydd *eg* dulliau rhydd
free tenant tenant rhydd *eg* tenantiaid rhydd
free thinker rhydd-feddyliwr *eg* rhydd-feddylwyr
free throw tafliad rhydd *eg* tafliadau rhydd
free trade masnach rydd *eb*
free will ewyllys rydd *eb*
Free Will Defence Amddiffyniad Ewyllys Rydd *eg*
free-body diagram diagram gwrthrych rhydd *eg*
freedom of a city rhyddfraint dinas *eb*
freedom of belief rhyddid cred *eg*
freedom of contract rhyddid contract *eg*
freedom of thought rhyddid meddwl *eg*
freedom to withdraw rhyddid i dynnu nôl *eg*
free -fall disgyn yn rhydd *be*
freehand llawrydd *ans*
freehand curve cromlin lawrydd *eb* cromliniau llawrydd
freehand design dyluniad llawrydd *eg* dyluniadau llawrydd
freehand diagram diagram llawrydd *eg* diagramau llawrydd
freehand drawing lluniad llawrydd *eg* lluniadau llawrydd
freehand sketch braslun llawrydd *eg* brasluniau llawrydd
freehold rhydd-ddaliad *eg* rhydd-ddaliadau
freehold land tir rhydd-ddaliol *eg* tiroedd rhydd-ddaliol
freehold property eiddo rhydd-ddaliol *eg*
freeholder rhydd-ddeiliad *eg* rhydd-ddeiliaid
freely pivot colynnu'n rhydd *be*
freeman rhyddfreiniwr *eg* rhyddfreinwyr
freemason saer rhydd *eg* seiri rhyddion
freenet rhadrwyd *eb*
freephone rhadffôn *eg*
freeplay chwarae rhydd *eg*
free-range egg wy maes *eg* wyau maes
free-range hen iâr faes *eb* ieir maes
free-response question cwestiwn penagored *eg* cwestiynau penagored
free-standing rhydd-sefyll *ans*
free-standing carcass sgerbwd rhydd-sefyll *eg* sgerbydau rhydd-sefyll
freeware rhadwedd *eg/b*
freeway traffordd *eb* traffyrdd
freeze rhewi *be*
freeze-dry sychrewi *be*
freezer rhewgell *eb* rhewgelloedd
freezer (cabinet) cwpwrdd rhew *eg* cypyrddau rhew
freezer burn llosg rhewgell *eg*
freeze-thaw action gwaith rhewi-dadmer *eg*; gwaith rhewi-dadlaith *eg*
freezing compartment (in fridge) blwch rhewi *eg* blychau rhewi
freezing point rhewbwynt *eg* rhewbwyntiau
freezing rain glasrew *eg*
freight line lein nwyddau *eb* leiniau nwyddau
freight rate tâl cludo *eg* taliadau cludo
freight train trên llwythi *eg* trenau llwythi
French beans ffa Ffrengig *ell*
French bread bara Ffrengig *eg*
French bun picen Ffrengig *eb* picau Ffrengig
French chalk sialc Ffrengig *eg*
French curve templed tro *eg* templedi tro
French dressing blaslyn Ffrengig *eg*
French harp organ geg *eb* organau ceg
French horn corn Ffrengig *eb* cyrn Ffrengig
French horn player canwr corn Ffrengig *eg* canwyr corn Ffrengig
French knot cwlwm Ffrengig *eg* clymau Ffrengig
French nail hoelen gron *eb* hoelion crwn
French overture agorawd Ffrengig *eb* agorawdau Ffrengig
French pitch traw safonol *eg*
French polish llathrydd Ffrengig *eg*
French polish finish gorffeniad llathrydd Ffrengig *eg*
French Revolution Chwyldro Ffrengig *eg*
French seam sêm Ffrengig *eb* semau Ffrengig
French sixth chweched Ffrengig *eg* chwechedau Ffrengig
French sixth chord cord y chweched Ffrengig *eg*
French suite cyfres Ffrengig *eb* cyfresi Ffrengig
French window ffenestr Ffrengig *eb* ffenestri Ffrengig
frequency (=commonness of occurrence) amlder *eg*
frequency (=rate of recurrence of vibration etc) amledd *eg* amleddau
frequency distribution (of statistics) dosraniad amlder *eg* dosraniadau amlder
frequency division multiplexing amlblecsu rhaniad amledd *be*
frequency of beat amledd curiad *eg*
frequency of discharge of water amlder gollwng dŵr *eg*
frequency polygon polygon amlder *eg* polygonau amlder
frequency shift keying allweddu syfliad amledd *be*
frequency table (in statistics) tabl amlder *eg* tablau amlder
frequently asked questions FAQ cwestiynau cyffredin *ell*
fresco ffresgo *eg* ffresgoau
fresh ffres *ans*
fresh bread bara ffres *eg*
fresh breeze awel ffres *eb* awelon ffres
freshwater dŵr croyw *eg* dyfroedd croyw
fret cribell *eb* cribellau

eg/b enw gwrywaidd/benywaidd, *masculine/feminine noun* ***ell*** enw lluosog, *plural noun* ***v*** berf, *verb* ***n*** enw, *noun* ►wedi newid, *changed*

fret nut talfran *eb* talfrain
fretsaw llif ffret *eb* llifiau ffret
fretted (of musical instrument) cribellog *ans*
fretted (of pattern) rhwyllog *ans*
fretwork rhwyllwaith *eg*
Freudian Freudaidd *ans*
friable hyfriw *ans*
friar brawd *eg* brodyr
friary tŷ'r brodyr *eg* tai'r brodyr
fricassée fricassée *eb* fricassées
friction ffrithiant *eg* ffrithiannau
friction clutch cydiwr ffrithiant *eg* cydwyr ffrithiant
friction drive gyriad ffrithiant *eg* gyriadau ffrithiant
friction washing golchi ffrithiant *be*
frictional grip gafael ffrithiannol *eb*
frictional unemployment diweithdra ffrithiannol *eg*
friction-compensated ffrithiant-gydadferedig *eg*
frictionless diffrithiant *ans*
frictionless roller rholer diffrithiant *eg* rholeri diffrithiant
Friendly Society Cymdeithas Gyfeillgar *eb* Cymdeithasau Cyfeillgar
Friends of the Earth Cyfeillion y Ddaear *ell*
frieze (architectural) ffris *eg* ffrisiau
frieze (material) brethyn tewban *eg* brethynnau tewban
frieze paper papur ffris *eg* papurau ffris
friezeman masnachwr brethyn *eg* masnachwyr brethyn
frigate ffrigad *eb* ffrigadau
frigid zone cylchfa rew *eb* cylchfaoedd rhew
frill ffrilen *eb* ffriliau
fringe *v* rhidennu *be*
fringe (=border of loose threads) *n* rhidens *ell*
fringe (=outer edge) *n* ymyl *eg/b* ymylon
fringe (in physics) *n* eddi *eg* eddïau
fringe (of town etc) *n* cwr *eg* cyrion
fringe benefit cilfantais *eb* cilfanteision
fringe separation gwahaniad eddïau *eg*
fringing reef ymylriff *eg* ymylriffiau
frit (glaze) ffrit *eg* ffritiau
fritted glaze gwydredd ffrit *eg*
fritter ffriter *eg* ffriterau
fritter batter cytew ffriterau *eg*
frizzling ffrislio *be*
frock ffrog *eb* ffrogiau
frog jump naid broga *eb* neidiau broga
frog spawn grifft broga *eg*
frond ffrond *eg* ffrondau
front (of position) blaen *eg*
front (of weather) ffrynt *eg* ffryntiau
front bodice bodis blaen *eg* bodisiau blaen
front clearance cliriad blaen *eg* cliriadau blaen
front elevation blaenolwg *eg* blaenolygon
front facing wynebyn blaen *eg* wynebynnau blaen
front foot troed flaen *eb* traed blaen
front loader peiriant blaen-lwytho *eg* peiriannau blaen-lwytho
front loading kiln odyn blaen-lwytho *eb* odynnau blaen-lwytho
front office service gwasanaeth blaen swyddfa *eg*
front opening agoriad blaen *eg* agoriadau blaen
front panel panel blaen *eg* paneli blaen
front rake gwyredd blaen *eg* gwyreddau blaen
front roller rholer blaen *eg* rholeri blaen
front row rheng flaen *eb* rhengoedd blaen
front support (in athletics) ymgynnal blaen *be*
front suspension hongiad blaen *eg* hongiadau blaen
front wall mur blaen *eg* muriau blaen
front wall out of court line ffin flaen *eb* ffiniau blaen
frontal apron ffedog flaen *eb* ffedogau blaen
frontal bone asgwrn talcen *eg* esgyrn talcen
frontal fog niwl ffrynt *eg*
frontal lobe llabed flaen *eb* llabedau blaen
frontal rain glaw ffrynt *eg*
frontality blaenluniad *eg* blaenluniadau
front-end pen blaen *eg* pennau blaen
front-end processor blaen-brosesydd *eg* blaen-brosesyddion
frontier ffin *eb* ffiniau
frontier district ardal ffiniol *eb* ardaloedd ffiniol
frontier state cyffinwlad *eb* cyffinwledydd
frontier zone parth ffiniol *eg* parthau ffiniol
frontispiece wynebddarlun *eg* wynebddarluniau
frontogenesis ffryntdarddiad *eg*
frontolysis ffryntwasgariad *eg*
frontoparietal blaenbaredol *ans*
frontosphenoidal blaensffenoidol *ans*
frost rhew *eg* rhewogydd
frost action gwaith rhew *eg*
frost attack ymosodiad gan rew *eg* ymosodiadau gan rew
frost bite ewinrhew *eg*
frost heaving gwthiad rhew *eg* gwthiadau rhew
frost hollow pant rhew *eg* pantiau rhew
frost line rhewlin *eg* rhewlinau
frost shattered rhewfriw *ans*
frosted barugog *ans*
frothy ewynnog *ans*
frottage *v* ffroteisio *be*
frottage (rubbing) *n* ffrotais *eg*
frotterism ffroteriaeth *eb*
frozen food market marchnad y bwydydd rhewedig *eb*
fructose ffrwctos *eg*
fruit (a single) ffrwythyn *eg* ffrwythynnau
fruit (in general) ffrwyth *eg* ffrwythau
fruit and vegetables ffrwythau a llysiau
fruit bowl ffiol ffrwythau *eb* ffiolau ffrwythau
fruit cake teisen ffrwythau *eb* teisennau ffrwythau
fruit crumble crymbl ffrwythau *eg* crymblau ffrwythau
fruit fool ffŵl ffrwythau *eg*

fruit juice sudd ffrwythau *eg*
fruit snow eirffrwyth *eg*
fruiting body ffrwythgorff *eg* ffrwythgyrff
fruity ffrwythus *ans*
frustrate (hopes) drysu *be*
frustrated rhwystredig *ans*
frustration rhwystredigaeth *eb* rhwystredigaethau
frustum ffrwstwm *eg* ffrwstymau
frustum of cone ffrwstwm côn *eg*
frustum of pyramid ffrwstwm pyramid *eg*
fry ffrio *be*
frying pan padell ffrio *eb* pedyll ffrio
fucoxanthin ffwcosanthin *eg*
fudge (confectionery) cyffug *eg*
fuel tanwydd *eg* tanwyddau
fuel cell cell danwydd *eb* celloedd tanwydd
fuel consumption traul tanwydd *eb*
fuel supply cyflenwad tanwydd *eg* cyflenwadau tanwydd
fugal ffiwgaidd *ans*
fugato ffiwgato
fughetta ffiwgeta *eb* ffiwgetau
fugitive ffoadur *eg* ffoaduriaid
fugitive colour lliw diflan *eg* lliwiau diflan
fugue ffiwg *eb* ffiwgiau
fugue form ffurf ffiwg *eb* ffurfiau ffiwg
fulcrum ffwlcrwm *eg* ffwlcrymau
fulfil cyflawni *be*
fulfilling life bywyd boddhaus *eg*
full anthem anthem lawn *eb* anthemau llawn
full back (female) cefnwraig *eb* cefnwragedd
full back (male) cefnwr *eg* cefnwyr
full bilingualism dwyieithrwydd llawn *eg*
full central heating gwres canolog llawn *eg*
full control rheolaeth lawn *eb*
full cost price pris llawn *eg*
full drop llithr llawn *eg*
full employment cyflogaeth lawn *eb*
full helix helics llawn *eg* helicsau llawn
full immersion trochiad llawn *eg*
full knees bend gliniau'n blyg i'r eithaf *ell*
full moon lleuad lawn *eb*
full organ organ lawn *eb*
full radiation (black body) pelydriad cyflawn *eg*
full range of ability ystod lawn o allu *eb*
full score sgôr lawn *eb* sgorau llawn
full screen editor sgrin-olygydd *eg* sgrin-olygyddion
full screen size maint sgrin lawn
full size maint llawn *eg*
full size court cwrt llawn maint *eg* cyrtiau llawn maint
full stop atalnod llawn *eg* atalnodau llawn
full time amser llawn *eg*
full toss pelen lawn *eb* pelenni llawn
full version fersiwn llawn *eg* fersiynau llawn
full weight rope rhaff bwysau llawn *eb* rhaffau pwysau llawn

full-adder adydd cyflawn *eg* adyddion cyflawn
full-duplex dwplecs cyflawn *eg* dwplecsau cyflawn
fuller pannwr *eg* panwyr
fullering pannu *be*
fullering tool erfyn pannu *eg* offer pannu
fuller's earth pridd y pannwr *eg*
fulling pannu *be*
fulling mill pandy *eg* pandai
full-length portrait portread hyd llawn *eg* portreadau hyd llawn
fullness llawnder *eg*
full-screen llond sgrin *ans*
fullsize mock-up brasfodel maint llawn *eg* brasfodelau maint llawn
full-time llawn amser *ans*
full-time equivalent cyfatebiaeth llawn amser *eb*
fully justified (with feminine nouns) wedi'i hunioni'n llawn *ans* wedi'u hunioni'n llawn
fully justified (with masculine nouns) wedi'i unioni'n llawn *ans* wedi'i hunioni'n llawn
fulminic acid asid ffwlminig *eg*
fumarole mygdwll *eg* mygdyllau
fumble ymbalfalu *be*
fume *n* mygdarth *eg* mygdarthau
fume *v* mygdarthu *be*
fume cupboard cwpwrdd gwyntyllu *eg* cypyrddau gwyntyllu
fumigate mygdarthu *be*
fuming mygdarthol *ans*
fun song cân hwyl *eb* caneuon hwyl
function (in general) swyddogaeth *eb* swyddogaethau
function (in mathematics) ffwythiant *eg* ffwythiannau
function code cod swyddogaeth *eg* codau swyddogaeth
function key bysell swyddogaeth *eb* bysellau swyddogaeth
functional (of mathematical functions) ffwythiannol *ans*
functional (of purpose or task) swyddogaethol *ans*
functional (of working or operating) gweithredol *ans*
functional area adran swyddogaethol *eb* adrannau swyddogaethol
functional art celfyddyd swyddogaethol *eb*
functional assessment asesiad perfformiad *eg* asesiadau perfformiad
functional design dylunio swyddogaethol *be*
functional difference gwahaniaeth gweithredol *eg* gwahaniaethau gweithredol
functional group (in chemistry) grŵp gweithredol *eg* grwpiau gweithredol
functional hemisphere asymmetry anghymesuredd swyddogaethau hemisfferau *eg*
functional illiteracy anllythrennedd gweithredol *eg*
functional literacy llythrennedd gweithredol *eg*
functional magnetic resonance imaging (fMRI) delweddu cyseiniant magnetig gweithredol *be*

functional niche cilfach weithredol *eb* cilfachau gweithredol
functional reading darllen gweithredol *eg*
functional surface arwyneb swyddogaethol *eg* arwynebau swyddogaethol
functional tool offeryn swyddogaethol *eg* offer swyddogaethol
functional word gair swyddogaethol *eg* geiriau swyddogaethol
▶ **functionalism** (in psychology) swyddogaetholdeb *eg*
functionalist swyddogaethwr *eg* swyddogaethwyr
fund cronfa *eb* cronfeydd
fundamental *adj* sylfaenol *ans*
fundamental *n* sylfaen *eg/b* sylfeini
fundamental attribution bias tuedd priodoli sylfaenol
fundamental attribution error cyfeiliornad priodoliad sylfaenol *eg* cyfeiliornadau priodoli sylfaenol
fundamental circuit cylched sylfaenol *eb* cylchedau sylfaenol
fundamental discord anghytgord sylfaenol *eg* anghytgordiau sylfaenol
fundamental dominant chord cord sylfaenol y llywydd *eg* cordiau sylfaenol y llywydd
fundamental dominant discord anghytgord sylfaenol y llywydd *eg* anghytgordiau sylfaenol y llywydd
fundamental interval cyfwng sylfaenol *eg* cyfyngau sylfaenol
fundamental note nodyn sylfaenol *eg* nodau sylfaenol
fundamental shape ffurf sylfaenol *eb* ffurfiau sylfaenol
fundamental temperature tymheredd sylfaenol *eg*
fundamentalism ffwndamentaliaeth *eb*
fundus ffwndws *eg* ffwndi
funeral march ymdeithgan angladd *eb* ymdeithganau angladd
fungal ffwngaidd *ans*
fungal attack ymosodiad ffwng *eg*
fungicide ffwngleiddiad *eg* ffwngleiddiaid
fungus ffwng *eg* ffyngau
funicular rheilffordd halio *eb* rheilffyrdd halio
funicular polygon polygon rhaff *eg* polygonau rhaff
funnel twndis *eg* twndisau; twmffat *eg* twmffedi
funnel stake bonyn twndis *eg* bonion twndis; bonion twmffat *eg*
fur (in pipes etc) cen *eg* cennau
fur (of animals) ffwr *eg*
fur fabric ffabrig ffwr *eg* ffabrigau ffwr
furlong ystaden *eb* ystadenni
furnace ffwrnais *eb* ffwrneisi
furnished accommodation llety wedi'i ddodrefnu *eg* lletyau wedi'u dodrefnu
furnishing fabric ffabrig dodrefnu *eg* ffabrigau dodrefnu
furniture dodrefn *ell*
furniture beetle chwilen ddodrefn *eb* chwilod dodrefn
furniture polish llathrydd dodrefn *eg*
furniture store siop ddodrefn *eb* siopau dodrefn
furniture wax cwyr dodrefn *eg*
furrow cwys *eb* cwysi
further education addysg bellach *eb*
Further Education Unit (FEU) Uned Addysg Bellach *eb*
further recognised stroke strôc gydnabyddedig bellach *eb* strociau cydnabyddedig pellach
fuse (=melt) *n* ymdoddiad *eg* ymdoddiadau
fuse (=melt) *v* ymdoddi *be*
fuse (of device) *n* ffiws *eg* ffiwsiau
fuse (when a fuse blows) *v* ffiwsio *be*
fused ymdoddedig *ans*
fusible ymdoddadwy *ans*
fusible alloy aloi ymdoddadwy *eg*
fusible clay clai ymdoddadwy *eg*
fusiform gwerthydffurf *eb*
fusing factor ffactor ymdoddi *eb*
fusing point ymdoddbwynt *eg* ymdoddbwyntiau
fusion (=melting) ymdoddiad *eg* ymdoddiadau
fusion (nuclear, cells etc) ymasiad *eg* ymasiadau
future generations cenedlaethau i ddod *ell*
future teaching addysgu pellach *be*
futurism dyfodoliaeth *eb*
futuristic dyfodolaidd *ans*
Futurists Dyfodolwyr *ell*
fuzzification niwlo *be*
fuzzy logic rhesymeg niwlog *eb*
fuzzy set set niwlog *eb* setiau niwlog

G

g (=balance) cydbwysedd *eg* cydbwyseddau
G clef cleff G *eg*
G cramp cramp G *eg*
g factor ffactor g *eb*
G major G fwyaf *eb*
G minor G leiaf *eb*
gabbro gabro *eg*
gaberdine gaberdîn *ans*
gable end talcen *eg* talcenni
gadget dyfais *eb* dyfeisiau
gadolinium (Gd) gadoliniwm *eg*
Gag Acts Deddfau Ffrwyno *ell*
gain (=increase) cynnydd *eg*
gain (=profit) ennill *eg* enillion
gain access cael mynediad *be*
gain confidence ennill hyder *be*
gain control rheolydd cynnydd *eg* rheolyddion cynnydd
gain ground ennill tir *be*
gainful worker gweithiwr cyflog *eg* gweithwyr cyflog
gait cerddediad *eg*
gaiter coesarn *eg* coesarnau
galactagogue blithogydd *eg* blithogyddion
galactic galaethog *ans*
galactosaemia galactosaemia *eg*
galactose galactos *eg*
Galapagos Islands Ynysoedd y Galapagos *ell*
galaxy galaeth *eb* galaethau
gale tymestl *eb* tymhestloedd
galena galena *eg*
Galilee (porch) galilca *eg*
gall (bile) bustl *eg* bustlau
gall (on plants) ardyfiant planhigol *eg*
gall-bladder coden y bustl *eb* codennau y bustl
galleon galiwn *eg* galiynau
gallery (in quarrying) ponc *eb* ponciau
gallery (in the arts) oriel *eb* orielau
gallery forest coedwig galeri *eb* coedwigoedd galeri
galley gali *eg* galïau
galliard galliard *eg* galliards
Gallican *adj* Galicanaidd *ans*
Gallican *n* Galicaniad *eg* Galicaniaid
Gallicanism Galicaniaeth *eb*
gallipot pot golchdrwyth *eg* potiau golchdrwyth
gallium (Ga) galiwm *eg*
gallon galwyn *eg/b* galwyni
gallop *n* carlam *eg*
gallop *v* carlamu *be*
gallstone carreg y bustl *eb* cerrig bustl
galvanic galfanig *ans*
galvanization galfaneiddiad *eg*
galvanize galfanu *be*
galvanized galfanedig *ans*
galvanized iron haearn galfanedig *eg*
galvanized window ffenestr alfanedig *eb* ffenestri galfanedig
galvanized wire gwifren alfanedig *eb* gwifrau galfanedig
galvanometer galfanomedr *eg* galfanomedrau
gamba (organ stop) gamba *eg*
gamboge tint arlliw gamboge *eg*
game gêm *eb* gemau
game form ffurf ar gêm *eb* ffurfiau ar gemau
game laws deddfau helwriaeth *ell*
game theory damcaniaeth gemau *eb*
gamekeeper ciper *eg* ciperiaid
games equipment offer chwaraeon *ell*
games teacher (female) athrawes chwaraeon *eb* athrawesau chwaraeon
games teacher (male) athro chwaraeon *eg* athrawon chwaraeon
gamete gamet *eg* gametau
gametocyte gametocyt *eg* gametocytau
gametogenesis gametogenesis *eg*
gametophore gametoffor *eg* gametofforau
gametophyte gametoffyt *eg* gametoffytau
gamgee gwlân *eg*
gamma radiation pelydriad gama *eg*
gamma ray pelydryn gama *eg* pelydrau gama
gamopetalous gamopetalog *ans*
gamosepalous gamosepalog *ans*
gamut gamwt *eg*
Ganesh / Ganesha / Ganapati Ganesh / Ganesha / Ganapati *eg*
gang gang *eg/b* gangiau
ganglion ganglion *eg* ganglia
ganglion cell cell ganglion *eb* celloedd ganglion
ganglionic ganglionig *ans*
gangrene madredd *eg*
Gannt chart siart Gannt *eg* siartiau Gannt
gap (in general) bwlch *eg* bylchau
gap (made for a purpose) adwy *eb* adwyau
gap town tref adwy *eb* trefi adwy
gapped bylchog *ans*
gapped edge ymyl fylchog *eb* ymylon bylchog
garage (of commercial enterprise) modurdy *eg* modurdai

garage (with a private dwelling) garej *eg* garejis
garaging cadw car *be*
garbage sbwriel *eg*
garden *n* gardd *eb* gerddi
garden *v* garddio *be*
garden city gardd-ddinas *eb* gardd-ddinasoedd
gargoyle gargoil *eg* gargoiliau
garland garlant *eg* garlantau
garment dilledyn *eg* dilladau
garnet paper papur garnet *eg* papurau garnet
garrison garsiwn *eg/b* garsiynau
garter gardys *eg* gardyson
garter stitch pwyth gardys *eg* pwythau gardys
gas nwy *eg* nwyon
gas cylinder silindr nwy *eg* silindrau nwy
gas exchange cyfnewid nwyon *be*
gas fire tân nwy *eg* tanau nwy
gas law deddf nwyon *eb*
gas lighter taniwr nwy *eg* tanwyr nwy
gas phase gwedd nwy *eb*
gas poker pocer nwy *eg* poceri nwy
Gascon Gascon *eg* Gasconiaid
gaseous nwyol *ans*
gaseous exchange cyfnewid nwyol *eg*
gash vein craig-wythïen *eb* craig-wythiennau
gashed edge ymyl wedi'i niweidio *eb* ymylon wedi'u niweidio
gasket gasged *eg* gasgedi
gas-liquid chromatography cromatograffaeth hylif nwy *eb*
gas-ring cylch nwy *eg* cylchoedd nwy
gastight nwyglos *ans*
gastric gastrig *ans*
gastric gland chwarren gastrig *eb* chwarennau gastrig
gastric juice sudd gastrig *eg* suddion gastrig
gastric pit mân-bant gastrig *eg* mân-bantiau gastrig
gastrocnemius croth y goes *eb*
gastro-enteritis gastro-enteritis *eg*
gastro-enterology gastro-enteroleg *eb*
gastrointestinal (tract) pibell gastroberfeddol *eb* pibellau gastroberfeddol
gastrula gastrwla *eg* gastrwlae
gastrulation gastrwliad *eg*
gat morddrws *eg* morddrysau
gate (=hurdle) clwyd *eb* clwydi
gate (in electronics, computing) adwy *eb* adwyon
gate (in metallurgy) porthell *eb* porthelli
gate (of garden) llidiart *eb* llidiardau
gate and knife tool erfyn porthellu a chyllell *eg* offer porthellu a chyllell
gate delay oediad adwy *eg* oediadau adwy
gate latch clicied llidiart *eb* cliciedau llidiart
gate tool erfyn porthellu *eg* offer porthellu
gate vault llofnaid glwyd *eb* llofneidiau clwyd
gated adwyog *ans*
gatekeeping (in administration of cases) didoli *be*
gate-leg table bwrdd coes gât *eg* byrddau coes gât
gateway porth *eg* pyrth
gather *n* crych *eg* crychau
gather *v* crychdynnu *be*
gathered fullness llawnder wedi'i grychdynnu *eg*
gathered lace les wedi'i grychdynnu *eg*
gathered skirt sgert grychog *eb* sgertiau crychog
gatherer (in general) casglwr *eg* casglwyr
gatherer (machine attachment) crychell *eb* crychellau
gathering (in material) crychiad *eg* crychiadau
gathering note nodyn casglu *eg* nodau casglu
gauge *v* medryddu *be*
gauge (=instrument) *n* medrydd *eg* medryddion
gauge (of railway) lled rheilffordd *eg* lledau rheilffyrdd
gauge block bloc medrydd *eg* blociau medrydd
gauze *adj* rhwyllog *ans*
gauze *n* rhwyllen *eb* rhwyllenni
gauze cloth lliain rhwyllog *eg* llieiniau rhwyllog
gauze swab swab rhwyllog *eg* swabiau rhwyllog
gavelkind cyfran *eb*
gavotte gavotte *eg* gavottes
GCSE Extended Welsh TGAU Cymraeg Estynedig
GCSE Extended Welsh Second Language TGAU Cymraeg Ail Iaith Estynedig
gear (=equipment) taclau *ell*
gear (of vehicle, lathe) gêr *eg/b* gerau
gear mechanism mecanwaith gêr *eg*
gear ratio cymhareb gêr *eb* cymarebau gêr
gear tooth dant gêr *eg* dannedd gêr
gear train trên gêr *eg* trenau gêr
gear wheel olwyn gêr *eb* olwynion gêr
gearbox blwch gêr *eg* blychau gêr
gearing ratio cymhareb geriad *eb*
gel gel *eg* geliau
gel coat araen gel *eb* araenau gel
gel medium cyfrwng gel *eg*
gelatine gelatin *eg* gelatinau
gelatine size seis gelatin *eg*
gelatinous gelaidd *ans*
gelatinous state cyflwr gelaidd *eg*
gelation geliad *eg*
gelifluction oerlif *eg* oerlifau
gem gem *eb* gemau
Gemara Gemara *eg*
gemma blaguryn *eg* blagur
gemmule gemwl *eg* gemylau
gemshorn gemshorn *eg*
gender rhyw y person *eg*
gender (=sex) rhyw *eg/b*
gender (in grammar) cenedl *eb*
gender bias gogwydd o ran rhyw *eg*
gender/sexual identity hunaniaeth rhyw *eb*
gender-stereotyped stereoteipio o ran rhyw
gene genyn *eg* genynnau
gene complex cymhlygyn genynnol *eg*

gene frequency amlder genynnol *eg*
gene locus locws genyn *eg*
gene pool cyfanswm genynnol *eg*
gene recombination adgyfuno genynnol *be*
gene therapy therapi genynnau *eg*
genealogical achyddol *ans*
genealogy achyddiaeth *eb*
general *adj* cyffredinol *ans*
general *n* cadfridog *eg* cadfridogion
general ability gallu cyffredinol *eg*
general ability test prawf gallu cyffredinol *eg* profion gallu cyffredinol
general adaption syndrome (GAS) syndrom addasu cyffredinol *eg*
General Agreement on Tariffs and Trade (GATT) Cytundeb Cyffredinol ar Dollau a Masnach *eg*
general anaesthetic anaesthetig cyffredinol *eg*
General Assembly Cynulliad Cyffredinol *eg*
General Certificate of Secondary Education (GCSE) Tystysgrif Gyffredinol Addysg Uwchradd *eb*
general Christian character cymeriad cyffredinol Cristnogol *eg*
general defence amddiffyniad cyffredinol *eg* amddiffyniadau cyffredinol
general degree gradd gyffredinol *eb* graddau cyffredinol
general election etholiad cyffredinol *eg* etholiadau cyffredinol
general feature nodwedd gyffredinol *eb* nodweddion cyffredinol
general gas equation hafaliad cyffredinol nwy *eg* hafaliadau cyffredinol nwy
general hospital ysbyty cyffredinol *eg* ysbytai cyffredinol
general improvement area ardal gwelliannau cyffredinol *eb* ardaloedd gwelliannau cyffredinol
general language discrimination hypothesis rhagdybiaeth gwahaniaethu iaith gyffredinol *eb*
general medicine meddygaeth gyffredinol *eb*
general method dull cyffredinol *eg*
General National Vocational Qualification (GNVQ) Cymhwyster Galwedigaethol Cenedlaethol Cyffredinol *eg* Cymwysterau Galwedigaethol Cenedlaethol Cyffredinol
general objective amcan cyffredinol *eg* amcanion cyffredinol
general pause (of orchestra) daliant cyffredinol *eg* daliannau cyffredinol
general post office prif swyddfa'r post *eb*
general practitioner meddyg teulu *eg* meddygon teulu
general purpose area llecyn at ddibenion cyffredinol *eg* llecynnau at ddibenion cyffredinol
general sales gwerthiant cyffredinol *eg*
general schools budget cyllideb gyffredinol i ysgolion *eb* cyllidebau cyffredinol i ysgolion
general session sesiwn gyffredinol *eg* sesiynau cyffredinol
general space gofod cyffredinol *eg*
general staff staff milwrol *ell*
general store siop bob peth *eb* siopau pob peth
general strike streic gyffredinol *eb* streiciau cyffredinol
general subject level lefel gyffredinol y pwnc *eb*
general surgery llawfeddygaeth gyffredinol *eb*
generalisation cyffredinoliad *eg* cyffredinoliadau
generalised cyffredinoledig *eg*
generalised animal cell cyffredinoliad o gell anifail *eg*
generality cyffredinolrwydd *eg*
generalizability gallu i gyffredinoli *eg*
generalize cyffredinoli *be*
generalized anxiety disorder anhwylder pryder cyffredinol *eg*
generate (in general) cynhyrchu *be*
generate (with generator) generadu *be*
generating capacity gallu cynhyrchu *eg* galluoedd cynhyrchu
generation (=age-group) cenhedlaeth *eb* cenedlaethau
generation (of heat, light) generadiad *eg* generadiadau
generation time (in biology) amser mitotig *eg*
generative cenhedlol *ans*
generative grammar gramadeg cynhyrchiol *eg*
generator generadur *eg* generaduron
generator of sound generadur sain *eg* generaduron sain
generic generig *ans*
generic convention confensiwn generig *eg* confensiynau generig
generic skills sgiliau generig *ell*
generic theme thema generig *eb* themâu generig
genetic genetig *ans*
genetic code cod genynnol *eg*
genetic counselling cynghori geneteg *be*
genetic disorder anhwylder genynnau *eg* anhwylderau genynnau
genetic drift symudiad genetig *eg*
genetic engineering peirianneg genetig *eb*
genetic epistemology epistemoleg geneteg *eb*
genetic equilibrium cydbwysedd genetig *eg*
genetic factor ffactor genetig *eb* ffactorau genetig
genetic fingerprinting adnabod ôl bys genynnol *be*
genetic isolation arwahaniad genynnau *eg*
genetic variant amrywiolyn genetig *eg*
genetic variation amrywiad genetig *eg* amrywiadau genetig
genetically modified a'u genynnau wedi'u haddasu
genetics geneteg *eb*
genital cenhedlol *ans*
genital stage cyfnod organau cenhedlu *eg*
genitals organau cenhedlu *ell*
genitive genidol *ans*
genius athrylith *eb*
genocide hil-laddiad *eg*
genome genom *eg* genomau

genomer genomer *eg* genomerau
genosome genosom *eg* genosomau
genotype genoteip *eg* genoteipiau
genotypic genoteipaidd *ans*
genotypic frequency amlder genoteipaidd *eg*
genre genre *eg* genres
gentle curve cromlin raddol *eb* cromliniau graddol
gentleman bonheddwr *eg* bonheddwyr
Gentleman at Arms Bonheddwr y Gwarchodlu *eg* Bonheddwyr y Gwarchodlu
Gentleman of the Bedchamber Bonheddwr y Siambr Wely *eg* Bonheddwyr y Siambr Wely
gentlemen's agreement cytundeb rhwng cyfeillion *eg*
gently rounded slope llethr esmwyth crwn *eg* llethrau esmwyth crwn
gentry bonedd *eg*
genus genws *eg* genera
geoanticline geoanticlin *eg* geoanticlinau
geoboard geofwrdd *eg* geofyrddau
geochemical geocemegol *ans*
geochronology geocronoleg *eb*
geochronometry geocronometreg *eb*
geode geod *eg* geodau
geodesic geodesig *ans*
geodesy geodedd *eg*
geodetic geodetig *ans*
geodimeter geodimedr *eg* geodimedrau
Geoffrey of Monmouth Sieffre o Fynwy *eg*
geographical concept cysyniad daearyddol *eg* cysyniadau daearyddol
geographical context cyd-destun daearyddol *eg*
geographical enquiry ymholiad daearyddol *eg* ymholiadau daearyddol
geographical feature nodwedd ddaearyddol *eb* nodweddion daearyddol
geographical information system system gwybodaeth ddaearyddol *eb*
geography daearyddiaeth *eb*
geoid geoid *eg* geoidau
geology daeareg *eb*
geometric geometrig *ans*
geometric concept cysyniad geometrig *eg* cysyniadau geometrig
geometric construction lluniad geometrig *eg* lluniadau geometrig
geometric design dyluniad geometrig *eg* dyluniadau geometrig
geometric grid grid geometrig *eg* gridiau geometrig
geometric mean cymedr geometrig *eg* cymedrau geometrig
geometric pattern patrwm geometrig *eg* patrymau geometrig
geometric progression dilyniant geometrig *eg*
geometric series cyfres geometrig *eb*
geometric shape siâp geometrig *eg* siapiau geometrig
geometric tolerancing goddefiannu geometrig *be*
geometrical geometregol *ans*
geometrical method dull geometregol *eg* dulliau geometregol
geometrical proportion cyfrannedd geometregol *eg*
geometry geometreg *eb* geometregau
geomorphic environment amgylchedd geomorffig *eg*
geomorphic process proses geomorffig *eb*
geomorphological geomorffolegol *ans*
geomorphological process proses geomorffolegol *eb*
geomorphology geomorffoleg *eb*
geon geon *eg* geonau
geophysics geoffiseg *eb*
geophyte geoffyt *eg* geoffytau
geopolitics geowleidyddiaeth *eb*
georgette georgette *eg*
Georgian Sioraidd *ans*
geostrophic geostroffig *ans*
geosyncline geosynclin *eg* geosynclinau
geotaxis geotacsis *eg*
geothermal geothermol *ans*
geotropism geotropedd *eg*
Gerald of Wales Gerallt Cymro *eg*
Geraldines Geraldiaid *ell*
geraniol geraniol *eg*
gerbil gerbil *eg* gerbilod
geriatric geriatrig *ans*
geriatrician geriatregydd *eg* geriatregwyr
geriatrification heneiddiad *eg*
germ germ *eg* germau
germ layer (embryo) haenen ymrannu *eb* haenau ymrannu
German Confederation Cydffederasiwn Almaenig *eg*
German Democratic Republic Gweriniaeth Dwyrain yr Almaen *eb*
German Empire Ymerodraeth yr Almaen *eb*
German Federal Republic Gweriniaeth Ffederal yr Almaen *eb*
German ladder ysgol Almaenig *eb* ysgolion Almaenig
German measles brech Almaenig *eb*
German offensive ymosodiad yr Almaenwyr *eg*
German Reformation Diwygiad Protestannaidd yn yr Almaen *eg*
German sixth chweched Almaenig *eg* chwechedau Almaenig
German sixth chord cord y chweched Almaenig *eg*
German suite cyfres Almaenig *eb* cyfresi Almaenig
German unification uno'r Almaen *be*
germanium (Ge) germaniwm *eg*
germanium(IV) oxide germaniwm(IV) ocsid *eg*
germ-cell cell genhedlu *eb* celloedd cenhedlu
germinal (relating to reproduction) cenhedlol *ans*
germinal epithelium epitheliwm cenhedlol *eg* epithelia cenhedlol
germinal ridge crib genhedlol *eb* cribau cenhedlol
germinal stage cyfnod eginol *eg*

germinate egino *be*
germinating seed hedyn eginol *eg* hadau eginol
germinating temperature tymheredd egino *eg* tymereddau egino
germination eginiad *eg* eginiadau
gerontology gerontoleg *eb*
gesso geso *eg*
GEST (Grants for Education Support and Training) Grantiau Cefnogi a Hyfforddi Addysg *ell*
Gestalt psychology seicoleg Gestalt *eb*
Gestalt therapy therapi Gestalt *eg*
Gestapo Gestapo *ell*
gestation period (of animal) cyfnod cyfebru *eg*
gestation period (of woman) cyfnod cario *eg*
gesture *n* ystum *eg/b* ystumiau
gesture *v* ystumio *be*
get (files etc on computer) estyn *be*
getting started dechrau arni *be*
geyser geiser *eg* geiserau
ghetto geto *eg* getos
Ghibelline Gibeliniad *eg* Gibeliniaid
ghost site gwefan farw *eb* gwefannau marw
giant *n* cawr *eg* cewri
giant (cells, chromosomes etc) *adj* enfawr *ans*
giant chromosome cromosom enfawr *eg* cromosomau enfawr
giant molecular moleciwlaidd enfawr *ans*
giant star seren gawr *eb* sêr cawr
giant structure adeiledd enfawr *eg* adeileddau enfawr
gib strip stribed gib *eg* stribedi gib
gibberellic acid asid giberelig *eg*
gibberellin giberelin *eg* giberelinau
giddiness pendro *eb*
Giffen goods nwyddau Giffen *ell*
gifted dawnus *ans*
gifted child plentyn dawnus *eg* plant dawnus
gigabyte (Gb) gigabeit *eg* gigabeitiau
gigantic anferth *ans*
gigue gigue *eb* gigues
gild euro *be*
gilded goreurog *ans*
gilding metal metel euro *eg*
gill *adj* tagellog *ans*
gill (of fish, mushrooms etc) *n* tagell *eb* tagellau
gill arch bwa tagell *eg* bwâu tagell
gill filament ffilament tagell *eg* ffilamentau tagell
gill plate plât tagell *eg* platiau tagell
gill raker cribin dagell *eb* cribiniau tagell
gill slit agen y dagell *eb* agennau tagellau
Gilles de la Tourette's syndrome syndrom Gilles de la Tourette *eg*
gilt goreurog *ans*
gilt glass gwydr goreurog *eg*
gimlet gimbil *eb* gimbilion
gimlet point pwynt gimbil *eg* pwyntiau gimbil
gimp pin pìn gimp *eg* pinnau gimp
ginger biscuit bisged sinsir *eb* bisgedi sinsir
gingham gingham *eg*
ginnery melin gotwm *eb* melinau cotwm
girder hytrawst *eg* hytrawstiau
girdle gwregys *eg* gwregysau
girdle scar craith gylchog *eb* creithiau cylchog
girth cwmpas *eg*
given instant ennyd benodol *eb* enydau penodol
gizzard glasog *eb* glasogau
glabrous llyfn *ans*
glacé cherry ceiriosen glacé *eb* ceirios glacé
glacial rhewlifol *ans*
glacial chronology cronoleg rewlifol *eb*
glacial drift drifft rhewlifol *eg*
glacial erosion erydiad rhewlifol *eg*
glacial lake rhewlyn *eg* rhewlynnoedd
glacial maximum uchafbwynt rhewlifol *eg* uchafbwyntiau rhewlifol
glaciate rhewlifo *be*
glaciation rhewlifiant *eg* rhewlifiannau
glacier milk llaeth rhewlif *eg*
glacier snout blaen rhewlif *eg* blaenau rhewlif
glacier sole gwadn rhewlif *eg* gwadnau rhewlif
glaciologist rhewlifwr *eg* rhewlifwyr
glaciology rhewlifeg *eb*
gladiator gladiator *eg* gladiatoriaid
Gladstonian liberalism rhyddfrydiaeth Gladstone *eb*
glair *n* glaer *eg*
glair *v* glaeru *be*
glance (=ricochet) *n* adlam *eg* adlamau
glance (in batting) *v* gwyro *be*
gland chwarren *eb* chwarennau
glandular chwarennol *ans*
glans penis blaen pidyn *eg*
glare llachared *eg*
glass (=mirror) drych *eg* drychau
glass (of material or object) gwydr *eg* gwydrau
glass blowing gwydr-chwythu *be*
glass chime clychsain gwydr *eb* clychseiniau gwydr
glass fibre gwydrffibr *eg*
glass mat mat gwydr *eg* matiau gwydr
glass mosaic mosaig gwydr *eg*
glass panel panel gwydr *eg* paneli gwydr
glass rod rhoden wydr *eb* rhodeni gwydr
glass slab slab gwydr *eg* slabiau gwydr
glass wool gwlân gwydr *eg*
glasscloth brethyn llyfnu *eg*
glasshouse tŷ gwydr *eg* tai gwydr
glass-reinforced fibre ffibr wedi'i atgyfnerthu â gwydr *eg*
glassware llestri gwydr *ell*
glassy gwydrog *ans*
glaucous llwydwyrdd *ans*
glaucous gull gwylan y gogledd *eb* gwylanod y gogledd
glaze (=glassy covering) *n* gwydredd *eg* gwydreddau
glaze (=shine) *n* sglein *eg* sgleiniau

glaze (=shine) *v* sgleinio *be*
glaze (with glassy covering) *v* gwydro *be*
glaze firing tanio gwydrog *be*
glaze stain staen gwydredd *eg* staeniau gwydredd
glazed (=shiny) sglein *ans*
glazed (with glassy covering) gwydrog *ans*
glazed cotton cotwm sglein *eg*
glazed crockery llestri wedi'u gwydro *ell*
glazed door drws gwydrog *eg* drysau gwydrog
glazed paper papur sglein *eg*
glazed surface arwyneb gwydrog *eg* arwynebau gwydrog
glazing bar bar gwydro *eg* barrau gwydro
glebeland clastir *eg* clastiroedd
glee club clwb glee *eg* clybiau glee
glenoid cavity crau glenoid *eg* creuau glenoid
gley glei *eg*
gleying gleio *be*
glia /glial cell cell glial *eb* celloedd glial
glial gliaidd *eg*
glide *n* llithriad *eg* llithriadau
glide *v* llithro *be*
glide (sliding door) *n* llithrydd *eg* llithryddion
glider gleider *eg* gleiderau
gliding joint cymal llithro *eg* cymalau llithro
glint-line lake llyn glintlin *eg* llynnoedd glintlin
glissade glissade *eg*
Glisson's capsule cwpan Glisson *eg*
global (=worldwide) byd-eang *ans*
global (in computing) eang *ans*
global (within document etc, with feminine nouns) drwyddi *ans* drwyddynt
global (within document etc, with masculine nouns) drwyddo *ans* drwyddynt
global distribution of population dosbarthiad byd-eang poblogaeth *eg*
global energy egni'r byd *eg*
global environment amgylchedd byd-eang *eg*
global pattern patrwm byd-eang *eg* patrymau byd-eang
global sport chwaraeon byd-eang *ell*
global system for mobile system fyd-eang cyfathrebu symudol *eb*
global tectonic process proses dectonig fyd-eang *eb*
global trial function ffwythiant prawf globaidd *eg*
global variable newidyn eang *eg* newidynnau eang
global variable newidyn drwy'r cyfan *eg* newidynnau drwy'r cyfan
global warming cynhesu byd-eang *be*
globalization globaleiddio *be*
globe glôb *eg* globau
globe artichoke artisiog glôb *eg* artisiogau glôb
globular crwn *ans*
globular clusters clystyrau crwn *ell*
globule globwl *eg* globylau
globulin globwlin *eg*
glockenspiel glockenspiel *eg* glockenspiele
glomerular filtrate hidlif glomerwlaidd *eg*
glomerulus glomerwlws *eg* glomerwlysau
Glorious Revolution Chwyldro Gogoneddus *eg*
gloss sglein *eg*
gloss paint paent sglein *eg*
glossopharyngeal glosoffaryngeal *ans*
glossy sgleiniog *ans*
glossy cane gwialen loyw *eb* gwialennau gloyw
glossy finish gorffeniad sgleiniog *eg* gorffeniadau sgleiniog
glossy paper papur sglein *eg* papurau sglein
glossy surface arwyneb sglein *eg* arwynebau sglein
glottal glotol *ans*
glottis glotis *eg* glotisau
gloup mordwll *eg* mordyllau
glove maneg *eb* menig
glove-puppet pyped maneg *eg* pypedau maneg
glove-puppet movement symudiad pyped maneg *eg* symudiadau pyped maneg
glow *n* tywyn *eg* tywynnau
glow *v* tywynnu *be*
glowing tywynnol *ans*
glowing splint (in chemistry) prennyn yn mudlosgi *eg* prenynnau yn mudlosgi
glucagon glwcagon *eg*
glucocorticoid glwcocorticoid *eg* glwcocorticoidau
glucose glwcos *eg*
glucose oxidase glwcos ocsidas *eg*
glucose tolerance test prawf goddefiad glwcos *eg* profion goddefiad glwcos
glucose-1-phosphate glwcos-1-ffosffad *eg*
glucostat glwcostat *eg* glwcostatau
glucostatic hypothesis rhagdybiaeth glwcostatig *eb*
glucosuria glwcoswria *eg*
glue *n* glud *eg* gludion
glue *v* gludio *be*
glue block bloc glud *eg* blociau glud
glue brush brwsh glud *eg* brwshys glud
glue ear gormod o gwyr yn y glust
glue kettle tegell glud *eg* tegellau glud
glue pot pot glud *eg* potiau glud
glue size seis glud *eg*
glue sniffing arogli glud *be*
glued blocks blociau wedi'u gludio *ell*
glued-on panel panel wedi'i ludio *eg* paneli wedi'u gludio
gluing surface arwyneb gludio *eg* arwynebau gludio
gluon glwon *eg* glwonau
glutamic acid asid glwtamig *eg*
glutamine glwtamin *eg*
glycerine glyserin *eg*
glycerol glyserol *eg*
glycine glycin *eg*
glycogen glycogen *eg*
glycogen synthetase glycogen synthetas *eg*
glycolysis glycolysis *eg*
glycoprotein glycoprotein *eg*

glycoside glycosid *eg*
glycosidic glycosidaidd *ans*
glyptic art celfyddyd glyptig *eb*
gnomonic projection tafluniad nomonig *eg* tafluniadau nomonig
go (on command button) mynd *be*
go about (in sport) ogamu *be*
go back nôl *adf*
go back one page nôl un dudalen *adf*
go forward ymlaen
go forward one page ymlaen un dudalen *adf*
goal (=aim) cyrchnod *eg* cyrchnodau
goal (in sport) gôl *eb* goliau
goal area cwrt y gôl *eg* cyrtiau'r goliau
goal board bwrdd gôl *eg* byrddau gôl
goal kick cic gôl *eb* ciciau gôl
goal line llinell gôl *eb* llinellau gôl
goal net rhwyd gôl *eb* rhwydi gôl
goal post postyn gôl *eg* pyst gôl
goal setting (in policy making) gosod nod *be*
goal shooter saethwr *eg* saethwyr
goalkeeper gôl-geidwad *eg* gôl-geidwaid
goalpost postyn *eg* pyst
goat-hair brush brwsh blew gafr *eg* brwshys blew gafr
gobelin stitch pwyth gobelin *eg* pwythau gobelin
goblet gobled *eg* gobledi
goblet cell cell gobled *eb* celloedd gobled
God Duw *eg*
god duw *eg* duwiau
godet godet *eg* godets
goffering goffro *be*
▶ **goggles** goglau *ell*
going (stairs) gofod llorwedd *eg*
goitre gwen, y wen *eb*
gold (Au) aur *eg*
gold cushion clustog aur *eb* clustogau aur
gold leaf deilen aur *eb* dail aur
gold leaf electroscope electrosgop deilen aur *eg* electrosgopau deilen aur
gold medal medal aur *eb* medalau aur
gold size seis aur *eg*
Gold Standard Safon Aur *eb*
gold thread edau aur *eb* edafedd aur
gold tooling foil ffoil offeru aur *eg*
gold tooling leaf deilen offeru aur *eb* dail offeru aur
Golden Age Oes Aur *eb*
golden bread crumbs briwsion cras *ell*
Golden Bull Bwla Aur *eg*
Golden Fleece Cnu Aur *eg*
Golden Horde Llu Euraidd *eg*
Golden Mean Cymedr Euraid *eg*
golden rectangle petryal euraid *eg* petryalau euraid
golden rule rheol euraidd *eb*
golden section adran euraid *eb* adrannau euraid
Golden Temple Teml Aur *eb*
goldsmith gof aur *eg* gofaint aur
golf links maes golff *eg* meysydd golff
Golgi apparatur organigyn Golgi *eg*
gomarist *adj* gomaraidd *ans*
gomarist *n* gomarwr *eg* gomarwyr
gonad gonad *eg* gonadau
gonadotrophic gonadotroffig *ans*
gonadotrophic hormone hormon gonadotroffig *eg*
gonadotrophin gonadotroffin *eg*
▶ **gonorrhoea** gonorea *eg*
good balance cydbwysedd da *eg*
good ball pêl dda *eb*
good continuation dilyniant da *eg*
Good Friday Dydd Gwener y Groglith *eg*
good length hyd da *eg*
good length ball bowliad hyd da *eg*
good loser collwr da *eg* collwyr da
Good Parliament Senedd Dda *eb*
good posture ymddaliad da *eg*
good practice ymarfer da *eg*
good proportion cyfrannedd da *eg*
good quality wood pren o ansawdd da *eg*
good saving practice arferiad cadw da *eg*
good sporting behaviour ymddygiad da wrth chwarae *eg*
good technique techneg dda *eb* technegau da
good timing amseru da *be*
good works gweithredoedd da *ell*
good-enough parenting magu digon da *be*
Goodhart's law deddf Goodhart *eb*
goodness of fit llwyddiant y ffit *eg*
goods nwyddau *ell*
goods and chattels nwyddau a meddiannau *ell*
goods or services nwyddau neu wasanaethau
good-subject role rôl cyfrannwr da *eb*
goodwill ewyllys da *eg*
googly gwgli *eg* gwglis
goose gŵydd *eg* gwyddau
goose pimples croen gŵydd *eg*
gooseberries eirin Mair *ell*
gooseneck *n* mynwydd *eg*
gooseneck *v* mynwyddu *be*
gore gôr *eb*
gored skirt sgert gôr *eb* sgertiau gôr
gorge ceunant *eg* ceunentydd
gospel efengyl *eb* efengylau
Gothic Gothig *ans*
Gothic architecture pensaernïaeth Gothig *eb*
Gothic art celfyddyd Gothig *eb*
Gothic sculpture cerflunwaith Gothig *eg*
gouache gouache *eg*
gouge *n* gaing gau *eb* geingiau cau
gouge *v* cafnu *be*
gouge cut toriad gaing gau *eg* toriadau gaing gau
gouged out lake llyn cafnog *eg* llynnoedd cafnog
govern llywodraethu *be*
governance trefn lywodraethol *eb*

governing body corff llywodraethol *eg* cyrff llywodraethol
government llywodraeth *eb* llywodraethau
government by decree llywodraeth drwy ordinhad *eb*
government of Wales llywodraeth Cymru *eb*
government ombudsman ombwdsmon llywodraeth *eg*
government spending gwariant llywodraeth *eg*
government training centre canolfan hyfforddi'r llywodraeth *eb* canolfannau hyfforddi'r llywodraeth
governor llywodraethwr *eg* llywodraethwyr
governorship swydd llywodraethwr *eb* swyddi llywodraethwyr
Graafian follicle ffoligl Graaf *eg* ffoliglau Graaf
graben (=rift valley) dyffryn hollt *eg* dyffrynnoedd hollt
grace gras *eg*
grace note addurnod *eg* addurnodau
Grace of Alais Pardwn Alais *eg*
graceful degradation diraddiad gosgeiddig *eg*
Gracious Aid Cymhorthdreth Wirfoddol *eb*
gradation graddiad *eg* graddiadau
gradation of accents graddiad acenion *eg* graddiadau acenion
gradation of contraction graddio cyfangiad *be*
gradation of dissonance graddoliad anghyseinedd *eg*
gradation of volume graddiad sain *eg* graddiadau sain
grade *n* gradd *eb* graddau
grade (=arrange in grades, sort) *v* graddio *be*
grade (=pass gradually between grades, blend) *v* graddoli *be*
grade description disgrifiad graddau *eg* disgrifiadau graddau
grade of pencil gradd o bensil *eb* graddau o bensiliau
grade review adolygu graddau *be*
graded graddedig *ans*
graded profile proffil graddedig *eg* proffiliau graddedig
graded test prawf graddedig *eg* profion graddedig
graded word reading test prawf graddedig darllen geiriau *eg* profion graddedig darllen geiriau
▶ **grade-related criterion** maen prawf gradd berthynol *eg* meini prawf gradd berthynol
gradient graddiant *eg* graddiannau
gradients of graphs graddiannau graffiau *ell*
grading test prawf graddio *eg* profion graddio
gradual *adj* graddol *ans*
gradual (in church service) *n* graddolen *eg* graddolennau
graduate *n* person graddedig *eg* graddedigion
graduate *v* graddio *be*
graduate teacher (female) athrawes raddedig *eg* athrawesau graddedig
graduate teacher (male) athro graddedig *eg* athrawon graddedig
graduated (in general) graddedig *ans*
graduated (of thermometer) graddnodedig *ans*
graduated flask fflasg raddedig *eb* fflasgiau graddedig
graduated pension pensiwn graddedig *eg* pensiynau graddedig
graduation (of thermometer) graddnod *eg* graddnodau
graduation ceremony seremoni graddio *eb* seremonïau graddio
Graeco-Roman Groeg-Rufeinig *ans*
graffito graffito *eg*
graft *n* impiad *eg* impiadau
graft *v* impio *be*
graft hybrid croesryw impiedig *eg* croesrywiau impiedig
grafted shoot cyffyn impiedig *eg* cyffynnau impiedig
grain (=particle) gronyn *eg* gronynnau
grain (food crop) grawn *eg*
grain (in rock, wood, cloth) graen *eg*
grain direction cyfeiriad y graen *eg*
grain markings marciau graen *ell*
graining graenio *be*
graining comb crib graenio *eb* cribau graenio
grainy surface arwyneb graenog *eg* arwynebau graenog
gram gram *eg* gramau
grammar gramadeg *eg/b*
grammar school ysgol ramadeg *eb* ysgolion gramadeg
grammatical gender cenedl ramadegol *eb*
gramophone gramoffon *eg* gramoffonau
granal granaidd *ans*
granary granar *eg* graneri
granary bread bara brown garw *eg*
granary flour blawd brown garw *eg*
Grand Alliance Cynghrair Fawr *eb*
grand barré (of the guitar) grand barré *eg*
grand canonical ensemble ensemble canonaidd mawreddog *eg* ensembles canonaidd mawreddog
grand duke archddug *eg* archddugiaid
grand inquisitor uchel chwilyswr *eg* uchel chwilyswyr
grand larceny lladrad mawr *eg* lladradau mawr
grand master uchel feistr *eg* uchel feistri
Grand National Consolidated Union Undeb Llafur Unedig Cenedlaethol *eg*
grand opera opera fawreddog *eb* operâu mawreddog
Grand Pensionary (Netherlands) Prif Swyddwr *eg* Prif Swyddwyr
grand period of growth prif gyfnod tyfiant *eg*
grand piano piano traws *eg* pianos traws
grand prince uchel dywysog *eg* uchel dywysogion
Grand Remonstrance Gwrthdystiad Mawr *eg*
granddaughter wyres *eb* wyresau
Grandees Mawrion, y *ell*
grandfather tad-cu *eg* tadau cu; taid *eg* teidiau
grandfather tape nain-dâp *eg* nain-dapiau

grandfather-father-son principle egwyddor-nain-mam-merch *eb*
grandmother mam-gu *eb* mamau cu; nain *eb* neiniau
grandson ŵyr *eg* wyrion
grange maenor *eb* maenorau
granite gwenithfaen *eg*
grant grant *eg/b* grantiau
grant maintained school ysgol a gynhelir â grant *eb* ysgolion a gynhelir â grant
grant sanctuary rhoi noddfa *be*
granular gronynnog *ans*
granulated gronynnog *ans*
granulation gronyniad *eg*
granulation tissue meinwe ronynnog *eb* meinweoedd gronynnog
granule gronigyn *eg* gronigion
granulocyte granwlocyt *eg* granwlocytau
granum granwm *eg* grana
grapefruit grawnffrwyth *eg* grawnffrwythau
graph graff *eg* graffiau
graph paper papur graff *eg* papurau graff
graph plotter plotydd graff *eg* plotyddion graff
grapheme graffem *eg* graffemau
grapheme-phoneme correspondence (GPC) **rule** rheol cyfatebiad graffem-ffonem *eb* rheolau cyfatebiad graffem-ffonem
graphic graffig *ans*
graphic *n* graffigyn *eg* graffigau
graphic art celfyddyd graffig *eb* celfyddydau graffig
graphic design dylunio graffig *be*
graphic designer dylunydd graffig *eg* dylunwyr graffig
graphic image delwedd graffig *eb* delweddau graffig
graphic notation nodiant graffig *eg*
graphic score sgôr graffig *eb* sgorau graffig
graphical graffigol *ans*
graphical differentiation differiad graffigol *eg* differiadau graffigol
graphical display unit (GDU) uned arddangos graffigol *eb* unedau arddangos graffigol
graphical form ffurf graffigol *eb* ffurfiau graffigol
graphical integration integriad graffigol *eg* integriadau graffigol
► **graphical technique** techneg graffigol *eb* technegau graffigol
graphical user interface rhyngwyneb defnyddiwr graffigol *eg*
graphics (=graphical work) graffigwaith *eg*
graphics (in general) graffeg *eb*
graphics pad pad graffeg *eg* padiau graffeg
graphics program rhaglen graffeg *eb* rhaglenni graffeg
graphics tablet llechen graffeg *eb* llechi graffeg
graphics terminal terfynell graffeg *eb* terfynellau graffeg
graphite graffit *eg* graffitiau
graptolite graptolit *eg* graptolitau
grasp *n* gafael *eg/b*
grasp *v* gafael *be*
grass gwair *eg* gweiriau
grass green (enamelling colour) gwyrdd porfa *eg*
grassland glaswelltir *eg* glaswelltiroedd
grated crayon creon mâl *eg* creonau mâl
graticule (in optical instruments) graticiwl *eg* graticiwlau
graticule (on maps) rhwyll map *eb* rhwyllau map
graticule intersection llinellau rhwyllog yn croesi *ell*
grating gratin *eg* gratinau
grave bedd *eg* beddau
grave goods nwyddau claddu *ell*
gravel *n* graean *eg*
gravel *v* graeanu *be*
gravelly graeanog *ans*
graver crafell *eb* crafellau
graveyard mynwent *eb* mynwentydd
gravimetric result canlyniad grafimetrig *eg*
gravitate disgyrchu *be*
gravitation disgyrchedd *eg* disgyrcheddau
gravitational disgyrchol *ans*
gravitational attraction atyniad disgyrchiant *eg*
gravitational equipotential surface arwyneb unbotensial disgyrcheddisgyrchiant *eg*
gravitational field maes disgyrchiant *eg*
gravitational field line llinell faes disgyrchiant *eb*
gravitational force grym disgyrchiant *eg* grymoedd disgyrchiant
gravitational potential potensial disgyrchiant *eg*
gravitational potential difference gwahaniaeth potensial disgyrchiant *eg*
gravitational pull tynfa disgyrchiant *eb*
gravitational slumping cylchlithriad disgyrchiant *eg* cylchlithriadau disgyrchiant
gravitational unit uned disgyrchiant *eb* unedau disgyrchiant
graviton disgyrchon *eg* disgyrchonau
gravity disgyrchiant *eg* disgyrchiannau
gravity flow llif disgyrchiant *eg*
gravity moulding moldio disgyrchol *be*
gravity slope llethr disgyrchiant *eg* llethrau disgyrchiant
graze (=feed on grass) *v* pori *be*
graze (=scrape) *n* crafiad *eg* crafiadau
graze (=scrape) *v* crafu *be*
graze (of wound) *n* clwyf crafiad *eg* clwyfau crafiad
grazier porfäwr *eg* porfawyr
grazing incidence (in physics) prin drawiad *eg* prin drawiadau
grazing land tir pori *eg* tiroedd pori
grease *n* saim *eg* seimiau
grease *v* iro *be*
grease box blwch saim *eg* blychau saim
grease gun gwn saim *eg* gynnau saim
grease solvent hydoddydd saim *eg* hydoddyddion saim
greasy seimlyd *ans*
great circle cylch mawr *eg* cylchoedd mawr
Great Circle Route Llwybr Cylch Mawr *eg*

Great Contract Cytundeb Mawr *eg*
Great Council Cyngor Mawr *eg*
Great Depression Dirwasgiad Mawr *eg*
Great Elector Etholydd Mawr *eg*
Great Exhibition Arddangosfa Fawr *eb*
Great Fire of London Tân Mawr Llundain *eg*
Great Leap Forward (in China) Naid Fawr Ymlaen *eb*
Great Northern War Rhyfel Mawr y Gogledd *eg*
great organ prif organ *eb* prif organau
Great Plague Pla Mawr *eg*
Great Powers Pwerau Mawrion *ell*
Great Purges Carthu Mawr *be*
Great Schism Sgism Mawr *eg*
Great Seal Sêl Fawr *eb*
Great Sessions Sesiwn Fawr *eb*
Great Society Cymdeithas Fawrfrydig *eb*
Great Trek Mudo Mawr *eg*
great white shark siarc mawr gwyn *eg* siarcod mawr gwyn
greatest common divisor (=highest common factor) rhannydd cyffredin mwyaf *eg*
great-grandchild gorwyr *eg* gorwyrion
greave coesarf *eg* coesarfau
Grecian harp telyn Roegaidd *eb* telynau Groegaidd
Greek *adj* Groegaidd *ans*
Greek art celfyddyd Groeg *eb*
Greek cadence diweddeb amen *eb* diweddebau amen
Greek Orthodox Church Eglwys Uniongred Roegaidd *eb*
green belt llain las *eb* lleiniau glas
green belt site safle tir glas *eg* safleoedd tir glas
green field (in planning etc) tir glas *eg*
▸ **green field site** safle tir glas *eg* safleoedd tir glas
green sand tywod llaith *eg*
green sand mould mowld tywod llaith *eg* mowldiau tywod llaith
green sand moulding mowldio tywod llaith *be*
green sward glastir *eg* glastiroedd
green timber (unseasoned) pren heb ei sychu *eg*
green ware crochenwaith heb ei danio *eg*
greengrocer (person) gwerthwr llysiau *eg* gwerthwyr llysiau
greengrocer (shop) siop lysiau *eb* siopau llysiau
greenhouse tŷ gwydr *eg* tai gwydr
greenhouse effect effaith tŷ gwydr *eb*
greens (=environmentalists) gwyrddion *ell*
greensand tywodfaen gwyrdd *eg* tywodfeini gwyrdd
Greenwich Mean Time Amser Safonol Greenwich *eg*
greeting card cerdyn cyfarch *eg* cardiau cyfarch
gregarious (of animals) heidiol *ans*
gregarious (of people) cymdeithasgar *ans*
gregariousness (of animals) heidioledd *eg*
gregariousness (of people) cymdeithasgarwch *eg*
Gregorian Gregoraidd *ans*
Gregorian Calendar Calendr Gregori *eg*
Gregory Gregori *eg*
grenade grenâd *eg* grenadau
grey (=darken) *v* tywyllu *be*
grey (enamelling colour) *n* llwyd *eg*
grey area ardal lwyd *eb* ardaloedd llwyd
grey board bwrdd llwyd *eg* byrddau llwyd
grey cardboard cardbord llwyd *eg*
grey cast iron haearn bwrw llwyd *eg*
grey dune twyn llwyd *eg* twyni llwyd
Grey Friar brawd llwyd *eg* Brodyr Llwydion
grey iron haearn llwyd *eg*
grey matter (brain) breithell *eb*
grey modelling clay clai modelu llwyd *eg*
grey powdered clay clai powdr llwyd *eg*
greyed out gwelw *ans*
greyscale graddlwyd *eg*
grid grid *eg* gridiau
grid bias bias grid *eg*
grid colour lliw grid *eg* lliwiau grid
grid line llinell grid *eb* llinellau grid
grid north gogledd grid *eg*
grid reference cyfeirnod grid *eg* cyfeirnodau grid
grid resistor gwrthydd grid *eg* gwrthyddion grid
grid system system grid *eb* systemau grid
grid to front grid i'r blaen
grid work gwaith grid *eg*
gridiron sgwarog *ans*
grief galar *eg*
grief reaction adwaith galar *eg* adweithiau galar
grievance cwyn *eg* cwynion
grievance procedure dull gweithredu cwynion *eg*
grieving process proses o alaru *eb*
grike greic *eg* greiciau
grill gridyll *eg/b* gridyllau
grille (of car) gril *eg* griliau
grille (ventilation) dellt awyru *eb* delltiau awyru
grilled chop golwyth o'r gridyll *eg* golwython o'r gridyll
grimace *n* ystum *eg/b* ystumiau
grimace *v* tynnu wyneb *be*
grind (=crush) malu *be*
grind (=reduce, sharpen or smooth) llifanu *be*
grind in a mortar malu mewn morter *be*
grinder llifanydd *eg* llifanwyr
grinding angle ongl lifanu *eb* onglau llifanu
grinding bevel befel llifanu *eg* befelau llifanu
grinding machine peiriant llifanu *eg* peiriannau llifanu
grinding paste past llifanu *eg*
grinding wheel olwyn lifanu *eb* olwynion llifanu
grindstone maen llifanu *eg* meini llifanu
grindstone truer cywirwr maen llifanu *eg* cywirwyr maen llifanu
grip *n* gafael *eg/b* gafaelion
grip *v* gafael *be*
grit grut *eg* grutiau
gritaceous grutiog *ans*
gritstone carreg grut *eb* cerrig grut

gritty grutiog *ans*
groan *n* ochenaid *eb* ocheneidiau
groan *v* griddfan *be*
grocer groser *eg* groseriaid
grog grog *eg*
groin cesail y forddwyd *eb*
grommet gromed *eg* gromedau
groove rhigol *eb* rhigolau
groove punch pwnsh sêm *eg* pynsiau sêm
groove punch seaming tool erfyn semio rhigol *eg* offer semio rhigolau
grooved rhigolog *ans*
grooved frame ffrâm rigolog *eb* fframiau rhigolog
grooved nut nyten rigolog *eb* nytiau rhigolog
grooved panel panel rhigolog *eg* paneli rhigolog
grooved seam sêm rigolog *eb* semau rhigolog
grooved stile cledren rigolog *eb* cledrau rhigolog
groover rhigolydd *eg* rhigolyddion
grooving rhigoli *be*
grooving plane plaen rhigoli *eg* plaeniau rhigoli
grosgrain (of silk) sidan rib *eg* sidanau rib
gross (=144) deuddeg dwsin *eg*
gross (of income etc) crynswth *eg*
gross box office takings crynswth arian am docynnau *eg*
gross capital cyfalaf crynswth *eg*
Gross Domestic Product Cynnyrch Mewnwladol Crynswth *eg*
gross income incwm crynswth *eg*
gross investment buddsoddiad gros *eg* buddsoddiadau gros
gross loss colled grynswth *eb* colledion crynswth
gross manipulative skills sgiliau llawdrin bras *ell*
gross motor skills sgiliau echddygol bras *ell*
Gross National Product Cynnyrch Gwladol Crynswth *eg*
gross pay cyflog crynswth *eg*
gross product lluoswm crynswth *eg*
gross profit elw crynswth *eg*
gross-motor movement symudiad echddygol bras *eg* symudiadau echddygol bras
grotesque grotesg *ans*
grotto groto *eg* grotos
ground (=floor) llawr *eg* lloriau
ground (in art) grwnd *eg*
ground (surface of land) daear *eb*
ground almonds almonau mâl *ell*
ground bass grwndfas *eg*
ground coat araen grwnd *eb* araenau grwnd
ground coffee coffi mâl *eg*
ground floor llawr gwaelod *eg* lloriau gwaelod
ground moraine marian llusg *eg* marianau llusg
ground photograph ffotograff lefel y tir *eg* ffotograffau lefel y tir
ground plan cynllun llawr *eg* cynlluniau llawr
ground plate grwndblat *eg* grwndblatiau
ground state cyflwr isaf *eg* cyflyrau isaf
ground swell ymchwydd y don *eg*
ground the ball turio'r bêl *be*
ground tissue meinwe daear *eg*
ground water (=phreatic water) dŵr daear *eg* dyfroedd daear
grounded theory damcaniaeth seiliedig *eb*
ground-rent rhent safle *eg* rhenti safle
groundsman tirmon *eg* tirmoniaid
groundsmanship tirmonaeth *eb*
groundwater dŵr daear *eg*
group (=huddle) twr *eg* tyrrau
group (in formal context) grŵp *eg* grwpiau
group (in informal context) cylch *eg* cylchoedd
group activity gweithgaredd grŵp *eg* gweithgareddau grŵp
group activity session sesiwn gweithgaredd grŵp *eb*
group box blwch grŵp *eg* blychau grŵp
group draw object gwrthrych lluniadu grŵp *eg* gwrthrychau lluniadu grŵp
group dynamics dynameg grŵp *eb*
group family teulu grŵp *eg* teuluoedd grŵp
group interaction rhyngweithio grŵp *be*
group leader arweinydd grŵp *eg* arweinwyr grŵp
group object gwrthrych grŵp *eg*
group of objects grŵp o wrthrychau *eg*
group piece darn grŵp *eg* darnau grŵp
group psychotherapy seicotherapi grŵp *eg*
group test prawf grŵp *eg* profion grŵp
group test of mental ability prawf grŵp o allu ymenyddol *eg* profion grŵp o allu ymenyddol
group therapy therapi grŵp *eg*
group view golwg grŵp *eg*
grouping not possible (screen message) nid yw grwpio'n bosibl
grouping of notes cyfosod nodau *eg*
grouping of rests cyfosod tawnodau *be*
groupthink meddwl grŵp *be*
grouse grugiar *eb* grugieir
grout *n* growt *eg* growtiau
grout *v* growtio *be*
grove llwyn *eb* llwyni
grow tyfu *be*
growing point tyfbwynt *eg* tyfbwyntiau
growing season tymor tyfu *eg* tymhorau tyfu
growth (act or process of) twf *eg*
growth (something grown / growing) tyfiant *eg*
growth and development twf a datblygiad
growth curve cromlin dyfiant *eb*
growth cycle cylchred dyfiant *eb* cylchredau tyfiant
growth formation ffurf tyfiant *eb* ffurfiau tyfiant
growth hormone hormon twf *eg* hormonau twf
growth industry diwydiant twf *eg* diwydiannau twf
growth medium cyfrwng cynnal twf *eg* cyfryngau cynnal twf
growth rate cyfradd twf *eb* cyfraddau twf
growth response twf-ymateb *eg*
growth ring cylch tyfiant *eg* cylchoedd tyfiant

groyne argor *eg* argorau
grub bolt bollt ddigopa *eb* bolltau digopa
grubber kick cic bwt *eb* ciciau pwt
grub-screw sgriw ddigopa *eb* sgriwiau digopa
guanine gwanin *eg*
guano giwana *eg*
guarantee *n* gwarant *eb* gwarantau
guarantee *v* gwarantu *be*
guaranteed goods nwyddau gwarantiedig *ell*
guarantor gwarantwr *eg* gwarantwyr
guard *v* gwarchod *be*
guard (=body of troops) *n* gwarchodlu *eg* gwarchodluoedd
guard (of person or device) *n* gard *eg* gardiau
guard cell cell warchod *eb* celloedd gwarchod
guard plate plât gwarchod *eg* platiau gwarchod
guard position safiad gwarchod *eg* safiadau gwarchod
guard rail rheilen warchod *eb* rheiliau gwarchod
guardian gwarcheidwad *eg* gwarcheidwaid
guardian angel angel gwarcheidiol *eg* angylion gwarcheidiol
guardianship gwarcheidwaeth *eb*
guerrilla milwr gerila *eg* milwyr gerila
guerrilla warfare rhyfel gerila *eg* rhyfeloedd gerila
guest gwestai *eg* gwesteion
guest house gwesty *eg* gwestai
guest speaker siaradwr gwadd *eg* siaradwyr gwadd
guidance (=advice) arweiniad *eg*
guidance (=instruction) cyfarwyddyd *eg* cyfarwyddiadau
guide (in general) *v* tywys *be*
guide (behaviour etc) llywio *be*
guide (=guideline) *n* canllaw *eg/b* canllawiau
guide (of instrument) *n* cyfeirydd *eg* cyfeiryddion
guide (of person) *n* tywysydd *eg* tywyswyr
guide book arweinlyfr *eg* arweinlyfrau
guide distance pellter canllaw *eg*
guide line (of diagram) tywyslinell *eb* tywyslinellau
guide pin pìn arwain *eg* pinnau arwain
guide plate plât tywys *eg* platiau tywys
guide screw sgriw gyfeirio *eb* sgriwiau cyfeirio
guideline canllaw *eg/b* canllawiau
guidelines of good practice canllawiau ymarfer da *ell*
guides to front canllawiau i'r blaen *ell*
guild (historical, ecological) gild *eg* gildiau
guild (in association titles etc) urdd *eb* urddau
Guild for the Promotion of Welsh Music Urdd er Hyrwyddo Cerddoriaeth yng Nghymru *eb*
guildhall neuadd y dref *eb*
guillemot gwylog *eb* gwylogod
guillotine gilotin *eg* gilotinau
guillotine shears gwellaif gilotin *eg* gwelleifiau gilotin
guilt euogrwydd *eg*
Guinevere Gwenhwyfar *eb*
guitar gitâr *eb* gitarau
guitarist gitarydd *eg* gitarwyr
gulch ceunant *eg* ceunentydd
gulf gwlff *eg* gylffiau
Gulf Stream Llif y Gwlff *eg*
gullet llwnc *eg* llynciau
gullet (of saw) gwddf *eg* gyddfau
gullied gylïog *ans*
gully gyli *eg* gylïau
gum *v* gymio *be*
gum (=glue) *n* gwm *eg* gymiau
gum (holding teeth) *n* deintgig *eg*
gum arabic gwm arabig *eg*
gum eraser dilëwr gwm *eg* dilewyr gwm
gum paper papur gwm *eg* papurau gwm
gum shield tarian geg *eb* tariannau ceg
gummed gymedig *ans*
gummed binding rhwymyn gwm *eg* rhwymynnau gwm
gummed tape tâp glud *eg*
gun gwn *eg* gynnau
gunmetal gwnfetel *eg*
gunpowder powdr gwn *eg*
Gunpowder Plot Cynllwyn y Powdwr Gwn *eg*
gunshot wound clwyf ergyd gwn *eg* clwyfau ergyd gwn
gunwale gynwal *eg* gynwalau
Gurdwara Gurdwara *eg*
gurmukhi gurmukhi *eg*
guru (general usage) gwrw *eg* gwrws
Guru (in Sikhism) Guru *eg*
Guru Granth Sahib Guru Granth Sahib *eg*
gush out ffrydio *be*
gusset cwysed *eb* cwysedi
gust hwrdd *eg* hyrddiau
gustation blasu *be*
gustatory hair blewyn blasu *eg* blew blasu
gut coludd *eg* coluddion
gut fret cribell goludd *eb* cribellau coludd
gut string tant coludd *eg* tannau coludd
guttate ymddafnu *be*
guttation ymddafniad *eg*
gutter (in street) cwter *eb* cwteri
gutter (on roof) cafn *eg* cafnau
Guy Fawkes Guto Ffowc *eg*
guyot mynydd guyot *eg* mynyddoedd guyot
gybe *n* starn ogam *eb* starnau ogam
gybe *v* starn ogamu *be*
gymnasium campfa *eb* campfeydd
gymnast gymnastwr *eg* gymnastwyr
gymnastic action gweithred gymnastig *eb* gweithredoedd gymnastig
gymnastic activity gweithgaredd gymnastig *eg* gweithgareddau gymnastig
gymnastics gymnasteg *eb*
gymnosperm gymnosberm *eg* gymnosbermau
gymnospore gymnosbor *eg* gymnosborau
gynaecium gynaeciwm *eg*

gynaecologist gynaecolegydd *eg* gynaecolegwyr
gynaecology gynaecoleg *eb*
gynoecium gynoeciwm *eg*
gypsum gypswm *eg*
gypsum plaster plastr gypswm *eg*
gypsy sipsi *eg* sipsiwn
gyration chwyrliant *eg* chwyrliannau
gyre cylchgerrynt *eg* cylchgerhyntau
gyri gyri *ell*
gyro compass cwmpawd gyro *eg* cwmpawdau gyro
gyroscope gyrosgop *eg* gyrosgopau

H

Haber process proses Haber *eb*
haberdashery manion gwnïo *ell*
habit (=custom) arfer *eg/b* arferion
habit (=dress) abid *eg/b* abidau
habitable trigiadwy *ans*
habitat cynefin *eg* cynefinoedd
habitation annedd *eg/b* anheddau
habitual abortion erthylu cyson *be*
habituation cynefino *be*
hack hacio *be*
hacking hacio *be*
hacksaw haclif *eb* haclifiau
hacksaw blade llafn haclif *eg* llafnau haclif
hacksaw frame ffrâm haclif *eb* fframiau haclif
Hadith Hadith *eg*
haematite haematit *eg*
haematite iron haearn haematit *eg*
haematitic haematitig *ans*
haematologist haematolegydd *eg* haematolegwyr
haematology haematoleg *eb*
haematuria haematwria *eg*
haemocoel ceudod gwaed *eg*
haemocyanin haemocyanin *eg*
haemocytometer haemocytomedr *eg*
haemoglobin haemoglobin *eg*
haemolysis haemolysis *eg*
haemophilia haemoffilia *eg*
haemoptysis gwaedboer *eg*
haemorrhage gwaedlif *eg*
haff morlyn *eg* morlynnoedd
hafnium (Hf) haffniwm *eg*
hagiography buchedd sant *eg* bucheddau saint
hair (on body) blewyn *eg* blew
hair (on head) gwallt *ell*
hair canvas cynfas rhawn *eg* cynfasau rhawn
hair cell cell flewyn *eb* celloedd blew
hair follicle ffoligl blewyn *eg* ffoliglau blew
hair shirt rhawnbais *eb* rhawnbeisiau
hairdryer sychwr gwallt *eg* sychwyr gwallt
Hajj Hajj *eg*
halberd gwayw fwyell *eb* gwayw fwyeill
half hanner *eg* haneri
half arch hanner bwa *eg* hanner bwâu
half cell hanner cell *eg* hanner celloedd
half centre hanner canol *eg* hanner canolau
half close diweddeb amherffaith *eb* diweddebau amherffaith
half court line llinell hanner cwrt *eb* llinellau hanner cwrt
half knees bend gliniau'n blyg i'r hanner *ell*
half moon hanner lleuad *eb*
half moon chisel cŷn hanner crwn *eg* cynion hanner crwn; gaing hanner crwn *eb* geingiau hanner crwn
half moon stake bonyn hanner crwn *eg* bonion hanner crwn
half rotary-cut veneer argaen toriad hanner cylchdro *eg* argaenau toriad hanner cylchdro
half round hanner crwn *eg*
half round chisel cŷn hanner crwn *eg* cynion hanner crwn; gaing hanner crwn *eb* geingiau hanner crwn
half round file ffeil hanner crwn *eb* ffeiliau hanner crwn
half round moulding mowldin hanner crwn *eg* mowldinau hanner crwn
half round rasp rhathell hanner crwn *eb* rhathellau hanner crwn
half round scraper sgrafell hanner crwn *eb* sgrafelli hanner crwn
half section hanner trychiad *eg* hanner trychiadau
half size hanner maint llawn *eg*
half time hanner amser *eg*
half turn hanner tro *eg* hanner troeon
half value period cyfnod hanner actifedd *eg*
half-adder hanner adydd *eg* hanner adyddion
half-back (female) hanerwraig *eb* hanerwragedd
half-back (male) hanerwr *eg* hanerwyr
half-bound hanner rhwym *ans*
half-day hanner diwrnod *eg*
half-drop pattern patrwm hanner disgyn *eg* patrymau hanner disgyn
half-duplex hanner dwplecs *eg* hanner dwplecsau
half-kneeling penlinio un glin *be*
half-lap joint goruniad hanerog *eg* goruniadau hanerog
half-length hanner hyd *eg*
half-length portrait portread hanner hyd *eg* portreadau hanner hyd
half-life hanner oes *eg*
half-mask hanner masg *eg* hanner masgiau
half-recessed join uniad hanner cilannog *eg* uniadau hanner cilannog
half-ripping hanner rhwygo *be*
half-sectional hanner trychiadol *ans*
half-sectional elevation golwg hanner trychiadol *eg* golygon hanner trychiadol
half-sectional end elevation ochrolwg hanner trychiadol *eg* ochrolygon hanner trychiadol

half-sectional front elevation blaenolwg hanner trychiadol *eg* blaenolygon hanner trychiadol
half-sectional plan uwcholwg hanner trychiadol *eg* uwcholygon hanner trychiadol
half-sectional side elevation ochrolwg hanner trychiadol *eg* ochrolygon hanner trychiadol
half-sectional view golwg hanner trychiadol *eg* golygon hanner trychiadol
half-space key bysell hanner bwlch *eb* bysellau hanner bwlch
half-term hanner tymor *eg*
half-timber trawst bras wedi'i haneru *eg* trawstiau bras wedi'u haneru
half-tone hanner tôn *eg* hanner tonau
half-volley hanner foli *eg*
half-wave hanner ton *eb* hanner tonnau
half-wave rectified power supply cyflenwad pŵer gydag unioniad hanner ton *eg*
half-wave rectifier meter mesurydd unioni hanner ton *eg*
halfway line llinell hanner *eb* llinellau hanner
halide halid *eg* halidau
halitosis halitosis *eg*
Hall effect proximity switch switsh agosrwydd effaith Hall *eg*
hall mark nod gwarant *eg* nodau gwarant
Hall probe chwiliwr Hall *eg*
Hall voltage foltedd Hall *eg*
hallmote halmwd *eg*
hallucinate gweld rhithiau *be*
hallucination rhithweledigaeth *eb* rhithweledigaethau
halo (of moon) lleugylch *eg* lleugylchoedd
halo (of saint) eurgylch *eg* eurgylchoedd
halogen halogen *eg* halogenau
halogenated halogenaidd *ans*
halogenation halogeniad *eg*
halogenoalkane halogenoalcan *eg*
halogeno-compound cyfansoddyn halogenaidd *eg* cyfansoddion halogenaidd
halophobe haloffob *eg* haloffobau
halophyte haloffyt *eg* haloffytau
halophytic haloffytig *ans*
halt *n* ataliad *eg* ataliadau
halt *v* atal *be*
halter neck gwddf tennyn *eg* gyddfau tennyn
halter top top tennyn *eg* topiau tennyn
halve haneru *be*
halving joint uniad haneru *eg* uniadau haneru
hamlet pentrefan *eg* pentrefannau
hammer *n* morthwyl *eg* morthwylion
hammer *v* morthwylio *be*
hammer beam trawst gordd *eg* trawstiau gordd
hammer beam roof to trawst gordd *eg* toeon trawst gordd
hammer drill dril morthwyl *eg* driliau morthwyl
hammer handle coes morthwyl *eb* coesau morthwylion
hammer mark marc morthwyl *eg* marciau morthwyl
hammer part rhan morthwyl *eb* rhannau morthwyl
hammer stone carreg forthwylio *eb* cerrig morthwylio
hammer-head tenon tyno pen morthwyl *eg* tynoau pen morthwyl
Hamming code cod Hamming *eg*
hand llaw *eb* dwylo
hand axe bwyell law *eb* bwyeill llaw
hand ball pêl law *eb* peli llaw
hand basin basn ymolchi *eb* basnau ymolchi
hand cards cardiau gwlân *ell*
hand drawn lettering llythrennu â llaw *be*
hand drill dril llaw *eg* driliau llaw
hand embroidery brodwaith llaw *eg*
hand file ffeil law *eb* ffeiliau llaw
hand flat file ffeil law fflat *eb* ffeiliau llaw fflat
hand hot (water) gwres llaw *ans*
hand jam clo llaw *eg* cloeon llaw
hand lens chwyddwydr *eg* chwyddwydrau
hand loom gwŷdd llaw *eg* gwyddau llaw
hand machine peiriant llaw *eg* peiriannau llaw
hand made o waith llaw *ans*
hand made buttonhole twll botwm llaw *eg* tyllau botymau llaw
hand off hwp llaw *eg*
hand organ organ law *eb* organau llaw
hand painting (of painted picture) paentiad llaw *eg* paentiadau llaw
hand painting (of process or art) peintio llaw *be*
hand puppet pyped llaw *eg* pypedau llaw
hand rail canllaw *eg/b* canllawiau
hand reamer agorell law *eb* agorellau llaw
hand saw llawlif *eb* llawlifiau
hand scraper sgrafell law *eb* sgrafelli llaw
hand screw sgriw law *eb* sgriwiau llaw
hand sketch braslun llaw *eg* brasluniau llaw
hand taper tapr llaw *eg* taprau llaw
hand tools offer llaw *ell*
hand vice feis law *eb* feisiau llaw
hand walking llaw gerdded *be*
hand washable golchadwy â llaw *ans*
hand wrench tyndro llaw *eg* tyndroeon llaw
handbag bag llaw *eg* bagiau llaw
handbill hysbyslen fach *eb* hysbyslenni bach
handbook llawlyfr *eg* llawlyfrau
hand-breadth (=4 inches) dyrnfedd *eg* dyrnfeddi
handedness llawdueddiad *eg*
hand-eye coordination cydsymud llaw a llygad *eg*
hand-held cup anemometer anemomedr llaw *eg* anemomedrau llaw
handicap anfantais *eb* anfanteision
handicapped child plentyn dan anfantais *eg* plant dan anfantais
handicraft gwaith llaw *eg*
hand-in (=server) serfiwr *eg* serfwyr
handkerchief hances *eg/b* hancesi
handle (data, goods, ball etc) *v* trafod *be*

eg/b enw gwrywaidd/benywaidd, *masculine/feminine noun* ***ell*** enw lluosog, *plural noun* ***v*** berf, *verb* ***n*** enw, *noun* ► wedi newid, *changed*

handle (of bat, brush, hammer, saucepan etc) *n* coes *eb* coesau
handle (of jug, cup etc) *n* dolen *eb* dolennau
handle (of knife, screwdriver etc) *n* carn *eg* carnau
handle (on computer graphics) *n* dolen *eb* dolennau
handle cane gwialen ddolen *eb* gwialennau dolenni
handle head pen coes *eg* pennau coesau
handle the ball (when it's an offence) llawio'r bêl *be*
handling (=discussion) ymdriniaeth *eb* ymdriniaethau
handling (=treatment) triniaeth *eb* triniaethau
handling (of ball in sport) llawio *be*
handling errors (of the ball in sport) camdrafod *be*
handlist llawrestr *eb* llawrestri
hand-operated gweithredu â llaw *ans*
hand-out dalen hysbysebu *eb* dalennau hysbysebu
handout taflen *eb* taflenni
hands across (in dancing) seren *eb* sêr
hands four cylch pedwar *eg*
hands three cylch tri pedwar *eg*
hands! (in sport) llaw!
handset set law *eb* setiau llaw
hands-free heb ddwylo *ans*
hand-shaking ysgwyd llaw *be*
handsign (for pitch) arwydd llaw *eg* arwyddion llaw
hands-on ymarferol *ans*
handspring sbring llaw *eg* sbringiau llaw
handstand *n* llawsafiad *eg* llawsafiadau
handstand *v* llawsefyll *be*
handwork gwaith llaw *eg*
handwriting llawysgrifen *eb*
hang *v* hongian *be*
hang (a person etc) crogi *be*
hang, draw and quarter crogi, diberfeddu a phedrannu
hanger (for hanging clothes) cambren *eg/b* cambrenni
hanger (of tapestry etc) hongiwr *eg* hongwyr
hanging *adj* crog *ans*
hanging bowl powlen grog *eb* powlenni crog
hanging carcass sgerbwd crog *eg* sgerbydau crog
hanging end pen crog *eg* pennau crog
hanging garden gardd grog *eb* gerddi crog
hanging indent mewnoliad crog *eg* mewnoliadau crog
hanging loop dolen grog *eb* dolennau crog
hanging paragraph paragraff crog *eg* paragraffau crog
hanging stile cledren hongian *eb* cledrau hongian
hanging valley crognant *eb* crognentydd
hanging wall crogfur *eg* crogfuriau
hank twysgen *eg* twysgenni
Hanoverian succession olyniaeth Hanoferaidd *eb*
Hanseatic cities dinasoedd Hansa *ell*
Hanseatic League Cynghrair Hansa *eb*
haploid haploid *ans*
haploidy haploidi *eg*
Hapsburg *adj* Hapsbwrgaidd *ans*
Hapsburg *n* Hapsbwrg *eg* Hapsbwrgiaid
Hapsburg empire ymerodraeth Hapsbwrgaidd *eb*
harbour harbwr *eg*
hard caled *ans*
hard copy copi caled *eg* copïau caled
hard cover clawr caled *eg* cloriau caled
hard disk disg caled *eg* disgiau caled
hard flooring llawr caled *eg* lloriau caled
hard landscaping tirlunio caled *be*
hard news newyddion caled *ell*
hard return dychweliad caled *eg* dychweliadau caled
hard rock craig galed *eb* creigiau caled
hard sectored sectoriad caled *eg*
hard silver solder sodr arian caled *eg*
hard soap sebon caled *eg*
hard solder sodr caled *eg*
hard space bwlch caled *eg* bylchau caled
hard water dŵr caled *eg*
hard wired gwifredig *ans*
hardboard caledfwrdd *eg*
hardboard plane plaen caledfwrdd *eg* plaeniau caledfwrdd
hardcore craidd caled *eg*
harden caledu *be*
hardener caledwr *eg* caledwyr
hardening and tempering caledu a thymheru
hardening hammer morthwyl caledu *eg*
hardening material defnydd caledu *eg* defnyddiau caledu
hardie cŷn eingion *eg* cynion eingion; gaing eingion *eb* geingiau eingion
hardie hole twll offer *eg* tyllau offer
hardiest tree coeden wytnaf *eb* coed gwytnaf
hardiness gwydnwch *eg*
hardness caledwch *eg*
hardness of water caledwch dŵr *eg*
hardness scale graddfa galedwch *eb* graddfeydd caledwch
hardness test prawf caledwch *eg* profion caledwch
hardpan cletir *eg* cletiroedd
hardware (of computers) caledwedd *eg/b*
hardware shop siop nwyddau metel *eb* siopau nwyddau metel
hardwearing yn gwisgo'n dda *adf*
hardwood pren caled *eg* prennau caled
hardwood cell cell pren caled *eb* celloedd pren caled
hardwood fillet ffiled pren caled *eb* ffiledau pren caled
hardwood mallet gordd pren caled *eb* gyrdd pren caled
hardwood wedging lletemu pren caled *be*
hardy personality personoliaeth wydn *eb*
haricot beans ffa haricot *ell*
Harijan Harijan *ell*
Harimandir Sahib Harimandir Sahib *eb*
harmattan harmatan *eg*
harmful niweidiol *ans*

harmful bacteria bacteria niweidiol *ell*
harmonic *adj* harmonig *ans*
harmonic *n* harmonig *eg* harmonigau
harmonic chromatic scale graddfa gromatig harmonig *eb* graddfeydd cromatig harmonig
harmonic colour lliw harmonig *eg* lliwiau harmonig
harmonic interval cyfwng harmonig *eg* cyfyngau harmonig
harmonic mean cymedr harmonig *eg* cymedrau harmonig
harmonic minor scale graddfa leiaf harmonig *eb* graddfeydd lleiaf harmonig
harmonic motion mudiant harmonig *eg*
harmonic movement rhediad harmonig *eg* rhediadau harmonig
harmonic proportion cyfrannedd harmonig *eg* cyfraneddau harmonig
harmonic sequence dilyniant harmonig *eg* dilyniannau harmonig
harmonic series cyfres harmonig *eb* cyfresi harmonig
harmonica harmonica *eg* harmonicâu
harmonious cydseiniol *ans*
harmonious colour lliw cydnaws *eg* lliwiau cydnaws
harmonium harmoniwm *eg* harmonia
harmonium player harmonydd *eg* harmonyddion
harmonize harmoneiddio *be*
harmony (figurative sense) cytgord *eg*
harmony (in music) harmoni *eg* harmonïau
harp telyn *eb* telynau
harp stop stop telyn *eg* stopiau telyn
harpist (female) telynores *eb* telynoresau
harpist (male) telynor *eg* telynorion
harpsichord harpsicord *eg* harpsicordiau
harvest cynhaeaf *eg* cynaeafau
harvest moon lleuad fedi *eb*
harvest service cyfarfod diolchgarwch *eg* cyfarfodydd diolchgarwch
harvest thanksgiving diolch am y cynhaeaf *be*
hash (in general) stwnsh *eg*
hash (of # symbol) clwyd *eb* clwydi
hash character nod clwyd *eg* nodau clwyd
▸ **hash symbol** symbol clwyd *eg* symbolau clwyd
hash table tabl stwnsh *eg* tablau stwnsh
hash total cyfanswm stwnsh *eg* cyfansymiau stwnsh
hashed random file organization trefn hap-ffeil stwnshlyd *eb*
hashing stwnsio *be*
hashing algorithm algorithm stwnsio *eg*
hasp and staple hasb a stwffwl hasbiau a styffylau
hatch (=mark with lines) *v* lliniogi *be*
hatch (for serving) *n* agoriad gweini *eg* agoriadau gweini
hatch (of egg) *v* deor *be*
hatchery deorfa *eb* deorfeydd
hatchet bwyell *eb* bwyeill
hatchet bit haearn sodro bwyell *eg* heyrn sodro bwyell
hatchet stake bonyn ongl lem *eg* bonion ongl lem
hauberk llurig *eb* llurigau
haulage cludiant *eg*
haulage contractor cludwr nwyddau *eg* cludwyr nwyddau
haulier halier *eg* halwyr
haunch *v* hansio *be*
haunched mortise and tenon mortais a thyno hansiedig
haunched mortise and tenon joint uniad mortais a thyno hansiedig *eg* uniadau mortais a thyno hansiedig
haunched tenon tyno hansiedig *eg* tynoau hansiedig
haustorium hawstoriwm *eg* hawstoria
haven hafan *eb* hafanau
Haversian canal sianel Havers *eb* sianeli Havers
Haversian space gwagle Havers *eg* gwagleoedd Havers
hawking heboga *be*
hawthorn draenen wen *eb* drain gwynion
Hawthorne effect effaith Hawthorne *eb*
hay infusion trwyth gwair *eg*
haybote perthfudd *eg*
hayward caegeidwad *eg* caegeidwaid
hazard perygl *eg* peryglon
hazardous substance sylwedd peryglus *eg*
haze (atmospheric pollution etc) tawch *eg*
haze (depth perception) tarth *eg*
head (in general) pen *eg* pennau
head (in geology) wynebyn *eg* wynebynnau
head boy prif fachgen *eg* prif fechgyn
head girl prif ferch *eb* prif ferched
head injury anaf i'r pen *eg* anafiadau i'r pen
head motif motiff pen *eg* motiffau pen
head movement symudiad y pen *eg* symudiadau'r pen
head of department pennaeth adran *eg* penaethiaid adran
▸ **head of faculty** pennaeth cyfadran *eg* penaethiaid cyfadrannau
head of lower school pennaeth yr ysgol isaf *eg* penaethiaid ysgolion isaf
head of middle school pennaeth yr ysgol ganol *eg* penaethiaid ysgolion canol
head of navigation terfyn mordwyo *eg* terfynau mordwyo
head of subject pennaeth pwnc *eg* penaethiaid pwnc
head of upper school pennaeth yr ysgol uchaf *eg* penaethiaid ysgolion uchaf
head of year pennaeth blwyddyn *eg* penaethiaid blwyddyn
head office prif swyddfa *eb* prif swyddfeydd
head register llais y pen *eg*
head the ball penio'r bêl *be*
head voice llais y pen *eg*
head wall recession enciliad cefnfur *eg*
head wear gwisg pen *eb* gwisgoedd pen
headache cur pen *eg*
header (of ball) peniad *eg* peniadau

header (on paper) pennyn *eg* penynnau
header and footer pennyn a throedyn
header left pennyn chwith *eg* penynnau chwith
header on (in football) peniad ymlaen *eg*
header right pennyn de *eg* penynnau de
header tape blaen-dâp *eg* blaen-dapiau
headers and footers penynnau a throedynnau *ell*
heading pennawd *eg* penawdau
headland pentir *eg* pentiroedd
headline pennawd *eg* penawdau
headmaster prifathro *eg* prifathrawon
headmistress prifathrawes *eb* prifathrawesau
head-on ben-ben
headphone ffôn pen *eg* ffonau pen
headphones clustffonau *ell*
headquarters pencadlys *eg* pencadlysoedd
Heads of Proposals Pennau'r Awgrymiadau *ell*
headslide penlithryn *eg* penlithrynnau
headspring sbring pen *eg* sbringiau pen
headstand *n* pensafiad *eg* pensafiadau
headstand *v* pensefyll *be*
headstock (of lathe) pen byw *eg* pennau byw
headstock centre canol tro *eg* canolau tro
headteacher pennaeth ysgol *eg* penaethiaid ysgolion
headward erosion blaen erydu *be*
headwater blaenddwr *eg* blaenddyfroedd
headword prif air *eg* prif eiriau
heal gwella *be*
health iechyd *eg*
Health & Morals of Apprentices Act Deddf Iechyd a Moesau Prentisiaid *eb*
health action process approach dull proses gweithredu iechyd *eg*
health and fitness officer swyddog iechyd a ffitrwydd *eg* swyddogion iechyd a ffitrwydd
health and safety iechyd a diogelwch
Health And Safety at Work Act Deddf Iechyd a Diogelwch yn y Gwaith *eb*
health and safety legislation deddfwriaeth iechyd a diogelwch *eb*
health and safety officer swyddog iechyd a diogelwch *eg* swyddogion iechyd a diogelwch
health and social care iechyd a gofal cymdeithasol *eg*
health and social care setting sefyllfa iechyd a gofal cymdeithasol *eb*
health authority awdurdod iechyd *eg* awdurdodau iechyd
health belief model model cred iechyd *eg*
health care assistant cynorthwyydd gofal iechyd *eg* cynorthwywyr gofal iechyd
health care provider darparwr gofal iechyd *eg* darparwyr gofal iechyd
health care purchaser prynwr gofal iechyd *eg* prynwyr gofal iechyd
health care support worker gweithiwr cynnal gofal iechyd *eg* gweithwyr cynnal gofal iechyd
health care system cyfundrefn gofal iechyd *eb* cyfundrefnau gofal iechyd
health centre canolfan iechyd *eb* canolfannau iechyd
health club clwb iechyd *eg* clybiau iechyd
health education addysg iechyd *eb*
health education authority awdurdod addysg iechyd *eg*
Health Education Council Cyngor Addysg Iechyd *eg*
health improvement gwella iechyd *be*
health improvement plan cynllun gwella iechyd *eg* cynlluniau gwella iechyd
Health Improvement Programmes Rhaglenni Gwella Iechyd *ell*
health index mynegai iechyd *eg*
health maintenance cynnal iechyd *be*
health promotion hybu iechyd *be*
health promotion activity gweithgaredd hybu iechyd *eg*
Health Promotion Authority for Wales Awdurdod Hybu Iechyd Cymru *eg*
health promotion campaign ymgyrch hybu iechyd *eb* ymgyrchoedd hybu iechyd
health promotion material deunydd hybu iechyd *eg*
Health Promotion Wales Hybu Iechyd Cymru *be*
health psychology seicoleg iechyd *eb*
health risk perygl iechyd *eg* peryglon iechyd
health screening sgrinio iechyd *be*
health service gwasanaeth iechyd *eg* gwasanaethau iechyd
health status statws iechyd *eg*
health team tîm iechyd *eg* timau iechyd
health visitor ymwelydd iechyd *eg* ymwelwyr iechyd
health-related exercise ymarfer cysylltiedig ag iechyd *eg* ymarferion cysylltiedig ag iechyd
healthy iach *ans*
healthy diet deiet iachus
healthy lifestyle ffordd iach o fyw *eb* ffyrdd iach o fyw
healthy plate plât o fwyd iachus *eg*
hearing (=ability to hear) clyw *eg*
hearing (of a case) gwrandawiad *eg* gwrandawiadau
hearing aid teclyn clywed *eg* teclynnau clywed
hearing loss colli clyw *be*
heart calon *eb* calonnau
heart attack trawiad ar y galon *eg*
heartbeat curiad calon *eg*
heart disease clefyd y galon *eg* clefydau'r galon
heart failure methiant y galon *eg*
heart murmur murmur y galon *eg*
heart rate cyfradd curiad y galon *eb*
heart rate training zone cylchfa ymarfer cyfradd curiad y galon *eb*
heart shake hollt calon *eg* holltau calon
heart sounds synau'r galon *ell*
heartbeat curiad calon *eg*
hearth aelwyd *eb* aelwydydd
hearth body corff yr aelwyd *eg*
hearth tax treth aelwyd *eb*
hearth trowel trywel aelwyd *eb* trywelion aelwyd

heartland perfeddwlad *eb* perfeddwledydd
heartwood rhuddin *eg*
heat *v* gwresogi *be*
heat (=condition of being hot) *n* gwres *eg*
heat (=preliminary race) *n* rhagras *eb* rhagrasys
heat and energy foods bwydydd gwres ac egni *ell*
heat capacity cynhwysedd gwres *eg* cynwyseddau gwres
heat haze tes *eg*
heat of combustion gwres hylosgi *eg*
heat of formation gwres ffurfio *eg*
heat of neutralisation gwres niwtralu *eg*
heat of reaction gwres adweithio *eg*
heat of vaporization gwres anweddu *eg*
heat resistant gwrthiannol i wres *ans*
heat sink suddfan gwres *eg*
heat treatment triniaeth wres *eb*
heater gwresogydd *eg* gwresogyddion
heater circuit cylched wresogi *eb* cylchedau gwresogi
heater current cerrynt gwresogi *eg* ceryntau gwresogi
heath rhos *eb* rhosydd
heathland rhostir *eg* rhostiroedd
heating element elfen wresogi *eb* elfennau gwresogi
heat-resisting varnish farnais gwrth-wres *eg*
heatstroke trawiad gwres *eg* trawiadau gwres
heatwave ton wres *eb* tonnau gwres
heave (a rope) *v* halio *be*
heave (in geological fault) *n* gwthiad *eg* gwthiadau
heave (of rope) *n* haliad *eg* haliadau
heave (on a bar) *n* ymgodiad *eg* ymgodiadau
heave (on a bar) *v* ymgodi *be*
heave hanging hongian halio *be*
heave swing swing ymhalio *eg* swingiau ymhalio
heaven (in religious sense) nefoedd *eb*
heavenly body corff wybrennol *eg* cyrff wybrennol
heavens (=sky) wybren *eb* wybrennau
heavy trwm *ans*
heavy colour lliw trwm *eg* lliwiau trwm
heavy damping gwanychiad trwm *eg*
heavy duty detergent glanedydd cryf *eg* glanedyddion cryf
heavy duty drilling machine peiriant drilio gwaith trwm *eg* peiriannau drilio gwaith trwm
heavy impasto impasto trwm *eg*
heavy industry diwydiant trwm *eg* diwydiannau trwm
heavy metal metel trwm *eg* metelau trwm
heavy oil olew trwchus *eg*
heavy water dŵr trwm *eg*
heavy weight pwysau trwm *ell*
Hebrew (language) Hebraeg *eb*
hectare hectar *eg* hectarau
heddle brwyd *eg* brwydau
hedge perth *eb* perthi
hedonic calculus calcwlws hedonig *eg*
hedonic relevance perthnasedd hedonig *eg*
heel *n* sawdl *eg/b* sodlau
heel *v* sodli *be*
heel and toe step step sawdl a bawd *eb* stepiau sawdl a bawd
heel clearance cliriad sawdl *eg*
heel of a bow sawdl bwa *eb* sodlau bwâu
heel of glove sawdl y faneg *eb* sodlau menig
heelball cwyr rhwbio *eg*
hegemony penarglwyddiaeth *eb*
height (=elevation) uchder *eg* uchderau
height (of person) taldra *eg*
height /time graph graff uchder /amser *eg*
height adjusting nut nyten gymhwyso uchder *eb* nytiau cymhwyso uchder
height gauge medrydd uchder *eg* medryddion uchder
heights are to the nearest metre above mean sea level uchderau i'r metr agosaf uwchlaw lefel y môr cymedrig
heir etifedd *eg* etifeddion
heir apparent edling *eg* edlingod
heir presumptive etifedd tebygol *eg* etifeddion tebygol
helical heligol *ans*
helical flute ffliwt heligol *eb* ffliwtiau heligol
helical path llwybr heligol *eg* llwybrau heligol
helical spring sbring heligol *eg* sbringiau heligol
helical thread edau heligol *eb* edafedd heligol
helicoid helicoid *eg* helicoidau
helicoidal helicoidol *ans*
helicopter hofrennydd *eg* hofrenyddion
heliotropic heliotropig *ans*
heliotropism heliotropedd *eg*
heliport maes hofrenyddion *eg*
helium (He) heliwm *eg*
helix helics *eg* helicsau
helix angle ongl helics *eb* onglau helics
helix clearance cliriad helics *eg* cliriadau helics
hell uffern *eb*
Hellenic Helenaidd *ans*
helm roof to helm *eg* toeon helm
helmet helm *eg* helmau
helmsman llywiwr *eg* llywyr
help cymorth *eg*
help channel sianel cymorth *eb* sianeli cymorth
help content cynnwys cymorth *eg*
help file ffeil cymorth *eb* ffeiliau cymorth
help file name enw ffeil cymorth *eg* enwau ffeiliau cymorth
help index mynegai cymorth *eg* mynegeion cymorth
help information gwybodaeth cymorth *eb*
help menu dewislen cymorth *eb* dewislenni cymorth
help on help cymorth ar gymorth
help system system cymorth *eb* systemau cymorth
help text testun cymorth *eg* testunau cymorth
helplessness diymadferthedd *eg*
Helvetic Helfetig *ans*

hem *n* hem *eb* hemiau
hem *v* hemio *be*
hem allowance lwfans hem *eg* lwfansau hem
hem depth lled hem *eg* lledau hem
hem finish gorffeniad hem *eg* gorffeniadau hem
hem line llinell hem *eb* llinellau hem
hem marker marciwr hem *eg* marcwyr hem
hem stitch pwyth hemio *eg* pwythau hemio
hem stitching hembwytho *be*
hemicellulose hemicellwlos *eg*
hemiparesis lled-barlys un ochr *eg*
hemiplegia parlys un ochr *eg*
hemisphere hemisffer *eg* hemisfferau
hemispherical bowl bowlen hemisffer *eb* bowlenni hemisffer
hemispherical shell cragen hemisffer *eb* cregyn hemisffer
hemmer (machine attachment) hemell *eb* hemelli
hemp cywarch *eg*
hemp twine cortyn cywarch *eg* cortynnau cywarch
henge cylch pridd *eg* cylchoedd pridd
Henle's loop dolen Henle *eb*
henotheism henotheistiaeth *eb*
Henrician Reformation, The Diwygiad Harri VIII *eg*
Henry the Lion Harri'r Llew *eg*
Henry the Navigator Harri'r Mordwywr *eg*
Henry Tudor Harri Tudur *eg*
Henry VII Harri VII *eg*
Henry VIII Harri VIII *eg*
hepatic portal vein gwythïen bortal hepatig *eb* gwythiennau portal hepatig
hepatic vein gwythïen hepatig *eb*
hepatitis hepatitis *eg*
heptagon heptagon *eg* heptagonau
heptagonal heptagonal *ans*
heptaoxodiphosphate(V) ion ïon heptaocsodeuffosffad(V) *eg* ïonau heptaocsodeuffosffad(V)
Her Majesty's Inspectorate (HMI) Arolygiaeth ei Mawrhydi *eb*
herald herodr *eg* herodrau
heraldic herodrol *ans*
heraldic banner lluman herodrol *eg/b* llumanau herodrol
heraldic bard arwyddfardd *eg* arwyddfeirdd
heraldic colour lliw herodrol *eg* lliwiau herodrol
heraldic lettering llythrennu herodrol *be*
heraldic purse pwrs herodrol *eg* pyrsiau herodrol
heraldry herodraeth *eb*
herb llysieuyn *eg* llysiau
herbaceous llysieuol *ans*
herbal (book) llysieulyfr *eg*
herbarium herbariwm *eg*
herbicide chwynladdwr *eg* chwynladdwyr
herbivore llysysydd *eg* llysysyddion
herbivorous llysysol *ans*
herd (of cattle) gyr *eg* gyrroedd
herd (of dairy cows) buches *eb* buchesau
herd immunity imiwnedd poblogaeth *eg*
hereditament etifeddiant *eg* etifeddiannau
hereditary etifeddol *ans*
hereditary fief ffiff etifeddol *eb* ffiffiau etifeddol
hereditary monarchy brenhiniaeth etifeddol *eb* breniniaethau etifeddol
heredity etifeddeg *eb*
heresy heresi *eb* heresïau
Heresy Act Deddf Heresi *eb*
heretic heretic *eg* hereticiaid
heretical hereticaidd *ans*
Hereward the Wake Hereward Effro *eg*
heriot ebediw *eg* ebediwiau
heritage etifeddiaeth *eb*
hermaphrodite *n* deurywiad *eg* deurywiaid
hermaphroditic deurywiol *ans*
hermaphroditism deurywiaeth *eb*
hermetically sealed cwbl seliedig *ans*
hermit meudwy *eg* meudwyiaid
hermitage cell meudwy *eb* celloedd meudwy
hero arwr *eg* arwyr
heroic society cymdeithas arwrol *eb* cymdeithasau arwrol
herpes herpes *eg*
herring bone strut cynheiliad saethben *eg* cynheiliaid saethben
herring-bone banding bandin saethben *eg* bandinau saethben
herring-bone pattern patrwm saethben *eg* patrymau saethben
herring-bone stitch pwyth saethben *eg* pwythau saethben
herring-bone weave gwehyddiad saethben *eg* gwehyddiadau saethben
hertz (Hz) herts *eg*
hessian hesian *eg*
heterodyne heterodein *eg* heterodeiniau
heterogametic heterogametaidd *ans*
heterogeneity heterogenedd *eg*
heterogeneous heterogenaidd *ans*
heterolytic fission ymholltiad heterolytig *eg*
heterophony heteroffoni *eg*
heterosexual heterorywiol *ans*
heterosporous heterosboraidd *ans*
heterospory heterosboredd *eg*
heterostyly heterostyledd *eg*
heterotroph heterotroff *eg* heterotroffau
heterozygous heterosygaidd *ans*
heuristic hewristig *ans*
heuristic play chwarae hewristig *eg*
heuristic program rhaglen hewristig *eb* rhaglenni hewristig
heuristic proof prawf hewristig *eg* profion hewristig
hex hecs *ell*
hex digit digid hecs *eg* digidau hecs
hexaaquaaluminium ion ïon hecsaacwaalwminiwm *eg* ïonau hecsaacwaalwminiwm

hexaaquaaluminium(III) ion
ïon hecsaacwaalwminiwm(III) *eg*
ïonau hecsaacwaalwminiwm(III)
hexaaquacopper(II) ion ïon hecsaacwacopr(II) *eg*
ïonau hecsaacwacopr(II)
1,2,3,4,5,6-hexachlorocyclohexane
1,2,3,4,5,6-hecsaclorocylchohecsan *eg*
hexachloroplatinate(IV) ion
ïon hecsacloroplatinad(IV) *eg*
ïonau hecsacloroplatinad(IV)
hexachloroplumbate(IV) ion
ïon hecsacloroplwmbad(IV) *eg*
ïonau hecsacloroplwmbad(IV)
hexachlorostannate(IV) ion
ïon hecsaclorostanad(IV) *eg*
ïonau hecsaclorostanad(IV)
hexacyanocobaltate(III) ion
ïon hecsacyanocobaltad(III) *eg*
ïonau hecsacyanocobaltad(III)
hexacyanoferrate ion ïon hecsacyanofferad *eg*
ïonau hecsacyanofferad
hexacyanoferrate(II) ion ïon hecsacyanofferad(II) *eg*
ïonau hecsacyanofferad(II)
hexacyanoferrate(III) ion
ïon hecsacyanofferad(III) *eg*
ïonau hecsacyanofferad(III)
hexadecanoic acid asid hecsadecanöig *eg*
hexadecan-1-ol hecsadecan-1-ol *eg*
hexadecimal hecsadegol *ans*
hexadecimal counting system
system rifo hecsadegol *eb*
hexadecimal notation nodiant hecsadegol *eg*
hexafluoroaluminate(III) ion
ïon hecsafflworoalwminad(III) *eg*
ïonau hecsafflworoalwminad(III)
hexafluorosilicate(IV) ion
ïon hecsafflworosilicad(IV) *eg*
ïonau hecsafflworosilicad(IV)
hexagon hecsagon *eg* hecsagonau
hexagonal hecsagonol *ans*
hexagonal close-packing pacio tyn hecsagonol
hexagonal head bolt bollt ben hecsagonol *eb*
bolltau pen hecsagonol
hexagonal head screw sgriw ben hecsagonol *eb*
sgriwiau pen hecsagonol
hexagonal nut nyten hecsagonol *eb*
nytiau hecsagonol
hexagonal prism prism hecsagonol *eg*
prismau hecsagonol
hexagonal pyramid pyramid hecsagonol *eg*
pyramidiau hecsagonol
hexagonal section material defnydd trychiad hecsagonol *eg* defnyddiau trychiad hecsagonol
hexahedron hecsahedron *eg* hecsahedronau
hexamethylene tetramine
hecsamethylen tetramin *eg*
hexane hecsan *eg*
hexane-1,6-diamine hecsan-1,6-deuamin *eg*
hexanedioic acid asid hecsandeuöig *eg*
hexanedioyl dichloride hecsandeuoyl deuclorid *eg*
hexanitrocobaltate(III) ion
ïon hecsanitrocobaltad(III) *eg*
ïonau hecsanitrocobaltad(III)
hexanoic acid asid hecsanöig *eg*
hexaoxoiodic(VII) acid asid hecsaocsoïodig(VII) *eg*
hexose hecsos *eg* hecsosau
hey hai *eg/b*
hey between hai traws *eg*
hey with your own hai unrhyw *eg*
hiatus bwlch *eg* bylchau
hibernate gaeafgysgu *be*
hibernation gaeafgwsg *eg*
hiccup igian *be*
hidden cudd *ans*
hidden control rheolydd cudd *eg* rheolyddion cudd
hidden costs costau cudd *ell*
hidden curriculum cwricwlwm cudd *eg*
hidden detail manylion cudd *ell*
hidden detail line llinell manylion cudd *eb*
llinellau manylion cudd
hidden eighth wythfed cudd *eg* wythfedau cudd
hidden fifth pumed cudd *eg* pumedau cudd
hidden instrument offeryn cudd *eg* offerynnau cudd
hidden line llinell gudd *eb* llinellau cudd
hidden paragraph paragraff cudd *eg*
paragraffau cudd
hidden slide sleid gudd *eb* sleidiau cudd
hidden text testun cudd *eg*
hide *v* cuddio *be*
hide (=camouflaged shelter) *n* cuddfan *eb*
cuddfannau
hide (=skin) *n* croen *eg* crwyn
hide all cuddio popeth *be*
hide author cuddio'r awdur *be*
hide autofilter cuddio awtohidlydd *be*
hide column cuddio colofn *be*
hide errors cuddio gwallau *be*
hide field cuddio maes *be*
hide fontwork outline
cuddio amlinell gwaith ffont *be*
hide formula cuddio fformiwla *be*
hide mallet gordd ledr *eb* gyrdd lledr
hide note cuddio nodyn *be*
hide picture cuddio llun *be*
hide rows cuddio rhesi *be*
hide sheet cuddio dalen *be*
hide subject cuddio pwnc *be*
hide subpoints cuddio isbwyntiau *be*
hide thread cuddio trywydd *be*
hide when printing cuddio wrth argraffu *be*
hierarchical hierarchaidd *ans*
hierarchical database cronfa ddata hierarchaidd *eb*
cronfeydd data hierarchaidd
hierarchical model model hierarchaidd *eg*
modelau hierarchaidd
hierarchical organisational structure
fframwaith rheoli hierarchaidd *eg*

Hierarchies of Throne Hierarchaethau Gorseddau *ell*
hierarchy hierarchaeth *eb* hierarchaethau
hierarchy of needs hierarchaeth anghenion *eb*
hierarchy of the courts hierarchaeth y llysoedd *eb*
hieroglyphic writing ysgrifen hieroglyffig *eb*
high uchel *ans*
high altar prif allor *eb* prif allorau
high ball pêl uchel *eb* peli uchel
high blood pressure pwysedd gwaed uchel*eb*
high carbon steel dur carbon uchel *eg*
high chair cadair uchel *be* cadeiriau uchel
High Church Uchel Eglwysig *ans*
high clarinet uwchglarinét *eg* uwchglarinetau
high class area ardal dosbarth uchaf *eb* ardaloedd dosbarth uchaf
high colour lliw uchel *eg*
High Commission Uchel Gomisiwn *eg*
High Constable Uchel Gwnstabl *eg*
High Court Uchel Lys *eg*
high density building adeiladu clos *be*
high dive deifio'n uchel *be*
high fidelity cywair-bur *ans*
high foaming detergent glanedydd llawndrochion *eg* glanedyddion llawndrochion
high forward roll rhôl uchel ymlaen *eb* rholiau uchel ymlaen
high frequency (of oscillations) amledd uchel *eg* amleddau uchel
high frequency induction furnace ffwrnais anwytho amledd uchel *eb* ffwrneisi anwytho amledd uchel
high jump naid uchel *eb* neidiau uchel
high level lefel uchel *eb* lefelau uchel
high limit terfan uchel *eb* terfannau uchel
high line llinell uchel *eb* llinellau uchel
high neck gwddf uchel *eg* gyddfau uchel
high place uchelfa *eb* uchelfeydd
high population density dwysedd poblogaeth uchel *eg* dwyseddau poblogaeth uchel
high pressure gwasgedd uchel *eg*
high pressure system system gwasgedd uchel *eb*
high register nodau uchel *ell*
high relief (=alto relievo) cerfwedd uchel *eb*
high Renaissance uchel Ddadeni *eg*
high resolution cydraniad uchel *ans*
high sales gwerthiant mawr *eg*
high sea cefnfor *eg* cefnforoedd
High Sheriff Uchel Siryf *eg* Uchel Siryfion
high spin amlsbin *ans*
high standard safon uchel *eb* safonau uchel
high street bank banc stryd fawr *eg* banciau stryd fawr
high tensile uchel dynnol *ans*
high tensile steel dur ucheldynnol *eg*
high tide llanw uchel *eg*
high treason uchel frad *eg*
high vacuum gwactod eithaf *eg*
high voltage foltedd uchel *eg*
high water penllanw *eg*
high water mark marc penllanw *eg* marciau penllanw
highboard llwyfan uchel *eg* llwyfannau uchel
higher uwch *ans*
higher clergy uwch glerigwyr *ell*
higher degree gradd uwch *eb* graddau uwch
higher education addysg uwch *eb*
higher order polynomial equation uwch-hafaliad polynomaidd *eg* uwch-hafaliadau polynomaidd
highest common factor ffactor gyffredin fwyaf *eb*
Highest Order Urdd Uchaf *eb*
highest point pwynt uchaf *eg* pwyntiau uchaf
highland ucheldir *eg* ucheldiroedd
Highland Clearances Cliriadau'r Ucheldiroedd *ell*
high-level language iaith lefel uchel *eb* ieithoedd lefel uchel
high-level programming language iaith rhaglennu lefel uchaf *eb*
highlight uchafbwynt *eg* uchafbwyntiau
highlight (=bring into prominence) amlygu *be*
highlight (=mark with a highlighter) lliwddangos *be*
highlight (in art) goleubwyntio *be*
highlight bar bar amlygu *eg* barrau amlygu
highlight changes amlygu newidiadau *be*
highlighter amlygwr *eg* amlygwyr
highlighting (in art) goleubwyntio *be*
highly skilled tra medrus *ans*
highly specialised tra arbenigol *ans*
high-order uwch-werth *ans*
high-quality colour image delwedd lliw ansawdd uchel *eb* delweddau lliw ansawdd uchel
high-speed bit ebill cyflym iawn *eg* ebillion cyflym iawn
high-speed drill dril cyflym iawn *eg* driliau cyflym iawn
highway priffordd *eb* priffyrdd
Highway Code Rheolau'r Ffordd Fawr *ell*
highwayman lleidr pen-ffordd *eg* lladron pen-ffordd
hijack herwgipio *be*
Hijra Hijra *eg*
hill bryn *eg* bryniau
hill country bryndir *eg* bryndiroedd
hill fog niwl mynydd *eg*
hill fort bryngaer *eb* bryngaerau
hill shading arlliwio llethrau *be*
hill station brynfa *eb* brynfeydd
hillock bryncyn *eg* bryncynnau
hilly bryniog *ans*
hilt carn *eg* cyrn
hilum hadgraith *eb* hadgreithiau
hind brain ôl-ymennydd *eg* ôl-ymenyddiau
hind gut ôl-berfeddyn *eg* ôl-berfedd
hind leg coes ôl *eb* coesau ôl
hind-milk armel *eg*

Hindu *adj* Hindŵaidd *ans*
Hindu *n* Hindŵ *eg* Hindŵiaid
Hinduism Hindŵaeth *eb*
hinge *n* colfach *eg* colfachau
hinge *v* colfachu *be*
hinge bracket braced colfach *eb* bracedi colfach
hinge knuckle cymal colfach *eg* cymalau colfach
hinge leaf dalen golfach *eb* dalennau colfach
hinge pin pin colfach *eg* pinnau colfach
hinge-bound clofach-glwm *ans*
hinged colfachog *ans*
hinged arm braich golfachog *eb* breichiau colfachog
hinterland cefnwlad *eb*
hip clun *eb* cluniau
hip carry cario wrth glun *be*
hip joint cymal y glun *eg* cymalau'r glun
hip line llinell glun *eb* llinellau cluniau
hip measurement mesuriad clun *eg* mesuriadau cluniau
hip rafter ceibr talcen *eg* ceibrau talcen
hip roof talcendo *eg* talcendoeon
hip roof rafter cwpl talcen *eg* cyplau talcen
hippocampus hipocampws *eg*
hire llogi *be*
hire-purchase *n* hurbwrcas *eg*
hire-purchase *v* hurbwrcasu *be*
hirsute blewog *ans*
His bundle sypyn His *eg* sypynnau His
histidine histidin *eg*
histogram histogram *eg* histogramau
histology histoleg *eb*
histone histon *eg* histonau
histopathology histopatholeg *eb*
historian hanesydd *eg* haneswyr
historical hanesyddol *ans*
historical data data hanesyddol *ell*
historical feature nodwedd hanesyddol *eb*
historical method dull yr hanesydd *eg*
historical period cyfnod hanesyddol *eg* cyfnodau hanesyddol
historical perspective persbectif hanesyddol *eg*
historical source ffynhonnell hanesyddol *eb* ffynonellau hanesyddol
historical theme thema hanesyddol *eb* themâu hanesyddol
historical topic topig hanesyddol *eg* topigau hanesyddol
historicism hanesiaeth *eb*
historicity hanesoldeb *eg*
historiographer (=authority on historiography) hanesyddiaethwr *eg* hanesyddiaethwyr
historiographer (=historian) hanesydd *eg* haneswyr
historiography hanesyddiaeth *eb*
history hanes *eg* hanesion
hit (=a stroke with a bat) *n* ergyd *eg/b* ergydion
hit (=reach a target) *v* taro *be*
hit (=strike with a bat) *v* ergydio *be*
hit (in general) *n* trawiad *eg* trawiadau
hit a boundary (for four runs) taro pedwar *be*
hit a boundary (for six runs) taro chwech *be*
hit back *n* trawiad nôl *eg* trawiadau nôl
hit back *v* taro nôl *be*
hit for six taro chwech *be*
hit rate cyfradd taro *eb* cyfraddau taro
hit the ball twice taro'r bêl eilwaith *be*
hit the target taro'r targed *be*
hit wicket taro'r wiced *be*
hitch clymu *be*
hi-tech technoleg uwch *eb*
hit-out *n* ergyd ochr *eb* ergydion ochr
hoar frost barrug *eg*; llwydrew *eg*
hoard celc *eg* celciau
hoarding (castle) oriel bren *eb* orielau pren
hob pentan *eg* pentanau
hobby hobi *eg* hobïau
hockey hoci *eg*
hodograph hodograff *eg* hodograffau
hogback hopgefn *eg* hopgefnau
hoghair brush brwsh blew mochyn *eg* brwshys blew mochyn
hoist *n* teclyn codi *eg* teclynnau codi
hoist *v* codi *be*
hold charges cadw'r un prisiau mynediad
holder daliwr *eg* dalwyr
holdfast (=clamp) dalbren *eg* dalbrennau
holdfast (of algae) gludafael *eg* gludafaelion
holding (of land, shares etc) daliad *eg* daliadau
holding device dyfais ddal *eb* dyfeisiau dal
holding hands cydio dwylo *be*
holding power (nails and screws) pwerddaliad *eg*
holding tools offer gafael *ell*
holding washer wasier gynnal *eb* wasieri cynnal
hole twll *eg* tyllau
hole in the heart twll yn y galon *eg*
hole saw llif dwll *eb* llifiau twll
Holi Holi *eg*
holiday brochure taflen wyliau *eb*
holiday camp gwersyll gwyliau *eg* gwersylloedd gwyliau
holiday centre canolfan wyliau *eb* canolfannau gwyliau
holiday insurance yswiriant gwyliau *eg*
holiday village pentref gwyliau *eg* pentrefi gwyliau
holidays gwyliau *ell*
holistic cyfannol *ans*
holistic model model cyfannol *eg*
hollow *v.intrans* pantio *be*
hollow *v.trans* cafnu *be*
hollow *adj* gwag *ans*
hollow *n* pant *eg* pantiau
hollow back somersault trosben ceugefn *eg* trosbennau ceugefn
hollow bit tongs gefel gegron *eb* gefeiliau cegrwn
hollow head pen cau *eg* pennau cau

hollow mandrel (lathe) mandrel cau *eg* mandreli cau
hollow moulding mowldin cau *eg* mowldinau cau
hollow plane plaen cafnu *eg* plaeniau cafnu
hollow saddle key allwedd gyfrwy cau *eb* allweddi cyfrwy cau
hollow set set gau *eb* setiau cau
hollow square bit tongs gefel gegsgwar *eb* gefeiliau cegsgwar
hollow tree coeden gau *eb* coed cau
hollow ware ceunwyddau *ell*
hollowing cafnu *be*
hollowing block bloc cafnu *eg* blociau cafnu
hollowing hammer morthwyl cafnu *eg* morthwylion cafnu
holmium (Ho) holmiwm *eg*
holocaust holocost *eg*
holomorphic holomorffig *ans*
holophytic holoffytig *ans*
holozoic holosöig *ans*
holy sanctaidd *ans*
Holy Alliance Cynghrair Sanctaidd *eb*
holy book llyfr bendigaid *eg* llyfrau bendigaid
holy communion cymun bendigaid *eg*
holy day dydd gŵyl *eg* dyddiau gŵyl
Holy Office Gwasanaeth Sanctaidd *eg*
Holy Orders Urddau Eglwysig *ell*
Holy Places Mannau Cysegredig *ell*
Holy Roman Emperor Ymerawdwr Rhufeinig Sanctaidd *eg*
Holy See Pabaeth *eb*
Holy Sepulchre Beddrod Sanctaidd *eg*
Holy Spirit Ysbryd Glân *eg*
Holy Week Wythnos y Pasg *eb*
homage gwrogaeth *eb*
home *n* cartref *eg* cartrefi
home *v* hafanu *be*
home army byddin gartref *eb* byddinoedd cartref
home background cefndir cartref *eg*
home button botwm cartref *eg*
home computer market marchnad y cyfrifiaduron cartref *eb*
home cured bacon cig moch cartref *eg*
home directory cyfeiriadur cartref *eg*
home economics economeg y cartref *eb*
home economist economegydd cartref *eg*
home education addysg gartref *eb*
home farm fferm y plas *eb* ffermydd plasau
home front ffrynt cartref *eg*
Home Guard Gwarchodlu Cartref *eg*
home help (person) cynorthwyydd cartref *eg* cynorthwywyr cartref
home help (service) cymorth cartref *eg*
home help organizer trefnydd cymorth cartref *eg* trefnyddion cymorth cartref
HOME key bysell HOME *eb* bysellau HOME
home key (of musical notes) cywair gwreiddiol *eg*
home market marchnad gartref *eb* marchnadoedd cartref
home ownership perchentyaeth *eb*
home page tudalen gartref *eb* tudalennau cartref
home rule ymreolaeth *eb*
home ruler ymreolwr *eg* ymreolwyr
home run rhediad adref *eg* rhediadau adref
home shopping siopa o'r cartref *be*
home tonic tonydd cysefin *eg*
home visit ymweliad cartref *eg* ymweliadau cartref
home worker gweithiwr cartref *eg* gweithwyr cartref
homebanking bancio cartref *be*
homegrown timber coed cartref *ell*
homegrown vegetables llysiau cartref *ell*
homeland mamwlad *eb* mamwledydd
homeless digartref *ans*
homelessness bod yn ddigartref *be*
home-made goods nwyddau cartref *ell*
homeopathy homeopathi *eg*
homeostasis homeostasis *eg*
homeostatic mechanism mecanwaith homeostatig *eg*
homeothermic homeothermig *ans*
homespun brethyn cartref *eg*
homestead tyddyn *eg* tyddynnod
homework gwaith cartref *eg*
homily homili *eb* homilïau
homocyclic homoseiclig *ans*
homogeneity homogenedd *eg*
homogeneous homogenaidd *ans*
homography homograffeg *eb*
homologous homologaidd *ans*
homologous series cyfres homologaidd *eb* cyfresi homologaidd
homologue homolog *eg* homologau
homology homoleg *eb*
homolytic fission ymholltiad homolytig *eg*
homomorphic homomorffig *ans*
homomorphism homomorffedd *eg* homomorffeddau
homophonic homoffonig *ans*
▶ **homosexual** cyfunrywiol *ans*
homosporous homosboraidd *ans*
homothetic homothetig *ans*
homozygous homosygaidd *ans*
hone hôn *eg* honau
hone *n* carreg hogi *eb* cerrig hogi
hone *v* hogi *be*
honest competition cystadlu gonest *be*
honey guide dynodyn mêl *eg* dynodion mêl
honeycomb diliau mêl *ell*
honeycomb smocking smocwaith crwybr *eg*
honeycomb stitch pwyth crwybr *eg* pwythau crwybr
honeycombed crwybrog *ans*
honeycombed door drws crwybr gwenyn *eg* drysau crwybr gwenyn
honeycombing crwybro *be*
honeysuckle pattern patrwm gwyddfid *eg* patrymau gwyddfid

adf, adv adferf, *adverb* ***ans, adj*** ansoddair, *adjective* ***be*** berf, *verb* ***eb*** enw benywaidd, *feminine noun* ***eg*** enw gwrywaidd, *masculine noun*

honing guide tywyswr hogi *eg* tywyswyr hogi
honorary degree gradd er anrhydedd *eb* graddau er anrhydedd
honour (in general) *n* anrhydedd *eb* anrhydeddau
honour (in general) *v* anrhydeddu *be*
honour (feudal) *n* arglwyddiaeth freiniol *eb*
honour system system anrhydedd *eb*
honours degree gradd anrhydedd *eb* graddau anrhydedd
hood (above fire etc) lwfer *eg* lwfrau
hood (on garment) cwfl *eg* cyflau
hoof foot troed garn *eb* traed carn
hook *v* bachu *be*
hook (=act of hooking) *n* bachiad *eg* bachiadau
hook (=harp peg) *n* gwrach *eb* gwrachïod
hook (of implement) *n* bach *eg* bachau
hook and bolt bach a bollt
hook and eye bach a llygad
hook shot bachiad *eg*
hook wrench tyndro bach *eg* tyndroeon bach
hooked spit tafod bachog *eg* tafodau bachog
hooker (in rugby) bachwr *eg* bachwyr
Hooke's law deddf Hooke *eb*
hooliganism hwliganiaeth *eb*
hoop *n* cylch *eg* cylchoedd
hoop (a wheel) *v* cylchu *be*
hooper daliwr *eg* dalwyr
hop *n* herc *eg* herciau
hop *v* hercian *be*
hop, skip and jump herc, cam a naid
hopeless anobeithiol *ans*
hopper hopran *eb* hoprau
hops hopys *ell*
hopsack hopsac *eb*
horde llu *eg*
horizon gorwel *eg* gorwelion
horizon line llinell orwel *eb*
horizontal *adj* llorweddol *ans*
horizontal *n* llorwedd *eg* llorweddau
horizontal astride vault llofnaid hir ar led *eb* llofneidiau hir ar led
horizontal axis echelin lorweddol *eb* echelinau llorweddol
horizontal bar bar llorweddol *eg* barrau llorweddol
horizontal boring borio llorweddol *be*
horizontal branch pipe peipen gangen lorweddol *eb* peipiau cangen llorweddol
horizontal buttonhole twll botwm llorweddol *eg* tyllau botymau llorweddol
horizontal centring canoli llorweddol *be*
horizontal chiselling naddu llorweddol *be*
horizontal control rheolaeth lorweddol *eb*
horizontal equivalent cywerth llorwedd *eg* cywerthoedd llorwedd
horizontal force grym llorweddol *eg* grymoedd llorweddol
horizontal grouping grwpio llorweddol *be*
horizontal integration integreiddio llorweddol *be*
horizontal kneeling penlinio llorweddol *be*
horizontal line llinell lorweddol *eb* llinellau llorweddol
horizontal line llinell lorwedd *eb* llinellau llorweddol
horizontal milling machine peiriant melino llorwedd *eg* peiriannau melino llorwedd
horizontal paring naddu llorweddol *be*
horizontal pitch gogwydd llorweddol *eg*
horizontal plane (H.P.) plân llorweddol *eg* planau llorweddol
horizontal pug mill melin gleio lorweddol *eb* melinau cleio llorweddol
horizontal range cyrhaeddiad llorweddol *eg*
horizontal relationship perthynas lorweddol *eb*
horizontal ruler mesurydd llorweddol *eg* mesuryddion llorweddol
horizontal scale graddfa lorweddol *eb* graddfeydd llorweddol
horizontal scroll sgrolio llorweddol *be*
horizontal scroll bar bar sgrolio llorweddol *eg* barrau sgrolio llorweddol
horizontal section trychiad llorweddol *eg* trychiadau llorweddol
horizontal shadow outline amlinell cysgod llorweddol *eb* amlinellau cysgod llorweddol
horizontal stripe rhes lorweddol *eb* rhesi llorweddol
horizontal text anchor angor testun llorweddol *eg* angorau testun llorweddol
horizontal through vault llofnaid fwlch hir *eb* llofneidiau bwlch hir
horizontal traces olinau llorweddol *ell*
horizontality llorwedd-dra *eg*
hormonal hormonaidd *ans*
hormone hormon *eg* hormonau
hormone replacement therapy therapi amnewid hormonau *eg*
horn corn *eg* cyrn
horn passage caniad y cyrn *eg* caniadau'r cyrn
horn player canwr corn *eg* canwyr corn
hornbook llyfr corn *eg* llyfrau corn
hornpipe (dance) cornddawns *eb* cornddawnsiau
hornpipe (instrument) pibgorn *eg* pibgyrn
horny texture gwead cornaidd *eg* gweadau cornaidd
horoscope horosgop *eg* horosgopau
horror arswyd *eg*
horse (for airing clothes) hors *eg/b* horsys
horse (of animal) ceffyl *eg* ceffylau
horse latitudes lledredau'r meirch *ell*
horseshoe pedol ceffyl *eb* pedolau ceffyl
horseshoe arch bwa pedol *eg* bwâu pedol
horseshoe magnet magnet pedol *eg* magnetau pedol
horse with pommels ceffyl â chorfau *eg*
horsepower marchnerth *eg*
horst horst *eg* horstau
hose pipe peipen ddŵr rwber *eb* peipiau dŵr rwber
hosiery hosanwaith *eg*
hospice hosbis *eb* hosbisau

hospital ysbyty *eg* ysbytai
hospital play specialist arbenigwr chwarae ysbyty *eg*
hospitalize anfon i'r ysbyty *be*
Host Hostia *eg*
host (a web site) *v* gwesteia *be*
host (at hotel) gwestywr *eg* gwestywyr
host (of person or computer) *n* gwesteiwr *eg* gwesteiwyr
host (organism) organeb letyol *eb* organebau lletyol
host cell cell letyol *eb*
hostage gwystl *eg* gwystlon
hostel hostel *eg* hosteli
hostility gelyniaeth *eb*
hot poeth *ans*
hot (in metalworking) gorgynnes *ans*
hot blast chwythiad gorgynnes *eg* chwythiadau gorgynnes
hot colour (in metalworking) lliw gorgynnes *eg* lliwiau gorgynnes
hot cross bun picen y Grog *eb* picau'r Grog
hot dip galvanizing galfanu dip poeth *be*
hot dipping dipio poeth *be*
hot iron haearn poeth *eg*
hot metal (in metalworking) metel gorgynnes *eg* metelau gorgynnes
hot sand tywod gorgynnes *eg*
hot set set boeth *eb* setiau poeth
hot shortness poeth freuder *ans*
hot spot man poeth *eg* mannau poeth
hot spring tarddell boeth *eb* tarddellau poeth
hot strip mill melin strip boeth *eb* melinau strip poeth
hot water dye llifyn dŵr poeth *eg* llifynnau dŵr poeth
hot water starch startsh dŵr poeth *eg*
hot wire gwifren boeth *eb*
hotbed magwrfa *eb* magwrfeydd
hotel gwesty *eg* gwestai
hotel chain cadwyn o westai *eb*
hotel management rheolaeth gwesty *eb*
hot-housing (=overstimulation) gorysgogi *be*
hotkey bysell frys *eb* bysellau brys
hotness poethder *eg*
hour awr *eb* oriau
hour angle ongl awr *eb* onglau awr
hourly rate tâl yn ôl yr awr *eg*
hours of labour oriau o lafur *ell*
house tŷ *eg* tai
house church eglwys dŷ *eb* eglwysi tai
house contents policy polisi cynnwys y tŷ *eg* polisïau cynnwys y tŷ
House of Commons Tŷ'r Cyffredin *eg*
House of Lancaster Teulu Lancaster *eg*
House of Lords Tŷ'r Arglwyddi *eg*
House of Orange Teulu Orange *eg*
House of Representatives Tŷ'r Cynrychiolwyr *eg*
House of York Teulu Iorc *eg*
house officer meddyg tŷ *eg* meddygon tŷ
house price pris tŷ *eg* prisiau tai
house to let tŷ ar osod *eg*
housebote anheddfudd *eg*
housebound caeth i'r tŷ *ans*
housecraft crefft cadw tŷ *eb*
housed shelf silff rigolog *eb* silffoedd rhigolog
houseflies clêr *ell*
household (=a house and its affairs) tŷ *eg* tai
household (=home) cartref *eg* cartrefi
household (=retinue) gosgordd *eb* gosgorddion
household goods nwyddau tŷ *ell*
household linen llieiniau tŷ *ell*
household soap sebon golchi *eg*
householder deiliad y tŷ *eg* deiliad y tai
housekeeping cadw tŷ *be*
housekeeping (=tidying up of files etc on computer) cymhennu *be*
housekeeping allowance lwfans cadw tŷ *eg*
housemaid morwyn tŷ *eb* morwynion tŷ
housewife gwraig tŷ *eb* gwragedd tŷ
housewifery crefft cadw tŷ *eb*
housing (for track, joint) rhigol *eb* rhigolau
housing (in general) tai *ell*
housing action area ardal weithredu ar dai *eb* ardaloedd gweithredu ar dai
housing association cymdeithas tai *eb* cymdeithasau tai
housing benefit budd-dal tai *eg* budd-daliadau tai
housing benefit supplement atodiad budd-dal tai *eg* atodiadau budd-dal tai
housing circlip cylchglip mewn rhigol *eg* cylchglipiau mewn rhigol
housing department adran dai *eb* adrannau tai
housing estate stad o dai *eb* stadau o dai
housing joint uniad rhigol draws *eg* uniadau rhigolau traws
housing problems problemau cartrefu *ell*
housing provision darparu tai *be*
housing subsidy cymhorthdal tai *eg* cymorthdaliadau tai
hovercraft hofrenfad *eg* hofrenfadau
how's that? howsat?
H-shaped stretcher estynnwr ffurf H *eg* estynwyr ffurf H
hub both *eg* bothau
hue arlliw *eg* arlliwiau
hue and cry gwaedd ac ymlid
hug *v* cofleidio *be*
hug the ball cofleidio'r bêl *be*
hug the knees cofleidio'r pengliniau *be*
Hugh the Fat Huw Fras *eg*
Huguenot *adj* Hiwgenotaidd *ans*
Huguenot *n* Hiwgenot *eg* Hiwgenotiaid
hulk (=prison ship) llong garchar *eb* llongau carchar
hull corff llong *eg* cyrff llongau
hum (in geography) tas galch *eb* teisi calch
human *adj* dynol *ans*
human *n* bod dynol *eg* bodau dynol

human activity gweithgarwch dynol *eg*
human behaviour ymddygiad dynol *eg*
human body corff dynol *eg* cyrff dynol
human capital cyfalaf dynol *eg*
human character cymeriad dynol *eg* cymeriadau dynol
human computer interface rhyngwyneb dynol y cyfrifiadur *eg*
human development datblygiad dynol *eg*
human development index (HDI) mynegrif datblygiad dynol *eg*
human digestive system system dreulio ddynol *eb*
human editor golygydd dynol *eg* golygyddion dynol
human environment amgylchedd dynol *eg*
human error gwall dynol *eg* gwallau dynol
human features nodweddion dynol *ell*
human figure ffigur dynol *eg* ffigurau dynol
human form ffurf ddynol *eb* ffurfiau dynol
human genetics geneteg dyn *eb*
human geography daearyddiaeth ddynol *eb*
human processes prosesau dynol *ell*
human resource planning cynllunio adnoddau dynol *be*
human resources adnoddau dynol *ell*
human resources function swyddogaeth adnoddau dynol *eb*
human resources manager rheolwr adnoddau dynol *eg* rheolwyr adnoddau dynol
human rights iawnderau dynol *ell*
Human Rights Act Deddf Hawliau Dynol *eb*
human speech lleferydd dynol *eg*
humanisitic art celfyddyd ddyneiddiol *eb*
humanism dyneiddiaeth *eb*
humanist dyneiddiwr *eg* dyneiddwyr
humanistic dyneiddiol *ans*
humanistic approach dull dyneiddiol *eg*
humanistic education addysg ddyneiddiol *eb*
humanistic psychology seicoleg ddyneiddiol *eb*
humanistic therapy therapi dyneiddiol *eg*
humanitarian *adj* dyngarol *ans*
humanitarian *n* dyngarwr *eg* dyngarwyr
humanitarianism dyngarwch *eg*
humanities dyniaethau *ell*
humanity dynoliaeth *eb*
Humble Petition and Advice Deiseb a Chyngor Gostyngedig
humerus hwmerws *eg*
humid llaith *ans*
humidification lleithiad *eg*
humidifier lleithydd *eg* lleithyddion
humidity lleithder *eg*
humification llufadredd *eg*
humiliation cywilydd *eg*
hummock ponc *eb* ponciau
hummocky ponciog *ans*
humus hwmws *eg*
hundred (=100) cant *eg* cannoedd
hundred (=administrative area) cantref *eg* cantrefi
hundred court llys y cantref *eg* llysoedd cantrefi
hundred metres can metr *eg*
hundred metres race ras gan metr *eb* rasys can metr
hundred square sgwâr cant *eg*
Hundred Years War Rhyfel Can Mlynedd *eg*
hundredth canfed *eg* canfedau
Hungry Forties Pedwardegau Newynog *ell*
hunter heliwr *eg* helwyr
hunter-gatherer heliwr-gasglwr *eg*
hunter's moon lleuad hela *eb*
Huntington's chorea corea Huntington *eg*
hurdle clwyd *eb* clwydi
hurdle race ras glwydi *eb* rasys clwydi
hurdler clwydwr *eg* clwydwyr
hurricane corwynt *eg* corwyntoedd
husbandry hwsmonaeth *eb*
husk plisgyn *eg* plisg
hussar hwsâr *eg* hwsariaid
Hussite *adj* Husaidd *ans*
Hussite *n* Husiad *eg* Husiaid
hustings hysting *eg* hystingau
hyaline cartilage cartilag hyalin *eg*
hyaluronic acid asid hyalwronig *eg*
hybrid *adj* croesryw *ans*
hybrid *n* croesryw *eg* croesrywiau
hybrid vigour ymnerth croesryw *eg*
hybridisation croesrywedd *eg*
hydathode hydathod *eg* hydathodau
hydrate *n* hydrad *eg* hydradau
hydrate *v* hydradu *be*
hydrated hydradol *ans*
hydrated aluminium hydroxide alwminiwm hydrocsid hydradol *eg*
hydrated aluminium oxide (bauxite) alwminiwm ocsid hydradol (bocsit) *eg*
hydration hydradiad *eg*
hydraulic hydrolig *ans*
hydraulic lift lifft hydrolig *eg* lifftiau hydrolig
hydraulic organ chwythorgan ddŵr *eb* chwythorganau dŵr
hydraulic press gwasgydd hydrolig *eg* gwasgyddion hydrolig
hydraulics hydroleg *eb*
hydrazine hydrasin *eg*
hydrazinium chloride hydrasiniwm clorid *eg*
hydrazoic acid asid hydrasöig *eg*
hydride hydrid *eg*
hydride ion ïon hydrid *eg* ïonau hydrid
hydriodic acid asid hydrïodig *eg*
hydrobromic acid asid hydrobromig *eg*
hydrocarbon hydrocarbon *eg* hydrocarbonau
hydrocarbon fuel tanwydd hydrocarbon *eg*
hydrocephalic hydroceffalig *ans*
hydrochloric acid asid hydroclorig *eg*
hydrodynamics hydrodynameg *eb*
hydroelectric trydan dŵr *eg*
hydroelectric power pŵer trydan dŵr *eg*

hydrofluoric acid asid hydrofflworig *eg*
hydrofoil hydroffoil *eg* hydroffoilau
hydrogen (H) hydrogen *eg*
hydrogen acceptor derbynnydd hydrogen *eg* derbynyddion hydrogen
hydrogen bromide hydrogen bromid *eg*
hydrogen chloride hydrogen clorid *eg*
hydrogen fluoride hydrogen fflworid *eg*
hydrogen halide halid hydrogen *eg* halidau hydrogen
hydrogen iodide hydrogen ïodid *eg*
hydrogen ion ïon hydrogen *eg* ïonau hydrogen
hydrogen peroxide hydrogen perocsid *eg*
hydrogenate hydrogenu *be*
hydrogenated hydrogenaidd *ans*
hydrogenation hydrogeniad *eg*
hydrogencarbonate hydrogencarbonad *eg*
hydrogencarbonate ion ïon hydrogencarbonad *eg* ïonau hydrogencarbonad
hydrogendifluoride ion ïon hydrogendeufflworid *eg* ïonau hydrogendeufflworid
hydrogenethanedioate ion ïon hydrogenethandeuoad *eg* ïonau hydrogenethandeuoad
hydrogenize hydrogenu *be*
hydrogenphosphate(V) ion ïon hydrogenffosffad(V) *eg* ïonau hydrogenffosffad(V)
hydrogensulfate(IV) ion ïon hydrogensylffad(IV) *eg* ïonau hydrogensylffad(IV)
hydrogensulfate(VI) hydrogensylffad(VI) *eg*
hydrogensulfate(VI) ion ïon hydrogensylffad(VI) *eg* ïonau hydrogensylffad(VI)
hydrogensulfide ion ïon hydrogensylffid *eg* ïonau hydrogensylffid
hydrograph hydrograff *eg* hydrograffau
hydrography hydrograffeg *eb*
hydrolapse cwymp gwlithbwynt *eg* cwympoedd gwlithbwynt
hydrological cycle cylchred hydrolegol *eb*
hydrology hydroleg *eb*
hydrolyse hydrolysu *be*
hydrolysis hydrolysis *eg*
hydrometer hydromedr *eg* hydromedrau
hydrophilic hydroffilig *ans*
hydrophobic hydroffobig *eg*
hydropool hydrobwll *eg* hydrobyllau
hydroscopic hydrosgopig *ans*
hydrosphere hydrosffer *eg*
hydrostatic hydrostatig *ans*
hydrostatics hydrostateg *eb*
hydrothermal hydrothermol *ans*
hydrotropism hydrotropedd *eg*
hydroxide hydrocsid *eg*
hydroxide ion ïon hydrocsid *eg* ïonau hydrocsid
hydroxo- (a ligand) hydrocso-
hydroxy- hydrocsi-
2-hydroxybenzenecarbaldehyde 2-hydrocsibensencarbaldehyd *eg*
2-hydroxybenzenecarboxylic acid asid 2-hydrocsibensencarbocsylig *eg*
3-hydroxybutanal 3-hydrocsibwtanal *eg*
2-hydroxybutanedioic acid asid 2-hydrocsibwtandeuöig *eg*
3-hydroxybut-2-enoic acid asid 3-hydrocsibwt-2-enöig *eg*
2-hydroxy-1,2-diphenylethanone 2-hydrocsi-1,2-deuffenylethanon *eg*
hydroxyethanoic acid asid hydrocsiethanöig *eg*
hydroxyl group grŵp hydrocsyl *eg*
hydroxylamine hydrocsylamin *eg*
hydroxylammonium ion ïon hydrocsylamoniwm *eg* ïonau hydrocsylamoniwm
4-hydroxy-4-methylpentan-2-one 4-hydrocsi-4-methylpentan-2-on *eg*
2-hydroxy-2-methylpropanenitrile 2-hydrocsi-2-methylpropannitril *eg*
2-hydroxyphenylmethanol 2-hydrocsiffenylmethanol *eg*
hydroxyproline hydrocsiprolin *eg*
2-hydroxypropanenitrile 2-hydrocsipropannitril *eg*
2-hydroxypropane-1,2,3-tricarboxylic acid asid 2-hydrocsipropan-1,2,3-tricarbocsylig *eg*
2-hydroxypropanoic acid asid 2-hydrocsipropanöig *eg*
hyetograph hyetograff *eg* hyetograffau
hygiene hylendid *eg*
hygienic hylan *ans*
hygrogram hygrogram *eg* hygrogramau
hygrometer hygromedr *eg* hygromedrau
hygroscopic hygrosgopig *ans*
hymn emyn *eg* emynau
hymn tune emyn-dôn *eb* emyn-donau
hypabyssal rock craig hypabysol *eb* creigiau hypabysol
hyper major gorfwyaf *eg*
hyperactive child plentyn gorfywiog *eg* plant gorfywiog
hyperactivity gorfywiogrwydd *eg*
hyperbola hyperbola *eg* hyperbolâu
hyperbole gormodiaith *eb*
hyperbolic hyperbolig *ans*
hyperbolic function ffwythiant hyperbolig *eg*
hyperboloid hyperboloid *eg* hyperboloidau
HyperCard HyperCard *eg*
hypergeometric hypergeometrig *ans*
hyperinflation gorchwyddiant *eg*
hyperlink hypergyswllt *eg* hypergysylltiadau
hypermarket archfarchnad *eb* archfarchnadoedd
hypermedia hypergyfryngau *ell*
hyperplasia gordyfiant *eg*
hypertension(blood pressure) gorbwysedd *eg*
hypertension(in psychology) gordensiwn *eg*
hypertext hyperdestun *eg*
hypertext knowledge gwybodaeth hyperdestun *eb*
hypertext link cyswllt hyperdestun *eg*
hypertext mark-up language iaith farcio hyperdestun *eb*

hypertext transfer protocol protocol trosglwyddo hyperdestun *eg*
hypertonic hypertonig *ans*
hypertrochoid hypertrocoid *eg* hypertrocoidau
hypertrophy hypertroffedd *eg*
hyperventilation goranadlu *be*
hypha hyffa *eg* hyffâu
hyphal hyffaidd *ans*
hyphen cysylltnod *eg* cysylltnodau
hyphenation cysylltnodi *be*
hyphenation exception eithriad cysylltnodi *eg* eithriadau cysylltnodi
hyphenation zone cylchfa gysylltnodi *eb*
hypnosis hypnosis *eg*
hypnotic analgesia analgesia hypnotig *eg*
Hypoaeolian mode modd Hypoaeloiaidd *eg*
hypochlorite bleach cannydd hypoclorit *eg*
hypochondria anhwylder claf diglefyd *eg*
hypocycloid hypocylchoid *eg* hypocylchoidau
hypodermal hypodermaidd *ans*
hypodermic tangroenol *ans*
hypodermic needle theory damcaniaeth nodwydd hypodermig *eb*
Hypodorian mode modd Hypodoriaidd *eg*
hypogeal tanddaearol *ans*
hypoglossal isdafodol *ans*
Hypoionian mode modd Hypoioniaidd *eg*
Hypolocrian mode modd Hypolocriaidd *eg*
Hypomixolydian mode modd Hypomicsolydiaidd *eg*
hypomode modd deilliedig *eg*
Hypophrygian mode modd Hypophrygiaidd *eg*
hyposecretion hyposecretiad *eg*
hypotension isbwysedd *eg*
hypotenuse hypotenws *eg* hypotenysau
hypothalamus hypothalamws *eg*
hypothermia hypothermia *eg*
hypothesis rhagdybiaeth *eb* rhagdybiaethau
hypothesis test prawf rhagdybiaeth *eg*
hypothesis testing profi rhagdybiaethau *be*
hypothetico-deductive rhagdybiaethol-diddwythol *ans*
hypotonic to hypotonig i *ans*
hypsography hypsograffeg *eb*
hypsometer hypsomedr *eg* hypsomedrau
hypsometric hypsometrig *ans*
hysteresis hysteresis *eg*
hysteria hysteria *eg*

I

iambic dyrchafedig *ans*

iambus corfan dyrchafedig *eg* corfannau dyrchafedig

IBM-compatible IBM-gytûn *ans*

IBM-compatible computer cyfrifiadur IBM-gytûn *eg* cyfrifiaduron IBM-gytûn

ice iâ *eg*; rhew *eg*

Ice Age Oes Iâ *eb*

ice axe caib eira *eb* ceibiau eira

ice barrier bar iâ *eg* barrau iâ; bar rhew *eg* barrau rhew

ice bound rhewgaeth *ans*

ice cap cap iâ *eg* capiau iâ; cap rhew *eg* capiau rhew

ice cold wind rhewynt *eg*

ice dam argae iâ *eg* argaeau iâ; argae rhew *eg* argaeau rhew

ice edge ymyl iâ *eb* ymylon iâ; ymyl rhew*eb* ymylon rhew

ice fall rhewgwymp *eg*

ice floe ffloch iâ *eg* fflochiau iâ; ffloch rhew *eg* fflochiau rhew

ice fog niwl iâ *eg* niwloedd iâ; niwl rhew *eg* niwloedd rhew

ice front ffrynt iâ *eg* ffryntiau iâ; ffrynt rhew *eg* ffryntiau rhew

ice jam tagfa iâ *eb* tagfeydd iâ; tagfa rhew *eb* tagfeydd rhew

ice lobe llabed iâ *eb* llabedau iâ; llabed rhew *eb* llabedau rhew

ice marginal channel sianel iâ ymylol *eb* sianeli iâ ymylol; sianel rew ymylol *eb* sianeli rhew ymylol

ice peg peg iâ *eg* pegiau iâ; peg rhew *eg* pegiau rhew

ice shattered rhewddrylliog *ans*

ice sheet llen iâ *eb* llenni iâ; llen rew *eb* llenni rhew

ice shelf sgafell iâ *eb* sgafelli iâ; sgafell rew *eb* sgafelli rhew

ice wedge lletem iâ *eb* lletemau iâ; lletem rew *eb* lletemau rhew

iceberg mynydd iâ *eg* mynyddoedd iâ; mynydd rhew *eg* mynyddoedd rhew

ice-breaking exercise ymarfer torri'r garw *eg* ymarferion torri'r garw

Iceland spar grisial Gwlad yr Iâ *eg*

Icelandic 'low' gwasgedd isel Gwlad yr Iâ *eg*

icicle pibonwyen *eb* pibonwy

icon eicon *eg* eiconau

iconic eiconig *ans*

iconic memory cof eiconig *eg*

iconic representation portread eiconig *eg* portreadau eiconig

iconic thinking meddwl eiconig *be*

iconoclasm delwddrylliad *eg*

iconoclast delwddrylliwr *eg* delwddryllwyr

iconoclastic delwddrylliol *ans*

iconographic eiconograffig *ans*

► **iconography** eiconograffeg *eb*

iconography and practice eiconograffeg ac ymarfer

icosahedron icosahedron *eg* icosahedronau

ICT Resources and Software adnoddau a meddalwedd technoleg gwybodaeth a chyfathrebu

ICT system system technoleg gwybodaeth a chyfathrebu *eb*

icy cold rhewllyd *ans*

id id *eg*

ID card cerdyn adnabod *eg* cardiau adnabod

ID number rhif adnabod *eg* rhifau adnabod

idea syniad *eg* syniadau

Idea of Progress Syniad o Gynnydd *eg*

ideal (in general) *adj* delfrydol *ans*

ideal (in general) *n* delfryd *eb* delfrydau

ideal (in mathematics) *n* ideal *eg* idealau

ideal (in physics) *adj* perffaith *ans*

ideal gas nwy delfrydol *eg*

idealism (in general) delfrydiaeth *eb*

idealism (in psychology etc) idealaeth *eb*

idealist delfrydwr *eg* delfrydwyr

idealization delfrydiad *eg*

idemfactor idemffactor *eg* idemffactorau

idempotent idempotent *ans*

identical unfath *ans*

identical twin gefell unfath *eg* gefeilliaid unfath

identifiable canfyddadwy *ans*

identification adnabyddiaeth *eb*

identification (with someone) uniaethu *be*

identified need angen canfyddadwy *eg* anghenion canfyddadwy

identifier dynodwr *eg* dynodwyr

identify (=establish the identity of, recognize) adnabod *be*

identify (=note) nodi *be*

identify (by analysis of the circumstances) canfod *be*

identify the specimen enwi'r sbesimen *be*

identifying needs adnabod anghenion *be*

identity (=absolute sameness) unfathiant *eg* unfathiannau

identity (=personality) hunaniaeth *eb*

identity band band adnabod *eg* bandiau adnabod

identity card cerdyn adnabod *eg* cardiau adnabod

identity element elfen unfathiant *eb* elfennau unfathiant
ideogram ideogram *eg* ideogramau
ideologue ideolegwr *eg* ideolegwyr
ideology ideoleg *eb*
idle resources adnoddau segur *ell*
idle return stroke strôc ddychwel segur *eb* strociau dychwel segur
idle rich cyfoethogion segur *ell*
idler wheels olwynion cyswllt *ell*
idling speed cyflymder segura *eg*
idol eilun *eg* eilunod
idolatry eilunaddoliaeth *eb*
IEEE interface rhyngwyneb IEEE *eg* rhyngwynebau IEEE
igloo iglw *eg* iglŵau
igneous igneaidd *ans*
igneous rock craig igneaidd *eb* creigiau igneaidd
ignite cynnau *be*
ignition taniad *eg* taniadau
ignition system system danio *eb* systemau tanio
ignorance anwybodaeth *eb*
ignore anwybyddu *be*
ignore character nod anwybyddu *eg* nodau anwybyddu
Ik Onkar Ik Onkar
ileum ilewm *eg*
iliac iliag *ans*
iliac artery rhydweli iliag *eb* rhydwelïau iliag
iliac vein gwythïen iliag *eb*
iliolumbar artery rhydweli iliolymbar *eb*
ilium iliwm *eg*
illegal anghyfreithlon *ans*
illegal character nod anghyfreithlon *eg* nodau anghyfreithlon
illegality anghyfreithlondeb *eg*
illegitimate anghyfreithlon *ans*
illiteracy anllythrennedd *eg*
illiterate anllythrennog *ans*
illness afiechyd *eg*
illness behaviour ymddygiad afiechyd *eg*
illness cognition gwybyddiaeth afiechyd *eb*
illness perception canfyddiad afiechyd *eg*
illness perception questionnaire (IPQ) holiadur canfyddiadau afiechyd *eg* holiaduron canfyddiadau afiechyd
illuminant goleuydd *eg*
illuminate (=decorate a manuscript) goliwio *be*
illuminate (=light up) goleuo *be*
illuminated (of manuscript) goliwiedig *ans*
illuminated lettering llythrennu goliwiedig *be*
illuminated manuscript llawysgrif oliwiedig *eb* llawysgrifau goliwiedig
illuminated script sgript oliwiedig *eb* sgriptiau goliwiedig
illuminating power goleunerth *eg* goleunerthoedd
illumination (=light) golau *eg* goleuadau
illumination (of manuscript) goliwiad *eg* goliwiadau
illumination factor ffactor goleuo *eb*
illuminism ilwminiaeth *eb*
illuminist ilwminydd *eg* ilwminiaid
illusion rhith *eg* rhithiau
illusion of out-group homogeneity ffugddelwedd o allgrwp homogenaidd *eb*
illusionism rhithiolaeth *eb*
illusory correlation cydberthyniad gau *eg*
illustrate (=explain or make clear) egluro *be*
illustrate (with a drawing) darlunio *be*
illustrate (with an example) enghreifftio *be*
illustrated (with drawings) darluniadol *ans*
illustrated (with examples) eglurhaol *ans*
illustration (=act or instance of illustrating) darluniad *eg* darluniadau
illustration (=drawing or picture illustrating a book etc) darlun eglurhaol *eg* darluniau eglurhaol
illustration (=example) enghraifft *eb* enghreifftiau
illustration (=picture) darlun *eg* darluniau
illustrative (=containing drawing or pictures) darluniadol *ans*
illustrative (serving as an explanation or example) enghreifftiol *ans*
illuvial mewnlifol *ans*
illuviation mewnlif *eg*
image (=idol) delw *eb* delwau
image (=representation, idea) delwedd *eb* delweddau
image analysis dadansoddi delweddau *be*
image blocking rhwystro delwedd *be*
image capture cipio delweddau *be*
image editing golygu delwedd *be*
image file ffeil delwedd *eb* ffeiliau delwedd
image manipulation trin delweddau *be*
image map map delweddau *eg* mapiau delweddau
image processing prosesu delweddau *be*
imagery delweddaeth *eb*
imaginary dychmygol *ans*
imaginary background cefndir dychmygol *eg*
imaginary part rhan ddychmygol *eb* rhannau dychmygol
imaginary world byd dychmygol *eg* bydoedd dychmygol
imagination dychymyg *eg*
imaginative llawn dychymyg *ans*
imaginative composition cyfansoddiad llawn dychymyg *eg* cyfansoddiadau llawn dychymyg
imaginative play chwarae llawn dychymyg *eg*
imbalance anghydbwysedd *eg*
imbecile ynfytyn *eg* ynfydion
imbecility ynfydrwydd *eg*
imbed plannu *be*
imbricated structure adeiledd gorwthiad *eg* adeileddau gorwthiad
imitate dynwared *be*
imitation dynwarediad *eg* dynwarediadau
imitative dynwaredol *ans*
imitative learning dysgu drwy ddynwared *be*

imitative play chwarae efelychol *eg*
immature anaeddfed *ans*
immature soil pridd anaeddfed *eg* priddoedd anaeddfed
immediacy digyfryngedd *eg*
immediate access memory cof mynediad uniongyrchol *eg*
immediate access store storfa uniongyrchol *eb* storfeydd uniongyrchol
immediate operand operand uniongyrchol *eg* operandau uniongyrchol
immerse trochi *be*
immersion trochiad *eg* trochiadau
immersion heater gwresogydd troch *eg* gwresogyddion troch
immersion programme rhaglen drochi *eb* rhaglenni trochi
immigrant mewnfudwr *eg* mewnfudwyr
immigrant education addysg mewnfudwyr *eb*
immigrant labour llafur estron *eg*
immigrate mewnfudo *be*
immigration mewnfudiad *eg* mewnfudiadau
immiscible anghymysgadwy *ans*
immobilised enzyme ensym ansymudol *eg*
immobility ansymudoledd *eg*
immoral anfoesol *ans*
immorality anfoesoldeb *eg*
immortality anfarwoldeb *eg*
immunal suppression ataliad imiwnedd *eg*
immune imiwn *ans*
immune reaction adwaith imiwn *eg* adweithiau imiwn
immune system system imiwnedd *eb*
immunisation programme rhaglen imiwneiddio *eb* rhaglenni imiwneiddio
immunity imiwnedd *eg*
immunization imiwneiddiad *eg*
immunize imiwneiddio *be*
immunoglobulin imiwnoglobwlin *eg* imiwnoglobwlinau
immunologist imiwnolegydd *eg* imiwnolegwyr
immunology imiwnoleg *eb*
immunosuppression atal imiwnedd *be*
impact (=effect or influence) effaith *eg/b*
impact (=firm press) ardrawiad *eg* ardrawiadau
impact adhesive adlyn ardrawol *eg* adlynion ardrawol
impact glue glud ardrawol *eg*
impact printer argraffydd traw *eg* argraffyddion traw
impact resistance gwrthiant ardrawiad *eg*
impact sound sŵn gwrthdaro *eg*
impact strength nerth ardrawiad *eg*
impacted cywasgedig *ans*
impair amharu ar *be*
impaired diffygiol *ans*
impairment nam *eg* namau
impasto impasto *eg*
impeach uchelgyhuddo *be*
impeachment uchelgyhuddiad *eg* uchelgyhuddiadau
impedance rhwystriant *eg* rhwystriannau
impede rhwystro *be*
impediment nam *eg* namau
impeller (pulsator) pwlsadur *eg* pwlsaduron
imperfect cadence diweddeb amherffaith *eb* diweddebau amherffaith
imperfect competition cystadleuaeth amherffaith *eb*
imperfection amherffeithrwydd *eg* amherffeithiadau
imperial (measure) imperial *ans*
imperial (of empire) ymerodrol *ans*
imperial (of expansionist aims) imperialaidd *ans*
Imperial Chamber Siambr Ymerodraeth *eb*
imperial history hanes yr ymerodraeth *eg*
Imperial Knight Marchog yr Ymerodraeth *eg* Marchogion yr Ymerodraeth
Imperial Preference Blaenoriaeth i'r Ymerodraeth *eb*
Imperial unit uned Imperial *eb* unedau Imperial
imperialism imperialaeth *eb*
imperialist imperialydd *eg* imperialwyr
impermeable anathraidd *ans*
impermeable membrane pilen anathraidd *eb* pilenni anathraidd
impersonal amhersonol *ans*
impervious anhydraidd *ans*
impetus ysgogiad *eg* ysgogiadau
impinge ardaro *be*
implant *n* mewnblaniad *eg* mewnblaniadau
implant *v* mewnblannu *be*
implant a cell in the placenta mewnblannu cell yn y brych *be*
implantation mewnblannu *be*
implement gweithredu *be*
implementation (in mathematics) gweithred *eb* gweithrediadau
implication goblygiad *eg* goblygiadau
implication of trend goblygiad y duedd *eg*
implicit ymhlyg *ans*
implicit function ffwythiant ymhlyg *eg*
implicit memory cof ymhlyg *eg*
implied ymhlyg *ans*
implied terms telerau dealledig *ell*
implosion mewnffrwydrad *eg* mewnffrwydradau
implosion therapy therapi mewnffrwydrad *eg*
imply ymhlygu *be*
impolder polderu *be*
import *n* mewnforyn *eg* mewnforion
import *v* mewnforio *be*
import duty toll mewnforio *eb* tollau mewnforio
import objects mewnforio gwrthrychau *be*
import replacement amnewid mewnforion *be*
import tariff toll mewnforio *eb* tollau mewnforio
import text mewnforio testun *be*
imported timber coed sy'n cael eu mewnforio *ell*
importer mewnforiwr *eg* mewnforwyr
impose gosod *be*
impost treth *eb* trethi

impound powndio *be*
impoverish tlodi *be*
impoverishment tlodi *eg*
impregnate (=saturate) trwytho *be*
impregnate (in biology) ffrwythloni *be*
impregnated wadding wadin trwythedig *eg*
impregnation (=saturation) trwythiad *eg*
impregnation (in biology) ffrwythloniad *eg*
impresario impresario *eg* impresari
impression argraff *eb* argraffiadau
impression formation ffurfio argraffiadau *be*
impressionable argraffadwy *ans*
impressionism argraffiadaeth *eb*
impressionist argraffiadydd *eg* argraffiadwyr
impressionistic argraffiadol *ans*
impressive nodedig *ans*
impressment gorfodaeth *eb*
imprimatur imprimatur *eg*
imprimatura imprimatura *eg*
imprint (of knurling tool) gwasgnod *eg* gwasgnodau
impromptu *adj* byrfyfyr *ans*
impromptu *n* impromptu *eg* impromptus
improper afreolaidd *ans*
improper fraction ffracsiwn pendrwm *eg* ffracsiynau pendrwm
impropriate amfeddu *be*
impropriate tithe degwm amfedd *eg* degymau amfedd
impropriation amfeddiad *eg* amfeddiadau
impropriator amfeddwr *eg* amfeddwyr
improve gwella *be*
improve performance gwella perfformiad *be*
improved land tir wedi ei wella *eg*
improved varieties gwell amrywogaethau *ell*
improvement gwelliant *eg* gwelliannau
Improvement Commissioners Comisiynwyr Gwelliannau *ell*
improvement grant grant gwella *eg* grantiau gwella
improving the school grounds gwella tir yr ysgol *be*
improvisation creu'n fyrfyfyr *be*
improvise (=adapt) addasu byrfyfyr *be*
improvise (in music playing) chwarae'n fyrfyfyr *be*
improvised byrfyfyr *ans*
improvised apparatus offer byrfyfyr *ell*
improvised testing profi byrfyfyr *be*
impulse ergyd *eg/b* ergydion
impulse (=mental incitement) symbyliad *eg* symbyliadau
impulse (nervous) ysgogiad *eb* ysgogiadau
impulse buying prynu byrbwyll *be*
impulsive ergydiol *ans*
impulsive tension tensiwn ergydiol *eg*
impure amhur *ans*
impurity amhuredd *eg* amhureddau
imputed cost cost briodoledig *eb* costau priodoledig
in care mewn gofal *ans*
in good proportion mewn cyfrannedd da
in her personal capacity dan ei henw ei hun *adf*
in his personal capacity dan ei enw ei hun *adf*
in parallax mewn paralacs
in proportion mewn cyfrannedd *adf*
in register mewn iawn luniad
in reserve wrth gefn *ans*
in sequence yn olynol
in series mewn cyfres
in the course of employment yng nghwrs cyflogaeth
in the nude yn noethlymun *adf*
in the proportion yn y gyfrannedd
in the round yn dri dimensiwn *adf*
in twos yn ddeuoedd *adf*
in vitro in vitro
in vitro fertilization (IVF) ffrwythloni in vitro *be*
in vivo in vivo
in vogue mewn bri *adf*
inability anallu *eg*
inaccessibility anhygyrchedd *eg*
inaccessible anhygyrch *ans*
inaccuracy anghywirdeb *eg* anghywirdebau
inaccurate gwallus *ans*
inaccurate size maint gwallus *eg* meintiau gwallus
inactivate anactifadu *be*
inactive (in chemistry) anactif *ans*
inactive (in general) anweithredol *ans*
inactive window ffenestr anweithredol *eb* ffenestri anweithredol
inactivity anactifedd *eg*
inadequate annigonol *ans*
inanimate difywyd *ans*
inappropriate clothing dillad anaddas *ell*
inaudible anhyglyw *ans*
inaugural agoriadol *ans*
inaugural lecture darlith sefydlu *eb* darlithoedd sefydlu
inaugural speech araith sefydlu *eb* areithiau sefydlu
inaugurate sefydlu *be*
inblowing wind gwynt mewnchwyth *eg* gwyntoedd mewnchwyth
inborn cynhenid *ans*
inborn capacity gallu cynhenid *eg* galluoedd cynhenid
inborn errors of metabolism gwallau cynhenid metabolaeth *ell*
inbound (of flights, traffic etc) i mewn *adf*
inbox mewnflwch *eg*
inbreed mewnfridio *be*
incandescence gwyniasedd *eg* gwyniaseddau
incandescent gwynias *ans*
incandescent cloud cwmwl gwynias *eg* cymylau gwynias
incantation swyngan *eb* swynganeuon
incarcerate carcharu *be*
incarnation ymgnawdoliad *eg*
incendiarism llosgyddiaeth *eb*

incendiary (bomb) bom tân *eg* bomiau tân
incense (=enrage) *v* cynhyrfu *be*
incense (sweet smelling gum or spice) *n* arogldarth *eg* arogldarthau
incentive cymhelliad *eg* cymhellion
incentive travel teithio cymhellol *be*
incentre mewnganol *eg* mewnganolau
incest llosgach *eg*
inch modfedd *eb* modfeddi
incidence (in physics) trawiad *eg* trawiadau
incidence (of cases) nifer *eg*
incidence of rainfall dygwydd glawiad *eg*
incident (=occurrence) *n* digwyddiad *eg* digwyddiadau
incident (=striking) *adj* trawol *ans*
incident (feudal) *n* treth *eb* trethi
incident radiation pelydriad trawol *eg*
incident ray pelydryn trawol *eg* pelydrau trawol
incipient plasmolysis plasmolysis cychwynnol *eg*
incircle (inscribed circle) mewngylch *eg* mewngylchoedd
incise endorri *be*
incised alphabet gwyddor endoredig *eb* gwyddorau endoredig
incised carving cerfiad endorri *eg* cerfiadau endorri
incised meander ystum rhychog *eg* ystumiau rhychog
incised moulding mowldin endoredig *eg*
incised wound clwyf toriad *eg* clwyfau toriad
incising knife cyllell endorri *eb* cyllyll endorri
incision endoriad *eg* endoriadau
incisor blaenddant *eg* blaenddannedd
incline *n* goledd *eg* goleddau
incline *v* goleddu *be*
incline (in a slate quarry) *n* inclein *eg* incleiniau
incline of difficulty goledd anhawster *eg*
inclined ar oledd *ans*
inclined face wyneb ar oledd *eg* wynebau ar oledd
inclined plane plân ar oledd *eg* planau ar oledd
inclined rope rhaff ar oledd *eb* rhaffau ar oledd
inclined solids solidau ar oledd *ell*
include cynnwys *be*
included angle ongl gynwysedig *eb* onglau cynwysedig
inclusion cynhwysiad *eg*
inclusive cynhwysol *ans*
inclusive fitness ffitrwydd cynhwysol *eg*
income incwm *eg* incymau
income elasticity elastigedd incwm *eg*
income group grŵp incwm *eg* grwpiau incwm
income support cymhorthdal incwm *eg*
income tax treth incwm *eb*
incommensurable anghymesur *ans*
incompatible (of objects) anghydnaws *ans*
incompatible (of people) anghymarus *ans*
incompetence anghymwyster *eg* anghymwysterau
incompetence model model anallu *eg* modelau anallu
incomplete anghyflawn *ans*
incomplete dominance trechedd anghyflawn *eg*
incomplete view golwg anghyflawn *eg* golygon anghyflawn
incompressible anghywasg *ans*
incongruence anghyfathiant *eg*
inconsistency anghysondeb *eg* anghysonderau
inconsistent anghyson *ans*
incontinence anymataliaeth *eb*
incontinent anymataliol *ans*
inconvenience anhwylustod *eg*
inconvenient position safle anghyfleus *eg*
incorrect anghywir *ans*
increase *n* cynnydd *eg*
increase *v* cynyddu *be*
increase rate cyfradd cynnydd *eb* cyfraddau cynnydd
increase stitches cynyddu pwythau *be*
increased magnification chwyddo pellach *be*
increasing control rheolaeth gynyddol *eb*
increasing cost cost gynyddol *eb* costau cynyddol
increasing fluency rhwyddineb cynyddol *eg*
increasing sequence dilyniant cynyddol *eg* dilyniannau cynyddol
increment (in computing) cynyddiad *eg* cynyddiadau
incremental cynyddol *ans*
incrustation crameniad *eg* crameniadau
incrusted cramennog *ans*
incubation period (of disease) cyfnod magu *eg*
incubation period (of egg) cyfnod deori *eg*
incubator (for babies) crud cynnal *eg* crudiau cynnal
incubator (for eggs) deorydd *eg* deoryddion
incumbency periglorïaeth *eb* periglorïaethau
incumbent (of any office) deiliad *eg* deiliaid
incumbent (of ecclesiastical office) periglor *eg* periglorion
incursion cipgyrch *eg* cipgyrchoedd
incus eingion *eg*
indathrene blue glas indathrin *eg*
indebted dyledus *ans*
indefinite amhendant *ans*
indefinite integral integryn amhendant *eg* integrynnau amhendant
indefinite length hyd amhendant *eg* hydoedd amhendant
indehiscent anymagorol *ans*
indelible ink inc parhaol *eg*
indemnify rhyddarbed *be*
indemnity (=compensation) digolledaid *eg*
indemnity (=protection or exemption) indemniad *eg* indemniadau
indent (a margin) *v* mewnoli *be*
indent (legal documents) *v* indeintio *be*
indent (of margin) *n* mewnoliad *eg* mewnoliadau
indent marker marciwr mewnoli *eg* marcwyr mewnoli
indentation (=dent) pantiad *eg* pantiadau
indentation (=toothlike notches) danheddiad *eg* daneddiadau

indentation (of legal documents) indeintiad *eg* indeintiadau
indented (with toothlike notches) danheddus *ans*
indented paragraph paragraff wedi'i fewnoli *eg* paragraffau wedi'u mewnoli
indented text testun wedi'i fewnoli *eg* testunau wedi'u mewnoli
indenture indeintur *eg* indeinturau
indentured labour llafur ymrwymedig *eg*
independence annibyniaeth *eb* annibyniaethau
independent annibynnol *ans*
independent (of television companies) cwmni annibynnol *eg* cwmnïau annibynnol
► **independent assortment of genes** rhydd-ddosraniad y genynnau *eg*
independent chuck crafanc gafael annibynnol *eb* crafangau gafael annibynnol
independent gentry bonedd annibynnol *eg*
independent groups design cynllun grwpiau annibynnol *eg* cynlluniau grwpiau annibynnol
Independent Labour Party (ILP) Plaid Lafur Annibynnol *eb*
independent learning dysgu annibynnol *be*
independent reading level lefel darllen annibynnol *eb*
independent school ysgol annibynnol *eb* ysgolion annibynnol
independent section adran annibynnol *eb* adrannau annibynnol
independent shop siop annibynnol *eb*
independent study astudio annibynnol *be*
independent suspension hongiad annibynnol *eg* hongiadau annibynnol
Independent Television Commission Comisiwn Teledu Annibynnol *eg*
independent university prifysgol annibynnol *eb* prifysgolion annibynnol
independent variable newidyn annibynnol *eg* newidynnau annibynnol
independently assorting rhydd-ddosrannol *ans*
indeterminacy amhenodrwydd *eg*
indeterminate (in economics) amhenderfynedig *ans*
indeterminate key cywair amhenodol *eg*
index (=alphabetical list with references) *n* mynegai *eg* mynegeion
index (in mathematics and science) *n* indecs *eg* indecsau
Index (Librorum Prohibitorum) Indecs, Yr *eg*
index (list alphabetically with references) *v* mynegeio *be*
index finger mynegfys *eg* mynegfysedd
index linked indecs gyswllt *ans*
index mode modd mynegai *eg*
index notation nodiant indecs *eg*
index number mynegrif *eg* mynegrifau
index of proportionality indecs cyfranoledd *eg*
index pin pìn cyfeirio *eg* pinnau cyfeirio
index register cofrestr mynegai *eb* cofrestri mynegai
indexed address cyfeiriad mynegedig *eg* cyfeiriadau mynegedig
indexed addressing cyfeirio mynegedig *be*
indexed field maes wedi'i fynegeio *eg* meysydd wedi'u mynegeio
indexed sequential file ffeil ddilyniannol fynegedig *eb* ffeiliau dilyniannol mynegedig
indexes window ffenestr mynegeion *eb* ffenestri mynegeion
indexical sign arwydd mynegeiol *eg*
India-corn India corn *eg*
Indian art celfyddyd India *eb*
Indian Empire Ymerodraeth India *eb*
Indian ink inc India *eg*
Indian oilstone carreg hogi India *eb* cerrig hogi India
Indian raga raga Indiaidd *eg*
Indian red coch India *eg*
Indian summer Haf Bach Mihangel *eg*
indicate dangos *be*
indicate dynamics dangos dynameg *be*
indication arwydd *eg/b* arwyddion
indicator dangosydd *eg* dangosyddion
indicator of abuse dangosydd camdriniaeth *eg* dangosyddion camdriniaeth
indict ditio *be*
indictable ditiadwy *ans*
indictable offence trosedd dditiadwy *eb* troseddau ditiadwy
indictment ditiad *eg*
indifference curves cromliniau diwahaniaeth *ell*
indiffusible anhryledadwy *ans*
indigenous brodorol *ans*
indigenous industry diwydiant brodorol *eg*
indigestible anhydraul *ans*
indigestion diffyg traul *eg*
indirect anuniongyrchol *ans*
indirect addressing cyfeirio anuniongyrchol *be*
indirect care gofal anuniongyrchol *eg*
indirect carer gofalydd anuniongyrchol *eg*
indirect contact cyswllt anuniongyrchol *eg*
indirect free kick cic rydd anuniongyrchol *eb* ciciau rhydd anuniongyrchol
indirect lighting golau anuniongyrchol *eg*
indirect tax treth anuniongyrchol *eb* trethi anuniongyrchol
indiscriminate diwahân *ans*
indissoluble residue gwaddod annhoddadwy *eg* gwaddodion annhoddadwy
indistinguishability anwahaniaethrwydd *eg*
indium (In) indiwm *eg*
individual *adj* unigol *ans*
individual *n* unigolyn *eg* unigolion
individual activities (in sport) gweithgareddau fel unigolyn *ell*
individual demand curve cromlin galw unigol *eb*
individual difference gwahaniaeth rhwng unigolion *eg*

individual game gêm unigol *eb* gemau unigol
individual performance review adolygiad perfformiad unigol *eg* adolygiadau perfformiad unigol
individual possession meddiant unigol *eg*
individual test prawf unigol *eg* profion unigol
individual training and assessment programme rhaglen hyfforddi ac asesu unigol *eb* rhaglenni hyfforddi ac asesu unigol
individual user defnyddiwr unigol *eg* defnyddwyr unigol
individualism unigoliaeth *eb*
individualist unigolydd *eg* unigolyddion
individuality unigoliaeth *eb*
individualized education programme rhaglen addysg unigol *eb* rhaglenni addysg unigol
individualized reading programme rhaglen ddarllen i'r unigolyn *eb* rhaglenni darllen i'r unigolyn
indivisibility anwahanadrwydd *eg*
indivisible anwahanadwy *ans*
indoctrinate cyflyru *be*
Indo-European Indo-Ewropeaidd *ans*
indole indol *eg*
indole acetic acid asid indol asetig *eg*
indole butyric acid (IBA) asid indol bwtyrig (IBA) *eg*
indol-3-yl-acetic acid (IAA) asid indol-3-yl-asetig IAA *eg*
indoor dan do *ans*
indoor environment amgylchedd dan do *eg*
indoor use defnydd dan do *eg*
indoor work gwaith dan do *eg*
Indo-Sumerian Indo-Swmeraidd *ans*
induce (=cause) peri *be*
induce (birth) prysuro *be*
induce (in logic, physics etc) anwytho *be*
induced anwythol *ans*
induced charge gwefr anwythol *eb*
induced fit ffit anwythol *eb*
induct sefydlu *be*
inductance anwythiant *eg*
induction (=inference) casgliad *eg* casgliadau
induction (in logic, physics etc) anwythiad *eg* anwythiadau
induction (of a person) sefydliad *eg* sefydliadau
induction coil coil anwythiad *eg* coiliau anwythiad
induction course cwrs sefydlu *eg* cyrsiau sefydlu
induction meeting cyfarfod sefydlu *eg* cyfarfodydd sefydlu
induction stroke strôc anwythiad *eb* strociau anwythiad
induction training hyfforddiant sefydlu *eg*
induction year blwyddyn sefydlu *eb*
inductive anwythol *ans*
inductive proof prawf anwythol *eg*
inductive reasoning rhesymu casgliadol *be*
inductive sensor synhwyrydd anwythol *eg*
inductor anwythydd *eg* anwythyddion
indulgence (papal) maddeueb *eb* maddeuebau
indurated (with feminine nouns) wedi'i chaledu *ans* wedi'u caledu
indurated (with masculine nouns) wedi'i galedu *ans* wedi'u caledu
induration calediant *eg*
indusium indwsiwm *eg*
industrial diwydiannol *ans*
industrial action gweithredu diwydiannol *be*
industrial area ardal ddiwydiannol *eb* ardaloedd diwydiannol
industrial complex cymhlyg diwydiannol *eg* cymhlygau diwydiannol
industrial conflict gwrthdaro diwydiannol *be*
industrial estate stad ddiwydiannol *eb* stadau diwydiannol
industrial history hanes diwydiannol *eg*
industrial marketing marchnata diwydiannol *be*
industrial melanism melanedd diwydiannol *eg*
industrial practice arfer diwydiannol *eg* arferion diwydiannol
industrial relations cysylltiadau diwydiannol *ell*
industrial retraining ailhyfforddi diwydiannol *be*
Industrial Revolution Chwyldro Diwydiannol *eg*
industrial sector sector diwydiannol *eg*
industrial training hyfforddiant diwydiannol *eg*
industrial training board bwrdd hyfforddi diwydiannol *eg* byrddau hyfforddi diwydiannol
industrial tribunal tribiwnlys diwydiannol *eg*
industrial waste gwastraff diwydiannol *eg*
industrialization diwydiannaeth *eb*
industrialize diwydianeiddio *be*
industry diwydiant *eg* diwydiannau
industry lead body corff arwain diwydiant *eg* cyrff arwain diwydiant
ineducable anaddysgadwy *ans*
ineffective aneffeithiol *ans*
ineffectiveness aneffeithioldeb *eg*
inefficiency aneffeithlonrwydd *eg*
inefficient aneffeithlon *ans*
inelastic anelastig *ans*
inelastic collision gwrthdrawiad anelastig *eg*
inelastic scattering gwasgariad anelastig *eg*
inequalities in health anghydraddoldebau iechyd *ell*
inequality (in mathematics) anhafaledd *eg* anhafaleddau
inequality (of status) anghydraddoldeb *eg*
inequation anhafaliad *eg* anhafaliadau
inert (=without inherent power, sluggish) difywyd *ans*
inert (without active chemical etc properties) anadweithiol *ans*
inert colour lliw difywyd *eg*
inert gas nwy anadweithiol *eg* nwyon anadweithiol
inert pair effect effaith pâr anadweithiol *eb*
inert substance sylwedd anadweithiol *eg* sylweddau anadweithiol
inertia (=sloth) syrthni *eg*
inertia (of property of matter) inertia *eg* inertiau

inertial inertiaidd *ans*
inertial frame of reference ffrâm gyfeirio inertiaidd *eb*
inessentials anhanfodion *ell*
inevitable accident damwain anochel *eb*
inextensible anestynadwy *ans*
infacing scarp sgarp mewnwynebol *eg* sgarpiau mewnwynebol
infallible anffaeledig *ans*
infancy babandod *eg*
infant baban *eg* babanod
infant baptism bedydd plant *eg*
infant mortality marwolaethau babanod *ell*
infant psychology seicoleg babanod *eb*
infant school ysgol babanod *eb* ysgolion babanod
infant welfare lles babanod *eg*
infanticide babanladdiad *eg*
infantile babanaidd *ans*
infantile amnesia amnesia babandod *eg*
infantry gwŷr traed *ell*
infect heintio *be*
infected heintiedig *ans*
infection (=infectious disease) haint *eb* heintiau
infection (act or process) heintiad *eg* heintiadau
infectious heintus *ans*
infectious disease clefyd heintus *eg* clefydau heintus
infer casglu *be*
inference casgliad *eg* casgliadau
► **inferential statistics** ystadegau casgliadol *eb*
inferior (=lower and therefore not as good) israddol *ans*
inferior (in anatomy) isaf *ans*
inferior (of quality) gwael *ans*
inferior (of rank) is *ans*
inferior goods nwyddau gwael *ell*
inferior resonance cyseiniant israddol *eg* cyseiniannau israddol
inferiority complex cymhleth israddoldeb *eg*
infertile anffrwythlon *ans*
infertility anffrwythlondeb *eg*
infest bod yn bla *be*
infestation pla *eg* plâu
infidel (=unbeliever) anghrediniwr *eg* anghredinwyr
infield maes agos *eg* meysydd agos
infilling mewnlenwad *eg* mewnlenwadau
infiltrate ymdreiddio *be*
infimum inffimwm *ans*
infinite anfeidraidd *ans*
infinite canon cylchganon *eb/g* cylchganonau
infinite decimal degolyn diddiwedd *eg* degolion diddiwedd
infinite loop dolen ddiddiwedd *eb* dolennau diddiwedd
infinitely yn anfeidraidd *adf*
infinitesimal *adj* gorfychan *ans*
infinitesimal *n* gorfychanyn *eg* gorfychanion
infinity anfeidredd *eg* anfeidreddau
infirm methedig *ans*
infirmary clafdy *eg* clafdai
infix *n* mewnddodiad *eg* mewnddodiaid
infix *v* mewnddodi *be*
infix notation nodiant mewnddodol *eg*
inflamed llidus *ans*
inflammable fflamadwy *ans*
inflammable liquid hylif fflamadwy *eg* hylifau fflamadwy
inflammable vapour anwedd fflamadwy *eg* anweddau fflamadwy
inflammation (medical) llid *eg*
inflate (in finance) chwyddo *be*
inflate (in physics) enchwythu *be*
inflated enchwythedig *ans*
inflation (=distention with air etc) enchwythiad *eg* enchwythiadau
inflation (of currency) chwyddiant *eg* chwyddiannau
inflation target targed chwyddiant *eg*
inflationary chwyddiannol *ans*
► **inflection** ffurfdro *eg* ffurfdroadau
inflexibility anhyblygrwydd *eg*
inflexible anhyblyg *ans*
inflexion goslef *eb* goslefau
inflorescence fflurgainc *eb* fflurgeinciau
inflow llifo i mewn *be*
influence *n* dylanwad *eg* dylanwadau
influence *v* dylanwadu *be*
influenza ffliw *eg*
influenza virus firws y ffliw *eg*
influx dylifiad *eg*
infold mewnblygu *be*
informal anffurfiol *ans*
informal approach dull anffurfiol *eg* dulliau anffurfiol
informal care gofal anffurfiol *eg*
informal carer gofalydd anffurfiol *eg*
informal communication cyfathrebu anffurfiol *be*
informal education addysg anffurfiol *eb*
informal group grŵp anffurfiol *eg*
informal method dull anffurfiol *eg* dulliau anffurfiol
informal reading inventory rhestr ddarllen anffurfiol *eb* rhestri darllen anffurfiol
informal teaching addysgu anffurfiol *be*
information gwybodaeth *eb*
information age oes wybodaeth *eb*
Information and Communication Technology Strategy Strategaeth Technoleg Gwybodaeth a Chyfathrebu *eb*
information bit did gwybodaeth *eg* didau gwybodaeth
information channel sianel wybodaeth *eb* sianeli gwybodaeth
information desk desg gwybodaeth *eb* desgiau gwybodaeth
information handbook llawlyfr gwybodaeth *eg* llawlyfrau gwybodaeth
information handling trin gwybodaeth *be*

information management and technology rheoli gwybodaeth a thechnoleg *be*
information mapping mapio gwybodaeth *be*
information network rhwydwaith gwybodaeth *eg*
information packet pecyn gwybodaeth *eg/b* pecynnau gwybodaeth
information probability field maes tebygolrwydd gwybodaeth *eg*
information processing prosesu gwybodaeth *be*
information retrieval adalw gwybodaeth *be*
information science gwyddor gwybodaeth *eb* gwyddorau gwybodaeth
information society cymdeithas wybodaeth *eb*
information source ffynhonnell gwybodaeth *eb* ffynonellau gwybodaeth
information superhighway traffordd wybodaeth *eb*
information system system wybodaeth *eb* systemau gwybodaeth
information technology (IT) technoleg gwybodaeth *eb*
information technology centre (ITEC) canolfan technoleg gwybodaeth *eb* canolfannau technoleg gwybodaeth
information test prawf gwybodaeth *eg* profion gwybodaeth
information theory theori gwybodaeth *eb* theorïau gwybodaeth
informative advertising hysbysebu er gwybodaeth *be*
informative label label gwybodaeth *eg* labeli gwybodaeth
informed choice dewis gwybodus *eg* dewisiadau gwybodus
informed consent cydsyniad gwybodus *eg*
infra-basal iswaelodol *ans*
infraorbital gland chwarren islygadol *eb* chwarennau islygadol
infrared *n* isgoch *eg*
infrared grill gridyll isgoch *eg* gridyllau isgoch
infrared wave ton isgoch *eb* tonnau isgoch
infrastructure isadeiledd *eg* isadeileddau
infringement trosedd *eg/b* troseddau
infuse trwytho *be*
infusion (=liquid or admixture) trwyth *eg* trwythau
infusion (of action) arllwysiad *eg* arllwysiadau
ingate trowel trywel gât *eb* trywelion gât
ingenious dyfeisgar *ans*
ingenuity dyfeisgarwch *eg*
ingest amlyncu *be*
ingestion amlynciad *eg*
ingot ingot *eg* ingotau
ingot mould mowld ingot *eg* mowldiau ingot
ingredient cynhwysyn *eg* cynhwysion
ingress mynediad *eg* mynediadau
ingrowing toenail casewin *eg* casewinedd
ingrown meander ystum lledrych *eg* ystumiau lledrych
inhabitant trigolyn *eg* trigolion
inhabited cyfannedd *ans*
inhalant siphon siffon mewnanadlu *eg* siffonau mewnanadlu
inhalation mewnanadliad *eg* mewnanadliadau
inhale mewnanadlu *be*
inhaled gases nwyon mewnanadledig *ell*
inhaler mewnanadlydd *eg* mewnanadlwyr
inherit etifeddu *be*
inheritance (of characteristics) etifeddiad *eg*
inherited etifeddol *ans*
inherited defect nam etifeddol *eg* namau etifeddol
inhibit (=hinder) llesteirio *be*
inhibit (in biochemistry, psychology) atal *be*
inhibiting ataliol *ans*
inhibition (=shyness) swildod *eg*
inhibition (e.g. enzyme and psychological) ataliad *eg* ataliadau
inhibitor atalydd *eg* atalyddion
inhibitory ataliol *ans*
inhibitory centre canolfannyn ataliol *eg*
inhibitory post-synaptic potential (**IPSP**) potensial ôl-synaptig ataliol *eg*
inhospitable digroeso *ans*
in-house mewnol *ans*
INIST: initial and in-service training HCMS: hyfforddiant cychwynnol ac mewn swydd *eg*
initial cychwynnol *ans*
initial ability level lefel gallu cychwynnol *eb*
initial concentration crynodiad cychwynnol *eg*
initial conditions amodau cychwynnol *ell*
initial curvature crymedd cychwynnol *eg* crymeddau cychwynnol
initial cycle cylchred gychwynnol *eb* cylchredau cychwynnol
initial line llinell gychwynnol *eb*
initial proposal cynnig cyntaf *eg* cynigion cyntaf
initial rate cyfradd gychwynnol *eb*
initial teacher training hyfforddiant cychwynnol i athrawon *eg*
initial velocity cyflymder cychwynnol *eg* cyflymderau cychwynnol
initialization procedure trefn ymgychwyn *eb*
initialize (disc) ymgychwyn *be*
initiate (=open) agor *be*
initiate (=start) cychwyn *be*
initiate proceedings cychwyn achos *be*
initiation (into a religion) derbyn *be*
initiation reaction adwaith cychwynnol *eg* adweithiau cychwynnol
initiative (=enterprise) menter *eb* mentrau
initiative (=first step) cam cyntaf *eg* camau cyntaf
initiator cychwynnydd *eg* cychwynyddion
inject (a person) rhoi pigiad *be*
inject (into a receptacle) chwistrellu *be*
injection (into a receptacle) chwistrelliad *eg* chwistrelliadau
injection (into person) pigiad *eg* pigiadau
injection moulding mowldio chwistrellu *be*
injective mapping mapio mewnsaethol *be*

injunction (=judicial order of compulsion) gorfodeb *eb* gorfodebion
injunction (=judicial order of restraint) gwaharddeb *eb* gwaharddebion
injury anaf *eg* anafiadau
ink *n* inc *eg* inciau
ink *v* incio *be*
ink drier sychydd inc *eg* sychwyr inc
ink roller rholer inc *eg* rholeri inc
ink sac coden inc *eb* codennau inc
ink thinner teneuydd inc *eg* teneuwyr inc
inking in incio *be*
inking slab slab incio *eg* slabiau incio
ink-jet printer argraffydd chwistrell *eg* argraffyddion chwistrell
inkle loom gwŷdd incl *eg* gwyddau incl
inland mewndirol *ans*
Inland Revenue Cyllid y Wlad *eg*
inlay *n* mewnosodiad *eg* mewnosodiadau
inlay *v* mewnosod *be*
inlay strings llinynnau mewnosod *ell*
inlet (=intake) mewnfa *eb* mewnfeydd
inlet (of sea, lake) cilfach *eb* cilfachau
inlet-head blaen cilfach *eg* blaenau cilfachau
inlier mewngraig *eb* mewngreigiau
in-line mewn llinell *ans*
inline image delwedd fewnol *eb* delweddau mewnol
in-line point follower dilynwr pwynt mewn-llinell *eg* dilynwyr pwynt mewn-llinell
in-line production cynhyrchu mewn llinell *be*
in-line roller rholer mewn-llinell *eg* rholeri mewn-llinell
inn of court neuadd brawdlys *eb* neuaddau brawdlys
innate cynhenid *ans*
inner mewnol *ans*
inner bead glain mewnol *eg* gleiniau mewnol
► **inner city** *n* dinas fewnol *eb*
► **inner city school** ysgol dinas fewnol *eb* ysgolion dinas fewnol
inner core craidd mewnol *eg* creiddiau mewnol
inner ear clust fewnol *eb*
inner face wyneb mewnol *eg*
Inner London Council Cyngor Llundain Fewnol *eg*
inner parts rhannau mewnol *ell*
inner pedal pedal mewnol *eg* pedalau mewnol
Inner Temple Ysbyty'r Inner Temple *eg*
innermost nesaf i mewn
innervate nerfogi *be*
innervation nerfogaeth *eb*
innings batiad *eg* batiadau
innominate (of artery) anenwol *ans*
innovate arloesi *be*
innovation arloesedd *eg*
innovation (=alteration) cyfnewidiad *eg* cyfnewidiadau
innovation (=new development) datblygiad newydd *eg* datblygiadau newydd
innovation (=new thing) newyddbeth *eg* newyddbethau
Inns of Court Ysbytai'r Brawdlys *ell*
inoculate brechu *be*
inoculation brechiad *eg* brechiadau
inoculation theory damcaniaeth brechu *eb*
inorganic anorganig *ans*
in-patient claf mewnol *eg* cleifion mewnol
inphase cydwedd *ans*
input *v* mewnbynnu *be*
input (=contribution of information) *n* cyfraniad *eg* cyfraniadau
input (=information fed into a computer) *n* mewnbwn *eg* mewnbynnau
input (in finance) *n* mewngyrch *eg*
Input/Output (I/O) Mewnbwn/Allbwn
input/output buffer byffer mewnbwn/allbwn *eg* bytferau mewnbwn/allbwn
input/output device dyfais mewnbwn/allbwn *eb* dyfeisiau mewnbwn/allbwn
input/output routine rheolwaith mewnbwn/allbwn *eg* rheolweithiau mewnbwn/allbwn
input/output stream mewnlif/all-lif *eg* mewnlifoedd/all-lifoedd
input and output mewnbwn ac allbwn
input control system system reoli mewnbwn *eb* systemau rheoli mewnbwn
input device dyfais fewnbynnu *eb* dyfeisiau mewnbynnu
input field maes mewnbwn *eg* meysydd mewnbwn
input help cymorth mewnbwn *eg*
input in tables mewnbwn mewn tablau *eg*
input line llinell mewnbwn *eb* llinellau mewnbwn
input options dewisiadau mewnbwn *ell*
input required mewnbwn angenrheidiol *eg*
input stream mewnlif *eg* mewnlifoedd
input unit uned fewnbynnu *eb* unedau mewnbynnu
inquest cwest *eg* cwestau
inquiry (=investigation) ymchwiliad *eg* ymchwiliadau
inquiry (=question) ymholiad *eg* ymholiadau
inquisition (=ecclesiastical court) chwilys *eg* chwilysoedd
inquisition (=enquiry) ymchwiliad *eg* ymchwiliadau
Inquisitor General Arch-chwilyswr *eg* Arch-chwilyswyr
inquisitorial system system holgar *eb*
in-range mewn amrediad *ans*
insane gwallgof *ans*
inscribe arysgrifio *be*
inscribed circle (in-circle) mewngylch *eg* mewngylchoedd
inscription arysgrif *eg* arysgrifau
insect pryfyn *eg* pryfed
insect attack ymosodiad trychfilod *eg*
insect bite pigiad pryfyn *eg* pigiadau pryfyn
insecticide pryfleiddiad *eg* pryfleiddiaid
insectivorous pryfysol *ans*

insemination ymhadiad *eg* ymhadiadau
insequent *n* haplif *eg*
insequent stream ffrwd haplif *eb* ffrydiau haplif
insert mewnosodiad *eg* mewnosodiadau
insert mewnosod *be*
insert applet mewnosod rhaglennig *be*
insert as copy mewnosod fel copi *be*
insert as hyperlink mewnosod fel hypergyswllt *be*
insert as link mewnosod fel cyswllt *be*
insert author field mewnosod maes awdur *be*
insert autotext mewnosod awtodestun *be*
insert bibliography entry mewnosod cofnod llyfryddiaeth *be*
insert bookmark mewnosod nod tudalen *be*
insert break mewnosod toriad *be*
insert business cards mewnosod cardiau busnes *be*
insert cells mewnosod celloedd *be*
insert cells down mewnosod celloedd i lawr *be*
insert cells right mewnosod celloedd i'r dde *be*
insert chart mewnosod siart *be*
insert column mewnosod colofn *be*
insert column break mewnosod toriad colofn *be*
insert command mewnosod gorchymyn *be*
insert comment mewnosod sylw *be*
insert controls mewnosod rheolyddion *be*
insert data mewnosod data *be*
insert data caption mewnosod egluryn data *be*
insert data label mewnosod label data *be*
insert database columns mewnosod colofnau cronfa ddata *be*
insert date mewnosod dyddiad *be*
insert document mewnosod dogfen *be*
insert document title mewnosod teitl dogfen *be*
insert endnote directly mewnosod ôl-nodyn yn uniongyrchol *be*
insert envelope mewnosod amlen *be*
insert field reference mewnosod cyfeirnod maes *be*
insert file mewnosod ffeil *be*
insert file field mewnosod maes ffeil *be*
insert footer mewnosod troedyn *be*
insert footnote mewnosod troednodyn *be*
insert footnote directly mewnosod troednodyn yn uniongyrchol *be*
insert formula mewnosod fformiwla *be*
insert frame mewnosod ffrâm *be*
insert frame manually mewnosod ffrâm â llaw *be*
insert function mewnosod swyddogaeth *be*
insert glue point mewnosod pwynt glud *be*
insert graphics mewnosod graffigau *be*
insert group mewnosod grŵp *be*
insert header mewnosod pennyn *be*
insert horizontal mewnosod y llorweddol *be*
insert horizontal ruler mewnosod mesurydd llorweddol *be*
insert horizontally mewnosod yn llorweddol *be*
insert hyperlink mewnosod hypergyswllt *be*
insert image mewnosod delwedd *be*
insert in container mewnosod mewn cynhwysydd *be*
insert index mewnosod mynegai *be*
insert index entry mewnosod cofnod mynegai *be*
insert index marker mewnosod nod mynegai *be*
insert join mewnosod uniad *be*
INSERT key bysell INSERT *eb* bysellau INSERT
insert label ranges mewnosod ystodau labeli *be*
insert layer mewnosod haen *be*
insert legend mewnosod allwedd *be*
insert link mewnosod cyswllt *be*
insert manual break mewnosod toriad â llaw *be*
insert matrix formula mewnosod fformiwla matrics *be*
insert merge field mewnosod maes cyfun *be*
insert mode modd mewnosod *eg*
insert name mewnosod enw *be*
insert new row mewnosod rhes newydd *be*
insert non-breaking hyphen mewnosod cysylltnod di-dor *be*
insert non-breaking space mewnosod bwlch di-dor *be*
insert note mewnosod nodyn *be*
insert object mewnosod gwrthrych *be*
insert optional hyphen mewnosod cysylltnod dewisol *be*
insert other objects mewnosod gwrthrychau eraill *be*
insert page mewnosod tudalen *be*
insert page field mewnosod maes tudalen *be*
insert page number mewnosod rhif tudalen *be*
insert paragraph mewnosod paragraff *be*
insert plug-in mewnosod ategyn *be*
insert point pwynt mewnosod *eg* pwyntiau mewnosod
insert primary key mewnosod allwedd gynradd *be*
insert query data mewnosod data ymholiad *be*
insert reference mewnosod cyfeirnod *be*
insert result mewnosod canlyniad *be*
insert row mewnosod rhes *be*
insert row break mewnosod toriad rhes *be*
insert ruler mewnosod mesurydd *be*
insert script mewnosod sgript *be*
insert section mewnosod adran *be*
insert sheet mewnosod dalen *be*
insert signature mewnosod llofnod *be*
insert slide mewnosod sleid *be*
insert slide direct mewnosod sleid yn uniongyrchol *be*
insert snap point mewnosod pwynt snap *be*
insert sound mewnosod sain *be*
insert sound plug-in mewnosod ategyn sain *be*
insert source text mewnosod testun ffynhonnell *be*
insert special character mewnosod nod arbennig *be*
insert subject mewnosod pwnc *be*
insert table mewnosod tabl *be*
insert text mewnosod testun *be*

insert text frame mewnosod ffrâm testun *be*
insert time mewnosod amser *be*
insert title mewnosod teitl *be*
insert unnumbered entry mewnosod cofnod heb rif *be*
insert URL button mewnosod botwm URL *be*
insert version comment mewnosod sylw ar y fersiwn *be*
insert vertical mewnosod fertigol *be*
insert video mewnosod fideo *be*
insert video plug-in mewnosod ategyn fideo *be*
inserted stitch pwyth cyswllt *eg* pwythau cyswllt
insertion mewniad *eg* mewniadau
insertion sort trefniad mewnosod *eg* trefniadau mewnosod
in-service education addysg mewn swydd *eb*
in-service training course cwrs hyfforddiant mewn swydd *eg* cyrsiau hyfforddiant mewn swydd
inset mewnosodiad *eg* mewnosodiadau
INSET: in-service training HMS: hyfforddiant mewn swydd *eg*
inshore gyda'r glannau *ans*
inshore fishing pysgota'r glannau *be*
inside tu mewn *eg*
inside callipers caliperau mewnol *ell*
inside diameter diamedr mewnol *eg* diamedrau mewnol
inside forward mewnwr *eg* mewnwyr
inside half mewnwr *eg* mewnwyr
inside left mewnwr chwith *eg* mewnwyr chwith
inside leg coes fewnol *eb*
inside micrometer micromedr mewnol *eg* micromedrau mewnol
inside of glove cledr y faneg *eb*
inside right (of player) mewnwr de *eg* mewnwyr de
inside the circle tu mewn i'r cylch *eg*
insight mewnwelediad *eg* mewnwelediadau
insolation darheulad *eg*
insolubility anhydoddedd *eg*
insoluble anhydawdd *ans*
insolvency methdaliad *eg* methdaliadau
insolvent methdalwr *eg* methdalwyr
insomnia anhunedd *eg*
inspect arolygu *be*
inspection arolygiad *eg* arolygiadau
inspection chamber siambr archwilio *eb* siambrau archwilio
inspector arolygwr *eg* arolygwyr
inspectorate arolygiaeth *eb* arolygiaethau
inspiration (of air) mewnanadliad *eg*
inspiration (poetic etc) ysbrydoliaeth *eb*
inspiratory reserve volume cyfaint mewnanadlol wrth gefn *eg*
inspire (of air) mewnanadlu *be*
inspire (poetic etc) ysbrydoli *be*
inspired air aer mewnanadledig *eg*
instability (of economy, society etc) ansefydlogrwydd *eg*
instability (of object) ansadrwydd *eg*
install (machinery, software etc) gosod *be*
install dictionaries gosod geiriaduron *be*
installation gosodiad *eg* gosodiadau
installation program rhaglen osod *eb* rhaglenni gosod
installation wizard dewin gosod *eg*
installer gosodwr *eg*
instalment rhandal *eg* rhandaliadau
instant ennyd *eg/b* enydau
instant grip wrench tyndro gafael ebrwydd *eg* tyndroeon gafael ebrwydd
instant messaging negeseua sydyn *be*
instantaneous (in general) ebrwydd *ans*
instantaneous (in physics) enydaidd *ans*
instantaneous centre of rotation canol enydaidd y cylchdro *eg*
instantaneous grip gafael ebrwydd *eb*
instantaneous grip vice feis gafael ebrwydd *eb* feisiau gafael ebrwydd
instantaneous water-heater gwresogydd dŵr ebrwydd *eg* gwresogyddion dŵr ebrwydd
instep cefn troed *eg* cefnau traed
instinct greddf *eb* greddfau
instinctive behaviour ymddygiad greddfol *eg*
institute sefydliad *eg* sefydliadau
institute of education athrofa *eb* athrofeydd
Institute of International Economics Sefydliad Economeg Ryngwladol *eg*
institute of legal executives sefydliad y gweithredwyr cyfreithlon *eg*
institution sefydliad *eg* sefydliadau
institutional sefydliadol *ans*
institutional care gofal mewn sefydliad *eg*
institutional determinant penderfynyn sefydliadol *eg*
institutional discrimination gwahaniaethu sefydliadol *be*
institutional history hanes sefydliadau *eg*
institutionalize sefydliadu *be*
instruction cyfarwyddyd *eg* cyfarwyddiadau
instruction address cyfeiriad cyfarwyddyd *eg* cyfeiriadau cyfarwyddyd
instruction cycle cylchred gyfarwyddyd *eb* cylchredau cyfarwyddyd
instruction decoder datgodiwr cyfarwyddyd *eg* datgodwyr cyfarwyddyd
instruction format fformat cyfarwyddyd *eg* fformatau cyfarwyddyd
instruction register cofrestr gyfarwyddyd *eb* cofrestri cyfarwyddyd
instruction set set gyfarwyddiadau *eb* setiau cyfarwyddiadau
instruction sheet taflen gyfarwyddiadau *eb* taflenni cyfarwyddiadau
instruction word gair cyfarwyddiadol *eg* geiriau cyfarwyddiadol
instructional programme rhaglen hyfforddi *eb* rhaglenni hyfforddi

instructor hyfforddwr *eg* hyfforddwyr
instrument (=implement) offeryn *eg* offer
instrument (of music) offeryn *eg* offerynnau
Instrument of Government Offeryn Llywodraeth *eg*
instrumental (of music) offerynnol *ans*
instrumental ostinato ostinato offerynnol *eg*
instrumental part rhan offerynnol *eb* rhannau offerynnol
instrumental writing ysgrifennu ar gyfer offerynnau *be*
instrumentalist offerynnwr *eg* offerynwyr
instrumentation offeryniaeth *eb* offeryniaethau
insular ynysol *ans*
insulate ynysu *be*
insulated ynysedig *ans*
insulating board bwrdd ynysu *eg* byrddau ynysu
insulating material defnydd ynysu *eg* defnyddiau ynysu
insulation ynysiad *eg* ynysiadau
insulator ynysydd *eg* ynysyddion
insulin inswlin *eg*
insulin-dependent diabetes mellitus diabetes mellitus dibynnol ar inswlin *eg*
insurance yswiriant *eg* yswiriannau
insurance policy polisi yswiriant *eg* polisïau yswiriant
insure yswirio *be*
insured yswiriedig *ans*
insured population poblogaeth yswiriedig *eb* poblogaethau yswiriedig
insurer yswiriwr *eg* yswirwyr
insurrection gwrthryfel *eg* gwrthryfeloedd
intact spurs sbardunau didoriad *ell*
intaglio intaglio *eg*
intaglio engraving ysgythriad intaglio *eg* ysgythriadau intaglio
intake nifer a dderbynnir *eg* niferoedd a dderbynnir
intake (flow) mewnlif *eg* mewnlifoedd
intake (land) ffridd *eb* ffriddoedd
intake (of food) cymeriant *eg*
intake and output cymeriant ac allgynnyrch *eg*
intarsia intarsia *eg*
integer cyfanrif *eg* cyfanrifau
integer arithmetic rhifyddeg cyfanrifau *eb*
integer value gwerth cyfanrifol *eg* gwerthoedd cyfanrifol
integer variable newidyn cyfanrifol *eg* newidynnau cyfanrifol
integral (of calculus) *adj* integrol *ans*
integral (of calculus) *n* integryn *eg* integrynnau
integral (of integer) *adj* cyfannol *ans*
integral (part of something) *adj* annatod *ans*
integral calculus calcwlws integrol *eg*
integral diagram diagram integrol *eg* diagramau integrol
integral domain parth integrol *eg* parthau integrol
integral multiple lluosrif cyfannol *eg* lluosrifau cyfannol
integral value gwerth cyfannol *eg* gwerthoedd cyfannol
integrand integrand *eg* integrandau
integrate (=bring into equal participation) integreiddio *be*
integrate (=combine into a whole or complete by the addition of parts) cyfannu *be*
integrate (=find the integral of) integru *be*
integrate children integreiddio plant *be*
integrate society cyfannu cymdeithas *be*
integrated (of children, people) integredig *ans*
integrated (of objects) cyfannol *ans*
integrated circuit cylched gyfannol *eb* cylchedau cyfannol
integrated circuit (IC) cylched gyfannol *eb* cylchedau cyfannol
integrated course cwrs cyfannol *eg* cyrsiau cyfannol
integrated curriculum cwricwlwm cyfannol *eg*
integrated day diwrnod cyfannol *eg*
integrated learning dysgu cyfannol *be*
integrated package pecyn cyfannol *eg* pecynnau cyfannol
integrated school ysgol gyfannol *eb* ysgolion cyfannol
Integrated Services Digital Network Rhwydwaith Digidol Gwasanaethau Integredig *eg*
integrated studies astudiaethau cyfannol *ell*
integrated support service gwasanaeth cefnogi cyfannol *eg* gwasanaethau cefnogi cyfannol
integrated syllabus maes llafur cyfannol *eg* meysydd llafur cyfannol
integrated training hyfforddiant cyfannol *eg*
integration integreiddiad *eg*
integration (in calculus) integriad *eg* integriadau
integration (of parts into a whole) cyfannu *be*
integration (of people) integreiddio *be*
integration by parts integru fesul rhan *be*
integration time amser integru *eg*
integrative integreiddiol *ans*
integrity (=moral uprightness) unplygrwydd *eg*
integrity (=wholeness) cyfanrwydd *eg*
integument pilyn *eg* pilynnau
intellectual *adj* deallusol *ans*
intellectual development datblygiad deallusol *eg*
intellectual experience profiad deallusol *eg* profiadau deallusol
intellectual factor ffactor ddeallusol *eb* ffactorau deallusol
intellectual property rights hawliau eiddo deallusol *ell*
intellectual rigour (as a criterion) trylwyredd deallusol *eg*
intelligence deallusrwydd *eg*
intelligence quotient (I.Q.) cyniferydd deallusrwydd *eg*
intelligence test prawf deallusrwydd *eg* profion deallusrwydd
intelligent deallus *ans*

intelligent knowledge based systems (IKBS) systemau deallus yn seiliedig ar wybodaeth *ell*
intelligent terminal terfynell ddeallus *eb* terfynellau deallus
intelligentsia deallusion *ell*
intense dwys *ans*
intense (of feeling) angerddol *ans*
intense (of light) tanbaid *ans*
intensity (in physics) arddwysedd *eg* arddwyseddau
intensity (of feeling) angerdd *eg*
intensity (of light) tanbeidrwydd *eg*
intensive (in physics) arddwys *ans*
intensive care gofal dwys *eg*
intention bwriad *eg* bwriadau
interact rhyngweithio *be*
interaction rhyngweithiad *eg* rhyngweithiadau
interactionism rhyngweithedd *eb*
interactive rhyngweithiol *ans*
interactive game gêm ryngweithiol *eb* gemau rhyngweithiol
interactive video fideo rhyngweithiol *eg* fideos rhyngweithiol
interagency work gwaith rhwng asiantaethau *eg*
interbedded rhynghaenol *ans*
inter-block gap bwlch rhyngfloc *eg* bylchau rhyngfloc
interbreed rhyngfridio *be*
intercalary rhyngosodol *ans*
intercede eiriol *be*
intercellular rhyng-gellol *ans*
intercellular spaces gwagleoedd rhyng-gellol *ell*
intercept *n* rhyng-gipiad *eg* rhyng-gipiadau
intercept (a ball in sport) *v* rhyng-gipio *be*
intercept (e.g. of aeroplanes) *v* rhyng-gyfarfod *be*
intercept (in mathematics) *n* rhyngdoriad *eg* rhyngdoriadau
intercept (in mathematics) *v* rhyngdorri *be*
interception (e.g. of aeroplanes) rhyng-gyfarfyddiad *eg* rhyng-gyfarfyddiadau
interception (of a ball in sport) rhyng-gipiad *eg* rhyng-gipiadau
intercession eiriolaeth *eb*
interchange (in mathematics) cydgyfnewid *be*
interchange (of data) ymgyfnewid *be*
interchangeable (in mathematics) cydgyfnewidiol *ans*
interconvertibility rhyngdrawsnewidioldeb *eg*
intercorrelation rhyng-gydberthyniad *eg* rhyng-gydberthyniadau
intercostal rhyngasennol *ans*
intercourse (sexual) cyfathrach rywiol *eb*
interdepartmental rhyngadrannol *ans*
interdependence cyd-ddibyniaeth *eb*
interdependent cyd-ddibynnol *ans*
interdependent variable newidyn rhyngddibynnol *eg* newidynnau rhyngddibynnol
interdict gwaharddiad *eg* gwaharddiadau
interdrumlin rhyngdrymlinol *ans*
interest (=advantage or profit) budd *eg* buddiannau
interest (=concern, curiosity, pastime) diddordeb *eg* diddordebau
interest (=money paid for money lent) llog *eg* llogau
interest area maes diddordeb *eg* meysydd diddordeb
interest rate cyfradd llog *eb* cyfraddau llog
interest-getting question cwestiwn i ddenu diddordeb *eg* cwestiynau i ddenu diddordeb
interesting diddorol *ans*
interface *n* rhyngwyneb *eg* rhyngwynebau
interface *v* rhyngwynebu *be*
interfacial rhyngwynebol *ans*
interfacing (of fabric) wynebyn cudd *eg* wynebynnau cudd
interfascicular rhyngffasgellol *ans*
interference (as a scientific phenomenon) ymyriant *eg*
interference (in general) ymyrraeth *eb* ymyraethau
interference fit ffit ymyrryd *eb* ffitiau ymyrryd
interference fringe eddi ymyriant *eg* eddïau ymyriant
interfering ymyrrol *ans*
interferometer ymyradur *eg* ymyraduron
interferon interfferon *eg*
interfluve tir rhyngafonol *eg* tiroedd rhyngafonol
intergalactic rhyngalaethog *ans*
interglacial rhyngrewlifol *ans*
inter-granal rhyng-granaidd *ans*
intergroup discrimination gwahaniaethu ar sail grŵp *be*
interim interim *ans*
interim report adroddiad interim *eg* adroddiadau interim
interior (=inside) *n* tu mewn *eg*
interior (in general) *adj* mewnol *ans*
interior (of land) *adj* mewndirol *ans*
interior (of land) *n* mewndir *eg*
interior angle ongl fewnol *eb* onglau mewnol
interior decorating addurno mewnol *be*
interior decoration addurn mewnol *eg* addurniadau mewnol
interior plywood pren haenog mewnol *eg*
interlace *n* rhyngles *eg*
interlace *v* rhynglesio *be*
interlining leinin cudd *eg*
interlink cydgysylltu *be*
interlinked cydgysylltiol *ans*
interlock cydgloi *be*
interlocked grain graen rhyng-gloëdig *eg*
interlocking cydgloi *be*
interlocking device dyfais gydgloëdig *eb* dyfeisiau cydgloëdig
interlocking spurs sbardunau pleth *ell*
interlude (in a performance) egwyl *eb* egwylion
intermanual conflict gwrthdaro dwy-law *be*
intermediary *n* cyfryngwr *eg* cyfryngwyr

intermediary compound rhyng-gyfansoddyn *eg* rhyng-gyfansoddion
intermediary metabolism metabolaeth ryngol *eb*
intermediate (in biology) *n* rhyngolyn *eg* rhyngolynnau
intermediate (in education) *adj* canolradd *ans*
intermediate area (=grey area) ardal lwyd *eb* ardaloedd llwyd
intermediate condition rhyng-gyflwr *eg* rhyng-gyflyrau
intermediate education addysg ganolradd *eb*
intermediate goods nwyddau rhyngol *ell*
intermediate layer haen ryngol *eb* haenau rhyngol
intermediate repeater radio station gorsaf aildrosglwyddo yn y canol *eb* gorsafoedd aildrosglwyddo yn y canol
intermediate school ysgol ganolradd *eb* ysgolion canolradd
intermediate state (in mathematics) rhyng-gyflwr *eg* rhyng-gyflyrau
intermezzo intermezzo *eg* intermezzi
intermittent ysbeidiol *ans*
intermittent feed porthiant ysbeidiol *eg*
intermittent reinforcement atgyfnerthiad ysbeidiol *eg*
intermittent stream ffrwd ysbeidiol *eb* ffrydiau ysbeidiol
intermix *n* cydgymysgiad *eg*
intermix *v* cydgymysgu *be*
intermixable rhyng-gymysgadwy *ans*
intermixture cydgymysgedd *eg* cydgymysgeddau
intermont rhyngfynyddig *ans*
internal mewnol *ans*
internal assessment asesu mewnol *be*
internal assessor aseswr mewnol *eg* aseswyr mewnol
internal bisector hanerydd mewnol *eg* hanerwyr mewnol
internal bleeding gwaedu mewnol *be*
internal capsule cwpan mewnol *eg*
internal circlip cylchglip mewnol *eg* cylchglipiau mewnol
internal combustion engine peiriant tanio mewnol *eg* peiriannau tanio mewnol
internal comfort cynhesrwydd mewnol *eg*
internal communication cyfathrebu mewnol *be*
internal degree gradd fewnol *eb* graddau mewnol
internal diameter diamedr mewnol *eg* diamedrau mewnol
internal environment amgylchedd mewnol *eg* amgylcheddau mewnol
internal examination arholiad mewnol *eg* arholiadau mewnol
internal examiner arholwr mewnol *eg* arholwyr mewnol
internal fabric ffabrig mewnol *eg*
internal growth twf mewnol *eg*
internal illumination golau mewnol *eg*
internal inquiry ymchwiliad mewnol *eg* ymchwiliadau mewnol
internal locus of control locws rheolaeth fewnol *eg*
internal pressure gwasgedd mewnol *eg*
internal recruitment recriwtio mewnol *be*
internal resistance gwrthiant mewnol *eg*
internal respiration resbiradaeth fewnol *eb*
internal secretion secretiad mewnol *eg* secretiadau mewnol
internal step cam mewnol *eg* camau mewnol
internal validity dilysrwydd mewnol *eg*
internal verifier dilysydd mewnol *eg* dilyswyr mewnol
internal wall wal fewnol *eb* waliau mewnol
internalization mewnoli *be*
internalize mewnoli *be*
international rhyngwladol *ans*
International (=L'internationale) Undeb Rhyngwladol *eg*
International Atomic Energy Agency Asiantaeth Ryngwladol Egni Niwclear *eb*
International Brigade Brigâd Ryngwladol *eb*
International Court of Justice Llys Barn Rhyngwladol *eg*
International Date Line Dyddlinell *eb*
international dimension dimensiwn rhyngwladol *eg* dimensiynau rhyngwladol
international ferry terminal terminws llongau fferi rhyngwladol *eg*
international history hanes rhyngwladol *eg*
international hotel chain cadwyn ryngwladol o westai *eb*
International Labour Organization Mudiad Llafur Rhyngwladol *eg*
international level lefel ryngwladol *eb* lefelau rhyngwladol
international market marchnad ryngwladol *eb*
international marketing marchnata rhyngwladol *be*
International Monetary Fund Cronfa Ariannol Ryngwladol *eb*
international paper sizes meintiau papur rhyngwladol *ell*
international phonetic alphabet (IPA) gwyddor ffonetig ryngwladol *eb*
International Red Cross Mudiad y Groes Goch Ryngwladol *eg*
International Refugee Organization Cyfundrefn Ryngwladol y Ffoaduriaid *eb*
international relations cydberthynas y gwledydd *eb*
international runner rhedwr rhyngwladol *eg* rhedwyr rhyngwladol
international sport chwaraeon rhyngwladol *ell*
International Standards Organization Cyfundrefn Safonau Rhyngwladol *eb*
international tension tensiwn rhyngwladol *eg*
international trade masnach ryngwladol *eb*
International Trade Commission Comisiwn Masnach Ryngwladol *eg*
internationalism rhyngwladoliaeth *eb*

internecine cyd-ddinistriol *ans*
internet rhyngrwyd *eb*
internet account cyfrif rhyngrwyd *eg* cyfrifon rhyngrwyd
internet banking bancio rhyngrwyd *be*
internet browser porwr rhyngrwyd *eg* porwyr rhyngrwyd
internet connection cysylltiad rhyngrwyd *eg*
internet server gweinydd rhyngrwyd *eg* gweinyddion rhyngrwyd
Internet Service Provider Cyflenwr Gwasanaeth Rhyngrwyd *eg* Cyflenwyr Gwasanaeth Rhyngrwyd
interneuron rhyngniwron *eg* rhyngniwronau
internodal rhyngnodol *ans*
internode internod *eg* internodau
interobserver agreement cytundeb rhwng arsylwyr *eg* cytundebau rhwng arsylwyr
interobserver reliability dilysrwydd rhwng arsylwyr *eg*
interoperability gallu i ryngweithredu *eg*
interpenetrate cydymdreiddio *be*
interpenetration cyd-dreiddiad *eg* cyd-dreiddiadau
interpersonal rhyngbersonol *ans*
interpersonal attraction atyniad rhyngbersonol *eg*
interpersonal communication cyfathrebu rhyngbersonol *be*
interpersonal relations cydberthynas rhwng pobl *eb*
interpersonal skills sgiliau rhyngbersonol *ell*
interphase rhyngwedd *eg*
interplay cydadwaith *be*
interpolate rhyngosod *be*
interpolation rhyngosodiad *eg* rhyngosodiadau
interposition rhyngsafle *eg* rhyngsafleoedd
interpret dehongli *be*
interpretation dehongliad *eg* dehongliadau
Interpretation Act 1978 Deddf Dehongliad 1978 *eb*
interpreted language iaith ddeongledig *eb* ieithoedd deongledig
interpreter (=computing program) dehonglydd *eg* dehonglwyr
interpreter (=translator) cyfieithydd *eg* cyfieithwyr
interpretive code cod deongliadol *eg* codau deongliadol
interquartile rhyngchwartel *eg* rhyngchwartelau
interquartile range amrediad rhyngchwartel *eg* amrediadau rhyngchwartel
interrater reliability dilysrwydd rhyng-gyfraddwyr *eg*
interregnum interregnum *eg*
interrelate cydberthyn *be*
interrelated variables newidynnau sy'n rhyngberthyn *ell*
interrelationship cydberthynas *eg/b* cydberthnasau
interrogate holi *be*
interrogatory *adj* holiadol *ans*
interrogatory *n* cwestiyneb *eb* cwestiynebau
interrupt *n* ymyriad *eg* ymyriadau
interrupt *v* ymyrryd *be*
interrupt event digwyddiad ymyriadol *eg* digwyddiadau ymyriadol
interrupt line lein ymyriadol *eb* leiniau ymyriadol
interrupt service routine rheolwaith trin ymyriadau *eg* rheolweithiau trin ymyriadau
interrupt trap magl ymyriadol *eb* maglau ymyriadol
interrupted cadence diweddeb annisgwyl *eb* diweddebau annisgwyl
interschool competition cystadleuaeth rhwng ysgolion *eb* cystadlaethau rhwng ysgolion
intersect croestorri *be*
intersecting prisms prismau croestoriadol *eg*
intersection croestoriad *eg* croestoriadau
intersection of sets croestoriad setiau *eg*
interspecific rhyngrywogaethol *ans*
interstellar accretion ymgasgliad rhyngserol *eg* ymgasgliadau rhyngserol
interstitial interstitaidd *ans*
interstitial cells celloedd interstitaidd *ell*
interstitial condensation cyddwysiad interstitaidd *eg*
intertextuality rhyngdestuniaeth *eb*
intertidal zone parth rhynglanw *eg*
intertropical rhyngdrofannol *ans*
intertropical front ffrynt rhyngdrofannol *eg*
interval (=break time) egwyl *eb* egwylion
interval (=intervening time) ysbaid *eb* ysbeidiau
interval (in music, mathematics) cyfwng *eg* cyfyngau
interval scale graddfa cyfyngau *eb* graddfeydd cyfyngau
interval timer amserydd cyfwng *eg* amseryddion cyfwng
interval training hyfforddiant egwyl *eg*
intervene ymyrryd *be*
intervening rhyngol *ans*
intervening variable newidyn cysylltiol *eg* newidynnau cysylltiol
intervention ymyriad *eg* ymyriadau
intervention price pris ymyrrol *eg* prisiau ymyrrol
intervertebral disc disg rhyngfertebrol *eg*
interview *n* cyfweliad *eg* cyfweliadau
interview *v* cyfweld *be*
interviewee cyfwelai *eg* cyfweleion
interviewer cyfwelydd *eg* cyfwelwyr
intestinal coluddol *ans*
intestine coluddyn *eg* coluddion
intimacy agosatrwydd *eg*
into function ffwythiant i mewn *eg*
intolerance anoddefgarwch *eg*
intonation (in plainsong) rhagnod *eg* rhagnodau
intonation (of instrument or voice) tonyddiaeth *eb*
intone goslefu *be*
intracellular mewngellol *ans*
intractable anhydrin *ans*
intrada intrada *eb* intradau
intradermal injection pigiad mewngroenol *eg* pigiadau mewngroenol

intrados of an arch cromlin fewnol bwa *eb* cromliniau mewnol bwâu
intramolecular mewnfoleciwlaidd *ans*
intramuscular injection pigiad mewngyhyrol *eg* pigiadau mewngyhyrol
intranet mewnrwyd *eb*
intransitive (in mathematics) anhrosaidd *ans*
intrapleural drainage draeniad mewnblewrol *eg*
intraspecies aggression ymosodedd mewnrywogaethol *eg*
intraspecific mewnrywogaethol *ans*
intrauterine loop dolen fewngroth *eb* dolennau mewngroth
intravenous mewnwythiennol *ans*
intravenous infusion (of action) arllwysiad mewnwythiennol *eg* arllwysiadau mewnwythiennol
intravenous infusion (of liquid) trwyth mewnwythiennol *eg* trwythau mewnwythiennol
intrazonal cydgylchfaol *ans*
intricate cymhleth *ans*
intricate pattern patrwm cymhleth *eg* patrymau cymhleth
intricate shape ffurf gymhleth *eb* ffurfiau cymhleth
intricate work gwaith cymhleth *eg*
intrigue cynllwyn *eg* cynllwynion
intrinsic cynhenid *ans*
intrinsic energy egni cynhenid *eg*
intrinsic movement symudiad cynhenid *eg* symudiadau cynhenid
intrinsic spin troelliad cynhenid *eg* troelliadau cynhenid
introduce cyflwyno *be*
introduction (=explanatory section of book) rhagymadrodd *eg* rhagymadroddion
introduction (in music etc) rhagarweiniad *eg* rhagarweiniadau
introduction (of person to another) cyflwyniad *eg* cyflwyniadau
introductory activity gweithgaredd rhagarweiniol *eg*
introductory screen sgrin ragarweiniol *eb* sgriniau rhagarweiniol
introspection mewnsyllu *be*
introvert mewnblyg *ans*
intrude ymwthio *be*
intrusion (in general) ymwthiad *eg*
intrusion (of rock) mewnwthiad *eg* mewnwthiadau
intrusive (of rock) mewnwthiol *ans*
intrusive rock craig fewnwthiol *eb* creigiau mewnwthiol
intubation mewndiwbio *be*
intuition greddf *eb* greddfau
intuitive sythweledol *ans*
intuitive stage cyfnod sythweledol *eg* cyfnodau sythweledol
intuitive thought meddwl sythweledol *eg*
intuitive understanding dealltwriaeth sythweledol *eb*
inundate gorlifo *be*
invade goresgyn *be*
invader goresgynnwr *eg* goresgynwyr
invaginate ymweinio *be*
invagination ymweiniad *eg* ymweiniadau
invalid *n* claf *eg* cleifion
invalid (of passport etc) *adj* annilys *ans*
invalid (of person) *adj* methedig *ans*
invalidate dirymu *be*
invalidity benefit budd-dal y methedig *eg*
invariant *adj* sefydlog *ans*
invariant *n* sefydlyn *eg* sefydlynnau
invasion goresgyniad *eg* goresgyniadau
invasion game gêm goresgyn *eb* gemau goresgyn
invasive procedure gweithred fewnwthiol *eb* gweithredoedd mewnwthiol
invent dyfeisio *be*
invention dyfais *eb* dyfeisiau
inventive dyfeisgar *ans*
inventor dyfeisiwr *eg* dyfeiswyr
inventory rhestr eiddo *eb* rhestri eiddo
inventory management rheolaeth restru *eb*
inverse gwrthdro *eg* gwrthdroeon
inverse element elfen wrthdro *eb* elfennau gwrthdro
inverse functions ffwythiannau gwrthdro *ell*
inverse matrix matrics gwrthdro *eg*
inverse operation gweithrediad gwrthdro *eg* gweithrediadau gwrthdro
inverse ratio cymhareb wrthdro *eb* cymarebau gwrthdro
inverse square law deddf sgwâr gwrthdro *eb*
inverse variation amrywiad gwrthdro *eg* amrywiadau gwrthdro
inversion (in general) gwrthdroad *eg* gwrthdroadau
inversion (in music) gwrthdro *eg* gwrthdroeon
inversion of chord gwrthdro cord *eg* gwrthdroeon cordiau
inversion of temperature gwrthdroad tymheredd *eg* gwrthdroadau tymheredd
invert gwrthdroi *be*
invert level lefel wrthdro *eb*
invert sugar siwgr gwrthdroëdig *eg*
invertase infertas *eg*
invertebral rhyngfertebrol *ans*
invertebrate infertebrat *eg* infertebratau
inverted gwrthdroedig *ans*
inverted gwrthdro *ans*
inverted answer ateb wyneb i waered *eg* atebion wyneb i waered
inverted cone côn gwrthdro *eg* conau gwrthdro
inverted image delwedd wrthdro *eb* delweddau gwrthdro
inverted mordent isfordent *eg* isfordentau
inverted pleat plet wrthdro *eb* pletiau gwrthdro
inverted pyramid pyramid gwrthdro *eg* pyramidiau gwrthdro
inverted relief tirwedd wrthdro *eb* tirweddau gwrthdro
inverted tuck twc gwrthdro *eg* tyciau gwrthdro
inverting amplifier mwyhadur gwrthdroadol *eg*

invertor gwrthdröydd *eg* gwrthdroyddion
invest (=clothe) arwisgo *be*
invest (=lay siege) gosod gwarchae *be*
invest (financial) buddsoddi *be*
investigate ymchwilio *be*
investigate scientific questions ymchwilio i gwestiynau gwyddonol *be*
investigation (=study) astudiaeth *eb* astudiaethau
investigation (medical) archwiliad *eg* archwiliadau
investigation (of crime etc) ymchwiliad *eg* ymchwiliadau
investigative ymchwiliol *ans*
investigative geography daearyddiaeth ymchwiliol *eb*
investigative method dull ymchwiliol *eg* dulliau ymchwiliol
investigative psychology seicoleg ymchwiliol *eb*
investigative work gwaith ymchwilio *eg*
investiture arwisgo *be*
Investiture Contest Ymryson yr Arwisgo *eb*
investment (of money) buddsoddiad *eg* buddsoddiadau
investment (of power) arwisgiad *eg*
investment appraisal gwerthuso buddsoddiad *be*
investment casting castio patrwm aberthol *be*
investor buddsoddwr *eg* buddsoddwyr
Investors in People Buddsoddwyr mewn Pobl
Investors in People award gwobr Buddsoddwyr mewn Pobl *eb*
inviable anhyfyw *ans*
invigilator goruchwyliwr *eg* goruchwylwyr
invigorating bywiogus *ans*
inviscid anludiog *ans*
invisible (=hidden) cudd *ans*
invisible (in general) anweledig *ans*
invisible earnings enillion anweledig *ell*
invisible exports allforion anweledig *ell*
invisible hemming hemio cudd *be*
invisible hinge colfach cudd *eg* colfachau cudd
invisible line llinell gudd *eb* llinellau cudd
invisible mending cyweirio cudd *be*
invisible zip sip cudd *eg* sipiau cudd
invitation to treat gwahoddiad i drafod *eg*
invite *v* gwahodd *be*
invocation of saints ymbil ar y saint *be*
invoice anfoneb *eb* anfonebau
invoice number rhif yr anfoneb *eg*
invoicing anfonebu *be*
involatile ananweddol *ans*
involucre cylchamlen *eb* cylchamlenni
involuntary anwirfoddol *ans*
involuntary action gweithred anwirfoddol *eb* gweithredoedd anwirfoddol
involuntary muscle cyhyr anrheoledig *eg* cyhyrau anrheoledig
involute infoliwt *eg* infoliwtiau
involute gear gêr infoliwt *eg* gerau infoliwt
involute gear rack rac gêr infoliwt *eb* raciau gêr infoliwt
involution infolytedd *eg* infolyteddau
inward mewnol *ans*
inward grasp mewnafael *eb*
inward investment buddsoddiad o'r tu allan *eg* buddsoddiadau o'r tu allan
inwards tuag i mewn *adf*
iodate(V) ion ïon ïodad(V) *eg* ïonau ïodad(V)
iodate(VII) ion ïon ïodad(VII) *eg* ïonau ïodad(VII)
iodic(V) acid asid ïodig(V) *eg*
iodic(VII) acid asid ïodig(VII) *eg*
iodide ion ïon ïodid *eg* ïonau ïodid
iodine (I) ïodin *eg*
iodine monochloride ïodin monoclorid *eg*
iodine(I) ion ïon ïodin(I) *eg* ïonau ïodin(I)
iodine(V) oxide ïodin(V) ocsid *eg*
iodomethane ïodomethan *eg*
ion ïon *eg* ïonau
ion channel sianel ïonau *eb* sianeli ïonau
ion exchange resin resin cyfnewid ïonau *eg*
ion transporter cludydd ïonau *eg* cludwyr ïonau
Ionian mode modd Ionaidd *eg*
ionic ïonig *ans*
ionic bond bond ïonig *eg* bondiau ïonig
ionic equation hafaliad ïonig *eg*
ionisation energy egni ïoneiddiad *eg*
ionizable ïonadwy *ans*
ionization ïoneiddiad *eg* ïoneiddiadau
ionization chamber llestr ïoneiddiad *eg*
ionize ïoneiddio *be*
ionosphere ïonosffer *eg* ïonosfferau
IP address cyfeiriad IP *eg* cyfeiriadau IP
IQ testing profi IQ *be*
Irenaean theodicy theodiciaeth Irenaeus *eb*
iridium (Ir) iridiwm *eg*
iris (eye) iris *eg* irisau
Irish (person) Gwyddel *eg* Gwyddelod
Irish harp telyn Wyddelig *eb* telynau Gwyddelig
Irish Question Pwnc Iwerddon *eg*
Irish Sea Môr Iwerddon *eg*
iron *v* smwddio *be*
iron (appliance) *n* haearn smwddio *eg* heyrn smwddio
iron (Fe) haearn *eg* heyrn
Iron Age Oes Haearn *eb*
iron cored solenoid solenoid craidd haearn *eg*
Iron Curtain Llen Haearn *eb*
iron filings naddion haearn *ell*
iron ion ïon haearn *eg* ïonau haearn
iron mould rhwd haearn *eg*
iron nipping press gwasg haearn nipio *eb* gweisg haearn nipio
iron on gwreslynu *be*
iron on interfacing wynebyn cudd gwreslyn *eg* wynebynnau cudd gwreslyn
iron ore mwyn haearn *eg* mwynau haearn

iron oxide haearn ocsid *eg*
iron pan cletir haearn *eg* cletiroedd haearn
iron pyrites pyrit haearn *eg*
iron setting gosodiad haearn *eg* gosodiadau haearn
iron tubing tiwbin haearn *eg* tiwbiau haearn
iron wire gwifren haearn *eb* gwifrau haearn
ironclad llong haearn *eb* llongau haearn
iron-cored coil coil craidd haearn *eg*
iron(II) diiron(III) oxide haearn(II) deuhaearn(III) ocsid *eg*
iron(II) diiron(III) oxide (magnetite) haearn(II) deuhaearn(III) ocsid (magnetit) *eg*
iron(II) disulfide (pyrites) haearn(II) deusylffid (pyritau) *eg*
iron(II) ion ïon haearn(II) *eg* ïonau haearn(II)
iron(III) chloride haearn(III) clorid *eg*
iron(III) ion ïon haearn(III) *eg* ïonau haearn(III)
iron(III) oxide (haematite) haearn(III) ocsid (haematit) *eg*
ironing board bwrdd smwddio *eg* byrddau smwddio
ironing pad pad smwddio *eg* padiau smwddio
ironmongery (hardware) nwyddau haearn *ell*
iron-on transfer trosglwyddyn gwreslynol *eg* trosglwyddynnau gwreslynol
irradiate arbelydru *be*
irradiation arbelydriad *eg* arbelydriadau
irrational (=unreasonable) afresymol *ans*
irrational (in mathematics) anghymarebol *ans*
irrational number rhif anghymarebol *eg* rhifau anghymarebol
irrecoverable error gwall anadferadwy *eg* gwallau anadferadwy
irredeemable (in economics) diatbryn *ans*
irredeemable bonds bondiau diatbryn *ell*
irredentism iredentiaeth *eb*
irreducible anostyngadwy *ans*
irregular afreolaidd *ans*
irregular cadence diweddeb annisgwyl *eb* diweddebau annisgwyl
irregular crust cramen afreolaidd *eb*
irregular solid solid afreolaidd *eg* solidau afreolaidd
irregularity afreoleidd-dra *eg*
irrelevant amherthnasol *ans*
irreversible (of reaction) anghildroadwy *ans*
irrigate dyfrhau *be*
irrigated dyfredig *ans*
irrigation dyfrhad *eg*
irrigation ditch ffos ddyfrhau *eb* ffosydd dyfrhau
irritability sensitifedd *eg*
irritation (of itchy skin) cosi poenus *be*
irrotational anghylchdro *ans*
Irwin twist bit ebill tro Irwin *eg* ebillion tro Irwin
isallobar isalobar *eg* isalobarrau
isanomalous line llinell anomaledd *eb* llinellau anomaledd
ischaemic (heart disease) ischaemig *ans*
ischium ischiwm *eg* ischia
isentropic isentropig *ans*
Islam Islam *eb*
Islamic Islamaidd *ans*
Islamic calligraphy caligraffeg Islamaidd *eb*
Islamic law cyfraith Islamaidd *eb*
Islamic state gwladwriaeth Islamaidd *eb*
islet ynysig *eb* ynysigau
islets of Langherans ynysoedd Langerhans *ell*
isobar isobar *eg* isobarrau
isobaric isobarig *ans*
isobath isobath *eg* isobathau
isobathytherm isobathytherm *eg* isobathythermau
isobront isobront *eg* isobrontau
isochrone isocron *eg* isocronau
isochronous isocronus *ans*
isoclinal folding plygiant isoclinol *eg*
isocline isoclin *eg* isoclinau
isocyanobenzene isocyanobensen *eg*
isocyano-compound cyfansoddyn isocyano *eg* cyfansoddion isocyano
isocyanoethane isocyanoethan *eg*
isoenzyme isoensym *eg* isoensymau
isogamy isogamedd *eg*
isogeotherm isogeotherm *eg* isogeothermau
isogloss isoglos *eg* isoglosau
isogon isogon *eg* isogonau
isogonal isogonol *ans*
isohaline isohalaidd *ans*
isohel isohel *eg* isohelau
isohyet glawlin *eg* glawlinau
isohypse (contour) cyfuchlin *eg* cyfuchlinau
isokinetic isocinetig *ans*
isokinetic muscle contraction cyfangiad cyhyrol isocinetig *eg* cyfangiadau cyhyrol isocinetig
isolate (a chemical) *v* arunigo *be*
isolate (in economics) *v* neilltuo *be*
isolate (of child) *n* unigyn *eg* unigion
isolated (of chemical) arunig *ans*
isolation arwahanrwydd *eg*
isolation aphasia affasia arunigedd *eg*
isolation hospital ysbyty heintiau *eg* ysbytai heintiau
isolation valve falf ynysu *eb* falfiau ynysu
isolation ward ward arwahanu *eb* wardiau arwahanu
isolationism ymneilltuedd *eg*
isolationist arwahanydd *eg* arwahanwyr
isolator arunigydd *eg* arunigwyr
isoleucine isolewcin *eg*
isomer isomer *eg* isomerau
isomerism isomeredd *eg*
isomerization isomeru *be*
isometric isometrig *ans*
isometric axis echelin isometrig *eb* echelinau isometrig
isometric drawing lluniad isometrig *eg*
isometric muscle contraction cyfangiad cyhyrol isometrig *eg* cyfangiadau cyhyrol isometrig
isometric plane plân isometrig *eg* planau isometrig

isometric projection tafluniad isometrig *eg* tafluniadau isometrig
isometric scale graddfa isometrig *eb* graddfeydd isometrig
isometric view golwg isometrig *eg* golygon isometrig
isometry isometreg *eg*
isomorphic isomorffig *ans*
isomorphism isomorffedd *eg*
isomorphous isomorffus *ans*
isoneph isoneff *eg* isoneffau
isoperimetric isoperimetrig *ans*
isophene isoffen *eg* isoffenau
isopleth isopleth *eg* isoplethau
isorhythmic isorhythmig *ans*
isoryme rhewlin *eg* rhewlinau
isosceles isosgeles *ans*
isosceles triangle triongl isosgeles *eg* trionglau isosgeles
isoseismal isoseismol *ans*
isoseismic isoseismig *ans*
isostade isostad *eg* isostadau
isostasy isostasi *eg*
isostatic adjustment cymhwysiad isostatig *eg* cymwysiadau isostatig
isostatic anomaly anomaledd isostatig *eg* anomaleddau isostatig
isostatic equilibrium cydbwysedd isostatig *eg*
isotach isotach *eg* isotachau
isotactic isotactig *ans*
isotherm isotherm *eg* isothermau
isothermal *n* isothermal *eb* isothermalau
isothermic isothermig *ans*
isotonic isotonig *ans*
isotonicity isotonedd *eg*
isotope isotop *eg* isotopau
isotopic isotopig *ans*
isotropic surface arwyneb isotropig *eg* arwynebau isotropig
isovaline isofalin *eg*
Israelite Israeliad *eg* Israeliaid
issue (=important topic) *n* mater *eg* materion
issue (=publish) *v* cyhoeddi *be*
issue (of a gas) *n* tarddiad *eg*
issue (of a gas) *v* tarddu *be*
issue (provide) *v* dyroddi *be*
isthmus culdir *eg* culdiroedd
IT and Administration Manager Rheolwr TG a Gweinyddu *eg*
IT coordinator cydgysylltydd TG *eg*
IT Skills Academy Academi Sgiliau TG *eb*
Italian overture agorawd Eidalaidd *eb* agorawdau Eidalaidd
Italian painting (of painted picture) paentiad Eidalaidd *eg* paentiadau Eidalaidd
Italian painting (of process or art) peintio Eidalaidd *be*
Italian quilting cwiltio Eidalaidd *be*
Italian serenade serenâd Eidalaidd *eg* serenadau Eidalaidd
Italian sixth chweched Eidalaidd *eg* chwechedau Eidalaidd
Italian sixth chord cord y chweched Eidalaidd *eg*
Italian unification uno'r Eidal *be*
italic italig *ans*
italic alphabet gwyddor italig *eb*
italic letter llythyren italig *eb* llythrennau italig
italic pen pen italig *eg* pennau italig
italic writing pen ysgrifbin italig *eg* ysgrifbinnau italig
italicize italeiddio *be*
italics italig
itch cosi *be*
item eitem *eb* eitemau
item bank cronfa eitemau *eb* cronfeydd eitemau
item of expenditure eitem gwariant *eb* eitemau gwariant
item testing profi eitemau *be*
itemize eitemeiddio *be*
iterate iteru *be*
iteration iteriad *eg* iteriadau
iterative iterus *ans*
iterative method dull iterus *eg* dulliau iterus
iterative routine rheolwaith iterus *eg* rheolweithiau iterus
iterative search chwiliad iterus *eg* chwiliadau iterus
itinerant teacher (female) athrawes deithiol *eg* athrawesau teithiol
itinerant teacher (male) athro teithiol *eg* athrawon teithiol
itinerary amserlen teithio *eb*
Ivan the Great Ifan Fawr *eg*
Ivan the Terrible Ifan Arswydus *eg*
ivory ifori *eg*
ivory black du ifori *eg*
ivory tower tŵr ifori *eg* tyrau ifori
ivy stem coesyn iorwg *eg* coesynnau iorwg

J

J curve effect effaith cromlin J *eb*
jabot jabot *eg*
jack *n* jac *eg* jaciau
jack *v* jacio *be*
jack rafter ceibr byr *eg* ceibrau byr
jacket siaced *eb* siacedi
jackplane plaen jac *eg* plaeniau jac
Jacob chuck crafanc Jacob *eb* crafangau Jacob
Jacobean Jacobeaidd *ans*
Jacobean couching cowtsio Jacobeaidd *be*
Jacobin *adj* Jacobinaidd *ans*
Jacobin *n* Jacobin *eg* Jacobiniaid
Jacobinism Jacobiniaeth *eb*
Jacquard weave gwehyddiad Jacquard *eg*
jam (of traffic etc) tagfa *eb* tagfeydd
jamb ystlysbost *eg* ystlysbyst
James (king) Iago *eg*
James-Lange theory damcaniaeth James-Lange *eb*
jamming cloi *be*
Janam Sakhis Janam Sakhis
janizary Janisariad *eg* Janisariaid
Jansenism Janseniaeth *eb*
Jansenist Jansenydd *eg* Janseniaid
jap silk sidan jap *eg*
Japanese Japaneaidd *ans*
Japanese print print Japaneaidd *eg* printiau Japaneaidd
Japanese school ysgol Japaneaidd *eb* ysgolion Japaneaidd
Japji Japji
jar jar *eb* jariau
jargon jargon *eg*
Jarrow Crusade Crwsâd Jarrow *eg*
jasper maen iasbis *eg* meini iasbis
jaundice clefyd melyn *eg*
javelin gwaywffon *eb* gwawyffyn
javelin pass pàs gwaywffon *eb* pasiau gwaywffyn
jaw safn *eb* safnau
jaw *adj* genol *ans*
jaw *n* gên *eb* genau
jaw plate plât safn *eg* platiau safn
jawbone genogl *eg* genoglau
jealous cenfigennus *ans*
jealousy cenfigen *eb*
jeans jîns *eg*
jejunum jejwnwm *eg*
jelly jeli *eg* jelïau
jelly block bloc jeli *eg* blociau jeli
jelly medium cyfrwng jeli *eg*
jelly-fish sglefren fôr *eb* sglefrod môr
jelly-like jelïaidd *ans*
jemmy (=short crowbar) bar haearn cwta *eg* barrau haearn cwta
Jennings twist bit ebill tro Jennings *eg* ebillion tro Jennings
jenny callipers caliperau jenni *ell*
jersey defnydd jersi *eg*
Jerusalem artichoke artisiog Jerwsalem *eg* artisiogau Jerwsalem
Jesuit *adj* Jeswitaidd *ans*
Jesuit *n* Jeswit *eg* Jeswitiaid
Jesuit Order Urdd y Jeswitiaid *eb*
Jesuitism Jeswitiaeth *eb*
Jesus Christ Iesu Grist *eg*
jet (of water, steam etc) jet *eg* jetiau
jet (stone) muchudd *eg*
jet engine peiriant jet *eg* peiriannau jet
jet stream jetlif *eg* jetlifau
jetty glanfa *eb* glanfeydd
jeweller gemydd *eg* gemyddion
jeweller's rouge rhuddliw gemydd *eg*
jewellery gemwaith *ell*
jewellery enamel enamel gemwaith *eg* enamelau gemwaith
Jewish Easter Pasg yr Iddewon *eg*
jib (of crane) braich fawr *eb* breichiau mawr
jib-headed key allwedd ben-gib *eb* allweddi pen-gib
jig *n* jig *eb* jigiau
jig *v* jigio *be*
jig music cerddoriaeth jig *eb*
jig rhyme rhythm jig *eg* rhythmau jig
jig saw herclif *eb* herclifiau
jigger jiger *eg* jigeri
jigsaw cut toriad herclif *eg* toriadau herclif
jigsaw puzzle pos jigso *eg* posau jigso
jingle *n* tincialyn *eg* tincialau
jingle *v* tincial *be*
jingoism jingoistiaeth *eb*
jink ochrgamu *be*
Joan (wife of Llywelyn the Great) Siwan *eb*
Joan of Arc Jeanne d'Arc *eb*
job (=occupation) swydd *eb* swyddi
job (=task) gorchwyl *eg* gorchwylion
job (=work) gwaith *eg*
job applicant ymgeisydd am swydd *eg* ymgeiswyr am swyddi
Job Centre Canolfan Gwaith *eb* Canolfannau Gwaith

Job Control Language (JCL) Iaith Rheoli Gorchwylion *eb*
job creation scheme cynllun creu gwaith *eg* cynlluniau creu gwaith
job description disgrifiad swydd *eg* disgrifiadau swydd
job interview cyfweliad am swydd *eg* cyfweliadau am swyddi
job placement lleoliad mewn swydd *eg* lleoliadau mewn swyddi
job production cynhyrchu yn ôl y gwaith *be*
job related ynglŷn â'r gwaith *ans*
job satisfaction bodlonrwydd swydd *eg*
job share *v* rhannu swydd *be*
job specification manyleb swydd *eb* manylebau swyddi
job stream llif gorchwylion *eg*
job turnaround gweithdroad *eg* gweithdroadau
job vacancy swydd wag *eb* swyddi gwag
jobber's drill dril jobwr *eg* driliau jobwr
jockey joci *eg* jociau
jog loncian *be*
Johansson's block bloc Johansson *eg* blociau Johansson
John (king) John *eg*
John (pope) Ioan *eg*
join *n* uniad *eg* uniadau
join *v* uno *be*
join in the worship ymuno yn yr addoliad *be*
join lace uno les *be*
join together cysylltu â'i gilydd *be*
joiner asiedydd *eg* asiedyddion
joiner's brad hoelen saer *eb* hoelion saer
joinery gwaith asiedydd *eg*
joining stitch pwyth uno *eg* pwythau uno
joint (=connect by joints) *v* uniadu *be*
joint (=divide into joints) *v* cymalu *be*
joint (in body) *n* cymal *eg* cymalau
joint (in object) *n* uniad *eg* uniadau
joint account cyfrif ar y cyd *eg* cyfrifon ar y cyd
joint and several cyd ac unigol
joint and several liability atebolrwydd ar y cyd ac yn unigol *eg*
joint distribution function ffwythiant cyd-ddosbarthiad *eg*
joint honours degree gradd gydanrhydedd *eb* graddau cydanrhydedd
joint liability cydatebolrwydd *eg*
joint project cywaith *eg* cyweithiau
joint replacement amnewid cymal *eg* amnewidiadau cymal
joint stock company cwmni cydgyfalaf *eg* cwmnïau cydgyfalaf
joint variation cydamrywiad *eg* cydamrywiadau
jointed cymalog *ans*
jointed arm braich gymalog *eb* breichiau cymalog
jointed figure ffigur cymalog *eg* ffigurau cymalog
jointed leg coes gymalog *eb* coesau cymalog
jointed marionette marionét cymalog *eg* marionetau cymalog
jointed puppet pyped cymalog *eg* pypedau cymalog
join-up charge tâl ymuno *eg* taliadau ymuno
joist dist *eg* distiau
jongleur jongleur *eg* jongleurs
Josephson junction cyswllt Josephson *eg*
joule (J) joule *eg* jouleau
journalism newyddiaduriaeth *eb*
journalist newyddiadurwr *eg* newyddiadurwyr
journey taith *eb* teithiau
journeyman jermon *eg* jermoniaid
joust ymryson twrnamaint *eb* ymrysonau twrnamaint
joystick ffon reoli *eb* ffyn rheoli
jubilant gorfoleddus *ans*
Judaism Iddewiaeth *eb*
judge barnwr *eg* barnwyr
judge (in sports) beirniad *eg* beirniaid
judgement (of tribunal etc) dyfarniad *eg* dyfarniadau
Judgement Day Dydd y Farn *eg*
Judgement, Last Barn, Y Farn Fawr *eb*
judgement of performance barnu perfformiad *be*
judges' law cyfraith llys *eb*
judicature barnweiniad *eg*
Judicature Acts Deddfau Barnweiniad *ell*
judicial cyfreithiol *ans*
judicial body corff barnwriaethol *eg* cyrff barnwriaethol
Judicial Committee of the Privy Council Pwyllgor Barnwrol y Cyfrin Gyngor *eg*
judicial power pŵer barnwrol *eg* pwerau barnwrol
judicial precedent cynsail farnwrol *eb*
judiciary barnwriaeth *eb*
jug jwg *eb* jygiau
juggle jyglo *be*
juggle the ball jyglo'r bêl *be*
juggler jyglwr *eg* jyglwyr
jugular vein gwythïen y gwddf *eb* gwythiennau'r gwddf
juice sudd *eg* suddion
Julian Calendar Calendr Julius *eg*
Julius Caesar Iŵl Cesar *eg*
July Monarchy Brenhiniaeth Gorffennaf *eb*
July Plot Cynllwyn Gorffennaf *eg*
jumbo print argraffu jymbo *be*
jump *n* naid *eb* neidiau
jump *v* neidio *be*
jump ball cydnaid *eb* cydneidiau
jump for the ball neidio am y bêl *be*
jump instruction cyfarwyddyd neidio *eg* cyfarwyddiadau neidio
jump suit siwt undarn *eb* siwtiau undarn
jump table tabl neidiau *eg* tablau neidiau
jump with a rebound naid ac adlam
jumper (of garment) siwmper *eb* siwmperi
jumper (of person) neidiwr *eg* neidwyr
jumping pit pwll neidio *eg* pyllau neidio

junction (in physics, chemistry) cysylltle *eg* cysylltleoedd
junction (of pipes etc) cydiad *eg* cydiadau
junction (of point of joining) cyswllt *eg* cysylltau
junction (of rivers /glaciers) cymer *eg* cymerau
junction (of roads, railways) cyffordd *eb* cyffyrdd
junction box blwch cyswllt *eg* blychau cyswllt
juncus brwynen *eb* brwyn
June days dyddiau Mehefin *ell*
jungle jyngl *eg* jyngls
junior counsel barrister bargyfreithiwr ieuaf *eg*
junior hacksaw haclif fach *eb* haclifiau bach
junior school ysgol gynradd *eb* ysgolion cynradd
junior secondary school ysgol iau *eb* ysgolion iau
junior stage cyfnod cynradd *eg* cyfnodau cynradd
junk mail post sothach *eg*
junk mail llythyrau sothach *ell*
junk playground maes chwarae sbwriel *eg*
Junker Junker *eg* Junkeriaid
Jupiter Iau *eg*
jurassic jwrasig *ans*
jurisdiction awdurdodaeth *eg* awdurdodaethau
jurisprudence cyfreitheg *eb*
jurist arbenigwr cyfreithiol *eg* arbenigwyr cyfreithiol
juror rheithiwr *eg* rheithwyr
juror bias scale graddfa tuedd rheithiwr *eb*
jury rheithgor *eg* rheithgorau
jury of presentment rheithgor cyflwyno *eg*
just (=barely) prin *adf*
just (=righteous) cyfiawn *ans*
just clear prin glirio *be*
just in time mewn union bryd
just in time production cynhyrchu mewn union bryd *be*
just miss prin osgoi *be*
just war rhyfel cyfiawn *eg* rhyfeloedd cyfiawn
just world hypothesis damcaniaeth byd cyfiawn *eb*
justice (=judge) ustus *eg* ustusiaid
justice (=justness) cyfiawnder *eg* cyfiawnderau
justice (=magistrate) ynad *eg* ynadon
justice in eyre ustus cylch *eg* ustusiaid cylch
justice of gaol delivery ustus gwacáu'r carcharau *eg*
Justice of the Peace (J.P.) Ynad Heddwch *eg*
justice of the quorum ustus cworwm *eg* ustusiaid cworwm
justiciar prif ustus *eg* prif ustusiaid
justiciary gweinyddwr cyfiawnder *eg* gweinyddwyr cyfiawnder
justification (in general) cyfiawnhad *eg*
justification (of lines of type) unioniad *eg* unioniadau
justification (of text edges) unioni *be*
justification by faith cyfiawnhad drwy ffydd *eg*
justify (in general) cyfiawnhau *be*
justify (lines of type) unioni *be*
just-noticeable difference gwahaniaeth lleiaf a welir *eg*
jut ymwthio allan *be*
jute jiwt *eg*
jute canvas cynfas jiwt *eg*
Jutes Jiwtiaid *ell*
jutting ymwthiol *ans*
juvenile *adj* ifanc *ans*
juvenile *n* person ifanc *eg* pobl ifanc
juvenile court llys plant *eg* llysoedd plant
juvenile hormone hormon ieuangedd *eg* hormonau ieuangedd
juvenile relief tirwedd ifanc *eb* tirweddau ifanc
juvenility ieuengrwydd *eg*
juxtapose cyfosod *be*
juxtaposition cyfosodiad *eg* cyfosodiadau

K

kaccha kaccha *eg*
Kaiser, The Kaiser, Y *eg*
kale cêl *ell*
Kali Kali *eb*
Kamares ware crochenwaith Kamares *eg*
kame cnwc gro *eg* cnyciau gro
kame and kettle country tirlun cnwc a thegell *eg*
kame moraine marian cnwc gro *eg* marianau cnwc gro
kamma (=karma) kamma *eg*
kangaroo rat llygoden fawr godog *eb* llygod mawr codog
Kangha Kangha *eg*
kaolin caolin *eg*
kapellmeister kapellmeister *eg*
kapok capoc *eg*
kapparot kapparot *ell*
Karah Prashad /Prasad Karah Prashad /Prasad *eg*
karma (=kamma) karma *eg*
karre clint *eg* clintiau
karrenfeld calchbalmant *eg* calchbalmentydd
karst carst *eg* carstiau
karstic carstig *ans*
karyotype caryoteip *eg* caryoteipiau
kashrut kashrut *ell*
Kathina Kathina *eg*
kayak caiac *eg* caiacau
keel cilbren *eg* cilbrennau
keen edge ymyl awchlym *eb* ymylon awchlym
keen edged awchlym *ans*
keep (of castle) gorthwr *eg* gorthwyr
keep filter criteria cadw meini prawf hidlo *be*
keep fit cadw'n heini *be*
keep formatting cadw fformatio *be*
keep one's balance cadw cydbwysedd *be*
keep order cadw trefn *be*
keep ratio cadw cymhareb *be*
keep records cadw cofnodion *be*
keep scale cadw graddfa *be*
keep size cadw maint *be*
keep spacing interval cadw maint bylchau *be*
keep wicket cadw wiced *be*
keep your head high cadw eich pen yn uchel *be*
keeper (in general) ceidwad *eg* ceidwaid
keeper (on magnet) cadwrydd *eg* cadwryddion
Keeper of the Rolls Ceidwad y Rholiau *eg* Ceidwaid y Rholiau
Keeper of the Seals Ceidwad y Seliau *eg*
keepers of our peace ceidwaid yr heddwch *ell*
kelvin (K) celfin *eg*
kemp saethflew *ell*
keratin ceratin *eg*
kerf llifdoriad *eg* llifdoriadau
kernel cnewyllyn *eg* cnewyll
kerning gorgyffwrdd *be*
kerosene cerosin *eg*
kersey cersi *eg*
kesh /kes kesh /kes *eg*
keto- ceto-
ketone ceton *eg* cetonau
Kett rebellion gwrthryfel Kett *eg*
kettle hole pwll tegell *eg* pyllau tegell
key *adj* allweddol *ans*
key (=cay) *n* cai *eg* caion
key (=system of notes) *n* cywair *eg* cyweiriau
key (for tuning piano) *n* morthwyl tiwnio *eg* morthwylion tiwnio
key (in general) *n* allwedd *eb* allweddi
key (of a musical instrument) *n* nodyn *eg* nodau
key (of a switch) *n* agoriad *eg* agoriadau
key (on computer or typewriter) *n* bysell *eb* bysellau
key age oedran allweddol *eg* oedrannau allweddol
key block bloc allwedd *eg* blociau allweddi
key drift drifft allwedd *eg* drifftiau allwedd
key field maes allweddol *eg* meysydd allweddol
key objective amcan allweddol *eg* amcanion allweddol
key press (keyboard) trawiad *eg* trawiadau
key principle egwyddor allweddol *eb* egwyddorion allweddol
key ring torch allwedd *eg* torchau allwedd
key signature arwydd cywair *eg* arwyddion cywair
key stage cyfnod allweddol *eg* cyfnodau allweddol
key string cyweirdant *eg* cyweirdannau
key strip stribed bysell *eg* stribedi bysell
key stroke trawiad *eg* trawiadau
key vocabulary geirfa allweddol *eb*
key word gair allweddol *eg* geiriau allweddol
key worker gweithiwr allweddol *eg* gweithwyr allweddol
keyboard (musical instrument) allweddellau *ell*
keyboard (of computer) bysellfwrdd *eg* bysellfyrddau
keyboard drive gyrrwr bysellfwrdd *eg* gyrwyr bysellfyrddau
keyboard instrument offeryn allweddellau *eg* offerynnau allweddellau

keyboard layout cynllun bysellfwrdd *eg* cynlluniau bysellfyrddau
keyboard shortcut llwybr byr bysellfwrdd *eg*
keyed *adj* bysellog *ans*
keyed joint uniad cloëdig *eg* uniadau cloëdig
keyed mitre meitr clo *eg* meitrau clo
keyed mitre joint uniad meitr clo *eg* uniadau meitr clo
keyed tenon tyno cloëdig *eg* tynoau cloëdig
keyhole saw llif dwll clo *eb* llifiau twll clo
keying allweddu *be*
Keynesian (of person) Keynesiad *eg* Keynesiaid
keynote cyweirnod *eg* cyweirnodau
keynote speaker prif siaradwr *eg* prif siaradwyr
keypad bysellbad *eg* bysellbadiau
keypunch tyllfwrdd *eg* tyllfyrddau
key-seat clamp clamp sedd glo *eg* clampiau sedd glo
key-seat milling cutter melinwr sedd glo *eg* melinwyr sedd glo
keystone maen clo *eg* meini clo
keystroke logger cofnodwr trawiadau bysellau *eg* cofnodwyr trawiadau bysellau
► **key-to-disk** bysell i ddisg *ans*
keyway allweddfa *eb* allweddfâu
keyword allweddair *eg* allweddeiriau
Khalsa Khalsa *eg*
khamsin camsin *eg* camsinau
khan khan *eg* khaniaid
khanate khanaeth *eb*
khandha khandha *eg*
Kharijite views syniadau'r Kharijitiaid *ell*
khurchatovium (Kh) curchatofiwm *eg*
kibbutz cibwts *eg* cibwtsau
kick *n* cic *eb* ciciau
kick *v* cicio *be*
kick ahead cic ymlaen *eb* ciciau ymlaen
kick for touch cic am ystlys *eb*
kick pleat plet gic *eb* pletiau cic
kickback ôl-gic *eb* ôl-giciau
kicker pad cicio *eg* padiau cicio
kicking strap strap gicio *eb* strapiau cicio
kick-off cic gychwyn *eb* ciciau cychwyn
kickwheel olwyn gic *eb* olwynion cic
kid (type of leather) croen myn *eg* crwyn myn
kidnap herwgipio *be*
kidney aren *eb* arennau
kidney artery rhydweli arennol *eb* rydwelïau arennol
kidney beans ffa Ffrengig *ell*
kidney shape arennog *ans*
kidney tubule tiwbyn aren *eg*
Kids' Club Clwb Plant *eg*
Kids' Club Leader Arweinydd Clybiau Plant *eg* Arweinwyr Clybiau Plant
killed spirits gwirodydd tyner *ell*
killer whale morfil danheddog *eg* morfilod danheddog
kiln odyn *eb* odynnau
kiln furniture dodrefn odyn *ell*
kiln seasoning sychu mewn odyn *be*
kiln shelf silff odyn *eb* silffoedd odyn
kiln-dry *adj* odyn-sych *ans*
kiln-dry *v* odyn-sychu *be*
kilobyte cilobeit *eg* cilobeitiau
kilocalorie cilocalori *eg* cilocalorïau
kilocycle ciloseicl *eg* ciloseiclau
kilogram (kg) cilogram *eg* cilogramau
kilometre (km) cilometr *eg* cilometrau
kilowatt (kW) cilowat *eg* cilowatiau
kilowatt hour (kW h) cilowat awr *eg*
kilt cilt *eg* ciltiau
kin perthynas *eb* perthnasau
kin selection detholiad ceraint *eg*
kindred carennydd *eg*
kinematics cinemateg *eb*
kinesthetic cinesthetig *ans*
kinetic cinetig *ans*
kinetic art celfyddyd ginetig *eb*
kinetic energy egni cinetig *eg*
kinetic energy of translation egni cinetig trawsfudiad *eg*
kinetic foci ffocysau cinetig *ell*
kinetic order gradd ginetig *eb*
kinetic theory of gases damcaniaeth ginetig nwyon *eb*
kinetics cineteg *eb*
kinetin cinetin *eg*
king brenin *eg* brenhinoedd
King Consort Brenin Cydweddog *eg*
king post roof truss cwpl brenhinbost *eg* cyplau brenhinbost
kingdom teyrnas *eb* teyrnasoedd
Kingdom of the Two Sicilies Teyrnas y Ddwy Sisilia *eb*
kingpost brenhinbost *eg* brenhinbyst
King's Evil Haint y Brenin *eb*
King's Peace Heddwch y Brenin *eg*
kingship brenhiniaeth *eb*
kink *n* cinc *eg* cinciau
kink *v* cincio *be*
kinship perthynas *eb* perthnasau
kiosk caban *eg* cabanau
Kirchoff's first law deddf gyntaf Kirchoff *eb*
Kirpan Kirpan *eg*
kirtan kirtan *eg*
kiss of life cusan adfer *eb*
kit cit *eg* citiau
kitchen cegin *eb* ceginau
kitchen foil papur arian *eg*
kitchen paper papur cegin *eg*
kitchen unit uned gegin *eb* unedau cegin
kite barcut *eg* barcutiaid
Kite Mark Nod Barcut *eg*
Klangforme seinwedd *eb* seinweddau
knead tylino *be*

knee pen-glin *eg/b* pengliniau
knee bracket braced pen-glin *eb* bracedi pen-glin
knee cap padell pen-glin *eb* pedyll pengliniau
knee joint cymal y pen-glin *eg* cymalau pengliniau
kknee-jerk reflex atgyrch plwc pen-glin *eg*
kneel penlinio *be*
kneel sitting penlinio eistedd *be*
knicker nicer *eg* nicers
knickpoint cnicyn *eg* cnicynnau
knife cyllell *eb* cyllyll
knife blade llafn cyllell *eg* llafnau cyllyll
knife edge (in general) min cyllell *eg*
knife edge (in physics, chemistry) arfin *eg* arfiniau
knife file ffeil cyllell *eb* ffeiliau cyllell
knife handle carn cyllell *eg* carnau cyllyll
knife pleat plet llafn *eb* pletiau llafn
knife stroke strôc gyllell *eb* strociau cyllell
knife tool erfyn cyllell *eg* offer cyllell
knife tool (of lathe tools) cyllell *e* cyllyll
knife-cut veneer argaen toriad cyllell *eg* argaenau toriad cyllell
knight *n* marchog *eg* marchogion
knight *v* urddo'n farchog *be*
knight errant marchog crwydrol *eg* marchogion crwydrol
Knight Hospitaller Marchog Ysbytaidd *eg* Marchogion Ysbytaidd
Knight of the Shire Marchog Sir *eg* Marchogion Sir
Knight Templar Marchog Temlaidd *eg* Marchogion Temlaidd
Knight Teutonic Marchog Tiwtonig *eg* Marchogion Tiwtonig
knightage corff urddau'r marchogion *eg*
knight's fee ffi marchog *eb*
knight's service gwasanaeth marchog *eg*
Knights' War Rhyfel y Marchogion *eg*
knit gwau *be*
knit two together gwau dau bwyth ynghyd *be*
knitted carpet carped wedi'i wau *eg* carpedi wedi'u gwau
knitted fabric ffabrig wedi'i wau *eg* ffabrigau wedi'u gwau
knitted fabric darn craith ffabrig wedi'i wau *eb* creithiau ffabrig wedi'i wau
knitted lace les wedi'i wau *eg*
knitted textiles tecstilau wedi'u gwau *ell*
knitting instructions cyfarwyddiadau gwau *ell*
knitting machine peiriant gwau *eg* peiriannau gwau
knitting needle gwaell *eb* gweill
knitwear gweuwaith *eg*
knob bwlyn *eg* byliau
knock down taro i lawr *be*
knock inhibitor atalydd cnocio *eg* atalyddion cnocio
knock on *n* trawiad ymlaen *eg* trawiadau ymlaen
knock on *v* taro ymlaen *be*
knockdown fittings ffitiadau datgysylltiol *ell*
knockdown furniture dodrefn datgysylltiol *ell*
knocked up bottom gwaelod gweflog *eg* gwaelodion gweflog
knocking down iron haearn fflatio *eg* heyrn fflatio
knoll cnwc *eg* cnyciau
knot *n* cwlwm *eg* clymau
knot *v* clymu *be*
knot (=measure of speed) *n* not *eb* notiau
knot (in wood) *n* cainc *eb* ceinciau
knot (wood) *v* cuddio ceinciau *be*
knotted stitch pwyth clwm *eg* pwythau clwm
knotting *n* cuddiwr ceinciau *eg* cuddwyr ceinciau
knotting *v* cuddio ceinciau *be*
knowledge gwybodaeth *eb*
knowledge base cronfa wybodaeth *eb* cronfeydd gwybodaeth
known concentration crynodiad diffiniedig *eg* crynodiadau diffiniedig
knuckle (=hinge) cymal *eg* cymalau
knuckle (in anatomy) cwgn *eg* cygnau
knuckle joint uniad cymal *eg* uniadau cymal
knuckle thread edau gymal *eb* edafedd cymal
knurl nwrl *eg* nwrliau
knurled grip gafael nwrl *eb* gafaelion nwrl
knurled nut nyten nwrl *eb* nytiau nwrl
knurled screw sgriw nwrl *eb* sgriwiau nwrl
knurling (of lathe tools) nwrlio *be*
knurling tools (of lathe accessories) offer nwrlio *ell*
kolkhoz colchos *eg*
kosher kosher *ans*
kraal cral *eg* cralau
kraft paper papur llwyd *eg*
Krebs cycle cylchred fetabolaidd Krebs *eb*
Krishna /Krsna Krishna /Krsna *eg*
Kruger telegram telegram Kruger *eg*
krypton (Kr) crypton *eg*
Kshatriya /Ksatriya Kshatriya /Ksatriya *ell*
kulak cwlac *eg* cwlaciaid
Kupffer cell cell Kupffer *eb* celloedd Kupffer
kurtosis cwrtosis *eg*

eg/b enw gwrywaidd/benywaidd, *masculine/feminine noun* ***ell*** enw lluosog, *plural noun* ***v*** berf, *verb* ***n*** enw, *noun* ▸ wedi newid, *changed*

L

label *n* label *eg/b* labeli
label *v* labelu *be*
label merge cyfuno labelau *be*
labelled wedi'i labelu *ans*
labelled diagram diagram wedi'i labelu *eg* diagramau wedi'u labelu
labelling paper papur labelu *eg*
labelling scheme cynllun labelu *eg* cynlluniau labelu
labelling theory damcaniaeth labelu *eb*
labial gwefusol *ans*
labile ansefydlog *ans*
labium labiwm *eg* labia
laboratory labordy *eg* labordai
laboratory experiment arbrawf labordy *eg* arbrofion labordy
laboratory test prawf labordy *eg* profion labordy
labour llafur *eg*
labour (=process of childbirth) esgor *be*
labour charge costau llafur *ell*
labour force gweithlu *eg*
labour intensive llafur-ddwys *ans*
labour market marchnad lafur *eb*
labour market failure methiant marchnad lafur *eg*
labour pains gwewyr esgor *eg*
Labour Party Plaid Lafur *eb*
labour pool pŵl llafur *eg*
labour productivity cynhyrchaeth llafur *eb*
labour saving arbed llafur *be*
labour stages camau geni *ell*
labour turnover trosiant llafur *eg*
labourer labrwr *eg* labrwyr
labour-intensive production cynhyrchu llafur-ddwys *be*
labour-saving device dyfais arbed gwaith *eb* dyfeisiau arbed gwaith
labrum labrwm *eg* labra
labyrinth labyrinth *eg* labyrinthau
laccolith lacolith *eg* lacolithau
lace les *eg*
lace (thong) carrai *eb* careiau
lace beading gleinwaith les *eg*
lace curtains llenni les *ell*
lace insertion les wedi'i fewnosod *eg*
lacemaking sideru *be*
lacerated wound clwyf rhwygiad *eg* clwyfau rhwygiad
laceration rhwygiad *eg* rhwygiadau
lacquer *n* lacr *eg* lacrau
lacquer *v* lacro *be*
lacquer finish gorffeniad lacr *eg* gorffeniadau lacr
lacquer paint paent lacr *eg*
lacquer solvent hydoddydd lacr *eg* hydoddyddion lacr
lacquering (in finishing metal) lacro *be*
lacrimal duct dwythell ddagrau *eb* dwythellau dagrau
lacrimatory peri dagrau *ans*
lactase lactas *eg*
lactate lactad *eg*
lactate llaetha *be*
lactation llaethiad *eg*
lactation period cyfnod llaetha *eg*
lacteal lacteal *eg* lactealau
lactogenic hormone hormon lactogenig *eg* hormonau lactogenig
lactophenol lactoffenol *eg*
lactose lactos *eg*
lactose intolerance anoddefgarwch lactos *eg*
lacuna ceudod *eg* ceudodau
lacunary bylchus *ans*
lacustrine llynnol *ans*
ladder (for climbing) ysgol *eb* ysgolion
ladder (in tights) rhediad *eg* rhediadau
ladder logic rhesymeg ysgol ddringo *eb*
ladder rung ffon ysgol *eb* ffyn ysgol
ladies chain cadwyn y merched *eb* cadwyni'r merched
ladle lletwad *eb* lletwadau
Lady chapel capel y Forwyn *eg* capeli'r Forwyn
Lady of the Bedchamber Boneddiges y Siambr Wely *eb* Boneddigesau'r Siambr Wely
lady's slipper orchid tegeirian esgid Fair *eg*
Laffer curve cromlin Laffer *eb*
lag (=wrap up) *v* lagio *be*
lag (of time) *n* oediad *eg* oediadau
lag and lead dilyn ac arwain *be*
lag deposits ôl-ddyddodion *ell*
lag phase (bacteria) cyfnod oedi *eg*
laggard (in geography) ymdrŵwr *ell* ymdrowyr
lagged ynysedig *ans*
lagging ynysydd *eg* ynysyddion
lagoon lagŵn *eg/b* lagwnau
lair gwâl *eb* gwalau
laissez-faire leader arweinydd laissez-faire *eg*
laissez-faire model model laissez-faire *eg*
laity lleygwyr *ell*
lake llyn *eg* llynnoedd
Lake District Ardal y Llynnoedd *eb*
lake dwelling crannog *eg* cranogau

lake head delta delta penllyn *eg* deltâu penllyn
lake plateau llwyfandir llynnoedd *eg* llwyfandiroedd llynnoedd
lakeside delta delta glanllyn *eg* deltâu glanllyn
Lakshmi /Laxmi Lakshmi /Laxmi *eb*
lamb's wool mop mop gwlân oen *eg* mopiau gwlân oen
lamina (in botany) llafn deilen *eg* llafnau dail
lamina (in general) lamina *eg* laminâu
laminar laminaidd *ans*
laminar flow llif laminaidd *eg*
laminarin laminarin *eg*
laminate *adj* laminedig *ans*
laminate *n* laminiad *eg* laminiadau
laminate *v* laminiadu *be*
laminate joint uniad laminiad *eg* uniadau laminiad
laminated laminedig *ans*
laminated core craidd laminedig *eg*
laminboard astell lafnog *eb* estyll llafnog
lamp lamp *eb* lampau
lamp black du lamp *eg*
lampshade cysgod lamp *eg* cysgodion lampau
Lancashire cheese caws Swydd Gaerhirfryn *eg*
Lancastrian *adj* Lancastraidd *ans*
Lancastrian *n* Lancastrydd *eg* Lancastriaid
lance gwaywffon *eb* gwaywffyn
lance corporal is-gorporal *eg* is-gorporaliaid
Lancelot Lawnslot *eg*
lancer gwaywr *eg* gwaywyr
lancet arch bwa lanset *eg* bwâu lanset
land tir *eg* tiroedd
land *v* glanio *be*
land (drill part) glan *eb* glannau
land agent stiward tir *eg* stiwardiaid tir
land animal anifail tir *eg* anifeiliaid tir
land breeze awel o'r tir *eb* awelon o'r tir
land enclosures cau tiroedd *be*
land question pwnc y tir *eg*
land surveyor syrfëwr tir *eg* syrfewyr tir
land tenure tirddaliadaeth *eb*
land use defnydd tir *eg* defnyddiau tir
Land Use Survey (LUS) Arolwg Defnydd Tir *eg*
land utilization map map defnydd tir *eg*
landed gentry bonedd *eg* boneddigion
landes rhostir *eg* rhostiroedd
landfill *v* tirlenwi *be*
landfill (of site) *n* safle tirlenwi *eg* safleoedd tirlenwi
landfill site *n* safle tirlenwi *eg* safleoedd tirlenwi
landform tirffurf *eg* tirffurfiau
landing (=top of stairs) pen grisiau *eg* pennau grisiau
landing (on land) glanio *be*
landing area ardal lanio *eb* ardaloedd glanio
landing strip llain lanio *eb* lleiniau glanio
landline llinell tir *eb* llinellau tir
Ländler Ländler *eg* Ländler
landlocked tirgaeedig *ans*
landlord perchennog *eg* perchenogion
landlordism landlordiaeth *eb*
landmap map tir *eg* mapiau tir
landmark tirnod *eg* tirnodau
landmass ehangdir *eg* eangdiroedd
landowner tirfeddiannwr *eg* tirfeddianwyr
landownership tirfeddiannaeth *eb*
landscape (geographical) tirwedd *eb* tirweddau
landscape (in art) tirlun *eg* tirluniau
landscape consultant ymgynghorydd tirwedd *eg* ymgynghorwyr tirwedd
landscape features nodweddion tirwedd *ell*
landscape painting (of painted picture) paentiad tirlun *eg* paentiadau tirlun
landscape painting (of process or art) peintio tirlun *be*
landslide tirlithriad *eg* tirlithriadau
landward tua'r tir *ans*
lane lôn *eb* lonydd
langar langar *eg*
language iaith *eb* ieithoedd
language ability gallu ieithyddol *eg*
language acquisition device dyfais caffael iaith *eb*
language centre canolfan iaith *eb* canolfannau iaith
language development datblygiad iaith *eg*
► **language disorder** anhwylder iaith *eg* anhwylderau iaith
language encoding amgodio iaith *be*
language experience profiad iaith *eg*
language formation ffurfiad iaith *eg*
language interaction rhyngweithiad iaith *eg*
language laboratory labordy iaith *eg* labordai iaith
language learning dysgu iaith *eg*
language of art iaith weledol celf *eb*
language shift dyfudiad iaith *eg*
language skills sgiliau iaith *ell*
language test prawf iaith *eg* profion iaith
lantern llusern *eb* llusernau
lanthanoid lanthanoid *eg*
lanthanum (La) lanthanwm *eg*
lap *n* lap *eg* lapiau
lap *v* lapio *be*
lap scorer rhifwr lapiau *eg* rhifwyr lapiau
lap seam sêm lap *eb* semau lap
lapel llabed *eb* llabedau
lapel badge bathodyn lapél *eg* bathodynnau lapél
lapiaz calchbalmant *eg* calchbalmentydd
lapidary lapidari *eg*
lapie clint *eg* clintiau
lapilli lapili *eg*
lapis blue (enamelling colour) glas lapis *eg*
lapped butt joint goruniad bôn ac ysgwydd *eg* goruniadau bôn ac ysgwydd
lapped dovetail joint goruniad cynffonnog *eg* goruniadau cynffonnog
lapped joint goruniad *eg* goruniadau
lapped seam sêm drosblyg *eb* semau trosblyg
lapping goruniad *eg*

lapping cane gwialen blethu *eb* gwialennau plethu
lapping line llinell goruniad *eb* llinellau goruniad
lapse rate cyfradd newid *eb* cyfraddau newid
laptop (computer) gliniadur *eg* gliniaduron
larceny lladrad *eg*
lard *n* bloneg *eg*
lard *v* blonegu *be*
lard oil olew lard *eg*
large apparatus offer mawr *ell*
large cabbage white glöyn gwyn mawr *eg* glöynnod gwyn mawr
large court cwrt mawr *eg* cyrtiau mawr
large face milling cutter melinwr wyneb mawr *eg* melinwyr wyneb mawr
large icon eicon mawr *eg* eiconau mawr
large intestine coluddyn mawr *eg* coluddion mawr
large print book llyfr print bras *eg* llyfrau print bras
large scale graddfa fawr *eb*
large scale integration (LSI) cyfannu graddfa eang *be*
large triangle triongl mawr *eg* trionglau mawr
large-scale ar raddfa fawr *ans*
large-scale production cynhyrchu ar raddfa fawr *be*
larva larfa *eg* larfâu
larynx laryncs *eg*
laser laser *eg* laserau
laser alignment equipment offer alinio gyda laser *ell*
laser beam pelydr laser *eg* pelydrau laser
laser printer argraffydd laser *eg* argraffyddion laser
laser scanner sganiwr laser *eg* sganwyr laser
laser store storfa laser *eb* storfeydd laser
last Ice Age Oes Iâ ddiwethaf *eb*
last in-first out (LIFO) olaf i mewn-cyntaf allan *eg*
last modified addaswyd ddiwethaf
last step cam olaf *eg* camau olaf
latch clicied *eb* cliciedau
late adolescence llencyndod hwyr *eg*
late adopter mabwysiadwr hwyr *eg* mabwysiadwyr hwyr
Late Bronze Age Oes Efydd Ddiweddar *eb*
late cut toriad hwyr *eg*
late developer datblygwr hwyr *eg* datblygwyr hwyr
late development datblygiad diweddar *eg*
late maturity aeddfedrwydd diweddar *eg*
latecomer hwyrddyfodiad *eg* hwyrddyfodiaid
latency cuddni *eg*
latency period cyfnod cudd *eg*
latent cudd *ans*
latent content cynnwys cudd *eg*
latent heat gwres cudd *eg*
latent heat capacity cynhwysedd gwres cudd *eg* cynwyseddau gwres cudd
latent heat of fusion gwres cudd ymdoddi *eg*
latent heat of vaporization gwres cudd anweddu *eg*
latent inhibition ataliad cudd *eg*
latent period (nerve /muscle) cyfnod diddigwydd *eg*
lateral ochrol *ans*
lateral adjustment cymhwysiad ochrol *eg* cymwysiadau ochrol
lateral adjustment lever lifer cymhwyso ochrol *eg* liferi cymhwyso ochrol
lateral bud blaguryn ochrol *eg* blagur ochrol
lateral dominance trechedd ochrol *eg*
lateral exercise ymarfer ochrol *eg* ymarferion ochrol
lateral force grym ochrol *eg*
lateral hazard llestair ochrol *eg*
lateral inversion gwrthdroad ochrol *eg* gwrthdroadau ochrol
lateral joint uniad ochrol *eg* uniadau ochrol
lateral line llinell ochrol *eb* llinellau ochrol
lateral moraine marian ochrol *eg* marianau ochrol
lateral root gwreiddyn ochrol *eg* gwreiddiau ochrol
lateral surfaces arwynebau ochrol *ell*
lateral view ochrolwg *eg* ochrolygon
lateralization swyddogaeth ochrol *eb*
Lateran Council Cyngor Lateran *eg*
Lateran Pacts Cytundebau Lateran *ell*
laterite laterit *eg* lateritau
lateritic lateritig *ans*
laterization latereiddio *be*
laterized latereiddiedig *ans*
latex latecs *eg*
latex mould mowld latecs *eg* mowldiau latecs
lath latsen *eb* lats
lathe turn *eg* turniau
lathe accessories cyfarpar turn *eg*
lathe centre canol turn *eg* canolau turn
lathe chisel cŷn turnio *eg* cynion turnio; gaing durnio *eb* geingiau turnio
lathe gouge gaing gau turn *eb* geingiau gau turn
lathe parts rhannau'r turn *ell*
lathe saddle cyfrwy turn *eg* cyfrwyau turn
lathe tools offer turn *ell*
lather *n* trochion sebon *ell*
lather *v* seboni *be*
lather stabilizer sefydlogydd trochion *eg* sefydlogyddiontrochion
lathework gwaith turn *eg*
Latin Lladin *eb*
Latin Christendom Gwledydd Cred Rhufeinig *ell*
Latin quarter rhan Ladinaidd *eb* rhannau Lladinaidd
Latin square design cynllun sgwâr Lladin *eg* cynlluniau sgwâr Lladin
latitude lledred *eg* lledredau
latitudinarian eang-gredwr *eg* eang-gredwyr
latitudinarianism eang-grededd *eg*
lattice dellten *eb* dellt
lattice breaking enthalpy enthalpi torri dellt *eg*
lattice energy egni dellt *eg* egnïon dellt
lattice formation ffurfiant dellt *eg*
lattice space gofod dellt *eg*
lattice work delltwaith *eg*
latus-rectum latws-rectwm *eg*

laudanum lodnwm *eg*
lauds moliannau *ell*
launch (a boat) lansio *be*
launch (an attack) cychwyn *be*
launder golchi a smwddio
launderette golchfa *eb* golchfeydd
laundress golchwraig *eb* golchwragedd
laundry golchdy *eg* golchdai
laundry appliances offer golchwaith *ell*
lava lafa *eg* lafâu
lava block bloc lafa *eg* blociau lafa
lava cone côn lafa *eg* conau lafa
lava flow llif lafa *eg* llifoedd lafa
lava outflow gorlif lafa *eg* gorlifau lafa
lava spine nodwydd lafa *eb* nodwyddau lafa
lavant lafant *eg* lafantau
lavatory brush brwsh tŷ bach *eg* brwshys tŷ bach
lavender blue (enamelling colour) glas lafant *eg*
law (=a single law) deddf *eb* deddfau
law (as a system) cyfraith *eb* cyfreithiau
law and order cyfraith a threfn
law book llyfr y gyfraith *eg*
law code cod cyfraith *eg*
Law Commission, the Comisiwn y Gyfraith *eg*
law of absorption deddf amsugniad *eb*
law of closure deddf cau *eb*
law of common fate deddf tynged gyffredin *eb*
law of complementation deddf gyflenwadol *eb*
law of conservation of mass deddf cadwraeth màs *eb*
law of constant composition deddf cyfansoddiad cyson *eb*
law of diminishing returns deddf adenillion lleihaol *eb*
law of effect deddf effaith *eb*
law of gravitation deddf disgyrchiant *eb*
law of gravity deddf disgyrchiant *eb*
law of mass action deddf adweithio masau *eb*
law of multiple motions deddf cyfraneddau lluosol *eg*
law of multiple proportions deddf cyfraneddau lluosol *eb*
law of retail gravitation deddf disgyrchiant adwerthol *eb*
law of succession cyfraith etifeddu *eb*
law reform diwygio'r gyfraith *be*
lawbreaking torcyfraith *be*
lawday diwrnod llys barn *eg* diwrnodau llys barn
lawful cyfreithlon *ans*
lawgiver deddfroddwr *eg* deddfroddwyr
lawn lawnt *eb* lawntiau
lawn cotton cotwm main *eg*
lawning rhidyllu *be*
lawrencium (Lr) lawrenciwm *eg*
laxative carthydd *eg* carthyddion
lay *adj* lleyg *ans*
lay *n* cân *eb* caneuon
lay (table) gosod *be*
lay brother brawd lleyg *eg* brodyr lleyg
lay figure ffigur gosod *eg* ffigurau gosod
lay out a pattern gosod patrwm *be*
layback ôl-gripian *be*
layer *n* haen *eb* haenau
layer *v* haenu *be*
layer colouring haenliwio *be*
layered structure adeiledd haenog *eg*
layette layette *eg*
lay-in mewn-osod *be*
laying up gosod haenau *be*
laying-on (of colour) rhagliwio *be*
layman lleygwr *eg* lleygwyr
layout cynllun *eg* cynlluniau
layout (=design) dyluniad *eg*
layout (of page) gosodiad *eg* gosodiadau
layout feature nodwedd gosodiad *eb* nodweddion gosodiad
layout grid grid cynllun *eg* gridiau cynllun
lazy daisy stitch pwyth llygad y dydd *eg* pwythau llygad y dydd
lazy eye llygad diog *eg* llygaid diog
LEA: local education authority AALL: awdurdod addysg lleol *eg*
leach trwytholchi *be*
leaching trwytholchiad *eg*
lead (=guide) *v* arwain *be*
lead (electrical) *n* lid *eb* lidiau
lead (in orchestra) *v* blaenu *be*
lead (Pb) *n* plwm *eg*
lead blocks blociau plwm *ell*
lead body corff arweiniol *eg* cyrff arweiniol
lead bronze efydd plwm *eg*
lead bush bwsh plwm *eg* bwshys plwm
lead carbonate hydroxide plwm carbonad hydrocsid *eg*
lead down arwain i lawr *be*
lead flashing lapiad plwm *eg* lapiadau plwm
lead glaze gwydredd plwm *eg*
lead paragraph paragraff agoriadol *eg* paragraffau agoriadol
lead professional officer swyddog proffesiynol arweiniol *eg* swyddogion proffesiynol arweiniol
lead screw (lathe part) sgriw dywys *eb* sgriwiau tywys
lead screw bearing beryn sgriw dywys *eg* berynnau sgriwiau tywys
lead sculpture cerflunwaith plwm *eg*
lead solder sodr plwm *eg* sodrau plwm
lead story prif stori *eb*
lead teacher (female) athrawes arweiniol *eb* athrawesau arweiniol
lead teacher (male) athro arweiniol *eg* athrawon arweiniol
lead up arwain i fyny *be*
leaded window ffenestr blwm *eb* ffenestri plwm
leader (in general) arweinydd *eg* arweinwyr
leader (in orchestra) blaenwr *eg* blaenwyr

leadership arweinyddiaeth *eb*
lead-free di-blwm *ans*
lead(II) carbonate (cerussite) plwm(II) carbonad (cerwsit) *eg*
lead(II) carbonate hydroxide plwm(II) carbonad hydrocsid *eg*
lead(II) ethanoate plwm(II) ethanoad *eg*
lead(II) ion ïon plwm(II) *eg* ïonau plwm(II)
lead(II) oxide (litharge, or massicot) plwm(II) ocsid (litharg, neu masicot) *eg*
leading edge blaenymyl *ans* blaenymylon
leading leg coes flaen *eb*
leading seventh seithfed arweiniol *eg* seithfedau arweiniol
leading tray (mosaics) hambwrdd gosod *eg* hambyrddau gosod
lead(IV) compound cyfansoddyn plwm(IV) *eg* cyfansoddion plwm(IV)
lead(IV) ethanoate plwm(IV) ethanoad *eg*
lead(IV) oxide plwm(IV) ocsid *eg*
leaf (of paper) dalen *eb* dalennau
leaf (of plant) deilen *eb* dail
leaf green gwyrdd y ddeilen *eg*
leaf mosaic mosaig dail *eg*
leaf node cwgn deilen *eg* cygnau dail
leaf print print deilen *eg* printiau dail
leaf scar craith deilen *eb* creithiau dail
leaf shaped arrowhead pen saeth ar ffurf deilen *eg* pennau saeth ar ffurf deilen
leaf stitch pwyth deilen *eg* pwythau deilen
leaf trace deildres *eb* deildresi
leaf-eating insects pryfed deilysol *ell*
leaflet (=small leaf) deiliosen *eb* deilios
leaflet (of paper) taflen *eb* taflenni
leaflet cover clawr taflen *eg* cloriau taflenni
leafy deiliog *ans*
leafy shoot brigyn deiliog *eg* brigau deiliog
league cynghrair *eg/b* cynghreiriau
League of Armed Neutrality Cynghrair Niwtral Arfog *eb*
League of Nations Cynghrair y Cenhedloedd *eb*
league table tabl cynghrair *eg* tablau cynghrair
leakage datgeliad anfwriadol *eg* datgeliadau anfwriadol
leakage current cerrynt gollwng *eg*
lean gwyro *be*
lean meat cig coch *eg*
lean paint paent tenau *eg*
lean pigment pigment tenau *eg*
lean production cynhyrchu main *be*
lean-to roof to ar oledd *eg* toeon ar oledd
leap *n* llam *eg* llamau
leap *v* llamu *be*
leap frog llam llyffant *eg*
leap year blwyddyn naid *eb* blynyddoedd naid
learn dysgu *be*
learned helplessness diymadferthedd wedi'i ddysgu *eb*
learner dysgwr *eg* dysgwyr
learning dysg *eb*
learning centre canolfan dysgu *eb* canolfannau dysgu
learning community cymuned ddysgu *eb* cymunedau dysgu
learning difficulty anhawster dysgu *eg* anawsterau dysgu
learning disability anabledd dysgu *eg* anableddau dysgu
learning materials deunyddiau dysgu *ell*
learning method dull dysgu *eg* dulliau dysgu
learning plateau gwastad dysgu *eg*
learning resource adnodd dysgu *eg* adnoddau dysgu
learning style arddull dysgu *eg* arddulliau dysgu
lease *n* prydles *eb* prydlesi
lease *v* rhentu ar brydles *be*
leased line llinell ar log *eb* llinellau ar log
▸ **leased line connection** cysylltiad llinell ar log *eg* cysylltiadau llinell ar log
leasehold prydlesol *ans*
leasehold reform diwygio cyfraith prydlesi *be*
Leasehold Reform Act Deddf Diwygio Cyfraith Prydlesi *eb*
leaseholder prydleswr *eg* prydleswyr
Lease-Lend Act Deddf Les-Fenthyg *eb*
least lleiaf *ans*
least significant bit (LSB) did lleiaf arwyddocaol *eg* didau lleiaf arwyddocaol
least square line llinell sgwariau lleiaf *eb* llinellau sgwariau lleiaf
least-squares estimate amcangyfrif swm lleiaf sgwariau *eg* amcangyfrifon swm lleiaf sgwariau
leather lledr *eg* lledrau
leather apron ffedog ledr *eb* ffedogau lledr
leather ball pêl ledr *eb* peli lledr
leather cloth lliain lledr *eg* llieiniau lledr
leather hammer morthwyl lledr *eg* morthwylion lledr
leather joint cymal lledr *eg* cymalau lledr
leather mallet gordd ledr *eb* gyrdd lledr
leather needle nodwydd lledr *eb* nodwyddau lledr
leather punch tyllydd lledr *eg* tyllwyr lledr
leather thong carrai ledr *eb* careiau lledr
leather washer wasier ledr *eb* wasieri lledr
leather webbing webin lledr *eg* webinau lledr
lecithin lecithin *eg*
lectern darllenfa *eb* darllenfeydd
lectionary llithlyfr *eg* llithlyfrau
lecture darlith *eb* darlithoedd
lecture theatre darlithfa *eb* darlithfeydd
lecturer darlithydd *eg* darlithwyr
ledge ysgafell *eb* ysgafelloedd
ledged and braced ysgafellog a chleddog
ledged door drws ysgafellog *eg* drysau ysgafellog
ledger (=plank) planc *eg* planciau
ledger (in accounting) cyfriflyfr *eg* cyfriflyfrau
ledger (in scaffolding) polyn llorwedd *eg* polion llorwedd

ledger line llinell estyn *eb* llinellau estyn
lee boards byrddau'r tu clytaf *ell*
lee side of ice ochr wrthrew *eb* ochrau gwrthrew
leech gelen *eb* gelenod
leeward cysgodol *ans*
leeward side ochr gysgodol *eb* ochrau cysgodol
left chwith *ans*
left arm bowling bowlio braich chwith *be*
left associative (in computer programming) chwith gysylltiadol *ans*
left court cwrt chwith *eg* cyrtiau chwith
left cross chwith draws *ans*
left eye llygad chwith *eg* llygaid chwith
left foot troed chwith *eb* traed chwith
left hand llaw chwith *eb* dwylo chwith
left indent mewnoli ar y chwith *be*
left justify unioni ar y chwith *be*
left outfielder ffildiwr chwith *eg* ffildwyr chwith
left over food bwyd dros ben *eg*
left pedal pedal chwith *eg* pedalau chwith
left shift syfliad chwith *eg* syfliadau chwith
left side ochr chwith *eb*
left side of the court ochr chwith y cwrt *eb*
left wing (in sport) asgell chwith *eb* esgyll chwith
left-align alinio ar y chwith *be*
left-click chwith-glicio *be*
left-half hanerwr chwith *eg* hanerwyr chwith
left-hand lock clo llaw chwith *eg* cloeon llaw chwith
left-hand screw sgriw llaw chwith *eb* sgriwiau llaw chwith
left-hand screw thread edau sgriw llaw chwith *eb* edafedd sgriw llaw chwith
left-hand side ochr chwith *eb*
left-hand thread edau llaw chwith *eb* edafedd llaw chwith
left-hand tools offer llaw chwith *ell*
left-hand turn tro chwith *eg* troeon chwith
left-handed llawchwith *ans*
left-handed batsman batiwr llaw chwith *eg* batwyr llaw chwith
leg coes *eb* coesau
leg and rail construction adeiladwaith coes a rheilen *eg*
leg before wicket (l.b.w.) coes o flaen wiced
leg break bowling troi o'r goes *be*
leg bye heibiad coes *eg*
leg glance cyffyrddiad coes *eg*
leg of mutton sleeve llawes goes dafad *eb* llewys coes dafad
leg side ochr goes *eb*
leg slip slip coes *eg*
leg stump stwmp coes *eg* stympiau coes
leg vice feis goes *eb* feisiau coes
legacy (=inheritance) etifeddiaeth *eb*
legacy (=sum or article bequeathed) cymynrodd *eb* cymynroddion
legacy translation cyfieithiad o'r gorffennol *eg* cyfieithiadau o'r gorffennol
legal cyfreithiol *ans*
legal aid cymorth cyfreithiol *eg*
legal capacity gallu cyfreithiol *eg*
legal consequences goblygiadau cyfreithiol *ell*
legal constraint cyfyngiad cyfreithiol *eg* cyfyngiadau cyfreithiol
legal history hanes cyfraith *eg*
legal liability atebolrwydd cyfreithiol *eg*
legal position safbwynt cyfreithiol *eg*
legal system system gyfreithiol *eb* systemau cyfreithiol
legalism cyfreithyddiaeth *eb*
legality cyfreithlondeb *eg*
legally binding cyfreithiol-rwym *ans*
legate legad *eg*
leg-break troelliad ochr goes *eg*
legend chwedl *eb* chwedlau
legibility darllenadwyaeth *eb*
legible darllenadwy *ans*
legion lleng *eg* llengoedd
Legion of Honour Lleng Anrhydedd *eb*
legislate deddfu *be*
legislation deddfwriaeth *eb* deddfwriaethau
legislation for the construction project deddfwriaeth i'r project adeiladu *eb*
legislative assembly cynulliad deddfu *eg* cynulliadau deddfu
legislative body corff deddfwriaethol *eg* cyrff deddfwriaethol
legislator deddfwr *eg* deddfwyr
legislature (=body of laws) corff o ddeddfau *eg* cyrff o ddeddfau
legislature (=legislative body) corff deddfwriaethol *eg* cyrff deddfwriaethol
legislature (=parliament) senedd *eb* seneddau
legitimacy cyfreithlondeb *eg*
legitimate cyfreithlon *ans*
legitimism cyfreithloniaeth *eb*
legitimist cyfreithlonydd *eg* cyfreithlonwyr
legume codlys *eg* codlysiau
leguminous codlysol *ans*
legwarmers legins gweu *ell*
leisure hamdden *eb*
leisure and recreation hamdden ac adloniant
leisure and recreation facility cyfleuster hamdden ac adloniant *eg* cyfleusterau hamdden ac adloniant
leisure and tourism hamdden a thwristiaeth
leisure centre canolfan hamdden *eb* canolfannau hamdden
leisure clothes dillad hamdden *ell*
leisure time amser hamdden *eg*
lemiscate loop dolen lemnisgat *eb* dolennau lemnisgat
lemma lema *eg* lemata
lemming leming *eg* lemingiaid
lemon lemon *eg* lemonau
lemon curd ceuled lemon *eg*
lending rate cyfradd fenthyg *eb* cyfraddau benthyg

lend-lease les-fenthyg *eb*
length hyd *eg* hydoedd
length (of thread) pwythyn *eg* pwythynnau
lengthen estyn *be*
lengthen ymestyn *be*
lengthen (skirt etc) llaesu *be*
lengthen a pattern estyn patrwm *be*
lengthening bars barrau ymestyn *ell*
lengthwise *adv* yn ei hyd *adf*
lens power (dioptre) nerth lens *eg*
Lent Grawys *eg*
lenticel *adj* lenticelaidd *ans*
lenticel *n* lenticel *eg* lenticelau
lenticular lensaidd *ans*
Lenz's law deddf Lenz *eb*
leptin leptin *eg* leptinau
leptokurtic leptocwrtig *ans*
leptotene leptoten *eg/b*
lesbian lesbiad *eb* lesbiaid
lesion nam *eg* namau
less economically developed countries (LEDCs) gwledydd llai economaidd ddatblygedig (LEDCs) *ell*
lessee prydleswr *eg* prydleswyr
lesser spoken language iaith lai arferedig *eb* ieithoedd llai arferedig
lesson (=instruction) gwers *eb* gwersi
lesson (=suite) cyfres *eb* cyfresi
lesson observation arsylwi gwersi *be*
lesson plan cynllun gwers *eg* cynlluniau gwersi
let (house) gosod *be*
lethal marwol *ans*
lethal gene genyn marwol *eg* genynnau marwol
lethargic swrth *ans*
letraset letraset *eg*
letter (=correspondence) llythyr *eg* llythyrau
letter (of alphabet) llythyren *eb* llythrennau
letter coordinates cyfesurynnau llythrennau *ell*
letter plate plât llythyrau *eg* platiau llythyrau
lettering *n* llythreniad *eg* llythreniadau
lettering *v* llythrennu *be*
lettering brush brwsh llythrennu *eg* brwshys llythrennu
lettering chalk sialc llythrennu *eg*
lettering nib nib llythrennu *eg* nibiau llythrennu
lettering paper papur llythrennu *eg*
lettering pen pen llythrennu *eg* pennau llythrennu
lettering pencil pensil llythrennu *eg* pensiliau llythrennu
lettering quill cwilsen lythrennu *eb* cwils llythrennu
lettering work *n* gwaith llythrennu *eg*
letters of denizenship llythyrau dinasyddiaeth *ell*
leucine lewcin *eg*
leucocyte lewcocyt *eg* lewcocytau
leucocyte count cyfrifiad lewcocytau *eg*
leucoplast lewcoplast *eg* lewcoplastau
Levant Company Cwmni'r Lefant *eg*
levee llifglawdd *eg* llifgloddiau

level *adj* gwastad *ans*
level *n* lefel *eg/b* lefelau
level *v* lefelu *be*
level bedded rocks creigiau llorhaenol *ell*
level crossing croesfan wastad *eb* croesfannau gwastad
level description disgrifiad lefel *eg* disgrifiadau lefel
level of activity lefel gweithgaredd *eb* lefelau gweithgaredd
level of attainment lefel cyrhaeddiad *eb* lefelau cyrhaeddiad
level of difficulty lefel anhawster *eb* lefelau anhawster
level of privilege lefel braint *eb* lefelau braint
level over trosoli *be*
leveller *adj* lefelaidd *ans*
Leveller *n* Lefelwr *eg* Lefelwyr
levels of demand lefelau'r galw *ell*
levels of dental decay lefelau o bydredd dannedd *ell*
levels of skill lefelau o fedrusrwydd *ell*
lever lifer *eg* liferi
lever bar trosolfar *eg* trosolfarrau
lever cap cap trosoli *eg* capiau trosoli
lever system system liferi *eb* systemau liferi
lever tools offer trosoli *ell*
leverage (act of) trosoliad *eg* trosoliadau
leverage (principle of) trosoledd *eg* trosoleddau
lever-frame fretsaw llif ffret lifer *eb* llifiau ffret lifer
levy (in finance) ardoll *eb* ardollau
levy (in general) treth *eb* trethi
levy, levies (of soldiers) milwyr a gasglwyd *ell*
levy rates codi trethi *be*
lexical geiriadurol *ans*
lexical analysis dadansoddiad geiriadurol *eg*
lexical awareness ymwybyddiaeth o'r lecsicon *eb*
lexicographic geiriadurol *ans*
lexicon lecsicon *eg* lecsiconau
ley gwndwn *eg*
ley farming ffermio gwndwn *be*
liability atebolrwydd *eg*
liana liana *eg* lianau
libel enllib *eg* enllibion
liberal *n* rhyddfrydwr *eg* rhyddfrydwyr
liberal democrat *adj* democrataidd rhyddfrydol *ans*
liberal democrat *n* democrat rhyddfrydol *eg* democratiaid rhyddfrydol
Liberal Democrat Party Plaid y Democratiaid Rhyddfrydol *eb*
liberal empire ymerodraeth ryddfrydol *eb*
Liberal Party Plaid Ryddfrydol *eb*
liberal Tory Tori rhyddfrydol *eg* Toriaid rhyddfrydol
liberal Toryism Toriaeth ryddfrydol *eb*
Liberal Unionist Rhyddfrydwr Unoliaethol *eg* Rhyddfrydwyr Unoliaethol
liberalisation rhyddfrydoli *be*
liberalism rhyddfrydiaeth *eb*
liberate rhyddhau *be*

Liberate Roll Rhôl Pensiwn a Lwfans *eb* Rholiau Pensiwn a Lwfans
liberation rhyddhad *eg*
liberation theology diwinyddiaeth rhyddhad *eb*
liberator rhyddhäwr *eg* rhyddhawyr
libertarian rhyddewyllyswr *eg* rhyddewyllyswyr
liberty (=domain or property) libart *eg* libartiau
liberty (=freedom) rhyddid *eg*
liberty of conscience rhyddid cydwybod *eg*
libido libido *eg/b*
librarian llyfrgellydd *eg* llyfrgellwyr
library llyfrgell *eb* llyfrgelloedd
library program rhaglen lyfrgell *eb* rhaglenni llyfrgell
library resource centre canolfan adnoddau llyfrgell *eb* canolfannau adnoddau llyfrgell
library routine rheolwaith llyfrgell *eg* rheolweithiau llyfrgell
library sub-routine is-reolwaith llyfrgell *eg* is-reolweithiau llyfrgell
libration mantoliad *eg* mantoliadau
librettist libretydd *eg* libretyddwyr
libretto libreto *eg* libreti
lice llau *ell*
licence (=absolute freedom) penrhyddid *eg*
licence (=freedom) rhyddid *eg*
licence (=permit) trwydded *eb* trwyddedau
licence agreement cytundeb trwyddedu *eg* cytundebau trwyddedu
licenced premises tŷ trwyddedig *eg* tai trwyddedig
licensed trwyddedig *ans*
Licensing Acts Deddfau Trwyddedu *ell*
lichen cen *eg* cennau
lichenometry cenfetreg *eb*
lid clawr *eg* cloriau
lido traeth ymdrochi *eg*
lie gorweddiad *eg*
Lied Lied *eg* Lieder
liege-lord uwch-arglwydd *eg* uwch-arglwyddi
lieutenant is-gapten *eg* is-gapteiniaid
lieutenant governor dirprwy lywodraethwr *eg* dirprwy lywodraethwyr
lieutenant-colonel is-gyrnol *eg*
lieutenant-general is-gadfridog *eg* is-gadfridogion
life after death bywyd ar ôl marwolaeth *eg*
life assurance aswiriant bywyd *eg*
life crisis argyfwng bywyd *eg*
life cycle (in biology) cylchred bywyd *eb*
life cycle (in economics) cylchred oes *eb*
life drawing bywluniad *eg* bywluniadau
life expectancy disgwyliad oes *eg* disgwyliadau oes
life experiences profiadau bywyd *ell*
life insurance yswiriant bywyd *eg*
life jacket siaced achub *eb* siacedi achub
life process proses bywyd *eb* prosesau bywyd
life skills sgiliau byw *ell*
life span rhychwant oes *eg*
life span experiment arbrawf goroesi *eg* arbrofion goroesi
life stage cam bywyd *eg* camau bywyd
lifelike real *ans*
lifelong learning dysgu gydol oes *be*
life-peer arglwydd am oes *eg*
life-saving achub bywyd *ans*
life-saving leg kick cic achub bywyd *eb* ciciau achub bywyd
life-sentence dedfryd am oes *eb* dedfrydau am oes
life-size gwir faint *eg*
life-size proportion cyfrannedd maint iawn *eg*
► **lifestyle** ffordd o fyw *eb* ffyrdd o fyw
lifestyle factors affecting health ffactor ffordd o fyw sy'n effeithio ar ar iechyd *eb* ffactorau ffordd o fyw sy'n effeithio iechyd
life-support system system cynnal bywyd *eb* systemau cynnal bywyd
lifetime hyd oes *eg*
lift *n* codiad *eg* codiadau
lift *v* codi *be*
lift pump pwmp codi *eg* pympiau codi
lift the body codi'r corff *be*
lifting tongs gefel godi *eb* gefeiliau codi
ligado ligado *eg* ligados
ligament gewyn *eg* gewynnau
ligamentous gewynnol *ans*
ligand ligand *eg*
ligation clymu *be*
ligature (for clarinet) rhwymyn *eg* rhwymynnau
ligature (in general) cwlwm *eg* clymau
ligature (in plainsong) cysylltnod *eg* cysylltnodau
light (=illuminate) *v* goleuo *be*
light (=illumination) *n* golau *eg* goleuadau
light (=natural agent that stimulates sight) *n* goleuni *eg*
light (in colour) *adj* golau *ans*
light (of weight) *adj* ysgafn *ans*
light and shade tywyll a golau
light breeze awel ysgafn *eb* awelon ysgafn
light brown (enamelling colour) brown golau *eg*
light colour lliw golau *eg* lliwiau golau
light damping gwanychiad ysgafn *eg*
light duty detergent glanedydd ysgafn *eg* glanedyddion ysgafn
light emitting diode deuod allyrru golau *eg* deuodau allyrru golau
light fast pigment pigment golau anniflan *eg* pigmentau golau anniflan
light fittings ffitiadau goleuo *ell*
light heavy weight pwysau go drwm *ell*
light industry diwydiant ysgafn *eg* diwydiannau ysgafn
light microscope microsgop golau *eg* microsgopau golau
light oil olew tenau *eg*
light opera opera ysgafn *eb* operâu ysgafn
light pen pen golau *eg* pennau golau

light plastic ball pêl blastig ysgafn *eb* peli plastig ysgafn
light pulley pwli ysgafn *eg* pwlïau ysgafn
light racket raced ysgafn *eb*
light reaction adwaith golau *eg*
light red coch golau *eg*
light ruby (enamelling colour) rhuddgoch golau *eg*
light source ffynhonnell goleuni *eb* ffynonellau goleuni
light straw (tempering colour) melyn golau *eg*
light string llinyn ysgafn *eg* llinynnau ysgafn
light tone (of colour) tôn golau *eg* tonau golau
light turning (of lathe tools) turnio ysgafn *be*
light weight pwysau ysgafn *ell*
light year blwyddyn golau *eb* blynyddoedd golau
light-chaser effect effaith erlid-golau *eb*
light-dependent golau-ddibynnol *ans*
light-dependent resistor (LDR) gwrthydd goleuni-ddibynnol *eg* gwrthyddion goleuni-ddibynnol
lightening (of weight) ysgafnhad *eg*
lighthouse goleudy *eg* goleudai
lighthouse in use and disused goleudy yn gweithio, yn segur *eg*
light-independent golau-annibynnol *ans*
light-sensitive cell cell oleusensitif *eb* celloedd goleusensitif
lightship goleulong *eb* goleulongau
lightweight ysgafn *ans*
ligneous lignaidd *ans*
lignification ligneiddiad *eg*
lignify ligneiddio *be*
lignin lignin *eg*
lignite lignit *eg*
like charge gwefr debyg *eb*
likelihood tebygoliaeth *eb* tebygoliaethau
likely tebygol *ans*
Likert scale graddfa Likert *eb*
liking hoffter *eg*
limb (of body) aelod *eg* aelodau
limb (of cross) braich *eb*
limb (structural) ystlys *eb* ystlysau
limbic cortex cortecs limbig *eg*
limbic system system limbig *eb*
lime calch *eg*
lime deficiency prinder calch *eg*
lime deficient prin o galch *ans*
lime kiln odyn galch *eb* odynnau calch
lime soap sebon calch *eg*
lime water dŵr calch *eg*
limepan cletir calch *eg* cletiroedd calch
limestone calchfaen *eg* calchfeini
limestone kiln odyn galch *eb* odynnau calch
limestone pavement calchbalmant *eg* calchbalmentydd
limestone pillar calchbost *eg* calchbyst
liminal trothwyol *ans*
liming calchu *be*
limit *v* cyfyngu *be*
limit (=boundary) *n* terfyn *eg* terfynau
limit (in physics and mathematics) *n* terfan *eg/b* terfannau
limit (on numbers etc) *n* cyfyngiad *eg* cyfyngiadau
limit gauge medrydd terfan *eg* medryddion terfan
limit of elasticity terfan elastigedd *eb*
limit of proportionality terfan gyfrannol *eb*
limit of tolerance terfan goddefiant *eb*
limit on entry (in electronic records) cyfyngiad ar gofnod *eg*
limit pricing prisio cyfyngol *be*
limitation cyfyngiad *eg* cyfyngiadau
limitations of the method cyfyngiadau'r dull *ell*
limited cyfyngedig *ans*
limited company (ltd.) cwmni cyfyngedig *eg* cwmnïau cyfyngedig
limited liability atebolrwydd cyfyngedig *eg*
limited movement symudiad cyfyngedig *eg* symudiadau cyfyngedig
limited vocal range cwmpas lleisiol cyfyngedig *eg*
limiting (in general) cyfyngol *ans*
limiting (in physics and mathematics) terfannol *ans*
limiting case achos terfannol *eg*
limiting conditions amodau cyfyngol *ell*
limiting density dwysedd terfannol *eg* dwyseddau terfannol
limiting factor ffactor gyfyngol *eb* ffactorau cyfyngol
limits of visibility terfannau gwelediad *ell*
limnology llynoleg *eb*
limonite limonit *eg* limonitau
limp *n* cloffni *eg*
limp (=not stiff or firm) *adj* llipa *ans*
line (=mark on a surface) llinell *eb* llinellau
line (=row) rhes *eb* rhesi
line (for railway, clothes etc) lein *eb* leiniau
line absorption spectrum sbectrwm amsugno llinell *eg*
line and wash llinell a golchiad
line break toriad llinell *eg* toriadau llinell
line chart siart llinell *eg* siartiau llinell
line editor llinolygydd *eg* llinolygyddion
line engraving ysgythriad llinell *eg* ysgythriadau llinell
line feed *n* llinborthiad *eg* llinborthiadau
line feed *v* llinborthi *be*
line feed character nod llin-borthiad *eg* nodau llin-borthiad
line feed key llinborthwr *eg* llinborthwyr
line filament lamp lamp ffilament llinell *eg*
line fill llanw llinell *be*
line graph graff llinell *eg* graffiau llinell
line in the rhyme llinell rhigwm *eb* llinellau rhigwm
line manager rheolwr llinell *eg* rheolwyr llinell
line of best fit llinell ffit orau *eb* llinellau ffit gorau
line of descent llinach *eb* llinachau
line of enquiry trywydd ymholi *eg* trywyddau ymholi
line of force llinell grym *eb* llinellau grym

line of intersection llinell croestoriad *eb* llinellau croestoriad
line of regression llinell atchwel *eb* llinellau atchwel
line of symmetry llinell cymesuredd *eb* llinellau cymesuredd
line of the ball llwybr y bêl *eg*
line of the stump llwybr y stwmp *eg*
line of the wicket llwybr y wiced *eg*
line out lein *eb* leiniau
line printer llin-argraffydd *eg* llin-argraffyddion
line space llinell gwagle *eb* llinellau gwagle
line spacing bylchiad llinellau *eg* bylchiadau llinellau
line spectrum sbectrwm llinell *eg* sbectra llinell
line stitch pwyth llinell *eg* pwythau llinell
line under the stave gorlinell *eb* gorlinellau
line up (print, pictures etc) unioni *be*
lineage llinach *eb* llinachau
linear (=consisting of lines) llinellog *ans*
linear (involving one dimension only) llinol *ans*
linear composition cyfansoddiad llinol *eg* cyfansoddiadau llinol
linear counterpoint gwrthbwynt llinellog *eg* gwrthbwyntiau llinellog
linear dependence dibyniaeth linol *eb*
linear equation hafaliad llinol *eg* hafaliadau llinol
linear factor ffactor linol *eb* ffactorau llinol
linear flow llif llinol *eg*
linear independence annibyniaeth linol *eb*
linear materials defnyddiau llinol *ell*
linear measurement mesuriadau llinol *ell*
linear momentum momentwm llinol *eg* momenta llinol
linear motion mudiant llinol *eg*
linear movement symudiad llinol *eg* symudiadau llinol
linear narrative stori linellol *eb*
linear programming rhaglennu llinol *be*
linear regression atchwel llinol *eg*
linear velocity cyflymder llinol *eg*
linearity llinoledd *eg*
linearly dependent llinol ddibynnol *ans*
linearly independent llinol annibynnol *ans*
lined in wedi'i leinio *ans*
lined pocket poced wedi'i leinio *eb* pocedi wedi'u leinio
lined yoke iau â leinin *eb* ieuau â leinin
linen lliain *eg* llieiniau
linen basket basged ddillad *eb* basgedi dillad
linen button botwm lliain *eg* botymau lliain
linen fold lliein-blyg *ans*
linen scrim lliain sgrim *eg* llieiniau sgrim
linen thread edau lin *eb* edafedd llin
linen-fold panel panel lliein-blyg *eg* panelau lliein-blyg
liner leiner *eg* leineri
liner train trên leiner *eg* trenau leiner
lines of communication ffyrdd cyswllt *ell*
lines of force llinellau grym *ell*
lines of supply ffyrdd cyflenwi *ell*
lines per minute (lpm) llinellau y funud
linesman llumanwr *eg* llumanwyr
linesman's flag lluman *eg/b* llumanau
ling brenhinbysg *eg* breninbysgod
lingerie lingerie *eg*
linguistic ieithyddol *ans*
linguistic method dull ieithyddol *eg* dulliau ieithyddol
linguistic relativity perthnasedd ieithyddol *eb*
linguistics ieithyddiaeth *eb*
lining leinin *eg* leininau
lining tool erfyn llinellu *eg* offer llinellu
lining wheel olwyn linellu *eb* olwynion llinellu
link *v* cysylltu *be*
link (=loop or ring of chain) *n* dolen *eb* dolennau
link (of person or connecting thing) *n* cyswllt *eg* cysylltau
link between voice and character cysylltiad rhwng y llais a'r cymeriad *eg*
link button botwm cyswllt *eg* botymau cyswllt
link for automatic feed dolen borthiant awtomatig *eb* dolennau porthiant awtomatig
link mechanism mecanwaith dolen *eg* mecanweithiau dolen
link polygon polygon cyswllt *eg* polygonau cyswllt
link simple skills cysylltu medrau syml *be*
linkage cysylltedd *eg* cysyllteddau
linkage editor golygydd cysylltedd *eg*
linked group grŵp cysylltiedig *eg* grwpiau cysylltiedig
linked list rhestr gysylltiedig *eb* rhestri cysylltiedig
linked sub-routine is-reolwaith cysylltiedig *eg* is-reolweithiau cysylltiedig
link-edit cyswllt-olygu *be*
link-editor cyswllt-olygydd *eg* cyswllt-olygyddion
linker cysylltwr *eg* cysylltwyr
link-loader cyswllt-lwythydd *eg* cyswllt-lwythwyr
lino leino *eg*
lino cut torlun leino *eg* torluniau leino
lino cutter torrell leino *eb* torellau leino
lino cutting nib nib torri leino *eg* nibiau torri leino
lino knife cyllell leino *eb* cyllyll leino
lino print print leino *eg* printiau leino
lino printing printio leino *be*
lino roller rholer leino *eg* rholeri leino
lino-block printing printio bloc leino *be*
linoleum linoliwm *eg*
lino-printing ink inc printio leino *eg* inciau printio leino
linseed oil olew had llin *eg*
linson linson *eg*
lintel capan drws *eg* capanau drysau
lip *v* gosod ymyl *be*
lip (corrie) *n* min *eg* minion
lip (drill part) *n* gwefus *eb* gwefusau
lip clearance angle (drill part) ongl cliriad gwefus *eb*

lip reading darllen gwefusau *be*
lipase lipas *eg*
lipid lipid *eg* lipidau
lipid molecule moleciwl lipid *eg* moleciwlau lipid
lipogenesis lipogenesis *eg*
lipoid lipoid *eg*
lipotropy lipotropi *eg*
lipped edge ymyl osod *eb* ymylon gosod
liquefaction hylifiad *eg* hylifiadau
liquefiable hylifadwy *ans*
liquefied hylifedig *ans*
liquefy hylifo *be*
liquid *adj* hylifol *ans*
liquid *n* hylif *eg* hylifau
liquid assets asedau hylifol *ell*
liquid colour lliw hylifol *eg* lliwiau hylifol
liquid colourant lliwydd hylif *eg* lliwyddion hylif
liquid core craidd hylifol *eg* creiddiau hylifol
liquid crystal display (LCD) arddangosiad grisial hylif *eg* arddangosiadau grisial hylif
liquid crystals grisialau hylif *ell*
liquid detergent glanedydd hylif *eg* glanedyddion hylif
liquid form ffurf hylifol *eb* ffurfiau hylifol
liquid measure mesur hylif *eg* mesurau hylif
liquid medium cyfrwng hylif *eg*
liquid metal polish llathrydd metel hylifol *eg*
liquid soap sebon hylif *eg*
liquid wax polish llathr cwyr hylif *eg*
liquidate difodi *be*
liquidated damages clause cymal iawndal penodedig *eg*
liquidation (=annihilation) difodiant *eg*
liquidation (=bankruptcy) methdaliad *eg*
liquidity hylifedd *eg*
liquidity preference theory damcaniaeth ffafriaeth hylifedd *eb*
liquidizer hylifydd *eg* hylifyddion
list rhestr *eb* rhestri
list processing prosesu rhestri *be*
listen gwrando *be*
listen attentively gwrando'n astud *be*
listening comprehension gwrando a deall
listening test prawf gwrando *eg* profion gwrando
litany litani *eb* litanïau
literacy llythrennedd *eg*
literal *adj* llythrennol *ans*
literal (symbol in computing) *n* symbol llythrennol *eg* symbolau llythrennol
literal rule rheol lythrennol *eb*
literal translation cyfieithiad llythrennol *eg* cyfieithiadau llythrennol
literary llenyddol *ans*
literary art celfyddyd lenyddol *eb*
literate llythrennog *ans*
literature llenyddiaeth *eb*
literature survey arolwg llenyddol *eg* arolygon llenyddol
litharge litharg *eg*
lithium (Li) lithiwm *eg*
lithium carbonate lithiwm carbonad *eg*
lithium ion ïon lithiwm *eg* ïonau lithiwm
lithium tetrahydridoaluminate(III) lithiwm tetrahydridoalwminad(III) *eg*
lithograph lithograff *eg* lithograffau
lithography lithograffi *eg*
lithology litholeg *eb* litholegau
lithosere lithoser *eg*
lithosol lithosol *eg*
lithosphere lithosffer *eg*
litigant achwynwr *eg* achwynwyr
litigate ymgyfreithio *be*
litigation cyfreitha *be*
litigious cyfreithgar *ans*
litigiousness cyfreithgarwch *eg*
litmus litmws *eg*
litre litr *eg* litrau
litter (=animal bedding) gwasarn *eg* gwasarnau
litter (of animals) torllwyth *eb* torllwythi
Little Hans Hans Fychan *eg*
littoral *adj* arfordirol *ans*
littoral *n* arfordir *eg* arfordiroedd
liturgical litwrgaidd *ans*
liturgy litwrgi *eg/b* litwrgïau
live *adj* byw *ans*
live *v* byw *be*
live action (in film and television) ffilmio byw *be*
live birth genedigaeth fyw *eb* genedigaethau byw
live centre (headstock) canol tro *eg*
live knot cainc fyw *eb* ceinciau byw
live music cerddoriaeth fyw *eb*
live record cofnod byw *eg* cofnodion byw
live vaccine brechlyn byw *eg*
live wire gwifren fyw *eb* gwifrau byw
liver afu *eg* afuoedd; iau *eg* ieuoedd
liver fluke (disease) clefyd yr euod *eg*
liver fluke (organism) llyngyren yr afu *eb* llyngyr yr afu; llyngyren yr iau *eb* llyngyr yr iau
liverwort llys yr afu *eg*; llys yr iau
livery lifrai *eg* lifreion
livery and maintenance lifrai a chynhaliaeth
livestock da byw *ell*
livestock farming ffermio da byw *be*
living *adj* byw *ans*
living *n* bywoliaeth *eb* bywoliaethau
living cell cell fyw *eb* celloedd byw
living thing peth byw *eg* pethau byw
Llandaff Reel Dawns Llandaf *eb*
Llanover Reel Dawns Llanofer *eb*
load *n* llwyth *eg* llwythi
load *v* llwytho *be*
load bearing surface arwyneb sy'n dal pwysau *eg* arwynebau sy'n dal pwysau
load current cerrynt llwyth *eg*
load font llwytho ffont *be*

load point pwynt llwyth *eg* pwyntiau llwyth
load-bearing wall wal cynnal pwysau *eb* waliau cynnal pwysau
loader (program) llwythwr *eg* llwythwyr
loading bay man llwytho *eg* mannau llwytho
loafing yard lloc cadw *eg* llociau cadw
loam lom *eg* lomau
loamy lomog *ans*
loan *n* benthyciad *eg* benthyciadau
loan *v* benthyca *be*
lob *n* lob *eb*
lob *v* lobio *be*
lobate bar bar clustennog *eg* barrau clustennog
lobby *v* lobïo *be*
lobby (hall in parliament, a body of lobbyists) *n* lobi *eb* lobïau
lobby correspondent gohebydd lobi *eg* gohebwyr lobi
lobbyist lobïwr *eg* lobïwyr
lobe llabed *eb* llabedau
lobed llabedog *ans*
lobule llabeden *eb* llabedennau
local lleol *ans*
local agreed syllabus maes llafur cytûn lleol *eg* meysydd llafur cytûn lleol
local anaesthetic anaesthetig lleol *eg*
local area ardal leol *eb* ardaloedd lleol
local area network (LAN) rhwydwaith ardal leol *eg*
local authority awdurdod lleol *eg* awdurdodau lleol
local colour lliw lleol *eg*
local education authority awdurdod addysg lleol *eg* awdurdodau addysg lleol
local environment amgylchedd lleol *eg*
local government llywodraeth leol *eb*
local history hanes lleol *eg*
local management of schools rheolaeth leol ysgolion *eb*
local relief tirwedd leol *eb* tirweddau lleol
local variable newidyn lleol *eg* newidynnau lleol
localization (in economics) lleoleiddiad *eg*
localization of function lleoliad swyddogaeth *eg*
localized lleoledig *ans*
localized activity gweithgaredd lleoledig *eg* gweithgareddau lleoledig
localized unemployment diweithdra lleol *eg*
locate lleoli *be*
locate position lleoli safle *be*
locating jig jig lleoli *eg* jigiau lleoli
locating pin pìn lleoli *eg* pinnau lleoli
locating plate plât lleoli *eg* platiau lleoli
location lleoliad *eg* lleoliadau
location bar bar lleoliad *eg*
location in space safle mewn gwagle *eg*
location of activities lleoliad gweithgareddau *eg*
location of features lleoliad nodweddion *eg*
locational lleoliadol *ans*
locational analysis dadansoddiad lleoliad *eg* dadansoddiadau lleoliad
locational control rheoli lleoliad *be*
locational framework fframwaith lleoliadol *eg*
locational quotient cyniferydd lleoliad *eg* cyniferyddion lleoliad
lock *v* cloi *be*
lock (on canal) *n* loc *eb* lociau
lock (on door etc) *n* clo *eg* cloeon
lock block (flush door) bloc clo *eg* blociau clo
lock knit gweuglwm *ans*
lock nut nyten gloi *eb* nytiau cloi
lock out cau allan *be*
lock rail rheilen glo *eb* rheiliau clo
lock stitch pwyth clo *eg* pwythau clo
locking device dyfais gloi *eb* dyfeisiau cloi
locking plate plât cloi *eg* platiau cloi
locking stile cledren gloi *eb* cledrau cloi
locking washer wasier gloi *eb* wasieri cloi
locking wedge lletem gloi *eb* lletemau cloi
lockjaw genglo *eg*
lock-seat clamp clamp sedd glo *eg* clampiau sedd glo
lockshield valve falf gloi *eb* falfiau cloi
locomotion ymsymudiad *eg* ymsymudiadau
locomotive locomotif *eg* locomotifau
Locrian mode modd Locriaidd *eg* moddau Locriaidd
locus locws *eg* loci
locus of control locws rheolaeth *eg*
locust locust *eg* locustiaid
lode (mineral) gwythïen *eb* gwythiennau
lodestone tynfaen *eg* tynfeini
lodge cyfrinfa *eb* cyfrinfeydd
lodgement till til glyniad *eg*
lodger lletywr *eg* lletywyr
lodging house llety *eg* lletyau
lodgings llety *eg* lletyau
lodicule lodicwl *eg* lodicwlau
loft llofft *eg* llofftydd
lofted drive dreif uchel *eb* dreifiau uchel
log (=record) log *eg* logiau
log (of wood) boncyff *eg* boncyffion
log book llyfr log *eg* llyfrau log
log file ffeil cofnodi *eb* ffeiliau cofnodi
log in (=log on) mewngofnodi *be*
log jam tagfa goed *eb* tagfeydd coed
log off (=log out) allgofnodi *be*
log on (=log in) mewngofnodi *be*
log out (=log off) allgofnodi *be*
log phase gwedd log *eb*
log roll troi'n unionsyth *be*
log/exponential phase gwedd log/esbonyddol *eb*
logarithm logarithm *eg* logarithmau
logarithmic logarithmig *ans*
logarithmic table tabl logarithmig *eg* tablau logarithmig
logic rhesymeg *eb*
logic board bwrdd rhesymeg *eg* byrddau rhesymeg

logic circuit cylched resymeg *eb* cylchedau rhesymeg

logic design cynllun rhesymeg *eg* cynlluniau rhesymeg

logic diagram diagram rhesymeg *eg* diagramau rhesymeg

logic element elfen resymeg *eb* elfennau rhesymeg

logic gate adwy resymeg *eb* adwyon rhesymeg

logic system system resymeg *eb*

logical rhesymegol *ans*

logical deduction diddwythiad rhesymegol *eg*

logical operator gweithredydd rhesymegol *eg* gweithredwyr rhesymegol

logical record cofnod rhesymegol *eg* cofnodion rhesymegol

logical shift syfliad rhesymegol *eg* syfliadau rhesymegol

logical symbol symbol rhesymegol *eg* symbolau rhesymegol

logical unit uned resymegol *eb* unedau rhesymegol

logistics logisteg *eb*

logo logo *eg*

logogram logogram *eg* logogramau

Lollard *adj* Lolardaidd *ans*

Lollard *n* Lolard *eg* Lolardiaid

Lollardy Lolardiaeth *eb*

London Corresponding Society Cymdeithas Ohebu Llundain *eb*

London pattern hammer morthwyl patrwm Llundain *eg* morthwylion patrwm Llundain

Londoner Llundeiniwr *eg* Llundeinwyr

lone pair pâr unig *eg* parau unig

lone parent family teulu un rhiant *eg*

long hir *ans*

long and short shoulder mortise and tenon joint uniad mortais a thyno ag ysgwydd hir a byr *eg* uniadau mortais a thyno ag ysgwydd hir a byr

long and short shouldered tenon tyno ysgwydd hir a byr *eg* tynoau ysgwydd hir a byr

long and short stitch hirbwyth a byrbwyth

long arm practice ymarfer o hyd braich *eg*

long auger taradr hir *eg* terydr hir

long broken line llinell hir doredig *eb* llinellau hir toredig

long chain carboxylic acid asid carbocsylig cadwyn hir *eg*

long corner (in sport) cornel bell *eb* corneli pell

long distance pellter hir *eg*

long division rhannu hir *be*

long grain graen hir *eg*

long head stake bonyn pen hir *eg* bonion pen hir

long high pass pàs hir uchel *eb* pasiau hir uchel

long hop (in cricket) pelen fer iawn *eb* peli byr iawn

long innings batiad hir *eg* batiadau hir

long jump naid hir *eb* neidiau hir

long jumper neidiwr hir *eg* neidwyr hir

long leaf dalen hir *eb* dalennau hir

long leg coeswr pell *eg* coeswyr pell

long low pass pàs hir isel *eb* pasiau hir isel

Long March Ymdaith Faith *eb*

long metre mesur hir *eg* mesurau hir

long multiplication lluosi hir *be*

long nose pliers gefelen drwyn hir *eb* gefeiliau trwyn hir

long off pellwr agored *eg* pellwyr agored

long on pellwr coes *eg* pellwyr coes

long parliament senedd faith *eb*

long pitch nail hoelen bitsh hir *eb* hoelion pitsh hir

long profile (of a river) hydbroffil *eg* hydbroffiliau

long range forces grymoedd amrediad pell *ell*

long range plane awyren taith hir *eb* awyrennau taith hir

long round nose pliers gefelen drwyn crwn hir *eb* gefeiliau trwyn crwn hir

long section (of a river) hyd-doriad *eg* hyd-doriadau

long ship llong hir *eb* llongau hir

long sight golwg hir *eg*

long snipe nose pliers gefelen drwyn crwn main hir *eb* gefeiliau trwyn crwn main hir

long stay bed gwely arhosiad hir *eg* gwelyau arhosiad hir

long step cam hir *eg* camau hir

long waisted hirwasg *ans*

long wall (of building) talcen hir *eg* talcenni hir

long-arm stapler styffylwr hir *eg* styffylwyr hir

long-armed cross stitch pwyth croes hirfraich *eg* pwythau croes hirfraich

longbow bwa hir *eg* bwâu hir

long-chain cadwyn-hir *ans*

longevity hirhoedledd *eg*

longitude hydred *eg* hydredau

longitude and latitude hydred a lledred

longitudinal hydredol *ans*

longitudinal distance pellter hydredol *eg* pellterau hydredol

longitudinal feed porthiant hydredol *eg*

longitudinal method dull hydredol *eg*

longitudinal movement symudiad hydredol *eg* symudiadau hydredol

longitudinal muscle cyhyryn hydredol *eg* cyhyrynnau hydredol

longitudinal profile proffil hydredol *eg* proffiliau hydredol

longitudinal section toriad hydredol *eg* toriadau hydredol

► **longitudinal vibration** dirgryniad hydredol *eg* dirgryniadau hydredol

longitudinal wave ton hydredol *eb* tonnau hydredol

long-life lamp lamp hir oes *eb* lampau hir oes

long-ray rheidden-hir *eb*

longshore current cerrynt y glannau *eg*

longshore drift drifft y glannau *eg*

long-tailed skua sgiwen lostfain *eb* sgiwennod llostfain

long-term tymor hir *ans*

long-term effects of abuse effeithiau tymor hir camdriniaeth *ell*

long-term liabilities rhwymedigaethau tymor hir *ell*
long-term memory cof tymor hir *eg*
long-term study astudiaeth dymor hir *eb* astudiaethau tymor hir
long-term training ymarfer tymor hir *eg*
longways for as many as will ar hyd i bawb a fynno
longways set set ar hyd *eb* setiau ar hyd
look edrych *be*
look and say method dull edrych a dweud *eg*
look-at ar-edrych *ans*
look-at table tabl ar-edrych *eg* tablau ar-edrych
look-up am-edrych *ans*
look-up table tabl am-edrych *eg* tablau am-edrych
loom gwŷdd *eg* gwyddiau
loom darning creithio gwŷdd *be*
loop dolen *eb* dolennau
loop and tie dolen a chwlwm
loop of Henle ascending limb aelod esgynnol dolen Henle *eg*
loop of Henle descending limb aelod disgynnol dolen Henle *eg*
loop stop dolen atal *eb* dolennau atal
looped cotton cotwm dolennog *eg*
looped fabric ffabrig dolennog *eg* ffabrigau dolennog
looped stitch pwyth dolen *eg* pwythau dolen
looped weave gwehyddiad dolennog *eg*
loose llac *ans*
loose cover gorchudd rhydd *eg* gorchuddion rhydd
loose dye llifyn llac *eg* llifynnau llac
loose feather tafod rhydd *eg* tafodau rhydd
loose fit ffit lac *eb* ffitiau llac
loose head pen rhydd *eg*
loose joint uniad llac *eg* uniadau llac
loose knitting gwau llac *be*
loose maul sgarmes rydd *eb* sgarmesoedd rhydd
loose rivet rhybed llac *eg* rhybedion llac
loose riveting rhybedu llac *be*
loose scrum sgrym rydd *eb* sgrymiau rhydd
loose tongue tafod rhydd *eg* tafodau rhydd
loose tongue joint uniad tafod rhydd *eg* uniadau tafod rhydd
loose-leaf book llyfr dalennau rhydd *eg* llyfrau dalennau rhydd
loosen rhyddhau *be*
looseness llacrwydd *eg*
loosing (the bow) gollwng *be*
lop tocio *be*
lop-eared clustlipa *ans*
lopolith lopolith *eg* lopolithau
lopsided cam *ans*
lord arglwydd *eg* arglwyddi
Lord Advocate Arglwydd Adfocad *eg*
Lord Chancellor Arglwydd Ganghellor *eg*
Lord Chief Justice Arglwydd Brif Ustus *eg*
Lord High Admiral Arglwydd Uchel Lyngesydd *eg*
Lord High Treasurer Arglwydd Uchel Drysorydd *eg*
Lord Keeper Arglwydd Geidwad *eg*
Lord Keeper of the Great Seal Arglwydd Geidwad y Sêl Fawr *eg*
Lord Lieutenant Arglwydd Raglaw *eg*
Lord Mayor Arglwydd Faer *eg*
lord of the manor arglwydd y faenor *eg* arglwyddi'r maenorau
Lord Penrhyn Arglwydd Penrhyn, Yr *eg*
Lord President Arglwydd Lywydd *eg*
Lord Protector Arglwydd Amddiffynnydd *eg*
Lord Shiva Arglwydd Shiva, Yr *eg*
Lords Marcher Arglwyddi'r Gororau *ell*
Lords of the Congregation Arglwyddi'r Gynulleidfa *ell*
Lords Ordainers Arglwyddi Ordeinwyr *ell*
Lord's Supper Swper yr Arglwydd *eg*
Lords Temporal and Spiritual Arglwyddi Lleyg ac Eglwysig *ell*
lordship arglwyddiaeth *eb* arglwyddiaethau
Lorenzo the Magnificent Lorenzo Ysblennydd *eg*
lose colour (enamelling colour) bwrw lliw *be*
lose colour (in general) colli lliw *be*
lose control of the ball colli rheolaeth ar y bêl *be*
lose possession of the ball colli meddiant o'r bêl *be*
loss colled *eg/b* colledion
lost ball pêl goll *eb* peli coll
lost village pentref diflan *eg* pentrefi diflan
lost-wax process proses cwyr coll *eb*
lot and scot lot a scot
lotion trwyth *eg* trwythau
Lotus Sutra Lotus Sutra *eg*
loud (of sound) cryf *ans*
loud sound sain gref *eb* seiniau cryf
loudness (of sound) cryfder *eg*
loudspeaker uchelseinydd *eg* uchelseinyddion
loudspeaker seinydd *eg* seinyddion
lough loch *eg* lochau
Louis the Pious Louis Dduwiol *eg*
lounge lolfa *eb* lolfeydd
louvre lwfer *eg* lwferau
louvre window ffenestr louvre *eb* ffenestri louvre
love cariad *eg*
love (tennis score) dim sgôr
love all (tennis score) dim dim
love feast (=Christian feast) cariadwledd *eb* cariadwleddoedd
love game gêm i ddim
low isel *ans*
low angle ongl isel *eb* onglau isel
low ball pêl isel *eb* peli isel
low carbon carbon isel *eg*
Low Church Isel Eglwysig *ans*
low cost labour llafur rhad *eg*
low dive deifio'n isel *be*
low foaming detergent glanedydd prindrochion *eg* glanedyddion prindrochion
low frequency (of oscillations) amledd isel *eg*
low key (in old Welsh music) isgywair *eg*

low latitude lledred isel *eg* lledredau isel
low level lefel isel *eb* lefelau isel
low limit terfan isel *eb*
low line llinell isel *eb*
low net rhwyd isel *eb* rhwydi isel
low population density dwysedd poblogaeth isel *eg* dwyseddau poblogaeth isel
low power drawing lluniad chwyddhad isel *eg* lluniadau chwyddhad isel
low pressure gwasgedd isel *eg*
low register nodau isel *ell*
low relief cerfwedd isel *eb* cerfweddau isel
low resolution cydraniad isel *eg*
low self-esteem hunan-barch isel *eg*
low spin troelliad paredig *eg* troelliadau paredig
low step cam isel *eg* camau isel
low voltage foltedd isel *eg*
low water distyll *eg*
low water mark marc distyll *eg*
low-angle plane plaen ongl-isel *eg* plaeniau ongl-isel
lower *v* gostwng *be*
lower attaining pupil disgybl is ei gyrhaeddiad *eg* disgyblion is eu cyrhaeddiad
lower bound arffin isaf *eg* arffiniau isaf
lower case letter llythyren fach *eb* llythrennau bach
lower class dosbarth isaf *eg* dosbarthiadau isaf
lower ground islawr *eg* isloriau
lower jaw gên isaf *eb* genau isaf
lower mordent isfordent *eg* isfordentau
lower order (in geology) haen isaf *eb* haenau isaf
lower register isgwmpasran *eb*
lower school ysgol isaf *eb* ysgolion isaf
lower the body gostwng y corff *be*
lower tier rhes isaf *eb* rhesi isaf
lowest common multiple lluosrif cyffredin lleiaf *eg*
lowest order gradd isaf *eb*
lowest terms ffurf symlaf *eb*
lowland iseldir *eg* iseldiroedd
low-level language iaith lefel isel *eb* ieithoedd lefel isel
low-lying plain gwastadedd isel *eg* gwastadeddau isel
low-order is-werth *ans*
low-order position safle is-werth *eg* safleoedd is-werth
low-pass pas-isel *ans*
low-pass filter hidlen pasio seiniau isel *eb* hidlenni pasio seiniau isel
loxodrome (=rhumb line) locsodrom *eg* locsodromau
loyal teyrngar *ans*
loyalist teyrngarwr *eg* teyrngarwyr
loyalty teyrngarwch *eg*
loyalty card cerdyn ffyddlondeb *eg* cardiau ffyddlondeb
lozenge graver crafell losin *eb* crafellau losin
lubricant iraid *eg* ireidiau
lubricate iro *be*
lubricating nipples niplau iro *ell*
lubricating point pwynt iro *eg* pwyntiau iro
lubrication iriad *eg* iriadau
lucerne maglys *eg*
lucid eglur *ans*
Luddite *adj* Ludaidd *ans*
Luddite *n* Ludiad *eg* Ludiaid
ludo liwdo *eg*
lug clust *eg/b* clustiau
lukewarm claear *ans*
lukewarm water dŵr claear *eg*
lullaby hwiangerdd *eb* hwiangerddi
lumbar *adj* meingefnol *ans*
lumbar puncture tynnu hylif madruddyn y cefn *be*
lumbar region adran y meingefn *eb*
lumbar vertebra fertebra meingefnol *eg* fertebrâu meingefnol
lumber coed *ell*
lumbering coetmona *be*
lumberjack coetmon *eg* coetmyn
lumen lwmen *eg* lwmina
Luminarists Goleueddwyr *ell*
luminescence ymoleuedd *eg*
luminosity goleuedd *eg* goleueddau
luminous goleuol *ans*
luminous intensity arddwysedd goleuol *eg* arddwyseddau goleuol
lump lwmp *eg* lympiau
lump sum lwmp-swm *eg* lymp-symiau
lumpsucker pysgodyn clytsiwr *eg* pysgod clytsiwr
lunar day diwrnod lleuad *eg*
lunar eclipse diffyg ar y lleuad *eg* diffygion ar y lleuad
lunar month mis lleuad *eg* misoedd lleuad
lunatic gwallgofddyn *eg*
lunatic fringe ymylwyr gwallgof *ell*
lunch cinio canol dydd *eg*
lunch interval amser cinio *eg*
lune lŵn *eg* lynau
lung ysgyfant *eg* ysgyfaint
lung capacity cynhwysedd yr ysgyfaint *eg* cynwyseddau'r ysgyfaint
lung deflation dadchwythiant yr ysgyfaint *eg*
lung fish pysgodyn ysgyfeiniog *eg* pysgod ysgyfeiniog
lung volume cyfaint ysgyfaint *eg*
lunge rhagwth *eg* rhagwthion
lunge forward rhagwth ymlaen *eg* rhagwthion ymlaen
lunge in low line rhagwth ar linell isel *eg* rhagwthion ar linell isel
lunge outward rhagwth allan *eg* rhagwthion allan
lunge sideways rhagwth ochr *eg* rhagwthion ochr
lunula lwnwla *eg* lwnwlau
Lurex Lurex *eg*
lurk llercian *be*
lurker llerciwr *eg* llercwyr
lustre gloywedd *eg* gloyweddau
lustre pottery crochenwaith gloywedd *eg*

lustrous (finish) gloyw *ans*
lustrous material defnydd gloyw *eg* defnyddiau gloyw
lute liwt *eg/b* liwtiau
luteal cells celloedd lwteal *ell*
luteinizing hormone hormon lwteineiddio *eg* hormonau lwteineiddio
lutenist liwtydd *eg* liwtwyr
lutetium (Lu) lwtetiwm *eg*
Lutheran *adj* Lutheraidd *ans*
Lutheran *n* Lutheriad *eg* Lutheriaid
Lutheranism Lutheriaeth *eb*
luting liwtio *be*
lux lwcs *eg* lycsau
luxurious moethus *ans*
luxury moeth *eg* moethau
luxury goods nwyddau moeth *ell*
lychgate porth mynwent *eg* pyrth mynwent
lying down gorweddol *ans*
lying press gwasg osod *eb* gweisg gosod
lyme grass clymwellt *ell*
lymph lymff *eg*
lymph gland chwarren lymff *eb* chwarennau lymff
lymph node nod lymff *eg* nodau lymff
lymph vessel pibell lymff *eb* pibellau lymff
lymphatic lymffatig *ans*
lymphatic gland chwarren lymffatig *eb*
lymphatic system system lymffatig *eb*
lymphocyte lymffocyt *eg* lymffocytau
lynchet glaslain *eb* glasleiniau
lynx lyncs *eg/eb* lyncsod
lyre lyra *eb* lyrâu
lyric drama drama delynegol *eb* dramâu telynegol
lyric opera opera delynegol *eb* operâu telynegol
lyric tenor tenor ysgafn *eg* tenoriaid ysgafn
lysergic acid diethylamide (LSD) deuethylamid asid lysergig *eg*
lysine lysin *eg*
lysis lysis *eg*
lysogeny lysogenedd *eg*
lysosome lysosom *eg* lysosomau
lysozyme lysosym *eg* lysosymau
lytic lytig *ans*

M

macaroni cheese caws macaroni *eg*
mace byrllysg *eg* byrllysgau
macerate briwio *be*
machine *n* peiriant *eg* peiriannau
machine *v* peiriannu *be*
machine architecture saernïaeth peiriant *eb*
machine attachments atodion peiriant *ell*
machine code cod peiriant *eg* codau peiriant
machine code language iaith cod peiriant *eb*
machine cycle cylchred peiriant *eb* cylchredau peiriant
machine darn craith peiriant *eb* creithiau peiriant
machine darn patch clwt craith peiriant *eg* clytiau craith peiriant
machine embroidery brodwaith peiriant *eg*
machine fell seam sêm ffel ddwbl *eb* semau ffel ddwbl
machine gather crychdynnu â pheiriant *be*
machine gun gwn peiriant *eg* gynau peiriant
machine heads ebillres *eb* ebillresi
machine independent annibynnol ar y peiriant *ans*
machine language iaith peiriant *eb* ieithoedd peiriant
machine made buttonhole twll botwm peiriant *eg* tyllau botymau peiriant
machine needle nodwydd peiriant *eb* nodwyddau peiriant
machine operating system (MOS) system weithredu peiriant *eb*
machine operator gweithiwr peiriannau *eg* gweithwyr peiriannau
machine screw sgriw beiriant *eb* sgriwiau peiriant
machine shop gweithdy peiriannau *eg* gweithdai peiriannau
machine tools offer peiriannau *ell*
machine translation cyfieithu peirianyddol *be*
machine vice feis peiriant *eb* feisiau peiriant
machine washable golchadwy â pheiriant *ans*
machine word gair peiriant *eg* geiriau peiriant
machine-aided translation cyfieithu drwy gymorth cyfrifiadur *be*
machined component cydran wedi'i pheiriannu *eb* cydrannau wedi'u peiriannu
machinery peirianwaith *eg* peirianweithiau
machining allowance lwfans peiriannu *eg* lwfansau peiriannu
mackerel sky traeth awyr *eg*
macramé macramé *eg*
macramé twine cortyn macramé *eg* cortynnau macramé
macro macro *ans*
macro macro *eg* macros
macro factor macro ffactor *eg*
macro nutrient macrofaethyn *eg* macrofaethynnau
macro programming rhaglennu macro *be*
macroassembler macrogydosodydd *eg* macrogydosodyddion
macro-climate macrohinsawdd *eg* macrohinsoddau
macrocosm macrocosm *eg* macrocosmau
macroeconomic macro economaidd *ans*
macroeconomic issue mater macroeconomaidd *eg* materion macroeconomaidd
macroeconomic objective amcan macroeconomaidd *eg* amcanion macroeconomaidd
macroeconomic policy polisi macroeconomaidd *eg*
macroeconomic theory theori facroeconomaidd *eb*
macrophage macroffag *eg* macroffagau
macula macwla *eg* macwlau
made environment amgylchedd gwneud *eg* amgylcheddau gwneud
made form ffurf wneud *eb* ffurfiau gwneud
Madinah Madinah *eg*
madrigal madrigal *eb* madrigalau
magazine cylchgrawn *eg* cylchgronau
magazine cover clawr cylchgrawn *eg* cloriau cylchgronau
magazine rack rhesel gylchgronau *eb* rheseli cylchgronau
magenta magenta *eg*
maggot cynrhonyn *eg* cynrhon
magic hud *eg*
magic chain stitch pwyth cadwyn hud *eg* pwythau cadwyn hud
magician dewin *eg* dewiniaid
Maginot Line Llinell Maginot *eb*
magistracy ynadaeth *eb*
magistrate ynad *eg* ynadon
magistrates court llys ynadon *eg* llysoedd ynadon
magma magma *eg* magmâu
magmatic magmatig *ans*
Magna Carta Magna Carta *eg*
magnesian magnesaidd *ans*
magnesium (Mg) magnesiwm *eg*
magnesium bicarbonate magnesiwm deucarbonad *eg*
magnesium carbonate magnesiwm carbonad *eg*
magnesium ion ïon magnesiwm *eg* ïonau magnesiwm
magnet magnet *eg* magnetau

magnetic magnetig *ans*
magnetic bearing cyfeiriant magnetig *eg*
magnetic board bwrdd magnetig *eg* byrddau magnetig
magnetic bubble memory cof bwrlwm magnetig *eg*
magnetic card cerdyn magnetig *eg* cardiau magnetig
magnetic catch clicied fagnetig *eb*
magnetic core store storfa craidd magnetig *eb* storfeydd craidd magnetig
magnetic disk disg magnetig *eg* disgiau magnetig
magnetic field maes magnetig *eg* meysydd magnetig
magnetic field line llinell faes magnetig *eb*
magnetic flux fflwcs magnetig *eg*
magnetic flux density dwysedd fflwcs magnetig *eg*
magnetic ink character recognition (MICR) adnabod nodau inc magnetig *be*
magnetic medium cyfrwng magnetig *eg* cyfryngau magnetig
magnetic moment moment magnetig *eg*
magnetic north gogledd magnetig *eg*
magnetic pole pôl magnetig *eg* polau magnetig
magnetic resonance imaging (MRI) delweddu cyseiniant magnetig *be*
magnetic stirrer tröydd magnetig *eg* troyddion magnetig
magnetic tape tâp magnetig *eg* tapiau magnetig
magnetically coated disk disg wedi'i orchuddio â haen fagnetig *eg* disgiau wedi'u gorchuddio â haen fagnetig
magnetism (of property) magnetedd *eg*
magnetism (study of) magneteg *eb*
magnetization magneteiddiad *eg* magneteiddiadau
magnetize magneteiddio *be*
magneto magneto *eg* magnetoeon
magnetometer magnetomedr *eg* magnetomedrau
magnetron magnetron *eg* magnetronau
magnification chwyddhad *eg* chwyddadau
magnifier chwyddhadur *eg* chwyddaduron
magnify chwyddo *be*
magnifying glass chwyddwydr *eg* chwyddwydrau
magnitude maint *eg* meintiau
magnitude and direction maint a chyfeiriad
magnitude of linear motion maint mudiant llinol *eg*
magnocellular pathway llwybr magnogellog *eg*
Magnus Maximus Macsen Wledig *eg*
magyar sleeve llawes magyar *eb* llewys magyar
Mahabharata Mahabharata *eb*
Mahayana Mahayana *eg*
Mahayana Buddhism Bwdhaeth Mahayana *eb*
mahlstick ffon peintiwr *eb* ffyn peintwyr
mahogany mahogani *eg*
Maid of Kent Morwyn Caint *eb*
maiden name enw cyn priodi *eg* enwau cyn priodi
maiden over pelawd ddi-sgôr *eb* pelawdau di-sgôr
mail post *eg*
mail boat llong bost *eb* llongau post
mail merge postgyfuno *be*
mail order *n* archeb drwy'r post *eb* archebion drwy'r post
mail order *v* archebu drwy'r post *be*
mail server gweinydd post *eg* gweinyddion post
mailcoach coets y post *eb* coetsys y post
mail-filter hidlydd post *eg* hidlyddion post
mailing group grŵp postio *eg* grwpiau postio
mailing list rhestr bostio *eb* rhestri postio
mail-order archebion post
mail-shot post-dafliad *eg* post-dafliadau
main axis prif echelin *eb*
main body text prif gorff y testun *eg*
main colour prif liw *eg*
main competitor prif gystadleuydd *eg* prif gystadleuwyr
main criterion prif faen prawf *eg* prif feini prawf
main dimensions prif ddimensiynau *ell*
main effect prif effaith *eb*
main entrance (of church) porth *eg* pyrth
main frame prif gyfrifiadur *eg* prif gyfrifiaduron
main mast prif hwylbren *eb* prif hwylbrennau
main memory prif gof *eg*
main menu prif ddewislen *eb* prif ddewislenni
main pipe prif bibell *eb* prif bibellau
main rafter prif geibr *eg* prif geibrau
main religion prif grefydd *eb* prif grefyddau
main screen prif sgrin *eb* prif sgriniau
main sequence stars sêr prif ddilyniant *ell*
main spindle (lathe part) prif werthyd *eg* prif werthydau
main store prif storfa *eb* prif storfeydd
main stream prif ffrwd *eb* prif ffrydiau
main subject prif destun *eg* prif destunau
main trend prif duedd *eb*
mainframe computer cyfrifiadur prif ffrâm *eg* cyfrifiaduron prif ffrâm
mainland tir mawr *eg*
mains prif gyflenwad *eg* prif gyflenwadau
mains electricity supply prif gyflenwad trydan *eg*
mainsail hwyl fawr *eb* hwyliau mawr
mainsheet prif raff *eb* prif raffau
mainstream film ffilm brif ffrwd *eb* ffilmiau prif ffrwd
mainstreaming prif ffrydio *be*
maintain a part cynnal rhan *be*
maintain possession cadw meddiant *be*
maintain possession of the ball cadw meddiant o'r bêl *be*
maintained school ysgol a gynhelir *eb* ysgolion a gynhelir
maintainer cynheiliad *eg* cynheiliaid
maintenance (of buildings etc) cynnal a chadw
maintenance cost cost cynnal *eb* costau cynnal
maintenance documentation dogfennaeth cynnal *eb*
maintenance grant (for students) grant cynnal *eg* grantiau cynnal
maintenance of growth cynnal twf *be*
maintenance operation gweithrediad cynnal *eg*

maintenance rehearsal ymarfer er mwyn cynnal *eg*
maize India corn *eg*
maize oil olew corn *eg*
majestic mawreddog *ans*
majesty mawrhydi *eg*
majolica (enamelled pottery) majolica *eg*
major *adj* mwyaf *ans*
major *n* uwch-gapten *eg* uwch-gapteniaid
major aftershock prif ôl-gryniad *eg*
major and minor games prif a mân chwaraeon
major axis echelin hwyaf *eb* echelinau hwyaf
major chord cord mwyaf *eg* cordiau mwyaf
major common chord cord cyffredin mwyaf *eg* cordiau cyffredin mwyaf
major depression iselder dwys *eg*
major diameter diamedr mwyaf *eg*
major health problem problem iechyd o bwys *eb* problemau iechyd o bwys
major incident digwyddiad mawr *eg* digwyddiadau mawr
major interval cyfwng mwyaf *eg* cyfyngau mwyaf
major key cywair mwyaf *eg*
major life change newid pwysig i fywyd *eg*
major order prif urdd *eb* prif urddau
major scale graddfa fwyaf *eb* graddfeydd mwyaf
major-general uwch-frigadydd *eg* uwch-frigadwyr
majority mwyafrif *eg*
majuscule llythrennau bras *ell*
make gwneud *be*
make a bridge gwneud pont *be*
make a circle gwneud cylch *be*
make a dance creu dawns *be*
make a decision penderfynu *be*
make a dummy pass (in rugby) ffugbasio *be*
make a sketch-map llunio llinfap *be*
make fast clymwch
make judgement barnu *be*
make observations cynnig arsylwadau *be*
make patterns gwneud patrymau *be*
make the transition (linguistically) croesi'r bont *be*
make up (=devise) dyfeisio *be*
make up (a solution) paratoi *be*
make up to the mark llenwi hyd at y graddnod *be*
make-believe *adj* ffug *ans*
make-believe *n* dychymyg *eg* dychmygion
make-believe *v* smalio *be*
make-up (cosmetics) *n* colur *eg*
make-up (cosmetics) *v* coluro *be*
make-up box blwch coluro *eg* blychau coluro
Makkah Makkah *eb*
mako shark morgi trwynfain *eg* morgwn trwynfain
maladjusted child plentyn heb ymaddasu *eg* plant heb ymaddasu
maladjustment diffyg ymaddasiad *eg*
maladministration camweinyddu *be*
malaria malaria *eg*
malarial swamps gwernydd malaria *ell*
male *adj* gwrywol *ans*
male *n* gwryw *eg* gwrywod
male gamete gamet gwryw *eg* gametau gwryw
male reproductive cell cell atgenhedlol wrywol *eb* celloedd atgenhedlol gwrywol
male sexual dysfunction camweithredu rhywiol mewn dynion *eg*
male voice choir côr meibion *eg* corau meibion
maleness gwrywedd *eg*
malformation camffurfiad *eg* camffurfiadau
malfunction *n* diffyg *eg* diffygion
malfunction *v* camweithio *be*
malic acid asid malig *eg*
malicious damage difrod maleisus *eg*
malignant malaen *ans*
malleability hydrinedd *eg* hydrineddau
malleable hydrin *ans*
malleable cast iron haearn bwrw hydrin *eg*
malleable iron haearn hydrin *eg*
malleable iron (ferrous metal) dur canol *eg*
malleable nail hoelen hydrin *eb* hoelion hydrin
mallee malî *eg*
mallet gordd *eb* gyrdd
malleus morthwyl y glust *eg*
malnutrition diffyg maeth *eg*
malonic acid asid malonig *eg*
Malpighian body corffyn Malpighi *eg*
Malpighian corpuscle corffilyn Malpighi *eg*
Malpighian layer haen Malpighi *eb*
Malpighian tubule tiwbyn Malpighi *eg*
malt brag brag *eg* bragau
malt bread bara brag *eg*
Malthusianism Malthwsiaeth *eb*
maltose maltos *eg*
mamillated bronennog *ans*
mammal mamolyn *eg* mamolion
mammalian mamolaidd *ans*
mammalian skeleton sgerbwd mamolaidd *eg* sgerbydau mamolaidd
mammary bronnol *ans*
mammary gland chwarren laeth *eb* chwarennau llaeth
mammatocumulus brongwmwl *eg* brongymylau
mammoth mamoth *eg* mamothiaid
man to man defence amddiffyn dyn am ddyn *be*
manage rheoli *be*
manage and control rheoli a chadw trefn
manage environments rheoli amgylcheddau *be*
manage expenditure rheoli gwariant *be*
manageable hylaw *ans*
managed exchange rate cyfradd cyfnewid reoledig *eb*
management (=managers) rheolwyr *ell*
management (act of) rheolaeth *eb* rheolaethau
management information gwybodaeth rheoli *eb*
manager rheolwr *eg* rheolwyr
manageress rheolwraig *eb* rheolwragedd

managerial rheolaethol *ans*
managerial post swydd reoli *eb* swyddi rheoli
managerial skills sgiliau rheoli *ell*
managerial studies astudiaethau rheoli *ell*
managing director rheolwr-gyfarwyddwr *eg*
managing unwanted behaviour rheoli ymddygiad digroeso *be*
man-at-arms milwr arfog *eg* milwyr arfog
manciple swyddog cyflenwi *eg* swyddogion cyflenwi
mandarin collar coler mandarin *eg* coleri mandarin
mandarin ink inc mandarin *eg*
mandate mandad *eg* mandadau
mandated mandedig *ans*
mandated territory tiriogaeth fandadol *eb* tiriogaethau mandadol
mandatory gorfodol *ans*
mandatory exception eithriad gorfodol *eg* eithriadau gorfodol
mandatory grant grant gorfodol *eg* grantiau gorfodol
mandatory unit uned orfodol *eb* unedau gorfodol
man-day dydd gweithiwr *eg* dyddiau gweithiwr
mandible mandibl *eg* mandiblau
mandibular arch bwa'r mandibl *eg*
mandolin mandolin *eg* mandolinau
mandorla mandorla *eg*
mandrel (lathe part) mandrel *eg* mandrelau
manganate(VI) ion ïon manganad(VI) *eg* ïonau manganad(VI)
manganate(VII) ion ïon manganad(VII) *eg* ïonau manganad(VII)
manganese (Mn) manganîs *eg*
manganese(II) carbonate manganis(II) carbonad *eg*
manganese(II) dimanganese(III) oxide manganîs(II) deumanganîs(III) ocsid *eg*
manganese(II) ion ïon manganîs(II) *eg* ïonau manganîs(II)
manganese(III) ion ïon manganîs(III) *eg* ïonau manganîs(III)
manganese(IV) oxide manganîs(IV) ocsid *eg*
manganese(VII) oxide manganîs(VII) ocsid *eg*
mangle *n* mangl *eg*
mangle *v* manglo *be*
mango mango *eg*
mangrove swamp gwern fangrof *eb* gwernydd mangrof
manhole twll archwilio *eg* tyllau archwilio
manhood suffrage pleidlais gwŷr *eb*
mania mania *eg*
manic manig *ans*
manic depression iselder manig *eg*
manifest amlygu *be*
manifest content cynnwys amlwg *eg*
manifest destiny arfaeth amlwg *eb*
manifesto maniffesto *eg*
manifold maniffold *eg* maniffoldau
manikin manicin *eg*
manilla manila *eg*
manilla paper papur manila *eg*
manipulate (data etc) trin *be*
manipulate (with hands) llawdrin *be*
manipulation llawdriniaeth *eb* llawdriniaethau
manipulative play chwarae trin â'r dwylo *be*
manipulative skill sgìl llawdriniol *eg* sgiliau llawdriniol
man-machine interface rhyngwyneb peiriant-dyn *eg* rhyngwynebau peiriant-dyn
man-made fibre ffibr gwneud *eg* ffibrau gwneud
man-made materials defnyddiau gwneud *ell*
man-made object gwrthrych gwneud *eg* gwrthrychau gwneud
manna manna *eg*
mannerism (in art) darddulliaeth *eb*
mannerist *adj* darddullaidd *ans*
mannerist *n* darddullwr *eg* darddullwyr
mannerist style arddull darddullaidd *eg*
Mann-Whitney U test prawf U Mann-Whitney *eg*
manoeuvres ymarferion *ell*
man-of-war llong arfog *eb* llongau arfog
manometer manomedr *eg* manomedrau
manor maenor *eb* maenorau
manor house maenordy *eb* maenordai
manorial system trefn faenorol *eb*
manpower (=labour force) gweithlu *eg*
manpower (of resources) adnoddau llafur *ell*
manpower planning cynllunio nifer y gweithlu *be*
Manpower Services Commission Comisiwn Gwasanaethau'r Gweithlu *eg*
mansard roof to mansard *eg* toeon mansard
mansion plas *eg* plasau
mansion house plasty *eg* plastai
mantel shelf silff fantell *eb* silffoedd mantell
mantelpiece silff ben tân *eb* silffoedd pen tân
mantissa mantisa *eg* mantisâu
mantle *n* mantell *eb* mentyll
mantle *v* mantellu *be*
mantle cavity ceudod mantell *eg* ceudodau mantell
mantle rock creicaen *eb* creicaenau
mantra mantra *eg*
manual (book) llawlyfr *eg* llawlyfrau
manual (on instrument) seinglawr *eg* seingloriau
manual sphygmomanometer teclyn mesur pwysau gwaed llaw *eg*
manual worker gweithiwr llaw *eg* gweithwyr llaw
manufacture cynhyrchu *be*
manufactured apparatus offer parod *ell*
manufactured board pren cyfansawdd *eg* prennau cyfansawdd
manufactured cloth defnydd gwneud *eg* defnyddiau gwneud
manufactured goods gweithgynhyrchion *ell*
manufacturer gwneuthurwr *eg* gwneuthurwyr
manufacturing industry diwydiant gweithgynhyrchu *eg* diwydiannau gweithgynhyrchu
manumission rhyddhau *eg*
manure *n* tail *eg*
manure *v* teilo *be*

manuscript llawysgrif *eb* llawysgrifau
manuscript ink inc llawysgrif *eg*
manuscript lettering llythrennu llawysgrif *be*
manuscript music book llyfr erwydd *eg* llyfrau erwydd
manuscript paper (for music) papur erwydd *eg* papurau erwydd
manuscript sheet (for music) taflen erwydd *eb* taflenni erwydd
many-many correspondence cyfatebiaeth llawer-i-lawer *eb*
many-one correspondence cyfatebiaeth llawer-i-un *eb*
many-to-many llawer-i-lawer
many-valued lluoswerth *ans*
map *n* map *eg* mapiau
map *v* mapio *be*
map analysis dadansoddiad map *eg*
map reference cyfeirnod map *eg* cyfeirnodau map
map sheet dalen fap *eb* dalennau map
mapping pen pen mapio *eg* pennau mapio
maquette maquette *eg* maquettes
marathon marathon *eg*
marauder ysbeiliwr *eg* ysbeilwyr
marble marmor *eg*
marble marblen *eb* marblis
marble chips sglodion marmor *ell*
marbling marmori *be*
marbling colour lliw marmori *eg*
marbling comb crib farmori *eb* cribau marmori
marbling effects effeithiau marmori *ell*
marbling technique techneg marmori *eb* technegau marmori
marbling trough cafn marmori *eg* cafnau marmori
march (=border) *n* goror *eg* gororau
march (=journey) *n* ymdaith *eb* ymdeithiau
march (=journey) *v* ymdeithio *be*
march (=procession) *n* gorymdaith *eb* gorymdeithiau
march (=walk in procession) *v* gorymdeithio *be*
march (music) *n* ymdeithgan *eb* ymdeithganau
March on Rome Ymdaith i Rufain *eb*
marcher customs arferion y Mers *ell*
marcher Lords Arglwyddi'r Mers *ell*
Marches Mers *eg*
marching camp gwersyll dros dro *eg* gwersylloedd dros dro
margarine margarin *eg*
margin (of page) ymyl *eg/b* ymylon
margin (of profit) maint *eg*
margin guide canllaw ymyl *eg* canllawiau ymyl
margin of error lled y gwall *eg*
margin release datglöwr *eg* datglowyr
margin setting gosodiad ymyl *eg* gosodiadau ymyl
margin stop stop ymyl *eg* stopiau ymyl
marginal ymylol *ans*
▶ **marginal cost** cost ymylol *eb* costau ymylol
marginal costing costio ymylol *be*
▶ **marginal distribution function** ffwythiant dosraniad ymylol *eg*
marginal efficiency of capital effeithlonrwydd ymylol cyfalaf *eg*
marginal land tir ymylol *eg* tiroedd ymylol
marginal product cynnyrch ymylol *eg*
marginal propensity to consume tuedd ymylol i dreulio *eb*
marginal propensity to import tuedd ymylol i fewnforio *eb*
marginal propensity to save tuedd ymylol i gynilo *eb*
marginal rate of tax cyfradd ymylol treth *eb*
marginal revenue refeniw ymylol *eg*
marginal revenue product cynnyrch refeniw ymylol *eg*
marginal utility budd ymylol *eg*
marginalize ymyleiddio *be*
Marian Marïaidd *ans*
Marian exiles alltudion Mari *ell*
Marian martyrs merthyron Mari *ell*
Marian persecution erledigaeth Mari *eb*
marina marina *eg* marinas
marine *adj* morol *ans*
marine *n* môr-filwr *eg* môr-filwyr
marine grade plywood pren haenog gradd morol *eg*
marine painting (of picture) môr-baentiad *eg* môr-baentiadau
marine painting (of process or art) môr-beintio *be*
marine varnish farnais morol *eg*
marionette pyped *eg* pypedau
marital priodasol *ans*
maritime (=coastal) arforol *ans*
maritime (=seafaring) morwrol *ans*
Maritime Code Cod y Môr *eg*
maritime law cyfraith forwrol *eb*
mark *v* marcio *be*
mark (numerical or alphabetical award) *n* marc *eg* marciau
mark (trace or symbol) *n* nod *eg* nodau
mark of expression marc mynegiant *eg* marciau mynegiant
mark out marcio *be*
mark scheme cynllun marcio *eg* cynlluniau marcio
mark sensing synhwyro marc *be*
mark sheet taflen farciau *eb* taflenni marciau
mark the opponent marcio'r gwrthwynebwr *be*
mark weighting pwysiad marciau *eg*
marked price pris dangosol *eg* prisiau dangosol
marker marciwr *eg* marcwyr
market *n* marchnad *eb* marchnadoedd
market *v* marchnata *be*
market analysis dadansoddiad o'r farchnad *eg*
market characteristic nodwedd farchnad *eb*
market conditions cyflwr y farchnad *eg*
market demand curve cromlin galw marchnad *eb*
market economy economi marchnad *eg*
market failure methiant y farchnad *eg*

market force grym y farchnad *eg* grymoedd y farchnad
market garden gardd fasnachol *eb* gerddi masnachol
market gardening garddio masnachol *be*
market place marchnad *eb*
market pull tyniad y farchnad *eg*
market research ymchwil marchnata *eg*
market research strategy strategaeth ymchwil farchnata *eb*
market segment segment o'r farchnad *eg*
market segmentation segmentiad y farchnad *eg*
market share cyfran marchnad *eb*
market square sgwâr marchnad *eg*
market town tref farchnad *eb* trefi marchnad
market value gwerth y farchnad *eg*
marketable gwerthadwy *ans*
marketable wealth cyfoeth gwerthadwy *eg*
marketing communications cyfathrebu marchnata *be*
marketing department adran farchnata *eb* adrannau marchnata
marketing manager rheolwr marchnata *eg* rheolwyr marchnata
marketing mix cymysgedd marchnata *eg*
marketing plan cynllun marchnata *eg* cynlluniau marchnata
marketing research ymchwil i farchnata *eg*
marketing research agency asiantaeth ymchwil marchnata *eb* asiantaethau ymchwil marchnata
marketing strategy strategaeth farchnata *eb* strategaethau marchnata
marking gauge medrydd marcio *eg* medryddion marcio
marking knife cyllell farcio *eb* cyllyll marcio
marking medium cyfrwng marcio *eg* cyfryngau marcio
marking out fluid llifydd marcio *eg* llifyddion marcio
marking table bwrdd marcio *eg* byrddau marcio
markup language iaith tagio *eb* ieithoedd tagio
marl *n* marl *eg* marlau
marl *v* marlio *be*
marly marlog *ans*
marouflage marouflage *eg*
marquetry argaenwaith *eg*
marquis ardalydd *eg* ardalyddion
marram grass moresg *ell*
marriage priodas *eb* priodasau
marriage by proxy priodas ddirprwyol *eb* priodasau dirprwyol
marriage portion gwaddol priodferch *eg*
marriage settlement cytundeb priodas *eg* cytundebau priodas
marrow mêr *eg*
Mars Mawrth *eg*
marsh fritillary brith y gors *eg*
marsh or salting mignen neu halwyndir
marsh orchid tegeirian rhuddgoch *eg* tegeirianau rhuddgoch
marshal marsial *eg* marsialiaid
marshalling yard iard drefnu *eb* iardiau trefnu
Marshall-Lerner condition amod Marshall-Lerner *eg* amodau Marshall-Lerner
mart marchnad *eb* marchnadoedd
martensite martensit *eg*
martial law cyfraith rhyfel *eb*
martyr *n* merthyr *eg* merthyron
martyr *v* merthyru *be*
martyrdom merthyrdod *eg*
martyrology merthyroleg *eb*
Marxism Marcsaeth *eb*
Marxist *adj* Marcsaidd *ans*
Marxist *n* Marcsydd *eg* Marcswyr
Mary, Queen of Scots Mari, Brenhines y Sgotiaid *eb*
Mary Stuart Mari Stiwart *eb*
Mashiach Meseia *eg*
mashlum amyd *eg*
mask *n* mwgwd *eg* mygydau
mask (=hide) *v* cuddio *be*
mask (with masking tape) *v* masgio *be*
maskable interrupt ymyriad cuddiadwy *eg* ymyriadau cuddiadwy
masked sprite ciplun cuddiedig *eg* cipluniau cuddiedig
masking masgio *be*
masking tape tâp masgio *eg*
Maslow's hierarchy of needs hierarchaeth anghenion Maslow *eb*
mason saer maen *eg* seiri maen
masonry bit ebill maen *eg* ebillion maen
masonry drill dril gwaith maen *eg* driliau gwaith maen
masonry nail hoelen gwaith maen *eb* hoelion gwaith maen
masque masque *eg* masques
mass offeren *eb* offerennau
mass (of matter) màs *eg* masau
mass defect diffyg màs *eg*
mass flow màs-lifiad *eg*
mass for the dead offeren i'r meirw *eb*
mass media cyfryngau torfol *ell*
mass movement (in physics) màs-symudiad *eg*
mass movement (of people) symudiad torfol *eg*
mass number rhif màs *eg* rhifau màs
mass of solid màs y solid *eg*
mass priest periglor *eg* perigloriaid
mass produce masgynhyrchu *be*
mass produced goods nwyddau masgynnyrch *ell*
mass production masgynhyrchu *be*
mass spectrograph sbectrograff màs *eg* sbectrograffau màs
mass spectrometer sbectromedr màs *eg*
mass spectrometry sbectromedreg màs *eb*
mass spectrum sbectrwm màs *eg*
mass storage storfa fàs *eb* storfeydd màs
massacre (in general especially in plural) lladdfa *eb* lladdfeydd

massacre (of specific historical instances) cyflafan *eb*
Massacre of St Bartholomew Cyflafan Gwylnos Bartholomeus *eb*
Massacre of the Sicilian Vespers Cyflafan y Gosberau Sisilaidd *eb*
massage tylino'r corff *be*
masses, the gwerin, y werin *eb*
masseter muscle cyhyryn maseter *eg* cyhyrynnau maseter
massif masiff *eg* masiffau
massive (=enormous) enfawr *ans*
massive (in physics) masfawr *ans*
mass-wasting masddarfodiant *eg*
mast hwylbren *eg* hwylbrennau
mast cell mastgell *eb* mastgelloedd
master (to make copies from) *adj* meistr *ans*
master(=main) *adj* prif *ans*
master *n* meistr *eg* meistri
master *v* meistroli *be*
master / slave system system meistr / gwas *eb* systemau meistr / gwas
master cast cast gwreiddiol *eg* castiau gwreiddiol
master copy copi gwreiddiol *eg* copïau gwreiddiol
▶ **master disk** meistr-ddisg *eg/b* meistrddisgiau
master document meistrddogfen *eb* meistrddogfenni
▶ **master file** meistr-ffeil *eb* meistrffeiliau
master of the rolls meistr y roliau *eg*
master page prif dudalen *eb* prif dudalennau
▶ **master program** meistr-raglen *eb* meistr-raglenni
master slide meistr-sleid *eg* meistrsleidiau
▶ **master tape** meistr-dâp *eg* meistrdapiau
master view meistrolwg *eb*
master's degree gradd meistr *eb* graddau meistr
Mastersinger Meistersinger *eg* Meistersinger
mastery meistrolaeth *eb*
mastery learning dysgu meistrolaeth *be*
mastery test prawf meistrolaeth *eg* profion meistrolaeth
masthead teitl *eg*
mastic mastig *eg*
masticate cnoi *be*
mastoid process cnepyn mastoid *eg* cnepynnau mastoid
masturbate mastyrbio *be*
masturbation mastyrbiad *eg*
mat mat *eg* matiau
match *v.intrans* cydweddu *be*
match (=game) *n* gêm *eb* gemau
match boards byrddau cydwedd *ell*
match play chwarae gornest *eg*
match point pwynt gornest *eg*
matchboarding estyll cydwedd *ell*
matchboarding panel panel estyll cydwedd *eg*
matched group design cynllun grwpiau tebyg *eg* cynlluniau grwpiau tebyg
matching cydweddu *be*
matching accessories cyfwisgoedd cydwedd *ell*
matching plane plaen cydweddu *eg* plaeniau cydweddu
matching sides ochrau cyfatebol *ell*
matching-to-sample cydweddu sampl *be*
matchstick coes matsen *eb* coesau matsys
mate cyplu *be*
material *adj* materol *ans*
material (=fabric, objects with physical presence) *n* defnydd *eg* defnyddiau
material (=information and other abstractions) *n* deunydd *eg* deunyddiau
material characteristics nodweddion defnyddiau *ell*
material object gwrthrych materol *eg* gwrthrychau materol
material weave gwehyddiad defnydd *eg*
materialism materoliaeth *eb*
materials and components defnyddiau a chydrannau
materials list rhestr ddefnyddiau *eb* rhestri defnyddiau
maternal mamol *ans*
maternal chromosome cromosom o du'r fam *eg* cromosomau o du'r fam
maternal deprivation theory damcaniaeth amddifadaeth mam *eb*
maternity mamolaeth *eb*
maternity allowance lwfans mamolaeth *eg*
maternity grant grant mamolaeth *eg* grantiau mamolaeth
maternity home cartref mamolaeth *eg* cartrefi mamolaeth
maternity hospital ysbyty mamolaeth *eg* ysbytai mamolaeth
maternity leave absenoldeb mamolaeth *eg*
mathematical mathemategol *ans*
mathematical argument dadl fathemategol *eb* dadleuon mathemategol
mathematical convention confensiwn mathemategol *eg* confensiynau mathemategol
mathematical explanation esboniad mathemategol *eg* esboniadau mathemategol
mathematical induction anwythiad mathemategol *eg*
mathematical language iaith fathemategol *eb*
mathematical similarity cyflunedd mathemategol *eg*
mathematical symbol symbol mathemategol *eg* symbolau mathemategol
mathematical techniques technegau mathemategol *ell*
mathematics mathemateg *eb*
matinée coat cot matinée *eb* cotiau matinée
mating instinct greddf baru *eb*
mating parts rhannau paru *ell*
matins boreol weddi *eb*
matriarchal matriarchaidd *ans*
matrilineal o linach y fam

matrimonial priodasol *ans*
matrimonial matter achos priodasol *eg* achosion priodasol
matrimony priodas *eb*
matrix matrics *eg* matricsau
matrix board bwrdd matrics *eg* byrddau matrics
matrix operator gweithredydd matrics *eg* gweithredwyr matrics
matrix product lluoswm matrics *eg* lluosymiau matrics
matron metron *eb* metronau
matt mat *ans*
matt fibreglass ffibrwydr mat *eg*
matt finish gorffeniad mat *eg*
matt glaze gwydredd mat *eg*
matt surface arwyneb mat *eg*
matt varnish farnais mat *eg*
matted matiog *ans*
matter mater *eg*
matting punch pwnsh matio *eg* pynsiau matio
matting tool erfyn matio *eg* offer matio
mattress matres *eb* matresi
mattress cover gorchudd matres *eg* gorchuddion matres
maturation aeddfediad *eg*
maturational aeddfedol *ans*
mature *adj* aeddfed *ans*
mature *v* aeddfedu *be*
mature and or semi-retired people pobl aeddfed a/neu wedi lled-ymddeol *eb*
mature insect pryfyn llawn-dwf *eg*
maturity aeddfedrwydd *eg*
maul sgarmes *eb* sgarmesoedd
Maundy Thursday Dydd Iau Cablyd *eg*
mauve (enamelling colour) porffor gwelw *eg*
maxilla macsila *eg* macsilâu
maxillo-facial surgeon llawfeddyg y genau a'r wyneb *eg* llawfeddygon y genau a'r wyneb
maxim gwireb *eb*
maxima (the note) macsima *eg* nodau macsima
maximal mwyafsymaidd *ans*
maximise profit gwneud yr elw mwyaf posibl *be*
maximize mwyhau *be*
maximize (in mathematics) uchafsymio *be*
maximum (=highest point) *n* uchafbwynt *eg* uchafbwyntiau
maximum (=largest) *adj* mwyaf *ans*
maximum (of amount) *n* uchafswm *eg* uchafsymiau
maximum agitation cynnwrf hwyaf *eg*
maximum delegation dirprwyo eithaf *be*
maximum dimensions dimensiynau mwyaf *ell*
maximum exploitation ymelwad mwyaf *eg* ymelwadau mwyaf
maximum footnote height mwyafswm uchder troednodyn *eg*
maximum height uchder mwyaf *eg*
maximum multiplicity rule egwyddor lluosogrwydd macsimwm *eb*
maximum negative negatif mwyaf *eg*
maximum positive positif mwyaf *eg*
maximum pressure gwasgedd mwyaf *eg*
maximum price control rheoli uchafbris *be*
maximum speed (of car) cyflymder eithaf *eg*
maximum strength cryfder mwyaf *eg*
maximum temperature uchafbwynt tymheredd *eg*
maximum temperature rise codiad tymheredd uchaf *eg*
maximum thermometer thermomedr uchafbwynt *eg* thermomedrau uchafbwynt
maximum weight pwysau mwyaf *ell*
mayor maer *eg* meiri
Mayor of the Palace Maer y Llys *eg*
mayoress maeres *eb* maeresau
maypole bedwen Fai *eb* bedw Mai
mazarin blue (enamelling colour) glas masarin *eg*
maze drysfa *eb*
mazurka mazurka *eg* mazurkas
McCarthyism McCarthiaeth *eb*
meadow dôl *eb* dolydd
meadow soils dolbriddoedd *ell*
meals on wheels pryd ar glud *eg*
mean (in statistics) *adj* cymedrig *ans*
mean (in statistics) *n* cymedr *eg* cymedrau
mean bond energy egni bond cymedrig *eg*
mean deviation gwyriad cymedrig *eg*
mean diameter circle cylch diamedr cymedrig *eg*
mean difference gwahaniaeth cymedrig *eg*
mean error cyfeiliornad cymedrig *eg*
mean free path llwybr rhydd cymedrig *eg*
Mean Information Field (MIF) Maes Gwybodaeth Gymedrig *eg*
mean length of utterance (MLU) hyd cymedrig ymadrodd *eg*
mean proportional cymedr cyfrannol *eg*
mean relative atomic mass màs atomig cymharol cymedrig *eg*
mean score sgôr gymedrig *eb*
mean sea level lefel môr cymedrig *eb*
mean square sgwâr cymedrig *eg*
mean temperature tymheredd cymedrig *eg*
mean time amser cymedrig *eg*
mean tone temperament ardymer trydydd cyfartal *eg*
mean value gwerth cymedrig *eg* gwerthoedd cymedrig
mean weight pwysau cymedrig *ell*
mean wind speed cyflymdra cyfartalog y gwynt *eg*
meander *n* ystum afon *eg* ystumiau afon
meander *v* dolennu *be*
meander belt llain ystumiau *eb* lleiniau ystumiau
meander scar craith ystum *eb* creithiau ystumiau
meaning ystyr *eg* ystyron
meaningless diystyr *ans*
means modd *eg* moddion

means of communication dull o gyfathrebu *eg* dulliau o gyfathrebu
means of improvement ffordd o wella *eb* ffyrdd o wella
means of payment modd talu *eg*
means of production modd cynhyrchu *eg*
means of propulsion dull symud *eg* dulliau symud
means test prawf modd *eg* profion modd
means testing profi modd *be*
measles brech goch *eb*
measurable mesuradwy *ans*
measure *n* mesur *eg* mesurau
measure *v* mesur *be*
measure (=bar) bar *eg* barrau
measure distances mesur pellteroedd *be*
measure of central tendency mesur canolduedd *be*
measure of spread mesur o wasgariad *eg*
measure of turn mesur troi *eg*
measure of variability mesur amrywiant *be*
measure unit display dangosydd uned mesur *eg* dangosyddion uned mesur
measurement mesuriad *eg* mesuriadau
measurement unit uned mesur *eb* unedau mesur
measurements of energy mesuriadau egni *ell*
measuring and marking out mesur a marcio *be*
measuring cylinder silindr mesur *eg* silindrau mesur
measuring device dyfais fesur *eb* dyfeisiau mesur
measuring instruments offer mesur *ell*
measuring methods dulliau mesur *ell*
measuring tape tâp mesur *eg* tapiau mesur
meat cig *eg* cigoedd
mechanical mecanyddol *ans*
mechanical advantage mantais fecanyddol *eb* manteision mecanyddol
mechanical agitation cynnwrf mecanyddol *eg*
mechanical arithmetic rhifyddeg fecanyddol *eb*
mechanical concept cysyniad mecanyddol *eg*
mechanical cutting torri mecanyddol *be*
mechanical drawing lluniadu mecanyddol *be*
mechanical exercise ymarfer mecanyddol *eg* ymarferion mecanyddol
mechanical form ffurf beiriannol *eb* ffurfiau peiriannol
mechanical principle egwyddor fecanyddol *eb* egwyddorion mecanyddol
mechanical structure ffurfiad mecanyddol *eg* ffurfiadau mecanyddol
mechanics mecaneg *eb*
mechanism mecanwaith *eg* mecanweithiau
mechanism of breathing mecanwaith anadlu *eg*
mechanization mecaneiddiad *eg*
mechanize mecaneiddio *be*
mechanoreceptor mecanodderbynnydd *eg* mecanodderbynyddion
meconium meconiwm *eg*
medal medal *eb* medalau
media cyfryngau *ell*
media companies cwmnïau'r cyfryngau *ell*
media concepts cysyniadau'r cyfryngau *ell*
media imperialism imperialaeth gyfryngol *eb*
media industries diwydiannau'r cyfryngau *ell*
media language iaith y cyfryngau *eb*
media producer cynhyrchydd cyfryngau *eg* cynhyrchwyr cyfryngau
media production cynnyrch cyfryngol *eg*
media saturation gorlwytho cyfryngol *be*
media text testun cyfryngol *eg*
medial medial *ans*
medial fin asgell ganol *eb* esgyll canol
medial moraine marian canol *eg* marianau canol
median canolrifau *eg*
median (in anatomy) canolwedd *eb* canolweddau
median (in geometry) llin ganol *eb* lliniau canol
median (in statistics) canolrif *eg* canolrifau
median fin asgell ganol *eb* esgyll canol
mediant meidon *eb* meidonau
mediastinum mediastinwm *eg*
mediate (ideas etc) cyfryngu *be*
mediation (in disputes) cyflafareddu *be*
mediation (with intermediate agency, also in plainsong) cyfryngiad *eg*
mediator cyfryngwr *eg* cyfryngwyr
medical meddygol *ans*
medical assessment asesiad meddygol *eg* asesiadau meddygol
medical audit archwiliad meddygol *eg* archwiliadau meddygol
medical certificate tystysgrif feddygol *eb* tystysgrifau meddygol
medical condition cyflwr meddygol *eg* cyflyrau meddygol
medical model model meddygol *eg* modelau meddygol
medical model of disability model meddygol o anabledd *eg*
Medical Officer of Health Prif Swyddog Iechyd *eg*
medical photography ffotograffiaeth feddygol *eb*
medical physics ffiseg feddygol *eb*
medical school ysgol feddygol *eb* ysgolion meddygol
medication meddyginiaeth *eb* meddyginiaethau
medicinal leech gelen feddyginiaethol *eb*
medicine (=drug or preparation) moddion *eg*
medicine (science of) meddygaeth *eb*
medieval canoloesol *ans*
meditation myfyrdod *eg* myfyrdodau
Mediterranean Mediteranaidd *ans*
Mediterranean scrub prysgwydd rhanbarth Môr y Canoldir *ell*
Mediterranean woodland coetir Môr y Canoldir *eg*
medium *adj* canolig *ans*
medium *n* cyfrwng *eg* cyfryngau
medium agitation cynnwrf cymedrol *eg*
medium carbon carbon canolig *eg*
medium carbon steel dur carbon canolig *eg*
medium grain graen canol *eg*
medium grit grit canolig *eg*

medium knurl nwrl canolig *eg* nyrliau canolig
medium of education cyfrwng addysg *eg*
medium oilstone carreg hogi gradd ganol *eb* cerrig hogi gradd ganol
medium pace bowling bowlio canolig *be*
medium scale integration (MSI) cyfannu graddfa ganolig *be*
medium size scissors siswrn canolig *eg* sisyrnau canolig
medley relay race ras gyfnewid dulliau cymysg *eb* rasys cyfnewid dulliau cymysg
medley swimming nofio dulliau cymysg *be*
medulla medwla *eg*
medulla oblongata medwla oblongata *eg*
medullary medwlaidd *ans*
medullary ray rheidden greiddiol *eb* rheiddennau creiddiol
medullated nerve fibre edefyn nerf myelinedig *eg*
meet cyfarfod *be*
meeting cyfarfod *eg* cyfarfodydd
meeting rail rheilen gwrdd *eb* rheiliau cwrdd
meeting stile cledren gwrdd *eb* cledrau cwrdd
megabyte (Mb) megabeit *eg* megabeitiau
megakaryocyte megacaryocyt *eg* megacaryocytau
megalith megalith *eg* megalithiau
megalopolis megalopolis *eg* megalopolisiau
meganucleus megacnewyllyn *eg*
megaspore megasbor *eg* megasborau
megatherm megatherm *eg* megathermau
megavolt (MV) megafolt *eg* megafoltiau
Megillah Megillah *eg* Megillot
megohm megohm *eg* megohmau
meiosis meiosis *eg*
meiotic meiotig *ans*
melamine melamin *eg*
melamine base sylfaen melamin *eb*
melamine formaldehyde melamin fformaldehyd *eg*
melancholy lleddf *ans*
Melanesian Melanesaidd *ans*
Melanesian art celfyddyd Felanesaidd *eb*
melanin melanin *eg*
melanocyte melanocyt *eg* melanocytau
melanophore melanoffor *eg* melanofforau
melisma melisma *eg* melismata
melismatic melismataidd *ans*
melodic (form) melodig *ans*
melodic (in contrast to harmonic) alawol *ans*
melodic (quality) melodaidd *ans*
melodic chromatic scale graddfa gromatig felodig *eb*
melodic interval cyfwng melodaidd *eg* cyfyngau melodaidd
melodic line llinell felodig *eb* llinellau melodig
melodic pattern patrwm melodig *eg* patrymau melodig
melodic sequence dilyniant alawol *eg* dilyniannau alawol
melodic shape siâp melodig *eg* siapiau melodig
melodrama melodrama *eb* melodramâu
melody alaw *eb* alawon
melody (=sweet music, tunefulness) melodi *eb* melodïau
melody by condensation alaw wedi'i chywasgu *eb* alawon wedi'u cywasgu
melt *v. intrans* ymdoddi *be*
melt *v. transt* toddi *be*
melt water dŵr tawdd *eg* dyfroedd tawdd
melting method (in cooking) dull toddi *eg*
melting point ymdoddbwynt *eg*
melting pot (figurative use) pair *eg* peiriau
member aelod *eg* aelodau
Member of Parliament (MP) aelod seneddol *eg* aelodau seneddol
member of the team aelod o'r tîm *eg*
membership aelodaeth *eb*
membrane pilen *eb* pilenni
membraneous pilennog *ans*
memo memo *eg* memos
memo file ffeil memo *eb* ffeiliau memo
memoirs (=autobiography) hunangofiant *eg* hunangofiannau
memorandum memorandwm *eg* memoranda
memorandum of association memorandwm sefydlu *eg* memoranda sefydlu
memorize dysgu ar y cof *be*
memory cof *eg* cofion
► **memory address register** cofrestr cofgyfeiriad *eb* cofrestri cofgyfeiriad
memory cache storfa cof *eb* storfeydd cof
memory chip sglodyn cof *eg* sglodion cof
memory circle cofgylchred *eb* cofgylchredau
► **memory data register** cofrestr cofddata *eb* cofrestri cofddata
memory expansion ehangiad cof *eg* ehangiadau cof
memory map map y cof *eg*
► **memory overlay** cofdroshaen *eb* cofdroshaenau
memory span cyfnod cofio *eg*
mend trwsio *be*
mendelevium (Md) mendelefiwm *eg*
Mendelian Mendelaidd *ans*
Mendelian inheritance etifeddiad Mendelaidd *eg*
mendicant *adj* cardotaidd *ans*
mendicant *n* cardotyn *eg* cardotwyr
mendicant friar brawd cardod *eg* brodyr cardod
mending wool gwlân cyweirio *eg*
► **meninges** pilenni'r ymennydd *ell*
meningitis llid yr ymennydd *eg*
meniscus menisgws *eg* menisgi
menopause diwedd y mislif *eg*
Menshevik *adj* Mensiefigaidd *ans*
Menshevik *n* Mensiefig *eg* Mensiefigiaid
menstrual cycle cylchred fislifol *eb*
menstrual synchrony mislif cydamseredig *eg*
menstruation mislif *eg*
mensuration mesureg *eb*
mental meddyliol *ans*

mental ability gallu meddyliol *eg*
mental activity gweithgaredd meddyliol *eg*
mental age oed meddyliol *eg*
mental arithmetic rhifyddeg pen *eb*
mental arithmetic test prawf rhifyddeg pen *eg* profion rhifyddeg pen
mental capacity gallu meddyliol *eg*
mental deficiency nam meddyliol *eg*
mental development datblygiad meddyliol *eg*
mental disability anabledd meddyliol *eg*
mental disorder anhwylder meddwl *eg* anhwylderau meddwl
mental disturbance aflonyddwch meddwl *eg*
mental handicap anfantais meddwl *eb*
mental health iechyd meddwl *eg*
Mental Health Act Deddf Iechyd Meddwl *eb*
mental health nurse nyrs iechyd meddwl *eb* nyrsys iechyd meddwl
mental health nursing nyrsio iechyd meddwl *be*
mental illness afiechyd meddwl *eg* afiechydon meddwl
mental lexicon lecsicon y meddwl *eg*
mental model model meddyliol *eg*
mental retardation arafwch meddwl *eg*
mental space gofod meddyliol *eg*
mentally handicapped child plentyn â nam meddyliol *eg* plant â nam meddyliol
mentor mentor *eg* mentoriaid
mentoring mentora *be*
mentorship mentoriaeth *eb* mentoriaethau
menu (of choices) dewislen *eb* dewislenni
menu (of food) bwydlen *eb* bwydlenni
menu bar bar dewislenni *eg* barrau dewislenni
menu box blwch dewislen *eg* blychau dewislen
menu card cerdyn bwydlen *eg* cardiau bwydlen
menu-driven system system ddewisyriad *eb* systemau dewisyriad
mercantile quality safon gwerthu *eb*
mercantilism mercantiliaeth *eb*
mercenary hurfilwr *eg* hurfilwyr
mercerization sgleiniad *eg*
mercerized (finish) sglein *ans*
mercerized cord cortyn sglein *eg* cortynnau sglein
mercerized cotton cotwm sglein *eg*
merchandise (of goods) nwyddau *ell*
merchant masnachwr *eg* masnachwyr
Merchant Adventurers Mentrwyr Masnachol *ell*
merchant bank banc masnachol *eg* banciau masnachol
merchant guild gild y masnachwyr *eg* gildiau'r masnachwyr
merchant shipping llongau masnach *ell*
Merchant Shipping Act Deddf Llongau Masnach *eb*
merchet amobr *eg* amobrau
Merciless Parliament Senedd Ddidostur *eb*
mercuric mercwrig *ans*
mercurous chloride clorid mercwrus *eg*
Mercury Mercher *eg*
mercury (Hg) mercwri *eg*
mercury(II) ion ïon mercwri(II) *eg* ïonau mercwri(II)
mere exposure effect effaith dangos yn unig *eb*
merge (files etc) cyfuno *be*
merge (in economics) cydsoddi *be*
merge cells cyfuno celloedd *be*
merge documents cyfuno dogfennau *be*
merge sort *n* trefniad cyfunol *eg* trefniadau cyfunol
merge sort *v* trefnu cyfunol *be*
merge tables cyfuno tablau *be*
merged cyfun *ans*
merge-filing cyfun-ffeilio *be*
merger (in economics) cydsoddiad *eg* cydsoddiadau
meridian meridian *eg* meridianau
meristem meristem *eb* meristemau
meristematic meristematig *ans*
merit teilyngdod *eg*
merit goods nwyddau rhinweddol *ell*
merit pay rise cynnydd cyflog teilyngdod *eg*
meritocracy meritocratiaeth *eb*
Merlin Myrddin *eg*
meromorphic meromorffig *ans*
Merovingian Merofingaidd *ans*
Merseyside Glannau Merswy *ell*
Merthyr rising terfysg Merthyr *eg*
mesa mesa *eg* mesâu
mesenteric mesenterig *ans*
mesenteric artery rhydweli fesenterig *eb*
mesenteric vein gwythïen fesenterig *eb* gwythiennau mesenterig
mesentery mesenteri *eg*
mesh (cogs) *n* masg *eg* masgiau
mesh (cogs) *v* masgio *be*
mesh (of wire etc) rhwyll *eb* rhwyllau
mesh refinement manylu'r rhwydwaith *be*
mesmerism mesmeriaeth *eb*
mesoderm mesoderm *eg* mesodermau
mesodermic mesodermig *ans*
meso-2,3-dihydroxybutanedioic acid asid meso-2,3-deuhydrocsibwtandeuöig *eg*
mesogloea mesogloea *eg*
mesokurtic mesocwrtig *ans*
mesolithic mesolithig *ans*
meson meson *eg* mesonau
mesophyll mesoffyl *eg* mesoffylau
mesophyllous mesoffylaidd *ans*
mesophyte mesoffyt *eg* mesoffytau
mesoscale graddfa ganol *eb*
mesosternum mesosternwm *eg* mesosterna
mesostome mesostom *eg* mesostomau
mesothorax mesothoracs *eg*
message neges *eb* negeseuon
message board negesfwrdd *eg* negesfyrddau
message ID dynodiad neges *eg* dynodiadau neges
message switching switsio neges *be*
message text testun neges *eg*
message thread edefyn neges *eg* edafedd neges

message window ffenestr neges *eb* ffenestri negeseuon
messenger mRNA mRNA negeseuol *eg*
messenger RNA RNA negeseuol *eg*
Messiah Meseia *eg*
mestizo mestiso *eg* mestisos
meta-analysis metaddadansoddi *be*
metabolic metabolaidd *ans*
metabolic breakdown ymddatod metabolaidd *be*
metabolism metabolaeth *eb*
metabolite metabolyn *eg* metabolynnau
metacarpal metacarpol *ans*
metacarpus metacarpws *eg*
metacentre metabwynt *eg* metabwyntiau
metacentric metasentrig *ans*
metacognition metawybyddiaeth *eb*
meta-ethics metafoeseg *eb*
metafile metaffeil *eb* metaffeiliau
metal metel *eg* metelau
metal beater curwr metel *eg* curwyr metel
metal bending plygu metel *be*
metal casting castio metel *be*
metal caul gwasgblat metel *eg* gwasgblatiau metel
metal cladding gwisgo metel *be*
metal cutting torri metel *be*
metal fabrication ffabrigo metel *be*
metal fastener ffasnydd metel *eg* ffasnyddion metel
metal filler llenwad metel *eg* llenwadau metel
metal foil ffoil metel *eg*
metal forging gofannu metel *be*
metal jackplane plaen jac metel *eg* plaeniau jac metel
metal oxide ocsid metel *eg* ocsidau metelau
metal plane plaen metel *eg* plaeniau metel
metal plug plwg metel *eg* plygiau metel
metal pouring arllwys metel *be*
metal sawing llifio metel *be*
metal shearing torri metel *be*
metal spokeshave rhasgl fetel *eb* rhasglau metel
metalinguistic metaieithyddol *ans*
metalinguistics metaieithyddiaeth *eb*
metallic metelig *ans*
metallic cloth defnydd metelig *eg*
metallic element elfen fetelig *eb* elfennau metelig
metallic thread edau fetelig *eb* edafedd metelig
metallicized material defnydd wedi'i feteleiddio *eg*
metalliferous metelifferaidd *ans*
metalling (road) metlin *eg*
metallizing meteleiddio *be*
metalloid meteloid *ans*
metallurgical metelegol *ans*
metallurgical industry diwydiant metelegol *eg* diwydiannau metelegol
metallurgy meteleg *eb*
metalwork gwaith metel *eg*
metamemory meta-gof *eb*
metamerism metameraeth *eb*
metamorphic metamorffig *ans*
metamorphism metamorffeg *eb*
metamorphosed metamorffedig *ans*
metamorphosis metamorffosis *eg*
metamorphy metamorffedd *eb*
metaphase metaffas *eg* metaffasau
metaphor trosiad *eg* trosiadau
metaphysical metaffisegol *ans*
metapleural folds plygion metaplewraidd *ell*
Metasoa Metasoa *ell*
metastable metasefydlog *ans*
metasternum metasternwm *eg*
metatarsal metatarsol *ans*
metatarsus metatarsws *eg*
metathesis metathesis *eg*
metathorax metathoracs *eg*
metaxylem metasylem *eb*
meteor meteor *eg* meteorau
meteoric meteorig *ans*
meteorite meteoryn *eg* meteorynnau
meteorologic meteorolegol *ans*
meteorology meteoroleg *eb*
meter (for measuring) mesurydd *eg* mesuryddion
methanal methanal *eg*
methanamide methanamid *eg*
methane methan *eg*
methanoic acid asid methanöig *eg*
methanol methanol *eg*
methionine methionin *eg*
method dull *eg* dulliau
method of colour mixing dull cymysgu lliwiau *eg* dulliau cymysgu lliwiau
method of composition dull cyfansoddi *eg* dulliau cyfansoddi
method of loci dull loci *eg*
method of transport math o gludiant
Methodism Methodistiaeth *eb*
Methodist *adj* Methodistaidd *ans*
Methodist *n* Methodist *eg* Methodistiaid
methodology methodoleg *eb*
methoxybenzene methocsibensen *eg*
methoxyethane methocsiethan *eg*
methoxymethane methocsimethan *eg*
2-methoxy-2-methylpropane 2-methocsi-2-methylpropan *eg*
methyl 2-hydroxybenzenecarboxylate methyl 2-hydrocsibensencarbocsylad *eg*
methyl orange methyl oren *eg*
methylamine methylamin *eg*
methylammoniumchloride methylamoniwmclorid *eg*
methylate methylu *be*
methylated spirits gwirod methyl *eg*
methylbenzene methylbensen *eg*
2-methylbenzenecarboxylic acid asid 2-methylbensencarbocsylig *eg*
2-methylbenzenesulfonic acid asid 2-methylbensensylffonig *eg*

2-methylbuta-1,3-diene 2-methylbwta-1,3-deuen *eg*
2-methylbutenedioic acid asid 2-methylbwtendeuöig *eg*
methylbutyl methylbwtyl *eg*
3-methylbutyl- 3-methylbwtyl- *eg*
1-methyl-2-nitrobenzene 1-methyl-2-nitrobensen *eg*
4-methylpent-3-en-2-one 4-methylpent-3-en-2-on *eg*
2-methylphenol 2-methylffenol *eg*
2-methylphenylamine 2-methylffenylamin *eg*
2-methylpropane 2-methylpropan *eg*
2-methylpropanoic acid asid 2-methylpropanöig *eg*
2-methylpropan-1-ol 2-methylpropan-1-ol *eg*
2-methylpropan-2-ol 2-methylpropan-2-ol *eg*
2-methylpropan-2-yl 2-methylpropan-2-yl *eg*
2-methylpropene 2-methylpropen *eg*
2-methylpropenoic acid asid 2-methylpropenöig *eg*
2-methylpropyl 2-methylpropyl *eg*
2-methyl-1,3,5-trinitrobenzene 2-methyl-1,3,5-trinitrobensen *eg*
meticulous gofalus iawn *ans*
metonym trawsenw *eg*
metre (in verse, music) mesur *eg* mesurau
metre (of metric unit) metr *eg* metrau
metre stick pren metr *eg* prennau metr
metric metrig *ans*
metric measure mesur metrig *eg*
metric rule riwl fetrig *eb* riwliau metrig
metric scale graddfa fetrig *eb*
metric system system fetrig *eb*
metric thread edau fetrig *eb* edafedd metrig
metric unit uned fetrig *eb* unedau metrig
metrical mydryddol *ans*
metrical foot corfan *eg* corfannau
metrical psalms salmau cân *ell*
metronome metronom *eg* metronomau
Metropolitan Police Act Deddf Heddlu Metropolitan *eb*
mezzo-soprano mezzo-soprano *eb* lleisiau mezzo-soprano
mezzo-soprano clef cleff mezzo-soprano *eg* cleffiau mezzo-soprano
mezzotint mesotint *eg* mesotintiau
mica mica *eg*
mica flake fflaw mica *eg* fflawiau mica
micella micela *eg* micelau
micelle misel *eg*
micro micro *ans*
microbe microb *eg* microbau
microbial fermentation eplesiad microbaidd *eg*
microbiologist microbiolegydd *eg* microbiolegwyr
microbiology microbioleg *eb*
microburin microbwyntil *eg* microbwyntilau
microcard microgerdyn *eg* microgardiau
microchip microsglodyn *eg* microsglodion
microcircuit microgylched *eb* microgylchedau
microclimate microhinsawdd *eg*
microclimatology microhinsoddeg *eb*
microcode microgod *eg* microgodau
microcomputer microgyfrifiadur *eg* microgyfrifiaduron
microcosm microcosm *eg* microcosmau
micro-crystalline microgrisialog *ans*
micro-crystalline wax cwyr microgrisialog *eg*
Microelectronic Education Programme (MEP) Rhaglen Addysg Microelectroneg *eb*
microelectronics microelectroneg *eb*
microfarad microffarad *eg* microffaradau
microffibril microffibrolyn *eg*
microfiche microffish *eg* microffishau
microfilm microffilm *eb* microffilmiau
microhm microhm *eg* microhmau
microlith microlith *eg* microlithiau
micrometer micromedr *eg* micromedrau
micrometer parts rhannau micromedr *ell*
micrometer reading darlleniad micromedr *eg* darlleniadau micromedr
micrometre micrometr *eg* micrometrau
micron micron *eg* micronau
micronucleus microcnewyllyn *eg*
micronutrient microfaethyn *eg* microfaethion
micro-organism micro-organeb *eb* micro-organebau
microphone microffon *eg* microffonau
microprocessor microbrosesydd *eg* microbrosesyddion
microprocessor control rheolaeth microbrosesydd *eb*
microprogramming microraglennu *be*
micropyle micropyl *eg* micropylau
microscope microsgop *eg* microsgopau
microscopic microsgopig *ans*
microscopy microsgopeg *eb*
microsecond microeiliad *eg/b* microeiliadau
microsome microsom *eg* microsomau
microspore microsbor *eg*
microsporophyll microsboroffyl *eg*
microswitch microswitsh *eg* microswitshis
microtechnology microdechnoleg *eb*
Microtex llestri Microtex *ell*
microtherm microtherm *eg* microthermau
microtonal microtonawl *ans*
microtonality microtonyddiaeth *eg* microtonyddiaethau
microtone microtôn *eg* microtonau
microtubule microdiwbyn *eg* microdiwbynnau
microvillus microfilws *eg* microfili
microwave microdon *eb* microdonnau
microworld microfyd *eg* microfydoedd
micturate troethi *be*
micturition troethiad *eg*
micturition reflexes atgyrchion troethi *ell*
mid blue (enamelling colour) glas canol *eg*
mid brown (enamelling colour) brown canol *eg*
mid cadmium yellow melyn cadmiwm canol *eg*

mid chrome yellow melyn crôm canol *eg*
mid off canolwr agored *eg* canolwyr agored
mid on canolwr coes *eg* canolwyr coes
mid wicket canol wiced *eg*
midbrain ymennydd canol *eg*
middle canol *eg*
Middle Ages Oesoedd Canol *ell*
middle C C ganol *eb*
middle childhood plentyndod canol *eg*
middle class dosbarth canol *eg*
middle cut file ffeil orfras *eb* ffeiliau gorfras
middle distance pellter canol *eg*
middle distance runner rhedwr pellter canol *eg* rhedwyr pellter canol
middle ear clust ganol *eb*
Middle East Dwyrain Canol *eg*
middle lamella lamela ganol *eb*
middle oil olew canol *eg*
middle passage mordaith ganol *eb*
middle rail rheilen ganol *eb* rheiliau canol
middle register nodau canol *ell*
middle school ysgol ganol *eb* ysgolion canol
middle stump stwmp canol *eg*
middle tuit tuit canol *eg*
middle weight pwysau canol *ell*
middleman dyn canol *eg* dynion canol
middleman's knot cwlwm canolwr *eg*
mid-feather slip rhannu *eg* slipiau rhannu
midfield canol cae *eg*
midget state corwlad *eb* corwledydd
midland canolbarth *eg* canolbarthau
Midlands Canolbarth Lloegr *eg*
mid-latitudes lledredau canol *ell*
mid-line llinell ganol *eb*
mid-ordinate mesuryn canol *eg* mesurynnau canol
mid-ordinate rule dull y mesuryn canol *eg*
mid-point canolbwynt *eg* canolbwyntiau
Midrash Midrash *eg* Midrashim
midrib (of leaf) gwythïen ganol *eb* gwythiennau canol
midterm break gwyliau hanner tymor *eg*
midway-upwards hanner ffordd i fyny
mid-west gorllewin canol *eg*
midwife bydwraig *eb* bydwragedd
midwifery gwaith bydwraig *eg*
mig welding weldio mig *be*
migrant labour llafur mudol *eg*
migrate mudo *be*
migration mudiad *eg*
migratory mudol *ans*
mild (=gentle) mwyn *ans*
mild (=not serious) ysgafn *ans*
mild disability anabledd ysgafn *eg* anableddau ysgafn
mild hardwood pren lled galed *eg*
mild learning disability anabledd dysgu ysgafn *eg* anableddau dysgu ysgafn
mild steel dur meddal *eg*
mildew llwydni *eg*
mildew resistant (finish) gwrthlwydni *ans*
mile milltir *eb* milltiroedd
mile castle caer filltir *eb* caerau milltir
mile race ras filltir *eb* rasys milltir
milepost postyn milltir *eg*
milestone carreg filltir *eb* cerrig milltir
milestone ritual defod carreg filltir *eb* defodau cerrig milltir
militant milwriaethus *ans*
militarism militariaeth *eb*
militarist militarydd *eg* militarwyr
military milwrol *ans*
military architecture pensaernïaeth filwrol *eb*
military base canolfan filwrol *eb* canolfannau milwrol
military history hanes milwrol *eg*
military service gwasanaeth milwrol *eg*
militia milisia *eg*
milium miliwm *eg*
milk and dairy foods llaeth a bwydydd llaeth
Milk Marketing Board Bwrdd Marchnata Llaeth *eg*
milk products cynnyrch llaeth *eg* cynhyrchion llaeth
milk tooth dant sugno *eg* dannedd sugno
milky (of lime water) llaethog *ans*
milky suspension daliant llaethog *eg*
Milky Way Llwybr Llaethog *eg*
mill *n* melin *eb* melinau
mill *v* melino *be*
mill race ffrwd melin *eb* ffrydiau melinau
millboard bwrdd melin *eg* byrddau melin
millenarianism milflwyddiaeth *eb*
Millenary Petition Deiseb y Fil *eb*
millenium mileniwm *eg*
miller melinydd *eg* melinwyr
millet milet *eg*
millibar milibar *eg* milibarrau
millilitre mililitr *eg* mililitrau
millimetre (mm) milimetr *eg* milimetrau
milling cutter melinwr *eg* melinwyr
milling machine peiriant melino *eg* peiriannau melino
million miliwn *eb* miliynau
million city dinas filiwn *eb* dinasoedd miliwn
Millon's Reagent Adweithydd Millon *eg*
millstone grit grut melinfaen *eg*
mimetic dynwaredol *ans*
mimicry (in biology) dynwarededd *eg*
mind meddwl, y meddwl *eg*
mind-body relationship perthynas meddwl-corff *eb*
mine *v* mwyngloddio *be*
mine (explosive) *n* ffrwydryn *eg* ffrwydrynnau
minelayer llong osod ffrwydrynnau *eb* llongau gosod ffrwydrynnau
miner (of any mineral) mwynwr *eg* mwynwyr
miner (of coal) glöwr *eg* glowyr
mineral mwyn *eg* mwynau
mineral oil olew mwynol *eg* olewau mwynol

mineral origin tarddiad mwynol *eg* tarddiadau mwynol
mineral railway rheilffordd fwynau *eb* rheilffyrdd mwynau
mineral resources adnoddau mwynol *ell*
mineral salts halwynau mwynol *ell*
mineral water dŵr mwynol *eg* dyfroedd mwynol
mineralization mwyneiddiad *eg*
mineralogy mwynoleg *eb*
miner's cramp cramp y mwynwr *eg*
Mines Act Deddf Mwyngloddiau *eb*
minesweeper llong glirio ffrwydrynnau *eb* llongau clirio ffrwydrynnau
mini mini *ans*
miniature (for film work) model *eg* modelau
miniature camera camera mini *eg*
miniature painting (of painted picture) mân-ddarlun *eg* mân-ddarluniau
miniature painting (of process or art) mân-ddarlunio *be*
miniature score sgôr boced *eb* sgorau poced
minicomputer minigyfrifiadur *eg* minigyfrifiaduron
mini-enterprise mini-menter *eb* mini-mentrau
mini-floppy disk disg hyblyg bychan *eg* disgiau hyblyg bychain
minimal minimol *ans*
minimalism minimaliaeth *eb*
minimalist *adj* minimalaidd *ans*
minimalist *n* minimalydd *eg* minimalwyr
minimize lleihau *be*
minimize (=lessen) lleihau *be*
minimize (in mathematics) lleiafsymio *be*
minimize all lleihau popeth *be*
minimize all windows lleihau pob ffenestr *be*
minimize window lleihau ffenestr *be*
minimum (=lowest point) isafbwynt *eg* isafbwyntiau
▸ **minimum** (=lowest sum) isafswm *eg* isafsymiau
minimum (=smallest) lleiaf *ans*
minimum agitation cynnwrf byrraf *eg*
minimum care (finish) lledofal *ans*
minimum change newid lleiaf *eg*
minimum installation gosodiad lleiaf *eg*
minimum iron (finish) smwddio ysgafn *be*
minimum length hyd lleiaf *eg*
minimum size maint lleiaf *eg*
minimum spacing bylchiad lleiaf *eg* bylchiadau lleiaf
minimum temperature isafbwynt tymheredd *eg*
minimum thermometer thermomedr isafbwynt *eg* thermomedrau isafbwynt
▸ **minimum wage** isafswm cyflog *eg*
mining mwyngloddio *be*
mining industry diwydiant mwyngloddio *eg*
mini-project mini-project *eg* mini-projectau
minister gweinidog *eg* gweinidogion
Minister for Education Gweinidog Addysg *eg*
minister of public enlightenment and propaganda gweinidog goleuo'r cyhoedd a phropaganda *eg* gweinidogion goleuo'r cyhoedd a phropaganda
Minister of State Gweinidog Gwladol *eg*
Minister of State for Wales Gweinidog Gwladol dros Gymru *eg*
minister's account cyfrif swyddwr *eg* cyfrifon swyddwr
ministry (=government department) gweinyddiaeth *eb* gweinyddiaethau
ministry (of chapel) gweinidogaeth *eb*
ministry (of church) offeiriadaeth *eb*
Ministry of Defence range maes tanio'r Weinyddiaeth Amddiffyn *eg* meysydd tanio'r Weinyddiaeth Amddiffyn
Minnesota multiphasic personality inventory (MMPI) prawfrestr personoliaeth amlwedd Minnesota *eb*
Minoan Minoaidd *ans*
Minoan art celfyddyd Finoaidd *eb*
▸ **minor** *n* (of child) plentyn dan oed *eg* plant dan oed
minor (of musical key) *adj* lleiaf *ans*
minor (of musical mood and feeling) *adj* lleddf *ans*
minor axis echelin leiaf *eb* echelinau lleiaf
minor chord cord lleiaf *eg* cordiau lleiaf
minor common chord cord cyffredin lleiaf *eg* cordiau cyffredin lleiaf
minor diameter diamedr lleiaf *eg* diamedrau lleiaf
minor fold plyg bychan *eg* plygion bychan
minor illnesses mân anhwylderau *ell*
minor interval cyfwng lleiaf *eg* cyfyngau lleiaf
minor key (in music in general) cywair lleiaf *eg*
minor key (in penillion singing) lleddf gywair *eg*
minor order urdd leiaf *eb*
minor road untarred and minor road in towns isffordd heb dar ac isffordd mewn trefi
minor scale graddfa leiaf *eb* graddfeydd lleiaf
minority lleiafrif *eg* lleiafrifoedd
minority audience cynulleidfa leiafrifol *eb* cynulleidfaoedd lleiafrifol
minority group grŵp lleiafrifol *eg* grwpiau lleiafrifol
minority language iaith leiafrifol *eb* ieithoedd lleiafrifol
minority subject pwnc lleiafrifol *eg* pynciau lleiafrifol
minstrel clerwr *eg* clerwyr
minstrels' gallery oriel y clerwyr *eb* orielau clerwyr
minstrelsy clerwriaeth *eb*
mint *adj* bath *ans*
mint *n* bathdy *eg*
mint *v* bathu *be*
minuend minwend *eg* minwendau
minuet miniwét *eg* minwetau
minus minws *eg* minysau
minus box blwch minws *eg* blychau minws
minus sign arwydd minws *eg* arwyddion minws
minuscule miniscwl *ans*
minuscule (lower case) llythrennau bach *ell*
minute (=record) *n* cofnod *eg* cofnodion

minute (=very small) *adj* bach iawn *ans*
minute (of time) *n* munud *eg/b* munudau
minute book llyfr cofnodion *eg* llyfrau cofnodion
minutes template templed cofnodion *eg* templedi cofnodion
minutes type math o gofnodion *eg*
minute-timer cloc munudau *eg* clociau munudau
miracle gwyrth *eb* gwyrthiau
miracle play drama firagl *eb* dramâu miragl
mirage rhithlun *eg* rhithluniau
mire cramp cramp meir *eg* crampiau meir
mirror drych *eg* drychau
mirror *v* drychweddu *be*
mirror archive drych-archif *eg* drych-archifau
mirror canon drychganon *eb/g* drychganonau
mirror finish gorffeniad drych *eg*
mirror fugue ffiwg ddrych *eb* ffiwgiau drych
mirror image drychddelwedd *eb* drychddelweddau
mirror line llinell ddrych *eb* llinellau drych
mirror plate plât drych *eg* platiau drych
mirror writing drych-ysgrifennu *be*
mirrorsite drych-safle *eg* drych-safleoedd
misbehave camymddwyn *be*
miscarriage erthyliad naturiol *eg* erthyliadau naturiol
miscarry erthylu'n naturiol *be*
miscegenation croeshilio *be*
miscellaneous options dewisiadau amrywiol *ell*
miscellaneous symbols symbolau amrywiol *ell*
mischief rule rheol drygioni *eb*
miscibility cymysgadwyaeth *eb*
miscible cymysgadwy *ans*
miscue analysis dadansoddi'r camddarllen *be*
misdemeanour camymddygiad *eg* camymddygiadau
mise meis *eb* meisiau
misericord misericord *eg* misericordiau
misfit river afon afrwydd *eb* afonydd afrwydd
Mishnah Mishnah *eg*
mislay camosod *be*
mispare cambaru *be*
misrule camreoli *be*
missal llyfr offeren *eg* llyfrau offeren
misshapen di-lun *ans*
missile taflegryn *eg* taflegrau
missile tip treiddiwr taflegryn *eg*
missing component cydran goll *eb* cydrannau coll
missing element elfen goll *eb* elfennau coll
missing tooth dant ar goll *eg*
mission statement datganiad o genhadaeth *eg* datganiadau o genhadaeth
missionary *adj* cenhadol *ans*
missionary *n* cenhadwr *eg* cenhadon
mist *n* niwlen *eb* niwlenni
mist *v* niwlo *be*
mistake camgymeriad *eg*
mistress meistres *eb* meistresi
misuse *n* camddefnydd *eg*
misuse *v* camddefnyddio *be*
misuse of alcohol camddefnyddio alcohol *be*
Misuse of Drugs Act Deddf Camddefnydd Cyffuriau *eb*
mite (arachnid) gwiddonyn *eg* gwiddon
Mithraism Mithraeth *eb*
mitochondrion mitocondrion *eg* mitocondria
mitosis mitosis *eg*
mitotic mitotig *ans*
mitotic index indecs mitotig *eg* indecsau mitotig
mitral valve falf feitrol *eb* falfiau meitrol
mitre *n* meitr *eg* meitrau
mitre *v* meitro *be*
mitre block bloc meitr *eg* blociau meitr
mitre box blwch meitro *eg* blychau meitro
mitre bridle bagl meitr *eb* baglau meitr
mitre cramp cramp meitr *eg* crampiau meitr
mitre dovetail meitr cynffonnog *eg* meitrau cynffonnog
mitre gauge medrydd meitr *eg* medryddion meitr
mitre joint uniad meitr *eg* uniadau meitr
mitre shooting board bwrdd plaenio meitr *eg* byrddau plaenio meitr
mitre square sgwâr meitro *eg* sgwariau meitro
mitre template patrymlun meitr *eg* patrymluniau meitr
mitred meitrog *ans*
mitred corner cornel feitrog *eb* corneli meitrog
mitred dovetail bridle joint uniad bagl cynffonnog meitrog *eg* uniadau bagl cynffonnog meitrog
mitred dovetail joint uniad cynffonnog meitrog *eg* uniadau cynffonnog meitrog
mitred halving joint uniad haneru meitrog *eg* uniadau haneru meitrog
mitred joint uniad meitrog *eg* uniadau meitrog
mitred tenon tyno meitrog *eg* tynoau meitrog
mitten mit *eb* mits
mitzvah mitzvah *eg* mitzvot
mix cymysgu *be*
mix and match cyfun-cydwedd *ans*
mixed cymysg *ans*
mixed ability gallu cymysg *eg*
mixed ability class dosbarth gallu cymysg *eg* dosbarthiadau gallu cymysg
mixed cereal bread bara amyd *eg*
mixed design cynllun cymysg *eg* cynlluniau cymysg
mixed dried fruits ffrwythau sych cymysg *eg*
mixed economy economi cymysg *eg*
mixed feeding bwydo cymysg *be*
mixed key (in old Welsh music) bragod gywair *eb*
mixed method dull cymysg *eg* dulliau cymysg
mixed number rhif cymysg *eg* rhifau cymysg
mixed school ysgol gymysg *eb* ysgolion cymysg
mixed sex rhyw cymysg *ans*
mixer (in acoustics) cymysgwr sain *eg* cymysgwyr sain
mixing medium cyfrwng cymysgu *eg* cyfryngau cymysgu
mixing palette palet cymysgu *eg* paletau cymysgu

mixing tray hambwrdd cymysgu *eg* hambyrddau cymysgu
mixture cymysgedd *eg* cymysgeddau
mixture stop stop cymysg *eg* stopiau cymysg
mizzen mast hwylbren canol *eg* hwylbrennau canol
mnemonic cofrif *eg* cofrifau
mnemonic operation code cod gweithredu cofrif *eg* codau gweithredu cofrif
mnemonic system system mnemonig *eb*
moat ffos *eb* ffosydd
mobile *adj* symudol *ans*
mobile *n* symudyn *eg* symudion
mobile classroom ystafell ddosbarth symudol *eb* ystafelloedd dosbarth symudol
mobile clinic clinig teithiol *eg* clinigau teithiol
mobile home cartref symudol *eg* cartrefi symudol
mobile learning dysgu symudol *be*
mobile library llyfrgell deithiol *eb* llyfrgelloedd teithiol
mobile phone ffôn symudol *eg* ffonau symudol
mobile phone card cerdyn ffôn symudol *eg* cardiau ffôn symudol
mobile shop siop deithiol *eb* siopau teithiol
mobilistic mobilistig *ans*
mobility symudedd *eg*
mobility and flexibility symudedd a hyblygrwydd
mobilize (of army) ymfyddino *be*
mobilizing movement symudiad llacio *eg* symudiadau llacio
mock examination ffug arholiad *eg* ffug arholiadau
mock-up brasfodel *eg* brasfodelau
modal moddol *ans*
modal class dosbarth modd *eg*
modality moddolrwydd *eg*
mode modd *eg* moddau
mode of address dull cyfarch *eg*
mode of durations and intensities (Messiaen) modd gwerth hyd a dwyster *eg*
model *v* modelu *be*
model (of female person) *n* model *eb* modelau
model (of male person, object) *n* model *eg* modelau
model of nursing model nyrsio *eg* modelau nyrsio
model town tref fodel *eb* trefi model
modelling modelu *be*
modelling assumption tybiaeth fodelu *eb*
modelling board bwrdd modelu *eg* byrddau modelu
modelling cement sment modelu *eg*
modelling clay clai modelu *eg*
modelling compound cyfansoddyn modelu *eg* cyfansoddion modelu
modelling material defnydd modelu *eg* defnyddiau modelu
modelling stand stand modelu *eg* standiau modelu
modelling tools offer modelu *ell*
modelling wax cwyr modelu *eg*
modelling wheel olwyn fodelu *eb* olwynion modelu
modem modem *eg* modemau
moderate *v* safoni *be*
moderate (=avoiding extremes) *adj* cymedrol *ans*
moderate (=middling) *adj* canolig *ans*
moderate breeze awel gymedrol *eb* awelon cymedrol
moderate learning difficulty anhawster dysgu canolig *eg* anawsterau dysgu canolig
moderate rainfall glawiad cymedrol *eg*
moderated mailing list rhestr drafod gyda chymedrolwr *eb* rhestri trafod gyda chymedrolwr
moderation (of examinations) safoni *be*
moderation committee pwyllgor safoni *eg* pwyllgorau safoni
moderation meeting cyfarfod safoni *eg* cyfarfodydd safoni
moderator (in physics) cymedrolydd *eg* cymedrolyddion
moderator (of person) cymedrolwr *eg* cymedrolwyr
modern modern *ans*
modern construction adeiladwaith cyfoes *eg*
modern educational dance dawnsio addysgol modern *be*
modern foreign language iaith dramor fodern *eb* ieithoedd tramor modern
modern history hanes modern *eg*
modern language iaith fodern *eb* ieithoedd modern
modern song cân fodern *eb* caneuon modern
modernize moderneiddio *be*
modification addasiad *eg* addasiadau
modified (with feminine nouns) wedi'i haddasu *ans* wedi'u haddasu
modified (with masculine nouns) wedi'i addasu *ans* wedi'u haddasu
modified version fersiwn a addaswyd *eg* fersiynau a addaswyd
modify addasu *be*
modify cell addasu cell *be*
modify colour depth addasu dyfnder lliw *be*
modify curve smoothing addasu llyfnhau cromlin *be*
modify data range addasu ystod data *be*
modify field addasu maes *be*
modular modiwlaidd *ans*
modular arithmetic rhifyddeg fodiwlaidd *eb*
modular course cwrs modiwlaidd *eg* cyrsiau modiwlaidd
modular programme rhaglen fodiwlaidd *eb* rhaglenni modiwlaidd
modular programming rhaglennu modiwlaidd *be*
modular scheme cynllun modiwlaidd *eg* cynlluniau modiwlaidd
modularity modiwlaeth *eb*
modularize modiwleiddio *be*
modulate (amplitude or frequency) modylu *be*
modulate (courses etc) modiwleiddio *be*
modulate (key in music) trawsgyweirio *be*
modulate (the speaking voice) goslefu *be*
modulated (amplitude or frequency) modyledig *ans*
modulated carrier wave ton gario wedi'i modylu *eb*

modulation (of amplitude or frequency) modyliad *eg* modyliadau
modulation (of key in music) trawsgyweiriad *eg* trawsgyweiriadau
modulator (=diagram for teaching sol-fa) cyweiriadur *eg* cyweiriaduron
modulator (=electronic device) modylydd *eg* modylyddion
module modiwl *eg* modiwlau
modulo modwlo *eg*
modulus modwlws *eg* modwli
modulus of elasticity modwlws elastigedd *eg*
mogul mogwl *eg*
mohair moher *eg*
moist llaith *ans*
moisture lleithder *eg* lleithderau
moisture content cynnwys lleithder *eg*
moisture expansion ymlediad lleithder *eg*
moksha /moksa moksha /moksa *eg*
mol dm-3 môl dm-3 *eg*
molal molal *ans*
molality molaledd *eg*
molar (in chemistry) *adj* molar *ans*
molar (tooth) *n* cilddant *eg* cilddannedd
molar mass màs molar *eg*
molar ratio cymhareb folar *eb*
molar volume cyfaint molar *eg* cyfeintiau molar
molarity molaredd *eg*
mole (=small mammal) gwahadden *eb* gwahaddod; twrch daear *eg* tyrchod daear
mole (unit in chemistry) môl *eg* molau
mole wrench tyndro hunanafael *eg* tyndroeon hunanafael
molecular moleciwlaidd *ans*
molecular chaos caos moleciwlaidd *eg*
molecular formula fformiwla foleciwlaidd *eb* fformiwlâu moleciwlaidd
molecular mass màs moleciwlaidd *eg*
molecular structure adeiledd moleciwlaidd *eg* adeileddau moleciwlaidd
molecularity moleciwledd *eg*
molecule moleciwl *eg* moleciwlau
molinia gwellt y gweunydd *eg*
mollusc molwsg *eg* molwsgiaid
molten (of metal) tawdd *ans*
molten iron haearn tawdd *eg*
molten lava lafa tawdd *eg*
molten metal metel tawdd *eg*
molten salts (cooling media) halwynau tawdd *ell*
molybdate(VI) ion ïon molybdad(VI) *eg* ïonau molybdad(VI)
molybdenum (Mo) molybdenwm *eg*
moment (=turning effect of force) moment *eg* momentau
moment of inertia moment inertia *eg*
moment of momentum moment momentwm *eg*
momentary enydol *ans*
momentum momentwm *eg* momenta
monadnock monadnoc *eg* monadnocau
monamine oxidase inhibitor (MAOIs) atalydd monoamin ocsidas *eg* atalyddion monoamin ocsidas
monarch (female) brenhines *eb* breninesau
monarch (male) brenin *eg* brenhinoedd
monarch (of butterfly) glöyn y llaethlys *eg* glöynnod y llaethlys
monarchism brenhiniaeth *eb*
monarchist brenhinwr *eg* brenhinwyr
monarchy brenhiniaeth *eb*
monastery mynachlog *eb* mynachlogydd
monastic mynachaidd *ans*
monasticism mynachaeth *eb*
monatomic monatomig *ans*
Monel Monel *eg*
monestial blue glas monestial *eg*
monetarism arianolaeth *eb*
monetarist arianyddwr *eg* arianyddwyr
monetary ariannol *ans*
monetary policy polisi ariannol *eg*
Monetary Policy Committee Pwyllgor Polisi Ariannol *eg*
money arian *eg*
money allocated to schools arian a ddyrennir i ysgolion *eg*
money economy economi arian *eg*
money order archeb arian *eb* archebion arian
monic monig *ans*
monism monyddiaeth *eb*
monitor *v* monitro *be*
monitor (=screen) *n* monitor *eg* monitorau
monitor (of person) *n* monitor *eg* monitoriaid
monk mynach *eg* mynachod
monk-bishop mynach-esgob *eg* mynach-esgobion
monkish mynachaidd *ans*
monk's belt pattern patrwm gwregys y mynach *eg* patrymau gwregys y mynach
mono mono *ans*
monochromatic monocromatig *ans*
monochrome monocrom *eg* monocromau
monocline monoclin *eg* monoclinau
monocormic monocormig *ans*
monocotyledon monocotyledon *eg* monocotyledonau
monoculture ungnwd *eg*
monocyte monocyt *eg* monocytau
monodic monodig *ans*
monodrama monodrama *eb* monodramâu
monodromy monodromi *eg* monodromïau
monoecious monoecaidd *ans*
▶ **monogamy** monogami *eg*
monogenic monogenig *eg*
monogram monogram *eg* monogramau
monograph monograff *eg* monograffau
monohybrid monohybrid *eg*
monohybrid inheritance etifeddiad monocroesryw *eg*
monohydrogen monohydrogen *eg*

monolingual uniaith *ans*
monolith monolith *eg* monolithiau
monolithic monolithig *ans*
monomer monomer *eg*
monomeric monomerig *ans*
monomial *adj* monomaidd *ans*
monomial *n* monomial *eg* monomialau
mononitrogen mononitrogen *eg*
monophonic monoffonig *ans*
monophony monoffoni *eg*
monopolise monopoleiddio *be*
monopolistic competition cystadleuaeth fonopolistaidd *eb*
monopoly monopoli *eg* monopoliau
monopsony monopsoni *eg*
monosaccharide monosacarid *eg*
monosomy monosomi *eg*
monospaced unlled *ans*
monostable unsad *ans*
monotheism undduwiaeth *eb*
monotone monoton *ans*
monotonic monotonig *ans*
monotreme monotrem *eg*
monotropic monotropig *ans*
monotype monoteip *eg* monoteipiau
monozygotic monosygotig *ans*
monozygotic (MZ) twin gefell monosygotig *eg* efeilliaid monosygotig
Monroe Doctrine Athrawiaeth Monroe *eb*
monsoon monsŵn *eg* monsynau
montage montage *eg* montages
Montessori school ysgol Montessori *eb* ysgolion Montessori
monument cofadail *eg* cofadeiladau
mood (in art, music etc) naws *eb*
mood (in dance) awyrgylch *eg/b*
mood (of person) hwyl *eb* hwyliau
mood disorder anhwylder hwyliau *eg*
Mool /Mul Mantar Mool /Mul Mantar
moon lleuad *eb* lleuadau
moon in orbit lleuad mewn orbit *eb*
moon wane ciliad y lleuad *eg*
moon wax cynnydd y lleuad *eg*
moonquake lloergryn *eg* lloergrynfeydd
Moor Mŵr *eg* Mwriaid
mooring angorfa *eb* angorfeydd
Moorish Mwraidd *ans*
moorland *n* gweundir *eg* gweundiroedd
moorland *adj* gweundirol *ans*
moorpan cletir hwmws *eg* **moose** elc *eg* elciaid
mop mop *eg* mopiau
moraine marian *eg* marianau
moraine dammed lake cronlyn marian *eg* cronlynnoedd marian
moral moesol *ans*
moral aspect agwedd foesol *eb* agweddau moesol
moral development datblygiad moesol *eg*
moral education addysg foesol *eb*
moral evil drygioni moesol *eg*
moral force grym moesol *eg*
moral matter mater moesol *eg* materion moesol
moral panic panig moesol *eg*
moral realism realaeth foesol *eb*
moral standard safon foesol *eb* safonau moesol
moral tutor tiwtor moesol *eg* tiwtoriaid moesol
morality moesoldeb *eg*
morality of co-operation moesoldeb cydweithio *eb*
morals moesau *ell*
morbidity morbidrwydd *eg*
morbidity rate cyfradd morbidrwydd *eb*
mordant mordant *eg* mordantau
mordent mordent *eg* mordentau
more economically developed countries (MEDCs) gwledydd mwy economaidd ddatblygedig *ell*
Mormon *adj* Mormonaidd *ans*
Mormon *n* Mormon *eg* Mormoniaid
Moroccan crisis argyfwng Moroco *eg*
morpheme morffem *eg* morffemau
morphological morffolegol *ans*
morphology morffoleg *eb*
morphophonology morffoffonoleg *eb*
morris dance dawns forris *eb* dawnsiau morris
morris dancer dawnsiwr morris *eg* dawnswyr morris
Morse drill dril Morse *eg* driliau Morse
Morse taper tapr Morse *eg* taprau Morse
mortality marwoldeb *eg*
mortality rate cyfradd marwolaethau *eb*
mortar morter *eg* morterau
mortgage morgais *eg* morgeisiau
mortgage repayment ad-daliad morgais *eg* ad-daliadau morgais
mortgager morgeisydd *eg* morgeiswyr
morticing machine peiriant morteisio *eg* peiriannau morteisio
mortise mortais *eb* morteisiau
mortise and tenon joint uniad mortais a thyno *eg* uniadau mortais a thyno
mortise chisel cŷn mortais *eg* cynion mortais; gaing fortais *eb* geingiau mortais
mortise lock clo mortais *eg* cloeon mortais
mortlake ystumllyn *eg* ystumllynnoedd
mortmain tir llaw farw *eg* tiroedd llaw farw
mortuary corffdy *eg* corffdai
mortuary fee ffi gladdu *eb* ffioedd claddu
mosaic *adj* mosaig *ans*
mosaic *n* mosaig *eg*
mosaic image delwedd fosaig *eb* delweddau mosaig
mosaic tile teilsen fosaig *eb* teils mosaig
mosque mosg *eg* mosgiau
moss mwsogl *eg* mwsoglau
moss size preservative cadwolyn seis mwsogl *eg* cadwolion seis mwsogl
moss stitch pwyth mwsogl *eg* pwythau mwsogl

most significant bit (MSB)
did mwyaf arwyddocaol *eg*
didau mwyaf arwyddocaol
motel motel *eg* motelau
motet motét *eg* motetau
moth gwyfyn *eg* gwyfynod
moth balls peli camffor *ell*
mother cell mamgell *eb* mamgelloedd
mother country mamwlad *eb* mamwledydd
mother liquor hylif bwrw *eg* hylifau bwrw
Mother of God Mam Duw *eb*
mother of pearl cloud cwmwl symudliw *eg*
cymylau symudliw
mother tongue mamiaith *eb* mamieithoedd
mother-abbey mam-abaty *eg* mam-abatai
motherboard mamfwrdd *eg* mamfyrddau
mother-church mam-eglwys *eb* mam-eglwysi
mothercraft crefft y fam *eb*
motherese siarad syml â phlant *be*
mothproof *adj* gwrthwyfyn *ans*
mothproof *v* gwrthwyfynu *be*
mothproofing gwrthwyfynu *be*
motif motiff *eg* motiffau
motile mudol *ans*
motion mudiant *eg* mudiannau
motion in a circle mudiant mewn cylch *eg*
motion parallax symudiad paralacs *eg*
motionless llonydd *ans*
motivate symbylu *be*
motivation (=impulse) symbyliad *eg* symbyliadau
motivation (incentive or encouragement)
cymhelliant *eg*
motivational factor ffactor cymhelliant *eb*
ffactorau cymhelliant
motivational theory damcaniaeth cymhelliant *eb*
motive cymhelliad *eg* cymhellion
motivism cymhelliaeth *eb*
motor (=efferent) echddygol *ans*
motor (=machine) modur *eg* moduron
motor association cortex
cortecs cyswllt echddygol *eg*
motor bicycle beic modur *eg* beiciau modur
motor control rheolaeth dros symudiadau *eb*
motor defect diffyg echddygol *eg* diffygion echddygol
motor end-plate terfynblat echddygol *eg*
motor impulse ysgogiad echddygol *eg*
motor nerve nerf echddygol *eg* nerfau echddygol
motor neuron niwron echddygol *eg*
niwronau echddygol
motor pathway llwybr echddygol *eg*
motor root gwreiddyn echddygol *eg*
gwreiddiau echddygol
motor skill sgil symud *eg* sgiliau symud
motor terminal terfynell echddygol *eb*
motor traffic trafnidiaeth foduron *eb*
motorised blower peiriant chwythu *eg*
peiriannau chwythu
motorway traffordd *eb* traffyrdd

motorway under construction
traffordd yn cael ei hadeiladu *eb*
motte and bailey tomen a beili
motte and bailey castle castell tomen a beili *eg*
cestyll tomen a beili
mottled brith *ans*
mottling (in finishing metal) brychu *be*
mould *v* mowldio *be*
mould (=fungal growth) *n* llwydni *eg*
mould (=hollow container) *n* mowld *eg* mowldiau
moulded shank button botwm garan fowld *eg*
botymau garan fowld
moulder's tools arfau mowldiwr *ell*
moulding mowldin *eg* mowldinau
moulding bench mainc fowldio *eb*
meinciau mowldio
moulding board bwrdd mowldio *eg*
byrddau mowldio
moulding box blwch mowldio *eg* blychau mowldio
moulding flask fflasg fowldio *eb* fflasgiau mowldio
moulding plane plaen mowldio *eg* plaeniau mowldio
moulding sand tywod mowldio *eg*
mouldy bread bara wedi llwydo *eg*
moult bwrw *be*
moulting glands chwarennau ecdysaidd *ell*
mount *n* mownt *eg* mowntiau
mount *v* mowntio *be*
mountain pasture porfa fynydd *eb* porfeydd mynydd
mountain range cadwyn o fynyddoedd *eb*
cadwyni o fynyddoedd
mountain rescue post safle achub ar fynydd *eg*
safleoedd achub ar fynydd
mountaineering mynydda *be*
mountaineering association
cymdeithas fynydda *eb* cymdeithasau mynydda
mounted mowntiedig *ans*
mounted lino block bloc leino mowntiedig *eg*
blociau leino mowntiedig
mounting mowntin *eg* mowntinau
mounting board bwrdd mowntio *eg*
byrddau mowntio
mounting plate plât mowntio *eg* platiau mowntio
mourn galaru *be*
mouse llygoden *eb* llygod
mouse mat mat llygoden *eg* matiau llygoden
mouse over object (of object) gwrthrych dan
lygoden *eg* gwrthrychau dan lygoden
mouse pointer pwyntydd llygoden *eg*
pwyntyddion llygoden
mouse positioning lleoli llygoden *be*
mouse wheel olwyn llygoden *eb*
mouse's tail cynffon llygoden *eb* cynffonnau llygod
mouse-tail file ffeil fach fain gron *eb*
ffeiliau bach main crwn
mouth (in general) ceg *eb* cegau
mouth (of river) aber *eg* aberoedd
mouth organ organ geg *eb* organau ceg
mouth-moving pliers gefelen geg-symudol *eb*
gefeiliau ceg-symudol

mouthparts gên-rannau *ell*
mouthpiece (=spokesperson) llefarydd *eg* llefarwyr
mouthpiece (of musical instrument) ceg offeryn *eb* cegau offerynnau
mouth-to-mouth respiration anadlu ceg wrth geg *be*
mouth-to-mouth resuscitation adfywio ceg wrth geg *be*
mouth-to-mouth ventilation awyru ceg i geg *eg*
mouthwash cegolch *eg* cegolchion
movable symudol *ans*
movable guide cyfeirydd symudol *eg* cyfeiryddion symudol
movable jaw safn symudol *eb* safnau symudol
movable joint cymal symudol *eg* cymalau symudol
movable pin pìn symudol *eb* pinnau symudol
move symud *be*
move around the court symud o gwmpas y cwrt *eg*
move data series symud cyfres ddata *be*
move database object symud gwrthrych cronfa ddata *be*
move down symud i lawr *be*
move fluently symud yn rhwydd *be*
move frame symud ffrâm *be*
move horizontally symud yn llorweddol *be*
move left symud i'r chwith *be*
move outline symud amlinell *be*
move page break symud toriad tudalen *be*
move paragraph symud paragraff *be*
move point symud pwynt *be*
move right symud i'r dde *be*
move sheet symud dalen *be*
move slide symud sleid *be*
move table symud tabl *be*
move table window symud ffenestr tabl *be*
move up symud i fyny *be*
move vertically symud yn fertigol *be*
movement (=locomotion) ymsymudiad *eg* ymsymudiadau
movement (in general) symudiad *eg* symudiadau
movement allowance lwfans symudiad *eg* lwfansau symudiad
mover symudydd *eg* symudyddion
moving average cyfartaledd newidiol *eg*
moving coil coil symudol *eg* coiliau symudol
moving coil galvanometer galfanomedr coil symudol *eg* galfanomedrau coil symudol
moving coil microphone microffon coil symudol *eg* microffonau coil symudol
moving in pairs symud mewn parau *be*
moving in time symud mewn amser *be*
moving jaw safn symudol *eb* safnau symudol
moving phase symudwedd *eb*
moving shadows cysgodion symudol *ell*
moving steady sadydd symudol *eg* sadyddion symudol
moving window ffenestr symudol *eb* ffenestri symudol
moving-iron repulsion meter mesurydd gwrthyriad haearn symudol *eg*
mucilage mwcilag *eg* mwcilagau
mucin mwcin *eg* mwcinau
mucoprotein mwcoprotein *eg* mwcoproteinau
mucosa mwcosa *eg* mwcosau
mucous mwcaidd *ans*
mucous gland chwarren fwcaidd *eb* chwarennau mwcaidd
mucous membrane pilen fwcaidd *eb* pilenni mwcaidd
mud llaid *eg*
mud flats fflatiau llaid *ell*
mud pellet pelen laid *eb* pelenni llaid
mud-flow lleidlif *eg* lleidlifau
mudstone carreg laid *eb* cerrig llaid
muffle furnace ffwrnais fwffwl *eb* ffwrneisi mwffwl
muffle loading kiln odyn fwffl-lwytho *eb* odynnau mwffl-lwytho
muggy mwll *ans*
Muhammad Muhammad *eg*
mulberry paper papur morwydd *eg*
mulga mylga *eg* mylgâu
mull (soil) mwl *eg*
Müllerian duct dwythell Müller *eb* dwythellau Müller
mullion mwliwn *eg* mwliynau
multi skilled workforce gweithlu sgiliau lluosog *eg*
multi-access amlfynediad *ans*
multicellular amlgellog *ans*
multi-chrome lluosliw *ans*
multichrome amryliw *ans*
multicultural amlddiwylliannol *ans*
multicultural aspects of sport agweddau amlddiwylliannol ar chwaraeon *ell*
multicultural society cymdeithas amlddiwylliannol *eb* cymdeithasau amlddiwylliannol
multidigit amlddigid *ans*
multidisciplinary team tîm amlddisgyblaethol *eg* timau amlddisgyblaethol
multi-ethnic amlhiliol *ans*
multifactorial amlffactoraidd *ans*
multifactorial inheritance etifeddiad amlffactoraidd *eg*
multifill aml-lenwi *be*
multiflash amlfflach *eg*
multifunctional amlswyddogaethol *ans*
multi-infarct dementia gorddryswch amlgnawdnychol *eg*
multilateral amlochrog *ans*
multilevel aml-lefel *ans*
multiline input mewnbwn aml-linell *eg* mewnbynnau aml-linell
multilingual amlieithog *ans*
multilist box blwch amlrestr *eg* blychau amlrestr
multi-lobed aml-labedog *ans*
multi-lobed nucleus cnewyllyn aml-labedog *eg* cnewyll aml-labedog

multimedia amlgyfrwng *ans*
multimedia computer cyfrifiadur amlgyfrwng *eg* cyfrifiaduron amlgyfrwng
multi-media course cwrs amlgyfrwng *eg* cyrsiau amlgyfrwng
multimedia program rhaglen amlgyfrwng *eb* rhaglenni amlgyfrwng
multimeter amlfesurydd *eg* amlfesuryddion
multimodal amlfodd *ans*
multinational rhyngwladol *ans*
multinational company cwmni amlwladol *eg* cwmnïau amlwladol
multinominal *adj* lluosnomaidd *ans*
multinominal *n* lluosnominal *eg* lluosnominalau
multi-page aml-dudalen
multi-part memory cof amlran *eg*
multi-part paper papur amlran *eg* papurau amlran
multi-peninsular amlbenrhynnol *ans*
multiple *adj* lluosol *ans*
multiple *n* lluosrif *eg* lluosrifau
multiple (and various) amryfal *ans*
multiple allelomorph alelomorff lluosrif *eg* alelomorffau lluosrif
multiple angles onglau cyfansawdd *ell*
multiple bond bond lluosol *eg*
multiple choice dewis lluosog *eg* dewisiadau lluosog
multiple correlation aml gydberthyniad *eg*
multiple disabilities anableddau amryfal *ell*
multiple graver crafell luosbig *eb* crafellau lluosbig
multiple injuries anafiadau niferus *ell*
multiple operations gweithrediadau amryfal *ell*
multiple personality disorder anhwylder personoliaeth luosog *eg*
multiple poles pegynau cyfansawdd *ell*
multiple proportion cyfrannedd lluosol *eg*
multiple quick search chwilio cyflym amryfal *be*
multiple regression atchweliad lluosog *eg*
multiple search chwilio amryfal *be*
multiple store siop gadwyn *eb* siopau cadwyn
multiple track amldrac *eg* amldraciau
multiple-choice question cwestiwn dewis lluosog *eg* cwestiynau dewis lluosog
multiplex (digital compression of tv channels) amlbleth *ans*
multiplex cinema sinema aml-sgrîn *eg*
multiplexer amlblecsydd *eg* amlblecsyddion
multiplexing amlblecsu *be*
multiplicand lluosyn *eg* lluosion
multiplication lluosiad *eg* lluosiadau
multiplication sign arwydd lluosi *eg* arwyddion lluosi
multiplicative lluosol *ans*
multiplicity lluosogrwydd *eg*
multiplier lluosydd *eg* lluosyddion
multiplier effect effaith luosydd
multi-ply pren amlhaenog *eg*
multiply lluosi *be*
multi-ply door drws pren amlhaenog *eg* drysau pren amlhaenog
multi-plywood pren amlhaenog *eg*
multi-precision arithmetic rhifyddeg amldrachywiredd *eb*
multiprocessor system system amlbrosesydd *eb* systemau amlbrosesydd
multi-programming amlraglennu *be*
Multipurpose Internet Mail Extension Estyniad Post Rhyngrwyd Aml-ddefnydd *eg* Estyniadau Post Rhyngrwyd Aml-ddefnydd
multi-purpose pattern patrwm amlbwrpas *eg* patrymau amlbwrpas
multiracial amlhiliol *ans*
multi-range amlamrediad *ans*
multiseeded amlhadog *ans*
multi-sensory amlsynhwyraidd *ans*
multi-sensory deprivation diffyg amlsynhwyraidd *eg*
multi-size pattern patrwm amlfaint *eg* patrymau amlfaint
multi-stage amlran *ans*
multi-storey amrylawr *ans*
multistranded amledau *ans*
multi-tasking amlorchwyl *ans*
multi-textured amlwead *ans*
multi-tone amldon *ans*
multi-tool post post amlerfyn *eg* pyst amlerfyn
multi-track amldrac *ans*
multi-user amlddefnyddiwr *eg* amlddefnyddwyr
multi-valued lluoswerth *ans*
multi-valved amlfalfog *ans*
multivariate analysis dadansoddiad amlamrywedd *eg* dadansoddiadau amlamrywedd
multivibrator amlddirgrynydd *eg* amlddirgrynyddion
multiview amlolwg *ans*
multivoque amlddrychigaeth *eb*
mung beans ffa mwng *ell*
municipal trefol *ans*
Municipal Corporations Act Deddf Corfforaethau Trefol *eb*
munitions arfau rhyfel *ell*
Munro's foramen fforamen Munro *eg*
muntin mwntin *eg* mwntinau
Muntz metal metel Muntz *eg*
muon miwon *eg* miwonau
murage murdreth *eb* murdrethi
mural *adj* murol *ans*
mural *n* murlun *eg* murluniau
mural brush brwsh murlun *eg* brwshys murlun
mural composition cyfansoddiad murol *eg* cyfansoddiadau murol
mural decorations addurniadau murol *ell*
mural ground grwnd murol *eg*
murder llofruddiaeth *eb* llofruddiaethau
murderer llofrudd *eg* llofruddion
muscle *adj* cyhyrol *ans*

muscle (a specific one /type) *n* cyhyryn *eg* cyhyrynnau
muscle (in general) *n* cyhyr *eg* cyhyrau
muscle attachment cydfan cyhyrau *eg*
muscle contraction cyfangiad cyhyrol *eg*
muscle fatigue lludded cyhyrol *eg*
muscle fibre ffibr cyhyrau *eg*
muscle fibre type math o ffibr cyhyrau *eg* mathau o ffibrau cyhyrau
muscle mass màs y cyhyrau *eg*
muscle tissue meinwe cyhyrau *eg*
Muscovite *adj* Moscofaidd *ans*
Muscovite *n* Moscofwr *eg* Moscofiaid
muscular dystrophy nychdod cyhyrol *eg*
muscular endurance dygnwch y cyhyrau *eg*
muscular strength cryfder cyhyrau *eg*
muscular system system gyhyrol *eb*
musculature cyhyredd *eg*
musculocutaneous cyhyr-groenol *ans*
musette musette *eg* musettes
museum amgueddfa *eb* amgueddfeydd
museum school service gwasanaeth amgueddfa i ysgolion *eg* gwasanaethau amgueddfa i ysgolion
mushroom madarchen *eb* madarch
mushroom head rivet rhybed pen madarch *eg* rhybedion pen madarch
mushroom heads pennau madarch *ell*
mushroom stake bonyn madarchen *eg* bonion madarch
mushrooming madarchu *be*
mushroom-like madarchaidd *ans*
music cerddoriaeth *eb*
music adjudicator beirniad cerdd *eg* beirniaid cerdd
music drama drama gerdd *eb* dramâu cerdd
music hall theatr gerdd *eb* theatrau cerdd
music of Wales cerddoriaeth Cymru *eb*
music stand stand cerddoriaeth *eg* standiau cerddoriaeth
music synthesis synthesis cerddoriaeth *eg*
musical *adj* cerddorol *ans*
musical *n* sioe gerdd *eb* sioeau cerdd
musical accompaniment cyfeiliant cerddorol *eg*
musical comedy comedi gerdd *eb* comedïau cerdd
musical element elfen gerddorol *eb* elfennau cerddorol
musical heritage treftadaeth gerddorol *eb*
musical idea syniad cerddorol *eg* syniadau cerddorol
musical instruction cyfarwyddyd cerddorol *eg* cyfarwyddiadau cerddorol
musical instrument offeryn cerdd *eg* offerynnau cerdd
musical pattern patrwm cerddorol *eg* patrymau cerddorol
musical scene maes cerddorol *eg* meysydd cerddorol
musical stimulus ysgogiad cerddorol *eg* ysgogiadau cerddorol
musical style arddull cerddorol *eg* arddulliau cerddorol
musician cerddor *eg* cerddorion
musk mwsg *eg*
muskeg mysceg *eg* myscegau
musket mysged *eg* mysgedau
musketeer mysgedwr *eg* mysgedwyr
Muslim *adj* Mwslimaidd *ans*
Muslim *n* Mwslim *eg/b* Mwslimiaid
Muslim theology diwinyddiaeth Fwslimaidd *eb*
muslin mwslin *eg* mwslinau
mustelid carlymoliad *eg* carlymoliaid
muster *n* mwstwr *eg*
muster *v* mwstro *be*
muster master meistr mwstro *eg* meistri mwstro
Muster Roll Rhôl Fwstro *eb* Rholiau Mwstro
mutagen mwtagen *eg* mwtagenau
mutagenesis mwtagenedd *eg*
mutagenic mwtagenaidd *ans*
mutant mwtan *eg* mwtanau
mutate mwtanu *be*
mutation treiglad *eg* treigladau
mutation (in genetics) mwtaniad *eg* mwtaniadau
Mu'tazili Mu'tazilitiad *eg* Mu'tazilitiaid
Mu'tazilite views syniadau'r Mu'tazilitiaid *ell*
mute *adj* mud *ans*
mute (device in music) *n* mudydd *eg* mudyddion
mute (in music, of drums) *v* pylu *be*
mute (in music, of stringed instruments) *v* rhoi mudydd ar *be*
mute (of person) *n* mud *eg* mudion
muted (of colour) tawel *ans*
muted colour lliw tawel *eg* lliwiau tawel
mutilate anffurfio *be*
mutiny miwtini *eg*
Mutiny Act Deddf Miwtini *eb*
mutual electrostatic repulsion cyd-wrthyriant electrostatig *eg*
mutual inductance cydanwythiant *eg*
mutual induction cydanwythiad *eg*
mutualism cydymddibyniaeth *eb*
mutually perpendicular cydberpendicwlar *ans*
muzzle trwyn *eg* trwynau
mycelium myceliwm *eg* mycelia
mycology mycoleg *eb*
mycorrhiza mycorhisa *eg*
mycorrhizal mycorhisol *ans*
myelin myelin *eg*
▶ **myelin sheath** pilen fyelin *eb* pilenni myelin
myelinated myelinedig *ans*
myelinated fibre edefyn myelinedig *eg*
myeloid myeloid *ans*
myocardial infarction cnawdnychiad myocardiaidd *eg*
myofibrol myoffibrolyn *eg*
myogenic myogenig *ans*
myoglobin myoglobin *eg*
myomer myomer *eg*
myopia myopia *eg*

myopic byr yr olwg *ans*
myosin myosin *eg*
mystery play drama firagl *eb* dramâu miragl
mystic cyfriniwr *eg* cyfrinwyr
mystical cyfriniol *ans*
mysticism cyfriniaeth *eb*
myth myth *eg* mythau
mythical mytholegol *ans*
mythology mytholeg *eb*
myxoedema mycsoedema *eg*
myxovirus mycsofirws *eg*

N

NAB: National Advisory Body for Higher Education in the Public Sector CYC: Corff Ymgynghorol Cenedlaethol ar gyfer Addysg Uwch yn y Sector Cyhoeddus *eg*
nacreous cloud cwmwl symudliw *eg* cymylau symudliw
nadir nadir *eg*
nail *n* hoelen *eb* hoelion
nail *v* hoelio *be*
nail punch pwnsh hoelion *eg* pynsiau hoelion
nail-head ornament addurn pen hoelen *eg* addurniadau pen hoelen
naïve diniwed *ans*
naked noeth *ans*
naked figure ffigur noeth *eg* ffigurau noeth
Nam Simaran Nam Simaran
named activity gweithgaredd a enwir *eg*
named nurse nyrs benodol *eb* nyrsys penodol
named person person a enwir *eg* personau a enwir
NAND NIAC
NAND gate adwy NIAC *eb* adwyon NIAC
nano-ammeter nano-amedr *eg* nano-amedrau
nanometre nanometr *eg* nanometrau
nanosecond nano-eiliad *eg/b* nano-eiliadau
nap (textile) *n* ceden *eb* cedennau
nap (textile) *v* cedenu *be*
nape-to-waist o'r gwegil i'r wasg
naphtha nafftha *eg*
naphthalen-1-amine nafffthalen-1-amin *eg*
naphthalene nafffthalen *eg*
naphthalene acetic acid (NAA) asid nafffthalen asetig (ANA) *eg*
naphthalene-1-carboxylic acid asid nafffthalen-1-carbocsylig *eg*
naphthalen-1-ol nafffthalen-1-ol *eg*
naphthalen-2-ol nafffthalen-2-ol *eg*
napkin napcyn *eg* napcynnau
Naples yellow melyn Napoli *eg*
Napoleonic Code Cod Napoleon *eg*
nappy cewyn *eg* cewynnau; clwt *eg* clytiau
nappy rash brech cewyn *eb*; brech clwt *eb*
narcissism hunan-serch *eg*
nardus cawnen ddu *eb* cawn duon
narration adroddiad *eg* adroddiadau
narrative *adj* traethiadol *ans*
narrative *n* naratif *eg*
narrative analysis dadansoddi naratif *be*
narrative art celfyddyd draethiadol *eb*
narrative code cod naratif *eg*
narrative film ffilm naratif *eb* ffilmiau naratif
narrative method dull naratif *eg*
narrative sequencing dilyniant naratif *eg*
narrative structure strwythur y naratif *eg*
narrative tradition traddodiad storïol *eg*
narrator adroddwr *eg* adroddwyr
narrow *adj* cul *ans*
narrow *v* culhau *be*
narrow gauge railway lein fach *eb* leiniau bach
narrow gauge track trac cul *eg* traciau cul
narrow leaved cul-ddeiliog *ans*
narrow road with passing places ffordd gul gyda lleoedd pasio *eb*
narrow stroke strôc gul *eb* strociau cul
narrowband band cul *eg*
narrowcasting targedu cyfyng *be*
narrowing the angle culhau'r ongl *be*
narrowness culni *eg*
narrows culfa *eb* culfeydd
nasal trwynol *ans*
nasal cavity ceudod trwynol *eg* ceudodau trwynol
nasal tone sain drwynol *eb* seiniau trwynol
nascent genedigol *ans*
Nashim Nashim *ell*
nasopharyngeal nasoffaryngeal *ans*
nastic nastig *ans*
nastic movement symudiad nastig *eg* symudiadau nastig
nation cenedl *eb* cenhedloedd
nation state gwladwriaeth genedlaethol *eb* gwladwriaethau cenedlaethol
national (of nation, not state) cenedlaethol *ans*
national (of state) gwladol *ans*
national account cyfrif gwladol *eg* cyfrifon gwladol
national anthem anthem genedlaethol *eb* anthemau cenedlaethol
National Assembly Cynulliad Cenedlaethol *eg*
National Assistance Cymorth Gwladol *eg*
national average cyfartaledd gwladol *eg*
national awareness ymwybyddiaeth genedlaethol *eb*
national context cyd-destun cenedlaethol *eg*
national costume gwisg genedlaethol *eb* gwisgoedd cenedlaethol
national curriculum cwricwlwm cenedlaethol *eg*
National Curriculum Council (NCC) Cyngor y Cwricwlwm Cenedlaethol *eg*
national dances dawnsiau cenedlaethol *ell*
national debt dyled wladol *eb* dyledion gwladol

National Foundation for Education Research (NFER) Sefydliad Cenedlaethol ar gyfer Ymchwil mewn Addysg *eg*
National Government Llywodraeth Genedlaethol *eb*
National Guard (US) Gwarchodlu Cenedlaethol *eg*
National Health Insurance Act Deddf Yswiriant Iechyd Gwladol *eb*
National Health Service (NHS) Gwasanaeth Iechyd Gwladol *eg*
national identity hunaniaeth genedlaethol *eb*
national income incwm gwladol *eg*
National Insurance Yswiriant Gwladol *eg*
National Insurance Act Deddf Yswiriant Gwladol *eb*
national literacy strategy strategaeth llythrennedd cenedlaethol *eb*
National Political Union Undeb Gwleidyddol Cenedlaethol *eg*
national register cofrestr genedlaethol *eb*
National Savings Cynilion Gwladol *ell*
National School Ysgol Genedlaethol *eb* Ysgolion Cenedlaethol
national standard safon genedlaethol *eb* safonau cenedlaethol
National Trust Ymddiriedolaeth Genedlaethol *eb*
National Unemployment Insurance Act Deddf Yswiriant y Di-waith *eb*
National Union of Students Undeb Cenedlaethol y Myfyrwyr *eg*
nationalism cenedlaetholdeb *eg*
nationalist *adj* cenedlaethol *ans*
nationalist *adj* cenedlaetholgar *ans*
nationalist *n* cenedlaetholwr *eg* cenedlaetholwyr
Nationalist Party Plaid Genedlaethol *eb*
nationality (=citizenship) dinasyddiaeth *eb*
nationalization gwladoliad *eg*
nationalize gwladoli *be*
nationalized industry diwydiant gwladoledig *eg* diwydiannau gwladoledig
nationally prescribed test prawf a osodir yn genedlaethol *eg* profion a osodir yn genedlaethol
nationhood cenedligrwydd *eg*
native *adj* brodorol *ans*
native *n* brodor *eg* brodorion
native ability gallu cynhenid *eg*
native language recognition hypothesis rhagdybiaeth adnabod iaith frodorol *eb*
native protein protein cynhenid *eg* proteinau cynhenid
native resistance gwrthsafiad y brodorion *eg*
nativism cynhenidiaeth *eb*
nativist cynhenidydd *eg* cynhenidwyr
natural *adj* naturiol *ans*
natural boundary conditions amodau ffin naturiol *ell*
natural colour lliw naturiol *eg* lliwiau naturiol
natural concept cysyniad naturiol *eg*
natural defects (in timber) diffygion naturiol *ell*
natural defence amddiffynfa naturiol *eb* amddiffynfeydd naturiol
natural environment amgylchedd naturiol *eg* amgylcheddau naturiol
natural evil drygioni naturiol *eg*
natural fibre ffibr naturiol *eg* ffibrau naturiol
natural finish gorffeniad naturiol *eg* gorffeniadau naturiol
natural form ffurf naturiol *eb* ffurfiau naturiol
natural gas nwy naturiol *eg*
natural grass gwair naturiol *eg*
natural grit grit naturiol *eg*
natural immunity imiwnedd cynhenid *eg*
natural justice cyfiawnder cynhenid *eg*
natural language iaith naturiol *eb*
natural law deddf naturiol *eb* deddfau naturiol
natural light golau naturiol *eg*
natural logarithm logarithm naturiol *eg* logarithmau naturiol
natural monopoly monopoli naturiol *eg*
natural note nodyn naturiol *eg* nodau naturiol
natural number rhif naturiol *eg* rhifau naturiol
natural object gwrthrych naturiol *eg* gwrthrychau naturiol
natural regions rhanbarthau naturiol *ell*
natural resources adnoddau naturiol *ell*
natural seasoning (of wood) sychu naturiol *be*
natural selection dethol naturiol *be*
natural sign arwydd naturiol *eg* arwyddion naturiol
natural teaching medium cyfrwng addysgu naturiol *eg* cyfryngau addysgu naturiol
Natural Theology Diwinyddiaeth Natur *eb*
natural trumpet utgorn naturiol *eg* utgyrn naturiol
natural twine cortyn naturiol *eg* cortynnau naturiol
natural wastage gwastraff naturiol *eg*
naturalism naturoliaeth *eb*
naturalistic naturiolaidd *ans*
naturalistic observation arsylwi mewn sefyllfa naturiol *be*
naturalize (=accept as citizen) derbyn yn ddinesydd *be*
naturalize (in biology) cynefino *be*
nature natur *eb*
Nature Conservancy Council Cyngor Gwarchod Natur *eg*
nature of scientific activity natur gweithgaredd gwyddonol *eb*
nature reserve gwarchodfa natur *eb* gwarchodfeydd natur
nature table bwrdd natur *eg* byrddau natur
nature trail llwybr natur *eg* llwybrau natur
nature/nurture debate dadl natur/magwraeth *eb*
nausea cyfog *eg*
nautical mile (knot) morfilltir *eb* morfilltiroedd
naval llyngesol *ans*
naval base canolfan llynges *eb* canolfannau llynges
naval blockade gwarchae o'r môr *eg*
naval history hanes llyngesol *eg*

naval officer swyddog y llynges *eg* swyddogion y llynges
naval power grym llyngesol *eg*
naval ship llong y llynges *eb* llongau'r llynges
nave (of wheel) both *eb* bothau
navigable mordwyol *ans*
navigate (around a site) llywio *be*
navigate (on the web) gwe-lywio *be*
navigation mordwyo *be*
Navigation Act Deddf Mordwyo *eb*
navigation bar bar llywio *eg* barrau llywio
navigator (on site) llywiwr *eg* llywyr
navigator (on web) gwe-lywiwr *eg* gwe-lywyr
navy llynges *eb* llyngesau
naze trwyn *eg* trwynau
Nazi *n* Natsi *eg* Natsïaid
Nazi *adj* Natsïaidd *ans*
Nazi Germany Almaen Natsïaidd *eb*
Nazi Party Plaid Natsïaidd *eb*
Nazi political system cyfundrefn wleidyddol y Natsïaid *eb*
Nazify Natsïeiddio *be*
neap tide llanw bach *eg*
near abstract lled-haniaethol *ans*
near bankful gogyforlan *eb* gogyforlannau
Near East Dwyrain Agos *eg*
near future dyfodol agos *eg*
near point agosbwynt *eg* agosbwyntiau
near side ochr agosaf *eb* ochrau agosaf
nearest neighbour cymydog agosaf *eg* cymdogion agosaf
nearest neighbour analysis dadansoddiad cymydog agosaf *eg* dadansoddiadau cymydog agosaf
neat appearance ymddangosiad destlus *eg*
neatness taclusrwydd *eg*
nebula nifwl *eg* nifylau
nebulizer nebiwlydd *eg* nebiwlyddion
nebulous niwlog *ans*
necessaries angenrheidiau *ell*
necessary angenrheidiol *ans*
necessary and sufficient angenrheidiol a digonol
necessity rheidrwydd *eg*
neck *v* gyddfu *be*
neck (in general) *n* gwddf *eg* gyddfau
neck (of harp) *n* crib *eg/b* cribau
neck of racket gwddf y raced *eg* gyddfau'r racedi
necking gyddfu *be*
necklace neclis *eb* neclisau
neckline llinell gwddf *eb* llinellau gwddf
neckspring sbring gwar *eg* sbringiau gwar
neck-to-waist o'r gwddf i'r wasg
nectar neithdar *eg* neithdarau
nectary neithdarle *eg* neithdarleoedd
need angen *eg* anghenion
needle nodwydd *eb* nodwyddau
needle clamp (of machine part) clamp nodwydd *eg* clampiau nodwydd
needle file ffeil nodwydd *eb* ffeiliau nodwydd
needle leaves dail nodwydd *ell*
needle point blaen nodwydd *eg* blaenau nodwyddau
needle position control (of machine part) rheolydd safle'r nodwydd *eg* rheolyddion safle'r nodwydd
needle threader edefydd nodwydd *eg* edefyddion nodwydd
needlecord melfaréd main *eg*
needled carpet carped nodwyddog *eg* carpedi nodwyddog
needlecraft crefft nodwydd *eb*
needlepoint gwaith blaen nodwydd *eg*
needlepoint edging ymylwaith blaen nodwydd *eg*
needleweaving gwehyddwaith nodwydd *eg*
needlework gwniadwaith *eg*
needs analysis dadansoddiad o anghenion *eg*
needs assessment asesiad o anghenion *eg* asesiadau o anghenion
needs of the user gofynion y defnyddiwr *ell*
negate negyddu *be*
negation of time (Messiaen) negyddiad amser *eg*
negative (in general sense) *adj* negyddol *ans*
negative (in photography) *n* negatif *eg* negatifau
negative (of charge) *adj* negatif *ans*
negative affectivity affeithioldeb negyddol *eg*
negative after image ôl-ddelwedd negyddol *eb*
negative allesthesia alesthesia negyddol *eg*
negative carving cerfio negatif *be*
negative charge gwefr negatif *eb* gwefrau negatif
negative deviation gwyriad negyddol *eg*
negative externality allanoldeb negatif *eg* allanoldebau negatif
negative feedback (of criticism) adborth negyddol *eg*
negative feedback (of signal) adborth negatif *eg*
negative image delwedd negyddol *eb* delweddau negyddol
negative number rhif negatif *eg* rhifau negatif
negative polarity polaredd negatif *eg*
negative rake gwyredd negatif *eg*
negative reinforcement atgyfnerthu negyddol *be*
negative response ymateb negyddol *eg* ymatebion negyddol
negative self-concept hunanddelwedd negyddol *eb*
negative skew sgiw negatif *eb*
negative symptom symptom negyddol *eg* symptomau negyddol
negative variance amrywiant negyddol *eg* amrywiannau negyddol
negativistic subject role rôl cyfrannwr negyddol *eb*
negativity negatifedd *eg*
neglect *n* esgeulustod *eg*
neglect *v* esgeuluso *be*
negligence esgeulustod *eg*
negligible dibwys *ans*
negligible thickness trwch y gellir ei anwybyddu *eg*
negotiate a settlement trafod telerau cytundeb *be*
negotiation trafodaeth *eb* trafodaethau

nehrung (=barrier beach) bardraeth *eg* bardraethau
neighbour cymydog *eg* cymdogion
neighbour test prawf cymydog *eg*
neighbourhood cymdogaeth *eb* cymdogaethau
neighbourhood unit uned gymdogaeth *eb* unedau cymdogaeth
neighbouring cyfagos *ans*
neighbourliness cymdogrwydd *eg*
nematocyst nematocyst *eg* nematocystau
nematode nematod *eg* nematodau
neobehaviourism / radical behaviourism neo-ymddygiadaeth / ymddygiadaeth radical *eb*
neoclassical neoglasurol *ans*
▶ **neoclassicism** neoglasuriaeth *eb*
neodymium (Nd) neodymiwm *eg*
neoglaciation neorewlifiant *eg*
neo-Gothic neo-Gothig *ans*
neo-impressionism neoargraffiadaeth *eb*
neolithic neolithig *ans*
neo-Malthusianism neo-Malthwsiaeth *eb*
neon (Ne) neon *eg*
neonatal newydd-anedig *ans*
neonatal jaundice clefyd melyn y newydd-anedig *eg*
neonate newydd-anedig *eg*
neo-Romantic neo-Ramantaidd *ans*
nephridium neffridiwm *eg* neffridia
nephron neffron *eg* neffronau
nepotism nepotistiaeth *eb*
nepotist nepotydd *eg* nepotyddion
Neptune Neifion *eg*
neptunium (Np) neptwniwm *eg*
neritic deposits dyddodion neritig *ell*
nerve nerf *eg/b* nerfau
nerve cell nerfgell *eb*
nerve deafness byddardod nerfol *eg*
nerve ending terfyn nerf *eg* terfynau nerfau
nerve fibre edefyn nerf *eg* edafedd nerf
nerve impulse ysgogiad nerfol *eg* ysgogiadau nerfol
nerve net nerfrwyd *eb* nerfrwydau
nerve root nerfwreiddyn *eg* nerfwreiddiau
nerve supply cyflenwad nerfol *eg* cyflenwadau nerfol
nervous (of anatomy) nerfol *ans*
nervous (of person) nerfus *ans*
nervous conduction dargludiad nerfol *eg*
nervous system system nerfol *eb*
nervous tissue meinwe nerfol *eb*
nervule nerfolyn *eg* nerfolynnau
ness trwyn *eg* trwynau
nest nythu *be*
nest *n* nyth *eb* nythod
nest egg wy addod *eg* wyau addod
nest of tables (in computing) nythaid o dablau *eb*
nest of tables (of furniture) nythaid o fyrddau *eb*
nested hierarchy hierarchaeth nythog *eb* hierarchaethau nythog
nested loop dolen nythol *eb* dolennau nythol
net *n* rhwyd *eb* rhwydi
net (=after deductions) *adj* net *ans*
net access (in computing) mynediad i'r rhwyd *eg*
net assets asedau net *ell*
net book value gwerth net ar bapur *eg*
net capital cyfalaf net *eg*
net cord cortyn rhwyd *eg* cortynnau rhwyd
net count rate cyfrif cyfradd net *eg*
net current gwir gerrynt *eg*
net drift (=drift in minus drift out) drifft canlyniadol *eg*
net effect gwir effaith *eb*
net energy gain cynnydd egni net *eg*
net export allforyn net *eg* allforion net
net force gwir rym *eg*
net gain enillion net *ell*
net income incwm net *eg*
net investment buddsoddiad net *eg* buddsoddiadau net
net loss colled net *eb*
net movement gwir symudiad *eg*
net pay cyflog net *eg*
net present value gwerth presennol net *eg*
net profit elw net *eg*
net profit figure ffigwr elw net *eg*
net register tonnage tunelledd cofrestredig net *eg* tunelleddau cofrestredig net
net the ball rhwydo'r bêl *be*
net weight pwysau net *ell*
netball pêl-rwyd *eb*
netiquette rhwydfoesau *ell*
netizen rhwyd-ddinesydd *eg* rhwyd-ddinasyddion
network *n* rhwydwaith *eg/b* rhwydweithiau
network *v* rhwydweithio *be*
network architecture saernïaeth rwydwaith *eb* saerniaethau rhwydwaith
network computer cyfrifiadur rhwydwaith *eg* cyfrifiaduron rhwydwaith
network connection cyswllt rhwydwaith *eg* cysylltau rhwydwaith
network flows dylifiadau rhwydwaith *ell*
network installation gosodiad rhwydwaith *eg* gosodiadau rhwydwaith
network management administration team tîm gweinyddu rheoli'r rhwydwaith *eg*
network of blood-vessels rhwydwaith pibellau gwaed *eg*
network operating system system weithredu rhwydwaith *eb* systemau gweithredu rhwydwaith
network system system rwydwaith *eb* systemau rhwydwaith
neume niwm *eg* niwmau
neural niwral *ans*
neural arch bwa niwral *eg* bwâu niwral
neural network rhwydwaith niwral *eg* rhwydweithiau niwral
neural spine (vertebra) pigyn niwral *eg* pigynnau niwral
neural streak rhes niwral *eb*
neural transmitter trawsyrrydd niwral *eg* trawsyryddion niwral

neural tube tiwb niwral *eg*
neurogenic niwrogenig *ans*
neuroglia niwroglia *eg*
neuroglial niwrogliaidd *ans*
neuroimaging niwroddelweddu *be*
neurological niwrolegol *ans*
neurological observation arsylw niwrolegol *eg* arsylwadau niwrolegol
neurologist niwrolegydd *eg* niwrolegwyr
neurology niwroleg *eb*
neuromodulator niwrofodylydd *eg* niwrofodylyddion
neuromuscular niwrogyhyrol *ans*
neuro-muscular control rheolaeth nerf-gyhyr *eb*
neuron niwron *eg* niwronau
neuron theory damcaniaeth niwronau *eb*
neuropsychological assessment asesiad niwroseicolegol *eg* asesiadau niwroseicolegol
neuropsychological rehabilitation adsefydlu niwroseicolegol *be*
neuropsychology/neuroscience niwroseicoleg/niwrowyddoniaeth *eb*
neurosecretory niwrosecretol *ans*
neurosis niwrosis *eg*
neuroticism niwrotiaeth *eb*
neurotransmitter niwrodrosglwyddydd *eg* niwrodrosglwyddyddion
neutral niwtral *ans*
neutral axis echelin niwtral *eb* echelinau niwtral
neutral colour lliw niwtral *eg* lliwiau niwtral
neutral equilibrium cydbwysedd niwtral *eg*
neutral wire gwifren niwtral *eb* gwifrau niwtral
neutrality niwtraliaeth *eb*
neutralization niwtraliad *eg* niwtraliadau
neutralization of acids niwtralu asidau *be*
neutralize niwtraleiddio *be*
neutralized niwtraledig *ans*
neutrino niwtrino *eg* niwtrinoeon
neutron niwtron *eg* niwtronau
neutrophil niwtroffil *eg* niwtroffilau
never been alive erioed wedi bod yn fyw
new newydd *ans*
new blue glas newydd *eg*
new classical economist economegwr clasurol newydd *eg* economegwyr clasurol newydd
new composer window ffenestr cyfansoddwr newydd *eb* ffenestri cyfansoddwr newydd
new content cynnwys newydd *eg*
new data source ffynhonnell data newydd *eb* ffynonellau data newydd
new database cronfa ddata newydd *eb* cronfeydd data newydd
new database title teitl cronfa ddata newydd *eg* teitlau cronfa ddata newydd
New Deal Bargen Newydd *eb*
New Deal Policy Polisi'r Fargen Newydd *eg*
new dialog deialog newydd *eb* deialogau newydd
new dictionary geiriadur newydd *eg* geiriaduron newydd
new DIR CYF newydd *eg*
new document dogfen newydd *eb* dogfennau newydd
New Economic Policy Polisi Economaidd Newydd *eg*
new event digwyddiad newydd *eg* digwyddiadau newydd
new folder ffolder newydd *eb* ffolderi newydd
new form ffurflen newydd *eb* ffurflenni newydd
new frameset fframset newydd *eb* fframsetiau newydd
new gallery oriel newydd *eb* orielau newydd
new group grŵp newydd *eg* grwpiau newydd
New Learning Dysg Newydd *eb*
new library llyfrgell newydd *eb* llyfrgelloedd newydd
new line llinell newydd *eb* llinellau newydd
new link cyswllt newydd *eg* cysylltiadau newydd
new mail e-bost newydd *eg* e-byst newydd
new menu dewislen newydd *eb* dewislenni newydd
New Model Army Byddin Model Newydd *eb*
new module modiwl newydd *eg* modiwlau newydd
new moon lleuad newydd *eb*
new music cerddoriaeth newydd *eb*
new name enw newydd *eg* enwau newydd
new outbox blwch allan newydd *eg* blychau allan newydd
new paragraph paragraff newydd *eg* paragraffau newydd
new pattern centre bit ebill canoli patrwm newydd *eg* ebillion canoli patrwm newydd
new record cofnod newydd *eg* cofnodion newydd
New Stone Age Oes Neolithig *eb*
New Testament Testament Newydd *eg*
New World Byd Newydd *eg*
New Year Blwyddyn Newydd *eb*
Newall limits terfannau Newall *ell*
newcomer newydd-ddyfodiad *eg* newydd-ddyfodiaid
newel post post ystlys *eg* pyst ystlys
newly developed newydd eu datblygu *ans*
newly industrialized country (NIC) gwlad newydd ei diwydianeiddio *eb* gwledydd newydd eu diwydianeiddio
news newyddion *ell*
news bulletin bwletin newyddion *eg* bwletinau newyddion
news media cyfryngau newyddion *ell*
news server gweinydd newyddion *eg* gweinyddion newyddion
news values gwerthoedd newyddion *ell*
newsagent siop bapurau *eb* siopau papurau
newsfeed cyflenwad newyddion *eg* cyflenwadau newyddion
newsgroup grŵp newyddion *eg* grwpiau newyddion
newsletter cylchlythyr *eg* cylchlythyrau
newspaper papur newydd *eg* papurau newydd
newspaper front page tudalen flaen papur newydd *eb* tudalennau blaen papurau newydd

newsreader darllenydd newyddion *eg*
news-sheet newyddlen *eb* newyddlenni
newton (N) newton *eg* newtonau
newtonmeter mesurydd newton *eg* mesuryddion newton
Newton-Raphson formula fformiwla Newton-Raphson *eb*
Newton's laws of motion deddfau mudiant Newton *ell*
next nesaf *ans*
next bookmark nod tudalen nesaf *eg*
next control rheolydd nesaf *eg*
next drawing llun nesaf *eg*
next error gwall nesaf *eg*
next footnote troednodyn nesaf *eg*
next heading pennawd nesaf *eg* penawdau nesaf
next index entry cofnod mynegai nesaf *eg*
next link cyswllt nesaf *eg*
next marker marciwr nesaf *eg*
next message neges nesaf *eb*
next note nodyn nesaf *eg*
next object gwrthrych nesaf *eg*
next of kin perthynas agosaf *eg/b* perthnasau agosaf
next page tudalen nesaf *eb*
next picture darlun nesaf *eg*
next record cofnod nesaf *eg*
next reminder nodyn atgoffa nesaf *eg*
next section adran nesaf *eb*
next selection dewis nesaf *eg*
next slide sleid nesaf *eb*
next style arddull nesaf *eg*
next table tabl nesaf *eg*
next table formula fformiwla tabl nesaf *eb* fformiwlâu tabl nesaf
next text frame ffrâm testun nesaf *eb* fframiau testun nesaf
next to nesaf at
next unread message neges nesaf heb ei darllen *eb*
next update diweddariad nesaf *eg*
next window ffenestr nesaf *eb* ffenestri nesaf
Nezikin Nezikin *eg*
n-fold degenerate dirywiedig n-blyg *ans*
nibbana (=nirvana) nibbana *eg*
niche (architecture) cloer *eg* cloerau
niche (in ecology) cilfach *eb* cilfachau
niche differentiation gwahaniaethu cilfachau *be*
niche marketing marchnata arbenigol *be*
Nichiren Buddhism Bwdhaeth Nichiren *eb*
nick rhic *eg*
nickel (Ni) nicel *eg*
nickel bronze efydd nicel *eg*
nickel plated plât nicel *eg*
nickel silver arian nicel *eg*
nickel(II) ion ïon nicel(II) *eg* ïonau nicel(II)
nicotinamide adenine dineucleotide (NAD) nicotinamid adenin deuniwcliotid *eg*
nicotinamide adenine dineucleotide phosphate (NAPD) nicotinamid adenin deuniwlcliotid ffosffad *eg*
nicotinic acid asid nicotinig *eg*
nictitating membrane pilen amrannol *eb* pilenni amrannol
night blindness dallineb nos *eg*
night school ysgol nos *eb* ysgolion nos
night shift shifft nos *eg*
night soil carthion nos *ell*
night stairs grisiau nos *ell*
night terrors ofnau'r nos *ell*
nightdress gŵn nos *eg* gwn nosys; coban *eb* cobanau
nightingale eos *eb* eosiaid
nightshirt crys nos *eg* crysau nos
nightwear dillad nos *ell*
nihilism nihiliaeth *eb*
nihilist nihilydd *eg* nihilwyr
nilpotent nilpotent *ans*
nimbostratus nimbostratus *eg*
nimbus (halo) lleugylch *eg* lleugylchoedd
nine o'clock watershed trothwy naw o'r gloch *eg*
nineteenth century pedwaredd ganrif ar bymtheg *eb*
Ninety Five Theses (of Luther) Naw Deg a Phum Pwnc *eg*
ninhydrin ninhydrin *eg*
ninth nawfed *eg* nawfedau
niobium (Nb) niobiwm *eg*
nipper niper *eg* niperi
nipping pliers gefelen nipio *eb* gefeiliau nipio
nipping press gwasg nipio *eb* gweisg nipio
nipple (in engineering) nipl *eg* niplau
nippy vice feis fach *eb* feisiau bach
nirvana (=nibbana) nirvana *eg*
Nissl granules gronynnau Nissl *ell*
nitrate nitrad *eg* nitradau
nitrate(III) ion ïon nitrad(III) *eg* ïonau nitrad(III)
nitrate(V) ion ïon nitrad(V) *eg* ïonau nitrad(V)
nitration nitradiad *eg*
nitric acid asid nitrig *eg*
nitric(III) acid asid nitrig(III) *eg*
nitric(V) acid asid nitrig(V) *eg*
nitride ion ïon nitrid *eg* ïonau nitrid
nitriding nitrido *be*
nitrification nitreiddiad *eg*
nitrify nitreiddio *be*
nitrifying bacteria bacteria nitreiddio *ell*
nitrites nitraid *eg* nitreidiau
nitrobenzene nitrobensen *eg*
nitro-cellulose nitro-cellwlos *eg*
nitro-compound nitro-gyfansoddyn *eg* nitro-gyfansoddion
nitrogen (N) nitrogen *eg*
nitrogen cycle cylchred nitrogen *eb*
nitrogen dioxide nitrogen deuocsid *eg*
nitrogen fixation sefydlogiad nitrogen *eg*
nitrogen monoxide nitrogen monocsid *eg*

nitrogen oxide nitrogen ocsid *eg*
nitrogenous excretory system
system ysgarthu sylweddau nitrogenaidd *eb* systemau ysgarthu sylweddau nitrogenaidd
nitrogenous waste product sylwedd gwastraff nitrogenaidd *eg* sylweddau gwastraff nitrogenaidd
nitromethane nitromethan *eg*
2-nitrophenol 2-nitroffenol *eg*
4-nitrophenylamine 4-nitroffenylamin *eg*
1-nitro-2-phenylethene 1-nitro-2-ffenylethen *eg*
nitroso- nitroso-
nitrosyl cation catïon nitrosyl *eg* catïonau nitrosyl
nitrous acid asid nitrus *eg*
nitryl cation catïon nitryl *eg* catïonau nitryl
nivation eirdreulio *be*
NLQ (near letter quality) ansawdd llythyr *ans*
no (on computer button) na
no action dim gweithred
no additional information
dim gwybodaeth ychwanegol
no additional properties
dim priodweddau ychwanegol
no assignment heb ei neilltuo
no automatic positioning dim lleoli awtomatig
no ball pelen wallus *eb* pelenni gwallus
no break dim toriad
no changes dim newidiadau
no changes discovered heb ganfod newidiadau
no character style dim arddull nodau
no drop dim llithriad *eg*
no duplication dim dyblygu
no effect dim effaith
no entry dim cofnod
no field dim maes
no fields specified dim meysydd wedi'u pennu
no format dim fformat
no formula specified dim fformiwla wedi'i phennu
no function dim swyddogaeth
no further files dim ffeiliau pellach
no header dim pennyn
no heading dim teitl
no hyphenation dim cysylltnodi
no indicators dim dangosyddion
no language set dim iaith wedi'i phennu
no liability without fault dim atebolrwydd heb fai
no logo dim logo
no mercy dim trugaredd *ans*
no outline dim amlinelliad
no page break dim toriad tudalen
no page end dim diwedd tudalen
no pair kerning dim pâr yn gorgyffwrdd
no pattern dim patrwm
no printer driver dim adnoddau argraffu
no room dim lle
nobelium (No) nobeliwm *eg*
nobility pendefigaeth *eb*
noble pendefig *eg* pendefigion
noble atmosphere awyrgylch urddasol *eg*
noble gas nwy nobl *eg*
noble metal metel nobl *eg*
nobleman (=aristocrat) pendefig *eg* pendefigion
nobleman (=gentry) uchelwr *eg* uchelwyr
nociceptor nociganfyddwr *eg* nociganfyddwyr
nock hic *eg* hiciau
nocking hicio *be*
nocking point man hicio *eg* mannau hicio
nocturnal nosol *ans*
nodal nodol *ans*
nodality nodaledd *eg*
node (in anatomy, physics and mathematics) nod *eg* nodau
node (on plant) cwgn *eg* cygnau
nodular cnepynnaidd *ans*
nodule cnepyn *eg* cnepynnau
noise sŵn *eg* synau
noise level lefel sŵn *eb* lefelau sŵn
noise pollution llygredd sŵn *eg*
nomad nomad *eg* nomadiaid
nomadic nomadig *ans*
nomadism nomadiaeth *eb*
no-man's land tir neb *eg*
nominal enwol *ans*
nominal fallacy twyllresymeg enwi *eb*
nominal interest llog enwol *eg*
nominal ledger llyfr enwol *eg* llyfrau enwol
nominal scale graddfa enwol *eb*
nominal size maint enwol *eg* meintiau enwol
nominal value gwerth enwol *eg*
nominalism enwolaeth *eb*
nominalist *adj* enwolaidd *ans*
nominalist *n* enwolwr *eg* enwolwyr
nominate enwebu *be*
nomination enwebiad *eg* enwebiadau
nominator enwebwr *eg* enwebwyr
nomogram nomogram *eg* nomogramau
non aggression pact cytundeb di-drais *eg* cytundebau di-drais
non aqueous annyfrllyd *ans*
non-accidental injury anaf annamweiniol *eg* anafiadau annamweiniol
non-adherence diffyg ymlyniad *eg*
nonagon nonagon *eg* nonagonau
non-aligned anymochrol *ans*
non-alignment anymochredd *eg*
non-basic ansylfaenol *ans*
non-biodegradable anfiodiraddadwy *ans*
non-calculator digyfrifiannell *ans*
non-calculator method dull digyfrifiannell *eg* dulliau digyfrifiannell
non-cellular anghellog *ans*
non-chronological writing
ysgrifennu anghronolegol *be*
non-classical anghlasurol *ans*
non-cognitive anwybyddol *ans*

nonconformist anghydffurfiwr *eg* anghydffurfwyr
nonconformity (in dissenting religion) ymneilltuaeth *eb*
nonconformity (in general) anghydffurfiaeth *eb*
non-contentious digynnen *ans*
non-contributory pension pensiwn anghyfrannol *eg* pensiynau anghyfrannol
non-corrosive anghyrydol *ans*
non-crystalline anghrisialog *ans*
non-cyclic photophosphorylation ffotoffosfforeiddiad anghylchol *eg*
nondecreasing anleihaol *ans*
non-denominational school ysgol anenwadol *eb* ysgolion anenwadol
non-destructive annistrywiol *ans*
non-destructive cursor cyrchwr annistrywiol *eg* cyrchwyr annistrywiol
non-diatonic anniatonig *ans*
nondiegetic sound sain anghynefin *eb*
non-directional anghyfeiriadol *ans*
non-directive play therapy therapi chwarae anghyfeiriol *eg*
non-disjunction anwahaniad *eg*
non-ecumene byd anghyfannedd *eg*
non-electrolyte anelectrolyt *eg* anelectrolytau
non-empty anwag *ans*
nonequilibrium anghydbwysedd *eg*
nonequivalent control group grŵp rheolydd anghywerth *eg* grwpiau rheolydd anghywerth
nones nonau *ell*
non-essential (of amino acid) dianghenraid *ans*
nonet noned *eb* nonedau
non-evolving anesblygol *ans*
non-excitable anghyffroadwy *ans*
non-existent nad yw'n bod *ans*
non-ferrous anfferrus *ans*
non-ferrous alloy aloi anfferrus *eg* aloion anfferrus
non-ferrous metal metel anfferrus *eg* metelau anfferrus
non-fiction ffeithiol *ans*
non-figurative work gwaith anffigurol *eg*
non-flammable anfflamadwy *ans*
non-flowering anflodeuol *ans*
non-flowering plant planhigyn anflodeuol *eg* planhigion anflodeuol
non-fluent (Broca's) aphasia affasia anhawster ynganu (Broca) *eg*
non-fraying gwrthraflog *ans*
non-government organisation sefydliad anllywodraethol *eg*
non-homologous anhomologaidd *ans*
non-homologue anhomolog *eg*
non-hydrous anhydrus *ans*
non-identical (of twins) heb fod yn unfath *ans*
non-impact printing argraffu di-draw *eg*
non-indictively wound dirwyniad an-anwythaidd *eg*
non-inflammable anfflamadwy *ans*
non-integrated anghyfannol *ans*
non-intervention anymyrraeth *eb*
non-inverting anwrthdroadol *ans*
non-ionic di-ïonig *ans*
non-iron (finish) dismwddio *ans*
non-judgemental yn peidio barnu *adf*
non-juror annhyngwr *eg* annhyngwyr
non-kicking foot troed segur *eb* traed segur
non-linear aflinol *ans*
non-linear function ffwythiant aflinol *eg* ffwythiannau aflinol
non-linear programming rhaglennu aflinol *be*
non-live vaccines brechlyn anfyw *eg*
non-living anfyw *ans*
non-luminous anoleuol *ans*
non-magnetic anfagnetig *ans*
non-manufactured goods nwyddau crai *ell*
non-maskable interrupt (NMI) ymyriad anghuddiadwy *eg* ymyriadau anghuddiadwy
non-metal anfetel *eg* anfetelau
non-metallic anfetelaidd *ans*
non-negative annegyddol *ans*
non-numeric anrhifaidd *ans*
non-ohmic anomig *ans*
non-paint finish gorffeniad heblaw paent *eg* gorffeniadau heblaw paent
non-parametric amharametrig *ans*
non-parametric statistic ystadegyn amharametrig *eg* ystadegau amharametrig
non-phosphoric anffosfforig *ans*
non-polar amholar *ans*
non-polar solvent hydoddydd amholar *eg* hydoddyddion amholar
non-porous difandwll *ans*
non-porous woods coed difandwll *ell*
non-positive drive gyriad amhositif *eg* gyriadau amhositif
non-procedural anhrefniadol *ans*
non-proliferation treaty cytundeb atal-lledaenu *eg* cytundebau atal-lledaenu
non-protein dibrotein *ans*
non-quantifiable anfesuradwy *ans*
non-reactive anadweithiol *ans*
non-reciprocal anghilyddol *ans*
non-relativistic amherthnaseddol *ans*
non-renewable anadnewyddadwy *ans*
non-renewable resource adnodd anadnewyddadwy *eg* adnoddau anadnewyddadwy
non-representational anghynrychiadol *ans*
non-resistance anwrthwynebiad *eg*
non-Roman anrhufeinig *ans*
non-scratch gwrthgrafiad *ans*
non-selective school ysgol annetholiadol *eb* ysgolion annetholiadol
nonsense syllable sillaf diystyr *eg* sillafau diystyr
non-separation anwahaniad *eg*
non-singular anhynod *ans*
non-singular matrix matrics anhynod *eg* matricsau anhynod

non-slip gwrth-lithr *ans*
non-slip rule riwl wrthslip *eb* riwliau gwrthslip
non-smudge di-staen *ans*
non-smudge crayon creon di-staen *eg* creonau di-staen
non-specialist anarbenigol *ans*
non-splitting hardwood pren caled nad yw'n hollti *eg*
non-statutory guidance canllawiau anstatudol *ell*
non-stick gwrthlud *ans*
non-stretch (finish) diymestyn *ans*
non-striker anergydiwr *eg* anergydwyr
non-systematic ansystematig *ans*
non-teaching staff staff nad ydynt yn addysgu *ell*
non-terminating annherfynus *ans*
non-terminating loop dolen annherfynus *eb*
non-toxic diwenwyn *ans*
non-toxic dye llifyn diogel *eg* llifynnau diogel
nontrivial annistadl *ans*
non-uniform anunffurf *ans*
nonuplet nawpled *eg* nawpledau
non-verbal communication cyfathrebu dieiriau *be*
non-viscous anludiog *ans*
non-vitreous anwydrog *ans*
non-volatile anehedol *ans*
non-volcanic anfolcanig *ans*
nonword / pseudoword ffugair *eg* ffugeiriau
non-zero ansero *ans*
non-zero acceleration cyflymiad ansero *eg*
noon canol dydd *eg*
NOR NIEU
NOR gate adwy NIEU *eb* adwyon NIEU
noradrenaline noradrenalin *eg*
Nordic Llychlynnaidd *ans*
Norfolk Crop Rotation Cylchdro Cnydau Norfolk *eg*
norm norm *eg* normau
normal *adj* normal *ans*
normal *n* normal *eg* normalau
normal construction adeiladwaith normal *eg*
normal curve cromlin normal *eb* cromliniau normal
▸ **normal distribution** gwasgariad normal *eg* gwasgariadau normal
normal goods nwyddau cyffredin *ell*
normal pitch pitsh normal *eg*
normal profit elw cyffredin *eg*
normal screwdriver tyrnsgriw cyffredin *eg* tyrnsgriwiau cyffredin
normal tidal limit terfyn arferol y llanw *eg* terfynau arferol y llanw
normalization normaleiddiad *eg*
normalize normaleiddio *be*
normalizer normalydd *eg* normalyddion
Norman *adj* Normanaidd *ans*
Norman (of person) *n* Norman *eg* Normaniaid
Norman castle castell Normanaidd *eg* cestyll Normanaidd
Norman conquest concwest Normanaidd *eb*
Norman-French *adj* Ffrengig Normanaidd *ans*
Norman-French (language) *n* Ffrangeg Normanaidd *eb*
Normanisation Normaneiddio *be*
normative development datblygiad normadol *eg*
normative ethics moeseg normadol *eb*
normed normedig *ans*
norm-referenced norm-gyfeiriol *ans*
norm-referenced assessment asesiad norm-gyfeiriol *eg* asesiadau norm-gyfeiriol
Norse *adj* Llychlynnaidd *ans*
Norse (language) *n* Norseg *eb*
Norseman Llychlynnwr *eg* Llychlynwyr
north gogledd *eg*
North Atlantic Drift Drifft Gogledd Iwerydd *eg*
North Atlantic Treaty Organization (NATO) Cyfundrefn Cytundeb Gogledd Iwerydd *eb*
north celestial pole pegwn wybrennol y gogledd *eg*
North German Confederation Cydffederasiwn Gogledd yr Almaen *eg*
north magnetic pole pôl magnetig y gogledd *eg*
north pole (geographic) pegwn y gogledd *eg*
north pole (of a magnet) pôl gogledd *eg*
north seeking pole (of a magnet) pôl sy'n cyrchu tua'r gogledd *eg*
North-East Passage Tramwyfa'r Gogledd-Ddwyrain *eb*
North-West Passage Tramwyfa'r Gogledd-Orllewin *eb*
northing gogleddiad *eg*
Norway spruce pyrwydden Norwy *eb* pyrwydd Norwy
nose trwyn *eg* trwynau
nose angle ongl drwyn *eb* onglau trwyn
nosing ymyl step *eb* ymylon stepiau
nostril ffroen *eb* ffroenau
NOT NID
NOT gate adwy NID *eb* adwyon NID
not in phase yn anghydweddu
not necessarily rights of way nid hawliau tramwy o angenrheidrwydd
not out ddim allan
not to scale heb fod wrth raddfa
not up (of lob) i lawr *adf*
NOT valve falf NID *eb* falfiau NID
nota cambiata nota cambiata *eg*
notary notari *eg* notarïaid
notate nodiannu *eg*
notation nodiant *eg* nodiannau
notch *v* rhicio *be*
notch (in blade) *n* bwlch *eg* bylchau
notch (in general) *n* rhic *eg* rhiciau
notch and strip bwlch a strip
notched bylchog *ans*
notched joint uniad bylchog *eg* uniadau bylchog
notched saw set gosodydd llif bylchog *eg* gosodyddion llif bylchog
note (=brief record) *n* nodyn *eg* nodiadau

note (=record) *v* nodi *be*
note (=take note) *v* sylwi *be*
note (in music) *n* nodyn *eg* nodau
note pad pad ysgrifennu *eg* padiau ysgrifennu
notebook nodiadur *eg* nodiaduron
notice (=announcement) hysbysiad *eg* hysbysiadau
notice (=warning) rhybudd *eg* rhybuddion
notice to quit rhybudd i adael *eg*
notice-board hysbysfwrdd *eg* hysbysfyrddau
notifiable disease clefyd hysbysadwy *eg* clefydau hysbysadwy
notification hysbysiad *eg*
notions (in sewing) gofynion ychwanegol *ell*
notochord notochord *eg*
no-touch technique techneg ddigyffwrdd *eb*
nought (=nothing) dim *eg*
nought (symbol) gwagnod *eg* gwagnodau
nourishing maethol *ans*
nourishment maeth *eg*
nova nofa *eg* nofâu
novel stimulus ysgogiad anghyfarwydd *eg*
novice nofis *eg* nofisiaid
noviciate tymor prawf *eg*
noxious trades masnach atgas *eb* masnachau atgas
nozzle ffroenell *eb* ffroenellau
NROVA: National Record of Vocational Achievement Cofnod Cenedlaethol Cyrhaeddiad Galwedigaethol *eg*
N-stage N-cam *eg*
N-terminal analysis dadansoddiad N-terfynol *eg*
nth nfed
nucellus niwcellws *eg*
nuclear niwclear *ans*
nuclear energy egni niwclear *eg*
nuclear envelope amlen gnewyllol *eb*
nuclear family teulu cnewyllol *eg* teuluoedd cnewyllol
nuclear fission ymholltiad niwclear *eg*
nuclear fusion ymasiad niwclear *eg*
nuclear magnetic resonance cyseiniant magnetig niwclear *eg*
nuclear magnetic resonance spectrum sbectrwm niwclear cyseiniant magnetig *eg*
nuclear mass màs niwclear *eg*
► **nuclear membrane** pilen gnewyllol *eb* pilenni cnewyllol
nuclear missile taflegryn niwclear *eg* taflegrau niwclear
nuclear power pŵer niwclear *eg*
nuclear power station atomfa *eb* atomfeydd
nuclear species math niwclear *eg*
Nuclear Test Ban Treaty Cytundeb Atal Profion Niwclear *eg*
nucleated (in biology) cnewyllol *ans*
nucleated (of atom) niwcledig *ans*
nucleated pattern patrwm cnewyllol *eg* patrymau cnewyllol
nucleated settlement anheddiad cnewyllol *eg* aneddiadau cnewyllol
nucleic acid asid niwclëig *eg*
nucleohistone niwcliohiston *eg*
nucleolar organiser meinwe patrymu'r cnewyllan *eg*
nucleolar organising region ardal meinwe patrymu'r cnewyllan *eb*
nucleolus cnewyllan *eg*
nucleon niwcleon *eg* niwcleonau
nucleophile *adj* niwclioffilig *ans*
nucleophile *n* niwclioffil *eg*
nucleophilic substitution amnewid niwclioffilig *be*
nucleoprotein niwclioprotein *eg*
nucleoside niwcliosid *eg*
nucleotide niwcliotid *eg*
nucleus (in biology) cnewyllyn *eg* cnewyll
nucleus (of an atom) niwclews *eg* niwclysau
nuclide niwclid *eg*
nude (=painting, sculpture etc of nude figure) noethlun *eg* noethluniau
nudging pwnio *be*
nuisance niwsans *eg*
null nwl *eg* nyliau
null & void di-rym *ans*
null character nylnod *eg* nylnodau
null hypothesis rhagdybiaeth nwl *eb* rhagdybiaethau nwl
null point nwlbwynt *eg* nwlbwyntiau
null pointer nylbwyntydd *eg* nylbwyntyddion
null result canlyniad nwl *eg* canlyniadau nwl
null set set wag *eb* setiau gwag
nullify dirymu *be*
numb dideimlad *ans*
number *v* rhifo *be*
number (=arithmetical value; word, symbol or figure representing this) *n* rhif *eg* rhifau
number (=total count or aggregate) *n* nifer *eg* niferoedd
number base bôn rhif *eg* bonau rhif
number coordinates cyfesurynnau rhifau *ell*
number generator generadur rhifau *eg* generaduron rhifau
number line llinell rif *eb* llinellau rhif
number of visits nifer yr ymweliadau *eg*
number on roll nifer ar y gofrestr *eg* niferoedd ar y gofrestr
number operations gweithrediadau rhif *ell*
number scale graddfa rif *eb* graddfeydd rhif
number sequence dilyniant rhif *eg*
number system system rifau *eb* systemau rhifau
number wheels olwynion rhif *ell*
number work gwaith rhif *eg*
numeracy rhifedd *eg*
numeral rhifolyn *eg* rhifolion
numerate rhifoli *be*
numeration cyfrifiad *eg* cyfrifiadau
numerator rhifiadur *eg* rhifiaduron
numeric rhifol *ans*

numeric control rheolaeth rifol *eb*
numeric keypad bysellbad rhifol *eg* bysellbadiau rhifol
numerical rhifiadol *ans*
numerical data data rhifiadol *ell*
numerical integration integru rhifiadol *be*
numerical modelling modelu rhifiadol *be*
numerical problem problem rifiadol *eb* problemau rhifiadol
numinous nwmenaidd *ans*
numismatics niwmismateg *eb*
nun lleian *eb* lleianod
nunatak nynatac *eg* nynatacau
nuncio cennad y Pab *eb* cenhadon y Pab
nunnery lleiandy *eg* lleiandai
nurse *n* nyrs *eb* nyrsys
nurse *v* nyrsio *be*
nursery meithrinfa *eb* meithrinfeydd
nursery assistant gweinyddes feithrin *eb* gweinyddesau meithrin
nursery class dosbarth meithrin *eg* dosbarthiadau meithrin
nursery education addysg feithrin *eb*
nursery nurse nyrs feithrin *eb* nyrsys meithrin
nursery rhyme hwiangerdd *eb* hwiangerddi
nursery school ysgol feithrin *eb* ysgolion meithrin
nursery supervisor goruchwyliwr y feithrinfa *eg*
nursing nyrsio *be*
nursing audit archwiliad nyrsio *eg* archwiliadau nyrsio
nursing auxiliary nyrs ategol *eb* nyrsys ategol
nursing care gofal nyrsio *eg*
nursing diagnosis diagnosis nyrsio *eg*
nursing home cartref nyrsio *eg* cartrefi nyrsio
nursing model model nyrsio *eg* modelau nyrsio
nursing officer swyddog nyrsio *eg* swyddogion nyrsio
nurture magwraeth *eb*
nurture group grŵp rhoi magwraeth *eg* grwpiau rhoi magwraeth
nurture theorist damcaniaethwr magwraeth *eg* damcaniaethwyr magwraeth
nut nyten *eb* nytiau
nut with nylon insert nyten â mewniad neilon *eb* nytiau â mewniad neilon
nut with rubber insert nyten â mewniad rwber *eb* nytiau â mewniad rwber
nut with sawn collar nyten â choler wedi'i llifio *eb* nytiau â choleri wedi'u llifio
nutate troelli *be*
nutation troelliad *eg* troelliadau
nutrient maetholyn *eg* maetholion
nutrient cycle cylchred faetholion *eb*
nutrient cycling cylchu maetholion *be*
nutrient jelly jeli meithrin *eg*
nutriment maeth *eg* maethion
nutrition (=mode of using food) maethiad *eg*
nutrition (in general) maeth *eg*
nutrition (science of) maetheg *eb*
nutritional maethol *ans*
nutritional analysis dadansoddiad maeth *eg*
nutritional composition cyfansoddiad maethion *eg*
nutritional content cynnwys maethol *eg*
nutritional needs anghenion maeth *ell*
nutritional value gwerth maethol *eg*
nutritious maethlon *ans*
nutritive maethol *ans*
nuts and bolts nytiau a bolltau
NVQ framework fframwaith CGC *eg*
NVQ: National Vocational Qualification CGC: Cymhwyster Galwedigaethol Cenedlaethol *eg* Cymwysterau Galwedigaethol Cenedlaethol
nyctinasty nyctinasedd *eg*
nylon neilon *eg*
Nylon (trade name) Nylon *eg*
nylon brush brwsh neilon *eg* brwshys neilon
nylon cutter torrell neilon *eb* torrellau neilon
nylon fishing line lein bysgota neilon *eb* leiniau pysgota neilon
nylon hinge colfach neilon *eg* colfachau neilon
nylon screw sgriw neilon *eb* sgriwiau neilon
nylon string tant neilon *eg* tannau neilon
nylon stud styden neilon *eb* stydiau neilon
nylon thread edau neilon *eb* edafedd neilon
nylon track trac neilon *eg* traciau neilon
nymph nymff *eb* nymffod

O

oak bark rhisgl derwen *eg*
oak gall afal derw *eg* afalau derw
oakum ocwm *eg*
oar rhwyf *eb* rhwyfau
oasis gwerddon *eb* gwerddonau
oatcakes bara ceirch *eg*
oath llw *eg* llwon
oath of allegiance llw teyrngarwch *eg* llwon teyrngarwch
oath of celibacy llw ymgadw'n ddibriod *eg*
oats ceirch *ell*
obedience ufudd-dod *eg*
obelisk obelisg *eg* obelisgau
obese gordew *ans*
obese people pobl ordew *eb*
obesity gordewdra *eg*
obey ufuddhau *be*
object gwrthrych *eg* gwrthrychau
object language nodiaith *eb* nodieithoedd
object menu dewislen gwrthrychau *eb* dewislenni gwrthrychau
object permanence sefydlogrwydd gwrthrych *eg*
object program nod-raglen *eb* nod-raglenni
objective (=something sought or aimed at) *n* amcan *eg* amcanion
objective (=uncoloured by feelings and opinions) *adj* gwrthrychol *ans*
objective (microscope) *n* gwrthrychiadur *eg* gwrthrychiaduron
objective art celfyddyd wrthrychol *eb*
objective function ffwythiant diben *eg*
objective judgement barn wrthrychol *eb* barnau gwrthrychol
▶ **objective lens** lens y gwrthrychiadur *eg* lensiau'r gwrthrychiadur
objective mirror drych y gwrthrychiadur *eg* drychau'r gwrthrychiadur
objective naturalism naturiolaeth wrthrychol *eb*
objective personality test prawf personoliaeth gwrthrychol *eg* profion personoliaeth gwrthrychol
objective question cwestiwn gwrthrychol *eg* cwestiynau gwrthrychol
objectivity gwrthrychedd *eg*
object-orientated programme rhaglen gwrthrych-gyfeiriadol *eb*
object-orientated programming rhaglennu gwrthrych-gyfeiriadol *be*
oblate (=person in religious order) *n* oblad *eg/b*
oblate (of spheroid, with feminine nouns) *adj* byrgron *ans*
oblate (of spheroid, with masculine nouns) *adj* byrgrwn *ans*
oblation offrwm *eg* offrymau
obligation rhwymedigaeth *eb* rhwymedigaethau
Obligations Court Cwrt Ymrwymiadau *eg*
oblique arosgo *ans*
oblique angle ongl arosgo *eb* onglau arosgo
oblique aspect agwedd arosgo *eb* agweddau arosgo
oblique axis echelin arosgo *eb* echelinau arosgo
oblique branch pipe peipen gangen arosgo *eb* peipiau cangen arosgo
oblique cylinder silindr arosgo *eg* silindrau arosgo
oblique line llinell arosgo *eb* llinellau arosgo
oblique nailing hoelio arosgo *be*
oblique photograph ffotograff arosgo *eg* ffotograffau arosgo
oblique plane plân arosgo *eg* planau arosgo
oblique prism prism arosgo *eg* prismau arosgo
oblique projection tafluniad arosgo *eg* tafluniadau arosgo
oblique reverse pen pen arosgo croes *eg* pennau arosgo croes
oblique section trychiad arosgo *eg* trychiadau arosgo
oblique stroke strôc arosgo *eb* strociau arosgo
oblique surface arwyneb arosgo *eg* arwynebau arosgo
oblique view golwg arosgo *eg* golygon arosgo
obliqueness arosgedd *eg*
obliquity (of rays) arosgedd *eg*
oblong *adj* petryal *ans*
oblong *n* petryal *eg* petryalau
oblong base sylfaen betryal *eb* sylfeini petryal
oblong palette palet petryal *eg* paletau petryal
oboe obo *eg* oboi
oboist oböydd *eg* oböwyr
obscurantism gwrtholeuaeth *eb*
obscurantist gwrtholeuwr *eg* gwrtholeuwyr
obscuration (in physics) amguddiad *eg* amguddiadau
obscure (of meaning) tywyll *ans*
obsequent *adj* gwrthlif *ans*
obsequent *n* gwrthlif *eg* gwrthlifau
obsequent stream ffrwd wrthlif *eb* ffrydiau gwrthlif
observable arsylladwy *ans*
Observant Cadwrydd *eg* Cadwryddion
observation arsylwi *be*
observation (=comment) sylw *eg* sylwadau
observation (technical usage) arsylw *eg* arsylwadau

observation skill sgìl arsylwi *eg* sgiliau arsylwi
observation technique techneg arsylwi *eb* technegau arsylwi
observational learning dysgu trwy arsylwi *be*
observational method dull arsylwi *eg* dulliau arsylwi
observational research ymchwil arsylwadol *eg*
observational skill sgìl arsylwi *eg* sgiliau arsylwi
observation-treatment-observation arsylwi-triniaeth-arsylwi *be*
observatory arsyllfa *eb* arsyllfeydd
observe (by telescope /microscope) arsyllu *be*
observe (non-technical usage) sylwi *be*
observe (technical usage) arsylwi *be*
observe phenomena arsylwi ffenomenau *be*
observed dan sylw *ans*
observed forms ffurfiau dan sylw *ell*
observed objects gwrthrychau dan sylw *ell*
observer (non-technical usage) gwyliwr *eg* gwylwyr
observer (technical usage) arsylwr *eg* arsylwyr
obsession obsesiwn *eg* obsesiynau
obsessive compulsive disorder anhwylder gorfodaeth obsesiynol *eg*
obsidian gwydrfaen *eg*
obsolete anarferedig *ans*
obstacle rhwystr *eg* rhwystrau
obstacle race ras rwystrau *eb* rasys rhwystrau
obstetrician obstetregydd *eg* obstetregwyr
obstetrics obstetreg *eb*
obstructing the field rhwystro'r maeswyr *be*
obstruction rhwystr *eg* rhwystrau
obtain (in physics etc) darganfod *be*
obtain evidence dod o hyd i dystiolaeth *be*
obtain measurements dod o hyd i fesuriadau *be*
obtuse (with feminine nouns) aflem *ans*
obtuse (with masculine nouns) aflym *ans*
obtuse angle ongl aflem *eb* onglau aflym
obtuse angled triangle triongl ongl aflem *eg* trionglau onglau aflym
ocarina ocarina *eg* ocarinâu
occasional conformity cydymffurfio achlysurol *be*
Occasional Conformity Act Deddf Cydymffurfio Achlysurol *eb*
occasional holidays gwyliau achlysurol *ell*
occasional music cerddoriaeth achlysurol *eb*
occasional stream ffrwd ysbeidiol *eb* ffrydiau ysbeidiol
occasional table bwrdd achlysurol *eg* byrddau achlysurol
occipital lobe llabed yr ocsipwt *eb* llabedau'r ocsipwt
occluded achludol *ans*
occluded front ffrynt achludol *eg* ffryntiau achludol
occlusion achludiad *eg* achludiadau
occulation arguddiad *eg* arguddiadau
occult cudd *ans*
occupation (=job) galwedigaeth *eb* galwedigaethau
occupation (military) meddiannaeth *eb*
occupation (of property) meddiannaeth *eb*
occupation number rhif meddiannaeth *eg*
occupational galwedigaethol *ans*
occupational field maes galwedigaethol *eg* meysydd galwedigaethol
occupational health iechyd galwedigaethol *eg*
occupational programme rhaglen alwedigaethol *eb* rhaglenni galwedigaethol
occupational therapist therapydd galwedigaethol *eg* therapyddion galwedigaethol
occupational therapy therapi galwedigaethol *eg*
occupied territory tiriogaeth feddianedig *eb*
occupier preswyliwr *eg* preswylwyr
occupy (in ecology) anheddu *be*
occupy (of military force) meddiannu *be*
occupying forces lluoedd y meddiannu *ell*
ocean cefnfor *eg* cefnforoedd
oceanic cefnforol *ans*
oceanography eigioneg *eb*
ocellus ocelws *eg* oceli
ochre ocr *eg* ocrau
octadecanoic acid asid octadecanöig *eg*
octagon octagon *eg* octagonau
octagonal wythonglog *ans*
octagonal bar bar wythonglog *eg* barrau wythonglog
octagonal table bwrdd wythonglog *eg* byrddau wythonglog
octahedron octahedron *eg* octahedronau
octal wythol *ans*
octal buffer byffer wythol *eg* byfferau wythol
octal notation nodiant wythol *eg*
octal system system wythol *eb* systemau wythol
octant octant *eg* octannau
octave wythfed *eg* wythfedau
octave step cam wythfed *eg* camau wythfed
octet wythawd *eg* wythawdau
octuplet wythpled *eg* wythpledi
ocular *adj* llygadol *ans*
ocular *n* ocwlar *eg* ocwlarau
odd function od-ffwythiant *eg*
odd leg callipers caliperau jenni *ell*
odd number odrif *eg* odrifau
odd parity odbaredd *eg*
odd side ochr od *eb* ochrau od
odd side pattern patrwm ochr od *eg* patrymau ochr od
oddments pethau dros ben *ell*
odd-parity check prawf odbaredd *eg* profion odbaredd
odds and ends tameidiau *ell*
ode (in free metre) cerdd *eb* cerddi
ode (in strict metre) awdl *eb* awdlau
odontoid process cnepyn deintffurf *eg* cnepynnau deintffurf
odour arogl *eg* aroglau
odourless diarogl *ans*
odourous aroglus *ans*
odour-resistant (finish) gwrtharogl *ans*
oedema oedema *eg*

Oedipus complex cymhleth Oedipws *eg*
oesophagus oesoffagws *eg*
oestrogen oestrogen *eg* oestrogenau
▸ **oestrous cycle** cylchred oestrws *eb*
oestrus oestrws *eg*
Of Noble Race was Shenkin
O Uchel Dras oedd Siencyn
Ofcom Office of (Communications) Ofcom *eg*
off (of light, fire, gas) wedi'i ddiffodd *ans*
wedi'u diffodd
off (of switch) i ffwrdd
off balance colli cydbwysedd *be*
off centre allan o'r canol
off drive dreif ochr agored *eb* dreifiau ochr agored
off licence siop drwyddedig *eb* siopau trwyddedig
off side ochr agored *eb*
off stump stwmp pellaf *eg* stympiau pellaf
off the school site oddi ar safle'r ysgol *adf*
Offa's Dyke Clawdd Offa *eg*
off-break bowling troelliad ochr agored *eg*
troelliadau ochr agored
off-cut torbren *eg* torbrennau
offence (civil) tramgwydd *eg* tramgwyddau
offence (criminal) trosedd *eg/b* troseddau
offences against the person
troseddau yn erbyn person *ell*
Offences Against the Person Act
Deddf Troseddau yn Erbyn Person *eb*
offender profiling proffilio troseddwyr *be*
offensive (=attack) *n* ymosodiad *eg* ymosodiadau
offensive (=attacking) *adj* ymosodol *ans*
offer cynnig *eg*
offer explanations cynnig esboniadau *be*
offering *n* offrwm *eg* offrymau
offertory (in music) offrymgan *eb* offrymganeuon
offertory (of church service) offrwm *eg* offrymau
off-hand grinder peiriant llifanu yn y llaw *eg*
peiriannau llifanu yn y llaw
off-hand grinding llifanu yn y llaw *be*
office (=post) swydd *eb* swyddi
office (of place) swyddfa *eb* swyddfeydd
office automation awtomeiddio swyddfa *eg*
office bar bar swyddfa *eg* barrau swyddfa
Office for Standards in Education (OFSTED)
Swyddfa Safonau mewn Addysg *eb*
Office of Fair Trading Swyddfa Masnachu Teg *eb*
Office of Her Majesty's Chief Inspector (OHMCI)
Swyddfa Prif Arolygydd ei Mawrhydi *eb*
office toolbar bar offer swyddfa *eg*
barrau offer swyddfa
office-holding swydd-ddaliad *eg*
officer swyddog *eg* swyddogion
Officer of the Royal Court Swyddog Llys y Brenin *eg*
official *adj* swyddogol *ans*
official *n* swyddog *eg* swyddogion
official opening agoriad swyddogol *eg*
agoriadau swyddogol

Official Secrets Act
Deddf Cyfrinachau Swyddogol *eb*
official statistics ystadegau swyddogol *ell*
off-line all-lein *ans*
off-line editing golygu all-lein *be*
off-line processing prosesu all-lein *be*
off-peak allfrig *ans*
offset *n* atred *eg* atredau
offset *v* ongli *be*
offset (against tax etc) gosod yn erbyn *be*
offset jaw spanner sbaner â safn atred *eg*
sbaneri â safn atred
offset peg peg atred *eg*
offset print printiad offset *eg* printiadau offset
offset printing argraffu offset *be*
offset roller rholer atred *eg* rholeri atred
offset screwdriver tyrnsgriw atred *eg*
tyrnsgriwiau atred
off-setting screw (lathe part) sgriw atredu *eb*
sgriwiau atredu
offshoot cangen *eb* canghennau
offshore (e.g. wind, bar) alltraeth *ans*
offside camsefyll *be*
offsite work gwaith oddi ar y safle *eg*
offspring epil *ell*
off-the-job training
hyfforddiant i ffwrdd o'r gwaith *eg*
ogee ogee *eg*
ogee arch bwa ogee *eg* bwâu ogee
ogee moulding mowldin ogee *eg* mowldinau ogee
ogee plane plaen ogee *eg* plaeniau ogee
ogham ogam *eg*
ogham characters llythrennau ogam *ell*
ogham stone maen ogam *eg* meini ogam
ogive ogif *eg* ogifau
ohm ohm *eg* ohmau
ohmeter ohmedr *eg* ohmedrau
Ohm's law deddf Ohm *eb*
oil *n* olew *eg* olewau
oil *v* iro *be*
oil based sail olew *ans*
oil based colour lliw sail olew *eg* lliwiau sail olew
oil based paint paent sail olew *eg* paentiau sail olew
oil blacking duo ag olew *be*
oil bluing glasu ag olew *be*
oil can can olew *eg* caniau olew
oil colour lliw olew *eg* lliwiau olew
oil crayon creon olew *eg* creonau olew
oil finish gorffeniad olew *eg* gorffeniadau olew
oil groove rhigol olew *eb* rhigolau olew
oil hardening olew galedu *be*
oil hole twll olew *eg* tyllau olew
oil nipple nipl olew *eg* niplau olew
oil of turpentine olew tyrpant *eg*
oil painting (of painted picture) paentiad olew *eg*
paentiadau olew
oil painting (of process or art) peintio olew *be*

oil palm kernels cnewyll palmwydd olew *ell*
oil paper papur olew *eg*
oil pastel pastel olew *eg* pasteli olew
oil reservoir cronfa olew *eb* cronfeydd olew
oil rig llwyfan olew *eg* llwyfannau olew
oil seed rape olew had rêp *eg*
oil stain staen olew *eg* staeniau olew
oil stencil paper papur olew stensil *eg*
oil well ffynnon olew *eb* ffynhonnau olew
oil-bearing rocks creigiau dal olew *ell*
oilfield maes olew *eg* meysydd olew
oil-immersion objective gwrthrychiadur mewn olew *eg*
oilproof gwrtholew *ans*
oilproof paper papur gwrtholew *eg*
oils and fats olewau a brasterau
oilseed hadau olew *ell*
oilstone carreg hogi *eb* cerrig hogi
oilstone slip carreg hogi gau *eb* cerrig hogi gau
oily olewog *ans*
ointment eli *eg* eliïau
old age henaint *eg*
old age pension pensiwn henoed *eg*
Old Age Pensions Act Deddf Pensiwn yr Henoed *eb*
old and infirm hen a methedig *ans*
Old Norse Hen Norseg *eb*
old people's home cartref henoed *eg* cartrefi henoed
old regime hen oruchwyliaeth *eb*
Old Stone Age Hen Oes y Cerrig *eb*
Old Testament Hen Destament *eg*
Old Testament prophetic literature llenyddiaeth broffwydol yr Hen Destament *eb*
Old World Yr Hen Fyd *eg*
older client cleient hŷn *eg* cleientiaid hŷn
oleaginous olewog *ans*
oleic acid asid olëig *eg*
▶ **oleum** olëwm *eg*
olfaction arogli *be*
olfactory arogleuol *ans*
olfactory bulb bwlb arogli *eg* bylbiau arogli
▶ **olfactory lobe** llabed arogli *eb* llabedau arogli
olfactory mucosa mwcosa arogli *eg*
oligarchy oligarchiaeth *eb*
oligopolistic market marchnad oligopolaidd *eb*
oligopoly oligopoli *eg* oligopoliïau
oligopsony oligopsoni *eg*
olive (of tree) olewydden *eb* olewydd
olive green (enamelling colour) gwyrdd olewydd *eg*
olive oil olew olewydd *eg*
Olympic Games Gemau Olympaidd *ell*
omasum omaswm *eg*
ombudsman ombwdsmon *eg* ombwdsmyn
ommatidium omatidiwm *eg* omatidia
omnipotent hollalluog *ans*
omnivore hollysydd *eg* hollysyddion
omnivorous hollysol *ans*
OMR form ffurflen DMG *eb* ffurflenni DMG
OMR: optical mark reader DMG: darllenydd marciau gweladwy *eg* darllenwyr marciau gweladwy
on (of light, fire, gas) ynghynn *ans*
on (of switch) ymlaen *adf*
on all pages ar bob tudalen
on average ar gyfartaledd *ans*
on drive dreif ochr goes *ç*
on even pages ar dudalennau eilrif
on heat (of bitch) cwnna *be*
on heat (of cow etc) gwasod *ans*
on odd pages ar dudalennau odrif
on position safle ymlaen *eg* safleoedd ymlaen
on probation ar brawf
on request ar gais
on screen encyclopaedia gwyddoniadur sgrin *eg* gwyddoniaduron sgrin
on side ochr goes *eb*
on the back ar y cefn *adf*
on the floor ar y llawr *adf*
on the front ar y tu blaen *adf*
on the rebound ar adlam *adf*
on the school site ar safle'r ysgol *adf*
on the wing ar yr ystlys *adf*
on toes ar flaenau'r traed *adf*
on your marks ar eich marciau
oncologist oncolegydd *eg* oncolegwyr
oncology oncoleg *eb*
one complete rotation un cylchdro cyflawn *eg*
one decimal place un lle degol
one minute gun ergyd munud *eb*
one parent family teulu un rhiant *eg* teuluoedd un rhiant
one piece pattern patrwm undarn *eg* patrymau undarn
one quarter chwarter *eg*
one religion worship addoliad un grefydd *eg*
one-brush stroke strôc brwsh un-strôc *eb* strociau brwsh un-strôc
one-eighth wythfed *eg*
one-fifth pumed *eg*
one-handed pass pàs unllaw *eb* pasiau unllaw
one-many correspondence cyfatebiaeth un-i-lawer *eb*
one-ninth nawfed *eg*
one-off mae angen un
one-one correspondence cyfatebiaeth un-i-un *eb*
one-pass system system unffordd *eb* systemau unffordd
one-piece development datblygiad undarn *eg* datblygiadau undarn
one's complement cyflenwad unol *eg*
one-seventh seithfed *eg*
one-side unochrol *ans*
one-sixth chweched *eg*
one-stroke brush brwsh un-strôc *eg* brwshys un-strôc
one-tailed test prawf ungynffon *eg* profion ungynffon

one-tenth degfed *eg*
one-third traean *eg* traeanau
one-to-one un-i-un
one-way classification dosbarthiad unffordd *eg* dosbarthiadau unffordd
one-way list rhestr unffordd *eb* rhestri unffordd
one-way street stryd unffordd *eb* strydoedd unffordd
onion nionyn *eg* nionod; winwnsyn *eg* winwns
on-line ar-lein *ans*
on-line access (through the internet) mynediad ar-lein *eg*
on-line facilities cyfleusterau ar-lein *ell*
on-line processing prosesu ar-lein *be*
on-line service provider darparwr gwasanaeth ar-lein *eg* darparwyr gwasanaeth ar-lein
on-line system system ar-lein *eb* systemau ar-lein
on-looking play (in child psychology) gwylio chwarae *be*
on-screen assistance cymorth sgrin *eg*
on-screen menu dewislen sgrin *eb* dewislenni sgrin
onset side of ice ochr atrew *eb* ochrau atrew
onshore atraeth *ans*
onside iawnochri *be*
on-the-job training hyfforddiant wrth y gwaith *eg*
on-the-spot dance dawns unfan *eb* dawnsiau unfan
onto function ffwythiant ar *eg*
onyx onics *eg*
oocyst oocyst *eg* oocystau
oocyt oocyt *eg*
oogamete oogamet *eg* oogametau
oogamous oogamus *ans*
oogamy oogamedd *eg*
oogenesis oogenesis *eg*
oogonium oogoniwm *eg*
oolitic oolitig *ans*
oology ooleg *eb*
oophore ooffor *eg* oofforau
oophyte ooffyt *eg* ooffytau
ooplast ooplast *eg*
OOPS (Object Orientated Programming System) OOPS *eb*
oosperm oosberm *eg* oosbermau
oosphere oosffer *eg* oosfferau
oosporangium oosborangiwm *eg* oosborangia
oospore oosbor *eg* oosborau
ootype ootyp *eg* ootypau
oozes (deep sea) morlaid *eg*
opacifier didreiddydd *eg* didreiddyddion
opacity didreiddedd *eg*
opalescent symudliw *ans*
opalescent enamel enamel symudliw *eg*
opaque di-draidd *ans*
opaque colour lliw di-draidd *eg* lliwiau di-draidd
opaque enamel enamel di-draidd *eg*
opaque glaze gwydredd di-draidd *eg*
opaque paste past di-draidd *eg*
open *adj* agored *ans*
open *v* agor *be*
open access mynediad agored *eg*
open adoption mabwysiadu agored *be*
open air awyr agored *eg*
open both ways agor y naill ffordd a'r llall *be*
open chain stitch pwyth cadwyn agored *eg* pwythau cadwyn agored
open cheque siec agored *eb* sieciau agored
open circulation cylchrediad agored *eg*
open clusters clystyrau agored *ell*
Open College Coleg Agored *eg*
open day diwrnod agored *eg* diwrnodau agored
open diapason diapason agored *eg* diapasonau agored
open eaves bondo agored *eg* bondoeau agored
open examination arholiad agored *eg* arholiadau agored
open factor ffactor agored *eb*
open field system cyfundrefn maes agored *eb* cyfundrefnau maes agored
open file agor ffeil *be*
open flat tongs gefel fflat agored *eb* gefeiliau fflat agored
open glove maneg agored *eb* menig agored
open grain graen agored *eg*
open hearth tân agored *eg* tanau agored
open interval cyfwng agored *eg* cyfyngau agored
open inwards and outwards agor tuag i mewn ac allan
open learning dysgu agored *be*
open market operations gweithrediadau marchnad agored *ell*
open merge-data-file agor ffeil ddata gyfun *be*
open note nodyn agored *eg* nodau agored
open pack pecyn agored *eg* pecynnau agored
open pipe (in music) pib agored *eb* pibau agored
open plan school ysgol cynllun agored *eb* ysgolion cynllun agored
open punctuation atalnodi agored *be*
open question cwestiwn agored *eg* cwestiynau agored
open score sgôr agored *eb* sgorau agored
open seam sêm agored *eb* semau agored
open side wing forward blaenasgell agored *eb*
open source cod agored *eg*
open staircase grisiau agored *ell*
open stance safiad agored *eg*
open string tant agored *eg* tannau agored
open system cyfundrefn agored *eb* cyfundrefnau agored
open texture gwead agored *eg*
open the bowling agor y bowlio *be*
open the tap agor y tap *be*
open traverse tramwy agored *eg*
Open University Prifysgol Agored *eb*
open web location agor lleoliad gwe *be*
opencast coal mining cloddio glo brig *be*
opencast coat glo brig *eg*

open-door policy polisi drws agored *eg*
open-end spanner sbaner ceg agored *eg* sbaneri ceg agored
open-ended question cwestiwn penagored *eg* cwestiynau penagored
openfield maes agored *eg* meysydd agored
openfield system trefn meysydd agored *eb*
open-flame kiln odyn fflam agored *eb* odynnau fflam agored
open-hearth furnace ffwrnais dân agored *eb* ffwrneisi tân agored
opening *adj* agoriadol *ans*
opening *n* agoriad *eg* agoriadau
opening balance balans agoriadol *eg*
opening stock stoc agoriadol *eb*
open-mouth tongs gefel gegagored *eb* gefeiliau cegagored
openness (=frankness) didwylledd *eg*
open-source operating system system weithredu cod agored *eb*
opera opera *eb* operâu
opéra buffe opéra buffe *eb* opéras bouffes
opera house tŷ opera *eg* tai opera
opera seria opera seria *eb* opere serie
opéra-ballet opéra-ballet *eg* opéras-ballet
opéra-comique opéra-comique *eb* opéras-comique
operand operand *eg* operandau
operant chamber siambr weithredol *eb* siambrau gweithredol
operant conditioning cyflyru gweithredol *be*
opera-oratorio opera-oratorio *eb* operâu-oratorio
operate gweithredu *be*
operating characteristic function ffwythiant nodwedd weithredol *eg*
operating system system weithredu *eb* systemau gweithredu
operating system software meddalwedd system weithredu *eb*
operation gweithrediad *eg* gweithrediadau
operation (military) ymgyrch *eb* ymgyrchoedd
operation (surgical) llawdriniaeth *eb* llawdriniaethau
operation code (op code) cod gweithredu *eg* codau gweithredu
operation mode modd gweithredu *eg* moddau gweithredu
operation of number gweithrediad rhif *eg*
operation table tabl gweithrediad *eg* tablau gweithrediad
operational (in economics) hywaith *ans*
operational (in general) gweithredol *ans*
operational area maes gweithredu *eg*
operational definition diffiniad gweithredol *eg* diffiniadau gweithredol
operational efficiency effeithlonrwydd gweithredol *eg*
operations manager rheolwr gweithrediadau *eg* rheolwyr gweithrediadau
operations of combination plane gweithrediadau'r plaen amlddefnydd *ell*
operative (in economics) gweithiol *ans*
operator (of person) gweithredwr *eg* gweithredwyr
operator (of symbol or function) gweithredydd *eg* gweithredyddion
operculum opercwlwm *eg* opercwla
operetta opereta *eb* operetau
operon operon *eg* operonau
ophthalmologist offthalmolegydd *eg* offthalmolegwyr
ophthalmology offthalmoleg *eb*
opinion barn *eb*
opinion poll arolwg barn *eg* arolygon barn
opioid opioid *eg* opioidau
opponent gwrthwynebwr *eg* gwrthwynebwyr
opponent process proses wrthwyneb *eb* prosesau gwrthwyneb
opportunism oportiwnistiaeth *eb*
opportunist oportiwnydd *eg* oportiwnwyr
opportunity cyfle *eg* cyfleoedd
opportunity cost cost cyfle *eb*
opposing gwrthwynebol *ans*
opposite (=contrary) *n* gwrthwyneb *eg*
opposite (=diametrically different) *adj* dirgroes *ans*
opposite (=facing) *adj* cyferbyn *ans*
opposite angle ongl gyferbyn *eb* onglau cyferbyn
opposite angles onglau cyferbyn *ell*
opposite bud blaguryn cyferbyn *eg* blagur cyferbyn
opposite direction cyfeiriad dirgroes *eg* cyfeiriadau dirgroes
opposite sides ochrau cyferbyn *ell*
opposite signs arwyddion dirgroes *ell*
opposition gwrthwynebiad *eg* gwrthwynebiadau
opposition (party) gwrthblaid *eb* gwrthbleidiau
oppress gormesu *be*
oppression gormes *eg/b*
oppressive gormesol *ans*
oppressor gormeswr *eg* gormeswyr
opt out eithrio *be*
opted out school ysgol sydd wedi eithrio *eb* ysgolion sydd wedi eithrio
optic chiasma ciasma optig *eg*
optic disk disg optig *eg* disgiau optig
optic lobe llabed optig *eb* llabedau optig
optic nerve nerf optig *eg* nerfau optig
optical optegol *ans*
optical activity actifedd optegol *eg*
optical angle ongl weledol *eb* onglau gweledol
optical art celfyddyd optegol *eb*
optical brightener disgleirydd optegol *eg* disgleiryddion optegol
optical character recognition (OCR) adnabod nodau gweledol *be*
optical compound microscope microsgop cyfansawdd optegol *eg*
optical disc disg optegol *eb* disgiau optegol
optical fibre ffibr optegol *eg* ffibrau optegol
optical illusion rhith optegol *eg* rhithiau optegol
optical isomer isomer optegol *eg* isomerau optegol

optical pyrometer pyromedr optegol *eg* pyromedrau optegol
optical square sgwâr optegol *eg* sgwariau optegol
optical system system optegol *eb* systemau optegol
optical white gwyn optegol *ans*
optician optegydd *eg* optegwyrr
optics opteg *eb*
optimal optimaidd *ans*
optimal level of skill performance perfformiad sgìl lefel optimaidd *eg* perfformiadau sgìl lefel optimaidd
optimal performance perfformiad optimaidd *eg*
optimism optimistiaeth *eb*
optimization optimeiddiaeth *eg*
optimize optimeiddio *be*
optimizer optimeiddiwr *eg* optimeiddwyr
optimizing compiler crynhoydd optimeiddio *eg* crynoyddion optimeiddio
optimum optimwm *eg* optima
optimum population poblogaeth optimwm *eb* poblogaethau optimwm
optimum-level hypothesis rhagdybiaeth lefel optimwm *eb*
option dewis *eg* dewisiadau
option mortgage morgais dewisol *eg* morgeisi dewisol
Option Mortgage Scheme Cynllun Morgais Dewisol *eg*
optional dewisol *ans*
opus opws *eg*
OR NEU
OR gate adwy NEU *eb* adwyon NEU
oracle oracl *eg*
oracy llefaredd *eg*
oral arithmetic rhifyddeg lafar *eb*
oral assessment asesu llafar *be*
oral description disgrifiad llafar *eg* disgrifiadau llafar
oral hygiene hylendid genau *eg*
oral infection haint trwy'r genau *eb*
oral report adroddiad llafar *eg* adroddiadau llafar
oral stage cyfnod y genau *eg*
oral surgeon llawfeddyg y geg *eg* llawfeddygon y geg
oral surgery llawfeddygaeth y geg *eb*
oral test prawf llafar *eg* profion llafar
oral toilet glanhau'r geg *be*
oral tradition traddodiad llafar *eg* traddodiadau llafar
oral vaccine brechlyn trwy'r genau *eg* brechlynnau trwy'r genau
oral vocabulary geirfa lafar *eb*
Orange Order Urdd Oren *eb*
orange red (vermilion) coch oren *eg*
orange shellac sielac oren *eg*
Orangeman Orenwr *eg* Orenwyr
oratorio oratorio *eb* oratorios
Oratory of Divine Love Oratori'r Cariad Dwyfol *eg*
orbit (of planets, satellite) *v* troi o gwmpas *be*
orbit (of planets, satellites) *n* orbit *eg* orbitau
orbit (of the eye) *n* crau'r llygad *eg*
orbital (of electron) *adj* orbitol *ans*
orbital (of electrons) *n* orbital *eg* orbitalau
orbital (of eye socket) *adj* creuol *ans*
orbital sander sandiwr orbitol *eg* sandwyr orbitol
orbital sinus sinws creuol *eg* sinysau creuol
orbitofrontal cortex cortecs craudalcennol *eg*
orchard perllan *eb* perllannau
orchestra cerddorfa *eb* cerddorfeydd
orchestral cerddorfaol *ans*
orchestral music cerddoriaeth gerddorfaol *eb*
orchestrate sgorio *be*
orchestration trefniant cerddorfaol *eg* trefniannau cerddorfaol
orchestrator sgoriwr *eg* sgorwyr
ordain ordeinio *be*
ordeal (=ancient test of guilt) diheurbrawf *eg* diheurbrofion
ordeal by fire diheurbrawf tân *eg*
ordeal by water diheurbrawf dŵr *eg*
order *n* gradd *eb* graddau
order (=body) *n* urdd *eb* urddau
order (=command) *n* gorchymyn *eg* gorchmynion
order (=place in sequence) *v* trefnu *be*
order (=sequence) *n* trefn *eb*
order (=something asked for) *n* archeb *eb* archebion
order of magnitude trefn maint *eb*
Order of the Day Trefn y Dydd *eb*
Order of the Garter Urdd y Gardys *eb*
order of work trefn gwaith *eb*
order statistics ystadegau trefn *ell*
ordered trefnedig *ans*
ordered list rhestr drefnedig *eb* rhestri trefnedig
ordered pairs parau trefnedig *ell*
Orders in Council Gorchmynion y Cyfrin Gyngor *ell*
orders of rotational symmetry trefnau cymesuredd cylchdro *ell*
ordinal trefnol *ans*
ordinal number rhif trefnol *eg* rhifau trefnol
ordinal scale graddfa drefnol *eb*
ordinance ordinhad *eg* ordinhadau
ordinary (=bishop) esgob *eg* esgobion
ordinary (=part of service) ordinari *eg*
ordinary truss cwpl cyffredin *eg* cyplau cyffredin
ordinate mesuryn *eg* mesurynnau
ordination ordeinio *be*
ordnance ordnans *eg*
Ordnance Bench Mark (OBM) Meincnod Ordnans *eg*
ordnance datum seilnod ordnans *eg* seilnodau ordnans
Ordnance Survey Arolwg Ordnans *eg*
Ordnance Survey map map Ordnans *eg*
Ordovician Ordoficaidd *ans*
ore mwyn *eg* mwynau
ore carrier mwynlong *eb* mwynlongau
organ (=musical instrument) organ *eb* organau
organ (of the body) organ *eg* organau
organ bellows megin organ *eb* meginau organ

organ console consol organ *eg* consolau organ
organ loft llofft organ *eb* llofftydd organ
organ mass offeren organ *eb* offerennau organ
organ of administration corff gweinyddol *eg* cyrff gweinyddol
organ of Corti organ Corti *eg* organau Corti
organ of government corff llywodraeth *eg* cyrff llywodraeth
organ sound board seinfwrdd organ *eg* seinfyrddau organ
organ transplantation (an instance of) trawsblaniad organ *eg* trawsblaniadau organ
organ transplantation (in general) trawsblannu organau *be*
organ wind chest cist wynt organ *eb* cistiau gwynt organ
organdie organdi *eg*
organelle organyn *eg* organynnau
organic organig *ans*
organic compound cyfansoddyn organig *eg* cyfansoddion organig
organic matter defnydd organig *eg* defnyddiau organig
organisational/occupational psychology seicoleg gyfundrefnol/alwedigaethol *eb*
organism organeb *eb* organebau
organist organydd *eg* organyddion
organization (=company) corff *eg* cyrff
organization (=society) mudiad *eg* mudiadau
organization (=system) cyfundrefn *eb* cyfundrefnau
organization (=systematic arrangement) trefniadaeth *eb*
organization chart siart trefniadaeth *eg* siartiau trefniadaeth
organization chart siart rheoli *eg* siartiau rheoli
Organization of Africa Unity Cyfundrefn Undod Affrica *eb*
Organization of American States Cyfundrefn Gwledydd America *eb*
organization structure strwythur trefniadaeth *eg*
organizational trefniadaethol *ans*
organizational chart siart trefniadaeth *eg* siartiau trefniadaeth
organizational effect effaith drefnu *eb*
organizational skills sgiliau trefnu *ell*
organize trefnu *be*
organize sounds trefnu seiniau *be*
organizer (of living tissue) meinwe patrymu *eb* meinweoedd patrymu
organizer (of person) trefnydd *eg* trefnyddion
organohalogen compounds cyfansoddion organohalogen *ell*
organum organwm *eg*
organza organsa *eg*
Orient, The Dwyrain, Y *eg*
orientated cyfeiriedig *ans*
orientation gogwydd *eg*
orientation cyfeiriadaeth *eg*
orienteering cyfeiriannu *be*
orienting response ymateb cyfeiriadol *eb* ymatebion cyfeiriadol
orifice agorfa *eb* agorfeydd
origin tarddiad *eg* tarddiadau
origin lleolbwynt *eg* lleolbwyntiau
origin (of graph) tarddbwynt *eg* tarddbwyntiau
origin myth myth tarddiad *eg*
origin of stars tarddiad sêr *eg*
origin of the universe dechreuad y bydysawd *eg*
original (in general) gwreiddiol *ans*
original (in serialism) sylfaenol *ans*
original cost cost wreiddiol *eb* costau gwreiddiol
original data data gwreiddiol *ell*
original design (of plan) cynllun gwreiddiol *eg* cynlluniau gwreiddiol
original design (of sketch etc) dyluniad gwreiddiol *eg* dyluniadau gwreiddiol
original equipment manufacturer (OEM) cynhyrchydd offer gwreiddiol *eg* cynhyrchwyr offer gwreiddiol
original place lle gwreiddiol *eg* lleoedd gwreiddiol
original shape ffurf wreiddiol *eb* ffurfiau gwreiddiol
originate tarddu *be*
originating web site gwefan wreiddiol *eb*
ornament addurn *eg* addurniadau
ornamental addurnol *ans*
ornamental hinge colfach addurniadol *eg* colfachau addurniadol
ornamentation addurniad *eg* addurniadau
ornate addurnol *ans*
orogenesis orogenesis *eg*
orogenetic orogenetig *ans*
orogeny orogeni *eg*
orographic orograffig *ans*
orographical orograffigol *ans*
orthininine orthinin *eg*
orthocentre orthograidd *eg* orthogreiddiau
orthodontics orthodonteg *eb*
orthodontist orthodeintydd *eg* orthodeintyddion
orthodox uniongred *ans*
Orthodox Jew Iddew Uniongred *eg* Iddewon Uniongred
orthodoxy uniongrededd *eg*
orthogonal orthogonol *ans*
orthogonal matrix matrics orthogonol *eg*
orthogonal orifice agorfa orthogonol *eb* agorfeydd orthogonol
orthogonality orthogonoledd *eg* orthogonoleddau
orthographic orthograffig *ans*
orthographic awareness ymwybyddiaeth orthograffig *eb*
orthographic drawing lluniad orthograffig *eg* lluniadau orthograffig
orthographic projection tafluniad orthograffig *eg* tafluniadau orthograffig
orthographic view golwg orthograffig *eg* golygon orthograffig
orthomorphic projection tafluniad orthomorffig *eg* tafluniadau orthomorffig

orthonormal orthonormal *ans*
orthopaedic orthopaedig *ans*
orthopaedics orthopaedeg *eb*
orthophosphate orthoffosffad *eg*
orthoptic orthoptig *ans*
orthoptist orthoptydd *eg* orthoptwyr
oscillate osgiliadu *be*
oscillating motion mudiant osgiliadol *eg*
oscillation osgiliad *eg* osgiliadau
oscillator osgiliadur *eg* osgiliaduron
oscillatory osgiliadol *ans*
oscillatory movement symudiad osgiliadol *eg* symudiadau osgiliadol
oscilloscope osgilosgop *eg* osgilosgopau
osculate minialu *be*
osculating minialaidd *ans*
osculation minialedd *eg* minialeddau
osmium (Os) osmiwm *eg*
osmoconformer osmogydymffurfiwr *eg*
osmoreceptor osmodderbynnydd *eg*
osmoregulation osmoreolaeth *eb*
osmoregulatory osmoreolaethol *ans*
osmosis osmosis *eg*
osmotic pressure gwasgedd osmotig *eg*
osmotic solute potential potensial toddyn osmotig *eg*
osmotically active osmotig weithredol *ans*
osprey gwalch y pysgod *eg* gweilch y pysgod
ossicle osigl *eg*
ossicle esgyrnyn *eg* esgyrnynnau
ossification asgwrneiddiad *eg*
ossify asgwrneiddio *be*
osteoporosis osteoporosis *eg*
ostinato ostinato *eg* ostinati
ostiole ostiol *eg*
ostium ostiwm *eg*
Ostwald theory theori Ostwald *eb*
Oswestry Croesoswallt *eb*
Oswestry Wake Dawns Croesoswallt *eb*
otherwise fel arall *adf*
otolith otolith *eg*
otter dyfrgi *eg* dyfrgwn
Ottoman *adj* Otomanaidd *ans*
Ottoman *n* Otoman *eg* Otomaniaid
Ottoman Empire Ymerodraeth Otomanaidd *eb*
Ottoman Turk Twrciad Otomanaidd *eg* Twrciaid Otomanaidd
out allan *adf*
out of bounds tu hwnt i'r ffin *eg*
out of court allan o'r cwrt
out of date wedi dyddio *ans*
out of phase anghydwedd *ans*
out of range (of statistics) tu allan i'r amrediad
outblowing wind gwynt allchwyth *eg* gwyntoedd allchwyth
outbound (of flights, traffic etc) allan *adf*
outbox blwch allan *eg* blychau allan
outbreak (of war) cychwyn *eg*
outbreed allfridio *be*
outburst echwythiad *eg* echwythiadau
outcast alltud *eg* alltudion
outcome canlyniad *eg* canlyniadau
outcrop brig *eg* brigiadau
outcropping brigo *be*
outdated ar ôl yr oes *ans*
outdoor activity gweithgaredd awyr agored *eg* gweithgareddau awyr agored
outdoor and adventurous activities gweithgareddau awyr agored ac antur *ell*
outdoor environment amgylchedd awyr agored *eg*
outdoor play chwarae awyr agored *eg*
outdoor sketching braslunio awyr agored *be*
outdoor sweeping brush brwsh cans *eg* brwshys cans
outdoor use defnydd yn yr awyr agored
outdoor work gwaith awyr agored *eg*
outdoors awyr agored *eg*
outer allanol *ans*
outer city cyrion dinas *ell*
outer country ring cylch gwledig y cyrion *eg*
outer ear clust allanol *eb*
outer face wyneb allanol *eg*
outer fringes cyrion allanol *ell*
outer parts rhannau allanol *ell*
outermost nesaf allan *ans*
outfield allfaes *eg* allfeysydd
outfielder ffildiwr *eg* ffildwyr
outfit gwisg gyflawn *eb* gwisgoedd cyflawn
outflow all-lif *eg* all-lifoedd
outflowing all-lifo *be*
outflows (of money) llif arian allan *eg*
out-group allgrwp *eg* allgrwpiau
outlaw *n* herwr *eg* herwyr
outlaw (a person) *v* rhoi ar herw *be*
outlaw (a practice) *v* gwahardd *be*
outlawry herwriaeth *eb*
outlay gwariant *eg*
outlet allfa *eb* allfeydd
outlier allgraig *eb* allgreigiau
outline *adj* amlinellol *ans*
outline *v* amlinellu *be*
outline (=lines of an object) *n* amlinell *eb* amlinellau
outline (=summary) *n* amlinelliad *eg* amlinelliadau
outline diagram diagram amlinellol *eg* diagramau amlinellol
outline drawing lluniad amlinell *eg* lluniadau amlinell
outline map map amlinell *eg* mapiau amlinell
outline section trychiad amlinell *eg* trychiadau amlinell
outline stitch pwyth amlinell *eg* pwythau amlinell
out-of-school activities gweithgareddau y tu allan i'r ysgol *ell*
out-of-town retail site safle adwerthu y tu allan i'r dref *eg* safleoedd adwerthu y tu allan i'r trefi
out-patient claf allanol *eg* cleifion allanol

outpatients' hospital ysbyty cleifion allanol *eg* ysbytai cleifion allanol
outport allborth *eg* allbyrth
outpost allbost *eg* allbyst
output *v* allbynnu *be*
output (=product) *n* cynnyrch *eg* cynhyrchion
output (of computer etc) *n* allbwn *eg* allbynnau
output buffer byffer allbwn *eg* byfferau allbwn
output device dyfais allbynnu *eb* dyfeisiau allbynnu
output stream all-lif *eg* all-lifoedd
output unit uned allbynnu *eb* unedau allbynnu
output voltage foltedd allbwn *eg*
outrelief cymorth allanol *eg*
outside tu allan *eg*
outside callipers caliperau allanol *ell*
outside diameter (o/d) diamedr allanol *eg* diamedrau allanol
outside forward asgellwr *eg* asgellwyr
outside left (of player) asgellwr chwith *eg* asgellwyr chwith
outside leg coes allanol *eb*
outside micrometer micromedr allanol *eg* micromedrau allanol
outside right (of player) asgellwr de *eg* asgellwyr de
outside wall wal allanol *eb* waliau allanol
outside-half maswr *eg* maswyr
outstep tu allan i'r droed *eg*
outswinger gwyriad allan *eg*
out-take alldoriad *eg* alldoriadau
outward allanol *ans*
outwash apron ffedog allolchi *eb* ffedogau allolchi
outwash deposits dyddodion allolchi *ell*
outwash plain sandur *eg* sandurau
outwork (industry) gwaith allanol *eg*
outwork (military) amddiffynfa allanol *eb*
outworker gweithiwr allanol *eg* gweithwyr allanol
oval hirgrwn *ans*
oval base sylfaen hirgrwn *eb* sylfeini hirgrwn
oval head stake bonyn pen cromen *eg* bonion pen cromen
oval lost head nail hoelen hirgron bengoll *eb* hoelion hirgrwn pengoll
oval nail hoelen hirgron *eb* hoelion hirgrwn
oval shape ffurf hirgron *eb* ffurfiau hirgrwn
oval window ffenestr hirgron *eb* ffenestri hirgrwn
ovarian ofaraidd *ans*
ovary ofari *eg* ofarïau
ovary wall mur yr ofari *eg* muriau'r ofari
oven ffwrn *eb* ffyrnau
oven cleaner defnydd glanhau ffwrn *eg*
ovenfire ffwrndanio *be*
over (in cricket) pelawd *eb* pelawdau
over arm bowling bowlio dros ysgwydd *be*
over bankful gorgyforlan *eb* gorgyforlannau
over distance training hyfforddi dros bellter *be*
over grasp trosafael *eb*
over thrust gorwthiad *eg* gorwthiadau
overall (=general) *adj* cyffredinol *ans*
overall (of measurements) *adj* o ben i ben *ans*
overall (of rate, reaction) *adj* cyflawn *ans*
overall (protective clothing) *n* oferôl *eb* oferôls
overall decrease lleihad trwodd a thro *eg*
overall dimensions mesuriadau o ben i ben *ell*
overall grade gradd ar gyfartaledd *eb*
overall length hyd o ben i ben *eg*
overarm pass pàs dros ysgwydd *eb* pasiau dros ysgwydd
overblanket carthen *eb* carthenni
overblouse trosflows *eb* trosflowsiau
overcast sky awyr gwbl gymylog *eb*
overcast stitch trawsbwyth *eg* trawsbwythau
overcharge gorgodi *be*
overcome goresgyn *be*
overcome difficulties goresgyn anawsterau *be*
overcrowded gorlawn *ans*
overcrowding gorlenwi *be*
overdeepen gorddyfnu *be*
overdeepened gorddwfn *ans*
overdose dos gormodol *eg* dosiau gormodol
overdraft gorddrafft *eg* gorddrafftiau
overdress *n* ffrog diwnig *eb* ffrogiau tiwnig
overestimate *n* goramcangyfrif *eg* goramcangyfrifon
overestimate *v* goramcangyfrif *be*
overextension gorestyniad *eg*
over-firing gordanio *be*
over-fishing gorbysgota *be*
overflow *n* gorlif *eg* gorlifoedd
overflow *v* gorlifo *be*
overflow bit did gorlif *eg* didau gorlif
overflow channel sianel orlif *eb* sianeli gorlif
overfold trosblyg *eg* trosblygion
overfolded seam sêm orlap *eb* semau gorlap
overgeneralization gorgyffredinoli *be*
overglaze *n* troswydryn *eg* troswydrau
overglaze *v* troswydro *be*
overhand knot cwlwm tros law *eg* clymau tros law
overhang *v* bargodi *be*
overhanging cave ogof ordo *eb* ogofâu gordo
overhanging window ffenestr fargod *eb* ffenestri bargod
overhaul atgyweirio *be*
overhead uwchben *adf*
overhead projector taflunydd dros ysgwydd *eg* taflunwyr dros ysgwydd
overhead valve falf uwchben *eb* falfiau uwchben
overhead wires gwifrau uwchben *ell*
overheads (in finance) gorbenion *ell*
overheat gorboethi *be*
overkill gor-ladd *be*
overland trostir *eg*
overlap *n* gorgyffyrddiad *eg* gorgyffyrddion
overlap *v* gorgyffwrdd *be*
overlapped seam sêm drosblyg *eb* semau trosblyg
overlapping top top gorymylol *eg* topiau gorymylol

overlay *n* troshaen *eb* troshaenau
overlay *v* troshaenu *be*
overlay keyboard bysellfwrdd droshaen *eg*
overload gorlwytho *be*
overlord mechdeyrn *eg* mechdeyrnedd
overlordship uwcharglwyddiaeth *eb* uwcharglwyddiaethau
overlying rock craig orchudd *eb* creigiau gorchudd
overmanning gorgyflogi *be*
overpainting trosbeintio *be*
overpopulate gorboblogi *be*
overpopulation gorboblogaeth *eb*
over-print tros-argraffu *be*
override gwrthwneud *be*
overrule goruwchreoli *be*
overseas tramor *ans*
overseas tourists twristiaid tramor *ell*
overseas visitor ymwelydd o wlad dramor *eg* ymwelwyr o wledydd tramor
oversecretion gorsecretiad *eg*
overseer goruchwyliwr *eg* goruchwylwyr
oversew amylu *be*
oversew stitch pwyth amylu *eg* pwythau amylu
overshot casting castin gorymyl *eg* castinau gorymyl
overshot wheel rhod uwchredol *eb* rhodau uwchredol
overspecialization gorarbenigo *be*
overspill *n* gorlif *eg* gorlifoedd
overspill *v* gorlifo *be*
overstimulation gorsymbyliad *eg*
oversubscribe gordanysgrifio *be*
overswing (bent arm) tros swing *eb* tros swingiau
overswing (long arm) tros swing freichsyth *eb* tros swingiau breichsyth
overt amlwg *ans*
overtake goddiweddyd *be*
overthrow of the monarchy dymchweliad y frenhiniaeth *eg*
overtighten gordynhau *be*
overtime goramser *eg*
overtone uwchdon *eb* uwchdonau
overtraining gorhyfforddi *be*
overture agorawd *eb* agorawdau
overtype *n* trosdeipiad *eg* trosdeipiadau
overtype *v* trosdeipio *be*
overutilize gorddefnyddio *be*
overview golwg cyffredinol *eg*
overview (as technical process) trosolwg *eg/b*
overweight *adj* dros bwysau *ans*
overweight *n* gorbwysedd *eg*
overwrap troslap *eg* troslapiau
overwrite trosysgrifo *be*
oviduct dwythell wyau *eb* dwythellau wyau
oviparous dodwyol *ans*
ovipositor wyddodydd *eg* wyddodyddion
ovolo ofolo *eg* ofoli
ovolo moulding mowldin ofolo *eg* mowldinau ofolo
ovolo plane plaen ofolo *eg* plaeniau ofolo
ovulate ofylu *be*
ovulation ofwliad *eg*
ovule ofwl *eg* ofwlau
ovum ofwm *eg* ofa
Owenism Oweniaeth *eb*
Owenite *adj* Owenaidd *ans*
Owenite *n* Owenydd *eg* Owenwyr
owner perchennog *eg* perchenogion
owner occupier perchennog preswyl *eg* perchenogion preswyl
ownership perchenogaeth *eb*
ox bow lake ystumllyn *eg* ystumllynnoedd
oxalic acid asid ocsalig *eg*
oxaloacetic acid asid ocsaloasetig *eg*
ox-blend blew ych *eg*
ox-blend brush brwsh blew ych *eg* brwshys blew ych
ox-ear hair brush brwsh blew clust ych *eg* brwshys blew clust ych
ox-gall bustl ych *eg*
ox-hair brush brwsh blew ych *eg* brwshys blew ych
oxidant ocsidydd *eg* ocsidyddion
oxidase ocsidas *eg*
oxidation ocsidiad *eg* ocsidiadau
oxidation number rhif ocsidiad *eg*
oxidation of fuels ocsidio tanwyddau *be*
oxidation state cyflwr ocsidiad *eg*
oxidative phosphorylation ffosfforyleiddiad ocsidiol *eg*
oxide ocsid *eg* ocsidau
oxidization ocsideiddiad *eg* ocsideiddiadau
oxidize ocsidio *be*
oxidized ocsidiedig *ans*
oxidizing agent ocsidydd *eg* ocsidyddion
oxidizing bleach cannydd ocsidio *eg*
oxidoreductase ocsidoredwctas *eg*
oxoacid ocsoasid *eg* ocsoasidau
3-oxobutanoic acid asid 3-ocsobwtanöig *eg*
oxoethanoic acid asid ocsoethanöig *eg*
oxonium ion ïon ocsoniwm *eg* ïonau ocsoniwm
2-oxopropanoic acid asid 2-ocsopropanöig *eg*
oxovanadium(IV) ion ïon ocsofanadiwm(IV) *eg* ïonau ocsofanadiwm(IV)
oxovanadium(IV) sulfate(VI) ocsofanadiwm(IV) sylffad(VI) *eg*
oxy-acetylene ocsi-asetylen *eg*
oxy-acetylene welding weldio ocsi-asetylen *be*
oxygen (O) ocsigen *eg*
oxygen converter furnace ffwrnais drawsnewidydd ocsigen *eb* ffwrneisi trawsnewidydd ocsigen
oxygen debt dyled ocsigen *eb*
oxygen difluoride ocsigen deufflworid *eg*
oxygen loading llwytho ocsigen *eg*
oxygen therapy therapi ocsigen *eg*
oxygenate ocsigenu *be*
oxygenated ocsigenedig *eg*

oxygenated blood gwaed ocsigenedig *eg*
oxygenation ocsigeniad *eg*
oxygen-haemoglobin dissociation curve
cromlin ddaduniad ocsigen-haemoglobin *eb*
oxygen-haemoglobin equilibrium curve
cromlin gydbwysedd ocsigen-haemoglobin *eb*
oxyhaemoglobin ocsihaemoglobin *eg*
oxytocin ocsitosin *eg*
ozone oson *eg*
ozone depletion darwagiad oson *eg*
ozone layer haen oson *eb*
ozonolysis osonolysis *eg*

P

pace (of lesson) rhediad *eg*
pacemaker (for heart) rheoliadur *eg* rheoliaduron
pacification heddychiad *eg*
pacifism heddychiaeth *eb*
pacifist heddychwr *eg* heddychwyr
pacify heddychu *be*
Pacinian corpuscle corffilyn Pacini *eg* corffilod Pacini
pack *n* pac *eg* paciau
pack *v* pacio *be*
pack animal anifail pwn *eg* anifeiliaid pwn
pack ice pacrew *eg*
package pac *eg* paciau
package *n* pecyn *eg* pecynnau
packaging defnydd pacio *eg*
packaging material deunyddiau pacio *ell*
packed paciedig *ans*
packet pecyn *eg* pecynnau
packet port pacedborth *eg* pacedbyrth
packet steamer pacedlong *eb* pacedlongau
packet switching switsio pecynnau *be*
packet switching cyfnewid pecynnau *be*
packet switching network rhwydwaith switsio pecynnau *eg*
packet switching network rhwydwaith cyfnewid pecynnau *eg* rhwydweithiau cyfnewid pecynnau
pack-horse pynfarch *eg* pynfeirch
packing *n* pacin *eg*
packing *v* pacio *be*
packing density dwysedd pacio *eg* dwyseddau pacio
packing waste gwastraff pacio *eg*
pact cytundeb *eg* cytundebau
Pact of Steel Cytundeb Dur *eg*
pad *n* pad *eg* padiau
pad *v* padio *be*
pad saw llif dwll clo *eb* llifiau twll clo
pad stitch pwyth pad *eg* pwythau pad
padding padin *eg*
padding stitch pwyth padio *eg* pwythau padio
paddle rhodlen *eb* rhodlenni
paddle *n* padl *eb* padlau
paddle *v* padlo *be*
paddle firm *v* padlo'n gadarn *be*
paddle light *v* padlo'n araf *be*
paddle steamer rhodlong *eb* rhodlongau
paddock padog *eg* padogau
paddy field cae padi *eg* caeau padi
padlock clo clwt *eg* cloeon clwt
paediatrician paediatregydd *eg* paediatregwyr
paediatrics paediatreg *eb*
paedophile paedoffilydd *eg*
paedophilia paedoffilia *eg*
pagan pagan *eg* paganiaid
paganism paganiaeth *eb*
page *n* tudalen *eg/b* tudalennau
page *v* tudalennu *be*
page boundary ffin tudalen *eb* ffiniau tudalen
page break toriad tudalen *eg* toriadau tudalen
page fault gwall tudalen *eg* gwallau tudalen
page jacking tudalengipio *be*
page lines canllawiau *ell*
page orientation cyfeiriadaeth tudalen *eb*
page setup gosodiad tudalen *eg* gosodiadau tudalen
page setup cysodi tudalen *be*
page swap cyfnewidiad tudalen *eg* cyfnewidiadau tudalen
pageant pasiant *eg* pasiantau
pageantry pasiantri *eg*
paged tudalennog *ans*
pager peiriant galw *eg* peiriannau galw
paginate tudalennu *be*
pagination tudaleniad *eg*
pagoda pagoda *eg* pagodau
pain poen *eg/b* poenau
pain receptor derbynnydd poen *eg* derbynyddion poen
painful poenus *ans*
painkiller cyffur lleddfu poen *eg*
paint *n* paent *eg* paentiau
paint *v* peintio *be*
paint brush brwsh paent *eg* brwshys paent
paint finish gorffeniad paent *eg* gorffeniadau paent
paint remover tynnwr paent *eg* tynwyr paent
paint solvent hydoddydd paent *eg* hydoddyddion paent
painted resist gwrthydd wedi'i beintio *eg* gwrthyddion wedi'u peintio
painter (=rope) rhaff glymu *eb* rhaffau clymu
painter (of house etc) peintiwr *eg* peintwyr
painter (of pictures) arlunydd *eg* arlunwyr
painting (=painted picture) paentiad *eg* paentiadau
painting (of process or art) peintio *be*
painting brush brwsh peintio *eg* brwshys peintio
painting knife cyllell beintio *eb* cyllyll peintio
painting medium cyfrwng peintio *eg* cyfryngau peintio
paintwork peintwaith *eg*

pair *n* pâr *eg* parau
pair *v* paru *be*
pair activities gweithgareddau mewn parau *ell*
paired fins esgyll paredig *ell*
paired reading darllen mewn pâr *be*
paired terraces cerlannau cyfatebol *ell*
pairing pariad *eg* pariadau
pairing (weaving with two canes) gwau â dwy wialen *be*
palaeography palaeograffeg *eb*
palaeolithic palaeolithig *ans*
palaeontology palaeontoleg *eb*
palate taflod *eb* taflodau
Palatine Earl Iarll Palatin *eg*
Palatine of the Rhine Etholaeth Balatin y Rhein *eb*
pale (in general) gwelw *ans*
Pale (Ireland) Rhanbarth Seisnig *eg*
pale (of colour) golau *ans*
pale cadmium yellow melyn cadmiwm golau *eg*
pale chrome yellow melyn crôm golau *eg*
pale colour lliw golau *eg* lliwiau golau
pale lemon yellow melyn lemwn golau *eg*
pale yellow (enamelling colour) melyn golau *eg*
paleoanthropology palaeoanthropoleg *eb*
Paleocene cyfnod Paleosen *eg*
Palestine Liberation Organization Mudiad Rhyddid Palesteina *eg*
palette palet *eg* paletau
palette knife cyllell balet *eb* cyllyll palet
Pali Canon Canon Pali *eg*
palindrome palindrom *eg* palindromau
paling ffens bolion *eb* ffensys polion
palisade palisâd *eg* palisadau
palisade cell cell balis *eb* celloedd palis
palisade layer haen balis *eb* haenau palis
pall cochl *eg* cochlau
palladium (Pd) paladiwm *eg*
palliative care gofal lliniarol *eg*
pallid llwydaidd *ans*
pallium paliwm *eg* palia
palm (of anchor) palf *eb* palfau
palm (of hand) cledr *eb* cledrau
palm (tree) palmwydden *eb* palmwydd
palm kernel cnewyllyn palmwydd *eg* cnewyll palmwydd
palm print cledrbrint *eg* cledrbrintiau
Palm Sunday Sul y Blodau *eg*
palmer palmwr *eg* palmwyr
palmtop (computer) cledriadur *eg* cledriaduron
palp palp *eg* palpiau
palpation teimlad cyffyrddol *eg* teimladau cyffyrddol
palpitation crychguriad *eg* crychguriadau
palpus palpws *eg* palpysau
palstave palstaf *eg* palstafau
pampas paith *eg* peithiau
pamphleteer pamffledwr *eg* pamffledwyr
pamphleteering pamffledu *be*
pan (=substratum of soil) cletir clai *eg* cletiroedd clai
pan (=vessel) padell *eb* pedyll
pan (of camera) tremio *be*
pan sensor ring alch hydeiml *eb* eilch hydeiml
panchromatic pancromatig *ans*
pancreas pancreas *eg*
pancreatic duct dwythell bancreatig *eb* dwythellau pancreatig
pane (of glass) cwarel *eg* cwarelau
panel panel *eg* paneli
panel construction adeiladwaith panel *eg*
panel gauge medrydd panel *eg* medryddion panel
panel infill llenwad panel *eg*
panel materials defnyddiau panel *ell*
panel of assessors panel o aseswyr *eg* paneli o aseswyr
panel pin pìn panel *eg* pinnau panel
panel saw llif banel *eb* llifiau panel
panelled door drws panelog *eg* drysau panelog
panelled skirt sgert baneli *eb* sgertiau paneli
panhandle estynwlad *eb* estynwledydd
pan-head rivet rhybed penpan *eg* rhybedion penpan
panic panig *eg*
panic disorder anhwylder panig *eg*
panicle panigl *eg* paniglau
paning hammer morthwyl twcio *eg* morthwylion twcio
Panj Kakka Panj Kakka
panj piare /panj pyare panj piare /panj pyare
pannage mesobr *eg* mesobrau
panorama panorama *eg* panoramâu
panoramic panoramig *ans*
panpipes pibau Pan *ell*
panplain llifwastadedd *eg* llifwastadeddau
panplanation llifwastadiant *eg*
panslavism panslafiaeth *eb*
pant dyhefod *be*
Panth Panth *eg*
pantile teilsen grom *eb* teils crwm
pantler pantler *eg* pantleriaid
pantograph pantograff *eg* pantograffau
pantomime pantomeim *eg* pantomeimau
pantonal pangyweiraidd *ans*
pantonality pangyweiredd *eg*
pants pants *ell*
papacy pabaeth *eb* pabaethau
papal pabaidd *ans*
papal consistory consistori'r Pab *eg*
papal encyclical cylchlythyr y Pab *eg*
papal legate legad y pab *eg* legadau'r Pab
papal notary notari'r Pab *eg* notarïau'r Pab
papal reaction adwaith y Pab *eg*
Papal Schism Sgism y Babaeth *eg*
Papal States Tiroedd y Babaeth *ell*
paper *n* papur *eg* papurau
paper *v* papuro *be*
paper back clawr papur *eg* cloriau papur

paper backed hessian hesian cefn papur *eg*
paper binding rhwymyn papur *eg* rhwymynnau papur
paper case cas papur *eg* casys papur
paper circle cylch papur *eg* cylchoedd papur
paper clip clip papur *eg* clipiau papur
paper cone côn papur *eg* conau papur
paper disc disg papur *eg* disgiau papur
paper fastener pìn clymu papur *eg* pinnau clymu papur
paper figure ffigur papur *eg* ffigurau papur
paper layer head pen haenau papur *eg* pennau haenau papur
paper low condition cyflwr papur isel *eg*
paper model model papur *eg* modelau papur
paper money arian papur *eg*
paper mosaic mosaig papur *eg*
paper plate plât papur *eg* platiau papur
paper pulp mwydion papur *ell*
paper shapes ffurfiau papur *ell*
paper sizes meintiau papur *ell*
paper tape tâp papur *eg* tapiau papur
paper tape reader darllenydd tâp papur *eg* darllenyddion tâp papur
paper varnish farnais papur *eg* farneisiau papur
paper-back edition argraffiad clawr papur *eg* argraffiadau clawr papur
papier mâché mwydion papur *ell*
papilla papila *eg* papilau
papillary papilaidd *ans*
papilliform papiliffurf *ans*
papist *adj* pabyddol *ans*
papist *n* pabydd *eg* pabyddion
pappus papws *eg*
papyrus papurfrwyn *ell*
par (=full value) llawn werth *eg*
parable dameg *eb* damhegion
parabola parabola *eg* parabolâu
parabolic curve cromlin barabolig *eb* cromliniau parabolig
parabolical parabolig *ans*
paraboloid paraboloid *eg* paraboloidau
parachute parasiwt *eg* parasiwtau
paraclete diddanydd *eg*
parade parêd *eg* paredau
paradigm shift syfliad paradeim *eg*
paradise paradwys *eb*
paradox paradocs *eg* paradocsau
paradox of thrift paradocs cynildeb *eg*
paraesthesia pigau mân *ell*
paraffin paraffin *eg*
paraffin wax cwyr paraffin *eg*
paragraph *n* paragraff *eg* paragraffau
paragraph *v* paragraffu *be*
paragraph break toriad paragraff *eg* toriadau paragraffau
paragraph format fformat paragraff *eg*
parallax paralacs *eg* paralacsau
parallel (in art and technology) *adj* cyflin *ans*
parallel (in general and in music) *adj* cyfochrog *ans*
parallel (in geometry and electronics) *adj* paralel *ans*
parallel (in geometry and electronics) *n* paralel *eg* paralelau
parallel adder adydd paralel *eg* adyddion paralel
parallel bars barrau cyflin *ell*
parallel circuit cylched baralel *eb* cylchedau paralel
parallel consecutive eighths wythfedau dilynol *ell*
parallel consecutive fifths pumedau cyfochrog dilynol *ell*
parallel distributed processing prosesu dosbarthu paralel *be*
parallel edges ymylon paralel *ell*
parallel fifths and octaves pumedau ac wythfedau cyfochrog
parallel flow llif cyfochrog *eg*
parallel form ffurf baralel *eb* ffurfiau paralel
parallel gutter cafn cyflin *eg* cafnau cyflin
parallel jaw vice feis safnau paralel *eb* feisiau safnau paralel
parallel key allwedd baralel *eb* allweddi paralel
parallel motion mudiant paralel *eg*
parallel nailing hoelio cyflin *be*
parallel octaves wythfedau cyfochrog *ell*
parallel of latitude paralel lledred *eg* paralelau lledred
parallel play (in child's development) chwarae cyfochrog *eg*
parallel port porth paralel *eg* pyrth paralel
parallel printer argraffydd paralel *eg* argraffyddion paralel
parallel processing prosesu paralel *be*
parallel processor prosesydd paralel *eg* prosesyddion paralel
parallel punch pwnsh paralel *eg* pynsiau paralel
parallel reamer agorell baralel *eb* agorellau paralel
parallel resistances gwrthiannau paralel *ell*
parallel resonant circuit cylched gysain baralel *eb* cylchedau cysain paralel
parallel shank garan baralel *eb* garanau paralel
parallel sides ochrau paralel *ell*
parallel transmission trawsyriant paralel *eg*
parallel turning turnio cyflin *be*
parallelepiped paralelepiped *eg* paralelepipedau
parallelism cyfochredd *eg*
parallelogram paralelogram *eg* paralelogramau
parallelogram of vectors' law deddf paralelogram fectorau *eb*
paralyse parlysu *be*
paralysis parlys *eg* parlysau
paramagnetism paramagnetedd *eg*
paramanu paramanw *eg*
paramedic parafeddyg *eg* parafeddygon
parameter paramedr *eg* paramedrau
parametric parametrig *ans*
parametric equation hafaliad parametrig *eg*

parametric statistic ystadegyn parametrig *eg* ystadegau parametrig
paramountcy principle egwyddor prif ystyriaeth *eb*
paranoia paranoia *eg*
paranoid schizophrenia sgitsoffrenia paranoid *eg*
parapet (of bridge) canllaw *eg* canllawiau
parapet (of castle) rhagfur *eg* rhagfuriau
parapet roof to erchwyn *eg* toeon erchwyn
paraphilia paraffilia *eg*
paraphrase aralleirio *be*
paraphrasing aralleirio *be*
parapodium parapodiwm *eg* parapodia
parapsychology paraseicoleg *eb*
parasite parasit *eg* parasitiaid
parasite population poblogaeth y parasit *eb*
parasitic parasitig *ans*
parasitic cone côn parasitig *eg* conau parasitig
parasitism parasitedd *eg*
parasitize parasiteiddio *be*
parasitoid ysglyfaethwr parasitaidd *eg*
parasympathetic paraymatebol *ans*
parasympathetic nervous system system nerfol barasympathetig *eb*
parathyroid parathyroid *eg* parathyroidau
paratroops awyrfilwyr *ell*
paraxial parechelin *ans*
parched cras *ans*
parchment memrwn *eg* memrynau
parchment lace ymylun memrwn *eg* ymyluniau memrwn
pardon pardwn *eg*
pardoned soul enaid rhydd *eg* eneidiau rhydd
pardoner pardynwr *eg* pardynwyr
parenchyma parencyma *eg*
parent rhiant *eg* rhieni
parent association cymdeithas rhieni *eb* cymdeithasau rhieni
parent cell rhiant-gell *eb*
parent company rhiant-gwmni *eg*
parent counselling cynghori rhieni *be*
parent element (radiation) elfen wreiddiol *eb*
parent isotope isotop gwreiddiol *eg*
parent plant rhiant-blanhigyn *eg*
parent population poblogaeth gysefin *eb*
parent rock mamgraig *eb* mamgreigiau
parental care gofal rhieni *eg*
parental characteristics nodweddion rhieni *ell*
parental choice dewis i rieni *eg*
parental genotype genoteip y rhieni *eg*
parental influence dylanwad rhieni *eg*
parental investment buddsoddiad rhieni *eg*
parentcraft crefft magu plant *eb*
parentheses ( ) cromfachau *ell*
parenthesis parenthesis *eg* parenthesisau
parent's charter siarter rhieni *eg* siarterau rhieni
parents' expectations disgwyliadau rhieni *ell*
parent's evening noson rieni *eb* nosweithiau rhieni
parent-teacher association cymdeithas rhieni athrawon *eb* cymdeithasau rhieni athrawon
parenxhymatous parencymol *ans*
Pareto efficiency effeithlonrwydd Pareto *eg*
parietal parwydol *ans*
parietal cell cell barwydol *eb* celloedd parwydol
parietal lobe llabed barwydol *eb* llabedau parwydol
paring naddu *be*
paring chisel cŷn hir *eg* cynion hir
paring gouge gaing gau hir *eb* geingiau cau hir
paring knife cyllell blicio *eb* cyllyll plicio
parinibbana (=parinirvana) parinibbana *eg*
parinirvana (=parinibbana) parinirvana *eg*
Paris binding rhwymyn Paris *eg* rhwymynnau Paris
Paris Peace Conference Cynhadledd Heddwch Paris *eb*
parish plwyf *eg* plwyfi
parish church eglwys blwyf *eb* eglwysi plwyf
parish relief cymorth plwyf *eg*
parishioner plwyfolyn *eg* plwyfolion
parity (in physics) paredd *eg* pareddau
parity (of status etc) cydraddoldeb *eg*
parity bit did paredd *eg* didau paredd
parity check prawf paredd *eg* profion paredd
park parc *eg* parciau
park or ornamental grounds parc neu erddi addurnol
Parkinson's disease clefyd Parkinson *eg*
parkland parcdir *eg* parcdiroedd
parkland avenue rhodfa parcdir *eb* rhodfeydd parcdir
parley cyd-drafod *be*
parliament senedd *eb* seneddau
Parliament Act Deddf y Senedd *eb*
parliamentarian seneddwr *eg* seneddwyr
parliamentary seneddol *ans*
parliamentary reform diwygio seneddol *eg*
Parliamentary Reform Act Deddf Diwygio'r Senedd *eb*
parliamentary sovereignty sofraniaeth y senedd *eb*
parochial plwyfol *ans*
parquet parquet *eg*
parquet floor llawr parquet *eg* lloriau parquet
parroting parota *be*
parry pario *be*
parry by detachment pario drwy ysgaru *be*
parry by opposition pario drwy wrthwynebu *be*
parse dosrannu *be*
parsimony cynildeb *eg*
parsing dosrannol *ans*
parsonage persondy *eg* persondai
part (=component, piece) darn *eg* darnau
part (in general) rhan *eb* rhannau
part book rhanlyfr *eg* rhanlyfrau
part exchange rhan-gyfnewid *eg*
part exchange allowance lwfans rhan-gyfnewid *eg*
part exchange item eitem ran-gyfnewid *eb* eitemau rhan-gyfnewid

part front elevation rhan flaenolwg *eb* rhannau blaenolwg
part time teacher (female) athrawes ran amser *eb* athrawesau rhan amser
part time teacher (male) athro rhan amser *eg* athrawon rhan amser
part view rhanolwg *eg/b* rhanolygon
partial rhannol *ans*
partial carry cario rhannol *be*
partial conversion trawsnewid rhannol *eg*
partial correlation cydberthyniad rhannol *eg*
partial differentiation differu rhannol *be*
partial exchange separation gwahaniad gwefr rhannol *eg*
partial fractions ffracsiynau rhannol *ell*
partial heating gwres rhannol *eg*
partial pressure gwasgedd rhannol *eg*
partially blind rhannol ddall *ans*
partially colour blind rhannol ddall i liwiau *ans*
partially completed rhannol orffenedig *ans*
partially deaf rhannol fyddar *ans*
partially miscible yn rhannol gymysgadwy *adf*
partible inheritance etifeddiaeth gyfrannol *eb*
participant cyfranogwr *eg* cyfranogwyr
participant observation arsylwi cyfranwyr *be*
participate cymryd rhan *be*
participation cyfranogiad *eg*
participation in sport cyfranogiad mewn chwaraeon *eg*
particle gronyn *eg* gronynnau
particle board bwrdd gronynnau *eg* byrddau gronynnau
particle-particle description disgrifiad gronyn-gronyn *eg*
particular *n* integryn *eg* integrynnau
particular (=singled out) *adj* neilltuol *ans*
particular (=specific) *adj* penodol *ans*
particular direction cyfeiriad penodol *eg* cyfeiriadau penodol
particular integral integryn neilltuol *eg* integrynnau neilltuol
particular matter mater penodol *eg* materion penodol
particular modelling technique techneg fodelu benodol *eb* technegau modelu penodol
particularism neilltuaeth daleithiol *eb*
particulate gronynnol *ans*
particulate inheritance etifeddiad gronynnol *eg*
particulate theory of inheritance damcaniaeth ronynnol etifeddiad *eb*
parting *n* rhaniad *eg* rhaniadau
parting *v* rhannu *be*
parting *n* (of lathe tools) partio *be*
parting bead glain rhannu *eg* gleiniau rhannu
parting off partio *be*
parting off tool erfyn partio *eg* offer partio
parting powder powdr partio *eg*
parting sand tywod partio *eg*
partisan partisan *eg* partisaniaid
partisanship pleidgarwch *eg*
partita partita *eg* partitâu
partition *v* rhannu *be*
partition (in mathematics) *n* dosraniad *eg* dosraniadau
partition (in mathematics) *v* dosrannu *be*
partition (of land etc) *n* rhaniad *eg* rhaniadau
partition (of structure) *n* pared *eg* parwydydd
partition aspect (of division) agwedd dosraniad *eb*
partition chromatography cromatograffaeth ddosrannol *eb*
partition coefficient cyfernod dosrannu *eg* cyfernodau dosrannu
partition function ffwythiant dosraniad *eg*
partition treaty cytundeb rhannu *eg* cytundebau rhannu
partition wall pared *eg* parwydydd
partly completed rhannol orffenedig *ans*
partly paid (with feminine nouns) wedi'i thalu'n rhannol *ans* wedi'u talu'n rhannol
partly paid (with masculine nouns) wedi'i dalu'n rhannol *ans* wedi'u talu'n rhannol
partner partner *eg* partneriaid
partner dance partner dawns *eg* partneriaid dawns
partnership partneriaeth *eb* partneriaethau
parts list rhestr ddarnau *eb* rhestri darnau
parts of a frame rhannau ffrâm *ell*
parts of file rhannau ffeil *ell*
parts of plane rhannau plaen *ell*
part-section rhandrychiad *eg* rhandrychiadau
part-sectional rhandrychiadol *ans*
part-sectional elevation golwg rhandrychiadol *eg*
part-sectional plan uwcholwg rhandrychiadol *eg*
part-sectional view golwg rhandrychiadol *eg*
part-time rhan amser *ans*
part-time education addysg ran amser *eb*
part-time labour llafur rhan amser *eg*
parturition esgoriad *eg* esgoriadau
party plaid *eb* pleidiau
Parvati Parvati *eb*
parvocellular pathway llwybr parfogellog *eg*
pasodoble pasodoble *eg* dawnsiau pasodoble
pass *v* pasio *be*
pass (=ticket or permit) *n* trwydded *eb* trwyddedau
pass (in mountains) *n* bwlch *eg* bylchau
pass (in sport) *n* pàs *eg/b* pasiau
pass back pasio am nôl *be*
pass laws (South Africa) deddfau trwydded *ell*
pass mark marc pasio *eg* marciau pasio
pass slip stitch over (p.s.s.o) pwyth dros bwyth
pass the ball pasio'r bêl *be*
passacaglia passacaglia *eg* passacaglie
passage (=journey) taith *eb* teithiau
passage (=route) tramwyfa *eb* tramwyfeydd
passage grave bedd cyntedd *eg* beddau cyntedd
passage of water llwybr y dŵr *eg*

passerine golfan *eb* golfanod
passing note nodyn camu *eg* nodau camu
passing of time treigl amser *eg*
Passion (of Christ) Dioddefaint *eg*
passion (of words, feelings) angerdd *eg*
passion (sexual) nwyd *eg* nwydau
Passion music cerddoriaeth y Dioddefaint *eb*
passionate love cariad angerddol *eg*
passive goddefol *ans*
passive abuse camdriniaeth oddefol *eb*
passive audience cynulleidfa oddefol *eb* cynulleidfaoedd goddefol
passive comprehension dealltwriaeth oddefol *eb*
passive flux fflwcs goddefol *eg* fflycsau goddefol
passive immunity imiwnedd goddefol *eg*
passive learning dysgu goddefol *be*
passive process proses oddefol *eb* prosesau goddefol
passive resistance gwrthwynebiad di-drais *eg*
passive transport cludiant goddefol *eg*
passive vocabulary geirfa oddefol *eb*
passivity goddefedd *eg*
Passover Pasg Iddewig *eg*
password cyfrinair *eg* cyfrineiriau
password protected diogelwyd gan gyfrinair
paste *n* past *eg* pastau
paste (in computing) *v* gludo *be*
paste (wallpaper) *v* pastio *be*
paste all gludo popeth *be*
paste brush brwsh past *eg* brwshys past
paste colour lliw past *eg* lliwiau past
paste colourant lliwydd past *eg* lliwyddion past
paste combing cribo past *be*
paste filler llenwad past *eg*
paste flux fflwcs past *eg* fflycsau past
paste powder powdr past *eg*
paste spreader lledaenydd past *eg* lledaenwyr past
pastel pastel *eg* pasteli
pastel fixative sefydlyn pastel *eg*
Pasteur effect effaith Pasteur *eb*
pasteurization pasteureiddiad *eg*
pasteurize pasteureiddio *be*
pastiche pastiche *eg* pastiches
pastime adloniant *eg* adloniannau
pastor (of church) gweinidog *eg* gweinidogion
pastoral *adj* bugeiliol *ans*
pastoral care gofal bugeiliol *eg*
pastoral curriculum cwricwlwm bugeiliol *eg*
pastoral farming ffermio bugeiliol *be*
pastoral symphony symffoni fugeiliol *eb*
pastoral tutor tiwtor bugeiliol *eg* tiwtoriaid bugeiliol
pastoralism bugeilyddiaeth *eb*
pastry board bwrdd crwst *eg* byrddau crwst
pasture porfa *eb* porfeydd
pasty (of soil) pastog *ans*
pat bounce tampio *be*
pat dry sychu'n dyner *be*
patch *n* clwt *eg* clytiau
patch *v* clytio *be*
patch pocket poced glwt *eb* pocedi clwt
patchwork clytwaith *eg* clytweithiau
patchy grass glaswellt clytiog *eg*
patella padell pen-glin *eb* pedyll pengliniau
patellar padellog *ans*
patent patent *eg*
patent fee ffi batent *eb* ffioedd patent
Patent Roll Rhôl Patent *eb* Rholiau Patent
paternal tadol *ans*
paternal chromosome cromosom o du'r tad *eg* cromosomau o du'r tad
paternalism agwedd dadol *eb*
path llwybr *eg* llwybrau
path of reaction llwybr adwaith *eg* llwybrau adwaith
pathname enw llwybr *eg*
pathogen *n* pathogen *eg* pathogenau
pathogenic pathogenaidd *ans*
pathological patholegol *ans*
pathologist patholegydd *eg* patholegwyr
pathology patholeg *eb*
pathway llwybr *eg* llwybrau
patient claf *eg* cleifion
patient appliances offer cleifion *ell*
patient satisfaction survey arolwg bodlonrwydd cleifion *eg*
patient-centred style arddull claf-ganolog *eg*
Patient's Charter Siarter y Claf *eg*
Patimokkha Patimokkha *eg*
patina (=sheen) patina *eg*
patriarch *n* patriarch *eg* patriarchiaid
patriarchal *adj* patriarchaidd *ans*
Patriarchal Narratives Hanesion Patriarchaidd *ell*
patriarchy patriarchaeth *eb*
patrician *adj* uchelwrol *ans*
patrician *n* uchelwr *eg*
patrilineal treftadol *ans*
patrimonial state gwladwriaeth dreftadol *eb* gwladwriaethau treftadol
patrimony treftadaeth *eb*
patriot gwladgarwr *eg* gwladgarwyr
patriotic gwlatgar *ans*
patriotism gwladgarwch *eg*
patrol patrôl *eg* patrolau
patron noddwr *eg* noddwyr
patronage nawdd *eg*
patronize noddi *be*
patronymic patronymig *ans*
patter song cân barablu *eb* caneuon parablu
pattern patrwm *eg* patrymau
pattern (in dance) ffigur *eg/b* ffigurau
pattern design *n* cynllun patrymol *eg* cynlluniau patrymol
pattern designer dylunydd patrymau *eg*
pattern layout cynllun gosod patrwm *eg* cynlluniau gosod patrwm

pattern markings marciau patrwm *ell*
pattern material defnydd patrymog *eg* defnyddiau patrymog
pattern of behaviour patrwm ymddygiad *eg* patrymau ymddygiad
pattern of economic activity patrwm o weithgarwch economaidd *eg* patrymau o weithgarwch economaidd
pattern piece darn patrwm *eg* darnau patrwm
patterned patrymog *ans*
patterned paper papur patrymog *eg* papurau patrymog
patterned surface arwyneb patrymog *eg* arwynebau patrymog
patterned weave gwehyddiad patrymog *eg* gwehyddiadau patrymog
patting patio *be*
Pauli exclusion principle egwyddor wahardd Pauli *eb*
Paulinus Pawl Hen *eg*
pauper tlotyn *eg* tlodion
pause (in general) saib *eg* seibiau
pause (sign in music) daliant *eg* daliannau
pause printing oedi'r argraffu *be*
pavane pavane *eg* pavanes
pavement palmant *eg* palmentydd
pavement epithelium epitheliwm palmantaidd *eg*
pavilion pafiliwn *eg* pafiliynau
Pavlovian conditioning cyflyru Pavlovaidd *be*
paw foot troed bawen *eb* traed pawen
pawl pawl *eg* polion
pawl and ratchet mechanism mecanwaith pawl a chlicied *eg*
pawn *v* gwystlo *be*
pawn (=of person) *n* gwystl *eg* gwystlon
pawn (in chess) *n* gwerinwr *eg* gwerinwyr
pawnbroker gwystlwr *eg* gwystlwyr
pay *n* cyflog *eg/b* cyflogau
pay *v* talu *be*
pay advice hysbysiad talu *eg*
Pay As You Earn Talu Wrth Ennill
pay attention rhoi sylw *be*
payable taladwy *ans*
PAYE Talu wrth Ennill *be*
payment tâl *eg* taliadau
payment on account tâl ar gyfrif *eg*
payment slip taleb *eb* talebau
payment system system dalu *eb* systemau talu
Payne's blue glas Payne *eg*
Payne's grey llwyd Payne *eg*
payroll rhestr gyflogau *eb* rhestri cyflogau
payroll program rhaglen cyflogres *eb* rhaglenni cyflogres
payroll system system gyflogau *eb* systemau cyflogau
paysage (landscape) tirlun *eg* tirluniau
pay-slip slip cyflog *eg* slipiau cyflog
P.B. silimanite silimanit P.B. *eg*

P.C.R. (pitch circle radius) radiws pitsh cylch *eg*
pdf file ffeil pdf *eb* ffeiliau pdf
peace (in general) heddwch *eg*
peace (of God) tangnefedd *eg*
peace offering hedd-offrwm *eg*
peace settlement ardrefniant heddwch *eg*
peace treaty cytundeb heddwch *eg* cytundebau heddwch
peaceable army byddin heddychlon *eb* byddinoedd heddychlon
peaceful co-existence cyd-fyw heddychlon *be*
peacemaker cymodwr *eg* cymodwyr
peak (=highest point in a curve /graph etc) brig *eg*
peak (=pointed part) pigyn *eg* pigynnau
peak (=time of greatest success) anterth *eg*
peak (of mountain) copa *eg* copaon
peak current cerrynt brig *eg*
peak demand galw brig *eg* galwadau brig
peak flow measurement mesuriad anterth llif *eg*
peak flow rate cyfradd anterth llif *eb*
peak hour awr frig *eb* oriau brig
peak input volts (piv) foltiau mewnbwn brig *ell*
peak period traffic trafnidiaeth oriau brig *eb*
peak population poblogaeth frig *eb*
peak value brigwerth *eg* brigwerthoedd
peak value intersection croestoriad uchafwerth *eg* croestoriadau uchafwerth
peak writing ysgrifennu uchafbwynt *be*
peak-to-peak brig i frig *eg*
peanuts cnau mwnci *ell*
pearl barley haidd gwyn *eg*
pearl button botwm perl *eg* botymau perl
pearl glue glud perl *eg* gludion perl
pearl lamp lamp berl *eb* lampau perl
pearlite perlit *eg*
Pearson r r Pearson *eg*
peasant gwerinwr *eg* gwerinwyr
peasantry gwerin wledig *eb*
Peasants' Revolt Gwrthryfel y Werin *eg*
Peasants' War Rhyfel y Werin *eg*
peat mawn *eg*
peat bog mawnog *eb* mawnogydd
peat hag torlan fawn *eb* torlannau mawn
pebble cerigyn *eg* cerigos
pebble dash gro chwipio *eg*
pectic acid asid pectig *eg*
pectin pectin *eg*
pectinase pectinas *eg*
pectoral fin asgell bectoral *eb* esgyll pectoral
pectoral girdle gwregys pectoral *eg* gwregysau pectoral
pedagogy pedagogeg *eb*
pedal *n* pedal *eg* pedalau
pedal *v* pedalu *be*
pedal harp telyn bedal *eb* telynau pedal
pedal loom gwŷdd pedal *eg* gwyddau pedal
pedal notch rhic pedal *eg* rhiciau pedal

pedal position safle'r pedal *eg* safle'r pedalau
pedestal pedestal *eg* pedestalau
pedestal drill dril pedestal *eg* driliau pedestal
pedestal drilling machine peiriant drilio pedestal *eg* peiriannau drilio pedestal
pedestal grinder llifanydd pedestal *eg* llifanwyr pedestal
pedestal rock craig gynnal *eb* creigiau cynnal
pedestrian cerddwr *eg* cerddwyr
pedestrian crossing croesfan gerddwyr *eb* croesfannau cerddwyr
pedicel pedicel *eg* pedicelau
pedicle pedicl *eg* pediclau
pedigree tras *eb* trasau
pedigree stock stoc o dras *eb* stociau o dras
pediment pediment *eg* pedimentau
pediplain pediplan *eg* pediplanau
pediplanation pediplaniant *eg*
pedological priddegol *ans*
pedology priddeg *eb*
peduncle pedwncl *eg* pedynclau
pedunculate pedynclaidd *ans*
peel (from block) pilio *be*
peeling pilio *be*
peeling movement (in sport) ôl-redeg *be*
peen pig morthwyl *eg* pigau morthwylion
peen end hammer morthwyl pigfain *eg* morthwylion pigfain
peer (=contemporary) cyfoed *eg* cyfoedion
peer (=lord) arglwydd *eg* arglwyddi
peer feedback adborth cymheiriaid *eg*
peer group (formal) grŵp cyfoedion *eg* grwpiau cyfoedion
peer group (informal) cylch cyfoedion *eg* cylchoedd cyfoedion
peer pressure pwysau gan gyfoedion *ell*
peer to peer cymar wrth gymar
peerage arglwyddi'r deyrnas *ell*
peg *n* peg *eg* pegiau
peg *v* pegio *be*
peg box blwch ebill *eg* blychau ebill
pegged tenon tyno wedi'i begio *eg* tynoau wedi'u pegio
peg-word method dull gair-peg *eg*
Pekingese stitch pwyth Pekin *eg* pwythau Pekin
pelagic eigionol *ans*
pelagic fishing pysgota'r wyneb *be*
pellagra pelagra *eg*
pellet pelen *eb* pelenni
pellicle pelicl *eg* peliclau
pelmet pelmet *eg* pelmetau
pelvic pelfig *ans*
pelvic cavity ceudod pelfig *eg*
pelvic girdle gwregys pelfig *eg* gwregysau pelfig
pelvic space gwagle pelfig *eg*
pelvis pelfis *eg* pelfisau
pen (for writing) ysgrifbin *eg* ysgrifbinnau
pen and ink pen ac inc
pen and wash pen a golchiad
pen drive cof pin *eg* cofion pin
pen lettering llythrennu pen *be*
Penal Code Cod Penyd *eg*
penal laws deddfau cosbi *ell*
penal reform diwygio'r deddfau cosbi *be*
penal system trefn gosbi *eb*
penalize cosbi *be*
penalty cosb *eb* cosbau
penalty (shot) bwli cosb *eg*
penalty area cwrt cosbi *eg* cyrtiau cosbi
penalty box blwch cosbi *eg* blychau cosbi
penalty bully bwli cosb *eg* bwlïau cosb
penalty clause cymal cosbi *eg*
penalty corner cornel gosb *eb* corneli cosb
penalty goal gôl gosb *eb* goliau cosb
penalty kick cic gosb *eb* ciciau cosb
penalty pass pàs gosb *eb* pasiau cosb
penalty spot smotyn gwyn *eg*
penalty try cais cosb *eg* ceisiau cosb
penance penyd *eg* penydiau
pencil pensil *eg* pensiliau
pencil bit haearn sodro pensil *eg*
pencil gauge medrydd pensil *eg* medryddion pensil
pencil sharpener miniwr *eg* minwyr
pencil slim skirt sgert gul *eb* sgertiau cul
pendant *adj* crog *ans*
pendant *n* tlws crog *eg*
pendant light golau crog *eg* goleuadau crog
pendulum pendil *eg* pendiliau
peneplanation lledwastadiad *eg* lledwastadiadau
penetrable treiddadwy *ans*
penetrance (genetic) treiddiad *eg*
penetrate treiddio *be*
penetrating treiddiol *ans*
penetrating powers pwerau treiddio *ell*
penetration treiddiad *eg* treiddiadau
penetration price pris treiddio *be* prisiau treiddio
penetration pricing prisiau treiddio *ell*
penicillin penisilin *eg*
penillion (cerdd dant) penillion *ell*
penillion singer canwr penillion *eg* cantorion penillion
peninsula gorynys *eb* gorynysoedd
peninsular India India orynysol *eb*
penis pidyn *eg* pidynnau
penis envy eiddigedd pidyn *eg*
penmanship crefft ysgrifennu *eb*
Penny Black stamp du ceiniog *eg* stampiau du ceiniog
penny post post ceiniog *eg*
penny rate treth geiniog *eb*
Penrhyn lockouts argyfyngau cau allan y Penrhyn *ell*
pension pensiwn *eg* pensiynau
pensioner pensiynwr *eg* pensiynwyr
pentacarbonyliron(0) pentacarbonylhaearn(0) *eg*

pentacyanonitrosylferrate(II) ion ïon pentacyanonitrosylfferad(II) *eg* ïonau pentacyanonitrosylfferad(II)
pentadecagon pentadecagon *eg* pentadecagonau
pentagon pentagon *eg* pentagonau
pentagonal pentagonol *ans*
pentagonal pyramid pyramid pentagonol *eg* pyramidiau pentagonol
pentagram pentagram *eg* pentagramau
pentane-2,4-dione pentan-2,4-deuon *eg*
pentanoic acid asid pentanöig *eg*
pentatonic pentatonig *ans*
pentatonic scale graddfa bentatonig *eb* graddfeydd pentatonig
Pentecost Pentecost *eg*
Pentecostal *adj* Pentecostalaidd *ans*
Pentecostal *n* Pentecostal *eg* Pentecostaliaid
penthouse penty *eg* pentai
pentomino pentomino *eg* pentominos
pentose pentos *eg*
pentosuria pentoswria *eg*
pentyl- pentyl-
penumbra penwmbra *eg* penwmbrâu
People's Charter Siarter y Bobl *eg*
peplum peplwm *eg*
pepper-pot pot pupur *eg* potiau pupur
peptide peptid *eg* peptidau
per capita allowance lwfansau'r pen *eg*
per capita grant grant y pen *eg*
per cent y cant
per head y pen
perborate perborad *eg*
perborate bleach cannydd perborad *eg*
perceive canfod *be*
percentage canran *eg* canrannau
percentage carbon content canran cynnwys carbon *eg*
percentage change newid yng nghanran *eg*
percentage composition canran cyfansoddiad *eg*
percentage moisture content canran cynnwys lleithder *eg*
percentage rise or fall canran y cynnydd neu'r gostyngiad *eg*
percentage yield arennill y cant *eg*
percentile canradd *eg* canraddau
percentile point pwynt canradd *eg* pwyntiau canradd
percentile ranking safle canraddol *eg*
perception canfyddiad *eg* canfyddiadau
perceptual canfyddiadol *ans*
perceptual difficulty anhawster canfyddiad *eg* anawsterau canfyddiad
perceptual disorder anhwylder canfyddiad *eg* anhwylderau canfyddiad
perch (=type of fish) draenog *eg* draenogiaid
perch (for bird) clwyd *eb* clwydi
perched block crogfaen *eg* crogfeini
perched water table lefel trwythiad dŵr clo *eb*
percolate trylifo *be*
percolated coffee coffi percoladur *eg*
percolation trylifiad *eg* trylifiadau
percolator percoladur *eg* percoladuron
percussion trawiad *eg* trawiadau
percussion band band taro *eg* bandiau taro
percussion headed flint callestr daro *eb* cellystr taro
percussion instrument offeryn taro *eg* offerynnau taro
percussion part rhan daro *eb* rhannau taro
percussion section adran daro *eb* adrannau taro
percussive ergydiol *ans*
peregrine falcon hebog tramor *eg* hebogau tramor
perennial (figuratively) parhaol *ans*
perennial (in biology) lluosflwydd *ans*
perennial flower blodyn lluosflwydd *eg* blodau lluosflwydd
perfect perffaith *ans*
perfect cadence diweddeb berffaith *eb* diweddebau perffaith
perfect competition cystadleuaeth berffaith *eb*
perfect interval cyfwng perffaith *eg* cyfyngau perffaith
perfect pitch traw perffaith *eg*
perfect square sgwâr perffaith *eg* sgwariau perffaith
perforate tyllu *be*
perforated tyllog *ans*
perforated pattern patrwm tyllog *eg* patrymau tyllog
perforating wheel olwyn dyllu *eb* olwynion tyllu
perforation (=hole) twll *eg* tyllau
perforation (on stamp) trydylliad *eg* trydylliadau
perforator tyllwr *eg* tyllwyr
perform perfformio *be*
perform structured tasks perfformio tasgau strwythuredig *be*
performance perfformiad *eg* perfformiadau
performance appraisal gwerthusiad perfformiad *eg*
performance criteria meini prawf perfformiad *ell*
performance fabric ffabrig perfformio *eg*
performance indicator dangosydd perfformiad *eg* dangosyddion perfformiad
performance test prawf perfformiad *eg* profion perfformiad
performance workshop gweithdy perfformio *eg* gweithdai perfformio
performer perfformiwr *eg* perfformwyr
performing arts celfyddydau perfformio *ell*
perfume *n* persawr *eg* persawrau
perfume *v* persawru *be*
perfuse darlifo *be*
perfusion darlifiad *eg* darlifiadau
pericardial cavity ceudod pericardiol *eg*
pericardium pericardiwm *eg*
pericarp pericarp *eg*
pericline periclin *eg* periclinau
pericycle periseicl *eg*
perigean tide (perigee) llanw perigeaidd *eg* llanwau perigeaidd
perigee perige *eg* perigeau

periglacial ffinrewlifol *ans*
perihelion perihelion *eg* perihelionau
perilymph perilymff *eg*
perimeter (in geometry) perimedr *eg* perimedrau
perimeter of the sector perimedr y sector *eg*
perimeters of simple shapes perimedrau siapiau syml *ell*
perinatal amenedigol *ans*
period cyfnod *eg* cyfnodau
period costume gwisg cyfnod *eb*
period of concrete operations cyfnod gweithredu diriaethol *eg*
period of formal operations cyfnod gweithredu ffurfiol *eg*
period of oscillation cyfnod yr osgiliad *eg*
period play drama gyfnod *eb* dramâu cyfnod
periodic cyfnodol *ans*
periodic changes newidiadau cyfnodol *ell*
periodic table tabl cyfnodol *eg*
periodical cyfnodolyn *eg* cyfnodolion
periodicity cyfnodedd *eg* cyfnodeddau
peri-operative care gofal yn ystod y llawdriniaeth *eg*
peripatetic cylchynol *ans*
peripatetic teacher (female) athrawes gylchynol *eg* athrawesau cylchynol
peripatetic teacher (male) athro cylchynol *eg* athrawon cylchynol
peripediment peripediment *eg* peripedimentau
peripheral (in geometry) *adj* amgantol *ans*
peripheral (in geometry) *n* amgantydd *eg* amgantyddion
peripheral (of computer) *adj* perifferol *ans*
peripheral (of computer) *n* perifferolyn *eg* perifferolion
peripheral area ardal ymylol *eb* ardaloedd ymylol
peripheral device dyfais berifferol *eb*
peripheral interface rhyngwyneb perifferol *eg* rhyngwynebau perifferol
peripheral interface adaptor (PIA) addasydd rhyngwyneb perifferol *eg* addasyddion rhyngwyneb perifferol
peripheral interrupt ymyriad perifferol *eg* ymyriadau perifferol
▸ **peripheral nervous system** system nerfol berifferol *eb*
peripheral route llwybr perifferol *eg*
▸ **peripheral speed** buanedd perifferol *eg*
periphery perifferi *eg* perifferïau
periphery (in geometry) amgant *eg* amgantau
periscope perisgop *eg* perisgopau
perishable darfodus *ans*
perishable goods nwyddau darfodus *ell*
peristalsis peristalsis *eg*
perithecium peritheciwm *eg*
peritoneal dialysis dialysis peritoneaidd *eg*
perivitelline space gwagle perifitelin *eg*
perjure tyngu anudon *be*
perjury anudoniaeth *eb*
permafrost rhew parhaol *eg*
permanence (=stability) sefydlogrwydd *eg*
permanent (in general) parhaol *ans*
permanent (of colour) sefydlog *ans*
permanent colour lliw sefydlog *eg* lliwiau sefydlog
permanent grazing pori parhaol *be*
permanent hardness caledwch parhaol *eg*
permanent joining uno parhaol *be*
permanent joint uniad parhaol *eg* uniadau parhaol
permanent pasture porfa barhaol *eb* porfeydd parhaol
permanent pleating pletio parhaol *be*
permanent press pres parhaol *eg*
permanent tooth dant parhaol *eg* dannedd parhaol
permanently stiffened (finish) cyfnerthu parhaol *be*
permeability athreiddedd *eg* athreiddeddau
permeability of free space athreiddedd gofod rhydd *eg*
permeable athraidd *ans*
permeable membrane pilen athraidd *eb*
Permian Permaidd *ans*
permissible caniataol *ans*
permissive goddefol *ans*
permissive legislation deddfwriaeth ganiataol *eb*
permissive society cymdeithas oddefol *eb*
permit *n* caniatâd *eg*
permit *v* caniatáu *be*
permittivity permitifedd *eg* permitifeddau
permittivity constant cysonyn permitifedd *eg*
permittivity of free space permitifedd gofod rhydd *eg*
permutation trynewid *eg* trynewidion
pernicious anaemia anaemia aflesol *eg*
peroxoacid perocsoasid *eg* perocsoasidau
peroxoborate(III) ion ïon perocsoborad(III) *eg* ïonau perocsoborad(III)
peroxodisulfate(VI) ion ïon perocsodeusylffad(VI) *eg* ïonau perocsodeusylffad(VI)
peroxodisulfuric(VI) acid asid perocsodeusylffwrig(VI) *eg*
peroxoethanoic acid asid perocsoethanöig *eg*
peroxosulfuric(VI) acid asid perocsosylffwrig(VI) *eg*
perpendicular *adj* perpendicwlar *ans*
perpendicular *n* perpendicwlar *eg* perpendicwlarau
perpendicular arch bwa perpendicwlar *eg* bwâu perpendicwlar
perpendicular bisector hanerydd perpendicwlar *eg* hanerwyr perpendicwlar
perpendicular distance pellter perpendicwlar *eg*
perpendicular height uchder perpendicwlar *eg*
perpendicular line llinell blwm *eb*
perpetual parhaol *ans*
perpetual edict cyhoeddeb barhaol *eb* cyhoeddebau parhaol
perpetual peace heddwch parhaol *eg*
perpetual variation amrywiad parhaol *eg* amrywiadau parhaol

perpetuate bytholi *be*
persecute erlid *eg*
persecution erledigaeth *eb*
perseverance dyfalbarhad *eg*
perseveration gorbarhad *eg*
persistance of vision darlunio parhaus *be*
person specification manyleb person *eb* manylebau person
person variable newidyn person *eg* newidynnau person
persona persona *eg*
personal personol *ans*
personal achievement record cofnod cyrhaeddiad personol *eg*
personal belief cred bersonol *eb* credoau personol
personal capability gallu personol *eg*
personal computer cyfrifiadur personol *eg* cyfrifiaduron personol
personal computer disc operating system (PC / DOS) system weithredu disg cyfrifiadur personol *eb*
personal construct lluniad personol *eg* lluniadau personol
personal data data personol *ell*
personal development datblygiad personol *eg*
personal education addysg bersonol *eb*
personal foul ffowl personol *eg*
personal health iechyd personol *eg*
personal hygiene hylendid personol *eg*
personal information gwybodaeth bersonol *eb*
personal letter llythyr personol *eg* llythyrau personol
personal liability atebolrwydd personol *eg*
personal loan benthyciad personol *eg* benthyciadau personol
personal programme rhaglen bersonol *eb* rhaglenni personol
personal record cofnod personol *eg* cofnodion personol
personal reflection myfyrdod personol *eg*
personal religious experience profiad crefyddol personol *eg*
personal rule llywodraeth bersonol *eb*
personal safety diogelwch personol *eg*
personal space gofod personol *eg*
personal survival goroesiad personol *eg*
personal training schedule amserlen hyfforddiant personol *eb* amserlenni hyfforddiant personol
personal tutor tiwtor personol *eg* tiwtoriaid personol
personalism personolyddiaeth *eb*
personality personoliaeth *eb* personoliaethau
personality disorder anhwylder personoliaeth *eg* anhwylderau personoliaeth
personality trait nodwedd personoliaeth *eb* nodweddion personoliaeth
personality type math o bersonoliaeth *eg* mathau o bersonoliaeth
personnel personél *eg*
personnel records cofnodion personél *ell*
perspective persbectif *eg* persbectifau
perspective drawing lluniadu mewn persbectif *be*
perspective view golwg persbectif *eg*
perspectivity persbectifedd *eg*
perspex persbecs *eg*
perspex cement sment persbecs *eg*
perspire chwysu *be*
persuasive advertising hysbysebu er perswâd *be*
persuasive message neges er perswâd *eb* negeseuon er perswâd
perturbation aflonyddiad *eg* aflonyddiadau
perturbation theory damcaniaeth aflonyddiad *eb*
Peruvian coast arfordir Periw *eg*
pervious hydraidd *ans*
pessary pesari *eg* pesarïau
pessimism pesimistiaeth *eb*
pessimistic pesimistaidd *ans*
pest pla *eg* plâu
pesticide plaleiddiad *eg* plaleiddiaid
pestilence haint *eb* heintiau
pestle pestl *eg* pestlau
pestle and mortar pestl a morter pestlau a morterau
petal petal *eg* petalau
Peter Pan collar coler Peter Pan *eg* coleri Peter Pan
Peter Scot Ceiniogau'r Pab *ell*
Peter the Great Pedr Fawr *eb*
Peter the Hermit Pedr Feudwy *eg*
Peter's Pence Ceiniogau Pedr *ell*
petersham petersham *eg*
petiole petiol *eg* petiolau
petition deiseb *eb* deisebau
Petition of Right Deiseb Iawnderau *eb*
Petri dish dysgl Petri *eb* dysglau Petri
petrification pedreiddiad *eg*
petrified forest fforest betraidd *eb* fforestydd petraidd
petrochemical industry diwydiant petrocemegol *eg* diwydiannau petrocemegol
petrol engine peiriant petrol *eg* peiriannau petrol
petroleum petroliwm *eg*
petroleum spirit gwirod petroliwm *eg*
petrology petroleg *eb*
petroselenic acid asid petroselenig *eg*
petticoat pais *eb* peisiau
petty cash arian mân *eg*
Petty Constable Is-Gwnstabl *eg* Is-Gwnstabliaid
petty larceny mân ladrad *eg* mân ladradau
petty officer is-swyddog *eg* is-swyddogion
petty sessions cwrt bach *eg*
petty theft mân ladrad *eg* mân ladradau
pewter piwter *eg*
peytrel mwclis pres *eg*
pH pH
pH value gwerth pH *eg* gwerthoedd pH
phaeophytin ffaeoffytin *eg*
phage ffag *eg*
phagocyte ffagocyt *eg* ffagocytau
phagocytic ffagocytig *ans*
phagocytosis ffagocytosis *eg*

phalange ffalang *eg* ffalangau
phalanx ffalancs *eg*
phallic stage cyfnod ffalig *eg*
phantom limb rhithaelod *eg* rhithaelodau
phantom line llinell manylion cudd *eb* llinellau manylion cudd
pharmaceutical fferyllol *ans*
pharmacist fferyllydd *eg* fferyllwyr
pharmacy fferyllfa *eb* fferyllfeydd
pharyngeal ffaryngeal *ans*
pharyngeal cavity ceudod y gwddf *eg*
pharynx ffaryncs *eg*
phase (=period or stage in process) cyfnod *eg* cyfnodau
phase (of matter, moon) gwedd *eb* gweddau
phase (of waves) cydwedd *eb* cydweddau
phase change newid gwedd *eg*
phase control rheolaeth gweddau *eb*
phase difference gwahaniaeth gwedd *eg*
phase linked gwedd-gysylltiedig *ans*
phase shift symudiad cydwedd *eg*
phase transition trawsnewidiad gwedd *eg*
phased introduction cyflwyno graddol *be*
phases of heart cycle gweddau cylchred y galon *ell*
phases of the moon gweddau'r lleuad *ell*
phasor diagram gwedd *eg*
phellogen ffelogen *eg*
phenol ffenol *eg*
phenol liquid hylif ffenol *eg*
phenolic ffenolig *ans*
phenolics (thermosetting plastics) ffenoligion *ell*
phenology ffenoleg *eb*
phenolphthalein ffenolffthalein *eg*
phenomenon ffenomen *eb* ffenomenau
phenotype ffenoteip *eg* ffenoteipiau
phenotypic ffenoteipaidd *ans*
phenyl- (as a substituent group) ffenyl-
phenyl thiourea ffenyl thiowrea *eg*
phenylalanine ffenylalanin *eg*
phenylalanine hydroxylase ffenylalanin hydrocsylas *eg*
phenylamine ffenylamin *eg*
phenylammonium chloride ffenylamoniwm clorid *eg*
phenylethanone ffenylethanon *eg*
phenylethene ffenylethen *eg*
phenylhydrazine ffenylhydrasin *eg*
phenylketonuria ffenylcetonwria *eg*
phenylketonuric ffenylcetonwrig *ans*
phenylmethanol ffenylmethanol *eg*
(phenylmethyl)amine (ffenylmethyl)amin *eg*
3-phenylpropenoic acid asid 3-ffenylpropenöig *eg*
pheromone fferomon *eg* fferomonau
phial ffiol *eb* ffiolau
philanthropic dyngarol *ans*
philanthropist dyngarwr *eg* dyngarwyr
philanthropy dyngarwch *eg*
Philip Augustus Philip Awgwstws *eg*
Philip the Fair Philip Deg *eg*
Philip the Handsome Philip Olygus *eg*
Phillips curve cromlin Phillips *eb*
Phillips screwdriver tyrnsgriw Phillips *eg*
philology ieitheg *eb*
philosophical problem problem athronyddol *eb* problemau athronyddol
philosophy athroniaeth *eb*
phlegm fflem *eg*
phloem ffloem *eb*
pH-meter mesurydd pH *eg*
phobia ffobia *eg*
phone dialer deialydd ffôn *eg* deialwyr ffôn
phoneme ffonem *eg/b* ffonemau
phonemics ffonemeg *eb*
phonetic reading darllen ffonetig *be*
phonetics seineg *eb*
Phoney War Rhyfel Ffug *eg*
phonic ffonig *ans*
phonic method dull ffonig *eg* dulliau ffonig
phonocardiogram ffonocardiogram *eg*
phonological awareness ymwybyddiaeth ffonolegol *eb*
phonological dyslexia dyslecsia ffonolegol *eg*
phonological loop cylch ffonolegol *eg*
phonology ffonoleg *eb*
phosphate ffosffad *eg* ffosffadau
phosphate(V) ion ïon ffosffad(V) *eg*
phosphinate ion ïon ffosffinad *eg* ïonau ffosffinad
phosphine ffosffin *eg*
phosphocreatine ffosffocreatin *eg*
phosphoglyceraldehyde ffosffoglyseraldehyd *eg*
phosphoglyseric acid asid ffosffoglyserig *eg*
phosphokinase ffosffocinas *eg*
phospholipid ffosffolipid *eg*
phosphonate ion ïon ffosffonad *eg* ïonau ffosffonad
phosphonic acid asid ffosffonig *eg*
phosphonium ion ïon ffosffoniwm *eg* ïonau ffosffoniwm
phosphor ffosffor *eg* ffosfforau
phosphor bronze (non-ferrous alloys) ffosfforefydd *eg*
phosphorescence ffosfforesgedd *eg*
phosphorescent ffosfforesgol *ans*
phosphoric acid asid ffosfforig *eg*
phosphoric(V) acid asid ffosfforig(V) *eg*
phosphorus (P) ffosfforws *eg*
phosphorus pentahalide ffosfforws pentahalid *eg* ffosfforws pentahalidau
phosphorus trichloride ffosfforws triclorid *eg*
phosphorus trichloride oxide ffosfforws triclorid ocsid *eg*
phosphorus trihalide ffosfforws trihalid *eg* ffosfforws trihalidau
phosphorus(III) oxide ffosfforws(III) ocsid *eg*
phosphorus(V) chloride ffosfforws(V) clorid *eg*
phosphorus(V) oxide ffosfforws(V) ocsid *eg*

phosphorylase ffosfforylas *eg*
photo story ffotostori *eb* ffotostorïau
photocell ffotogell *eb* ffotogelloedd
photochemistry ffotocemeg *eb*
photocopier llungopïwr *eg* llungopiwyr
photocopy *n* llungopi *eg* llungopïau
photocopy *v* llungopïo *be*
photodiode ffotodeuod *eg*
photoelectric ffotodrydanol *ans*
photoelectric effect effaith ffotodrydanol *eb*
photoelectricity ffotodrydan *eg*
photo-emission ffoto-allyriant *eg* ffoto-allyriannau
photogrammetry ffotogrametreg *eb*
photograph ffotograff *eg* ffotograffau
photographic ffotograffig *ans*
photographic image delwedd ffotograffig *eb* delweddau ffotograffig
photography ffotograffiaeth *eb*
photogravure ffoto-ysgythru *be*
photometer ffotomedr *eg* ffotomedrau
photometric ffotometrig *ans*
photometry ffotometreg *eb*
photomontage montage ffotograffig *eg*
photon ffoton *eg* ffotonau
photon energy egni ffoton *eg*
photoperiodism ffotogyfnodedd *eg*
photopigment ffotopigment *eg*
photoreceptor goleudderbynnydd *eg* goleudderbynyddion
photosensitivity goleusensitifedd *eg*
photosphere ffotosffer *eg* ffotosfferau
photostat ffotostat *eg* ffotostatau
photosynthesis ffotosynthesis *eg*
photosynthetic ffotosynthetig *ans*
phototransistor ffototransistor *eg*
phototropism ffototropedd *eg*
photovoltaic ffotofoltaidd *ans*
phrase *v* brawddegu *be*
phrase read-only memory (PHROM) cof cymal darllen yn unig *eg*
phreatic water dŵr daear *eg* dyfroedd daear
phrenic ffrenig *ans*
Phrygian Phrygiaidd *ans*
phylogenetic esblygol *ans*
phylum ffylwm *eg* ffyla
physical (=bodily) corfforol *ans*
physical (=of physics) ffisegol *ans*
physical activity gweithgaredd corfforol *eg* gweithgareddau corfforol
physical area maes ffisegol *eg*
physical care gofal corfforol *eg*
physical change newid corfforol *eg*
physical defect nam corfforol *eg* namau corfforol
physical dependence dibyniaeth gorfforol *eb*
physical development datblygiad corfforol *eg*
physical disability anabledd corfforol *eg* anableddau corfforol
physical education addysg gorfforol *eb*
physical effect effaith gorfforol *eb* effeithiau corfforol
physical environment amgylchedd ffisegol *eg*
physical exercise ymarfer corff *eg*
physical factor ffactor gorfforol *eb* ffactorau corfforol
physical features nodweddion ffisegol *ell*
physical fitness ffitrwydd corfforol *eg*
physical force grym corfforol *eg*
physical handicap anfantais gorfforol *eb* anfanteision corfforol
physical impairment nam corfforol *eg* namau corfforol
physical maturity aeddfedrwydd corfforol *eg*
physical measurement mesuriad corfforol *eg* mesuriadau corfforol
physical play chwarae corfforol *eg*
physical processes prosesau ffisegol *ell*
physical property priodwedd ffisegol *eb* priodweddau ffisegol
physical recreation ymarfer corff *eg*
physical resource adnodd ffisegol *eg* adnoddau ffisegol
physically active corfforol weithgar *ans*
physically handicapped child plentyn â nam corfforol *eg* plant â nam corfforol
physician meddyg *eg* meddygon
physics ffiseg *eb*
physiognomics ffisionomeg *eb*
physiological ffisiolegol *ans*
physiological change newid ffisiolegol *eg*
physiological measurement mesuriad ffisiolegol *eg* mesuriadau ffisiolegol
physiological psychology seicoleg ffisiolegol *eb*
physiological saline heli ffisiolegol *eg*
physiological status statws ffisiolegol *eg*
physiologist ffisiolegydd *eg* ffisiolegwyr
physiology ffisioleg *eb*
physiotherapist ffisiotherapydd *eg* ffisiotherapyddion
physiotherapy ffisiotherapi *eg*
physique corffoledd *eb*
phytoplankton ffytoplancton *eg*
phytotoxin llyswenwyn *eg* llyswenwynau
pianist pianydd *eg* pianyddion
piano piano *eg* pianos
piano accordion acordion piano *eg* acordiynau piano
piano hinge colfach hir *eg* colfachau hir
piano key nodyn piano *eg* nodau piano
piano lock clo piano *eg* cloeon piano
piano score sgôr biano *eb* sgorau piano
piano stool stôl biano *eb* stolion piano
piano trio triawd piano *eg* triawdau piano
piano tuner tiwniwr piano *eg* tiwnwyr piano
pibgorn pibgorn *eg* pibgyrn
piccolo player canwr picolo *eg* canwyr picolo
pick up a stitch codi pwyth *be*

picket *n* picedwr *eg* picedwyr
picket *v* picedu *be*
pickle *n* picl *eg* piclau
pickle *v* piclo *be*
pickle-bath tongs gefel fath picl *eb* gefeiliau bath picl
pickup cipyn *eg* cipynnau
pick-up tongs gefel godi *eb* gefeiliau codi
picot picot *eg*
picot edging ymylwaith picot *eg*
pictogram pictogram *eg* pictogramau
pictograph pictograff *eg* pictograffau
pictography pictograffeg *eb*
pictorial darluniadol *ans*
pictorial art celfyddyd ddarluniol *eb*
pictorial drawing lluniad darluniol *eg* lluniadau darluniol
pictorial plan uwcholwg darluniol *eg* uwcholwg darluniadol
pictorial projection tafluniad darluniol *eg* tafluniadau darluniol
pictorial representation portread darluniol *eg* portreadau darluniol
pictorial sketch braslun darluniol *eg* brasluniau darluniol
pictorial space gofod darluniol *eg* gofodau darluniol
pictorial view golwg darluniol *eg*
pictorialism darluniadaeth *eb*
picture darlun *eg* darluniau
picture llun *eg* lluniau
picture frame ffrâm ddarlun *eb* fframiau darluniau
picture messaging llun-negesu *be*
picture placeholder dalfan llun *eg* dalfannau llun
picture plane plân darlun *eg* planau darlun
picture rail rheilen bictiwr *eb* rheiliau pictiwr
picture varnish farnais darlun *eg*
picture window ffenestr lydan *eb* ffenestri llydan
picturesque darluniaidd *ans*
pie chart siart cylch *eg* siartiau cylch
pie graph (=wheel graph) graff olwyn *eg* graffiau olwyn
piece darn *eg* darnau
piece rate (in economics) cyfradd yn ôl y gwaith *eb*
piece work (remuneration) tâl yn ôl y gwaith *eg*
Piepowder Court Cwrt Marchnad *eg*
pierce (=stab) trywanu *be*
pierce (in metalwork) rhwyllo *be*
pierced panel panel rhwyllog *eg* paneli rhwyllog
pierced work rhwyllwaith *eg*
piercer gwanydd *eg* gwanyddion
piercing saw llif rwyllo *eb* llifiau rhwyllo
pietism pietistiaeth *eb*
pietist *adj* pietistaidd *ans*
pietist *n* pietist *eg* pietistiaid
piety duwioldeb *eg*
piezo electric effect effaith piesodrydanol *eb*
pig iron (ferrous metal) haearn crai *eg*
pigment pigment *eg* pigmentau
pigmentation pigmentiad *eg*
pike picell *eb* picellau
pike dive deif blygu *eb* deifiau plygu
pikeman picellwr *eg* picellwyr
pilaster pilastr *eg* pilastrau
pile (of fabric) peil *eg*
pile foundation sylfaen bileri *eb* sylfeini pileri
piles clwyf y marchogion *eg*
pileus pilews *eg*
pilgrim pererin *eg* pererinion
Pilgrim Fathers Tadau Pererin *ell*
Pilgrim Festivals Gwyliau'r Pererinion *ell*
pilgrimage pererindod *eb* pererindodau
pill pilsen *eb* pils
pillage ysbeilio *be*
pillar piler *eg* pileri
pillar and stall mining gweithio talcennau *be*
pillar drill dril piler *eg* driliau piler
pillar drilling machine peiriant drilio piler *eg* peiriannau drilio piler
pillar type machine peiriant pilerog *eg* peiriannau pilerog
pillaring (in slate quarries) pileru *be*
pilling pellennu *be*
pillory rhigod *eg* rhigodau
pillow gobennydd *eg* gobenyddion
pillow lava lafa clustog *eg* lafâu clustog
pillow structure adeiledd clustog *eg* adeileddau clustog
pillowcase cas gobennydd *eg* casys gobennydd
pilot *adj* peilot *ans*
pilot (a scheme etc) *v* cynnal peilot *be*
pilot drill dril arwain *eg* driliau arwain
pilot drilling drilio arwain *be*
pilot hole twll arwain *eg* tyllau arwain
pilot project project peilot *eg* projectau peilot
pilot research ymchwil peilot *eg*
pilot test prawf peilot *eg* profion peilot
pimple ploryn *eg* plorod
pin *n* pìn *eg* pinnau
pin *v* pinio *be*
pin (for tuning) ebill *eg* ebillion
pin and slot cynffon a bwlch
pin and string method dull pìn a llinyn *eg*
pin drill dril pìn *eg* driliau pìn
pin hammer morthwyl pìn *eg* morthwylion pìn
pin lock clo pìn *eg* cloeon pìn
pin mark marc pìn *eg* marciau pìn
pin plate pinblat *eg* pinblatiau
pin punch pwnsh pìn *eg* pynsiau pìn
pin stitch pwyth pìn *eg* pwythau pìn
pin tuck twc pìn *eg* tyciau pìn
pin vice feis pìn *eb* feisiau pìn
pinafore dress ffrog biner *eb* ffrogiau piner
pincers pinsiwrn *eg* pinsiyrnau
pinch *n* pinsiad *eg* pinsiadau
pinch *v* pinsio *be*

pinch pleat mân-blet *eg* mân-bletiau
pinch pottery crochenwaith pinsiad *eg*
pincushion pincas *eg* pincasau
pingo pingo *eg* pingoau
pinhole twll pìn *eg* tyllau pìn
pinion (=cog-wheel or spindle) piniwn *eg* piniynau
pin-jointed framework fframwaith uniad-pìn *eg* fframweithiau uniad-pìn
pinking pincio *be*
pinking scissors siswrn pincio *eg* sisyrnau pincio
pinking shears gwellaif pincio *eg* gwelleifiau pincio
pinna pinna *eg* pinnâu
pinnace pinnas *eg* pinasau
pinnate drainage draeniad pluog *eg*
pinned mortise and tenon joint uniad mortais a thyno niferus *eg* uniadau mortais a thyno niferus
pinning (of file) pinio *be*
pinocytosis pinocytosis *eg*
pin-pointed mechanism mecanwaith uniad-pìn *eg*
pint peint *eg* peintiau
pinto beans ffa pinto *ell*
pioneer *adj* arloesol *ans*
pioneer *n* arloeswr *eg* arloeswyr
pioneer *v* arloesi *be*
pipe (=play the pipe) *v* canu pib *be*
pipe (in general) pibell *eb* pibellau
pipe (in music etc) *n* pib *eb* pibau
pipe (in plumbing etc) *n* peipen *eb* peipiau
pipe (in plumbing etc) *v* peipio *be*
pipe bending machine peiriant plygu peipen *eg* peiriannau plygu peipiau
pipe bending wrench tyndro plygu peipen *eg* tyndroeon plygu peipiau
pipe clamp clamp peipen *eg* clampiau peipen
pipe cleaner glanhawr pibell *eg* glanhawyr pibell
pipe grips gafaelydd peipen *eg* gafaelyddion peipiau
pipe line lein bibell *eb*
pipe organ organ bib *eb* organau pib
Pipe Roll Rhôl Siecr *eb* Rholiau Siecr
pipe tongs gefel beipen *eb* gefeiliau peipen
pipe vice feis beipen *eb* feisiau peipen
pipe wrench tyndro peipen *eg* tyndroeon peipen
piped buttonhole twll botwm wedi'i beipio *eg* tyllau botymau wedi'u peipio
piped light golau drwy beipen *eg*
piped seam sêm wedi'i pheipio *eb* semau wedi'u peipio
pipelining blaenbeipio *be*
piper (machine attachment) peipell *eb* peipellau
pipette *n* pibed *eb* pibedau
pipette *v* pibedu *be*
piping (shrinkage) peipio *be*
piping cord cortyn peipio *eg* cortynnau peipio
pipkrake nodwyddau iâ *ell*; nodwyddau rhew *ell*
pippin pipin *eg*
pique pique *eg*
piracy (=river capture) afonladrad *eg*
piracy (in general) lladrad *eg* lladradau
piracy (on sea) môr-ladrad *eg*
pirate môr-leidr *eg* môr-ladron
pirate stream lleidr *eg* lladron
pistil pistil *eg* pistiliau
pistol grip (hacksaw frame) gafael llawddryll *eb* gafaelion llawddryll
piston piston *eg* pistonau
piston rings cylchau piston *ell*
pit (=deep hole in ground) pwll *eg* pyllau
pit (in sport) pwll neidio *eg* pyllau neidio
pit (on plant or animal body) mân-bant *eg* mân-bantiau
pit dwelling annedd bant *eb* anheddau pant
pitch (=playing field) *n* maes *eg* meysydd
pitch (=tar) *n* pyg *eg*
pitch (a ball) *v* pitsio *be*
pitch (a note) *v* taro *be*
pitch (for playing cricket) *n* llain *eb* lleiniau
pitch (in geology) *n* gogwydd *eg* gogwyddau
pitch (in geology) *v* gogwyddo *be*
pitch (in mountaineering) *n* dringen *eb* dringennau
pitch (of ball) *n* pitsh *eg*
pitch (of roof) *n* codiad to *eg*
pitch (of sound) *n* traw *eg* trawiau
pitch angle (plane) ongl bitsh *eb* onglau pitsh
pitch angle (saw teeth) pitsh *eg*
pitch block blocyn pyg *eg* blociau pyg
pitch circle diameter (P.C.D.) diamedr pitsh cylch *eg*
pitch of screw danheddiad sgriw *eg*
pitch of the ball disgynfan y bêl *eg*
pitched roof to ar ongl *eg* toeon ar ongl
pitcher pitsiwr *eg* pitswyr
pitcher's plate plât y pitsiwr *eg*
pitchstone pygfaen *eg* pygfeini
pith bywyn *eg* bywynnau
piton piton *eg* pitonau
pitprop postyn pwll *eg* pyst pwll
pitted mân-bantiog *ans*
pitting pyllu *be*
pituitary gland chwarren bitwidol *eb* chwarennau pitwidol
pivot *n* colyn *eg* colynnau
pivot (in general) *v* colynnu *be*
pivot (on a needle) *v* troi ar y nodwydd *be*
pivot element elfen golyn *eb* elfennau colyn
pivot hinge colfach colyn *eg* colfachau colyn
pivot joint (in anatomy) cymal cylchdroi *eg* cymalau cylchdroi
pivot joint (in woodwork) uniad colyn *eg* uniadau colyn
pivot turn troad ar golyn *eg* troadau ar golyn
pivotal colynnol *ans*
pivoted ar golyn *ans*
pivoted arm braich ar golyn *eb* breichiau ar golyn
pivoted sash window ffenestr ar golyn dalennog *eb* ffenestri ar golyn dalennog

pixel picsel *eg* picseli
pixel colour lliw picsel *eg* lliwiau picsel
pixel edit golygu picsel *be*
pixel editor golygydd picseli *eg* golygyddion picseli
pixel mode modd picseli *eg*
pixelation picseleiddio *be*
place *n* lle *eg* lleoedd
place *v* gosod *be*
place kick cic osod *eb* ciciau gosod
place mat mat bwrdd *eg* matiau bwrdd
place of interest lle diddorol *eg* lleoedd diddorol
place of worship man addoli *eg* mannau addoli
place value gwerth lle *eg* gwerthoedd lle
placebo plasebo *eg*
placebo effect effaith blasebo *eb*
place-dependent memory cof lle-ddibynnol *eg*
placeholder dalfan *eg/b* dalfannau
placeholder expression mynegiad dalfan *eg* mynegiadau dalfan
placement lleoliad *eg* lleoliadau
placement log log lleoliad *eg*
placement officer swyddog lleoliadau *eg* swyddogion lleoliadau
placenta brych *eg* brychau
placer gold aur banc tywod *eg*
place-setting gosodiad bwrdd *eg* gosodiadau bwrdd
placing gosodiad *eg*
placket placed *eg* placedau
plagal cadence diweddeb amen *eb* diweddebau amen
plagal mode modd deilliedig *eg* moddau deilliedig
► **plagiarism** llên-ladrad *eg*
plagioclimax plagioclimacs *eg*
plague pla *eg* plâu
plaid plad *eg*
Plaid Cymru Plaid Cymru *eb*
plain *adj* plaen *ans*
plain *n* gwastadedd *eg* gwastadeddau
plain butt ymyl blaen *eb* ymylon plaen
plain centre canol plaen *eg*
plain cutter torrell blaen *eb* torellau plaen
plain drawstroke strôc dynnu *eb* strociau tynnu
plain finish gorffeniad plaen *eg* gorffeniadau plaen
plain flour blawd plaen *eg*
plain material defnydd plaen *eg* defnyddiau plaen
plain milling cutter melinwr plaen *eg* melinwyr plaen
plain mitred joint uniad meitrog plaen *eg* uniadau meitrog plaen
plain panel panel plaen *eg* paneli plaen
plain quartering llifio plaen chwarteru *be*
plain sawing llifio trwodd *be*
plain scale graddfa syml *eb* graddfeydd syml
plain seam sêm agored *eb* semau agored
plain stitch pwyth plaen *eg* pwythau plaen
plain text testun plaen *eg*
plain tile teilsen blaen *eb* teils plaen
plain tract gwastatir afon *eg* gwastatiroedd afonydd
plain washer wasier blaen *eb* wasieri plaen
plain weather-boarding byrddau hindraul cyffredin *ell*
plain weave gwehyddiad plaen *eg*
plainsong plaengan *eb* plaenganau
plaintiff pleintydd *eg* pleintyddion
plaintiff achwynydd *eg* achwynyddion
plait *n* pleth *eb* plethau
plait *v* plethu *be*
plan *v* cynllunio *be*
plan (=scheme) *n* cynllun *eg* cynlluniau
plan, do and review cynllunio, gwneud ac adolygu
plan environments cynllunio amgylcheddau *be*
plan view uwcholwg *eg* uwcholygon
planar planar *ans*
planar engraving ysgythriad planar *eg* ysgythriadau planar
planation gwastadiant *eg*
plane (geometrical) *n* plân *eg* planau
plane (of tool) *n* plaen *eg* plaeniau
plane (with tool) *v* plaenio *be*
plane and solid geometry geometreg plân a solid *eb*
plane figure ffigur plân *eg* ffigurau plân
plane geometry geometreg plân *eb*
plane of reference plân cyfeirnod *eg*
plane of symmetry plân cymesuredd *eg*
plane picture darlun plân gwastad *eg* darluniau plân gwastad
plane polarized light golau plân polar *eg*
plane polarized wave ton blân bolar *eb* tonnau plân polar
plane solids solidau plân *ell*
plane surface arwyneb plân *eg* arwynebau plân
► **planed all round** (of wood) wedi'i blaenio i gyd *ans*
planed size maint wedi'i blaenio *eg* meintiau wedi'u plaenio
planer plaeniwr *eg* plaenwyr
planet planed *eb* planedau
planing machine peiriant plaenio *eg*
planishing planisio *be*
planishing hammer morthwyl planisio *eg* morthwylion planisio
planisphere planisffer *eg* planisfferau
plank planc *eg* planciau
plankton plancton *eg* planctonau
planned economy economi cynlluniedig *eg*
planning cynllunio *be*
planning trend ffasiwn cynllunio *eg* ffasiynau cynllunio
plant *adj* planhigol *ans*
plant (=equipment) *n* peiriannau *ell*
plant (=factory) *n* gwaith *eg* gweithfeydd
plant (=place in ground) *v* plannu *be*
plant (trees, flowers etc) *n* planhigyn *eg* planhigion
plant association cydgymuned blanhigion *eb* cydgymunedau planhigion
plant cell wall cellfur planhigion *eg*

plant gum gwm planhigol *eg* gymiau planhigol
plant hormone hormon planhigol *eg* hormonau planhigol
plant tissue meinwe planhigion *eb* meinweoedd planhigion
plant tissue culture *v* meithrin meinweoedd planhigol *be*
plantain llyriad *eg* llyriaid
plantarflexion gwadnblygiad *eg* gwadnblygiadau
plantation (of people) trefedigaeth *eb* trefedigaethau
plantation (of plants) planhigfa *eb* planhigfeydd
planted bead glain gosod *eg* gleiniau gosod
planted moulding mowldin gosod *eg* mowldinau gosod
planted top (table) top gosod *eg* topiau gosod
planum temporale planum temporale *eg*
plaque plac *eg* placiau
plasma membrane pilen blasmaidd *eb* pilenni plasmaidd
plasmolyse plasmolysu *be*
plaster *n* plastr *eg* plastrau
plaster *v* plastro *be*
plaster and bandage plastr a rhwymyn
plaster bat bat plastr *eg* batiau plastr
plaster cast cast plastr *eg* castiau plastr
plaster casting castin plastr *eg* castinau plastr
plaster figure ffigur plastr *eg* ffigurau plastr
plaster head pen plastr *eg* pennau plastr
plaster of Paris plastr Paris *eg*
plasterboard bwrdd plastr *eg*
plastic *adj* plastig *ans*
plastic *n* plastig *eg* plastigion
plastic art celfyddyd blastig *eb*
plastic bead glain plastig *eg* gleiniau plastig
plastic beaker bicer plastig *eg* biceri plastig
plastic bending plygu plastig *be*
plastic carving (of action) cerfio plastig *be*
plastic carving (of object) cerfiad plastig *eg* cerfiadau plastig
plastic coating araen blastig *eb* araenau plastig
plastic colour lliw plastig *eg* lliwiau plastig
plastic container cynhwysydd plastig *eg* cynwysyddion plastig
plastic emulsion emwlsiwn plastig *eg*
plastic figure ffigur plastig *eg* ffigurau plastig
plastic filler llenwad plastig *eg* llenwadau plastig
plastic fitting gosodydd plastig *eg* gosodyddion plastig
plastic foil ffoil plastig *eg*
plastic hammer morthwyl plastig *eg* morthwylion plastig
plastic heating gwresogi plastig *be*
plastic laminate laminiad plastig *eg* laminiadau plastig
plastic machining peiriannu plastig *be*
plastic mallet gordd blastig *eb* gyrdd plastig
plastic material defnydd plastig *eg* defnyddiau plastig
plastic mould mowld plastig *eg* mowldiau plastig
plastic racket raced blastig *eb* racedi plastig
plastic ruler riwl blastig *eb* riwliau plastig
plastic saucer soser blastig *eb* soseri plastig
plastic sheeting llen blastig *eb* llenni plastig
plastic spoon llwy blastig *eb* llwyau plastig
plastic starch startsh plastig *eg*
plastic surgery llawfeddygaeth blastig *eb*
plastic track trac plastig *eg* traciau plastig
plastic tube tiwb plastig *eg* tiwbiau plastig
plastic webbing webin plastig *eg*
plasticine plastisin *eg* plastisinau
plasticity plastigrwydd *eg*
plasticizer plastigydd *eg* plastigyddion
plastid plastid *eg* plastidau
plate *n* plât *eg* platiau
plate *v* platio *be*
plate glass platwydr *eg* platwydrau
plate tectonic theory damcaniaeth tectoneg platiau *eb*
plate tectonics tectoneg platiau *eb*
plateau llwyfandir *eg* llwyfandiroedd
plateau block bloclwyfandir *eg* bloclwyfandiroedd
plateau phase gwedd lwyfandir *eb*
platelet (blood) platen *eb* platennau
platen platen *eb* platennau
platform llwyfan *eg/b* llwyfannau
plating platio *be*
platinize platinio *be*
platinum (Pt) platinwm *eg*
platoon platŵn *eg* platwnau
platykurtic platycwrtig *ans*
play (=drama) *n* drama *eb* dramâu
play (=recreation) *n* chwarae *eg*
play (a piece) *v* chwarae *be*
play (an instrument) *v* canu *be*
play (of games) *v* chwarae *be*
play a simple ostinato chwarae ostinato syml
play activities gweithgareddau chwarae *ell*
play area lle chwarae *eg* llefydd chwarae
play by ear chwarae yn ôl y glust *be*
play centre canolfan chwarae *eb* canolfannau chwarae
play ethos ethos chwarae *eg*
play fighting chwarae ymladd *be*
play in full chwarae'n llawn *be*
play leader arweinydd chwarae *eg* arweinwyr chwarae
play school cylch chwarae *eg* cylchoedd chwarae
play sound chwarae sain *be*
play stool stôl fach *eb* stolion bach
play tennis chwarae tennis *be*
play therapist therapydd chwarae *eg* therapyddion chwarae
play therapy therapi chwarae *eg*
play time amser chwarae *eg*
play tutoring tiwtora chwarae *be*

play unit uned chwarae *eb* unedau chwarae
playa playa *eg* playâu
play-back trosglwyddo *be*
play-based assessment asesiad seiliedig ar chwarae *eg* asesiadau seiliedig ar chwarae
playboard (puppet stage) bwrdd chwarae *eg* byrddau chwarae
playcare gofal-chwarae
player chwaraewr *eg* chwaraewyr
playground (in general) lle chwarae *eg* llefydd chwarae
playground (of school) buarth chwarae *eg* buarthau chwarae
playgroup cylch chwarae *eg* cylchoedd chwarae
playgroup worker gweithiwr cylch chwarae *eg* gweithwyr cylch chwarae
playing field cae chwarae *eg* caeau chwarae
playing music chwarae cerddoriaeth *be*
play-pen corlan chwarae *eb* corlannau chwarae
play-scheme cynllun chwarae *eg* cynlluniau chwarae
playwork gwaith-chwarae *eg*
plea ple *eg/b* pledion
plead pledio *be*
pleader plediwr *eg* pledwyr
pleas of the Crown pledion y Goron *ell*
pleasing dymunol *ans*
pleasing appearance ymddangosiad dymunol *eg*
pleasure principle egwyddor pleser *eb*
pleat plet *eg/b* pletiau
pleated edge ymyl bletiog *eb* ymylon pletiog
pleated skirt sgert bletiog *eb* sgertiau pletiog
pleating pletio *be*
plebeian *adj* gwerinol *ans*
plebeian *n* gwerinwr Rhufeinig *eg* gwerinwyr Rhufeinig
plebiscite pleidlais gwlad *eb* pleidleisiau gwlad
plectrum plectrwm *eg* plectrymau
pledge (given as security) gwystl *eg* gwystlon
pleion pleion *eg*
pleiotropy pleiotropedd *eg*
Pleistocene Pleistosen *eg*
plenary llawn *ans*
plenary session sesiwn lawn *eb* sesiynau llawn
plenipotentiary plenipotensiwr *eg* plenipotenswyr
pleura *n* eisbilen *eb* eisbilennau
pleural eisbilennol *ans*
pleural cavity ceudod eisbilennol *eg* ceudodau eisbilennol
pleural fluid hylif eisbilennol *eg*
pleural membrane pilen eisbilennol yr ysgyfaint *eb* pilenni eisbilennol yr ysgyfaint
pliability hyblygedd *eg*
pliable hyblyg *ans*
pliancy ystwythder *eg*
pliant ystwyth *ans*
plication plygiant *eg* plygiannau
pliers gefelen *eb* gefeiliau
pliers-type saw set gosodydd llif teip gefelen *eg* gosodyddion llif teip gefelen
plinth plinth *eg* plinthiau
plinth block bloc plinth *eg* blociau plinth
plosive ffrwydrol *ans*
plot (=conspiracy) *n* cynllwyn *eg* cynllwynion
plot (=conspiracy) *v* cynllwynio *be*
plot (a point) *v* plotio *be*
plot (of land) *n* llain *eb* lleiniau
plot (of story etc) *n* plot *eg* plotiau
plotter plotydd *eg* plotyddion
plough (bookbinder's) plaen llyfr-rwymwr *eg* plaeniau llyfr-rwymwr
plough plane plaen rhigoli *eg* plaeniau rhigoli
ploughbote aradfudd *eg*
ploughing (in technology) rhigoli *be*
plug hys-bys *eg*
plug *n* plwg *eg* plygiau
plug *v* plygio *be*
plug compatible plwg-gytûn *ans*
plug gauge medrydd plwg *eg* medryddion plwg
plug tap tap plwg *eg* tapiau plwg
plugging chisel cŷn plygio *eg* cynion plygio; gaing blygio *eb* geingiau plygio
plug-in ategyn *eg* ategion
plug-in bar bar ategion *eg*
plug-in unit uned blygio *eb* unedau plygio
plumb plwm *ans*
plumb line llinyn plwm *eg* llinynnau plwm
plumbago (graphite + clay) plwmbago *eg*
plumbane plwmban *eg*
plumbate(II) ion ïon plwmbad(II) *eg* ïonau plwmbad(II)
plumbate(IV) ion ïon plwmbad(IV) *eg* ïonau plwmbad(IV)
plumber plymwr *eg* plymwyr
plumber's solder sodr plymwr *eg* sodrau plymwr
plumule (in botany) cyneginyn *eg* cynegin
plunge *n* plymiad *eg* plymiadau
plunge *v* plymio *be*
plunge pool plymbwll *eg* plymbyllau
plunger plymiwr *eg* plymwyr
plural society cymdeithas luosryw *eb* cymdeithasau lluosryw
pluralism (=holding more than one benefice) amlblwyfaeth *eb*
pluralism (of cultural diversity) plwraliaeth *eb*
pluralist amlblwyfydd *eg* amlblwyfyddion
pluralistic amlblwyfol *ans*
plurality amlblwyfaeth *eb*
plus plws *eg* plysau
plus sign arwydd plws *eg*
Pluto Plwton *eg*
plutocracy pliwtocratiaeth *eb*
plutocrat pliwtocrat *eg* pliwtocratiaid
plutonic rocks creigiau plwtonig *ell*
plutonium (Pu) plwtoniwm *eg*
pluvial glawog *ans*

ply (=layer) haen *eb* haenau
3 plywood pren tair haen *eg*
plywood pren haenog *eg*
plywood panel panel pren haenog *eg* paneli pren haenog
p-n junction cyswllt p-n *eg* cysylltau p-n
pneumatic niwmatig *ans*
pneumatic system system niwmatig *eb* systemau niwmatig
pneumatic tools offer niwmatig *ell*
pneumatics niwmateg *eb*
► **pneumonia** niwmonia *eg*
pneumotaxis niwmotacsis *eg*
poached egg wy wedi'i botsio *eg* wyau wedi'u potsio
poacher potsiwr *eg* potswyr
pocket *n* poced *eb* pocedi
pocket *v* pocedu *be*
pocket beach (bay head beach) cildraeth *eg* cildraethau
pocket borough bwrdeistref boced *eb* bwrdeistrefi poced
pocket money arian poced *eg*
pocket screwing sgriwio poced *be*
pocketbook (of portable computer) pocediadur *eg* pocediaduron
pod coden *eb* codennau
podiatrist podiatregydd *eg* podiatregwyr
podiatry podiatreg *eb*
podsol podsol *eg* podsolau
podsolic podsolig *ans*
poem cerdd *eb* cerddi
Poet Laureate Bardd y Brenin *eg*
poetic tradition traddodiad barddol *eg*
poetry barddoniaeth *eb*
poikilothermic poicilothermig *ans*
point *v* pwyntio *be*
point (in general) *n* pwynt *eg* pwyntiau
point (of bow) *n* blaen *eg*
point (topographic) *n* trwyn *eg* trwynau
point angle (drill part) ongl bwynt *eb* onglau pwynt
point attack ymosod â'r pwynt *be*
point charge gwefr bwynt *eb* gwefrau pwynt
point circle cylch pwynt *eg* cylchoedd pwynt
point collocation cydleoliad pwyntiol *eg*
point graph graff pwyntiau *eg* graffiau pwynt
point mass màs pwynt *eg* masau pwynt
point of articulation pwynt cymal *eg* pwyntiau cymal
point of contact pwynt cyffwrdd *eg* pwyntiau cyffwrdd
point of delay pwynt oedi *eg* pwyntiau oedi
point of detail pwynt manylyn *eg*
point of infinity pwynt anfeidredd *eg*
point of inflection pwynt ffurfdro *eg*
point of insertion mewnfan *eg* mewnfannau
► **point of intersection** pwynt croestoriad *eg* pwyntiau croestoriad
point of origin (muscle) tarddle *eg* tarddleoedd
point of sale terminal (POS) terfynell pwynt talu *eb* terfynellau pwyntiau talu
point of tangency pwynt tangiadaeth *eg* pwyntiau tangiadaeth
point of the jaw pwynt yr ên *eg*
point of view safbwynt *eg* safbwyntiau
point pattern analysis dadansoddi patrwm pwyntiau *be*
point sample samplu pwynt *be*
point size maint pwynt *eg*
point source tarddle pwynt *eg* tarddleoedd pwynt
point symmetry cymesuredd pwynt *eg*
pointed pigfain *ans*
pointed arch bwa pigfain *eg* bwâu pigfain
pointed collar coler pig *eg* coleri pig
pointed scissors siswrn pigfain *eg* sisyrnau pigfain
pointer pwyntydd *eg* pwyntyddion
point-of-sale item eitem pwynt talu *eb* eitemau pwynt talu
points of the compass pwyntiau'r cwmpawd *ell*
poise (=balance) cydbwysedd *eg*
poise (=carriage of body) osgo *eg*
poison *n* gwenwyn *eg* gwenwynau
poison *v* gwenwyno *be*
poisoning gwenwyniad *eg*
poisonous gases nwyon gwenwynig *ell*
Poisson distribution dosraniad Poisson *eg*
poker pocer *eg* poceri
poker work gwaith pocer *eg*
polar *n* pegynlin *eg* pegynliniau
polar (geographic) *adj* pegynol *ans*
polar (of magnet, electricity) *adj* polar *ans*
polar axis echelin begynol *eb* echelinau pegynol
polar body corffyn pegynol *eg* corffynnau pegynol
polar covalent cofalent polar *eg*
polar front ffrynt pegynol *eg* ffryntiau pegynol
polar projection tafluniad pegynol *eg* tafluniadau pegynol
polar solvent hydoddydd polar *eg* hydoddyddion polar
polar-continental pegynol-gyfandirol *ans*
polarimeter polarimedr *eg* polarimedrau
polarimetry polarimedreg *eb*
polarity polaredd *eg* polareddau
polarization polareiddiad *eg* polareiddiadau
► **polarize** polareiddio *be*
polarized polar *ans*
polarized light golau polar *eg*
polarizer polarydd *eg* polaryddion
polar-maritime pegynol-arforol *ans*
polder polder *eg* polderau
pole (=long, slender piece of wood, metal etc) polyn *eg* polion
pole (geographic) pegwn *eg* pegynau
pole (of magnet) pôl *eg* polau
pole lathe turn polyn *eg* turniau polyn
pole of development pegwn datblygiadol *eg* pegynau datblygiadol

pole piece darn pôl *eg* darnau pôl
pole star seren y gogledd *eb*
pole strength poledd *eg* poleddau
pole vault naid bolyn *eb* neidiau polyn
poleward tua'r pegwn *ans*
police heddlu *eg* heddluoedd
Police and Criminal Evidence Act Deddf Heddlu a Thystiolaeth Droseddol *eb*
police protection amddiffyniad heddlu *eg*
police state gwladwriaeth heddlu *eb*
police station gorsaf heddlu *eb* gorsafoedd heddlu
policy polisi *eg* polisïau
policy framework fframwaith polisi *eg*
polio polio *eg*
polish *v* llathru *be*
polish (=shine) *n* llathredd *eg*
polish (material) *n* llathrydd *eg* llathryddion
polish (style, performance etc) *v* caboli *be*
Polish Corridor Coridor Pwylaidd *eg*
polished (style, performance etc) caboledig *ans*
polished (surface) llathredig *ans*
polished stone axe bwyell garreg wedi'i llathru *eb*
polisher (equipment) llathrydd *eg* llathryddion
polishing buff bwff llathru *eg* bwffiau llathru
polishing cloth cadach llathru *eg* cadachau llathru
polishing compound cyfansoddyn llathru *eg* cyfansoddion llathru
polishing head pen llathru *eg* pennau llathru
polishing mop mop llathru *eg* mopiau llathru
polishing pad pad llathru *eg* padiau llathru
polishing process proses lathru *eb* prosesau llathru
polishing rag clwtyn llathru *eg* clytiau llathru
polishing wheel olwyn lathru *eb* olwynion llathru
political gwleidyddol *ans*
political and electoral reform diwygio gwleidyddol ac etholiadol *be*
political and religious radicalism radicaliaeth wleidyddol a chrefyddol *eb*
political asylum lloches wleidyddol *eb*
political balance cydbwysedd gwleidyddol *eg*
political economy economeg wleidyddol *eb*
political history hanes gwleidyddol *eg*
political party plaid wleidyddol *eb* pleidiau gwleidyddol
political structure strwythur gwleidyddol *eg*
political thought syniadaeth wleidyddol *eb*
political unification uno gwleidyddol *be*
politics gwleidyddiaeth *eb*
politics and society gwleidyddiaeth a chymdeithas
polka polca *eg* polcâu
polka step step bolca *eb* stepiau polca
poll search (in computing) chwiliad polau *eg* chwiliadau polau
poll tax treth y pen *eb*
pollack morleisiad *eg* morleisiaid
pollard tocbren *eg* tocbrennau
pollen paill *eg*
pollen analysis dadansoddi paill *be*
pollinate peillio *be*
pollutant llygrydd *eg* llygryddion
pollute llygru *be*
pollution llygredd *eg* llygreddau
polo neck gwddf polo *eg* gyddfau polo
polonaise polonaise *eg* polonaises
polonium (Po) poloniwm *eg*
polyandry amlwriaeth *eb*
polycarbonate polycarbonad *eg* polycarbonadau
poly(2-chlorobuta-1,3-diene) poly(2-clorobwta-1,3-deuen) *eg*
poly(chloroethene) poly(cloroethen) *eg*
polyclens polyclens *eg*
polycormic amlgormig *ans*
polyculture *n* amlgnwd *eg*
polyculture *v* amlgnydio *be*
polycycle amlgylchred *eg* amlgylchredau
polycyclic amlgylchredol *ans*
polydioxoboric(III) acid asid polydeuocsoborig(III) *eg*
polyester polyester *eg*
polyester lacquer lacr polyester *eg* lacrau polyester
polyester resin resin polyester *eg*
polyesters (thermosetting plastics) polyesterau *ell*
poly(ethene) poly(ethen) *eg*
poly(ethenol) poly(ethenol) *eg*
polyether foam ewyn polyether *eg*
polyethylene polyethylen *eg*
polyfilla polyffila *eg*
polyfluorocarbon polyfflworocarbon *eg*
polygamy (in zoology) amlweddogrwydd *eg*
polyglot *adj* amlieithog *ans*
polyglot *n* amlieithydd *eg* amlieithwyr
polygon polygon *eg* polygonau
polygon of forces polygon grymoedd *eg*
polygon shape siâp polygon *eg* siapiau polygon
polygynandry amlbariaeth *eb*
polygyny amlwreiciaeth *eb*
polyhedral polyhedrol *ans*
polyhedron polyhedron *eg* polyhedronau
polymer polymer *eg* polymerau
polymer emulsion emwlsiwn polymer *eg*
polymerization polymeriad *eg*
polymerize polymeru *be*
poly(methanal) poly(methanal) *eg*
poly(methyl 2-methylpropenoate) poly(methyl 2-methylpropenoad) *eg*
polynomial *adj* polynomaidd *ans*
polynomial *n* polynomial *eg* polynomialau
polynomial equation hafaliad polynomaidd *eg* hafaliadau polynomaidd
polynomial function ffwythiant polynomaidd *eg* ffwythiannau polynomaidd
polyomino polyomino *eg* polyominos
polypeptide polypeptid *eg*
poly(phenylethene) poly(ffenylethen) *eg*

polyphosphate polyffosffad *eg*
poly(propene) poly(propen) *eg*
polypropylene polypropylen *eg*
polysaccharide polysacarid *eg*
polysemic amlystyr *ans*
polystyrene polystyren *eg*
polystyrene casting castio polystyren *be*
poly(tetrafluoroethene) poly(tetrafflworoethen) *eg*
polytheism amldduwiaeth *eb*
polythene polythen *eg*
polythene bag bag polythen *eg* bagiau polythen
polytonal amlgywair *ans*
polytonality amlgyweiredd *eg* amlgyweireddau
polytope polytop *eg* polytopau
polytrioxophosphate(V) polytriocsoffosffad(V) *eg*
polytrioxovanadate(V) polytriocsofanadad(V) *eg*
polyunsaturated amlannirlawn *ans*
polyunsaturated fatty acid asid brasterog amlannirlawn *eg*
polyurethane polywrethan *eg*
polyurethane finish gorffeniad polywrethan *eg*
polyurethane varnish farnais polywrethan *eg*
polyvinyl acetate polyfinyl asetad *eg*
polyvinyl acetate glue glud polyfinyl asetad *eg*
polyvinyl chloride polyfinyl clorid *eg*
polyvinylidene polyfinyliden *eg*
pomarine skua sgiwen gynffondro *eb* sgiwennod cynffondro
pommel cnap *eg* cnapiau
pompom pompom *eg* pompomau
ponderous trwm *ans*
ponor (=swallow hole) llyncdwll *eg* llyncdyllau
pons pons *eg*
pontage pontreth *eb* pontrethi
ponticello ponticello *adf*
pontiff pontiff *eg* pontiffau
pontifical llyfr esgobol *eg* llyfrau esgobol
pontificate teyrnasiad pab *eg*
pony trekker merlotwr *eg* merlotwyr
pony trekking merlota *be*
pony-hair brush brwsh blew merlen *eg* brwshys blew merlen
pool (=fund) cronfa *eb* cronfeydd
pool (for swimming) pwll *eg* pyllau
pool resources cyfuno adnoddau *be*
poor tlawd *ans*
poor law cyfraith y tlodion *eb*
Poor Law Amendment Act Deddf Newydd y Tlodion *eb*
poor quality housing tai o ansawdd gwael *ell*
poor relief cymorth y tlodion *eg*
pop *n* pop *eg*
pop *v* popio *be*
pop art celfyddyd bop *eb*
pop rivet rhybed pop *eg* rhybedion pop
pop song cân boblogaidd *eb* caneuon poblogaidd
pope pab *eg* pabau

popish pabaidd *ans*
Popish Plot Cynllwyn Pabaidd *eg*
poplin poplin *eg*
popping crease cris batio *eg* crisiau batio
poppy oil olew pabi *eg*
popular poblogaidd *ans*
popular front ffrynt y bobl *eg*
popular protest protestiadau'r bobl *ell*
popular sovereignty sofraniaeth y bobl *eb*
popularity and appeal poblogrwydd ac apêl
populated country gwlad boblog *eb* gwledydd poblog
population poblogaeth *eb* poblogaethau
population cycle cylchred poblogaeth *eb*
population explosion ffrwydrad poblogaeth *eg*
population potential potensial poblogaeth *eg*
population regulation rheoli poblogaeth *be*
population variance amrywiant poblogaeth *eg*
populism poblyddiaeth *eb*
populist poblyddwr *eg* poblyddwyr
pop-up menu naidlen *eb* naidlenni
porbeagle shark corgi môr *eg* corgwn môr
porcelain porslen *eg*
porch porth *eg* pyrth
pore mandwll *eg* mandyllau
porosity mandylledd *eg*
porous mandyllog *ans*
porous ground (in art) grwnd mandyllog *eg*
porous ring cylch hydraidd *eg* cylchoedd hydraidd
porous surface arwyneb mandyllog *eg* arwynebau mandyllog
porphyritic porffyritig *ans*
porphyry porffyri *eg*
porpoise llamhidydd *eg* llamhidyddion
port porth *eg* pyrth
port (side) port *eg*
port of call porthladd galw *eg* porthladdoedd galw
port tack tacio port *be*
portability cludadwyedd *eg*
portable cludadwy *ans*
portable apparatus offer cludol *ell*
portable computer cyfrifiadur cludadwy *eg* cyfrifiaduron cludadwy
portable drill dril cludadwy *eg* driliau cludadwy
portable easel îsl cludadwy *eg* islau cludadwy
portable electric drill dril trydan cludadwy *eg* driliau trydan cludadwy
portable forge gefail gludadwy *eb* gefeiliau cludadwy
portable grinder llifanydd cludadwy *eg* llifanyddion cludadwy
portable plane plaen cludadwy *eg* plaeniau cludadwy
portable planer plaeniwr cludadwy *eg* plaenwyr cludadwy
portable power tools offer pŵer cludadwy *ell*
portable sander sandiwr cludadwy *eg* sandwyr cludadwy

portable screen sgrin gludadwy *eb* sgriniau cludadwy
portable vice feis gludadwy *eb* feisiau cludadwy
portal dolmen dolmen porth *eg*
portal framed building adeilad ffrâm bortal *eg*
portal vein gwythïen bortal *eb* gwythiennau portal
portamento portamento *eg* portamenti
portative organ organ gludadwy *eb* organau cludadwy
portcullis porthcwlis *eg*
porter porthor *eg* porthorion
portering porthora *be*
portfolio portffolio *eg*
porting trosglwyddo *be*
porting (=carrying the canoe) cario *be*
portion cyfran *eb* cyfrannau
portionary church eglwys gyd-gyfranedig *eb* eglwysi cyd-gyfranedig
Portland cement sment Portland *eg*
portrait portread *eg* portreadau
portrait painter paentiwr portreadau *eg* paentwyr portreadau
portrait painting (of painted picture) paentiad portreadol *be* paentiadau portreadol
portrait painting (of process or art) peintio portreadol *be*
portrait study astudiaeth bortreadol *eb* astudiaethau portreadol
portray portreadu *be*
port-reeve porthfaer *eg* porthfeiri
Portuguese (language) Portiwgaleg *eb*
Portuguese (person) Portiwgalydd *eg* Portiwgaliaid
PoS: programme of study RhA: rhaglen astudio *eb* rhaglenni astudio
pose *n* ystum *eg/b* ystumiau
pose *v* sefyll mewn ystum *be*
posed model model mewn ystum arbennig *eg* modelau mewn ystum arbennig
position (=place) *v* lleoli *be*
position (=situation) *n* sefyllfa *eb* sefyllfaoedd
position (of place) *n* safle *eg* safleoedd
position (oneself) *v* cymryd safle *be*
position of the feet safle'r traed *eg*
position of the sun safle'r haul
position vector fector safle *eg*
positive (in general) cadarnhaol *ans*
positive (in mathematics, science) positif *ans*
positive aspect agwedd gadarnhaol *eb* agweddau cadarnhaol
positive attitude agwedd gadarnhaol *eb*
positive charge gwefr bositif *eb* gwefrau positif
positive constant cysonyn positif *eg*
positive discrimination gwahaniaethu'n gadarnhaol *be*
positive drive gyriad positif *eg* gyriadau positif
positive externalities allanoldeb positif *eg* allanoldebau positif
positive feedback (from people) ymateb cadarnhaol *eg*
positive feedback (of signal) adborth positif *eg*
positive image (in photography etc) delwedd bositif *eb* delweddau positif
positive image (of people etc) delwedd gadarnhaol *eb* delweddau cadarnhaol
positive rake gwyredd positif *eg*
positive reinforcement atgyfnerthiad cadarnhaol *eg*
positive skew sgiw bositif *eb* sgiwiau positif
positive symptom symptom cadarnhaol *eg* symptomau cadarnhaol
positive variance amrywiant cadarnhaol *eg* amrywiannau cadarnhaol
positive whole number rhif cyfan positif *eg*
positively bounded below yn ffinedig bositif oddi tanodd
positivism positifiaeth *eb*
positron positron *eg* positronau
positron emission tomography (PET) tomograffeg gollwng positronau *eg*
possession meddiant *eg* meddiannau
possession of the ball meddiant o'r bêl *eg*
possessions (=belongings) eiddo *eg*
possessive meddiannol *ans*
posset llaeth baban *eg*
possibilism posibiliaeth *eb*
possibilist posibiliedydd *eg* posibiliedwyr
possible impact effaith bosibl *eb* effeithiau posibl
post postio *be*
post postyn *eg* pyst
post glacial olrewlifol *ans*
Post Graduate Certificate of Education (PGCE) Tystysgrif Addysg i Raddedigion *eb*
post hoc post hoc
post impressionism ôl-argraffiadaeth *eb*
post office swyddfa'r post *eb*
Post Office box blwch Swyddfa'r Post *eg* blychau Swyddfa'r Post
post synaptic membrane pilen ôl-synaptig *eb*
postage stamp stamp post *eg* stampiau post
postal post *ans*
postal order archeb bost *eb* archebion post
postal services gwasanaethau post *ell*
post-anaesthetic recovery adfer wedi'r anaesthetig *be*
postcard cerdyn post *eg* cardiau post
postconventional level lefel ôl-gonfensiynol *eb*
post-dissolution wedi'r diddymiad *ans*
poster poster *eg* posteri
poster colour lliw posteri *eg* lliwiau posteri
poster paint paent posteri *eg* paentiau posteri
poster pen pen posteri *eg* pennau posteri
poster-brush brwsh poster *eg* brwshys poster
posterior *adj* ôl *ans*
posterior part of the parietal cortex (PPC) rhan ôl y cortecs parwydol *eb*
posterior probability ôl debygolrwydd *eg*
postfix *n* olddodiad *eg* olddodiaid
postfix *v* olddodi *be*

posthypnotic amnesia amnesia ôl-hypnosis *eg*
posthypnotic suggestibility awgrymiadedd ôl-hypnosis *eb*
postlude postliwd *eg* postliwdiau
post-mortem post-mortem *eg*
post-multiply ôl-luosi *be*
post-natal ôl-enedigol *ans*
post-natal care gofal ôl-eni *eg*
post-natal clinic clinig ôl-eni *eg* clinigau ôl-eni
post-operative care gofal wedi'r llawdriniaeth *eg*
postsynaptic neuron niwron ôl-synaptig *eg* niwronau ôl-synaptig
post-traumatic stress disorder (PTSD) anhwylder pryder ôl-drawmatig *eg*
postulate cynosod *be*
postulation cynosodiad *eg* cynosodiadau
postural sense synnwyr o osgo *eg*
posture (in gymnastics) ymddaliad *eg* ymddaliadau
pot llestr *eg* llestri
pot life oes defnydd *eg*
potassium (K) potasiwm *eg*
potassium iodide potasiwm iodid *eg*
potassium ion ïon potasiwm *eg* ïonau potasiwm
potassium nitrate potasiwm nitrad *eg*
potassium sodium 2,3-dihydroxybutanedioate potasiwm sodiwm 2,3-deuhydrocsibwtandeuoad *eg*
potassium tetracyanocuprate(I) potasiwm tetracyanocwprad(I) *eg*
potato blight malltod tatws *eg*
potato cut torlun taten *eg* torluniau tatws
potato printing printio â thaten *be*
potency nerth *eg*
potential potensial *eg* potensialau
potential customer darpar gwsmer *eg* darpar gwsmeriaid
potential difference gwahaniaeth potensial *eg* gwahaniaethau potensial
potential divider rhannwr potensial *eg* rhanwyr potensial
potential energy egni potensial *eg*
potential growth twf posibl *eg*
potential hazard perygl posibl *eg*
potential market marchnad botensial *eb*
potentiometer potensiomedr *eg* potensiomedrau
pothole ceubwll *eg* ceubyllau
potted sports mabolgampau bach *ell*
potter crochenydd *eg* crochenwyr
potter's apron ffedog crochenydd *eb* ffedogau crochenydd
potter's clay clai crochenydd *eg*
potter's wheel olwyn crochenydd *eb* olwynion crochenydd
pottery (object) crochenwaith *eg*
pottery (workshop) crochendy *eg* crochendai
pottery glaze gwydredd crochenwaith *eg*
potty training hyfforddiant toiled *eg*
poultice powltis *eg*
poultry dofednod *ell*
pounce (=powder) *n* panlwch *eg*
pounce (=powder) *v* panlychu *be*
pound (money) *n* punt *eb* punnoedd
pound (weight) *n* pwys *eg* pwysi
pound key bysell punt *eb* bysellau punt
pour arllwys *be*
pouring basin basn arllwys *eg* basnau arllwys
pouring batter cytew tenau *eg*
pouring gate porthell arllwys *eb* porthelli arllwys
pouring method dull arllwys *eg*
poussette poussette *eb*
poverty tlodi *eg*
powder powdr *eg* powdrau
powder colour powdrliw *eg* powdrliwiau
powder form ffurf bowdr *eb*
powder glaze gwydredd powdr *eg*
powder pigment pigment powdr *eg* pigmentau powdr
powdered clay clai powdr *eg*
powdered enamel enamel powdrog *eg*
powdered glue glud powdr *eg*
powdery powdrog *ans*
power (=strength) nerth *eg* nerthoedd
power (in physics) pŵer *eg* pwerau
power (of capability) gallu *eg* galluoedd
power amp mwyhadur pŵer *eg* mwyaduron pŵer
power cut toriad pŵer *eg* toriadau pŵer
power drive gyriad pŵer *eg* gyriadau pŵer
power factor ffactor pŵer *eb*
power function ffwythiant pŵer *eg* ffwythiannau pŵer
power hacksaw haclif bŵer *eb* haclifiau pŵer
power jig saw herclif bŵer *eb* herclifiau pŵer
power loom gwŷdd peiriannol *eg* gwyddau peiriannol
power (of a statistical test) pŵer (prawf ystadegol) *eg*
power pack pecyn pŵer *eg* paecynnau pŵer
power plane plaen pŵer *eg* plaeniau pŵer
power point soced trydan *eg* socedi trydan
power politics gwleidyddiaeth grym *eb*
power sander sandiwr pŵer *eg* sandwyr pŵer
power station gorsaf drydan *eb* gorsafoedd trydan
power supply cyflenwad pŵer *eg* cyflenwadau pŵer
power surge ymchwydd pŵer *eg* ymchwyddiadau pŵer
power tool erfyn pŵer *eg* offer pŵer
powerful grymus *ans*
powerful serve serfio grymus *be*
powers of 10 pwerau o 10 *ell*
pox brech *eb* brechau
Pozidrive screw sgriw Pozidrive *eb* sgriwiau Pozidrive
Pozidrive screwdriver tyrnsgriw Pozidrive *eg* tyrnsgriwiau Pozidrive
PP number publications cyhoeddiadau rhif PP *ell*
practical ymarferol *ans*
practical activity gweithgaredd ymarferol *eg* gweithgareddau ymarferol

practical approach agwedd ymarferol *eb*
practical ethics moeseg ymarferol *eb*
practical test prawf ymarferol *eg* profion ymarferol
practical work gwaith ymarferol *eg*
practice (=exercise) *n* ymarfer *eg* ymarferion
practice (=habit) *n* arfer *eg/b* arferion
practice enamel enamel ymarfer *eg*
practice nurse nyrs practis *eb* nyrsys practis
practice period cyfnod ymarfer *eg* cyfnodau ymarfer
practise *v* ymarfer *be*
practitioner ymarferwr *eg* ymarferwyr
pragmatic pragmatig *ans*
Pragmatic Sanction Datganiad Pragmatig *eg*
pragmatism pragmatiaeth *eb*
pragmatist pragmatydd *eg* pragmatyddion
prairie paith *eg* peithiau
prairie soils peithbriddoedd *ell*
pram pram *eg* pramiau
pram hood cwfl pram *eg* cyflau pram
praseodymium (Pr) praseodymiwm *eg*
pratitya-samutpada pratitya-samutpada *eg*
pray gweddïo *be*
prayer gweddi *eb* gweddïau
preach pregethu *be*
preacher pregethwr *eg* pregethwyr
preamble rhaglith *eg* rhaglithoedd
pre-amp rhagfwyhadur *eg*
preamplifier rheolydd ton
prebend prebend *eg* prebendau
prebendary prebendari *eg* prebendariaid
pre-budget statement datganiad cyn y gyllideb *eg*
pre-Cambrian cyn-Gambriaidd *ans*
precaution rhagofal *eg* rhagofalon
precedence blaenoriaeth *eb* blaenoriaethau
precedent cynsail *eb* cynseiliau
preceptor preceptor *eg* preceptoriaid
preceptorship preceptoriaeth *eb* preceptoriaethau
precess presesu *be*
precession presesiad *eg* presesiadau
precession of the equinoxes blaenoriad y cyhydnosau *eg*
precinct cyffin *eg* cyffiniau
precipice dibyn *eg* dibynnau
precipitate (=sediment) gwaddod *eg* gwaddodion
precipitation (of insoluble compound) dyddodiad *eg*
precipitation (of rain, snow or hail) dyodiad *eg*
precise (in science) trachywir *ans*
precision (in human activity etc) manwl gywirdeb *eg*
precision (of instruments etc) trachywiredd *eg*
precision instruments offer trachywir *ell*
precision measuring tool erfyn mesur trachywir *eg* offer mesur trachywir
precision trimmer trimiwr trachywir *eg* trimwyr trachywir
precocious (of fruit, flower etc) rhagaeddfed *ans*
pre-conceptual thought meddwl cyn-gysyniadol *eg* meddyliau cyn-gysyniadol
precondition rhag-amod *eg* rhag-amodau
preconventional level lefel gyngonfensiynol *eb*
predation ysglyfaethu *be*
predator ysglyfaethwr *eg* ysglyfaethwyr
predatory pricing prisio rheibus *be*
predecessor rhagflaenydd *eg* rhagflaenwyr
predestinarian rhagordeiniadol *ans*
predestinarianism rhagordeiniadaeth *eb*
predestination rhagordeiniad *eg*
predict (in non-technical usage) rhagweld *be*
predict (in science) rhagfynegi *be*
predicting rhagfynegi *be*
prediction rhagfynegiad *eg* rhagfynegiadau
predictive validity dilysrwydd rhagfynegi *eg*
predictor daroganwr *eg* daroganwyr
predisposing factors ffactor rhagdueddu *eb* ffactorau rhagdueddu
predisposition rhagdueddiad *eg*
predominant prif *ans*
predominate (=excel) rhagori *be*
pre-eclampsia cyneclampsia *eg*
pre-emptive strike rhagymosodiad *eg* rhagymosodiadau
pre-existing valley dyffryn cynfodol *eg* dyffrynnoedd cynfodol
prefabricate (preform) rhagffurfio *be*
prefabricated house tŷ parod *eg* tai parod
prefect (in French administration) rhaglaw *eg* rhaglawiaid
preference blaenoriaeth *eb* blaenoriaethau
preference dewis *eg* dewisiadau
preferences (=preferred settings) dewisiadau *ell*
preferential discharge dadwefru blaenoriaethol *be*
preferential tariff toll fantais *eb* tollau mantais
preferment dyrchafiad *eg* dyrchafiadau
preferred reading (of audience response) dehongliad dewisol *eg*
prefix *n* rhagddodiad *eg* rhagddodiaid
prefix *v* rhagddodi *be*
preform rhagffurfio *be*
prefrontal cortex cortecs cyndalcennol *eg*
pre-glacial cynrewlifol *ans*
pregnancy beichiogrwydd *eg*
pregnant beichiog *ans*
preheat rhagboethi *be*
prehistoric cynhanes *ans*
prehistoric trackway llwybr cynhanes *eg* llwybrau cynhanes
prehistory cynhanes *eg*
pre-ignition cyn-daniad *eg*
prejudice rhagfarn *eb* rhagfarnau
prelate prelad *eg* preladiaid
preliminary rhagarweiniol *ans*
preliminary coat cot gyntaf *eb* cotiau cyntaf
preliminary drawing lluniad rhagarweiniol *eg* lluniadau rhagarweiniol
preliminary sketch braslun rhagarweiniol *eg* brasluniau rhagarweiniol

preliminary test rhagbrawf *eg* rhagbrofion
prelude preliwd *eg* preliwdiau
premature cynamserol *ans*
premedication rhagfoddion *eg*
premenstrual tension tyndra cyn mislif *eg*
premises adeiladau *ell*
premium premiwm *eg* premiymau
Premium Bond Bond Premiwm *eg* Bondiau Premiwm
premium price pris premiwm *eg*
pre-mix blaen-gymysgiad *eg*
premolar gogilddant *eg* gogilddannedd
Premonstratensians Canoniaid Premonstratensiaidd *ell*
pre-multiply blaen-luosi *be*
prenatal cyn-geni *ans*
prenatal period cyfnod cyn geni *eg*
prenursing course cwrs cyn-nyrsio *eg*
preoperational stage cyfnod cynweithredol *eg*
preoperative care gofal cyn llawdriniaeth *eg*
preoptic area ardal gynoptig *eb*
prepack blaenbacio *be*
prepacked food bwyd wedi'i bacio'n barod *eg*
preparation paratoad *eg* paratoadau
preparation of a discord paratoi anghytsain *be*
preparatory paratoadol *ans*
preparatory beat blaenguriad *eg* blaenguriadau
preparatory work gwaith paratoadol *eg*
prepare paratoi *be*
prepared piano piano paratoëdig *eg* pianos paratoëdig
prepared slide sleid wedi'i pharatoi *eb*
preparing children for hospital paratoi plant i'r ysbyty *be*
prepay rhagdalu *be*
prepayment meter mesurydd rhagdal *eg* mesuryddion rhagdal
pre-prepare paratoi ymlaen llaw *be*
pre-prepared a baratowyd ymlaen llaw *ans*
preprinted paper papur cynargraffedig *eg*
preproduction rhag-gynhyrchu *be*
Pre-Raphaelite *adj* Cyn-Raffaelaidd *ans*
Pre-Raphaelite *n* Cyn-Raffaeliad *eg* Cyn-Raffaeliaid
Pre-Raphaelite Brotherhood Brawdoliaeth y Cyn-Raffaeliaid *eb*
prerecorded tape tâp parod *eg* tapiau parod
prerogative *adj* uchelfreiniol *ans*
prerogative *n* uchelfraint *eb* uchelfreintiau
Prerogative Court Llys Uchelfraint *eg*
presbyter presbyter *eg* presbyteriaid
Presbyterian *adj* Presbyteraidd *ans*
Presbyterian *n* Presbyteriad *eg* Presbyteriaid
presbytery presbytri *eg* presbytriau
preschool dan oed ysgol *ans*
preschool child plentyn dan oed ysgol *eg* plant dan oed ysgol
prescribe (=impose authoritatively) rhagnodi *be*
prescribed limits cyfyngiadau penodedig *ell*
prescription presgripsiwn *eg* presgripsiynau
prescription charge tâl presgripsiwn *eg* taliadau presgripsiwn
prescriptive rhagnodol *ans*
preselective rhagddetholiadol *ans*
presence presenoldeb *eg*
present the worship cyflwyno'r addoliad *be*
present worth gwerth presennol *eg*
presentation cyflwyniad *eg* cyflwyniadau
presentation mode modd cyflwyno *eg* moddau cyflwyno
presentation style arddull cyflwyno *eb* arddulliau cyflwyno
presentation technique techneg gyflwyno *eb* technegau cyflwyno
presenting information cyflwyno gwybodaeth *be*
preservative (=preserving substance) cadwolyn *eg* cadwolion
preservative (of foodstuffs) cyffeithydd *eg* cyffeithyddion
preserve cadw *be*
preset rhagosod *be*
pre-shrink rhagbannu *be*
pre-shrunk (finish) rhagbanedig *ans*
presidency (of society etc) llywyddiaeth *eb*
presidency (of state) arlywyddiaeth *eb*
president (of society etc) llywydd *eg* llywyddion
president (of state) arlywydd *eg* arlywyddion
presidium presidiwm *eg*
press (=apply pressure) *v* pwyso *be*
press (=force) *v* gorfodi *be*
press (=squeeze) *v* gwasgu *be*
press (for printing, journalists) *n* gwasg *eb* gweisg
press a key pwyso bysell *be*
press cloth lliain presio *eg* llieiniau presio
press clothes presio dillad *be*
Press Complaints Commission Comisiwn Cwynion y Wasg *eg*
press conference cynhadledd i'r wasg *eb* cynadleddau i'r wasg
press fit gwasgffit *eg*
press gang près, y *ell*
press release datganiad i'r wasg *eg* datganiadau i'r wasg
press stud styden wasg *eb* stydiau gwasg
press stud tool erfyn styden wasg *eg* offer stydiau gwasg
pressed gwasgedig *ans*
pressed clay clai gwasgedig *eg*
pressed hinge colfach gwasgedig *eg* colfachau gwasgedig
presser foot (of machine part) gwasgell *eb* gwasgelli
presser lever (of machine part) lifer gwasgell *eg* liferi gwasgell
pressing cloth lliain presio *eg* llieiniau presio
pressing pad pad presio *eg* padiau presio
pressing roller rholer presio *eg* rholeri presio
press-up byrfraich *eg* byrfreichiau

pressure (in physics etc) gwasgedd *eg* gwasgeddau
pressure (of work etc) pwysau *ell*
pressure area man gwasgu *eg* mannau gwasgu
pressure belt belt wasgedd *eb* beltiau gwasgedd
pressure block bloc gwasgu *eg* blociau gwasgu
pressure cooker sosban frys *eb* sosbannau brys
pressure die casting deigastio gwasgol *be*
pressure forming ffurfio dan wasgedd *be*
pressure gauge medrydd gwasgedd *eg* medryddion gwasgedd
pressure gradient graddiant gwasgedd *eg* graddiannau gwasgedd
pressure group carfan bwyso *eb* carfannau pwyso
pressure level lefel gwasgedd *eb*
pressure point gwasgbwynt *eg* gwasgbwyntiau
pressure sore dolur gwasgu *eg* doluriau gwasgu
pressure tendency tueddiad gwasgedd *eg* tueddiadau gwasgedd
pressure valve falf gwasgedd *eb* falfiau gwasgedd
pressurize gwasgeddu *be*
pressurized gwasgeddedig *ans*
prestige bri *eg*
prestige industries diwydiannau bri *ell*
prestige myth myth bri *eg*
presumption rhagdybiaeth *eb* rhagdybiaethau
presynaptic rhagsynaptig *ans*
presynaptic neuron niwron cynsynaptig *eg* niwronau cynsynaptig
pretend play chwarae dychmygu *be*
pretender (to the throne) ymhonnwr *eg* ymhonwyr
pre-test *v* cynbrofi *be*
pre-test *n* cyn-brawf *eg* cynbrofion
pre-trial cyndreialu *be*
prevailing wind prifwynt *eg* prifwyntoedd
prevalence mynychder *eg*
prevent atal *be*
preventative model model ataliol *eg*
prevention ataliad *eg*
prevention rhwystro *be*
preventive care gofal ataliol *eg*
preventive medicine meddygaeth ataliol *eb*
previously prepared document dogfen barod *eb* dogfennau parod
pre-wash cynolchi *be*
prey *n* ysglyfaeth *eb* ysglyfaethau
prey *v* ysglyfaethu *be*
prey insect pryfyn ysglyfaeth *eg* pryfed ysglyfaeth
prey population poblogaeth yr ysglyfaeth
price pris *eg* prisiau
price and income elasticity elastigedd pris ac incwm *eg*
price control rheoli prisiau *be*
price differentiation priswahaniaethu *be*
price discrimination gwahaniaethu prisiau *be*
price elasticity elastigedd pris *eg*
price elasticity of demand elastigedd pris y galw *eg*
price elasticity of supply elastigedd pris y cyflenwad *eg*
price revolution chwyldro prisiau *eg*
Prices Act Deddf Prisiau *eb*
prices and incomes policy polisi prisiau ac incwm *eg*
pricing policy polisi prisio *eg*
pricing strategy strategaeth brisio *eb* strategaethau prisio
prick and pounce pricio a phanlychu *be*
priest offeiriad *eg* offeiriaid
priesthood of all believers offeiriadaeth yr holl saint *eb*
primacy uchafiaeth *eb*
primacy effect effaith blaenoriaeth *eb*
primal gwreiddiol *ans*
primarrumpf lledwastad dechreuol *eg*
primary (=basic) sylfaenol *ans*
primary (=first tier) cynradd *ans*
primary (=initial) cychwynnol *ans*
primary (=original) gwreiddiol *ans*
primary (=principal) prif *ans*
primary alcohol alcohol cynradd *eg*
primary appraisal gwerthusiad cychwynnol *eg* gwerthusiadau cychwynnol
primary auditory cortex prif gortecs y clyw *eg*
primary clay clai sylfaenol *eg*
primary coil coil cynradd *eg* coiliau cynradd
primary colour lliw sylfaenol *eg* lliwiau sylfaenol
primary consumer ysydd cynradd *eg* ysyddion cynradd
primary education addysg gynradd *eb*
primary election (US) rhagetholiad *eg* rhagetholiadau
primary evidence tystiolaeth wreiddiol *eb*
primary feather prif bluen *eb* prif blu
primary hazard perygl cynradd *eg*
▸ **primary health care** gofal iechyd cychwynnol *eg*
primary industry diwydiant cynradd *eg* diwydiannau cynradd
▸ **primary key** prif allwedd *eb* prif allweddi
▸ **primary memory** prif gof *eg*
primary motor cortex prif gortecs echddygol *eg*
primary nurse nyrs sylfaenol *eb* nyrsys sylfaenol
primary nursing nyrsio sylfaenol *be*
primary productivity cynhyrchedd cynradd *eg*
primary punisher cosbydd sylfaenol *eg* cosbyddion sylfaenol
primary reinforcer atgyfnerthydd sylfaenol *eg* atgyfnerthwyr sylfaenol
primary research ymchwil cynradd *eg*
primary school ysgol gynradd *eb* ysgolion cynradd
primary school child plentyn ysgol gynradd *eg* plant ysgol gynradd
primary sector sector cynradd *eg*
primary socialization cymdeithasoli cynradd *be*
primary somatosensory cortex prif gortecs corfforol-synhwyraidd *eg*
primary source ffynhonnell wreiddiol *eb* ffynonellau gwreiddiol

primary stem coesyn cynradd *eg* coesynnau cynradd
primary storage and secondary storage storio cynradd a storio eilaidd
primary visual cortex prif gortecs y golwg *eg*
primate (=archbishop) archesgob *eg* archesgobion
primate (of mammal) primat *eg* primatiaid
primate city archddinas *eb* archddinasoedd
prime *adj* cysefin *ans*
prime *v* preimio *be*
prime (monastic) *n* awr brim *eb* oriau prim
prime factor ffactor gysefin *eb* ffactorau cysefin
prime meridian prif feridian *eb*
prime minister prif weinidog *eg* prif weinidogion
prime number *n* rhif cysefin *eg* rhifau cysefin
prime time oriau brig *ell*
primed canvas cynfas wedi'i breimio *eg* cynfasau wedi'u preimio
primer paint paent preimio *eg* paentiau preimio
primeval cynoesol *ans*
priming preimio *be*
primitive cyntefig *ans*
Primitive Methodism Methodistiaeth Gyntefig *eb*
primitive music cerddoriaeth gyntefig *eb*
primitivism cyntefigedd *eg*
primogeniture cyntaf-anedigaeth *eb*
primordial meristem meristem brimordiol *eb*
primrose yellow melyn y friallen *eg*
prince tywysog *eg* tywysogion
Prince Consort Tywysog Cydweddog *eg*
Prince Elector Etholydd Tywysogol *eg*
prince of the blood tywysog o waed *eg* tywysogion o waed
Prince Regent Rhaglyw Dywysog *eg*
Princess Elizabeth's Fancy Ffansi Lisa *eb*
principal *adj* prif *ans*
principal (=chief person) *n* pennaeth *eg* penaethiaid
principal (of money) *n* prifswm *eg* prifsymiau
Principal Component Analysis Dadansoddiad Prif Gydrannau *eg*
principal contractor prif gontractwr *eg* prif gontractwyr
principal focus prif ffocws *eg*
principal planes prif blanau *ell*
principal station prif orsaf *eb* prif orsafoedd
principal value penrhif *eg* penrhifau
principality tywysogaeth *eb* tywysogaethau
principle egwyddor *eb* egwyddorion
principle of continuity egwyddor didoriant *eg*
principles of diet egwyddorion deiet *ell*
principles of levers egwyddorion liferi *ell*
principles of movement egwyddorion symudiad *ell*
print (=printed picture, fabric) *n* print *eg* printiau
print (pictures, designs) *v* printio *be*
print (text) *v* argraffu *be*
print format fformat argraffu *eg*
print patch clwt print *eg* clytiau print
print position cysodfan *eg* cysodfannau
print preview rhagolwg argraffu *eg* rhagolygon argraffu
print thimble gwniadur argraffu *eg* gwniaduron argraffu
print wheel olwyn argraffu *eb* olwynion argraffu
printed printiedig *ans*
printed circuit cylched brintiedig *eb* cylchedau printiedig
printed circuit board bwrdd cylched brintiedig *eg* byrddau cylched brintiedig
printed fabric ffabrig printiedig *eg* ffabrigau printiedig
printed image delwedd brintiedig *eb* delweddau printiedig
printed pattern patrwm print *eg* patrymau print
printed source ffynhonnell brintiedig *eb* ffynonellau printiedig
printed textile tecstil printiedig *eg* tecstilau printiedig
printed title block bloc teitl printiedig *eg* blociau teitl printiedig
printer argraffydd *eg* argraffyddion
printer driver gyrrwr argraffydd *eg*
printer port porth argraffydd *eg* pyrth argraffyddion
printer window ffenestr argraffydd *eb* ffenestri argraffyddion
printer-friendly version fersiwn hwylus i'w argraffu *eg* fersiynau hwylus i'w hargraffu
printer's ink inc argraffydd *eg* inciau argraffydd
printing equipment offer argraffu *ell*
printing ink inc argraffu *eg* inciau argraffu
printing material defnydd argraffu *eg* defnyddiau argraffu
printing method dull argraffu *eg* dulliau argraffu
printing press gwasg argraffu *eb* gweisg argraffu
printing roller rholer printio *eg* rholeri printio
printing speed cyflymder argraffu *eg*
printing stick ffon argraffu â phren *eb* ffyn argraffu â phren
printing unit uned argraffu *eb* unedau argraffu
printout allbrint *eg* allbrintiau
prior *adj* blaenorol *ans*
prior (of religious order) *n* prior *eg* prioriaid
prior learning dysgu blaenorol *be*
prior probability rhagdebygolrwydd *eg*
prioress priores *eb* prioresau
prioritize blaenoriaethu *be*
priority blaenoriaeth *eb* blaenoriaethau
priority interrupt ymyriad blaenoriaethol *eg* ymyriadau blaenoriaethol
priorship prioriaeth *eb* prioriaethau
priory priordy *eg* priordai
prise preis *eg*
prism prism *eg* prismau
prismatic prismatig *ans*
prismatic compass cwmpawd prismatig *eg* cwmpawdau prismatig
prismatoid prismatoid *eg* prismatoidau
prismoid prismoid *eg* prismoidau

prismoidal prismoidol *ans*
prison reform diwygio'r carcharau *be*
prison simulation efelychu carchar *be*
prisoner of war camp
gwersyll carcharorion rhyfel *eg*
gwersylloedd carcharorion rhyfel
pritchel hole twll pwnsh *eg* tyllau pwnsh
private *adj* preifat *ans*
private (soldier) *n* milwr cyffredin *eg* milwyr cyffredin
private benefits buddiannau preifat *ell*
private costs costau preifat *ell*
private enterprise menter breifat *eb* mentrau preifat
private health care gofal iechyd preifat *eg*
private limited company
cwmni cyfyngedig preifat *eg*
private sale gwerthu'n breifat *be*
private school ysgol breifat *eb* ysgolion preifat
private sector sector preifat *eg*
privateer preifatîr *eg* preifatiriaid
privation amddifadrwydd *eg*
privatization preifateiddio *be*
privatize preifateiddio *be*
privilege braint *eb* breintiau
privity of contract preifatrwydd contract *eg*
Privy Chamber Siambr Gyfrin *eb*
Privy Council Cyfrin Gyngor *eg*
Privy Purse Pwrs Cyfrin *eg*
Privy Seal Sêl Gyfrin *eb*
prize day diwrnod gwobrwyo *eg*
diwrnodau gwobrwyo
proactive rhagweithiol *ans*
proactive interference ymyrraeth ragweithiol *eb*
probabilism tebygoliaeth *eb*
probability tebygolrwydd *eg* tebygolrwyddau
probability curve cromlin debygolrwydd *eb*
cromliniau tebygolrwydd
probability density dwysedd tebygolrwydd *eg*
probability density function
ffwythiant dwysedd tebygolrwydd *eg*
probable tebygol *ans*
probable error cyfeiliornad tebygol *eg*
cyfeiliornad tebygo
proban proban *eg*
probate (=copy of will) profeb *eb* profebau
probate (=proving of a will) profiant *eg*
Probate Court Llys Profiant *eg*
probation prawf *eg*
probation (in strict legal context) profiannaeth *eb*
probation officer swyddog prawf *eg*
swyddogion prawf
probation order gorchymyn prawf *eg*
gorchmynion prawf
probationary period cyfnod prawf *eg*
cyfnodau prawf
probationer un ar brawf *eg/b* rhai ar brawf
problem problem *eb* problemau
problem definition diffiniad problem *eg*
diffiniadau problem
problem description disgrifiad problem *eg*
disgrifiadau problem
problem orientated problem gyfeiriedig *ans*
problem solving datrys problemau *eg*
problem solving process
proses datrys problemau *eb*
prosesau datrys problemau
problem specification manyleb problem *eb*
manylebau problemau
problem-focused coping ymdopi drwy
ganolbwyntio ar y broblem *be*
procedural trefniadol *ans*
procedural instruction cyfarwyddyd gweithredu *eg*
cyfarwyddiadau gweithredu
procedural language iaith drefniadol *eb*
procedure (=general method) trefn *eb* trefnau
procedure (of series of actions) dull gweithredu *eg*
dulliau gweithredu
procedure sheet dalen drefn *eb* dalennau trefn
proceedings (=action at law) achos *eg* achosion
proceedings (=published report) trafodion *ell*
proceeds (sales) derbyniadau *ell*
process *n* proses *eb* prosesau
process *v* prosesu *be*
process (anatomical) *n* cnap *eg* cnapiau
process control rheolaeth ar broses *eb*
process costing costio prosesau *be*
process journal dyddiadur proses *eg*
process model model proses *eg*
process production proses gynhyrchu *eb*
process schizophrenia sgitsoffrenia proses *eg*
Process Theology Diwinyddiaeth Proses *eb*
processed cheese caws proses *eg* cawsiau proses
processional *adj* gorymdeithiol *ans*
processor prosesydd *eg* prosesyddion
processor speed cyflymder y prosesydd *eg*
proclamation cyhoeddiad *eg* cyhoeddiadau
proconsul rhaglaw *eg* rhaglawiaid
proctor proctor *eg* proctorion
procuration (church history) tâl esgobol *eg*
taliadau esgobol
procurator procuradur *eg* procuraduron
procurement methods dulliau caffael *ell*
produce *n* cynnyrch *eg* cynhyrchion
produce (a line in geometry) *v* estyn *be*
produce (in general) *v* cynhyrchu *be*
produce backwards (of line) estyn tuag yn ôl *be*
producer cynhyrchydd *eg* cynhyrchwyr
producer gas nwy aer *eg*
producer goods nwyddau cynhyrchydd *ell*
product (in general) cynnyrch *eg* cynhyrchion
product (of multiplication) lluoswm *eg* lluosymiau
product design dylunio cynnyrch *be*
product designer dylunydd cynhyrchion *eg*
dylunwyr cynhyrchion
product differentiation
gwahaniaethu rhwng cynnyrch *be*
product life cycle cylchred oes cynnyrch *eb*

product moment correlation cydberthyniad moment lluoswm *eg*
product placement lleoli cynnyrch *be*
product range ystod cynnyrch *eb*
production cynhyrchiad *eg* cynyrchiadau
production control rheolaeth ar gynhyrchu *eb*
production department adran gynhyrchu *eb* adrannau cynhyrchu
production of voice cynhyrchu'r llais *be*
production piece darn cynhyrchu *eg*
production plan cynllun cynhyrchu *eg* cynlluniau cynhyrchu
production planning cynllunio cynhyrchu *be*
production possibility curve cromlin posibilrwydd cynhyrchu *eb*
production possibility frontier ffin eithaf posibilrwydd cynhyrchu *eb*
production specification manyleb y cynnyrch *eb*
productive cynhyrchiol *ans*
productive capacity gallu cynhyrchu *eg* galluoedd cynhyrchu
productive efficiency effeithlonrwydd cynhyrchiol *eg*
productive investment buddsoddiad cynhyrchiol *eg* buddsoddiadau cynhyrchiol
productivity cynhyrchedd *eg*
products of cracking cynnyrch y cracio *eg*
profess different creeds arddel credoau gwahanol *be*
profession proffesiwn *eg* proffesiynau
professional *ans* proffesiynol *ans*
professional *n* gweithiwr proffesiynol *eg* gweithwyr proffesiynol
professional care gofal proffesiynol *eg*
professional carer gofalydd proffesiynol *eg*
professional player chwaraewr proffesiynol *eg* chwaraewyr proffesiynol
professional sport chwaraeon proffesiynol *ell*
professionalism proffesiynoldeb *eg*
proficiency hyfedredd *eg*
profile *n* proffil *eg* proffiliau
profile *v* proffilio *be*
profile board bwrdd proffil *eg*
profile component cydran broffil *eb* cydrannau proffil
profile of equilibrium proffil cydbwysedd *eg* proffiliau cydbwysedd
profile view golwg cernlun *eg*
profilm proffilm *eg* proffilmiau
profit elw *eg*
profit and loss account cyfrif elw a cholled *eg*
profit and loss statement cyfriflen elw a cholled *eb* cyfriflenni elw a cholled
profit margin maint yr elw *eg*
profit maximisation gwneud yr elw mwyaf *be*
profit summary crynodeb elw *eg*
profitability proffidioldeb *eg*
profitable (=beneficial) buddiol *ans*
profitable (financially) proffidiol *ans*
profiteer budrelwa *be*
profits elw *eg*
profound handicap anfantais ddifrifol *eb* anfanteision difrifol
progenitor hynafiad *eg* hynafiaid
progeny disgynyddion *ell*
progesterone progesteron *eg*
proglacial lake llyn cyfrewlifol *eg* llynnoedd cyfrewlifol
prognosis argoel *eb* argoelion
progradation allraddiad *eg* allraddiadau
program *n* rhaglen *eb* rhaglenni
program *v* rhaglennu *be*
program code cod rhaglen *eg*
program counter rhifydd rhaglen *eg* rhifyddion rhaglen
program design cynllun rhaglen *eg* cynlluniau rhaglen
program disk disg y rhaglen *eg* disgiau'r rhaglenni
program documentation dogfennaeth rhaglen *eg*
program generator generadur rhaglen *eg* generaduron rhaglen
program library llyfrgell raglenni *eb* llyfrgelloedd rhaglenni
program maintenance cynnal rhaglen *be*
program modification addasu rhaglen *be*
program overlay troshaen rhaglen *eb* troshaenau rhaglen
program proving profi rhaglen *be*
program specification manyleb rhaglen *eb* manylebau rhaglenni
program testing rhoi prawf ar raglen *be*
programmable read-only memory (PROM) cof rhaglenadwy darllen yn unig *eg*
programme *n* rhaglen *eb* rhaglenni
programme *v* rhaglennu *be*
Programme Evaluation and Review Technique (PERT) Techneg Gwerthuso ac Adolygu Rhaglen *eb*
programme music *n* cerddoriaeth destunol *eb*
programme note nodyn rhaglen *eg* nodiadau rhaglen
programmer rhaglennydd *eg* rhaglenwyr
programming key allwedd raglennu *eb* allweddi rhaglennu
programming language iaith rhaglennu *eb* ieithoedd rhaglennu
programming of leisure activities rhaglennu gweithgareddau hamdden *be*
progress cynnydd *eg*
progression dilyniant *eg* dilyniannau
progressive (=advancing) cynyddol *ans*
progressive (=innovative) blaengar *ans*
progressive exercise ymarfer graddedig *eg* ymarferion graddedig
progressive relaxation technique techneg ymlacio cynyddol *eb*
progressive resistance gwrthiant cynyddol *eg*
progressive school ysgol flaengar *eb* ysgolion blaengar
progressive taxes treth gynyddol *eb* trethi cynyddol

progressive wave ton gynyddol *eb* tonnau cynyddol
prohibit gwahardd *be*
prohibition (US) gwahardd *be*
project *n* project *eg* projectau
project (=extend oneself) *v.intrans* ymestyn *be*
project (=extend something) *v.trans* estyn *be*
project (=forecast, estimate) *v* rhagamcanu *be*
project (optical) *v* taflunio *be*
project objective amcan y project *eg*
project planning cynllunio projectau *be*
project Washoe project Washoe *eg*
project work gwaith project *eg* gweithiau project
projected profile proffil estynedig *eg* proffiliau estynedig
projectile taflegryn *eg* taflegrau
projectile vomiting chwydu hyrddiol *be*
projecting eaves bondo ymestynnol *eg* bondoeau ymestynnol
projecting lugs clustiau estynedig *ell*
projection (=forecast or estimate) rhagamcaniad *eg* rhagamcaniadau
projection (=image projected) tafluniad *eg* tafluniadau
projection (=thing that obtrudes) ymestyniad *eg* ymestyniadau
projection (graph) estyniad *eg* estyniadau
projection line llinell dafluniad *eb* llinellau tafluniad
projective tafluniol *ans*
projective illusionism rhithiolaeth dafluniol *eb*
projective realism realaeth dafluniol *eb*
projective test prawf alldaflu *eg* profion alldaflu
projectivity taflunedd *eg*
projector taflunydd *eg* taflunyddion
prolate prolad *ans*
prolation proladiad *eg*
proletarian gwerinol *ans*
proletariat proletariat *eg*
proline prolin *eg*
prologue prolog *eg* prologau
prolong estyn *be*
prolongation estyniad *eg* estyniadau
promenade promenâd *eg* promenadau
promethium (Pm) promethiwm *eg*
prominence amlygrwydd *eg*
prominent amlwg *ans*
promontory pentir *eg* pentiroedd
promontory fort caer bentir *eb* caerau pentir
promote hybu *be*
promote respect hybu parch *be*
promote understanding hybu dealltwriaeth *be*
promoting client independence hybu annibyniaeth cleientiaid *be*
promotion (in the media) hyrwyddo *be*
promotional activity gweithgaredd hyrwyddo *eg*
promotional plan cynllun hyrwyddo *eg* cynlluniau hyrwyddo
promotional technique techneg hyrwyddo *eb* technegau hyrwyddo
prompt *v* annog *be*
prompt (in computing) *n* anogwr *eg* anogwyr
pro-natalist (policies etc) geni-bleidiol *ans*
pronation (of foot motion) pronadiad *eg* pronadiadau
prone wyneb i lawr *adf*
prone-lying tor-orwedd *be*
prong fforch *eb* ffyrch
prong centre canol fforch *eg* canolau fforch
prong chuck crafanc fforch *eb* crafangau fforch
prong key allwedd fforch *eb* allweddi fforch
proof (=evidence) prawf *eg* profion
proof (=trial impression) proflen *eb* proflenni
proof-read darllen proflenni *be*
prop (=rigid support) ateg *eb* ategion
prop (in rugby) prop *eg* propiau
prop shaft siafft yrru *eb* siafftiau gyrru
propadiene (or, as generic name, no change) propadeuen *eg*
propaganda propaganda *eg*
propagate lledaenu *be*
propagation lledaeniad *eg* lledaeniadau
Propagation of the Gospel Taenu'r Efengyl *be*
propanal propanal *eg*
propane propan *eg*
propanedioic acid asid propandeuöig *eg*
propanenitrile propannitril *eg*
propane-1,2,3-triol propan-1,2,3-triol *eg*
propane-1,2,3-triyl trinitrate propan-1,2,3-triyl trinitrad *eg*
propane-1,2,3-triyl trisoctadecanoate propan-1,2,3-triyl trisoctadecanoad *eg*
propan-1-ol propan-1-ol *eg*
propan-2-ol propan-2-ol *eg*
propanone propanon *eg*
propanone oxime propanon ocsim *eg*
propan-2-yl- propan-2-yl- *eg*
prop-2-anylbenzene prop-2-anylbensen *eg*
propan-2-ylbenzene propan-2-ylbensen *eg*
propel gyrru ymlaen *be*
propeller llafn gwthio *eg* llafnau gwthio
propenal propenal *eg*
propenenitrile propennitril *eg*
propenoic acid asid propenöig *eg*
prop-2-en-1-ol prop-2-en-1-ol *eg*
proper priodol *ans*
proper fraction ffracsiwn bondrwm *eg* ffracsiynau bondrwm
proper motion mudiant priodol *eg*
proper time amser priodol *eg*
property (=attribute) priodwedd *eb* priodweddau
property (=something owned) eiddo *eg*
property conveyance trosglwyddo eiddo *be*
property of metals priodwedd metelau *eb* priodweddau metelau
property qualification cymhwyster eiddo *eg* cymwysterau eiddo
property rights hawliau perchenogaeth *ell*

prophase proffas *eg*
prophecy proffwydoliaeth *eb* proffwydoliaethau
prophet proffwyd *eg* proffwydi
prophetic proffwydol *ans*
prophetic activity gweithgaredd proffwydol *eg*
prophetic literature llenyddiaeth broffwydol *eb*
prophylaxis proffylacsis *eg*
proportion (=comparative part) cyfran *eb* cyfrannau
proportion (=symmetry, equality of ratios in mathematics) cyfrannedd *eg* cyfraneddau
proportional cyfraneddol *ans*
proportional characters nodau cyfrannol *ell*
proportional limit terfan gyfrannol *eb* terfannau cyfrannol
proportional parts cyfrannau *ell*
proportional printing argraffu cyfrannol *be*
proportional representation cynrychiolaeth gyfrannol *eb*
proportional spacing bylchu cyfrannol *be*
proportional symbols symbolau cyfrannol *ell*
proportionalism cyfranoliaeth *eb*
proposal cynnig *eg* cynigion
proposed changes newidiadau arfaethedig *ell*
proposed new housing estate stad o dai newydd arfaethedig *eb* stadau o dai newydd arfaethedig
proposed target targed arfaethedig *eg* targedau arfaethedig
proposition gosodiad *eg* gosodiadau
proprioception propriodderbyniaeth *eb*
propulsion gwthio *be*
prorogue gohirio *be*
proscenium prosceniwm *eg*
prosecute erlyn *eg*
prosecution erlyniad *eg* erlyniadau
prosecutor erlynydd *eg* erlynwyr
proselyte proselyt *eb* proselytiaid
proselytism proselytiaeth *eb*
pro-social disposition rhagduedd cymdeithasol *eb*
prosody mydryddiaeth *eb*
prosopagnosia prosopagnosia *eg*
prospective memory darpar gof *eg*
prospectus prosbectws *eg* prosbectysau
prosperity ffyniant *eg*
prosthesis prosthesis *eg*
protagonist ymgyrchwr *eg* ymgyrchwyr
protanopia protanopia *eg*
protect (=defend) amddiffyn *be*
protect (=keep safe) diogelu *be*
protect tab tab diogelu *eg* tabiau diogelu
protected software meddalwedd wedi'i diogelu *eb*
protected tenancy tenantiaeth warchodedig *eb*
protecting data gwarchod data *be*
protection (=defence) amddiffyniad *eg* amddiffyniadau
protection (=safety) diogelwch *eg*
protection from harm amddiffyn rhag niwed *be*
protection mechanism dull diogelu *eg* dulliau diogelu
protection motivation theory damcaniaeth cymhelliad gwarchod *eb*
Protection of Sea Life Act Deddf Gwarchod Bywyd y Môr *eb*
protection order gorchymyn amddiffyn *eg* gorchmynion amddiffyn
protectionism diffynnaeth *eb*
protectionist policy polisi diffynnaeth *eg* polisïau diffynnaeth
protective amddiffynnol *ans*
protective clothing dillad gwarchod *ell*
protective coating araen ddiogelu *eb* araenau diogelu
protective colouration lliwiad gwarchodol *eg*
protective edging ymyl amddiffyn *eb* ymylon amddiffyn
protective factor ffactor amddiffynnol *eb* ffactorau amddiffynnol
protective film ffilm warchod *eb* ffilmiau gwarchod
protective finish gorffeniad diogelu *eg* gorffeniadau diogelu
protective foods bwydydd amddiffyn *ell*
protective wear gwisg warchodol *eb* gwisgoedd gwarchodol
protector amddiffynnydd *eg* amddiffynwyr
protectorate protectoriaeth *eb* protectoriaethau
protein protein *eg* proteinau
proteinaceous stain staen protein *eg* staeniau protein
proteinase proteinas *eg*
protest *n* protest *eb* protestiadau
protest *v* protestio *be*
protest movement mudiad protest *eg* mudiadau protest
Protestant *adj* Protestannaidd *ans*
Protestant *n* Protestant *eg* Protestaniaid
Protestant Ascendancy Goruchafiaeth Brotestannaidd *eb*
Protestant denomination enwad Protestannaidd *eg* enwadau Protestannaidd
Protestant establishment sefydliad Protestannaidd *eg*
Protestant Reformation Diwygiad Protestannaidd *eg*
Protestant settlement ardrefniant Protestannaidd *eg*
Protestant Succession Olyniaeth Brotestannaidd *eb*
Protestantism Protestaniaeth *eb*
protestation protestiad *eg* protestiadau
protocol protocol *eg* protocolau
protoctinium (Pa) protoctiniwm *eg*
proton proton *eg* protonau
proton pump pwmp proton *eg* pympiau proton
protonotary protonoteri *eg*
prototype prototeip *eg*
prototype solution ateb prototeip *eg*
prototype system system brototeip *eb*
protoword protoair *eg* protoeiriau
protozoan protosoad *eg* protosoaid

protractor onglydd *eg* onglyddion
protrude ymwthio allan *be*
protrusion ymwthiad allan *eg* ymwthiadau allan
prove profi *be*
provenance tarddiad *eg*
Provençal *adj* Profensaidd *ans*
Provençal *n* Profenswr *eg* Profenswyr
Provençal (language) Profensaleg *eg*
provide darparu *be*
providence rhagluniaeth *eb*
province talaith *eb* taleithiau
provincial taleithiol *ans*
provision darpariaeth *eb* darpariaethau
provision (papal) cyflwyniad *eg* cyflwyniadau
provisional dros dro *ans*
provisional ball pêl ddarpar *eb* peli darpar
provisional government llywodraeth dros dro *eb* llywodraethau dros dro
Provisions of Clarendon Gosodiadau Clarendon *ell*
Provisions of Oxford Gosodiadau Rhydychen *ell*
Provisions of Westminster Gosodiadau San Steffan *ell*
Provisors Act Deddf Atal Enwebu *eb*
provost profost *eg* profostiaid
provost marshal profost-farsial *eg* profost-farsialiaid
proximal procsimol *ans*
proximate cause achos agos *eg* achosion agos
proximity principle egwyddor agosrwydd *eb*
proxy dirprwyol *ans*
proxy server gweinydd dirprwyol *eg* gweinyddion dirprwyol
Prussian *adj* Prwsiaidd *ans*
Prussian *n* Prwsiad *eg* Prwsiaid
Prussian blue glas Prwsia *eg*
psalm salm *eb* salmau
psalter sallwyr *eg* sallwyrau
psammosere samoser *eg* samoserau
pseudo-code ffug-god *eg* ffug-godau
pseudohomophone ffughomoffon *eg* ffughomoffonau
pseudo-instruction ffug-gyfarwyddyd *eg* ffug-gyfarwyddiadau
pseudo-operation ffugweithrediad *eg* ffugweithrediadau
pseudo-random ffug-hap *eg*
pseudo-server ffugweinydd *eg* ffugweinyddion
psychiatric seiciatrig *ans*
psychiatric hospital ysbyty meddwl *eg* ysbytai meddwl
psychiatrist seiciatrydd *eg* seiciatryddion
psychiatry seiciatreg *eb*
psychoactive substance use disorder anhwylder defnyddio sylweddau seicoweithredol *eg*
psychoanalysis seicdreiddiad *eg*
psychoanalyze seicdreiddio *be*
psychobiology seicobioleg *eb*
psychodynamic seicodynamig *ans*
psychodynamic play therapy therapi chwarae seicodynamig *eg*
psychodynamic therapy therapi seicodynamig *eg*
psychogenic seicogenig *ans*
psychogenic amnesia amnesia seicogenig *eg*
psychogenic fugue ffiwg seicogenig *eb*
psychogeriatrician seicogeriatregydd *eg* seicogeriatregwyr
psycholegal study astudiaeth seico-gyfreithiol *eb*
psycholinguistics seicoieithyddiaeth *eb*
psychological seicolegol *ans*
psychological autopsy awtopsi seicolegol *eg*
psychological intervention ymyriad seicolegol *eg*
psychological model model seicolegol *eg*
psychologist seicolegydd *eg* seicolegwyr
psychology seicoleg *eb*
psychometric testing profi seicometrig *be*
psychomotor skill sgil seicoechddygol *eg* sgiliau seicoechddygol
psychoneuronimmunology seiconiwronimiwnoleg *eb*
psychopath seicopath *eg* seicopathiaid
psychophysics seicoffiseg *eb*
psychophysiology seicoffisioleg *eb*
psychosexual seicorywiol *ans*
psychosis seicosis *eg*
psychosocial seicogymdeithasol *ans*
psychosomatic seicosomatig *ans*
psychosurgery seicolawdriniaeth *eb*
psychotherapy seicotherapi *eg*
psychotic art celfyddyd seicotig *eb*
psychoticism seicotiaeth *eb*
puberty glasoed *eg*
public cyhoeddus *ans*
public body corff cyhoeddus *eg*
public building adeilad cyhoeddus *eg* adeiladau cyhoeddus
public convenience cyfleusterau cyhoeddus *ell*
public domain software meddalwedd parth cyhoeddus *eb*
public goods nwyddau cyhoeddus *ell*
public health iechyd y cyhoedd *eg*
Public Health Act Deddf Iechyd Cyhoeddus *eb*
public house tŷ tafarn *eg* tai tafarnau
public inquiry ymchwiliad cyhoeddus *eg* ymchwiliadau cyhoeddus
public limited company (p.l.c.) cwmni cyfyngedig cyhoeddus *eg* cwmnïau cyfyngedig cyhoeddus
public notary notari'r cyhoedd *eg* notarïaid y cyhoedd
public ownership perchnogaeth gyhoeddus *eb*
public path llwybr cyhoeddus *eg* llwybrau cyhoeddus
public policy polisi cyhoeddus *eg*
Public Record Office Archifdy Gwladol *eg*
public relations cysylltiadau cyhoeddus *ell*
public relations officer swyddog cysylltiadau cyhoeddus *eg* swyddogion cysylltiadau cyhoeddus

public right of way hawl tramwy cyhoeddus *eg* hawliau tramwy cyhoeddus
public school ysgol fonedd *eb* ysgolion bonedd
public sector sector cyhoeddus *eg*
public sector net cash requirements gofynion arian parod net y sector cyhoeddus *ell*
public sector venture menter sector cyhoeddus *eb*
public service gwasanaeth cyhoeddus *eg* gwasanaethau cyhoeddus
public transport cludiant cyhoeddus *eg*
public transport service gwasanaeth cludiant cyhoeddus *eg* gwasanaethau cludiant cyhoeddus
public utilities gwasanaethau cyhoeddus *ell*
publication cyhoeddiad *eg* cyhoeddiadau
publicity flyer taflen cyhoeddusrwydd *eb* taflenni cyhoeddusrwydd
publish cyhoeddi *be*
publisher cyhoeddwr *eg* cyhoeddwyr
pucker rhychu *be*
puddle *n* pwll *eg* pyllau
puddle *v* pwdlo *be*
puddler pydlwr *eg* pydlwyr
puddling furnace ffwrnais bwdlo *eb* ffwrneisi pwdlo
puffed sleeve llawes bwff *eb* llewys pwff
pug cleio *be*
pug mill melin gleio *eb* melinau cleio
puja puja *eg*
pull *n* tyniad *eg* tyniadau
pull *v* tynnu *be*
pull a muscle tynnu cyhyr *be*
pull down tynnu lawr *be*
pull shot tyniad *eg* tyniadau
pull the ball tynnu'r bêl *be*
pulley pwli *eg* pwlïau
pulley block bloc pwli *eg* blociau pwli
pulley guide cyfeirydd pwli *eg* cyfeiryddion pwli
pulley housing rhigol bwli *eb* rhigolau pwli
pulley stile cledren bwli *eb* cledrau pwli
pulling the punch lleddfu'r ddyrnod *be*
pullover pwlofer *eg/b* pwloferau
pulmonary ysgyfeiniol *ans*
pulmonary system system ysgyfeiniol *eb*
pulp (=soft thick wet mass) mwydion *ell*
pulp (from wood) mwydion coed *ell*
pulp (of fruit) pwlp *eg*
pulp (of tooth) bywyn *eg* bywion
pulpit pulpud *eg* pulpudau
pulpitum croglofft *eb* croglofftydd
pulsate pylsadu *be*
pulsating star seren guriadol *eb* sêr curiadol
pulsation curiad *eg* curiadau
pulsator pylsadur *eg* pylsaduron
pulse (in general) curiad *eg* curiadau
pulse (in technical usage) pwls *eg* pylsiau
pulse detector canfodydd curiadau *eg* canfodwyr curiadau
pulse pattern (pulse train) patrwm curiadau *eg* patrymau curiadau
pulse position modulation modyliad safle pwls *eg*
pulse rate cyfradd curiad y galon *eb*
pulse width lled pwls *eg*
pulverization pylori *be*
pumice pwmis *eg*
pumice powder powdr pwmis *eg*
pump pwmp *eg* pympiau
pump storage storfa bwmp *eb* storfeydd pwmp
pun gair mwys *eg* geiriau mwys
pun *v* chwarae ar eiriau *be*
puna pwna *eg*
punch (=blow) *n* dyrnod *eb* dyrnodiau
punch (=make holes) *v* pwnsio *be*
punch (=strike) *v* dyrnu *be*
punch (for making holes) *n* pwnsh *eg* pynsiau
punch bag bag dyrnu *eg* bagiau dyrnu
punch ball pêl ddyrnu *eb* peli dyrnu
punch hole twll pwnsh *eg* tyllau pwnsh
punch pad pad dyrnu *eg* padiau dyrnu
punch stitch pwyth tyllog *eg* pwythau tyllog
punch strip banden dyllog *eb* bandiau tyllog
punched card cerdyn tyllog *eg* cardiau tyllog
punched cards cardiau tyllog *ell*
punched hole twll wedi'i bwnsio *eg* tyllau wedi'u pwnsio
punched paper tape tâp papur tyllog *eg* tapiau papur tyllog
punching (forging process) pwnsio *be*
punctuation atalnodi *be*
puncture wound clwyf trywaniad *eg* clwyfau trywaniad
punishment cosb *eb* cosbau
punitive cosbol *ans*
punitive expedition ymgyrch gosbi *eb* ymgyrchoedd cosbi
punt *n* pwnt *eg* pyntiau
punt (kick) *v* pyntio *be*
punteado punteado *eg*
pupil (=schoolchild) disgybl *eg* disgyblion
pupil (of eye) cannwyll llygad *eb*
pupil profile proffil disgybl *eg* proffiliau disgyblion
pupil-teacher ratio cymhareb disgybl-athro *eb* cymarebau disgybl-athro
puppet pyped *eg* pypedau
puppet regime llywodraeth byped *eb* llywodraethau pyped
puppet stage llwyfan pypedau *eg* llwyfannau pypedau
puppet state gwladwriaeth byped *eb* gwladwriaethau pyped
puppet theatre theatr bypedau *eb* theatrau pypedau
puppeteer pypedwr *eg* pypedwyr
purchase prynu *be*
► **purchase ledger** llyfr pryniadau *eg* llyfrau pryniadau
purchase order archeb prynu *eb* archebion prynu
purchase tax treth bryniant *eb*
purchasing cycle cylchred prynu *eb*

purchasing power gallu prynu *eg* galluoedd prynu
pure pur *ans*
pure colour lliw pur *eg* lliwiau pur
pure culture of bacteria meithriniad pur o facteria *eg*
pure ellipse gwir elips *eg*
Pure Land Tir Pur *eg*
pure mathematics mathemateg bur *eb*
pure white surface arwyneb purwyn *eg* arwynebau purwyn
pure word deafness byddardod geiriau *eg*
purgatory purdan *eg*
purge carthu *be*
purism purdebaeth *eb*
▶ **purist** purydd *eg* purwyr
puritan *adj* piwritanaidd *ans*
puritan *n* piwritan *eg* piwritaniaid
Puritan Choir Carfan Biwritanaidd *eb*
Puritan Revolution Chwyldro Piwritanaidd *eg*
puritanism piwritaniaeth *eb*
purl stitch pwyth o chwith *eg* pwythau o chwith
purled edge ymyl pwyth o chwith *eb* ymylon pwyth o chwith
purlin trawslath *eg* trawslathau
purlin roof to trawslath *eg* toeon trawslath
purple (tempering colour) porffor *eg*
purple brown (tempering colour) porffor brown *eg*
purpose built resort canolfan wyliau sydd wedi'i hadeiladu'n bwrpasol *eb*
purposeful concurrent use of language trawsieithu *be*
purposive behaviourism ymddygiadaeth fwriadus *eb*
pursuit movement symudiad dilyn *eg*
pursuivant pwrswifant *eg*
purvey arlwyo *be*
purveyance arlwyaeth *eb*
purveyor arlwywr *eg* arlwywyr
pus crawn *eg*
push *n* gwthiad *eg* gwthiadau
push *v* gwthio *be*
push fit gwthffit *eb* gwthffitiau
push moraine marian gwthio *eg* marianau gwthio
push pass gwrthbas *eb* gwrthbasiau
push rod rhoden wthio *eb* rhodenni gwthio
push stick ffon wthio *eb* ffyn gwthio
push stick (power sawing) pren gwthio *eg* prennau gwthio
push-chair cadair wthio *eb* cadeiriau gwthio
push-down *adj* cywasgedig *ans*
push-down *v* cywasgu *be*
push-up *adj* gwrthwasgedig *ans*
push-up *v* gwrthwasgu *be*
put rhoi *be*
put on a collar gosod coler *be*
put on probation rhoi ar brawf *be*
put the switch off (=open the switch) agor y switsh *be*
put the switch on (=close the switch) cau'r switsh *be*
putt pytio *be*
putting the shot gwthio'r pwysau *be*
putty pwti *eg*
PVA PVA *eg*
PVC (polyvinyl chloride) PVC *eg*
pygmy pigmi *eg* pigmiaid
pyjamas pyjamas *ell*
pylon peilon *eg* peilonau
pyramid pyramid *eg* pyramidiau
pyramidal pyramidaidd *ans*
pyramidal face wyneb pyramidaidd *eg* wynebau pyramidaidd
pyramidal peak pigyn pyramidaidd *eg* pigynnau pyramidaidd
pyramids of biomass pyramidiau biomas *ell*
pyramids of numbers (in ecology) pyramidiau niferoedd *ell*
pyre (in funeral ceremony) coelcerth *eb*
Pyrex ware llestri Pyrex *ell*
pyrexia gwres *eg*
pyridine pyridin *eg*
pyrites pyrit *eg* pyritau
Pyroceram llestri Pyroceram *ell*
Pyrocil llestri Pyrocil *ell*
pyroclast pyroclast *eg* pyroclastau
pyroclastian pyroclastaidd *ans*
pyroclastic pyroclastig *ans*
pyrocouple pyrocwpl *eg*
pyrometer pyromedr *eg* pyromedrau
pyrometric pyrometrig *ans*
pyrometric cone côn pyrometrig *eg* conau pyrometrig
pyrometry pyrometreg *eb*
pyroxylin pyrocsilin *eg*
Pythagoras Pythagoras *eg*
Pythagoras theorem theorem Pythagoras *eb*

Q

qanat canat *eg* canatau
quadrangle pedrongl *eg/b* pedronglau
quadrant pedrant *eg* pedrannau
quadrant arch bwa pedrant *eg* bwâu pedrant
quadrant moulding mowldin pedrant *eg* mowldinau pedrant
quadrat cwadrad *eg* cwadradau
quadrate cwadrat *eg* cwadratau
quadratic cwadratig *ans*
quadratic equation hafaliad cwadratig *eg* hafaliadau cwadratig
quadrennial pob pedair blynedd
quadriceps cwadriceps *eg*
quadrilateral *adj* pedrochr *ans*
quadrilateral *n* pedrochr *eg/b* pedrochrau
quadrille cwadril *eg* cwadriliau
quadriplegia parlys pedwar aelod *eg*
quadruped pedwartroedyn *eg* pedwartroedion
quadruple pedwarplyg *ans*
quadruple stopping gwasgiad pedwarplyg *eg* gwasgiadau pedwarplyg
quadruplet pedrybled *eg* pedrybledau
quagmire siglen *eb* siglennydd
Quaker Crynwr *eg* Crynwyr
Quakerism Crynwriaeth *eb*
qualification cymhwyster *eg* cymwysterau
qualified cymwysedig *ans*
qualifier (in grammar) goleddfwr *eg* goleddfwyr
qualify (in a competition) ennill lle *be*
qualify (oneself for a job) ymgymhwyso *be*
qualitative ansoddol *ans*
qualitative analysis dadansoddi ansoddol *be*
qualitative analysis dadansoddiad ansoddol *eg* dadansoddiadau ansoddol
qualitative data data ansoddol *ell*
qualitative evidence tystiolaeth ansoddol *eb*
qualitative research ymchwil ansoddol *eg*
qualitative work gwaith ansoddol *eg*
quality ansawdd *eg* ansoddau
► **quality assurance** sicrhau ansawdd *eg*
quality assurance procedure dull sicrhau ansawdd *eg* dulliau sicrhau ansawdd
quality circle cylch ansawdd *eg* cylchoedd ansawdd
quality control rheoli ansawdd *be*
quality of life ansawdd bywyd *eg*
quality of the environment ansawdd yr amgylchedd *eg*
quality system system ansawdd *eb* systemau ansawdd
quality variation amrywiaeth ansawdd *eb*
quango cwango *eg* cwangos
quantifiable mesuradwy *ans*
quantify (in non-technical usage) mesur *be*
quantify (in technical usage) meintioli *be*
quantisation error gwall cwanteiddio *eg* gwallau cwanteiddio
quantitative meintiol *ans*
quantitative analysis dadansoddiad meintiol *eg* dadansoddiadau meintiol
quantitative approach dull meintiol *eg* dulliau meintiol
quantitative evidence tystiolaeth feintiol *eb*
quantitative research ymchwil meintiol *eg*
quantitative treatment triniaeth feintiol *eb*
quantities of data meintiau o ddata *ell*
quantity (=how much) maint *eg*
quantity (=property of thing that is measurable) mesur *eg* mesurau
quantity (unspecified, e.g. of soil) rhywfaint *eg*
quantity demanded maint y galw *eg*
quantity supplied maint y cyflenwad *eg*
quantity surveyor syrfëwr meintiau *eg* syrfewyr meintiau
quantity theory damcaniaeth maint *eb*
quantization cwanteiddiad *eg*
quantize cwanteiddio *be*
quantized cwanteiddiedig *ans*
quantum cwantwm *eg* cwanta
quantum theory damcaniaeth cwantwm *eb*
quarantine cwarantin *eg*
quarantine period cyfnod cwarantin *eg*
quark cwarc *eg* cwarciau
quarry chwarel *eb* chwareli
quarry tile teilsen chwarel *eb* teils chwarel
quarrying chwarela *be*
quarter (=one fourth) chwarter *eg* chwarteri
quarter (=part of town etc) rhan *eb* rhannau
quarter full size chwarter maint llawn *eg*
quarter moon chwarter lleuad *eg*
quarter of a whole chwarter un cyfan *eg* chwarteri un cyfan
quarter round moulding mowldin chwarter crwn *eg* mowldinau chwarter crwn
quarter sawn llifiad rheiddiol *eg* llifiadau rheiddiol
Quarter Sessions Llys Chwarter *eg*
quarter turn (right angle) chwarter tro *eg* chwarter troeon

quarter-comma mean-tone tuning tiwnio tôn-gymedr chwarter-coma *be*
quartered oak derw rheidd-dor *eg*
quartered panel panel rheiddiol *eg* paneli rheiddiol
quartering chwarteru *be*
quartermaster swyddog cyflenwi *eg* swyddogion cyflenwi
quartet pedwarawd *eg* pedwarawdau
quartic cwartig *ans*
quartic equation hafaliad cwartig *eg* hafaliadau cwartig
quartile chwartel *eg* chwartelau
quartile point pwynt chwartel *eg* pwyntiau chwartel
quarto cwarto *eg*
quartz cwarts *eg* cwartsiau
quartzite cwartsit *eg*
quasi-experiment lled-arbrawf *eg* lledarbrofion
quasi-field cwasi-faes *eg* cwasi-feysydd
quasi-group cwasi-grŵp *eg* cwasi-grwpiau
quasistatic cwasistatig *ans*
quaternary cwaternaidd *ans*
quaternary pedryddol *ans*
quaternion cwaternion *eg*
quaver (eighth-note) cwafer *eg* cwaferau
quay cei *eg* ceiau
Queen Consort Brenhines Gydweddog *eb*
queen dowager gweddw'r brenin *eb*
queenpost banonbost *eg* banonbyst
Queen's Bench Division Adran Mainc y Frenhines *eb*
quench trochoeri *be*
quern breuan *eb* breuanau
query *n* ymholiad *eg* ymholiadau
query *v* ymholi *be*
query language iaith ymholi *eb* ieithoedd ymholi
question cwestiwn *eg* cwestiynau
question and answer a data file holi ac ateb ffeil ddata
question bank cronfa gwestiynau *eb* cronfeydd cwestiynau
question mark gofynnod *eg* gofynodau
questioning (=asking) holi *be*
questioning (as a teaching method, doubting) cwestiynu *be*
questionnaire holiadur *eg* holiaduron
queue ciw *eg* ciwiau
queuing theory theori ciwio *eb* theorïau ciwio
quick cyflym *ans*
quick adjustment cymhwysiad cyflym *eg* cymwysiadau cyflym
quick change post post newid cyflym *eg* pyst newid cyflym
quick drying sychu'n gyflym *be*
quick frozen food bwyd wedi'i rewi'n gyflym *eg*
quick response and mental calculation cards cardiau ymatebion cyflym a chyfrifiadau pen
quick silver arian byw *eg*
quick unpick datodydd *eg* datodyddion
quick-action nut nyten chwimwth *eb* nytiau chwimwth
quickening (of foetus) bywiocáu *be*
quicklime calch brwd *eg*
quick-release mechanism mecanwaith rhyddhau cyflym *eg*
quick-return mechanism mecanwaith dychwel cyflym *eg*
quicksands sugndraeth *eg* sugndraethau
quickstep quickstep *eg* dawnsiau quickstep
quiet distaw *ans*
quietism tawelyddiaeth *eb*
quietist tawelwr *eg* tawelwyr
quill (lathe part) cwilsen *eb* cwils
quill brush brwsh cwilsen *eg* brwshys cwils
quill pen pen cwilsen *eg* pennau cwils
quilt *n* cwilt *eg* cwiltiau
quilt *v* cwiltio *be*
quilter (machine attachments) cwiltell *eb* cwiltellau
quilting cwiltio *be*
quilting frame ffrâm gwiltio *eb* fframiau cwiltio
quincentennial pumcanmlwyddiant *eg*
quinine cwinin *eg*
quinquennial pob pum mlynedd
quintet pumawd *eg* pumawdau
quintuplet pumled *eg* pumledi
quire cwir *eg* cwiroedd
quirk cwirc *eg* cwirciau
quirk bead glain cwirc *eg* gleiniau cwirc
quit gadael *be*
quit claim ildio hawl *be*
quiver cawell saethau *eg* cewyll saethau
quiz cwis *eg* cwisiau
quoin conglfaen *eg* conglfeini
quoit *n* coeten *eb* coetiau
quoit *v* coetio *be*
quorum cworwm *eg* cworymau
quota cwota *eg* cwotâu
quota reduction gostwng cwotâu *be*
quotation dyfyniad *eg* dyfyniadau
quotation aspect (of division) agwedd mesuriad *eb*
quotation mark dyfynnod *eg* dyfynodau
quotient cyniferydd *eg* cyniferyddion
quotient rule rheol cyniferydd *eb*
Qur'an Qur'an *eg*
QWERTY keyboard bysellfwrdd QWERTY *eg* bysellfyrddau QWERTY

R

rabbet *n* rabad *eg* rabadau
rabbet *v* rabedu *be*
rabbet joint uniad rabad *eg* uniadau rabad
rabbet plane plaen rabad *eg* plaeniau rabad
rabbeted stile cledren rabedog *eb* cledrau rabedog
rabbeted weather boarding byrddau hindraul rabedog *ell*
rabbi rabbi *eg*
Rabbinical Judaism Iddewiaeth Rabbinaidd *eb*
rabbit punch dyrnod gwar *eb* dyrnodiau gwar
rabble ciwed *eb*
rabies y gynddaredd *eb*
race hil *eb* hilion
race *n* ras *eb* rasys
race *v* rasio *be*
race relations cysylltiadau hiliol *ell*
Race Relations Act Deddf Cysylltiadau Hiliol *eb*
racemate racemad *eg* racemadau
raceme racem *eb* racemau
racemic (in chemistry) racemig *ans*
racemization racemeiddiad *eg*
racemose racemaidd *ans*
rachis rachis *eg* rachisau
racial hiliol *ans*
racial community cymuned hiliol *eb* cymunedau hiliol
racial conflict gwrthdaro hiliol *be*
racial discrimination gwahaniaethu hiliol *be*
racial segregation arwahanu hiliol *be*
racing dive deif ras *eb* deifiau ras
racism hiliaeth *eb*
racist hiliwr *eg* hilwyr
rack (=shelf) rhesel *eb* rheseli
rack (for torture) arteithglwyd *eb* arteithglwydi
rack (lathe part) rac *eb* raciau
rack and pinion rac a phiniwn
rack and pinion railway rheilffordd rac a phiniwn *eb* rheilffyrdd rac a phiniwn
racket raced *eb* racedi
racket parts rhannau o'r raced *ell*
racket weight pwysau'r raced *ell*
racketeer llwgr-fasnachwr *eg* llwgr-fasnachwyr
rack-rent rhacrentu *be*
radar radar *eg*
raddle radl *eg* radlau
Radha Radha *eb*
radial rheiddiol *ans*
radial easel îsl rheiddiol *eg* islau rheiddiol
radial flute ffliwt reiddiol *eb* ffliwtiau rheiddiol
radial line llinell reiddiol *eb* llinellau rheiddiol
radial sawcut llifiad rheiddiol *eg* llifiadau rheiddiol
radial section toriad rheiddiol *eg* toriadau rheiddiol
radial shake hollt rheiddiol *eg* holltau rheiddiol
radial symmetry cymesuredd rheiddiol *eg*
radian radian *eg* radianau
radiant pelydrol *ans*
radiant heat gwres pelydrol *eg*
radiate pelydru *be*
radiating line llinell belydrol *eb* llinellau pelydrol
radiation (in general) pelydriad *eg* pelydriadau
radiation (radioactive) ymbelydredd *eg*
radiation fog niwl pelydriad *eg*
radiation pyrometer pyromedr pelydriad *eg* pyromedrau pelydriad
radiation sickness salwch ymbelydredd *eg*
radiator (of heating system) rheiddiadur *eg* rheiddiaduron
radiator (of light, heat) pelydrydd *eg* pelydryddion
radical radical *eg* radicalau
radical cadence diweddeb cordiau gwreiddiol *eb* diweddebau cordiau gwreiddiol
radical philosopher athronydd radicalaidd *eg* athronwyr radicalaidd
radicalism radicaliaeth *eb*
radicle cynwreiddyn *eg* cynwreiddiau
radio radio *eg* radios
radio or tv mast mast radio neu deledu *eg*
radio receiver derbynnydd radio *eg* derbynyddion radio
radio star seren radio *eb* sêr radio
radio wave ton radio *eb* tonnau radio
radioactive ymbelydrol *ans*
radioactive decay dadfeiliad ymbelydrol *eg*
radioactive emission allyriad ymbelydrol *eg* allyriadau ymbelydrol
radioactive fallout alldafliad ymbelydrol *eg*
radioactive particle gronyn ymbelydrol *eg* gronynnau ymbelydrol
radioactive source ffynhonnell ymbelydrol *eb* ffynonellau ymbelydrol
radioactive substance sylwedd ymbelydrol *eg* sylweddau ymbelydrol
radioactivity ymbelydredd *eg*
radioastronomy radioseryddiaeth *eb*
radiograph radiograff *eg* radiograffau
radiographer radiograffydd *eg* radiograffwyr
radiography radiograffeg *eb*

radiologist radiolegydd *eg* radiolegwyr
radiology radioleg *eb*
radiotherapy radiotherapi *eg*
radium (Ra) radiwm *eg*
radius (in botany) rhaidd *eg* rheiddiau
radius (in geometry etc) radiws *eg* radiysau
radius gauge medrydd radiws *eg* medryddion radiws
radius of gyration radiws chwyrliant *eg* radiysau chwyrliant
radiused corner cornel gron *eb* corneli crwn
radiusing (lathe tool) radiysu *be*
radix radics *eg* radicsau
radon (Rn) radon *eg*
radon gas nwy radon *eg*
raffia raffia *eg*
raffia weaving plethu raffia *be*
raffia work gwaith raffia *eg*
raft foundation sylfaen rafft *eb* sylfeini rafft
rafter ceibr *eg* ceibrau
rafting rafftio *be*
rag cerpyn *eg* carpiau
rag bag bag carpiau *eg* bagiau carpiau
rag bolt bollt sylfaen *eb* bolltau sylfaen
rag paper papur lliain *eg*
rag week wythnos rag *eb* wythnosau rag
ragged school ysgol y tlodion *eb* ysgolion y tlodion
ragged shores glannau bylchog *ell*
raglan sleeve llawes raglan *eb* llewys raglan
ragtime ragtime *eg*
raid cyrch *eg* cyrchoedd
rail rheilen *eb* rheiliau
rail junction cyffordd trenau *eb* cyffyrdd trenau
railway rheilffordd *eb* rheilffyrdd
railway siding lein aros *eb* leiniau aros
railway station gorsaf drenau *eb* gorsafoedd trenau
rain proof gwrthlaw *ans*
rain shadow cysgod glaw *eg* cysgodion glaw
rainbow enfys *eb* enfysau
rainfall glawiad *eg*
rainfall regime patrymedd glawiad *eg*
▸ **rainfall reliability** dibynadwyedd glawiad *eg*
rainfall variability amrywioldeb glawiad *eg*
rainforest coedwig law *eb* coedwigoedd glaw
rainwash glawred *eg* glawrediadau
rainwater dŵr glaw *eg*
raise codi *be*
raise a perpendicular codi perpendicwlar *be*
raise or lower codi neu ostwng
raise stitches (scorping) codi pwythau *be*
raised beach cyfordraeth *eg* cyfordraethau
raised bog cyforgors *eb* cyforgorsydd
raised cliff cyforglogwyn *eg* cyforglogwyni
raised head (machine screws) copog uchel *ans*
raised head screw sgriw gopog *eb* sgriwiau copog
raised panel panel wedi'i godi *eg* paneli wedi'u codi
raised work gwaith codi *eg*
raising hammer morthwyl codi *eg* morthwylion codi
raising mallet gordd godi *eb* gyrdd codi
rake (implement) *n* cribin *eg/b* cribinau; rhaca *eg/b* rhacanau
rake (of sloping angle) *n* gwyredd *eg* gwyreddau
rake (with implement) *v* cribinio *be*; rhacanu *be*
rake angle (drill part) ongl wyredd *eb* onglau gwyredd
raking out glanhau allan *be*
raking shore ateg ogwydd *eb* ategion gogwydd
raku racw *eg*
rally rali *eb* ralïau
ram hwrdd *eg* hyrddod; maharen *eg* meheryn
Rama Rama *eg*
Ramadan Ramadan *eg*
Ramayana Ramayana *eg*
rammer hyrddwr *eg* hyrddwyr
ramming blocks blociau hyrddu *ell*
ramp ramp *eg* rampiau
rampart rhagfur *eg* rhagfuriau
ranch *n* ransh *eb* ransiau
ranch *v* ransio *be*
ranch style bungalow byngalo dull ransh *eg* byngalos dull ransh
ranch-house tŷ ransh *eg* tai ransh
randing plethu *be*
random hap *ans*
random access *n* hapgyrch *eg* hapgyrchoedd
random access *v* hapgyrchu *be*
random access file ffeil hapgyrchu *eb* ffeiliau hapgyrchu
random access memory (RAM) cof hapgyrch *eg*
random access store storfa hapgyrch *eb* storfeydd hapgyrch
random assignment aseinio ar hap *be*
random choice hapddewis *be*
random error hapgyfeiliornad *eg* hapgyfeiliornadau
random event hapddigwyddiad *eg* hapddigwyddiadau
random experiment haparbrawf *eg* haparbrofion
random file ffeil hapgyrchu *eb* ffeiliau hapgyrchu
random groups design cynllun grwpiau ar hap *eg* cynlluniau grwpiau ar hap
random length hap-hyd *eg* haphydoedd
random motion mudiant afreolus *eg*
random number haprif *eg* haprifau
random number generator generadur haprifau *eg* generaduron haprifau
random pattern hapbatrwm *eg* hapbatrymau
random sample hapsampl *eg* hapsamplau
random scale value gwerth hapraddfa *eg* gwerthoedd hapraddfa
random selection hapddethol *be*
random variable hapnewidyn *eg* hapnewidynnau
random walk hapgerddediad *eg* hapgerddediadau
randomly select dethol ar hap *be*
range (=maximum travel distance) cwmpas *eg*
range (=extent) amrediad *eg* amrediadau
range (=reach) cyrhaeddiad *eg* cyraeddiadau

range (=variety) amrywiaeth *eb*
range (of ability etc) ystod *eb* ystodau
range (of products) dewis *eg*
range of gymnastic action amrywiaeth o weithrediadau gymnastig *eb*
range of mountains cadwyn o fynyddoedd *eb* cadwyni o fynyddoedd
range of music amrywiaeth o gerddoriaeth *eb*
range of performance ystod o berfformiad *eb*
range of tide amrediad llanw *eg*
range of variations amrediad yr amrywiadau *eg*
range statements datganiadau ystod *ell*
ranger ceidwad *eg* ceidwaid
ranging pole polyn anelu *eg* polion anelu
rank (=position in general) *n* safle *eg* safleoedd
rank (=position in hierarchy) *n* gradd *eb* graddau
rank (=row or line) *n* rheng *eb* rhengoedd
rank (in economics) *v* graddio *be*
rank (on organ) *n* set o bibau *eb* setiau o bibau
rank correlation cydberthyniad rhestrol *eg*
rank order trefn restrol *eb* trefnau rhestrol
rank size rule rheol gradd a maint *eb* rheolau gradd a maint
ranking method dull graddio *eg* dulliau graddio
ranks of windows rhesi o ffenestri *ell*
ransom *n* pridwerth *eg*
rap (=knock) *n* cnoc *eg/b* cnociau
rap (=knock) *v* cnocio *be*
rap (in music) *v* rapio *be*
rap (of music) *n* rap *eg*
rape *n* trais rhywiol *eg*
rape *v* treisio *be*
rapid eye movement (REM) sleep cwsg symudiad llygaid cyflym *eg*
rapid eye movement sleep behaviour disorder anhwylder ymddygiad cwsg symudiad llygaid cyflym *eg*
rapid hardening cement sment cyflym-galedu *eg*
rapier cleddyf main *eg* cleddyfau main
rapping iron haearn cnocio *eg* heyrn cnocio
rapping tool erfyn cnocio *eg* offer cnocio
rare earth prinfwyn *eg* prinfwynau
rare gas nwy prin *eg*
rarefaction teneuad *eg* teneuadau
rash brech *eb* brechau
rasp *n* rhathell *eb* rhathellau
rasp *v* rhathellu *be*
rasp cut toriad rhathell *eg* toriadau rhathell
raspberries mafon *ell*
rasqueado rasqueado *eg*
Rastafarian Rastaffariad *eg* Rastaffariaid
Rastafarianism Rastaffariaeth *eb*
ratchet clicied ddannedd *eb* cliciedau dannedd
ratchet and pawl clicied a phawl
ratchet brace carntro clicied *eg* carntroeon clicied
ratchet drill dril clicied *eg* driliau clicied
ratchet easel îsl clicied *eg* islau clicied
ratchet pawl pawl clicied *eg* polion clicied
ratchet screwdriver tyrnsgriw clicied *eg* tyrnsgriwiau clicied
ratchet stop stop clicied *eg* stopiau clicied
ratchet teeth dannedd clicied *ell*
ratchet wheel olwyn glicied *eb* olwynion clicied
rate (=numerical proportion) cyfradd *eb* cyfraddau
rate of decrease cyfradd lleihad *eb*
rate of exchange cyfradd cyfnewid *eb* cyfraddau cyfnewid
rate of feed cyfradd porthiant *eb*
rate of growth cyfradd twf *eb*
rate of interest cyfradd llog *eb* cyfraddau llog
rate of mutations cyfradd mwtaniadau *eb*
rate of photosynthesis cyfradd ffotosynthesis *eb*
rate of progress cyfradd cynnydd *eb* cyfraddau cynnydd
rate of reaction cyfradd adwaith *eb*
rate of return on capital employed cyfradd yr adenillion ar y cyfalaf a ddefnyddiwyd *eb*
rate of striking amseriad taro *eg* amseriadau taro
rate of transferring energy cyfradd trosglwyddo egni *eb*
rate of water loss cyfradd colli dŵr *eb*
rate of weight loss cyfradd colli pwysau *eb*
rate of working cyfradd gweithio *eb*
rate payer trethdalwr *eg* trethdalwyr
rate per cent cyfradd y cant *eb*
rate rebate ad-daliad treth *eg* ad-daliadau treth
rate subsidy cymhorthdal trethi *eg*
rateable ardrethol *ans*
rateable value gwerth ardrethol *eg* gwerthoedd ardrethol
rate-support grant grant cynnal trethi *eg*
ratify cadarnhau *be*
ratings (=audience size) maint cynulleidfa *eg*
ratio cymhareb *eb* cymarebau
ratio analysis (in general) dadansoddi cymarebau *be*
ratio analysis (of individual instances) dadansoddiad cymarebau *eg*
ratio IQ IQ cymarebol *eg*
ratio scale graddfa gymarebol *eb*
ration *n* dogn *eg* dognau
ration *v* dogni *be*
ration book llyfr dogni *eg* llyfrau dogni
rational (=based on reason) rhesymol *ans*
rational (of ratios) cymarebol *ans*
rational choice theory theori dewis rhesymegol *eb*
Rational Dissenter anghydffurfiwr rhesymol *eg* anghydffurfwyr rhesymol
rational emotive therapy therapi rhesymoli emosiwn *eg*
rational function ffwythiant cymarebol *eg*
rational number rhif cymarebol *eg*
rationale sail resymegol *eb* seiliau rhesymegol
rationalisation rhesymoliad *eg* rhesymoliadau
rationalism rhesymoliaeth *eb*
rationalization rhesymoli *be*

rattan corsen *eb* cyrs
rattan palm palmwydden corsen *eb* palmwydd cyrs
rattle *n* rhuglen *eb* rhuglenni
rattle *v* rhuglo *be*
ravage anrheithio *be*
ravine dyfnant *eb* dyfnentydd
raw crai *ans*
raw data data crai *ell*
raw edge ymyl grai *eb* ymylon crai
raw fibre ffibr crai *eg* ffibrau crai
raw glaze gwydredd crai *eg*
raw material deunyddiau crai *ell*
raw sienna sienna crai *eg*
raw silk sidan crai *eg*
raw steel dur crai *eg*
raw umber wmber crai *eg*
rawhide mallet gordd lledr crai *eb* gyrdd lledr crai
rawlbolt rawlfollt *eg* rawlfolltau
ray paladr *eg* pelydr
ray (in chemistry and physics) pelydryn *eg* pelydrau
ray (in physiology and biology) rheidden *eb* rheiddennau
ray box blwch pelydru *eg* blychau pelydru
ray diagram diagram pelydrol *eg* diagramau pelydrol
rayon reion *eg*
rayon acetate reion asetad *eg*
rayon cord cord reion *eg*
razorbill gwalch y penwaig *eg* gweilch y penwaig
reabsorption (renal) adamsugniad *eg*
reach *n* cyrhaeddiad *eg* cyraeddiadau
reach *v* cyrraedd *be*
reach (of river) estyniad *eg* estyniadau
reach one's majority dod i oed *be*
react (of chemical) adweithio *be*
react (of person) ymateb *be*
reactance adweithedd *eg* adweitheddau
reactant adweithydd *eg* adweithyddion
reaction (=person's response) ymateb *eg* ymatebion
reaction (physiological or chemical) adwaith *eg* adweithiau
reaction activator actifadydd adwaith *eg*
reaction formation ffurfio ymateb *be*
reaction kinetics cineteg adweithiau *eb*
reaction mixture cymysgedd adwaith *eg*
reaction rate cyfradd adwaith *eb*
reaction rate expression mynegiad cyfradd adwaith *eg*
reaction speed cyflymder adwaith *eg*
reaction time amser adweithio *eg*
reaction timer amserydd adweithio *eg* amseryddion adweithio
reactionary policy polisi adweithiol *eg* polisïau adweithiol
reactive adweithiol *ans*
reactive depression iselder adweithiol *eg*
reactive dye llifyn adweithiol *eg* llifynnau adweithiol
reactive schizophrenia sgitsoffrenia adweithiol *eg*
reactivity adweithedd *eg* adweitheddau
reactivity series cyfres adweithedd *eb* cyfresi adweithedd
reactor adweithydd *eg* adweithyddion
read darllen *be*
read /write channel sianel darllen ac ysgrifennu *eb* sianeli darllen ac ysgrifennu
read /write head pen darllen ac ysgrifennu *eg* pennau darllen ac ysgrifennu
read head pen darllen *eg* pennau darllen
read speed cyflymder darllen *eg*
read time amser darllen *eg* amserau darllen
reader darllenydd *eg* darllenyddion
reader profile proffil darllenydd *eg*
readers newsletter cylchlythyr darllenwyr *eg* cylchlythyrau darllenwyr
reading darlleniad *eg* darlleniadau
reading age oed darllen *eg*
reading comprehension darllen a deall
reading corner cornel ddarllen *eb* corneli darllen
reading scheme cynllun darllen *eg* cynlluniau darllen
reading span rhychwant darllen *eg*
reading test prawf darllen *eg* profion darllen
readjust ailgymhwyso *be*
read-only memory (ROM) cof darllen yn unig *eg*
readout allddarlleniad *eg* allddarlleniadau
ready veneer board bwrdd argaen parod *eg* byrddau argaen parod
ready-made parod *ans*
ready-reckoner cyfrifydd parod *eg* cyfrifwyr parod
ready-to-assemble furniture dodrefn parod i'w cydosod *ell*
reafforestation ailgoedwigo *be*
reagent adweithydd *eg* adweithyddion
real (in general) gwir *ans*
real (in mathematics) real *ans*
real book llyfr dewis *eg* llyfrau dewis
real capital gwir gyfalaf *eg*
real depth gwir ddyfnder *eg*
real estate eiddo tiriog *eg*
real fugue ffiwg wir *eb* ffiwgiau gwir
real gas nwy real *eg* nwyon real
real image delwedd real *eb* delweddau real
real number rhif real *eg* rhifau real
real part rhan real *eb* rhannau real
real time amser real *eg* amserau real
real time clock cloc amser real *eg* clociau amser real
real time processing prosesu amser real *be*
real value gwerth real *eg* gwerthoedd real
real variable newidyn real *eg* newidynnau real
real world byd go iawn *eg*
realised niche cilfach wedi'i chyflawni *eb* cilfachau wedi'u cyflawni
realism realaeth *eb*
realistic realistig *ans*
reality realiti *eg*
reality orientation atgoffa o realaeth *be*

reality principle egwyddor realaeth *eb*
reality television teledu realaeth *eg*
realization of a plan gwireddu cynllun *be*
reallocate ailddyrannu *be*
realm teyrnas *eb* teyrnasoedd
ream rîm *eg* rimau
reamer agorell *eb* agorellau
reaming agorellu *be*
reappraisal ailwerthusiad *eg*
rear access ôl-fynedfa *eb* ôl-fynedfeydd
rear projection (act of) ôl-daflunio *be*
rear projection (of backdrop) ôl-dafluniau
rear suspension hongiad ôl *eg*
rear-admiral dirprwy lyngesydd *eg* dirprwy lyngeswyr
rearguard action ymladd i gadw'r cefn *be*
rearrangement reaction adwaith ad-drefnu *eg*
reason rhesymu *be*
reasonable rhesymol *ans*
reasonable foreseeability rhagweladwyaeth resymol *eb*
reasonable to foresee rhesymol i ragweld
reasonableness rhesymolrwydd *eg*
reasonably dust-proof yn weddol rydd o lwch *adf*
reasoning ymresymu *be*
reassurance cysur *eg*
reassure tawelu meddwl *be*
rebate ad-daliad *eg* ad-daliadau
rebec rebec *eg* rebecau
Rebecca riots terfysgoedd Beca *ell*
rebel gwrthryfelwr *eg* gwrthryfelwyr
rebellion gwrthryfel *eg* gwrthryfeloedd
rebellious gwrthryfelgar *ans*
rebind ailrwymo *be*
reboot (in computing) ailgychwyn *be*
rebound *n* adlam *eg* adlamau
rebound *v* adlamu *be*
rebuild ailadeiladu *be*
recall galw i gof *be*
recall musical patterns galw i gof batrymau cerddorol *be*
recant gwadu *be*
recantation gwadiad *eg* gwadiadau
recede encilio *be*
receding colour lliw enciliol *eg* lliwiau enciliol
receipt derbynneb *eb* derbynebau
receive derbyn *be*
receive into membership derbyn yn aelod *be*
receive poor relief byw ar y plwyf *be*
receiver derbynnydd *eg* derbynyddion
receiver (feudal) rhysyfwr *eg* rhysyfwyr
Receiver General Rhysyfwr Cyffredinol *eg* Rhysyfwyr Cyffredinol
recency effect effaith diweddaredd *eb*
recent incomer hwyrddyfodiad *eg* hwyrddyfodiaid
recentred projection tafluniad atganolog *eg* tafluniadau atganolog
receptacle llestr *eg* llestri
receptacle (flower) cynheilydd *eg* cyneilyddion
reception (act of, formal occasion) derbyniad *eg* derbyniadau
reception (of place) derbynfa *eb* derbynfeydd
receptionist croesawydd *eg* croesawyr
receptor derbynnydd *eg* derbynyddion
receptor cell cell dderbyn *eb* celloedd derbyn
receptor molecule moleciwl derbyn *eg* moleciwlau derbyn
recess *v* cilannu *be*
recess (drill part) *n* cilan *eb* cilannau
recess (in a wall etc) *n* cilfach *eb* cilfachau
recessed cilannog *ans*
recessed joint uniad cilannog *eg* uniadau cilannog
recessed lighting golau cilannog *eg* goleuadau cilannog
recessed window ffenestr gilannog *eb* ffenestri cilannog
recessing (of lathe tools) rhigoli *be*
recession (economical) dirwasgiad *eg* dirwasgiadau
recession (geographical etc) enciliad *eg* enciliadau
recessional moraine marian enciliol *eg* marianau enciliol
recessive enciliol *ans*
recessive allele alel enciliol *eg* alelau enciliol
recessive attribute priodwedd enciliol *eb* priodweddau enciliol
recessive factor ffactor enciliol *eb* ffactorau enciliol
recharge ailwefru *be*
rechargeable ailwefradwy *ans*
recheck ailwirio *be*
recipe rysáit *eb* ryseitiau
reciprocal (in general) *adj* dwyochrog *ans*
reciprocal (in mathematics) *adj* cilyddol *ans*
reciprocal (in mathematics) *n* cilydd *eg* cilyddion
reciprocal altruism allgaredd cilyddol *eg*
reciprocal arrangement telerau cytbwys *ell*
reciprocal determinism penderfyniaeth ddwyochrog *eb*
reciprocate (in mathematics) cilyddu *be*
reciprocating motion mudiant cilyddol *eg*
reciprocity dwyochredd *eb*
Reciprocity of Duties Act Deddf Cydbwyso Tollau *eb*
recirculate ailgylchredeg *be*
recirculating cooker hood lwfer ailgylchredol *eg* lwfrau ailgylchredol
recital datganiad *eg* datganiadau
reciting note adroddnod *eg* adroddnodau
reclaim adennill *be*
recluse meudwy *eg* meudwyaid
recognition (=acknowledgement) cydnabyddiaeth *eb*
recognition (=identification) adnabyddiad *eg* adnabyddiadau
recognizance ymrwymiad *eg* ymrwymiadau
recognize (=accept, admit) cydnabod *be*

recognize (=identify) adnabod *be*
recognized form ffurf gydnabyddedig *eb* ffurfiau cydnabyddedig
recognized standard safon gydnabyddedig *eb* safonau cydnabyddedig
recognized stroke strôc gydnabyddedig *eb* strociau cydnabyddedig
recognized version fersiwn cydnabyddedig *eg* fersiynau cydnabyddedig
recoil *n* adlam *eg* adlamau
recoil *v* adlamu *be*
recombination ailgyfuniad *eg* ailgyfuniadau
recommend (=advise as a course of action) argymell *be*
recommend (=commend) cymeradwyo *be*
recommendation (=advice) argymhelliad *eg* argymhellion
recommendation (=commendation) cymeradwyaeth *eg*
recommended daily allowance (food etc) lwfans beunyddiol argymelledig *eg*
recommended daily amount (of a nutrient) maint beunyddiol argymelledig *eg*
reconcile (facts) cysoni *be*
reconcile (people) cymodi *be*
reconciliation cymod *eg*
recondition adnewyddu *be*
reconnaissance archwiliad strategol *eg*
reconnoitre archwilio strategol *be*
reconsider ailystyried *be*
reconstruct (=rebuild) ailadeiladu *be*
reconstruct (=recreate) ail-lunio *be*
reconstruction ail-luniad *eg* ail-luniadau
reconstructive memory cof ailadeiladol *eg*
record (=best attempt) *n* record *eb* recordiau
record (=evidence or information) *n* cofnod *eg* cofnodion
record (=plastic disc carrying recorded sound) *n* record *eb* recordiau
record (evidence etc on paper, computer etc) *v* cofnodi *be*
record (music etc on disc) *v* recordio *be*
record card cerdyn cofnod *eg* cardiau cofnod
record count cyfrif cofnodion *be*
record format fformat cofnod *eg*
record keeping cadw cofnodion *be*
record length hyd cofnod *eg*
record of achievement cofnod cyrhaeddiad *eg* cofnodion cyrhaeddiad
record office archifdy *eg* archifdai
record phenomena cofnodi ffenomenau *be*
record sheet taflen gofnodi *eb* taflenni cofnodi
recorder (=keeper of records) cofnodwr *eg* cofnodwyr
recorder (=machine for recording) recordydd *eg* recordwyr
recorder (=type of judge) cofiadur *eg* cofiaduron
recorder (=wind instrument) recorder *eg* recorderau
recording recordiad *eg* recordiadau
recording equipment offer recordio *ell*
recording head pen recordio *eg* pennau recordio
recording station gorsaf gofnodi *eb* gorsafoedd cofnodi
recording surface arwyneb recordio *eg* arwynebau recordio
record-structured database cronfa ddata cofnod-strwythuredig *eb* cronfeydd data cofnod-strwythuredig
recoup adennill *be*
recover adfer *be*
recoverable adferadwy *ans*
recovered memory atgof wedi'i adfer *eg* atgofion wedi'u hadfer
recovery adferiad *eg* adferiadau
recovery order gorchymyn adfer *eg*
recovery position ystum adferol *eg*
recovery rate cyfradd adfer *eb*
recreation adloniant *eg* adloniannau
recreational activity gweithgaredd adloniadol *eg* gweithgareddau adloniadol
recreational drug cyffur adloniant *eg* cyffuriau adloniant
recreational facilities cyfleusterau adloniadol *ell*
recriminate gwrthgyhuddo *be*
recruit *n* recriwt *eg* recriwtiaid
recruit *v* recriwtio *be*
recruitment method dull recriwtio *eg* dulliau recriwtio
recruitment system system recriwtio *eb* systemau recriwtio
recrystallization ailgrisialiad *eg*
recrystallize ailgrisialu *be*
rectangle petryal *eg* petryalau
rectangle method dull petryal *eg*
rectangular petryal *ans*
rectangular Cartesian coordinates cyfesurynnau Cartesaidd petryal *ell*
rectangular channel sianel betryal *eb* sianeli petryal
rectangular die dei petryal *eg* deiau petryal
rectangular duct dwythell betryal *eb* dwythellau petryal
rectangular end pen petryal *eg* pennau petryal
rectangular hyperbola hyperbola petryal *eg* hyperbolâu petryal
rectangular key allwedd betryal *eb* allweddi petryal
rectangular matrix matrics petryal *eg*
rectangular prism prism petryal *eg* prismau petryal
rectangular section material defnydd trychiad petryal *eg*
rectangular solid solid petryal *eg* solidau petryal
rectangular table bwrdd petryal *eg* byrddau petryal
rectification unioniad *eg* unioniadau
rectified spirit gwirod coeth *eg*
rectifier (of electric current) unionydd *eg* unionwyr
rectify unioni *be*
rectilinear unionlin *ans*
rectilinear coordinate cyfesuryn unionlin *eg* cyfesurynnau unionlin

rectilinear coordinate ordinate cyfesuryn unionlin mesuryn *eg* cyfesurynnau unionlin mesurynnau
rectilinear figure ffigur unionlin *eg* ffigurau unionlin
rectilinear motion mudiant unionlin *eg*
rector rheithor *eg* rheithorion
rectorate rheithoriaeth *eb* rheithoriaethau
rectory rheithordy *eg* rheithordai
rectum rectwm *eg*
recumbent gorweddol *ans*
recumbent fold plyg gorweddol *eg* plygion gorweddol
recurrance dychweliad *eg* dychweliadau
recurring cylchol *ans*
recurring decimal degolyn cylchol *eg* degolion cylchol
recursion dychweliad *eg* dychweliadau
recursive dychweliadol *ans*
recursive algorithm algorithm dychweliadol *eg* algorithmau dychweliadol
recurved atro *ans*
recusancy reciwsantiaeth *eb*
recusancy list rhestr reciwsantiaid *eb* rhestri reciwsantiaid
recusancy rolls rholiau reciwsantiaid *ell*
recusant reciwsant *eg* reciwsantiaid
recycle ailgylchu *be*
recycling of rocks ailgylchu creigiau *be*
red (enamelling colour) coch *eg*
red blood cell cell goch y gwaed *eb* celloedd coch y gwaed
red blood cell count cyfrifiad celloedd coch y gwaed *eg*
red blood corpuscle corffilyn coch y gwaed *eg* corffilod coch y gwaed
red blood corpuscle count cyfrifiad corffilod coch y gwaed *eg*
red cell ghost gweddillyn corffilyn coch *eg* gweddillion corffilod coch
red clay clai coch *eg*
Red Cross, The Groes Goch, Y *eb*
red earth pridd coch *eg* priddoedd coch
red heat gwres coch *eg*
red hot poethgoch *ans*
red kidney beans ffa coch *ell*
red ochre ocr coch *eg*
red sable sabl coch *eg*
red sable brush brwsh sabl coch *eg* brwshys sabl coch
red shift rhuddiad *eg* rhuddiadau
reddish cochlyd *ans*
redefine ailddiffinio *be*
redemption achubiaeth *eb*
re-deposit ailddyddodi *be*
redistribute ailddosbarthu *be*
redoubt amddiffynfa allanol *eb* amddiffynfeydd allanol
redox rhydocs *eg*
redox process proses rhydocs *eb* prosesau rhydocs
reduce (=curtail) cwtogi *be*
reduce (=make smaller) lleihau *be*
reduce (=subdue) darostwng *be*
reduce (=thin) teneuo *be*
reduce (in chemistry) rhydwytho *be*
reduce (price, temperature) gostwng *be*
reduce a pattern lleihau patrwm *be*
reduce bulk lleihau swmp *be*
reduced goods nwyddau pris gostyngol *ell*
reduced level (in physics) lefel seiliedig *eb*
reduced mass màs gostyngol *eg*
reduced pressure gwasgedd gostyngol *eg*
reduced price pris gostyngol *eg* prisiau gostyngol
reduced size maint llai *eg*
reducible gostyngadwy *ans*
reducing agent rhydwythydd *eg* rhydwythyddion
reducing medium (thinners) cyfrwng teneuo *eg* cyfryngau teneuo
reduction (in chemistry) rhydwythiad *eg*
reduction (in numbers) lleihad *eg*
reduction (in price, temperature) gostyngiad *eg* gostyngiadau
reduction box blwch gostyngiad *eg*
reduction division ymraniad lleihaol *eg*
reductionism lleihadaeth *eb*
reductionist lleihaol *ans*
redundancy colli gwaith *be*
redundancy check gwiriad afreidrwydd *eg* gwiriadau afreidrwydd
redundancy pay tâl colli gwaith *eg*
redundant (=not needed) diangen *ans*
redundant (=unemployed) di-waith *ans*
redwoods coedydd coch *ell*
reed (=type of plant) corsen *eb* cyrs
reed (in wind instruments) brwynen *eb* brwyn
reed hook bach corsen *eg* bachau cyrs
reed organ organ gyrs *eb* organau cyrs
reed pen pen corsen *eg* pennau cyrs
reeding corsenwaith *eg*
reef creigres *eb* creigresi
reef riff *eg* riffiau
reefing (the sail) riffio *be*
reel ril *eb* riliau
re-enter (in computing) adfewnio *be*
re-entrant (in computing) adfewniadol *ans*
re-entrant (in geography) adfewnol *ans*
re-entrant contour line cyfuchlin adfewnol *eg* cyfuchliniau adfewnol
re-entry (in computing) adfewniad *eg* adfewniadau
re-equip ailgyfarparu *be*
re-establish ailsefydlu *be*
reeve (=chief magistrate) prif ynad *eg* prif ynadon
reeve (=manorial supervisor) maer *eg* meiri
re-export ailallforio *be*
refectory ffreutur *eg* ffreuturau
refectory table bwrdd ffreutur *eg* byrddau ffreutur
refer cyfeirio *be*

referee (female, in sport) dyfarnwraig *eb* dyfarnwragedd
referee (for references) canolwr *eg* canolwyr
referee (male, in sport) dyfarnwr *eg* dyfarnwyr
referee's book llyfr bach *eg*
reference (=testimonial) geirda *eg*
reference (in book) cyfeiriad *eg* cyfeiriadau
reference (mark or number) cyfeirnod *eg* cyfeirnodau
reference book cyfeirlyfr *eg* cyfeirlyfrau
reference drawing lluniad cyfeirio *eg* lluniadau cyfeirio
reference plane plân cyfeirnod *eg* planau cyfeirnod
reference section adran gyfeirio *eb* adrannau cyfeirio
referendum refferendwm *eg* refferenda
referral cyfeiriad *eg* cyfeiriadau
referral procedures trefn gyfeirio *eb*
referral route llwybr cyfeirio *eg* llwybrau cyfeirio
referred pain poen allgyfeiriol *eg*
refill *n* adlenwad *eg* adlenwadau
refill *v* adlenwi *be*
refine (metal, sugar) coethi *be*
refine (oil) puro *be*
refine technique gwella perfformiad *be*
refined (of metal, sugar) coeth *ans*
refined linseed oil olew had llin puredig *eg*
refined oil olew puredig *eg*
refined sugar siwgr coeth *eg*
refinement coethder *eg* coethderau
refinery purfa *eb* purfeydd
reflation atchwyddiant *eg*
reflect (=consider) ystyried *be*
reflect (light) adlewyrchu *be*
reflected adlewyrchedig *ans*
reflected (light, sound wave) adlewyrch *ans*
reflected colour lliw adlewyrchedig *eg* lliwiau adlewyrchedig
reflected light golau adlewyrchedig *eg*
reflection adlewyrchiad *eg* adlewyrchiadau
reflection in a line adlewyrchiad mewn llinell *eg*
reflective practitioner ymarferwr adfyfyriol *eg* ymarferwyr adfyfyriol
reflective symmetry cymesuredd adlewyrchiad *eg*
reflector adlewyrchydd *eg* adlewyrchyddion
reflex *adj* atgyrchol *ans*
reflex *n* atgyrch *eg* atgyrchau
reflex action gweithred atgyrch *eb* gweithredoedd atgyrch
reflex angle ongl atblyg *eb* onglau atblyg
reflex arc llwybr atgyrch *eg* llwybrau atgyrch
reflexive relation perthynas ymatblyg *eb*
reflux *adj* adlifol *ans*
reflux *n* adlifiad *eg* adlifiadau
reflux *v* adlifo *be*
reflux condenser cyddwysydd adlifol *eg* cyddwysyddion adlifol
refoot troedio *be*
reform *n* diwygiad *eg* diwygiadau
reform (=form again) *v* ailffurfio *be*
reform (=improve) *v* diwygio *be*
Reform Act Deddf Ddiwygio *eb*
Reform Bill Mesur Diwygio *eg*
Reform Bill Crisis Argyfwng y Mesur Diwygio *eg*
Reform Jew Iddew Diwygiedig *eg* Iddewon Diwygiedig
reformation diwygiad *eg* diwygiadau
Reformation Diwygiad Protestannaidd *eg*
reformatory ysgol benyd *eb* ysgolion penyd
reformed diwygiedig *ans*
reformer diwygiwr *eg* diwygwyr
reformer (chemical) ailffurfydd *eg* ailffurfyddion
refract (light) plygu *be*
refracted (light, sound wave) plyg *ans*
refracted angle ongl blygiant *eb* onglau plygiant
refracted light golau plyg *eg* goleuadau plyg
refraction plygiant *eg*
refractive index indecs plygiant *eg* indecsau plygiant
refractivity plygiannedd *eg*
refractometer reffractomedr *eg* reffractomedrau
refractory (of substance) gwrthsafol *ans*
refractory brick bricsen wrthsafol *eb* brics gwrthsafol
refractory lining leinin gwrthsafol *eg*
refractory period (of nerve) cyfnod diddigwydd *eg*
refractory priest offeiriad gwrthnysig *eg* offeiriaid gwrthnysig
refrain byrdwn *eg* byrdynau
refresh rate cyfradd adnewyddu *eb*
refrigerant rhewydd *eg* rhewyddion
refrigerate rheweiddio *be*
refrigerated rheweiddiedig *ans*
refrigeration rheweiddiad *eg*
refrigeration ship llong rewi *eb* llongau rhewi
refrigerator oergell *eb* oergelloedd
refuge village pentref noddfa *eg* pentrefi noddfa
refugee ffoadur *eg* ffoaduriaid
refugee camp gwersyll ffoaduriaid *eg* gwersylloedd ffoaduriaid
refugee centre canolfan ffoaduriaid *eb* canolfannau ffoaduriaid
refund *n* ad-daliad *eg* ad-daliadau
refund *v* ad-dalu *be*
refuse sbwriel *eg*
refuse bin bin sbwriel *eg* biniau sbwriel
refuse collector casglwr sbwriel *eg* casglwyr sbwriel
refuse disposal gwaredu sbwriel *be*
refuse tip tomen sbwriel *eb* tomenni sbwriel
refute gwrthbrofi *be*
regain adennill *be*
regain balance adennill cydbwysedd *be*
regain the ball adennill y bêl *be*
regal *adj* brenhinol *ans*
regal *n* organ rigol *eb* organau rhigol
regalia regalia *eg*
regalian teyrnaidd *ans*

regalian rights hawliau teyrnaidd *ell*
regality breninoldeb *eg*
regelation adrewiad *eg*
regency rhaglywiaeth *eb*
regency council cyngor rhaglywiaeth *eg*
regenerate (economy) adfywio *be*
regenerate (tissue etc) atffurfio *be*
regenerated atgynyrchiedig *ans*
regenerated fibre ffibr atgynyrchiedig *eg* ffibrau atgynyrchiedig
regeneration (e.g. organ) atffurfiant *eg*
regenerator atffurfydd *eg* atffurfyddion
regent rhaglyw *eg* rhaglywiaid
regicide (crime) teyrnladdiad *eg* teyrnladdiadau
regicide (of person) teyrnleiddiad *eg* teyrnleiddiaid
regime (in physics) patrymedd *eg*
regime (in politics) cyfundrefn *eb* cyfundrefnau
regiment catrawd *eb* catrodau
region (geographical) rhanbarth *eg* rhanbarthau
region (in music) ardal *eb* ardaloedd
region of space rhanbarth gofod *eg* rhanbarthau gofod
regional rhanbarthol *ans*
regional airport maes awyr rhanbarthol *eg* meysydd awyr rhanbarthol
regional level lefel ranbarthol *eb* lefelau rhanbarthol
regional tourist board bwrdd croeso rhanbarthol *eg* byrddau croeso rhanbarthol
regional variety amrywiaeth ranbarthol *eb*
regionalism rhanbarthiaeth *eb*
register *v* cofrestru *be*
register (=device controlling organ pipes) *n* stop *eg* stopiau
register (book or database etc) *n* cofrestr *eb* cofrestri
register (of language) *n* cywair *eg* cyweiriau
register (printing) *n* iawn luniad *eg* iawn luniadau
registered child minder gwarchodwr plant cofrestredig *eg* gwarchodwyr plant cofrestredig
registered general nurse nyrs gofrestredig gyffredinol *eb* nyrsys cofrestredig cyffredinol
registered nursery meithrinfa drwyddedig *eb* meithrinfeydd trwyddedig
registered office swyddfa gofrestredig *eb* swyddfeydd cofrestredig
registered protocol protocol wedi'i gofrestru *eg* protocolau wedi'u cofrestru
registrar cofrestrydd *eg* cofrestryddion
registration cofrestriad *eg* cofrestriadau
registration fee tâl cofrestru *eg* taliadau cofrestru
Registration of Births, Marriages and Deaths Act Deddf Cofrestru Genedigaethau, Priodasau a Marwolaethau *eb*
registry cofrestrfa *eb* cofrestrfeydd
Registry Office Swyddfa Gofrestru *eb* Swyddfeydd Cofrestru
regolith (=mantle rock) creicaen *eb* creicaenau
regrade ailraddio *be*
regress atchwelyd *be*
regression atchweliad *eg* atchweliadau
regression analysis dadansoddiad atchwel *eg* dadansoddiadau atchwel
regression line llinell atchwel *eb* llinellau atchwel
regression model model atchwel *eg* modelau atchwel
regression technique techneg atchwel *eb*
regression to the mean atchweliad at y cymedr *eg*
regressive tax treth atchwel *eb* trethi atchwel
regular rheolaidd *ans*
regular canon canon rheolaidd *eg* canoniaid rheolaidd
regular clergy clerigaeth reolaidd *eb*
regular cleric clerigwr rheolaidd *eg* clerigwyr rheolaidd
regular prism prism rheolaidd *eg* prismau rheolaidd
regular solid solid rheolaidd *eg* solidau rheolaidd
regular value gwerth rheolaidd *eg*
regular word gair cyson *eg* geiriau cyson
regularity rheoleidd-dra *eg*
regulate rheoli *be*
regulation rheoliad *eg* rheoliadau
regulator rheolydd *eg* rheolyddion
regulatory behaviour ymddygiad rheoleiddio *eg*
regur regur *eg* regurau
regurgitation ailchwydiad *eg* ailchwydiadau
rehabilitate ailsefydlu *be*
rehabilitation adferiad *eg* adferiadau
rehabilitation centre canolfan adfer *eb* canolfannau adfer
rehearsal ymarfer *eg* ymarferiadau
rehearsal technique techneg ymarfer *eb* technegau ymarfer
rehearse ymarfer *be*
reheat aildwymo *be*
Reich Concordat Concordat y Reich *eg*
Reichstag Fire Tân y Reichstag *eg*
reign teyrnasiad *eg* teyrnasiadau
reincarnation ailymgnawdoliad *eg* ailymgnawdoliadau
reindeer carw Llychlyn *eg* ceirw Llychlyn
reindeer moss mwsogl carw *eg*
reinforce atgyfnerthu *be*
reinforced concrete concrit cyfnerth *eg*
reinforced corner cornel gyfnerth *eb* corneli cyfnerth
reinforced heel sawdl gaerog *eb* sodlau caerog
reinforcement atgyfnerthiad *eg* atgyfnerthiadau
reinforcing square sgwâr cryfhau *eg* sgwariau cryfhau
reinstall ailosod *be*
Reinsurance Treaty Cytundeb Ailyswirio *eg*
reiterated notes nodau mynych *ell*
reject gwrthod *be*
rejection gwrthodiad *eg* gwrthodiadau
rejection ratio cymhareb wrthod *eb*
rejector circuit cylched wrthod *eb* cylchedau gwrthod

rejoin ailuno *be*
rejoinder gwrthateb *eg* gwrthatebion
rejuvenate adnewyddu *be*
rejuvenated adnewyddedig *ans*
relate perthnasu *be*
related perthynol *ans*
related concepts cysyniadau cysylltiedig *ell*
related shapes ffurfiau perthynol *ell*
relation (=connection) cysylltiad *eg* cysylltiadau
relation (=relative) perthynas *eg* perthnasau
relational perthynol *ans*
relational database cronfa ddata berthynol *eb* cronfeydd data perthynol
relational research ymchwil perthynol *eg*
relationship perthynas *eg/b* perthnasoedd
relative (=comparative) *adj* cymharol *ans*
relative (=related) *adj* perthynol *ans*
relative (=relation) *n* perthynas *eg/b* perthnasau
relative abundance digonedd cymharol *eg*
relative addressing cyfeirio perthynol *be*
relative atomic mass màs atomig cymharol *eg*
relative density dwysedd cymharol *eg* dwyseddau cymharol
relative dimensions dimensiynau perthynol *ell*
relative flatness gwastadrwydd cymharol *eg*
relative humidity lleithder cymharol *eg*
relative key cywair perthynol *eg* cyweiriau perthynol
relative major cywair perthynol mwyaf *eg*
relative major scale graddfa berthynol fwyaf *eb*
relative minor cywair perthynol lleiaf *eg*
relative minor scale graddfa berthynol leiaf *eb*
relative molecular mass màs moleciwlaidd cymharol *eg*
relative permeability athreiddedd perthynol *eg*
relative pitch traw perthynol *eg*
relative price pris cymharol *eg*
relative proportions cyfrannau cymharol *ell*
▸ **relative velocity** cyflymder perthynol *eg*
relativism perthynoliaeth *eb*
relativistic perthnaseddol *ans*
relativity perthnasedd *eg*
relax (a muscle) llaesu *be*
relax (oneself) ymlacio *be*
relaxation oscillator osgiliadur llaciad *eg*
relaxed (in general) wedi ymlacio *ans*
relaxed (of muscle) yn llaes ac yn llac *adf*
relay (in electronics) relái *eg* releiau
relay (race) ras gyfnewid *eb* rasys cyfnewid
release rhyddhau *be*
release agent cyfrwng rhyddhau *eg*
release and rescue rhyddhau ac achub
release key rhyddhäwr *eg* rhyddhawyr
release valve falf ryddhau *eb* falfiau rhyddhau
relevance perthnasedd *eg*
relevant perthnasol *ans*
relevant legislation deddfwriaeth berthnasol *eb*
relevant parts rhannau perthnasol *ell*
relevant safety procedure trefn diogelwch perthnasol *eg*
reliability dibynadwyedd *eg*
reliable dibynadwy *ans*
reliable supply cyflenwad dibynadwy *eg* cyflenwadau dibynadwy
reliable supply of energy cyflenwad dibynadwy o egni *eg*
relic crair *eg* creiriau
relict landscape tirwedd greiriol *eb* tirweddau creiriol
relict structure adeiledd creiriol *eg* adeileddau creiriol
relief (=freedom) *n* rhyddhad *eg*
relief (fine) *n* dirwy etifedd *eb*
relief (from pain etc) *n* gollyngdod *eg*
relief (in economics) *n* gostyngiad *eg* gostyngiadau
relief (income tax) *n* cymorth *eg* cymhorthion
relief (of land) *n* tirwedd *eb* tirweddau
relief (on design) *adj* cerfweddol *ans*
relief (sculpture) *n* cerfwedd *eb* cerfweddau
relief carving cerfiad cerfwedd *eg* cerfiadau cerfwedd
relief engraving ysgythriad cerfwedd *eg* ysgythriadau cerfwedd
relief etching ysgythru cerfweddol *be*
relief feature nodwedd tirwedd *eb* nodweddion tirwedd
relief map map tirwedd *eg* mapiau tirwedd
relief mould mowld cerfwedd *eg* mowldiau cerfwedd
relief road ffordd liniaru *eb* ffyrdd lliniaru
relief sculpture cerflunwaith cerfweddol *eg*
relieve (symptoms etc) lliniaru *be*
religion crefydd *eb* crefyddau
religiosity crefyddoldeb *eg*
religious crefyddol *ans*
religious character of a school cymeriad crefyddol ysgol *eg*
religious commitment ymrwymiad crefyddol *eg*
religious concept cysyniad crefyddol *eg* cysyniadau crefyddol
religious conversion tröedigaeth grefyddol *eb* tröedigaethau crefyddol
religious denomination enwad crefyddol *eg* enwadau crefyddol
religious education addysg grefyddol *eb*
religious experience profiad crefyddol *eg*
religious freedom rhyddid crefyddol *eg*
religious group grŵp crefydd *eg* grwpiau crefydd
religious house tŷ crefydd *eg* tai crefydd
religious intolerance anoddefgarwch crefyddol *eg*
religious language iaith grefyddol *eb*
religious leader arweinydd crefyddol *eg* arweinwyr crefyddol
religious order urdd grefyddol *eb* urddau crefyddol
religious revival diwygiad crefyddol *eg* diwygiadau crefyddol
religious song cân grefyddol *eb* caneuon crefyddol
religious teacher (female) athrawes crefydd *eb* athrawesau crefydd

religious teacher (male) athro crefydd *eg* athrawon crefydd
religious teaching dysgeidiaeth grefyddol *eb*
religious tradition traddodiad crefyddol *eg* traddodiadau crefyddol
religious worship cydaddoli crefyddol *be*
reliquary creirfa *eb* creirfâu
reload ail-lwytho *be*
relocatable adleoladwy *ans*
relocate adleoli *be*
relocator adleolydd *eg* adleolyddion
reluctance gwrthiant *eg* gwrthiannau
reluctant learner dysgwr amharod *eg* dysgwyr amharod
remainder gweddill *eg* gweddillion
remainder theorem theorem y gweddill *eb*
remand *n* remand *eg*
remand (in custody) *v* cadw yn y ddalfa *be*
remand centre canolfan remand *eb* canolfannau remand
remand fostering scheme cynllun maethu remand *eg* cynlluniau maethu remand
remark sylw *eg* sylwadau
remedial class dosbarth adfer *eg* dosbarthiadau adfer
remedial exercise ymarferiad adfer *eg* ymarferion adfer
remedial work gwaith adfer *eg*
remedy the fault cywiro'r diffyg *be*
remember cofio *be*
remember-to-know shift symudiad cofio-i-wybod *eg*
Remembrance Day Dydd y Cofio *eg*
remembrancer swyddog dyledion y Goron *eg* swyddogion dyledion y Goron
reminiscence therapy therapi hel atgofion *eg*
remission gwellhad dros dro *eg*
remittance advice nodyn talu *eg*
remnant sbaryn *eg* sbarion
remodel adlunio *be*
remonstrance gwrthdystiad *eg* gwrthdystiadau
remonstrant haerwr *eg* haerwyr
remonstrate gwrthdystio *be*
remote pell *ans*
remote access cyrchiad pell *eg* cyrchiadau pell
remote console consol pell *eg* consolau pell
remote control rheolaeth bell *eb*
remote control panel panel pell-reoli *eg* paneli pell-reoli
remote data station gorsaf ddata pell *eb* gorsafoedd data pell
remote data terminal terfynell ddata pell *eb* terfynellau data pell
remote debugging dadfygio pell *be*
remote enquiry ymholiad pell *eg* ymholiadau pell
remote job entry (RJE) mewnbynnu gorchwyl pell *be*
remote processing prosesu pell *be*
remote testing profi pell *be*
remotely sensed data data a synhwyrir o bell *ell*
removable symudadwy *ans*
removal agent codydd staen *eg* codyddion staen
remove (=cancel) *v* diddymu *be*
remove (=move) *v* symud *be*
remove (in music) *n* gwyriad *eg* gwyriadau
remove brackets diddymu cromfachau *be*
remove fullness cael gwared â llawnder *be*
removing harmful consequences gwaredu canlyniadau niweidiol *be*
Renaissance Dadeni *eg*
renal arennol *ans*
renal medicine meddygaeth arennau *eb*
renal vein gwythïen arennol *eb* gwythiennau arennol
render (=sandy mixture) rendrad *eg* rendradau
rendering (in music) datganiad *eg* datganiadau
rendering (on wall) rendro *be*
rendition datganiad *eg* datganiadau
rendzina rendsina *eg*
renegade gwrthgiliwr *eg* gwrthgilwyr
renew adnewyddu *be*
renewable adnewyddadwy *ans*
renewable energy egni adnewyddadwy *eg*
renewable resource adnodd adnewyddadwy *eg* adnoddau adnewyddadwy
renewable resources adnoddau adnewyddol *ell*
renewal adnewyddiad *eg* adnewyddiadau
rennin rennin *eg*
renounce diarddel *be*
renovate adnewyddu *be*
renovation adnewyddiad *eg* adnewyddiadau
rent *n* rhent *eg* rhenti
rent *v* rhentu *be*
Rent Act Deddf Rhenti *eb* Deddfau Rhenti
rent control rheolaeth rhent *eb*
rent of assize rhent aseis *eg*
rent rebate ad-daliad rhent *eg* ad-daliadau rhent
rent roll rhôl rhent *eb* rholiau rhent
rental rhent *eg* rhenti
rentier rhentwr *eg* rhentwyr
rentier class dosbarth rhentyddol *eg*
reorientation ailgyfeiriadaeth *eb*
repair *n* atgyweiriad *eg* atgyweiriadau
repair *v* atgyweirio *be*
repair grant grant atgyweirio *eg* grantiau atgyweirio
repair kit cit atgyweirio *eb* citiau atgyweirio
reparation iawndal *eg* iawndaliadau
repatriate *n* dychweledig *eg* dychweledigion
repay ad-dalu *be*
repayable ad-daladwy *ans*
repayment ad-daliad *eg* ad-daliadau
repeal diddymu *be*
repeal of the Corn Laws diddymu'r Deddfau Ŷd *be*
repeat *n* ailadroddiad *eg* ailadroddiadau
repeat *v* ailadrodd *be*
repeat alignment ailadrodd aluniad *be*

repeat column ailadrodd colofn *be*
repeat header ailadrodd pennyn *be*
repeat heading ailadrodd teitl *be*
repeat mark marc ailadrodd *eg* marciau ailadrodd
repeat pattern patrwm ailadroddol *eg* patrymau ailadroddol
repeat row ailadrodd rhes *be*
repeat search ailadrodd chwiliad *be*
repeated measures design cynllun ailadrodd mesurau *eg* cynlluniau ailadrodd mesurau
repel gwrthyrru *be*
repel text gwrthyrru testun *be*
repertoire repertoire *eg* repertoires
repertoire requirements gofynion repertoire *ell*
répétiteur répétiteur *eg* répétiteurs
repetition ailadroddiad *eg* ailadroddiadau
replace newid *be*
replace amnewid *be*
replace all newid popeth *be*
replace control newid rheolydd *be*
replace custom styles newid arddulliau addasu *be*
replace dashes newid llinellau toredig *be*
replace existing libraries newid llyfrgelloedd presennol *be*
replace graphics newid graffigau *be*
replace with background newid gyda chefndir *be*
replacement amnewidyn *eg* amnewidynnau
replacement series cyfres amnewidiad *eb*
replacement table tabl amnewid *eg* tablau amnewid
replay ailchwarae *be*
replay the point ailchwarae'r pwynt *be*
replica replica *eg* replicâu
replicate dyblygu *be*
replication dyblygiad *eg* dyblygiadau
replication dyblygu *be*
replies and comments ymatebion a sylwadau
reply path llwybr ateb *eg* llwybrau ateb
reply to all ateb i bawb *be*
reply to group ateb i grŵp *be*
reply to mail ateb i e-bost *be*
reply to sender ateb yr anfonwr *be*
report *n* adroddiad *eg* adroddiadau
report (formally) *v* adrodd *be*
report (informally) *v* rhoi gwybod *be*
report back adrodd yn ôl *be*
report design cynllun adroddiad *eg*
report footer troedyn adroddiad *eg* troedynnau adroddiad
report generator generadur adroddiadau *eg* generaduron adroddiadau
report header pennyn adroddiad *eg* penynnau adroddiad
report name enw adroddiad *eg* enwau adroddiadau
report type math o adroddiad *eg*
report wizard dewin adroddiadau *eg* dewiniaid adroddiadau
Reporting of Injuries, Diseases and Dangerous Occupations Adrodd am Anafiadau, Afiechydon a Galwedigaethau Peryglus *be*
reposition ail-leoli *be*
repository ystorfa *eb* ystorfeydd
repoussé (decorative processes) repoussé *ans*
repoussé hammer morthwyl repoussé *eg*
repoussé punch pwnsh repoussé *eg* pynsiau repoussé
represent (=portray) portreadu *be*
represent (in general) cynrychioli *be*
represent a landscape cynrychioli tirlun *be*
representation (=portrait) portread *eg* portreadau
representation (in mathematics) cynrychioliad *eg* cynrychioliadau
representation (of people) cynrychiolaeth *eb* cynrychiolaethau
representation fraction ffracsiwn cynrychioliadol *eg* ffracsiynau cynrychioliadol
Representation of the People Act Deddf Cynrychiolaeth y Bobl *eb*
representation theorem theorem gynrychioliad *eb*
representational (=seeking to portray) portreadol *ans*
representational art celfyddyd gynrychioliadol *eb*
representative *adj* cynrychiadol *ans*
representative *n* cynrychiolydd *eg* cynrychiolwyr
representative assembly cynulliad cynrychiadol *eg* cynulliadau cynrychiadol
representative fraction (R.F.) ffracsiwn cynrychiadol *eg* ffracsiynau cynrychiadol
representative sample sampl gynrychioliadol *eb* samplau cynrychioliadol
representativeness heuristic hewristig cynrychioldeb *eg*
representing the past cynrychioli'r gorffennol *be*
repression (of enzyme etc) cynyrchluddiant *eg*
repression (political) gormes *eg/b*
repression (psychological) ataliad *eg*
repressive (of regime) gormesol *ans*
reprieve (from capital punishment) atal dienyddio *be*
reprisal dial *eg* dialon
reprise (historical) atbreis *eg*
reprocess ailbrosesu *be*
reproduce (in general) atgynhyrchu *be*
reproduce (sexually) atgenhedlu *be*
reproducer (in computing) dyblygydd *eg* dyblygwyr
reproduction (in general) atgynhyrchiad *eg* atgynhyrchiadau
reproduction (sexual) atgenhedliad *eg*
reproductive organs organau atgenhedlu *ell*
reproductive rate cyfradd atgenhedlu *eb* cyfraddau atgenhedlu
reproductive strategy strategaeth atgenhedlu *eb* strategaethau atgenhedlu
reproductive success llwyddiant atgenhedlu *eg*
reproductive system system genhedlu *eb*
reptile ymlusgiad *eg* ymlusgiaid

republic gweriniaeth *eb* gweriniaethau
republican *adj* gweriniaethol *ans*
republican *n* gweriniaethwr *eg* gweriniaethwyr
Republican Party Plaid Weriniaethol *eb*
repulsion gwrthyriad *eg* gwrthyriadau
repulsive force grym gwrthyrru *eg* grymoedd gwrthyrru
request cais *eg* ceisiadau
require gofyn *be*
required gofynnol *ans*
required height uchder gofynnol *eg*
requirement gofyniad *eg* gofynion
requisition (=official claim on land or materials) meddiant gorfodol *eg*
requisition (=order) archeb *eb* archebion
reredorter geudy *eg* geudai
resale *n* adwerthiant *eg* adwerthiannau
resale *v* adwerthu *be*
rescue achub *be*
rescue equipment cyfarpar achub *eg*
research *n* ymchwil *eg*
research *v* ymchwilio *be*
research and development ymchwil a datblygu
research assistant cynorthwyydd ymchwil *eg* cynorthwywyr ymchwil
research data data ymchwil *ell*
research fellow cymrawd ymchwil *eg* cymrodyr ymchwil
research grant grant ymchwil *eg* grantiau ymchwil
research method dull ymchwil *eg* dulliau ymchwil
research objective amcan ymchwil *eg* amcanion ymchwil
research student myfyriwr ymchwil *eg* myfyrwyr ymchwil
researcher ymchwilydd *eg* ymchwilwyr
researcher bias tuedd ymchwilydd *eb*
reselect ailddewis *be*
resemblance tebygrwydd *eg*
resequent (stream) *n* adlif *eg* adlifau
resequent stream ffrwd adlif *eb* ffrydiau adlif
reservation tiriogaeth frodorol *eb* tiriogaethau brodorol
reservation fee ffi cadw *eb* ffioedd cadw
reservations manager rheolwr bwcio *eg* rheolwyr bwcio
reservations staff staff bwcio *ell*
reserve *v* neilltuo *be*
reserve (for nature) *n* gwarchodfa *eb* gwarchodfeydd
reserve (of food) *n* storfa fwyd *eb* storfeydd bwyd
reserve player chwaraewr wrth gefn *eg* chwaraewyr wrth gefn
reserved word gair cadw *eg* geiriau cadw
reserves (financial) cronfa wrth gefn *eb* cronfeydd wrth gefn
reserves (military) milwyr wrth gefn *ell*
reservoir (in general) cronfa *eb* cronfeydd
reservoir (of water) cronfa ddŵr *eb* cronfeydd dŵr
reset ailosod *be*
reset attribute priodoledd ailosod *eg* priodoleddau ailosod
reset cell ailosod cell *be*
reset default ailosod rhagosodiadau *be*
reset font attributes ailosod priodoleddau ffont *be*
reset routing ailosod llwybrydd *be*
reset scale ailosod graddfa *be*
reset tip list ailosod rhestr cyngor *be*
resettle ailgyfanheddu *be*
resettlement (of place) ailgyfanheddiad *eg* ailgyfaneddiadau
resettlement of offenders ailsefydlu troseddwyr *be*
reshuffle ad-drefnu *be*
residence annedd *eg/b* anheddau
resident *adj* preswyl *ans*
resident *n* preswyliwr *eg* preswylwyr
resident alien estron preswyl *eg* estroniaid preswyl
residential care gofal preswyl *eg*
residential care home cartref gofal preswyl *eg* cartrefi gofal preswyl
residential home cartref preswyl *eg* cartrefi preswyl
residential social worker gweithiwr cymdeithasol preswyl *eg* gweithwyr cymdeithasol preswyl
residential zone cylchfa breswyl *eb* cylchfaoedd preswyl
residual *adj* gweddillol *ans*
residual (in mathematics) *n* gweddilleb *eb* gweddillebau
residual air aer gweddillol *eg*
▶ **residual deposits** dyddodion gweddillol *ell*
residual hearing gweddill clyw *eg*
residual vision gweddill golwg *eg*
residue gweddill *eg* gweddillion
resign ymddiswyddo *be*
resignation ymddiswyddiad *eg*
resilient (of person) gwydn *ans*
resilient (of substance) adlamol *ans*
resin resin *eg* resinau
resin adhesive adlyn resin *eg* adlynion resin
resin cored solder sodr plymwr *eg*
resin duct pibell ystôr *eb* pibellau ystôr
resin glaze sglein resin *eg*
resin glue glud resin *eg* gludion resin
resinous resinaidd *ans*
resinous ground grwnd resinaidd *eg*
resist gwrthsefyll *be*
resist printing gwrthbrintio *be*
resistance gwrthwynebedd *eg*
resistance (=ability to withstand adverse conditions) gwydnwch *eg*
resistance (=hindering the conduction of electricity etc) gwrthiant *eg* gwrthiannau
resistance (=refusal to comply) gwrthwynebiad *eg*
Resistance (in France, World War II) Byddin Gêl *eb*
resistance movement mudiad gwrthwynebu *eg* mudiadau gwrthwynebu
resistance to motion gwrthiant i'w fudiant *eg*

resistance wire technique techneg gwrthiant gwifren *eb*
resistant (=tough) gwydn *ans*
resistant (to electricity etc) gwrthiannol *ans*
resistant attachment ymlyniad gwrthwynebol *eg*
resistant materials defnyddiau gwrthiannol *ell*
resistive circuit cylched gwrtheddol *eb*
resistivity gwrthedd *eg* gwrtheddau
resistor gwrthydd *eg* gwrthyddion
resizable ailfeintiol *ans*
resize ailfeintio *be*
resize frame ailfeintio'r ffrâm *be*
resize table window ailfeintio ffenestr tabl *be*
reslant ailogwyddo *be*
resolute (=component) cydran *eb* cydrannau
resolution (=decision) penderfyniad *eg* penderfyniadau
resolution (of discord in music) adferiad *eg* adferiadau
resolution (of resolving power in physics) datrysyn *eg* datrysynnau
resolution (of vectors) cydraniad *eg* cydraniadau
resolve (a discord) adfer *be*
resolve (problems) datrys *be*
resolve (vectors: force, velocity etc) cydrannu *be*
resolve a force into components cydrannu grym *be*
resolve horizontally cydrannu'n llorweddol *be*
resolve vertically cydrannu'n fertigol *be*
resolved (of components) cydrannol *ans*
resolvent *adj* datrysol *ans*
resolvent *n* cydrennydd *eg* cydrenyddion
resolvent kernel cnewyllyn datrysol *eg* cnewyll datrysol
resonance cyseiniant *eg* cyseiniannau
resonance chord cord cyseinio *eg* cordiau cyseinio
resonance curve cromlin gyseinio *eb*
resonant *adj* cyseiniol *ans*
resonant *n* cysain *eg* cyseiniau
resonant frequency amledd cysain *eg*
resonate cyseinio *be*
resonator cyseinydd *eg* cyseinyddion
resort area ardal wyliau *eb* ardaloedd gwyliau
resource adnodd *eg* adnoddau
resource allocation formula fformiwla dyrannu adnoddau *eb*
resource centre canolfan adnoddau *eb* canolfannau adnoddau
resource exhausted adnoddau wedi dod i ben
resource folder ffolder adnoddau *eb*
resource implications goblygiadau adnoddol *ell*
resource management rheoli adnoddau *be*
resource materials deunyddiau adnoddau *ell*
resource partitioning rhaniad adnoddau *eg*
resource planning cynllunio adnoddau *be*
resource selection dewis adnoddau *be*
respectability parchusrwydd *eg*
respective priodol *ans*
respectively yn ôl eu trefn *adf*
respiration resbiradaeth *eb* resbiradaethau
respirator peiriant anadlu *eg* peiriannau anadlu
respiratory resbiradol *ans*
respiratory device dyfais resbiradol *eb* dyfeisiau resbiradol
respiratory gas nwy resbiradol *eg*
respiratory quotient (R.Q.) cyniferydd resbiradol *eg*
respiratory surface arwyneb resbiradol *eg*
respiratory system system resbiradaeth *eb*
respiratory system system resbiradol *eb*
respire resbiradu *be*
respite seibiant *eg*
respite care gofal seibiant *eg*
respond ymateb *be*
respond readily ymateb yn barod *be*
responsa responsa *ell*
response ymateb *eg* ymatebion
response acquiescence ymateb cydsyniol *eg*
response bias gogwydd ymateb *eg*
response cost cost ymateb *eb*
response curve cromlin ymateb *eg*
response deviation ymateb gwyrol *eg*
response style arddull ymateb *eb* arddulliau ymateb
response time amser ymateb *eg*
response to set tasks ymateb i dasgau *be*
responsibility cyfrifoldeb *eg* cyfrifoldebau
responsible government llywodraeth gyfrifol *eb*
rest (=musical silence) *n* saib *eg* seibiau
rest (=non movement in physics) *n* disymudedd *eg*
rest (=repose) *v* gorffwys *be*
rest (=support or prop) *n* cynhaliwr *eg* cynhalwyr
rest in water gorffwys yn y dŵr *be*
rest mass màs disymudedd *eg*
rest sign tawnod *eg* tawnodau
rest stroke symudiad gorffwysol *eg* symudiadau gorffwysol
restart ailgychwyn *be*
restart numbering ailgychwyn rhifo *be*
restaurant tŷ bwyta *eg* tai bwyta
restaurant manager rheolwr y tŷ bwyta *eg*
resting pin (on harp) gorffwysbin *eb* gorffwysbinau
restitute adfer *be*
restitution adferiad *eg*
restless aflonydd *ans*
restoration adferiad *eg*
restore (in general) adfer *be*
restore button botwm adfer *eg* botymau adfer
restore damaged environments adfer amgylcheddau sydd wedi'u difrodi *be*
restore data source adfer ffynhonnell y data *be*
restore editing view adfer golwg golygu *be*
restore expand state adfer cyflwr ehangu *be*
restore view adfer golwg *be*
restoring components adfer cydrannau *be*
restoring force grym adferol *eg* grymoedd adferol
restrain atal *be*

restraining circle cylch atal *eg* cylchoedd atal
restraint (of trade etc) ataliad *eg*
restrict cyfyngu *be*
restriction cyfyngiad *eg* cyfyngiadau
restrictive practice arfer cyfyngol *eg* arferion cyfyngol
restrictive practices court llys arferion cyfyngol *eg*
rest-stick ffon peintiwr *eb* ffyn peintwyr
result canlyniad *eg* canlyniadau
result register cofrestr ganlyniadau *eb* cofrestri canlyniadau
resultant force grym cydeffaith *eg*
resultant tone cyfundon *eb* cyfundonau
resulting canlynol *ans*
resurface (of ideas etc) brigo i'r wyneb *be*
resurrection atgyfodiad *eg*
resuscitate adfywio *be*
retable (ledge) ysgafell *eb* ysgafelloedd
retail *v* adwerthu *be*
retail (in finance) *adj* adwerthol *ans*
retail and distributive service gwasanaeth adwerthu a dosbarthu *eg* gwasanaethau adwerthu a dosbarthu
retail market marchnad adwerthu *eb*
retail outlet allfa adwerthu *eb*
retail price index mynegai nwyddau adwerthu *eg*
retail psychology seicoleg adwerthu *eb*
retail services gwasanaethau adwerthu *ell*
retail trade masnach adwerthu *eb*
retailer adwerthwr *eg* adwerthwyr
retain (in biology) dargadw *be*
retain its shape cadw'i siâp
retainer (fee) tâl ar gadw *eg*
retainer (of land) daliedydd *eg* daliedyddion
retainer (of person) gŵr ar gadw *eg* gwŷr ar gadw
retaliatory tariff toll ddial *eb* tollau dial
retard arafu *be*
retardation (in music) gohiriad *eg* gohiriadau
retardation (of mind) arafwch *eg*
retardation (of tides etc) arafiad *eg* arafiadau
retarded araf *ans*
retarder arafwr *eg* arafwyr
retching cyfogi gwag *be*
retention (e.g. of iron by the tissues) dargadwedd *eg*
retention interval ysbaid dargadw *eb* ysbeidiau dargadw
retention of urine ataliad dŵr *eg*
re-texture adweadu *be*
reticulate rhwydol *ans*
reticulocyte reticwlocyt *eg* reticwlocytau
reticuloendothelial system system reticwloendothelaidd *eb*
reticulum reticwlwm *eg*
retina retina *eg* retinâu
retinal disparity gwahaniaeth retinâu *eg*
retinue gosgordd *eb* gogorddion
retire (from a place) cilio *be*
retire (from work) ymddeol *be*
retire injured gadael oherwydd anaf *be*
retirement ymddeoliad *eg*
retirement benefit budd-dal ymddeol *eg*
retort retort *eg* retortâu
retort stand stand retort *eg* standiau retort
retouch atgyffwrdd *be*
re-touching varnish farnais aildrwsio *eg*
retreat *v* encilio *be*
retreat (=act of retreating) *n* enciliad *eg* enciliadau
retreat (place or period) *n* encil *eg* encilion
retrievable adalwadwy *ans*
retrieval adalwad *eb* adalwadau
retrieval cue ciw adalw *eg* ciwiau adalw
retrieve adalw *be*
retrieve all records adalw pob cofnod *be*
retrieve information adalw gwybodaeth *be*
retrieve work adalw gwaith *be*
retrieving and restoring adalw ac adfer
retroactive interference ymyrraeth ôl-weithredol *eb*
retrogradable olraddadwy *ans*
retrogradation olraddiad *eg*
retrograde (movement) olrediad *eg* olrediadau
retrograde amnesia amnesia ôl-redol *eg*
retrograde canon canon ôl-redol *eb* canonau ôl-redol
retrospective (=looking back) ôl-syllol *ans*
retrospective (=taking effect from a date in the past) ôl-weithredol *ans*
retrospective legislation deddfwriaeth ôl-weithredol *eb*
retrospective study astudiaeth ôl-syllol *eb* astudiaethau ôl-syllol
retry ceisio eto *be*
return *n* dychweliad *eg* dychweliadau
return *v* dychwelyd *be*
return address cyfeiriad dychwelyd *eg* cyfeiriadau dychwelyd
return crease cris ochrol *eg* crisiau ochrol
return earnings adenillion *ell*
return function ffwythiant adenillion *eg*
return key dychwelwr *eg* dychwelwyr
return on capital employed adenillion ar y cyfalaf a ddefnyddiwyd *ell*
return on net assets adenillion ar asedau net *ell*
return stroke strôc ddychwel *eb* strociau dychwel
reuptake ailgydio *be*
revaluation ailbrisiad *eg* ailbrisiadau
reveal *n* dadlen *eb* dadlennau
reveal *v* dadlennu *be*
revelation datguddiad *eg* datguddiadau
revenue (=income from the sale of goods or services) refeniw *eg* refeniwiau
revenue (in general) cyllid *eg* cyllidau
revenue men gwŷr yr ecseis *ell*
revenue support grant grant cynnal incwm *eg*
reverberation datseinedd *eg* datseineddau
reverberation time amser datseinedd *eg*

reverberatory datseiniol *ans*
reverberatory furnace ffwrnais adlewyrchol *eb* ffwrneisi adlewyrchol
revers llabed *eb* llabedi
revers collar coler llabed *eg* coleri llabed
reversal (of letters, words) trawsosod *be*
reversal ABA design cynllun gwrthdro ABA *eg* cynlluniau gwrthdro ABA
reverse (in computing etc) *n* cildroad *eg* cildroadau
reverse (in computing etc) *v* cildroi *be*
reverse (in general) *n* gwrthdro *eg* gwrthdroeon
reverse (in general) *v* gwrthdroi *be*
▶ **reverse a pattern** cildroi patrwm *be*
reverse arc cilarc *eb* cilarcau
reverse astride vault llofnaid ar led wysg y cefn *eb* llofneidiau ar led wysg y cefn
reverse barrier nursing nyrsio rhwystrol gwrthol *be*
reverse bias bias yn ôl *eg*
reverse control (of machine part) rheolydd cyflymder *eg* rheolyddion cyflymder
reverse cycle gwrthdroi cylchred *be*
reverse horizontal astride vault llofnaid hir ar led wysg y cefn *eb* llofneidiau hir ar led wysg y cefn
reverse order trefn wrthdro *eb*
reverse paddling stroke strôc badlo'n ôl *eb*
reverse pass pàs wrthol *eb* pasiau gwrthol
reverse pivot colyn ôl *eg* colynnau ôl
Reverse Polish Notation Nodiant Cil-Bwyl *eg*
reverse side tu chwith *eg*
reverse stick ffon wrthdro *eb* ffyn gwrthdro
reverse stick dribble driblo gwrthdro *be*
reverse stick pass pàs wrthdro *eb* pasiau gwrthdro
reversed (in computing) cildro *ans*
reversed beam trawst o chwith *eg* trawstiau o chwith
reversed hanging hongian pen i lawr *be*
reversed stream nant gildro *eb* nentydd cildro
reversibility cildroadedd *eg*
reversible (in science) cildroadwy *ans*
reversible (of garment) dwyffordd *ans*
reversible garment dilledyn dwyffordd *eg* dillad dwyffordd
reversible reaction adwaith cildroadwy *eg* adweithiau cildroadwy
reversing motion mudiant tu chwith *eg*
reversion cildroad *eg* cildroadau
revert dychwelyd *be*
revetment gwrthglawdd *eg* gwrthgloddiau
review *n* adolygiad *eg* adolygiadau
review *v* adolygu *be*
review of results adolygu canlyniadau *be*
reviewer adolygydd *eg* adolygwyr
revise adolygu *be*
revise mode modd addasu *eg*
revisionism glastwreiddio *be*
revival diwygiad *eg* diwygiadau
revocation dirymiad *eg* dirymiadau
revoke dirymu *be*
revolt gwrthryfel *eg* gwrthryfeloedd
Revolt of the Camisards Gwrthryfel y Camisardiaid *eg*
revolution (=overthrow of system) chwyldro *eg* chwyldroadau
revolution (of circular motion) cylchdro *eg* cylchdroeon
revolution counter rhifydd cylchdroeon *eg* rhifyddion cylchdroeon
revolutionary (of person) chwyldroadwr *eg* chwyldroadwyr
revolutionary settlement ardrefniant chwyldroadol *eg*
revolve cylchdroi *be*
revolving centre canol cylchdro *eg* canolau cylchdro
revolving head pen cylchdro *eg* pennau cylchdro
revolving hearth aelwyd dro *eb* aelwydydd tro
revolving stage llwyfan tro *eg* llwyfannau tro
revs/min cylchdro'r funud
revue rifiw *eg* rifiwiau
rewind ailddirwyn *be*
rhenium (Re) rheniwm *eg*
rheostat rheostat *eg* rheostatau
rhesus factor ffactor rhesws *eb*
rhesus negative rhesws negatif *eg*
rhesus positive rhesws positif *eg*
rhetorical question cwestiwn rhethregol *eg* cwestiynau rhethregol
rheumatic fever twymyn gwynegon *eb*
rheumatism gwynegon *ell*
rheumatologist rhiwmatolegydd *eg* rhiwmatolegwyr
rheumatology rhiwmatoleg *eb*
rhizobium rhisobiwm *eg* rhisobia
rhizoid rhisoid *eg*
rhizome rhisom *eg* rhisomau
rhodium (Rh) rhodiwm *eg*
rhodopsin rhodopsin *eg*
rhomb rhomb *eg* rhombau
rhombohedron rhombohedron *eg* rhombohedronau
rhomboid rhomboid *eg* rhomboidau
rhombus rhombws *eg* rhombi
rhumb line rhymlin *eg* rhymliniau
rhyme rhigwm *eg* rhigymau
rhyolite rhiolit *eg*
rhyolitic rhiolitig *ans*
rhythm rhythm *eg* rhythmau
rhythm pattern patrwm rhythm *eg* patrymau rhythm
rhythmic rhythmig *ans*
rhythmic accompaniment cyfeiliant rhythmig *eg*
rhythmic cell cell rythmig *eb* celloedd rhythmig
rhythmic 'fun' music cerddoriaeth rythmig hwylgar *eb*
rhythmic jump naid rythmig *eb* neidiau rhythmig
rhythmic motion (thread cutting) mudiant rhythmig *eg*
rhythmic movement symudiad rhythmig *eg* symudiadau rhythmig
rhythmic music cerddoriaeth rythmig *eb*

rhythmic response ymateb rhythmig *eg* ymatebion rhythmig
rhythmic stimulus ysgogiad rhythmig *eg* ysgogiadau rhythmig
rhythmically spoken word pattern patrwm geiriol wedi'i lefaru'n rhythmig *eg* patrymau geiriol wedi'u llefaru'n rhythmig
ria ria *eg* riau
rib asen *eb* asennau
rib cage cawell asennau *eg* cewyll asennau
rib weave gwehyddiad rhesog *eg*
ribbed (in general) asennog *ans*
ribbed (of weave) rhesog *ans*
ribbed G cramp cramp G asennog *eg* crampiau G asennog
ribbon rhuban *eg* rhubanau
ribbon back chair cadair gefn rhuban *eb* cadeiriau cefn rhuban
ribbon development datblygiad hirgul *eg* datblygiadau hirgul
ribbon lake llyn hirgul *eg* llynnoedd hirgul
ribbon settlement anheddiad hirgul *eg* aneddiadau hirgul
ribbon-end scroll sgrôl pen rhuban *eb* sgroliau pen rhuban
riboflavin ribofflafin *eg*
ribonucleic acid asid riboniwcleig *eg*
ribosome ribosom *eg* ribosomau
rice paper papur reis *eg*
rice stitch pwyth reis *eg* pwythau reis
ricercare ricercare *eg*
rich cyfoethog *ans*
rich (of food etc) bras *ans*
rich text format fformat testun cyfoethog *eg* fformatau testun cyfoethog
Richard the Lionheart Rhisiart Lewgalon *eg*
richness cyfoeth *eg*
rickets llech, y *eb*
ricrac braid brêd ricrac *eg* brediau ricrac
riddle *n* rhidyll *eg* rhidyllau
riddle *v* rhidyllu *be*
rider atodeg *eb* atodegau
ridge (of arable land) gwrym *eg* gwrymiau
ridge (of hilltop, barometric pressure) cefnen *eb* cefnenau
ridge (of roof or similar) crib *eg/b* cribau
ridge and furrow relief tirwedd cefnen a rhych *eb* tirweddau cefnen a rhych
ridge board bwrdd crib *eg* byrddau crib
ridge of high pressure cefnen o wasgedd uchel *eb*
ridge tree nenbren *eg* nenbrennau
ridges and swales cefnau a phantiau
riffle riffl *eg* rifflau
riffler rifflwr *eg* rifflwyr
riffler file ffeil rifflwr *eb* ffeiliau rifflwr
rift hollt *eg/b* holltau
rift (=slot, slit) agen *eb* agennau
rift sawn (quarter sawn) llifiad rheiddiol *eg*
rift valley dyffryn hollt *eg* dyffrynnoedd hollt
rig llwyfan tyllu *eg* llwyfannau tyllu
riggers rigeri *ell*
rigging rigin *eg*
right (=correct) *adj* cywir *ans*
right (=entitlement) *n* hawl *eg/b* hawliau
right (as opposed to left) *n* de *eb*
right amount maint cywir *eg*
right angle ongl sgwâr *eb* onglau sgwâr
right arm bowler bowliwr braich dde *eg* bowlwyr braich dde
Right Ascension (RA) Esgyniad Cywir *eg*
right bank glan dde *eb*
right bank tributary llednant glan dde *eb* llednentydd glan dde
right circular cone côn crwn union *eg* conau crwn union
right court cwrt de *eg* cyrtiau de
right cross de draws *eb*
right hand llaw dde *eb* dwylo de
right indent mewnoli ar y dde *be*
right justify unioni ar y dde *be*
right of way hawl tramwy *eg* hawliau tramwy
right outfielder maeswr de *eg* maeswyr de
right prism prism union *eg* prismau union
right pyramid pyramid union *eg* pyramidiau union
right section toriad union *eg* toriadau union
right shift syfliad de *eg* syfliadau de
right shift theory damcaniaeth syfliad i'r dde *eb*
right side (=correct side) ochr gywir *eb* ochrau cywir
right side (as opposed to left side) ochr dde *eb*
right type math cywir *eg* mathau cywir
right wing (in politics) adain dde *eb*
right wing (in sport) asgell dde *eb* esgyll de
right-aligned aliniedig ar y dde *ans*
right-angled sgwaronglog *ans*
right-angled triangle triongl ongl sgwâr *eg* trionglau ongl sgwâr
right-click de-glicio *be*
right-half hanerwr de *eg* hanerwyr de
right-hand lock clo ochr dde *eg* cloeon ochr dde
right-hand screw thread edau sgriw llaw dde *eb* edafedd sgriw llaw dde
right-hand side ochr dde *eb*
right-hand thread edau llaw dde *eb* edafedd llaw dde
right-hand turn tro de *eg* troeon de
right-handed batsman batiwr llaw dde *eg* batwyr llaw dde
rights iawnderau *ell*
rights charter siarter hawliau *eg* siarterau hawliau
rigid anhyblyg *ans*
rigid wire gwifren anhyblyg *eb* gwifrau anhyblyg
rigidity anhyblygedd *eg*
rigorous trwyadl *ans*
rigorous justification cyfiawnhad trylwyr *eg*
rigour manwl gywirdeb *eg*
rill cornant *eb* cornentydd

rim ymyl *eg/b* ymylon
rim (of drum) cantel *eg* cantelau
rim latch clicied ymyl *eb* cliciedau ymyl
rim lock clo ymyl *eg* cloeon ymyl
rindless bacon cig moch digrofen *eg*
ring (=circle) cylch *eg* cylchoedd
ring (on finger) modrwy *eb* modrwyau
ring and star dance dawns cylch a seren *eb* dawnsiau cylch a seren
ring gauge medrydd torch *eg* medryddion torch
ring headed pin pìn cylchog *eg* pinnau cylchog
ring nebula nifwl modrwy *eg* nifylau modrwy
ring road cylchffordd *eb* cylchffyrdd
ring shake hollt cylch *eg* holltau cylch
ring spanner sbaner cylch *eg* sbaneri cylch
ring-binder ffeil fodrwy *eb* ffeiliau modrwy
ringed cylchog *ans*
Ringers solution hydoddiant Ringer *eg*
rings right and left cylchoedd bach i bedwar *ell*
ringshank hoelen garan gylch *eb* hoelion garan cylch
ringshank tongs (casting) gefel garan gylch *eb* gefeiliau garan cylch
ringwork amddiffynfa gylch *eb* amddiffynfeydd cylch
ringworm tarwden *eb* tarwdenni
rinse *n* rins *eg* rinsiau
rinse *v* rinsio *be*
riot terfysg *eg* terfysgoedd
Riot Act Deddf Terfysg *eb*
rip current cerrynt terfol *eg*
rip saw rhwyglif *eb* rhwyglifau
rip tide llanw terfol *eg*
riparian torlannol *ans*
ripieno ripieno *eg* ripieni
riposte riposte *eg*
ripping fence ffens rwygo *eb* ffensys rhwygo
ripple (in general) *n* crych *eg* crychau
ripple (small wave) *v* crychdon *eb* crychdonnau
ripple *v* crychdonni *be*
ripple blanking output (RBO) allbwn blancio crychdon *eg*
ripple counter rhifydd crychdon *eg* rhifydd crychdon
ripple tank tanc crychdonni *eg* tanciau crychdonni
risalah risalah *eg*
rise and fall table bwrdd codi a gostwng *eg* byrddau codi a gostwng
rise of Prussia esgyniad Prwsia *eg*
rise-and-fall light golau codi a gostwng *eg*
riser codwr *eg* codwyr
riser pin pìn codi *eg* pinnau codi
rising gwrthryfel *eg* gwrthryfeloedd
rising butt hinge colfach codi *eg* colfachau codi
risk *n* risg *eg* risgiau
risk *v* mentro *be*
risk assessment asesiad risg *eg* asesiadau risg
rite defod *eb* defodau
rite of passage defod newid byd *eb* defodau newid byd

ritornello ritornello *eg* ritornelli
ritual *adj* defodol *ans*
ritual *n* defod *eb* defodau
ritual myth myth defodol *eg*
ritualism defodaeth *eb*
rival *n* cydymgeisydd *eg* cydymgeiswyr
rival *v* cydymgeisio *be*
rivalry cystadleuaeth *eb*
river afon *eb* afonydd
river basin basn afonydd *eg* basnau afonydd
river capture afonladrad *eg*
river floods llifogydd afonydd *ell*
river mist tarth *eg* tarthau
river regime patrymedd afon *eg*
river system system afonydd *eb* systemau afonydd
river terrace cerlan *eb* cerlannau
river valley dyffryn afon *eg* dyffrynnoedd afonydd
riverine afonol *ans*
riverlands afondiroedd *ell*
rivet *n* rhybed *eg* rhybedion
rivet *v* rhybedu *be*
rivet set set rybed *eb* setiau rhybed
rivet snap snap rhybed *eg* snapiau rhybed
riveted rhybedog *ans*
riveted joint uniad rhybedog *eg* uniadau rhybedog
riveted lap joint goruniad rhybedog *eg* goruniadau rhybedog
riveted plate plât rhybedog *eg* platiau rhybedog
riveted stay gwanas rhybedog *eg* gwanasau rhybedog
riveting hammer morthwyl rhybedu *eg* morthwylion rhybedu
riving rhannu *be*
riving knife (saw bench) cyllell rannu *eb* cyllyll rhannu
rivulet afonig *eb* afonigau
road ffordd *eb* ffyrdd
road construction adeiladu ffordd *be*
road fund licence trwydded modur *eb* trwyddedau modur
road junction cyffordd *eb* cyffyrdd
road system rhwydwaith ffyrdd *eg*
road traffic accident damwain ffordd *eb* damweiniau ffordd
road tunnel twnnel ffordd *eg* twnelau ffordd
road used as public path ffordd a ddefnyddir yn llwybr cyhoeddus *eb*
roads and paths ffyrdd a llwybrau
roadstead angorle *eg* angorleoedd
roaring forties deugeiniau gwyllt *ell*
roaring twenties dauddegau gwyllt *eg*
robber economy economi disbyddol *eg* economïau disbyddol
robber industry diwydiant disbyddol *eg* diwydiannau disbyddol
robbery lladrad *eg*
robe mantell *eb* mentyll
robot robot *eg* robotiaid
robotics roboteg *eb*

robust cadarn *ans*
roche moutonée craig follt *eb* creigiau myllt
rock craig *eb* creigiau
rock basin lake llyn creicafn *eg* llynnoedd creicafn
rock features arweddion craig *ell*
rock flour blawd craig *eg*
rock hollow lakeland llyndir creicafn *eg*
rock salt halen craig *eg*
rocket roced *eb* rocedi
rocket (tool post) siglydd *eg* siglyddion
rockfish pysgodyn carreg *eg* pysgod cerrig
rocking chair cadair siglo *eb* cadeiriau siglo
rococo rococo *ans*
rod rhoden *eb* rhodenni
rod and glove puppet pyped rod a maneg *eg* pypedau rod a maneg
rod puppet pyped rod *eg* pypedau rod
rodent cnofil *eg* cnofilod
rodent control rheoli cnofilod *be*
rodent infestation pla cnofilod *eg* plâu cnofilod
rods and cones rhodenni a chonau
roe (of fish - hard) bola caled *eg*
roe (of fish - soft) bola meddal *eg*
rogue value gwalchwerth *eg* gwalchwerthoedd
rolag (teased wool) gwlân *eg*
role swyddogaeth *eb* swyddogaethau
role conflict gwrthdaro rhwng swyddogaethau *be*
role model delfryd ymddwyn *eb* delfrydau ymddwyn
role of health educators rôl addysgwyr iechyd *eb*
role of microbes swyddogaeth microbau *eb*
role play chwarae rhan *be*
roll *n* rholyn *eg* rholiau
roll *v* rholio *be*
roll call galw cofrestr *be*
roll collar coler rhôl *eg* coleri rhôl
roll in rholio mewn *be*
roll on/roll off gyrru mewn ac allan *be*
roll over trosglwyddo ymlaen *be*
roll sulphur sylffwr rhôl *eg*
roller rholer *eg* rholeri
roller bearing rholferyn *eg* rholferynnau
roller blind llen rholer *eg* llenni rholer
roller follower dilynwr rholer *eg* dilynwyr rholer
roller loom gwŷdd rholer *eg* gwyddau rholer
roller shuttle gwennol rholer *eb* gwenoliaid rholer
rollers (of waves) gwanegau *ell*
rolling downland twyndir tonnog *eg* twyndiroedd tonnog
rolling pin rholbren *eg* rholbrennau
rolling review adolygiad treigl *eg* adolygiadau treigl
rolling stock rholstoc *eg*
Roman *adj* Rhufeinig *ans*
Roman *n* Rhufeinwr *eg* Rhufeinwyr
roman alphabet gwyddor Rufeinig *eb*
Roman Catholic Church Eglwys Babyddol *eb*
Roman Church Eglwys Rufain *eb*
Roman Empire Ymerodraeth Rufeinig *eb*
Roman Inquisition Chwilys Rhufain *eg*
Roman Law Cyfraith Rufain *eb*
Roman town house tŷ tref Rhufeinig *eg* tai tref Rhufeinig
romance rhamant *eb* rhamantau
Romanism Pabyddiaeth *eb*
Romanization Rhufeinio *be*
Romanize Rhufeinio *be*
romantic rhamantaidd *ans*
romantic art celfyddyd ramantaidd *eb*
romantic love cariad rhamantus *eg*
romantic music cerddoriaeth ramantaidd *eb*
Romantic period cyfnod Rhamantaidd *eg*
romanticism rhamantiaeth *eb*
Rome Scot Ceiniogau'r Pab *ell*
romper romper *eb* romperi
rondeau rondeau *eg*
rondo rondo *eb* rondoau
rondo form ffurf rondo *eb*
rood crog *eb* crogau
rood loft croglofft *eb* croglofftydd
rood screen croglen *eb* croglenni
roof to *eg* toeon
roof cladding cladin to *eg*
roof line llinell doeau *eb*
roof pitch serthiant to *eg*
roof truss cwpl to *eg* cyplau to
roofing felt ffelt toi *eg*
roofing tile teilsen to *eb* teils to
room divider rhannwr ystafell *eg* rhanwyr ystafelloedd
room heater gwresogydd ystafell *eg* gwresogyddion ystafell
room occupancy deiliadaeth ystafelloedd *eb*
room temperature tymheredd (yr) ystafell *eg*
roost clwyd *eb* clwydi
root (in mathematics) isradd *eg* israddau
root (of plant) gwreiddyn *eg* gwreiddiau
Root & Branch Petition Deiseb Wreiddyn a Changen *eb*
root cap gwreiddgapan *eg* gwreiddgapanau
root chord cord gwreiddnod *eg* cordiau gwreiddnod
root crop cnwd gwraidd *eg* cnydau gwraidd
root directory cyfeiriadur gwraidd *eg* cyfeiriaduron gwraidd
root hair gwreiddflewyn *eg* gwreiddflew
root hair cell cell wreiddflew *eb* celloedd gwreiddflew
root mean square isradd sgwâr cymedrig *eg*
root node cwgn gwreiddyn *eg* cygnau gwraidd
root nodule gwreiddgnepyn *eg* gwreiddgnepynnau
root of the equation gwreiddyn yr hafaliad *eg* gwreiddiau'r hafaliadau
root position safle gwreiddiol *eg* safleoedd gwreiddiol
root pressure gwasgedd gwraidd *eg*
root tip blaenwreiddyn *eg* blaenwreiddiau
root vegetable gwreiddlysieuyn *eg* gwreiddlysiau

rooted plant planhigyn gwreiddiog *eg* planhigion gwreiddiog
rootless harmony harmoni di-wraidd *eg* harmonïau di-wraidd
rootlet gwreiddiosyn *eg* gwreiddios
rope rhaff *eb* rhaffau
rope ladder ysgol raff *eb* ysgolion rhaff
rope stitch pwyth rheffyn *eg* pwythau rheffyn
ropeway rhaffordd *eb* rhaffyrdd
Rorschach inkblot test prawf blotiau inc Rorschach *eg* profion blotiau inc Rorschach
rosary llaswyr *eg* llaswyrau
rose (enamelling colour) rhosyn *eg*
rose bit rhosebill *eg* rhosebillion
rose countersink bit ebill gwrthsoddi rhychog *eg* ebillion gwrthsoddi rhychog
rose path pattern patrwm lôn y rhosyn *eg* patrymau lôn y rhosyn
rose reamer rhosagorell *eb* rhosagorellau
rose window ffenestr ros *eb* ffenestri rhos
▶ **rosette** rhosglwm *eb* rhosenni
rosette chain stitch pwyth cadwyn rhosyn *eg* pwythau cadwyn rhosyn
rosewood rhosbren *ans*
rosewood handle carn rhosbren *eg* carnau rhosbren
rostrum rostrwm *eg* rostra
rot pydredd *eg*
rotary cylchdro *ans*
rotary clothes line lein ddillad gylchdro *eb* leiniau dillad cylchdro
rotary converter trawsnewidydd cylchdro *eg* trawsnewidyddion cylchdro
rotary iron peiriant smwddio cylchdro *eg* peiriannau smwddio cylchdro
rotary motion mudiant cylchdro *eg*
rotary movement symudiad cylchdro *eg* symudiadau cylchdro
rotary quern breuan droi *eb* breuanau troi
rotary valve falf drogylch *eb* falfiau trogylch
rotary-cut veneer argaen toriad cylchdro *eg* argaenau toriad cylchdro
rotate cylchdroi *be*
rotate by hand cylchdroi â llaw *be*
rotate colours cylchdroi lliwiau *be*
rotate freely cylchdroi'n rhydd *be*
rotation cylchdro *eg* cylchdroeon
rotation of crops cylchdro cnydau *eg* cylchdroeon cnydau
rotational energy egni cylchdroi *eg*
rotational grazing pori cylchdro *be*
rotational motion mudiant cylchdro *eg*
rotational movement symudiad cylchdro *eg* symudiadau cylchdro
rotational slip cylchlithriad *eg* cylchlithriadau
rotational symmetry cymesuredd cylchdro *eg*
rotor rotor *eg* rotorau
rotten pwdr *ans*
rotten borough bwrdeistref bwdr *eb* bwrdeistrefi pwdr
rouge rhuddliw *eg*
rough (=approximate) bras *ans*
rough (of surface, land) garw *ans*
rough and tumble chwarae sgarmes *be*
rough answer ateb bras *eg* atebion bras
rough cut file ffeil frasddant *eb* ffeiliau brasddant
rough dimensions dimensiynau lled agos *ell*
rough draft drafft bras *eg* drafftiau bras
rough drawing lluniad lled gywir *eg* lluniadau lled gywir
rough dry *adj* bras-sych *ans*
rough dry *v* bras-sychu *be*
rough metric equivalent cywerth metrig bras *eg* cywerthoedd metrig bras
rough open garw agored *eg*
rough pasture porfa arw *eb* porfeydd garw
rough sawn braslifiad *ans*
rough surface arwyneb garw *eg* arwynebau garw
roughage bwyd garw *eg*
roughening tool brasnaddell *eb* brasnaddellau
roughing (of lathe tools) brasnaddu *be*
roughing reamer agorell frasnaddu *eb* agorellau brasnaddu
roughness garwedd *eg*
rouleau loop dolen rouleau *eb* dolennau rouleau
round *adj* crwn *ans*
round (in penillion singing) *n* cylch *eg* cylchoedd
round (in sport etc) *n* rownd *eb* rowndiau
round (of music) *n* pennill *eg* penillion
round arch bwa crwn *eg* bwâu crwn
round base sylfaen gron *eb* sylfeini crwn
round bottomed flask fflasg fongron *eb* fflasgiau bongrwn
round centre cane gwialen ganol crwn *eb* gwialennau canol crwn
round down talgrynnu i lawr *be*
round edge ymyl gron *eb* ymylon crwn
round end pen crwn *eg* pennau crwn
round faced spokeshave rhasgl wyneb crwn *eb* rhasglau wyneb crwn
round file ffeil gron *eb* ffeiliau crwn
round head stake bonyn pengrwn *eg* bonion pengrwn
round leg coes gron *eb* coesau crwn
round lost head nail hoelen gron bengoll *eb* hoelion crwn pengoll
round nail hoelen gron *eb* hoelion crwn
round neck gwddf crwn *eg* gyddfau crwn
round nose (of lathe tools) trwyn crwn *eg* trwynau crwn
round nose pliers gefelen drwyn crwn *eb* gefeiliau trwyn crwn
round off talgrynnu *be*
round plane plaen crwn *eg* plaeniau crwn
round section material defnydd trychiad crwn *eg*
round up talgrynnu i fyny *be*

round vault llofnaid gylch *eb* llofneidiau cylch
round window ffenestr gron *eb* ffenestri crwn
roundabout cylchfan *eg/b* cylchfannau
rounded (=finished) gorffenedig *ans*
rounded (of hills) llyfngrwn *ans*
rounded drawer slip drôr-gryfhawr crwm *eg* drôr-gryfhawyr crwm
rounders rownderi *ell*
Roundhead Pengrynwr *eg* Pengrynwyr
roundhead bolt bollt bengron *eb* bolltau pengrwn
roundhead rivet rhybed pengrwn *eg* rhybedion pengrwn
roundhead scissors siswrn pig crwn *eg* sisyrnau pig crwn
roundhead screw sgriw bengron *eb* sgriwiau pengrwn
round-headed key allwedd ben crwn *eb* allweddi pen crwn
rounding crymu *be*
rounding error cyfeiliornad talgrynnu *eg* cyfeiliornadau talgrynnu
roundness crynrwydd *eg*
roundness index indecs crymder *eg* indecsau crymder
rousing jig jig cyffrous *eg* jigiau cyffrous
rout gyrru ar ffo *eg*
route *n* llwybr *eg* llwybrau
route *v* llwybro *be*
router llwybrydd *eg* llwybryddion
router plane plaen dyfnder *eg* plaeniau dyfnder
routeway llwybr *eg* llwybrau
routine (=regular procedure) trefn *eb*
routine (=set sequence) rheolwaith *eg* rheolweithiau
roving harmony cynghanedd gyfnewidiol *eb*
row (=line) *n* rhes *eb* rhesi
row (in sport) *n* rheng *eb* rhengoedd
row (with oars) *v* rhwyfo *be*
row matrix matrics rhes *eg*
row reduction newidiadau rhes *ell*
row vector fector rhes *eg*
rowlock roloc *eg*
royal brenhinol *ans*
Royal Academy of Arts,The Academi Frenhinol y Celfyddydau *eb*
Royal Cambrian Academy of Arts Academi Gelf Frenhinol Cymru *eb*
royal estates ystadau brenhinol *ell*
royal minister gweinidog y brenin *eg* gweinidogion y brenin
royal power pŵer y brenin *eg* pwerau'r brenin
royal prerogative uchelfraint y brenin *eg* uchelfreintiau'r brenin
royal progress taith frenhinol *eb*
Royal Society of Mines Cymdeithas Frenhinol y Mwyngloddiau *eb*
royalist brenhinwr *eg* brenhinwyr
royalty (payment) breindal *eg* breindaliadau
R.P.M. (revolutions per minute) cylchdroeon y funud

rub rhwbio *be*
rub out diddymu *be*
rubbed joint uniad rhwbiedig *eg* uniadau rhwbiedig
rubber rwber *eg* rwberi
rubber band band rwber *eg* bandiau rwber
rubber bung topyn rwber *eg* topynnau rwber
rubber hammer morthwyl rwber *eg* morthwylion rwber
rubber squeegee gwesgi rwber *eg* gwesgïau rwber
rubber washer wasier rwber *eb* wasieri rwber
rubber webbing webin rwber *eg*
rubbing (frottage) ffrotais *eg* ffroteisiau
rubbing (in general) rhwbiad *eg* rhwbiadau
rubbing board bwrdd rhwbio *eg* byrddau rhwbio
rubbing down rhwbio *be*
rubbing method dull rhwbio *eg*
rubbing stick ffon rwbio *eb* ffyn rhwbio
rubbing strips stribedi rhwbio *ell*
rubbish sbwriel *eg*
rubble rwbel *eg*
rubeanic acid asid rwbeanig *eg*
rubella rwbela *eb*
rubidium (Rb) rwbidiwm *eg*
rubric cyfarwyddyd *eg* cyfarwyddiadau
ruck ryc *eg* ryciau
rudder llyw *eg*
rudderlines rhaffau llyw *ell*
rudimentary (organ etc) elfennol *ans*
rudimentary level lefel elfennol *eb*
ruffle *n* ryffl *eg* ryfflau
ruffle *v* ryfflo *be*
ruffled neck gwddf ryffl *eg* gyddfau ryffl
ruffler (machine attachments) rhyfflydd *eg* rhyfflyddion
rug ryg *eg/b* rygiau
rugby rygbi *eg*
rugby ball pêl rygbi *eb* peli rygbi
rugby shirt crys rygbi *eg* crysau rygbi
rugged individualism unigolyddiaeth rymus *eb*
ruggedness garwedd *eg*
ruin adfail *eg* adfeilion
rule (=government, dominion) rheolaeth *eb*
rule (for measuring, getting straight lines) riwl *eb* riwliau
rule (of order, law) rheol *eb* rheolau
rule and thumb gauge medrydd riwl a bawd *eg* medryddion riwl a bawd
rule joint uniad riwl *eg* uniadau riwl
rule joint hinge colfach uniad riwl *eg* colfachau uniad riwl
rule of law rheolaeth cyfraith *eb*
rule of procedure rheol trefniadaeth *eb* rheolau trefniadaeth
rule of Stalin llywodraeth Stalin *eb*
rule of thirds rheol traeanau *eb*
rule of three rheol tri *eb*
rule off gwahanu *be*

rule utilitarianism (with parallel lines) iwtilitariaeth rheol *eb*
rule-based seiliedig ar reolau *ans*
ruled llinellog *ans*
ruler (=graduated straight measure) riwl *eb* riwliau
ruler (=person who rules) rheolwr *eg* rheolwyr
ruler (=strip of wood for measuring) pren mesur *eg* prennau mesur
ruler (on computer screen) mesurydd *eg* mesuryddion
rules and conventions rheolau a chonfensiynau
rules of indices rheolau indecsau *ell*
rules of precedence rheolau blaenoriaeth *ell*
ruling class dosbarth llywodraethol *eg*
ruling pen pen riwlio *eg* pennau riwlio
rumba rhwmba *eg* dawnsiau rhwmba
rumen rwmen *eg* rwmenau
ruminant anifail cnoi cil *eg* anifeiliaid cnoi cil
Rump Parliament Senedd y Gweddill *eb*
run *v* rhedeg *be*
run (=enclosed yard) *n* libart *eg* libartau
run (in sport etc) *n* rhediad *eg* rhediadau
run out *n* rhediad allan *eg* rhediadau allan
run out *v* rhedeg allan *be*
run with the ball rhedeg â'r bêl *be*
rundale (=runrig) lleiniau cytal *ell*
rune llythyren rwnig *eb* llythrennau rwnig
rung ffon ysgol *eb* ffyn ysgol
runic alphabet gwyddor rwnig *eb*
runnel corffrwd *eb* corffrydiau
runner (cricket) cydredwr *eg* cydredwyr
runner (in botany) ymledydd *eg* ymledyddion
runner (of drawer) rhedwr drôr *eg* rhedwyr drôr
runner (of person) rhedwr *eg* rhedwyr
runner beans ffa dringo *ell*
runner cup cwpan ymledu *eg* cwpanau ymledu
runner peg (casting) peg rhedwr *eg* pegiau rhedwyr
running angle ongl redeg *eb* onglau rhedeg
running commentary sylwebaeth ar y pryd *eb*
running cost cost rhedeg *eb* costau rhedeg
running fit ffit redegog *eb* ffitiau rhedegog
running method dull o redeg *eg*
running oblique back vault llofnaid wellaif *eb* llofneidiau gwellaif
running order trefn rhaglen *eb*
running shoe esgid redeg *eb* esgidiau rhedeg
running stitch pwyth rhedeg *eg* pwythau rhedeg
running technique techneg rhedeg *eb* technegau rhedeg
running track trac rhedeg *eg* traciau rhedeg
running true rhedeg yn gywir *be*
running vest fest redeg *eb* festiau rhedeg
run-off dŵr ffo *eg* dyfroedd ffo
runrig lleiniau cytal *ell*
run-time amser rhedeg *eg*
runway rhedfa *eb* rhedfeydd
rupture (in general) *n* rhwyg *eg* rhwygiadau
rupture (medical) *n* torlengig *eg*
rupture (medical) *v.trans* torri llengig *be*
rupture (of cell) *v.intrans* ymdorri *be*
rural gwledig *ans*
rural area ardal wledig *eb* ardaloedd gwledig
rural dean deon gwlad *eg* deoniaid gwlad
rural deanery deoniaeth wlad *eb* deoniaethau gwlad
rural history hanes cefn gwlad *eg*
rural school ysgol wledig *eb* ysgolion gwledig
► **rural-urban continuum** continwwm gwledig-trefol *eg*
rurban fringe cyrion gwledig trefol *ell*
rush brwynen *eb* brwyn
rush hour awr frys *eb* oriau brys
rusk rhysgen *eb* rhysgenni
Russification Rwsianeiddio *be*
rust *v* rhydu *be*
rust (in chemistry) *n* rhwd *eg*
rust (plant disease) *n* cawod goch, y gawod goch *eb*
rust inhibitor atalydd rhwd *eg* atalyddion rhwd
rusted rhydlyd *ans*
rustic gwledig *ans*
rustic furniture celfi gwledig *ell*
rustification creigwaith *eg*
rustless nail hoelen wrthrwd *eb* hoelion gwrthrwd
rustless screw sgriw wrthrwd *eb* sgriwiau gwrthrwd
rustproof gwrthrwd *ans*
rusty rhydlyd *ans*
ruthenium (Ru) rwtheniwm *eg*
rye bread bara rhyg *eg*
ryegrass rhygwellt *ell*
ryot raiot *eg* raiotiaid

S

S factor ffactor S *eb*
Sabath (in technical Jewish usage) Shabbat *eg*
Sabbatarianism Sabathyddiaeth *eb*
Sabbath (Jewish) Sabath *eg* Sabathau
sabbatical sabothol *ans*
sable sabl *eg*
sable brush brwsh sabl *eg* brwshys sabl
sabre sabr *eg* sabrau
sabre saw llif sabr *eb* llifiau sabr
sac coden *eb* codennau
saccadic movement symudiad ysmiciog *eg*
saccharin sacarin *eg*
saccular codennog *ans*
sacculate codennaidd *ans*
saccule codennyn *eg* codenynnau
sacerdotal offeiriadol *ans*
sacerdotalism offeiriadolaeth *eb*
sack (=destruction) *n* anrhaith *eg*
sack (=large bag) *n* sach *eb* sachau
sack (=plunder and destroy) *v* anrheithio *be*
Sack of Rome Anrhaith Rhufain *eg*
sacral vertebra fertebra'r sacrwm *eg* fertebrâu'r sacrwm
sacrament (=consecrated elements) sagrafen *eb* sagrafennau
sacrament (=religious ceremony or act) sacrament *eg* sacramentau
SACRE: Standing Advisory Council Council for Religious Education CYSAG: Cyngor Ymgynghorol Sefydlog Addysg Grefyddol *eg*
sacred (=consecrated) cysegredig *ans*
sacred (=holy) sanctaidd *ans*
sacred monogram monogram sanctaidd *eg* monogramau sanctaidd
sacred thread edau sanctaidd *eb* edafedd sanctaidd
sacred writings ysgrifeniadau cysegredig *ell*
sacrifice aberth *eg/b* aberthau
sacring bell cloch aberth *eb* clychau aberth
sacristan sacristan *eg* sacristaniaid
sacristy sacristi *eg* sacristiau
sacrum sacrwm *eg* sacra
saddle cyfrwy *eg* cyfrwyau
saddle key allwedd gyfrwy *eb* allweddi cyfrwy
saddle quern breuan gyfrwy *eb* breuanau cyfrwy
saddle stitch pwyth cyfrwy *eg* pwythau cyfrwy
saddle yoke iau cyfrwy *eb* ieuau cyfrwy
saddlepoint (=col) col *eg* colau
sadism sadistiaeth *eb*
safe diogel *ans*
safe edge (file part) ymyl ddiogel *eb* ymylon diogel
safe practice ymarfer diogel *eg*
safe working practices arferion gweithio diogel *ell*
safety diogelwch *eg*
safety and security diogelwch pobl ac eiddo *eg*
safety belt gwregys diogelwch *eg* gwregysau diogelwch
safety device dyfais ddiogelwch *eb* dyfeisiau diogelwch
safety equipment offer diogelwch *ell*
safety guard gard diogelwch *eg* gardiau diogelwch
safety ladle lletwad ddiogelwch *eb* lletwadau diogelwch
safety mark marc diogelwch *eg*
safety net rhwyd ddiogelwch *eb* rhwydi diogelwch
safety pin pìn cau *eg* pinnau cau
safety precautions rhagofalon diogelwch *ell*
safety procedure dull gweithredu diogel *eg* dulliau gweithredu diogel
safety regulations rheoliadau diogelwch *ell*
safety requirements gofynion diogelwch *ell*
safety risk perygl i ddiogelwch *eg*
safety screen sgrin ddiogelu *eb* sgriniau diogelu
safety standards safonau diogelwch *ell*
safety switch switsh diogelu *eg* switshis diogelu
safety valve falf ddiogelu *eb* falfiau diogelu
safety-barrier clwyd ddiogelwch *eb* clwydi diogelwch
safety-harness harnais diogelwch *eg* harneisi diogelwch
sag *n* ysigiad *eg* ysigiadau
sag *v* ysigo *be*
saga saga *eb* sagâu
sage bush llwyn saets *eg* llwyni saets
sagebrush prysgwydd saets *ell*
sagger sager *eg* sageri
sagittal saethol *ans*
sagittal section toriad saethol *eg* toriadau saethol
sahel sahel *eg*
sahelian sahelaidd *ans*
sail hwylio *be*
sailcloth defnydd hwyliau *eg*
saint sant *eg* seintiau
Saint Augustine Awstin Sant *eg*
Saint David's Day Dydd Gŵyl Dewi *eg*
Saint George's Channel Sianel San Siôr *eb*
Saint James Sant Iago *eg*
Saint John Sant Ioan *eg*
Saint Patrick Sant Padrig *eg*
saint's day gŵyl mabsant *eb* gwyliau mabsant

saithe celog *eb* celogiaid
sal ammoniac sal amoniac *eg*
Salab Salab *eg*
salad bowl bowlen salad *eb* bowlenni salad
salad dressing blaslyn salad *eg*
salary cyflog *eg/b* cyflogau
salbutamol salbwtamol *eg*
sale gwerthiant *eg* gwerthiannau
sale by sample gwerthiant wedi dod trwy sampl *eg*
Sale of Goods Act Deddf Gwerthu Nwyddau *eb*
sales cost cost gwerthiant *eb* costau gwerthiant
sales figures ffigurau gwerthu *ell*
sales floor llawr gwerthu *eg* lloriau gwerthu
sales forecasting rhagolygu gwerthiant *be*
sales growth twf gwerthiant *eg*
sales invoice anfoneb gwerthiant *eb* anfonebau gwerthiant
sales ledger llyfr gwerthiant *eg* llyfrau gwerthiant
sales manager rheolwr gwerthu *eg* rheolwyr gwerthu
sales person gwerthwr *eg* gwerthwyr
sales personnel personél gwerthu *eg*
sales promotion hyrwyddo gwerthiant *be*
sales returns dychweliadau gwerthiant *ell*
sales revenue refeniw gwerthiant *eg*
sales staff staff gwerthu *eg*
sales turnover trosiant gwerthu *eg* trosiannau gwerthu
sales volumes maint y gwerthiant *eg*
salesman gwerthwr *eg* gwerthwyr
Salic Law Cyfraith Salig *eb*
salient amlwg *ans*
salina salina *eg* salinau
saline *adj* halwynog *ans*
saline *n* heli *eg*
saline solution hydoddiant halwynog *eg*
salinity halwynedd *eg*
saliva poer *eg*
saliva gland chwarren boer *eb* chwarennau poer
salivary poerol *ans*
salivary amylase amylas poerol *eg*
salivary gland chwarren boer *eb* chwarennau poer
sally port cyrchborth *eg* cyrchbyrth
salon salon *eg* salonau
salt (=sodium chloride) halen *eg*
salt (in chemistry) halwyn *eg* halwynau
salt cellar llestr halen *eg* llestri halen
salt content cynnwys halen *eg*
salt deposits dyddodion halen *ell*
salt flat gwastad heli *eg*
salt lake llyn halen *eg* llynnoedd halen
salt marsh morfa heli *eg* morfeydd heli
salt pan pant heli *eg* pantiau heli
salt water heli *eg*
saltarello saltarelo *eg* saltarelau
saltation neidiant *eg*
saltatory neidiol *ans*
saltings halwyndir *eg*
saltpetre solpitar *eg*
salts of lemon halwynau lemwn *ell*
salty hallt *ans*
salute *n* saliwt *eg* saliwtiau
salute *v* saliwtio *be*
salvation iachawdwriaeth *eb*
Salvation Army Byddin yr Iachawdwriaeth *eb*
Salvationist aelod o Fyddin yr Iachawdwriaeth *eg* aelodau o Fyddin yr Iachawdwriaeth
samadhi samadhi *eg*
samarium (Sm) samariwm *eg*
samatha samatha *eg*
samba samba *eg* dawnsiau samba
sample *n* sampl *eg/b* samplau
sample *v* samplu *be*
sample area ardal samplu *eb* ardaloedd samplu
sample space gofod sampl *eg*
sample study astudiaeth sampl *eb* astudiaethau sampl
sampler sampler *eg* sampleri
sampling distribution dosraniad samplu *eg*
sampling errors cyfeiliornadau samplu *ell*
sampling gate adwy samplu *eb*
sampling method dull samplu *eg* dulliau samplu
sampling technique techneg samplu *eb* technegau samplu
samsara samsara *eg*
sanctification sancteiddhad *eg*
sanctions (economic) sancsiynau *ell*
sanctuary (=refuge) noddfa *eb* noddfeydd
sanctuary (for animals) gwarchodfa *eb* gwarchodfeydd
sanctuary (in temple etc) seintwar *eb* seintwarau
sand tywod *eg*
sand bank banc tywod *eg* banciau tywod
sand bar bar tywod *eg* barrau tywod
sand bin bin tywod *eg* biniau tywod
sand box blwch tywod *eg* blychau tywod
sand bunker byncer tywod *eg* bynceri tywod
sand dune twyn tywod *eg* twyni tywod
sand inclusions cynhwysion tywod *ell*
sand spit tafod tywod *eg* tafodau tywod
sandbag bag tywod *eg* bagiau tywod
sander sandiwr *eg* sandwyr
sanding disc disg llyfnu *eg* disgiau llyfnu
sandpaper papur gwydrog *eg*
sandpit pwll tywod *eb* pyllau tywod
sandstone tywodfaen *eg* tywodfeini
sandur sandur *eg* sandurau
sandwich construction adeiladwaith llafnog *eg*
sandwich construction chipboard bwrdd sglodion adeiladwaith llafnog *eg*
sane in insane places call o dan amgylchiadau gwallgof
Sangha Sangha *eg*
sanitary protection darpariaeth mislif *eg*

sanitation iechydaeth *eb*
sans-culottes sans-culottes *ell*
sap nodd *eg* noddion
sap green gwyrdd sudd *eg*
Sapir-Whorf hypothesis rhagdybiaeth Sapir-Whorf *eb*
sapling glasbren *eg* glasbrennau
saponification seboneiddiad *eg*
saponify seboneiddio *be*
sapper cloddiwr *eg* cloddwyr
saprophage saproffag *eg*
saprophyte *adj* saproffytig *ans*
saprophyte *n* saproffyt *eg* saproffytau
sapwood (alburnum) gwynnin *eg*
Saracen Sarasen *eg* Saraseniaid
sash sash *eg* sasiau
sash bar bar gwydriad *eg* barrau gwydriad
sash catch clicied sash *eb* cliciedau sash
sash cramp cramp hir *eg* crampiau hir
sash fastener ffasnydd sash *eg* ffasnyddion sash
sash joint uniad ffrâm *eg* uniadau ffrâm
sash pivot colyn sash *eg* colynnau sash
sash weight pwysyn sash *eg* pwysynnau sash
sash window ffenestr ddalennog *eb* ffenestri dalennog
Sat Nam Sat Nam *eg*
sateen satîn *eg*
satellite lloeren *eb* lloerenni
satellite broadcasting darlledu lloeren *be*
satellite state gwlad ddibynnol *eb* gwledydd dibynnol
satellite town tref ddibynnol *eb* trefi dibynnol
satin satin *eg*
satin finish gorffeniad satin *eg* gorffeniadau satin
satin stitch pwyth satin *eg* pwythau satin
satin weave gwehyddiad satin *eg*
satisfaction boddhad *eg*
satisfactory boddhaol *ans*
satisfier bodlonwr *eg* bodlonwyr
satisfy bodloni *be*
saturate dirlenwi *be*
saturated dirlawn *ans*
saturated fat braster dirlawn *eg*
saturated fatty acid asid brasterog dirlawn *eg*
saturated solution hydoddiant dirlawn *eg* hydoddiannau dirlawn
saturated vapour pressure gwasgedd anwedd dirlawn *eg*
saturation dirlawnder *eg*
saturation point pwynt dirlawnder *eg*
saturation zone cylchfa ddirlawnder *eb* cylchfaoedd dirlawnder
Saturn Sadwrn *eg*
saucer soser *eb* soseri
savannah safana *eg* safanau
savannah grassland tir glas y safana *eg* tiroedd glas y safana
savant savant *eg* savants
save (=make economies) cynilo *be*
save (=rescue) arbed *be*
save (in computing) cadw *be*
save a shot arbed ergyd *be*
save as cadw fel *be*
save screen cadw sgrin *be*
savers cynilwyr *ell*
saving arbediad *eg* arbedion
savings (=money saved) cynilion *ell*
savings account cyfrif cynilo *eg* cyfrifon cynilo
savings bank banc cynilo *eg* banciau cynilo
savings box cadw-mi-gei *eg*
savings scheme cynllun cynilo *eg* cynlluniau cynilo
saw *n* llif *eb* llifiau
saw *v* llifio *be*
saw set llifosodiad *eg* llifosodiadau
saw teeth dannedd llif *ell*
saw vice feis hogi llif *eb* feisiau hogi llif
saw-cut llifdoriad *eg* llifdoriadau
saw-cut veneer argaen llifdoriad *eg* argaenau llifdoriad
sawdust blawd llif *eg*
saw-fence ffens lif *eb* ffensys llif
saw-frame ffrâm lif *eb* fframiau llif
sawing board bwrdd llifio *eg* byrddau llifio
Sawm Sawm *eg*
sawmill melin lifio *eb* melinau llifio
sawn nut nyten wedi'i llifio *eb* nytiau wedi'u llifio
sawn timber pren wedi'i lifio *eg*
saw-setting anvil eingion gosod llif *eb* eingionau gosod llif
saw-setting hammer morthwyl gosod llif *eg* morthwylion gosod llif
saw-setting pliers gefelen osod llif *eb* gefeiliau gosod llif
sawyer llifiwr *eg* llifwyr
Saxon *adj* Sacsonaidd *ans*
Saxon *n* Sacson *eg* Sacsoniaid
Saxon place name enw lle Sacsonaidd *eg* enwau lleoedd Sacsonaidd
SCAA: School Curriculum and Assessment Authority ACAY: Awdurdod Cwricwlwm ac Asesu Ysgolion *eg*
scab crachen *eb* crach
scabies clefyd crafu *eg*
scabland garwdir basalt *eg* garwdiroedd basalt
scaffold (=gallows) crocbren *eg* crocbrennau
scaffold (for construction purposes) sgaffald *eg* sgaffaldau
scaffolding sgaffaldio *be*
scalar *adj* sgalar *ans*
scalar *n* sgalar *eg* sgalarau
scalar multiplication lluosiad sgalar *eg*
scalar product lluoswm sgalar *eg*
scalar quantity mesur sgalar *eg* mesurau sgalar
scald sgaldiad *eg* sgaldiadau
scalding sgaldanu *be*
scale *v* graddio *be*

scale (=series of degrees, ratio) *n* graddfa *eb* graddfeydd
scale (for weighing) *n* clorian *eb* cloriannau
scale (in furnace or on plants) *n* cen *eg* cennau
scale drawing lluniad wrth raddfa *eg* lluniadau wrth raddfa
scale factor ffactor graddfa *eb* ffactorau graddfa
scale leaf cenddeilen *eb* cenddail
scale mock-up brasfodel wrth raddfa *eg* brasfodelau wrth raddfa
scale of hardness graddfa galedwch *eb* graddfeydd caledwch
scale of three graddfa tri *eb*
scale of two graddfa dau *eb*
scale picture graddio llun *be*
scale sprite graddio ciplun *be*
scale working model model gweithio i raddfa *eg*
scale-attenuation effect effaith cyfyngu graddfa *eb*
scaled copy copi graddfa *eg* copïau graddfa
scalene anghyfochrog *ans*
scalene triangle triongl anghyfochrog *eg* trionglau anghyfochrog
scaliform thickening tewychiad sgalaraidd *eg*
scaling factor ffactor graddio *eb* ffactorau graddio
scallop *n* sgolop *eg* sgolopiau
scallop *v* sgolopio *be*
scalloped edge ymyl sgolop *eb* ymylon sgolop
scalpel cyllell llawfeddyg *eb* cyllyll llawfeddyg
scaly cennog *ans*
scan *n* sgan *eg* sganiau
scan *v* sganio *be*
scandal sgandal *eg* sgandalau
Scandinavian Union Undeb Llychlyn *eg*
scandium (Sc) scandiwm *eg*
scanner sganiwr *eg* sganwyr
scapegoat bwch dihangol *eg* bychod dihangol
scapula padell yr ysgwydd *eb* pedyll ysgwyddau
scapular sgapwlar *eg* sgapwlarau
scar craith *eb* creithiau
scar tissue meinwe craith *eb*
scarce resources adnoddau prin *ell*
scarcity prinder *eg*
scarf *n* sgarff *eg/b* sgarffiau
scarf *v* sgarffio *be*
scarf joint uniad sgarff *eg* uniadau sgarff
scarlet fever twymyn goch *eb*
scarlet lake llif sgarlad *eg*
scarlet madder madr sgarlad *eg*
scarp sgarp *eg* sgarpiau; tarren *eb* tarenni
scarp fault sgarp ffawt *eg* sgarpiau ffawt
scarp slope llethr sgarp *eg* llethrau sgarp
scarpland sgarpdir *eg* sgarpdiroedd
scatter gwasgaru *be*
scatter cushions mân glustogau *ell*
scatter diagram diagram gwasgariad *eg* diagramau gwasgariad
scatter graph graff gwasgariad *eg* graffiau gwasgariad
scattered particles gronynnau gwasgarog *ell*
scattered pattern patrwm gwasgarog *eg* patrymau gwasgarog
scattered settlement annedd wasgarog *eb* anheddau gwasgarog
scattering gwasgariad *eg* gwasgariadau
scatterplot plot gwasgariad *eg* plotiau gwasgariad
scavenge carthysu *be*
scavenger carthysydd *eg* carthysyddion
scene golygfa *eb* golygfeydd
scene designer cynllunydd golygfeydd *eb* cynllunwyr golygfeydd
scene painter peintiwr golygfeydd *eg* peintwyr golygfeydd
scene painting (of process or art) peintio golygfa *be*
scenery golygfa *eb* golygfeydd
scenic beauty golygfeydd prydferth *ell*
scenic route ffordd hynod o hardd *eb* ffyrdd hynod o hardd
scent mark arwydd sawr *eg* arwyddion sawr
sceptre teyrnwialen *eb* teyrnwialennau
schattenseite cil haul *eg*
schedule (=appendix to a document) atodlen *eb* atodlenni
schedule (=inventory) rhestr *eb* rhestri
schedule (=programme) rhaglen *eb* rhaglenni
schedule (=timetable) amserlen *eb* amserlenni
schema sgema *eg* sgemâu
schematic sgematig *ans*
schematic diagram diagram cynllunio *eg* diagramau cynllunio
scheme cynllun *eg* cynlluniau
scheme of assessment cynllun asesu *eg* cynlluniau asesu
scheme of work cynllun gwaith *eg* cynlluniau gwaith
scherzo scherzo *eg* scherzi
scherzo and trio scherzo a thrio
schism sgism *eg* sgismau
Schism Act Deddf Sgism *eb*
schismatic sgismatig *ans*
schist sgist *eg* sgistau
schistosity sgistedd *eg*
schizocarp sgitsocarp *eg* sgitsocarpau
schizophrenia sgitsoffrenia *eg*
Schlieffen Plan Cynllun Schlieffen *eg*
Schmalkaldic League Cynghrair Schmalkalden *eb*
Schmitt inverter gwrthdröydd Schmitt *eg*
Schmitt Trigger *eg* Triger Schmitt
scholarship (=award of money) ysgoloriaeth *eb* ysgoloriaethau
scholarship (=learning) ysgolheictod *eg*
scholastic sgolastig *ans*
scholasticism sgolastigiaeth *eb*
school ysgol *eb* ysgolion
school budget cyllideb ysgol *eb* cyllidebau ysgolion
school catchment area dalgylch ysgol *eg* dalgylchoedd ysgolion

school championships pencampwriaethau ysgolion *ell*
school child plentyn ysgol *eg* plant ysgol
school consortium consortiwm ysgolion *eg* consortia ysgolion
school counsellor cynghorwr ysgol *eg* cynghorwyr ysgol
school development plan cynllun datblygu ysgol *eg* cynlluniau datblygu ysgol
school dinner cinio ysgol *eg* ciniawau ysgol
school fund cronfa ysgol *eb* cronfeydd ysgol
school governor llywodraethwr ysgol *eg* llywodraethwyr ysgol
school ground tir yr ysgol *eg*
school leaving certificate tystysgrif gadael ysgol *eb* tystysgrifau gadael ysgol
school library llyfrgell ysgol *eb* llyfrgelloedd ysgol
school meals prydau ysgol *ell*
school nurse nyrs ysgol *eb* nyrsys ysgol
school of composition traddodiad cyfansoddi *eg* traddodiadau cyfansoddi
school performance table tabl perfformiad ysgolion *eg* tablau perfformiad ysgolion
school report adroddiad ysgol *eg* adroddiadau ysgol
school site safle'r ysgol *eg*
school uniform gwisg ysgol *eb*
school year blwyddyn ysgol *eb* blynyddoedd ysgol
school-based indicator dangosydd yn yr ysgol *eg* dangosyddion yn yr ysgol
schoolman ysgolwr *eg* ysgolwyr
Schumpeter's theory of creative destruction damcaniaeth distryw creadigol Schumpeter *eb*
Schwann cell cell Schwann *eb*
sciatic (of nerve) clunol *ans*
sciatic nerve nerf clunol *eg* nerfau clunol
science (=systematic and formulated body of knowledge) gwyddor *eb* gwyddorau
science (especially concerned with material and functions of physical universe) gwyddoniaeth *eb*
science fiction ffuglen wyddonol *eb*
science of navigation mordwyeg *eb*
science working group gweithgor gwyddoniaeth *eg* gweithgorau gwyddoniaeth
scientific claims honiadau gwyddonol *ell*
scientific concept cysyniad gwyddonol *eg* cysyniadau gwyddonol
scientific convention confensiwn gwyddonol *eg* confensiynau gwyddonol
scientific idea syniad gwyddonol *eg* syniadau gwyddonol
scientific knowledge gwybodaeth wyddonol *eb*
scientific method dull gwyddonol *eg* dulliau gwyddonol
scientific model model gwyddonol *eg* modelau gwyddonol
scientific principle egwyddor wyddonol *eb* egwyddorion gwyddonol
Scientific Revolution Chwyldro Gwyddonol *eg*
scientific symbol symbol gwyddonol *eg* symbolau gwyddonol
scintillate fflachennu *be*
scion brigyn impiedig *eg* brigau impiedig
scission toriant *eg* toriannau
scissors (implement) siswrn *eg* sisyrnau
scissors (method) dull siswrn *eg*
scissors control rheolaeth siswrn *eb*
scissors kick cic siswrn *eg* ciciau siswrn
scissors movement symudiad siswrn *eg* symudiadau siswrn
scissors vault llofnaid siswrn *eb* llofneidiau siswrn
sclera sglera *eg*
sclerenchyma sglerencyma *eg*
sclerosis sglerosis *eg*
sclerotic sglerotig *ans*
sclerous sglerws *ans*
scolex sgolecs *eg*
scoop *n* sgŵp *eg* sgwpiau
scoop *v* sgwpio *be*
scope cwmpas *eg* cwmpasau
scorbutic sgorbwtig *ans*
scorch deifio *be*
scorched earth policy polisi ymddiffeithio *eg*
score (=notch or line) *n* rhic *eg* rhiciau
score (number of points, goals etc) *n* sgôr *eb* sgorau
score (=cut or scratch a notch etc) *v* rhicio *be*
score (points, goals etc) *v* sgorio *be*
score a goal sgorio gôl *be*
score a try sgorio cais *be*
score event cystadleuaeth sgôr *eb* cystadlaethau sgôr
scoreboard bwrdd sgôr *eg* byrddau sgôr
scorer sgoriwr *eg* sgorwyr
score-sheet taflen sgorio *eb* taflenni sgorio
scoria scoria *be*
scoring system system sgorio *eb* systemau sgorio
scorper sgorper *eg* sgorperau
scot and lot borough bwrdeistref scot a lot *eb* bwrdeistrefi scot a lot
Scotch Baptist Bedyddiwr Albanaidd *eg* Bedyddwyr Albanaidd
Scotch Cattle Teirw Scotch *ell*
Scotch glue glud Scotch *eg*
Scotch snap clec Sgotaidd *eb* cleciadau Sgotaidd
scotia sgotia *eg*
scotia moulding mowldin sgotia *eg*
scotopic sensitivity syndrome syndrom sensitifedd sgotopig *eg*
scour sgwrio *be*
scourer sgwrydd *eg* sgwryddion
scouring sgwriad *eg* sgwriadau
scouring powder powdr sgwrio *eg*
Scramble for Africa Ymgiprys am Affrica *eg*
scrambled egg wy wedi'i sgramblo *eg* wyau wedi'u sgramblo
scrap sgrap *eg* sgrapiau
scrap book llyfr lloffion *eg* llyfrau lloffion
scrap iron haearn sgrap *eg*

scrap material defnydd sgrap *eg* defnyddiau sgrap
scrap metal metel sgrap *eg* metelau sgrap
scrap wood pren gwastraff *eg* prennau gwastraff
scrape sgrafellu *be*
scraper sgrafell *eb* sgrafelli
scraper cutter torrell grafu *eb* torellau crafu
scraper equipment taclau sgrafellu *ell*
scraper plane plaen crafu *eg* plaeniau crafu
scraper sharpener hogwr sgrafell *eg* hogwyr sgrafell
scraperboard sgraffwrdd *eg* sgraffyrddau
scraping (in finishing metal) sgrafellu *be*
scrapings crafion *ell*
scratch *n* crafiad *eg* crafiadau
scratch (=delete) *v* dileu *be*
scratch (in general) *v* crafu *be*
scratch brush brwsh crafu *eg* brwshys crafu
scratch disk disg dros dro *eg* disgiau dros dro
scratch memory cof dros dro *eg*
scratch stock crafwr addurn *eg* crafwyr addurn
scrawl sgriblo *be*
scree sgri *eg* sgrïau
screen *n* sgrin *eb* sgriniau
screen *v* cysgodi *be*
screen capture (=screen grab, screen shot) ciplun *eg* cipluniau
screen dump argraffu sgrin *be*
screen filler llenwad sgrin *eg*
screen frame ffrâm sgrin *eb* fframiau sgrin
screen grab (=screen capture, screen shot) ciplun *eg* cipluniau
screen layout cynllun sgrin *eg*
screen material defnydd sgrin *eg*
screen resolution cydraniad sgrin *eg*
screen saver arbedwr sgrin *eg* arbedwyr sgrin
screen shot (=screen capture, screen grab) ciplun *eg* cipluniau
screen the ball cysgodi'r bêl *be*
screen turtle crwban sgrin *eg* crwbanod sgrin
screenful sgriniad *eg* sgrineidiau
screening sgrinio *be*
screenplay sgript ffilm *eb* sgriptiau ffilm
screen-printing sgrin-brintio *be*
screenshot sgrinlun *eg* sgrinluniau
screw *n* sgriw *eb* sgriwiau
screw *v* sgriwio *be*
screw cup cwpan sgriw *eg* cwpanau sgriw
screw eye sgriw lygad *eb* sgriwiau llygad
screw gauge medrydd sgriw *eg* medryddion sgriw
screw hook bach sgriw *eg* bachau sgriw
screw pitch gauge medrydd pitsh sgriw *eg* medryddion pitsh sgriw
screw point pwynt sgriw *eg* pwyntiau sgriw
screw thread edau sgriw *eb* edafedd sgriw
screwbinder rhwymyn sgriw *eg* rhwymau sgriw
screw-bound sgriwglwm *ans*
screwdriver tyrnsgriw *eg* tyrnsgriwiau
screwdriver bit ebill tyrnsgriw *eg* ebillion tyrnsgriw
screwing block bloc sgriwio *eg* blociau sgriwio
screw-jack jac sgriw *eg* jaciau sgriw
screw-plate plât sgriwio *eg* platiau sgriwio
scribble sgriblo *be*
scribe *v* sgrifellu *be*
scribe (=copyist) *n* copïwr *eg* copïwyr
scribe (Biblical) *n* ysgrifennydd *eg* ysgrifenyddion
scribed joint uniad sgrifellog *eg* uniadau sgrifellog
scribed line llinell wedi'i sgrifellu *eb* llinellau wedi'u sgrifellu
scriber sgrifell *eb* sgrifelli
scribing block medrydd arwyneb *eg* medryddion arwyneb
scribing gouge gaing gau wyneb *eb* geingiau cau wyneb
scrim sgrim *eg*
script (=handwriting) llawysgrifen *eb*
script (of film, play etc) sgript *eb* sgriptiau
script pen pen sgript *eg* pennau sgript
scriptorium sgriptoriwm *eg* sgriptoria
scripture ysgrythur *eb* ysgrythurau
scrivener ysgrifner *eg* ysgrifneriaid
scroll rhôl *eb* rholiau
scroll *n* sgrôl *eg* sgroliau
scroll *v* sgrolio *be*
scroll a page up or a page down sgrolio i fyny tudalen neu i lawr *be*
scroll bar bar sgrolio *eg* barrau sgrolio
scroll moulding mowldin sgrôl *eg* mowldinau sgrôl
scroll tongs gefel sgrôl *eb* gefeiliau sgrôl
scroll wrench tyndro sgrôl *eg* tyndroeon sgrôl
scroll-bar bar-rholio *eg* bariau-rholio
scroll-down rholio i lawr *be*
scrolling (forging process) sgrolio *be*
scrolling tool erfyn sgrolio *eg* offer sgrolio
scroll-up rholio i fyny *be*
scrotum ceillgwd *eg* ceillgydau
scrub *n* prysg *eg*
scrub *v* sgrwbio *be*
scrub land tir prysg *eg*
scrum *n* sgrym *eb* sgrymiau
scrum *v* sgrymio *be*
scrum-half mewnwr *eg* mewnwyr
scull *v* sgwlio *be*
sculpt metal metel cerfiedig *eg*
sculptor cerflunydd *eg* cerflunwyr
sculptural cerfluniol *ans*
sculptural form ffurf gerfluniol *eb* ffurfiau cerfluniol
sculptural unit uned gerfluniol *eb* unedau cerfluniol
sculpture cerflunwaith *eg*
sculpturesque cerflunaidd *ans*
scum llysnafedd *eg* llysnafeddau
scumble *n* sgwmbl *eg* sgymblau
scumble *v* sgwmblo *be*
scurf cen *eg*
scurvy llwg, y llwg *eg*
scutage ysgwtreth *eb*

adf, adv adferf, *adverb* ***ans, adj*** ansoddair, *adjective* ***be*** berf, *verb* ***eb*** enw benywaidd, *feminine noun* ***eg*** enw gwrywaidd, *masculine noun*

scutcheon pais arfau *eb*
scutellum sgwtelwm *eg*
SDP-Liberal Alliance Cynghrair y Rhyddfrydwyr a'r Democratiaid Cymdeithasol *eb*
sea môr *eg* moroedd
Sea Beggars Cardotwyr y Môr *ell*
sea breeze awel o'r môr *eb* awelon o'r môr
sea buckthorn helygen y môr *eb* helyg y môr
sea coal glo môr *eg*
sea ford moryd *eb* morydau
sea front glan y môr *eg*
sea green gwyrdd y môr *eg*
sea lane llwybr môr *eg* llwybrau môr
sea level lefel môr *eb* lefelau môr
sea lion morlew *eg* morlewod
sea lyme-grass amdowellt *eg*
sea power (naval) grym morwrol *eg*
sea scorpion scorpion môr *eg* scorpionnau môr
SEAC: School Examinations and Assessment Council CAAY: Cyngor Arholiadau ac Asesu Ysgolion *eg*
sea-coast arfordir *eg* arfordiroedd
sea-gate morddrws *eg* morddrysau
seagrass morwellt *eg*
seal (=sea mammal) morlo *eg* morloi
seal (=symbol stamped in wax etc.) *n* sêl *eb* seliau
seal *v* selio *be*
seal swimming nofio morlo *be*
sealer seliwr *eg* selwyr
sealing work gwaith selio *eg*
seam (in dressmaking) sêm *eb* semau
seam (of coal) gwythïen *eb* gwythiennau
seam (of wrinkle, scar) gwrym *eg* gwrymiau
seam allowance lwfans sêm *eg* lwfansau sêm
seam binding rhwymyn sêm *eg* rhwymynnau sêm
seam finish gorffeniad sêm *eg* gorffeniadau sêm
seam joint uniad sêm *eg* uniadau sêm
seam set gosodydd sêm *eg* gosodyddion sêm
seamed gwrymiog *ans*
seaming semio *be*
seaming pliers gefelen semio *eb* gefeiliau semio
seaming tool erfyn semio *eg* offer semio
seamless ferrule amgarn ddi-sêm *eb* amgarnau di-sêm
seamount morfynydd *eg* morfynyddoedd
seaquake morgryn *eg* morgrynfeydd
search *n* chwiliad *eg* chwiliadau
search *v* chwilio *be*
search and replace chwilio a newid
search coil coil chwilio *eg*
search directory cyfeiriadur chwilio *eg* cyfeiriaduron chwilio
search engine peiriant chwilio *eg* peiriannau chwilio
search result canlyniad chwiliad *eg* canlyniadau chwiliad
search time amser chwilio *eg*
search word (in net searches) gair chwilio *eg* geiriau chwilio
seascape morlun *eg* morluniau
seashore glan y môr *eb*
seasickness salwch môr *eg*
seaside resort cyrchfan glan-môr *eb* cyrchfannau glan-môr
seasonal affective disorder anhwylder affeithiol tymhorol *eg*
seasonal changes newidiadau tymhorol *ell*
seasonal constellation cytser tymhorol *eg* cytserau tymhorol
seasonal entertainment adloniant tymhorol *eg*
seasonal song cân dymhorol *eb* caneuon tymhorol
seasonal star seren dymhorol *eb* sêr tymhorol
seasoning (of timber) sychu *be*
seat (of emotions etc) eisteddle *eg* eisteddleoedd
seat (to sit on) sedd *eb* seddau
seat of power canolfan grym *eb* canolfannau grym
sea-urchin draenog môr *eg* draenogod môr
seaward atfor *ans*
sea-water dŵr y môr *eg*
seaway morffordd *eb* morffyrdd
seaweed gwymon *eg*
sebaceous gland chwarren sebwm *eb* chwarennau sebwm
sebkha sebca *eg* sebcâu
secant (sec) secant *eg* secannau
secco secco *ans*
secede ymwahanu *be*
secession ymwahaniad *eg*
secessionist ymwahanwr *eg* ymwahanwyr
sech sech *eg*
second (=sixtieth of a minute) *n* eiliad *eg/b* eiliadau
second (interval) *n* eilfed *eg* eilfedau
second (a motion) *v* eilio *be*
second cut file ffeil eildor *eb* ffeiliau eildor
second degree equation hafaliad deuradd *eg* hafaliadau deuradd
second fold ail blyg *eg*
second generation ail genhedlaeth *eb*
second German empire ail ymerodraeth yr Almaen *eb*
second growth ail dyfiant *eg*
second inversion ail wrthdro *eg* ail wrthdroeon
second leg ail gymal *eg*
second lieutenant is-lifftenant *eg* is-lifftenantiaid
second mortgage ail forgais *eg*
second order (in mathematics) trefn dau *eb*
second order (of reaction, in geography) gradd dau *eb*
second order equation hafaliad trefn dau *eg* hafaliadau trefn dau
second order reaction adwaith gradd dau *eg*
second order spectrum sbectrwm trefn dau *eg*
second point ail bwynt *eg*
second row ail reng *eb*
second run ail rediad *eg*
second service ail gynnig serfio *eg*
second slip ail slip *eg*

Second Socialist International (Working-Men's Association) Ail Gymdeithas Sosialaidd Ryngwladol y Gweithwyr *eb*
second tap ail dap *eg*
Second World War Ail Ryfel Byd *eg*
secondary (=less important) eilradd *ans*
secondary (in general) eilaidd *ans*
secondary (of schools) uwchradd *ans*
secondary alcohol alcohol eilaidd *eg*
secondary appraisal gwerthuso eilaidd *be* gwerthuso eilaidd
secondary clay clai eilaidd *eg*
secondary coil coil eilaidd *eg* coiliau eilaidd
secondary colour lliw eilaidd *eg* lliwiau eilaidd
secondary consumer ysydd eilaidd *eg* ysyddion eilaidd
secondary depression dirwasgedd dilynol *eg*
secondary education addysg uwchradd *eb*
secondary evidence tystiolaeth eilaidd *eb*
secondary growth eildwf *eg*
secondary hazard perygl eilaidd *eg* peryglon eilaidd
secondary health care gofal iechyd eilaidd *eg*
secondary industry diwydiant eilaidd *eg* diwydiannau eilaidd
secondary meristem meristem eilaidd *eg*
secondary plumage plu eilaidd *ell*
secondary productions cynhyrchion eilaidd *ell*
secondary punisher cosbydd eilaidd *eb* cosbwyr eilaidd
secondary reinforcer atgyfnerthydd eilaidd *eg* atgyfnerthwyr eilaidd
secondary research ymchwil eilaidd *eg*
secondary research data data ymchwil eilaidd *ell*
secondary road ffordd eilaidd *eb* ffyrdd eilaidd
secondary sector sector eilaidd *eg*
secondary sexual character nodwedd rywiol eilaidd *eb* nodweddion rhywiol eilaidd
secondary socialisation cymdeithasoli eilaidd *be*
secondary source ffynhonnell eilaidd *eb* ffynonellau eilaidd
secondary storage storfa eilaidd *eb* storfeydd eilaidd
secondary thickening tewychu eilaidd *be*
secondary voltage foltedd eilaidd *eg*
secondary windings dirwyniad eilaidd *eg*
secondary window ffenestr eilaidd *eb* ffenestri eilaidd
secondhand goods nwyddau ail-law *ell*
secondment secondiad *eg* secondiadau
secret *n* cyfrinach *eb* cyfrinachau
secret (=confidential) *adj* cyfrinachol *ans*
secret (=hidden) *adj* cudd *ans*
secret ballot pleidlais gudd *eb*
Secret Ballot Act Deddf y Bleidlais Gudd *eb*
secret dovetail joint uniad cynffonnog cudd *eg* uniadau cynffonnog cudd
secret haunch hansh cudd *eg* hanshys cudd
secret haunched hansiedig cudd *ans*
secret haunched mortise and tenon joint uniad mortais a thyno hansiedig cudd *eg* uniadau mortais a thyno hansiedig cudd
secret haunched tenon tyno hansiedig cudd *eg*
secret lap dovetail goruniad cynffonnog cudd *eg* goruniadau cynffonnog cudd
secret lapped dovetail joint goruniad cudd cynffonnog *eg* goruniadau cudd cynffonnog
secret mitre dovetail meitr cynffonnog cudd *eg* meitrau cynffonnog cudd
secret mitre dovetail joint uniad cynffonnog meitr cudd *eg* uniadau cynffonnog meitr cudd
secret nailing hoelio cudd *be*
secret screwing sgriwio cudd *be*
secret service gwasanaeth cudd *eg* gwasanaethau cudd
secret society cymdeithas gudd *eb* cymdeithasau cudd
secret treaty cytundeb dirgel *eg* cytundebau dirgel
secretarial course cwrs ysgrifenyddol *eg* cyrsiau ysgrifenyddol
secretariat ysgrifenyddiaeth *eb*
secretary of state ysgrifennydd gwladol *eg* ysgrifenyddion gwladol
Secretary of State for Education Ysgrifennydd Gwladol dros Addysg *eg*
Secretary of State for Wales Ysgrifennydd Gwladol Cymru *eg*
secretary-general ysgrifennydd cyffredinol *eg*
secrete secretu *be*
secretin secretin *eg*
secretion secretiad *eg* secretiadau
secretory immunoglobulin A (sIgA) imiwnoglobwlin secretu A *eg*
sect sect *eb* sectau
sectarian sectyddol *ans*
sectary sectydd *eg* sectyddion
section (a plan, drawing) *v* trychu *be*
section (in biology) *n* toriad *eg* toriadau
section (in book, orchestra etc) *n* adran *eb* adrannau
section (of DNA) *n* darn *eg* darnau
section (of plan, drawing) *n* trychiad *eg* trychiadau
section line llinell drychu *eb* llinellau trychu
section plane plân trychu *eg*
sectional (=made in parts) adrannol *ans*
sectional (of drawing) trychiadol *ans*
sectional area arwynebedd trychiadol *eg* arwynebeddau trychiadol
sectional drawing trychlun *eg* trychluniau
sectional elevation golwg trychiadol *eg* golygon trychiadol
sectional end view ochrolwg trychiadol *eg* ochrolygon trychiadol
sectional front elevation blaenolwg trychiadol *eg* blaenolygon trychiadol
sectional paper papur adrannol *eg*
sectional plan uwcholwg trychiadol *eg* uwcholygon trychiadol

sectional view golwg trychiadol *eg* golygon trychiadol
sectionalism triniaeth adrannol *eb*
sectioning line llinell drychu *eb* llinellau trychu
sector sector *eg/b* sectorau
sector angle ongl sector *eb* onglau sector
sector theory damcaniaeth sector *eb* damcaniaethau sector
secular seciwlar *ans*
secular clergy clerigaeth seciwlar *eb*
secularism seciwlariaeth *eb*
secularizations meddiannau a seciwlareiddiwyd *ell*
secularize seciwlareiddio *be*
secure (=fasten) *v* cysylltu *be*
secure (=make safe) *v* diogelu *be*
secure (=safe) *adj* diogel *ans*
secure attachment ymlyniad diogel *eg*
secure school ysgol gadarn *eb* ysgolion cadarn
secure server gweinydd diogel *eg*
secure unit uned gadarn *eb* unedau cadarn
security (=safety) diogelwch *eg*
security (as deposit or pledge) gwarant *eb* gwarantau
security (in computing) gwarchodaeth *eb*
security (of latch etc) sicrwydd *eg*
security alarm larwm diogelwch *eg* larymau diogelwch
security check gwiriad diogelwch *eg* gwiriadau diogelwch
Security Council Cyngor Diogelwch *eg*
security of tenure sicrwydd daliadaeth *eg*
security tab tab gwarchod *eg* tabiau gwarchod
sedarim sedarim *ell*
sedative tawelydd *eg* tawelyddion
sedentary eisteddog *ans*
sedentary community cymuned sefydlog *eb* cymunedau sefydlog
sedentary lifestyle ffordd o fyw eisteddog *eb*
sedentary occupation galwedigaeth eisteddog *eb* galwedigaethau eisteddog
sedentary work gwaith eisteddog *eg*
sedentary worker gweithiwr eisteddog *eg* gweithwyr eisteddog
sedge hesgen *eb* hesg
sediment gwaddod *eg* gwaddodion
sedimentary gwaddodol *ans*
sedimentary rocks creigiau gwaddod *ell*
sedimentation gwaddodiad *eg*
sedition cynnwrf *eg*
Seditious Meetings Act Deddf Cyfarfodydd Terfysglyd *eb*
Seditious Publications Act Deddf Cyhoeddiadau Terfysglyd *eb*
see esgobaeth *eb* esgobaethau
seed hedyn *eg* had, hadau
seed (in sport) detholyn *eg* detholion
seed coat hadgroen *eg*
seed dispersion gwasgariad hadau *eg*
seed dressing dresin had *eg*
seed drill dril hau *eg* driliau hau
seed propagation lluosogi hadau *be*
seed vessel hadlestr *eg* hadlestri
seed-eater hadysydd *eg* hadysyddion
seed-eating hadysol *ans*
seeded player chwaraewr dethol *eg* chwaraewyr dethol
seedling eginblanhigyn *eg* eginblanhigion
seek *n* ymofyniad *eg* ymofyniadau
seek (in computing) *v* ymofyn *be*
seek (in mathematics and physics) *v* cyrchu *be*
seek sanctuary ceisio noddfa *be*
seek time amser ymofyn *eg* amserau ymofyn
seep tryddiferu *be*
seepage tryddiferiad *eg*
seersucker seersucker *eg*
see-saw sigl adenydd *eg* siglion adenydd
Seger cone côn Seger *eg*
segment *n* segment *eg* segmentau
segment *v* segmentu *be*
segmental arch bwa segmentol *eg* bwâu segmentol
segmentation segmentiad *eg* segmentiadau
segmented segmentiedig *ans*
segregate (in biology) arwahanu *be*
segregate (in general) gwahanu *be*
seif seiff *eg*
seigneurial arglwyddiaethol *ans*
seigniorage hawl arglwydd *eg*
seigniory arglwyddiaeth *eb* arglwyddiaethau
seigniory homage gwrogaeth arglwyddiaeth *eb*
seisin meddiant *eg* meddiannau
seismic seismig *ans*
seismic wave ton seismig *eb* tonnau seismig
seismograph seismograff *eg* seismograffau
seismology seismoleg *eb*
seismonasty seismonastedd *eg*
select (in computing) dewis *be*
select (in general) dethol *be*
► **select all** dewis y cyfan *be*
select all sheets dewis pob dalen *be*
select an autolayout dewis awtogynllun *be*
select autotext dewis awtodestun *be*
select button style dewis arddull botwm *be*
select cell styles dewis arddulliau celloedd *be*
select character left dewis nod i'r chwith *be*
select character right dewis nod i'r dde *be*
select colour scheme dewis cynllun lliw *be*
select column dewis colofn *be*
select committee pwyllgor dethol *eg* pwyllgorau dethol
select currency cells dewis celloedd arian *be*
select data area dewis ardal data *be*
select data source dewis ffynhonnell data *be*
select database range dewis ystod cronfa ddata *be*
select directory dewis cyfeiriadur *be*
select down dewis i lawr *be*

select file dewis ffeil *be*
select filter dewis hidlydd *be*
select font dewis ffont *be*
select form dewis ffurflen *be*
select graphics dewis graffigau *be*
select installation directory dewis cyfeiriadur gosod *be*
select installation type dewis y math o osodiad *be*
select language dewis iaith *be*
select left dewis chwith *be*
select logo dewis logo *be*
select macro dewis macro *be*
select module dewis modiwl *be*
select object dewis gwrthrych *be*
select outline level dewis lefel amlinelliad *be*
select output medium dewis cyfrwng allbwn *be*
select page down dewis tudalen i lawr *be*
select page left dewis tudalen i'r chwith *be*
select page up dewis tudalen i fyny *be*
select paragraph dewis paragraff *be*
select path dewis llwybr *be*
select range dewis ystod *be*
select right dewis de *be*
select root directory dewis cyfeiriadur gwraidd *be*
select row dewis rhes *be*
select source dewis ffynhonnell *be*
select style dewis arddull *be*
select table dewis tabl *be*
select target directory dewis cyfeiriadur targed *be*
select title graphics dewis graffigau teitl *be*
select tool dewis offeryn *be*
select up dewis i fyny *be*
select word dewis gair *be*
selection detholiad *eg* detholiadau
selection bias tuedd wrth ddethol *eb*
selective detholus *ans*
selective absorption amsugniad detholus *eg*
selective advantage mantais ddetholus *eb* manteision detholus
selective attention sylw dethol *eg*
selective benefit budd-dal dethol *eg* budd-daliadau dethol
selective breeding bridio detholus *be*
Selective Employment Tax (SET) Treth Gyflogi Dethol *eb*
selective erosion erydu dethol *be*
selective heating gwres detholus *eg*
selective membrane pilen ddetholus *eb* pilenni detholus
selectivist detholus *ans*
selectivity detholedd *eg*
selector (in general) detholydd *eg* detholyddion
selector (in sport) dewiswr *eg* dewiswyr
selenium (Se) seleniwm *eg*
self hunan *eg*
self-acting (function of a centre lathe) hunanweithredu *be*
self-action hunanweithredol *ans*
self-actualisation hunansylweddoli *be*
self-adhesive hunanadlynol *ans*
self-administration hunan-roi *be*
self-appraisal hunanwerthusiad *eg* hunanwerthusiadau
self-assessment hunanasesiad *eg* hunanasesiadau
self-awareness hunanymwybyddiaeth *eb*
self-booting CD CD byw *eg*
self-care hunanofal *eg*
self-centering chuck crafanc hunanganoli *eb* crafangau hunanganoli
self-cleaning hunanlanhau *be*
self-concept hunangysyniad *eg*
self-confidence hunanhyder *eg*
self-conscious hunanymwybodol *ans*
self-contained hunangynhaliol *ans*
self-control hunanreolaeth *eb*
self-correcting hunangywiro *be*
self-denial hunanymwadiad *eg*
Self-Denying Ordinance Deddf Hunanymwadiad *eb*
self-defence hunanamddiffyniad *eg*
self-differentiation hunan wahaniaethiad *eg*
self-disclosure hunanddatgelu *be*
self-efficacy hunaneffeithiolrwydd *eg*
self-employed hunangyflogedig *ans*
self-empowerment ymrymuso *be*
self-esteem hunan-barch *eg*
self-examination hunanarchwiliad *eg* hunanarchwiliadau
self-fertilization hunanffrwythloniad *eg*
self-fulfilling prophecy proffwydoliaeth hunangyflawnol *eb*
self-government hunanlywodraeth *eg*
self-gratification hunanfoddhad *eg*
self-grip wrench tyndro hunanafael *eg*
self-help hunangymorth *eg*
self-help group grŵp hunangymorth *eg* grwpiau hunangymorth
self-image hunanddelwedd *eb* hunanddelweddau
self-interest hunan-les *eg*
self-inverse element elfen hunanwrthdro *eb*
self-medication hunanddosio *be*
self-perception theory damcaniaeth hunanganfyddiad *eb*
self-pollination hunanbeilliad *eg*
self-portrait hunanbortread *eg* hunanbortreadau
self-protection hunanamddiffyniad *eg*
self-raising flour blawd codi *eg*
self-referral hunangyfeirio *be*
self-regulatory model model hunanreoleiddio *eg*
self-report hunanadrodd *be*
self-schema hunansgema *eg*
self-serving attribution bias tuedd priodoliad hunangyflenwol *eb*
self-serving bias tuedd hunanlesol *eb*
self-service store siop hunanwasanaeth *eb* siopau hunanwasanaeth

self-sterilization hunananffrwythloniad *eg*
self-study materials adnoddau astudio unigol *ell*
self-sufficiency hunangynhaliaeth *eb*
self-sufficient hunangynhaliol *ans*
self-tapping screw sgriw hunandapio *eb* sgriwiau hunandapio
selihot selihot *ell*
seller gwerthwr *eg* gwerthwyr
selling cost cost gwerthu *eb* costau gwerthu
selling price pris gwerthu *eg*
selva selfa *eg* selfâu
selvage selfais *eg* selfeisiau
selvage thread edau selfais *eb* edafedd selfais
semantic memory cof semantig *eg*
semantic priming preimio semantig *be*
semantics semanteg *eb*
semaphore semaffor *eg* semafforau
semen semen *eg*
semi rhannol *ans*
semi abstract lled haniaethol *ans*
semi bold rhannol drwm *ans*
semi chorus rhangor *eg* rhangorau
semi light (of colour) rhannol olau *ans*
semi permeable lledathraidd *ans*
semi-arid lletgras *ans*
semi-automatic lled awtomatig *ans*
semicarbazide semicarbasaid *eg*
semicarbazidium chloride semicarbasaidiwm clorid *eg*
semicarbazone semicarbason *eg*
semicircle hanner cylch *eg* hanner cylchoedd
semicircular hanner crwn *ans*
semicircular arch bwa hanner crwn *eg* bwâu hanner crwn
semicircular canal sianel hanner cylch *eb* sianeli hanner cylch
semicircular canal (in the inner ear) tiwb hanner cylch *eg* tiwbiau hanner cylch
semicolon hanner colon *eg* haneri colon
semiconductor lled-ddargludydd *eg* lled-ddargludyddion
semi-desert lled-ddiffeithwch *eg*
semi-detached house tŷ pâr *eg* tai pâr
semi-direct lighting golau lled uniongyrchol *eg*
semi-elliptic hanner eliptig *ans*
semi-elliptical arch bwa hanner eliptig *eg* bwâu hanner eliptig
semi-final *adj* cynderfynol *ans*
semi-independent lled annibynnol *ans*
semilunar valve falf gilgant *eb* falfiau cilgant
seminal semenol *ans*
seminal fluid hylif semenol *eg*
seminal vesicle fesigl semenol *eg*
seminary coleg offeiriadol *eg* colegau offeiriadol
seminiferous tubule tiwbyn semen *eg* tiwbynnau semen
semiology semioleg *eb*
semi-opaque rhannol ddi-draidd *ans*
semi-opera lled opera *eb* lled operâu
semi-permeable membrane pilen ledathraidd *eb* pilenni lledathraidd
semiquaver hanner cwafer *eg* hanner cwaferau
semi-retired wedi lled-ymddeol *ans*
semi-sheer lled-dryloyw *ans*
semi-skilled lled-fedrus *ans*
semi-skilled craftsman crefftwr lled-fedrus *eg* crefftwyr lled fedrus
semi-skilled labour llafur lled-grefftus *eg*
semi-skilled worker gweithiwr lled-grefftus *eg* gweithwyr lled grefftus
semi-structured interview cyfweliad lled-strwythuredig *eg* cyfweliadau lled-strwythuredig
semi-submerged lled soddedig *ans*
Semitism Semitiaeth *eb*
semitonal hanner tonol *ans*
semitone hanner tôn *eg* hanner tonau
semi-vertical hanner fertigol *ans*
senate senedd *eb* seneddau
senator seneddwr *eg* seneddwyr
send anfon *be*
send again anfon eto *eb*
send and receive messages anfon a derbyn negesau *be*
send as e-mail anfon fel e-bost *eb*
send default fax anfon ffacs rhagosodedig *be*
send document anfon dogfen *be*
send mail anfon e-bost *be*
send message anfon neges *be*
send news anfon newyddion *be*
send off anfon o'r cae *be*
send to back anfon i'r cefn *be*
sender anfonwr *eg* anfonwyr
senescence heneiddedd *eg*
senescent heneiddol *ans*
seneschal senysgal *eg* senysgaliaid
senile dementia gorddryswch henaint *eg*
senile dune hen dwyn *eg* hen dwyni
senior mentor uwch fentor *eg* uwch fentoriaid
senior (of position) uwch *eg*
senior management uwch reolwyr *ell*
senior mentor uwch fentor *eg* uwch fentoriaid
sensation (=feeling) teimlad *eg* teimladau
sensation (in biology) synhwyriad *eg* synwyriadau
sense (=meaning) ystyr *eg* ystyron
sense (of bodily faculties) synnwyr *eg* synhwyrau
sense (plus and minus etc) cyfeiriad *eg* cyfeiriadau
sense of rhythm ymdeimlad â rhythm *eg*
sense of touch synnwyr cyffwrdd *eg*
sense organ organ synhwyro *eg* organau synhwyro
sensibility synwyrusrwydd *eg*
sensing synhwyro *be*
sensitive sensitif *ans*
sensitive drilling machine peiriant drilio sensitif *eg* peiriannau drilio sensitif
sensitive feed porthiant sensitif *eg*

eg/b enw gwrywaidd/benywaidd, *masculine/feminine noun* ***ell*** enw lluosog, *plural noun* ***v*** berf, *verb* ***n*** enw, *noun* ► wedi newid, *changed*

sensitivity (in general) sensitifrwydd *eg*
sensitivity (in mathematics and biology) sensitifedd *eg*
sensor synhwyrydd *eg* synwyryddion
sensorimotor period cyfnod synhwyraidd-weithredol *eb*
sensory synhwyraidd *ans*
sensory association cortex cortecs synhwyraidd-gysylltiol *eg*
sensory deprivation amddifadu'r synhwyrau *be*
sensory disability anabledd synhwyraidd *eg*
sensory memory cof synhwyraidd *eg*
sensory motor intelligence deallusrwydd echddygol synhwyraidd *eg*
sensory nerve nerf synhwyraidd *eg* nerfau synhwyraidd
sensory neuron niwron synhwyraidd *eg* niwronau synhwyraidd
sensory specific satiety llawnder synhwyraidd-benodol *eg*
sensory-motor synhwyraidd-weithredol *ans*
sentence *v* dedfrydu *be*
sentence (=decision of law court) *n* dedfryd *eb* dedfrydau
sentence (=set of words) *n* brawddeg *eb* brawddegau
sentencing option opsiwn dedfrydu *eg* opsiynau dedfrydu
sentimental sentimental *ans*
sepal sepal *eg* sepalau
separable gwahanadwy *ans*
separate *adj* ar wahân *ans*
separate *v* gwahanu *be*
separate compartments adrannau ar wahân *ell*
separate out (animals, information) didoli *be*
separate parts rhannau ar wahân *ell*
separate piece darn ar wahân *eg* darnau ar wahân
separated gwahanedig *ans*
separates amrywion *ell*
separating funnel twndis gwahanu *eg* twndisau gwahanu; twmffat gwahanu *eg* twmffedi gwahanu
separating hyperplane hyperplân sy'n gwahanu *eg*
separation gwahaniad *eg* gwahaniadau
separation anxiety pryder gwahanu *eg*
separation into spherical polars gwahaniad i begynliniau sfferig *eg*
separation of powers gwahaniad pwerau *eg*
separatism ymwahaniaeth *eb*
separatist ymwahanwr *eg* ymwahanwyr
separator ymwahanydd *eg* ymwahanyddion
sepia sepia *ans*
Septennial Act Deddf Seithmlwydd *eb*
septet seithawd *eg* seithawdau
septic tank tanc septig *eg* tanciau septig
septum gwahanfur *eg* gwahanfuriau
septuplet seithpled *eg* seithpledi
sequence dilyniant *eg* dilyniannau
sequence generator generadur dilyniant *eg*
sequence of images cyfres o ddelweddau *eb* cyfresi o ddelweddau
sequence of instructions dilyniant o gyfarwyddiadau *eg* dilyniannau o gyfarwyddiadau
sequence of movements dilyniant o symudiadau *eg* dilyniannau o symudiadau
sequence of operations trefn y gweithrediadau *eb*
sequential dilyniannol *ans*
sequential access cyrchiad dilyniannol *eg* cyrchiadau dilyniannol
sequential access file ffeil cyrchu dilyniannol *eg*
sequential control rheolaeth ddilyniannol *eb*
sequential file ffeil ddilyniannol *eb* ffeiliau dilyniannol
sequential process proses ddilyniannol *eb* prosesau dilyniannol
sequential search chwiliad dilyniannol *eg* chwiliadau dilyniannol
sequester atafaelu *be*
sequestrant secwestrydd *eg*
sequestration atafaeliad *eg* atafaeliadau
sequestrator atafaelwr *eg* atafaelwyr
sequin secwin *eg* secwinau
serac serac *eg* seracau
sere dilyniant *eg* dilyniannau
serenade *n* serenâd *eg* serenadau
serenade *v* serenadu *be*
serf taeog *eg* taeogion
serfdom taeogaeth *eb*
serge serge *eg*
sergeant (historically and colloquially) sarsiant *eg*
sergeant (in modern usage) rhingyll *eg* rhingyllod
sergeant-at-arms sarsiant wrth arfau *eg*
sergeant-at-law sarsiant wrth gyfraith *eg*
sergeant-major uwch-ringyll *eg*
sergeantry sarsiantaeth *eb*
serial *adj* cyfresol *ans*
serial *n* cyfres *eb* cyfresi
serial access *n* cyrchiad cyfresol *eg* cyrchiadau cyfresol
serial access *v* cyrchu cyfresol *be*
serial adder adydd cyfresol *eg* adyddion cyfresol
serial drama drama gyfres *eb*
serial interface rhyngwyneb cyfresol *eg* rhyngwynebau cyfresol
serial port porth cyfresol *eg* pyrth cyfresol
serial transfer trosglwyddiad cyfresol *eg* trosglwyddiadau cyfresol
serialism cyfresiaeth *eb*
serialize cyfresu *be*
sericulture sidaniaeth *eb*
series cyfres *eb* cyfresi
series circuit cylched gyfres *eb* cylchedau cyfres
series of airs (in penillion singing) gosteg *eb* gostegion
series resonant circuit cylched gysain gyfres *eb* cylchedau cysain cyfres
series wound dirwyniad cyfres *eg* dirwyniadau cyfres

serif seriff *eb* seriffau
serif font ffont seriff *eg*
serigraphy printio â sgrin sidan *be*
serine serin *eg*
sermon pregeth *eb* pregethau
serotonin-specific reuptake inhibitor atalydd ailafael serotonin-benodol *eg* atalyddion ailafael serotonin-benodol
serous serws *ans*
serous membrane pilen serws *eb* pilenni serws
serpentine *adj* dolennog *ans*
serpentine *n* sarff-faen *eb* sarff-feini
serpentine front blaen dolennog *eg* blaenau dolennog
serrated danheddog *ans*
serrated edge ymyl ddanheddog *eb* ymylon danheddog
serrated jaw safn ddanheddog *eb* safnau danheddog
serum serwm *eg* sera
serum cholesterol colesterol serwm *eg*
serve *n* serf *eb* serfiau
serve (in tennis) *v* serfio *be*
serve pattern patrwm y serfio *eg* patrymau'r serfio
server (in general) gweinydd *eg* gweinyddion
server (in tennis) serfiwr *eg* serfwyr
server administration gweinyddiaeth gweinydd *eb*
server farm (collection of servers serving other computers) fferm gwasanaethwyr *eb* ffermydd gwasanaethwyr
server not available nid yw'r gweinydd ar gael
server timeout terfyn amser gweinydd *eg*
server user installation gosodiad defnyddiwr gweinydd *eg* gosodiadau defnyddiwr gweinydd
server/client network rhwydwaith gweinydd/cleient *eg* rhwydweithiau gweinydd/cleient
server-side ochr y gweinydd *eb*
service serfiad *eg* sefiadau
service *n* gwasanaeth *eg* gwasanaethau
service *v* gwasanaethu *be*
service and maintenance schedule manyleb cynnal a chadw *eb*
service area ardal wasanaeth *eb* ardaloedd gwasanaeth
service industry diwydiant gwasanaethu *eg* diwydiannau gwasanaethu
service provider darparwr gwasanaeth *eg* darparwyr gwasanaeth
service road ffordd wasanaeth *eb* ffyrdd gwasanaeth
service routine rheolwaith gwasanaethu *eg* rheolweithiau gwasanaethu
serving box sgwâr serfio *eg* sgwariau serfio
serving line llinell serfio *eb* llinellau serfio
serving square sgwâr serfio *eg* sgwariau serfio
sesamum sesamwm *eg*
sessile digoes *ans*
session sesiwn *eb* sesiynau
set *n* set *eb* setiau
set (=place in sets) *v* setio *be*
set (tasks, homework etc) *v* gosod *be*
set a saw gosod llif *be*
set a table gosod bwrdd *be*
set as default gosod fel rhagosodiad *be*
set book llyfr gosod *eg* llyfrau gosod
set colours gosod lliwiau *be*
set cursor gosod cyrchwr *be*
set dance dawns osod *eb* dawnsiau gosod
set default rhagosod *be*
set home page gosod tudalen gartref *be*
set of a saw gosodiad llif *eg* gosodiadau llif
set of common values set o werthoedd cyffredin *eb*
set of data set o ddata *eb* setiau o ddata
set of instructions set o gyfarwyddiadau *eb* setiau o gyfarwyddiadau
set of objects set o wrthrychau *eb* setiau o wrthrychau
set of punched cards set o gardiau tyllog *eb* setiau o gardiau tyllog
set operations gosod gweithrediadau *be*
set out trefnu *be*
set page number (unfair) gosod rhif tudalen *be*
set point pwynt gosod *eg* pwyntiau gosod
set reference gosod cyfeirnod *be*
set reminder gosod nodyn atgoffa *be*
set root gosod y gwraidd *be*
set screw sgriw set *eb* sgriwiau set
set scrum sgrym osod *eb* sgrymiau gosod
set square sgwaryn *eg* sgwarynnau
set tab order gosod trefn tabiau *be*
set task tasg osod *eb* tasgau gosod
set to music gosod i gerddoriaeth *be*
set up (apparatus) cydosod *be*
set up conditions gosod amodau dechreuol *be*
set-in sleeve llawes osod *eb* llewys gosod
set-on collar coler gosod *eg* coleri gosod
setting gosodiad *eg* gosodiadau
setting (of a film, story) lleoliad *eg* lleoliadau
setting boundaries gosod ffiniau *be*
setting hammer morthwyl gosod *eg* morthwylion gosod
setting in a sleeve gosod llawes *be*
setting out foundations gosod seiliau *be*
settle cyfanheddu *be*
settlement (=agreement) ardrefniant *eg* ardrefniannau
settlement (of new country) gwladychiad *eg* gwladychiadau
settlement (of place by people) anheddiad *eb* aneddiadau
settlement (of water treatment) setliad *eg*
settlement pattern patrwm anheddu *eg* patrymau anheddu
settler cyfaneddwr *eg* cyfaneddwyr
seven a side saith bob ochr
seven yard line llinell seithlath *eb* llinellau seithlath

seven-segment display arddangosydd saith-segment *eg* arddangosyddion saith-segment
seventh seithfed *eg* seithfedau
sever torri *be*
severe caled *ans*
severe (=serious) difrifol *ans*
severe learning difficulty anhawster dysgu difrifol *eg* anawsterau dysgu difrifol
severe learning disability anabledd dysgu difrifol *eg* anableddau dysgu difrifol
Severn bore eger Hafren *eg*
sew gwnïo *be*
sewa / seva sewa / seva *eg*
sewage carthion *ell*
sewage works gwaith carthion *eg* gweithfeydd carthion
sewerage carthffosiaeth *eb*
sewing foot (of machine part) troed wnïo *eb* traed gwnïo
sewing frame ffrâm wnïo *eb* fframiau gwnïo
sewing needle nodwydd wnïo *eb* nodwyddau gwnïo
sewing press gwasg wnïo *eb* gweisg gwnïo
sewing process proses wnïo *eb* prosesau gwnïo
sex *adj* rhywiol *ans*
sex *n* rhyw *eg/b* rhywiau
sex before marriage rhyw cyn priodas *eg*
sex chromosome cromosom rhyw *eg* cromosomau rhyw
sex discrimination (in general) gwahaniaethu ar sail rhyw *be*
sex discrimination (unfair) camwahaniaethu ar sail rhyw *be*
Sex Discrimination Act Deddf Gwahaniaethu ar Sail Rhyw *eb*
Sex Disqualification (Removal) Act 1919 Deddf (Dileu) Anghymwysterau Rhyw 1919 *eb*
sex education addysg rhyw *eb*
sex linkage cysylltedd rhyw *eg*
sex linked rhyw-gysylltiedig *ans*
sex role rôl rhyw *eb*
sex stereotype stereoteip rhyw *eg* stereoteipiau rhyw
sexagesimal secsagesimol *ans*
sex-influenced gene genyn rhyw-ddylanwadedig *eg* genynnau rhyw-ddylanwadedig
sex-linked gene genyn rhyw-gysylltiedig *eg* genynnau rhyw-gysylltiedig
sext secsdens *eg*
sextant secstant *eg* secstantau
sextet chwechawd *eg* chwechawdau
sextic secstig *ans*
sexton clochydd *eg* clochyddion
sextuplet chwephled *eg* chwephledi
sexual rhywiol *ans*
sexual abuse camdriniaeth rywiol *eb*
sexual intercourse cyfathrach rywiol *eb*
sexual masochism masocistiaeth rywiol *eb*
sexual reproduction atgenhedliad rhywiol *eg*
sexual sadism sadistiaeth rywiol *eb*
sexual selection (as a count noun) detholiad rhywiol *eg*
sexual selection (as a mass noun) dethol rhyw *be*
sexually transmitted disease clefyd cysylltiad rhywiol *eg* clefydau cysylltiad rhywiol
sgraffito sgraffito *eg*
shackle gefyn *eg* gefynnau
shackle pin pìn gefyn *eg* pinnau gefyn
shade (=darken) *v* tywyllu *be*
shade (=object which gives shade) *n* cysgodlen *eb* cysgodlenni
shade (in drawing etc) *n* cysgod *eg* cysgodion
shading graddliwio *be*
shadow *n* cysgod *eg* cysgodion
shadow (=follow) *v* dilyn *be*
shadow puppet pyped cysgod *eg* pypedau cysgod
shadow tuck twc cysgod *eg* tyciau cysgod
shadow work cysgodwaith *eg*
shaduf siadwff *eg* siadwffau
shaft (=handle) coes *eb* coesau
shaft (in general) siafft *eb* siafftiau
shag mulfran *eb* mulfrain
Shahadah Shahadah *eg*
Shaivism / Śaivism Shaiviaeth / Śaiviaeth *eg*
shake *v* ysgwyd *be*
shake (=split) *n* hollt *eg/b* holltau
shake hands ysgwyd llaw *be*
shake left hand ysgwyd llaw chwith *be*
shake right hand ysgwyd llaw dde *be*
shake-proof washer wasier wrthgryn *eb* wasieri gwrthgryn
Shaker Siglwr *eg* Siglwyr
shale siâl *eg* sialau
shallow *adj* bas *ans*
shallow *n* basddwr *eg* basddyfroedd
shallow end of the bath pen bas y baddon *eg*
shallow frying ffrio bas *be*
shallow processing prosesu bas *be*
shank garan *eg/b* garanau
shank and ring garan a chylch
shantung shantung *eg*
shanty town tref sianti *eb* trefi sianti
shape *n* siâp *eg* siapiau
shape *v* siapio *be*
shape designer dylunydd siâp *eg* dylunwyr siâp
shape work gwaith ar siâp *eg*
shaped ffurfiedig *ans*
shaped caul gwasgblat ffurfiedig *eg* gwasgblatiau ffurfiedig
shaped facing wynebyn wedi'i siapio *eg* wynebynnau wedi'u siapio
shaped front ffrynt ffurfiedig *eg* ffryntiau ffurfiedig
shaped leg coes siapog *eb* coesau siapog
shaped stretchers estynwyr ffurfiedig *ell*
shaper (machine) peiriant llunio *eg* peiriannau llunio

shaper tools offer peiriant llunio *ell*
shaping siapio *be*
shaping clay siapio clai *be*
shard darn crochenwaith *eg* darnau crochenwaith
share *v* rhannu *be*
share (in general) *n* rhan *eb* rhannau
share (stock market) *n* cyfranddaliad *eg* cyfranddaliadau
share capital cyfalaf cyfranddaliadau *eg*
share certificate tystysgrif cyfranddaliadau *eb* tystysgrifau cyfranddaliadau
share cropping cyfran-gnydio *be*
shared electrons electronau cydranedig *ell*
shareholder cyfranddaliwr *eg* cyfranddalwyr
shareholder dividend buddran cyfranddalwyr *eb*
shareware rhanwedd *eg/b*
Shari'ah Shari'ah *eg*
shark siarc *eg* siarcod
sharp (in general) *adj* llym *ans*
sharp (note in music) *n* llonnod *eg* llonnodau
sharp (when singing too high) *adj* uwchben y nodyn *ans*
sharp blade llafn llym *eg* llafnau llym
sharp corner cornel lem *eb* corneli llym
sharp key (in old Welsh music) crasgywair *eg*
sharp knife cyllell finiog *eb* cyllyll miniog
sharp point pwynt llym *eg* pwyntiau llym
sharp switching action gweithrediad switsio cyflym iawn
sharp value gwerth pendant *eg* gwerthoedd pendant
sharp-edged awchlym *ans*
sharp-edged orifice flow meter mesurydd llif agorfa awchlym *eg* mesuryddion llif agorfa awchlym
sharpen hogi *be*
sharpener hogwr *eg* hogwyr
sharpening (exaggerating difference) gwahaniaethu *be*
sharpening angle ongl hogi *eb* onglau hogi
sharpening bevel befel hogi *eg* befelau hogi
shatter dryllio *be*
shave eillio *be*
shavings naddion *ell*
Shavuot Shavuot *eg*
shawl siôl *eb* sioliau
shawm shawm *eg* shawms
sheaf ysgub *eb* ysgubau
shear (=cut off) *v* torri *be*
shear (=cut sheep's wool) cneifio *be*
shear (=strain produced by pressure) *n* croeswasgiad *eg* croeswasgiadau
shear (=strain produced by pressure) *v* croeswasgu *be*
shear strength cryfder croeswasgiad *eg*
shearforce croesrym *eg* croesrymoedd
shearforce diagram diagram croesrym *eg* diagramau croesrym
shearing force croesrym *eg* croesrymoedd
shearing machine peiriant llafnu *eg* peiriannau llafnu
shearing stress diriant croesrym *eg*
shears gwellaif *eg* gwelleifiau
sheath gwain *eb* gweiniau
sheave olwyn bwli *eb* olwynion pwli
shed stick ffon barthu *eb* ffyn parthu
shedding parthiad *eg*
sheen llewyrch *eg*
sheep dafad *eb* defaid
sheep fold corlan *eb* corlannau
sheep walk cynefin defaid *eg* cynefinoedd defaid
sheepskin croen dafad *eg* crwyn defaid
sheer tryloyw *ans*
sheet (of bedlinen) cynfas *eb* cynfasau
sheet (of ice, basalt, steel etc) llen *eg/b* llenni
sheet (of paper) dalen *eb* dalennau
sheet decking decin llen *eg*
sheet erosion llen erydiad *eg*
sheet flood llenlif *eg* llenlifiau
sheet glass gwydr gwastad *eg*
sheet metal llenfetel *eg* llenfetelau
sheet metalwork gwaith llenfetel *eg*
sheet of map dalen map *eb* dalennau map
sheet saw llif len *eb* llifiau llen
sheet steel llenddur *eg*
sheet wash llen olchiad *eg*
sheet-feeder porthydd dalennau *eg* porthyddion dalennau
sheeting defnydd cynfasau *eg*
Sheffield plate arian Sheffield
shelf silff *eb* silffoedd
shelf life oes silff *eb*
shelf support cynhaliad silff *eg* cynhaliaid silff
shell (of eggs, vegetables, electrons) plisgyn *eg* plisg
shell (of shellfish, snails) cragen *eb* cregyn
shell and husk carving cerfiad cragen a phlisgyn *eg* cerfiadau cragen a phlisgyn
shell bit ebill cragen *eg* ebillion cragen
shell edging ymylwaith cragen *eg*
shell milling cutter melinwr cragen *eg* melinwyr cragen
shell tuck twc cragen *eg* tyciau cragen
shellac sielac *eg*
shellac knotting cuddiwr ceinciau sielac *eg*
shellac sealer seliwr sielac *eg*
shellac varnish farnais sielac *eg*
shelly cregynnog *ans*
shelter lloches *eb* llochesau
shelter belt llain gysgodi *eb* lleiniau cysgodi
shelter seeking cysgotgar *ans*
sheltered accommodation llety cysgodol *eg* lletyau cysgodol
sheltered accommodation unit uned llety cysgodol *eb* unedau llety cysgodol
sheltered housing cartrefi gwarchodol *ell*
shepherd *n* bugail *eg* bugeiliaid

shepherd *v* bugeilio *be*
shepherd castor castor bugail *eg* castorau bugail
shepherd's pie pastai'r bugail *eb*
sherardize sierardeiddio *be*
sheriff siryf *eg* siryfion
Sheriff's Tourn Llys y Siryf *eg*
Shi'ah Shi'ah *eg*
shield tarian *eb* tariannau
shield back chair cadair gefn tarian *eb* cadeiriau cefn tarian
shield boss bogail tarian *eg* bogeiliau tarian
shield volcano llosgfynydd tarian *eg* llosgfynyddoedd tarian
shift (=displace) *v* syflyd *be*
shift (=displacement) *n* syfliad *eg* syfliadau
shift (=move) *v* symud *be*
shift (=movement) *n* symudiad *eg* symudiadau
shift in the demand curve newid yn y gromlin galw
SHIFT key bysell SHIFT *eg* bysellau SHIFT
shift lock key clo cyfnewid *eg* cloeon cyfnewid
shift register cofrestr syfliad *eb* cofrestri syfliad
shift supervisor goruchwyliwr y shifft *eg*
shifting cultivation triniad mudol *eg*
Shimbel Index Indecs Shimbel *eg*
shin crimog *eb* crimogau
shin muscle cyhyryn y grimog *eg* cyhyrynnau'r grimog
shine *n* sglein *eg* sgleiniau
shine (of polished objects) *v* sgleinio *be*
shine (of sun etc) disgleirio *be*
shingle (=pebbles) graean bras *eg*
shingle (=roof tile) estyllen do *eb* estyll to
shingle, mud or sand graean bras, llaid neu dywod
shiny paper papur sglein *eg*
shiny solids solidau sgleiniog *ell*
ship *v* cludo mewn llong *be*
Ship Money Treth Longau *eb*
ship yard iard llongau *eb* iardiau llongau
shipment llwyth llong *eg* llwythau llong
shipping llongau *ell*
shire (in England) swydd *eb*
shire (in Wales) sir *eb* siroedd
shire fee ffi sir *eb*
shirk shirk *eg*
shirr cygrychu *be*
shirring elastic elastig cygrychu *eg*
shirt crys *eg* crysau
shirt button botwm crys *eg* botymau crys
shirt collar coler crys *eg* coleri crysau
Shiva /Śiva Shiva /Śiva *eg*
Shiva Nataraja Shiva Nataraja *eg*
shiver crynu *be*
shoal (=shallow place in sea) basle *eg* basleoedd
shoal (of fish) haig *eb* heigiau
shock sioc *eb* siociau
shock absorber sioc laddwr *eg* sioc laddwyr
shock appeal apêl sioc *eb*
shoddy brethyn eilban *eg*
shoe esgid *eb* esgidiau
shoot blaguryn *eg* blagur
shoot (of plant) *n* cyffyn *eg* cyffion
shoot (with gun etc) *v* saethu *be*
shooting board bwrdd plaenio *eg* byrddau plaenio
shooting circle cylch saethu *eg* cylchoedd saethu
shooting line llinell saethu *eb* llinellau saethu
shop siop *eb* siopau
shop assistant gweithiwr siop *eg* gweithwyr siop
shop conversion trawsnewid siop *be*
shop front level lefel ffrynt siopau *eb*
shop manager rheolwr siop *eg* rheolwyr siop
shop steward swyddog undeb *eg* swyddogion undeb
shop-soiled goods nwyddau wedi'u baeddu yn y siop *ell*
shore (=prop) ateg *eb* ategion
shore (of sea etc) glan *eb* glannau
short back bacon cig moch cefn *eg*
short circuit cylched fer *eb* cylchedau byr
short clap clapio swta *be*
short corner cornel fer *eb* corneli byr
short dance dawns fer *eb* dawnsiau byr
short distance pellter byr *eg*
short division rhannu byr *be*
short eared owl tylluan glustiog *eb* tylluanod glustiog
short grain graen byr *eg*
short haul destination cyrchfan pellter byr *eb*
short haul destination canolfan wyliau tramor agos *eb*
short haul market marchnad cyrchfannau agos *eb*
short hurdle race ras clwydi byr *eb* rasys clwydi byr
short leaf dalen fer *eb* dalennau byr
short leg coeswr agos *eg* coeswyr agos
short line llinell fer *eb* llinellau byr
short mid wicket canolwr wiced agos *eg* canolwyr wiced agos
short nose pliers gefelen drwyn byr *eb* gefeiliau trwyn byr
short pitch nail hoelen bitsh byr *eb* hoelion pitsh byr
short pitched delivery pêl fer *eb* peli byr
short punch dyrnod bwt *eb* dyrnodiau pwt
short race ras fer *eb* rasys byr
short range plane awyren taith fer *eb* awyrennau taith fer
short relay race ras gyfnewid fer *eb* rasys cyfnewid byr
short route llwybr byr *eg* llwybrau byr
short run rhediad byr *eg*
short score sgôr fer *eb* sgorau byrion
short series of movements cyfres fer o symudiadau *eb* cyfresi byr o symudiadau
short service serfiad byr *eg* serfiadau byr
short sight golwg byr *eg*
short, slow ball pêl fer ac araf *eb*
short square leg coeswr byr sgwâr *eg* coeswyr byr sgwâr
short stop ataliwr *eg* atalwyr

short taper tapr byr *eg* taprau byr
short term change newid tymor byr *eg* newidiadau tymor byr
short time amser byr *eg*
short volley foli gwta *eb* foliau cwta
short waisted byrwasg *ans*
short-answer question cwestiwn ateb byr *eg* cwestiynau ateb byr
shortbread biscuit teisen Berffro *eb* teisennau Berffro
shortcut llwybr byr *eg* llwybrau byr
shorten (a dress etc) cwtogi *be*
shorten a pattern byrhau patrwm *be*
shortened form byrfodd *eg* byrfoddau
shortest generator generadur byrraf *eg* generaduron byrraf
shortest route llwybr byrraf *eg* llwybrau byrraf
shortfall diffyg *eg* diffygion
shortie pyjamas pyjamas cwta *ell*
shortlist rhestr fer *eb*
shorts siorts *ell*
short-term tymor byr *ans*
short-term care gofal tymor byr *eg*
short-term effect effaith tymor byr *eb* effeithiau tymor byr
short-term memory cof tymor byr *eg*
shot (=heavy ball in athletics) pwysau *ell*
shot (in a film) saethiad *eg*
shot (with ball, gun etc) ergyd *eg/b* ergydion
shot of steam iron haearn â chwythell ager *eg* heyrn â chwythelli ager
shotgun dryll *eb* drylliau
shoulder *v* ysgwyddo *be*
shoulder (of person, bat, harp etc) *n* ysgwydd *eb* ysgwyddau
shoulder blade palfais *eb* palfeisiau
shoulder carry cario ar ysgwydd *be*
shoulder charge hyrddiad ysgwydd *eg* hyrddiadau ysgwydd
shoulder girdle gwregys yr ysgwydd *eg* gwregysau ysgwyddau
shoulder line llinell ysgwydd *eb* llinellau ysgwydd
shoulder pad pad ysgwydd *eg* padiau ysgwydd
shoulder pass pàs o'r ysgwydd *eb* pasiau o'r ysgwydd
shoulder plane plaen ysgwydd *eg* plaeniau ysgwydd
shoulder strap strap ysgwydd *eb* strapiau ysgwydd
shouldered dowel hoelbren ysgwyddog *eb* hoelbrennau ysgwyddog
shovel rhaw *eb* rhofiau
show sioe *eb* sioeau
show clipboard dangos clipfwrdd *be*
show invisibles dangos anweledigion *be*
show page guides dangos canllawiau tudalen *be*
show ruler dangos mesurydd *be*
shower cawod *eb* cawodydd
shower bath baddon cawod *eg* baddonau cawod
shower-proof (finish) gwrthgawod *ans*
shred *n* cerpyn *eg* carpion
shred *v* carpio *be*
shredded paper carpion papur *ell*
shrew chwistlen *eb* chwistlod
shrievalty siryfiaeth *eb*
shrine (for relics) creirfa *eb* creirfâu
shrine (in general) cysegr *eg* cysegrau
shrink (=narrow) culhau *be*
shrink (=shrivel) crebachu *be*
shrink (of textiles) pannu *be*
shrink fit ffitio poeth *be*
shrink wrapping lapio poeth *be*
shrinkage culhad *eg* culhadau
shrinkage allowance lwfans culhad *eg* lwfansau culhad
shrinkage plate plât culhad *eg* platiau culhad
shrink-resistant (finish) gwrthbannu *ans*
shroud panel panel gordo *eg* paneli gordo
shrouds rhaffau mast *ell*
shrub llwyn *eg* llwyni
Shudra /Śudra Shudra /Śudra *eg*
shunt siynt *eg* siyntiau
shunt wound siyntweindiog *ans*
shutter caead *eg* caeadau
shuttering caeedydd *eg*
shuttle gwennol *eb* gwenoliaid
shuttle bobbin bobin gwennol *eg* bobinau gwennol
shuttle relay race ras gyfnewid nôl a mlaen *eb* rasys cyfnewid nôl a mlaen
shuttlecock gwennol *eb* gwenoliaid
SI unit uned SI *eb* unedau SI
sibling brawd neu chwaer
siccative sychydd *eg* sychyddion
Sicilian circle cylch Sisili *eg* cylchoedd Sisili
sick (=ill) gwael *ans*
sickle cryman *eg* crymannau
sickle cell anaemia anaemia cryman-gell *eg*
sickness benefit budd-dal afiechyd *eg* budd-daliadau afiechyd
sick-role behaviour ymddygiad rôl-salwch *eg*
side ochr *eg/b* ochrau
side and face milling cutter melinwr ochr ac wyneb *eg* melinwyr ochr ac wyneb
side by side ochr yn ochr *adf*
side clearance cliriad ochr *eg* cliriadau ochr
side cutting pliers gefel ochr dorri *eb* gefeiliau ochr dorri
side drum drwm ochr *eg* drymiau ochr
side elevation ochrolwg *eg* ochrolygon
side left i'r ochr chwith
side of the racket ochr y raced *eb*
side product sgil gynnyrch *eg* sgil gynhyrchion
side rabbet plane plaen rabad ochr *eg* plaeniau rabad ochr
side rail rheilen ochr *eb* rheiliau ochr
side rake gwyredd ochr *eg*
side right i'r ochr dde

side seam pocket poced sêm ochr *eb* pocedi sêm ochr
side serving line llinell serfio ochr *eb* llinellau serfio ochr
side support (in athletics) ymgynnal ochr *be*
side table bwrdd ochr *eg* byrddau ochr
side tool erfyn ochr *eg* offer ochr
side valve falf ochr *eb* falfiau ochr
side vault llofnaid ochrol *eb* llofneidiau ochrol
side view ochrolwg *eg* ochrolygon
side wall mur ochr *eg* muriau ochr
side wall out of court line ffin ochr *eb* ffiniau ochr
side-block tackle tacl floc o'r ochr *eb* taclau bloc o'r ochr
sideboard seld *eb* seldiau
side-cutters torrell ochr *eb* torellau ochr
side-cutting ochr-dorri *be*
side-cutting pliers gefelen ochr-dorri *eb* gefeiliau ochr-dorri
sided ochrog *ans*
side-effect sgil effaith *eb* sgil effeithiau
sidefoot ochr y droed *eb*
sideline llinell ochr *eb* llinellau ochr
side-mouth tongs gefel gegochr *eb* gefeiliau cegochr
sidereal day diwrnod sêr *eg*
sidereal time amser y sêr *eg*
sidereal year blwyddyn serol *eb* blynyddoedd serol
sidespin troelli ochr y bêl *be*
side-step *n* cam i'r ochr *eg*
side-step *v* ochrgamu *be*
sidestroke nofio ar yr ochr *be*
sideways i'r ochr
sideways pressure gwasgedd ochrol *eg*
sideways RAM RAM ochr *eg*
sideways ROM ROM ochr *eg*
sideways-upward i'r ochr ac i fyny
siding lein aros *eb* leiniau aros
siege gwarchae *eg* gwarchaeau
sieve *n* gogr *eg* gograu
sieve *v* gogru *be*
sieve plate plât hidlo *eg* platiau hidlo
sieving brush brwsh rhidyllu *eg* brwshys rhidyllu
sift rhidyllu *be*
sifted sand tywod wedi'i ridyllu *eg*
sifter rhidyll *eg* rhidyllau
sifter jar jar ridyllu *eb* jariau rhidyllu
sight golwg *eg/b* golygon
sight rails alidad
sight singing canu ar yr olwg gyntaf *be*
sign arwydd *eg/b* arwyddion
sign and magnitude code cod maint ac arwydd *eg*
sign bit did arwydd *eg* didau arwydd
sign extension estyniad arwydd *eg* estyniadau arwydd
sign language iaith arwyddion *eb*
sign language arwyddiaith *eb* arwyddieithoedd
sign painting (of painted picture) paentiad arwydd *eg* paentiadau arwydd
sign painting (of process or art) peintio arwydd *be*
signal (mechanical, electrical etc) signal *eg* signalau
signal (non-technical) arwydd *eg/b* arwyddion
signal detection theory damcaniaeth signal-ganfyddiad *eb*
signal generator generadur signalau *eg* generaduron signalau
signatory llofnodydd *eg* llofnodyddion
signature (of key or time) arwydd *eg/b* arwyddion
signed (in maths, physics) (with feminine nouns) wedi'i harwyddo *ans* wedi'u harwyddo
signed (in maths, physics) (with masculine nouns) wedi'i arwyddo *ans* wedi'u harwyddo
signed (with handwritten name) (with feminine nouns) wedi'i llofnodi *ans* wedi'u llofnodi
signed (with handwritten name) (with masculine nouns) wedi'i lofnodi *ans* wedi'u llofnodi
signed integer cyfanrif arwyddedig *eg* cyfanrifau arwyddedig
signed language iaith arwyddion *eb*
significance arwyddocâd *eg*
significance level lefel arwyddocâd *eb*
significant (in general) arwyddocaol *ans*
significant (of figures) ystyrlon *ans*
significant difference gwahaniaeth arwyddocaol *eg*
significant figure ffigur ystyrlon *eg* ffigurau ystyrlon
significant testing profi ystyrlon *be*
signified (of image) arwyddedig *eg*
signifier (of image or word) arwyddwr *eg*
signing (in sign language) arwyddo *be*
signs of the Zodiac arwyddion y Sidydd *ell*
signum signwm *eg* signa
Sikh sikhaidd *ans*
Sikh Sikh *eg/b* Sikhiaid
Sikh identity hunaniaeth y Sikhiaid *eb*
Sikhism Sikhiaeth *eb*
silane silan *eg*
silence distawrwydd *eg*
silencer tawelydd *eg* tawelyddion
silhouette silwét *eg* silwetau
silica silica *eg* silicâu
silica gel silica sychu *eg*
silicate silicad *eg*
silicate ion ïon silicad *eg* ïonau silicad
silicon (Si) silicon *eg*
silicon carbide paper papur silicon carbid *eg*
silicon crucible crwsibl silicon *eg* crwsiblau silicon
silicon dioxide silicon deuocsid *eg*
silicon tetrachloride silicon tetraclorid *eg*
silicone (compounds) silicôn *eg* siliconau
silicone polish llathrydd silicôn *eg* llathryddion silicôn
silicone spray chwistrelliad silicôn *eg* chwistrelliadau silicôn
silicon(IV) oxide silicon(IV) ocsid *eg*
siliqua silicwa *eg*

silk sidan *eg* sidanau
silk finish paper papur sglein sidan *eg*
silkscreen sgrin sidan *eb* sgriniau sidan
silk-screen printing printio â sgrin sidan *be*
silkscreen process proses sgrin sidan *eb* prosesau sgrin sidan
silkworm pryf sidan *eg* pryfed sidan
sill sil *eg* siliau
silly mid-off mentrwr agored *eg* mentrwyr agored
silly mid-on mentrwr coes *eg* mentrwyr coes
silt *n* silt *eg*
silt *v* siltio *be*
silt stone carreg silt *eb* cerrig silt
Silurian Silwraidd *ans*
silver arian *eg*
silver foil ffoil arian *eg*
silver grain (oak) graen arian *eg*
silver money arian gwynion *ell*
silver nitrate arian nitrad *eg*
silver plate plât arian *eg*
silver solder sodr arian *eg*
silver soldering ariansodro *be*
silver steel dur arian *eg*
silver tooling leaf dalen offer arian *eb* dalennau offer arian
silver-braze arianbresyddu *be*
silver(I) ion ïon arian(I) *eg* ïonau arian(I)
silversmith gof arian *eg* gofaint arian
silversmithing operations gweithrediadau gofannu arian *eg*
similar (in general) tebyg *ans*
similar (in mathematics) cyflun *ans*
similar ability gallu cyffelyb *eg*
similar figure (in mathematics) ffigur cyflun *eg* ffigurau cyflun
similar triangles trionglau cyflun *ell*
similarities (in general) nodweddion sy'n debyg *ell*
similarity (in general) tebygrwydd *eg*
similarity (in mathematics) cyflunedd *eg* cyfluneddau
similarity of colour tebygrwydd lliw *eg*
similarity of tone tebygrwydd tôn *eg*
similarity principle egwyddor tebygrwydd *eb*
similitude cyfluniant *eg* cyfluniannau
Simmonds nut nyten Simmonds *eb* nytiau Simmonds
simoniac seimonydd *eg* seimonyddion
simoniacal seimonaidd *ans*
simonist seimonwr *eg* seimonwyr
simony seimoniaeth *eb*
simoom simwm *eg*
simple syml *ans*
simple a.c. generator generadur cerrynt eiledol *eg* generaduron cerrynt eiledol
simple accompaniment cyfeiliant syml *eg*
simple action gweithred syml *eb* gweithredoedd syml
simple attack ymosod syml *eg*
simple camera camera syml *eg* camerâu syml
simple circuit cylched syml *eb* cylchedau syml
simple dance dawns syml *eb* dawnsiau syml
simple drive gyriad syml *eg* gyriadau syml
simple equation hafaliad syml *eg* hafaliadau syml
simple fee ffi rydd *eb*
simple form ffurf syml *eb* ffurfiau syml
simple fraction ffracsiwn syml *eg* ffracsiynau syml
simple fracture torasgwrn syml *eg* toresgyrn syml
simple harmonic harmonig syml *eg* harmonigau syml
simple harmonic motion mudiant harmonig syml *eg*
simple instrument offeryn syml *eg* offerynnau syml
simple interest llog syml *eg*
simple linear simultaneous equations hafaliadau cydamserol llinol syml *ell*
simple melody alaw syml *eb* alawon syml
simple movement symudiad syml *eg* symudiadau syml
simple movement phrase cymal syml o symudiadau *eg* cymalau syml o symudiadau
simple parry pario syml *be*
simple pattern patrwm syml *eg* patrymau syml
simple pendulum pendil syml *eg* pendiliau syml
simple pits mân-bantiau syml *ell*
simple plain brace carntro cyffredin *eg* carntroeon cyffredin
simple rhyme rhigwm syml *eg* rhigymau syml
simple rhythm rhythm syml *eg* rhythmau syml
simple rhythmic response ymateb rhythmig syml *eg* ymatebion rhythmig syml
simple rondo rondo syml *eb* rondoau syml
simple shape siâp syml *eg* siapiau syml
simple sketch braslun syml *eg* brasluniau syml
simple song cân syml *eb* caneuon syml
simple technical language iaith dechnegol syml *eb*
simple text testun syml *eg* testunau syml
simple train trên syml *eg* trenau syml
simplest form ffurf symlaf *eb* ffurfiau symlaf
simplest formula fformiwla symlaf *eb* fformiwlâu symlaf
simplex simplecs *eg*
simplicity symlrwydd *eg*
simplification symleiddiad *eg* symleiddiadau
simplified symledig *ans*
simplified version fersiwn syml *eg* fersiynau syml
simplify symleiddio *be*
simply supported beam trawst wedi'i gynnal yn syml *eg* trawstiau wedi'u cynnal yn syml
Simpson's rule dull Simpson *eg*
simulate efelychu *be*
simulated ffug *ans*
simulated experiment ffug arbrawf *eg* ffug arbrofion
simulation efelychiad *eg* efelychiadau
simulator efelychydd *eg* efelychyddion
simultaneous cydamserol *ans*

simultaneous equations hafaliadau cydamserol *ell*
simultaneous translation cyfieithu ar y pryd *be*
sin *n* pechod *eg* pechodau
sin *v* pechu *be*
sine (sin) sin *eg* sinau
sine wave ton sin *eb* tonnau sin
sinecure segurswydd *eb* segurswyddi
sinew gewyn *eg* gewynnau
sinewy (=ligamentous) gewynnol *ans*
sinfonia sinffonia *eg* sinffonïau
sinfonietta sinffonieta *eb* sinffonietau
sing canu *be*
sing a round canu tôn gron *be*
sing songs canu caneuon *be*
sing to the accompaniment of the harp canu gyda'r tannau *be*
singable canadwy *ans*
singer (female) cantores *eb* cantorion
singer (male) canwr *eg* cantorion
singing the rhyme canu'r rhigwm *be*
single *adj* sengl *ans*
single action harp telyn arwaith sengl *eb* telynau arwaith sengl
Single Award Dyfarniad Sengl *eg*
single celled ungellog *ans*
single circle cylch sengl *eg* cylchoedd sengl
single cream hufen sengl *eg*
single currency arian sengl *eg*
single density dwysedd sengl *eg*
single digit multiples lluosrifau un-digid *ell*
single distribution dosbarthiad sengl *eg*
single European currency arian cyfred Ewropeaidd sengl *eg*
single faggot stitch pwyth ffagod sengl *eg* pwythau ffagod sengl
single gate-leg bwrdd coes gât sengl *eg* byrddau coes gât sengl
single layer chipboard bwrdd sglodion haen sengl *eg* byrddau sglodion haen sengl
single open-end spanner sbaner ceg agored sengl *eg* sbaneri ceg agored sengl
single parent rhiant sengl *eg* rhieni sengl
single quote dyfynnod sengl *eg* dyfynodau sengl
single roof to sengl *eg* toeon sengl
single section book llyfr un-darn *eg* llyfrau un-darn
single seeded unhadog *ans*
single seeded succulent fruit ffrwythyn suddlon unhadog *eg* ffrwythynnau suddlon unhadog
single set set sengl *eb* setiau sengl
single sex un rhyw *ans*
single sheet cynfas sengl *eb* cynfasau sengl
single spacing bylchiad sengl *ans*
single take-off esgyn untroed *be*
single thread edau sengl *eb* edafedd sengl
single tonguing tafodi sengl *be*
single tub machine peiriant twb sengl *eg* peiriannau twb sengl
single turning troad sengl *eg* troadau sengl
single weight pwysyn *eg* pwysynnau
single-blind study astudiaeth sengl-ddall *eb* astudiaethau sengl-ddall
single-breasted coat cot â chaead sengl *eb* cotiau â chaead sengl
single-coil lamp lamp coil sengl *eb* lampau coil sengl
single-cut file ffeil toriad sengl *eb* ffeiliau toriad sengl
single-lap tile teilsen lap sengl *eb* teils lap sengl
singles senglau *ell*
single-section un-darn *eg*
single-sheet dalen sengl *ans*
single-step camu *be*
single-subject research ymchwil un cyfrannwr *eg*
single-track untrac *ans*
single-valued unwerth *ans*
Singspiel Singspiel *eg* Singspiele
singular (e.g. matrix) hynod *ans*
singular matrix matrics hynod *eg*
singularity hynodyn *eg* hynodion
sinh sinh *eg*
sink *v* suddo *be*
sink (for absorbing water, energy etc) *n* suddfan *eg/b* suddfannau
sink (for washing) *n* sinc *eg* sinciau
sink hole llyncdwll *eg* llyncdyllau
sinking and matting punch pwnsh suddo a matio *eg* pynsiau suddo a matio
sinking fund cronfa ad-dalu *eb* cronfeydd ad-dalu
sinking hammer morthwyl suddo *eg* morthwylion suddo
sinking of the Lusitania suddo'r Lusitania *be*
sinter *n* sinter *eg*
sinter *v* sinteru *be*
sinuosity dolennedd *eb*
sinus sinws *eg* sinysau
sinusoid sinwsoid *eg*
sinusoidal sinwsoidaidd *ans*
sinusoidal alternating potential difference gwahaniaeth potensial eiledol sinwsoidaidd *eg*
sinusoidal waveform tonffurf sinwsoidaidd *eb*
siphon siffon *eg* siffonau
Sir (title of nobleman) Syr *eg*
sirocco siroco *eg* sirocos
sister (in nursing) prif weinyddes nyrsio *eb* prif weinyddesau nyrsio
Sistine Chapel Capel Sistin *eg*
sit (an examination) sefyll *be*
Sita Sita *eb*
sitar sitar *eg* sitarau
site safle *eg* safleoedd
site conditions cyflwr safle *eg*
site evaluation gwerthusiad safle *eg*
site evaluation procedure trefn o werthuso safle *eb*
site map map safle *eg* mapiau safle
site-specific safle-benodol *ans*
Sitka spruce pyrwydden Sitca *eb* pyrwydd Sitca
situation sefyllfa *eb* sefyllfaoedd

situation ethics moeseg sefyllfa *eb*
situational attribution priodoliad sefyllfaol
situational factor ffactor sefyllfa *eb* ffactorau sefyllfa
six chwech *eg* chwechau
Six Articles, The Chwe Erthygl, Y *eb*
six-figure grid references cyfeirnodau grid chwe-ffigur *ell*
sixteen yard hit-out ergyd gylch *eb* ergydion cylch
sixth chweched *eg* chwechedau
sixth form chweched dosbarth *eg*
sixth former disgybl chweched dosbarth *eg* disgyblion chweched dosbarth
sixth sense chweched synnwyr *eg*
sixth-form college coleg chweched dosbarth *eg* colegau chweched dosbarth
sixty-fourth-note nodyn chwe deg pedwar *eg* nodau chwe deg pedwar
sixway punch pwnsh chweffordd *eg* pynsiau chweffordd
size (=extent of a thing) *n* maint *eg* meintiau
size (=gelatinous solution) *n* seis *eg*
size (glue) *v* seisio *be*
skandha (=khandha) skandha *eg*
skating (canework) bonynnu *be*
skein sgein *eg* sgeiniau
skeletal ysgerbydol *ans*
skeletal system system ysgerbydol *eb* systemau ysgerbydol
skeletal traction hydyniad ar yr ysgerbwd *eg*
skeleton ysgerbwd *eg* ysgerbydau
skeleton framework bras fframwaith *eg*
skeleton score sgôr fras *eb* sgorau bras
skeleton weeds chwyn ysgerbwd *ell*
skerry sgeri *eg* sgerïau
sketch *v* braslunio *be*
sketch (=rough draft) *n* braslun *eg* brasluniau
sketch (of composition) *n* darlun *eg* darluniau
sketch block bloc cynllunio *eg* blociau cynllunio
sketch map llinfap *eg* llinfapiau
sketch of elevation braslun golwg *eg* brasluniau golwg
sketch of point of detail braslun pwynt manylyn *eg*
sketch pad pad braslunio *eg* padiau braslunio
sketch paper papur braslunio *eg* papurau braslunio
sketch plan braslun cynllunio *eg* brasluniau cynllunio
sketch section llindoriad *eg* llindoriadau
sketch-book llyfr braslunio *eg* llyfrau braslunio
sketching charcoal siarcol braslunio *eg*
sketching easel îsl braslunio *eg* islau braslunio
skew *adj* sgiw *ans*
skew *n* sgiw *eb* sgiwiau
skew chisel cŷn goledd *eg* cynion goledd; gaing oledd *eb* geingiau goledd
skew line llinell sgiw *eb* llinellau sgiw
skew mouth plane plaen ceg sgiw *eg* plaeniau ceg sgiw
skew nailing hoelio arosgo *be*
skewed distribution gwasgariad sgiw *eg* gwasgariadau sgiw
skewness sgiwedd *eg*
skilful medrus *ans*
skilful movement symud medrus *be*
skill sgìl *eg* sgiliau
skill mix cymysgedd o sgiliau *eb*
skilled medrus *ans*
skilled craftsman crefftwr medrus *eg* crefftwyr medrus
skilled labour llafur crefftus *eg*
skilled worker gweithiwr medrus *eg* gweithwyr medrus
skills in measuring sgiliau mesur *ell*
skills of water safety sgiliau diogelwch yn y dŵr *ell*
skim sgimio *be*
skimmer sgimiwr *eg* sgimwyr
skimming price pris hufennu *eg*
skin croen *eg* crwyn
skin care gofal croen *eg*
skin traction hydyniad ar y croen *eg*
skip *n* sgip *eb*
skip *v* sgipio *be*
skip jump naid sgip *eb* neidiau sgip
skip step step sgip *eb* stepiau sgip
skipped stitch pwyth coll *eg* pwythau coll
skipping dance dawns sgipio *eb* dawnsiau sgipio
skipping rope rhaff sgipio *eb* rhaffau sgipio
skirmish ysgarmes *eb* ysgarmesoedd
skirt sgert *eb* sgertiau
skirting sgyrtin *eg* sgyrtinau
skirting board bwrdd sgyrtin *eg* byrddau sgyrtin
skittle ceilysyn *eg* ceilys
skiver sgifer *eg*
skiving knife cyllell sgifio *eb* cyllyll sgifio
skua sgiwen *eb* sgiwennod
skull penglog *eg* penglogau
skunk drewgi *eg* drewgwn
sky blue (enamelling colour) glas y nen *eg*
skylight ffenestr do *eb* ffenestri to
slab slab *eg* slabiau
slab milling cutter melinwr slab *eg* melinwyr slab
slab pottery crochenwaith slab *eg*
slack *adj* llac *ans*
slack *v* llacio *be*
slack (=small coal) *n* glo mân *eg*
slack fit ffit lac *eb*
slack tide slac-lanw *eg*
slack variable newidyn llacrwydd *eg* newidynnau llacrwydd
slacken (ligament) llacio *be*
slackness llacrwydd *eg*
slag slag *eg*
slake (lime) slecio *be*
slaked lime calch tawdd *eg*
slalom slalom *eg*
slander *n* athrod *eg* athrodion

slander *v* athrodi *be*
slant *n* goledd *eg* goleddau
slant *v* goleddu *be*
slant edge ymyl oledd *eb* ymylon goledd
slant height uchder oledd *eg* uchderau goledd
slanting ar oledd *ans*
slash *n* slaes *eg* slaesau
slash *v* slaesu *be*
slash sawn tangiad llifiol *ans*
slat slat *eb* slatiau
slate (for roofing, writing) llechen *eb* llechi
slate (rock) llechfaen *eg* llechfeini
slate nail hoelen lechen *eb* hoelion llechi
slave caethwas *eg* caethweision
slave trade masnach gaethion *eb*
slavery caethwasiaeth *eb*
sledge hammer gordd *eb* gyrdd
sleep apnoea apnoea cwsg *eg*
sleep wall wal gynnal *eb* waliau cynnal
sleeper effect effaith gwsg *eb*
sleeping-bag sach gysgu *eb* sachau cysgu
sleeptalking siarad yn eich cwsg *be*
sleepwalking cerdded yn eich cwsg *be*
sleet eirlaw *eg*
sleeve llawes *eb* llewys
sleeve board bwrdd llawes *eg* byrddau llewys
sleeveless dilawes *ans*
sleigh bells clychau car llusg *ell*
slice sleis *eb* sleisiau
slice *n* tafell *eb* tafellau
slice *v* tafellu *be*
slicing action arwaith tafellu *eg*
slick bit ebill slic *eg* ebillion slic
slickensides llyfnochrau *ell*
slide *adj* llithr *ans*
slide *v* llithro *be*
slide (for microscope) *n* sleid *eb* sleidiau
slide (for projector) *n* tryloywder *eg* tryloywderau
slide (in music) *n* llithryn *eg* llithrynnau
slide (in playground) llithren *eb* llithrennau
slide rest rest llithr *eg* restiau llithr
slide rule llithriwl *eb* llithriwliau
slide sequence dilyniant sleidiau *eg* dilyniannau sleidiau
slide valve falf lithr *eb* falfiau llithr
slide-frame transition trosi rhwng fframiau *be*
slider llithrydd *eg* llithryddion
sliding llithr *ans*
sliding action arwaith llithr *eg* arweithiau llithr
sliding bevel befel llithr *eg* befelau llithr
sliding block bloc llithr *eg* blociau llithr
sliding component cydran lithr *eb* cydrannau llithr
sliding door drws llithro *eg* drysau llithro
sliding feed porthiant llithr *eg*
sliding fence ffens lithr *eb* ffensys llithr
sliding fit (transition fit) ffit lithr *eb* ffitiau llithr
sliding friction ffrithiant llithro *eg*
sliding jaw safn lithr *eb* safnau llithr
sliding key allwedd lithr *eb* allweddi llithr
sliding scale graddfa symudol *eb* graddfeydd symudol
sliding seat sedd lithro *eb* seddi llithro
sliding tackle tacl lithriad *eb* taclau llithriad
sliding top (table) top llithr *eg* topiau llithr
sliding-door lock clo drws llithr *eg* cloeon drysau llithro
slight (a castle) dinistrio *be*
slim main *ans*
slim knife cyllell fain *eb* cyllyll main
slime llysnafedd *eg* llysnafeddau
slime fungi ffyngau llysnafedd *ell*
sling (for shooting) ffon dafl *eb* ffyn tafl
sling (for supporting arm etc) sling *eg* slingiau
slip (=mistake, slide) *n* llithriad *eg* llithriadau
slip (=petticoat) *n* pais *eb* peisiau
slip (in carpentry) *n* cryfhawr *eg* cryfhawyr
slip (of cricket fielder) *n* slip *eg* slipwyr
slip (of cricket position) *n* slip *eg* slipiau
slip (pottery) *n* slip *eg*
slip (the ball) *v* slipio *be*
slip casting castin slip *eg*
slip clay clai slip *eg*
slip gauge medrydd slip *eg* medryddion slip
slip hemming hemio slip *be*
slip hemming stitch pwyth hemio slip *eg* pwythau hemio slip
slip plane plân slip *eg* planau slip
slip road slipffordd *eb* slipffyrdd
slip stain staen slip *eg*
slip tracer dargopïwr slip *eg* dargopïwyr slip
slip tracing llwybro slip *be*
slip ware crochenwaith slip *eg*
slip-off slope llethr slip *eg* llethrau slip
slippery llithrig *ans*
slip-step *n* cam llithro *eg* camau llithro
slip-step *v* llithro *be*
slip-step in a circle cam llithro mewn cylch *eg* camau llithro mewn cylch
slip-stepping clockwise llithro gyda'r cloc *be*
slipway llithrfa *eb* llithrfeydd
slit agen *eb* agennau
slitting agennu *be*
slitting saw llif agennu *eb* llifiau agennu
slocombe drill dril canoli *eg* driliau canoli
slogan slogan *eg* sloganau
slope *v* goleddu *be*
slope (=inclined position or direction) *n* goledd *eg* goleddau
slope (=measure of gradient) *n* graddiant *eg* graddiannau
slope (=piece of rising or falling ground) *n* llethr *eg/b* llethrau
slope of line goledd llinell *eg*
sloping face wyneb goleddol *eg* wynebau goleddol
sloping haunch hansh ar oledd *eg* hanshys ar oledd

slot (=slit) agen *eb* agennau
slot (in general) slot *eg* slotiau
slot (of screwhead etc) rhych *eb* rhychau
slot screwing rhych sgriwio *be*
slotted agennog *ans*
slotted link dolen rych *eb* dolennau rhych
slotted nut nyten rych *eb* nytiau rhych
slotting drill dril rhychio *eg* driliau rhychio
slotting milling cutter melinwr agennu *be* melinwyr agennu
slotting saw llif agennu *eb* llifiau agennu
slough cen *eg*
slow araf *ans*
slow ball pêl araf *eb* peli araf
slow bowler bowliwr araf *eg* bowlwyr araf
slow bowling bowlio araf *be*
slow casserole caserol araf *eg* caserolau araf
slow down arafu *be*
slow left arm bowler bowliwr araf braich chwith *eg* bowlwyr araf braich chwith
slow motion (in films) arafu lluniau *be*
slow run rhedeg araf *be*
slow-wave sleep cwsg tonfedd araf *eg*
slub yarn edafedd slyb *ell*
sludging (=solifluction) priddlif *eg* priddlifau
slug (in mathematics) slyg *eg* slygiau
slug (of mollusc) gwlithen *eb* gwlithod
sluice lle golchi *eg* llefydd golchi
slum slym *eg* slymiau
slum clearance clirio slymiau *be*
slump dirwasgiad *eg*
slump (land) cylchlithriad *eg*
slumped cliff clogwyn cylchlithriad *eg* clogwyni cylchlithriad
slumping cylchlithro *be*
slur *n* llithriad *eg* llithriadau
slur *v* llithro *be*
slush enamel enamel llaid *eg*
slype tramwyfa *eb* tramwyfeydd
small circle cylch bychan *eg* cylchoedd bychain
small claims court llys mân ddyledion *eg*
small court cwrt bychan *eg*
small holding mân ddaliad *eg* mân ddaliadau
small intestine coluddyn bach *eg* coluddion bach
small letter llythyren fach *eb* llythrennau bach
small scale production cynhyrchu ar raddfa fach *be*
small world play chwarae byd bach *eg*
smaller-scale map map graddfa lai *eg* mapiau graddfa lai
small-scale graddfa fach *eb*
smallholding tyddyn *eg* tyddynnod
small-n design cynllun n-fechan *eg* cynlluniau n-fechan
smallpox y frech wen *eb*
small-sided game gêm timau bach *eb* gemau timau bach
smart smart *ans*
smart materials defnyddiau clyfar *ell*
smash ergyd galed *eb* ergydion caled
smash shot pwyad *eg* pwyadau
smear iriad *eg* iriadau
smell arogl *eg* aroglau
smelt mwyndoddi *be*
smelter ffwrnais fwyndoddi *eb* ffwrneisi mwyndoddi
smock *n* smoc *eb* smociau
smock *v* crychu *be*
smocking smocwaith *eg*
smocking transfer trosglwyddyn smocwaith *eg* trosglwyddynnau smocwaith
smog mwrllwch *eg*
smoke *n* mwg *eg*
smoke *v* ysmygu *be*
smoke controlled area rhanbarth rheoli mwg *eg* rhanbarthau rheoli mwg
smoked bacon cig moch wedi'i gochi *eg*
smokeless fuel tanwydd di-fwg *eg*
smoking (cigarettes, pipe) ysmygu *be*
smoking (of fire etc) yn mygu *adf*
smooth *adj* llyfn *ans*
smooth *v* llyfnu *be*
smooth curve cromlin lefn *eb* cromliniau llyfn
smooth cut file ffeil lefn *eb* ffeiliau llyfn
smooth finish gorffeniad llyfn *eg* gorffeniadau llyfn
smooth muscle cyhyr anrhesog *eg* cyhyrau anrhesog
smooth surface arwyneb llyfn *eg* arwynebau llyfn
smooth texture gwead llyfn *eg*
smoothing capacitor cynhwysydd llyfnhau *eg*
smoothing plane plaen llyfnhau *eg* plaeniau llyfnhau
smother mygu *be*
smother tackle tacl goflaid *eb* taclau coflaid
smudge smwtsio *be*
smut penddu *eg*
smutted wheat gwenith penddu *eg*
snack bar bar byrbryd *eg* barrau byrbryd
snail bit ebill gwrthsoddi malwen *eg* ebillion gwrthsoddi malwen
snail's trail pattern patrwm ôl y falwen *eg* patrymau ôl y falwen
snake bite brathiad neidr *eg* brathiadau neidr
snap snap *eg* snapiau
snap (string) torri *be*
snap (to grid) clecian *be*
snap fastener ffasnydd snap *eg* ffasnyddion snap
snap grid grid snap *eg* gridiau snap
snap line llinell snap *eb* llinellau snap
snap lines visible dangos llinellau snap *be*
snap point pwynt snap *eg* pwyntiau snap
snap position safle snap *eg* safleoedd snap
snap range ystod snap *eb* ystodau snap
snap riveting rhybedu snap *be*
snap to grid snapio i'r grid *be*
snap-head rivet rhybed pengrwn *eg* rhybedion pengrwn
snaplink (Karabiner) clesbyn *eg* clasbiau

snare drum drwm gwifrau *eg* drymiau gwifrau
snarling (=tangle) cafflo *be*
snarling iron haearn cafflo *eg* heyrn cafflo
snatch cipio *be*
sneeze tisian *be*
sniff (glue etc) arogli *be*
snip snip *eg* snipiau
snipping snipio *be*
snips snipiwr *eg* snipwyr
snow bridge pont eira *eb* pontydd eira
snow drift lluwch eira *eg* lluwchfeydd eira
snow fed river afon eira tawdd *eb* afonydd eira tawdd
snow glasses sbectol eira *eb* sbectolau eira
snow goose gŵydd yr eira *eb* gwyddau yr eira
snow line eirlin *eg* eirlinau
snowfield maes eira *eg* meysydd eira
snowy owl tylluan yr eira *eb* tylluanod yr eira
soak (dried food etc) mwydo *be*
soakaway suddfan dŵr *eg* suddfannau dŵr
soaked peas pys wedi'u mwydo *ell*
soaker darn gwrthddwr *eg* darnau gwrthddwr
soap sebon *eg* sebonau
soap flakes fflochion sebon *ell*
soap opera opera sebon *eb* operâu sebon
soap powder powdr golchi *eg*
soaped pad pad sebon *eg* padiau sebon
soapless disebon *ans*
soapless detergent glanedydd disebon *eg* glanedyddion disebon
soapy sebonllyd *ans*
soapy water dŵr sebon *eg*
socage socaeth *eb*
socalization cymdeithasoliad *eg*
soccer shirt crys pêl-droed *eg* crysau pêl-droed
sociability cymdeithasgarwch *eg*
social cymdeithasol *ans*
social and economic factors affecting health ffactorau cymdeithasol ac economaidd sy'n effeithio ar iechyd *ell*
social area analysis dadansoddiad ardaloedd cymdeithasol *eg*
social assessment asesiad cymdeithasol *eg* asesiadau cymdeithasol
social benefit budd cymdeithasol *eg*
social buffering hypothesis rhagdybiaeth byffro cymdeithasol *eb*
social care gofal cymdeithasol *eg*
social class dosbarth cymdeithasol *eg* dosbarthiadau cymdeithasol
social cognition gwybyddiaeth gymdeithasol *eb*
social comparison cymhariaeth gymdeithasol *eb*
social constructivist adeileddwr cymdeithasol *eg*
social cost cost gymdeithasol *eb*
Social Democrat Sosialydd Democrataidd *eg* Sosialwyr Democrataidd
social democrat *adj* democrataidd cymdeithasol *ans*
social democrat *n* democrat cymdeithasol *eg* democratiaid cymdeithasol
Social Democratic Party (SDP) Plaid y Democratiaid Cymdeithasol *eb*
social desirability dymunolrwydd cymdeithasol *eg*
social development datblygiad cymdeithasol *eg*
social economic group grŵp economaidd cymdeithasol *eg*
social engineering teilwrio cymdeithasol *be*
social exclusion all-gau cymdeithasol *be*
social facilitation hwyluso cymdeithasol *be*
social factor ffactor gymdeithasol *eb* ffactorau cymdeithasol
social history hanes cymdeithasol *eg*
social identity hunaniaeth gymdeithasol *eb*
social impact effaith gymdeithasol *eb* effeithiau cymdeithasol
social implications arwyddocâd cymdeithasol *eg*
social judgeability gallu barnu cymdeithasol *be*
social learning theory damcaniaeth dysgu cymdeithasol *eb*
social loafing diogi cymdeithasol *eg*
social model model cymdeithasol *eg*
social norm norm cymdeithasol *eg* normau cymdeithasol
social order trefn cymdeithas *eb*
social organization cyfundrefn gymdeithasol *eb*
social phobia ffobia cymdeithasol *eg*
social policy polisi cymdeithasol *eg* polisïau cymdeithasol
social policy development datblygiad polisi cymdeithasol *eg*
social practice arfer cymdeithasol *eg* arferion cymdeithasol
social pressures pwysau cymdeithasol *ell*
social psychology seicoleg gymdeithasol *eb*
social referencing cyfeirio cymdeithasol *be*
social reform diwygio cymdeithasol *be*
social relationship perthynas gymdeithasol *eb*
social representation cynrychiolaeth gymdeithasol *eb*
social role valorization rhoi gwerth ar swyddogaeth gymdeithasol *be*
social security nawdd cymdeithasol *eg*
social services gwasanaethau cymdeithasol *ell*
social services department adran gwasanaethau cymdeithasol *eb* adrannau gwasanaethau cymdeithasol
social skill sgil cymdeithasol *eg* sgiliau cymdeithasol
social skills sgiliau cymdeithasol *ell*
social skills training hyfforddi sgiliau cymdeithasol *be*
social space gofod cymdeithasol *eg* gofodau cymdeithasol
social status statws cymdeithasol *eg*
social structure strwythur cymdeithasol *eg*
social studies astudiaethau cymdeithasol *ell*
social support cefnogaeth gymdeithasol *eb*
social trend tuedd gymdeithasol *eb* tueddiadau cymdeithasol
social unrest aflonyddwch cymdeithasol *eg*

social welfare lles cymdeithasol *eg*
social withdrawal encilio cymdeithasol *be*
social work gwaith cymdeithasol *eg*
social worker gweithiwr cymdeithasol *eg* gweithwyr cymdeithasol
socialism sosialaeth *eb*
socialist *adj* sosialaidd *ans*
socialist *n* sosialydd *eg* sosialwyr
Socialist Party Plaid Sosialaidd *eb*
socialization cymdeithasoli *be*
socially clean cymdeithasol lân *ans*
society cymdeithas *eb* cymdeithasau
Society of Christ Cymdeithas yr Iesu *eb*
Society of Friends Cymdeithas y Cyfeillion *eb*
sociobiology bioleg gymdeithasol *eb*
socio-cultural impact effaith ddiwylliannol gymdeithasol *eb* effeithiau diwylliannol cymdeithasol
socio-dramatic play chwarae dramatig-gymdeithasol *eg*
socio-economic economaidd gymdeithasol *ans*
socio-economic status statws cymdeithasol-economaidd *eg*
sociolinguistics ieithyddiaeth gymdeithasegol *eb*
sociology cymdeithaseg *eb*
sociology of childhood cymdeithaseg plentyndod *eb*
sociology of education cymdeithaseg addysg *eb*
sock hosan fer *eb* sanau byr
socket (electrical etc) soced *eg/b* socedi
socket (of eye) twll *eg* tyllau
socket (of joint) crau *eg* creuau
socket screw sgriw soced *eb* sgriwiau soced
socket spanner sbaner soced *eg* sbaneri soced
socketed axe bwyell greuog *eb* bwyeill creuog
socketed sickle cryman creuog *eg* crymanau creuog
soda soda *eg*
soda (washing soda) soda golchi *eg*
soda lime (as reagent) calch soda *eb*
sodium (Na) sodiwm *eg*
sodium aluminate sodiwm alwminad *eg*
sodium azide sodiwm asid *eg*
sodium bicarbonate sodiwm deucarbonad *eg*
sodium carbonate sodiwm carbonad *eg*
sodium chloride sodiwm clorid *eg*
sodium ethoxide sodiwm ethocsid *eg*
sodium hexafluoroaluminate(III) (cryolite) sodiwm hecsafflworoalwminad(III) (cryolit) *eg*
sodium hydroxide sodiwm hydrocsid *eg*
sodium hydroxide solution hydoddiant sodiwm hydrocsid *eg*
sodium ion ïon sodiwm *eg* ïonau sodiwm
sodium lauryl sulphonate sodiwm lawryl sylffonad *eg*
sodium phenoxide sodiwm ffenocsid *eg*
sodium thiosulphate solution hydoddiant sodiwm thiosylffad *eg*
soffit bondo *eg* bondoeau
soffit bearer cynheiliad bondo *eg* cynheiliaid bondo
soffit board astell fondo *eg* estyll bondo
soft meddal *ans*
soft board plane plaen meddalfwrdd *eg* plaeniau meddalfwrdd
soft cloth cadach meddal *eg* cadachau meddal
soft consistency ansawdd meddal *eg*
soft copy copi meddal *eg* copïau meddal
soft drug cyffur ysgafn *eg* cyffuriau ysgafn
soft flour blawd meddal *eg*
soft furnishings dodrefn meddal *ell*
soft ground etching ysgythru ar rwnd meddal *be*
soft hair brush brwsh blew meddal *eg* brwshys blew meddal
soft hammer morthwyl meddal *eg* morthwylion meddal
soft head pen meddal *eg* pennau meddal
soft iron core craidd haearn meddal *eg*
soft iron keeper cadwrydd haearn meddal *eg* cadwryddion haearn meddal
soft landscaping tirlunio meddal *be*
soft option dewis hawdd *eg* dewisiadau hawdd
soft pedal pedal chwith *eg* pedalau chwith
soft pleating pletio ysgafn *be*
soft sectored sectoriad meddal *eg*
soft soap sebon meddal *eg*
soft solder sodr meddal *eg*
soft soldering sodro meddal *be*
soft table bwrdd meddal *eg* byrddau meddal
soft texture gwead meddal *eg*
soft tissue meinwe feddal *eb* meinweoedd meddal
soft touch cyffyrddiad ysgafn *eg* cyffyrddiadau ysgafn
soft toy tegan meddal *eg* teganau meddal
soften meddalu *be*
softener meddalydd *eg* meddalyddion
softness meddalwch *eg*
software meddalwedd *eg/b*
software engineer peiriannydd meddalwedd *eg* peirianwyr meddalwedd
software house tŷ meddalwedd *eg* tai meddalwedd
software protection diogelwch meddalwedd *eg*
software update diweddariad meddalwedd *eg* diweddariadau meddalwedd
softwood pren meddal *eg* prennau meddal
softwood cell cell pren meddal *eb* celloedd pren meddal
softwood wedging lletemu pren meddal *be*
soil (=dirt) baw *eg*
soil (=earth) pridd *eg* priddoedd
soil creep ymgripiad pridd *eg*
soil erosion erydiad pridd *eg*
soil fertility ffrwythlondeb pridd *eg*
soil horizon haenlin pridd *eb* haenlinau pridd
soil micro-organisms micro-organebau'r pridd *ell*
soil profile proffil pridd *eg*
soil structure adeiledd pridd *eg*
soil suspending agent cyfrwng dal baw *eg*
soil texture gwead pridd *eg*

soil type math o bridd *eg*
soiled wedi baeddu *ans*
solar (central heating system) solar *ans*
solar activity gweithgaredd yr haul *eg*
solar day diwrnod haul *eg*
solar eclipse diffyg ar yr haul *eg*
solar energy egni solar *eg*
solar eruption echdoriad yr haul *eg* echdoriadau'r haul
solar heating gwres solar *eg*
solar radiation pelydriad heulog *eg*
solar system cysawd yr haul *eg* cysodau yr haul
solar time amser yr haul *eg*
solar year blwyddyn haul *eb* blynyddoedd haul
solder *n* sodr *eg* sodrau
solder *v* sodro *be*
solder and braze sodro a phresyddu
solder panel panel sodr *eg* paneli sodr
soldered sodrog *ans*
soldering bench mainc sodro *eb* meinciau sodro
soldering bit haearn sodro *eg* heyrn sodro
soldering iron haearn sodro *eg* heyrn sodro
soldering process proses sodro *eb*
sole gwadn *eg* gwadnau
sole of the foot gwadn troed *eg* gwadnau traed
sole trader unig fasnachwr *eg*
Solemn League & Covenant Cynghrair Sanctaidd a Chyfamod *eb*
solenoid solenoid *eg* solenoidau
soleplate (of iron) platwadn *eg* platwadnau
sol-fa *v* solffeuo *be*
sol-fa hand sign arwydd llaw sol-ffa *eg* arwyddion llaw sol-ffa
sol-faist (female) solffeuwraig *eb* solffeuwragedd
sol-faist (male and general) solffeuwr *eg* solffeuwyr
solfatara solffatara *eg* solffatarau
solicitor cyfreithiwr *eg* cyfreithwyr
Solicitor General Cyfreithiwr Cyffredinol *eg*
Solicitors Act 1971 Deddf y Twrneiod 1971 *eb*
solid *adj* solet *ans*
solid *n* solid *eg* solidau
solid auger bit ebill taradr solet *eg* ebillion taradr solet
solid cleated door drws cleddog solet *eg* drysau cleddog solet
solid drawn hinge colfach solet *eg* colfachau solet
solid figure ffigur solet *eg* ffigurau solet
solid floor llawr solet *eg* lloriau solet
solid fuel tanwydd solet *eg*
solid moulding mowldin solet *eg*
solid of revolution solid cylchdro *eg* solidau cylchdro
solid panel panel solet *eg* paneli solet
solid state cyflwr solet *eg*
solid strut cynheiliad solet *eg* cynheiliaid solet
solid strutting cynheilio solet *be*
solid timber pren solet *eg*
solid wall wal solet *eb* waliau solet
solid wood pren solet *eg*
solid wood door drws pren solet *eg* drysau pren solet
solidarity cydlyniad *eg*
Solidarity (movement) Mudiad Solidarność *eg*
solidification solidiad *eg* solidiadau
solidify (in physics etc) ymsolido *be*
solidify (non-technical usage) caledu *be*
solidity (in chemistry etc) solidedd *eg*
solidity (of argument etc) cadernid *eg*
solifluction priddlif *eg* priddlifau
solitary play chwarae unigol *eg*
solo unawd *eb* unawdau
solo instrument offeryn unawd *eg* offerynnau unawd
solo organ organ solo *eb* organau solo
solo stop stop solo *eg* stopiau solo
soloist unawdydd *eg* unawdwyr
solonchak solontshac *eg*
solonetz solonets *eg*
solstice heuldro *eg* heuldroadau
solubility hydoddedd *eg* hydoddeddau
solubility product constant cysonyn lluoswm hydoddedd *eg*
soluble hydawdd *ans*
soluble in water hydawdd mewn dŵr *ans*
soluble oil olew hydawdd *eg*
soluble varnish farnais hydawdd *eg*
solute hydoddyn *eg* hydoddion
solution (=answer) ateb *eg* atebion
solution (=solving) datrysiad *eg* datrysiadau
solution (of dissolved state) hydoddiant *eg* hydoddiannau
solution of salts hydoddiant halwynau *eg* hydoddiannau halwynau
solution set set ddatrysiad *eb* setiau datrysiad
solvated hydoddedig *ans*
solvation hydoddiant *eg*
solve datrys *be*
solve a problem datrys problem *be*
solve the equation datrys yr hafaliad *be*
solvency hyfywedd *eg*
solvent hydoddydd *eg* hydoddyddion
solvent abuse camddefnyddio hydoddyddion *eg*
solvent extraction echdyniad â hydoddydd *eg*
solvent front ffin hydoddydd *eb* ffiniau hydoddyddion
solvent sniffing arogli hydoddyddion *be*
soma soma *eg*
somatic somatig *ans*
somatic marker hypothesis rhagdybiaeth marciwr somatig *eb*
somatic mutation mwtaniad somatig *eg* mwtaniadau somatig
somatoform disorder anhwylder somatoffurf *eg*
somatosense synnwyr corfforol *eg*
somatotype somatoteip *eg*
sombre tywyll *ans*

sombre atmosphere awyrgylch prudd *eg*
somersault *n* trosben *eg* trosbennau
somersault *v* trosbennu *be*
somersault dive deif drosben *eb* deifiau trosben
son tape merch-dâp *eg* merchdapiau
sonarized sonaredig *ans*
sonata sonata *eb* sonatau
sonata form ffurf sonata *eb*
sonata rondo rondo sonata *eb* rondoau sonata
sonatina sonatina *eb* sonatinau
song cân *eb* caneuon
sonnenseite (=adret) llygad haul *eg*
sonometer sainfesurydd *eg* sainfesuryddion
sonority seinlawnder *eg* seinlawnderau
sonorous soniarus *ans*
soothe lleddfu *be*
sophistication soffistigeiddrwydd *eg*
soprano soprano *eb* lleisiau soprano
sorbite sorbit *eg*
sore briw *eg* briwiau
sore throat dolur gwddf *eg*
soroche salwch mynydd *eg*
sort *n* trefniad *eg* trefniadau
sort (=arrange) *v* trefnu *be*
sort (=separate) *v* didoli *be*
sort ascending trefniad esgynnol *eg* trefniadau esgynnol
sort descending trefniad disgynnol *eg* trefniadau disgynnol
sort in alphabetical order gosod yn nhrefn y wyddor
sorted trefnedig *ans*
sough lefel *eb* lefelau
sound (=dive) *v* plymio *be*
sound (=noise) *n* sŵn *eg* synau
sound (=passage of water) *n* swnt *eg* swntiau
sound (musical) *n* sain *eb* seiniau
sound board seinfwrdd *eg* seinfyrddau
sound box seinflwch *eg* seinflychau
sound card cerdyn sain *eg* cardiau sain
sound collage collage o seiniau *eg*
sound effects effeithiau sain *ell*
sound generator generadur sain *eg* generaduron sain
sound hole seindwll *eg* seindyllau
sound insulation ynysu rhag sŵn *be*
sound judgment barn gadarn *eb*
sound level meter mesurydd lefelau sain *eg*
sound path llwybr sain *eg* llwybrau sain
sound picture seinlun *eg* seinluniau
sound player chwaraeydd sain *eg* chwaraewyr sain
sound processing prosesu sain *be*
sound source ffynhonnell sain *eb* ffynonellau sain
sound table bwrdd sain *eg* byrddau sain
sound wave seindon *eb* seindonnau
soundbite sylw bachog *eg*
soundcard cerdyn sain *eg* cardiau sain
soundproof gwrthsain *ans*
soundtrack trac sain *eg* traciau sain
source (in general) ffynhonnell *eb* ffynonellau
source (of specific point) tarddle *eg* tarddleoedd
source (of stream etc) tarddiad *eg* tarddiadau
source code cod ffynhonnell *eg* codau ffynhonnell
source colour lliw ffynhonnell *eg* lliwiau ffynhonnell
source directory cyfeiriadur ffynhonnell *eg* cyfeiriaduron ffynhonnell
source disk disg ffynhonnell *eg* disgiau ffynhonnell
source document dogfen ffynhonnell *eb* dogfennau ffynhonnell
source drive gyrriant ffynhonnell *eg* gyriannau ffynhonnell
source file ffeil ffynhonnell *eb* ffeiliau ffynhonnell
source language iaith ffynhonnell *eb* ieithoedd ffynhonnell
source of authority ffynhonnell awdurdod *eb*
source of light tarddiad goleuni *eg*
source of variation tarddle amrywiant *eb* tarddleoedd amrywiannau
source program rhaglen ffynhonnell *eb* rhaglenni ffynhonnell
sources of finance ffynonellau cyllid *ell*
south de *eg*
south celestial pole pegwn wybrennol y de *eg*
south magnetic pole pôl magnetig y de *eg*
south pole (of a magnet) pôl de *eg*
South Sea Bubble Swigen Môr y De *eb*
south seeking pole (of a magnet) pôl sy'n cyrchu tua'r de *eg*
South Wales Miner's Federation Ffederasiwn Glowyr De Cymru *eg*
southing deheuad *eg*
sovereign (=gold coin) sofren *eb* sofrenni
sovereign (=supreme ruler) sofran *eg* sofraniaid
sovereign state gwladwriaeth sofran *eb* gwladwriaethau sofran
sovereignty sofraniaeth *eb* sofraniaethau
sovereignty homage gwrogaeth sofraniaeth *eb*
sovereignty of the people sofraniaeth y bobl *eb*
sovlet sofiet *eg* sofietau
soviet montage montage sofiet *eg*
soya beans ffa soia *ell*
spa sba *eg* sbâu
space *v* bylchu *be*
space (=empty place) lle gwag *eg* lleoedd gwag
space (=gap) bwlch *eg* bylchau
space (around a person, beyond Earth's atmosphere) gofod *eg*
space (between cells etc) gwaglyn *eg* gwaglynnau
space awareness ymwybyddiaeth ofodol *eb*
space bar bylchwr *eg* bylchwyr
space domain parth gofod *eg* parthau gofod
space shuttle gwennol ofod *eb* gwenoliaid gofod
spaced warp ystof wahanedig *eb* ystofau gwahanedig
space-filling model model llenwi-gofod *eg*

spaceman gofodwr *eg* gofodwyr
spacer gwahanydd *eg* gwahanyddion
space-saving table bwrdd arbed lle *eg* byrddau arbed lle
space-time gofod-amser *eg*
spacing bylchiad *eg* bylchiadau
spadix sbadics *eg*
spalt rhigol *eb* rhigolau
spam *n* sbam *eg*
spam *v* sbamio *be*
spam filter hidlydd sbam *eg*
span *n* rhychwant *eg* rhychwantau
span *v* rhychwantu *be*
span of control rhychwant rheoli *eg*
Spanish Fury Cynddaredd y Sbaenwyr *eb*
Spanish Inquisition Chwilys Sbaen *eg*
Spanish Main Môr Sbaenaidd *eg*
Spanish ulcer aflwydd Sbaenaidd, yr *eg*
spanner sbaner *eg* sbaneri
spanning pontio *be*
spare blade llafn sbâr *eg* llafnau sbâr
spark *n* gwreichionen *eb* gwreichion
spark *v* gwreichioni *be*
spark test prawf gwreichionen *eg*
sparking plug plwg tanio *eg* plygiau tanio
sparkling pefriol *ans*
sparring sbarian *be*
sparring partner partner sbarian *eg* partneriaid sbarian
sparrowhawk gwalch glas *eg* gweilch glas
spars (common rafters) ceibrennau cyffredin *ell*
sparse gwasgarog *ans*
Spartacist revolt gwrthryfel y Spartaciaid *eg*
spastic child plentyn sbastig *eg* plant sbastig
spate llifeiriant *eg* llifeiriaint
spathe fflurwain *eb* fflurweiniau
spatial gofodol *ans*
spatial ability gallu gofodol *eg*
spatial configuration ffurfwedd ofodol *eb* ffurfweddau gofodol
spatial context cyd-destun gofodol *eg*
spatial data data gofodol *ell*
spatial distribution dosbarthiad gofodol *eg*
spatial feature nodwedd ofodol *eb* nodweddion gofodol
spatial margins ymylon gofodol *ell*
spatial neglect diystyru gofodol *be*
spatial organisation trefnu gofod *be*
spatial orientation cyfeiriadaeth ofodol *eb*
spatial puzzle pos gofodol *eg* posau gofodol
spatial reasoning rhesymu gofodol *be*
spatial relationship cydberthynas ofodol *eb* cydberthnasau gofodol
spatula sbatwla *eg* sbatwlâu
spawn *v* silio *be*
spawn (of fish etc) *n* sil *eg* silod
spawn (of frogs) *n* grifft *eg*
spawning area silfa *eb* silfeydd
speaker (=sound unit) seinydd *eg* seinyddion
speaker (at a conference etc) siaradwr *eg* siaradwyr
speaker (of House of Commons) llefarydd *eg* llefarwyr
speaker key cwgn sain *eg* cygnau sain
spear *n* gwaywffon *eb* gwaywffyn
spear *v* trywanu *be*
Spearman rank correlation coefficient cyfernod cydberthyniad rhestrol Spearman *eg*
Special Areas Act Deddf yr Ardaloedd Arbennig *eb*
special care baby unit uned gofal arbennig i fabanod *eb* unedau gofal arbennig i fabanod
special care unit uned gofal arbennig *eb* unedau gofal arbennig
special development area ardal ddatblygu arbennig *eb* ardaloedd datblygu arbennig
special diet deiet arbennig *eg*
special education addysg arbennig *eb*
special educational needs anghenion addysgol arbennig *ell*
special effect effaith arbennig *eb* effeithiau arbennig
special grant grant arbennig *eg* grantiau arbennig
special juror rheithiwr arbennig *eg* rheithwyr arbennig
special needs anghenion arbennig *ell*
special needs support service gwasanaeth cefnogi anghenion arbennig *eg* gwasanaethau cefnogi anghenion arbennig
special school ysgol arbennig *eb* ysgolion arbennig
special support assistant cynorthwyydd cefnogaeth arbennig *eg* cynorthwywyr cefnogaeth arbennig
special unit uned arbennig *eb* unedau arbennig
specialised equipment offer arbenigol *ell*
specialism arbenigedd *eg*
specialist arbenigwr *eg* arbenigwyr
specialist care worker gweithiwr gofal arbenigol *eg* gweithwyr gofal arbenigol
specialist magazine cylchgrawn arbenigol *eg* cylchgronau arbenigol
specialist shop siop arbenigol *eb* siopau arbenigol
speciality arbenigedd *eg* arbenigeddau
specialization arbenigaeth *eb* arbenigaethau
specialize arbenigo *be*
specialized arbenigol *ans*
speciation ffurfiant rhywogaethau *eg*
specie arian bath *eg*
species rhywogaeth *eb* rhywogaethau
species of bacteria rhywogaeth o facteria *eb*
speciesism rhywogaethiaeth *eg*
species-typical behaviour ymddygiad rhywogaeth-nodweddiadol *eg*
specific (=definite, particular etc) penodol *ans*
specific (=per unit mass) sbesiffig *ans*
specific dynamic action gweithred ddynamig benodol *eb*
specific factor ffactor benodol *eb* ffactorau penodol

specific heat capacity cynhwysedd gwres sbesiffig *eg* cynwyseddau gwres sbesiffig
specific language impairment nam ieithyddol penodol *eg*
specific learning difficulty anhawster dysgu penodol *eg* anawsterau dysgu penodol
specific material defnydd penodol *eg* defnyddiau penodol
specific memory cof penodol *eg*
specific performance cyflwyniad penodol *eg*
specific phobia ffobia penodol *eg*
specification manyleb *eb* manylebau
specification grid grid manyleb *eg* gridiau manyleb
specification language iaith manyleb *eb*
specificity (enzyme) penodolrwydd *eg*
specify enwi *be*
specify location pennu lleoliad *be*
specimen sbesimen *eg* sbesimenau
speckle *n* brychni *eg*
speckle *v* brychu *be*
spectator gwyliwr *eg* gwylwyr
spectator ion ïon segur *eg* ïonau segur
spectral sbectrol *ans*
spectrometer sbectromedr *eg* sbectromedrau
spectrometry sbectromedreg *eb*
spectrophotometer sbectroffotomedr *eg* sbectroffotomedrau
spectroscope sbectrosgop *eg* sbectrosgopau
spectroscopic sbectrosgopig *ans*
spectroscopic technique techneg sbectrosgopig *eb* technegau sbectrosgopig
spectroscopy sbectrosgopeg *eb*
spectrum sbectrwm *eg* sbectra
spectrum palette palet sbectrwm *eg* paletau sbectrwm
speculate (in finance) hapfasnachu *be*
speculation (in finance) hapfasnach *eb*
speculative (in finance) hapfasnachol *ans*
speculator (in finance) hapfasnachwr *eg* hapfasnachwyr
speech (=faculty of speaking) lleferydd *eg*
speech (=oration) araith *eb* areithiau
speech act gweithred siarad *eb*
speech and language therapy therapi lleferydd ac iaith *eg*
speech development datblygu'r gallu i siarad *be*
speech difficulty anhawster llefaru *eg* anawsterau llefaru
speech impediment nam ar y lleferydd *eg* namau ar y lleferydd
speech recognition adnabod lleferydd *be*
speech synthesis synthesis lleferydd *eg*
speech therapist therapydd lleferydd *eg* therapyddion lleferydd
speech therapy therapi lleferydd *eg*
speed (in general) cyflymder *eg*
speed (scalar quantity) buanedd *eg* buaneddau
speed /time diagram diagram buanedd /amser *eg* diagramau buanedd /amser
speed of light cyflymder goleuni *eg*
speed of the ball cyflymder y bêl *eg*
speed ratio cymhareb buanedd *eb*
speed regulator (of machine part) rheolydd cyflymder *eg* rheolyddion cyflymder
speed up cyflymu *be*
speedometer sbidomedr *eg* sbidomedrau
speleologist ogofwr *eg* ogofwyr
speleology ogofeg *eb*
spell *v* sillafu *be*
spell check *v* gwirio sillafu *be*
spell checker gwirydd sillafu *eg* gwirwyr sillafu
spelling option dewisiad sillafu *eg* dewisiadau sillafu
spelling test prawf sillafu *eg* profion sillafu
spelter sbelter *eg*
spend (money) gwario *be*
spend (time) treulio *be*
spending gwariant *eg*
sperm sberm *eg* sbermau
spermatogenesis sbermatogenesis *eg*
spermatozoon sbermatosoon *eg* sermatosoa
spermicidal sbermleiddiol *ans*
spermicide sbermleiddiad *eg* sbermleiddiaid
spermocyte sbermocyt *eg* sbermocytau
sphagnum (moss) migwyn *eg*
sphalerite sffalerit *eg*
sphere sffêr *eg* sfferau
sphere of influence cylch dylanwad *eg* cylchoedd dylanwad
spherical sfferig *ans*
spherical triangle triongl sfferig *eg* trionglau sfferig
spherical vacuum cleaner sugnwr llwch crwn *eg* sugnwyr llwch crwn
spheroid sfferoid *eg* sfferoidau
spheroidal sfferoidol *ans*
spherometer sfferomedr *eg* sfferomedrau
sphincter sffincter *eg* sffinctrau
sphygmomanometer teclyn mesur pwysau gwaed *eg* teclynnau mesur pwysau gwaed
spice sbeis *eg* sbeisiau
spider corryn *eg* corynod; pry cop *eg* pryfed cop
spigot sbigot *eg* spigotau
spike sbigyn *eg* sbigynnau
spiked shoe esgid sbeic *eb* esgidiau sbeic
spikelet sbigolyn *eg* sbigolion
spillway gorlifan *eb* gorlifannau
spin (in general) *n* troelliad *eg* troelliadau
spin (in general) *v* troelli *be*
spin (of elementary particles) *n* sbin *eg* sbiniau
spin (of elementary particles) *v* sbinio *be*
spin (wool) *v* nyddu *be*
spin drier sychwr dillad *eg* sychwyr dillad
spin of racket troelliad raced *eg*
spin of the Earth troelliad y Ddaear *eg* troelliadau'r Ddaear

spin resonance cyseiniant sbin *eg*
spin the ball troelli'r bêl *be*
spina bifida spina bifida *eg*
spinal sbinol *ans*
spinal cord madruddyn y cefn *eg*
spinal nerve nerf yr asgwrn cefn *eg*
spinal reflex atgyrch sbinol *eg*
spindle gwerthyd *eb* gwerthydau
spindle attachment atodyn gwerthyd *eg* atodion gwerthyd
spindle back chair cadair gefn gwerthyd *eb* cadeiriau cefn gwerthyd
spindle moulder mowldiwr gwerthyd *eg* mowldwyr gwerthyd
spindle nut nyten werthyd *eb* nytiau gwerthyd
spine (of book) meingefn *eg* meingefnau
spine (of plants, fish, hedgehogs etc) draenen *eb* drain
spine (spinal column) asgwrn cefn *eg* esgyrn cefn
spinet spined *eb* spinedau
spinneret nyddolyn *eg* nyddolynnau
spinning jenny siani nyddu *eb*
spinning top top troi *eg* topiau troi
spinning wheel troell nyddu *eb* troellau nyddu
spin-off deilliedig *ans*
spin-off industries diwydiannau deilliedig *ell*
spinous processes cnapiau asgwrn cefn *ell*
spiracle sbiragl *eg* sbiraglau
spiral *adj* troellog *ans*
spiral *n* sbiral *eb* sbiralau
spiral cleavage ymraniad troellog *eg* ymraniadau troellog
spiral curriculum cwricwlwm sbiral *eg*
spiral flute ffliwt sbiral *eb* ffliwtiau sbiral
spiral milling cutter melinwr sbiral *eg* melinwyr sbiral
spiral screwdriver tyrnsgriw sbiral *eg* tyrnsgriwiau sbiral
spiral spring sbring sbiral *eg* sbringiau sbiral
spiral staircase grisiau tro *ell*
spiral thickening tewychiad troellog *eg* tewychiadau troellog
spiral valve falf droellog *eb* falfiau troellog
spire meindwr *eg* meindyrau
spirit (of alcohol) gwirod *eg* gwirodydd
spirit (of person, ghost) ysbryd *eg*
spirit level lefel wirod *eb* lefelau gwirod
spirit marker marciwr gwirod *eg* marcwyr gwirod
spirit stain staen gwirod *eg* staeniau gwirod
spirit varnish farnais gwirod *eg* farneisiau gwirod
spirits of turpentine gwirod tyrpant *eg*
spiritual *adj* ysbrydol *ans*
spiritual *n* cân ysbrydol *eb* caneuon ysbrydol
spiritual and moral education addysg ysbrydol a moesol *eb*
spiritual aspect agwedd ysbrydol *eb* agweddau ysbrydol
spiritual development datblygiad ysbrydol *eg*
spiritual man dyn ysbrydol *eg* dynion ysbrydol
spiritual power awdurdod ysbrydol *eg*
spiritual values gwerthoedd ysbrydol *ell*
spiritualities eiddo ysbrydol *eg*
spirochaete sbirochaet *eg* sbirochaetau
spirometer traces trywydd sbiromedr *eg*
spit (for roasting) bêr *eg* berau
spit (of sand etc) tafod *eg* tafodau
splanchnic perfeddol *ans*
splash tasgu *be*
splash page rhagdudalen *eb* rhagdudalennau
splashback cefnfwrdd *eg* cefnfyrddau
splay goledd *eg*
splay legs coesau sblae *ell*
splayed sblae *ans*
splayed joint uniad sblae *eg* uniadau sblae
spleen dueg *eb* duegau
splendid isolation arwahanrwydd gogoneddus *eg*
splenic duegol *ans*
splenic nerve nerf duegol *eg* nerfau duegol
splice *n* sbleis *eg* sbleisiau
splice *v* sbleisio *be*
spline sblein *eg* sbleiniau
splint sblint *eg* sblintiau
splinter fflewyn *eg* fflawiau
split *n* hollt *eg/b* holltau
split *v* hollti *be*
split bearing beryn hollt *eg* berynnau hollt
split brain ymennydd hollt *eg*
split die dei hollt *eg* deiau hollt
split keyboard bysellfwrdd hollt *eg* bysellfyrddau hollt
split pattern patrwm hollt *eg* patrymau hollt
split pin pin hollt *eg* pinnau hollt
split ring commutator cymudadur modrwy hollt *eg* cymudaduron modrwy hollt
split style of drawing arddull arlunio rhanedig *eb*
split washer wasier hollt *eb* wasieri hollt
split-brain surgery llawdriniaeth hollti'r ymennydd *eb*
split-half reliability dibynadwyedd hollt dau hanner *eg*
split-level cooker stof ddeuddarn *eb* stofiau deuddarn
split-level house tŷ amryw lefel *eg* tai amryw lefel
splitting hollti *be*
splitting ymraniadau *ell*
spoil difetha *be*
spoil heap tomen sbwriel *eb* tomenni sbwriel
spoiling of food difetha bwyd *be*
spoiling tactic tacteg sbwylio *eb* tactegau sbwylio
spoke adain olwyn *eb* adenydd olwyn
spoken word gair llafar *eg* geiriau llafar
spokeshave rhasgl *eb* rhasglau
spokesman llefarydd *eg* llefarwyr
spondee corfan cytbwys *eg* corfannau cytbwys
sponge *n* sbwng *eg* sbyngiau

sponge *v* sbwngio *be*
sponge ball pêl sbwng *eb* peli sbwng
sponge rubber rwber sbwng *eg*
spongeable wallpaper papur sychadwy *eg*
spongophyll sbwngoffyl *eg*
spongy layer haen sbwngaidd *eb* haenau sbwngaidd
sponsor noddwr *eg* noddwyr
sponsorship nawdd *eg*
sponsored spell sillafu noddedig *be*
spontaneous digymell *ans*
spontaneous generation ymdarddiad digymell *eg* ymdarddiadau digymell
spontaneous play chwarae digymell *eg*
spontaneous recovery adferiad digymell *eg*
spontaneous response ymateb digymell *eg* ymatebion digymell
spool sbŵl *eg* sbwliau
spool pin pìn sbŵl *eg* pinnau sbŵl
spool rack rac sbwliau *eb* raciau sbwliau
spooled printer argraffydd sbŵl *eg* argraffyddion sbŵl
spooler sbwliwr *eg* sbwlwyr
spooling sbwlio *be*
spoon llwy *eb* llwyau
spoon bit ebill llwy *eg* ebillion llwy
spoon tool erfyn llwy *eg* offer llwy
sporadic attendance presenoldeb ysbeidiol *eg*
sporangium sborangiwm *eg* sborangia
spore sbôr *eg* sborau
sporogonium sborogoniwm *eg* sborogonia
sporophore sboroffor *eg*
sporophyte sboroffyt *eg*
sport (in general) chwaraeon *ell*
sport (of individual sports) camp *eb* campau
sport and exercise psychology seicoleg chwaraeon ac ymarfer corff *eb*
sport scientist gwyddonydd chwaraeon *eg* gwyddonwyr chwaraeon
sporting culture diwylliant chwaraeon *eg*
sporting example enghraifft o fyd chwaraeon *eb* enghreifftiau o fyd chwaraeon
sporting industry diwydiant chwaraeon *eg*
sports (in general) chwaraeon *eg*
Sports Council Cyngor Chwaraeon *eg*
sports day mabolgampau *ell*
sports hall neuadd chwaraeon *eb* neuaddau chwaraeon
sports therapist therapydd chwaraeon *eg* therapyddion chwaraeon
sportsman mabolgampwr *eg* mabolgampwyr
sportswoman mabolgampwraig *eb* mabolgampwragedd
spot *n* smotyn *eg* smotiau
spot *v* smotio *be*
spot (on the) unfan *eg*
spot drop glass diferwydr *eg* diferwydrau
spot facing sbotwynebu *be*
spot galvanometer galfanomedr smotyn *eg* galfanomedrau smotyn
spot height pwynt uchder *eg* pwyntiau uchder
spot lamp lamp oleugylch *eb* lampau goleugylch
spot welding sbotweldio *be*
spotlight golau cylch *eg*
spotted smotiog *ans*
spotting (in finishing metal) sbotio *be*
spout pig *eg/b* pigau
sprain ysigiad *eg* ysigiadau
spraint baw dyfrgi *eg*
sprawl blerdwf *eg*
spray *v* chwistrellu *be*
spray (of act) *n* chwistrelliad *eg* chwistrelliadau
spray (of object) *n* chwistrell *eb* chwistrelli
spray booth bwth chwistrellu *eg* bythod chwistrellu
spray bottle potel chwistrellu *eb* poteli chwistrellu
spray cover gorchudd trochion *eg* gorchuddion trochion
spray diffuser tryledwr chwistrell *eg* tryledwyr chwistrell
spray gun gwn chwistrellu *eg* gynnau chwistrellu
spray iron haearn chwistrellu *eg* heyrn chwistrellu
spray nozzle (of iron) twll chwistrellu *eg* tyllau chwistrellu
spray painting (of painted picture) paentiad chwistrell *eg* paentiadau chwistrell
spray painting (of process or art) peintio chwistrell *be*
spray polish llathr chwistrell *eg*
spray starch startsh chwistrell *eg*
sprayer chwistrellwr *eg* chwistrellwyr
spread lledaenu *be*
spread the ball wide (in rugby) lledu'r bêl *be*
spreader lledaenydd *eg* lledaenwyr
spreadsheet *n* taenlen *eb* taenlenni
spreadsheet *v* taenlennu *be*
spreadsheet package pecyn taenlen *eg* pecynnau taenlen
spreadsheet software meddalwedd taenlen *eb*
sprig sbrig *eb* sbrigiau
sprightly yn sionc *adf*
spring sbring *eg* sbringiau
spring (=season of year) gwanwyn *eg*
spring (of water) tarddell *eb* tarddellau
spring balance clorian sbring *eb* cloriannau sbring
spring constant cysonyn sbring *eg*
spring dividers cwmpas sbring *eg* cwmpasau sbring
spring green (enamelling colour) gwyrdd y gwanwyn *eg*
spring line tarddlin *eb* tarddlinau
spring line settlement anheddiad tarddlin *eg* aneddiadau tarddlin
spring punch pwnsh sbring *eg* pynsiau sbring
spring squill serennyn y gwanwyn *eg* sêr y gwanwyn
spring term tymor y gwanwyn *eg*
spring tide llanw mawr *eg*
spring toggle togl sbring *eg* toglau sbring

spring washer wasier sbring *eb* wasieri sbring
spring wood pren y gwanwyn *eg*
springboard astell ddeifio *eb* estyll deifio
springboard diving deifio o'r astell *be*
spring-cleaning glanhau blynyddol *be*
spring-loaded sbring-lwythog *ans*
spring-loaded catch clicied sbring-lwythog *eb* cliciedau sbring-lwythog
spring-sapping tarddell-danseilio *be*
springy sbringar *ans*
springy turfs tywyrch sbringar *ell*
sprinkle ysgeintio *be*
sprinkler ysgeintell *eb* ysgeintellau
sprint *n* gwibiad *eg* gwibiadau
sprint *v* gwibio *be*
sprint (in swimming) *n* nofio cyflym *be*
sprint start cychwyn cyflym *eg*
sprinter gwibiwr *eg* gwibwyr
sprite corlun *eg* corluniau
sprocket sbroced *eg* sbrocedi
sprocket and chain sbroced a chadwyn
sprocket hole twll cocos *eg* tyllau cocos
sprocket wheel olwyn ddannedd *eb* olwynion dannedd
spruce pyrwydden *eb* pyrwydd
sprue hole twll sbriw *eg* tyllau sbriw
sprue pin pìn sbriw *eg* pinnau sbriw
spun metal metel trowasg *eg*
spun rayon reion cyfrodedd *eg*
spun wool edafedd gwlân *ell*
spur (=trace) trywydd *eg* trywyddau
spur (in general) sbardun *eg* sbardunau
spur (of wiring) cainc *eb* ceinciau
spur gear gêr sbardun *eg* gerau sbardun
spur wheel olwyn sbardun *eb* olwynion sbardun
spurious modes moddau ffug *ell*
spurt *n* hyrddiad *eg* hyrddiadau
spurt *v* hyrddio *be*
sputum crachboer *eg*
spy hole twll sbïo *eg* tyllau sbïo
spyware ysbïwedd *eg/b*
squadron sgwadron *eb* sgwadronau
squall sgol *eg* sgoliau
squalor aflendid *eg*
square *adj* sgwâr *ans*
square *n* sgwâr *eg* sgwariau
square *v* sgwario *be*
square angle ongl sgwâr *eb* onglau sgwâr
square bar bar sgwâr *eg* barrau sgwâr
square brackets bachau petryal *ell*
square centimetre centimetr sgwâr *eg* centimetrau sgwâr
square cut trawsergyd sgwâr *eb* trawsergydion sgwâr
Square Dance Dawns Sgwâr *eb* Dawnsiau Sgwâr
square deal policy polisi chwarae teg *eg*
square drift drifft sgwâr *eg* drifftiau sgwâr
square edged ymyl sgwâr *eb* ymylon sgwâr
square file ffeil sgwâr *eb* ffeiliau sgwâr
square haunch hansh sgwâr *eg* hanshys sgwâr
square haunched hansiedig sgwâr *ans*
square haunched mortise and tenon joint uniad mortais a thyno hansiedig sgwâr *eg* uniadau mortais a thyno hansiedig sgwâr
square haunched tenon tyno hansiedig sgwâr *eg* tynoau hansiedig sgwâr
square head (machine screws) pensgwar *ans*
square head bolt bollt bensgwar *eb* bolltau pensgwar
square head screw sgriw bensgwar *eb* sgriwiau pensgwar
square head stake bonyn pensgwar *eg* bonion pensgwar
square integrable integradwy sgwâr *ans*
square leg (of person) coeswr sgwâr *eg* coeswyr sgwâr
square leg (of table etc) coes sgwâr *eb* coesau sgwâr
square matrix matrics sgwâr *eg*
square mouth plane plaen ceg sgwâr *eg* plaeniau ceg sgwâr
square mouth tongs gefel ceg sgwâr *eb* gefeiliau ceg sgwâr
square neck gwddf sgwâr *eg* gyddfau sgwâr
square nose pliers gefelen trwyn sgwâr *eb* gefeiliau trwyn sgwâr
square nosed tool erfyn trwyn sgwâr *eg* offer trwyn sgwâr
square number rhif sgwâr *eg* rhifau sgwâr
square nut nyten sgwâr *eb* nytiau sgwâr
square pass pàs sgwâr *eb* pasiau sgwâr
square prism prism sgwâr *eg* prismau sgwâr
square pyramid pyramid sgwâr *eg* pyramidiau sgwâr
square root ail isradd *eg*
square section bar bar toriad sgwâr *eg* barrau toriad sgwâr
square section material defnydd trychiad sgwâr *eg* defnyddiau trychiad sgwâr
square set set sgwâr *eb* setiau sgwâr
square stance safiad sgwâr *eg*
square thread edau sgwâr *eb* edafedd sgwâr
square trowel trywel sgwâr *eb* trywelion sgwâr
square up sgwario *be*
square-box tongs gefel flwch sgwâr *eb* gefeiliau blwch sgwâr
squared paper papur sgwariau *eg*
squaretail carrier cariwr cynffon sgwâr *eg* carwyr cynffon sgwâr
squaring up sgwario *be*
squash *n* sboncen *eb*
squash *v* gwasgu *be*
squat *n* cwrcwd *eg*
squat *v* cyrcydu *be*
squat flask fflasg fyrdew *eb* fflasgiau byrdew
squatter sgwatiwr *eg* sgwatwyr
squatter settlement anheddiad sgwatwyr *eg*
squeegee gwesgi *eg* gwesgïau
squeeze gwasgu *be*
squiggle sgwigl *eg/b* sgwiglau

squill serennyn *eg* sêr
squint llygad croes *eg* llygaid croes
squire yswain *eg* ysweiniaid
squirearchical ysweiniol *ans*
squirearchy ysweiniaeth *eb*
squirrel hair brush brwsh blew gwiwer *eg* brwshys blew gwiwer
squirt *n* chwistrelliad *eg* chwistrelliadau
squirt *v* chwistrellu *be*
St John Ambulance Ambiwlans Sant Ioan
St Louis Louis Sant *eg*
stab stitch pwyth taro *eg* pwythau taro
stability (of economy, society etc) sefydlogrwydd *eg*
stability (of object) sadrwydd *eg*
stabilization technique techneg sefydlogi *eb*
stabilize sefydlogi *be*
stabilizer sefydlogydd *eg* sefydlogyddion
stable sefydlog *ans*
stable equilibrium cydbwysedd sefydlog *eg*
staccato stacato *ans*
stack (=coastal islet) *n* stac *eg* staciau
stack (=pile) *n* pentwr *eb* pentyrrau
stack (=pile up) *v* pentyrru *be*
stack (of hay, wood) *n* tas *eb* teisi
stack base sail stac *eb* seiliau staciau
stack overflow gorlif stac *eg*
stack top pen stac *eg* pennau staciau
stack underflow islif stac *eg*
staff (=persons employed) staff *ell*
staff (in music) erwydd *eg*
staff development datblygiad staff *eg*
staff development programme rhaglen ddatblygu staff *eb* rhaglenni datblygu staff
staff meeting (of teachers) cyfarfod athrawon *eg* cyfarfodydd athrawon
staff mix cymysgedd o staff *eb*
staff notation hen nodiant *eg*
staff nurse nyrs staff *eb* nyrsys staff
staff turnover trosiant staff *eg*
staff-student ratio cymhareb staff-myfyrwyr *eb*
stage (=form in insect's life cycle) ffurf *eb* ffurfiau
stage (=period of time) cyfnod *eg* cyfnodau
stage (=platform) llwyfan *eg/b* llwyfannau
stage (=point of time) pwynt *eg* pwyntiau
stage (=step in development) cam *eg* camau
stage (in psychology) stad *eb* stadau
stage coach coets fawr *eb* coetsys mawr
stage craft crefft llwyfan *eb*
stage micrometer micrometr llwyfan *eg*
stage of development cyfnod datblygiad *eg* cyfnodau datblygiad
stage presentation cyflwyniad ar lwyfan *eg*
stages of change model model cyfnodau newid *eg*
stages of dyeing camau'r llifo *ell*
stages of play cyfnodau chwarae *ell*
stagger darwahanu *be*
stagger nails darwahanu hoelion *be*
staggered conformation cydffurfiad alldro *eg* cydffurfiadau alldro
staggered start hwnt gychwyniad *eg* hwnt gychwyniadau
staging inn tafarn y goets *eb* tafarnau'r goets
stagnant disymud *ans*
stagnant pond merllyn *eg* merllynnoedd
stagnant water merddwr *eg* merddyfroedd
stagnation marweidd-dra *eg*
stain *n* staen *eg* staeniau
stain *v* staenio *be*
stain finish gorffeniad staen *eg* gorffeniadau staen
stain removal codi staen *be*
stain remover codwr staen *eg* codwyr staen
stain setting setio staen *be*
stained glass gwydr lliw *eg* gwydrau lliw
stained glaze gwydredd lliw *eg*
stained preparation gwrthrych staenedig *eg*
stainless gwrthstaen *ans*
stainless steel dur gwrthstaen *eg*
stainless steel screw sgriw ddur wrthstaen *eb* sgriwiau dur gwrthstaen
stair gris *eg* grisiau
stair lift cadair esgyn *eb* cadeiriau esgyn
staircase grisiau *ell*
stairway grisffordd *eb* grisffyrdd
stake (=stout stick) polyn *eg* polion
stake (in metalworking) bonyn *eg* bonion
stake-boat bad clwm *eg* badau clwm
stakeholder rhanddeiliad *eg* rhanddeiliaid
staking cane gwialen fonynnu *eb* gwialennau bonynnu
stalactite stalactid *eg* stalactidau
stalagmite stalagmid *eg* stalagmidau
stale bread hen fara *eg*
Stalinist Stalinydd *eg* Stalinyddion
stalk (=support) cynheilydd *eg* cyneilyddion
stalk (of flower, leaf, etc) coesyn *eg* coesynnau
stallage stondiniaeth *eb*
stamen briger *eb* brigerau
stamina stamina *eg*
staminate brigerog *ans*
staminode gau friger *eb* gau frigerau
stammer atal dweud *eg*
stamp *n* stamp *eg* stampiau
stamp (with foot) *v* taro troed *be*
Stamp Act Deddf Stamp *eb*
stamp duty treth stamp *eb*
stance safiad *eg* safiadau
stanchion annel *eg* anelau
stand *v* sefyll *be*
stand (for spectators) *n* eisteddle *eg* eisteddleoedd
stand (of trees) *n* clwstwr *eg* clystyrau
stand (target) *n* stand *eg/b* standiau
stand-alone arunig *ans*
stand-alone system system arunig *eb* systemau arunig

standard *adj* safonol *ans*
standard *n* safon *eg/b* safonau
Standard Assessment Task (SAT) Tasg Asesu Safonol *eb* Tasgau Asesu Safonol
standard atmospheric pressure gwasgedd atmosfferig safonol *eg*
standard attainment tasks tasgau asesu safonol *ell*
standard bearer llumanwr *eg* llumanwyr
standard business document dogfen fusnes safonol *eb* dogfennau busnes safonol
standard conditions of trading amodau safonol masnachu *ell*
standard cost card cerdyn costio safonol *eg* cardiau costio safonol
standard costs costau safonol *ell*
standard deviation gwyriad safonol *eg* gwyriadau safonol
standard electrode potential potensial electrod safonol *eg*
standard enthelapy change newid enthelapi safonol *be*
standard error cyfeiliornad safonol *eg* cyfeiliornadau safonol
standard error of the mean cyfeiliornad safonol o'r cymedr *eg* cyfeiliornadau safonol o'r cymedr
standard form (of customary method) ffurf safonol *eb* ffurfiau safonol
standard form (of document) ffurflen safonol *eb* ffurflenni safonol
standard form contract contract ffurf safonol *eg* contractau ffurf safonol
standard gauge lled safonol *eg*
standard interface rhyngwyneb safonol *eg* rhyngwynebau safonol
standard interview technique dull cyfweld safonol *eg*
standard mathematical notation nodiant mathemategol safonol *eg*
standard molar enthalpy enthalpi molar safonol *eg*
standard normal distribution gwasgariad normal safonol *eg*
standard of care safon gofal *eb* safonau gofal
standard of living safon byw *eb* safonau byw
standard of play safon y chwarae *eb*
standard parallel cyflin safonol *eb* cyfliniau safonol
standard pitch traw safonol *eg*
standard random variable hapnewidyn safonol *eg* hapnewidynnau safonol
standard rate cyfradd safonol *eb* cyfraddau safonol
standard score sgôr safonol *eb* sgorau safonol
standard section trychiad safonol *eg*
standard size maint safonol *eg* meintiau safonol
standard size court cwrt maint safonol *eg* cyrtiau maint safonol
standard state (thermodynamics) cyflwr safonol *eg* cyflyrau safonol
Standard Temperature and Pressure (STP) Tymheredd a Gwasgedd Safonol *eg*
standard test prawf safonol *eg* profion safonol
Standard Tests and Assessment Implementation Research (STAIR) Ymchwil Gweithredu Profion ac Asesu Safonol *eg*
standard thread edau safonol *eb* edafedd safonol
standard Welsh Cymraeg safonol *eg*
standardization test prawf safoni *eg* profion safoni
standardize safoni *be*
standardized safonedig *ans*
standardized assessment asesu safonedig *be*
standardized intelligence test prawf deallusrwydd safonedig *eg* profion deallusrwydd safonedig
standardized marks marciau safonedig *ell*
standardized test prawf safonedig *eg* profion safonedig
standby mode modd segur *eg*
standing army byddin sefydlog *eb* byddinoedd sefydlog
standing committee pwyllgor sefydlog *eg* pwyllgorau sefydlog
standing jump naid stond *eb* neidiau stond
standing orders rheolau sefydlog *ell*
standing press gwasg unionsyth *eb* gweisg unionsyth
standing tall sefyll yn syth a thal *be*
standpoint safbwynt *eg* safbwyntiau
Stanford-Binet scale graddfa Stanford-Binet *eb*
stannane stanan *eg*
stannate(II) ion ïon stanad(II) *eg* ïonau stanad(II)
stannate(IV) ion ïon stanad(IV) *eg* ïonau stanad(IV)
stapes gwarthol *eg* gwartholion
staple *v* styffylu *be*
staple (=fibre) *n* edefyn *eg* edafedd
staple (e.g. staple industry) *adj* prif *ans*
staple (for fastening) *n* stwffwl *eg* styffylau
staple gun gwn styffylu *eg* gynnau styffylu
staple industries prif ddiwydiannau *ell*
staple yarn edafedd toredig *ell*
stapler (of object) styffylwr *eg* styffylwyr
star seren *eb* sêr
star (hands across) seren llaw dde/chwith *eb*
Star Chamber Siambr y Seren *eb*
Star of David Seren Dafydd *eb*
star shake hollt seren *eg* holltau seren
starboard starbord *eg*
starboard tack tacio starbord *be*
starch *n* startsh *eg*
starch *v* startsio *be*
starch reduced flour blawd startsh gostyngol *eg*
starchy foods bwydydd startsh *ell*
star-head screw sgriw ben-seren *eb* sgriwiau pen-seren
star-rating marciau sêr *ell*
start cychwyn *be*
start area man cychwyn *eg* mannau cychwyn
start button botwm cychwyn *eg*
start of dance cychwyn dawns *eg*
start time amser cychwyn *eg* amserau cychwyn
starter cychwynnwr *eg* cychwynwyr

starter switch switsh cychwyn *eg* switshis cychwyn
starting bloc bloc cychwyn *eg* blociau cychwyn
starting flag lluman cychwyn *eg* llumanau cychwyn
starting gun ergyd cychwyn *eb*
starting line llinell gychwyn *eb* llinellau cychwyn
starting place man cychwyn *eg* mannau cychwyn
starting position safle cychwynnol *eg* safleoedd cychwynnol
starting software meddalwedd cychwyn *eb*
start-up cychwynnol *ans*
start-up conditions amodau dechreuol *ell*
start-up disk disg cychwynnol *eg* disgiau cychwynnol
starvation newyn *eg*
starve newynu *be*
state (=condition) *n* cyflwr *eg* cyflyrau
state (in USA etc) *n* talaith *eb* taleithiau
state (of political community) *n* gwladwriaeth *eb* gwladwriaethau
state capitalism cyfalafiaeth wladol *eb*
State Department Adran Wladol *eb* Adrannau Gwladol
state farm fferm y wladwriaeth *eb* ffermydd y wladwriaeth
state function ffwythiant cyflyrol *eg*
state school ysgol y wladwriaeth *eb* ysgolion y wladwriaeth
statecraft gwladweinyddiaeth *eb*
state-dependent memory cof cyflwr-ddibynnol *eg*
statement (=declaration) datganiad *eg* datganiadau
statement (=expression in words) gosodiad *eg* gosodiadau
statement (in computing) mynegiad *eg* mynegiadau
statement number rhif mynegiad *eg* rhifau mynegiad
statement of account datganiad o gyfrif *eg*
statement of attainment datganiad o gyrhaeddiad *eg* datganiadau o gyrhaeddiad
statement of competence datganiad o gymhwysedd *eg* datganiadau o gymhwysedd
statement of incompatibility datganiad o anghymarusrwydd *eg* datganiadau o anghymarusrwydd
statement of special educational needs datganiad anghenion addysgol arbennig *eg* datganiadau anghenion addysgol arbennig
statemented pupil disgybl sy'n destun datganiad *eg* disgyblion sy'n destun datganiad
states of matter cyflyrau mater *ell*
statesman gwladweinydd *eg* gwladweinwyr
static statig *ans*
static electricity trydan statig *eg*
static screen sgrin statig *eb* sgriniau statig
static store stôr statig *eb* storau statig
statics stateg *eb*
stationary (=fixed) sefydlog *ans*
stationary knife (veneer cutting) cyllell sefydlog *eb* cyllyll sefydlog
stationary phase (of bacteria) cyfnod digyfnewid *eg* cyfnodau digyfnewid
stationary wave ton unfan *eb* tonnau unfan
stationer gwerthwr papurau *eg* gwerthwyr papurau
stationery papur ysgrifennu *eg*
Stations of the Cross (of places) Gorsafoedd y Groes *ell*
Stations of the Cross (of service) Ffordd y Groes *eb*
statistic ystadegyn *eg* ystadegau
statistical ystadegol *ans*
statistical analysis dadansoddi ystadegol *be*
statistical inference casgliad ystadegol *eg* casgliadau ystadegol
statistical significance arwyddocâd ystadegol *eg*
statistical table tabl ystadegol *eg* tablau ystadegol
statistical test prawf ystadegol *eg* profion ystadegol
statistically significant ystadegol bwysig *ans*
statistician ystadegydd *eg* ystadegwyr
statistics (=data) ystadegau *ell*
statistics (science of) ystadegaeth *eb*
stator stator *eg* statorau
statue cerflun *eg* cerfluniau
statuette cerflun bach *eg* cerfluniau bach
stature (of towns) maintioli *eg*
status statws *eg*
status line llinell statws *eb* llinellau statws
status symbol symbol o statws *eg*
status word cyflyrair *eg* cyflyreiriau
statute statud *eg* statudau
statute book llyfr statud *eg*
statute law cyfraith statud *eb*
Statute of Proclamations Statud Proclamasiwn *eg*
Statute of Retainers Statud Gwŷr ar Gadw *eg*
Statute of Rhuddlan Statud Rhuddlan *eg*
Statute of Uses Statud Defnyddiau *eg*
Statute of Wales Statud Cymru *eg*
Statute of Westminster Statud Westminster *eg*
statute roll rhôl statud *eb* rholiau statud
statutory statudol *ans*
statutory authority awdurdod statudol *eg*
statutory body corff statudol *eg* cyrff statudol
statutory instrument offeryn statudol *eg* offerynnau statudol
statutory interpretation dehongliad statudol *eg*
statutory law deddf statudol *eb*
statutory national minimum wage isafswm cyflog gwladol statudol *eg*
statutory organization corff statudol *eg* cyrff statudol
statutory presumption rhagdybiaeth statudol *eb*
statutory requirement gofyniad statudol *eg* gofynion statudol
stave erwydd *eg* erwyddi
stay (rule joint) gwanas *eg/b* gwanasau
stay stitch pwyth cynnal *eg* pwythau cynnal
staying on (at school) aros ymlaen *be*
staying visitor ymwelydd sy'n aros *eg*
steady (lathe accessories) sadydd *eg* sadyddion

steady beat curiad cyson *eg* curiadau cyson
steady build-up adeiladu'n bwyllog *be*
steady current cerrynt cyson *eg*
steady state cyflwr sefydlog *eb* cyflyrau sefydlog
steadycam sadio-cam *eg*
steam *n* ager *eg*
steam *v* ageru *be*
steam and spray iron haearn ager a chwistrell *eg* heyrn ager a chwistrell
steam bending agerblygu *be*
steam chest agergist *eb* agergistiau
steam cleaning glanhau gydag ager *be*
steam coal glo rhydd *eg*
steam de-waxing digwyro gydag ager *be*
steam distillation distyllu ag ager *be*
steam drum drwm ager *eg* drymiau ager
steam engine injan stêm *eb*
steam iron haearn ager *eg* heyrn ager
steam pump pwmp ager *eg*
steam turbine tyrbin ager *eg* tyrbinau ager
steamroller stêm-roler *eg* stêm-roleri
steamship llong ager *eb* llongau ager
steel dur *eg* duroedd
steel back saw llif gefn ddur *eb* llifau cefn dur
steel column colofn ddur *eb* colofnau dur
steel filings durlifion *ell*
steel framing fframwaith dur *eg* fframweithiau dur
steel mesh rhwyddur *eg*
steel racket raced ddur *eb* racedi dur
steel screw sgriw ddur *eb* sgriwiau dur
steel spur sbardun dur *eg* sbardunau dur
steel tape tâp dur *eg*
steel wool gwlân dur *eg*
steel-spring cramp cramp sbring dur *eg* crampiau sbring dur
steelyard stiliard *eg*
steep mwydo *be*
steep pitch codiad serth *eg* codiadau serth
steep slope llethr serth *eg* llethrau serth
steeplechase ras ffos a pherth *eb* rasys ffos a pherth
steepsided serthochrog *ans*
steering a course llywio cwrs *be*
steering committee pwyllgor llywio *eg* pwyllgorau llywio
steering wheel llyw *eg* llywiau
Steiner philosophy athroniaeth Steiner *eb*
stellar serol *ans*
stellar year blwyddyn serol *eb* blynyddoedd serol
stellite (alloying elements) stelit *eg*
stem (of gauge etc) coes *eb* coesau
stem (of multiple choice question) datganiad *eg* datganiadau
stem (of plant) coesyn *eg* coesynnau
stem (of tree) cyff *eg* cyffion
stem stitch pwyth conyn *eg* pwythau conyn
stencil stensil *eg* stensiliau
stencil brush brwsh stensil *eg* brwshys stensil
stencil cutter torrell stensil *eb* torellau stensil
stencil knife cyllell stensil *eb* cyllyll stensil
stencil paper papur stensil *eg*
stencil pattern patrwm stensil *eg* patrymau stensil
step (in dance) *v* stepio *be*
step (on stairs, in dance) *n* gris *eg* grisiau
step (when walking and figuratively) *n* cam *eg* camau
step by step cam wrth gam
step counter rhifydd camau *eg* rhifyddion camau
step cutting torri step *be*
step out camu allan *be*
step round *v* camu o amgylch *be*
step-down transformer newidydd gostwng *eg* newidyddion gostwng
stepfather llystad *eg*
stepladder ysgol fach *eb* ysgolion bach
stepmother llysfam *eb* llysfamau
steppe soils step-briddoedd *ell*
stepped cliffs gris-glogwyni *ell*
stepping reflex atgyrch camu *eg* atgyrchion camu
step-up-transformer newidydd codi *eg* newidyddion codi
steradian steradian *eg* steradiannau
stereochemical formula fformiwla stereocemegol *eb*
stereographic stereograffig *ans*
stereographic projection tafluniad stereograffig *eg*
stereophonic stereoffonig *ans*
stereopsis stereopsis *eg*
stereoscopic stereosgopig *ans*
stereotaxic apparatus cyfarpar stereotacsig *eg*
stereotype stereoteip *eg* stereoteipiau
stereotyping stereoteipio *be*
sterile (=free of micro-organisms) di-haint *ans*
sterile (of reproduction) anffrwythlon *ans*
sterile dressing gorchudd di-haint *eg* gorchuddion di-haint
sterile equipment cyfarpar di-haint *eg*
sterile field maes di-haint *eg* meysydd di-haint
sterile glove maneg ddi-haint *eb* menig di-haint
sterility anffrwythlondeb *eg*
sterilize (=make free of micro-organisms) diheintio *be*
sterilize (in medical physiology) diffrwythloni *be*
sterilizer diheintydd *eg* diheintyddion
sterilizing techniques technegau diheintio *ell*
sterling sterling *eg*
sterling area cylch sterling *eg*
stern starn *eb* starnau
sternum sternwm *eg* sterna
steroid steroid *eg* steroidau
sterol sterol *eg* sterolau
stethoscope stethosgop *eg* stethosgopau
Stevenson screen sgrin Stevenson *eb* sgriniau Stevenson
steward stiward *eg* stiwardiaid
stewardship stiwardiaeth *eb* stiwardiaethau

stewed apple afal wedi'i stiwio *eg* afalau wedi'u stiwio
stibine stibin *eg*
stick *n* ffon *eb* ffyn
stick (adhere) *v* glynu *be*
stick printing printio â phren *be*
stick puppet pyped pren *eg* pypedau pren
stickleback crothell *eb* crethyll
sticky gludiog *ans*
sticky tape tâp glynu *eg*
stiff anystwyth *ans*
stiff board bwrdd caled *eg* byrddau caled
stiff cover clawr caled *eg* cloriau caled
stiff nut nyten glwm *eb* nytiau clwm
stiff wire gwifren anystwyth *eb* gwifrau anystwyth
stiffen (=strengthen) cyfnerthu *be*
stiffened waistband band gwasg wedi'i gyfnerthu *eg* bandiau gwasg wedi'u cyfnerthu
stiffening cyfnerthydd *eg* cyfnerthyddion
stiffness anhyblygedd *eg*
stigma (=mark on skin or butterfly wing) stigma *eg* stigmata
stigma (=part of a pistil) stigma *eg* stigmâu
stile cledren *eb* cledrau
stiletto stileto *eg*
still llonydd *ans*
still birth geni'n farw *be*
still water dŵr llonydd *eg*
stillborn marw-anedig *ans*
still-life bywyd llonydd *eg*
stillness llonyddwch *eg*
stilt stilt *eg* stiltiau
stimulant symbylydd *eg* symbylyddion
stimulate ysgogi *be*
stimulating play chwarae ysgogol *eg*
stimulus ysgogiad *eg* ysgogiadau
stimulus equivalence cywerthedd ysgogiadau *eg*
stimulus material deunydd ysgogi *eg*
sting *n* pigiad *eg* pigiadau
sting *v* pigo *be*
sting cell cell golyn *eb* celloedd colyn
stipe coes *eb* coesau
stipend tâl offeiriad *eg*
stipendiary magistrate ynad cyflogedig *eg* ynadon cyflogedig
stipple *n* dotwaith *eg*
stipple *v* dotweithio *be*
stipple drawing lluniad dotwaith *eg* lluniadau dotwaith
stipple engraving ysgythriad dotwaith *eg* ysgythriadau dotwaith
stipule stipwl *eg* stipylau
stir troi *be*
stirrer tröydd *eg* troyddion
stirrer fan gwyntyll droelli *eb* gwyntyllau troelli
stirring (of music etc) cyffrous *ans*
stirring rod rhoden droi *eb* rhodenni troi
stirrup gwarthol *eb* gwartholion
stirrup strap strap warthol *eb* strapiau gwarthol
stitch *n* pwyth *eg* pwythau
stitch *v* pwytho *be*
stitch holder pìn cadw pwythau *eg* pinnau cadw pwythau
stitch length adjustment (of machine part) rheolydd hyd pwyth *eg* rheolyddion hyd pwyth
stitched calico mop mop calico wedi'i bwytho *eg* mopiau calico wedi'u pwytho
stitchery pwythwaith *eg*
stitching frame ffrâm bwytho *eb* fframiau pwytho
stitching press gwasg bwytho *eb* gweisg pwytho
stitching tool erfyn pwytho *eg* offer pwytho
stochastic stocastig *ans*
stock (=line of ancestry) llinach *eb*
stock (in finance) stoc *eb* stociau
stock (of machine) dwrn *eg* dyrnau
stock (of tree etc) cyff *eg* cyffion
stock and dies cyffion a deiau
stock control rheolaeth stoc *eb*
stock control rheoli stoc *be*
stock exchange cyfnewidfa stoc *eb* cyfnewidfeydd stoc
stock market marchnad stoc *eb* marchnadoedd stoc
stock pile *n* pentwr stoc *eg* pentyrrau stoc
stock pile *v* pentyrru stoc *be*
stock turnover trosiant stoc *eg*
stockbroker brocer stoc *eg* broceriaid stoc
stockhorn pibgorn *eg* pibgyrn
stockinette stocinét *eb*
stocking hosan *eb* sanau
stocking stitch pwyth plaen *eg* pwythau plaen
stocks cyffion traed *ell*
stoichiometric stoichiometrig *ans*
stoichiometric equation hafaliad stoichiometrig *eg*
stoichiometry stoichiometreg *eb*
stole (of church vestment) ystola *eb* ystolau
stole (of costume) stôl *eb* stoliau
stoloniferous stolonog *ans*
stoma stoma *eg* stomata
stomach stumog *eb* stumogau
stomach acid asid y stumog *eg*
stomach bile bustl y stumog *eg*
stomach ulcer briw'r stumog *eg*
stomium stomiwm *eg* stomia
stone carreg *eb* cerrig
Stone Age Oes y Cerrig *eb*
stone architecture gwaith carreg pensaernïol *eg*
stone axe bwyell garreg *eb* bwyeill cerrig
stone carving cerfio carreg *be*
stone cell cell garreg *eb* celloedd cerrig
stone fruit ffrwyth carreg *eg* ffrwythau cerrig
Stonehenge Côr y Cewri *eg*
stone-tumbling carreg-dwmblo *be*
stoneware crochenwaith caled *eg*
stoneware glaze gwydredd crochenwaith *eg*

stonework gwaith carreg *eg*
stool (=faeces) carthion *ell*
stool (for sitting on) stôl *eb* stolion
stool construction adeiladwaith stôl *eg*
stop (=prevent) *v* atal *be*
stop (a note on musical intrument) *v* atal *be*
stop (on organ) *n* stop *eg* stopiau
stop dead stopio'n stond *be*
stop motion stop-symudiad *eg*
stop the ball atal y bêl *be*
stop volley foli stop *eb* folïau stop
stop-clock stopgloc *eg* stopglociau
stoppage ataliad *eg*
stopped (of note on organ, wind and string instrument) wedi'i atal *ans* wedi'u hatal
stopped chamfer siamffer cau *eg* siamfferi cau
stopped dovetail housing joint uniad rhigol drawsgynffonnog gau *eg* uniadau rhigol trawsgynffonnog cau
stopped housing rhigol gau *eb* rhigolau cau
stopped housing joint uniad rhigol draws gau *eg* uniadau rhigol traws gau
▶ **stopped mortise and tenon joint** uniad mortais a thyno cau *eg* uniadau mortais a thyno cau
▶ **stopped rabbet** rabad cau *eg* rabadau cau
▶ **stopped tenon** tyno cau *eg* tynoau cau
stopper caead *eg* caeadau
stoppered bottle potel â thopyn *eb* poteli â thopiau
stopping distance pellter stopio *eg*
stopping the ball by kneeling atal y bêl drwy benlinio *be*
stopping-out varnish farnais atal *eg* farneisiau atal
stop-start atal a chychwyn
storage (of action) storio *be*
storage (of place) storfa *eb* storfeydd
storage allocation dyraniad storfa *eg*
storage capacity cynhwysedd storio *eg*
storage cupboard cwpwrdd storio *eg* cypyrddau storio
storage device dyfais storio *eb* dyfeisiau storio
storage drawer drôr storio *eg* droriau storio
storage heater gwresogydd stôr *eg* gwresogyddion stôr
storage jar cawg storio *eg* cawgiau storio
storage organ organ storio *eg* organau storio
storage space lle storio *eg*
storage tank tanc storio *eg* tanciau storio
store *v* storio *be*
store (=place of storage) *n* storfa *eb* storfeydd
store (=shop) *n* siop *eb* siopau
store (=supply) *n* stôr *eb* storau
store a composition storio cyfansoddiad *be*
store control unit uned rheoli storfa *eb* unedau rheoli storfa
store information storio gwybodaeth *be*
stored carbohydrate carbohydrad stôr *eg*
stored point pwynt stôr *eg* pwyntiau stôr
storey llawr *eg* lloriau
storing food storio bwyd *be*
storm beach stormdraeth *eg* stormdraethau
stormtroopers stormfilwyr *ell*
story stori *eb* straeon
story book llyfr stori *eg* llyfrau stori
story method dull storïol *eg* dulliau storïol
story order trefn y stori *eb*
storyboard bwrdd stori *eg* byrddau stori
stoss and lee llyfn a sgythrog *ans*
stoutheart plywood pren haenog canol trwchus *eg*
stove stof *eb* stofiau
stow stow *eg* stowiau
straddle llednaid *eb*
straddle jump naid fforchog *eb* neidiau fforchog
straddler lledneidiwr *eg* lledneidwyr
straight syth *ans*
straight angle ongl syth *eb* onglau syth
straight bit haearn sodro syth *eg*
straight bodkin botgin syth *eg* botginau syth
straight collar coler syth *eg* coleri syth
straight drive dreif syth *eb* dreifiau syth
straight edge ymyl syth *eb* ymylon syth
straight flute drill dril ffliwt syth *eg* driliau ffliwt syth
straight grain graen union *eg*
straight handle (hacksaw frame) dolen syth *eb* dolennau syth
straight knurl nwrl syth *eg* nwrliau syth
straight left chwith syth *ans*
straight line llinell syth *eb* llinellau syth
straight pass pàs syth *eb* pasiau syth
straight peen wyneb syth *eg* wynebau syth
straight peen hammer morthwyl wyneb syth *eg* morthwylion wyneb syth
straight right de syth *eb*
straight shank garan syth *eb* garanau syth
straight shank drill dril garan syth *eg* driliau garan syth
straight skirt sgert syth *eb* sgertiau syth
straight snips snipiwr syth *eg* snipwyr syth
straight taper tapr syth *eg* taprau syth
straight tinsnips snipiwr tun syth *eg* snipwyr tun syth
straighten unioni *be*
straight-toothed milling cutter melinwr dant union *eg* melinwyr dant union
strain (=piece of music) *n* cainc *eb* ceinciau
strain (emotional, in physics, mathematics) *n* straen *eg*
strain (in biology) *n* rhywogaeth *eb* rhywogaethau
strain (liquid) *v* hidlo *be*
strain (physical) *n* ysigiad *eg* ysigiadau
strain (physical) *v* ysigo *be*
strain gauge medrydd straen *eg* medryddion straen
strained foods bwydydd wedi'u hidlo *ell*
strainer hidlen *eb* hidlenni
straining pliers gefelen dynhau *eb* gefeiliau tynhau
strait culfor *eg* culforoedd

Straits Convention Cytundeb y Culfor *eg*
strand *v* ceincio *be*
strand (of beach) *n* traethell *eb* traethellau
strand (of cotton etc) *n* cainc *eb* ceinciau
strand (to argument etc) *n* llinyn *eg* llinynnau
strand of DNA edefyn DNA *eg* edafedd DNA
stranded (of cotton etc) ceinciog *ans*
stranding ceincio *be*
strandline traethlin *eb* traethlinau
strange situation sefyllfa ddieithr *eb* sefyllfaoedd dieithr
stranger anxiety pryder rhag dieithriaid *eg*
strap strap *eb* strapiau
strap hinge colfach strap *eg* colfachau strap
strategic strategol *ans*
strategic alliance cysylltiad strategol *eg*
Strategic Intent for Health Services in Wales Bwriad Strategol Gwasanaethau Iechyd Cymru *eg*
strategy strategaeth *eb* strategaethau
strath ystrad *eg* ystradau
Strathspey step step Strathspey *eb*
stratification haeniad *eg* haeniadau
stratified haenedig *ans*
stratified epithelium epitheliwm haenedig *eg*
stratified random sampling hapsamplu haenedig *be*
stratified sample sampl haenedig *eb* samplau haenedig
stratified sampling samplu haenedig *be*
stratiform haenol *ans*
stratigraphical table tabl stratigraffig *eg* tablau stratigraffig
stratigraphy stratigraffeg *eb*
stratosphere stratosffer *eg* stratosfferau
stratospheric stratosfferig *ans*
stratum stratwm *eg* strata
straw gwelltyn *eg* gwellt
strawberries mefus *ell*
strawboard bwrdd gwellt *eg* byrddau gwellt
streaky bacon cig moch brith *eg*
stream (=flow) *n* llif *eg* llifoedd
stream (=small river) *n* nant *eb* nentydd
stream (in school) *v* ffrydio *be*
stream (used figuratively) *n* ffrwd *eb* ffrydiau
stream orders graddau ffrwd *ell*
stream source tarddiad nant *eg*
streamflow ffrydlif *eg*
streaming ffrydio *be*
streamless di-ffrwd *ans*
streamline *n* llilin *eb* llilíniau
streamline *v* llilinio *be*
streamline flow llif llilin *eg*
streamlined llyfn *ans*
street scape strydlun *eg* strydluniau
strength (in general) cryfder *eg* cryfderau
strength (of sound) nerth *eg*
strengthen cryfhau *be*
strengthen the body cryfhau'r corff *be*
strengthening movement symudiad cryfhau *eg* symudiadau cryfhau
stress straen *eg*
stress (=accent) acen *eb* acenion
stress (in biology) tyndra *eg*
stress (in general) straen *eg*
stress (in physics and chemistry) diriant *eg* diriannau
stress buffer byffer straen *eg*
stress inoculation training hyfforddiant gwrthsefyll straen *eg*
stress response ymateb straen *eg*
stressor straenachoswr *eg* straenachoswyr
stretch *v.intrans* ymestyn *be*
stretch *v.trans* estyn *be*
stretch (of water) *n* darn *eg* darnau
stretch fabric ffabrig ymestyn *eg*
stretch receptor derbynnydd ymestynnedd *eg* derbynyddion ymestynnedd
stretch the muscles llaesu'r cyhyrau *be*
stretched estynedig *ans*
stretcher (=frame) estynnwr *eg* estynwyr
stretcher (for injured person) stretsier *eg* stretsieri
stretcher piece darn estyn *eg* darnau estyn
stretcher pliers gefelen estyn *eb* gefeiliau estyn
stretcher rail rheilen gynnal *eb* rheiliau cynnal
strewing gwasgaru *be*
striated rhychedig *ans*
striated (=striped muscle) rhesog *ans*
striation rhychiad *eg* rhychiadau
strickle striclo *be*
strickle bar bar striclo *eg* barrau striclo
strickling tool erfyn striclo *eg* offer striclo
strict caeth *ans*
strict counterpoint gwrthbwynt caeth *eg*
strict liability atebolrwydd caeth *eg*
strict metre mesur caeth *eg* mesurau caeth
stricture (medical) culfan *eg/b* culfannau
stride camu *be*
stridulation grillian *be*
strike (=blow) *n* ergyd *eg/b* ergydion
strike (=cease work as protest) *v* streicio *be*
strike (=cessation of work as protest) *n* streic *eb* streiciau
strike (=hit) *v* taro *be*
strike breaker torrwr streic *eg* torwyr streic
striker (in cricket) ergydiwr *eg* ergydwyr
striker (in football) saethwr *eg* saethwyr
striker (in industrial dispute) streiciwr *eg* streicwyr
striker's plate plât yr ergydiwr *eg* platiau ergydwyr
strike-slip streic-rwyg *eg*
strikethrough *n* llinell drwodd *eb* llinellau drwodd
striking button botwm taro *eg* botymau taro
striking circle cylch saethu *eg* cylchoedd saethu
striking game gêm daro *eb* gemau taro
striking head trawben *eg* trawbennau
striking plate plât taro *eg* platiau taro

striking tool erfyn taro *eg* offer taro
string *v* llinynnu *be*
string (=narrow cord) *n* llinyn *eg* llinynnau
string (on musical instrument, racket) *n* tant *eg* tannau
string board (stairs) bwrdd cynnal *eg* byrddau cynnal
string course llin-gwrs *eg* llin-gyrsiau
string cramp cramp cortyn *eg* crampiau cortyn
string handling trin llinynnau *be*
string marionette marionét llinyn *eg* marionetau llinyn
string puppet pyped llinyn *eg* pypedau llinyn
string quartet pedwarawd llinynnol *eg* pedwarawdau llinynnol
string section adran llinynnau *eb* adrannau llinynnau
string solo unawd llinynnol *eb* unawdau llinynnol
string variable newidyn llinynnol *eg* newidynnau llinynnol
stringed instrument offeryn llinynnol *eg* offerynnau llinynnol
stringer ochr grisiau *eb* ochrau grisiau
stringers stringeri *ell*
strings (in orchestra, inlaying) llinynnau *ell*
strip *v* stripio *be*
strip (in agriculture) *n* llain *eb* lleiniau
strip (of material) *n* stribed *eg* stribedi
strip cartoon cartŵn stribed *eg* cartwnau stribed
strip cultivation llaindriniad *eg* llaindriniadau
strip development datblygiad hirgul *eg* datblygiadau hirgul
strip foundation sylfaen stribed *eb* sylfeini stribed
strip holding llainddaliad *eg* llainddaliadau
strip lighting golau stribed *eg*
strip mill melin strip *eb* melinau strip
strip opening agoriad di-dor *eg* agoriadau di-dor
stripe rhes *eb* rhesi
striped rhesog *ans*
stripping stripio *be*
striving for superiority ymdrechu at oruchafiaeth *be*
strobe pulse curiad strôb *eg* curiadau strôb
stroboscope strobosgop *eg* strobosgopau
stroke *v* ergydio *be*
stroke (=mode of swimming) *n* dull *eg* dulliau
stroke (=the whole of the motion) *n* strôc *eb* strociau
stroke (medical condition) strôc *eb* strociau
stroke (with bat or racket) *n* ergyd *eg/b* ergydion
stroke play chwarae strôc *be*
stroke side ochr strôc *eb*
stroke side under ochr strôc dani *eb*
stroke technique techneg strôc *eb*
stroked gathers crychau nodwydd *eg*
strong cryf *ans*
strong acid asid cryf *eg*
strong base bas cryf *eg* basau cryf
strong flour blawd cryf *eg*
strong inference casgliad cryf *eg*
strong racket raced gref *eb* racedi cryf
strong runner rhedwr cryf *eg* rhedwyr cryf
stronghold cadarnle *eg* cadarnleoedd
strontium (Sr) strontiwm *eg*
strontium carbonate strontiwm carbonad *eg*
strontium ion ïon strontiwm *eg* ïonau strontiwm
strontium sulphate strontiwm sylffad *eg*
Stroop effect effaith Stroop *eb*
strop strapen hogi *eb* strapiau hogi
strophic stroffig *ans*
structural (of administration) strwythurol *ans*
structural (of buildings) adeileddol *ans*
structural basin basn adeileddol *eg* basnau adeileddol
structural difference gwahaniaeth adeileddol *eg*
structural formula fformiwla adeileddol *eb*
structural isomerism isomeredd adeileddol *eg*
structural member rhan strwythurol *eb*
structural reason rheswm adeileddol *eg*
structural unemployment diweithdra strwythurol *eg*
structural weakness gwendid adeileddol *eg* gwendidau adeileddol
structuralism strwythuriaeth *eb*
structure (=framework) fframweithiau *eg*
structure (=way in which something is constructed) adeiladwaith *eg*
structure (a single, definable) ffurfiad *eg* ffurfiadau
structure (in administration etc) strwythur *eg* strwythurau
structure (of constructed objects) adeiledd *eg*
structure elucidation egluro adeiledd *be*
structure plan cynllun fframwaith *eg*
structured strwythuredig *ans*
structured health related exercise programme rhaglen ymarfer strwythuredig sy'n gysylltiedig ag iechyd *eb* rhaglenni ymarfer strwythuredig sy'n gysylltiedig ag iechyd
structured interview cyfweliad strwythuredig *eg* cyfweliadau strwythuredig
structured language iaith strwythuredig *eb*
structured play chwarae strwythuredig *be*
structured programming rhaglennu strwythurol *be*
Structured Query Language Iaith Ymholiadau Strwythuredig *eb*
structured question cwestiwn strwythuredig *eg* cwestiynau strwythuredig
structure-process-stage adeiledd-proses-cam *eg*
struggle brwydro *be*
struggle for existence ymdrech i fodoli *eb*
struggle for survival ymdrech i oroesi *eb*
strut pwyslath *eb* pwyslathau
strut (e.g. on guitar) eisen *eb* ais
strutted instrument offeryn eisedig *eg* offerynnau eisedig
strutting cynheilio croes *be*
Stuarts Stiwartiaid *ell*
stub bonyn *eg* bonion
stub axle echel bwt *eb* echelau pwt

stub mortise and tenon joint uniad mortais a thyno pwt *eg* uniadau mortais a thyno pwt
stub tenon tyno pwt *eg* tynoau pwt
stubborn ystyfnig *ans*
stubnose trwyn byr *eg* trwynau byr
stucco stwco *eg*
stuck moulding mowldin solet *eg*
stud styden *eb* stydiau
stud anchor angor styden *eb* angorau stydiau
stud box blwch stydiau *eg* blychau stydiau
student (female) myfyrwraig *eb* myfyrwragedd
student (male and general) myfyriwr *eg* myfyrwyr
student loan benthyciad i fyfyrwyr *eg* benthyciadau i fyfyrwyr
student nurse myfyriwr nyrsio *eg* myfyrwyr nyrsio
student record cofnod myfyriwr *eg* cofnodion myfyrwyr
Student's T test prawf T Student *eg*
students' union undeb myfyrwyr *eg* undebau myfyrwyr
studies (academic) efrydiau *ell*
studies director cyfarwyddwr astudiaethau *eg* cyfarwyddwyr astudiaethau
studio stiwdio *eb* stiwdios
studio easel îsl stiwdio *eg* islau stiwdio
study *n* astudiaeth *eb* astudiaethau
study *v* astudio *be*
study in depth astudiaeth fanwl *eb* astudiaethau manwl
stuff stwffio *be*
stuffed fabric ffabrig wedi'i stwffio *eg* ffabrigau wedi'u stwffio
stumbling block maen tramgwydd *eg* meini tramgwydd
stump *n* stwmp *eg* stympiau
stump *v* stympio *be*
stumper stympiwr *eg* stympwyr
stunted corachaidd *ans*
sturdy beggars cardotwyr holliach *ell*
style (=idiom) arddull *eg/b* arddulliau
style (in botany) colofnig *eb* colofnigau
style (in zoology) styl *eg* stylau
style name enw arddull *eg* enwau arddull
style of accompaniment arddull y cyfeiliant *eg*
style sheet dalen arddull *eb* dalennau arddull
stylistic arddulliadol *ans*
styrene styren *eg*
styrofoam ewyn styro *eg*
subacute cymedrol ddifrifol *ans*
subadults is-oedolion *eg*
subalpine government llywodraeth isalpaidd *eb*
subaerial isawyrol *ans*
subcellular isgellog *ans*
subclass isddosbarth *eg*
subclavian isglafiglaidd *ans*
subcommittee is-bwyllgor *eg* is-bwyllgorau
subcontract *n* is-gontract *eg* is-gontractau
subcontract *v* is-gontractio *be*
subculture isddiwylliant *eg* isddiwylliannau
subcutaneous isgroenol *ans*
subdirectory is-gyfeiriadur *eg* is-gyfeiriaduron
subdivide isrannu *be*
subdivision israniad *eg* israniadau
subdominant is-lywydd *eg* is-lywyddion
subduction tansugno *be*
subdue darostwng *be*
subdued relief tirwedd iselaidd *eb* tirweddau iselaidd
suberin swberin *eg*
subfactorial is-ffactorial *eg*
subfile is-ffeil *eb* is-ffeiliau
subglacial channel sianel danrewlifol *eb* sianeli tanrewlifol
subglacial moraine marian tanrewlifol *eg* marianau tanrewlifol
subglacial stream ffrwd danrewlifol *eb* ffrydiau tanrewlifol
subgroup is-grŵp *eg* is-grwpiau
subharmonic is-harmonig *eg* is-harmonigau
subheading is-bennawd *eg* is-benawdau
subhumid islaith *ans*
subinfeudate is-ffeodu *be*
subinfeudation is-ffeodaeth *eb*
subject (=department or field of study) pwnc *eg* pynciau
subject (=theme) testun *eg* testunau
subject (in grammar) goddrych *eg* goddrychau
subject (to a monarch) deiliad *eg* deiliaid
subject attrition athreuliad cyfranwyr *eg*
subject content cynnwys pwnc *eg*
subject representativeness cynrychioldeb cyfranwyr *eg*
subject role rôl cyfrannwr *eb*
subject teacher (female) athrawes pwnc *eb* athrawesau pwnc
subject teacher (male) athro pwnc *eg* athrawon pwnc
subject to contract yn ôl cytundeb
subject variable newidyn cyfrannwr *eg* newidynnau cyfranwyr
subject working group gweithgor pwnc *eg* gweithgorau pwnc
subject-centred pwnc-ganolog *ans*
subjectivation goddrychiad *eg*
subjective goddrychol *ans*
subjective assessment asesiad goddrychol *eg* asesiadau goddrychol
subjective probability tebygolrwydd goddrychol *eg* tebygolrwyddau goddrychol
subjectivity goddrychedd *eg*
subject-specific pwnc-benodol *ans*
subjugate darostwng *be*
sub-let is-osod *be*
sublimate *n* sychdarth *eg*
sublimate *v* sychdarthu *be*
sublimation (in chemistry) sychdarthiad *eg*
sublimation (in psychology) trosgyfeirio *be*

subliminal perception canfyddiad isdrothwyol *eg*
sublingual isdafodol *ans*
sub-machine gun peirianddryll bychan *eg* peirianddrylliau bychain
submandibular isfandiblaidd *ans*
submarine *adj* tanfor *ans*
submarine *n* llong danfor *eb* llongau tanfor
submature isaeddfed *ans*
submaxillary isfacsilaidd *ans*
submediant isfeidion *eb* isfeidonau
sub-menu isddewislen *eb* isddewislenni
submerge soddi *be*
submerged soddedig *ans*
submerged forest coedwig soddedig *eb* coedwigoedd soddedig
submerged leaf deilen soddedig *eb* dail soddedig
submission (=proposal) argymhelliad *eg* argymhellion
submission (=surrender) ymostyngiad *eg*
Submission of the Clergy Ymostyngiad y Glerigaeth *eg*
submissive ymostyngol *ans*
sub-multiple angles onglau ffracsiynol *ell*
subneural isniwral *ans*
subnormal isnormal *ans*
suboctave iswythfed *eg* iswythfedau
suborder is-urdd *eb*
subordinate concept cysyniad darostyngol *eg*
subpharyngeal isffaryngeal *ans*
sub-program is-raglen *eb* is-raglenni
subprogram library llyfrgell israglen *eb*
subregion isranbarth *eg* isranbarthau
sub-routine is-reolwaith *eg* is-reolweithiau
subroutine is-reolwaith NEU
subscribe (to a magazine etc) tanysgrifio *be*
subscribe (to an opinion) cefnogi *be*
subscriber tanysgrifiwr *eg* tanysgrifwyr
subscript is-nod *eg* is-nodau
subscript isysgrif *eg* isysgrif
subscription tanysgrifiad *eg* tanysgrifiadau
subsequence is-ddilyniant *eg* is-ddilyniannau
subsequent (in general) *adj* dilynol *ans*
subsequent (stream) *adj* trawslif *ans*
subsequent (stream) *n* trawslif *eg* trawslifau
subsequent stream ffrwd drawslif *eb* ffrydiau trawslif
subservience gwaseidd-dra *eg*
subservient gwasaidd *ans*
subset is-set *eb* is-setiau
subside ymsuddo *be*
subsidence (of land) ymsuddiant *eg*
subsidiarity cyfrifolaeth *eb*
subsidiary atodol *ans*
subsidiary is-gwmni *eg* is-gwmnïau
subsidiary course cwrs atodol *eg* cyrsiau atodol
subsidiary grant grant atodol *eg* grantiau atodol
subsidiary subject pwnc atodol *eg* pynciau atodol
subsidy cymhorthdal *eg* cymorthdaliadau
Subsidy Roll Rhôl Cymorth *eb*
subsistence *adj* ymgynhaliol *ans*
subsistence *n* cynhaliaeth *eb*
subsistence allowance lwfans cynnal *eg* lwfansau cynnal
subsistence crop cnwd cynnal *eg* cnydau cynnal
subsistence farming ffermio ymgynhaliol *be*
subsoil isbridd *eg* isbriddoedd
subsonic is-sonig *ans*
subspecies isrywogaeth *eb* isrywogaethau
substance sylwedd *eg* sylweddau
substance accumulation in tissue sylwedd yn ymgasglu mewn meinwe *eg*
substandard is-safonol *ans*
sub-station is-orsaf *eb* is-orsafoedd
substitute (a person) *v* dirprwyo *be*
substitute (a player in a game) *v* eilyddio *be*
substitute (a substance) *v* amnewid *be*
substitute (of person) *n* eilydd *eg* eilyddion
substitute (of substance) *n* amnewidyn *eg* amnewidion
substitute clausula dirprwy glawswla *eg*
substitute x for y amnewid y am x *be*
substitution (in sport) eilyddio *be*
substitution (of substance) amnewidiad *eg* amnewidiadau
substitution reaction adwaith amnewid *eg*
substrate (in physics) is-haen *eb* is-haenau
substrate (in relation to enzymes) swbstrad *eg* swbstradau
substratum is-haen *eb* is-haenau
sub-string is-linyn *eg* is-linynnau
sub-system is-system *eb* is-systemau
subtangent istangiad *eg* istangiadau
subtend cynnal *be*
subtended angle ongl a gynhelir *eb* onglau a gynhelir
subterranean tanddaearol *ans*
subtitle isdeitl *eg* isdeitlau
subtle cynnil *ans*
subtle change newid cynnil *eg* newidiadau cynnil
subtle movement symudiad cynnil *eg* symudiadau cynnil
subtotal isgyfanswm *eg*
subtown istref *eb* istrefi
subtract tynnu *be*
subtraction tynnu *be*
subtraction problem problem dynnu *eb* problemau tynnu
subtractive tynnol *ans*
subtractive bilingualism dwyieithrwydd gostyngol *eg*
subtractive printing printio tynnol *be*
sub-tree is-goeden *eb* is-goed
subtropical istrofannol *ans*
suburb maestref *eb* maestrefi
suburban maestrefol *ans*

suburban history hanes maestrefol *eg*
suburbia maestrefi *ell*
subversion tanseilio *be*
subversive *adj* tanseiliol *ans*
subversive *n* tanseiliwr *eg* tanseilwyr
subvert tanseilio *be*
subvert gwyrdroi *be*
subvocal articulation ynganu isleisiol *be*
subway tanlwybr *eg* tanlwybrau
subway Samaritans Samariaid y trenau tanddaearol *ell*
succeed (=come after) olynu *be*
succeed (=have success) llwyddo *be*
succentor ail gantor *eg* ail gantorion
success llwyddiant *eg* llwyddiannau
succession olyniaeth *eb* olyniaethau
succession of rocks olyniaeth creigiau *eb*
Succession States Gwladwriaethau'r Olyniaeth *ell*
successive olynol *ans*
successor olynydd *eg* olynwyr
succinic sycsinig *ans*
succulence suddlonedd *eg*
succulent suddlon *ans*
succulent plant planhigyn suddlon *eg* planhigion suddlon
suck sugno *be*
sucker sugnolyn *eg* sugnolynau
sucking reflex atgyrch sugno *eg*
suckle *v.intrans* sugno'r fron *be*
suckle *v.trans* rhoi'r fron *be*
sucrose swcros *eg*
sucrose solution hydoddiant swcros *eg*
suction sugnedd *eg* sugneddau
suction pressure gwasgedd sugno *eg*
suction pump pwmp sugno *eg* pympiau sugno
suction tube tiwb sugno *eg* tiwbiau sugno
sudd swd *eg* swdiau
sudden change newid sydyn *eg* newidiadau sydyn
suds trochion *ell*
suds sensitive machine peiriant sensitif i drochion *eg* peiriannau sensitif i drochion
suds tolerant machine peiriant goddef trochion *eg* peiriannau goddef trochion
suede finish gorffeniad swêd *eg*
sufficient digon *ans*
suffix olddodiad *eg* olddodiaid
suffocate mygu *be*
suffragan swffragan *eg* swffraganiaid
suffrage pleidlais *eb* pleidleisiau
suffragette swffragét *eb* swffragetiaid
suffragist swffragydd *eg* swffragwyr
Sufi Sufi *eg*
sugar siwgr *eg* siwgrau
sugar beet betys siwgr *ell*
sugar loaf torth siwgr *eb* torthau siwgr
sugar paper papur siwgr *eg*
sugar-loaf mandrel mandrel côn *eg* mandreli côn
suggest awgrymu *be*
suggestion awgrym *eg* awgrymiadau
suicide hunanladdiad *eg*
suicide troops milwyr hunanleiddiol *ell*
suit of armour arfwisg *eb* arfwisgoedd
suit of court dyledogaeth llys *eb*
suitability cyfaddasrwydd *eg*
suitable background cefndir addas *eg* cefndiroedd addas
suitable material defnydd addas *eg* defnyddiau addas
suite cyfres *eb* cyfresi
suite de danses dawns gyfres *eb* dawns gyfresi
suited addas *ans*
suiting siwtin *eg*
suitor cwynwr *eg* cwynwyr
Sukkot Sukkot
Suleiman the Magnificent Swleiman Ysblennydd *eg*
sulfate(IV) ion ïon sylffad(IV) *eg* ïonau sylffad(IV)
sulfate(VI) ion ïon sylffad(VI) *eg* ïonau sylffad(VI)
sulfinate ion ïon sylffinad *eg* ïonau sylffinad
sulfur sylffwr *eg*
sulfur dichloride dioxide sylffwr deuclorid deuocsid *eg*
sulfur dichloride oxide sylffwr deuclorid ocsid *eg*
sulfur dioxide sylffwr deuocsid *eg*
sulfur trioxide sylffwr triocsid *eg*
sulfuric(IV) acid asid sylffwrig(IV) *eg*
sulfuric(VI) acid asid sylffwrig(VI) *eg*
sulphate sylffad *eg*
sulphate attack ymosodiad sylffad *eg*
sulphide sylffid *eg*
sulphur (S) sylffwr *eg*
sulphuric sylffwrig *eg*
sulphuric acid asid sylffwrig *eg*
Sultan Swltan *eg*
sum swm *eg* symiau
sum (=elementary arithmetical problem) *n* sym *eb* symiau
sum of squares (SS) swm sgwariau *eg*
sum total cyfanswm *eg* cyfansymiau
summable symadwy *ans*
summary crynodeb *eg/b* crynodebau
summary offence trosedd ddiannod *eb* troseddau diannod
summation symiant *eg* symiannau
summative assessment asesiad crynodol *eg* asesiadau crynodol
summative project project crynodol *eg*
summer camp gwersyll haf *eg* gwersylloedd haf
summer holidays gwyliau haf *ell*
summer house tŷ haf *eg* tai haf
summer months misoedd yr haf *ell*
summer representative cynrychiolydd haf *eg* cynrychiolwyr haf
summer school ysgol haf *eb* ysgolion haf
summer season tymor yr haf *eg*

summer solstice heuldro'r haf *eg*
summer term tymor yr haf *eg*
summer wood pren yr haf *eg*
summit copa *eg* copaon
summit conference uwchgynhadledd *eb* uwchgynadleddau
summit plain gwastadedd copa *eg* gwastadeddau copaon
summoner gwysiwr *eg* gwyswyr
sump swmp *eg* swmpau
sumptuary laws deddfau cyfyngu *ell*
sun haul *eg* heuliau
sun proof gwrth-haul *ans*
sun terrace teras haul *eg* terasau haul
sunburn llosg haul *eg*
Sunday school ysgol Sul *eb* ysgolion Sul
sunflower blodyn yr haul *eg* blodau'r haul
sunk moulding mowldin suddo *eg*
sunk panel panel wedi'i suddo *eg* paneli wedi'u suddo
sunlight golau haul *eg*
sunna sunna *eg*
Sunni Sunni *eg*
sunray pleating pletio pelydrog *be*
sunrise pattern patrwm codiad yr haul *eg* patrymau codiad yr haul
sunshine heulwen *eb*
sunspots brychau haul *ell*
sunstroke twymyn haul *eb*
sun-suit gwisg haul *eb* gwisgoedd haul
sun-top top haul *eg* topiau haul
super giant star seren orgawr *eb*
super powers pwerau mawr *ell*
super state archwladwriaeth *eb*
super video graphics array arae graffeg fideo uwch *eb* araeau graffeg fideo uwch
superannuation budd-dal ymddeol *eg*
superconductivity uwchddargludedd *eg*
superconductivity gorddargludedd *eg*
supercool *adj* goroer *ans*
supercool *v* goroeri *be*
supercooled goroeredig *ans*
superego uwch-ego *eg*
superficial deposits dyddodion arwynebol *ell*
superfluidity uwchlifedd *eg*
supergrid uwchgrid *eg* uwchgridiau
superhet uwch-heterodein *ans*
superimpose arosod *be*
superimposed arosod *ans*
superimposed drainage draeniad arosod *eg*
superintendent uwch-arolygydd *eg* uwch-arolygyddion
superior uwch *ans*
superior (of anatomy) uwch *ans*
superiority rhagoriaeth *eb*
supermarket uwchfarchnad *eb* uwchfarchnadoedd
supermarket chain cadwyn o uwchfarchnadoedd *eb*
supernatant uwchwaddod *eg* uwchwaddodion
supernatural goruwchnaturiol *ans*
supernormal profit elw goruwchnormal *eg*
supernova uwchnofa *eb* uwchnofâu
superoctave uwchwythfed *eb* uwchwythfedau
superordinate concept cysyniad uwchraddol *eg* cysyniadau uwchraddol
superosculate uwchfinialu *be*
superosculating uwchfinialaidd *ans*
superpose arosod *be*
superposed fourths pedweryddau arosodedig *ell*
superposition arosodiad *eg* arosodiadau
supersaturate gorddirlenwi *be*
supersaturated gorddirlawn *ans*
supersaturation gorddirlawnder *eg*
superscript uwchysgrif *eb* uwchysgrifau
superset uwchset *eb* uwchsetiau
supersonic uwchsonig *ans*
superstition (in general) ofergoeliaeth *eb*
superstition (of specific instance) ofergoel *eb* ofergoelion
superstructure aradeiledd *eg* aradeileddau
supertonic uwch donydd *eg*
supervised study astudio dan oruchwyliaeth *be*
supervision goruchwyliaeth *eb*
supervision order gorchymyn goruchwyliaeth *eg*
supervisor goruchwyliwr *eg* goruchwylwyr
supervisory attentional system (SAS) system rheoli sylw goruchwyliol *eb*
Superwash wool gwlân 'Superwash' *eg*
supination (in Latin grammar) dyleddfiad *eg*
supination (of foot motion) swpinadiad *eg* swpinadiadau
supine (with feminine nouns) ar wastad ei chefn *ans*
supine (with masculine nouns) ar wastad ei gefn *ans*
supple ystwyth *ans*
supple twig brigyn ystwyth *eg* brigau ystwyth
supplement (in food) ychwanegyn *eg* ychwanegion
supplementary atodol *ans*
supplementary allocation dyraniad atodol *eg* dyraniadau atodol
supplementary angle ongl atodol *eb* onglau atodol
supplementary benefit budd-dal atodol *eg* budd-daliadau atodol
supplementary sketches brasluniau atodol *ell*
supplementation atchwanegiad *eg* atchwanegiadau
suppleness ystwythder *eg*
Supplication against the Ordinaries Ymbil yn erbyn yr Ordinariaid *eg*
supplied quantity (in economics) maint y cyflenwad *eg*
supply *v* cyflenwi *be*
supply (mains) *n* prif gyflenwad *eg*
supply (of food etc) *n* cyflenwad *eg* cyflenwadau
supply and demand cyflenwad a galw
supply and demand graph graff cyflenwad a galw *eg* graffiau cyflenwad a galw
supply curve cromlin gyflenwad *eb*

supply lines ffyrdd cyflenwi *ell*
Supply of Goods Act Deddf Cyflenwi Nwyddau *eb*
supply teacher (female) athrawes lanw *eb* athrawesau llanw
supply teacher (male) athro llanw *eg* athrawon llanw
supply-side policies polisi ochr gyflenwi *eg* polisïau ochr gyflenwi
support (=prop, skeletal function) *n* cynhaliad *eg*
support (active) *n* cymorth *eg*
support (active) *v* cynorthwyo *be*
support (an argument) *v* ategu *be*
support (of piece of equipment) *n* cynhalydd *eg* cynalyddion
support (oneself) *v* ymgynnal *be*
support (passive) *n* cefnogaeth *eb*
support (passive) *v* cefnogi *be*
support (structures etc) *v* cynnal *be*
support booklet llyfryn cymorth *eg* llyfrynnau cymorth
support group grŵp cefnogi *eg* grwpiau cefnogi
support materials deunyddiau atodol *ell*
support position safle cynnal *eg* safleoedd cynnal
supported self-study astudio unigol gyda chymorth *be*
supporter cefnogwr *eg* cefnogwyr
supporting stool (for cabinet) stôl gynnal *eb* stolion cynnal
supporting tissue meinwe gynhaliol *eb* meinweoedd cynhaliol
supportive cefnogol *ans*
suppository tawddgyffur *eg* tawddgyffuriau
suppress atal *be*
suppressed immunity imiwnedd ataliedig *eg*
suppression ataliad *eg* ataliadau
suprapharyngeal uwchffaryngeal *ans*
supremacist goruchafwr *eg* goruchafwyr
supremacy goruchafiaeth *eb*
supreme goruchaf *ans*
Supreme Court Llys Goruchaf *eg*
Supreme Court of Judicature Goruchaf Lys y Farnwriaeth *eg*
Supreme Governor Uchaf-Lywodraethwr *eg*
Supreme Head Goruchaf Ben *eg*
Supreme Soviet Sofiet Goruchaf *eg*
supremum swpremwm *ans*
surachiasmatic nucleus (SCN) niwclews uwchaciasmatig *eg*
surah surah *eg*
surazo swraso *eg* swrasoau
surcharge tâl ychwanegol *eg* taliadau ychwanegol
surcoat crysbais *eb*
surd swrd *eg* syrdiau
surety mach *eg* meichiau
surety bail mechnïaeth *eb*
suretyship mechnïaeth *eb*
surf *n* ewyn môr *eg*
surf *v* syrffio *be*
surface arwyneb *eg* arwynebau
surface area arwynebedd arwyneb *eg*
surface decoration addurn arwyneb *eg* addurniadau arwyneb
surface development datblygiad arwyneb *eg* datblygiadau arwyneb
surface dive deif arwyneb *eb* deifiau arwyneb
surface dyslexia dyslecsia arwynebol *eg*
surface embroidery brodwaith arwyneb *eg*
surface engraving ysgythriad arwyneb *eg* ysgythriadau arwyneb
surface finish gorffeniad arwyneb *eg*
surface finishing gorffen arwyneb *be*
surface gauge medrydd arwyneb *eg*
surface membrane pilen arwyneb *eb*
surface of revolution arwyneb cylchdro *eg*
surface plate plât arwyneb *eg* platiau arwyneb
surface scratches crafiadau arwyneb *ell*
surface stain staen arwyneb *eg*
surface storage storfa arwyneb *eb*
surface table bwrdd arwyneb *eg*
surface tension tyniant arwyneb *eg* tyniannau arwyneb
surface treatment triniaeth arwyneb *eb* triniaethau arwyneb
surface view uwcholwg *eg* uwcholygon
surface water dŵr wyneb *eg*
surfactant (surface active agent) arwynebydd *eg* arwynebyddion
surfer brigdonnwr *eg* brigdonwyr
Surform blade llafn Surform *eg* llafnau Surform
surge dygyfor *be*
surge ymchwydd *eg* ymchwyddiadau
surgeon llawfeddyg *eg* llawfeddygon
surgery (=branch of medicine) llawfeddygaeth *eb*
surgery (of place) meddygfa *eb* meddygfeydd
surjective mapping mapio arsaethol *be*
surplice gwenwisg *eb* gwenwisgoedd
surplus (=amount left over) gweddill *eg* gweddillion
surplus (in accounting) gwarged *eg* gwargedion
surplus variable newidyn gweddill *eg* newidynnau gweddill
surprise cadence diweddeb annisgwyl *eb* diweddebau annisgwyl
surrealism swrealaeth *eb*
surrealist swrealydd *eg* swrealwyr
surrender ildio *be*
surround *n* amgylchyn *eg* amgylchynau
surround *v* amgylchynu *be*
surtax gordreth *eb* gordrethi
surtitle uwchdeitl *eg* uwchdeitlau
survey (in general) *v* gwneud arolwg *eb*
survey (of evidence etc) *n* arolwg *eg* arolygon
survey (of land) *v* tirfesur *be*
survey research ymchwil arolwg *eg*
surveying equipment offer tirfesur *ell*
surveyor (in general) syrfëwr *eg* syrfewyr
surveyor (of land) tirfesurydd *eg* tirfesurwyr
surveyor's levels lefelau syrfëwr *ell*

survival goroesiad *eg* goroesiadau
survival of the fittest goroesiad y cymhwysaf *eg*
survival rate cyfradd goroesi *eb*
survival value gwerth goroesol *eg* gwerthoedd goroesol
survive goroesi *be*
survivor goroeswr *eg* goroeswyr
survivorship goroesedd *eg*
susceptibility rhagdueddiad *eg*
susceptibility derbynnedd *eg* derbyneddau
suspend diarddel *be*
suspend (=hang) hongian *be*
suspend (from school) gwahardd dros dro *be*
suspended ynghrog *ans*
suspended (=hanging) crog *ans*
suspended cadence diweddeb ohiriedig *eb* diweddebau gohiriedig
suspended drawer drôr crog *eg* droriau crog
suspended floor llawr crog *eg* lloriau crog
suspended light golau crog *eg* goleuadau crog
suspended note gohirnod *eg* gohirnodau
suspended sculpture cerflunwaith crog *eg*
suspended sentence dedfryd ohiriedig *eb* dedfrydau gohiriedig
suspending agent cyfrwng daliant *eg* cyfryngau daliant
suspending power (from work etc) hawl atal *eg* hawliau atal
suspension (from school) gwaharddiad dros dro *eg* gwaharddiadau dros dro
suspension (in music) gohiriant *eg* gohiriannau
suspension (of car) hongiad *eg* hongiadau
suspension (of objects) crogiant *eg* crogiannau
suspension (particles in liquid, etc) daliant *eg* daliannau
suspension bridge pont grog *eb* pontydd crog
suspensory cynhaliol *ans*
suspensory ligament gewyn cynhaliol *eg* gewynnau cynhaliol
sustain activity cynnal gweithgarwch *be*
sustainable cynaliadwy *ans*
sustainable development datblygiad cynaliadwy *eg*
sustainable economic growth twf economaidd cynaliadwy *eg*
sustained event camp hir ei pharhad *eb* campau hir eu parhad
suture (in nature) asiad *eg* asiadau
suture (in surgery) pwyth *eg* pwythau
suture line (in nature) llinell asio *eb* llinellau asio
suture line (in surgery) llinell bwytho *eb* llinellau pwytho
suzerain penarglwydd *eg* penarglwyddi
suzerainty penarglwyddiaeth *eb* penarglwyddiaethau
suzerainty agreement cytundeb penarglwyddiaethol *eg*
swab *n* swab *eg* swabiau
swab (=clean wound etc) *v* glanhau *be*
swage *n* darfath *eg* darfathau
swage *v* darfathu *be*
swage block bloc darfath *eg* blociau darfath
swale traethbant *eg* traethbantau
swallow *n* gwennol *eb* gwenoliaid
swallow *v* llyncu *be*
swallow dive deif wennol *eb* deifiau gwennol
swallow hole llyncdwll *eg* llyncdyllau
swamp gwern *eb* gwernydd
swamp forest gwern goedwig *eb* gwern goedwigoedd
swan neck (on boat) *v* mynwyddu *be*
swan neck (on harp) *n* gwyriad ar y grib *eg*
swan-neck (on boat) *n* mynwydd *eg*
swan-necked pin pin gwddf alarch *eg* pinnau gwddf alarch
swansdown mop mop manblu alarch *eg* mopiau manblu alarch
swap cyfnewid *be*
swarf naddion *ell*
swash torddwr *eg* torddyfroedd
swastika (Hindu symbol) swastika *eg* swastikas
swastika (Nazi symbol) swastica *eg* swasticas
swatch casgliad patrymau *eg* casgliadau patrymau
swathe *n* amrwym *eg* amrwymau
swathe *v* amrwymo *be*
sweat *n* chwys *eg*
sweat *v* (=perspire) chwysu *be*
sweat *v* (=soldering) cysodro *be*
sweat gland chwarren chwys *eb* chwarennau chwys
sweatshirt crys chwys *eg* crysau chwys
Swede Swediad *eg* Swediaid
swede erfinen *eb* erfin; meipen *eb* maip
Swedish *adj* Swedaidd *ans*
Swedish (language) *n* Swedeg *eb*
Swedish iron haearn Sweden *eg*
sweep (of brace) ehangylch *eg* ehangylchoedd
sweep shot ysgubiad *eg*
sweeper ysgubwr *eg* ysgubwyr
sweet container cynhwysydd melysion *eg* cynwysyddion melysion
swell (in general) *v* chwyddo *be*
swell (of waves, sowing sections) *n* ymchwydd *eg* ymchwyddiadau
swell and swale bryn a phant
swelling chwydd *eg* chwyddiadau
swerve gwyro *be*
swimming nofio *be*
swimming bladder chwysigen nofio *eb* chwysigod nofio
swimming gala gala nofio *eg* galâu nofio
swimming pool pwll nofio *eg* pyllau nofio
swimming stroke dull nofio *eg* dulliau nofio
swimsuit gwisg nofio *eb* gwisgoedd nofio
swing (=seat slung on ropes) *n* siglen *eb* siglenni
swing (in cricket) *v* swingio *be*
swing (in politics) *n* gogwydd *eg*
swing (of movement) *n* osgiliad *eg* osgiliadau

swing (of winds) *n* mudiad *eg* mudiadau
swing (on rope etc) *v* siglo *be*
swing on a bar swingio ar far *be*
swing on a rope siglo ar raff *be*
swing the arms backward and forward swingio'r breichiau yn ôl ac ymlaen *be*
swirl chwyrlïad *eg* chwyrliadau
swirled pattern patrwm chwyrlïog *eg* patrymau chwyrlïog
swirling motion mudiant chwyrlïog *eg*
Swiss darn craith Swisaidd *eb* creithiau Swisaidd
switch *n* switsh *eg* switshis
switch *v* switsio *be*
switch node trosnod *eg* trosnodau
switch off diffodd *be*
switch on (light, fire) cynnau *be*
switch on (motor etc) cychwyn *be*
switchboard switsfwrdd *eg* switsfyrddau
switching algebra algebra switsio *eg*
switching circuit cylched switsio *eb* cylchedau switsio
swivel *n* bwylltid *eg* bwylltidau
swivel *v* bwylltidio *be*
swivel base gwaelod bwylltid *eg* gwaelodion bwylltid
swivel castor castor bwylltid *eg* castorau bwylltid
swivel head pen bwylltid *eg* pennau bwylltid
swivel joint cymal bwylltid *eg* cymalau bwylltid
swivel shoe (G cramp) esgid fwylltid *eb* esgidiau bwylltid
swivel vice feis fwylltid *eb* feisiau bwylltid
sword cleddyf *eg* cleddyfau
sword belt gwregys cleddyf *eg* gwregysau cleddyf
sword fight gornest gleddyfau *eb* gornestau cleddyfau
sword shape brush brwsh siâp cleddyf *eg* brwshys siâp cleddyf
sylko edau sglein *eb* edafedd sglein
syllabus maes llafur *eg* meysydd llafur
syloxdex sylocsdecs *eg*
symbiosis symbiosis *eg*
symbol symbol *eg* symbolau
symbolic symbolaidd *ans*
symbolic address cyfeiriad symbolaidd *eg* cyfeiriadau symbolaidd
symbolic character cymeriad symbolaidd *eg* cymeriadau symbolaidd
symbolic play chwarae symbolaidd *be*
symbolic thinking meddwl symbolaidd *be*
symbolism symbolaeth *eb*
symbolist *adj* symbolaidd *ans*
symbolist movement mudiad symbolaidd *eg*
symbolize symboleiddio *be*
symmetric cymesur *ans*
symmetric fold plyg cymesur *eg* plygion cymesur
symmetrical cymesur *ans*
symmetrical effect effaith gymesur *eb*
symmetrization cymesuro *be*
symmetry cymesuredd *eg* cymesureddau

sympathetic (of nervous system) sympathetig *ans*
sympathetic (of person) llawn cydymdeimlad *ans*
sympathetic branch cangen sympathetig *eb*
► **sympathetic nervous system** system nerfol sympathetig *eb*
sympathetic strings (acoustics) tannau cydseiniol *ell*
sympathy cydymdeimlad *eg*
symphonic symffonig *ans*
symphonic poem cathl symffonig *eg* cathlau symffonig
symphony symffoni *eb* symffonïau
symposium symposiwm *eg* symposia
symptom symptom *eg* symptomau
symptom substitution amnewid symptomau *be*
synaesthesia synaesthesia *eg*
synaesthete synaesthetwr *eg* synaesthetwyr
synagogue synagog *eb* synagogau
synapse synaps *eg* synapsau
synaptic synaptig *ans*
synaptic cleft hollt synaptig *eb* holltau synaptig
synchromesh cyd-ddant *eg*
synchronization cydamseriad *eg* cydamseriadau
synchronize cydamseru *be*
synchronizer cydamserydd *eg* cydamseryddion
synchronous cydamseredig *ans*
synchronous counter rhifydd cydamseredig *eg*
synchrotron syncrotron *eg*
synclinal synclinol *ans*
syncline synclin *eg* synclinau
synclinorium synclinoriwm *eg* synclinoria
syncopation trawsacen *eb* trawsacenion
syncope llesmair *eg* llesmeiriau
syncytium syncytiwm *eg* syncytia
syndicalism syndicaliaeth *eb*
syndiotactic syndiotactig *ans*
syndrome syndrom *eg* syndromau
synergism synergedd *eg* synergeddau
synergist synergydd *eg* synergyddion
synergistic synergaidd *ans*
synod synod *eg* synodau
synodal synodaidd *ans*
synonym-antonym test prawf cyfystyr-gwrthystyr *eg* profion cyfystyr-gwrthystyr
synopsis crynodeb *eg/b* crynodebau
synoptic synoptig *ans*
synoptic chart siart synoptig *eg* siartiau synoptig
synovial synofaidd *ans*
synovial fluid hylif synofaidd *eg*
synovial joint cymal synofaidd *eg* cymalau synofaidd
syntactical cystrawennol *ans*
syntagm syntagm *eg*
syntax cystrawen *eb* cystrawennau
syntax analysis dadansoddiad cystrawen *eg* dadansoddiadau cystrawen
syntax error gwall cystrawen *eg* gwallau cystrawen

syntax rules rheolau cystrawen *ell*
synthesis *n* synthesis *eg* synthesisau
synthesize *v* syntheseiddio *be*
synthesize information syntheseiddio gwybodaeth *be*
synthesizer syntheseiddydd *eg* syntheseiddwyr
synthetic *adj* synthetig *ans*
synthetic *n* synthetigyn *eg* synthetigion
synthetic adhesive adlyn synthetig *eg* adlynion synthetig
synthetic bass (stop) bas synthetig *eg*
synthetic cane gwialen synthetig *eb* gwialennau synthetig
synthetic chemist cemegydd synthetig *eg*
synthetic detergent glanedydd synthetig *eg* glanedyddion synthetig
synthetic fibre ffibr synthetig *eg* ffibrau synthetig
synthetic glue glud synthetig *eg* gludion synthetig
synthetic lacquer lacr synthetig *eg*
synthetic paint paent synthetig *eg*
synthetic resin resin synthetig *eg* resinau synthetig
synthetic resin glue glud resin synthetig *eg*
synthetic route llwybr synthetig *eg*
synthetic speech llefaru synthetig *be*
synthetic track trac synthetig *eg* traciau synthetig
synthetic wood pren synthetig *eg* prennau synthetig
syphilis syffilis *eg*
syringe *n* chwistrell *eb* chwistrelli
syringe *v* chwistrellu *be*
syringe driver gyrrwr chwistrell *eg* gyrwyr chwistrell
syrup syryp *eg* syrypau
syrup form ffurf driog *eb*
syrupy syrypaidd *ans*
system (of body organs, computers, numbers) system *eb* systemau
system (of organization, administration) cyfundrefn *eb* cyfundrefnau
system maintenance cynnal system *be*
system of measurement system fesur *eb* systemau mesur
system software meddalwedd system *eb*
system specification manyleb system *eb* manylebau system
system tray cilfach *eb* (TG)
system variable newidyn system *eg* newidynnau system
systematic (=orderly) systematig *ans*
systematic (belonging to a system) cyfundrefnol *ans*
systematic desensitization dadsensiteiddio systematig *be*
systematic error cyfeiliornad systematig *eg* cyfeiliornadau systematig
systematic replication dyblygu systematig *be*
systematic sampling samplu systematig *be*
systemic (e.g. of insecticides) hollgorffol *ans*
systemic arch bwa systemig *eg* bwâu systemig
systems analysis dadansoddiad systemau *eg*
systems analyst dadansoddwr systemau *eg* dadansoddwyr systemau
systems and control technology systemau a thechnoleg rheoli
systems flowchart siart llif systemau *eg* siartiau llif systemau
systems programmer rhaglennwr systemau *eg* rhaglenwyr systemau
systole systole *eg*

T

T lymphocyte lymffocyt T *eb* lymffocytau T
T test prawf T *eg*
tab tab *eg* tabiau
tab key bysell tab *eb* bysellau tab
tab setting gosodiad tab *eg* gosodiadau tab
tab washer wasier dafod *eb* wasieri tafod
tabard tabard *eg* tabardau
tabby loom gwŷdd tabi *eg* gwyddau tabi
tabernacle tabernacl *eg* tabernaclau
table (e.g. of numbers /data) tabl *eg* tablau
table (e.g. on guitar) seinfwrdd *eg* seinfyrddau
table (furniture) bwrdd *eg* byrddau
table adjustment shaft siafft gymhwyso bwrdd *eb* siafftiau cymhwyso byrddau
table easel îsl bwrdd *eg* islau bwrdd
table lectern darllenfa fwrdd *eb* darllenfeydd bwrdd
table mat mat bwrdd *eg* matiau bwrdd
table of logarithms tabl logarithmau *eg* tablau logarithmau
table of three tabl tri *eg*
table steady sadydd bwrdd *eg* sadwyr byrddau
table top top bwrdd *eg* topiau byrddau
table vice feis fwrdd *eb* feisiau bwrdd
table with drawer bwrdd â drôr ynddo *eg* byrddau â drôr ynddynt
tablecloth lliain bwrdd *eg* llieiniau bwrdd
tableland tirfwrdd *eg* tirfyrddau
table-linen llieiniau bwrdd *ell*
table-napkin napcyn *eg* napcynau
tablet tabled *eb* tabledi
tablet loom gwŷdd tabled *eg* gwyddau tabled
tablet weaving gwehyddu tabled *be*
table-top fixing sicrhau top bwrdd *be*
table-top hinge colfach top bwrdd *eg* colfachau top bwrdd
tableware llestri bwrdd *ell*
tabloid papur poblogaidd *eg*
taboo tabŵ *eg* tabwau
tabor tabwrdd *eg* tabyrddau
Taborites Taboriaid *ell*
tabular (broad and flat) byrddol *ans*
tabular (of data) tablaidd *ans*
tabular ice iâ byrddol *eg*; rhew byrddol *eg*
tabular relief tirwedd fyrddol *eb* tirweddau byrddol
tabulate tablu *be*
tabulated tabledig *ans*
tachism tasiaeth *eg*
tachistoscope tacistosgop *eg* tacistosgopau
tachycardia cyflymedd y galon *eg*
tack *v* tacio *be*
tack (=nail) *n* hoelen fer *eb* hoelion byr
tack (=stickiness) *n* gludedd *eg*
tack (of ship, in sewing) *n* tac *eg* taciau
tacker taciwr *eg* tacwyr
tacking stitch pwyth tacio *eg* pwythau tacio
tackle *n* tacl *eb* taclau
tackle *v* taclo *be*
tackler taclwr *eg* taclwyr
tacky gludiog *ans*
tacnode tacnod *eg* tacnodau
tactic tacteg *eb* tactegau
tactile cyffyrddol *ans*
tactile agnosia agnosia cyffwrdd *eg*
tactile consciousness ymwybyddiaeth gyffyrddol *eb*
tactile imagination dychymyg cyffyrddol *eg*
tactile sensation synhwyriad cyffyrddol *eg*
tadpole penbwl *eg* penbyliaid
Taff Vale Case Achos Dyffryn Taf *eg*
taffeta taffeta *eg*
tag *n* tag *eg* tagiau
tag *v* tagio *be*
tag lace carrai tag *eb* careiau tag
tag question cwestiwn tag *eg* cwestiynau tag
taiga taiga *eg*
tail cynffon *eb* cynffonnau
tailored suit siwt wedi'i theilwra *eb* siwtiau wedi'u teilwra
tailoring teilwrio *be*
tailor's canvas cynfas teiliwr *eg*
tailor's chalk sialc teiliwr *eg*
tailor's tack tac teiliwr *eg* taciau teiliwr
tailpiece cynffon *eb* cynffonnau
tailstock (lathe) pen llonydd *eg* pennau llonydd
tailstock die holder daliwr dei pen llonydd *eg* dalwyr dei pen llonydd
take exercise ymarfer *be*
take loose datod *be*
take off (in jumping and vaulting) *v* esgyn *be*
take part cymryd rhan *be*
take the blade (prise de fer) cymryd y llafn *be*
take up (fugue) cydio yn *be*
take weight on hands cymryd pwysau ar y dwylo *be*
takeaway siop prydau parod *eb* siopau prydau parod
take-home pay *n* cyflog clir *eg*
take-off (jumping /vaulting) *n* esgynfa *eb* esgynfeydd
take-over *n* trosfeddiant *eg* trosfeddiannau

take-over *v* trosfeddiannu *be*
take-up (gas fluid) cymryd i mewn *be*
take-up lever (of machine part) codell *eb* codellau
taking in slack tynnu slac *be*
talc talc *eg* talciau
talented talentog *ans*
talk board (on the web) bwrdd siarad *eg* byrddau siarad
talk show sioe siarad *eb*
talking head pen sy'n siarad *eg* pennau sy'n siarad
tall organisation structre strwythur trefniadaeth tal *eg*
tallage treth ffiwdal *eb*
tallow gwêr *eg* gwerau
tally (of stick) rhicbren *eg* rhicbrennau
tally chart siart cyfrif *eg* siartiau cyfrif
tally mark marc rhifo *eg* marciau rhifo
Talmud Talmud *eg*
talwind talwynt *eg* talwyntoedd
tamarind tamarind *eg* tamarindau
tambora tambora *eg* tamborâu
tambour tabwrdd *eg* tabyrddau
tambour de Basque (musical instrument) tambwrîn *eg* tambwrinau
tambour door drws tabwrdd *eg* drysau tabwrdd
tambour frame (embroidery) ffrâm frodio gron *eb* fframiau brodio crwn
tambour front ffrynt tabwrdd *eg* ffryntiau tabwrdd
tambour shutter clawr tabwrdd *eg* cloriau tabwrdd
tambour slat slat dabwrdd *eb* slatiau tabwrdd
tambourin (type of music or dance) tambwrîn *eg* tambwrinau
tambourine (musical instrument) tambwrîn *eg* tambwrinau
tan (leather) *v* barcio *be*
tandem corrie peiran tandem *eg* peirannau tandem
tang (of chisel, file) colsaid *eg* colseidiau
tangency tangiadaeth *eb* tangiadaethau
tangent tangiad *eg* tangiadau
tangent plane plân tangiad *eg* planau tangiad
tangential tangiadol *ans*
tangential arc arc dangiadol *eb* arcau tangiadol
tangential follower dilynwr tangiadol *eg* dilynwyr tangiadol
tangential plane plân tangiadol *eg* planau tangiadol
tangential sawcut tanglifiad *eg* tanglifiadau
tangential sawing llifio tangiadol *be*
tangential section trychiad tangiadol *eg* trychiadau tangiadol
tango tango *eg* dawnsiau tango
tangram tangram *eg* tangramau
tanh tanh *eg*
tanha tanha *eg*
tank tanc *eg* tanciau
tank cutter torrwr tanc *eg* torwyr tanc
tank drill dril tanc *eg* driliau tanc
tanker tancer *eg* tanceri
tanner (of leather) barcer *eg* barceriaid
tannery tanerdy *eg* tanerdai
tannic acid asid tannig *eg*
tannin tanin *eg*
tantalum (Ta) tantalwm *eg*
tantrum stranc *eb* stranciau
Taoist *adj* Taoaidd *ans*
Taoist *n* Taoydd *eg* Taoyddion
tap *n* tap *eg* tapiau
tap *v* tapio *be*
tap dancing dawnsio tap *be*
tap root prif wreiddyn *eg* prif wreiddiau
tap wrench tyndro tap *eg* tyndroeon tap
tape *n* tâp *eg* tapiau
tape deck dec tâp *eg* deciau tâp
tape drive tâp-yrrwr *eg* tâp-yrwyr
tape feed *n* tâp-borthydd *eg* tâp-borthwyr
tape feed *v* tâp-borthi *be*
tape file ffeil tâp *eb* ffeiliau tâp
tape library llyfrgell dapiau *eb* llyfrgelloedd tapiau
tape mark marc tâp *eg* marciau tâp
tape punch tyllydd tâp *eg* tyllwyr tâp
tape reader darllenydd tâp *eg* darllenyddion tâp
tape sequence dilyniant tâp *eg* dilyniannau tâp
tape serial number rhif cyfresol tâp *eg* rhifau cyfresol tâp
tape transport cludydd tâp *eg* cludwyr tâp
tape unit uned tâp *eb* unedau tâp
taped music cerddoriaeth dâp *eb*
tape-measure tâp mesur *eg* tapiau mesur
taper *n* tapr *eg* taprau
taper *v* tapro *be*
taper drift drifft tapr *eg* drifftiau tapr
taper lead arweiniad tapr *eg*
taper pin pìn tapr *eg* pinnau tapr
taper reamer agorell dapr *eb* agorellau tapr
taper shank garan dapr *eb* garanau tapr
taper shank drill dril garan dapr *eg* driliau garanau tapr
taper sleeve llawes dapr *eb* llewys tapr
taper tap tap tapr *eg* tapiau tapr
taper turning turnio tapr *be*
taper turning attachment atodyn turnio tapr *eg* atodion turnio tapr
tapered taprog *ans*
tapered former ffurfydd taprog *eg* ffurfwyr taprog
tapered gutter cafn taprog *eg* cafnau taprog
tapered handle coes daprog *eb* coesau taprog
tapered housing joint uniad rhigol draws daprog *eg* uniadau rhigolau traws taprog
tapered key allwedd daprog *eb* allweddi taprog
tapered leg coes daprog *eb* coesau taprog
tapered part rhan daprog *eb* rhannau taprog
tapered shaft siafft daprog *eb* siafftau taprog
tapered stake bonyn taprog *eg* bonion taprog
tapered tread gris taprog *eg* grisiau taprog
tapered trowel trywel taprog *eg* trywelion taprog
tapering blaenfain *ans*

tapering *adj* pigfain *ans*
tapering fold plyg pigfain *eg* plygion pigfain
tapestry tapestri *eg* tapestrïau
tapestry needle nodwydd tapestri *eb* nodwyddau tapestri
tapestry wool edafedd tapestri *ell*
tapetum tapetwm *eg* tapeta
tapeworm llyngyren *eb* llyngyr
tapped hole twll wedi'i dapio *eg* tyllau wedi'u tapio
tappet taped *eg* tapedi
tappet clearance cliriad taped *eg* cliriadau taped
tapping drill dril tapio *eg* driliau tapio
tapping hole twll tapio *eg* tyllau tapio
taps and dies tapiau a deiau
tarantella tarantela *eg* tarantelâu
tardive dyskinesia dyscinesia camsymud araf *eg*
target targed *eg* targedau
target audience cynulleidfa darged *eb* cynulleidfaoedd targed
target cell cell darged *eb* celloedd targed
target criteria meini prawf targed *ell*
target game gêm darged *eb* gemau targed
target group grŵp targed *eg* grwpiau targed
target language iaith darged *eb* ieithoedd targed
target organ cyrch-organ *eb* cyrch-organau
targeted programme rhaglen a dargedwyd *eb* rhaglenni a dargedwyd
tariff (=tax) toll *eb* tollau
tariff wall mur tollau *eg* muriau tollau
tarmac tarmac *eg*
tarn llyn mynydd *eg* llynnoedd mynydd
tarnish *n* tarnais *eg* tarneisiau
tarnish *v* tarneisio *be*
tarsal tarsol *ans*
tarsus tarsws *eg*
Tartar *adj* Tartaraidd *ans*
Tartar *n* Tartar *eg* Tartariaid
tartaric acid asid tartarig *eg*
task tasg *eb* tasgau
task force cyrchlu *eg* cyrchluoedd
task orientated care gofal yn ôl tasgau *eg*
tassel tasel *eg* taselau
taste *v* blasu *be*
taste (=discernment) *n* chwaeth *eb*
taste (of food etc) *n* blas *eg*
taste bud blasbwynt *eg* blasbwyntiau
tatting tatio *be*
tattoo tatŵ *eg* tatŵau
taurine tawrin *eg*
taurocholic acid asid tawrocolig *eg*
taut tynn *ans*
tautology tawtoleg *eb*
tautomeric tawtomerig *ans*
tautomerism tawtomeredd *eg*
tawhid tawhid *eg*
tax *n* treth *eb* trethi
tax *v* trethu *be*
tax allowance lwfans trethi *eg* lwfansau trethi
tax exemption eithriad o dreth *eg*
tax gatherer casglwr trethi *eg* casglwyr trethi
tax rebate ad-daliad treth *eg* ad-daliadau treth
tax relief gostyngiad yn y dreth *eg*
taxable trethadwy *ans*
taxable income incwm trethadwy *eg*
taxation trethiad *eg* trethiadau
taxation rates cyfraddau trethiad *ell*
taxi tacsi *eg* tacsis
taxonomic tacsonomaidd *ans*
taxonomic constraint cyfyngiad tacsonomi *eg*
taxonomy tacsonomeg *eb*
tca cycle cylched tca *eb* cylchedau tca
tea break amser paned *eg*
tea cosy gorchudd tebot *eg* gorchuddion tebot
teach *v* addysgu *be*
teacher (female) athrawes *eb* athrawesau
teacher (male) athro *eg* athrawon
teacher assessment (when the teacher is assessed) asesu athrawon *be*
teacher assessment (when the teacher is the assessor - of female teacher) asesiad yr athrawes *eb*
teacher assessment (when the teacher is the assessor - of male teacher) asesiad yr athro *eg*
teacher centre canolfan athrawon *eb* canolfannau athrawon
teacher education addysg athrawon *eb*
teacher placement service gwasanaeth lleoli athrawon *eg*
teacher support programme rhaglen cefnogi athrawon *eb* rhaglenni cefnogi athrawon
teacher training hyfforddi athrawon *be*
teaching dysgeidiaeth *eb*
teaching hospital ysbyty athrofaol *eg* ysbytai athrofaol
teaching load baich dysgu *eg* beichiau dysgu
teaching materials deunyddiau addysgu *ell*
teaching methods dulliau addysgu *ell*
teaching practice ymarfer dysgu *eg*
teaching style arddull addysgu *eg* arddulliau addysgu
teaching unit uned ddysgu *eb* unedau dysgu
teak tîc *eg*
teak oil olew tîc *eg*
team tîm *eg* timau
team event camp tîm *eb* campau tîm
team game gêm i dîm *eb* gemau tîm
team leader arweinydd tîm *eg* arweinwyr tîm
team member aelod o dîm *eg* aelodau o dîm
team nursing nyrsio tîm *be*
team teaching addysgu tîm *be*
teamwork gwaith tîm *eg*
tear (drop of liquid) *n* deigryn *eg* dagrau
tear (hole or damage) *n* rhwyg *eg* rhwygau
tear (pull apart) *v* rhwygo *be*
tear duct dwythell ddagrau *eb* dwythellau dagrau
tear-off roll rholen rwygo *eb* rholiau rhwygo

tease (wool) cribo gwlân *be*
teaser (of wool) cribwr *eg* cribwyr
teaser campaign ymgyrch ragflas *eb*
teat teth *eb* tethi
teat pipette diferydd *eg* diferyddion
TEC: Training and Enterprise Councils Cynghorau Hyfforddi a Menter *ell*
technetium (Tc) technetiwm *eg*
technical technegol *ans*
technical code cod technegol *eg* codau technegol
technical college coleg technegol *eg* colegau technegol
technical designer cynllunydd technegol *eg* cynllunwyr technegol
technical drawing *n* lluniad technegol *eg* lluniadau technegol
technical education addysg dechnegol *eb*
technical production skill sgil cynhyrchu technegol *eg* sgiliau cynhyrchu technegol
technical staff staff technegol *ell*
technician technegydd *eg* technegwyr
technique techneg *eb* technegau
technological technolegol *ans*
technological change newid technolegol *eg* newidiadau technolegol
technologist technolegydd *eg* technolegwyr
technology technoleg *eb* technolegau
technology push gwthiad technoleg *eg*
tectonic tectonig *ans*
tectonic activity gweithgaredd tectonig *eg*
tectonic event digwyddiad tectonig *eg* digwyddiadau tectonig
tectonic hazard perygl tectonig *eg* peryglon tectonig
tectonic plate movement symudiad platiau tectonig *eg* symudiadau platiau tectonig
tectonic process proses dectonig *eb* prosesau tectonig
tectorial membrane pilen dectoraidd *eb* pilenni tectoraidd
tee *n* ti *eg* tiau
tee *v* tio *be*
tee bolt bollt T *eb* bolltau T
tee bridle bagl T *eb* baglau T
tee bridle joint uniad bagl T *eg* uniadau bagl T
tee halving haneru T *be*
teenage magazine cylchgrawn ar gyfer yr arddegau *eg* cylchgronau ar gyfer yr arddegau
teens arddegau *ell*
tee-slot milling cutter melinwr rhigol T *eg* melinwyr rhigol T
teething torri dannedd *be*
teething-ring cylch cnoi *eg* cylchoedd cnoi
teetotaller llwyrymwrthodwr *eg* llwyrymwrthodwyr
telecommunication telathrebu *be*
teleological teleolegol *ans*
teleological argument dadl deleolegol *eb*
teleology teleoleg *eb*
telephone ffôn *eg* ffonau
telephone banking bancio ffôn *be*
telephone survey arolwg ffôn *eg* arolygon ffôn
teleprinter tele-argraffydd *eg* tele-argraffyddion
telescope telesgop *eg* telesgopau
teletext teledestun *eg*
teletype teledeip *eg* teledeipiau
television teledu *eg* setiau teledu
television documentary rhaglen ddogfen teledu *eb* rhaglenni dogfen teledu
television drama drama deledu *eb* dramâu teledu
television programme rhaglen deledu *eb* rhaglenni teledu
television set set deledu *eb* setiau teledu
television technique techneg deledu *eb* technegau teledu
tellurium (Te) telwriwm *eg*
telophase teloffas *eg*
temper *n* tymer *eg*
temper (a musical instrument) *v* ardymheru *be*
tempera tempera *eg*
tempera colour lliw tempera *eg* lliwiau tempera
tempera painting (of painted picture) paentiad tempera *eg* paentiadau tempera
tempera painting (of process or art) peintio tempera *be*
temperament (in music) ardymer *eg/b*
temperament (of character) anianawd *eg*
temperance movement mudiad dirwest *eg*
temperate tymherus *ans*
temperate forest coedwig dymherus *eb* coedwigoedd tymherus
temperate grassland glaswelltir tymherus *eg* glaswelltiroedd tymherus
temperate zone cylchfa dymherus *eb* cylchfaoedd tymherus
temperature tymheredd *eg* tymereddau
temperature coefficient of resistance cyfernod tymheredd gwrthiant *eg* cyfernodau tymheredd gwrthiant
temperature colour guide cyfarwyddyd lliwiau tymheredd *eg*
temperature range amrediad tymheredd *eg* amrediadau tymheredd
temperature scale graddfa tymheredd *eb* graddfeydd tymheredd
tempering tymheru *be*
tempering colours lliwiau tymheru *ell*
template (in computing) templed *eg* templedi
template (pattern in wood etc) patrymlun *eg* patrymluniau
template directory cyfeiriadur templedi *eg* cyfeiriaduron templedi
template file name enw ffeil templedi *eg* enwau ffeiliau templedi
template management rheoli templedi *be*
template path llwybr templed *eg* llwybrau templedi
temple teml *eb* temlau

tempo tempo *eg*
tempo marking arwydd tempo *eg*
temporal (=secular) tymhorol *ans*
temporal (of time) amseryddol *ans*
temporal coding codio amseryddol *be*
temporal data data amseryddol *ell*
temporal lobe llabed yr arlais *eb* llabedau'r arlais
temporal power pŵer tymhorol *eg*
temporary dros dro *ans*
Temporary Bench Mark (TBM) Meincnod Dros Dro (TBM) *eg*
Ten Articles, The Deg Erthygl, Y *eb*
Ten Commandments, The Deg Gorchymyn, Y
ten point scale graddfa deg pwynt *eb*
Tenakh Tenakh *eg*
tenancy tenantiaeth *eb*
tenant tenant *eg* tenantiaid
tenant farmer tenant fferm *eg* tenantiaid fferm
tenant-at-will tenant wrth ewyllys *eg* tenantiaid wrth ewyllys
tenant-in-chief prif denant *eg* prif denantiaid
tenantry tenantiaid *ell*
tendency tuedd *eb* tueddiadau
tender tendr *eg*
tender tyner *ans*
tenderness (emotion) tynerwch *eg*
tendon tendon *eg* tendonau
tendons of origin and insertion tendonau tarddol a thendonau mewniad *ell*
tendril tendril *eg* tendrilau
tenement tenement *eg* tenementau
tennis tennis *eg*
tennis ball pêl dennis *eb* peli tennis
tennis shoe esgid dennis *eb* esgidiau tennis
tenon tyno *eg* tynoau
tenon saw llif dyno *eb* llifiau tyno
tenoned clamp clamp tyno *eg* clampiau tyno
tenor tenor *eg* tenoriaid
tenor horn corn tenor *eg* cyrn tenor
tenor stave erwydd tenor *eg*
tenor viol feiol denor *eb* feiolau tenor
tens and units degau ac unedau
tensile tynnol *ans*
tensile bolt bollt tynnol *eb* bolltau tynnol
tensile force grym tynnol *eg*
tensile strain straen tynnol *eg*
tensile strength cryfder tynnol *eg*
tensile stress diriant tynnol *eg* diriannau tynnol
tension (mechanical) tyniant *eg* tyniannau
tension (of muscles, nerves etc) tyndra *eg* tyndrau
tension bar bar tyniant *eg* barrau tyniant
tension bolt bollt tyniant *eb* bolltau tyniant
tension disc (machine part) disg tyniant *eg* disgiau tyniant
tension force grym tyniant *eg*
tension spring sbring tyniant *eg* sbringiau tyniant
tension stress diriant tyniant *eg* diriannau tyniant
tensioner tyniannwr *eg* tynianwyr
tensor tensor *eg* tensorau
tent pabell *eb* pebyll
tent stitch pwyth pabell *eg* pwythau pabell
tentacle tentacl *eg* tentaclau
tenter frame ffrâm ddeintur *eb* fframiau deintur
tenter hook bach deintur *eg* bachau deintur
tenth degfed *eg* degfedau
Tenth Penny Y Ddegfed Geiniog *eb*
tenure daliadaeth *eb* daliadaethau
tepid claear *ans*
tepid sponging sbwngio â dŵr claear *be*
terabyte terabeit *eg* terabeitiau
teratogen teratogen *eg* teratogenau
terazzo terazzo *ans*
terbium (Tb) terbiwm *eg*
terce awr anterth *eb*
tercimal *adj* triol *ans*
tercimal *n* triolyn *eg* triolion
tercimal point pwynt triol *eg*
term (=period of time) tymor *eg* tymhorau
term (in language) term *eg* termau
term assurance aswiriant cyfnod *eg*
terminal (=end of term) *adj* pen tymor *ans*
terminal (=every term) *adj* tymhorol *ans*
terminal (=final) *adj* terfynol *ans*
terminal (e.g. computer terminal) *n* terfynell *eb* terfynellau
terminal bud penflaguryn *eg* penflagur
terminal button botwm terfynol *eg* botymau terfynol
terminal illness afiechyd marwol *eg* afiechydon marwol
terminal mode modd terfynell *eg* moddau terfynell
terminal moraine marian terfynol *eg* marianau terfynol
terminal oxidase ocsidas terfynol *eg*
terminalization terfyneiddiad *eg* terfyneiddiadau
terminate terfynu *be*
terminating terfynus *ans*
termination reaction adwaith terfynu *eg*
terms (=conditions) telerau *ell*
terms of reference cylch gorchwyl *eg*
terms of trade telerau masnach *ell*
ternary triaidd *ans*
ternary number rhif triaidd *eg* rhifau triaidd
terne plate plât tern *eg* platiau tern
terra cotta terra cotta *eg*
terrace *v* terasu *be*
terrace (on a slope) *n* teras *eg* terasau
terrace (relief feature) *n* rhes *eb* rhesi
terrace house tŷ rhes *eg* tai rhes
terraced house tŷ teras *eg* tai teras
terracette teraset *eg* terasetau
terracing (topographical) cerlan *eb* cerlannau
terrain tir *eg* tiroedd
terrestrial daearol *ans*
terrestrial magnetism magnetedd daear *eg*

terrestrial television teledu daearol *eg*
terret ring cylch genfa *eg* cylchoedd genfa
terrier (book) tirlyfr *eg* tirlyfrau
territorial tiriogaethol *ans*
territorial army byddin diriogaethol *eb* byddinoedd tiriogaethol
territorial expansion ehangiad tiriogaethol *eg*
territorial integrity tiriogaeth gydnabyddedig *eb*
territorial waters dyfroedd tiriogaethol *ell*
territory tiriogaeth *eb* tiriogaethau
terrorism terfysgaeth *eb*
terrorist terfysgwr *eg* terfysgwyr
terrorize (=frighten) brawychu *be*
terrorize (=use terrorism) terfysgu *be*
tertiary trydyddol *ans*
tertiary health care gofal iechyd trydyddol *eg*
tertiary sector sector trydyddol *eg*
Terylene Terylene *eg*
terylene gauze rhwyllen derylen *eb* rhwyllau terylen
tessellation brithwaith *eg* brithweithiau
test *n* prawf *eg* profion
test (in general) *v* profi *be*
test (put something to the test) rhoi prawf ar *be*
Test Act Deddf Brawf *eb*
Test and Corporation Acts Deddfau Prawf a Chorfforaeth *ell*
test battery casgliad o brofion *eg* casgliadau o brofion
test data prawf-ddata *ell*
test development manager rheolwr datblygu profion *eg* rheolwyr datblygu profion
test game gêm brawf *eb* gemau prawf
test marketing prawf-farchnata *be*
test of significance prawf arwyddocâd *eg* profion arwyddocâd
test paper papur prawf *eg* papurau prawf
test pilot peilot profi *eg* peilotiaid profi
test reliability dibynadwyedd prawf *eg*
test run rhediad arbrofol *eg* rhediadau arbrofol
test text testun prawf *eg* testunau prawf
test transmission trawsyriant prawf *eg*
testa hadgroen *eg* hadgrwyn
testability profadwyedd *eg*
testable hypothesis rhagdybiaeth brofadwy *eb*
testaceous cragennaidd *ans*
testament testament *eg* testamentau
testee profedigai *eg* profedigeion
testicles ceilliau *ell*
testicular cancer canser y ceilliau *eg*
testicular self-examination hunanarchwiliad o'r ceilliau *eg* hunanarchwiliadau o'r ceilliau
testimonial tysteb *eb* tystebau
testing procedure dull gweithredu i brofi *eg*
testing protocols protocolau profi *ell*
testing question cwestiwn profi *eg* cwestiynau profi
testing strategy strategaeth brofi *eb*
testis caill *eg* ceilliau
testosterone testosteron *eg*
test-retest reliability dibynadwyedd prawf-ailbrawf *eg*
test-tube tiwb profi *eg* tiwbiau profi
test-tube rack rhesel tiwbiau profi *eb* rheseli tiwbiau profi
tetanus tetanws *eg*
tetany tetanedd *eg*
tête de boeuf stitch pwyth tête de boeuf *eg* pwythau tête de boeuf
tetraalkoxymethane tetraalcocsimethan *eg*
tetraamminecopper(II) ion ïon tetraamincopr(II) *eg* ïonau tetraamincopr(II)
1,1,2,2-tetrabromoethane 1,1,2,2-tetrabromoethan *eg*
tetracarbonylnickel(0) tetracarbonylnicel(0) *eg* tetracarbonylnicel(0)
tetrachlorocuprate(II) ion ïon tetraclorocwprad(II) *eg* ïonau tetraclorocwprad(II)
1,1,2,2-tetrachloroethane 1,1,2,2-tetracloroethan *eg*
tetrachloromethane tetracloromethan *eg*
tetrachord tetracord *eg* tetracordiau
tetracyanonickelate(II) ion ïon tetracyanonicelad(II) *eg* ïonau tetracyanonicelad
tetracyclic pedwarcylchol *ans*
tetraethoxymethane tetraethocsimethan *eg*
tetraethyllead(IV) tetraethylplwm(IV) *eg*
tetrahedral tetrahedrol *ans*
tetrahedron tetrahedron *eg* tetrahedronau
tetrahydridoaluminate(III) ion ïon tetrahydridoalwminad(III) *eg* ïonau tetrahydridoalwminad(III)
tetrahydridoborate(III) ion ïon tetrahydridoborad(III) *eg* ïonau tetrahydridoborad(III)
tetraiodomercurate(II) ion ïon tetraïodomercwrad(II) *eg* ïonau tetraïodomercwrad(II)
tetrathioantimonate(V) ion ïon tetrathioantimonad(V) *eg* ïonau tetrathioantimonad(V)
tetrathioarsenate(V) ion ïon tetrathioarsenad(V) *eg* ïonau tetrathioarsenad(V)
tetrathionate ion ïon tetrathionad *eg* ïonau tetrathionad
tetrode tetrod *eg* tetrodau
tetromino tetromino *eg* tetrominos
text *n* testun *eg* testunau
text *v* tecstio *be*
text animation animeiddio testun *be*
text attribute priodoledd testun *eg* priodoleddau testun
text body corff testun *eg*
text body indent mewnoliad corff testun *eg* mewnoliadau corff testun
text body justfied unioni corff testun *be*
text boundary ffin testun *eb* ffiniau testun
text box blwch testun *eg* blychau testun
text colour lliw testun *eg* lliwiau testun

text compression technique dull cywasgu testun *eg* dulliau cywasgu testun
text compression techniques dulliau cywasgu testun *ell*
text contour amlinell testun *eb* amlinellau testun
text delimiter amffinydd testun *eg* amffinyddion testun
text direction cyfeiriad y testun *eg*
text display dangos testun *be*
text document dogfen testun *eb* dogfennau testun
text editing golygu testun *be*
text editor golygydd testun *eg* golygyddion testun
text file ffeil testun *eb* ffeiliau testun
text flow llif testun *eg*
text format fformat testun *eg* fformatau testun
text formula fformiwla testun *eb* fformiwlâu testun
text frame ffrâm testun *eb* fframiau testun
text length hyd testun *eg*
text limit terfyn testun *eg* terfynau testun
text mode modd testun *eg*
text object gwrthrych testun *eg* gwrthrychau testun
text object bar bar gwrthrych testun *eg* barrau gwrthrych testun
text only testun yn unig
text overflow gorlif testun *eg*
text placeholder dalfan testun *eg* dalfannau testun
text position safle testun *eg*
text processing gairbrosesu *be*
text screen sgrin destun *eb* sgriniau testun
text separator gwahanydd testun *eg* gwahanyddion testun
text size maint testun *eg*
text status statws testun *eg*
text style arddull testun *eb* arddulliau testun
text wrap amlapio testun *be*
text zoom chwyddo'r testun *be*
textbook gwerslyfr *eg* gwerslyfrau
textile *n* tecstil *eg* tecstilau
textile colour lliw tecstil *eg* lliwiau tecstil
textile industry diwydiant tecstilau *eg*
textiles and surface pattern tecstilau a phatrwm ar yr wyneb
textphone ffôn testun *eg* ffonau testun
text-to-speech synthesizer syntheseiddydd llefaru testun *eg* syntheseiddwyr llefaru testun
textual testunol *ans*
textual analysis dadansoddiad testunol *eg*
textural gweadeddol *ans*
texture gwead *eg* gweadau
texture gweadedd *eb*
texture (of wood) gwedd *eb*
texture rubbing ffrotais gwead *eg* ffroteisiau gwead
textured material defnydd gweadog *eg* defnyddiau gweadog
textured surface arwyneb gweadog *eg* arwynebau gweadog
textured thread edau weadog *eb* edafedd gweadog
textured yarn edafedd gweadog *ell*
texturing gweadeddu *be*
textwrap lapio testun *be*
TGAT: Task Group on Assessment and Testing GAP: Gweithgor ar Asesu a Phrofi *eg*
thalamus thalamws *eg*
thallium (Tl) thaliwm *eg*
thallus thalws *eg* thali
T-halving joint uniad haneru T *eg* uniadau haneru T
thane brëyr *eg* brehyrion
thatched roof to gwellt *eg* toeon gwellt
thaw dadmer *be*
Theatine Theatiad *eg/b* Theatiaid
theatre theatr *eb* theatrau
theatre design dylunio ar gyfer y theatr *be*
theatre gown gŵn theatr *eg* gynau theatr
theatre music cerddoriaeth theatr *eb*
theatre practitioners ymarferwyr theatr *ell*
theatrical theatraidd *ans*
theatrical convention confensiwn theatrig *eg* confensiynau theatrig
theatrical production cynhyrchiad theatraidd *eg* cynyrchiadau theatraidd
theism theistiaeth *eb*
thematic apperception test (TAT) prawf cyfarganfod thematig *eg*
thematic approach dull thematig *eg* dulliau thematig
thematic element elfen thematig *eb* elfennau thematig
thematic extension study astudiaeth estyn thematig *eb* astudiaethau estyn thematig
thematic work gwaith thematig *eg*
theme thema *eb* themâu
theme and variations thema ac amrywiadau
theme park parc thema *eg* parciau thema
theocracy theocratiaeth *eb*
theodicy theodiciaeth *eb*
theodolite theodolit *eg* theodolitau
theology diwinyddiaeth *eb*
theorbo theorbo *eg* theorboi
theorem theorem *eb* theoremau
theoretical damcaniaethol *ans*
theorize damcaniaethu *be*
theory (=exposition of the principles of a science) theori *eb*
theory (of individual examples) damcaniaeth *eb* damcaniaethau
theory of development damcaniaeth datblygiad *eb*
theory of evolution damcaniaeth esblygiad *eb*
theory of games theori gemau *eb*
theory of mind theori o feddwl *eb*
theory of mind damcaniaeth darogan meddwl *eb*
theory of music theori cerddoriaeth *eb*
theory of planned behaviour damcaniaeth cynllunio ymddygiad *eb*
theory of reasoned action damcaniaeth gweithredu rhesymegol *eb*
theory of relativity damcaniaeth perthnasedd *eb*
therapeutic therapiwtig *ans*

therapeutic play chwarae therapiwtig *eg*
therapist therapydd *eg* therapyddion
therapy therapi *eg* therapïau
Theravada Theravada *eb*
therefore felly *adf*
therm therm *eg* thermau
thermal thermol *ans*
thermal conductivity dargludedd thermol *eg*
thermal decomposition dadelfennu thermol *be*
thermal dissociation daduniad thermol *eg* daduniadau thermol
thermal energy egni thermol *eg*
thermal equator cyhydedd thermol *eg*
thermal equilibrium cydbwysedd thermol *eg*
thermal insulation ynysiad thermol *eg*
thermal insulator ynysydd thermol *eg* ynysyddion thermol
thermionic thermionig *ans*
thermionic valve falf thermionig *eb* falfiau thermionig
thermistor thermistor *eg* thermistorau
thermit reaction adwaith thermit *eg*
thermo forming thermoffurfio *be*
thermocline thermoclein *eg* thermocleinau
thermocouple thermocwpl *eg* thermocyplau
thermocouple pyrometer pyromedr thermocwpl *eg* pyromedrau thermocwpl
thermo-dummy teth dymheredd *eb* tethi tymheredd
thermodynamic thermodynamig *ans*
thermodynamics thermodynameg *eb*
thermoelectric thermodrydanol *ans*
thermoelectricity thermodrydan *eg*
thermogram thermogram *eg* thermogramau
thermo-hardening adhesive adlyn thermo-galedu *eg*
thermojunction thermogydiad *eg* thermogydiadau
thermometer thermomedr *eg* thermomedrau
thermometric thermometrig *ans*
thermometric titration titradiad thermometrig *eg*
thermometry thermometreg *eg*
thermopile thermopil *eg* thermopiliau
thermoplastic *adj* thermoplastig *ans*
thermoplastic *n* thermoplastig *eg* thermoplastigau
thermoscope thermosgop *eg* thermosgopau
thermosetting *adj* thermosodol *ans*
thermosetting plastic plastig thermosodol *eg*
thermostat thermostat *eg* thermostatau
thermostatic control rheolaeth thermostatig *eb*
thesaurus thesawrws *eg* thesawrysau
thesis (=dissertation) traethawd *eg* traethodau
thesis (=proposition, argument) thesis *eg* theses
thesis (=research essay) traethawd ymchwil *eg* traethodau ymchwil
theta activity gweithgarwch theta *eg*
Thevenin's theorem theorem Thevenin *eb*
thiamine thiamin *eg*
thick (of liquids, materials) trwchus *ans*
thick (of thread, rope etc) tew *ans*
thick flank ystlys dew *eb* ystlysau tew
thick line llinell dew *eb* llinellau tew
thick plate glass platwydr trwchus *eg*
thicken tewychu *be*
thickener tewychydd *eg* tewychwyr
thicket dryslwyn *eg* dryslwyni
thickly populated country gwlad boblog iawn *eb* gwledydd poblog iawn
thickness trwch *eg*
thickenssing attachment atodyn tewychu *eg* atodion tewychu
thicknessing machine peiriant tewychu *eg* peiriannau tewychu
thief lleidr *eg* lladron
thief vault llofnaid lleidr *eb* llofneidiau lleidr
thigh morddwyd *eb* morddwydydd
thimble gwniadur *eg* gwniaduron
thin tenau *ans*
thin card disk disg cerdyn tenau *eg* disgiau cerdyn tenau
thin chain line llinell gadwyn denau *eb* llinellau cadwyn denau
thin flank ystlys denau *eb* ystlysau tenau
thin line llinell denau *eb* llinellau tenau
thin metal metel tenau *eg*
thin place darn craith man gwan *eb* creithiau man gwan
T-hinge colfach T *eg* colfachau T
thinking meddwl *be*
thin-layer chromatography cromatograffaeth haen-denau *eb*
thinly populated country gwlad denau ei phoblogaeth *eb* gwledydd tenau eu poblogaeth
thinner teneuydd *eg* teneuwyr
thinning medium cyfrwng teneuo *eg*
thiocarbamide thiocarbamid *eg*
thiocyanate ion ïon thiocyanad *eg* ïonau thiocyanad
thiol (generic name) thiol *eg* thiolau
thiosulfate ion ïon thiosylffad *eg* ïonau thiosylffad
third (fraction =one third) traean *eg* traeanau
third (ordinal number) trydydd *eg* trydyddau
third angle projection tafluniad trydedd ongl *eg* tafluniadau trydedd ongl
third degree equation hafaliad gradd tri *eg* hafaliadau gradd tri
Third Estate y Drydedd Stad *eb*
third inversion trydydd gwrthdro *eg*
third man (sport) trydydd *eg*
third order gradd tri *eb*
third order reaction adwaith gradd tri *eg*
third party insurance yswiriant trydydd person *eg*
third person trydydd person *eg*
Third Reich Trydedd Reich *eb*
Third Republic Trydedd Weriniaeth *eb*
thirsty sychedig *ans*
Thirteen Articles Tair Erthygl ar Ddeg *eb*
thirteenth trydydd ar ddeg *eg*

Thirty Nine Articles Deugain Erthygl Namyn Un *eb*
Thirty Years War Rhyfel Deng Mlynedd ar Hugain *eg*
thistle funnel twndis ysgall *eg* twndisau ysgall; twmffat ysgall *eg* twmffedi ysgall
thixotropic thicsotropig *ans*
Thomas the Tank Engine Tomos y Tanc *eg*
Thomism Tomistiaeth *eb*
Thomistic Tomistig *ans*
thong carrai *eb* careiau
thoracic thorasig *ans*
thorax thoracs *eg*
thorium (Th) thoriwm *eg*
thorn forest coedwig ddrain *eb* coedwigoedd drain
thorough trylwyr *ans*
thorough bass continuo *eg*
thorough cleaning glanhau trylwyr *be*
thoroughfare tramwyfa *eb* tramwyfeydd
thought meddwl *eg* meddyliau
thousand mil *eb* miloedd
thousandth milfed *eg* milfedau
thrashing machine peiriant dyrnu *eg* peiriannau dyrnu
thread *v* edafu *be*
thread (of argument, discussion etc) *n* trywydd *eg*
thread (of yarn, screw etc) *n* edau *eb* edafedd
thread angle gauge medrydd ongl edau *eg* medryddion ongl edau
thread cell edeugell *eb* edeugelloedd
thread chaser siaswr edafedd *eg* siaswyr edafedd
thread cutter (of machine part) torrwr edau *eg* torwyr edau
thread cutting (of lathe tools) torri edau *be*
thread guide (of machine part) bachyn tywys edau *eg* bachau tywys edau
thread hole twll edau *eg* tyllau edau
thread parts rhannau edau *ell*
thread pitch pitsh edau *eg*
thread pitch gauge medrydd pitsh edau *eg* medryddion pitsh edau
thread-cutting screw sgriw torri edau *eb* sgriwiau torri edau
threaded hole twll ag edau ynddo *eg* tyllau ag edau ynddynt
threader (machine attachments) edefydd *eg* edefyddion
thread-forming screw sgriw ffurfio edau *eb* sgriwiau ffurfio edau
threading hook bach edafu *eg* bachau edafu
threat gesture ystum bygwth *eg* ystumiau bygwth
three arm stake bonyn teirbraich *eg* bonion teirbraich
three dimensional design dylunio tri dimensiwn *be*
Three Jewels, the Tair Gem, y
three outs tri allan
three point plug plwg tri phìn *eg* plygiau tri phìn
three quarters (fraction) tri chwarter *eg*
Three Resolutions (1629) Tri Phenderfyniad *eg*
three second rule rheol tair eiliad *eb*
three-digit tri-digid *ans*
three-dimensional tri dimensiwn *ans*
three-dimensional construction adeiladwaith tri dimensiwn *eg*
three-dimensional modelling modelu tri dimensiwn *be*
three-division saucer soser deir-ran *eb* soseri teir-ran
three-field system trefn drimaes *eb*
three-handed reel ril deirllaw *eb* riliau teirllaw
three-jaw chuck crafanc tair safn *eb* crafangau tair safn
three-line banding bandin tair llinell *eg* bandinau tair llinell
three-ply wood pren tairhaenog *eg*
three-ply wool edafedd tair cainc *ell*
three-quarter (in rugby) trichwarterwr *eg* trichwarterwyr
three-sided stitch pwyth triongl *eg* pwythau triongl
threesome triawd *eg* triawdau
three-square *adj* tairongl *ans*
three-square file ffeil dairongl *eb* ffeiliau tairongl
three-stage reaction adwaith tri cham *eg* adweithiau tri cham
three-term contingency amodoldeb tri-thymor *eg*
three-way tap tap teirffordd *eg* tapiau teirffordd
threshold trothwy *eg* trothwyau
threshold energy egni trothwy *eg* egnïon trothwy
threshold frequency amledd trothwy *eg*
thrift (=sea pink) clustog Fair *eb*
thrift (being careful with money etc) darbodaeth *eb*
thro' ball pàs hollti *eb* pasiau hollti
throat gwddf *eg* gyddfau
throat plate (of machine part) plât bobin *eg* platiau bobin
throating (window) gwrthyrrwr dŵr *eg* gwrthyrwyr dŵr
throb curo *be*
thrombocyte thrombocyt *eg* thrombocytau
thrombosis thrombosis *eb*
thrombus thrombws *eg* thrombysau
throne gorsedd *eb* gorseddau
throttle *n* sbardun *eg* sbardunau
throttle *v* tagu *be*
through chamfer siamffer trwodd *eg* siamfferi trwodd
through dovetail housing joint uniad rhigol draws gynffonnog trwodd *eg* uniadau rhigolau traws cynffonnog trwodd
through dovetail joint uniad cynffonnog trwodd *eg* uniadau cynffonnog trwodd
through housing rhigol trwodd *eb* rhigolau trwodd
through housing joint uniad rhigol draws trwodd *eg* uniadau rhigolau traws trwodd
through mortise and tenon joint uniad mortais a thyno trwodd *eg* uniadau mortais a thyno trwodd
through sawcut llifiad trwodd *eg* llifiadau trwodd
through tenon tyno trwodd *eg* tynoau trwodd
through traffic trafnidiaeth drwodd *eb*

through vault llofnaid fwlch *eb* llofneidiau bwlch
through vault with double beat llofnaid fwlch ddeuglap *eb* llofneidiau bwlch deuglap
throughput trwybwn *eg* trwybynnau
throw *n* tafliad *eg* tafliadau
throw *v* taflu *be*
throw down the wicket torri'r wiced *be*
throw forward taflu ymlaen *be*
throw in taflu i mewn *be*
thrower taflwr *eg* taflwyr
throwing the discus taflu'r ddisgen *be*
throwing the hammer taflu'r ordd *be*
throwing the javelin taflu'r waywffon *be*
thrown shape siâp a daflwyd *eg* siapiau a daflwyd
throw-up (jump) cydnaid *eb* cydneidiau
thrum tynnu *be*
thrush (throat infection) llindag *eg*
thrust (=push) *n* gwthiad *eg* gwthiadau
thrust (=push) *v* gwthio *be*
thrust (of sword) *n* gwaniad *eg* gwaniadau
thrust (of sword) *v* gwanu *be*
thrust bearing gwthferyn *eg* gwthferynnau
thrust cap cap gwthio *eg* capiau gwthio
thrust direction cyfeiriad gwthiad *eg*
thulium (Tm) thwliwm *eg*
thumb bawd *eg* bodiau
thumb gauge medrydd bawd *eg* medryddion bawd
thumb latch clicied fawd *eb* cliciedau bawd
thumb piston piston bawd *eg* pistonau bawd
thumb position safle'r bawd *eg* safleoedd y bawd
thumbnail sketch braslun bawd *eg* brasluniau bawd
thumbnail version fersiwn mân-lun *eg* fersiynau mân-lun
thumbscrew sgriw fawd *eb* sgriwiau bawd
thunder taran *eb* taranau
thunder machine peiriant taranau *eg* peiriannau taranau
thunder shake hollt taran *eg* holltau taran
thunderbolt taranfollt *eb* taranfolltau
thunderstorm storm fellt a tharanau *eb* stormydd mellt a tharanau
thus felly *adf*
thwart (=boat seat) sedd ystlys *eb* seddi ystlys
thymus thymws *eg*
thyristor thyristor *eg*
thyroglobulin thyroglobwlin *ans*
thyroid thyroid *eg*
thyroid gland chwarren thyroid *eb* chwarennau thyroid
thyroxin thyrocsin *eg*
tibia tibia *eg*
tic gwingiad *eg* gwingiadau
ticker tape tâp ticio *eg* tapiau ticio
ticker timer amserydd ticio *eg* amseryddion ticio
ticket tocyn *eg* tocynnau
ticket board bwrdd tocynnau *eg* byrddau tocynnau
tidal air (of respiration) aer cyfnewid *eg*
tidal bore eger llanw *eg* egerau llanw
tidal current cerrynt llanw *eg* ceryntau llanw
tidal datum seilnod llanw *eg* seilnodau llanw
tidal energy egni llanw *eg*
tidal flat fflat llanw *eg* fflatiau llanw
tidal lagoon morlyn llanw *eg* morlynnoedd llanw
tidal range amrediad llanw *eg* amrediadau llanw
tidal scour sgwrfa llanw *eg*
tidal volume (of respiration) cyfaint cyfnewid *eg*
tidal wave ton llanw *eb* tonnau llanw
tide llanw *eg* llanwau
tide race eger *eg* egerau
tie *v* clymu *be*
tie (=drawn game) *n* gêm gyfartal *eb* gemau cyfartal
tie (a knot or attachment etc) *n* cwlwm *eg* clymau
tie (article of clothing) *n* tei *eg* teis
tie and dye clymu a llifo
tie-beam tynlath *eb* tynlathau
tie-break (in tennis) torri'r ddadl *be*
tied clwm *ans*
tied cottage bwthyn clwm *eg* bythynnod clwm
tied fret cribell glwm *eb* cribellau clwm
tied house tŷ clwm *eg* tai clwm
tied note nodyn clwm *eg* nodau clwm
tie-line clymlin *eb* clymliniau
tie-off screw sgriw gwlwm *eb* sgriwiau cwlwm
tier (=layer) haen *eb* haenau
tier (=row) rhes *eb* rhesi
tier (of seats etc) rhenc *eb* rhenciau
tierce de Picardie tierce de Picardie *eg* tierces de Picardie
tiered skirt sgert renciog *eb* sgertiau rhenciog
tierra caliente tir poeth *eg*
tierra fria tir oer *eg*
tierra templada tir tymherus *eg*
tierspoint arch bwa tiersbwynt *eg* bwâu tiersbwynt
tight tynn *ans*
tight fit ffit dynn *eb*
tight head (in rugby) pen tynn *eg*
tighten tynhau *be*
tightening loop dolen dynhau *eb* dolennau tynhau
tightness tyndra *eg*
tile *n* teilsen *eb* teils
tile *v* teilsio *be*
tile cement sment teils *eg*
till (glacial) *n* til *eg*
till (land) *v* trin *be*
tiller (of boat) llyw *eg* llywiau
tillering tileru *be*
tillite tilfaen *eg* tilfeini
tilt (slope or inclination) *n* gogwydd *eg* gogwyddau
tilt (slope or incline) *v* gogwyddo *be*
tilted ar ogwydd *ans*
tilth tir rhywiog *eg*
timber *n* coed *ell*
timber conversion trosiad coed *eg*
timber defects diffygion coed *ell*

timber framing fframwaith coed *eg* fframweithiau coed
timber preservation cadwraeth coed *eb*
timber stacking tasu coed *be*
timbre (=quality) ansawdd *eg*
timbre (of musical sound) soniaredd *eg*
time *v* amseru *be*
time (=period) *n* cyfnod *eg* cyfnodau
time (in general) *n* amser *eg* amserau
time average cyfartaledd amser *eg*
time constant cysonyn amser *eg*
time delay oediad amser *eg*
time division multiplexing amlblethu rhaniadau amser *be*
time field maes amser *eg* meysydd amser
time format fformat amser *eg* fformatau amser
time frame ffrâm amser *eb* fframiau amser
time keeper amserwr *eg* amserwyr
time lag oediad amser *eg*
time left amser yn weddill *eg*
time of arrival amser cyrraedd *eg*
time of flight amser hedfan *eg*
Time of Troubles Cyfnod y Cynnwrf *eg*
time off (time out) saib *eg* seibiau
time out saib *eg* seibiau
time sheet taflen amser *eb* taflenni amser
time slice tafell amser *eb* tafelli amser
time taken amser a gymerwyd *eg*
time zone cylchfa amser *eb* cylchfaoedd amser
time-base amserlin *eg* amserliniau
time-lag design cynllun oedi amser *eg* cynlluniau oedi amser
time-line programme rhaglen llinell-amser *eb* rhaglenni llinell-amser
timeout terfyn amser *eg*
timer amserydd *eg* amseryddion
time-scale graddfa amser *eb* graddfeydd amser
time-sharing (computing) cydrannu amser *be*
timetable *n* amserlen *eb* amserlenni
timetable *v* amserlennu *be*
timing (=tempo) amseriad *eg* amseriadau
tin *v* tunio *be*
tin (of container) *n* tun *eg* tuniau
tin (Sn) *n* tun *eg*
Tinbergen's rule rheol Tinbergen *eb*
tinctorial trwythol *ans*
tincture trwyth *eg*
tinder box blwch tân *eg* blychau tân
tinge gwawr *eb*
tin(II) ion ïon tun(II) *eg* ïonau tun(II)
tin(IV) compound cyfansoddyn tun(IV) *eg* cyfansoddion tun(IV)
tin(IV) ion ïon tun(IV) *eg* ïonau tun(IV)
tin(IV) oxide tun(IV) ocsid *eg*
tinned food bwyd tun *eg* bwydydd tun
tinplate tunplat *eg*
tinsel tinsel *eg*
tinsnips snipiwr tun *eg* snipwyr tun
tint *n* arlliw *eg* arlliwiau
tint *v* arlliwio *eb*
tinted arlliwedig *ans*
tinted paper papur arlliwedig *eg*
tip (=penetrator) *n* treiddiwr *eg*
tip (extremity or end) *n* blaen *eg* blaenau
tip (money) *n* cildwrn *eg*
tip (of rubbish etc) *n* tomen *eb* tomennydd
tip *v* tipio *be*
tip of the tongue phenomenon ffenomen blaen y tafod *eb*
tirando tirando *eg*
tiredness blinder *eg*
Tironian Tironiad *eg* Tironiaid
tissue (=paper hankie) hances bapur *eb* hancesi papur
tissue (in animals, plants) meinwe *eg/b* meinweoedd
tissue culture meithriniad meinwe *eg* meithriniadau meinwe
tissue fluid hylif meinweol *eg* hylifau meinweol
tissue paper papur sidan *eg*
titanium (Ti) titaniwm *eg*
titanium white gwyn titaniwm *eg*
titanium(II) chloride titaniwm(II) clorid *eg*
titanium(II) ion ïon titaniwm(II) *eg* ïonau titaniwm(II)
titanium(III) compound cyfansoddyn titaniwm(III) *eg* cyfansoddion titaniwm(III)
titanium(III) ion ïon titaniwm(III) *eg* ïonau titaniwm(III)
titanium(IV) compound cyfansoddyn titaniwm(IV) *eg* cyfansoddion titaniwm(IV)
titanium(IV) ion ïon titaniwm(IV) *eg* ïonau titaniwm(IV)
titanium(IV) oxide titaniwm(IV) ocsid *eg*
tithe degwm *eg* degymau
tithe barn ysgubor ddegwm *eb* ysguboriau degwm
Tithe Commutation Act Deddf Cyfnewid y Degwm *eb*
Tithe War Rhyfel y Degwm *eg*
tithing degymiad *eg* degymiadau
title teitl *eg* teitlau
title (to land etc) hawl *eg/b*
title background cefndir teitl *eg*
title bar bar teitl *eg* barrau teitl
title block bloc teitl *eg* blociau teitl
title font ffont y teitl *eg* ffontiau'r teitl
title only teitl yn unig
title page wynebddalen *eb* wynebddalennau
title row rhes teitl *eb* rhesi teitlau
title screen sgrin agoriadol *eb* sgriniau agoriadol
title slide sleid y teitl *eb*
title text testun y teitl *eg*
titrate titradu *be*
titre titr *eg* titrau
titrimetric titradaethol *ans*
titrimetry titradaeth *eb*

to a scale of (1:1) wrth raddfa (1:1)
to a suitable scale wrth raddfa addas
toaster tostiwr *eg* tostwyr
tobacco tybaco *eg*
toccata tocata *eg* tocatâu
toddler plentyn bach *eg* plant bach
toddlers' wear dillad plant bach *ell*
toe bys troed *eg* bysedd traed
toe (in dancing) blaen y droed *eg* blaenau'r traed
toe piston piston troed *eg* pistonau troed
toe tapping tapio sawdl blaen *be*
toe-cap blaen yr esgid *eg*
toga toga *eb* togâu
toggle *n* togl *eg* toglau
toggle *v* toglo *be*
toggle clamp clamp togl *eg* clampiau togl
toilet toiled *eg* toiledau
token taleb *eg* talebau
token (in truck system) arian tryc *eg*
token economy rhaglen atgyfnerthu â thalebau *eb* rhaglenni atgyfnerthu â thalebau
tokenism tocynistiaeth *eb*
tolerance (of measurements etc) goddefiant *eg* goddefiannau
tolerance (of people) goddefgarwch *eg*
tolerance (to drugs etc) goddefedd *eg*
toleranced drawing lluniad goddefiannol *eg*
tolerancing goddefiannu *be*
tolerate goddef *be*
toleration (of people) goddefgarwch *eg*
Toleration Act Deddf Goddefiad *eb*
toll toll *eb* tollau
tollage tollaeth *eb*
toll-bridge tollbont *eb* tollbontydd
toll-gate tollborth *eg* tollbyrth
toll-road tollffordd *eb* tollffyrdd
Tolpuddle Martyrs Merthyron Tolpuddle *ell*
tom tom tom tom *eg* tom tomau
tomb bedd *eg* beddau
tommy-bar twmfar *eg* twmfarrau
tommy-shop siop dryc *eb* siopau tryc
ton tunnell *eb* tunelli
tonal cyweiraidd *ans*
tonality cyweiredd *eg* cyweireddau
tone (of sound) tôn *eb* tonau
tone (of colour) tôn *eg* tonau
tone painting seinliwio *be*
tone quality ansawdd y dôn *eb*
tone value gwerth tôn *eb* gwerthoedd tôn
tone-deaf tôn-fyddar *ans*
tongs gefel *eb* gefeiliau
tongue *n* tafod *eg* tafodau
tongue *v* tafodi *be*
tongue and groove tafod a rhych
tongue and groove joint uniad tafod a rhych *eg* uniadau tafod a rhych
tongue depressor gwasgwr tafod *eg* gwasgwyr tafod
tongued mitre joint uniad meitr tafod *eg* uniadau meitr tafod
tonic (=a thing that invigorates) tonig *eg* tonigau
tonic (musical) tonydd *eg* tonyddion
tonic chord cord y tonydd *eg* cordiau'r tonydd
tonic major scale graddfa fwyaf y tonydd *eb*
tonic minor scale graddfa leiaf y tonydd *eb*
tonic seventh chord cord seithfed y tonydd *eg* cordiau seithfed y tonydd
tonic sol-fa sol-ffa *eg*
tonicity tonedd *eg*
Tonk strip (shelf) stribed Tonk *eg* stribedi Tonk
Tonk's fitting ffitiad Tonk *eg*
tonnage tunelledd *eg* tunelleddau
tonne tunnell fetrig *eb* tunelli metrig
tonsil tonsil *eg* tonsilau
tonsillitis tonsilitis *eg*
tonsure tonsur *eg* tonsuriau
too remote rhy bellennig *ans*
tool erfyn *eg* offer
tool bit erfyn turn *eg* offer turn
tool box blwch offer *eg* blychau offer
tool chatter sgrytian erfyn *be*
tool for work offeryn ar gyfer gwaith *eg* offer ar gyfer gwaith
tool holder daliwr offer *eg* dalwyr offer
tool post postyn offer *eg* pyst offer
tool set steel dur offer *eg*
toolbar bar offer *eg* barrau offer
toolbar button botwm bar offer *eg* botymau bar offer
toolbar configuration ffurfweddiad bar offer *eg* ffurfweddiadau bar offer
tooling gouge gaing gau offeru *eb* geingiau gau offeru
toolmaker's clamp clamp offerwr *eg* clampiau offerwr
toolmaker's vice feis offerwr *eb* feisiau offerwr
tools offer llaw *ell*
tooth dant *eg* dannedd
toothing plane plaen danheddog *eg* plaeniau danheddog
top (=surface) wyneb *eg* wynebau
top (in general) top *eg* topiau
top (of mountain etc) pen *eg* pennau
top (of page, tree etc) brig *eg*
top bit did uchaf *eg* didau uchaf
top drawer rail rheilen uchaf drôr *eb* rheiliau uchaf drôr
top fuller pannydd uchaf *eg* panwyr uchaf
top half of page hanner uchaf y dudalen *eg*
top loader peiriant top-lwytho *eg* peiriannau top-lwytho
top loading kiln odyn dop-lwytho *eb* odynnau top-lwytho
top of baseline brig y gwaelodlin *eg*
top of character brig y nod *eg*
top of line brig y llinell *eg*
top part darn uchaf *eg* darnau uchaf

top priority prif flaenoriaeth *eg*
top quality o'r ansawdd gorau *ans*
top rail rheilen uchaf *eb* rheiliau uchaf
top rake gwyredd cefn *eg*
top rest briglithryn *eg*
top row rhes uchaf *eb* rhesi uchaf
top slide llithryn uchaf *eg*
top speed buanedd uchaf *eg*
top stitch wyneb-bwyth *eg* wyneb-bwythau
top stitching wyneb-bwytho *be*
top swage darfath uchaf *eg*
top to bottom o'r brig i'r gwaelod
top-down processing prosesu o'r pen i'r gwaelod *be*
top-down programming rhaglennu dadelfennol *be*
topical (=on skin) argroenol *ans*
topical preparation cymysgedd ar gyfer y croen *eb* cymysgeddau ar gyfer y croen
topographic topograffig *ans*
topographical topograffigol *ans*
topography topograffi *eg*
topological topolegol *ans*
topology topoleg *eb*
topping (saw teeth) topio *be*
topple dymchwel *be*
topset bed gwely uwch-haen *eg* gwelyau uwch-haen
topsoil uwchbridd *eg* uwchbriddoedd
topspin troelli'r bêl tros ben *be*
tor twr *eg* tyrrau
Torah Torah *eg*
torch (light) tortsh *eb* tortshys
tornado tornado *cg* tornados
torque (=necklace) torch *eg* torchau
torque (=rotational effect of force) trorym *eg* trorymoedd
torque wrench tyndro trorym *eg* tyndroeon trorym
torrent cenllif *eg* cenllifau
torrent llifeiriant *eg* llifeiriaint
torrent tract blaendir afon *eg* blaendiroedd afon
torrid crasboeth *ans*
torrid zone cylchfa grasboeth *eb*
torsion *n* dirdro *eg* dirdroeon
torsion balance clorian ddirdro *eb* cloriannau dirdro
torsion bar trofar *eg* trofarrau
torsion free diddirdro *ans*
torsional dirdroadol *ans*
torso torso *eg* torsoau
tort (civil wrong) camwedd *eg*
tortious liability atebolrwydd camweddus *eg*
torture *v* arteithio *be*
torus torws *eg* torysau
torus moulding mowldin torws *eg* mowldinau torws
Tory Party Plaid Doriaidd *eb*
Tory reform diwygiad y Toriaid *eg* diwygiadau y Toriaid
total (complete) *adj* cyflawn *ans*
total (number) *n* cyfanswm *eg* cyfansymiau
total columns cyfanswm colofnau *eg*
total contents cyfanswm cynnwys *eg*
total cost cyfanswm cost *eg*
total costs cyfanswm costau *eg*
total internal reflection adlewyrchiad mewnol cyflawn *eg*
total output cyfanswm cynnyrch *eg*
total payments cyfanswm taliadau *eg*
total probability cyfanswm tebygolrwydd *eg*
total quality management rheolaeth lwyr ar ansawdd *eb*
total receipts cyfanswm derbyniadau *eg*
total replacement amnewid cyflawn *eg*
total revenue cyfanswm refeniw *eg*
Total Station Gweithfan Gyfansawdd *eg*
total war rhyfel diarbed *eg*
totalitarian totalitaraidd *ans*
totality crynswth *eg*
totem totem *eg* totemau
touch *n* cyffyrddiad *eg* cyffyrddiadau
touch *v* cyffwrdd *be*
touch down (in ball games) llorio'r bêl *be*
touch in goal ystlys cwrt cais *eb* ystlysau cwrt cais
touch in goal line ystlys gwsg *eb* ystlysau cwsg
touch judge llumanwr *eg* llumanwyr
touch latch clicied gyffwrdd *eb* cliciedau cyffwrdd
touch rugby rygbi bach *eg*
touch screen sgrin gyffwrdd *eb* sgriniau cyffwrdd
touch sensitive sensitif i gyffyrddiad *ans*
touchdown (in rugby) *v* tirio'r bêl *be*
touched out allan drwy gyffwrdd
touchline llinell ystlys *eb* llinellau ystlys
touchpad pad cyffwrdd *eg* padiau cyffwrdd
touch-screen information kiosk caban gwybodaeth sgrin gyffwrdd *eb* cabanau gwybodaeth sgrin gyffwrdd
tough gwydn *ans*
toughness gwydnwch *eg*
tour *n* taith *eb* teithiau
tour operator trefnydd teithiau *eg* trefnwyr teithiau
tourism twristiaeth *eb*
tourism development datblygiad twristiaeth *eg*
tourism development plan cynllun datblygu twristiaeth *eg*
tourism facilities cyfleusterau twristiaeth *ell*
tourism officer swyddog twristiaeth *eg* swyddogion twristiaeth
tourist ymwelydd *eg* ymwelwyr
tourist board bwrdd croeso *eg* byrddau croeso
tourist centre canolfan croeso *eb* canolfannau croeso
tourist industry diwydiant ymwelwyr *eg*
tourist information gwybodaeth i ymwelwyr *eb*
tourist information assistant cynorthwyydd gwybodaeth i ymwelwyr *eg* cynorthwywyr gwybodaeth i ymwelwyr
tournament twrnamaint *eg* twrnameintiau
tourniquet rhwymyn tynhau *eg* rhwymynnau tynhau
tourniquet (bowsaw) tynhawr *eg* tynhawyr
towards the harp (in dance) gwrogaeth i'r delyn *eb*

towel tywel *eg* tywelion
towel rail rheilen dywelion *eb* rheiliau tywelion
towelling tywelin *eg*
tower tŵr *eg* tyrau
tower case cas tŵr *eg* casys tŵr
towering cloud cwmwl tyrog *eg* cymylau tyrog
town tref *eb* trefi
Town and Country Planning Act Deddf Cynllunio Gwlad a Thref *eb*
town crier cyhoeddwr *eg* cyhoeddwyr
town planning cynllunio tref *be*
townscape treflun *eg* trefluniau
township trefgordd *eb* trefgorddau
toxaemia tocsaemia *eg*
toxic gwenwynig *ans*
toxicity gwenwyndra *eg*
toxin tocsin *eg* tocsinau
toy tegan *eg* teganau
T.P.I. (teeth per inch) dannedd i'r fodfedd
trace (=copy over) *v* dargopïo *be*
trace (=discover) *v* olrhain *be*
trace (of line) *n* olin *eg* olinau
trace (of particle) *n* mymryn *eg* mymrynnau
trace element elfen hybrin *eb* elfennau hybrin
trace error olrhain gwall *be*
trace precedent olrhain cynsail *be*
tracer olinydd *eg* olinyddion
tracery treswaith *eg* tresweithiau
trachea tracea *eg* traceau
tracheal traceuol *ans*
tracheid (softwood) traceid *eg* traceidiau
tracheostomy care gofal y traceostomi *eg*
tracing cloth lliain dargopïo *eg* llieiniau dargopïo
tracing paper papur dargopïo *eg*
tracing punch pwnsh olinio *eg* pynsiau olinio
tracing wheel olwyn ddargopïo *eb* olwynion dargopïo
track (=path) llwybr *eg* llwybrau
track (in sport, of sliding door etc) trac *eg* traciau
track event cystadleuaeth drac *eb* cystadlaethau trac
track junction cyffordd traciau *eb* cyffyrdd traciau
track multiple or single amldrac neu untrac
track rod rhoden lwybro *eb* rhodenni llwybro
trackball pelen lwybro *eg* peli llwybro
tracking (with camera on tracks) cledru *be*
tracking device dyfais lwybro *eb* dyfeisiau llwybro
tracking sheet dalen lwybro *eb*
tracking system system lwybro *eb* systemau llwybro
tracks olion traed *ell*
tracksuit tracwisg *eb* tracwisgoedd
tract (of land) darn o dir *eg* darnau o dir
Tractarianism Tractariaeth *eb*
traction tyniant *eg*
traction feed porthi cocos *be*
tractive force grym tynnol *eg* grymoedd tynnol
tractrix tractrics *eg* tractricsau
trade *v* masnachu *be*
trade (=commerce) *n* masnach *eb* masnachau
trade (=craft) *n* crefft *eb* crefftau
trade association cymdeithas masnachu *eb* cymdeithasau masnachu
trade bloc bloc masnach *eg* blociau masnach
trade creditor credydwr masnach *eg* credydwyr masnach
trade customer cwsmer masnach *eg* cwsmeriaid masnach
trade debtor dyledwr masnach *eg* dyledwyr masnach
Trade Descriptions Act Deddf Disgrifiadau Masnach *eb*
trade directory cyfarwyddiadur masnachol *eg* cyfarwyddiaduron masnachol
trade discount disgownt masnach *eg* disgowntiau masnach
Trade Disputes Act Deddf Anghydfodau Undebol *eb*
trade liberalisation measure mesur rhyddfrydoli masnach *eg* mesurau rhyddfrydoli masnach
trade press gwasg fasnachol *eb*
trade restriction cyfyngiad masnach *eg* cyfyngiadau masnach
trade supplier cyflenwr masnach *eg* cyflenwyr masnach
trade union undeb llafur *eg* undebau llafur
Trade Union Congress Cyngres yr Undebau Llafur *eb*
trade union legislation deddfwriaeth undebau llafur *eb*
trade unionism undebaeth lafur *eb*
trade wind gwynt cyson *eg* gwyntoedd cyson
trademark nod masnach *eg* nodau masnach
trader masnachwr *eg* masnachwyr
trade-route llwybr masnach *eg* llwybrau masnach
Trades Union Amendment Act Deddf Newid yr Undebau Llafur *eb*
trading estate stad fasnachol *eb* stadau masnachol
trading post canolfan fasnachol *eb* canolfannau masnachol
trading profit and loss account cyfrif masnachu, elw a cholled *eg*
trading quarter (=zone) rhan masnach *eb* rhannau masnach
trading restriction cyfyngiad masnachol *eg* cyfyngiadau masnachol
trading stamp stamp masnachu *eg* stampiau masnachu
trading standards safonau masnachu *ell*
Trading Standards Department Adran Safonau Masnachu *eb*
tradition traddodiad *eg* traddodiadau
traditional traddodiadol *ans*
traditional construction adeiladwaith traddodiadol *eg*
traditional design cynllun traddodiadol *eg* cynlluniau traddodiadol
traditional instrument offeryn traddodiadol *eg* offerynnau traddodiadol
traditional material defnydd traddodiadol *eg* defnyddiau traddodiadol

traditional morality moesoldeb traddodiadol *eg*
traditional set dance dawns set draddodiadol *eb* dawnsiau set traddodiadol
traffic trafnidiaeth *eb*
traffic congestion tagfeydd trafnidiaeth *ell*
traffic jam tagfa drafnidiaeth *eb* tagfeydd trafnidiaeth
traffic offence trosedd drafnidiol *eb* troseddau trafnidiol
tragacanth gwm tragacanth *eg*
tragedy trasiedi *eg* trasiedïau
trail *n* llwybr *eg* llwybrau
trail *v* llwybro *be*
trail angle ongl ddilyn *eb* onglau dilyn
trail enamel enamel llusg *eg*
trail enamelling enamlo llusg *be*
trailer (before a film) rhaghysbyseb *eb* rhaghysbysebion
train *v* hyfforddi *be*
train (gear) *n* trên *eg* trenau
train (of waves) *n* dilyniant *eg* dilyniannau
trainee hyfforddai *eg* hyfforddeion
trainee teacher (female) athrawes dan hyfforddiant *eb* athrawesau dan hyfforddiant
trainee teacher (male) athro dan hyfforddiant *eg* athrawon dan hyfforddiant
trainer hyfforddwr *eg* hyfforddwyr
training hyfforddiant *eg*
training agency asiantaeth hyfforddi *eb* asiantaethau hyfforddi
training centre canolfan hyfforddi *eb* canolfannau hyfforddi
training college coleg hyfforddi *eg* colegau hyfforddi
training day diwrnod hyfforddi *eg* diwrnodau hyfforddi
training grant grant hyfforddi *eg* grantiau hyfforddi
training hospital ysbyty hyfforddi *eg* ysbytai hyfforddi
training initiative menter hyfforddi *eb*
training method dull hyfforddi *eg* dulliau hyfforddi
training officer swyddog hyfforddi *eg* swyddogion hyfforddi
training programme rhaglen hyfforddi *eb* rhaglenni hyfforddi
training session sesiwn hyfforddi *eb* sesiynau hyfforddi
training zone cylchfa ymarfer *eb*
traitor bradwr *eg* bradwyr
trajectory taflwybr *eg* taflwybrau
tramline (in tennis) ystlyslin *eb* ystlyslinau
trampette trampét *eg* trampetau
trampoline trampolîn *eg* trampolinau
tramroad tramffordd *eb* tramffyrdd
tranquillizer tawelydd *eg* tawelyddion
transaction trafod *eg* trafodion
transaction cost cost trafod *eb* costau trafod
transaction file ffeil drafod *eb* ffeiliau trafod
transaction processing prosesu trafodion *be*
transactional analysis dadansoddi trafodol *be*
transactional model of stress model rhyngweithredol o straen *eg*
transamination trawsamineiddiad *eg*
transatlantic trawsiwerydd *ans*
transcendental trosgynnol *ans*
transcontinental trawsgyfandirol *ans*
transcribe trawsgrifio *be*
transcription trawsgrifiad *eg* trawsgrifiadau
transcription error gwall trawsysgrifol *eg* gwallau trawsysgrifol
transducer trawsddygiadur *eg* trawsddygiaduron
transduction trosglwyddiad *eg* trosglwyddiadau
transduction trawsddygiad *eg* trawsddygiadau
transect *n* trawslun *eg* trawsluniau
transect *v* trawslunio *be*
transept croesfa *eb* croesfâu
transfer (=coloured picture) *n* troslun *eg* trosluniau
transfer (=reallocation) *n* trosglwyddiad *eg* trosglwyddiadau
transfer (=transferable design) *n* trosglwyddyn *eg* trosglwyddynnau
transfer (blood) *v* trallwyso *be*
transfer (in general) *v* trosglwyddo *be*
transfer age (between schools) oed symud *eg*
transfer cost *n* cost trosglwyddo *eb* costau trosglwyddo
transfer cost *v* trosglwyddo'r gost *be*
transfer deed *n* gweithred drosglwyddo *eb* gweithredoedd trosglwyddo
transfer earnings *n* enillion trosglwyddo *ell*
transfer energy *v* trosglwyddo egni *be*
transfer ink *n* inc troslunio *eg* inciau troslunio
transfer matter *v* trosglwyddo mater *be*
transfer paper *n* papur troslunio *eg*
transfer payment taliad trosglwyddo *eg* taliadau trosglwyddo
transfer RNA RNA trosglwyddol *eg*
transferability trosglwyddedd *eg*
transferable trosglwyddadwy *ans*
transference trosglwyddo *be*
transfinite trawsfeidraidd *ans*
transfluence trawslifiant *eg*
transform *n* trawsffurf *eb* trawsffurfiau
transform *v* trawsffurfio *be*
transform integral equation hafaliad integrol trawsffurfiol *eg* hafaliadau integrol trawsffurfiol
transformation trawsffurfiad *eg* trawsffurfiadau
transformation geometry geometreg trawsffurfiadau *eb*
transformation of functions trawsffurfio ffwythiannau *be*
transformational grammar gramadeg trawsffurfio *eg*
transformer newidydd *eg* newidyddion
transfuse trallwyso *be*
transfusion trallwysiad *eg* trallwysiadau
transgression tresmasiad *eg* tresmasiadau

transhumance trawstrefa *be*
transistor transistor *eg* transistorau
Transistor-Transistor logic rhesymeg Transistor-Transistor *eb*
transit croesiad *eg* croesiadau
transit camp gwersyll dros dro *eg* gwersylloedd dros dro
transit region rhanbarth trawstaith *eg* rhanbarthau trawstaith
transition (=change) trawsnewidiad *eg* trawsnewidiadau
transition (=connecting passage in music) pont *eb* pontydd
transition (in physics) trosiad *eg* trosiadau
transition (into another key) trawsgyweiriad *eg* trawsgyweiriadau
transition element elfen drosiannol *eb* elfennau trosiannol
transition metal metel trosiannol *eg* metelau trosiannol
transition metal complex cymhlyg metelau trosiannol *eg*
transition piece darn cyfnewid *eg* darnau cyfnewid
transition state cyflwr trosiannol *eg* cyflyrau trosiannol
transitional (=changing) trawsnewidiol *ans*
transitional zone (geographic) cylchfa ryngbarthol *eb* cylchfaoedd rhyngbarthol
transitive trosaidd *ans*
transitory dros dro *ans*
translate (=move) symud *be*
translate (energy etc) trawsfudo *be*
translate (from one language to another) cyfieithu *be*
translate (in biochemistry) trosi *be*
translation (between places) trawsfudiad *eg* trawsfudiadau
translation (from one language to another) cyfieithiad *eg* cyfieithiadau
translation (of bishop etc) symudiad *eg* symudiadau
translation (of ideas) trosiad *eg* trosiadau
translation memory cof cyfieithu *eg* cofion cyfieithu
translation software meddalwedd cyfieithu *eb*
translational trawsfudol *ans*
translational energy egni trawsfudol *eg* egnïon trawsfudol
translator cyfieithydd *eg* cyfieithwyr
transliterate trawslythrennu *be*
translocated weed killer chwynladdwr trawsleoledig *eg* chwynladdwyr trawsleoledig
translocation trawsleoliad *eg* trawsleoliadau
translucency tryleuedd *eg*
translucent tryleu *ans*
translucent china tsieni tryleu *eg*
translucent colour lliw tryleu *eg* lliwiau tryleu
translucent enamel enamel tryleu *eg*
translucent materials defnyddiau tryleu *ell*
transmission (of heat, sound) trawsyriant *eg* trawsyriannau
transmission (of message, parcel) trosglwyddiad *eg* trosglwyddiadau
transmission model model trosglwyddo *eg*
transmission of sound waves trawsyriant tonnau sain *eg*
transmit (heat, sound) trawsyrru *be*
transmit (message, parcel) trosglwyddo *be*
transmitter (for broadcasting) trosglwyddydd *eg* trosglwyddyddion
transmitter (of heat, sound) trawsyrrydd *eg* trawsyryddion
transmutation trawsnewidiad *eg* trawsnewidiadau
transparency tryloywder *eg* tryloywderau
transparency colour lliw tryloywder *eg* lliwiau tryloywderau
transparency window ffenestr dryloyw *eb* ffenestri tryloyw
transparent tryloyw *ans*
transparent brown brown tryloyw *eg*
transparent colour lliw tryloyw *eg* lliwiau tryloyw
transparent enamel enamel tryloyw *eg*
transparent glaze gwydredd tryloyw *eg*
transparent gradient graddiad tryloyw *eg* graddiadau tryloyw
transparent gummed paper papur gwm tryloyw *eg*
transparent material defnydd tryloyw *eg* defnyddiau tryloyw
transparent paper papur tryloyw *eg*
transparent pixel picsel tryloyw *eg* picseli tryloyw
transparent ruler riwl dryloyw *eb* riwliau tryloyw
transpiration trydarthiad *eg*
transpiration rate cyfradd trydarthu *eb*
transpiration stream llif trydarthol *eg*
transpire trydarthu *be*
transplant *n* trawsblaniad *eg* trawsblaniadau
transplant *v* trawsblannu *be*
transplantation trawsblaniad *eg* trawsblaniadau
transplanted trawsblanedig *ans*
transport *v* cludo *be*
transport (mechanism) *n* cludydd *eg* cludyddion
transport (of goods etc) *n* cludiant *eg* cludiannau
transport link cysylltiad cludiant *eg*
transport medium cyfrwng cludo *eg* cyfryngau cludo
transport route ffordd gludiant *eb* ffyrdd cludiant
transportation trawsgludiad *eg*
transpose (in algebra) *n* trawsddodyn *eg* trawsddodynnau
transpose (in algebra) *v* trawsddodi *be*
transpose (in music) *v* trawsnodi *be*
transposing instrument offeryn trawsnodi *eg* offerynnau trawsnodi
transposition (in algebra) trawsddodiad *eg* trawsddodiadau
transposition (in music) trawsnodiad *eg* trawsnodiadau
transshipment point pwynt trawslwytho *eg* pwyntiau trawslwytho

transtheoretical model model trawsddamcaniaethol *eg*
transubstantiation traws-sylweddiad *eg*
transversal ardrawslin *eb* ardrawsliniau
transverse ardraws *ans*
transverse coastline morlin ardraws *eg* morlinau ardraws
transverse flute ffliwt draws *eb* ffliwtiau traws
transverse flute player canwr ffliwt draws *eg* canwyr ffliwt draws
transverse process cnepyn traws *eg* cnepynnau traws
transverse projection tafluniad ardraws *eg*
transverse section toriad ardraws *eg* toriadau ardraws
transverse vibration dirgryniad ardraws *eg* dirgryniadau ardraws
transverse wave ton ardraws *eb* tonnau ardraws
transvestic fetishism ffetisiaeth drawswisgo *eb*
transvestite trawswisgwr *eg* trawswisgwyr
trap (=snare) *n* magl *eb* maglau
trap (=snare) *v* maglu *be*
trap (for water, oil etc) *n* trap *eg* trapiau
trap (the ball) *v* trapio *be*
trapezium trapesiwm *eg* trapesiymau
trapezoid trapesoid *eg* trapesoidau
traste cribell *eb* cribellau
trauma trawma *eg* trawmâu
travel teithio *be*
travel agent asiantaeth deithio *eb* asiantaethau teithio
travel agent trefnwr teithiau *eg* trefnwyr teithiau
travel destination cyrchfan teithio *eb* cyrchfannau teithio
travel supplement atodiad teithio *eg* atodiadau teithio
travel through a space (in dance etc) teithio i mewn ac allan o ofod
travelling dance dawns deithiol *eb* dawnsiau teithiol
travelling microscope microsgop teithiol *eg* microsgopau teithiol
travelling step step deithio *eb* stepiau teithio
traverse (in mountaineering) trawstaith *eb* trawsteithiau
traverse (of lathe carriage) tramwy *eg* tramwyon
travertine trafertin *eg* trafertinau
trawl treillio *be*
trawl net treillrwyd *eb* treillrwydi
trawler (ship) treillong *eb* treillongau
tray hambwrdd *eg* hambyrddau
tray base sylfaen hambwrdd *eb* sylfeini hambwrdd
tray cloth lliain hambwrdd *eg* llieiniau hambwrdd
treachery brad *eg*
Treachery of the Blue Books Brad y Llyfrau Gleision *eg*
tread (of stairs) gris *eg* grisiau
tread and riser gris ac wyneb
tread water troedio'r dŵr *be*
treadle troedlath *eb* troedlathau
treadmill melin droedlath *eb* melinau troedlath
treason brad *eg*
Treason of the Blue Books Brad y Llyfrau Gleision *eg*
treasure basket basged drysor *eb* basgedi trysor
treasury trysorlys *eg*
Treasury Bill Bil Trysorlys *eg*
treat *v* trin *be*
treatise traethawd *eg* traethodau
treatment triniaeth *eb* triniaethau
treatment room ystafell driniaeth *eb* ystafelloedd triniaeth
treaty cytundeb *eg* cytundebau
treble trebl *eg* treblau
treble boost atgyfnerthiad trebl *eg*
treble cut toriad trebl *eg*
treble instrument offeryn trebl *eg* offerynnau trebl
tree coeden *eb* coed
tree branch cangen coeden *eb* canghennau coed
tree diagram diagram canghennog *eg* diagramau canghennog
tree line coedlin *eg* coedlinau
tree trunk boncyff *eg* boncyffion
trellis smocking smocwaith dellt *eg*
trellised delltog *ans*
tremolando tremolando *adf*
tremolo tremolo *eg* tremoli
tremor cryndod *eg* cryndodau
trench ffos *eb* ffosydd
trench foundation sylfaen ffos *eb* sylfeini ffos
trenching rhigoli *be*
trend tuedd *eb* tueddiadau
trend surface analysis dadansoddiad arwyneb tuedd *eg* dadansoddiadau arwyneb tuedd
trental trental *eg* trentalau
trespass *n* tresmasiad *eg* tresmasiadau
trespass *v* tresmasu *be*
trespasser tresmaswr *eg* tresmaswyr
trestle trestl *eg* trestlau
triad triad *eg* triadau
triage brysbennu *be*
trial (=experiment) *n* arbrawf *eg* arbrofion
trial (=experimental) *adj* arbrofol *ans*
trial (=test beforehand) *v* rhagbrofi *be*
trial (in sport) *n* treial *eg* treialon
trial balance mantolen brawf *eb* mantolenni prawf
trial by battle prawf trwy ornest *eg*
trial by his peers prawf gan ei gydradd *eg*
trial by jury treial gan reithgor *eg*
trial by ordeal diheurbrawf *eg* diheurbrofion
trial print print arbrofol *eg* printiau arbrofol
trial printing prawf-brintio *be*
trialkoxymethane trialcocsimethan *eg*
triangle triongl *eg* trionglau
triangle of forces triongl grymoedd *eg* trionglau grymoedd

triangle of velocities triongl cyflymderau *eg* trionglau cyflymderau
triangular trionglog *ans*
triangular arch bwa trionglog *eg* bwâu trionglog
triangular bandage rhwymyn trionglog *eg* rhwymynnau trionglog
triangular cleat (sash window) cledd trionglog *eg* cleddau trionglog
triangular file ffeil dairongl *eb* ffeiliau tairongl
triangular number rhif triongl *eg* rhifau triongl
triangular prism prism triongl *eg* prismau triongl
triangular pyramid pyramid trionglog *eg* pyramidiau trionglog
triangular scraper sgrafell dairongl *eb* sgrafelli tairongl
triangularity trionglogrwydd *eg*
triangulation triongliant *eg* triongliannau
triangulation pillar piler triongli *eg* pileri triongli
triarchic theory damcaniaeth dri-bwa *eb*
Triassic Triasig *ans*
tribal llwythol *ans*
tribalism llwytholdeb *eg*
tribe llwyth *eg* llwythau
tribromomethane tribromomethan *eg*
tribunal tribiwnlys *eg* tribiwnlysoedd
Tribunals and Inquiries Act Deddf Tribiwnlysoedd ac Ymchwiliadau *eb*
tribune tribiwn *eg* tribiwnau
tributary llednant *eb* llednentydd
tributary region rhanbarth ategol *eg* rhanbarthau ategol
tribute (=payment) treth *eb* trethi
tribute (of respect or affection) teyrnged *eb* teyrngedau
tricel tricel *eg*
triceps cyhyryn triphen *eg* cyhyrynnau triphen
trichlorocuprate(I) ion ïon triclorocwprad(I) *eg* ïonau triclorocwprad(I)
trichloroethanal tricloroethanal *eg*
2,2,2-trichloroethanediol 2,2,2-tricloroethandeuol *eg*
trichloromethane tricloromethan *eg*
(trichloromethyl)benzene (tricloromethyl)bensen *eg*
trichloronitromethane tricloronitromethan *eg*
trichromatic theory damcaniaeth drigromatig *eb*
trick marionette marionét tric *eg* marionetau tric
trickle *v* diferynnu *be*
tricolour baner drilliw *eb* baneri trilliw
tricuspid valve falf deirlen *eb* falfiau teirlen
tricyclic antidepressant gwrthiselydd trichylch *eg* gwrthiselyddion trichylch
trident tryfer *eg* tryferi
Tridentine Tridentaidd *ans*
triennial teirblwydd *ans*
Triennial Act Deddf Deirblwydd *eb*
trier profwr *eg* profwyr
triethoxymethane triethocsimethan *eg*
triethylamine triethylamin *eg*
triforium trifforiwm *eg* trifforia
trig point piler triongli *eg* pileri triongli
trigger triger *eg* trigeri
trigger hyperlink cychwyn hypergyswllt *be*
triglyceride triglyserid *eg* triglyseridau
trigonal trigonol *ans*
trigonal bipyramid deubyramid trigonol *eg* deubyramidiau trigonol
trigonometric trigonometrig *ans*
trigonometric function ffwythiant trigonometrig *eg* ffwythiannau trigonometrig
trigonometrical trigonometregol *ans*
trigonometry trigonometreg *eb*
trihedral trihedrol *ans*
3,4,5-trihydroxybenzenecarboxylic acid asid 3,4,5-trihydrocsibensencarbocsylig *eg*
triiodomethane triiodomethan *eg*
trikaya trikaya *eg*
trim *v* trimio *be*
trim and snip trimio a snipio
trim with lace addurno â les *be*
trimer trimer *eg* trimerau
trimester tymor *eg* tymhorau
trimethylaluminium trimethylalwminiwm *eg*
1,3,5-trimethylbenzene 1,3,5-trimethylbensen *eg*
2,2,4-trimethylpentane 2,2,4-trimethylpentan *eg*
trimetric projection tafluniad trimetrig *eg* tafluniadau trimetrig
trimmer trimiwr *eg* trimwyr
trimming (decoration) addurn *eg* addurniadau
trimming knife cyllell drimio *eb* cyllyll trimio
2,4,6-trinitrophenol 2,4,6-trinitroffenol *eg*
Trinity Trindod *eb*
trinket box blwch tlysau *eg* blychau tlysau
trinomial *adj* trinomaidd *ans*
trinomial *n* trinomial *eg* trinomialau
trio (group) triawd *eg* triawdau
trio (movement) trio *eg* trios
trio sonata sonata drio *eb* sonatau trio
triode triod *eg* triodau
trioxoboric acid asid triocsoborig *eg*
trioxygen triocsigen *eg*
trip *v* baglu *be*
trip (of long duration) *n* taith *eb* teithiau
trip (of short duration) *n* trip *eg* tripiau
tripartite tridarn *ans*
Tripartite Indenture Cytundeb Tridarn *eg*
triple *adj* triphlyg *ans*
triple (in general) *n* triphlyg *eg* triphlygion
triple (=set of three) *n* triawd *eg* triawdau
Triple Alliance Cynghrair Driphlyg *eb*
triple bond bond triphlyg *eg* bondiau triphlyg
triple counterpoint gwrthbwynt triphlyg *eg*
triple curve integral cromlin gyfannol driphlyg *eb* cromliniau cyfannol triphlyg
triple dot dot triphlyg *eg* dotiau triphlyg

triple fugue ffiwg driphlyg *eb* ffiwgiau triphlyg
triple glazed window ffenestr gwydr triphlyg *eb* ffenestri gwydr triphlyg
triple harp telyn deires *eb* telynau teires
triple immunization imiwneiddiad triphlyg *eg*
triple jump naid driphlyg *eb* neidiau triphlyg
triple point pwynt triphlyg *eg* pwyntiau triphlyg
triple roof to fframiog *eg* toeon fframiog
triple tonguing tafodi triphlyg *be*
triple vaccine brechlyn triphlyg *eg* brechlynnau triphlyg
triple-point stilts stiltiau tri-phwynt *ell*
triplet tripled *eb* tripledi
tripod trybedd *eb* trybeddau
Tripoli compound sebon Tripoli *eg*
triratna triratna *eg*
trisect (equal parts) traeannu *be*
trisect (in general) teirannu *be*
trisection (in equal parts) traeaniad *eg* traeaniadau
trisection (in general) teiraniad *eg* teiraniadau
tris(2-hydroxyethyl)amine tris(2-hydrocsiethyl)amin *eg*
tris(pentane-2,4-dionato)cobalt(III) tris(pentan-2,4-deuonato)cobalt(III) *eg*
TRIST: TVEI Related In-Service Training HMS-ADAG: Hyfforddiant Mewn Swydd yn gysylltiedig ag ADAG *eg*
tritanopia tritanopia *eg*
trithioantimonate(III) ion ïon trithioantimonad(III) *eg* ïonau trithioantimonad(III)
trithioarsenate(III) ion ïon trithioarsenad(III) *eg* ïonau trithioarsenad(III)
trithiostannate(IV) ion ïon trithiostanad(IV) *eg* ïonau trithiostanad(IV)
triumphant gorfoleddus *ans*
triumvir triwr *eg* triwyr
triumvirate triwriaeth *eb* triwriaethau
trivet trybedd *eb* trybeddau
trivial distadl *ans*
trochoid trocoid *eg* trocoidau
troll *n* trôl *eg* troliau
troll *v* trolio *be*
trolley troli *eg* trolïau
trolley bed gwely troli *eg* gwelyau troli
trolley jack jac troli *eg* jaciau troli
trombone trombôn *eg* trombonau
trombone tenor trombôn tenor *eg* trombonau tenor
trombonist trombonydd *eg* trombonwyr
tromino tromino *eg* trominos
troop ship llong filwyr *eb* llongau milwyr
trophic troffig *ans*
trophic level lefel droffig *eb* lefelau troffig
trophy tlws *eg* tlysau
tropic trofan *eg* trofannau
Tropic of Cancer Trofan Cancr *eg*
Tropic of Capricorn Trofan Capricorn *eg*
tropical trofannol *ans*
tropical continental trofannol-gyfandirol *ans*
tropical desert diffeithdir trofannol *eg*
tropical maritime trofannol-arforol *ans*
tropical rainforest coedwig law drofannol *eb* coedwigoedd glaw trofannol
tropical zone cylchfa drofannol *eb* cylchfaoedd trofannol
tropics trofannau *ell*
tropism tropedd *eg* tropeddau
tropopause tropoffin *eg* tropoffiniau
troposphere troposffer *eg* troposfferau
trot *n* tuth *eb* tuthiau
trot *v* tuthio *be*
Trotskyism Trotscïaeth *eb*
Trotskyist Trotscïad *eg/b* Trotsciaid
troubadour trwbadŵr *eg* trwbadwriaid
trough cafn *eg* cafnau
trough (pressure) cafn o wasgedd isel *eg*
trough shaped valley dyffryn cafnog *eg* dyffrynnoedd cafnog
trough's end blaen cafn *eg*
trousers trowsus *eg* trowsusau
trowel trywel *eg* trywelion
truancy triwantiaeth *eb*
truant *adj* triwant *ans*
truant *n* triwant *eg* triwantiaid
truce cadoediad *eg* cadoediadau
truck tryc *eg* tryciau
truck shop siop dryc *eb* siopau tryc
truckle bed gwely treigl *eg* gwelyau treigl
true (=correct, accurate) cywir *ans*
true (=veracious, real) gwir *ans*
true bearing cyfeiriant cywir *eg*
true bias gwir fias *eg*
true colour gwir liw *eg* gwir liwiau
true discount gwir ddisgownt *eg*
true ellipse gwir elips *eg*
true fruit gwir ffrwythyn *eg* gwir ffrwythynnau
true length hyd cywir *eg*
true magnetic magnetig cywir *eg*
true north gogledd cywir *eg*
true or false (in exam questions) cywir neu anghywir
true rate of interest gwir gyfradd llog *eb*
true shape gwir siâp *eg* gwir siapiau
true size maint cywir *eg* meintiau cywir
true string tant cywirsain *eg* tannau cywirsain
true vertical height uchder fertigol cywir *eg*
trueness to type gwirdeiprwydd *eg*
trumpet utgorn *eg* utgyrn
trumpeter trwmpedwr *eg* trwmpedwyr
truncate blaendorri *be*
truncated blaendor *ans*
truncated (of soil) uwchdor *ans*
truncated cone côn blaendor *eg* conau blaendor
truncated cylinder silindr blaendor *eg* silindrau blaendor

truncated prism prism blaendor *eg* prismau blaendor
truncated pyramid pyramid blaendor *eg* pyramidiau blaendor
truncated soil pridd uwchdor *eg* priddoedd uwchdor
truncated spur sbardun blaendor *eg* sbardunau blaendor
truncation blaendoriad *eg* blaendoriadau
truncation error gwall blaendorri *eg* gwallau blaendorri
truncheon pastwn *eg* pastynau
trunk (of body) bongorff *eg* bongyrff
trunk exercise ymarfer bongorff *eg* ymarferion bongorff
trunk road cefnffordd *eb* cefnffyrdd
trunk stream prif ffrwd *eb* prif ffrydiau
trunks (for swimming) trowsus nofio *eg* trowsusau nofio
trunnion trynion *eg* trynionau
truss cwpl *eg* cyplau
trussed cypledig *ans*
trussed rafter ceibr cypledig *eg* ceibrau cypledig
trust *n* ymddiriedolaeth *eb* ymddiriedolaethau
trust *v* ymddiried *be*
trust deed dogfen ymddiriedolaeth *eb* dogfennau ymddiriedolaeth
trust status statws ymddiriedolaeth *eg*
Trust Territory Tiriogaeth Ymddiriedig *eb*
trustee ymddiriedolwr *eg* ymddiriedolwyr
Trustee Savings Bank Banc Cynilo Ymddiriedol *eg*
trusteeship ymddiriedolaeth *eb* ymddiriedolaethau
trusteeship council cyngor ymddiriedolaeth *eg*
trusteeship territory tiriogaeth ymddiriedol *eb* tiriogaethau ymddiriedol
truth table gwirlen *eb* gwirlenni
try (in rugby) *n* cais *eg* ceisiau
try square sgwâr profi *eg* sgwariau profi
trying plane plaen hir *eg* plaeniau hir
tryptophan tryptoffan *eg*
Tsar of all the Russians Tsar yr holl Rwsiaid *eg*
Tsardom Tsaraeth *eb*
tsarism tsariaeth *eb*
T-shaped stretcher estynnwr ffurf T *eg* estynwyr ffurf T
T-shirt crys T *eg* crysau T
T-slot agen T *eb* agennau T
tsunami tsunami *eg*
tub *n* twb *eg* tybiau
tub *v* twbio *be*
tub four twb pedwar *eg*
tub pair twb pâr *eg*
tuba tiwba *eg* tiwbâu
tuba player canwr tiwba *eg* canwyr tiwba
tube tiwb *eg* tiwbiau
tuber cloronen *eb* cloron
► **tuberculosis** twbercwlosis *eg*
tubing tiwbin *eg* tiwbinau
tubular tiwbaidd *ans*
tubular aluminium alwminiwm tiwbaidd *eg*
tubular bells tiwbglychau *ell*
tubular brass pres tiwbaidd *eg*
tubular bridge pont diwb *eb* pontydd tiwb
tubular gauze rhwyllen diwb *eb* rhwyllenni tiwb
tubular heater gwresogydd tiwb *eg* gwresogyddion tiwb
tubular steel dur tiwbaidd *eg*
tubule tiwbyn *eg* tiwbynnau
tuck twc *eg* tyciau
tucked hem hem dwc *eb* hemiau twc
Tudor dynasty llinach y Tuduriaid *eb*
Tudor rebellions gwrthryfeloedd cyfnod y Tuduriaid *ell*
Tudor settlement ardrefniant Tuduraidd *eg*
Tudors Tuduriaid *ell*
tufa twffa *eg* twffâu
tuff twff *eg* twffau
tuffaceous tyffaidd *ans*
tuft cudyn *eg* cudynnau
tufted cudynnog *ans*
tufted carpet carped cudynnog *eg* carpedi cudynnog
tug tynfad *eg* tynfadau
tug o war tynnu rhaff *be*
tuition fees ffïoedd dysgu *ell*
tulle tulle *eg*
tumble drier peiriant sychu dillad *eg* peiriannau sychu dillad
tumble dry sychu mewn peiriant *be*
tumble gear gêr twmblo *eg* gerau twmblo
tumbler drive barrel casgen gyriant twmblo *eb* casgiau gyriant twmblo
tumbrel trol *eb* troliau
tumour tyfiant *eg* tyfiannau
tumulus gwyddfa *eb* gwyddfeydd
tuna tiwna *eg* tiwnaod
tundra twndra *eg* twndrâu
tune alaw *eb* alawon
tuned circuit cylched gysain *eb* cylchedau cysain
tuned instrument offeryn traw *eg* offerynnau traw
tuned percussion instrument offeryn taro tiwniedig *eg* offerynnau taro tiwniedig
tuner tiwniwr *eg* tiwnwyr
tungstate(VI) ion ïon twngstad(VI) *eg* ïonau twngstad(VI)
tungsten (W) twngsten *eg*
tungsten carbide twngsten carbid *eg*
tungsten carbide paper papur twngsten carbid *eg*
tungsten steel dur twngsten *eg*
tungsten tipped (lathe toll forms) blaen twngsten *eg*
tunic tiwnig *eb* tiwnigau
tuning fork trawfforch *eb* trawffyrch
tuning hammer morthwyl cyweirio *eg* morthwylion cyweirio
tuning key allwedd diwnio *eb* allweddi tiwnio
tuning note cyweirdant *eg* cyweirdannau
tuning pin ebill cyweirio *eg* ebillion cyweirio
tuning string cyweirdant *eg* cyweirdannau
tunnage & poundage treth gasgen a phwysau *eb*

tunnel twnnel *eg* twnelau
turban twrban *eg* twrbanau
turbary (of land) mawnog *eb* mawnogydd
turbid cymylog *ans*
turbidity cymylogrwydd *eg*
turbidity current cerrynt tyrfedd *eg* ceryntau tyrfedd
turbine tyrbin *eg* tyrbinau
turbo-generator generadur tyrbo *eg* generaduron tyrbo
turbulence (in general) cynnwrf *eg*
turbulence (in meteorology) tyrfedd *eg* tyrfeddau
turbulent (in general) cynhyrfus *ans*
turbulent (in meteorology) tyrfol *ans*
turbulent flow llif tyrfol *eg* llifoedd tyrfol
turgid chwydd-dynn *ans*
turgidity chwydd-dyndra *eg*
Turk Twrc *eg* Twrciaid
Turkish Twrcaidd *ans*
Turkish Empire Ymerodraeth Twrci *eb*
Turkish stitch pwyth Twrcaidd *eg* pwythau Twrcaidd
turn *n* tro *eg* troeon
turn (ideas) *v* trosi *be*
turn (in general) *v* troi *be*
turn (lathe) *v* turnio *be*
turn a partner troi partner *be*
turn and give troi a rhoi
turn in a coil tro mewn coil *eg* troadau mewn coil
turn off (power supply) diffodd *be*
turn on (power supply) cynnau *be*
turn on an engine cychwyn injan *be*
turn on the ball troi ar y bêl *be*
turn out the light diffodd y golau *be*
turn single tro unfan *eg* troeon unfan
turn the electric fire off diffodd y tân trydan *be*
turn the electric fire on cynnau'r tân trydan *be*
turn the heel troi'r sawdl *be*
turn the scrum olwyno'r sgrym *be*
turn the tap off cau'r tap *be*
turn the tap on agor y tap *be*
turner turniwr *eg* turnwyr
Turner's syndrome syndrom Turner *eg*
turnery turnwriaeth *eb*
turning (=bend) troad *eg* troadau
turning allowance lwfans troi *eg* lwfansau troi
turning between centres turnio rhwng canolau *be*
turning chisel cŷn turnio *eg* cynion turnio; gaing turnio *eb* geingiau turnio
turning force grym troi *eg*
turning point trobwynt *eg* trobwyntiau
turning tool erfyn turnio *eg* offer turnio
turnip meipen *eb* maip; erfinen *eb* erfin
turnkey system system osodedig *eb* systemau gosodedig
turnover trosiant *eg* trosiannau
turnover board bwrdd dymchwel *eg* byrddau dymchwel
turnpike tyrpeg *eg* tyrpegau
turnpike company cwmni tyrpeg *eg* cwmnïau tyrpeg
turntable bwrdd tro *eg* byrddau tro
turn-taking cymryd tro *be*
turpentine tyrpant *eg*
turps substitute amnewidyn tyrpant *eg* amnewidion tyrpant
turquoise (enamelling colour) glaswyrdd *eg*
turret twred *eg* tyredau
turtle crwban *eg* crwbanod
turtle graphics graffeg crwban *eg*
turtle neck gwddf crwban *eg*
tusk tenon tyno ysgithr *eg* tynoau ysgithr
tusk tenon joint uniad tyno ysgithr *eg* uniadau tyno ysgithr
tussock (bunch grass) sypwellt *eg*
tussore tussore *ans*
tutelage gwarchodaeth *eb*
tutor tiwtor *eg* tiwtoriaid
tutor group grŵp tiwtor *eg* grwpiau tiwtoriaid
tutorial tiwtorial *eg* tiwtorialau
tutor-organiser tiwtor drefnydd *eg* tiwtor drefnyddion
tuyére tuyére *eg*
TV listings amserlenni teledu *ell*
TVEI: Technical Vocational Education Initiative ADAG: Addysg Dechnegol a Galwedigaethol *eb*
tweed brethyn caerog *eg* brethynnau caerog
tweezers gefel fach *eg* gefeiliau bach
twelfth deuddegfed *eg* deuddegfedau
twelfth man deuddegfed dyn *eg*
Twelve Articles Deuddeg Erthygl *eb*
twelve note technique techneg deuddeg nodyn *eb*
twentieth century ugeinfed ganrif *eb*
twenty five yards pum llath ar hugain *eg*
twice full size dwywaith maint llawn
twig brigyn *eg* brigau
twilight zone cylchfa gyfnosi *eb* cylchfaoedd cyfnosi
twill twil *eg*
twill weave gwehyddiad caerog *eg*
twin (female) gefeilles *eb* gefeilliaid
twin (male) gefell *eg* gefeilliaid
twin haunched dwbl hansiedig *ans*
twin needle (of machine part) nodwydd ddwbl *eb* nodwyddau dwbl
twin tenon tyno dwbl *eg* tynoau dwbl
twin town gefeilldref *eb* gefeilldrefi
twin tub machine peiriant twb dwbl *eg* peiriannau twb dwbl
twine *n* cortyn *eg* cortynnau
twine (as in climbing plants) *v.intrans* ymgordeddu *be*
twine (in general) *v.trans* cordeddu *be*
twinning (of schools) gefeillio *be*
twinning (of towns) trefeillio *be*
twist (=give spiral form to) *v* dirdroi *be*
twist (=turn) *n* tro *eg* troeon
twist (in general) *v* troelli *be*
twist (of spiral) *n* dirdroad *eg* dirdroadau

twist (of strands) *v.intrans* ymgordeddu *be*
twist (strands) *v.trans* cordeddu *be*
twist bit ebill tro *eg* ebillion tro
twist drill dril dirdro *eg* driliau dirdro
twist drill parts rhannau dril dirdro *ell*
twisted dirdro *ans*
twisted chain stitch pwyth cadwyn dro *eg* pwythau cadwyn dro
twisted cord cortyn dirdro *eg* cortynnau dirdro
twisted grain graen tro *eg*
twisted shank hoelen garan ddirdro *eb* hoelion garan dirdro
twisting (forging process) dirdroi *be*
twitch *n* plwc *eg* plyciau
twitch *v* plycio *be*
two dau *eg* deuoedd
two bails dwy gaten *eb*
two by two factorial design cynllun ffactoraidd dau wrth ddau *eg* cynlluniau ffactoraidd dau wrth ddau
two dimensional modelling modelu dau ddimensiwn *be*
two hands clean and jerk plwc dwy law
two hands snatch cipiad dwy law *eg* cipiadau dwy law
two on the ball (of females) dwy ar y bêl *eb*
two on the ball (of males) dau ar y bêl *eg*
two plywood fillets dau ffiled pren haenog *eg*
two step flow theory damcaniaeth llif dau gam *eb*
two way switch switsh dwyffordd *eg* switshis dwyffordd
two-digit dau ddigid *ans*
two-dimensional dau ddimensiwn *ans*
two-hand turn tro dwy law *eg* troeon dwy law
two-part dwyran *ans*
two-part (in singing) deulais *ans*
two-phase dwywedd *ans*
two-ply wool edafedd dwy gainc *ell*
two-point discrimination threshold trothwy gwahaniaethu deubwynt *eg*
two-pronged chuck crafanc fforch ddwbl *eb* crafangau fforch ddwbl
two-pronged fork fforch ddeubig *eb* ffyrch deubig
twos deuoedd *ell*
two's complement cyflenwad deuol *eg*
two-storey deulawr *ans*
two-stroke dwystroc *ans*
two-tailed test prawf dwygynffon *eg* profion dwygynffon
two-way loom gwŷdd dwyffordd *eg* gwyddau dwyffordd
tympanic membrane tympan y glust *eg* tympanau clustiau
tympanym tympanwm *eg*
type (=kind or sort) *n* math *eg* mathau
type (=write with a typewriter) *v* teipio *be*
type (in printing) *n* teip *eg* teipiau
type A personality personoliaeth math A *eb*
type B personality personoliaeth math B *eb*
type C (cancer-prone) personality personoliaeth math C (tuedd tuag at ganser) *eb*
type checking math-wirio *be*
type 1 error cyfeiliornad math 1 *eg* cyfeiliornadau math 1
type 2 error cyfeiliornad math 2 *eg* cyfeiliornadau math 2
type holder daliwr teip *eg* dalwyr teip
type metal metel teip *eg*
type of farming math o ffermio *eg* mathau o ffermio
type of performance math o berfformiad *eg* mathau o berfformiad
type of throw natur y tafliad *eb*
type station gorsaf deip *eb* gorsafoedd teip
typeface ffurfdeip *eg* ffurfdeipiau
typefont ffont-deip *eb* ffontdeipiau
types of files mathau o ffeiliau
types of finishes dulliau o orffeniadau *ell*
types of food mathau o fwyd *ell*
types of support mathau o gymorth *ell*
typeset teiposod *be*
typewriter teipiadur *eg* teipiaduron
typhoon teiffŵn *eg* teiffwnau
typing error gwall teipio *eg* gwallau teipio
typography teipograffeg *eb*
typology teipoleg *eb*
tyramine cheese reaction adwaith caws tyramin *eg*
tyrannical gormesol *ans*
tyrannicide (=person who kills a tyrant) teyrnleiddiad *eg* teyrnleiddiaid
tyrannicide (crime) teyrnladdiad *eg* teyrnladdiadau
tyranny gormes *eg/b*
tyrant teyrn *eg* teyrnedd
tyrosine tyrosin *eg*

U

U shaped valley dyffryn ffurf U *eg* dyffrynnoedd ffurf U

ubac cil haul *eg*

U-bend pibell U *eb* pibellau U

U-boat llong danfor Almaenig *eb* llongau tanfor Almaenig

UCCA Cyngor Canolog ar gyfer Mynediad i'r Prifysgolion *eg*

udder pwrs *eg* pyrsiau; cadair *eb* cadair

UK energy policy polisi egni'r Deyrnas Unedig *eg*

ukelele iwcalili *eg* iwcalilis

Ukrainian *adj* Wcrainaidd *ans*

Ukrainian *n* Wcrainiad *eg* Wcrainiaid

ulcer briw *eg* briwiau

ulcerate briwio *be*

ulna wlna *eg* wlnâu

ulnar nerve nerf wlnar *eg* nerfau wlnar

Ulster Loyalist Teyrngarwr Ulster *eg* Teyrngarwyr Ulster

Ulster plantations trefedigaethau Ulster *ell*

Ulster Unionist Unoliaethwr Ulster *eg* Unoliaethwyr Ulster

Ulster Volunteer Gwirfoddolwr Ulster *eg* Gwirfoddolwyr Ulster

ultimate attribution error cyfeiliornad priodoli eithaf *eg* cyfeiliornadau priodoli eithaf

ultimate cause achos eithaf *eg* achosion eithaf

ultimatum wltimatwm *eg*

ultra bold (of type) trwm iawn *ans*

ultra thin (of line) tenau iawn *ans*

ultra violet lamp lamp uwchfioled *eb* lampau uwchfioled

ultra violet light golau uwchfioled *eg*

ultrabasic wltrabasig *ans*

ultracentrifuge uwchallgyrchydd *eg* uwchallgyrchwyr

ultra-fashionable tra ffasiynol *ans*

ultrafiltration uwch-hidlo *be*

ultrafine dashed (of line) toredig mân iawn *ans*

ultrafine dotted (of line) dotiog mân iawn *ans*

ultramarine dulas *eg*

Ultra-Royalist Uchel Frenhinwr *eg* Uchel Frenhinwyr

ultrasonic uwchsain *ans*

ultrasonics (of science) uwchseineg *eb*

ultrasound uwchsain *eg* uwchseiniau

ultraviolet uwchfioled *eg*

ultraviolet wave ton uwchfioled *eb* tonnau uwchfioled

umbel wmbel *eg* wmbelau

umber wmber *eg*

umbilical wmbilig *ans*

umbilical cord llinyn bogail *eg* llinynnau bogeiliau

umbilicus bogail *eg* bogeiliau

umma umma *eg*

ummah ummah *eg*

umpire dyfarnwr *eg* dyfarnwyr

UN convention on the rights of the child confensiwn yr UN ar hawliau plant *eg*

unaccented diacen *ans*

unacceptable behaviour ymddygiad annerbyniol *eg*

unaccompanied digyfeiliant *ans*

unaided heb gymorth *adf*

unambiguous diamwys *ans*

unauthorized absence absenoldeb heb ei awdurdodi *eg* absenoldebau heb eu hawdurdodi

unauthorized access absenoldeb heb ei awdurdodi *eg*

unbalanced diet deiet anghytbwys *eg*

unbalanced forces grymoedd anghytbwys *ell*

unbeneficed difywoliaeth *ans*

unbiased (in physics) di-fias *ans*

unbiased (in statistics) diduedd *ans*

unbiased estimate amcangyfrif diduedd *eg* amcangyfrifon diduedd

unbiased estimator amcangyfrifyn diduedd *eg*

unbleached heb ei gannu *ans*

unbleached calico calico heb ei gannu *eg*

unbounded diarffin *ans*

unbroken line llinell ddi-dor *eb* llinellau di-dor

unburnt heb losgi *ans*

uncertainty principle egwyddor ansicrwydd *eb*

unchanged heb newid *ans*

uncheck (=get rid of tick in box) dad-dicio *be*

unchristian anghristnogol *ans*

uncial wnsial *eg* wnsialau

unclassified annosbarthedig *ans*

unclear aneglur *ans*

unconditional diamod *ans*

unconditional branch instruction cyfarwyddyd canghennu diamod *eg* cyfarwyddiadau canghennu diamod

unconditional jump naid ddiamod *eb* neidiau diamod

unconditional jump instruction cyfarwyddyd neidio diamod *eg* cyfarwyddiadau neidio diamod

unconditional positive regard agwedd gadarnhaol ddiamod *eb*

unconditional positive regard parch cadarnhaol diamod *eg*
unconditional response ymateb heb ei gyflyru *eg*
unconditional stimulus ysgogiad heb ei gyflyru *eg*
unconditional surrender ildio diamod *be*
unconditional transfer instruction gorchymyn trosglwyddo diamod *eg* gorchmynion trosglwyddo diamod
unconditioned stimulus pre-exposure effect effaith cyn-amlygiad ysgogiad heb ei gyflyru *eb*
unconformable beds haenau anghyffurfiadwy *ell*
unconformity anghydffurfedd *eg*
unconscious *adj* anymwybodol *ans*
unconscious *n* anymwybod *eg*
unconscious inference rhesymu anymwybodol *be*
unconstitutional anghyfansoddiadol *ans*
unconventional anghonfensiynol *ans*
uncorrelated anghydberthnasol *ans*
uncover dadorchuddio *be*
uncover from bottom dadorchuddio o'r gwaelod *be*
uncover from left dadorchuddio o'r chwith *be*
uncover from right dadorchuddio o'r dde *be*
uncover from top dadorchuddio o'r brig *be*
uncrushable (finish) anghrychadwy *ans*
unction eneiniad olaf *eg*
undefined anniffiniedig *ans*
under arm bowling bowlio dan ysgwydd *be*
under construction ar y gweill
under grasp tanafael *be*
under stitching tanbwytho *be*
under the action of gravity o dan effaith disgyrchiant
underachieve tangyflawni *be*
underachiever (of child) plentyn sy'n tangyflawni *eg* plant sy'n tangyflawni
underarm cesail *eb* ceseiliau
underarm pass pàs dan ysgwydd *eb* pasiau dan ysgwydd
underarm throw tafliad dan ysgwydd *eg* tafliadau dan ysgwydd
underblanket isflanced *eb* isflancedi
underclothing dillad isaf *ell*
undercoat *v* tanbeintio *be*
undercoat (of paint) *n* tanbaent *eg* tanbaentiau
undercolour tanliw *eg*
undercover cudd *ans*
undercurrent islif *eg* islifogydd
undercut *n* tandoriad *eg* tandoriadau
undercut *v* tandorri *be*
undercut bank torlan *eb* torlannau
underdeveloped (of child) heb ddatblygu digon *ans*
underdeveloped (of country etc) tanddatblygedig *ans*
under-employ tangyflogi *be*
underemployment tangyflogaeth *eb*
underextension tanestyn *be*
underface *n* tanwyneb *eg* tanwynebau
underface *v* tanwynebu *be*
underfire tan ffwrndanio *be*
underfloor tanlawr *ans*
underflow islif *eg* islifoedd
underframe ffrâm isaf *eb* fframiau isaf
underframe rail rheilen isaf *eb* rheiliau isaf
underfur isflew *eg*
undergarments dillad isaf *ell*
underglaze *n* tanwydredd *eg*
underglaze *v* tanwydro *be*
underglaze colour lliw tanwydredd *eg*
underground tanddaearol *ans*
underground movement (=secret movement) mudiad cyfrin *eg* mudiadau cyfrin
undergrowth isdyfiant *eg*
underlay (of carpet) haen waelodol *eb* haenau gwaelodol
underline tanlinellu *be*
underline key tanlinellwr *eg* tanlinellwyr
underlying gwaelodol *ans*
underlying bedrock creigwely gwaelodol *eg* creigwelyau gwaelodol
underlying pattern patrwm gwaelodol *eg* patrymau gwaelodol
undermine tanseilio *be*
under-nourish tanfaethu *be*
under-nourished heb ddigon o faeth *ans*
undernourishment diffyg maeth *eg*
underpaid heb dâl digonol *ans*
underpaint tanbaent *eg* tanbaentiau
under-pass tanffordd *eb* tanffyrdd
underpin tanategu *be*
underpinning knowledge gwybodaeth greiddiol *eb*
underpopulated tanboblog *ans*
underprivileged difreintiedig *ans*
underprivileged group grŵp llai breintiedig *eg* grwpiau llai breintiedig
underscoring tanlinellu *be*
undersheet isgynfas *eg* isgynfasau
undershot wheel rhod isredol *eb* rhodau isredol
underside ochr isaf *eb* ochrau isaf
underskirt pais *eb* peisiau
underspend *n* tanwariant *eg*
underspend *v* tanwario *be*
understand deall *be*
understand the principles deall egwyddorion *be*
understanding dealltwriaeth *eb*
understanding of style dealltwriaeth o arddull *eb*
understated bank balance mantolen fanc rhy isel *eb*
understudy dirprwy *eg* dirprwyon
undertake cyflawni *be*
undertaker ymgymerwr *eg* ymgymerwyr
undertaking ymgymeriad *eg* ymgymeriadau
underutilize tanddefnyddio *be*
underwater seal drainage draenio sêl tanddwr *be*
underwear dillad isaf *ell*
underwrap islap *eg* islapiau
underwrite gwarantu *be*

undetermined amhendant *ans*
undetermined coefficient cyfernod amhendant *eg* cyfernodau amhendant
undifferentiated schizophrenia sgitsoffrenia diwahaniaeth *eg*
undo (knot, shoes etc) datod *be*
undo (work, mistake etc) dadwneud *be*
undo data entry dadwneud cofnodi data *be*
undo data input dadwneud mewnbwn data *be*
undo entry dadwneud cofnod *be*
undo print range dadwneud ystod argraffu *be*
undoing formatting dadwneud fformatio *be*
undress dadwisgo *be*
undulate ymdonni *be*
undulation ymdoniad *eg* ymdoniadau
unearned income incwm heb ei ennill *eg*
unearned investment income incwm eiddo *eg*
unemployable anghyflogadwy *ans*
unemployed di-waith *ans*
unemployment diweithdra *eg*
unenforceable anorfodadwy *ans*
unequal (in general) anghyfartal *ans*
unequal (in mathematics) anhafal *ans*
unerisis wnerisis *eg*
unethical anfoesegol *ans*
uneven anwastad *ans*
uneven growth rings cylchoedd tyfiant anwastad *ell*
uneven plaid plad anghyson *eg*
uneven surface arwyneb anwastad *eg* arwynebau anwastad
unexpected character nod annisgwyl *eg* nodau annisgwyl
unexploited anghyffwrdd *ans*
unfair annheg *ans*
Unfair Contract Terms Act Deddf Telerau Contract Annheg *eb*
unfair play chwarae annheg *eg*
unfamiliar anghyfarwydd *ans*
unfamiliar context cyd-destun anghyfarwydd *eg* cyd-destunau anghyfarwydd
unfamiliar environment amgylchedd anghyfarwydd *eg* amgylcheddau anghyfarwydd
unfasten agor *be*
unfenced di-ffens *ans*
unfit anffit *ans*
unforested di-goed
unformatted (with plural nouns) heb eu fformatio *ans*
unformatted (with singular nouns) heb ei fformatio *ans*
unformatted text testun heb ei fformatio *eg*
ungentlemanly conduct ymddygiad anfonheddig *eg*
ungraded anraddedig *ans*
ungroup dadgrwpio *be*
ungroup drawing objects dadgrwpio gwrthrychau lluniadu *be*
ungroup metafiles dadgrwpio metaffeiliau *be*
ungulate *adj* carnol *ans*
ungulate *n* carnolyn *eg* carnolion
unhappy customer cwsmer anfodlon *eg* cwsmeriaid anfodlon
unhitch datglymu *be*
Uniate Church Eglwys Uniadol *eb*
unicellular ungellog *ans*
unicorn uncorn *eg*
unicursal uncwrsaidd *ans*
unidentified species rhywogaeth anhysbys *eb* rhywogaethau anhysbys
unification uniad *eg* uniadau
unification of Italy uno'r Eidal *be*
unified unedig *ans*
unified thread edau unol *eb* edafedd unol
uniform *adj* unffurf *ans*
uniform (for school) *n* gwisg ysgol *eb*
uniform (military) *n* lifrai *eg*
uniform benefit budd-dal unffurf *eg* budd-daliadau unffurf
uniform fields meysydd unffurf *ell*
uniform pitch pitsh unffurf *eg*
Uniform Resource Locator Lleolydd Adnoddau Unffurf *eg*
uniform strength cryfder cyson *eg* cryfderau cyson
uniformitarianism unffurfiadaeth *eb*
uniformity unffurfiaeth *eb*
unify uno *be*
unilateral unochrog *ans*
Unilateral Declaration of Independence Datganiad Annibyniaeth Unochrog *eg*
unimodular unfodiwlaidd *ans*
unimolecular unfoleciwlaidd *ans*
unindented annanheddus *ans*
uninhabitable annrhigiadwy *ans*
uninhabited anghyfannedd *ans*
uninstall dadosod *be*
unintentional anfwriadol *ans*
uninterruptible power supply cyflenwad trydan annhoradwy *eg* cyflenwadau trydan annhoradwy
uninverted relief tirwedd ddiwrthdro *eb* tirweddau diwrthdro
union (=trade union, association etc) undeb *eg/b* undebau
union (act or instance of uniting) uniad *eg* uniadau
union (join in mathematics) cyswllt *eg* cysylltau
Union Jack Jac yr Undeb *eg*
union of England and Wales uno Cymru a Lloegr *be*
union of sets uniad setiau *eg*
union officer swyddog undeb *eg* swyddogion undeb
unionism undebaeth *eb*
unionist (N. Ireland) unoliaethwr *eg* unoliaethwyr
unionist (trade) undebwr *eg* undebwyr
Unionist Party Plaid yr Unoliaethwyr *eb*
unique unigryw *ans*
unique factorization domain parth ffactoriad unigryw *eg*
unique God Duw unigryw *eg*

uniqueness unigrywiaeth *eb*
unisexual unrhywiol *ans*
unison unsain *ans*
unit *adj* unedol *ans*
unit *n* uned *eb* unedau
unit credit credyd uned *eg* credydau uned
unit mould mowld uned *eg* mowldiau uned
unit of account uned cyfrif *eg* unedau cyfrif
unit of competence uned cymhwysedd *eb* unedau cymhwysedd
unit of design uned batrymu *eb* unedau patrymu
unit of heat uned wres *eb* unedau gwres
unit pole pegwn uned *eg* pegynau uned
unit price pris uned *eg*
unit vector fector uned *eg* fectorau uned
unitarian *adj* undodaidd *ans*
unitarian *n* undodwr *eg* undodiaid
unitarianism undodiaeth *eb*
unitary unedol *ans*
unitary authority awdurdod unedol *eg* awdurdodau unedol
unitary method dull uned *eg*
United Brotherhood Brawdoliaeth Unedig *eb*
united company cwmni unol *eg* cwmnïau unol
United Irishmen Cymdeithas y Gwyddelod Unedig *eb*
United Kingdom (=the countries of Britain) gwledydd Prydain *ell*
United Kingdom (as defined in law) Teyrnas Unedig, y Deyrnas Unedig *eb*
United Nations Cenhedloedd Unedig *ell*
United Nations International Children's Fund (UNICEF) Cronfa Ryngwladol Plant y Cenhedloedd Unedig *eb*
United Reformed Church Eglwys Ddiwygiedig Unedig *eb*
univalent unfalent *ans*
universal cyffredinol *ans*
universal benefit budd-dal cyffredinol *eg* budd-daliadau cyffredinol
universal donor rhoddwr cyffredinol *eg* rhoddwyr cyffredinol
universal feature nodwedd gyffredinol *eb* nodweddion cyffredinol
universal grammar gramadeg cynhenid *eg*
universal indicator dangosydd cyffredinol *eg*
universal joint cymal cyffredinol *eg* cymalau cyffredinol
universal recipient derbynnydd cyffredinol *eg* derbynyddion cyffredinol
universal set set gynhwysol *eb* setiau cynhwysol
universal snips snipiwr cyffredinol *eg* snipwyr cyffredinol
universal square sgwâr cyffredinol *eg* sgwariau cyffredinol
universal suffrage pleidlais gyffredinol *eb*
universal tinsnips snipiwr tun cyffredinol *eg* snipwyr tun cyffredinol
universal tongs gefel gyffredinol *eb* gefeiliau cyffredinol
universal understanding dealltwriaeth gyffredinol *eb*
universe bydysawd *eg*
university prifysgol *eb* prifysgolion
University Tests Acts Deddfau Prawf y Prifysgolion *ell*
unknown *adj* anhysbys *ans*
unknown (in mathematics) *n* anhysbysyn *eg* anhysbysion
unknown attribute priodoledd anhysbys *eg* priodoleddau anhysbys
unknown error gwall anhysbys *eg* gwallau anhysbys
unknown file format fformat ffeil anhysbys *eg* fformatau ffeil anhysbys
unknown file type math anhysbys o ffeil *eg* mathau anhysbys o ffeil
unknown filter hidlydd anhysbys *eg* hidlyddion anhysbys
unknown graphic format fformat graffig anhysbys *eg* fformatau graffig anhysbys
unknown source ffynhonnell anhysbys *eb* ffynonellau anhysbys
unlawful interference ymyrraeth anghyfreithiol *eb*
Unlawful Oaths Act Deddf Llwon Anghyfreithlon *eb*
unleavened bread bara croyw *eg*
unlimited liability atebolrwydd llawn *eg*
unmarried dibriod *ans*
unmetered access mynediad heb ei fesur *eg*
unmodulated anfodyledig *ans*
unmodulated carrier wave ton gario heb ei modylu *eb* tonnau cario heb eu modylu
unobtrusive measures mesurau anymwthiol *be*
unobtrusive observation arsylwi anymwthiol *eg* arsylliadau anymwthiol
unpack dadbacio *be*
unpaired (of electrons) digymar *ans*
unpaired electron electron heb bâr *eg* electronau heb bâr
unpaired terrace cerlannau anghyfatebol *ell*
unparliamentary anseneddol *ans*
unpick datod *be*
unplug datgysylltu plwg *be*
unpolluted (with feminine nouns) heb ei llygru *ans*
unpolluted (with masculine nouns) heb ei lygru *ans*
unpolluted (with plural nouns) heb eu llygru *ans*
unpredictable annarogan *ans*
unpressed pleating pletio rhydd *be*
unprimed di-breim *ans*
unproductive anghynhyrchiol *ans*
unprovoked direswm *ans*
unreactive anadweithiol *ans*
unrealistic optimism optimistiaeth afrealistig *eb*
unrelenting didostur *ans*
unrest aflonyddwch *eg*
unroll dadrolio *be*

unroof di-doi *be*
unsafe practice ymarferion anniogel
unsaturated annirlawn *ans*
unsaturated fatty acid asid brasterog annirlawn *eg*
unscrew dadsgriwio *be*
unseasoned timber pren heb ei sychu *eg*
unsegmented ansegmennol *ans*
unset dadosod *be*
unsigned integer cyfanrif diarwydd *eg* cyfanrifau diarwydd
unskilled (of worker) di-grefft *ans*
unskilled labour llafur di-grefft *eg*
unskilled manual gweithiwr llaw di-grefft *ell* gweithwyr llaw di-grefft
unskilled worker gweithiwr di-grefft *eg* gweithwyr di-grefft
Unsolicited Goods & Services Act Deddf Nwyddau a Gwasanaethau nas Archebwyd *eb*
unsorted anhrefnedig *ans*
unstable ansefydlog *ans*
unstable equilibrium cydbwysedd ansefydlog *eg*
unstiffened waistband band gwasg heb ei gyfnerthu *eg* bandiau gwasg heb eu cyfnerthu
unstitched calico mop mop calico heb ei bwytho *eg* mopiau calico heb eu pwytho
unstratified dihaenedig *ans*
unstretched diestyn *ans*
unstrutted di-ais *ans*
untempered nas tymherwyd *ans*
untouchables anghyffyrddedigion *ell*
untuned percussion instruments offerynnau taro di-draw *ell*
untwist fibres gwahanu ffibrau *be*
unweighted amhwysol *ans*
unweighted sample sampl amhwysol *eg* samplau amhwysol
unwind (wool) dad-ddirwyn *be*
unwound (of wool) wedi'i ddad-ddirwyn *ans*
up and over door drws esgyn *eg* drysau esgyn
up and under (in rugby) cic a chwrs
up arrow saeth i fyny *eb*
up to date cyfoes *ans*
up-beat curiad i fyny *eg*
up-count cyfrif i fyny *eg*
update *n* diweddaraf, y diweddaraf *eg*
update *v* diweddaru *be*
upfold plyg i fyny *eg* plygion i fyny
upgrade uwchraddio *be*
upholstered (with feminine nouns) wedi'i chlustogi *ans* wedi'u clustogi
upholstered (with masculine nouns) wedi'i glustogi *ans* wedi'u clustogi
upholstery clustogwaith *eg*
upholstery nail hoelen glustogwaith *eb* hoelion clustogwaith
upholstery needle nodwydd glustogwaith *eb* nodwyddau clustogwaith
upholstery spring sbring clustogwaith *eg* sbringiau clustogwaith
upland uwchdir *eg* uwchdiroedd
uplift *adj* ymgodol *ans*
uplift *n* ymgodiad *eg* ymgodiadau
uplift *v* ymgodi *be*
upload llwytho i fyny *be*
upper air aer uchaf *eg*
upper boundary arffin uchaf *eg* arffiniau uchaf
upper case llythrennau bras *ell*
upper case letter priflythyren *eb* priflythrennau
upper class dosbarth uchaf *eg* dosbarthiadau uchaf
upper floor llawr uchaf *eg* lloriau uchaf
upper school ysgol uchaf *eb* ysgolion uchaf
upper sixth chweched uchaf *eg*
upright unionsyth *ans*
upright mortise lock clo mortais unionsyth *eg* cloeon mortais unionsyth
upright piano piano syth *eg* pianos syth
upright position safle unionsyth *eg* safleoedd unionsyth
upright posture ymddaliad unionsyth *eg* ymddaliadau unionsyth
upright vacuum cleaner sugnwr llwch unionsyth *eg* sugnwyr llwch unionsyth
uprising gwrthryfel *eg* gwrthryfeloedd
upset (=a shake) hollt *eg/b* holltau
upset grain graen cymysg *eg*
upsetting (jumping up - forging process) clopáu *be*
upside down wyneb i waered *adf*
upslope llethr gorifyny *eg* llethrau gorifyny
upstream i fyny'r afon
upstroke blaenstroc *eb* blaenstrociau
uptake (of salts by a root) mewnlifiad *eg* mewnlifiadau
upthrow side ochr esgynedig *eb* ochrau esgynedig
upthrust brigwth *eg* brigwthiadau
uptime amser mynd *eg* amserau mynd
upward pressure gwasgedd i fyny *eg*
upward sloping curve cromlin esgynnol *eb* cromliniau esgynnol
upwarp crychiad i fyny *eg* crychiadau i fyny
upwelling ymchwydd *eg* ymchwyddiadau
uracil wracil *eg*
uranate(VI) ion ïon wranad(VI) *eg* ïonau wranad(VI)
uranium (U) wraniwm *eg*
Uranus Wranws *eg*
uranyl(VI) ion ïon wranyl(VI) *eg* ïonau wranyl(VI)
urban trefol *ans*
urban area ardal drefol *eb* ardaloedd trefol
urban community cymuned drefol *eb* cymunedau trefol
urban environment amgylchedd trefol *eg*
urban field cylch trefol *eg* cylchoedd trefol
urban fringe cyrion trefol *ell*
urban hierarchy hierarchaeth drefol *eb*
urban history hanes trefol *eg*
urban land use defnydd tir trefol *eg*
urban renewal adnewyddiad trefol *eg*
urban sprawl blerdwf trefol *eg*

urbanism trefolaeth *eb*
urbanize trefoli *be*
urbanized trefoledig *ans*
urbanrural trefol-wledig *ans*
urea wrea *eg*
urea cycle cylchred wrea *eb*
urea formaldehyde wrea fformaldehyd *eg*
urea formaldehyde glue glud wrea fformaldehyd *eg*
urease wreas *eg*
ureter wreter *eg* wreterau
urethra wrethra *eg/b* wrethrâu
urge *n* cymhelliad *eg* cymhellion
urge *v* annog *be*
uric acid asid wrig *eg*
uricotelic wricotelig *ans*
urinals wrinalau *ell*
urine troeth *eg*
urine test prawf troeth *eg* profion troeth
uriniferous tubule tiwbyn troeth *eg* tiwbynnau troeth
urn wrn *eg* yrnau
urnfield yrnfaes *eg* yrnfeysydd
urology wroleg *eb*
use *v* defnyddio *be*
use (=being used) *n* defnydd *eg* defnyddiau
use (=benefit or profit of lands) *n* mwyniant *eg* mwyniannau
use (=custom) *n* arfer *eg/b* arferion
use and gratification defnydd a boddhad
use of land defnyddio tir *be*
use of sources defnyddio ffynonellau *be*
U-section trychiad U *eg* trychiadau U
useful defnyddiol *ans*
use-height uchder defnydd *eg*
user defnyddiwr *eg* defnyddwyr
user dictionary geiriadur defnyddiwr *eg* geiriaduron defnyddwyr
user disk disg defnyddiwr *eg* disgiau defnyddwyr
user documentation dogfennaeth defnyddiwr *eb*
user group grŵp defnyddwyr *eg* grwpiau defnyddwyr
user interface rhyngwyneb defnyddiwr *eg* rhyngwynebau defnyddwyr
user-friendly cyfeillgar *ans*
user-hostile package pecyn anghyfeillgar *eg* pecynnau anghyfeillgar
username enw defnyddiwr *eg* enwau defnyddiwr
users and potential users defnyddwyr a defnyddwyr posibl
user-unfriendly anghyfeillgar *ans*
U-shaped ar ffurf U *ans*
U-shaped kitchen cegin ar ffurf U *eb* ceginau ar ffurf U
U.S.S.R. Undeb Sofietaidd, yr *eg*
usurp trawsfeddiannu *be*
usurpation trawsfeddiannaeth *eb*
usurper trawsfeddiannwr *eg* trawsfeddianwyr
usury usuriaeth *eb*
utensils offer *ell*
uterine crothol *ans*
uterus croth *eb*
utilitarian *adj* iwtalitaraidd *ans*
utilitarian *n* iwtilitariad *eg* iwtilitariaid
utilitarianism iwtilitariaeth *eb*
utility defnyddioldeb *eg*
utility (of public utility) gwasanaeth *eg* gwasanaethau
utility disk disg gwasanaethu *eg* disgiau gwasanaethu
utility program rhaglen wasanaethu *eb* rhaglenni gwasanaethu
utilization defnydd *eg* defnyddiau
utilize defnyddio *be*
U-tool erfyn U *eg* offer U
Utopia Iwtopia *eb* Iwtopiâu
Utraquism Wtraciaeth *eb*
Utraquist (of person) Wtracwr *eg* Wtracwyr
utricle wtrigl *eg* wtriglau
u-turn tro pedol *eg* troeon pedol
uvala wfala *eg* wfalau
uvinial wfinial *ans*

V

V base gwaelod V *eg* gwaelodau V
V blocks and clamps blociau V a chlampiau
V pulley pwli V *eg* pwlïau V
vacancy (for a job) swydd wag *eb* swyddi gwag
vacation gwyliau *ell*
vaccinate brechu *be*
vaccination brechiad *eg* brechiadau
vaccine brechlyn *eg* brechlynnau
vacuole gwagolyn *eg* gwagolynnau
vacuum gwactod *eg* gwactodau
vacuum bottle potel wactod *eg* poteli gwactod
vacuum chamber siambr wactod *eb* siambrau gwactod
vacuum cleaner sugnwr llwch *eg* sugnwyr llwch
vacuum flask fflasg wactod *eb* fflasgiau gwactod
vacuum forming ffurfio â gwactod *be*
vacuum tools offer sugnwr llwch *ell*
vadose uwch-lefel-trwythiad *eb*
vagabond crwydryn *eg* crwydriaid
vagabondage crwydraeth *eb*
vagina (of cow, mare etc) llawes goch *eb*
vagina (of woman) gwain *eb* gweiniau
vagrancy crwydraeth *eb*
vagrant crwydryn *eg* crwydriaid
vagus nerve nerf fagws *eg*
Vaishnavism/Vaisnavism Vaishnaviaeth/Vaisnaviaeth *eb*
Vaishya/Vaisya Vaishya/Vaisya *eg*
vale dyffryndir *eg* dyffryndiroedd
valence falens *eg* falensau
valence bond theory damcaniaeth bond falens *eb*
valence shell electron pair repulsion gwrthyriad parau electron plisgyn falens *eg*
valency falens *eg* falensau
valid dilys *ans*
valid screen sgrin ddilys *eb* sgriniau dilys
validate dilysu *be*
validation dilysiad *eg* dilysiadau
validation routine rheolwaith dilysu *eg*
validation suite cyfres ddilysu *eb* cyfresi dilysu
validity dilysrwydd *eg*
validity check prawf dilysrwydd *eg* profion dilysrwydd
valine falin *eg*
valley dyffryn *eg* dyffrynnoedd
valley floor llawr y dyffryn *eg*
valley glacier rhewlif dyffryn *eg* rhewlifau dyffryn
valley head pen y dyffryn *eg* pennau dyffrynnoedd
valley rafter ceibr cafn *eg* ceibrau cafn
valley roof to cafnog *eg* toeon cafnog
valley tract dyffryndir afon *eg* dyffryndiroedd afon
valley train rhes dyffryn *eb* rhesi dyffrynnoedd
valorisation sefydlu gwerth *be*
valse valse *eb* valses
valuables pethau gwerthfawr *ell*
valuation prisiant *eg* prisiannau
valuation list rhestr brisiant *eb* rhestri prisiant
valuation officer swyddog prisio *eg* swyddogion prisio
value *n* gwerth *eg* gwerthoedd
value added tax (VAT) treth ar werth *eb*
value base seiliau gwerth *ell*
value base sylfaen gwerthoedd *eb*
value for money gwerth eich arian *eg*
value judgement barn ar werth *eb*
value of a constant gwerth cysonyn *eg*
value of the beat gwerth y curiad *eg*
valuer prisiwr *eg* priswyr
valve falf *eb* falfiau
valve clearance cliriad falf *eg* cliriadau falf
valve instrument offeryn falf *eg* offerynnau falf
valve seat eisteddle falf *eg* eisteddleoedd falf
valve trumpet utgorn falfiau *eg* utgyrn falfiau
vamp fampio *be*
vanadate(IV) ion ïon fanadad(IV) *eg* ïonau fanadad(IV)
vanadate(V) ion ïon fanadad(V) *eg* ïonau fanadad(V)
vanadium (V) fanadiwm *eg*
vanadium(II) ion ïon fanadiwm(II) *eg* ïonau fanadiwm(II)
vanadium(III) ion ïon fanadiwm(III) *eg* ïonau fanadiwm(III)
vanadium(V) oxide fanadiwm(V) ocsid *eg*
vandal fandal *eg* fandaliaid
vandalism fandaliaeth *eb*
Vandyke brown brown Vandyke *eg*
Vandyke crystals grisialau Vandyke *ell*
Vandyke smocking smocwaith Vandyke *eg*
vane (of arrow) asgell *eb* esgyll
vane (of turbine, feather etc) llafn *eg/b* llafnau
vanguard blaengad *eb* blaengadau
vanish diflannu *be*
vanished diflan *ans*
vanishing line llinell ddiflannol *eb* llinellau diflannol
vanishing point diflanbwynt *eg* diflanbwyntiau
vanity unit uned ymolchi *eb* unedau ymolchi
vaporization anweddiad *eg* anweddiadau
vaporize anweddu *be*

vaporized anweddol *ans*
vapour (water) anwedd *eg* anweddau
vapour density dwysedd anwedd *eg*
vapour pressure gwasgedd anwedd *eg*
variability amrywioldeb *eg*
variable *adj* newidiol *ans*
variable *n* newidyn *eg* newidynnau
variable address cyfeiriad newidiol *eg* cyfeiriadau newidiol
variable cost cost newidiol *eb* costau newidiol
variable current cerrynt newidiol *eg* ceryntau newidiol
variable error cyfeiliornad newidyn *eg* cyfeiliornadau newidyn
variable field maes newidiol *eg* meysydd newidiol
variable form (=diverse types) ffurf amrywiol *eb* ffurfiau amrywiol
variable interval schedule amserlen ysbeidiau newidiol *eb*
variable length hyd newidiol *eg* hydoedd newidiol
variable length records cofnodion hyd newidiol *ell*
variable overheads gorbenion newidiol *ell*
variable ratio schedule amserlen cymarebau newidiol *eb*
variable resistor gwrthydd newidiol *eg* gwrthyddion newidiol
variable star seren newidiol *eb* sêr newidiol
variable string llinyn newidiol *eg* llinynnau newidiol
variable type math newidiol *eg* mathau newidiol
variable word length hyd gair newidiol *eg*
variable-width font ffont newidiol ei led *eg* ffontiau newidiol eu lled
variance amrywiant *eg* amrywiannau
variant amrywiolyn *eg* amrywiolion
variate amryweb *eb* amrywebau
variates amryweddau *ell*
variation amrywiad *eg* amrywiadau
variation of rhythm amrywiad rythm *eg* amrywiadau rythm
variation of tension amrywiad tyndra *eg* amrywiadau tyndra
variation sonata sonata amrywiad *eb* sonatau amrywiad
variational amrywiadol *ans*
varied diet deiet amrywiol *eg*
variegated leaf deilen fraith *eb* dail brith
variegation brithedd *eg*
variety amrywiaeth *eb* amrywiaethau
variety of media amrywiaeth o gyfryngau *eb*
varna varna *eg*
varnashramadharma varnashramadharma *eg*
varnish *n* farnais *eg*
varnish *v* farneisio *be*
varnish finish gorffeniad farnais *eg*
varnished wedi'i farneisio *ans* wedi'u farneisio
varnished surface arwyneb farnais *eg* arwynebau farnais
varve farf *eg* farfau
vary amrywio *be*
vary timing amrywio amseriad *be*
vascular fasgwlar *ans*
vascular bundle sypyn fasgwlar *eg* sypynnau fasgwlar
vasculum fasgwlwm *eg* fasgwla
vase ffiol *eb* ffiolau
vase shape siâp ffiol *eg* siapiau ffiol
Vaseline Vaseline *eg*
vasoconstriction fasogyfyngiad *eg*
vasoconstrictor fasogyfyngydd *eg* fasogyfyngwyr
vasodilation fasoymlediad *eg*
vasodilator fasoymledydd *eg* fasoymledwyr
Vassa Vassa *eg*
vassal deiliad *eg* deiliaid
vassalage deiliadaeth ffiwdal *eb*
Vatican Fatican *eg*
Vauclusian spring tarddell Vaucluse *eb* tarddellau Vaucluse
vaudeville vaudeville *eg* vaudevilles
vault (of chamber) cromgell *eb* cromgelloedd
vault (of jump) llofnaid *eb* llofneidiau
vault with a double beat llofnaid ddeuglap *eb* llofneidiau deuglap
vault with foot assisting llofnaid milwr *eb* llofneidiau milwr
vavasour fafasor *eg* fafasoriaid
V-cut toriad V *eg* toriadau V
Veblen goods nwyddau Veblen *ell*
vector *n* fector *eg* fectorau
vector *v* fectoru *be*
vector and bitmap graphics graffigwaith fector a didfap *eg*
vector equation hafaliad fector *eg*
vector multiplication lluosiad fector *eg*
vector quantity mesur fector *eg* mesurau fector
vectorial fectoraidd *ans*
vectorize fectoreiddio *be*
vee belt gwregys 'V' *eg* gwregysau 'V'
vee groove locking nut nyten gloi rhigol V *eb* nytiau cloi rhigol V
vee-bit tongs gefel geg 'V' *eb* gefeiliau ceg 'V'
veer and back gwyro a gwrthwyro
vegetable dye llifyn llysiau *eg* llifynnau llysiau
vegetable fibre ffibr llysiau *eg* ffibrau llysiau
vegetable glue glud llysiau *eg*
vegetable oil olew llysiau *eg*
vegetable origin tarddiad llysieuol *eg*
vegetarian llysieuwr *eg* llysieuwyr
vegetation llystyfiant *eg*
vegetative reproduction atgynhyrchiad llystyfol *eg*
vehicle (=car, lorry etc) cerbyd *eg* cerbydau
vehicle (=medium for suspending pigments etc) cludydd *eg* cludyddion
vehicular traffic trafnidiaeth gerbydol *eb*
vein gwythïen *eb* gwythiennau
vein of ore gwythïen fwyn *eb* gwythiennau mwyn
veiner erfyn cerfio ffurf U *eg* offer cerfio ffurf U

velcro felcro *eg*
veld ffeld *eg*
vellum felwm *eg*
vellum glaze gwydredd felwm *eg*
vellum paper papur felwm *eg*
velocity (vector quantity) cyflymder *eg* cyflymderau
velocity /acceleration graph graff cyflymder /cyflymiad *eg* graffiau cyflymder /cyflymiad
velocity /time diagram diagram cyflymder /amser *eg* diagramau cyflymder /amser
velocity diagram diagram cyflymder *eg* diagramau cyflymder
velocity graph graff cyflymder *eg* graffiau cyflymder
velocity of circulation cyflymder cylchrediad *eg*
velocity ratio cymhareb cyflymder *eb* cymarebau cyflymder
velour felôr *eg*
velvet melfed *eg* melfedau
velvet board bwrdd melfed *eg* byrddau melfed
velveteen melfedîn *eg* melfediniau
venal llygredig *ans*
venation (of a leaf) gwythieniad *eg*
vending-machine peiriant gwerthu *eg* peiriannau gwerthu
vendor gwerthwr *eg* gwerthwyr
veneer *n* argaen *eg* argaenau
veneer *v* argaenu *be*
veneer board bwrdd argaen *eg* byrddau argaen
veneer hammer morthwyl argaenu *eg* morthwylion argaenu
veneer key allwedd argaen *eb* allweddi argaen
veneer pin pin argaen *eg* pinnau argaen
veneered chipboard bwrdd sglodion argaen *eg* byrddau sglodion argaen
veneered ply door drws pren haenog *eg* drysau pren haenog
veneered ply wood pren haenog wedi'i argaenu *eg*
venepuncture tynnu gwaed *be*
venereal disease clefyd gwenerol *eg*
Venetian Fenisaidd *ans*
venetian blind llen ddelltog *eb* llenni delltog
Venetian red coch Fenis *eg*
venison cig carw *eg*
Venn diagram diagram Venn *eg* diagramau Venn
vent (=finger hole of musical instrument) *n* twll bys *eg* tyllau bysedd
vent (=opening in general) *n* agorfa *eb* agorfeydd
vent (for air circulation) *n* awyrell *eb* awyrellau
vent (for air circulation) *v* awyrellu *be*
vent hole twll awyr *eg* tyllau awyr
vent window ffenestr awyru *eb* ffenestri awyru
ventifact carreg wyntraul *eb* cerrig gwyntraul
ventilate awyru *be*
ventilating fan gwyntyll awyru *eb* gwyntyllau awyru
ventilation awyriad *eg*
ventilation brick bricsen awyru *eb* brics awyru
ventilation grill dellt awyru *eb* delltiau awyru
ventilation movement symudiad awyru *eg*
ventilation rate cyfradd anadlu *eb*
ventilator (=respirator) peiriant anadlu *eg* peiriannau anadlu
ventilator (for ventilating a room etc) awyrydd *eg* awyryddion
ventral fentrol *ans*
ventral fin asgell fentrol *eb* esgyll fentrol
ventral root gwreiddyn fentrol *eg* gwreiddiau fentrol
ventricle fentrigl *eg* fentriglau
ventricular volume cyfaint fentriglaidd *eg*
venture menter *eb* mentrau
venture capital cyfalaf menter *eg*
Venturi meter mesurydd Venturi *eg*
venule gwythiennig *eb* gwythienigau
Venus Gwener *eb*
verbal geiriol *ans*
verbal ability gallu geiriol *eg*
verbal protocol analysis dadansoddi protocolau llafar *eg*
verderer gwyrddmon *eg* gwyrddmyn
verdict rheithfarn *eb* rheithfarnau
verdigris rhwd copr *eg*
verge ymyl *eg/b* ymylon
verglas glasrew *eg*
verifiable gwiriadwy *ans*
verisimilitude hygrededd *eg*
vermiform llyngyraidd *ans*
vermilion fermiliwn *eg*
vermin fermin *ell*
vernacular *adj* brodorol *ans*
vernacular *n* iaith frodorol *eb* ieithoedd brodorol
vernal equinox cyhydnos y gwanwyn *eb*
vernalization gwanwyneiddiad *eg*
vernicle fernagl *eb*
vernier *adj* fernier *ans*
vernier *n* fernier *eg* fernieri
vernier callipers caliperau fernier *eg*
vernier height gauge medrydd uchder fernier *eg* medryddion uchder fernier
vernier protractor onglydd fernier *eg* onglyddion fernier
vernier reading darlleniad fernier *eg* darlleniadau fernier
vernier scale graddfa fernier *eb* graddfeydd fernier
verruca ferwca *eg* ferwcau
Versailles settlement ardrefniant Versailles *eg*
versatile (of object) amlbwrpas *ans*
versatile (of person) amryddawn *ans*
verse (in Bible) adnod *eb* adnodau
verse (in song etc) pennill *eg* penillion
verse anthem anthem wersi *eb* anthemau gwersi
versine fersin *eg* fersinau
version fersiwn *eg* fersiynau
vertebra fertebra *eg* fertebrâu
vertebral fertebrol *ans*

vertebral column asgwrn cefn *eg* esgyrn cefn
vertebrate *adj* fertebraidd *ans*
vertebrate *n* fertebrat *eg* fertebratau
vertex fertig *eg* fertigau
vertical fertigol *ans*
vertical alignment aliniad fertigol *eg*
vertical arrangement trefniant fertigol *eg*
vertical axis echelin fertigol *eb* echelinau fertigol
vertical blind llen stribed *eb* llenni stribed
vertical boring borio fertigol *be*
vertical branch pipe peipen gangen fertigol *eb* peipiau cangen fertigol
vertical buttonhole twll botwm fertigol *eg* tyllau botwm fertigol
vertical centre line llinell ganol fertigol *eb* llinellau canol fertigol
vertical centring canoli fertigol *be*
vertical chiselling naddu fertigol *be*
vertical control rheolaeth fertigol *eb*
vertical exaggeration gormodaeth fertigol *eb*
vertical feed porthiant fertigol *eg*
vertical force grym fertigol *eg*
vertical grouping grwpio fertigol *be*
vertical height uchder fertigol *eg*
vertical integration integreiddiad fertigol *eg*
vertical interval cyfwng fertigol *eg* cyfyngau fertigol
vertical line llinell fertigol *eb* llinellau fertigol
vertical milling machine peiriant melino fertigol *eg* peiriannau melino fertigol
vertical mortise lock clo mortais fertigol *eg* cloeon mortais fertigol
vertical paring naddu fertigol *be*
vertical pen pin fertigol *eg* pinnau fertigol
vertical perspective persbectif fertigol *eg* persbectifau fertigol
vertical photograph ffotograff fertigol *eg* ffotograffau fertigol
vertical pitch gogwydd fertigol *eg*
vertical plane (V.P.) plân fertigol *eg* planau fertigol
vertical projection line llinell dafluniadol fertigol *eb* llinellau tafluniadol fertigol
vertical pug mill melin gleio fertigol *eb* melinau cleio fertigol
vertical ruler mesurydd fertigol *eg* mesuryddion fertigol
vertical ruler hydlin *eg* hydlinau
vertical scroll sgrolio fertigol *be*
vertical scroll bar bar sgrolio fertigol *eg* barrau sgrolio fertigol
vertical section toriad fertigol *eg* toriadau fertigol
vertical shadow outline amlinell cysgod fertigol *eb* amlinellau cysgod fertigol
vertical stack pentwr fertigol *eg* pentyrrau fertigol
vertical stripe rhes fertigol *eb* rhesi fertigol
vertical text anchor angor testun fertigol *eg* angorau testun fertigol
vertical trace olin fertigol *eg* olinau fertigol
verticality fertigoledd *eg*
vertically opposite angles onglau croesfertigol *ell*
vertices of a rectangle fertigau petryal *ell*
very difficult anodd iawn *ans*
very fine grit grit mân iawn *eg*
very large scale integration (VLSI) cyfannu graddfa eang iawn *be*
vesicular cavity ceudod pothellog *eg* ceudodau pothellog
vesper gosber *eg* gosberau
vessel llestr *eg* llestri
vest fest *eb* festiau
Vestiarian Controversy Ymryson yr Urddwisgoedd *eb*
vestibular apparatus offer cyntedd y glust *eg*
vestibular sac sach cyntedd y glust *eb*
vestibule cyntedd *eg* cynteddau
vestigial organ organ gweddilliol *eg* organau gweddilliol
vestment urddwisg *eb* urddwisgoedd
vestry festri *eb* festrïoedd
veto pleidlais atal *eb* pleidleisiau atal
viability hyfywdra *eg*
viable (of living thing) hyfyw *ans*
viable (of plan etc) dichonadwy *ans*
viaduct traphont *eb* traphontydd
vibraphone fibraffon *eg* fibraffonau
vibrate dirgrynu *be*
vibrating dirgrynol *ans*
vibrating reed brwynen ddirgrynol *eb* brwyn dirgrynol
vibration dirgryniad *eg* dirgryniadau
vibration wave ton ddirgrynol *eb* tonnau dirgrynol
vibrational dirgrynol *ans*
vibrato vibrato *eg*
vibratory dirgrynol *ans*
vicar ficer *eg* ficeriaid
vicarage ficerdy *eg* ficerdai
vicar-choral ficer corawl *eg* ficeriaid corawl
vicar-general ficer cyffredinol *eg* ficeriaid cyffredinol
vicariate ficeriaeth *eb* ficeriaethau
vicarious dirprwyol *ans*
vicarious liability atebolrwydd dirprwyol *eg*
vice feis *eb* feisiau
vice clamps arbedion feis *ell*
vice jaw safn feis *eb* safnau feis
vice-admiral is-lyngesydd *eg* is-lyngeswyr
vice-consul is-gonswl *eg* is-gonswliaid
viceroy rhaglaw *eg* rhaglawiaid
victim dioddefwr *eg* dioddefwyr
victim survey arolwg dioddefwyr *eg*
victimisation erledigaeth *eb* erledigaethau
Victorian Fictoraidd *ans*
Victorian middle-class family teulu dosbarth canol Fictoraidd *eg* teuluoedd dosbarth canol Fictoraidd
Victorian terraced house tŷ teras Fictoraidd *eg* tai teras Fictoraidd
victorious buddugoliaethus *ans*
victory buddugoliaeth *eb* buddugoliaethau

video fideo *eg* fideos
video card cerdyn fideo *eg* cardiau fideo
video clip clip fideo *eg* clipiau fideo
video conferencing fideo-gynadledda *be*
video disk disg fideo *eg* disgiau fideo
video editing golygu fideo *be*
video extract darn o glip fideo *eg*
video file ffeil fideo *eb* ffeiliau fideo
video nasty fideo ffiaidd *eg* fideos ffiaidd
video production cynhyrchiad fideo *eg*
video programme rhaglen fideo *eb* rhaglenni fideo
video recorder recordydd fideo *eg* recordyddion fideo
video recording recordiad fideo *eg* recordiadau fideo
video rental store siop rhentu fideos *eb*
video renting shop siop llogi fideos *eb*
video shop siop fideo *eb*
video still camera camera fideo unllun *eg* camerâu fideo unllun
video streaming ffrydio fideo *be*
videoscope fideosgop *eg* fideosgopau
Vietnam Fietnam *eb*
view *n* golwg *eb* golygon
view (=scene) golygfa *eb* golygfeydd
view (=sight of something) golwg *eg/b* golygon
view mode modd gweld *eg*
view of frankpledge cwrt tangwystl *eg* cyrtiau tangwystl
view options golwg dewisiadau *eg*
viewdata gweldata *ell*
viewed from X yn edrych o gyfeiriad X *adf*
viewpoint safbwynt *eg* safbwyntiau
vigorous egnïol *ans*
vigorous activity gweithgarwch egnïol *eg*
vihara vihara *eg*
Viking *adj* Llychlynnaidd *ans*
Viking *n* Llychlynnwr *eg* Llychlynwyr
villa fila *eb* filâu
village pentref *eg* pentrefi
villainy anfadwaith *eg*
villein bilain *eg* bileiniaid
villeinage bileiniaeth *eb*
villus filws *eg* filysau
Vinaya Vinaya *eg*
vine charcoal siarcol gwinwydd *eg*
vinegar finegr *eg*
vinyl finyl *eg* finylau
vinyl polymer polymer finyl *eg* polymerau finyl
vinyl resin resin finyl *eg* resinau finyl
vinyl tile teilsen finyl *eb* teils finyl
vinyl wallpaper papur finyl *eg*
viol feiol *eb* feiolau
viol player feiolydd *eg* feiolyddion
viola fioal *eb* fiolâu
viola da gamba viola da gamba *eb* violas da gamba
viola da gamba player chwaraewr viola da gamba *eg* chwaraewyr viola da gamba
viola player fiolydd *eg* fiolyddion
violate (a law) torri *be*
violate (a temple) halogi *be*
violate (a woman) treisio *be*
violate (convention) troseddu yn erbyn *be*
violence trais *eg*
violent treisgar *ans*
violin feiolin *eb* feiolinau
violinist feiolinydd *eg* feiolinwyr
violoncellist sielydd *eg* sielyddion
vipassana vipassana *eg*
viral firaol *ans*
virement hawl trosglwyddo arian *eg*
virgate firgat *eg* firgatau
virgin *adj* gwyryfol *ans*
virgin *n* gwyryf *eb* gwyryfon
virgin birth geni o forwyn *be*
virgin lands (USSR) tiroedd newydd *ell*
virginalist firdsinalydd *eg* firdsinalyddion
virginals (=musical instrument) firdsinal *eb* firdsinalau
viridian firidian *eg*
virology firoleg *eb*
virtual (in computing) rhith *ans*
virtual community rhithgymuned *eb* rhithgymunedau
virtual image rhithddelwedd *eb* rhithddelweddau
virtual machine rhithbeiriant *eg* rhithbeiriannau
virtual memory rhith-gof *eg*
virtual reality rhithwirionedd *eg*
virtual storage rhithstorfa *eb* rhith storfeydd
virtual work rhith-waith *eg*
virtue rhinwedd *eb* rhinweddau
virus firws *eg* firysau
virus checking gwirio firysau *be*
virus checking software meddalwedd gwirio firysau *eb*
virus scanner sganiwr firysau *eg*
viscera ymysgaroedd *ell*
visceral organs organau perfeddol *ell*
viscose fiscos *eg*
viscose rayon reion fiscos *eg*
viscosity gludedd *eg* gludeddau
viscount is-iarll *eg* is-ieirll
viscous gludiog *ans*
Vishnu /Visnu Vishnu /Visnu *eg*
visibility gwelededd *eg*
visible gweladwy *ans*
visible light golau gweladwy *eg*
vision (=foresight) gweledigaeth *eb* gweledigaethau
vision (=sight) golwg *eg/b* golygon
visionary *adj* breuddwydiol *ans*
visionary *n* gweledydd *eg* gweledyddion
visit *v* ymweld â *be*
visitation ymweliad *eg* ymweliadau
visitor ymwelydd *eg* ymwelwyr

visitor attraction atyniad i ymwelwyr *eg* atyniadau i ymwelwyr
vista golygfa *eb* golygfeydd
visual gweledol *ans*
visual agnosia agnosia'r golwg *eg*
visual aid cymhorthyn gweledol *eg* cymhorthion gweledol
visual axis echelin weledol *eb* echelinau gweledol
visual concept cysyniad gweledol *eg* cysyniadau gweledol
visual display unit (VDU) uned arddangos weledol *eb* unedau arddangos gweledol
visual evidence tystiolaeth weledol *eb*
visual image delwedd weledol *eb* delweddau gweledol
visual impairment nam ar y golwg *eg*
visual language iaith weledol *eb*
visual nature natur weledol *eb*
visual note nodiad gweledol *eg* nodiadau gweledol
visual purple porffor gweledol *eg*
visual sign arwydd gweledol *eg* arwyddion gweledol
visual stimulation ysgogiad gweledol *eg*
visual stimulus ysgogiad gweledol *eg* ysgogiadau gweledol
visual system system golwg *eb*
visualize delweddu *be*
visually pleasing dymunol yr olwg *ans*
visuo-motor ability gallu gweld-echddygol *eg*
visuospatial scratchpad pad gweledol-gofodol *eg*
vital capacity (of lungs) cyfaint anadlol *eg*
vital organ organ hanfodol *eg* organau hanfodol
vital signs arwyddion bywyd *ell*
vital statistics ystadegau bywyd *ell*
vitamin fitamin *eg* fitaminau
vitamin C fitamin C *eg*
vitamin deficiency prinder fitamin *eg*
vitamin drop defnyn fitamin *eg* defnynau fitamin
vitamin supplement fitaminau atodol *ell*
viticulture gwinwyddaeth *eb*
vitreous gwydrog *ans*
vitreous enamel enamel gwydrog *eg*
vitreous humour hylif gwydrog *eg*
vitrifiable gwydreiddiadwy *ans*
vitrifiable clay clai gwydreiddiadwy *eg*
vitrified gwydredig *ans*
vitrify troi'n wydr *be*
vitriol fitriol *eg*
viva voce viva voce *ans*
vivid llachar *ans*
vivid colour lliw llachar *eg* lliwiau llachar
viviparity bywesgoredd *eg*
viviparous bywesgorol *ans*
vivisection bywddyraniad *eg* bywddyraniadau
Viyella Viyella *eg*
V-joint uniad V *eg* uniadau V
vocabulary geirfa *eb* geirfâu
vocal lleisiol *ans*
vocal advice cyngor lleisiol *eg*
vocal cords tannau llais *ell*
vocal interpretation dehongliad lleisiol *eg*
vocal music cerddoriaeth leisiol *eb*
vocal part rhan leisiol *eb* rhannau lleisiol
vocal range cwmpas lleisiol *eg*
vocal technique techneg leisiol *eb* technegau lleisiol
vocalize lleisio *be*
vocation galwedigaeth *eb* galwedigaethau
vocational galwedigaethol *ans*
vocational counselling cynghori galwedigaethol *be*
vocational education addysg alwedigaethol *eb*
vocational test prawf galwedigaethol *eg* profion galwedigaethol
vocational training hyfforddiant galwedigaethol *eg*
vogue ffasiwn *eg/b* ffasiynau
voice llais *eg* lleisiau
voice data entry (VDE) cofnodi data llais *be*
voice production cynhyrchu'r llais *be*
voice-onset time oediad dechrau lleisio *eg*
voiceover trosleisio *be*
voiceover *n* troslais *eg* trosleisiau
voicing lleisio *be*
void di-rym *ans*
voile voile *eg*
volatile (=flighty) cyfnewidiol *ans*
volatile (in chemistry) anweddol *ans*
volatile (in cooking) ehedol *ans*
volatile (in technology) hedegog *ans*
volatility anweddolrwydd *eg*
volcanic folcanig *ans*
volcanic activity gweithgaredd folcanig *eg*
volcanic ash lludw folcanig *eg*
volcanic bomb bom folcanig *eg* bomiau folcanig
volcanic breccia breccia folcanig *eg*
volcanic cinders marwor folcanig *ell*
volcanic cone côn folcanig *eg* conau folcanig
volcanic crater crater folcanig *eg* crateri folcanig
volcanic dome cromen folcanig *eb* cromenni folcanig
volcanic dust llwch folcanig *eg*
volcanic eruption echdoriad folcanig *eg* echdoriadau folcanig
volcanic filler llenwad folcanig *eg* llenwadau folcanig
volcanic hazard perygl folcanig *eg* peryglon folcanig
volcanic mud llaid folcanig *eg*
volcanic neck gwddf folcanig *eg* gyddfau folcanig
volcanic pipe pibell folcanig *eb* pibellau folcanig
volcanic plug plwg folcanig *eg* plygiau folcanig
volcanic spine nodwydd folcanig *eb* nodwyddau folcanig
volcanicity folcanigrwydd *eg*
volcanism folcanigrwydd *eg*
volcano llosgfynydd *eg* llosgfynyddoedd
volley *n* foli *eb* folïau
volley *v* folïo *be*
volley ball pêl foli *eb* peli foli
volt folt *eg* foltiau

voltage foltedd *eg* folteddau
voltage amplifier mwyhadur foltedd *eg*
voltage comparator cymharydd foltedd *eg*
voltage divider rhannydd foltedd *eg*
voltage gain cynnydd mewn foltedd *eg*
voltage source ffynhonnell foltedd *eb*
voltameter foltamedr *eg* foltamedrau
voltmeter foltmedr *eg* foltmedrau
volume (=fullness of tone) llais *eg* lleisiau
volume (=measurement) cyfaint *eg* cyfeintiau
volume (=noise) sŵn *eg*
volume (of a book) cyfrol *eb* cyfrolau
volume of solids cyfaint solidau *eg*
volumetric cyfeintiol *ans*
volumetric flask fflasg safonol *eb* fflasgiau safonol
volumetric work gwaith cyfeintiol *eg*
voluntarism gwirfoddoliaeth *eb*
voluntary *adj* gwirfoddol *ans*
voluntary *n* offrymddarn *eg* offrymddarnau
voluntary action gweithred wirfoddol *eb* gweithredoedd gwirfoddol
voluntary admission derbyniad gwirfoddol *eg* derbyniadau gwirfoddol
voluntary aided school ysgol wirfoddol dan gymorth *eb* ysgolion gwirfoddol dan gymorth
voluntary care gofal gwirfoddol *eg*
voluntary carer gofalydd gwirfoddol *eg*
voluntary controlled school ysgol wirfoddol dan reolaeth *eb* ysgolion gwirfoddol dan reolaeth
voluntary education addysg wirfoddol *eb*
voluntary muscle cyhyr rheoledig *eg* cyhyrau rheoledig
voluntary organization mudiad gwirfoddol *eg* mudiadau gwirfoddol
voluntary redundancy colli gwaith yn wirfoddol *be*
voluntary school ysgol wirfoddol *eb* ysgolion gwirfoddol
voluntary sector sector gwirfoddol *eg*
voluntary service gwasanaeth gwirfoddol *eg* gwasanaethau gwirfoddol
volunteer gwirfoddolwr *eg* gwirfoddolwyr
volunteer problem problem gwirfoddolwyr *eb*
vomit *n* chwyd *eg*
vomit *v* chwydu *be*
vortex fortecs *eg* fortecsau
vorticist forteisydd *eg* forteisyddion
vorticity forteisedd *eg*
vote *n* pleidlais *eb* pleidleisiau
vote *v* pleidleisio *be*
vote of censure pleidlais gerydd *eb* pleidleisiau cerydd
voting by proxy pleidleisio dirprwyol *be*
votive mass offeren addunedol *eb* offerennau addunedol
votive offering offrwm addunedol *eg* offrymau addunedol
voucher taleb *eb* talebau
vox pop vox pop *eg*
voyeur sbeciwr *eg* sbecwyr
V-section toriad V *eg* toriadau V
V-shape ffurf V *eb*
V-shaped ar ffurf V *ans*
V-tool erfyn V *eg* offer V
vulcanicity fwlcanigrwydd *eg*
vulcanize fwlcaneiddio *be*
vulcanology fwlcanoleg *eb*
vulgar fraction ffracsiwn cyffredin *eg* ffracsiynau cyffredin
Vulgate Fwlgat *eg*
Vulgate Bible Beibl Fwlgat *eg*
vulnerable archolladwy *ans*
vulva (of woman) fwlfa *eg* fwlfâu
V-weapons arfau V *ell*
Vygotskian tutorial tiwtorial Vygotskian *eg*

W

wad box blwch wad *eg* blychau wad
wadding wadin *eg*
wadi wadi *eg/b* wadïau
waffle pattern patrwm waffl *eg* patrymau waffl
wage cyflog *eg/b* cyflogau
wagon chamfer siamffer wagen *eg* siamfferi wagen
Waheguru /Vahiguru Waheguru /Vahiguru *eg*
Wailing Wall Mur Wylofain *eg*
wainscot wensgot *ans*
waist gwasg *eb* gweisg
waist slip pais wasg *eb* peisiau gwasg
waist tie cwlwm gwasg *eg* clymau gwasg
waistband band gwasg *eg* bandiau gwasg
waistcoat gwasgod *eb* gwasgodau
waistline llinell wasg *eb* llinellau gwasg
waiting list rhestr aros *eb* rhestri aros
waiting room ystafell aros *eb* ystafelloedd aros
waiting time amser aros *eg* amserau aros
waits carolwyr *ell*
wake (in Ireland) gwylnos *eb* gwylnosau
wake (of ship) ôl llong *eg* olion llongau
Waldenses Waldensiaid *ell*
Waldensian Waldensaidd *ans*
Wales Herald of Arms Extraordinary Herodr Arbenigol Cymru *eg*
Wales regions rhanbarthau Cymru *ell*
walk cerdded *be*
walk backwards cerdded wysg y cefn *be*
walker ffrâm gerdded *eb* fframiau cerdded
walking stick ffon *eb* ffyn
walkthrough (in computer programming) archwiliad rhaglen *eg*
wall (in formal usage) mur *eg* muriau
wall (in modern, every day usage) wal *eb* waliau
wall bar bar wal *eg* barrau wal
wall cladding cladin wal *eg*
wall display arddangosfa mur *eb* arddangosfeydd mur
wall hanging croglun *eg* crogluniau
wall light golau wal *eg* goleuadau wal
wall panel panel wal *eg* paneli wal
wall plaque plac mur *eg* placiau mur
Wallace's Line Llinell Wallace *eb*
wall-attachment device dyfais gydio wrth wal *eb* dyfeisiau cydio wrth wal
walled muriog *ans*
walled town tref gaerog *eb* trefi caerog
Wallerian degeneration ymddatod Walleraidd *be*
wallet waled *eb* waledi
wall-hanging unit uned i'w hongian *eb* unedau i'w hongian
wall-painting murlun *eg* murluniau
wallpaper *n* papur wal *eg*
wallpaper *v* papuro *be*
wallplate gwarblat *eg* gwarblatiau
wall-thickness (of pipe) trwch wal *eg*
walnut cneuen Ffrengig *eb* cnau Ffrengig
walrus walrws *eg* walrysod
waltz *v* waltsio *be*
wander crwydro *be*
wandering cell cell grwydrol *eb* celloedd crwydrol
waney edge ymyl ddi-lif *eb* ymylon di-lif
waning trai *eg*
waning of the moon lleuad ar ei chil *eb*
wants (of consumers) chwenychiadau *ell*
war rhyfel *eg/b* rhyfeloedd
war axe bwyell ryfel *eb* bwyeill rhyfel
war communism comiwnyddiaeth ryfel *eb*
war crime trosedd ryfel *eb* troseddau rhyfel
war crimes trial achos llys troseddau rhyfel *eg* achosion llys troseddau rhyfel
war criminal troseddwr rhyfel *eg* troseddwyr rhyfel
war guilt euogrwydd rhyfel *eg*
war lord arglwydd rhyfel *eg* arglwyddi rhyfel
War of Austrian Succession Rhyfel Olyniaeth Awstria *eg*
War of League of Augsburg Rhyfel Cynghrair Augsburg *eg*
War of Polish Succession Rhyfel Olyniaeth Pwyl *eg*
War of Spanish Succession Rhyfel Olyniaeth Sbaen *eg*
warbler telor *eg* teloriaid
ward ward *eb* wardiau
wardenship gwardeiniaeth *eb* gwardeiniaethau
warding wardio *be*
warding file ffeil wardio *eb* ffeiliau wardio
wardrobe wardrob *eb* wardrobau
wardship gwardiaeth *eb*
ware (of ceramics) crochenwaith *eg*
warehouse warws *eg* warysau
warfare rhyfela *be*
warhead pen ffrwydrol *eg* pennau ffrwydrol
warm *adj* cynnes *ans*
warm *v* cynhesu *be*
warm air (central heating system) aer cynnes *eg*
warm blooded animal anifail gwaed cynnes *eg* anifeiliaid gwaed cynnes
warm colour lliw cynnes *eg* lliwiau cynnes

warm front ffrynt cynnes *eg* ffryntiau cynnes
warm iron haearn cynnes *eg*
warm sector sector cynnes *eg* sectorau cynnes
warm temperate tymherus cynnes *ans*
warm temperate zone cylchfa dymherus gynnes *eb* cylchfaoedd tymherus cynnes
warm tone (of colour) tôn cynnes *eg* tonau cynnes
warm up cynhesu *be*
warm up activity gweithgaredd cynhesu *eg* gweithgareddau cynhesu
warm up exercise ymarfer ystwytho *eg* ymarferion ystwytho
warm up movement symudiad ystwytho *eg* symudiadau ystwytho
warm up the muscles cynhesu cyhyrau *be*
warming house ystafell gynhesu *eb* ystafelloedd cynhesu
warmonger rhyfelgi *eg* rhyfelgwn
warmth cynhesrwydd *eg*
warm-up ymgynhesu *be*
warn rhybuddio *be*
warning rhybudd *eg* rhybuddion
warning colouration lliwiad rhybuddiol *eg* lliwiadau rhybuddiol
warp (in wood) *n* camdroad *eg* camdroadau
warp (of land, in geography) *n* crychiad *eg* crychiadau
warp (of land, in geography) *v* crychu *be*
warp (of threads on loom) *n* ystof *eb* ystofau
warp (textiles) *v* ystofi *be*
warp (wood) *v* camdroi *be*
warp and weft ystof ac anwe
warp board bwrdd ystofi *eg* byrddau ystofi
warp grain graen ystof *eg*
warp stick ffon ystofi *eb* ffyn ystofi
warp thread edau ystof *eb* edafedd ystof
warpage ystofiad *eg* ystofiadau
warping (=distortion) camdroad *eg* camdroadau
warping clamp clamp ystofi *eg* clampiau ystofi
warping frame ffrâm ystofi *eb* fframiau ystofi
warping post postyn ystofi *eg* pyst ystofi
warpland crychdir *eg* crychdiroedd
warp-weighted loom gwŷdd pwysau *eg* gwyddau pwysau
warrant gwarant *eb* gwarantau
warrant officer swyddog gwarant *eg* swyddogion gwarant
warranty gwarant *eb* gwarantau
warren cwningar *eg* cwningaroedd
Warrington pattern hammer morthwyl patrwm Warrington *eg* morthwylion patrwm Warrington
warrior rhyfelwr *eg* rhyfelwyr
wars of Scottish independence rhyfeloedd dros annibyniaeth yr Alban *ell*
Wars of the Roses Rhyfeloedd y Rhosynnod *ell*
wart dafaden *eb* defaid
wash *n* golch *eg/b* golchion
wash *v* golchi *be*
wash basin basn ymolchi *eb* basnau ymolchi
wash code cod golchi *eg* codau golchi
wash slope golch-lethr *eg* golch-lethrau
wash tub symbol symbol twb golchi *eg* symbolau twb golchi
washability golchadwyaeth *eb*
washable golchadwy *ans*
washable wallpaper papur golchadwy *eg*
wash-drawing golchlun *eg* golchluniau
washer wasier *eb* wasieri
washing cycle cylchred olchi *eb* cylchredau golchi
washing machine peiriant golchi *eg* peiriannau golchi
washing powder powdr golchi *eg* powdrau golchi
washing process proses olchi *eb* prosesau golchi
washing products nwyddau golchi *ell*
washing programme rhaglen olchi *eb* rhaglenni golchi
washing soda soda golchi *eg*
washing solution hydoddiant golchi *eg* hydoddiannau golchi
Washita oilstone carreg hogi Washita *eb*
wasp gwenynen feirch *eb* gwenyn meirch
waste *n* gwastraff *eg* gwastraffau
waste *v* gwastraffu *be*
waste (land) *n* gorest *eb* gorestau
waste disposal gwaredu sbwriel *be*
waste land tir diffaith *eg* tiroedd diffaith
waste material defnydd gwastraff *eg* defnyddiau gwastraff
waste mould mowld gwastraff *eg* mowldiau gwastraff
waste product isgynnyrch diwerth *eg* isgynhyrchion diwerth
waste side (of line) ochr wastraff *eb*
waste wood pren gwastraff *eg*
waste-disposal unit uned gwaredu sbwriel *eb* unedau gwaredu sbwriel
waste-mantle caen erydion *eg* caenau erydion
wasting process proses wastraffu *eb* prosesau gwastraffu
watch the ball gwylio'r bêl *be*
watch-glass gwydryn oriawr *eg* gwydrau oriawr
watchman gwyliwr *eg* gwylwyr
water *n* dŵr *eg* dyfroedd
water *v* dyfrhau *be*
water attracting molecule moleciwl sy'n atynnu dŵr *eg* moleciwlau sy'n atynnu dŵr
water bath baddon dŵr *eg* baddonau dŵr
water circulation (central heating system) dŵr cylchredol *eg*
water cistern seston ddŵr *eb* sestonau dŵr
water closet toiled *eg* toiledau
water closet closed dŵr *eg* closedau dŵr
water colour dyfrlliw *eg* dyfrlliwiau
water colour brush brwsh dyfrlliw *eg* brwshys dyfrlliw
water colour painting (of painted picture) paentiad dyfrlliw *eg* paentiadau dyfrlliw

water colour painting (of process or art) peintio dyfrlliw *be*
water colour paper papur dyfrlliw *eg*
water content cynhwysiad dŵr *eg*
water course cwrs dŵr *eg* cyrsiau dŵr
water cress berwr dŵr *eg*
water culture dwrfeithriniad *eg*
water cycle cylchred ddŵr *eb*
water deficit diffyg dŵr *eg*
water dispersal gwasgariad gan ddŵr *eg*
water extraction echdynnu dŵr *be*
water features arweddion dŵr *ell*
water frame ffrâm ddŵr *eb* fframiau dŵr
water gas nwy dŵr *eg*
water glass dŵr silicad *eg*
water hole pwll dŵr *eg* pyllau dŵr
water level lefel dŵr *eb* lefelau dŵr
water management rheoli dŵr *be*
water meadow llifddol *eb* llifddolydd
Water of Ayr stone carreg Ayr *eb*
water of crystallization dŵr grisialu *eg*
water parting gwahanfa ddŵr *eb* gwahanfeydd dŵr
water paste past dŵr *eg*
water plant planhigyn dŵr *eg* planhigion dŵr
water potential potensial dŵr *eg*
water repelling molecule moleciwl sy'n gwrthyrru dŵr *eg* moleciwlau sy'n gwrthyrru dŵr
water sac coden ddŵr *eb* codennau dŵr
water safety diogelwch yn y dŵr *eg*
water softener meddalydd dŵr *eg* meddalyddion dŵr
water stain staen dŵr *eg* staeniau dŵr
water supply cyflenwad dŵr *eg*
water survival goroesi yn y dŵr *be*
water table lefel trwythiad *eb* lefelau trwythiad
water treatment trin dŵr *be*
water vapour anwedd dŵr *eg*
water vascular system system fasgwlar ddyfrol *eb*
water vole llygoden y dŵr *eb* llygod y dŵr
water wheel rhod ddŵr *eb* rhodau dŵr
water work gwaith dŵr *eg*
water-based (in technical usage) dyfrsail *ans*
water-based activity gweithgaredd dŵr *eg*
water-based emulsion polish llathr emwlsiwn dŵr *eg*
water-based medium cyfrwng sylfaen ddŵr *eg*
waterfall rhaeadr *eb* rhaeadrau
water-heater gwresogydd dŵr *eg* gwresogyddion dŵr
watering place dyfrfan *eg* dyfrfannau
waterlogged dwrlawn *ans*
watermark dyfrnod *eg* dyfrnodau
water-polo polo'r dŵr *eg*
waterproof *v* diddosi *be*
waterproof (=snug from the weather) *adj* diddos *ans*
waterproof (in technical usage) *adj* dal dŵr *ans*
waterproof dressing gorchudd dal dŵr *eg* gorchuddion dal dŵr
waterproof ink inc gwrth-ddŵr *eg*
waterproof paper papur gwrth-ddŵr *eg*
waterproof sheet cynfas dal dŵr *eb* cynfasau dal dŵr
water-repellent gwrth-ddŵr *ans*
water-resistant dŵr-wrthiannol *ans*
watershed gwahanfa ddŵr *eb* gwahanfeydd dŵr
water-softening plant cyfarpar meddalu dŵr *eg*
waterspout colofn ddŵr *eb* colofnau dŵr
watertight dwrglos *ans*
waterway dyfrffordd *eb* dyfrffyrdd
watt (W) wat *eg* watiau
wattage watedd *eg* wateddau
wattle and daub plethwaith a chlai
wattle fence ffens bleth *eb* ffensys pleth
wave ton *eb* tonnau
wave (of sound) seindon *eb* seindonnau
wave machine peiriant tonnau *eg* peiriannau tonnau
wave mechanics tonfecaneg *eb*
wave motion mudiant ton *eg*
wave refraction plygiant tonnau *eg*
wave-cut platform llyfndir tonnau *eg* llyfndiroedd tonnau
waveform *adj* tonffurf *ans*
waveform *n* tonffurf *eg* tonffurfiau
wave-front blaendon *eb* blaendonnau
wavelength tonfedd *eb* tonfeddi
wavelength of a wave tonfedd ton *eb* tonfeddi tonnau
wavelet tonnell *eb* tonellau
wavy tonnog *ans*
wavy grain graen tonnog *eg*
wax cwyr *eg* cwyrau
wax crayon creon cwyr *eg* creonau cwyr
wax finish gorffeniad cwyr *eg*
wax painting (of process or art) peintio cwyr *be*
wax paper papur cwyr *eg*
wax pastel pastel cwyr *eg* pasteli cwyr
wax polish (material) llathrydd cwyr *eg* llathryddion cwyr
wax polish (shine) llathredd cwyr *eg*
wax resistant gwrth-gwyr *ans*
wax shine llathredd cwyr *eg*
wax varnish farnais cwyr *eg* farneisiau cwyr
waxing cwyro *be*
waxing and waning cynnydd a chiliad
waxing of the moon lleuad ar ei chynnydd *eb*
wax-resist decoration addurn gwrthgwyr *eg* addurniadau gwrthgwyr
waxy cwyraidd *ans*
waxy surface arwyneb cwyraidd *eg* arwynebau cwyraidd
way leave hawl tramwy *eg* hawliau tramwy
weak gwan *ans*
weak acid asid gwan *eg* asidau gwan
weak base bas gwan *eg* basau gwan
weak field ligand ligand maes gwan *eg*
weaker side ochr wanaf *eb* ochrau gwanaf

weakly singular hynod wannaidd *ans*
weakness gwendid *eg* gwendidau
wealth cyfoeth *eg*
wealth tax treth ar gyfoeth *eb*
wean diddyfnu *be*
weapon arf *eg* arfau
weapon focus ffocws arf *eg*
weapon hand llaw'r arf *eb*
wear traul *eb*
wear and tear traul a gwisgo
weasel gwenci *eb* gwencïod
weather tywydd *eg*
weather board (bargeboard) bwrdd hindraul *eg* byrddau hindraul
weather forecast rhagolygon y tywydd *ell*
weather forecaster (female) merch y tywydd *eb* merched tywydd
weather forecaster (male and in general) dyn y tywydd *eg* dynion y tywydd
weather map map tywydd *eg* mapiau tywydd
weather pattern patrwm y tywydd *eg*
weather report adroddiad tywydd *eg* adroddiadau tywydd
weathered hindreuliedig *ans*
weathering *n* hindreuliad *eg*
weathering *v* hindreulio *be*
weathering agent cyfrwng hindreulio *eg* cyfryngau hindreulio
weave *n* gwehyddiad *eg* gwehyddiadau
weave *v* gwehyddu *be*
weave in and out (in dancing) plethu *be*
weaver gwehydd *eg* gwehyddion
weaving (in Lord of Caernarfon dance) gwau drwy'r gwŷdd *be*
weaving (in Oswestry Wake) gwau igam-ogam *be*
weaving cotton cotwm sglein *eg*
weaving dance dawns weu *eb* dawnsiau gweu
weaving pattern patrwm gwehyddu *eg* patrymau gwehyddu
weaving shuttle gwennol y gwehydd *eb* gwenoliaid gwehyddion
web gwe *eb* gweoedd
web browser porwr gwe *eg* porwyr gwe
web cam gwe-gam *eg*
web crawler gwe-ymlusgwr *eg*
web hosting gwe-letya *be*
web location lleoliad gwe *eg* lleoliadau gwe
web mining gwe-gloddio *eg*
web page tudalen we *eb* tudalennau gwe
web page font ffont tudalen gwe *eg* ffontiau tudalen gwe
web site gwefan *eb* gwefannau
web site address cyfeiriad gwefan *eg*
web site design dylunio gwefannau *be*
web site still image delwedd lonydd gwefan *eb*
web site video clip clip fideo gwefan *eg*
web style arddull gwe *eg*
webbed gweog *ans*
webbing webin *eg* webinau
webbing stretcher estynnwr webin *eg* estynwyr webin
webcast *n* gwe-ddarllediad *eg* gwe-ddarllediadau
webcast *v* gwe-ddarlledu *be*
weber weber *eg* weberau
weblog gwe-log *eg* gwe-logiau
webmaster gwefeistr *eg* gwefeistri
webzine gwegrawn *eg* gwegronau
Wechsler Abbreviated Scale of Intelligence (WASI) Graddfa Deallusrwydd Gryno Wechsler *eb*
Wechsler Adult Intelligence Scale (WAIS) Graddfa Deallusrwydd Oedolion Wechsler *eb*
Wechsler Intelligence Scale for Children (WISC) Graddfa Deallusrwydd Plant Wechsler *eb*
wedge *n* lletem *eb* lletemau
wedge *v* lletemu *be*
wedged (with feminine nouns) wedi'i lletemu *ans* wedi'u lletemu
wedged (with masculine nouns) wedi'i letemu *ans* wedi'u lletemu
wedged tenon tyno wedi'i letemu *eg* tynoau wedi'u lletemu
wedging lletemiad *eg*
weed chwynnyn *eg* chwyn
weekly wash golch wythnosol *eb*
weekwork wythnoswaith *eg*
weft anwe *eb*
weft grain graen anwe *eg*
weft thread edau anwe *eb* edafedd anwe
weigh pwyso *be*
weigh in pwyso *be*
weighbridge pont bwyso *eb* pontydd pwyso
weighed (with feminine nouns) wedi'i phwyso *ans* wedi'u pwyso
weighed (with masculine nouns) wedi'i bwyso *ans* wedi'u pwyso
weighman pwyswr *eg* pwyswyr
weight (=object for weighing) pwysyn *eg* pwysynnau
weight (in general) pwysau *ell*
weight training hyfforddiant gyda phwysau *eg*
weighted pwysol *ans*
weighted average cyfartaledd pwysol *eg* cyfartaleddau pwysol
weighted mean cymedr pwysol *eg* cymedrau pwysol
weighting pwysiad *eg* pwysiadau
weightlifting codi pwysau *be*
Weights & Measures Act Deddf Pwysau a Mesurau *eb*
weir cored *eb* coredau
Welch Whim Chwiw Gymreig *eb*
weld *n* weldiad *eg* weldiadau
weld *v* weldio *be*
weld line llinell weldio *eb* llinellau weldio
welding rod rhoden weldio *eb* rhodenni weldio
welding torch tortsh weldio *eg* tortshys weldio
welfare lles *eg*
welfare food bwyd lles *eg* bwydydd lles

welfare loss colled les *eb* colledion lles
welfare officer swyddog lles *eg* swyddogion lles
welfare payment taliad lles *eg* taliadau lles
welfare state gwladwriaeth les *eb* gwladwriaethau lles
well man clinic clinig dynion iach *eg* clinigau dynion iach
well of bench cafn mainc *eg* cafnau mainc
well woman clinic clinig merched iach *eg* clinigau merched iach
well-balanced cytbwys *ans*
well-being lles *eg*
well-defined clir-ddiffiniedig *ans*
well-groomed (=carefully tended) graenus *ans*
well-groomed (of dress etc) trwsiadus *ans*
well-known adnabyddus *ans*
well-proportioned (=symmetrical) cymesur *ans*
well-proportioned (in art etc) o gyfrannedd da *ans*
well-proportioned drawing lluniad o gyfrannedd da *eg* lluniadau o gyfrannedd da
well-proportioned sketch braslun o gyfrannedd da *eg* brasluniau o gyfrannedd da
Welsh Bible Beibl Cymraeg *eg*
Welsh Church Temporalities Act Deddf Eiddo Bydol Eglwys Cymru *eb*
Welsh Folk Dance Society Cymdeithas Ddawns Werin Cymru *eb*
Welsh folk dancing dawnsio gwerin Cymreig *be*
Welsh gentry bonedd Cymreig *eg*
Welsh harp telyn Gymreig *eb* telynau Cymreig
Welsh language policy polisi Cymraeg *eg* polisïau Cymraeg
Welsh law Cyfraith Hywel *eb*
Welsh League of Youth Urdd Gobaith Cymru *eb*
Welsh National Board (WNB) Bwrdd Cenedlaethol Cymru *eg*
Welsh Nationalist Party Plaid Genedlaethol Cymru *eb*
Welsh Office Swyddfa Gymreig *eb*
Welsh quilting cwiltio Cymreig *be*
Welsh Trust Ymddiriedolaeth Gymreig *eb*
Welsh wool gwlân Cymru *eg*
Welsh-medium cyfrwng Cymraeg *ans*
Welsh-medium education addysg cyfrwng Cymraeg *eb*
Welshness Cymreictod *eg*
welshry brodoriaeth *eb*
welt gwald *eg* gwaldiau
welt pocket poced wald *eb* pocedi wald
welter weight pwysau welter *ell*
Wendicote loom gwŷdd Wendicote *eg* gwyddau Wendicote
Wendy loom gwŷdd Wendy *eg* gwyddau Wendy
Wernicke's aphasia affasia Wernicke *eg*
Wernicke's area rhan Wernicke *eb*
Wesleyan Weslead *eg* Wesleaid
Wesleyan Methodism Methodistiaeth Wesleaidd *eb*
Wesleyanism Wesleaeth *eb*
west gorllewin *eg*
West Bank Glan Orllewinol *eb*
westerlies gwyntoedd y gorllewin *ell*
western margins glandiroedd gorllewinol *ell*
Western religions crefyddau'r Gorllewin *ell*
Western roll (in gymnastics) rhôl y Gorllewin *eb*
Western values gwerthoedd y Gorllewin *ell*
westernization gorllewiniad *eg*
westernize gorllewino *be*
westing gorllewiniad *eg*
wet gwlyb *ans*
wet and dry gwlyb a sych
wet and dry paper papur gwlyb a sych *eg*
wet bulb thermometer thermomedr bwlb gwlyb *eg* thermomedrau bwlb gwlyb
wet media cyfryngau gwlyb *ell*
wet rot gwlyb-bydredd *eg*
wet spin gwlybnyddu *be*
wet weather tywydd gwlyb *eg*
wetting gwlychu *be*
wetting agent cyfrwng gwlychu *eg* cyfryngau gwlychu
wetting power pŵer gwlychu *eg*
whale morfil *eg* morfilod
whale back cefn morfil *eg* cefnau morfil
wharf cei *eg* ceiau
Wharton's jelly jeli Wharton *eg*
wheatmeal bread bara gwenith *eg*
wheatmeal flour blawd bywyn gwenith *eg*
Wheatstone's bridge circuit cylched pont Wheatstone *eb* cylchedau pont Wheatstone
wheel *n* olwyn *eb* olwynion
wheel *v* olwyno *be*
wheel castor castor olwyn *eg* castorau olwynion
wheel dresser erfyn trin olwyn *eg* offer trin olwyn
wheel dressing trin olwyn *be*
wheel of fortune pattern patrwm olwyn ffawd *eg* patrymau olwyn ffawd
wheel-back chair cadair gefn olwyn *eb* cadeiriau cefn olwyn
wheelbarrow berfa *eb* berfâu
wheelbrace carntro olwyn *eg* carntroeon olwyn
wheelchair cadair olwyn *eb* cadeiriau olwyn
wheeling the scrummage olwyno'r sgrym *be*
wheelwright saer troliau *eg* seiri troliau
wheezing gwichian *be*
whet hogi *be*
whetstone carreg hogi *eb* cerrig hogi
Whig *adj* Chwigaidd *ans*
Whig *n* Chwig *eg* Chwigiaid
Whig Party Plaid y Chwigiaid *eb*
whip *v* chwipio *be*
whip (as in a long shaft or beam) *n* ysgogiad *eg*
whip (in general) *n* chwip *eb* chwipiau
whip a hem chwipio hem *be*
whipping cream hufen chwipio *eg*
whipping stitch pwyth chwipio *eg* pwythau chwipio

whirl *n* chwyrlïad *eg* chwyrliadau
whirl *v* chwyrlïo *be*
whirler chwyrlïwr *eg* chwyrlïwyr
whirling wheel olwyn chwyrlïo *eb* olwynion chwyrlïo
whirlpool trobwll *eg* trobyllau
whirlwind chwyrlwynt *eg* chwyrlwyntoedd
whisking method dull chwisgio *eg*
whisper *n* sibrwd *eg* sibrydion
whisper *v* sibrwd *be*
whistle *n* chwiban *eg/b* chwibanau
whistle *v* chwibanu *be*
whistling sand tywod sïo *eg*
white (enamelling colour) gwyn *eg*
white apron ffedog wen *eb* ffedogau gwyn
white blood cell cell wen y gwaed *eb* celloedd gwyn y gwaed
white board bwrdd gwyn *eg* byrddau gwyn
white bread bara gwyn *eg*
white cardboard cardbord gwyn *eg*
white chalk sialc gwyn *eg*
white check banding bandin siec gwyn *eg*
white collar worker gweithiwr swyddfa *eg* gweithwyr swyddfa
white dune twyn gwyn *eg* twyni gwyn
white foundation gwyn sylfaenol *eg*
white heat gwres gwynias *eg*
White House Tŷ Gwyn *eg*
white jumper siwmper wen *eb* siwmperi gwyn
white light golau gwyn *eg*
white line llinell wen *eb* llinellau gwyn
white man's burden baich y dyn gwyn *eg*
white matter (brain) gwynnin *eg*
white metal alloy aloi metel gwyn *eg* aloion metel gwyn
white meter mesurydd gwyn *eg* mesuryddion gwyn
white monk mynach gwyn *eg* mynachod gwyn
white paste past gwyn *eg*
white shellac sielac gwyn *eg*
white spirit gwirod gwyn *eg*
white supremacy goruchafiaeth y dyn gwyn *eb*
white tissue paper papur sidan gwyn *eg*
white-cast iron (ferrous metal) haearn bwrw gwyn *eg*
white-collar worker gweithiwr coler wen *eg* gweithwyr coler wen
whitefly pryf gwyn *eg* pryfed gwyn
whiten gwynnu *be*
whitener gwynnydd *eg* gwynyddion
whitewood pren gwyn *eg*
whiting powdr sialc *eg*
whitlow ffelwm *eg*
Whitsun Sulgwyn *eg*
whittle naddu *be*
Whitworth thread edau Whitworth *eb*
whole consort consort offerynnau tebyg *eg* consortiau offerynnau tebyg
whole curriculum cwricwlwm cyflawn *eg*
whole number rhif cyfan *eg* rhifau cyfain
whole school policy polisi ysgol gyfan *eg*
wholemeal bread bara cyflawn *eg*
whole-number system system rhifau cyfain *eb*
wholesale cyfanwerth *eg*
wholesale and retail distribution dosbarthu cyfanwerth ac adwerth *be*
wholesale market marchnad gyfanwerthu *eb* marchnadoedd cyfanwerthu
wholesale store siop gyfanwerthu *eb* siopau cyfanwerthu
wholesaler cyfanwerthwr *eg* cyfanwerthwyr
whole-word reading darllen gair cyfan *be*
whooping cough (pertussis) pas, y *eg*
whorl sidell *eb* sidelli
whorled sidellog *ans*
wicker gwiail *ell*
wickerwork basgedwaith *eg*
wicket wiced *eb* wicedi
wicket-keeper wicedwr *eg* wicedwyr
wide llydan *ans*
wide area (WAN) ardal eang *eb*
wide area network (WAN) rhwydwaith ardal eang *eg*
wide area publishing cyhoeddi ardal eang *be*
wide ball pelen lydan *eb* pelenni llydan
wide open llydan agored *ans*
wide range of ability ystod eang o allu *eb*
wide stroke strôc lydan *eb* strociau llydan
wide text testun llydan *eg*
wideband band canolig *eg*
widely spaced valleys dyffrynnoedd pell oddi wrth ei gilydd *ell*
widen lledu *be*
widen a pattern lledu patrwm *be*
widening joint uniad lledu *eg* uniadau lledu
widescreen sgrin lydan *eb* sgriniau llydan
widow gweddw *eb* gweddwon
width lled *eg* lledau
wiggle nail hoelen rychiog *eb* hoelion rhychiog
Wilcoxon signed-ranks test prawf arwyddion graddedig Wilcoxon *eg*
wild card *n* nodchwiliwr *eg* nodchwilwyr
wild card *v* nodchwilio *be*
wild card search nodchwiliad *eg* nodchwiliadau
wild scape gwylltlun *eg* gwylltluniau
wild silk sidan gwyllt *eg*
Wild West Gorllewin Gwyllt *eg*
wildcard character nod chwilio *eg* nodau chwilio
wildcard symbol symbol nodchwilio *eg* symbolau nodchwilio
wildlife bywyd gwyllt *eg*
will ewyllys *eg/b* ewyllysiau
William of Orange Gwilym o Orange *eg*
William the Conqueror Gwilym Goncwerwr *eg*
William the Silent Gwilym Dawedog *eg*
willow helygen *eb* helyg
willow charcoal siarcol helyg *eg*

wilt gwywo *be*
wilting coefficient cyfernod gwywo *eg* cyfernodau gwywo
win *v* ennill *be*
win a game ennill gêm *be*
win by a canvas ennill o gynfas *be*
win by a length ennill o un hyd *be*
win by an innings ennill o fatiad *be*
win by 3 wickets ennill o dair wiced *be*
win easily ennill o ddigon *be*
win possession ennill meddiant *be*
winch *n* winsh *eb* winshis
winch *v* winsio *be*
Winchester disk disg Winchester *eg* disgiau Winchester
wind (cord, rope etc) *v* dirwyn *be*
wind (in timber) *n* camdroad *eg* camdroadau
wind (that blows) *n* gwynt *eg* gwyntoedd
wind chest cist wynt *eb* cistiau gwynt
wind dispersal gwasgariad gan y gwynt *eg*
wind erosion erydiad gwynt *eg*
wind instrument chwythbren *eg* chwythbrennau
wind machine peiriant gwynt *eg* peiriannau gwynt
wind of change gwynt cyfnewid *eg*
wind quartet pedwarawd chwyth *eg* pedwarawdau chwyth
wind sacks codennau awyr *ell*
wind solo unawd chwythbrennau *eb* unawdau chwythbrennau
wind speed buanedd y gwynt *eg*
windband band chwyth *eg* bandiau chwyth
wind-break atalfa wynt *eb* atalfeydd gwynt
winder dirwynydd *eg* dirwynyddion
windgap bwlch gwynt *eg* bylchau gwynt
winding *n* dirwyniad *eg* dirwyniadau
windmill melin wynt *eb* melinau gwynt
window ffenestr *eb* ffenestri
window button botwm ffenestr *eg*
window ladder ysgol ffenestr *eb* ysgolion ffenestr
windowing ffenestru *be*
window-sill silff ffenestr *eb* silffoedd ffenestri
windproof (finish) gwyntglos *ans*
windproof clothing dillad gwyntglos *ell*
windpump pwmp gwynt *eg* pympiau gwynt
windrose seren wynt *eb* sêr gwynt
windscreen sgrin wynt *eb* sgriniau gwynt
windvane ceiliog y gwynt *eg* ceiliogod y gwynt
windward atwynt *ans*
windward side ochr atwynt *eb* ochrau atwynt
wine bar bar gwin *eg*
wing (in general) adain *eb* adenydd
wing (in sports etc) asgell *eb* esgyll
wing attack ymosodwr asgell *eg* ymosodwyr asgell
wing compass cwmpas adeiniog *eg* cwmpasau adeiniog
wing defence gwarchodwr asgell *eg* gwarchodwyr asgell
wing forward blaenasgellwr *eg* blaenasgellwyr
wing nut nyten asgellog *eb* nytiau asgellog
wing three quarter asgellwr *eg* asgellwyr
winged (of insect, fruit) adeiniog *ans*
winger asgellwr *eg* asgellwyr
wing-half hanerwr asgell *eg* hanerwyr asgell
Winifred Gwenffrewi *eb*
winning stroke ergyd ennill *eb* ergydion ennill
winter solstice heuldro'r gaeaf *eg*
winter sports chwaraeon y gaeaf *ell*
winterbourne nant hafesb *eb* nentydd hafesb
wipe (in film-editing etc) disodli *be*
wiper sychwr *eg* sychwyr
wire *n* gwifren *eb* gwifrau
wire *v* gwifro *be*
wire brush brwsh gwifrau *eg* brwshys gwifrau
wire coil coil gwifren *eg* coiliau gwifren
wire edge ymyl wifrog *eb* ymylon gwifrog
wire foundation sylfaen wifren *eb* sylfeini gwifren
wire frame ffrâm wifren *eb* fframiau gwifren
wire gauge medrydd gwifren *eg* medryddion gwifren
wire loop dolen wifren *eb* dolennau gwifren
wire mesh rhwyll wifrog *eb* rhwyllau gwifrog
wire mesh guard gard rhwyll wifrog *eg* gardiau rhwyll wifrog
wire mesh support cynhaliwr rhwyll wifrog *eg* cynhalwyr rhwyll wifrog
wire nail hoelen gron *eb* hoelion crwn
wire pliers gefelen wifrau *eb* gefeiliau gwifrau
wire printer argraffydd gwifren *eg* argraffyddion gwifren
wire safety cage cawell diogelwch gwifrau *eg* cewyll diogelwch gwifrau
wire staples styffylau gwifren *ell*
wire wool gwlân dur *eg*
wired gwifrog *ans*
wireless diwifr *ans*
wireless network rhwydwaith diwifr *eg* rhwydweithiau diwifr
wire-stripping pliers gefelen stripio gwifrau *eb* gefeiliau stripio gwifrau
wisdom literature llenyddiaeth doethineb *eb*
wisdom tooth cilddant ôl *eg* cilddannedd ôl
WISE: Women in Science and Engineering Merched mewn Gwyddoniaeth a Pheirianneg *ell*
witch hunt erledigaeth *eb*
witch of Agnesi cromlin Agnesi *eb*
witchcraft dewiniaeth *eb*
witchcraze gwrachdwymyn *eb*
with the grain gyda'r graen
withdraw cilio *be*
withdraw a child from religious education tynnu plentyn yn ôl o addysg grefyddol *be*
withdrawal (of money) alldyniad *eg* alldyniadau
withdrawal symptom symptom diddyfnu *eg* symptomau diddyfnu
withdrawal tool erfyn tynnu allan *eg* offer tynnu allan
withdrawn encilgar *ans*

wither gwywo *be*
within-groups design cynllun mewn-grwpiau *eg* cynlluniau mewn-grwpiau
within-groups variance amrywiant mewn-grwpiau *eg* amrywiannau mewn-grwpiau
within-subjects design cynllun mewn-gyfranwyr *eg* cynlluniau mewn-gyfranwyr
without contact heb gyffwrdd *adf*
without loss of generality heb golli cyffredinolrwydd
witness *n* tyst *eg* tystion
witness *v* tystio *be*
witness order gorchymyn tystiolaeth *eg* gorchmynion tystiolaeth
witness punch pwnsh tyst *eg* pynsiau tyst
witness punching tystbwnsio *be*
witness statement datganiad gan dyst *eg*
Witton high frequency furnace ffwrnais amledd uchel Witton *eb* ffwrneisi amledd uchel Witton
WJEC: Welsh Joint Education Committee CBAC: Cyd-bwyllgor Addysg Cymru *eg*
woad glaslys *eg*
wobbler wobler *eg*
WOED: Welsh Office Department of Education Adran Addysg y Swyddfa Gymreig *eb*
wolf note nodyn blaidd *eg* nodau blaidd
wolf vault llofnaid blaidd *eb* llofneidiau blaidd
womb croth *eb* crothau
Women's Institute Sefydliad y Merched *eg*
women's liberation movement mudiad rhyddid merched *eg*
Women's Social and Political Union Undeb Cymdeithasol a Gwleidyddol y Merched *eg*
wood (=forest) coed *ell*
wood (=material) pren *eg*
wood ash lludw pren *eg*
wood bending plygu coed *eg*
wood block bloc pren *eg* blociau pren
wood carving *n* cerfiad pren *eg* cerfiadau pren
wood carving *v* cerfio pren *be*
wood dye llifyn pren *eg* llifynnau pren
wood engraving *n* ysgythriad pren *eg* ysgythriadau pren
wood fibre ffibr coed *eg* ffibrau coed
wood grain graen pren *eg*
wood jackplane plaen jac pren *eg* plaeniau jac pren
wood joint uniad pren *eg* uniadau pren
wood mallet gordd bren *eb* gyrdd pren
wood of light colour pren golau ei liw *eg*
wood plug plwg pren *eg* plygiau pren
wood pulp mwydion coed *ell*
wood scraper sgrafell goed *eb* sgrafelli coed
wood screw sgriw bren *eb* sgriwiau pren
wood sealer seliwr coed *eg* selwyr coed
wood shavings naddion pren *ell*
wood shot taro'r pren *be*
wood turning turnio coed *be*
wood turning gouge gaing gau durnio *eb* geingiau cau turnio
wood work gwaith coed *eg*
wood-boring insect pryfyn tyllu coed *eg* pryfed tyllu coed
woodchip wallpaper papur sglodion pren *eg*
woodcut torlun pren *eg* torluniau pren
wooden bead glain pren *eg* gleiniau pren
wooden cleat (used in seasoning) cledd pren *eg* cleddau pren
wooden frame ffrâm bren *eb* fframiau pren
wooden handle (of brush) coes bren *eb* coesau pren
wooden marionette marionét pren *eg* marionetau pren
wooden racket raced bren *eb* racedi pren
wooden shuttle gwennol bren *eb* gwenoliaid pren
wooden spokeshave rhasgl bren *eb* rhasglau pren
wooden spoon llwy bren *eb* llwyau pren
woodland coetir *eg* coetiroedd
woodpecker cnocell y coed *eb* cnocellod y coed
Woodruff key allwedd Woodruff *eb* allweddi Woodruff
woodwind section adran chwythbrennau *eb* adrannau chwythbrennau
woodworm pryfed pren *ell*
woody prennaidd *ans*
woof anwe *eb*
wool gwlân *eg* gwlanoedd
woollen gwlân *ans*
woollen garments dillad gwlân *ell*
woollen industry diwydiant gwlân *eg*
woollen mill melin wlân *eb* melinau gwlân
woollen thread edau wlân *eb* edafedd gwlân
woollens nwyddau gwlân *ell*
woolly gwlanog *ans*
Woolmark Nod Gwlân *eg*
woolsack sach wlân *eb* sachau gwlân
word gair *eg* geiriau
word class dosbarth geiriau *eg*
word equation hafaliad geiriau *eg* hafaliadau geiriau
word length hyd gair *eg*
word orientated geiriol gyfeiriedig *ans*
word painting lliwio geiriau *be*
word processing prosesu geiriau *be*
word processing software meddalwedd prosesu geiriau *eb*
word processor prosesydd geiriau *eg* prosesyddion geiriau
word search chwilair *eg* chwileiriau
words with numbers geiriau gyda rhifau *ell*
wordwrap geirlap *eg* geirlapiau
work *n* gwaith *eg* gweithiau
work *v* gweithio *be*
work area ardal waith *eb* ardaloedd gwaith
work bench mainc waith *eb* meinciau gwaith
work box basged wnïo *eb* basgedi gwnïo
work card cerdyn gwaith *eg* cardiau gwaith
work experience profiad gwaith *eg* profiadau gwaith

work experience scheme cynllun profiad gwaith *eg* cynlluniau profiad gwaith
work hardening gwaith galedu *be*
work of art gwaith celfyddydol *eg* gweithiau celfyddydol
work opportunity service gwasanaeth cyfle am waith *eg*
work pattern patrwm gwaith *eg*
work placement lleoliad gwaith *eg* lleoliadau gwaith
work sheet dalen waith *eb* dalennau gwaith
work tape tâp gwaith *eg* tapiau gwaith
work to rule gweithio i reol *be*
work-based assessment asesu yn y gweithle *be*
work-board (basketry) bwrdd gweithio basgedi *eg* byrddau gweithio basgedi
worked buttonhole twll botwm pwythog *eg* tyllau botymau pwythog
worked loop dolen edau *eb* dolennau edau
worked scalloping sgolop wedi'i weithio *eg* sgolopiau wedi'u gweithio
worker gweithiwr *eg* gweithwyr
Workers' Education Association (WEA) Cymdeithas Addysg y Gweithwyr *eg*
workforce gweithlu *eg*
workhouse tloty *eg* tlotai
working area rhan weithio *eb* rhannau gweithio
working capital cyfalaf gweithio *eg*
working class dosbarth gwaith *eg*
working conditions amodau gwaith *ell*
working draft drafft gweithio *eg*
working drawing lluniad gweithio *eg* lluniadau gweithio
working edge ymyl weithio *eb* ymylon gweithio
working face wyneb gweithio *eg* wynebau gweithio
Working Families' Tax Credit Credyd Treth Teuluoedd sy'n Gweithio *eg*
working group gweithgor *eg* gweithgorau
working line llinell waith *eb* llinellau gwaith
working memory cof gweithredol *eg*
working party gweithgor *eg* gweithgorau
working population poblogaeth weithio *eb*
working property priodwedd gweithio *eb* priodweddau gweithio
working to capacity gweithio i'r eithaf *be*
working-out (development) datblygiad *eg* datblygiadau
workload baich gwaith *eg*
workpiece darn gwaith *eg* darnau gwaith
workplace gweithle *eg* gweithleoedd
work-related education (WRE) addysg gysylltiedig â gwaith *eb*
works manager rheolwr gweithiau *eg* rheolwyr gweithiau
worksheet taflen waith *eb* taflenni gwaith
workshop gweithdy *eg* gweithdai
workshop approach dull gweithdy *eg* dulliau gweithdy
workshop of the world gweithdy'r byd *eg*
workspace gweithle *eg* gweithleoedd
workstation gweithfan *eg* gweithfannau
worktop (kitchen) wyneb gweithio *eg* wynebau gweithio
workweek wythnos waith *eb*
World Bank, The Banc y Byd *eg*
world context cyd-destun byd-eang *eg*
World Cup Cwpan y Byd *eg*
world development datblygiad y byd *eg*
world economic growth twf economaidd byd-eang *eg*
World Health Organization (WHO) Mudiad Iechyd y Byd *eg*
world of fantasy byd ffantasi *eg* bydoedd ffantasi
World Trade Organisation (WTO) Cyfundrefn Masnach y Byd (WTO) *eb*
world war rhyfel byd *eg* rhyfeloedd byd
World Wide Web We Fyd-eang, y *eb*
worldwide byd-eang *ans*
worm mwydyn *eg* mwydod
worm drive gyriad cripian *eg* gyriadau cripian
worm eaten pryf-dyllog *ans*
worm gears gerau cripian *ell*
worm wheel olwyn gripian *eb* olwynion cripian
worn wedi treulio *ans*
worn oilstone carreg hogi wedi treulio *eb* cerrig hogi wedi treulio
worn threadbare (with feminine nouns) wedi'i gwisgo at yr edau *ans* wedi'u gwisgo at yr edau
worn threadbare (with masculine nouns) wedi'i wisgo at yr edau *ans* wedi'u gwisgo at yr edau
worship *n* addoliad *be* addoliadau
worship *v* addoli *be*
worsted wstid *ans*
worthlessness (of person) diffyg hunan-werth *eg*
wound *adj* wedi'i weindio *ans* wedi'u weindio
wound *n* clwyf *eg* clwyfau
wound *v* clwyfo *be*
wound dressing gorchudd clwyf *eg* gorchuddion clwyfau
woven (with feminine nouns) wedi'i gwehyddu *ans* wedi'u gwehyddu
woven (with masculine nouns) wedi'i wehyddu *ans* wedi'u gwehyddu
woven carpet carped wedi'i wehyddu *eg* carpedi wedi'u gwehyddu
woven lace les wedi'i wehyddu *eg*
woven textiles tecstilau wedi'u gwehyddu *ell*
wrap (in computing) amlapio *be*
wrap (in general) lapio *be*
wrap contour on amlinell amlapio ymlaen
wrap first paragraph amlapio'r paragraff cyntaf *be*
wrap left amlapio i'r chwith *be*
wrap off diffodd amlapio *be*
wrap on amlapio ymlaen *be*
wrap right amlapio i'r dde *be*
wrap through amlapio drwodd *be*
wrap transparent amlapio tryloyw *be*
wrap-around *n* amlap *eg* amlapiau

wrap-around *v* amlapio *be*
wrap-over skirt sgert lapio *eb* sgertiau lapio
wrapping cane gwialen lapio *eb* gwialennau lapio
wrapping paper papur lapio *eg*
wrasse gwrachen y môr *eb* gwrachod y môr
wreathed torchog *ans*
wreck *n* drylliad *eg* drylliadau
wreck *v* dryllio *be*
wreck (legal) hawl broc *eg*
wreckers dryllwyr *ell*
wrench *n* tyndro *eg* tyndroeon
wrench *v* tyndroi *be*
wrest-board bwrdd ebillion *eg* byrddau ebillion
wrest-pin ebill *eg* ebillion
wring gwasgu *be*
wringer (for clothes) gwasgwr dillad *eg* gwasgwyr dillad
wrinkle *n* crych *eg* crychau
wrinkle *v* crychu *be*
wrist arddwrn *eg* arddyrnau
wrist band band llawes *eg* bandiau llewys
wrist bowler bowliwr arddwrn *eg* bowlwyr arddwrn
wrist guard gorchudd arddwrn *eg* gorchuddion arddwrn
writ gwrit *eg* gwritiau
write ysgrifennu *be*
write error gwall ysgrifennu *eg*
write head pen ysgrifennu *eg* pennau ysgrifennu
write inhibit ring cylch atal ysgrifennu *eg* cylchoedd atal ysgrifennu
write permit ring cylch caniatáu ysgrifennu *eg* cylchoedd caniatáu ysgrifennu
write protect diogelu rhag ysgrifennu *be*
write protected (of disk) wedi'i ddiogelu *ans* wedi'u diogelu
write protection diogelu rhag ysgrifennu *be*
write time amser ysgrifennu *eg* amserau ysgrifennu
write-protected darllen yn unig
writing configuration files ysgrifennu ffeiliau ffurfweddiad *be*
writing house ysgrifendy *eg* ysgrifendai
writing paper papur ysgrifennu *eg*
writing skills sgiliau ysgrifennu *ell*
written ysgrifenedig *ans*
written alphabet gwyddor ysgrifenedig *eb* gwyddorau ysgrifenedig
written communication cyfathrebu ysgrifenedig *be*
written description disgrifiad ysgrifenedig *eg* disgrifiadau ysgrifenedig
wrong anghywir *ans*
wrong check amount swm gwirio anghywir *eg*
wrong parameter paramedr anghywir *eg* paramedrau anghywir
wrong password cyfrinair anghywir *eg* cyfrineiriau anghywir
wrong side (W.S.) ochr anghywir *eb* ochrau anghywir
wrong table formula fformiwla tabl anghywir *eb* fformiwlâu tabl anghywir
Wronskian Wronskian *eg* Wronskianau
wrought iron haearn gyr *eg*
wrought iron body corff haearn gyr *eg*
wrought iron bolt bollt haearn gyr *eb* bolltau haearn gyr
wrought iron bracket braced haearn gyr *eb* bracedi haearn gyr
wrought iron nail hoelen haearn gyr *eb* hoelion haearn gyr
wrought iron strap strap haearn gyr *eb*
Wycliffite *adj* Wycliffaidd *ans*
Wycliffite *n* Wycliffiad *eg* Wycliffiaid
Wyndham's Land Purchase Act Deddf Wyndham ar Bwrcasu Tir *eb*

X

X axis echelin X *eb*

X chromosome cromosom X *eg*

X square test prawf sgwâr X *eg*

xanthophyll santhoffyl *eg*

X-efficiency effeithlonrwydd-X *eg*

xenon (Xe) senon *eg*

xenophobia senoffobia *eg*

xenophobic senoffobig *ans*

xenotape alldap *eg* alldapiau

xerographic serograffig *ans*

xerographic printer argraffydd serograffig *eg* argraffyddion serograffig

xerophyte seroffyt *eg* seroffytau

xerosere seroser *eg*

xerotherm serotherm *eg*

X-ray pelydr X *eg* pelydrau X

X-shift symudydd X *eg*

xylem sylem *eg*

xylem vessel tiwb sylem *eg* tiwbiau sylem

xylophone seiloffon *eg* seiloffonau

xylorimba seilorimba *eg* seilorimbau

xylose sylos *eg*

Y

Y adjusting lever lifer cymhwyso Y *eg* liferi cymhwyso Y
'Y' alloy aloi 'Y' *eg*
Y axis echelin Y *eb*
Y chromosome cromosom Y *eg*
Yahweh Yahweh *eg*
Yankee Ianci *eg* Iancis
yard llathen *eb* llathenni
yardang iardang *eg* iardangau
yardarm hwyldrawst *eg* hwyldrawstiau
yarn edau *eb* edafedd
Yarrel blenny llyfrothen Yarrel *eb* llyfrothod Yarrel
yawn dylyfu gên *be*
year book blwyddlyfr *eg* blwyddlyfrau
year coordinator cydgysylltydd blwyddyn *eg* cydgysylltwyr blwyddyn
year group grŵp blwyddyn *eg* grwpiau blwyddyn
year of publication blwyddyn cyhoeddi *eb*
year overview trosolwg blwyddyn *eb*
year planner blwyddiadur *eg* blwyddiaduron
year tutor tiwtor blwyddyn *eg* tiwtoriaid blwyddyn
yeast burum *eg* burumau
yellow (enamelling colour) melyn *eg*
yellow beans ffa melyn *ell*
yellow ochre ocr melyn *eg*
yellowing (of fabric) melynu *be*
yellows and oranges melynion ac orenau *ell*
yeoman iwmon *eg* iwmyn
Yeoman of the Guard Iwmon y Gard *eg* Iwmyn y Gard
yeoman service gwasanaeth iwmon *eg*
yeomanry rhydd-ddeiliaid *ell*
Yeomanry Battalion Bataliwn yr Iwmyn *eg*
yes (on computer button) iawn *adf*
yield (=produce) *n* cynnyrch *eg* cynhyrchion
yield (=produce) *v* cynhyrchu *be*
yield (=surrender) *v* ildio *be*
yield per head cynnyrch y pen *eg*
yield per hectare cynnyrch yr hectar *eg*
yield point pwynt ildio *eg* pwyntiau ildio
yodel *n* iodl *eg* iodlau
yoke iau *eb* ieuau
yoke lining leinin iau *eg*
yolk melynwy *eg*
yolk gland chwarren felynwy *eb* chwarennau melynwy
yolk sac cwd melynwy *eg* cydau melynwy
yorker iorcer *eg*
Yorkist *adj* Iorcaidd *ans*
Yorkist *n* Iorcydd *eg* Iorciaid
Yorkist monarchy brenhiniaeth Iorc *eb*
Young England Movement Mudiad Lloegr Ieuanc *eg*
Young Ireland Movement Mudiad Iwerddon Ieuanc *eg*
Young Italy (movement) Eidal Ifanc
young mountain mynydd ifanc *eg* mynyddoedd ifanc
young offender troseddwr ifanc *eg* troseddwyr ifanc
Young Wales Cymru Fydd *eb*
Young Wales Movement Mudiad Cymru Fydd *eg*
youth ieuenctid *ell*
youth centre canolfan ieuenctid *eb* canolfannau ieuenctid
youth club clwb ieuenctid *eg* clybiau ieuenctid
youth dependency dibyniaeth ieuenctid *eb*
youth employment scheme cynllun cyflogi'r ifanc *eg* cynlluniau cyflogi'r ifanc
youth hostel hostel ieuenctid *eg* hosteli ieuenctid
youth justice cyfiawnder i'r ifanc *eg*
youth leader arweinydd ieuenctid *eg* arweinwyr ieuenctid
youth section adran ieuenctid *eb* adrannau ieuenctid
youth training scheme cynllun hyfforddi'r ifanc *eg* cynlluniau hyfforddi'r ifanc
Y-shift symudydd Y *eg*
ytterbium (Yb) yterbiwm *eg*
yttrium (Y) ytriwm *eg*

Z

zakah zakah *eg*
Zakat Zakat *eg*
zambo sambo *eg* sambos
zazen zazen *eg*
zealot (=extremist) eithafwr *eg* eithafwyr
zealot (member of Jewish sect) selot *eg* selotiaid
zealous eithafol *ans*
Zener diode deuod Zener *eg* deuodau Zener
zenith anterth *eg*
zenithal anterthol *ans*
zenithal projection tafluniad anterthol *eg* tafluniadau anterthol
zeolite seolit *eg*
zeotrope seotrop *eg*
zero sero *eg* seroau
zero blanking gwynnu sero *be*
zero fill sero-lenwi *be*
zero filled sero-lawn *ans*
zero mark marc sero *eg* marciau sero
zero point energy egni tymheredd sero *eg*
zero suppressed sero-lethedig *ans*
zero suppression sero-lethiad *eg* sero-lethiadau
zero tolerance policy polisi goddef dim *eg*
zeroize seroeiddio *be*
zeroth serofed *ans*
zigzag *adj* igam ogam *ans*
zigzag *v* igam ogamu *be*
zigzag riveting rhybedu igam ogam *be*
zigzag stitch pwyth igam ogam *eg* pwythau igam ogam
zigzag width control (of machine part) rheolydd lled pwyth igam ogam *eg* rheolyddion lled pwyth igam ogam
zimbalom simbalom *eg* simbalomau
zinc (Zn) sinc *eg*
zinc blende sinc blend *eg*
zinc carbonate (calamine) sinc carbonad (calamin) *eg*
zinc chloride (killed spirits) sinc clorid *eg*
zinc cutting plate plât torri sinc *eg* platiau torri sinc
zinc ion ïon sinc *eg* ïonau sinc
zinc ore mwyn sinc *eg* mwynau sinc
zinc oxide sinc ocsid *eg*
zinc silicate sinc silicad *eg*
zinc white gwyn sinc *eg*
zincate ion ïon sincad *eg* ïonau sincad
Zionism Seioniaeth *eb*
Zionist *adj* Seionaidd *ans*
Zionist *n* Seionydd *eg* Seionyddion
zip sip *eg* sipiau
zip drive gyriant sip *eg* gyriannau sip
zip fastener ffasnydd sip *eg* ffasnyddion sip
zipper foot (machine attachments) sipell *eb* sipelli
zirconium (Zr) sirconiwm *eg*
zither sither *eg* sitherau
Zodiac Sidydd *eg*
zona pellucida zona pellucida *eb*
zona reticularis zona reticularis *eb*
zonal cylchfaol *ans*
zonation dosbarthiad mewn cylchfaoedd *eg*
zonation cylchfäedd *eg*
zone (=horizontal band in geography, geometry etc) cylchfa *eb* cylchfaoedd
zone (=region) rhanbarth *eg* rhanbarthau
zone (for pedestrians etc) parth *eg* parthau
zone (in histology) haenen *eb* haenau
zone defence amddiffyn rhanbarth *be*
zone in transition cylchfa sy'n trawsnewid *eb*
zone of accumulation cylchfa gronni *eb* cylchfaoedd cronni
zone of advance and assimilation cylchfa cynnydd a chymathu *eb* cylchfaoedd cynnydd a chymathu
zone of discard cylchfa wrthod *eb* cylchfaoedd gwrthod
Zone of Proximal Development Parth Datblygu Procsimol *eg*
zone of proximal development parth datblygiad procsimol *eg*
zone of proximal development cylchfa datblygiad procsimol *eb*
zone refining coethi cylchfaol *be*
zoning cylchfaeo *be*
zoo sw *eg* swau
zoo format fformat sŵ *eg*
zoologist swolegydd *eg* swolegwyr
zoology swoleg *eb*
zoom chwyddo *be*
zoom control rheolydd chwyddo *eg* rheolyddion chwyddo
zoom in chwyddo mewn *be*
zoom in (in camera work) tynhau'r lens *be*
zoom next chwyddo nesaf *be*
zoom out chwyddo allan *be*
zoom out (in camera work) llacio'r lens *be*
zoom page chwyddo tudalen *be*
zoom page width chwyddo lled tudalen *be*
zoom previous chwyddo blaenorol *be*

zooplankton swoplancton *eg*
zoospore swosbor *eg* swosborau
zwitterion switerïon *eg* switerïonau
zygospore sygosbor *eg* sygosborau
zygote sygot *eg* sygotau

notes

Y TERMIADUR

Cymraeg – Saesneg

ISBN 1-86112-588-7 £15

9 781861 125880

Y TERMIADUR

Termau wedi'u safoni

Cymraeg – Saesneg

Saesneg – Cymraeg

Yn ddiáu, o ddydd i ddydd – y mae'r hen
Iaith Gymraeg ar gynnydd;
Cadarnhau holl dermau'r dydd
A wna'r Termiadur newydd.

Iolo Wyn Williams

Lluniwyd gan
Delyth Prys J P M Jones Owain Davies Gruffudd Prys
Prifysgol Cymru, Bangor

accac

Noddir gan
Lywodraeth Cynulliad Cymru

2006

Cyhoeddwyd gan
Awdurdod Cymwysterau, Cwricwlwm ac Asesu Cymru

Mae cofnod catalogio'r gyfrol hon ar gael
gan y Llyfrgell Brydeinig

ISBN 1 86112 588 7
Cyf ACCAC: AC/OM/0609

Dyluniwyd a chosodwyd yng Nghymru gan MAGMA ✆ 01248 810833

Argraffwyd gan Clays Ltd

Rhagair

Yn 1998 cyhoeddwyd *Y Termiadur Ysgol* gan Awdurdod Cymwysterau, Cwricwlwm ac Asesu Cymru (ACCAC). Ei brif bwrpas oedd safoni'r termau Cymraeg a ddefnyddid yn ein hysgolion ym mhynciau'r Cwricwlwm Cenedlaethol hyd at safon Tystysgrif Gyffredinol Addysg Uwchradd. Roedd hyn yn sicrhau cysondeb yn yr iaith a ddefnyddid mewn arholiadau ac yn y tasgau a'r profion a gynhelid bryd hynny i asesu disgyblion 7, 11 a 14 mlwydd oed.

Bu newidiadau ym myd y cwricwlwm ac mewn asesu yn ystod y blynyddoedd ers cyhoeddi'r gyfrol honno. Nid oes profi statudol bellach ar ddisgyblion 7, 11 na 14 mlwydd oed ac mae cylch y cwricwlwm wedi ehangu ers hynny. Mae rhagor o ddysgu ar byncíau galwedigaethol yn yr ysgolion yn ogystal ag yn y colegau ac mae dysgu pynciau Safon Uwch drwy'r Gymraeg hefyd yn ehangu o ran eu meysydd astudio.

O'r herwydd, bu galw am safoni'r termau a ddefnyddir yn y pynciau galwedigaethol ac mewn pynciau Safon Uwch. Yn y gyfrol hon, felly, ceir termau'r meysydd newydd hyn yn ogystal â'r termau gwreiddiol. Manteisiwyd ar y cyfle hwn i gywiro neu ddiweddaru ambell i gofnod yn *Y Termiadur Ysgol* gwreiddiol ac fe nodir hyn yn eglur ► yn y testun.

Unwaith eto, Prifysgol Cymru, Bangor fu'n ymgymryd â'r gwaith gyda Delyth Prys yn brif olygydd. Lleolwyd y gwaith gwreiddiol yn y Ganolfan Safoni Termau yn yr Ysgol Addysg, ond erbyn hyn mae'n rhan o Ganolfan Bedwyr yn y Brifysgol. Aelodau eraill y tîm golygyddol oedd Owain Davies a Gruffudd Prys, gydag Owain Gwilym a Sioned Roberts hefyd yn cynorthwyo ar y project. Gwnaed y gwaith cyfrifiadurol gan Dewi Bryn Jones, a gweithredodd Dr J Prys Morgan Jones fel ymgynghorydd i'r project.

Ar ôl cyhoeddi *Y Termiadur Ysgol* gwreiddiol, paratowyd disg CD-ROM oedd yn cynnwys y termau ynghyd â rhai diweddariadau. Bu'r ddisg honno ar werth yn y siopau. Erbyn heddiw, mae disg yn cael ei chynnwys gyda'r fersiwn papur. Gellir

llwytho'r holl dermau hyn ar ffurf electronig o'r ddisg yn syth i gof y cyfrifiadur er mwyn hwyluso'r gwaith o'u cyrchu.

Unwaith eto wrth gyflwyno'r gyfrol newydd hon i ddisgyblion, athrawon, myfyrwyr a darlithwyr Cymru, dymunwn yn dda iddynt hwythau ac i ddyfodol addysg drwy gyfrwng y Gymraeg.

Canllawiau

1. Sut i chwilio am derm
2. Dangos rhannau ymadrodd
3. Cenedl a lluosogion enwau
4. Cyfatebiaeth berfau ac enwau yn y Gymraeg a'r Saesneg
5. Meini prawf safoni termau
6. Orgraff safonol
7. Deall ystyr term
8. Cyfystyron a chywair iaith
9. Amrywiadau tafodieithol
10. Enwau lleoedd mewn daearyddiaeth
11. Termau addysg grefyddol
12. Dyfynnu termau estron
13. Acronymau

1 Sut i chwilio am derm

Dilynir trefn y wyddor Gymraeg i restru'r termau Cymraeg a'r wyddor Saesneg i restru'r termau Saesneg. Ceir cofnod annibynnol ar gyfer pob term, felly dylid chwilio am dermau sy'n cynnwys mwy nag un gair o dan air cyntaf y term bob amser, e.e. daw 'deddf disgyrchiant' yn y rhestr ar ôl 'deddf' ac nid fel isgofnod i 'disgyrchiant'.

Lle ceir mwy nag un ystyr i air, mae cofnod ar wahân ar gyfer pob ystyr, ac mae dadamwysydd yn dilyn y prifair. Mae'r dadamwysydd yn ddiffiniad byr rhwng cromfachau sy'n dod ar ôl term er mwyn gwahaniaethu rhwng geiriau sydd yn

edrych yn debyg i'w gilydd ond yn wahanol o ran ystyr. Mae termau sy'n cynnwys un gair a dadamwysydd wedi'u rhestru cyn termau sy'n cynnwys mwy nag un gair. Er enghraifft, daw 'asgell (mewn chwaraeon)', 'asgell (pysgodyn etc.)' ac 'asgell (saeth)' o flaen 'asgell bectoral', 'asgell chwith', 'asgell dde', 'asgell ddorsal' ac yn y blaen.

2 Dangos rhannau ymadrodd

Mae'r rhestr hon yn dangos rhannau ymadrodd termau yn Gymraeg pan fônt yn enwau, berfau neu ansoddeiriau, gan fod y wybodaeth honno yn ddefnyddiol i wybod a ddylid treiglo ac ati. Nid yw'n eu dangos fel arfer gyda geiriau eraill na gyda chymalau ac ymadroddion hirach, ond mae'n labelu ymadroddion enwol fel enwau oherwydd y gall yr ymadrodd cyfan achosi treiglad, e.e. gyda 'sbectol haul' mae 'sbectol' yn fenywaidd a 'haul' yn wrywaidd, ond labelir yr ymadrodd cyfan yn fenywaidd am ei fod yn treiglo'n feddal unrhyw ansoddeiriau sy'n ei dilyn, h.y. 'sbectol haul dywyll' nid 'sbectol haul tywyll'.

Ni ddangosir rhannau ymadrodd y Saesneg ond pan fo'n rhaid gwahaniaethu rhwng berf ac enw ac ansoddair – yn debyg, felly, i swyddogaeth y diffiniadau a geir weithiau rhwng cromfachau yn dilyn term. Er enghraifft, gall 'call' yn Saesneg fod yn enw neu'r ferf ('a call' neu 'to call').

Dangosir y ddau gofnod yn *Y Termiadur* fel:

call *n* galwad *eb* galwadau
call *v* galw *be*

3 Cenedl a lluosogion enwau

Mae nifer o eiriau yn Gymraeg sy'n medru bod yn fenywaidd neu'n wrywaidd, gan amrywio gan amlaf yn ôl tafodiaith. Ceisiwyd dangos y rhain gydag *eg/b* gan adael i unigolion ddefnyddio'r ffurfiau sy'n swnio'n iawn iddynt hwy. Fodd bynnag, pan fo gair sy'n *eg/b* yn codi mewn term sy'n cynnwys mwy nag un gair, dewiswyd dangos un ffurf yn unig, rhag gorfod ailadrodd termau lle ceid treiglad. Er enghraifft, gall 'diweddeb' fod yn enw gwrywaidd neu fenywaidd. Pan fo'n enw gwrywaidd ceir y ffurf 'diweddeb perffaith' a phan fo'n fenywaidd ceir y ffurf 'diweddeb berffaith'. Dewiswyd trin 'diweddeb' fel enw benywaidd yn *Y Termiadur*, felly mae'n peri treiglo'n feddal mewn enwau cyfansawdd. Dylid derbyn y ffurf wrywaidd hefyd os hynny sy'n dod yn naturiol i'r glust, a'r un modd gyda geiriau eraill sy'n amrywio o ran cenedl.

Cofier fodd bynnag fod dyrnaid bach o enwau yn Gymraeg lle ceir ystyr gwahanol yn ôl cenedl y gair. Er enghraifft, yn *Y Termiadur* mae 'y tôn' (enw gwrywaidd) yn cael ei gyfieithu fel 'the tone' ac mae 'y de' (enw gwrywaidd) yn rhoi 'the south' i ni yn Saesneg, ac 'y dde' (enw benywaidd) yn rhoi 'the right [side]' i ni yn Saesneg.

Weithiau hefyd bydd ystyr gwahanol i luosogion enwau er bod yr enw unigol yn edrych yr un fath, e.e. llwyth (=tribe) lluosog: llwythau; llwyth (=load) lluosog: llwythi.

4 Cyfatebiaeth berfau ac enwau yn y Gymraeg a'r Saesneg

Defnyddir berfau a berfenwau yn Gymraeg yn aml lle mae'r Saesneg yn tueddu i ddefnyddio enw. Er enghraifft, lle ceir 'do a headstand' yn Saesneg, mae'r Gymraeg yn fwy tueddol o ddweud 'sefwch ar eich pen'. Mae rhai geiriaduron cyfoes Cymraeg yn rhoi berfenw i gyfieithu enw Saesneg er mwyn atgoffa'r Cymro i beidio ag efelychu'r gystrawen Saesneg. Ond mae adegau pan fo angen enw yn Gymraeg i gyfateb i enw yn Saesneg, yn enwedig gyda rhifolion. Felly, os ceir rhestr o symudiadau ymarfer corff yn nodi sawl gwaith y mae'n rhaid i ddisgybl wneud symudiad arbennig, e.e. '10 headstands', gellir defnyddio gair gwneud fel 'pensafiad'. Mae *Y Termiadur* yn ceisio cadw cyfatebiaeth rhannau ymadrodd hyd y bo modd, ond yn annog cyfieithwyr i gofio bod sawl cyd-destun lle dylid newid enw yn ferfenw wrth gyfieithu o'r Saesneg i'r Gymraeg er mwyn cadw cystrawen naturiol Gymraeg.

5 Meini prawf safoni termau

Dilynwyd meini prawf gwrthrychol wrth lunio *Y Termiadur*. Seiliwyd y rhain ar safonau'r Gyfundrefn Safonau Rhyngwladol (International Standards Organization), gan gynnwys ISO 704 ar Safoni Termau ac ISO 860 ar Harmoneiddio Cysyniadau a Thermau. Y mae'r rhain yn nodi, ymhlith pethau eraill:

- Dylai term fod yn ieithyddol gywir.
- Dylai term adlewyrchu, hyd y gall, nodweddion y cysyniad y mae'n ei gynrychioli.
- Dylai term fod yn gryno.
- Dylai term fedru esgor ar ffurfiau eraill.
- Dylai un cysyniad gyfateb i un term yn unig.

6 Orgraff safonol

Dilynwyd orgraff *Geiriadur Prifysgol Cymru* (Gwasg Prifysgol Cymru, 1950–2001) hyd yr oedd modd, ac mae'r geiriadur hwnnw yn ei dro yn dilyn canllawiau *Orgraff yr Iaith Gymraeg* (Gwasg Prifysgol Cymru, Rhan II, Geirfa 1987). Weithiau mae dewis o sillafiad yn y Gymraeg, gyda'r ddwy ffurf yn cael eu cyfrif yn gywir. Enghraifft o hyn yw *project* a *prosiect*. Mewn achosion fel hyn, mater o gysondeb ac arddull tŷ, nid cywirdeb, yw dewis y naill ffurf yn lle'r llall.

O ran orgraff, ceisiwyd cadw at lythrennau'r wyddor Gymraeg, ac felly 'cilo' a 'sinc' a geir yn y Gymraeg yn y Termiadur hwn, ac nid 'kilo' a 'zinc'. Y mae'r symbolau rhyngwladol wrth gwrs, megis y 'k' am 'cilo' a'r symbolau am yr elfennau cemegol, yn aros yn ddigyfnewid. Yr unig eithriadau i hyn yw enwau priod a thermau crefyddol, sy'n cadw'u sillafiad gwreiddiol, neu'r trawslythreniad cydnabyddedig i'r ysgrif Rufeinig os ydynt wedi'u trawslythrennu o ryw ysgrif arall (gweler adran 11 isod).

7 Deall ystyr term

Mae'n bwysig deall ystyr y termau sy'n cael eu defnyddio. Gall camgyfieithu ddigwydd wrth chwilio mewn geiriadur a chael hyd i derm sy'n edrych fel cyfieithiad, ond sydd mewn gwirionedd yn cyfieithu ystyr cwbl wahanol. Felly gall gair megis 'grain' yn Saesneg fod â nifer o ystyron iddo ac nid yr un peth yw 'a grain of sand' (gronyn), 'the grain of wood' (graen), a 'grain grown for food' (grawn). Weithiau gall dewis yr ystyr anghywir arwain at gamgymeriad difrifol, fel wrth gamddeall ystyr 'seal' mewn ymadrodd fel 'the seal of Edward I', a'i gyfieithu fel 'morlo Edward I', yn hytrach na 'sêl Edward I'. Y peth pwysicaf i'w gofio felly wrth gyfieithu termau yw na ellir byth gyfieithu gair am air heb ystyried y cysyniad sy'n cael ei fynegi, h.y.

nid term Saesneg = term Cymraeg

ond yn hytrach term Saesneg = cysyniad = term Cymraeg.

Mae *Y Termiadur* yn defnyddio diffiniadau byr mewn cromfachau ar ôl term Saesneg er mwyn gwahaniaethu rhwng geiriau sy'n edrych yr un fath ond sydd ag ystyron gwahanol iddynt. Yr enw technegol ar y diffiniadau cryno hyn yw dadamwyswyr. Weithiau fodd bynnag dim ond un ystyr fydd yn *Y Termiadur*, a bryd hynny, does dim dadamwysydd wedi'i gynnwys. Mae angen defnyddio synnwyr cyffredin, felly, os yw'r cynnig yn *Y Termiadur* i'w weld yn anaddas i'r

cyd-destun, a chwilio a oes ystyr arall posib i'r term. Gall geiriadur uniaith Saesneg da sy'n esbonio'r cysyniad roi arweiniad ar wahanol ystyron termau a fydd yn gymorth i'w cyfieithu i'r Gymraeg.

8 Cyfystyron a chywair iaith

Weithiau mae'n anodd iawn dewis rhwng dau neu fwy o dermau am eu bod yn gyfystyron agos. Yn yr iaith bob dydd, mae rhyddid i ddefnyddio amrywiaeth o eiriau sy'n agos o ran ystyr. Fodd bynnag, ceir cyd-destunau technegol lle mae manwl-gywirdeb cysyniadol yn bwysicach. Yr enw technegol ar y cywair hwn yw 'iaith at ddibenion arbennig'. Po fwyaf technegol y cyd-destun, mwyaf o ofal sydd ei angen i sicrhau cysondeb y ffurfiau safonol. Mae *Y Termiadur* bellach yn rhychwantu ystod eang o bynciau ysgol o oed cynradd hyd at Safon Uwch, a bydd angen mesur o ddoethineb ar ddefnyddwyr i wybod pryd mae'n briodol defnyddio termau technegol a phryd nad oes angen gwneud hynny. Er enghraifft, mae 'munud' mewn ystyr technegol yn golygu ysbaid benodol o amser (60 eiliad). Wrth siarad yn anffurfiol, fodd bynnag, bydd rhywun yn dweud 'aros funud' heb olygu 'aros union 60 eiliad'. Gellid dweud 'aros ychydig', 'aros foment', 'aros eiliad' heb newid ystyr. Mae'n bwysig deall nad oes raid glynu at dermau technegol y tu allan i gywair iaith at ddibenion arbennig, a bod mesur o hyblygrwydd ar gyfer cyd-destunau annhechnegol ac anffurfiol.

Gall fod yn anodd mewn sefyllfa ysgol benderfynu pa mor dechnegol yw cyd-destun arbennig ac, felly, pa mor dechnegol y dylai'r eirfa fod, yn enwedig yn yr ysgol gynradd a gwaelod yr ysgol uwchradd. Fel rheol gyffredinol, os nad oes angen dysgu'r cysyniad technegol, nid oes angen yr eirfa ychwaith. Felly, wrth drafod 'cyflymder' a 'buanedd' ('velocity' a 'speed') nid oes angen gwahaniaethu rhyngddynt ond yng nghyd-destun technegol gwyddoniaeth a mathemateg. Nid oes angen newid 'cyflymder' yn 'buanedd' felly mewn cyd-destunau cyffredinol, annhechnegol.

9 Amrywiadau tafodieithol

Yr unig adeg y ceir eithriad i'r arfer o gynnig un term yn unig yn y Gymraeg ar gyfer term Saesneg yw pan fo gwahaniaeth pendant yn arfer de a gogledd Cymru, e.e. defnyddir 'gwahadden' yn ne Cymru a 'twrch daear' yn y gogledd am y creadur 'mole'. Bryd hynny barnwyd nad oedd yn deg rhoi'r flaenoriaeth i un ardal dros un arall, ac mae'r ddau derm wedi'u cynnwys. Argymhellir bod y ddau derm

yn cael eu cynnwys gyda'i gilydd mewn deunyddiau asesu, ond bod athrawon a disgyblion yn defnyddio'r term sydd yn fwyaf cyfarwydd iddynt hwy. Nid geiriadur tafodieithol yw hwn, fodd bynnag, a, lle barnwyd bod un ffurf yn ddigon derbyniol i fod yn ffurf safonol, nid aethpwyd ati i gynnwys ffurfiau eraill sydd ar gael yn y gwahanol dafodieithoedd.

10 Enwau lleoedd mewn daearyddiaeth

Mae enwau lleoedd ac enwau priod yn peri problemau neilltuol o fewn y cwricwlwm ysgol. Barn athrawon daearyddiaeth ers blynyddoedd yw mai'r ateb gorau yw dilyn y ffurfiau brodorol wrth gyfeirio at enwau lleoedd y tu allan i Gymru, gan ddefnyddio *Yr Atlas Cymraeg Newydd* (CBAC, 1999) fel safon. Lle mae'r ffurfiau brodorol wedi'u hysgrifennu mewn gwyddor wahanol i'r ysgrif Rufeinig, mae'r Atlas yn defnyddio trawslythreniad rhyngwladol yr ysgrif Rufeinig ar gyfer yr enwau hynny. Argymhellir parhau i ddilyn y safon hon wrth ddysgu daearyddiaeth fel pwnc.

Ond mewn cyd-destun cyffredin y tu allan i gylchoedd defnydd technegol gellir dilyn arfer traddodiadol y Gymraeg. Er enghraifft, defnyddir y ffurf Eidalaidd 'Roma' ar brifddinas yr Eidal yn *Yr Atlas Cymraeg Newydd* ac, yng nghyd-destun technegol daearyddol, dylid defnyddio'r ffurf honno. Fodd bynnag, wrth sôn am y ddinas yn gyffredinol, dyweder mewn cyd-destun hanesyddol neu gerddorol, mae'n dal yn dderbyniol cyfeirio at y ddinas fel 'Rhufain'.

11 Termau addysg grefyddol

Mae problem arbennig hefyd gydag enwau sy'n perthyn i grefyddau ar wahân i Gristnogaeth lle mae'r iaith wreiddiol yn defnyddio ysgrif wahanol i'r ysgrif Rufeinig. Mae gan rai o'r ysgrifau hyn fwy o lythrennau na'r ysgrif Rufeinig, a rhaid defnyddio mwy nag un llythyren yn yr ysgrif Rufeinig i'w cyfleu. Er enghraifft, ceir deugain llythyren yn y Gurumukhi, ysgrif sanctaidd y Sikhiaid, a thrawslythrennir un llythyren yn kh, un arall yn k, un arall yn c ac un arall yn ch. Ni cheir y llythrennau 'k', 'q', 'v' a 'x' yn y wyddor Gymraeg, ond mae'r Gymraeg yn dilyn y dull rhyngwladol o Rufeineiddio ysgrifau eraill (er enghraifft ISO 233 ar drawslythrennu llythrennau Arabaidd i lythrennau Rhufeinig). Gellir cymharu hyn â'r ffordd y mae'r Gymraeg yn derbyn enwau priod sy'n cynnwys y llythrennau hyn, er enghraifft, Keller, Quentin a Vivian. Byddai'n gamarweiniol rhoi'r llythyren 'c' yn lle'r llythyren 'k' yn Gymraeg wrth sôn, er enghraifft, am bum 'k' sanctaidd y

Sikhiaid. Ni ddylid ystyried y termau hyn sydd wedi'u benthyg o ieithoedd eraill yn dermau Saesneg, ond yn hytrach fel dyfyniadau o ieithoedd eraill wedi'u trawslythrennu i ysgrif Rufeinig. Yn 1994 cyhoeddwyd *Religious Education: Glossary of Terms* gan yr Awdurdod Cwricwlwm ac Asesu Ysgolion (ACAY) gyda sêl bendith y gwahanol gymunedau crefyddol, a cheir ynddo'r trawslythreniadau derbyniol o eirfa sy'n perthyn i'r gwahanol grefyddau.

Fodd bynnag, fel yn achos enwau lleoedd mewn daearyddiaeth, mewn cyd-destunau cyffredinol, y tu allan i gyfyngiadau defnydd technegol, gellir dilyn arfer traddodiadol y Gymraeg. Er enghraifft, mewn addysg grefyddol, dylid cyfeirio at sefydlydd Islam fel 'Muhammed', ond mewn cyd-destun cyffredinol, gellir defnyddio'r ffurf Gymraeg draddodiadol 'Mohamed'.

12 Dyfynnu termau estron

Mae'n arferol dyfynnu term o iaith arall heb ei gyfieithu i'r Gymraeg mewn cyd-destunau eraill ar wahân i addysg grefyddol. Mae hyn yn gyffredin mewn cerddoriaeth, er enghraifft, lle defnyddir termau Eidaleg megis 'appoggiatura' neu rai Almaeneg megis 'Lied' yn Gymraeg. Yr arfer traddodiadol yn Gymraeg yw defnyddio print italig gyda geiriau estron i ddangos nad geiriau Cymraeg mohonynt. Fodd bynnag, nid oes ffontiau italig ar gael bob amser: gall fod traethawd wedi'i ysgrifennu mewn llawysgrifen, neu gall gwasg fod eisoes wedi clustnodi'r ffont italig at ryw ddiben arall, megis teitlau cyhoeddiadau. Nid yw *Y Termiadur* yn defnyddio print italig ar gyfer geiriau estron.

13 Acronymau

Mae acronymau yn peri problem arbennig yn Gymraeg, ym myd addysg fel mewn llawer maes arall, oherwydd eu dieithrwch, yr angen i dreiglo a hefyd oherwydd bod y llythrennau 'C' a 'G' yn codi mor aml a llafariaid yn llawer llai aml. Oherwydd hyn, ni ddylid cyfieithu acronymau i'r Gymraeg, ac eithrio'r dyrnaid enghreifftiau, megis CBAC (Cyd-bwyllgor Addysg Cymru) a WJEC (Welsh Joint Education Committee), lle mae'r acronym Cymraeg wedi hen blwyfo, neu'r eithriadau prinnach byth (megis ACCAC) lle defnyddir yr acronym Cymraeg (Awdurdod Cymwysterau, Cwricwlwm ac Asesu Cymru) yn Gymraeg ac yn Saesneg. Yr arfer naturiol yn Gymraeg yw defnyddio enw'r corff yn llawn y tro cyntaf mewn sgwrs neu ddogfen ac wedyn gyfeirio at 'yr Awdurdod', 'y Gymdeithas' ac ati os yw hi'n glir pa awdurdod, cymdeithas, corff, undeb ac ati sydd dan sylw.

A

a baratowyd ymlaen llaw *ans* pre-prepared
a cappella *adf* a cappella
â chaead dwbl (am got) *ans* double-breasted
A fwyaf *eb* A major
A leiaf *eb* A minor
â lle gwag cyfartal equispaced
a posteriori (o'r effaith i'r achos) a posteriori
a priori (o'r achos i'r effaith) a priori
a reolir gan gyfrifiadur *ans* computer-controlled
AALL: awdurdod addysg lleol *eg* LEA: local education authority
AB wedi ei estyn *eg* AB produced
ABA neu ABAB ABA or ABAB
abacws *eg* abaci abacus
abad *eg* abadau abbot
abadaeth *eb* abadaethau abbacy
abades *eb* abadesau abbess
abaty *eg* abatai abbey
abdomen *eg* abdomenau abdomen
abdomenol *ans* abdominal
Abendlied *eg* Abendlieder Abendlied
aber *eg* aberoedd mouth
aberth *eg/b* aberthau sacrifice
abid *eg/b* abidau habit
abladiad *eg* abladiadau ablation
abladu *be* ablate
abomaswm *eg* abomasum
abozzo *eg* abozzo
abseil *eg* abseiliau abseil
abseilio *be* abseil
absennol *ans* absent
absenoldeb *eg* absence
absenoldeb heb ei awdurdodi *eg* absenoldebau heb eu hawdurdodi unauthorized absence
absenoldeb mamolaeth *eg* maternity leave
absenoliaeth *eb* absenteeism
absenolwr *eg* absenolwyr absentee
absgisa *eg* abscissa
absgisedd *eg* abscission
absoliwt *ans* absolute
absoliwtiaeth *eb* absolutism
absoliwtiaeth oleuedig *eb* enlightened absolutism
AC AND
academaidd *ans* academic
academi *eb* academïau academy
Academi Frenhinol y Celfyddydau *eb* Royal Academy of Arts, The
Academi Gelf Frenhinol Cymru *eb* Royal Cambrian Academy of Arts
Academi Sgiliau TG *eb* IT Skills Academy
academiaeth *eb* academicism
academydd *eg* academyddion academician
ACAY: Awdurdod Cwricwlwm ac Asesu Ysgolion *eg* SCAA: School Curriculum and Assessment Authority
ACCAC: Awdurdod Cymwysterau, Cwricwlwm ac Asesu Cymru *eg* ACCAC: Qualifications, Curriculum and Assessment Authority for Wales
acciaccatura *eg* acciaccature acciaccatura
acen *eb* acenion (=pwyslais) stress
acen *eb* acenion (yn gyffredinol) accent
acen grom *eb* acenion crwm circumflex
acennog *ans* accented
acennu *be* accent
aciwbigo *be* acupuncture
acme *eg* acme
acolit *eg* acolitiaid acolyte
acordion *eg* acordiynau accordion
acordion piano *eg* acordiynau piano piano accordion
Acrilan *eg* Acrilan
acrobat *eg* acrobatiaid acrobat
acromatig *ans* achromatic
acromatopsia *eg* achromatopsia
acronym *eg* acronymau acronym
acrosentrig *ans* acrocentric
acrosom *eg* acrosome
acrostig *ans* acrostic
acrylig *ans* acrylic
acrylig *eg* acryligion acrylic
acryloid *eg* acryloid
acsis *eg* axis
acson *eg* acsonau axon
actif *ans* active
actifadu *be* activate
actifadydd *eg* actifadyddion activator
actifadydd adwaith *eg* reaction activator
actifadydd ensym *eg* actifadyddion ensym enzyme activator
actifedig *ans* activated
actifedd *eg* actifeddau activity
actifedd ensymig *eg* enzyme activity
actifedd optegol *eg* optical activity
actifiant *eg* actifiannau activation
actiniwm *eg* actinium
actinoid *ans* actinoid
actinomorffig *ans* actinomorphic
acwafeithrin *be* aquaculture

acwariwm *eg* acwaria aquarium
acwatint *eg* aquatint
acwsteg *eb* acoustics
acwstig *ans* acoustic
achen *eg* achenau achene
achludiad *eg* achludiadau occlusion
achludol *ans* occluded
achos (=peth enwog) *eg* achosion affair
achos (llys etc) *eg* achosion proceedings
achos (yn gyffredinol) *eg* achosion case
achos agos *eg* achosion agos proximate cause
achos all-gontract *eg* achosion all-gontract extra contractual referral
achos anrheolaidd *eg* achosion anrheolaidd anomaly
achos cyntaf *eg* first cause
Achos Dyffryn Taf *eg* Taff Vale Case
achos effeithlon *eg* efficient cause
achos eithaf *eg* achosion eithaf ultimate cause
achos ffiniol *eg* achosion ffiniol borderline case
achos llygredd *eg* achosion llygredd cause of pollution
achos llys troseddau rhyfel *eg* achosion llys troseddau rhyfel war crimes trial
achos priodasol *eg* achosion priodasol matrimonial matter
achos sifil *eg* civil proceedings
achos terfannol *eg* limiting case
achos terfynol *eg* final cause
achoseg *eb* aetiology
achosegol *ans* aetiological
achosi *be* cause
achosiad *eg* causation
achosiaeth *eb* causality; causation
achosiaeth gronnus *eb* cumulative causation
achosion afiechyd *ell* causes of ill health
achosol *ans* causal
achrediad *eg* achrediadau accreditation
achredu *be* accredit
achredu dysgu blaenorol *be* accreditation of prior learning
achub *be* rescue
achub bywyd *ans* life-saving
achubiaeth *eb* redemption
achwynwr *eg* achwynwyr litigant
achwynydd *eg* achwynyddion plaintiff
achyddiaeth *eb* genealogy
achyddol *ans* genealogical
ad hoc *ans* ad hoc
ad lib *eg* ad lib
ad libio *be* ad lib
ADAG: Addysg Dechnegol a Galwedigaethol *eb* TVEI: Technical Vocational Education Initiative
adain *eb* adenydd wing
adain dde *eb* right wing
adain olwyn *eb* adenydd olwyn spoke
adalw *be* retrieve
adalw ac adfer retrieving and restoring
adalw data *be* data retrieval
adalw gwaith *be* retrieve work
adalw gwybodaeth *be* retrieve information
adalw gwybodaeth *be* information retrieval
adalw pob cofnod *be* retrieve all records
adalwad *eb* adalwadau retrieval
adalwadwy *ans* retrievable
adamsugniad *eg* reabsorption
adborth *eg* adborthion feedback
adborth cwsmeriaid *eg* customer feedback
adborth cymheiriaid *eg* peer feedback
adborth negatif *eg* negative feedback
adborth negyddol (beirniadaeth) *eg* negative feedback
adborth o'r ystafell ddosbarth *eg* classroom feedback
adborth positif *eg* positive feedback
adborthi *be* feedback
adbryniad ecwitïol *eg* equitable redemption
ad-daladwy *ans* repayable
ad-daliad *eg* ad-daliadau refund, rebate, repayment
ad-daliad morgais *eg* ad-daliadau morgais mortgage repayment
ad-daliad rhent *eg* ad-daliadau rhent rent rebate
ad-daliad treth *eg* ad-daliadau treth tax rebate
ad-daliad treth *eg* ad-daliadau treth rate rebate
ad-dalu *be* repay, refund
ad-drefnu *be* reshuffle
ad-drefnu llawnder *be* dispose of fullness
adechelinol *ans* adaxial
adeilad *eg* adeiladau building
adeilad barics *eg* adeiladau barics barrack building
adeilad cyhoeddus *eg* adeiladau cyhoeddus public building
adeilad ffrâm bortal *eg* portal framed building
adeiladau *ell* premises
adeiladau ac adeileddau buildings and structures
adeiladol *ans* constructive
adeiladu *be* build
adeiladu clos *be* high density building
adeiladu ffordd *be* road construction
adeiladu'n bwyllog *be* steady build-up
adeiladwaith *eg* adeiladweithiau construction; structure
adeiladwaith blwch *eg* box construction
adeiladwaith coes a rheilen *eg* leg and rail construction
adeiladwaith cyfoes *eg* modern construction
adeiladwaith drôr *eg* drawer construction
adeiladwaith ffrâm *eg* frame construction
adeiladwaith ffrâm *eg* framed construction
adeiladwaith hoelbren *eg* dowel construction
adeiladwaith llafnog *eg* sandwich construction
adeiladwaith normal *eg* normal construction
adeiladwaith panel *eg* panel construction
adeiladwaith sgerbwd *eg* carcass construction
adeiladwaith stôl *eg* stool construction

adeiladwaith sylfaenol *eg* basic construction
adeiladwaith traddodiadol *eg* traditional construction
adeiladwaith tri dimensiwn *eg* three-dimensional construction
adeiledd *eg* structure
adeiledd cellog *eg* adeileddau cellog cellular structure
adeiledd cemegol *eg* chemical structure
adeiledd clustog *eg* adeileddau clustog pillow structure
adeiledd cordiol *eg* adeileddau cordiol chordal structure
adeiledd creiriol *eg* adeileddau creiriol relict structure
adeiledd electronig *eg* adeileddau electronig electronic structure
adeiledd enfawr *eg* adeileddau enfawr giant structure
adeiledd gorwthiad *eg* adeileddau gorwthiad imbricated structure
adeiledd haenog *eg* layered structure
adeiledd moleciwlaidd *eg* adeileddau moleciwlaidd molecular structure
adeiledd oedran *eg* adeileddau oedran age structure
adeiledd pridd *eg* soil structure
adeiledd yr atom *eg* atomic structure
adeileddiaeth (mewn mathemateg, celf) *eb* constructivism
adeileddol (yn gyffredinol) *ans* structural
adeileddol (mewn mathemateg, celf) *ans* constructivist
adeiledd-proses-cam *eg* structure-process-stage
adeileddwr *eg* adeileddwyr constructivist
adeileddwr cymdeithasol *eg* social constructivist
adeiniog *ans* winged
adend *eg* adendau addend
adendriad *eg* attainder
adendro *be* attaint
adendwm *eg* adenda addendum
adenillion *ell* return earnings
adenillion ar asedau net *ell* return on net assets
adenin *eg* adenine
adennill *be* regain; recoup; reclaim
adennill costau *be* break even
adennill cydbwysedd *be* regain balance
adennill y bêl *be* regain the ball
adenosin *eg* adenosine
adenosin deuffosffad *eg* adenosine diphosphate (ADP)
adenosin monoffosffad *eg* adenosine monophosphate (AMP)
adenosin triffosffad (ATP) *eg* adenosine triphosphate
adenyl cyclas *eg* adenyl cyclase
aderyn pysgysol *eg* adar pysgysol fish eating bird
adfach *eg* adfachau barb
adfachyn *eg* adfachau barbule
adfail *eg* adfeilion ruin
adfeddiad *eg* adfeddiadau appropriation
adfeddu *be* appropriate
Adfent *eg* Advent
adfer (anghytgord mewn cerddoriaeth) *be* resolve
adfer (yn gyffredinol) *be* restore; recover; restitute
adfer amgylcheddau sydd wedi'u difrodi *be* restore damaged environments
adfer cydrannau *be* restoring components
adfer cyflwr ehangu *be* restore expand state
adfer ffeil *be* file recovery
adfer ffynhonnell y data *be* restore data source
adfer golwg *be* restore view
adfer golwg golygu *be* restore editing view
adfer wedi'r anaesthetig *be* post-anaesthetic recovery
adferadwy *ans* recoverable
adferiad (=gwellhad) *eg* adferiadau rehabilitation
adferiad (anghytgord) *eg* adferiadau resolution
adferiad (yn gyffredinol) *eg* adferiadau restoration; recovery; restitution
adferiad digymell *eg* spontaneous recovery
adferiad economaidd *eg* economic recovery
adferiad gwybyddol *eg* cognitive rehabilitation
adferiad y Bourboniaid *eg* Bourbon restoration
adfewniad *eg* adfewniadau re-entry
adfewniadol *ans* re-entrant
adfewnio *be* re-enter
adfewnol *ans* re-entrant
adfocad *eg* adfocadau advocate
adfowri *eg* adfowrïau advowry
adfowswn *eg* adfowsynau advowson
adfywio (ardal etc) *be* regenerate
adfywio (claf) *be* resuscitate
adfywio ceg wrth geg *be* mouth-to-mouth resuscitation
adfywio'r galon a'r ysgyfaint *be* cardiopulmonary resuscitation
adgyfuno genynnol *be* gene recombination
Adi Granth *eg* Adi Granth
adiabatig *ans* adiabatic
adiad *eg* adiadau addition
adiad electroffilig *eg* electrophilic addition
adict *eg* adictiaid addict
adio *be* add
adiol *ans* additive
adiolyn *eg* adiolion additive
adlach *eb* adlachau backlash
adlam *eg* adlamau recoil; rebound, glance; bounce back
adlam y cysylltau *eg* adlamau'r cysylltau contact bounce
adlamiad elastig *eg* elastic recoil
adlamol *ans* resilient
adlamu *be* recoil; rebound, glance; bounce back
adlamu allan *be* drop out
adlenwad *eg* adlenwadau refill
adlenwi *be* refill

adleoladwy *ans* relocatable
adleoli *be* relocate
adleolydd *eg* adleolyddion relocator
adlewyrch *ans* reflected
adlewyrchedig *ans* reflected
adlewyrchiad *eg* adlewyrchiadau reflection
adlewyrchiad mewn llinell *eg* reflection in a line
adlewyrchiad mewnol cyflawn *eg* total internal reflection
adlewyrchu *be* reflect
adlewyrchydd *eg* adlewyrchyddion reflector
adlif *eg* adlifau resequent
adlifiad *eg* adlifiadau reflux
adlifo *be* reflux
adlifol *ans* reflux
adlithro oed *be* age regression
adlog *eg* adlogau compound interest
adloniant *eg* adloniannau entertainment: recreation; pastime
adloniant cefn gwlad *eg* countryside recreation
adloniant tymhorol *eg* seasonal entertainment
adluniad arlunydd *eg* adluniadau arlunydd artist's reconstruction
adlunio *be* remodel
adlyn *eg* adlynion adhesive
adlyn ardrawol *eg* adlynion ardrawol impact adhesive
adlyn bondio *eg* bonding adhesive
adlyn resin *eg* adlynion resin resin adhesive
adlyn synthetig *eg* adlynion synthetig synthetic adhesive
adlyn thermo-galedu *eg* thermo-hardening adhesive
adlyniad *eg* adlyniadau adhesion
adlyniad *eg* adlyniadau adherence
adlynol *ans* adhesive
adlynu *be* adhere
adnabod (yn gyffredinol) *be* recognize
adnabod (=sefydlu pwy yw rhywun etc) *be* identify
adnabod anghenion *be* identifying needs
adnabod awtodeip *be* autotype recognition
adnabod lleferydd *be* speech recognition
adnabod nodau *be* character recognition
adnabod nodau gweledol *be* optical character recognition
adnabod nodau inc magnetig *be* magnetic ink character recognition
adnabod ôl bys genynnol *be* genetic fingerprinting
adnabyddiad *eg* adnabyddiadau recognition
adnabyddiaeth *eb* identification
adnabyddus *ans* well-known
adnau *eg* adneuon deposit
adneuwr *eg* adneuwyr depositor
adnewyddadwy *ans* renewable
adnewyddedig *ans* rejuvenated
adnewyddiad *eg* adnewyddiadau renewal; renovation
adnewyddiad trefol *eg* urban renewal
adnewyddu (a gwneud yn ifanc eto) *be* rejuvenate
adnewyddu (a thrwsio) *be* recondition
adnewyddu (hen adeilad etc) *be* renovate
adnewyddu (yn gyffredinol) *be* renew
adnod *eb* adnodau verse
adnodd *eg* adnoddau resource
adnodd adnewyddadwy *eg* adnoddau adnewyddadwy renewable resource
adnodd anadnewyddadwy *eg* adnoddau anadnewyddadwy non-renewable resource
adnodd dysgu *eg* adnoddau dysgu learning resource
adnodd ffisegol *eg* adnoddau ffisegol physical resource
adnoddau a meddalwedd technoleg gwybodaeth a chyfathrebu ICT Resources and Software
adnoddau adnewyddol *ell* renewable resources
adnoddau astudio unigol *ell* self-study materials
adnoddau clyweled *ell* audio visual aids
adnoddau dynol *ell* human resources
adnoddau llafur *ell* manpower
adnoddau mwynol *ell* mineral resources
adnoddau naturiol *ell* natural resources
adnoddau prin *ell* scarce resources
adnoddau segur *ell* idle resources
adnoddau wedi dod i ben resource exhausted
adolygiad *eg* adolygiadau review
adolygiad perfformiad unigol *eg* adolygiadau perfformiad unigol individual performance review
adolygiad treigl *eg* adolygiadau treigl rolling review
adolygu (=asesu'n ffurfiol) *be* review
adolygu (ar gyfer arholiad etc) *be* revise
adolygu canlyniadau *be* review of results
adolygu graddau *be* grade review
adolygu'r achosion ffiniol *be* borderline reviewing
adolygydd *eg* adolygwyr reviewer; critic
adraddiant *eg* aggradation
adraddu *be* aggrade
adran (=rhaniad gweinyddol) *eb* adrannau department
adran (=rhaniad daearyddol) *eb* adrannauarea
adran (COBOL) *eb* adrannau division
adran (mewn cynghrair etc) *eb* adrannau division
adran (mewn cynhwysydd) *eb* adrannau compartment
adran (mewn llyfr etc) *eb* adrannau section
Adran Addysg a Chyflogaeth *eb* Department for Education and Employment
Adran Addysg y Swyddfa Gymreig *eb* WOED: Welsh Office Department of Education
adran annibynnol *eb* adrannau annibynnol independent section
adran arfog *eb* adrannau arfog armoured division
adran bres *eb* adrannau pres brass section
adran brosesu data *eb* adrannau prosesu data data processing department
adran cyfeiriadau *eb* adrannau cyfeiriadau address area

adran chwythbrennau *eb* adrannau chwythbrennau woodwind section
adran dai *eb* adrannau tai housing department
adran daro *eb* adrannau taro percussion section
Adran Diwydiant a Masnach *eb* Department of Trade and Industry
adran ddamweiniau ac achosion brys *eb* adrannau damweiniau ac achosion brys accident and emergency department
adran euraid *eb* adrannau euraid golden section
adran farchnata *eb* adrannau marchnata marketing department
Adran Gwarchod Defnyddwyr *eb* Consumer Protection Department
adran gwasanaethau cymdeithasol *eb* adrannau gwasanaethau cymdeithasolsocial services department
adran gyfeirio *eb* adrannau cyfeirio reference section
adran gyfredol *eb* adrannau cyfredol current section
adran gynhyrchu *eb* adrannau cynhyrchu production department
Adran Iechyd yr Amgylchedd *eb* Environmental Health Department
adran ieuenctid *eb* adrannau ieuenctid youth section
adran lanweithio *eb* adrannau glanweithio cleansing department
adran llinynnau *eb* adrannau llinynnau string section
adran nesaf *eb* next section
adran o'r fyddin *eb* adrannau'r fyddin army division
adran oeri *eb* adrannau oeri chilling compartment
Adran Safonau Masnachu *eb* Trading Standards Department
adran swyddogaethol *eb* adrannau swyddogaethol functional area
adran weinyddu *eb* adrannau gweinyddu administration department
adran weithredol *eb* adrannau gweithredol executive
Adran Wladol *eb* Adrannau Gwladol State Department
adran y meingefn *eb* lumbar region
adrannau ar wahân *ell* separate compartments
adrannau'r wyddor *ell* alphabet agencies
adrannol (=a wnaed mewn rhannau) *ans* sectional
adrannol (am ysgolion etc) *ans* departmental
adrenalin *eg* adrenalin
adrewiad *eg* regelation
adrodd *be* report
adrodd yn ôl *be* report back
adrodd yn ôl *be* debriefing
adroddiad (=darn adrodd) *eg* adroddiadau narration
adroddiad (=disgrifiad) *eg* adroddiadau account
adroddiad (am ddogfen etc) *eg* adroddiadau report
adroddiad cynhadledd *eg* adroddiadau cynhadledd conference report
adroddiad gwaith maes *eg* adroddiadau gwaith maes fieldwork report
adroddiad interim *eg* adroddiadau interim interim report
adroddiad llafar *eg* adroddiadau llafar oral report
adroddiad terfynol *eg* adroddiadau terfynol final report
adroddiad tywydd *eg* adroddiadau tywydd weather report
adroddiad ysgol *eg* adroddiadau ysgol school report
adroddnod *eg* adroddnodau reciting note
adroddwr *eg* adroddwyr narrator
adsefydlu niwroseicolegol *be* neuropsychological rehabilitation
Adulamiaid *ell* Adullamites
adwaith *eg* adweithiau reaction
adwaith ad-drefnu *eg* rearrangement reaction
adwaith adio *eg* addition reaction
adwaith alergaidd *eg* adweithiau alergaidd allergic reaction
adwaith amnewid *eg* substitution reaction
adwaith cadwynol *eg* adweithiau cadwynol chain reaction
adwaith caws tyramin *eg* tyramine cheese reaction
adwaith cemegol *eg* adweithiau cemegol chemical reaction
adwaith cildroadwy *eg* adweithiau cildroadwy reversible reaction
adwaith cychwynnol *eg* adweithiau cychwynnol initiation reaction
adwaith cyddwyso *eg* condensation reaction
adwaith cyflym *eg* adweithiau cyflym fast reaction
adwaith cyfnewid *eg* exchange reaction
adwaith dadleoli *eg* displacement reaction
adwaith dileu *eg* adweithiau dileu elimination reaction
adwaith electrolytig *eg* adweithiau electrolytig electrolytic reaction
adwaith galar *eg* adweithiau galar grief reaction
adwaith golau *eg* light reaction
adwaith gradd dau *eg* second order reaction
adwaith gradd tri *eg* third order reaction
adwaith gradd un *eg* first order reaction
adwaith imiwn *eg* adweithiau imiwn immune reaction
adwaith terfynu *eg* termination reaction
adwaith tri cham *eg* adweithiau tri cham three-stage reaction
adwaith thermit *eg* thermit reaction
adwaith y Pab *eg* papal reaction
adwaith ymholltiad *eg* fission reaction
adweadu *be* re-texture
adweithedd *eg* adweitheddau reactance
adweithedd *eg* adweitheddau reactivity
adweithio *be* react
adweithiol *ans* reactive
adweithydd *eg* adweithyddion reactor; reagent; reactant

adweithydd Benedict *eg* Benedict reagent
adweithydd bridiol *eg* adweithyddion bridiol breeder reactor
Adweithydd Millon *eg* Millon's Reagent
adweithydd nwy-oeredig uwch *eg* adweithyddion nwy-oeredig uwch advanced gas-cooler reactor
adwerthiant *eg* adwerthiannau resale
adwerthol *ans* retail
adwerthu *be* retail; resale
adwerthwr *eg* adwerthwyr retailer
adwreiddyn *eg* adwreiddiau adventitious root
adwy *eb* adwyau gap
adwy (mewn electroneg, cyfrifiadureg) *eb* adwyon gate
adwy AC *eb* adwyon AC AND gate
adwy NEU *eb* adwyon NEU OR gate
adwy NIAC *eb* adwyon NIAC NAND gate
adwy NID *eb* adwyon NID NOT gate
adwy NIEU *eb* adwyon NIEU NOR gate
adwy resymeg *eb* adwyon rhesymeg logic gate
adwy samplu *eb* sampling gate
adwyog *ans* gated
adydd *eg* adyddion adder
adydd cyflawn *eg* adyddion cyflawn full-adder
adydd cyfresol *eg* adyddion cyfresol serial adder
adydd paralel *eg* adyddion paralel parallel adder
Adda *eg* Adam
Adda o Frynbuga *eg* Adam of Usk
addas *ans* suited
addas *ans* appropriate
addas o ran datblygiad *ans* developmentally appropriate
addasadwy *ans* adaptable
addasiad *eg* addasiadau modification
addasiad *eg* addasiadau adaptation
addasiad patrwm *eg* addasiadau patrwm adaptation of pattern
addasol *ans* adaptive
addasu (at ddiben arbennig) *be* customize
addasu (yn gyffredinol) *be* adapt; modify; adjust
addasu byrfyfyr *be* improvise
addasu cell *be* modify cell
addasu cyfeiriad *be* address modification
addasu dwysedd *be* adjust intensity
addasu dyfnder lliw *be* modify colour depth
addasu i'r tywyllwch *be* dark adaption
addasu llyfnhau cromlin *be* modify curve smoothing
addasu maes *be* modify field
addasu rhaglen *be* program modification
addasu ymddygiad *be* behaviour modification
addasu ystod data *be* modify data range
addasu'r barrau offer *be* customize toolbars
addasu'r botymau *be* customize buttons
addasu'r gyllideb *be* adjust the budget
addaswyd ddiwethaf last modified
addasydd *eg* addasyddion adaptor
addasydd rhyngwyneb perifferol *eg* addasyddion rhyngwyneb perifferol peripheral interface adaptor
addewid manteisiol *eg* advantageous promise
addoli *be* worship
addoli ar y cyd *be* collective worship
addoli cyndadau *be* ancestor worship
addoliad (mewn cywair hynafol, eglwysig) *eg* adoration
addoliad (yn gyffredinol) *be* addoliadau worship
addoliad amgen *eg* addoliadau amgen alternative worship
addoliad un grefydd *eg* one religion worship
addurn *eg* addurniadau decoration; ornament; trimming; adornment
addurn arwyneb *eg* addurniadau arwyneb surface decoration
addurn cromlinog *eg* addurniadau cromlinog curvilinear decoration
addurn glain *eg* addurniadau glain bead trimming
addurn gosod *eg* addurniadau gosod applied ornament
addurn gwaelod *eg* addurniadau gwaelod base moulding
addurn gwrthgwyr *eg* addurniadau gwrthgwyr wax-resist decoration
addurn mewnol *eg* addurniadau mewnol interior decoration
addurn pen hoelen *eg* addurniadau pen hoelen nail-head ornament
addurn wy a saethell *eg* egg and dart treatment
addurnedig *ans* decorated
addurniad *eg* addurniadau ornamentation: embellishment
addurniadau murol *ell* mural decorations
addurno *be* decorate; adorn
addurno â les *be* trim with lace
addurno mewnol *be* interior decorating
addurnod *eg* addurnodau grace note
addurnol *ans* decorative: ornate; ornamental
addysg *eb* education
addysg alwedigaethol *eb* vocational education
addysg amgylcheddol *eb* environmental education
addysg anffurfiol *eb* informal education
addysg arbennig *eb* special education
addysg athrawon *eb* teacher education
addysg barhaus *eb* continuing education
addysg bellach *eb* further education
addysg bellach uwch *eb* advanced further education
addysg bersonol *eb* personal education
addysg cyfrwng Cymraeg *eb* Welsh-medium education
addysg dechnegol *eb* technical education
addysg defnyddwyr *eb* consumer education
addysg drwy gymorth cyfrifiadur *eb* computer aided education
addysg drwy'r post *eb* correspondence education
addysg ddwyieithog *eb* bilingual education
addysg ddyneiddiol *eb* humanistic education

addysg elfennol *eb* elementary education
addysg elusennol *eb* charity education
addysg fasnachol *eb* commercial education
addysg feithrin *eb* nursery education
addysg foesol *eb* moral education
addysg ganolradd *eb* intermediate education
addysg gartref *eb* home education
addysg gorfforol *eb* physical education
addysg grefyddol *eb* religious education
addysg grefyddol enwadol *eb* denominational religious education
addysg gydadferol *eb* compensatory education
addysg gyfun *eb* comprehensive education
addysg gymunedol *eb* community education
addysg gynradd *eb* primary education
addysg gyrfaoedd *eb* careers education
addysg gysylltiedig â gwaith (AGG) *eb* work-related education
addysg iechyd *eb* health education
addysg mewn swydd *eb* in-service education
addysg mewnfudwyr *eb* immigrant education
addysg o bell *eb* distance education
addysg oedolion *eb* adult education
addysg orfodol *eb* compulsory education
addysg plant ganolog *eb* child-centred education
addysg ran amser *eb* part-time education
addysg rhyw *eb* sex education
addysg uwch *eb* higher education
addysg uwchradd *eb* secondary education
addysg wirfoddol *eb* voluntary education
addysg wrth-hiliol *eb* anti-racist education
addysg wyddonol ffurfiol *eb* formal science education
addysg ymaddasol *eb* adaptive education
addysg ysbrydol a moesol *eb* spiritual and moral education
addysgadwy *ans* educable
addysgedd *eg* educability
addysgiadol *ans* educative
addysgol *ans* educational
addysgu *be* teach
addysgu am foeseg *be* ethical teaching
addysgu anffurfiol *be* informal teaching
addysgu cefnogol *be* companion teaching
addysgu cydweithredol *be* cooperative teaching
addysgu drwy weithgaredd *be* activity teaching
addysgu o bell *be* distance teaching
addysgu pellach *be* future teaching
addysgu plant ganolog *be* child-centred teaching
addysgu tîm *be* team teaching
addysgwr *eg* addysgwyr educationalist
aeddfed *ans* mature
aeddfediad *eg* maturation
aeddfedol *ans* maturational
aeddfedrwydd *eg* maturity
aeddfedrwydd corfforol *eg* physical maturity
aeddfedrwydd datblygiad *eg* developmental maturity
aeddfedrwydd diweddar *eg* late maturity
aeddfedu *be* mature
ael *eb* aeliau eyebrow; brow
aelod (o gymdeithas, tîm etc) *eg* aelodau member
aelod (o'r corff) *eg* aelodau limb
► **aelod artiffisial** *eg* aelodau artiffisial artificial limb
aelod cyfetholedig *eg* aelodau cyfetholedig co-opted member
aelod cyswllt *eg* aelodau cyswllt affiliated member
aelod cysylltiol *eg* aelodau cysylltiol associate member
aelod disgynnol dolen Henle *eg* loop of Henle descending limb
aelod esgynnol dolen Henle *eg* loop of Henle ascending limb
aelod o dîm *eg* aelodau o dîm team member
aelod o Fyddin yr Iachawdwriaeth *eg* aelodau o Fyddin yr Iachawdwriaeth Salvationist
aelod o fframwaith *eg* aelodau o fframwaith framework member
aelod o gôr *eg* aelodau o gôr chorister
aelod o'r tîm *eg* member of the team
Aelod Seneddol (AS) *eg* Aelodau Seneddol Member of Parliament
aelodaeth *eb* membership
aelwyd *eb* aelwydydd hearth
aelwyd bresyddu *eb* aelwydydd presyddu brazing hearth
aelwyd dro *eb* aelwydydd tro revolving hearth
aeolaidd *ans* aeolian
aeon *eg* aeon
aer *eg* air
aer arctig *eg* arctic air
aer cyfnewid *eg* tidal air
aer cynnes *eg* warm air
aer cywasgedig *eg* compressed air
aer gwacáu *eg* exhaust air
aer gweddillol *eg* residual air
aer mewnanadledig *eg* inspired air
aer uchaf *eg* upper air
aerdymheru *be* air-condition
aerdymherus *ans* air-conditioned
aerdymherydd *eg* aerdymherwyr air-conditioner
aergaledu *be* air hardening
aerglo *eg* aergloeon air lock
aerglos *ans* airtight
aergorff *eg* aergyrff air-mass
aerobeg *eb* aerobics
aerobig *ans* aerobic
aerodynameg *eb* aerodynamics
aerograffiaeth *eb* aerography
aeroleg *eb* aerology
aeronen *eb* aeron berry
aerosol *eg* aerosolau aerosol
aersgriw *eb* aersgriwiau airscrew

afal bwyta *eg* afalau bwyta dessert apple
afal coginio *eg* afalau coginio cooking apple
afal derw *eg* afalau derw oak gall
afal pob *eg* afalau pob baked apple
afal wedi'i stiwio *eg* afalau wedi'u stiwio stewed apple
afentwrin *eg* aventurine
afiach *ans* diseased
afiechyd *eg* illness
afiechyd llym *eg* acute illness
afiechyd marwol *eg* afiechydon marwol terminal illness
afiechyd meddwl *eg* afiechydon meddwl mental illness
afiechyd y galon *eg* cardiac disease
aflem *ans* obtuse
aflendid *eg* squalor
afleoli *be* dislocate
afleoliad *eg* afleoliadau dislocation
aflinol *ans* non-linear
afliwiad *eg* afliwiadau discolouration
afliwio *be* discolour
aflonydd *ans* restless
aflonydd *ans* disturbed
aflonyddgar *ans* disruptive
aflonyddiad *eg* aflonyddiadau perturbation
aflonyddu *be* disrupt
aflonyddwch *eg* disruption; disturbance; unrest; disruptiveness
aflonyddwch cymdeithasol *eg* social unrest
aflonyddwch meddwl *eg* mental disturbance
afluniad *eg* afluniadau distortion
afluniad clipio *eg* clipping distortion
aflunio *be* distort
► **aflunio corlun** *be* distort sprite
aflwydd Sbaenaidd, yr *eg* Spanish ulcer
aflym *ans* obtuse
afocado *eg* afocados avocado pear
afon *eb* afonydd river
afon afrwydd *eb* afonydd afrwydd misfit river
afon blethog *eb* afonydd plethog braided river
afon eira tawdd *eb* afonydd eira tawdd snow fed river
afondiroedd *ell* riverlands
afonig *eb* afonigau rivulet
afonladrad *eg* river capture
afonladrad *eg* piracy
afonol *ans* fluvial; riverine
afradlonedd *eg* afradloneddau dissipation
afradloni *be* dissipate
afreolaidd *ans* improper; irregular; anomalous
afreoleidd-dra *eg* irregularity
afresymol *ans* absurd; irrational
afrlladen *eb* afrlladau consecrated wafer
afu *eg* afuoedd liver
AFF (ar draws fflatiau nyten hecsagonol) AF
affaith *eg* affeithiau affect
affasia *eg* aphasia
affasia anhawster ynganu (Broca) *eg* non-fluent (Broca's) aphasia
affasia arunigedd *eg* isolation aphasia
affasia Wernicke *eg* Wernicke's aphasia
affeithio *be* affect
affeithiol *ans* affective
affeithioldeb negyddol *eg* negative affectivity
affeithiolrwydd *eg* affectivity
affelion *eg* aphelion
afferol *ans* afferent
affin *eg* affine
affinedd *eg* affineddau affinity
affinedd electronol *eg* electron affinity
affwys *eg* affwysau abyss
affwysol *ans* abysmal
agape *eg* agape
agat *eg* agatau agate
agen (hir a chul) *eb* agennau slit
agen (mewn peiriant) *eb* agennau slot
agen (mewn craig) *eb* agennau fissure
agen ehangu *eb* agennau ehangu expansion slot
agen saethu *eb* agennau saethu arrowloop
agen T *eb* agennau T T-slot
agen y dagell *eb* agennau tagellau gill slit
agenda *eg* agendâu agenda
agenda awtobeilot *eg* agendâu awtobeilot autopilot agenda
agendor *eb* agendorau chasm
agennog *ans* slotted
agennu *be* slitting
ager *eg* steam
agerblygu *be* steam bending
agergist *eb* agergistiau steam chest
ageru *be* steam
agnawd *ans* agnate
agnosia *eg* agnosia
agnosia cyfarganfod *eg* apperceptive agnosia
agnosia cyffwrdd *eg* tactile agnosia
agnosia cysylltiadol *eg* associative agnosia
agnosia'r golwg *eg* visual agnosia
agnosticiaeth *eb* agnosticism
agnostig *ans* agnostic
agor (=datod) *be* unfasten
agor (mewn chwarel) *eg* agorydd chamber
agor (rhoi cychwyn ar) *be* initiate
agor (yn gyffredinol) *be* open
agor ffeil *be* open file
agor ffeil ddata gyfun *be* open merge-data-file
agor lleoliad gwe *be* open web location
agor tuag i mewn ac allan open inwards and outwards
agor y bowlio *be* open the bowling
agor y naill ffordd a'r llall *be* open both ways
agor y switsh *be* put the switch off
agor y tap *be* turn the tap on, open the tap
agoraffobia *eg* agoraphobia

agorawd *eb* agorawdau overture
agorawd cyngerdd *eb* agorawdau cyngerdd concert overture
agorawd Eidalaidd *eb* agorawdau Eidalaidd Italian overture
agorawd Ffrengig *eb* agorawdau Ffrengig French overture
agored (=heb gysgod) *ans* exposed
agored (yn gyffredinol) *ans* open
agorell *eb* agorellau reamer
agorell baralel *eb* agorellau paralel parallel reamer
agorell dapr *eb* agorellau tapr taper reamer
agorell frasnaddu *eb* agorellau brasnaddu roughing reamer
agorell gymwysadwy *eb* agorellau cymwysadwy adjustable reamer
agorell gymwysadwy *eb* agorellau cymwysadwy expanding reamer
agorell law *eb* agorellau llaw hand reamer
agorell maint sefydlog *eb* agorellau maint sefydlog fixed size reamer
agorell rychiog *eb* agorellau rhychiog fluted reamer
agorellu *be* reaming
agorfa (ar gyfer aer, nwy etc) *eb* agorfeydd vent
agorfa (mewn teclyn) *eb* agorfeydd aperture
agorfa (yn y corff) *eb* agorfeydd orifice
agorfa fach *eb* agorfeydd bach fine orifice
agorfa orthogonol *eb* agorfeydd orthogonol orthogonal orifice
agoriad (=mynedfa) *eg* agoriadau entrance
agoriad (switsh) *eg* agoriadau key
agoriad (yn gyffredinol) *eg* agoriadau opening
agoriad blaen *eg* agoriadau blaen front opening
agoriad cefn *eg* agoriadau cefn back opening
agoriad cudd *eg* agoriadau cudd concealed opening
agoriad di-dor *eg* agoriadau di-dor strip opening
agoriad di-dor *eg* agoriadau di-dor continuous lap
agoriad drôr *eg* agoriadau drôr drawer opening
agoriad gweini *eg* agoriadau gweini hatch
agoriad placed ffrog *eg* dress placket opening
agoriad plet bocs *eg* agoriadau pletiau bocs box pleat opening
agoriad rhwymog *eg* agoriadau rhwymog bound opening
agoriad swyddogol *eg* agoriadau swyddogol official opening
agoriad wedi'i wynebu *eg* agoriadau wedi'u hwynebu faced opening
agoriadol (am araith/darlith) *ans* inaugural
agoriadol (yn gyffredinol) *ans* opening
agos *ans* close
agosatrwydd *eg* intimacy
agosáu *be* approach
agosbwynt *eg* agosbwyntiau near point
agoslun *eg* agosluniau close-up
agramadegiaeth *eb* agrammatism
agranwlocyt *eg* agranwlocytau agranulocyte
agreg *eg* agregau aggregate
agregau concrit *ell* concrete aggregates
agregu *be* aggregate
agwedd *eb* agweddau attitude; aspect
agwedd arosgo *eb* agweddau arosgo oblique aspect
agwedd dadol *eb* paternalism
agwedd dosraniad *eb* partition aspect
agwedd ddiwylliannol *eb* agweddau diwylliannol cultural aspect
agwedd foesol *eb* agweddau moesol moral aspect
agwedd gadarnhaol *eb* agweddau cadarnhaol positive attitude
agwedd gadarnhaol *eb* agweddau cadarnhaol positive aspect
agwedd gadarnhaol ddiamod *eb* unconditional positive regard
agwedd greadigol *eb* agweddau creadigol creative approach
agwedd mesuriad *eb* quotation aspect
agwedd natur ffugiadwy *eb* falsifiability view
agwedd ymarferol *eb* practical approach
agwedd ysbrydol *eb* agweddau ysbrydol spiritual aspect
agweddau amlddiwylliannol ar chwaraeon *ell* multicultural aspects of sport
agweddau ar ddawnsiau *ell* aspects of dance
Angefin *eg* Angefiniaid Angevin
angel *eg* angylion angel
angel gwarcheidiol *eg* angylion gwarcheidiol guardian angel
angel syrthiedig *eg* angylion syrthiedig fallen angel
angelica *eg* angelica
angen *eg* anghenion need
angen canfyddadwy *eg* anghenion canfyddadwy identified need
angen dynol sylfaenol *eg* anghenion dynol sylfaenol basic human need
angenrheidiau *ell* necessaries
angenrheidiol *ans* necessary
angenrheidiol a digonol necessary and sufficient
angerdd *eg* passion; intensity
angerddol *ans* intense
anghellog *ans* non-cellular
anghellog *ans* acellular
anghenion addysgol *ell* educational needs
anghenion addysgol arbennig *ell* special educational needs
anghenion arbennig *ell* special needs
anghenion gofal *ell* care needs
anghenion maeth *ell* nutritional needs
anghildroadwy *ans* irreversible
anghilyddol *ans* non-reciprocal
anghirol *ans* achiral
anghlasurol *ans* non-classical
anghonfensiynol *ans* unconventional
anghrediniwr *eg* anghredinwyr infidel

anghrisialog *ans* non-crystalline
Anghrist *eg* Antichrist
anghristnogol *ans* unchristian
anghrychadwy *ans* uncrushable
anghydamseredig *ans* asynchronous
anghydberthnasol *ans* uncorrelated
anghydbwysedd *eg* imbalance
anghydbwysedd *eg* nonequilibrium
anghydfod *eg* dispute
anghydffurfedd *eg* unconformity
anghydffurfiaeth *eb* dissent
anghydffurfiaeth *eb* nonconformity
anghydffurfiol *ans* dissenting
anghydffurfiwr *eg* anghydffurfwyr nonconformist
anghydffurfiwr *eg* anghydffurfwyr dissenter
anghydffurfiwr rhesymol *eg* anghydffurfwyr rhesymol Rational Dissenter
anghydnaws *ans* incompatible; discordant
anghydraddoldeb *eg* inequality
anghydraddoldebau iechyd *ell* inequalities in health
anghydwedd *ans* out of phase
anghyfannedd *ans* uninhabited
anghyfannol *ans* non-integrated
anghyfansoddiadol *ans* unconstitutional
anghyfartal *ans* unequal
anghyfarwydd *ans* unfamiliar
anghyfathiant *eg* incongruence
anghyfeillgar *ans* user-unfriendly
anghyfeiriadol *ans* non-directional
anghyflawn *ans* incomplete
anghyflogadwy *ans* unemployable
anghyfochrog *ans* scalene
anghyfreithlon *ans* illegitimate
anghyfreithlon *ans* illegal
anghyfreithlondeb *eg* illegality
anghyffroadwy *ans* non-excitable
anghyffwrdd *ans* unexploited
anghyffyrddedigion *ell* untouchables
anghylchdro *ans* irrotational
anghymarebol *ans* irrational
anghymarus *ans* incompatible
anghymesur *ans* asymmetric; incommensurable
anghymesuredd *eg* anghymesureddau asymmetry
anghymesuredd swyddogaethau hemisfferau *eg* functional hemisphere asymmetry
anghymesurol *ans* asymmetrical
anghymhelliad *eg* anghymelliadau disincentive
anghymwyster *eg* anghymwysterau incompetence
anghymysgadwy *ans* immiscible
anghynhenid extrinsic
anghynhwysol *ans* exclusive
anghynhyrchiol *ans* unproductive
anghynrychiadol *ans* non-representational
anghyrydol *ans* non-corrosive
anghyseinedd *eg* dissonance
anghyseiniol *ans* dissonant
anghyson *ans* inconsistent
anghysondeb *eg* anghysondebau inconsistency; anomaly
anghytgord *eg* anghytgordiau discord
anghytgord sylfaenol *eg* anghytgordiau sylfaenol fundamental discord
anghytgord sylfaenol y llywydd *eg* anghytgordiau sylfaenol y llywydd fundamental dominant discord
anghytgordiol *ans* discordant
anghytûn *ans* discordant
anghywasg *ans* incompressible
anghywir *ans* incorrect, wrong
anghywirdeb *eg* anghywirdebau inaccuracy
Anglicaniaeth *eb* Anglicanism
angor *eg/b* angorau anchor
angor ôl-nodyn *eg* angorau ôl-nodyn endnote anchor
angor styden *eb* angorau stydiau stud anchor
angor testun fertigol *eg* angorau testun fertigol vertical text anchor
angor testun llorweddol *eg* angorau testun llorweddol horizontal text anchor
angora *eg* angora
angorfa *eb* angorfeydd mooring
angorfa *eb* angorfâu anchorage
angori i'r dudalen *be* anchor to page
angori i'r ffrâm *be* anchor to frame
angori i'r nod *be* anchor to character
angori i'r paragraff *be* anchor to paragraph
angorle *eg* angorleoedd roadstead
► **AIDS** *eg* AIDS
ail blyg *eg* second fold
ail bwynt *eg* second point
ail dap *eg* second tap
ail dyfiant *eg* second growth
ail forgais *eg* second mortgage
ail gantor *eg* ail gantorion succentor
ail genhedlaeth *eb* second generation
ail gymal *eg* second leg
Ail Gymdeithas Sosialaidd Ryngwladol y Gweithwyr *eb* Second Socialist International (Working-Men's Association)
ail gynnig serfio *eg* second service
ail isradd *eg* square root
ail rediad *eg* second run
ail reng *eb* second row
Ail Ryfel Byd *eg* Second World War
ail slip *eg* second slip
ail wrthdro *eg* ail wrthdroeon second inversion
ail ymerodraeth yr Almaen *eb* second German empire
ailadeiladu *be* rebuild, reconstruct
ailadrodd *be* repeat
ailadrodd aluniad *be* repeat alignment
ailadrodd colofn *be* repeat column
ailadrodd chwiliad *be* repeat search
ailadrodd pennyn *be* repeat header
ailadrodd rhes *be* repeat row

ailadrodd teitl *be* repeat heading
ailadroddiad *eg* ailadroddiadau repeat; repetition
ailallforio *be* re-export
ailbrisiad *eg* ailbrisiadau revaluation
ailbrosesu *be* reprocess
ailchwarae *be* replay
ailchwarae'r pwynt *be* replay the point
ailchwydiad *eg* ailchwydiadau regurgitation
aildwymo *be* reheat
ailddewis *be* reselect
ailddiffinio *be* redefine
ailddirwyn *be* rewind
ailddosbarthu *be* redistribute
ailddyddodi *be* re-deposit
ailddyrannu *be* reallocate
Ailfedyddiwr *eg* Ailfedyddwyr Anabaptist
ailfeintio *be* resize
ailfeintio ffenestr tabl *be* resize table window
ailfeintiol *ans* resizable
ailfeintio'r ffrâm *be* resize frame
ailffurfio *be* reform
ailffurfydd *eg* ailffurfyddion reformer
ailgoedwigo *be* reafforestation
ailgrisialiad *eg* recrystallization
ailgrisialu *be* recrystallize
ailgychwyn (cyfrifiadur) *be* reboot
ailgychwyn (yn gyffredinol) *be* restart
ailgychwyn rhifo *be* restart numbering
ailgychwyniad oer *eg* ailgychwyniadau oer cold restart
ailgydio *be* reuptake
ailgyfanheddiad *eg* ailgyfaneddiadau resettlement
ailgyfanheddu *be* resettle
ailgyfarparu *be* re-equip
ailgyfeiriadaeth *eb* reorientation
ailgyfuniad *eg* ailgyfuniadau recombination
ailgylchredeg *be* recirculate
ailgylchu *be* recycle
ailgylchu creigiau *be* recycling of rocks
ailgymhwyso *be* readjust
ailhyfforddi diwydiannol *be* industrial retraining
ail-leoli *be* reposition
ail-luniad *eg* ail-luniadau reconstruction
ail-lunio *be* reconstruct
ail-lwytho *be* reload
ailogwyddo *be* reslant
ailosod (rhaglen) *be* reinstall
ailosod (yn gyffredinol) *be* reset
ailosod cell *be* reset cell
ailosod graddfa *be* reset scale
ailosod llwybrydd *be* reset routing
ailosod priodoleddau ffont *be* reset font attributes
ailosod rhagosodiadau *be* reset default
ailosod rhestr cyngor *be* reset tip list
ailraddio *be* regrade
ailrwymo *be* rebind
ailsefydlu (ac adfer) *be* rehabilitate
ailsefydlu (yn gyffredinol) *be* re-establish
ailsefydlu troseddwyr *be* resettlement of offenders
ailstrwythuro gwybyddol *be* cognitive restructuring
ailuno *be* rejoin
ailwefradwy *ans* rechargeable
ailwefru *be* recharge
ailwerthusiad *eg* reappraisal
ailwirio *be* recheck
ailymgnawdoliad *eg* ailymgnawdoliadau reincarnation
ailystyried *be* reconsider
ailystyried gwybyddol *be* cognitive reappraisal
akirah *ell* akirah
alabastr *eg* alabaster
alalia *eg* alalia
alanin *eg* alanine
alantois *eg* allantois
alaw *eb* alawon melody, tune
alaw ag amrywiadau *eb* alawon ag amrywiadau air with variations
alaw syml *eb* alawon syml simple melody
alaw wedi'i chywasgu *eb* alawon wedi'u cywasgu melody by condensation
alawol *ans* melodic
alb *eb* alb
albatros *eg* albatrosiaid albatross
albedo *eg* albedo
Albigensaidd *ans* Albigensian
Albigensiad *eg* Albigensiaid Albigensian
albinaidd *ans* albino
albinedd *eg* albinism
albino *eg* albinoaid albino
alborada *eg* alboradas alborada
Albumblatt *eg* Albumblätter Albumblatt
albwm *eg* albymau album
albwmen *eg* albumen
alcali *eg* alcalïau alkali
alcalïaidd *ans* alkaline
alcalinedd *eg* alkalinity
► **alcan** *eg* alcanau alkane
alcaptonwria *eg* alkaptonuria
alcemeg *eb* alchemy
alcemydd *eg* alcemyddion alchemist
► **alcen** *eg* alcenau alkene
alclad *eg* alclad
alcof *eb* alcofau alcove
alcohol *eg* alcoholau alcohol
alcohol cynradd *eg* primary alcohol
alcohol eilaidd *eg* secondary alcohol
alcohol pur *eg* absolute alcohol
alcoholiaeth *eb* alcoholism
alcoholig *ans* alcoholic
alcoholig *eg* alcoholigion alcoholic
alcybensen *eg* alcybensenau alkybenzene
alcyl *eg* alcylau alkyl
alcyleiddiad *eg* alkylation

alcyleiddio *be* alkylate
alcylmagnesiwm halid *eg* alcylmagnesiwm halidau alkylmagnesium halide
alcyn *eg* alcynau alkyne
alch *eb* eilch cooker ring
alch hydeiml *eb* eilch hydeiml pan sensor ring
aldehyd *eg* aldehydau aldehyde
aleatoraidd *ans* aleatory
Alecsander Fawr *eg* Alexander the Great
Alecsandraidd *ans* Alexandrine
alegori *eg* alegorïau allegory
alegorïaidd *ans* allegorical
alel *eg* alelau allele
alel enciliol *eg* alelau enciliol recessive allele
alel trechol *eg* alelau trechol dominant allele
alelomorff *eg* alelomorffau allelomorph
alelomorff lluosrif *eg* alelomorffau lluosrif multiple allelomorph
alelopathi *eg* alellopathy
alergaidd *ans* allergic
alergedd *eg* alergeddau allergy
alesthesia *eg* allesthesia
alesthesia negyddol *eg* negative allesthesia
alewron *eg* aleurone
alfeolaidd *ans* alveolar
alfeolws *eg* alfeoli alveolus
alffa *eg* alpha
alffamerig *ans* alphameric
alffaniwmerig *ans* alphanumeric
Alffred Fawr *eg* Alfred the Great
alga *eg* algâu alga
algebra *eg/b* algebra
algebra Boole *eg* Boolean algebra
algebra ffurfiol *eg* formal algebra
algebra switsio *eg* switching algebra
ALGOL ALGOL
algorithm *eg* algorithmau algorithm
algorithm dychweliadol *eg* algorithmau dychweliadol recursive algorithm
algorithm Ewclid *eg* Euclid's algorithm
algorithm stwnsio *eg* hashing algorithm
algorithmig *ans* algorithmic
alicwot *eg* aliquot
alidad *eg* alidadau alidade; sight rails
aliffatig *ans* aliphatic
aligylchol *ans* alicyclic
aliniad *eg* aliniadau alignment
aliniad fertigol *eg* vertical alignment
aliniedig *ans* aligned
aliniedig ar y dde *ans* right-aligned
alinio *be* align
alinio ar y chwith *be* left-align
alinio dotiau i lawr *be* align dots down
alinio ffynhonnell y data *be* align data source
alinio i'r brig *be* align to top
alinio i'r canol *be* align middle
alinio i'r canol fertigol *be* align vertical centre
alinio i'r chwith *be* align left
alinio i'r dde *be* align right
alinio i'r grid *be* align to grid
alinio i'r gwaelod *be* align to bottom
alinio'r canol *be* align centre
alinio'r canol yn fertigol *be* align centre vertically
alinio'r canol yn llorweddol *be* align centre horizontally
alinio'r gwaelod *be* align bottom
Almaen Natsïaidd *eb* Nazi Germany
almonau mâl *ell* ground almonds
alocryl *eg* alocryl
aloffon *eg* aloffonau allophone
alogenig *ans* allogenic
aloi *eg* aloion alloy
aloi alwminiwm *eg* aloion alwminiwm aluminium alloy
aloi anfferrus *eg* aloion anfferrus non-ferrous alloy
aloi 'E' *eg* 'E' alloy
aloi efydd *eg* bronze alloy
aloi metel gwyn *eg* aloion metel gwyn white metal alloy
aloi 'Y' *eg* 'Y' alloy
aloi ymdoddadwy *eg* fusible alloy
aloi'r Iseldiroedd *eg* Dutch metal
alomorff *eg* alomorffau allomorph
alopolyploid *ans* allopolyploid
alopolyploidi *eg* allopolyploidy
alotetraploid *ans* allotetraploid
alotrop *eg* alotropau allotrope
alotropaeth *eb* allotropy
alotropig *ans* allotropic
alp *eg* alpau alp
alpaidd *ans* alpine
Alpau *ell* Alps
alpgorn *eg* alpgyrn alpenhorn
al-Qad'r *eg* al-Qad'r
alternativo *eg* alternativi alternativo
altimedr *eg* altimedrau altimeter
alto *eg/b* altos alto
altocumulus *eg* altocumulus
altostratus *eg* altostratus
alwm *eg* alum
alwmina *eg* alumina
alwminiwm *eg* aluminium
alwminiwm amoniwm sylffad(III)-12-dŵr *eg* aluminium ammonium sulfate(III)-12-water
alwminiwm amoniwm sylffad(V)-12-dŵr *eg* aluminium ammonium sulfate(V)-12-water
alwminiwm bromid *eg* aluminium bromide
alwminiwm clorid *eg* aluminium chloride
alwminiwm ethanoad basig *eg* basic aluminium ethanoate
alwminiwm ffosffad(V) *eg* aluminium phosphate(V)
alwminiwm hydrocsid *eg* aluminium hydroxide
alwminiwm hydrocsid hydradol *eg* hydrated aluminium hydroxide
alwminiwm nitrad(V) *eg* aluminium nitrate(V)

alwminiwm ocsid *eg* aluminium oxide
alwminiwm ocsid (corundwm) *eg* aluminium oxide (corundum)
alwminiwm ocsid hydradol (bocsit) *eg* hydrated aluminium oxide (bauxite)
alwminiwm potasiwm sylffad(VI)-12-dŵr *eg* aluminium potassium sulfate(VI)-12-water
alwminiwm sylffad(VI) *eg* aluminium sulfate(VI)
alwminiwm tiwbaidd *eg* tubular aluminium
alwminiwm(III) bromid *eg* aluminium(III) bromide
alylicion *ell* allylics
alla cappella *adf* alla cappella
allafon *eb* allafonydd distributary
Allah *eg* Allah
allan *adf* out
allan (am awyren, traffig etc) *adf* outbound
allan drwy ddal caught out
allan drwy gyffwrdd touched out
allan o'r canol off centre
allan o'r cwrt out of court
allanadliad *eg* expiration
allanadlu *be* exhale; expire
allanfa *eb* allanfeydd exit
allanol (=yn wynebu allan) *ans* outward
allanol (am arholwr etc) *ans* external
allanol (am fur etc) *ans* outer
allanol (o ran lleoliad) *ans* exterior
allanol (o ran tarddiad) *ans* extraneous
allanoldeb negatif *eg* allanoldebau negatif negative externality
allanoldeb positif *eg* allanoldebau positif positive externalities
allblyg *ans* extrovert
allblygedd *eg* extroversion
allborth *eg* allbyrth outport
allbost *eg* allbyst outpost
allbrint *eg* allbrintiau printout
allbrint cyfrifiadurol *eg* allbrintiau cyfrifiadurol computer printout
allbriordy *eg* allbriordai alien priory
allbwn *eg* allbynnau output
allbwn blancio crychdon (ABC) *eg* ripple blanking output
allbwn byfferog *eg* allbynnau byfferog buffered output
allbwn y galon *eg* cardiac output
allbynnu *be* output
alldafliad (mewn ffisioleg) *eg* alldafliadau ejaculation
alldafliad ymbelydrol *eg* radioactive fallout
alldaflol *ans* ejaculatory
alldaflu (mewn ffisioleg) *be* ejaculate
alldaith *eb* alldeithiau expedition
alldap *eg* alldapiau xenotape
alldardd *eg* exotic
alldarddiad *eg* exogenesis
alldarddol *ans* exogenous; exogenic
alldiriogaethol *ans* extraterritorial
alldoriad *eg* alldoriadau out-take
alldyniad *eg* alldyniadau withdrawal
alldynnu *be* abstract
alldystiolaethol *ans* extra-evidential
allddarlleniad *eg* allddarlleniadau readout
allddarlleniad distrywiol *eg* allddarlleniadau distrywiol destructive readout
allddodol *ans* emergent
allechelinol *ans* abaxial
allemande *eb* allemandes allemande
allembryonig *ans* extra-embryonic
allfa *eb* allfeydd outlet
allfa adwerthu *eb* retail outlet
allfa fwyd *eb* allfeydd bwyd food outlet
allfaes *eg* allfeysydd outfield
allforio *be* export
allforion anweledig *ell* invisible exports
allforiwr *eg* allforwyr exporter
allforyn *eg* allforion export
allforyn net *eg* allforion net net export
allfridio *be* outbreed
allfrig *ans* off-peak
allfwriad *eg* allfwriadau ejection
allfwrw *be* egestion
allganol *ans* excentric
allganol *eg* allganolau eccentric centre
allgaredd *eg* altruism
allgaredd cilyddol *eg* reciprocal altruism
all-gau cymdeithasol *be* social exclusion
allgellog *ans* extracellular
allglofan *eg* allglofannau exclave
allgofnodi *be* log off; log out
allgraig *eb* allgreigiau outlier
allgrwp *eg* allgrwpiau out-group
allgylch *eg* allgylchoedd escribed circle; eccentric circle; excircle
allgyrchol *ans* centrifugal
allgyrchu *be* centrifuge
allgyrchu graddiant dwysedd *be* density gradient centrifugation
allgyrchydd *eg* allgyrchion centrifuge
all-lein *ans* off-line
all-lif (mewn cyfrifiadureg etc) *eg* all-lifoedd output stream
all-lif (yn gyffredinol)*eg* all-lifoedd outflow
all-lifo *be* outflowing
allniwclear *ans* extra-nuclear
allor *eb* allorau altar
allorau mawr eu braint *ell* altars once so privileged
allordal *eg* allordaliadau altarage
allorlun *eg* allorluniau altar piece
allosod *be* extrapolate
allosodiad *eg* allosodiadau extrapolation
allraddiad *eg* allraddiadau progradation
allrwyd *eb* allrwydi extranet
allsianel *eb* allsianeli distributary channel
alltraeth *ans* offshore

alltud *eg* alltudion exile, outcast
alltudiad *eg* alltudiadau expulsion
alltudiaeth *eb* deportation
alltudio (mewnfudwr anghyfreithlon) *be* deport
alltudio (yn gyffredinol) *be* exile; expel
alltudion Mari *ell* Marian exiles
allwedd *eb* allweddi key
allwedd Allen *eb* allweddi Allen Allen key
allwedd argaen *eb* allweddi argaen veneer key
allwedd baralel *eb* allweddi paralel parallel key
allwedd ben crwn *eb* allweddi pen crwn round-headed key
allwedd ben-gib *eb* allweddi pen-gib jib-headed key
allwedd betryal *eb* allweddi petryal rectangular key
allwedd bluen *eb* allweddi pluen feather key
allwedd daprog *eb* allweddi taprog tapered key
allwedd diwnio *eb* allweddi tiwnio tuning key
allwedd estron *eb* foreign key
allwedd fforch *eb* allweddi fforch prong key
allwedd grafanc *eb* allweddi crafanc chuck key
allwedd gyfansawdd *eb* allweddi cyfansawdd compound key
allwedd gyfrwy *eb* allweddi cyfrwy saddle key
allwedd gyfrwy cau *eb* allweddi cyfrwy cau hollow saddle key
allwedd gynffonnog *eb* allweddi cynffonnog dovetailed key
allwedd lithr *eb* allweddi llithr sliding key
allwedd raglennu *eb* allweddi rhaglennu programming key
allwedd Woodruff *eb* allweddi Woodruff Woodruff key
allwedd y bariton *eb* allweddau'r bariton baritone-clef
allweddair *eg* allweddeiriau keyword
allweddair addasu *eg* allweddeiriau addasu custom keyword
allweddell electronig *eb* allweddellau electronig electronic keyboard
allweddellau *ell* keyboard
allweddfa *eb* allweddfâu keyway
allweddi cyrhaeddiad *ell* attainment keys
allweddol *ans* key; critical
allweddu *be* keying
allweddu syfliad amledd *be* frequency shift keying
allweiniad *eg* evagination
allwthiad *eg* allwthiadau extrusion
allwthio *be* extrude
allwthiol *ans* extrusive
allwyriad *eg* allwyriadau deflection
allwyriadol *ans* deflecting
allwyro *be* deflect
allyriad *eg* allyriadau emission; discharge emission
allyriad ymbelydrol *eg* allyriadau ymbelydrol radioactive emission
allyrredd *ans* emissivity
allyrru *be* emit
allyrrydd *eg* allyrwyr emitter
amaethyddiaeth *eb* agriculture
amaethyddiaeth gyfalafol *eb* capitalist agriculture
amaethyddol *ans* agrarian
amalgam *eg* amalgamau amalgam
amatur *eg* amaturiaid amateur
amaturiaeth *eb* amateurism
ambiwlans *eg* ambiwlansys ambulance
Ambiwlans Sant Ioan St John Ambulance
ambr *eg* amber
amcan *eg* amcanion objective
amcan allweddol *eg* amcanion allweddol key objective
amcan asesu *eg* amcanion asesu assessment objective
amcan busnes *eg* business objective
amcan cyffredinol *eg* amcanion cyffredinol general objective
amcan gwybyddol *eg* amcanion gwybyddol cognitive objective
amcan gyrfaol *eg* amcanion gyrfaol career objective
amcan macroeconomaidd *eg* amcanion macroeconomaidd macroeconomic objective
amcan y project *eg* project objective
amcan ymchwil *eg* amcanion ymchwil research objective
amcangyfrif *be* estimate
amcangyfrif *eg* amcangyfrifon estimate; estimation
amcangyfrif â thuedd *eg* biased estimate
amcangyfrif cyfeiliornad *eg* estimation of error
amcangyfrif diduedd *eg* amcangyfrifon diduedd unbiased estimate
amcangyfrif swm lleiaf sgwariau *eg* amcangyfrifon swm lleiaf sgwariau least-squares estimate
amcangyfrifyn *eg* amcangyfrifynnau estimator
amcangyfrifyn diduedd *eg* unbiased estimator
amcanion ymddygiad *ell* behaviour objectives
amdowellt *eg* sea lyme-grass
amddifadedd *eg* deprivation
amddifadiad diwylliannol *eg* cultural deprivation
amddifadiad emosiynol *eg* emotional deprivation
amddifadrwydd *eg* privation
amddifadu *be* deprive
amddifadu'r synhwyrau *be* sensory deprivation
amddifadus *ans* deprived
amddiffyn *be* defend; protect
amddiffyn *eg* defence
amddiffyn dyn am ddyn *be* man to man defence
amddiffyn oddi ar y droed flaen *be* defend off the front leg
amddiffyn rhag niwed *be* protection from harm
amddiffyn rhanbarth *be* zone defence
amddiffyn sifil *eg* civil defence
amddiffyn y gôl *be* defend the goal
amddiffyn y wiced *be* defend the wicket
amddiffyn yr amgylchedd *be* environmental protection

amddiffynfa *eb* amddiffynfeydd defence
amddiffynfa allanol *eb* amddiffynfeydd allanol redoubt; outwork
amddiffynfa gylch *eb* amddiffynfeydd cylch ringwork
amddiffynfa naturiol *eb* amddiffynfeydd naturiol natural defence
amddiffyniad *eg* amddiffyniadau defence; protection
amddiffyniad cyffredinol *eg* amddiffyniadau cyffredinol general defence
Amddiffyniad Ewyllys Rydd *eg* Free Will Defence
amddiffyniad heddlu *eg* police protection
amddiffynnol *ans* defensive; protective
amddiffynnydd *eg* amddiffynwyr protector
Amddiffynnydd y Ffydd *eg* Defender of the Faith
amedr *eg* amedrau ammeter
am-edrych *ans* look-up
amen *eg* ameniau amen
amenedigol *ans* perinatal
americiwm (Am) *eg* americium
amersiad *eg* amersiadau amercement
amersu *be* amerce
amfae *eg* amfaeau embayment
amfeddiad *eg* amfeddiadau impropriation
amfeddu *be* impropriate
amfeddwr *eg* amfeddwyr impropriator
amffibiad *eg* amffibiaid amphibian
amffibiaidd *ans* amphibious
amffictyoni *eg* amphictyony
amffinio *be* delimit
amffinydd *eg* amffinyddion delimiter
amffinydd testun *eg* amffinyddion testun text delimiter
amffipathig *ans* amphipathic
amffiprostyl *eg* amffiprostylau amphiprostyle
amffitheatr *eg* amffitheatrau amphitheatre
amffoterig *ans* amphoteric
amgaead cwmpawd *eg* amgaeadau cwmpawdau compass housing
amgaeedig *ans* enclosed
amganol *eg* amganolau circumcentre
amgant *eg* amgantau periphery
amgantol *ans* peripheral
amgantydd *eg* amgantyddion peripheral
amgarn *eg/b* amgarnau ferrule
amgarn ddi-sêm *eb* amgarnau di-sêm seamless ferrule
amgáu *be* enclose
amgen *ans* alternative
amgodio *be* encode
amgodio iaith *be* language encoding
amgodio penodol *be* encoding specificity
amgrwm *ans* convex
amgrymedd *eg* amgrymeddau convexity; convex curvature
amgryptiad *eg* amgryptiadau encryption
amgryptio *be* encrypt
amgryptio data *be* data encryption
amguddiad *eg* amguddiadau obscuration
amgueddfa *eb* amgueddfeydd museum
amgylch *eg* amgylchoedd circumcircle; circumscribed circle
amgylchedd *eg* amgylcheddau environment
amgylchedd anghyfarwydd *eg* amgylcheddau anghyfarwydd unfamiliar environment
amgylchedd awyr agored *eg* outdoor environment
amgylchedd busnes *eg* business environment
amgylchedd bwrdd gwaith *eg* amgylcheddau bwrdd gwaith desktop environment
amgylchedd byd-eang *eg* global environment
amgylchedd dan do *eg* indoor environment
amgylchedd dynol *eg* human environment
amgylchedd ffisegol *eg* physical environment
amgylchedd geomorffig *eg* geomorphic environment
amgylchedd gwneud *eg* amgylcheddau gwneud made environment
amgylchedd lleol *eg* local environment
amgylchedd mewnol *eg* amgylcheddau mewnol internal environment
amgylchedd naturiol *eg* amgylcheddau naturiol natural environment
amgylchedd trefol *eg* urban environment
amgylchedd yr ystafell ddosbarth *eg* classroom environment
amgylcheddol *ans* environmental
amgylchol *ans* circumscribed
amgylchu *be* circumscribe
amgylchyn *eg* amgylchynau surround
amgylchyniad *eg* amgylchyniadau encirclement
amgylchynu *be* surround; encircle
amharametrig *ans* non-parametric
amharhaol *ans* discontinuous
amharu ar *be* impair
amhendant *ans* undetermined; indefinite
amhenderfynedig *ans* indeterminate
amhenodrwydd *eg* indeterminacy
amherffeithrwydd *eg* amherffeithiadau imperfection
amhersonol *ans* impersonal
amherthnaseddol *ans* non-relativistic
amherthnasol *ans* irrelevant
amholar *ans* non-polar
amhur *ans* impure
amhuredd *eg* amhureddau impurity; dross
amhureddu *be* doping
amhwysol *ans* unweighted
amid *eg* amide
amin *eg* aminau amine
amineiddiad *eg* amination
4-aminobensensylffonamid *eg* 4-aminobenzenesulfonamide
aminoblastigion *ell* amino plastics
2-aminoethanol *eg* 2-aminoethanol
2-aminoffenol *eg* 2-aminophenol

4-aminoffenylamoniwm clorid *eg* 4-aminophenylammonium chloride
amis *eg* amice
amitosis *eg* amitosis
aml gydberthyniad *eg* multiple correlation
amlamrediad *ans* multi-range
amlannirlawn *ans* polyunsaturated
amlap *eg* amlapiau wrap-around
amlap awtomatig *eg* amlapiau awtomatig automatic wrap-around
amlapio *be* wrap; wrap-around
amlapio drwodd *be* wrap through
amlapio i'r chwith *be* wrap left
amlapio i'r dde *be* wrap right
amlapio testun *be* text wrap
amlapio tryloyw *be* wrap transparent
amlapio ymlaen *be* wrap on
amlapio'r paragraff cyntaf *be* wrap first paragraph
amlbariaeth *eb* polygynandry
amlbenrhynnol *ans* multi-peninsular
amlblecsu *be* multiplexing
amlblecsu rhaniad amledd *be* frequency division multiplexing
amlblecsydd *eg* amlblecsyddion multiplexer
amlbleth *ans* multiplex
amlblethu rhaniadau amser *be* time division multiplexing
amlblwyfaeth *eb* pluralism; plurality
amlblwyfol *ans* pluralistic
amlblwyfydd *eg* amlblwyfyddion pluralist
amlbwrpas *ans* versatile
amlder *eg* frequency
amlder alel *eg* allele frequency
amlder cronnus *eg* amlderau cronnus cumulative frequency
amlder genoteipaidd *eg* genotypic frequency
amlder genynnol *eg* gene frequency
amlder gollwng dŵr *eg* frequency of discharge of water
amldon *ans* multi-tone
amldrac *ans* multi-track
amldrac *eg* amldraciau multiple track
amldrac neu untrac track multiple or single
aml-dudalen *ans* multi-page
amlddefnyddiwr *eg* amlddefnyddwyr multi-user
amlddigid *ans* multidigit
amlddirgrynydd *eg* amlddirgrynyddion multivibrator
amlddirgrynydd gwrthsefydlog *eg* amlddirgrynwyr gwrthsefydlog astable multivibrator
amlddiwylliannol *ans* multicultural
amlddrychigaeth *eb* multivoque
amldduwiaeth *eb* polytheism
amledau *ans* multistranded
amledd *eg* amleddau frequency
amledd awdio *eg* audio frequency
amledd curiad *eg* frequency of beat
amledd curiad *eg* amleddau curiad beat frequency
amledd cylchdro *eg* angular frequency
amledd cysain *eg* resonant frequency
amledd isel *eg* low frequency
amledd torri *eg* break frequency
amledd trothwy *eg* threshold frequency
amledd uchel *eg* amleddau uchel high frequency
amlen *eb* amlenni envelope
amlen gnewyllol *eb* nuclear envelope
amlen llinellau syth *eb* amlenni llinellau syth envelope of straight lines
amlfalfog *ans* multi-valved
amlfesurydd *eg* amlfesuryddion multimeter
amlfodd *ans* multimodal
amlfynediad *ans* multi-access
amlffactoraidd *ans* multifactorial
amlfflach *eg* multiflash
amlgellog *ans* multicellular
amlgenhedlig *ans* cosmopolitan
amlgnwd *eg* polyculture
amlgnydio *be* polyculture
amlgormig *ans* polycormic
amlgyfrwng *ans* multimedia
amlgylchred *eg* amlgylchredau polycycle
amlgylchredol *ans* polycyclic
amlgywair *ans* polytonal
amlgyweiredd *eg* amlgyweireddau polytonality
amlhadog *ans* multiseeded
amlhiliol *ans* multiracial; multi-ethnic
amlieithog *ans* multilingual, polyglot
amlieithydd *eg* amlieithwyr polyglot
amlin *eb* amliniau contour
amlinell (ar fap) *eb* amlinellau contour
amlinell (yn gyffredinol) *eb* amlinellau outline
amlinell amlapio ymlaen wrap contour on
amlinell cysgod fertigol *eb* amlinellau cysgod fertigol vertical shadow outline
amlinell cysgod llorweddol *eb* amlinellau cysgod llorweddol horizontal shadow outline
amlinell testun *eb* amlinellau testun text contour
amlinelliad *eg* amlinelliadau outline
amlinelliad byr *eg* amlinelliadau byr brief outline
amlinellol *ans* outline
amlinellu *be* outline
aml-labedog *ans* multi-lobed
aml-lefel *ans* multilevel
aml-lenwi *be* multifill
amlochrog *ans* multilateral
amlolwg *ans* multiview
amlorchwyl *ans* multi-tasking
amlosgiad *eg* amlosgiadau cremation
amlraglennu *be* multi-programming
amlran *ans* multi-stage
amlsbin *ans* high spin
amlswyddogaethol *ans* multifunctional
amlsynhwyraidd *ans* multi-sensory
amlwead *ans* multi-textured

amlweddogrwydd *eg* polygamy
amlwg (ac agored) *ans* overt
amlwg (am bwynt mewn dadl) *ans* salient
amlwg (=hawdd ei ganfod) *ans* apparent
amlwg (=yn sefyll allan) *ans* prominent; distinct
amlwreiciaeth *eb* polygyny
amlwriaeth *eb* polyandry
amlwythiant *eg* containerization
amlygrwydd *eg* prominence
amlygu (=dod i'r amlwg) *be* manifest
amlygu (yn gyffredinol) *be* highlight
amlygu newidiadau *be* highlight changes
amlygwr *eg* amlygwyr highlighter
amlynciad *eg* ingestion
amlyncu (=gorchuddio'n llwyr) *be* engulf
amlyncu (bwyd, diod etc) *be* ingest
amlystyr *ans* polysemic
amnesia *eg* amnesia
amnesia anterograd *eg* anterograde amnesia
amnesia babandod *eg* infantile amnesia
amnesia ôl-hypnosis *eg* posthypnotic amnesia
amnesia ôl-redol *eg* retrograde amnesia
amnesia seicogenig *eg* psychogenic amnesia
amnest *eg* amnestau amnesty
Amnest Rhyngwladol *eg* Amnesty International
amnewid *be* substitute; replace
amnewid cyflawn *eg* total replacement
amnewid cymal *eg* amnewidiadau cymal joint replacement
amnewid mewnforion *be* import replacement
amnewid niwclioffilig *be* nucleophilic substitution
amnewid symptomau *be* symptom substitution
amnewid y am x *be* substitute x for y
amnewidiad *eg* amnewidiadau substitution
amnewidyn *eg* amnewidion substitute; replacement
amnewidyn tyrpant *eg* amnewidion tyrpant turps substitute
amnion *eg* amnion
amobr *eg* amobrau merchet
amod *eg* amodau condition
amod gwasanaeth *eg* amodau gwasanaeth condition of service
amod gwerth *eg* amodau gwerth condition of worth
amod gwerthu *eg* amodau gwerthu condition of sale
amod Marshall-Lerner *eg* amodau Marshall-Lerner Marshall-Lerner condition
amodau atmosfferig *ell* atmospheric conditions
amodau cychwynnol *ell* initial conditions
amodau cyfyngol *ell* limiting conditions
amodau cysur *ell* comfort conditions
amodau dechreuol *ell* start-up conditions
amodau ffin *ell* boundary conditions
amodau ffin hanfodol *ell* essential boundary conditions
amodau ffin naturiol *ell* natural boundary conditions
amodau gwaith *ell* working conditions
amodau masnach *ell* conditions of trading
amodau safonol masnachu *ell* standard conditions of trading
amodol *ans* conditional
amodoldeb *eb* contingency
amodoldeb tri-thymor *eg* three-term contingency
amoebaidd *ans* amoeboid
amoneiddio *be* ammonification
amonia *eg* ammonia
amonia dyfrllyd *eg* aqueous ammonia
amoniac *ans* ammoniac
amoniwm bensencarbocsylad (neu bensoad) *eg* ammonium benzenecarboxylate (or benzoate)
amoniwm ceriwm(IV) sylffad(VI) *eg* ammonium cerium(IV) sulfate(VI)
amoniwm clorid *eg* ammonium chloride
amoniwm copr(II) sylffad(VI)-6-dŵr *eg* ammonium copper(II) sulfate(VI)-6-water
amoniwm deucromad *eg* ammonium dichromate
amoniwm deucromad(VI) *eg* ammonium dichromate(VI)
amoniwm deuhydrogenffosffad(V) *eg* ammonium dihydrogenphosphate(V)
amoniwm ethandeuoad *eg* ammonium ethanedioate
amoniwm ethanoad *eg* ammonium ethanoate
amoniwm ffosffad(V) *eg* ammonium phosphate(V)
amoniwm haearn(II) sylffad(VI)-6-dŵr *eg* ammonium iron(II) sulfate(VI)-6-water
amoniwm haearn(III) sylffad(VI)-12-dŵr *eg* ammonium iron(III) sulfate(VI)-12-water
amoniwm hydrogencarbonad *eg* ammonium hydrogencarbonate
amoniwm hydrogenffosffad(V) *eg* ammonium hydrogenphosphate(V)
amoniwm hydrogensylffad(VI) *eg* ammonium hydrogensulfate(VI)
amoniwm methanoad *eg* ammonium methanoate
amoniwm nicel(II) sylffad(VI)-6-dŵr *eg* ammonium nickel(II) sulfate(VI)-6-water
amoniwm nitrad(V) *eg* ammonium nitrate(V)
amoniwm perocsodeusylffad(VI) *eg* ammonium peroxodisulfate(VI)
amoniwm polytriocsofanadad(V) *eg* ammonium polytrioxovanadate(V)
amoniwm sodiwm hydrogenffosffad(V) *eg* ammonium sodium hydrogenphosphate(V)
amoniwm sylffad(VI) *eg* ammonium sulfate(VI)
amoniwm sylffid *eg* ammonium sulphide
amoniwm thiocyanad *eg* ammonium thiocyanate
amonolysis *eg* ammonolysis
amorffaidd *ans* amorphous
AMP cylchol *eg* cyclic AMP
amper *eg* amperau ampere
ampersand (&) *eg* ampersand
ampwl *eg* ampylau ampoule
amrediad *eg* amrediadau range
amrediad clywadwy *eg* audible range

amrediad critigol *eg* amrediadau critigol critical range
amrediad gwallau *eg* amrediadau gwallau error range
amrediad llanw *eg* amrediadau llanw tidal range
amrediad llanw *eg* range of tide
amrediad lliw *eg* colour range
amrediad rhyngchwartel *eg* amrediadau rhyngchwartel interquartile range
amrediad tymheredd *eg* amrediadau tymheredd temperature range
amrediad yr amrywiadau *eg* range of variations
Amrit-dhari *eg* Amrit-dhari
Amrit-sanskar *eg* Amrit-sanskar
amrwd *ans* crude
amrwym *eg* amrwymau swathe
amrwymo *be* swathe
amryddawn *ans* versatile
amryddawn *ans* facultative
amryfal *ans* multiple
amrylawr *ans* multi-storey
amryliw *ans* multichrome
amryweb *eb* amrywebau variate
amryweddau *ell* variates
amrywiad *eg* amrywiadau variation
amrywiad ffinedig *eg* amrywiadau ffinedig bounded variation
amrywiad genetig *eg* amrywiadau genetig genetic variation
amrywiad gwrthdro *eg* amrywiadau gwrthdro inverse variation
amrywiad parhaol *eg* amrywiadau parhaol perpetual variation
amrywiad rhythm *eg* amrywiadau rhythm variation of rhythm
amrywiad tyndra *eg* amrywiadau tyndra variation of tension
amrywiad union *eg* amrywiadau union direct variation
amrywiadau *ell* divisions
amrywiadol *ans* variational
amrywiaeth *eb* amrywiaethau variety; assortment; range; diversity
amrywiaeth ansawdd *eb* quality variation
amrywiaeth defnyddiau *eb* assortment of materials
amrywiaeth ddiwylliannol *eb* cultural diversity
amrywiaeth o gerddoriaeth *eb* range of music
amrywiaeth o gleientiaid *eb* client diversity
amrywiaeth o gyfryngau *eb* variety of media
amrywiaeth o weithrediadau gymnastig *eb* range of gymnastic action
amrywiaeth ranbarthol *eb* regional variety
amrywiaethu *be* diversify
amrywiant *eg* amrywiannau variance
amrywiant cadarnhaol *eg* amrywiannau cadarnhaol positive variance
amrywiant mewn-grwpiau *eg* amrywiannau mewn-grwpiau within-groups variance
amrywiant negyddol *eg* amrywiannau negyddol negative variance
amrywiant poblogaeth *eg* population variance
amrywiant rhwng grwpiau *eg* between groups variance
amrywio *be* vary
amrywio amseriad *be* vary timing
amrywiol *ans* assorted
amrywioldeb *eg* variability
amrywioldeb glawiad *eg* rainfall variability
amrywiolion nodwedd *ell* feature variants
amrywiolyn *eg* amrywiolion variant
amrywiolyn genetig *eg* genetic variant
amrywion *ell* separates
amrywion cydwedd *ell* coordinated separates
amser *eg* amserau time
amser a aeth heibio *eg* elapsed time
amser a gymerwyd *eg* time taken
amser adweithio *eg* reaction time
amser aros *eg* amserau aros waiting time
amser bwydo *eg* feeding-time
amser byr *eg* short time
amser cinio *eg* lunch interval
amser cychwyn *eg* amserau cychwyn start time
amser cyfartalog ail-wneud *eg* average rep time
amser cyffredin *eg* common time
amser cymedrig *eg* mean time
amser cyrchu *eg* amserau cyrchu access time
amser cyrraedd *eg* time of arrival
amser cyswllt *eg* amserau cyswllt contact time
amser cysylltu *eg* connect time
amser chwarae *eg* play time
amser chwilio *eg* search time
amser darllen *eg* amserau darllen read time
amser datseinedd *eg* reverberation time
amser dau *eg* duple time
amser di-fynd *eg* amserau di-fynd down time
amser dwyran *eg* binary time
amser gorau *eg* amserau gorau best time
amser gweithredu *eg* amserau gweithredu execution time
amser hamdden *eg* leisure time
amser haul *eg* apparent time
amser hedfan *eg* time of flight
amser integru *eg* integration time
amser llawn *eg* full time
amser mitotig *eg* generation time
amser mynd *eg* amserau mynd uptime
amser paned *eg* coffee break, tea break
amser parhad (curiad y galon) *eg* duration
amser priodol *eg* proper time
amser real *eg* amserau real real time
amser rhedeg *eg* run-time
Amser Safonol Greenwich *eg* Greenwich Mean Time
amser sychu *eg* amserau sychu drying time
amser y cwricwlwm *eg* curriculum time

amser y sêr *eg* sidereal time
amser ymateb *eg* response time
amser ymofyn *eg* amserau ymofyn seek time
amser yn weddill *eg* time left
amser yr haul *eg* solar time
amser ysgrifennu *eg* amserau ysgrifennu write time
amseriad *eg* amseriadau timing
amseriad taro *eg* amseriadau taro rate of striking
amserlen *eb* amserlenni timetable, schedule
amserlen cymarebau newidiol *eb* variable ratio schedule
amserlen cymarebau sefydlog *eb* fixed ratio schedule
amserlen hyfforddiant personol *eb* amserlenni hyfforddiant personol personal training schedule
amserlen teithio *eb* itinerary
amserlen ysbeidiau newidiol *eb* variable interval schedule
amserlen ysbeidiau sefydlog *eb* fixed interval schedule
amserlenni teledu *ell* TV listings
amserlennu *be* timetable
amserlin *eg* amserliniau time-base
amseru *be* time
amseru da *be* good timing
amserwr *eg* amserwyr time keeper
amserydd *eg* amseryddion timer
amserydd adweithio *eg* amseryddion adweithio reaction timer
amserydd cyfwng *eg* amseryddion cyfwng interval timer
amserydd ticio *eg* amseryddion ticio ticker timer
amseryddol *ans* temporal
amsugnedd *eg* absorbance; absorbency
amsugniad *eg* amsugniadau absorption
amsugniad detholus *eg* selective absorption
amsugno *be* absorb
amsugnol *ans* absorbent
amsugnydd *eg* amsugnyddion absorber
amsugnydd *eg* amsugnyddion absorbent
amwys *ans* ambiguous
amyd *eg* mashlum
amygdala *eg* amygdala
amyl asetad *eg* amyl acetate
amylas *eg* amylase
amylas poerol *eg* salivary amylase
amyloplast *eg* amyloplastau amyloplast
amylu *be* oversew
anabatig *ans* anabatic
anabl *ans* disabled
anabledd *eg* anableddau disability; disablement
anabledd corfforol *eg* anableddau corfforol physical disability
anabledd dysgu *eg* anableddau dysgu learning disability
anabledd dysgu difrifol *eg* anableddau dysgu difrifol severe learning disability
anabledd dysgu ysgafn *eg* anableddau dysgu ysgafn mild learning disability
anabledd meddyliol *eg* mental disability
anabledd synhwyraidd *eg* sensory disability
anabledd ysgafn *eg* anableddau ysgafn mild disability
anableddau amryfal *ell* multiple disabilities
anabolaeth *eb* anabolism
anabolig *ans* anabolic
anacrwsis *eg* anacrwses anacrusis
anacrwstig *ans* anacrustic
anactif *ans* inactive
anactifadu *be* inactivate
anactifedd *eg* inactivity
anadl *eg/b* anadliadau breath
anadliad *eg* anadliadau afflation
anadlu *be* breathe
anadlu ceg wrth geg *be* mouth-to-mouth respiration
anadlydd aerosol *eg* anadlyddion aerosol aerosol inhaler
anadnewyddadwy *ans* non-renewable
anadweithiol *ans* inert; non-reactive; unreactive
anaddysgadwy *ans* ineducable
anaeddfed (=heb raniadau eto) *ans* azonal
anaeddfed (yn gyffredinol) *ans* immature
anaemia *eg* anaemia
anaemia aflesol *eg* pernicious anaemia
anaemia cryman-gell *eg* sickle cell anaemia
anaerobig *ans* anaerobic
anaestheteg *eb* anaesthetics
anaesthetegydd *eg* anaesthetegyddion anaesthetist
anaesthetig *eg* anaesthetigion anaesthetic
anaesthetig cyffredinol *eg* general anaesthetic
anaesthetig lleol *eg* local anaesthetic
anaf *eg* anafiadau injury
anaf annamweiniol *eg* anafiadau annamweiniol non-accidental injury
anaf i'r pen *eg* anafiadau i'r pen head injury
anaf mathru *eg* anafiadau mathru crush injury
anafedig *eg* anafedigion casualty
anafiadau niferus *ell* multiple injuries
anaffas *eg* anaphase
analgesia hypnotig *eg* hypnotic analgesia
analog *ans* analogue
analog *eg* analogau analogue
analogaidd *ans* analogous
anallu *eg* inability
analluogi *be* disable
analluogi cwcis *be* disable cookies
analluogi ymyriadau *be* disable interruptions
ananweddol *ans* involatile
anarbenigol *ans* non-specialist
anarchaidd *ans* anarchist
anarchiaeth *eb* anarchy; anarchism
anarchydd *eg* anarchwyr anarchist

anarferedig *ans* obsolete
anastomosis *eg* anastomoses anastomosis
anatman *eg* anatman
anatomeg *eb* anatomy
anatomegol *ans* anatomical
anatomi *eg* anatomy
anatta *eg* anatta
anathraidd *ans* impermeable
anawsterau ymddygiad *ell* behaviour difficulties
anawsterau ymddygiad ac emosiwn *ell* emotional and behavioural difficulties
ancr *eg* ancriaid anchorite
androeciwm *eg* androecium
androgen *eg* androgenau androgen
androgynedd *eg* androgyny
aneffeithiol *ans* ineffective
aneffeithioldeb *eg* ineffectiveness
aneffeithlon *ans* inefficient
aneffeithlonrwydd *eg* inefficiency
aneglur *ans* unclear
anehedol *ans* non-volatile
anelastig *ans* inelastic
anelectrolyt *eg* anelectrolytau non-electrolyte
aneliad *eg* aneliadau aim
anelid *eg* anelidau annelid
anelio *be* anneal
anelu *be* aim
anelu at y glwyd *be* aim for the hurdle
anelu ergyd *be* aim a stroke
anelu'r bêl *be* aim the ball
anelu'r foli *be* aim the volley
anemoffiledd *eg* anemophily
anemomedr *eg* anemomedrau anemometer
anemomedr llaw *eg* anemomedrau llaw hand-held cup anemometer
anenwol *ans* innominate
anerchiad *eg* anerchiadau address
anergydiwr *eg* anergydwyr non-striker
aneroid *ans* aneroid
aneroid *eg* aneroidau aneroid
anesblygol *ans* non-evolving
anestynadwy *ans* inextensible
anewploid *eg* anewploidau aneuploid
anewrin *eg* aneurine
anfadwaith *eg* villainy
anfagnetig *ans* non-magnetic
anfantais *eb* anfanteision handicap
anfantais ddifrifol *eb* anfanteision difrifol profound handicap
anfantais gorfforol *eb* anfanteision corfforol physical handicap
anfantais meddwl *eb* mental handicap
anfarwoldeb *eg* immortality
anfeidraidd *ans* infinite
anfeidredd *eg* anfeidreddau infinity
anferth *ans* gigantic
anfesuradwy *ans* non-quantifiable
anfetel *eg* anfetelau non-metal
anfetelaidd *ans* non-metallic
anfioddiraddadwy *ans* non-biodegradable
anfiotig *ans* abiotic
anflodeuol *ans* non-flowering
anfodyledig *ans* unmodulated
anfoesegol *ans* unethical
anfoesol *ans* immoral
anfoesoldeb *eg* immorality
anfolcanig *ans* non-volcanic
anfon *be* send
anfon a derbyn negesau *be* send and receive messages
anfon dogfen *be* send document
anfon e-bost *be* send mail
anfon eto *be* send again
anfon fel e-bost *be* send as e-mail
anfon ffacs rhagosodedig *be* send default fax
anfon i'r cefn *be* send to back
anfon i'r ysbyty *be* hospitalize
anfon neges *be* send message
anfon newyddion *be* send news
anfon o'r cae *be* send off
anfoneb *eb* anfonebau invoice
anfoneb gwerthiant *eb* anfonebau gwerthiant sales invoice
anfonebu *be* invoicing
anfonwr *eg* anfonwyr sender
anfwriadol *ans* unintentional
anfyw *ans* non-living
anffaeledig *ans* infallible
anfferrus *ans* non-ferrous
anffit *ans* unfit
anfflamadwy *ans* non-flammable; non-inflammable
anffosfforig *ans* non-phosphoric
anffrwythlon *ans* infertile; sterile
anffrwythlondeb *eg* infertility; sterility
anffurfiad *eg* anffurfiadau disfigurement; deformation; deformity
anffurfiad onglog *eg* anffurfiadau onglog angular deformation
anffurfio *be* deform; mutilate
anffurfiol *ans* informal
anffyddiaeth *eb* atheism
anffyddiwr *eg* anffyddwyr atheist
angiosberm *eg* angiosbermau angiosperm
Anglican *eg* Anglicaniaid Anglican
Anglicanaidd *ans* Anglican
anhafal *ans* unequal
anhafaledd *eg* anhafaleddau inequality
anhafaliad *eg* anhafaliadau inequation
anhanfodion (diwinyddol) *ell* accidents
anhanfodion (yn gyffredinol) *ell* inessentials
anharmonig *ans* anharmonic
anharmonig *eg* anharmonigau anharmonic
anhawster *eg* anawsterau difficulty

anhawster canfyddiad *eg* anawsterau canfyddiad perceptual difficulty
anhawster cyfathrebu *eg* anawsterau cyfathrebu communication difficulty
anhawster dysgu *eg* anawsterau dysgu learning difficulty
anhawster dysgu canolig *eg* anawsterau dysgu canolig moderate learning difficulty
anhawster dysgu difrifol *eg* anawsterau dysgu difrifol severe learning difficulty
anhawster dysgu penodol *eg* anawsterau dysgu penodol specific learning difficulty
anhawster llefaru *eg* anawsterau llefaru speech difficulty
anhedonia *eg* anhedonia
anheddeg *eb* ekistics
anheddfudd *eg* housebote
anheddiad *eb* aneddiadau settlement
anheddiad cnewyllol *eg* aneddiadau cnewyllol nucleated settlement
anheddiad hirgul *eg* aneddiadau hirgul ribbon settlement
anheddiad sgwatwyr *eg* squatter settlement
anheddiad sifil *eb* aneddiadau sifil civil settlement
anheddiad tarddlin *eg* aneddiadau tarddlin spring line settlement
anheddu *be* occupy
anhomolog *eg* non-homologue
anhomologaidd *ans* non-homologous
anhrefn *eg/b* disorder
anhrefn *eg/b* chaos
anhrefnedig *ans* unsorted
anhrefniadol *ans* non-procedural
anhrosaidd *ans* intransitive
anhryledadwy *ans* indiffusible
anhuddo (tân) *be* banking up
anhunedd *eg* insomnia
anhwylder (meddygol) *eg* anhwylderau disorder; ailment
anhwylder affeithiol *eg* anhwylderau affeithiol affective disorder
anhwylder affeithiol tymhorol *eg* seasonal affective disorder
anhwylder awtistig *eg* autistic disorder
anhwylder canfyddiad *eg* anhwylderau canfyddiad perceptual disorder
anhwylder cardiofasgwlar *eg* anhwylderau cardiofasgwlar cardiovascular disorder
anhwylder claf diglefyd *eg* hypochondria
anhwylder cylchthymig *eg* cyclothymic disorder
anhwylder datgysylltiol *eg* anhwylderau datgysylltiol dissociative disorder
anhwylder defnyddio sylweddau seicoweithredol *eg* psychoactive substance use disorder
anhwylder deubegwn *eg* bipolar disorder
anhwylder diffyg canolbwyntio *eg* attention deficit disorder
anhwylder diffyg canolbwyntio a gorfywiogrwydd *eg* attention deficit hyperactivity disorder
anhwylder dysthymig *eg* dysthymic disorder
anhwylder genynnau *eg* anhwylderau genynnau genetic disorder
anhwylder gorbryder *eg* anxiety disorder
anhwylder gorfodaeth obsesiynol *eg* obsessive compulsive disorder
anhwylder gwybyddol *eg* anhwylderau gwybyddol cognitive disorder
anhwylder hunaniaeth datgysylltiol *eg* dissociative identity disorder
anhwylder hwyliau *eg* mood disorder
► **anhwylder iaith** *eg* anhwylderau iaith language disorder
anhwylder meddwl *eg* anhwylderau meddwl mental disorder
anhwylder panig *eg* panic disorder
anhwylder personoliaeth *eg* anhwylderau personoliaeth personality disorder
anhwylder personoliaeth anghymdeithasol *eg* antisocial personality disorder
anhwylder personoliaeth luosog *eg* multiple personality disorder
anhwylder pryder cyffredinol *eg* generalized anxiety disorder
anhwylder pryder ôl-drawmatig *eg* post-traumatic stress disorder (PTSD)
anhwylder somatoffurf *eg* somatoform disorder
anhwylder syndrom awtistiaeth *eg* autistic syndrome disorder
anhwylder trosi *eg* conversion disorder
anhwylder ymddygiad *eg* anhwylderau ymddygiad conduct disorder
anhwylder ymddygiad cwsg symudiad llygaid cyflym *eg* rapid eye movement sleep behaviour disorder
anhwylustod *eg* inconvenience
anhyblyg *ans* rigid; inflexible
anhyblygedd *eg* rigidity; stiffness
anhyblygrwydd *eg* inflexibility
anhydawdd *ans* insoluble
anhydoddedd *eg* insolubility
anhydrad *eg* anhydradau anhydrate
anhydraidd *ans* impervious
anhydraul *ans* indigestible
anhydrid *eg* anhydridau anhydride
anhydrin *ans* intractable
anhydrus *ans* anhydrous; non-hydrous
anhyfyw *ans* inviable
anhyglyw *ans* inaudible
anhygyrch *ans* inaccessible
anhygyrchedd *eg* inaccessibility
anhynod *ans* non-singular
anhysbys *ans* unknown
anhysbysrwydd *eg* anonymity
anhysbysyn *eg* anhysbysion unknown
anianawd *eg* temperament

anicca *eg* anicca
anifail *eg* anifeiliaid animal
anifail cnoi cil *eg* anifeiliaid cnoi cil ruminant
anifail gwaed cynnes *eg* anifeiliaid gwaed cynnes warm blooded animal
anifail gwedd *eg* anifeiliaid gwedd draught animal
anifail pwn *eg* anifeiliaid pwn pack animal
anifail pwn *eg* anifeiliaid pwn beast of burden
anifail tir *eg* anifeiliaid tir land animal
anifeilaidd *ans* animal
anilin *eg* aniline
animeiddiad *eg* animeiddiadau animation
animeiddio *be* animate; animation
animeiddio testun *be* text animation
animeiddydd *eg* animeiddwyr animator
animistaidd *ans* animistic
animistiad *eg/b* animistiaid animist
animistiaeth *eb* animism
anion *eg* anionau anion
anionig *ans* anionic
anitya *eg* anitya
anleihaol *ans* nondecreasing
anludiog *ans* non-viscous; inviscid
anllythrennedd *eg* illiteracy
anllythrennedd gweithredol *eg* functional illiteracy
anllythrennog *ans* illiterate
annanheddus *ans* unindented
annarbodion maint *ell* diseconomies of scale
annarogan *ans* unpredictable
annatblygedig *ans* backward
annatod *ans* integral
annedd *eg/b* anheddau dwelling; habitation; residence
annedd bant *eb* anheddau pant pit dwelling
annedd wasgarog *eb* anheddau gwasgarog scattered settlement
annegyddol *ans* non-negative
annel *eg* anelau stanchion
annerch (cyfarfod) *be* address
annheg *ans* unfair
annherfynus *ans* non-terminating
annheyrngarwch *eg* disaffection
annhyngwr *eg* annhyngwyr non-juror
anniatonig *ans* non-diatonic
annibyniaeth *eb* annibyniaethau independence
annibyniaeth data *eb* data independence
annibyniaeth feirniadol *eb* critical autonomy
annibyniaeth linol *eb* linear independence
Annibynnol (am yr enwad) *ans* Congregationalist
annibynnol (ac ar wahân) *ans* discrete
annibynnol (yn gyffredinol) *ans* independent
annibynnol ar y peiriant *ans* machine independent
Annibynnwr *eg* Annibynwyr Congregationalist
anniddigrwydd *eg* discontent
anniflan *ans* fast
anniflanedd *eg* fastness
anniffiniedig *ans* undefined
annigonol *ans* inadequate
annilys *ans* invalid
annirlawn *ans* unsaturated
annistadl *ans* nontrivial
annistrywiol *ans* non-destructive
annog *be* urge; prompt; encourage
annormal *ans* abnormal
annormaledd *eg* abnormality
annosbarthedig *ans* unclassified
annrhigiadwy *ans* uninhabitable
annwyd *eg* anwydau cold; common cold
annyfrllyd *ans* non aqueous
anobeithiol *ans* hopeless
anocsia *eg* anoxia
anod *eg* anodau anode
anodau *ell* annates
anodeiddio *be* anodize
anodi *be* annotate
anodiad *eg* anodiadau annotation
anodig *ans* anodic
anodd *ans* difficult
anoddefgarwch *eg* intolerance
anoddefgarwch bwyd *eg* food intolerance
anoddefgarwch crefyddol *eg* religious intolerance
anoddefgarwch lactos *eg* lactose intolerance
anogwr *eg* anogwyr prompt
anoleuol *ans* non-luminous
anomaledd *eg* anomaly
anomaledd isostatig *eg* anomaleddau isostatig isostatic anomaly
anomalus *ans* anomalous
anomig *ans* non-ohmic
anorecsia nerfosa *eg* anorexia nervosa
anorecsig *ans* anorexic
anorfodadwy *ans* unenforceable
anorganig *ans* inorganic
anostyngadwy *ans* irreducible
anraddedig *ans* ungraded
anrhaith *eg* sack
Anrhaith Rhufain *eg* Sack of Rome
anrheithio *be* sack
anrheithio *be* ravage
anrheolaidd *ans* anomalous
anrhifaidd *ans* non-numeric
anrhufeinig *ans* non-Roman
anrhydedd *eb* anrhydeddau honour
anrhydeddu *be* honour
anrhywiol *ans* asexual
ansadrwydd *eg* instability
ansawdd (mewn cerddoriaeth) *eg* timbre
ansawdd (o ran trwch, gludiogrwydd etc) *eg* consistency
ansawdd (yn gyffredinol) *eg* ansoddau quality
ansawdd bywyd *eg* quality of life
ansawdd darlledu *eg* broadcast quality
ansawdd hufennog *eg* creamy consistency
ansawdd lliw *eg* ansoddau lliw colour quality

ansawdd llythyr *ans* NLQ
ansawdd meddal *eg* soft consistency
ansawdd tôn *eg* tone quality
ansawdd yr amgylchedd *eg* quality of the environment
ansefydlog (=hawdd eu torri i lawr) *ans* labile
ansefydlog (yn gyffredinol) *ans* unstable
ansefydlogrwydd *eg* instability
ansegmennol *ans* unsegmented
anseneddol *ans* unparliamentary
ansensitifrwydd i androgenau *eg* androgen insensitivity
ansero *ans* non-zero
ansicrwydd amcangyfrifol *eg* estimated uncertainty
ansoddol *ans* qualitative
ansoddyn *eg* ansoddau constituent
ansylfaenol *ans* non-basic
ansymudoledd *eg* immobility
ansystematig *ans* non-systematic
Antarctig *eg* Antarctic
antena *eg* antenau antenna
antennyn *eg* antenynnau antennule
anterth (am lif etc) *eg* peak
anterth (mewn seryddiaeth) *eg* zenith
anterthol *ans* zenithal
anticlin *eg* anticlinau anticline
anticlinol *ans* anticlinal
anticlinoriwm *eg* anticlinoria anticlinorium
antiffon *eb* antiffonau antiphon
antigen *eg* antigenau antigen
antimoni *eg* antimony
antimoni(III) clorid *eg* antimony(III) chloride
antimoni(III) clorid ocsid *eg* antimony(III) chloride oxide
antimoni(III) ocsid *eg* antimony(III) oxide
antimoni(III) potasiwm *eg* antimony(III) potassium
antimoni(V) ocsid *eg* antimony(V) oxide
antinod *eg* antinodau antinode
antinodol *ans* antinodal
antinomaidd *ans* antinomian
antinomiad *eg* antinomiaid antinomian
antinomiaeth *eb* antinomianism
Antiochaidd *ans* Antiochene
antiproton *eg* antiprotonau antiproton
antiseiclon *eg* antiseiclonau anticyclone
antiseiclon rhwystrol *eg* antiseiclonau rhwystrol blocking anticyclone
antiseiclonig *ans* anticyclonic
antiseptig *ans* antiseptic
antiseptig *eg* antiseptic
antithesis *eg* antithesis
anthem *eb* anthemau anthem
anthem genedlaethol *eb* anthemau cenedlaethol national anthem
anthem lawn *eb* anthemau llawn full anthem
anthem wersi *eb* anthemau gwersi verse anthem
anther *eg* antheri anther
anthocsanthin *eg* anthocsanthinau anthoxanthin
anthocyanin *eg* anthocyaninau anthocyanin
anthrasen *eg* anthracene
anthrasen-9,10-deuon *eg* anthracene-9,10-dione
anthropogenig *ans* anthropogenic
anthropoid *eg* anthropoidau anthropoid
anthropoleg *eb* anthropology
anthropometreg *eb* anthropometrics
anthropometrig *ans* anthropometric
anthropomorffaeth *eb* anthropomorphism
anthropomorffaidd *ans* anthropomorphic
anudoniaeth *eb* perjury
anufudd *ans* disobedient
anufudd-dod *eg* disobedience
anufudd-dod sifil *eg* civil disobedience
anunffurf *ans* non-uniform
anuniongyrchol *ans* indirect
anwadal *ans* fluctuating
anwadaliad *eg* anwadaliadau fluctuation
anwadalu *be* fluctuate
anwag *ans* non-empty
anwahanadwy *ans* indivisible
anwahanadwyedd *eg* indivisibility
anwahaniad (mewn geneteg) *eg* non-disjunction
anwahaniad (yn gyffredinol) *eg* non-separation
anwahaniaethrwydd *eg* indistinguishability
anwastad *ans* uneven
anwe *eb* weft, woof
anwedd (=hylif wedi troi yn nwy) *eg* anweddau vapour
anwedd dŵr *eg* water vapour
anwedd fflamadwy *eg* anweddau fflamadwy inflammable vapour
anwedd-drydarthiad *eg* evapotranspiration
anweddiad *eg* anweddiadau evaporation; vaporization
anweddol (=hawdd ei anweddu) *ans* volatile
anweddol (wedi'i anweddu) *ans* vaporized
anweddolrwydd *eg* volatility
anweddu *be* evaporate; vaporize
anweithredol *ans* inactive
anweledig *ans* invisible
anwesu *be* cuddle
anwirfoddol *ans* involuntary
anwlar *ans* annular
anwlws *eg* anwli annulus
anwria *eg* anuria
anwrthdroadol *ans* non-inverting
anwrthwynebiad *eg* non-resistance
anws *eg* anus
anwybodaeth *eb* ignorance
anwybyddol *ans* non-cognitive
anwybyddu *be* ignore
anwydrog *ans* non-vitreous
anwyldeb *eg* affection
anwythiad *eg* anwythiadau induction

anwythiad electromagnetig *eg* electromagnetic induction
anwythiad electrostatig *eg* electrostatic induction
anwythiad mathemategol *eg* mathematical induction
anwythiant *eg* inductance
anwytho *be* induce
anwythol *ans* inductive; induced
anwythydd *eg* anwythyddion inductor
anymagorol *ans* indehiscent
anymataliaeth *eb* incontinence
anymataliaeth ddwbl *eb* double incontinence
anymataliol *ans* incontinent
anymochredd *eg* non-alignment
anymochrol *ans* non-aligned
anymwybod *eg* unconscious
anymwybod cyffredinol *eg* collective unconscious
anymwybodol *ans* unconscious
anymyrraeth *eb* non-intervention
anystwyth *ans* stiff
aorta *eg* aorta
apartheid *eg* apartheid
apathi *eg* apathy
apêl *eb* apeliadau appeal
apêl sioc *eb* shock appeal
apelio *be* appeal
apelydd *eg* apelyddion appellant
apig *eb* apigau apex
apigol *ans* apical
▶ **apnoea** *eg* apnoea
apnoea cwsg *eg* sleep apnoea
apocalyptaidd *ans* apocalyptic
apocalypteg *eb* apocalyptic
apocarpog *ans* apocarpous
apocryffa *eg* apocrypha
apoge *eg* apogee
apoplast *eg* apoplast
apostol *eg* apostolion apostle
apostolaidd *ans* apostolic
apostoliaeth *eb* apostleship
apostoligrwydd *eg* apostolicity
apoyando *eg* apoyando
appliqué *eg* appliqué
appoggiatura *eg* appoggiature appoggiatura
apracsia *eg* apraxia
apresoriwm *eg* appresorium
apwyntiad *eg* apwyntiadau appointment
âr *ans* arable
âr *eg* arau are
ar adlam *adf* on the rebound
ar bob tudalen on all pages
ar brawf on probation
ar bremiwm at a premium
ar draws y graen across the grain
ar dudalennau eilrif on even pages
ar dudalennau odrif on odd pages
ar ddisgownt at a discount
ar ei orau cyn best before
ar eich marciau on your marks
ar flaenau'r traed *adf* on toes
ar ffurf U *ans* U-shaped
ar ffurf V *ans* V-shaped
ar ffurf wy *ans* egg shape
ar gael *ans* available
ar gais on request
ar gau *ans* closed
ar golyn *ans* pivoted
ar gyfartaledd *ans* on average
ar hap at random
ar hyd i bawb a fynno longways for as many as will
ar hyd y graen along the grain
ar lawn werth at par
ar letraws *ans* askew
ar ogwydd *ans* tilted
ar ongl at an angle
ar ongl 35° at an angle of 35°
ar ôl yr oes *ans* outdated
ar oledd *ans* inclined, slanting
ar raddfa fawr *ans* large-scale
ar safle'r ysgol *adf* on the school site
ar wahân *ans* apart, separate
ar wastad ei chefn *ans* supine
ar wastad ei gefn *ans* supine
ar y cefn *adf* on the back
ar y llawr *adf* on the floor
ar y tu blaen *adf* on the front
ar yr ystlys *adf* on the wing
arabésg *eg* arabesgau arabesque
aradeiledd *eg* aradeileddau superstructure
aradfudd *eg* ploughbote
arae *eb* araeau array
arae data *eb* araeau data data array
arae graffeg fideo uwch *eb* araeau graffeg fideo uwch super video graphics array
araen (haenen allanol) *eb* araenau coat
araen blastig *eb* araenau plastig plastic coating
araen ddiogelu *eb* araenau diogelu protective coating
araen gel *eb* araenau gel gel coat
araen grwnd *eb* araenau grwnd ground coat
araenu *be* coat
araf (o ran datblygiad corfforol etc) *ans* retarded
araf (o ran datblygiad economaidd) *ans* backward
araf (yn gyffredinol) *ans* slow
arafiad (cyflymder teithio) *eg* arafiadau deceleration
arafiad (twf) *eg* arafiadau retardation
arafu (cyflymder teithio) *be* decelerate
arafu (twf) *be* retard
arafu (yn gyffredinol) *be* slow down
arafu lluniau *be* slow motion
arafwch (datblygiad meddyliol, corfforol etc) *eg* retardation
arafwch (o ran datblygiad) *eg* backwardness
arafwch meddwl *eg* mental retardation

arafwr *eg* arafwyr retarder
araith *eb* areithiau speech
araith sefydlu *eb* areithiau sefydlu inaugural speech
arall *ans* alternative
aralleirio *be* paraphrase
aralleirio *be* paraphrasing
aralliad *eg* alienation
arallu (eiddo) *be* alienate
Aramaeg *eb* Aramaic
Aramaegeb *eb* Aramaegebau Aramaism
Arameaidd *ans* Aramaic
arbed *be* save
arbed ergyd *be* save a shot
arbed llafur *be* labour saving
arbediad *eg* arbedion saving
arbedion effeithlonrwydd *ell* efficiency savings
arbedion feis *ell* vice clamps
arbedwr sgrin *eg* arbedwyr sgrin screen saver
arbelydriad *eg* arbelydriadau irradiation
arbelydru *be* irradiate
arbenigaeth *eb* arbenigaethau specialization
arbenigedd *eg* arbenigeddau speciality; expertise; specialism
arbenigo *be* specialize
arbenigol *ans* specialized
arbenigwr *eg* arbenigwyr expert, specialist
arbenigwr cyfreithiol *eg* arbenigwyr cyfreithiol jurist
arbenigwr chwarae ysbyty *eg* hospital play specialist
arbor *eg* arborau arbor
arbrawf *eg* arbrofion experiment; trial
arbrawf cymharu *eg* control experiment
arbrawf dall *eg* arbrofion dall blind experiment
arbrawf dwbl-ddall *eg* arbrofion dwbl-ddall double-blind experiment
arbrawf goroesi *eg* arbrofion goroesi life span experiment
arbrawf labordy *eg* arbrofion labordy laboratory experiment
arbrawf maes *eg* arbrofion maes field experiment
arbrisiant *eg* arbrisiannau appreciation
arbrofi *be* experiment
arbrofol *ans* experimental; trial
arbwsciwl *eg* arbuscule
arc *eb* arcau arc
arc dangiadol *eb* arcau tangiadol tangential arc
arc flaen *eb* arcau blaen forward arc
arc gyffwrdd *eb* arcau cyffwrdd arc of contact
arc y gornel *eb* corner arc
arcêd *eb* arcedau arcade
Arctig *eg* Arctic
arctig alpinaidd *eg* arctic alpine
arc-weldio *be* arc welding
Arch y Cyfamod *eb* Arch of Covenant, the
archaeoleg *eb* archaeology
archangel *eg* archangylion archangel
Arch-chwilyswr *eg* Arch-chwilyswyr Inquisitor General
archdeip *eg* archdeipiau archetype
archddinas *eb* archddinasoedd primate city
archddug *eg* archddugiaid grand duke
archdduges *eb* archddugesau archduchess
archddugiaeth *eb* archddugiaethau archduchy
archddyfarniad *eg* archddyfarniadau decree
archddyfarniad absoliwt *eg* decree absolute
archddyfarniad amodol *eg* decree nisi
archddyfarniadau Carlsbad *ell* Carlsbad decrees
archddyfarnu *be* decree
archeb (swyddogol, milwrol etc) *eb* archebion requisition
archeb (yn gyffredinol) *eb* archebion order
archeb arian *eb* archebion arian money order
archeb banc *eb* archebion banc banker's order
archeb bost *eb* archebion post postal order
archeb drwy'r post *eb* archebion drwy'r post mail order
archeb prynu *eb* archebion prynu purchase order
archebion post *ell* mail-order
archebu *be* book
archebu drwy'r post *be* mail order
archegoniwm *eg* archegonium
Archentaidd *ans* Argentine
Archentwr *eg* Archentwyr Argentine
archesgob (yn gyffredinol) *eg* archesgobion archbishop
archesgob (yn nheitl prif esgob talaith) *eg* archesgobion primate
archfarchnad *eb* archfarchnadoedd hypermarket
archif *eg* archifau archive
archifdy *eg* archifdai record office
Archifdy Gwladol *eg* Public Record Office
archifdy'r sir *eg* archifdai'r siroedd county record office
archifo *be* archive
archifydd *eg* archifyddion archivist
architraf *eg* architrafau architrave
archoll *eg* archollion cut
archolladwy *ans* vulnerable
archwaeth *eb* appetite
archwiliad (ariannol etc) *eg* archwiliadau audit
archwiliad (claf etc) *eg* archwiliadau examination
archwiliad (dadansoddol) *eg* archwiliadau exploration
archwiliad (meddygol) *eg* archwiliadau check-up
archwiliad (yn gyffredinol) *eg* archwiliadau investigation
archwiliad clinigol *eg* archwiliadau clinigol clinical audit
archwiliad cod *eg* code walkthrough
archwiliad dan anaesthetig *eg* archwiliadau dan anaesthetig examination under anaesthetic
archwiliad meddygol *eg* archwiliadau meddygol medical audit

archwiliad nyrsio *eg* archwiliadau nyrsio nursing audit
archwiliad rhaglen *eg* walkthrough
archwiliad strategol *eg* reconnaissance
archwiliadol *ans* exploratory
archwilio (a dadansoddi) *be* explore
archwilio (ariannol etc) *be* audit
archwilio (yn feddygol etc) *be* examine
archwilio strategol *be* reconnoitre
archwiliwr *eg* archwilwyr auditor
archwiliwr cyfrifon *eg* archwilwyr cyfrifon auditor of accounts
archwladwriaeth *eb* super state
archwys *eg* exudate
archwysiad *eg* archwysiadau exudation
archwysu *be* exude
ardal (yn gyffredinol) *eb* ardaloedd area
ardal (mewn cerddoriaeth) *eb* ardaloedd region
ardal (=cymdogaeth) *eb* ardaloedd district
ardal (=rhanbarth penodol) *eb* ardaloedd belt
ardal â golygfeydd prydferth *eb* ardaloedd â golygfeydd prydferth area of scenic beauty
ardal adeiledig *eb* ardaloedd adeiledig built-up area
ardal amaethyddol *eb* ardaloedd amaethyddol agricultural area
ardal arafgynnydd *eb* ardaloedd arafgynnydd backward area
Ardal Corn a Moch *eb* Corn Hog Belt
ardal dosbarth uchaf *eb* ardaloedd dosbarth uchaf high class area
ardal drefol *eb* ardaloedd trefol urban area
▸ **ardal ddadfilwroledig** *eb* ardaloedd dadfilwroledig demilitarized zone
ardal ddatblygu *eb* ardaloedd datblygu development area
ardal ddatblygu arbennig *eb* ardaloedd datblygu arbennig special development area
ardal ddifreintiedig *eb* ardaloedd difreintiedig deprived area
ardal ddirwasgedig *eb* ardaloedd dirwasgedig depressed area
ardal ddiwydiannol *eb* ardaloedd diwydiannol industrial area
ardal eang *eb* wide area
ardal electronig *eb* ardaloedd electronig electronic area
ardal ethnograffig *eb* ardaloedd ethnograffig ethnographic area
Ardal Fasnach Rydd Ewropeaidd *eb* European Free Trade Area
ardal fenter *eb* ardaloedd menter enterprise zone
ardal ffiniol *eb* ardaloedd ffiniol frontier district
ardal ffocws *eb* ardaloedd ffocws focus area
ardal gadwraeth *eb* ardaloedd cadwraeth conservation area
ardal gadwraeth sefydledig *eb* ardaloedd cadwraeth sefydledig established conservation area
ardal gofalon canolog *eb* ardaloedd gofalon canolog central care area
ardal gotwm *eb* ardaloedd cotwm cotton belt
ardal gwelliannau cyffredinol *eb* ardaloedd gwelliannau cyffredinol general improvement area
ardal gyferbyniol *eb* ardaloedd cyferbyniol contrasting locality
ardal gynoptig *eb* preoptic area
ardal gynorthwyedig *eb* ardaloedd cynorthwyedig assisted area
ardal hynod o hardd *eb* ardaloedd hynod o hardd area of scenic attraction
ardal lanio *eb* ardaloedd glanio landing area
ardal leol *eb* ardaloedd lleol local area
ardal lwyd *eb* ardaloedd llwyd grey area; intermediate area
ardal meinwe patrymu'r cnewyllan *eb* nucleolar organising region
ardal o dangynhyrchu amaethyddol *eb* ardaloedd o dangynhyrchu amaethyddol agricultural deficiency area
ardal o flaenoriaeth addysgol *eb* ardaloedd o flaenoriaeth addysgol education priority area
ardal o orgynhyrchu amaethyddol *eb* ardaloedd o orgynhyrchu amaethyddol agricultural surplus area
ardal o werth amgylcheddol mawr *eb* ardaloedd o werth amgylcheddol mawr area of great environmental value
ardal samplu *eb* ardaloedd samplu sample area
ardal waith *eb* ardaloedd gwaith work area
ardal wasanaeth *eb* ardaloedd gwasanaeth service area
ardal wedi'i diboblogi *eb* ardaloedd wedi'u diboblogi depopulated area
ardal weithredu ar dai *eb* ardaloedd gweithredu ar dai housing action area
ardal wledig *eb* ardaloedd gwledig rural area, countryside area
ardal wyliau *eb* ardaloedd gwyliau resort area
Ardal y Llynnoedd *eb* Lake District
ardal ymylol *eb* ardaloedd ymylol peripheral area
ardalydd *eg* ardalyddion marquis
ardaro *be* impinge
ardoll *eb* ardollau levy
ardrawiad *eg* ardrawiadau impact
ardraws *ans* transverse
ardrawslin *eb* ardrawsliniau transversal
ardrefniant *eg* ardrefniannau settlement
ardrefniant chwyldroadol *eg* revolutionary settlement
Ardrefniant Edward *eg* Edwardian Settlement
Ardrefniant Eglwysig Elizabeth *eg* Elizabethan Church Settlement
ardrefniant heddwch *eg* peace settlement
ardrefniant Protestannaidd *eg* Protestant settlement
ardrefniant Tuduraidd *eg* Tudor settlement
ardrefniant Versailles *eg* Versailles settlement

ardrethol *ans* rateable
ardyfiant planhigol *eg* gall
ardymer *eg/b* temperament
ardymer cyfartal *eg* equal temperament
ardymer trydydd cyfartal *eg* mean tone temperament
ardymheru *be* temper
ardystio *be* certification
ardystio *be* certify
ardywallt *be* decant
arddangosiaeth *eb* exhibitionism
arddangosydd saith-segment *eg* arddangosyddion saith-segment seven-segment display
arddangos *be* exhibit; display; demonstrate
arddangosfa *eb* arddangosfeydd exhibition; display
arddangosfa ddawnsio *eb* arddangosfeydd dawnsio display of dancing
Arddangosfa Fawr *eb* Great Exhibition
arddangosfa mur *eb* arddangosfeydd mur wall display
arddangosiad *eg* arddangosiadau demonstration; display (act of); exhibition
arddangosiad grisial hylif *eg* arddangosiadau grisial hylif liquid crystal display
arddangoswr *eg* arddangoswyr exhibitor
arddegau *ell* teens
arddel credoau gwahanol *be* profess different creeds
arddelw *eb* arddelwau effigy
arddull *eg/b* arddulliau style
arddull addysgu *eg* arddulliau addysgu teaching style
arddull arlunio rhanedig *eg* split style of drawing
arddull border *eg* arddulliau border border style
arddull cerddorol *eg* arddulliau cerddorol musical style
arddull claf-ganolog *eg* patient-centred style
arddull cyflwyno *eg* arddulliau cyflwyno presentation style
arddull cyfoes *eg* arddulliau cyfoes contemporary style
arddull dysgu *eg* arddulliau dysgu learning style
arddull darddullaidd *eg* mannerist style
arddull clasurol *eg* classic style
arddull gwe *eg* web style
arddull meddyg-ganolog *eg* doctor-centred style
arddull nesaf *eg* next style
arddull pensaernïol *eg* arddulliau pensaernïol architectural style
arddull saeth *eg* arddulliau saeth arrow style
arddull testun *eg* arddulliau testun text style
arddull wedi'i addasu *eg* custom style
arddull y cyfeiliant *eg* style of accompaniment
arddull ymateb *eg* arddulliau ymateb response style
arddulliadol *ans* stylistic
arddwrn *eg* arddyrnau wrist
arddwrn cadarn *eg* arddyrnau cadarn firm wrist
arddwys *ans* intensive
arddwysedd *eg* arddwyseddau intensity
arddwysedd goleuol *eg* arddwyseddau goleuol luminous intensity
ar-edrych *ans* look-at
aren *eb* arennau kidney
aren *eg* arenau arene
aren artiffisial *eb* arennau artiffisial artificial kidney
arena *eb* arenau arena
arennill y cant *eg* percentage yield
arennog *ans* kidney shape
arennol *ans* renal
arestiad *eg* arestiadau arrest
arestio (cywair hynafol) *be* attach
arestio (yn gyffredinol) *be* arrest
arf *eg* arfau weapon
arf ataliol *eg* arfau ataliol deterrent
arfaeth amlwg *eb* manifest destiny
arfau *ell* armaments
arfau mowldiwr *ell* moulder's tools
arfau rhyfel *ell* munitions
arfau V *ell* V-weapons
arfbais *eb* arfbeisiau coat of arms
arfbib *eb* arfbibau armoured hose
arfdy *eg* arfdai arsenal
arfer *eg/b* arferion practice; habit; use; custom
arfer bwyd *eg* arferion bwyd food-related custom
arfer cyfyngol *eg* arferion cyfyngol restrictive practice
arfer cymdeithasol *eg* arferion cymdeithasol social practice
arfer diwydiannol *eg* arferion diwydiannol industrial practice
arfer gwael *eg* arferion gwael bad practice
arfer gwahaniaethol *eg* arferion gwahaniaethol discriminatory practice
arfer y faenor *eg* custom of the manor
arferiad cadw da *eg* good saving practice
arferion bwyta *ell* feeding habits
arferion gofal *ell* care practice
arferion gweithio diogel *ell* safe working practices
arferion y Mers *ell* marcher customs
arfin *eg* arfiniau knife edge
arfloyw *ans* armour bright
arfogaeth *eb* armour
arfogi *be* arm
arfordir *eg* arfordiroedd coast; sea-coast; littoral
arfordir cyfodol *eg* arfordiroedd cyfodol coast of emergence
arfordir Periw *eg* Peruvian coast
arfordir yr Iwerydd *eg* Atlantic coast
arfordirol *ans* coastal; littoral
arforol *ans* maritime
arfwisg *eb* arfwisgoedd suit of armour
arffin *eb* arffiniau bound
arffin isaf *eb* arffiniau isaf lower bound
arffin uchaf *eb* arffiniau uchaf upper boundary

arg *eg* argiau amplitude
arg *eg* argiau argument
argae *eg* argaeau dam
argae iâ *eg* argaeau iâ ice dam
argae rhew *eg* argaeau rhew ice dam
argaeledd *eg* availability
argaen *eg* argaenau veneer
argaen addurnol *eg* argaenau addurnol decorative veneer
argaen cydbwyso *eg* balancer veneer
argaen llifdoriad *eg* argaenau llifdoriad saw-cut veneer
argaen toriad cylchdro *eg* argaenau toriad cylchdro rotary-cut veneer
argaen toriad cyllell *eg* argaenau toriad cyllell knife-cut veneer
argaen toriad hanner cylchdro *eg* argaenau toriad hanner cylchdro half rotary-cut veneer
argaen wyneb *eg* argaenau wyneb face veneer
argaenu *be* veneer
argaenu gwasgblat *be* caul veneering
argaenwaith *eg* marquetry
argenin *eg* argenine
arginin *eg* arginine
arglwydd (â hawl i sedd yn Nhŷ'r Arglwyddi) *eg* arglwyddi peer
arglwydd (yn gyffredinol) *eg* arglwyddi lord
Arglwydd Adfocad *eg* Lord Advocate
arglwydd am oes *eg* life-peer
Arglwydd Amddiffynnydd *eg* Lord Protector
Arglwydd Brif Ustus *eg* Lord Chief Justice
Arglwydd Faer *eg* Lord Mayor
Arglwydd Ganghellor *eg* Lord Chancellor
Arglwydd Geidwad *eg* Lord Keeper
Arglwydd Geidwad y Sêl Fawr *eg* Lord Keeper of the Great Seal
Arglwydd Lywydd *eg* Lord President
Arglwydd Penrhyn, Yr *eg* Lord Penrhyn
Arglwydd Raglaw *eg* Lord Lieutenant
arglwydd rhyfel *eg* arglwyddi rhyfel war lord
Arglwydd Shiva, Yr *eg* Lord Shiva
Arglwydd Uchel Drysorydd *eg* Lord High Treasurer
Arglwydd Uchel Lyngesydd *eg* Lord High Admiral
arglwydd y faenor *eg* arglwyddi'r maenorau lord of the manor
Arglwyddi Apelyddol *ell* Appellant Lords
Arglwyddi Lleyg ac Eglwysig *ell* Lords Temporal and Spiritual
Arglwyddi Ordeinwyr *ell* Lords Ordainers
arglwyddiaeth (ffiwdal) *eb* arglwyddiaethau seigniory
arglwyddiaeth (yn gyffredinol) *eb* arglwyddiaethau lordship
arglwyddiaeth freiniol *eb* honour
arglwyddiaethol *ans* seigneurial
arglwyddi'r deyrnas *ell* peerage
Arglwyddi'r Gororau *ell* Lords Marcher
Arglwyddi'r Gynulleidfa *ell* Lords of the Congregation
Arglwyddi'r Mers *ell* marcher Lords
argoel *eb* argoelion prognosis
argon *eg* argon
argor *eg* argorau groyne
argraff *eb* argraffiadau impression
argraff craidd *eb* core impression
argraffadwy *ans* impressionable
argraffiad *eg* argraffiadau edition
argraffiad clawr papur *eg* argraffiadau clawr papur paper-back edition
argraffiad craidd *eg* argraffiadau craidd core print
argraffiadaeth *eb* impressionism
argraffiadol *ans* impressionistic
argraffiadydd *eg* argraffiadwyr impressionist
argraffu *be* print
argraffu cyfrannol *be* proportional printing
argraffu di-draw *eg* non-impact printing
argraffu jymbo *be* jumbo print
argraffu offset *be* offset printing
argraffu sgrin *be* screen dump
argraffu ychwanegol *be* additive printing
argraffydd *eg* argraffyddion printer
argraffydd cadwyn *eg* argraffyddion cadwyn chain printer
argraffydd celwrn *eg* argraffyddion celwrn barrel printer
argraffydd chwistrell *eg* argraffyddion chwistrell ink-jet printer
argraffydd drwm *eg* argraffyddion drwm drum printer
argraffydd gwifren *eg* argraffyddion gwifren wire printer
argraffydd laser *eg* argraffyddion laser laser printer
argraffydd matrics *eg* argraffyddion matrics dot matrix printer
argraffydd nodau *eg* argraffyddion nodau character printer
argraffydd olwyn *eb* argraffyddion olwyn daisy-wheel printer
argraffydd paralel *eg* argraffyddion paralel parallel printer
argraffydd rhagosodedig *eg* argraffyddion rhagosodedig default printer
argraffydd sbŵl *eg* argraffyddion sbŵl spooled printer
argraffydd serograffig *eg* argraffyddion serograffig xerographic printer
argraffydd traw *eg* argraffyddion traw impact printer
argragen *eb* carapace
argroenol *ans* topical
arguddiad *eg* arguddiadau occulation
argyfwng *eg* argyfyngau emergency; crisis
argyfwng bywyd *eg* life crisis
argyfwng clwy'r traed a'r genau *eg* foot and mouth crisis
argyfwng dyledion *eg* debt crisis

argyfwng Fashoda *eg* Fashoda crisis
argyfwng Moroco *eg* Moroccan crisis
argyfwng Tsiecoslofacia *eg* Czech crisis
Argyfwng y Gwahardd *eg* Exclusion Crisis
Argyfwng y Mesur Diwygio *eg* Reform Bill Crisis
argyfwng yr ymddiorseddiad *eg* abdication crisis
argyfyngau cau allan y Penrhyn *ell* Penrhyn lockouts
argyfyngus *ans* critical
argymell *be* recommend
argymhelliad *eg* argymhellion recommendation; submission
argymhelliad B.S. *eg* B.S. recommendation
arhant /arahant arhant /arahant
arhat arhat
arholi *be* examine
arholiad *eg* arholiadau examination
arholiad agored *eg* arholiadau agored open examination
arholiad cyffredinol proffesiynol *eg* arholiadau cyffredinol proffesiynol common professional examination
arholiad gwahaniaethol *eg* arholiadau gwahaniaethol differentiated examination
arholiad mewnol *eg* arholiadau mewnol internal examination
arholiadau terfynol *ell* finals
arholwr allanol *eg* arholwyr allanol external examiner
arholwr mewnol *eg* arholwyr mewnol internal examiner
arhythmig *ans* arhythmic
aria *eb* ariâu aria
Ariad *eg* Ariaid Aryan
Ariaidd *ans* Aryan
arian (=cyfrwng cyfnewid) *eg* money
arian (Ag) *eg* silver
arian a ddyrennir i ysgolion *eg* money allocated to schools
arian bath *eg* coinage; specie
arian byw *eg* quick silver
arian cochion *ell* copper money
arian cwmni *eg* company finance
arian cyfred *eg* currency
arian cyfred Ewropeaidd sengl *eg* single European currency
arian cywir *eg* exact money
arian degol *ell* decimal coinage
arian gwynion *ell* silver money
arian mân *eg* petty cash
arian nicel *eg* nickel silver
arian nitrad *eg* silver nitrate
arian nitrad dyfrllyd *eg* aqueous silver nitrate
arian nitrad(V) amoniaidd *eg* ammoniacal silver nitrate(V)
arian papur *eg* paper money; banknotes
arian parod *eg* cash
arian poced *eg* pocket money
arian sengl *eg* single currency
arian Sheffield Sheffield plate
arian treigl *eg* current money
arian tryc *eg* token
arianbresyddu *be* silver-braze
arian(I) nitrad(V) amoniaidd *eg* ammoniacal silver(I) nitrate(V)
ariannol (=cyllidol) *ans* financial
ariannol (yn gyffredinol) *ans* monetary
ariannu *be* finance
ariannu'r gweithgareddau *be* finance the activities
ariannwr *eg* arianwyr financier
arianolaeth *eb* monetarism
ariansodro *be* silver soldering
arianyddwr *eg* arianyddwyr monetarist
arioso *eg* ariosi arioso
ar-lein *ans* on-line
arloesedd *eg* innovation
arloesi *be* innovate; pioneer
arloesol *ans* pioneer
arloeswr *eg* arloeswyr pioneer
arlunydd *eg* arlunwyr painter, artist
arlunydd gwlad *eg* arlunwyr gwlad artisan painter
arlwyaeth *eb* purveyance
arlwyo *be* cater; catering; purvey
arlwywr *eg* arlwywyr caterer; purveyor
arlywydd *eg* arlywyddion president
arlywyddiaeth *eb* presidency
arlliw *eg* arlliwiau tint; hue
arlliw gamboge *eg* gamboge tint
arlliwedig *ans* tinted
arlliwio *eb* tint
arlliwio llethrau *be* hill shading
arllwys (=rhyddhau hylif) *be* discharge
arllwys (yn gyffredinol) *be* pour
arllwys metel *be* metal pouring
arllwysiad (meddygol) *eg* arllwysiadau infusion
arllwysiad (wrth ryddhau hylif) *eg* arllwysiadau discharge
arllwysiad mewnwythiennol *eg* arllwysiadau mewnwythiennol intravenous infusion
arllwysiad parhaus *eg* arllwysiadau parhaus continuous infusion
armada *eb* armadau armada
armatwr *eg* armatyrau armature
armel *eg* hind-milk
Arminaidd *ans* Arminian
Arminiad *eg* Arminiaid Arminian
Arminiaeth *eb* Arminianism
armonica *eg* armonicau armonica
arnodedig *ans* endorsed
arnodi *be* endorse
arnodiad *eg* arnodiadau endorsement
arnofiad *eg* arnofiadau flotation
arnofio *be* float
Arnwlff *eg* Arnulph
arogl (yn arbennig arogl da) *eg* aroglau aroma

arogl (yn arbennig arogl drwg) *eg* aroglau odour
arogl (yn gyffredinol) *eg* aroglau smell
arogldarth *eg* arogldarthau incense
arogleuol *ans* olfactory
arogli *be* sniff; smell
arogli (am y synnwyr o arogli) *be* olfaction
arogli glud *be* glue sniffing
arogli hydoddyddion *be* solvent sniffing
aroglus *ans* odourous
arolwg *eg* arolygon survey
arolwg adeiladu *eg* arolygon adeiladu building survey
arolwg awyr *eg* arolygon awyr air survey
arolwg barn *eg* arolygon barn opinion poll
arolwg bodlonrwydd cleifion *eg* patient satisfaction survey
arolwg cyflwr *eg* arolygon cyflwr condition survey
arolwg cyfforddusrwydd *eg* arolygon cyfforddusrwydd comfort survey
arolwg cynulleidfa *eg* arolygon cynulleidfa audience survey
Arolwg Defnydd Tir (ADT) *eg* Land Use Survey
arolwg defnyddio adeiladau *eg* arolygon defnyddio adeiladau building use survey
arolwg dioddefwyr *eg* victim survey
arolwg ffôn *eg* arolygon ffôn telephone survey
Arolwg Gwariant Teulu *eg* Family Expenditure Survey
arolwg llenyddol *eg* arolygon llenyddol literature survey
Arolwg Ordnans *eg* Ordnance Survey
Arolwg Trosedd Prydain *eg* British Crime Survey
arolygiad *eg* arolygiadau inspection
arolygiaeth *eb* arolygiaethau inspectorate
Arolygiaeth ei Mawrhydi (AEM) *eb* Her Majesty's Inspectorate
arolygu *be* inspect
arolygwr *eg* arolygwyr inspector
aromatig *ans* aromatic
arorwt *eg* arrowroot
aros ymlaen *be* staying on
arosgedd *eg* obliqueness; obliquity
arosgo *ans* oblique
arosod *ans* superimposed
arosod *be* superimpose
arosod *be* superpose
arosodiad *eg* arosodiadau superposition
arpeggio *eg* arpeggi arpeggio
arsenal *eg* arsenalau arsenal
arsenig *eg* arsenic
arsenig triclorid *eg* arsenic trichloride
arsenig(III) ocsid *eg* arsenic(III) oxide
arsenig(V) ocsid *eg* arsenic(V) oxide
arsin *eg* arsine
arsugnedd *eg* adsorbency
arsugniad *eg* adsorption
arsugno *be* adsorb
arsugnydd *eg* arsugnyddion adsorbent
arsugnyn *eg* arsugnynnau adsorbate
arswyd *eg* horror
arsylw *eg* arsylwadau observation
arsylw niwrolegol *eg* arsylwadau niwrolegol neurological observation
arsylwi *be* observe; observation
arsylwi anymwthiol *be* unobtrusive observation
arsylwi cyfranwyr *be* participant observation
arsylwi disgrifiadol *be* descriptive observation
arsylwi ffenomenau *be* observe phenomena
arsylwi gwersi *be* lesson observation
arsylwi mewn sefyllfa naturiol *be* naturalistic observation
arsylwi yn yr ystafell ddosbarth *be* classroom observation
arsylwi-triniaeth-arsylwi *be* observation-treatment-observation
arsylwr *eg* arsylwyr observer
arsylladwy *ans* observable
arsyllfa *eb* arsyllfeydd observatory
arsyllu *be* observe
Art Nouveau *eb* Art Nouveau
arteffact *eg* arteffactau artefact
arteithglwyd *eb* arteithglwydi rack
arteithio *be* torture
arteriosglerosis *eg* arteriosclerosis
artiffisial *ans* artificial
artisiog *eg* artisiogau artichoke
artisiog glôb *eg* artisiogau glôb globe artichoke
artisiog Jerwsalem *eg* artisiogau Jerwsalem Jerusalem artichoke
artist *eg* artistiaid artist
artistig *ans* artistic
arthritis *eg* arthritis
arthropod *eg* arthropodau arthropod
arunig *ans* isolated
arunig *ans* stand-alone
arunigo (cemegyn) *be* isolate
arunigydd *eg* arunigwyr isolator
arwahaniad genynnau *eg* genetic isolation
arwahanol *ans* discrete
arwahanrwydd *eg* isolation
arwahanrwydd gogoneddus *eg* splendid isolation
arwahanu *be* isolate; segregate
arwahanu hiliol *be* racial segregation
arwahanydd *eg* arwahanwyr isolationist
arwain (cerddorfa etc) *be* conduct
arwain (yn gyffredinol) *be* lead
arwain i fyny *be* lead up
arwain i lawr *be* lead down
arwaith *eg* arweithiau action
arwaith ac adwaith action and reaction
arwaith crampio *eg* cramping action
arwaith llithr *eg* arweithiau llithr sliding action
arwaith sgraffinio *eg* abrasive action
arwaith tafellu *eg* slicing action
arwaith torri *eg* arweithiau torri cutting action

arwedd *eb* arweddion feature
arwedd arfordirol *eb* arweddion arfordirol coastal feature
arwedd nodweddiadol *eb* arweddion nodweddiadol characteristic feature
arweddion craig *ell* rock features
arweddion dŵr *ell* water features
arweiniad *eg* guidance
arweiniad ar ddatblygiad *eg* developmental guidance
arweiniad ar yrfa *eg* career guidance
arweiniad parhaus *eg* continuous guidance
arweiniad tapr *eg* taper lead
arweinlyfr *eg* arweinlyfrau guide book
arweinwyr Catholig *ell* Catholic leadership
arweinydd (cerddorfa etc) *eg* arweinyddion conductor
arweinydd (yn gyffredinol) *eg* arweinwyr leader
Arweinydd Clybiau Plant *eg* Arweinwyr Clybiau Plant Kids' Club Leader
arweinydd crefyddol *eg* arweinwyr crefyddol religious leader
arweinydd cwricwlwm *eg* arweinwyr cwricwlwm curriculum leader
arweinydd chwarae *eg* arweinwyr chwarae play leader
arweinydd democrataidd *eg* arweinwyr democrataidd democratic leader
arweinydd grŵp *eg* arweinwyr grŵp group leader
arweinydd ieuenctid *eg* arweinwyr ieuenctid youth leader
arweinydd laissez-faire *eg* laissez-faire leader
arweinydd tîm *eg* arweinwyr tîm team leader
arweinydd unbenaethol *eg* autocratic leader
arweinyddiaeth *eb* leadership
arwerthiant *eg* arwerthiannau auction sale
arwerthiant electronig dwyffordd *eg* electronic reverse auction
arwerthwr *eg* arwerthwyr auctioneer
arwisgiad *eg* investment
arwisgo *be* invest; investiture
arwr *eg* arwyr hero
arwrgerdd *eg* arwrgerddi epic
arwrol *ans* epic
arwydryn *eg* arwydrau coverslip
arwydd (=addurn ar do neu fur) *eg/b* arwyddion cresting
arwydd (=dangosydd) *eg/b* arwyddion indication
arwydd (cywair neu amser) *eg/b* arwyddion signature
arwydd (sain neu weithred) *eg/b* arwyddion signal
arwydd (yn gyffredinol) *eg/b* arwyddion sign
arwydd confensiynol *eg* arwyddion confensiynol conventional sign
arwydd cyfyngder *eg* arwyddion cyfyngder distress signal
arwydd cywair *eg* arwyddion cywair key signature
arwydd gweledol *eg* arwyddion gweledol visual sign
arwydd llaw *eg* arwyddion llaw handsign
arwydd llaw sol-ffa *eg* arwyddion llaw sol-ffa sol-fa hand sign
arwydd lluosi *eg* arwyddion lluosi multiplication sign
arwydd minws *eg* arwyddion minws minus sign
arwydd mynegeiol *eg* indexical sign
arwydd naturiol *eg* arwyddion naturiol natural sign
arwydd plws *eg* plus sign
arwydd sawr *eg* arwyddion sawr scent mark
arwydd tempo *eg* tempo marking
arwyddedig (am ddelwedd) *eg* signified
arwyddfardd *eg* arwyddfeirdd heraldic bard
arwyddiaith *eb* arwyddieithoedd sign language
arwyddion bywyd *ell* vital signs
arwyddion dirgroes *ell* opposite signs
arwyddion y Sidydd *ell* signs of the Zodiac
arwyddlun *eg* arwyddluniau emblem
arwyddo *be* signing
arwyddo baban *be* baby signing
arwyddocâd *eg* significance; connotation
arwyddocâd addasu *eg* adaptive significance
arwyddocâd cymdeithasol *eg* social implications
arwyddocâd ystadegol *eg* statistical significance
arwyddocaol *ans* significant
arwyddwr (am ddelwedd neu air) *eg* signifier
arwyneb *eg* arwynebau surface
arwyneb anwastad *eg* arwynebau anwastad uneven surface
arwyneb arosgo *eg* arwynebau arosgo oblique surface
arwyneb bondiog *eg* arwynebau bondiog bonded surface
arwyneb bras *eg* arwynebau bras coarse surface
arwyneb cesiwm *eg* caesium surface
arwyneb ceugrwm *eg* arwynebau ceugrwm concave surface
arwyneb crwm *eg* arwynebau crwm curved surface
arwyneb cwyraidd *eg* arwynebau cwyraidd waxy surface
arwyneb cyfwyneb *eg* arwynebau cyfwyneb flush surface
arwyneb cylchdro *eg* surface of revolution
arwyneb erydiad *eg* arwynebau erydiad erosion surface
arwyneb erydog *eg* arwynebau erydog eroded surface
arwyneb farnais *eg* arwynebau farnais varnished surface
arwyneb garw *eg* arwynebau garw rough surface
arwyneb gludio *eg* arwynebau gludio gluing surface
arwyneb gorffenedig *eg* arwynebau gorffenedig finished surface
arwyneb graenog *eg* arwynebau graenog grainy surface
arwyneb gweadog *eg* arwynebau gweadog textured surface

arwyneb gwydrog *eg* arwynebau gwydrog glazed surface
arwyneb isotropig *eg* arwynebau isotropig isotropic surface
arwyneb llyfn *eg* arwynebau llyfn fine surface
arwyneb llyfn *eg* arwynebau llyfn smooth surface
arwyneb mandyllog *eg* arwynebau mandyllog porous surface
arwyneb mat *eg* matt surface
arwyneb patrymog *eg* arwynebau patrymog patterned surface
arwyneb plân *eg* arwynebau plân plane surface
arwyneb purwyn *eg* arwynebau purwyn pure white surface
arwyneb recordio *eg* arwynebau recordio recording surface
arwyneb resbiradol *eg* respiratory surface
arwyneb sglein *eg* arwynebau sglein glossy surface
arwyneb swyddogaethol *eg* arwynebau swyddogaethol functional surface
arwyneb sy'n dal pwysau *eg* arwynebau sy'n dal pwysau load bearing surface
arwyneb unbotensial disgyrchedd *eg* gravitational equipotential surface
arwyneb wedi tagu *eg* arwynebau wedi tagu clogged surface
arwyneb y gell *eg* cell surface
arwyneb y toriad *eg* cut surface
arwynebau ochrol *ell* lateral surfaces
arwynebedd *eg* arwynebeddau area
arwynebedd arwyneb *eg* surface area
arwynebedd crwm *eg* arwynebeddau crwm curved area
arwynebedd cyfartal *eg* arwynebeddau cyfartal equal area
arwynebedd cywerth *eg* arwynebeddau cywerth equivalent area
arwynebedd triongl *eg* area of triangle
arwynebedd trychiadol *eg* arwynebeddau trychiadol sectional area
arwynebedd y sector *eg* area of the sector
arwynebydd *eg* arwynebyddion surfactant
aryl *eg* aryl
aryneilio *be* alternate
arysgrif *eg* arysgrifau inscription
arysgrifio *be* inscribe
asart *eg* asartau assart
asasin *eg* asasiniaid assassin
asbaragws *eg* asparagus
asbartas *eg* aspartase
asbestos *eg* asbestos
asbig *eg* aspic
ased *eg* asedau asset
ased sefydlog *eg* asedau sefydlog fixed asset
asedau cyfredol *ell* current assets
asedau hylifol *ell* liquid assets
asedau net *ell* net assets
aseiniad *eg* aseiniadau assignment
aseiniad a fercir â chyfrifiadur *eg* aseiniadau a fercir â chyfrifiadur computer-marked assignment
aseinio ar hap *be* random assignment
aséis arfau *eg* assize of arms
asen *eb* asennau rib
asen flaen *eb* asennau blaen fore-rib
asen y fainc *eb* asennau'r fainc bench rib
asennog *ans* ribbed
asennol *ans* costal
aseotrop *eg* aseotropau azeotrope
asepsis *eg* asepsis
aseptig *ans* aseptic
asesiad *eg* asesiadau assessment
asesiad clinigol *eg* asesiadau clinigol clinical assessment
asesiad crynodol *eg* asesiadau crynodol summative assessment
asesiad cymdeithasol *eg* asesiadau cymdeithasol social assessment
asesiad cyntaf nad yw'n destun adroddiad *eg* first unreported assessment
asesiad cyntaf sy'n destun adroddiad *eg* first reported assessment
asesiad diagnostig *eg* asesiadau diagnostig diagnostic assessment
asesiad ffurfiannol *eg* asesiadau ffurfiannol formative assessment
asesiad goddrychol *eg* asesiadau goddrychol subjective assessment
asesiad gwaelodlin *eg* asesiadau gwaelodlin baseline assessment
asesiad maen prawf gyfeiriol *eg* asesiadau maen prawf gyfeiriol criterion-referenced assessment
asesiad meddygol *eg* asesiadau meddygol medical assessment
asesiad niwroseicolegol *eg* asesiadau niwroseicolegol neuropsychological assessment
asesiad norm-gyfeiriol *eg* asesiadau norm-gyfeiriol norm-referenced assessment
asesiad o anghenion *eg* asesiadau o anghenion needs assessment
asesiad perfformiad *eg* asesiadau perfformiad functional assessment
asesiad risg *eg* asesiadau risg risk assessment
asesiad seiliedig ar chwarae *eg* asesiadau seiliedig ar chwarae play-based assessment
asesiad yr athrawes *eb* teacher assessment
asesiad yr athro *eg* teacher assessment
asesu *be* assess
asesu allanol *be* external assessment
asesu athrawon *be* teacher assessment
asesu llafar *be* oral assessment
asesu mewnol *be* internal assessment
asesu parhaus *be* continuous assessment
asesu safonedig *be* standardized assessment
asesu sylfaen *be* baseline assessment
asesu symudedd *be* assessment of mobility
asesu yn y gweithle *be* work-based assessment
aseswr *eg* aseswyr assessor

aseswr allanol *eg* aseswyr allanol external assessor
aseswr mewnol *eg* aseswyr mewnol internal assessor
asetabwlaidd *ans* acetabular
asetabwlwm *eg* acetabulum
asetad *eg* asetadau acetate
asetal *eg* asetalau acetal
asetig *ans* acetic
aseton *eg* acetone
asetyl *eg* acetyl
asetyl CoA *eg* acetyl CoA
asetylcolin *eg* acetylcholine
asetylcolinesteras *eg* acetylcholinesterase
asetyleiddio *be* acetylation
asetylen *eg* acetylene
asetyn *eg* asetynnau acetate sheet
asffalt *eg* asphalt
asgell (ar saeth etc) *eb* esgyll vane
asgell (mewn chwaraeon) *eb* esgyll wing
asgell (pysgodyn etc) *eb* esgyll fin
asgell bectoral *eb* esgyll pectoral pectoral fin
asgell chwith *eb* esgyll chwith left wing
asgell dde *eb* esgyll de right wing
asgell ddorsal *eb* esgyll dorsal dorsal fin
asgell fentrol *eb* esgyll fentrol ventral fin
asgell ganol *eb* esgyll canol medial fin
asgell ganol *eb* esgyll canol median fin
asgellwr *eg* asgellwyr winger; outside forward; wing three quarter
asgellwr chwith *eg* asgellwyr chwith outside left
asgellwr de *eg* asgellwyr de outside right
asgetig *ans* ascetic
asgetigiaeth *eb* asceticism
asgites *eg* ascites
asgwrn *eg* esgyrn bone
asgwrn atodol *eg* esgyrn atodol accessory bone
asgwrn cefn *eg* esgyrn cefn backbone; spine; vertebral column
asgwrn cynffon *eg* esgyrn cynffon coccyx
asgwrn talcen *eg* esgyrn talcen frontal bone
asgwrn y forddwyd *eg* femur
asgwrn y gorfant *eg* alveolar bone
asgwrneiddiad *eg* ossification
asgwrneiddio *be* ossify
asgws *eg* asgi ascus
Asharitiad *eg* Asharitiaid Asharite
ashrama / aśrama *ell* ashrama / aśrama
asiad *eg* asiadau suture
asiant *eg* asiantiaid agent
asiant hysbysebu *eg* asiantiaid hysbysebu advertising agent
asiantaeth *eb* asiantaethau agency
asiantaeth archwilio *eb* asiantaethau archwilio audit agency
asiantaeth deithio *eb* asiantaethau teithio travel agent
asiantaeth ddatblygu *eb* asiantaethau datblygu development agency
asiantaeth fabwysiadu *eb* asiantaethau mabwysiadu adoption agency
asiantaeth hyfforddi *eb* asiantaethau hyfforddi training agency
asiantaeth hysbysebu *eb* advertising agency
Asiantaeth Ryngwladol Egni Niwclear *eb* International Atomic Energy Agency
asiantaeth ymchwil marchnata *eb* asiantaethau ymchwil marchnata marketing research agency
asid *eg* asidau acid
asid absgisig *eg* abscisic acid
asid alcanöig (enw generig) *eg* asidau alcanöig alkanoic acid
asid amino *eg* asidau amino amino acid
asid 2-aminobensencarbocsylig *eg* 2-aminobenzenecarboxylic acid
asid 4-aminobensencarbocsylig *eg* 4-aminobenzenecarboxylic acid
asid 4-aminobensensylffonig *eg* 4-aminobenzenesulfonic acid
asid aminobwtandeuöig *eg* aminobutanedioic acid
asid aminoethanöig *eg* aminoethanoic acid
asid 2-aminopentandeuöig *eg* 2-aminopentanedioic acid
asid 2-aminopropanöig *eg* 2-aminopropanoic acid
asid aminosylffonig *eg* aminosulfonic acid
asid anthranilig *eg* anthranilic acid
asid asbartig *eg* aspartic acid
asid asetig *eg* asidau asetig acetic acid
asid asgorbig *eg* ascorbic acid
asid bensencarbocsylig *eg* benzenecarboxylic acid
asid bensen-1,2-deucarbocsylig *eg* benzene-1,2-dicarboxylic acid
asid bensen-1,3-deucarbocsylig *eg* benzene-1,3-dicarboxylic acid
asid bensen-1,4-deucarbocsylig *eg* benzene-1,4-dicarboxylic acid
asid bensenperocsocarbocsylig *eg* benzeneperoxocarboxylic acid
asid bensensylffonig *eg* benzenesulfonic acid
asid bensöig *eg* benzoic acid
asid borig *eg* boric acid
asid brasterog *eg* asidau brasterog fatty acid
asid brasterog amlannirlawn *eg* polyunsaturated fatty acid
asid brasterog annirlawn *eg* unsaturated fatty acid
asid brasterog dirlawn *eg* saturated fatty acid
asid bromig(I) *eg* bromic(I) acid
asid bromig(V) *eg* bromic(V) acid
asid bwtandeuöig *eg* butanedioic acid
asid bwtanöig *eg* butanoic acid
asid bwtyrig *eg* butyric acid
asid carbamig *eg* carbamic acid
asid carbocsylig *eg* asidau carbocsylig carboxylic acid
asid carbocsylig cadwyn hir *eg* long chain carboxylic acid
asid carbonig *eg* carbonic acid

asid citrig *eg* citric acid
asid clorig(I) *eg* chloric(I) acid
asid clorig(III) *eg* chloric(III) acid
asid clorig(V) *eg* chloric(V) acid
asid clorig(VII) *eg* chloric(VII) acid
asid cloroethanöig *eg* chloroethanoic acid
asid clorosylffonig *eg* chlorosulfonic acid
asid colig *eg* cholic acid
asid cromig(VI) *eg* chromic(VI) acid
asid cryf *eg* strong acid
asid crynodedig *eg* asidau crynodedig concentrated acid
asid cyfieuol *eg* asidau cyfieuol conjugate acid
asid decandeuöig *eg* decanedioic acid
asid (-)-2,3-deuhydrocsibwtandeuöig *eg* (-)-2,3-dihydroxybutanedioic acid
asid (±)-2,3-deuhydrocsibwtandeuöig *eg* (±)-2,3-dihydroxybutanedioic acid
asid 2,4-dicloroffenocsiasetig *eg* 2,4-dichlorophenoxyacetic acid
asid ethandeuöig *eg* ethanedioic acid
asid ethanöig *eg* ethanoic acid
asid 2-ethanoylocsibensencarbocsylig *eg* 2-ethanoyloxybenzenecarboxylic acid
asid 3-ffenylpropenöig *eg* 3-phenylpropenoic acid
asid fformig *eg* formic acid
asid ffosffoglyserig *eg* phosphoglyseric acid
asid ffosffonig *eg* phosphonic acid
asid ffosfforig *eg* phosphoric acid
asid ffosfforig(V) *eg* phosphoric(V) acid
asid ffwlminig *eg* fulminic acid
asid glwtamig *eg* glutamic acid
asid gwan *eg* asidau gwan weak acid
asid gwanedig *eg* dilute acid
asid hecsadecanöig *eg* hexadecanoic acid
asid hecsandeuöig *eg* hexanedioic acid
asid hecsanöig *eg* hexanoic acid
asid hecsaocsoïodig(VII) *eg* hexaoxoiodic(VII) acid
asid hyalwronig *eg* hyaluronic acid
asid hydrasöig *eg* hydrazoic acid
asid hydrïodig *eg* hydriodic acid
asid hydrobromig *eg* hydrobromic acid
asid hydroclorig *eg* hydrochloric acid
asid 2-hydrocsibensencarbocsylig *eg* 2-hydroxybenzenecarboxylic acid
asid 2-hydrocsibwtandeuöig *eg* 2-hydroxybutanedioic acid
asid 3-hydrocsibwt-2-enöig *eg* 3-hydroxybut-2-enoic acid
asid hydrocsiethanöig *eg* hydroxyethanoic acid
asid 2-hydrocsipropanöig *eg* 2-hydroxypropanoic acid
asid 2-hydrocsipropan-1,2,3-tricarbocsylig *eg* 2-hydroxypropane-1,2,3-tricarboxylic acid
asid hydrofflworig *eg* hydrofluoric acid
asid indol bwtyrig (IBA) *eg* indole butyric acid (IBA)
asid indol-3-yl-asetig (IAA) *eg* indol-3-yl-acetic acid (IAA)
asid ïodig(V) *eg* iodic(V) acid
asid ïodig(VII) *eg* iodic(VII) acid
asid malonig *eg* malonic acid
asid meso-2,3-deuhydrocsibwtandeuöig *eg* meso-2,3-dihydroxybutanedioic acid
asid methanöig *eg* methanoic acid
asid 2-methylbensencarbocsylig *eg* 2-methylbenzenecarboxylic acid
asid 2-methylbensensylffonig *eg* 2-methylbenzenesulfonic acid
asid 2-methylbwtendeuöig *eg* 2-methylbutenedioic acid
asid 2-methylpropanöig *eg* 2-methylpropanoic acid
asid 2-methylpropenöig *eg* 2-methylpropenoic acid
asid naffthalen asetig (ANA) *eg* naphthalene acetic acid (NAA)
asid naffthalen-1-carbocsylig *eg* naphthalene-1-carboxylic acid
asid nicotinig *eg* nicotinic acid
asid nitrig *eg* nitric acid
asid nitrig(III) *eg* nitric(III) acid
asid nitrig(V) *eg* nitric(V) acid
asid nitrus *eg* nitrous acid
asid niwclëig *eg* nucleic acid
asid ocsalig *eg* oxalic acid
asid ocsaloasetig *eg* oxaloacetic acid
asid 3-ocsobwtanöig *eg* 3-oxobutanoic acid
asid ocsoethanöig *eg* oxoethanoic acid
asid 2-ocsopropanöig *eg* 2-oxopropanoic acid
asid octadecanöig *eg* octadecanoic acid
asid olëig *eg* oleic acid
asid pectig *eg* pectic acid
asid pentanöig *eg* pentanoic acid
asid perocsodeusylffwrig(VI) *eg* peroxodisulfuric(VI) acid
asid perocsoethanöig *eg* peroxoethanoic acid
asid perocsosylffwrig(VI) *eg* peroxosulfuric(VI) acid
asid petroselenig *eg* petroselenic acid
asid polydeuocsoborig(III) *eg* polydioxoboric(III) acid
asid propandeuöig *eg* propanedioic acid
asid propenöig *eg* propenoic acid
asid riboniwcleig (RNA) *eg* ribonucleic acid
asid rwbeanig *eg* rubeanic acid
asid sylffwrig *eg* sulphuric acid
asid sylffwrig gwanedig *eg* dilute sulphuric acid
asid sylffwrig(IV) *eg* sulfuric(IV) acid
asid sylffwrig(VI) *eg* sulfuric(VI) acid
asid tannig *eg* tannic acid
asid tartarig *eg* tartaric acid
asid tawrocolig *eg* taurocholic acid
asid 3,4,5-trihydrocsibensencarbocsylig *eg* 3,4,5-trihydroxybenzenecarboxylic acid

asid triocsoborig *eg* trioxoboric acid
asid wrig *eg* uric acid
asid y stumog *eg* stomach acid
asidau bustlog *ell* bile acids
asid-bas *ans* acid-base
asidedd *eg* acidity
asidiedig *ans* acidulated
asidiedig *ans* acidified
asidig *ans* acidic
asidio *be* acidify
asidosis *eg* acidosis
asiedydd *eg* asiedyddion joiner
asiento *eg* asiento
asimwth *eg* asimwthau azimuth
asio *be* blend
asomethan *eg* azomethane
asparagin *eg* asparagine
astatin *eg* astatine
Astec *eg* Asteciaid Aztec
Astecaidd *ans* Aztec
astell (ar gyfer lloriau) *eb* estyll floorboard
astell (i ddal rhywbeth yn ei le) *eb* estyll batten
astell (yn gyffredinol) *eb* estyll board
astell dywydd *eb* estyll tywydd fascia board; barge-board
astell ddeifio *eb* estyll deifio springboard
astell ddiferu *eb* estyll diferu draining board
astell fondo *eg* estyll bondo soffit board
astell lafnog *eb* estyll llafnog laminboard
astell stribed *eb* estyll stribed batten board
astellog *ans* boarded
asteroid *eg* asteroidau asteroid
astigmatedd *eg* astigmatism
astragal *eg* astragalau astragal
astroffiseg *eb* astrophysics
astrolab *eg* astrolabe
astudiaeth (=archwiliad) *eb* astudiaethau investigation
astudiaeth (yn gyffredinol) *eb* astudiaethau study
astudiaeth achos *eb* astudiaethau achos case study
astudiaeth bortreadol *eb* astudiaethau portreadol portrait study
astudiaeth dichonoldeb *eb* astudiaethau dichonoldeb feasibility study
astudiaeth drawsddiwylliannol *eb* astudiaethau trawsddiwylliannol cross-culture study
astudiaeth drawstoriadol *eb* astudiaethau trawstoriadol cross-sectional study
astudiaeth dymor hir *eb* astudiaethau tymor hir long-term study
astudiaeth ddadansoddol *eb* analytical study
astudiaeth ddwbl-ddall *eb* astudiaethau dwbl-ddall double-blind study
astudiaeth estyn *eb* astudiaethau estyn extension study
astudiaeth estyn thematig *eb* astudiaethau estyn thematig thematic extension study
astudiaeth fanwl *eb* astudiaethau manwl study in depth
astudiaeth gefndir *eb* astudiaethau cefndir background study
astudiaeth glinigol *eb* astudiaethau clinigol clinical study
astudiaeth gyd-destunol *eg* astudiaethau cyd-destunol contextual study
astudiaeth gymharol *eb* astudiaethau cymharol comparative study
astudiaeth ôl-syllol *eb* astudiaethau ôl-syllol retrospective study
astudiaeth sampl *eb* astudiaethau sampl sample study
astudiaeth sengl-ddall *eb* astudiaethau sengl-ddall single-blind study
astudiaeth seico-gyfreithiol *eb* psycholegal study
astudiaethau beirniadol a chyd-destunol *ell* critical and contextual studies
astudiaethau cartref *ell* domestic studies
astudiaethau clasurol *ell* classical studies
astudiaethau cyfannol *ell* integrated studies
astudiaethau cyfrifiadur *ell* computer studies
astudiaethau cymdeithasol *ell* social studies
astudiaethau rheoli *ell* managerial studies
astudiaethau'r amgylchedd *ell* environmental studies
astudiaethau'r cwricwlwm *ell* curriculum studies
astudio *be* study
astudio annibynnol *be* independent study
astudio dan oruchwyliaeth *be* supervised study
astudio unigol gyda chymorth *be* supported self-study
asthma *eg* asthma
aswiriant bywyd *eg* life assurance
aswiriant cyfnod *eg* term assurance
aswiriant gwaddol *eg* endowment assurance
asygotig *ans* azygotic
asyl *ans* acyl
asyl halid *eg* asyl halidau acyl halide
asyleiddiad *eg* acylation
asyleiddio *be* acylate
asymptot *eg* asymptotau asymptote
asymptotig *ans* asymptotic
atacsia *eg* ataxia
atactig *ans* atactic
atafaeliad *eg* atafaeliadau sequestration; distraint
atafaelu *be* sequester; distrain
atafaelwr *eg* atafaelwyr sequestrator
atal (=rhwystro) *be* prevent
atal (=stopio'n sydyn) *be* halt
atal (ensymau etc) *be* inhibit
atal (gweithred sydd wedi dechrau) *be* abort
atal (mewn seicoleg) *be* suppress
atal (nodyn ar offeryn cerddorol) *be* stop
atal (rhywun rhag gwneud rhywbeth) *be* restrain
atal a chychwyn stop-start
atal cenhedlu *be* contraception

atal dienyddio *be* reprieve
atal dweud *eg* stammer
atal imiwnedd *be* immunosuppression
atal y bêl *be* stop the ball
atal y bêl drwy benlinio *be* stopping the ball by kneeling
atalfa wynt *eb* atalfeydd gwynt wind-break
ataliad (=rhwystriad) *eg* prevention
ataliad (=stopiad sydyn) *eg* ataliadau halt
ataliad (ensymau etc) *eg* ataliadau inhibition
ataliad (mewn seicoleg) *eg* ataliadau suppression
ataliad (nodyn ar offeryn cerddorol) *eg* stoppage
ataliad (rhywun rhag gwneud rhywbeth) *eg* restraint
ataliad cudd *eg* latent inhibition
ataliad dŵr *eg* retention of urine
ataliad ensym *eg* enzyme inhibition
ataliad gan gynnyrch terfynol *eg* end product inhibition
ataliad imiwnedd *eg* immunal suppression
ataliad y galon *eg* asystole
ataliad y galon *eg* ataliadau'r galon cardiac arrest
ataliol (rhag troseddu etc) *ans* deterrent
ataliol (yn gyffredinol) *ans* inhibitory; inhibiting
ataliwr *eg* atalwyr short stop
atalnod llawn *eg* atalnodau llawn full stop
atalnodi *be* punctuation
atalnodi agored *be* open punctuation
atalydd *eg* atalyddion inhibitor
atalydd ailafael serotonin-benodol *eg* atalyddion ailafael serotonin-benodol serotonin-specific reuptake inhibitor
atalydd cnocio *eg* atalyddion cnocio knock inhibitor
atalydd monoamin ocsidas *eg* atalyddion monoamin ocsidas monamine oxidase inhibitor (MAOIs)
atalydd rhwd *eg* atalyddion rhwd rust inhibitor; corrosion inhibitor
atbreis *eg* reprise
atchwanegiad *eg* atchwanegiadau supplementation
atchwel llinol *eg* linear regression
atchweliad *eg* atchweliadau regression
atchweliad at y cymedr *eg* regression to the mean
atchweliad lluosog *eg* multiple regression
atchwelyd *be* regress
atchwyddiant *eg* reflation
ateb *be* answer
ateb *eg* atebion answer; solution
ateb bras *eg* atebion bras approximate answer; rough answer
ateb cyfrifiadurol *eg* atebion cyfrifiadurol computer solution
ateb i bawb *be* reply to all
ateb i e-bost *be* reply to mail
ateb i grŵp *be* reply to group
ateb prototeip *eg* prototype solution
Ateb Terfynol *eg* Final Solution
ateb wyneb i waered *eg* atebion wyneb i waered inverted answer
ateb yr anfonwr *be* reply to sender
atebol (i) *ans* accountable
atebolrwydd (cyfreithiol) *eg* liability
atebolrwydd (yn gyffredinol) *eg* accountability
atebolrwydd ar y cyd ac yn unigol *eg* joint and several liability
atebolrwydd caeth *eg* strict liability
atebolrwydd camweddus *eg* tortious liability
atebolrwydd cyfreithiol *eg* legal liability
atebolrwydd cyfyngedig *eg* limited liability
atebolrwydd dirprwyol *eg* vicarious liability
atebolrwydd llawn *eg* unlimited liability
atebolrwydd personol *eg* personal liability
ateg *eb* ategion prop; abutment; shore
ateg fwa *eb* ategion bwa flying shore
ateg gastellaidd *eb* ategion castellaidd castellated prop
ateg gôn *eb* ategion côn cone stand
ateg ogwydd *eb* ategion gogwydd raking shore
ateg unionsyth *eb* ategion unionsyth dead shore
ategiad *eg* ategiadau back-up support
ategol (=cefnogol) *ans* ancillary
ategol (i wisg etc) *ans* accessory
ategol (yn gyffredinol) *ans* auxiliary
ategolyn *eg* ategolion accessory
ategu (dadl) *be* support
ategwaith *eg* ategweithiau abutment
ategyn *eg* ategion plug-in
atfor *ans* seaward
atffurfiant *eg* regeneration
atffurfio *be* regenerate
atffurfydd *eg* atffurfyddion regenerator
atgan *eb* atganau episode
atganol *ans* episodical
atgenhedliad *eg* reproduction
atgenhedliad rhywiol *eg* sexual reproduction
atgenhedlu *be* reproduce
atgof echblyg *eg* atgofion echblyg explicit memory
atgof wedi'i adfer *eg* atgofion wedi'u hadfer recovered memory
atgofio rhydd *be* free recall
atgoffa o realaeth *be* reality orientation
atgyd *eg* atgydion adjoint
atgydiol *ans* adjugate
atgyfnerthiad *eg* atgyfnerthiadau reinforcement
atgyfnerthiad bas *eg* bass boost
atgyfnerthiad cadarnhaol *eg* positive reinforcement
atgyfnerthiad trebl *eg* treble boost
atgyfnerthiad ysbeidiol *eg* intermittent reinforcement
atgyfnerthol *ans* booster
atgyfnerthu *be* reinforce; fortify
atgyfnerthu negyddol *be* negative reinforcement
atgyfnerthydd cyflyrol *eg* atgyfnerthwyr cyflyrol conditioned reinforcer

atgyfnerthydd eilaidd *eg* atgyfnerthwyr eilaidd secondary reinforcer
atgyfnerthydd sylfaenol *eg* atgyfnerthwyr sylfaenol primary reinforcer
atgyfodiad *eg* resurrection
atgyffwrdd *be* retouch
atgynhyrchiad *eg* atgynhyrchiadau reproduction
atgynhyrchiad llystyfol *eg* vegetative reproduction
atgynhyrchu *be* reproduce
atgynhyrchu anrhywiol *be* asexual reproduction
atgynhyrchu cysyniad *be* conceptual replication
atgynhyrchu uniongyrchol *be* direct replication
atgynyrchiedig *ans* regenerated
atgyrch *eg* atgyrchion reflex
atgyrch cadwynol *eg* chain reflex
atgyrch camu *eg* atgyrchion camu stepping reflex
atgyrch cyflyredig *eg* conditioned reflex
atgyrch plwc pen-glin *eg* knee-jerk reflex
atgyrch sbinol *eg* spinal reflex
atgyrch sugno *eg* sucking reflex
atgyrchion troethi *ell* micturition reflexes
atgyrchol *ans* reflex
atgyweiriad *eg* atgyweiriadau repair
atgyweirio *be* repair; overhaul
atlas *eg* atlasau atlas
atman *eg* atman
atmosffer *eg* atmosfferau atmosphere
atmosffer di-lwch *eg* dust free atmosphere
atmosfferig *ans* atmospheric
atodeg *eb* atodegau rider
atodi (i ddogfen) *be* append
atodi (i e-bost) *be* attach
atodi dalen *be* append sheet
atodi data *be* attach data
atodi ffeil *be* attach file
atodi gofod *be* append space
atodi llyfrgelloedd *be* append libraries
atodiad (i ddogfen) *eg* atodiadau appendix; annexe
atodiad (i e-bost) *eg* atodiadau attachment
atodiad budd-dal tai *eg* atodiadau budd-dal tai housing benefit supplement
atodiad e-bost *eg* atodiadau e-bost e-mail attachment
Atodiad Incwm Teulu *eg* Family Income Supplement
atodiad teithio *eg* atodiadau teithio travel supplement
atodion peiriant *ell* machine attachments
atodlen *eb* atodlenni schedule
atodol *ans* supplementary; subsidiary; added
atodyn *eg* atodion attachment
atodyn cymwysadwy *eg* atodion cymwysadwy adjustable attachment
atodyn gwerthyd *eg* atodion gwerthyd spindle attachment
atodyn tewychu *eg* atodion tewychu thicknessing attachment
atodyn turnio tapr *eg* atodion turnio tapr taper turning attachment
atojoule *eg* atojouleau attojoule
atol *eb* atolau atoll
atom *eg/b* atomau atom
atom canol-yr-wyneb *eg* atomau canol-yr-wyneb centre-face atom
atom copr *eg* atomau copr copper atom
atom derbyn *eg* atomau derbyn acceptor atom
atomadur *eg* atomaduron atomizer
atomedd *eg* atomicity
atomeiddiad *eg* atomization
atomeiddio *be* atomize
atomfa *eb* atomfeydd nuclear power station
atomig *ans* atomic
atraeth *ans* onshore
atred *eg* atredau offset
atredeg *be* approach run
atrediad *eg* atrediadau approach run
atrïaidd *ans* atrial
atriwm *eg* atrium
atro *ans* recurved
atsain *eb* atseiniau echo
atseinio *be* echo
atwynt *ans* windward
atyniad *eg* atyniadau attraction
atyniad disgyrchedd *eg* gravitational attraction
atyniad electrostatig *eg* electrostatic attraction
atyniad i ymwelwyr *eg* atyniadau i ymwelwyr visitor attraction
atyniad rhyngbersonol *eg* interpersonal attraction
atyniadol *ans* attractive
atynnol *ans* attractive
atynnu *be* attract
athematig *ans* athematic
atherosglerosis *eg* atherosclerosis
athletaidd *ans* athletic
athletau *ell* athletics
athletwr *eg* athletwyr athlete
athletwr sy'n ymarfer *eg* athletwyr sy'n ymarfer athlete in training
athraidd *ans* permeable
athrawes *eb* athrawesau teacher
athrawes arweiniol *eb* athrawesau arweiniol lead teacher
athrawes crefydd *eb* athrawesau crefydd religious teacher
athrawes chwaraeon *eb* athrawesau chwaraeon games teacher
athrawes dan hyfforddiant *eb* athrawesau dan hyfforddiant trainee teacher
athrawes deithiol *eb* athrawesau teithiol itinerant teacher
athrawes ddosbarth *eb* athrawesau dosbarth form teacher
athrawes gylchynol *eb* athrawesau cylchynol peripatetic teacher

athrawes gynorthwyol *eb* athrawesau cynorthwyol auxiliary teacher
athrawes lanw *eb* athrawesau llanw supply teacher
athrawes pwnc *eb* athrawesau pwnc subject teacher
athrawes raddedig *eb* athrawesau graddedig graduate teacher
athrawes ran amser *eb* athrawesau rhan amser part time teacher
athrawes ymgynghorol a chylchynol *eb* athrawesau ymgynghorol a chylchynol advisory and peripatetic teacher
athrawes yrfaoedd *eb* athrawesau gyrfaoedd careers teacher
athrawiaeth *eb* athrawiaethau doctrine
Athrawiaeth Anffaeledigrwydd y Pab *eb* Doctrine of Papal Infallibility
athrawiaeth cyfarganfod *eb* doctrine of apperception
athrawiaeth cysylltu syniadau *eb* doctrine of association of ideas
athrawiaeth egnïon nerfau arbennig *eb* doctrine of specific nerve energies
Athrawiaeth Gwrthod Cydnabod *eb* Doctrine of Non-recognition
Athrawiaeth Monroe *eb* Monroe Doctrine
Athrawiaeth yr Iawn *eb* Doctrine of Atonement
athreiddedd *eg* athreiddeddau permeability
athreiddedd gofod rhydd *eg* permeability of free space
athreiddedd gwahaniaethol *eg* differential permeability
athreiddedd perthynol *eg* relative permeability
athreuliad *eg* attrition
athreuliad cyfranwyr *eg* subject attrition
athro *eg* athrawon teacher
athro arweiniol *eg* athrawon arweiniol lead teacher
athro crefydd *eg* athrawon crefydd religious teacher
athro cylchynol *eg* athrawon cylchynol peripatetic teacher
athro cynorthwyol *eg* athrawon cynorthwyol auxiliary teacher
athro chwaraeon *eg* athrawon chwaraeon games teacher
athro dan hyfforddiant *eg* athrawon dan hyfforddiant trainee teacher
athro dosbarth *eg* athrawon dosbarth form teacher
athro graddedig *eg* athrawon graddedig graduate teacher
athro gyrfaoedd *eg* athrawon gyrfaoedd careers teacher
athro llanw *eg* athrawon llanw supply teacher
athro pwnc *eg* athrawon pwnc subject teacher
athro rhan amser *eg* athrawon rhan amser part time teacher
athro teithiol *eg* athrawon teithiol itinerant teacher
athro ymgynghorol a chylchynol *eg* athrawon ymgynghorol a chylchynol advisory and peripatetic teacher
athrod *eg* athrodion slander
athrodi *be* slander
athrofa *eb* athrofeydd institute of education
athroniaeth *eb* philosophy
athroniaeth Steiner *eb* Steiner philosophy
athronydd radicalaidd *eg* athronwyr radicalaidd radical philosopher
athrylith *eb* genius
athyrru *be* agglomerate
a'u genynnau wedi'u haddasu genetically modified
au gratin *ans* au gratin
aubade *eg* aubades aubade
aur (Au) *eg* gold
aur banc tywod *eg* placer gold
auteur *eg* auteurs auteur
auteur sinema *eg* auteurs sinema cinema auteur
avant-garde *eg/b* avant-garde
avatar / avatara *eg* avatar / avatara
awcsin *eg* awcsinau auxin
awchlym *ans* sharp-edged, keen-edged
awdiogram *eg* awdiogramau audiogram
awdiomedr *eg* awdiomedrau audiometer
awdiometreg *eb* audiometry
awdl *eb* awdlau ode
awdur *eg* awduron author
awdurdod (=rheolaeth, sofraniaeth) *eg* dominion
awdurdod (yn gyffredinol) *eg* awdurdodau authority
awdurdod addysg *eg* awdurdodau addysg education authority
awdurdod addysg iechyd *eg* health education authority
awdurdod addysg lleol *eg* awdurdodau addysg lleol local education authority
awdurdod caffaelol *eg* acquiring authority
awdurdod Esgobaethol *eg* awdurdodau Esgobaethol Episcopal authority
Awdurdod Gwasanaethau Iechyd Teulu (AGIT) *eg* Family Health Services Authority
awdurdod gweinyddol *eg* awdurdodau gweinyddol administrative authority
Awdurdod Hybu Iechyd Cymru *eg* Health Promotion Authority for Wales
awdurdod iechyd *eg* awdurdodau iechyd health authority
Awdurdod Iechyd Dosbarth (AID) *eg* District Health Authority
awdurdod lleol *eg* awdurdodau lleol local authority
awdurdod statudol *eg* statutory authority
awdurdod unedol *eg* awdurdodau unedol unitary authority
awdurdod ysbrydol *eg* spiritual power
awdurdodaeth (=hawl i wneud penderfyniadau cyfreithiol) *eg* awdurdodaethau jurisdiction
awdurdodaeth (=yn ffafrio ufudd-dod llwyr i awdurdod) *eb* authoritarianism
awdurdodaeth sifil *eb* civil jurisdiction
awdurdodaidd *ans* authoritarian
awdurdodedig *ans* authorized
awdurdodi *be* empower

awdurdodi *be* authorize
awdurdodiad *eg* awdurdodiadau authorization
awdurdodol *ans* authoritative
awduro *be* authoring
awel *eb* awelon breeze
awel ffres *eb* awelon ffres fresh breeze
awel gymedrol *eb* awelon cymedrol moderate breeze
awel o'r môr *eb* awelon o'r môr sea breeze
awel o'r tir *eb* awelon o'r tir land breeze
awel ysgafn *eb* awelon ysgafn light breeze
awgend *eg* awgendau augend
awgrym *eg* awgrymiadau suggestion
awgrymiadedd ôl-hypnosis *eb* posthypnotic suggestibility
awgrymu *be* suggest
awlos *eg* awloi aulos
awr *eb* oriau hour
awr anterth *eb* terce
awr brim (mynachlogydd) *eb* oriau prim prime
awr frig *eb* oriau brig peak hour
awr frys *eb* oriau brys rush hour
awra *eb* aura
awrigl *eg* awriglau auricle
awrora *eg* awrorau aurora
awroraidd *ans* auroral
awstenit *eg* awstenitiau austenite
Awstin Sant *eg* Saint Augustine
Awstinaidd *ans* Augustinian
Awstiniad *eg* Awstiniaid Augustinian
Awstiniaeth *eb* Augustinianism
Awstria *eb* Austria
awtarchiaeth *eb* autarchy
awtecoleg *eb* autecology
awtistiaeth *eb* autism
awtistig *ans* autistic
awto *ans* auto
awtoadnewyddu *be* autorefresh
awtoailadrodd *be* autorepeat
awtoail-lwytho *be* autoreload
awto-alinio *be* autoalign
awtoamlinelliad *eg* awtoamlinelliadau autooutline
awtobeilot *eg* autopilot
awtobost *eg* automail
awtocatalysis *ans* autocatalysis
awtodestun *eg* awtodestunau autotext
awtodrefnu *be* autoarrange
awtoddiweddaru *be* autoupdate
awtofertigol *ans* autovertical
awtofewnbwn *eg* awtofewnbynnau autoinput
awtoffitio *be* autofit
awtofformat *eg* awtofformatau autoformat
awtogadw *be* autosave
awtoganfod *be* auto detect
awto-gau *be* auto closing
awtogrynhoi ar gyfer cyflwyniad *be* autoabstract to presentation
awtogychwyn *be* autostart
awtogynnwys *be* autoinclude
awtogynyddiad *eg* awtogynyddiadau autoincrement
► **awtogysylltnodi** *be* autohyphenate
awtogywiro *be* autocorrect
awtohidlydd *eg* awtohidlyddion autofilter
awtoimiwnedd *eg* autoimmunity
awtolanw *be* autofill
awtoled *eg* autowidth
awtolorweddol *ans* autohorizontal
awtolwytho *be* autoload
awtomatedd *eb* automatism
awtomatiaeth *eb* automation
awtomatig *ans* automatic
awtomeiddio *be* automate
awtomeiddio swyddfa *eg* office automation
awtomorffig *ans* automorphic
awtonewid *be* autoswitch
awtonomig *ans* autonomic
awtopolyploid *eg* autopolyploid
awtopolyploidi *eg* autopolyploidy
awtopsi *eg* autopsy
awtopsi seicolegol *eg* psychological autopsy
awtorifo *be* autonumbering
awtosiapio testun *be* autosize text
awtosom *eg* awtosomau autosome
awtosomaidd *ans* autosomal
awtotopagnosia *eg* autotopagnosia
awto-uchder *eg* autoheight
awto-werth *eg* awtowerthoedd autovalue
awtowirio sillafu *be* autospellcheck
awthigenig *ans* authigenic
awydd i gystadlu *eg* competitiveness
awyddus *ans* eager
awyr *eg* air
awyr afluniaidd *eb* chaotic sky
awyr agored *eg* open air; outdoors
awyr gwbl gymylog *eb* overcast sky
awyrell *eb* awyrellau vent
awyrellu *be* vent
awyren taith fer *eb* awyrennau taith fer short range plane
awyren taith hir *eb* awyrennau taith hir long range plane
awyrennaeth *eb* aeronautics
awyrfilwyr *ell* paratroops, air-borne troops
awyrgludiad *eg* awyrgludiadau airlift
awyrgludiad Berlin *eg* Berlin airlift
awyrgylch *eg/b* atmosphere; mood
awyrgylch comig *eg* comic atmosphere
awyrgylch prudd *eg* sombre atmosphere
awyrgylch urddasol *eg* noble atmosphere
awyriad *eg* aeration; ventilation
awyr-ladrad *eg* air piracy
awyrlun *eg* awyrluniau aerial photograph
awyr-oeri *be* air cool

awyrofod *eg* aerospace
awyrog *ans* aerated
awyrol *ans* aerial
awyru *be* aerate; ventilate
awyru artiffisial *be* artificial ventilation
awyrydd *eg* awyryddion ventilator
ayah *eg* ayat ayah
ayre *eb* ayres ayre

B

B fwyaf *eb* B major
B leiaf *eb* B minor
baban *eg* babanod infant
baban glas *eg* babanod glas blue baby
baban wedi'i guro *eg* babanod wedi'u curo battered baby
babanaidd *ans* infantile
babandod *eg* infancy; babyhood
babanladdiad *eg* infanticide
bacbib *eb* bacbibau bagpipe
bacteria dadnitreiddio *ell* denitrifying bacteria
bacteria nitreiddio *ell* nitrifying bacteria
bacteria niweidiol *ell* harmful bacteria
bacterioffag *eg* bacterioffagau bacteriophage
bacteriol *ans* bacterial
bacterioleg *eb* bacteriology
bacteriolegydd *eg* bacteriolegwyr bacteriologist
bacterioleiddiol *ans* bactericidal
bacteriostat *eg* bacteriostat
bacteriostatig *ans* bacteriostatic
bacteriwm *eg* bacteria bacterium
bach *eg* bachau hook
bach a bollt hook and bolt
bach a llygad hook and eye
bach caban *eg* bachau caban cabin hook
bach corsen *eg* bachau cyrs reed hook
bach crosio *eg* bachau crosio crochet hook
bach deintur *eg* bachau deintur tenter hook
bach edafu *eg* bachau edafu threading hook
bach iawn *ans* minute
bach sgriw *eg* bachau sgriw screw hook
bachau cyrliog { } *ell* curly brackets
bachau petryal *ell* square brackets
bachau petryal dwbl *ell* double square brackets
bachgen *eg* bechgyn boy
bachgen côr *eg* bechgyn côr choir boy
bachgen y bêl *eg* bechgyn y bêl ball boy
bachiad (yn gyffredinol) *eg* bachiadau hook
bachiad (mewn chwaraeon) *eg* hook shot
bachu (er mwyn clymu, cau) *be* fasten
bachu (er mwyn dal) *be* hook
bachwr *eg* bachwyr hooker
bachyn mainc *eg* bachau mainc bench hook
bachyn tywys edau *eg* bachau tywys edau thread guide
bad *eg* badau boat; craft
bad clwm *eg* badau clwm stake-boat
badminton *eg* badminton
baddon *eg* baddonau bath
baddon asid *eg* baddonau asid acid bath
baddon cawod *eg* baddonau cawod shower bath
baddon dŵr *eg* baddonau dŵr water bath
baddon llifo *eg* baddonau llifo dyebath
baddon traed *eg* baddonau traed footbath
baddondy *eg* baddondai bath building
bae *eg* baeau bay
Bafaraidd *ans* Bavarian
Bafariad *eg* Bafariaid Bavarian
bag *eg* bagiau bag
bag carpiau *eg* bagiau carpiau rag bag
bag draenio *eg* bagiau draenio drainage bag
bag dyrnu *eg* bagiau dyrnu punch bag
bag ffa *eg* bagiau ffa bean bag
bag hynofedd *eg* bagiau hynofedd buoyancy bag
bag llaw *eg* bagiau llaw handbag
bag polythen *eg* bagiau polythen polythene bag
bag tywod *eg* bagiau tywod sandbag
bagatelle *eg* bagatelles bagatelle
bagl (ffon esgob) *eb* baglau crook; crosier
bagl (mewn cyd-destun meddygol) *eb* baglau crutch
bagl gynffonnog *eb* baglau cynffonnog dovetail bridle
bagl meitr *eb* baglau meitr mitre bridle
bagl ongl *eb* baglau ongl angle bridle
bagl T *eb* baglau T tee bridle
bagloriaeth *eb* baccalaureate
baglu *be* trip
bai *eg* beiau fault
baich *eg* beichiau burden
baich achosion *eg* beichiau achosion case load
baich dysgu *eg* beichiau dysgu teaching load
baich gwaith *eg* workload
baich y dyn gwyn *eg* white man's burden
bain-marie *eg* bains-marie bain-marie
Baisakhi /Vaisakhi Baisakhi /Vaisakhi
Bakelite *eg* Bakelite
balalaica *eg* balalaicau balalaika
balans agoriadol *eg* opening balance
balans dyledus *eg* balance due
balans terfynol *eg* balansau terfynol closing balance
balans yn y banc *eg* bank balance
▶ **Balcanau, y** *ell* Balkans
balconi *eg* balconïau balcony
baldordd *eg* babble

bale *eg* dawnsiau bale ballet
baled *eb* baledi ballad
balet *eb* baletau ballett
balisteg *eb* ballistics
balistig *ans* ballistic
balog *eb* balogau fly opening
balsa *eg* balsa
balŵn *eg/b* balwnau balloon
balwster *eg* balwsterau baluster
balwstrad *eg* balwstradau balustrade
ballade *eg* ballades ballade
bambŵ *eg* bamboo
ban *eg* bannau beacon
banana *eb* bananas banana
banc *eg* banciau bank
banc canolog *eg* banciau canolog central bank
banc clirio *eg* banciau clirio clearing bank
banc cydweithredol *eg* banciau cydweithredol cooperative bank
banc cynilo *eg* banciau cynilo savings bank
Banc Cynilo Ymddiriedol *eg* Trustee Savings Bank
banc data *eg* banciau data data bank
banc gwaed *eg* banciau gwaed blood bank
Banc Lloegr *eg* Bank of England
banc masnachol *eg* banciau masnachol commercial bank
banc masnachol *eg* banciau masnachol merchant bank
banc o ddroriau *eg* banciau o ddroriau bank of drawers
banc stryd fawr *eg* banciau stryd fawr high street bank
banc tywod *eg* banciau tywod sand bank
Banc y Byd *eg* World Bank, The
Banc yr Alban *eg* Bank of Scotland
bancio *be* banking
bancio cartref *be* homebanking
bancio ffôn *be* telephone banking
bancio rhyngrwyd *be* internet banking
band *eg* bandiau band
band adnabod *eg* bandiau adnabod identity band
band amsugno *eg* absorption band
band canolig *eg* wideband
band cul *eg* narrowband
band chwyth *eg* bandiau chwyth windband
band dawns *eg* bandiau dawns dance-band
Band Eang Cymru (enw rhaglen) *eg* Broadband Wales
Band Eang Cymru Ar-lein *eg* BECA Network
band elastig *eg* bandiau elastig elastic band
band gwasg *eg* bandiau gwasg waistband
band gwasg heb ei gyfnerthu *eg* bandiau gwasg heb eu cyfnerthu unstiffened waistband
band gwasg wedi'i gyfnerthu *eg* bandiau gwasg wedi'u cyfnerthu stiffened waistband
band llawes *eg* bandiau llewys wrist band
band llydan *eg* broadband
band rwber *eg* bandiau rwber rubber band
band taro *eg* bandiau taro percussion band
banden dyllog *eb* bandiau tyllog punch strip
bandin *eg* bandinau banding
bandin ceibr *eg* bandinau ceibr chevron banding
bandin croes *eg* bandinau croes cross banding
bandin diemwnt *eg* bandinau diemwnt diamond banding
bandin domino *eg* bandinau domino domino banding
bandin saethben *eg* bandinau saethben herring-bone banding
bandin siec du *eg* black check banding
bandin siec gwyn *eg* white check banding
bandin tair llinell *eg* bandinau tair llinell three-line banding
bandog *ans* banded
baner *eb* baneri flag
baner *eb* baneri banner
baner drilliw *eb* baneri trilliw tricolour
banjo *eg* banjos banjo
banonbost *eg* banonbyst queenpost
bar (=mesur) *eg* barrau measure
bar (yn gyffredinol) *eg* barrau bar
bar amlygu *eg* barrau amlygu highlight bar
bar ategion *eg* plug-in bar
bar bae *eg* barrau baeau bay bar
bar byrbryd *eg* barrau byrbryd snack bar
bar canol *eg* barrau canol centre bar
bar cloch *eg* barrau clych chime bar
bar clustennog *eg* barrau clustennog lobate bar
bar cronfa ddata *eg* barrau cronfa ddata database bar
bar dewislenni *eg* barrau dewislenni menu bar
bar du *eg* barrau du black bar
bar dwbl *eg* barrau dwbl double bar
bar gwin *eg* wine bar
bar gwrthrych lluniadu *eg* barrau gwrthrych lluniadu drawing object bar
bar gwrthrych testun *eg* barrau gwrthrych testun text object bar
bar gwydriad *eg* barrau gwydriad sash bar
bar gwydro *eg* barrau gwydro glazing bar
bar haearn cwta *eg* barrau haearn cwta jemmy
bar hidlo *eg* barrau hidlo filter bar
bar iâ *eg* barrau iâ ice barrier
bar lleoliad *eg* location bar
bar lliwiau *eg* barrau lliwiau colour bar
bar llorweddol *eg* barrau llorweddol horizontal bar
bar llywio *eg* barrau llywio navigation bar
bar o wydr ffibr *eg* barrau o wydr ffibr fibreglass bar
bar offer *eg* barrau offer toolbar
bar offer fformatio *eg* barrau offer fformatio formatting toolbar
bar offer swyddfa *eg* barrau offer swyddfa office toolbar
bar plygu *eg* barrau plygu bending bar
bar rheoli *eg* barrau rheoli control bar
bar rhew *eg* barrau rhew ice barrier

bar rhynnu *eg* barrau rhynnu chill bar
bar sgrolio *eg* barrau sgrolio scroll bar
bar sgrolio fertigol *eg* barrau sgrolio fertigol vertical scroll bar
bar sgrolio llorweddol *eg* barrau sgrolio llorweddol horizontal scroll bar
bar sgwâr *eg* barrau sgwâr square bar
bar siart *eg* barrau siart chart bar
bar striclo *eg* barrau striclo strickle bar
bar swyddfa *eg* barrau swyddfa office bar
bar teitl *eg* barrau teitl title bar
bar toriad sgwâr *eg* barrau toriad sgwâr square section bar
bar torri *eg* barrau torri cutter bar
bar tyllu *eg* barrau tyllu boring bar
bar tyniant *eg* barrau tyniant tension bar
bar tywod *eg* barrau tywod sand bar
bar wal *eg* barrau wal wall bar
bar wythonglog *eg* barrau wythonglog octagonal bar
bara *eg* bread
bara amyd *eg* mixed cereal bread
bara brag *eg* malt bread
bara brith *eg* currant bread
bara brown *eg* brown bread
bara brown garw *eg* granary bread
bara ceirch *eg* oatcakes
bara croyw *eg* unleavened bread
bara cyflawn *eg* wholemeal bread
bara Ffrengig *eg* French bread
bara ffres *eg* fresh bread
bara gwenith *eg* wheatmeal bread
bara gwyn *eg* white bread
bara haidd *eg* barley bread
bara menyn *eg* bread and butter
bara rhyg *eg* rye bread
bara wedi llwydo *eg* mouldy bread
barathea *eg* barathea
barbitwrad *eg* barbitwradau barbiturate
barbola *eg* barbola
barcaról *eg* barcarolau barcarolle
barcer *eg* barceriaid tanner
barcio *be* tan
barcut *eg* barcutiaid kite
barchan *eg* barchanau barchan
bardraeth *eg* bardraethau barrier beach; nehrung
bardd llys *eg* beirdd llys court poet
Bardd y Brenin *eg* Poet Laureate
barddoniaeth *eb* poetry
bared *eg* baredau barrage
barette *eb* barettes barette
barf *eb* barfau beard
barfagnet *eg* barfagnetau bar magnet
bargeinio rhydd *be* free bargaining
bargen *eb* bargeinion bargain
bargen *eb* bargeinion deal
Bargen Newydd *eb* New Deal
bargod llinell dimensiwn *eg* bargodion llinell dimensiwn dimension line overhang
bargodfaen *eg* bargodfeini dripstone
bargodi *be* overhang
bargyfreithiwr *eg* bargyfreithwyr barrister
bargyfreithiwr ieuaf *eg* junior counsel barrister
baricêd *eg* baricedau barricade
barics *ell* barracks
baril *eb* barilau barrel
barilfollt *eb* barilfolltau barrel bolt
bariton *eg* baritonwyr baritone
bariwm *eg* barium
bariwm perocsid *eg* barium peroxide
barlyn *eg* barlynnoedd barrier lake
barn *eb* opinion; estimation
barn ar werth *eb* value judgement
barn gadarn *eb* sound judgment
barn glinigol *eb* clinical judgement
barn gytbwys *eb* balanced judgement
barn wrthrychol *eb* barnau gwrthrychol objective judgement
Barn, Y Farn Fawr *eb* Judgement, Last
barnu *be* make judgement
barnu perfformiad *be* judgement of performance
barnweiniad *eg* judicature
barnwr *eg* barnwyr judge
barnwr cylchdaith *eg* barnwyr cylchdaith circuit judge
barnwriaeth *eb* judiciary
baróc *ans* baroque
barograff *eg* barograffau barograph
barogram *eg* barogramau barogram
baromedr *eg* baromedrau barometer
baromedr aneroid *eg* baromedrau aneroid aneroid barometer
► **barometrig** *ans* barometric
barrau cyflin *ell* parallel bars
barrau gloyw *ell* bright drawn bars
barrau plygu *ell* folding bars
barrau ymestyn *ell* lengthening bars
barre *eg* barres barre
barriff *eg* barriffiau barrier reef
barrug *eg* hoar frost
bar-rholio *eg* barrau-rholio scroll-bar
Bartholomeus *eg* Bartholomew
barugog *ans* frosted
barwn *eg* barwniaid baron
barwni *eb* barwnïau barony
barwnigaeth *eb* barwnigaethau baronetcy
barwnol *ans* baronial
barysffer *eg* barysfferau barysphere
baryton *eg* barytonau baryton
bas (=heb fod yn ddwfn) *ans* shallow
bas (=llais isaf mewn cerddoriaeth) *eg* basau bass
bas (mewn cemeg) *eg* basau base
bas acwstig *eg* acoustic bass
bas Alberti *eg* Alberti bass

bas cryf *eg* basau cryf strong base
bas cyfieuol *eg* basau cyfieuol conjugate base
bas drôn *eg* basau drôn drone bass
bas dwbl *eg* basau dwbl double bass; contra bass
bas gwan *eg* basau gwan weak base
bas rhifoledig *eg* figured bass
bas synthetig *eg* synthetic bass
basalt *eg* basalt
basar *eg* basarau bazaar
bas-asid *eg* base-acid
bas-drombonydd *eg* bas-drombonwyr bass trombonist
basddwr *eg* basddyfroedd shallow
basfar *eg* basfarrau bass-bar
basged *eb* basgedi basket
basged drysor *eb* basgedi trysor treasure basket
basged ddillad *eb* basgedi dillad clothes basket, linen basket
basged wnïo *eb* basgedi gwnïo work box
basgedwaith *eg* basket work; wickerwork
bas-glarinetydd *eg* bas-glarinetwyr bass clarinettist
BASIC *eb* BASIC
basidiomycet *eg* basidiomycetau basidiomycete
basidiosbor *eg* basidiosborau basidiospore
basidiwm *eg* basidia basidium
basig *ans* basic
basigedd *eg* basicity
basil *eg* basil
basilica *eg* basilicâu basilica
basipetalaidd *ans* basipetal
basle *eg* basleoedd shoal
basn *eg* basnau basin
basn adeileddol *eg* basnau adeileddol structural basin
basn afonydd *eg* basnau afonydd river basin
basn arllwys *eg* basnau arllwys pouring basin
basn derbyn *eg* basnau derbyn basin of reception
basn ymolchi *eb* basnau ymolchi wash basin
basn ymolchi *eb* basnau ymolchi hand basin
basoffil *eg* basoffiliau basophil
basoffilig *ans* basophilic
basso ostinato *eg* basso ostinato
bast *eg* bast
bastid *eg* bastidau bastide
baswn *eg* baswnau bassoon
baswn dwbl *eg* baswnau dwbl contra bassoon
baswn dwbl *eg* baswnau dwbl double bassoon
baswnydd *eg* baswnwyr bassoonist
baswr *eg* baswyr baseman
bat *eg* batiau bat
bat plastr *eg* batiau plastr plaster bat
bataliwn *eg* bataliynau battalion
Bataliwn yr Iwmyn *eg* Yeomanry Battalion
bateloedd *ell* battels
batiad *eg* batiadau innings
batiad hir *eg* batiadau hir long innings
batic *eg* batik
batio *be* bat
batiwr *eg* batwyr batsman
batiwr llaw chwith *eg* batwyr llaw chwith left-handed batsman
batiwr llaw dde *eg* batwyr llaw dde right-handed batsman
batri *eg* batrïau battery
batwn *eg* batynau baton
bath *ans* mint
bathdy *eg* mint
bathio *be* bath
bathodyn *eg* bathodynnau badge
bathodyn lapél *eg* bathodynnau lapél lapel badge
batholith *eg* batholithau batholith
batholithig *ans* batholithic
bathu *be* mint
bathygraff *eg* bathygraffau bathygraph
bathymetreg *eb* bathymetry
bathymetrig *ans* bathymetric
bathysffer *eg* bathysphere
baud *eg* baud
baw *eg* soil
baw dyfrgi *eg* spraint
bawd *eg* bodiau thumb
beaumontage *eg* beaumontage
Bebung *eg* Bebung
Beda Ddoeth *eg* Bede, the Venerable
bedel *eg* bedeliaid beadle
bedwen *eb* bedw birch
bedwen Fai *eb* bedw Mai maypole
Bedwin *eg* Bedwiniaid Bedouin
Bedwyr *eg* Bedivere
bedydd *eg* baptism
bedydd cred *eg* believer's baptism
bedydd esgob *eg* confirmation
bedydd plant *eg* infant baptism
bedyddfa *eb* bedyddfeydd baptistry
bedyddfaen *eb* bedyddfeini baptismal font
bedyddfaen *eg* bedyddfeini font
Bedyddiwr *eg* Bedyddwyr Baptist
Bedyddiwr Albanaidd *eg* Bedyddwyr Albanaidd Scotch Baptist
bedd *eg* beddau grave; tomb
bedd cyntedd *eg* beddau cyntedd passage grave
beddargraff *eg* beddargraffiadau epitaph
Beddrod Sanctaidd *eg* Holy Sepulchre
beddrod siambr *eg* beddrodau siambr chamber tomb
befel *eg* befelau bevel
befel cymwysadwy *eg* befelau cymwysadwy adjustable bevel
befel hogi *eg* befelau hogi sharpening bevel
befel llifanu *eg* befelau llifanu grinding bevel
befel llithr *eg* befelau llithr sliding bevel
befelu *be* bevel
beias *eg* baize
beiau sgraffinio *ell* abrasive faults

Beibl *eg* Beiblau Bible
Beibl Cymraeg *eg* Welsh Bible
Beibl Fwlgat *eg* Vulgate Bible
Beiblaidd *ans* Biblical
beic modur *eg* beiciau modur motor bicycle
beichiog *ans* pregnant
beichiogi *be* conceive
beichiogrwydd *eg* pregnancy
beili *eg* beilïau bailey
beirniad (mewn cystadleuaeth) *eg* beirniaid critic
beirniad (yn gyffredinol) *eg* beirniaid adjudicator; judge
beirniad cerdd *eg* beirniaid cerdd music adjudicator
beirniadaeth (mewn cystadleuaeth) *eb* beirniadaethau adjudication
beirniadaeth (yn gyffredinol) *eb* beirniadaethau criticism
beirniadol *ans* critical
beit *eg* beitiau byte
bel *eg* belau bel
belai *eg* belaiau belay
belt *eb* beltiau belt
belt wasgedd *eb* beltiau gwasgedd pressure belt
belt yrru *eb* beltiau gyrru driving belt
ben-ben head-on
bendith *eb* bendithion blessing
bendith *eb* bendithion benediction
Bendith Aaron *eb* Aaronic Blessing
Benedictiad *eg* Benedictiaid Benedictine
bensen *eg* benzene
bensencarbaldehyd *eg* benzenecarbaldehyde
bensencarbaldehyd ocsim *eg* benzenecarbaldehyde oxime
bensencarbocsamid *eg* benzenecarboxamide
bensencarbonitril *eg* benzenecarbonitrile
bensencarbonyl clorid *eg* benzenecarbonyl chloride
bensen-1,4-deuamin *eg* benzene-1,4-diamine
bensen-1,4-deuamoniwm clorid *eg* benzene-1,4-diammonium chloride
bensen-1,2-deucarbocsimid *eg* benzene-1,2-dicarboximide
bensen-1,2-deucarbocsylig anhydrid *eg* benzene-1,2-dicarboxylic anhydride
bensen-1,2-deuol *eg* benzene-1,2-diol
bensen-1,3-deuol *eg* benzene-1,3-diol
bensen-1,4-deuol *eg* benzene-1,4-diol
bensen-1,2,3-triol *eg* benzene-1,2,3-triol
bensen-1,3,5-triol *eg* benzene-1,3,5-triol
bensodiasepin *eg* benzodiazepine
benthig *ans* benthic
benthos *eg* benthos
benthyca (cael benthyg) *be* borrow
benthyca (rhoi benthyg) *be* loan
benthyciad *eg* benthyciadau loan
benthyciad banc *eg* benthyciadau banc bank loan
benthyciad cyfeillgar *eg* benthyciadau cyfeillgar amicable loan
benthyciad dros dro *eg* benthyciadau dros dro bridging loan
benthyciad gorfodol *eg* benthyciadau gorfodol benevolence
benthyciad gorfodol *eg* benthyciadau gorfodol forced loan
benthyciad i fyfyrwyr *eg* benthyciadau i fyfyrwyr student loan
benthyciad personol *eg* benthyciadau personol personal loan
benthyciwr *eg* benthycwyr borrower
benyw *eb* benywod female
benywaidd *ans* feminine
benywol *ans* female
bêr (troi) *eg* berau spit
berceliwm *eg* berkelium
berceuse *eb* berceuses berceuse
beret *eg* berets beret
berfa *eb* berfâu barrow
berfa *eb* berfâu wheelbarrow
bergamasca *eg* bergamasce bergamask
bergwynt *eg* bergwyntoedd bergwind
berw *ans* boiling
berwbwynt *eg* boiling point
berwi *be* boil
berwr *eg* cress
berwr dŵr *eg* water cress
beryliwm (Be) *eg* beryllium
beryliwm ethanoad basig *eg* basic beryllium ethanoate
beryn *eg* berynnau bearing
beryn hollt *eg* berynnau hollt split bearing
beryn sgriw dywys *eg* berynnau sgriwiau tywys lead screw bearing
beryn y pen mawr *eg* berynnau y pen mawr big end bearing
betain *eg* betaine
betws *eg* betysau beadhouse
betys siwgr *ell* sugar beet
betysen *eg* betys beetroot
Bhagavad Gita *eg* Bhagavad Gita
bhakti *eg* bhakti
bias *eg* biasau bias
bias grid *eg* grid bias
bias yn ôl *eg* reverse bias
biasu *be* bias
bib *eg* bibiau bib
bicer *eg* biceri beaker
bicer plastig *eg* biceri plastig plastic beaker
bicerwyr *ell* beaker folk
bicini *eg* bicinis bikini
bidog *eb* bidogau bayonet
biffenyl-4,4'-deuamin *eg* biphenyl-4,4'-diamine
bil *eg* biliau bill
bil cyfnewid *eg* biliau cyfnewid bill of exchange
bil ditio *eg* biliau ditio bill of indictment
bil gwerthiant *eg* biliau gwerthiant bill of sale
bil llwytho *eg* biliau llwytho bill of loading

bil priodweddau *eg* biliau priodweddau bill of quantities
Bil Trysorlys *eg* Treasury Bill
bilain *eg* bileiniaid villein
bileiniaeth *eb* villeinage
biliferdin *eg* biliverdin
bilirwbin *eg* bilirubin
biliwn *eg* biliynau billion
bilwg *eg* bilygau billhook
bin *eg* biniau bin
bin clai *eg* biniau clai clay bin
bin sbwriel *eg* biniau sbwriel dustbin, refuse bin
bin tywod *eg* biniau tywod sand bin
binomaidd *ans* binomial
binomial *eg* binomialau binomial
bioadborth *eg* biofeedback
bioargaeledd *eg* bioavailability
biocemeg *eb* biochemistry
biocemegydd *eg* biocemegwyr biochemist
biocemegyn *eg* biocemegion biochemical
bïocor *eg* biocorau biochore
bioddaeargemegol *ans* biogeochemical
bioddaearyddiaeth *eb* biogeography
bioddiraddadwy *ans* biodegradable
biogenesis *eg* biogenesis
biogynyddiad *eg* bioaccumulation
biohinsoddeg *eb* bioclimatology
bioleg *eb* biology
bioleg gymdeithasol *eb* sociobiology
biolegol *ans* biological
bïom *eg* bïomau biome
biomas *eg* biomass
biomecaneg *eb* biomechanics
biosffer *eg* biosphere
biosom *eg* biosome
biosynhwyrydd *eg* biosynwyryddion biosensor
biosynthesu *be* biosynthesize
biotechnoleg *eb* biotechnology
biotig *ans* biotic
biotrawsffurfiant *eg* biotrawsffurfiannau biotransformation
bioymoleuedd *eb* bioluminescence
1,2-bis[bis(carbocsimethyl)amino]ethan *eg* 1,2-bis[bis(carboxymethyl)amino]ethane
bis(bwtandeuon deuocsimato)nicel(II) *eg* bis(butanedione dioximato)nickel(II)
bisged *eb* bisgedi biscuit
bisged ddigestif *eb* bisgedi digestif digestive biscuit
bisged gracer *eb* bisgedi cracer cream cracker
bisged sinsir *eb* bisgedi sinsir ginger biscuit
bismwth *eg* bismuth
bismwth(III) clorid *eg* bismuth(III) chloride
bismwth(III) clorid ocsid *eg* bismuth(III) chloride oxide
bitwmen *eg* bitumen
biwgl *eg* biwglau bugle
biwret *eg* biuret
biwro *eg* biwroau bureau
biwrocrat *eg* biwrocratiaid bureaucrat
biwrocrataidd *ans* bureaucratic
biwrocratiaeth *eb* bureaucracy
blacjac *eg* blackjack
blacleg *eg* blaclegwyr blackleg
blaen *ans* anterior; fore
blaen (am ben eithaf) *eg* blaenau tip
blaen (bwa) *eg* point
blaen (yn gyffredinol) *eg* front; forward
blaen cafn *eg* trough's end
blaen carbid *ans* carbide tipped
blaen cilfach *eg* blaenau cilfachau inlet-head
blaen diemwnt *ans* diamond tipped
blaen dolennog *eg* blaenau dolennog serpentine front
blaen erydu *be* headward erosion
blaen nodwydd *eg* blaenau nodwyddau needle point
blaen pidyn *eg* glans penis
blaen rhewlif *eg* blaenau rhewlif glacier snout
blaen siop electronig *eg* electronic storefront
blaen twngsten *eg* tungsten tip
blaen y droed *eg* blaenau'r traed toe
blaen yr esgid *eg* toe-cap
blaenadwaith *eg* forward reaction
blaenasgell agored *eb* open side wing forward
blaenasgell dywyll *eb* blind side wing forward
blaenasgellwr *eg* blaenasgellwyr wing forward
blaenbacio *be* prepack
blaenbaredol *ans* frontoparietal
blaenbeipio *be* pipelining
blaenbrosesu *be* foreground processing
blaen-brosesydd *eg* blaen-brosesyddion front-end processor
blaendal *eg* blaendaliadau deposit; down payment
blaen-dâp *eg* blaen-dapiau header tape
blaendir *eg* blaendiroedd foreground
blaendir afon *eg* blaendiroedd afon torrent tract
blaendon *eb* blaendonnau wave-front
blaendor *ans* truncated
blaendoriad *eg* blaendoriadau truncation
blaendorri *be* truncate
blaendraeth *eg* blaendraethau foreshore
blaenddant *eg* blaenddannedd incisor
blaenddwfn *eg* blaenddyfnion foredeep
blaenddwr *eg* blaenddyfroedd headwater
blaenfain *ans* tapering
blaenffrwyth *eg* first fruits
blaengad *eb* blaengadau vanguard
blaengar *ans* advanced; progressive
blaen-gau *be* foreclose
blaengroen *eg* blaengrwyn foreskin
blaengrwm *ans* bow-fronted
blaenguriad *eg* blaenguriadau preparatory beat
blaen-gymysgiad *eg* pre-mix

blaenlaniad *eg* blaenlaniadau beachhead; bridgehead
blaenluniad *eg* blaenluniadau frontality
blaen-luosi *be* pre-multiply
blaenllaw *eg* forehand
blaenolwg *eg* blaenolygon front elevation
blaenolwg ategol *eg* blaenolygon ategol auxiliary front elevation
blaenolwg hanner trychiadol *eg* blaenolygon hanner trychiadol half-sectional front elevation
blaenolwg trychiadol *eg* blaenolygon trychiadol sectional front elevation
blaenoriad y cyhydnosau *eg* precession of the equinoxes
blaenoriaeth *eb* blaenoriaethau priority; precedence; preference
blaenoriaeth i'r trefedigaethau *eb* colonial preference
Blaenoriaeth i'r Ymerodraeth *eb* Imperial Preference
blaenoriaethu *be* prioritize
blaenorol *ans* prior
blaensffenoidol *ans* frontosphenoidal
blaenslaes *eg* blaenslaesau forward slash
blaenstroc *eb* blaenstrociau upstroke
blaenswm *eg* blaensymiau advance
blaenu (cerddorfa) *be* lead
blaenu (yn gyffredinol) *be* advance
blaenwr (mewn cerddorfa) *eg* blaenwyr leader
blaenwr (mewn chwaraeon) *eg* blaenwyr forward
blaenwraig *eb* blaenwragedd forward
blaenwreiddyn *eg* blaenwreiddiau root tip
blaen-ymennydd *eg* fore-brain
blaenymyl *ans* blaenymylon leading edge
blaguro *be* bud
blaguryn *eg* blagur bud; gemma; shoot
blaguryn apigol *eg* blagur apigol apical bud
blaguryn atodol *eg* blagur atodol accessory bud
blaguryn ceseilaidd *eg* blagur ceseilaidd axillary bud
blaguryn cwsg *eg* blagur cwsg dormant bud
blaguryn cyferbyn *eg* blagur cyferbyn opposite bud
blaguryn eiledol *eg* blagur eiledol alternate bud
blaguryn ochrol *eg* blagur ochrol lateral bud
blanc copr *eg* copper blank
blanc crymdo *eg* blanciau crymdo domed blank
blanc dysglog *eg* blanciau dysglog dished blank
blanced *eb* blancedi blanket
blanced dân *eb* blancedi tân fire blanket
blanced drydan *eb* blancedi trydan electric blanket
Blancedwyr *ell* Blanketeers
blansio *be* blanch
blas *eg* flavour, taste
blasbwynt *eg* blasbwyntiau taste bud
blaslyn Ffrengig *eg* French dressing
blaslyn salad *eg* salad dressing
blastocoel *eg* blastocoelau blastocoel
blastocyt *eg* blastocytau blastocyte
blastoderm *eg* blastodermau blastoderm
blastoffor *eg* blastofforau blastophore
blastomer *eg* blastomerau blastomere
blastwla *eg* blastwlâu blastula
blasu *be* taste; gustation
blasus *ans* appetizing
blasyn *eg* blasynnau appetizer
blawd *eg* blodiau flour
blawd brown garw *eg* granary flour
blawd bywyn gwenith *eg* wheatmeal flour
blawd codi *eg* self-raising flour
blawd corn *eg* cornflour
blawd craig *eg* rock flour
blawd cryf *eg* strong flour
blawd llif *eg* sawdust
blawd meddal *eg* soft flour
blawd plaen *eg* plain flour
blawd pysgod *eg* fish meal
blawd startsh gostyngol *eg* starch reduced flour
blawd sylffwr *eg* flowers of sulphur
blend *eg* blende
blerdwf *eg* sprawl
blerdwf trefol *eg* urban sprawl
blew ych *eg* ox-blend
blewog *ans* hirsute
blewyn (mochyn etc) *eg* blew bristle
blewyn (yn gyffredinol) *eg* blew hair
blewyn amrant *eg* blew amrant eyelash
blewyn blasu *eg* blew blasu gustatory hair
blinder *eg* tiredness
blipiwr *eg* blipwyr bleeper
Blitz, Y *eg* Blitz, The
blithogydd *eg* blithogyddion galactagogue
bliw *eg* blue
bloc *eg* blociau block
bloc allwedd *eg* blociau allweddi key block
bloc bodis *eg* blociau bodis bodice block
bloc brêc *eg* blociau brêc brake block
bloc bris *eg* blociau bris breeze block
bloc cafnu *eg* blociau cafnu hollowing block
bloc clo *eg* blociau clo lock block
bloc corc *eg* blociau corc cork block
bloc cordiau *eg* blociau cordiau chordal block
bloc cornel *eg* blociau cornel corner block
bloc cychwyn *eg* blociau cychwyn starting bloc
bloc cynllunio *eg* blociau cynllunio sketch block
bloc darfath *eg* blociau darfath swage block
bloc glud *eg* blociau glud glue block
bloc gwasgu *eg* blociau gwasgu pressure block
bloc jeli *eg* blociau jeli jelly block
bloc Johansson *eg* blociau Johansson Johansson's block
bloc lafa *eg* blociau lafa lava block
bloc lafa *eg* blociau lafa block lava
bloc leino mowntiedig *eg* blociau leino mowntiedig mounted lino block
bloc llithr *eg* blociau llithr sliding block

bloc lliw *eg* blociau lliw colour block
bloc masnach *eg* blociau masnach trade bloc
bloc medrydd *eg* blociau medrydd gauge block
bloc meitr *eg* blociau meitr mitre block
bloc plinth *eg* blociau plinth plinth block
bloc pren *eg* blociau pren wood block
bloc pwli *eg* blociau pwli pulley block
bloc sglodi *eg* blociau sglodi chipping block
bloc sgriwio *eg* blociau sgriwio screwing block
bloc teitl *eg* blociau teitl title block
bloc teitl printiedig *eg* blociau teitl printiedig printed title block
bloc torri *eg* blociau torri cutter block
bloc Tsieineaidd *eg* blociau Tsieineaidd Chinese block
bloc ysgythru *eg* blociau ysgythru engraving block
blocdorrwr *eg* blocdorwyr block cutter
blocfwrdd *eg* blocfyrddau blockboard
blocfynydd *eg* blocfynyddoedd block mountain
blociau a chlampiau blocks and clamps
blociau crampio *ell* cramping blocks
blociau hap *ell* block randomization
blociau hyrddu *ell* ramming blocks
blociau plwm *ell* lead blocks
blociau V a chlampiau V blocks and clamps
blociau wedi'u gludio *ell* glued blocks
blocio *be* block
bloclwyfandir *eg* bloclwyfandiroedd plateau block
blocyn pyg *eg* blociau pyg pitch block
blodeuo *be* flourish
blodeuog *ans* flowery; floral; florid
blodfresych caws *ell* cauliflower cheese
blodfresychen *eb* blodfresych cauliflower
blodigyn *eg* blodigion floret
blodiog *ans* floury
blodyn *eg* blodau flower
blodyn eilflwydd *eg* blodau eilflwydd biennial flower
blodyn lluosflwydd *eg* blodau lluosflwydd perennial flower
blodyn unflwydd *eg* blodau unflwydd annual
blodyn yr haul *eg* blodau'r haul sunflower
blog *eg* blogiau blog
blogio *be* blog
blogiwr *eg* blogwyr blogger
bloneg *eg* lard
blonegog *ans* adipose
blonegrwydd *eg* adiposity
blonegu *be* lard
blows *eb* blowsys blouse
blowson *eb* blowsonau blouson
blues *ell* blues
blwch *eg* blychau box
blwch allan *eg* blychau allan outbox
blwch allan newydd *eg* blychau allan newydd new outbox
blwch amlrestr *eg* blychau amlrestr multilist box
blwch clepian *eg* blychau clepian clapper box
blwch coluro *eg* blychau coluro make-up box
blwch cosbi *eg* blychau cosbi penalty box
blwch craidd *eg* blychau craidd core box
blwch cyswllt *eg* blychau cyswllt junction box
blwch deialog *eg* blychau deialog dialog box
blwch dewislen *eg* blychau dewislen menu box
blwch ebill *eg* blychau ebill peg box
blwch gemau *eg* blychau gemau casket
blwch gêr *eg* blychau gêr gearbox
blwch gostyngiad *eg* reduction box
blwch grŵp *eg* blychau grŵp group box
blwch lliw *eg* blychau lliw colour box
blwch llwch *eg* blychau llwch ash tray
blwch meitro *eg* blychau meitro mitre box
blwch minws *eg* blychau minws minus box
blwch mowldio *eg* blychau mowldio moulding box
blwch offer *eg* blychau offer tool box
blwch offer lluniadu *eg* blychau offer lluniadu draw toolbox
blwch pelydru *eg* blychau pelydru ray box
blwch penderfyniad *eg* blychau penderfyniad decision box
blwch rhewi *eg* blychau rhewi freezing compartment
blwch saim *eg* blychau saim grease box
blwch stydiau *eg* blychau stydiau stud box
blwch Swyddfa'r Post *eg* blychau Swyddfa'r Post Post Office box
blwch tân *eg* blychau tân tinder box
blwch testun *eg* blychau testun text box
blwch ticio *eg* blychau ticio check box
blwch tlysau *eg* blychau tlysau trinket box
blwch tyllu *eg* blychau tyllu bore box
blwch tywod *eg* blychau tywod sand box
blwch wad *eg* blychau wad wad box
blwff *eg* blyffiau bluff
blwm *eg* blymau bloom
blwydd-dal *eg* blwydd-daliadau annuity
blwyddiadur *eg* blwyddiaduron year planner
blwyddlyfr *eg* blwyddlyfrau year book
blwyddnod *eg* blwyddnodau annal
blwyddyn academaidd *eb* blynyddoedd academaidd academic year
blwyddyn ariannol *eb* financial year
blwyddyn cyhoeddi *eb* year of publication
blwyddyn golau *eb* blynyddoedd golau light year
blwyddyn haul *eb* blynyddoedd haul solar year
blwyddyn naid *eb* blynyddoedd naid leap year
Blwyddyn Newydd *eb* New Year
blwyddyn sefydlu *eb* induction year
blwyddyn serol *eb* blynyddoedd serol sidereal year
blwyddyn serol *eb* blynyddoedd serol stellar year
blwyddyn ysgol *eb* blynyddoedd ysgol school year
blynyddoedd cynnar *ell* early years
blynyddol *ans* annual
bob *eg* bobiau bob

bob tro *adf* always
bob yn ail *ans* alternate
bobin *eg* bobinau bobbin
bobin gwennol *eg* bobinau gwennol shuttle bobbin
bocs *eg* bocsys box
bocs ar groes *eg* box crosswise
bocs ar hyd *eg* box lengthwise
bocsio *be* box
bocsit *eg* bauxite
boch *eb* bochau cheek
bod *eg* bodau being
bod dynol *eg* bodau dynol human
bod yn bla *be* infest
bod yn ddigartref *be* homelessness
bod yn fwy na *be* exceed
Bodhisattva *eg* Bodhisattva
bodis *eg* bodisiau bodice
bodis blaen *eg* bodisiau blaen front bodice
bodis cefn *eg* bodisiau cefn back bodice
bodlon *ans* content
bodloni *be* satisfy
bodlonrwydd swydd *eg* job satisfaction
bodlonwr *eg* bodlonwyr satisfier
bodolaeth *eb* bodolaethau existence
bodolaeth Duw *eb* existence of God
boddhad *eg* satisfaction
boddhaol *ans* satisfactory
boeler *eg* boeleri boiler
Boer *eg* Boeriaid Boer
bogail *eg* bogeiliau umbilicus
bogail *eg* bogeiliau boss
bogail tarian *eg* bogeiliau tarian shield boss
boglynnog *ans* embossed
boglynnu *be* emboss
boglynwaith *eg* boglynweithiau embossing
Boiar *eg* Boiariaid Boyar
boicotio *be* boycott
bol *eg* bolïau belly
bola caled *eg* roe
bola meddal *eg* roe
boladdawnswraig *eb* boladdawnswragedd belly-dancer
bolero *eg* boleros bolero
bolio *be* bulge; dishing
Bolsiefig *eg* Bolsiefigiaid Bolshevik
Bolsiefigaidd *ans* Bolshevik
bolson *eg* bolsonau bolson
bolster *eg* bolsteri bolster
bolws *eg* bolysau bolus
bollt *eb* bolltau bolt
bollt ben gwrthsodd *eb* bolltau pen gwrthsodd countersunk head bolt
bollt ben hecsagonol *eb* bolltau pen hecsagonol hexagonal head bolt
bollt bencosyn *eb* bolltau pencosyn cheese-head bolt
bollt bengron *eb* bolltau pengrwn round head bolt
bollt bensgwar *eb* bolltau pensgwar square head bolt
bollt ddeuben *eb* bolltau deuben double-ended bolt
bollt ddigopa *eb* bolltau digopa grub bolt
bollt ddolen *eb* bolltau dolen eye bolt
bollt goets *eb* bolltau coets coach bolt
bollt gwpwrdd *eb* bolltau cwpwrdd cupboard bolt
bollt gyfwyneb *eb* bolltau cyfwyneb flush bolt
bollt haearn gyr *eb* bolltau haearn gyr wrought iron bolt
bollt sylfaen *eb* bolltau sylfaen rag bolt
bollt sylfaen *eb* bolltau sylfaen foundation bolt
bollt T *eb* bolltau T tee bolt
bollt tyniant *eb* bolltau tyniant tension bolt
bollt tynnol *eb* bolltau tynnol tensile bolt
bollt wagen *eb* bolltau wagen carriage bolt
bollt ymestyn *eb* bolltau ymestyn expansion bolt
bolltio *be* bolt
bolltiog *ans* bolted
bom folcanig *eg* bomiau folcanig volcanic bomb
bom tân *eg* bomiau tân incendiary
bombardon *eg* bombardonau bombardon
bôn *eg* bonau base; butt
bôn rhif *eg* bonau rhif number base
bôn y sgrym *eg* base of scrum
Bonapartiaeth *eb* Bonapartism
boncyff *eg* boncyffion tree trunk; log; bole
bond *eg* bondiau bond
bond cam *eg* bent bond
bond cofalent *eg* bondiau cofalent covalent bond
bond cyd-drefnol *eg* coordinate bond
bond dwbl *eg* bondiau dwbl double bond
bond egnioledig *eg* bondiau egnioledig energy-rich bond
bond ïonig *eg* bondiau ïonig ionic bond
bond lluosol *eg* multiple bond
Bond Premiwm *eg* Bondiau Premiwm Premium Bond
bond triphlyg *eg* bondiau triphlyg triple bond
Bondiau Amddiffyn *ell* Defence Bonds
Bondiau Cynilo Prydeinig *ell* British Savings Bonds
bondiau diatbryn *ell* irredeemable bonds
bondin *eg* bonding
bondin du *eg* black bonding
bondin Ffleminaidd *eg* Flemish bond
bondin Ffleminaidd wal gardd *eg* Flemish garden wall bonding
bondin Seisnig *eg* English bond
bondin Seisnig wal gardd *eg* English garden wall bonding
bondio *be* bond
bondiog *ans* bonded
bondo *eg* bondoeau eaves
bondo *eg* bondoeau soffit
bondo agored *eg* bondoeau agored open eaves
bondo caeedig *eg* bondoeau caeedig closed eaves
bondo cyfwyneb *eg* bondoeau cyfwyneb flush eave

bondo ymestynnol *eg* bondoeau ymestynnol projecting eaves
boned *eb* bonedau bonnet
bonedd *eg* boneddigion landed gentry
bonedd *eg* gentry
bonedd annibynnol *eg* independent gentry
bonedd Cymreig *eg* Welsh gentry
Boneddiges y Siambr Wely *eb* Boneddigesau'r Siambr Wely Lady of the Bedchamber
bongo *eg* bongos bongo
bongorff *eg* bongyrff trunk
bonheddwr *eg* bonheddwyr gentleman
Bonheddwr y Gwarchodlu *eg* Bonheddwyr y Gwarchodlu Gentleman at Arms
Bonheddwr y Siambr Wely *eg* Bonheddwyr y Siambr Wely Gentleman of the Bedchamber
bonws *eg* bonus
bonyn (tocyn etc) *eg* bonion counterfoil; stub
bonyn (pren etc) *eg* bonion stake
bonyn crychu *eg* bonion crychu creasing stake
bonyn gwaelodi *eg* bonion gwaelodi bottoming stake
bonyn hanner crwn *eg* bonion hanner crwn half moon stake
bonyn hirbig *eg* bonion hirbig extinguisher stake
bonyn madarchen *eg* bonion madarch mushroom stake
bonyn ongl lem *eg* bonion ongl lem hatchet stake
bonyn pen cromen *eg* bonion pen cromen oval head stake
bonyn pen hir *eg* bonion pen hir long head stake
bonyn pengrwn *eg* bonion pengrwn ball-head stake; round head stake
bonyn pensgwar *eg* bonion pensgwar square head stake
bonyn pig *eg* bonion pig bick iron
bonyn tafod buwch *eg* bonion tafod buwch cow's tongue stake
bonyn taprog *eg* bonion taprog tapered stake
bonyn teirbraich *eg* bonion teirbraich three arm stake
bonyn twmffat *eg* bonion twmffedi funnel stake
bonyn twndish *eg* bonion twndis funnel stake
bonynnu *be* skating
Boole *ans* Boolean
boracs *eg* borax
bordar *eg* bordariaid borderer
border *eg* borderi border
boreol weddi *eb* matins
borio fertigol *be* vertical boring
borio llorweddol *be* horizontal boring
boron *eg* boron
boron triffllworid *eg* boron trifluoride
boron(III) ocsid *eg* boron(III) oxide
botgin *eg* botginau bodkin
botgin cam *eg* botginau cam bent bodkin
botgin crwm *eg* botginau crwm curved bodkin
botgin fflat cam *eg* botginau fflat cam bent flat bodkin
► **botgin gweithiwr gwiail** *eg* botginau gweithwyr gwiail caneworker's bodkin
botgin pengrwn *eg* botginau pengrwn ball pointed bodkin
botgin syth *eg* botginau syth straight bodkin
botwliaeth *eb* botulism
botwm *eg* botymau button
botwm adfer *eg* botymau adfer restore button
botwm bar offer *eg* botymau bar offer toolbar button
botwm cartref *eg* home button
botwm cau dogfen *eg* botymau cau dogfen document close button
botwm cromen *eg* botymau cromen domed button
botwm crys *eg* botymau crys shirt button
botwm cychwyn *eg* start button
botwm cyswllt *eg* botymau cyswllt link button
botwm ffenestr *eg* window button
botwm garan fowld *eg* botymau garan fowld moulded shank button
botwm gorchudd *eg* botymau gorchudd covered button
botwm gorchymyn *eg* botymau gorchymyn command button
botwm lliain *eg* botymau lliain linen button
botwm perl *eg* botymau perl pearl button
botwm rhagosodedig *eg* botymau rhagosodedig default button
botwm taro *eg* botymau taro striking button
botwm terfynol *eg* botymau terfynol terminal button
botwm yn ôl *eg* botymau yn ôl back button
botymell *eb* botymellau buttonholer
botymu *be* button
both (olwyn) *eb* bothau nave; hub
bouclé *eg* bouclé
bouquet garni *eg* bouquets garnis bouquet garni
Bourboniaid *ell* Bourbons
bourgeois *ans* bourgeois
bourgeoisie *eg* bourgeoisie
bourrée *eg* bourrées bourrée
bowlen hemisffer *eb* bowlenni hemisffer hemispherical bowl
bowlen salad *eb* bowlenni salad salad bowl
bowliad *eg* bowliadau bowl
bowliad hyd da *eg* good length ball
bowlin *eb* bowliniau bowline
bowlio *be* bowl
bowlio allan *be* bowl out
bowlio amddiffynnol *be* defensive bowling
bowlio araf *be* slow bowling
bowlio braich chwith *be* left arm bowling
bowlio canolig *be* medium pace bowling
bowlio cyflym *be* fast bowling
bowlio dan ysgwydd *be* underarm bowling
bowlio dros y wiced *be* bowl over the wicket

bowlio dros ysgwydd *be* overarm bowling
bowlio rownd y wiced *be* bowl round the wicket
bowliwr *eg* bowlwyr bowler
bowliwr araf *eg* bowlwyr araf slow bowler
bowliwr araf braich chwith *eg* bowlwyr araf braich chwith slow left arm bowler
bowliwr arddwrn *eg* bowlwyr arddwrn wrist bowler
bowliwr braich dde *eg* bowlwyr braich dde right arm bowler
bowliwr cyflym *eg* bowlwyr cyflym fast bowler
bowt *eg* bowtiau bout
braced *eg/b* bracedi bracket
braced angor *eb* bracedi angor anchor bracket
braced colfach *eb* bracedi colfach hinge bracket
braced haearn gyr *eb* bracedi haearn gyr wrought iron bracket
braced ongl *eb* bracedi ongl angle bracket
braced pen-glin *eb* bracedi pen-glin knee bracket
bracedu *be* bracketing
bract *eg* bractau bract
bractolyn *eg* bractolynnau bracteole
brad (yn erbyn gwlad, brenin etc) *eg* treason
brad (yn gyffredinol) *eg* treachery
Brad y Llyfrau Gleision *eg* Treason of the Blue Books; Treachery of the Blue Books
bradwr *eg* bradwyr traitor
bradycardia *eg* bradycardia
braenar *eg* fallow
braenaru *be* fallow
brafwra *eg* bravura
brag *eg* bragau malt brag
bragod gywair *eb* mixed key
bragu *be* brew
Brahman *eg* Brahman
Brahmin *eg* Brahmin
braich (deilen, offer mesur etc) *eb* limb
braich (yn gyffredinol) *eb* breichiau arm
braich ar golyn *eb* breichiau ar golyn pivoted arm
braich fawr (craen) *eb* breichiau mawr jib
braich golfachog *eb* breichiau colfachog hinged arm
braich gymalog *eb* breichiau cymalog jointed arm
braich gymwysadwy *eb* breichiau cymwysadwy adjustable arm
braich rydd *eb* breichiau rhydd free arm
braich sadio *eb* breichiau sadio anti-snake bar
braich ymladd *eb* breichiau ymladd fighting arm
braich-gerdded *be* arm walking
braich-neidio *be* arm jumping
braint (eglwysig) *eb* breintiau benefit
braint (yn gyffredinol) *eb* breintiau privilege
braint clerigwyr *eb* benefit of clergy
braint fasnachol *eb* breintiau masnachol commercial privilege
bran *eg* bran
brand *eg* brandiau brand
brandi *eg* brandy
brandio *be* brand
brandro *be* brandering
branell *eb* branellau capotasto
bras (=garw) *ans* rough; coarse
bras (=llawn braster) *ans* rich
bras (=tua) *ans* approximate
bras fframwaith *eg* skeleton framework
brasamcan *eg* brasamcanion approximation
brasamcanu *be* approximate
brasbwyth *eg* brasbwythau basting stitch
brasbwytho *be* baste
brasfodel *eg* brasfodelau mock-up
brasfodel maint llawn *eg* brasfodelau maint llawn fullsize mock-up
brasfodel wrth raddfa *eg* brasfodelau wrth raddfa scale mock-up
brasgopi *eg* brasgopïau engrossment
brasgopïo *be* engross
braslifiad *ans* rough sawn
braslun *eg* brasluniau sketch
braslun anodedig *eg* brasluniau anodedig annotated sketch
braslun bawd *eg* brasluniau bawd thumbnail sketch
braslun cynllunio *eg* brasluniau cynllunio sketch plan
braslun darluniol *eg* brasluniau darluniol pictorial sketch
braslun datblygiad *eg* brasluniau datblygiad development sketch
braslun dimensiynol *eg* brasluniau dimensiynol dimensional sketch
braslun eglur *eg* brasluniau eglur clear sketch
braslun golwg *eg* brasluniau golwg sketch of elevation
braslun llaw *eg* brasluniau llaw hand sketch
braslun llawrydd *eg* brasluniau llawrydd freehand sketch
braslun maes *eg* brasluniau maes field sketch
braslun o gyfrannedd da *eg* brasluniau o gyfrannedd da well-proportioned sketch
braslun pwynt manylyn *eg* sketch of point of detail
braslun rhagarweiniol *eg* brasluniau rhagarweiniol preliminary sketch
braslun syml *eg* brasluniau syml simple sketch
braslun taenedig *eg* brasluniau taenedig exploded sketch
brasluniau atodol *ell* supplementary sketches
braslunio *be* sketch
braslunio awyr agored *be* outdoor sketching
braslythreniad *eg* engrossment
braslythrennu *be* engross
brasnaddell *eb* brasnaddellau roughening tool
brasnaddu *be* roughing
bras-sych *ans* rough dry
bras-sychu *be* rough dry
braster *eg* brasterau fat
braster anifail *eg* animal fat
braster dirlawn *eg* saturated fat
braster menyn *eg* butterfat

brasterog *ans* fatty
brasteru *be* baste
brathiad neidr *eg* brathiadau neidr snake bite
brau *ans* brittle, fragile
brawd *eg* brodyr friar
brawd cardod *eg* brodyr cardod mendicant friar
Brawd Carmelaidd *eg* Brodyr Carmelaidd Carmelite Friar
Brawd Cycyllog *eg* Brodyr Cycyllog Capuchin Friar
Brawd Du *eg* Brodyr Duon Black Friar
brawd lleyg *eg* brodyr lleyg lay brother
Brawd Llwyd *eg* Brodyr Llwydion Grey Friar
brawd neu chwaer brodyr neu chwiorydd sibling
Brawd y Groes *eg* Brodyr y Groes Crutched Friar
Brawd-Bregethwr *eg* Brawd-Bregethwyr Brother Preacher
brawdgarwch *eg* fraternity
brawd-laddiad *eg* fratricide
brawdlys *eg* brawdlysoedd assize
Brawdlys *eg* Courts of Assize
Brawdlys Gwaedlyd *eg* Bloody Assizes
brawdoliaeth *eb* brawdoliaethau fraternity; brotherhood
Brawdoliaeth Dysgeidiaeth Gristnogol *eb* Confraternity of Christian Doctrine
Brawdoliaeth Unedig *eb* United Brotherhood
Brawdoliaeth y Cyn-Raffaeliaid *eb* Pre-Raphaelite Brotherhood
Brawdoliaeth y Ffeniaid *eb* Fenian Brotherhood
brawddeg *eb* brawddegau sentence
brawddegu *be* phrase
brawychu *be* terrorize
brêc *eg* breciau brake
breccia folcanig *eg* volcanic breccia
brecwast *eg* brecwastau breakfast
brech (am y clefyd) *eb* brechau pox
brech (yn gyffredinol) *eb* brechau rash
brech Almaenig *eb* German measles
brech cewyn *eb* nappy rash
brech clwt *eb* nappy rash
brech goch *eb* measles
brech yr ieir *eb* chicken-pox
brechiad *eg* brechiadau vaccination; inoculation
brechlyn *eg* brechlynnau vaccine
brechlyn anfyw *eg* non-live vaccines
brechlyn byw *eg* live vaccine
brechlyn triphlyg *eg* brechlynnau triphlyg triple vaccine
brechlyn trwy'r genau *eg* brechlynnau trwy'r genau oral vaccine
brechu *be* vaccinate; inoculate
brêd *eg* brediau braid
brêd gosod *eg* brediau gosod applied braid
brêd ricrac *eg* brediau ricrac ricrac braid
bregus *ans* frail
breichiau ar led arms sideways
breichiau i fyny arms upwards
breichiau'n blyg arms bend
breichio *be* arm
breichiol *ans* brachial
breichydd *eg* breichwyr bracer
breindal *eg* breindaliadau royalty
breiniwr *eg* breinwyr franchisor
breithell *eb* grey matter
brenhinbost *eg* brenhinbyst kingpost
brenhinbysg *eg* breninbysgod ling
brenhines *eb* brenhinesau queen
Brenhines Gydweddog *eb* Queen Consort
brenhiniaeth *eb* kingship; monarchy
brenhiniaeth absoliwt *eb* absolute monarchy
Brenhiniaeth Ddeuol *eb* Dual Monarchy
brenhiniaeth etifeddol *eb* breniniaethau etifeddol hereditary monarchy
brenhiniaeth etholedig *eb* elective monarchy
Brenhiniaeth Gorffennaf *eb* July Monarchy
brenhiniaeth Iorc *eb* Yorkist monarchy
brenhinol *ans* royal; regal
brenhinwr *eg* brenhinwyr royalist; monarchist
brenin *eg* brenhinoedd king; monarch
Brenin Cydweddog *eg* King Consort
breninoldeb *eg* regality
brest *eb* brestiau chest; breast
bresychen *eb* bresych cabbage
brethyn *eg* brethynnau cloth
brethyn caerog *eg* brethynnau caerog tweed
brethyn cartref *eg* homespun
brethyn Dhootie *eg* Dhootie cloth
brethyn eilban *eg* shoddy
brethyn llyfnu *eg* glasscloth
brethyn tewban *eg* brethynnau tewban frieze
brethynnwr *eg* brethynwyr clothier
breuan *eb* breuanau quern
breuan droi *eb* breuanau troi rotary quern
breuan gyfrwy *eb* breuanau cyfrwy saddle quern
breuder *eg* brittleness
breuddwydiol *ans* visionary
brëyr *eg* brehyrion thane
bri *eg* prestige
bric-bridd *eg* brick earth
bric-glai *eg* brick clay
bricolage *eg* bricolage
bricsen *eb* brics brick
bricsen awyru *eb* brics awyru ventilation brick
bricsen beirianneg *eb* brics peirianneg engineering brick
bricsen dân *eb* brics tân firebrick
bricsen focsit *eb* brics bocsit bauxite brick
bricsen wrthsafol *eb* brics gwrthsafol refractory brick
bricwaith *eg* brickwork
bricyllen *eb* bricyll apricot
brid *eg* bridiau breed
bridio *be* breed
bridio detholus *be* selective breeding
brif *eg* brifiau breve

briff *eg* briffiau brief
briff dylunio *eg* briffiau dylunio design brief
brig (graff, cromlin) *eg* peak
brig (haen o lo etc mewn craig) *eg* brigiadau outcrop
brig (ton, bryn) *eg* brigau crest
brig (tudalen etc) *eg* top
brig i frig *eg* peak-to-peak
brig y gwaelodlin *eg* top of baseline
brig y llinell *eg* top of line
brig y nod *eg* top of character
brigâd *eb* brigadau brigade
Brigâd Ryngwladol *eb* International Brigade
Brigadydd *eg* Brigadyddion Brigadier
brigdonnwr *eg* brigdonwyr surfer
briger *eb* brigerau stamen
brigerog *ans* staminate
briglin cyson *eg* briglinau cyson even crestline
briglithryn *eg* top rest
brigo *be* outcropping
brigo i'r wyneb *be* resurface
brigwerth *eg* brigwerthoedd peak value
brigwth *eg* brigwthiadau upthrust
brigyn *eg* brigau twig
brigyn deiliog *eg* brigau deiliog leafy shoot
brigyn impiedig *eg* brigau impiedig scion
brigyn ystwyth *eg* brigau ystwyth supple twig
bril *eg* brill
brioche *eb* brioches brioche
brisged *eb* brisket
brith *ans* mottled
brith y gors *eg* marsh fritillary
brithedd *eg* variegation
brithlen *eb* brithlenni arras
brithwaith *eg* brithweithiau tessellation
brithyll Mair pumbarf *eg* brithyllod Mair pumbarf five bearded rockling
briw *eg* briwiau ulcer; sore
briw gorwedd *eg* briwiau gorwedd bedsore
briwio *be* ulcerate
briwio *be* macerate
briw'r stumog *eg* stomach ulcer
briwsion bara *ell* bread crumbs
briwsion cras *ell* golden bread crumbs
briwsioni *be* crumble
briwsionllyd *ans* crumbly
briwsionyn *eg* briwsion crumb
broc (môr) *eg* driftwood
brocêd *eg* brocade
brocer *eg* broceriaid broker
brocer stoc *eg* broceriaid stoc stockbroker
broceriaeth *eb* brokerage
brocoli *ell* broccoli
broderie anglaise *eb* broderie anglaise
brodio *be* embroider
brodor *eg* brodorion native
brodoriaeth *eb* welshry
brodorol *ans* native; indigenous; autochthonous; vernacular
brodwaith *eg* embroidery
brodwaith arwyneb *eg* surface embroidery
brodwaith Assisi *eg* Assisi embroidery
brodwaith cynfas *eg* canvas embroidery
brodwaith eglwysig *eg* ecclesiastical embroidery
brodwaith eglwysig *eg* church embroidery
brodwaith ffabrig *eg* drawn fabric embroidery
brodwaith llaw *eg* hand embroidery
brodwaith peiriant *eg* machine embroidery
brodwaith rhydd *eg* free embroidery
brodwaith rhydd â pheiriant *eg* free machine embroidery
brodwaith tynnu edau *eg* drawn thread embroidery
Brodyr Bohemia *ell* Bohemian Brethren
brodyr lleyg *ell* conversi
Brodyr Sant Awstin *ell* Augustinian Friars
Brodyr y Bywyd Cyffredin *ell* Brethren of the Common Life
bromin (Br) *eg* bromine
bromin triffîworid *eg* bromine trifluoride
bromineiddiad *eg* bromination
bromineiddio *be* brominate
bromobensen *eg* bromobenzene
bromoethan *eg* bromoethane
bron *eb* bronnau breast
bronciolyn *eg* bronciolynnau bronchiole
broncitis *eg* bronchitis
broncws *eg* bronci bronchus
bronennog *ans* mamillated
brongwmwl *eg* brongymylau mammatocumulus
bronnol *ans* mammary
brown *eg* browniau brown
brown alisarin *eg* alizarin brown
brown canol *eg* mid brown
brown copr *eg* copper brown
brown golau *eg* light brown
brown tryloyw *eg* transparent brown
brown tywyll *eg* dark brown
brown Vandyke *eg* Vandyke brown
brownaidd *ans* brownish
brownio *be* brown
brwsh *eg* brwshys brush
brwsh aer *eg* brwshys aer air brush
brwsh blew *eg* brwshys blew bristle brush
brwsh blew camel *eg* brwshys blew camel camel hair brush
brwsh blew clust ych *eg* brwshys blew clust ych ox-ear hair brush
brwsh blew cymysg *eg* brwshys blew cymysg blended-hair brush
brwsh blew ffwlbart *eg* brwshys blew ffwlbart fitch hog brush
brwsh blew gafr *eg* brwshys blew gafr goat-hair brush
brwsh blew gwiwer *eg* brwshys blew gwiwer squirrel hair brush

brwsh blew meddal *eg* brwshys blew meddal soft hair brush
brwsh blew merlen *eg* brwshys blew merlen pony-hair brush
brwsh blew mochyn *eg* brwshys blew mochyn hoghair brush
brwsh blew ych *eg* brwshys blew ych ox-hair brush; ox-blend brush
brwsh canllaw grisiau *eg* brwshys canllaw grisiau banister brush
brwsh cans *eg* brwshys cans outdoor sweeping brush
brwsh crafu *eg* brwshys crafu scratch brush
brwsh cwilsen *eg* brwshys cwils quill brush
brwsh dyfrlliw *eg* brwshys dyfrlliw water colour brush
brwsh ffeil *eg* brwshys ffeil carding brush
brwsh glud *eg* brwshys glud glue brush
brwsh gwifrau *eg* brwshys gwifrau wire brush
brwsh llythrennu *eg* brwshys llythrennu lettering brush
brwsh murlun *eg* brwshys murlun mural brush
brwsh neilon *eg* brwshys neilon nylon brush
brwsh paent *eg* brwshys paent paint brush
brwsh past *eg* brwshys past paste brush
brwsh peintio *eg* brwshys peintio painting brush
brwsh poster *eg* brwshys poster poster-brush
brwsh rhidyllu *eg* brwshys rhidyllu sieving brush
brwsh sabl *eg* brwshys sabl sable brush
brwsh sabl coch *eg* brwshys sabl coch red sable brush
brwsh siâp cleddyf *eg* brwshys siâp cleddyf sword shape brush
brwsh siâp cneuen *eg* brwshys siâp cneuen filbert shape brush
brwsh stensil *eg* brwshys stensil stencil brush
brwsh sych *eg* brwshys sych dry brush
brwsh tŷ bach *eg* brwshys tŷ bach lavatory brush
brwsh un-strôc *eg* brwshys un-strôc one-stroke brush
brwshwaith *eg* brushwork
brwsio *be* brush
brwyd *eg* brwydau heddle
brwydr *eb* brwydrau battle
brwydr Lepanto *eb* battle of Lepanto
brwydr lled y cledrau *eb* battle of the gauges
Brwydr Prydain *eb* Battle of Britain
Brwydr y Somme *eb* Battle of the Somme
brwydro *be* struggle
brwynen (mewn offeryn chwyth) *eb* brwyn reed
brwynen (y planhigyn) *eb* brwyn rush; juncus
brwynen ddirgrynol *eb* brwyn dirgrynol vibrating reed
brwynen ddwbl *eb* brwyn dwbl double reed
brwyniad *eg* brwyniaid anchovy
brwysio *be* braise
brych *eg* brychau afterbirth; placenta
brychau haul *ell* sunspots
brycheuyn *eg* brychau blemish; blur
brychni *eg* fleck; speckle
brychu *be* fleck; speckle; mottling
bryn *eg* bryniau hill
bryn a phant swell and swale
bryncyn *eg* bryncynnau hillock
bryncyn acson *eg* axon hillock
bryndir *eg* bryndiroedd hill country
brynfa *eb* brynfeydd hill station
bryngaer *eb* bryngaerau hill fort
bryniog *ans* hilly
bryoffyt *eg* bryoffytau bryophyte
brys *ans* emergency
brysbennu *be* triage
Brython *eg* Brythoniaid Briton
Brythonaidd *ans* Brythonic
buanedd *eg* buaneddau speed
▶ **buanedd perifferol** *eg* peripheral speed
buanedd uchaf *eg* top speed
buanedd y gwynt *eg* wind speed
buarth chwarae *eg* buarthau chwarae playground
buchedd sant *eg* bucheddau saint hagiography
buches *eb* buchesau herd
budrelwa *be* profiteer
budd (=mantais etc) *eg* buddiannau interest
budd (ariannol etc) *eg* buddion benefit; bote
budd allanol *eg* buddlon allanol external benefit
budd cymdeithasol *eg* social benefit
budd ymylol *eg* marginal utility
buddai (gorddi) *eb* buddeiau churn
budd-dal *eg* budd-daliadau benefit
budd-dal afiechyd *eg* budd-daliadau afiechyd sickness benefit
budd-dal atodol *eg* budd-daliadau atodol supplementary benefit
budd-dal cyffredinol *eg* budd-daliadau cyffredinol universal benefit
budd-dal dethol *eg* budd-daliadau dethol selective benefit
budd-dal plant *eg* child allowance
budd-dal tai *eg* budd-daliadau tai housing benefit
budd-dal unffurf *eg* budd-daliadau unffurf uniform benefit
budd-dal y methedig *eg* invalidity benefit
budd-dal ymddeol *eg* retirement benefit
budd-dal ymddeol *eg* superannuation
buddiannau preifat *ell* private benefits
buddiol *ans* profitable
buddioldeb *eb* expediency
buddran *eb* buddrannau dividend
buddran cyfranddalwyr *eb* shareholder dividend
buddsoddi *be* invest
buddsoddiad *eg* buddsoddiadau investment
buddsoddiad cyflawnedig *eg* buddsoddiadau cyflawnedig actual investment
buddsoddiad cynhyrchiol *eg* buddsoddiadau cynhyrchiol productive investment

buddsoddiad gros *eg* buddsoddiadau gros gross investment
buddsoddiad net *eg* buddsoddiadau net net investment
buddsoddiad o'r tu allan *eg* buddsoddiadau o'r tu allan inward investment
buddsoddiad rhieni *eg* parental investment
buddsoddwr *eg* buddsoddwyr investor
Buddsoddwyr mewn Pobl Investors in People
Buddug *eb* Boadicea
buddugoliaeth *eb* buddugoliaethau victory
buddugoliaethus *ans* victorious
bufedd *eb* bufeddi bovate
bugail *eg* bugeiliaid shepherd
bugeilgerdd *eb* bugeilgerddi eclogue
bugeilio *be* shepherd
bugeiliol *ans* pastoral
bugeilyddiaeth *eb* pastoralism
burum *eg* burumau yeast
busnes *eg* busnesau business
busnes cydweithredol *eg* busnesau cydweithredol cooperative business
bustl *eg* bile; gall
bustl y stumog *eg* stomach bile
bustl ych *eg* ox-gall
bustlog *ans* bilious
bwa *eg* bwâu bow; arch; fan
bwa aortig *eg* bwâu aortig aortic arch
bwa cangell *eg* bwâu cangell chancel arch
bwa cambr *eg* bwâu cambr camber arch
bwa corbelaidd *eg* bwâu corbelaidd corbelled arch
bwa croes *eg* bwâu croes crossbow
bwa crwn *eg* bwâu crwn round arch; circular arch
bwa eliptigol *eg* bwâu eliptigol elliptical arch
bwa hafalochrog *eg* bwâu hafalochrog equilateral arch
bwa hanner crwn *eg* bwâu hanner crwn semicircular arch
bwa hanner eliptig *eg* bwâu hanner eliptig semi-elliptical arch
bwa hir *eg* bwâu hir longbow
bwa i fyny bow up
bwa i lawr bow down
bwa lanset *eg* bwâu lanset lancet arch
bwa llifwaddod *eg* bwâu llifwaddod alluvial fan
bwa malurion *eg* bwâu malurion fanglomerate
bwa niwral *eg* bwâu niwral neural arch
bwa ogee *eg* bwâu ogee ogee arch
bwa pedol *eg* bwâu pedol horseshoe arch
bwa pedrant *eg* bwâu pedrant quadrant arch
bwa pedwar canolbwynt *eg* bwâu pedwar canolbwynt four-centred arch
bwa perpendicwlar *eg* bwâu perpendicwlar perpendicular arch
bwa pigfain *eg* bwâu pigfain pointed arch
bwa rhededog *eg* bwâu rhededog arch in situ
bwa segmentol *eg* bwâu segmentol segmental arch
bwa systemig *eg* bwâu systemig systemic arch
bwa tagell *eg* bwâu tagell gill arch
bwa tiersbwynt *eg* bwâu tiersbwynt tierspoint arch
bwa trionglog *eg* bwâu trionglog triangular arch
bwa-nodi *be* bowing
bwaog *ans* arcuate
bwa'r mandibl *eg* mandibular arch
bwced *eg* bwcedi bucket
bwciad *eg* bwciadau booking
bwcl *eg* byclau buckle
bwcler *eg* bwcleri buckler
bwclo *be* buckle
bwcram *eg* buckram
bwch dihangol *eg* bychod dihangol scapegoat
Bwdha *eg* Buddha
Bwdhadod *eg* Buddhahood
Bwdhaeth *eb* Buddhism
Bwdhaeth Mahayana *eb* Mahayana Buddhism
Bwdhaeth Nichiren *eb* Nichiren Buddhism
Bwdhaidd *ans* Buddhist
Bwdhydd *eg* Bwdhyddion Buddhist
bwff *eg* bwffiau buff
bwff calico *eg* bwffiau calico calico buff
bwff ffelt *eg* bwffiau ffelt felt buff
bwff llathru *eg* bwffiau llathru polishing buff
bwffe *eg* bwffes buffet
bwffio *be* buff
bwgi-wgi *eg* boogie-woogie
bwi *eg* bwiau buoy
bwla *eg* bwlaon bull
Bwla Aur *eg* Golden Bull
bwlb *eg* bylbiau bulb
bwlb arogli *eg* bylbiau arogli olfactory bulb
bwlch (=gofod) *eg* bylchau space
bwlch (=lle gwag) *eg* bylchau blank
bwlch (ar lafn) *eg* bylchau notch
bwlch (mewn amser) *eg* bylchau hiatus
bwlch (mewn mur neu amddiffyniad) *eg* bylchau breach
bwlch (rhwng dau fynedd) *eg* bylchau pass
bwlch (yn gyffredinol) *eg* bylchau gap
bwlch a strip notch and strip
bwlch caled *eg* bylchau caled hard space
bwlch gwynt *eg* bylchau gwynt windgap
bwlch llinell dimensiwn *eg* bylchau llinell dimensiwn dimension line space
bwlch rhyngfloc *eg* bylchau rhyngfloc inter-block gap
bwled *eg* bwledi bullet
bwletin *eg* bwletinau bulletin
bwletin newyddion *eg* bwletinau newyddion news bulletin
bwli *eg* bwlïau bully
bwli cam *eg* bwlïau cam faulty bully
bwli cosb *eg* bwlïau cosb penalty bully
bwli cosb *eg* penalty
bwlimia *eg* bulimia
bwlïo *be* bully off

bwliwn *eg* bullion
bwlyn *eg* byliau knob
bŵm *eg* bwmau boom
bwmbamau *ell* boombams
bwnd *eg* byndiau bund
bwnt *eg* bunt hit
bwr *eg* burr
bwrán *eg* buran
bwrdais *eg* bwrdeisiaid burgher
bwrdeisiol *ans* burghol
bwrdeistref *eb* bwrdeistrefi borough
bwrdeistref boced *eb* bwrdeistrefi poced pocket borough
bwrdeistref bwdr *eb* bwrdeistrefi pwdr rotten borough
bwrdeistref fwrgais *eb* burgage borough
bwrdeistref scot a lot *eb* bwrdeistrefi scot a lot scot and lot borough
bwrdd (=darn o bren) *eg* byrddau board
bwrdd (=dodrefnyn) *eg* byrddau table
bwrdd â drôr ynddo *eg* byrddau â drôr ynddynt table with drawer
bwrdd ac îsl board and easel
bwrdd academi *eg* byrddau academi academy board
bwrdd acwstig *eg* byrddau acwstig acoustic board
bwrdd achlysurol *eg* byrddau achlysurol occasional table
Bwrdd Addysg *eg* Board of Education
bwrdd arbed lle *eg* byrddau arbed lle space-saving table
bwrdd arddangos *eg* byrddau arddangos display board
bwrdd argaen *eg* byrddau argaen veneer board
bwrdd argaen parod *eg* byrddau argaen parod ready veneer board
bwrdd arholi *eg* byrddau arholi examinations board
bwrdd arlunio *eg* byrddau arlunio art board
bwrdd arwyneb *eg* surface table
bwrdd bara *eg* byrddau bara breadboard
bwrdd Bryste *eg* Bristol board
bwrdd bwyd *eg* byrddau bwyd dining table
bwrdd caled *eg* byrddau caled stiff board
bwrdd canol *eg* byrddau canol centreboard
Bwrdd Canol Cymreig *eg* Central Welsh Board
bwrdd caws *eg* byrddau caws cheeseboard
bwrdd cefn *eg* byrddau cefn backboard
bwrdd cefnu *eg* byrddau cefnu backing board
Bwrdd Cenedlaethol Cymru *eg* Welsh National Board
bwrdd cerdded *eg* byrddau cerdded duck-board
bwrdd clawr *eg* byrddau clawr cover board
bwrdd codi a gostwng *eg* byrddau codi a gostwng rise and fall table
bwrdd coes gât *eg* byrddau coes gât gate-leg table
bwrdd coes gât sengl *eg* byrddau coes gât sengl single gate-leg
bwrdd coffi *eg* byrddau coffi coffee table
bwrdd coleg *eg* byrddau coleg college board
bwrdd crib *eg* byrddau crib ridge board
bwrdd croeso *eg* byrddau croeso tourist board
bwrdd croeso rhanbarthol *eg* byrddau croeso rhanbarthol regional tourist board
bwrdd crwst *eg* byrddau crwst pastry board
bwrdd cylched brintiedig *eg* byrddau cylched brintiedig printed circuit board
Bwrdd Cymeradwyo Trydan Prydain (BEAB) *eg* British Electrical Approvals Board
bwrdd cymwysadwy *eg* byrddau cymwysadwy adjustable table
bwrdd cynfas *eg* byrddau cynfas canvas board
bwrdd cynnal *eg* byrddau cynnal string board
bwrdd chwarae *eg* byrddau chwarae playboard
bwrdd dalen blyg *eg* byrddau dalenni plyg drop-leaf table
bwrdd dalen estynedig *eg* byrddau dalenni estynedig draw leaf table
bwrdd drilio *eg* byrddau drilio drill table
bwrdd du *eg* byrddau du blackboard
bwrdd dymchwel *eg* byrddau dymchwel turnover board
bwrdd ebillion *eg* byrddau ebillion wrest-board
bwrdd ffibr *eg* byrddau ffibr fibreboard
bwrdd ffreutur *eg* byrddau ffreutur refectory table
bwrdd gôl *eg* byrddau gôl goal board
bwrdd goleddu *eg* byrddau goleddu canting table
bwrdd gronynnau *eg* byrddau gronynnau particle board
bwrdd gwaith *eg* byrddau gwaith desktop
Bwrdd Gwarcheidwaid *eg* Board of Guardians
bwrdd gweithio basgedi *eg* byrddau gweithio basgedi work-board
bwrdd gwellt *eg* byrddau gwellt strawboard
bwrdd gwisgo *eg* byrddau gwisgo dressing table
bwrdd gwyn *eg* byrddau gwyn white board
bwrdd hindraul *eg* byrddau hindraul weather board
bwrdd hyfforddi diwydiannol *eg* byrddau hyfforddi diwydiannol industrial training board
Bwrdd Iechyd *eg* Board of Health
bwrdd llawes *eg* byrddau llewys sleeve board
Bwrdd Lleol Gorboblogaeth *eg* Congested Local Board
bwrdd llifio *eg* byrddau llifio sawing board
bwrdd lluniadu *eg* byrddau lluniadu drawing-board
bwrdd llwch *eg* byrddau llwch dust board
bwrdd llwyd *eg* byrddau llwyd grey board
bwrdd magnetig *eg* byrddau magnetig magnetic board
bwrdd marcio *eg* byrddau marcio marking table
Bwrdd Marchnata Llaeth *eg* Milk Marketing Board
bwrdd matrics *eg* byrddau matrics matrix board
bwrdd meddal *eg* byrddau meddal soft table
bwrdd melfed *eg* byrddau melfed velvet board
bwrdd melin *eg* byrddau melin millboard
bwrdd modelu *eg* byrddau modelu modelling board

bwrdd mowldio *eg* byrddau mowldio moulding board
bwrdd mowntio *eg* byrddau mowntio mounting board
bwrdd natur *eg* byrddau natur nature table
bwrdd ochr *eg* byrddau ochr side table
bwrdd petryal *eg* byrddau petryal rectangular table
bwrdd plaenio *eg* byrddau plaenio shooting board
bwrdd plaenio meitr *eg* byrddau plaenio meitr mitre shooting board
bwrdd plastr *eg* plasterboard
bwrdd proffil *eg* profile board
bwrdd pylu *eg* byrddau pylu dimmer board
bwrdd rhesymeg *eg* byrddau rhesymeg logic board
bwrdd rhwbio *eg* byrddau rhwbio rubbing board
bwrdd sain *eg* byrddau sain sound table
bwrdd sefydlog *eg* byrddau sefydlog fixed table
bwrdd seiliedig *ans* board based
bwrdd sglodion *eg* byrddau sglodion chipboard
bwrdd sglodion adeiladwaith llafnog *eg* sandwich construction chipboard
bwrdd sglodion argaen *eg* byrddau sglodion argaen veneered chipboard
bwrdd sglodion haen sengl *eg* byrddau sglodion haen sengl single layer chipboard
bwrdd sgôr *eg* byrddau sgôr scoreboard
bwrdd sgyrtin *eg* byrddau sgyrtin skirting board
bwrdd siarad *eg* byrddau siarad talk board
bwrdd smwddio *eg* byrddau smwddio ironing board
bwrdd stori *eg* byrddau stori storyboard
bwrdd tocynnau *eg* byrddau tocynnau ticket board
bwrdd torri *eg* byrddau torri cutting board, chopping board
bwrdd trafod *eg* byrddau trafod discussion board
bwrdd tro *eg* byrddau tro turntable
bwrdd wythonglog *eg* byrddau wythonglog octagonal table
bwrdd y cymun *eg* communion table
Bwrdd y Morlys *eg* Board of Admiralty
bwrdd ynysu *eg* byrddau ynysu insulating board
bwrdd ystofi *eg* byrddau ystofi warp board
bwred *eb* bwredau burette
Bwrgwynaidd *ans* Burgundian
Bwrgwyniad *eg* Bwrgwyniaid Burgundian
bwriad *eg* bwriadau intention
bwriad artistig *eg* bwriadau artistig artistic intention
Bwriad Strategol Gwasanaethau Iechyd Cymru *eg* Strategic Intent for Health Services in Wales
bwrlap *eg* burlap
bwrlesg *eg* burlesque
bwrlwm drwm *eg* bwrlwm drymiau drum roll
bwrn *eg* byrnau bale
bwrnais *eg* bwrneisiau burnish
bwrneisio *be* burnish
bwrneisydd *eg* bwrneisyddion burnisher
bwrsar *eg* bwrsariaid bursar
bwrsari *eg* bwrsarïau bursary
bwrw (metel) *be* cast
bwrw (plu /croen /blew) *be* moult
bwrw allan *be* eject; eliminate; exorcise
bwrw ffrwyth *be* brew
bwrw haearn *be* founding
bwrw lliw *be* lose colour
bws *eg* bysiau bus
bws deugyfeiriadol *eg* bysiau deugyfeiriadol bidirectional bus
bws moethus *eg* bysiau moethus coach
bwsh *eg* bwshys bush
bwsh plwm *eg* bwshys plwm lead bush
bwsh pres *eg* bwshys pres brass bush
bwta-1,3-deuen *eg* buta-1,3-diene
bwtan *eg* butane
bwtan-2-al *eg* butan-2-al
bwtanal *eg* butanal
bwtandeual *eg* butanedial
bwtandeuöig anhydrid *eg* butanedioic anhydride
bwtandeuon *eg* butanedione
bwtandeuon deuocsim *eg* butanedione dioxime
bwtan-1-ol *eg* butan-1-ol
bwtan-2-ol *eg* butan-2-ol
bwtanon *eg* butanone
bwtan-2-yl *eg* butan-2-yl
bwt-2-en *eg* but-2-ene
bwt-1-en *eg* but-1-ene
bwtres *eg/b* bwtresi buttress
bwtres llyfrau *eg* bwtresi llyfrau book-end
bwtyl- butyl-
bwtyleiddio *be* butylate
bwtyrad *eg* butyrate
bwth *eg* bythod booth
bwth chwistrellu *eg* bythod chwistrellu spray booth
bwthyn clwm *eg* bythynnod clwm tied cottage
bwyd *eg* bwydydd food; foodstuff
bwyd cyfleus *eg* bwydydd cyfleus convenience food
bwyd cyflym *eg* fast food
bwyd dros ben *eg* left over food
bwyd garw *eg* roughage
bwyd lles *eg* bwydydd lles welfare food
bwyd tun *eg* bwydydd tun canned food, tinned food
bwyd wedi'i bacio'n barod *eg* prepacked food
bwyd wedi'i rewi'n gyflym *eg* quick frozen food
bwydlen *eb* bwydlenni menu
bwydlestr *eg* bwydlestri food vessel
bwydo *be* feed
bwydo ar alw *be* demand feeding
bwydo cymysg *be* mixed feeding
bwydo gyda thiwb *be* enteral tube feeding
bwydo o'r botel *be* bottle feeding
bwydo o'r fron *be* breast feeding
bwydydd amddiffyn *ell* protective foods
bwydydd cryfhau'r corff *ell* body building foods
bwydydd gwres ac egni *ell* heat and energy foods

bwydydd masnachol i fabanod *ell* commercial baby foods
bwydydd startsh *ell* starchy foods
bwydydd wedi'u hidlo *ell* strained foods
bwyell (=bwyell fach) *eb* bwyeill hatchet
bwyell (yn gyffredinol) *eb* bwyeill axe
bwyell fetel fflat *eb* bwyeill metel fflat flat metal axe
bwyell garreg *eb* bwyeill cerrig stone axe
bwyell garreg wedi'i llathru *eb* polished stone axe
bwyell gig *eb* bwyeill cig chopper
bwyell greuog *eb* bwyeill creuog socketed axe
bwyell law *eb* bwyeill llaw hand axe
bwyell ryfel *eb* bwyeill rhyfel war axe
bwylltid *eg* bwylltidau swivel
bwylltidio *be* swivel
bwysel *eg* bwyseli bushel
bwytawyr dyfrol *ell* aquatic feeders
bycanîr *eg* bycaniriaid buccaneer
byd anghyfannedd *eg* non-ecumene
byd cyfannedd, y *eg* ecumene
byd dychmygol *eg* bydoedd dychmygol imaginary world
byd ffantasi *eg* bydoedd ffantasi world of fantasy
byd go iawn *eg* real world
byd modern cynnar *eg* early modern world
Byd Newydd *eg* New World
byd-eang *ans* worldwide, global
bydwraig *eb* bydwragedd midwife
bydysawd *eg* universe
byddar *ans* deaf
byddardod *eg* deafness
byddardod geiriau *eg* pure word deafness
byddardod nerfol *eg* nerve deafness
byddin *eb* byddinoedd army; force
byddin diriogaethol *eb* byddinoedd tiriogaethol territorial army
byddin gartref *eb* byddinoedd cartref home army
Byddin Gêl *eb* Resistance
byddin heddychlon *eb* byddinoedd heddychlon peaceable army
Byddin Model Newydd *eb* New Model Army
byddin sefydlog *eb* byddinoedd sefydlog standing army
Byddin yr Iachawdwriaeth *eb* Salvation Army
byffer *eg* byfferau buffer
byffer allbwn *eg* byfferau allbwn output buffer
byffer cylchol *eg* byfferau cylchol circular buffer
byffer mewnbwn /allbwn *eg* byfferau mewnbwn / allbwn input /output buffer
byffer straen *eg* stress buffer
byffer wyth did *eg* eight bit buffer
byffer wythol *eg* byfferau wythol octal buffer
byffro *be* buffer
byffro dwbl *be* double buffering
byg *eg* bygiau bug
bylchfuriau *ell* battlements
bylchiad *eg* bylchiadau spacing
bylchiad colofnau *eg* bylchiadau colofnau column spacing
bylchiad dwbl *eg* bylchiadau dwbl double spacing
bylchiad lleiaf *eg* bylchiadau lleiaf minimum spacing
bylchiad llinellau *eg* bylchiadau llinellau line spacing
bylchiad llinellau dwbl *eg* bylchiadau llinellau dwbl double-line spacing
bylchiad sengl *ans* single spacing
bylchog (am lafn) *ans* notched
bylchog (am fur) *ans* breached
bylchog (yn gyffredinol) *ans* gapped
bylchu (mewn prosesu geiriau) *be* space
bylchu (mur) *be* breach
bylchu cyfrannol *be* proportional spacing
bylchu dwbl *be* double spacing
bylchus *ans* lacunary
bylchwr *eg* bylchwyr space bar
bymper *eg* bymperi bumper
byncer tywod *eg* bynceri tywod sand bunker
bynen *eb* byns bun
bynen Chelsea *eb* byns Chelsea Chelsea bun
byngalo *eg* byngalos bungalow
byngalo dull ransh *eg* byngalos dull ransh ranch style bungalow
byr *ans* brief
byr ei anadl *ans* byr eu hanadl breathless
byr ei hanadl *ans* byr eu hanadl breathless
byr yr olwg *ans* myopic
byrdwn *eg* byrdynau refrain
byrddau cydwedd *ell* match boards
byrddau hindraul cyffredin *ell* plain weather-boarding
byrddau hindraul rabedog *ell* rabbeted weather boarding
byrddau'r tu clytaf *ell* lee boards
byrddio *be* embark
byrddol *ans* tabular
byrfodd *eg* byrfoddau abbreviation; shortened form
byrfraich *eg* byrfreichiau press-up
byrfyfyr *ans* improvised; impromptu; extempore
byrgnwd *eg* byrgnydau catch crop
byrgron *ans* oblate
byrgrwn *ans* oblate
byrhau patrwm *be* shorten a pattern
byrhoedlog *ans* caducous
byrlymu *be* bubble; ebullition
byrllysg *eg* byrllysgau mace
byrnwr *eg* byrnwyr baler
byrwasg *ans* short waisted
bys *eg* bysedd finger
bys pysgodyn *eg* bysedd pysgod fish finger
bys troed *eg* bysedd traed toe
Bysantaidd *ans* Byzantine
bysedig *ans* fingered
byseddiad *eg* byseddiadau digitation
byseddu *be* finger; fingering

bysell *eb* bysellau key
▶ **bysell BACKSPACE** *eb* bysellau BACKSPACE BACKSPACE key
bysell BREAK *eb* bysellau BREAK BREAK key
bysell CANSLO *eb* bysellau CANSLO CANCEL key
bysell CTRL *eb* bysellau CTRL CTRL key
bysell doler *eb* bysellau doler dollar key
bysell ESCAPE *eb* bysellau ESCAPE ESCAPE key
bysell EXECUTE *eb* bysellau EXECUTE EXECUTE key
bysell frys *eb* bysellau brys hotkey
bysell gopïo *eb* bysellau copïo copy key
bysell hanner bwlch *eb* bysellau hanner bwlch half-space key
bysell HOME *eb* bysellau HOME HOME key
▶ **bysell i ddisg** *ans* key-to-disk
bysell INSERT *eb* bysellau INSERT INSERT key
bysell punt *eb* bysellau punt pound key
bysell reoli *eb* bysellau rheoli control key
bysell saeth *eb* bysellau saeth arrow key
bysell SHIFT *eb* bysellau SHIFT SHIFT key
bysell swyddogaeth *eb* bysellau swyddogaeth function key
bysell tab *eb* bysellau tab tab key
bysell y cyrchwr *eb* bysellau'r cyrchwr cursor key
bysellbad *eg* bysellbadiau keypad
bysellbad rhifol *eg* bysellbadiau rhifol numeric keypad
bysellfwrdd *eg* bysellfyrddau keyboard
bysellfwrdd droshaen *eg* overlay keyboard
bysellfwrdd hollt *eg* bysellfyrddau hollt split keyboard
bysellfwrdd QWERTY *eg* bysellfyrddau QWERTY QWERTY keyboard
bysellog *ans* keyed
bytio *be* butt
bytholi *be* perpetuate
bythwyrdd *ans* evergreen
byw *ans* live; living
byw *be* live
byw ar y plwyf *be* receive poor relief
bywddyraniad *eg* bywddyraniadau vivisection
bywesgoredd *eg* viviparity
bywesgorol *ans* viviparous
bywiocáu *be* quickening
bywiog *ans* active
bywiogus *ans* invigorating
bywluniad *eg* bywluniadau life drawing
bywoliaeth (eglwysig) *eb* bywoliaethau benefice
bywoliaeth (yn gyffredinol) *eb* bywoliaethau living
bywyd ar ôl marwolaeth *eg* life after death
bywyd boddhaus *eg* fulfilling life
bywyd gwyllt *eg* wildlife
bywyd llonydd *eg* still-life
bywyd oedolyn *eg* adult life
bywyd teuluol *eg* family life
bywyn *eg* bywynnau pith
bywyn (dant) *eg* bywion pulp

C

C fwyaf *eb* C major
C ganol *eb* middle C
C leiaf *eb* C minor
CAAY: Cyngor Arholiadau ac Asesu Ysgolion *eg* SEAC: School Examinations and Assessment Council
caban *eg* cabanau kiosk
caban codi *eg* cabanau codi cabin lift
caban gwybodaeth sgrin gyffwrdd *eb* cabanau gwybodaeth sgrin gyffwrdd touch-screen information kiosk
cabidwl *eg* cabidylau chapter
cabidyldy *eg* cabidyldai chapterhouse
cabidylwr *eg* cabidylwyr capitular
cabinet *eg* cabinetau cabinet
cabinet llestri *eg* cabinetau llestri china cabinet
cabinet ystafell ymolch *eg* cabinetau ystafell ymolch bathroom cabinet
cabledd *eg* cableddau blasphemy
caboledig *ans* polished
caboli *be* polish
cacen *eb* cacennau cake
cacen bysgod *eb* cacennau pysgod fishcake
cacen Dundee *eb* cacennau Dundee Dundee cake
cacen gaws *eb* cacennau caws cheesecake
cacoffoni *eg* cacophony
cacoffonig *ans* cacophonous
cactws *eg* cacti cactus
cadach llathru *eg* cadachau llathru polishing cloth
cadach meddal *eg* cadachau meddal soft cloth
cadair (=pwrs buwch) *eb* cadeiriau udder
cadair (yn gyffredinol) *eb* cadeiriau chair
cadair bren plyg *eb* cadeiriau pren plyg bentwood chair
cadair esgyn *eb* cadeiriau esgyn stair lift
cadair freichiau *eb* cadeiriau breichiau armchair
cadair gefn crwth *eb* cadeiriau cefn crwth fiddle back chair
cadair gefn gwerthyd *eb* cadeiriau cefn gwerthyd spindle back chair
cadair gefn olwyn *eb* cadeiriau cefn olwyn wheel-back chair
cadair gefn rhuban *eb* cadeiriau cefn rhuban ribbon back chair
cadair gefn tarian *eb* cadeiriau cefn tarian shield back chair
cadair godi *eb* cadeiriau codi chair lift
cadair olwyn *eb* cadeiriau olwyn wheelchair
cadair siglo *eb* cadeiriau siglo rocking chair
cadair uchel *be* cadeiriau uchel high chair
cadair wthio *eb* cadeiriau gwthio push-chair
cadair ystafell fwyta *eb* cadeiriau ystafell fwyta dining chair
cadarn *ans* firm; robust
cadarnhad *eg* confirmation; affirmation; endorsement
cadarnhaol *ans* positive
cadarnhau *be* confirm; ratify; endorse
cadarnhau cyfrinair *be* confirm password
cadarnhau derbyn *be* confirm receipt
cadarnhau dileu *be* confirm delete
cadarnle *eg* cadarnleoedd stronghold
cadarnwedd *ell* firmware
cadbennaeth *eg* cadbenaethiaid commander-in-chief
cadeirio *be* chair
cadenza *eg* cadenze cadenza
cadernid *eg* solidity
cadfridog *eg* cadfridogion general
cadfwyell *eb* cadfwyeill battle axe
cadlywydd *eg* cadlywyddion commander
cadmiwm (Cd) *eg* cadmium
cadoediad *eg* cadoediadau armistice
cadoediad *eg* cadoediadau truce
cadw (=diogelu) *be* preserve
cadw (ar gyfrifiadur) *be* save
cadw at *be* adhere
cadw car *be* garaging
cadw cofnodion *be* keep records
cadw cofnodion *be* record keeping
cadw cydbwysedd *be* balance; keep one's balance
cadw cymhareb *be* keep ratio
cadw eich pen yn uchel *be* keep your head high
cadw fel *be* save as
cadw fformatio *be* keep formatting
cadw graddfa *be* keep scale
cadw maint *be* keep size
cadw maint bylchau *be* keep spacing interval
cadw meddiant *be* maintain possession
cadw meddiant o'r bêl *be* maintain possession of the ball
cadw meini prawf hidlo *be* keep filter criteria
cadw sgrin *be* save screen
cadw trefn *be* keep order
cadw trefn (ar) *be* control
cadw tŷ *be* housekeeping
cadw wiced *be* keep wicket
cadw yn y ddalfa *be* remand
cadw'i siâp retain its shape

cadw-mi-gei *eg* savings box
cadw'n heini *be* keep fit
cadwolyn *eg* cadwolion preservative
cadwolyn seis mwsogl *eg* cadwolion seis mwsogl moss size preservative
cadw'r un prisiau mynediad hold charges
cadwraeth *eb* cadwraethau conservation
cadwraeth coed *eb* timber preservation
cadwraeth egni *eb* conservation of energy
cadwraeth gwefr *eb* conservation of charge
cadwraeth momentwm *eb* conservation of momentum
cadwraeth rhif *eb* conservation of number
cadwrol *ans* conservative
Cadwrydd *eg* Cadwryddion Observant
cadwrydd *eg* cadwryddion keeper
cadwrydd haearn meddal *eg* cadwryddion haearn meddal soft iron keeper
cadwyn *eb* cadwynau chain
cadwyn awdurdod *eb* chain of command
cadwyn bydredd *eb* decay chain
cadwyn fwyd *eb* cadwynau bwydydd food chain
cadwyn gynhyrchu *eb* chain of production
cadwyn o fynyddoedd *eb* cadwyni o fynyddoedd mountain range; cordillera
cadwyn o uwchfarchnadoedd *eb* supermarket chain
cadwyn o westai *eb* hotel chain
cadwyn ryngwladol o westai *eb* international hotel chain
cadwyn y merched *eb* cadwyni'r merched ladies chain
cadwynedd *eg* cadwyneddau catenation
cadwyn-hir *ans* long-chain
cadwyno (moliciwlau) *be* catenate
cadwyno (yn gyffredinol) *be* chain
cadwyno ymlaen *be* forward chaining
cadwynog *ans* chained
cadwyno'n ôl *be* backward chaining
cae *eg* caeau field
cae chwarae *eg* caeau chwarae playing field
cae padi *eg* caeau padi paddy field
cae pêl-droed *eg* caeau pêl-droed football pitch
caead *eg* caeadau stopper; shutter
caecwm *eg* caecum
caeedig *ans* closed
caeedydd *eg* shuttering
caefa *eb* caefeydd closure
caegeidwad *eg* caegeidwaid hayward
cael at *be* access
cael gwared â llawnder *be* remove fullness
cael mynediad *be* gain access
caen *eg* caenau coat
caen erydion *eg* caenau erydion waste-mantle
caenu *be* coat
caer *eb* caerau fort; fortress; fortification
caer bentir *eb* caerau pentir promontory fort
caer ddinesig *eb* caerau dinesig citadel
caer filltir *eb* caerau milltir mile castle
caetae *ell* chaetae
caeth (i gyffuriau etc) *ans* addicted
caeth (mesurau barddonol) *ans* strict
caeth i'r tŷ *ans* housebound
Caethglud *eb* Exile
caethiwed (=dibyniaeth) *eb* dependence
caethiwed (i gyffuriau etc) *eb* addiction
caethiwed i gyffuriau *eb* drug addiction
caethiwus *ans* addictive
caethwas *eg* caethweision slave
caethwasiaeth *eb* slavery
cafalîr *eg* cafaliriaid cavalier
cafaliraidd *ans* cavalier
cafalri caerog *eg* cavalry twill
cafatina *eg* cafatinâu cavatina
cafiar *eg* caviare
cafn (=sianel wneud) *eg* cafnau flume
cafn (ar ymyl to) *eg* cafnau gutter
cafn (yn gyffredinol) *eg* cafnau trough
cafn cyflin *eg* cafnau cyflin parallel gutter
cafn llyfrau *eg* cafnau llyfrau book trough
cafn mainc *eg* cafnau mainc well of bench
cafn mainc *eg* cafnau mainc bench well
cafn marmori *eg* cafnau marmori marbling trough
cafn o wasgedd isel *eg* trough
cafn taprog *eg* cafnau taprog tapered gutter
cafnu *be* hollow; gouge
caffael *be* acquire
caffaeledig *ans* acquired
caffaeliad (iaith, sgiliau) *eg* acquisition
caffein *eg* caffeine
caffi *eg* café
caffi'r we *eg* caffis y we cybercafé
cafflo *be* snarling
cangell *eb* canghellau chancel
cangen (=cainc ar goeden) *eb* canghennau bough
cangen (=tyfiant ochr; sgil-gynnyrch) *eb* canghennau offshoot
cangen (o fynachlog) *eb* canghennau daughter house
cangen (yn gyffredinol) *eb* canghennau branch
cangen banc *eb* canghennau banc bank branch
cangen coeden *eb* canghennau coed tree branch
cangen sympathetig *eb* sympathetic branch
canghellor *eg* cangellorion chancellor
Canghellor y Trysorlys *eg* Chancellor of the Exchequer
canghennu *be* branch
cai *eg* caion cay
cai *eg* caion key
CAI: hyfforddiant drwy gymorth cyfrifiadur *eg* CAI: computer aided instruction
caiac *eg* caiacau kayak
caib eira *eb* ceibiau eira ice axe
caill *eg* ceilliau testis
cain *ans* delicate

cainc (=alaw) *eb* ceinciau air
cainc (=cangen ochr) *eb* ceinciau spur
cainc (=llinyn mewn rhaff etc) *eb* ceinciau strand
cainc (lle bu cangen ar bren) *eb* ceinciau knot
cainc farw *eb* ceinciau marw dead knot
cainc fyw *eb* ceinciau byw live knot
cais (=gofyn) *eg* ceisiadau request
cais (am swydd etc) *eg* ceisiadau application
cais (mewn rygbi) *eg* ceisiau try
cais cosb *eg* ceisiadau cosb penalty try
calamin *eg* calamine
calasa *eg* chalaza
calcio *be* caulk
calcopyrit *eg* chalcopyrite
calcwlws *eg* calculus
calcwlws amrywiad *eg* calculus of variation
calcwlws differol *eg* differential calculus
calcwlws hedonig *eg* hedonic calculus
calcwlws integrol *eg* integral calculus
calch *eg* lime
calch brwd *eg* quicklime
calch soda (fel adweithydd) *eg* soda lime
calch tawdd *eg* slaked lime
calchaidd *ans* calcareous
calchbalmant *eg* calchbalmentydd limestone pavement; karrenfeld; lapiaz
calchbost *eg* calchbyst limestone pillar
calcheiddiad *eg* calcification
calcheiddio *be* calcify
calchfaen *eg* calchfeini limestone
calchfaen carbonifferaidd *eg* carboniferous limestone
calchgar *ans* calciphile
calchgas *ans* calciphobe; calcifuge
calchit *eg* calcite
calchu *be* liming
calchyniad *eg* calchyniadau calcination
calchynnu *be* calcinate
caled (=llym) *ans* severe
caled (yn gyffredinol) *ans* hard
caleden *eb* caledennau callus
caledfwrdd *eg* hardboard
caledfwrdd rhychiog *eg* caledfyrddau rhychiog fluted hardboard
calediant *eg* induration
Caledonaidd *ans* Caledonian
caledu (dillad) *be* air
caledu (glud) *be* cure
caledu (o hylif i solid) *be* solidify
caledu (yn gyffredinol) *be* harden
caledu a thymheru hardening and tempering
caledwch *eg* hardness
caledwch dŵr *eg* hardness of water
caledwch parhaol *eg* permanent hardness
caledwedd *eg/b* hardware
caledwr *eg* caledwyr hardener
calendr *eg* calendrau calendar
Calendr Gregori *eg* Gregorian Calendar
Calendr Julius *eg* Julian Calendar
Calfin *eg* Calvin
Calfiniaeth *eb* Calvinism
calgon *eg* calgon
calico *eg* calicoau calico
calico can *eg* bleached calico
calico gwyn can *eg* bleached white calico
calico heb ei gannu *eg* unbleached calico
califforniwm (Cf) *eg* californium
caligraffeg *eb* calligraphy
caligraffeg Islamaidd *eb* Islamic calligraphy
caligraffig *ans* calligraphic
caligraffydd *eg* caligraffwyr calligraphist
caliper *eg* caliperau calliper
caliper cymal cadarn *eg* caliperau cymal cadarn firm joint calliper
caliperau allanol *ell* outside callipers
caliperau cwmpas *ell* compass callipers
caliperau cyfunol *ell* combination callipers
caliperau fernier *eg* vernier callipers
caliperau jenni *ell* odd leg callipers
caliperau jenni *ell* jenny callipers
caliperau mewnol *ell* inside callipers
calon *eb* calonnau heart
caloreiddio *be* calorizing
calori *eg* caloriau calorie
caloriffig *ans* calorific
caloriffydd *eg* caloriffyddion calorifier
calorimedr *eg* calorimedrau calorimeter
calorimedr bom *eg* bomb calorimeter
calorimetreg *eb* calorimetry
calsitonin *eg* calcitonin
calsiwm (Ca) *eg* calcium
calsiwm carbid *eg* calcium carbide
calsiwm carbonad *eg* calcium carbonate
calsiwm cyanamid *eg* calcium cyanamide
calsiwm deucarbid *eg* calcium dicarbide
calsiwm deuethyndeuid *eg* calcium diethynediide
calsiwm ethyndeuid *eg* calcium ethynediide
calsiwm hydrocsid *eg* calcium hydroxide
calsiwm hydrocsid dyfrllyd *eg* aqueous calcium hydroxide
calsiwm magnesiwm biscarbonad (dolomit) *eg* calcium magnesium biscarbonate (dolomite)
calsiwm ocsid *eg* calcium oxide
calsiwm octadecanoad *eg* calcium octadecanoate
calsiwm silicad *eg* calcium silicate
calsiwm sylffad(VI) (anhydrit) *eg* calcium sulfate(VI) (anhydrite)
calsiwm sylffad(VI)-Ω-dŵr *eg* calcium sulfate(VI)-Ω-water
calsiwm sylffad(VI)-2-dŵr (gypswm) *eg* calcium sulfate(VI)-2-water (gypsum)
calycs *eg* calyx
call o dan amgylchiadau gwallgof *ans* sane in insane places
callestr daro *eb* cellystr taro percussion headed flint

callor *eg* callorau caldera
cam *ans* lopsided; cranked
cam (=cyfnod datblygiad) *eg* camau stage
cam (ar beiriant) *eg* camau cam
cam (yn gyffredinol) *eg* camau step
cam baril *eg* camau baril barrel cam
cam bywyd *eg* camau bywyd life stage
cam cyntaf *eg* camau cyntaf initiative
cam datblygiadol *eg* camau datblygiadol developmental stage
cam ergyd *eb* cam ergydion foul shot
cam hir *eg* camau hir long step
cam i'r ochr *eg* side-step
cam isel *eg* camau isel low step
cam llithro *eg* camau llithro slip-step
cam llithro mewn cylch *eg* camau llithro mewn cylch slip-step in a circle
cam mewnol *eg* camau mewnol internal step
cam olaf *eg* camau olaf last step
cam wrth gam step by step
cam wythfed *eg* camau wythfed octave step
camau geni *ell* labour stages
camau i ddisgyblu *ell* disciplinary action
camau'r llifo *ell* stages of dyeing
cambaru *be* mispare
cambiata *eg* cambiatâu cambiata
cambiwm *eg* cambium
cambr *eg* cambrau camber
cambren *eg/b* cambrenni hanger
cambren dillad *eb* cambrenni dillad clothes hanger
Cambriaidd *ans* Cambrian
cambrig *eg* cambrigau cambric
cambro *be* camber
camdaflu *be* foul throw
camdrafod (y bêl) *be* handling errors
cam-drin *be* abuse
cam-drin plant *be* child abuse
camdriniaeth *eb* abuse
camdriniaeth emosiynol *eb* emotional abuse
camdriniaeth oddefol *eb* passive abuse
camdriniaeth rywiol *eb* sexual abuse
camdroad *eg* camdroadau warp; warping; wind
camdroi *be* warp; cast
camddefnydd *eg* abuse; misuse
camddefnyddio *be* abuse; misuse
camddefnyddio alcohol *be* misuse of alcohol
camddefnyddio cyffuriau *be* drug abuse
camddefnyddio hydoddyddion *eg* solvent abuse
camddehongliad catastroffig *eg* camddeongliadau catastroffig catastrophic misinterpretation
cameo *eg* cameos cameo
camera *eg* camerâu camera
camera digidol *eg* camerâu digidol digital camera
camera fideo unllun *eg* camerâu fideo unllun video still camera
camera mini *eg* miniature camera
camera syml *eg* camerâu syml simple camera
camfaethol *ans* dystrophic
camffor *eg* camphor
camffurfiad *eg* camffurfiadau malformation
camffurfiad cynhenid *eg* camffurfiadau cynhenid congenital malformation
camgydiad *eg* camgydiadau false entry
camgymeriad *eg* mistake
camil *eb* camomile
camisol *eg* camisolau camisole
camlas *eb* camlesi canal
camlas, lloc a llwybr tynnu canal, lock and towpath
camlesyn *eg* camlesynnau canalicus
camlesynnaidd *ans* canalicular
camog *eg* camogau felloe
camosod *be* mislay
camp (=gwyddor unigol mewn chwaraeon) *eb* campau sport
camp (=llwyddiant) *eb* campau achievement
camp hir ei pharhad *eb* campau hir eu parhad sustained event
camp tîm *eb* campau tîm team event
campanoleg *eb* campanology
Campau Conwy *ell* Conway Races
campfa *eb* campfeydd gymnasium
campwaith *eg* campweithiau chef-d'oeuvre
campws *eg* campysau campus
camreoli *be* misrule
camsefyll *be* offside
camsiafft *eg* camsiafftiau camshaft
camsin *eg* camsinau khamsin
camu *be* stride; single-step
camu allan *be* step out
camu o amgylch *be* step round
camwahaniaethu ar sail rhyw *be* sex discrimination
camwedd *eg* tort
camweinyddu *be* maladministration
camweithio *be* malfunction
camweithrediad *eg* camweithrediadau dysfunction
camweithredu rhywiol mewn dynion *eg* male sexual dysfunction
camweithredu rhywiol mewn merched *eg* female sexual dysfunction
camymddwyn *be* misbehave
camymddygiad *eg* camymddygiadau misdemeanour
can *ans* bleached
cân (baled hanesyddol) *eb* caneuon lay
cân (yn gyffredinol) *eb* caneuon song
cân actol *eb* caneuon actol action song
cân barablu *eb* caneuon parablu patter song
cân boblogaidd *eb* caneuon poblogaidd pop song
cân dymhorol *eb* caneuon tymhorol seasonal song
cân fodern *eb* caneuon modern modern song
cân galypso *eb* caneuon calypso calypso
cân grefyddol *eb* caneuon crefyddol religious song
cân gronnus *eb* caneuon cronnus cumulative song

cân gyfrif *eb* caneuon cyfrif counting song
cân hwyl *eb* caneuon hwyl fun song
can llaeth *eg* caniau llaeth churn
can metr *eg* hundred metres
can olew *eg* caniau olew oil can
cân syml *eb* caneuon syml simple song
cân werin *eb* caneuon gwerin folk song
cân ysbrydol *eb* caneuon ysbrydol spiritual
canadwy *ans* singable
canapés *ell* canapés
canat *eg* canatau qanat
cancr *eg* canker
cancrizans *ell* cancrizans
candi pîl *eg* candied peel
canerdy *eg* canerdai cannery
canfasio *be* canvass
canfed *eg* canfedau hundredth
canfod (=adnabod ac enwi) *be* identify
canfod (=darganfod) *be* detect
canfod (=gweld mewn ffordd arbennig) *be* perceive
canfod (yn gyffredinol) *be* find
canfod a newid *be* find and replace
canfod cofnod *be* find record
canfod cromfachau *be* find parentheses
canfod cyfeiriad *be* find address
canfod ffeil *be* find file
canfod graffigau *be* find graphics
canfod sŵn *be* auditory perception
canfod y gwreiddiol *be* find original
canfod ymyl *be* edge detection
canfodydd *eg* canfodyddion detector
canfodydd curiadau *eg* canfodyddion curiadau pulse detector
canfyddadwy *ans* identifiable
canfyddiad *eg* canfyddiadau perception
canfyddiad afiechyd *eg* illness perception
canfyddiad allsynhwyraidd *eg* extra-sensory perception
canfyddiad clywedol *eg* aural perception
canfyddiad isdrothwyol *eg* subliminal perception
canfyddiad o ddyfnder *eg* depth perception
canfyddiadol *ans* perceptual
canghennog *ans* branched; dendritic
canhwyllbren *eg* canwyllbrennau candlestick
canhwyllnerth *eg* candle-power
canhwyllyr *eg* canwyllyriau chandelier
caniad *eg* caniadau entry
caniad y cyrn *eg* caniadau'r cyrn horn passage
caniatâd *eg* permit
caniataol *ans* permissible
caniatáu *be* allow; permit
caniatáu cadw cefndir *be* allow background save
caniatáu cadw cyflym *be* allow fast save
caniatáu effeithiau *be* allow effects
caniatáu golygu cyflym *be* allow quick editing
caniatáu lle gwag *be* allow blank
caniatáu newidiadau *be* allow modifications
caniatáu rhyngweithio *be* allow interaction
caniatáu ychwanegiadau *be* allow additions
canig *eb* canigau ditty
canio *be* canning
canion *eg* canionau canyon
caniwla *eg* cannula
canlyneb *eb* canlynebau corollary
canlyniad (=dilyniant annymunol) *eg* aftermath
canlyniad (yn gyffredinol) *eg* canlyniadau result; outcome; consequence
canlyniad chwiliad *eg* canlyniadau chwiliad search result
canlyniad databeilot *eg* canlyniadau databeilot datapilot result
canlyniad grafimetrig *eg* gravimetric result
canlyniad nwl *eg* canlyniadau nwl null result
canlyniadaeth *eb* consequentialism
canlyniadau cyfanredol *ell* aggregate results
canlynol *ans* consequent; resulting
canllaw (ar gyfer gweithredu) *eg/b* canllawiau guideline; guide
canllaw (i afael ynddo) *eg/b* canllawiau hand rail
canllaw (pont) *eg/b* canllawiau parapet
canllaw asesu *eg* canllawiau asesu assessment guide
canllaw grisiau *eg* canllawiau grisiau banister
canllaw pellach *eg* canllawiau pellach additional guidance
canllaw ymyl *eg* canllawiau ymyl margin guide
canllawiau *ell* page lines
canllawiau anstatudol *ell* non-statutory guidance
canllawiau i'r blaen *ell* guides to front
canllawiau ymarfer da *ell* guidelines of good practice
canmlwyddiant *eg* centenary
cannu *be* bleach
cannwyll *eb* canhwyllau candle
cannwyll llygad *eb* pupil
cannydd *eg* canyddion bleach; bleaching agent
cannydd hypoclorit *eg* hypochlorite bleach
cannydd ocsidio *eg* oxidizing bleach
cannydd perborad *eg* perborate bleach
canol *eg* canolau centre; middle
canol blaen *eg* centre front
canol busnes y dref (C.B.D.) *eg* central business district
canol cae *eg* midfield
canol cefn (C.C.) *eg* centre back
canol côn *eg* canolau côn cone centre
canol cylchdro *eg* canolau cylchdro centre of rotation; revolving centre
canol cymesuredd *eg* centre of symmetry
canol dydd *eg* noon
canol enydaidd y cylchdro *eg* instantaneous centre of rotation
canol fforch *eg* canolau fforch prong centre; fork centre
canol llonydd *eg* canolau llonydd dead centre

canol pendant *eg* clear middle
canol plaen *eg* plain centre
canol tref *eg* downtown
canol tro *eg* canolau tro live centre; headstock centre
canol turn *eg* canolau turn lathe centre
canol wiced *eg* mid wicket
canol y cwrt *eg* centre of the court
canol y ddinas *eg* city centre
canol y nod *eg* centre of character
canol y waelodlin *eg* centre of baseline
canolbarth *eg* canolbarthau midland
Canolbarth Lloegr *eg* Midlands
canolbopio *be* centre popping
canolbwnsio *be* centre punching
canolbwynt (pellter) *eg* canolbwyntiau mid-point; centre point; centre
canolbwynt (sylw) *eg* canolbwyntiau focus; focal point
canolbwynt gwasgedd *eg* canolbwyntiau gwasgedd centre of pressure
canolbwyntiedig *ans* focused
canolbwyntio *be* concentrate; focus
canolduedd *eb* central tendency
canoledig *ans* centralized
canolfan *eg/b* canolfannau centre; base
canolfan actif *eb* active centre
canolfan adfer *eb* canolfannau adfer rehabilitation centre
canolfan adnoddau *eb* canolfannau adnoddau resource centre
canolfan adnoddau llyfrgell *eb* canolfannau adnoddau llyfrgell library resource centre
canolfan asesu *eb* canolfannau asesu assessment centre
Canolfan Astudiaethau Polisi *eb* Centre for Policy Studies
canolfan athrawon *eb* canolfannau athrawon teacher centre
canolfan croeso *eb* canolfannau croeso tourist centre
canolfan cyddwysiad *eb* condensation centre
canolfan cyfarwyddo plant *eb* canolfannau cyfarwyddo plant child guidance centre
canolfan chwarae *eb* canolfannau chwarae play centre
canolfan deialog *eb* canolfannau deialog dialog centre
canolfan dysgu *eb* canolfannau dysgu learning centre
canolfan ddydd *eb* canolfannau dydd day centre
canolfan fancio *eb* canolfannau bancio banking centre
canolfan fasnachol *eb* canolfannau masnachol trading post
canolfan filwrol *eb* canolfannau milwrol military base
canolfan fynychu *eb* canolfannau mynychu attendance centre
canolfan ffoaduriaid *eb* canolfannau ffoaduriaid refugee centre
canolfan gadw *eb* canolfannau cadw detention centre
canolfan gofal *eb* canolfannau gofal care centre
canolfan gost *eb* canolfannau cost cost centre
canolfan grym *eb* canolfannau grym seat of power
Canolfan Gwaith *eb* Canolfannau Gwaith Job Centre
canolfan gydgysylltiol *eb* canolfannau cydgysylltiol association centre
Canolfan Gynghori *eb* Canolfannau Cynghori Citizens Advice Bureau
canolfan gymunedol *eb* canolfannau cymunedol community centre
canolfan hamdden *eb* canolfannau hamdden leisure centre
canolfan hyfforddi *eb* canolfannau hyfforddi training centre
canolfan hyfforddi oedolion *eb* canolfannau hyfforddi oedolion adult training centre
canolfan hyfforddi'r llywodraeth *eb* canolfannau hyfforddi'r llywodraeth government training centre
canolfan iaith *eb* canolfannau iaith language centre
canolfan iechyd *eb* canolfannau iechyd health centre
canolfan ieuenctid *eb* canolfannau ieuenctid youth centre
canolfan llynges *eb* canolfannau llynges naval base
canolfan maes *eb* canolfannau maes field centre
canolfan remand *eb* canolfannau remand remand centre
canolfan rhagoriaeth *eb* canolfannau rhagoriaeth centre of excellence
canolfan technoleg gwybodaeth *eb* canolfannau technoleg gwybodaeth information technology centre
canolfan wyliau *eb* canolfannau gwyliau holiday centre
canolfan wyliau sydd wedi'i hadeiladu'n bwrpasol *eb* purpose built resort
canolfan wyliau tramor agos *eb* short haul destination
canolfannyn *eg* canolfanynnau centre
canolfannyn ataliol *eg* inhibitory centre
canolfannyn cardiofasgwlar (yr ymennydd) *eg* cardiovascular centre
canolfannyn cyffroadol *eg* excitatory centre
canolfannyn ymborthi *eg* canolfanynnau ymborthi appetite centre
canolfarcio *be* centre dotting
canoli (=dwyn pethau i fan canolog) *be* centralize
canoli (=gosod yn y canol) *be* centre
canoli diwedd saeth *be* centre arrowend
canoli dotiau *be* centre dots
canoli fertigol *be* vertical centring
canoli llorweddol *be* horizontal centring
canoli pensaeth *be* centre arrowhead
canolig (=cymhedrol) *ans* moderate

canolig (=safon cyffredin) *ans* average
canolig (=yn y canol) *ans* medium
canoli'r bêl *be* centre the ball
canoli'r llorweddol *be* centre horizontal
canoloesol *ans* medieval
canolog *ans* central
canolradd *ans* intermediate
canolrif *eg* canolrifau median
canolrifau *eg* median
canolrwydd *eg* centrality
canolwedd *eb* canolweddau median
canolwr *eg* canolwyr referee
canolwr *eg* canolwyr centre; centre-half
canolwr agored *eg* canolwyr agored mid off
canolwr coes *eg* canolwyr coes mid on
canolwr wiced agos *eg* canolwyr wiced agos short mid wicket
canolwr wiced bell *eg* canolwyr wiced bell deep mid wicket
canon (=cyfraith) *eg* canonau canon
canon (am offeiriaid) *eg* canoniaid canon
canon (mewn cerddoriaeth) *eg/b* canonau canon
canon â chyfeiliant *eb* canonau â chyfeiliant accompanied canon
canon bedwar yn un *eb* canonau pedwar yn un four in one canon
canon drwy estyniad *eb* canonau drwy estyniad canon by augmentation
canon drwy gywasgiad *eb* canonau drwy gywasgiad canon by diminution
canon drwy wrthdro *eb* canonau drwy wrthdro canon by inversion
canon eglwysig *eg* canonau eglwysig ecclesiastical canon
canon gyfanedig *eb* canonau cyfanedig finite canon
canon ôl-redol *eb* canonau ôl-redol retrograde canon
Canon Pali *eg* Pali Canon
canon per arsin et thesin *eb* canonau per arsin et thesin canon per arsin et thesin
canon recte et retro *eb* canonau recte et retro canon recte et retro
canon rectus et inversus *eb* canonau rectus et inversus canon rectus et inversus
canon rheolaidd *eg* canoniaid rheolaidd regular canon
canon unsain *eb* canonau unsain canon at the unison
canon yn y pumed *eb* canonau yn y pumed canon at the fifth
canon yn yr wythfed *eb* canonau yn yr wythfed canon at the octave
canonaidd *ans* canonical
canoneiddio *be* canonize
canoniaeth *eb* canoniaethau canonry
Canoniaid Awstinaidd *ell* Augustinian Canons
Canoniaid Premonstratensiaidd *ell* Premonstratensians
canopi *eg* canopïau canopy
canradd (am boblogaeth) *eg* canraddau percentile; centile
canradd (graddfa Celsius) *ans* centigrade
canran *eg* canrannau percentage
canran cyfansoddiad *eg* percentage composition
canran cynnwys carbon *eg* percentage carbon content
canran cynnwys lleithder *eg* percentage moisture content
canran y cynnydd neu'r gostyngiad *eg* percentage rise or fall
canrif *eb* canrifoedd century
cansen fambŵ *eb* cansenni bambŵ bamboo cane
canser *eg* canserau cancer
canser gwddf y groth *eg* cervical cancer
canser y ceilliau *eg* testicular cancer
canser y colon *eg* colon cancer
canser y coluddyn *eg* cancer of the bowel
canser y fron *eg* breast cancer
canslad *eg* cansladau cancellation
canslo *be* cancel
canslo awtobeilot *be* cancel autopilot
cant *eg* cannoedd hundred
cantata *eg* cantatau cantata
cantel *eg* cantelau rim
cantigl *eg/b* cantiglau canticle
cantilena *eg* cantilenâu cantilena
cantilifer *eg* cantilifrau cantilever
canton *eg* cantonau canton
cantor *eg* cantoriaid cantor
cantores *eb* cantorion singer
cantoris *eg* cantoris
cantref *eg* cantrefi hundred
cantus fermus *eg* cantus fermus
canu (yn gyffredinol) *be* sing
canu (offeryn) *be* play
canu ar yr olwg gyntaf *be* sight singing
canu caneuon *be* sing songs
canu glân *be* articulation
canu gwlad *eg* country and western
canu gyda'r tannau *be* sing to the accompaniment of the harp
canu pib *be* pipe
canu tôn gron *be* sing a round
canu'n lân *be* articulate
canu'r felan *be* blues singing
canu'r rhigwm *be* singing the rhyme
canŵ *eg* canŵod canoe
canwr *eg* cantorion singer
canwr bas dwbl *eg* canwyr bas dwbl double bass player; contra bass player
canwr baswn dwbl *eg* canwyr baswnau dwbl double bassoonist
canwr baswn dwbl *eg* canwyr baswn dwbl contra bassoonist
canwr corn *eg* canwyr corn horn player

canwr corn bas *eg* canwyr corn bas bass horn player
canwr corn baset *eg* canwyr corn baset basset horn player
canwr corn Ffrengig *eg* canwyr corn Ffrengig French horn player
canwr cornet *eg* canwyr cornet cornetist
canwr ffliwt draws *eg* canwyr ffliwt draws transverse flute player
canwr penillion *eg* cantorion penillion penillion singer
canwr picolo *eg* canwyr picolo piccolo player
canwr tiwba *eg* canwyr tiwba tuba player
canzona *eg* canzone canzona
canzonetta *eg* canzonette canzonet
caolin *eg* kaolin; china clay
caos moleciwlaidd *eg* molecular chaos
cap *eg* capiau cap
cap gwthio *eg* capiau gwthio thrust cap
cap iâ *eg* capiau iâ ice cap
cap inc clystyrog *eg* crumble cap
cap rhew *eg* capiau rhew ice cap
cap trosoli *eg* capiau trosoli lever cap
capan drws *eg* capanau drysau lintel
capel *eg* capeli chapel
capel anwes *eg* capeli anwes chapel of ease
capel heb dŵr na meindwr *eg* chapel without tower or spire
Capel Sistin *eg* Sistine Chapel
capel y Forwyn *eg* capeli'r Forwyn Lady chapel
capeliaeth *eb* capeliaethau chapelry
Capetaidd *ans* Capetian
capgraig *eb* capgreigiau cap rock
capilaredd *eg* capilareddau capillarity
capilari *eg* capilarïau capillary
caplan *eg* caplaniaid chaplain
caplaniaeth *eb* chaplaincy
capoc *eg* kapok
cappella *eg* cappella
capriccio *eg* capricci capriccio
caprwn *eg* capryniaid capon
capryn *eg* caprau caper
capsiwl *eg* capsiwlau capsule
capsiwlaidd *ans* capsular
capten *eg* capteiniaid captain
capteniaeth *eb* captaincy
capwt *eg* caput
CAPY: Consortiwm Asesu a Phrofi mewn Ysgolion *eg* CATS: Consortium for Assessment and Testing in Schools
carac *eg* caracau carrack
Caradog *eg* Caractacus
carafel *eg* carafelau caravel
caramel *eg* caramel
carameleiddio *be* caramelization
carbamid *eg* carbamide
carbanion *eg* carbanion
carbocsihaemoglobin *eg* carboxyhaemoglobin
(carbocsimethyl)amoniwm clorid *eg* (carboxymethyl)ammonium chloride
carbocsimethyl-cellwlos *eg* carboxymethyl-cellulose
carbocsyleiddiad *eg* carboxylation
carbocsylig *ans* carboxylic
carbohydrad *eg* carbohydradau carbohydrate
carbohydrad stôr *eg* stored carbohydrate
carbon (C) *eg* carbonau carbon
carbon canolig *eg* medium carbon
carbon cyfunol *eg* combined carbon
carbon (deiamwnt) *eg* carbon (diamond)
carbon deuocsid *eg* carbon dioxide
carbon deusylffid *eg* carbon disulfide
carbon fulleren *eg* carbon fullerene
carbon (golosg) *eg* carbon (charcoal)
carbon (golosg anifail) *eg* carbon (animal charcoal)
carbon (golosg pren) *eg* carbon (wood charcoal)
carbon (graffit) *eg* carbon (graphite)
carbon isel *eg* low carbon
carbon monocsid *eg* carbon monoxide
carbon rhydd *eg* free carbon
carbon tetraclorid *eg* carbon tetrachloride
carbonad *eg* carbonadau carbonate
carbonadu *be* carbonation
Carbonariaid *ell* Carbonari
carbonedig *ans* carbonated
carboneiddiad *eg* carbonization
carboneiddio *be* carbonize
carbonifferaidd *ans* carboniferous
carbonig anhydras *ans* carbonic anhydrase
carbonyl deuclorid *eg* carbonyl dichloride
carborwndwm *eb* carborundum
carbwradur *eg* carbwraduron carburettor
carbwreiddio *be* carburize
Carchar Dyledwyr *eg* Debtor's Prison
carcharu *be* incarcerate
cardbord *eg* cardboard
cardbord gwyn *eg* white cardboard
cardbord lliw *eg* coloured cardboard
cardbord llwyd *eg* grey cardboard
cardiaidd *ans* cardiac
cardiau gwlân *ell* hand cards
cardiau tyllog *ell* punched cards
cardiau ymatebion cyflym a chyfrifiadau pen quick response and mental calculation cards
cardigan *eb* cardiganau cardigan
cardinal *eg* cardinaliaid cardinal
cardioid *eg* cardioidau cardioid
cardioleg *eb* cardiology
cardiolegydd *eg* cardiolegyddion cardiologist
cardotaidd *ans* mendicant
cardotwyr holliach *ell* sturdy beggars
Cardotwyr y Môr *ell* Sea Beggars
cardotyn *eg* cardotwyr beggar; mendicant
caregl *eg* careglau chalice
carennydd *eg* kindred

carfan (mewn plaid etc) *eb* carfanau faction
carfan (o' un oed etc) *eb* carfanau cohort
Carfan Biwritanaidd *eb* Puritan Choir
carfan bwyso *eb* carfannau pwyso pressure group
carfanyddiaeth *eb* factionalism
cariad *eg* love
cariad angerddol *eg* passionate love
cariad cymar *eg* companionate love
cariad rhamantus *eg* romantic love
cariadwledd *eb* cariadwleddoedd love feast
caricot *eg* caricotau carrycot
carilon *eg/b* carilonau carillon
cario *be* carry
cario *be* porting
cario ar ysgwydd *be* shoulder carry
cario rhannol *be* partial carry
cario wrth glun *be* hip carry
cario'r batwn *be* carry the baton
carismataidd *ans* charismatic
cariwr (ar durn) *eg* carwyr driving dog
cariwr (yn gyffredinol) *eg* carwyr carrier
cariwr cynffon plyg *eg* carwyr cynffon plyg bent-tail carrier
cariwr cynffon sgwâr *eg* carwyr cynffon sgwâr squaretail carrier
carlam *eg* gallop
carlamu *be* gallop
carlwm *eg* carlymiaid ermine
carlymoliad *eg* carlymoliaid mustelid
carmin *eg* carmine
carn (ar gleddyf) *eg* carnau hilt
carn (ar gyllell) *eg* carnau handle
carn cyllell *eg* carnau cyllyll knife handle
carn rhosbren *eg* carnau rhosbren rosewood handle
carnedd *eb* carneddau cairn
carnol *ans* ungulate
carnolyn *eg* carnolion ungulate
carntro *eg* carntroeon brace
carntro ac ebill brace and bit
carntro clicied *eg* carntroeon clicied ratchet brace
carntro cyffredin *eg* carntroeon cyffredin simple plain brace
carntro olwyn *eg* carntroeon olwyn wheelbrace
carob *eg* carob
carol *eb* carolau carol
Carolingaidd *ans* Carolingian
carolwyr *ell* waits
caroten *eg* carotene
carotenyn *eg* carotenau carotenoid
carp *eg* carpiaid carp
carpal *eg* carpalau carpal
carped *eg* carpedi carpet
carped cudynnog *eg* carpedi cudynnog tufted carpet
carped ffeltiog *eg* carpedi ffeltiog felted carpet
carped ffloc *eg* carpedi ffloc flocked carpet
carped nodwyddog *eg* carpedi nodwyddog needled carpet
carped treuliedig *eg* carpedi treuliedig frayed carpet
carped wedi'i wau *eg* carpedi wedi'u gwau knitted carpet
carped wedi'i wehyddu *eg* carpedi wedi'u gwehyddu woven carpet
carpel *eg* carpelau carpel
carpio *be* shred
carpion papur *ell* shredded paper
carpogoniwm *eg* carpogonia carpogonium
carrai *eb* careiau lace; thong
carrai ledr *eb* careiau lledr leather thong
carrai liw *eb* careiau lliw coloured lace
carrai tag *eb* careiau tag tag lace
carreg *eb* cerrig stone
carreg Ayr *eb* Water of Ayr stone
carreg ddylif *eb* cerrig dylif flowstone
carreg filltir *eb* cerrig milltir milestone
carreg forthwylio *eb* cerrig morthwylio hammer stone
carreg ffug *eb* cerrig ffug artificial stone
carreg gopa *eb* cerrig copa coping stone
carreg grut *eb* cerrig grut gritstone
carreg hogi *eb* cerrig hogi whetstone
carreg hogi *eb* cerrig hogi oilstone
carreg hogi *eb* cerrig hogi hone
carreg hogi *eg* cerrig hogi carborundum stone
carreg hogi Arkansas *eb* Arkansas oilstone
carreg hogi ddwbl *eb* cerrig hogi dwbl combination oilstone
carreg hogi gau *eb* cerrig hogi gau oilstone slip
carreg hogi gradd arw *eg* cerrig hogi gradd arw coarse oilstone
carreg hogi gradd ganol *eb* cerrig hogi gradd ganol medium oilstone
carreg hogi India *eb* cerrig hogi India Indian oilstone
carreg hogi Washita *eb* Washita oilstone
carreg hogi wedi treulio *eb* cerrig hogi wedi treulio worn oilstone
carreg hogi wneud *eb* cerrig hogi gwneud artificial whetstone
carreg laid *eb* cerrig llaid mudstone
carreg lorio *eb* cerrig llorio flagstone
carreg nadd *eb* cerrig nadd ashlar
carreg silt *eb* cerrig silt silt stone
carreg wyntraul *eb* cerrig gwyntraul ventifact
carreg y bustl *eb* cerrig bustl gallstone
carreg-dwmblo *be* stone-tumbling
car-rif *eg* car-rifau carry
carsinogen *eg* carsinogenau carcinogen
carsinogenaidd *ans* carcinogenic
carst *eg* carstiau karst
carstig *ans* karstic
cart achau *eg* cartiau achau family tree
cartel *eg* cartelau cartel

carteleiddio *be* cartelize
Cartesaidd *ans* Cartesian
cartilag *eg* cartilage
cartilag hyalin *eg* hyaline cartilage
cartilagaidd *ans* cartilaginous
cartograffeg *eb* cartography
cartograffig *ans* cartographic
carton *eg* cartonau carton
cartref *ans* domiciliary
cartref (a'r bobl sy'n byw yno) *eg* cartrefi household
cartref (yn gyffredinol) *eg* cartrefi home
cartref cymuned *eg* cartrefi cymuned community home
cartref gofal *eg* cartrefi gofal care home
cartref gofal preswyl *eg* cartrefi gofal preswyl residential care home
cartref henoed *eg* cartrefi henoed old people's home
cartref maeth *eg* cartrefi maeth foster home
cartref mamolaeth *eg* cartrefi mamolaeth maternity home
cartref nyrsio *eg* cartrefi nyrsio nursing home
cartref plant *eg* cartrefi plant children's home
cartref preswyl *eg* cartrefi preswyl residential home
cartref symudol *eg* cartrefi symudol mobile home
cartref y cyrchwr *eg* cursor home position
cartrefi gwarchodol *ell* sheltered housing
cartwlari *eg* cartwlarïau cartulary
cartŵn *eg* cartwnau cartoon
cartŵn stribed *eg* cartwnau stribed strip cartoon
carthbwll *eg* carthbyllau cesspool
carthen *eb* carthenni overblanket
carthffosiaeth *eb* sewerage
carthffosiaeth *eb* drainage
carthffrwd *eb* carthffrydiau effluent
carthiad *eg* egestion
carthion *ell* sewage
carthion nos *ell* night soil
carthu (ffos etc) *be* dredge
carthu (yn ffigurol) *be* purge
Carthu Mawr *be* Great Purges
Carthwsiad *eg* Carthwsiaid Carthusian
carthydd *eg* carthyddion laxative; aperient; cathartic
carthysu *be* scavenge
carthysydd *eg* carthysyddion coprophage; scavenger
carw Llychlyn *eg* ceirw Llychlyn reindeer
carwgad *eg* carwgadau carucate
carwngl *eg* carynglau caruncle
caryatid *eg* caryatidau caryatid
caryoteip *eg* caryoteipiau karyotype
cas *eg* casys case
cas bobin *eg* casys bobiniau bobbin case
cas bwa *eg* casys bwa bow case
cas bwrdd gwaith *eg* casys bwrdd gwaith desktop case
cas gobennydd *eg* casys gobennydd pillowcase
cas papur *eg* casys papur paper case
cas tŵr *eg* casys tŵr tower case
casafa *eg* cassava
casein *eg* casein
caseinogen *eg* caseinogen
caserol *eg* caserolau casserole
caserol araf *eg* caserolau araf slow casserole
casét *eg* casetiau cassette
casewin *eg* casewinedd ingrowing toenail
casgen *eb* casgenni barrel
casgen gyriant twmblo *eb* casgiau gyriant twmblo tumbler drive barrel
casgliad (=canlyniad rhesymegol) *eg* casgliadau conclusion; inference; deduction
casgliad (o arian, eitemau) *eg* casgliadau collection
casgliad (o bobl) *eg* casgliadau assemblage
casgliad cryf *eg* strong inference
casgliad data *eg* casgliadau data data collection
casgliad o brofion *eg* casgliadau o brofion test battery
casgliad patrymau *eg* casgliadau patrymau swatch
casgliad ystadegol *eg* casgliadau ystadegol statistical inference
casgliadau *ell* findings
casglifiad *eg* colluvium
casglifol *ans* colluvial
casglu (=barnu drwy resymu) *be* infer
casglu (=hel) *be* collect
casglu credydau *be* credit accumulation
casglu data *be* data collection
casglu gwybodaeth *be* collect information
casglu'r bêl *be* collect the ball
casglwr *eg* casglwyr gatherer
casglwr sbwriel *eg* casglwyr sbwriel refuse collector
casglwr trethi *eg* casglwyr trethi tax gatherer
casin *eg* casinau casing
casiterit *eg* cassiterite
casog *eb* casogau cassock
cast *eg* castiau caste
cast gwreiddiol *eg* castiau gwreiddiol master cast
cast plastr *eg* castiau plastr plaster cast
castanét *eg* castanetau castanet
castell *eg* cestyll castle
castell Normanaidd *eg* cestyll Normanaidd Norman castle
castell tomen a beili *eg* cestyll tomen a beili motte and bailey castle
castellaidd *ans* castellated
castelliad *eg* castelliadau castellation
castellog *ans* castellated
castellydd *eg* castellwyr castellan
Castilaidd *ans* Castilian
Castiliad *eg* Castiliaid Castilian
castin *eg* castinau casting

castin gorymyl *eg* castinau gorymyl overshot casting
castin plastr *eg* castinau plastr plaster casting
castin plastr *eg* casting plaster
castin slip *eg* slip casting
castio *be* casting
castio allgyrchol *be* centrifugal casting
castio i fyny *be* casting up
castio i lawr *be* casting down
castio metel *be* metal casting
castio môr-gyllell *be* cuttlefish casting
castio patrwm aberthol *be* investment casting
castio polystyren *be* polystyrene casting
castor *eg* castorau castor
castor bugail *eg* castorau bugail shepherd castor
castor bwylltid *eg* castorau bwylltid swivel castor
castor cromen *eg* castorau cromen dome castor
castor olwyn *eg* castorau olwynion wheel castor
castor pêl *eg* castorau pêl ball castor
casul *eg* casuliau chasuble
catabatig *ans* catabatic
catabolaeth *eb* catabolism
catabolig *ans* catabolic
catabolyn *eg* catabolynnau catabolite
catalas *eg* catalase
catalog *eg* catalogau catalogue
catalogio *be* catalogue
catalydd *eg* catalyddion catalyst
catalyddu *be* catalyse
catalysis *eg* catalysis
catalytig *ans* catalytic
cataplecsi *eg* cataplexy
cataract *eg* cataractau cataract
catecism *eg* catecismau catechism
catecolamin *eg* catecholamine
categoreiddio *be* categorize
categori *eg* categorïau category
categori databeilot *eg* categorïau databeilot datapilot category
categori gwallau *eg* categorïau gwallau error category
caten *eb* catiau bail
catena *eb* catenâu catena; catenary
catenoid *eg* catenoidau catenoid
catïon *eg* catïonau cation
catïon nitrosyl *eg* catïonau nitrosyl nitrosyl cation
catïon nitryl *eg* catïonau nitryl nitryl cation
cationig *ans* cationic
catod *eg* catodau cathode
catodig *ans* cathodic
catrawd *eb* catrodau regiment
Catrin *eb* Catherine
Catrin Fawr *eb* Catherine the Great
Cathariad *eg* Cathariaid Cathar
catharsis *eg* catharsis
cathetr *eg* cathetrau catheter
cathl symffonig *eg* cathlau symffonig symphonic poem
catholig *ans* catholic
cau (tir etc) *be* enclose
cau (yn gyffredinol) *be* close
cau allan *be* exclude; lock out
cau pob ffeil *be* close all files
cau pob ffenestr *be* close all windows
cau popeth *bc* close all
cau pwythau *be* cast off
cau tiroedd *be* land enclosures
caul *eg* chyle
cau'n fertigol *be* close vertically
cau'n llorweddol *be* close horizontally
cau'r agoriad *be* close the key
cau'r batiad *be* declare the innings closed
cau'r dasg *be* close task
cau'r ddeialog *be* close dialog
cau'r ddogfen *be* close document
cau'r e-bost *be* close mail
cau'r ffenestr *be* close window
cau'r ffenestr weithredol *be* close active window
cau'r gwrthrych *be* close object
cau'r polygon *be* close polygon
cau'r rhaglen *be* close application
cau'r switsh *be* put the switch on
cau'r switsh *be* close the switch
cau'r tap *be* close the tap
cau'r tap *be* turn the tap off
cawc (pedol ceffyl) *eg* cawciau calkin
cawell *eb* cewyll cage; crate; crating
cawell asennau *eg* cewyll asennau rib cage
cawell diogelwch gwifrau *eg* cewyll diogelwch gwifrau wire safety cage
cawell saethau *eg* cewyll saethau quiver
cawellog *ans* clathrate
cawellu *be* crating
cawg storio *eg* cawgiau storio storage jar
cawnen ddu *eb* cawn duon nardus
cawod *eb* cawodydd shower
cawod drom *eg* cawodydd trwm downpour
cawod goch, y gawod goch *eb* rust
cawr *eg* cewri giant
caws *eg* cawsiau cheese
caws Caer *eg* Cheshire cheese
caws Caerffili *eg* Caerffili cheese
caws colfran *eg* cottage cheese
caws Cheddar *eg* Cheddar cheese
caws macaroni *eg* macaroni cheese
caws proses *eg* cawsiau proses processed cheese
caws Swydd Gaerhirfryn *eg* Lancashire cheese
cawsio *be* curdle
cayenne *eg* cayenne
CBAC: Cyd-bwyllgor Addysg Cymru *eg* WJEC: Welsh Joint Education Committee
CC (Cyn Crist) BC
CD byw *eg* self-booting CD

cebl *eg* ceblau cable
cebl cyfechelog *eg* ceblau cyfechelog coaxial cable
cêc gwartheg *eg* cattle cake
ceden *eb* cedennau nap
cedenu *be* nap
cedrwydden *eb* cedrwydd cedar
cefn *eg* cefnau back
cefn crwth *ans* fiddle back
cefn cynfas *eg* cefnau cynfas canvas backing
cefn ffyn *ell* back sticks
cefn gwlad *eg* countryside
cefn morfil *eg* cefnau morfil whale back
cefn pres *eg* cefnau pres brass backed
cefn tlws *eg* cefnau tlysau brooch back
cefn troed *eg* cefnau traed instep
cefn wrth gefn *adf* back to back
cefnau a phantiau ridges and swales
cefnblat *eg* cefnblatiau backplate
cefnblygiad *eg* dorsiflexion
cefndir *eg* cefndiroedd background
cefndir addas *eg* cefndiroedd addas suitable background
cefndir cartref *eg* home background
cefndir dychmygol *eg* imaginary background
cefndir teitl *eg* title background
cefndorrol *ans* dorsiventral
cefndraeth *eg* cefndraethau backshore
cefnell *eb* cefnellau backrest
cefnen *eb* cefnenau ridge
cefnen o wasgedd uchel *eb* ridge of high pressure
cefnfor (defnydd cyfreithiol) *eg* cefnforoedd high sea
cefnfor (yn gyffredinol) *eg* cefnforoedd ocean
cefnforol *ans* oceanic
cefnfur *eg* cefnfuriau backwall
cefnfwrdd *eg* cefnfyrddau back board; splashback
cefnffordd *eb* cefnffyrdd trunk road
cefngefn *ans* back to back
cefnlen *eb* cefnlenni back drop; backcloth
cefnlethr *eg* cefnlethrau backslope
cefnliain gorchuddio *eg* cefnlieiniau gorchuddio draped backcloth
cefnlun *eg* cefnluniau back view
cefnogaeth (yn gyffredinol) *eb* support; backing
cefnogaeth (wrth gefn) *eb* back-up
cefnogaeth ategol *eb* ancillary support
cefnogaeth gymdeithasol *eb* social support
cefnogaeth i ffurflenni *eb* form support
cefnogi *be* support
cefnogol *ans* supportive
cefnogwr *eg* cefnogwyr supporter
cefnsbwng *ans* foambacked
cefnu *be* backing off
cefnwlad *eb* cefnwledydd hinterland; backland
cefnwr *eg* cefnwyr full back; defender
cefnwraig *eb* cefnwragedd full back
cefnyn *eg* cefnynnau backing
ceffaleiddiad *eg* cephalisation
ceffalig *ans* cephalic
ceffalo- cephalo-
ceffyl *eg* ceffylau horse
ceffyl â chorfau *eg* horse with pommels
ceg *eb* cegau mouth
ceg aderyn *eb* birdsmouth
ceg offeryn *eb* cegau offerynnau mouthpiece
cegin *eb* ceginau kitchen
cegin ar ffurf U *eb* ceginau ar ffurf U U-shaped kitchen
cegin hirgul *eb* ceginau hirgul corridor kitchen
cegolch *eg* cegolchion mouthwash
cei *eg* ceiau quay; wharf
ceibr *eg* ceibrau rafter
ceibr byr *eg* ceibrau byr jack rafter
ceibr cafn *eg* ceibrau cafn valley rafter
ceibr cypledig *eg* ceibrau cypledig trussed rafter
ceibr talcen *eg* ceibrau talcen hip rafter
ceibrennau cyffredin *ell* spars
ceidwad (mewn parc gwledig etc) *eg* ceidwaid ranger
ceidwad (yn gyffredinol) *eg* ceidwaid keeper; custodian
Ceidwad Bow Street *eg* Ceidwaid Bow Street Bow Street Runner
Ceidwad y Rholiau *eg* Ceidwaid y Rholiau Keeper of the Rolls
Ceidwad y Seliau *eg* Keeper of the Seals
ceidwadaeth *eb* conservatism
ceidwadol *ans* conservative
ceidwadwr *eg* ceidwadwyr conservative
ceidwaid yr heddwch *ell* keepers of our peace
ceiliog y gwynt *eg* ceiliogod y gwynt windvane
ceilysyn *eg* ceilys skittle
ceillgwd *eg* ceillgydau scrotum
ceilliau *ell* testicles
ceincio *be* strand; stranding
ceinciog *ans* stranded
Ceiniogau Pedr *ell* Peter's Pence
Ceiniogau'r Pab *ell* Rome Scot; Peter Scot
ceirch *ell* oats
ceirios *eg* cerise
ceiriosen *eb* ceirios cherry
ceiriosen glacé *eb* ceirios glacé glacé cherry
ceisio eto *be* retry
ceisio noddfa *be* seek sanctuary
cejuela *eg* cejuelas cejuela
cêl *ell* kale
celadiad *eg* chelation
celadu *be* chelate
celain *eb* celanedd cadaver
celc *eg* celciau hoard
celc arian bath *eg* celciau arian bath coin hoard
celc efydd *eg* celciau efydd bronze hoard
celedig *ans* chelated
celf *eb* art

celfi drws *ell* door furniture
celfi gwledig *ell* rustic furniture
celfin (K) *eg* kelvin
celfydd *ans* artistic
celfyddyd *eb* celfyddydau art
celfyddyd addurnol *eb* decorative art
celfyddyd bensaernïol *eb* architectural art
celfyddyd blastig *eb* plastic art
celfyddyd bop *eb* pop art
Celfyddyd Cristnogaeth Gynnar *eb* Early Christian art
celfyddyd draethiadol *eb* narrative art
celfyddyd ddarluniol *eb* pictorial art
celfyddyd ddeilliadol *eb* derivative art
celfyddyd ddiriaethol *eb* concrete art
celfyddyd ddyneiddiol *eb* humanisitic art
celfyddyd Etrwsgaidd *eb* Etruscan art
celfyddyd faróc *eb* baroque art
celfyddyd fasnachol *eb* commercial art
celfyddyd Felanesaidd *eb* Melanesian art
celfyddyd Finoaidd *eb* Minoan art
celfyddyd Fflorens *eb* Florentine art
celfyddyd gain *eb* celfyddydau cain fine art
celfyddyd Garolingaidd *eb* Carolingian art
celfyddyd Geltaidd *eb* Celtic art
celfyddyd ginetig *eb* kinetic art
celfyddyd glyptig *eb* glyptic art
celfyddyd gonfensiynol *eb* conventional art
celfyddyd Gothig *eb* Gothic art
celfyddyd graffig *eb* celfyddydau graffig graphic art
celfyddyd Groeg *eb* Greek art
celfyddyd gyfoes *eb* contemporary art
celfyddyd gymhwysol *eb* celfyddydau cymhwysol applied art
celfyddyd gynfrodorol *eb* aboriginal art
celfyddyd gynrychioliadol *eb* representational art
celfyddyd haniaethol *eb* abstract art
celfyddyd India *eb* Indian art
celfyddyd lenyddol *eb* literary art
celfyddyd optegol *eb* optical art
celfyddyd ramantaidd *eb* romantic art
celfyddyd seicotig *eb* psychotic art
celfyddyd storïol *eb* anecdotal art
celfyddyd swyddogaethol *eb* functional art
celfyddyd wrthrychol *eb* objective art
celfyddydau ac adloniant arts and entertainment
celfyddydau creadigol *ell* creative arts
celfyddydau mynegiannol *ell* expressive arts
celfyddydau perfformio *ell* performing arts
cêl-liwiad *eg* cryptic coloration
celog *eb* celogiaid saithe; coley
Celsius *ans* Celsius
Celtaidd *ans* Celtic
Celteg *eb* Celtic
cell *eb* celloedd cell
cell adlynol *eb* celloedd adlynol adhesive cell
cell amsugno *eb* celloedd amsugno absorptive cell
cell atgenhedlol wrywol *eb* celloedd atgenhedlol gwrywol male reproductive cell
cell balis *eb* celloedd palis palisade cell
cell barwydol *eb* celloedd parwydol parietal cell
cell blewyn y clyw *eb* celloedd blew y clyw auditory hair cell
cell danwydd *eb* celloedd tanwydd fuel cell
cell darged *eb* celloedd targed target cell
cell dderbyn *eb* celloedd derbyn receptor cell
cell ddeuaidd *eb* celloedd deuaidd binary cell
cell ddeubegwn *eb* celloedd deubegwn bipolar cell
cell farw *eb* celloedd marw dead cell
cell flewyn *eb* celloedd blew hair cell
cell fyw *eb* celloedd byw living cell
cell fflam *eb* celloedd fflam flame cell
cell fformiwla *eb* celloedd fformiwla formula cell
cell ganglion *eb* celloedd ganglion ganglion cell
cell gapan *eb* celloedd capan cap cell
cell garreg *eb* celloedd cerrig stone cell
cell genhedlu *eb* celloedd cenhedlu germ-cell
cell glial *eb* celloedd glial glia/glial cell
cell gobled *eb* celloedd gobled goblet cell
cell goch y gwaed *eb* celloedd coch y gwaed red blood cell
cell golyn *eb* celloedd colyn sting cell
cell grwydrol *eb* celloedd crwydrol wandering cell
cell Kupffer *eb* celloedd Kupffer Kupffer cell
cell letyol *eb* host cell
cell meudwy *eb* celloedd meudwy hermitage
cell oleusensitif *eb* celloedd goleusensitif light-sensitive cell
cell pren caled *eb* celloedd pren caled hardwood cell
cell pren meddal *eb* celloedd pren meddal softwood cell
cell rythmig *eb* celloedd rhythmig rhythmic cell
cell Schwann *eb* Schwann cell
cell warchod *eb* celloedd gwarchod guard cell
cell wen y gwaed *eb* celloedd gwyn y gwaed white blood cell
cell wreiddflew *eb* celloedd gwreiddflew root hair cell
cell yrru *eb* celloedd gyrru driver cell
cellbilen *eb* cellbilenni cell membrane
cellblat *eg* cellblatiau cell plate
celldwll *eg* celldyllau cell pore
cellfur *eg* cellfuriau cell wall
cellfur planhigion *eg* plant cell wall
cellgorff *eg* cellgyrff cell body
cellnodd *eg* cell sap
celloedd interstitaidd *ell* interstitial cells
celloedd lwteal *ell* luteal cells
celloedd meithrin *ell* culture cells
cellog *ans* cellular
cellraniad *eg* cellraniadau cell division
cellwloid *eg* celluloid
cellwlos *eg* cellulose
cellwlos asetad *eg* acetate cellulose

cellwlosigion *ell* cellulosics
cembalo *eg* cembali cembalo
cemeg *eg/b* chemistry
cemeg bwyd *eb* chemistry of food
cemeg ddadansoddol *eb* analytical chemistry
cemegion aeddfedu blawd *ell* flour improvers
cemegol *ans* chemical
cemegydd *eg* cemegwyr chemist
cemegydd synthetig *eg* synthetic chemist
▶ **cemegyn** *eg* cemegion chemical
cemodderbynnydd *eg* cemodderbynyddion chemoreceptor
cemosynhwyraidd *ans* chemosensory
cemosynnwyr *eg* chemosense
cemosynthesis *eg* chemosynthesis
cemotacsis *eg* chemotaxis
cemotropedd *eg* chemotropism
cemotherapi *eg* chemotherapy
cemsugniad *eg* chemisorption
cen (ar garreg) *eg* cennau lichen
cen (ar groen) *eg* slough; scurf
cen (mewn ffwrnais, ar blanhigion) *eg* cennau scale
cen (mewn pibau etc) *eg* cennau fur
cen ar y pen *eg* dandruff
cen blaguro *eg* cennau blaguro bud scale
cen bract *eg* cennau bract bract scales
cenau *eg* cenawon cub
cenddeilen *eb* cenddail scale leaf
cenedl (=pobl un wlad) *eb* cenhedloedd nation
cenedl (mewn gramadeg) *eb* gender
cenedl ddatblygol *eb* cenhedloedd datblygol emergent nation
cenedl ramadegol *eb* grammatical gender
cenedl wleidyddol *eb* body politic
cenedlaethau i ddod *ell* future generations
cenedlaethol *ans* national
cenedlaetholdeb *eg* nationalism
cenedlaetholgar *ans* nationalist
cenedlaetholwr *eg* cenedlaetholwyr nationalist
cenedligrwydd *eg* nationhood
cenfetreg *eb* lichenometry
cenfigen *eb* jealousy
cenfigennus *ans* jealous
cenhadol *ans* missionary
cenhadwr *eg* cenhadon missionary
cenhedlaeth *eb* cenedlaethau generation
cenhedlaeth gyntaf *eb* first generation
cenhedliad *eg* conception
Cenhedloedd Unedig *ell* United Nations
cenhedlol (=cynhyrchiol) *ans* generative
cenhedlol (am gam cyntaf datblygiad) *ans* germinal
cenhedlol (am organau cenhedlu) *ans* genital
cenhedlu *be* conceive
cenllif *eg* cenllifau torrent
cennad *eg* cenhadon envoy
cennad y Pab *eb* cenhadon y Pab nuncio
cennin syfi *ell* chives
cennog *ans* scaly
centilitr *eg* centilitrau centilitre
centimetr *eg* centimetrau centimetre
centimetr sgwâr *eg* centimetrau sgwâr square centimetre
centriol *eg* centriolau centriole
centromer *eg* centromerau centromere
centrosom *eg* centrosomau centrosome
centuria (uned o filwyr) *eb* century
cerameg *eb* ceramics
ceramig *ans* ceramic
ceratin *eg* keratin
cerbyd *eg* cerbydau vehicle
cerbyd rhyfel *eg* cerbydau rhyfel chariot
cerdyn *eg* cardiau card
cerdyn adnabod *eg* cardiau adnabod identity card, ID card
cerdyn bwydlen *eg* cardiau bwydlen menu card
cerdyn cofnod *eg* cardiau cofnod record card
cerdyn costio safonol *eg* cardiau costio safonol standard cost card
cerdyn credyd *eg* cardiau credyd credit card
cerdyn cyfarch *eg* cardiau cyfarch greeting card
cerdyn fideo *eg* cardiau fideo video card
cerdyn fflachio *eg* cardiau fflachio flash card
cerdyn ffôn symudol *eg* cardiau ffôn symudol mobile phone card
cerdyn ffyddlondeb *eg* cardiau ffyddlondeb loyalty card
cerdyn gwaith *eg* cardiau gwaith work card
cerdyn lliw *eg* cardiau lliw coloured card
cerdyn magnetig *eg* cardiau magnetig magnetic card
cerdyn post *eg* cardiau post postcard
cerdyn rheoli *eg* cardiau rheoli control card
cerdyn rhychiog *eg* cardiau rhychiog corrugated card
cerdyn sain *eg* cardiau sain sound card
cerdyn tyllog *eg* cardiau tyllog punched card
cerdd *eb* cerddi poem; ode
cerdd dant *eg* cerdd dant
cerdded *be* walk
cerdded wysg y cefn *be* walk backwards
cerdded yn eich cwsg *be* sleepwalking
cerddedfa *eb* cerddedfeydd ambulatory
cerddediad *eg* gait
cerddor *eg* cerddorion musician
cerddorfa *eb* cerddorfeydd orchestra
cerddorfaol *ans* orchestral
cerddoriaeth *eb* music
cerddoriaeth absoliwt *eb* absolute music
cerddoriaeth achlysurol *eb* occasional music
cerddoriaeth curiad cryf *eb* down beat music
cerddoriaeth Cymru *eb* music of Wales
cerddoriaeth dâp *eb* taped music
cerddoriaeth destunol *eb* programme music
cerddoriaeth ddiriaethol *eb* concrete music
cerddoriaeth ddisgrifiadol *eb* descriptive music

cerddoriaeth ddrymio Affricanaidd *eb* African drumming music
cerddoriaeth fale *eb* ballet music
cerddoriaeth Fysantaidd *eb* Byzantine music
cerddoriaeth fyw *eb* live music
cerddoriaeth gefndir *eb* background music
cerddoriaeth gerddorfaol *eb* orchestral music
cerddoriaeth glasurol *eb* classical music
cerddoriaeth gyfrifiadur *eb* computer music
cerddoriaeth gyntefig *eb* primitive music
cerddoriaeth haniaethol *eb* abstract music
cerddoriaeth jig *eb* jig music
cerddoriaeth leisiol *eb* vocal music
cerddoriaeth newydd *eb* new music
cerddoriaeth ramantaidd *eb* romantic music
cerddoriaeth rythmig *eb* rhythmic music
cerddoriaeth rythmig hwylgar *eb* rhythmic 'fun' music
cerddoriaeth siambr *eb* chamber music
cerddoriaeth traed *eb* foot music
cerddoriaeth theatr *eb* theatre music
cerddoriaeth y Dioddefaint *eb* Passion music
cerddorol *ans* musical
cerddwr *eg* cerddwyr baby-walker
cerddwr *eg* cerddwyr pedestrian
cerebelwm *eg* cerebellum
cerebrol *ans* cerebral
cerebrosbinol *ans* cerebrospinal
cerebrwm *eg* cerebra cerebrum
cerfiad *eg* cerfiadau carving
cerfiad acanthws *eg* cerfiadau acanthws acanthus carving
cerfiad cerfwedd *eg* cerfiadau cerfwedd relief carving
cerfiad cragen a phlisgyn *eg* cerfiadau cragen a phlisgyn shell and husk carving
cerfiad endorri *eg* cerfiadau endorri incised carving
cerfiad plastig *eg* cerfiadau plastig plastic carving
cerfiad pren *eg* cerfiadau pren wood carving
cerfiedig *ans* carved
cerfigol *ans* cervical
cerfio *be* carve
cerfio carreg *be* stone carving
cerfio negatif *be* negative carving
cerfio plastig *be* plastic carving
cerfio pren *be* wood carving
cerfiwr *eg* cerfwyr carver
cerflun *eg* cerfluniau statue
cerflun bach *eg* cerfluniau bach statuette
cerflunaidd *ans* sculpturesque
cerfluniol *ans* sculptural
cerflunwaith *eg* sculpture
cerflunwaith cerfweddol *eg* relief sculpture
cerflunwaith crog *eg* suspended sculpture
cerflunwaith deiliant *eg* foliage sculpture
cerflunwaith Gothig *eg* Gothic sculpture
cerflunwaith plwm *eg* lead sculpture
cerflunydd *eg* cerflunwyr sculptor
cerfwedd *eb* cerfweddau relief
cerfwedd addurnol *eb* cerfweddau addurnol decorative relief
cerfwedd glai *eb* cerfweddau clai clay relief
cerfwedd isel *eb* cerfweddau isel bas-relief; low relief
cerfwedd uchel *eb* high relief; alto-relievo
cerfweddol *ans* relief
cerigyn *eg* cerigos pebble
ceriwm *eg* cerium
cerlan *eb* cerlannau river terrace
cerlan *eb* cerlannau terracing
cerlannau anghyfatebol *ell* unpaired terrace
cerlannau cyfatebol *ell* paired terraces
cerosin *eg* kerosene
cerpyn *eg* carpiau rag; shred
cerrynt *eg* ceryntau current
cerrynt aer *eg* ceryntau aer air current
cerrynt arfordirol *eg* ceryntau arfordirol coastal current
cerrynt brig *eg* peak current
cerrynt cyson *eg* steady current
cerrynt eiledol (C.E.) *eg* alternating current
cerrynt gollwng *eg* leakage current
cerrynt gwresogi *eg* ceryntau gwresogi heater current
cerrynt llanw *eg* ceryntau llanw tidal current
cerrynt llwyth *eg* load current
cerrynt newidiol *eg* ceryntau newidiol variable current
cerrynt terfol *eg* rip current
cerrynt trolif *eg* ceryntau trolif eddy current
cerrynt trydan *eg* ceryntau trydan electric current
cerrynt tyrfedd *eg* ceryntau tyrfedd turbidity current
cerrynt union (C.U.) *eg* direct current
cerrynt y casglydd *eg* collector current
cerrynt y glannau *eg* longshore current
cerrynt y sail *eg* base current
cersi *eg* kersey
cerydd *eg* ceryddon censure
Cerydd i'r Senedd *eg* Admonition to the Parliament
cesail (mewn botaneg) *eb* ceseiliau axil
cesail (y corff) *eb* ceseiliau armpit; underarm
cesail y forddwyd *eb* groin
Cesar *eg* Caesar
ceseilaidd *ans* axillary
CESIL *eb* CESIL
cesiwm (Cs) *eg* caesium
cesiwm clorid *eg* caesium chloride
ceto- keto-
ceton *eg* cetonau ketone
cetrisen *eb* cetris cartridge
cetrisen data *eb* cetris data data cartridge
ceubwll *eg* ceubyllau pothole
ceudod *eg* ceudodau cavity; lacuna

ceudod abdomenol *eg* abdominal cavity
ceudod bochaidd *eg* ceudodau bochaidd buccal cavity
ceudod cyflymu *eg* ceudodau cyflymu accelerating cavity
ceudod eisbilennol *eg* ceudodau eisbilennol pleural cavity
ceudod gwaed *eg* haemocoel
ceudod mantell *eg* ceudodau mantell mantle cavity
ceudod pelfig *eg* pelvic cavity
ceudod pericardiol *eg* pericardial cavity
ceudod pothellog *eg* ceudodau pothellog vesicular cavity
ceudod trwynol *eg* ceudodau trwynol nasal cavity
ceudod y corff *eg* body cavity
ceudod y gwddf *eg* pharyngeal cavity
ceudod ysgarthiol *eg* excretory cavity
ceudwll *eg* ceudyllau cavern
ceudyllog *ans* cavernous
ceugrwm *ans* concave
ceugrymedd *eg* ceugrymeddau concavity; concave curvature
ceulad *eg* coagulation
ceuled *eg* curd
ceuled a maidd curds and whey
ceuled caws *eg* cheese curd
ceuled lemon *eg* lemon curd
ceuledig *ans* coagulated
ceulo *be* clot; coagulate
ceulomicron *eg* ceulomicronau chylomicron
ceulo'r gwaed *be* blood clotting
ceunant *eg* ceunentydd gorge; gulch; flume
ceunwyddau *ell* hollow ware
cewyn *eg* cewynnau nappy
cewyn parod *eg* cewynnau parod disposable nappy
CFCau *ell* CFCs
CGC: Cymhwyster Galwedigaethol Cenedlaethol *eg* Cymwysterau Galwedigaethol Cenedlaethol NVQ: National Vocational Qualification
ciasma *eg* ciasmata chiasma
ciasma optig *eg* optic chiasma
cibwts *eg* cibwtsau kibbutz
cic *eb* ciciau kick
cic a chwrs up and under
cic achub bywyd *eb* ciciau achub bywyd life-saving leg kick
cic adlam *eb* ciciau adlam drop kick
cic am ystlys *eb* kick for touch
cic bwt *eb* ciciau pwt grubber kick
cic dolffin *eb* ciciau dolffin dolphin kick
cic gôl *eb* ciciau gôl goal kick
cic gornel *eb* ciciau cornel corner kick
cic gosb *eb* ciciau cosb penalty kick
cic groes *eb* ciciau croes cross kick
cic gychwyn *eb* ciciau cychwyn kick-off
cic letraws *eb* ciciau lletraws diagonal kick
cic osod *eb* ciciau gosod place kick
cic rydd *eb* ciciau rhydd free kick
cic rydd anuniongyrchol *eb* ciciau rhydd anuniongyrchol indirect free kick
cic rydd uniongyrchol *eb* ciciau rhydd uniongyrchol direct free kick
cic siswrn *eb* ciciau siswrn scissors kick
cic wib *eb* ciciau gwib fly kick
cic ymlaen *eb* ciciau ymlaen kick ahead
cicio (yn galed) *be* boot
cicio (yn gyffredinol) *be* kick
ciclid *eg* ciclidiaid cichlid
cig *eg* cigoedd meat
cig carw *eg* venison
cig coch *eg* lean meat
cig eidion *eg* beef
cig gwyn *eg* fatty meat
cig moch *eg* bacon
cig moch brith *eg* streaky bacon
cig moch cartref *eg* home cured bacon
cig moch cefn *eg* short back bacon
cig moch digrofen *eg* rindless bacon
cig moch wedi'i gochi *eg* smoked bacon
cigydd *eg* cigyddion butcher
cigysol *ans* carnivorous
cigysydd *eg* cigysyddion carnivore
cingwlotomi *eg* cingulotomy
cil fonynnau *ell* bye-stakes
cil haul *eg* schattenseite; ubac
cilan *eb* cilannau recess
cilannog *ans* recessed
cilannu *be* recess
cilarc *eb* cilarcau reverse arc
cilbren *eg* cilbrennau keel
cilbren plygu *eg* cilbrennau plygu folding keel
cilbren sadio *eg* cilbrennau sadio bilge keel
cildoriad *eg* cildoriadau chop
cildorri *be* chop
cildraeth *eg* cildraethau cove; bay-head beach; pocket beach
cildro *ans* reversed
cildroad *eg* cildroadau reverse; reversion
cildroadedd *eg* reversibility
cildroadwy *ans* reversible
cildroi *be* reverse
▶ **cildroi patrwm** *be* reverse a pattern
cildwrn *eg* tip
cilddant *eg* cilddannedd molar
cilddant ôl *eg* cilddannedd ôl wisdom tooth
cilfa *eb* cilfâu escapement
cilfach (mewn wal etc) *eb* cilfachau recess; niche
cilfach (môr, llyn) *eb* cilfachau creek; inlet
cilfach (TG) *eb* cilfachau system tray
cilfach wedi'i chyflawni *eb* cilfachau wedi'u cyflawni realised niche
cilfach weithredol *eb* cilfachau gweithredol functional niche
cilfae *eg* cilfaeau cut-off bay
cilfantais *eb* cilfanteision fringe benefit

cilffordd *eb* cilffyrdd byway
cilffordd yn agored i bob trafnidiaeth *eb* cilffyrdd yn agored i bob trafnidiaeth byway open to all traffic
cilgant *eg* cilgantau crescent
Cilgant Ffrwythlon *eg* Fertile Crescent
cilgantaidd *ans* crescentic
ciliad y lleuad *eg* moon wane
ciliaraidd *ans* ciliary
cilio *be* withdraw; retire
ciliwm *eg* cilia cilium
cilobeit *eg* cilobeitiau kilobyte
cilocalori *eg* cilocaloriau kilocalorie
cilogram (kg) *eg* cilogramau kilogram
cilometr (km) *eg* cilometrau kilometre
ciloseicl *eg* ciloseiclau kilocycle
cilowat (kW) *eg* cilowatiau kilowatt
cilowat awr (kW awr) *eg* kilowatt hour
cilt *eg* ciltiau kilt
cilydd *eg* cilyddion reciprocal
cilyddol *ans* reciprocal
cilyddu *be* reciprocate
cilyddu awtomatig *be* automatic reciprocation
cimwch coch *eg* cimychiaid coch crawfish
cimwch yr afon *eg* cimychiaid yr afon crayfish
cinc *eg* cinciau kink
cincio *be* kink
cinemateg *eb* kinematics
cinesthetig *ans* kinesthetic
cineteg *eb* kinetics
cineteg adweithiau *eb* reaction kinetics
cineteg gemegol *eb* chemical kinetics
cinetig *ans* kinetic
cinetin *eg* kinetin
cinio canol dydd *eg* lunch
cinio ysgol *eg* ciniawau ysgol school dinner
ciper *eg* ciperiaid gamekeeper
cipgyrch *eg* cipgyrchoedd incursion
cipiad dwy law *eg* cipiadau dwy law two hands snatch
cipio *be* snatch; capture
cipio data *be* data capture
cipio delweddau *be* image capture
ciplun *eg* cipluniau screen shot; screen grab; screen capture
cipyn *eg* cipynnau pickup
cirol *ans* chiral
ciroledd *eg* chirality
ciropodydd *eg* ciropodyddion chiropodist
cirrocumulus *eg* cirrocumulus
cirrostratus *eg* cirrostratus
cirrus *eg* cirrus
cis *eg* cis
cisoid *eg* cisoidau cissoid
cist *eb* cistiau chest
cist o ddroriau *eb* cistiau o ddroriau chest of drawers
cist o feiolau *eb* cistiau o feiolau chest of viols
cist wynt *eb* cistiau gwynt wind chest
cist wynt organ *eb* cistiau gwynt organ organ wind chest
cistfaen *eb* cistfeini cist
cistron *eg* cistronau cistron
cit *eg* citiau kit
cit atgyweirio *eb* citiau atgyweirio repair kit
citin *eg* chitin
citrwlin *eg* citrulline
citrws *eg* citrus
ciw *eg* ciwiau queue
ciw (snwcer, pŵl) *eg* ciwiau cue
ciw adalw *eg* ciwiau adalw retrieval cue
ciwb *eg* ciwbiau cube
Ciwbaidd *ans* Cubist
ciwbiaeth *eb* cubism
ciwbig *ans* cubic
ciwbig corff-ganolog *ans* body-centred cubic
ciwbig wyneb-ganolog *ans* face-centred cubic
ciwbigol *ans* cubical
ciwboid *eg* ciwboidau cuboid
Ciwbydd *eg* Ciwbwyr Cubist
ciwcymer *eg* ciwcymerau cucumber
ciwed *eb* rabble
cladin *eg* cladinau cladding
cladin to *eg* roof cladding
cladin wal *eg* wall cladding
claddedigaeth *eb* claddedigaethau burial
claddu cwrcwd *be* crouched burial
claear *ans* cool; tepid; lukewarm
claearu *be* cool
claf *eg* cleifion patient; invalid
claf allanol *eg* cleifion allanol out-patient
claf mewnol *eg* cleifion mewnol in-patient
clafdy *eg* clafdai infirmary
clafesin *eg* clavecin
clafiau *ell* claves
claficord *eg* claficordiau clavichord
clafisymbal *eg* clafisymbalau clavicymbal
clai *eg* cleiau clay
clai â challestr *eg* clay with flints
clai coch *eg* red clay
clai crochenydd *eg* potter's clay
clai eilaidd *eg* secondary clay
clai gwasgedig *eg* pressed clay
clai gwydreiddiadwy *eg* vitrifiable clay
clai modelu *eg* modelling clay
clai modelu llwyd *eg* grey modelling clay
clai modelu uniongyrchol *eg* direct moulding clay
clai pêl *eg* ball clay
clai powdr *eg* powdered clay
clai powdr llwyd *eg* grey powdered clay
clai slip *eg* slip clay
clai sylfaenol *eg* primary clay
clai tân *eg* fireclay
clai ymdoddadwy *eg* fusible clay
clais *eg* cleisiau bruise

clamp *eg* clampiau clamp
clamp bloc *eg* clampiau bloc block clamp
clamp bwrdd lluniadu *eg* clampiau bwrdd lluniadu drawing-board clamp
clamp nodwydd *eg* clampiau nodwydd needle clamp
clamp offerwr *eg* clampiau offerwr toolmaker's clamp
clamp peipen *eg* clampiau peipen pipe clamp
clamp presyddu *eg* clampiau presyddu brazing clamp
clamp sedd glo *eg* clampiau sedd glo key-seat clamp; lock-seat clamp
clamp togl *eg* clampiau togl toggle clamp
clamp tyno *eg* clampiau tyno tenoned clamp
clamp ystofi *eg* clampiau ystofi warping clamp
clampio *be* clamp
clamydosbor *eg* chlamydospore
clan *eg* claniau clan
clap *eg* clapiau clap
clapio *be* clap
clapio clir *be* crisp claps
clapio curiad cyson *be* clap a steady beat
clapio swta *be* short clap
clarinét *eg* clarinetau clarinet
clarinét alto *eg* clarinetau alto alto clarinet
clarinét bas *eg* clarinetau bas bass clarinet
clarinét tenor *eg* clarinetau tenor basset horn clarinet
clarinetydd *eg* clarinetwyr clarinettist
clarsach *eg* clarsachau clarsach
clasper *eg* clasperi clasper
clastig *ans* clastic
clastir *eg* clastiroedd glebeland
clasuriaeth *eb* classicism
clasurol *ans* classical
clasuron *ell* classics
clasurwr *eg* clasurwyr classicist
clathrad *eg* clathradau clathrate
clawdd *eg* cloddiau dyke; bank
Clawdd Offa *eg* Offa's Dyke
clawr *eg* cloriau cover; lid
clawr biwro *eg* cloriau biwro bureau fall
clawr caled *eg* cloriau caled hard cover; stiff cover
clawr cylchgrawn *eg* cloriau cylchgronau magazine cover
clawr papur *eg* cloriau papur paper back
clawr tabwrdd *eg* cloriau tabwrdd tambour shutter
clawr taflen *eg* cloriau taflenni leaflet cover
clebran baban *be* babbling
clec Sgotaidd *eb* cleciadau Sgotaidd Scotch snap
clecian (i'r grid) *be* snap
cledr (llaw) *eb* cledrau palm
cledr y faneg *eb* inside of glove
cledrau (ar durn) *ell* bedways
cledrbrint *eg* cledrbrintiau palm print
cledren *eb* cledrau stile
cledren bwli *eb* cledrau pwli pulley stile
cledren gau *eb* cledrau cau closing stile
cledren gloi *eb* cledrau cloi locking stile
cledren gwrdd *eb* cledrau cwrdd meeting stile
cledren hongian *eb* cledrau hongian hanging stile
cledren rabedog *eb* cledrau rabedog rabbeted stile
cledren rigolog *eb* cledrau rhigolog grooved stile
cledriadur *eg* cledriaduron palmtop
cledru (gyda chamera) *be* tracking
cledd *eg* cleddau brace; cleat
cledd cynffonnog *eg* cleddau cynffonnog dovetail cleat
cledd pren *eg* cleddau pren wooden cleat
cledd trionglog *eg* cleddau trionglog triangular cleat
cleddog *ans* braced
cleddu *be* brace; cleat
cleddu croeslinol *be* diagonal bracing
cleddyf *eg* cleddyfau sword
cleddyf main *eg* cleddyfau main rapier
clefyd *eg* clefydau disease
clefyd Alzheimer *eg* Alzheimer's disease
clefyd coronaidd y galon *eg* coronary heart disease
clefyd crafu *eg* scabies
clefyd crynu *eg* ague
clefyd cyffwrdd-ymledol *eg* clefydau cyffwrdd-ymledol contagious disease
clefyd cysylltiad rhywiol *eg* clefydau cysylltiad rhywiol sexually transmitted disease
clefyd diffyg *eg* clefydau diffyg deficiency disease
clefyd dirywiol *eg* clefydau dirywiol degenerative disease
clefyd gwenerol *eg* venereal disease
clefyd heintus *eg* clefydau heintus infectious disease
clefyd hysbysadwy *eg* clefydau hysbysadwy notifiable disease
clefyd llwyfen yr Iseldiroedd *eg* Dutch elm disease
clefyd melyn *eg* jaundice
clefyd melyn y newydd-anedig *eg* neonatal jaundice
clefyd Parkinson *eg* Parkinson's disease
clefyd y galon *eg* clefydau'r galon heart disease
clefyd yr euod *eg* liver fluke
cleff *eg* cleffiau clef
cleff bas *eg* cleffiau bas bass clef
cleff C *eg* C clef
cleff F *eg* F clef
cleff G *eg* G clef
cleff mezzo-soprano *eg* cleffiau mezzo-soprano mezzo-soprano clef
clegyr *eg* clegyrau crag
clegyr a chynffon crag and tail
clegyrog *ans* craggy
cleient *eg* cleientiaid client
cleient hŷn *eg* cleientiaid hŷn older client
cleientaeth *eb* clientage
cleient-ganolog *ans* client-centred

cleio *be* pug
cleiog *ans* argillaceous
cleisio *be* bruise
clensio (hoelen, rhybed) *be* clench
clêr *ell* houseflies
clerc *eg* clercod clerk
clerc cyfrifon *eg* clercod cyfrifon accounts clerk
clerc y maes *eg* clercod y maes clerk of the course
clerigaeth reolaidd *eb* regular clergy
clerigaeth seciwlar *eb* secular clergy
clerigiaeth *eb* clericalism
clerigol *ans* clerical
clerigwr *eg* clerigwyr cleric; clergyman
clerigwr rheolaidd *eg* clerigwyr rheolaidd regular cleric
clerigwyr rheolaidd *ell* clerks regular
clerwr *eg* clerwyr minstrel
clerwriaeth *eb* minstrelsy
clesbyn (Karabiner) *eg* clasbiau snaplink
clesbyn (yn gyffredinol) *eg* clasbiau clasp
cletir *eg* cletiroedd hardpan
cletir calch *eg* cletiroedd calch limepan
cletir clai *eg* cletiroedd clai pan
cletir haearn *eg* cletiroedd haearn iron pan
cletir hwmws *eg* moorpan
clic *eg* cliciau click
clic dwbl *eg* cliciau dwbl double click
clicied *eb* cliciedau latch; catch
clicied a phawl ratchet and pawl
clicied bêl *eb* cliciedau pêl ball catch
clicied drws *eb* cliciedau drws door latch
clicied ddannedd *eb* cliciedau dannedd ratchet
clicied fagnetig *eb* magnetic catch
clicied fawd *eb* cliciedau bawd thumb latch
clicied follt *eb* cliciedau bollt bolt catch
clicied gyffwrdd *eb* cliciedau cyffwrdd touch latch
clicied llidiart *eb* cliciedau llidiart gate latch
clicied sash *eb* cliciedau sash sash catch
clicied sbring-lwythog *eb* cliciedau sbring-lwythog spring-loaded catch
clicied ymyl *eb* cliciedau ymyl rim latch
clicio *be* click
clincer *eg* clinceri clinker
clincer pedwar *eg* clinker four
clincer wyth *eg* clinker eight
clindarddach *be* decrepitate
clinig *eg* clinigau clinic
clinig clyw *eg* clinigau clyw audiology clinic
clinig cyfarwyddo plant *eg* clinigau cyfarwyddo plant child guidance clinic
clinig cyn-geni *eg* clinigau cyn-geni antenatal clinic
clinig cynllunio teulu *eg* family planning clinic
clinig dynion iach *eg* clinigau dynion iach well man clinic
clinig lles plant *eg* clinigau lles plant child welfare clinic
clinig merched iach *eg* clinigau merched iach well woman clinic
clinig ôl-eni *eg* clinigau ôl-eni post-natal clinic
clinig teithiol *eg* clinigau teithiol mobile clinic
clinigol *ans* clinical
clinigol lân *ans* clinically clean
clinomedr *eg* clinomedrau clinometer
clint *eg* clintiau clint; lapie; karre
clip *eg* clipiau clip
clip bwrdd lluniadu *eg* clipiau bwrdd lluniadu drawing-board clip
clip fideo *eg* clipiau fideo video clip
clip fideo camcordor *eg* clipiau fideo camcordor camcorder video clip
clip fideo gwefan *eg* web site video clip
clip papur *eg* clipiau papur paper clip
clipfwrdd *eg* clipfyrddau clipboard
clipio *be* clip
cliplun *eg* clipluniau clip art
clir *ans* clear
clir-ddiffiniedig *ans* well-defined
clirffordd *eb* clirffyrdd clearway
cliriad *eg* cliriadau clearance
cliriad blaen *eg* cliriadau blaen front clearance
cliriad falf *eg* cliriadau falf valve clearance
cliriad helics *eg* cliriadau helics helix clearance
cliriad ochr *eg* cliriadau ochr side clearance
cliriad sawdl *eg* heel clearance
cliriad taped *eg* cliriadau taped tappet clearance
cliriad torri *eg* cliriadau torri cutting clearance
cliriad y dril *eg* body clearance
Cliriadau'r Ucheldiroedd *ell* Highland Clearances
clirio *be* clear
clirio slymiau *be* slum clearance
clirio storfa'r cof *be* clear memory cache
clirio storfa'r disg *be* clear disk cache
clirio'r storfa *be* clear cache
clirio'r ymholiad *be* clear query
clirio'r ystod argraffu *be* clear print range
clitelwm *eg* clitellum
clo *eg* cloeon lock
clo blwch *eg* cloeon blychau box lock
clo CAPS *eg* CAPS lock
clo clwt *eg* cloeon clwt padlock
clo cwpwrdd *eg* cloeon cwpwrdd cupboard lock
clo cyfnewid *eg* cloeon cyfnewid shift lock key
clo cynffonnog *eg* cloeon cynffonnog dovetail key
clo drôr *eg* cloeon drôr drawer lock
clo drws *eg* cloeon drws door lock
clo drws llithr *eg* cloeon drysau llithro sliding-door lock
clo llaw *eg* cloeon llaw hand jam
clo llaw chwith *eg* cloeon llaw chwith left-hand lock
clo mortais *eg* cloeon mortais mortise lock
clo mortais fertigol *eg* cloeon mortais fertigol vertical mortise lock

clo mortais unionsyth *eg* cloeon mortais unionsyth upright mortise lock
clo ochr dde *eg* cloeon ochr dde right-hand lock
clo piano *eg* cloeon piano piano lock
clo pìn *eg* cloeon pìn pin lock
clo ymyl *eg* cloeon ymyl rim lock
cloaca *eg* cloaca
cloc *eg* clociau clock
cloc amser real *eg* clociau amser real real time clock
cloc munudau *eg* clociau munudau minute-timer
clocsen *eb* clocsiau clog
clocwedd *ans* clockwise
cloch *eb* clychau bell
cloch aberth *eb* clychau aberth sacring bell
clochdy *eg* clochdai bell tower; belfry
clochen *eb* clochenni bell-jar
clochydd *eg* clochyddion sexton
clodrestr *eb* credits
cloddfa *eb* cloddfeydd dig
cloddiad *eg* cloddiadau excavation
cloddio (archaeolegol) *be* excavate
cloddio (yn gyffredinol) *be* dig
cloddio data *be* data mining
cloddio glo brig *be* opencast coal mining
cloddiwr *eg* cloddwyr sapper
Cloddwyr *ell* Diggers
cloer *eg* cloerau niche
clof *eg* clofau clove
clofach-glwm *ans* hinge-bound
clofan *eg* clofannau enclave
cloffni *eg* limp
clogfaen *eg* clogfeini boulder
clog-glai *eg* boulder clay
clogwyn *eg* clogwyni cliff
clogwyn cylchlithriad *eg* clogwyni cylchlithriad slumped cliff
clogwyn yn syrthio *eg* cliff collapse
clogyn *eg* clogynnau cloak; cape
cloi *be* lock
clôn *eg* clonau clone
clonio *be* clone
clopáu *be* upsetting
cloramin *eg* chloramine
clorian *eb* cloriannau scale; balance
clorian drawst *eb* cloriannau trawst beam balance
clorian ddirdro *eb* cloriannau dirdro torsion balance
clorian gerrynt *eb* cloriannau cerrynt current balance
clorian sbring *eb* cloriannau sbring spring balance
cloriannu (=gwerthuso) *be* evaluate
cloriannu (=pwyso) *be* balance
clorid *eg* chloride
clorid mercwrus *eg* mercurous chloride
clorin (Cl) *eg* chlorine
clorin deuocsid *eg* chlorine dioxide
clorinedig *ans* chlorinated
clorineiddio *be* chlorinate
2-clorobwta-1,3-deuen *eg* 2-chlorobuta-1,3-diene
cloroethan *eg* chloroethane
2-cloroethanol *eg* 2-chloroethanol
cloroethen *eg* chloroethene
clorofform *eg* chloroform
cloroffyl *eg* chlorophyll
cloromethan *eg* chloromethane
(cloromethyl)bensen *eg* (chloromethyl)benzene
1-cloro-2-methylbensen *eg* 1-chloro-2-methylbenzene
cloronen *eb* cloron tuber
cloroplast *eg* cloroplastau chloroplast
cloropropan *eg* chloropropane
3-cloroprop-1-en *eg* 3-chloroprop-1-ene
clorosis *eg* chlorosis
clos eglwys gadeiriol *eg* closydd eglwysi cadeiriol cathedral close
clos pen-glin *eg* breeches
closed dŵr *eg* closedau dŵr water closet
clown *eg* clowniaid clown
cludadwy *ans* portable
cludadwyedd *eg* portability
cludadwyedd data *eg* data portability
cludair *eg* cludeiriau block field
cludfelt *eg* cludfeltiau conveyor belt
cludiant *eg* cludiannau transport; conveyance; haulage; carriage
cludiant actif *eg* active transport
cludiant cyhoeddus *eg* public transport
cludiant cynorthwyedig *eg* facilitated transport
cludiant cynorthwyedig *eg* assisted transport
cludiant goddefol *eg* passive transport
cludo *be* transport; convey
cludo mewn llong *be* ship
cludwr nwyddau *eg* cludwyr nwyddau haulage contractor
cludydd *eg* cludyddion carrier; conveyor
cludydd electronau *eg* cludyddion electronau electron carrier
cludydd ïonau *eg* cludwyr ïonau ion transporter
cludydd tâp *eg* cludwyr tâp tape transport
clun *eb* cluniau hip
clunol *ans* sciatic
clust (ar lestr etc) *eg/b* clustiau lug
clust (yn gyffredinol) *eg/b* clustiau ear
clust allanol *eb* outer ear
clust dost *eb* clustiau tost earache
clust fewnol *eb* inner ear
clust ganol *eb* middle ear
clust, trwyn a gwddf ear, nose and throat
clustdlws *eg* clustdlysau earring
clustffonau *ell* headphones
clustiau estynedig *ell* projecting lugs
clustlipa *ans* lop-eared
clustnodi *be* earmark
clustog *eb* clustogau cushion

clustog aer *eb* clustogau aer air-cushion
clustog aur *eb* clustogau aur gold cushion
clustog Fair *eb* thrift
clustogwaith *eg* upholstery
clwb *eg* clybiau club
clwb ar ôl ysgol *eg* clybiau ar ôl ysgol after-school club
clwb athletau *eg* clybiau athletau athletics club
clwb criced *eg* clybiau criced cricket club
clwb glee *eg* clybiau glee glee club
clwb iechyd *eg* clybiau iechyd health club
clwb ieuenctid *eg* clybiau ieuenctid youth club
Clwb Plant *eg* Kids' Club
clwbfwsogl *eg* clwbfwsoglau club-moss
clwm *ans* tied
clwstwr (o goed) *eg* clystyrau stand
clwstwr (o syniadau) *eg* clystyrau constellation
clwstwr (yn gyffredinol) *eg* clystyrau cluster
clwstwr deiciau *eg* clystyrau deiciau dyke swarm
clwstwr o drefi *eg* clystyrau o drefi constellation of towns
clwt (=cewyn baban) *eg* clytiau nappy
clwt (ar gyfer mopio etc) *eg* clytiau cloth
clwt (i drwsio dilledyn) *eg* clytiau patch
clwt brethyn *eg* clytiau brethyn cloth patch
clwt calico *eg* clytiau calico calico patch
clwt craith peiriant *eg* clytiau craith peiriant machine darn patch
clwt emeri *eg* clytiau emeri emery cloth
clwt gwlanen *eg* clytiau gwlanen flannel patch
clwt parod *eg* clytiau parod disposable nappy
clwt print *eg* clytiau print print patch
clwtyn llathru *eg* clytiau llathru polishing rag
clwyd (i aderyn glwydo arni) *eb* clwydi perch; roost
clwyd (mewn chwaraeon) *eb* clwydi hurdle
clwyd (symbol #) *eb* clwydi hash
clwyd (yn gyffredinol) *eb* clwydi gate
clwyd ddiogelwch *eb* clwydi diogelwch safety-barrier
clwydwr *eg* clwydwyr hurdler
clwyf *eg* clwyfau wound
clwyf crafiad *eg* clwyfau crafiad graze
clwyf ergyd gwn *eg* clwyfau ergyd gwn gunshot wound
clwyf rhwygiad *eg* clwyfau rhwygiad lacerated wound
clwyf toriad *eg* clwyfau toriad incised wound
clwyf trywaniad *eg* clwyfau trywaniad puncture wound
clwyf y marchogion *eg* piles
clwyfo *be* wound
clwystredig *ans* cloistered
clwystrol *ans* claustral
clwysty *eg* clwystai cloister
clybodol *ans* auditory
clychau *ell* carillon
clychau car llusg *ell* sleigh bells
clychau gwartheg *ell* cowbells
clychsain *eb* clychseiniau chime
clychsain gwydr *eb* clychseiniau gwydr glass chime
clymblaid *eb* clymbleidiau coalition
clymfaen *eg* clymfeini conglomerate
clymlin *eb* clymliniau tie-line
clymu *be* tie; knot; bind
clymu a llifo tie and dye
clymwch make fast
clymwellt *ell* lyme grass
clystyrau agored *ell* open clusters
clystyrau crwn *ell* globular clusters
clystyru *be* cluster
clytio *be* patch
clytwaith *eg* clytweithiau patchwork
clyw *eg* hearing
clywadwy *ans* audible
clywadwyedd *eg* audibility
clywdeipio *be* audiotyping
clywedol *ans* aural; audio
clywieithol *ans* audiolingual
cnap *eg* cnapiau pommel; boss; process
cnapiau asgwrn cefn *ell* spinous processes
cnau mwnci *ell* peanuts
cnawdnychiad myocardiaidd *eg* myocardial infarction
cneifio *be* shear
cnepyn *eg* cnepynnau nodule
cnepyn deintffurf *eg* cnepynnau deintffurf odontoid process
cnepyn mastoid *eg* cnepynnau mastoid mastoid process
cnepyn traws *eg* cnepynnau traws transverse process
cnepynnaidd *ans* nodular
cneuen almon *eb* cnau almon almond
cneuen Ffrengig *eb* cnau Ffrengig walnut
cneuen gastan *eb* cnau castan chestnut
cneuen goco *eb* cnau coco coconut
cnewyll palmwydd olew *ell* oil palm kernels
cnewyllan *eg* nucleolus
cnewyllol *ans* nucleated
cnewyllyn (canol cneuen etc) *eg* cnewyll kernel
cnewyllyn (mewn bioleg) *eg* cnewyll nucleus
cnewyllyn aml-labedog *eg* cnewyll aml-labedog multi-lobed nucleus
cnewyllyn datrysol *eg* cnewyll datrysol resolvent kernel
cnewyllyn palmwydd *eg* cnewyll palmwydd palm kernel
cnewyllyn wy *eg* egg nucleus
cnicyn *eg* cnicynnau knickpoint
cnoad *eg* bite
cnoc *eg/b* cnociau rap
cnocell y coed *eb* cnocellod y coed woodpecker
cnocio *be* rap
cnodiog *ans* fleshy
cnofil *eg* cnofilod rodent

cnoi *be* masticate
cnu *eg* cnuoedd fleece
Cnu Aur *eg* Golden Fleece
cnufiog *ans* fleecy
cnwc *eg* cnyciau knoll
cnwc gro *eg* cnyciau gro kame
cnwd *eg* cnydau crop
cnwd bresych *eg* cnydau bresych brassica crop
cnwd cynnal *eg* cnydau cynnal subsistence crop
cnwd gorchudd *eg* cnydau gorchudd cover crop
cnwd gwraidd *eg* cnydau gwraidd root crop
cnwd porthiant *eg* cnydau porthiant fodder crop
cnwd saib *eg* cnydau saib break crop
cnwd trin *eg* cnydau trin cultivated crop
cnydio dwbl *be* double cropping
coaserfad *eg* coaserfadau coacervate
coaserfadiad *eg* coacervation
cobalt *eg* cobalt
cobalt(II) deucobalt(III) ocsid *eg* cobalt(II) dicobalt(III) oxide
coban *eb* cobanau nightdress
cobl *eg* coblau cobble
COBOL *eb* COBOL
coco *eg* cocoa
coconyt mân *eg* desiccated coconut
cocosen *eb* cocos cockle
cocotte *eb* cocottes cocotte
cocs *eg* cocsys cox
cocsen *eb* cocs cog
cocsidiosis *eg* coccidiosis
cocsio *be* cox
coctel *eg* coctels cocktail
cocŵn *eg* cocynau cocoon
cocws *eg* coci coccus
coch *eg* red
coch cadmiwm *eg* cadmium red
coch Fenis *eg* Venetian red
coch glas (rhuddgoch) *eg* blue red
coch golau *eg* light red
coch India *eg* Indian red
coch oren (fermiliwn) *eg* orange red
cochddu *ans* chestnut brown
cochi (pysgod) *be* curing
cochl *eg* cochlau pall
cochlea *eg* cochlea
cochlyd *ans* reddish
cod *eg* codau code
cod agored *eg* open source
cod archwilio gwallau *eg* codau archwilio gwallau error checking code
cod ASCII *eg* ASCII code
► **cod bar** *eg* codau bar bar code
cod cerdyn *eg* codau cerdyn card code
cod cyflwr *eg* codau cyflwr condition code
cod cyfraith *eg* law code
cod cywiro gwallau *eg* codau cywiro gwallau error correcting code
cod darganfod gwallau *eg* codau darganfod gwallau error detecting code
cod deongliadol *eg* codau deongliadol interpretive code
cod deuaidd *eg* codau deuaidd binary code
cod diogelu ffeil *eg* codau diogelu ffeiliau file protection code
cod EBCDIC *eg* EBCDIC code
cod ffynhonnell *eg* codau ffynhonnell source code
cod genynnol *eg* genetic code
cod golchi *eg* codau golchi wash code
cod gorchymyn *eg* codau gorchymyn command code
cod gwallau *eg* codau gwallau error code
cod gweithredu *eg* codau gweithredu operation code
cod gweithredu cofrif *eg* codau gweithredu cofrif mnemonic operation code
cod Hamming *eg* Hamming code
cod lliwiau *eg* colour coding
cod maint ac arwydd *eg* sign and magnitude code
Cod Masnach *eg* Commercial Code
Cod Napoleon *eg* Napoleonic Code
cod naratif *eg* narrative code
cod nodau *eg* codau nodau character code
cod peiriant *eg* codau peiriant machine code
Cod Penyd *eg* Penal Code
cod rhaglen *eg* program code
cod rheoli *eg* codau rheoli control code
Cod Sifil *eg* Civil Code
cod swyddogaeth *eg* codau swyddogaeth function code
cod technegol *eg* codau technegol technical code
Cod Troseddol *eg* Criminal Code
Cod y Caethion Du *eg* Black Code
Cod y Môr *eg* Maritime Code
cod ymarfer *eg* codau ymarfer code of practice
cod ymarfer da *eg* codau ymarfer da code of good practice
cod ymddygiad *eg* codau ymddygiad code of conduct
cod ymddygiad *eg* code of behaviour
coda *eg* codâu coda
CODASYL *eb* CODASYL
codecs *eg* codecsau codex
codeiddiad *eg* codification
codeiddio *be* codify
codeiddiwr *eg* codeiddwyr codifier
codell *eb* codellau take-up lever
coden *eb* codennau sac; pod; cyst
coden aer *eb* codennau aer air sac
coden ddŵr *eb* codennau dŵr water sac
coden embryo *eb* codennau embryo embryo sac
coden inc *eb* codennau inc ink sac
coden y bustl *eb* codennau y bustl gall-bladder
codennaidd *ans* sacculate
codennau awyr *ell* wind sacks
codennog *ans* saccular

codennyn *eg* codenynnau saccule
codeta *eg* codetâu codetta
codi (=adeiladu) *be* erect
codi (gyda chraen etc) *be* hoist
codi (yn gyffredinol) *be* raise; lift
codi llifyn *be* dye pick-up
codi neu ostwng raise or lower
codi perpendicwlar *be* raise a perpendicular
codi pwysau *be* weightlifting
codi pwyth *be* pick up a stitch
codi pwythau (sgorpio) *be* raise stitches
codi staen *be* stain removal
codi tâl *be* charge
codi trethi *be* levy rates
codi ymwybyddiaeth *be* consciousness-raising
codiad (rhywiol) *eg* codiadau erection
codiad (yn gyffredinol) *eg* codiadau lift
codiad (y berwbwynt) *eg* elevation
codiad capilari *eg* codiadau capilari capillary rise
codiad serth *eg* codiadau serth steep pitch
codiad to *eg* pitch
codiad tymheredd uchaf *eg* maximum temperature rise
codio *be* code; coding
codio amseryddol *be* temporal coding
codio anatomegol *be* anatomical coding
codio nod *be* character coding
codi'r corff *be* lift the body
codlys *eg* codlysiau legume
codlysol *ans* leguminous
codwr *eg* codwyr riser; elevator
codwr byrnau *eg* codwyr byrnau bale loader
codwr staen *eg* codwyr staen stain remover
codydd *eg* codyddion coder
codydd staen *eg* codyddion staen removal agent
coed *ell* wood; timber; lumber
coed cartref *ell* homegrown timber
coed difandwll *ell* non-porous woods
coed sy'n cael eu mewnforio *ell* imported timber
coeden *eb* coed tree
coeden benderfyniadau *eb* decision tree
coeden cyfeiriaduron *eb* coed cyfeiriaduron directory tree
coeden ddeuaidd *eb* coed deuaidd binary tree
coeden fythwyrdd *eb* coed bythwyrdd evergreen
coeden gau *eb* coed cau hollow tree
coeden gollddail *eb* coed collddail deciduous tree
coeden lydanddail *eb* coed llydanddail broadleaved tree
coeden wytnaf *eb* coed gwytnaf hardiest tree
coeden ymwthiol *eb* coed ymwthiol emergent tree
coedlan *eb* coedlannau coppice
coedlin *eg* coedlinau tree line
coedwig *eb* coedwigoedd forest
coedwig dymherus *eb* coedwigoedd tymherus temperate forest
coedwig ddrain *eb* coedwigoedd drain thorn forest
coedwig galeri *eb* coedwigoedd galeri gallery forest
coedwig gonwydd *eb* coedwigoedd conwydd coniferous forest
coedwig law *eb* coedwigoedd glaw rainforest
coedwig law drofannol *eb* coedwigoedd glaw trofannol tropical rainforest
coedwig soddedig *eb* coedwigoedd soddedig submerged forest
coedwigaeth *eb* forestry
coedwigo *be* afforestation
coedwigwr *eg* coedwigwyr forester
coedydd coch *ell* redwoods
coedyddiaeth *eb* arboriculture
coelcerth (angladdol) *eb* pyre
coeliag *ans* coeliac
coelom *eg* coelomau coelom
coenobia *eg* coenobiaid coenobites
coes (arf) *eb* coesau shaft
coes (brwsh etc)) *eb* coesau handle
coes (gwymon neu ffwng) *eb* coesau stipe
coes (planhigyn) *eb* coesau stem
coes (rhan o'r corff) *eb* coesau leg
coes allanol *eb* outside leg
coes bren *eb* coesau pren wooden handle
coes brwsh *eb* coesau brwsh brush handle
coes daprog *eb* coesau taprog tapered handle
coes daprog *eb* coesau taprog tapered leg
coes fewnol *eb* inside leg
coes flaen *eb* leading leg
coes flaen *eb* coesau blaen fore-limb
coes gabriol *eb* coesau cabriol cabriole leg
coes gron *eb* coesau crwn round leg
coes gymalog *eb* coesau cymalog jointed leg
coes matsen *eb* coesau matsys matchstick
coes morthwyl *eb* coesau morthwylion hammer handle
coes o flaen wiced (c.o.f.) leg before wicket
coes oddfog *eb* coesau oddfog bulbous leg
coes ôl *eb* coesau ôl hind leg
coes sgwâr *eb* coesau sgwâr square leg
coes siapog *eb* coesau siapog shaped leg
coes ysgubell *eb* coesau ysgubell broomstick
coesarf *eg* coesarfau greave
coesarn *eg* coesarnau gaiter
coesau sblae *ell* splay legs
coesgroes *ans* cross-legged
coeswr agos *eg* coeswyr agos short leg
coeswr byr sgwâr *eg* coeswyr byr sgwâr short square leg
coeswr cul *eg* coeswyr cul fine leg
coeswr pell *eg* coeswyr pell long leg
coeswr pell sgwâr *eg* coeswyr pell sgwâr deep square leg
coeswr sgwâr *eg* coeswyr sgwâr square leg
coesyn *eg* coesynnau stem; stalk
coesyn a dorrwyd o blanhigyn *eg* coesynnau a dorrwyd o blanhigion cut stem

coesyn cynradd *eg* coesynnau cynradd primary stem
coesyn iorwg *eg* coesynnau iorwg ivy stem
coesyn yr ymennydd *eg* coesynnau'r ymennydd brain stem
coeten *eb* coetiau quoit
coetio *be* quoit
coetir *eg* coetiroedd woodland
coetir collddail *eg* coetiroedd collddail deciduous woodland
coetir Môr y Canoldir *eg* Mediterranean woodland
coetmon *eg* coetmyn lumberjack
coetmona *be* lumbering
coets baban *eb* coetsys babanod baby buggy
coets fawr *eb* coetsys mawr stage coach
coets y post *eb* coetsys y post mailcoach
coeth (am fetel, siwgr) *ans* refined
coeth (am waith celf) *ans* elaborate
coethder *eg* coethderau refinement
coethi (gwaith celf) *be* elaborate
coethi (metel, siwgr) *be* refine
coethi cylchfaol *be* zone refining
cof *eg* cofion memory
cof adleisiol *eg* echoic memory
cof ailadeiladol *eg* reconstructive memory
cof allanol *eg* external memory
cof amlran *eg* multi-part memory
cof bwrlwm magnetig *eg* magnetic bubble memory
cof clywedol *eg* auditory memory
cof clyweled tymor byr *eg* audio-visual scratchpad
cof craidd *eg* cofion craidd core memory
cof cyfieithu *eg* cofion cyfieithu translation memory
cof cyflwr-ddibynnol *eg* state-dependent memory
cof cyfnodol *eg* episodic memory
cof cymal darllen yn unig (PHROM) *eg* phrase read-only memory
cof cysylltiadol *eg* associative memory
cof darllen yn unig (ROM) *eg* read-only memory
cof dros dro *eg* cache memory; scratch memory
cof dynamig *eg* cofion dynamig dynamic memory
cof eiconig *eg* iconic memory
cof fflachfwlb *eg* flashbulb memory
cof gweithredol *eg* working memory
cof hapgyrch (RAM) *eg* random access memory
cof hapgyrch dynamig (DRAM) *eg* dynamic random access memory
cof hunangofiannol *eg* autobiographical memory
cof lle-ddibynnol *eg* place-dependent memory
cof mynediad uniongyrchol *eg* immediate access memory
cof penodol *eg* specific memory
cof pin *eg* cofion pin pen drive
cof rhaglenadwy darllen yn unig (PROM) *eg* programmable read-only memory
cof rheoli *eg* cofion rheoli control memory
cof semantig *eg* semantic memory
cof synhwyraidd *eg* sensory memory
cof tymor byr *eg* short-term memory
cof tymor hir *eg* long-term memory
cof ymhlyg *eg* implicit memory
cofadail *eg* cofadeiladau monument
cofalens *eg* cofalensau covalency
cofalent *ans* covalent
cofalent polar *eg* polar covalent
► **cofdroshaen** *eb* cofdroshaenau memory overlay
cofgylchred *eb* cofgylchredau memory circle
cofiadur *eg* cofiaduron recorder
cofio *be* remember
cofleidio *be* hug
cofleidio'r bêl *be* hug the ball
cofleidio'r pengliniau *be* hug the knees
cofnod *eg* cofnodion record; minute; entry
cofnod achos *eg* cofnodion achos case record
cofnod archifol *eg* cofnodion archifol archive record
cofnod byw *eg* cofnodion byw live record
Cofnod Cenedlaethol Cyrhaeddiad Galwedigaethol *eg* NROVA: National Record of Vocational Achievement
cofnod cronnus *eg* cofnodion cronnus cumulative record
cofnod cyfrinachol *eg* cofnodion cyfrinachol confidential record
cofnod cyrhaeddiad *eg* cofnodion cyrhaeddiad record of achievement
cofnod cyrhaeddiad cronnus *eg* cofnodion cyrhaeddiad cronnus cumulative achievement record
cofnod cyrhaeddiad personol *eg* personal achievement record
cofnod cywir *eg* cofnodion cywir accurate record
cofnod data *eg* cofnodion data data entry
cofnod ffosil *eg* fossil record
cofnod hyd penodol *eg* cofnodion hyd penodol fixed length record
cofnod marw *eg* cofnodion marw dead record
cofnod myfyriwr *eg* cofnodion myfyrwyr student record
cofnod mynegai nesaf *eg* next index entry
cofnod mynychu *eg* cofnodion mynychu attendance record
cofnod nesaf *eg* next record
cofnod newydd *eg* cofnodion newydd new record
cofnod personol *eg* cofnodion personol personal record
cofnod rhesymegol *eg* cofnodion rhesymegol logical record
cofnodi *be* record
cofnodi data *be* data entering
cofnodi data llais *be* voice data entry
cofnodi data uniongyrchol *be* direct data entry
cofnodi ffenomenau *be* record phenomena
cofnodi ffurfiannol *be* formative recording
cofnodion gweledol gyda nodiadau *ell* annotated visual records
cofnodion hyd newidiol *ell* variable length records
cofnodion personél *ell* personnel records

cofnodwr *eg* cofnodwyr recorder
cofnodwr trawiadau bysellau *eg* cofnodwyr trawiadau bysellau keystroke logger
cofrestr *eb* cofrestri register
cofrestr amddiffyn plant *eb* cofrestri amddiffyn plant child protection register
► **cofrestr cofddata** *eb* cofrestri cofddata memory data register
► **cofrestr cofgyfeiriad** *eb* cofrestri cofgyfeiriad memory address register
cofrestr cyfeiriadau *eb* cofrestri cyfeiriadau address register
cofrestr ganlyniadau *eb* cofrestri canlyniadau result register
cofrestr genedlaethol *eb* national register
cofrestr gyfarwyddyd *eb* cofrestri cyfarwyddyd instruction register
cofrestr mynegai *eb* cofrestri mynegai index register
cofrestr plant a gamdriniwyd *eb* cofrestri plant a gamdriniwyd child abuse register
cofrestr syfliad *eb* cofrestri syfliad shift register
cofrestr un pwrpas *eb* cofrestri un pwrpas dedicated register
cofrestrfa *eb* cofrestrfeydd registry
cofrestriad *eg* cofrestriadau registration; enrolment
cofrestru *be* register; enrol
cofrestrydd *eg* cofrestryddion registrar
cofrestrydd academaidd *eg* cofrestryddion academaidd academic registrar
cofrif *eg* cofrifau mnemonic
coffi *eg* coffee
coffi mâl *eg* ground coffee
coffi percoladur *eg* percolated coffee
coffi wedi'i hidlo *eg* filtered coffee
coffr *eg* coffrau coffer
cogail *eg* cogeiliau distaff
coginio *be* cook
cogyddio (defnyddio panyddion) *be* cogging
conglfaen *eg* conglfeini quoin
congren *eb* congrod conger eel
coil *eg* coiliau coil
coil anwythiad *eg* coiliau anwythiad induction coil
coil craidd aer *eg* air-cored coil
coil craidd haearn *eg* iron-cored coil
coil cynradd *eg* coiliau cynradd primary coil
coil chwilio *eg* search coil
coil eilaidd *eg* coiliau eilaidd secondary coil
coil gwifren *eg* coiliau gwifren wire coil
coil maes *eg* field coil
coil symudol *eg* coiliau symudol moving coil
coïonig *ans* co-ionic
col (gweiryn neu ddeilen) *eg* colion awn
col (ar fynydd) *eg* colau col; saddlepoint
col legno *adf* col legno
coladiad *eg* coladiadau collation
coladu *be* collate
coladydd *eg* coladwyr collator
colagen *eg* collagen
colandr *eg* colandrau colander
colchos *eg* kolkhoz
colecalchifferol *eg* cholecalciferol
coleg *eg* colegau college
coleg addysg *eg* colegau addysg college of education
coleg addysg bellach *eg* colegau addysg bellach college of further education
coleg addysg uwch *eg* colegau addysg uwch college of higher education
Coleg Agored *eg* Open College
coleg cymunedol *eg* colegau cymunedol community college
coleg chweched dosbarth *eg* colegau chweched dosbarth sixth-form college
coleg hyfforddi *eg* colegau hyfforddi training college
coleg offeiriadol *eg* colegau offeiriadol seminary
coleg technegol *eg* colegau technegol technical college
Coleg Technegol Dinas *eg* City Technology College
colencyma *eg* collenchyma
coleoptil *eg* coleoptilau coleoptile
coleorhisa *eg* coleorhisâu coleorhiza
coler *eg/b* coleri collar
coler â band *eg* coleri â band collar with band
coler crys *eg* coleri crysau shirt collar
coler cwfl *eg* coleri cwfl cowl collar
coler gosod *eg* coleri gosod set-on collar
coler llabed *eg* coleri llabed revers collar
coler mandarin *eg* coleri mandarin mandarin collar
coler Peter Pan *eg* coleri Peter Pan Peter Pan collar
coler pig *eg* coleri pig pointed collar
coler rhôl *eg* coleri rhôl roll collar
coler rhydd *eg* coleri rhydd detachable collar
coler syth *eg* coleri syth straight collar
colera *eg* cholera
coleru *be* collaring
coleslaw *eg* coleslaw
colesterol *eg* cholesterol
colesterol serwm *eg* serum cholesterol
colesystocinin *eg* cholecystokinin
colet *eg* coletau collet
colfach *eg* colfachau hinge
colfach addurniadol *eg* colfachau addurniadol ornamental hinge
colfach canol *eg* colfachau canol centre hinge
colfach canol camdro *eg* colfachau canol camdro cranked centre hinge
colfach codi *eg* colfachau codi rising butt hinge
colfach colyn *eg* colfachau colyn pivot hinge
colfach cudd *eg* colfachau cudd invisible hinge
colfach cyfunol *eg* colfachau cyfunol combination hinge
colfach estyn *eg* colfachau estyn extension hinge

colfach glöyn byw *eg* colfachau glöyn byw butterfly hinge
colfach gwasgedig *eg* colfachau gwasgedig pressed hinge
colfach hir *eg* colfachau hir piano hinge
colfach llydan *eg* colfachau llydan backflap hinge
colfach neilon *eg* colfachau neilon nylon hinge
colfach solet *eg* colfachau solet solid drawn hinge
colfach strap *eg* colfachau strap strap hinge
colfach T *eg* colfachau T T-hinge
colfach top bwrdd *eg* colfachau top bwrdd table-top hinge
colfach uniad riwl *eg* colfachau uniad riwl rule joint hinge
colfach ymyl *eg* colfachau ymyl butt hinge
colfachog *ans* hinged
colfachu *be* hinge
colig *eg* colic
colinergig *ans* cholinergic
colinesteras *eg* cholinesterase
colitig *ans* colitic
colofn *eb* colofnau column
colofn aer *eb* colofnau aer air column
colofn arffin *eb* colofnau arffin bound column
colofn bresennol *eb* colofnau presennol existing column
colofn cronfa ddata *eb* colofnau cronfa ddata database column
colofn cyfnewid catïonau *eb* colofnau cyfnewid catïonau cation exchange column
colofn drioedd *eb* column of threes
colofn ddur *eb* colofnau dur steel column
colofn ddŵr *eb* colofnau dŵr waterspout
colofn ffracsiynu *eb* colofnau ffracsiynu fractionating column
colofn ganolog *eb* colofnau canolog central column
colofn gerdyn *eb* colofnau cerdyn card column
colofn gyswllt *eb* colofnau cyswllt engaged column
colofn wag *eb* colofnau gwag blank column
colofnig *eb* colofnigau style
coloid *eg* coloidau colloid
coloidaidd *ans* colloidal
colon *eg* colonau colon
colon disgynnol *eg* descending colon
colon esgynnol *eg* ascending colon
coloratwra *ans* coloratura
colorimedr *eg* colorimedrau colorimeter
colosterolaemia *eg* cholosterolaemia
colostomi *eg* colostomïau colostomy
colostrwm *eg* colostrum
colsaid *eg* colseidiau tang
col-tar *eg* coal tar
coltario *be* coal tar
coludd (ar gyfer tannau cerdd) *eg* coluddion catgut
coludd (yn gyffredinol) *eg* coluddion gut
coluddol *ans* intestinal
coluddyn *eg* coluddion intestine
coluddyn bach *eg* coluddion bach small intestine
coluddyn mawr *eg* coluddion mawr large intestine
colur *eg* make-up
coluro *be* make-up
colyn *eg* colynnau pivot
colyn blaen *eg* colynnau blaen forward pivot
colyn ôl *eg* colynnau ôl reverse pivot
colyn sash *eg* colynnau sash sash pivot
colynnol *ans* pivotal
colynnu *be* pivot
colynnu'n rhydd *be* freely pivot
coll geiriau *eg* ellipsis
collage *eg* collage
collage brodwaith *eg* embroidered collage
collage o seiniau *eg* sound collage
collddail *ans* deciduous
colled *eg/b* colledion loss
colled grynswth *eb* colledion crynswth gross loss
colled les *eb* colledion lles welfare loss
colled net *eb* net loss
colli clyw *be* hearing loss
colli clyw yn y glust ganol conductive hearing loss
colli cydbwysedd *be* off balance
colli gwaith *be* redundancy
colli gwaith yn wirfoddol *be* voluntary redundancy
colli llifyn *be* dye loss
colli lliw *be* fade; lose colour
colli meddiant o'r bêl *be* lose possession of the ball
colli rheolaeth ar y bêl *be* lose control of the ball
collnod *eg* collnodau apostrophe
collwr da *eg* collwyr da good loser
coma *eg* comas comma
comander *eg* comanderiaid commander
comed *eb* comedau comet
comedi gerdd *eb* comedïau cerdd musical comedy
Cominfform *eg* Cominform
comisar *eg* comisariaid commissar
comisari'r esgob *eg* bishop's commissary
comisiwn *eg* comisiynau commission
comisiwn aráe *eg* commission of array
Comisiwn Coedwigaeth *eg* Forestry Commission
Comisiwn Cystadleuaeth *eg* Competition Commission
Comisiwn Diarfogi *eg* Disarmament Commission
Comisiwn Gwasanaethau'r Gweithlu *eg* Manpower Services Commission
Comisiwn Masnach Ryngwladol *eg* International Trade Commission
comisiwn oyer a terminer *eg* commission of oyer and terminer
Comisiwn Rheoli'r Gynghrair *eb* Alliance Control Commission
Comisiwn y Gyfraith *eg* Law Commission, the
comisiynu *be* commission
Comisiynwyr Gwelliannau *ell* Improvement Commissioners
Comisiynwyr yr Atafaeliad *ell* Commissions for Sequestration

comisiynydd *eg* comisiynwyr commissioner
comisiynydd gwarchod data *eg* comisiynwyr gwarchod data data protection commissioner
comiwn *eg* comiwnau commune
comiwnydd *eg* comiwnyddion communist
comiwnyddiaeth *eb* communism
comiwnyddiaeth ryfel *eb* war communism
comiwnyddol *ans* communist
comôd *eg* comodau commode
comodor *eg* comodoriaid commodore
compot *eg* compotau compote
côn *eg* conau cone
côn blaendor *eg* conau blaendor truncated cone
côn boracs *eg* conau boracs borax cone
côn crwn union *eg* conau crwn union right circular cone
côn folcanig *eg* conau folcanig volcanic cone
côn gwrthdro *eg* conau gwrthdro inverted cone
côn lafa *eg* conau lafa lava cone
côn lludw *eg* conau lludw cinder cone
côn papur *eg* conau papur paper cone
côn parasitig *eg* conau parasitig adventive cone
côn parasitig *eg* conau parasitig parasitic cone
côn pyrometrig *eg* conau pyrometrig pyrometric cone
côn Seger *eg* Seger cone
con sordino *eg* con sordini con sordino
concertante *eg* concertanti concertante
concertino *eg* concertini concertino
concerto *eg* concerti concerto
concerto dwbl *eg* concerti dwbl double concerto
concerto grosso *eg* concerti grossi concerto grosso
concoid *eg* concoidau conchoid
concoidaidd *ans* conchoidal
concordat *eg* concordatiau concordat
Concordat y Reich *eg* Reich Concordat
concretiad *eg* concretion
concrit *eg* concrete
concrit cyfnerth *eg* reinforced concrete
concwest *eg/b* concwestau conquest
concwest Normanaidd *eb* Norman conquest
condom *eg* condomau condom
condominiwm *eg* condominia condominium
condroid *ans* chondroid
condroitin *eg* chondroitin
condrol *ans* chondral
condyl *eg* condylau condyle
confensiwn *eg* confensiynau convention
Confensiwn Ewropeaidd ar Hawliau Dynol *eg* European Convention on Human Rights
confensiwn generig *eg* confensiynau generig generic convention
confensiwn gwyddonol *eg* confensiynau gwyddonol scientific convention
confensiwn lluniadu *eg* drawing convention
confensiwn mathemategol *eg* confensiynau mathemategol mathematical convention
confensiwn theatrig *eg* confensiynau theatrig theatrical convention
confensiwn yr UN ar hawliau plant *eg* UN convention on the rights of the child
confensiynau chwarae teg *ell* conventions of fair play
confensiynol *ans* conventional
confentigl *eb* confentiglau conventicle
confocasiwn *eg* confocasiynau convocation
confylsiwn *eg* confylsiynau convulsion
Conffiwsaidd *ans* Confucian
Conffiwsiad *eg/b* Conffiwsiaid Confucian
conga *eg* congâu conga
conicoid *eg* conicoidau conicoid
conig *ans* conic
conigol *ans* conical
conoid *eg* conoidau conoid
consenswS *eg* consensus
consenswS ffug *eg* false consensus
conseptagl *eg* conseptaglau conceptacle
consertina *eg* consertinâu concertina
conservatoire *eg* conservatoires conservatoire
consesiwn *eg* consesiynau concession
consgripsiwn *eg* conscription
consistoraidd *ans* consistorial
consistori *eg* consistorïau consistory
consistori'r Pab *eg* papal consistory
consol *eg* consolau console
consol organ *eg* consolau organ organ console
consol pell *eg* consolau pell remote console
consommé *eg* consommé
consort *eg* consortiau consort
consort cymysg *eg* broken consort
consort feiolau *eg* consortiau feiolau consort of viols
consort offerynnau tebyg *eg* consortiau offerynnau tebyg whole consort
consortiwm *eg* consortia consortium
consortiwm ysgolion *eg* consortia ysgolion school consortium
conswl *eg* conswliaid consul
conswliaeth *eb* consulate
continuo *eg* continui continuo; thorough bass
continwwm *eg* continwa continuum
continwwm gwledig-trefol *eg* rural-urban continuum
contract *eg* contractau contract
contract cyflogaeth *eg* contractau cyflogaeth employment contract
contract ffurf safonol *eg* contractau ffurf safonol standard form contract
contractau ymlyniad *ell* contracts of adhesion
contractwr *eg* contractwyr contractor
contralto *eb* contraltos contralto
conws arteriosws *eg* conus arteriosus
conwydden *eb* conwydd conifer; coniferous tree
copa *eg* copaon peak; summit
copa *eg* copâu cope

copa a drag cope and drag
copi *eg* copïau copy
copi caled *eg* copïau caled hard copy
copi dyblyg *eg* copïau dyblyg duplicate
copi graddfa *eg* copïau graddfa scaled copy
copi gwreiddiol *eg* copïau gwreiddiol master copy
copi meddal *eg* copïau meddal soft copy
copi wrth gefn *eg* copïau wrth gefn back-up
copi wrth gefn *eg* copïau wrth gefn back-up copy
copiddeiliad *eg* copiddeiliaid copyholder
copin *eg* copinau coping
copïo *be* copy
copïo a gludo copy and paste
copïo fformatio *be* copy formatting
copïo lleoliad y cyswllt *be* copy link location
copïo lleoliad y ddelwedd *be* copy image location
copïo mesurydd *be* copy ruler
copïo, torri a gludo copy, cut and paste
copis *eg* copisau fly opening
copïwr (yn hanesyddol) *eg* copïwyr scribe
copïwr (yn gyffredinol) *eg* copïwyr copier
copog uchel *ans* raised head
copr *eg* copper
copr pothell *eg* blister copper
copr sylffad *eg* copper sulphate
copr(I) clorid *eg* copper(I) chloride
copr(I) clorid amoniaidd *eg* ammoniacal copper(I) chloride
copr(II) carbonad deuhydrocsid (malachit) *eg* copper(II) carbonate dihydroxide (malachite)
copr(II) haearn(II) deusylffid (calcopyrit) *eg* copper(II) iron(II) disulfide (chalcopyrite)
copr(II) sylffad(VI) *eg* copper(II) sulfate(VI)
coprosterol *eg* coprosterol
côr *eg* corau choir; chorus
cor anglais *eg* cors anglais cor anglais; English horn
côr atsain *eg* corau atsain echo chorus
côr dwbl *eg* corau dwbl double chorus
côr meibion *eg* corau meibion male voice choir
Côr y Cewri *eg* Stonehenge
corachaidd *ans* stunted
corachedd *eg* dwarfism
corâl *eg* coralau chorale
corbel *eg* corbelau corbel
corbennog *eg* corbenogiaid brisling
corblanhigyn *eg* corblanhigion dwarf plant
corbysen *eb* corbys dwarf pea
corc *ans* cork
corcaidd *ans* corky
corcyn *eg* cyrc cork
cord *eg* cordiau chord
cord 6/4 arpeggio *eg* cordiau 6/4 arpeggio arpeggio 6/4 chord
cord 6/4 diweddebol *eg* cordiau 6/4 diweddebol cadential 6/4 chord
cord 6/4 tonnog *eg* cordiau 6/4 tonnog auxiliary 6/4 chord
cord ail wrthdro *eg* cordiau ail wrthdro chord in second inversion
cord cromatig *eg* cordiau cromatig chromatic chord
cord cyffredin *eg* cordiau cyffredin common chord
cord cyffredin lleiaf *eg* cordiau cyffredin lleiaf minor common chord
cord cyffredin mwyaf *eg* cordiau cyffredin mwyaf major common chord
cord cyseinio *eg* cordiau cyseinio resonance chord
cord cywasg *eg* cordiau cywasg diminished chord
cord diweddeb *eg* cordiau diweddeb cadence chord
cord estynedig *eg* cordiau estynedig augmented chord
cord gwasgar *eg* cordiau gwasgar broken chord
cord gwreiddnod *eg* cordiau gwreiddnod root chord
cord gwrthdro cyntaf *eg* cordiau gwrthdro cyntaf chord in first inversion
cord lleiaf *eg* cordiau lleiaf minor chord
cord mwyaf *eg* cordiau mwyaf major chord
cord reion *eg* rayon cord
cord safle gwreiddiol *eg* cordiau safle gwreiddiol chord in root position
cord seithfed *eg* cordiau seithfed chord of the seventh
cord seithfed cywasg *eg* cordiau seithfed cywasg diminished seventh chord
cord seithfed y llywydd *eg* dominant seventh chord
cord seithfed y tonydd *eg* cordiau seithfed y tonydd tonic seventh chord
cord sylfaenol y llywydd *eg* cordiau sylfaenol y llywydd fundamental dominant chord
cord trydydd gwrthdro *eg* cordiau trydydd gwrthdro chord in third inversion
cord y chweched Almaenig *eg* German sixth chord
cord y chweched atodol *eg* added sixth chord
cord y chweched Eidalaidd *eg* Italian sixth chord
cord y chweched estynedig *eg* cordiau'r chweched estynedig augmented sixth chord
cord y chweched Ffrengig *eg* French sixth chord
cord y seithfed estynedig *eg* cordiau'r seithfed estynedig augmented seventh chord
cord y tonydd *eg* cordiau'r tonydd tonic chord
cordat *eg* cordatau chordate
cordeddu *be* twist; twine
cordial *eg* cordial
cordio *be* chord
corddi *be* churn
corea Huntington *eg* Huntington's chorea
cored *eb* coredau weir
coreograffi *eg* choreography
coreograffydd *eg* coreograffwyr choreographer
corfan *eg* corfannau metrical foot
corfan amgyrch *eg* corfannau amgyrch amphibrach
corfan cyrch dyrchafedig *eg* corfannau cyrch dyrchafedig anapaest
corfan cytbwys *eg* corfannau cytbwys spondee

corfan dyrchafedig *eg* corfannau dyrchafedig iambus
côr-feistr *eg* côr-feistri chorus master
côr-ferch *eb* côr-ferched chorus girl
côr-fynach *eg* côr-fynaich choir-monk
corff (=sefydliad) *eg* cyrff organization
corff (yn gyffredinol) *eg* cyrff body
corff arwain diwydiant *eg* cyrff arwain diwydiant industry lead body
corff arweiniol *eg* cyrff arweiniol lead body
corff barnwriaethol *eg* cyrff barnwriaethol judicial body
corff cyhoeddus *eg* public body
corff deddfwriaethol *eg* cyrff deddfwriaethol legislature
corff deddfwriaethol *eg* cyrff deddfwriaethol legislative body
corff dilysu *eg* cyrff dilysu authenticating body
corff dyfarnu *eg* cyrff dyfarnu awarding body
corff dynol *eg* cyrff dynol human body
corff gweinyddol *eg* cyrff gweinyddol organ of administration
corff gweithredol *eg* cyrff gweithredol executive body
corff haearn gyr *eg* wrought iron body
corff lliain *eg* cyrff lliain cloth body
corff llong *eg* cyrff llongau hull
corff llywodraeth *eg* cyrff llywodraeth organ of government
corff llywodraethol *eg* cyrff llywodraethol governing body
corff o ddeddfau *eg* cyrff o ddeddfau legislature
corff statudol *eg* cyrff statudol statutory body; statutory organization
corff testun *eg* text body
corff urddau'r marchogion *eg* knightage
corff wybrennol *eg* cyrff wybrennol heavenly body
corff y testun *eg* body text
corff yr aelwyd *eg* hearth body
corffdy *eg* corffdai mortuary
corffgell *eb* corffgelloedd body cell
corffilyn *eg* corffilod corpuscle
corffilyn coch y gwaed *eg* corffilod coch y gwaed red blood corpuscle; erythrocyte
corffilyn Malpighi *eg* Malpighian corpuscle
corffilyn Pacini *eg* corffilod Pacini Pacinian corpuscle
corffilyn y gwaed *eg* corffilod y gwaed blood corpuscle
corffoledd *eb* physique
corfforaeth *eb* corfforaethau corporation
corfforaeth y fwrdeistref *eb* corfforaethau'r bwrdeistrefi borough corporation
corfforaethol *ans* corporate
corfforol *ans* physical
corfforol weithgar *ans* physically active
corffrwd *eb* corffrydiau runnel
corffyn aortig *eg* corffynnau aortig aortic body
corffyn carotid *eg* corffynnau carotid carotid body
corffyn ciliaraidd *eg* corffynnau ciliaraidd ciliary body
corffyn estron *eg* corffynnau estron foreign body
corffyn gwaelodol *eg* corffynnau gwaelodol basal body
corffyn Malpighi *eg* Malpighian body
corffyn pegynol *eg* corffynnau pegynol polar body
côr-gân *eb* corganau chant
corgi môr *eg* corgwn môr porbeagle shark
corhelygen *eb* corhelyg dwarf willow
coriander *eg* coriander
coridor *eg* coridorau corridor
coridor awyr *eg* coridorau awyr air corridor
Coridor Pwylaidd *eg* Polish Corridor
corion *eb* chorion
corlan *eb* corlannau sheep fold; corral
corlan chwarae *eb* corlannau chwarae play-pen
corlan gyfredol *eb* corlannau cyfredol current band
corlannu *be* band
corlun *eg* corluniau sprite
corlun cuddiedig *eg* corluniau cuddiedig masked sprite
► **corlun cyfredol** *eg* corluniau cyfredol current sprite
corm *eg* cormau corm
cormaidd *ans* cormoid
corn (am y cnwd) *eg* corn
corn (anifail etc) *eg* cyrn horn
corn bas *eg* cyrn bas bass horn
corn baset *eg* cyrn baset basset horn
corn cerbyd *eg* cyrn cerbyd coach horn
corn Ffrengig *eb* cyrn Ffrengig French horn
corn gwartheg *eg* cyrn gwartheg cow horn
corn hufen *eg* cyrn hufen cream horn
corn tenor *eg* cyrn tenor tenor horn
cornant *eb* cornentydd rill
cornbiff *eg* corn-beef
cornbilen *eg* cornbilennau cornea
cornbilennol *ans* corneal
cornddawns *eb* cornddawnsiau hornpipe
cornel *eg/b* corneli corner
cornel bell *eb* corneli pell long corner
cornel databeilot *eb* corneli databeilot datapilot corner
cornel ddarllen *eb* corneli darllen reading corner
cornel feitrog *eb* corneli meitrog mitred corner
cornel fer *eb* corneli byr short corner
cornel gosb *eb* corneli cosb penalty corner
cornel gron *eb* corneli crwn radiused corner
cornel gyfnerth *eb* corneli cyfnerth reinforced corner
cornel lem *eb* corneli llym sharp corner
cornelu *be* corner
cornet *eg* cornetau cornet
cornetto *eg* cornetti cornetto
cornfaen *eg* cornfeini chert
cornis *eg* cornisiau cornice

cornopean *eg* cornopeanau cornopean
cornwyd *eg* cornwydydd boil
coro *eg* cori coro
coroid *ans* choroid
corola *eg* corolae corolla
coron *eb* coronau crown
corona *eg* coronâu corona
coronaidd *ans* coronary
coronbleth *eb* coronblethau chaplet
coronomedr *eg* cronomedrau chronometer
coropleth *eg* choropleth
corporal *eg* corporaliaid corporal
corpws *eg* corpus
corpws cafernoswm *eg* corpus cavernosum
corpws caloswm *eg* corpus callosum
corpws lwtewm *eg* corpus luteum
corpws spongioswm *eg* corpus spongiosum
corpws striatwm *eg* corpus striatum
corryn *eg* corynod spider
cors *eb* corsydd bog
corsen *eb* cyrs reed
corsen *eb* cyrs rattan
corsenwaith *eg* reeding
cortecs *eg* cortex
cortecs cerebrol *eg* cerebral cortex
cortecs craudalcennol *eg* orbitofrontal cortex
cortecs cyndalcennol *eg* prefrontal cortex
cortecs cyswllt echddygol *eg* motor association cortex
cortecs limbig *eg* limbic cortex
cortecs synhwyraidd-gysylltiol *eg* sensory association cortex
cortecs y chwarren adrenal *eg* adrenal cortex
corticosteron *eg* corticosterone
corticotroffin *eg* corticotrophin
cortyn *eg* cortynnau cord; twine
cortyn cotwm *eg* cortynnau cotwm cotton twine
cortyn cywarch *eg* cortynnau cywarch hemp twine
cortyn dirdro *eg* cortynnau dirdro twisted cord
cortyn llin *eg* cortynnau llin flax cord
cortyn macramé *eg* cortynnau macramé macramé twine
cortyn naturiol *eg* cortynnau naturiol natural twine
cortyn peipio *eg* cortynnau peipio piping cord
cortyn rhwyd *eg* cortynnau rhwyd net cord
cortyn sglein *eg* cortynnau sglein mercerized cord
corun (=**rhan uchaf y pen**) *eg* corunau crown
corwlad *eb* corwledydd midget state
corwrych *eg* corwrychoedd dwarf shrub
corws *eg* corysau chorus
corwynt *eg* corwyntoedd hurricane
Cosac *eg* Cosaciaid Cossack
cosb *eb* cosbau punishment; penalty
cosb eithaf *eb* death penalty; capital punishment
cosb gorfforol *eb* cosbau corfforol corporal punishment
cosbi *be* penalize
cosbol *ans* punitive
cosbydd cyflyrol *eg* cosbyddion cyflyrol conditioned punisher
cosbydd eilaidd *eb* cosbwyr eilaidd secondary punisher
cosbydd sylfaenol *eg* cosbyddion sylfaenol primary punisher
cosecant (cosec) *eg* cosecannau cosecant
cosech *eg* cosechau cosech
cosh *eg* coshau cosh
cosi *be* itch
cosi poenus *be* irritation
cosin (cos) *eg* cosinau cosine
cosmetigau *ell* cosmetics
cosmig *ans* cosmic
cosmoleg *eb* cosmology
cosmolegol *ans* cosmological
cost *eb* costau cost; charge
cost allanol *eb* costau allanol external cost
cost briodoledig *eb* costau priodoledig imputed cost
cost cyfle *eb* opportunity cost
cost cynnal *eb* costau cynnal maintenance cost
cost economaidd *eg* economic cost
cost effeithiol *ans* cost-effective
cost gwerthiant *eb* costau gwerthiant sales cost
cost gwerthu *eb* costau gwerthu selling cost
cost gyfartalog *eb* costau cyfartalog average cost
cost gyfrifyddol *eb* costau cyfrifyddol accounting cost
cost gymdeithasol *eb* social cost
cost gymharol *eb* costau cymharol comparative cost
cost gynyddol *eb* costau cynyddol increasing cost
cost newidiol *eb* costau newidiol variable cost
cost ostyngol *eb* costau gostyngol decreasing cost
cost rhedeg *eb* costau rhedeg running cost
cost sefydlog *eb* costau sefydlog fixed cost
cost trafod *eb* costau trafod transaction cost
cost trosglwyddo *eb* costau trosglwyddo transfer cost
cost wirioneddol *eb* costau gwirioneddol actual cost
cost wreiddiol *eb* costau gwreiddiol original cost
cost ymateb *eb* response cost
► **cost ymylol** *eb* costau ymylol marginal cost
costau cudd *ell* hidden costs
costau llafur *ell* labour charge
costau preifat *ell* private costs
costau safonol *ell* standard costs
costiad *eg* costiadau costing
costio amsugno *be* absorption costing
costio contractau *be* contract costing
costio prosesau *be* process costing
costio ymylol *be* marginal costing
cosyn pen *eg* cosynnau pen brawn
cot *eb* cotiau coat

cot â chaead sengl *eb* cotiau â chaead sengl single-breasted coat
cot ffibrog *eb* cotiau ffibrog fibrous coat
cot ffrog *eb* cotiau ffrog coat-dress
cot gyntaf *eb* cotiau cyntaf preliminary coat
cot matinée *eb* cotiau matinée matinée coat
cotangiad (cot) *eg* cotangiadau cotangent
coter *eg* coteri cotter
cotwm *eg* cotton
cotwm dolennog *eg* looped cotton
cotwm gwlanog *eg* brushed cotton
cotwm main *eg* lawn cotton
cotwm sglein *eg* mercerized cotton
cotwm sglein *eg* glazed cotton
cotwm sglein *eg* weaving cotton
cotyledon *eb* cotyledonau cotyledon
cotywr *eg* cotywyr cottar
coth *eg* cothau coth
coulomb *eg* coulombau coulomb
coulombmedr *eg* coulombmeter
courante *eg* courantes courante
courgettes *ell* courgettes
courtelle *eg* courtelle
cownt gorfod *eg* compulsory count
Cownt Palatin *eg* Count Palatine
cowper *eg* cowperiaid cooper
cowstio *be* coasting
cowtsio *be* couching
cowtsio Bokhara *be* Bokhara couching
cowtsio Jacobeaidd *be* Jacobean couching
cowyll *eg* cowyllion bride-price
crac *eg* craciau crack
cracellu *be* crackle
cracellu *be* crazing
cracio *be* crack
cracydd *eg* cracyddion cracker
crachboer *eg* sputum
crachen *eb* crach scab
craen *eg* craeniau crane
crafangu *be* chucking
crafanc (ar beiriant) *eb* crafangau chuck
crafanc (yn gyffredinol) *eb* crafangau claw
crafanc arbor *eb* crafangau arbor arbor chuck
crafanc colet *eb* crafangau colet collet chuck
crafanc dril *eb* crafangau dril drill chuck
crafanc fforch *eb* crafangau fforch fork chuck
crafanc fforch *eb* crafangau fforch prong chuck
crafanc fforch ddwbl *eb* crafangau fforch ddwbl two-pronged chuck
crafanc gafael annibynnol *eb* crafangau gafael annibynnol independent chuck
crafanc gloch *eb* crafangau clychau bell chuck
crafanc gwpan *eb* crafangau cwpan cup chuck
crafanc gyfunol *eb* crafangau cyfunol combination chuck
crafanc hunanganoli *eb* crafangau hunanganoli self-centering chuck
crafanc Jacob *eb* crafangau Jacob Jacob chuck
crafanc pedair safn *eb* crafangau pedair safn four-jaw chuck
crafanc tair safn *eb* crafangau tair safn three-jaw chuck
crafell *eb* crafellau graver
crafell losin *eb* crafellau losin lozenge graver
crafell luosbig *eb* crafellau lluosbig multiple graver
crafiad *eg* crafiadau scratch; graze; abrasion
crafiadau arwyneb *ell* surface scratches
crafion *ell* scrapings
crafu *be* scratch; graze
crafwr addurn *eg* crafwyr addurn scratch stock
crafwr asgwrn *eg* crafwyr asgwrn bone scraper
craffter *eg* acuity
cragen *eb* cregyn shell
cragen feryn *eb* cregyn beryn bearing shell
cragen hemisffer *eb* cregyn hemisffer hemispherical shell
cragen long *eb* cregyn llong barnacle
cragennaidd *ans* testaceous
crai *ans* crude; raw
craidd (mewn mathemateg) *eg* creiddiau centroid
craidd (yn gyffredinol) *eg* creiddiau core
craidd afal *eg* creiddiau afalau apple core
craidd caled *eg* hardcore
craidd canolog *eg* creiddiau canolog central core
craidd crymedd *eg* creiddiau crymedd centre of curvature
craidd disgyrchiant *eg* creiddiau disgyrchiant centre of gravity
craidd fferrit *eg* creiddiau fferrit ferrite core
craidd fferrus *eg* ferrous core
craidd haearn meddal *eg* soft iron core
craidd hylifol *eg* creiddiau hylifol liquid core
craidd laminedig *eg* laminated core
craidd màs *eg* creiddiau màs centre of mass
craidd mewnol *eg* creiddiau mewnol inner core
craidd silindrog *eg* creiddiau silindrog cylindrical core
craidd taro *eg* creiddiau taro centre of percussion
craiddfwrdd *eg* craiddfyrddau coreboard
craidd-parth-cylch *eg* core-domain-sphere
craig *eb* creigiau rock
craig allwthiol *eb* creigiau allwthiol extrusive rock
craig fasig *eb* creigiau basig basic rock
craig fewnwthiol *eb* creigiau mewnwthiol intrusive rock
craig follt *eb* creigiau myllt roche moutonée
craig galed *eb* creigiau caled hard rock
craig gynnal *eb* creigiau cynnal pedestal rock
craig gysefin *eb* creigiau cysefin country rock
craig hypabysol *eb* creigiau hypabysol hypabyssal rock
craig igneaidd *eb* creigiau igneaidd igneous rock
craig orchudd *eb* creigiau gorchudd overlying rock
craig-wythïen *eb* craig-wythiennau gash vein
crair *eg* creiriau relic

crair ffug *eg* creiriau ffug feigned relic
craith (wedi trwsio defnydd) *eb* creithiau darn
craith (yn gyffredinol) *eb* creithiau scar
craith deilen *eb* creithiau dail leaf scar
craith ffabrig wedi'i wau *eb* creithiau ffabrig wedi'i wau knitted fabric darn
craith gylchog *eb* creithiau cylchog girdle scar
craith man gwan *eb* creithiau man gwan thin place darn
craith peiriant *eb* creithiau peiriant machine darn
craith rhwyg cornel *eb* creithiau rhwyg cornel corner tear darn
craith Swisaidd *eb* creithiau Swisaidd Swiss darn
craith trawstoriad *eb* creithiau trawstoriad cross-cut darn
craith ystum *eb* creithiau ystumiau meander scar
cral *eg* cralau kraal
cramen *eb* cramennau crust
cramen afreolaidd *eb* irregular crust
cramen galed *eb* cramennau caled duricrust
crameniad *eg* crameniadau incrustation
cramennog *ans* crustaceous; incrusted
cramennog *eg* cramenogion crustacean
cramennol *ans* crustal
cramp *eg* crampiau cramp
cramp cortyn *eg* crampiau cortyn string cramp
cramp G *eg* G cramp
cramp G asennog *eg* crampiau G asennog ribbed G cramp
cramp G dyfnwddf *eg* crampiau G dyfnwddf deep throat G cramp
cramp hir *eg* crampiau hir sash cramp
cramp meir *eg* crampiau meir mire cramp
cramp meitr *eg* crampiau meitr mitre cramp
cramp sbring dur *eg* crampiau sbring dur steel-spring cramp
cramp y mwynwr *eg* miner's cramp
crampio *be* cramp
crampon *eg* cramponau crampon
cramwythen *eb* cramwyth crumpet
cranc (=cramennog) *eg* crancod crab
cranc (ar beiriant) *eg* cranciau crank
cranca *be* catch a crab
crancbin *eg* crancbinnau crank pin
crancgolyn *eg* crancgolynnau crank pivot
crancsiafft *eg* crancsiafftiau crankshaft
crannog *eg* cranogau lake dwelling
cras *ans* arid; parched
crasboeth *ans* torrid
crasgywair *eg* sharp key
crasu *be* air
crater *eg* craterau crater
crater folcanig *eg* crateri folcanig volcanic crater
crau *eg* creuau socket
crau (twll mewn nodwydd etc) *eg* creuau eye
crau glenoid *eg* creuau glenoid glenoid cavity
crau morthwyl *eg* creuau morthwylion eye of hammer
crau nodwydd *eg* creuau nodwyddau eye of needle
crau'r llygad *eg* orbit
crawn *eg* pus
crawniad *eg* crawniadau abscess
creadigaeth *eb* creadigaethau creation
creadigaeth y dychymyg *eb* creadigaethau'r dychymyg figment of imagination
creadigol *ans* creative
creadigrwydd *eg* creativity
creawdwr *eg* creawdwyr creator
crebachiad *eg* atrophy
crebachu *be* shrink; contract; atrophy
cred bersonol *eb* credoau personol personal belief
cred Gristnogol *eb* Christian belief
cred mewn byd cyfiawn *eb* belief in a just world
credo *eb* credoau creed; belief
credu *be* believe
credyd *eg* credydau credit
credyd teulu *eg* family credit
Credyd Treth Teuluoedd sy'n Gweithio *eg* Working Families' Tax Credit
credyd uned *eg* credydau uned unit credit
credydwr *eg* credydwyr creditor
credydwr masnach *eg* credydwyr masnach trade creditor
crefas *eg* crefasau crevasse
crefydd *eb* crefyddau religion
crefyddau'r Dwyrain *ell* Eastern religions
crefyddau'r Gorllewin *ell* Western religions
crefyddol *ans* religious
crefyddoldeb *eg* religiosity
crefft *eb* crefftau craft; trade
crefft adeiladu *eb* construction craft
crefft cadw tŷ *eb* housewifery
crefft cadw tŷ *eb* housecraft
Crefft Dylunio a Thechnoleg (CDT) Craft Design Technology
crefft ffabrig *eb* crefftau ffabrig fabric craft
crefft llwyfan *eb* stagecraft
crefft llyfrau *eb* book craft
crefft magu plant *eb* parentcraft
crefft nodwydd *eb* needlecraft
crefft y fam *eb* mothercraft
crefft ysgrifennu *eb* penmanship
crefftwaith creadigol *eg* creative craftwork
crefftwr *eg* crefftwyr craftsman; craftworker; artisan
crefftwr lled-fedrus *eg* crefftwyr lled fedrus semi-skilled craftsman
crefftwr medrus *eg* crefftwyr medrus skilled craftsman
crefftwriaeth *eb* craftsmanship
cregynnog *ans* shelly
creicaen *eb* creicaenau mantle rock; regolith
creigiau â glo *ell* coal-bearing rocks
creigiau dal olew *ell* oil-bearing rocks
creigiau gwaddod *ell* sedimentary rocks
creigiau llorhaenol *ell* level bedded rocks

creigiau plwtonig *ell* plutonic rocks
creigres *eb* creigresi reef
creigwaith *eg* rustification
► **creigwely** *eg* creigwelyau bedrock
creigwely gwaelodol *eg* creigwelyau gwaelodol underlying bedrock
creirfa *eb* creirfâu reliquary
creirfa *eb* creirfâu shrine
creision tatws *ell* crisps
creision ŷd *ell* cornflakes
creisionllyd *ans* crunchy
creithio gwŷdd *be* loom darning
crempog *eb* crempogau crêpe
Creol *eg* Creoliaid Creole
creon *eg* creonau crayon
creon cwyr *eg* creonau cwyr wax crayon
creon di-staen *eg* creonau di-staen non-smudge crayon
creon mâl *eg* creonau mâl grated crayon
creon olew *eg* creonau olew oil crayon
crêp *eg* crêpe
crêpe de chine *eg* crêpe de chine
Creta *eb* Crete
cretasig *ans* cretaceous
cretinedd *eg* cretinism
creu *be* create
creu adran newydd *be* create new section
creu allwedd gynradd *be* create primary key
creu arddull *be* create style
creu awtogrynodeb *be* create autoabstract
creu copi wrth gefn *be* create back-up
creu credyd *be* credit creation
creu crynodeb *be* create summary
creu cyfeiriadur *be* create directory
creu cyfeiriadur targed *be* create target directory
creu cymeriadau *be* create characters
creu cyswllt *be* create link
creu dawns *be* make a dance
creu dogfen *be* create document
creu ffeil *be* file creation
creu ffolder newydd *be* create new folder
creu ffurflen *be* create form
creu grŵp *be* create group
creu gwrthrych allwthiad *be* create extrusion object
creu gwrthrych troi *be* create rotation object
creu meistrddogfen *be* create master document
creu o ffeil *be* create from file
creu parhaus *be* continuous creation
creu rheolydd *be* create control
creu tabl *be* create table
creu tabl databeilot *be* create datapilot table
creu templed *be* create template
creu templed newydd *be* create new template
creu tudalen deitl *be* create title page
creu'n fyrfyfyr *be* improvisation
creuan *eb* creuanau cranium
creuanol *ans* cranial
creuol *ans* orbital
crib (aderyn) *eg/b* cribau crest
crib (ar do, ar fynydd) *eg/b* cribau ridge; arête
crib (i drin gwallt) *eg/b* cribau comb
crib (telyn) *eg/b* cribau neck
crib ddeltoid *eb* cribau deltoid deltoid ridge
crib farmori *eb* cribau marmori marbling comb
crib genhedlol *eb* cribau cenhedlol germinal ridge
crib graenio *eb* cribau graenio graining comb
crib telyn *eb* cribau telynau comb of harp
cribddeiliaeth *eb* extortion
cribddeilio *be* extort
cribddeiliwr *eg* cribddeilwyr extorter
cribell *eb* cribellau fret; traste
cribell glwm *eb* cribellau clwm tied fret
cribell goludd *eb* cribellau coludd gut fret
cribell osod *eb* cribellau gosod fixed fret
cribellog *ans* fretted
cribin *eg/b* cribinau rake
cribin dagell *eb* cribiniau tagell gill raker
cribinio *be* rake
cribo (gwallt) *be* comb
cribo (ffibrau) *be* card
cribo gwlân *be* tease
cribo past *be* paste combing
cribwr *eg* cribwyr carder; teaser
criced *eg* cricket
cricedwr *eg* cricedwyr cricketer
crimog *eb* crimogau shin
crimpen frandi *eb* crimp brandi brandy snap
crimpio *be* crimp
Crimplene *eg* Crimplene
cris *eg* crisiau crease
cris batio *eg* crisiau batio batting crease; popping crease
cris bowlio *eg* crisiau bowlio bowling crease
cris ochrol *eg* crisiau ochrol return crease
Crist *eg* Christ
crista *eg* cristâu crista
cristabolit *eg* crystabolite
Cristion *eg* Cristnogion Christian
Cristnogaeth *eb* Christianity
Cristnogol *ans* Christian
critigol *ans* critical
crocbren *eg* crocbrennau scaffold
crochendy *eg* crochendai pottery
crochenwaith *eg* pottery; ware
crochenwaith agat *eg* agate ware
crochenwaith basalt *eg* basalt ware
crochenwaith caled *eg* stoneware
crochenwaith Delft *eg* Delft ware
crochenwaith gloywedd *eg* lustre pottery
crochenwaith heb ei danio *eg* green ware
crochenwaith Kamares *eg* Kamares ware
crochenwaith pinsiad *eg* pinch pottery
crochenwaith slab *eg* slab pottery

crochenwaith slip *eg* slip ware
crochenydd *eg* crochenwyr potter
croen (anifail i'w drin) *eg* crwyn hide
croen (yn gyffredinol) *eg* crwyn skin
croen dafad *eg* crwyn defaid sheepskin
croen gŵydd *eg* goose pimples
croen myn *eg* crwyn myn kid
croenol *ans* cutaneous
croenol *ans* dermal
croes *ans* contravening
croes (delw'r groes gyda'r Iesu arni) *eb* croesau crucifix
croes (yn gyffredinol) *eb* croesau cross
croes Geltaidd *eb* croesau Celtaidd Celtic cross
Croes Goch, Y Groes Goch *eb* Red Cross, The
croesacen *eb* croesacenion cross-accent
croesawydd *eg* croesawyr receptionist
croesbylu *be* cross-fade
croesbylu o'r brig *be* cross-fade from top
croesbylu o'r chwith *be* cross-fade from left
croesbylu o'r dde *be* cross-fade from right
croesbylu o'r gwaelod *be* cross-fade from bottom
croesedig *ans* decussate
croesfa *eb* croesfâu transept
croesfan *eb* croesfannau crossing
croesfan gerddwyr *eb* croesfannau cerddwyr pedestrian crossing
croesfan wastad *eb* croesfannau gwastad level crossing
croesfar *eg* croesfarrau crossbar
croesfridio *be* cross-breeding
croesfur *eg* croesfuriau cross wall
croesffeilio *be* cross-filing
croesffurf *ans* cruciform
croesgad *eb* croesgadau crusade
Croesgad y Plant *eb* Children's Crusade
Croesgad yn erbyn yr Albigensiaid *eb* Albigensian Crusade
croesgornel *ans* diagonal
croesgornel sgwariog *ans* checkered diagonal
croeshilio *be* miscegenation
croeshoeliad *eg* crucifixion
croesi *be* cross
croesiad *eg* croesiadau transit; cross
croesi'r bont *be* make the transition
croesi'r llinell *be* cross the line
croesi'r llinell gôl *be* cross the goal line
croeslin (ar gyfrifiadur) *eb* croeslinau cross-hair
croeslin (yn gyffredinol) *eb* croeslinau diagonal
▸ **croeslinellu** *be* cross hatching
croeslinol *ans* diagonal
Croesoswallt *eb* Oswestry
croesresog *ans* cross-striated
croesrym *eg* croesrymoedd shearing force; shearforce
croesryw *ans* hybrid
croesryw *eg* croesrywiau hybrid
croesryw impiedig *eg* croesrywiau impiedig graft hybrid
croesrywedd *eg* hybridisation
croestoriad *eg* croestoriadau intersection
croestoriad setiau *eg* intersection of sets
croestoriad uchafwerth *eg* croestoriadau uchafwerth peak value intersection
croestorri *be* intersect
croeswasgiad *eg* croeswasgiadau shear
croeswasgu *be* shear
croeswifrau *ell* cross wires
croesymgroes *eg* criss-cross
crofen *eb* crofennau bacon rind
crofennu *be* case hardening
crofft *eg* crofftau croft
crofftwr *eg* crofftwyr crofter
crog *ans* hanging; suspended; pendant
crog *eb* crogau rood
crogfaen *eg* crogfeini perched block
crogfur *eg* crogfuriau hanging wall
crogi *be* hang
crogi, diberfeddu a phedrannu hang, draw and quarter
crogiant *eg* crogiannau suspension
croglen *eb* croglenni rood screen
croglin ddwbl *eb* crogliniau dwbl bifilar suspension
croglofft *eb* croglofftydd rood loft
croglofft *eb* croglofftydd pulpitum
croglun *eg* crogluniau wall hanging
crognant *eb* crognentydd hanging valley
crom *ans* curved
crôm *eg* chrome
cromatid *eg* cromatidau chromatid
cromatig *ans* chromatic
cromatin *eg* chromatin
cromatograffaeth *eb* chromatography
cromatograffaeth ddosrannol *eb* partition chromatography
cromatograffaeth haen-denau *eb* thin-layer chromatography
cromatograffaeth hylif nwy *eb* gas-liquid chromatography
cromatograffig *ans* chromatographic
cromatyddiaeth *eb* chromaticism
cromeiddio *be* chromising
cromen *eb* cromenni dome
cromen folcanig *eb* cromenni folcanig volcanic dome
cromennog *ans* domed
cromennu *be* dome
cromfach *eg* cromfachau bracket
cromfachau *ell* parentheses ( )
cromfan *eb* cromfannau apse
cromfannol *ans* apsidal
cromgell *eb* cromgelloedd vault
cromiwm (Cr) *eg* chromium
cromiwm(III) ocsid *eg* chromium(III) oxide

cromiwm(III) potasiwm sylffad(VI)-12-dŵr *eg* chromium(III) potassium sulfate(VI)-12-water
cromiwm(VI) deuclorid deuocsid *eg* chromium(VI) dichloride dioxide
cromiwm(VI) ocsid *eg* chromium(VI) oxide
cromlin *eb* cromliniau curve
cromlin Agnesi *eb* witch of Agnesi
cromlin allanol bwa *eb* cromliniau allanol bwa extrados of an arch
cromlin amgrwm *eb* cromliniau amgrwm convex curve
cromlin amlder cronnus *eb* cromliniau amlder cronnus cumulative frequency curve
cromlin barabolig *eb* cromliniau parabolig parabolic curve
cromlin Bezier *eb* Bezier curve
cromlin cymhareb gyson *eb* constant ratio curve
cromlin debygolrwydd *eb* cromliniau tebygolrwydd probability curve
cromlin dyfiant *eb* growth curve
cromlin ddaduniad *eb* dissociation curve
cromlin ddaduniad ocsigen-haemoglobin *eb* oxygen-haemoglobin dissociation curve
cromlin ddi-dor *eb* cromliniau di-dor continuous curve
cromlin ddisgynnol *eb* cromliniau disgynnol downward sloping curve
cromlin ddosraniad *eb* distribution curve
cromlin esgynnol *eb* cromliniau esgynnol upward sloping curve
cromlin fewnol bwa *eb* cromliniau mewnol bwâu intrados of an arch
cromlin galw *eb* cromliniau galw demand curve
cromlin galw marchnad *eb* market demand curve
cromlin galw unigol *eb* individual demand curve
cromlin gawstig *eb* cromliniau cawstig caustic curve
cromlin geugrwm *eb* cromliniau ceugrwm concave curve
cromlin groestoriad *eb* cromliniau croestoriad curve of intersection
cromlin gydbwysedd ocsigen-haemoglobin *eb* oxygen-haemoglobin equilibrium curve
cromlin gyfannol driphlyg *eb* cromliniau cyfannol triphlyg triple curve integral
cromlin gyfansawdd *eb* cromliniau cyfansawdd compound curve
cromlin gyflenwad *eb* supply curve
cromlin gyseinio *eb* resonance curve
cromlin Laffer *eb* Laffer curve
cromlin lawrydd *eb* cromliniau llawrydd freehand curve
cromlin lefn *eb* cromliniau llyfn smooth curve
cromlin lefn ddi-dor *eb* cromliniau llyfn di-dor continuous smooth curve
cromlin nodweddiadol *eb* cromliniau nodweddiadol characteristic curve
cromlin normal *eb* cromliniau normal normal curve
cromlin posibilrwydd cynhyrchu *eb* production possibility curve
cromlin Phillips *eb* Phillips curve
cromlin raddol *eb* cromliniau graddol gentle curve
cromlin rydd *eb* cromliniau rhydd free curve
cromlin rydd ddi-dor *eb* cromliniau rhydd di-dor continuous free curve
cromlin rhent cynnig *eb* cromliniau rhent cynnig bid-rent curve
cromlin ymateb *eb* response curve
cromliniau cylchoidol *ell* cycloidal curves
cromliniau diwahaniaeth *ell* indifference curves
cromlinog *ans* curvilinear
cromoffor *eg* chromophore
cromomer *eg* cromomerau chromomer
cromosffer *eg* cromosfferau chromosphere
cromosom *eg* cromosomau chromosome
cromosom enfawr *eg* cromosomau enfawr giant chromosome
cromosom o du'r fam *eg* cromosomau o du'r fam maternal chromosome
cromosom o du'r tad *eg* cromosomau o du'r tad paternal chromosome
cromosom rhyw *eg* cromosomau rhyw sex chromosome
cromosom X *eg* X chromosome
cromosom Y *eg* Y chromosome
cromosomaidd *ans* chromosomal
cronedd hidlo *eb* filter accumulation
cronfa (o arian) *eb* cronfeydd fund
cronfa (o bethau i'w rhannu) *eb* cronfeydd pool
cronfa (o ddŵr) *eb* cronfeydd reservoir
cronfa ad-dalu *eb* cronfeydd ad-dalu sinking fund
Cronfa Ariannol Ryngwladol *eb* International Monetary Fund
cronfa banc *eb* cronfeydd banciau bank reserve
cronfa ddata *eb* cronfeydd data database
cronfa ddata Access *eb* cronfeydd data Access Access database
cronfa ddata berthynol *eb* cronfeydd data perthynol relational database
cronfa ddata cofnod-strwythuredig *eb* cronfeydd data cofnod-strwythuredig record-structured database
cronfa ddata ganghennog *eb* cronfeydd data canghennog branching database
cronfa ddata gyfredol *eb* cronfeydd data cyfredol current database
cronfa ddata hierarchaidd *eb* cronfeydd data hierarchaidd hierarchical database
cronfa ddata newydd *eb* cronfeydd data newydd new database
cronfa ddŵr *eb* cronfeydd dŵr reservoir
cronfa eitemau *eb* cronfeydd eitemau item bank
cronfa gwestiynau *eb* cronfeydd cwestiynau question bank
cronfa olew *eb* cronfeydd olew oil reservoir
Cronfa Ryngwladol Plant y Cenhedloedd Unedig *eb* United Nations International Children's Fund
cronfa sylwadau *eb* cronfeydd sylwadau comment bank

cronfa wrth gefn *eb* cronfeydd wrth gefn reserves
cronfa wybodaeth *eb* cronfeydd gwybodaeth knowledge base
cronfa ysgol *eb* cronfeydd ysgol school fund
croniad *eg* croniadau accumulation
croniad eira *eg* alimentation
croniadur *eg* croniaduron accumulator
croniant *eg* croniannau accretion
Croniclau'r Eingl-Sacsoniaid *ell* Anglo-Saxon Chronicles
cronig *ans* chronic
cronlyn *eg* cronlynnoedd dammed lake
cronlyn marian *eg* cronlynnoedd marian moraine dammed lake
cronnedd cyfalaf *eg* capital accumulation
cronni (=hel) *be* accumulate
cronni (dŵr) *be* dam
cronnol *ans* accumulative
cronnus *ans* cumulative
cronoleg *eb* chronology
cronoleg rewlifol *eb* glacial chronology
cronoleg treuliant *eb* denudation chronology
cronolegol *ans* chronological
cropian *be* crawl
croquette *eb* croquettes croquette
crosiet *eg* crosietau crotchet
crosio *be* crochet
crotalau *ell* crotales
croth *eb* crothau womb; uterus
croth y goes *eb* calf; gastrocnemius
crothell *eb* crethyll stickleback
crothol *ans* uterine
crouton *eg* croutons crouton
croyw (am siarad) *ans* articulate
crud *eg* crudiau cradle;cot
crud cynnal *eg* crudiau cynnal incubator
crud V *eg* cradle V
crudgen *eg* cradle cap
crudiad *eg* crudiadau cradling
crudo *be* cradle
crug *eg* crugiau barrow
crugiad *eg* crugiadau conglomeration
crwban *eg* crwbanod turtle
crwban llawr *eg* crwbanod llawr floor turtle
crwban sgrin *eg* crwbanod sgrin screen turtle
crwcddarn *eg* crwcddarnau bit
crwm *ans* curved
crwmgorn *eg* crwmgyrn crum horn
crwn *ans* round; circular; globular
crwner *eg* crwneriaid coroner
crwnod *eg* crwnodau crunode
Crwsâd Jarrow *eg* Jarrow Crusade
crwsibl *eg* crwsiblau crucible
crwsibl silicon *eg* crwsiblau silicon silicon crucible
crwst *eg* croute
crwst haenog *eg* flaky pastry
crwth *eg* crythau crwth; crowd
crwybro *be* honeycombing
crwybrog *ans* honeycombed
crwydraeth *eb* vagrancy
crwydraeth *eb* vagabondage
crwydro *be* wander
crwydryn *eg* crwydriaid vagabond; vagrant
crych (ar ddŵr) *eg* crychau ripple
crych (mewn defnydd) *eg* crychau crease; wrinkle
crych (mewn gwaith llaw) *eg* crychau gather
crychau nodwydd *eg* stroked gathers
crychdir *eg* crychdiroedd warpland
crychdon *eb* crychdonnau ripple
crychdonni *be* ripple
crychdynnu *be* gather
crychdynnu â pheiriant *be* machine gather
crychell *eb* crychellau gatherer
crychguriad *eg* crychguriadau palpitation
crychiad (ar y tir) *eg* crychiadau warp
crychiad (mewn gwaith llaw) *eg* crychiadau gathering
crychiad i fyny *eg* crychiadau i fyny upwarp
crychiad i lawr *eg* crychiadau i lawr downwarp
crychu (=gwneud smocwaith) *be* smock
crychu (yn gyffredinol) *be* crease; wrinkle; crinkle
cryf (am sain) *ans* loud
cryf (yn gyffredinol) *ans* strong
cryfder (sain) *eg* loudness
cryfder (yn gyffredinol) *eg* cryfderau strength
cryfder asid *eg* acid strength
cryfder bas *eg* base strength
cryfder bond *eg* bond strength
cryfder croeswasgiad *eg* shear strength
cryfder cyhyrau *eg* muscular strength
cryfder cyson *eg* cryfderau cyson uniform strength
cryfder maes *eg* field strength
cryfder mwyaf *eg* maximum strength
cryfder tynnol *eg* tensile strength
cryfhau *be* strengthen
cryfhau'r corff *be* strengthen the body
cryfhawr *eg* cryfhawyr slip
cryman *eg* crymannau sickle
cryman creuog *eg* crymanau creuog socketed sickle
crymbl ffrwythau *eg* crymblau ffrwythau fruit crumble
crymedd *eg* crymeddau curvature
crymedd cychwynnol *eg* crymeddau cychwynnol initial curvature
crymu *be* curve; bow; rounding
cryndafodi *be* flutter tonguing
cryndod *eg* cryndodau tremor
crynhoad *eg* crynoadau compilation
crynhoi (=adrodd yn fyr) *be* abstract
crynhoi (=casglu) *be* compile
crynhoydd *eg* crynoyddion compiler
crynhoydd optimeiddio *eg* crynoyddion optimeiddio optimizing compiler

cryno *ans* concise; brief; compact
crynodeb *eg/b* crynodebau summary; synopsis; abstract
crynodeb elw *eg* profit summary
crynodeb (o) ffilm *eg* film synopsis
crynodedig *ans* concentrated
crynoder *eg* compactness
crynodi *be* concentrate
crynodiad *eg* crynodiadau concentration
crynodiad cychwynnol *eg* initial concentration
crynodiad diffiniedig *eg* crynodiadau diffiniedig known concentration
crynodiad ecwilibriwm *eg* equilibrium concentration
crynodiadur *eg* crynodiaduron compactor
crynrwydd *eg* roundness
crynswth *eg* gross; totality
crynswth arian am docynnau *eg* gross box office takings
crynu *be* shiver
Crynwr *eg* Crynwyr Quaker
Crynwriaeth *eb* Quakerism
cryoffil *eg* cryophil
cryoffilig *ans* cryophilic
cryogeneg *eb* cryogenics
cryolit *eg* cryolite
cryosgopi *eg* cryoscopy
cryptau Lieberkuhn *ell* crypts of Lieberkuhn
cryptig *ans* cryptic
cryptoffyt *eg* cryptoffytau cryptophyte
crypton (Kr) *eg* krypton
crys *eg* crysau shirt
crys chwys *eg* crysau chwys sweatshirt
crys nos *eg* crysau nos nightshirt
crys pêl-droed *eg* crysau pêl-droed soccer shirt
crys rygbi *eg* crysau rygbi rugby shirt
crys T *eg* crysau T T-shirt
crysau brown *ell* brownshirts
crysau duon *eg* blackshirts
crysbais *eb* surcoat
crythor *eg* crythorion crwth player
cudyn *eg* cudynnau tuft
cudynnog *ans* tufted
cudd (=anweledig) *ans* invisible
cudd (=cyfrinachol) *ans* secret
cudd (=heb ei amlygu eto) *ans* latent
cudd (am heddlu etc) *ans* undercover
cudd (yn gyffredinol) *ans* hidden; concealed
cuddfan *eb* cuddfannau hide
cuddio *be* hide; disguise; mask; conceal
cuddio amlinell gwaith ffont *be* hide fontwork outline
cuddio awtohidlydd *be* hide autofilter
cuddio ceinciau *be* knot; knotting
cuddio colofn *be* hide column
cuddio dalen *be* hide sheet
cuddio fformiwla *be* hide formula
cuddio gwallau *be* hide errors
cuddio isbwyntiau *be* hide subpoints
cuddio llun *be* hide picture
cuddio maes *be* hide field
cuddio nodyn *be* hide note
cuddio popeth *be* hide all
cuddio pwnc *be* hide subject
cuddio rhesi *be* hide rows
cuddio trywydd *be* hide thread
cuddio wrth argraffu *be* hide when printing
cuddio'r awdur *be* hide author
cuddiwr ceinciau *eg* cuddwyr ceinciau knotting
cuddiwr ceinciau sielac *eg* shellac knotting
cuddliw *eg* cuddliwiau camouflage
cuddliwio *be* camouflage
cuddni *eg* latency
cufydd *eg* cufyddau cubit
cul *ans* narrow
culdir *eg* culdiroedd isthmus
cul-ddeiliog *ans* narrow leaved
culfa *eb* culfeydd narrows
culfan *eg/b* culfannau stricture
culfor *eg* culforoedd strait
culhad *eg* culhadau shrinkage
culhau (a lleihau) *be* shrink
culhau (a thynhau) *be* constrict
culhau (yn gyffredinol) *be* narrow
culhau'r ongl *be* narrowing the angle
culni *eg* narrowness
cummerbund *eg* cummerbund
cur pen *eg* headache
curchatofiwm (Kh) *eg* khurchatovium
curiad (y galon) *eg* curiadau pulse
curiad (cerddorol) *eg* curiadau beat
curiad calon *eg* heartbeat
curiad cloc *eg* curiadau cloc clock pulse
curiad cyson *eg* curiadau cyson steady beat
curiad i fyny *eg* upbeat
curiad i lawr *eg* curiadau i lawr downbeat
curiad stond *eg* curiadau stond deadbeat
curiad strôb *eg* curiadau strôb strobe pulse
curiadau'r don gario *ell* carrier pulse train
curiwm (Cm) *eg* curium
curo (hoelen) *be* drive
curo (drwm etc) *be* beat
curo (am boen etc) *be* throb
curo amser *be* beating time
curo dwylo *be* clap hands
curo dwylo partner *be* clap partner's hands
curriculum vitae *eg* curriculum vitae
curwr *eg* curwyr beater
curwr metel *eg* curwyr metel metal beater
cusan adfer *eb* kiss of life
cwadrad *eg* cwadradau quadrat
cwadrat *eg* cwadratau quadrate
cwadratig *ans* quadratic
cwadriceps *eg* quadriceps

cwadril *eg* cwadriliau quadrille
cwafer *eg* cwaferau quaver
cwango *eg* cwangos quango
cwanteiddiad *eg* quantization
cwanteiddiedig *ans* quantized
cwanteiddio *be* quantize
cwantwm *eg* cwanta quantum
cwarantin *eg* quarantine
cwarc *eg* cwarciau quark
cwarel *eg* cwarelau pane
cwartig *ans* quartic
cwarto *eg* quarto
cwarts *eg* cwartsiau quartz
cwartsit *eg* quartzite
cwasi-faes *eg* cwasi-feysydd quasi-field
cwasi-grŵp *eg* cwasi-grwpiau quasi-group
cwasistatig *ans* quasistatic
cwaternaidd *ans* quaternary
cwaternion *eg* quaternion
cwbl seliedig *ans* hermetically sealed
cwblhau *be* complete
cwblhau geiriau awtomatig *be* automatic word completion
cwblhau'r sgwâr *be* complete the square
cwci *eg* cwcis cookie
cwch sianel *eg* cychod sianel cross-channel boat
▸ **cwd amniotig** *eg* amniotic sac
cwd melynwy *eg* cydau melynwy yolk sac
cwest *eg* cwestau inquest
cwest crwner *eg* coroner's inquest
cwestiwn *eg* cwestiynau question
cwestiwn agored *eg* cwestiynau agored open question
cwestiwn ateb byr *eg* cwestiynau ateb byr short-answer question
cwestiwn caeedig *eg* cwestiynau caeedig closed question
cwestiwn cydgyfeiriol *eg* cwestiynau cydgyfeiriol convergent question
cwestiwn dargyfeiriol *eg* cwestiynau dargyfeiriol divergent question
cwestiwn dewis lluosog *eg* cwestiynau dewis lluosog multiple-choice question
cwestiwn gwrthrychol *eg* cwestiynau gwrthrychol objective question
cwestiwn i ddenu diddordeb *eg* cwestiynau i ddenu diddordeb interest-getting question
cwestiwn marwol *eg* bloody question
cwestiwn penagored *eg* cwestiynau penagored free-response question
cwestiwn penagored *eg* cwestiynau penagored open-ended question
cwestiwn profi *eg* cwestiynau profi testing question
cwestiwn rhethregol *eg* cwestiynau rhethregol rhetorical question
cwestiwn strwythuredig *eg* cwestiynau strwythuredig structured question
cwestiwn tag *eg* cwestiynau tag tag question
Cwestiwn y Dwyrain *eg* Eastern Question
cwestiwn ymholi *eg* cwestiynau ymholi enquiry question
cwestiynau cyffredin *ell* frequently asked questions
cwestiyneb *eb* cwestiynebau interrogatory
cwestiynu *be* questioning
cwfeiniad *eg* cwfeiniaid conventual
cwfeiniol *ans* conventual
cwfl *eg* cyflau hood; cowl
cwfl pram *eg* cyflau pram pram hood
cwgn *eg* cygnau knuckle
cwgn *eg* cygnau node
cwgn deilen *eg* cygnau dail leaf node
cwgn gwreiddyn *eg* cygnau gwraidd root node
cwgn sain *eg* cygnau sain speaker key
cwilsen *eb* cwils quill
cwilsen lythrennu *eb* cwils llythrennu lettering quill
cwilt *eg* cwiltiau quilt
cwiltell *eb* cwiltellau quilter
cwiltio *be* quilting
cwiltio *be* quilt
cwiltio Cymreig *be* Welsh quilting
cwiltio Eidalaidd *be* Italian quilting
cwiltio Seisnig *be* English quilting
cwinin *eg* quinine
cwir *eg* cwiroedd quire
cwirc *eg* cwirciau quirk
cwis *eg* cwisiau quiz
cwlac *eg* cwlaciaid kulak
cwlwm *eg* clymau knot; tie; ligature
cwlwm agosrwydd *eg* bond
cwlwm canolwr *eg* alpine butterfly
cwlwm canolwr *eg* middleman's knot
Cwlwm Cydweithred *eg* Bond of Association
cwlwm dolen *eg* clymau dolen bow knot
cwlwm Ffrengig *eg* clymau Ffrengig French knot
cwlwm glyn *eg* clymau glyn clove hitch
cwlwm gwasg *eg* clymau gwasg waist tie
cwlwm pysgotwr *eg* clymau pysgotwr fisherman's joining knot
cwlwm tros law *eg* clymau tros law overhand knot
cwlltwr *eg* cylltyrau coulter
cwm *eg* cymoedd cirque; cwm
cwmgraig *eb* cwmgreigiau coombe rock
cwmni *eg* cwmnïau company; firm
cwmni amlwladol *eg* cwmnïau amlwladol multinational company
cwmni annibynnol *eg* cwmnïau annibynnol independent company
Cwmni Cathay *eg* Cathay Company
cwmni cydgyfalaf *eg* cwmnïau cydgyfalaf joint stock company
cwmni cyfyngedig (cyf.) *eg* cwmnïau cyfyngedig limited company
cwmni cyfyngedig trwy warant *eg* cwmnïau cyfyngedig trwy warant company limited by guarantee

cwmni datblygu *eg* cwmnïau datblygu development company
cwmni hedfan *eg* cwmnïau hedfan airline
cwmni hur *eg* cwmnïau hur free company
Cwmni India'r Dwyrain *eg* East India Company
cwmni tyrpeg *eg* cwmnïau tyrpeg turnpike company
cwmni unol *eg* cwmnïau unol united company
cwmnïau'r cyfryngau *ell* media companies
Cwmni'r Lefant *eg* Levant Company
cwmpas *eg* cwmpasau compass
cwmpas *eg* cwmpasau scope
cwmpas *eg* girth
cwmpas (=uchafswm pellter teithio) *eg* range
cwmpas adeiniog *eg* cwmpasau adeiniog wing compass
cwmpas lleisiol *eg* vocal range
cwmpas lleisiol cyfyngedig *eg* limited vocal range
cwmpas mesur *eg* cwmpasau mesur dividers
cwmpas sbring *eg* cwmpasau sbring spring dividers
▶ **cwmpasu** *be* encompass
cwmpawd *eg* cwmpawdau compass
cwmpawd gyro *eg* cwmpawdau gyro gyro compass
cwmpawd prismatig *eg* cwmpawdau prismatig prismatic compass
cwmplin *eg* compline
cwmwd *eg* cymydau commote
cwmwl *eg* cymylau cloud
cwmwl electronau *eg* cymylau electronau electron cloud
cwmwl gwynias *eg* cymylau gwynias incandescent cloud
cwmwl symudliw *eg* cymylau symudliw mother of pearl cloud
cwmwl symudliw *eg* cymylau symudliw nacreous cloud
cwmwl tyrog *eg* cymylau tyrog towering cloud
cwmwlonimbws *eg* cumulonimbus
cwmwlws *eg* cumulus
cwndid *eg* cwndidau conduit
cwningar *eg* cwningaroedd warren
cwnna *be* on heat
Cwnsler Dysgedig yn y Gyfraith *eg* Counsel Learned in the Law
cwnstabl *eg* cwnstabliaid constable
cworwm *eg* cworymau quorum
cwota *eg* cwotâu quota
cwpan (mewn bioleg) *eg* cwpanau capsule
cwpan Bowman *eg* Bowman's capsule
cwpan Glisson *eg* Glisson's capsule
cwpan mewnol *eg* internal capsule
cwpan sgriw *eg* cwpanau sgriw screw cup
cwpan wy *eg* cwpanau wy egg cup
Cwpan y Byd *eg* World Cup
cwpan y glust *eg* auditory capsule
cwpan ymledu *eg* cwpanau ymledu runner cup
cwpanaid *eg/b* cwpaneidiau cupful
cwpanu *be* cupping
cwpl *eg* cyplau truss; couple
cwpl brenhinbost *eg* cyplau brenhinbost king post roof truss
cwpl bwaog *eg* cyplau bwaog bow-stringed truss
cwpl cleddog *eg* cyplau cleddog braced truss
cwpl cyffredin *eg* cyplau cyffredin ordinary truss
cwpl talcen *eg* cyplau talcen hip roof rafter
cwpl to *eg* cyplau to roof truss
cwpled *eg* cwpledi couplet
cwplws *eg* cyplysau chevron
cwpola *eg* cwpolau cupola
cwpon *eg* cwponau coupon
cwpwla *eg* cupula
cwpwrdd caledu *eg* cypyrddau caledu airing cupboard
cwpwrdd *eg* cypyrddau cupboard
cwpwrdd crasu dillad *eg* cypyrddau crasu dillad airing cupboard
cwpwrdd gosod *eg* built-in cupboard
cwpwrdd gwyntyllu *eg* cypyrddau gwyntyllu fume cupboard
cwpwrdd llyfrau *eg* cypyrddau llyfrau bookcase
cwpwrdd rhew *eg* cypyrddau rhew deep freeze cabinet
cwpwrdd rhew *eg* cypyrddau rhew freezer
cwpwrdd storio *eg* cypyrddau storio storage cupboard
cwpwrdd sychu *eg* cypyrddau sychu drying cabinet
cwr *eg* cyrion fringe
cwrcwd *eg* squat
cwrcwd *eg* crouch
cwrel *eg* cwrelau coral
cwrelaidd *ans* coralline
cwricwlaidd *ans* curricular
cwricwlwm *eg* cwricwla curriculum
cwricwlwm bugeiliol *eg* pastoral curriculum
cwricwlwm cenedlaethol *eg* national curriculum
cwricwlwm clasurol *eg* classical curriculum
cwricwlwm craidd *eg* core curriculum
cwricwlwm cudd *eg* hidden curriculum
cwricwlwm cyfannol *eg* integrated curriculum
cwricwlwm cyflawn *eg* whole curriculum
cwricwlwm cyfnod sylfaen *eg* foundation stage curriculum
cwricwlwm cyffredin *eg* common curriculum
cwricwlwm datblygiadol *eg* developmental curriculum
cwricwlwm gwahaniaethol *eg* differentiated curriculum
cwricwlwm sbiral *eg* spiral curriculum
cwricwlwm sylfaenol *eg* basic curriculum
cwrl *eg* cyrlau curl
cwrlid *eg* cwrlidau bedspread; coverlet
cwrlid plu *eg* cwrlidau plu eiderdown
cwrs *eg* cyrsiau course

cwrs amlgyfrwng *eg* cyrsiau amlgyfrwng multi-media course
cwrs atodol *eg* cyrsiau atodol subsidiary course; accessory course
cwrs blaenwyr *eg* cyrsiau blaenwyr forward rush
cwrs breiniol *eg* cyrsiau breiniol franchised course
cwrs carlam *eg* cyrsiau carlam crash course; accelerated course
cwrs cyfannol *eg* cyrsiau cyfannol integrated course
cwrs cyn-nyrsio *eg* prenursing course
cwrs drwy'r post *eg* cyrsiau drwy'r post correspondence course
cwrs dŵr *eg* cyrsiau dŵr water course
cwrs galwedigaethol y bar *eg* bar vocational course
cwrs gwrthleithder *eg* damp-proof course
cwrs hyfforddiant mewn swydd *eg* cyrsiau hyfforddiant mewn swydd in-service training course
cwrs modiwlaidd *eg* cyrsiau modiwlaidd modular course
cwrs mynediad *eg* cyrsiau mynediad access course
cwrs pontio *eg* cyrsiau pontio bridging course
cwrs sefydlu *eg* cyrsiau sefydlu induction course
cwrs sylfaen *eg* cyrsiau sylfaen foundation course
cwrs traed *eg* cyrsiau traed foot-rush
cwrs ymarfer cyffredinol *eg* cyrsiau ymarfer cyffredinol common practice course
cwrs ysgrifenyddol *eg* cyrsiau ysgrifenyddol secretarial course
cwrt *eg* cyrtiau court
Cwrt Anodau a Degawdau *eg* Court of First Fruits and Tenths
Cwrt Archwilwyr Cyffredinol *eg* Court of General Surveyors
cwrt bach *eg* petty sessions
cwrt barwn *eg* court-baron
cwrt bychan *eg* small court
cwrt cosbi *eg* cyrtiau cosbi penalty area
cwrt chwith *eg* cyrtiau chwith left court
cwrt de *eg* cyrtiau de right court
Cwrt Ecwiti *eg* Equity Court
Cwrt Eglwysig *eg* Christian Court
Cwrt Gward a Lifrai *eg* Court of Wards & Liveries
Cwrt Gwrandawiad *eg* Audience Court
cwrt lit *eg* court leet
cwrt llawn maint *eg* cyrtiau llawn maint full size court
Cwrt Mainc y Brenin *eg* Court of King's Bench
cwrt maint safonol *eg* cyrtiau maint safonol standard size court
Cwrt Marchnad *eg* Piepowder Court
cwrt mawr *eg* cyrtiau mawr large court
Cwrt Pledion Cyffredin *eg* Court of Common Pleas
Cwrt Siawnsri *eg* Court of Chancery
cwrt tangwystl *eg* cyrtiau tangwystl view of frankpledge
Cwrt y Bwâu *eg* Court of Arches
Cwrt y Deisyfion *eg* Court of Requests
cwrt y gôl *eg* cyrtiau'r goliau goal area
Cwrt y Siecr *eg* Court of Exchequer
Cwrt Ymrwymiadau *eg* Obligations Court
Cwrt yr Uchel Gomisiwn *eg* Court of High Commission
Cwrt yr Ychwanegiadau *eg* Augmentations Court
cwrtosis *eg* kurtosis
cwrw *eg* beer
cwsb *eg* cysbau cusp
cwsg *ans* dormant
cwsg symudiad llygaid cyflym *eg* rapid eye movement (REM) sleep
cwsg tonfedd araf *eg* slow-wave sleep
cwsmer *eg* cwsmeriaid customer
cwsmer anfodlon *eg* cwsmeriaid anfodlon unhappy customer
cwsmer masnach *eg* cwsmeriaid masnach trade customer
cwstard *eg* custard
cwstard wy *eg* egg custard
cwter *eb* cwteri gutter
cwtigl *eg* cwtiglau cuticle
cwtogi *be* reduce
cwtogi *be* shorten
cwymp (organ o'r corff etc) *eg* cwympiadau collapse
cwymp (y farchnad stoc etc) *eg* cwympiadau drop
cwymp (yn gyffredinol) *eg* cwympiadau fall
cwymp gwlithbwynt *eg* cwympoedd gwlithbwynt hydrolapse
cwymplen *eb* cwymplenni drop-down menu
cwympo (am organ o'r corff etc) *be* collapse
cwympo coed *be* felling
cwympol *ans* caducous
cwympo'r sgrym *be* collapse the scrum
cwyn *eb* cwynion complaint
cwyn *eg* cwynion grievance
cwyno *be* complain
cwynwr *eg* cwynwyr suitor
cwyr *eg* cwyrau wax
cwyr batic *eg* batik wax
cwyr carnawba *eg* carnauba wax
cwyr coll *eg* cire perdue
cwyr dodrefn *eg* furniture wax
cwyr gwenyn *eg* beeswax
cwyr microgrisialog *eg* micro-crystalline wax
cwyr modelu *eg* modelling wax
cwyr paraffîn *eg* paraffin wax
cwyr rhwbio *eg* heelball
cwyraidd *ans* waxy
cwyro *be* waxing
cwys *eb* cwysi furrow
cwysed *eb* cwysedi gusset
cyanid *eg* cyanide
cyanidin *eg* cyanidin
cyanogen *eg* cyanogen
cybydd-dod *eg* avarice
cybyddlyd *ans* avaricious

CYC: Corff Ymgynghorol Cenedlaethol ar gyfer Addysg Uwch yn y Sector Cyhoeddus *eg* NAB: National Advisory Body for Higher Education in the Public Sector
cychwyn (=cynau) *be* switch on
cychwyn (cyfrifiadur) *be* boot
cychwyn (proses) *be* initiate
cychwyn (rhyfel) *eg* outbreak
cychwyn (yn gyffredinol) *be* start
cychwyn achos *be* initiate proceedings
cychwyn cyflym *eg* sprint start
cychwyn dawns *eg* start of dance
cychwyn hypergyswllt *be* trigger hyperlink
cychwyn injan *be* turn on an engine
cychwynnol (am fusnesau) *ans* start-up
cychwynnol (am wasanaethau iechyd) *ans* primary
cychwynnol (yn gyffredinol) *ans* initial
cychwynnwr *eg* cychwynwyr starter
cychwynnwr cyflym *eg* cychwynwyr cyflym fast starter
cychwynnydd *eg* cychwynyddion initiator
cyd ac unigol joint and several
cydadwaith *be* interplay
cydadweithiol *ans* co-reactive
cydaddoli *be* corporate worship
cydaddoli crefyddol *be* religious worship
cydaddoliad *eg* corporate act of worship
cydaddoliad dyddiol *eg* daily collective worship
cydaddysg *eb* co-education
cydamrywiad *eg* cydamrywiadau joint variation
cydamrywiad *eg* cydamrywiadau covariance
cydamseredig *ans* synchronous
cydamseriad *eg* cydamseriadau synchronization
cydamserol *ans* concurrent
cydamserol *ans* simultaneous
cydamseru *be* synchronize
cydamserydd *eg* cydamseryddion synchronizer
cydanwythiad *eg* mutual induction
cydanwythiant *eg* mutual inductance
cydatebolrwydd *eg* joint liability
cydatebydd *eg* cydatebyddion co-respondent
cydberpendicwlar *ans* mutually perpendicular
cydberthyn *be* correlate
cydberthyn *be* interrelate
cydberthynas *eg/b* cydberthnasau interrelationship
cydberthynas ofodol *eb* cydberthnasau gofodol spatial relationship
cydberthynas rhwng pobl *eb* interpersonal relations
cydberthynas y gwledydd *eb* international relations
cydberthyniad *eg* correlate
cydberthyniad *eg* cydberthyniadau correlation
cydberthyniad gau *eg* illusory correlation
cydberthyniad moment lluoswm *eg* product moment correlation
cydberthyniad panel dros amser *eg* cross-lagged panel correlation
cydberthyniad rhannol *eg* partial correlation
cydberthyniad rhestrol *eg* rank correlation
cydberthynol *ans* correlate
cydbwyntiol *ans* copunctual
cydbwysedd *eg* cydbwyseddau balance; poise
cydbwysedd ansefydlog *eg* unstable equilibrium
cydbwysedd asid bas *eg* acid base balance
cydbwysedd cymuned *eg* balance of community
cydbwysedd da *eg* good balance
cydbwysedd egni *eg* energy balance
cydbwysedd genetig *eg* genetic equilibrium
cydbwysedd grym *eg* balance of power
cydbwysedd gwleidyddol *eg* political balance
cydbwysedd isostatig *eg* isostatic equilibrium
cydbwysedd natur *eg* balance of nature
cydbwysedd niwtral *eg* neutral equilibrium
cydbwysedd sefydlog *eg* stable equilibrium
cydbwysedd thermol *eg* thermal equilibrium
cydbwyso *be* balance
cydbwyso hafaliad *be* balance an equation
cydbwysol *ans* balancing
cyd-daro *be* coincide
cyd-derfynol *ans* coterminal
cyd-destun *eg* cyd-destunau context
cyd-destun anghyfarwydd *eg* cyd-destunau anghyfarwydd unfamiliar context
cyd-destun byd-eang *eg* world context
cyd-destun cenedlaethol *eg* national context
cyd-destun cyfarwydd *eg* familiar context
cyd-destun daearyddol *eg* geographical context
cyd-destun diwylliannol *eg* cyd-destunau diwylliannol cultural context
cyd-destun Ewropeaidd *eg* European context
cyd-destun gofodol *eg* spatial context
cyd-destun priodol *eg* appropriate setting
cyd-drafod *be* parley
cyd-drawol *ans* coincident
cyd-drechedd *eg* co-dominance
► **cyd-drechol** *ans* co-dominant
cyd-drechydd *eg* cyd-drechyddion co-dominant
cyd-drefniant *eg* coordination
cyd-drefnol *ans* coordinate
cyd-drefnu *be* coordinate
cyd-dreiddiad *eg* cyd-dreiddiadau interpenetration
cyd-dyriad *eg* cyd-dyriadau conglomeration
cyd-dyriad defnyddwyr *eg* consumer conglomerate
cyd-dyrru *be* conglomerate
cyd-ddant *eg* synchromesh
cyd-ddarpariaeth *eb* coordinated provision
cyd-ddibyniaeth *eb* interdependence
cyd-ddibyniaeth *eb* co-dependency
cyd-ddibynnol *ans* interdependent
cyd-ddinistriol *ans* internecine
cydensym *eg* cydensymau co-enzyme

cydfan *eg* cydfannau attachment
cydfan cyhyrau *eg* muscle attachment
cydfargeinio *be* collective bargaining
cydfwytäedd *eg* commensalism
cydfwytaol *ans* commensal
cyd-fyw heddychlon *be* peaceful co-existence
cydffederasiwn *eg* cydffederasiynau confederation
Cydffederasiwn Almaenig *eg* German Confederation
Cydffederasiwn Gogledd yr Almaen *eg* North German Confederation
Cydffederasiwn y Rhein *eg* Confederation of the Rhine
cydffocal *ans* confocal
cydffurf *ans* conformal
cydffurfiad *eg* cydffurfiadau conformation
cydffurfiad alldro *eg* cydffurfiadau alldro staggered conformation
cydffurfiad gorchuddiedig *eg* cydffurfiadau gorchuddiedig eclipsed conformation
cydffurfiadwy *ans* conformable
cydffurfiol *ans* conformational
cydgadwynedd *eg* concatenation
cydgadwyno *be* concatenate
cydganol *ans* concentric
cydgasglu *be* aggregate
cydgloi *be* interlock
cydglymu *be* colligate
cydgordiol *ans* concordant
cydgroesi *be* concur
cydgrynhoad *eg* agglomeration
cydgyfeiriant *eg* cydgyfeiriannau convergence
cydgyfeiriant o ran cymedr cwadratig *eg* convergence in quadratic mean
cydgyfeiriant o ran dosraniad *eg* convergence in distribution
cydgyfeiriant o ran tebygolrwydd *eg* convergence in probability
cydgyfeirio *be* converge
cydgyfeiriol *ans* convergent
cydgyferbyniol *ans* contralateral
cydgyfnewid *be* interchange
cydgyfnewidiol *ans* interchangeable
cydgylchfaol *ans* intrazonal
cydgylchol *ans* concyclic
cydgymuned (ecolegol) *eb* cydgymunedau association
cydgymuned blanhigion *eb* cydgymunedau planhigion plant association
cydgymysgedd *eg* cydgymysgeddau intermixture
cydgymysgiad *eg* intermix
cydgymysgu *be* intermix
cydgynllwynio *be* collusion
cydgysylltedd troadau fflwcs *eg* flux-turns interlinkage
cydgysylltiol *ans* interlinked
cydgysylltu *be* coordinate; interlink
cydgysylltwr *eg* cydgysylltwyr coordinator
cydgysylltydd blwyddyn *eg* cydgysylltwyr blwyddyn year coordinator
cydgysylltydd TG *eg* IT coordinator
cyd-hynafiad *eg* cyd-hynafiaid common ancestor
cydiad *eg* cydiadau junction; entry
cydiad pibell gangen *eg* cydiadau pibellau cangen branch pipe junction
cydiedig *ans* adjoined
cydio (wrth) *be* attach
cydio dwylo *be* holding hands
cydio yn (y ffiwg) *be* take up
cydiwr *eg* cydwyr clutch
cydiwr crafanc *eg* cydwyr crafanc claw clutch
cydiwr ffrithiant *eg* cydwyr ffrithiant friction clutch
cydleoliad pwyntiol *eg* point collocation
cydlif *eg* cydlifau consequent
cydlifiad *eg* cydlifiadau confluence
cydlifiad gohiriedig *eg* cydlifiadau gohiriedig deferred confluence
cydlinol *ans* co-linear
cydlyniad *eg* cydlyniadau cohesion
cydlyniad *eg* coherence; solidarity
cydlynol *ans* cohesive; coherent
cydlynrwydd *eg* cohesiveness
cydlynydd canolfan *eg* cydlynwyr canolfannau centre coordinator
cydlywodraeth *eb* cydlywodraethau condominium
cydnabod *be* recognize; acknowledge
cydnabyddiaeth *eb* recognition
cydnaid *eb* cydneidiau jump ball; throw-up
cydnaws *ans* compatible
cydnawsedd *eg* compatibility
cyd-newidyn *eg* cyd-newidynnau covariate
cydosod *be* assemble; set up
cydosodiad *eg* cydosodiadau assembly
cydosodiad differyn *eg* cydosodiadau differyn differential assembly
cydosodydd *eg* cydosodyddion assembler
cydraddoldeb (statws etc) *eg* parity
cydraddoldeb (yn gyffredinol) *eg* equality
cydran *eb* cydrannau component; resolute
cydran arholiad *eb* cydrannau arholiad examination component
cydran broffil *eb* cydrannau proffil profile component
cydran cyflymder *eb* cydrannau cyflymder component of velocity
cydran drydanol *eb* cydrannau trydanol electrical component
cydran electronig *eb* cydrannau electronig electronic component
cydran goll *eb* cydrannau coll missing component
cydran grym *eb* cydrannau grym component of a force
cydran gwerth gofal *eb* cydrannau gwerth gofal care value component
cydran gyffredin *eb* cydrannau cyffredin common component

cydran lithr *eb* cydrannau llithr sliding component
cydran modur *eb* cydrannau moduron automobile component
cydran wedi'i pheiriannu *eb* cydrannau wedi'u peiriannu machined component
cydran ychwanegol *eb* cydrannau ychwanegol additional component
cydraniad *eg* cydraniadau resolution
cydraniad isel *eg* low resolution
cydraniad lliw *eg* cydraniadau lliw colour resolution
cydraniad sgrin *eg* screen resolution
cydraniad uchel *ans* high resolution
cydrannau bwyd *ell* food components
cydrannol *ans* resolved
cydrannu *be* resolve
cydrannu amser *be* time-sharing
cydrannu enw parth *be* domain name resolution
cydrannu grym *be* resolve a force into components
cydrannu'n fertigol *be* resolve vertically
cydrannu'n llorweddol *be* resolve horizontally
cydredol *ans* concomitant
cydredwr *eg* cydredwyr runner
cydrennydd *eg* cydrenyddion resolvent
cydrifol *ans* aliquot
cydseiniol *ans* harmonious
cydsoddi *be* merge
cydsoddiad *eg* cydsoddiadau merger
cydsylweddiad *eg* consubstantiation
cydsymud *be* coordination
cydsymud llaw a llygad *be* hand-eye coordination
cydsyniad *eg* consent
cydsyniad gwybodus *eg* informed consent
Cydsyniad y Bobl *eg* Agreement of the People
cydwedd (am donnau) *ans* in-phase
cydwedd (yn gyffredinol) *ans* compatible
cydwedd *eb* cydweddau phase
cydweddiad *eg* cydweddiadau analogy
cydweddiad *eg* compatibility
cydweddiad *eg* assimilation
cydweddiadol *ans* analogical
cydweddog *eg/b* cydweddogion consort
cydweddol *ans* analogous
cydweddu *be* match; coordinate
cydweddu sampl *be* matching-to-sample
cydweddyn *eg* cydweddion coordinate
cydweithrediad *eg* cydweithrediadau cooperation
cydweithredol *ans* cooperative
cydweithredu *be* cooperate
cydweithredwr *eg* cydweithredwyr collaborator
cyd-wrthyriant electrostatig *eg* mutual electrostatic repulsion
cydwybod *eb* conscience
cydwybodolrwydd *eg* conscientiousness
cydymdeimlad *eg* sympathy
cydymdreiddio *be* interpenetrate
cydymddibyniaeth *eb* mutualism
cydymffurfiad *eg* conformity; compliance
cydymffurfio achlysurol *be* occasional conformity
cydymgeisio *be* rival
cydymgeisydd *eg* cydymgeiswyr rival
cyddwysedig *ans* condensed
cyddwysiad *eg* condensation
cyddwysiad interstitaidd *eg* interstitial condensation
cyddwyso *be* condense
cyddwysydd *eg* cyddwysyddion condenser
cyddwysydd adlifol *eg* cyddwysyddion adlifol reflux condenser
CYF newydd *eg* new DIR
cyfadran *eb* cyfadrannau faculty
cyfaddasrwydd *eg* suitability
cyfaddawd *eg* cyfaddawdau compromise
cyfaddawd Avranches *eg* compromise of Avranches
cyfaddefiad *eg* cyfaddefiadau confession
cyfaddefiad *eg* cyfaddefiadau admission
cyfagos *ans* neighbouring
cyfagos *ans* adjacent
cyfagosrwydd *eg* contiguity
cyfangiad *eg* cyfangiadau contraction
cyfangiad cyhyrol *eg* muscle contraction
cyfangiad cyhyrol isocinetig *eg* cyfangiadau cyhyrol isocinetig isokinetic muscle contraction
cyfangiad cyhyrol isometrig *eg* cyfangiadau cyhyrol isometrig isometric muscle contraction
cyfangol *eg* contractile
cyfangu *be* contract
cyfaint *eg* cyfeintiau volume
cyfaint anadlol *eg* vital capacity
cyfaint cyfnewid (yr ysgyfaint) *eg* tidal volume
cyfaint fentriglaidd *eg* ventricular volume
cyfaint mewnanadlol wrth gefn *eg* inspiratory reserve volume
cyfaint molar *eg* cyfeintiau molar molar volume
cyfaint solidau *eg* volume of solids
cyfaint ysgyfaint *eg* lung volume
cyfalaf *eg* capital
cyfalaf crynswth *eg* gross capital
cyfalaf cyfartalog *eg* average capital
cyfalaf cyfranddaliadau *eg* share capital
cyfalaf cylchredol *eg* circulating capital
cyfalaf dynol *eg* human capital
cyfalaf gweithio *eg* working capital
cyfalaf menter *eg* venture capital
cyfalaf net *eg* net capital
cyfalaf sefydlog *eg* fixed capital
cyfalaf ychwanegol *eg* additional capital
cyfalaf-ddwys *ans* capital intensive
cyfalafiaeth *eb* capitalism
cyfalafiaeth fasnach *eb* commercial capitalism
cyfalafiaeth wladol *eb* state capitalism
cyfalafol *ans* capitalist
cyfalafwr *eg* cyfalafwyr capitalist

cyfalaw *eb* cyfalawon countermelody
cyfamod *eg* cyfamodau covenant
cyfamserol *ans* concurrent
cyfan *ans* entire
cyfanbwynt *eg* cyfanbwyntiau attachment site
cyfandir *eg* cyfandiroedd continent
cyfandir Ewrop *eg* continental Europe
cyfandiroledd *eg* continentality
cyfaneddwr *eg* cyfaneddwyr settler
cyfanheddu *be* settle
cyfannedd *ans* inhabited
cyfannol *ans* holistic; integral; integrated
cyfannu *be* integrate; integration
cyfannu cymdeithas *be* integrate society
cyfannu graddfa eang *be* large scale integration
cyfannu graddfa eang iawn *be* very large scale integration
cyfannu graddfa ganolig *be* medium scale integration
cyfanred *eg* cyfanredau aggregate
cyfanredol *ans* aggregate
cyfanrif *eg* cyfanrifau integer
cyfanrif arwyddedig *eg* cyfanrifau arwyddedig signed integer
cyfanrif diarwydd *eg* cyfanrifau diarwydd unsigned integer
cyfanrwydd *eg* entirety; integrity
cyfansawdd *ans* composite; compound
cyfansoddi *be* compose
cyfansoddi dilyniannau *be* compose sequences
cyfansoddiad (=corff o egwyddorion) *eg* cyfansoddiadau constitution
cyfansoddiad (=gosodiad pethau ynghyd) *eg* cyfansoddiadau composition
cyfansoddiad bwyd *eg* food composition
cyfansoddiad dawns *eg* cyfansoddiadau dawns dance composition
cyfansoddiad gradd *eg* cyfansoddiadau gradd degree exercise
cyfansoddiad gwaed *eg* composition of blood
cyfansoddiad llawn dychymyg *eg* cyfansoddiadau llawn dychymyg imaginative composition
cyfansoddiad llinol *eg* cyfansoddiadau llinol linear composition
cyfansoddiad maethion *eg* nutritional composition
cyfansoddiad murol *eg* cyfansoddiadau murol mural composition
cyfansoddiad sefydlog *eg* fixed composition
cyfansoddiad sifil *eg* civil constitution
cyfansoddiadol (am gorff o egwyddorion) *ans* constitutional
cyfansoddiadol (am osodiad pethau ynghyd) *ans* compositional
cyfansoddiaeth *eb* constitutionalism
cyfansoddion organohalogen *ell* organohalogen compounds
cyfansoddwr *eg* cyfansoddwyr composer
cyfansoddyn (niwclews) *eg* cyfansoddion constituent
cyfansoddyn (yn gyfredinol) *eg* cyfansoddion compound
cyfansoddyn halogenaidd *eg* cyfansoddion halogenaidd halogeno-compound
cyfansoddyn isocyano *eg* cyfansoddion isocyano isocyano-compound
cyfansoddyn llathru *eg* cyfansoddion llathru polishing compound
cyfansoddyn modelu *eg* cyfansoddion modelu modelling compound
cyfansoddyn organig *eg* cyfansoddion organig organic compound
cyfansoddyn plwm(IV) *eg* cyfansoddion plwm(IV) lead(IV) compound
cyfansoddyn sylfaenol *ell* cyfansoddion sylfaenol basic constituent
cyfansoddyn titaniwm(III) *eg* cyfansoddion titaniwm(III) titanium(III) compound
cyfansoddyn titaniwm(IV) *eg* cyfansoddion titaniwm(IV) titanium(IV) compound
cyfansoddyn tun(IV) *eg* cyfansoddion tun(IV) tin(IV) compound
cyfanswm *eg* cyfansymiau total; amount; sum total
cyfanswm colofnau *eg* total columns
cyfanswm cost *eg* total cost
cyfanswm costau *eg* total costs
cyfanswm cronnus *eg* cyfansymiau cronnus cumulative total
cyfanswm cynnwys *eg* total contents
cyfanswm cynnyrch *eg* total output
cyfanswm derbyniadau *eg* total receipts
cyfanswm genynnol *eg* gene pool
cyfanswm refeniw *eg* total revenue
cyfanswm stwnsh *eg* cyfansymiau stwnsh hash total
cyfanswm taliadau *eb* total payments
cyfanswm tebygolrwydd *eg* total probability
cyfanwerth *eg* wholesale
cyfanwerthwr *eg* cyfanwerthwyr wholesaler
cyfar *eg* cover point
cyfarch *be* address
cyfarchiad *eg* cyfarchiadau annunciation
cyfarfod *be* meet
cyfarfod *eg* cyfarfodydd meeting
cyfarfod athrawon *eg* cyfarfodydd athrawon staff meeting
cyfarfod diolchgarwch *eg* cyfarfodydd diolchgarwch harvest service
cyfarfod safoni *eg* cyfarfodydd safoni moderation meeting
cyfarfod sefydlu *eg* cyfarfodydd sefydlu induction meeting
Cyfarfodydd Cyngres *ell* Congregations of Congress
cyfarganfod *be* apperception
cyfarpar *eg* apparatus; equipment
cyfarpar achub *eg* rescue equipment
cyfarpar atal cenhedlu *eg* contraceptive device
cyfarpar castio *eg* casting apparatus

cyfarpar didactig *eg* didactic apparatus
cyfarpar di-haint *eg* sterile equipment
cyfarpar electroacwstig *eg* electroacoustic equipment
cyfarpar meddalu dŵr *eg* water-softening plant
cyfarpar stereotacsig *eg* stereotaxic apparatus
cyfarpar turn *eg* lathe accessories
cyfartal *ans* equal
cyfartaledd *eg* cyfartaleddau average
cyfartaledd amser *eg* time average
cyfartaledd gwladol *eg* national average
cyfartaledd newidiol *eg* moving average
cyfartaledd pwysol *eg* cyfartaleddau pwysol weighted average
cyfartalog *ans* average
cyfartalu *be* equalize
cyfarwyddeb *eb* cyfarwyddebau directive
cyfarwyddiadau gwau *ell* knitting instructions
cyfarwyddiadau sgrin *ell* on-screen instructions
cyfarwyddiadur masnachol *eg* cyfarwyddiaduron masnachol trade directory
cyfarwyddo plant *be* child guidance
cyfarwyddwr *eg* cyfarwyddwyr director
cyfarwyddwr addysg *eg* cyfarwyddwyr addysg director of education
cyfarwyddwr astudiaethau *eg* cyfarwyddwyr astudiaethau studies director
Cyfarwyddwr Erlyniadau Cyhoeddus *eg* Director of Public Prosecutions
cyfarwyddwr gwasanaethau nyrsio *eg* cyfarwyddwyr gwasanaethau nyrsio director of nursing services
cyfarwyddyd (=arweiniad) *eg* cyfarwyddiadau guidance
cyfarwyddyd (ar bapur arholiad) *eg* cyfarwyddiadau rubric
cyfarwyddyd (yn gyffredinol) *eg* cyfarwyddiadau instruction
cyfarwyddyd addysgol *eg* educational guidance
cyfarwyddyd canghennu *eg* cyfarwyddiadau canghennu branch instruction
cyfarwyddyd canghennu amodol *eg* cyfarwyddiadau canghennu amodol conditional branch instruction
cyfarwyddyd canghennu diamod *eg* cyfarwyddiadau canghennu diamod unconditional branch instruction
cyfarwyddyd cerddorol *eg* cyfarwyddiadau cerddorol musical instruction
cyfarwyddyd gweithredu *eg* cyfarwyddiadau gweithredu procedural instruction
cyfarwyddyd gwirioneddol *eg* cyfarwyddiadau gwirioneddol actual instruction
cyfarwyddyd gwneud dim *eg* cyfarwyddiadau gwneud dim do nothing instruction
cyfarwyddyd lliwiau tymheredd *eg* temperature colour guide
cyfarwyddyd neidio *eg* cyfarwyddiadau neidio jump instruction
cyfarwyddyd neidio diamod *eg* cyfarwyddiadau neidio diamod unconditional jump instruction
cyfateb *be* correspond
cyfatebiaeth *eb* cyfatebiaethau correspondence
cyfatebiaeth llawer-i-lawer *eb* many-many correspondence
cyfatebiaeth llawer-i-un *eb* many-one correspondence
cyfatebiaeth llawn amser *eb* full-time equivalent
cyfatebiaeth oed *eb* age equivalent
cyfatebiaeth un-i-lawer *eb* one-many correspondence
cyfatebiaeth un-i-un *eb* one-one correspondence
cyfatebol *ans* corresponding
cyfatebolrwydd *eg* complementarity
cyfath *ans* congruent
cyfathiant *eg* cyfathiannau congruence
cyfathrach rywiol *eb* sexual intercourse
cyfathrach rywiol *eb* intercourse
cyfathrebiad *eg* cyfathrebiadau communication
cyfathrebiad data *eg* cyfathrebiadau data data communication
cyfathrebol *ans* communicational
cyfathrebu *be* communicate
cyfathrebu addas i'r plentyn *be* child-directed speech
cyfathrebu allanol *be* external communication
cyfathrebu anffurfiol *be* informal communication
cyfathrebu dieiriau *be* non-verbal communication
cyfathrebu marchnata *be* marketing communications
cyfathrebu mewnol *be* internal communication
cyfathrebu rhyngbersonol *be* interpersonal communication
cyfathrebu ysgrifenedig *be* written communication
cyfathrebwr electronig *eg* cyfathrebwyr electronig electronic communicator
cyfbilen *eb* cyfbilennau conjunctiva
cyfdro *eg* cyfdroeon converse
cyfechelog *ans* coaxial
cyfeddiannu *be* annex
cyfeddiant *eg* annexation
cyfeiliant *eg* backing
cyfeiliant *eg* cyfeiliannau accompaniment
cyfeiliant cerddorol *eg* musical accompaniment
cyfeiliant drôn *eg* drone accompaniment
cyfeiliant rhythmig *eg* rhythmic accompaniment
cyfeiliant syml *eg* simple accompaniment
cyfeiliant ychwanegol *eg* additional accompaniment
cyfeilio *be* accompany
cyfeiliornad *eg* cyfeiliornadau error
cyfeiliornad cymedrig *eg* mean error
cyfeiliornad math 1 *eg* cyfeiliornadau math 1 type 1 error
cyfeiliornad math 2 *eg* cyfeiliornadau math 2 type 2 error

► **cyfeiliornad mewn arbrawf** *eg* cyfeiliornadau mewn arbrawf experimental error
cyfeiliornad newidyn *eg* cyfeiliornadau newidyn variable error
cyfeiliornad priodoli eithaf *eg* cyfeiliornadau priodoli eithaf ultimate attribution error
cyfeiliornad priodoli sylfaenol *eg* cyfeiliornadau priodoli sylfaenol fundamental attribution error
cyfeiliornad safonol *eg* cyfeiliornadau safonol standard error
cyfeiliornad safonol o'r cymedr *eg* cyfeiliornadau safonol o'r cymedr standard error of the mean
cyfeiliornad systematig *eg* cyfeiliornadau systematig systematic error
cyfeiliornad talgrynnu *eg* cyfeiliornadau talgrynnu rounding error
cyfeiliornad tebygol *eg* cyfeiliornadau tebygol probable error
cyfeiliornadau samplu *ell* sampling errors
cyfeilydd *eg* cyfeilyddion accompanist
cyfeillgar (am fudiad elusennol) *ans* benevolent
cyfeillgar (i'r defnyddiwr) *ans* user-friendly
Cyfeillion y Ddaear *ell* Friends of the Earth
cyfeintiol *ans* volumetric
cyfeireb ddu *eb* cyfeirebau du black rubric
cyfeirgylch *eg* cyfeirgylchoedd director circle
cyfeiriad (=cyfeirio rhywun at arbenigwr) *eg* cyfeiriadau referral
cyfeiriad (=crybwylliad) *eg* cyfeiriadau reference
cyfeiriad (=y ffordd i gyrraedd rhywle) *eg* cyfeiriadau direction
cyfeiriad (ar lythyr etc) *eg* cyfeiriadau address
cyfeiriad (mewn mathemateg) *eg* cyfeiriadau sense
cyfeiriad (wrth fesur o bwynt sefydlog) *eg* cyfeiriadau bearings
cyfeiriad absoliwt *eg* cyfeiriadau absoliwt absolute address
cyfeiriad anatomegol *eg* anatomical direction
cyfeiriad clocwedd *eg* clockwise direction
cyfeiriad cyfarwyddyd *eg* cyfeiriadau cyfarwyddyd instruction address
cyfeiriad cyrchwr *eg* cursor address
cyfeiriad dirgroes *eg* cyfeiriadau dirgroes opposite direction
cyfeiriad dychwelyd *eg* cyfeiriadau dychwelyd return address
cyfeiriad gadael *eg* exit direction
cyfeiriad gadael i'r brig *eg* exit direction top
cyfeiriad gadael i'r chwith *eg* exit direction left
cyfeiriad gadael i'r dde *eg* exit direction right
cyfeiriad gadael i'r gwaelod *eg* exit direction bottom
cyfeiriad gwefan *eg* web site address
cyfeiriad gwrthglocwedd *eg* anticlockwise direction
cyfeiriad gwthiad *eg* thrust direction
cyfeiriad IP *eg* cyfeiriadau IP IP address
cyfeiriad mynegedig *eg* cyfeiriadau mynegedig indexed address
cyfeiriad newidiol *eg* cyfeiriadau newidiol variable address
cyfeiriad penodol *eg* cyfeiriadau penodol particular direction
cyfeiriad porthiant *eg* direction of feed
cyfeiriad priodol *eg* cyfeiriadau priodol appropriate direction
cyfeiriad saeth A *eg* direction of arrow A
cyfeiriad symbolaidd *eg* cyfeiriadau symbolaidd symbolic address
cyfeiriad symudiad *eg* direction of movement
cyfeiriad y bêl *eg* direction of the ball
cyfeiriad y cylchdro *eg* direction of rotation
cyfeiriad y graen *eg* direction of grain
cyfeiriad y tafliad *eg* direction of throw
cyfeiriad y testun *eg* text direction
cyfeiriad y toriad *eg* direction of cut
cyfeiriadaeth *eg* orientation
cyfeiriadaeth ofodol *eb* spatial orientation
cyfeiriadaeth sylfaenol *eb* basic orientation
cyfeiriadaeth tudalen *eb* page orientation
cyfeiriadol *ans* directional
cyfeiriadur *eg* cyfeiriaduron directory
cyfeiriadur awtodestun *eg* cyfeiriaduron awtodestun autotext directory
cyfeiriadur cartref *eg* home directory
cyfeiriadur chwilio *eg* cyfeiriaduron chwilio search directory
cyfeiriadur ffynhonnell *eg* cyfeiriaduron ffynhonnell source directory
cyfeiriadur gwraidd *eg* cyfeiriaduron gwraidd root directory
cyfeiriadur templedi *eg* cyfeiriaduron templedi template directory
cyfeiriannu *be* orienteering
cyfeiriant cywir *eg* true bearing
cyfeiriant magnetig *eg* magnetic bearing
cyfeiriedig *ans* orientated
cyfeirio (at wybodaeth etc) *be* refer
cyfeirio (llythyr) *be* address
cyfeirio anuniongyrchol *be* indirect addressing
cyfeirio at feini prawf *be* criteria referencing
cyfeirio cof *eg* address a memory
cyfeirio cymdeithasol *be* social referencing
cyfeirio mynegedig *be* indexed addressing
cyfeirio perthynol *be* relative addressing
cyfeirio uniongyrchol *be* direct addressing
cyfeirlin *eb* cyfeirlinau bearing line
cyfeirlin *eb* cyfeirlinau directrix
cyfeirlyfr *eg* cyfeirlyfrau reference book
cyfeirnod *eg* cyfeirnodau reference
cyfeirnod absoliwt *eg* cyfeirnodau absoliwt absolute reference
cyfeirnod cell *eg* cyfeirnodau cell cell reference
cyfeirnod didoli *eg* cyfeirnodau didoli discrimination index
cyfeirnod grid *eg* cyfeirnodau grid grid reference
cyfeirnod map *eg* cyfeirnodau map map reference

cyfeirnodau grid chwe-ffigur *ell* six-figure grid references

cyfeirydd *eg* cyfeiryddion guide; direct

cyfeirydd hoelbren *eg* cyfeiryddion hoelbren dowel guide

cyfeirydd pwli *eg* cyfeiryddion pwli pulley guide

cyfeirydd symudol *eg* cyfeiryddion symudol movable guide

cyferbyn *ans* opposite; contrary

cyferbyniad *eg* cyferbyniadau contrast

cyferbyniad disgleirdeb *eg* brightness contrast

cyferbyniad lefel *eg* contrast of level

cyferbyniad maint *eg* contrast of size

cyferbyniad parhad *eg* contrast of continuity

cyferbyniad siâp *eg* contrast of shape

cyferbyniad tyndra *eg* contrast of tension

cyferbyniol *ans* contrasting

cyferbynnedd *eg* cyferbyneddau contrast

cyferbynnu *be* contrast

cyferbynnu deuaidd *be* binary opposition

cyfernod *eg* cyfernodau coefficient

cyfernod actifedd *eg* cyfernodau actifedd activity coefficient

cyfernod adfer *eg* cyfernodau adfer coefficient of restitution

cyfernod amhendant *eg* cyfernodau amhendant undetermined coefficient

cyfernod amrywiad *eg* cyfernodau amrywiad coefficient of variation

cyfernod amsugno *eg* cyfernodau amsugno absorption coefficient

cyfernod atchwel *eg* cyfernodau atchwel coefficient of regression

cyfernod cydberthyniad *eg* cyfernodau cydberthyniad correlation coefficient

cyfernod cydberthyniad rhestrol Spearman *eg* Spearman rank correlation coefficient

cyfernod differol *eg* cyfernodau differol differential coefficient

cyfernod dosraniad *eg* cyfernodau dosraniad distribution coefficient

cyfernod dosrannu *eg* cyfernodau dosrannu partition coefficient

cyfernod ehangiad *eg* cyfernodau ehangiad coefficient of expansion

cyfernod ehangiad llinol *eg* cyfernodau ehangiad llinol coefficient of linear expansion

cyfernod ffrithiant *eg* cyfernodau ffrithiant coefficient of friction

cyfernod gwrthiant *eg* cyfernodau gwrthiant coefficient of resistance

cyfernod gwywo *eg* cyfernodau gwywo wilting coefficient

cyfernod pendant *eg* cyfernodau pendant determined coefficient

cyfernod treuliadwyedd *eg* cyfernodau treuliadwyedd digestibility coefficient

cyfernod tymheredd gwrthiant *eg* cyfernodau tymheredd gwrthiant temperature coefficient of resistance

cyfersin *eg* cyfersinau coversine

cyfesur *ans* commensurable

cyfesuryn *eg* cyfesurynnau coordinate

cyfesuryn unionlin *eg* cyfesurynnau unionlin rectilinear coordinate

cyfesuryn unionlin mesuryn *eg* cyfesurynnau unionlin mesurynnau rectilinear coordinate ordinate

cyfesurynnau Cartesaidd *ell* Cartesian coordinates

cyfesurynnau Cartesaidd petryal *ell* rectangular Cartesian coordinates

cyfesurynnau llythrennau *ell* letter coordinates

cyfesurynnau rhifau *ell* number coordinates

cyfethol *be* co-opt

cyfiau *eg* cyfieuau conjugate

cyfiau cymhlyg *eg* cyfieuau cymhlyg complex conjugate

cyfiawn *ans* just

cyfiawnder *eg* cyfiawnderau justice

cyfiawnder cynhenid *eg* natural justice

cyfiawnder i'r ifanc *eg* youth justice

cyfiawnder troseddol *eg* criminal justice

cyfiawnhad *eg* justification

cyfiawnhad drwy ffydd *eg* justification by faith

cyfiawnhad trylwyr *eg* rigorous justification

cyfiawnhad y Senedd *eg* apology of the Commons

cyfiawnhau *be* justify

cyfieithiad *eg* cyfieithiadau translation

cyfieithiad llythrennol *eg* cyfieithiadau llythrennol literal translation

cyfieithiad o'r gorffennol *eg* cyfieithiadau o'r gorffennol legacy translation

cyfieithu *be* translate

cyfieithu ar y pryd *be* simultaneous translation

cyfieithu drwy gymorth cyfrifiadur *be* machine-aided translation

cyfieithu peirianyddol *be* machine translation

cyfieithydd *eg* cyfieithwyr interpreter; translator

cyfieuol *ans* conjugate

cyflafan *eb* massacre

Cyflafan Gwylnos Bartholomeus *eb* Massacre of St Bartholomew

Cyflafan y Gosberau Sisilaidd *eb* Massacre of the Sicilian Vespers

cyflafareddiad *eg* cyflafareddiadau arbitration

cyflafareddu *be* arbitrate

cyflafareddwr *eg* cyflafareddwyr arbitrator

cyflaith menyn *eg* butterscotch

cyflasyn *eg* cyflasynnau flavouring

cyflawn *ans* total; complete; overall

cyflawni (=llwyddo i wneud) *be* achieve; fulfil

cyflawni (=ymgymryd â) *be* undertake

cyflawni (gweithred) *be* execute

cyflawni amcan *be* achieve an objective

cyflawni amcanion *be* attainment of objectives

cyflawni hunanladdiad *be* commit suicide

cyflawniad (yn y Cwricwlwm Cenedlaethol) *eg* cyflawniadau achievement

cyflawniad (yn gyffredinol) *eg* cyflawniadau accomplishment
cyflawnrwydd *eg* completeness
cyfle *eg* cyfleoedd opportunity
cyfle cyfartal *eg* cyfleoedd cyfartal equal opportunity
cyfle gyrfaol *eg* cyfleoedd gyrfaol career opportunity
cyfledred *eg* cyfledredion co-latitude
cyflenwad (=digonedd) *eg* abundance
cyflenwad (i wneud yn gyflawn) *eg* cyflenwadau complement
cyflenwad (yn gyffredinol) *eg* cyflenwadau supply
cyflenwad a galw supply and demand
cyflenwad bwyd *eg* cyflenwadau bwyd food supplies
cyflenwad cyfanredol *eg* cyflenwadau cyfanredol aggregate supply
cyflenwad deuol *eg* two's complement
cyflenwad dibynadwy *eg* cyflenwadau dibynadwy reliable supply
cyflenwad dibynadwy o egni *eg* reliable supply of energy
cyflenwad dŵr *eg* water supply
cyflenwad nerfol *eg* cyflenwadau nerfol nerve supply
cyflenwad newyddion *eg* cyflenwadau newyddion newsfeed
cyflenwad pŵer *eg* cyflenwadau pŵer power supply
cyflenwad pŵer gydag unioniad hanner ton *eg* half-wave rectified power supply
cyflenwad pŵer wrth gefn *eg* cyflenwadau pŵer wrth gefn back-up power supply
cyflenwad tanwydd *eg* cyflenwadau tanwydd fuel supply
cyflenwad trydan *eg* electricity supply
cyflenwad unol *eg* one's complement
cyflenwadau sylweddol *ell* bulk supplies
cyflenwi (yn gyffredinol) *be* supply
cyflenwi (=gwneud yn gyflawn) *be* complement
cyflenwol *ans* complementary
cyflenwr masnach *eg* cyflenwyr masnach trade supplier
cyflenwydd *eg* cyflenwyddion feeder
cyfleu *be* communicate
cyfleu gwybodaeth *be* communicate information
cyfleu syniadau *be* communicate ideas
cyfleu ystyr *be* communicate meaning
cyfleus *ans* convenient
cyfleuster *eg* cyfleusterau facility
cyfleuster hamdden ac adloniant *eg* cyfleusterau hamdden ac adloniant leisure and recreation facility
cyfleusterau *ell* facilities
cyfleusterau a mwynderau facilities and amenities
cyfleusterau adloniadol *ell* recreational facilities
cyfleusterau addysgol *ell* educational facilities
cyfleusterau ar-lein *ell* on-line facilities
cyfleusterau cyhoeddus *ell* public convenience
cyfleusterau twristiaeth *ell* tourism facilities
cyflin *ans* parallel
cyflin safonol *eb* cyfliniau safonol standard parallel
cyflinydd *eg* cyflinyddion collimator
cyflog *eg/b* cyflogau salary; wage; pay
cyflog blynyddol *eg* annual wage
cyflog clir *eg* take-home pay
cyflog crynswth *eg* gross pay
cyflog cydradd *eg* equal pay
cyflog net *eg* net pay
cyflog sylfaenol *eg* cyflogau sylfaenol basic salary; basic wage
cyflogadwy *ans* employable
cyflogadwyedd *eg* employability
cyflogaeth *eb* employment
cyflogaeth lawn *eb* full employment
cyflogarithm *eg* cyflogarithmau cologarithm
cyflogedig *ans* employed
cyflogi *be* employ
cyflogwr *eg* cyflogwyr employer
cyfludedig *ans* agglutinated
cyfludiad *eg* cyfludiadau agglutination
cyfludo *be* agglutinate
cyflun *ans* similar
cyflunedd *eg* cyfluneddau similarity
cyflunedd mathemategol *eg* mathematical similarity
cyfluniant *eg* cyfluniannau similitude
cyflwr *eg* cyflyrau condition; state
cyflwr cynhyrfol *eg* cyflyrau cynhyrfol excited state
cyflwr dryslyd cronig *eg* chronic confusional state
cyflwr dryslyd llym *eg* acute confusional state
cyflwr gelaidd *eg* gelatinous state
cyflwr isaf *eg* cyflyrau isaf ground state
cyflwr meddygol *eg* cyflyrau meddygol medical condition
cyflwr ocsidiad *eg* oxidation state
cyflwr papur isel *eg* paper low condition
cyflwr rheolydd *eg* control condition
cyflwr safle *eg* site conditions
cyflwr safonol *eg* cyflyrau safonol standard state
cyflwr sefydlog *eb* cyflyrau sefydlog steady state
cyflwr solet *eg* solid state
cyflwr trosiannol *eg* cyflyrau trosiannol transition state
cyflwr y farchnad *eg* market conditions
cyflwyniad (=darpariaeth) *eg* cyflwyniadau provision
cyflwyniad (=neilltuad) *eg* cyflwyniadau dedication
cyflwyniad (i berson, i lyfr) *eg* cyflwyniadau introduction
cyflwyniad (yn gyffredinol) *eg* cyflwyniadau presentation
cyflwyniad ar lwyfan *eg* stage presentation
cyflwyniad penodol *eg* specific performance
cyflwyno (=neilltuo) *be* dedicate
cyflwyno (yn gyffredinol) *eg be* introduce
cyflwyno graddol *be* phased introduction

cyflwyno gwybodaeth *be* presenting information
cyflwyno'r addoliad *be* present the worship
cyflym *ans* quick; fast
cyflymder (mesur fector) *eg* cyflymderau velocity
cyflymder (yn gyffredinol) *eg* speed
cyflymder adwaith *eg* reaction speed
cyflymder argraffu *eg* printing speed
cyflymder bws *eg* bus speed
cyflymder cychwynnol *eg* cyflymderau cychwynnol initial velocity
cyflymder cylchrediad *eg* velocity of circulation
cyflymder cyson *eg* constant velocity
cyflymder darllen *eg* read speed
cyflymder dianc *eg* escape velocity
cyflymder drifft *eg* drift velocity
cyflymder eithaf *eg* maximum speed
cyflymder goleuni *eg* speed of light
cyflymder llinol *eg* linear velocity
cyflymder onglaidd *eg* cyflymderau onglaidd angular velocity
▶ **cyflymder perthynol** *eg* relative velocity
cyflymder segura *eg* idling speed
cyflymder terfynol *eg* final velocity
cyflymder y bêl *eg* speed of the ball
cyflymder y bowlio *eg* bowling speed
cyflymder y prosesydd *eg* processor speed
cyflymdra cyfartalog y gwynt *eg* mean wind speed
cyflymedig *ans* accelerated
cyflymedd y galon *eg* tachycardia
cyflymiad *eg* cyflymiadau acceleration
cyflymiad ansero *eg* non-zero acceleration
cyflymiad cyson *eg* constant acceleration
cyflymiad disgyrchiant *eg* acceleration due to gravity
cyflymu *be* accelerate; speed up
cyflymydd *eg* cyflymyddion accelerator
cyflyrair *eg* cyflyreiriau status word
cyflyrau mater *ell* states of matter
cyflyredig *ans* conditioned
cyflyru (mewn seicoleg) *be* conditioning
cyflyru (i dderbyn cred heb gwestiynu) *be* indoctrinate
cyflyru clasurol *be* classical conditioning
cyflyru dysgu osgoi-blas *be* conditioned flavour-aversion learning
cyflyru gweithredol *be* operant conditioning
cyflyru Pavlovaidd *be* Pavlovian conditioning
cyflyrydd *eg* cyflyrwyr conditioner
cyflyrydd ffabrig *eg* cyflyryddion ffabrig fabric softener
cyflyrydd ffabrig *eg* cyflyryddion ffabrig fabric conditioner
cyflythreniad alliteration
cyfnerthedig *ans* consolidated
cyfnerthu (defnydd) *be* stiffen
cyfnerthu (yn gyffredinol) *be* consolidate
cyfnerthu medrau *be* consolidate skills
cyfnerthu parhaol *be* permanently stiffened
cyfnerthydd *eg* cyfnerthyddion stiffening
cyfnerthydd (pŵer trydan etc) *eg* cyfnerthyddion booster
cyfnewid *be* exchange
cyfnewid *be* swap
cyfnewid cronfa ddata *be* exchange database
cyfnewid ffynhonnell *be* exchange source
cyfnewid nodau *be* exchange characters
cyfnewid nwyol *eg* gaseous exchange
cyfnewid nwyon *be* gas exchange
cyfnewid pecynnau *be* packet switching
cyfnewid tudalen gefndir *be* exchange background page
cyfnewidfa *eb* cyfnewidfeydd exchange
cyfnewidfa dramor *eb* cyfnewidfeydd tramor foreign exchange
cyfnewidfa stoc *eb* cyfnewidfeydd stoc stock exchange
cyfnewidiad *eg* cyfnewidiadau innovation
cyfnewidiad tudalen *eg* cyfnewidiadau tudalen page swap
cyfnewidiadwy *ans* exchangeable
cyfnewidiol *ans* volatile
cyfnifer *eg* cyfniferoedd aliquot
cyfnod (=amser) *eg* cyfnodau time
cyfnod (mewn hanes) *eg* cyfnodau epoch
cyfnod (mewn proses) *eg* cyfnodau phase
cyfnod (yn y cwricwlwm) *eg* cyfnodau stage
cyfnod (yn gyffredinol) *eg* cyfnodau period
cyfnod achosol *eg* cyfnodau achosol causal phase
cyfnod allweddol *eg* cyfnodau allweddol critical period
cyfnod allweddol (yn y Cwricwlwm Cenedlaethol) *eg* cyfnodau allweddol key stage
cyfnod canolbwyntio *eg* cyfnodau canolbwyntio attention span
cyfnod cario *eg* gestation period
cyfnod cofio *eg* memory span
cyfnod cudd *eg* latency period
cyfnod cwarantin *eg* quarantine period
cyfnod cyfebru *eg* gestation period
cyfnod cylchdro *eg* angular period
cyfnod cyn geni *eg* prenatal period
cyfnod cynradd *eg* cyfnodau cynradd junior stage
cyfnod cynweithredol *eg* preoperational stage
cyfnod datblygiad *eg* cyfnodau datblygiad stage of development
cyfnod deori *eg* incubation period
cyfnod diddigwydd *eg* refractory period
cyfnod diddigwydd *eg* latent period
cyfnod digyfnewid *eg* cyfnodau digyfnewid stationary phase
cyfnod dysgu allweddol *eg* cyfnodau dysgu allweddol critical learning period
cyfnod eginol *eg* germinal stage
cyfnod embryo *eg* embryo stage
cyfnod ffalig *eg* phallic stage
cyfnod ffetws *eg* fetal stage

cyfnod geni *eg* confinement
cyfnod gweithredu diriaethol *eg* period of concrete operations
cyfnod gweithredu ffurfiol *eg* period of formal operations
cyfnod gwella *eg* convalescence
cyfnod hanesyddol *eg* cyfnodau hanesyddol historical period
cyfnod hanner actifedd *eg* half value period
cyfnod llaetha *eg* lactation period
cyfnod magu *eg* incubation period
cyfnod modern cynnar *eg* early modern period
cyfnod oedi *eg* lag phase
cyfnod organau cenhedlu *eg* genital stage
cyfnod Paleosen *eg* Paleocene
cyfnod peri-blodeuo *eg* flower-inducing period
cyfnod prawf *eg* cyfnodau prawf probationary period
cyfnod Rhamantaidd *eg* Romantic period
cyfnod sail *eg* base period
cyfnod synhwyraidd-weithredol *eg* sensorimotor period
cyfnod sythweledol *eg* cyfnodau sythweledol intuitive stage
Cyfnod y Cynnwrf *eg* Time of Troubles
cyfnod y genau *eg* oral stage
cyfnod ymarfer *eg* cyfnodau ymarfer practice period
cyfnod yr anws *eg* anal stage
cyfnod yr osgiliad *eg* period of oscillation
cyfnodau chwarae *ell* stages of play
cyfnodedd *eg* cyfnodeddau periodicity
cyfnodol *ans* periodic
cyfnodolyn *eg* cyfnodolion periodical
cyfochredd *eg* parallelism
cyfochrog *ans* parallel
cyfodol *ans* emerged
cyfoed *eg* cyfoedion peer
cyfoes *ans* contemporary; up to date
cyfoeswr *eg* cyfoeswyr contemporary
cyfoeth *eg* wealth; richness
cyfoeth gwerthadwy *eg* marketable wealth
cyfoethog *ans* rich
cyfoethogi *be* enrichment
cyfoethogion segur *ell* idle rich
cyfog *eg* nausea
cyfogi gwag *be* retching
cyfoglyn *eg* cyfoglynnau emetic
cyfordraeth *eg* cyfordraethau raised beach
cyforglogwyn *eg* cyforglogwyni raised cliff
cyforgors *eb* cyforgorsydd raised bog
cyforlan *eb* cyforlannau bankful
cyfosod *be* juxtapose
cyfosod nodau *eg* grouping of notes
cyfosod tawnodau *be* grouping of rests
cyfosodiad *eg* cyfosodiadau juxtaposition
cyfradd *eb* cyfraddau rate
cyfradd adfer *eb* recovery rate
cyfradd adnewyddu *eb* refresh rate
cyfradd adwaith *eb* reaction rate
cyfradd adwaith *eb* rate of reaction
cyfradd anadlu *eb* breathing rate
cyfradd anadlu *eb* ventilation rate
cyfradd anterth llif *eb* peak flow rate
cyfradd atgenhedlu *eb* cyfraddau atgenhedlu reproductive rate
cyfradd banc *eb* cyfraddau banc bank rate
cyfradd baud *eb* cyfraddau baud baud rate
cyfradd cloc *eb* cyfraddau cloc clock rate
cyfradd colli dŵr *eb* rate of water loss
cyfradd colli pwysau *eb* rate of weight loss
cyfradd curiad y galon *eb* heart rate
cyfradd curiad y galon *eb* pulse rate
cyfradd cyfnewid *eb* cyfraddau cyfnewid rate of exchange
cyfradd cyfnewid arnawf *eb* floating exchange rate
cyfradd cyfnewid reoledig *eb* managed exchange rate
cyfradd cyfrif *eb* count rate
cyfradd cyfrif cefndir *eb* background count rate
cyfradd cynnydd *eb* cyfraddau cynnydd rate of progress; increase rate
cyfradd diffygion *eb* cyfraddau diffygion fault rate
cyfradd ddidol *eb* cyfraddau didol bit rate
cyfradd echdynnol blawd *eb* extraction rate of flour
cyfradd fenthyg *eb* cyfraddau benthyg lending rate
cyfradd ffotosynthesis *eb* rate of photosynthesis
cyfradd ffrwythlondeb *eb* fertility rate
cyfradd genedigaethau *eb* birth rate
cyfradd geni /marw syml *eb* crude birth /death rate
cyfradd goroesi *eb* survival rate
cyfradd gweithio *eb* rate of working
cyfradd gychwynnol *eb* initial rate
cyfradd gyfartalog *eb* cyfraddau cyfartalog average rate
cyfradd gyfnewid *eb* cyfraddau cyfnewid exchange rate
cyfradd gyfnewid osodedig *eb* fixed exchange rate
cyfradd gyfredol *eb* cyfraddau cyfredol current rate
cyfradd lleihad *eb* rate of decrease
cyfradd llifiant *eb* flow rate
cyfradd llog *eb* cyfraddau llog interest rate; rate of interest
cyfradd marwolaethau *eb* death rate; mortality rate
Cyfradd Metabolaeth Waelodol (CMW) *eb* Basal Metabolic Rate
cyfradd morbidrwydd *eb* morbidity rate
cyfradd mwtaniadau *eb* rate of mutations
cyfradd newid *eb* cyfraddau newid lapse rate
cyfradd porthiant *eb* rate of feed
cyfradd safonol *eb* cyfraddau safonol standard rate
cyfradd sylfaenol *eb* cyfraddau sylfaenol basic rate
cyfradd taro *eb* cyfraddau taro hit rate

cyfradd trosglwyddo data *eb* cyfraddau trosglwyddo data data transfer rate
cyfradd trosglwyddo egni *eb* rate of transferring energy
cyfradd trydarthu *eb* transpiration rate
cyfradd twf *eb* rate of growth; growth rate
cyfradd y cant *eb* rate per cent
cyfradd ymylol treth *eb* marginal rate of tax
cyfradd yn ôl y gwaith *eb* piece rate
cyfradd yr adenillion ar y cyfalaf a ddefnyddiwyd *eb* rate of return on capital employed
cyfraddau trethiad *ell* taxation rates
cyfraith *eb* cyfreithiau law
cyfraith a threfn law and order
cyfraith achosion *eb* case law
Cyfraith Defod *eb* Customary Law
Cyfraith Ecwiti *eb* Equity Law
cyfraith eglwysig *eb* canon law
Cyfraith Eingl-Normanaidd *eb* Anglo-Norman Law
Cyfraith Eingl-Sacsonaidd *eb* Anglo-Saxon Law
cyfraith etifeddu *eb* law of succession
cyfraith Ewrop *eb* European law
cyfraith fasnachol *eb* commercial law
cyfraith forwrol *eb* maritime law
cyfraith fforest *eb* forest law
Cyfraith Ganonaidd *eb* Canon Law
cyfraith gwlad *eb* common law
Cyfraith Gwlad Lloegr *eb* English Common Law
Cyfraith Hywel *eb* Welsh law
cyfraith Islamaidd *eb* Islamic law
Cyfraith Loegr *eb* English Law
cyfraith llys *eb* judges' law
Cyfraith Rufain *eb* Roman Law
cyfraith rhyfel *eb* martial law
Cyfraith Salig *eb* Salic Law
Cyfraith Sifil *eb* Civil Law
cyfraith statud *eb* statute law
cyfraith trosedd *eb* criminal law
cyfraith troseddau a chyfiawnder criminal law and justice
cyfraith y tlodion *eb* poor law
cyfran (mewn cyfrannedd) *eb* cyfrannau proportion
cyfran (yng Nghyfraith Hywel) *eb* gavelkind
cyfran (yn gyffredinol) *eb* cyfrannau portion
cyfran marchnad *eb* market share
cyfran o'r gyllideb *eb* cyfrannau o'r gyllideb budget share
cyfranddaliad *eg* cyfranddaliadau share
cyfranddaliwr *eg* cyfranddalwyr shareholder
cyfraneddol *ans* proportional
cyfran-gnydio *be* share cropping
cyfraniad *eg* cyfraniadau contribution; input
cyfrannau *ell* proportional parts
cyfrannau cymharol *ell* relative proportions
cyfrannedd *eg* cyfraneddau proportion
cyfrannedd cywir *eg* cyfraneddau cywir correct proportion
cyfrannedd da *eg* good proportion
cyfrannedd geometregol *eg* geometrical proportion
cyfrannedd harmonig *eg* cyfraneddau harmonig harmonic proportion
cyfrannedd lluosol *eg* multiple proportion
cyfrannedd maint iawn *eg* life-size proportion
cyfrannedd union *eg* cyfraneddau union direct proportion
cyfrannu *be* contribute
cyfrannwr *eg* cyfranwyr contributor
cyfrannydd electronau *eg* cyfranwyr electronau electron donor
cyfranogiad *eg* participation
cyfranogiad mewn chwaraeon *eg* participation in sport
cyfranogwr *eg* cyfranogwyr participant
cyfranoliaeth *eb* proportionalism
cyfredol *ans* current
cyfreitha *be* litigation
cyfreithadwy per se *ans* actionable per se
cyfreitheg *eb* jurisprudence
cyfreithgar *ans* litigious
cyfreithgarwch *eg* litigiousness
cyfreithiol *ans* legal; judicial
cyfreithiol-rwym *ans* legally binding
cyfreithiwr *eg* cyfreithwyr solicitor
Cyfreithiwr Cyffredinol *eg* Solicitor General
cyfreithlon *ans* lawful; legitimate
cyfreithlondeb *eg* legality; legitimacy
cyfreithloniaeth *eb* legitimism
cyfreithlonydd *eg* cyfreithlonwyr legitimist
cyfreithyddiaeth *eb* legalism
cyfres *eb* cyfresi serial; series; suite
cyfres adweithedd *eb* cyfresi adweithedd reactivity series
cyfres Almaenig *eb* cyfresi Almaenig German suite
cyfres amnewidiad *eb* replacement series
cyfres ddadfeiliad *eb* decay series
cyfres ddargyfeiriol *eb* cyfresi dargyfeiriol divergent series
cyfres ddilysu *eb* cyfresi dilysu validation suite
cyfres fer o symudiadau *eb* cyfresi byr o symudiadau short series of movements
cyfres Ffrengig *eb* cyfresi Ffrengig French suite
cyfres ffyrnau golosg *eb* cyfresi ffyrnau golosg coke oven batteries
cyfres geometrig *eb* geometric series
cyfres gydgyfeiriol *eb* cyfresi cydgyfeiriol convergent series
cyfres harmonig *eb* cyfresi harmonig harmonic series
cyfres homologaidd *eb* cyfresi homologaidd homologous series
cyfres o ddelweddau *eb* cyfresi o ddelweddau sequence of images
cyfres pob cyfwng *eb* cyfresi pob cyfwng all-interval series
cyfres Seisnig *eb* cyfresi Seisnig English suite

cyfresiaeth *eb* serialism
cyfresol *ans* serial
cyfresu *be* serialize
cyfrif *be* count
cyfrif (yn gyffredinol) *eg* cyfrifon count
cyfrif (yn y banc etc) *eg* cyfrifon account
cyfrif allan *be* count out
cyfrif ar y cyd *eg* cyfrifon ar y cyd joint account
cyfrif banc *eg* cyfrifon banc bank account
cyfrif busnes *eg* cyfrifon busnes business account
cyfrif cadw *eg* cyfrifon cadw deposit account
cyfrif cefndir *eg* background count
cyfrif cofnodion *be* record count
cyfrif cyfalaf *eg* cyfrifon cyfalaf capital account
cyfrif cyfradd net *eg* net count rate
cyfrif cyfredol *eg* cyfrifon cyfredol current account
cyfrif cyllido *eg* cyfrifon cyllido budget account
cyfrif cynilo *eg* cyfrifon cynilo savings account
cyfrif debyd *eg* cyfrifon debyd debit account
cyfrif deialu *eg* cyfrifon deialu dial-up account
cyfrif dogfennau *be* document count
cyfrif elw a cholled *eg* profit and loss account
cyfrif gwaed *eg* blood count
cyfrif gwaharddedig *eg* cyfrifon gwaharddedig blocked account
cyfrif gwladol *eg* cyfrifon gwladol national account
cyfrif i fyny *eg* up-count
cyfrif i lawr *eg* down-count
cyfrif masnachu, elw a cholled *eg* trading profit and loss account
cyfrif rhyngrwyd *eg* cyfrifon rhyngrwyd internet account
cyfrif swyddwr *eg* cyfrifon swyddwr minister's account
cyfrif yn gredyd *be* credit
cyfrifeg *eb* accountancy
cyfrifiad (arolwg o boblogaeth) *eg* cyfrifiadau census
cyfrifiad (=proses o gyfrifo) *eg* cyfrifiadau numeration
cyfrifiad (mewn mathemateg) *eg* cyfrifiadau calculation
cyfrifiad celloedd coch y gwaed *eg* red blood cell count
cyfrifiad corffilod coch y gwaed *eg* red blood corpuscle count
cyfrifiad lewcocytau *eg* leucocyte count
cyfrifiadau syrfeo sylfaenol *ell* basic surveying calculations
cyfrifiadur *eg* cyfrifiaduron computer
cyfrifiadur amlgyfrwng *eg* cyfrifiaduron amlgyfrwng multimedia computer
cyfrifiadur analog *eg* cyfrifiaduron analog analogue computer
cyfrifiadur cludadwy *eg* cyfrifiaduron cludadwy portable computer
cyfrifiadur digidol *eg* cyfrifiaduron digidol digital computer
cyfrifiadur electronig *eg* cyfrifiaduron electronig electronic computer
cyfrifiadur IBM-gytûn *eg* cyfrifiaduron IBM-gytûn IBM-compatible computer
cyfrifiadur personol *eg* cyfrifiaduron personol personal computer
cyfrifiadur prif ffrâm *eg* cyfrifiaduron prif ffrâm mainframe computer
cyfrifiadur rhwydwaith *eg* cyfrifiaduron rhwydwaith network computer
cyfrifiadur un pwrpas *eg* cyfrifiaduron un pwrpas dedicated computer
cyfrifiadura *be* computing
cyfrifiadureg *eb* computer science
cyfrifiaduro *be* computerize
cyfrifiadurol *ans* computer; computerized
cyfrifiadurol lythrennog *ans* computer-literate
cyfrifiadurwr *eg* cyfrifiadurwyr computer scientist
cyfrifiadurwr *eg* cyfrifiadurwyr computer operator
cyfrifiannell *eg* cyfrifianellau calculator
cyfrifiannell sylfaenol *eb* cyfrifianellau sylfaenol basic calculator
cyfrifiannu *be* compute
cyfrifiant *eg* cyfrifiannau computation
cyfriflen *eb* cyfriflenni bank statement
cyfriflen elw a cholled *eb* cyfriflenni elw a cholled profit and loss statement
cyfriflyfr *eg* cyfriflyfrau ledger
cyfrifo *be* calculate
cyfrifolaeth *eb* subsidiarity
cyfrifoldeb *eg* cyfrifoldebau responsibility
cyfrifo'r dewis *be* calculate selection
cyfrifo'r tabl *be* calculate table
cyfrifydd *eg* cyfrifwyr accountant
cyfrifydd parod *eg* cyfrifwyr parod ready-reckoner
Cyfrin Gyngor *eg* Privy Council
cyfrinach *eb* cyfrinachau secret
cyfrinachedd *eg* confidentiality
cyfrinachedd cleient *eg* client confidentiality
cyfrinachol *ans* secret; confidential
cyfrinair *eg* cyfrineiriau password
cyfrinair anghywir *eg* cyfrineiriau anghywir wrong password
cyfrinair cronfa ddata *eg* cyfrineiriau cronfeydd data database password
cyfrinfa *eb* cyfrinfeydd lodge
cyfriniaeth *eb* mysticism
cyfriniol *ans* mystical
cyfriniwr *eg* cyfrinwyr mystic
cyfro *be* cover
cyfrol *eb* cyfrolau volume
cyfrwng *eg* cyfryngau medium
cyfrwng *eg* cyfryngau agent
cyfrwng acrylig *eg* acrylic medium
cyfrwng addysg *eg* medium of education
cyfrwng addysgu naturiol *eg* cyfryngau addysgu naturiol natural teaching medium
cyfrwng alocryl *eg* alocryl medium

cyfrwng bondio *eg* cyfryngau bondio bonding agent
cyfrwng cludo *eg* cyfryngau cludo transport medium
cyfrwng Cymraeg *ans* Welsh-medium
cyfrwng cymysgu *eg* cyfryngau cymysgu mixing medium
cyfrwng cynnal twf *eg* cyfryngau cynnal twf growth medium
cyfrwng dal baw *eg* soil suspending agent
cyfrwng daliant *eg* cyfryngau daliant suspending agent
cyfrwng ffabrig *eg* cyfryngau ffabrig fabric medium
cyfrwng fflycsio *eg* fluxing agent
cyfrwng gel *eg* gel medium
cyfrwng gwasgaru *eg* cyfryngau gwasgaru disperse medium
cyfrwng gwlychu *eg* cyfryngau gwlychu wetting agent
cyfrwng gwrthdalpio *eg* cyfryngau gwrthdalpio anti-caking agent
cyfrwng gwrthgyrydu *eg* anti-corrosion agent
cyfrwng hindreulio *eg* cyfryngau hindreulio weathering agent
cyfrwng hylif *eg* liquid medium
cyfrwng jeli *eg* jelly medium
cyfrwng lliw *eg* colour medium
cyfrwng lliwio *eg* cyfryngau lliwio colouring agent
cyfrwng magnetig *eg* cyfryngau magnetig magnetic medium
cyfrwng marcio *eg* cyfryngau marcio marking medium
cyfrwng meithrin *eg* cyfryngau meithrin culture medium
cyfrwng peintio *eg* cyfryngau peintio painting medium
cyfrwng rhwymo *eg* cyfryngau rhwymo binding medium
cyfrwng rhyddhau *eg* release agent
cyfrwng sychu *eg* drying agent
cyfrwng sylfaen ddŵr *eg* water-based medium
cyfrwng teneuo *eg* cyfryngau teneuo reducing medium
cyfrwng teneuo *eg* thinning medium
cyfrwy *eg* cyfrwyau saddle
cyfrwy trawst *eg* cyfrwyau trawst beam saddle
cyfrwy turn *eg* cyfrwyau turn lathe saddle
cyfryngau *ell* media
cyfryngau gwlyb *ell* wet media
cyfryngau hysbysebu *ell* advertising media
cyfryngau newyddion *ell* news media
cyfryngau oeri *ell* cooling media
cyfryngau torfol *ell* mass media
cyfryngiad *eg* mediation
cyfryngu *be* mediate
cyfryngwr *eg* cyfryngwyr mediator; intermediary
cyfuchedd copaon *eg* accordance of summit levels
cyfuchlin *eg* cyfuchlinau contour line; isohypse
cyfuchlin adfewnol *eg* cyfuchliniau adfewnol re-entrant contour line
cyfuchlinedd *eg* cyfuchlineddau contour
cyfun (=cyffredinol) *ans* comprehensive
cyfun (=wedi cyfuno) *ans* merged
cyfun-cydwedd *ans* mix and match
cyfundon *eb* cyfundonau resultant tone
cyfundrefn *eb* cyfundrefnau regime
cyfundrefn *eb* cyfundrefnau system
cyfundrefn *eb* cyfundrefnau organization
cyfundrefn agored *eb* cyfundrefnau agored open system
Cyfundrefn Cytundeb Gogledd Iwerydd *eb* North Atlantic Treaty Organization
cyfundrefn faeth *eb* fosterage
cyfundrefn fancio *eb* cyfundrefnau bancio banking system
cyfundrefn Fismarcaidd *eb* Bismarckian system
Cyfundrefn Fwyd ac Amaeth *eb* Food & Agriculture Organization
cyfundrefn gaeedig *eb* cyfundrefnau caeedig closed system
cyfundrefn gast *eb* caste system
cyfundrefn gofal iechyd *eb* cyfundrefnau gofal iechyd health care system
cyfundrefn grofftio *eb* crofting system
Cyfundrefn Gwledydd America *eb* Organization of American States
Cyfundrefn Gyngresol *eb* Congress System
cyfundrefn gymdeithasol *eb* social organization
Cyfundrefn Hyfforddi Gydnabyddedig *eb* Accredited Training Organization
cyfundrefn maes agored *eb* cyfundrefnau maes agored open field system
Cyfundrefn Masnach y Byd (WTO) *eb* World Trade Organisation (WTO)
Cyfundrefn Ryngwladol y Ffoaduriaid *eb* International Refugee Organization
Cyfundrefn Safonau Rhyngwladol *eb* International Standards Organization
Cyfundrefn Undod Affrica *eb* Organization of Africa Unity
cyfundrefn wleidyddol y Natsïaid *eb* Nazi political system
cyfundrefnol *ans* systematic
cyfunedig *ans* conjugated
cyfunedd *eg* conjugation
cyfun-ffeilio *be* merge-filing
cyfuniad *eg* cyfuniadau coalescence
cyfuniad *eg* cyfuniadau combination; coalescence; amalgamation
cyfuniad dyrnodau *eg* combination punches
cyfuniad o unedau *eg* combination of units
cyfuniad o'r ddau *eg* combination of the two
cyfuniadau o liwiau *ell* colour combinations
cyfuniadol *ans* combinatorial
cyfun-nwyddau *ell* complements
cyfuno *be* combine; amalgamate; merge; fold in; coalesce; conjugate

cyfuno adnoddau *be* pool resources
cyfuno celloedd *be* merge cells
cyfuno data *be* combining data
cyfuno dogfennau *be* merge documents
cyfuno fectorau *be* compounding vectors
cyfuno labelau *be* label merge
cyfuno paragraffau *be* combine paragraphs
cyfuno tablau *be* merge tables
cyfuno testun *be* combining text
cyfunol *ans* combined
cyfunol *ans* combination
cyfunoliad *eg* collectivization
cyfunoliaeth *eb* collectivism
▶ **cyfunrywiol** *ans* homosexual
cyfunsain *eg* cyfunseiniau combination tone
cyfuwch (â) *ans* accordant
cyfuwch â *ans* as high as
cyfwelai *eg* cyfweleion interviewee
cyfweld *be* interview
cyfweliad *eg* cyfweliadau interview
cyfweliad am swydd *eg* cyfweliadau am swyddi job interview
cyfweliad gwybyddol *eg* cyfweliadau gwybyddol cognitive interview
cyfweliad lled-strwythuredig *eg* cyfweliadau lled-strwythuredig semi-structured interview
cyfweliad strwythuredig *eg* cyfweliadau strwythuredig structured interview
cyfwelydd *eg* cyfwelwyr interviewer
cyfwerth egni bwyd *eg* energy value of food
cyfwng *eg* cyfyngau interval
cyfwng agored *eg* cyfyngau agored open interval
cyfwng anghyseiniol *eg* cyfyngau anghyseiniol dissonant interval
cyfwng caeedig *eg* cyfyngau caeedig closed interval
cyfwng cyfansawdd *eg* cyfyngau cyfansawdd compound interval
cyfwng cyfuchlinol *eg* cyfyngau cyfuchlinol contour interval
cyfwng cyseiniol *eg* cyfyngau cyseiniol consonant interval
cyfwng cywasg *eg* cyfyngau cywasg diminished interval
cyfwng dosbarth *eg* cyfyngau dosbarth class interval
cyfwng enharmonig *eg* cyfyngau enharmonig enharmonic interval
cyfwng estynedig *eg* cyfyngau estynedig augmented interval
cyfwng fertigol *eg* cyfyngau fertigol vertical interval
cyfwng hafal *eg* cyfyngau hafal equal interval
cyfwng harmonig *eg* cyfyngau harmonig harmonic interval
cyfwng hyder *eg* cyfyngau hyder confidence interval
cyfwng lleiaf *eg* cyfyngau lleiaf minor interval
cyfwng melodaidd *eg* cyfyngau melodaidd melodic interval
cyfwng mwyaf *eg* cyfyngau mwyaf major interval
cyfwng perffaith *eg* cyfyngau perffaith perfect interval
cyfwng sylfaenol *eg* cyfyngau sylfaenol fundamental interval
cyfwisg *eb* cyfwisgoedd accessory
cyfwisgoedd cydwedd *ell* matching accessories
cyfwyd *eg* cyfwydydd accompaniment
cyfwyneb *ans* flush
cyfyng *eg* cyfyngoedd defile
cyfyngder *eg* distress
cyfyngedig *ans* limited
cyfyng-gyngor *eg* dilemma
cyfyngiad *eg* cyfyngiadau constraint
cyfyngiad *eg* cyfyngiadau limit
cyfyngiad *eg* cyfyngiadau restriction
cyfyngiad *eg* cyfyngiadau limitation
cyfyngiad ar gofnod *eg* limit on entry
cyfyngiad arian *eg* cyfyngiadau arian cash limit
cyfyngiad cyfreithiol *eg* cyfyngiadau cyfreithiol legal constraint
cyfyngiad masnach *eg* cyfyngiadau masnach trade restriction
cyfyngiad masnachol *eg* cyfyngiadau masnachol trading restriction
cyfyngiad tacsonomi *eg* taxonomic constraint
cyfyngiadau penodedig *ell* prescribed limits
cyfyngiadau'r dull *ell* limitations of the method
cyfyngiant *eg* containment
cyfyngol *ans* limiting
cyfyngu *be* restrict; limit
cyfyngu drwy gefn y pwyth *be* decrease through back of stitch
cyfyngydd *eg* cyfyngyddion constraint
cyff *eg* cyffion stem; stock
cyffeithio bwyd *be* food preservation
cyffeithydd *eg* cyffeithyddion preservative
cyffeithydd bwyd *eg* cyffeithyddion bwyd food preservative
cyffen *eb* cyffiau cuff
cyffes *eb* cyffesion confession
Cyffes Augsburg *eb* Confession of Augsburgh
cyffes ffydd *eb* confession of faith
cyffes gudd *eb* cyffesion cudd auricular confession
cyffesgell *eb* cyffesgelloedd confessional
cyffesu *be* confess
cyffeswr *eg* cyffeswyr confessor
cyffiau silindrog *ell* cylindrical cuffs
cyffin *eg* cyffiniau precinct
cyffindir *eg* cyffindiroedd ecotone
cyffinwlad *eb* cyffinwledydd frontier state
cyffion a deiau stock and dies
cyffion traed *ell* stocks
cyffordd *eb* cyffyrdd junction
cyffordd *eb* cyffyrdd road junction
cyffordd dail meillion *eb* cyffyrdd dail meillion clover leaf junction
cyffordd traciau *eb* cyffyrdd traciau track junction

cyffordd trenau *eb* cyffyrdd trenau rail junction
cyffredin *ans* common
cyffredinol *ans* general; universal; overall
cyffredinoledig *eg* generalised
cyffredinoli *be* generalize
cyffredinoliad *eg* cyffredinoliadau generalisation
cyffredinoliad o gell anifail *eg* generalised animal cell
cyffredinolrwydd *eg* generality
cyffroad *eg* excitation
cyffroad clywedol *eg* aural stimulation
cyffroadwy *ans* excitable
cyffrous *ans* stirring
cyffrwyth meddal *eg* conserve
cyffug *eg* fudge
cyffur *eg* cyffuriau drug
cyffur adloniant *eg* cyffuriau adloniant recreational drug
cyffur atal epilepsi *eg* cyffuriau atal epilepsi antiepileptic
cyffur cytotocsig *eg* cyffuriau cytotocsig cytotoxic drug
cyffur erthylu *eg* cyffuriau erthylu abortifacient
cyffur gwrthfania *eg* cyffuriau gwrthfania anti-manic drug
cyffur gwrthgeulo *eg* cyffuriau gwrthgeulo anti-coagulant
cyffur gwrthiselder *eg* cyffuriau gwrthiselder antidepressant drug
cyffur gwrthseicotig *eg* cyffuriau gwrthseicotig antipsychotic drug
cyffur lleddfu poen *eg* painkiller
cyffur lleihau gorbryder *eg* cyffuriau lleihau gorbryder anti-anxiety drug
cyffur rheoledig *eg* cyffuriau rheoledig controlled drug
cyffur ysgafn *eg* cyffuriau ysgafn soft drug
cyffuriau ac alcohol drugs and alcohol
cyffwrdd *be* touch
cyffwrdd-ymledol *ans* contagious
cyffyn *eg* cyffion shoot
cyffyn a dorrwyd o blanhigyn *eg* cyffion a dorrwyd o blanhigion cut shoot
cyffyn cymharu *eg* control shoot
cyffyn impiedig *eg* cyffynnau impiedig grafted shoot
cyffyrddell *eb* cyffyrddellau concept keyboard
cyffyrddiad *eg* cyffyrddiadau touch; contact
cyffyrddiad coes *eg* leg glance
cyffyrddiad ysgafn *eg* cyffyrddiadau ysgafn soft touch
cyffyrddol *ans* tactile
cyffyrddus *ans* comfortable
cygrychu *be* shirr
cyngerdd *eg/b* cyngherddau concert
cynghanedd gyfnewidiol *eb* roving harmony
cynghoraidd *ans* conciliar
Cynghorau Hyfforddi a Menter *ell* TEC: Training and Enterprise Councils
cynghori *be* counsel
cynghori academaidd *be* academic counselling
cynghori galwedigaethol *be* vocational counselling
cynghori geneteg *be* genetic counselling
cynghori rhieni *be* parent counselling
cynghorwr *eg* cynghorwyr counsellor
cynghorwr ysgol *eg* cynghorwyr ysgol school counsellor
cynghorydd *eg* cynghorwyr councillor
cynghorydd sir *eg* cynghorwyr sir county councillor
cynghrair *eg/b* cynghreiriau league
cynghrair *eg/b* cynghreiriau alliance
Cynghrair Arabaidd *eb* Arab League
Cynghrair Driphlyg *eb* Triple Alliance
cynghrair ddeublyg *eb* cynghreiriau deublyg dual alliance
Cynghrair er Cynnydd *eb* Alliance for Progress
Cynghrair er Diddymu'r Deddfau Ŷd *eb* Anti-Corn Law League
Cynghrair Fawr *eb* Grand Alliance
Cynghrair Hansa *eb* Hanseatic League
Cynghrair Niwtral Arfog *eb* League of Armed Neutrality
Cynghrair Sanctaidd *eb* Holy Alliance
Cynghrair Sanctaidd a Chyfamod *eb* Solemn League & Covenant
Cynghrair Schmalkalden *eb* Schmalkaldic League
Cynghrair y Cenhedloedd *eb* League of Nations
Cynghrair y Rhyddfrydwyr a'r Democratiaid Cymdeithasol *eb* SDP-Liberal Alliance
Cynghrair y Tri Brenin *eb* Dreikaiserbund
cynghreiriad *eg* cynghreiriaid ally
cynghreiriol *ans* allied
cyngor (=barn a gynigir) *eg* cynghorion advice
cyngor (=corff o bobl) *eg* cynghorau council
Cyngor Addysg a Thechnoleg *eg* Council for Educational Technology
Cyngor Addysg Iechyd *eg* Health Education Council
cyngor ar dribiwnlysoedd *eg* council on tribunals
Cyngor Canolog ar gyfer Mynediad i'r Prifysgolion *eg* UCCA
Cyngor Chwaraeon *eg* Sports Council
Cyngor Diogelwch *eg* Security Council
cyngor dosbarth *eg* cynghorau dosbarth district council
Cyngor Dyfarniadau Academaidd Cenedlaethol *eg* CNAA
Cyngor Economaidd a Chymdeithasol *eg* Economic & Social Council
Cyngor Gofal Cymru *eg* Care Council for Wales
Cyngor Gwaedlyd *eg* Council of Blood
Cyngor Gwarchod Natur *eg* Nature Conservancy Council
Cyngor Iechyd Cymdeithas *eg* Cynghorau Iechyd Cymdeithas Community Health Council
Cyngor Lateran *eg* Lateran Council
cyngor lleisiol *eg* vocal advice

Cyngor Llundain Fewnol *eg* Inner London Council
Cyngor Mawr *eg* Great Council
cyngor rhaglywiaeth *eg* regency council
Cyngor y Cwricwlwm Cenedlaethol *eg* National Curriculum Council
Cyngor y Gogledd *eg* Council of the North
Cyngor y Rhaglywiaeth *eg* Council of Regency
cyngor ymddiriedolaeth *eg* trusteeship council
cyngor ymgynghorol *eg* cynghorau ymgynghorol advisory council
Cyngor yr Henoed *eg* Age Concern
cyngres *eb* cyngresau congress
Cyngres Berlin *eb* Berlin Congress
Cyngres Berlin *eb* Congress of Berlin
Cyngres yr Undebau Llafur *eb* Trade Union Congress
cyngresol *ans* congressional
cyhoeddeb *eb* cyhoeddebau edict
Cyhoeddeb Adferiad *eb* Edict of Restitution
cyhoeddeb barhaol *eb* cyhoeddebau parhaol perpetual edict
Cyhoeddeb Brawdgarwch *eb* Edict of Fraternity
Cyhoeddeb Rhyddfreiniad *eb* Edict of Emancipation
cyhoeddi *be* publish; issue
cyhoeddi ardal eang *be* wide area publishing
cyhoeddi bwrdd gwaith *be* desktop publishing
cyhoeddi diddordeb *be* declare an interest
cyhoeddi rhyfel *be* declaration of war
cyhoeddiad (ar goedd) *eg* cyhoeddiadau proclamation
cyhoeddiad (=llyfr, cylchgrawn) *eg* cyhoeddiadau publication
cyhoeddiadau rhif PP *ell* PP number publications
cyhoeddus *ans* public
cyhoeddwr (llyfrau) *eg* cyhoeddwyr publisher
cyhoeddwr (y dref) *eg* cyhoeddwyr town crier
cyhuddo *be* arraign
cyhydedd *eg* cyhydeddau equator
cyhydedd thermol *eg* thermal equator
cyhydedd wybrennol *eg* celestial equator
cyhydeddol *ans* equatorial
cyhydnos *eb* cyhydnosau equinox
cyhydnos y gwanwyn *eb* vernal equinox
cyhydnos yr hydref *eb* autumn equinox
cyhyr *eg* cyhyrau muscle
cyhyr anrheoledig *eg* cyhyrau anrheoledig involuntary muscle
cyhyr anrhesog *eg* cyhyrau anrhesog smooth muscle
cyhyr ciliaraidd *eg* cyhyrau ciliaraidd ciliary muscle
cyhyr croth y goes *eg* cyhyrau croth y goes calf muscle
cyhyr llygad *eg* cyhyrau llygad eye muscle
cyhyr rheoledig *eg* cyhyrau rheoledig voluntary muscle
cyhyredd *eg* musculature
cyhyr-groenol *ans* musculocutaneous
cyhyrol *ans* muscle
cyhyryn *eg* cyhyrynnau muscle
cyhyryn crwn *eg* cyhyrynnau crwn circular muscle
cyhyryn deuben *eg* cyhyrynnau deuben biceps
cyhyryn estyn *eg* cyhyrynnau estyn extensor muscle
cyhyryn hydredol *eg* cyhyrynnau hydredol longitudinal muscle
cyhyryn maseter *eg* cyhyrynnau maseter masseter muscle
cyhyryn sythu *eg* cyhyrynnau syth erector muscle
cyhyryn triphen *eg* cyhyrynnau triphen triceps
cyhyryn y grimog *eg* cyhyrynnau'r grimog shin muscle
cylch (=criw o bobl) *eg* cylchoedd group
cylch (=modrwy) *eg* cylchoedd ring
cylch (mewn canu penillion) *eg* cylchoedd round
cylch (mewn chwaraeon) *eg* cylchoedd hoop
cylch (o ganeuon, cerddi) *eg* cylchoedd cycle
cylch (yn gyffredinol) *eg* cylchoedd circle
cylch anfantais *eb* cycle of disadvantage
cylch ansawdd *eg* cylchoedd ansawdd quality circle
cylch atal *eg* cylchoedd atal restraining circle
cylch atal ysgrifennu *eg* cylchoedd atal ysgrifennu write inhibit ring
cylch ategol *eb* cylchoedd ategol auxiliary circle
cylch blynyddol *eg* cylchoedd blynyddol annual ring
cylch bychan *eg* cylchoedd bychain small circle
cylch caniatáu ysgrifennu *eg* cylchoedd caniatáu ysgrifennu write permit ring
cylch canol *eg* cylchoedd canol centre circle
cylch cnoi *eg* cylchoedd cnoi teething-ring
cylch corc *eg* cork ring
cylch creithio *eg* cylchoedd creithio darning hoop
cylch cyfoedion *eg* cylchoedd cyfoedion peer group
cylch chwarae *eg* cylchoedd chwarae playgroup; play school
cylch dedendwm *eg* cylchoedd dedendwm dedendum circle
cylch diamedr cymedrig *eg* mean diameter circle
cylch dylanwad *eg* cylchoedd dylanwad sphere of influence
cylch ffelt *eg* cylchoedd ffelt felt ring
cylch fflan *eg* cylchoedd fflan flan ring
cylch fflan rhychiog *eg* cylchoedd fflan rhychiog fluted flan ring
cylch ffonolegol *eg* phonological loop
cylch genfa *eg* cylchoedd genfa terret ring
cylch gorchwyl *eg* terms of reference
cylch gwledig y cyrion *eg* outer country ring
cylch hydraidd *eg* cylchoedd hydraidd porous ring
cylch llygad *eg* cylchoedd llygaid eye ring
cylch mawr *eg* cylchoedd mawr great circle
cylch nwy *eg* cylchoedd nwy gas-ring
cylch papur *eg* cylchoedd papur paper circle

cylch pedwar *eg* hands four
cylch pridd *eg* cylchoedd pridd henge
cylch pumedau *eg* cylchoedd pumedau cycle of fifths; circle of fifths
cylch pwynt *eg* cylchoedd pwynt point circle
cylch rhedeg *eg* cylchoedd rhedeg circuit
cylch saethu *eg* cylchoedd saethu shooting circle
cylch saethu *eg* cylchoedd saethu striking circle
cylch sengl *eg* cylchoedd sengl single circle
cylch Sisili *eg* cylchoedd Sisili Sicilian circle
cylch sterling *eg* sterling area
cylch trafod *eg* cylchoedd trafod discussion group
cylch trefol *eg* cylchoedd trefol urban field
cylch tri pedwar *eg* hands three
cylch tyfiant *eg* cylchoedd tyfiant growth ring
cylch ynganu *eg* articulatory loop
cylchamlen *eb* cylchamlenni involucre
cylchau piston *ell* piston rings
cylchbais *eb* cylchbeisiau farthingale
cylchdaith (barnwr) *eb* cylchdeithiau eyre
cylchdaith (yn gyffredinol) *eb* cylchdeithiau circuit
cylchdro *ans* rotary
cylchdro *eg* cylchdroeon rotation; revolution
cylchdro cnydau *eg* cylchdroeon cnydau rotation of crops
cylchdro cnydau *eg* cylchdroeon cnydau crop rotation
Cylchdro Cnydau Norfolk *eg* Norfolk Crop Rotation
cylchdro cyflawn *eg* cylchdroeon cyflawn complete revolution
cylchdroeon clocwedd olynol *ell* clockwise consecutive revolutions
cylchdroeon dilynol *ell* consecutive revolutions
cylchdroeon y funud (c.y.f.) R.P.M.
cylchdroi *be* rotate; revolve
cylchdroi â llaw *be* rotate by hand
cylchdroi lliwiau *be* rotate colours
cylchdroi'n rhydd *be* rotate freely
cylchdro'r funud revs/min
cylchddwytho *be* circumduction
cylched *eb* cylchedau circuit
cylched AC *eb* cylchedau AC AND circuit
cylched baralel *eb* cylchedau paralel parallel circuit
cylched bont *eb* cylchedau pont bridge circuit
cylched brintiedig *eb* cylchedau printiedig printed circuit
cylched drydanol *eb* cylchedau trydanol electric circuit
cylched dderbyn *eb* cylchedau derbyn acceptor circuit
cylched electronig *eb* cylchedau electronig electronic circuit
cylched fer *eb* cylchedau byr short circuit
cylched gaeedig *eb* cylchedau caeedig closed circuit
cylched gwrtheddol *eb* resistive circuit
cylched gyfannol *eb* cylchedau cyfannol integrated circuit
cylched gyflawn *eb* cylchedau cyflawn complete circuit
cylched gyfres *eb* cylchedau cyfres series circuit
cylched gysain *eb* cylchedau cysain tuned circuit
cylched gysain baralel *eb* cylchedau cysain paralel parallel resonant circuit
cylched gysain gyfres *eb* cylchedau cysain cyfres series resonant circuit
cylched gywerth *eb* cylchedau cywerth equivalent circuit
cylched pont Wheatstone *eb* cylchedau pont Wheatstone Wheatstone's bridge circuit
cylched ragfynegi car-rif *eb* cylchedau rhagfynegi car-rif carry prediction circuit
cylched resymeg *eb* cylchedau rhesymeg logic circuit
cylched switsio *eb* cylchedau switsio switching circuit
cylched sylfaenol *eb* cylchedau sylfaenol fundamental circuit
cylched syml *eb* cylchedau syml simple circuit
cylched tca *eb* cylchedau tca tca cycle
cylched wresogi *eb* cylchedau gwresogi heater circuit
cylched wrthod *eb* cylchedau gwrthod rejector circuit
cylched yrru *eb* cylchedau gyrru driver circuit
cylchedd *eg* cylcheddau circumference
cylchedd cangen *eg* branch circumference
cylchfa *eb* cylchfaoedd zone
cylchfa amser *eb* cylchfaoedd amser time zone
cylchfa breswyl *eb* cylchfaoedd preswyl residential zone
cylchfa cynnydd a chymathu *eb* cylchfaoedd cynnydd a chymathu zone of advance and assimilation
cylchfa datblygiad procsimol *eb* zone of proximal development
cylchfa drofannol *eb* cylchfaoedd trofannol tropical zone
cylchfa dymherus *eb* cylchfaoedd tymherus temperate zone
cylchfa dymherus glaear *eb* cool temperate zone
cylchfa dymherus gynnes *eb* cylchfaoedd tymherus cynnes warm temperate zone
cylchfa ddirlawnder *eb* cylchfaoedd dirlawnder saturation zone
cylchfa fathyal *eb* cylchfaoedd bathyal bathyal zone
cylchfa ffawtio *eb* cylchfaoedd ffawtio fault zone
cylchfa grasboeth *eb* torrid zone
cylchfa gronni *eb* cylchfaoedd cronni zone of accumulation
cylchfa gyfnosi *eb* cylchfaoedd cyfnosi twilight zone
cylchfa gyswllt *eb* cylchfaoedd cyswllt contact zone
cylchfa gysylltnodi *eb* hyphenation zone
cylchfa rew *eb* cylchfaoedd rhew frigid zone

cylchfa ryngbarthol *eb* cylchfaoedd rhyngbarthol transitional zone
cylchfa sy'n trawsnewid *eb* zone in transition
cylchfa wrthod *eb* cylchfaoedd gwrthod zone of discard
cylchfa ymarfer *eb* training zone
cylchfa ymarfer cyfradd curiad y galon *eb* heart rate training zone
cylchfäedd *eg* zonation
cylchfaeo *be* zoning
cylchfan *eg/b* cylchfannau roundabout
cylchfaol *ans* zonal
cylchfordaith *eb* cylchfordeithiau circumnavigation
cylchfordeithio *be* circumnavigate
cylchforwr *eg* cylchforwyr circumnavigator
cylchffordd *eb* cylchffyrdd ring road
cylchganon *eb/g* cylchganonau infinite canon
cylchgerrynt *eg* cylchgerhyntau gyre
cylchglip *eg* cylchglipiau circlip
cylchglip allanol *eg* cylchglipiau allanol external circlip
cylchglip mewn rhigol *eg* cylchglipiau mewn rhigol housing circlip
cylchglip mewnol *eg* cylchglipiau mewnol internal circlip
cylchgrawn *eg* cylchgronau magazine
cylchgrawn ar gyfer yr arddegau *eg* cylchgronau ar gyfer yr arddegau teenage magazine
cylchgrawn arbenigol *eg* cylchgronau arbenigol specialist magazine
cylchgymesuredd *eg* cylchgymesureddau cyclosymmetry
cylchlif *eb* cylchlifiau bandsaw
cylchlithriad *eg* cylchlithriadau slump; rotational slip
cylchlithriad disgyrchol *eg* cylchlithriadau disgyrchol gravitational slumping
cylchlithro *be* slumping
cylchlythyr *eg* cylchlythyrau newsletter; circular
cylchlythyr darllenwyr *eg* cylchlythyrau darllenwyr readers newsletter
cylchlythyr y Pab *eg* cylchlythyrau'r Pab encyclical; papal encyclical
cylchoalcan *eg* cylchoalcanau cylchoalkane
cylchoalcen *eg* cylchoalcenau cylchoalkene
cylchoedd bach i bedwar *ell* rings right and left
cylchoedd cydganol *ell* concentric circles
cylchoedd cyfechelin *ell* coaxial circles
cylchoedd tyfiant anwastad *ell* uneven growth rings
cylchog *ans* ringed
cylchohecsadeuen-1,4-deuon *eg* cyclohexadiene-1,4-dione
cylchohecsan *eg* cyclohexane
cylchohecsanol *eg* cyclohexanol
cylchoid *eg* cylchoidau cycloid
cylchol (=yn ailadrodd e i hun) *ans* recurring
cylchol (mewn cemeg) *ans* cyclic
cylchol (o ran ffurf) *ans* circular
▶ **cylchotron** *eg* cylchotronau cyclotron
cylchred *eg/b* cylchredau cycle
cylchred bywyd *eb* life cycle
cylchred Calvin *eb* Calvin cycle
cylchred cywain /gweithredu *eb* cylchredau cywain /gweithredu fetch /execute cycle
cylchred dyfiant *eb* cylchredau tyfiant growth cycle
cylchred ddŵr *eb* water cycle
cylchred erydu *eb* cylchredau erydu cycle of erosion
cylchred faetholion *eb* nutrient cycle
cylchred fetabolaidd Krebs *eb* Krebs cycle
cylchred fislifol *eb* menstrual cycle
cylchred fridio *eb* cylchredau bridio breeding cycle
cylchred fwyd *eb* cylchredau bwydydd food cycle
cylchred garbon *eb* carbon cycle
cylchred gardiaidd *eb* cardiac cycle
cylchred gychwynnol *eb* cylchredau cychwynnol initial cycle
cylchred gyfarwyddyd *eb* cylchredau cyfarwyddyd instruction cycle
cylchred hydrolegol *eb* hydrological cycle
cylchred nitrogen *eb* nitrogen cycle
cylchred oes *eb* life cycle
cylchred oes cynnyrch *eb* product life cycle
▶ **cylchred oestrws** *eb* oestrous cycle
cylchred olchi *eb* cylchredau golchi washing cycle
cylchred pedair strôc *eb* cylchredau pedair strôc four-stroke cycle
cylchred peiriant *eb* cylchredau peiriant machine cycle
cylchred poblogaeth *eb* population cycle
cylchred prosesu data *eb* cylchredau prosesu data data processing cycle
cylchred prynu *eb* purchasing cycle
cylchred weithredu *eb* cylchredau gweithredu execute cycle
cylchred wrea *eb* urea cycle
cylchredeg *be* circulate
cylchrediad *eg* cylchrediadau circulation
cylchrediad agored *eg* open circulation
cylchrediad atmosfferig *eg* atmospheric circulation
cylchrediad caeedig *eg* closed circulation
cylchrediad dwbl *eg* double circulation
cylchrediad y gwaed *eg* blood circulation
cylchredol *ans* circulating
cylchtherm *ans* cyclotherm
cylchu (olwyn) *be* hoop
cylchu (troed, breichiau) *be* circling
cylchu (yn gyffredinol) *be* circle
cylchu maetholion *be* nutrient cycling
cylchyn *eg* cylchynnau circumference
cylchynol *ans* peripatetic
cylchynu *be* cycling
cyllell *eb* cyllyll knife; knife tool
cyllell balet *eb* cyllyll palet palette knife

cyllell balet gam *eb* cyllyll palet cam cranked palette knife
cyllell beintio *eb* cyllyll peintio painting knife
cyllell blicio *eb* cyllyll plicio paring knife
cyllell dorri *eb* cyllyll torri cutting knife
cyllell drimio *eb* cyllyll trimio trimming knife
cyllell ddeugarn *eb* cyllyll deugarn drawknife
cyllell endorri *eb* cyllyll endorri incising knife
cyllell fain *eb* cyllyll main slim knife
cyllell farcio *eb* cyllyll marcio marking knife
cyllell finiog *eb* cyllyll miniog sharp knife
cyllell gât a thrywel calon cyfunol combined gate knife and heart trowel
cyllell gerfio *eb* cyllyll cerfio carver
cyllell grefft *eb* cyllyll crefft craft knife
cyllell leino *eb* cyllyll leino lino knife
cyllell llawfeddyg *eb* cyllyll llawfeddyg scalpel
cyllell rannu *eb* cyllyll rhannu riving knife
cyllell sefydlog *eb* cyllyll sefydlog fixed knife
cyllell sefydlog (torri argaen) *eb* cyllyll sefydlog stationary knife
cyllell sgifio *eb* cyllyll sgifio skiving knife
cyllell stensil *eb* cyllyll stensil stencil knife
cyllell torri cerdyn *eb* cyllyll torri cerdyn card knife
cyllid (yn dod i mewn) *eg* cyllidau revenue
cyllid (yn gyffredinol) *eg* finance
cyllid a glustnodwyd *eg* earmarked funding
Cyllid y Wlad *eg* Inland Revenue
cyllideb *eb* cyllidebau budget
cyllideb arian cyfyngedig *eb* cyllidebau arian cyfyngedig cash limited budget
cyllideb ddirprwyedig *eb* cyllidebau dirprwyedig delegated budget
cyllideb fantoledig *eb* cyllidebau mantoledig balanced budget
cyllideb gyfanredol ysgolion *eb* cyllidebau cyfanredol ysgolion aggregate schools budget
cyllideb gyffredinol i ysgolion *eb* cyllidebau cyffredinol i ysgolion general schools budget
cyllideb ysgol *eb* cyllidebau ysgolion school budget
cyllidebu *be* budget
cyllidol *ans* budgetary
cyllidol *ans* fiscal
cyllyll a ffyrc cutlery
cymal (=colfach) *eg* cymalau knuckle
cymal (mewn dogfen) *eg* cymalau clause
cymal (yn y corff) *eg* cymalau joint
cymal bwylltid *eg* cymalau bwylltid swivel joint
cymal colfach *eg* cymalau colfach hinge knuckle
cymal cosbi *eg* penalty clause
cymal cyffredinol *eg* cymalau cyffredinol universal joint
cymal cylchdroi *eg* cymalau cylchdroi pivot joint
cymal eithrio *eg* cymalau eithrio exclusion clause
cymal eithrio *eg* cymalau eithrio exemption clause
cymal hyblyg *eg* cymalau hyblyg flexible joint
cymal iawndal penodedig *eg* liquidated damages clause
cymal lledr *eg* cymalau lledr leather joint
cymal llithro *eg* cymalau llithro gliding joint
cymal pelen a chrau *eg* cymalau pelen a chrau ball and socket joint
cymal penelin *eg* cymalau penelin elbow joint
cymal syml o symudiadau *eg* cymalau syml o symudiadau simple movement phrase
cymal symudol *eg* cymalau symudol movable joint
cymal synofaidd *eg* cymalau synofaidd synovial joint
cymal y glun *eg* cymalau'r glun hip joint
cymal y pen-glin *eg* cymalau pengliniau knee joint
cymalog *ans* jointed; articulated
cymalu *be* joint
cymanfa *eb* cymanfaoedd conclave
cymanfa *eb* cymanfaoedd assembly
cymanfa'r cardinaliaid *eb* conclave of cardinals
cymanfa'r hynodion *eb* assembly of notables
Cymanwlad y Gwladwriaethau Annibynnol *eb* Commonwealth of Independent States
Cymanwlad: y Gymanwlad (Brydeinig) *eb* Commonwealth, the
cymar wrth gymar peer to peer
cymaradwy *ans* comparable
cymarebol *ans* rational
cymargell *eb* cymargelloedd companion cell
cymaroldeb *eg* comparability
cymathiad *eg* assimilation
▶ **cymathol** *ans* assimilative
cymathu *be* assimilate
cymathyn *eg* cymathion assimilator
cymdaith *eg* cymdeithiau convoy
cymdeithas *eb* cymdeithasau society; association
cymdeithas adeiladu *eb* cymdeithasau adeiladu building society
Cymdeithas Addysg y Gweithwyr *eg* Workers' Education Association
cymdeithas amgen *eb* alternative society
cymdeithas amlddiwylliannol *eb* cymdeithasau amlddiwylliannol multicultural society
cymdeithas arwrol *eb* cymdeithasau arwrol heroic society
Cymdeithas Ddawns Werin Cymru *eb* Welsh Folk Dance Society
cymdeithas fasnach *eb* cymdeithasau masnach chamber of trade
Cymdeithas Fawrfrydig *eb* Great Society
cymdeithas feddiangar *eb* cymdeithasau meddiangar acquisitive society
Cymdeithas Frenhinol y Mwyngloddiau *eb* Royal Society of Mines
cymdeithas fynydda *eb* cymdeithasau mynydda mountaineering association
cymdeithas Gatholig *eb* cymdeithasau Catholig Catholic association
cymdeithas gefnog *eb* cymdeithasau cefnog affluent society
cymdeithas Geltaidd *eb* cymdeithasau Celtaidd Celtic society

cymdeithas gudd *eb* cymdeithasau cudd secret society
cymdeithas gydweithredol *eb* cymdeithasau cydweithredol cooperative society
Cymdeithas Gyfeillgar *eb* Cymdeithasau Cyfeillgar Friendly Society
cymdeithas gyfoes *eb* contemporary society
cymdeithas heb arian parod *eb* cashless society
cymdeithas i weithwyr *eb* cymdeithasau i weithwyr employee organisation
cymdeithas luosryw *eb* cymdeithasau lluosryw plural society
cymdeithas masnachu *eb* cymdeithasau masnachu trade association
cymdeithas oddefol *eb* permissive society
cymdeithas ohebu *eb* cymdeithasau gohebu corresponding society
Cymdeithas Ohebu Llundain *eb* London Corresponding Society
Cymdeithas Ryngwladol Gyntaf (y Gweithwyr) *eb* First International
cymdeithas rhieni *eb* cymdeithasau rhieni parent association
cymdeithas rhieni athrawon *eb* cymdeithasau rhieni athrawon parent-teacher association
cymdeithas tai *eb* cymdeithasau tai housing association
cymdeithas wâr *eb* cymdeithasau gwâr civilized society
cymdeithas wybodaeth *eb* information society
Cymdeithas y Cyfeillion *eb* Society of Friends
Cymdeithas y Ffabiaid *eb* Fabian Society
Cymdeithas y Gwyddelod Unedig *eb* United Irishmen
Cymdeithas yr Iesu *eb* Society of Christ
cymdeithaseg *eb* sociology
cymdeithaseg addysg *eb* sociology of education
cymdeithaseg plentyndod *eb* sociology of childhood
cymdeithasgar *ans* gregarious
cymdeithasgarwch *eg* sociability
cymdeithasgarwch *eg* gregariousness
cymdeithasiad syniadau *eg* association of ideas
cymdeithasol *ans* social
cymdeithasol lân *ans* socially clean
cymdeithasoli *be* socialization
cymdeithasoli cynradd *be* primary socialization
cymdeithasoli eilaidd *be* secondary socialisation
cymdeithasoliad *eg* socalization
cymdogaeth *eb* cymdogaethau neighbourhood
cymdogrwydd *eg* neighbourliness
cymedr *eg* cymedrau mean
cymedr cyfrannol *eg* mean proportional
Cymedr Euraid *eg* Golden Mean
cymedr geometrig *eg* cymedrau geometrig geometric mean
cymedr harmonig *eg* cymedrau harmonig harmonic mean
cymedr pwysol *eg* cymedrau pwysol weighted mean
cymedr rhifyddol *eg* arithmetic mean
cymedrig *ans* mean
cymedrol *ans* moderate; equable
cymedrol ddifrifol *ans* subacute
cymedrolwr *eg* cymedrolwyr moderator
cymedrolwr archwilio *eg* cymedrolwyr archwilio audit moderator
cymedrolydd *eg* cymedrolyddion moderator
cymer *eg* cymerau junction
cymeradwyaeth *eb* commendation; recommendation
cymeradwyo *be* recommend
cymeriad *eg* cymeriadau character
cymeriad comig *eg* cymeriadau comig comic character
cymeriad crefyddol ysgol *eg* religious character of a school
cymeriad cyffredinol Cristnogol *eg* general Christian character
cymeriad dynol *eg* cymeriadau dynol human character
cymeriad pyped *eg* cymeriadau pyped character of a puppet
cymeriad symbolaidd *eg* cymeriadau symbolaidd symbolic character
cymeriadaeth *eb* characterization
cymeriant *eg* consumption
cymeriant *eg* intake
cymeriant ac allgynnyrch *eg* intake and output
cymesur *ans* symmetric; symmetrical; well-proportioned
cymesuredd *eg* cymesureddau symmetry
cymesuredd adlewyrchiad *eg* reflective symmetry
cymesuredd cylchdro *eg* rotational symmetry
cymesuredd dwyochrol *eg* bilateral symmetry
cymesuredd pwynt *eg* point symmetry
cymesuredd rheiddiol *eg* radial symmetry
cymesuro *be* symmetrization
cymhareb *eb* cymarebau ratio
cymhareb ariannol *eb* financial ratio
cymhareb buanedd *eb* speed ratio
cymhareb cyflymder *eb* cymarebau cyflymder velocity ratio
cymhareb disgybl-athro *eb* cymarebau disgybl-athro pupil-teacher ratio
cymhareb draws *eb* cymarebau traws cross-ratio
cymhareb ddeufforchio *eb* cymarebau deufforchio bifurcation ratio
cymhareb F *eb* F ratio
cymhareb folar *eb* molar ratio
cymhareb gêr *eb* cymarebau gêr gear ratio
cymhareb geriad *eb* gearing ratio
cymhareb gritigol *eb* cymarebau critigol critical ratio
cymhareb grym *eb* cymarebau grym force ratio
cymhareb gyffredin *eb* cymarebau cyffredin common ratio

cymhareb prawf asid *eb* acid test ratio
cymhareb staff-myfyrwyr *eb* staff-student ratio
cymhareb union *eb* cymarebau union direct ratio
cymhareb wrthdro *eb* cymarebau gwrthdro inverse ratio
cymhareb wrthod *eb* rejection ratio
cymhareb wrthod modd-cyffredin *eb* common mode rejection ratio
cymhariaeth *eb* cymariaethau comparison
cymhariaeth gymdeithasol *eb* social comparison
cymharol *ans* comparative; relative
cymharu *be* compare
cymharu canlyniadau *be* compare results
cymharydd *eg* cymaryddion comparator
cymharydd foltedd *eg* voltage comparator
cymhelliad *eg* cymhellion incentive; motive; urge
cymhelliad a gweithred cymeriad character motivation and action
cymhelliaeth *eb* motivism
cymhelliant *eg* motivation
cymhellwr *eg* cymhellwyr exhorter
cymhennu *be* housekeeping
cymhlan *ans* coplanar
cymhleth *ans* complex; intricate
cymhleth Electra *eg* Electra complex
cymhleth israddoldeb *eg* inferiority complex
cymhleth Oedipws *eg* Oedipus complex
cymhlethdod *eg* cymhlethdodau complication; complexity
cymhlethu *be* compound
cymhlitho *be* blend
cymhlyg *ans* complex
cymhlyg diwydiannol *eg* cymhlygau diwydiannol industrial complex
cymhlyg metelau trosiannol *eg* transition metal complex
cymhlygu *be* complex
cymhlygyn *eg* cymhlygion complex
cymhlygyn genynnol *eg* gene complex
cymhorthdal *eg* cymorthdaliadau subsidy
cymhorthdal ad valorem *eg* ad valorem subsidy
cymhorthdal incwm *eg* income support
cymhorthdal tai *eg* cymorthdaliadau tai housing subsidy
cymhorthdal trethi *eg* rate subsidy
cymhorthdreth *eb* cymorthdrethi aid
cymhorthdreth ffiwdal *eb* feudal aid
Cymhorthdreth Wirfoddol *eb* Gracious Aid
cymhorthiad (addysgol) *eg* cymhorthiaid aide
cymhorthion clywedol *ell* aural aids
cymhorthion ergonomig *ell* ergonomic aids
cymhorthyn gweledol *eg* cymhorthion gweledol visual aid
cymhwysedd (=gallu i wneud y gwaith) *eg* cymwyseddau competence
cymhwysedd (=perthnasedd) *eg* applicability
cymhwysedd gwybyddol *eg* cognitive competence
cymhwysedd sylfaenol *eg* cymwyseddau sylfaenol basic competence
cymhwysiad (=addasiad bach) *eg* cymwysiadau adjustment; accommodation
cymhwysiad (=y defnydd a wneir o rywbeth) *eg* cymwysiadau application
cymhwysiad bras *eg* cymwysiadau bras coarse adjustment
cymhwysiad cyflym *eg* cymwysiadau cyflym quick adjustment
cymhwysiad isostatig *eg* cymwysiadau isostatig isostatic adjustment
cymhwysiad manwl *eg* cymwysiadau manwl fine adjustment
cymhwysiad masnachol *eg* cymwysiadau masnachol commercial application
cymhwysiad o wyddoniaeth *eg* application of science
cymhwysiad ochrol *eg* cymwysiadau ochrol lateral adjustment
cymhwyso (=addasu ychydig) *be* adjust; accommodate
cymhwyso (at) (=defnyddio pel peth addas) *be* apply
cymhwyso gosodiad *be* adjusting setting
cymhwysol *ans* applied
cymhwyso'r sbectromedr *be* adjust the spectrometer
cymhwyster (afon) *eg* competence
cymhwyster (yn gyffredinol) *eg* cymwysterau qualification
cymhwyster eiddo *eg* cymwysterau eiddo property qualification
Cymhwyster Galwedigaethol Cenedlaethol Cyffredinol (GNVQ) *eg* Cymwysterau Galwedigaethol Cenedlaethol Cyffredinol General National Vocational Qualification
cymhwysydd *eg* cymwysyddion adjuster
cymod *eg* reconciliation
cymodi *be* reconcile
cymodwr *eg* cymodwyr peacemaker
cymorth *eg* cymhorthion help; aid; assistance; support
cymorth a masnach aid and trade
cymorth allanol *eg* outrelief
cymorth ar gymorth help on help
cymorth cartref *eg* home help
cymorth cefn (drysau tabwrdd) *eg* cymhorthion cefn backing
cymorth cyfreithiol *eg* legal aid
cymorth cyntaf *eg* first aid
cymorth estynedig *eg* extended help
Cymorth Gwladol *eg* National Assistance
cymorth mewnbwn *eg* input help
cymorth plwyf *eg* parish relief
cymorth sgrin *eg* on-screen assistance
cymorth y tlodion *eg* poor relief
cymosin *eg* chymosin
cymotrypsin *eg* chymotrypsin

Cymraeg safonol *eg* standard Welsh
cymrawd *eg* cymrodyr comrade
cymrawd *eg* cymrodorion fellow
cymrawd ymchwil *eg* cymrodyr ymchwil research fellow
Cymreictod *eg* Welshness
cymrodoriaeth *eb* cymrodoriaethau fellowship
Cymru Fydd *eb* Young Wales
cymryd i mewn *be* take-up
cymryd pwysau ar y dwylo *be* take weight on hands
cymryd rhan *be* participate; take part
cymryd safle *be* position
cymryd tro *be* turn-taking
cymryd y llafn *be* take the blade
cymudadur *eg* cymudaduron commutator
cymudadur modrwy hollt *eg* cymudaduron modrwy hollt split ring commutator
cymudiad *eg* commutation
cymudo *be* commute
cymudol *ans* commutative
cymudwr *eg* cymudwyr commuter
cymun bendigaid *eg* holy communion
cymun bendigaid *eg* blessed sacrament
cymundeb *eg* communion
cymuned *eb* cymunedau community
cymuned amaethyddol *eb* cymunedau amaethyddol farming community
cymuned drefol *eb* cymunedau trefol urban community
cymuned dwyni *eb* cymunedau twyni dune community
cymuned ddysgu *eb* cymunedau dysgu learning community
Cymuned Glo a Dur Ewrop *eb* European Coal & Steel Community
cymuned hiliol *eb* cymunedau hiliol racial community
cymuned sefydlog *eb* cymunedau sefydlog sedentary community
cymuned sirol *eb* cymunedau sirol county community
cymunedol *ans* communal
cymwys (am berson sydd **â'r cymwyseddau**) *ans* competent
cymwys (am rywbeth ellir ei gymhwyso) *ans* applicable
cymwys (yn bodloni'r amodau) *ans* eligible
cymwysadwy *ans* adjustable
cymwysedig *ans* qualified
cymydog *eg* cymdogion neighbour
cymydog agosaf *eg* cymdogion agosaf nearest neighbour
cymyledd *eg* cloudiness
cymylog *ans* turbid
cymylogrwydd *eg* turbidity
cymylyn *eg* cymylynnau cloudlet
cymynaeth *eb* cymynaethau demise by will
cymynrodd *eb* cymynroddion bequest
cymynrodd *eb* cymynroddion legacy
cymynroddi *be* bequeath
cymysg *ans* mixed
cymysgadwy *ans* miscible
cymysgadwyaeth *eb* miscibility
cymysgedd *eg* cymysgeddau mixture; blend
cymysgedd adwaith *eg* reaction mixture
cymysgedd ar gyfer y croen *eb* cymysgeddau ar gyfer y croen topical preparation
cymysgedd ewtectig *eb* eutectic mixture
cymysgedd marchnata *eg* marketing mix
cymysgedd o sgiliau *eb* skill mix
cymysgedd o staff *eb* staff mix
cymysgedd pwynt berwi cyson *eb* constant boiling mixture
cymysgiad *eg* cymysgiadau admixture
cymysgu (=drysu) *be* confuse
cymysgu (mewn coginio) *be* blend
cymysgu (mewn metereoleg) *be* diffuse
cymysgu (yn gyffredinol) *be* mix
cymysgu clai *be* blunging
cymysgu lliwiau *be* colour mixing
cymysgwr sain *eg* cymysgwyr sain mixer
cymysgydd *eg* cymysgyddion blender
cymysgydd bwyd *eg* cymysgyddion bwyd food mixer
cŷn *eg* cynion chisel
cŷn befel *eg* cynion befel bevel chisel
cŷn caled *eg* cynion caled cold chisel
cŷn cerfio *eg* cynion cerfio carving chisel
cŷn clo drôr *eg* cynion clo drôr drawer lock chisel
Cyn Crist (CC) Before Christ
cŷn eingion *eg* cynion eingion hardie
cŷn ffyrf *eg* cynion ffyrf firmer chisel
cŷn goledd *eg* cynion goledd skew chisel
cŷn hanner crwn *eg* cynion hanner crwn half round chisel
cŷn hedegog *eg* cynion hedegog fly cutter
cŷn hir *eg* cynion hir paring chisel
cŷn main *eg* cynion main broach
cŷn mortais *eg* cynion mortais mortise chisel
cŷn plygio *eg* cynion plygio plugging chisel
cŷn sglodi *eg* cynion sglodi chipping chisel
cŷn trawstor *eg* cynion trawstor cross-cut chisel
cŷn trwyn diemwnt *eg* cynion trwyn diemwnt diamond point chisel
cŷn turnio *eg* cynion turnio lathe chisel
cŷn turnio *eg* cynion turnio turning chisel
cyn tynnu treth before tax
Cyn y Presennol (CP) Before Present
cynaliadwy *ans* sustainable
cynamserol *ans* premature
cyn-brawf *eg* cynbrofion pre-test
cynbrofi *be* pre-test
cyn-daniad *eg* pre-ignition
cynderfynol *ans* semi-final
cyndreialu *be* pre-trial

cyn-dwyn *eg* cyn-dwyni foredune
Cynddaredd y Sbaenwyr *eb* Spanish Fury
cyneclampsia *eg* pre-eclampsia
cynefin *eg* cynefinoedd habitat
cynefin defaid *eg* cynefinoedd defaid sheep walk
cynefino (mewn bioleg) *be* naturalize
cynefino (mewn seicoleg) *be* habituation
cyneginyn *eg* cynegin plumule
cynfas *eb* cynfasau sheet
cynfas *eg* cynfasau canvas
cynfas acrylig *eg* cynfasau acrylig acrylic canvas
cynfas arlunio *eg* cynfasau arlunio artist's canvas
cynfas dal dŵr *eb* cynfasau dal dŵr waterproof sheet
cynfas dynnu *eb* cynfasau tynnu drawsheet
cynfas ddwbl *eb* cynfasau dwbl double sheet
cynfas ffitiedig *eb* cynfasau ffitiedig fitted sheet
cynfas jiwt *eg* jute canvas
cynfas rhawn *eg* cynfasau rhawn hair canvas
cynfas sengl *eb* cynfasau sengl single sheet
cynfas teiliwr *eg* tailor's canvas
cynfas wedi'i breimio *eg* cynfasau wedi'u preimio primed canvas
cynfrodor *eg* cynfrodorion aborigine
cynfrodorol *ans* aboriginal
cynffon (gwisg) *eb* cynffonnau tailpiece
cynffon (yn gyffredinol) *eb* cynffonnau tail
cynffon a bwlch pin and slot
cynffon oen bach *eg* cynffonnau ŵyn bach catkin
cynffon llygoden *eb* cynffonnau llygod mouse's tail
cynffonnol *ans* caudal
cynffurf *ans* cuneiform
cyn-Gambriaidd *ans* pre-Cambrian
cyn-genl *ans* antenatal
cyn-geni *ans* prenatal
cynhadledd *eb* cynadleddau conference
cynhadledd achos *eb* cynadleddau achos case conference
Cynhadledd Heddwch Paris *eb* Paris Peace Conference
cynhadledd i'r wasg *eb* cynadleddau i'r wasg press conference
cynhaeaf *eg* cynaeafau harvest
cynhaliad *eg* support
cynhaliad silff *eg* cynhaliaid silff shelf support
cynhaliaeth *eb* subsistence
cynhaliol *ans* suspensory
cynhaliwr *eg* cynhalwyr rest
cynhaliwr rhwyll wifrog *eg* cynhalwyr rhwyll wifrog wire mesh support
cynhalydd *eg* cynalyddion bearer
cynhalydd *eg* cynalyddion support
cynhalydd drôr *eg* cynalyddion drôr drawer bearer
cynhanes *ans* prehistoric
cynhanes *eg* prehistory
cynheiliad *eg* cynheiliaid maintainer
cynheiliad bondo *eg* cynheiliaid bondo soffit bearer
cynheiliad saethben *eg* cynheiliaid saethben herring bone strut
cynheiliad silffoedd cymwysadwy *eg* cynheiliaid silffoedd cymwysadwy adjustable shelf support
cynheiliad solet *eg* cynheiliaid solet solid strut
cynheilio croes *be* strutting
cynheilio solet *be* solid strutting
cynheilydd (blodyn) *eg* cyneilyddion receptacle
cynheilydd (coesyn) *eg* cyneilyddion stalk
cynhenid *ans* intrinsic; innate; inborn
cynhenidiaeth *eb* nativism
cynhenidydd *eg* cynhenidwyr nativist
cynhennus *ans* contentious
cynhesrwydd *eg* warmth
cynhesrwydd mewnol *eg* internal comfort
cynhesu *be* warm; warm up
cynhesu byd-eang *be* global warming
cynhesu cyhyrau *be* warm up the muscles
cynhwysaidd *ans* capacitive
cynhwysedd *eg* cynwyseddau capacity
cynhwysedd cludo *eg* carrying capacity
cynhwysedd gwres *eg* cynwyseddau gwres heat capacity
cynhwysedd gwres cudd *eg* cynwyseddau gwres cudd latent heat capacity
cynhwysedd gwres sbesiffig *eg* cynwyseddau gwres sbesiffig specific heat capacity
cynhwysedd storio *eg* storage capacity
cynhwysedd yr ysgyfaint *eg* cynwyseddau yr ysgyfaint lung capacity
cynhwysfawr *ans* comprehensive
cynhwysiad *eg* inclusion
cynhwysiad dŵr *eg* water content
cynhwysiant *eg* cynwysiannau capacitance
cynhwysion paent *ell* contents of paint
cynhwysion tywod *ell* sand inclusions
cynhwysol *ans* inclusive
cynhwysydd *eg* cynwysyddion container
cynhwysydd *eg* cynwysyddion condenser
cynhwysydd *eg* cynwysyddion capacitor
cynhwysydd addurnol *eg* cynwysyddion addurnol decorative container
cynhwysydd electrolytig *eg* cynwysyddion electrolytig electrolytic capacitor
cynhwysydd electronig *eg* cynwysyddion electronig electronic container
cynhwysydd llyfnhau *eg* smoothing capacitor
cynhwysydd melysion *eg* cynwysyddion melysion sweet container
cynhwysydd plastig *eg* cynwysyddion plastig plastic container
cynhwysydd wedi'i wefru *eg* cynwysyddion wedi'u gwefru charged condenser
cynhwysydd-llwyth *eg* capacitor-load
cynhwysyn *eg* cynhwysion ingredient
cynhyrchaeth llafur *eb* labour productivity
cynhyrchedd *eg* productivity
cynhyrchedd cynradd *eg* primary productivity

cynhyrchiad *eg* cynyrchiadau production
cynhyrchiad fideo *eg* video production
cynhyrchiad theatraidd *eg* cynyrchiadau theatraidd theatrical production
cynhyrchiol *ans* productive
cynhyrchion eilaidd *ell* secondary productions
cynhyrchu (=creu mewn diwydiant) *be* manufacture
cynhyrchu (=datblygu) *be* evolve
cynhyrchu (cynnyrch amaethyddol etc) *be* yield
cynhyrchu (trydan) *be* generate
cynhyrchu (yn gyffredinol) *be* produce
cynhyrchu ar raddfa fach *be* small-scale production
cynhyrchu ar raddfa fawr *be* large-scale production
cynhyrchu celloedd *be* cell production
cynhyrchu cod *be* code generation
cynhyrchu cyfeiriad *be* address generation
cynhyrchu llafur-ddwys *be* labour-intensive production
cynhyrchu llinell gydosod *be* assembly-line production
cynhyrchu main *be* lean production
cynhyrchu mewn-llinell *be* in-line production
cynhyrchu mewn union bryd *be* just in time production
cynhyrchu yn ôl y gwaith *be* job production
cynhyrchu'r llais *be* voice production
cynhyrchydd *eg* cynhyrchwyr producer
cynhyrchydd cyfryngau *eg* cynhyrchwyr cyfryngau media producer
cynhyrchydd offer gwreiddiol *eg* cynhyrchwyr offer gwreiddiol original equipment manufacturer
cynhyrfu *be* excite; agitate; incense
cynhyrfus *ans* exciting; turbulent
cynhyrfwr *eg* cynhyrfwyr agitator
cynhyrfydd canolog *eg* cynhyrfwyr canolog central agitator
cyniferydd *eg* cyniferyddion quotient
cyniferydd addysgol *eg* cyniferyddion addysgol educational quotient
cyniferydd datblygiad *eg* developmental quotient
cyniferydd deallusrwydd *eg* intelligence quotient
cyniferydd lleoliad *eg* cyniferyddion lleoliad locational quotient
cyniferydd resbiradol *eg* respiratory quotient
cynildeb *eg* parsimony
cynilion *ell* savings
Cynilion Gwladol *ell* National Savings
cynilo (arian) *be* save
cynilo (egni) *be* conserve
cynilwyr *ell* savers
cynlyn *eg* cynlynnoedd former lake
cynllun *eg* cynlluniau plan; scheme; design
cynllun (=y ffordd mae rhywbeth wedi'i osod) *eg* cynlluniau layout
cynllun AB *eg* AB design
cynllun adroddiad *eg* report design
cynllun ailadrodd mesurau *eg* cynlluniau ailadrodd mesurau repeated measures design
cynllun arbrawf *eg* cynlluniau arbrofion experimental design
cynllun asesu *eg* cynlluniau asesu assessment plan; cheme of assessment
cynllun busnes *eg* business plan
cynllun bysellfwrdd *eg* cynlluniau bysellfyrddau keyboard layout
Cynllun Casglu a Throsglwyddo Credydau *eg* CATS: Credit Accumulation and Transfer Scheme
cynllun creadigol *eg* cynlluniau creadigol creative design
cynllun credydau *eg* cynlluniau credydau credit scheme
cynllun creu gwaith *eg* cynlluniau creu gwaith job creation scheme
cynllun cydaddysgol *eg* cynlluniau cydaddysgol co-educational scheme
cynllun cyflogi'r ifanc *eg* cynlluniau cyflogi'r ifanc youth employment scheme
cynllun cyfnewid *eg* cynlluniau cyfnewid exchange scheme
cynllun cyfoes *eg* cynlluniau cyfoes contemporary design
cynllun cyfuchlin *eg* contour plan
cynllun cymysg *eg* cynlluniau cymysg mixed design
cynllun cynhyrchu *eg* cynlluniau cynhyrchu production plan
cynllun cynilo *eg* cynlluniau cynilo savings scheme
cynllun chwarae *eg* cynlluniau chwarae play-scheme
cynllun darllen *eg* cynlluniau darllen reading scheme
cynllun datblygu twristiaeth *eg* tourism development plan
cynllun datblygu ysgol *eg* cynlluniau datblygu ysgol school development plan
cynllun ffactoraidd *eg* cynlluniau ffactoraidd factorial design
cynllun ffactoraidd dau wrth ddau *eg* cynlluniau ffactoraidd dau wrth ddau two by two factorial design
cynllun fflat *eg* cynlluniau fflat flatplan
cynllun fframwaith *eg* structure plan
cynllun gofal yn y gymuned *eg* community care plan
cynllun gofalu *eg* cynlluniau gofalu care plan
cynllun gosod patrwm *eg* cynlluniau gosod patrwm pattern layout
cynllun grwpiau annibynnol *eg* cynlluniau grwpiau annibynnol independent groups design
cynllun grwpiau ar hap *eg* cynlluniau grwpiau ar hap random groups design
cynllun grwpiau tebyg *eg* cynlluniau grwpiau tebyg matched group design
cynllun gwaith *eg* cynlluniau gwaith scheme of work
cynllun gweithredu *eg* cynlluniau gweithredu action plan

cynllun gwella iechyd *eg* cynlluniau gwella iechyd health improvement plan
cynllun gwers *eg* cynlluniau gwersi lesson plan
cynllun gwerthuso *eg* cynlluniau gwerthuso appraisal scheme
cynllun gwreiddiol *eg* cynlluniau gwreiddiol original design
cynllun gwrthdro ABA *eg* cynlluniau gwrthdro ABA reversal ABA design
cynllun gwrthgyfnewid *eg* cynlluniau gwrthgyfnewid counterchange design
cynllun haniaethol *eg* cynlluniau haniaethol abstract design
cynllun hyfforddi'r ifanc *eg* cynlluniau hyfforddi'r ifanc youth training scheme
cynllun hyrwyddo *eg* cynlluniau hyrwyddo promotional plan
cynllun labelu *eg* cynlluniau labelu labelling scheme
cynllun llawr *eg* cynlluniau llawr ground plan
cynllun llawr sylfaenol *eg* cynlluniau llawr sylfaenol basic ground plan
cynllun lliw *eg* cynlluniau lliw colour scheme
cynllun maethu remand *eg* cynlluniau maethu remand remand fostering scheme
cynllun marcio *eg* cynlluniau marcio mark scheme
cynllun marchnata *eg* cynlluniau marchnata marketing plan
cynllun mewn-grwpiau *eg* cynlluniau mewn-grwpiau within-groups design
cynllun mewn-gyfranwyr *eg* cynlluniau mewn-gyfranwyr within-subjects design
cynllun modiwlaidd *eg* cynlluniau modiwlaidd modular scheme
Cynllun Morgais Dewisol *eg* Option Mortgage Scheme
cynllun n-fechan *eg* cynlluniau n-fechan small-n design
cynllun oedi amser *eg* cynlluniau oedi amser time-lag design
cynllun oriau hyblyg *eg* cynlluniau oriau hyblyg flexible hours scheme
cynllun patrymol *eg* cynlluniau patrymol pattern design
cynllun presennol *eg* cynlluniau presennol existing design
cynllun profiad gwaith *eg* cynlluniau profiad gwaith work experience scheme
cynllun pum mlynedd *eg* cynlluniau pum mlynedd five year plan
cynllun rhaglen *eg* cynlluniau rhaglen program design
cynllun rhesymeg *eg* cynlluniau rhesymeg logic design
cynllun rhyng-grwpiau *eg* cynlluniau rhyng-gyfranwyr between-subjects design
cynllun rhyng-gyfranwyr *eg* cynlluniau rhyng-grwpiau between-groups design
Cynllun Schlieffen *eg* Schlieffen Plan
cynllun sgrin *eg* screen layout
cynllun sgwâr Lladin *eg* cynlluniau sgwâr Lladin Latin square design
cynllun traddodiadol *eg* cynlluniau traddodiadol traditional design
cynllun trawsddilynol *eg* cynlluniau trawsddilynol cross-sequential design
cynllun wrth gefn *eg* cynlluniau wrth gefn contingency plan
▶ **cynllun ymarfer corff** *eg* cynlluniau ymarfer corff exercise plan
cynllunio *be* plan; planning; design
cynllunio adnoddau *be* resource planning
cynllunio adnoddau dynol *be* human resource planning
cynllunio amgylcheddau *be* plan environments
cynllunio ar gyfer gyrfa *be* career planning
cynllunio cyfoes *be* contemporary design
cynllunio cynhyrchu *be* production planning
cynllunio drwy gymorth cyfrifiadur *be* computer aided design
cynllunio gweithredol *be* active planning
cynllunio, gwneud ac adolygu plan, do and review
cynllunio nifer y gweithlu *be* manpower planning
cynllunio projectau *be* project planning
cynllunio rhaglen *be* designing of programme
cynllunio rhyddhau *be* discharge planning
cynllunio system *be* design a system
cynllunio teulu *be* family planning
cynllunio tref *be* town planning
cynllunio'r cwricwlwm *be* curriculum planning
cynllunydd golygfeydd *eb* cynllunwyr golygfeydd scene designer
cynllunydd technegol *eg* cynllunwyr technegol technical designer
cynllwyn *eg* cynllwynion plot; conspiracy; intrigue
Cynllwyn Gorffennaf *eg* July Plot
Cynllwyn Pabaidd *eg* Popish Plot
Cynllwyn y Cydraddolion *eg* Conspiracy of Equals
Cynllwyn y Powdwr Gwn *eg* Gunpowder Plot
cynllwynio *be* plot; conspire
cynnal (arbrawf) *be* conduct
cynnal (arbrawf ar) *be* carry out
cynnal (blodyn) *be* subtend
cynnal (yn gyffredinol) *be* support
cynnal a chadw maintenance
cynnal ffeiliau *be* file maintenance
cynnal gweithgarwch *be* sustain activity
cynnal iechyd *be* health maintenance
cynnal peilot *be* pilot
cynnal prawf teg *be* carry out a fair test
cynnal rhaglen *be* program maintenance
cynnal rhan *be* maintain a part
cynnal system *be* system maintenance
cynnal twf *be* maintenance of growth
cynnau (golau, peiriant) *be* switch on
cynnau (tân) *be* ignite
cynnau (cyflenwad pŵer) *be* turn on
cynnau'r tân trydan *be* turn the electric fire on

cynneddf *eb* cyneddfau faculty
cynnen *eb* cynhennau feud
cynnen waed *eb* blood feud
cynnes *ans* warm
cynnig *eg* cynigion offer; proposal
cynnig arsylwadau *be* make observations
cynnig cyntaf *eg* cynigion cyntaf initial proposal
cynnig esboniadau *be* offer explanations
cynnig hidlo *eg* cynigion hidlo filter proposal
cynnil *ans* subtle
cynnwrf (=terfysg) *eg* cynhyrfau disturbance
cynnwrf (mewn hylif) *eg* agitation
cynnwrf (mewn aer etc) *eg* turbulence
cynnwrf (yn erbyn yr awdurdodau) *eg* sedition
cynnwrf (yn gyffredinol) *eg* excitement
cynnwrf byrraf *eg* minimum agitation
cynnwrf cymedrol *eg* medium agitation
cynnwrf hwyaf *eg* maximum agitation
cynnwrf mecanyddol *eg* mechanical agitation
cynnwys *be* include; contain
cynnwys *eg* cynhwysion content
cynnwys amlwg *eg* manifest content
cynnwys bwyd *eg* food content
cynnwys celloedd *eg* cell contents
cynnwys cronfa ddata *eg* database content
cynnwys cudd *eg* latent content
cynnwys cyfeiriadur *eg* directory contents
cynnwys cymorth *eg* help content
cynnwys dogfen *eg* document contents
cynnwys egni *eg* energy content
cynnwys ffibr *eg* fibre content
cynnwys gwyddoniaeth *eg* content of science
cynnwys halen *eg* salt content
cynnwys lleithder *eg* moisture content
cynnwys lludw *eg* ash content
cynnwys maethol *eg* nutritional content
cynnwys newydd *eg* new content
cynnwys pwnc *eg* subject content
cynnydd (=ennill) *eg* gain
cynnydd (=symudiad ymlaen) *eg* progress; advance
cynnydd (=twf) *eg* increase
cynnydd a chiliad waxing and waning
cynnydd cyflog teilyngdod *eg* merit pay rise
cynnydd egni net *eg* net energy gain
cynnydd mewn foltedd *eg* voltage gain
cynnydd unradd *eg* flat-rate increase
cynnydd y lleuad *eg* moon wax
cynnydd ymenyddol *eg* encephalization
cynnyrch (swm yr hyn a gynhyrchir) *eg* cynhyrchion yield; output
cynnyrch (yn gyffredinol) *eg* cynhyrchion product; produce
cynnyrch bwyd *eg* food product
cynnyrch cyfartalog *eg* average product
cynnyrch cyfryngol *eg* media production
cynnyrch egni *eg* energy yield
cynnyrch gorffenedig *eg* cynhyrchion gorffenedig finished product
Cynnyrch Gwladol Crynswth *eg* Gross National Product
cynnyrch llaeth *eg* cynhyrchion llaeth milk products; dairy products
Cynnyrch Mewnwladol Crynswth *eg* Gross Domestic Product
cynnyrch refeniw ymylol *eg* marginal revenue product
cynnyrch terfynol *eg* end product
cynnyrch y cracio *eg* products of cracking
cynnyrch y pen *eg* yield per head
cynnyrch ymhollti *eg* cynhyrchion ymhollti fission product
cynnyrch ymylol *eg* marginal product
cynnyrch yr hectar *eg* yield per hectare
cynoesol *ans* primeval
cynolchi *be* pre-wash
cynorthwyo *be* aid; assist; support
cynorthwyol *ans* auxiliary
cynorthwyydd *eg* cynorthwywyr assistant
cynorthwyydd cartref *eg* cynorthwywyr cartref home help
cynorthwyydd cefnogaeth arbennig *eg* cynorthwywyr cefnogaeth arbennig special support assistant
cynorthwyydd cinio *eg* cynorthwywyr cinio dinner lady
cynorthwyydd gofal iechyd *eg* cynorthwywyr gofal iechyd health care assistant
cynorthwyydd gofal plant *eg* cynorthwywyr gofal plant child care assistant
cynorthwyydd gwybodaeth i ymwelwyr *eg* cynorthwywyr gwybodaeth i ymwelwyr tourist information assistant
cynorthwyydd ymchwil *eg* cynorthwywyr ymchwil research assistant
cynosod *be* postulate
cynosodiad *eg* cynosodiadau postulation
cynradd *ans* primary
Cyn-Raffaelaidd *ans* Pre-Raphaelite
Cyn-Raffaeliad *eg* Cyn-Raffaeliaid Pre-Raphaelite
cynrewlifol *ans* pre-glacial
cynrychiadol *ans* representative
cynrychiolaeth *eb* cynrychiolaethau representation
cynrychiolaeth etholiadol *eb* electoral representation
cynrychiolaeth gyfrannol *eb* proportional representation
cynrychiolaeth gymdeithasol *eb* social representation
cynrychioldeb cyfranwyr *eg* subject representativeness
cynrychioli *be* represent
cynrychioli tirlun *be* represent a landscape
cynrychioliad *eg* cynrychioliadau representation
cynrychioliad data *eg* cynrychioliadau data data representation

cynrychioliad diagramatig *eg* cynrychioliadau diagramatig diagrammatic representation
cynrychioli'r gorffennol *be* representing the past
cynrychiolydd *eg* cynrychiolwyr delegate
cynrychiolydd *eg* cynrychiolwyr representative
cynrychiolydd haf *eg* cynrychiolwyr haf summer representative
Cynrychiolydd Tasglu Band Eang Cymru *eg* Broadband Wales Taskforce Representative
cynrhonyn *eg* cynrhon maggot
cynsail *eb* cynseiliau precedent
cynsail farnwrol *eb* judicial precedent
cynsail rwymol *eb* binding precedent
cyntaf i mewn - cyntaf allan *ans* first in - first out
cyntaf-anedigaeth *eb* primogeniture
cyntedd *eg* cynteddau vestibule
cyntedd y glust *eg* auditory meatus
cyntefig *ans* primitive
cyntefigedd *eg* primitivism
cynulleidfa (mewn oedfa grefyddol) *eb* cynulleidfaoedd congregation
cynulleidfa (mewn theatr, cyngerdd etc) *eb* cynulleidfaoedd audience
cynulleidfa darged *eb* cynulleidfaoedd targed target audience
cynulleidfa leiafrifol *eb* cynulleidfaoedd lleiafrifol minority audience
cynulleidfa oddefol *eb* cynulleidfaoedd goddefol passive audience
cynulleidfa weithredol *eb* active audience
Cynulleidfaoedd Crist *ell* Congregations of Christ
cynulliad *eg* cynulliadau assembly; convention; colloquy
Cynulliad Cenedlaethol *eg* National Assembly
cynulliad cyfansoddol *eg* constituent assembly
Cynulliad Cyffredinol *eg* General Assembly
cynulliad cynrychiadol *eg* cynulliadau cynrychiadol representative assembly
cynulliad deddfu *eg* cynulliadau deddfu legislative assembly
cynullydd *eg* cynullyddion convener
cynwreiddyn *eg* cynwreiddiau radicle
cynyddiad *eg* cynyddiadau increment
cynyddol *ans* progressive; incremental
cynyddu *be* increase
cynyddu pwythau *be* increase stitches
cynyrchluddiant *eg* repression
cypledig *ans* trussed
cypledig *ans* coupled
cyplu (rhywiol) *be* mate
cyplu (yn gyffrednol) *be* couple
cyplydd *eg* cyplyddion coupler; coupling
cyplydd acwstig *eg* cyplyddion acwstig acoustic coupler
cyplydd belt *eg* cyplyddion belt belt coupling
cyplydd dwyffordd *eg* cyplyddion dwyffordd double-acting coupler
cyplydd hyblyg *eg* cyplyddion hyblyg flexible coupling
cyplysu falfiau *be* coupling of valves
cyplysydd *eg* cyplyswyr brace
cyrathiad *eg* corrasion
cyrcydu *be* squat; crouch
cyrch *eg* cyrchoedd raid; fetch
cyrch awyr *eg* cyrchoedd awyr air raid
cyrch milwrol *eg* engagement
cyrchborth *eg* cyrchbyrth sally port
cyrchddisg *eg* cyrchddisgiau destination disk
cyrchfan *eg/b* cyrchfannau destination
cyrchfan glan-môr *eb* cyrchfannau glan-môr seaside resort
cyrchfan pellter byr *eb* short haul destination
cyrchfan teithio *eb* cyrchfannau teithio travel destination
cyrchfraint *eg* cyrchfreintiau access privilege
cyrchiad *eg* cyrchiadau access
cyrchiad cyfresol *eg* cyrchiadau cyfresol serial access
cyrchiad dilyniannol *eg* cyrchiadau dilyniannol sequential access
cyrchiad pell *eg* cyrchiadau pell remote access
cyrchlu *eg* cyrchluoedd task force
cyrchnod *eg* cyrchnodau goal
cyrch-organ *eb* cyrch-organau target organ
cyrchu (ffeil, data etc) *be* access
cyrchu (yn gyffredinol) *be* fetch; seek
cyrchu cyfresol *be* serial access
cyrchu o ffeil *be* file access
cyrchu uniongyrchol *be* direct access
cyrchu'r wybodaeth *be* access information
cyrchwr *eg* cyrchwyr cursor
cyrchwr annistrywiol *eg* cyrchwyr annistrywiol non-destructive cursor
cyrchwr fflachiog *eg* cyrchwyr fflachiog flashing cursor
cyrchwr traws *eg* cyrchwyr traws cross-hair cursor
cyrchwr uniongyrchol *eg* cyrchwyr uniongyrchol direct cursor
cyrens duon *ell* blackcurrants
cyrensen *eb* cyrens currant
cyrhaeddiad (=pa mor bell y gellir estyn) *eg* cyraeddiadau range; reach
cyrhaeddiad (yn y Cwricwlwm Cenedlaethol) *eg* cyraeddiadau attainment
cyrhaeddiad ar gyfartaledd *eg* average attainment
cyrhaeddiad llorweddol *eg* horizontal range
cyri *eg* curry
cyrion allanol *ell* outer fringes
cyrion dinas *ell* outer city
cyrion gwledig trefol *ell* rurban fringe
cyrion trefol *ell* urban fringe
cyrlio *be* curl
cyrnol *eg* cyrnolau colonel
cyrraedd (=dod i rywle) *be* arrive
cyrraedd (=estyn) *be* reach
cyrraedd a gadael arrival and departure
cyrraedd ei arffiniau *be* attain its bounds

cyrtsi *eg* cyrtsïau curtsy
cyrydiad *eg* cyrydiadau corrosion
cyrydol *ans* corrosive
cyrydu *be* corrode
cyrydu haearn *be* corrosion of iron
CYSAG: Cyngor Ymgynghorol Sefydlog Addysg Grefyddol *eg* SACRE: Standing Advisory Council for Religious Education
cysain *eg* cyseiniau resonant
cysawd yr haul *eg* cysodau yr haul solar system
cysefin *ans* prime
cysegr *eg* cysegrau shrine
cysegredig *ans* consecrated
cysegredig *ans* sacred
cysegriad *eg* consecration
cysegriad *eg* cysegriadau dedication
cysegru *be* consecrate; dedicate
cyseinedd *eg* consonance
cyseiniant *eg* cyseiniannau resonance
cyseiniant israddol *eg* cyseiniannau israddol inferior resonance
cyseiniant magnetig niwclear *eg* nuclear magnetic resonance
cyseiniant sbin *eg* spin resonance
cyseiniau gwneud *ell* artificial harmonics
cyseinio *be* resonate
cyseiniol *ans* resonant
cyseinydd *eg* cyseinyddion resonator
cysgiad *eg* dormancy
cysgod *eg* cysgodion shadow; shade
cysgod glaw *eg* cysgodion glaw rain shadow
cysgod lamp *eg* cysgodion lampau lampshade
cysgodi *be* screen
cysgodion symudol *ell* moving shadows
cysgodi'r bêl *be* screen the ball
cysgodlen *eb* cysgodlenni blind; shade
cysgodol *ans* leeward
cysgodwaith *eg* shadow work
cysgotgar *ans* shelter seeking
cysodfan *eg* cysodfannau print position
cysodi tudalen *be* page setup
cysodro *be* sweat
cyson *ans* consistent; constant; equable
cysondeb *eg* consistency
cysondeb disgleirdeb *eg* brightness constancy
cysondeb ffurf *eg* form constancy
cysoni *be* reconcile
cysonyn *eg* cysonion constant
cysonyn amser *eg* time constant
cysonyn cyfrannol *eg* constant of proportionality
cysonyn dadfeilio *eg* decay constant
cysonyn daduniad *eg* dissociation constant
cysonyn daduniad asid *eg* acid dissociation constant
cysonyn deuelectrig *eg* cysonion deuelectrig dielectric constant
cysonyn ecwilibriwm *eg* equilibrium constant
cysonyn graddnodiad *eg* calibration constant
cysonyn grym *eg* force constant
cysonyn lluoswm hydoddedd *eg* solubility product constant
cysonyn mympwyol *eg* cysonion mympwyol arbitrary constant
cysonyn permitifedd *eg* permittivity constant
cysonyn positif *eg* positive constant
cysonyn sbring *eg* spring constant
cystadleuaeth (i gael y trechaf) *eb* rivalry
cystadleuaeth (yn gyffredinol) *eb* cystadlaethau competition; contest; event
cystadleuaeth amherffaith *eb* imperfect competition
cystadleuaeth berffaith *eb* perfect competition
cystadleuaeth drac *eb* cystadlaethau trac track event
cystadleuaeth draws gwlad *eb* cystadlaethau traws gwlad cross country event
cystadleuaeth faes *eb* cystadlaethau maes field event
cystadleuaeth fasnachol *eb* commercial rivalry
cystadleuaeth fonopolistaidd *eb* monopolistic competition
cystadleuaeth rhwng ysgolion *eb* cystadlaethau rhwng ysgolion interschool competition
cystadleuaeth sgôr *eb* cystadlaethau sgôr score event
cystadleuol *ans* competitive
cystadleuydd *eg* cystadleuwyr contender
cystadleuydd *eg* cystadleuwyr competitor
cystadlu *be* compete
cystadlu am adnoddau *be* competition for resources
cystadlu am y bêl *be* compete for the ball
cystadlu gonest *be* honest competition
cystein *eg* cysteine
Cystennin Fawr *eg* Constantine the Great
cystiedig *ans* encysted
cystig *ans* cystic
cystin *eg* cystine
cystradau glo *ell* coal measures
cystrawen *eb* cystrawennau syntax
cystrawennol *ans* syntactical
cysur *eg* cysuron comfort; reassurance
cysuro *be* comfort
cyswllt (am feinwe etc) *ans* connective
cyswllt (am aelod, cymdeithas etc) *ans* affiliated
cyswllt *eg* cysylltau link; union; contact; junction
cyswllt anuniongyrchol *eg* indirect contact
cyswllt cyfathrebu *eg* cysylltau cyfathrebu communication link
cyswllt hyperdestun *eg* hypertext link
cyswllt Josephson *eg* Josephson junction
cyswllt llygaid *eg* eye contact
cyswllt nesaf *eg* next link
cyswllt newydd *eg* cysylltiadau newydd new link
cyswllt p-n *eg* cysylltau p-n p-n junction

cyswllt rhwydwaith *eg* cysylltau rhwydwaith network connection
cyswllt uniongyrchol *eg* direct contact
cyswllt ymgyfnewid data electronig (EDI) *eg* electronic data interchange (EDI) link
▸ **cyswllt-dorrwr** *eg* cyswllt-dorwyr contact breaker
cyswllt-lwythydd *eg* cyswllt-lwythwyr link-loader
cyswllt-olygu *be* link-edit
cyswllt-olygydd *eg* cyswllt-olygyddion link-editor
cysylltedd *eg* cysylltedau linkage; connectivity
cysylltedd fflwcs *eg* flux linkage
cysylltedd rhyw *eg* sex linkage
cysylltiad *eg* cysylltiadau connection; relation
cysylltiad cludiant *eg* transport link
cysylltiad drwy briodas *eg* cysylltiadau drwy briodas affinity
▸ **cysylltiad llinell ar log** *eg* cysylltiadau llinell ar log leased line connection
cysylltiad parhaol *ans* always on connection
cysylltiad rhwng y llais a'r cymeriad *eg* link between voice and character
cysylltiad rhyngrwyd *eg* internet connection
cysylltiad sain *eg* clang association
cysylltiad strategol *eg* strategic alliance
cysylltiadau cyhoeddus *ell* public relations
cysylltiadau diwydiannol *ell* industrial relations
cysylltiadau gyda'r gymuned *ell* community links
cysylltiadau hiliol *ell* race relations
cysylltiadau rhwng y cyflogwr a'r gweithwyr *ell* employer employee relations
cysylltiadol *ans* associative
cysylltiedig *ans* accompanying
cysylltiol *ans* associated
cysylltle *eg* cysylltleoedd junction
cysylltnod *eg* cysylltnodau hyphen; ligature
cysylltnodi *be* hyphenation
cysylltnodi awtomatig *be* automatic hyphenation
cysylltu (=gwneud yn sownd) *be* secure
cysylltu (=uno) *be* connect; link
cysylltu (â rhywun) *be* contact
cysylltu (cymdeithas etc) *be* affiliate
cysylltu â'i gilydd *be* join together
cysylltu medrau syml *be* link simple skills
cysylltwr *eg* cysylltwyr linker
cysylltydd *eg* cysylltyddion connector
cysylltydd ffrâm *eg* cysylltwyr ffrâm frame connector
cysylltyn *eg* cysylltion connective
cysyniad *eg* cysyniadau concept
cysyniad crefyddol *eg* cysyniadau crefyddol religious concept
cysyniad cynhwysiant *eg* concept of capacitance
cysyniad daearyddol *eg* cysyniadau daearyddol geographical concept
cysyniad darostyngol *eg* subordinate concept
cysyniad ffurfiol *eg* cysyniadau ffurfiol formal concept
cysyniad geometrig *eg* cysyniadau geometrig geometric concept
cysyniad gweledol *eg* cysyniadau gweledol visual concept
cysyniad gwyddonol *eg* cysyniadau gwyddonol scientific concept
cysyniad haniaethol *eg* cysyniadau haniaethol abstract concept
cysyniad lefel sylfaenol *eg* basic-level concept
cysyniad mecanyddol *eg* mechanical concept
cysyniad naturiol *eg* natural concept
cysyniad o dduw *eg* concept of god
cysyniad uwchraddol *eg* cysyniadau uwchraddol superordinate concept
cysyniadau cysylltiedig *ell* related concepts
cysyniadau hamdden *ell* concepts of leisure
cysyniadau'r cyfryngau *ell* media concepts
cysyniadol *ans* conceptual
cytawl pori *eb* common of pasture
cytbell *ans* equidistant
cytbell *ans* equally spaced
cytbwys *ans* balanced; well-balanced
cytbwys ddwyieithog *ans* balanced bilingual
cytew *eg* batter
cytew caenu *eg* coating batter
cytew ffriterau *eg* fritter batter
cytew tenau *eg* pouring batter
cytgan *eg/b* cytganau chorus
cytgord *eg* cytgordiau harmony; concord
Cytgord Ewrop *eg* Concert of Europe
cytgroes *ans* concurrent
cytocinesis *eg* cytokinesis
cytocinin *eg* cytocininau cytokinin
cytoleg *eb* cytology
cytoplasm *eg* cytoplasm
cytosgerbwd *eg* cytoskeleton
cytosol *eg* cytosol
cytosom *eg* cytosome
cytref *eb* cytrefi colony; conurbation
cytrefu *be* colonize
cytser *eg* cytserau constellation
cytser ambegynol *eg* cytserau ambegynol circumpolar constellation
cytser tymhorol *eg* cytserau tymhorol seasonal constellation
cytûn *ans* agreed
cytundeb (rhwng gwladwriaethau) *eg* cytundebau treaty; pact; concord
cytundeb (yn gyffredinol) *eg* cytundebau agreement
Cytundeb Ailyswirio *eg* Reinsurance Treaty
Cytundeb Atal Profion Niwclear *eg* Nuclear Test Ban Treaty
cytundeb atal-lledaenu *eg* cytundebau atal-lledaenu non-proliferation treaty
cytundeb credyd *eg* cytundebau credyd credit agreement

Cytundeb Cyffredinol ar Dollau a Masnach *eg* General Agreement on Tariffs and Trade
cytundeb dirgel *eg* cytundebau dirgel secret treaty
Cytundeb Dur *eg* Pact of Steel
Cytundeb Eingl-Wyddelig *eg* Anglo-Irish Treaty
cytundeb heddwch *eg* cytundebau heddwch peace treaty
cytundeb i beidio ag ymosod *eg* cytundebau i beidio ag ymosod non-aggression pact
cytundeb iawndal *eg* cytundebau iawndal compensation agreement
Cytundeb Iawnderau Dynol Ewrop *eg* European Law Convention on Human Rights
Cytundeb Mawr *eg* Great Contract
cytundeb penarglwyddiaethol *eg* suzerainty agreement
cytundeb priodas *eg* cytundebau priodas marriage settlement
cytundeb rhannu *eg* cytundebau rhannu partition treaty
cytundeb rhwng arsylwyr *eg* cytundebau rhwng arsylwyr interobserver agreement
cytundeb rhwng cyfeillion *eg* gentlemen's agreement
cytundeb terfynol *eg* cytundebau terfynol final concord
Cytundeb Tridarn *eg* Tripartite Indenture
cytundeb trwyddedu *eg* cytundebau trwyddedu licence agreement
Cytundeb y Culfor *eg* Straits Convention
Cytundebau Lateran *ell* Lateran Pacts
cythraul *eg* cythreuliaid demon
cythraul llwch *eg* cythreuliaid llwch dust devil
cythraul môr *eg* cythreuliaid môr angler fish
cythrwfl emosiynol *eg* emotional disturbance
cythryblus *ans* disturbed
cyw brwylio *eg* cywion brwylio broiler
cyw iâr *eg* cywion ieir chicken; fowl
cywain (gorchymyn cyfrifiadurol) *be* fetch
cywair (yn gerddorol) *eg* cyweiriau key
cywair (yn ieithyddol) *eg* cyweiriau register
cywair amhenodol *eg* indeterminate key
cywair gwreiddiol *eg* home key
cywair lleiaf *eg* minor key
cywair mwyaf *eg* major key
cywair penodol *eg* cyweiriau penodol determinate key
cywair perthynol *eg* cyweiriau perthynol relative key
cywair perthynol lleiaf *eg* relative minor
cywair perthynol mwyaf *eg* relative major
cywair-bur *ans* high fidelity
cywaith *eg* cyweithiau joint project
cywarch *eg* hemp
cywasg *ans* diminished
cywasgadwy *ans* compressible
cywasgadwyedd *eg* compressibility
cywasgedig *ans* compressed; impacted; push-down
cywasgedd *eg* cywasgeddau compression
cywasgfwrdd *eg* cywasgfyrddau compoboard
cywasgiad (mewn cerddoriaeth) *eg* cywasgiadau diminution
cywasgiad (yn gyffredinol) *eg* cywasgiadau compression; compaction
cywasgiad allanol ar y frest *eg* cywasgiadau allanol ar y frest external chest compression
cywasgol *eg* compressive
cywasgran *eb* cywasgrannau crumple zone
cywasgu (mewn cerddoriaeth) *be* diminish
cywasgu (yn gyffredinol) *be* compress; compact; push-down
cywasgu data *be* data compression
cywasgu ffeiliau *be* file compression
cywasgu'r frest *be* chest compression
cywasgydd *eg* cywasgyddion compressor
cyweddiad *eg* cyweddiadau engagement
cyweddiad dwbl *eg* double engagement
cyweddu *be* engage
cyweiraidd *ans* tonal
cyweirdant *eg* cyweirdannau tuning note
cyweirdant *eg* cyweirdannau tuning string; key string
cyweiredd *eg* cyweireddau tonality
cyweiriadur *eg* cyweiriaduron modulator
cyweiriadur mawr *eg* cyweiriaduron mawr extended modulator
cyweiriau perthynol *ell* attendant keys
cyweirio (lledr) *be* curing
cyweirio cudd *be* invisible mending
cyweirio cylched *be* circuit tuning
cyweirnod *eg* cyweirnodau keynote
cywerth *ans* equivalent
cywerth electrocemegol *eg* cywerthoedd electrocemegol electrochemical equivalent
cywerth llorwedd *eg* cywerthoedd llorwedd horizontal equivalent
cywerth metrig bras *eg* cywerthoedd metrig bras rough metric equivalent
cywerthedd *eg* equivalence
cywerthedd ysgogiadau *eg* stimulus equivalence
cywerthydd *eg* cywerthyddion equivalent
cywilydd *eg* humiliation
cywir (=gwir) *ans* true
cywir (=iawn) *ans* right
cywir (=manwlgywir) *ans* accurate
cywir (yn gyffredinol) *ans* correct
cywir neu anghywir true or false
cywirdeb *eg* accuracy
cywirdeb y perfformiad *eg* accuracy of the performance
cywiriad *eg* cywiriadau correction
cywiro *be* correct
cywiro'r diffyg *be* remedy the fault
cywirwr maen llifanu *eg* cywirwyr maen llifanu grindstone truer

Ch

chaconne *eg* chaconnes chaconne
chalet *eg* chalets chalet
chalumeau *eg* chalumeaux chalumeau
champlevé *eg* champlevé
chanson *eb* chansons chanson
Charlotte afal *eg* apple Charlotte
chaudfroid *ans* chaudfroid
chi (χ) **sgwâr** *eg* chi (χ) square
chiaroscuro *eg* chiaroscuro
chilli *eg* chilli
chintz *eg* chintz
chwa *eb* chwaon breeze
chwaeth *eb* taste
chwaeth gwisgo *eb* dress sense
chwalfa *eb* chwalfeydd crash
chwalfa disg *eb* disk crash
chwalu (=disgyn yn ddarnau) *be* disintegrate
chwalu (adeilad etc) *be* demolish
chwalu (gweithred ar gyfrifiadur) *be* crash
chwalu'n llwyr *be* annihilate
chwannen *eg* chwain flea
chwant *eg* craving
chwarae (darn) *be* play
chwarae (yn gyffredinol) *be* play
chwarae (yn gyffredinol) *eg* play
chwarae annheg *eg* unfair play
chwarae antur *eg* adventure play
chwarae ar eiriau *be* pun
chwarae archwiliadol *be* exploratory play
chwarae awyr agored *eg* outdoor play
chwarae brwnt *eg* foul play
chwarae byd bach *eg* small world play
chwarae cerddoriaeth *be* playing music
chwarae corfforol *eg* physical play
chwarae creadigol *eg* creative play
chwarae cydweithredol *eg* cooperative play
chwarae cyfochrog *eg* parallel play
chwarae cystadleuol *eg* competitive play
chwarae cysylltiadol *eg* associative play
chwarae digymell *eg* spontaneous play
chwarae dramatig-gymdeithasol *eg* socio-dramatic play
chwarae dychmygu *be* pretend play
chwarae efelychol *eg* imitative play
chwarae ffantasi *eg* fantasy play
chwarae gornest *eg* match play
chwarae hewristig *eg* heuristic play
chwarae llawn dychymyg *eg* imaginative play
chwarae llif rhydd *eg* free flow play
chwarae ostinato syml play a simple ostinato
chwarae peryglus *eg* dangerous play
chwarae rhan *be* role play
chwarae rhydd *eg* freeplay
chwarae sain *be* play sound
chwarae sgarmes *be* rough and tumble
chwarae strôc *be* stroke play
chwarae strwythuredig *eg* structured play
chwarae symbolaidd *eg* symbolic play
chwarae teg *eg* fair play
chwarae tennis *be* play tennis
chwarae trin â'r dwylo *be* manipulative play
chwarae therapiwtig *eg* therapeutic play
chwarae unigol *eg* solitary play
chwarae ymladd *be* play fighting
chwarae yn ôl y glust *be* play by ear
chwarae ysgogol *eg* stimulating play
chwarae'n fyrfyfyr *be* improvise
chwarae'n llawn *be* play in full
chwaraeon *ell* sport
chwaraeon byd-eang *ell* global sport
chwaraeon proffesiynol *ell* professional sport
chwaraeon rhyngwladol *ell* international sport
chwaraeon y gaeaf *ell* winter sports
chwaraewr *eg* chwaraewyr player
chwaraewr amryddawn *eg* chwaraewyr amryddawn all-rounder
chwaraewr clafesin *eg* chwaraewyr clafesin claveciniste
chwaraewr dethol *eg* chwaraewyr dethol seeded player
chwaraewr proffesiynol *eg* chwaraewyr proffesiynol professional player
chwaraewr viola da gamba *eg* chwaraewyr viola da gamba viola da gamba player
chwaraewr wrth gefn *eg* chwaraewyr wrth gefn reserve player
chwaraeydd casét *eg* chwaraewyr casét cassette player
chwaraeydd sain *eg* chwaraewyr sain sound player
chwarel *eb* chwareli quarry
chwarela *be* quarrying
chwarennau ecdysaidd *ell* moulting glands
chwarennol *ans* glandular
chwarren *eb* chwarennau gland
chwarren adrenal *eb* chwarennau adrenal adrenal gland

chwarren bitwidol *eb* chwarennau pitwidol pituitary gland
chwarren boer *eb* chwarennau poer saliva gland; salivary gland
chwarren Cowper *eb* Cowper's gland
chwarren chwys *eb* chwarennau chwys sweat gland
chwarren ddiddwythell *eb* chwarennau diddwythell ductless gland
chwarren ecsocrin *eb* chwarennau ecsocrin exocrine gland
chwarren endocrin *eb* chwarennau endocrin endocrine gland
chwarren felynwy *eb* chwarennau melynwy yolk gland
chwarren fwcaidd *eb* chwarennau mwcaidd mucous gland
chwarren gastrig *eb* chwarennau gastrig gastric gland
chwarren islygadol *eb* chwarennau islygadol infraorbital gland
chwarren laeth *eb* chwarennau llaeth mammary gland
chwarren lymff *eb* chwarennau lymff lymph gland
chwarren lymffatig *eb* lymphatic gland
chwarren sebwm *eb* chwarennau sebwm sebaceous gland
chwarren thyroid *eb* chwarennau thyroid thyroid gland
chwartel *eg* chwartelau quartile
chwarter *eg* chwarteri quarter; one quarter
chwarter cwafer *eg* chwarteri cwafer demi semiquaver
chwarter lleuad *eg* quarter moon
chwarter maint llawn *eg* quarter full size
chwarter tro (ongl sgwâr) *eg* chwarter troeon quarter turn
chwarter un cyfan *eg* chwarteri un cyfan quarter of a whole
chwarteru *be* quartering
Chwe Erthygl, Y *eb* Six Articles, The
chwech *eg* chwechau six
chwechawd *eg* chwechawdau sextet
chweched *eg* chwechedau sixth; one-sixth
chweched Almaenig *eg* chwechedau Almaenig German sixth
chweched atodol *eg* chwechedau atodol added sixth
chweched dosbarth *eg* sixth form
chweched Eidalaidd *eg* chwechedau Eidalaidd Italian sixth
chweched Ffrengig *eg* chwechedau Ffrengig French sixth
chweched synnwyr *eg* sixth sense
chweched uchaf *eg* upper sixth
chwedl *eb* chwedlau legend
chwedl achosegol *eb* chwedlau achosegol aetiological legend
chwedl Arthuraidd *eb* chwedlau Arthuraidd Arthurian legend
chwedl ethnolegol *eb* ethnological legend
chwenychiadau *ell* wants
chwephled *eg* chwephledi sextuplet
chwerw *ans* bitter
chwerwedd *eg* bitterness
chwiban *eg/b* chwibanau whistle
chwibanu *be* whistle
chwifio *be* flapping
Chwig *eg* Chwigiaid Whig
Chwigaidd *ans* Whig
chwilair *eg* chwileiriau word search
chwilen *eb* chwilod beetle
chwilen ddodrefn *eb* chwilod dodrefn furniture beetle
chwiler *eg* chwilerod chrysalis
chwilfriw *ans* disintegrated
chwilfriwiant *eg* disintegration
chwiliad *eg* chwiliadau search
chwiliad Boole *eg* chwiliadau Boole Boolean search
chwiliad cyfrifiadurol o lenyddiaeth *eg* chwiliadau cyfrifiadurol o lenyddiaeth computerized literature search
chwiliad deuaidd *eg* chwiliadau deuaidd binary search
chwiliad dilyniannol *eg* chwiliadau dilyniannol sequential search
chwiliad estynedig *eg* chwiliadau estynedig extended search
chwiliad iterus *eg* chwiliadau iterus iterative search
chwiliad polau *eg* chwiliadau polau poll search
chwiliad uwch *eg* chwiliadau uwch advanced search
chwiliedydd fflam *eg* chwiliedyddion fflam flame probe
chwilio *be* search
chwilio a newid search and replace
chwilio amryfal *be* multiple search
chwilio cyflym amryfal *be* multiple quick search
chwiliwr Hall *eg* Hall probe
chwilota *be* foraging
chwilys *eg* chwilysoedd inquisition
Chwilys Rhufain *eg* Roman Inquisition
Chwilys Sbaen *eg* Spanish Inquisition
chwip *eb* chwipiau whip
chwipio *be* whip
chwipio hem *be* whip a hem
chwistlen *eb* chwistlod shrew
chwistrell *eb* chwistrelli spray; syringe
chwistrell aerosol *eb* chwistrelli aerosol aerosol spray
chwistrell sefydlogi *eg* chwistrellau sefydlogi fixative spray
chwistrelliad (=pigiad) *eg* chwistrelliadau injection
chwistrelliad (yn gyffredinol) *eg* chwistrelliadau spray; squirt
chwistrelliad silicôn *eg* chwistrelliadau silicôn silicone spray
chwistrellu (=rhoi pigiad) *be* inject; syringe

chwistrellu (yn gyffredinol) *be* spray; squirt
chwistrellwr *eg* chwistrellwyr sprayer
chwitlyn glas *eg* chwitlyniaid glas coalfish
chwith *ans* left
chwith draws *ans* left cross
chwith gysylltiadol *ans* left associative
chwith syth *ans* straight left
chwith-glicio *be* left-click
chwiw *eb* chwiwiau fad
Chwiw Gymreig *eb* Welch Whim
chwyd *eg* vomit
chwydu *be* vomit
chwydu hyrddiol *be* projectile vomiting
chwydd *eg* chwyddiadau swelling
chwydd-amlen *eb* chwydd-amlenni amplitude envelope
chwyddbedal cytbwys *eg* chwyddbedalau cytbwys balanced swell pedal
chwydd-dyndra *eg* turgidity
chwydd-dynn *ans* turgid
chwyddedig *ans* distended
chwyddhad *eg* chwyddadau magnification
chwyddhad onglog *eg* chwyddadau onglog angular magnification
chwyddhadur *eg* chwyddaduron magnifier
chwyddiannol *ans* inflationary
chwyddiant (ariannol) *eg* chwyddiannau inflation
chwyddiant (y stumog) *eg* distention
chwyddiant cynnydd cost *eg* cost push inflation
chwyddiant cynnydd galw *eg* demand pull inflation
chwyddo (gydag aer etc) *be* swell; inflate
chwyddo (gyda chamera, cyfrifiadur) *be* magnify; zoom
chwyddo allan *be* zoom out
chwyddo blaenorol *be* zoom previous
chwyddo lled tudalen *be* zoom page width
chwyddo mewn *be* zoom in
chwyddo nesaf *be* zoom next
chwyddo pellach *be* increased magnification
chwyddo tudalen *be* zoom page
chwyddo'r testun *be* text zoom
chwyddwydr *eg* chwyddwydrau magnifying glass; hand lens
chwyldro *eg* chwyldroadau revolution
Chwyldro Amaethyddol *eg* Agricultural Revolution
Chwyldro Americanaidd *eg* American Revolution
chwyldro demograffig *eg* demographic revolution
chwyldro di-drais *eg* bloodless revolution
Chwyldro Diwydiannol *eg* Industrial Revolution
Chwyldro Ffrengig *eg* French Revolution
Chwyldro Gogoneddus *eg* Glorious Revolution
Chwyldro Gwyddonol *eg* Scientific Revolution
Chwyldro Môr Iwerydd *eg* Atlantic Revolution, The
Chwyldro Piwritanaidd *eg* Puritan Revolution
chwyldro prisiau *eg* price revolution
chwyldroadwr *eg* chwyldroadwyr revolutionary
chwylrod *eb* chwylrodau flywheel
chwyn ysgerbwd *ell* skeleton weeds
chwynladdwr *eg* chwynladdwyr herbicide
chwynladdwr cemegol *eg* chwynladdwyr cemegol chemical weed killer
chwynladdwr trawsleoledig *eg* chwynladdwyr trawsleoledig translocated weed killer
chwynnyn *eg* chwyn weed
chwyrlïad *eg* chwyrliadau swirl; whirl
chwyrliant *eg* chwyrliannau gyration
chwyrlïo *be* whirl
chwyrlïwr *eg* chwyrlïwyr whirler
chwyrlwynt *eg* chwyrlwyntoedd whirlwind
chwys *eg* sweat
chwysigen *eb* chwysigod bladder
chwysigen aer *eb* chwysigod aer air bladder
chwysigen nofio *eb* chwysigod nofio swimming bladder
chwysu *be* sweat
chwysu *be* perspire
chwyth *ans* blast
chwythbib *eb* chwythbibau blowpipe
chwythbren *eg* chwythbrennau wind instrument
chwythdwll *eg* chwythdyllau blast hole
chwythdyllau (castio) *ell* blow holes
chwythellu *be* blast
chwythfowldio *be* blow moulding
chwythiad *eg* chwythiadau blast
chwythiad gorgynnes *eg* chwythiadau gorgynnes hot blast
chwythlamp *eb* chwythlampau blowlamp
chwythorgan ddŵr *eb* chwythorganau dŵr hydraulic organ
chwythu *be* blow
chwythu EPROM *be* blow an EPROM
chwythu plwc *be* burn-out
chwythwr *eg* chwythwyr blower

D

D fwyaf *eb* D major
D leiaf *eb* D minor
da byw *ell* livestock
dab *eg* dabiau dab
dabio *be* dab
Dada *eg* Dada
dadadeiladu *be* deconstruct
dadadlamu *be* debouncing
dadagregu *be* disaggregate
Dadaiaeth *eb* Dadaism
dadaminas *eg* deaminase
dadamineiddiad *eg* deamination
dadamineiddio *be* deaminate
dadansoddi *be* analyse
dadansoddi achos-gwyredig *be* deviant-case analysis
dadansoddi ansoddol *be* qualitative analysis
dadansoddi clwstwr *be* cluster analysis
dadansoddi cymarebau *be* ratio analysis
dadansoddi cynnwys *be* content analysis
dadansoddi delweddau *be* image analysis
dadansoddi disgwrs *be* discourse analysis
dadansoddi ffactorau *be* factor analysis
dadansoddi gwallau *be* error analysis
dadansoddi naratif *be* narrative analysis
dadansoddi paill *be* pollen analysis
dadansoddi patrwm pwyntiau *be* point pattern analysis
dadansoddi protocolau llafar *eg* verbal protocol analysis
dadansoddi trafodol *be* transactional analysis
dadansoddi ymddygiad cymhwysol *be* applied behaviour analysis
dadansoddi ystadegol *be* statistical analysis
dadansoddiad *eg* dadansoddiadau analysis
dadansoddiad amlamrywedd *eg* dadansoddiadau amlamrywedd multivariate analysis
dadansoddiad amrywiant *eg* analysis of variance
dadansoddiad ansoddol *eg* dadansoddiadau ansoddol qualitative analysis
dadansoddiad ardaloedd cymdeithasol *eg* social area analysis
dadansoddiad arwyneb tuedd *eg* dadansoddiadau arwyneb tuedd trend surface analysis
dadansoddiad atchwel *eg* dadansoddiadau atchwel regression analysis
dadansoddiad cost a budd *eg* dadansoddiadau cost a budd cost-benefit analysis
dadansoddiad costau *eg* dadansoddiadau costau cost analysis
dadansoddiad cost-bygythiad *eg* analysis of cost-threat
dadansoddiad cydffurfiol *eg* dadansoddiadau cydffurfiol conformational analysis
dadansoddiad cyfanredol *eg* dadansoddiadau cyfanredol aggregate analysis
dadansoddiad cymarebau *eg* ratio analysis
dadansoddiad cymydog agosaf *eg* dadansoddiadau cymydog agosaf nearest neighbour analysis
dadansoddiad cystrawen *eg* dadansoddiadau cystrawen syntax analysis
dadansoddiad geiriadurol *eg* lexical analysis
dadansoddiad lleoliad *eg* dadansoddiadau lleoliad locational analysis
dadansoddiad llwybr critigol *eg* critical path analysis
dadansoddiad maeth *eg* nutritional analysis
dadansoddiad map *eg* map analysis
dadansoddiad meintiol *eg* dadansoddiadau meintiol quantitative analysis
dadansoddiad N-terfynol *eg* N-terminal analysis
dadansoddiad o anghenion *eg* needs analysis
dadansoddiad o'r farchnad *eg* market analysis
Dadansoddiad Prif Gydrannau *eg* Principal Component Analysis
dadansoddiad safle trosedd *eg* dadansoddiadau safle trosedd crime scene analysis
dadansoddiad systemau *eg* systems analysis
dadansoddiad testunol *eg* textual analysis
dadansoddi'r camddarllen *be* miscue analysis
dadansoddol *ans* analytical
dadansoddwr *eg* dadansoddwyr analyst
dadansoddwr systemau *eg* dadansoddwyr systemau systems analyst
dadansoddydd *eg* dadansoddyddion analyser
dadansoddydd awtomatig *eg* dadansoddyddion awtomatig auto-analyser
dadbacio *be* unpack
dadbersonoli *be* depersonalization
dadbigmentiad *eg* depigmentation
dadbolariad *eg* dadbolariadau depolarization
dadbolaru *be* depolarize
dadbolarydd *eg* dadbolaryddion depolarizer
dadchwyddiant *eg* deflation
dadchwyddo *be* deflate
dadchwythedig *ans* deflated
dadchwythiad *eg* dadchwythiadau deflation

dadchwythiant yr ysgyfaint *eg* lung deflation
dadchwythu *be* deflate
dad-dicio *be* uncheck
dad-drefedigaethu *be* decolonize
dad-ddarnio *be* defragment
dad-ddewis *be* deselect
dad-ddirwyn *be* unwind
dad-ddiweddaru *be* downdate
dad-ddyneiddio *be* dehumanize
dadelfeniad *eg* dadelfeniadau decomposition
dadelfeniad asomethan *eg* decomposition of azomethane
dadelfeniad dwbl *eg* double decomposition
dadelfennu *be* decompose
dadelfennu thermol *be* thermal decomposition
dadelfennydd *eg* dadelfenyddion decomposer
Dadeni *eg* Renaissance
dadfagneteiddio *be* demagnetize
dadfeiliad *eg* dadfeiliadau decay
dadfeiliad ymbelydrol *eg* radioactive decay
dadfeilio *eg* decay
dadfilwrio *be* demilitarize
dadflocio *be* deblocking
dadfodiwliad *eg* dadfodiwliadau demodulate
dadfodylydd *eg* dadfodylyddion demodulator
dadfygio *be* debug
dadfygio *be* debugging
dadfygio pell *be* remote debugging
dadfygiwr *eg* dadfygwyr debugger
dadgennu *be* desloughing
dadgodio *be* decode
dadgrwpio *be* ungroup
dadgrwpio gwrthrychau lluniadu *be* ungroup drawing objects
dadgrwpio metaffeiliau *be* ungroup metafiles
dadgrynhoi *be* decompile
dadgryptio *be* decryption
dadgydosod *be* disassemble
dadgydosodydd *eg* dadgydosodyddion disassembler
dadgyfraniad *eg* dadgyfraniadau disproportionation
dadgyplu *be* decouple
dadhydradiad *eg* dehydration
dadhydradu *be* dehydrate
dadhydradydd *eg* dadhydradyddion dehydration agent
dadhydredig *ans* dehydrated
dadhydrogenas *eg* dehydrogenase
dadhydrogeniad *eg* dehydrogenation
dadhydrogenu *be* dehydrogenate
dadl (=anghydweld) *eb* dadleuon disputation
dadl (=ffrae) *eb* dadleuon argument
dadl (=trafodaeth) *eb* dadleuon debate
dadl deleolegol *eb* teleological argument
dadl fathemategol *eb* dadleuon mathemategol mathematical argument
dadl gosmolegol *eb* cosmological argument
dadl natur/magwraeth *eb* nature/nurture debate
dadlaminadu *be* delamination
dadlen *eb* dadlennau reveal
dadlennu *be* reveal
dadleoledig *ans* delocalized
dadleoli *be* displace; delocalize
dadleoliad *eg* displacement; delocalization
dadleoliad electronau *eg* electron delocalization
dadlercian *be* delurk
dadleuwr *eg* dadleuwyr disputant
dadliwio *be* decolourize
dadlwytho *be* dismount
dadlygru *be* decontaminate
dadmer *be* thaw
dadnatsieiddio *be* denatzification
dadnatureiddiad *eg* denaturation
dadnatureiddio *be* denature
dadnerfogi *be* denervate
dadnitreiddiad *eg* denitrification
dadnitreiddio *be* denitrify
dadniwlo *be* defuzzification
dado *eg* dado
dadorchuddio *be* uncover
dadorchuddio o'r brig *be* uncover from top
dadorchuddio o'r chwith *be* uncover from left
dadorchuddio o'r dde *be* uncover from right
dadorchuddio o'r gwaelod *be* uncover from bottom
dadosod *be* uninstall; unset
► **dadreoleiddio** *be* deregulate
dadreoli *be* decontrol
dadrewi *be* defrost
dadrewlifiant *eg* dadrewlifiannau deglaciation
dadrithio *be* disillusion
dadrolio *be* unroll
dadryddfreinio *be* disenfranchise
dadsensiteiddio systematig *be* systematic desensitization
dadsgriwio *be* unscrew
dadstalineiddio *be* de-Stalinization
dadstartsio *be* destarch
daduniad *eg* dissociation
daduniad thermol *eg* daduniadau thermol thermal dissociation
dadunigoleiddio *be* deindividuation
daduno *be* dissociate
dadwaddoli *be* disendow
dadwaddoliad *eg* disendowment
dadwahanu *be* desegregation
dadwefriad *eg* dadwefriadau discharge
dadwefru *be* discharge
dadwefru blaenoriaethol *be* preferential discharge
dadwefrydd *eg* dadwefryddion discharger
dadwenwyniad *eg* detoxication
dadwenwyno *be* detoxicate
dadwisgo *be* undress

dadwladoli *be* denationalize
dadwneud *be* undo
dadwneud cofnod *be* undo entry
dadwneud cofnodi data *be* undo data entry
dadwneud fformatio *be* undoing formatting
dadwneud mewnbwn data *be* undo data input
dadwneud ystod argraffu *be* undo print range
daear (=cartref llwynog etc) *eb* daeërydd burrow
daear (=llawr) *eb* ground
daear (=tir) *eb* daearoedd earth
Daear (am y blaned) *eb* Earth
daeareg *eb* geology
daeargryd *eg* daeargrydiau earth tremor
daeargryn *eg* daeargrynfeydd earthquake
daearol *ans* terrestrial
daearu *be* earth; earthing
daearyddiaeth *eb* geography
daearyddiaeth ddynol *eb* human geography
daearyddiaeth gymhwysol *eb* applied geography
daearyddiaeth ymchwiliol *eb* investigative geography
dafad *eb* defaid sheep
dafaden *eb* defaid wart
dafnau gwaed *ell* drops of blood
dafnau hylif *ell* drops of moisture
dagr *eg* dagerau dagger
dangosiad *eg* dangosiadau exposition
dangosiad dwbl *eg* dangosiadau dwbl double exposition
dail nodwydd *ell* needle leaves
dal (gronyn) *be* capture
dal (yn gyffredinol) *be* catch
dal dŵr *ans* waterproof
Dalai Lama *eg* Dalai Lama
dalbren *eg* dalbrennau holdfast
dalbren mainc *eg* dalbrennau mainc bench holdfast
dalen *eb* dalennau sheet; leaf
dalen adborth *eb* dalennau adborth feedback sheet
dalen drefn *eb* dalennau trefn procedure sheet
dalen ddata *eb* dalennau data data sheet
dalen fap *eb* dalennau map map sheet
dalen fer *eb* dalennau byr short leaf
dalen frig *eb* dalennau brig fly-leaf
dalen gefnu *eb* dalennau cefnu backing sheet
dalen golfach *eb* dalennau colfach hinge leaf
dalen hir *eb* dalennau hir long leaf
dalen hysbysebu *eb* dalennau hysbysebu hand-out
dalen lwybro *eb* tracking sheet
dalen map *eb* dalennau map sheet of map
dalen offer arian *eb* dalennau offer arian silver tooling leaf
dalen offeru lliw *eb* dalennau offeru lliw colour tooling leaf
dalen sengl *ans* single-sheet
dalen sgraffinio *eb* dalennau sgraffinio abrasive sheet
dalen waith *eb* dalennau gwaith work sheet
dalen-borthi *be* form-feed
dalen-borthiad *eg* dalen-borthiadau form-feed
dalfan *eg/b* dalfannau placeholder
dalfan llun *eg* dalfannau llun picture placeholder
dalfan testun *eg* dalfannau testun text placeholder
dalgylch *eg* dalgylchoedd catchment area
dalgylch afon *eg* dalgylchoedd afonydd drainage basin
dalgylch ysgol *eg* dalgylchoedd ysgolion school catchment area
daliad (pêl etc) *eg* daliadau catch
daliad (yn gyffredinol) *eg* daliadau holding
daliad glân *eg* daliadau glân fair catch
daliadaeth *eb* daliadaethau tenure
daliadaeth fwrgeisiol *eb* burgage tenure
daliant (mewn cerddoriaeth) *eg* daliannau pause; fermata
daliant (gronynnau mewn hylif etc) *eg* daliannau suspension
daliant cyffredinol *eg* daliannau cyffredinol general pause
daliant llaethog *eg* milky suspension
daliedydd *eg* daliedyddion retainer
Dalit *eg* Dalit
daliwr (=teclyn i ddal) *eg* dalwyr holder; hooper
daliwr (mewn chwaraeon) *eg* dalwyr catcher
daliwr dei pen llonydd *eg* dalwyr dei pen llonydd tailstock die holder
daliwr dogfen *eg* dalwyr dogfen document holder
daliwr offer *eg* dalwyr offer tool holder
daliwr teip *eg* dalwyr teip type holder
dall *ans* blind
dall i liwiau *ans* colour blind
dallbwynt *eg* dallbwyntiau blind spot
dallineb *eg* blindness
dallineb geiriau caffaeledig *eg* acquired word blindness
dallineb lliw *eg* colour blindness
dallineb nos *eg* night blindness
dallolwg *eb* blindsight
damasg *eg* damask
damasgin *eg* damascene
damasgu *be* damascene
damcaniaeth *eb* damcaniaethau theory
damcaniaeth aflonyddiad *eb* perturbation theory
damcaniaeth agwedd ddwbl *eb* double aspect theory
damcaniaeth anghyseinedd gwybyddol *eb* cognitive dissonance theory
damcaniaeth amddifadaeth mam *eb* maternal deprivation theory
damcaniaeth bond falens *eb* valence bond theory
damcaniaeth brechu *eb* inoculation theory
damcaniaeth byd cyfiawn *eb* just world hypothesis
damcaniaeth cwantwm *eb* quantum theory
damcaniaeth cyflymu *eb* accelerator theory

damcaniaeth cymhelliad gwarchod *eb* protection motivation theory
damcaniaeth cymhelliant *eb* motivational theory
damcaniaeth cynllunio ymddygiad *eb* theory of planned behaviour
damcaniaeth cysondeb troseddau *eb* criminal consistency hypothesis
damcaniaeth darogan meddwl *eb* theory of mind
damcaniaeth datblygiad *eb* theory of development
damcaniaeth distryw creadigol Schumpeter *eb* Schumpeter's theory of creative destruction
damcaniaeth dri-bwa *eb* triarchic theory
damcaniaeth drigromatig *eb* trichromatic theory
damcaniaeth dysgu cymdeithasol *eb* social learning theory
damcaniaeth efelychu *eb* damcaniaethau efelychu copycat theory
damcaniaeth esblygiad *eb* theory of evolution
damcaniaeth foesegol *eb* damcaniaethau moesegol ethical theory
damcaniaeth ffafriaeth hylifedd *eb* liquidity preference theory
damcaniaeth gemau *eb* game theory
damcaniaeth ginetig nwyon *eb* kinetic theory of gases
damcaniaeth gweithredu rhesymegol *eb* theory of reasoned action
damcaniaeth gwrthyriad parau electron *eb* electron pair repulsion theory
damcaniaeth hunanganfyddiad *eb* self-perception theory
damcaniaeth James-Lange *eb* James-Lange theory
damcaniaeth labelu *eb* labelling theory
damcaniaeth llif dau gam *eb* two step flow theory
damcaniaeth maint *eb* quantity theory
Damcaniaeth Man Canol *eb* Central Place Theory
damcaniaeth niwronau *eb* neuron theory
damcaniaeth nodwydd hypodermig *eb* hypodermic needle theory
damcaniaeth perthnasedd *eb* theory of relativity
damcaniaeth priodoli *eb* attribution theory
damcaniaeth reoli *eb* control theory
damcaniaeth ronynnol etifeddiad *eb* particulate theory of inheritance
damcaniaeth sector *eb* damcaniaethau sector sector theory
damcaniaeth seiliedig *eb* grounded theory
damcaniaeth signal-ganfyddiad *eb* signal detection theory
damcaniaeth syfliad i'r dde *eb* right shift theory
damcaniaeth tectoneg platiau *eb* plate tectonic theory
damcaniaeth ymddygiad *eb* behavioural theory
damcaniaethol *ans* theoretical
damcaniaethu *be* theorize
damcaniaethwr magwraeth *eg* damcaniaethwyr magwraeth nurture theorist
dameg *eb* damhegion parable
damper *eg* damperau damper
damwain *eb* damweiniau accident
damwain *eb* damweiniau casualty
damwain ac argyfwng accident and emergency
damwain anochel *eb* inevitable accident
damwain ffordd *eb* damweiniau ffordd road traffic accident
damwain gerebrofasgwlar *eb* cerebrovascular accident
dan anfantais *ans* disadvantaged
dan anfantais ddiwylliannol culturally disadvantaged
dan anfantais gymdeithasol disadvantaged socially
dan do *ans* indoor
dan ei enw ei hun *adf* in his personal capacity
dan ei henw ei hun *adf* in her personal capacity
dan oed ysgol *ans* preschool
dan sylw *ans* observed
dan y belt *adf* below the belt
dana *eg* dana
Danaidd *ans* Danish
Daneg *eb* Danish
dangos *be* indicate
dangos anweledigion *be* show invisibles
dangos ategion *be* display plug-ins
dangos bwledi *be* display bullets
dangos canllawiau tudalen *be* show page guides
dangos clipfwrdd *be* show clipboard
dangos cofnodion anweithredol *be* display inactive records
dangos dogfennau *be* display documents
dangos dynameg *be* indicate dynamics
dangos graddlwyd *be* display grayscale
dangos grid *be* display grid
dangos gwybodaeth ychwanegol *be* display additional information
dangos llinellau snap *be* snap lines visible
dangos lliwiau *be* display colours
dangos maes *be* display field
dangos mesurydd *be* show ruler
dangos popeth *be* display all
dangos priflythrennau bach *be* display drop caps
dangos priodweddau *be* display properties
dangos rhybudd *be* display warning
dangos testun *be* text display
dangosydd (sgrin cyfrifiadur etc) *eg* dangosyddion display
dangosydd (yn gyffredinol) *eg* dangosyddion indicator
dangosydd camdriniaeth *eg* dangosyddion camdriniaeth indicator of abuse
dangosydd cyfrifiannell *eg* dangosyddion cyfrifiannell calculator display
dangosydd cyffredinol *eg* universal indicator
dangosydd gwall *eg* dangosyddion gwall error indicator
dangosydd llif *eg* flow indicator

adf, adv adferf, *adverb* ***ans, adj*** ansoddair, *adjective* ***be*** berf, *verb* ***eb*** enw benywaidd, *feminine noun* ***eg*** enw gwrywaidd, *masculine noun*

dangosydd perfformiad *eg* dangosyddion perfformiad performance indicator
dangosydd uned mesur *eg* dangosyddion uned mesur measure unit display
dangosydd yn yr ysgol *eg* dangosyddion yn yr ysgol school-based indicator
danheddiad *eg* daneddiadau indentation
danheddiad sgriw *eg* pitch of screw
danheddog (am olwyn) *ans* cogged
danheddog (llafn etc) *ans* serrated
danheddus *ans* indented
Daniad *eg* Daniaid Dane
dannedd *ell* feed dog
dannedd clicied *ell* ratchet teeth
dannedd dodi *ell* dentures
dannedd gosod *ell* dentures
dannedd i'r fodfedd T.P.I.
dannedd llif *ell* saw teeth
dannedd mân *ell* fine teeth
dant *eg* dannedd tooth
dant â llenwad *eg* filled tooth
dant ar goll *eg* missing tooth
dant cyntaf *eg* dannedd cyntaf deciduous tooth
dant gêr *eg* dannedd gêr gear tooth
dant gêr cylchoidol *eg* dannedd gêr cylchoidol cycloidal gear tooth
dant gosod *eg* dannedd gosod false tooth
dant llygad *eg* dannedd llygad canine tooth
dant llygad *eg* dannedd llygad eye tooth
dant parhaol *eg* dannedd parhaol permanent tooth
dant sugno *eg* dannedd sugno milk tooth
dant wedi pydru *eg* dannedd wedi pydru decayed tooth
darbodaeth *eb* thrift
darbodion maint *ell* economies of scale
darbodus *ans* economical
darddullaidd *ans* mannerist
darddulliaeth *eb* mannerism
darddullwr *eg* darddullwyr mannerist
darfath *eg* darfathau swage
darfath isaf *eg* bottom swage
darfath uchaf *eg* top swage
darfathu *be* swage
darfodedigaeth *eb* consumption
darfodus *ans* perishable
darforio *be* drawboring
darfudiad *eg* darfudiadau convection
darfudol *ans* convectional
darffeilio *be* drawfiling
dargadw *be* retain
dargadwedd (haearn gan y meinweoedd) *eg* retention
darganfod (=cael hyd i) *be* obtain
darganfod (=pennu) *be* determine
darganfod (yn gyffredinol) *be* find
darganfod atebion *be* find solutions
darganfyddiad *eg* darganfyddiadau find; discovery
dargludedd *eg* dargludeddau conductivity
dargludedd thermol *eg* thermal conductivity
dargludiad *eg* dargludiadau conduction
dargludiad electronig *eg* electronic conduction
dargludiad nerfol *eg* nervous conduction
dargludiant *eg* dargludiannau conductance
dargludo *be* conduct
dargludo drwy'r asgwrn *be* bone conduction
dargludol *ans* conducting
dargludydd *eg* dargludyddion conductor
dargludydd gwres *eg* dargludyddion gwres conductor of heat
dargopïo *be* trace
dargopïwr slip *eg* dargopïwyr slip slip tracer
dargyfeiriad *eb* dargyfeiriadau detour; diversion; divergence
dargyfeirio *be* diverge
dargyfeiriol *ans* divergent
darlifiad *eg* darlifiadau perfusion
darlifo *be* perfuse
darlith *eb* darlithoedd lecture
darlith sefydlu *eb* darlithoedd sefydlu inaugural lecture
darlithfa *eb* darlithfeydd lecture theatre
darlithydd *eg* darlithwyr lecturer
darlun (=braslun) *eg* darluniau sketch
darlun (i egluro rhywbeth) *eg* darluniau illustration
darlun (yn gyffredinol) *eg* darluniau picture
darlun eglurhaol *eg* darluniau eglurhaol illustration
darlun nesaf *eg* next picture
darlun plân gwastad *eg* darluniau plân gwastad plane picture
darlun ymddiddan *eg* darluniau ymddiddan conversation piece
darluniad *eg* darluniadau illustration
darluniad pwrpasol *eg* darluniadau pwrpasol appropriate illustration
darluniadaeth *eb* pictorialism
darluniadol *ans* illustrated;pictorial; illustrative
darluniaidd *ans* picturesque
darlunio *be* illustrate
darlunio parhaus *be* persistance of vision
darllediad *eg* darllediadau broadcast
darlledu *be* broadcast
darlledu lloeren *be* satellite broadcasting
darllen *be* read
darllen a chywiro corrective reading
darllen a deall reading comprehension
darllen cymharol *eg* comparative reading
darllen dan oruchwyliaeth *eg* controlled reading
darllen datblygiadol *eg* developmental reading
darllen eang *be* extensive reading
darllen estynedig *eg* extended reading
darllen ffonetig *be* phonetic reading
darllen gair cyfan *be* whole-word reading
darllen gwefusau *be* lip reading
darllen gweithredol *be* active reading

darllen gweithredol *eg* functional reading
darllen mewn pâr *be* paired reading
darllen proflenni *be* proof-read
darllen yn unig write-protected
darllenadwy *ans* legible
darllenadwy i gyfrifiadur *ans* computer readable
darllenadwyaeth *eb* legibility
darllenfa *eb* darllenfeydd lectern
darllenfa fwrdd *eb* darllenfeydd bwrdd table lectern
darlleniad *eg* darlleniadau reading
darlleniad fernier *eg* darlleniadau fernier vernier reading
darlleniad micromedr *eg* darlleniadau micromedr micrometer reading
darllenydd *eg* darllenyddion reader
darllenydd annibynnol *eg* darllenwyr annibynnol autonomous reader
darllenydd bathodynnau *eg* darllenyddion bathodynnau badge reader
darllenydd cardiau *eg* darllenyddion cardiau card reader
▸ **darllenydd codau bar** *eg* darllenwyr codau bar bar code reader
darllenydd dogfennau *eg* darllenyddion dogfennau document reader
darllenydd newyddion *eg* newsreader
darllenydd nodau *eg* darllenwyr nodau character reader
darllenydd tâp *eg* darllenyddion tâp tape reader
darllenydd tâp papur *eg* darllenyddion tâp papur paper tape reader
darn *eg* darnau piece; part; fragment; section
darn ar wahân *eg* darnau ar wahân separate piece
darn arian *eg* darnau arian coin
darn byrfyfyr *eg* darnau byrfyfyr extemporization passage
darn crafangu *eg* darnau crafangu chucking piece
darn crochenwaith *eg* darnau crochenwaith shard
darn croes *eg* darnau croes cross piece
darn crudiad (aelwyd) *eg* cradling piece
darn cydrannol *eg* darnau cydrannol component part
darn cyfagos *eg* darnau cyfagos adjacent part
darn cyfnewid *eg* darnau cyfnewid transition piece
darn cynhyrchu *eg* production piece
darn estyn *eg* darnau estyn stretcher piece
darn grŵp *eg* darnau grŵp group piece
darn gwaelod *eg* darnau gwaelod bottom part
darn gwaith *eg* darnau gwaith workpiece
darn gwrthddwr *eg* darnau gwrthddwr soaker
darn lletemu *eg* darnau lletemu firming piece
darn o dir *eg* darnau o dir tract
darn o ffilm *eg* footage
darn o glip fideo *eg* video extract
darn patrwm *eg* darnau patrwm pattern piece
darn pellter *eg* darnau pellter distance piece
darn pôl *eg* darnau pôl pole piece
darn uchaf *eg* darnau uchaf top part
darn ychwanegol *eg* darnau ychwanegol additional piece
darniad *eg* darniadau fragmentation
darnio ffermydd *be* fragmentation of holdings
darniog *ans* fragmentary
darogan *eg* daroganau augury
daroganwr *eg* daroganwyr predictor
darostwng *be* subjugate; subdue; reduce
darostyngiad *eg* abasement
darpar *ans* designate
darpar gadeirydd *eg* darpar gadeiryddion chairman designate
darpar gof *eg* prospective memory
darpar gwsmer *eg* darpar gwsmeriaid potential customer
darpariaeth *eb* darpariaethau provision
darpariaeth mislif *eg* sanitary protection
darparu *be* provide; cater
darparu tai *be* housing provision
darparwr gofal iechyd *eg* darparwyr gofal iechyd health care provider
darparwr gwasanaeth *eg* darparwyr gwasanaeth service provider
darparwr gwasanaeth ar-lein *eg* darparwyr gwasanaeth ar-lein on-line service provider
dart *eg* dartiau dart
dart deubwynt *eg* dartiau deubwynt double pointed dart
dart deubwynt *eg* dartiau deubwynt double ended dart
darwagiad oson *eg* ozone depletion
darwagio *be* deplete
darwahanu *be* stagger
darwahanu hoelion *be* stagger nails
darwasgedig *ans* constricted
darwasgiad *eg* darwasgiadau constriction
darwasgu *be* constrict
Darwiniaeth *eb* Darwinism
darheulad *eg* insolation
data *ell* data
data a synhwyrir o bell *ell* remotely sensed data
data amseryddol *ell* temporal data
data annormal *ell* abnormal data
data ansoddol *ell* qualitative data
data arbrofion *ell* experimental data
data arwahanol *ell* discrete data
data busnes *ell* business data
data crai *ell* raw data
data cyfrifiad *ell* census data
data cyffredin *ell* common data
data di-dor *ell* continuous data
data epidemiolegol *ell* epidemiological data
data gofodol *ell* spatial data
▸ **data gwaelodlin** *ell* baseline data
data gwreiddiol *ell* original data
data hanesyddol *ell* historical data
data maes *ell* field data
data personol *ell* personal data

data rhifiadol *ell* numerical data
data siart *ell* chart data
data ymchwil *ell* research data
data ymchwil eilaidd *ell* secondary research data
databeilot *eg* databeilotiaid datapilot
datawyru *be* de-airing
datblygedig *ans* advanced
datblygiad *eg* datblygiadau development; working-out
datblygiad addysgol *eg* datblygiadau addysgol educational development
datblygiad arwyneb *eg* datblygiadau arwyneb surface development
datblygiad cangen *eg* branch development
datblygiad corfforol *eg* physical development
datblygiad cymdeithasol *eg* social development
datblygiad cymunedol *eg* datblygiadau cymunedol community development
datblygiad cynaliadwy *eg* sustainable development
datblygiad cynllun *eg* datblygiadau cynllun design development
datblygiad cysyniadol *eg* datblygiadau cysyniadol conceptual development
datblygiad deallusol *eg* intellectual development
datblygiad diweddar *eg* late development
datblygiad diwylliannol *eg* cultural development
datblygiad dynol *eg* human development
datblygiad emosiynol *eg* emotional development
datblygiad emosiynol a chymdeithasol *eg* emotional and social development
datblygiad gwybyddol *eg* cognitive development
datblygiad hirgul *eg* datblygiadau hirgul ribbon development; strip development
datblygiad iaith *eg* language development
datblygiad meddyliol *eg* mental development
datblygiad moesol *eg* moral development
datblygiad newydd *eg* datblygiadau newydd innovation
datblygiad normadol *eg* normative development
datblygiad personol *eg* personal development
datblygiad plant *eg* child development
datblygiad polisi cymdeithasol *eg* social policy development
datblygiad silindrog *eg* datblygiadau silindrog cylindrical development
datblygiad staff *eg* staff development
datblygiad twristiaeth *eg* tourism development
datblygiad undarn *eg* datblygiadau undarn one-piece development
datblygiad y byd *eg* world development
datblygiad ymaddasol *eg* adaptive development
datblygiad ysbrydol *eg* spiritual development
datblygiadol *ans* developmental
datblygu *be* develop; evolve; exploit
datblygu adnoddau *be* exploitation of resources
datblygu busnes *be* business development
datblygu cynllun *be* evolve a design
datblygu economaidd *be* economic development
datblygu gwybodaeth *be* develop knowledge
datblygu perfformiad *be* develop performance
datblygu rhagdybiaethau *be* develop hypotheses
datblygu rheol *be* develop rule
datblygu'r gallu i siarad *be* speech development
datblygwr hwyr *eg* datblygwyr hwyr late developer
datgalchiad *eg* decalcification
datgalchu *be* decalcify
datgan *be* declare
datganiad (=cyhoeddiad) *eg* datganiadau declaration
datganiad (=perfformiad cerddorol) *eg* datganiadau recital
datganiad (=perfformiad dramatig) *eg* datganiadau rendition; rendering
datganiad (cyhoeddiad i'r wasg etc) *eg* datganiadau statement
datganiad (mewn cwestiwn dewis lluosog) *eg* datganiadau stem
datganiad (mewn ffiwg) *eg* datganiadau entry
datganiad anghenion addysgol arbennig *eg* datganiadau anghenion addysgol arbennig statement of special educational needs
Datganiad Annibyniaeth *eg* Declaration of Independence
Datganiad Annibyniaeth Unochrog *eg* Unilateral Declaration of Independence
datganiad ar y pryd *eg* datganiadau ar y pryd extemporization
datganiad cyn y gyllideb *eg* pre-budget statement
datganiad gan dyst *eg* witness statement
Datganiad Iawnderau *eg* Declaration of Rights
datganiad i'r wasg *eg* datganiadau i'r wasg press release
datganiad o anghymarusrwydd *eg* datganiadau o anghymarusrwydd statement of incompatibility
datganiad o genhadaeth *eg* datganiadau o genhadaeth mission statement
datganiad o gyfrif *eg* statement of account
datganiad o gymhwysedd *eg* datganiadau o gymhwysedd statement of competence
datganiad o gyrhaeddiad *eg* datganiadau o gyrhaeddiad statement of attainment
Datganiad Pardwn *eg* Declaration of Indulgence
Datganiad Pragmatig *eg* Pragmatic Sanction
datganiadau ystod *ell* range statements
datganoli *be* decentralize; devolution
datganoliad *eg* decentralization
datganu ar y pryd *be* extemporize
datgarbocsyleiddio *be* decarboxylate
datgarboneiddio *be* decarbonize
datgeliad *eg* datgeliadau disclosure
datgeliad anfwriadol *eg* datgeliadau anfwriadol leakage
datgelu (=dinoethi) *be* expose
datgelu (gwybodaeth etc) *be* disclose
datgilyddu *be* demutualization
datgladdedig *ans* exhumed
datglöwr *eg* datglowyr margin release

datglymu *be* unhitch
datglystyriad *eg* deflocculation
datglystyru *be* deflocculate
datgodiwr *eg* datgodwyr decoder
datgodiwr cyfarwyddyd *eg* datgodwyr cyfarwyddyd instruction decoder
datgoedwigo *be* deforestate
datgrychu *be* crease recovery
datguddiad (i aer, golau etc) *eg* exposure
datguddiad (gwybodaeth newydd) *eg* datguddiadau revelation
datguddiad (yn y Beibl Fwlgat) *eg* datguddiadau apocalypse
datgymhwysiad *eg* datgymwysiadau disapplication
datgymhwyso *be* disapply
datgysylltiad *eg* disestablishment
datgysylltiedig *ans* detached
datgysylltiol *ans* detachable
datgysylltu *be* disconnect
datgysylltu (=tynnu'n rhydd oddi wrth) *be* detach
datgysylltu (a thynnu i lawr) *be* dismantle
datgysylltu (yr Eglwys) *be* disestablish
datgysylltu plwg *be* unplug
datgywasgiad *eg* decompression
datgywasgu *be* decompress
datgyweddiad *eg* datgyweddiadau disengagement
datgyweddiad ffug *eg* datgyweddiadau ffug feint of disengagement
datgyweddu *be* disengage
datod *be* undo; unpick; take loose
datodydd *eg* datodyddion quick unpick
datrys *be* resolve; solve
datrys problem *be* solve a problem
datrys problemau *eg* problem solving
datrys yr hafaliad *be* solve the equation
datrysiad *eg* datrysiadau solution
datrysiad cyflawn *eg* datrysiadau cyflawn complete primitive
datrysiad dichonadwy *eg* datrysiadau dichonadwy feasible solution
datrysiad dichonadwy sylfaenol (dds) *eg* basic feasible solution
datrysol *ans* resolvent
datrysyn *eg* datrysynnau resolution
datseimio *be* degrease
datseimydd *eg* datseimyddion degreasant
datseinedd *eg* datseineddau reverberation
datseiniol *ans* reverberatory
datwm *eg* data datum
datysen *eb* datys date
dathliad *eg* dathliadau celebration
dathlu *be* celebrate
dau *eg* deuoedd two
dau ar y bêl *eg* two on the ball
dau ddigid *ans* two-digit
dau ddimensiwn *ans* two-dimensional
dau ffiled pren haenog *eg* two plywood fillets
dau lanw *eg* double tide
dauddegau gwyllt *eg* roaring twenties
dawn (=gallu) *eb* doniau facility
dawns (=achlysur i ddawnsio) *eb* dawnsfeydd dance
dawns (=cyfres o symudiadau) *eb* dawnsiau dance
Dawns Croesoswallt *eb* Oswestry Wake
dawns cylch a seren *eb* dawnsiau cylch a seren ring and star dance
Dawns Dafydd Gain *eb* Dainty Davy dance
dawns deithiol *eb* dawnsiau teithiol travelling dance
dawns Esgob Bangor *eb* Bishop of Bangor's jig
dawns fer *eb* dawnsiau byr short dance
dawns forris *eb* dawnsiau morris morris dance
dawns gyfres *eb* dawns gyfresi suite de danses
dawns gylch *eb* dawnsiau cylch circular dance
Dawns Ifan *eb* Evans' Jig
Dawns Llandaf *eb* Llandaff Reel
Dawns Llanofer *eb* Llanover Reel
dawns neuadd *eb* dawnsiau neuadd ballroom dance
dawns osod *eb* dawnsiau gosod set dance
dawns set draddodiadol *eb* dawnsiau set traddodiadol traditional set dance
dawns sgipio *eb* dawnsiau sgipio skipping dance
Dawns Sgwâr *eb* Dawnsiau Sgwâr Square Dance
dawns syml *eb* dawnsiau syml simple dance
dawns unfan *eb* dawnsiau unfan on-the-spot dance
dawns werin *eb* dawnsiau gwerin folk dance
dawns weu *eb* dawnsiau gweu weaving dance
dawns wledig *eb* dawnsiau gwledig country dance
dawns y glocsen *eb* dawnsiau'r glocsen clog dance
dawnsdrefn *eb* dawnsdrefnau dance routine
dawnsgor bale *eb* dawnsgorau bale ballet chorus
dawnsiau cenedlaethol *ell* national dances
dawnsio *be* dance
dawnsio addysgol modern *be* modern educational dance
dawnsio gwerin *be* folk dancing
dawnsio gwerin Cymreig *be* Welsh folk dancing
dawnsio rhydd *be* free dancing
dawnsio tap *be* tap dancing
dawnsio yn yr unfan *be* dance on the spot
dawnsio'n rhydd *be* dance freely
dawnsiwr bale *eg* dawnswyr bale ballet dancer
dawnsiwr morris *eg* dawnswyr morris morris dancer
dawnus *ans* gifted
de (o'i chyferbynnu â'r chwith) *eb* right
de (o'i gyferbynnu â'r gogledd) *eg* south
de draws *eb* right cross
De Eithaf (yr UD) *eg* Deep South
de syth *eb* straight right
deall *be* understand
deall egwyddorion *be* understand the principles
dealladwy *ans* coherent
dealltwriaeth *eb* understanding

dealltwriaeth *eb* comprehension
dealltwriaeth economaidd a diwydiannol *eb* economic and industrial understanding
dealltwriaeth gronolegol *eb* chronological understanding
dealltwriaeth gyd-destunol *eb* contextual intelligence
dealltwriaeth gydrannol *eb* componential intelligence
dealltwriaeth gyffredinol *eb* universal understanding
dealltwriaeth gysyniadol *eb* conceptual understanding
dealltwriaeth o arddull *eb* understanding of style
dealltwriaeth oddefol *eb* passive comprehension
dealltwriaeth sythweledol *eb* intuitive understanding
deallus *ans* intelligent
deallusion *ell* intelligentsia
deallusol *ans* intellectual
deallusrwydd *eg* intelligence
deallusrwydd drwy brofiadau *eg* experiential intelligence
deallusrwydd echddygol synhwyraidd *eg* sensory motor intelligence
début *eg* débuts début
debyd *eg* debydau debit
▸ **debydu** *be* debit
dec *eg* deciau deck
dec tâp *eg* deciau tâp tape deck
decagon *eg* decagonau decagon
decandeuoyl deuclorid *eg* decanedioyl dichloride
decani *eg* decani
decilitr *eg* decilitrau decilitre
decimetr *eg* decimetrau decimetre
decin llen *eg* sheet decking
decoladydd *eg* decoladwyr decollator
décor *eg* décor
decretal *eg* decretal
decstros *eg* dextrose
dechrau *be* begin
dechrau *eg* dechreuadau beginning
dechrau arni *be* getting started
dechrau pendant *eg* clear beginning
dechreuad y bydysawd *eg* origin of the universe
dechreuwr *eg* dechreuwyr beginner
dedfryd *eb* dedfrydau sentence
dedfryd am oes *eb* dedfrydau am oes life-sentence
dedfryd ohiriedig *eb* dedfrydau gohiriedig suspended sentence
dedfrydu *be* sentence
deddf (=cyfraith unigol) *eb* deddfau act
deddf (mewn gwyddoniaeth, economeg etc) *eb* deddfau law
Deddf Adendro *eb* Act of Attainder
deddf adenillion lleihaol *eb* law of diminishing returns
deddf adio *eb* addition law
Deddf Adran Gwarchod Defnyddwyr *eb* Consumer Protection Department Act
deddf adweithio masau *eb* law of mass action
Deddf Addysg *eb* Education Act
Deddf Anghydfodau Undebol *eb* Trade Disputes Act
deddf alluogi *eb* deddfau galluogi enabling act
Deddf Amddiffyn yr Amgylchedd *eb* Environmental Protection Act
Deddf Amodol Atal Anodau *eb* Act in Conditional Restraint of Annates
deddf amsugniad *eb* law of absorption
Deddf Anheddau'r Gweithwyr *eb* Artisans' Dwelling Act
Deddf Anodau *eb* Act of Annates
Deddf Apeliadau *eb* Act of Appeals
Deddf Ardrefnu *eb* Act of Settlement
Deddf Atal Enwebu *eb* Provisors Act
Deddf Awdurdod Apeliadol *eb* Appelate Jurisdiction Act
Deddf Blaenffrwyth a Degadau *eb* First Fruits and Tenths Act
Deddf Brad *eb* Act of Treasons
Deddf Brawf *eb* Test Act
Deddf Bwyd a Chyffuriau *eb* Food and Drugs Act
deddf cadwraeth màs *eb* law of conservation of mass
Deddf Camddefnydd Cyffuriau *eb* Misuse of Drugs Act
deddf cau *eb* law of closure
Deddf Cau Tir Comin *eb* Enclosure of Common Land Act
Deddf Cofrestru Genedigaethau, Priodasau a Marwolaethau *eb* Registration of Births, Marriages and Deaths Act
Deddf Corfforaeth *eb* Corporation Act
Deddf Corfforaethau Trefol *eb* Municipal Corporations Act
Deddf Credyd Defnyddwyr *eb* Consumer Credit Act
Deddf Cydbwyso Tollau *eb* Reciprocity of Duties Act
Deddf Cydymffurfio Achlysurol *eb* Occasional Conformity Act
deddf cyfansoddiad cyson *eb* law of constant composition
Deddf Cyfarfodydd Terfysglyd *eb* Seditious Meetings Act
Deddf Cyflenwi Nwyddau *eb* Supply of Goods Act
Deddf Cyflogwyr a Gweithwyr *eb* Employers' and Workmen's Act
Deddf Cyfnewid y Degwm *eb* Tithe Commutation Act
Deddf Cyfraith Trosedd *eb* Criminal Law Act
deddf cyfraneddau lluosol *eb* law of multiple proportions
deddf cyfraneddau lluosol *eb* law of multiple motions
Deddf Cyfrinachau Swyddogol *eb* Official Secrets Act

eg/b enw gwrywaidd/benywaidd, *masculine/feminine noun* ***ell*** enw lluosog, *plural noun* ***v*** berf, *verb* ***n*** enw, *noun* ▸ wedi newid, *changed*

Deddf Cyfuno *eb* Combination Act
Deddf Cyhoeddiadau Terfysglyd *eb* Seditious Publications Act
Deddf Cymhwyso Amaethyddiaeth *eb* Agricultural Adjustments Act
Deddf Cynllunio Gwlad a Thref *eb* Town and Country Planning Act
Deddf Cynllwyn a Diogelu Eiddo *eb* Conspiracy & Protection of Property Act
Deddf Cynrychiolaeth y Bobl *eb* Representation of the People Act
Deddf Cysylltiadau Hiliol *eb* Race Relations Act
Deddf Datganiad *eb* Declaratory Act
Deddf Dehongliad 1978 *eb* Interpretation Act 1978
Deddf Deirblwydd *eb* Triennial Act
Deddf Diarddel Gweinidogion Gwarthus *eb* Ejection of Scandalous Ministers Act
Deddf (Dileu) Anghymwysterau Rhyw 1919 *eb* Sex Disqualification (Removal) Act 1919
Deddf Dileu Caethwasiaeth *eb* Abolition of Slavery Act
Deddf Dirymiad *eb* Act of Revocation
Deddf Disgrifiadau Masnach *eb* Trade Descriptions Act
deddf disgyrchiant *eb* law of gravity; law of gravitation
deddf disgyrchiant adwerthol *eb* law of retail gravitation
Deddf Diwygio Addysg *eb* Education Reform Act
Deddf Diwygio Cyfraith Prydlesi *eb* Leasehold Reform Act
Deddf Diwygio'r Senedd *eb* Parliamentary Reform Act
Deddf Ddiwygio *eb* Reform Act
deddf ddosbarthol *eb* distributive law
deddf effaith *eb* law of effect
Deddf Eiddo Bydol Eglwys Cymru *eb* Welsh Church Temporalities Act
Deddf Estroniaid *eb* Aliens Act
Deddf Goddefiad *eb* Toleration Act
Deddf Gofal Plant *eb* Child Care Act
deddf Goodhart *eb* Goodhart's law
Deddf Gorfodaeth *eb* Coercion Act
Deddf Goruchafiaeth *eb* Act of Supremacy
Deddf Gwahaniaethu ar Sail Rhyw *eb* Sex Discrimination Act
Deddf Gwahardd *eb* Exclusion Act
Deddf Gwarchod Bywyd y Môr *eb* Protection of Sea Life Act
Deddf Gwarchod Data *eb* Data Protection Act
Deddf Gwarchod Defnyddwyr 1987 *eb* Consumer Protection Act 1987
Deddf Gweithrediadau Llwgr *eb* Corrupt Practices Act
Deddf Gwerthu Nwyddau *eb* Sale of Goods Act
deddf gyflenwadol *eb* law of complementation
deddf gymudol *eb* deddfau cymudol commutative law
deddf gyntaf Kirchoff *eb* Kirchoff's first law
deddf gyntaf thermodynameg *eb* first law of thermodynamics
deddf gysylltiadol *eb* deddfau cysylltiadol associative law
Deddf Hawliau Dynol *eb* Human Rights Act
Deddf Heddlu a Thystiolaeth Droseddol *eb* Police and Criminal Evidence Act
Deddf Heddlu Metropolitan *eb* Metropolitan Police Act
Deddf Heresi *eb* Heresy Act
deddf Hooke *eb* Hooke's law
Deddf Hunanymwadiad *eb* Self-Denying Ordinance
Deddf i Lwyr Atal Anodau *eb* Act in Absolute Restraint of Annates
Deddf Iechyd a Moesau Prentisiaid *eb* Health & Morals of Apprentices Act
Deddf Iechyd Cyhoeddus *eb* Public Health Act
Deddf Iechyd Meddwl *eb* Mental Health Act
deddf Lenz *eb* Lenz's law
deddf leol *eb* deddfau lleol by-law
Deddf Les-Fenthyg *eb* Lease-Lend Act
Deddf Llongau Masnach *eb* Merchant Shipping Act
Deddf Llwon Anghyfreithlon *eb* Unlawful Oaths Act
Deddf Llysoedd a Gwasanaethau Cyfreithiol *eb* Courts and Legal Services Act
Deddf Mabwysiadu *eb* Adoption Act
Deddf Miwtini *eb* Mutiny Act
Deddf Mordwyo *eb* Navigation Act
Deddf Mwyngloddiau *eb* Mines Act
Deddf Mynediad i Gyfiawnder *eb* Access to Justice Act
deddf naturiol *eb* deddfau naturiol natural law
Deddf Newid y Gyfraith Trosedd *eb* Criminal Law Amendment Act
Deddf Newid yr Undebau Llafur *eb* Trades Union Amendment Act
Deddf Newydd y Tlodion *eb* Poor Law Amendment Act
Deddf Nwyddau a Gwasanaethau nas Archebwyd *eb* Unsolicited Goods & Services Act
deddf nwyon *eb* gas law
deddf Ohm *eb* Ohm's law
deddf paralelogram fectorau *eb* parallelogram of vectors' law
Deddf Pensiwn yr Henoed *eb* Old Age Pensions Act
Deddf Prisiau *eb* Prices Act
Deddf Pum Milltir *eb* Five Mile Act
Deddf Pwysau a Mesurau *eb* Weights & Measures Act
Deddf Rhenti *eb* Deddfau Rhenti Rent Act
Deddf Rhyddfreinio *eb* Emancipation Act
Deddf Rhyddfreinio'r Pabyddion *eb* Catholic Emancipation Act
Deddf Seithmlwydd *eb* Septennial Act

deddf seneddol *eb* deddfau seneddol act of parliament
Deddf Sgism *eb* Schism Act
deddf sgwâr gwrthdro *eb* inverse square law
Deddf Siarter y Banc *eb* Bank Charter Act
Deddf Stamp *eb* Stamp Act
deddf statudol *eb* statutory law
Deddf Swyddfa Masnachu Teg *eb* Fair Trading Office Act
Deddf Taenu'r Efengyl *eb* Act for the Propagation of the Gospel
Deddf Telerau Contract Annheg *eb* Unfair Contract Terms Act
Deddf Terfysg *eb* Riot Act
Deddf Trefi a Chorfforaethau *eb* Corporations & Municipalities Act
Deddf Tribiwnlysoedd ac Ymchwiliadau *eb* Tribunals and Inquiries Act
Deddf Troseddau yn Erbyn Person *eb* Offences Against the Person Act
Deddf Trwyddedau *eb* Act of Dispensations
deddf tynged gyffredin *eb* law of common fate
Deddf Unffurfiaeth *eb* Act of Uniformity
Deddf Uno *eb* Deddfau Uno Act of Union
Deddf Wyndham ar Bwrcasu Tir *eb* Wyndham's Land Purchase Act
Deddf y Bleidlais Gudd *eb* Secret Ballot Act
Deddf y Confentiglau *eb* Conventigles Act
Deddf y Chwe Erthygl *eb* Act of Six Articles
Deddf y Senedd *eb* Parliament Act
Deddf y Twrneiod 1971 *eb* Solicitors Act 1971
Deddf ŷd *eb* Deddfau Ŷd Corn Law
Deddf Ymostyngiad y Clerigwyr *eb* Act of Submission of the Clergy
Deddf yn Erbyn Amlblwyfiaeth *eb* Act Against Pluralities
Deddf yr Ardaloedd Arbennig *eb* Special Areas Act
Deddf Yswiriant Gwladol *eb* National Insurance Act
Deddf Yswiriant Iechyd Gwladol *eb* National Health Insurance Act
Deddf Yswiriant y Di-waith *eb* National Unemployment Insurance Act
Deddfau Barnweiniad *ell* Judicature Acts
Deddfau Cau Tiroedd *ell* Enclosure Acts
deddfau cosbi *ell* penal laws
deddfau cyfyngu *ell* sumptuary laws
Deddfau Duon *ell* Black Acts
Deddfau Ffatri *ell* Factory Acts
Deddfau Ffrwyno *ell* Gag Acts
deddfau helwriaeth *ell* game laws
deddfau mudiant Newton *ell* Newton's laws of motion
Deddfau Prawf a Chorfforaeth *ell* Test and Corporation Acts
Deddfau Prawf y Prifysgolion *ell* University Tests Acts
deddfau trwydded (De Affrica) *ell* pass laws
Deddfau Trwyddedu *ell* Licensing Acts
deddfroddwr *eg* deddfroddwyr lawgiver
deddfu *be* legislate
deddfwr *eg* deddfwyr legislator
deddfwriaeth *eb* deddfwriaethau legislation
deddfwriaeth berthnasol *eb* relevant legislation
deddfwriaeth ddirprwyedig *eb* delegated legislation
deddfwriaeth ffatri *eb* factory legislation
deddfwriaeth ganiataol *eb* permissive legislation
deddfwriaeth gwarchod data *eb* deddfwriaethau gwarchod data data protection legislation
deddfwriaeth iechyd a diogelwch *eb* health and safety legislation
deddfwriaeth i'r project adeiladu *eb* legislation for the construction project
deddfwriaeth ôl-weithredol *eb* retrospective legislation
deddfwriaeth undebau llafur *eb* trade union legislation
defnydd (y weithred o ddefnyddio, pwrpas) *eg* defnyddiau use; utilization
defnydd (ffabrig, gwrthrychau ffisegol etc) *eg* defnyddiau material
defnydd a boddhad use and gratification
defnydd addas *eg* defnyddiau addas suitable material
defnydd amsugnol *eg* defnyddiau amsugnol absorbent material
defnydd argraffu *eg* defnyddiau argraffu printing material
defnydd caledu *eg* defnyddiau caledu hardening material
defnydd cymysg *eg* blended material
defnydd cynfasau *eg* sheeting
defnydd dan do *eg* indoor use
defnydd glanhau *eg* defnyddiau glanhau cleaner
defnydd glanhau ffwrn *eg* oven cleaner
defnydd gloyw *eg* defnyddiau gloyw lustrous material
defnydd gwastraff *eg* defnyddiau gwastraff waste material
defnydd gweadog *eg* defnyddiau gweadog textured material
defnydd gwneud *eg* defnyddiau gwneud manufactured cloth
defnydd gwrthdan *eg* defnyddiau gwrthdan fireproof material
defnydd hapgael *eg* defnyddiau hapgael found material
defnydd hwyliau *eg* sailcloth
defnydd jersi *eg* jersey
defnydd lapio bwyd *eg* defnyddiau lapio bwyd food wrap
defnydd llifo *eg* dyestuff
defnydd metelig *eg* metallic cloth
defnydd modelu *eg* defnyddiau modelu modelling material
defnydd organig *eg* defnyddiau organig organic matter

defnydd pacio *eg* packaging
defnydd patrymog *eg* defnyddiau patrymog pattern material
defnydd penodol *eg* defnyddiau penodol specific material
defnydd plaen *eg* defnyddiau plaen plain material
defnydd plastig *eg* defnyddiau plastig plastic material
defnydd presennol *eg* existing use
defnydd sgrap *eg* defnyddiau sgrap scrap material
defnydd sgrin *eg* screen material
defnydd siec *eg* defnyddiau siec checked material
defnydd sylfaenol *eg* defnyddiau sylfaenol basic material
defnydd tir *eg* defnyddiau tir land use
defnydd tir trefol *eg* urban land use
defnydd traddodiadol *eg* defnyddiau traddodiadol traditional material
defnydd trychiad crwn *eg* round section material
defnydd trychiad hecsagonol *eg* defnyddiau trychiad hecsagonol hexagonal section material
defnydd trychiad petryal *eg* rectangular section material
defnydd trychiad sgwâr *eg* defnyddiau trychiad sgwâr square section material
defnydd tryloyw *eg* defnyddiau tryloyw transparent material
defnydd wedi'i feteleiddio *eg* metallicized material
defnydd yn yr awyr agored outdoor use
defnydd ynysu *eg* defnyddiau ynysu insulating material
defnyddiau a chydrannau materials and components
defnyddiau arlunio *ell* artist's materials
defnyddiau bwyd *oll* food materials
defnyddiau celf *ell* art materials
defnyddiau clyfar *ell* smart materials
defnyddiau cyfansawdd *ell* composite materials
defnyddiau ffrwdrewlifol *ell* fluvioglacial material
defnyddiau gwneud *ell* man-made materials
defnyddiau gwrthiannol *ell* resistant materials
defnyddiau llinol *ell* linear materials
defnyddiau panel *ell* panel materials
defnyddiau swmp *ell* bulk materials
defnyddiau traeth *ell* beach material
defnyddiau traul *ell* consumables
defnyddiau tryleu *ell* translucent materials
defnyddio *be* use; utilize
defnyddio ffynonellau *be* use of sources
defnyddio tir *be* use of land
defnyddiol *ans* useful
defnyddioldeb *eg* utility
defnyddio'r corff yn briodol *be* appropriate use of the body
defnyddiwr *eg* defnyddwyr user; consumer
defnyddiwr annibynnol *eg* defnyddwyr annibynnol autonomous user
defnyddiwr busnes *eg* defnyddwyr busnes business user
defnyddiwr cyfrifiadur *eg* defnyddwyr cyfrifiadur computer user
defnyddiwr parth *eg* defnyddwyr parth domain user
defnyddiwr unigol *eg* defnyddwyr unigol individual user
defnyddwyr a defnyddwyr posibl users and potential users
defnyn *eg* defnynnau droplet
defnyn fitamin *eg* defnynnau fitamin vitamin drop
defod *eb* defodau rite; ritual
defod carreg filltir *eb* defodau cerrig milltir milestone ritual
defod newid byd *eb* defodau newid byd rite of passage
defodaeth *eb* ritualism
defodol *ans* ritual
Deg Erthygl, Y *eb* Ten Articles, The
Deg Gorchymyn, Y Ten Commandments, The
degaidd *ans* denary
degau ac unedau tens and units
degawd *eg/b* degawdau decade
degfed *eg* degfedau tenth
degfed *eg* one-tenth
de-glicio *be* right-click
degol *ans* decimal
degoli *be* decimalize
degolyn *eg* degolion decimal
degolyn cod deuaidd *eg* degolion cod deuaidd binary coded decimal
degolyn cylchol *eg* degolion cylchol recurring decimal
degolyn diddiwedd *eg* degolion diddiwedd infinite decimal
degradd *eg* degraddau decile
degwm *eg* degymau tithe
degwm adfedd *eg* degymau adfedd appropriated tithe
degwm amfedd *eg* degymau amfedd impropriate tithe
degymiad *eg* degymiadau tithing
degymu *be* decimation
dengwriad *eg* dengwriaid decurion
deheuad *eg* southing
deheurwydd *eg* dexterity
dehongli *be* interpret
dehongliad *eg* dehongliadau interpretation
dehongliad dewisol (am ymateb cynulleidfa) *eg* preferred reading
dehongliad lleisiol *eg* vocal interpretation
dehongliad statudol *eg* statutory interpretation
dehonglydd *eg* dehonglwyr interpreter
dei *eg* deiau die
dei crwn *eg* deiau crwn circular die
dei crwn hollt *eg* deiau crwn hollt circular split die
dei hollt *eg* deiau hollt split die
dei petryal *eg* deiau petryal rectangular die
deial *eg* deialau dial

deialog *eb* deialogau dialogue
deialog *eb* deialogau dialog
deialog amlinell *eb* deialogau amlinell contour dialog
deialog newydd *eb* deialogau newydd new dialog
deialwr *eg* deialwyr dialer
deialydd ffôn *eg* deialwyr ffôn phone dialer
deic *eg* deiciau dyke
▶ **deiet** *eg* deietau diet
deiet anghytbwys *eg* unbalanced diet
deiet amrywiol *eg* varied diet
deiet arbennig *eg* special diet
deiet cytbwys *eg* balanced diet
▶ **deiet gwella** *eg* convalescent diet
deiet iachus healthy diet
deieteg *eb* dietetics
▶ **deietegol** *ans* dietary
▶ **deietegydd** *eg* deietegwyr dietitian
deif *eb* deifiau dive
deif arwyneb *eb* deifiau arwyneb surface dive
deif blygu *eb* deifiau plygu pike dive
deif drosben *eb* deifiau trosben somersault dive
deif hwyaden *eb* deifiau hwyaden duck dive
deif ras *eb* deifiau ras racing dive
deif wennol *eb* deifiau gwennol swallow dive
deifio (llosgi etc) *be* scorch
deifio (nofio tanddwr etc) *be* dive
deifio am y bêl *be* dive for the ball
deifio o'r astell *be* springboard diving
deifio wrth draed ymosodwr *be* dive at a striker's feet
deifio'n isel *be* low dive
deifio'n uchel *be* high dive
deifrol ymlaen *eb* deifroliau ymlaen dive forward roll
deigastio *be* die-casting
deigastio gwasgol *be* pressure die casting
deigryn *eg* dagrau tear
deildres *eb* deildresi leaf trace
deilen *eb* dail leaf
deilen arnawf *eb* dail arnawf floating leaf
deilen aur *eb* dail aur gold leaf
deilen fraith *eb* dail brith variegated leaf
deilen gyfansawdd *eb* dail cyfansawdd compound leaf
deilen llawryf *eb* dail llawryf bayleaf
deilen offeru aur *eb* dail offeru aur gold tooling leaf
deilen soddedig *eb* dail soddedig submerged leaf
deiliad (swydd) *eg* deiliaid incumbent
deiliad (brenin neu frenhines) *eg* deiliaid subject
deiliad (ffiwdal) *eg* deiliaid vassal
deiliad braint *eg* deiliaid braint franchisee
deiliad y tŷ *eg* deiliad y tai householder
deiliadaeth ffiwdal *eb* vassalage
deiliadaeth ystafelloedd *eb* room occupancy
deiliant *eg* deiliannau foliage
deiliog *ans* leafy; foliated; folar
deiliogrwydd *eg* foliation
deiliosen *eb* deilios leaflet
deilliad *eg* deilliadau derivative
deilliadol *ans* derivative; derived
deilliant *eg* deilliannau derivation
deilliedig *ans* spin-off
deillio *be* derive
deillio mynegiad *be* derive an expression
deintgig *eg* gum
deintigl *eg* deintiglau denticle
deintiol *ans* dental
deintydd *eg* deintyddion dentist
deintyddiaeth *eb* dentistry
deiseb *eb* deisebau petition
Deiseb a Chyngor Gostyngedig Humble Petition and Advice
Deiseb Iawnderau *eb* Petition of Right
Deiseb Wreiddyn a Changen *eb* Root & Branch Petition
Deiseb y Fil *eb* Millenary Petition
deisio *be* dice
dëistiaeth *eb* deism
delfryd *eb* delfrydau ideal
delfryd ymddwyn *eb* delfrydau ymddwyn role model
delfrydiad *eg* idealization
delfrydiaeth *eb* idealism
delfrydol *ans* ideal
delfrydwr *eg* delfrydwyr idealist
delio *be* deal
delio â chwsmeriaid *be* dealing with customers
deliriwm *eg* delirium
delta *eg* deltâu delta
delta bwaog *eg* deltâu bwaog dearcuate delta
delta crafanc *eg* deltâu crafanc bird's foot delta
delta glanllyn *eg* deltâu glanllyn lakeside delta
delta penllyn *eg* deltâu penllyn lake head delta
deltaidd *ans* deltaic
delw *eb* delwau image
delw ofannu *be* drop forging
delwddrylliad *eg* iconoclasm
delwddrylliol *ans* iconoclastic
delwddrylliwr *eg* delwddryllwyr iconoclast
delwedd *eb* delweddau image
delwedd bositif *eb* delweddau positif positive image
delwedd brand *eb* delweddau brand brand image
delwedd brintiedig *eb* delweddau printiedig printed image
delwedd cerdyn *eb* delweddau cerdyn card image
delwedd ddeuaidd *eb* delweddau deuaidd binary image
delwedd fewnol *eb* delweddau mewnol inline image
delwedd fosaig *eb* delweddau mosaig mosaic image
delwedd fwy *eb* delweddau mwy enlarged image

delwedd ffotograffig *eb* delweddau ffotograffig photographic image
delwedd gadarnhaol *eb* delweddau cadarnhaol positive image
delwedd gorfforaethol *eb* corporate image
delwedd graffig *eb* delweddau graffig graphic image
delwedd lai *eb* delweddau llai diminished image
delwedd lonydd gwefan *eb* web site still image
delwedd lliw *eb* delweddau lliw colour image
delwedd lliw ansawdd uchel *eb* delweddau lliw ansawdd uchel high-quality colour image
delwedd negyddol *eb* delweddau negyddol negative image
delwedd real *eb* delweddau real real image
delwedd unionsyth *eb* delweddau unionsyth erect image
delwedd weledol *eb* delweddau gweledol visual image
delwedd wrthdro *eb* delweddau gwrthdro inverted image
delwedd y corff *eb* body image
delweddaeth *eb* imagery
delweddau camera llonydd *ell* camera still images
delweddu *be* visualize
delweddu cyseiniant magnetig *be* magnetic resonance imaging (MRI)
delweddu cyseiniant magnetig gweithredol *be* functional magnetic resonance imaging (fMRI)
dellt awyru *eb* delltiau awyru ventilation grill
dellt awyru *eb* delltiau awyru grille
dellten *eb* dellt lattice
dellten giwbig gorff-ganolog *eb* delltiau ciwbig corff-ganolog body-centred cubic lattice
dellten giwbig wyneb-ganolog *eb* delltiau ciwbig wyneb-ganolog face-centred cubic lattice
delltog *ans* trellised
delltwaith *eg* lattice work
dem *eg* demau dem
demagog *eg* demagogiaid demagogue
demen *eg* demenau demesne
► **dementia** *eg* dementia
democrat *eg* democratiaid democrat
democrat cymdeithasol *eg* democratiaid cymdeithasol social democrat
democrat rhyddfrydol *eg* democratiaid rhyddfrydol liberal democrat
democrataidd *ans* democratic
democrataidd cymdeithasol *ans* social democrat
democrataidd rhyddfrydol *ans* liberal democrat
democratiaeth *eb* democracy
demograffeg *eb* demography
demograffeg *eb* demographics
demograffig *ans* demographic
dendrid *eg* dendridau dendrite
dendrocronoleg *eb* dendrochronology
deniadol *ans* attractive
denier *eg* denier
denim *eg* denim
dentiad *eg* dentage
dentin *eg* dentine
dentio *be* denting
deocsigenedig *ans* deoxygenated
deocsiribos *eg* deoxyribose
deon *eg* deoniaid dean
deon gwlad *eg* deoniaid gwlad rural dean
deondy *eg* deondai deanery
deoniaeth wlad *eb* deoniaethau gwlad rural deanery
deontolegol *ans* deontological
deor *be* hatch
deorfa *eb* deorfeydd hatchery
deorydd *eg* deoryddion incubator
depo amlwytho *eg* depos amlwytho container depot
deponiad *eg* deponiadau deposition
derbyn (=cael, croesawu) *be* receive
derbyn (=cymryd yr hyn a gynigir, cydnabod) *be* accept; receive
derbyn (yn aelod, fel arfer gyda seremoni) *be* initiation
derbyn (mesur) *be* adopt
derbyn nifer cytbwys *be* balanced intake
derbyn yn aelod *be* receive into membership
derbyn yn ddinesydd *be* naturalize
derbynfa *eb* derbynfeydd reception
derbyniad (=achlysur ffurfiol etc) *eg* derbyniadau reception
derbyniad (=ateb cadarnhaol) *eg* acceptance
derbyniad (i gwrs, ysbyty etc) *eg* derbyniadau admission
derbyniad cynulleidfa *eg* audience reception
derbyniad gwirfoddol *eg* derbyniadau gwirfoddol voluntary admission
derbyniadau (gwerthiant) *ell* proceeds
derbyniadwy *ans* admissible
derbynneb *eb* derbynebau receipt
derbynnedd *eg* derbyneddau susceptibility
derbynnydd (hydrogen, electronau) *eg* derbynyddion acceptor
derbynnydd (mewn ffisioleg etc) *eg* derbynyddion receptor
derbynnydd (yn gyffredinol) *eg* derbynyddion receiver
derbynnydd cyffredinol *eg* derbynyddion cyffredinol universal recipient
derbynnydd electronau *eg* derbynyddion electronau electron acceptor
derbynnydd hydrogen *eg* derbynyddion hydrogen hydrogen acceptor
derbynnydd poen *eg* derbynyddion poen pain receptor
derbynnydd radio *eg* derbynyddion radio radio receiver
derbynnydd ymestynnedd *eg* derbynyddion ymestynnedd stretch receptor
deric *eg* dericiau derrick
dermatitis *eg* dermatitis

dermatoleg *eb* dermatology
dermatolegydd *eg* dermatolegwyr dermatologist
derw rheidd-dor *eg* quartered oak
derwen gorc *eb* derw corc cork oak
derwydd *eg* derwyddon druid
derwyddiaeth *eb* druidism
desg *eb* desgiau desk
desg gwybodaeth *eb* desgiau gwybodaeth information desk
desg talu *eb* desgiau talu checkout
desgant *eg* desgantau descant
desibel *eg* desibelau decibel
desmomom *eg* desmomomau desmomome
determinant *eg* determinannau determinant
detritws *eg* detritus
detritysydd *eg* detritysyddion detritivore
dethol *be* select
dethol ar hap *be* randomly select
dethol naturiol *be* natural selection
dethol rhyw *be* sexual selection
detholedd *eg* selectivity
detholiad *eg* detholiadau selection; extract
detholiad ceraint *eg* kin selection
detholiad cyfeiriadol *eg* directional selection
detholiad rhwygol *eg* disruptive selection
detholiad rhywiol *eg* sexual selection
detholus *ans* selective; selectivist
detholydd *eg* detholyddion selector
detholyn *eg* detholion seed
deuad *eg* deuadau dyad
deuaidd *ans* binary
deuamgrwm *ans* biconvex
deuamincopr(I) clorid *eg* diamminecopper(I) chloride
deuarian(I) ethyndeuid *eg* disilver(I) ethynediide
deuatomig *ans* diatomic
deuawd *eb* deuawdau duet
deubegwn *ans* bipolar
deu(bensencarbonyl) perocsid *eg* di(benzenecarbonyl) peroxide
1,1-deubromoethan *eg* 1,1-dibromoethane
1,2-deubromoethan *eg* 1,2-dibromoethane
deubyramid trigonol *eg* deubyramidiau trigonol trigonal bipyramid
deuclorin ocsid *eg* dichlorine oxide
Deucloro Deuffenyl Tricloroethan (DDT) *eg* Dichloro Diphenyl Trichloroethane (DDT)
4-deuclorobensen *eg* 4-dichlorobenzene
1,4-deuclorobensen *eg* 1,4-dichlorobenzene
1,2-deucloroethen *eg* 1,2-dichloroethene
(deucloromethyl)bensen *eg* (dichloromethyl)benzene
deucopr(I) ethyndeuid *eg* dicopper(I) ethynediide
deucromiwm(III) copr(II) ocsid *eg* dichromium(III) copper(II) oxide
deu(dodecanoyl) perocsid *eg* di(dodecanoyl) peroxide
deuddeg dwsin *eg* gross
Deuddeg Erthygl (Gwrthryfel y Werin) *eb* Twelve Articles
deuddegfed *eg* deuddegfedau twelfth
deuddegfed dyn *eg* twelfth man
deuddegol *ans* duodecimal
deuddiwylliannol *ans* bicultural
deuelectrig *ans* dielectric
deuelectryn *eg* deuelectrynnau dielectric
1,1-deuethocsiethan *eg* 1,1-diethoxyethane
deuethylamid asid lysergig *eg* lysergic acid diethylamide (LSD)
deuethylamin *eg* diethylamine
deufalent *ans* bivalent
deufetel *ans* bimetallic
deufodd *ans* bimodal
deufoleciwlaidd *ans* bimolecular
1,2-deuffenylethandeuon *eg* 1,2-diphenylethanedione
1,2-deuffenylethen *eg* 1,2-diphenylethene
deuffenylmethanon *eg* diphenylmethanone
deuffocal *ans* bifocal
deufforchiad *eg* deufforchiadau bifurcation
deufforchiog *ans* bifurcated
deuffosffan *eg* diphosphane
Deugain Erthygl Namyn Un *eb* Thirty Nine Articles
deugeiniau gwyllt *ell* roaring forties
deugellog *ans* bicellular
deugeugrwm *ans* biconcave
deuglust *ans* binaural
deugotyledon *eg* dicotyledon
deugotyledonaidd *ans* dicotyledonous
deugraff *eg* deugraffau digraph
deugywair *ans* bitonal
deugyweiredd *eg* bitonality
deuhedrol *ans* dihedral
deuhybrid *eg* dihybrid
2,3-deuhydrocsibwtandeuoad ocsid *eg* 2,3-dihydroxybutanedioate oxide
deuïodin hecsaclorid *eg* diiodine hexachloride
2,4-deuisocyanato-1-methylbensen *eg* 2,4-diisocyanato-1-methylbenzene
deulais *ans* two-part
deulawr *ans* two-storey
deulinol *ans* bilinear
deulygad *ans* binocular
deumer *eg* deumerau dimer
deumethyl bensen-1,2-deucarbocsylad *eg* dimethyl benzene-1,2-dicarboxylate
1,2-deumethylbensen *eg* 1,2-dimethylbenzene
3,3-deumethylbiffenyl-4,4'-deuamin *eg* 3,3-dimethylbiphenyl-4,4'-diamine
2,2-deumethylbwtan *eg* 2,2-dimethylbutane
2,3-deumethylbwtan-2,3-deuol *eg* 2,3-dimethylbutane-2,3-diol
3,3-deumethylbwtanon *eg* 3,3-dimethylbutanone
deumethylethandeuoad *eg* dimethylethanedioate
2,2-deumethylpropan-1-ol *eg* 2,2-dimethylpropan-1-ol

1,3-deunitrobensen *eg* 1,3-dinitrobenzene
deunitrogen ocsid *eg* dinitrogen oxide
deuniwcliotid *eg* deuniwcliotidau dinucleotide
deunydd *eg* deunyddiau material
deunydd cartograffig *eg* cartographic material
deunydd hybu iechyd *eg* health promotion material
deunydd ysgogi *eg* stimulus material
deunyddiau adnoddau *ell* resource materials
deunyddiau addysgu *ell* teaching materials
deunyddiau atodol *ell* support materials
deunyddiau crai *ell* raw material
deunyddiau dysgu *ell* learning materials
deunyddiau pacio *ell* packaging material
deuocsid *eg* dioxide
deuocsigenedig *ans* dioxygenated
deuocsowraniwm(VI) sinc ethanoad *eg* dioxouranium(VI) zinc ethanoate
deuod *eg* deuodau diode
deuod allyrru golau *eg* deuodau allyrru golau light emitting diode
deuod Zener *eg* deuodau Zener Zener diode
deuoecaidd *ans* dioecious
deuoedd *ell* twos
deuol *ans* dual; bicimal
deuol (enw generig) *eg* deuolau diol
deuoliaeth *eb* dualism
deuoliaeth Gartesaidd *eb* Cartesian dualism
deuolyn *eg* deuolion bicimal
deuplwm(II) plwm(IV) ocsid *eg* dilead(II) lead(IV) oxide
deupol *eg* deupolau dipole
deurannol *ans* bipartite
deurywiad *eg* deurywiaid hermaphrodite
deurywiaeth *eb* hermaphroditism
deurywiol *ans* bisexual; hermaphroditic
deusacarid *eg* deusacaridau disaccharide
deusad *eg* deusadau bistable
deusentrig *ans* dicentric
deusodiwm tetraborad(III)-10-dŵr *eg* disodium tetraborate(III)-10-water
deusygotig (DS) *ans* dizygotic (DZ)
deusylffwr deuclorid *eg* disulfur dichloride
deuwraeth *eb* duumvirate
deuwriad *eg* deuwriaid duumvir
dewin *eg* dewiniaid magician
dewin adroddiadau *eg* dewiniaid adroddiadau report wizard
dewin gosod *eg* installation wizard
dewiniaeth *eb* witchcraft
dewis *be* select
dewis (=hoff ddewis) *eg* dewisiadau preference
dewis (arall) *eg* dewisiadau alternative
dewis (o gynnyrch) *eg* range
dewis (yn gyffredinol) *eg* dewisiadau choice; option
dewis adnoddau *be* resource selection
dewis ardal data *be* select data area
dewis arddull *be* select style
dewis arddull botwm *be* select button style
dewis arddulliau celloedd *be* select cell styles
dewis awtodestun *be* select autotext
dewis awtogynllun *be* select an autolayout
dewis celloedd arian *be* select currency cells
dewis colofn *be* select column
dewis cyfeiriadur *be* select directory
dewis cyfeiriadur gosod *be* select installation directory
dewis cyfeiriadur gwraidd *be* select root directory
dewis cyfeiriadur targed *be* select target directory
dewis cyfrwng allbwn *be* select output medium
dewis cynllun lliw *be* select colour scheme
dewis chwith *be* select left
dewis de *be* select right
dewis dogfen *be* document selection
dewis doliau *eg* doll choice
dewis ffeil *be* select file
dewis ffont *be* select font
dewis ffurflen *be* select form
dewis ffynhonnell *be* select source
dewis ffynhonnell data *be* select data source
dewis gair *be* select word
dewis graffigau *be* select graphics
dewis graffigau teitl *be* select title graphics
dewis gwrthrych *be* select object
dewis gwybodus *eg* dewisiadau gwybodus informed choice
dewis gyrfa *eg* dewisiadau gyrfa career choice
dewis hawdd *eg* dewisiadau hawdd soft option
dewis hidlydd *be* select filter
dewis i fyny *be* select up
dewis i lawr *be* select down
dewis i rieni *eg* parental choice
dewis iaith *be* select language
dewis lefel amlinelliad *be* select outline level
dewis logo *be* select logo
dewis lliw *be* colour selection
dewis lluosog *eg* dewisiadau lluosog multiple choice
dewis llwybr *be* select path
dewis macro *be* select macro
dewis modiwl *be* select module
dewis nesaf *eg* next selection
dewis nod i'r chwith *be* select character left
dewis nod i'r dde *be* select character right
dewis offeryn *be* select tool
dewis paragraff *be* select paragraph
dewis peidio â siarad *be* elective mutism
dewis pob dalen *be* select all sheets
dewis rhes *be* select row
dewis tabl *be* select table
dewis tudalen i fyny *be* select page up
dewis tudalen i lawr *be* select page down
dewis tudalen i'r chwith *be* select page left
► **dewis y cyfan** *be* select all
dewis y math o osodiad *be* select installation type

dewis ystod *be* select range
dewis ystod cronfa ddata *be* select database range
dewisiad sillafu *eg* dewisiadau sillafu spelling option
dewisiadau *ell* preferences
dewisiadau amrywiol *ell* miscellaneous options
dewisiadau hidlo *ell* filter options
dewisiadau lluniadu *ell* drawing options
dewisiadau mewnbwn *ell* input options
dewisiadau porwr *ell* browser options
dewisiadau siart *ell* chart options
dewislen *eb* dewislenni menu
dewislen cymorth *eb* dewislenni cymorth help menu
dewislen ffeilio *eb* dewislenni ffeilio filing menu
dewislen ffurfweddu *eb* dewislenni ffurfweddu configuration menu
dewislen gopïo *eb* dewislenni copïo copy menu
dewislen gorlannu *eb* dewislenni corlannu banding menu
dewislen gwrthrychau *eb* dewislenni gwrthrychau object menu
dewislen newydd *eb* dewislenni newydd new menu
dewislen sgrin *eb* dewislenni sgrin on-screen menu
dewisol *ans* optional; discretionary
dewiswr *eg* dewiswyr selector
(+)-(D)-glwcos *eg* (+)-(D)-glucose
dhamma *eg* dhamma
dharma *eg* dharma
diabas *eg* diabasau diabase
► **diabetes** *eg* diabetes
diabetes mellitus dibynnol ar inswlin *eg* insulin-dependent diabetes mellitus
diabetig *ans* diabetic
diacen *ans* unaccented
diacinesis *eg* diakinesis
diacon *eg* diaconiaid deacon
diacones *eb* diaconesau deaconess
diaffram *eg* diafframau diaphragm
diagnosis *eg* diagnosau diagnosis
diagnosis nyrsio *eg* nursing diagnosis
diagnosteg *eb* diagnostics
diagnosteg gwallau *eb* error diagnostics
diagnostig *ans* diagnostic
diagram *eg* diagramau diagram
diagram amlder cronnus *eg* diagramau amlder cronnus cumulative frequency diagram
diagram amlinellol *eg* diagramau amlinellol outline diagram
diagram Argand *eg* Argand diagram
diagram bloc *eg* diagramau bloc block diagram
diagram buanedd /amser *eg* diagramau buanedd / amser speed /time diagram
diagram canghennog *eg* diagramau canghennog tree diagram
diagram croesrym *eg* diagramau croesrym shearforce diagram
diagram cyflymder *eg* diagramau cyflymder velocity diagram
diagram cyflymder /amser *eg* diagramau cyflymder /amser velocity /time diagram
diagram cyflymiad /amser *eg* diagramau cyflymiad /amser acceleration /time diagram
diagram cylched *eg* diagramau cylched circuit diagram
diagram cynllunio *eg* diagramau cynllunio schematic diagram
diagram dadleoliad *eg* diagramau dadleoliad displacement diagram
diagram dadleoliad /amser *eg* diagramau dadleoliad /amser displacement /time diagram
diagram eglurhaol *eg* diagramau eglurhaol explanatory diagram
diagram fflurol *eg* diagramau fflurol floral diagram
diagram gwasgariad *eg* diagramau gwasgariad scatter diagram
diagram gwedd *eg* phasor
diagram gwrthrych rhydd *eg* free-body diagram
diagram integrol *eg* diagramau integrol integral diagram
diagram llawrydd *eg* diagramau llawrydd freehand diagram
diagram llif *eg* diagramau llif flow diagram
diagram llif data *eg* diagramau llif data data flow diagram
diagram pelydrol *eg* diagramau pelydrol ray diagram
diagram perthynas endidau *eg* diagramau perthynas endidau entity-relationship diagram
diagram rhesymeg *eg* diagramau rhesymeg logic diagram
diagram saeth *eg* diagramau saeth arrow diagram
diagram Venn *eg* diagramau Venn Venn diagram
diagram wedi'i labelu *eg* diagramau wedi'u labelu labelled diagram
diangen *ans* redundant
dianghenraid *ans* non-essential
di-ais *ans* unstrutted
dial *eg* dialon reprisal
dialysad *eg* dialysate
dialysis *eg* dialysis
dialysis peritoneaidd *eg* peritoneal dialysis
diamagnetedd *eg* diamagnetism
diamedr *eg* diamedrau diameter
diamedr allanol *eg* diamedrau allanol outside diameter
diamedr craidd *eg* diamedrau craidd core diameter
diamedr lleiaf *eg* diamedrau lleiaf minor diameter
diamedr mewnol *eg* diamedrau mewnol inside diameter
diamedr mewnol *eg* diamedrau mewnol internal diameter
diamedr mwyaf *eg* major diameter
diamedr pitsh cylch *eg* pitch circle diameter
diamedrol *ans* diametral
diamod *ans* unconditional

diamwys *ans* unambiguous
diapason *eg* diapasonau diapason
diapason agored *eg* diapasonau agored open diapason
diapason agored dwbl *eg* double open diapason
diapason dwbl *eg* double diapason
diaper *eg* diaper
diarddel *be* suspend
diarddel *be* renounce
diarddel *be* expel
diarddel *be* disqualify
diarddel o'r ras *be* disqualify from the race
diarddeliad *eg* diarddeliadau disqualification
diarddeliad *eg* diarddeliadau expulsion
diarfogi *be* disarm
diarffin *ans* unbounded
diarogl *ans* odourless
diarogli *be* deodorize
diaroglydd *eg* diaroglyddion deodorant
diastas *eg* diastase
diastole *eg* diastole
diastolig *ans* diastolic
diastroffedd *eg* diastrophism
diatbryn (mewn economeg) *ans* irredeemable
diatom *eg* diatomau diatom
diatonig *ans* diatonic
diatonyddiaeth *eb* diatonicism
diathesis *eg* diathesis
► **dibetal** *ans* apetalous
di-blwm *ans* lead-free
diboblogaeth *eb* depopulation
diboblogi *be* depopulate
di-breim *ans* unprimed
dibriod *ans* unmarried
dibrisiad *eg* dibrisiadau devaluation; depreciation
dibrisiad cyfalaf *eg* capital depreciation
dibrisiant *eg* depreciation
dibrisio *be* depreciate
dibrisio'r bunt *be* devaluation of the pound
dibrotein *ans* non-protein
dibwys *ans* negligible
dibyn *eg* dibynnau precipice
dibynadwy *ans* reliable
dibynadwyedd *eg* reliability
► **dibynadwyedd glawiad** *eg* rainfall reliability
dibynadwyedd hollt dau hanner *eb* split-half reliability
dibynadwyedd prawf *eg* test reliability
dibynadwyedd prawf-ailbrawf *eg* test-retest reliability
dibyniaeth *eb* dependence; dependency
dibyniaeth ar gyffuriau *eb* drug dependency
dibyniaeth gorfforol *eb* physical dependence
dibyniaeth ieuenctid *eb* youth dependency
dibyniaeth linol *eb* linear dependence
dibyniaeth maes *eb* field dependence
dibynnol *ans* dependent
dibynnydd *eg* dibynyddion dependant
dichonadwy *ans* feasible; viable
dichonoldeb masnachol *eg* commercial viability
did (digid deuaidd) *eg* didau bit
did arwydd *eg* didau arwydd sign bit
did cario *eg* didau cario carry bit
did deuaidd *eg* didau deuaidd binary bit
did gorlif *eg* didau gorlif overflow bit
did gwybodaeth *eg* didau gwybodaeth information bit
did lleiaf arwyddocaol *eg* didau lleiaf arwyddocaol least significant bit
did mwyaf arwyddocaol *eg* didau mwyaf arwyddocaol most significant bit
did paredd *eg* didau paredd parity bit
did uchaf *eg* didau uchaf top bit
didau yr eiliad bits per second
dideimlad *ans* numb
didfap *eg* didfapiau bitmap
di-doi *be* unroof
didol borthi *be* creep feeding
didol borthi moch bach creep feeding of suckling pigs
didol borthi ŵyn bach creep feeding of lambs
didoli (a threfnu) *be* sort
didoli (anifeiliaid, gwybodaeth) *be* separate out
didoli (mewn cwestiynau arholiad) *be* discrimination
didoli (wrth weinyddu achosion) *be* gatekeeping
didolnod *eg* didolnodau diaeresis
di-dor *ans* continuous
didostur *ans* unrelenting
di-draidd *ans* opaque
didreiddedd *eg* opacity
didreiddydd *eg* didreiddyddion opacifier
diduedd *ans* unbiased
didwyll *ans* candid
didwylledd *eg* openness
didyniad *eg* didyniadau deduction
didynnu *be* deduct
diddanydd *eg* paraclete
diddeilio *be* defoliate
diddirdro *ans* torsion free
diddordeb *eg* diddordebau interest
diddorol *ans* interesting
diddos *ans* waterproof
diddosi *be* waterproof
diddwythell *ans* ductless
diddwythiad *eg* diddwythiadau deduction
diddwythiad rhesymegol *eg* logical deduction
diddwytho *be* deduce
diddyfnu *be* wean
diddymiad (mewn cerddoriaeth) *eg* diddymiadau cancellation
diddymiad (mynachlog, senedd etc) *eg* diddymiadau dissolution
diddymu (mewn cerddoriaeth) *be* cancel
diddymu (=symud yn llwyr) *be* remove

diddymu (deddf) *be* repeal
diddymu (mynachlog, senedd etc) *be* dissolve
diddymu cromfachau *be* remove brackets
diddymu'r Deddfau Ŷd *be* repeal of the Corn Laws
diddymu'r mynachlogydd *be* dissolution of the monasteries
diemwnt *eg* diemyntau diamond
dienyddio *be* execute
diestyn *ans* unstretched
Diet Worms *eg* Diet of Worms
diewynnu *be* defoaming
difandwll *ans* non-porous
difateroli *be* dematerialize
difeddiannu *be* expropriate
difenwad *eg* defamation
diferu *be* drop
diferwydr *eg* diferwydrau spot drop glass
diferydd *eg* diferyddion dropper; teat pipette
diferyn *eg* diferion drop
diferynnu *be* trickle
difetha *be* spoil
difetha bwyd *be* spoiling of food
di-fias *ans* unbiased
diflan *ans* vanished
diflanbwynt *eg* diflanbwyntiau vanishing point
diflanedig *ans* extinct
diflannu *be* vanish
diflas *ans* boring; bored
diflastod *eg* boredom
diflewio *be* depilate
difodi *be* annihilate; annihilate; liquidate
difodiant *eg* extinction; liquidation
difreintiedig *ans* deprived; underprivileged
difrifol *ans* severe
difrod *eg* damage
difrod i'r haen oson *eg* damage to the ozone layer
difrod maleisus *eg* malicious damage
difrodi *be* damage
difwyniad *eg* adulteration
difwyno *be* adulterate
difydio *be* deprive
difywoliaeth *ans* unbeneficed
difywyd *ans* inanimate; inert
diffaith *ans* desolate; derelict
diffeithdir *eg* diffeithdiroedd desert
diffeithdir trofannol *eg* tropical desert
diffeithdiro *be* desertification
diffeithdra *eg* dereliction
diffeithle *eg* diffeithleoedd desert place
di-ffens *ans* unfenced
differadwy *ans* differentiable
differadwyedd *eg* differentiability
differiad *eg* differiadau differentiation
differiad graffigol *eg* differiadau graffigol graphical differentiation
differol *ans* differential
differol athraidd differentially permeable
differu *be* differentiate
differu rhannol *be* partial differentiation
differyn *eg* differynnau differential
diffiniad *eg* diffiniadau definition
diffiniad esbonyddol *eg* exponential definition
diffiniad gweithredol *eg* diffiniadau gweithredol operational definition
diffiniad problem *eg* diffiniadau problem problem definition
diffinio *be* define
diffinio cofnod llyfryddiaeth *be* define bibliography entry
diffinio priodoleddau testun *be* define text attributes
diffinio ystod *be* define range
diffinio ystod argraffu *be* define print range
diffinio ystod cronfa ddata *be* define database range
diffinio ystod enwau *be* define range names
diffinio ystod labeli *be* define label range
diffodd *be* switch off
diffodd (cyflenwad pŵer) *be* turn off
diffodd amlapio *be* wrap off
diffodd y golau *be* turn out the light
diffodd y tân trydan *be* turn the electric fire off
diffoddwr tân *eg* diffoddwyr tân fire extinguisher
diffreithiant *eg* diffreithiannau diffraction
diffreithiant electronau *eg* electron diffraction
diffreithio *be* diffract
diffrithiant *ans* frictionless
di-ffrwd *ans* streamless
diffrwyth *ans* barren
diffrwythloni *be* sterilize
difftheria *eg* diphtheria
diffyg (=heb fod yn gweithio'n iawn) *eg* diffygion malfunction
diffyg (=nam) *eg* diffygion defect; fault; flaw
diffyg (=prinder) *eg* diffygion deficiency; shortfall
diffyg (ar yr haul, y lleuad) *eg* eclipse
diffyg (ariannol) *eg* diffygion deficit
diffyg amlsynhwyraidd *eg* multi-sensory deprivation
diffyg ar y lleuad *eg* diffygion ar y lleuad lunar eclipse
diffyg ar yr haul *eg* solar eclipse
diffyg cydbwysedd *eg* disequilibrium
diffyg cyllidol *eg* diffygion cyllidol budget deficit
diffyg cynnydd *eg* failure to thrive
diffyg dŵr *eg* water deficit
diffyg echddygol *eg* diffygion echddygol motor defect
diffyg golau *eg* absence of light
diffyg gwybyddol *eg* diffygion gwybyddol cognitive deficit
diffyg hunan-werth *eg* worthlessness
diffyg hylif *eg* dehydration
diffyg maeth *eg* malnutrition; undernourishment
diffyg màs *eg* mass defect

diffyg mynegiant llafar *eg* expressive language disorder
diffyg parhad *eg* discontinuity
diffyg rhuglder *eg* dysfluency
diffyg traul *eg* indigestion; dyspepsia
diffyg ymaddasiad *eg* maladjustment
diffyg ymlyniad *eg* non-adherence
diffygiol *ans* deficient; defective; impaired; faulty
diffygion coed *ell* timber defects
▸ **diffygion deiet** *ell* dietary deficiencies
diffygion naturiol (mewn pren) *ell* natural defects
diffyniad *eg* diffyniadau apology
diffyniadaeth *eb* apologetics
diffyniadol *ans* apologetic
diffynnaeth *eb* protectionism
diffynnydd (=dadleuwr rhesymegol) *eg* diffynwyr apologetist
diffynnydd (mewn llys) *eg* diffynyddion defendant
digartref *ans* homeless
di-gell *ans* cell-free
digennu *be* descale
digid *eg* digidau digit
digid cod deuaidd *eg* digidau cod deuaidd binary coded digit
digid deuaidd *eg* digidau deuaidd binary digit
digid hecs *eg* digidau hecs hex digit
▸ **digideiddiad** *eg* digideiddiadau digitation
digido *be* digitize
digidol *ans* digital
digidydd *eg* digidyddion digitizer
di-goed *ans* unforested
digoes *ans* sessile
digollediad *eg* indemnity
digolledu *be* compensate
digon *ans* sufficient
digonedd *eg* abundance
digonedd cymharol *eg* relative abundance
digonol *ans* adequate
digorff *ans* bodyless
digornio *be* dehorning
digramennu *be* debridement
di-grefft *ans* unskilled
digreiddiwr *eg* digreiddwyr corer
digreiddiwr afal *eg* digreiddwyr afalau apple corer
digroeso *ans* inhospitable
digwyddiad *eg* digwyddiadau event
digwyddiad *eg* digwyddiadau incident
digwyddiad achosol *eg* digwyddiadau achosol causal event or determinant
digwyddiad critigol *eg* digwyddiadau critigol critical incident
digwyddiad cymhleth *eg* digwyddiadau cymhleth complex event
digwyddiad mawr *eg* digwyddiadau mawr major incident
digwyddiad newydd *eg* digwyddiadau newydd new event
digwyddiad tectonig *eg* digwyddiadau tectonig tectonic event
digwyddiad ymyriadol *eg* digwyddiadau ymyriadol interrupt event
digwyddiadau ar y pryd *ell* actuality
digwyro *be* de-waxing
digwyro gydag ager *be* steam de-waxing
digyfeiliant *ans* unaccompanied
digyfnod *ans* aperiodic
digyfrifiannell *ans* non-calculator
digyfryngedd *eg* immediacy
digymar (am electronau) *ans* unpaired
digymell *ans* spontaneous
digynnen *ans* non-contentious
digywair *ans* atonal
digyweiredd *eg* atonality
digyweirydd *eg* digyweirwyr atonalist
dihaenedig *ans* unstratified
dihaenu *be* delayer
di-haint *ans* sterile
dihalwyno *be* desalination
diheintiad *eg* disinfection
diheintiedig *ans* disinfected
diheintio *be* sterilize; disinfect
diheintydd *eg* diheintyddion sterilizer; disinfectant
diheurbrawf *eg* diheurbrofion ordeal
diheurbrawf *eg* diheurbrofion trial by ordeal
diheurbrawf dŵr *eg* ordeal by water
diheurbrawf tân *eg* ordeal by fire
di-ïonig *ans* non-ionic
dilawes *ans* sleeveless
dilead (=rhwbiad allan) *eg* dileadau erasure
dilead (deddfau etc) *eg* dileadau abolition
dilead (mewn cemeg) *eg* dileadau elimination
dilead (yn gyffredinol) *eg* dileadau deletion
dilechdid *eg* dialectic
dileu (=rhwbio allan) *be* erase
dileu (deddfau etc) *be* abolish
dileu (mewn cemeg) *be* eliminate
dileu (yn gyffredinol) *be* delete
dileu adran *be* delete section
dileu arddull llinell *be* delete line style
dileu awtofformat *be* delete autoformat
dileu caethwasiaeth *be* abolition of slavery
dileu cofnod (mewn cronfa ddata) *be* delete record
dileu cofnod (yn gyffredinol) *be* delete entry
dileu colofn *be* delete column
dileu croeslinellu *be* delete hatching
dileu cyfeiriaduron *be* delete directories
dileu cynllun ddewiswyd *be* delete selected design
dileu cynnwys *be* delete contents
dileu dalen *be* delete sheet
dileu data *be* delete data
dileu defnyddiwr *be* delete user
dileu delwedd *be* delete image
dileu dewisiadau *be* delete options
dileu diwedd llinell *be* delete line end

dileu drwy amnewid *be* elimination by substitution
dileu eicon *be* delete icon
dileu ffeil *be* delete file
dileu ffenestr dalen *be* delete sheet window
dileu ffrâm *be* delete frame
dileu ffynhonnell data *be* delete data source
dileu gosodiadau lleol *be* delete local settings
dileu graddiant *be* delete gradient
dileu graffigau *be* delete graphics
dileu grŵp *be* delete group
dileu gwrthrych *be* delete object
dileu gwrthrychau lluniadu *be* delete drawing objects
dileu hanes *be* delete history
dileu llinell snap *be* delete snap line
dileu lliw *be* delete colour
dileu mynegai *be* delete index
dileu neges *be* delete message
dileu nod tudalen *be* delete bookmark
dileu pob ffeil *be* delete all files
dileu popeth *be* delete all
dileu pwynt snap *be* delete snap point
dileu rhes *eb* delete row
dileu rhifo *be* delete numbering
dileu sleid *be* delete slide
dileu tabl databeilot *be* delete datapilot table
dileu toriad colofn *be* delete column break
dileu toriad llaw *be* delete manual break
dileu toriad rhes *be* delete row break
dileu toriadau tudalen *be* delete page breaks
dileu tudalen *be* delete page
dileu uniad *be* delete join
dileubrint *eg* dileubrintiau elimination print
dileubrintio *be* elimination printing
dilëwr (bysell cyfrifiadur) *eg* dilewyr delete key
dilëwr (yn gyffredinol) *eg* dilewyr eraser
dilëwr gwm *eg* dilewyr gwm gum eraser
dilëydd *eg* dilëyddion eliminant
diliau mêl *ell* honeycomb
di-liw *ans* colourless
diloywi *be* delustre
di-lun *ans* misshapen
di-lwch *ans* dust-free
dilyn *be* follow; shadow
dilyn ac arwain *be* lag and lead
dilyn drwodd *be* follow through
dilyn llwybrau *be* following routes
dilyn ymlaen *be* follow on
dilyniad cordiau *eg* dilyniadau cordiau chord progression
dilyniannol *ans* sequential
dilyniant (=gweithred, profiad dilynol) *eg* dilyniannau follow-up
dilyniant (cymuned o anifeiliaid neu blanhigion) *eg* dilyniannau sere
dilyniant (mewn cerddoriaeth) *eg* dilyniannau sequence
dilyniant (mewn rhifyddeg) *eg* dilyniannau progression
dilyniant (train) *eg* dilyniannau train
dilyniant alawol *eg* dilyniannau alawol melodic sequence
dilyniant bas *eg* base sequence
dilyniant cymhleth o symudiadau *eg* dilyniannau cymhleth o symudiadau complex sequence of movements
dilyniant cynyddol *eg* dilyniannau cynyddol increasing sequence
dilyniant da *eg* good continuation
dilyniant galw *eg* dilyniannau galw calling sequence
dilyniant geometrig *eg* geometric progression
dilyniant harmonig *eg* dilyniannau harmonig harmonic sequence
dilyniant mewn gofal continuity of care
dilyniant naratif *eg* narrative sequencing
dilyniant o gordiau *eg* dilyniannau o gordiau chord sequence
dilyniant o gyfarwyddiadau *eg* dilyniannau o gyfarwyddiadau sequence of instructions
dilyniant o symudiadau *eg* dilyniannau o symudiadau sequence of movements
dilyniant rhif *eg* number sequence
dilyniant rhifyddol *eg* arithmetical progression
dilyniant sleidiau *eg* dilyniannau sleidiau slide sequence
dilyniant tâp *eg* dilyniannau tâp tape sequence
dilynol *ans* consecutive; subsequent; follow-up
dilynolion *ell* consecutives
dilynwr *eg* dilynwyr follower
dilynwr Barrow *eg* dilynwyr Barrow Barrowist
dilynwr cam *eg* dilynwyr cam cam follower
dilynwr ffurfiedig *eg* dilynwyr ffurfiedig formed follower
dilynwr pwynt mewn-llinell *eg* dilynwyr pwynt mewn-llinell in-line point follower
dilynwr rholer *eg* dilynwyr rholer roller follower
dilynwr tangiadol *eg* dilynwyr tangiadol tangential follower
dilys *ans* valid; authentic
dilysiad *eg* dilysiadau validation; authentication
dilysiad data *eg* dilysiadau data data validation
dilysrwydd *eg* validity
dilysrwydd *eg* authenticity
dilysrwydd allanol *eg* external validity
dilysrwydd ecolegol *eg* ecological validity
dilysrwydd lluniad *eg* construct validity
dilysrwydd mewnol *eg* internal validity
dilysrwydd rhagfynegi *eg* predictive validity
dilysrwydd rhwng arsylwyr *eg* interobserver reliability
dilysrwydd rhyng-gyfraddwyr *eg* interrater reliability
dilysu *be* authenticate; validate
dilysu data *be* data validation
dilysydd allanol *eg* dilyswyr allanol external validator

dilysydd mewnol *eg* dilyswyr mewnol internal verifier
dillad *ell* clothes
dillad anaddas *ell* inappropriate clothing
dillad gwarchod *ell* protective clothing
dillad gwely *ell* bedding
dillad gwely *ell* bed linen
dillad gwlân *ell* woollen garments
dillad gwyntglos *ell* windproof clothing
dillad hamdden *ell* leisure clothes
dillad isaf *ell* underwear; undergarments; underclothing
dillad nos *ell* nightwear
dillad plant bach *ell* toddlers' wear
dillad segura *ell* casuals
dillad traeth *ell* beachwear
dilladaeth *eb* drapery
dilledydd *eg* dilledyddion draper
dilledyn *eg* dilladau garment
dilledyn babygro *eg* dillad babygro babygro
dilledyn dwyffordd *eg* dillad dwyffordd reversible garment
dilledyn llac *eg* dillad llac flowing garment
dilledyn sail *eg* dillad sail foundation garment
dim *eg* nought
dim adnoddau argraffu no printer driver
dim amlinelliad no outline
dim arddull nodau no character style
dim atebolrwydd heb fai no liability without fault
dim cofnod no entry
dim cysylltnodi no hyphenation
dim dangosyddion no indicators
dim dim love all
dim diwedd tudalen no page end
dim dyblygu no duplication
dim effaith no effect
dim ffeiliau pellach no further files
dim fformat no format
dim fformiwla wedi'i phennu no formula specified
dim gweithred no action
dim gwybodaeth ychwanegol no additional information
dim iaith wedi'i phennu no language set
dim logo no logo
dim lle no room
dim lleoli awtomatig no automatic positioning
dim llithriad *eg* no drop
dim maes no field
dim meysydd wedi'u pennu no fields specified
dim newidiadau no changes
dim pâr yn gorgyffwrdd no pair kerning
dim patrwm no pattern
dim pennyn no header
dim priodweddau ychwanegol no additional properties
dim sgôr love
dim swyddogaeth no function
dim teitl no heading
dim toriad no break
dim toriad tudalen no page break
dim trugaredd *ans* no mercy
dimensiwn *eg* dimensiynau dimension
dimensiwn dyfnder *eg* depth dimension
dimensiwn Ewropeaidd *eg* European dimension
dimensiwn rhyngwladol *eg* dimensiynau rhyngwladol international dimension
dimensiynau gorffenedig *ell* finished dimensions
dimensiynau hanfodol *ell* essential dimensions
dimensiynau lled agos *ell* rough dimensions
dimensiynau mwyaf *ell* maximum dimensions
dimensiynau perthynol *ell* relative dimensions
dimensiynol *ans* dimensional
dimensiynu *be* dimension
dinas *eb* dinasoedd city
▶ **dinas fewnol** *eb* inner city
dinas filiwn *eb* dinasoedd miliwn million city
dinasoedd Hansa *ell* Hanseatic cities
dinasyddiaeth *eb* citizenship; denizenship
dinesig *ans* civic
dinesydd *eg* dinasyddion citizen
dinistrio (yn gyffredinol) *be* destroy
dinistrio (castell) *be* slight
dinistriol *ans* devastating
diniwed *ans* naïve
dinoethi *be* expose
dinoethiad *eg* dinoethiadau exposure
dinosor *eg* dinosoriaid dinosaur
dinwyo *bc* degassing
diod *eb* diodydd beverage
diod feddwol *eb* diodydd meddwol alcoholic drink
Dioddefaint *eg* Passion
dioddefaint anifeiliaid *eg* animal suffering
dioddefwr *eg* dioddefwyr victim
diofynnu *be* default
diogel *ans* safe; secure
diogelu *be* protect; secure
diogelu ffeil *be* file protection
diogelu plant *be* child protection
diogelu rhag ysgrifennu *be* write protect
diogelu rhag ysgrifennu *be* write protection
diogelwch *eg* safety; security; protection
diogelwch meddalwedd *eg* software protection
diogelwch personol *eg* personal safety
diogelwch pobl ac eiddo *eg* safety and security
diogelwch rhag tân *eg* fire protection
diogelwch yn y dŵr *eg* water safety
diogelwyd gan gyfrinair password protected
diogi cymdeithasol *eg* social loafing
diolch am y cynhaeaf *be* harvest thanksgiving
diorama *eg* dioramau diorama
diorit *eg* diorite
diorseddiad *eg* diorseddiadau deposition
diorseddu *be* depose
dip *eg* dipiau dip

dip gloywi *eg* dipiau gloywi bright dip
dipell *eb* dipelli dipper
dipell ddwbl *eb* dipelli dwbl double dipper
dipio *be* dip
dipio poeth *be* hot dipping
diploid *ans* diploid
diploidi *eg* diploidy
diploma *eg* diplomau diploma
diplomateg *eb* diplomatics
diplomydd *eg* diplomyddion diplomat
diplomyddiaeth *eb* diplomacy
diplomyddol *ans* diplomatic
diraddedig *ans* degraded
diraddiad *eg* diraddiadau degradation
diraddiad gosgeiddig *eg* graceful degradation
diraddio *be* degrade
dirdro *ans* twisted
dirdro *eg* dirdroeon torsion
dirdroad *eg* dirdroadau twist
dirdroadol *ans* torsional
dirdroi *be* twist; twisting
Directoire *eg* Directory
direswm *ans* unprovoked
dirgroes *ans* opposite
dirgryniad *eg* dirgryniadau vibration; convulsion
dirgryniad ardraws *eg* dirgryniadau ardraws transverse vibration
dirgryniad gorfod *eg* dirgryniadau gorfod forced vibration
dirgryniad gwanychol *eg* dirgryniadau gwanychol damped vibration
► **dirgryniad hydredol** *eg* dirgryniadau hydredol longitudinal vibration
dirgrynol *ans* vibratory; vibrational; vibrating
dirgrynu *be* vibrate
diriaethol *ans* concrete
diriaetholi *be* concretization
diriant *eg* diriannau stress
diriant croesrym *eg* shearing stress
diriant tyniant *eg* diriannau tyniant tension stress
diriant tynnol *eg* diriannau tynnol tensile stress
dirinwedd *ans* demerit
dirlawn *ans* saturated
dirlawnder *eg* saturation
dirlenwi *be* saturate
dirmyg llys *eg* contempt of court
dirnad *be* apprehend
dirnadaeth *eb* dirnadaethau discrimination; apprehension
dirprwy (ym myd y theatr etc) *eg* dirprwyon understudy
dirprwy (yn gyffredinol) *eg* dirprwyon deputy
dirprwy bennaeth (ysgol) *eg* dirprwy benaethiaid deputy head
dirprwy brifathrawes *eb* dirprwy brifathrawesau deputy headmistress
dirprwy cyffredinol *eg* dirprwyaid cyffredinol commissary general
dirprwy glawswla *eg* substitute clausula
dirprwy lyngesydd *eg* dirprwy lyngeswyr rear-admiral
dirprwy lywodraethwr *eg* dirprwy lywodraethwyr lieutenant governor
dirprwy raglaw *eg* dirprwy raglawiaid deputy lieutenant
dirprwyaeth *eb* dirprwyaethau delegation; deputation
dirprwyo *be* delegate; substitute
dirprwyo cyllidebau *be* delegation of budgets
dirprwyo eithaf *be* maximum delegation
dirprwyo gofynion *be* delegation of requirements
dirprwyo rheolaeth *be* delegate the management of
dirprwyol *ans* proxy; vicarious
dirwasgedd dilynol *eg* secondary depression
dirwasgiad *eg* dirwasgiadau depression; recession; slump
Dirwasgiad Mawr *eg* Great Depression
dirwy *eb* dirwyon fine
dirwy etifedd *eb* relief
dirwyn *be* wind
dirwyniad *eg* dirwyniadau winding
dirwyniad an-anwythaidd *eg* non-indictively wound
dirwyniad cyfansawdd *eg* dirwyniadau cyfansawdd compound wound
dirwyniad cyfres *eg* dirwyniadau cyfres series wound
dirwyniad eilaidd *eg* secondary windings
dirwynydd *eg* dirwynyddion winder
dirwyo *be* fine
di-rym (=heb fod yn ddilys) *ans* void
di-rym (yn gyfreithiol) *ans* null & void
dirymiad *eg* dirymiadau revocation; annulment
dirymu *be* annul; revoke; invalidate; nullify
dirywiad *eg* dirywiadau decline; deterioration; degeneracy
dirywiad bwyd *eg* food spoilage
dirywiaeth *eb* decadence
dirywiedig *ans* degenerate
dirywiedig n-blyg *ans* n-fold degenerate
dirywio *be* deteriorate; degenerate
dirywiol *ans* degenerating
dis *eg* disiau dice
dis digidol *eg* disiau digidol digital dice
disbyddadwy *ans* exhaustible
disbyddedig *ans* exhausted
disbyddiad *eg* disbyddiadau depletion
disbyddu *be* exhaust
disebon *ans* soapless
disg (mewn cyd-destun cyfrifiadurol) *eg/b* disgiau disk
disg (yn gyffredinol) *eg/b* disgiau disc
disg caled *eg* disgiau caled hard disk
disg caled allanol *eg* disgiau caled allanol external hard disk

disg cerdyn tenau *eg* disgiau cerdyn tenau thin card disk
disg cetrisen *eg* disgiau cetris cartridge disk
disg cychwynnol *eg* disgiau cychwynnol start-up disk
disg cyfnewidiadwy *eg* disgiau cyfnewidiadwy exchangeable disk
disg defnyddiwr *eg* disgiau defnyddwyr user disk
disg dros dro *eg* disgiau dros dro scratch disk
disg echreiddig *eg* disgiau echreiddig eccentric disc
disg fideo *eg* disgiau fideo video disk
disg fflans *eg* disgiau fflans flange disc
disg ffynhonnell *eg* disgiau ffynhonnell source disk
disg gwag *eg* disgiau gwag blank disk
disg gwasanaethu *eg* disgiau gwasanaethu utility disk
disg gyrru *eg* disgiau gyrru driving disk
disg hyblyg *eg* disgiau hyblyg floppy disk
disg hyblyg bychan *eg* disgiau hyblyg bychain mini-floppy disk
disg llyfnu *eg* disgiau llyfnu sanding disc
disg magnetig *eg* disgiau magnetig magnetic disk
disg optegol *eg* disgiau optegol optical disc
disg optig *eg* disgiau optig optic disk
disg papur *eg* disgiau papur paper disc
disg rhyngfertebrol *eg* intervertebral disc
disg tyniant *eg* disgiau tyniant tension disc
disg wedi'i orchuddio â haen fagnetig *eg* disgiau wedi'u gorchuddio â haen fagnetig magnetically coated disk
disg Winchester *eg* disgiau Winchester Winchester disk
disg y rhaglen *eg* disgiau'r rhaglenni program disk
disgen *eb* disgiau discus
disgleirdeb *eg* brightness
disgleirdeb *eg* brilliance
disgleirdeb lliw *eg* brilliance of colour
disgleirio *be* shine
disgleirydd optegol *eg* disgleiryddion optegol optical brightener
disgo *eg* disgos disco
disgownt *eg* disgowntiau discount
disgownt masnach *eg* disgowntiau masnach trade discount
disgresiwn *eg* discretion
disgrifiad (o ddigwyddiad etc) *eg* disgrifiadau account
disgrifiad (yn gyffredinol) *eg* disgrifiadau description
disgrifiad graddau *eg* disgrifiadau graddau grade description
disgrifiad gronyn-gronyn *eg* particle-particle description
disgrifiad lefel *eg* disgrifiadau lefel level description
disgrifiad llafar *eg* disgrifiadau llafar oral description
disgrifiad o fath *eg* description of type
disgrifiad o'r gwall *eg* disgrifiadau o'r gwallau error description
disgrifiad o'r rheolfan *eg* disgrifiadau o'r rheolfan control description
disgrifiad problem *eg* disgrifiadau problem problem description
disgrifiad swydd *eg* disgrifiadau swydd job description
disgrifiad ysgrifenedig *eg* disgrifiadau ysgrifenedig written description
disgrifiadol *ans* descriptive
disgrifio *be* describe
disgrifydd *eg* disgfrifwyr descriptor
disgwyliad *eg* expectancy
disgwyliad oes *eg* disgwyliadau oes life expectancy
disgwyliadau cynulleidfa *ell* audience expectations
disgwyliadau oedolion *ell* adult expectations
disgwyliadau rhieni *ell* parents' expectations
disgwyliedig *ans* expected
disgybl *eg* disgyblion pupil
disgybl aflonyddgar *eg* disgyblion aflonyddgar disruptive pupil
disgybl anystywallt *eg* disgyblion anystywallt disorderly pupil
disgybl breiniol *eg* disgyblion breiniol franchised pupil
disgybl cythryblus *eg* disgyblion cythryblus disturbed pupil
disgybl chweched dosbarth *eg* disgyblion chweched dosbarth sixth former
disgybl dall *eg* disgyblion dall blind pupil
disgybl iaith gyntaf *eg* disgyblion iaith gyntaf first language pupil
disgybl is ei gyrhaeddiad *eg* disgyblion is eu cyrhaeddiad lower attaining pupil
disgybl sy'n destun datganiad *eg* disgyblion sy'n destun datganiad statemented pupil
disgybl sy'n gaeth i'w gadair *eg* disgyblion sy'n gaeth i'w cadair chairbound pupil
disgyblaeth *eb* disgyblaethau discipline
disgybledig *ans* disciplined
disgyblwr *eg* disgyblwyr disciplinarian
disgyddiaeth *eb* disgyddiaethau discography
disgyn *be* descend
disgyn yn rhydd *be* free-fall
disgynfan y bêl *eg* pitch of the ball
disgyniad *eg* descent
disgynnol *ans* descending
disgynnydd *eg* disgynyddion descendant
disgynyddion *ell* progeny
disgyrchedd *eg* disgyrcheddau gravitation
disgyrchiant *eg* disgyrchiannau gravity
disgyrchol *ans* gravitational
disgyrchon *eg* disgyrchonau graviton
disgyrchu *be* gravitate
disgyrrwr *eg* disgyrwyr disk drive
dismwddio *ans* non-iron
disodli (wrth olygu ffilmiau etc) *be* wipe

dist *eg* distiau joist
distadl *ans* trivial
di-staen *ans* non-smudge
distain *eg* disteiniaid comptroller
distal *ans* distal
distaw *ans* quiet
distawrwydd *eg* silence
distemper *eg* distemper
distrywiol *ans* destructive
distyll *eg* low water
distyllad *eg* distylladau distillate
distyllu *be* distil
distyllu ag ager *be* steam distillation
distyllu ffracsiynol *be* fractional distillation
diswyddiad *eg* diswyddiadau deposition
diswyddo *be* depose
disymud *ans* stagnant
disymudedd *eg* rest
ditiad *eg* indictment
ditiadwy *ans* indictable
ditio *be* indict
divertimento *eg* divertimenti divertimento
diwahân *ans* indiscriminate
di-waith *ans* unemployed; redundant
Diwali *eg* Diwali
► **diwasgedd** *eg* diwasgeddau depression
diwedd *eg* finish
diwedd cofnod *eg* end of record
diwedd dawns *eg* end of dance
diwedd ffeil *eg* end of file
diwedd gorchwyl *eg* end of job
diwedd maes *eg* end of field
diwedd pendant *eg* clear end
diwedd rhediad *eg* end of run
diwedd tâp *eg* end of tape
diwedd y data *eg* end of data
diwedd y mislif *eg* menopause
diwedd y ras *eg* end of the race
diweddariad meddalwedd *eg* diweddariadau meddalwedd software update
diweddariad nesaf *eg* next update
diweddaru *be* update
diweddbwynt *eg* diweddbwyntiau end-point
diweddbwynt (titradiad) *eg* diwedd bwyntiau end point (titration)
diweddeb *eg/b* diweddebau cadence; clausula; close
diweddeb 6/4 *eb* diweddebau 6/4 cadential 6/4
diweddeb amen *eb* diweddebau amen amen cadence; plagal cadence; church cadence; Greek cadence
diweddeb amherffaith *eb* diweddebau amherffaith demi-cadence; imperfect cadence; half close; dominant cadence
diweddeb annisgwyl *eb* diweddebau annisgwyl interrupted cadence; surprise cadence; deceptive cadence; evaded cadence; avoided cadence; irregular cadence; broken cadence; false close
diweddeb berffaith *eb* diweddebau perffaith perfect cadence; complete cadence
diweddeb cordiau gwreiddiol *eb* diweddebau cordiau gwreiddiol radical cadence
diweddeb ohiriedig *eb* diweddebau gohiriedig suspended cadence
diweddeb swta *eb* diweddebau swta abrupt cadence
diweddebol *ans* cadential
diweirdeb *eg* chastity
diweithdra *eg* unemployment
diweithdra cylchol *eg* cyclical unemployment
diweithdra ecwilibriwm *eg* equilibrium unemployment
diweithdra ffrithiannol *eg* frictional unemployment
diweithdra heb gydbwysedd *eg* disequilibrium unemployment
diweithdra lleol *eg* localized unemployment
diweithdra strwythurol *eg* structural unemployment
diweithdra ysbeidiol *eg* casual unemployment
diwenwyn *ans* non-toxic
diwifr (=heb wifren) *ans* cordless
diwifr (yn defnyddio tonfeddi radio) *ans* wireless
diwinyddiaeth *eb* theology
Diwinyddiaeth Asgetig *eb* Ascetic Theology
diwinyddiaeth Fwslimaidd *eb* Muslim theology
diwinyddiaeth ffeministaidd *eb* feminist theology
Diwinyddiaeth Natur *eb* Natural Theology
Diwinyddiaeth Proses *eb* Process Theology
diwinyddiaeth rhyddhad *eb* liberation theology
diwretig *ans* diuretic
diwretig *eg* diwretigion diuretic
diwrnod *eg* diwrnodau day
diwrnod agored *eg* diwrnodau agored open day
diwrnod cyfannol *eg* integrated day
diwrnod estynedig *eg* diwrnodau estynedig extended day
diwrnod gwobrwyo *eg* diwrnodau gwobrwyo prize day
diwrnod haul *eg* solar day
diwrnod hyfforddi *eg* diwrnodau hyfforddi training day
diwrnod lleuad *eg* lunar day
diwrnod llys barn *eg* diwrnodau llys barn lawday
diwrnod sêr *eg* sidereal day
diwrnodau o rybudd *ell* days of notification
diws *eg* deuce
diwteranopia *eg* deuteranopia
diwteron *eg* diwteronau deuteron
diwydianeiddio *be* industrialize
diwydiannaeth *eb* industrialization
diwydiannau bri *ell* prestige industries
diwydiannau deilliedig *ell* spin-off industries
diwydiannau'r cyfryngau *ell* media industries
diwydiannol *ans* industrial
diwydiant *eg* diwydiannau industry

diwydiant aelwyd *eg* diwydiannau aelwyd domestic industry
diwydiant arfau *eg* diwydiannau arfau armament industry
diwydiant ategol *eg* diwydiannau ategol ancillary industry
diwydiant awyrennau *eg* aircraft industry
diwydiant awyrennau *eg* aeronautics industry
diwydiant awyrennau *eg* aviation industry
diwydiant awyrofod *eg* aerospace industry
diwydiant bancio *eg* banking industry
diwydiant brodorol *eg* indigenous industry
diwydiant canio *eg* canning industry
diwydiant cartref *eg* diwydiannau cartref cottage industry
diwydiant ceir *eg* diwydiannau ceir car industry
▸ **diwydiant cemegion** *eg* diwydiannau cemegion chemical industry
diwydiant cynorthwyol *eg* diwydiannau cynorthwyol auxiliary industry
diwydiant cynradd *eg* diwydiannau cynradd primary industry
diwydiant chwaraeon *eg* sporting industry
diwydiant disbyddol *eg* diwydiannau disbyddol robber industry
diwydiant echdynnol *eg* diwydiannau echdynnol extractive industry
diwydiant ehangol *eg* diwydiannau ehangol expanding industry
diwydiant eilaidd *eg* diwydiannau eilaidd secondary industry
diwydiant enciliol *eg* diwydiannau enciliol contracting industry
diwydiant ffilm Prydain *eg* British film industry
diwydiant glo *eg* coal industry
diwydiant gwasanaethu *eg* diwydiannau gwasanaethu service industry
diwydiant gweithgynhyrchu *eg* diwydiannau gweithgynhyrchu manufacturing industry
diwydiant gwladoledig *eg* diwydiannau gwladoledig nationalized industry
diwydiant gwlân *eg* woollen industry
diwydiant llaethdy *eg* dairy industry
diwydiant metelegol *eg* diwydiannau metelegol metallurgical industry
diwydiant mwyngloddio *eg* mining industry
diwydiant nwyddau traul *eg* diwydiannau nwyddau traul consumer industry
diwydiant peirianneg *eg* engineering industry
diwydiant petrocemegol *eg* diwydiannau petrocemegol petrochemical industry
▸ **diwydiant rhyddsymudol** *eg* diwydiannau rhyddsymudol foot-loose industry
diwydiant sylfaen *eg* diwydiannau sylfaen basic industry
diwydiant sy'n dirywio *eg* diwydiannau sy'n dirywio declining industry
diwydiant tecstilau *eg* textile industry
diwydiant trwm *eg* diwydiannau trwm heavy industry
diwydiant twf *eg* diwydiannau twf growth industry
diwydiant ymwelwyr *eg* tourist industry
diwydiant ysgafn *eg* diwydiannau ysgafn light industry
diwydriad *eg* devitrification
diwygiad (=adfywiad crefyddol) *eg* diwygiadau revival
diwygiad (am y Diwygiad Protestannaidd) *eg* diwygiadau reformation
diwygiad (yn gyffredinol) *eg* diwygiadau reform
diwygiad crefyddol *eg* diwygiadau crefyddol religious revival
Diwygiad Harri VIII *eg* Henrician Reformation, The
Diwygiad Protestannaidd *eg* Reformation; Protestant Reformation
Diwygiad Protestannaidd yn yr Almaen *eg* German Reformation
diwygiad y Torïaid *eg* diwygiadau y Torïaid Tory reform
diwygiedig *ans* reformed
diwygio *be* reform; amend
diwygio amaethyddol *be* agrarian reform
diwygio cyfraith prydlesi *be* leasehold reform
diwygio cymdeithasol *be* social reform
diwygio etholiadol *be* electoral reform
diwygio gwleidyddol ac etholiadol *be* political and electoral reform
diwygio seneddol *eg* parliamentary reform
diwygio'r carcharau *be* prison reform
diwygio'r deddfau cosbi *be* penal reform
diwygio'r gyfraith *be* law reform
diwygiwr *eg* diwygwyr reformer
diwylliannol *ans* cultural
diwylliannu *be* culturalization
diwylliant *eg* diwylliannau culture
diwylliant corfforaethol *eg* corporate culture
diwylliant craidd *eg* diwylliannau craidd core culture
diwylliant chwaraeon *eg* sporting culture
diwylliant ffilmiau *eg* film culture
diwylliant fflawiau *eg* flake culture
diwylliedig *ans* cultured
diymadferthedd *eg* helplessness
diymadferthedd wedi'i ddysgu *eb* learned helplessness
diymestyn *ans* non-stretch
diystyr *ans* meaningless
diystyru gofodol *be* spatial neglect
DMG: darllenydd marciau gweladwy *eg* darllenwyr marciau gweladwy OMR: optical mark reader
docfa *eb* docfâu berth
docio *be* berth
dod allan *be* emerge
dod i aros *be* come to rest
dod i ben *be* expire
dod i oed *be* reach one's majority
dod o hyd i dystiolaeth *be* obtain evidence

dod o hyd i fesuriadau *be* obtain measurements
dodecaffoni *eg* dodecaphony
dodecaffonig *ans* dodecaphonic
dodecagon *eg* dodecagonau dodecagon
dodecahedron *eg* dodecahedronau dodecahedron
dodecanal *eg* dodecanal
dodecan-1-ol *eg* dodecan-1-ol
dodrefn *ell* furniture
dodrefn datgysylltiol *ell* knockdown furniture
dodrefn fflatpac *ell* flatpack furniture
dodrefn meddal *ell* soft furnishings
dodrefn odyn *ell* kiln furniture
dodrefn parod-i'w-cydosod *ell* ready to assemble furniture
dodrefn pren plyg *ell* bentwood furniture
dodrefnyn sefydlog *eg* dodrefn sefydlog fitment
dodwyol *ans* oviparous
doethair *eg* doetheiriau apophthegm
doethuriaeth *eb* doctorate
dofednod *ell* poultry
dofi *be* domesticate
dogfen *eb* dogfennau document
dogfen ariannol *eb* dogfennau ariannol financial document
dogfen barod *eb* dogfennau parod previously prepared document
dogfen braint filwrol *eb* dogfennau braint filwrol brevet
dogfen busnes *eb* dogfennau busnes business document
dogfen ddrafft *eb* dogfennau drafft draft document
dogfen fel e-bost document as e-mail
dogfen fusnes safonol *eb* dogfennau busnes safonol standard business document
dogfen ffynhonnell *eb* dogfennau ffynhonnell source document
dogfen newydd *eb* dogfennau newydd new document
dogfen o grynodeb *eb* document from abstract
dogfen testun *eb* dogfennau testun text document
dogfen wag *eb* dogfennau gwag blank document
dogfen ymddiriedolaeth *eb* dogfennau ymddiriedolaeth trust deed
dogfennaeth *eb* documentation
dogfennaeth cynnal *eb* maintenance documentation
dogfennaeth defnyddiwr *eb* user documentation
dogfennaeth rhaglen *eg* program documentation
dogfennu *be* document
dogfennu system *be* document a system
dogn *eg* dognau ration
dogni *be* ration
dogni bwyd *be* food rationing
doili *eg* doilis doily
dôl *eb* dolydd meadow
dolbriddoedd *ell* meadow soils
doldrymau *ell* doldrums
dolen *eb* dolennau bow
dolen *eb* dolennau loop
dolen *eb* dolennau handle
dolen (ar gwpan etc) *eb* dolennau handle
dolen (mewn cadwyn etc) *eb* dolennau link
dolen a chwlwm loop and tie
dolen adborth *eb* dolennau adborth feedback loop
dolen adborth a rheoli *eb* feedback control loop
dolen annherfynus *eb* non-terminating loop
dolen atal *eb* dolennau atal loop stop
dolen belt *eb* dolennau belt belt carrier
dolen borthiant awtomatig *eb* dolennau porthiant awtomatig link for automatic feed
dolen botwm *eb* dolennau botwm buttonhole loop
dolen bres *eb* dolennau pres brass handle
dolen dynhau *eb* dolennau tynhau tightening loop
dolen ddiddiwedd *eb* dolennau diddiwedd infinite loop
dolen ddylunio *eb* dolennau dylunio design loop
dolen edau *eb* dolennau edau worked loop
dolen fasged *eb* dolennau basged basket handle
dolen fewngroth *eb* dolennau mewngroth intrauterine loop
dolen frêc *eb* dolennau brêc brake handle
dolen gadwyn *eb* dolennau cadwyn chain link
dolen gaeedig *eb* dolennau caeedig closed loop
dolen gamdro *eb* dolennau camdro cranked handle
dolen grog *eb* dolennau crog hanging loop
dolen gwpan *eb* dolennau cwpan cup handle
dolen Henle *eb* Henle's loop
dolen lawes *eb* dolennau llawes cufflink
dolen lemnisgat *eb* dolennau lemnisgat lemiscate loop
dolen llenni *eb* dolennau llenni curtain ring
dolen nythol *eb* dolennau nythol nested loop
dolen rouleau *eb* dolennau rouleau rouleau loop
dolen rych *eb* dolennau rhych slotted link
dolen syth *eb* dolennau syth straight handle
dolen wifren *eb* dolennau gwifren wire loop
dolennau droriau a chypyrddau *ell* drawer and cupboard pulls
dolennedd *eb* sinuosity
dolennog *ans* serpentine
dolennu *be* meander
doler *eb* doleri dollar
dolerit *eg* doleritau dolerite
dolffin *eg* dolffiniaid dolphin
doli *eb* doliau dolly
dolin *eg* dolinau dolina
dolmen *eb* dolmenni dolmen
dolmen porth *eg* portal dolmen
dolomit *eg* dolomitiau dolomite
dolur gwasgu *eg* doluriau gwasgu pressure sore
dolur gwddf *eg* sore throat
dolur rhydd *eg* diarrhoea
domestig *ans* domestic
Dominicaidd *ans* Dominican
Dominiciad *eg* Dominiciaid Dominican

dominiwn *eg* dominiynau dominion
domino *eg* dominos domino
dopamin *eg* dopamine
dorsal *ans* dorsal
dortur *eg* dorturiau dorter
dortur *eg* dorturiau dormitory
dos *eg* dosiau dose
dos angheuol *eg* dosau angheuol fatal dose
dos atgyfnerthol *eg* dosau atgyfnerthol booster dose
dos gormodol *eg* dosiau gormodol overdose
dosbarth (is-raniad o sir) *eg* dosbarthiadau district
dosbarth (yn gyffredinol) *eg* dosbarthiadau class
dosbarth adfer *eg* dosbarthiadau adfer remedial class
dosbarth canol *eg* middle class
dosbarth cymdeithasol *eg* dosbarthiadau cymdeithasol social class
dosbarth gallu cymysg *eg* dosbarthiadau gallu cymysg mixed ability class
dosbarth geiriau *eg* word class
dosbarth gwaith *eg* working class
dosbarth isaf *eg* dosbarthiadau isaf lower class
dosbarth llywodraethol *eg* ruling class
dosbarth meithrin *eg* dosbarthiadau meithrin nursery class
dosbarth modd *eg* modal class
dosbarth nos *eg* dosbarthiadau nos evening class
dosbarth rhentyddol *eg* rentier class
dosbarth uchaf *eg* dosbarthiadau uchaf upper class
dosbarthfa *eb* dosbarthfeydd dispensary
dosbarthiad (=dyraniad) *eg* dosbarthiadau allocation
dosbarthiad (=ffordd o drefnu llyfrau etc) *eg* dosbarthiadau classification
dosbarthiad (yn gyffredinol) *eg* distribution
dosbarthiad byd-eang poblogaeth *eg* global distribution of population
dosbarthiad cyfoeth *eg* distribution of wealth
dosbarthiad dwysedd electronau *eg* electron density distribution
dosbarthiad gofodol *eg* spatial distribution
dosbarthiad mewn cylchfaoedd *eg* zonation
dosbarthiad sengl *eg* single distribution
dosbarthiad unffordd *eg* dosbarthiadau unffordd one-way classification
dosbarthol *ans* distributive
dosbarthu (=rhannu allan) *be* distribute
dosbarthu (=trefnu) *be* classify
dosbarthu (e.e. myfyrwyr) *be* allocate
dosbarthu cyfanwerth ac adwerth *be* wholesale and retail distribution
dosbarthu gwybodaeth *be* classify information
dosbarthydd *eg* dosbarthwyr distributor
do-si-do *eg* do-se-do
dosraniad (=dosbarthiad) *eg* distribution
dosraniad (mewn mathemateg) *eg* dosraniadau partition
dosraniad amlder *eg* dosraniadau amlder frequency distribution
dosraniad amlder cronnus *eg* cumulative frequency distribution
dosraniad binomaidd *eg* binomial distribution
dosraniad di-dor *eg* dosraniadau di-dor continuous distribution
dosraniad Poisson *eg* Poisson distribution
dosraniad samplu *eg* sampling distribution
dosraniad samplu union *eg* exact sampling distribution
dosraniadol *ans* distributional
dosrannol *ans* parsing
dosrannu (=trefnu) *be* assort
dosrannu (mewn cyfrifiadureg) *be* parse
dosrannu (mewn mathemateg) *be* partition
dosrannu (mewn ystadegaeth) *be* distribute
dosrannu cyfartal *be* equal partition
dot *eg* dotiau dot
dot dwbl *eg* dotiau dwbl double dot
dot llinell doriad *eg* dotiau llinell doriad dot dash
dot triphlyg *eg* dotiau triphlyg triple dot
dotbwnsio *be* dot punching
dotiau i'r brig *ell* dots to top
dotiau'n fertigol *ell* dots vertically
dotio *be* dot
dotiog *ans* dotted
dotiog mân iawn *ans* ultrafine dotted
dotwaith *eg* stipple
dotweithio *be* stipple
dowcio *be* ducking
draen *eg* draenlau drain
draenen *eb* drain spine
draenen wen *eb* drain gwynion hawthorn
draeniad *eg* drainage
draeniad arosod *eg* superimposed drainage
draeniad datgymalog *eg* dismembered drainage
draeniad dryslyd *eg* draeniadau dryslyd confused drainage
draeniad mewnblewrol *eg* intrapleural drainage
draeniad pluog *eg* pinnate drainage
draenio *be* drain
draenio sêl tanddwr *be* underwater seal drainage
draenog (pysgodyn) *eg* draenogiaid perch
draenog môr *eg* draenogod môr sea-urchin
draenogiad y môr *eg* draenogiaid y môr bass
drafft *eg* drafftiau draft; draught
drafft bras *eg* drafftiau bras rough draft
drafft gweithio *eg* working draft
drafftio *be* draft
drafftio patrwm *be* draft a pattern
drafftsmon *eg* drafftsmyn draughtsman
drafftsmonaeth *eb* draughtsmanship
dragŵn *eg* dragwniaid dragoon
drama (mewn opera) *eb* action

drama (yn gyffredinol) *eb* dramâu drama; play
drama deledu *eb* dramâu teledu television drama
drama delynegol *eb* dramâu telynegol lyric drama
drama firagl *eb* dramâu miragl miracle play; mystery play
drama gerdd *eb* dramâu cerdd music drama
drama gyfnod *eb* dramâu cyfnod period play
drama gyfres *eb* serial drama
drama mewn addysg *eb* drama in education
dramateiddio *be* dramatize
dramatig *ans* dramatic
dreif *eb* dreifiau drive
dreif gyfar *eb* dreifiau cyfar cover drive
dreif ochr agored *eb* dreifiau ochr agored off drive
dreif ochr goes *eb* on drive
dreif syth *eb* dreifiau syth straight drive
dreif uchel *eb* dreifiau uchel lofted drive
dreifio'r bêl *be* drive the ball
dreser *eb* dreserau dresser
dresin *eg* dresins dressing
dresin belt *eg* belt dressing
dresin had *eg* seed dressing
drewgi *eg* drewgwn skunk
dribl *eg* dribble
dribl dwbl *eg* double dribble
driblo *be* dribble
driblo gwrthdro *be* reverse stick dribble
driblwr *eg* driblwyr dribbler
drifft *eg* drifftiau drift
drifft allwedd *eg* drifftiau allwedd key drift
drifft canlyniadol *eg* net drift
drifft cyfandirol *eg* continental drift
Drifft Gogledd Iwerydd *eg* North Atlantic Drift
drifft llacio *eg* ejector drift
drifft rhewlifol *eg* glacial drift
drifft sgwâr *eg* drifftiau sgwâr square drift
drifft tapr *eg* drifftiau tapr taper drift
drifft y glannau *eg* longshore drift
driffter *eb* driffterau drifter
drifftio *be* drift; drifting
dringen *eb* dringennau pitch
dringo *be* climb
dringo'n uchel *be* climb high
dril *eg* driliau drill
dril Archimedes *eg* driliau Archimedes Archimedean drill
dril arwain *eg* driliau arwain pilot drill
dril brest *eg* driliau brest breast drill
dril canoli *eg* driliau canoli centre drill; slocombe drill
dril canoli cyfunol *eg* driliau canoli cyfunol combination drill
dril clicied *eg* driliau clicied ratchet drill
dril cliriad *eg* driliau cliriad clearance drill
dril cludadwy *eg* driliau cludadwy portable drill
dril cyflym iawn *eg* driliau cyflym iawn high-speed drill
dril dirdro *eg* driliau dirdro twist drill
dril dymchwel *eg* driliau dymchwel capsize drill
dril ffliwt syth *eg* driliau ffliwt syth straight flute drill
dril garan dapr *eg* driliau garanau tapr taper shank drill
dril garan syth *eg* driliau garan syth straight shank drill
dril gwaith maen *eg* driliau gwaith maen masonry drill
dril gwrthsoddi *eg* driliau gwrthsoddi countersink drill
dril hau *eg* driliau hau seed drill
dril jobwr *eg* driliau jobwr jobber's drill
dril llaw *eg* driliau llaw hand drill
dril mainc *eg* driliau mainc bench drill
dril Morse *eg* driliau Morse Morse drill
dril morthwyl *eg* driliau morthwyl hammer drill
dril pedestal *eg* driliau pedestal pedestal drill
dril piler *eg* driliau piler pillar drill
dril pìn *eg* driliau pìn pin drill
dril rhychio *eg* driliau rhychio slotting drill
dril tanc *eg* driliau tanc tank drill
dril tapio *eg* driliau tapio tapping drill
dril trydan *eg* driliau trydan electric drill
dril trydan cludadwy *eg* driliau trydan cludadwy portable electric drill
drilio *be* drill
drilio arwain *be* pilot drilling
drilio cadwynol *be* chain drilling
driliwr *eg* drilwyr driller
dripsych *ans* drip-dry
dripsychu *be* drip-dry
drôn *eg* drone
drôr *eg* droriau drawer
drôr crog *eg* droriau crog suspended drawer
drôr storio *eg* droriau storio storage drawer
drôr-gryfhawr *eg* drôr-gryfhawyr drawer slip
drôr-gryfhawr crwm *eg* drôr-gryfhawyr crwm rounded drawer slip
drôr-gryfhawr cyfwyneb *eg* drôr-gryfhawyr cyfwyneb flush drawer slip
drôr-gryfhawr fflat *eg* drôr-gryfhawyr fflat flat drawer slip
dros bwysau *ans* overweight
dros dro *ans* provisional; temporary; transitory
drwm *eg* drymiau drum
drwm a ffyn drum and sticks
drwm ager *eg* drymiau ager steam drum
drwm bas *eg* drymiau bas bass drum
drwm brêc *eg* drymiau brêc brake drum
drwm gwifrau *eg* drymiau gwifrau snare drum
drwm ochr *eg* drymiau ochr side drum
drŵp *eg* drwpiau drupe
drws *eg* drysau door
drws barrog *eg* drysau barrog barred door
drws cefn *eg* drysau cefn backdoor
drws cleddog *eg* drysau cleddog braced door

drws cleddog solet *eg* drysau cleddog solet solid cleated door
drws craidd wedi'i ymylu a'i argaenu *eg* drysau craidd wedi'u hymylu a'u hargaenu core lipped and veneered door
drws crwybr gwenyn *eg* drysau crwybr gwenyn honeycombed door
drws cyfwyneb *eg* drysau cyfwyneb flush door
drws dwbl-wydrog *eg* drysau dwbl-wydrog double-glazed door
drws esgyn *eg* drysau esgyn up and over door
drws fframiog *eg* drysau fframiog framed door
drws gostwng *eg* drysau gostwng drop-down door
drws gwydrog *eg* drysau gwydrog glazed door
drws llithro *eg* drysau llithro sliding door
drws panelog *eg* drysau panelog panelled door
drws pren amlhaenog *eg* drysau pren amlhaenog multi-ply door
drws pren haenog *eg* drysau pren haenog veneered ply door
drws pren solet *eg* drysau pren solet solid wood door
drws tabwrdd *eg* drysau tabwrdd tambour door
drws ysgafellog *eg* drysau ysgafellog ledged door
drwyddi *ans* drwyddynt global
drwyddo *ans* drwyddynt global
drych *eg* drychau mirror; glass
drych y gwrthrychiadur *eg* drychau'r gwrthrychiadur objective mirror
drych-archif *eg* drych-archifau mirror archive
drychddelwedd *eb* drychddelweddau mirror image
drychganon *eb/g* drychganonau mirror canon
drych-safle *eg* drych-safleoedd mirrorsite
drychweddu *be* mirror
drych-ysgrifennu *be* mirror writing
drygioni *eg* evil
drygioni a dioddefaint evil and suffering
drygioni moesol *eg* moral evil
drygioni naturiol *eg* natural evil
dryll *eb* drylliau shotgun
drylliad *eg* drylliadau wreck
drylliad cardiau *eg* drylliadau cardiau card wreck
dryllio *be* shatter; wreck
dryllwyr *ell* wreckers
drymiwr *eg* drymwyr drummer
drymlin *eb* drymlinau drumlin
drysfa *eb* maze
dryslwyn *eg* dryslwyni thicket
drysu (gobeithion) *be* frustrate
drysu (yn gyffredinol) *be* confuse; confound
du *eg* black
du ifori *eg* ivory black
du lamp *eg* lamp black
dueg *eb* duegau spleen
duegol *ans* splenic
dug *eg* dugiaid duke
Dug Efrog *eg* Duke of York
Dug Lancaster *eg* Duke of Lancaster
dugaeth *eb* dugaethau duchy; dukedom
duges *eb* dugesau duchess
dugol *ans* ducal
dukha *eg* dukha
dukka *eg* dukka
dulas *eg* ultramarine
dulasedd *eg* cyanosis
dulciana *eg* dulciana
dull (nofio) *eg* dulliau stroke
dull (yn gyffredinol) *eg* dulliau method; approach
dull a, b, c *eg* alphabetic method
dull a priori *eg* a priori method
dull adio cyfartal *eg* equal addition method
dull adio cyflenwol *eg* complementary addition method
▶ **dull addysgol** *eg* dulliau addysgol educational approach
dull anffurfiol *eg* dulliau anffurfiol informal method; informal approach
dull arbrofol *eg* dulliau arbrofol experimental method
dull archwilio *eg* dulliau archwilio exploration method
dull argraffu *eg* dulliau argraffu printing method
dull arllwys *eg* pouring method
dull arsylwi *eg* dulliau arsylwi observational method
dull asesu *eg* dulliau asesu assessment tool
dull atal cenhedlu *eg* dulliau atal cenhedlu contraceptive method
dull cau *eg* dulliau cau fastenings
dull confensiynol *eg* dulliau confensiynol conventional method
dull cyfannu *eg* dulliau cyfannu cloze procedure
dull cyfansoddi *eg* dulliau cyfansoddi method of composition
dull cyfarch *eg* mode of address
dull cyfrifiadurol *eg* dulliau cyfrifiadurol computer based method
dull cyfrifiannu *eg* dulliau cyfrifiannu computational method
dull cyfrifo *eg* dulliau cyfrifo calculating method
dull cyfweld safonol *eg* standard interview technique
dull cyffredinol *eg* general method
dull cylch ategol *eg* auxiliary circle method
dull cymysg *eg* dulliau cymysg mixed method
dull cymysgu lliwiau *eg* dulliau cymysgu lliwiau method of colour mixing
dull cywasgu testun *eg* dulliau cywasgu testun text compression technique
dull chwisgio *eg* whisking method
dull dadelfennu *eg* decomposition method
dull diagramatig *eg* dulliau diagramatig diagrammatic approach
dull digyfrifiannell *eg* dulliau digyfrifiannell non-calculator method
dull diogelu *eg* dulliau diogelu protection mechanism
dull dyddiadur *eg* diary method

dull dyneiddiol *eg* humanistic approach
dull dysgu *eg* dulliau dysgu learning method
dull dysgu drwy weithgaredd *eg* dulliau dysgu drwy weithgaredd activity method
dull eclectig *eg* eclectic approach
dull edrych a dweud *eg* look and say method
dull empirig *eg* dulliau empirig empirical method
dull enwi binomaidd *eg* binomial nomenclature
dull ffonig *eg* dulliau ffonig phonic method
dull gair-peg *eg* peg-word method
dull geometregol *eg* dulliau geometregol geometrical method
dull gorchymyn ac ymateb *eg* command-response method
dull graddio *eg* dulliau graddio ranking method
dull gweithdy *eg* dulliau gweithdy workshop approach
dull gweithredu *eg* dulliau gweithredu procedure
dull gweithredu abc *eg* abc procedure
dull gweithredu cwynion *eg* complaints procedure; grievance procedure
dull gweithredu diogel *eg* dulliau gweithredu diogel safety procedure
dull gweithredu i brofi *eg* testing procedure
dull gwyddonol *eg* dulliau gwyddonol scientific method
dull hufennu *eg* creaming method
dull hydredol *eg* longitudinal method
dull hyfforddi *eg* dulliau hyfforddi training method
dull ieithyddol *eg* dulliau ieithyddol linguistic method
dull iterus *eg* dulliau iterus iterative method
dull loci *eg* method of loci
dull llwybr critigol *eg* critical path method
dull meintiol *eg* dulliau meintiol quantitative approach
dull naratif *eg* narrative method
dull nofio *eg* dulliau nofio swimming stroke
dull o fowlio *eg* dulliau o fowlio bowling method
dull o fyw bywiog *eg* active lifestyle
dull o gyfathrebu *eg* dulliau o gyfathrebu means of communication
dull o redeg *eg* running method
dull o weithredu arbrawf *eg* dulliau o weithredu arbrawf experimental procedure
dull petryal *eg* rectangle method
dull pìn a llinyn *eg* pin and string method
dull plentyn ganolog *eg* dulliau plentyn ganolog child-centred approach
dull priodol *eg* dulliau priodol appropriate method
dull proses gweithredu iechyd *eg* health action process approach
dull recriwtio *eg* dulliau recriwtio recruitment method
dull rhwbio *eg* rubbing method
dull rhwystrol *eg* dulliau rhwystrol barrier method
dull rhydd *eg* dulliau rhydd free style
dull samplu *eg* dulliau samplu sampling method
dull sicrhau ansawdd *eg* dulliau sicrhau ansawdd quality assurance procedure
dull Simpson *eg* Simpson's rule
dull siswrn *eg* scissors
dull storïol *eg* dulliau storïol story method
dull symud *eg* dulliau symud means of propulsion
dull toddi *eg* melting method
dull thematig *eg* dulliau thematig thematic approach
dull uned *eg* unitary method
dull uniongyrchol *eg* dulliau uniongyrchol direct method
dull wedi'i gyfeirio at y cleient *eg* client-directed approach
dull y mesuryn canol *eg* mid-ordinate rule
dull ymchwil *eg* dulliau ymchwil research method
dull ymchwiliol *eg* dulliau ymchwiliol investigative method
dull yr hanesydd *eg* historical method
dulliau addysgu *ell* teaching methods
dulliau caffael *ell* procurement methods
dulliau cywasgu testun *ell* text compression techniques
dulliau mesur *ell* measuring methods
dulliau o orffeniadau *ell* types of finishes
duo *be* blacking
duo ag olew *be* oil blacking
duon a gwynion blacks and whites
dur *eg* duroedd steel
dur aloi *eg* alloy steel
dur arian *eg* silver steel
dur bwrw *eg* cast steel
dur canol *eg* malleable iron
dur carbon *eg* carbon steel
dur carbon canolig *eg* medium carbon steel
dur carbon uchel *eg* high carbon steel
dur crai *eg* raw steel
dur crwsibl *eg* crucible steel
dur gwrthstaen *eg* stainless steel
dur meddal *eg* mild steel
dur meddal du *eg* black mild steel
dur meddal gloyw *eg* bright mild steel
dur meddal gloyw wedi'i dynnu *eg* bright drawn mild steel
dur offer *eg* tool set steel
dur pothell *eg* blister steel
dur tiwbaidd *eg* tubular steel
dur twngsten *eg* tungsten steel
dur ucheldynnol *eg* high tensile steel
Durga *eb* Durga
Durga Puja *eb* Durga Puja
durlifion *ell* steel filings
duvet *eg* duvet
duw *eg* duwiau god
Duw *eg* God
Duw unigryw *eg* unique God
duwioldeb *eg* piety
duxelles *ell* duxelles

dwbl *ans* double
dwbl *eg* dyblau double
dwbl hansiedig *ans* double haunched; twin haunched
dwbled (=set o ddau) *eg* dwbledau duplet
dwbled (=siaced fer) *eb* dwbledi doublet
dwbl-glicio *be* double click
dwdlan *be* doodling
dwfn *ans* deep
dwlsimer *eg* dwlsimerau dulcimer
dwma *eg* duma
dwnsiwn *eg* dwnsiynau dungeon
dwodenwm *eg* duodenum
dwplecs *eg* dwplecsau duplex
dwplecs cyflawn *eg* dwplecsau cyflawn full-duplex
dŵr *eg* dyfroedd water
dŵr achlysurol *eg* casual water
dŵr berw *eg* boiling water
dŵr bromin *eg* bromine water
dŵr calch *eg* lime water
dŵr caled *eg* hard water
dŵr claear *eg* lukewarm water
dŵr croyw *eg* dyfroedd croyw freshwater
dŵr cylchredol *eg* water circulation
dŵr daear *eg* dyfroedd daear groundwater; phreatic water
dŵr distyll *eg* distilled water
dŵr ffo *eg* dyfroedd ffo run-off
dŵr glaw *eg* rainwater
dŵr grisialu *eg* water of crystallization
dŵr haldd *eg* barley water
dŵr lled hallt *eg* dyfroedd lled hallt brackish water
dŵr llonydd *eg* still water
dŵr mwynol *eg* dyfroedd mwynol mineral water
dŵr rhedegog *eg* flowing water
dŵr sebon *eg* soapy water
dŵr silicad *eg* water glass
dŵr tawdd *eg* dyfroedd tawdd melt water
dŵr trwm *eg* heavy water
dŵr wedi'i ferwi *eg* boiled water
dŵr wyneb *eg* surface water
dŵr y môr *eg* sea-water
dwralwmin *eg* duralumin
dwramen *eg* duramen
dwrfeithriniad *eg* water culture
dwrglos *ans* watertight
dwrlawn *ans* waterlogged
dwrn (ar beiriant) *eg* dyrnau stock
dwrn (yn gyffredinol) *eg* dyrnau fist
dwrn addurnedig *eg* dyrnau addurnedig boss
dŵr-wrthiannol *ans* water-resistant
dwy ar y bêl *eb* two on the ball
Dwy Erthygl a Deugain *eb* Forty Two Articles
dwy gaten *eb* two bails
dwy law i ffurfio pont double arch
dwy linell drwodd *eb* double strikethrough
Dwyfol Hawl Brenhinoedd *eb* Divine Right of Kings
dwyffordd *ans* reversible
dwygragennog *ans* bivalve
dwyieithog *ans* bilingual
dwyieithrwydd *eg* bilingualism
dwyieithrwydd cynyddol *eg* additive bilingualism
dwyieithrwydd gostyngol *eg* subtractive bilingualism
dwyieithrwydd llawn *eg* full bilingualism
dwyn i'r blaen *be* bring to front
dwyochredd *eb* reciprocity
dwyochrog *ans* reciprocal
dwyochrol *ans* bilateral
dwyochrol gymesur *ans* bilaterally symmetrical
dwyrain (Dn) *eg* east
Dwyrain Agos *eg* Near East
Dwyrain Canol *eg* Middle East
Dwyrain Ewrop *eb* Eastern Europe
Dwyrain Pell *eg* Far East
Dwyrain, Y *eg* Orient, The
dwyran *ans* two-part
dwyrannu *be* bisect
dwyreiniad *eg* dwyreiniaid easting
dwys (am ansawdd sain, ffiseg etc) *ans* dense
dwys (yn gyffredinol) *ans* intense
dwysáu (concentrate) *be* concentrate
dwysáu (am wrthdaro) *be* escalate
dwysedd *eg* dwyseddau density
dwysedd anwedd *eg* vapour density
dwysedd cymharol *eg* dwyseddau cymharol relative density
dwysedd data *eg* dwyseddau data data density
dwysedd didol *eg* dwyseddau didol bit density
dwysedd dwbl *eg* double density
dwysedd fflwcs *eg* flux density
dwysedd fflwcs magnetig *eg* magnetic flux density
dwysedd pacio *eg* dwyseddau pacio packing density
dwysedd poblogaeth isel *eg* dwyseddau poblogaeth Isel low population density
dwysedd poblogaeth uchel *eg* dwyseddau poblogaeth uchel high population density
dwysedd sengl *eg* single density
dwysedd tebygolrwydd *eg* probability density
dwysedd terfannol *eg* dwyseddau terfannol limiting density
dwystroc *ans* two-stroke
dwythell *eb* dwythellau duct
dwythell bancreatig *eb* dwythellau pancreatig pancreatic duct
dwythell betryal *eb* dwythellau petryal rectangular duct
dwythell ddagrau *eb* dwythellau dagrau lacrimal duct
dwythell ddagrau *eb* dwythellau dagrau tear duct
dwythell echdynnu aer *eb* dwythellau echdynnu aer air extraction duct

dwythell Müller *eb* dwythellau Müller Müllerian duct
dwythell wyau *eb* dwythellau wyau oviduct
dwythell y bustl *eb* bile duct
dwywaith maint llawn twice full size
dwywedd *ans* two-phase
dyblu *be* double
dyblyg *ans* duplicate; duple
dyblygeb *eb* dyblygebau duplicate
dyblygiad *eg* dyblygiadau duplication; replication
dyblygiad cadwrol *eg* conservative replication
dyblygu *be* duplicate; replicate
dyblygu systematig *be* systematic replication
dyblygydd *eg* dyblygwyr reproducer
dyblygydd cardiau *eg* dyblygyddion cardiau card reproducer
dychmygol *ans* imaginary; fictitious
dychweledig *eg* dychweledigion repatriate
dychweliad *eg* dychweliadau return; recurrance; recursion
dychweliad caled *eg* dychweliadau caled hard return
dychweliad lletraws *eg* dychweliadau lletraws angled return
dychweliadau gwerthiant *ell* sales returns
dychweliadol *ans* recursive
dychwelwr *eg* dychwelwyr return key
dychwelyd *be* return; revert
dychwelydd *eg* dychwelyddion carriage return
dychymyg *eg* dychmygion imagination; make-believe
dychymyg cyffyrddol *eg* tactile imagination
dydd *eg* dyddiau day
dydd a nos day and night
dydd gweithiwr *eg* dyddiau gweithiwr man-day
Dydd Gwener Du *eg* Black Friday
Dydd Gwener y Groglith *eg* Good Friday
dydd gŵyl *eg* dyddiau gŵyl holy day; feast day
Dydd Gŵyl Dewi *eg* Saint David's Day
Dydd Iau Cablyd *eg* Maundy Thursday
Dydd Iau Dyrchafael *eg* Ascension Thursday
Dydd Mercher Lludw *eg* Ash Wednesday
dydd Mers *eg* day of the March
Dydd y Baricedau *eg* Day of Barricades
Dydd y Cofio *eg* Remembrance Day
Dydd y Cymod *eg* Day of Atonement
Dydd y Farn *eg* Judgement Day
Dydd y Twyllo *eg* Day of Dupes
dyddiad *eg* dyddiadau date
dyddiad ac amser date and time
dyddiad creu *eg* dyddiadau creu creation date
dyddiad cychwyn *eg* dyddiadau cychwyn commencement date
dyddiad cyfredol *eg* dyddiadau cyfredol current date
► **dyddiad trosglwyddo** *eg* dyddiadau trosglwyddo delivery date
dyddiadur *eg* dyddiaduron diary
dyddiadur proses *eg* process journal
Dyddiau Llawenydd *ell* Days of Gladness
dyddiau Mehefin *ell* June days
dyddiedig *ans* dated
dyddio carbon *be* carbon dating
dyddiol *ans* diurnal
Dyddlinell *eb* International Date Line
dyddlyfr *eg* dyddlyfrau day book
dyddlyfr arian *eg* dyddlyfrau arian cash book
dydd-niwtral *ans* day-neutral
dyddodi *be* deposit
dyddodiad *eg* dyddodiadau deposition; precipitation
dyddodion affwys (y cefnfor) *ell* abyssal deposits
dyddodion allolchi *ell* outwash deposits
dyddodion arwynebol *ell* superficial deposits
► **dyddodion gweddillol** *ell* residual deposits
dyddodion halen *ell* salt deposits
dyddodion neritig *ell* neritic deposits
dyddodol *ans* depositional
dyddodyn *eg* dyddodion deposit
dyfais *eb* dyfeisiau device; gadget; invention
dyfais ailgynnau fflam *eb* dyfeisiau ailgynnau fflam flame-failure device
dyfais allbynnu *eb* dyfeisiau allbynnu output device
dyfais arbed gwaith *eb* dyfeisiau arbed gwaith labour-saving device
dyfais berifferol *eb* peripheral device
dyfais caffael iaith *eb* language acquisition device
dyfais drydanol *eb* dyfeisiau trydanol electrical appliance
dyfais ddal *eb* dyfeisiau dal holding device
dyfais ddiogelwch *eb* dyfeisiau diogelwch safety device
dyfais fesur *eb* dyfeisiau mesur measuring device
dyfais fewnbynnu *eb* dyfeisiau mewnbynnu input device
dyfais ffitio *eb* dyfeisiau ffitio fitting device
dyfais glampio *eb* dyfeisiau clampio clamping device
dyfais gloi *eb* dyfeisiau cloi locking device
dyfais gydgloëdig *eb* dyfeisiau cydgloëdig interlocking device
dyfais gydio wrth wal *eb* dyfeisiau cydio wrth wal wall-attachment device
dyfais gymhwyso *eb* dyfeisiau cymhwyso adjusting device
dyfais gysylltu *eb* dyfeisiau cysylltu connecting device
dyfais lanhau *eb* dyfeisiau glanhau cleaning appliance
dyfais lwybro *eb* dyfeisiau llwybro tracking device
dyfais mewnbwn /allbwn *eb* dyfeisiau mewnbwn / allbwn input /output device
dyfais reoli *eb* dyfeisiau rheoli control device
dyfais resbiradol *eb* dyfeisiau resbiradol respiratory device
dyfais sicrhau *eb* dyfeisiau sicrhau fastening device
dyfais storio *eb* dyfeisiau storio storage device

dyfais wrthderfysgol *eb* dyfeisiau gwrthderfysgol anti-terrorist device
dyfalbarhad *eg* perseverance; application
dyfaliad *eg* dyfaliadau conjecture
dyfarniad *eg* dyfarniadau award; judgement
dyfarniad dwbl *eg* dyfarniadau dwbl double award
Dyfarniad Sengl *eg* Single Award
dyfarnu *be* award
dyfarnu iawndal *be* award damages
dyfarnwr *eg* dyfarnwyr referee; umpire
dyfarnwraig *eb* dyfarnwragedd referee
dyfeisgar *ans* inventive; ingenious
dyfeisgarwch *eg* ingenuity
dyfeisio *be* invent; devise; make up
dyfeisiwr *eg* dyfeiswyr inventor
dyfnant *eb* dyfnentydd ravine
dyfnder *eg* dyfnderau depth
dyfnder draeniau *eg* drainage runs
dyfnder ffocws *eg* depth of field
dyfnder lliw *eg* colour depth
dyfnhau *be* deepen
dyfodfa *eb* dyfodfeydd approach
dyfodiad *eg* dyfodiaid arrival
dyfodol agos *eg* near future
dyfodolaidd *ans* futuristic
dyfodoliaeth *eb* futurism
Dyfodolwyr *ell* Futurists
dyfredig *ans* irrigated
dyfrfan *eg* dyfrfannau watering place
dyfrffordd *eb* dyfrffyrdd waterway
dyfrgi *eg* dyfrgwn otter
dyfrhad *eg* irrigation
dyfrhau *be* irrigate; water
dyfrlawn *ans* waterlogged
dyfrlliw *eg* dyfrlliwiau water colour
dyfrllyd *ans* aqueous
dyfrnod *eg* dyfrnodau watermark
dyfroedd cylchredol *ell* circulating waters
dyfroedd tiriogaethol *ell* territorial waters
dyfrol *ans* aquatic
dyfrsail *ans* water-based
▶ **dyfrhaen** *eb* dyfrhaenau aquifer
dyfudiad iaith *eg* language shift
dyfyniad *eg* dyfyniadau quotation
dyfynnod *eg* dyfynodau quotation mark
dyfynnod dwbl *eg* dyfynodau dwbl double quote
dyfynnod sengl *eg* dyfynodau sengl single quote
dyffryn *eg* dyffrynnoedd valley
dyffryn afon *eg* dyffrynnoedd afonydd river valley
dyffryn boddedig *eg* dyffrynnoedd boddedig drowned valley
dyffryn cafnog *eg* dyffrynnoedd cafnog trough shaped valley
dyffryn cynfodol *eg* dyffrynnoedd cynfodol pre-existing valley
dyffryn ffurf U *eg* dyffrynnoedd ffurf U U shaped valley
dyffryn hollt *eg* dyffrynnoedd hollt rift valley; graben
dyffryn sych *eg* dyffrynnoedd sych dry valley
dyffryndir *eg* dyffryndiroedd vale
dyffryndir afon *eg* dyffryndiroedd afon valley tract
dyffryndir clai *eg* dyffryndiroedd clai clay vale
dyffrynnoedd pell oddi wrth ei gilydd *ell* widely spaced valleys
dygnwch *eg* endurance
dygnwch y cyhyrau *eg* muscular endurance
dygwydd glawiad *eg* incidence of rainfall
dygyfor *be* surge
dyngarîs *eg* dungarees
dyhead *eg* dyheadau aspiration
dyhefod *be* pant
dyhuddiad *eg* dyhuddiadau appeasement
dyhuddo *be* appease
dylanwad *eg* dylanwadau influence
dylanwad rhieni *eg* parental influence
dylanwadu *be* influence
dyled *eb* dyledion debt
dyled ocsigen *eb* oxygen debt
dyled wladol *eb* dyledion gwladol national debt
dyledogaeth llys *eb* suit of court
dyledus *ans* indebted
dyledwr *eg* dyledwyr debtor
dyledwr masnach *eg* dyledwyr masnach trade debtor
dyleddfiad *eg* supination
dyletswydd gofal *eb* duty of care
dylifiad *eg* influx
dylifiadau rhwydwaith *ell* network flows
dylsiton *eg* dylsitonau dulcitone
dyluniad *eg* dyluniadau design; layout
dyluniad batik *eg* dyluniadau batik design of a batik
dyluniad border *eg* dyluniadau borderi border design
dyluniad cefndir *eg* dyluniadau cefndir background design
dyluniad geometrig *eg* dyluniadau geometrig geometric design
dyluniad gwreiddiol *eg* dyluniadau gwreiddiol original design
dyluniad haniaethol *eg* dyluniadau haniaethol abstract design
dyluniad llawrydd *eg* dyluniadau llawrydd freehand design
dylunio *be* design
dylunio a thechnoleg design and technology
dylunio ar gyfer y theatr *be* theatre design
dylunio cynnyrch *be* product design
dylunio graffig *be* graphic design
dylunio gwefannau *be* web site design
dylunio swyddogaethol *be* functional design
dylunio tri dimensiwn *be* three dimensional design
dylunydd *eg* dylunyddion designer
dylunydd Bauhaus *eg* dylunwyr Bauhaus Bauhaus designer

dylunydd cynhyrchion *eg* dylunwyr cynhyrchion product designer
dylunydd cynhyrchion bwyd *eg* dylunwyr cynhyrchion bwyd food product designer
dylunydd graffig *eg* dylunwyr graffig graphic designer
dylunydd patrymau *eg* pattern designer
dylunydd siâp *eg* dylunwyr siâp shape designer
dylyfu gên *be* yawn
dymchwel (cwch etc) *be* capsize
dymchwel (yn gyffredinol) *be* topple
dymchweliad y frenhiniaeth *eg* overthrow of the monarchy
dymi *eg* dymïau dummy
dymp *eg* dympiau dump
dymp deuaidd *eg* dympiau deuaidd binary dump
dympio *be* dump
dympio deuaidd *be* binary dump
dymunol *ans* pleasing
dymunol yr olwg *ans* visually pleasing
dymunolrwydd cymdeithasol *eg* social desirability
dyn canol *eg* dynion canol middleman
dyn hysbys *eg* dynion hysbys cunning man
dyn y tywydd *eg* dynion y tywydd weather forecaster
dyn ysbrydol *eg* dynion ysbrydol spiritual man
dynameg *eb* dynamics
dynameg grŵp *eb* group dynamics
dynamegol *ans* dynamical
dynameit *eg* dynamite
dynamig *ans* dynamic
dynamo *eg* dynamoau dynamo
dynamometr *eg* dynamometrau dynamometer
dynatron *eg* dynatronau dynatron
dyneiddiaeth *eb* humanism
dyneiddiol *ans* humanistic
dyneiddiwr *eg* dyneiddwyr humanist
dyngarol *ans* humanitarian; philanthropic
dyngarwch *eg* humanitarianism; philanthropy
dyngarwr *eg* dyngarwyr humanitarian; philanthropist
dyniaethau *ell* humanities
dynodedig *ans* designated
dynodi *be* designate; denote
dynodi *be* designate
dynodi cord *be* chord indication
dynodiad *eg* denotation
dynodiad neges *eg* dynodiadau neges message ID
dynodwr *eg* dynodwyr identifier
dynodyn mêl *eg* dynodion mêl honey guide
dynol *ans* human
dynoliaeth *eb* humanity
dynwared *be* imitate
dynwaredd *eg* mimicry
dynwarediad *eg* dynwarediadau imitation
dynwarediad Batesaidd *eg* dynwarediadau Batesaidd Batesian mimicry
dynwarediad canonaidd *eg* dynwarediadau canonaidd canonic imitation
dynwaredol *ans* imitative; mimetic
dyodiad *eg* precipitation
dyraniad (adnoddau etc) *eg* dyraniadau allocation
dyraniad (mewn bioleg etc) *eg* dyraniadau dissection
dyraniad arian *eg* dyraniadau arian cash allocation
dyraniad atodol *eg* dyraniadau atodol supplementary allocation
dyraniad storfa *eg* storage allocation
dyrannu (adnoddau etc) *be* allocate
dyrannu (mewn bioleg etc) *be* dissect
dyrannu dynamig *be* dynamic allocation
dyrchafedig *ans* iambic
dyrchafiad *eg* dyrchafiadau preferment
dyrnfedd *eg* dyrnfeddi hand-breadth
dyrnod *eb* dyrnodiau punch
dyrnod bwt *eb* dyrnodiau pwt short punch
dyrnod gwar *eb* dyrnodiau gwar rabbit punch
dyrnu *be* punch
dyrnwr medi *eg* dyrnwyr medi combine harvester
dyroddi *be* issue
dyscinesia camsymud araf *eg* tardive dyskinesia
dysentri *eg* dysentery
dysffasia *eg* dysphasia
dysg *eb* learning
Dysg Newydd *eb* New Learning
dysgeidiaeth *eb* teaching
dysgeidiaeth grefyddol *eb* religious teaching
dysgeidiaeth Gristnogol *eb* Christian teaching
dysgl *eb* dysglau dish
dysgl anweddu *eb* dysglau anweddu evaporating basin
dysgl Petri *eb* dysglau Petri Petri dish
dysgu *be* learn
dysgu agored *be* open learning
dysgu annibynnol *be* independent learning
dysgu antur *be* adventure learning
dysgu ar y cof *be* memorize
dysgu blaenorol *be* prior learning
dysgu blynyddoedd cynnar *be* early years learning
dysgu cyfannol *be* integrated learning
dysgu dan arweiniad cyfrifiadur *be* computer managed learning
dysgu drwy brofiadau *be* experiential learning
dysgu drwy ddynwared *be* imitative learning
dysgu drwy gymorth cyfrifiadur *be* computer aided learning
dysgu drwy gymorth cyfrifiadur *be* computer assisted learning
dysgu drwy weithgaredd *be* activity learning
dysgu goddefol *be* passive learning
dysgu gwybyddol *be* cognitive learning
dysgu gydol oes *be* lifelong learning
dysgu iaith *eg* language learning
dysgu meistrolaeth *be* mastery learning
dysgu o bell *be* distance learning

dysgu symudol *be* mobile learning
dysgu tra'n ffetws *be* fetal learning
dysgu trwy arsylwi *be* observational learning
dysgu uniongyrchol *be* direct instruction
dysgwr *eg* dysgwyr learner
dysgwr amharod *eg* dysgwyr amharod reluctant learner
dysgwr uwch *eg* dysgwyr uwch advanced learner
dyslecsia *eg* dyslexia
dyslecsia arwynebol *eg* surface dyslexia
dyslecsia caffaeledig *eg* acquired dyslexia
dyslecsia datblygiad *eg* developmental dyslexia
dyslecsia dwfn *eg* deep dyslexia
dyslecsia ffonolegol *eg* phonological dyslexia
dyslecsig *ans* dyslexic
dyspeptig *ans* dyspeptic
dyspnoea *eg* dyspnoea
dysprosiwm (Dy) *eg* dysprosium
dysychedig *ans* desiccated
dysychiad *eg* desiccation
dysychu *be* desiccate
dyweddïad *eg* dyweddiadau engagement; betrothal

Dd

ddim allan not out

E

E fwyaf *eb* E major
E leiaf *eb* E minor
eang (mewn cyfrifiadureg) *ans* global
eang (yn gyffredinol) *ans* extensive
eang-grededd *eg* latitudinarianism
eang-gredwr *eg* eang-gredwyr latitudinarian
eangolrwydd *eg* expansivity
e-alluogi *be* e-enable
ebediw *eg* ebediwiau heriot
ebill (ar offeryn cerdd) *eg* ebillion pin; wrest-pin
ebill (darn o ddril etc) *eg* ebillion bit
ebill canoli *eg* ebillion canoli centre bit
ebill canoli patrwm newydd *eg* ebillion canoli patrwm newydd new pattern centre bit
ebill cobra *eg* ebillion cobra cobra bit
ebill cragen *eg* ebillion cragen shell bit
ebill cyflym iawn *eg* ebillion cyflym iawn high-speed bit
ebill cyweirio *eg* ebillion cyweirio tuning pin
ebill dril *eg* ebillion dril drill bit
ebill Forstner *eg* ebillion Forstner Forstner bit
ebill gwastad *eg* ebillion gwastad flat bit
ebill gwrthsoddi *eg* ebillion gwrthsoddi countersink bit
ebill gwrthsoddi malwen *eg* ebillion gwrthsoddi malwen snail bit
ebill gwrthsoddi rhychog *eg* ebillion gwrthsoddi rhychog rose countersink bit
ebill hoelbren *eg* ebillion hoelbren dowel bit
ebill llwy *eg* ebillion llwy spoon bit
ebill maen *eg* ebillion maen masonry bit
ebill slic *eg* ebillion slic slick bit
ebill taradr *eg* ebillion taradr auger bit
ebill taradr solet *eg* ebillion taradr solet solid auger bit
ebill tro *eg* ebillion tro twist bit
ebill tro Irwin *eg* ebillion tro Irwin Irwin twist bit
ebill tro Jennings *eg* ebillion tro Jennings Jennings twist bit
ebill tyrnsgriw *eg* ebillion tyrnsgriw screwdriver bit
ebill ymledu *eg* ebillion ymledu expansive bit
ebillres *eb* ebillresi machine heads
ebol *eg* ebolion buck
ebol ar groes *eg* ebolion ar groes buck crosswise
eboneiddio *be* ebonizing
eboni *eg* ebony
e-bost *eg* e-mail
e-bost newydd *eg* e-byst newydd new mail
e-bostio *be* e-mail
ebrwydd *ans* instantaneous
ebwliosgopaeth *eg* ebullioscopy
ebwliosgopig *ans* ebullioscopic
ebychiad *eg* ebychiadau burst
ebychnod *eg* ebychnodau exclamation mark
ecdysis *eg* ecdysis
eciwmenaidd *ans* ecumenical
eciwmeniaeth *eb* ecumenism
eclair *eb* eclairs eclair
eclectig *ans* eclectic
ecliptig *ans* ecliptic
ecoclin *eg* ecocline
ecolalia *eg* echolalia
ecoleg *eb* ecology
ecoleg ffactoraidd *eb* factorial ecology
ecolegol *ans* ecological
economaidd *ans* economic
economaidd gymdeithasol *ans* socio-economic
economeg *eb* economics
economeg addysgu *eb* economics of education
economeg wleidyddol *eb* political economy
economeg y cartref *eb* home economics
economegwr clasurol newydd *eg* economegwyr clasurol newydd new classical economist
economegydd *eg* economegwyr economist
economegydd cartref *eg* home economist
econometreg *eb* econometrics
economi *eg/b* economïau economy
economi arian *eg* money economy
economi cymysg *eg* mixed economy
economi cynlluniedig *eg* planned economy
economi cytbwys *eg* economïau cytbwys balanced economy
economi disbyddol *eg* economïau disbyddol robber economy
economi du *eg* black economy
economi gorfodol *eg* forced economy
economi marchnad *eg* market economy
economi marchnad rydd *eg* free market economy
ecorywogaeth *eb* ecospecies
ecosystem *eb* ecosystemau ecosystem
ecoteip *eg* ecoteipiau ecotype
ecotôn *eg* ecotonau ecotone
ecsbloetiaeth *eb* exploitation
► **ecsbloetio** *be* exploit
ecseis *eg* excise
ecseismon *eg* ecseismyn exciseman
ecsema *eg* eczema

ecsergonig *ans* exergonic
ecsocrin *eg* exocrine
ecsothermig *ans* exothermic
ectoderm *eg* ectoderm
ectoparasit *eg* ectoparasitiaid ectoparasite
ectoplasm *eg* ectoplasm
ecwilibreiddio *be* equilibrate
ecwilibriwm *eg* equilibrium
ecwilibriwm dynamig *eg* dynamic equilibrium
ecwiti *eg* equity
echalaethog *ans* extra galactic
echblyg *ans* explicit
echdoriad *eg* eruption
echdoriad folcanig *eg* echdoriadau folcanig volcanic eruption
echdoriad yr haul *eg* echdoriadau'r haul solar eruption
echdorri *be* erupt
echdroad *eg* eversion
echdyniad *eg* echdyniadau extraction
echdyniad â hydoddydd *eg* solvent extraction
echdynnol *ans* extractive
echdynnu *be* extract
echdynnu adnodd *be* extract a resource
echdynnu dŵr *be* extract water
echdynnu dŵr *be* water extraction
echdynnwr *eg* echdynwyr extractor
echdynnyn *eg* echdynion extract
echddygol *ans* motor
echddygol *ans* efferent
echel *eb* echelau axle
echel bwli *eb* echelau pwli axle pulley
echel bwt *eb* echelau pwt stub axle
echelin *eb* echelinau axis
echelin arosgo *eb* echelinau arosgo oblique axis
echelin begynol *eb* echelinau pegynol polar axis
echelin cymesuredd *eb* axis of symmetry
echelin ddifferyn *eb* echelinau differyn differential axis
echelin fertigol *eb* echelinau fertigol vertical axis
echelin hwyaf *eb* echelinau hwyaf major axis
echelin isometrig *eb* echelinau isometrig isometric axis
echelin leiaf *eb* echelinau lleiaf minor axis
echelin lorweddol *eb* echelinau llorweddol horizontal axis
echelin niwtral *eb* echelinau niwtral neutral axis
echelin plyg *eb* echelinau plyg axis of fold
echelin weledol *eb* echelinau gweledol visual axis
echelin X *eb* X axis
echelin Y *eb* Y axis
echelinau cyfesurynnol *ell* coordinate axes
echelinau lleoli *ell* axes of reference
echelinol *ans* axial
echelon *eg* echelon
echinoderm *eg* echinodermau echinoderm
echlifiant *eg* eluviation
echlifol *ans* eluvial
echludiad *eg* echludiadau elution
echludo *be* elute
echludydd *eg* eluent
echreiddiad *eg* echreiddiadau eccentricity
echreiddig *ans* eccentric
echwythiad *eg* echwythiadau outburst
edafedd bouclé *ell* bouclé yarn
edafedd craidd *ell* core yarn
edafedd di-dor *ell* continuous yarn
edafedd dwy gainc *ell* two-ply wool
edafedd gweadog *ell* textured yarn
edafedd gwlân *ell* spun wool
edafedd rhaffog *ell* cable yarn
edafedd slyb *ell* slub yarn
edafedd tair cainc *ell* three-ply wool
edafedd tapestri *ell* tapestry wool
edafedd toredig *ell* staple yarn
edafedd wedi'u swmpuso *ell* bulked yarn
edafu *be* thread
edaffig *ans* edaphic
edau *eb* edafedd yarn
edau *eb* edafedd thread
edau acme *eb* edafedd acme acme thread
edau anwe *eb* edafedd anwe weft thread
edau aur *eb* edafedd aur gold thread
edau chwil *eb* edafedd chwil drunken thread
edau ddeintiol *eb* edafedd deintiol dental floss
edau ddwbl *eb* edafedd dwbl double thread
edau enamel *eb* edafedd enamel enamel thread
edau fenyw *eb* edafedd benyw female thread
edau fetelig *eb* edafedd metelig metallic thread
edau fetrig *eb* edafedd metrig metric thread
edau fras *eb* edafedd bras coarse thread
edau frodio *eb* edafedd brodio embroidery thread
edau frodwaith *eb* edafedd brodwaith embroidery cotton
edau fwtres *eb* edafedd bwtres buttress thread
edau ffilament *eb* edafedd ffilament filament yarn
edau gotwm *eb* edafedd cotwm cotton thread
edau gyfrodedd *eb* edafedd cyfrodedd buttonhole thread
edau gyffredin *eb* edafedd cyffredin common thread
edau gymal *eb* edafedd cymal knuckle thread
edau heligol *eb* edafedd heligol helical thread
edau lân *eb* edafedd glân clean thread
edau lin *eb* edafedd llin linen thread
edau llaw chwith *eb* edafedd llaw chwith left-hand thread
edau llaw dde *eb* edafedd llaw dde right-hand thread
edau neilon *eb* edafedd neilon nylon thread
edau onglog *eb* edafedd onglog angular thread
edau safonol *eb* edafedd safonol standard thread
edau sanctaidd *eb* edafedd sanctaidd sacred thread

edau sengl *eb* edafedd sengl single thread
edau selfais *eb* edafedd selfais selvage thread
edau sglein *eb* edafedd sglein sylko
edau sgriw *eb* edafedd sgriw screw thread
edau sgriw llaw chwith *eb* edafedd sgriw llaw chwith left-hand screw thread
edau sgriw llaw dde *eb* edafedd sgriw llaw dde right-hand screw thread
edau sgwâr *eb* edafedd sgwâr square thread
edau unol *eb* edafedd unol unified thread
edau weadog *eb* edafedd gweadog textured thread
edau Whitworth *eb* Whitworth thread
edau wlân *eb* edafedd gwlân woollen thread
edau ystof *eb* edafedd ystof warp thread
edefydd *eg* edefyddion threader
edefydd nodwydd *eg* edefyddion nodwydd needle threader
edefyn (=ffeibr) *eg* edafedd staple
edefyn DNA *eg* edafedd DNA strand of DNA
edefyn myelinedig *eg* myelinated fibre
edefyn neges *eg* edafedd neges message thread
edefyn nerf *eg* edafedd nerf nerve fibre
edefyn nerf myelinedig *eg* medullated nerve fibre
edeuffurf *ans* filiform
edeugell *eb* edeugelloedd thread cell
edling *eg* edlingod heir apparent
edmygedd *eg* admiration
edmygu *be* admire
edrych *be* look
Edward Gyffeswr *eg* Edward the Confessor
Edward yr Hynaf *eg* Edward the Elder
Edwardaidd *ans* Edwardian
edwythiad *eg* eduction
edwytho *be* educe
eddi *eg* eddïau fringe
eddi ymyriant *eg* eddïau ymyriant interference fringe
e-ddysgu *be* e-learning
e-fasnach *eb* e-commerce
efengyl *eb* efengylau gospel
efengylaidd *ans* evangelical
efengylwr *eg* efengylwyr evangelist
efelychiad *eg* efelychiadau simulation
efelychiad cyfrifiadurol *eg* efelychiadau cyfrifiadurol computer simulation
efelychu *be* simulate
efelychu *be* emulate
efelychu carchar *be* prison simulation
efelychydd *eg* efelychwyr emulator
efelychydd *eg* efelychyddion simulator
eferwad *eg* effervescence
eferwi *be* effervesce
eferwol *ans* effervescing
efoliwt *eg* efoliwtiau evolute
efrydiau *ell* studies
efydd *eg* bronze
efydd alwminiwm *eg* aluminium bronze
efydd nicel *eg* nickel bronze
efydd plwm *eg* lead bronze
efyddlifion *ell* brass filings
effaith *eg/b* impact
effaith *eg/b* effeithiau action
effaith *eg/b* effeithiau effect
effaith actor-gwyliwr *eb* actor-observer effect
effaith allanoldeb *eb* effeithiau allanoldeb externality effect
effaith amgylcheddol *eb* effeithiau amgylcheddol environmental impact
effaith amledd *eb* effect of frequency
effaith animeiddio *eb* effeithiau animeiddio animation effect
effaith arbennig *eb* effeithiau arbennig special effect
effaith asid ar gopr *eb* action of acid on copper
effaith Barnum *eb* Barnum effect
effaith blaenoriaeth *eb* primacy effect
effaith blasebo *eb* placebo effect
effaith bosibl *eb* effeithiau posibl possible impact
effaith cario drosodd *eb* effeithiau cario drosodd carryover effect
effaith croesbylu *eb* cross-fade effect
effaith cromlin J *eb* J curve effect
effaith cyfyngu graddfa *eb* scale-attenuation effect
effaith cyn-amlygiad ysgogiad heb ei gyflyru *eb* unconditioned stimulus pre-exposure effect
effaith cyn-amlygiad ysgogiad wedi'i gyflyru *eb* conditioned stimulus pre-exposure effect
effaith dangos yn unig *eb* mere exposure effect
effaith diweddaredd *eb* recency effect
effaith drefnu *eb* organizational effect
effaith ddiwylliannol gymdeithasol *eb* effeithiau diwylliannol cymdeithasol socio-cultural impact
effaith erlid-golau *eb* light-chaser effect
effaith ffotodrydanol *eb* photoelectric effect
effaith gemegol *eb* effeithiau cemegol chemical action
effaith gorfforol *eb* effeithiau corfforol physical effect
effaith gwsg *eb* sleeper effect
effaith gymdeithasol *eb* effeithiau cymdeithasol social impact
effaith gymesur *eb* symmetrical effect
effaith Hawthorne *eb* Hawthorne effect
effaith luosydd multiplier effect
effaith llygredd *eb* effeithiau llygredd effect of pollution
effaith nenfwd *eb* ceiling effect
effaith pâr anadweithiol *eb* inert pair effect
effaith Pasteur *eb* Pasteur effect
effaith piesodrydanol *eb* piezo electric effect
effaith Stroop *eb* Stroop effect
effaith trans-cis *eb* cis-trans effect
effaith tŷ gwydr *eb* greenhouse effect
effaith tymor byr *eb* effeithiau tymor byr short-term effect

effaith waelodi *eb* floor effect
effaith ysgogi *eb* activational effect
effeithiau marmori *ell* marbling effects
effeithiau tymor hir camdriniaeth *ell* long-term effects of abuse
effeithiol *ans* effective
effeithiolrwydd *eg* effectiveness
effeithiolrwydd *eg* efficacy
effeithiolrwydd cost *eg* cost effectiveness
effeithlon *ans* efficient
effeithlonedd *eg* efficiency
effeithlonrwydd *eg* efficiency
▶ **effeithlonrwydd ac effeithiolrwydd** efficiency and effectiveness
effeithlonrwydd cynhyrchiol *eg* productive efficiency
effeithlonrwydd dyrannol *eg* allocative efficiency
▶ **effeithlonrwydd egni** *eg* energy efficiency
effeithlonrwydd gweithredol *eg* operational efficiency
effeithlonrwydd Pareto *eg* Pareto efficiency
▶ **effeithlonrwydd sianel** *eg* channel efficiency
effeithlonrwydd ymylol cyfalaf *eg* marginal efficiency of capital
effeithlonrwydd-X *eg* X-efficiency
effeithydd *eg* effeithyddion effector
effemera *eg* ephemera
effermeris *eg* ephermeris
effro *ans* active
egalitaraidd *ans* egalitarian
egalitariad *eg* egalitariaid egalitarian
egalitariaeth *eb* egalitarianism
eger (ton lanw) *eg* egerau bore; tide race
eger Hafren *eg* Severn bore
eger llanw *eg* egerau llanw tidal bore
egin ffa *ell* bean sprouts
eginblanhigyn *eg* eginblanhigion seedling
egin-dwyn *eg* egin-dwyni embryo dune
eginiad *eg* eginiadau germination
egino *be* germinate
eglur *ans* clear; lucid
eglurder *eg* clarity; comprehensibility
eglurder siâp y corff *eg* clarity of body shape
eglurder y nodiant *eg* clarity of the notation
eglureb bwrpasol *eb* eglurebau pwrpasol appropriate illustration
eglurhaol *ans* illustrated
egluro (gan ddarlunio) *be* illustrate
egluro (yn gyffredinol) *be* explain
egluro adeiledd *be* structure elucidation
eglwys *eb* eglwysi church
Eglwys Babyddol *eb* Roman Catholic Church
eglwys blwyf *eb* eglwysi plwyf parish church
eglwys dŷ *eb* eglwysi tai house church
Eglwys Ddiwygiedig Unedig *eb* United Reformed Church
eglwys gadeiriol *eb* eglwysi cadeiriol cathedral
eglwys Gatholig *eb* eglwysi Catholig Catholic church
eglwys golegaidd *eb* eglwysi colegaidd collegiate church
eglwys Gristnogol *eb* eglwysi Cristnogol Christian church
Eglwys Gristnogol, yr *eb* Christian Church
eglwys gyda thŵr *eb* church with tower
eglwys gyd-gyfranedig *eb* eglwysi cyd-gyfranedig portionary church
Eglwys Loegr *eb* Church of England
Eglwys Rufain *eb* Roman Church
eglwys rydd *eb* eglwysi rhyddion free church
Eglwys Uniadol (Dwyrain Ewrop) *eb* Uniate Church
Eglwys Uniongred Roegaidd *eb* Greek Orthodox Church
Eglwys yng Nghymru, yr *eb* Church in Wales
eglwysig *ans* ecclesiastical
eglwysyddiaeth *eb* ecclesiasticism
egni *eg* egnïon energy
egni actifadu *eg* activation energy
egni adnewyddadwy *eg* renewable energy
egni bond cymedrig *eg* mean bond energy
egni cinetig *eg* kinetic energy
egni cinetig trawsfudiad *eg* kinetic energy of translation
egni clymu *eg* egnïon clymu binding energy
egni cylchdroi *eg* rotational energy
egni cynhenid *eg* intrinsic energy
egni daduno bond *eg* bond dissociation energy
egni dellt *eg* egnïon dellt lattice energy
egni elastig *eg* elastic energy
egni ffoton *eg* photon energy
egni ïoneiddiad *eg* ionisation energy
egni llanw *eg* tidal energy
egni niwclear *eg* nuclear energy
egni parod *eg* egnïon parod free energy
egni potensial *eg* potential energy
egni potensial elastig *eg* elastic potential energy
egni solar *eg* solar energy
egni trawsfudol *eg* egnïon trawsfudol translational energy
egni trothwy *eg* egnïon trothwy threshold energy
egni tymheredd sero *eg* zero point energy
egni thermol *eg* thermal energy
egnïeg *eb* energetics
egnïol *ans* energetic; vigorous
egnioledig *ans* energized
egnioli *be* energize
egni'r byd *eg* global energy
ego *eg* ego
e-grawn *eg* e-gronau e-zine
egsotig *ans* exotic
egwyddor *eb* egwyddorion principle
egwyddor agosrwydd *eb* proximity principle
egwyddor allweddol *eb* egwyddorion allweddol key principle
egwyddor ansicrwydd *eb* uncertainty principle

egwyddor anthropig *eb* anthropic principle
egwyddor cyfagosrwydd *eb* adjacency principle
egwyddor didoriant *eb* principle of continuity
egwyddor fecanyddol *eb* egwyddorion mecanyddol mechanical principle
egwyddor lluosogrwydd macsimwm *eb* maximum multiplicity rule
egwyddor pleser *eb* pleasure principle
egwyddor prif ystyriaeth *eb* paramountcy principle
egwyddor realaeth *eb* reality principle
egwyddor tebygolrwydd hafal *eb* equally likely principle
egwyddor tebygrwydd *eb* similarity principle
egwyddor wahardd *eb* exclusion principle
egwyddor wahardd Pauli *eb* Pauli exclusion principle
egwyddor wyddonol *eb* egwyddorion gwyddonol scientific principle
egwyddorion deiet *ell* principles of diet
egwyddorion liferi *ell* principles of levers
egwyddorion symudiad *ell* principles of movement
egwyddor-nain-mam-merch *eb* grandfather-father-son principle
egwyl *eb* egwylion interval; interlude
egwyriant *eg* egwyriannau aberration
e-gyfnodolyn *eg* e-gyfnodolion e-journal
e-gyhoeddi *be* e-publishing
enghraifft (=darlun) *eb* enghreifftiau illustration
enghraifft (yn gyffredinol) *eb* enghreifftiau example
enghraifft batrymol *eb* enghreifftiau patrymol exemplar
enghraifft o fyd chwaraeon *eb* enghreifftiau o fyd chwaraeon sporting example
enghreifftio *be* illustrate
enghreifftiol *ans* illustrative
engreinio *be* engrain
ehangdir *eg* eangdiroedd landmass
ehangedig *ans* expanded
ehangiad *eg* ehangiadau expansion
ehangiad cof *eg* ehangiadau cof memory expansion
ehangiad tiriogaethol *eg* territorial expansion
ehangu *be* expand
ehangu fformatio *be* expand formatting
ehangu gair unigol *be* expand single word
ehangu sleid *be* expand slide
ehangylch *eg* ehangylchoedd sweep
ehebiaeth *eb* electronic mail
ehebu *be* correspond by e-mail
ehedol *ans* volatile
eicon *eg* eiconau icon
eicon mawr *eg* eiconau mawr large icon
eiconig *ans* iconic
▸ **eiconograffeg** *eb* iconography
eiconograffeg ac ymarfer iconography and practice
eiconograffig *ans* iconographic
Eidal Ifanc (mudiad) Young Italy
eidionyn *eg* eidionod beefburger
▸ **eidionyn caws** *eg* eidionod caws cheeseburger
eiddigedd pidyn *eg* penis envy
eiddil *ans* delicate
eiddo *eg* property; possessions
eiddo rhydd-ddaliol *eg* freehold property
eiddo tiriog *eg* real estate
eiddo ysbrydol *eg* spiritualities
Eifftoleg *eb* Egyptology
eigioneg *eb* oceanography
eigionol *ans* pelagic
Eingl-Norman *eg* Eingl-Normaniaid Anglo-Norman
Eingl-Normanaidd *ans* Anglo-Norman
Eingl-Sacsonaidd *ans* Anglo-Saxon
Eingl-Sacsoneg *eb* Anglo-Saxon
eil *eb* eiliau aisle
eilaidd *ans* secondary
eilbaredd *eg* eilbareddau even parity
eildwf *eg* secondary growth
eiledEDD cenedlaethau *eg* alternation of generations
eiledol *ans* alternate; alternating
eilfed *eg* eilfedau second
eilflwydd *ans* biennial
eilflwyddiad *eg* eilflwyddiadau biennial
eilfodd *eg* altmode
eil-ffwythiant *eg* eil-ffwythiannau even function
eiliad *eg/b* eiliadau second
eiliadur *eg* eiliaduron alternator
eilio *be* second
eiliog *ans* aisled
eilradd *ans* secondary
eilrif *eg* eilrifau even number
eilun *eg* eilunod idol
eilunaddoliaeth *eb* idolatry
eilydd *eg* eilyddion substitute
eilyddio *be* substitute; substitution
eillio *be* shave
eingion (=asgwrn yn y glust) *eg* incus
eingion (yn gyffredinol) *eb* eingionau anvil
eingion gosod llif *eb* eingionau gosod llif saw-setting anvil
einsteiniwm *eg* einsteinium
Einstellung *eg* Einstellung
eirdreulio *be* nivation
eirffrwyth *eg* fruit snow
eirin duon *ell* damsons
eirin Mair *ell* gooseberries
eiriol *be* intercede
eiriolaeth *eb* intercession
eiriolaeth *eb* eiriolaethau advocacy
eiriolwr *eg* eiriolwyr advocate
eirlaw *eg* sleet
eirlin *eg* eirlinau snow line
eirlithrad *eg* eirlithradau avalanche
eisbilen *eb* eisbilennau pleura
eisbilennol *ans* pleural

eisen *eb* ais strut
eisteddfod *eb* eisteddfodau eisteddfod
eisteddle (ar gyfer gwylwyr chwaraeon etc) *eg* eisteddleoedd stand
eisteddle falf *eg* eisteddleoedd falf valve seat
eisteddog *ans* sedentary
eitem *eb* eitemau item
eitem ddirprwyedig *eb* eitemau dirprwyedig delegated item
eitem gwariant *eb* eitemau gwariant item of expenditure
eitem o ddata *eb* eitemau o ddata data item
eitem pwynt talu *eb* eitemau pwynt talu point-of-sale item
eitem ran-gyfnewid *eb* eitemau rhan-gyfnewid part exchange item
eitem wedi'i thicio *eb* eitemau wedi'u ticio checked item
eitemeiddio *be* itemize
eithaf *ans* extreme
eithafion *ell* extremes
eithafion hinsawdd *ell* climatic extremes
eithafion tywydd *ell* extremes of weather
eithafoedd *ell* extremities
eithafol *ans* extremist; zealous
eithafwr *eg* eithafwyr extremist; zealot
eithriad *eg* eithriadau exception
eithriad cysylltnodi *eg* eithriadau cysylltnodi hyphenation exception
eithriad dewisol *eg* eithriadau dewisol discretionary exception
eithriad gorfodol *eg* eithriadau gorfodol mandatory exception
eithriad o dreth *eg* tax exemption
eithrio *be* opt out; except
El Nino *eg* El Nino
elastig *ans* elastic
elastig *eg* elastic
elastig cygrychu *eg* shirring elastic
elastigedd *eg* elastigeddau elasticity
elastigedd incwm *eg* income elasticity
elastigedd pris *eg* price elasticity
elastigedd pris ac incwm *eg* price and income elasticity
elastigedd pris y cyflenwad *eg* price elasticity of supply
elastigedd pris y galw *eg* price elasticity of demand
elastigedd y galw *eg* elasticity of demand
elastin *eg* elastine
elastomerau *ell* elastomers
elastomerig *ans* elastomeric
elc *eg* elciaid moose
electrocemegol *ans* electrochemical
electrocemegyn *eg* electrocemegau electrochemical
electrod *eg* electrodau electrode
electrofalent *ans* electrovalent
electroffil *eg* electroffiliau electrophile
electrofforesis *eg* electrophoresis
electrofforws *eg* electroffori electrophorus
electroleiddio *be* electrolyse
electrolysis *eg* electrolysis
electrolyt *eg* electrolytau electrolyte
electrolytig *ans* electrolytic
electromagnetedd *eg/b* electromagnetism
electromagneteg *eb* electromagnetism
electromagnetig *ans* electromagnetic
electromedr *eg* electromedrau electrometer
electromyogram *eg* electromyogramau electromyogram
electron *eg* electronau electron
electron heb bâr *eg* electronau heb bâr unpaired electron
electron mewn cyflwr rhwym *eg* electronau mewn cyflwr rhwym electron in bound state
electron rhydd *eg* electronau rhydd free electron
electronau cydranedig *ell* shared electrons
electrondderbynydd *eg* electrodderbynyddion electroreceptor
electron-ddiffygiol *ans* electron-deficient
electroneg *eb* electronics
electronegatif *ans* electronegative
electronegatifedd *eg* electronegativity
electronig *ans* electronic
electronmicrograff *eg* electronmicrograffau electronmicrograph
electronmicrosgop *eg* electronmicrosgopau electron microscope
electro-ocwlogram *eg* electro-ocwlogramau electro-oculogram
electroplat *eg* electroplatiau electroplate
electroplatio *be* electroplate
electropositif *ans* electropositive
electropositifedd *eg* electropositivity
electrosgop *eg* electrosgopau electroscope
electrosgop deilen aur *eg* electrosgopau deilen aur gold leaf electroscope
electrostateg *eb* electrostatics
electrostatig *ans* electrostatic
elfen *eb* elfennau element
elfen AC *eb* elfennau AC AND element
elfen ansoddol *eb* elfennau ansoddol constituent element
elfen cymhwysedd *eb* elfennau cymhwysedd element of competence
elfen drosiannol *eb* elfennau trosiannol transition element
elfen drydan *eb* elfennau trydan electric element
elfen ddiwylliannol *eb* elfennau diwylliannol culture element
elfen ddryslyd *eb* elfennau dryslyd confound
elfen fetelig *eb* elfennau metelig metallic element
elfen ffitrwydd *eb* elfennau ffitrwydd fitness component
elfen gerddorol *eb* elfennau cerddorol musical element
elfen golyn *eb* elfennau colyn pivot element

elfen goll *eb* elfennau coll missing element
elfen grŵp awtobeilot *eb* elfennau grŵp awtobeilot autopilot group element
elfen hunanwrthdro *eb* self-inverse element
elfen hybrin *eb* elfennau hybrin trace element
elfen resymeg *eb* elfennau rhesymeg logic element
elfen tabl awtobeilot *eb* elfennau tabl awtobeilot autopilot table element
elfen thematig *eb* elfennau thematig thematic element
elfen unfathiant *eb* elfennau unfathiant identity element
elfen wreiddiol *eb* parent element
elfen wresogi *eb* elfennau gwresogi heating element
elfen wrthdro *eb* elfennau gwrthdro inverse element
elfennaidd *ans* elemental
elfennau aloi *ell* alloying elements
elfennau peintio *ell* elements of painting
elfennol *ans* rudimentary
elfennol *ans* elementary
eli *eg* eliau ointment
eli rhwystrol *eg* barrier cream
elifiant *eg* elifiannau effluence
elifol *ans* effluent
elifyn *eg* elifion effluent
elin *eb* elinau forearm
elin ladrad *eb* elin ladradau elbow of capture
eliniad *eg* forearm deflection
elinwisg *eb* elinwisgoedd forearm shield
elips *eg* elipsau ellipse
elipsoid *eg* elipsoidau ellipsoid
elipsoidol *ans* ellipsoidal
eliptig *ans* elliptic
eliptigol *ans* elliptical
Elisabethaidd *ans* Elizabethan
elit *eg* elitau elite
elitaeth *eb* elitism
elitaidd *ans* elite
elitydd *eg* elitwyr elitist
Elizabeth I *eb* Elizabeth I
Elohim Elohim
elusen *eb* elusennau alms
elusen *eb* elusennau charity
elusendir *eg* frankalmoign
elusendy *eg* elusendai almshouse
elusenfa *eb* elusenfeydd almonry
elusennwr *eg* elusenwyr almoner
elw *eg* profits
elw *eg* profit
elw crynswth *eg* gross profit
elw cyffredin *eg* normal profit
elw goruwchnormal *eg* supernormal profit
elw net *eg* net profit
e-lywodraeth *eb* e-government
ellyllbren *eg* elfinwood
Emaniwel Ffodus *eg* Emmanuel the Fortunate
embryo *eg* embryonau embryo
embryo datblygol *eg* embryonau datblygol developing embryo
emeri *eg* emery
emffysema *eg* emphysema
emosiwn *eg* emosiynau emotion
emosiynol *ans* emotional
empathi *eg* empathy
► **empiriaeth** *eb* empiricism
empirig *ans* empirical
empirydd *eg* empirwyr empiricist
emrallt *eg* emerald
Emrys *eg* Ambrose
emwlseiddio *be* emulsification
emwlsio *be* emulsify
emwlsiwn plastig *eg* plastic emulsion
emwlsiwn polymer *eg* polymer emulsion
emwlsydd *eg* emwlsyddion emulsifier
emyn *eg* emynau hymn
emyn-dôn *eb* emyn-donau hymn tune
enaid rhydd *eg* eneidiau rhydd absolved soul
enaid rhydd *eg* eneidiau rhydd pardoned soul
enamel *eg* enamelau enamel
enamel cefndir *eg* counter enamel
enamel cefndir *eg* background enamel
enamel cloisonné *eg* cloisonné enamel
enamel cracellu *eg* cracked enamel
enamel cras *eg* baked enamel
enamel di-draidd *eg* opaque enamel
enamel gemwaith *eg* enamelau gemwaith jewellery enamel
enamel gwydrog *eg* vitreous enamel
enamel llaid *eg* slush enamel
enamel llusg *eg* crawl enamel
enamel llusg *eg* trail enamel
enamel mâl *eg* crushed enamel
enamel powdrog *eg* powdered enamel
enamel symudliw *eg* opalescent enamel
enamel tryleu *eg* translucent enamel
enamel tryloyw *eg* transparent enamel
enamel ymarfer *eg* practice enamel
enamlo *be* enamel
enamlo llusg *be* crawl enamelling
enamlo llusg *be* trail enamelling
enamlog *ans* enamelled
enantiomer *eg* enantiomerau enantiomer
enantiomorff *eg* enantiomorffau enantiomorph
enceffalitis *eg* encephalitis
encil *eg* encilion retreat
encilgar *ans* withdrawn
enciliad *eg* enciliadau retreat
enciliad (mewn daearyddiaeth etc) *eg* enciliadau recession
enciliad cefnfur *eg* head wall recession
enciliad clogwyn *eg* enciliadau clogwyn cliff recession

encilio *be* recede
encilio *be* retreat
encilio cymdeithasol *be* social withdrawal
enciliol *ans* recessive
enciliwr *eg* encilwyr deserter
enchwythedig *ans* inflated
enchwythiad *eg* enchwythiadau inflation
enchwythu *be* inflate
endemig *ans* endemic
endergonig *ans* endergonic
endid *eg* endidau entity
endid DIFFYG *eg* entity FAULT
endif *eg* endive
endocarp *eg* endocarp
endocrinaidd *ans* endocrine
endocrinoleg *eb* endocrinology
endocyst *eg* endocyst
endodermaidd *ans* endodermal
endolymff *eg* endolymph
endometriwm *eg* endometrium
endomorffig *ans* endomorphic
endorffin *eg* endorffinau endorphin
endoriad *eg* endoriadau incision
endorri *be* incise
endosberm *eg* endosperm
endoseicl *eg* endocycle
endosgop *eg* endosgopau endoscope
endotheliwm *eg* endothelium
endothermig *ans* endothermic
eneiniad *eg* anointing
eneiniad olaf *eg* extreme unction
eneiniad olaf *eg* unction
eneinio *be* anoint
eneinio *be* chrismation
eneiniog *ans* anointed
enema *eg* enemâu enema
enfawr *ans* massive
enfawr *ans* giant
enfys *eb* enfysau rainbow
enffeodu *be* enfeoff
enharmonig *ans* enharmonic
enigma *eg* enigma
enillion *ell* earnings
enillion anweledig *ell* invisible earnings
enillion cyfalaf *ell* capital gain
enillion lleihaol *ell* diminishing returns
enillion net *ell* net gain
enillion trosglwyddo *ell* transfer earnings
enillydd y bêl *eg* enillwyr y bêl ball-winner
enllib *eg* enllibion libel
ennill *be* win
ennill *be* achieve
ennill *eg* enillion gain
ennill gêm *be* win a game
ennill hyder *be* gain confidence
ennill lle *be* qualify
ennill meddiant *be* win possession
ennill o dair wiced *be* win by 3 wickets
ennill o ddigon *be* win easily
ennill o fatiad *be* win by an innings
ennill o gynfas *be* win by a canvas
ennill o un hyd *be* win by a length
ennill tir *be* gain ground
ennyd *eg/b* enydau instant
ennyd benodol *eb* enydau penodol given instant
ennyn *be* elicit
enrhifiad *eg* enrhifiadau evaluation
enrhifo *be* evaluate
enrhifo mynegiadau *be* evaluate expressions
ensemble *eg* ensembles ensemble
ensemble canonaidd mawreddog *eg* ensembles canonaidd mawreddog grand canonical ensemble
ensemble dosbarth *eg* ensembles dosbarth classroom ensemble
ensym *eg* ensymau enzyme
ensym ansymudol *eg* immobilised enzyme
ensym treulio *eg* ensymau treulio digestive enzyme
entael *eg* enteiliau entail
enteilio *be* entail
entemoffilaidd *ans* entemophilous
entente *eb* entente
enteritis *eg* enteritis
enterocinas *eg* enterokinase
entomoleg *eb* entomology
entr'acte *eg* entr'actes entr'acte; act tune
entrepreneur *eg* entrepreneuriaid entrepreneur
entropi *eg* entropy
enthalpi *eg* enthalpïau enthalpy
enthalpi anweddiad *eg* enthalpy of vaporization
enthalpi molar safonol *eg* standard molar enthalpy
enthalpi torri dellt *eg* lattice breaking enthalpy
enw adroddiad *eg* enwau adroddiadau report name
enw arall *eg* enwau eraill alias
enw arddull *eg* enwau arddull style name
enw brand *eg* enwau brand brand name
enw colofn *eg* enwau colofnau column name
enw cronfa ddata *eg* enwau cronfeydd data database name
enw cyn priodi *eg* enwau cyn priodi maiden name
enw defnyddiwr *eg* enwau defnyddiwr username
enw ffeil *eg* enwau ffeiliau file name
enw ffeil cymorth *eg* enwau ffeiliau cymorth help file name
enw ffeil templedi *eg* enwau ffeiliau templedi template file name
enw lle Sacsonaidd *eg* enwau lleoedd Sacsonaidd Saxon place name
enw llwybr *eg* pathname
enw newydd *eg* enwau newydd new name
enw parth *eg* enwau parth domain name
enwad (crefyddol) *eg* enwadau denomination
enwad crefyddol *eg* enwadau crefyddol religious denomination

enwad Protestannaidd *eg* enwadau Protestannaidd Protestant denomination
enwaediad *eg* circumcision
enwebiad *eg* enwebiadau nomination
enwebu *be* nominate
enwebwr *eg* enwebwyr nominator
enwi *be* specify
enwi'r sbesimen *be* identify the specimen
enwol *ans* nominal
enwolaeth *eb* nominalism
enwolaidd *ans* nominalist
enwolwr *eg* enwolwyr nominalist
enw'r cyfrif *eg* account name
enwresis *eg* enuresis
enydaidd *ans* instantaneous
enydol *ans* momentary
eos *eb* eosiaid nightingale
Ëosen *eb* Eocene
eosin *eg* eosin
eosinoffil *eg* eosinoffilau eosinophil
epaulette *eg* epaulettes epaulette
epée *eg* epées epée
epeirogenetig *ans* epeirogenetic
epicotyl *eg* epicotyl
epidemig *eg* epidemigau epidemic
epidemig colera *eg* epidemigau colera cholera epidemic
epidemioleg *eb* epidemiology
epidermaidd *ans* epidermal
epidwral *ans* epidural
epiffysis *eg* epiphysis
epiffyt *eg* epiphyte
epiffytig *ans* epiphytic
epigeal *ans* epigeal
epiglotis *eg* epiglottis
epigynol *ans* epigynous
epil *ell* offspring
epilepsi *eg* epilepsy
epileptig *ans* epileptic
epilgell *eb* epilgelloedd daughter cell
epilgentriol *eg* epilgentriolau daughter centriole
epilgnewyllyn *eg* epilgnewyll daughter nucleus
▶ **epilgynnyrch** *eg* epilgynhyrchion daughter product
epilisotop *eg* epilisotopau daughter isotope
epilniwclid *eg* daughter nuclide
epimeredd *eg* epimerism
epimeru *be* epimerization
epimorffig *ans* epimorphic
epipetalog *ans* epipetalous
episeiclig *ans* epicyclic
episeicloid *eg* episeicloidau epicycloid
episiotomi *eg* episiotomïau episiotomy
epistemoleg *be* epistemology
epistemoleg geneteg *eb* genetic epistemology
epistol *eg* epistolau epistle
epitrocoid *eg* epitrocoidau epitrochoid
epithelaidd *ans* epithelial
epitheliwm *eg* epithelia epithelium
epitheliwm cenhedlol *eg* epithelia cenhedlol germinal epithelium
epitheliwm ciliedig *eg* ciliated epithelium
epitheliwm ciwboid *eg* cuboid epithelium
epitheliwm colofnog *eg* columnar epithelium
epitheliwm haenedig *eg* stratified epithelium
epitheliwm palmantaidd *eg* pavement epithelium
eples *eg* ferment
epleseg *eb* fermentation science
eplesiad *eg* eplesiadau fermentation
eplesiad microbaidd *eg* microbial fermentation
eplesol *ans* fermentative
eplesydd *eg* fermenter
eplesydd swp-feithrin *eg* batch culture fermenter
epocsi *eg* epocsiau epoxy
epocsiethan *eg* epoxyethane
epocsipropan *eg* epoxypropane
er gwaeth *adf* adversely
Erasmiaeth *eb* Erasmianism
Erastiaeth *eb* Erastianism
erbiwm (Er) *eg* erbium
erchyllter *eg* erchyllterau atrocity
erfinen *eb* erfin turnip; swede
erfyn *eg* offer tool
erfyn calcio *eg* offer calcio caulking tool
erfyn cerfio ffurf U *eg* offer cerfio ffurf U veiner
erfyn cnocio *eg* offer cnocio rapping tool
erfyn crychu *eg* offer crychu creasing tool
erfyn cyllell *eg* offer cyllell knife tool
erfyn diemwnt *eg* offer diemwnt diamond tool
erfyn ffurfio *eg* offer ffurfio forming tool
erfyn llinellu *eg* offer llinellu lining tool
erfyn llwy *eg* offer llwy spoon tool
erfyn matio *eg* offer matio matting tool
erfyn mesur trachywir *eg* offer mesur trachywir precision measuring tool
erfyn modelu clai *eg* offer modelu clai clay modelling tool
erfyn ochr *eg* offer ochr side tool
erfyn pannu *eg* offer pannu fullering tool
erfyn partio *eg* offer partio parting off tool
erfyn porthellu *eg* offer porthellu gate tool
erfyn porthellu a chyllell *eg* offer porthellu a chyllell gate and knife tool
erfyn pŵer *eg* offer pŵer power tool
erfyn pwytho *eg* offer pwytho stitching tool
erfyn semio *eg* offer semio seaming tool
erfyn semio rhigol *eg* offer semio rhigolau groove punch seaming tool
erfyn sgrolio *eg* offer sgrolio scrolling tool
erfyn striclo *eg* offer striclo strickling tool
erfyn styden wasg *eg* offer stydiau gwasg press stud tool
erfyn taro *eg* offer taro striking tool
erfyn trin olwyn *eg* offer trin olwyn wheel dresser

erfyn trwyn sgwâr *eg* offer trwyn sgwâr square nosed tool
erfyn turn *eg* offer turn tool bit
erfyn turnio *eg* offer turnio turning tool
erfyn tyllu *eg* offer tyllu boring tool
erfyn tynnu allan *eg* offer tynnu allan withdrawal tool
erfyn U *eg* offer U U-tool
erfyn V *eg* offer V V-tool
erfyn wynebu *eg* offer wynebu facing tool
erfyn ysgythru *eg* offer ysgythru engraving tool
erfyn ysgythru *eg* offer ysgythru block cutting tool
ergodig *ans* ergodic
ergonomeg *eb* ergonomics
ergyd (=trawiad) *eg/b* ergydion strike
ergyd (gyda bat etc) *eg/b* ergydion hit
ergyd (gyda gwn etc) *eg/b* ergydion shot
ergyd (gyda raced etc) *eg/b* ergydion stroke
ergyd (yn gyffredinol) *eg/b* ergydion blow
ergyd amddiffynnol *eb* ergydion amddiffynnol defensive shot
ergyd amddiffynnol *eb* ergydion amddiffynnol defensive stroke
ergyd cychwyn *eb* starting gun
ergyd ennill *eb* ergydion ennill winning stroke
ergyd flaenllaw *eb* ergydion blaenllaw forehand stroke
ergyd galed *eb* ergydion caled smash
ergyd gornel *eb* ergydion cornel corner hit
ergyd gwta *eb* ergydion cwta drop shot
ergyd gylch *eb* ergydion cylch sixteen yard hit-out
ergyd munud *eb* one minute gun
ergyd ochr *eb* ergydion ochr hit-out
ergyd onglog *eb* ergydion onglog angle shot
ergyd pum munud *eb* five-minute gun
ergyd rydd *eb* ergydion rhydd free hit
ergyd wrthlaw *eb* ergydion gwrthlaw backhand stroke
ergyd ymosodol *eb* ergydion ymosodol attacking stroke
ergydio *be* hit; stroke
ergydiol *ans* percussive; impulsive
ergydiwr *eg* ergydwyr striker
erial *eb* erialau aerial
erioed wedi bod yn fyw never been alive
erledigaeth *eb* persecution; witch hunt
erledigaeth *eb* erledigaethau victimisation
erledigaeth filwrol *eb* dragonnade
erledigaeth Mari *eb* Marian persecution
erlid *eg* persecute
erlyn *eg* prosecute
erlyniad *eg* erlyniadau prosecution
erlynydd *eg* erlynwyr prosecutor
erlynydd y goron *eg* crown prosecution
ermid *eg* ermidion eremite
ernes *eb* ernesau deposit
ers eiliad (am orffen dogfen) elapsed seconds
erthygl *eb* erthyglau article
erthygl nodwedd *eb* erthyglau nodwedd feature
erthyglau cymdeithasiad *ell* articles of association
erthyglau cytundeb Rhufain *ell* articles of the treaty of Rome
erthyliad *eg* erthyliadau abortion
erthyliad naturiol *eg* erthyliadau naturiol miscarriage
erthylu *be* abort
erthylu cyson *be* habitual abortion
erthylu'n naturiol *be* miscarry
eruv *eg* eruv
erw *eb* erwau acre
erwydd *eg* erwyddi stave; staff
erwydd tenor *eg* tenor stave
erydiad *eg* erosion
erydiad gwahaniaethol *eg* differential erosion
erydiad gwynt *eg* wind erosion
erydiad pridd *eg* soil erosion
erydiad rhewlifol *eg* glacial erosion
erydol *ans* erosive
erydu *be* erode
erydu dethol *be* selective erosion
erydydd *eg* erydyddion erosive agent
esblygiad *eg* esblygiadau evolution
esblygiad biolegol *eg* biological evolution
esblygiad diwylliannol *eg* cultural evolution
esblygiadol *ans* evolutionary
esblygol *ans* phylogenetic
esblygu *be* evolve
esboniad (=nodiadau esboniadol) *eg* esboniadau commentary
esboniad (yn gyffredinol) *eg* esboniadau explanation
esboniad mathemategol *eg* esboniadau mathemategol mathematical explanation
esboniwr *eg* esbonwyr commentator
esbonydd *eg* esbonyddion exponent
esbonyddol *ans* exponential
escalope *eb* escalopes escalope
eschatoleg *eb* eschatology
esgair *eb* esgeiriau esker
esgair gnapiog *eb* esgeiriau cnapiog beaded esker
esgeuluso *be* neglect
esgeulustod *eg* neglect; negligence
esgid (ar gyfer rygbi etc) *eb* esgidiau boot
esgid (yn gyffredinol) *eb* esgidiau shoe
esgid brêc *eb* esgidiau brêc brake shoe
esgid dennis *eb* esgidiau tennis tennis shoe
esgid fwylltid *eb* esgidiau bwylltid swivel shoe
esgid griced *eb* esgidiau criced cricket shoe
esgid gynfas *eb* esgidiau cynfas canvas boot
esgid redeg *eb* esgidiau rhedeg running shoe
esgid sbeic *eb* esgidiau sbeic spiked shoe
esgidiau *ell* footwear
esgidiau hoelion clincer *ell* clinker nailed boots
esgob *eg* esgobion bishop
Esgob William Morgan *eg* Bishop William Morgan

esgobaeth *eb* esgobaethau bishopric; episcopacy; episcopate; diocese; see
esgobaethol *ans* diocesan; episcopalian
esgobol *ans* episcopal
esgobwr *eg* esgobwyr episcopalian
esgobwriaeth *eb* episcopalianism
esgor *be* labour
esgoriad *eg* esgoriadau parturition
esgoriad ffolennol *eg* esgoriadau ffolennol breech birth
esgusodi rhag credyd *be* credit exemption
esgusodiad *eg* esgusodiadau exemption
esgyll paredig *ell* paired fins
esgyn *be* ascend; take off
esgyn untroed *be* single take-off
esgynfa *eb* esgynfeydd take-off
esgyniad *eg* esgyniadau ascent; ascension
Esgyniad Cywir *eg* Right Ascension
esgyniad deudroed *eg* double take-off
esgyniad Prwsia *eg* rise of Prussia
esgynlawr *eg* esgynloriau dais
esgynnol *ans* ascending
esgynnwr *eg* esgynwyr ascender
esgynnydd *eg* esgynyddion ascender
esgyrnyn *eg* esgyrnynnau ossicle
esgyrnyn y glust *eg* esgyrnynnau'r glust ear ossicle
esgytsiwn *eg* esgytsiynau escutcheon
esmwythder *eg* ease
esmwytho (llawnder) *be* ease
esparto *eg* esparto
ester *eg* esterau ester
esteriad *eg* esterification
esteru *be* esterify
estraddodi *be* extradition
estron *ans* foreign; alien; extraneous
estron *eg* estroniaid alien
estron preswyl *eg* estroniaid preswyl resident alien
estroniaid *ell* advenae
estyll croglofft *ell* ashlaring
estyll cydwedd *ell* matchboarding
estyllen do *eb* estyll to shingle
estyllu *be* batten
estyn (=cyrchu) *be* get
estyn (amser) *be* prolong
estyn (hyd rhywbeth) *be* lengthen
estyn (mewn cerddoriaeth) *be* augment
estyn (mewn geometreg) *be* produce
estyn (mewn graff) *be* project
estyn (rhywbeth elastig) *be* stretch
estyn (yng nghyd-destun haenau iâ etc) *be* advance
estyn (yn gyffredinol) *be* extend
estyn ac encilio advance and retreat
estyn patrwm *be* lengthen a pattern
estyn tuag yn ôl *be* produce backwards
estynadwy *ans* extensible
estynedig (am rywbeth elastig) *ans* stretched
estynedig (mewn cerddoriaeth) *ans* augmented
estynedig (yn gyffredinol) *be* extended
estyniad (=pellter y gellir ei estyn) *eg* estyniadau reach
estyniad (amser) *eg* estyniadau prolongation
estyniad (mewn cerddoriaeth) *eg* estyniadau augmentation
estyniad (mewn graff) *eg* estyniadau projection
estyniad (yng nghyd-destun haenau iâ etc) *eg* estyniadau advance
estyniad (yn gyffredinol) *eg* estyniadau extension
estyniad arwydd *eg* estyniadau arwydd sign extension
estyniad bias *eg* estyniadau bias bias extension
estyniad enw ffeil *eg* estyniadau enw ffeil filename extension
estyniad ffeil *eg* estyniadau ffeil file extension
estynnwr *eg* estynwyr stretcher
estynnwr belt *eg* estynwyr belt belt stretcher
estynnwr croes *eg* estynwyr croes cross stretcher
estynnwr croeslinol *eg* estynwyr croeslinol diagonal stretcher
estynnwr crwm *eg* estynwyr crwm curved stretcher
estynnwr cynfas *eg* estynwyr cynfas canvas stretcher
estynnwr ffurf H *eg* estynwyr ffurf H H-shaped stretcher
estynnwr ffurf T *eg* estynwyr ffurf T T-shaped stretcher
estynnwr webin *eg* estynwyr webin webbing stretcher
estynnydd *eg* estynyddion extender
estynwlad *eb* estynwledydd panhandle
estynwyr ffurfiedig *ell* shaped stretchers
estheteg *eb* aesthetics
esthetig *ans* aesthetic
esthetigaeth *eb* aestheticism
etifedd *eg* etifeddion heir
etifedd tebygol *eg* etifeddion tebygol heir presumptive
etifeddeg *eb* heredity
etifeddiad (nodweddion) *eg* inheritance
etifeddiad amlffactoraidd *eg* multifactorial inheritance
etifeddiad gronynnol *eg* particulate inheritance
etifeddiad Mendelaidd *eg* Mendelian inheritance
etifeddiad monocroesryw *eg* monohybrid inheritance
etifeddiaeth *eb* heritage; legacy
etifeddiaeth ddiwylliannol *eb* cultural heritage
etifeddiaeth Gristnogol *eb* Christian heritage
etifeddiaeth gyfrannol *eb* partible inheritance
etifeddiaeth gymhlith *eb* blended inheritance
etifeddiant *eg* etifeddiannau hereditament
etifeddol *ans* hereditary; inherited
etifeddu *be* inherit
étude *eb* études étude
ethan *eg* ethane
ethanal *eg* ethanal

ethanal ocsim *eg* ethanal oxime
ethanal tetramer *eg* ethanal tetramer
ethanal trimer *eg* ethanal trimer
ethanamid *eg* ethanamide
ethandeual *eg* ethanedial
ethandeuamid *eg* ethanediamide
ethan-1,2-deuamin *eg* ethane-1,2-diamine
ethan-1,2-deuol *eg* ethane-1,2-diol
ethanenitril *eg* ethanenitrile
ethanenitril deumethyl ether *eg* ethanenitrile dimethyl ether
ethanoad *eg* ethanoadau ethanoate
► **ethanöig** *ans* ethanoic
ethanöig anhydrid *eg* ethanoic anhydride
ethanöig methanöig anhydrid *eg* ethanoic methanoic anhydride
ethanol *ans* ethanol
ethanoyl clorid *eg* ethanoyl chloride
ethanthiol *eg* ethanethiol
Ethelred y Digyngor *eg* Ethelred the Unready
ethen *eg* ethene
ethen osonid *eg* ethene ozonide
ethenon *eg* ethenone
ethenyl- ethenyl-
ethenyl ethanoad *eg* ethenyl ethanoate
ether *eg* ether
ether-rwyd *eb* ethernet
etherydd *eg* etheryser
ethnig *ans* ethnic
ethnigedd *eg* ethnicity
ethnoganolog *ans* ethnocentric
ethnogerddoleg *eb* ethnomusicology
ethnograffeg *eb* ethnography
ethnoleg *eb* ethnology
ethocsibensen *eg* ethoxybenzene
ethocsiethan *eg* ethoxyethane
ethogram *eg* ethogramau ethogram
ethol *be* elect
Etholaeth Balatin y Rhein *eb* Palatine of the Rhine
etholaethau cyfartal *ell* equal constituencies
etholedig *ans* elect
etholedig rai *ell* elect
etholeg *eb* ethology
etholfraint *eb* etholfreintiau franchise
etholfraint fwrdeistrefol *eb* borough franchise
etholiad *eg* etholiadau election
etholiad cyffredinol *eg* etholiadau cyffredinol general election
Etholiad y Cwpon *eg* Coupon Election
etholiadol *ans* electoral
etholwr *eg* etholwyr elector
etholwyr *ell* electorate
Etholydd *eg* Etholyddion Elector
Etholydd Archesgob *eg* Elector Archbishop
Etholydd Mawr *eg* Great Elector
Etholydd Palatin *eg* Elector Palatine
Etholydd Tywysogol *eg* Prince Elector
ethos *eg* ethos
ethos cyffredin *eg* common ethos
ethos chwarae *eg* play ethos
ethyl alcohol *eg* ethyl alcohol
ethyl bensencarbocsylad *eg* ethyl benzenecarboxylate
ethyl bensoad *eg* ethyl benzoate
ethyl ethanoad *eg* ethyl ethanoate
ethyl 3-ocsobwtanoad *eg* ethyl 3-oxobutanoate
ethylamin *eg* ethylamine
ethylamoniwm clorid *eg* ethylammonium chloride
ethylbensen *eg* ethylbenzene
ethyl-lithiwm *eg* ethyl-lithium
ethylmagnesiwm bromid *eg* ethylmagnesium bromide
ethyn *eg* ethyne
ethyndeuid *eg* ethynediide
Eu Mawrhydi Catholig *ell* Catholic Majesties
euogrwydd *eg* guilt
euogrwydd rhyfel *eg* war guilt
eurgylch *eg* eurgylchoedd halo
euro *be* gild
ewcaryot *eg* ewcaryotau eukaryote
ewcaryotig *ans* eukaryotic
Ewclidaidd *ans* Euclidean
Ewcharist *eg* Eucharist
e-Weinidog *eg* e-Weinidogion e-Minister
ewinrhew *eg* frostbite
ewlychiad *eg* ewlychiadau efflorescence
ewlychol *ans* efflorescent
ewro *eg* ewros euro
Ewrodir *eg* Eurozone
Ewrofaint (am gartonau) *ans* Eurosize
Ewropeiddio *be* Europeanization
ewropiwm (Eu) *eg* europium (Eu)
ewstatig *ans* eustatic
ewtecteg *eb* eutectics
ewtroffig *ans* eutrophic
ewtroffigedd *eg* eutrophication
ewthanasia *eg* euthanasia
ewtheraidd *ans* eutherian
ewyllys *eg/b* ewyllysiau will
ewyllys dda *eb* good will
ewyllys rydd *eb* free will
ewyn *eg* ewynnau foam
ewyn môr *eg* surf
ewyn polyether *eg* polyether foam
ewyn styro *eg* styrofoam
ewynnog *ans* frothy
ewynnu *be* foam
ex post facto ex post facto
Exodus (llyfr yn y Beibl) Exodus

F

F fwyaf *eb* F major
F leiaf *eb* F minor
Fablon *eg* Fablon
faciwî *eg/b* faciwîs evacuee
fafasor *eg* fafasoriaid vavasour
fagotto *eg* fagotti fagotto
faience *eg* faience
Fainc, y *eb* Bench, the
falens *eg* falensau valence; valency
falf *eb* falfiau valve
falf deirlen *eb* falfiau teirlen tricuspid valve
falf droellog *eb* falfiau troellog spiral valve
falf drogylch *eb* falfiau trogylch rotary valve
falf ddiogelu *eb* falfiau diogelu safety valve
falf ddwylen *eb* falfiau dwylen bicuspid valve
falf feitrol *eb* falfiau meitrol mitral valve
falf ganfod *eb* falfiau canfod detector valve
falf gilgant *eb* falfiau cilgant semilunar valve
falf gloi *eb* falfiau cloi lockshield valve
falf gwasgedd *eb* falfiau gwasgedd pressure valve
falf lithr *eb* falfiau llithr slide valve
falf NID *eb* falfiau NID NOT valve
falf ochr *eb* falfiau ochr side valve
falf ryddhau *eb* falfiau rhyddhau release valve
falf thermionig *eb* falfiau thermionig thermionic valve
falf uwchben *eb* falfiau uwchben overhead valve
falf ynysu *eb* falfiau ynysu isolation valve
falin *eg* valine
fampio *be* vamp
fanadiwm (V) *eg* vanadium
fanadiwm(V) ocsid *eg* vanadium(V) oxide
fandal *eg* fandaliaid vandal
fandaliaeth *eb* vandalism
farf *eg* farfau varve
farnais *eg* varnish
farnais aildrwsio *eg* re-touching varnish
farnais atal *eg* farneisiau atal stopping-out varnish
farnais barbola *eg* barbola varnish
farnais clir *eg* farneisiau clir clear varnish
farnais copal *eg* copal varnish
farnais cwyr *eg* farneisiau cwyr wax varnish
farnais darlun *eg* picture varnish
farnais gwirod *eg* farneisiau gwirod spirit varnish
farnais gwrthasid *eg* farneisiau gwrthasid acid resisting varnish
farnais gwrth-wres *eg* heat-resisting varnish
farnais hydawdd *eg* soluble varnish
farnais mat *eg* matt varnish
farnais morol *eg* marine varnish
farnais papur *eg* farneisiau papur paper varnish
farnais polywrethan *eg* polyurethane varnish
farnais sielac *eg* shellac varnish
farnais y diffeithdir *eg* desert varnish
farneisio *be* varnish
fasgwlar *ans* vascular
fasgwlwm *eg* fasgwla vasculum
fasogyfyngiad *eg* vasoconstriction
fasogyfyngydd *eg* fasogyfyngwyr vasoconstrictor
fasoymlediad *eg* vasodilation
fasoymledydd *eg* fasoymledwyr vasodilator
Fatican *eg* Vatican
faux bourdon *eg* faux bourdons faux bourdon
fector *eg* fectorau vector
fector colofn *eg* fectorau colofn column vector
fector eigen *eg* fectorau eigen eigen vector
fector rhes *eg* row vector
fector safle *eg* position vector
fector uned *eg* fectorau uned unit vector
fectoraidd *ans* vectorial
fectoreiddio *be* vectorize
fectoru *be* vector
feiol *eb* feiolau viol
feiol denor *eb* feiolau tenor tenor viol
feiol ddesgant *eb* feiolau desgant descant viol
feiol fas *eb* feiolau bas bass viol
feiolin *eb* feiolinau violin
feiolinydd *eg* feiolinwyr violinist
feiolydd *eg* feiolyddion viol player
feis *eb* feisiau vice
feis beipen *eb* feisiau peipen pipe vice
feis ben mainc *eb* feisiau pen mainc bench end vice
feis fach *eb* feisiau bach nippy vice
feis fainc *eb* feisiau mainc bench vice
feis fwrdd *eb* feisiau bwrdd table vice
feis fwylltid *eb* feisiau bwylltid swivel vice
feis gafael ebrwydd *eb* feisiau gafael ebrwydd instantaneous grip vice
feis gludadwy *eb* feisiau cludadwy portable vice
feis goes *eb* feisiau coes leg vice
feis haearn bwrw *eb* feisiau haearn bwrw cast iron vice
feis hogi llif *eb* feisiau hogi llif saw vice
feis law *eb* feisiau llaw hand vice
feis offerwr *eb* feisiau offerwr toolmaker's vice

feis peiriannydd *eb* feisiau peiriannydd engineer's vice
feis peiriant *eb* feisiau peiriant machine vice
feis pìn *eb* feisiau pìn pin vice
feis safnau paralel *eb* feisiau safnau paralel parallel jaw vice
fel arall *adf* otherwise
fel y dangosir gan as indicated by
fel y mae (am gyflwr) as is
felcro *eg* velcro
felôr *eg* velour
felwm *eg* vellum
felly *adf* therefore
felly *adf* accordingly
felly *adf* thus
Fenisaidd *ans* Venetian
fentrigl *eg* fentriglau ventricle
fentrol *ans* ventral
fermiliwn *eg* vermilion
fermin *ell* vermin
fernagl *eb* vernicle
fernier *ans* vernier
fernier *eg* fernieri vernier
fersin *eg* fersinau versine
fersiwn *eg* fersiynau version
fersiwn a addaswyd *eg* fersiynau a addaswyd modified version
fersiwn awdurdodedig *eg* authorized version
fersiwn cydnabyddedig *eg* fersiynau cydnabyddedig recognized version
fersiwn hwylus i'w argraffu *eg* fersiynau hwylus i'w hargraffu printer-friendly version
fersiwn llawn *eg* fersiynau llawn full version
fersiwn mân-lun *eg* fersiynau mân-lun thumbnail version
fersiwn presennol *eg* fersiynau presennol existing version
fersiwn syml *eg* fersiynau syml simplified version
fertebra *eg* fertebrâu vertebra
fertebra cynffonnol *eg* fertebrâu cynffonnol caudal vertebra
fertebra gyddfol *eg* fertebrâu gyddfol cervical vertebra
fertebra meingefnol *eg* fertebrâu meingefnol lumbar vertebra
fertebraidd *ans* vertebrate
fertebra'r sacrwm *eg* fertebrâu'r sacrwm sacral vertebra
fertebrat *eg* fertebratau vertebrate
fertebrol *ans* vertebral
fertig *eg* fertigau vertex
fertigau petryal *ell* vertices of a rectangle
fertigol *ans* vertical
fertigol i lawr *ans* downward vertical
fertigoledd *eg* verticality
ferwca *eg* ferwcau verruca
fesigl semenol *eg* seminal vesicle
fest *eb* festiau vest
fest redeg *eb* festiau rhedeg running vest
festri *eb* festrïoedd vestry
fesul rhandal by instalment
fibraffon *eg* fibraffonau vibraphone
ficer *eg* ficeriaid vicar
ficer corawl *eg* ficeriaid corawl vicar-choral
ficer cyffredinol *eg* ficeriaid cyffredinol vicar-general
ficerdy *eg* ficerdai vicarage
ficeriaeth *eb* ficeriaethau vicariate
Fictoraidd *ans* Victorian
fideo *eg* fideos video
fideo ffiaidd *eg* fideos ffiaidd video nasty
fideo rhyngweithiol *eg* fideos rhyngweithiol interactive video
fideo-gynadledda *be* video conferencing
fideosgop *eg* fideosgopau videoscope
Fietnam *eb* Vietnam
fila *eb* filâu villa
filws *eg* filysau villus
finale *eg* finales finale
finegr *eg* vinegar
finyl *eg* finylau vinyl
fiola *eb* fiolâu viola
fioled alisarin *eg* alizarin violet
fioled cobalt *eg* cobalt violet
fiolydd *eg* fiolyddion viola player
firaol *ans* viral
firdsinal *eb* firdsinalau virginals
firdsinal ddwbl *eb* firdsinalau dwbl double virginal
firdsinalydd *eg* firdsinalyddion virginalist
firgat *eg* firgatau virgate
firidian *eg* viridian
firoleg *eb* virology
firws *eg* firysau virus
firws hidladwy *eg* filterable virus
firws y ffliw *eg* influenza virus
fiscos *eg* viscose
fitamin *eg* fitaminau vitamin
fitamin braster-hydawdd *eg* fitaminau braster-hydawdd fat soluble vitamin
fitamin C *eg* vitamin C
fitaminau atodol *ell* vitamin supplement
fitriol *eg* vitriol
flambé *ans* flambé
folcanig *ans* volcanic
folcanigrwydd *eg* volcanism
folcanigrwydd *eg* volcanicity
foli *eb* folïau volley
foli gwta *eb* folïau cwta short volley
foli stop *eb* folïau stop stop volley
folio *be* volley
folt *eg* foltiau volt
foltamedr *eg* foltamedrau voltameter
foltedd *eg* folteddau voltage
foltedd allbwn *eg* output voltage
foltedd eilaidd *eg* secondary voltage

foltedd Hall *eg* Hall voltage
foltedd isel *eg* low voltage
foltedd uchel *eg* high voltage
foltiau mewnbwn brig *ell* peak input volts
foltmedr *eg* foltmedrau voltmeter
fortecs *eg* fortecsau vortex
forteisedd *eg* vorticity
forteisydd *eg* forteisyddion vorticist
fortepiano *eg* fortepianos fortepiano
foulard *eg* foulard
Freudaidd *ans* Freudian
fricassée *eb* fricassées fricassée
FTP anhysbys *eg* anonymous FTP
fwlcaneiddio *be* vulcanize
fwlcanigrwydd *eg* vulcanicity
fwlcanoleg *eb* vulcanology
fwlfa *eg* fwlfâu vulva (of woman)
Fwlgat *eg* Vulgate

Ff

ffa *ell* broad beans
ffa adwci *ell* aduki beans
ffa coch *ell* red kidney beans
ffa coffi *ell* coffee beans
ffa dringo *ell* runner beans
ffa du *ell* black beans
ffa flageolet *ell* flageolet beans
ffa Ffrengig *ell* French beans
ffa Ffrengig *ell* kidney beans
ffa haricot *ell* haricot beans
ffa llygatddu *ell* black-eyed beans
ffa melyn *ell* yellow beans
ffa menyn *ell* butter beans
ffa mwng *ell* mung beans
ffa pinto *ell* pinto beans
ffa pob *ell* baked beans
ffa soia *ell* soya beans
Ffabiaeth *eb* Fabianism
ffabrig *eg* ffabrigau fabric
ffabrig amsugnol *eg* ffabrigau amsugnol absorbent fabric
ffabrig bondiog *eg* ffabrigau bondiog bonded fabric
ffabrig cymysg *eg* blended fabric
ffabrig dodrefnu *eg* ffabrigau dodrefnu furnishing fabric
ffabrig dolennog *eg* ffabrigau dolennog looped fabric
ffabrig ffwr *eg* ffabrigau ffwr fur fabric
ffabrig gwead clos *eg* ffabrigau gwead clos close woven fabric
ffabrig mewnol *eg* internal fabric
ffabrig perfformio *eg* performance fabric
ffabrig printiedig *eg* ffabrigau printiedig printed fabric
ffabrig wedi'i stwffio *eg* ffabrigau wedi'u stwffio stuffed fabric
ffabrig wedi'i wau *eg* ffabrigau wedi'u gwau knitted fabric
ffabrig ymestyn *eg* stretch fabric
ffabrigedig *ans* fabricated
ffabrigo *be* fabricate
ffabrigo metel *be* metal fabrication
ffacs *eg* ffacsys fax
ffacs awtobeilot *eg* ffacsys awtobeilot autopilot fax
ffacsimili *eg* ffacsimilïau facsimile
ffacsio *be* fax
ffactor *eg/b* ffactorau factor
ffactor achosol *eb* ffactorau achosol causative factor
ffactor agored *eb* open factor
ffactor amddiffynnol *eb* ffactorau amddiffynnol protective factor
ffactor amgylcheddol *eb* ffactorau amgylcheddol environmental factor
ffactor annibynnol ar ddwysedd *eb* density independent factor
ffactor benodol *eb* ffactorau penodol specific factor
ffactor cymhelliant *eb* ffactorau cymhelliant motivational factor
ffactor drechol *eb* ffactorau trechol dominant factor
ffactor ddeallusol *eb* ffactorau deallusol intellectual factor
ffactor economaidd *eb* ffactorau economaidd economic factor
ffactor enciliol *eb* ffactorau enciliol recessive factor
ffactor flocio *eb* ffactorau blocio blocking factor
ffactor ffordd o fyw sy'n effeithio ar iechyd *eb* ffactorau ffordd o fyw sy'n effeithio ar iechyd lifestyle factors affecting health
ffactor g *eb* g factor
ffactor genetig *eb* ffactorau genetig genetic factor
ffactor golau dydd *eb* daylight factor
ffactor goleuo *eb* illumination factor
ffactor gorfforol *eb* ffactorau corfforol physical factor
ffactor graddfa *eb* ffactorau graddfa scale factor
ffactor graddfa gyfartalog *eb* average scale factor
ffactor graddio *eb* ffactorau graddio scaling factor
ffactor gyfyngol *eb* ffactorau cyfyngol limiting factor
ffactor gyffredin fwyaf *eb* highest common factor
ffactor gymdeithasol *eb* ffactorau cymdeithasol social factor
ffactor gysefin *eb* ffactorau cysefin prime factor
ffactor linol *eb* ffactorau llinol linear factor
ffactor pŵer *eb* power factor
ffactor rhagdueddu *eb* ffactorau rhagdueddu predisposing factors
ffactor rhesws *eb* rhesus factor
ffactor S *eb* S factor
ffactor sefyllfa *eb* ffactorau sefyllfa situational factor
ffactor ymdoddi *eb* fusing factor
ffactoraidd *ans* factorial
ffactorau cymdeithasol ac economaidd sy'n effeithio ar iechyd *ell* social and economic factors affecting health

ffactorau cynhyrchu *ell* factors of production
ffactoriad *eg* ffactoriadau factorization
▸ **ffactoriadwy** *ans* factorizable
ffactoriaeth *eb* factorizing
ffactorial *eg* ffactorialau factorial
ffactorio *be* factorize
ffactorio yn llwyr *be* factorize completely
ffaeoffytin *eg* phaeophytin
ffafrio *be* favour
ffag *eg* phage
ffagocyt *eg* ffagocytau phagocyte
ffagocytig *ans* phagocytic
ffagocytosis *eg* phagocytosis
ffagodwaith *eg* faggotting
ffagotsen *eb* ffagots faggot
ffaith *eb* ffeithiau fact
ffalang *eg* ffalangau phalange
ffalancs *eg* phalanx
ffaltwng *eg* ffaltyngau faltung
ffaltwng *eg* ffaltyngau convolution
ffan (=dilynwr brwd) *eg* ffaniau fan
ffanfer *eg* ffanferau fanfare
ffanfowt *eg* ffanfowtiau fan vaulting
ffanffer *eg* ffanfferau flourish
ffansi *ans* fancy
Ffansi Lisa *eb* Princess Elizabeth's Fancy
ffansîn *eg* fanzine
ffantasi *eb* ffantasïau fantasy
ffantasia *eb* ffantasïau fantasia
ffantasia rydd *eb* ffantasïau rhydd free fantasia
ffarad *eg* ffaradau farad
ffaryngeal *ans* pharyngeal
ffaryncs *eg* pharynx
ffasâd *eg* ffasadau facade
ffased *eg* ffasedau facet
ffasgaeth *eb* fascism
ffasgaidd *ans* fascist
ffasgau *ell* fascia
ffasgedd *eg* fasciation
ffasgell *eb* ffasgellau fascicle
ffasgellol *ans* fascicular
ffasgol *ans* fasciated
ffasgydd *eg* ffasgwyr fascist
ffasiwn *eg/b* ffasiynau fashion; vogue
ffasiwn cynllunio *eg* ffasiynau cynllunio planning trend
ffasnydd *eg* ffasnyddion fastener
ffasnydd ffenestr adeiniog *eg* ffasnyddion ffenestr adeiniog casement fastener
ffasnydd metel *eg* ffasnyddion metel metal fastener
ffasnydd rhychiog *eg* ffasnyddion rhychiog corrugated fastener
ffasnydd sash *eg* ffasnyddion sash sash fastener
ffasnydd sip *eg* ffasnyddion sip zip fastener
ffasnydd snap *eg* ffasnyddion snap snap fastener
ffatri *eb* ffatrïoedd factory
ffatri barod *eb* ffatrïoedd parod advance factory
ffatri gangen *eb* ffatrïoedd cangen branch
ffawna *ell* fauna
ffawt *eg/b* ffawtiau fault
ffawt ddwbl *eb* ffawtiau dwbl double fault
ffawt troed *eb* ffawtiau traed foot fault
ffawtio *be* fault
ffawtlin *eg* ffawtlinau fault line
ffawydden *eb* ffawydd beech
ffawydden *eb* ffawydd beech tree
ffederal *ans* federal
ffederaleiddio *be* federate
ffederaliaeth *eb* federalism
ffederasiwn *eg* federation
Ffederasiwn Glowyr De Cymru *eg* South Wales Miner's Federation
ffedog *eb* ffedogau apron
ffedog allolchi *eb* ffedogau allolchi outwash apron
ffedog crochenydd *eb* ffedogau crochenydd potter's apron
ffedog flaen *eb* ffedogau blaen frontal apron
ffedog gotwm *eb* ffedogau cotwm cotton apron
ffedog ledr *eb* ffedogau lledr leather apron
ffedog wen *eb* ffedogau gwyn white apron
ffefryn *eg* ffefrynnau favourite
ffeil *eb* ffeiliau file
ffeil Abra *eb* ffeiliau Abra Abra file
ffeil archif *eb* ffeiliau archif archive file
ffeil cofnodi *eb* ffeiliau cofnodi log file
ffeil cronfa ddata *eb* ffeiliau cronfa ddata database file
ffeil cyllell *eb* ffeiliau cyllell knife file
ffeil cymorth *eb* ffeiliau cymorth help file
ffeil cyrchu dilyniannol *eg* sequential access file
ffeil dairongl *eb* ffeiliau tairongl three-square file
ffeil dairongl *eb* ffeiliau tairongl triangular file
ffeil delwedd *eb* ffeiliau delwedd image file
ffeil drafod *eb* ffeiliau trafod transaction file
ffeil ddata *eb* ffeiliau data data file
ffeil ddilyniannol *eb* ffeiliau dilyniannol sequential file
ffeil ddilyniannol fynegedig *eb* ffeiliau dilyniannol mynegedig indexed sequential file
ffeil eildor *eb* ffeiliau eildor second cut file
ffeil electronig *eb* ffeiliau electronig electronic file
ffeil fach fain gron *eb* ffeiliau bach main crwn mouse-tail file
ffeil fastard *eb* ffeiliau bastard bastard file
ffeil fastard *eb* ffeiliau bastard bastard cut file
ffeil fideo *eb* ffeiliau fideo video file
ffeil fodrwy *eb* ffeiliau modrwy ring-binder
ffeil frasddant *eb* ffeiliau brasddant rough cut file
ffeil ffurfweddu *eb* ffeiliau ffurfweddu configuration file
ffeil ffynhonnell *eb* ffeiliau ffynhonnell source file
ffeil gabinet *eb* ffeiliau cabinet cabinet file
ffeil gron *eb* ffeiliau crwn round file
ffeil gyffredin *eb* ffeiliau cyffredin common file
ffeil gyrchfan *eb* ffeiliau cyrchfan destination file

ffeil hanner crwn *eb* ffeiliau hanner crwn half round file
ffeil hapgyrchu *eb* ffeiliau hapgyrchu random access file
ffeil hapgyrchu *eb* ffeiliau hapgyrchu random file
ffeil i'w throsi *eb* ffeiliau i'w trosi file to convert
ffeil law *eb* ffeiliau llaw hand file
ffeil law fflat *eb* ffeiliau llaw fflat hand flat file
ffeil lefn *eb* ffeiliau llyfn smooth cut file
ffeil memo *eb* ffeiliau memo memo file
ffeil nodwydd *eb* ffeiliau nodwydd needle file
ffeil orfras *eb* ffeiliau gorfras middle cut file
ffeil orlefn *eb* ffeiliau gorlyfn dead smooth file
ffeil pdf *eb* ffeiliau pdf pdf file
ffeil rifflwr *eb* ffeiliau rifflwr riffler file
ffeil sain *eb* ffeiliau sain audio file
ffeil sgwâr *eb* ffeiliau sgwâr square file
ffeil tâp *eb* ffeiliau tâp tape file
ffeil testun *eb* ffeiliau testun text file
ffeil toriad dwbl *eb* ffeiliau toriad dwbl double-cut file
ffeil toriad sengl *eb* ffeiliau toriad sengl single-cut file
ffeil wardio *eb* ffeiliau wardio warding file
ffeil wedi'i llwytho i lawr *eb* ffeiliau wedi'u llwytho i lawr downloaded file
ffeil wrth gefn *eb* ffeiliau wrth gefn file backup
ffeilio *be* file
ffeirio *be* barter
ffeithiol *ans* non-fiction
ffeld *eg* veld
ffeld prysglwyni *eg* ffeldiau prysglwyni bushveld
ffelogen *eg* phellogen
ffelon *eg* ffeloniaid felon
ffelonaidd *ans* felonious
ffeloniaeth *eb* ffeloniaethau felony
ffelsbar *eg* feldspar
ffelsenmer *eg* felsenmeer
ffelspathig *ans* feldspathic
ffelt *eg* felt
ffelt lliw *eg* coloured felt
ffelt toi *eg* roofing felt
ffeltin *eg* felting
ffelwm *eg* whitlow
ffeminist *eg* ffeministiaid feminist
ffeministaidd *ans* feminist
ffeministiaeth *eb* feminism
ffen *eg* ffeniau fen; carr
ffendiroedd *ell* fenlands
ffenestr *eb* ffenestri window
ffenestr adeiniog *eb* ffenestri adeiniog casement window
ffenestr alfanedig *eb* ffenestri galfanedig galvanized window
ffenestr anweithredol *eb* ffenestri anweithredol inactive window
ffenestr ar golyn dalennog *eb* ffenestri ar golyn dalennog pivoted sash window
ffenestr argraffydd *eb* ffenestri argraffyddion printer window
ffenestr awyru *eb* ffenestri awyru vent window
ffenestr blwm *eb* ffenestri plwm leaded window
ffenestr cyfansoddwr newydd *eb* ffenestri cyfansoddwr newydd new composer window
ffenestr do *eb* ffenestri to dormer window; skylight
ffenestr dogfen *eb* ffenestri dogfen document window
ffenestr dryloyw *eb* ffenestri tryloyw transparency window
ffenestr ddalennog *eb* ffenestri dalennog sash window
ffenestr eilaidd *eb* ffenestri eilaidd secondary window
ffenestr fargod *eb* ffenestri bargod overhanging window
ffenestr fwa *eb* ffenestri bwa bow window
ffenestr Ffrengig *eb* ffenestri Ffrengig French window
ffenestr gilannog *eb* ffenestri cilannog recessed window
ffenestr grom *eb* ffenestri crwm bay window
ffenestr gron *eb* ffenestri crwn round window; fenstra rotunda
ffenestr gwydr dwbl *eb* ffenestri gwydr dwbl double-glazed window
ffenestr gwydr triphlyg *eb* ffenestri gwydr triphlyg triple-glazed window
ffenestr gyfredol *eb* ffenestri cyfredol current window
ffenestr hirgron *eb* ffenestri hirgrwn oval window; fenestra ovalis
ffenestr louvre *eb* ffenestri louvre louvre window
ffenestr lydan *eb* ffenestri llydan picture window
ffenestr mynegeion *eb* ffenestri mynegeion indexes window
ffenestr neges *eb* ffenestri negeseuon message window
ffenestr nesaf *eb* ffenestri nesaf next window
ffenestr ros *eb* ffenestri rhos rose window
ffenestr symudol *eb* ffenestri symudol moving window
ffenestr weithredol *eb* ffenestri gweithredol active window
ffenestr y rhaglen *eb* ffenestri'r rhaglen application window
ffenestru *be* windowing
Ffeniad *eg* Ffeniaid Fenian
ffenigl *eg* fennel
ffenol *eg* phenol
ffenoleg *eb* phenology
ffenolffthalein *eg* phenolphthalein
ffenolig *ans* phenolic
ffenoligion *ell* phenolics
ffenomen *eb* ffenomenau phenomenon
ffenomen blaen y tafod *eb* tip of the tongue phenomenon
ffenomen electrostatig *eb* ffenomenau electrostatig electrostatic phenomenon

ffenomen parti coctels *eb* cocktail-party phenomenon
ffenoteip *eg* ffenoteipiau phenotype
ffenoteipaidd *ans* phenotypic
ffens *eb* ffensys fence
ffens bleth *eb* ffensys pleth wattle fence
ffens bolion *eb* ffensys polion paling
ffens gymwysadwy *eb* ffensys cymwysadwy adjustable fence
ffens lif *eb* ffensys llif saw-fence
ffens lithr *eb* ffensys llithr sliding fence
ffens rwygo *eb* ffensys rhwygo ripping fence
ffensio *be* fence
ffensiwr *eg* ffenswyr fencer
ffenyl- (fel grŵp dirprwyol) phenyl-
ffenyl thiowrea *eg* phenyl thiourea
ffenylalanin *eg* phenylalanine
ffenylalanin hydrocsylas *eg* phenylalanine hydroxylase
ffenylamin *eg* phenylamine
ffenylamoniwm clorid *eg* phenylammonium chloride
ffenylcetonwrig *ans* phenylketonuric
ffenylethanon *eg* phenylethanone
ffenylethen *eg* phenylethene
ffenylhydrasin *eg* phenylhydrazine
ffenylmethanol *eg* phenylmethanol
(ffenylmethyl)amin *eg* (phenylmethyl)amine
ffeodai *eg* ffeodeion feoffee
ffeodariad *eg* ffeodariaid feodary
ffeodeion amfeddiad *ell* feoffees for impropriation
ffeodiad *eg* ffeodiadau feoffment
ffeodwr *eg* ffeodwyr feoffor
ffêr *eb* fferau ankle
Fferdinand *eg* Ferdinand
fferi *eb* fferïau ferry
fferm *eb* ffermydd farm
fferm gwasanaethwyr *eb* ffermydd gwasanaethwyr server farm
fferm gyfunol *eb* ffermydd cyfunol collective farm
fferm laeth *eb* ffermydd llaeth dairy farm
fferm y plas *eb* ffermydd plasau home farm
fferm y wladwriaeth *eb* ffermydd y wladwriaeth state farm
ffermio *be* farm
ffermio bugeiliol *be* pastoral farming
ffermio da byw *be* livestock farming
ffermio gorddwys *be* factory farming
ffermio gwndwn *be* ley farming
ffermio ymgynhaliol *be* subsistence farming
ffermiwm (Fm) *eg* fermium
ffermwr *eg* ffermwyr farmer
fferoconcrit *eg* ferro-concrete
fferomagnetedd *eg* ferromagnetism
fferomon *eg* fferomonau pheromone
fferrig *ans* ferric
fferrig clorid *eg* ferric chloride
fferrit *eg* ferrite
fferrus *ans* ferrous
fferyllfa *eb* fferyllfeydd pharmacy
fferyllol *ans* pharmaceutical
fferyllydd *eg* fferyllwyr chemist
fferyllydd *eg* fferyllwyr pharmacist
► **ffetish** *eg* ffetisiau fetish
ffetisiaeth *eb* fetishism
ffetisiaeth drawswisgo *eb* transvestic fetishism
ffetlo *be* fettle
ffetws *eg* ffetysau fetus
ffeuen *eb* ffa bean
ffi *eb* ffioedd fee
ffi amodol *eb* ffioedd amodol conditional fee
ffi batent *eb* ffioedd patent patent fee
ffi cadw *eb* ffioedd cadw reservation fee
ffi entael *eb* ffioedd entael entail fee
ffi gladdu *eb* ffioedd claddu mortuary fee
ffi marchog *eb* knight's fee
ffi rydd *eb* simple fee
ffi sir *eb* shire fee
ffiard *eg* ffiardau fjard
ffibr *eg* ffibrau fibre
ffibr anifail *eg* ffibrau anifail animal fibre
ffibr atgynyrchiedig *eg* ffibrau atgynyrchiedig regenerated fibre
ffibr coed *eg* ffibrau coed wood fibre
ffibr crai *eg* ffibrau crai raw fibre
ffibr cyhyrau *eg* muscle fibre
ffibr cymysg *eg* blended fibre
► **ffibr deietegol** *eg* dietary fibre
ffibr di-dor *eg* ffibrau di-dor continuous fibre
ffibr elastig *eg* ffibrau elastig elastic fibre
ffibr gwneud *eg* ffibrau gwneud man-made fibre
ffibr llin *eg* ffibrau llin flax fibre
ffibr llysiau *eg* ffibrau llysiau vegetable fibre
ffibr naturiol *eg* ffibrau naturiol natural fibre
ffibr optegol *eg* ffibrau optegol optical fibre
ffibr synthetig *eg* ffibrau synthetig synthetic fibre
ffibr synthetig *eg* man-made fibre
ffibr wedi'i atgyfnerthu â gwydr *eg* glass-reinforced fibre
ffibriliad *eg* ffibriliadau fibrillation
ffibrin *eg* fibrin
ffibrinogen *eg* fibrinogen
ffibroblast *eg* fibroblast
ffibrocyt *eg* ffibrocytau fibrocyte
ffibrog *ans* fibrous
ffibrolyn *eg* ffibrolion fibril
ffibrosis y bledren *eg* cystic fibrosis
ffibrwydr mat *eg* matt fibreglass
ffibwla *eg* ffibwlâu fibula
ffidil *eb* ffidlau fiddle
ffidlwr *eg* ffidlwyr fiddler
ffieiddiwr *eg* ffieiddwyr abhorrer
ffiff *eg* ffiffiau fief
ffiff etifeddol *eb* ffiffiau etifeddol hereditary fief

ffigur (mewn dawns) *eg/b* ffigurau pattern
ffigur (yn gyffredinol) *eg/b* ffigurau figure
ffigur academi *eg* ffigurau academi academy figure
ffigur cyflun *eg* ffigurau cyflun similar figure
ffigur cymalog *eg* ffigurau cymalog jointed figure
ffigur dawns *eg* ffigurau dawns dance figure
ffigur dynol *eg* ffigurau dynol human figure
ffigur ffantasi *eg* ffigurau ffantasi fantasy figure
ffigur gosod *eg* ffigurau gosod lay figure
ffigur i'w gario *eg* ffigurau i'w cario carrying figure
ffigur noeth *eg* ffigurau noeth naked figure
ffigur papur *eg* ffigurau papur paper figure
ffigur plân *eg* ffigurau plân plane figure
ffigur plastig *eg* ffigurau plastig plastic figure
ffigur plastr *eg* ffigurau plastr plaster figure
ffigur solet *eg* ffigurau solet solid figure
ffigur tywyll *eg* ffigurau tywyll dark figure
ffigur unionlin *eg* ffigurau unionlin rectilinear figure
ffigur wyth *eg* ffigurau wyth figure eight
ffigur ystyrlon *eg* ffigurau ystyrlon significant figure
ffigurau gwerthu *ell* sales figures
ffigur-grwnd *eg* figure-ground
ffigurol *ans* figurative
ffiguryn *eg* ffigurynnau figurine
ffigwr costau sefydlog *eg* fixed costs figure
ffigwr elw net *eg* net profit figure
ffigysen *eb* ffigys fig
ffilament *eg* ffilamentau filament
ffilament tagell *eg* ffilamentau tagell gill filament
ffilamentog *ans* filamentous
ffildiwr *eg* ffildwyr outfielder
ffildiwr chwith *eg* ffildwyr chwith left outfielder
ffiled *eb* ffiledau fillet
ffiled pren caled *eb* ffiledau pren caled hardwood fillet
ffiled wynebu *eb* ffiledau wynebu facing fillet
ffiledu *be* fillet
ffiligri *eg* filigree
ffilm *eb* ffilmiau film
ffilm arbrofol *eb* ffilmiau arbrofol experimental film
ffilm brif ffrwd *eb* ffilmiau prif ffrwd mainstream film
ffilm ffocws *eb* ffilmiau ffocws focus film
ffilm naratif *eb* ffilmiau naratif narrative film
ffilm warchod *eb* ffilmiau gwarchod protective film
ffilmio byw *be* live action
ffin *eb* ffiniau boundary; frontier; borderline
ffin eithaf posibilrwydd cynhyrchu *eb* production possibility frontier
ffin flaen *eb* ffiniau blaen front wall out of court line
ffin gefn *eb* ffiniau cefn back wall out of court line
ffin hyder *eb* ffiniau hyder confidence limit
ffin hydoddydd *eb* ffiniau hydoddyddion solvent front
ffin ochr *eb* ffiniau ochr side wall out of court line
ffin testun *eb* ffiniau testun text boundary
ffin tudalen *eb* ffiniau tudalen page boundary
ffinedig *ans* bounded
ffin-ganllaw *eg* ffin-ganllawiau edge guide
ffinio â *be* abut
ffiniol *ans* borderline
ffinrewlifol *ans* periglacial
ffïoedd dysgu *ell* tuition fees
ffiol (=potel fach wydr i ddal ffisig etc) *eb* ffiolau phial
ffiol (yn gyffredinol) *eb* ffiolau vase
ffiol ffrwythau *eb* ffiolau ffrwythau fruit bowl
ffiord *eg* ffiordau fiord
ffirn *eg* ffirniau firn
ffiseg *eb* physics
ffiseg feddygol *eb* medical physics
ffisegol *ans* physical
ffisioleg *eb* physiology
ffisiolegol *ans* physiological
ffisiolegydd *eg* ffisiolegwyr physiologist
ffisionomeg *eb* physiognomics
ffisiotherapi *eg* physiotherapy
ffisiotherapydd *eg* ffisiotherapyddion physiotherapist
ffit *ans* fit
ffit *eb* ffitiau fit
ffit anwythol *eb* induced fit
ffit dynn *eb* tight fit
ffit lac *eb* slack fit
ffit lac *eb* ffitiau llac loose fit
ffit lithr *eb* ffitiau llithr sliding fit
ffit orau *eb* best fit
ffit orwasg *eb* ffitiau gorwasg force fit
ffit orwasg *eb* ffitiau gorwasg driving fit
ffit redegog *eb* ffitiau rhedegog running fit
ffit ymyrryd *eb* ffitiau ymyrryd interference fit
ffitiad Tonk *eg* Tonk's fitting
ffitiadau cabinet *ell* cabinet fittings
ffitiadau datgysylltiol *ell* knockdown fittings
ffitiadau goleuo *ell* light fittings
ffitiau a therfynau fits and limits
ffitio *be* fit
ffitio poeth *be* shrink fit
ffitiwr *eg* ffitwyr fitter
ffitrwydd (corfforol) *eg* fitness
ffitrwydd corfforol *eg* physical fitness
ffitrwydd cynhwysol *eg* inclusive fitness
ffiwdal *ans* feudal
ffiwdaleiddio *be* feudalize
ffiwdaliaeth *eb* feudalism
ffiwg *eb* ffiwgiau fugue
ffiwg â chyfeiliant *eb* ffiwgiau â chyfeiliant accompanied fugue
ffiwg driphlyg *eb* ffiwgiau triphlyg triple fugue
ffiwg ddrych *eb* ffiwgiau drych mirror fugue
ffiwg ddwbl *eb* ffiwgiau dwbl double fugue
ffiwg seicogenig *eb* psychogenic fugue
ffiwg wir *eb* ffiwgiau gwir real fugue
ffiwgaidd *ans* fugal
ffiwgato fugato

ffiwgeta *eb* ffiwgetau fughetta
ffiws *eg* ffiwsiau fuse
ffiws trydan *eg* ffiwsys trydan electric fuse
ffiwsio *be* fuse
fflach *eb* fflachiau flash
fflachbwynt *eg* fflachbwyntiau flash point
fflachedig *ans* flashed
fflachennu *be* scintillate
fflachiad *eg* fflachiadau flashover
fflachlif *eg* fflachlifau flash flood
fflafonoid *eg* fflafonoidau flavonoid
fflagelwm *eg* fflagela flagellum
fflangell *eb* fflangellau cat-o'-nine-tails
fflam *eg* fflamau flame
fflamadwy *ans* flammable; inflammable
fflamadwyedd *eg* flammability
fflamdorrwr *eg* fflamdorwyr flame cutter
fflamio *be* flame
fflan *eb* fflaniau flan
fflaneléd *eg* flannelette
fflans *eg/b* fflansiau flange
fflans eliptigol *eb* fflansiau eliptigol elliptical flange
fflans gyplydd *eb* fflansiau cyplydd coupling flange
fflansio *be* flange
fflap *eg* fflapiau flap
fflapjacs *ell* flapjacks
fflasg *eb* fflasgiau flask
fflasg fongron *eb* fflasgiau bongrwn round bottomed flask
fflasg fowldio *eb* fflasgiau mowldio moulding flask
fflasg fyrdew *eb* fflasgiau byrdew squat flask
fflasg gonigol *eb* fflasgiau conigol conical flask
fflasg raddedig *eb* fflasgiau graddedig graduated flask
fflasg safonol *eb* fflasgiau safonol volumetric flask
fflasg wactod *eb* fflasgiau gwactod vacuum flask
fflat *ans* flat
fflat (=lle i fyw) *eb* fflatiau apartment
fflat (=tir isel) *eg* fflatiau flat
fflat llanw *eg* fflatiau llanw tidal flat
fflat un ystafell *eg* fflatiau un ystafell bedsitter
fflatiau llaid *ell* mud flats
fflatio *be* flatting
fflatiwr *eg* fflatwyr flatter
fflatws *eg* flatus
fflaw *eg* fflawiau flake
fflaw mica *eg* fflawiau mica mica flake
fflawiog *ans* flaked
fflecnod *eg* fflecnodau flecnode
fflecs drydan *eb* fflecsys trydan electric flex
fflem *eg* phlegm
fflêr *eb* fflerau flare
fflerio *be* flare
fflewyn *eg* fflawiau splinter
fflic *eg* ffliciau flick
fflic-fflac *eg* flick-flack
fflicio *be* flick
ffliw *eb* ffliwiau flue
ffliw *eg* influenza
ffliw gytbwys *eb* ffliwiau cytbwys balanced flue
ffliwt *eb* ffliwtiau flute
ffliwt alto *eb* ffliwtiau alto alto flute
ffliwt draws *eb* ffliwtiau traws transverse flute
ffliwt fas *eb* ffliwtiau bas bass flute
ffliwt glir *eb* ffliwtiau clir clear flute
ffliwt heligol *eb* ffliwtiau heligol helical flute
ffliwt reiddiol *eb* ffliwtiau rheiddiol radial flute
ffliwt sbiral *eb* ffliwtiau sbiral spiral flute
ffliwtydd *eg* ffliwtwyr flute player
ffliwtydd *eg* ffliwtwyr flautist
ffloch iâ *eg* fflochiau iâ ice floe
ffloch rhew *eg* fflochiau rhew ice floe
fflochion sebon *ell* soap flakes
ffloem *eb* phloem
fflora *ell* flora
fflorigen *eg* florigen
fflôt *eg* fflotiau float
fflowns *eb* fflownsiau flounce
fflowns osod *eb* fflownsiau gosod applied flounce
fflurben *eg* fflurbennau flower head
fflurben *eg* fflurbennau capitate flower
fflurgainc *eb* fflurgeinciau inflorescence
fflurgainc gyfansawdd *eb* fflurgeinciau cyfansawdd compound inflorescence
fflurol *ans* floral
fflurwain *eb* fflurweiniau spathe
fflwcs *eg* fflycsau flux
fflwcs goddefol *cg* fflycsau goddefol passive flux
fflwcs gweithredol *eg* fflycsau gweithredol active flux
fflwcs magnetig *eg* magnetic flux
fflwcs past *eg* fflycsau past paste flux
fflwcsocarbon *eg* fluxocarbon
fflwff *eg* fluff
fflwffio *be* fluffing
fflworeiddiad *eg* fluoridation
fflworesin *eg* fluorescein
fflworesydd *eg* fflworesyddion fluorescer
fflworid *eg* fluoride
fflworimedr *eg* fflworimedrau fluorimeter
fflworin (F) *eg* fluorine
fflworoblastigion *ell* fluoroplastics
fflworosis *eg* fluorosis
fflwrolau *eg* fflwroleuadau fluorescent lighting
fflwroleuedd *eg* fluorescence
fflwroleuo *be* fluoresce
fflwroleuol *ans* fluorescent
fflycsiwn *eg* fflycsiynau fluxion
ffoadur (rhag rhyfel etc) *eg* ffoaduriaid refugee
ffoadur (rhag y gyfraith etc) *eg* ffoaduriaid fugitive
ffobia *eg* phobia
ffobia cymdeithasol *eg* social phobia
ffobia penodol *eg* specific phobia
ffocal *ans* focal

ffocstrot *eg* dawnsiau ffocstrot foxtrot
ffocws *eg* ffocysau focus
ffocws arf *eg* weapon focus
ffocysau cinetig *ell* kinetic foci
ffocysu *be* focus
ffoetws *eg* ffoetysau foetus
ffofea *eg* fovea
ffogara *eg* ffogarau foggara
ffoil *eg* ffoiliau foil
ffoil alwminiwm *eg* aluminium foil
ffoil arian *eg* silver foil
ffoil metel *eg* metal foil
ffoil offeru aur *eg* gold tooling foil
ffoil plastig *eg* plastic foil
► **ffolder** *eb* ffolderi folder
ffolder adnoddau *eb* resource folder
ffolder cyrchfan *eb* ffolderi cyrchfan destination folder
ffolder eitemau wedi'u dileu *eb* ffolderi eitemau wedi'u dileu deleted items folder
ffolder newydd *eb* ffolderi newydd new folder
ffolen *eb* ffolennau buttock
ffoligl *eg* ffoliglau follicle
ffoligl blewyn *eg* ffoliglau blew hair follicle
ffoligl Graaf *eg* ffoliglau Graaf Graafian follicle
ffoliglaidd *ans* follicular
ffolio *eg* ffolios folio
ffolio dylunio *eg* ffolios dylunio design folio
ffoliwm *eg* ffolia folium
ffon (ar gyfer cerdded) *eb* ffyn walking stick
ffon (yn gyffredinol) *eb* ffyn stick
ffôn *eg* ffonau telephone
ffon argraffu â phren *eb* ffyn argraffu â phren printing stick
ffon barthu *eb* ffyn parthu shed stick
ffôn clust *eg* ffonau clust earphone
ffon dafl *eb* ffyn tafl sling
ffon gotwm *eb* ffyn cotwm cottonbud
ffon lliw *eb* ffyn lliw colour stick
ffon peintiwr *eb* ffyn peintwyr rest-stick
ffon peintiwr *eb* ffyn peintwyr mahlstick
ffôn pen *eg* ffonau pen headphone
ffon reoli *eb* ffyn rheoli joystick
ffon rwbio *eb* ffyn rhwbio rubbing stick
ffôn symudol *eg* ffonau symudol mobile phone
ffôn testun *eg* ffonau testun textphone
ffon wasgu *eb* ffyn gwasgu back stick
ffon wrthdro *eb* ffyn gwrthdro reverse stick
ffon wthio *eb* ffyn gwthio push stick
ffon ysgol *eb* ffyn ysgol ladder rung
ffon ysgol *eb* ffyn ysgol rung
ffon ystofi *eb* ffyn ystofi warp stick
ffondant *eg* fondant
ffonem *eg/b* ffonemau phoneme
ffonemeg *eb* phonemics
ffonig *ans* phonic
ffonocardiogram *eg* phonocardiogram
ffonoleg *eb* phonology
ffont *eg* ffontiau font
ffont cyfredol *eg* ffontiau cyfredol current font
ffont newidiol ei led *eg* ffontiau newidiol eu lled variable-width font
ffont nodau *eg* ffontiau nodau character font
ffont rhagosodedig *eg* ffontiau rhagosodedig default font
ffont seriff *eg* serif font
ffont tudalen gwe *eg* ffontiau tudalen gwe web page font
ffont y teitl *eg* ffontiau'r teitl title font
ffontanél *eg* ffontanelau fontanelle
ffont-deip *eb* ffontdeipiau typefont
fforamen *eg* fforamina foramen
fforamen Munro *eg* Munro's foramen
fforc *eb* ffyrc fork
fforch *eb* ffyrch fork; prong
fforch danio *eb* ffyrch tanio firing fork
fforch ddeubig *eb* ffyrch deubig two-pronged fork
fforchog *ans* forked
ffordd *eb* ffyrdd road
ffordd a ddefnyddir yn llwybr cyhoeddus *eb* road used as public path
ffordd brifwythiennol *eb* ffyrdd prifwythiennol arterial road
ffordd ddeuol *eb* ffyrdd deuol dual carriageway
ffordd eilaidd *eb* ffyrdd eilaidd secondary road
ffordd fawr pedair lôn *eb* ffyrdd mawr pedair lôn four lane highway
ffordd fynediad *eb* ffyrdd mynediad access road
ffordd gerbydau *eb* ffyrdd cerbydau carriageway
ffordd gludiant *eb* ffyrdd cludiant transport route
ffordd gul gyda lleoedd pasio *eb* narrow road with passing places
ffordd gyflym *eb* ffyrdd cyflym expressway
ffordd hynod o hardd *eb* ffyrdd hynod o hardd scenic route
ffordd iach o fyw *eb* ffyrdd iach o fyw healthy lifestyle
ffordd liniaru *eb* ffyrdd lliniaru relief road
► **ffordd o fyw** *eb* ffyrdd o fyw lifestyle
ffordd o fyw eisteddog *eb* sedentary lifestyle
ffordd o wella *eb* ffyrdd o wella means of improvement
ffordd osgoi aneddiadau *eb* ffyrdd osgoi aneddiadau bypass around a settlement
ffordd wasanaeth *eb* ffyrdd gwasanaeth service road
Ffordd y Groes *eb* Stations of the Cross
fforest betraidd *eb* fforestydd petraidd petrified forest
fforestbriddoedd *ell* forest soils
fforffediad *eg* fforffediadau forfeiture
fforiad *eg* fforiadau exploration
fforio *be* explore
fforio Ewropeaidd *be* European exploration
fforiwr *eg* fforwyr explorer

fformaldehyd *eg* formaldehyde
fformant *eg* fformantau formant
fformat *eg* fformatau format
fformat amser *eg* fformatau amser time format
fformat analog *eg* fformatau analog analogue format
fformat APA *eg* APA format
fformat argraffu *eg* print format
fformat cerdyn *eg* fformatau cerdyn card format
fformat cofnod *eg* record format
fformat cyfarwyddyd *eg* fformatau cyfarwyddyd instruction format
fformat data *eg* fformatau data data format
fformat disg *eg* fformatau disg disk format
fformat dyddiad *eg* fformatau dyddiad date format
fformat ffeil anhysbys *eg* fformatau ffeil anhysbys unknown file format
fformat graffig anhysbys *eg* fformatau graffig anhysbys unknown graphic format
fformat gwerth dimensiwn *eg* fformatau gwerth dimensiwn dimension value format
fformat lliw *eg* fformatau lliw colour format
fformat paragraff *eg* paragraph format
fformat sŵ *eg* zoo format
fformat testun *eg* fformatau testun text format
fformatio *be* format
fformatydd *eg* fformatyddion formatter
fformica *eg* formica
fformiwla *eb* fformiwlâu formula
fformiwla adeileddol *eb* structural formula
fformiwla dyrannu adnoddau *eb* resource allocation formula
fformiwla empirig *eb* fformiwlâu empirig empirical formula
fformiwla foleciwlaidd *eb* fformiwlâu moleciwlaidd molecular formula
fformiwla fflurol *eb* fformiwlâu fflurol floral formula
fformiwla graffig *eb* fformiwlâu graffig displayed formula
fformiwla Newton-Raphson *eb* Newton-Raphson formula
fformiwla stereocemegol *eb* stereochemical formula
fformiwla symlaf *eb* fformiwlâu symlaf simplest formula
fformiwla tabl anghywir *eb* fformiwlâu tabl anghywir wrong table formula
fformiwla tabl nesaf *eb* fformiwlâu tabl nesaf next table formula
fformiwla testun *eb* fformiwlâu testun text formula
fformiwlari *eg* formulary
fforwm *eg* fforymau forum
ffos (o amgylch castell) *eb* ffosydd moat
ffos (yn gyffredinol) *eb* ffosydd trench
ffos (i gario dŵr) *eb* ffosydd dyke
ffos ddyfrhau *eb* ffosydd dyfrhau irrigation ditch
ffosffad *eg* ffosffadau phosphate
ffosffin *eg* phosphine
ffosffocinas *eg* phosphokinase
ffosffocreatin *eg* phosphocreatine
ffosffoglyseraldehyd *eg* phosphoglyceraldehyde
ffosffolipid *eg* phospholipid
ffosffor *eg* ffosfforau phosphor
ffosfforefydd *eg* phosphor bronze
ffosfforesgedd *eg* phosphorescence
ffosfforesgol *ans* phosphorescent
ffosfforws (P) *eg* phosphorus
ffosfforws pentahalid *eg* ffosfforws pentahalidau phosphorus pentahalide
ffosfforws triclorid *eg* phosphorus trichloride
ffosfforws triclorid ocsid *eg* phosphorus trichloride oxide
ffosfforws trihalid *eg* ffosfforws trihalidau phosphorus trihalide
ffosfforws(V) clorid *eg* phosphorus(V) chloride
ffosfforws(III) ocsid *eg* phosphorus(III) oxide
ffosfforws(V) ocsid *eg* phosphorus(V) oxide
ffosfforylas *eg* phosphorylase
ffosfforyleiddiad ocsidiol *eg* oxidative phosphorylation
ffosil *eg* ffosiliau fossil
ffosilaidd *ans* fossil
ffosileiddiad *eg* fossilation
ffosileiddio *be* fossilize
ffosilifferaidd *ans* fossiliferous
ffoto-allyriant *eg* ffoto-allyriannau photo-emission
ffotocemeg *eb* photochemistry
ffotodeuod *eg* photodiode
ffotodrydan *eg* photoelectricity
ffotodrydanol *ans* photoelectric
ffotofoltaidd *ans* photovoltaic
ffotoffosfforyleiddiad anghylchol *eg* non-cyclic photophosphorylation
ffotogell *eb* ffotogelloedd photocell
ffotograff *eg* ffotograffau photograph
ffotograff arosgo *eg* ffotograffau arosgo oblique photograph
ffotograff fertigol *eg* ffotograffau fertigol vertical photograph
ffotograff lefel y tir *eg* ffotograffau lefel y tir ground photograph
ffotograffiaeth *eb* photography
ffotograffiaeth feddygol *eb* medical photography
ffotograffig *ans* photographic
ffotogrametreg *eb* photogrammetry
ffotogyfnodedd *eg* photoperiodism
ffotomedr *eg* ffotomedrau photometer
ffotometreg *eb* photometry
ffotometrig *ans* photometric
ffoton *eg* ffotonau photon
ffotopigment *eg* photopigment
ffotosffer *eg* ffotosfferau photosphere
ffotostat *eg* ffotostatau photostat
ffotostori *eb* ffotostorïau photo story
ffotosynthesis *eg* photosynthesis
ffotosynthetig *ans* photosynthetic
ffototransistor *eg* phototransistor

ffototropedd *eg* phototropism
ffoto-ysgythru *be* photogravure
ffowl personol *eg* personal foul
ffowlio *be* fouling
ffowndri *eb* ffowndrïau foundry
ffracsiwn *eg* ffracsiynau fraction
ffracsiwn bondrwm *eg* ffracsiynau bondrwm proper fraction
ffracsiwn cyffredin *eg* ffracsiynau cyffredin common fraction
ffracsiwn cyffredin *eg* ffracsiynau cyffredin vulgar fraction
ffracsiwn cynrychiadol *eg* ffracsiynau cynrychiadol representative fraction
ffracsiwn cynrychioliadol *eg* ffracsiynau cynrychioladol representation fraction
ffracsiwn degol *eg* ffracsiynau degol decimal fraction
ffracsiwn pendrwm *eg* ffracsiynau pendrwm improper fraction
ffracsiwn syml *eg* ffracsiynau syml simple fraction
ffracsiynau cywerth *ell* equivalent fractions
ffracsiynau o dro cyflawn *ell* fractions of a complete turn
ffracsiynau rhannol *ell* partial fractions
ffracsiynol *ans* fractional
ffractal *eg* ffractalau fractal
Ffrangeg Normanaidd *eb* Norman-French
ffrâm *eb* fframiau frame
ffrâm Abra *eb* fframiau Abra Abra frame
ffrâm amser *eb* fframiau amser time frame
ffrâm blyg *eb* fframiau plyg bent frame
ffrâm bocs *eg* fframiau bocs box frame
ffrâm bren *eb* fframiau pren wooden frame
ffrâm bwytho *eb* fframiau pwytho stitching frame
ffrâm ddannedd *eb* fframiau dannedd brace; dental brace
ffrâm ddarlun *eb* fframiau darluniau picture frame
ffrâm ddeintur *eb* fframiau deintur tenter frame
ffrâm ddringo *eb* fframiau dringo climbing frame
ffrâm ddrws *eb* fframiau drws door frame
ffrâm ddŵr *eb* fframiau dŵr water frame
ffrâm falŵn *eb* fframiau balŵn balloon framing
ffrâm fasged *eb* fframiau basged basket frame
ffrâm frodio *eb* fframiau brodio embroidery frame
ffrâm frodio gron *eb* fframiau brodio crwn tambour frame
ffrâm gerdded *eb* fframiau cerdded walker
ffrâm gwiltio *eb* fframiau cwiltio quilting frame
ffrâm gyfeirio *eb* fframiau cyfeirio frame of reference
ffrâm gyfeirio inertiaidd *eb* inertial frame of reference
ffrâm gymwysadwy *eb* fframiau cymwysadwy adjustable frame
ffrâm haclif *eb* fframiau haclif hacksaw frame
ffrâm holi *eb* fframiau holi enquiry frame
ffrâm isaf *eb* fframiau isaf underframe
ffrâm lif *eb* fframiau llif saw-frame
ffrâm rigolog *eb* fframiau rhigolog grooved frame
ffrâm sgrin *eb* fframiau sgrin screen frame
ffrâm siasi *eb* fframiau siasi chassis frame
ffrâm testun *eb* fframiau testun text frame
ffrâm testun nesaf *eb* fframiau testun nesaf next text frame
ffrâm waelod *eb* fframiau gwaelod bottom frame
ffrâm wifren *eb* fframiau gwifren wire frame
ffrâm wnïo *eb* fframiau gwnïo sewing frame
ffrâm ystofi *eb* fframiau ystofi warping frame
fframgipiwr *eg* fframgipwyr frame grabber
fframio *be* frame
fframset newydd *eb* fframsetiau newydd new frameset
fframwaith *eg* fframweithiau framework; structure
fframwaith CGC *eg* NVQ framework
fframwaith coed *eg* fframweithiau coed timber framing
fframwaith cysyniadol *eg* fframweithiau cysyniadol conceptual framework
fframwaith dosbarth *eg* class structure
fframwaith dur *eg* fframweithiau dur steel framing
fframwaith dylunio *eg* design framework
fframwaith gofal *eg* framework of care
fframwaith lleoliadol *eg* locational framework
fframwaith polisi *eg* policy framework
fframwaith rheoli hierarchaidd *eg* hierarchical organisational structure
fframwaith uniad-pìn *eg* fframweithiau uniad-pin pin-jointed framework
Ffrancaidd *ans* Frankish
Ffranciaid *ell* Franks
ffranciwm (Fr) *eg* francium
Ffrancwyr Rhydd *ell* Free French
Ffransis *eg* Francis
Ffransisgaidd *ans* Franciscan
Ffransisiad *eg* Ffransisiaid Franciscan
ffrasil *eg* ffrasilau frazil
Ffredric *eg* Frederick
Ffredric Fawr *eg* Frederick the Great
Ffrengig Normanaidd *ans* Norman-French
ffrenig *ans* phrenic
ffres *ans* fresh
ffresgo *eg* ffresgoau fresco
ffreutur (mewn mynachlog) *eg* ffreuturiau frater
ffreutur (yn gyffredinol) *eg* ffreuturau canteen; refectory
ffridd *eb* ffriddoedd intake
ffrigad *eb* ffrigadau frigate
ffrilen *eb* ffriliau frill
ffrio *be* fry
ffrio bas *be* shallow frying
ffrio dwfn *be* deep fat frying
ffrio sych *be* dry frying
ffris *eg* ffrisiau frieze
ffrislio *be* frizzling
ffrit *eg* ffritiau frit

ffriter *eg* ffriterau fritter
ffrithiant *eg* ffrithiannau friction
ffrithiant llithro *eg* sliding friction
ffrithiant peiriant *eg* ffrithiannau peiriant engine friction
ffrithiant-gydadferedig *eg* friction-compensated
ffroen *eb* ffroenau nostril
ffroenell *eb* ffroenellau nozzle
ffrog *eb* ffrogiau dress; frock
ffrog biner *eb* ffrogiau piner pinafore dress
ffrog diwnig *eb* ffrogiau tiwnig overdress
ffrog fin nos *eb* ffrogiau fin nos evening dress
ffrond *eg* ffrondau frond
ffrotais (=rhwbiad) *eg* ffroteisiau rubbing; frottage
ffrotais gwead *eg* ffroteisiau gwead texture rubbing
ffroteisio *be* frottage
ffroteriaeth *eb* frotterism
ffrwctos *eg* fructose
ffrwd *eb* ffrydiau stream
ffrwd adlif *eb* ffrydiau adlif resequent stream
ffrwd bengoll *eb* ffrydiau pengoll beheaded stream
ffrwd danrewlifol *eb* ffrydiau tanrewlifol subglacial stream
ffrwd drawslif *eb* ffrydiau trawslif subsequent stream
ffrwd ddi-dor *eb* ffrydiau di-dor continuous stream
ffrwd gradd un *eb* ffrydiau gradd un first order stream
ffrwd gydlif *eb* ffrydiau cydlif consequent stream
ffrwd haplif *eb* ffrydiau haplif insequent stream
ffrwd melin *eb* ffrydiau melinau mill race
ffrwd wrthlif *eb* ffrydiau gwrthlif obsequent stream
ffrwd ysbeidiol *eb* ffrydiau ysbeidiol intermittent stream; occasional stream
ffrwstwm *eg* ffrwstymau frustum
ffrwstwm côn *eg* frustum of cone
ffrwstwm pyramid *eg* frustum of pyramid
ffrwydrad *eg* ffrwydradau explosion; blast
ffrwydrad poblogaeth *eg* population explosion
ffrwydriad *eg* ffrwydriaid burster
ffrwydro *be* explode
ffrwydrol (mewn seineg) *ans* plosive
ffrwydrol (yn gyffredinol) *ans* explosive
ffrwydryn *eg* ffrwydron explosive; mine
ffrwydryn tanddwr *eg* ffrwydrynnau tanddwr depth charge
ffrwyn *eb* ffrwynau bridle
ffrwyno *be* bridle
ffrwyth *eg* ffrwythau fruit
ffrwyth carreg *eg* ffrwythau cerrig stone fruit
ffrwyth citrws *eg* ffrwythau citrws citrus fruit
ffrwythau a llysiau fruit and vegetables
ffrwythau grisialog *ell* crystallized fruit
ffrwythau sych *ell* dried fruits
ffrwythau sych cymysg *eg* mixed dried fruits
ffrwythgorff *eg* ffrwythgyrff fruiting body
ffrwythlon *ans* fertile
ffrwythlondeb *eg* fertility
ffrwythlondeb pridd *eg* soil fertility
ffrwythlonedig *ans* fertilised
ffrwythlonedd *eg* fecundity
ffrwythloni *be* impregnate
ffrwythloni *be* fertilize
ffrwythloni in vitro *be* in vitro fertilization
ffrwythloniad *eg* impregnation
ffrwythloniad *eg* fertilization
ffrwythus *ans* fruity
ffrwythyn *eg* ffrwythynnau fruit
ffrwythyn suddlon unhadog *eg* ffrwythynnau suddlon unhadog single seeded succulent fruit
ffrydio *be* stream; streaming; gush out
ffrydio fideo *be* video streaming
ffrydlif *eg* streamflow
ffrynt *eg* ffryntiau front
ffrynt achludol *eg* ffryntiau achludol occluded front
ffrynt cartref *eg* home front
ffrynt cynnes *eg* ffryntiau cynnes warm front
ffrynt ffug (drôr) *eg* ffryntiau ffug false front
ffrynt ffurfiedig *eg* ffryntiau ffurfiedig shaped front
ffrynt iâ *eg* ffryntiau iâ ice front
ffrynt oer *eg* ffryntiau oer cold front
ffrynt pegynol *eg* ffryntiau pegynol polar front
ffrynt rhew *eg* ffryntiau rhew ice front
ffrynt rhyngdrofannol *eg* intertropical front
ffrynt tabwrdd *eg* ffryntiau tabwrdd tambour front
ffrynt y bobl *eg* popular front
ffryntdarddiad *eg* frontogenesis
ffryntwasgarlad *eg* frontolysis
ffug *ans* artificial; fake; false; simulated
ffug arbrawf *eg* ffug arbrofion simulated experiment
ffug arholiad *eg* ffug arholiadau mock examination
ffug ffiwdaliaeth *eb* bastard feudalism
ffug ffrwythyn *eg* ffug ffrwythau false fruit
ffug haenau *ell* false bedding
ffug ymosod *be* false attack
ffugair *eg* ffugeiriau nonword/pseudoword
ffug-bàs *eg/b* ffugbasiau dummy
ffugbasio *be* make a dummy pass
ffugddelwedd o allgrwp homogenaidd *eb* illusion of out-group homogeneity
ffug-god *eg* ffug-godau pseudo-code
ffug-gyfarwyddyd *eg* ffug-gyfarwyddiadau pseudo-instruction
ffug-hap *eg* pseudo-random
ffughomoffon *eg* ffughomoffonau pseudohomophone
ffugiad *eg* ffugiadau forgery
ffugiad (=ffug-bas) *eg* ffugiadau dummy
ffugio (mewn bocsio etc) *be* feint
ffugio (yn gyffredinol) *be* fake
ffugio (=ffug-basio) *be* dummy
ffuglen wyddonol *eb* science fiction
ffugwaith *eg* ffugweithiau fake
ffugweinydd *eg* ffugweinyddion pseudo-server

ffugweithrediad *eg* ffugweithrediadau pseudo-operation
ffurf *eb* ffurfiau form
ffurf a chynnwys form and content
ffurf amrywiol *eb* ffurfiau amrywiol variable form
ffurf anifeiliaid *eb* animal form
ffurf ar gêm *eb* ffurfiau ar gemau game form
ffurf baralel *eb* ffurfiau paralel parallel form
ffurf beiriannol *eb* ffurfiau peiriannol mechanical form
ffurf bloc *eb* ffurfiau bloc block form
ffurf bowdr *eb* powder form
ffurf bwa *eb* ffurfiau bwa arch form
ffurf dawns *eb* ffurfiau dawns dance form
ffurf driog *eb* syrup form
ffurf ddeuaidd *eb* ffurfiau deuaidd binary form
ffurf ddigidol *eb* ffurfiau digidol digital form
ffurf ddramatig *eb* dramatic form
ffurf ddwyran gyfansawdd *eb* ffurfiau dwyran cyfansawdd compound binary form
ffurf ddynol *eb* ffurfiau dynol human form
ffurf echelon *eb* ffurfiau echelon echelon form
ffurf electronig *eb* ffurfiau electronig electronic form
ffurf ffilm *eb* film form
ffurf ffiwg *eb* ffurfiau ffiwg fugue form
ffurf ganonaidd *eb* ffurfiau canonaidd canonical form
ffurf gelf *eb* ffurfiau celf art form
ffurf Geltaidd *eb* ffurfiau Celtaidd Celtic form
ffurf gerfluniol *eb* ffurfiau cerfluniol sculptural form
ffurf graffigol *eb* ffurfiau graffigol graphical form
ffurf gydnabyddedig *eb* ffurfiau cydnabyddedig recognized form
ffurf gymhleth *eb* ffurfiau cymhleth intricate shape
ffurf gytbwys *eb* ffurfiau cytbwys balanced shape
ffurf hirgron *eb* ffurfiau hirgrwn oval shape
ffurf hylifol *eb* ffurfiau hylifol liquid form
ffurf naturiol *eb* ffurfiau naturiol natural form
ffurf oedolyn *eb* ffurfiau oedolyn adult stage
ffurf rondo *eb* rondo form
ffurf safonol *eb* ffurfiau safonol standard form
ffurf sonata *eb* sonata form
ffurf sylfaenol *eb* ffurfiau sylfaenol basic form
ffurf sylfaenol *eb* ffurfiau sylfaenol fundamental shape
ffurf syml *eb* ffurfiau syml simple form
ffurf symlaf *eb* ffurfiau symlaf simplest form; lowest terms
ffurf symudiad cyntaf *eb* first movement form
ffurf tyfiant *eb* ffurfiau tyfiant growth formation
ffurf V *eb* V-shape
ffurf wneud *eb* ffurfiau gwneud made form
ffurf wreiddiol *eb* ffurfiau gwreiddiol original shape
ffurfdeip *eg* ffurfdeipiau typeface
► **ffurfdro** *eg* ffurfdroadau inflection
ffurfiad *eg* ffurfiadau structure
ffurfiad grisialog *eg* ffurfiadau grisialog crystalline structure
ffurfiad iaith *eg* language formation
ffurfiad mecanyddol *eg* ffurfiadau mecanyddol mechanical structure
ffurfiannol *ans* formative
ffurfiant *eg* ffurfiannau formation
ffurfiant dellt *eg* lattice formation
ffurfiant rhywogaethau *eg* speciation
ffurfiant wy *eg* egg formation
ffurfiau dan sylw *ell* observed forms
ffurfiau gosod *ell* applied forms
ffurfiau hafaliad y cylch *ell* forms of equation of the circle
ffurfiau papur *ell* paper shapes
ffurfiau perthynol *ell* related shapes
ffurfiedig *ans* shaped
ffurfio *be* form
ffurfio â gwactod *be* vacuum forming
ffurfio argraffiadau *be* impression formation
ffurfio dan wasgedd *be* pressure forming
ffurfio dilyniannau *be* form sequences
ffurfio seren *be* form a star
ffurfio ymateb *be* reaction formation
ffurfiol *ans* formal
ffurfiolaeth *eb* formalism
ffurfio'n oer *be* cold-forming
ffurfiwr ffilm *eg* ffurfwyr ffilm film former
ffurflen *eb* ffurflenni form
ffurflen awtobeilot *eb* ffurflenni awtobeilot autopilot form
ffurflen bwcio *eb* booking form
ffurflen DMG *eb* ffurflenni DMG OMR form
ffurflen electronig *eb* ffurflenni electronig electronic form
ffurflen gais *eb* ffurflenni cais application form
ffurflen gydsynio *eb* ffurflenni cydsynio consent form
ffurflen gyfrifiad *eb* ffurflenni cyfrifiad census return
ffurflen hawlio'r llys sirol *eb* ffurflenni hawlio'r llys sirol county court claim form
ffurflen newydd *eb* ffurflenni newydd new form
ffurflen safonol *eb* ffurflenni safonol standard form
ffurflin *eg* ffurflinau form-line
ffurfwaith *eg* ffurfweithiau formwork
ffurfwedd electronau *eb* ffurfweddau electronau electron configuration
ffurfwedd electronig *eb* electronic configuration
ffurfwedd ofodol *eb* ffurfweddau gofodol spatial configuration
ffurfweddiad *eg* ffurfweddiadau configuration
ffurfweddiad awtofformat *eg* ffurfweddiadau awtofformat autoformat configuration
ffurfweddiad awtogywiro *eg* ffurfweddiadau awtogywiro autocorrect configuration
ffurfweddiad bar offer *eg* ffurfweddiadau bar offer toolbar configuration

ffurfweddiad colofn *eg* ffurfweddiadau colofnau column configuration
ffurfweddu *be* configure
ffurfydd *eg* ffurfwyr former
ffurfydd silindrog *eg* ffurfyddion silindrog cylindrical former
ffurfydd taprog *eg* ffurfwyr taprog tapered former
ffwcosanthin *eg* fucoxanthin
ffwng *eg* ffyngau fungus
ffwngaidd *ans* fungal
ffwngleiddiad *eg* ffwngleiddiaid fungicide
ffŵl ffrwythau *eg* fruit fool
ffwlcrwm *eg* ffwlcrymau fulcrum; centre of balance
ffwlsgap *eg* ffwlsgapau foolscap
ffwndamentaliaeth *eb* fundamentalism
ffwndws *eg* ffwndi fundus
ffwr *eg* fur
ffwrn *eb* ffyrnau oven
ffwrn aerglos *eb* ffyrnau aerglos autoclave
ffwrnais *eb* ffwrneisi furnace
ffwrnais adlewyrchol *eb* ffwrneisi adlewyrchol reverberatory furnace
ffwrnais amledd uchel Witton *eb* ffwrneisi amledd uchel Witton Witton high frequency furnace
ffwrnais anwytho amledd uchel *eb* ffwrneisi anwytho amledd uchel high frequency induction furnace
ffwrnais arc drydan *eb* ffwrneisi arc trydan electric arc furnace
ffwrnais bwdlo *eb* ffwrneisi pwdlo puddling furnace
ffwrnais chwyth *eb* ffwrneisi chwyth blast furnace
ffwrnais dân agored *eb* ffwrneisi tân agored open-hearth furnace
ffwrnais drawsnewidydd Bessemer *eb* Bessemer converter furnace
ffwrnais drawsnewidydd ocsigen *eb* ffwrneisi trawsnewidydd ocsigen oxygen converter furnace
ffwrnais fwffwl *eb* ffwrneisi mwffwl muffle furnace
ffwrnais fwyndoddi *eb* ffwrneisi mwyndoddi smelter
ffwrnais grwsibl *eb* ffwrneisi crwsibl crucible furnace
ffwrnais gwpola *eb* ffwrneisi cwpola cupola furnace
ffwrndanio *be* fire
ffwrndanio *be* ovenfire
ffwyl *eg* ffwyliau foil
ffwyliwr *eg* ffwylwyr foilist
ffwythiannau esbonyddol *ell* exponential functions
ffwythiannau gwrthdro *ell* inverse functions
ffwythiannol *ans* functional
ffwythiant *eg* ffwythiannau function
ffwythiant adenillion *eg* return function
ffwythiant aflinol *eg* ffwythiannau aflinol non-linear function
ffwythiant ar *eg* onto function
ffwythiant AVERAGE *eg* fwythiannau AVERAGE AVERAGE function
ffwythiant cyd-ddosbarthiad *eg* joint distribution function
ffwythiant cyflyrol *eg* state function
ffwythiant cymarebol *eg* rational function
ffwythiant cymhlyg *eg* ffwythiannau cymhlyg complex function
ffwythiant deilliadol *eg* ffwythiannau deilliadol derived function
ffwythiant diben *eg* objective function
ffwythiant dosraniad *eg* partition function
ffwythiant dosraniad cronnus *eg* cumulative distribution function
► **ffwythiant dosraniad ymylol** *eg* marginal distribution function
ffwythiant dwysedd tebygolrwydd *eg* probability density function
ffwythiant echblyg *eg* explicit function
ffwythiant eigen *eg* ffwythiannau eigen eigen function
ffwythiant hyperbolig *eg* hyperbolic function
ffwythiant i mewn *eg* into function
ffwythiant nodwedd weithredol *eg* operating characteristic function
ffwythiant polynomaidd *eg* ffwythiannau polynomaidd polynomial function
ffwythiant prawf globaidd *eg* global trial function
ffwythiant pŵer *eg* ffwythiannau pŵer power function
ffwythiant siâp cydffurfiol *eg* ffwythiannau siâp cydffurfiol conforming shape function
ffwythiant trigonometrig *eg* ffwythiannau trigonometrig trigonometric function
ffwythiant ymhlyg *eg* implicit function
ffydd *eb* faith
ffydd Gristnogol *eb* Christian faith
ffyngau llysnafedd *ell* slime fungi
ffylwm *eg* ffyla phylum
ffynhonnell *eb* ffynonellau source
ffynhonnell anhysbys *eb* ffynonellau anhysbys unknown source
ffynhonnell awdurdod *eb* source of authority
ffynhonnell brintiedig *eb* ffynonellau printiedig printed source
ffynhonnell briodol *eb* ffynonellau priodol appropriate source
ffynhonnell data *eb* ffynonellau data data source
ffynhonnell data newydd *eb* ffynonellau data newydd new data source
ffynhonnell egni *eb* ffynonellau egni energy source
ffynhonnell eilaidd *eb* ffynonellau eilaidd secondary source
ffynhonnell foltedd *eb* voltage source
ffynhonnell goleuni *eb* ffynonellau goleuni light source
ffynhonnell gwybodaeth *eb* ffynonellau gwybodaeth information source
ffynhonnell hanesyddol *eb* ffynonellau hanesyddol historical source
ffynhonnell sain *eb* ffynonellau sain sound source
ffynhonnell wreiddiol *eb* ffynonellau gwreiddiol primary source

ffynhonnell ymbelydrol *eb* ffynonellau ymbelydrol
radioactive source
ffyniannus *ans* booming
ffyniant *eg* prosperity; boom
ffyniant ariannol *eg* financial boom
ffyniant defnyddwyr *eg* consumer boom
ffyniant economaidd *eg* economic prosperity
ffynnon artesaidd *eb* ffynhonnau artesaidd
artesian well
ffynnon olew *eb* ffynhonnau olew oil well
ffynonellau cyllid *ell* sources of finance
ffyrdd a llwybrau roads and paths
ffyrdd cyflenwi *ell* supply lines
ffyrdd cyswllt *ell* lines of communication
ffytoplancton *eg* phytoplankton

G

G fwyaf *eb* G major
G leiaf *eb* G minor
gaberdîn *ans* gaberdine
gabro *eg* gabbro
gadael (=mynd allan) *be* exit
gadael (=mynd i ffwrdd) *be* depart
gadael (=rhoi'r gorau i rywun neu rywbeth) *be* abandon
gadael (yn barhaol) *be* quit
gadael grŵp *be* exit group
gadael modd llanw *be* exit fill mode
gadael oherwydd anaf *be* retire injured
gadael pob grŵp *be* exit all groups
gadael y cyflwyniad *be* exit presentation
gadael y recordiad *be* exit recording
gadoliniwm (Gd) *eg* gadolinium
gaeafgwsg *eg* hibernation
gaeafgysgu *be* hibernate
gafael *be* grip; grasp; clutch
gafael *eg/b* gafaelion grip; grasp
gafael bob yn ail *be* alternate grasp
gafael bwyell *eb* gafaelion bwyeill chopper grip
gafael ebrwydd *eb* instantaneous grip
gafael ffrithiannol *eb* frictional grip
gafael llawddryll *eb* gafaelion llawddryll pistol grip
gafael nwrl *eb* gafaelion nwrl knurled grip
gafael troed *eb* gafaelion traed foothold
gafael y flaen-llaw *eb* Eastern grip
gafaelgar *ans* catchy
gafaelion bysedd *ell* finger holds
gafaelydd bwlb *eg* gafaelyddion bylbiau bulb holder
gafaelydd peipen *eg* gafaelyddion peipiau pipe grips
gang *eg/b* gangiau gang
ganglia gwaelodol *ell* basal ganglia
ganglionig *ans* ganglionic
gaing *eb* geingiau chisel
gaing befel *eb* geingiau befel bevel chisel
gaing blygio *eb* geingiau plygio plugging chisel
gaing drawstor *eb* geingiau trawstor cross cut chisel
gaing drwyn diemwnt *eb* geingiau trwyn diemwnt diamond point chisel
gaing durnio *eb* geingiau turnio lathe chisel; turning chisel
gaing eingion *eb* geingiau eingion hardie
gaing fortais *eb* geingiau mortais mortise chisel
gaing fferf *eb* geingiau ffyrf firmer gouge
gaing galed *eb* geingiau caled cold chisel
gaing gau *eb* geingiau cau gouge
gaing gau blyg *eb* geingiau cau plyg bent gouge
gaing gau durnio *eb* geingiau cau turnio wood turning gouge
gaing gau gefn *eb* geingiau gau cefn firmer gouge
gaing gau hir *eb* geingiau cau hir paring gouge
gaing gau offeru *eb* geingiau gau offeru tooling gouge
gaing gau turn *eb* geingiau gau turn lathe gouge
gaing gau wyneb *eb* geingiau cau wyneb scribing gouge
gaing gerfio *eb* geingiau cerfio carving chisel
gaing glo drôr *eb* geingiau clo drôr drawer lock chisel
gaing hanner crwn *eb* geingiau hanner crwn half round chisel
gaing hanner crwn *eb* geingiau hanner crwn half moon chisel
gaing hedegog *eb* geingiau hedegog fly cutter
gaing hir *eb* geingiau hir paring chisel
gaing oledd *eb* geingiau oledd skew chisel
gaing sglodi *eb* geingiau sglodi chipping chisel
gair *eg* geiriau word
gair allweddol *eg* geiriau allweddol key word
gair cadw *eg* geiriau cadw reserved word
gair cyfarwyddiadol *eg* geiriau cyfarwyddiadol instruction word
gair cynnwys *eg* geiriau cynnwys content word
gair cyson *eg* geiriau cyson regular word
gair chwilio *eg* geiriau chwilio search word
gair eithriad *eg* geiriau eithriad exception word
gair gorchymyn *eg* geiriau gorchymyn command word
gair llafar *eg* geiriau llafar spoken word
gair mwys *eg* geiriau mwys pun
gair peiriant *eg* geiriau peiriant machine word
gair swyddogaethol *eg* geiriau swyddogaethol functional word
gairbrosesu *be* text processing
gala nofio *eg* galâu nofio swimming gala
galactos *eg* galactose
galactosaemia *eg* galactosaemia
galaeth *eb* galaethau galaxy
galaethog *ans* galactic
galanas *eb* blood feud
Galanas Stockholm *eb* Blood Bath of Stockholm
galar *eg* grief
galargan *eb* galarganeuon elegy

galaru *be* mourn
galena *eg* galena
galeri (telyn Gothig) *eg* galerïau capital
galfanedig *ans* galvanized
galfaneiddiad *eg* galvanization
galfanig *ans* galvanic
galfanomedr *eg* galfanomedrau galvanometer
galfanomedr coil symudol *eg* galfanomedrau coil symudol moving coil galvanometer
galfanomedr smotyn *eg* galfanomedrau smotyn spot galvanometer
galfanu *be* galvanize
galfanu dip poeth *be* hot dip galvanizing
gali *eg* galïau galley
Galicanaidd *ans* Gallican
Galicaniad *eg* Galicaniaid Gallican
Galicaniaeth *eb* Gallicanism
Galilea *eg* Galilee
galiwm *eg* gallium
galiwn *eg* galiynau galleon
galw (=mynnu) *be* demand
galw (yn gyffredinol) *be* call
galw *eg* galwadau demand
galw brig *eg* galwadau brig peak demand
galw cofrestr *be* roll call
galw cyfanredol *eg* aggregate demand
galw cyfansawdd *eg* composite demand
galw i gof *be* recall
galw i gof batrymau cerddorol *be* recall musical patterns
galw mewnol *eg* domestic demand
galw mewnol terfynol *eg* final domestic demand
galw wrth enw *be* call by name
galw wrth werth *be* call by value
galwad *eb* galwadau call
galwedigaeth *eb* galwedigaethau occupation
galwedigaeth *eb* galwedigaethau vocation
galwedigaeth eisteddog *eb* galwedigaethau eisteddog sedentary occupation
galwedigaethol *ans* vocational
galwedigaethol *ans* occupational
galwyn *eg/b* galwyni gallon
galliard *eg* galliards galliard
gallu *eg* galluoedd capability
gallu *eg* galluoedd ability; capability; power
gallu barnu cymdeithasol *be* social judgeability
gallu canolig *eg* average ability
gallu cyd-drefnu *eg* coordinating power
gallu cyfreithiol *eg* legal capacity
gallu cyffelyb *eg* similar ability
gallu cyffredinol *eg* general ability
gallu cymysg *eg* mixed ability
gallu cynhenid *eg* galluoedd cynhenid inborn capacity; native ability
gallu cynhyrchu *eg* galluoedd cynhyrchu generating capacity; productive capacity
gallu geiriol *eg* verbal ability
gallu gofodol *eg* spatial ability
gallu gweld-echddygol *eg* visuo-motor ability
gallu gwybyddol *eg* galluoedd gwybyddol cognitive ability
gallu i dalu sylw *eg* attentiveness
gallu i gyffredinoli *eg* generalizability
gallu i ryngweithredu *eg* interoperability
gallu ieithyddol *eg* language ability
gallu meddyliol *eg* mental ability; mental capacity
gallu personol *eg* personal capability
gallu prynu *eg* galluoedd prynu purchasing power
galluog *ans* able; capable
galluogi *be* enable
galluogi cwcis *be* enable cookies
galluogi nodweddion *be* enable features
galluogi ymyriadau *be* enable interrupts
galluogwr *eg* galluogwyr enabler
gamba *eg* gamba
gamet *eg* gametau gamete
gamet benyw *eg* gametau benyw female gamete
gamet gwryw *eg* gametau gwryw male gamete
gametocyt *eg* gametocytau gametocyte
gametoffor *eg* gametofforau gametophore
gametoffyt *eg* gametoffytau gametophyte
gametogenesis *eg* gametogenesis
gamopetalog *ans* gamopetalous
gamosepalog *ans* gamosepalous
gamwt *eg* gamut
Ganesh /Ganesha /Ganapati *eg* Ganesh /Ganesha /Ganapati
ganglion *eg* ganglia ganglion
GAP: Gweithgor ar Asesu a Phrofi *eg* TGAT: Task Group on Assessment and Testing
garan *eg/b* garanau shank
garan a chylch shank and ring
garan baralel *eb* garanau paralel parallel shank
garan dapr *eb* garanau tapr taper shank
garan syth *eb* garanau syth straight shank
gard *eg* gardiau guard
gard diogelwch *eg* gardiau diogelwch safety guard
gard rhwyll wifrog *eg* gardiau rhwyll wifrog wire mesh guard
gard tân *eg* gardiau tân fireguard
gard uchaf *eg* gardiau uchaf crown guard
gardys *eg* gardyson garter
gardd *eb* gerddi garden
gardd fasnachol *eb* gerddi masnachol market garden
gardd grog *eb* gerddi crog hanging garden
gardd-ddinas *eb* gardd-ddinasoedd garden city
garddio *be* garden
garddio masnachol *be* market gardening
garej *eg* garejis garage
gargoil *eg* gargoiliau gargoyle
garlant *eg* garlantau garland
garsiwn *eg/b* garsiynau garrison
gartref at home

garw *ans* rough; coarse
garw agored *eg* rough open
garwdir basalt *eg* garwdiroedd basalt scabland
garwdiroedd *ell* badlands
garwdirol *ans* badland
garwedd *eg* roughness; coarseness; ruggedness
Gascon *eg* Gasconiaid Gascon
gasged *eg* gasgedi gasket
gastrig *ans* gastric
gastro-enteritis *eg* gastro-enteritis
gastro-enteroleg *eb* gastro-enterology
gastrwla *eg* gastrwlae gastrula
gastrwliad *eg* gastrulation
gau *ans* false
gau berthynas *eb* gau berthnasau false relation
gau friger *eb* gau frigerau staminode
gavotte *eg* gavottes gavotte
gefail *eb* gefeiliau forge
gefail gludadwy *eb* gefeiliau cludadwy portable forge
gefail gof *eg* gefeiliau gof blacksmith's forge
gefeilldref *eb* gefeilldrefi twin town
gefeilles *eb* gefeilliaid twin
gefeilliaid annhebyg *ell* fraternal twins
gefeillio (ysgolion etc) *be* twinning
gefel *eb* gefeiliau forceps
gefel *eb* gefeilau tongs
gefel beipen *eb* gefeiliau peipen pipe tongs
gefel ceg sgwâr *eb* gefeiliau ceg sgwâr square mouth tongs
gefel dynnu *eb* gefeiliau tynnu draw tongs
gefel fach *eg* gefeiliau bach tweezers
gefel fath plcl *eb* gefeiliau bath picl pickle-bath tongs
gefel flwch *eb* gefeiliau blwch box tongs
gefel flwch sgwâr *eb* gefeiliau blwch sgwâr square-box tongs
gefel follt *eb* gefeiliau bollt bolt tongs
gefel fflat agored *eb* gefeiliau fflat agored open flat tongs
gefel garan gylch (castio) *eb* gefeiliau garan cylch ringshank tongs
gefel geg 'V' *eb* gefeiliau ceg 'V' vee-bit tongs
gefel gegagored *eb* gefeiliau cegagored open-mouth tongs
gefel gegdyn *eb* gefeiliau cegdyn close-mouth tongs
gefel gegochr *eb* gefeiliau cegochr side-mouth tongs
gefel gegron *eb* gefeiliau cegrwn hollow bit tongs
gefel gegron ddwbl *eb* gefeiliau cegrwn dwbl double hollow-bit tongs
gefel gegsgwar *eb* gefeiliau cegsgwar hollow square bit tongs
gefel godi *eb* gefeiliau codi pick-up tongs
gefel godi *eb* gefeiliau codi lifting tongs
gefel grwsibl *eb* gefeiliau crwsibl crucible tongs
gefel gyffredinol *eb* gefeiliau cyffredinol universal tongs
gefel ochr dorri *eb* gefeiliau ochr dorri side cutting pliers
gefel ofannu *eb* gefeiliau gofannu forging tongs
gefel sgrôl *eb* gefeiliau sgrôl scroll tongs
gefelen *eb* gefeiliau pliers
gefelen dorri *eb* gefeiliau torri cutting pliers
gefelen dorri croeslin *eb* gefeiliau torri croeslin diagonal cutting pliers
gefelen drwyn byr *eb* gefeiliau trwyn byr short nose pliers
gefelen drwyn cam *eb* gefeiliau trwyn cam bent nose pliers
gefelen drwyn crwn *eb* gefeiliau trwyn crwn round nose pliers
gefelen drwyn crwn hir *eb* gefeiliau trwyn crwn hir long round nose pliers
gefelen drwyn crwn main hir *eb* gefeiliau trwyn crwn main hir long snipe nose pliers
gefelen drwyn hir *eb* gefeiliau trwyn hir long nose pliers
gefelen dynhau *eb* gefeiliau tynhau straining pliers
gefelen estyn *eb* gefeiliau estyn stretcher pliers
gefelen geg-symudol *eb* gefeiliau ceg-symudol mouth-moving pliers
gefelen gweithiwr gwiail *eb* gefeiliau gweithwyr gwiail caneworker's pliers
gefelen gyfunol *eb* gefeiliau cyfunol combination pliers
gefelen llygaden *eb* gefeiliau llygaden eyelet pliers
gefelen nipio *eb* gefeiliau nipio nipping pliers
gefelen ochr-dorri *eb* gefeiliau ochr-dorri side-cutting pliers
gefelen osod llif *eb* gefeiliau gosod llif saw-setting pliers
gefelen semio *eb* gefeiliau semio seaming pliers
gefelen stripio gwifrau *eb* gefeiliau stripio gwifrau wire-stripping pliers
gefelen trwyn sgwâr *eb* gefeiliau trwyn sgwâr square nose pliers
gefelen wifrau *eb* gefeiliau gwifrau wire pliers
gefelen ynysedig trydanwr *eb* gefeiliau ynysedig trydanwr electrician's insulated pliers
gefell *eg* gefeilliaid twin
gefell deusygotig *eg* gefeilliaid deusygotig dizygotic twin
gefell monosygotig *eg* efeilliaid monosygotig monozygotic (MZ) twin
gefell unfath *eg* gefeilliaid unfath identical twin
gefyn *eg* gefynnau shackle
geilwad *eg* geilwaid folk dance caller
geirda *eg* reference
geirda cymeriad *eg* character reference
geirfa *eb* geirfâu vocabulary
geirfa allweddol *eb* key vocabulary
geirfa briodol *eb* appropriate vocabulary
geirfa gelf *eb* art vocabulary
geirfa graidd *eb* geirfâu craidd core vocabulary

geirfa lafar *eb* oral vocabulary
geirfa oddefol *eb* passive vocabulary
geirfa sylfaenol *eb* basic vocabulary
geirfa weledol sylfaenol *eb* basic sight vocabulary
geiriadur *eg* geiriaduron dictionary
geiriadur data *eg* geiriaduron data data dictionary
geiriadur defnyddiwr *eg* geiriaduron defnyddwyr user dictionary
geiriadur newydd *eg* geiriaduron newydd new dictionary
geiriadurol *ans* lexicographic
geiriadurol *ans* lexical
geiriau gyda rhifau *ell* words with numbers
geiriol *ans* verbal
geiriol gyfeiriedig *ans* word orientated
geirlap *eg* geirlapiau wordwrap
geiser *eg* geiserau geyser
gel *eg* geliau gel
gelaidd *ans* gelatinous
gelatin *eg* gelatinau gelatine
gelen *eb* gelenod leech
gelen feddyginiaethol *eb* medicinal leech
geliad *eg* gelation
gelyn *eg* gelynion enemy
gelyniaeth *eb* hostility
gelyniaethiad *eg* alienation
gelyniaethu *be* alienate
gem *eb* gemau gem
gêm *eb* gemau game; match
gêm atsain *eb* gemau atsain echo game
gêm brawf *eb* gemau prawf test game
gêm cyfrifiadur *eb* gemau cyfrifiadur computer game
gêm darged *eb* gemau targed target game
gêm daro *eb* gemau taro striking game
gêm goresgyn *eb* gemau goresgyn invasion game
gêm gyfartal *eb* gemau cyfartal drawn game
gêm gyfartal *eb* gemau cyfartal tie
gêm gystadleuol *eb* gemau cystadleuol competitive game
gêm i barau *eb* gemau i barau doubles game
gêm i dîm *eb* gemau tîm team game
gêm i ddim love game
gêm ryngweithiol *eb* gemau rhyngweithiol interactive game
gêm timau bach *eb* gemau timau bach small-sided game
gêm un ar ddeg bob ochr *eb* gemau un ar ddeg bob ochr eleven a side game
gêm unigol *eb* gemau unigol individual game
Gemara *eg* Gemara
Gemau Olympaidd *ell* Olympic Games
gemau tîm cystadleuol *ell* competitive team games
Gemau'r Gymanwlad *ell* Commonwealth Games
gemshorn *eg* gemshorn
gemwaith *ell* jewellery
gemwl *eg* gemylau gemmule
gemydd *eg* gemyddion jeweller
gên *eb* genau jaw; chin
gên isaf *eb* genau isaf lower jaw
gên-bwys *eg* genbwysau chin rest
genedigaeth *eb* genedigaethau childbirth
genedigaeth *eb* genedigaethau birth
genedigaeth *eb* genedigaethau delivery
genedigaeth fyw *eb* genedigaethau byw live birth
genedigaeth Gesaraidd *eb* genedigaethau Cesaraidd Caesarean birth
genedigaeth-fraint *eb* birthright
genedigol *ans* nascent
generadiad *eg* generadiadau generation
generadol feidraidd *ans* finitely generated
generadu *be* generate
generadur *eg* generaduron generator
generadur adroddiadau *eg* generaduron adroddiadau report generator
generadur byrraf *eg* generaduron byrraf shortest generator
generadur cerrynt eiledol *eg* generaduron cerrynt eiledol a.c. generator
generadur cerrynt eiledol *eg* generaduron cerrynt eiledol simple a.c. generator
generadur curiadau cloc *eg* generaduron curiadau cloc clock pulse generator
generadur dilyniant *eg* sequence generator
generadur haprifau *eg* generaduron haprifau random number generator
generadur rhaglen *eg* generaduron rhaglen program generator
generadur rhifau *eg* generaduron rhifau number generator
generadur sain *eg* generaduron sain sound generator
generadur signalau *eg* generaduron signalau signal generator
generadur trydan *eg* generaduron trydan electrical generator
generadur tyrbo *eg* generaduron tyrbo turbo-generator
generig *ans* generic
geneteg *eb* genetics
geneteg dyn *eb* human genetics
geneteg ymddygiad *eb* behaviour genetics
genetig *ans* genetic
geneufor *eg* geneuforoedd bight
genfa ffrwyn *eb* genfeydd ffrwyn bridle bit
genglo *eg* lockjaw
geni o forwyn *be* virgin birth
geni-bleidiol *ans* pro-natalist
genidol *ans* genitive
geni'n farw *be* still birth
genogl *eg* genoglau jawbone
genol *ans* jaw
genom *eg* genomau genome
genomer *eg* genomerau genomer
genosom *eg* genosomau genosome
genoteip *eg* genoteipiau genotype

genoteip y rhieni *eg* parental genotype
genoteipaidd *ans* genotypic
gên-rannau *ell* mouthparts
genre *eg* genres genre
genws *eg* genera genus
genyn *eg* genynnau gene
genyn marwol *eg* genynnau marwol lethal gene
genyn rhyw-ddylanwadedig *eg* genynnau rhyw-ddylanwadedig sex-influenced gene
genyn rhyw-gysylltiedig *eg* genynnau rhyw-gysylltiedig sex-linked gene
geoanticlin *eg* geoanticlinau geoanticline
geocemegol *ans* geochemical
geocronoleg *eb* geochronology
geocronometreg *eb* geochronometry
geod *eg* geodau geode
geodedd *eg* geodesy
geodesig *ans* geodesic
geodetig *ans* geodetic
geodimedr *eg* geodimedrau geodimeter
geofwrdd *eg* geofyrddau geoboard
geoffiseg *eb* geophysics
geoffyt *eg* geoffytau geophyte
geoid *eg* geoidau geoid
geometreg *eb* geometregau geometry
geometreg gyfesurynnol *eb* coordinate geometry
geometreg plân *eb* plane geometry
geometreg plân a solid *eb* plane and solid geometry
geometreg trawsffurfiadau *eb* transformation geometry
geometregol *ans* geometrical
geometrig *ans* geometric
geomorffoleg *eb* geomorphology
geomorffolegol *ans* geomorphological
geon *eg* geonau geon
georgette *eg* georgette
geostroffig *ans* geostrophic
geosynclin *eg* geosynclinau geosyncline
geotacsis *eg* geotaxis
geotropedd *eg* geotropism
geothermol *ans* geothermal
geowleidyddiaeth *eb* geopolitics
gêr *eg/b* gerau gear
gêr infoliwt *eg* gerau infoliwt involute gear
gêr isaf *eg* bottom gear
gêr sbardun *eg* gerau sbardun spur gear
gêr twmblo *eg* gerau twmblo tumble gear
Geraldiaid *ell* Geraldines
Gerallt Cymro *eg* Gerald of Wales
geraniol *eg* geraniol
gerau befel *ell* bevel gears
gerau cripian *ell* worm gears
gerbil *eg* gerbilod gerbil
gerbocs awtomatig *eg* gerbocsys awtomatig automatic gearbox
geriatregydd *eg* geriatregwyr geriatrician
geriatrig *ans* geriatric
germ *eg* germau germ
germaniwm (Ge) *eg* germanium
germaniwm(IV) ocsid *eg* germanium(IV) oxide
gerontoleg *eb* gerontology
geso *eg* gesso
Gestapo *ell* Gestapo
geto *eg* getos ghetto
geudy *eg* geudai reredorter
gewyn *eg* gewynnau sinew
gewyn *eg* gewynnau ligament
gewyn cynhaliol *eg* gewynnau cynhaliol suspensory ligament
gewynnol *ans* sinewy
gewynnol *ans* ligamentous
Gibeliniad *eg* Gibeliniaid Ghibelline
giberelin *eg* giberelinau gibberellin
gigabeit (Gb) *eg* gigabeitiau gigabyte
gigue *eb* gigues gigue
gingham *eg* gingham
gild *eg* gildiau guild
gild crefft *eg* gildiau crefft craft guild
gild y masnachwyr *eg* gildiau'r masnachwyr merchant guild
gilotîn *eg* gilotinau guillotine
gimbil *eb* gimbilion gimlet
gitâr *eb* gitarau guitar
gitâr acwstig *eb* gitarau acwstig acoustic guitar
gitâr drydan *eb* gitarau trydan electric guitar
gitarydd *eg* gitarwyr guitarist
giwana *eg* guano
gladiator *eg* gladiatoriaid gladiator
glaer *eg* glair
glaeru *be* glair
glafoerio *be* dribble
glain *eg* gleiniau bead
glain a rîl bead and reel
glain cwirc *eg* gleiniau cwirc quirk bead
glain gosod *eg* gleiniau gosod planted bead
glain lliw *eg* gleiniau lliw coloured bead
glain mewnol *eg* gleiniau mewnol inner bead
glain ongl *eg* gleiniau ongl angle bead
glain plastig *eg* gleiniau plastig plastic bead
glain pren *eg* gleiniau pren wooden bead
glain rhannu *eg* gleiniau rhannu parting bead
glân *ans* clean
glan (afon) *eb* glannau bank
glan (môr) *eb* glannau shore
glan dde *eb* right bank
glan gylchol (agorell) *eb* glannau cylchol circular land
Glan Orllewinol *eb* West Bank
glan y môr *eb* seashore; sea front
glandiroedd dwyreiniol *ell* eastern margins
glandiroedd gorllewinol *ell* western margins
glanedwaith *eg* detergency
glanedydd *eg* glanedyddion detergent

glanedydd biolegol *eg* glanedyddion biolegol biological detergent
glanedydd cryf *eg* glanedyddion cryf heavy duty detergent
glanedydd disebon *eg* glanedyddion disebon soapless detergent
glanedydd ensym *eg* glanedyddion ensym enzyme detergent
glanedydd hylif *eg* glanedyddion hylif liquid detergent
glanedydd llawndrochion *eg* glanedyddion llawndrochion high foaming detergent
glanedydd prindrochion *eg* glanedyddion prindrochion low foaming detergent
glanedydd synthetig *eg* glanedyddion synthetig synthetic detergent
glanedydd ysgafn *eg* glanedyddion ysgafn light duty detergent
glanfa *eb* glanfeydd jetty
glanhau (clwyf etc) *be* cleanse
glanhau (gyda swab) *be* swab
glanhau allan *be* raking out
glanhau blynyddol *be* spring-cleaning
glanhau dyddiol *be* daily cleaning
glanhau gydag ager *be* steam cleaning
glanhau trylwyr *be* thorough cleaning
glanhau'r geg *be* oral toilet
glanhawr *eg* glanhawyr cleaner
glanhawr pibell *eg* glanhawyr pibell pipe cleaner
glanhawraig *eb* glanhawragedd cleaner
glaniad y cynghreiriaid *eg* allied landing
glaniadau D-Day *ell* D-Day landings
glanio *be* land; disembark
glannau bylchog *ell* ragged shores
Glannau Merswy *ell* Merseyside
glanweithydd *eg* glanweithyddion cleanser
glas *eg* blue
glas canol *eg* mid blue
glas indathrin *eg* indathrene blue
glas lafant *eg* lavender blue
glas lapis *eg* lapis blue
glas llachar *eg* brilliant blue
glas masarin *eg* mazarin blue
glas monestial *eg* monestial blue
glas newydd *eg* new blue
glas Payne *eg* Payne's blue
glas Prwsia *eg* Prussian blue
glas trydan *eg* electric blue
glas y nen *eg* cerulean blue
glas y nen *eg* sky blue
glasbren *eg* glasbrennau sapling
glasbrint *eg* glasbrintiau blueprint
glaslain *eb* glasleiniau lynchet
glaslys *eg* woad
glasoed *eg* puberty
glasog *eb* glasogau gizzard
glasrew *eg* freezing rain
glasrew *eg* verglas
glastir *eg* glastiroedd green sward
glastwreiddio *be* revisionism
glasu *be* bluing
glasu ag olew *be* oil bluing
glaswellt clytiog *eg* patchy grass
glaswelltir *eg* glaswelltiroedd grassland
glaswelltir tymherus *eg* glaswelltiroedd tymherus temperate grassland
glaswyrdd *eg* turquoise
glaw asid *eg* acid rain
glaw darfudol *eg* convectional rain
glaw ffrynt *eg* frontal rain
glaw mân *eg* drizzle
glawiad *eg* rainfall
glawiad blynyddol *eg* annual rainfall
glawiad cyfartalog *eg* glawiadau cyfartalog average rainfall
glawiad cymedrol *eg* moderate rainfall
glawiad effeithiol *eg* effective rainfall
glawlin *eg* glawlinau isohyet
glawlin cymarebol *eg* glawlinau cymarebol equipluve
glawog *ans* pluvial
glawred *eg* glawrediadau rainwash
glei *eg* gley
gleider *eg* gleiderau glider
gleinio *be* bead
gleinwaith *eg* beading
gleinwaith *eg* beadwork
gleinwaith les *eg* lace beading
gleio *be* gleying
gleision a fioledau blues and violets
glendid *eg* cleanliness
gliaidd *eg* glial
gliniadur *eg* gliniaduron laptop
gliniau'n blyg i'r eithaf *ell* full knees bend
gliniau'n blyg i'r hanner *ell* half knees bend
glissade *eg* glissade
glo *eg* coal
glo brig *eg* opencast coat
glo brown *eg* brown coal
glo cannwyll *eg* cannel coal
glo carreg *eg* anthracite
glo golosg *eg* coking coal
glo mân *eg* slack
glo môr *eg* sea coal
glo rhwym *eg* bituminous coal
glo rhydd *eg* steam coal
glôb *eg* globau globe
globaleiddio *be* globalization
globwl *eg* globylau globule
globwl braster *eg* globylau braster fat globule
globwlin *eg* globulin
glockenspiel *eg* glockenspiele glockenspiel
glomerwlws *eg* glomerwlysau glomerulus
glosoffaryngeal *ans* glossopharyngeal
glotis *eg* glotisau glottis

glotol *ans* glottal
glöwr *eg* glowyr miner
glöyn byw *eg* glöynnod byw butterfly
glöyn gwyn mawr *eg* glöynnod gwyn mawr large cabbage white
glöyn y llaethlys *eg* glöynnod y llaethlys monarch
gloyw *ans* lustrous
gloywedd *eg* gloyweddau lustre
gloywi *be* clarify
gloywi *be* clearing
gloywydd *eg* gloywyddion clearing agent
glud *eg* gludion glue
glud anifail *eg* animal glue
glud ardrawol *eg* impact glue
glud asgwrn a chroen *eg* bone and hide glue
glud casein *eg* casein glue
glud cyswllt *eg* contact glue
glud dŵr oer *eg* cold water glue
glud llysiau *eg* vegetable glue
glud oer *eg* cold glue
glud oer ystwyth *eg* flexible cold glue
glud perl *eg* gludion perl pearl glue
glud polyfinyl asetad *eg* polyvinyl acetate glue
glud powdr *eg* powdered glue
glud resin *eg* gludion resin resin glue
glud resin epocsi *eg* epoxy resin glue
glud resin synthetig *eg* synthetic resin glue
glud Scotch *eg* Scotch glue
glud slab *eg* cake glue
glud synthetig *eg* gludion synthetig synthetic glue
glud wrea fformaldehyd *eg* urea formaldehyde glue
gludafael *eg* gludafaelion holdfast
gludedd *eg* tack
gludedd *eg* gludeddau viscosity
gludio *be* glue
gludiog *ans* tacky
gludiog *ans* viscous
gludiog *ans* sticky
gludo *be* paste
gludo popeth *be* paste all
gludydd *eg* gludyddion adhesive
gludydd cellog *eg* gludyddion cellog cellular adhesive
gludydd cyswllt *eg* gludyddion cyswllt contact adhesive
glwcagon *eg* glucagon
glwcocorticoid *eg* glwcocorticoidau glucocorticoid
glwcos *eg* glucose
glwcos gwaed *eg* blood glucose
glwcos ocsidas *eg* glucose oxidase
glwcos-1-ffosffad *eg* glucose-1-phosphate
glwcostat *eg* glwcostatau glucostat
glwcoswria *eg* glucosuria
glwon *eg* glwonau gluon
glwtamin *eg* glutamine
glycin *eg* glycine
glycogen *eg* glycogen
glycogen synthetas *eg* glycogen synthetase
glycolysis *eg* glycolysis
glycoprotein *eg* glycoprotein
glycosid *eg* glycoside
glycosidaidd *ans* glycosidic
glynu (wrth) *be* stick; adhere
glyserin *eg* glycerine
glyserol *eg* glycerol
gobennydd *eg* gobenyddion pillow
gobled *eg* gobledi goblet
goblygiad *eg* goblygiadau implication
goblygiad y duedd *eg* implication of trend
goblygiadau adnoddol *ell* resource implications
goblygiadau cyfreithiol *ell* legal consequences
godet *eg* godets godet
godineb *eg* adultery
godrefryniau *ell* foothills
godre'r gwaelodlin *eg* bottom of baseline
goddef *be* tolerate
goddefedd *eg* passivity
goddefedd *eg* tolerance
goddefgarwch *eg* toleration
goddefgarwch *eg* tolerance
goddefiannu *be* tolerancing
goddefiannu geometrig *be* geometric tolerancing
goddefiant *eg* goddefiannau tolerance
goddefol *ans* passive
goddefol *ans* permissive
goddiweddyd *be* overtake
goddiwylliannu *be* acculturation
goddrych *eg* goddrychau subject
goddrychedd *eg* subjectivity
goddrychiad *eg* subjectivation
goddrychol *ans* subjective
gof *eg* gofaint blacksmith
gof arian *eg* gofaint arian silversmith
gof aur *eg* gofaint aur goldsmith
gofal *eg* gofalon care; caution
gofal ac ôl-ofal care and after-care
gofal am yr amgylchedd *eg* care of the environment
gofal anffurfiol *eg* informal care
gofal anuniongyrchol *eg* indirect care
gofal ataliol *eg* preventive care
gofal brwsh *eg* brush care
gofal bugeiliol *eg* pastoral care
gofal corfforol *eg* physical care
gofal croen *eg* skin care
gofal cymdeithasol *eg* social care
gofal cyn llawdriniaeth *eg* preoperative care
gofal cyn-geni *eg* antenatal care
gofal dwys *eg* intensive care
gofal dydd *eg* day care
gofal gwirfoddol *eg* voluntary care
► **gofal iechyd cychwynnol** *eg* primary health care
gofal iechyd eilaidd *eg* secondary health care
gofal iechyd preifat *eg* private health care

gofal iechyd trydyddol *eg* tertiary health care
gofal lliniarol *eg* palliative care
gofal maeth *eg* foster care
gofal mewn sefydliad *eg* institutional care
gofal nyrsio *eg* nursing care
gofal ôl-eni *eg* post-natal care
gofal plant *eg* child care
gofal preswyl *eg* residential care
gofal proffesiynol *eg* professional care
gofal rhieni *eg* parental care
gofal seibiant *eg* respite care
gofal tymor byr *eg* short-term care
gofal uniongyrchol *eg* direct care
gofal wedi'r llawdriniaeth *eg* post-operative care
gofal y traceostomi *eg* tracheostomy care
gofal yn ôl tasgau *eg* task orientated care
gofal yn y gymuned *eg* community care
gofal yn ystod y llawdriniaeth *eg* peri-operative care
gofal yr henoed *eg* care of the elderly
gofalaeth *eb* gofalaethau cure
gofal-chwarae playcare
gofalus iawn *ans* meticulous
gofalwr *eg* gofalwyr caretaker
gofalwr *eg* gofalwyr carer
gofalwr maeth *eg* gofalwyr maeth foster carer
gofalydd *eg* gofalwyr caregiver
gofalydd anffurfiol *eg* informal carer
gofalydd anuniongyrchol *eg* indirect carer
gofalydd ffurfiol *eg* gofalwyr ffurfiol formal carer
gofalydd gwirfoddol *eg* voluntary carer
gofalydd proffesiynol *eg* professional carer
gofaniad *eg* gofaniadau forging
gofannu *be* forge
gofannu metel *be* metal forging
gofod *eg* space
gofod cyffredinol *eg* general space
gofod cymdeithasol *eg* gofodau cymdeithasol social space
gofod darluniol *eg* gofodau darluniol pictorial space
gofod dellt *eg* lattice space
gofod gwag *eg* free space
gofod gweithredu *eg* action-space
gofod llorwedd *eg* going
gofod meddyliol *eg* mental space
gofod personol *eg* personal space
gofod sampl *eg* sample space
gofod-amser *eg* space-time
gofodol *ans* spatial
gofodwr *eg* gofodwyr spaceman
gofyn *be* require
gofyniad *eg* gofynion requirement
gofyniad statudol *eg* gofynion statudol statutory requirement
gofynion arian parod net y sector cyhoeddus *ell* public sector net cash requirements
gofynion diogelwch *ell* safety requirements
gofynion egni *ell* energy demands
gofynion repertoire *ell* repertoire requirements
gofynion sy'n gwrthdaro *ell* conflicting demands
gofynion y defnyddiwr *ell* needs of the user
gofynion ychwanegol *ell* notions
gofynnod *eg* gofynodau question mark
gofynnol *ans* required
goffro *be* goffering
gogilddant *eg* gogilddannedd premolar
▸ **goglau** *ell* goggles
gogledd *eg* north
gogledd cwmpawd *eg* compass north
gogledd cywir *eg* true north
gogledd grid *eg* grid north
gogledd magnetig *eg* magnetic north
gogleddiad *eg* northing
gogoneddiad *eg* ascription
gogoneddu Duw *be* ascribe glory to God
gogr *eg* gograu sieve
gogru *be* sieve
gogwydd *eg* swing
gogwydd *eg* gogwyddiadau bias
gogwydd *eg* orientation
gogwydd *eg* gogwyddau pitch
gogwydd *eg* gogwyddau tilt
gogwydd dadansoddol *eg* analytical orientation
gogwydd fertigol *eg* vertical pitch
gogwydd ffasiwn *eg* fashion trend
gogwydd llorweddol *eg* horizontal pitch
gogwydd o ran rhyw *eg* gender bias
gogwydd rhagosodedig *eg* default orientation
gogwydd ymateb *eg* response bias
gogwyddiad *eg* gogwyddiadau declination
gogwyddiad *eg* gogwyddiadau dip
gogwyddo *be* tilt
gogwyddo *be* pitch
gogwyddo'n ôl *be* backward tilt
gogyforlan *eb* gogyforlannau near bankful
gohebiaeth *eb* gohebiaethau correspondence
gohebydd lobi *eg* gohebwyr lobi lobby correspondent
gohiriad (mewn cerddoriaeth) *eg* gohiriadau retardation
gohiriad (mewn achos llys etc) *eg* gohiriadau adjournment
gohiriant *eg* gohiriannau suspension
gohiriant dwbl *eg* gohiriannau dwbl double suspension
gohirio (eisteddiad senedd etc) *be* prorogue
gohirio (yn gyffredinol) *be* adjourn
gohirnod *eg* gohirnodau suspended note
gôl *eb* goliau goal
gôl adlam *eb* goliau adlam drop goal
gôl gosb *eb* goliau cosb penalty goal
golau *ans* pale
golau *ans* light

golau *eg* goleuadau light
golau *eg* goleuadau illumination
golau adlewyrchedig *eg* reflected light
golau anuniongyrchol *eg* indirect lighting
golau artiffisial *eg* artificial light
golau benthyg *eg* borrowed light
golau cilannog *eg* goleuadau cilannog recessed lighting
golau codi a gostwng *eg* rise-and-fall light
golau crog *eg* goleuadau crog pendant light
golau crog *eg* goleuadau crog suspended light
golau cudd *eg* concealed lighting
golau cylch *eg* spotlight
golau drwy beipen *eg* piped light
golau dydd *eg* daylight
golau gweladwy *eg* visible light
golau gwyn *eg* white light
golau haul *eg* sunlight
golau lled uniongyrchol *eg* semi-direct lighting
golau mewnol *eg* internal illumination
golau naturiol *eg* natural light
golau plân polar *eg* plane polarized light
golau plyg *eg* goleuadau plyg refracted light
golau polar *eg* polarized light
golau stribed *eg* strip lighting
golau tryledol *eg* diffused lighting
golau uniongyrchol *eg* direct lighting
golau uwchfioled *eg* ultra violet light
golau wal *eg* goleuadau wal wall light
golau-annibynnol *ans* light-independent
golau-ddibynnol *ans* light-dependent
golau'r amgylchedd *eg* ambient light
golau'r godre *eg* footlights
golch *eg/b* golchion wash
golch wythnosol *eb* weekly wash
golchadwy *ans* washable
golchadwy â llaw *ans* hand washable
golchadwy â pheiriant *ans* machine washable
golchadwyaeth *eb* washability
golchdy *eg* golchdai laundry
golchdy masnachol *eg* golchdai masnachol commercial laundry
golchfa *eb* golchfeydd launderette
golchi *be* wash; bathe
golchi a smwddio launder
golchi ffrithiant *be* friction washing
golchiad *eg* golchiadau ablution
golch-lethr *eg* golch-lethrau wash slope
golchlun *eg* golchluniau wash-drawing
golchwraig *eb* golchwragedd laundress
goledd (arwynebedd) *eg* splay
goledd (llethr) *eg* goleddau incline
goledd (llinell etc) *eg* goleddau slope
goledd (strata) *eg* dip
goledd (yn gyffredinol) *eg* goleddau slant
goledd anhawster *eg* incline of difficulty
goledd cynffonnog *eg* goleddau cynffonnog dovetail slope
goledd llinell *eg* slope of line
goleddfwr *eg* goleddfwyr qualifier
goleddu (am strata) *be* dip
goleddu (am linell etc) *be* slope
goleddu (yn gyffredinol) *be* slant
goleddu (am lethr) *be* incline
golethr *eg* golethrau dip slope
goleubwyntio *be* highlighting
goleubwyntio *be* highlight
goleudy *eg* goleudai lighthouse
goleudy yn gweithio, yn segur *eg* lighthouse in use and disused
goleudderbynnydd *eg* goleudderbynyddion photoreceptor
goleuedig *ans* enlightened
goleuedd *eg* goleueddau luminosity
Goleueddwyr *ell* Luminarists
goleufa *eg* goleufâu beacon
goleulong *eb* goleulongau lightship
goleunerth *eg* goleunerthoedd illuminating power
goleuni *eg* light
Goleuni'r De *eg* Aurora Australis
Goleuni'r Gogledd *eg* Aurora Borealis
goleuo *be* illuminate
Goleuo *be* Enlightenment
goleuo *be* light
goleuol *ans* luminous
goleusensitifedd *eg* photosensitivity
goleuydd *eg* illuminant
golfan *eb* golfanod passerine
gôl-geidwad *eg* gôl-geidwaid goalkeeper
goliwiad *eg* goliwiadau illumination
goliwiedig *ans* illuminated
goliwio *be* illuminate
golosg *eg* coke
golwg (=y gallu i weld) *eg/b* golygon sight; vision
golwg (=yr hyn a welir) *eg/b* golygon view
golwg (lluniad neu gynllun) *eg/b* golygon elevation
golwg acromatig *eg* achromatic vision
golwg anghyflawn *eg* golygon anghyflawn incomplete view
golwg anghyflawn *eg* golygon anghyflawn elevation view
golwg arosgo *eg* golygon arosgo oblique view
golwg ategol *eg* golygon ategol auxiliary view; auxiliary elevation
golwg byr *eg* short sight
golwg cernlun *eg* profile view
golwg cyfansawdd *eg* golygon cyfansawdd composite view
golwg cyflawn *eg* golygon cyflawn complete view
golwg cyffredinol *eg* overview
golwg darluniol *eg* pictorial view
golwg deulygad *eg* golygon deulygad binocular vision
golwg dewisiadau *eg* view options

golwg dogfen *eg* document view
golwg dylunio *eg* design view
golwg grŵp *eg* group view
golwg hanner trychiadol *eg* golygon hanner trychiadol half-sectional view
golwg hanner trychiadol *eg* golygon hanner trychiadol half-sectional elevation
golwg hir *eg* long sight
golwg isometrig *eg* golygon isometrig isometric view
golwg isometrig taenedig *eg* golygon isometrig taenedig exploded isometric view
golwg lliw *eg* colour vision
golwg lluniadu *eb* drawing view
golwg orthograffig *eg* golygon orthograffig orthographic view
golwg persbectif *eg* perspective view
golwg rhandrychiadol *eg* part-sectional elevation
golwg rhandrychiadol *eg* part-sectional view
golwg taenedig *eg* golygon taenedig exploded view
golwg trychiadol *eg* golygon trychiadol sectional view
golwg trychiadol *eg* golygon trychiadol sectional elevation
golwg trychiadol cyflawn *eg* golygon trychiadol cyflawn complete sectional elevation
golwyth *eg* golwython chop
golwyth o'r gridyll *eg* golwython o'r gridyll grilled chop
golygfa (=rhan o ddrama, ffilm etc) *eb* golygfeydd scene
golygfa (yn y tirlun naturiol, ac ategion yn y theatr) *eb* golygfeydd scenery
golygfa (=yr hyn a welir) *eb* golygfeydd view; vista
golygfa trem aderyn *eb* bird's eye view
golygfeydd prydferth *ell* scenic beauty
golygu *be* edit
golygu adrannau *be* edit sections
golygu all-lein *be* off-line editing
golygu allwedd *be* edit legend
golygu amlinell *be* edit contour
golygu arddull *be* edit style
golygu arddull cell *be* edit cell style
golygu arddull tudalen *be* edit page style
golygu awtodestun *be* edit autotext
golygu awtogywiro *be* edit autocorrect
golygu cofnod llyfryddiaeth *be* edit bibliography entry
golygu cofnod mynegai *be* edit index entry
golygu cyfres data *be* edit data series
golygu cysylltiadau *be* edit links
golygu data *be* edit data
golygu data siart *be* edit chart data
golygu delwedd *be* image editing
golygu disgrifiad colofn *be* edit column description
golygu echel *be* edit axis
golygu fideo *be* video editing
golygu ffeil *be* edit file
golygu ffeil mynegeiriau *be* edit concordance file
golygu fformat rhif *be* edit number format
golygu ffrâm *be* edit frame
golygu fframset *be* edit frameset
golygu ffurflenni *be* edit forms
golygu geiriadur addasu *be* edit custom dictionary
golygu gosodiadau hidlydd *be* edit filter settings
golygu graffigau *be* edit graphics
golygu grid *be* edit grid
golygu gwrthrych *be* edit object
golygu hypergyswllt *be* edit hyperlink
golygu isdeitl *be* edit subtitle
golygu labeli *be* edit labels
golygu llawr siart *be* edit chart floor
golygu llinell osod *be* edit snap line
golygu macros *be* edit macros
golygu maes *be* edit field
golygu math o siart *be* edit chart type
golygu mur siart *be* edit chart wall
golygu mynegai *be* edit index
golygu newidiadau *be* edit changes
golygu newidyn *be* edit variable
golygu nodau tudalen ffolder *be* edit folder bookmarks
golygu picsel *be* pixel edit
golygu pob echel *be* edit all axes
golygu pob teitl *be* edit all titles
golygu pwynt data *be* edit data point
golygu pwynt gosod *be* edit snap point
golygu rhaglennig *be* edit applet
golygu sgript *be* edit script
golygu sylw *be* edit comment
golygu symbolau *be* edit symbols
golygu tabl *be* edit table
golygu tabl databeilot *be* edit datapilot table
golygu teitl *be* edit title
golygu templed *be* edit template
golygu testun *be* text editing
golygu troednodyn *be* edit footnote
golygu ystod argraffu *be* edit print range
golygydd *eg* golygyddion editor
golygydd amlinell *eg* golygyddion amlinell contour editor
golygydd cysylltedd *eg* linkage editor
golygydd dynol *eg* golygyddion dynol human editor
golygydd picseli *eg* golygyddion picseli pixel editor
golygydd testun *eg* golygyddion testun text editor
gollwng (pêl) *be* drop
gollwng (y bwa) *be* loosing
gollwng aer allan *be* deflate
gollwng y bom atomig *be* dropping the atomic bomb
gollyngdod *eg* relief
gomaraidd *ans* gomarist
gomarwr *eg* gomarwyr gomarist

gonad *eg* gonadau gonad
gonadotroffig *ans* gonadotrophic
gonadotroffin *eg* gonadotrophin
▶ **gonorea** *eg* gonorrhoea
gôr *eb* gore
goralw *eg* excess demand
goramcangyfrif *be* overestimate
goramcangyfrif *eg* goramcangyfrifon overestimate
goramser *eg* overtime
goranadlu *be* hyperventilation
gorarbenigo *be* overspecialization
gorbarhad *eg* perseveration
gorbenion *ell* overheads
gorbenion newidiol *ell* variable overheads
gorboblogaeth *eb* overpopulation
gorboblogi *be* overpopulate
gorboethi *be* overheat
gorbryder *eg* anxiety
gorbryder rhagweledol *eg* anticipatory anxiety
gorbwysedd (am berson dros bwysau) *eg* overweight
gorbwysedd (am bwysedd gwaed) *eg* hypertension
gorbysgota *be* over-fishing
gorchfygwr *eg* gorchfygwyr conqueror
Gorchmynion y Cyfrin Gyngor *ell* Orders in Council
gorchudd (ar glwyf) *eg* gorchuddion dressing
gorchudd (yn gyffredinol) *eg* gorchuddion cover
gorchudd adlynol *eg* gorchuddion adlynol adhesive dressing
gorchudd arddwrn *eg* gorchuddion arddwrn wrist guard
gorchudd cefn cadair *eg* gorchuddion cefn cadair chair back
gorchudd clustog *eg* gorchuddion clustogau cushion cover
gorchudd clwyf *eg* gorchuddion clwyfau wound dressing
gorchudd cwmwl *eg* gorchuddion cwmwl cloud cover
gorchudd dal dŵr *eg* gorchuddion dal dŵr waterproof dressing
gorchudd di-haint *eg* gorchuddion di-haint sterile dressing
gorchudd ffabrig *eg* gorchuddion ffabrig fabric dressing
gorchudd matres *eg* gorchuddion matres mattress cover
gorchudd rhydd *eg* gorchuddion rhydd loose cover
gorchudd tebot *eg* gorchuddion tebot tea cosy
gorchudd trochion *eg* gorchuddion trochion spray cover
gorchuddio *be* cover; drape
gorchwyddiant *eg* hyperinflation
gorchwyl *eg* gorchwylion job
gorchymyn *be* command
gorchymyn *eg* gorchmynion command; order
gorchymyn adfer *eg* recovery order
gorchymyn amddiffyn *eg* gorchmynion amddiffyn protection order
gorchymyn amddiffyn brys *eg* gorchmynion amddiffyn brys emergency protection order
gorchymyn asesu plentyn *eg* gorchmynion asesu plant child assessment order
gorchymyn chwalu *eg* gorchmynion chwalu demolition order
gorchymyn dirywiad llwyr *eg* dereliction order
gorchymyn gofal *eg* gorchmynion gofal care order
gorchymyn goruchwyliaeth *eg* supervision order
gorchymyn prawf *eg* gorchmynion prawf probation order
gorchymyn prynu gorfodol *eg* gorchmynion prynu gorfodol compulsory purchase order
gorchymyn trosglwyddo diamod *eg* gorchmynion trosglwyddo diamod unconditional transfer instruction
gorchymyn tystiolaeth *eg* gorchmynion tystiolaeth witness order
gordanio *be* over-firing
gordanysgrifio *be* oversubscribe
gordensiwn *eg* hypertension
gordew *ans* obese
gordewdra *eg* obesity
gordo *eg* gordoeau cornice
gordreth *eb* gordrethi surtax
gordyfiant *eg* hyperplasia
gordynhau *be* overtighten
gordyrrog *ans* congested
gordyrru *be* congest
gordd (mewn chwaraeon) *eb* gyrdd mallet
gordd (yn gyffredinol) *eb* gyrdd sledge hammer
gordd ben wy *eb* gyrdd pen wy bossing mallet
gordd blastig *eb* gyrdd plastig plastic mallet
gordd bren *eb* gyrdd pren wood mallet
gordd bren ffawydd *eb* gyrdd pren ffawydd beech wood mallet
gordd brintio ffabrig *eb* gyrdd printio ffabrig fabric printing mallet
gordd ffawydd *eb* gyrdd ffawydd beech mallet
gordd gerfio *eb* gyrdd cerfio carving mallet
gordd godi *eb* gyrdd codi raising mallet
gordd ledr *eb* gyrdd lledr leather mallet; hide mallet
gordd lledr crai *eb* gyrdd lledr crai rawhide mallet
gordd pren bocs *eb* gyrdd pren bocs boxwood mallet
gordd pren caled *eb* gyrdd pren caled hardwood mallet
gorddargludedd *eg* superconductivity
gorddefnyddio *be* overutilize
gordderch *eb* gordderchadon concubine
gordderchaeth *eb* concubinage
gorddirlawn *ans* supersaturated
gorddirlawnder *eg* supersaturation
gorddirlenwi *be* supersaturate
gorddrafft *eg* gorddrafftiau overdraft
gorddryswch amlgnawdnychol *eg* multi-infarct dementia

gorddryswch henaint *eg* senile dementia
gorddwfn *ans* overdeepened
gorddyfnu *be* overdeepen
goresgyn (anawsterau etc) *be* overcome
goresgyn (gwlad) *be* invade
goresgyn anawsterau *be* overcome difficulties
goresgyniad *eg* goresgyniadau invasion
Goresgyniad Edward *eg* Edwardian Conquest
goresgynnwr *eg* goresgynwyr invader
gorest *eb* gorestau waste
gorestyniad *eg* overextension
goreurog *ans* gilded; gilt
gorfannol *ans* alveolar
gorfodaeth (yn gyffredinol) *eb* force; coercion; impressment
gorfodaeth (fewnol) *eb* gorfodaethau compulsion
gorfodeb *eb* gorfodebion injunction
gorfodi *be* force; coerce; press; constrain
gorfodi'r dilyn ymlaen *be* force the follow on
gorfodol *ans* compulsory; mandatory
gorfoleddus *ans* triumphant; jubilant
gorfwyaf *eg* hyper major
gorfychan *ans* infinitesimal
gorfychanyn *eg* gorfychanion infinitesimal
gorfywiogrwydd *eg* hyperactivity
gorffen *be* finish
gorffen arwyneb *be* surface finishing
gorffenedig *ans* finished
gorffenedig *ans* rounded
gorffeniad *eg* gorffeniadau finish
gorffeniad addurnol *eg* gorffeniadau addurnol decorative finish
gorffeniad arwyneb *eg* surface finish
gorffeniad cellwlos *eg* cellulose finish
gorffeniad cerrig nadd *eg* ashlar finish
gorffeniad clir *eg* gorffeniadau clir clear finish
gorffeniad cwyr *eg* wax finish
gorffeniad diogelu *eg* gorffeniadau diogelu protective finish
gorffeniad drych *eg* mirror finish
gorffeniad farnais *eg* varnish finish
gorffeniad heblaw paent *eg* gorffeniadau heblaw paent non-paint finish
gorffeniad hem *eg* gorffeniadau hem hem finish
gorffeniad lacr *eg* gorffeniadau lacr lacquer finish
gorffeniad llathrydd Ffrengig *eg* French polish finish
gorffeniad llyfn *eg* gorffeniadau llyfn smooth finish
gorffeniad mat *eg* matt finish
gorffeniad naturiol *eg* gorffeniadau naturiol natural finish
gorffeniad olew *eg* gorffeniadau olew oil finish
gorffeniad paent *eg* gorffeniadau paent paint finish
gorffeniad plaen *eg* gorffeniadau plaen plain finish
gorffeniad plisgyn wy *eg* eggshell finish
gorffeniad polywrethan *eg* polyurethane finish
gorffeniad satin *eg* gorffeniadau satin satin finish
gorffeniad sêm *eg* gorffeniadau sêm seam finish
gorffeniad sgleiniog *eg* gorffeniadau sgleiniog glossy finish
gorffeniad staen *eg* gorffeniadau staen stain finish
gorffeniad swêd *eg* suede finish
gorffeniadau yn y cynllun *ell* design refinements
gorffennu *be* finishing
gorffwys *be* rest
gorffwys gwely *eg* bedrest
gorffwys yn y dŵr *be* rest in water
gorffwysbin *eb* gorffwysbinau resting pin
gorffwysfan beryn *eg* gorffwysfannau beryn bearing rest
gorgodi *be* overcharge
gorgors *eb* gorgorsydd blanket bog
gorgyflogi *be* overmanning
gorgyforlan *eb* gorgyforlannau over bankful
gorgyffredinoli *be* overgeneralization
gorgyffwrdd (mewn teipograffeg) *be* kerning
gorgyffwrdd (yn gyffredinol) *be* overlap
gorgyffyrddiad *eg* gorgyffyrddion overlap
gorgyffyrddiad cymylau electronau *eg* electron cloud overlap
gorgynnes *ans* hot
goriwaered *eg* declivity
gor-ladd *be* overkill
gorlawn *ans* overcrowded
gorlenwad *eg* congestion
gorlenwi *be* overcrowding
gorlif *eg* gorlifoedd overflow; overspill
gorlif lafa *eg* gorlifoedd lafa lava outflow
gorlif pwynt arnawf *eg* floating point overflow
gorlif rhifyddol *eg* arithmetic overflow
gorlif stac *eg* stack overflow
gorlif testun *eg* text overflow
gorlifan *eb* gorlifannau spillway
gorlifdir *eg* flood plain
gorlifo *be* overflow; overspill; inundate
gorlinell *eb* gorlinellau line under the stave
gorliwiad *eg* gorliwiadau exaggeration
gorliwio *be* exaggerate
gorludded *eg* exhaustion
gorlwytho *be* overload
gorlwytho cyfryngol *be* media saturation
gorlwytho gwybyddol *be* cognitive overload
gorllewin *eg* west
gorllewin canol *eg* mid-west
gorllewin eithaf *eg* extreme west
Gorllewin Gwyllt *eg* Wild West
gorllewiniad (=mabwysiadu diwylliant y Gorllewin) *eg* westernization
gorllewiniad (=mesuriad pellter ar y môr) *eg* westing
gorllewino *be* westernize
gormes *eg/b* oppression; repression; tyranny
Gormes yr Un Mlwydd ar Ddeg *eb* Eleven Years Tyranny

gormesol *ans* oppressive; repressive; tyrannical
gormesu *be* oppress
gormeswr *eg* gormeswyr oppressor
gormod o gwyr yn y glust glue ear
gormodaeth fertigol *eb* vertical exaggeration
gormodedd *eg* gormodeddau excess
gormodedd egni *eg* excess energy
gormodedd gwasgedd *eg* excess pressure
gormodiaith *eb* hyperbole
gormodol *ans* excessive; extortionate
gornest (ymladd ffurfiol gydag arfau rhwng dau) *eb* gornestau duel
gornest derfynol (y cwpan) *eb* gornestau terfynol cup final
gornest (yn gyffredinol) *eb* gornestau contest; combat
gornest gleddyfau *eb* gornestau cleddyfau sword fight
gornest glos *eb* gornestau clos close combat
gornest gwpan *eb* gornestau cwpan cup-tie
goroer *ans* supercool
goroeredig *ans* supercooled
goroeri *be* supercool
goroesedd *eg* survivorship
goroesi *be* survive
goroesi yn y dŵr *be* water survival
goroesiad *eg* goroesiadau survival
goroesiad personol *eg* personal survival
goroesiad y cymhwysaf *eg* survival of the fittest
goroeswr *eg* goroeswyr survivor
goror *eg* gororau border; march
gorsaf aildrosglwyddo yn y canol *eb* gorsafoedd aildrosglwyddo yn y canol intermediate repeater radio station
gorsaf betrol *eb* gorsafoedd petrol filling station
gorsaf deip *eb* gorsafoedd teip type station
gorsaf drenau *eb* gorsafoedd trenau railway station
gorsaf drydan *eb* gorsafoedd trydan power station
gorsaf ddata pell *eb* gorsafoedd data pell remote data station
gorsaf ddocio *eb* gorsafoedd docio docking station
gorsaf gofnodi *eb* gorsafoedd cofnodi recording station
gorsaf heddlu *eb* gorsafoedd heddlu police station
Gorsafoedd y Groes *ell* Stations of the Cross
gorsecretiad *eg* oversecretion
gorsedd *eb* gorseddau throne
gorsymbyliad *eg* overstimulation
gorthwr *eg* gorthwyr keep
goruchaf *ans* supreme
Goruchaf Ben *eg* Supreme Head
Goruchaf Lys y Farnwriaeth *eg* Supreme Court of Judicature
goruchafiaeth *eb* ascendancy; supremacy; dominance
Goruchafiaeth Brotestannaidd *eb* Protestant Ascendancy
goruchafiaeth y dyn gwyn *eb* white supremacy
goruchafu *be* dominate
goruchafwr *eg* goruchafwyr supremacist
goruchwyliaeth *eb* supervision
goruchwyliwr (mewn arholiad) *eg* goruchwylwyr invigilator
goruchwyliwr (yn gyffredinol) *eg* goruchwylwyr supervisor; overseer
goruchwyliwr canolog *eg* goruchwylwyr canolog central executive
goruchwyliwr prosesu data *eg* goruchwylwyr prosesu data data processing supervisor
goruchwyliwr prosesu data *eg* goruchwylwyr prosesu data data processing manager
goruchwyliwr y feithrinfa *eg* nursery supervisor
goruchwyliwr y shifft *eg* shift supervisor
goruniad *eg* goruniadau lapped joint; lapping
goruniad bôn ac ysgwydd *eg* goruniadau bôn ac ysgwydd lapped butt joint
goruniad cudd cynffonnog *eg* goruniadau cudd cynffonnog secret lapped dovetail joint
goruniad cynffonnog *eg* goruniadau cynffonnog lapped dovetail joint
goruniad cynffonnog cudd *eg* goruniadau cynffonnog cudd secret lap dovetail
goruniad cynffonnog dwbl *eg* goruniadau cynffonnog dwbl double lapped dovetail joint
goruniad hanerog *eg* goruniadau hanerog half-lap joint
goruniad rhybedog *eg* goruniadau rhybedog riveted lap joint
goruwchnaturiol *ans* supernatural
goruwchreoli *be* overrule
gorweddiad *eg* lie
gorweddiad (brethyn) *eg* draping qualities
gorweddog *ans* bedridden
gorweddol (mewn botaneg) *ans* decumbent
gorweddol (yn gyffredinol) *ans* lying down; recumbent
gorwel *eg* gorwelion horizon
gorwthiad *eg* gorwthiadau over thrust
gorwyr *eg* gorwyrion great-grandchild
gorymdaith *eb* gorymdeithiau march
gorymdeithio *be* march
gorymdeithiol *ans* processional
gorynys *eb* gorynysoedd peninsula
gorysgogi *be* hot-housing
gorhyfforddi *be* overtraining
gosber *eg* gosberau vesper; evensong
gosgordd *eb* gosgorddion retinue; household
goslef *eb* goslefau inflexion
goslefu *be* intone; modulate
gosod *ans* applied; artificial
gosod (=lleoli) *be* place
gosod (=mynnu) *be* impose
gosod (=rhentu) *be* let
gosod (bwrdd) *be* lay
gosod (rhaglen, peiriant etc) *be* install
gosod (tasgau, arholiadau etc) *be* set

gosod amodau dechreuol *be* set up conditions
gosod bwrdd *be* set a table
gosod coler *be* put on a collar
gosod cyfeirnod *be* set reference
gosod cyrchwr *be* set cursor
gosod drws *be* door fitting
gosod fel rhagosodiad *be* set as default
gosod ffiniau *be* setting boundaries
gosod geiriaduron *be* install dictionaries
gosod gwarchae ar *be* besiege
gosod gweithrediadau *be* set operations
gosod haenau *be* laying up
gosod i gerddoriaeth *be* set to music
gosod llawes *be* setting in a sleeve
gosod llif *be* set a saw
gosod lliwiau *be* set colours
gosod nod *be* goal setting
gosod nodyn atgoffa *be* set reminder
gosod patrwm *be* lay out a pattern
gosod rhif tudalen *be* set page number
gosod seiliau *be* setting out foundations
gosod trefn *be* arrange order
gosod trefn tabiau *be* set tab order
gosod tudalen gartref *be* set home page
gosod y gwraidd *be* set root
gosod ymyl *be* lip
gosod yn erbyn *be* offset
gosod yn nhrefn y wyddor sort in alphabetical order
gosodedig *ans* fixed
gosodiad (=datganiad mewn geiriau) *eg* gosodiadau statement
gosodiad (=y ffordd mae tudalen etc wedi'i gosod) *eg* gosodiadau layout
gosodiad (am raglen) *eg* gosodiadau installation
gosodiad (yn gyffredinol) *eg* gosodiadau setting
gosodiad allforio *eg* gosodiadau allforio export setting
gosodiad bwrdd *eg* gosodiadau bwrdd place-setting
gosodiad cyfredol *eg* gosodiadau cyfredol current setting
gosodiad defnyddiwr gweinydd *eg* gosodiadau defnyddiwr gweinydd server user installation
gosodiad ffont *eg* gosodiadau ffont font setting
gosodiad haearn *eg* gosodiadau haearn iron setting
gosodiad hidlo *eg* gosodiadau hidlo filter setting
gosodiad lleiaf *eg* minimum installation
gosodiad llif *eg* gosodiadau llif set of a saw
gosodiad rhwydwaith *eg* gosodiadau rhwydwaith network installation
gosodiad rhyngrwyd awtobeilot *eg* gosodiadau rhyngrwyd awtobeilot autopilot internet setup
gosodiad tab *eg* gosodiadau tab tab setting
gosodiad tudalen *eg* gosodiadau tudalen page setup
gosodiad y dangosydd *eg* gosodiadau'r dangosydd display setting
gosodiad ymyl *eg* gosodiadau ymyl margin setting
Gosodiadau Apostolaidd, y *ell* Apostolic Constitutions, the
Gosodiadau Clarendon *ell* Provisions of Clarendon
gosodiadau gyrrwr *ell* driver settings
Gosodiadau Rhydychen *ell* Provisions of Oxford
Gosodiadau San Steffan *ell* Provisions of Westminster
gosodwr *eg* installer
gosodydd llif bylchog *eg* gosodyddion llif bylchog notched saw set
gosodydd llif teip gefelen *eg* gosodyddion llif teip gefelen pliers-type saw set
gosodydd plastig *eg* gosodyddion plastig plastic fitting
gosodydd sêm *eg* gosodyddion sêm seam set
gosodyn *eg* gosodion fixture
gosteg *eg* gostegau calm
gosteg (mewn canu penillion etc) *eb* gostegion series of airs
gostwng *be* lower; reduce
gostwng cwotâu *be* quota reduction
gostwng pwythau *be* decrease
gostwng traw *be* flatten
gostwng y corff *be* lower the body
gostyngadwy *ans* reducible
gostyngiad (=lleihad) *eg* gostyngiadau reduction
gostyngiad (=dirywiad) *eg* decline
gostyngiad (y rhewbwynt) *eg* depression of freezing point
gostyngiad mewn nifer *eg* falling rolls
gostyngiad yn y dreth *eg* tax relief
gostyngiadau *ell* cuts
gostyngol *ans* decreasing
gostyngydd *eg* gostyngwyr depressor
Gothig *ans* Gothic
gouache *eg* gouache
gradell *eb* gredyll bakestone
gradd (=cymhwyster a roddir gan brifysgol) *eb* graddau degree
gradd (=mesuriad, marc) *eb* graddau grade
gradd (=statws) *eb* graddau rank
gradd (=uned fesur onglau etc) *eb* graddau degree
gradd (=urdd, dosbarth) *eb* graddau order
gradd allanol *eb* graddau allanol external degree
gradd anrhydedd *eb* graddau anrhydedd honours degree
gradd ar gyfartaledd *eb* overall grade
gradd dau *eb* second order
gradd ddaduno *eb* degree of dissociation
gradd er anrhydedd *eb* graddau er anrhydedd honorary degree
gradd fewnol *eb* graddau mewnol internal degree
gradd ginetig *eb* kinetic order
gradd gydanrhydedd *eb* graddau cydanrhydedd joint honours degree

gradd gyffredinol *eb* graddau cyffredinol general degree
gradd isaf *eb* lowest order
gradd meistr *eb* graddau meistr master's degree
gradd o bensil *eb* graddau o bensiliau grade of pencil
gradd o ryddid *eb* graddau o ryddid degree of freedom
gradd tri *eb* third order
gradd uwch *eb* graddau uwch higher degree
graddau ffrwd *ell* stream orders
graddau rhyddid *ell* degrees of freedom
graddau sgraffinio *ell* abrasive grades
graddau'r raddfa *ell* degrees of the scale
graddedig (=gyda gradd brifysgol) *ans* graduated
graddedig (=wedi'i fesur a'i ddosbarthu) *ans* graded
gradden *eb* graddennau division
graddfa *eb* graddfeydd scale
graddfa amser *eb* graddfeydd amser time-scale
Graddfa Beaufort *eb* Beaufort Scale
graddfa bentatonig *eb* graddfeydd pentatonig pentatonic scale
graddfa berthynol fwyaf *eb* relative major scale
graddfa berthynol leiaf *eb* relative minor scale
graddfa Binet-Simon *eb* Binet-Simon scale
graddfa cyfyngau *eb* graddfeydd cyfyngau interval scale
graddfa dau *eb* scale of two
Graddfa Deallusrwydd Gryno Wechsler *eb* Wechsler Abbreviated Scale of Intelligence (WASI)
Graddfa Deallusrwydd Oedolion Wechsler *eb* Wechsler Adult Intelligence Scale (WAIS)
Graddfa Deallusrwydd Plant Wechsler *eb* Wechsler Intelligence Scale for Children (WISC)
graddfa deg pwynt *eb* ten point scale
graddfa drefnol *eb* ordinal scale
graddfa ddeilliadol *eb* graddfeydd deilliadol derived scale
graddfa ddisgyn *eb* graddfeydd disgyn descending scale
graddfa ddodecaffonig *eb* dodecaphonic scale
graddfa enwol *eb* nominal scale
graddfa esgyn *eb* graddfeydd esgyn ascending scale
graddfa fach *eb* small scale
graddfa fawr *eb* large scale
graddfa fernier *eb* graddfeydd fernier vernier scale
graddfa fetrig *eb* metric scale
graddfa fwyaf *eb* graddfeydd mwyaf major scale
graddfa fwyaf y tonydd *eb* tonic major scale
graddfa galedwch *eb* graddfeydd caledwch hardness scale
graddfa galedwch *eb* graddfeydd caledwch scale of hardness
graddfa ganol *eb* mesoscale
graddfa groeslinol *eb* graddfeydd croeslinol diagonal scale
graddfa gromatig *eb* graddfeydd cromatig chromatic scale
graddfa gromatig felodig *eb* melodic chromatic scale
graddfa gromatig harmonig *eb* graddfeydd cromatig harmonig harmonic chromatic scale
graddfa gymarebol *eb* ratio scale
graddfa gymharol *eb* graddfeydd cymharol comparative scale
graddfa isometrig *eb* graddfeydd isometrig isometric scale
graddfa leiaf *eb* graddfeydd lleiaf minor scale
graddfa leiaf harmonig *eb* graddfeydd lleiaf harmonig harmonic minor scale
graddfa leiaf y tonydd *eb* tonic minor scale
graddfa Likert *eb* Likert scale
graddfa lorweddol *eb* graddfeydd llorweddol horizontal scale
graddfa rif *eb* graddfeydd rhif number scale
graddfa Stanford-Binet *eb* Stanford-Binet scale
graddfa syml *eb* graddfeydd syml plain scale
graddfa symudol *eb* graddfeydd symudol sliding scale
graddfa tri *eb* scale of three
graddfa tuedd rheithiwr *eb* juror bias scale
graddfa tymheredd *eb* graddfeydd tymheredd temperature scale
graddfa tymheredd absoliwt *eb* absolute scale of temperature
graddiad *eg* graddiadau gradation
graddiad acenion *eg* graddiadau acenion gradation of accents
graddiad sain *eg* graddiadau sain gradation of volume
graddiad tryloyw *eg* graddiadau tryloyw transparent gradient
graddiannau graffiau *ell* gradients of graphs
graddiant *eg* graddiannau gradient; slope
▶ **graddiant barometrig** *eg* barometric gradient
graddiant crynodiad *eg* graddiannau crynodiad concentration gradient
graddiant gwasgedd *eg* graddiannau gwasgedd pressure gradient
graddio (gyda gradd brifysgol) *be* graduate
graddio (mewn graffeg) *be* scale
graddio (yn gyffredinol) *be* grade
graddio (yn ôl statws, safle) *be* rank
graddio ciplun *be* scale sprite
graddio cyfangiad *be* gradation of contraction
graddio llun *be* scale picture
graddliwio *be* shading
graddlwyd *eg* greyscale
graddnod *eg* graddnodau calibration mark; graduation
graddnodedig *ans* graduated
graddnodi *be* calibrate
graddnodiad *eg* graddnodiad calibration
graddol *ans* gradual
graddolen *eg* graddolennau gradual
graddoli *be* grade

graddoliad anghyseinedd *eg* gradation of dissonance
graean *eg* gravel
graean bras *eg* shingle
graean bras, llaid neu dywod shingle, mud or sand
graeanog *ans* gravelly
graeanu *be* gravel
graen *eg* grain
graen agored *eg* open grain
graen anwe *eg* weft grain
graen arian (derwen) *eg* silver grain
graen bras *eg* coarse grain
graen byr *eg* short grain
graen cam *eg* crooked grain
graen canol *eg* medium grain
graen clos *eg* close grain
graen croes *eg* cross grain
graen cymysg *eg* upset grain
graen cynfas *eg* canvas grain
graen hir *eg* long grain
graen llyfn *eg* even grain
graen mân *eg* fine grain
graen pen *eg* end grain
graen pren *eg* wood grain
graen rhyng-gloëdig *eg* interlocked grain
graen sglodion *eg* chipped grain
graen tonnog *eg* wavy grain
graen tro *eg* twisted grain
graen union *eg* straight grain
graen ystof *eg* warp grain
graenio *be* graining
graenus *ans* well-groomed
graff *eg* graffiau graph
graff amlder cronnus *eg* graffiau amlder cronnus cumulative frequency graph
graff bar *eg* graffiau bar bar graph
graff barlinell *eg* graffiau barlinell barline graph
graff bloc *eg* graffiau bloc block graph
graff colofn *eg* graffiau colofn column graph
graff cyflenwad a galw *eg* graffiau cyflenwad a galw supply and demand graph
graff cyflymder *eg* graffiau cyflymder velocity graph
graff cyflymder /cyflymiad *eg* graffiau cyflymder / cyflymiad velocity /acceleration graph
graff cyflymiad *eg* graffiau cyflymiad acceleration graph
graff gwasgariad *eg* graffiau gwasgariad scatter graph
graff llinell *eg* graffiau llinell line graph
graff llinell gyfansawdd *eg* graffiau llinellau cyfansawdd compound line graph
graff olwyn *eg* graffiau olwyn pie graph
graff pwyntiau *eg* graffiau pwynt point graph
graff trawsnewid *eg* graffiau trawsnewid conversion graph
graff uchder /amser *eg* height /time graph
graffeg *eb* graphics
graffeg crwban *eg* turtle graphics
graffem *eg* graffemau grapheme
graffig *ans* graphic
graffigol *ans* graphical
graffigwaith *eg* graphics
graffigwaith cyfrifiadurol *eg* computer graphics
graffigwaith fector a didfap *eg* vector and bitmap graphics
graffigyn *eg* graffigau graphic
graffigyn wedi'i animeiddio *eg* graffigau wedi'u hanimeiddio animated graphic
graffit *eg* graffitiau graphite
graffito *eg* graffito
gram *eg* gramau gram
gramadeg *eg/b* grammar
gramadeg cynhenid *eg* universal grammar
gramadeg cynhyrchiol *eg* generative grammar
gramadeg trawsffurfio *eg* transformational grammar
gramoffon *eg* gramoffonau gramophone
granaidd *ans* granal
granar *eg* graneri granary
grand barré *eg* grand barré
grant *eg/b* grantiau grant
grant arbennig *eg* grantiau arbennig special grant
grant atgyweirio *eg* grantiau atgyweirio repair grant
grant atodol *eg* grantiau atodol subsidiary grant
grant cynnal *eg* grantiau cynnal maintenance grant
grant cynnal addysg *eg* grantiau cynnal addysg educational support grant
grant cynnal incwm *eg* revenue support grant
grant cynnal trethi *eg* rate-support grant
grant datblygu *eg* grantiau datblygu development grant
grant dewisol *eg* grantiau dewisol discretionary grant
grant gorfodol *eg* grantiau gorfodol mandatory grant
grant gwella *eg* grantiau gwella improvement grant
grant gwirfoddol *eg* grantiau gwirfoddol amicable grant
grant hyfforddi *eg* grantiau hyfforddi training grant
grant mamolaeth *eg* grantiau mamolaeth maternity grant
grant marwolaeth *eg* grantiau marwolaeth death grant
grant y pen *eg* grantiau'r pen capitation grant; per capita grant
grant ymchwil *eg* grantiau ymchwil research grant
Grantiau Cefnogi a Hyfforddi Addysg *ell* GEST
granwlocyt *eg* granwlocytau granulocyte
granwm *eg* grana granum
graptolit *eg* graptolitau graptolite
gras *eg* grace
graticiwl *eg* graticiwlau graticule
gratin *eg* gratinau grating
gratin diffreithiant *eg* diffraction grating

grawn *eg* grain
grawnfwyd *eg* grawnfwydydd cereal
grawnfwyd brecwast *eg* grawnfwydydd brecwast breakfast cereal
grawnffrwyth *eg* grawnffrwythau grapefruit
Grawys *eg* Lent
greddf *eb* greddfau instinct; intuition
greddf baru *eb* mating instinct
Gregoraidd *ans* Gregorian
Gregori *eg* Gregory
greic *eg* greiciau grike
grenâd *eg* grenadau grenade
grid *eg* gridiau grid
grid asesu *eg* gridiau asesu assessment grid
grid cell *eg* gridiau cell cell grid
grid cynllun *eg* gridiau cynllun layout grid
grid geometrig *eg* gridiau geometrig geometric grid
grid i'r blaen grid to front
grid manyleb *eg* gridiau manyleb specification grid
grid pedwar ffigur *eg* gridiau pedwar ffigur four-figure grid
grid snap *eg* gridiau snap snap grid
gridyll *eg/b* gridyllau grill
gridyll cyswllt *eg* gridyllau cyswllt contact grill
gridyll isgoch *eg* gridyllau isgoch infrared grill
gridyll plygu *eg* gridyllau plygu fold-away grill
gridyll sefydlog *eg* gridyllau sefydlog fixed grill
gridyll uchel *eg* gridyllau uchel eye-level grill
griddfan *be* groan
grifft *eg* spawn
grifft broga *eg* frog spawn
gril *eg* griliau grille
grillian *be* stridulation
gris *eg* grisiau step; stair; tread
gris ac wyneb tread and riser
gris cytbwys *eg* grisiau cytbwys balanced step
gris taprog *eg* grisiau taprog tapered tread
grisffordd *eb* grisffyrdd stairway
gris-glogwyni *ell* stepped cliffs
grisial *eg* grisialau crystal
grisial Gwlad yr Iâ *eg* Iceland spar
grisialau hylif *ell* liquid crystals
grisialau Vandyke *ell* Vandyke crystals
grisialiad *eg* grisialiadau crystallization
grisialog *ans* crystalline
grisialograffaeth *eb* crystallography
grisialu *be* crystallize
grisialu ffracsiynol *be* fractional crystallization
grisiau *ell* staircase
grisiau agored *ell* open staircase
grisiau mynediad *ell* access staircase
grisiau nos *ell* night stairs
grisiau tro *ell* spiral staircase
grit bras *eg* coarse grit
grit canolig *eg* medium grit
grit mân *eg* fine grit
grit mân iawn *eg* very fine grit
grit naturiol *eg* natural grit
gro chwipio *eg* pebble dash
Groegaidd *ans* Greek
Groeg-Rufeinig *ans* Graeco-Roman
grog *eg* grog
gromed *eg* gromedau grommet
gronigyn *eg* gronigion granule
gronyn *eg* gronynnau particle; grain
gronyn alffa *eg* gronynnau alffa alpha particle
gronyn beta *eg* gronynnau beta beta particle
gronyn elfennol *eg* gronynnau elfennol elementary particle
gronyn llwch *eg* gronynnau llwch dust particle
gronyn wedi'i wefru *eg* gronynnau wedi'u gwefru charged particle
gronyn ymbelydrol *eg* gronynnau ymbelydrol radioactive particle
gronyniad *eg* granulation
gronynnau gwasgarog *ell* scattered particles
gronynnau Nissl *ell* Nissl granules
gronynnog *ans* granulated; granular
gronynnol *ans* particulate
groser *eg* groseriaid grocer
grotesg *ans* grotesque
groto *eg* grotos grotto
growt *eg* growtiau grout
growtio *be* grout
grugiar *eb* grugieir grouse
grut *eg* grutiau grit
grut melinfaen *eg* millstone grit
grutiog *ans* gritty
grutiog *ans* gritaceous
grwnd *eg* ground
grwnd bolws *eg* bolus ground
grwnd mandyllog *eg* porous ground
grwnd murol *eg* mural ground
grwnd resinaidd *eg* resinous ground
grwnd ysgythru *eg* grwndiau ysgythru etching ground
grwndblat *eg* grwndblatiau ground plate
grwndfas *eg* ground bass
grŵp *eg* grwpiau group
grŵp Abel *eg* Abelian group
grŵp anffurfiol *eg* informal group
grŵp animeiddio *eg* grwpiau animeiddio animation group
grŵp arbrofol *eg* grwpiau arbrofol experimental group
grŵp blwyddyn *eg* grwpiau blwyddyn year group
grŵp bwyd *eg* grwpiau bwyd food group
grŵp cefnogi *eg* grwpiau cefnogi support group
grŵp crefydd *eg* grwpiau crefydd religious group
grŵp cyfansoddol *eg* grwpiau cyfansoddol constituent group
grŵp cyfoedion *eg* grwpiau cyfoedion peer group
grŵp cylchol *eg* grwpiau cylchol cyclic group
grŵp cymudol *eg* grwpiau cymudol commutative group

grŵp cysylltiedig *eg* grwpiau cysylltiedig linked group
grŵp defnyddwyr *eg* grwpiau defnyddwyr user group
grŵp economaidd cymdeithasol *eg* social economic group
grŵp ethnig *eg* grwpiau ethnig ethnic group
grŵp ffocws *eg* grwpiau ffocws focus group
grŵp ffurfiol *eg* grwpiau ffurfiol formal group
grŵp gallu *eg* grwpiau gallu ability group
grŵp gwaed *eg* grwpiau gwaed blood group
grŵp gweithredol *eg* grwpiau gweithredol functional group
grŵp hunangymorth *eg* grwpiau hunangymorth self-help group
grŵp hydrocsyl *eg* hydroxyl group
grŵp incwm *eg* grwpiau incwm income group
grŵp llai breintiedig *eg* grwpiau llai breintiedig underprivileged group
grŵp lleiafrifol *eg* grwpiau lleiafrifol minority group
grŵp lleiafrifol ethnig *eg* grwpiau lleiafrifol ethnig ethnic minority group
grŵp moeseg *eg* grwpiau moeseg ethics group
grŵp newydd *eg* grwpiau newydd new group
grŵp newyddion *eg* grwpiau newyddion newsgroup
grŵp o gleientiaid *eg* client group
grŵp o wrthrychau *eg* group of objects
grŵp oedran *eg* grwpiau oedran age group
grŵp postio *eg* grwpiau postio mailing group
grŵp prosthetig ensym *eg* enzyme prosthetic group
grŵp rheolydd *eg* grwpiau rheolydd control group
grŵp rheolydd anghywerth *eg* grwpiau rheolydd anghywerth nonequivalent control group
grŵp rhoi magwraeth *eg* grwpiau rhoi magwraeth nurture group
grŵp rhydd *eg* grwpiau rhydd free group
grŵp sydd dan anfantais *eg* grwpiau sydd dan anfantais disadvantaged group
grŵp targed *eg* grwpiau targed target group
grŵp teulu *eg* grwpiau teulu family group
grŵp tiwtor *eg* grwpiau tiwtoriaid tutor group
grŵp trafod *eg* grwpiau trafod discussion group
grwpiau diagnosis perthynol *ell* diagnosis related groups
grwpio fertigol *be* vertical grouping
grwpio llorweddol *be* horizontal grouping
grwpio teuluol *be* family grouping
grwpio yn ôl gallu *be* ability grouping
grym *eg* grymoedd force
grym a roir force exerted
grym adferol *eg* grymoedd adferol restoring force
grym allgyrchol *eg* grymoedd allgyrchol centrifugal force
grym atyniad trydanol *eg* electric force of attraction
grym atynnol *eg* grymoedd atynnol attractive force
grym awyrennol *eg* air power
grym corfforol *eg* physical force
grym Coriolis *eg* Coriolis force
grym cydeffaith *eg* resultant force
grym cyffwrdd *eg* contact force
grym cywasgol *eg* grymoedd cywasgol compressive force
grym disgyrchiant *eg* grymoedd disgyrchiant force of gravity
grym disgyrchiant *eg* grymoedd disgyrchiant gravitational force
grym electro-gwan *eg* electro-weak force
grym electromotif *eg* electromotive force
grym fertigol *eg* vertical force
grym gosod *eg* applied force
grym gwrthyriad trydanol *eg* electric force of repulsion
grym gwrthyrru *eg* grymoedd gwrthyrru repulsive force
grym llorweddol *eg* grymoedd llorweddol horizontal force
grym llyngesol *eg* naval power
grym mewngyrchol *eg* grymoedd mewngyrchol centripetal force
grym moesol *eg* moral force
grym morwrol *eg* sea power
grym ochrol *eg* lateral force
grym troi *eg* turning force
grym tyniant *eg* tension force
grym tynnol *eg* grymoedd tynnol tractive force; tensile force
grym y farchnad *eg* grymoedd y farchnad market force
grym ychwanegol *eg* additional force
grymoedd anghytbwys *ell* unbalanced forces
grymoedd amrediad pell *ell* long range forces
grymoedd cymhlan *ell* coplanar forces
grymoedd cytbwys *ell* balanced forces
grymus *ans* powerful
Gurdwara *eg* Gurdwara
gurmukhi *eg* gurmukhi
Guru *eg* Guru
Guru Granth Sahib *eg* Guru Granth Sahib
Guto Ffowc *eg* Guy Fawkes
gwacáu *be* exhaust
gwacáu *be* flush
gwactod *eg* gwactodau vacuum
gwactod eithaf *eg* high vacuum
gwadiad *eg* gwadiadau recantation
gwadn *eg* gwadnau sole
gwadn rhewlif *eg* gwadnau rhewlif glacier sole
gwadn troed *eg* gwadnau traed sole of the foot
gwadnblygiad *eg* gwadnblygiadau plantarflexion
gwadu *be* deny; recant
gwaddod *eg* gwaddodion sediment; precipitate
gwaddod annhoddadwy *eg* gwaddodion annhoddadwy indissoluble residue
gwaddod glas *eg* blue precipitate
gwaddodiad *eg* sedimentation

gwaddodol *ans* sedimentary
gwaddol *eg* gwaddolion endowment; dowry
gwaddol priodferch *eg* marriage portion
gwaddoledig *ans* endowed
gwaddoledig *ans* dowried
gwaddoli *be* endow
gwaed *eg* blood
gwaed a haearn blood and iron
gwaed ocsigenedig *eg* oxygenated blood
gwaedboer *eg* haemoptysis
gwaedlif *eg* haemorrhage
gwaedlif ar yr ymennydd *eg* cerebral haemorrhage
gwaedu *be* bleeding
gwaedu mewnol *be* internal bleeding
gwaedd ac ymlid hue and cry
gwael (oherwydd afiechyd) *ans* sick
gwael (oherwydd safon is) *ans* inferior
► **gwaeledd cronig** *eg* chronic illness
gwaelod *eg* gwaelodion bottom; base
gwaelod bwylltid *eg* gwaelodion bwylltid swivel base
gwaelod crwn *eg* gwaelodion crwn circular base
gwaelod cwmwl *eg* gwaelodion cwmwl cloud base
gwaelod drôr *eg* gwaelodion droriau drawer bottom; drawer base
gwaelod dysglog *eg* gwaelodion dysglog dished base
gwaelod gweflog *eg* gwaelodion gweflog knocked up bottom
gwaelod V *eg* gwaelodau V V base
gwaelod y llinell *eg* bottom of line
gwaelod y nod *eg* bottom of character
gwaelod-danseilio *be* basal sapping
gwaelodfa *eb* gwaelodfeydd base level
gwaelodlin *eb* gwaelodliniau baseline
gwaelodol *ans* underlying; basal
gwaell *eb* gweill knitting needle
gwaethygiad *eg* exacerbation
gwag (=heb ddim y tu mewn iddo) *ans* hollow
gwag (am dudalen etc) *ans* blank
gwagio *be* evacuate
gwagle amddiffynnol *eg* defensible space
gwagle diddefnydd *eg* dead space
gwagle gwaed *eg* gwagleoedd gwaed blood space
gwagle Havers *eg* gwagleoedd Havers Haversian space
gwagle pelfig *eg* pelvic space
gwagle perifitelin *eg* perivitelline space
► **gwag-lenwad** *eg* gwag-lenwadau blank-fill
► **gwag-lenwi** *be* blank-fill
gwagleoedd rhyng-gellol *ell* intercellular spaces
gwaglyn *eg* gwaglynnau space
gwagnod *eg* gwagnodau nought
gwagolyn *eg* gwagolynnau vacuole
gwagolyn cyfangol *eg* gwagolynnau cyfangol contractile vacuole
gwahadden *eb* gwahaddod mole
gwahanadwy *ans* separable
gwahanedig *ans* separated
gwahanfa ddŵr *eb* gwahanfeydd dŵr divide
gwahanfa ddŵr *eb* gwahanfeydd dŵr watershed; divide; water parting
gwahanfur *eg* gwahanfuriau septum
gwahanfur gwaed-ymennydd *eg* blood-brain barrier
gwahanfur rhag yr hinsawdd *eg* climate barrier
gwahaniad *eg* gwahaniadau separation
gwahaniad atomig *eg* atomic spacing
gwahaniad dosbarth *eg* class separation
gwahaniad eddïau *eg* fringe separation
gwahaniad gwefr rhannol *eg* partial exchange separation
gwahaniad i begynliniau sfferig *eg* separation into spherical polars
gwahaniad pwerau *eg* separation of powers
gwahaniaeth *eg* gwahaniaethau difference
gwahaniaeth adeileddol *eg* structural difference
gwahaniaeth arwyddocaol *eg* significant difference
gwahaniaeth cyffredin *eg* common difference
gwahaniaeth cymedrau *eg* difference of means
gwahaniaeth cymedrig *eg* mean difference
gwahaniaeth dosbarth *eg* gwahaniaethau dosbarth class distinction
gwahaniaeth gwedd *eg* phase difference
gwahaniaeth gweithredol *eg* gwahaniaethau gweithredol functional difference
gwahaniaeth lleiaf a welir *eg* just-noticeable difference
gwahaniaeth potensial *eg* gwahaniaethau potensial potential difference
gwahaniaeth potensial cyflymu *eg* accelerating potential difference
gwahaniaeth potensial disgyrchedd *eg* gravitational potential difference
gwahaniaeth potensial eiledol sinwsoidaidd *eg* sinusoidal alternating potential difference
gwahaniaeth potensial trydanol *eg* electric potential difference
gwahaniaeth retinâu *eg* retinal disparity
gwahaniaeth rhwng dau sgwâr difference of two squares
gwahaniaeth rhwng unigolion *eg* individual difference
gwahaniaeth sylfaenol *eg* gwahaniaethau sylfaenol basic difference
gwahaniaethadwy *ans* distinguishable
gwahaniaethiad *eg* differentiation
gwahaniaethiad arwynebedd *eg* areal differentiation
gwahaniaethol *ans* differentiated
gwahaniaethol *ans* differential
gwahaniaethu (yn gyffredinol) *be* differentiate; distinguish;
gwahaniaethu (yn erbyn) *be* discriminate; discrimination

gwahaniaethu ar sail grŵp *be* intergroup discrimination
gwahaniaethu ar sail rhyw *be* sex discrimination
gwahaniaethu cilfachau *be* niche differentiation
gwahaniaethu hiliol *be* racial discrimination
gwahaniaethu prisiau *be* price discrimination
gwahaniaethu rhwng cynnyrch *be* product differentiation
gwahaniaethu sefydliadol *be* institutional discrimination
gwahaniaethu sŵn *be* auditory discrimination
gwahaniaethu yn ôl y canlyniad *be* differentiation by outcome
gwahaniaethu'n gadarnhaol *be* positive discrimination
gwahanol *ans* different
gwahanolrwydd *eg* distinctiveness
gwahanolyn *eg* gwahanolion discriminant
gwahanu *be* separate; segregate; rule off
gwahanu ffibrau *be* untwist fibres
gwahanydd *eg* gwahanyddion spacer
gwahanydd testun *eg* gwahanyddion testun text separator
gwahardd (a gwneud yn anghyfreithlon) *be* outlaw
gwahardd (o ysgol etc) *be* exclude
gwahardd (yn gyffredinol) *be* prohibit
gwahardd dros dro *be* suspend
gwaharddeb *eb* gwaharddebion injunction
gwaharddiad *eg* gwaharddiadau prohibition; embargo; interdict
gwaharddiad cystadleuol *eg* competitive exclusion
gwaharddiad dros dro *eg* gwaharddiadau dros dro suspension
gwaharddiad lliw *eg* colour bar
gwaharddle *eg* gwaharddleoedd exclosure
gwahodd *be* invite
gwahoddiad i drafod *eg* invitation to treat
gwain (cleddyf etc) *eb* gweiniau sheath
gwain (mewn anatomeg etc) *eb* gweiniau vagina
gwain sypyn *eb* bundle sheath
gwair *eg* gweiriau grass
gwair naturiol *eg* natural grass
gwaith (=ffatri) *eg* gweithfeydd plant
gwaith (yn gyffredinol) *eg* gweithiau work; job
gwaith adfer *eg* remedial work
gwaith allanol *eg* outwork
gwaith anffigurol *eg* non-figurative work
gwaith ansoddol *eg* qualitative work
gwaith ar siâp *eg* shape work
gwaith ar y llawr *eg* floorwork
gwaith arbrofi *eg* experimental work
gwaith asiedydd *eg* joinery
gwaith awyr agored *eg* outdoor work
gwaith barbola *eg* barbola work
gwaith basged *eg* basketry
gwaith blaen nodwydd *eg* needlepoint
gwaith bloc /blociau *eg* blockwork
gwaith blociau *eg* block work
gwaith bydwraig *eg* midwifery
gwaith carreg *eg* stonework
gwaith carreg pensaernïol *eg* stone architecture
gwaith cartref *eg* homework
gwaith carthion *eg* gweithfeydd carthion sewage works
gwaith celfyddydol *eg* gweithiau celfyddydol work of art
gwaith cerrig ffug *eg* artificial stonework
gwaith cerrig nadd *eg* ashlar
gwaith codi *eg* raised work
gwaith coed *eg* wood work
gwaith creadigol *eg* creative work
gwaith crosio *eg* crochet
gwaith cwrs *eg* coursework
gwaith cydosod *eg* gweithfeydd cydosod assembly plant
gwaith cyfeintiol *eg* volumetric work
gwaith cymdeithasol *eg* social work
gwaith cymhleth *eg* intricate work
gwaith dan do *eg* indoor work
gwaith dodrefn *eg* cabinet work
gwaith dŵr *eg* water work
gwaith dydd *eg* day-work
gwaith eisteddog *eg* sedentary work
gwaith ffelt *eg* felt work
gwaith galedu *be* work hardening
gwaith gof *eg* forgework
gwaith gosod *eg* directed work
gwaith grid *eg* grid work
gwaith gwiail *eg* canework
gwaith llaw *eg* handwork
gwaith llaw *eg* handicraft
gwaith llenfetel *eg* sheet metalwork
gwaith llythrennu *eg* lettering work
gwaith maes *eg* fieldwork
gwaith mainc *eg* bench work
gwaith metel *eg* metalwork
gwaith morthwyl *eg* beaten metalwork
gwaith oddi ar y safle *eg* offsite work
gwaith paratoadol *eg* preparatory work
gwaith plygu *eg* folding work
gwaith pocer *eg* poker work
gwaith project *eg* gweithiau project project work
gwaith raffia *eg* raffia work
gwaith rhew *eg* frost action
gwaith rhewi-dadlaith *eg* freeze-thaw action
gwaith rhewi-dadmer *eg* freeze-thaw action
gwaith rhif *eg* number work
gwaith rhwng asiantaethau *eg* interagency work
gwaith saer *eg* carpentry
gwaith saer ac asiedydd carpentry and joinery
gwaith selio *eg* sealing work
gwaith tîm *eg* teamwork
gwaith turn *eg* lathework
gwaith thematig *eg* thematic work
gwaith ymarferol *eg* practical work

gwaith ymchwilio *eg* investigative work
gwaith ysbeidiol *eg* casual employment
gwaith-chwarae *eg* playwork
gwâl *eb* gwalau lair
gwalch glas *eg* gweilch glas sparrowhawk
gwalch y penwaig *eg* gweilch y penwaig razorbill
gwalch y pysgod *eg* gweilch y pysgod osprey
gwalchwerth *eg* gwalchwerthoedd rogue value
gwald *eg* gwaldiau welt
gwall *eg* gwallau error
gwall angheuol *eg* gwallau angheuol fatal error
gwall amseru *eg* gwallau amseru error of timing
gwall anadferadwy *eg* gwallau anadferadwy irrecoverable error
gwall anelu *eg* aiming error
gwall anhysbys *eg* gwallau anhysbys unknown error
gwall blaendorri *eg* gwallau blaendorri truncation error
gwall creu gwrthrych *eg* error creating object
gwall crynhoi *eg* gwallau crynhoi compile error
gwall cwanteiddio *eg* gwallau cwanteiddio quantisation error
gwall cystrawen *eg* gwallau cystrawen syntax error
gwall dynol *eg* gwallau dynol human error
gwall geiriadur *eg* gwallau geiriadur dictionary error
gwall methiant *eg* gwallau methiant error of failure
gwall nesaf *eg* next error
gwall priflythrennu *eg* capitalization error
gwall teipio *eg* gwallau teipio typing error
gwall trawsysgrifol *eg* gwallau trawsysgrifol transcription error
gwall trefn *eg* gwallau trefn error of order
gwall trwy gamwaith *eg* gwallau trwy gamwaith error of commission
gwall tudalen *eg* gwallau tudalen page fault
gwall wrth ailenwi *eg* gwallau wrth ailenwi error while renaming
gwall wrth argraffu *eg* gwallau wrth argraffu error while printing
gwall ysgrifennu *eg* write error
gwallau cynhenid metabolaeth *ell* inborn errors of metabolism
gwallgof *ans* insane
gwallgofddyn *eg* lunatic
gwallnod *eg* gwallnodau error character
gwallt *ell* hair
gwallus *ans* defective
gwallus *ans* inaccurate
gwan *ans* weak
gwanas *eg/b* gwanasau buttress; stay
gwanas rhybedog *eg* gwanasau rhybedog riveted stay
gwanediad *eg* gwanediadau dilution
gwanedig *ans* dilute
gwanedu *be* dilute
gwanedydd *eg* gwanedyddion diluent
gwaneg Iwerydd *eb* gwanegau Iwerydd Atlantic roller
gwanegau *ell* rollers
gwangalon *ans* defeatist
gwangalonnwr *eg* gwangalonwyr defeatist
gwanhad *eg* attenuation
gwanhad-pellter *eg* distance-decay
gwanhadur *eg* gwanaduron attenuator
gwanhau *be* attenuate
gwaniad *eg* gwaniadau thrust
gwaniad union *eg* gwaniadau union direct thrust
gwanin *eg* guanine
gwanu *be* thrust
gwanwyn *eg* spring
gwanwyneiddiad *eg* vernalization
gwanychiad *eg* gwanychiadau damping
gwanychiad trwm *eg* heavy damping
gwanychiad ysgafn *eg* light damping
gwanychol *ans* damped
gwanychu (sain) *be* damp
gwanydd *eg* gwanyddion piercer
gwarant (am nwyddau etc) *eb* gwarantau guarantee; warranty
gwarant (i arestio rhywun) *eb* gwarantau warrant
gwarant (=sicrwydd) *eb* security
gwarant atafaelu *eg* gwarantau atafaelu distress warrant
gwarant dienyddio *eb* gwarantau dienyddio death warrant
gwarantu *be* guarantee; underwrite
gwarantwr *eg* gwarantwyr guarantor
gwarblat *eg* gwarblatiau wallplate
gwarchae *eg* gwarchaeon blockade; siege
gwarchae o'r môr *eg* naval blockade
gwarcheidwad *eg* gwarcheidwaid guardian
gwarcheidwaeth *eb* guardianship
gwarchod (gyda milwyr etc) *be* guard
gwarchod (plant) *be* babysit
gwarchod (yr amgylchedd etc) *be* conserve
gwarchod ac amddiffyn yr amgylchedd environmental conservation and protection
gwarchod data *be* data protection; protecting data
gwarchodaeth (=diogelwch) *eb* security
gwarchodaeth (=awdurdod gwarchodwr) *eb* tutelage
gwarchodaeth castell *eb* castleguard
gwarchodfa *eb* gwarchodfeydd reserve; sanctuary
gwarchodfa natur *eb* gwarchodfeydd natur nature reserve
gwarchodlu *eg* gwarchodluoedd guard
Gwarchodlu Cartref *eg* Home Guard
Gwarchodlu Cenedlaethol *eg* National Guard
gwarchodwr *eg* gwarchodwyr babysitter
gwarchodwr asgell *eg* gwarchodwyr asgell wing defence
gwarchodwr plant *eg* gwarchodwyr plant child minder

gwarchodwr plant cofrestredig *eg* gwarchodwyr plant cofrestredig registered child minder
gwardeiniaeth *eb* gwardeiniaethau wardenship
gwardiaeth *eb* wardship
gwarediad *eg* disposal
gwaredu (o'r corff) *be* elimination
gwaredu (yn gyffredinol) *be* discard; dispose
gwaredu canlyniadau niweidiol *be* removing harmful consequences
gwaredu sbwriel *be* waste disposal; refuse disposal
gwareiddiad *eg* gwareiddiadau civilization
gwarged *eb* gwargedion surplus
gwarged defnyddwyr *eb* consumer surplus
gwariant *eg* expenditure; outlay; spending
gwariant a gedwir yn ôl *eg* expenditure retained
gwariant cyfalaf *eg* capital expenditure
gwariant defnyddwyr *eg* consumer spending; consumer expenditure
gwariant dirprwyedig *eg* delegated expenditure
gwariant llywodraeth *eg* government spending
gwarineb *eg* civility
gwario (arian) *be* spend
gwarthnodi *be* brand
gwarthol *eb* gwartholion stirrup; stapes
gwas dirwyn *eg* gweision dirwyn bobbin winder
gwasaidd *ans* subservient
gwasanaeth (=cydgynulliad er mwyn addoli) *eg* gwasanaethau assembly
gwasanaeth (yn gyffredinol) *eg* gwasanaethau service
gwasanaeth (e.e. cyflenwad trydan, dŵr etc) *eg* gwasanaethau utility
gwasanaeth adwerthu a dosbarthu *eg* gwasanaethau adwerthu a dosbarthu retail and distributive service
gwasanaeth addysg blynyddoedd cynnar *eg* gwasanaethau addysg blynyddoedd cynnar early years education service
gwasanaeth amgueddfa i ysgolion *eg* gwasanaethau amgueddfa i ysgolion museum school service
gwasanaeth ariannol *eg* gwasanaethau ariannol financial service
gwasanaeth beunyddiol *eg* daily office
gwasanaeth blaen swyddfa *eg* front office service
gwasanaeth byw yn y gymuned *eg* gwasanaethau byw yn y gymuned community living service
gwasanaeth cartref *eg* gwasanaethau cartref domiciliary service
gwasanaeth cefnogi anghenion arbennig *eg* gwasanaethau cefnogi anghenion arbennig special needs support service
gwasanaeth cefnogi cyfannol *eg* gwasanaethau cefnogi cyfannol integrated support service
gwasanaeth cludiant cyhoeddus *eg* gwasanaethau cludiant cyhoeddus public transport service
gwasanaeth cludo *eg* gwasanaethau cludo carrying service
gwasanaeth cudd *eg* gwasanaethau cudd secret service
gwasanaeth cyfathrebu *eg* gwasanaethau cyfathrebu communication service
gwasanaeth cyfle am waith *eg* work opportunity service
gwasanaeth cynghori *eg* gwasanaethau cynghori advisory service; counselling service
Gwasanaeth Cynghori Defnyddwyr *eg* Consumer Advice Service
gwasanaeth cyngor a gwybodaeth *eg* gwasanaethau cyngor a gwybodaeth advice and information service
gwasanaeth cyhoeddus *eg* gwasanaethau cyhoeddus public service
Gwasanaeth Cymodi ACAS *eg* Advisory, Conciliation and Arbitration Service
gwasanaeth cynnal yn y gymuned *eg* gwasanaethau cynnal yn y gymuned community support service
Gwasanaeth Erlyn y Goron *eg* Crown Prosecution Service
gwasanaeth gwirfoddol *eg* gwasanaethau gwirfoddol voluntary service
gwasanaeth gyrfaoedd *eg* gwasanaethau gyrfaoedd career service
gwasanaeth i gwsmeriaid *eg* gwasanaethau i gwsmeriaid customer service
gwasanaeth iechyd *eg* gwasanaethau iechyd health service
Gwasanaeth Iechyd Gwladol *eg* National Health Service
gwasanaeth iwmon *eg* yeoman service
gwasanaeth lleoli athrawon *eg* teacher placement service
gwasanaeth marchog *eg* knight's service
gwasanaeth milwrol *eg* military service
gwasanaeth ôl-werthu *eg* gwasanaethau ôl-werthu after-sales service
Gwasanaeth Sanctaidd *eg* Holy Office
gwasanaeth sifil *eg* civil service
gwasanaethau adwerthu *ell* retail services
gwasanaethau cyhoeddus *ell* public utilities
gwasanaethau cymdeithasol *ell* social services
gwasanaethau gofal *ell* caring services
gwasanaethau post *ell* postal services
gwasanaethu *be* service
gwasarn *eg* litter; deep litter
gwaseidd-dra *eg* subservience
gwasg (ar gyfer argraffu) *eb* gweisg press
gwasg (canol corff) *eb* gweisg waist
Gwasg Aldus Manutius *eb* Aldine Press
gwasg argraffu *eb* gweisg argraffu printing press
gwasg bwytho *eb* gweisg pwytho stitching press
gwasg dorri *eb* gweisg torri cutting press
gwasg fasnachol *eb* trade press
gwasg haearn nipio *eb* gweisg haearn nipio iron nipping press
gwasg hedegog *eb* gweisg hedegog fly press

gwasg nipio *eb* gweisg nipio nipping press
gwasg orffennu *eb* gweisg gorffennu finishing press
gwasg osod *eb* gweisg gosod lying press
gwasg rhwymwr llyfrau *eb* gweisg rhwymwr llyfrau bookbinder's press
gwasg unionsyth *eb* gweisg unionsyth standing press
gwasg wnïo *eb* gweisg gwnïo sewing press
gwasg ysgythru *eb* gweisg ysgythru etching press
gwasgariad *eg* gwasgariadau dispersion; dispersal; scattering
gwasgariad anelastig *eg* inelastic scattering
gwasgariad binomial *eg* binomial distribution
gwasgariad cyfrifoldeb *eg* diffusion of responsibility
gwasgariad elastig *eg* elastic scattering
gwasgariad gan ddŵr *eg* water dispersal
gwasgariad gan y gwynt *eg* wind dispersal
gwasgariad hadau *eg* seed dispersion
▸ **gwasgariad normal** *eg* gwasgariadau normal normal distribution
gwasgariad normal safonol *eg* standard normal distribution
gwasgariad sborau *eg* dispersal of spores
gwasgariad sgiw *eg* gwasgariadau sgiw skewed distribution
gwasgarog *ans* dispersed; sparse
gwasgarol *ans* dispersive
gwasgaru *be* disperse; scatter
gwasgarwedd *eb* gwasgarweddau disperse phase
gwasgblat *eg* gwasgblatiau caul
gwasgblat ffurfiedig *eg* gwasgblatiau ffurfiedig shaped caul
gwasgblat metel *eg* gwasgblatiau metel metal caul
gwasgbwynt *eg* gwasgbwyntiau pressure point
gwasgedig *ans* pressed
gwasgedd *eg* gwasgeddau pressure
gwasgedd aer *eg* air pressure
gwasgedd allanol *eg* external pressure
gwasgedd anwedd *eg* vapour pressure
gwasgedd anwedd dirlawn *eg* saturated vapour pressure
gwasgedd atmosfferig *eg* atmospheric pressure
gwasgedd atmosfferig safonol *eg* standard atmospheric pressure
gwasgedd cyson *eg* constant pressure
gwasgedd gostyngol *eg* reduced pressure
gwasgedd gwraidd *eg* root pressure
gwasgedd i fyny *eg* upward pressure
gwasgedd isel *eg* low pressure
gwasgedd isel Gwlad yr Iâ *eg* Icelandic 'low'
gwasgedd llyfn *eg* even pressure
gwasgedd mewnol *eg* internal pressure
gwasgedd mwyaf *eg* maximum pressure
gwasgedd ochrol *eg* sideways pressure
gwasgedd osmotig *eg* osmotic pressure
gwasgedd rhannol *eg* partial pressure
gwasgedd sugno *eg* suction pressure
gwasgedd tuag i lawr *eg* downward pressure
gwasgedd uchel *eg* high pressure
gwasgedd uchel Azores *eg* Azores high
gwasgeddedig *ans* pressurized
gwasgeddu *be* pressurize
gwasgell *eb* gwasgelli presser foot
gwasgffit *eg* press fit
gwasgiad dwbl *eg* gwasgiadau dwbl double stopping
gwasgiad pedwarplyg *eg* gwasgiadau pedwarplyg quadruple stopping
gwasgnod (erfyn nwrlio) *eg* gwasgnodau imprint
gwasgod *eb* gwasgodau waistcoat
gwasgu *be* press; squeeze; depress; squash; wring
gwasgwr dillad *eg* gwasgwyr dillad wringer
gwasgwr tafod *eg* gwasgwyr tafod tongue depressor
gwasgydd hydrolig *eg* gwasgyddion hydrolig hydraulic press
gwasod *ans* on heat
gwastad *ans* flat; level; flattened
gwastad dysgu *eg* learning plateau
gwastad heli *eg* salt flat
gwastadedd *eg* gwastadeddau plain
gwastadedd arfordirol *eg* gwastadeddau arfordirol coastal plain
gwastadedd copa *eg* gwastadeddau copaon summit plain
gwastadedd isel *eg* gwastadeddau isel low-lying plain
gwastadedd ysgythru *eg* gwastadeddau ysgythru etch plain
gwastadiant *eg* planation
gwastadrwydd *eg* flatness
gwastadrwydd cymharol *eg* relative flatness
gwastatir afon *eg* gwastatiroedd afonydd plain tract
gwastatir llifwaddod *eg* gwastatiroedd llifwaddod alluvial plain
gwastraff *eg* gwastraffau waste
gwastraff cotwm *eg* cotton waste
gwastraff diwydiannol *eg* industrial waste
gwastraff naturiol *eg* natural wastage
gwastraff pacio *eg* packing waste
gwastraffu *be* waste
gwau *be* knit
gwau â dwy wialen *be* pairing
gwau dau bwyth ynghyd *be* knit two together
gwau drwy'r gwŷdd *be* weaving
gwau igam-ogam *be* weaving
gwau llac *be* loose knitting
gwawdlun *eg* gwawdluniau caricature
gwawdlunydd *eg* gwawdlunwyr caricaturist
gwawr *eb* tinge
gwayw fwyell *eb* gwayw fwyeill halberd
gwaywffon *eb* gwawyffyn javelin
gwaywffon *eb* gwaywffyn spear

gwaywffon *eb* gwaywffyn lance
gwaywr *eg* gwaywyr lancer
gwddf (rhan o lif) *eg* gyddfau gullet
gwddf (yn gyffredinol) *eg* gyddfau throat; neck
gwddf bad *eg* boat neck
gwddf crwban *eg* turtle neck
gwddf crwn *eg* gyddfau crwn round neck
gwddf cwfl *eg* cowl neck
gwddf folcanig *eg* gyddfau folcanig volcanic neck
gwddf polo *eg* gyddfau polo polo neck
gwddf ryffl *eg* gyddfau ryffl ruffled neck
gwddf sgwâr *eg* gyddfau sgwâr square neck
gwddf siamffrog *eg* chamfered neck
gwddf tennyn *eg* gyddfau tennyn halter neck
gwddf uchel *eg* gyddfau uchel high neck
gwddf y groth *eg* cervix
gwddf y raced *eg* gyddfau'r racedi neck of racket
gwe *eb* gweoedd web
gwe capilarïau *eb* gweoedd capilarïau capillary web
gwe fwydydd *eb* gweoedd bwydydd food web
gwead *eg* gweadau texture
gwead agored *eg* open texture
gwead basged *eg* basket weave
gwead bras *eg* coarse texture
gwead cornaidd *eg* gweadau cornaidd horny texture
gwead llyfn *eg* smooth texture
gwead llyfn *eg* gweadau llyfn even texture
gwead main *eg* fine texture
gwead meddal *eg* soft texture
gwead pridd *eg* soil texture
gweadedd *eb* texture
gweadeddol *ans* textural
gweadeddu *be* texturing
gwedd (mewn meddygaeth) *eb* gweddau facies
gwedd (pren) *eb* texture
gwedd (yn gyffredinol) *eb* gweddau phase
gwedd esbonyddol *eb* exponential phase
gwedd log *eb* log phase
gwedd log/esbonyddol *eb* log/exponential phase
gwedd lwyfandir *eb* plateau phase
gwedd nwy *eb* gas phase
gwedd orffenedig *eb* finished appearance
gwedd weithredu *eb* gweddau gweithredu execute phase
gwe-ddarllediad *eg* gwe-ddarllediadau webcast
gwe-ddarlledu *be* webcast
gweddau cylchred y galon *ell* phases of heart cycle
gweddau'r lleuad *ell* phases of the moon
gwedd-gysylltiedig *ans* phase linked
gweddi *eb* gweddïau prayer
gweddill (mewn cyfrif banc etc) *eg* gweddillion balance
gweddill (yn gyffredinol) *eg* gweddillion residue; remainder; surplus
gweddill clyw *eg* residual hearing
gweddill golwg *eg* residual vision
gweddilleb *eb* gweddillebau residual
gweddillol *ans* residual
gweddillyn corffilyn coch *eg* gweddillion corffilod coch red cell ghost
gweddïo *be* pray
gweddw *eb* gweddwon widow; dowager
gweddw'r brenin *eb* queen dowager
gwefan *eb* gwefannau web site
gwefan cwmni *eb* gwefannau cwmnïau company website
gwefan farw *eb* gwefannau marw ghost site
gwefan lychlyd *eb* gwefannau llychlyd cobweb site
gwefan wreiddiol *eb* originating web site
gwefeistr *eg* gwefeistri webmaster
gwefl *eb* gweflau bezel
gweflog *ans* bezelled
gweflogyn *eg* gweflogynion eelpout
gwefr *eb* gwefrau charge
gwefr anwythol *eb* induced charge
gwefr bositif *eb* gwefrau positif positive charge
gwefr bwynt *eb* gwefrau pwynt point charge
gwefr debyg *eb* like charge
gwefr electrostatig *eb* gwefrau electrostatig electrostatic charge
gwefr negatif *eb* gwefrau negatif negative charge
gwefru *be* charge
gwefus *eb* gwefusau lip
gwefusol *ans* labial
gwe-gam *eg* web cam
gwe-gloddio *eg* web mining
gwegrawn *eg* gwegronau webzine
gwehydd *eg* gwehyddion weaver
gwehyddiad *eg* gwehyddiadau weave
gwehyddiad caerog *eg* twill weave
gwehyddiad cordynnog *eg* corded weave
gwehyddiad defnydd *eg* material weave
gwehyddiad dolennog *eg* looped weave
gwehyddiad Jacquard *eg* Jacquard weave
gwehyddiad llyfn *eg* even weave
gwehyddiad patrymog *eg* gwehyddiadau patrymog patterned weave
gwehyddiad plaen *eg* plain weave
gwehyddiad rhesog *eg* rib weave
gwehyddiad saethben *eg* gwehyddiadau saethben herring-bone weave
gwehyddiad satin *eg* satin weave
gwehyddu *be* weave
gwehyddu tabled *be* tablet weaving
gwehyddwaith nodwydd *eg* needleweaving
gweini *be* administer
gweini cyffuriau *be* drug administration
gweiniad *eg* administration
gweinidog *eg* gweinidogion minister
gweinidog *eg* gweinidogion pastor
Gweinidog Addysg *eg* Minister for Education

gweinidog goleuo'r cyhoedd a phropaganda *eg* gweinidogion goleuo'r cyhoedd a phropaganda minister of public enlightenment and propaganda
Gweinidog Gwladol *eg* Minister of State
Gweinidog Gwladol dros Gymru *eg* Minister of State for Wales
gweinidog y brenin *eg* gweinidogion y brenin royal minister
gweinidogaeth *eb* ministry
gweinydd *eg* gweinyddion server
gweinydd canolog *eg* gweinyddion canolog central server
gweinydd diogel *eg* secure server
gweinydd dirprwyol *eg* gweinyddion dirprwyol proxy server
gweinydd ffeiliau *eg* gweinyddion ffeiliau file server
gweinydd newyddion *eg* gweinyddion newyddion news server
gweinydd post *eg* gweinyddion post mail server
gweinydd rhyngrwyd *eg* gweinyddion rhyngrwyd internet server
gweinyddes feithrin *eb* gweinyddesau meithrin nursery assistant
gweinyddiad *eg* administration
gweinyddiaeth *eb* gweinyddiaethau administration
gweinyddiaeth (=adran lywodraeth) *eb* gweinyddiaethau ministry
gweinyddiaeth gweinydd *eb* server administration
gweinyddol *ans* administrative
gweinyddu *be* administer
gweinyddwr *eg* gweinyddwyr administrator
gweinyddwr cyfiawnder *eg* gweinyddwyr cyfiawnder justiciary
gweithdroad *eg* gweithdroadau job turnaround
gweithdy *eg* gweithdai workshop
gweithdy peiriannau *eg* gweithdai peiriannau machine shop
gweithdy perfformio *eg* gweithdai perfformio performance workshop
gweithdy'r byd *eg* workshop of the world
gweithfan *eg* gweithfannau workstation
gweithfan cyfrifiadur *eb* computer workstation
Gweithfan Gyfansawdd *eg* Total Station
gweithgar *ans* active
gweithgaredd *eg* gweithgareddau activity
gweithgaredd a enwir *eg* named activity
gweithgaredd adloniadol *eg* gweithgareddau adloniadol recreational activity
gweithgaredd allgyrsiol *eg* gweithgareddau allgyrsiol extra-curricular activity
gweithgaredd antur *eg* gweithgareddau antur adventure activity
gweithgaredd antur *eg* gweithgareddau antur adventurous activity
gweithgaredd athletaidd *eg* gweithgareddau athletaidd athletic activity
gweithgaredd awyr agored *eg* gweithgareddau awyr agored outdoor activity
gweithgaredd benodol *ans* activity specific
gweithgaredd busnes *eg* gweithgareddau busnes business activity
gweithgaredd corfforol *eg* gweithgareddau corfforol physical activity
gweithgaredd corfforol dewisol *eg* gweithgareddau corfforol dewisol chosen physical activity
gweithgaredd cynhesu *eg* gweithgareddau cynhesu warm up activity
gweithgaredd chwilio *eg* gweithgareddau chwilio exploratory behaviour
gweithgaredd dadhydrogenas *eg* dehydrogenase activity
gweithgaredd dŵr *eg* water-based activity
gweithgaredd economaidd *eg* gweithgareddau economaidd economic activity
gweithgaredd egnïol *eg* gweithgareddau egnïol energetic activity
gweithgaredd estyn *eg* gweithgareddau estyn extension activity
gweithgaredd folcanig *eg* volcanic activity
gweithgaredd grŵp *eg* gweithgareddau grŵp group activity
gweithgaredd gymnastig *eg* gweithgareddau gymnastig gymnastic activity
gweithgaredd hybu iechyd *eg* health promotion activity
gweithgaredd hyrwyddo *eg* promotional activity
gweithgaredd lleoledig *eg* gweithgareddau lleoledig localized activity
gweithgaredd meddyliol *eg* mental activity
gweithgaredd priodol *eg* gweithgareddau priodol appropriate activity
gweithgaredd proffwydol *eg* prophetic activity
gweithgaredd rhagarweiniol *eg* introductory activity
gweithgaredd tectonig *eg* tectonic activity
gweithgaredd ymarfer corff *eg* exercise activity
gweithgaredd ymarferol *eg* gweithgareddau ymarferol practical activity
gweithgaredd yr haul *eg* solar activity
gweithgareddau awyr agored ac antur *ell* outdoor and adventurous activities
gweithgareddau byw bob dydd *ell* daily living activities
gweithgareddau cydgyfeiriol *ell* converging operations
gweithgareddau chwarae *ell* play activities
gweithgareddau fel unigolyn *ell* individual activities
gweithgareddau mewn parau *ell* pair activities
gweithgareddau peirianyddol *ell* engineering activities
gweithgareddau y tu allan i'r ysgol *ell* out-of-school activities
gweithgareddau ystafell ddosbarth *ell* classroom-based activities
gweithgarwch alffa *eg* alpha activity
gweithgarwch beta *eg* beta activity
gweithgarwch corfforol *eg* bodily activity

gweithgarwch delta *eg* delta activity
gweithgarwch dynol *eg* human activity
gweithgarwch egnïol *eg* vigorous activity
gweithgarwch theta *eg* theta activity
gweithgor *eg* gweithgorau working group; working party
gweithgor gwyddoniaeth *eg* gweithgorau gwyddoniaeth science working group
gweithgor pwnc *eg* gweithgorau pwnc subject working group
gweithgynhyrchion *ell* manufactured goods
gweithgynhyrchu drwy gymorth cyfrifiadur *be* computer aided manufacture
Gweithgynhyrchu drwy Integreiddio Cyfrifiaduron *be* Computer Integrated Manufacture
gweithio *be* work
gweithio defnyddiau'n oer *be* cold working of materials
gweithio i reol *be* work to rule
gweithio i'r eithaf *be* working to capacity
gweithio talcennau *be* pillar and stall mining
gweithiol *ans* operative
gweithio'n agos gyda *be* engage with
gweithiwr *eg* gweithwyr worker; employee
gweithiwr allanol *eg* gweithwyr allanol outworker
gweithiwr allweddol *eg* gweithwyr allweddol key worker
gweithiwr blynyddoedd cynnar *eg* gweithwyr blynyddoedd cynnar early years worker
gweithiwr cartref *eg* gweithwyr cartref home worker
gweithiwr coler las *eg* gweithwyr coler las blue-collar worker
gweithiwr coler wen *eg* gweithwyr coler wen white-collar worker
gweithiwr cyflog *eg* gweithwyr cyflog gainful worker
gweithiwr cyflogedig *eg* gweithwyr cyflogedig employee
gweithiwr cylch chwarae *eg* gweithwyr cylch chwarae playgroup worker
gweithiwr cymdeithasol *eg* gweithwyr cymdeithasol social worker
gweithiwr cymdeithasol preswyl *eg* gweithwyr cymdeithasol preswyl residential social worker
gweithiwr cynnal gofal iechyd *eg* gweithwyr cynnal gofal iechyd health care support worker
gweithiwr di-grefft *eg* gweithwyr di-grefft unskilled worker
gweithiwr eisteddog *eg* gweithwyr eisteddog sedentary worker
gweithiwr ffrâm wehyddu *eg* gweithwyr ffrâm wehyddu frame-weaving worker
gweithiwr gofal *eg* gweithwyr gofal care worker
gweithiwr gofal arbenigol *eg* gweithwyr gofal arbenigol specialist care worker
gweithiwr gofal plant *eg* gweithwyr gofal plant child care worker
gweithiwr gofal yn y gymuned *eg* gweithwyr gofal yn y gymuned community care worker
gweithiwr llaw *eg* gweithwyr llaw manual worker
gweithiwr llaw di-grefft *ell* gweithwyr llaw di-grefft unskilled manual
gweithiwr lled-grefftus *eg* gweithwyr lled-grefftus semi-skilled worker
gweithiwr maes *eg* gweithwyr maes field worker
gweithiwr medrus *eg* gweithwyr medrus skilled worker
gweithiwr peiriannau *eg* gweithwyr peiriannau machine operator
gweithiwr proffesiynol *eg* gweithwyr proffesiynol professional
gweithiwr siop *eg* gweithwyr siop shop assistant
gweithiwr swyddfa *eg* gweithwyr swyddfa white collar worker
gweithle *eg* gweithleoedd workspace; workplace
gweithlu *eg* workforce; labour force; manpower
gweithlu hyblyg *eg* flexible workforce
gweithlu sgiliau lluosog *eg* multi skilled workforce
gweithred *eb* gweithredoedd act
gweithred *eb* gweithredoedd deed; action;
gweithred *eb* gweithrediadau implementation
gweithred anwirfoddol *eb* gweithredoedd anwirfoddol involuntary action
gweithred atgyrch *eb* gweithredoedd atgyrch reflex action
gweithred drosglwyddo *eb* gweithredoedd trosglwyddo transfer deed
gweithred Duw *eb* act of God
gweithred ddynamig benodol *eb* specific dynamic action
gweithred fewnwthiol *eb* gweithredoedd mewnwthiol invasive procedure
gweithred gyfredol *eb* gweithredoedd cyfredol current operation
gweithred gymnastig *eb* gweithredoedd gymnastig gymnastic action
gweithred partneriaeth *eb* deed of partnership
gweithred siarad *eb* speech act
gweithred swmpuso *eb* bulking action
gweithred syml *eb* gweithredoedd syml simple action
gweithred wirfoddol *eb* gweithredoedd gwirfoddol voluntary action
gweithredadwy *ans* executable
gweithrediad *eg* gweithrediadau operation
gweithrediad AC *eg* gweithrediadau AC AND operation
gweithrediad Boole *eg* gweithrediadau Boole Boolean operation
gweithrediad cynnal *eg* maintenance operation
gweithrediad deuaidd *eg* gweithrediadau deuaidd binary operation
gweithrediad gwrthdro *eg* gweithrediadau gwrthdro inverse operation
gweithrediad rhif *eg* operation of number

gweithrediad rhifyddeg ddeuaidd *eg* gweithrediadau rhifyddeg ddeuaidd binary arithmetic operation
gweithrediad switsio cyflym iawn sharp switching action
gweithrediad sylfaenol *eg* gweithrediadau sylfaenol basic action
gweithrediadau amryfal *ell* multiple operations
gweithrediadau ar y llawr *ell* actions on the floor
gweithrediadau gofannu arian *eg* silversmithing operations
gweithrediadau marchnad agored *ell* open market operations
gweithrediadau rhif *ell* number operations
gweithrediadau'r plaen amlddefnydd *ell* operations of combination plane
gweithredoedd da *ell* good works
gweithredol *ans* active; functional; operational; executive
gweithredu (nodwedd) *be* apply
gweithredu (yn gyffredinol) *be* act; operate; execute; implement
gweithredu â llaw *ans* hand-operated
gweithredu arddull *be* apply style
gweithredu arddull cell *be* apply cell style
gweithredu arddull ffrâm *be* apply frame style
gweithredu arddull tudalen *be* apply page style
gweithredu bob tro *be* always execute
gweithredu border *be* apply border
gweithredu colofnau *be* apply columns
gweithredu data defnyddiwr *be* apply user data
gweithredu datganiad SQL *be* execute SQL statement
gweithredu dewisiadau awtofformat *be* apply autoformat options
gweithredu diwydiannol *be* industrial action
gweithredu enwau *be* apply names
gweithredu fformat maes *be* apply field format
gweithredu gosodiad cyflwyniad *be* apply presentation layout
gweithredu hidlydd *be* apply filter
gweithredu macro *be* execute macro
gweithredu mesurydd *be* apply ruler
gweithredu priodoleddau *be* apply attributes
gweithredu priodoleddau tabl *be* apply table attributes
gweithredu tabl newid *be* apply replacement table
gweithredu thema *be* apply theme
gweithredu ymholiad yn syth *be* execute query immediately
gweithredu'r rhaglen *be* execute program
gweithredwr (ar bwyllgor gweithredu) *eg* gweithredwyr executive
gweithredwr (peiriant etc) *eg* gweithredwyr operator
gweithredwr paratoi data *eg* gweithredwyr paratoi data data preparation operator
gweithredydd *eg* gweithredyddion operator
gweithredydd Boole *eg* gweithredyddion Boole Boolean operator
gweithredydd matrics *eg* gweithredwyr matrics matrix operator
gweithredydd rhesymegol *eg* gweithredwyr rhesymegol logical operator
gweithydd *eg* gweithyddion agonist
gweladwy *ans* visible
gweld rhithiau *be* hallucinate
gweldata *ell* viewdata
gwelededd *eg* visibility
gweledigaeth *eb* gweledigaethau vision
gweledol *ans* visual
gweledydd *eg* gweledyddion visionary
gwe-letya *be* web hosting
gwe-log *eg* gwe-logiau weblog
gwelw (ar sgrin cyfrfiadur) *ans* greyed out
gwelw (yn gyffredinol) *ans* pale
gwely *eg* gwelyau bed
gwely arhosiad hir *eg* gwelyau arhosiad hir long stay bed
gwely blaen-haen *eg* gwelyau blaen-haen foreset bed
gwely capilarïau *eg* gwelyau capilarïau capillary bed
gwely is-haen *eg* gwelyau is-haen bottom set bed
gwely llifol *eg* gwelyau llifol fluidized bed
gwely treigl *eg* gwelyau treigl truckle bed
gwely troli *eg* gwelyau troli trolley bed
gwely uwch-haen *eg* gwelyau uwch-haen topset bed
gwelyo *be* bed
gwe-lywio *be* navigate
gwe-lywiwr *eg* gwe-lywyr navigator
gwell *ans* enhanced
gwell amrywogaethau *ell* improved varieties
gwella (=mireinio) *be* improve; enhance
gwella (ar ôl salwch etc) *be* convalesce
gwella (briw, anaf etc) *be* heal
gwella iechyd *be* health improvement
gwella perfformiad *be* improve performance
gwella perfformiad *be* refine technique
gwella tir yr ysgol *be* improving the school grounds
gwellaif *eg* gwelleifiau shears
gwellaif gilotin *eg* gwelleifiau gilotin guillotine shears
gwellaif mainc *eg* gwelleifiau mainc bench shears
gwellaif pincio *eg* gwelleifiau pincio pinking shears
gwellhad dros dro *eg* remission
gwelliant (i gynnig etc) *eg* gwelliannau amendment
gwelliant (yn gyffredinol) *eg* gwelliannau improvement
gwellt y gweunydd *eg* molinia
gwelltyn *eg* gwellt straw; blade of grass
gwên Duchenne *eb* Duchenne smile
gwen, y wen *eb* goitre
gwenci *eb* gwencïod weasel
gwendid *eg* gwendidau weakness

gwendid adeileddol *eg* gwendidau adeileddol structural weakness
Gwener *eb* Venus
Gwenffrewi *eb* Winifred
Gwenhwyfar *eb* Guinevere
gwenith penddu *eg* smutted wheat
gwenith yr hydd *eg* buckwheat
gwenithfaen *eg* granite
gwennol (ar gyfer gwehyddu) *eb* gwenoliaid shuttle
gwennol (mewn badminton) *eb* gwenoliaid shuttlecock
gwennol (yr aderyn) *eb* gwenoliaid swallow
gwennol bren *eb* gwenoliaid pren wooden shuttle
gwennol hedegog *eb* gwenoliaid hedegog flying shuttle
gwennol ofod *eb* gwenoliaid gofod space shuttle
gwennol rholer *eb* gwenoliaid rholer roller shuttle
gwennol y gwehydd *eb* gwenoliaid gwehyddion weaving shuttle
gwenwisg *eb* gwenwisgoedd surplice
gwenwyn *eg* gwenwynau poison
gwenwyn bwyd *eg* food poisoning
gwenwyndra *eg* toxicity
gwenwyniad *eg* poisoning
gwenwynig *ans* toxic
gwenwyno *be* poison
gwenynen feirch *eb* gwenyn meirch wasp
gweog *ans* webbed
gwêr *eg* gwerau tallow
gwêr cannwyll *eg* candle grease
gwerddon *eb* gwerddonau oasis
gwerin gwyddbwyll *ell* chessmen
gwerin wledig *eb* peasantry
gwerin, y werin *eb* masses, the
gweriniaeth *eb* gweriniaethau republic
Gweriniaeth Dwyrain yr Almaen *eb* German Democratic Republic
gweriniaeth ffederal *eb* gweriniaethau ffederal federal republic
Gweriniaeth Ffederal yr Almaen *eb* German Federal Republic
Gweriniaeth Gyntaf *eb* First Republic
Gweriniaeth Isalpaidd *eb* Cisalpine Republic
gweriniaethol *ans* republican
gweriniaethwr *eg* gweriniaethwyr republican
Gwerinlywodraeth, y Werinlywodraeth (Cromwell) *eb* Commonwealth, the
gwerinol *ans* plebeian; proletarian
gwerinwr (mewn gwyddbwyll) *eg* gwerinwyr pawn
gwerinwr (yn gyffredinol) *eg* gwerinwyr peasant
gwerinwr Rhufeinig *eg* gwerinwyr Rhufeinig plebeian
gwern *eb* gwernydd swamp
gwern fangrof *eb* gwernydd mangrof mangrove swamp
gwern goedwig *eb* gwern goedwigoedd swamp forest
gwernen *eb* gwern alder
gwernydd malaria *ell* malarial swamps
gwers *eb* gwersi lesson
gwers ar ôl ysgol *eb* gwersi ar ôl ysgol after-school lesson
gwers ddwbl *eb* gwersi dwbl double lesson
gwers enghreifftiol *eb* gwersi enghreifftiol demonstration lesson
gwers rydd *eb* gwersi rhydd free period
gwerslyfr *eg* gwerslyfrau textbook
gwersyll *eg* gwersylloedd camp
gwersyll carcharorion rhyfel *eg* gwersylloedd carcharorion rhyfel prisoner of war camp
gwersyll crynhoi *eg* gwersylloedd crynhoi concentration camp
gwersyll difodi *eg* gwersylloedd difodi extermination camp
gwersyll dros dro *eg* gwersylloedd dros dro transit camp
gwersyll dros dro *eg* gwersylloedd dros dro marching camp
gwersyll ffoaduriaid *eg* gwersylloedd ffoaduriaid refugee camp
gwersyll gwyliau *eg* gwersylloedd gwyliau holiday camp
gwersyll haf *eg* gwersylloedd haf summer camp
gwersyll sarnau *eg* causeway camp
gwersyllfan *eg* gwersyllfannau encampment
gwerth *eg* gwerthoedd value
gwerth absoliwt *eg* gwerthoedd absoliwt absolute value
gwerth ardrethol *eg* gwerthoedd ardrethol rateable value
gwerth ariannol *eg* cash value
gwerth biolegol *eg* biological value
gwerth Boole *eg* gwerthoedd Boole Boolean value
gwerth caloriffig *eg* gwerthoedd caloriffig calorific value
gwerth cyfannol *eg* gwerthoedd cyfannol integral value
gwerth cyfanrifol *eg* gwerthoedd cyfanrifol integer value
gwerth cymedrig *eg* gwerthoedd cymedrig mean value
gwerth cysonyn *eg* value of a constant
gwerth databeilot *eg* gwerthoedd databeilot datapilot value
gwerth disgwyliedig *eg* gwerthoedd disgwyliedig expected value
gwerth egni *eg* energy value
gwerth eich arian *eg* value for money
gwerth eigen *eg* gwerthoedd eigen eigen value
gwerth eithaf *eg* gwerthoedd eithaf extreme value
gwerth enwol *eg* nominal value
gwerth goroesol *eg* gwerthoedd goroesol survival value
gwerth hapraddfa *eg* gwerthoedd hapraddfa random scale value
gwerth lle *eg* gwerthoedd lle place value
gwerth maethol *eg* nutritional value

gwerth net ar bapur *eg* net book value
gwerth pendant *eg* gwerthoedd pendant sharp value
gwerth presennol *eg* present worth
gwerth pH *eg* gwerthoedd pH pH value
gwerth real *eg* gwerthoedd real real value
gwerth rhagosodedig *eg* gwerthoedd rhagosodedig default value
gwerth rheolaidd *eg* regular value
gwerth tôn *eg* gwerthoedd tôn tone value
gwerth y curiad *eg* value of the beat
gwerth y farchnad *eg* market value
gwerthadwy *ans* marketable
gwerthfawrogi *be* appreciate
gwerthfawrogiad *eg* gwerthfawrogiadau appreciation
gwerthiant *eg* gwerthiannau sale
gwerthiant credyd *eg* credit sale
gwerthiant cyffredinol *eg* general sales
gwerthiant mawr *eg* high sales
gwerthiant rhydd *eg* free sale
gwerthiant wedi dod trwy sampl *eg* sale by sample
gwerthoedd cyffredin *ell* common values
gwerthoedd gofal *ell* care value
gwerthoedd newyddion *ell* news values
gwerthoedd y Gorllewin *ell* Western values
gwerthoedd ysbrydol *ell* spiritual values
gwerthu'n breifat *be* private sale
gwerthusiad *eg* gwerthusiadau appraisal; evaluation
gwerthusiad beirniadol *eg* critical evaluation
gwerthusiad cychwynnol *eg* gwerthusiadau cychwynnol primary appraisal
gwerthusiad ffurfiannol *eg* gwerthusiadau ffurfiannol formative evaluation
gwerthusiad gwybyddol *eg* gwerthusiadau gwybyddol cognitive appraisal
gwerthusiad perfformiad *eg* performance appraisal
gwerthusiad safle *eg* site evaluation
gwerthuso *be* appraise; evaluate
gwerthuso buddsoddiad *be* investment appraisal
gwerthuso cynllun *be* design evaluation
gwerthuso eilaidd *be* gwerthuso eilaidd secondary appraisal
gwerthuso tystiolaeth *be* evaluate evidence
gwerthwr *eg* gwerthwyr seller; vendor; sales person; salesman
gwerthwr eiddo *eg* gwerthwyr eiddo estate agent
gwerthwr llysiau *eg* gwerthwyr llysiau greengrocer
gwerthwr o ddrws i ddrws *eg* gwerthwyr o ddrws i ddrws door-to-door salesman
gwerthwr papurau *eg* gwerthwyr papurau stationer
gwerthwr pysgod *eg* gwerthwyr pysgod fishmonger
gwerthyd *eb* gwerthydau spindle
gwerthydffurf *eb* fusiform
gwesgi *eg* gwesgïau squeegee
gwesgi rwber *eg* gwesgïau rwber rubber squeegee
gwestai *eg* gwesteion guest
gwesteia *be* host
gwesteiwr (mewn TG) *eg* gwesteiwyr host
gwesty *eg* gwestai hotel; guest house
gwestywr *eg* gwestywyr host
gweuglwm *ans* lock knit
gweundir *eg* gweundiroedd moorland
gweundirol *ans* moorland
gweuwaith *eg* knitwear
gwewyr esgor *eg* labour pains
gwe-ymlusgwr *eg* web crawler
gwgli *eg* gwglis googly
gwiail *ell* wicker
gwialen *eb* gwialennau cane
gwialen blethu *eb* gwialennau plethu lapping cane
gwialen ddolen *eb* gwialennau dolenni handle cane
gwialen fonynnu *eb* gwialennau bonynnu staking cane
gwialen gan *eb* gwialennau can bleached cane
gwialen ganol *eb* gwialennau canol centre cane
gwialen ganol crwn *eb* gwialennau canol crwn round centre cane
gwialen lapio *eb* gwialennau lapio wrapping cane
► **gwialen liw** *eb* gwialennau lliw dyed cane
gwialen loyw *eb* gwialennau gloyw glossy cane
gwialen synthetig *eb* gwialennau synthetig synthetic cane
gwibiad *eg* gwibiadau sprint
gwibio *be* sprint; dart
gwibiwr *eg* gwibwyr sprinter
gwichian *be* wheezing
gwiddonyn *eg* gwiddon mite
gwifrau uwchben *ell* overhead wires
gwifredig *ans* hard wired
gwifren *eb* gwifrau wire
gwifren alfanedig *eb* gwifrau galfanedig galvanized wire
gwifren anhyblyg *eb* gwifrau anhyblyg rigid wire
gwifren anystwyth *eb* gwifrau anystwyth stiff wire
gwifren blyg *eb* gwifrau plyg bent wire
gwifren boeth *eb* hot wire
gwifren bres *eb* gwifrau pres brass wire
gwifren bres fain *eb* gwifrau pres main fine brass wire
gwifren bresyddu *eb* gwifrau presyddu brazing wire
gwifren dorri *eb* gwifrau torri cutting wire
gwifren ddaearu *eb* gwifrau daearu earth wire
gwifren fyw *eb* gwifrau byw live wire
gwifren gopr *eb* gwifrau copr copper wire
gwifren goprog *eb* gwifrau coprog coppered wire
gwifren gwerthwr blodau *eb* gwifrau gwerthwr blodau florist's wire
gwifren haearn *eb* gwifrau haearn iron wire
gwifren niwtral *eb* gwifrau niwtral neutral wire
gwifren noeth *eb* gwifrau noeth bare wire
gwifren rwymo *eb* gwifrau rhwymo binding wire

gwifro *be* wire
gwifrog *ans* wired
gwingiad *eg* gwingiadau tic
Gwilym Dawedog *eg* William the Silent
Gwilym Goncwerwr *eg* William the Conqueror
Gwilym o Orange *eg* William of Orange
gwinau *eg* chestnut brown
gwinwyddaeth *eb* viticulture
gwir *ans* true; real
gwir ddisgownt *eg* true discount
gwir ddyfnder *eg* real depth
gwir effaith *eb* net effect
gwir elips *eg* pure ellipse; true ellipse
gwir faint *eg* life-size
gwir fias *eg* true bias
gwir ffrwythyn *eg* gwir ffrwythynnau true fruit
gwir gerrynt *eg* net current
gwir gyfalaf *eg* real capital
gwir gyfradd llog *eb* true rate of interest
gwir liw *eg* gwir liwiau true colour
gwir rym *eg* net force
gwir siâp *eg* gwir siapiau true shape
gwir symudiad *eg* net movement
gwirdeiprwydd *eg* trueness to type
gwireb *eb* gwirebau axiom; maxim
gwirebol *ans* axiomatic
gwireddu cynllun *be* realization of a plan
gwireddu data *be* data verification
gwirfoddol *ans* voluntary
gwirfoddoliaeth *eb* voluntarism
gwirfoddolwr *eg* gwirfoddolwyr volunteer
Gwirfoddolwr Ulster *eg* Gwirfoddolwyr Ulster Ulster Volunteer
gwiriad *eg* gwiriadau check
gwiriad afreidrwydd *eg* gwiriadau afreidrwydd redundancy check
gwiriad desg *eg* gwiriadau desg desk check
gwiriad diogelwch *eg* gwiriadau diogelwch security check
gwiriad eilbaredd *eg* gwiriadau eilbaredd even parity check
gwiriadwy *ans* verifiable
gwirio *be* check
gwirio awtomatig *be* automatic checking
gwirio dewisiad *be* check selection
gwirio digid *eg* check digit
gwirio firysau *be* virus checking
gwirio oll *be* check all
gwirio sillafu *be* spell check
gwiriwr cardiau *eg* gwirwyr cardiau card verifier
gwirlen *eb* gwirlenni truth table
gwirod *eg* gwirodydd spirit
gwirod coeth *eg* rectified spirit
gwirod gwyn *eg* white spirit
gwirod methyl *eg* methylated spirits
gwirod petroliwm *eg* petroleum spirit
gwirod tyrpant *eg* spirits of turpentine
gwirodydd tyner *ell* killed spirits
gwirydd sillafu *eg* gwirwyr sillafu spell checker
gwisg *eb* gwisgoedd dress; costume
gwisg academaidd *eb* academic dress
gwisg briodol *eb* gwisgoedd priodol appropriate dress
gwisg cyfnod *eb* period costume
gwisg genedlaethol *eb* gwisgoedd cenedlaethol national costume
gwisg gyflawn *eb* gwisgoedd cyflawn outfit
gwisg haul *eb* gwisgoedd haul sun-suit
gwisg nofio *eb* gwisgoedd nofio swimsuit; bathing costume
gwisg pen *eb* gwisgoedd pen head wear
gwisg warchodol *eb* gwisgoedd gwarchodol protective wear
gwisg ysgol *eb* school uniform; uniform
gwisgo *be* dress; dressing up
gwisgo metel *be* metal cladding
gwisgo'r llwyfan *be* dress the stage
gwisgo'r set *be* dress the set
gwlad *eb* gwledydd country
Gwlad Belg *eb* Belgium
gwlad boblog *eb* gwledydd poblog populated country
gwlad boblog iawn *eb* gwledydd poblog iawn thickly populated country
gwlad denau ei phoblogaeth *eb* gwledydd tenau eu poblogaeth thinly populated country
gwlad ddatblygedig *eb* gwledydd datblygedig developed country
gwlad ddibynnol *eb* gwledydd dibynnol satellite state
Gwlad Ddu *eb* Black Country
gwlad newydd ei diwydianeiddio (GND) *eb* gwledydd newydd eu diwydianeiddio newly industrialized country
gwlad sy'n datblygu *eb* gwledydd sy'n datblygu developing country
gwlad sy'n datblygu'n economaidd *eb* gwledydd sy'n datblygu'n economaidd economically developing country
gwladgarwch *eg* patriotism
gwladgarwr *eg* gwladgarwyr patriot
gwladol *ans* national
gwladoli *be* nationalize
gwladoliad *eg* nationalization
gwladweinydd *eg* gwladweinwyr statesman
gwladweinydd hyn *eg* gwladweinwyr hyn elder statesman
gwladweinyddiaeth *eb* statecraft
gwladwriaeth *eb* gwladwriaethau state
gwladwriaeth byped *eb* gwladwriaethau pyped puppet state
gwladwriaeth dreftadol *eb* gwladwriaethau treftadol patrimonial state
gwladwriaeth ddibynnol *eb* gwladwriaethau dibynnol client state

gwladwriaeth ddinas *eb* gwladwriaethau dinas city state
gwladwriaeth genedlaethol *eb* gwladwriaethau cenedlaethol nation state
gwladwriaeth glustog *eb* gwladwriaethau clustog buffer state
gwladwriaeth gorfforaethol *eb* gwladwriaethau corfforaethol corporate state
gwladwriaeth heddlu *eb* police state
gwladwriaeth Islamaidd *eb* Islamic state
gwladwriaeth les *eb* gwladwriaethau lles welfare state
gwladwriaeth sofran *eb* gwladwriaethau sofran sovereign state
Gwladwriaethau'r Olyniaeth *ell* Succession States
gwladychiad *eg* gwladychiadau colonization
gwladychiad *eg* gwladychiadau settlement
gwlân *ans* woollen
gwlân (ar gyfer clwyf) *eg* gamgee
gwlân (wedi'i gribo) *eg* rolag
gwlân (yn gyffredinol) *eg* gwlanoedd wool
gwlân brodio *eg* embroidery wool
gwlân cotwm *eg* cotton wool
gwlân Cymru *eg* Welsh wool
gwlân cyweirio *eg* mending wool
gwlân dur *eg* wire wool
gwlân dur *eg* steel wool
gwlân gwydr *eg* glass wool
gwlân 'Superwash' *eg* Superwash wool
gwlanen *eb* gwlanenni flannel
gwlanog (gorffeniad) *ans* brushed
gwlanog (yn gyffredinol) *ans* woolly
gwlatgar *ans* patriotic
gwledig *ans* rural; rustic; country
Gwledydd Cred *ell* Christendom
Gwledydd Cred Rhufeinig *ell* Latin Christendom
gwledydd llai economaidd ddatblygedig (GLlEDd) *ell* less economically developed countries
gwledydd mwy economaidd ddatblygedig (GMEDd) *ell* more economically developed countries
gwledydd Prydain *ell* United Kingdom
gwledydd y Balcan *eg* Balkan countries
gwleidyddiaeth *eb* politics
gwleidyddiaeth a chymdeithas politics and society
gwleidyddiaeth grym *eb* power politics
gwleidyddol *ans* political
gwlff *eg* gylffiau gulf
gwlith *eg* gwlithoedd dew
gwlithbwll *eg* gwlithbyllau dewpond
gwlithbwynt *eg* gwlithbwyntiau dew point
gwlithen *eb* gwlithod slug
gwlyb *ans* wet
gwlyb a sych wet and dry
gwlyb-bydredd *eg* wet rot
gwlybnyddu *be* wet spin
gwlybyredd *eg* deliquescence
gwlybyrol *ans* deliquescent
gwlychu *be* wetting
gwlychu gwely *be* bed-wetting
gwm *eg* gymiau gum
gwm Arabig *eg* Arabic gum
gwm arabig *eg* gum arabic
gwm planhigol *eg* gymiau planhigol plant gum
gwm tragacanth *eg* tragacanth
gwn *eg* gynnau gun
gŵn bedydd *eg* gynau bedydd christening robe
gwn chwistrellu *eg* gynnau chwistrellu spray gun
gŵn nos *eg* gŵn nosys nightdress
gwn peiriant *eg* gynau peiriant machine gun
gwn saim *eg* gynnau saim grease gun
gwn styffylu *eg* gynnau styffylu staple gun
gŵn tŷ *eg* gynau tŷ dressing gown
gwn theatr *eg* gynau theatr theatre gown
gwndwn *eg* ley
gwneud *ans* artificial
gwneud *be* make
gwneud arbedion *be* economize
gwneud arolwg *eb* survey
gwneud cais *be* apply
gwneud cylch *be* make a circle
gwneud diagnosis *be* diagnose
gwneud iawn *be* atone
gwneud iawn *be* compensate
gwneud patrymau *be* make patterns
gwneud penderfyniadau clinigol *be* clinical decision-making
gwneud pont *be* make a bridge
gwneud tyllau *be* drifting
gwneud yr elw mwyaf *be* profit maximisation
gwneud yr elw mwyaf posibl *be* maximise profit
gwneuthurwr *eg* gwneuthurwyr manufacturer
gwneuthurwr basgedi *eg* gwneuthurwyr basgedi basket maker
gwnfetel *eg* gunmetal
gwnfetel Morlys *eg* Admiralty gunmetal
gwniadur *eg* gwniaduron thimble
gwniadur argraffu *eg* gwniaduron argraffu print thimble
gwniadwaith *eg* needlework
gwnio *be* sew
gwniyddes *eb* gwniyddesau dressmaker
gwobr *eb* gwobrau award
gwobr Buddsoddwyr mewn Pobl *eb* Investors in People award
gwobr y faner las *eb* blue flag award
gwobrwyo *be* award
gwr ar gadw *eg* gwyr ar gadw retainer
gŵr llys *eg* gwŷr llys courtier
gwrach *eb* gwrachïod hook
gwrachdwymyn *eb* witchcraze
gwrachen ddu *eb* gwrachod du bream
gwrachen y môr *eb* gwrachod y môr wrasse
gwraig gleisiog *eb* gwragedd cleisiog battered wife
gwraig tŷ *eb* gwragedd tŷ housewife

gwrandawiad *eg* gwrandawiadau hearing
gwrando *be* listen
gwrando a deall listening comprehension
gwrando deugotig *be* dichotic listening
gwrando eang *be* extensive listening
gwrando gweithredol *be* active listening
gwrando'n astud *be* listen attentively
gwregys *eg* gwregysau belt; girdle
gwregys cleddyf *eg* gwregysau cleddyf sword belt
gwregys diogelwch *eg* gwregysau diogelwch safety belt
gwregys pectoral *eg* gwregysau pectoral pectoral girdle
gwregys pelfig *eg* gwregysau pelfig pelvic girdle
gwregys 'V' *eg* gwregysau 'V' vee belt
gwregys yr ysgwydd *eg* gwregysau ysgwyddau shoulder girdle
gwrêng *eg* gwrengod commoner
gwreichionen *eb* gwreichion spark
gwreichioni *be* spark
gwreiddflewyn *eg* gwreiddflew root hair
gwreiddgapan *eg* gwreiddgapanau root cap
gwreiddgnepyn *eg* gwreiddgnepynnau root nodule
gwreiddiau cymhlyg *ell* complex roots
gwreiddiol *ans* original; primal; primary
gwreiddiosyn *eg* gwreiddios rootlet
gwreiddlysieuyn *eg* gwreiddlysiau root vegetable
gwreiddyn *eg* gwreiddiau root (of plant)
gwreiddyn cyfangol *eg* gwreiddiau cyfangol contractile root
gwreiddyn echddygol *eg* gwreiddiau echddygol motor root
gwreiddyn fentrol *eg* gwreiddiau fentrol ventral root
gwreiddyn ffibrog *eg* gwreiddiau ffibrog fibrous root
gwreiddyn ffug *eg* gwreiddiau ffug false root
gwreiddyn ochrol *eg* gwreiddiau ochrol lateral root
gwreiddyn yr hafaliad *eg* gwreiddiau'r hafaliadau root of the equation
gwres *eg* heat
gwres (mewn meddygaeth) *eg* pyrexia
gwres adweithio *eg* heat of reaction
gwres anweddu *eg* heat of vaporization
gwres canolog *eg* central heating
gwres canolog llawn *eg* full central heating
gwres cefndir *eg* background heat
gwres coch *eg* red heat
gwres cochias *eg* bright red heat
gwres cudd *eg* latent heat
gwres cudd anweddu *eg* latent heat of vaporization
gwres cudd ymdoddi *eg* latent heat of fusion
gwres detholus *eg* selective heating
gwres du *eg* black heat
gwres ecsothermig *eg* exothermic heat
gwres eirias *eg* bright yellow heat
gwres ffurfio *eg* heat of formation
gwres gwynias *eg* white heat
gwres hylosgi *eg* heat of combustion
gwres llaw (am ddŵr) *ans* hand hot
gwres niwtralu *eg* heat of neutralisation
gwres pelydrol *eg* radiant heat
gwres rhannol *eg* partial heating
gwres solar *eg* solar heating
gwreslynu *be* iron on
gwresogi *be* heat
gwresogi plastig *be* plastic heating
gwresogydd *eg* gwresogyddion heater
gwresogydd darfudol *eg* gwresogyddion darfudol convector heater
gwresogydd dŵr *eg* gwresogyddion dŵr water-heater
gwresogydd dŵr ebrwydd *eg* gwresogyddion dŵr ebrwydd instantaneous water-heater
gwresogydd potel *eg* gwresogyddion poteli bottle warmer
gwresogydd stôr *eg* gwresogyddion stôr storage heater
gwresogydd stôr trydan *eg* gwresogyddion stôr trydan electric storage heater
gwresogydd tiwb *eg* gwresogyddion tiwb tubular heater
gwresogydd troch *eg* gwresogyddion troch immersion heater
gwresogydd ystafell *eg* gwresogyddion ystafell room heater
gwrid *eg* flush
gwrit *eg* gwritiau writ
gwrogaeth *eb* homage
gwrogaeth arglwyddiaeth *eb* seigniory homage
gwrogaeth i'r delyn *eb* towards the harp
gwrogaeth llw ffyddlondeb *eb* fealty homage
gwrogaeth sofraniaeth *eb* sovereignty homage
gwrogaeth teyrngarwch *eb* allegiance homage
gwrtaith *eg* gwrteithiau fertilizer
gwrtaith artiffisial *eg* gwrteithiau artiffisial artificial manure
gwrteithio *be* fertilize
gwrthargaen *eg* gwrthargaenau counter veneer
gwrtharogl *ans* odour-resistant
gwrthasid *ans* acid resisting; antacid
gwrthateb *eg* gwrthatebion rejoinder
gwrthbab *eg* gwrthbabau antipope
gwrth-Babaidd *ans* antipapal
gwrth-Babyddol *ans* anti-catholic
gwrthbannu *ans* shrink-resistant
gwrthbaralel *ans* antiparallel
gwrthbario *be* counter parry
gwrthbas *eb* gwrthbasiau push pass
gwrthblaid *eb* gwrthbleidiau opposition
gwrthbrawf *eg* gwrthbrofion counterproof
gwrthbrintio *be* resist printing
gwrthbrofi *be* refute
gwrthbwynt *eg* gwrthbwyntiau counterpoint
gwrthbwynt caeth *eg* strict counterpoint
gwrthbwynt dwbl *eg* double counterpoint

gwrthbwynt llinellog *eg* gwrthbwyntiau llinellog linear counterpoint
gwrthbwynt rhydd *eg* gwrthbwyntiau rhydd free counterpoint
gwrthbwynt triphlyg *eg* triple counterpoint
gwrthbwyntiol *ans* contrapuntal
gwrthbwyntydd *eg* gwrthbwyntwyr contrapuntalist
gwrthbwyso *be* counterbalance
gwrthbwysyn *eg* gwrthbwysynnau counterweight
gwrthchwyddiannol *ans* anti-inflationary
gwrthchwyldro *eg* gwrthchwyldroadau counter revolution
gwrthchwyldroadol *ans* counter-revolutionary
gwrthdafod *eg* gwrthdafodau counter spit
gwrthdan *ans* fireproof
gwrthdangiad *eg* gwrthdangiadau arctangent
gwrthdaro *be* conflict
gwrthdaro *be* collide
gwrthdaro *be* confrontation
gwrthdaro *be* clash
gwrthdaro diwydiannol *be* industrial conflict
gwrthdaro dwy-law *be* intermanual conflict
gwrthdaro hiliol *be* racial conflict
gwrthdaro rhwng swyddogaethau *be* role conflict
gwrthderfysgaeth *eb* anti-terrorism
gwrthderfysgwr *eg* gwrthderfysgwyr anti-terrorist
gwrthdrawiad *eg* gwrthdrawiadau collision
gwrthdrawiad anelastig *eg* inelastic collision
gwrthdrawydd *eg* gwrthdrawyddion collider
gwrthdrefedigaethol *ans* anti-colonialist
gwrthdrefoli *be* counter-urbanisation
gwrthdro *ans* inverted
gwrthdro *eg* gwrthdroeon inversion; inverse; reverse
gwrthdro cord *eg* gwrthdroeon cordiau inversion of chord
gwrthdro cyntaf *eg* gwrthdroeon cyntaf first inversion
gwrthdroad *eg* gwrthdroadau inversion
gwrthdroad ochrol *eg* gwrthdroadau ochrol lateral inversion
gwrthdroad tymheredd *eg* gwrthdroadau tymheredd inversion of temperature
gwrthdroedig *ans* inverted
gwrthdroi *be* reverse; invert
gwrthdroi cylchred *be* reverse cycle
gwrthdröydd *eg* gwrthdroyddion invertor
gwrthdröydd Schmitt *eg* Schmitt inverter
gwrthdyllu *be* counterbore
gwrthdyniad *eg* gwrthdyniadau distraction
gwrthdynnu *be* distract
gwrthdynnwr *eg* gwrthdynwyr distractor
gwrthdystiad *eg* gwrthdystiadau demonstration; remonstrance
Gwrthdystiad Mawr *eg* Grand Remonstrance
gwrthdystio *be* demonstrate; remonstrate
gwrthddangosiad *eg* gwrthddangosiadau counter exposition
gwrthddiwretig *ans* antidiuretic
gwrthddiwygiad *eg* counter-reformation
gwrth-ddŵr *ans* water-repellent
gwrthddywediad *eg* gwrthddywediadau contradiction
gwrthedd *eg* gwrtheddau resistivity
gwrthedd brêc *eg* gwrtheddau brêc brake resistance
gwrthenghraifft *eb* gwrthenghreifftiau counter-example
gwrth-eni *ans* anti-natalist
gwrth-Ewropeaidd *ans* anti-European
gwrthfacteria *ans* anti-bacterial
gwrthfacteria *ans* bacteriostatic
gwrthfiotig *ans* antibiotic
gwrthfiotig *eg* gwrthfiotigau antibiotic
gwrthfondio *ans* anti bonding
gwrthfywddyraniad *eg* antivivisection
gwrthffactor *eg* gwrthffactorau counterfactor
gwrth-ffasgaidd *ans* anti-fascist
gwrth-fflam *ans* flame proof
gwrth-fflam *ans* anti-flame
gwrth-ffrithiant *ans* anti-friction
gwrthgawod *ans* shower-proof
► **gwrthgerrynt** *eg* gwrthgerhyntau counter-current
gwrthgiliad *eg* gwrthgiliadau apostasy
gwrthgilio *be* defect
gwrthgiliol *ans* apostate
gwrthgiliwr *eg* gwrthgilwyr renegade; apostate; defector
gwrthglawdd *eg* gwrthgloddiau earthwork; revetment
gwrthglerigaeth *eb* anti-clericalism
gwrthglerigol *ans* anticlerical
gwrthglocwedd *ans* anticlockwise
gwrthgodon *eg* anticodon
gwrthgorff *eg* gwrthgyrff antibody
gwrthgrafiad *ans* non-scratch
gwrthgrych *ans* crease-resistant
gwrth-gwyr *ans* wax resistant
gwrthgyfnewid *be* counterchange
gwrthgyfnewidiad *eg* gwrthgyfnewidiadau counterchange
gwrthgyfogydd *eg* gwrthgyfogyddion antiemetic
gwrthgyhuddo *be* recriminate
gwrthgymesur *ans* antisymmetric
gwrthgymesuredd *eg* gwrthgymesureddau antisymmetry
gwrthgyrydiad *ans* corrosion resistant
gwrthgytbwys *ans* counterbalanced
gwrthgytbwys *eg* gwrthgytbwysau counterbalance
Gwrth-Haerwyr *ell* Counter-Remonstrants
gwrth-haul *ans* sun proof
gwrth-hiliaeth *eb* anti-racism
gwrthiad *eg* gwrthiadau counter
gwrthiannau paralel *ell* parallel resistances
gwrthiannol *ans* resistant
gwrthiannol i wres *ans* heat resistant

gwrthiant *eg* gwrthiannau reluctance
gwrthiant *eg* gwrthiannau resistance
gwrthiant aer *eg* air resistance
gwrthiant ardrawiad *eg* impact resistance
gwrthiant cynyddol *eg* progressive resistance
gwrthiant i'w fudiant *eg* resistance to motion
gwrthiant mewnol *eg* internal resistance
gwrthiant sglodi *eg* chipping resistance
gwrthiant trydanol *eg* electrical resistance
gwrthio *be* counter
gwrthisbwysol *ans* antihypotensive
gwrthiselydd *eg* gwrthiselyddion antidepressant
gwrthiselydd deuweithredol *eg* gwrthiselyddion deuweithredol dual-action antidepressant
gwrthiselydd trichylch *eg* gwrthiselyddion trichylch tricyclic antidepressant
gwrthlaw *ans* rain proof
gwrthlaw *eb* backhand
gwrthlidiol *ans* anti-inflammatory
gwrthlif *ans* obsequent
gwrthlif *eg* gwrthlifau obsequent; counterflow
gwrth-lithr *ans* anti-slip; non-slip
gwrthliwio *be* countershading
gwrthlogarithm *eg* gwrthlogarithmau antilogarithm
gwrthlud *ans* non-stick
gwrthlwydni *ans* mildew resistant
gwrthocsidydd *eg* gwrthocsidyddion antioxidant
gwrthod *be* reject
gwrthod gafael *be* bond failure
gwrthodiad *eg* gwrthodiadau rejection
gwrtholeuaeth *eb* obscurantism
gwrtholeuwr *eg* gwrtholeuwyr obscurantist
gwrtholew *ans* oilproof
gwrthorbwysol *ans* antihypertensive
gwrthraflog *ans* non-fraying
gwrthran *eb* gwrthrannau counterpart
gwrthrwd *ans* rustproof
gwrthrybudd *eg* contra-indication
gwrthrych *eg* gwrthrychau object; body
gwrthrych allwthiad *eg* gwrthrychau allwthiad extrusion object
gwrthrych dan lygoden *eg* gwrthrychau dan lygoden mouse over object
gwrthrych grŵp *eg* group object
gwrthrych gwneud *eg* gwrthrychau gwneud man-made object
gwrthrych hapgael *eg* gwrthrychau hapgael found object
gwrthrych lluniadu *eg* gwrthrychau lluniadu draw object
gwrthrych lluniadu grŵp *eg* gwrthrychau lluniadu grŵp group draw object
gwrthrych materol *eg* gwrthrychau materol material object
gwrthrych naturiol *eg* gwrthrychau naturiol natural object
gwrthrych nesaf *eg* next object
gwrthrych siart *eg* gwrthrychau siart chart object
gwrthrych staenedig *eg* stained preparation
gwrthrych terfynol *eg* final outcome
gwrthrych testun *eg* gwrthrychau testun text object
gwrthrychau dan sylw *ell* observed objects
gwrthrychedd *eg* objectivity
gwrthrychiadur *eg* gwrthrychiaduron objective
gwrthrychiadur mewn olew *eg* oil-immersion objective
gwrthrychol *ans* objective
gwrthryfel *eg* gwrthryfeloedd uprising; rebellion; revolt; insurrection; rising
gwrthryfel Kett *eg* Kett rebellion
Gwrthryfel y Bocswyr *eg* Boxer Rising
Gwrthryfel y Camisardiaid *eg* Revolt of the Camisards
Gwrthryfel y Rhagfyrwyr *eg* Decembrists' Revolt
gwrthryfel y Spartaciaid *eg* Spartacist revolt
Gwrthryfel y Werin *eg* Peasants' Revolt
gwrthryfelgar *ans* rebellious
gwrthryfeloedd cyfnod y Tuduriaid *ell* Tudor rebellions
gwrthryfelwr *eg* gwrthryfelwyr rebel
gwrthsafiad y brodorion *eg* native resistance
gwrthsafol *ans* refractory
gwrthsain *ans* soundproof
gwrthsefyll *be* resist
gwrth-Semitiaeth *eb* anti-Semitism
gwrthsodd *ans* countersunk
gwrthsoddi *be* countersink
gwrthsoddydd *eg* gwrthsoddyddion countersink
gwrthstaen *ans* stainless
gwrthstatig *ans* antistatic
gwrthsymudiad *eg* gwrthsymudiadau contrary motion
gwrthwahaniaethol *be* anti-discrimination
gwrthwasgedig *ans* push-up
gwrthwasgu *be* push-up
gwrthwedd *ans* antiphase
gwrthweithio *be* counteract
gwrthweithiol *ans* antagonistic
gwrthweithydd *eg* gwrthweithyddion antagonist
gwrthwenwyn *eg* antidote
gwrthwneud *be* override
gwrthwyfyn *ans* mothproof; anti-moth
gwrthwyfynu *be* mothproof; mothproofing
gwrthwyneb *eg* opposite
gwrthwynebedd *eg* resistance
gwrthwynebiad *eg* gwrthwynebiadau resistance; opposition
gwrthwynebiad di-drais *eg* passive resistance
gwrthwynebol *ans* opposing
gwrthwynebwr *eg* gwrthwynebwyr opponent
gwrthwyntoedd cyson *ell* anti-trades
gwrthwyro *be* backing
gwrthydd *eg* gwrthyddion resistor
gwrthydd dabio *eg* gwrthyddion dabio dabbed resist

gwrthydd goleuni-ddibynnol *eg* gwrthyddion goleuni-ddibynnol light-dependent resistor
gwrthydd gosod *eg* applied resist
gwrthydd grid *eg* gwrthyddion grid grid resistor
gwrthydd newidiol *eg* gwrthyddion newidiol variable resistor
gwrthydd wedi'i beintio *eg* gwrthyddion wedi'u peintio painted resist
gwrthymosodiad *eg* gwrthymosodiadau counter-attack
gwrthyriad *eg* gwrthyriadau repulsion
gwrthyriad parau electron plisgyn falens *eg* valence shell electron pair repulsion
gwrthyrru *be* repel
gwrthyrru testun *be* repel text
gwrthyrrwr dŵr *eg* gwrthyrwyr dŵr throating
gwrw *eg* gwrws guru
gwrychyn *eg* gwrych bristle
gwryd *eg* gwrhydau fathom
gwrym (am chwydd) *eg* gwrymiau bulge
gwrym (ar dir) *eg* gwrymiau ridge
gwrym (crych neu graith) *eg* gwrymiau seam
gwrymiog *ans* seamed
gwryw *eg* gwrywod male
gwrywedd *eg* maleness
gwrywol *ans* male
gwthferyn *eg* gwthferynnau thrust bearing
gwthffit *eb* gwthffitiau push fit
gwthiad *eg* gwthiadau push; heave; thrust
gwthiad cyffwrdd *eg* contact push
gwthiad rhew *eg* gwthiadau rhew frost heaving
gwthiad technoleg *eg* technology push
gwthiad ymlaen *eg* forward thrust
gwthio *be* push; thrust; propulsion
gwthio'r pwysau *be* putting the shot
gwybodaeth (=dealltwriaeth o bwnc, swm yr hyn a ddysgwyd) *eb* knowledge
gwybodaeth (=rhywbeth a hysbysir i rywun) *eb* information
gwybodaeth ariannol *eb* financial information
gwybodaeth bersonol *eb* personal information
gwybodaeth cymorth *eb* help information
gwybodaeth electronig *eb* electronic information
gwybodaeth gartograffig *eb* cartographic information
gwybodaeth greiddiol *eb* underpinning knowledge
gwybodaeth gyfrifiadurol *eb* computer knowledge
gwybodaeth gyfrinachol *eb* confidential information
gwybodaeth hyperdestun *eb* hypertext knowledge
gwybodaeth i ymwelwyr *eb* tourist information
gwybodaeth rheoli *eb* management information
gwybodaeth wyddonol *eb* scientific knowledge
gwybyddiaeth *eb* cognition
gwybyddiaeth afiechyd *eb* illness cognition
gwybyddiaeth gymdeithasol *eb* social cognition
gwybyddol *ans* cognitive
gwydn *ans* tough; resilient; durable; resistant
gwydnwch *eg* toughness; hardiness; durability; resistance
gwydr *eg* gwydrau glass
gwydr crwm *eg* crown glass
gwydr ffibr *eg* fibreglass
gwydr goreurog *eg* gilt glass
gwydr gwastad *eg* sheet glass
gwydr lliw *eg* gwydrau lliw stained glass; coloured glass
gwydr-chwythu *be* glass blowing
gwydredig *ans* vitrified
gwydredd *eg* gwydreddau glaze
gwydredd alcalïaidd *eg* alkaline glaze
gwydredd borasig *eg* boracic glaze
gwydredd crai *eg* raw glaze
gwydredd crochenwaith *eg* pottery glaze
gwydredd crochenwaith *eg* stoneware glaze
gwydredd di-draidd *eg* opaque glaze
gwydredd felwm *eg* vellum glaze
gwydredd ffrit *eg* fritted glaze
gwydredd gloyw *eg* clear glaze
gwydredd grisialog *eg* crystalline glaze
gwydredd lliw *eg* stained glaze
gwydredd mat *eg* matt glaze
gwydredd plwm *eg* lead glaze
gwydredd powdr *eg* powder glaze
gwydredd tryloyw *eg* transparent glaze
gwydreiddiadwy *ans* vitrifiable
gwydrfaen *eg* obsidian
gwydrffibr *eg* glass fibre
gwydro *be* glaze
gwydro dwbl *be* double glazing
gwydrog *ans* glazed; vitreous; glassy
gwydryn cloc *eg* gwydrynnau cloc clock glass
gwydryn oriawr *eg* gwydrau oriawr watch-glass
gŵydd *eb* gwyddau goose
gŵydd fôr *eb* gwyddau môr barnacle
gŵydd yr eira *eb* gwyddau yr eira snow goose
gwŷdd *eg* gwyddiau loom
gwŷdd brêd *eg* gwyddiau brêd braid loom
gwŷdd bwrdd *eg* gwyddiau bwrdd board loom
gwŷdd bwthyn *eg* gwyddiau bwthyn cottage loom
gwŷdd cerdyn *eg* gwyddiau cerdyn card loom
gwŷdd dwyffordd *eg* gwyddiau dwyffordd two-way loom
gwŷdd incl *eg* gwyddiau incl inkle loom
gwŷdd llaw *eg* gwyddiau llaw hand loom
gwŷdd pedair siafft *eg* gwyddiau pedair siafft four-shaft loom
gwŷdd pedal *eg* gwyddiau pedal pedal loom
gwŷdd peiriannol *eg* gwyddiau peiriannol power loom
gwŷdd pwysau *eg* gwyddiau pwysau warp-weighted loom
gwŷdd rholer *eg* gwyddiau rholer roller loom
gwŷdd tabi *eg* gwyddiau tabi tabby loom
gwŷdd tabled *eg* gwyddiau tabled tablet loom

gwŷdd troedlath *eg* gwyddiau troedlath footpower loom
gwŷdd Wendicote *eg* gwyddiau Wendicote Wendicote loom
gwŷdd Wendy *eg* gwyddiau Wendy Wendy loom
Gwyddel *eg* Gwyddelod Irish
gwyddfa *eb* gwyddfeydd tumulus
gwyddoniadur *eg* gwyddoniaduron encyclopaedia
gwyddoniadur sgrin *eg* gwyddoniaduron sgrin on screen encyclopaedia
gwyddoniadurwr *eg* gwyddoniadurwyr encyclopaedist
gwyddoniaeth *eb* science
gwyddonydd chwaraeon *eg* gwyddonwyr chwaraeon sport scientist
gwyddor (=corff systematig o wybodaeth *eb* gwyddorau science
gwyddor (=yr abiéc) *eb* gwyddorau alphabet
gwyddor cartref *eb* domestic science
gwyddor endoredig *eb* gwyddorau endoredig incised alphabet
gwyddor ffonetig ryngwladol *eb* international phonetic alphabet (IPA)
gwyddor gwybodaeth *eb* gwyddorau gwybodaeth information science
gwyddor gwybyddiaeth *eb* cognitive science
gwyddor Gyrilig *eb* Cyrillic alphabet
gwyddor italig *eb* italic alphabet
gwyddor Rufeinig *eb* Roman alphabet
gwyddor rwnig *eb* runic alphabet
gwyddor ysgrifenedig *eb* gwyddorau ysgrifenedig written alphabet
gwyfyn *eg* gwyfynod moth
gŵyl *eb* gwyliau festival
gŵyl (yn y calendr Cristnogol etc) *eb* gwyliau feast
Gŵyl Badrig (17 Mawrth) *eb* Feast of St Patrick
Gŵyl Bawl (25 Ionawr) *eb* Feast of St Paul
Gŵyl Bedr a Phawl (29 Mehefin) *eb* Feast of Peter and Paul
Gŵyl Cecilia Wyryf (22 Tachwedd) *eb* Feast of St Cecilia
Gŵyl Ddewi (1 Mawrth) *eb* Feast of St David
Gŵyl Edward Frenin (13 Hydref) *eb* Feast of Edward, the Confessor
Gŵyl Eni'r Arglwyddes Fair *eb* Feast of St Mary, Nativity
Gŵyl Fair y Canhwyllau *eb* Candlemas
Gŵyl Fair ym Medi *eb* Feast of St Mary, September
Gŵyl Fair yn Awst *eb* Feast of St Mary, August
Gŵyl Fathew yr Apostol (21 Medi) *eb* Feast of Matthew the Apostle
Gŵyl Iago'r Apostol (25 Gorffennaf) *eb* Feast of James the Apostle
Gŵyl Ifan (24 Mehefin) *eb* Feast of John the Baptist
Gŵyl Ioan yr Apostol (27 Rhagfyr) *eb* Feast of John the Apostle
Gŵyl Luc Efengylwr (18 Hydref) *eb* Feast of St Luke the Evangelist
Gŵyl Lleuan Wyryf (13 Rhagfyr) *eb* Feast of Lucy
gŵyl mabsant *eb* gwyliau mabsant saint's day
Gŵyl San Steffan (26 Rhagfyr) *eb* Feast of Stephen the Martyr
Gŵyl Sant Andreas (30 Tachwedd) *eb* Feast of Andrew the Apostle
Gŵyl Sant Benedict (21 Mawrth) *eb* Feast of St Benedict
Gŵyl Sant Denis (9 Hydref) *eb* Feast of St Denis
Gŵyl Sant Hyllar (13 Ionawr) *eb* Feast of St Hilary
Gŵyl Sant Martin (11 Tachwedd) *eb* Feast of St Martin
Gŵyl Sant Mihangel (29 Medi) *eb* Feast of St Michael
Gŵyl Tomos yr Apostol (21 Rhagfyr) *eb* Feast of Thomas the Apostle
Gŵyl y Pab Calixtus (14 Hydref) *eb* Feast of Pope Calixtus
gwylan y gogledd *eb* gwylanod y gogledd glaucous gull
gwyliau *ell* holidays; vacation
gwyliau achlysurol *ell* occasional holidays
gwyliau haf *ell* summer holidays
gwyliau hanner tymor *eg* midterm break
Gwyliau'r Pererinion *ell* Pilgrim Festivals
gwylio chwarae *be* on-looking play
gwylio ffilmiau *be* film consumption
gwylio'r bêl *be* watch the ball
gwyliwr *eg* gwylwyr spectator; observer; watchman
gwyliwr y glannau *eg* gwylwyr y glannau coastguard
gwylnos *eb* gwylnosau wake
gwylog *eb* gwylogod guillemot
gwylliad *eg* gwylliaid brigand
gwylltgoed *ell* backwoods
gwylltlun *eg* gwylltluniau wild scape
gwymon *eg* seaweed
gwyn *eg* white
gwyn optegol *ans* optical white
gwyn plwm *eg* flake white
gwyn sinc *eg* zinc white
gwyn sylfaenol *eg* white foundation
gwyn titaniwm *eg* titanium white
gwyn Tsieina *eg* Chinese white
gwynegon *ell* rheumatism
Gwynfydedig *ans* Blessed
gwynias *ans* incandescent
gwyniasedd *eg* gwyniaseddau incandescence
gwynnin *eg* white matter
gwynnin (albwrnwm) *eg* sapwood
gwynnu *be* whiten
gwynnu sero *be* zero blanking
gwynnydd *eg* gwynyddion whitener
gwynnydd fflwroleuol *eg* fluorescent whitener
gwynt (nwy a gynhyrchir yn y stumog etc) *eg* flatulence
gwynt (yn gyffredinol) *eg* gwyntoedd wind
gwynt allchwyth *eg* gwyntoedd allchwyth outblowing wind

gwynt cryfaf *eg* dominant wind
gwynt cyfnewid *eg* wind of change
gwynt cyson *eg* gwyntoedd cyson trade wind
gwynt grym 10 *eg* force 10 wind
gwynt mewnchwyth *eg* gwyntoedd mewnchwyth inblowing wind
gwyntglos *ans* windproof
Gwyntoedd Grymus y Gorllewin *ell* Brave West Winds
gwyntoedd y gorllewin *ell* westerlies
gwyntyll *eb* gwyntyllau fan
gwyntyll awyru *eb* gwyntyllau awyru ventilating fan
gwyntyll droelli *eb* gwyntyllau troelli stirrer fan
gwyntyll echdynnu *eb* gwyntyllau echdynnu extractor fan
gwyntyll oeri *eb* gwyntyllau oeri cooling fan
gwŷr meirch *ell* cavalry
gwŷr traed *ell* infantry
gwŷr yr ecseis *ell* revenue men
gwyrdröedig *ans* deviant
gwyrdroi *be* subvert
gwyrdd alisarin *eg* alizarin green
gwyrdd bwdgerigar *eg* budgerigar green
gwyrdd cobalt *eg* cobalt green
gwyrdd crôm *eg* chrome green
gwyrdd efydd *eg* bronze green
gwyrdd llachar *eg* brilliant green
gwyrdd olewydd *eg* olive green
gwyrdd porfa *eg* grass green
gwyrdd sudd *eg* sap green
gwyrdd tywyll *eg* dark green
gwyrdd y ddeilen *eg* leaf green
gwyrdd y gwanwyn *eg* spring green
gwyrdd y môr *eg* sea green
gwyrddion *ell* greens
gwyrddmon *eg* gwyrddmyn verderer
gwyrddwst *eg* chlorosis
gwyredd *eg* gwyreddau rake
gwyredd blaen *eg* front rake
gwyredd cefn *eg* top rake
gwyredd gwaelod *eg* bottom rake
gwyredd negatif *eg* negative rake
gwyredd ochr *eg* side rake
gwyredd positif *eg* positive rake
gwyriad (ar ffordd etc) *eg* gwyriadau deviation
gwyriad (mewn cerddoriaeth) *eg* gwyriadau remove
gwyriad allan *eg* gwyriadau allan outswinger; awayswinger
gwyriad ar y grib *eg* swan neck
gwyriad cymedrig *eg* mean deviation
gwyriad negyddol *eg* negative deviation
gwyriad safonol *eg* gwyriadau safonol standard deviation
gwyriad y llonnod cyntaf *eg* first sharp remove
gwyriad yn y cromosom *eg* gwyriadau yn y cromosomau chromosomal aberration
gwyro (=pwyso i un ochr) *be* lean
gwyro (=symud i osgoi) *be* swerve
gwyro (=symud oddi ar y llwybr iawn) *be* deviate
gwyro (wrth fatio) *be* glance
gwyro a gwrthwyro veer and back
gwyrol *ans* aberrant
gwyro'r bêl *be* deflect the ball
gwyrth *eb* gwyrthiau miracle
gwyryf *eb* gwyryfon virgin
gwyryfol *ans* virgin
gwysiwr *eg* gwyswyr summoner
gwystl *eg* gwystlon hostage; pledge; pawn
gwystlo *be* pawn
gwystlwr *eg* gwystlwyr pawnbroker
gwythïen *eb* gwythiennau vein; seam; lode
gwythïen arennol *eb* gwythiennau arennol renal vein
gwythïen bortal *eb* gwythiennau portal portal vein
gwythïen bortal hepatig *eb* gwythiennau portal hepatig hepatic portal vein
gwythïen fesenterig *eb* gwythiennau mesenterig mesenteric vein
gwythïen fwyn *eb* gwythiennau mwyn vein of ore
gwythïen ganol *eb* gwythiennau canol midrib
gwythïen hepatig *eb* hepatic vein
gwythïen iliag *eb* iliac vein
gwythïen y gwddf *eb* gwythiennau'r gwddf jugular vein
gwythieniad *eg* venation
gwythiennig *eb* gwythienigau venule
gwywo *be* wither; wilt
gyda'r glannau *ans* inshore
gyda'r graen with the grain
gyddfu *be* neck; necking
gyli *eg* gylïau gully
gylïog *ans* gullied
gymedig *ans* gummed
gymio *be* gum
gymnasteg *eb* gymnastics
gymnasteg addysgol *eb* educational gymnastics
gymnasteg ffurfiol *eb* formal gymnastics
gymnastwr *eg* gymnastwyr gymnast
gymnosberm *eg* gymnosbermau gymnosperm
gymnosbor *eg* gymnosborau gymnospore
gynaeciwm *eg* gynaecium
gynaecoleg *eb* gynaecology
gynaecolegydd *eg* gynaecolegwyr gynaecologist
gynoeciwm *eg* gynoecium
gynwal *eg* gynwalau gunwale
gypswm *eg* gypsum
gyr *eg* gyrroedd herd
gyrfa *eb* gyrfaoedd career
gyri *ell* gyri
gyriad *eg* gyriadau drive
gyriad amhositif *eg* gyriadau amhositif non-positive drive
gyriad cripian *eg* gyriadau cripian worm drive

gyriad cyfansawdd *eg* gyriadau cyfansawdd compound drive
gyriad ffrithiant *eg* gyriadau ffrithiant friction drive
gyriad positif *eg* gyriadau positif positive drive
gyriad pŵer *eg* gyriadau pwer power drive
gyriad syml *eg* gyriadau syml simple drive
gyriad terfynol *eg* gyriadau terfynol final drive
gyriant *eg* gyriannau drive
gyriant cadwyn *eg* chain drive
gyriant CD ROM *eg* gyriannau CD ROM CD ROM drive
gyriant disg hyblyg *eg* gyriannau disg hyblyg floppy disk drive
gyriant dyfais *eg* gyriannau dyfais device driver
gyriant sip *eg* gyriannau sip zip drive
gyrosgop *eg* gyrosgopau gyroscope
gyrriant ffynhonnell *eg* gyriannau ffynhonnell source drive
gyrru *be* drive
gyrru a gyredig driver and driven
gyrru ar ffo *eg* rout
gyrru mewn ac allan *be* roll on /roll off
gyrru swigod drwy *be* bubble
gyrru ymlaen *be* propel
gyrrwr *eg* gyrwyr driver
gyrrwr ambiwlans *eg* gyrwyr ambiwlans ambulance driver
gyrrwr argraffydd *eg* printer driver
gyrrwr bysellfwrdd *eg* gyrwyr bysellfyrddau keyboard drive
gyrrwr chwistrell *eg* gyrwyr chwistrell syringe driver

H

hacio *be* hack; hacking
haclif *eb* haclifiau hacksaw
haclif bŵer *eb* haclifiau pŵer power hacksaw
haclif fach *eb* haclifiau bach junior hacksaw
had ardyst *eg* certified seed
hadau haidd *ell* barley seeds
hadau olew *ell* oilseed
hadgraith *eb* hadgreithiau hilum
hadgroen *eg* hadgrwyn testa
hadgroen *eg* seed coat
Hadith *eg* Hadith
hadlestr *eg* hadlestri seed vessel
hadysol *ans* seed-eating
hadysydd *eg* hadysyddion seed-eater
haearn (Fe) *eg* heyrn iron
haearn â chwythell ager *eg* heyrn â chwythelli ager shot of steam iron
haearn ager *eg* heyrn ager steam iron
haearn ager a chwistrell *eg* heyrn ager a chwistrell steam and spray iron
haearn bwrw *eg* cast iron
haearn bwrw gwyn *eg* white-cast iron
haearn bwrw hydrin *eg* blackheart cast iron
haearn bwrw hydrin *eg* malleable cast iron
haearn bwrw llwyd *eg* grey cast iron
haearn cafflo *eg* heyrn cafflo snarling iron
haearn cefn *eg* cap iron
haearn cefn *eg* heyrn cefn back iron
haearn claear *eg* cool iron
haearn cnocio *eg* heyrn cnocio rapping iron
haearn crai *eg* pig iron
haearn cynnes *eg* warm iron
haearn chwistrellu *eg* heyrn chwistrellu spray iron
haearn fflatio *eg* heyrn fflatio knocking down iron
haearn galfanedig *eg* galvanized iron
haearn gyr *eg* wrought iron
haearn haematit *eg* haematite iron
haearn hydrin *eg* malleable iron
haearn llwyd *eg* grey iron
haearn ocsid *eg* iron oxide
haearn ongl *eg* heyrn ongl angle iron
haearn poeth *eg* hot iron
haearn rhychiog *eg* corrugated iron
haearn sgrap *eg* scrap iron
haearn smwddio *eg* heyrn smwddio iron
haearn smwddio *eg* heyrn smwddio domestic iron
haearn smwddio *eg* heyrn smwddio flatiron
haearn sodro *eg* heyrn sodro soldering bit
haearn sodro *eg* heyrn sodro bit
haearn sodro *eg* heyrn sodro soldering iron
haearn sodro bwyell *eg* heyrn sodro bwyell hatchet bit
haearn sodro pensil *eg* pencil bit
haearn sodro syth *eg* straight bit
haearn Sweden *eg* Swedish iron
haearn tawdd *eg* molten iron
haearn trydan *eg* electric iron
haearn(II) deuhaearn(III) ocsid *eg* iron(II) diiron(III) oxide
haearn(II) deuhaearn(III) ocsid (magnetit) *eg* iron(II) diiron(III) oxide (magnetite)
haearn(II) deusylffid (pyritau) *eg* iron(II) disulfide (pyrites)
haearn(III) clorid *eg* iron(III) chloride
haearn(III) ocsid (haematit) *eg* iron(III) oxide (haematite)
haelfraint *eb* copyleft
haematit *eg* haematite
haematitig *ans* haematitic
haematoleg *eb* haematology
haematolegydd *eg* haematolegwyr haematologist
haematwria *eg* haematuria
haemocyanin *eg* haemocyanin
haemocytomedr *eg* haemocytometer
haemoffilia *eg* haemophilia
haemoglobin *eg* haemoglobin
haemolysis *eg* haemolysis
haen *eb* haenau layer; ply; tier; bed
haen balis *eb* haenau palis palisade layer
haen ddisbydd *eb* haenau disbydd depletion layer
haen ffin *eb* haenau ffin boundary layer
haen gambiwm *eb* haenau cambiwm cambium layer
haen hidlo *eb* haenau hidlo filter bed
haen isaf *eb* haenau isaf lower order
haen Malpighi *eb* Malpighian layer
haen oson *eb* ozone layer
haen ryngol *eb* haenau rhyngol intermediate layer
haen sail *eb* haenau sail base coat
haen sbwngaidd *eb* haenau sbwngaidd spongy layer
haen waelodol (carped) *eb* haenau gwaelodol underlay
haenau *ell* bedding
haenau anghyffurfiadwy *ell* unconformable beds
haenau cydffurfiadwy *ell* conformable beds
haenau eiledol *ell* alternate layers

haenau ffawtiedig *ell* faulted strata
haenau plyg *ell* folded beds
haenedig *ans* stratified
haenen *eb* haenau zone
haenen absgisaidd *eb* haenau absgisaidd abscission layer
haenen alewron *eb* haenau alewron aleurone layer
haenen goroid *eb* haenau coroid choroid layer
haenen lynu *eb* haenau glynu cling film
haenen ymrannu *eb* haenau ymrannu germ layer
haeniad *eg* haeniadau stratification
haenlin pridd *eb* haenlinau pridd soil horizon
haenliwio *be* layer colouring
haenol *ans* stratiform; bedding
haenu *be* layer
haerwr *eg* haerwyr remonstrant
Haf Bach Mihangel *eg* Indian summer
hafal *ans* equal
hafal a dirgroes equal and opposite
hafaledd *eg* hafaleddau equality
hafaliad *eg* hafaliadau equation
hafaliad ategol *eg* hafaliadau ategol auxiliary equation
hafaliad Cartesaidd *eg* Cartesian equation
hafaliad ciwbig *eg* hafaliadau ciwbig cubic equation
hafaliad cwadratig *eg* hafaliadau cwadratig quadratic equation
hafaliad cwartig *eg* hafaliadau cwartig quartic equation
hafaliad cyffredinol nwy *eg* hafaliadau cyffredinol nwy general gas equation
hafaliad deuradd *eg* hafaliadau deuradd second degree equation
hafaliad differol *eg* hafaliadau differol differential equation
hafaliad differol trefn un *eg* hafaliadau differol trefn un first order differential equation
hafaliad fector *eg* vector equation
hafaliad geiriau *eg* hafaliadau geiriau word equation
hafaliad gradd tri *eg* hafaliadau gradd tri third degree equation
hafaliad integrol trawsffurfiol *eg* hafaliadau integrol trawsffurfiol transform integral equation
hafaliad ïonig *eg* ionic equation
hafaliad llinol *eg* hafaliadau llinol linear equation
hafaliad parametrig *eg* parametric equation
hafaliad polynomaidd *eg* hafaliadau polynomaidd polynomial equation
hafaliad stoichiometrig *eg* stoichiometric equation
hafaliad syml *eg* hafaliadau syml simple equation
hafaliad trefn dau *eg* hafaliadau trefn dau second order equation
hafaliad unradd (llinol) *eg* hafaliadau unradd first degree equation
hafaliadau cydamserol *ell* simultaneous equations
hafaliadau cydamserol llinol syml *ell* simple linear simultaneous equations
hafalnod (=) *eg* hafalnodau equal sign
hafalochrog *eg* equilateral
hafalonglog *ans* equiangular
hafalu *be* equate
hafalu *be* equalize
hafal-ymraniad *eg* hafal-ymraniadau equi-partition
hafan *eb* hafanau haven
hafanu *be* home
haffniwm *eg* hafnium
hai *eg/b* hey
hai croes *eg* cross hey
hai cynnydd *eg* cumulative hey
hai traws *eg* hey between
hai unrhyw *eg* hey with your own
haidd *eg* barley
haidd gwyn *eg* pearl barley
haig (pysgod) *eb* heigiau shoal
haint *eb* heintiau infection
haint *eb* heintiau pestilence
haint trwy'r genau *eb* oral infection
Haint y Brenin *eb* King's Evil
Hajj *eg* Hajj
halen *eg* salt
halen *eg* common salt
halen craig *eg* rock salt
haliad *eg* haliadau heave
halid *eg* halidau halide
halid hydrogen *eg* halidau hydrogen hydrogen halide
halier *eg* halwyr haulier
halio *be* heave
halitosis *eg* halitosis
halmwd *eg* hallmote
haloffob *eg* haloffobau halophobe
haloffyt *eg* haloffytau halophyte
haloffytig *ans* halophytic
halogen *eg* halogenau halogen
halogenaidd *ans* halogenated
halogeniad *eg* halogenation
halogenoalcan *eg* halogenoalkane
halogi (teml) *be* violate
halogi (yn gyffredinol) *be* contaminate
halogiad *eg* contamination
halwyn *eg* halwynau salt
halwynau lemwn *ell* salts of lemon
halwynau mwynol *ell* mineral salts
halwynau tawdd *ell* molten salts
halwynau'r bustl *ell* bile salts
halwyndir *eg* saltings
halwynedd *eg* salinity
halwynog *ans* saline
hallt *ans* salty
halltu (mochyn) *be* curing
hambwrdd *eg* hambyrddau tray
hambwrdd cymysgu *eg* hambyrddau cymysgu mixing tray
hambwrdd diferu *eg* hambyrddau diferu drip tray

hambwrdd gosod *eg* hambyrddau gosod leading tray
hambwrdd îsl *eg* hambyrddau îsl easel tray
hamdden *eb* leisure
hamdden a thwristiaeth leisure and tourism
hamdden ac adloniant leisure and recreation
hances *eg/b* hancesi handkerchief
hances bapur *eb* hancesi papur tissue
haneru *be* halve; bisect
haneru cornel *be* corner halving
haneru croes *be* cross halving
haneru cynffonnog *be* dovetail halving
haneru ongl *be* angle halving
haneru T *be* Tee halving
hanerwr *eg* hanerwyr half-back
hanerwr asgell *eg* hanerwyr asgell wing-half
hanerwr chwith *eg* hanerwyr chwith left-half
hanerwr de *eg* hanerwyr de right-half
hanerwraig *eb* hanerwragedd half-back
hanerydd *eg* haneryddion bisector
hanerydd allanol *eg* hanerwyr allanol external bisector
hanerydd mewnol *eg* hanerwyr mewnol internal bisector
hanerydd perpendicwlar *eg* hanerwyr perpendicwlar perpendicular bisector
hanes *eg* hanesion history
hanes achos *eg* case history
hanes amaethyddiaeth *eg* agrarian history
hanes bwrdeistrefol *eg* borough history
hanes cefn gwlad *eg* rural history
hanes cyfansoddiadol *eg* constitutional history
hanes cyfraith *eg* legal history
hanes cymdeithasol *eg* social history
hanes cynnar *eg* early history
hanes diplomyddiaeth *eg* diplomatic history
hanes diwydiannol *eg* industrial history
hanes economaidd *eg* economic history
hanes eglwysig *eg* ecclesiastical history
hanes gweinyddol *eg* administrative history
hanes gwleidyddol *eg* political history
hanes lleol *eg* local history
hanes llyngesol *eg* naval history
hanes maestrefol *eg* suburban history
hanes milwrol *eg* military history
hanes modern *eg* modern history
hanes modern cynnar *eg* early modern history
hanes oes Elizabeth *eg* Elizabethan history
hanes rhyngwladol *eg* international history
hanes sefydliadau *eg* institutional history
hanes teuluol *eg* domestic history
hanes trefol *eg* urban history
hanes y trefedigaethau *eg* colonial history
hanes yr hen fyd *eg* ancient history
hanes yr ymerodraeth *eg* imperial history
hanesiaeth *eb* historicism
Hanesion Patriarchaidd *ell* Patriarchal Narratives
hanesoldeb *eg* historicity
hanesydd *eg* haneswyr historian; historiographer
hanesydd academaidd *eg* haneswyr academaidd academic historian
hanesyddiaeth *eb* historiography
hanesyddiaethwr *eg* hanesyddiaethwyr historiographer
hanesyddol *ans* historical
hanfodion *ell* essentials
hanfodol *ans* essential
haniaeth *eb* haniaethau abstract; abstraction
haniaethol *ans* abstract
haniaethu *be* abstract
hanner *eg* haneri half
hanner adydd *eg* hanner adyddion half-adder
hanner amser *eg* half time
hanner bwa *eg* hanner bwâu half arch
hanner canol *eg* hanner canolau half centre
hanner cell *eg* hanner celloedd half cell
hanner colon *eg* haneri colon semicolon
hanner crwn *ans* semicircular
hanner crwn *eg* half round
hanner cwafer *eg* hanner cwaferau semiquaver
hanner cylch *eg* hanner cylchoedd semicircle
hanner diwrnod *eg* half-day
hanner dwplecs *eg* hanner dwplecsau half-duplex
hanner eliptig *ans* semi-elliptic
hanner fertigol *ans* semi-vertical
hanner foli *eg* half-volley
hanner ffordd i fyny midway-upwards
hanner hyd *eg* half-length
hanner lleuad *eb* half moon
hanner maint llawn *eg* half size
hanner masg *eg* hanner masgiau half-mask
hanner oes *eg* half-life
hanner oes biolegol *eg* biological half life
hanner rhwygo *be* half-ripping
hanner rhwym *ans* half-bound
hanner ton *eb* **hanner tonnau** half-wave
hanner tôn *eg* hanner tonau semitone; half-tone
hanner tôn cromatig *eg* hanner tonau cromatig chromatic semitone
hanner tôn diatonig *eg* hanner tonau diatonig diatonic semitone
hanner tonol *ans* semitonal
hanner tro *eg* hanner troeon half turn
hanner trychiad *eg* hanner trychiadau half section
hanner trychiadol *ans* half-sectional
hanner tymor *eg* half-term
hanner uchaf y dudalen *eg* top half of page
► **hanner-adydd deuaidd** *eg* hanner-adyddion deuaidd binary half-adder
Hans Fychan *eg* Little Hans
hansh ar oledd *eg* hanshys ar oledd sloping haunch
hansh cudd *eg* hanshys cudd secret haunch
hansh sgwâr *eg* hanshys sgwâr square haunch
hansiedig cudd *ans* secret haunched

hansiedig sgwâr *ans* square haunched
hansio *be* haunch
hap *ans* random
haparbrawf *eg* haparbrofion random experiment
hapbatrwm *eg* hapbatrymau random pattern
hapddethol *be* random selection
hapddewis *be* random choice
hapddigwyddiad *eg* hapddigwyddiadau random event
hapfasnach *eb* speculation
hapfasnachol *ans* speculative
hapfasnachu *be* speculate
hapfasnachwr *eg* hapfasnachwyr speculator
hapgerddediad *eg* hapgerddediadau random walk
hapgyfeiliornad *eg* hapgyfeiliornadau random error
hapgyrch *eg* hapgyrchoedd random access
hapgyrchu *be* random access
hap-hyd *eg* haphydoedd random length
haplif *eg* insequent
haploid *ans* haploid
haploidi *eg* haploidy
hapnewidyn *eg* hapnewidynnau random variable
hapnewidyn arwahanol *eg* hapnewidynnau arwahanol discrete random variable
hapnewidyn di-dor *eg* hapnewidynnau di-dor continuous random variable
hapnewidyn safonol *eg* hapnewidynnau safonol standard random variable
hapnod *eg* hapnodau accidental
haprif *eg* haprifau random number
hapsampl *eg* hapsamplau random sample
hapsamplu haenedig *be* stratified random sampling
Hapsbwrg *eg* Hapsbwrgiaid Hapsburg
Hapsbwrgaidd *ans* Hapsburg
harbwr *eg* harbour
harddwch *eg* beauty
Harijan *ell* Harijan
Harimandir Sahib *eb* Harimandir Sahib
harmatan *eg* harmattan
harmoneiddio *be* harmonize
harmoni *eg* harmonïau harmony
harmoni anwadal *eg* harmonïau anwadal fluctuating harmony
harmoni clos *eg* close harmony
harmoni di-wraidd *eg* harmonïau di-wraidd rootless harmony
harmonica *eg* harmonicâu harmonica
harmonig *ans* harmonic
harmonig *eg* harmonigau harmonic
harmonig syml *eg* harmonigau syml simple harmonic
harmoniwm *eg* harmonia harmonium
harmonydd *eg* harmonyddion harmonium player
harnais diogelwch *eg* harneisi diogelwch safety-harness
harnesu egni *be* energy harnessing
harpsicord *eg* harpsicordiau harpsichord
Harri Tudur *eg* Henry Tudor
Harri VII *eg* Henry VII
Harri VIII *eg* Henry VIII
Harri'r Llew *eg* Henry the Lion
Harri'r Mordwywr *eg* Henry the Navigator
hasb a stwffwl hasbiau a styffylau hasp and staple
haul *eg* heuliau sun
hawdd *ans* easy
hawl (i dir etc) *eg/b* title
hawl (yn gyffredinol) *eg/b* hawliau right; claim; entitlement
hawl arglwydd *eg* seigniorage
hawl atal *eg* hawliau atal suspending power
hawl broc *eg* wreck
hawl cynuta *eg* hawliau cynuta fire bote
hawl ffiwdal *eg* hawliau ffiwdal feudal incident
hawl gweld *eg* access
hawl pledio *eg* cognizance of pleas
hawl torri mawn *eg* common of turbary
hawl tramwy *eg* hawliau tramwy right of way
hawl tramwy *eg* hawliau tramwy way leave
hawl tramwy cyhoeddus *eg* hawliau tramwy cyhoeddus public right of way
hawl trosglwyddo arian *eg* virement
hawlfraint *eb* copyright
hawliau cyfartal *ell* equal rights
hawliau defnyddwyr *ell* consumer rights
hawliau eiddo deallusol *ell* intellectual property rights
hawliau perchenogaeth *ell* property rights
hawliau teyrnaidd *ell* regalian rights
hawlio *be* demand; claim
hawstoriwm *eg* hawstoria haustorium
HCMS: hyfforddiant cychwynnol ac mewn swydd *eg* INIST: initial and in-service training
heb dâl digonol *ans* underpaid
heb ddatblygu digon *ans* underdeveloped
heb ddigon o faeth *ans* under-nourished
heb ddwylo *ans* hands-free
heb ei fformatio *ans* unformatted
heb ei gannu *ans* unbleached
heb ei lygru *ans* unpolluted
heb ei llygru *ans* unpolluted
heb ei neilltuo *ans* no assignment
heb eu fformatio *ans* unformatted
heb eu llygru *ans* unpolluted
heb fod wrth raddfa not to scale
heb fod yn unfath *ans* non-identical
heb ganfod colofn column not found
heb ganfod newidiadau no changes discovered
heb golli cyffredinolrwydd without loss of generality
heb gyffwrdd *adf* without contact
heb gymorth *adf* unaided
heb losgi *ans* unburnt
heb newid *ans* unchanged

hebog tramor *eg* hebogau tramor peregrine falcon
heboga *be* hawking
hebogydd *eg* hebogwyr falconer
Hebraeg *eb* Hebrew
hecs *ell* hex
1,2,3,4,5,6-hecsaclorocylchohecsan *eg* 1,2,3,4,5,6-hexachlorocyclohexane
hecsadecan-1-ol *eg* hexadecan-1-ol
hecsadegol *ans* hexadecimal
hecsagon *eg* hecsagonau hexagon
hecsagonol *ans* hexagonal
hecsahedron *eg* hecsahedronau hexahedron
hecsamethylen tetramin *eg* hexamethylene tetramine
hecsan *eg* hexane
hecsan-1,6-deuamin *eg* hexane-1,6-diamine
hecsandeuoyl deuclorid *eg* hexanedioyl dichloride
hecsos *eg* hecsosau hexose
hectar *eg* hectarau hectare
hedegog *ans* volatile
hedfan *be* aviation
hedyn *eg* had, hadau seed
hedyn carwe *eg* hadau carwe caraway seed
hedyn eginol *eg* hadau eginol germinating seed
heddlu *eg* heddluoedd police
hedd-offrwm *eg* peace offering
heddwch *eg* peace
heddwch parhaol *eg* perpetual peace
Heddwch y Brenin *eg* King's Peace
heddychiad *eg* pacification
heddychiaeth *eb* pacifism
heddychu *be* pacify
heddychwr *eg* heddychwyr pacifist
hegledd *eg* etiolation
heglog *ans* etiolated
heibiad *eg* heibiadau bye
heibiad coes *eg* leg bye
heidiol *ans* gregarious
heidioledd *eg* gregariousness
heintiad *eg* heintiadau infection
heintiad defnynnau *eg* droplet infection
heintiedig *ans* infected
heintio *be* infect
heintus *ans* infectious
helaethiad *eg* helaethiadau enlargement
helaethu *be* enlarge
helaethu a lleihau enlargement and reduction
helaethu patrwm *be* enlarge a pattern
Helenaidd *ans* Hellenic
helfa *eb* helfeydd chase
Helfetig *ans* Helvetic
heli *eg* brine; saline
heli *eg* salt water
heli ffisiolegol *eg* physiological saline
helicoid *eg* helicoidau helicoid
helicoidol *ans* helicoidal
helics *eg* helicsau helix
helics dwbl *eg* double helix
helics llawn *eg* helicsau llawn full helix
heligol *ans* helical
heliotropedd *eg* heliotropism
heliotropig *ans* heliotropic
heliwm *eg* helium
heliwr *eg* helwyr hunter
heliwr-gasglwr *eg* hunter-gatherer
helm *eg* helmau helmet
helygen *eb* helyg willow
helygen y môr *eb* helyg y môr sea buckthorn
helynt *eg* helyntion affair
helynt Dreyfus *eg* Dreyfus affair
hem *eb* hemiau hem
hem addurnol *eb* hemiau addurnol decorative hem
hem dwc *eb* hemiau twc tucked hem
hem ddwbl *eb* hemiau dwbl double hem
hem ffug *eb* hemiau ffug false hem
hem gudd *eb* hemiau cudd blind hem
hem pwyth cudd *eb* hemiau pwyth cudd catch stitched hem
hem wedi'i hwynebu *eb* hemiau wedi'u hwynebu faced hem
hembwytho *be* hem stitching
hemell *eb* hemelli hemmer
hemicellwlos *eg* hemicellulose
hemio *be* hem
hemio cudd *be* invisible hemming
hemio slip *be* slip hemming
hemisffer *eg* hemisfferau hemisphere
hemisffer cerebrol *eg* cerebral hemisphere
hen a methedig *ans* old and infirm
Hen Aifft *eb* Ancient Egypt
Hen Destament *eg* Old Testament
hen dwyn *eg* hen dwyni senile dune
Hen Ddihenydd *eg* Ancient of Days
hen fara *eg* stale bread
Hen Frythoniaid *ell* Ancient Britons
hen fyd *eg* antiquity
Hen Gynghrair *eb* Auld Alliance
hen nodiant *eg* staff notation
Hen Norseg *eb* Old Norse
Hen Oes y Cerrig *eb* Old Stone Age
hen oruchwyliaeth *eb* old regime
Hen Roeg *eb* Ancient Greece
henadur *eg* henaduriaid alderman
henaint *eg* old age
heneb *eb* henebion ancient monument
heneiddedd *eg* senescence
heneiddiad *eg* geriatrification
heneiddio *be* ageing
heneiddol *ans* senescent
henoed *ell* elderly
henotheistiaeth *eb* henotheism
henuriad *eg* henaduriaid elder
hepatitis *eg* hepatitis
heptagon *eg* heptagonau heptagon

heptagonal *ans* heptagonal
her *eb* challenge
her yr amgylchedd *eb* environmental challenge
herbariwm *eg* herbarium
herc *eg* herciau hop
herc, cam a naid hop, skip and jump
hercian *be* hop
herclif *eb* herclifiau jig saw
herclif bŵer *eb* herclifiau pŵer power jig saw
heresi *eb* heresïau heresy
heretic *eg* hereticiaid heretic
hereticaidd *ans* heretical
Hereward Effro *eg* Hereward the Wake
herio *be* challenge
heriwr *eg* herwyr challenger
herodr *eg* herodrau herald
Herodr Arbenigol Cymru *eg* Wales Herald of Arms Extraordinary
herodraeth *eb* heraldry
herodrol *ans* heraldic
herpes *eg* herpes
herts (Hz) *eg* hertz
herwgipio (awyren etc) *be* hijack
herwgipio (pobl) *be* kidnap
herwr *eg* herwyr outlaw
herwriaeth *eb* outlawry
hesgen *eb* hesg sedge
hesian *eg* hessian
hesian cefn papur *eg* paper backed hessian
hesian llifedig *eg* dyed hessian
heterodein *eg* heterodeiniau heterodyne
heteroffoni *eg* heterophony
heterogametaidd *ans* heterogametic
heterogenaidd *ans* heterogeneous
heterogenedd *eg* heterogeneity
heterorywiol *ans* heterosexual
heterosboraidd *ans* heterosporous
heterosboredd *eg* heterospory
heterostyledd *eg* heterostyly
heterosygaidd *ans* heterozygous
heterotroff *eg* heterotroffau heterotroph
heuldro *eg* heuldroadau solstice
heuldro'r gaeaf *eg* winter solstice
heuldro'r haf *eg* summer solstice
heulwen *eb* sunshine
hewristig *ans* heuristic
hewristig argaeledd *eg* availability heuristic
hewristig cynrychiolideb *eg* representativeness heuristic
heyrn sgrôl *ell* anvil horn scrolls
hic *eg* hiciau nock
hicio *be* nocking
hidlen *eb* hidlenni filter; strainer
hidlen fflwff *eb* hidlenni fflwff fluff filter
hidlen pasio seiniau isel *eb* hidlenni pasio seiniau isel low-pass filter
hidliad *eg* filtration
hidlif *eg* hidlifau filtrate
hidlif glomerwlaidd *eg* glomerular filtrate
hidlo *be* filter; strain
hidlo drwy ddewis *be* filter by selection
hidlydd *eg* hidlyddion filter
hidlydd aer *eg* hidlyddion aer air filter
hidlydd anhysbys *eg* hidlyddion anhysbys unknown filter
hidlydd cleient *eg* hidlyddion cleient client-based filter
hidlydd lliw *eg* hidlyddion lliw colour filter
hidlydd post *eg* hidlyddion post mail-filter
hidlydd rhagosodedig *eg* hidlyddion rhagosodedig default filter
hidlydd sbam *eg* spam filter
hierarchaeth *eb* hierarchaethau hierarchy
hierarchaeth anghenion *eb* hierarchy of needs
hierarchaeth anghenion Maslow *eb* Maslow's hierarchy of needs
hierarchaeth drefol *eb* urban hierarchy
hierarchaeth nythog *eb* hierarchaethau nythog nested hierarchy
hierarchaeth y llysoedd *eb* hierarchy of the courts
Hierarchaethau Gorseddau *ell* Hierarchies of Throne
hierarchaidd *ans* hierarchical
hieroglyffigau'r Eifftwyr *ell* Egyptian hieroglyphics
Hijra *eg* Hijra
hil *eb* hilion race
Hil Ariaidd *eb* Aryan Race
hiliaeth *eb* racism
hiliol *ans* racial
hiliwr *eg* hilwyr racist
hil-laddiad *eg* genocide
hindreuliad *eg* weathering
hindreuliedig *ans* weathered
hindreulio *be* weathering
Hindŵ *eg* Hindŵiaid Hindu
Hindŵaeth *eb* Hinduism
Hindŵaidd *ans* Hindu
hinsawdd *eb* climatic conditions
hinsawdd *eb* hinsoddau climate
hinsoddeg *eb* climatology
hipocampws *eg* hippocampus
hir *ans* long
hirbwyth a byrbwyth long and short stitch
hirgrwn *ans* oval
hirgul *ans* elongated
hirhoedledd *eg* longevity
hirwasg *ans* long waisted
histidin *eg* histidine
histogram *eg* histogramau histogram
histoleg *eb* histology
histon *eg* histonau histone
histopatholeg *eb* histopathology
Hiwgenot *eg* Hiwgenotiaid Huguenot
Hiwgenotaidd *ans* Huguenot

HMS: hyfforddiant mewn swydd *eg*
INSET: in-service training
HMS-ADAG: Hyfforddiant Mewn Swydd yn gysylltiedig ag ADAG *eg*
TRIST: TVEI Related In-Service Training
hobi *eg* hobïau hobby
hoci *eg* hockey
hodograff *eg* hodograffau hodograph
hoelbren *eg* hoelbrennau dowel
hoelbren ysgwyddog *eb* hoelbrennau ysgwyddog shouldered dowel
hoelen *eb* hoelion nail
hoelen ben pres *eb* hoelion pen pres brass head nail
hoelen benfawr *eb* hoelion penfawr clout nail
hoelen benfawr *eb* hoelion penfawr felt nail
hoelen bitsh byr *eb* hoelion pitsh byr short pitch nail
hoelen bitsh hir *eb* hoelion pitsh hir long pitch nail
hoelen bres *eb* hoelion pres brass nail
hoelen fain *eb* hoelion main brad
hoelen fer *eb* hoelion byr tack; cut tack
hoelen garan ddirdro *eb* hoelion garan dirdro twisted shank
hoelen garan gylch *eb* hoelion garan cylch ringshank
hoelen glustogwaith *eb* hoelion clustogwaith upholstery nail
hoelen gopr *eb* hoelion copr copper nail
hoelen gron *eb* hoelion crwn round nail; wire nail; French nail
hoelen gron bengoll *eb* hoelion crwn pengoll round lost head nail
hoelen gwaith maen *eb* hoelion gwaith maen masonry nail
hoelen haearn gyr *eb* hoelion haearn gyr wrought iron nail
hoelen hirgron *eb* hoelion hirgrwn oval nail
hoelen hirgron bengoll *eb* hoelion hirgrwn pengoll oval lost head nail
hoelen hydrin *eb* hoelion hydrin malleable nail
hoelen lechen *eb* hoelion llechi slate nail
hoelen lorio *eb* hoelion llorio clasp nail; cut clasp nail
hoelen rychiog *eb* hoelion rhychiog wiggle nail; corrugated fastener
hoelen saer *eb* hoelion saer joiner's brad
hoelen wrthrwd *eb* hoelion gwrthrwd rustless nail
hoelio *be* nail; fasten
hoelio arosgo *be* skew nailing
hoelio arosgo *be* oblique nailing
hoelio cudd *be* secret nailing
hoelio cyflin *be* parallel nailing
hoelio cynffonnog *be* dovetail nailing
hoelio dall *be* blind nailing
hofrenfad *eg* hofrenfadau hovercraft
hofrennydd *eg* hofrenyddion helicopter
hoffter *eg* liking
hogi *be* sharpen; hone; whet
hogwr *eg* hogwyr sharpener
hogwr sgrafell *eg* hogwyr sgrafell scraper sharpener
hongiad *eg* hongiadau suspension
hongiad annibynnol *eg* hongiadau annibynnol independent suspension
hongiad blaen *eg* hongiadau blaen front suspension
hongiad ôl *eg* rear suspension
hongian *be* suspend; hang
hongian halio *be* heave hanging
hongian ôl *be* backward hanging
hongian ôl plyg *be* bent backward hanging
hongian pen i lawr *be* reversed hanging
hongian yn rhydd *be* dangling
hongiwr *eg* hongwyr hanger
holi *be* interrogate; questioning
Holi *eg* Holi
holi ac ateb ffeil ddata question and answer a data file
holiadol *ans* interrogatory
holiadur *eg* holiaduron questionnaire
holiadur canfyddiadau afiechyd *eg* holiaduron canfyddiadau afiechyd illness perception questionnaire (IPQ)
holmiwm *eg* holmium
holocost *eg* holocaust
holoffytig *ans* holophytic
holomorffig *ans* holomorphic
holosöig *ans* holozoic
holwyddoreg *eb* holwyddoregau catechism
hollalluog *ans* omnipotent
hollalluog *ans* almighty
► **hollbwysig** *ans* all important
hollgorffol *ans* systemic
hollt (mewn craig) *eg/b* holltau cleft
hollt (mewn dyffryn) *eg/b* holltau rift
hollt (yn gyffredinol) *eg/b* holltau split
hollt calon *eg* holltau calon heart shake
hollt cwpan *eg* holltau cwpan cup shake
hollt cylch *eg* holltau cylch ring shake
hollt rheiddiol *eg* holltau rheiddiol radial shake
hollt seren *eg* holltau seren star shake
hollt synaptig *eb* holltau synaptig synaptic cleft
hollt taran *eg* holltau taran thunder shake
hollti *be* split
holltiad *eg* holltiadau cleavage
hollysol *ans* omnivorous
hollysydd *eg* hollysyddion omnivore
homeopathi *eg* homeopathy
homeostasis *eg* homeostasis
homeothermig *ans* homeothermic
homili *eb* homilïau homily
homoffonig *ans* homophonic
homogenaidd *ans* homogeneous
homogenedd *eg* homogeneity
homograffeg *eb* homography

homoleg *eb* homology
homolog *eg* homologau homologue
homologaidd *ans* homologous
homomorffedd *eg* homomorffeddau homomorphism
homomorffig *ans* homomorphic
homosboraidd *ans* homosporous
homoseiclig *ans* homocyclic
homosygaidd *ans* homozygous
homothetig *ans* homothetic
hôn *eg* honau hone
honiad *eg* honiadau allegation
honiadau gwyddonol *ell* scientific claims
honni *be* allege
hopgefn *eg* hopgefnau hogback
hopran *eb* hoprau hopper
hopran gardiau *eb* hopranau cardiau card hopper
hopsac *eb* hopsack
hopys *ell* hops
hormon *eg* hormonau hormone
hormon adrenocorticotroffig *eg* hormonau adrenocorticotroffig adrenocorticotrophic hormone
hormon gonadotroffig *eg* gonadotrophic hormone
hormon gwrthddiwretig *eg* antidiuretic hormone
hormon ieuangedd *eg* hormonau ieuangedd juvenile hormone
hormon lactogenig *eg* hormonau lactogenig lactogenic hormone
hormon lwteineiddio *eg* hormonau lwteineiddio luteinizing hormone
hormon planhigol *eg* hormonau planhigol plant hormone
hormon symbylu'r cortecs adrenal (HSCA) *eg* adrenal cortex stimulating hormone (HSCA)
hormon twf *eg* hormonau twf growth hormone
hormonaidd *ans* hormonal
Horn, Yr *eg* Cape Horn
horosgop *eg* horosgopau horoscope
hors *eg/b* horsys horse
hors ddillad *eb* horsys dillad clothes horse
horst *eg* horstau horst
hosan *eb* sanau stocking
hosan fer *eb* sanau byr sock
hosan wely *eb* sanau gwely bedsock
hosanwaith *eg* hosiery
hosbis *eb* hosbisau hospice
hostel *eg* hosteli hostel
hostel ieuenctid *eg* hosteli ieuenctid youth hostel
Hostia *eg* Host
howsat? how's that?
hud *eg* magic
hufen *eg* cream
hufen chwipio *eg* whipping cream
hufen dwbl *eg* double cream
hufen sengl *eg* single cream
hufen tolch *eg* clotted cream
hufennog *ans* creamy
hufennu *be* cream
hunan *eg* self
hunanadlynol *ans* self-adhesive
hunanadrodd *be* self-report
hunanamddiffyniad *eg* self-protection
hunanamddiffyniad *eg* self-defence
hunananffrwythloniad *eg* self-sterilization
hunanarchwiliad *eg* hunanarchwiliadau self-examination
hunanarchwiliad o'r ceilliau *eg* hunanarchwiliadau o'r ceilliau testicular self-examination
hunanarchwiliad o'r fron *eg* breast self-examination
hunanasesiad *eg* hunanasesiadau self-assessment
hunan-barch *eg* self-esteem
hunan-barch isel *eg* low self-esteem
hunanbeilliad *eg* self-pollination
hunanbortread *eg* hunanbortreadau self-portrait
hunanborthwr *eg* hunanborthwyr autotroph
hunanddatgelu *be* self-disclosure
hunanddelfryd *eg* ego-ideal
hunanddelwedd *eb* hunanddelweddau self-image
hunanddelwedd negyddol *eb* negative self-concept
hunanddigonedd *eg* self-sufficiency
hunanddosio *be* self-medication
hunaneffeithiolrwydd *eg* self-efficacy
hunanfoddhad *eg* self-gratification
hunanffrwythloniad *eg* self-fertilization
hunangenedledig *ans* autogenic
hunangofiant *eg* hunangofiannau memoirs
hunangydberthynas *eb* hunangydberthnasau autocorrelation
hunangyfeirio *be* self-referral
hunangyflogedig *ans* self-employed
hunangymorth *eg* self-help
hunangynhaliaeth *eb* self-sufficiency
hunangynhaliol *ans* self-sufficient
hunangynhaliol *ans* self-contained
hunangysyniad *eg* self-concept
hunangywiro *be* self-correcting
hunanhyder *eg* self-confidence
hunaniaeth *eb* identity
hunaniaeth genedlaethol *eb* national identity
hunaniaeth gorfforaethol *eb* corporate identity
hunaniaeth gymdeithasol *eb* social identity
hunaniaeth rhyw *eb* gender/sexual identity
hunaniaeth y Sikhiaid *eb* Sikh identity
hunanladdiad *eg* suicide
hunanlanhau *be* self-cleaning
hunan-les *eg* self-interest
hunanlywodraeth *eg* self-government
hunanofal *eg* self-care
hunanreolaeth *eb* self-control
hunan-roi *be* self-administration
hunan-serch *eg* narcissism
hunansgema *eg* self-schema
hunansylweddoli *be* self-actualisation

hunanwahaniaethiad *eg* self-differentiation
hunanweithredol *ans* self-action
hunanweithredu *be* self-acting
hunanwerthusiad *eg* hunanwerthusiadau self-appraisal
hunanymwadiad *eg* self-denial
hunanymwybodol *ans* self-conscious
hunanymwybyddiaeth *eb* self-awareness
hurbwrcas *eg* hire-purchase
hurbwrcasu *be* hire-purchase
hurfilwr *eg* hurfilwyr mercenary
Husaidd *ans* Hussite
Husiad *eg* Husiaid Hussite
Huw Fras *eg* Hugh the Fat
hwiangerdd *eb* hwiangerddi lullaby; nursery rhyme; cradle song
hwl amgrwm *eg* hyliau amgrwm convex hull
hwliganiaeth *eb* hooliganism
hwmerws *eg* humerus
hwmws *eg* humus
hwnt gychwyniad *eg* hwnt gychwyniadau staggered start
hwp llaw *eg* hand off
hwrdd (anifail) *eg* hyrddod ram
hwrdd (o wynt) *eg* hyrddiau gust
hwsâr *eg* hwsariaid hussar
hwsmonaeth *eb* husbandry
hwyaden *eb* hwyaid duck
hwyfo *be* fluttering
hwyhad *eg* hwyhadau elongation
hwyhau *be* elongate
hwyl *eb* hwyliau mood
hwyl fawr *eb* hwyliau mawr mainsail
hwyl flaen (jib) *eb* hwyliau blaen foresail
hwylbren *eg* hwylbrennau mast
hwylbren blaen *eg* hwylbrennau blaen foremast
hwylbren canol *eg* hwylbrennau canol mizzen mast
hwyldrawst *eg* hwyldrawstiau yardarm
hwylio *be* sail
hwylio yn agos i'r gwynt *be* brinkmanship
hwyluso *be* facilitate
hwyluso cymdeithasol *be* social facilitation
hwyluswr *eg* hwyluswyr facilitator
hwyr yn siarad *ans* delayed speech
hwyrddyfodiad *eg* hwyrddyfodiaid recent incomer
hwyrddyfodiad *eg* hwyrddyfodiaid latecomer
hwyrgloch *eb* hwyrglychau curfew
hyblyg *ans* flexible; pliable; adaptable
hyblygedd *eg* pliability
hyblygrwydd *eg* flexibility; adaptability
hybu *be* promote
hybu annibyniaeth cleientiaid *be* promoting client independence
hybu dealltwriaeth *be* promote understanding
hybu iechyd *be* health promotion
Hybu Iechyd Cymru *be* Health Promotion Wales
hybu parch *be* promote respect
hyd *eg* hydoedd length
hyd amhendant *eg* hydoedd amhendant indefinite length
hyd atodol *eg* added value
hyd bloc *eg* hydoedd bloc block length
hyd cofnod *eg* record length
hyd cymedrig ymadrodd *eg* mean length of utterance (MLU)
hyd cywir *eg* hydoedd cywir true length; exact length
hyd da *eg* good length
hyd dwbl *eg* double length
hyd ffocal *eg* hydoedd ffocal focal length
hyd gair *eg* word length
hyd gair newidiol *eg* variable word length
hyd gair penodol *eg* fixed word length
hyd lleiaf *eg* minimum length
hyd llinell awtomatig *eg* auto line length
hyd maes *eg* hydoedd maes field length
hyd newidiol *eg* hydoedd newidiol variable length
hyd o ben i ben *eg* overall length
hyd oes *eg* lifetime
hyd penodol *eg* hydoedd penodol fixed length
hyd testun *eg* text length
hyd yr oedi *eg* duration of pause
hydathod *eg* hydathodau hydathode
hydawdd *ans* soluble
hydawdd mewn dŵr *ans* soluble in water
hydbroffil *eg* hydbroffiliau long profile
hyd-doriad *eg* hyd-doriadau long section
hyder *eg* confidence
hyder mewn dŵr *eg* confidence in water
hydlin *eg* hydlinau vertical ruler
hydoddedig *ans* solvated
hydoddedd *eg* hydoddeddau solubility
hydoddi *be* dissolve
hydoddiant *eg* hydoddiannau solution; solvation
hydoddiant byffer *eg* buffer solution
hydoddiant cannu *eg* bleach solution
hydoddiant coloidaidd *eg* hydoddiannau coloidaidd colloidal solution
hydoddiant dirlawn *eg* hydoddiannau dirlawn saturated solution
hydoddiant dyfrllyd *eg* aqueous solution
hydoddiant Fehling *eg* Fehlings solution
hydoddiant golchi *eg* hydoddiannau golchi washing solution
hydoddiant halwynau *eg* hydoddiannau halwynau solution of salts
hydoddiant halwynog *eg* saline solution
hydoddiant iodomethan ethanolig *eg* ethanolic solution of iodomethane
hydoddiant litmws glas *eg* blue litmus solution
hydoddiant meithrin *eg* hydoddiannau meithrin culture solution
hydoddiant Ringer *eg* Ringers solution
hydoddiant sodiwm hydrocsid *eg* sodium hydroxide solution

hydoddiant sodiwm thiosylffad *eg* sodium thiosulphate solution
hydoddiant swcros *eg* sucrose solution
hydoddydd *eg* hydoddyddion solvent
hydoddydd amholar *eg* hydoddyddion amholar non-polar solvent
hydoddydd lacr *eg* hydoddyddion lacr lacquer solvent
hydoddydd paent *eg* hydoddyddion paent paint solvent
hydoddydd polar *eg* hydoddyddion polar polar solvent
hydoddydd saim *eg* hydoddyddion saim grease solvent
hydoddyn *eg* hydoddion solute
hydrad *eg* hydradau hydrate
hydradiad *eg* hydration
hydradol *ans* hydrated
hydradu *be* hydrate
hydraidd *ans* pervious
hydrasin *eg* hydrazine
hydrasiniwm clorid *eg* hydrazinium chloride
hydred *eg* hydredau longitude
hydred a lledred longitude and latitude
hydredol *ans* longitudinal
hydrid *eg* hydride
hydrin *ans* malleable
hydrinedd *eg* hydrineddau malleability
hydrobwll *eg* hydrobyllau hydropool
hydrocarbon *eg* hydrocarbonau hydrocarbon
hydroceffalig *ans* hydrocephalic
hydrocsi- hydroxy-
2-hydrocsibensencarbaldehyd *eg* 2-hydroxybenzenecarbaldehyde
3-hydrocsibwtanal *eg* 3-hydroxybutanal
hydrocsid *eg* hydroxide
2-hydrocsi-1,2-deuffenylethanon *eg* 2-hydroxy-1,2-diphenylethanone
2-hydrocsiffenylmethanol *eg* 2-hydroxyphenylmethanol
4-hydrocsi-4-methylpentan-2-on *eg* 4-hydroxy-4-methylpentan-2-one
2-hydrocsi-2-methylpropannitril *eg* 2-hydroxy-2-methylpropanenitrile
hydrocsiprolin *eg* hydroxyproline
2-hydrocsipropannitril *eg* 2-hydroxypropanenitrile
hydrocso- (math o ligand) hydroxo-
hydrocsylamin *eg* hydroxylamine
hydrodynameg *eb* hydrodynamics
hydroffilig *ans* hydrophilic
hydroffobig *eg* hydrophobic
hydroffoil *eg* hydroffoilau hydrofoil
hydrogen (H) *eg* hydrogen
hydrogen bromid *eg* hydrogen bromide
hydrogen clorid *eg* hydrogen chloride
hydrogen fflworid *eg* hydrogen fluoride
hydrogen ïodid *eg* hydrogen iodide
hydrogen perocsid *eg* hydrogen peroxide
hydrogenaidd *ans* hydrogenated
hydrogencarbonad *eg* hydrogencarbonate
hydrogeniad *eg* hydrogenation
hydrogeniad catalytig *eg* catalytic hydrogenation
hydrogensylffad(VI) *eg* hydrogensulfate(VI)
hydrogenu *be* hydrogenate; hydrogenize
hydrograff *eg* hydrograffau hydrograph
hydrograff llifogydd *eg* hydrograffau llifogydd flood hydrograph
hydrograffeg *eb* hydrography
hydroleg *eb* hydraulics; hydrology
hydrolig *ans* hydraulic
hydrolysis *eg* hydrolysis
hydrolysis alcalïaidd *eg* alkaline hydrolysis
hydrolysu *be* hydrolyse
hydromedr *eg* hydromedrau hydrometer
hydrosffer *eg* hydrosphere
hydrosgopig *ans* hydroscopic
hydrostateg *eb* hydrostatics
hydrostatig *ans* hydrostatic
hydrotropedd *eg* hydrotropism
hydrothermol *ans* hydrothermal
hydwyth *ans* ductile
hydwythedd *eg* ductility
hydyniad ar y croen *eg* skin traction
hydyniad ar yr ysgerbwd *eg* skeletal traction
hyetograff *eg* hyetograffau hyetograph
hyfedredd *eg* proficiency
hyfriw *ans* friable
hyfyw *ans* viable
hyfywdra *eg* viability
hyfywedd *eg* solvency
hyffa *eg* hyffâu hypha
► **hyffae cymathol** *ell* assimilative hyphae
hyffaidd *ans* hyphal
hyfforddai *eg* hyfforddeion trainee
hyfforddi *be* train; coach
hyfforddi athrawon *be* teacher training
hyfforddi cynghorwyr *be* counsellor training
hyfforddi dros bellter *be* over distance training
hyfforddi sgiliau cymdeithasol *be* social skills training
hyfforddiant *eg* training; coaching
hyfforddiant antur *eg* adventure training
hyfforddiant clinigol *eg* clinical training
hyfforddiant cychwynnol i athrawon *eg* initial teacher training
hyfforddiant cyfannol *eg* integrated training
hyfforddiant cylchol *eg* circuit training
hyfforddiant diwydiannol *eg* industrial training
hyfforddiant drwy gymorth cyfrifiadur *eg* computer aided instruction
hyfforddiant egwyl *eg* interval training
hyfforddiant galwedigaethol *eg* vocational training
hyfforddiant gwrando *eg* auditory training
hyfforddiant gwrthsefyll straen *eg* stress inoculation training

hyfforddiant gyda phwysau *eg* weight training
hyfforddiant i ffwrdd o'r gwaith *eg* off-the-job training
hyfforddiant pendantrwydd *eg* assertiveness training
hyfforddiant sefydlu *eg* induction training
hyfforddiant toiled *eg* potty training
hyfforddiant wrth y gwaith *eg* on-the-job training
hyfforddwr *eg* hyfforddwyr trainer; coach; instructor
hyfforddwraig *eb* hyfforddwragedd coach
hygrededd *eg* credibility; verisimilitude
hygrogram *eg* hygrogramau hygrogram
hygromedr *eg* hygromedrau hygrometer
hygrosgopig *ans* hygroscopic
hygyrch *ans* accessible
hygyrchedd *eg* accessibility
hygyrchedd tasg *eg* accessibility of task
hylan *ans* hygienic
hylaw *ans* manageable
hylendid *eg* hygiene
hylendid bwyd *eg* food hygiene
hylendid genau *eg* oral hygiene
hylendid personol *eg* personal hygiene
hylif *eg* hylifau liquid; fluid
hylif amniotig *eg* amniotic fluid
hylif Baker *eg* Baker's fluid
hylif brêc *eg* brake fluid
hylif bwrw *eg* hylifau bwrw mother liquor
hylif dyfrllyd *eg* aqueous humour
hylif eisbilennol *eg* pleural fluid
hylif ffenol *eg* phenol liquid
hylif fflamadwy *eg* hylifau fflamadwy inflammable liquid
hylif glanhau *eg* hylifau glanhau cleaning fluid
hylif gwydrog *eg* vitreous humour
hylif marcio glas *eg* engineer's marking blue
hylif meinweol *eg* hylifau meinweol tissue fluid
hylif semenol *eg* seminal fluid
hylif synofaidd *eg* synovial fluid
hylif torri *eg* hylifau torri cutting fluid
hylifadwy *ans* liquefiable
hylifau'r corff *ell* body fluids
hylifedig *ans* liquefied
hylifedd *eg* liquidity
hylifiad *eg* hylifiadau liquefaction
hylifo *be* liquefy; fluidization
hylifol *ans* liquid; fluid
hylifydd *eg* hylifyddion liquidizer; fluidizer
hylosg *ans* combustible
hylosgiad *eg* hylosgiadau combustion
hynafiad *eg* hynafiaid progenitor
hynafiad *eg* hynafiaid ancestor
hynafiadol *ans* ancestral
hynafiaeth *eb* hynafiaethau antiquity
hynafiaethol *ans* antiquarian
hynafiaethydd *eg* hynafiaethwyr antiquary
hynafol *ans* ancient; archaic; antique
hynafoliad *eg* archaism
hynafolyn *eg* hynafolion antique
hynawf *ans* buoyant
hynawsedd *eg* agreeableness
hynod *ans* singular
hynod ddiolchgar *adf* extremely thankful
hynod wannaidd *ans* weakly singular
hynodyn *eg* hynodion singularity
hynofedd *eg* buoyancy
hyperbola *eg* hyperbolâu hyperbola
hyperbola petryal *eg* hyperbolâu petryal rectangular hyperbola
hyperbolig *ans* hyperbolic
hyperboloid *eg* hyperboloidau hyperboloid
HyperCard *eg* HyperCard
hyperdestun *eg* hypertext
hypergeometrig *ans* hypergeometric
hypergyfryngau *ell* hypermedia
hypergyswllt *eg* hypergysylltiadau hyperlink
hyperplân sy'n gwahanu *eg* separating hyperplane
hypertonig *ans* hypertonic
hypertrocoid *eg* hypertrocoidau hypertrochoid
hypertroffedd *eg* hypertrophy
hypnosis *eg* hypnosis
hypnosis fforensig *eg* forensic hypnosis
hypocylchoid *eg* hypocylchoidau hypocycloid
hypodermaidd *ans* hypodermal
hyposecretiad *eg* hyposecretion
hypotenws *eg* hypotenysau hypotenuse
hypotonig i *ans* hypotonic to
hypothalamws *eg* hypothalamus
hypothermia *eg* hypothermia
hypsograffeg *eb* hypsography
hypsomedr *eg* hypsomedrau hypsometer
hypsometrig *ans* hypsometric
hyrddiad *eg* hyrddiadau spurt; charge; barge
hyrddiad ysgwydd *eg* hyrddiadau ysgwydd shoulder charge
hyrddio *be* spurt; charge; barge
hyrddwr *eg* hyrddwyr rammer
hyrddwr pen ôl *eg* hyrddwyr pen ôl butt end rammer
hyrwyddo (yn y cyfryngau) *be* promotion
hyrwyddo gwerthiant *be* sales promotion
hys-bys *eg* plug
hysbyseb *eb* hysbysebion advertisement
hysbyseb fras *eb* banner advert
hysbysebu *be* advertise
hysbysebu er gwybodaeth *be* informative advertising
hysbysebu er perswâd *be* persuasive advertising
hysbysebu uniongyrchol *be* direct advertising
hysbysfwrdd *eg* hysbysfyrddau notice-board; bulletin board
hysbysiad *eg* notification; notice
hysbysiad parhad *eg* hysbysiadau parhad continuation notice

hysbysiad talu *eg* pay advice
hysbyslen fach *eb* hysbyslenni bach handbill
hysteresis *eg* hysteresis
hysteria *eg* hysteria
hysting *eg* hystingau hustings
hytrawst *eg* hytrawstiau girder
hywaith *ans* operational

I

i fyny'r afon upstream
i ffwrdd off
i gyd wedi'u sgwario all squared
i lawr *adf* down; downward; not up
i lawr ac i'r ochr downward-sideways
i lawr y maes (am faes magnetig) down-field
i lawr yr afon downstream
i mewn (am awyren, traffig etc) *adf* inbound
iâ *eg* ice
iâ byrddol *eg* tabular ice
iâ du *eg* black ice
iach *ans* healthy
iachâd *eg* cure
iachawdwriaeth *eb* salvation
Iago (brenin) *eg* James
iaith *eb* ieithoedd language
iaith arwyddion *eb* sign language; signed language
iaith arwyddion America *eb* American sign language
iaith arwyddion Prydain *eb* British sign language
iaith cod peiriant *eb* machine code language
iaith Creol *eb* ieithoedd Creol Creole
iaith darged *eb* ieithoedd targed target language
iaith dechnegol syml *eb* simple technical language
iaith dogfen *eb* document language
iaith dramor fodern *eb* ieithoedd tramor modern modern foreign language
iaith drefniadol *eb* procedural language
iaith ddeongledig *eb* ieithoedd deongledig interpreted language
iaith ddisgrifiadol *eb* descriptive language
iaith estynedig *eb* extended language
iaith farcio hyperdestun *eb* hypertext mark-up language
iaith fathemategol *eb* mathematical language
iaith fodern *eb* ieithoedd modern modern language
iaith frodorol *eb* ieithoedd brodorol vernacular
iaith ffilm *eb* film language
iaith ffynhonnell *eb* ieithoedd ffynhonnell source language
iaith gaffaeledig *eb* ieithoedd caffaeledig acquired language
iaith grefyddol *eb* religious language
iaith grynoadol *eb* ieithoedd crynoadol compiled language
iaith gydosod *eb* ieithoedd cydosod assembly language
iaith gyfarwyddyd *eb* ieithoedd cyfarwyddyd carrier language
iaith gyffredin *eb* common speech
iaith lai arferedig *eb* ieithoedd llai arferedig lesser spoken language
iaith lefel isel *eb* ieithoedd lefel isel low-level language
iaith lefel uchel *eb* ieithoedd lefel uchel high level language
iaith leiafrifol *eb* ieithoedd lleiafrifol minority language
iaith manyleb *eb* specification language
iaith naturiol *eb* natural language
iaith peiriant *eb* ieithoedd peiriant machine language
iaith ragosodedig *eb* ieithoedd rhagosodedig default language
iaith rhaglennu *eb* ieithoedd rhaglennu programming language
iaith rhaglennu lefel uchaf *eb* high-level programming language
Iaith Rheoli Gorchwylion *eb* Job Control Language
iaith strwythur bloc *eb* block structured language
iaith strwythuredig *eb* structured language
iaith tagio *eb* ieithoedd tagio markup language
iaith trin data *eb* data manipulation language
iaith weledol *eb* visual language
iaith weledol celf *eb* language of art
iaith y corff *eb* body language
iaith y cyfryngau *eb* media language
iaith ymholi *eb* ieithoedd ymholi query language
Ianci *eg* Iancis Yankee
iâr faes *eb* ieir maes free-range hen
iâr fatri *eb* ieir batri battery hen
iâr i'w berwi *eb* ieir i'w berwi boiling fowl
iard *eb* iardiau courtyard
iard drefnu *eb* iardiau trefnu marshalling yard
iard llongau *eb* iardiau llongau ship yard
iardang *eg* iardangau yardang
iarll *eg* ieirll earl
Iarll Farsial *eg* Earl Marshall
Iarll Palatin *eg* Palatine Earl
iarllaeth *eb* iarllaethau earldom
iarllaeth balatin *eb* iarllaethau palatin county palatine
iarlles *eb* iarllesau countess
iau (=afu) *eg* ieuau liver
iau (ar gyfer cario neu dynnu) *eb* ieuau yoke
Iau (y blaned) *eg* Jupiter
iau â leinin *eb* ieuau â leinin lined yoke
iau cyfrwy *eb* ieuau cyfrwy saddle yoke

iawn *eg* atonement
iawn (ar fotwm cyfrifiadur) *adf* yes
iawn luniad *eg* iawn luniadau register
Iawn, Yr *eg* Atonement, The
iawndal *eg* iawndaliadau reparation
iawndal *eg* iawndaliadau compensation
iawndal *eg* damages
iawnderau *ell* rights
iawnderau dynol *ell* human rights
iawnderau sifil *ell* civil rights
iawnochri *be* onside
IBM-gytûn *ans* IBM-compatible
id *eg* id
ideal *eg* idealau ideal
idealaeth *eb* idealism
idemffactor *eg/b* idemffactorau idemfactor
idempotent *ans* idempotent
ideogram *eg* ideogramau ideogram
ideoleg *eb* ideology
ideolegwr *eg* ideolegwyr ideologue
Iddew Diwygiedig *eg* Iddewon Diwygiedig Reform Jew
Iddew Uniongred *eg* Iddewon Uniongred Orthodox Jew
Iddewiaeth *eb* Judaism
Iddewiaeth Rabbinaidd *eb* Rabbinical Judaism
iechyd *eg* health
iechyd a diogelwch health and safety
iechyd a gofal cymdeithasol *eg* health and social care
▸ **iechyd cardiofasgwlar** *eg* cardiovascular health
iechyd galwedigaethol *eg* occupational health
iechyd meddwl *eg* mental health
iechyd personol *eg* personal health
iechyd y cyhoedd *eg* public health
iechyd yr amgylchedd *eg* environmental health
iechydaeth *eb* sanitation
ieitheg *eb* philology
ieithyddiaeth *eb* linguistics
ieithyddiaeth gymdeithasegol *eb* sociolinguistics
ieithyddiaeth gymharol *eb* comparative linguistics
ieithyddol *ans* linguistic
Iesu Grist *eg* Jesus Christ
ieuenctid *ell* youth
ieuengrwydd *eg* juvenility
Ifan Arswydus *eg* Ivan the Terrible
Ifan Fawr *eg* Ivan the Great
ifanc *ans* juvenile
ifori *eg* ivory
igam ogam *ans* zigzag
igam ogamu *be* zigzag
igian *be* hiccup
iglw *eg* iglŵau igloo
igneaidd *ans* igneous
ing *eg* ingoedd agony
Ik Onkar Ik Onkar
ildio *be* surrender; yield; capitulate; cede;
ildio diamod *be* unconditional surrender
ildio hawl (ar dir) *be* quit claim
ildio'r goron *be* abdicate
ilewm *eg* ileum
iliag *ans* iliac
iliwm *eg* ilium
ilwminiaeth *eb* illuminism
ilwminydd *eg* ilwminiaid illuminist
imiwn *ans* immune
imiwnedd *eg* immunity
imiwnedd ataliedig *eg* suppressed immunity
imiwnedd caffaeledig *eg* acquired immunity
imiwnedd cynhenid *eg* natural immunity
imiwnedd goddefol *eg* passive immunity
imiwnedd gweithredol *eg* active immunity
imiwnedd poblogaeth *eg* herd immunity
imiwneiddiad *eg* immunization
imiwneiddiad triphlyg *eg* triple immunization
imiwneiddio *be* immunize
imiwnoglobwlin *eg* imiwnoglobwlinau immunoglobulin
imiwnoglobwlin secretu A *eg* secretory immunoglobulin A (sIgA)
imiwnoleg *eb* immunology
imiwnolegydd *eg* imiwnolegwyr immunologist
impasto *eg* impasto
impasto trwm *eg* heavy impasto
imperial *ans* imperial
imperialaeth *eb* imperialism
imperialaeth ddiwylliannol *eb* cultural imperialism
imperialaeth gyfryngol *eb* media imperialism
imperialaidd *ans* imperial
imperialydd *eg* imperialwyr imperialist
impiad *eg* impiadau graft
impio *be* graft
impresario *eg* impresari impresario
imprimatur *eg* imprimatur
imprimatura *eg* imprimatura
impromptu *eg* impromptus impromptu
in vitro in vitro
in vivo in vivo
inc argraffu *eg* inciau argraffu printing ink
inc argraffydd *eg* inciau argraffydd printer's ink
inc gwrth-ddŵr *eg* waterproof ink
inc India *eg* Indian ink
inc llawysgrif *eg* manuscript ink
inc lluniadu *eg* inciau lluniadu drawing ink
inc lluniadu lliw *eg* inciau lluniadu lliw coloured drawing ink
inc mandarin *eg* mandarin ink
inc parhaol *eg* indelible ink
inc printio leino *eg* inciau printio leino lino-printing ink
inc troslunio *eg* inciau troslunio transfer ink
incio *be* ink; inking in
inclein *eg* incleiniau incline
incwm *eg* incymau income

incwm crynswth *eg* gross income
incwm cyfartalog *eg* incymau cyfartalog average income
incwm eiddo *eg* unearned investment income
incwm gwaith *eg* earned income
incwm gwario *eg* disposable income
incwm gwladol *eg* national income
incwm heb ei ennill *eg* unearned income
incwm net *eg* net income
incwm trethadwy *eg* taxable income
incwm ychwanegol *eg* additional income
indecs *eg* indecsau index
indecs ceffalig *eg* cephalic index
indecs crymder *eg* indecsau crymder roundness index
indecs cyfranoledd *eg* index of proportionality
indecs gyswllt *ans* index linked
indecs màs y corff *eg* body mass index
indecs mitotig *eg* indecsau mitotig mitotic index
indecs plygiant *eg* indecsau plygiant refractive index
Indecs Shimbel *eg* Shimbel Index
Indecs, Yr *eg* Index
indeintiad *eg* indeintiadau indentation
indeintio *be* indent
indeintur *eg* indeinturau indenture
indemniad *eg* indemniadau indemnity
India corn *eg* India-corn; maize
India orynysol *eb* peninsular India
indiwm *eg* indium
Indo-Ewropeaidd *ans* Indo-European
indol *eg* indole
Indo-Swmeraidd *ans* Indo-Sumerian
indwsiwm *eg* indusium
inertia *eg* inertiau inertia
inertiaidd *ans* inertial
infertas *eg* invertase
infertebrat *eg* infertebratau invertebrate
infoliwt *eg* infoliwtiau involute
infolytedd *eg* infolyteddau involution
inffimwm *ans* infimum
ingot *eg* ingotau ingot
injan *eb* injans engine
injan stêm *eb* steam engine
inswlin *eg* insulin
intaglio *eg* intaglio
intarsia *eg* intarsia
integradwy sgwâr *ans* square integrable
integrand *eg* integrandau integrand
integredig *ans* integrated
integreiddiad *eg* integration
integreiddiad fertigol *eg* vertical integration
integreiddio *be* integrate; integration
integreiddio bwrdd gwaith *be* desktop integration
integreiddio llorweddol *be* horizontal integration
integreiddio plant *be* integrate children
integreiddiol *ans* integrative
integriad *eg* integriadau integration
integriad graffigol *eg* integriadau graffigol graphical integration
integrol *ans* integral
integru *be* integrate
integru fesul rhan *be* integration by parts
integru rhifiadol *be* numerical integration
integryn *eg* integrynnau particular
integryn *eg* integrynnau integral
integryn amhendant *eg* integrynnau amhendant indefinite integral
integryn dwbl *eg* integrynnau dwbl double integral
integryn neilltuol *eg* integrynnau neilltuol particular integral
integryn pendant *eg* integrynnau pendant definite integral
interfferon *eg* interferon
interim *ans* interim
intermezzo *eg* intermezzi intermezzo
internod *eg* internodau internode
interregnum *eg* interregnum
interstitaidd *ans* interstitial
intrada *eb* intradau intrada
Ioan (pab) *eg* John
ïodin (I) *eg* iodine
ïodin monoclorid *eg* iodine monochloride
ïodin(V) ocsid *eg* iodine(V) oxide
iodl *eg* iodlau yodel
ïodomethan *eg* iodomethane
ïon *eg* ïonau ion
ïon alwminad *eg* ïonau alwminad aluminate ion
ïon alwminiwm *eg* ïonau alwminiwm aluminium ion
ïon amoniwm *eg* ïonau amoniwm ammonium ion
ïon antimonad(III) *eg* ïonau antimonad(III) antimonate(III) ion
ïon antimonad(V) *eg* ïonau antimonad(V) antimonate(V) ion
ïon arian(I) *eg* ïonau arian(I) silver(I) ion
ïon arsenad(III) *eg* ïonau arsenad(III) arsenate(III) ion
ïon arsenad(V) *eg* ïonau arsenad(V) arsenate(V) ion
ïon asaid *eg* ïonau asaid azide ion
ïon bariwm *eg* ïonau bariwm barium ion
ïon bensendeuasoniwm *eg* ïonau bensendeuasoniwm benzenediazonium ion
ïon bismwthad(V) *eg* ïonau bismwthad(V) bismuthate(V) ion
ïon bismwth(III) *eg* ïonau bismwth(III) bismuth(III) ion
ïon borad *eg* ïonau borad borate ion
ïon bromad(I) *eg* ïonau bromad(I) bromate(I) ion
ïon bromad(V) *eg* ïonau bromad(V) bromate(V) ion
ïon cadmiwm *eg* ïonau cadmiwm cadmium ion
ïon calsiwm *eg* ïonau calsiwm calcium ion
ïon carbamad *eg* ïonau carbamad carbamate ion
ïon carbid *eg* ïonau carbid carbide ion
ïon carbonad *eg* ïonau carbonad carbonate ion

ïon cerad(IV) *eg* ïonau cerad(IV) cerate(IV) ion
ïon ceriwm(III) *eg* ïonau ceriwm(III) cerium(III) ion
ïon ceriwm(IV) *eg* ïonau ceriwm(IV) cerium(IV) ion
ïon cesiwm *eg* ïonau cesiwm caesium ion
ïon clorad (III) *eg* ïonau clorad (III) chlorate(III) ion
ïon clorad(I) *eg* ïonau clorad(I) chlorate(I) ion
ïon clorad(V) *eg* ïonau clorad(V) chlorate(V) ion
ïon clorad(VII) *eg* ïonau clorad(VII) chlorate(VII) ion
ïon clorid *eg* ïonau clorid chloride ion
ïon cobalt(II) *eg* ïonau cobalt(II) cobalt(II) ion
ïon cobalt(III) *eg* ïonau cobalt(III) cobalt(III) ion
ïon copr(I) *eg* ïonau copr(I) copper(I) ion
ïon copr(II) *eg* ïonau copr(II) copper(II) ion
ïon cromad(III) *eg* ïonau cromad(III) chromate(III) ion
ïon cromad(VI) *eg* ïonau cromad(VI) chromate(VI) ion
ïon cromiwm(II) *eg* ïonau cromiwm(II) chromium(II) ion
ïon cromiwm(III) *eg* ïonau cromiwm(III) chromium(III) ion
ïon cyanad *eg* ïonau cyanad cyanate ion
ïon cyanid *eg* ïonau cyanid cyanide ion
ïon deucromad(VI) *eg* ïonau deucromad(VI) dichromate(VI) ion
ïon deuhydrogenffosffad(V) *eg* ïonau deuhydrogenffosffad(V) dihydrogenphosphate(V) ion
ïon deumercwri(I) *eg* ïonau deumercwri(I) dimercury(I) ion
ïon deusylffad(IV) *eg* ïonau deusylffad(IV) disulfate(IV) ion
ïon deuthionad *eg* ïonau deuthionad dithionate ion
ïon fanadad(IV) *eg* ïonau fanadad(IV) vanadate(IV) ion
ïon fanadad(V) *eg* ïonau fanadad(V) vanadate(V) ion
ïon fanadiwm(II) *eg* ïonau fanadiwm(II) vanadium(II) ion
ïon fanadiwm(III) *eg* ïonau fanadiwm(III) vanadium(III) ion
ïon fflworid *eg* ïonau fflworid fluoride ion
ïon ffosffad(V) *eg* phosphate(V) ion
ïon ffosffinad *eg* ïonau ffosffinad phosphinate ion
ïon ffosffonad *eg* ïonau ffosffonad phosphonate ion
ïon ffosffoniwm *eg* ïonau ffosffoniwm phosphonium ion
ïon haearn *eg* ïonau haearn iron ion
ïon haearn(II) *eg* ïonau haearn(II) iron(II) ion
ïon haearn(III) *eg* ïonau haearn(III) iron(III) ion
ïon hecsaacwaalwminiwm *eg* ïonau hecsaacwaalwminiwm hexaaquaaluminium ion
ïon hecsaacwaalwminiwm(III) *eg* ïonau hecsaacwaalwminiwm(III) hexaaquaaluminium(III) ion
ïon hecsaacwacopr(II) *eg* ïonau hecsaacwacopr(II) hexaaquacopper(II) ion
ïon hecsacloroplatinad(IV) *eg* ïonau hecsacloroplatinad(IV) hexachloroplatinate(IV) ion
ïon hecsacloroplwmbad(IV) *eg* ïonau hecsacloroplwmbad(IV) hexachloroplumbate(IV) ion
ïon hecsaclorostanad(IV) *eg* ïonau hecsaclorostanad(IV) hexachlorostannate(IV) ion
ïon hecsacyanocobaltad(III) *eg* ïonau hecsacyanocobaltad(III) hexacyanocobaltate(III) ion
ïon hecsacyanofferad *eg* ïonau hecsacyanofferad hexacyanoferrate ion
ïon hecsacyanofferad(II) *eg* ïonau hecsacyanofferad(II) hexacyanoferrate(II) ion
ïon hecsacyanofferad(III) *eg* ïonau hecsacyanofferad(III) hexacyanoferrate(III) ion
ïon hecsafflworoalwminad(III) ïonau hecsafflworoalwminad(III)*eg* hexafluoroaluminate(III) ion
ïon hecsafflworosilicad(IV) *eg* ïonau hecsafflworosilicad(IV) hexafluorosilicate(IV) ion
ïon hecsanitrocobaltad(III) *eg* ïonau hecsanitrocobaltad(III) hexanitrocobaltate(III) ion
ïon heptaocsodeuffosffad(V) *eg* ïonau heptaocsodeuffosffad(V) heptaoxodiphosphate(V) ion
ïon hydrid *eg* ïonau hydrid hydride ion
ïon hydrocsid *eg* ïonau hydrocsid hydroxide ion
ïon hydrocsylamoniwm *eg* ïonau hydrocsylamoniwm hydroxylammonium ion
ïon hydrogen *eg* ïonau hydrogen hydrogen ion
ïon hydrogencarbonad *eg* ïonau hydrogencarbonad hydrogencarbonate ion
ïon hydrogendeufflworid *eg* ïonau hydrogendeufflworid hydrogendifluoride ion
ïon hydrogenethandeuoad *eg* ïonau hydrogenethandeuoad hydrogenethanedioate ion
ïon hydrogenffosffad(V) *eg* ïonau hydrogenffosffad(V) hydrogenphosphate(V) ion
ïon hydrogensylffad(IV) *eg* ïonau hydrogensylffad(IV) hydrogensulfate(IV) ion
ïon hydrogensylffad(VI) *eg* ïonau hydrogensylffad(VI) hydrogensulfate(VI) ion
ïon hydrogensylffid *eg* ïonau hydrogensylffid hydrogensulfide ion
ïon ïodad(V) *eg* ïonau ïodad(V) iodate(V) ion
ïon ïodad(VII) *eg* ïonau ïodad(VII) iodate(VII) ion
ïon ïodid *eg* ïonau ïodid iodide ion
ïon ïodin(I) *eg* ïonau ïodin(I) iodine(I) ion
ïon lithiwm *eg* ïonau lithiwm lithium ion
ïon magnesiwm *eg* ïonau magnesiwm magnesium ion
ïon manganad(VI) *eg* ïonau manganad(VI) manganate(VI) ion
ïon manganad(VII) *eg* ïonau manganad(VII) manganate(VII) ion
ïon manganîs(II) *eg* ïonau manganîs(II) manganese(II) ion
ïon manganîs(III) *eg* ïonau manganîs(III) manganese(III) ion
ïon mercwri(II) *eg* ïonau mercwri(II) mercury(II) ion
ïon molybdad(VI) *eg* ïonau molybdad(VI) molybdate(VI) ion

ïon nicel(II) *eg* ïonau nicel(II) nickel(II) ion
ïon nitrad(III) *eg* ïonau nitrad(III) nitrate(III) ion
ïon nitrad(V) *eg* ïonau nitrad(V) nitrate(V) ion
ïon nitrid *eg* ïonau nitrid nitride ion
ïon ocsofanadiwm(IV) *eg* ïonau ocsofanadiwm(IV) oxovanadium(IV) ion
ïon ocsoniwm *eg* ïonau ocsoniwm oxonium ion
ïon pentacyanonitrosylfferad(II) *eg* ïonau pentacyanonitrosylfferad(II) pentacyanonitrosylferrate(II) ion
ïon perocsoborad(III) *eg* ïonau perocsoborad(III) peroxoborate(III) ion
ïon perocsodeusylffad(VI) *eg* ïonau perocsodeusylffad(VI) peroxodisulfate(VI) ion
ïon plwmbad(II) *eg* ïonau plwmbad(II) plumbate(II) ion
ïon plwmbad(IV) *eg* ïonau plwmbad(IV) plumbate(IV) ion
ïon plwm(II) *eg* ïonau plwm(II) lead(II) ion
ïon potasiwm *eg* ïonau potasiwm potassium ion
ïon segur *eg* ïonau segur spectator ion
ïon silicad *eg* ïonau silicad silicate ion
ïon sinc *eg* ïonau sinc zinc ion
ïon sincad *eg* ïonau sincad zincate ion
ïon sodiwm *eg* ïonau sodiwm sodium ion
ïon stanad(II) *eg* ïonau stanad(II) stannate(II) ion
ïon stanad(IV) *eg* ïonau stanad(IV) stannate(IV) ion
ïon strontiwm *eg* ïonau strontiwm strontium ion
ïon sylffad(IV) *eg* ïonau sylffad(IV) sulfate(IV) ion
ïon sylffad(VI) *eg* ïonau sylffad(VI) sulfate(VI) ion
ïon sylffinad *eg* ïonau sylffinad sulfinate ion
ïon tetraamincopr(II) *eg* ïonau tetraamincopr(II) tetraamminecopper(II) ion
ïon tetraclorocwprad(II) *eg* ïonau tetraclorocwprad(II) tetrachlorocuprate(II) ion
ïon tetracyanonicelad(II) *eg* tetracyanonickelate(II) ion
ïon tetrahydridoalwminad(III) *eg* ïonau tetrahydridoalwminad(III) tetrahydridoaluminate(III) ion
ïon tetrahydridoborad(III) *eg* ïonau tetrahydridoborad(III) tetrahydridoborate(III) ion
ïon tetraïodomercwrad(II) *eg* ïonau tetraïodomercwrad(II) tetraiodomercurate(II) ion
ïon tetrathioantimonad(V) *eg* ïonau tetrathioantimonad(V) tetrathioantimonate(V) ion
ïon tetrathioarsenad(V) *eg* ïonau tetrathioarsenad(V) tetrathioarsenate(V) ion
ïon tetrathionad *eg* ïonau tetrathionad tetrathionate ion
ïon titaniwm(II) *eg* ïonau titaniwm(II) titanium(II) ion
ïon titaniwm(III) *eg* ïonau titaniwm(III) titanium(III) ion
ïon titaniwm(IV) *eg* ïonau titaniwm(IV) titanium(IV) ion
ïon triclorocwprad(I) *eg* ïonau triclorocwprad(I) trichlorocuprate(I) ion
ïon trithioantimonad(III) *eg* ïonau trithioantimonad(III) trithioantimonate(III) ion
ïon trithioarsenad(III) *eg* ïonau trithioarsenad(III) trithioarsenate(III) ion
ïon trithiostanad(IV) *eg* ïonau trithiostanad(IV) trithiostannate(IV) ion
ïon tun(II) *eg* ïonau tun(II) tin(II) ion
ïon tun(IV) *eg* ïonau tun(IV) tin(IV) ion
ïon twngstad(VI) *eg* ïonau twngstad(VI) tungstate(VI) ion
ïon thiocyanad *eg* ïonau thiocyanad thiocyanate ion
ïon thiosylffad *eg* ïonau thiosylffad thiosulfate ion
ïon wranad(VI) *eg* ïonau wranad(VI) uranate(VI) ion
ïon wranyl(VI) *eg* ïonau wranyl(VI) uranyl(VI) ion
ïonadwy *ans* ionizable
ïoneiddiad *eg* ïoneiddiadau ionization
ïoneiddio *be* ionize
ïonig *ans* ionic
ïonosffer *eg* ïonosfferau ionosphere
Iorcaidd *ans* Yorkist
iorcer *eg* yorker
Iorcydd *eg* Iorciaid Yorkist
IQ cymarebol *eg* ratio IQ
IQ gwyriad *eg* deviation IQ
i'r ochr sideways
i'r ochr ac i fyny sideways-upward
i'r ochr chwith side left
i'r ochr dde side right
iraid *eg* ireidiau lubricant
iredentiaeth *eb* irredentism
iriad *eg* iriadau smear; lubrication
iridiwm (Ir) *eg* iridium
iris *eg* irisau iris
iro *be* oil; grease; lubricate
is *ans* inferior
isadeiledd *eg* isadeileddau infrastructure
isadeiledd academaidd *eg* academic infrastructure
Is-adran Cymru Ar-lein *eb* Cymru Ar-lein Division
isaeddfed *ans* submature
isaf *ans* inferior
isafbwynt *eg* isafbwyntiau minimum
isafbwynt tymheredd *eg* minimum temperature
isafswm *eg* isafsymiau minimum
▸ **isafswm cyflog** *eg* minimum wage
isafswm cyflog gwladol statudol *eg* statutory national minimum wage
isalobar *eg* isalobarrau isallobar
isawyrol *ans* subaerial
is-bennawd *eg* is-benawdau subheading
isbridd *eg* isbriddoedd subsoil
is-bwyllgor *eg* is-bwyllgorau sub-committee
isbwysedd *eg* hypotension
ischaemig *ans* ischaemic
ischiwm *eg* ischia ischium
isdafodol *ans* sublingual
isdafodol *ans* hypoglossal
isdeitl *eg* isdeitlau subtitle
isdyfiant *eg* undergrowth

is-ddeddf *eg* is-ddeddfau by-law
isddewislen *eb* isddewislenni sub-menu
is-ddilyniant *eg* is-ddilyniannau subsequence
isddiwylliant *eg* isddiwylliannau subculture
isddosbarth *eg* subclass
isel *ans* low
Isel Eglwysig *ans* Low Church
iselder adweithiol *eg* reactive depression
iselder dwys *eg* major depression
iselder manig *eg* manic depression
▸ **iselder ysbryd** *eg* depression
iseldir *eg* iseldiroedd lowland
Iseldiraidd *ans* Dutch
Iseldireg *eb* Dutch
Iseldirwr *eg* Iseldirwyr Dutchman
isentropig *ans* isentropic
isetholiad *eg* isetholiadau by-election
isfacsilaidd *ans* submaxillary
isfandiblaidd *ans* submandibular
isfeidion *eb* isfeidonau submediant
isflanced *eb* isflancedi underblanket
isflew *eg* underfur
isfordent *eg* isfordentau inverted mordent
isfordent *eg* isfordentau lower mordent
is-ffactorial *eg* subfactorial
isffaryngeal *ans* subpharyngeal
is-ffeil *eb* is-ffeiliau subfile
is-ffeodaeth *eb* subinfeudation
is-ffeodu *be* subinfeudate
isffordd heb dar ac isffordd mewn trefi minor road untarred and minor road in towns
is-gadfridog *eg* is-gadfridogion lieutenant-general
is-gapten *eg* is-gapteiniaid lieutenant
isgarped *eg* isgarpedi carpet underlay
isgellog *ans* subcellular
isglafiglaidd *ans* subclavian
isgoch *eg* infrared
is-goeden *eb* is-goed sub-tree
is-gonswl *eg* is-gonswliaid vice-consul
is-gontract *eg* is-gontractau subcontract
is-gontractio *be* subcontract
is-gorporal *eg* is-gorporaliaid lance corporal
isgroenol *ans* subcutaneous
is-grŵp *eg* is-grwpiau subgroup
is-gwmni *eg* is-gwmnïau subsidiary
isgwmpasran *eb* lower register
Is-Gwnstabl *eg* Is-Gwnstabliaid Petty Constable
isgyfanswm *eg* subtotal
is-gyfeiriadur *eg* is-gyfeiriaduron subdirectory
isgynfas *eg* isgynfasau undersheet
isgyniferydd datblygiad *eg* developmental subquotient
isgynnyrch diwerth *eg* isgynhyrchion diwerth waste product
is-gyrnol *eg* lieutenant-colonel
isgywair *eg* low key
is-haen *eb* is-haenau substrate
is-haen *eb* is-haenau substratum
is-harmonig *eg* is-harmonigau subharmonic
is-iarll *eg* is-ieirll viscount
îsl *eg* islau easel
îsl braslunio *eg* islau braslunio sketching easel
îsl bwrdd *eg* islau bwrdd table easel
îsl clicied *eg* islau clicied ratchet easel
îsl cludadwy *eg* islau cludadwy portable easel
îsl cyfunol *eg* islau cyfunol combination easel
îsl rheiddiol *eg* islau rheiddiol radial easel
îsl stiwdio *eg* islau stiwdio studio easel
islaith *ans* subhumid
Islam *eb* Islam
Islamaidd *ans* Islamic
islap *eg* islapiau underwrap
islawr *eg* isloriau basement; lower ground
islif *eg* islifoedd underflow
islif *eg* islifogydd undercurrent
islif stac *eg* stack underflow
is-lifftenant *eg* is-lifftenantiaid second lieutenant
is-linyn *eg* is-linynnau sub-string
is-lyngesydd *eg* is-lyngeswyr vice-admiral
is-lywydd *eg* is-lywyddion subdominant
isniwral *ans* subneural
is-nod *eg* is-nodau subscript
isnormal *ans* subnormal
isobar *eg* isobarrau isobar
isobarig *ans* isobaric
isobath *eg* isobathau isobath
isobathytherm *eg* isobathythermau isobathytherm
isobront *eg* isobrontau isobront
isocinetig *ans* isokinetic
isoclin *eg* isoclinau isocline
isocron *eg* isocronau isochrone
isocronus *ans* isochronous
isocyanobensen *eg* isocyanobenzene
isocyanoethan *eg* isocyanoethane
is-oedolion *eg* subadults
isoensym *eg* isoensymau isoenzyme
isofalin *eg* isovaline
isoffen *eg* isoffenau isophene
isogamedd *eg* isogamy
isogeotherm *eg* isogeothermau isogeotherm
isoglos *eg* isoglosau isogloss
isogon *eg* isogonau isogon
isogonol *ans* isogonal
isohalaidd *ans* isohaline
isohel *eg* isohelau isohel
isolewcin *eg* isoleucine
isomer *eg* isomerau isomer
isomer optegol *eg* isomerau optegol optical isomer
isomeredd *eg* isomerism
isomeredd adeileddol *eg* structural isomerism
isomeru *be* isomerization
isometreg *eb* isometry
isometrig *ans* isometric
isometrig taenedig *eg* exploded isometric

isomorffedd *eg* isomorphism
isomorffig *ans* isomorphic
isomorffus *ans* isomorphous
isoneff *eg* isoneffau isoneph
isoperimetrig *ans* isoperimetric
isopleth *eg* isoplethau isopleth
is-orsaf *eb* is-orsafoedd sub-station
isorhythmig *ans* isorhythmic
isoseismig *ans* isoseismic
isoseismol *ans* isoseismal
isosgeles *ans* isosceles
is-osod *be* sub-let
isostad *eg* isostadau isostade
isostasi *eg* isostasy
isotactig *ans* isotactic
isotach *eg* isotachau isotach
isotonedd *eg* isotonicity
isotonig *ans* isotonic
isotop *eg* isotopau isotope
isotop gwreiddiol *eg* parent isotope
isotopig *ans* isotopic
isotherm *eg* isothermau isotherm
isothermal *eb* isothermalau isothermal
isothermig *ans* isothermic
isradd (mewn mathemateg) *eg* israddau root
isradd digidol *eg* israddau digidol digital root
isradd sgwâr cymedrig *eg* root mean square
israddol *ans* inferior
Israeliad *eg* Israeliaid Israelite
is-raglen *eb* is-raglenni sub-program
isranbarth *eg* isranbarthau subregion
israniad *eg* israniadau subdivision
isrannu *be* subdivide
is-reolwaith *eg* is-reolweithiau subroutine
is-reolwaith cysylltiedig *eg* is-reolweithiau cysylltiedig linked sub-routine
is-reolwaith llyfrgell *eg* is-reolweithiau llyfrgell library sub-routine
isrywogaeth *eb* isrywogaethau subspecies
is-safonol *ans* substandard
is-set *eb* is-setiau subset
is-sonig *ans* subsonic
is-swyddog *eg* is-swyddogion petty officer
is-system *eb* is-systemau sub-system
istangiad *eg* istangiadau subtangent
istref *eb* istrefi subtown
istrofannol *ans* subtropical
is-urdd *eb* suborder
iswaelodol *ans* infra-basal
is-werth *ans* low-order
iswythfed *eg* iswythfedau suboctave
isysgrif *eg* isysgrif subscript
italeiddio *be* italicize
italig italics
italig *ans* italic
iteriad *eg* iteriadau iteration
iteru *be* iterate
iterus *ans* iterative
Iŵl Cesar *eg* Julius Caesar
iwmon *eg* iwmyn yeoman
Iwmon y Gard *eg* Iwmyn y Gard Yeoman of the Guard
iwtalitaraidd *ans* utilitarian
iwtilitariad *eg* iwtilitariaid utilitarian
iwtilitariaeth *eb* utilitarianism
iwtilitariaeth gweithredoedd *eb* act utilitarianism
iwtilitariaeth rheol *eb* rule utilitarianism
Iwtopia *eb* Iwtopiâu Utopia

J

jabot *eg* jabot
jac *eg* jaciau jack
jac sgriw *eg* jaciau sgriw screw-jack
jac troli *eg* jaciau troli trolley jack
Jac yr Undeb *eg* Union Jack
jacio *be* jack
Jacobeaidd *ans* Jacobean
Jacobin *eg* Jacobiniaid Jacobin
Jacobinaidd *ans* Jacobin
Jacobiniaeth *eb* Jacobinism
Janam Sakhis Janam Sakhis
Janisariad *eg* Janisariaid janizary
Janseniaeth *eb* Jansenism
Jansenydd *eg* Janseniaid Jansenist
Japaneaidd *ans* Japanese
Japji Japji
jar *eb* jariau jar
jar ridyllu *eb* jariau rhidyllu sifter jar
jargon *eg* jargon
Jeanne d'Arc *eb* Joan of Arc
jejwnwm *eg* jejunum
jeli *eg* jelïau jelly
jeli meithrin *eg* nutrient jelly
jeli Wharton *eg* Wharton's jelly
jelïaidd *ans* jelly-like
jermon *eg* jermoniaid journeyman
Jeswit *eg* Jeswitiaid Jesuit
Jeswitaidd *ans* Jesuit
Jeswitiaeth *eb* Jesuitism
jet *eg* jetiau jet
jetlif *eg* jetlifau jet stream
jig *eb* jigiau jig
jig cyffrous *eg* jigiau cyffrous rousing jig
jig drilio *eg* jigiau drilio drilling jig
jig hoelbrennau *eg* jigiau hoelbrennau dowel jig
jig lleoli *eg* jigiau lleoli locating jig
jig plygu *eg* jigiau plygu bending jig
jiger *eg* jigeri jigger
jigio *be* jig
jingoistiaeth *eb* jingoism
jîns *eg* jeans
jiwt *eg* jute
Jiwtiaid *ell* Jutes
joci *eg* jociau jockey
John (brenin) *eg* John
jongleur *eg* jongleurs jongleur
joule (J) *eg* jouleau joule
Junker *eg* Junkeriaid Junker
jwg *eb* jygiau jug
jwrasig *ans* jurassic
jyglo *be* juggle
jyglo'r bêl *be* juggle the ball
jyglwr *eg* jyglwyr juggler
jyngl *eg* jyngls jungle

K

kaccha *eg* kaccha
Kangha *eg* Kangha
Kaiser, Y *eg* Kaiser, The
Kali *eb* Kali
kamma *eg* kamma
kapellmeister *eg* kapellmeister
kapparot *ell* kapparot
Karah Prashad / Prasad *eg* Karah Prashad / Prasad
karma *eg* karma
kashrut *ell* kashrut
Kathina *eg* Kathina
kesh / kes *eg* kesh / kes
Keynesiad *eg* Keynesiaid Keynesian
Khalsa *eg* Khalsa
khan *eg* khaniaid khan
khanaeth *eb* khanate
khandha *eg* khandha
Kirpan *eg* Kirpan
kirtan *eg* kirtan
kosher *ans* kosher
Krishna / Krsna *eg* Krishna / Krsna
Kshatriya / Ksatriya *ell* Kshatriya / Ksatriya

L

label *eg/b* labeli label
label Avery *eb* labelau Avery Avery label
► **label cod bar** *eg* labeli cod bar bar-coded label
label cymeradwyaeth *eg* labeli cymeradwyaeth approval label
label cynllun *eg* labeli cynllun design label
label gofal *eg* labeli gofal care label
label gwybodaeth *eg* labeli gwybodaeth informative label
labelu *be* label
labiwm *eg* labia labium
labordy *eg* labordai laboratory
labordy iaith *eg* labordai iaith language laboratory
labrwm *eg* labra labrum
labrwr *eg* labrwyr labourer
labyrinth *eg* labyrinthau labyrinth
lacolith *eg* lacolithau laccolith
lacr *eg* lacrau lacquer
lacr cellwlos *eg* lacrau cellwlos cellulose lacquer
lacr clir *eg* clear lacquer
lacr polyester *eg* lacrau polyester polyester lacquer
lacr synthetig *eg* synthetic lacquer
lacro *be* lacquer; lacquering
lactad *eg* lactate
lactas *eg* lactase
lacteal *eg* lactealau lacteal
lactoffenol *eg* lactophenol
lactos *eg* lactose
lafa *eg* lafâu lava
lafa clustog *eg* lafâu clustog pillow lava
lafa tawdd *eg* molten lava
lafant *eg* lafantau lavant
lagio *be* lag
lagŵn *eg/b* lagwnau lagoon
langar *eg* langar
Lakshmi /Laxmi *eb* Lakshmi /Laxmi
lamela ganol *eb* middle lamella
lamina *eg* laminâu lamina
laminaidd *ans* laminar
laminarin *eg* laminarin
laminedig *ans* laminate; laminated
laminiad *eg* laminiadau laminate
laminiad plastig *eg* laminiadau plastig plastic laminate
laminiadu *be* laminate
lamp *eb* lampau lamp
lamp berl *eb* lampau perl pearl lamp
lamp coil dwbl *eb* lampau coil dwbl double-coil lamp
lamp coil sengl *eb* lampau coil sengl single-coil lamp
lamp ffilament llinell *eg* line filament lamp
lamp glir *eb* lampau clir clear lamp
lamp gonsol *eb* lampau consol console light
lamp hir oes *eb* lampau hir oes long-life lamp
lamp oleugylch *eb* lampau goleugylch spot lamp
lamp uwchfioled *eb* lampau uwchfioled ultra violet lamp
Lancastraidd *ans* Lancastrian
Lancastrydd *eg* Lancastriaid Lancastrian
Ländler *eg* Ländler Ländler
landlordiaeth *eb* landlordism
lansio *be* launch
lanthanoid *eg* lanthanoid
lanthanwm (La) *eg* lanthanum
lap *eg* lapiau lap
lapiad plwm *eg* lapiadau plwm lead flashing
lapidari *eg* lapidary
lapili *eg* lapilli
lapio *be* wrap; lap
lapio poeth *be* shrink wrapping
lapio testun *be* textwrap
larfa *eg* larfâu larva
larwm *eg* larymau alarm
larwm diogelwch *eg* larymau diogelwch security alarm
laryncs *eg* larynx
laser *eg* laserau laser
latecs *eg* latex
latereiddiedig *ans* laterized
latereiddio *be* laterization
laterit *eg* lateritau laterite
lateritig *ans* lateritic
latsen *eb* lats lath
latws-rectwm *eg* latus-rectum
Lawnslot *eg* Lancelot
lawnt *eb* lawntiau lawn
lawrenciwm (Lr) *eg* lawrencium
layette *eg* layette
lecithin *eg* lecithin
lecsicon *eg* lecsiconau lexicon
lecsicon y meddwl *eg* mental lexicon
lefel (oed) *eg/b* lefelau age phase
lefel (yn gyffredinol) *eg/b* lefelau level
lefel alffa *eb* alpha level
lefel anhawster *eb* lefelau anhawster level of difficulty
lefel arwyddocâd *eb* significance level

lefel braint *eb* lefelau braint level of privilege
lefel cyfrinachedd *eb* lefelau cyfrinachedd confidentiality level
lefel cyrhaeddiad *eb* lefelau cyrhaeddiad attainment level
lefel cyrhaeddiad *eb* lefelau cyrhaeddiad level of attainment
lefel darllen annibynnol *eb* independent reading level
lefel droffig *eb* lefelau troffig trophic level
lefel dŵr *eb* lefelau dŵr water level
lefel egni *eb* lefelau egni energy level
lefel elfennol *eb* rudimentary level
lefel ffrynt siopau *eb* shop front level
lefel gallu cychwynnol *eb* initial ability level
lefel glwcos yn y gwaed *eb* blood glucose level
lefel gonfensiynol *eb* conventional level
lefel gwasgedd *eb* pressure level
lefel gweithgaredd *eb* lefelau gweithgaredd level of activity
lefel gyffredinol y pwnc *eb* general subject level
lefel gyngonfensiynol *eb* preconventional level
lefel hyder *eb* confidence level
lefel isel *eb* lefelau isel low level
lefel llawr *eb* lefelau llawr floor level
lefel môr *eb* lefelau môr sea level
lefel môr cymedrig *eb* mean sea level
lefel ôl-gonfensiynol *eb* postconventional level
lefel ranbarthol *eb* lefelau rhanbarthol regional level
lefel ryngwladol *eb* lefelau rhyngwladol international level
lefel seiliedig *eb* reduced level
lefel sŵn *eb* lefelau sŵn noise level
lefel trwythiad *eb* lefelau trwythiad water table
lefel trwythiad dŵr clo *eb* perched water table
lefel uchel *eb* lefelau uchel high level
lefel wirod *eb* lefelau gwirod spirit level
lefel wrthdro *eb* invert level
lefelaidd *ans* leveller
lefelau cyffuriau *ell* drug levels
lefelau o bydredd dannedd *ell* levels of dental decay
lefelau o fedrusrwydd *ell* levels of skill
lefelau syrfëwr *ell* surveyor's levels
lefelau'r galw *ell* levels of demand
lefelu *be* level
Lefelwr *eg* Lefelwyr Leveller
legad *eg* legate
legad y Pab *eg* legadau'r Pab papal legate
legins gweu *ell* legwarmers
lein (mewn rygbi) *eb* leiniau line out
lein (yn gyffredinol) *eb* leiniau line
lein aros *eb* leiniau aros siding; railway siding
lein bibell *eb* pipe line
lein bysgota neilon *eb* leiniau pysgota neilon nylon fishing line
lein ddillad *eb* leiniau dillad clothes line
lein ddillad gylchdro *eb* leiniau dillad cylchdro rotary clothes line
lein fach *eb* leiniau bach narrow gauge railway
lein gangen *eb* leiniau cangen branch line
lein gyfathrebu *eb* leiniau cyfathrebu communication line
lein nwyddau *eb* leiniau nwyddau freight line
lein trawsyrru trydan *eb* electricity transmission line
lein ymyriadol *eb* leiniau ymyriadol interrupt line
leiner *eg* leineri liner
leinin *eg* leininau lining
leinin cudd *eg* interlining
leinin gwrthsafol *eg* refractory lining
leinin iau *eg* yoke lining
leinio *be* form a line-out
leino *eg* lino
lema *eg* lemata lemma
leming *eg* lemingiaid lemming
lemon *eg* lemonau lemon
lens amgrwm *eg* lensiau amgrwm convex lens
lens ceugrwm *eg* lensiau ceugrwm concave lens
lens cydgyfeiriol *eg* lensiau cydgyfeiriol converging lens
lens cyddwyso *eg* lensys cyddwyso condenser lens
lens cywerth *eg* lensiau cywerth equivalent lens
lens dargyfeirio *eg* lensiau dargyfeirio diverging lens
lens deugeugrwm *eg* lensiau deugeugrwm biconcave lens
lens electron cydgyfeiriol *eg* lensiau electron cydgyfeiriol converging electron lens
lens electronau *eg* electron lens
lens grisialog *eg* lensiau grisialog crystalline lens
▸ **lens y gwrthrychiadur** *eg* lensiau'r gwrthrychiadur objective lens
lens y llygad *eg* lensiau'r llygad eye lens
lensaidd *ans* lenticular
lenticel *eg* lenticelau lenticel
lenticelaidd *ans* lenticel
leptin *eg* leptinau leptin
leptocwrtig *ans* leptokurtic
leptoten *eg/b* leptotene
les *eg* lace
les bobin *eg* bobbin lace
les rhychiog *eg* fluted lace
les wedi'i fewnosod *eg* lace insertion
les wedi'i frodio *eg* embroidered lace
les wedi'i grosio *eg* crocheted lace
les wedi'i grychdynnu *eg* gathered lace
les wedi'i wau *eg* knitted lace
les wedi'i wehyddu *eg* woven lace
lesbiad *eb* lesbiaid lesbian
les-fenthyg *eb* lend-lease
letraset *eg* letraset
lewcin *eg* leucine
lewcocyt *eg* lewcocytau leucocyte
lewcoplast *eg* lewcoplastau leucoplast

liana *eg* lianau liana
libart *eg* libartiau run; liberty
libido *eg/b* libido
libreto *eg* libreti libretto
libretydd *eg* libretyddwyr librettist
lid *eb* lidiau lead
Lied *eg* Lieder Lied
lifer *eg* liferi lever
lifer brêc *eg* liferi brêc brake lever
lifer cydiwr *eg* liferi cydiwr clutch lever
lifer cymhwyso ochrol *eg* liferi cymhwyso ochrol lateral adjustment lever
lifer cymhwyso Y *eg* liferi cymhwyso Y Y adjusting lever
lifer gwasgell *eg* liferi gwasgell presser lever
lifer trawsborthiant *eg* liferi trawsborthiant cross-feed lever
lifrai *eg* livery; uniform
lifrai a chynhaliaeth livery and maintenance
lifft *eg* lifftiau elevator
lifft hydrolig *eg* lifftiau hydrolig hydraulic lift
ligado *eg* ligados ligado
ligand *eg* ligand
ligand maes gwan *eg* weak field ligand
lignaidd *ans* ligneous
ligneiddiad *eg* lignification
ligneiddiad modrwyol *eg* annular lignification
ligneiddio *be* lignify
lignin *eg* lignin
lignit *eg* lignite
limonit *eg* limonitau limonite
lindysyn *eg* lindys caterpillar
lingerie *eg* lingerie
linoliwm *eg* linoleum
linson *eg* linson
linteri cotwm *ell* cotton linters
lipas *eg* lipase
lipid *eg* lipidau lipid
lipogenesis *eg* lipogenesis
lipoid *eg* lipoid
lipotropi *eg* lipotropy
litani *eb* litanïau litany
litmws *eg* litmus
litr *eg* litrau litre
litwrgaidd *ans* liturgical
litwrgi *eg/b* litwrgïau liturgy
litharg *eg* litharge
lithiwm (Li) *eg* lithium
lithiwm carbonad *eg* lithium carbonate
lithiwm tetrahydridoalwminad(III) *eg* lithium tetrahydridoaluminate(III)
lithograff *eg* lithograffau lithograph
lithograffi *eg* lithography
litholeg *eb* litholegau lithology
lithoser *eg* lithosere
lithosffer *eg* lithosphere
lithosol *eg* lithosol
liwdo *eg* ludo
liwt *eg/b* liwtiau lute
liwtio *be* luting
liwtydd *eg* liwtwyr lutenist
lob *eb* lob
lobi *eb* lobïau lobby
lobio *be* lob
lobïo *be* lobby
lobïwr *eg* lobïwyr lobbyist
loc *eb* lociau lock
locomotif *eg* locomotifau locomotive
locsodrom (=rhymlin) *eg* locsodromau loxodrome
locust *eg* locustiaid locust
locws *eg* loci locus
locws genyn *eg* gene locus
locws rheolaeth *eg* locus of control
locws rheolaeth allanol *eg* external locus of control
locws rheolaeth fewnol *eg* internal locus of control
loch *eg* lochau lough
lodicwl *eg* lodicwlau lodicule
lodnwm *eg* laudanum
log *eg* logiau log
log consol *eg* logiau consol console log
log lleoliad *eg* placement log
logarithm *eg* logarithmau logarithm
logarithm cyffredin *eg* logarithmau cyffredin common logarithm
logarithm naturiol *eg* logarithmau naturiol natural logarithm
logarithmig *ans* logarithmic
logio data *be* data logging
logisteg *eb* logistics
logo *eg* logo
logogram *eg* logogramau logogram
logo'r cwmni *eg* company logo
Lolard *eg* Lolardiaid Lollard
Lolardaidd *ans* Lollard
Lolardiaeth *eb* Lollardy
lolfa *eb* lolfeydd lounge
lom *eg* lomau loam
lomog *ans* loamy
lôn *eb* lonydd lane
loncian *be* jog
lopolith *eg* lopolithau lopolith
Lorenzo Ysblennydd *eg* Lorenzo the Magnificent
lot a scot lot and scot
Lotus Sutra *eg* Lotus Sutra
Louis Dduwiol *eg* Louis the Pious
Louis Sant *eg* St Louis
Ludaidd *ans* Luddite
Ludiad *eg* Ludiaid Luddite
Lurex *eg* Lurex
Lutheraidd *ans* Lutheran
Lutheriad *eg* Lutheriaid Lutheran
Lutheriaeth *eb* Lutheranism
lwcs *eg* lycsau lux

lwfans *eg* lwfansau allowance
lwfans beunyddiol argymelledig *eg* recommended daily allowance
lwfans cadw tŷ *eg* housekeeping allowance
lwfans culhad *eg* lwfansau culhad shrinkage allowance
lwfans cyfalaf *eg* lwfansau cyfalaf capital allowance
lwfans cynnal *eg* lwfansau cynnal subsistence allowance
lwfans ehangu *eg* lwfansau ehangu expansion allowance
lwfans gweini *eg* lwfansau gweini attendance allowance
lwfans hem *eg* lwfansau hem hem allowance
lwfans mamolaeth *eg* maternity allowance
lwfans peiriannu *eg* lwfansau peiriannu machining allowance
lwfans rhan-gyfnewid *eg* part exchange allowance
lwfans sêm *eg* lwfansau sêm seam allowance
lwfans symudiad *eg* lwfansau symudiad movement allowance
lwfans teulu *eg* family allowance
lwfans trethi *eg* lwfansau trethi tax allowance
lwfans troi *eg* lwfansau troi turning allowance
lwfans y pen *eg* lwfansau'r pen capitation allowance
lwfans y pen *eg* lwfansau'r pen per capita allowance
lwfans yr anabl *eg* lwfansau'r anabl disablement allowance
lwfer (uwchben tân etc) *eg* lwfrau hood
lwfer (yn gyffredinol) *eg* lwferau louvre
lwfer ailgylchredol *eg* lwfrau ailgylchredol recirculating cooker hood
lwfer popty *eg* lwfrau popty cooker hood
lwmen *eg* lwmina lumen
lwmp *eg* lympiau lump
lwmp-swm *eg* lymp-symiau lump sum
lŵn *eg* lynau lune
lwnwla *eg* lwnwlau lunula
lwtetiwm (Lu) *eg* lutetium
lymff *eg* lymph
lymffatig *ans* lymphatic
lymffocyt *eg* lymffocytau lymphocyte
lymffocyt B *eg* lymffocytau B B lymphocyte
lymffocyt T *eb* lymffocytau T T lymphocyte
lyncs *eg/eb* lyncsod lynx
lyra *eb* lyrâu lyre
lysin *eg* lysine
lysis *eg* lysis
lysogenedd *eg* lysogeny
lysosom *eg* lysosomau lysosome
lysosym *eg* lysosymau lysozyme
lytig *ans* lytic

Ll

llabed (ar ddilledyn) *eb* llabedau lapel; revers
llabed (morfil) *eg/eb* llabedau fluke
llabed (mewn anatomi) *eb* llabedau lobe
► **llabed arogli** *eb* llabedau arogli olfactory lobe
llabed barwydol *eb* llabedau parwydol parietal lobe
llabed flaen *eb* llabedau blaen frontal lobe
llabed iâ *eb* llabedau iâ ice lobe
llabed optig *eb* llabedau optig optic lobe
llabed rhew *eb* llabedau rhew ice lobe
llabed yr arlais *eb* llabedau'r arlais temporal lobe
llabed yr ocsipwt *eb* llabedau'r ocsipwt occipital lobe
llabeden *eb* llabedennau lobule
llabedog *ans* lobed
llac *ans* loose; slack
llac twyni *eg* llaciau twyni dune slack
llacio (gewyn) *be* slacken
llacio'r lens (mewn gwaith camera) *be* zoom out
llacrwydd *eg* slackness; looseness
llacrwydd gormodol *eg* excessive slackness
llacrwydd gormodol ar y pen *eg* excessive end play
llacrwydd y pen *eg* end play
llachar *ans* bright; vivid; brilliant
llachar *ans* vivid
llacharedd *eg* glare
Lladin *eb* Latin
lladrad *eg* lladradau robbery; piracy; larceny
lladrad mawr *eg* lladradau mawr grand larceny
lladdfa *eb* lladdfeydd massacre
llaesu (cyhyr) *be* relax
llaesu (yn gyffredinol) *be* lengthen
llaesu'r cyhyrau *be* stretch the muscles
llaeth a bwydydd llaeth milk and dairy foods
llaeth baban *eg* posset
llaeth cyddwysedig *eg* condensed milk
llaeth enwyn *eg* buttermilk
llaeth powdr *eg* dried milk
llaeth rhewlif *eg* glacier milk
llaetha *be* lactate
llaethdy *eg* llaethdai dairy
llaethiad *eg* lactation
llaethog *ans* milky
llafarganu *be* chant
llafarganu'n rhythmig *be* chanting rhythmically
llafn (cyllell, bat) *eg/b* llafnau blade
llafn (tyrbin, pluen etc) *eg/b* llafnau vane
llafn cwbl-galed *eg* llafnau cwbl-galed all-hard blade
llafn cyllell *eg* llafnau cyllyll knife blade
llafn cŷn *eg* llafnau cŷn chisel blade
llafn deilen *eg* llafnau dail lamina
llafn gaing *eg* llafnau gaing chisel blade
llafn gwthio *eg* llafnau gwthio propeller
llafn haclif *eg* llafnau haclif hacksaw blade
llafn haclif cwbl-galed *eg* llafnau haclif cwbl-galed all-hard hacksaw blade
llafn llym *eg* llafnau llym sharp blade
llafn sbâr *eg* llafnau sbâr spare blade
llafn Surform *eg* llafnau Surform Surform blade
llafn torri *eg* llafnau torri cutting blade; cutting iron
llafur *eg* labour
llafur crefftus *eg* skilled labour
llafur di-grefft *eg* unskilled labour
llafur estron *eg* immigrant labour
llafur gorfodol *eg* forced labour
llafur lled-grefftus *eg* semi-skilled labour
llafur mudol *eg* migrant labour
llafur rhad *eg* low cost labour
llafur rhan amser *eg* part-time labour
llafur ymrwymedig *eg* indentured labour
llafur ysbeidiol *eg* casual labour
llafur-ddwys *ans* labour intensive
llai *ans* diminished
llaid *eg* mud
llaid folcanig *eg* volcanic mud
llain (=stribyn o dir) *eb* lleiniau belt
llain (hir a chul) *eb* lleiniau strip
llain (mewn criced) *eb* lleiniau pitch
llain (o dir yn gyffredinol) *eb* lleiniau plot
llain gysgodi *eb* lleiniau cysgodi shelter belt
llain lanio *eb* lleiniau glanio landing strip
llain las *eb* lleiniau glas green belt
llain waharddedig *eb* lleiniau gwaharddedig danger area
llain ystumiau *eb* lleiniau ystumiau meander belt
llaindriniad *eg* llaindriniadau strip cultivation
llainddaliad *eg* llainddaliadau strip holding
llais (=sain uchel) *eg* lleisiau volume
llais (yn gyffredinol) *eg* lleisiau voice
llais y frest *eg* chest register
llais y pen *eg* head register; head voice
llais yn newid *eg* changing voice
llais yn torri breaking of voice
llaith *ans* damp; humid; moist

llam *eg* llamau leap; bound
llam llyffant *eg* leap frog
llamhidydd *eg* llamhidyddion porpoise
llamu (morfilod etc) *be* breach
llamu (yn gyffredinol) *be* leap; bound
llannerch *eb* llennyrch clearing
llanw *ans* filled
llanw *eg* llanwau tide
llanw a thrai forward and back a double
llanw apogeaidd *eg* apogean tide
llanw bach *eg* neap tide
llanw cyfres *be* fill series
llanw dalen *be* fill sheet
llanw i fyny *be* fill up
llanw i lawr *be* fill down
llanw i'r chwith *be* fill left
llanw i'r dde *be* fill right
llanw llinell *be* line fill
llanw mawr *eg* spring tide
llanw perigeaidd *eg* llanwau perigeaidd perigean tide
llanw rhes *be* fill row
llanw terfol *eg* rip tide
llanw uchel *eg* high tide
llanw'r dudalen gyfan *be* fill entire page
llaswyr *eg* llaswyrau rosary
llathen *eb* llathenni yard
llathr botwm *eg* button polish
llathr cwyr hylif *eg* liquid wax polish
llathr chwistrell *eg* spray polish
llathr disgleirsych *eg* dry-bright polish
llathr emwlsiwn *eg* emulsion polish
llathr emwlsiwn dŵr *eg* water-based emulsion polish
llathredig *ans* polished
llathredd *eg* polish
llathredd cwyr *eg* wax polish; wax shine
llathru *be* polish; apply polish
llathrydd *eg* llathryddion polisher; polish
llathrydd brwsh *eg* llathryddion brwsh brush polish
llathrydd clir *eg* llathryddion clir clear polish
llathrydd cwyr *eg* llathryddion cwyr wax polish
llathrydd cwyr gwenyn *eg* beeswax polish
llathrydd dodrefn *eg* furniture polish
llathrydd Ffrengig *eg* French polish
llathrydd metel hylifol *eg* liquid metal polish
llathrydd silicôn *eg* llathryddion silicôn silicone polish
llau *ell* lice
llaw *eb* dwylo hand
llaw chwith *eb* dwylo chwith left hand
llaw dde *eb* dwylo de right hand
Llaw Ddu *eb* Black Hand
llaw galigraffig *eb* calligraphic hand
llaw gerdded *be* hand walking
llaw! hands!
llawchwith *ans* left-handed
llawdrin *be* manipulate
llawdriniaeth (=trin â'r dwylo) *eb* llawdriniaethau manipulation
llawdriniaeth (mewn meddygaeth) *eb* llawdriniaethau operation
llawdriniaeth hollti'r ymennydd *eb* split-brain surgery
llawdueddiad *eg* handedness
llawer-i-lawer many-to-many
llawes *eb* llewys sleeve
llawes bwff *eb* llewys pwff puffed sleeve
llawes dapr *eb* llewys tapr taper sleeve
llawes ddolman *eb* llewys dolman dolman sleeve
llawes esgob *eb* llewys esgob bishop sleeve
llawes gap *eb* llewys cap cap sleeve
llawes gloch *eb* llewys cloch bell sleeve
llawes goch *eb* vagina
llawes goes dafad *eb* llewys coes dafad leg of mutton sleeve
llawes hirgul *eb* llewys hirgul fitted sleeve
llawes magyar *eb* llewys magyar magyar sleeve
llawes osod *eb* llewys gosod set-in sleeve
llawes raglan *eb* llewys raglan raglan sleeve
llawes ystlum *eb* llewys ystlum batwing sleeve
llawfeddyg *eg* llawfeddygon surgeon
llawfeddyg y geg *eg* llawfeddygon y geg oral surgeon
llawfeddyg y genau a'r wyneb *eg* llawfeddygon y genau a'r wyneb maxillo-facial surgeon
llawfeddygaeth *eb* surgery
llawfeddygaeth blastig *eb* plastic surgery
llawfeddygaeth gyffredinol *eb* general surgery
llawfeddygaeth y geg *eb* oral surgery
llawfwrdd *eg* llawfyrddau clavier
llawio *be* handling
llawio'r bêl *be* handle the ball
llawlif *eb* llawlifiau hand saw
llawlyfr *eg* llawlyfrau manual; handbook
llawlyfr gwybodaeth *eg* llawlyfrau gwybodaeth information handbook
llawn *ans* plenary
llawn amser *ans* full-time
llawn cydymdeimlad *ans* sympathetic
llawn dychymyg *ans* imaginative
llawn mynegiant *ans* expressive
llawn werth *eg* par
llawnder *eg* fullness
llawnder synhwyraidd-benodol *eg* sensory specific satiety
llawnder wedi'i grychdynnu *eg* gathered fullness
llawr (=y ddaear) *eg* lloriau ground
llawr (mewn adeilad aml-lawr) *eg* lloriau storey
llaw'r arf *eb* weapon hand
llawr caled *eg* lloriau caled hard flooring
llawr crog *eg* lloriau crog suspended floor
llawr cyntaf *eg* lloriau cyntaf first floor
llawr estyll dwbl *eg* lloriau estyll dwbl double-boarded floor

llawr gwaelod *eg* lloriau gwaelod ground floor
llawr gwerthu *eg* lloriau gwerthu sales floor
llawr parquet *eg* lloriau parquet parquet floor
llawr siart *eg* lloriau siart chart floor
llawr solet *eg* lloriau solet solid floor
llawr uchaf *eg* lloriau uchaf upper floor
llawr wedi'i fondio *eg* lloriau wedi'u bondio bonded floor
llawr y dyffryn *eg* valley floor
llawrestr *eb* llawrestri handlist
llawrydd *ans* freehand
llawsafiad *eg* llawsafiadau handstand
llawsefyll *be* handstand
llawysgrif *eb* llawysgrifau manuscript
llawysgrif oliwiedig *eb* llawysgrifau goliwiedig illuminated manuscript
llawysgrifen *eb* script
llawysgrifen *eb* handwriting
lle *eg* lleoedd place
lle ar gael ar ddisg *eg* available disk space
lle chwarae *eg* llefydd chwarae playground; play area
lle dangos *eg* llefydd dangos display area
lle degol *eg* lleoedd degol decimal place
lle diddorol *eg* lleoedd diddorol place of interest
lle golchi *eg* llefydd golchi sluice
lle gwag *eg* lleoedd gwag space
lle gwreiddiol *eg* lleoedd gwreiddiol original place
lle llwyd gwag *eg* llefydd llwyd gwag blank grey area
lle nad oes coetiroedd unforested
lle paratoi bwyd *eg* lleoedd paratoi bwyd food preparation area
lle storio *eg* storage space
lle tân *eg* lleoedd tân fireplace
llecyn at ddibenion cyffredinol *eg* llecynnau at ddibenion cyffredinol general purpose area
llech, y *eb* rickets
llechen *eb* llechi slate
llechen graffeg *eb* llechi graffeg graphics tablet
llechfaen *eg* llechfeini slate
llechfeddiannu *be* encroach
llechfeddiant *eg* encroachment
lled *eg* lledau width; breadth
lled annibynnol *ans* semi-independent
lled awtoffitio *eg* autofit width
lled awtomatig *ans* semi-automatic
lled band *eg* bandwidth
lled colofn *eg* column width
lled ffrâm awtoffitio *eg* autofit frame width
lled hem *eg* lledau hem hem depth
lled opera *eb* lled operâu semi-opera
lled pwls *eg* pulse width
lled rheilffordd *eg* lledau rheilffyrdd gauge
lled safonol *eg* standard gauge
lled soddedig *ans* semi-submerged
lled y gwall *eg* margin of error
lledaeniad *eg* lledaeniadau propagation
lledaeniad yr adwaith *eg* extent of reaction
lledaenu *be* disseminate; propagate; spread
lledaenu ymarfer da *be* dissemination of good practice
lledaenydd *eg* lledaenwyr spreader
lledaenydd past *eg* lledaenwyr past paste spreader
lled-arbrawf *eg* lledarbrofion quasi-experiment
lledathraidd *ans* semi permeable
lled-barlys un ochr *eg* hemiparesis
lled-dryloyw *ans* semi-sheer
lled-ddargludydd *eg* lled-ddargludyddion semiconductor
lled-ddiffeithwch *eg* semi-desert
lleden *eb* lledod flatfish; flounder
lled-fedrus *ans* semi-skilled
lled-haniaethol *ans* near abstract
lled-haniaethol *ans* semi abstract
llednaid *eb* straddle
llednant *eb* llednentydd affluent
llednant *eb* llednentydd tributary
llednant glan dde *eb* llednentydd glan dde right bank tributary
lledneidiwr *eg* lledneidwyr straddler
lledofal *ans* minimum care
lledr *eg* lledrau leather
lledr llyfr *eg* book leather
lledr siami *eg* chamois leather
lledred *eg* lledredau latitude
lledred isel *eg* lledredau isel low latitude
lledredau canol *ell* mid-latitudes
lledredau'r meirch *ell* horse latitudes
lledu *be* broaden; widen
lledu patrwm *be* widen a pattern
lledu'r bêl *be* spread the ball wide
lledwastad dechreuol *eg* primarrumpf
lledwastad terfynol *eg* lledwastadau terfynol endrumpf
lledwastadiad *eg* lledwastadiadau peneplanation
lleddf *ans* melancholy
lleddf (awyrgylch a theimlad cerddorol) *ans* minor
lleddf gywair (mewn canu penillion) *eg* minor key
lleddf gywair (mewn hen gerddoriaeth Gymreig) *eg* flat key
lleddfu *be* soothe
lleddfu *be* ease
lleddfu'r ddyrnod *be* pulling the punch
llefaredd *eg* oracy
llefaru synthetig *be* synthetic speech
llefarydd *eg* llefarwyr spokesman
llefarydd *eg* llefarwyr mouthpiece
llefarydd *eg* llefarwyr speaker
lleferydd *eg* speech
lleferydd dynol *eg* human speech
lleferydd ecolalig *eg* echolalic speech
lleng *eb* llengoedd legion
Lleng Anrhydedd *eb* Legion of Honour

lleiaf *ans* minimum
lleiaf *ans* least
lleiaf (cywair cerddorol) *ans* minor
lleiafrif *eg* lleiafrifoedd minority
lleiafswm *eg* lleiafsymiau minimum
lleiafsymio *be* minimize
lleian *eb* lleianod nun
Lleian Le Begue *eb* Lleianod Le Begue Beguine
lleiandy *eg* lleiandai nunnery
lleiandy *eg* lleiandai convent
lleidlif *eg* lleidlifau mud-flow
lleidr *eg* lladron thief
lleidr (am afon) *eg* lladron pirate stream
lleidr pen-ffordd *eg* lladron pen-ffordd highwayman
lleihad *eg* lleihadau decrement
lleihad *eg* lleihadau decrease
lleihad *eg* lleihadau diminution
lleihad *eg* reduction
lleihad trwodd a thro *eg* overall decrease
lleihadaeth *eb* reductionism
lleihadaeth fiolegol *eb* biological reductionism
lleihaol *ans* decreasing
lleihaol *ans* reductionist
lleihau *be* decrease
lleihau *be* reduce; decrease; minimize; diminish
lleihau bylchu *be* decrease spacing
lleihau ffenestr *be* minimize window
lleihau mewnoliad *be* decrease indent
lleihau patrwm *be* reduce a pattern
lleihau pob ffenestr *be* minimize all windows
lleihau popeth *be* minimize all
lleihau swmp *be* reduce bulk
lleiniau cytal *ell* rundale
lleiniau cytal *ell* runrig
lleinweldiad *eg* lleinweldiadau fillet weld
lleisio *be* vocalize; voicing
lleisiol *ans* vocal
lleithder *eg* lleithderau dampness; damp; moisture; humidity
lleithder absoliwt *eg* absolute humidity
lleithder cymharol *eg* relative humidity
lleithiad *eg* humidification
lleithio *be* dampen
lleithydd *eg* lleithyddion humidifier
llem *ans* acute
llen *eg/b* llenni curtain; sheet
llen blastig *eb* llenni plastig plastic sheeting
llen ddelltog *eb* llenni delltog venetian blind
llen erydiad *eg* sheet erosion
llên gwerin *eb* folklore
Llen Haearn *eb* Iron Curtain
llen iâ *eb* llenni iâ ice sheet
llen olchiad *eg* sheet wash
llen rhew *eb* llenni rhew ice sheet
llen rholer *eg* llenni rholer roller blind
llen stribed *eb* llenni stribed vertical blind
llencyndod *eg* adolescence
llencyndod cynnar *eg* early adolescence
llencyndod hwyr *eg* late adolescence
llencynnaidd *ans* adolescent
llenddur *eg* sheet steel
llenfetel *eg* llenfetelau sheet metal
llengig *eg* llengigoedd diaphragm
▸ **llên-ladrad** *eg* plagiarism
llenlif *eg* llenlifiau sheet flood
llenni les *ell* lace curtains
llenwad *eg* llenwyddion filler; filling; fill
llenwad folcanig *eg* llenwadau folcanig volcanic filler
llenwad metel *eg* llenwadau metel metal filler
llenwad panel *eg* panel infill
llenwad past *eg* paste filler
llenwad plastig *eg* llenwadau plastig plastic filler
llenwad sgrin *eg* screen filler
llenwi *be* fill
llenwi hyd at y graddnod *be* make up to the mark
llenwi'r mân dyllau *be* bodying-in
llenyddiaeth *eb* literature
llenyddiaeth apocalyptaidd *eb* apocalyptic literature
llenyddiaeth broffwydol *eb* prophetic literature
llenyddiaeth broffwydol yr Hen Destament *eb* Old Testament prophetic literature
llenyddiaeth doethineb *eb* wisdom literature
llenyddiaeth plant *eb* children's literature
llenyddol *ans* literary
lleol *ans* local
lleolbwynt *eg* lleolbwyntiau origin
lleoledig *ans* localized
lleoleiddiad *eg* localization
lleoli *be* locate; position
lleoli cynnyrch *be* product placement
lleoli llygoden *be* mouse positioning
lleoli safle *be* locate position
lleoliad (ffilm, stori) *eg* lleoliadau setting
lleoliad (rhywun ar ymarfer gwaith) *eg* lleoliadau placement
lleoliad (yn gyffredinol) *eg* lleoliadau location
lleoliad adlais *eg* echolocation
lleoliad did *eg* lleoliadau did bit location
lleoliad gwaith *eg* lleoliadau gwaith work placement
lleoliad gweithgareddau *eg* location of activities
lleoliad mewn bloc *eg* lleoliadau mewn bloc block placement
lleoliad mewn swydd *eg* lleoliadau mewn swyddi job placement
lleoliad nodweddion *eg* location of features
lleoliad swyddogaeth *eg* localization of function
lleoliadol *ans* locational
lleolnod *eg* lleolnodau caret
llercian *be* lurk
llerciwr *eg* llercwyr lurker
lles *eg* welfare
lles *eg* well-being

lles babanod *eg* infant welfare
Lles Cyffredin *eg* Common Weal
lles cymdeithasol *eg* social welfare
lles plant *eg* child welfare
llesgedd *eg* debility
llesmair *eg* llesmeiriau syncope
llestair ochrol *eg* lateral hazard
llesteirio *be* inhibit
llestr *eg* llestri vessel; pot; receptacle
llestr entrée *eg* llestri entrée entrée dish
llestr halen *eg* llestri halen salt cellar
llestr ïoneiddiad *eg* ionization chamber
llestr niwl *eg* llestri niwl cloud chamber
llestr niwl ehangiad *eg* expansion cloud chamber
llestr niwl tryllediad *eg* diffusion cloud chamber
llestri *ell* crockery
llestri bwrdd *ell* tableware
llestri gwydr *ell* glassware
llestri gwydr cerfiedig *ell* cut glassware
llestri gwydr lliw *ell* coloured glassware
llestri gwydr ysgythredig *ell* engraved glassware
llestri gwydr ysgythrog *ell* etched glassware
llestri Microtex *ell* Microtex
llestri pridd *ell* earthenware
llestri Pyrex *ell* Pyrex ware
llestri Pyroceram *ell* Pyroceram
llestri Pyrocil *ell* Pyrocil
llestri tsieni *ell* china ware
llestri wedi'u gwydro *ell* glazed crockery
lletchwith *ans* awkward
lletchwithdod *eg* clumsiness
lletem *eb* lletemau wedge
lletem gloi *eb* lletemau cloi locking wedge
lletem gyflin *eb* lletemau cyflin folding wedge
lletem iâ *eb* lletemau iâ ice wedge
lletem rew *eb* lletemau rhew ice wedge
lletemiad *eg* wedging
lletemu *be* wedge
lletemu croeslinol *be* diagonal wedging
lletemu cudd *be* fox wedging
lletemu pren caled *be* hardwood wedging
lletemu pren meddal *be* softwood wedging
lletgras *ans* semi-arid
lletraws *ans* diagonal
lletwad *eb* lletwadau ladle
lletwad ddiogelwch *eb* lletwadau diogelwch safety ladle
lletwad ffowndri *eb* lletwadau ffowndri foundry ladle
llety (=lle i fyw) *eg* lletyau accommodation
llety (dros dro fel arfer) *eg* lletyau lodging house; lodgings
llety cysgodol *eg* lletyau cysgodol sheltered accommodation
llety wedi'i ddodrefnu *eg* lletyau wedi'u dodrefnu furnished accommodation
lletya *be* accommodate
lletya milwyr *be* billet
lletywr *eg* lletywyr lodger
llethr *eg/b* llethrau slope
llethr amgrwm *eg* llethrau amgrwm convex slope
llethr ceugrwm *eg* llethrau ceugrwm concave slope
llethr cyson *eg* llethrau cyson constant slope
llethr disgyrchiant *eg* llethrau disgyrchiant gravity slope
llethr esmwyth crwn *eg* llethrau esmwyth crwn gently rounded slope
llethr gorifyny *eg* llethrau gorifyny upslope
llethr rhydd *eg* llethrau rhydd free slope
llethr serth *eg* llethrau serth steep slope
llethr sgarp *eg* llethrau sgarp scarp slope
llethr slip *eg* llethrau slip slip-off slope
lleuad *eb* lleuadau moon
lleuad ar ei chil *eb* waning of the moon
lleuad ar ei chynnydd *eb* waxing of the moon
lleuad fedi *eb* harvest moon
lleuad gilgant *eb* crescent moon
lleuad hela *eb* hunter's moon
lleuad lawn *eb* full moon
lleuad mewn orbit *eb* moon in orbit
lleuad newydd *eb* new moon
lleugylch *eg* lleugylchoedd aureole
lleugylch *eg* lleugylchoedd halo
lleugylch *eg* lleugylchoedd nimbus
llewyg *eg* faint
llewygu *be* faint
llewyrch *eg* sheen
llewyrch daear *eg* earthshine
lleyg *ans* lay
lleygwr *eg* lleygwyr layman
lleygwyr *ell* laity
lliain *eg* llieiniau cloth; linen
lliain bwrdd *eg* llieiniau bwrdd tablecloth
lliain caws *eg* llieiniau caws cheesecloth
lliain dargopïo *eg* llieiniau dargopïo tracing cloth
lliain hambwrdd *eg* llieiniau hambwrdd tray cloth
lliain lledr *eg* llieiniau lledr leather cloth
lliain llyfrau *eg* bookcloth
lliain presio *eg* llieiniau presio pressing cloth
lliain presio *eg* llieiniau presio press cloth
lliain rhwyllog *eg* llieiniau rhwyllog gauze cloth
lliain rhwymo llyfrau *eg* bookbinding cloth
lliain sgrim *eg* llieiniau sgrim linen scrim
llid *eg* inflammation
llid y bledren *eg* cystitis
llid y gyfbilen *eg* conjunctivitis
llid y pendics *eg* appendicitis
llid yr ymennydd *eg* meningitis
llidiart *eb* llidiardau gate
llidus *ans* inflamed
lliein-blyg *ans* linen fold
llieiniau bwrdd *ell* table-linen
llieiniau tŷ *ell* household linen
llif (=arf ar gyfer torri) *eb* llifiau saw

llif (=rhediad) *eg* llifoedd flow; stream
llif agennu *eb* llifiau agennu slitting saw
llif agennu *eb* llifiau agennu slotting saw
llif arian *eg* cash flow
llif arian allan *eg* outflows
llif awyru *eg* aeration stream
llif banel *eb* llifiau panel panel saw
llif cyfochrog *eg* parallel flow
llif cylchol incwm *eg* circular flow of income
llif chwil *eb* llifiau chwil drunken saw
llif disgyrchiant *eg* gravity flow
llif dwfn *be* llifio dwfn deep saw
llif dwll *eb* llifiau twll hole saw
llif dwll clo *eb* llifiau twll clo pad saw; keyhole saw
llif dyno *eb* llifiau tyno tenon saw
llif dyno fach *eb* llifiau tyno bach dovetail saw
llif egni *eg* energy flow
llif electronau *eg* electron flow
llif electronau *eg* llifoedd electronau electron stream
llif fwa *eb* llifiau bwa bow-saw
llif fwa fach *eb* llifiau bwa bach coping saw
llif ffens *eb* llifiau ffens fence saw
llif ffrâm *eb* llifiau ffrâm frame saw
llif ffret *eb* llifiau ffret fretsaw
llif ffret lifer *eb* llifiau ffret lifer lever-frame fretsaw
llif gefn *eb* llifiau cefn backsaw
llif gefn bres *eb* llifiau cefn pres brassback saw
llif gefn ddur *eb* llifau cefn dur steel back saw
llif gefn fetel plyg *eb* llifiau cefn metel plyg folded metal back saw
llif gorchwylion *eg* job stream
llif gron *eb* llifiau crwn circular saw
llif gwefr *eg* flow of charge
llif gweithgaredd *eg* activity flow
llif gwmpas *eb* llifiau cwmpas compass saw
llif gwrthgerrynt *eg* counter-current flow
llif hylifau *eg* fluid flow
llif lafa *eg* llifoedd lafa lava flow
llif laminaidd *eg* laminar flow
llif len *eb* llifiau llen sheet saw
llif lorio *eb* llifiau llorio flooring saw
llif llilin *eg* streamline flow
llif llinol *eg* linear flow
llif oleddu *eb* llifiau goleddu canting saw
llif porffor alisarin *eg* alizarin purple lake
llif rwyllo *eb* llifiau rhwyllo piercing saw
llif rhuddgoch *eg* crimson lake
llif sabr *eb* llifiau sabr sabre saw
llif sgarlad *eg* scarlet lake
llif testun *eg* text flow
llif trydarthol *eg* transpiration stream
llif tyrfol *eg* llifoedd tyrfol turbulent flow
llif y gwaed *eg* blood stream
Llif y Gwlff *eg* Gulf Stream
llifanu *be* grind
llifanu yn y llaw *be* off-hand grinding
llifanydd *eg* llifanwyr grinder
llifanydd aer *eg* llifanyddion aer air grinder
llifanydd cludadwy *eg* llifanyddion cludadwy portable grinder
llifanydd mainc *eg* llifanwyr mainc bench grinder
llifanydd pedestal *eg* llifanwyr pedestal pedestal grinder
llifdoriad *eg* llifdoriadau saw-cut; kerf
llifddalen *eb* llifddalenni flow sheet
llifddol *eb* llifddolydd water meadow
llifedig *ans* dyed
llifedd *eg* llifeddau fluidity
llifeiriant *eg* llifeiriaint torrent
llifeiriant *eg* llifeiriaint spate
llif-ffwythiant *eg* flow function
llifglawdd *eg* llifgloddiau levee
llif-gynhyrchu *be* flow production
llifhaenau *ell* current bedding
llifiad rheiddiol *eg* llifiadau rheiddiol radial sawcut; quarter sawn
llifiad trwodd *eg* llifiadau trwodd through sawcut
llifio *be* saw
llifio metel *be* metal sawing
llifio plaen chwarteru *be* plain quartering
llifio tangiadol *be* tangential sawing
llifio trwodd *be* plain sawing
llifion anilin *ell* aniline dyes
llifiwr *eg* llifwyr sawyer
lliflin *eb* llifliniau flow line
llifo (am hylif) *be* flow
llifo (lliwio brethyn etc) *be* dye
llifo batic *be* batik dyeing
llifo i mewn *be* inflow
llifogydd *ell* flood
llifogydd afonydd *ell* river floods
llifogydd arfordirol *ell* coastal flooding
llifosodiad *eg* llifosodiadau saw set
llifwaddod *eg* llifwaddodion alluvial deposit; alluvium
llifwaddodol *ans* alluvial
llifwastadedd *eg* llifwastadeddau panplain
llifwastadiant *eg* panplanation
llifydd *eg* llifyddion fluid
llifydd marcio *eg* llifyddion marcio marking out fluid
llifyddol *ans* fluid
llifyn *eg* llifynnau dye
llifyn adweithiol *eg* llifynnau adweithiol reactive dye
llifyn alisarin *eg* llifynnau alisarin alizarin dye
llifyn anniflan *eg* llifynnau anniflan fast dye
llifyn anniflan *eg* llifynnau anniflan colourfast dye
llifyn asid *eg* llifynnau asid acid dye
llifyn aso *eg* llifynnau aso azo dye
llifyn col-tar *eg* llifynnau col-tar coal tar dye
llifyn crefft *eg* llifynnau crefft craft dye
llifyn diogel *eg* llifynnau diogel non-toxic dye
llifyn dŵr oer *eg* llifynnau dŵr oer cold water dye

llifyn dŵr poeth *eg* llifynnau dŵr poeth hot water dye
llifyn ffabrig *eg* llifynnau ffabrig fabric dye
llifyn fflwroleuol *eg* llifynnau fflwroleuol fluorescent dye
llifyn llac *eg* llifynnau llac loose dye
llifyn llysiau *eg* llifynnau llysiau vegetable dye
llifyn pren *eg* llifynnau pren wood dye
► **llifyn uniongyrchol** *eg* llifynnau uniongyrchol direct dye
llifyn yn rhedeg bleeding of dye
llilin *eb* lliliniau streamline
llilinio *be* streamline
llin *eg* flax
llin ganol *eb* lliniau canol median
llinach (frenhinol) *eb* dynasty
llinach (yn gyffredinol) *eb* llinachau ancestry; lineage; stock; line of descent
llinach y Tuduriaid *eb* Tudor dynasty
llinachyddiaeth *eb* dynasticism
llinachyddol *ans* dynastic
llin-argraffydd *eg* llin-argraffyddion line printer
llinborthi *be* line feed
llinborthiad *eg* llinborthiadau line feed
llinborthwr *eg* llinborthwyr line feed key
llindag (gwddf) *eg* thrush
llindoriad *eg* llindoriadau sketch section
llinell *eb* llinellau line
llinell a golchiad line and wash
llinell anomaledd *eb* llinellau anomaledd isanomalous line
llinell ar log *eb* llinellau ar log leased line
llinell arosgo *eb* llinellau arosgo oblique line
llinell asio *eb* llinellau asio suture line
llinell atchwel *eb* llinellau atchwel line of regression
llinell bar *eb* llinellau bar bar line
llinell bar dwbl *eb* llinellau bar dwbl double bar line
llinell belydrol *eb* llinellau pelydrol radiating line
llinell blwm *eb* perpendicular line
llinell blygu *eb* llinellau plygu fold line; bend line
llinell bumllath *eb* five yard line
llinell bwytho *eb* llinellau pwytho suture line
llinell croestoriad *eb* llinellau croestoriad line of intersection
llinell cymesuredd *eb* llinellau cymesuredd line of symmetry
llinell dafluniad *eb* llinellau tafluniad projection line
llinell dafluniadol fertigol *eb* llinellau tafluniadol fertigol vertical projection line
llinell danysgrifio ddigidol anghymesur *eb* llinellau tanysgrifio digidol anghymesur asymmetric digital subscriber line
llinell denau *eb* llinellau tenau thin line
llinell dew *eb* llinellau tew thick line
llinell dimensiwn *eb* llinellau dimensiwn dimension line
llinell doeau *eb* roof line
llinell doredig *eb* llinellau toredig broken line; dashed line; dashed line
llinell doredig fân *eb* llinellau toredig mân fine dashed line
llinell doriad *eb* llinellau toriad break line; dash
llinell dorri *eb* llinellau torri cutting line
llinell drwodd *eb* llinellau drwodd strikethrough
llinell drychu *eb* llinellau trychu section line; sectioning line
llinell ddatwm *eb* llinellau datwm datum line
llinell ddi-dor *eb* llinellau di-dor continuous line; unbroken line
llinell ddiflannol *eb* llinellau diflannol vanishing line
llinell ddrych *eb* llinellau drych mirror line
llinell ddwbl *eb* llinellau dwbl double line
llinell ddyfnder *eb* llinellau dyfnder depth line
llinell estyn *eb* llinellau estyn ledger line
llinell estynedig *eb* llinellau estynedig extended line
llinell faes *eb* field line
llinell faes disgyrchedd *eb* gravitational field line
llinell faes drydanol *eb* llinellau maes trydanol electric field line
llinell faes magnetig *eb* magnetic field line
llinell felodig *eb* llinellau melodig melodic line
llinell fer *eb* llinellau byr short line
llinell fertigol *eb* llinellau fertigol vertical line
llinell fynwes *eb* llinellau mynwes bustline
llinell ffit orau *eb* llinellau ffit gorau line of best fit
llinell ffitio *eb* llinellau ffitio fitting line
llinell ffitio pen *eb* crown fitting line
llinell gadwyn *eb* llinellau cadwyn chain line
llinell gadwyn denau *eb* llinellau cadwyn denau thin chain line
llinell ganol *eb* llinellau canol centre line; mid-line
llinell ganol fertigol *eb* llinellau canol fertigol vertical centre line
llinell gefn *eb* llinellau cefn baseline
llinell glogwyn *eb* llinellau clogwyn cliff line
llinell glun *eb* llinellau cluniau hip line
llinell gôl *eb* llinellau gôl goal line
llinell goruniad *eb* llinellau goruniad lapping line
llinell grid *eb* llinellau grid grid line
llinell grom *eb* llinellau crwm curved line
llinell grym *eb* llinellau grym line of force
llinell gudd *eb* llinellau cudd hidden line; invisible line
llinell gwagle *eb* llinellau gwagle line space
llinell gwddf *eb* llinellau gwddf neckline
llinell gwsg *eb* llinellau cwsg dead ball line
llinell gwymp *eb* llinellau cwymp fall line
llinell gychwyn *eb* llinellau cychwyn starting line
llinell gychwynnol *eb* initial line
llinell gydbwysedd *eb* llinellau cydbwysedd balance line
llinell gydosod *eb* llinellau cydosod assembly line
llinell gyflanw *eb* llinellau cyflanw co-tidal line
llinell gyswllt *eb* llinellau cyswllt contact line

llinell gyswllt onglog *eb* llinellau cyswllt onglog angled connector line
llinell hanner *eb* llinellau hanner halfway line
llinell hanner cwrt *eb* llinellau hanner cwrt half court line
llinell hem *eb* llinellau hem hem line
llinell hir doredig *eb* llinellau hir toredig long broken line
llinell isel *eb* low line
llinell lorwedd *eb* llinellau llorweddol horizontal line
llinell lorweddol *eb* llinellau llorweddol horizontal line
llinell lunio *eb* llinellau llunio construction line
Llinell Maginot *eb* Maginot Line
llinell manylion cudd *eb* llinellau manylion cudd phantom line; hidden detail line
llinell mewnbwn *eb* llinellau mewnbwn input line
llinell newid *eb* llinellau newid alteration line
llinell newydd *eb* llinellau newydd new line
llinell ochr *eb* llinellau ochr sideline
llinell ochrol *eb* llinellau ochrol lateral line
llinell oedi *eb* llinellau oedi delay line
llinell onglog *eb* llinellau onglog angled line
llinell orwel *eb* llinellau gorwel horizon line; eye-level
llinell reiddiol *eb* llinellau rheiddiol radial line
llinell rif *eb* llinellau rhif number line
llinell rhediad *eb* llinellau rhediad flowline
llinell rhigwm *eb* llinellau rhigwm line in the rhyme
llinell rhydweli *eb* llinellau rhydwelïau arterial line
llinell saethu *eb* llinellau saethu shooting line
llinell seithlath *eb* llinellau seithlath seven yard line
llinell serfio *eb* llinellau serfio serving line
llinell serfio ganol *eb* llinellau serfio canol centre serving line
llinell serfio ochr *eb* llinellau serfio ochr side serving line
llinell sgiw *eb* llinellau sgiw skew line
llinell sgwariau lleiaf *eb* llinellau sgwariau lleiaf least square line
llinell snap *eb* llinellau snap snap line
llinell statws *eb* llinellau statws status line
llinell syth *eb* llinellau syth straight line
llinell tir *eb* llinellau tir landline
llinell uchel *eb* llinellau uchel high line
llinell waith *eb* llinellau gwaith working line
Llinell Wallace *eb* Wallace's Line
llinell wasg *eb* llinellau gwasg waistline
llinell wedi'i hongli *eb* llinellau wedi'u hongli double-angled line
llinell wedi'i neilltuo *eb* llinellau wedi'u neilltuo dedicated line
llinell wedi'i sgrifellu *eb* llinellau wedi'u sgrifellu scribed lines
llinell weldio *eb* llinellau weldio weld line
llinell wen *eb* llinellau gwyn white line
llinell y costau *eb* costs line
llinell ysgwydd *eb* llinellau ysgwydd shoulder line
llinell ystlys *eb* llinellau ystlys touchline
llinellau grym *ell* lines of force
llinellau rhwyllog yn croesi *ell* graticule intersection
llinellau y funud (llyf) lines per minute
llinellau'r gelyn *ell* enemy lines
llinelliad *eg* llinelliadau drawn line
llinellog (=yn cynnwys llinellau) *ans* linear
llinellog (am bapur) *ans* ruled
llinfap *eg* llinfapiau sketch map
llinfap wedi'i labelu â nodiadau *eg* annotated sketch map
llin-gwrs *eg* llin-gyrsiau string course
lliniaru *be* relieve
lliniogi *be* hatch
llinol *ans* linear
llinol annibynnol *ans* linearly independent
llinol ddibynnol *ans* linearly dependent
llinoledd *eg* linearity
llinolygydd *eg* llinolygyddion line editor
llinyn *eg* llinynnau strand
llinyn *eg* llinynnau string
llinyn bogail *eg* llinynnau bogeiliau umbilical cord
llinyn bwa *eg* llinynnau bwa bowstring
llinyn didau *eg* llinynnau didau bit string
llinyn llifedig *eg* llinynnau llifedig dyed string
llinyn newidiol *eg* llinynnau newidiol variable string
llinyn nodau *eg* llinynnau nodau character string
llinyn plwm *eg* bob line
llinyn plwm *eg* llinynnau plwm plumb line
llinyn tynnu *eg* llinynnau tynnu drawstring
llinyn ysgafn *eg* llinynnau ysgafn light string
llinynnau *ell* strings
llinynnau mewnosod *ell* inlay strings
llinynnu *be* string
llin-ysgythriad *eg* llin-ysgythriadau engraving line
llipa *ans* limp
llipa *ans* flaccid
llithlyfr *eg* llithlyfrau lectionary
llithr *ans* slide; sliding
llithr llawn *eg* full drop
llithren *eb* llithrennau slide
llithrfa *eb* llithrfeydd slipway
llithriad (=camgymeriad) *eg* llithriadau slip
llithriad (mewn nodiant cerddorol) *eg* llithriadau slur
► **llithriad fferi** *eg* llithriadau fferi ferry glide
llithrig *ans* slippery
llithriwl *eb* llithriwliau slide rule
llithro (mewn canu) *be* slur
llithro (mewn dawns) *be* slip-step
llithro (mewn nodiant cerddorol) *be* glide
llithro (yn gyffredinol) *be* slide
llithro gyda'r cloc *be* slip-stepping clockwise
llithrydd (ar ddrws llithro) *eg* llithryddion glide
llithrydd (yn gyffredinol) *eg* llithryddion slider
llithryn *eg* llithrynnau slide

llithryn cyfansawdd *eg* llithrynnau cyfansawdd compound slide
llithryn uchaf *eg* top slide
lliw *eg* lliwiau colour
lliw acrylig *eg* lliwiau acrylig acrylic colour
lliw adlewyrchedig *eg* lliwiau adlewyrchedig reflected colour
lliw anniflan *eg* lliwiau anniflan fast colour
lliw bloc *eg* lliwiau bloc block colour
lliw border *eg* lliwiau border border colour
lliw casein *eg* lliwiau casein casein colour
lliw cefndir *eg* lliwiau cefndir background colour
lliw cydnaws *eg* lliwiau cydnaws harmonious colour
lliw cyferbyniol *eg* lliwiau cyferbyniol contrasting colour
lliw cyflenwol *eg* lliwiau cyflenwol complementary colour
lliw cynnes *eg* lliwiau cynnes warm colour
lliw di-draidd *eg* lliwiau di-draidd opaque colour; body colour
lliw diflan *eg* lliwiau diflan fugitive colour
lliw difywyd *eg* inert colour
lliw eilaidd *eg* lliwiau eilaidd secondary colour
lliw enamlo *eg* lliwiau enamlo enamelling colour
lliw enciliol *eg* lliwiau enciliol receding colour
lliw ffabrig *eg* lliwiau ffabrig fabric colour
lliw fflwroleuol *eg* lliwiau fflwroleuol fluorescent colour
lliw ffynhonnell *eg* lliwiau ffynhonnell source colour
lliw golau *eg* lliwiau golau light colour; pale colour
lliw gorgynnes *eg* lliwiau gorgynnes hot colour
lliw grid *eg* lliwiau grid grid colour
lliw harmonig *eg* lliwiau harmonig harmonic colour
lliw herodrol *eg* lliwiau herodrol heraldic colour
lliw hylifol *eg* lliwiau hylifol liquid colour
lliw llachar *eg* lliwiau llachar bright colour; vivid colour; brilliant colour
lliw lleol *eg* local colour
lliw marmori *eg* marbling colour
lliw naturiol *eg* lliwiau naturiol natural colour
lliw niwtral *eg* lliwiau niwtral neutral colour
lliw oer *eg* lliwiau oer cold colour
lliw oeraidd *eg* lliwiau oeraidd cool colour
lliw olew *eg* lliwiau olew oil colour
lliw past *eg* lliwiau past paste colour
lliw picsel *eg* lliwiau picsel pixel colour
lliw plastig *eg* lliwiau plastig plastic colour
lliw posteri *eg* lliwiau posteri poster colour
lliw pur *eg* lliwiau pur pure colour
lliw sail olew *eg* lliwiau sail olew oil based colour
lliw sefydlog *eg* lliwiau sefydlog permanent colour
lliw siart *eg* lliwiau siart chart colour
lliw sylfaen *eg* lliwiau sylfaen foundation colour
lliw sylfaenol *eg* lliwiau sylfaenol basic colour; primary colour
lliw sy'n para *eg* lliwiau sy'n para durable colour
lliw tanwydredd *eg* underglaze colour
lliw tawel *eg* lliwiau tawel muted colour
lliw tecstil *eg* lliwiau tecstil textile colour
lliw tempera *eg* lliwiau tempera tempera colour
lliw testun *eg* lliwiau testun text colour
lliw trechol *eg* lliwiau trechol dominant colour
lliw trwm *eg* lliwiau trwm heavy colour
lliw tryleu *eg* lliwiau tryleu translucent colour
lliw tryloyw *eg* lliwiau tryloyw transparent colour
lliw tryloywder *eg* lliwiau tryloywderau transparency colour
lliw tywyll *eg* dark colour
lliw uchel *eg* high colour
lliwddangos *be* highlight
lliwiad *eg* lliwiadau colouration
lliwiad gwarchodol *eg* protective colouration
lliwiad rhybuddiol *eg* lliwiadau rhybuddiol warning colouration
lliwiau amrywiol *ell* assorted colours
lliwiau anilin *ell* aniline colours
lliwiau rhagosodedig *ell* default colours
lliwiau tymheru *ell* tempering colours
lliwio *be* colour
lliwio geiriau *be* word painting
lliwydd *eg* lliwyddion colourant
lliwydd hylif *eg* lliwyddion hylif liquid colourant
lliwydd past *eg* lliwyddion past paste colourant
lliwydd sych *eg* lliwyddion sych dry colourant
lloc *eg* llociau enclosure
lloc cadw *eg* llociau cadw loafing yard
lloches *eb* llochesau shelter
lloches cyrch awyr *eb* llochesau cyrch awyr air-raid shelter
lloches wleidyddol *eb* political asylum
lloeren *eb* lloerenni satellite
lloergryn *eg* lloergrynfeydd moonquake
llofnaid *eb* llofneidiau vault
llofnaid ar led *eb* llofneidiau ar led astride vault
llofnaid ar led wysg y cefn *eb* llofneidiau ar led wysg y cefn reverse astride vault
llofnaid blaidd *eb* llofneidiau blaidd wolf vault
llofnaid ddeuglap *eb* llofneidiau deuglap vault with a double beat
llofnaid fwlch *eb* llofneidiau bwlch through vault
llofnaid fwlch ddeuglap *eb* llofneidiau bwlch deuglap through vault with double beat
llofnaid fwlch hir *eb* llofneidiau bwlch hir horizontal through vault
llofnaid gefn *eb* llofneidiau cefn back vault
llofnaid glwyd *eb* llofneidiau clwyd gate vault
llofnaid gylch *eb* llofneidiau cylch round vault
llofnaid hir ar led *eb* llofneidiau hir ar led horizontal astride vault
llofnaid hir ar led wysg y cefn *eb* llofneidiau hir ar led wysg y cefn reverse horizontal astride vault
llofnaid lleidr *eb* llofneidiau lleidr thief vault
llofnaid milwr *eb* llofneidiau milwr vault with foot assisting
llofnaid ochrol *eb* llofneidiau ochrol side vault
llofnaid siswrn *eb* llofneidiau siswrn scissors vault

llofnaid wellaif *eb* llofneidiau gwellaif running oblique back vault
llofnaid wyneb *eb* llofneidiau wyneb face vault
llofneidiau cysylltiol *ell* combined vaults
llofnod *eg* llofnodion autograph
llofnodydd *eg* llofnodyddion signatory
llofrudd *eg* llofruddion murderer
llofruddiaeth *eb* llofruddiaethau murder; assassination
llofft *eg* llofftydd loft
llofft olau *eb* llofftydd golau clerestory
llofft organ *eb* llofftydd organ organ loft
llog *eg* llogau interest
llog ar ddebyd *eg* debit interest
llog cronedig *eg* accrued interest
llog enwol *eg* nominal interest
llog penodol *eg* fixed interest
llog syml *eg* simple interest
llogi *be* hire
llogi car *be* car hire
llongau *ell* shipping
llongau masnach *ell* merchant shipping
llong ager *eb* llongau ager steamship
llong arfog *eb* llongau arfog man-of-war
llong awyrennau *eb* llongau awyrennau aircraft carrier
llong bost *eb* llongau post mail boat
llong danfor *eb* llongau tanfor submarine
llong danfor Almaenig *eb* llongau tanfor Almaenig U-boat
llong filwyr *eb* llongau milwyr troop ship
llong garchar *eb* llongau carchar hulk
llong garthu *eb* llongau carthu dredger
llong glirio ffrwydrynnau *eb* llongau clirio ffrwydrynnau minesweeper
llong haearn *eb* llongau haearn ironclad
llong hir *eb* llongau hir long ship
llong osod ffrwydrynnau *eb* llongau gosod ffrwydrynnau minelayer
llong rewi *eb* llongau rhewi refrigeration ship
llong ryfel *eb* llongau rhyfel battleship
llong ryfel fechan *eb* llongau rhyfel bychain destroyer
llong ryfel gyflym *eb* llongau rhyfel cyflym cruiser
llong y llynges *eb* llongau'r llynges naval ship
llong y llyngesydd *eb* llongau'r llyngeswyr flagship
llond llwy bwdin *eg* llond llwyau pwdin dessertspoonful
llond sgrin *ans* full-screen
llonnod *eg* llonnodau sharp
llonnod dwbl *eg* llonnodau dwbl double sharp
llonydd *ans* still; motionless
llonyddwch *eg* stillness
llorestynnol *ans* decurrent
llorfudiant *eg* advection
llorio'r bêl *be* touch down
llorwedd *eg* llorweddau horizontal
llorwedd-dra *eg* horizontality
llorweddol *ans* horizontal
llosg *ans* burnt
llosg *eg* llosgiadau burn
llosg haul *eg* sunburn
llosg rhewgell *eg* freezer burn
llosgach *eg* incest
llosgadwy *ans* burnable
llosgfynydd *eg* llosgfynyddoedd volcano
llosgfynydd cwsg *eg* llosgfynyddoedd cwsg dormant volcano
llosgfynydd marw *eg* llosgfynyddoedd marw extinct volcano
llosgfynydd tarian *eg* llosgfynyddoedd tarian shield volcano
llosg-garnedd *eb* llosg-garneddau agglomerate
llosgi *be* burn
llosgi bwriadol *be* arson
llosgliw *ans* encaustic
llosgwayw *eg* causalgia
llosgydd *eg* llosgyddion burner
llosgydd Bunsen *eg* llosgyddion Bunsen Bunsen burner
llosgyddiaeth *eb* incendiarism
llu *eg* horde
llu awyr *eg* lluoedd awyr air force
Llu Euraidd *eg* Golden Horde
lludw *eg* ash
lludw folcanig *eg* volcanic ash
lludw pren *eg* wood ash
lludded *eg* fatigue
lludded cyhyrol *eg* muscle fatigue
llufadredd *eg* humification
llugaeron *ell* cranberries
lluman *eg/b* llumanau flag; linesman's flag; ensign
lluman cario *eg* llumanau cario carry flag
lluman cornel *eg* llumanau cornel corner flag
lluman cychwyn *eg* llumanau cychwyn starting flag
lluman herodrol *eg/b* llumanau herodrol heraldic banner
llumanu *be* flag
llumanwr (mewn byddin) *eg* llumanwyr standard bearer; ensign
llumanwr (mewn chwaraeon) *eg* llumanwyr touch judge; linesman
llun *eg* lluniau picture; drawing
llun lleoli *eg* lluniau lleoli establishing shot
llun nesaf *eg* next drawing
llun pen ffelt *eg* lluniau pen ffelt felt pen drawing
llun sialc *eg* lluniau sialc chalk drawing
llun siarcol *eg* lluniau siarcol charcoal drawing
Llundeiniwr *eg* Llundeinwyr Londoner
llungopi *eg* llungopïau photocopy
llungopïo *be* photocopy
llungopïwr *eg* llungopiwyr photocopier
lluniad (am lun wedi'i luniadu) *eg* lluniadau drawing
lluniad (yn y meddwl) *eg* lluniadau construct
lluniad adeiladu *eg* lluniadau adeiladu construction drawing

lluniad amlinell *eg* lluniadau amlinell outline drawing
lluniad anodedig *eg* annotated drawing
lluniad blwch *eg* lluniadau blwch box drawing
lluniad cydosod *eg* lluniadau cydosod assembly drawing
lluniad cydrannau *eg* lluniadau cydrannau component drawing
lluniad cyfeirio *eg* lluniadau cyfeirio reference drawing
lluniad chwyddhad isel *eg* lluniadau chwyddhad isel low power drawing
lluniad darluniol *eg* lluniadau darluniol pictorial drawing
lluniad dimensiynol *eg* lluniadau dimensiynol dimensioned drawing
lluniad dotwaith *eg* lluniadau dotwaith stipple drawing
lluniad ffurfiol *eg* lluniadau ffurfiol formal drawing
lluniad geometrig *eg* lluniadau geometrig geometric construction
lluniad goddefiannol *eg* toleranced drawing
lluniad gorffenedig *eg* lluniadau gorffenedig finished drawing
lluniad gweithio *eg* lluniadau gweithio working drawing
lluniad isometrig *eg* lluniadau isometrig isometric drawing
lluniad llawrydd *eg* lluniadau llawrydd freehand drawing
lluniad lled gywir *eg* lluniadau lled gywir rough drawing
lluniad manwl *eg* lluniadau manwl detailed drawing
lluniad manylion *eg* lluniadau manylion detail drawing
lluniad o gyfrannedd da *eg* lluniadau o gyfrannedd da well-proportioned drawing
lluniad orthograffig *eg* lluniadau orthograffig orthographic drawing
lluniad peirianegol *eg* lluniadau peirianegol engineering drawing
lluniad personol *eg* lluniadau personol personal construct
lluniad rhagarweiniol *eg* lluniadau rhagarweiniol preliminary drawing
lluniad taenedig *eg* lluniadau taenedig exploded drawing
lluniad technegol *eg* lluniadau technegol technical drawing
lluniad wrth raddfa *eg* lluniadau wrth raddfa scale drawing
lluniadaeth *eb* constructivism
lluniadu *be* draw
lluniadu cydosod *be* assembly drawing
lluniadu mecanyddol *be* mechanical drawing
lluniadu mewn persbectif *be* perspective drawing
lluniadu peirianegol *be* engineering drawing
lluniadu wrth raddfa *be* draw to scale
llunio *be* construct
llunio elips *be* constructing an ellipse
llunio llinfap *be* make a sketch-map
llunio siapiau *be* construct shapes
llunio trawstoriad *be* draw a cross-section
llun-negesu *be* picture messaging
lluoedd y meddiannu *ell* occupying forces
lluosflwydd *ans* perennial
lluosi *be* multiply
lluosi hir *be* long multiplication
lluosiad *eg* lluosiadau multiplication
lluosiad fector *eg* vector multiplication
lluosiad sgalar *eg* scalar multiplication
lluosliw *ans* multi-chrome
lluosnomaidd *ans* multinominal
lluosnominal *eg* lluosnominalau multinominal
lluosogi hadau *be* seed propagation
lluosogrwydd *eg* multiplicity
lluosol *ans* multiplicative
lluosol *ans* multiple
lluosrif *eg* lluosrifau multiple
lluosrif cyfannol *eg* lluosrifau cyfannol integral multiple
lluosrif cyffredin lleiaf *eg* lowest common multiple
lluosrifau un-digid *ell* single digit multiples
lluoswerth *ans* multi-valued; many-valued
lluoswm *eg* lluosymiau product
lluoswm crynswth *eg* gross product
lluoswm matrics *eg* lluosymiau matrics matrix product
lluoswm sgalar *eg* scalar product
lluosydd *eg* lluosyddion multiplier
lluosyn *eg* lluosion multiplicand
llurig *eb* llurigau hauberk
llus *ell* bilberries
llusern *eb* llusernau lantern
llusgiad *eg* llusgiadau drag
llusgiad cyllidol *eg* fiscal drag
llusgo *be* drag
llusgo a gollwng drag and drop
llusgo bar *be* drag bar
lluwch *eg* lluwchfeydd drift
lluwch eira *eg* lluwchfeydd eira snow drift
llw *eg* llwon oath
llw ffyddlondeb *eg* fealty
llw teyrngarwch *eg* llwon teyrngarwch oath of allegiance
llw ymgadw'n ddibriod *eg* oath of celibacy
Llw Ymwadiad *eg* Abjuration Oath
llwch *eg* dust
llwch brics *eg* brick dust
llwch folcanig *eg* volcanic dust
llwch mân *eg* fine dust
llwch ymbelydrol *eg* fallout
llwg, y llwg *eg* scurvy
llwgr *ans* corrupt
llwgr-fasnachwr *eg* llwgr-fasnachwyr racketeer
llwgrwobr *eb* llwgrwobrwyon bribe
llwgrwobrwyo *be* bribe

llwgrwobrwyo a llygru bribery and corruption
llwnc *eg* llynciau gullet
llwy *eb* llwyau spoon
llwy blastig *eb* llwyau plastig plastic spoon
llwy bren *eb* llwyau pren wooden spoon
llwy bwdin *eb* llwyau pwdin dessertspoon
llwy fwrdd *eb* llwyau bwrdd tablespoon
llwy ffaglu *eb* llwyau ffaglu deflagrating spoon
llwybr *eg* llwybrau pathway
llwybr *eg* llwybrau path; route; track; routeway; trail
llwybr adwaith *eg* llwybrau adwaith path of reaction
llwybr anadlu *eg* airway
llwybr ateb *eg* llwybrau ateb reply path
llwybr atgyrch *eg* llwybrau atgyrch reflex arc
llwybr awyr *eg* llwybrau awyr air route
llwybr byr *eg* llwybrau byr shortcut; short route
llwybr byr bysellfwrdd *eg* keyboard shortcut
llwybr byrraf *eg* llwybrau byrraf shortest route
llwybr canolog *eg* central route
llwybr cyfeiriadur *eg* llwybrau cyfeiriadur directory path
llwybr cyfeirio *eg* llwybrau cyfeirio referral route
llwybr cyhoeddus *eg* llwybrau cyhoeddus public path
Llwybr Cylch Mawr *eg* Great Circle Route
llwybr cynhanes *eg* llwybrau cynhanes prehistoric trackway
llwybr diffrwyth *eg* llwybrau diffrwyth blind alley
llwybr echddygol *eg* motor pathway
llwybr heligol *eg* llwybrau heligol helical path
Llwybr Llaethog *eg* Milky Way
llwybr magnogellog *eg* magnocellular pathway
llwybr masnach *eg* llwybrau masnach trade-route
llwybr môr *eg* llwybrau môr sea lane
llwybr natur *eg* llwybrau natur nature trail
llwybr parfogellog *eg* parvocellular pathway
llwybr perifferol *eg* peripheral route
llwybr rhydd cymedrig *eg* mean free path
llwybr sain *eg* llwybrau sain sound path
llwybr synthetig *eg* synthetic route
llwybr templed *eg* llwybrau templedi template path
llwybr troed *eg* llwybrau troed footpath
Llwybr Wythblyg (Bwdhaeth) *eg* Eightfold Path
llwybr y bêl *eg* line of the ball
llwybr y dŵr *eg* passage of water
llwybr y stwmp *eg* line of the stump
llwybr y wiced *eg* line of the wicket
llwybr ymborth *eg* alimentary canal
llwybro *be* route; trail
llwybro slip *be* slip tracing
llwybrydd *eg* llwybryddion router
llwyd *eg* grey
llwyd Payne *eg* Payne's grey
llwydaidd *ans* pallid
llwydlas *eg* dove grey
llwydni *eg* mildew
llwydni *eg* mould
llwydni mewn pren *eg* doatiness
llwydrew *eg* hoar frost
llwydwyrdd *ans* glaucous
llwyddiant *eg* llwyddiannau success; accomplishment
llwyddiant academaidd *eg* llwyddiannau academaidd academic success
llwyddiant atgenhedlu *eg* reproductive success
llwyddiant y ffit *eg* goodness of fit
llwyddo *be* succeed; achieve
llwyfan (mewn theatr etc) *eg/b* llwyfannau stage
llwyfan (yn gyffredinol) *eg/b* llwyfannau platform
llwyfan cludadwy *eg* llwyfannau cludadwy fit-up stage
llwyfan erydu *eg* llwyfannau erydu erosion platform
llwyfan ffedog *eg* llwyfannau ffedog apron stage
llwyfan olew *eg* llwyfannau olew oil rig
llwyfan pypedau *eg* llwyfannau pypedau puppet stage
llwyfan tro *eg* llwyfannau tro revolving stage
llwyfan tyllu *eg* llwyfannau tyllu rig
llwyfan uchel *eg* llwyfannau uchel highboard
llwyfandir *eg* llwyfandiroedd plateau
llwyfandir dyranedig *eg* llwyfandiroedd dyranedig dissected plateau
llwyfandir llynnoedd *eg* llwyfandiroedd llynnoedd lake plateau
llwyn *eg* llwyni bush; shrub; grove
llwyn saets *eg* llwyni saets sage bush
llwyrfoddi *be* flooding
llwyrglo *eg* llwyrgloeon deadlock
llwyrlosgi *be* burn out
llwyrlosgi *be* ash
llwyrymwrthodwr *eg* llwyrymwrthodwyr teetotaller
llwyth (=casgliad o bobl) *eg* llwythau tribe
llwyth (=yr hyn a ellir ei gario) *eg* llwythi load; consignment
llwyth dosbarthedig *eg* llwythi dosbarthedig distributed loading
llwyth llong *eg* llwythau llong shipment
llwytho (ffwrnais neu grwsibl) *be* charge
llwytho (yn gyffredinol) *be* load
llwytho cyflwyniad i lawr *be* download presentation
llwytho delwedd i lawr *be* download an image
llwytho ffont *be* load font
llwytho i fyny *be* upload
llwytho i lawr *be* download
llwytho ocsigen *eg* oxygen loading
llwytho rhagor i lawr *be* download more
llwythol *ans* tribal
llwytholdeb *eg* tribalism
llwythwr *eg* llwythwyr loader
llychlyd *ans* dusty
Llychlynnaidd *ans* Viking
Llychlynnaidd *ans* Nordic; Viking; Norse
Llychlynnwr *eg* Llychlynwyr Viking; Norseman
llydan *ans* broad; wide

llydan agored *ans* wide open
llydanddail *ans* broadleaved
llyfn (am ddail) *ans* glabrous
llyfn (am symudiad) *ans* fluid
llyfn (heb wrthiant i lif aer) *ans* streamlined
llyfn (yn gyffredinol) *ans* smooth
llyfn a sgythrog *ans* stoss and lee
llyfndir tonnau *eg* llyfndiroedd tonnau wave-cut platform
llyfngrwn *ans* rounded
llyfnhau *be* even down
llyfnochrau *ell* slickensides
llyfnu *be* smooth
llyfr *eg* llyfrau book
llyfr bach *eg* referee's book
llyfr bendigaid *eg* llyfrau bendigaid holy book
llyfr braslunio *eg* llyfrau braslunio sketch-book
llyfr cofnodion *eg* llyfrau cofnodion minute book
llyfr corn *eg* llyfrau corn hornbook
Llyfr Chwaraeon *eg* Book of Sports
llyfr dalennau rhydd *eg* llyfrau dalennau rhydd loose-leaf book
llyfr dewis *eg* llyfrau dewis real book
Llyfr Disgyblaeth *eg* Book of Discipline
llyfr dogni *eg* llyfrau dogni ration book
Llyfr Domesday *eg* Domesday Book
Llyfr Du Cyfrifon y Llys *eg* Black Book of the Household
llyfr enwol *eg* llyfrau enwol nominal ledger
llyfr erwydd *eg* llyfrau erwydd manuscript music book
llyfr esgobol *eg* llyfrau esgobol pontifical
Llyfr Gorchmynion *eg* Book of Orders
llyfr gosod *eg* llyfrau gosod set book
llyfr gwasanaeth *eg* llyfrau gwasanaeth breviary
llyfr gwerthiant *eg* llyfrau gwerthiant sales ledger
llyfr log *eg* llyfrau log log book
llyfr llafar *eg* llyfrau llafar audio book
llyfr lloffion *eg* llyfrau lloffion scrap book
Llyfr Merthyron *eg* Book of Martyrs
llyfr offeren *eg* llyfrau offeren missal
Llyfr Oriau *eg* Book of Hours
llyfr print bras *eg* llyfrau print bras large print book
► **llyfr pryniadau** *eg* llyfrau pryniadau purchase ledger
llyfr statud *eg* statute book
llyfr stori *eg* llyfrau stori story book
llyfr un-darn *eg* llyfrau un-darn single section book
llyfr y gyfraith *eg* law book
Llyfr yr Hysbysebion *eg* Book of Advertisements
llyfrgell *eb* llyfrgelloedd library
Llyfrgell Bodley *eb* Bodleian Library
llyfrgell dapiau *eb* llyfrgelloedd tapiau tape library
llyfrgell deithiol *eb* llyfrgelloedd teithiol mobile library
llyfrgell ffilmiau *eb* llyfrgelloedd ffilmiau film library
llyfrgell glipluniau *eb* llyfrgelloedd clipluniau clip art library
llyfrgell gyfredol *eb* llyfrgelloedd cyfredol current library
llyfrgell israglen *eb* subprogram library
llyfrgell newydd *eb* llyfrgelloedd newydd new library
llyfrgell raglenni *eb* llyfrgelloedd rhaglenni program library
llyfrgell ysgol *eb* llyfrgelloedd ysgol school library
llyfrgellydd *eg* llyfrgellwyr librarian
llyfrgellydd ffeiliau *eg* llyfrgellwyr ffeiliau file librarian
llyfrifo dwbl *be* double entry
llyfrothen *eb* llyfrothod butterfish
llyfrothen Yarrel *eb* llyfrothod Yarrel Yarrel blenny
llyfryddiaeth *eb* bibliography
llyfryn *eg* llyfrynnau brochure
llyfryn *eg* llyfrynnau booklet
llyfryn cymorth *eg* llyfrynnau cymorth support booklet
llyfryn ymestyn *eg* llyfrynnau ymestyn extension booklet
llygad *eg/b* llygaid eye
llygad aderyn (masarnen) *ans* bird's eye
llygad croes *eg* llygaid croes squint
llygad cyfansawdd *eg* llygaid cyfansawdd compound eye
llygad chwith *eg* llygaid chwith left eye
llygad diog *eg* llygaid diog lazy eye
llygad haul *eg* sonnenseite
llygad haul *eg* adret
llygaden *eb* llygadennau eyelet
llygaden bres *eb* llygadennau pres brass eyelet
llygaden liw *eb* llygadennau lliw coloured eyelet
llygadol *ans* ocular
llygoden *eb* llygod mouse
llygoden fawr ddyranedig *be* llygod mawr dyranedig dissected rat
llygoden fawr godog *eb* llygod mawr codog kangaroo rat
llygoden y dŵr *eb* llygod y dŵr water vole
llygredig *ans* venal
llygredd (moesol) *eg* corruption
llygredd (yn yr amgylchedd) *eg* llygreddau pollution
llygredd amgylcheddol *eg* environmental pollution
llygredd atmosfferig *eg* atmospheric pollution
llygredd sŵn *eg* noise pollution
llygriad (arian) *eg* debasement
llygru (moesol) *be* corrupt
llygru (yr amgylchedd) *be* pollute
llygru gwybodaeth electronig *be* corruption of electronic information
llygrydd *eg* llygryddion pollutant
llynges *eb* llyngesau navy
llynges fach *eb* llyngesau bach flotilla
llyngesol *ans* naval
llyngesydd *eg* llyngesyddion admiral
llyngyraidd *ans* vermiform
llyngyren yr afu *eb* llyngyr yr afu liver fluke

llyngyren yr iau *eb* lyngyr yr iau liver fluke
llyngyren *eb* llyngyr tapeworm
llym *ans* acute; sharp
llymder *eg* austerity
llyn *eg* llynnoedd lake
llyn cafnog *eg* llynnoedd cafnog gouged out lake
llyn creicafn *eg* llynnoedd creicafn rock basin lake
llyn cyfrewlifol *eg* llynnoedd cyfrewlifol proglacial lake
llyn chwerw *eg* llynnoedd chwerw bitter lake
llyn glintlin *eg* llynnoedd glintlin glint-line lake
llyn halen *eg* llynnoedd halen salt lake
llyn hirgul *eg* llynnoedd hirgul ribbon lake; finger lake
llyn mynydd *eg* llynnoedd mynydd tarn
llyncdwll *eg* llyncdyllau swallow hole; sink hole; ponor
llyncu *be* deglutition
llyncu *be* swallow
llyndir creicafn *eg* rock hollow lakeland
llynnol *ans* lacustrine
llynoleg *eb* limnology
llyriad *eg* llyriaid plantain
llys *eg* llysoedd court
llys a gwlad court and country
llys adrannol *eg* llysoedd adrannol divisional court
Llys Adrannol Mainc y Frenhines *eg* Divisional Court of the QBD
llys ag awdurdod digonol *eg* court of competent jurisdiction
Llys Anfonogion *eg* Delegates Court
llys apêl *eg* llysoedd apêl appeal court
Llys Apêl *eg* Court of Appeal
Llys Apêl Troseddol *eg* Court of Criminal Appeal
llys arferion cyfyngol *eg* restrictive practices court
llys awdurdod arbennig *eg* court of special jurisdiction
Llys Bach *eg* Court of Petty Sessions
Llys Barn Rhyngwladol *eg* International Court of Justice
Llys Chwarter *eg* Quarter Sessions
Llys Chwarter *eg* Court of Quarter Sessions
llys ffiwdal *eg* llysoedd ffiwdal feudal court
Llys Goruchaf *eg* Supreme Court
llys gwarchod *eg* court of protection
llys mân ddyledion *eg* small claims court
llys masnach *eg* commercial court
llys methdaliad *eg* bankruptcy court
llys morlys *eg* admiralty court
llys plant *eg* llysoedd plant juvenile court
Llys Profiant *eg* Probate Court
Llys Siambr y Seren *eg* Court of Star Chamber
llys sirol *eg* llysoedd sirol county court
Llys Troseddol Canolog *eg* Central Criminal Court
Llys Uchelfraint *eg* Prerogative Court
llys y cantref *eg* llysoedd cantrefi hundred court
Llys y Goron *eg* Crown Court
Llys y Morlys *eg* Court of Admiralty
Llys y Pab *eg* curia
Llys y Sesiwn Fawr *eb* Court of Great Sessions
Llys y Siecr *eg* Exchequer Court
Llys y Siryf *eg* Sheriff's Tourn
llys ynadon *eg* llysoedd ynadon magistrates court
llys yr afu *eg* liverwort
llys yr iau *eg* liverwort
llysfam *eb* llysfamau stepmother
llysgenhadaeth *eb* llysgenadaethau embassy
llysgennad *eg* llysgenhadon ambassador
llysiau cartref *ell* homegrown vegetables
llysieulyfr *eg* herbal
llysieuol *ans* herbaceous
llysieuwr *eg* llysieuwyr vegetarian
llysieuyn *eg* llysiau herb
llysnafedd *eg* llysnafeddau scum; slime
llystad *eg* stepfather
llystyfiant *eg* vegetation
llyswenwyn *eg* llyswenwynau phytotoxin
llysysol *ans* herbivorous
llysysydd *eg* llysysyddion herbivore
llysywen *eb* llyswennod eel
llythreniad *eg* llythreniadau lettering
llythrennau bach *ell* minuscule
llythrennau bras *ell* upper case; majuscule
llythrennau ogam *ell* ogham characters
llythrennedd *eg* literacy
llythrennedd cyfrifiadurol *eg* computer literacy
llythrennedd gweithredol *eg* functional literacy
llythrennog *ans* literate
llythrennol *ans* literal
llythrennu *be* lettering
llythrennu â llaw *be* hand drawn lettering
llythrennu goliwiedig *be* illuminated lettering
llythrennu herodrol *be* heraldic lettering
llythrennu llawysgrif *be* manuscript lettering
llythrennu pen *be* pen lettering
llythrennu pen llydan *be* broad pen lettering
llythrennu troslun sych *be* dry transfer lettering
llythyr *eg* llythyrau letter
llythyr awtobeilot *eg* llythyrau awtobeilot autopilot letter
llythyr busnes *eg* llythyrau busnes business letter
llythyr parod *eg* llythyrau parod form letter
llythyr personol *eg* llythyrau personol personal letter
llythyrau dinasyddiaeth *ell* letters of denizenship
llythyrau sothach *ell* junk mail
Llythyrau'r Blwch *ell* Casket Letters
llythyren *eb* llythrennau letter
llythyren fach *eb* llythrennau bach lower case letter; small letter
llythyren italig *eb* llythrennau italig italic letter
llythyren rwnig *eb* llythrennau rwnig rune
llyw (ar gefn llong) *eg* rudder
llyw (cwch) *eg* llywiau tiller
llyw (cerbyd modur) *eg* llywiau steering wheel

llywio *be* navigate; guide
llywio cwrs *be* steering a course
llywiwr *eg* llywyr navigator; helmsman
llywodraeth *eb* llywodraethau government
llywodraeth bersonol *eb* personal rule
llywodraeth byped *eb* llywodraethau pyped puppet regime
llywodraeth Cymru *eb* government of Wales
llywodraeth dros dro *eb* llywodraethau dros dro provisional government
llywodraeth drwy ordinhad *eb* government by decree
llywodraeth ganolog *eb* central government
Llywodraeth Genedlaethol *eb* National Government
llywodraeth gyfrifol *eb* responsible government
llywodraeth isalpaidd *eb* subalpine government
llywodraeth leol *eb* local government
llywodraeth ofalu *eb* llywodraethau gofalu caretaker government
llywodraeth Stalin *eb* rule of Stalin
llywodraethu *be* govern
llywodraethwr *eg* llywodraethwyr governor
llywodraethwr eglwysig *eg* llywodraethwyr eglwysig church governor
llywodraethwr ysgol *eg* llywodraethwyr ysgol school governor
llywydd (cymdeithas etc) *eg* llywyddion president
llywydd (mewn graddfa gerddorol) *eg* dominant
llywyddiaeth *eb* presidency

M

mabol *ans* filial
mabolgampau *ell* sports day
mabolgampau bach *ell* potted sports
mabolgampwr *eg* mabolgampwyr sportsman
mabolgampwraig *eb* mabolgampwragedd sportswoman
mabwysiad *eg* mabwysiadau adoption
mabwysiadaeth *eb* adoptionism
mabwysiadu *be* adopt
mabwysiadu agored *be* open adoption
mabwysiadwr cynnar *eg* mabwysiadwyr cynnar early adopter
mabwysiadwr hwyr *eg* mabwysiadwyr hwyr late adopter
mabwysiedig *ans* adopted
macramé *eg* macramé
macro *ans* macro
macro *eg* macros macro
macro economaidd *ans* macroeconomic
macro ffactor *eg* macro factor
macrocosm *eg* macrocosmau macrocosm
macrofaethyn *eg* macrofaethynnau macro nutrient
macroffag *eg* macroffagau macrophage
macrogydosodydd *eg* macrogydosodyddion macroassembler
macrohinsawdd *eg* macrohinsoddau macro-climate
Macsen Wledig *eg* Magnus Maximus
macsila *eg* macsilâu maxilla
macsima *eg* nodau macsima maxima
macwla *eg* macwlau macula
mach *eg* meichiau surety
madarchaidd *ans* mushroom-like
madarchen *eb* madarch mushroom
madarchu *be* mushrooming
Madinah *eg* Madinah
madr sgarlad *eg* scarlet madder
madredd *eg* gangrene
madrigal *eb* madrigalau madrigal
madruddyn y cefn *eg* spinal cord
maddau *be* forgive
maddeuant *eg* forgiveness; absolution
maddeueb *eb* maddeuebau indulgence
mae angen un one-off
maen *eg* meini bakestone
maen capan *eg* meini capan capstone
maen clo *eg* meini clo keystone
maen iasbis *eg* meini iasbis jasper
maen llifanu *eg* meini llifanu grindstone
maen ogam *eg* meini ogam ogham stone
maen prawf *eg* meini prawf criterion
maen prawf asesu *eg* meini prawf asesu assessment criterion
▸ **maen prawf gradd berthynol** *eg* meini prawf gradd berthynol grade-related criterion
maen prawf gwerthuso *eg* meini prawf gwerthuso evaluation criterion
maen prawf gyfeiriol *ans* criterion-referenced
maen tramgwydd *eg* meini tramgwydd stumbling block
maenor *eb* maenorau manor; grange
maenordy *eg* maenordai manor house
maenordy ag amddiffynfeydd *eg* maenordai ag amddiffynfeydd fortified manor house
maer *eg* meiri mayor; reeve
Maer y Llys *eg* Mayor of the Palace
maeres *eb* maeresau mayoress
maes (=cae chwarae) *eg* meysydd pitch
maes (=rhychwant diddordeb, gweithgaredd etc) *eg* meysydd area
maes (mewn cronfa ddata) *eg* meysydd field
maes (yn gyffredinol) *eg* meysydd field
maes affeithiol *eg* meysydd affeithiol affective domain
maes agored *eg* meysydd agored openfield
maes agos *eg* meysydd agos infield
maes allweddol *eg* meysydd allweddol key field
maes allwyriadol *eg* deflecting field
maes amser *eg* meysydd amser time field
maes ar gael *eg* meysydd ar gael available field
maes awyr *eg* meysydd awyr airport
maes awyr rhanbarthol *eg* meysydd awyr rhanbarthol regional airport
maes brwydr *eg* meysydd brwydr battlefield
maes cadwrol grym *eg* conservative field of force
maes cerdyn *eg* meysydd cerdyn card field
maes cerddorol *eg* meysydd cerddorol musical scene
maes craidd *eg* meysydd craidd core area
maes criced *eg* meysydd criced cricket field
maes cronfa ddata *eg* meysydd cronfa ddata database field
maes cyflymu *eg* accelerating field
▸ **maes chwarae antur** *eg* meysydd chwarae antur adventure playground
maes chwarae sbwriel *eg* junk playground
maes databeilot *eg* meysydd databeilot datapilot field

maes diddordeb *eg* meysydd diddordeb interest area
maes di-haint *eg* meysydd di-haint sterile field
maes disgyrchiant *eg* gravitational field
maes dyddiad *eg* meysydd dyddiad date field
maes dynodedig *eg* meysydd dynodedig designated area
maes eira *eg* meysydd eira snowfield
maes ffisegol *eg* physical area
maes galwedigaethol *eg* meysydd galwedigaethol occupational field
maes glanio *eg* meysydd glanio airfield
maes glo *eg* meysydd glo coalfield
maes glo cudd *eg* meysydd glo cudd concealed coalfield
maes golff *eg* meysydd golff golf links
maes grym *eg* field of force
maes gweithgaredd annibynnol *eg* meysydd gweithgaredd annibynnol discrete area of activity
maes gweithredu *eg* operational area
maes gweld *eg* meysydd gweld field of view
Maes Gwybodaeth Gronedig *eg* Accumulated Information Field
Maes Gwybodaeth Gymedrig *eg* Mean Information Field
maes gwybyddol *eg* cognitive domain
maes hofrenyddion *eg* heliport
maes llafur *eg* meysydd llafur syllabus
maes llafur craidd *eg* meysydd llafur craidd core syllabus
maes llafur cyfannol *eg* meysydd llafur cyfannol integrated syllabus
maes llafur cyffredin *eg* meysydd llafur cyffredin common syllabus
maes llafur cytûn *eg* meysydd llafur cytûn agreed syllabus
maes llafur cytûn lleol *eg* meysydd llafur cytûn lleol local agreed syllabus
maes llafur pwnc cyfun *eg* meysydd llafur pynciau cyfun combined subject syllabus
maes magnetig *eg* meysydd magnetig magnetic field
maes mewnbwn *eg* meysydd mewnbwn input field
maes newidiol *eg* meysydd newidiol variable field
maes olew *eg* meysydd olew oilfield
maes pêl-droed *eg* meysydd pêl-droed football field
maes presennol *eg* meysydd presennol existing field
maes sefydlog *eg* meysydd sefydlog fixed field
maes tanio *eg* meysydd tanio artillery range
maes tanio'r Weinyddiaeth Amddiffyn *eg* meysydd tanio'r Weinyddiaeth Amddiffyn Ministry of Defence range
maes tebygolrwydd gwybodaeth *eg* information probability field
maes wedi'i fynegeio *eg* meysydd wedi'u mynegeio indexed field
Maes y Brethyn Euraid *eg* Field of the Cloth of Gold
maeslywydd *eg* maeslywyddion field marshal
maestir gwartheg *eg* maestiroedd gwartheg cattle range
maestref *eb* maestrefi suburb
maestrefi *ell* suburbia
maestrefol *ans* suburban
maesu *be* field
maesu ar y ffin *be* field on the boundary
► **maes-uwchriaddadwy** *ans* field-upgradeable
maeswellt *eg* bent grass; agrostis
maeswr *eg* maeswyr fielder
maeswr canol *eg* maeswyr canol centre outfielder
maeswr de *eg* maeswyr de right outfielder
maeth *eg* maethion nourishment; nutriment; nutrition
maetheg *eb* nutrition
maethiad *eg* nutrition
maethlon *ans* nutritious
maethol *ans* nourishing; nutritional; nutritive
maetholyn *eg* maetholion nutrient
maethu *be* foster
mafon *ell* raspberries
magenta *eg* magenta
magl *eb* maglau trap
magl gwallau *eb* maglau gwallau error trap
magl ymyriadol *eb* maglau ymyriadol interrupt trap
magl-flwch *eb* magl-flychau box-trap
maglu *be* trap
maglu gwallau *be* error trapping
maglys *eg* alfalfa; lucerne
magma *eg* magmâu magma
magmatig *ans* magmatic
Magna Carta *eg* Magna Carta
magnel *eb* magnelau cannon
magnelaeth *eb* artillery; canonry
magnelwr *eg* magnelwyr artilleryman
magnesaidd *ans* magnesian
magnesiwm (Mg) *eg* magnesium
magnesiwm carbonad *eg* magnesium carbonate
magnesiwm deucarbonad *eg* magnesium bicarbonate
magnet *eg* magnetau magnet
magnet pedol *eg* magnetau pedol horseshoe magnet
magnetedd *eg* magnetism
magnetedd daear *eg* terrestrial magnetism
magneteg *eb* magnetism
magneteiddiad *eg* magneteiddiadau magnetization
magneteiddio *be* magnetize
magnetig *ans* magnetic
magnetig cywir *eg* true magnetic
magneto *eg* magnetoeon magneto
magnetomedr *eg* magnetomedrau magnetometer
magnetron *eg* magnetronau magnetron
magu awdurdodol *be* authoritative parenting
magu digon da *be* good-enough parenting
magu gorawdurdodol *be* authoritarian parenting

magwraeth *eb* nurture
magwrfa *eb* magwrfeydd hotbed
manganîs(II) carbonad *eg* manganese(II) carbonate
manganîs(II) deumanganîs(III) ocsid *eg* manganese(II) dimanganese(III) oxide
manganîs(IV) ocsid *eg* manganese(IV) oxide
manganîs(VII) ocsid *eg* manganese(VII) oxide
mangl *eg* mangle
manglo *be* mangle
mangoed *eg* chaparral
Mahabharata *eb* Mahabharata
maharen (anifail) *eg* meheryn ram
Mahayana *eg* Mahayana
mahogani *eg* mahogany
main (=mirain) *ans* delicate
main (=tenau) *ans* slim
main (am ddefnydd) *ans* fine
mainc *eb* meinciau bench
mainc fowldio *eb* meinciau mowldio moulding bench
mainc gefn *eb* meinciau cefn back bench
mainc rhwymo llyfrau *eb* meinciau rhwymo llyfrau bookbinder's bench
mainc sodro *eb* meinciau sodro soldering bench
mainc waith *eb* meinciau gwaith work bench
maint (=hyd a lled) *eg* meintiau size; magnitude; extent
maint (=nifer) *eg* quantity
maint (yr elw) *eg* margin
maint a chyfeiriad magnitude and direction
maint beunyddiol argymelledig *eg* recommended daily amount
maint critigol *eg* critical size
maint cynulleidfa *eg* ratings
maint cywir *eg* meintiau cywir true size; exact size; accurate size; right amount
maint digonol *eg* meintiau digonol adequate size
maint dril *eg* meintiau driliau drill size
maint drilio *be* drilling capacity
maint enwol *eg* meintiau enwol nominal size
maint ffeil *eg* meintiau ffeil file extent
maint ffont *eg* meintiau ffont font size
maint gorffenedig *eg* meintiau gorffenedig finished size
maint gwallus *eg* meintiau gwallus inaccurate size
maint iawn *eg* actual size
maint llai *eg* reduced size
maint llawn *eg* full size
maint lleiaf *eg* minimum size
maint mudiant llinol *eg* magnitude of linear motion
maint pwynt *eg* point size
maint safonol *eg* meintiau safonol standard size
maint sgrin lawn *eg* full screen size
maint sylfaenol *eg* meintiau sylfaenol basic size
maint testun *eg* text size
maint troed *eg* maint traed footprint
maint wedi'i blaenio *eg* meintiau wedi'u plaenio planed size
maint y cyflenwad *eg* quantity supplied; supplied quantity
maint y galw *eg* quantity demanded; demanded quantity
maint y gwerthiant *eg* sales volumes
maint yr elw *eg* profit margin
maintioli *eg* stature
majolica *eg* majolica
Makkah *eb* Makkah
malaen *ans* malignant
malaria *eg* malaria
malî *eg* mallee
maltos *eg* maltose
Malthwsiaeth *eb* Malthusianism
malu *be* grind
malu mewn morter *be* grind in a mortar
malu'n fân *be* crush
malurion *ell* debris; detritus; brash
malwr *eg* malwyr crusher
mallryg *eg* ergot
malltod *eg* blight
malltod tatws *eg* potato blight
Mam Duw *eb* Mother of God
mam faeth *eb* mamau maeth foster mother
mam feichiog *eb* mamau beichiog expectant mother
mam-abaty *eg* mam-abatai mother-abbey
mam-dâp *eg* mam-dapiau father tape
mam-eglwys *eb* mam-eglwysi mother-church
mamfwrdd *eg* mamfyrddau motherboard
mamgell *eb* mamgelloedd mother cell
mamgraig *eb* mamgreigiau parent rock
mam-gu *eb* mamau grandmother
mamiaith *eb* mamieithoedd mother tongue
mamol *ans* maternal
mamolaeth *eb* maternity
mamolaidd *ans* mammalian
mamolyn *eg* mamolion mammal
mamoth *eg* mamothiaid mammoth
mamwlad *eb* mamwledydd mother country; homeland
mân *ans* fine
man addoli *eg* mannau addoli place of worship
mân anhwylderau *ell* minor illnesses
man claddu *eg* mannau claddu burial ground
man cychwyn *eg* mannau cychwyn starting place; start area; baseline; entry point
mân daclau *ell* fittings
mân ddaliad *eg* mân ddaliadau smallholding
man geni *eg* mannau geni birthmark
mân glustogau *ell* scatter cushions
man gwasgu *eg* mannau gwasgu pressure area
man hicio *eg* mannau hicio nocking point
mân iawn *ans* extra fine
mân ladrad *eg* mân ladradau petty larceny

mân ladrad *eg* mân ladradau petty theft
man llwytho *eg* mannau llwytho loading bay
man poeth *eg* mannau poeth hot spot
man pontio *eg* mannau pontio bridge point
mân-adeiledd *eb* mân-adeileddau fine structure
mân-bant *eg* mân-bantiau pit
mân-bant gastrig *eg* mân-bantiau gastrig gastric pit
mân-bantiau gweflog *ell* bordered pits
mân-bantiau syml *ell* simple pits
mân-bantiog *ans* pitted
mân-blet *eg* mân-bletiau pinch pleat
mandad *eg* mandadau mandate
mandedig *ans* mandated
mandibl *eg* mandiblau mandible
mandolin *eg* mandolinau mandolin
mandorla *eg* mandorla
mandrel *eg* mandrelau mandrel
mandrel cau (turn) *eg* mandreli cau hollow mandrel
mandrel côn *eg* mandreli côn sugar-loaf mandrel
mandwll *eg* mandyllau pore
mandylledd *eg* porosity
mandyllog *ans* porous
mandyllog tryledol *ans* diffuse porous
mân-ddarlun *eg* mân-ddarluniau miniature painting
mân-ddarlunio *be* miniature painting
manedd *eg* fineness
maneg *eb* menig glove
maneg agored *eb* menig agored open glove
maneg asbestos *eb* menig asbestos asbestos glove
maneg ddi-haint *eb* menig di-haint sterile glove
maneg fatio *eb* menig batio batting glove
maneg siami *eb* menig siami chamois glove
manganîs *eg* manganese
mango *eg* mango
mania *eg* mania
manicin *eg* manikin
maniffesto *eg* manifesto
maniffold *eg* maniffoldau manifold
maniffold gwacáu *eg* maniffoldau gwacáu exhaust manifold
manig *ans* manic
manila *eg* manilla
manion gwnïo *ell* haberdashery
manna *eg* manna
Mannau Cysegredig *ell* Holy Places
manomedr *eg* manomedrau manometer
mantais *eb* manteision advantage
mantais addysgol *eb* manteision addysgol educational advantage
mantais ddetholus *eb* manteision detholus selective advantage
mantais fecanyddol *eb* manteision mecanyddol mechanical advantage
mantais gymharol *eb* manteision cymharol comparative advantage
mantais lwyr *eb* absolute advantage
mantell *eb* mentyll mantle; robe
mantellu *be* mantle
mantisa *eg* mantisâu mantissa
mantol daliadau *eb* balance of payments
mantol fasnach *eb* balance of trade
mantolen *eb* mantolenni balance sheet
mantolen brawf *eb* mantolenni prawf trial balance
mantolen fanc rhy isel *eb* understated bank balance
mantoli *be* balance
mantoliad *eg* mantoliadau libration
mantoli'r cyfrifon *be* balance the accounts
mantra *eg* mantra
manwl *ans* fine; detailed; elaborate
manwl gywir *ans* accurate
manwl gywirdeb *eg* precision; accuracy; exactness; rigour
manwl gywirdeb priodol *eg* appropriate accuracy
manyleb *eb* manylebau specification
manyleb cynnal a chadw *eb* service and maintenance schedule
manyleb person *eb* manylebau person person specification
manyleb problem *eb* manylebau problemau problem specification
manyleb rhaglen *eb* manylebau rhaglenni program specification
manyleb Safonau Prydeinig *eb* manylebau Safonau Prydeinig British Standard specification
manyleb swydd *eb* manylebau swyddi job specification
manyleb system *eb* manylebau system system specification
manyleb y cynnyrch *eb* production specification
manylion *ell* details
manylion addurnol *ell* decorative details
manylion cudd *ell* hidden detail
manylion y gwerthwr eiddo *ell* estate agent details
manylu *be* detail; elaborate
manylu'r rhwydwaith *be* mesh refinement
manylyn *eg* manylion detail
map *eg* mapiau map
map amlinell *eg* mapiau amlinell outline map
map anodedig *eg* mapiau anodedig annotated map
map cromosomau *eg* mapiau cromosomau chromosome map
map cyfuchlinol *eg* mapiau cyfuchlinol contour map
map defnydd tir *eg* land utilization map
map delweddau *eg* mapiau delweddau image map
map delweddau cliciadwy *be* mapiau delweddau cliciadwy clickable image map
map didau *eg* mapiau didau bit map
map graddfa lai *eg* mapiau graddfa lai smaller-scale map
map Ordnans *eg* mapiau Ordnans Ordnance Survey map
map safle *eg* mapiau safle site map
map sylfaen *eg* mapiau sylfaen base map

map tir *eg* mapiau tir landmap
map tirwedd *eg* mapiau tirwedd relief map
map tywydd *eg* mapiau tywydd weather map
map y cof *eg* memory map
mapio *be* map
mapio arsaethol *be* surjective mapping
mapio cydffurfiol *be* conformal mapping
mapio deusaethol *be* bijective mapping
mapio gwybodaeth *be* information mapping
mapio maes *be* field mapping
mapio mewnsaethol *be* injective mapping
mapio sydyn *be* fast mapping
maquette *eg* maquettes maquette
marathon *eg* marathon
marblen *eb* marblis marble
marc *eg* marciau mark
marc ailadrodd *eg* marciau ailadrodd repeat mark
marc anadlu *eg* marciau anadlu breath mark
marc canol *eg* marciau canol centre spot
marc diogelwch *eg* safety mark
marc distyll *eg* low water mark
marc dosbarth *eg* marciau dosbarth class mark
marc gwyn mewn pren *eg* marciau gwyn mewn pren druxiness
marc morthwyl *eg* marciau morthwyl hammer mark
marc mynegiant *eg* marciau mynegiant expression mark; mark of expression
marc pasio *eg* marciau pasio pass mark
marc penllanw *eg* marciau penllanw high water mark
marc pìn *eg* marciau pìn pin mark
marc rhifo *eg* marciau rhifo tally mark
marc sero *eg* marciau sero zero mark
marc tâp *eg* marciau tâp tape mark
marc ymyl *eg* marciau ymyl edge mark
marc ymyl wyneb *eg* marciau ymyl wyneb face edge mark
marciau cydbwysedd *ell* balance marks
marciau graen *ell* grain markings
marciau patrwm *ell* pattern markings
marciau safonedig *ell* standardized marks
marciau sêr *ell* star-rating
marcio *be* mark; mark out
marcio'r gwrthwynebwr *be* mark the opponent
marciwr *eg* marcwyr marker
marciwr ffelt *eg* marcwyr ffelt felt marker
marciwr gwirod *eg* marcwyr gwirod spirit marker
marciwr hem *eg* marcwyr hem hem marker
marciwr mewnoli *eg* marcwyr mewnoli indent marker
marciwr nesaf *eg* next marker
marciwr rheoli *eg* marcwyr rheoli control marker
Marcsaeth *eb* Marxism
Marcsaidd *ans* Marxist
Marcsydd *eg* Marcswyr Marxist
marchnad *eb* marchnadoedd market; market place; mart
marchnad adwerthu *eb* retail market
marchnad botensial *eb* potential market
marchnad cyrchfannau agos *eb* short haul market
marchnad defnyddwyr *eb* consumer market
marchnad ddu *eb* black market
marchnad electronig *eb* marchnadoedd electronig electronic mall
marchnad gartref *eb* marchnadoedd cartref home market
marchnad gyfanwerthu *eb* marchnadoedd cyfanwerthu wholesale market
marchnad lafur *eb* labour market
marchnad oligopolaidd *eb* oligopolistic market
marchnad rydd *eb* marchnadoedd rhydd free market
marchnad ryngwladol *eb* international market
marchnad stoc *eb* marchnadoedd stoc stock market
marchnad y bwydydd rhewedig *eb* frozen food market
marchnad y cyfrifiaduron cartref *eb* home computer market
marchnata *be* market
marchnata arbenigol *be* niche marketing
Marchnata Band Eang (enw rhaglen) *be* Broadband Marketing
marchnata diwydiannol *be* industrial marketing
marchnata rhyngwladol *be* international marketing
marchnata uniongyrchol *eg* direct marketing
marchnerth *eg* horsepower
marchnerth brêc *eg* brake horse power
marchog *eg* marchogion knight
marchog crwydrol *eg* marchogion crwydrol knight errant
Marchog Sir *eg* Marchogion Sir Knight of the Shire
Marchog Temlaidd *eg* Marchogion Temlaidd Knight Templar
Marchog Tiwtonig *eg* Marchogion Tiwtonig Knight Teutonic
Marchog yr Ymerodraeth *eg* Marchogion yr Ymerodraeth Imperial Knight
Marchog Ysbytaidd *eg* Marchogion Ysbytaidd Knight Hospitaller
marchwellt *ell* couch grass
margarin *eg* margarine
Mari, Brenhines y Sgotiaid *eb* Mary, Queen of Scots
Mari Stiwart *eb* Mary Stuart
Mari Waedlyd *eb* Bloody Mary
Marïaidd *ans* Marian
marian *eg* marianau moraine
marian canol *eg* marianau canol medial moraine
marian cnwc gro *eg* marianau cnwc gro kame moraine
marian enciliol *eg* marianau enciliol recessional moraine
marian gwthio *eg* marianau gwthio push moraine
marian llusg *eg* marianau llusg ground moraine
marian ochrol *eg* marianau ochrol lateral moraine

marian perfedd *eg* marianau perfedd englacial moraine
marian tanrewlifol *eg* marianau tanrewlifol subglacial moraine
marian terfynol *eg* marianau terfynol terminal moraine; end moraine
marina *eg* marinas marina
marionét anifail *eg* marionetau anifeiliaid animal marionette
marionét cymalog *eg* marionetau cymalog jointed marionette
marionét llinyn *eg* marionetau llinyn string marionette
marionét pren *eg* marionetau pren wooden marionette
marionét tric *eg* marionetau tric trick marionette
marl *eg* marlau marl
marlio *be* marl
marlog *ans* marly
marmor *eg* marble
marmor artiffisial *eg* artificial marble
marmori *be* marbling
marouflage *eg* marouflage
marsial *eg* marsialiaid marshal
martensit *eg* martensite
marw-anedig *ans* stillborn
marweidd-dra *eg* stagnation
marwol *ans* lethal
marwolaeth *eb* marwolaethau death
marwolaeth yn y crud *eb* marwolaethau yn y crud cot death
marwolaeth yr ymennydd *eg* brain death
marwolaethau babanod *ell* infant mortality
marwoldeb *eg* mortality
marwor folcanig *ell* volcanic cinders
màs *eg* masau mass
màs atomig *eg* atomic mass
màs atomig cymharol *eg* relative atomic mass
màs atomig cymharol cymedrig *eg* mean relative atomic mass
màs disymudedd *eg* rest mass
màs gostyngol *eg* reduced mass
màs molar *eg* molar mass
màs moleciwlaidd *eg* molecular mass
màs moleciwlaidd cymharol *eg* relative molecular mass
màs niwclear *eg* nuclear mass
màs penodol *eg* masau penodol fixed mass
màs penodol o nwy *eg* fixed mass of gas
màs pwynt *eg* masau pwynt point mass
màs y cyhyrau *eg* muscle mass
màs y solid *eg* mass of solid
masddarfodiant *eg* mass-wasting
masfawr *ans* massive
masg *eg* masgiau mesh
masgio *be* mask; mesh; masking
masgio am yn ôl *be* backward masking
masgl pigog *eg* masglau pigog bur
masgynhyrchu *be* mass produce; mass production
masiff *eg* masiffau massif
màs-lifiad *eg* mass flow
masnach *eb* masnachau trade; commerce
masnach adwerthu *eb* retail trade
masnach arlwyo a gwestya *eb* catering and hotel trade
masnach atgas *eb* masnachau atgas noxious trades
masnach dramor *eb* foreign trade
masnach ddosbarthu *eb* distributive trade
masnach frethyn *eb* cloth trade
masnach gaethion *eb* slave trade
masnach rydd *eb* free trade
masnach ryngwladol *eb* international trade
masnachdy *eg* masnachdai counter
masnachfraint *eb* masnachfreintiau franchise
masnachol *ans* commercial
masnachu *be* trade
masnachu teg *be* fair trading
masnachwr *eg* masnachwyr merchant; trader
masnachwr brethyn *eg* masnachwyr brethyn friezeman
masocistiaeth rywiol *eb* sexual masochism
masque *eg* masques masque
màs-symudiad *eg* mass movement
mast radio neu deledu *eg* radio or tv mast
mastgell *eb* mastgelloedd mast cell
mastig *eg* mastic
mastyrbiad *eg* masturbation
mastyrbio *be* masturbate
maswr *eg* maswyr outside-half
mat *ans* matt
mat *eg* matiau mat
mat asbestos *eg* matiau asbestos asbestos mat
mat bwrdd *eg* matiau bwrdd table mat; place mat
mat ffibr *eg* matiau ffibr fibre mat
mat gwydr *eg* matiau gwydr glass mat
mat llygoden *eg* matiau llygoden mouse mat
mater *eg* matter
mater *eg* materion affair; issue
mater cyd-destunol *eg* materion cyd-destunol contextual issue
mater macroeconomaidd *eg* materion macroeconomaidd macroeconomic issue
mater mewnol *eg* materion mewnol domestic affair
mater moesegol *eg* materion moesegol ethical issue
mater moesol *eg* materion moesol moral matter
mater penodol *eg* materion penodol particular matter
mater perthnasol i gyfrifiaduron *eg* materion perthnasol i gyfrifiaduron computer related matter
mater tramor *eg* materion tramor foreign affair
mater trawsgwricwlaidd *eg* materion trawsgwricwlaidd cross-curricular issue
materion egni *ell* energy issues
materol *ans* material

materoliaeth *eb* materialism
materoliaeth ddilechdidol *eb* dialectical materialism
matiau duchesse *ell* duchesse set
matiog *ans* matted
matres *eb* matresi mattress
matriarchaidd *ans* matriarchal
matrics *eg* matricsau matrix
matrics anhynod *eg* matricsau anhynod non-singular matrix
Matrics Ansoff *eg* Ansoff Matrix
matrics calcheiddiedig *eg* calcified matrix
matrics colofn *eg* matricsau colofn column matrix
matrics cydberthyniad *eg* matricsau cydberthyniad correlation matrix
matrics cyfansawdd *eg* matricsau cyfansawdd compound matrix
matrics gwrthdro *eg* inverse matrix
matrics hynod *eg* singular matrix
matrics orthogonol *eg* orthogonal matrix
matrics petryal *eg* rectangular matrix
matrics rhes *eg* row matrix
matrics sgwâr *eg* square matrix
math *eg* mathau type
math anhysbys o ffeil *eg* mathau anhysbys o ffeil unknown file type
math Boole *eg* mathau Boole Boolean type
math bws *eg* bus type
math cywir *eg* mathau cywir right type
math data *eg* mathau data data type
math newidiol *eg* mathau newidiol variable type
math niwclear *eg* nuclear species
math o adroddiad *eg* report type
math o berfformiad *eg* mathau o berfformiad type of performance
math o bersonoliaeth *eg* mathau o bersonoliaeth personality type
math o bridd *eg* soil type
math o fotwm *eg* button type
math o ffeil *eg* mathau o ffeil file type
math o ffermio *eg* mathau o ffermio type of farming
math o ffibr cyhyrau *eg* mathau o ffibrau cyhyrau muscle fibre type
math o gludiant method of transport
math o gofnodion *eg* minutes type
math o gorff *eg* mathau o gyrff body type
math o siart *eg* mathau o siart chart type
mathau eraill o ofal *ell* alternative forms of care
mathau o fwyd *ell* types of food; classes of food
mathau o ffeiliau types of files
mathau o gymorth *ell* types of support
mathemateg *eb* mathematics
mathemateg bur *eb* pure mathematics
mathemateg ddinesig *eb* civic mathematics
mathemateg gymhwysol *eb* applied mathematics
mathemategol *ans* mathematical
math-wirio *be* type checking
mawn *eg* peat
mawn amorffaidd *eg* amorphous peat
mawn ffibrog *eg* fibrous peat
mawnog *eb* mawnogydd turbary
mawnog *eb* mawnogydd peat bog
mawreddog *ans* majestic
mawrhydi *eg* majesty
Mawrion, y *ell* Grandees
Mawrth (y blaned) *eg* Mars
mazurka *eg* mazurkas mazurka
McCarthiaeth *eb* McCarthyism
mecaneg *eb* mechanics
mecaneiddiad *eg* mechanization
mecaneiddio *be* mechanize
mecanodderbynnydd *eg* mecanodderbynyddion mechanoreceptor
mecanwaith *eg* mecanweithiau mechanism
mecanwaith amddiffyn *eg* mecanweithiau amddiffyn defence mechanism
mecanwaith anadlu *eg* mechanism of breathing
mecanwaith cydbwysol *eg* balancing mechanism
mecanwaith cyswllt *eg* chain mechanism
mecanwaith cywiro *eg* mecanweithiau cywiro correctional mechanism
mecanwaith dolen *eg* mecanweithiau dolen link mechanism
mecanwaith dychwel cyflym *eg* quick-return mechanism
mecanwaith gêr *eg* gear mechanism
mecanwaith homeostatig *eg* homeostatic mechanism
mecanwaith pawl a chlicied *eg* pawl and ratchet mechanism
mecanwaith rhyddhau cyflym *eg* quick-release mechanism
mecanwaith uniad-pìn *eg* pin-pointed mechanism
mecanyddol *ans* mechanical
meconiwm *eg* meconium
mechdeyrn *eg* mechdeyrnedd overlord
mechnïaeth *eb* bail; surety bail; suretyship
medal *eb* medalau medal
medal aur *eb* medalau aur gold medal
medial *ans* medial
mediastinwm *eg* mediastinum
Mediteranaidd *ans* Mediterranean
medrus *ans* skilled; skilful
medrydd *eg* medryddion gauge
medrydd arwyneb *eg* medryddion arwyneb scribing block
medrydd arwyneb *eg* surface gauge
medrydd bawd *eg* medryddion bawd thumb gauge
medrydd bys *eg* medryddion bys finger gauge
medrydd caliper *eg* medryddion caliper calliper gauge
medrydd deial *eg* medryddion deial dial gauge
medrydd dyfnder *eg* medryddion dyfnder depth gauge
medrydd ffiled *eg* medryddion ffiled fillet gauge

medrydd gwasgedd *eg* medryddion gwasgedd pressure gauge
medrydd gwifren *eg* medryddion gwifren wire gauge
medrydd marcio *eg* medryddion marcio marking gauge
medrydd meitr *eg* medryddion meitr mitre gauge
medrydd ongl edau *eg* medryddion ongl edau thread angle gauge
medrydd panel *eg* medryddion panel panel gauge
medrydd pensil *eg* medryddion pensil pencil gauge
medrydd pitsh edau *eg* medryddion pitsh edau thread pitch gauge
medrydd pitsh sgriw *eg* medryddion pitsh sgriw screw pitch gauge
medrydd plwg *eg* medryddion plwg plug gauge
medrydd radiws *eg* medryddion radiws radius gauge
medrydd riwl a bawd *eg* medryddion riwl a bawd rule and thumb gauge
medrydd sgriw *eg* medryddion sgriw screw gauge
medrydd slip *eg* medryddion slip slip gauge
medrydd straen *eg* medryddion straen strain gauge
medrydd teimlo *eg* medryddion teimlo feeler gauge
medrydd terfan *eg* medryddion terfan limit gauge
medrydd torch *eg* medryddion torch ring gauge
medrydd torri *eg* medryddion torri cutting gauge
medrydd uchder *eg* medryddion uchder height gauge
medrydd uchder fernier *eg* medryddion uchder fernier vernier height gauge
medryddu *be* gauge
medwla *eg* medulla
medwla oblongata *eg* medulla oblongata
medwla y chwarren adrenal *eg* adrenal medulla
medwlaidd *ans* medullary
meddal *ans* soft
meddalnod *eg* meddalnodau flat
meddalnod dwbl *eg* meddalnodau dwbl double flat
meddalu *be* soften
meddalwch *eg* softness
meddalwedd *eg/b* software
meddalwedd arddangos *eb* demo software
meddalwedd beta *eb* beta software
meddalwedd cychwyn *eb* starting software
meddalwedd cyfieithu *eb* translation software
meddalwedd cyhoeddi bwrdd gwaith *eb* desktop publishing software
meddalwedd cyrsiau *eb* courseware
meddalwedd fasnachol *eb* commercial software
meddalwedd gwirio firysau *eb* virus checking software
meddalwedd gwrthfirysau *eg* anti-virus software
meddalwedd hidlo *eb* filtering software
meddalwedd parth cyhoeddus *eb* public domain software
meddalwedd prosesu geiriau *eb* word processing software
meddalwedd rhaglenni *eb* applications software
meddalwedd rhwystro *eb* blocking software
meddalwedd system *eb* system software
meddalwedd system weithredu *eb* operating system software
meddalwedd taenlen *eb* spreadsheet software
meddalwedd wedi'i diogelu *eb* protected software
meddalydd *eg* meddalyddion softener
meddalydd dŵr *eg* meddalyddion dŵr water softener
meddiannaeth (filwrol) *eb* occupation
meddiannau a seciwlareiddiwyd *ell* secularizations
meddiannol *ans* possessive
meddiannu *be* occupy
meddiant *eg* meddiannau possession; seisin
meddiant gorfodol *eg* requisition
meddiant o'r bêl *eg* possession of the ball
meddiant unigol *eg* individual possession
meddw *ans* drunk
meddwl *be* thinking
meddwl *eg* meddyliau thought
meddwl creadigol *be* creative thinking
meddwl cyn-gysyniadol *eg* meddyliau cyn-gysyniadol pre-conceptual thought
meddwl dargyfeiriol *eg* divergent thinking
meddwl eiconig *be* iconic thinking
meddwl enactif *be* enactive thinking
meddwl grŵp *be* groupthink
meddwl gweithredu diriaethol *eg* concrete operational thought
meddwl gweithredu ffurfiol *eg* formal operational thought
meddwl haniaethol *eg* abstract thought
meddwl symbolaidd *be* symbolic thinking
meddwl sythweledol *eg* intuitive thought
meddwl, y meddwl *eg* mind
meddwyn *eg* meddwon drunk
meddyg *eg* meddygon doctor; physician
meddyg cymuned *eg* meddygon cymuned community physician
meddyg teulu *eg* meddygon teulu family doctor; family practitioner
meddyg teulu *eg* meddygon teulu general practitioner
meddyg tŷ *eg* meddygon tŷ house officer
meddygaeth *eb* medicine
meddygaeth amgen *eb* alternative medicine
meddygaeth arennau *eb* renal medicine
meddygaeth ataliol *eb* preventive medicine
meddygaeth gyflenwol *eb* complementary medicine
meddygaeth gyffredinol *eb* general medicine
meddygaeth y frest *eb* chest medicine
meddygfa *eb* meddygfeydd surgery
meddyginiaeth *eb* meddyginiaethau medication
meddygol *ans* medical
meddyliau awtomatig *ell* automatic thoughts
meddyliol *ans* mental

meddyliwr beirniadol *eg* meddylwyr beirniadol critical thinker
mefus *ell* strawberries
megabeit *eg* megabeitiau megabyte
megacaryocyt *eg* megacaryocytau megakaryocyte
megacnewyllyn *eg* meganucleus
megafolt (MV) *eg* megafoltiau megavolt
megalith *eg* megalithiau megalith
megalopolis *eg* megalopolisiau megalopolis
megasbor *eg* megasborau megaspore
megatherm *eg* megathermau megatherm
Megillah *eg* Megillot Megillah
megin *eb* meginau bellows
megin droed *eb* meginau troed foot bellows
megin droed chwyth dwbl *eb* meginau troed chwyth dwbl double blast foot bellows
megin organ *eb* meginau organ organ bellows
megohm *eg* megohmau megohm
meic cyswllt *eg* meiciau cyswllt contact mike
meidon *eb* meidonau mediant
meidraidd *ans* finite
meillionen *eb* meillion clover
meinciwr *eg* meincwyr bencher
meincnod *eg* meincnodau benchmark
Meincnod Dros Dro *eg* Temporary Bench Mark (TBM)
Meincnod Ordnans *eg* Ordnance Bench Mark (OBM)
meincnodi *be* benchmarking
meinder *eg* fineness
meindwr *eg* meindyrau spire
meingefn (llyfr) *eg* meingefnau spine
meingefnol *ans* lumbar
meini prawf derbyn *ell* admissions criteria
meini prawf dylunio *ell* design criteria
meini prawf perfformiad *ell* performance criteria
meini prawf targed *ell* target criteria
meintiau o ddata *ell* quantities of data
meintiau papur *ell* paper sizes
meintiau papur rhyngwladol *ell* international paper sizes
meintiol *ans* quantitative
meintioli *be* quantify
meinwe *eg/b* meinweoedd tissue
meinwe areolaidd *eb* areolar tissue
meinwe bloneg *eb* meinweoedd bloneg adipose tissue
meinwe craith *eb* scar tissue
meinwe cyhyrau *eg* muscle tissue
meinwe daear *eg* ground tissue
meinwe feddal *eb* meinweoedd meddal soft tissue
meinwe gynhaliol *eb* meinweoedd cynhaliol supporting tissue
▶ **meinwe gyswllt** *eb* connective tissue
meinwe nerfol *eb* nervous tissue
meinwe patrymu *eb* meinweoedd patrymu organizer
meinwe patrymu'r cnewyllan *eg* nucleolar organiser
meinwe planhigion *eb* meinweoedd planhigion plant tissue
meinwe ronynnog *eb* meinweoedd gronynnog granulation tissue
meinwe sythu *eg* erectile tissue
meinweoedd meithrin *ell* culture tissues
meiosis *eg* meiosis
meiotig *ans* meiotic
meipen *eb* maip swede; turnip
meis *eb* meisiau mise
Meistersinger *eg* Meistersinger Mastersinger
meistr *ans* master
meistr *eg* meistri master
meistr mwstro *eg* meistri mwstro muster master
meistr y roliau *eg* master of the rolls
▶ **meistr-dâp** *eg* meistrdapiau master tape
▶ **meistr-ddisg** *eg/b* meistrddisgiau master disk
meistrddogfen *eb* meistrddogfenni master document
meistres *eb* meistresi mistress
meistres y bale *eb* meistresi'r bale ballet mistress
▶ **meistr-ffeil** *eb* meistrffeiliau master file
meistrolaeth *eb* mastery
meistroli *be* master
meistrolwg *eb* master view
▶ **meistr-raglen** *eb* meistr-raglenni master program
meistr-sleid *eg* meistrsleidiau master slide
meitr *eg* meitrau mitre
meitr clo *eg* meitrau clo keyed mitre
meitr cynffonnog *eg* meitrau cynffonnog mitre dovetail
meitr cynffonnog cudd *eg* meitrau cynffonnog cudd secret mitre dovetail
meitro *be* mitre
meitrog *ans* mitred
meithrin *be* culture
meithrin meinweoedd planhigol *be* plant tissue culture
meithrin rheolaeth *be* develop control
meithrin sgiliau *be* develop skills
meithrinfa *eb* meithrinfeydd nursery; crèche
meithrinfa drwyddedig *eb* meithrinfeydd trwyddedig registered nursery
meithrinfa ddydd *eb* meithrinfeydd dydd day nursery
meithriniad *eg* meithriniadau culture
meithriniad meinwe *eg* meithriniadau meinwe tissue culture
meithriniad pur o facteria *eg* pure culture of bacteria
melamin *eg* melamine
melamin fformaldehyd *eg* melamine formaldehyde
melan y ddinas *eb* city blues
melanedd diwydiannol *eg* industrial melanism
Melanesaidd *ans* Melanesian
melanin *eg* melanin

melanocyt *eg* melanocytau melanocyte
melanoffor *eg* melanofforau melanophore
melfaréd *eg* corduroy
melfaréd main *eg* needlecord
melfed *eg* melfedau velvet
melfedîn *eg* melfediniau velveteen
melin *eb* melinau mill
melin bêl *eb* melinau pêl ball mill
melin droedlath *eb* melinau troedlath treadmill
melin gleio *eb* melinau cleio pug mill
melin gleio fertigol *eb* melinau cleio fertigol vertical pug mill
melin gleio lorweddol *eb* melinau cleio llorweddol horizontal pug mill
melin gotwm *eb* melinau cotwm ginnery
melin lifio *eb* melinau llifio sawmill
melin strip *eb* melinau strip strip mill
melin strip boeth *eb* melinau strip poeth hot strip mill
melin strip ddi-dor *eb* melinau strip di-dor continuous strip mill
melin strip oer *eb* melinau strip oer cold strip mill
melin wlân *eb* melinau gwlân woollen mill
melin wynt *eb* melinau gwynt windmill
melino *be* mill
melino confensiynol *be* conventional milling
melino dringol *eg* climb milling
melinwr *eg* melinwyr milling cutter
melinwr agennu *be* melinwyr agennu slotting milling cutter
melinwr ceugrwm *eg* melinwyr ceugrwm concave milling cutter
melinwr cragen *eg* melinwyr cragen shell milling cutter
melinwr dant union *eg* melinwyr dant union straight-toothed milling cutter
melinwr hedegog *ans* melinwyr hedegog fly milling cutter
melinwr ochr *eg* melinwyr ochr end milling cutter
melinwr ochr ac wyneb *eg* melinwyr ochr ac wyneb side and face milling cutter
melinwr plaen *eg* melinwyr plaen plain milling cutter
melinwr rhigol T *eg* melinwyr rhigol tee-slot milling cutter
melinwr sbiral *eg* melinwyr sbiral spiral milling cutter
melinwr sedd glo *eg* melinwyr sedd glo key-seat milling cutter
melinwr slab *eg* melinwyr slab slab milling cutter
melinwr wyneb mawr *eg* melinwyr wyneb mawr large face milling cutter
melinydd *eg* melinwyr miller
melisma *eg* melismata melisma
melismataidd *ans* melismatic
melodaidd *ans* melodic
melodi *eb* melodïau melody
melodig *ans* melodic
melodrama *eb* melodramâu melodrama
melyn *eg* yellow
melyn alisarin *eg* alizarin yellow
melyn cadmiwm *eg* cadmium yellow
melyn cadmiwm canol *eg* mid cadmium yellow
melyn cadmiwm golau *eg* pale cadmium yellow
melyn crôm canol *eg* mid chrome yellow
melyn crôm dwfn *eg* deep chrome yellow
melyn crôm golau *eg* pale chrome yellow
melyn dwfn Napoli *eg* deep Naples yellow
melyn golau *eg* pale yellow
melyn golau *eg* light straw
melyn lemwn dwfn *eg* deep lemon yellow
melyn lemwn golau *eg* pale lemon yellow
melyn Napoli *eg* Naples yellow
melyn tywyll *eg* dark straw
melyn y friallen *eg* primrose yellow
melynfrown *eg* amber brown
melyngoch *eg* amber
melynion ac orenau *ell* yellows and oranges
melynu *be* yellowing
melynwy *eg* egg yolk; yolk
melysion *ell* confectionery
memo *eg* memos memo
memo awtobeilot *eg* memos awtobeilot autopilot memo
memorandwm *eg* memoranda memorandum
memorandwm sefydlu *eg* memoranda sefydlu memorandum of association
memrwn *eg* memrynau parchment
Mendelaidd *ans* Mendelian
mendelefiwm *eg* mendelevium
menisgws *eg* menisgi meniscus
Mensiefig *eg* Mensiefigiaid Menshevik
Mensiefigaidd *ans* Menshevik
menter *eb* mentrau enterprise; initiative; venture
menter breifat *eb* mentrau preifat private enterprise
menter hyfforddi *eb* training initiative
menter sector cyhoeddus *eb* public sector venture
mentor *eg* mentoriaid mentor
mentora *be* mentoring
mentoriaeth *eb* mentoriaethau mentorship
mentro *be* risk
mentrwr agored *eg* mentrwyr agored silly mid-off
mentrwr coes *eg* mentrwyr coes silly mid-on
Mentrwyr Masnachol *ell* Merchant Adventurers
menyn *eg* butter
menyn brandi *eg* brandy butter
mêr *eg* bone marrow; marrow
mêr brasterog *eg* fatty marrow
mercantiliaeth *eb* mercantilism
mercwri (Hg) *eg* mercury
mercwrig *ans* mercuric
merch y bêl *eb* merched y bêl ball girl
merch y tywydd *eb* merched tywydd weather forecaster
merch-dâp *eg* merchdapiau son tape

Merched mewn Gwyddoniaeth a Pheirianneg *ell* WISE: Women in Science and Engineering
Mercher (y blaned) *eg* Mercury
merddwr *eg* merddyfroedd backwater; stagnant water
meridian *eg* meridianau meridian
meristem *eb* meristemau meristem
meristem apigol *eg* apical meristem
meristem brimordiol *eb* primordial meristem
meristem eilaidd *eg* secondary meristem
meristematig *ans* meristematic
meritocratiaeth *eb* meritocracy
merlota *be* pony trekking
merlotwr *eg* merlotwyr pony trekker
merllyn *eg* merllynnoedd stagnant pond
Merofingaidd *ans* Merovingian
meromorffig *ans* meromorphic
Mers *eg* Marches
merthyr *eg* merthyron martyr
merthyrdod *eg* martyrdom
merthyroleg *eb* martyrology
merthyron Mari *ell* Marian martyrs
Merthyron Pabyddol *ell* Catholic Martyrs
Merthyron Tolpuddle *ell* Tolpuddle Martyrs
merthyru *be* martyr
mesa *eg* mesâu mesa
Meseia (mewn Cristnogaeth) *eg* Messiah
Meseia (mewn Iddewiaeth) *eg* Mashiach
mesenteri *eg* mesentery
mesenterig *ans* mesenteric
mesmeriaeth *eb* mesmerism
mesobr *eg* mesobrau pannage
mesocwrtig *ans* mesokurtic
mesoderm *eg* mesodermau mesoderm
mesodermig *ans* mesodermic
mesoffyl *eg* mesoffylau mesophyll
mesoffylaidd *ans* mesophyllous
mesoffyt *eg* mesoffytau mesophyte
mesogloea *eg* mesogloea
mesolithig *ans* mesolithic
meson *eg* mesonau meson
mesosternwm *eg* mesosterna mesosternum
mesostom *eg* mesostomau mesostome
mesotint *eg* mesotintiau mezzotint
mesothoracs *eg* mesothorax
mestiso *eg* mestisos mestizo
mesur *be* measure; quantify
mesur (maint) *eg* mesurau measure; quantity
mesur (mewn barddoniaeth etc) *eg* mesurau metre
mesur a marcio *be* measuring and marking out
mesur amrywiant *be* measure of variability
mesur caeth *eg* mesurau caeth strict metre
mesur canolduedd *be* measure of central tendency
mesur cyffredin (MC) *eg* common metre
Mesur Diwygio *eg* Reform Bill
mesur fector *eg* mesurau fector vector quantity
mesur gwrthfirysau *eg* mesurau gwrthfirysau anti-virus measure
mesur hir *eg* mesurau hir long metre
mesur hylif *eg* mesurau hylif liquid measure
Mesur Iawnderau *eg* Bill of Rights
mesur metrig *eg* metric measure
mesur o wasgariad *eg* measure of spread
mesur pellteroedd *be* measure distances
mesur rheoli *eg* mesuriadau rheoli control measure
mesur rhydd *eg* mesurau rhydd free metre
mesur rhyddfrydoli masnach *eg* mesurau rhyddfrydoli masnach trade liberalisation measure
mesur seneddol *eg* bill
mesur sgalar *eg* mesurau sgalar scalar quantity
mesur troi *eg* measure of turn
mesuradwy *ans* measurable; quantifiable
mesurau anymwthiol *be* unobtrusive measures
mesureg *eb* mensuration
mesuriad *eg* mesuriadau determination
mesuriad *eg* mesuriadau measurement
mesuriad anterth llif *eg* peak flow measurement
mesuriad bôn *eg* mesuriadau bôn butt measurement
mesuriad clun *eg* mesuriadau cluniau hip measurement
mesuriad corfforol *eg* mesuriadau corfforol physical measurement
mesuriad ffisiolegol *eg* mesuriadau ffisiolegol physiological measurement
mesuriad rheoli *eg* control measurement
mesuriadau llinol *ell* linear measurement
mesuriadau o ben i ben *ell* overall dimensions
mesuriadau egni *ell* measurements of energy
mesurydd (ar sgrin cyfrifiadur) *eg* mesuryddion ruler
mesurydd (yn gyffredinol) *eg* mesuryddion meter
mesurydd copïo *eg* mesuryddion copïo copy ruler
mesurydd digidol *eg* mesuryddion digidol digital meter
mesurydd dwysedd gwefr *eg* charge density meter
mesurydd fertigol *eg* mesuryddion fertigol vertical ruler
mesurydd grym *eg* mesuryddion grym forcemeter
mesurydd gwrthyriad haearn symudol *eg* moving-iron repulsion meter
mesurydd gwyn *eg* mesuryddion gwyn white meter
mesurydd lefelau sain *eg* sound level meter
mesurydd llif agorfa awchlym *eg* mesuryddion llif agorfa awchlym sharp-edged orifice flow meter
mesurydd llorweddol *eg* mesuryddion llorweddol horizontal ruler
mesurydd maes trydanol *eg* mesuryddion maes trydanol electric field meter
mesurydd newton *eg* mesuryddion newton newtonmeter
mesurydd pH *eg* pH-meter
mesurydd rhagdal *eg* mesuryddion rhagdal prepayment meter

mesurydd unioni hanner ton *eg* half-wave rectifier meter
mesurydd Venturi *eg* Venturi meter
mesuryn *eg* mesurynnau ordinate
mesuryn canol *eg* mesurynnau canol mid-ordinate
metabolaeth *eb* metabolism
metabolaeth ryngol *eb* intermediary metabolism
metabolaeth waelodol *eb* basal metabolism
metabolaidd *ans* metabolic
metabolyn *eg* metabolynnau metabolite
metabwynt *eg* metabwyntiau metacentre
metacarpol *ans* metacarpal
metacarpws *eg* metacarpus
metaddadansoddi *be* meta-analysis
metafoeseg *eb* meta-ethics
metaffas *eg* metaffasau metaphase
metaffeil *eb* metaffeiliau metafile
metaffisegol *ans* metaphysical
meta-gof *eb* metamemory
metaieithyddiaeth *eb* metalinguistics
metaieithyddol *ans* meta-linguistic
metameraeth *eb* metamerism
metamorffedig *ans* metamorphosed
metamorffedd *eb* metamorphy
metamorffeg *eb* metamorphism
metamorffig *ans* metamorphic
metamorffosis *eg* metamorphosis
metasefydlog *ans* metastable
metasentrig *ans* metacentric
Metasoa *ell* Metasoa
metasternwm *eg* metasternum
metasylem *eb* metaxylem
metatarsol *ans* metatarsal
metatarsws *eg* metatarsus
metathesis *eg* metathesis
metathoracs *eg* metathorax
metawybyddiaeth *eb* metacognition
metel *eg* metelau metal
metel alcalïaidd *eg* metelau alcalïaidd alkali metal
metel anfferrus *eg* metelau anfferrus non-ferrous metal
metel babbitt *eg* babbitt metal
metel Britannia *eg* Britannia metal
metel cerfiedig *eg* sculpt metal
metel ciwbig corff-ganolog *eg* metelau ciwbig corff-ganolog body-centred cubic metal
metel cloch *eg* bell metal
metel ehangedig *eg* metelau ehangedig expanded metal
metel euro *eg* gilding metal
metel fferrus *eg* metelau fferrus ferrous metal
metel gorgynnes *eg* metelau gorgynnes hot metal
metel gwrth-ffrithiant *eg* metelau gwrth-ffrithiant anti-friction metal
metel Muntz *eg* Muntz metal
metel mwynol alcalïaidd *eg* alkaline earth metal
metel nobl *eg* noble metal
metel sgrap *eg* metelau sgrap scrap metal
metel tawdd *eg* molten metal
metel teip *eg* type metal
metel tenau *eg* thin metal
metel trosiannol *eg* metelau trosiannol transition metal
metel trowasg *eg* spun metal
metel trwm *eg* metelau trwm heavy metal
meteleg *eb* metallurgy
metelegol *ans* metallurgical
meteleiddio *be* metallizing
metelifferaidd *ans* metalliferous
metelig *ans* metallic
meteloid *ans* metalloid
meteor *eg* meteorau meteor
meteorig *ans* meteoric
meteoroleg *eb* meteorology
meteorolegol *ans* meteorologic
meteoryn *eg* meteorynnau meteorite
metlin *eg* metalling
metr *eg* metrau metre
metr ciwbig *eg* metrau ciwbig cubic metre
metrig *ans* metric
metron *eb* metronau matron
metronom *eg* metronomau metronome
methan *eg* methane
methanal *eg* methanal
methanamid *eg* methanamide
methanol *eg* methanol
methdaliad *eg* methdaliadau bankruptcy
methdaliad *eg* methdaliadau bankruptcy; insolvency; liquidation
methdalwr *eg* methdalwyr bankrupt; insolvent; defaulter
methedig *ans* infirm; invalid
methiant *eg* methiannau failure; breakdown
methiant cyfrifiadurol *eg* methiannau cyfrifiadurol computer breakdown
methiant marchnad lafur *eg* labour market failure
methiant y farchnad *eg* market failure
methiant y galon *eg* heart failure
methionin *eg* methionine
methocsibensen *eg* methoxybenzene
methocsiethan *eg* methoxyethane
methocsimethan *eg* methoxymethane
2-methocsi-2-methylpropan *eg* 2-methoxy-2-methylpropane
Methodist *eg* Methodistiaid Methodist
Methodistaidd *ans* Methodist
Methodistiaeth *eb* Methodism
Methodistiaeth Galfinaidd *eb* Calvinistic Methodism
Methodistiaeth Gyntefig *eb* Primitive Methodism
Methodistiaeth Wesleaidd *eb* Wesleyan Methodism
methodoleg *eb* methodology
methodoleg ddwy-dasg *eb* dual-task methodology
methu adfer *be* can't restore

methu agor cyfeiriadur *be* can't open directory
methu agor ffeil *be* can't open file
methu ailwneud *be* can't redo
methu dadwneud *be* can't undo
methu dirymu *be* can't revoke
methyl 2-hydrocsibensencarbocsylad *eg* methyl 2-hydroxybenzenecarboxylate
methyl oren *eg* methyl orange
methylamin *eg* methylamine
methylamoniwmclorid *eg* methylammoniumchloride
methylbensen *eg* methylbenzene
2-methylbwta-1,3-deuen *eg* 2-methylbuta-1,3-diene
3-methylbwtyl- *eg* 3-methylbutyl-
methylbwtyl *eg* methylbutyl
2-methylffenol *eg* 2-methylphenol
2-methylffenylamin *eg* 2-methylphenylamine
1-methyl-2-nitrobensen *eg* 1-methyl-2-nitrobenzene
4-methylpent-3-en-2-on *eg* 4-methylpent-3-en-2-one
2-methylpropan *eg* 2-methylpropane
2-methylpropan-2-ol *eg* 2-methylpropan-2-ol
2-methylpropan-1-ol *eg* 2-methylpropan-1-ol
2-methylpropan-2-yl *eg* 2-methylpropan-2-yl
2-methylpropen *eg* 2-methylpropene
2-methylpropyl *eg* 2-methylpropyl
2-methyl-1,3,5-trinitrobensen *eg* 2-methyl-1,3,5-trinitrobenzene
methylu *be* methylate
meudwy *eg* meudwyiaid hermit; recluse
meudwyaidd *ans* eremitical
mewn amrediad *ans* in-range
mewn bri *ans* in vogue
mewn bywoliaeth *ans* beneficed
mewn cyfrannedd *adf* in proportion
mewn cyfrannedd da in good proportion
mewn cyfres in series
mewn gofal *ans* in care
mewn iawn luniad in register
mewn llinell *ans* in-line
mewn paralacs in parallax
mewn perygl at risk
mewn union bryd just in time
mewnafael *eb* inward grasp
mewnanadliad *eg* mewnanadliadau inhalation; inspiration
mewnanadlu *be* inhale; inspire
mewnanadlydd *eg* mewnanadlwyr inhaler
mewnblaniad *eg* mewnblaniadau implant
mewnblannu *be* implant; embed
mewnblannu cell yn y brych *be* implant a cell in the placenta
mewnblyg *ans* introvert
mewnblygu *be* infold
mewnbwn *eg* mewnbynnau input
Mewnbwn / Allbwn (M/A) Input / Output
mewnbwn ac allbwn input and output
mewnbwn angenrheidiol *eg* input required
mewnbwn aml-linell *eg* mewnbynnau aml-linell multiline input
mewnbwn byfferog *eg* mewnbynnau byfferog buffered input
mewnbwn cyfalaf *eg* capital input
mewnbwn mewn tablau *eg* input in tables
mewnbynnu *be* input
mewnbynnu data *be* data entering
mewnbynnu gorchwyl pell *be* remote job entry
mewndarddiad *eg* endogenesis
mewndarddol *ans* endogenous
mewndir *eg* interior
mewndirol *ans* inland; interior
mewndiwbio *be* intubation
mewnddodi *be* infix
mewnddodiad *eg* mewnddodiaid infix
mewnfa *eb* mewnfeydd inlet
mewnfan *eg* mewnfannau point of insertion
mewnflwch *eg* inbox
mewnfoleciwlaidd *ans* intramolecular
mewnforio *be* import
mewnforio gwrthrychau *be* import objects
mewnforio testun *be* import text
mewnforiwr *eg* mewnforwyr importer
mewnforyn *eg* mewnforion import
mewnfridio *be* inbreed
mewnfudiad *eg* mewnfudiadau immigration
mewnfudo *be* immigrate
mewnfudwr *eg* mewnfudwyr immigrant
mewnffrwydrad *eg* mewnffrwydradau implosion
mewnganol *eg* mewnganolau incentre
mewngapsiwleiddio *be* encapsulation
mewngellol *ans* intracellular
mewngofnodi *be* log in; log on
mewngraig *eb* mewngreigiau inlier
mewngylch *eg* mewngylchoedd incircle; inscribed circle
mewngyrch *eg* input
mewngyrchol *ans* centripetal
mewniad *eg* mewniadau insertion
mewnlenwad *eg* mewnlenwadau infilling
mewnlif *eg* mewnlifoedd intake; input stream; illuviation
mewnlif *eg* mewnlifoedd input stream
mewnlif / all-lif *eg* mewnlifoedd / all-lifoedd input / output stream
mewnlifiad *eg* mewnlifiadau uptake
mewnlifol *ans* illuvial
mewnol (=domestig) *ans* domestic
mewnol (=tu mewn i gorff) *ans* internal
mewnol (=tu mewn i adeilad) *ans* interior
mewnol (=tuag i mewn) *ans* inward
mewnol (=tu mewn i gwmni neu sefydliad) *ans* in-house
mewnol (am feddyliau, teimladau) *ans* inner

mewnoli (ymyl tudalen) *be* indent
mewnoli (yn gyffredinol) *be* internalize
mewnoli ar y chwith *be* left indent
mewnoli ar y dde *be* right indent
mewnoliad *eg* mewnoliadau indent
mewnoliad corff testun *eg* mewnoliadau corff testun text body indent
mewnoliad crog *eg* mewnoliadau crog hanging indent
mewnoliad llinell gyntaf *eg* mewnoliadau llinell gyntaf first-line indent
mewnosod (gwaith pren etc addurniedig) *be* inlay
mewnosod (yn gyffredinol) *be* insert
mewn-osod *be* lay-in
mewnosod adran *be* insert section
mewnosod allwedd *be* insert legend
mewnosod allwedd gynradd *be* insert primary key
mewnosod amlen *be* insert envelope
mewnosod amser *be* insert time
mewnosod ategyn *be* insert plug-in
mewnosod ategyn fideo *be* insert video plug-in
mewnosod ategyn sain *be* insert sound plug-in
mewnosod awtodestun *be* insert autotext
mewnosod botwm URL *be* insert URL button
mewnosod bwlch di-dor *be* insert non-breaking space
mewnosod canlyniad *be* insert result
mewnosod cardiau busnes *be* insert business cards
mewnosod celloedd *be* insert cells
mewnosod celloedd i lawr *be* insert cells down
mewnosod celloedd i'r dde *be* insert cells right
mewnosod cofnod heb rif *be* insert unnumbered entry
mewnosod cofnod llyfryddiaeth *be* insert bibliography entry
mewnosod cofnod mynegai *be* insert index entry
mewnosod colofn *be* insert column
mewnosod colofnau cronfa ddata *be* insert database columns
mewnosod cyfeirnod *be* insert reference
mewnosod cyfeirnod maes *be* insert field reference
mewnosod cyswllt *be* insert link
mewnosod cysylltnod dewisol *be* insert optional hyphen
mewnosod cysylltnod di-dor *be* insert non-breaking hyphen
mewnosod dalen *be* insert sheet
mewnosod data *be* insert data
mewnosod data ymholiad *be* insert query data
mewnosod delwedd *be* insert image
mewnosod dogfen *be* insert document
mewnosod dyddiad *be* insert date
mewnosod egluryn data *be* insert data caption
mewnosod enw *be* insert name
mewnosod fel copi *be* insert as copy
mewnosod fel cyswllt *be* insert as link
mewnosod fel hypergyswllt *be* insert as hyperlink
mewnosod fertigol *be* insert vertical
mewnosod fideo *be* insert video
mewnosod ffeil *be* insert file
mewnosod fformiwla *be* insert formula
mewnosod fformiwla matrics *be* insert matrix formula
mewnosod ffrâm *be* insert frame
mewnosod ffrâm â llaw *be* insert frame manually
mewnosod ffrâm testun *be* insert text frame
mewnosod gorchymyn *be* insert command
mewnosod graffigau *be* insert graphics
mewnosod grŵp *be* insert group
mewnosod gwrthrych *be* insert object
mewnosod gwrthrychau eraill *be* insert other objects
mewnosod haen *be* insert layer
mewnosod hypergyswllt *be* insert hyperlink
mewnosod label data *be* insert data label
mewnosod llofnod *be* insert signature
mewnosod llorweddol *be* insert horizontal
mewnosod maes awdur *be* insert author field
mewnosod maes cyfun *be* insert merge field
mewnosod maes ffeil *be* insert file field
mewnosod maes tudalen *be* insert page field
mewnosod mesurydd *be* insert ruler
mewnosod mesurydd llorweddol *be* insert horizontal ruler
mewnosod mewn cynhwysydd *be* insert in container
mewnosod mynegai *be* insert index
mewnosod nod arbennig *be* insert special character
mewnosod nod mynegai *be* insert index marker
mewnosod nod tudalen *be* insert bookmark
mewnosod nodyn *be* insert note
mewnosod ôl-nodyn yn uniongyrchol *be* insert endnote directly
mewnosod paragraff *be* insert paragraph
mewnosod pennyn *be* insert header
mewnosod pwnc *be* insert subject
mewnosod pwynt glud *be* insert glue point
mewnosod pwynt snap *be* insert snap point
mewnosod rhaglennig *be* insert applet
mewnosod rheolyddion *be* insert controls
mewnosod rhes *be* insert row
mewnosod rhes newydd *be* insert new row
mewnosod rhif tudalen *be* insert page number
mewnosod sain *be* insert sound
mewnosod sgript *be* insert script
mewnosod siart *be* insert chart
mewnosod sleid *be* insert slide
mewnosod sleid yn uniongyrchol *be* insert slide direct
mewnosod swyddogaeth *be* insert function
mewnosod sylw *be* insert comment
mewnosod sylw ar y fersiwn *be* insert version comment

mewnosod tabl *be* insert table
mewnosod teitl *be* insert title
mewnosod teitl dogfen *be* insert document title
mewnosod testun *be* insert text
mewnosod testun ffynhonnell *be* insert source text
mewnosod toriad *be* insert break
mewnosod toriad â llaw *be* insert manual break
mewnosod toriad colofn *be* insert column break
mewnosod toriad rhes *be* insert row break
mewnosod troednodyn *be* insert footnote
mewnosod troednodyn yn uniongyrchol *be* insert footnote directly
mewnosod troedyn *be* insert footer
mewnosod tudalen *be* insert page
mewnosod uniad *be* insert join
mewnosod yn llorweddol *be* insert horizontally
mewnosod ystodau labeli *be* insert label ranges
mewnosodiad *eg* mewnosodiadau insert
mewnosodiad (gwaith pren etc addurniedig) *eg* mewnosodiadau inlay
mewnosodiad (yn gyffredinol) *eg* mewnosodiadau inset
mewnrewlifol *ans* englacial
mewnrwyd *eb* intranet
mewnrywogaethol *ans* intraspecific
mewnsyllu *be* introspection
mewnwelediad *eg* mewnwelediadau insight
mewnwr (mewn pêl-droed) *eg* mewnwyr inside half
mewnwr (mewn pêl-droed) *eg* mewnwyr inside forward
mewnwr (mewn rygbi) *eg* mewnwyr scrum-half
mewnwr chwith *eg* mewnwyr chwith inside left
mewnwr de *eg* mewnwyr de inside right
mewnwthiad *eg* mewnwthiadau intrusion
mewnwthiol *ans* intrusive
mewnwythiennol *ans* intravenous
meysydd unffurf *ell* uniform fields
mezzo-soprano *eb* lleisiau mezzo-soprano mezzo-soprano
mica *eg* mica
micela *eg* micelau micella
micro *ans* micro
microb *eg* microbau microbe
microbioleg *eb* microbiology
microbiolegydd *eg* microbiolegwyr microbiologist
microbrosesydd *eg* microbrosesyddion microprocessor
microbwyntil *eg* microbwyntilau microburin
microcnewyllyn *eg* micronucleus
microcosm *eg* microcosmau microcosm
microdechnoleg *eb* microtechnology
microdiwbyn *eg* microdiwbynnau microtubule
microdon *eb* microdonnau microwave
microeiliad *eg/b* microeiliadau microsecond
microelectroneg *eb* microelectronics
microfaethyn *eg* microfaethion micronutrient
microfilws *eg* microfili microvillus
microfyd *eg* microfydoedd microworld
microffarad *eg* microffaradau microfarad
microffibrolyn *eg* microffibril
microffilm *eb* microffilmiau microfilm
microffilm o gyfrifiadur *eg* computer output to microfilm
microffish *eg* microffishau microfiche
microffon *eg* microffonau microphone
microffon coil symudol *eg* microffonau coil symudol moving coil microphone
microgerdyn *eg* microgardiau microcard
microgod *eg* microgodau microcode
microgrisialog *ans* micro-crystalline
microgyfrifiadur *eg* microgyfrifiaduron microcomputer
microgylched *eb* microgylchedau microcircuit
microhinsawdd *eg* microclimate
microhinsoddeg *eb* microclimatology
microhm *eg* microhmau microhm
microlith *eg* microlithiau microlith
micromedr *eg* micromedrau micrometer
micromedr allanol *eg* micromedrau allanol outside micrometer
micromedr mewnol *eg* micromedrau mewnol inside micrometer
micrometr *eg* micrometrau micrometre
micrometr llwyfan *eg* stage micrometer
micron *eg* micronau micron
micro-organeb *eb* micro-organebau micro-organism
micro-organebau'r pridd *ell* soil micro-organisms
micropyl *eg* micropylau micropyle
microraglennu *be* microprogramming
microsbor *eg* microspore
microsboroffyl *eg* microsporophyll
microsglodyn *eg* microsglodion microchip
microsgop *eg* microsgopau microscope
microsgop cyfansawdd optegol *eg* optical compound microscope
microsgop golau *eg* microsgopau golau light microscope
microsgop maes ïonau *eg* field ion microscope
microsgop teithiol *eg* microsgopau teithiol travelling microscope
microsgopeg *eb* microscopy
microsgopig *ans* microscopic
microsom *eg* microsomau microsome
microswitsh *eg* microswitshis microswitch
microtôn *eg* microtonau microtone
microtonawl *ans* microtonal
microtonyddiaeth *eg* microtonyddiaethau microtonality
microtherm *eg* microthermau microtherm
Midrash *eg* Midrashim Midrash
mignen neu halwyndir marsh or salting
migwyn *eg* sphagnum
migwyn *eg* bog moss
mil *eb* miloedd thousand

mileniwm *eg* millenium
milet *eg* millet
milfed *eg* milfedau thousandth
milflwyddiaeth *eb* millenarianism
milibar *eg* milibarrau millibar
mililitr *eg* mililitrau millilitre
milimetr *eg* milimetrau millimetre
milisia *eg* militia
militariaeth *eb* militarism
militarydd *eg* militarwyr militarist
miliwm *eg* milium
miliwn *eb* miliynau million
milwr arfog *eg* milwyr arfog man-at-arms
milwr cyffredin *eg* milwyr cyffredin private
milwr gerila *eg* milwyr gerila guerrilla
milwriaethus *ans* militant
milwrol *ans* military
milwyr a gasglwyd *ell* levy, levies
milwyr hunanleiddiol *ell* suicide troops
milwyr wrth gefn *ell* reserves
milltir *eb* milltiroedd mile
min (=gwefus) *eg* minion lip
min (=ymyl) *eg* minion edge
min (sgrafell) *eg* burr
min cyllell *eg* knife edge
mini *ans* mini
minialaidd *ans* osculating
minialedd *eg* minialeddau osculation
minialu *be* osculate
minigyfrifiadur *eg* minigyfrifiaduron minicomputer
minimalaidd *ans* minimalist
minimaliaeth *eb* minimalism
minimalydd *eg* minimalwyr minimalist
mini-menter *eb* mini-mentrau mini-enterprise
minimol *ans* minimal
mini-project *eg* mini-projectau mini-project
miniscwl *ans* minuscule
miniwét *eg* minwetau minuet
miniwr *eg* minwyr pencil sharpener
Minoaidd *ans* Minoan
mintai *eb* minteioedd cohort
minwend *eg* minwendau minuend
minws *eg* minysau minus
mis lleuad *eg* misoedd lleuad lunar month
misel *eg* micelle
misericord *eg* misericordiau misericord
Mishnah *eg* Mishnah
mislif *eg* menstruation
mislif cydamseredig *eg* menstrual synchrony
misoedd yr haf *ell* summer months
mit *eb* mits mitten
mitocondrion *eg* mitocondria mitochondrion
mitosis *eg* mitosis
mitotig *ans* mitotic
mitzvah *eg* mitzvot mitzvah
Mithraeth *eb* Mithraism
miwon *eg* miwonau muon
miwtini *eg* mutiny
mobilistig *ans* mobilistic
mochyn bacwn *eg* moch bacwn baconer
model (am ddyn neu wrthrych) *eg* modelau model
model (am ferch) *eb* modelau model
model (am gopi bach) *eg* modelau miniature
model anallu *eg* modelau anallu incompetence model
model anwrthdrawol *eg* modelau anwrthdrawol collisionless model
model ataliol *eg* preventative model
model atchwel *eg* modelau atchwel regression model
model biofeddygol *eg* biomedical model
model bioseicogymdeithasol *eg* biopsychosocial model
model cardbord *eg* modelau cardbord cardboard model
model cred iechyd *eg* health belief model
model cyfannol *eg* holistic model
model cyfnodau newid *eg* stages of change model
model cyfrifiadurol *eg* modelau cyfrifiadurol computer model
model cymdeithasol *eg* social model
model darllen deulwybr *eg* dual-route model of reading
model data *eg* modelau data data model
model diathesis *eg* diathesis model
model didactig *eg* didactic model
model diffyg *eg* modelau diffyg deficit model
model ffeministaidd *eg* feminist model
model gweithio i raddfa *eg* scale working model
model gwniyddes *eg* modelau gwniyddes dressmaker's dummy
model gwyddonol *eg* modelau gwyddonol scientific model
model hierarchaidd *eg* modelau hierarchaidd hierarchical model
model hunanreoleiddio *eg* self-regulatory model
model laissez-faire *eg* laissez-faire model
model llenwi-gofod *eg* space-filling model
model manylder tebygolrwydd *eg* elaboration likelihood model
model meddygol *eg* modelau meddygol medical model
model meddygol o anabledd *eg* medical model of disability
model meddyliol *eg* mental model
model mewn ystum arbennig *eg* modelau mewn ystum arbennig posed model
model mosaig hylifol *eg* fluid mosaic model
model nyrsio *eg* modelau nyrsio nursing model; model of nursing
model papur *eg* modelau papur paper model
model proses *eg* process model
model pum ffactor *eg* five factor model
model rhoi grym *eg* empowerment model
model rhyngweithredol o straen *eg* transactional model of stress

model seicolegol *eg* psychological model
model straen diathesis *eg* diathesis stress model
model trawsddamcaniaethol *eg* transtheoretical model
model trosglwyddo *eg* transmission model
modelu *be* model; modelling
modelu â chlai *be* clay modelling
modelu cyfrifiadurol *be* computer modelling
modelu dau ddimensiwn *be* two dimensional modelling
modelu rhifiadol *be* numerical modelling
modelu tri dimensiwn *be* three-dimensional modelling
modem *eg* modemau modem
modem cebl *eg* modemau cebl cable modem
modem deialu *eg* modemau deialu dial-up modem
modem ffacs *eg* modemau ffacs fax modem
modern *ans* modern
moderneiddio *be* modernize
modfedd *eb* modfeddi inch
modiwl *eg* modiwlau module
modiwl newydd *eg* modiwlau newydd new module
modiwlaeth *eb* modularity
modiwlaidd *ans* modular
modiwleiddio (=amrywio llais) *be* modulate
modiwleiddio (=troi'n fodiwlau) *be* modularize
modrwy (ar fys) *eb* modrwyau ring
modrwy (mewn bioleg) *eb* modrwyau annulus
modrwyau *ell* drip rings
modrwyol *ans* annular
modrwywedd *ans* annulate
modur *eg* moduron motor; automobile
modur cerrynt union *eg* direct current motor
modur trydan *eg* moduron trydan electric motor
modurdy *eg* modurdai garage
modwlo *eg* modulo
modwlws *eg* modwli modulus
modwlws elastigedd *eg* modulus of elasticity
modyledig *ans* modulated
modyliad *eg* modyliadau modulation
modyliad osgled *eg* modyliadau osgled amplitude modulation
modyliad safle pwls *eg* pulse position modulation
modylu *be* modulate
modylydd *eg* modylyddion modulator
modd *eg* moddion means
modd *eg* moddau mode
modd addasu *eg* revise mode
modd Aeolaidd *eg* Aeolian mode
modd amlinell *eg* contour mode
modd asesu *eg* moddau asesu assessment mode
modd creu *eg* create mode
modd cyfeirio *eg* addressing mode
modd cyflwyno *eg* moddau cyflwyno presentation mode
modd cynhyrchu *eg* means of production
modd deilliedig *eg* moddau deilliedig plagal mode
modd deilliedig *eg* hypomode
modd did *eg* bitwise
modd dogfen *eg* document mode
modd Doriaidd *eg* Dorian mode
modd eglwysig *eg* moddau eglwysig ecclesiastical mode
modd eglwysig *eg* moddau eglwysig church mode
modd fformat *eg* format-mode
modd gweithredu *eg* moddau gweithredu operation mode
modd gweld *eg* view mode
modd gwerth hyd a dwyster *eg* mode of durations and intensities
modd Hypoaeloiaidd *eg* Hypoaeolian mode
modd Hypodoriaidd *eg* Hypodorian mode
modd Hypoioniaidd *eg* Hypoionian mode
modd Hypolocriaidd *eg* Hypolocrian mode
modd Hypomicsolydiaidd *eg* Hypomixolydian mode
modd Hypophrygiaidd *eg* Hypophrygian mode
modd Ionaidd *eg* Ionian mode
modd Locriaidd *eg* moddau Locriaidd Locrian mode
modd llanw *eg* fill mode
modd lluniadu *eg* drawing mode
modd mewnosod *eg* insert mode
modd mynegai *eg* index mode
modd picseli *eg* pixel mode
modd segur *eg* standby mode
modd siart *eg* chart mode
modd sylfaenol *eg* moddau sylfaenol authentic mode
modd talu *eg* means of payment
modd terfynell *eg* moddau terfynell terminal mode
modd testun *eg* text mode
moddau ffug *ell* spurious modes
modd-cyffredin *ans* common mode
moddion *eg* medicine
moddol *ans* modal
moddolrwydd *eg* modality
moes a phryn bring-and-buy
moesau *ell* morals
moeseg *eb* ethics
moeseg busnes *eb* business ethics
moeseg gymhwysol *eb* applied ethics
moeseg normadol *eb* normative ethics
moeseg sefyllfa *eb* situation ethics
moeseg ymarferol *eb* practical ethics
moesegol *ans* ethical
moesgar *ans* civil
moesol *ans* moral
moesoldeb *eg* morality
moesoldeb cydweithio *eb* morality of co-operation
moesoldeb traddodiadol *eg* traditional morality
moeth *eg* moethau luxury
moethus *ans* luxurious
mogwl *eg* mogul

moher *eg* mohair
moksha /moksa *eg* moksha /moksa
môl *eg* molau mole
môl dm-3 *eg* mol dm-3
molal *ans* molal
molaledd *eg* molality
molar *ans* molar
molaredd *eg* molarity
moldio disgyrchol *be* gravity moulding
moleciwl *eg* moleciwlau molecule
moleciwl cludo *eg* moleciwlau cludo carrier molecule
moleciwl cydrannol *eg* moleciwlau cydrannol component molecule
moleciwl cyfrannol *eg* moleciwlau cyfrannol donor molecule
moleciwl derbyn *eg* moleciwlau derbyn receptor molecule
moleciwl lipid *eg* moleciwlau lipid lipid molecule
moleciwl sy'n atynnu dŵr *eg* moleciwlau sy'n atynnu dŵr water attracting molecule
moleciwl sy'n gwrthyrru dŵr *eg* moleciwlau sy'n gwrthyrru dŵr water repelling molecule
moleciwlaidd *ans* molecular
moleciwlaidd enfawr *ans* giant molecular
moleciwlau cadwynol *ell* chain molecules
moleciwledd *eg* molecularity
moliannau *ell* lauds
moltas *eg* molteisi archivolt
molwsg *eg* molwsgiaid mollusc
molybdenwm *eg* molybdenum
moment *eg* momentau moment
moment clocwedd *eg* clockwise moment
moment deupol *eg* dipole moment
moment inertia *eg* moment of inertia
moment magnetig *eg* magnetic moment
moment momentwm *eg* moment of momentum
moment plygu *eg* bending moment
momentwm *eg* momenta momentum
momentwm llinol *eg* momenta llinol linear momentum
momentwm onglaidd *eg* momenta onglaidd angular momentum
monadnoc *eg* monadnocau monadnock
monatomig *ans* monatomic
Monel *eg* Monel
monig *ans* monic
monitor (=sgrin) *eg* monitorau monitor
monitor (person) *eg* monitoriaid monitor
monitro *be* monitor
mono *ans* mono
monoclin *eg* monoclinau monocline
monocormig *ans* monocormic
monocotyledon *eg* monocotyledonau monocotyledon
monocrom *eg* monocromau monochrome
monocromatig *ans* monochromatic
monocyt *eg* monocytau monocyte
monodig *ans* monodic
monodrama *eb* monodramâu monodrama
monodromi *eg* monodromïau monodromy
monoecaidd *ans* monoecious
monoffoni *eg* monophony
monoffonig *ans* monophonic
▸ **monogami** *eg* monogamy
monogenig *eg* monogenic
monograff *eg* monograffau monograph
monogram *eg* monogramau monogram
monogram sanctaidd *eg* monogramau sanctaidd sacred monogram
monohybrid *eg* monohybrid
monohydrogen *eg* monohydrogen
monolith *eg* monolithiau monolith
monolithig *ans* monolithic
monomaidd *ans* monomial
monomer *eg* monomer
monomerig *ans* monomeric
monomial *eg* monomialau monomial
mononitrogen *eg* mononitrogen
monopoleiddio *be* monopolise
monopoli *eg* monopolïau monopoly
monopoli dwyffordd *eg* monopolïau dwyffordd bilateral monopoly
monopoli naturiol *eg* natural monopoly
monopsoni *eg* monopsony
monosacarid *eg* monosaccharide
monosomi *eg* monosomy
monosygotig *ans* monozygotic
monoteip *eg* monoteipiau monotype
monoton *ans* monotone
monotonig *ans* monotonic
monotrem *eg* monotreme
monotropig *ans* monotropic
monswn *eg* monsynau monsoon
montage *eg* montages montage
montage ffotograffig *eg* photomontage
montage sofiet *eg* soviet montage
monyddiaeth *eb* monism
Mool /Mul Mantar Mool /Mul Mantar
mop *eg* mopiau mop
mop bwffio *eg* mopiau bwffio buff mop
mop calico *eg* mopiau calico calico mop
mop calico heb ei bwytho *eg* mopiau calico heb eu pwytho unstitched calico mop
mop calico wedi'i bwytho *eg* mopiau calico wedi'u pwytho stitched calico mop
mop ffelt *eg* mopiau ffelt felt mop
mop gwlân oen *eg* mopiau gwlân oen lamb's wool mop
mop llathru *eg* mopiau llathru polishing mop
mop manblu alarch *eg* mopiau manblu alarch swansdown mop
môr *eg* moroedd sea
môr epeirig *eg* moroedd epeirig epeiric sea
Môr Iwerddon *eg* Irish Sea

Môr Sbaenaidd *eg* Spanish Main
môr-baentiad *eg* môr-baentiadau marine painting
môr-beintio *be* marine painting
morbidrwydd *eg* morbidity
mordaith ganol *eb* middle passage
mordant *eg* mordantau mordant
mordant asid (ysgythru) *eg* acid mordant
mordent *eg* mordentau mordent
mordwll *eg* mordyllau gloup
mordwll *eg* mordyllau blow-hole
mordwyeg *eb* science of navigation
mordwyo *be* navigation
mordwyol *ans* navigable
morddrws *eg* morddrysau sea-gate
morddwyd *eb* morddwydydd thigh
morddwydol *ans* femoral
moresg *ell* marram grass
morfa *eg/b* morfeydd coastal marsh
morfa heli *eg* morfeydd heli salt marsh
morfil *eg* morfilod whale
morfil danheddog *eg* morfilod danheddog killer whale
môr-filwr *eg* môr-filwyr marine
morfilltir *eb* morfilltiroedd nautical mile
morfynydd *eg* morfynyddoedd seamount
morffem *eg* morffemau morpheme
morffoffonoleg *eb* morphophonology
morffoleg *eb* morphology
morffolegol *ans* morphological
morffordd *eb* morffyrdd seaway
morgais *eg* morgeisiau mortgage
morgais dewisol *eg* morgeisi dewisol option mortgage
morgais gwaddol *eg* morgeisi gwaddol endowment mortgage
morgeisydd *eg* morgeiswyr mortgager
morgi *eg* morgwn dogfish
morgi trwynfain *eg* morgwn trwynfain mako shark
morglawdd *eg* morgloddiau breakwater; dyke
morgryn *eg* morgrynfeydd seaquake
môr-ladrad *eg* piracy
morlaid *eg* oozes
môr-leidr *eg* môr-ladron pirate
morleisiad *eg* morleisiaid pollack
morlew *eg* morlewod sea lion
morlin *eg* morlinau coastline
morlin ardraws *eg* morlinau ardraws transverse coastline
morlo *eg* morloi seal
morlun *eg* morluniau seascape
morlyn *eg* morlynnoedd haff
morlyn llanw *eg* morlynnoedd llanw tidal lagoon
Morlys *eg* Admiralty
Mormon *eg* Mormoniaid Mormon
Mormonaidd *ans* Mormon
morol *ans* marine
moronen *eb* moron carrot
mortais *eb* morteisiau mortise
mortais a thyno hansiedig haunched mortise and tenon
mortais a thyno unysgwyddog barefaced mortise and tenon
mortais botwm *eg* morteisiau botwm button mortise
mortais dall *eg* morteisiau dall blind mortise
morter *eg* morterau mortar
morthwyl *eg* morthwylion hammer
morthwyl argaenu *eg* morthwylion argaenu veneer hammer
morthwyl blocio *eg* morthwylion blocio blocking hammer
morthwyl cafnu *eg* morthwylion cafnu hollowing hammer
morthwyl caledu *eg* hardening hammer
morthwyl cefnu *eg* morthwylion cefnu backing hammer
morthwyl codi *eg* morthwylion codi raising hammer
morthwyl coleru *eg* morthwylion coleru collar hammer
morthwyl colet *eg* morthwylion colet collet hammer
morthwyl copr *eg* morthwylion copr copper hammer
morthwyl crafanc *eg* morthwylion crafanc claw hammer
morthwyl cromennu *eg* morthwylion cromennu doming hammer
morthwyl crychu *eg* morthwylion crychu creasing hammer
morthwyl cyweirio *eg* morthwylion cyweirio tuning hammer
morthwyl dau wyneb crwn *eg* morthwylion dau wyneb crwn double faced hammer
morthwyl gofannu *eg* forging hammer
morthwyl gosod *eg* morthwylion gosod setting hammer
morthwyl gosod llif *eg* morthwylion gosod llif saw-setting hammer
morthwyl gweithiwr gwiail *eg* morthwylion gweithwyr gwiail caneworker's hammer
morthwyl lledr *eg* morthwylion lledr leather hammer
morthwyl meddal *eg* morthwylion meddal soft hammer
morthwyl patrwm Exeter *eg* morthwylion patrwm Exeter Exeter pattern hammer
morthwyl patrwm Llundain *eg* morthwylion patrwm Llundain London pattern hammer
morthwyl patrwm Warrington *eg* morthwylion patrwm Warrington Warrington pattern hammer
morthwyl peiriannydd *eg* morthwylion peiriannydd engineer's hammer
morthwyl pigfain *eg* morthwylion pigfain peen end hammer
morthwyl pìn *eg* morthwylion pìn pin hammer
morthwyl planisio *eg* morthwylion planisio planishing hammer

morthwyl plastig *eg* morthwylion plastig plastic hammer
morthwyl repoussé *eg* repoussé hammer
morthwyl rwber *eg* morthwylion rwber rubber hammer
morthwyl rhybedu *eg* morthwylion rhybedu riveting hammer
morthwyl sglodi *eg* morthwylion sglodi chipping hammer
morthwyl siasio *eg* chasing hammer
morthwyl suddo *eg* morthwylion suddo sinking hammer
morthwyl tiwnio *eg* morthwylion tiwnio key
morthwyl twcio *eg* morthwylion twcio paning hammer
morthwyl wyneb croes *eg* morthwylion wyneb croes cross peen hammer
morthwyl wyneb crwn *eg* morthwylion wyneb crwn ball peen hammer
morthwyl wyneb syth *eg* morthwylion wyneb syth straight peen hammer
morthwyl y glust *eg* malleus
morthwylio *be* hammer
morwellt *eg* seagrass
morwellt llifedig *ell* dyed seagrass
morwrol *ans* maritime
Morwyn Caint *eb* Maid of Kent
Morwyn Fair Fendigaid *eb* Blessed Virgin Mary
morwyn tŷ *eb* morwynion tŷ housemaid
moryd *eb* morydau estuary; sea ford
moryd wneud *eb* morydau gwneud constructed estuary
moryn *eg* morynnau breaker
mosaig *ans* mosaic
mosaig *eg* mosaic
mosaig dail *eg* leaf mosaic
mosaig gwydr *eg* glass mosaic
mosaig hylifol *eg* fluid mosaic
mosaig papur *eg* paper mosaic
Moscofaidd *ans* Muscovite
Moscofwr *eg* Moscofiaid Muscovite
mosg *eg* mosgiau mosque
motel *eg* motelau motel
motét *eg* motetau motet
motiff *eg* motiffau motif
motiff pen *eg* motiffau pen head motif
mowld *eg* mowldiau mould
mowld blawd corn *eg* mowldiau blawd corn cornflour mould
mowld botwm *eg* mowldiau botwm button mould
mowld cerfwedd *eg* mowldiau cerfwedd relief mould
mowld dariol *eg* mowldiau dariol dariole mould
mowld ffowndri *eg* mowldiau ffowndri foundry mould
mowld glân *eg* mowldiau glân clean mould
mowld gwastraff *eg* mowldiau gwastraff waste mould
mowld ingot *eg* mowldiau ingot ingot mould
mowld latecs *eg* mowldiau latecs latex mould
mowld plastig *eg* mowldiau plastig plastic mould
mowld tywod llaith *eg* mowldiau tywod llaith green sand mould
mowld uned *eg* mowldiau uned unit mould
mowldin *eg* mowldinau moulding
mowldin architraf *eg* mowldinau architraf architrave moulding
mowldin astragal *eg* mowldinau astragal astragal moulding
mowldin bilet *eg* billet moulding
mowldin cafeto *eg* mowldinau cafeto cavetto moulding
mowldin cau *eg* mowldinau cau hollow moulding
mowldin cornis *eg* mowldinau cornis cornice moulding
mowldin cyfwyneb *eg* mowldinau cyfwyneb flush moulding
mowldin cywasgedd *eg* mowldinau cywasgedd compression moulding
mowldin chwarter crwn *eg* mowldinau chwarter crwn quarter round moulding
mowldin endoredig *eg* incised moulding
mowldin ffiled *eg* mowldinau ffiled fillet moulding
mowldin glain *eg* bead moulding
mowldin gosod *eg* mowldinau gosod planted moulding
mowldin gosod *eg* applied moulding
mowldin hanner crwn *eg* mowldinau hanner crwn half round moulding
mowldin ofolo *eg* mowldinau ofolo ovolo moulding
mowldin ogee *eg* mowldinau ogee ogee moulding
mowldin pedrant *eg* mowldinau pedrant quadrant moulding
mowldin sgotia *eg* scotia moulding
mowldin sgrôl *eg* mowldinau sgrôl scroll moulding
mowldin solet *eg* solid moulding; stuck moulding
mowldin suddo *eg* sunk moulding
mowldin torws *eg* mowldinau torws torus moulding
mowldio *be* mould
mowldio chwistrellu *be* injection moulding
mowldio tywod llaith *be* green sand moulding
mowldiwr gwerthyd *eg* mowldwyr gwerthyd spindle moulder
mownt *eg* mowntiau mount
mowntiedig *ans* mounted
mowntin *eg* mowntinau mounting
mowntio *be* mount
mRNA negeseuol *eg* messenger mRNA
muchudd *eg* jet
mud *ans* mute
mud *eg* mudion mute
mudiad (=corff neu gymdeithas) *eg* mudiadau organization
mudiad (=y weithred o fudo) *eg* migration
mudiad (gwyntoedd) *eg* mudiadau swing
mudiad cau tiroedd *eg* enclosure movement
mudiad cyfrin *eg* mudiadau cyfrin underground movement

Mudiad Cymru Fydd *eg* Young Wales Movement
mudiad dirwest *eg* temperance movement
mudiad eciwmenaidd *eg* mudiadau eciwmenaidd ecumenical movement
mudiad ffilmiau *eg* film movement
mudiad gwirfoddol *eg* mudiadau gwirfoddol voluntary organization
mudiad gwrthgaethwasiaeth *eg* anti-slavery movement
mudiad gwrthwynebu *eg* mudiadau gwrthwynebu resistance movement
Mudiad Iwerddon Ieuanc *eg* Young Ireland Movement
Mudiad Llafur Rhyngwladol *eg* International Labour Organization
Mudiad Lloegr Ieuanc *eg* Young England Movement
mudiad protest *eg* mudiadau protest protest movement
mudiad rhyddid merched *eg* women's liberation movement
Mudiad Rhyddid Palesteina *eg* Palestine Liberation Organization
Mudiad Solidarność *eg* Solidarity
mudiad symbolaidd *eg* symbolist movement
Mudiad y Cynghorau *eg* Conciliar Movement
Mudiad y Ffeniaid *eg* Fenian Movement
Mudiad y Groes Goch Ryngwladol *eg* International Red Cross
mudiad y Siartwyr *eg* Chartist movement
mudiant *eg* mudiannau motion
mudiant afreolus *eg* random motion
mudiant cilyddol *eg* reciprocating motion
mudiant cyfyngedig *eg* constrained motion
mudiant cylchdro *eg* rotational motion
mudiant cylchdro *eg* rotary motion
mudiant chwyrlïog *eg* swirling motion
mudiant harmonig *eg* harmonic motion
mudiant harmonig syml *eg* simple harmonic motion
mudiant llinol *eg* linear motion
mudiant mewn cylch *eg* circular motion
mudiant mewn cylch *eg* motion in a circle
mudiant osgiliadol *eg* oscillating motion
mudiant paralel *eg* parallel motion
mudiant priodol *eg* proper motion
mudiant rhythmig (torri edafedd) *eg* rhythmic motion
mudiant ton *eg* wave motion
mudiant tu chwith *eg* reversing motion
mudiant unionlin *eg* rectilinear motion
mudiant ymddangosol y lleuad *eg* apparent motion of the moon
mudo *be* migrate
Mudo Mawr *eg* Great Trek
mudol *ans* migratory; motile
mudydd *eg* mudyddion mute
Muhammad *eg* Muhammad
mulfran *eg/b* mulfrain shag
munud *eg* munudau minute
mur *eg* muriau wall
mur blaen *eg* muriau blaen front wall
mur cefn *eg* muriau cefn back wall
mur gwarchod *eg* muriau gwarchod firewall
mur ochr *eg* muriau ochr side wall
mur plyg y coluddyn *eg* muriau plyg y coluddion folded wall of the intestine
mur tollau *eg* muriau tollau tariff wall
Mur Wylofain *eg* Wailing Wall
mur yr ofari *eg* muriau'r ofari ovary wall
murdreth *eb* murdrethi murage
murfylchau *ell* battlements
muriog *ans* walled
murlen *eg* murlenni curtain wall
murlun *eg* murluniau mural
murlun *eg* murluniau wall-painting
murmur y galon *eg* heart murmur
murol *ans* mural
musette *eg* musettes musette
Mu'tazilitiad *eg* Mu'tazilitiaid Mu'tazili
mwcaidd *ans* mucous
mwcilag *eg* mwcilagau mucilage
mwcin *eg* mwcinau mucin
mwclis pres *eg* peytrel
mwcoprotein *eg* mwcoproteinau mucoprotein
mwcosa *eg* mwcosau mucosa
mwcosa arogli *eg* olfactory mucosa
mwg *eg* smoke
mwgwd *eg* mygydau mask
mwl *eg* mull
mwliwn *eg* mwliynau mullion
mwll *ans* muggy
mwntin *eg* mwntinau muntin
Mŵr *eg* Mwriaid Moor
Mwraidd *ans* Moorish
mwrllwch *eg* smog
mwsg *eg* musk
Mwslim *eg/b* Mwslimiaid Muslim
Mwslimaidd *ans* Muslim
mwslin *eg* mwslinau muslin
mwsogl *eg* mwsoglau moss
mwsogl Carragheen *eg* Carragheen moss
mwsogl carw *eg* reindeer moss
mwstro *be* muster
mwstwr *eg* muster
mwtagen *eg* mwtagenau mutagen
mwtagenaidd *ans* mutagenic
mwtagenedd *eg* mutagenesis
mwtan *eg* mwtanau mutant
mwtaniad *eg* mwtaniadau mutation
mwtaniad somatig *eg* mwtaniadau somatig somatic mutation
mwtanu *be* mutate
mwy na bigger than
mwyaf *ans* major; maximum
mwyafrif *eg* majority

mwyafswm uchder troednodyn *eg* maximum footnote height
mwyafsymaidd *ans* maximal
mwyar *ell* blackberries
mwydion *ell* pulp
mwydion coed *ell* pulp; wood pulp
mwydion papur *ell* paper pulp; papier mâché
mwydo *be* soak; steep
mwydro *be* dither
mwydyn *eg* mwydod worm
mwyhad *eg* amplification
mwyhadur *eg* mwyhaduron amplifier
mwyhadur allanol *eg* mwyhaduron allanol external amplifier
mwyhadur foltedd *eg* voltage amplifier
mwyhadur gwahaniaeth *eg* mwyhaduron gwahaniaeth difference amplifier
mwyhadur gwrthdroadol *eg* inverting amplifier
mwyhadur pŵer *eg* mwyaduron pŵer power amp
mwyhau (llun) *be* maximize
mwyhau (sain) *be* amplify
mwyn *ans* mild
mwyn *eg* mwynau mineral; ore
mwyn copr *eg* copper ore
mwyn haearn *eg* mwynau haearn iron ore
mwyn sinc *eg* mwynau sinc zinc ore
mwynder *eg* mwynderau amenity
mwyndoddi *be* smelt
mwyneiddiad *eg* mineralization
mwyngloddio *be* mine
mwyngloddio *be* mining
mwynhad *eg* enjoyment
mwynhau *be* enjoy
mwyniant *eg* mwyniannau pleasure; use
mwynlong *eb* mwynlongau ore carrier
mwynoleg *eb* mineralogy
mwynwr *eg* mwynwyr miner
myceliwm *eg* mycelia mycelium
mycoleg *eb* mycology
mycorhisa *eg* mycorrhiza
mycorhisol *ans* mycorrhizal
mycsoedema *eg* myxoedema
mycsofirws *eg* myxovirus
myctod *eg* asphyxia
mydryddiaeth *eb* prosody
mydryddol *ans* metrical
myelin *eg* myelin
myelinedig *ans* myelinated
myeloid *ans* myeloid
myfïaeth *eb* egocentricity
myfïol *ans* egocentric
myfyrdod *eg* myfyrdodau meditation
myfyrdod personol *eg* personal reflection
myfyriwr *eg* myfyrwyr student
myfyriwr nyrsio *eg* myfyrwyr nyrsio student nurse
myfyriwr ymchwil *eg* myfyrwyr ymchwil research student
myfyrwraig *eb* myfyrwragedd student
mygdarth *eg* mygdarthau fume
mygdarthol *ans* fuming
mygdarthu *be* fumigate; fume
mygdwll *eg* mygdyllau fumarole
mygu *be* smother; asphyxiate; suffocate
mylga *eg* mylgâu mulga
mympwy *eg* arbitrariness
mympwyol *ans* arbitrary
mymryn *eg* mymrynnau trace
mynach *eg* mynachod monk
mynach gwyn *eg* mynachod gwyn white monk
mynachaeth *eb* monasticism
mynachaidd *ans* monastic; monkish
mynach-esgob *eg* mynach-esgobion monk-bishop
mynachlog *eb* mynachlogydd monastery
mynawyd *eg* mynawydau awl; bradawl
mynawyd asgwrn *eg* bone awl
mynd *be* go
mynd at (berson) *be* approach
mynd gyda *be* accompany
mynd i mewn *be* enter
mynd i'r afael (â mater) *be* address
mynedfa *eb* mynedfeydd entrance; entry
mynediad *eg* mynediadau access; entry; ingress; admittance
mynediad agored *eg* open access
mynediad ar-lein *eg* on-line access
mynediad diwifr sefydlog band llydan *eg* broadband fixed wireless access
mynediad heb ei awdurdodi *eg* unauthorized access
mynediad heb ei fesur *eg* unmetered access
mynediad i'r rhwyd *eg* net access
mynediad uniongyrchol *eg* direct access
mynegai *eg* mynegeion index
mynegai cardiau *eg* mynegeion cardiau card index
mynegai costau byw *eg* cost of living index
mynegai cyfredol *eg* mynegeion cyfredol current index
mynegai cymorth *eg* mynegeion cymorth help index
mynegai hygyrchedd *eg* mynegeion hygyrchedd accessibility index
mynegai iechyd *eg* health index
mynegai nwyddau adwerthu *eg* retail price index
mynegeio *be* index
mynegfys *eg* mynegfysedd index finger; forefinger
mynegi *be* express
mynegiad *eg* mynegiadau expression; statement
mynegiad algebraidd *eg* mynegiadau algebraidd algebraic expression
mynegiad Boole *eg* mynegiadau Boole Boolean expression
mynegiad cyfradd adwaith *eg* reaction rate expression
mynegiad dalfan *eg* mynegiadau dalfan placeholder expression

mynegiad ecwilibriwm *eg* equilibrium expression
mynegiad emosiwn *eg* expressed emotion
mynegiadaeth *eb* expressionism
mynegiadaeth haniaethol *eb* abstract expressionism
mynegiadol *ans* expressionist
mynegiadwr *eg* mynegiadwyr expressionist
mynegiant *eg* mynegiannau expression
mynegiant creadigol *eg* creative expression
mynegolrwydd *eg* expressiveness
mynegrif *eg* mynegrifau index number
mynegrif dargyfeirio *eg* mynegrifau dargyfeirio detour index
mynegrif datblygiad dynol (MDD) *eg* human development index
mynwent *eb* mynwentydd graveyard
mynwent eglwys *eb* mynwentydd eglwysi churchyard
mynwes *eb* mynwesau bust
mynwydd *eg* gooseneck; swan-neck
mynwyddu *be* gooseneck; swan neck
mynychder *eg* prevalence
mynychu (ysgol) *be* attend
mynydd guyot *eg* mynyddoedd guyot guyot
mynydd iâ *eg* mynyddoedd iâ iceberg
mynydd ifanc *eg* mynyddoedd ifanc young mountain
mynydd rhew *eg* mynyddoedd rhew iceberg
mynydda *be* mountaineering
myoffibrolyn *eg* myofibrol
myogenig *ans* myogenic
myoglobin *eg* myoglobin
myomer *eg* myomer
myopia *eg* myopia
myosin *eg* myosin
Myrddin *eg* Merlin
mysceg *eg* myscegau muskeg
mysged *eg* mysgedau musket
mysgedwr *eg* mysgedwyr musketeer
myth *eg* mythau myth
myth bri *eg* prestige myth
myth cyltig *eg* cultic myth
myth defodol *eg* ritual myth
myth eschatolegol *eg* eschatological myth
myth tarddiad *eg* origin myth
mytholeg *eb* mythology
mytholegol *ans* mythical

N

na (ar fotwm cyfrifiadur) no
nad yw'n bod *ans* non-existent
nadir *eg* nadir
Nadolig *eg* Christmas
naddion *ell* shavings; filings; swarf
naddion copr *ell* copper filings
naddion haearn *ell* iron filings
naddion pren *ell* wood shavings
naddu *be* chisel; whittle; paring
naddu fertigol *be* vertical chiselling; vertical paring
naddu llorweddol *be* horizontal chiselling; horizontal paring
nafftha *eg* naphtha
nafflthalen *eg* naphthalene
nafflthalen-1-amin *eg* naphthalen-1-amine
nafflthalen-2-ol *eg* naphthalen-2-ol
nafflthalen-1-ol *eg* naphthalen-1-ol
naid *eb* neidiau jump
naid ac adlam jump with a rebound
naid amodol *eb* neidiau amodol conditional jump
naid ar led *eb* neidiau ar led astride jump
naid bolyn *eb* neidiau polyn pole vault
naid braich *eb* neidiau braich arm jump
naid broga *eb* neidiau broga frog jump
naid cath *eb* neidiau cath catspring
naid cwningen *eb* neidiau cwningen bunny jump
naid driphlyg *eb* neidiau triphlyg triple jump
naid ddeudroed *eb* neidiau deudroed fly spring
naid ddiamod *eb* neidiau diamod unconditional jump
naid fainc *eb* neidiau mainc bench jump
Naid Fawr Ymlaen (Tsieina) *eb* Great Leap Forward
naid fforchog *eb* neidiau fforchog straddle jump
naid gwrcwd *eb* neidiau cwrcwd crouch jump
naid hir *eb* neidiau hir long jump
naid rythmig *eb* neidiau rhythmig rhythmic jump
naid sgip *eb* neidiau sgip skip jump
naid stond *eb* neidiau stond standing jump
naid uchel *eb* neidiau uchel high jump
naid wasg *eb* neidiau gwasg burpee
naid yn ôl *eb* neidiau yn ôl backward spring
naidlen *eb* naidlenni pop-up menu
naidlen databeilot *eb* naidlenni databeilot datapilot pop-up menu
nain *eb* neiniau grandmother
nain-dâp *eg* nain-dapiau grandfather tape
nam (=gwall mewn rhaglen gyfrifiadur) *eg* namau bug
nam (ar leferydd) *eg* namau impediment
nam (ar organ neu feinwe) *eg* namau lesion
nam (ar synhwyrau) *eg* namau impairment
nam (yn gyffredinol) *eg* namau defect
nam ar ddau synnwyr *eg* dual sensory impairment
nam ar y golwg *eg* visual impairment
nam ar y lleferydd *eg* namau ar y lleferydd speech impediment
nam corfforol *eg* namau corfforol physical impairment; physical defect
nam etifeddol *eg* namau etifeddol inherited defect
nam geni *eg* namau geni birth defect
nam ieithyddol penodol *eg* specific language impairment
nam meddyliol *eg* mental deficiency
Nam Simaran Nam Simaran
nano-amedr *eg* nano-amedrau nano-ammeter
nano-eiliad *eg/b* nano-eiliadau nanosecond
nanometr *eg* nanometrau nanometre
nant *eb* nentydd stream; creek
nant gildro *eb* nentydd cildro reversed stream
nant hafesb *eb* nentydd hafesb bourn; winterbourne
napcyn *eg* napcynau napkin; table-napkin
naratif *eg* narrative
naratif arall *eg* naratifau eraill alternative narrative
nas tymherwyd *ans* untempered
Nashim *ell* Nashim
nasoffaryngeal *ans* nasopharyngeal
nastig *ans* nastic
Natsïeiddio *be* Nazify
Natsi *eg* Natsïaid Nazi
Natsïaidd *ans* Nazi
natur *eb* nature
natur gweithgaredd gwyddonol *eb* nature of scientific activity
natur weledol *eb* visual nature
natur y tafliad *eb* type of throw
naturiol *ans* natural
naturiolaeth wrthrychol *eb* objective naturalism
naturiolaidd *ans* naturalistic
naturoliaeth *eb* naturalism
Naw Deg a Phum Pwnc (Luther) *eg* Ninety Five Theses
nawdd *eg* patronage; sponsorship
nawdd cymdeithasol *eg* social security
nawfed *eg* nawfedau ninth; one-ninth
nawpled *eg* nawpledau nonuplet
naws *eb* mood; feel
naws yr ystafell ddosbarth *eb* classroom climate

N-cam *eg* N-stage
nebiwlydd *eg* nebiwlyddion nebulizer
neclis *eb* neclisau necklace
neddyf *eb* neddyfau adze
nefoedd *eb* heaven
neffridiwm *eg* neffridia nephridium
neffron *eg* neffronau nephron
negatif *ans* negative
negatif *eg* negatifau negative
negatif mwyaf *eg* maximum negative
negatifedd *eg* negativity
neges *eb* negeseuon message
neges er perswâd *eb* negeseuon er perswâd persuasive message
neges ffacs *eb* negeseuon ffacs facsimile message
▶ **neges gwall** *eb* negesau gwall error message
neges nesaf *eb* next message
neges nesaf heb ei darllen *eb* next unread message
negeseua sydyn *be* instant messaging
negesfwrdd *eg* negesfyrddau message board
negyddiad amser *eg* negation of time
negyddol *ans* negative
negyddu *be* negate
neidiant *eg* saltation
neidio *be* jump
neidio am y bêl *be* jump for the ball
neidiol *ans* saltatory
neidiwr *eg* neidwyr jumper
neidiwr hir *eg* neidwyr hir long jumper
Neifion *eg* Neptune
neilon *eg* nylon
neilon gwlanog *eg* brushed nylon
neilltuad *eg* neilltuadau assignment
neilltuaeth daleithiol *eb* particularism
neilltuo (=pennu) *be* assign
neilltuo (mewn economeg) *be* isolate
neilltuo (yn gyffredinol) *be* reserve
neilltuo gronyn i gell *be* assign particle to cell
neilltuol *ans* particular
neithdar *eg* neithdarau nectar
neithdarle *eg* neithdarleoedd nectary
nematocyst *eg* nematocystau nematocyst
nematod *eg* nematodau nematode
nenbren *eg* nenbrennau ridge tree
nenfwd *eg* nenfydau ceiling
nenfwd baril *eg* nenfydau baril barrel ceiling
nenfforch *eb* nenffyrch cruck
nenffyrchog *ans* crucked
neoargraffiadaeth *eb* neo-impressionism
neodymiwm *eg* neodymium
▶ **neoglasuriaeth** *eb* neoclassicism
neoglasurol *ans* neoclassical
neo-Gothig *ans* neo-Gothic
neolithig *ans* neolithic
neo-Malthwsiaeth *eb* neo-Malthusianism
neon *eg* neon
neo-Ramantaidd *ans* neo-Romantic
neorewlifiant *eg* neoglaciation
neo-ymddygiadaeth/ymddygiadaeth radical *eb* neobehaviourism/radical behaviourism
nepotistiaeth *eb* nepotism
nepotydd *eg* nepotyddion nepotist
neptwniwm *eg* neptunium
nerf *eg/b* nerfau nerve
nerf abdwcent *eg* abducent nerve
nerf atodol *eg* nerfau atodol accessory nerve
nerf clunol *eg* nerfau clunol sciatic nerve
nerf creuanol *eg* nerfau creuanol cranial nerve
nerf cyflymu *eg* accelerator nerve
nerf duegol *eg* nerfau duegol splenic nerve
nerf echddygol *eg* nerfau echddygol efferent nerve
nerf echddygol *eg* nerfau echddygol motor nerve
nerf fagws *eg* vagus nerve
nerf gostyngol *eg* nerfau gostyngol depressor nerve
nerf optig *eg* nerfau optig optic nerve
nerf synhwyraidd *eg* nerfau synhwyraidd sensory nerve
nerf wlnar *eg* nerfau wlnar ulnar nerve
nerf wynebol *eg* nerfau wynebol facial nerve
nerf y clyw *eg* auditory nerve
nerf yr asgwrn cefn *eg* spinal nerve
nerfgell *eb* nerve cell
nerfogaeth *eb* innervation
nerfogi *be* innervate
nerfol *ans* nervous
nerfolyn *eg* nerfolynnau nervule
nerfrwyd *eb* nerfrwydau nerve net
nerfus *ans* nervous
nerfwreiddyn *eg* nerfwreiddiau nerve root
nerfwreiddyn blaen *eg* nerfwreiddiau blaen anterior root
nerth (cyffur) *eg* potency
nerth (sain) *eg* strength
nerth (yn gyffredinol) *eg* nerthoedd power
nerth adlynol *eg* adhesive power
nerth ardrawiad *eg* impact strength
nerth gwasgaru *eg* nerthoedd gwasgaru dispersive power
nerth lens (dioptr) *eg* lens power
nerth plygiant *eg* flexure strength
nesâd agosaf *eg* closest approach
nesaf *ans* next
nesaf allan *ans* outermost
nesaf at next to
nesaf i mewn innermost
net *ans* net
NEU OR
NEU anghynhwysol (NEUA) *eg* exclusive OR
neuadd brawdlys *eb* neuaddau brawdlys inn of court
neuadd chwaraeon *eb* neuaddau chwaraeon sports hall
neuadd y dref *eb* guildhall

adf, adv adferf, *adverb* ***ans, adj*** ansoddair, *adjective* ***be*** berf, *verb* ***eb*** enw benywaidd, *feminine noun* ***eg*** enw gwrywaidd, *masculine noun*

newid *be* replace
newid (i destun) *eg* newidiadau amendment
newid (yn gyffredinol) *eg* newidiadau change; alteration
newid angor *be* change anchor
newid arddulliau addasu *be* replace custom styles
newid beunyddiol *eg* newidiadau beunyddiol daily change
newid bob tro *be* always replace
newid corfforol *eg* physical change
newid cronfa ddata *be* change database
newid cyfeiriad *be* change direction
newid cyflymdra *be* change of pace
newid cyfrinair *be* change password
newid cynnil *eg* newidiadau cynnil subtle change
newid cyweddiad *be* change of engagement
newid demograffig *eg* demographic change
newid diogelwch cyfrinair *be* change password protection
newid enharmonig *eg* newidiadau enharmonig enharmonic change
newid enthalpi *eg* enthalpy change
newid enthalpi atomeiddiad *be* enthalpy change of atomization
newid enthalpi ffurfiant *be* enthalpy change of formation
newid enthalpi hydradiad *be* enthalpy change of hydration
newid enthalpi hylosgiad *be* enthalpy change of combustion
newid enthalpi niwtraliad *be* enthalpy change of neutralization
newid enthalpi sychdarthiad *be* enthalpy change of sublimation
newid enthalpi toddiant *be* enthalpy change of solution
newid enthelapi safonol *be* standard enthelapy change
newid enw *be* change name
newid ffisiolegol *eg* physiological change
newid ffont *be* change font
newid graddfa *be* change scale
newid graffigau *be* replace graphics
newid gwedd *eg* phase change
newid gyda chefndir *be* replace with background
newid i ddogfen *eg* newidiadau i ddogfen change to a document
newid lleiaf *eg* minimum change
newid llinellau toredig *be* replace dashes
newid llyfrgelloedd presennol *be* replace existing libraries
newid modd *be* change mode
newid popeth *be* replace all
newid pwysig i fywyd *eg* major life change
newid rheolydd *be* replace control
newid rhif tudalen *be* change page number
newid safle *be* change position
newid sensitifrwydd *be* alter sensitivity
newid sleidiau â llaw *be* change slides manually
newid sydyn *eg* newidiadau sydyn sudden change
newid technolegol *eg* newidiadau technolegol technological change
newid tymor byr *eg* newidiadau tymor byr short term change
newid un ffactor *be* change one factor
newid yng nghanran *eg* percentage change
newid yn y gromlin galw shift in the demand curve
newid ystod cronfa ddata *be* change database range
newidiadau arfaethedig *ell* proposed changes
newidiadau cydadferol *ell* compensatory changes
newidiadau cyfnodol *ell* periodic changes
newidiadau enthalpi ffurfiant *ell* enthalpy changes of formation
newidiadau rhes *ell* row reduction
newidiadau tymhorol *ell* seasonal changes
newidiol *ans* variable
newidydd *eg* newidyddion transformer
newidydd codi *eg* newidyddion codi step-up-transformer
newidydd gostwng *eg* newidyddion gostwng step-down transformer
newidyn *eg* newidynnau variable
newidyn annibynnol *eg* newidynnau annibynnol independent variable
newidyn arwahanol *eg* newidynnau arwahanol discrete variable
newidyn Boole *eg* newidynnau Boole Boolean variable
newidyn cyfanrifol *eg* newidynnau cyfanrifol integer variable
newidyn cyfrannwr *eg* newidynnau cyfranwyr subject variable
newidyn cyfredol *eg* newidynnau cyfredol current variable
newidyn cymhlyg *eg* newidynnau cymhlyg complex variable
newidyn cysylltiol *eg* newidynnau cysylltiol intervening variable
newidyn deuaidd *eg* newidynnau deuaidd binary variable
newidyn dibynnol *eg* newidynnau dibynnol dependent variable
newidyn di-dor *eg* newidynnau di-dor continuous variable
newidyn drwy'r cyfan *eg* newidynnau drwy'r cyfan global variable
newidyn dryslyd *eg* newidynnau dryslyd confounding variable
newidyn eang *eg* newidynnau eang global variable
newidyn gweddill *eg* newidynnau gweddill surplus variable
newidyn llacrwydd *eg* newidynnau llacrwydd slack variable
newidyn lleol *eg* newidynnau lleol local variable
newidyn llinynnol *eg* newidynnau llinynnol string variable
newidyn person *eg* newidynnau person person variable

newidyn real *eg* newidynnau real real variable
newidyn rheolydd *eg* newidynnau rheolydd control variable
newidyn rhyngddibynnol *eg* newidynnau rhyngddibynnol interdependent variable
newidyn system *eg* newidynnau system system variable
newidynnau sy'n rhyngberthyn *ell* interrelated variables
newton *eg* newtonau newton
newydd *ans* new
newydd eu datblygu *ans* newly developed
newydd-anedig *ans* neonatal
newydd-anedig *eg* neonate
newyddbeth *eg* newyddbethau innovation
newydd-ddyfodiad *eg* newydd-ddyfodiaid newcomer
newyddiaduraeth *eb* journalism
newyddiaduraeth ffilm *eb* film journalism
newyddiadurwr *eg* newyddiadurwyr journalist
newyddion *ell* news
newyddion caled *ell* hard news
newyddion sy'n torri *ell* breaking news
newyddlen *eb* newyddlenni news-sheet
newyn *eg* starvation; famine
newynu *be* starve
Nezikin *eg* Nezikin
nfed nth
NIAC NAND
nib llythrennu *eg* nibiau llythrennu lettering nib
nib torri leino *eg* nibiau torri leino lino cutting nib
nibbana *eg* nibbana
nicel *eg* nickel
nicel coprog *eg* cupro-nickel
nicer *eg* nicers knicker
nicers cami *eg* camiknickers
nicotinamid adenin deuniwcliotid *eg* nicotinamide adenine dineucleotide (NAD)
nicotinamid adenin deuniwcliotid ffosffad *eg* nicotinamide adenine dineucleotide phosphate (NADP)
NID NOT
nid hawliau tramwy o angenrheidrwydd not necessarily rights of way
nid yw grwpio'n bosibl (neges ar sgrin) grouping not possible
nid yw'r gweinydd ar gael server not available
NIEU NOR
nifer (yn gyffredinol) *eg* niferoedd number
nifer (yr achosion) *eg* incidence
nifer a dderbynnir *eg* niferoedd a dderbynnir intake
nifer ar y gofrestr *eg* niferoedd ar y gofrestr number on roll
nifer yr ymweliadau *eg* number of visits
nifwl *eg* nifylau nebula
nifwl modrwy *eg* nifylau modrwy ring nebula
nihiliaeth *eb* nihilism
nihilydd *eg* nihilwyr nihilist
nilpotent *ans* nilpotent
nimbostratus *eg* nimbostratus
ninhydrin *eg* ninhydrin
niobiwm (Nb) *eg* niobium
nionyn *eg* nionod onion
niper *eg* niperi nipper
niper bandio *eg* niperi bandio band nipper
niper torri blaen *eg* niperi torri blaen end-cutting nipper
niper torri croeslinol *eg* niperi torri croeslinol diagonal-cutting nipper
nipl *eg* niplau nipple
nipl olew *eg* niplau olew oil nipple
niplau iro *ell* lubricating nipples
nirvana *eg* nirvana
nitrad *eg* nitradau nitrate
nitradiad *eg* nitration
nitraid *eg* nitreidiau nitrites
nitreiddiad *eg* nitrification
nitreiddio *be* nitrify
nitrido *be* nitriding
nitrobensen *eg* nitrobenzene
nitro-cellwlos *eg* nitro-cellulose
2-nitroffenol *eg* 2-nitrophenol
4-nitroffenylamin *eg* 4-nitrophenylamine
1-nitro-2-ffenylethen *eg* 1-nitro-2-phenylethene
nitrogen (N) *eg* nitrogen
nitrogen deuocsid *eg* nitrogen dioxide
nitrogen monocsid *eg* nitrogen monoxide
nitrogen ocsid *eg* nitrogen oxide
nitro-gyfansoddyn *eg* nitro-gyfansoddion nitro-compound
nitromethan *eg* nitromethane
nitroso- nitroso-
niwcellws *eg* nucellus
niwclear *ans* nuclear
niwcledig *ans* nucleated
niwcleon *eg* niwcleonau nucleon
niwclews *eg* niwclysau nucleus
niwclews diploid *eg* diploid nucleus
niwclews uwchaciasmatig *eg* surachiasmatic nucleus (SCN)
niwclid *eg* nuclide
niwclioffil *eg* nucleophile
niwclioffilig *ans* nucleophile
niwcliohiston *eg* nucleohistone
niwclioprotein *eg* nucleoprotein
niwcliosid *eg* nucleoside
niwcliotid *eg* nucleotide
niwed arbrofol i'r ymennydd *eg* experimental brain lesion
niwed i'r ymennydd *eg* brain damage
niweidiol *ans* harmful
niwl *eg* niwloedd fog; fogging
niwl ffrynt *eg* frontal fog
niwl iâ *eg* niwloedd iâ ice fog
niwl llorfudol *eg* advection fog

niwl mynydd *eg* hill fog
niwl pelydriad *eg* radiation fog
niwl rhew *eg* niwloedd rhew ice fog
niwlen *eb* niwlenni mist
niwlo *be* mist
niwlo *be* fog
niwlo *be* fuzzification
niwlog *ans* nebulous
niwm *eg* niwmau neume
niwmateg *eb* pneumatics
niwmatig *ans* pneumatic
niwmismateg *eb* numismatics
► **niwmonia** *eg* pneumonia
niwmotacsis *eg* pneumotaxis
niwral *ans* neural
niwrodrosglwyddydd *eg* niwrodrosglwyddyddion neurotransmitter
niwroddelweddu *be* neuroimaging
niwrofodylydd *eg* niwrofodylyddion neuromodulator
niwrogenig *ans* neurogenic
niwroglia *eg* neuroglia
niwrogliaidd *ans* neuroglial
niwrogyhyrol *ans* neuromuscular
niwroleg *eb* neurology
niwrolegol *ans* neurological
niwrolegydd *eg* niwrolegwyr neurologist
niwron *eg* niwronau neuron
niwron afferol *eg* afferent neuron
niwron cynsynaptig *eg* niwronau cynsynaptig presynaptic neuron
niwron cysylltiol *eg* niwronau cysylltiol associator
niwron echddygol *eg* niwronau echddygol efferent neuron
niwron echddygol *eg* niwronau echddygol motor neuron
niwron ôl-synaptig *eg* niwronau ôl-synaptig postsynaptic neuron
niwron synhwyraidd *eg* niwronau synhwyraidd sensory neuron
niwrosecretol *ans* neurosecretory
niwroseicoleg glinigol *eb* clinical neuropsychology
niwroseicoleg/niwrowyddoniaeth *eb* neuropsychology/neuroscience
niwrosis *eg* neurosis
niwrotiaeth *eb* neuroticism
niwrowyddoniaeth wybyddol *eb* cognitive neuroscience
niwsans *eg* nuisance
niwtral *ans* neutral
niwtraledig *ans* neutralized
niwtraleiddio *be* neutralize
niwtraliad *eg* niwtraliadau neutralization
niwtraliaeth *eb* neutrality
niwtraliaeth arfog *eb* armed neutrality
niwtraliaeth gyfeillgar *eb* benevolent neutrality
niwtralu asidau *be* neutralization of acids
niwtrino *eg* niwtrinoeon neutrino
niwtroffil *eg* niwtroffilau neutrophil
niwtron *eg* niwtronau neutron
nobeliwm (No) *eg* nobelium
nociganfyddwr *eg* nociganfyddwyr nociceptor
nod (=marc) *eg* nodau mark
nod (=symbol yn cynrychioli llythyren) *eg* nodau character
nod (=uchelgais, rhywbeth i gyrchu ato) *eg* nodau aim
nod (mewn anatomi, ffiseg a mathemateg) *eg* nodau node
nod anghyfreithlon *eg* nodau anghyfreithlon illegal character
nod annisgwyl *eg* nodau annisgwyl unexpected character
nod anwybyddu *eg* nodau anwybyddu ignore character
nod atrio-fentriglaidd (NAF) *eg* atrio-ventricular node (AVN)
Nod Barcut *eg* Kitemark
nod canslo *eg* nodau canslo cancel mark
nod clwyd *eg* nodau clwyd hash character
nod cod deuaidd *eg* nodau cod deuaidd binary coded character
nod chwilio *eg* nodau chwilio wildcard character
nod dalen-borthi *eg* nodau dalen-borthi form-feed character
nod egluryn *eg* nodau egluryn caption character
nod gwarant *eg* nodau gwarant hall mark
Nod Gwlân *eg* Woolmark
nod lymff *eg* nodau lymff lymph node
nod llin-borthiad *eg* nodau llin-borthiad line feed character
nod masnach *eg* nodau masnach trademark
nod prawf *eg* nodau prawf assay mark
nod rheoli *eg* nodau rheoli control character
nod tudalen *eg* nodau tudalen bookmark
nod tudalen nesaf *eg* next bookmark
nod wedi'i fewnblannu *eg* nodau wedi'u mewnblannu embedded character
nodaledd *eg* nodality
nodau ac amcanion aims and objectives
nodau ac amcanion ariannol financial aims and objectives
nodau 'blue' *ell* 'blue' notes
nodau canol *ell* middle register
nodau cyfnewid *ell* changing notes
nodau cyfrannol *ell* proportional characters
nodau isel *ell* low register
nodau mynych *ell* reiterated notes
nodau uchel *ell* high register
nodau yr eiliad (nye) *ell* characters per second
nodchwiliad *eg* nodchwiliadau wild card search
nodchwilio *be* wild card
nodchwiliwr *eg* nodchwilwyr wild card
nodedig *ans* distinctive; impressive
nodi *be* note; identify
nodiad gweledol *eg* nodiadau gweledol visual note

nodiadau dadansoddol *ell* analytical notes
nodiadau maes *ell* field notes
nodiadur *eg* nodiaduron notebook
nodiaith *eb* nodieithoedd object language
nodiannu *eg* notate
nodiant *eg* nodiannau notation
nodiant arluniol *eg* diagrammatic notation
nodiant Bow *eg* Bow's notation
Nodiant Cil-Bwyl *eg* Reverse Polish Notation
nodiant confensiynol *eg* conventional notation
nodiant degol *eg* decimal notation
nodiant degolion cod deuaidd *eg* binary coded decimal notation
nodiant deuaidd *eg* binary notation
nodiant graffig *eg* graphic notation
nodiant hecsadegol *eg* hexadecimal notation
nodiant indecs *eg* index notation
nodiant mathemategol confensiynol *eg* conventional mathematical notation
nodiant mathemategol safonol *eg* standard mathematical notation
nodiant mewnddodol *eg* infix notation
nodiant wythol *eg* octal notation
nodol *ans* nodal
nod-raglen *eb* nod-raglenni object program
nodwedd *eb* nodweddion character
nodwedd *eb* nodweddion feature
nodwedd *eb* nodweddion characteristic
nodwedd amffoterig *eb* nodweddion amffoterig amphoteric character
nodwedd awgrymu ymateb *eb* nodweddion awgrymu ymateb demand characteristic
nodwedd cyrchfan *eb* nodweddion cyrchfan destination feature
nodwedd diffyg *eb* deficiency characteristic
nodwedd drechol *eb* nodweddion trechol dominant feature
nodwedd ddaearyddol *eb* nodweddion daearyddol geographical feature
nodwedd ddemograffig *eb* nodweddion demograffig demographic characteristic
nodwedd farchnad *eb* market characteristic
nodwedd gaffaeledig *eb* nodweddion caffaeledig acquired feature
nodwedd gosodiad *eb* nodweddion gosodiad layout feature
nodwedd gyffredinol *eb* nodweddion cyffredinol general feature; universal feature
nodwedd hanesyddol *eb* historical feature
nodwedd hinsoddol *eb* nodweddion hinsoddol climatic feature
nodwedd llystyfiant *eb* nodweddion llystyfiant character of vegetation
nodwedd nodedig *eb* nodweddion nodedig distinctive feature
nodwedd ofodol *eb* nodweddion gofodol spatial feature
nodwedd personoliaeth *eb* nodweddion personoliaeth personality trait
nodwedd rywiol eilaidd *eb* nodweddion rhywiol eilaidd secondary sexual character
nodwedd tirwedd *eb* nodweddion tirwedd relief feature
nodwedd uwch *eb* nodweddion uwch advanced feature
nodweddiadol *ans* characteristic
nodweddion cyferbyniol *ell* contrasted characteristics
nodweddion defnyddiau *ell* material characteristics
nodweddion dynol *ell* human features
nodweddion ffisegol *ell* physical features
nodweddion hynafiadol *ell* ancestral traits
nodweddion rhieni *ell* parental characteristics
nodweddion sy'n debyg *ell* similarities
nodweddion tirwedd *ell* landscape features
nodweddrif *eg* nodweddrifau characteristic
nodwydd *eb* nodwyddau needle; aiguille
nodwydd belenbwynt *eb* nodwyddau pelenbwynt ball-point needle
nodwydd chenille *eb* nodwyddau chenille chenille needle
nodwydd ddwbl *eb* nodwyddau dwbl twin needle
nodwydd folcanig *eb* nodwyddau folcanig volcanic spine
nodwydd frodio *eb* nodwyddau brodio embroidery needle
nodwydd frodio *eb* nodwyddau brodio crewel needle
nodwydd gleinwaith *eb* nodwyddau gleinwaith beading needle
nodwydd glustogwaith *eb* nodwyddau clustogwaith upholstery needle
nodwydd greithio *eb* nodwyddau creithio darning needle
nodwydd lafa *eb* nodwyddau lafa lava spine
nodwydd lledr *eb* nodwyddau lledr leather needle
nodwydd llygad agored *eb* nodwyddau llygad agored calyx eye needle
nodwydd peiriant *eb* nodwyddau peiriant machine needle
nodwydd tapestri *eb* nodwyddau tapestri tapestry needle
nodwydd wnïo *eb* nodwyddau gwnïo sewing needle
nodwydd ysgythru *eb* nodwyddau ysgythru etching needle
nodwyddau iâ *ell* pipkrake
nodwyddau rhew *ell* pipkrake
nodwydden *eb* nodwyddennau between needle
nodyn (=cofnod byr) *eg* nodiadau note
nodyn (mewn cerddoriaeth) *eg* nodau note
nodyn agored *eg* nodau agored open note
nodyn anhepgor *eg* nodau anhepgor essential note
nodyn atgoffa nesaf *eg* next reminder
nodyn atodol *eg* nodau atodol added note
nodyn blaidd *eg* nodau blaidd wolf note
nodyn camu *eg* nodau camu passing note
nodyn camu acennog *eg* nodau camu acennog accented passing note

nodyn casglu *eg* nodau casglu gathering note
nodyn clwm *eg* nodau clwm tied note
nodyn credyd *eg* nodion credyd credit note
nodyn chwe deg pedwar *eg* nodau chwe deg pedwar sixty-fourth-note
nodyn dangos *eg* nodau dangos distinguishing note
nodyn deuddot *eg* nodau deuddot double dotted note
nodyn diogelu *eg* nodiadau diogelu cover note
nodyn dot *eg* nodau dot dotted note
nodyn enharmonig *eg* nodau enharmonig enharmonic note
nodyn hyd atodol *eg* nodau hyd atodol added value note
nodyn naturiol *eg* nodau naturiol natural note
nodyn nesaf *eg* next note
nodyn nodweddiadol *eg* nodau nodweddiadol characteristic note
nodyn piano *eg* nodau piano piano key
nodyn rhaglen *eg* nodiadau rhaglen programme note
nodyn sylfaenol *eg* nodau sylfaenol fundamental note
nodyn talu *eg* remittance advice
nodyn trosglwyddo *eg* delivery note
nodyn wyth *eg* nodau wyth eighth-note
nodd *eg* noddion sap
noddfa *eb* noddfeydd sanctuary
noddi *be* patronize
noddwr *eg* noddwyr patron; sponsor
noeth (=heb ddillad) *ans* naked
noeth (am goed, gwifrau etc) *ans* bare
noeth (mewn cerddoriaeth) *ans* exposed
noethlun *eg* noethluniau nude
nofa *eg* nofâu nova
nofio *be* swimming
nofio ar y cefn *be* backstroke; backcrawl
nofio ar yr ochr *be* sidestroke
nofio broga *be* breaststroke
nofio ci *be* dog paddle
nofio cyflym *be* sprint
nofio dulliau cymysg *be* medley swimming
nofio morlo *be* seal swimming
nofio pellter *be* distance swimming
nofio pilipala *be* butterfly stroke
nofis *eg* nofisiaid novice
nôl (=mynd yn ôl) *adf* go back
nôl (yn gryno) *adf* back
nôl i'r brif ddewislen back to main menu
nôl un dudalen *adf* go back one page
nomad *eg* nomadiaid nomad
nomadiaeth *eb* nomadism
nomadig *ans* nomadic
nomogram *eg* nomogramau nomogram
nonagon *eg* nonagonau nonagon
nonau *ell* nones
noned *eb* nonedau nonet
noradrenalin *eg* noradrenaline
norm *eg* normau norm
norm cymdeithasol *eg* normau cymdeithasol social norm
norm cysylltiol *eg* associated norm
norm oed *eg* age norm
normal *ans* normal
normal *eg* normalau normal
normaleiddiad *eg* normalization
normaleiddio *be* normalize
normalydd *eg* normalyddion normalizer
Norman *eg* Normaniaid Norman
Normanaidd *ans* Norman
Normaneiddio *be* Normanisation
normedig *ans* normed
norm-gyfeiriol *ans* norm-referenced
Norseg *eb* Norse
nosol *ans* nocturnal
noson rhieni *eb* nosweithiau rhieni parents' evening
not *eb* notiau knot
nota cambiata *eg* nota cambiata
notari *eg* notarïaid notary
notari'r cyhoedd *eg* notarïaid y cyhoedd public notary
notari'r Pab *eg* notarïau'r Pab papal notary
notochord *eg* notochord
nwl *eg* nyliau null
nwlbwynt *eg* nwlbwyntiau null point
nwmenaidd *ans* numinous
nwrl *eg* nwrliau knurl
nwrl bras *eg* nwrliau bras coarse knurl
nwrl canolig *eg* nyrliau canolig medium knurl
nwrl diemwnt *eg* nwrliau diemwnt diamond knurl
nwrl mân *eg* fine knurl
nwrl syth *eg* nwrliau syth straight knurl
nwrlio *be* knurling
nwy *eg* nwyon gas
nwy aer *eg* producer gas
nwy anadweithiol *eg* nwyon anadweithiol inert gas
nwy delfrydol *eg* ideal gas
nwy dŵr *eg* water gas
nwy gwacáu *eg* nwyon gwacáu exhaust gas
nwy naturiol *eg* natural gas
nwy nobl *eg* noble gas
nwy prin *eg* rare gas
nwy pwll glo *eg* fire damp
nwy radon *eg* radon gas
nwy real *eg* nwyon real real gas
nwy resbiradol *eg* respiratory gas
nwyd *eg* nwydau passion
nwydd *eg* nwyddau commodity
nwyddau *ell* goods; merchandise
nwyddau a meddiannau *ell* goods and chattels
nwyddau ail-law *ell* secondhand goods
nwyddau brand *ell* branded goods
nwyddau cartref *ell* home-made goods
nwyddau claddu *ell* grave goods

nwyddau crai *ell* non-manufactured goods
nwyddau cyfalaf *ell* capital goods
nwyddau cyfleus *ell* convenience goods
nwyddau cyffredin *ell* normal goods
nwyddau cyhoeddus *ell* public goods
nwyddau cymhariaeth *ell* comparison goods
nwyddau cynhyrchydd *ell* producer goods
nwyddau darfodus *ell* perishable goods
nwyddau diffygiol *ell* faulty goods
nwyddau di-gost *ell* free goods
nwyddau dirinwedd *ell* demerit goods
nwyddau economaidd *ell* economic goods
nwyddau Giffen *ell* Giffen goods
nwyddau golchi *ell* washing products
nwyddau gorffenedig *ell* finished goods
nwyddau gwael *ell* inferior goods
nwyddau gwarantiedig *ell* guaranteed goods
nwyddau gwlân *ell* woollens
nwyddau haearn *ell* ironmongery
nwyddau masgynnyrch *ell* mass produced goods
nwyddau moeth *ell* luxury goods
nwyddau neu wasanaethau goods or services
nwyddau pris gostyngol *ell* reduced goods
nwyddau rhinweddol *ell* merit goods
nwyddau rhyngol *ell* intermediate goods
nwyddau swmpus *ell* bulky goods
nwyddau sy'n para *ell* durable goods
nwyddau traul *ell* consumer goods
nwyddau tŷ *ell* household goods
nwyddau Veblen *ell* Veblen goods
nwyddau wedi'u baeddu yn y siop *ell* shop-soiled goods
nwyglos *ans* gastight
nwyol *ans* gaseous
nwyon allanadledig *ell* exhaled gases
nwyon cynyrchiedig *ell* evolved gases
nwyon gwenwynig *ell* poisonous gases
nwyon mewnanadledig *ell* inhaled gases
nyctinasedd *eg* nyctinasty
nychdod *eg* dystrophy
nychdod cyhyrol *eg* muscular dystrophy
nyddolyn *eg* nyddolynnau spinneret
nyddu *be* spin
nylbwyntydd *eg* nylbwyntyddion null pointer
nylnod *eg* nylnodau null character
Nylon (enw masnach) *eg* Nylon
nymff *eb* nymffod nymph
nynatac *eg* nynatacau nunatak
nyrs *eb* nyrsys nurse
nyrs ardal *eb* nyrsys ardal district nurse
nyrs ategol *eb* nyrsys ategol nursing auxiliary
nyrs benodol *eb* nyrsys penodol named nurse
nyrs cymuned *eb* nyrsys cymuned community nurse
nyrs cymuned, iechyd meddwl *eb* nyrsys cymuned, iechyd meddwl community nurse, mental health
nyrs feithrin *eb* nyrsys meithrin nursery nurse
nyrs gofrestredig gyffredinol *eb* nyrsys cofrestredig cyffredinol registered general nurse
nyrs gysylltiol *eb* nyrsys cysylltiol associate nurse
nyrs iechyd meddwl *eb* nyrsys iechyd meddwl mental health nurse
nyrs practis *eb* nyrsys practis practice nurse
nyrs restredig *eb* nyrsys rhestredig enrolled nurse
nyrs seiciatrig cymuned *eb* nyrsys seiciatrig cymuned community psychiatric nurse
nyrs staff *eb* nyrsys staff staff nurse
nyrs sylfaenol *eb* nyrsys sylfaenol primary nurse
nyrs ysgol *eb* nyrsys ysgol school nurse
nyrsio *be* nurse; nursing
nyrsio iechyd meddwl *be* mental health nursing
nyrsio rhwystrol *be* barrier nursing
nyrsio rhwystrol gwrthol *be* reverse barrier nursing
nyrsio sylfaenol *be* primary nursing
nyrsio tîm *be* team nursing
nyten *eb* nytiau nut
nyten â choler wedi'i llifio *eb* nytiau â choleri wedi'u llifio nut with sawn collar
nyten â mewniad neilon *eb* nytiau â mewniad neilon nut with nylon insert
nyten â mewniad rwber *eb* nytiau â mewniad rwber nut with rubber insert
nyten asgellog *eb* nytiau asgellog wing nut
nyten chwimwth *eb* nytiau chwimwth quick-action nut
nyten ddei *eb* nytiau dei die nut
nyten gastell *eb* nytiau castell castle nut
nyten gloi *eb* nytiau cloi check nut; lock nut
nyten gloi rhigol V *eb* nytiau cloi rhigol V vee groove locking nut
nyten glwm *eb* nytiau clwm stiff nut
nyten gymhwyso *eb* nytiau cymhwyso adjusting nut
nyten gymhwyso uchder *eb* nytiau cymhwyso uchder height adjusting nut
nyten hecsagonol *eb* nytiau hecsagonol hexagonal nut
nyten nwrl *eb* nytiau nwrl knurled nut
nyten rigolog *eb* nytiau rhigolog grooved nut
nyten rych *eb* nytiau rhych slotted nut
nyten sgwâr *eb* nytiau sgwâr square nut
nyten Simmonds *eb* nytiau Simmonds Simmonds nut
nyten wedi'i llifio *eb* nytiau wedi'u llifio sawn nut
nyten werthyd *eb* nytiau gwerthyd spindle nut
nytiau a bolltau nuts and bolts
nyth *eb* nythod nest
nythaid o dablau *eb* nest of tables
nythaid o fyrddau *eb* nest of tables
nythu *be* nest

O

o amgylch *adf* around
o ben i ben *ans* overall
o dan effaith disgyrchiant under the action of gravity
o dan ofal being cared for
o flaen before
o gyfrannedd da *ans* well-proportioned
o linach y fam matrilineal
O Uchel Dras oedd Siencyn Of Noble Race was Shenkin
o waith llaw *ans* hand made
obelisg *eg* obelisgau obelisk
oblad *eg/b* oblate
obo *eg* oboi oboe
oböydd *eg* obōwyr oboist
obsesiwn *eg* obsesiynau obsession; fixation
obstetreg *eb* obstetrics
obstetregydd *eg* obstetregwyr obstetrician
OC (Oed Crist) *eg* AD
ocarina *eg* ocarinâu ocarina
ocelws *eg* oceli ocellus
ocr *eg* ocrau ochre
ocr coch *eg* red ochre
ocr melyn *eg* yellow ochre
ocsi-asetylen *eg* oxy-acetylene
ocsid *eg* ocsidau oxide
ocsid metel *eg* ocsidau metelau metal oxide
ocsidas *eg* oxidase
ocsidas terfynol *eg* terminal oxidase
ocsideiddiad *eg* ocsideiddiadau oxidization
ocsidiad *eg* ocsidiadau oxidation
ocsidiad anodig *eg* anodic oxidation
ocsidiedig *ans* oxidized
ocsidio *be* oxidize
ocsidio tanwyddau *be* oxidation of fuels
ocsidoredwctas *eg* oxidoreductase
ocsidydd *eg* ocsidyddion oxidizing agent; oxidant
ocsigen (O) *eg* oxygen
ocsigen deufflworid *eg* oxygen difluoride
ocsigenedig *eg* oxygenated
ocsigeniad *eg* oxygenation
ocsigenu *be* oxygenate
ocsihaemoglobin *eg* oxyhaemoglobin
ocsitosin *eg* oxytocin
ocsoasid *eg* ocsoasidau oxoacid
ocsofanadiwm(IV) sylffad(VI) *eg* oxovanadium(IV) sulfate(VI)
octagon *eg* octagonau octagon
octahedron *eg* octahedronau octahedron
octant *eg* octannau octant
ocwlar *eg* ocwlarau ocular
ocwm *eg* oakum
ochenaid *eb* ocheneidiau groan
ochr *eg/b* ochrau side
ochr agored *eb* off side
ochr agosaf *eb* ochrau agosaf near side
ochr anghywir (O.A.) *eb* ochrau anghywir wrong side
ochr atrew *eb* ochrau atrew onset side of ice
ochr atwynt *eb* ochrau atwynt windward side
ochr bellaf *eb* ochrau pellaf far side
ochr chwith *eb* left-hand side; left side
ochr chwith y cwrt *eb* left side of the court
ochr dywyll *eb* ochrau tywyll blind side
ochr ddatwm *eb* ochrau datwm datum side
ochr dde (wrth rwyfo) *eb* bow side
ochr dde (yn gyffredinol) *eb* right side; right-hand side
ochr ddrôr *eb* ochrau drôr drawer side
ochr esgynedig *eb* ochrau esgynedig upthrow side
ochr flaenllaw *eb* forehand side
ochr goes *eb* leg side; on side
ochr grisiau *eb* ochrau grisiau stringer
ochr gyfagos *eb* ochrau cyfagos adjacent side
ochr gysgodol *eb* ochrau cysgodol leeward side
ochr gywir *eb* ochrau cywir right side
ochr isaf *eb* ochrau isaf underside
ochr od *eb* ochrau od odd side
ochr strôc *eb* stroke side
ochr strôc dani *eb* stroke side under
ochr syrthiedig *eb* ochrau syrthiedig downthrow side
ochr waered *eb* ochrau gwaered downhill side
ochr wanaf *eb* ochrau gwanaf weaker side
ochr wastraff (y llinell) *eb* waste side
ochr wrthlaw *eb* ochrau gwrthlaw backhand side
ochr wrthrew *eb* ochrau gwrthrew lee side of ice
ochr wyneb *eb* ochrau wyneb face side
ochr y droed *eb* sidefoot
ochr y gweinydd *eb* server-side
ochr y raced *eb* side of the racket
ochr yn ochr *adf* side by side
ochrau cyfatebol *ell* matching sides; corresponding sides
ochrau cyferbyn *ell* opposite sides
ochrau paralel *ell* parallel sides
ochr-dorri *be* side-cutting

ochr-gadwyn arginin *eb* arginine side-chain
ochrgamu *be* jink
ochrgamu *be* side-step
ochrog *ans* sided
ochrol *ans* lateral
ochrolwg *eg* ochrolygon side elevation; lateral view; side view
ochrolwg cyfansawdd *eg* ochrolygon cyfansawdd composite end view
ochrolwg hanner trychiadol *eg* ochrolygon hanner trychiadol half-sectional side elevation
ochrolwg trychiadol *eg* ochrolygon trychiadol sectional end view
odbaredd *eg* odd parity
od-ffwythiant *eg* odd function
odrif *eg* odrifau odd number
odyn *eb* odynnau kiln
odyn blaen-lwytho *eb* odynnau blaen-lwytho front loading kiln
odyn dop-lwytho *eb* odynnau top-lwytho top loading kiln
odyn drydan *eb* odynnau trydan electric kiln
odyn enamlo *eb* odynnau enamlo enamelling kiln
odyn fwffl-lwytho *eb* odynnau mwffl-lwytho muffle loading kiln
odyn fflam agored *eb* odynnau fflam agored open-flame kiln
odyn galch *eb* odynnau calch limestone kiln; lime kiln
odyn-sych *ans* kiln-dry
odyn-sychu *be* kiln-dry
oddfog *ans* bulbous
oddi ar safle'r ysgol *adf* off the school site
oed *eg* age
Oed Crist (OC) Anno Domini
oed cronolegol *eg* chronological age
oed cyrhaeddiad *eg* achievement age
oed darllen *eg* reading age
oed datblygiad *eg* developmental age
oed galedu *be* age hardening
oed meddyliol *eg* mental age
oed symud *eg* transfer age
oedema *eg* oedema
oedi *be* delay
oedi dynwared *be* deferred imitation
oediad *eg* oediadau delay; lag
oediad adwy *eg* oediadau adwy gate delay
oediad amser *eg* time delay
oediad amser *eg* time lag
► **oediad datblygiad** *be* developmental delay
oediad dechrau lleisio *eg* voice-onset time
oedi'r argraffu *be* pause printing
oedolyn *eg* oedolion adult
oedolyn y parasit *eg* adult form of the parasite
oedran allweddol *eg* oedrannau allweddol key age
oedrannus *ans* elderly; aged
oer *ans* cold; cool
oer freuder *eg* cold shortness
oerfel *eg* exposure
oergell *eb* oergelloedd refrigerator
oeri *be* chill; cool
oerlif *eg* oerlifau gelifluction
oerni *eg* cold
oerydd *eg* oeryddion coolant
oes (=cyfnod) *eb* oesau era
oes (yn gyffredinol) *eb* oesoedd age
Oes Aur *eb* Golden Age
Oes Cynnydd *eb* Age of Improvement
oes defnydd *eg* pot life
oes Edwardaidd *eb* Edwardian era
Oes Efydd *eb* Bronze Age
Oes Efydd Ddiweddar *eb* Late Bronze Age
Oes Efydd Gynnar *eb* Early Bronze Age
Oes Ffydd *eb* Age of Faith
Oes Haearn *eb* Iron Age
Oes Iâ *eb* Ice Age
Oes Iâ ddiwethaf *eb* last Ice Age
Oes Neolithig *eb* New Stone Age
Oes Rheswm *eb* Age of Reason
oes silff *eb* shelf life
oes wybodaeth *eb* information age
Oes y Cerrig *eb* Stone Age
Oes y Goleuo *eb* Age of Enlightenment
Oes y Llymder *eb* Age of Austerity
Oes y Saint *eb* Age of the Saints
Oesoedd Canol *ell* Middle Ages
Oesoedd Tywyll *ell* Dark Ages
oesoffagws *eg* oesophagus
oestrogen *eg* oestrogenau oestrogen
oestrws *eg* oestrus
ofaraidd *ans* ovarian
ofari *eg* ofarïau ovary
Ofcom *eg* Ofcom
ofergoel *eb* ofergoelion superstition
ofergoeliaeth *eb* superstition
oferôl *eb* oferôls overall
ofnau'r nos *ell* night terrors
ofolo *eg* ofoli ovolo
ofwl *eg* ofwlau ovule
ofwliad *eg* ovulation
ofwm *eg* ofa ovum
ofylu *be* ovulate
offeiriad *eg* offeiriaid priest
offeiriad gwrthnysig *eg* offeiriaid gwrthnysig refractory priest
offeiriad siantri *eg* offeiriaid siantri chantry priest
offeiriadaeth *eb* ministry
offeiriadaeth yr holl saint *eb* priesthood of all believers
offeiriadol *ans* sacerdotal
offeiriadolaeth *eb* sacerdotalism
offer *ell* equipment; utensils
offer alinio gyda laser *ell* laser alignment equipment
offer arbenigol *ell* specialised equipment

offer argraffu *ell* printing equipment
offer awtomatiaeth *ell* automation equipment
offer byrfyfyr *ell* improvised apparatus
offer clai *ell* clay tools
offer cleifion *ell* patient appliances
offer cludol *ell* portable apparatus
offer cyntedd y glust *eg* vestibular apparatus
offer chwaraeon *ell* games equipment
offer diogelwch *ell* safety equipment
offer drymiau *ell* drum kit
offer electronig *ell* electronic equipment
offer fferm *ell* farm implements
offer ffurfio *ell* form tools
offer gafael *ell* holding tools
offer golchwaith *ell* laundry appliances
offer gorffennu *ell* finishing tools
offer llaw *ell* hand tools
offer llaw chwith *ell* left-hand tools
offer lluniadu *ell* drawing instruments
offer llygadennu *ell* eyelet tools
offer mainc *ell* bench tools
offer mawr *ell* large apparatus
offer mesur *ell* measuring instruments
offer miniog *ell* edged tools
offer modelu *ell* modelling tools
offer niwmatig *ell* pneumatic tools
offer nwrlio *ell* knurling tools
offer parod *ell* manufactured apparatus
offer peiriannau *ell* machine tools
offer peiriant llunio *ell* shaper tools
offer plygu *ell* bending equipment
offer pŵer cludadwy *ell* portable power tools
offer recordio *ell* recording equipment
offer sugnwr llwch *ell* vacuum tools
offer tirfesur *ell* surveying equipment
offer torri *ell* cutting tools
offer trachywir *ell* precision instruments
offer trosoli *ell* lever tools
offer turn *ell* lathe tools
offeren *eb* offerennau mass
offeren addunedol *eb* offerennau addunedol votive mass
offeren Babyddol *eb* Catholic mass
offeren gylch *eb* offerennau cylch cyclic mass
offeren i'r meirw *eb* mass for the dead
offeren organ *eb* offerennau organ organ mass
offeryn *eg* offerynnau instrument
offeryn *eg* offer appliance
offeryn allweddellau *eg* offerynnau allweddellau keyboard instrument
offeryn ar gyfer gwaith *eg* offer ar gyfer gwaith tool for work
offeryn cerdd *eg* offerynnau cerdd musical instrument
offeryn cerdd trydan *eg* offerynnau cerdd trydan electric musical instrument
offeryn cudd *eg* offerynnau cudd hidden instrument
offeryn eisedig *eg* offerynnau eisedig strutted instrument
offeryn falf *eg* offerynnau falf valve instrument
offeryn golygu *eg* offer golygu editing tool
offeryn llawfwrdd *eg* offerynnau llawfwrdd clavier
offeryn llinynnol *eg* offerynnau llinynnol stringed instrument
Offeryn Llywodraeth *eg* Instrument of Government
offeryn meini prawf *eg* offer meini prawf criteria instrument
offeryn pres *eg* offerynnau pres brass instrument
offeryn statudol *eg* offerynnau statudol statutory instrument
offeryn swyddogaethol *eg* offer swyddogaethol functional tool
offeryn syml *eg* offerynnau syml simple instrument
offeryn taro *eg* offerynnau taro percussion instrument
offeryn taro tiwniedig *eg* offerynnau taro tiwniedig tuned percussion instrument
offeryn traddodiadol *eg* offerynnau traddodiadol traditional instrument
offeryn traw *eg* offerynnau traw tuned instrument
offeryn trawsnodi *eg* offerynnau trawsnodi transposing instrument
offeryn trebl *eg* offerynnau trebl treble instrument
offeryn unawd *eg* offerynnau unawd solo instrument
offeryniaeth *eb* offeryniaethau instrumentation
offerynnau taro di-draw *ell* untuned percussion instruments
offerynnol *ans* instrumental
offerynnwr *eg* offerynwyr instrumentalist
offrwm *eg* offrymau offering; oblation; offertory
offrwm addunedol *eg* offrymau addunedol votive offering
offrymddarn *eg* offrymddarnau voluntary
offrymgan *eb* offrymganeuon offertory
offthalmoleg *eb* ophthalmology
offthalmolegydd *eg* offthalmolegwyr ophthalmologist
ogam *eg* ogham
ogamu *be* go about
ogee *eg* ogee
ogif *eg* ogifau ogive
ogof *eb* ogofâu cave
ogof ordo *eb* ogofâu gordo overhanging cave
ogof-annedd *eb* ogof-anheddau cave dwelling
ogofeg *eb* speleology
ogofwr *eg* ogofwyr speleologist
ongl *eb* onglau angle
ongl a gynhelir *eb* onglau a gynhelir subtended angle
ongl adlewyrchiad *eb* onglau adlewyrchiad angle of reflection
ongl aflem *eb* onglau aflym obtuse angle
ongl allanol *eb* onglau allanol exterior angle
ongl arosgo *eb* onglau arosgo oblique angle
ongl atblyg *eb* onglau atblyg reflex angle

ongl atodol *eb* onglau atodol supplementary angle
ongl awr *eb* onglau awr hour angle
ongl benelin *eb* onglau penelin elbow angle
ongl bitsh *eb* onglau pitsh pitch angle
ongl blygiant *eb* onglau plygiant angle of refraction; refracted angle
ongl breswyl *eb* onglau preswyl dwell angle
ongl bwynt *eb* onglau pwynt point angle
ongl cliriad gwefus *eb* lip clearance angle
ongl critigol *eb* critical angle
ongl dafluniad *eb* onglau tafluniad angle of projection
ongl dorri *eb* onglau torri cutting angle
ongl drawiad *eb* onglau trawiad angle of incidence
ongl drwyn *eb* onglau trwyn nose angle
ongl ddadleoliad *eb* onglau dadleoliad displacement angle
ongl ddeuhedrol *eb* onglau deuhedrol dihedral angle
ongl ddilyn *eb* onglau dilyn trail angle
► **ongl eiledol** *eb* onglau eiledol alternate angle
ongl erfyn torri *eb* onglau offer torri angle of cutting tool
ongl erfyn turnio *eb* onglau offer turnio angle of turning tool
ongl fewnol *eb* onglau mewnol interior angle
ongl ffrithiant *eb* onglau ffrithiant angle of friction
ongl gliriad *eb* onglau cliriad clearance angle
ongl godiad *eb* onglau codiad angle of elevation
ongl groestoriad *eb* onglau croestoriad angle of intersection
ongl gyfagos *eb* onglau cyfagos adjacent angle
ongl gyferbyn *eb* onglau cyferbyn opposite angle
ongl gyflenwol *eb* onglau cyflenwol complementary angle
ongl gylchdro *eb* onglau cylchdro angle of rotation
ongl gynffonnog *eb* onglau cynffonnog dovetail angle
ongl gynwysedig *eb* onglau cynwysedig included angle
ongl gyswllt *eb* onglau cyswllt angle of contact
ongl gywir *eb* onglau cywir correct angle
ongl helics *eb* onglau helics helix angle
ongl hogi *eb* onglau hogi sharpening angle
ongl isel *eb* onglau isel low angle
ongl lem *eb* onglau llym acute angle
ongl letrawsedd *eb* onglau lletrawsedd angle of obliquity
ongl lifanu *eb* onglau llifanu grinding angle
ongl oledd *eb* onglau goledd angle of inclination
ongl ostwng *eb* onglau gostwng angle of depression
ongl prin drawiad *eb* onglau prin drawiad angle of grazing incidence
ongl redeg *eb* onglau rhedeg running angle
ongl sail *eb* onglau sail base angle
ongl sector *eb* onglau sector sector angle
ongl sgwâr *eb* onglau sgwâr right angle; square angle
ongl syth *eb* onglau syth straight angle
ongl weledol *eb* onglau gweledol optical angle
ongl wyredd *eb* onglau gwyredd rake angle
ongl wyriad *eb* onglau gwyriad angle of deviation
onglaidd *ans* angular
onglau croesfertigol *ell* vertically opposite angles
onglau cyfansawdd *ell* multiple angles
onglau cyfatebol *ell* corresponding angles
onglau cyferbyn *ell* opposite angles
onglau ffracsiynol *ell* sub-multiple angles
ongli *be* angle
ongli *be* offset
onglog *ans* angular
onglogrwydd *eg* angularity
onglydd *eg* onglyddion protractor
onglydd fernier *eg* onglyddion fernier vernier protractor
ohm *eg* ohmau ohm
ohmedr *eg* ohmedrau ohmeter
ôl *ans* posterior
ôl bys *eg* ôl bysedd fingerprint
ôl debygolrwydd *eg* posterior probability
ôl llong *eg* olion llongau wake
ôl troed *eg* olion traed footprint
ôl-adwaith *eg* backward reaction
olaf i mewn – cyntaf allan *eg* last in – first out
ôl-argraffiadaeth *eb* post impressionism
ôl-berfeddyn *eg* ôl-berfedd hind gut
ôl-brosesydd *eg* ôl-brosesyddion backend processor
ôl-bwynt *eg* ôl-bwyntiau backward point
ôl-bwyth *eg* ôl-bwythau backstitch
ôl-dafluniau rear projection
ôl-daflunio *be* rear projection
ôl-dâl *eg* back pay
ôl-daliad *eg* ôl-daliadau back-payment
ôl-dywyn *eg* ôl-dywynnau afterglow
ôl-ddarfodiant *eg* backwasting
ôl-ddelwedd *eb* after-image
ôl-ddelwedd negyddol *eb* negative after image
olddodi *be* postfix
olddodiad *eg* olddodiaid suffix; postfix
ôl-ddyddodion *ell* lag deposits
ôl-ddyled *eb* ôl-ddyledion arrears
ôl-ddylediaeth *eb* arrearage
ôl-ddyledion rhent *ell* arrears of rent
ôl-effaith *eb* ôl-effeithiau after-effect
ôl-enedigol *ans* post-natal
olew afu pysgod *eg* fish liver oil
olew *eg* olewau oil
olew canol *eg* middle oil
olew cedrwydden *eg* cedar oil
olew corn *eg* maize oil
olew corn *eg* corn oil
olew crai *eg* crude oil
olew creosot *eg* creosote oil
olew galedu *be* oil hardening

olew gwasgedd eithaf *eg* extreme pressure oil
olew had llin *eg* linseed oil
olew had llin puredig *eg* refined linseed oil
olew had llin wedi'i ferwi *eg* boiled linseed oil
olew had rêp *eg* oil seed rape
olew hydawdd *eg* soluble oil
olew iau pysgod *eg* fish liver oil
olew lard *eg* lard oil
olew llysiau *eg* vegetable oil
olew mwynol *eg* olewau mwynol mineral oil
olew olewydd *eg* olive oil
olew pabi *eg* poppy oil
olew puredig *eg* refined oil
olew tenau *eg* light oil
olew tîc *eg* teak oil
olew trwchus *eg* heavy oil
olew tyrpant *eg* oil of turpentine
olew wedi'i ferwi *eg* boiled oil
olewau a brasterau oils and fats
► **olëwm** *eg* oleum
olewog *ans* oleaginous
olewog *ans* oily
olewydden *eb* olewydd olive
ôl-fwtaniad *eg* ôl-fwtaniadau back mutation
ôl-fynedfa *eb* ôl-fynedfeydd rear access
ôl-fflach *eb* ôl-fflachiau flashback
ôl-gic *eb* ôl-giciau kickback
ôl-gripian *be* layback
ôl-groesiad *eg* ôl-groesiadau backcross
ôl-gryniad *eg* ôl-gryniadau aftershock
ôl-gyfeiriad *eg* ôl-gyfeiriadau backbearing
olifau cig eidion *ell* beef olives
oligarchiaeth *eb* oligarchy
oligopoli *eg* oligopolïau oligopoly
oligopsoni *eg* oligopsony
olin *eg* olinau trace
olin fertigol *eg* olinau fertigol vertical trace
olinau llorweddol *ell* horizontal traces
olinydd *eg* olinyddion tracer
olio *be* backspace
olion traed *ell* tracks
ôl-lenwi *be* back fill
ôl-lifiad *eg* ôl-lifiadau backflow
ôl-luosi *be* post-multiply
ôl-nodyn *eg* ôl-nodion endnote
ôl-ofal *eg* after-care
ôl-ogwydd *eg* batter
ôl-olwg *eg* back sight
olraddadwy *ans* retrogradable
olraddiad *eg* retrogradation
ôl-redeg *be* peeling movement
olrediad *eg* olrediadau retrograde
olrewlifol *ans* post glacial
ôl-rym electromotif *eg* back electromotive force
olrhain *be* trace
olrhain cynsail *be* trace precedent
olrhain gwall *be* trace error
► **ôl-slaes** *eg* ôl-slaesau backslash
ôl-sodli *be* back-heel
ôl-strôc *eb* down-stroke
ôl-syllol *ans* retrospective
ôl-weithredol *ans* retrospective
olwr *eg* olwyr back
olwyn *eb* olwynion wheel
olwyn argraffu *eb* olwynion argraffu print wheel
olwyn argraffu *eb* olwynion argraffu daisy-wheel
olwyn bwli *eb* olwynion pwli sheave
olwyn crochenydd *eb* olwynion crochenydd potter's wheel
olwyn cydbwysedd *eb* olwynion cydbwysedd balance wheel
olwyn chwyrlïo *eb* olwynion chwyrlïo whirling wheel
olwyn dro *eb* olwynion tro cartwheel
olwyn dyllu *eb* olwynion tyllu perforating wheel
olwyn ddannedd *eb* olwynion dannedd sprocket wheel
olwyn ddargopïo *eb* olwynion dargopïo tracing wheel
olwyn ddiemwnt *eb* olwynion diemwnt diamond wheel
olwyn emeri *eb* olwynion emeri emery wheel
olwyn fandio *eb* olwynion bandio banding wheel
olwyn fodelu *eb* olwynion modelu modelling wheel
olwyn frêc *eb* olwynion brêc brake wheel
olwyn fwffio *eb* olwynion bwffio buff wheel
olwyn gêr *eb* olwynion gêr gear wheel
olwyn gic *eb* olwynion cic kickwheel
olwyn glicied *eb* olwynion clicied ratchet wheel
olwyn gocos *eb* olwynion cocos cogwheel
olwyn gripian *eb* olwynion cripian worm wheel
olwyn lathru *eb* olwynion llathru polishing wheel
olwyn lifanu *eb* olwynion llifanu grinding wheel
olwyn linellu *eb* olwynion llinellu lining wheel
olwyn llygoden *eb* olwynion llygod mouse wheel
olwyn newid *eb* olwynion newid change wheel
olwyn sbardun *eb* olwynion sbardun spur wheel
olwyn strôc *eb* olwynion strôc bull wheel
olwyndroi *be* cartwheel
olwynion befel *ell* bevel wheels
olwynion cyswllt *ell* idler wheels
olwynion rhif *ell* number wheels
olwyno *be* wheel
olwyno'r sgrym *be* turn the scrum
olwyno'r sgrym *be* wheeling the scrummage
ôl-ymennydd *eg* ôl-ymenyddiau hind brain
olyniaeth *eb* olyniaethau succession
Olyniaeth Apostolaidd *eb* Apostolic Succession
Olyniaeth Brotestannaidd *eb* Protestant Succession
olyniaeth creigiau *eb* succession of rocks
olyniaeth Hanoferaidd *eb* Hanoverian succession
olynol *ans* successive
olynu *be* succeed
olynydd *eg* olynwyr successor

omaswm *eg* omasum
omatidiwm *eg* omatidia ommatidium
ombwdsmon *eg* ombwdsmyn ombudsman
ombwdsmon llywodraeth *eg* government ombudsman
oncoleg *eb* oncology
oncolegydd *eg* oncolegwyr oncologist
onics *eg* onyx
onnen *eb* ynn ash tree
oocyst *eg* oocystau oocyst
oocyt *eg* oocyt
ooffor *eg* oofforau oophore
ooffyt *eg* ooffytau oophyte
oogamedd *eg* oogamy
oogamet *eg* oogametau oogamete
oogamus *ans* oogamous
oogenesis *eg* oogenesis
oogoniwm *eg* oogonium
ooleg *eb* oology
oolitig *ans* oolitic
ooplast *eg* ooplast
OOPS (System Rhaglennu Gwrthrych Gyfeiriedig) *eb* OOPS
oosberm *eg* oosbermau oosperm
oosbor *eg* oosborau oospore
oosborangiwm *eg* oosborangia oosporangium
oosffer *eg* oosfferau oosphere
ootyp *eg* ootypau ootype
opera *eb* operâu opera
opéra buffe *eb* opéras bouffes opéra buffe
opera delynegol *eb* operâu telynegol lyric opera
opera faled *eb* operâu baled ballad opera
opera fawreddog *eb* operâu mawreddog grand opera
opera gomig *eb* operâu comig comic opera
opera sebon *eb* operâu sebon soap opera
opera seria *eb* opere serie opera seria
opera ysgafn *eb* operâu ysgafn light opera
opéra-ballet *eg* opéras-ballet opéra-ballet
opéra-comique *eb* opéras-comique opéra-comique
operand *eg* operandau operand
operand uniongyrchol *eg* operandau uniongyrchol immediate operand
opera-oratorio *eb* operâu-oratorio opera-oratorio
opercwlwm *eg* opercwla operculum
opereta *eb* operetau operetta
operon *eg* operonau operon
opioid *eg* opioidau opioid
oportiwnistiaeth *eb* opportunism
oportiwnydd *eg* oportiwnwyr opportunist
opsiwn dedfrydu *eg* opsiynau dedfrydu sentencing option
opteg *eb* optics
opteg ffibr *eb* fibre optics
optegol *ans* optical
optegydd *eg* optegwyr optician
optimaidd *ans* optimal
optimeiddiaeth *eg* optimization
optimeiddio *be* optimize
optimeiddiwr *eg* optimeiddwyr optimizer
optimistiaeth *eb* optimism
optimistiaeth afrealistig *eb* unrealistic optimism
optimwm *eg* optima optimum
opws *eg* opus
o'r ansawdd gorau *ans* top quality
o'r brig i'r gwaelod top to bottom
o'r gwaelod i'r brig bottom to top
o'r gwddf i'r wasg neck-to-waist
o'r gwegil i'r wasg nape-to-waist
oracl *eg* oracle
oratorio *eb* oratorios oratorio
Oratori'r Cariad Dwyfol *eg* Oratory of Divine Love
orbit *eg* orbitau orbit
orbital *eg* orbitalau orbital
orbitol *ans* orbital
ordeinio *be* ordain; decree
ordinari *eg* ordinary
ordinhad *eg* ordinhadau ordinance; decree
Ordinhadau Eglwysig *ell* Ecclesiastical Ordinances
ordnans *eg* ordnance
Ordoficaidd *ans* Ordovician
oren cadmiwm *eg* cadmium orange
oren crôm *eg* chrome orange
oren llachar *eg* bright orange
Orenwr *eg* Orenwyr Orangeman
organ (=offeryn cerdd) *eb* organau organ
organ (yn y corff) *eg* organau organ
organ Americanaidd *eb* organau Americanaidd American organ
organ atsain *eb* organau atsain echo organ
organ bib *eb* organau pib pipe organ
organ Corti *eg* organau Corti organ of Corti
organ drydan *eb* organau trydan electric organ
organ electronig *eb* organau electronig electronic organ
organ estyn *eb* organau estyn extension organ
organ geg *eb* organau ceg mouth organ; French harp
organ gelwrn *eb* organau celwrn barrel organ
organ gist *eb* organau cist cabinet organ
organ gludadwy *eb* organau cludadwy portative organ
organ gôr *eb* organau côr choir organ
organ gôr gaeedig *eb* organau côr caeedig enclosed choir organ
organ gweddilliol *eg* organau gweddilliol vestigial organ
organ gyrs *eb* organau cyrs reed organ
organ hanfodol *eg* organau hanfodol vital organ
organ law *eb* organau llaw hand organ
organ lawn *eb* full organ
organ rigol *eb* organau rhigol regal
organ solo *eb* organau solo solo organ
organ solo gaeedig *eb* organau solo caeedig enclosed solo organ

organ storio *eg* organau storio storage organ
organ synhwyro *eg* organau synhwyro sense organ
organ ysgarthu *eg* organau ysgarthu excretory organ
organau atgenhedlu *ell* reproductive organs
organau cenhedlu *ell* genitals
organau perfeddol *ell* visceral organs
organdi *eg* organdie
organeb *eb* organebau organism
organeb letyol *eb* organebau lletyol host
organig *ans* organic
organigyn Golgi *eg* Golgi apparatur
organsa *eg* organza
organwm *eg* organum
organydd *eg* organyddion organist
organyn *eg* organynnau organelle
oriau brig *ell* prime time
oriau cyswllt *ell* contact hours
oriau o lafur *ell* hours of labour
oriel *eb* orielau gallery
oriel bren *eb* orielau pren hoarding
oriel newydd *eb* orielau newydd new gallery
oriel y clerwyr *eb* orielau clerwyr minstrels' gallery
orogenesis *eg* orogenesis
orogenetig *ans* orogenetic
orogeni *eg* orogeny
orograffig *ans* orographic
orograffigol *ans* orographical
orthinin *eg* orthinine
orthodeintydd *eg* orthodeintyddion orthodontist
orthodonteg *eb* orthodontics
orthoffosffad *eg* orthophosphate
orthogonol *ans* orthogonal
orthogonoledd *eg* orthogonoleddau orthogonality
orthograffig *ans* orthographic
orthograidd *eg* orthogreiddiau orthocentre
orthonormal *ans* orthonormal
orthopaedeg *eb* orthopaedics
orthopaedig *ans* orthopaedic
orthoptig *ans* orthoptic
orthoptydd *eg* orthoptwyr orthoptist
osgiliad *eg* osgiliadau swing; oscillation; amplitude swing
osgiliad gorfod *eg* osgiliadau gorfod forced oscillation
osgiliad gwanychol *eg* osgiliadau gwanychol damped oscillation
osgiliadol *ans* oscillatory
osgiliadu *be* oscillate
osgiliadur *eg* osgiliaduron oscillator
osgiliadur amledd curiad *eg* osgiliaduron amledd curiad beat frequency oscillator
osgiliadur llaciad *eg* relaxation oscillator
osgilosgop *eg* osgilosgopau oscilloscope
osgled *eg* osgledau amplitude
osgo *eg* attitude; poise
osgoi *be* avoid; dodge
osigl *eg* ossicle
osmiwm (Os) *eg* osmium
osmodderbynnydd *eg* osmoreceptor
osmogydymffurfiwr *eg* osmoconformer
osmoreolaeth *eb* osmoregulation
osmoreolaethol *ans* osmoregulatory
osmosis *eg* osmosis
osmotig weithredol *ans* osmotically active
oson *eg* ozone
osonolysis *eg* ozonolysis
osteoporosis *eg* osteoporosis
ostinato *eg* ostinati ostinato
ostinato offerynnol *eg* instrumental ostinato
ostiol *eg* ostiole
ostiwm *eg* ostium
otolith *eg* otolith
Otoman *eg* Otomaniaid Ottoman
Otomanaidd *ans* Ottoman
Owenaidd *ans* Owenite
Oweniaeth *eb* Owenism
Owenydd *eg* Owenwyr Owenite

P

pab *eg* pabau pope
PAB: Partneriaeth Addysg Busnes *eb* EBP: Education Business Partnership
pabaeth *eb* pabaethau papacy
Pabaeth *eb* Holy See
Pabaeth Avignon *eb* Avignon Papacy
pabaidd *ans* papal; popish
pabell *eb* pebyll tent
pabwyrgotwm *eg* candlewick
Pabydd *eg* Pabyddion Catholic
pabydd *eg* pabyddion papist
Pabyddiaeth *eb* Catholicism
Pabyddiaeth *eb* Romanism
pabyddol *ans* catholic; papist
pac *eg* paciau package; pack
pacedborth *eg* pacedbyrth packet port
pacedlong *eb* pacedlongau packet steamer
paciedig *ans* packed
pacin *eg* packing
pacio *be* pack; packing
pacio tyn close-packing
pacio tyn ciwbig cubic close-packing
pacio tyn hecsagonol hexagonal close-packing
pacio'n dynn *be* close packing
pacrew *eg* pack ice
pact gwrth-Gomintern *eg* anti-Comintern pact
pad *eg* padiau pad
pad amsugnol *eg* padiau amsugnol absorbent pad
pad asbestos *eg* padiau asbestos asbestos pad
pad braslunio *eg* padiau braslunio sketch pad
pad cicio *eg* padiau cicio kicker
pad concrit *eg* padiau concrit concrete pad
pad cyffwrdd *eg* padiau cyffwrdd touchpad
pad chwys *eg* padiau chwys dress shield
pad dyrnu *eg* padiau dyrnu punch pad
pad ffelt *eg* padiau ffelt felt pad
pad graffeg *eg* padiau graffeg graphics pad
pad gweledol-gofodol *eg* visuospatial scratchpad
pad llathru *eg* padiau llathru polishing pad
pad presio *eg* padiau presio pressing pad
pad sebon *eg* padiau sebon soaped pad
pad smwddio *eg* padiau smwddio ironing pad
pad ysgrifennu *eg* padiau ysgrifennu note pad
pad ysgwydd *eg* padiau ysgwydd shoulder pad
padell *eb* pedyll pan
padell ffrio *eb* pedyll ffrio frying pan
padell lwch *eb* pedyll llwch dustpan
padell pen-glin *eb* pedyll pengliniau patella
padell pen-glin *eb* pedyll pengliniau knee cap
padell wely *eb* pedyll gwely bedpan
padell yr ysgwydd *eb* pedyll ysgwyddau scapula
padellog *ans* patellar
paderwr *eg* paderwyr beadsman
padin *eg* padding
padio *be* pad
padl *eb* padlau paddle
padlo *be* paddle
padlo'n araf *be* paddle light
padlo'n gadarn *be* paddle firm
padog *eg* padogau paddock
paediatreg *eb* paediatrics
paediatregydd *eg* paediatregwyr paediatrician
paedoffilia *eg* paedophilia
paedoffilydd *eg* paedophile
paent *eg* paentiau paint
paent acrylig *eg* paentiau acrylig acrylic paint
paent bitwmen *eg* bituminous paint
paent bys *eg* finger paint
paent crefft *eg* craft paint
paent distemper *eg* distemper paint
paent emwlsiwn *eg* emulsion paint
paent enamel *eg* enamel paint
paent lacr *eg* lacquer paint
paent plisgyn wy *eg* eggshell paint
paent posteri *eg* paentiau posteri poster paint
paent preimio *eg* paentiau preimio primer paint
paent sail olew *eg* paentiau sail olew oil based paint
paent sglein *eg* gloss paint
paent synthetig *eg* synthetic paint
paent tenau *eg* lean paint
paentiad *eg* paentiadau painting
paentiad arwydd *eg* paentiadau arwydd sign painting
paentiad bys *eg* paentiadau bys finger painting
paentiad chwistrell *eg* paentiadau chwistrell spray painting
paentiad dyfrlliw *eg* paentiadau dyfrlliw water colour painting
paentiad Eidalaidd *eg* paentiadau Eidalaidd Italian painting
paentiad ffigurol *eg* paentiadau ffigurol figurative painting
paentiad gweithredol *eg* paentiadau gweithredol action painting
paentiad haniaethol *eg* paentiadau haniaethol abstract painting
paentiad llaw *eg* paentiadau llaw hand painting

paentiad ogof *eg* paentiadau ogof cave painting
paentiad olew *eg* paentiadau olew oil painting
paentiad portreadol *be* paentiadau portreadol portrait painting
paentiad rhydd *eg* paentiadau rhydd free painting
paentiad tempera *eg* paentiadau tempera tempera painting
paentiad tirlun *eg* paentiadau tirlun landscape painting
paentiwr portreadau *eg* paentwyr portreadau portrait painter
pafiliwn *eg* pafiliynau pavilion
pagan *eg* paganiaid pagan
paganiaeth *eb* paganism
pagoda *eg* pagodau pagoda
pangyweiraidd *ans* pantonal
pangyweiredd *eg* pantonality
paill *eg* pollen
pair *eg* peiriau cauldron; melting pot
pais *eb* peisiau petticoat; underskirt; slip
pais arfau *eb* scutcheon
pais wasg *eb* peisiau gwasg waist slip
paith *eg* peithiau prairie; pampas
paladiwm *eg* palladium
paladr *eg* pelydr beam; ray
paladr allddodol *eg* pelydr allddodol emergent beam
paladr main *eg* fine beam
palaeoanthropoleg *eb* paleoanthropology
palaeograffeg *eb* palaeography
palaeolithig *ans* palaeolithic
palaeontoleg *eb* palaeontology
palas esgob *eg* palasau esgobion bishop's palace
palet *eg* paletau palette
palet boracs *eg* paletau boracs borax palette
palet braich *eg* arm palette
palet cymysgu *eg* paletau cymysgu mixing palette
palet hepgor *eg* paletau hepgor disposable palette
palet lliw *eg* paletau lliw colour palette
palet petryal *eg* paletau petryal oblong palette
palet sbectrwm *eg* paletau sbectrwm spectrum palette
palet tsieni *eg* paletau tsieni china palette
palf *eb* palfau palm
palfais *eb* palfeisiau shoulder blade
palindrom *eg* palindromau palindrome
palisâd *eg* palisadau palisade
paliwm *eg* palia pallium
palmant *eg* palmentydd pavement
palmwr *eg* palmwyr palmer
palmwydden *eb* palmwydd palm
palmwydden corsen *eb* palmwydd cyrs rattan palm
palp *eg* palpiau palp
palpws *eg* palpysau palpus
palstaf *eg* palstafau palstave
pamffledu *be* pamphleteering
pamffledwr *eg* pamffledwyr pamphleteer
pancreas *eg* pancreas
pancromatig *ans* panchromatic
pandy *eg* pandai fulling mill
panel *eg* paneli panel
panel addurnol *eg* paneli addurnol decorative panel
panel arddangos *eg* paneli arddangos display panel
panel befel *eg* paneli befel bevelled panel
panel befel *eg* paneli befel bevel panel
panel blaen *eg* paneli blaen front panel
panel cafeto *eg* paneli cafeto cavetto panel
panel cwricwlwm *eg* paneli cwricwlwm curriculum panel
panel cyfwyneb *eg* paneli cyfwyneb flush panel
panel drws *eg* paneli drws door panel
panel estyll cydwedd *eg* matchboarding panel
panel glain ac ymyl *eg* paneli glain ac ymyl bead and butt panel
panel gleinio cyfwyneb *eg* paneli gleinio cyfwyneb flush-beaded panel
panel gordo *eg* paneli gordo shroud panel
panel gwydr *eg* paneli gwydr glass panel
panel llien-blyg *eg* panelau llien-blyg linen-fold panel
panel o aseswyr *eg* paneli o aseswyr panel of assessors
panel pell-reoli *eg* paneli pell-reoli remote control panel
panel plaen *eg* paneli plaen plain panel
panel pren haenog *eg* paneli pren haenog plywood panel
panel rheiddiol *eg* paneli rheiddiol quartered panel
panel rheoli *eg* paneli rheoli control panel
panel rhigolog *eg* paneli rhigolog grooved panel
panel rhwyllog *eg* paneli rhwyllog pierced panel
panel sodr *eg* paneli sodr solder panel
panel solet *eg* paneli solet solid panel
panel wal *eg* paneli wal wall panel
panel wedi'i godi *eg* paneli wedi'u codi raised panel
panel wedi'i ludio *eg* paneli wedi'u gludio glued-on panel
panel wedi'i suddo *eg* paneli wedi'u suddo sunk panel
panig *eg* panic
panig moesol *eg* moral panic
panigl *eg* paniglau panicle
Panj Kakka Panj Kakka
panj piare /panj pyare panj piare /panj pyare
panlwch (=powdr) *eg* pounce
panlychu (=powdro) *be* pounce
pannu *be* fulling; shrink; fullering
pannwr *eg* panwyr fuller
► **pannydd isaf** *eg* panwyr isaf bottom fuller
pannydd uchaf *eg* panwyr uchaf top fuller
panorama *eg* panoramâu panorama
panoramig *ans* panoramic
panslafiaeth *eb* panslavism

pant *eg* pantiau hollow; depression
pant heli *eg* pantiau heli salt pan
pant rhew *eg* pantiau rhew frost hollow
pantiad *eg* pantiadau indentation
pantio *be* hollow; dishing
pantler *eg* pantleriaid pantler
pantograff *eg* pantograffau pantograph
pantomeim *eg* pantomeimau pantomime
pants *ell* pants
Panth *eg* Panth
papila *eg* papilau papilla
papilaidd *ans* papillary
papiliffurf *ans* papilliform
papur *eg* papurau paper
papur adeiladwaith *eg* construction paper
papur adrannol *eg* sectional paper
papur alwminiwm ocsid *eg* aluminium oxide paper
papur amlran *eg* papurau amlran multi-part paper
papur amsugnol *eg* papurau amsugnol absorbent paper
papur arholiad *eg* papurau arholiad examination paper
papur arian *eg* kitchen foil
papur arlliwedig *eg* tinted paper
papur blawd *eg* flour paper
papur boglynnog *eg* embossed wallpaper
papur bras *eg* antique paper
papur braslunio *eg* papurau braslunio sketch paper
papur carbon *eg* papurau carbon carbon paper
papur cegin *eg* kitchen paper
papur cetris *eg* cartridge paper
papur cetris lliw *eg* coloured cartridge paper
papur clawr *eg* cover paper
papur crêp *eg* crêpe paper
papur crych *eg* crinkled paper
papur cwyr *eg* wax paper
papur cynargraffedig *eg* preprinted paper
papur dargopïo *eg* tracing paper
papur di-dor *eg* continuous stationery
papur diferu *eg* draining paper
papur drafftio *eg* drafting paper
papur dyfrlliw *eg* water colour paper
papur erwydd *eg* papurau erwydd manuscript paper
papur estynedig *eg* papurau estynedig extension paper
papur felwm *eg* vellum paper
papur finyl *eg* vinyl wallpaper
papur ffris *eg* papurau ffris frieze paper
papur garnet *eg* papurau garnet garnet paper
papur golchadwy *eg* washable wallpaper
papur graff *eg* papurau graff graph paper
papur gwahaniaethol *eg* papurau gwahaniaethol differentiated paper
papur gwlyb a sych *eg* wet and dry paper
papur gwm *eg* papurau gwm gum paper
papur gwm tryloyw *eg* transparent gummed paper
papur gwrth-ddŵr *eg* waterproof paper
papur gwrtholew *eg* oilproof paper
papur gwydrog *eg* sandpaper
papur hidlo *eg* papurau hidlo filter paper
papur igam ogam *eg* fan-fold paper
papur labelu *eg* labelling paper
papur lapio *eg* wrapping paper
papur lliain *eg* rag paper
papur lliw *eg* coloured paper
papur lluniadu *eg* drawing-paper
papur llwyd *eg* kraft paper
papur llwyd *eg* papurau llwyd brown paper
papur llythrennu *eg* lettering paper
papur manila *eg* manilla paper
papur manylion *eg* detail paper
papur morwydd *eg* mulberry paper
papur newydd *eg* papurau newydd newspaper
papur olew *eg* oil paper
papur olew stensil *eg* oil stencil paper
papur patrymog *eg* papurau patrymog patterned paper
papur poblogaidd *eg* tabloid
papur prawf *eg* papurau prawf test paper
papur reis *eg* rice paper
papur rhychiog *eg* papurau rhychiog corrugated paper
papur safonol *eg* papurau safonol broadsheet
papur sglein *eg* papurau sglein glossy paper; shiny paper; glazed paper
papur sglein sidan *eg* silk finish paper
papur sglodion pren *eg* woodchip wallpaper
papur sgraffinio *eg* papurau sgraffinio abrasive paper
papur sgwariau *eg* squared paper
papur sidan *eg* tissue paper
papur sidan gwyn *eg* white tissue paper
papur sidan lliw *eg* coloured tissue paper
papur silicon carbid *eg* silicon carbide paper
papur siwgr *eg* sugar paper
papur stensil *eg* stencil paper
papur sugno *eg* blotting paper
papur sychadwy *eg* spongeable wallpaper
papur terfyn *eg* papurau terfyn end paper
papur torri allan *eg* cutting out paper
papur troslunio *eg* transfer paper
papur tryloyw *eg* transparent paper
papur twngsten carbid *eg* tungsten carbide paper
papur wal *eg* wallpaper
papur wedi'i dorri *eg* cut paper
papur ysgrifennu *eg* writing paper
papur ysgrifennu *eg* stationery
papurfrwyn *ell* papyrus
papuro *be* paper; wallpaper
papws *eg* pappus
pâr (yn gyffredinol) *eg* parau pair
pâr (yn rhwyfo) *eg* parau coxless pair
pâr a chocs coxed pair

pâr cyfiau *eg* conjugate pair
pâr cyflenwol o fasau *eg* complementary base pair
pâr unig *eg* parau unig lone pair
parabola *eg* parabolâu parabola
parabolig *ans* parabolical
paraboloid *eg* paraboloidau paraboloid
paradeim arbrawf *eg* paradeimau arbrawf experimental paradigm
paradeim oedi dynwared *eg* deferred imitation paradigm
paradocs *eg* paradocsau paradox
paradocs cynildeb *eg* paradox of thrift
paradwys *eb* paradise
parafeddyg *eg* parafeddygon paramedic
paraffilia *eg* paraphilia
paraffîn *eg* paraffin
paragraff *eg* paragraffau paragraph
paragraff agoriadol *eg* paragraffau agoriadol lead paragraph
paragraff crog *eg* paragraffau crog hanging paragraph
paragraff cudd *eg* paragraffau cudd hidden paragraph
paragraff newydd *eg* paragraffau newydd new paragraph
paragraff ochr *eg* paragraffau ochr block paragraph
paragraff wedi'i fewnoli *eg* paragraffau wedi'u mewnoli indented paragraph
paragraffu *be* paragraph
paralacs *eg* paralacsau parallax
paralel *ans* parallel
paralel *eg* paralelau parallel
paralel lledred *eg* paralelau lledred parallel of latitude
paralelepiped *eg* paralelepipedau parallelepiped
paralelogram *eg* paralelogramau parallelogram
paramagnetedd *eg* paramagnetism
paramanw *eg* paramanu
paramedr *eg* paramedrau parameter
paramedr anghywir *eg* paramedrau anghywir wrong parameter
paramedr animeiddio *eg* paramedrau animeiddio animation parameter
paramedr ffurfiol *eg* paramedrau ffurfiol formal parameter
paramedr gwirioneddol *eg* paramedrau gwirioneddol actual parameter
paramedr llanw *eg* paramedrau llanw fill parameter
parametrig *ans* parametric
paranoia *eg* paranoia
parapodiwm *eg* parapodia parapodium
paraseicoleg *eb* parapsychology
parasit *eg* parasitiaid parasite
parasitedd *eg* parasitism
parasiteiddio *be* parasitize
parasitig *ans* parasitic
parasiwt *eg* parasiwtau parachute
paratoad *eg* paratoadau preparation
paratoadol *ans* preparatory
paratoi *be* prepare; make up
paratoi anghytsain *be* preparation of a discord
paratoi data *be* data preparation
paratoi plant i'r ysbyty *be* preparing children for hospital
paratoi ymlaen llaw *be* pre-prepare
parathyroid *eg* parathyroidau parathyroid
parau *ell* doubles
parau gwrthweithiol o gyhyrau *ell* antagonistic muscle pairs
parau trefnedig *ell* ordered pairs
paraymatebol *ans* parasympathetic
parc *eg* parciau park
parc neu erddi addurnol park or ornamental grounds
parc thema *eg* parciau thema theme park
parcdir *eg* parcdiroedd parkland
parch *eg* deference
parch cadarnhaol diamod *eg* unconditional positive regard
parchusrwydd *eg* respectability
pardwn *eg* pardon
Pardwn Alais *eg* Grace of Alais
pardynwr *eg* pardynwyr pardoner
parechelin *ans* paraxial
parêd *eg* paredau parade
pared *eg* parwydydd partition; partition wall
paredd *eg* pareddau parity
parencyma *eg* parenchyma
parencymol *ans* parenxhymatous
parenthesis *eg* parenthesisau parenthesis
parhad *eg* continuation; continuity; duration
parhad dadansoddol *eg* analytical continuation
parhaol *ans* permanent; perpetual; perennial
parhau *be* continue
parhau i chwilio nôl *be* continue search backwards
parhau i chwilio ymlaen *be* continue search forward
pariad *eg* pariadau pairing
parinibbana *eg* parinibbana
parinirvana *eg* parinirvana
pario *be* parry
pario cylchol *be* circular parry
pario drwy wrthwynebu *be* parry by opposition
pario drwy ysgaru *be* parry by detachment
pario syml *be* simple parry
pario union *be* direct parry
parlys *eg* parlysau paralysis
parlys lleferydd *eg* dysarthria
parlys pedwar aelod *eg* quadriplegia
parlys un ochr *eg* hemiplegia
parlys yr ymennydd *eg* cerebral palsy
parlysu *be* paralyse
parod *ans* ready-made
parodrwydd esblygol *eg* evolutionary preparedness

parota *be* parroting
parquet *eg* parquet
partio *be* parting; parting off
partisan *eg* partisaniaid partisan
partita *eg* partitâu partita
partner *eg* partneriaid partner
partner dawns *eg* partneriaid dawns partner dance
partner sbarian *eg* partneriaid sbarian sparring partner
partneriaeth *eb* partneriaethau partnership
parth *eg* parthau domain; zone
parth datblygiad procsimol *eg* zone of proximal development
parth ffactoriad unigryw *eg* unique factorization domain
parth ffiniol *eg* parthau ffiniol frontier zone
parth gofod *eg* parthau gofod space domain
parth integrol *eg* parthau integrol integral domain
parth rhynglanw *eg* intertidal zone
parthiad *eg* shedding
paru *be* pair
Parvati *eb* Parvati
parwydol *ans* parietal
pàs *eg/b* pasiau pass
pàs dan ysgwydd *eb* pasiau dan ysgwydd underarm pass
pàs dros ysgwydd *eb* pasiau dros ysgwydd overarm pass
pàs glasurol *eb* pasiau clasurol classic pass
pàs gosb *eb* pasiau cosb penalty pass
pàs gwaywffon *eb* pasiau gwaywffyn javelin pass
pàs gyntaf *eb* pasiau cyntaf centre pass
pàs hir isel *eb* pasiau hir isel long low pass
pàs hir uchel *eb* pasiau hir uchel long high pass
pàs hollti *eb* pasiau hollti thro' ball
pàs letraws *eb* pasiau lletraws diagonal pass
pàs o'r frest *eb* pasiau o'r frest chest pass
pàs o'r ysgwydd *eb* pasiau o'r ysgwydd shoulder pass
pàs sboncio *eb* pasiau sboncio bounce pass
pàs sgwâr *eb* pasiau sgwâr square pass
pàs syth *eb* pasiau syth straight pass
pàs unllaw *eb* pasiau unllaw one-handed pass
pàs wrthdro *eb* pasiau gwrthdro reverse stick pass
pàs wrthol *eb* pasiau gwrthol reverse pass
pas, y *eg* whooping cough
pàs ymlaen *eb* pasiau ymlaen forward pass
Pasg *eg* Easter
Pasg Iddewig *eg* Passover
Pasg yr Iddewon *eg* Jewish Easter
pasiant *eg* pasiantau pageant
pasiantri *eg* pageantry
pasio *be* pass
pasio am nôl *be* pass back
pasio'r bêl *be* pass the ball
pas-isel *ans* low-pass
pasodoble *eg* dawnsiau pasodoble pasodoble
passacaglia *eg* passacaglie passacaglia
past *eg* pastau paste
past barbola *eg* barbola paste
past blawd *eg* flour paste
past cellwlos *eg* cellulose paste
past di-draidd *eg* opaque paste
past dŵr *eg* water paste
past dŵr oer *eg* cold water paste
past emeri *eg* emery paste
past gwyn *eg* white paste
past llifanu *eg* grinding paste
pastai Gernyw *eb* pasteiod Cernyw Cornish pasty
pastai'r bugail *eb* shepherd's pie
► **pastai'r bwthyn** *eb* pasteiod bwthyn cottage pie
pastel *eg* pasteli pastel
pastel cwyr *eg* pasteli cwyr wax pastel
pastel olew *eg* pasteli olew oil pastel
pasteureiddiad *eg* pasteurization
pasteureiddio *be* pasteurize
pastiche *eg* pastiches pastiche
pastio *be* paste
pastog *ans* pasty
pastwn *eg* pastynau truncheon
pat côn *eg* patiau côn cone pat
patent *eg* patent
Patimokkha *eg* Patimokkha
patina *eg* patina
patio *be* patting
patriarch *eg* patriarchiaid patriarch
patriarchaeth *eb* patriarchy
patriarchaidd *ans* patriarchal
patrôl *eg* patrolau patrol
patronymig *ans* patronymic
patrwm *eg* patrymau pattern
patrwm ailadroddol *eg* patrymau ailadroddol repeat pattern
patrwm amlbwrpas *eg* patrymau amlbwrpas multi-purpose pattern
patrwm amlfaint *eg* patrymau amlfaint multi-size pattern
patrwm anheddu *eg* patrymau anheddu settlement pattern
patrwm bloc *eg* patrymau bloc block pattern
patrwm byd-eang *eg* patrymau byd-eang global pattern
patrwm cerddorol *eg* patrymau cerddorol musical pattern
patrwm cnau menyn *eg* patrymau cnau menyn butter-nut pattern
patrwm cnewyllol *eg* patrymau cnewyllol nucleated pattern
patrwm codiad yr haul *eg* patrymau codiad yr haul sunrise pattern
patrwm craidd *eg* patrymau craidd core pattern
patrwm creiddig *eg* patrymau creiddig cored pattern
patrwm curiadau *eg* patrymau curiadau pulse pattern

patrwm cwlwm dolen *eg* patrymau cwlwm dolen bow knot pattern
patrwm cyfangiad *eg* patrymau cyfangiad contraction pattern
patrwm cymhleth *eg* patrymau cymhleth intricate pattern
patrwm cymudo *eg* patrymau cymudo commuting pattern
patrwm chwyrlïog *eg* patrymau chwyrlïog swirled pattern
patrwm dannedd *eg* dental formula
patrwm didol *eg* patrymau didol bit pattern
patrwm disgyn *eg* patrymau disgyn drop pattern
patrwm dosbarthiad *eg* patrymau dosbarthiad distribution pattern
patrwm draeniad *eg* patrymau draeniad drainage pattern
patrwm drafft *eg* patrymau drafft drafted pattern
patrwm ecolegol *eg* patrymau ecolegol ecological pattern
patrwm ffurfiol *eg* patrymau ffurfiol formal pattern
patrwm geiriol wedi'i lefaru'n rhythmig *eg* patrymau geiriol wedi'u llefaru'n rhythmig rhythmically spoken word pattern
patrwm geometrig *eg* patrymau geometrig geometric pattern
patrwm gwaelodol *eg* patrymau gwaelodol underlying pattern
patrwm gwaith *eg* work pattern
patrwm gwasgarog *eg* patrymau gwasgarog scattered pattern
patrwm gwehyddu *eg* patrymau gwehyddu weaving pattern
patrwm gwregys y mynach *eg* patrymau gwregys y mynach monk's belt pattern
patrwm gwrthgyfnewid *eg* patrymau gwrthgyfnewid counterchange pattern
patrwm gwyddfid *eg* patrymau gwyddfid honeysuckle pattern
patrwm haniaethol *eg* patrymau haniaethol abstract pattern
patrwm hanner disgyn *eg* patrymau hanner disgyn half-drop pattern
patrwm hollt *eg* patrymau hollt split pattern
patrwm lôn y rhosyn *eg* patrymau lôn y rhosyn rose path pattern
patrwm llif *eg* patrymau llif flow pattern
patrwm melodig *eg* patrymau melodig melodic pattern
patrwm o weithgarwch economaidd *eg* patrymau o weithgarwch economaidd pattern of economic activity
patrwm ochr od *eg* patrymau ochr od odd side pattern
patrwm ôl y falwen *eg* patrymau ôl y falwen snail's trail pattern
patrwm olwyn cerbyd *eg* patrymau olwyn cerbyd chariot wheel pattern
patrwm olwyn ffawd *eg* patrymau olwyn ffawd wheel of fortune pattern
patrwm parod *eg* patrymau parod commercial pattern
patrwm print *eg* patrymau print printed pattern
patrwm rhythm *eg* patrymau rhythm rhythm pattern
patrwm saethben *eg* patrymau saethben herring-bone pattern
patrwm siec *eg* patrymau siec check pattern
patrwm stensil *eg* patrymau stensil stencil pattern
patrwm sylfaenol *eg* patrymau sylfaenol basic pattern
patrwm syml *eg* patrymau syml simple pattern
patrwm trosodd *eg* all-over pattern
patrwm tyllog *eg* patrymau tyllog perforated pattern
patrwm undarn *eg* patrymau undarn one piece pattern
patrwm waffl *eg* patrymau waffl waffle pattern
patrwm y serfio *eg* patrymau'r serfio serve pattern
patrwm y tywydd *eg* weather pattern
patrwm ymddygiad *eg* patrymau ymddygiad pattern of behaviour
patrymau diffreithiant *ell* diffraction patterns
patrymedd *eg* regime
patrymedd afon *eg* river regime
patrymedd glawiad *eg* rainfall regime
patrymlun *eg* patrymluniau template
patrymlun cerdyn *eg* patrymluniau cerdyn card template
patrymlun cynffonnog *eg* patrymluniau cynffonnog dovetail template
patrymlun meitr *eg* patrymluniau meitr mitre template
patrymlun pennawd ffacs *eg* patrymluniau pennawd ffacs fax header template
patrymog *ans* patterned
pathogen *eg* pathogenau pathogen
pathogenaidd *ans* pathogenic
patholeg *eb* pathology
patholegol *ans* pathological
patholegydd *eg* patholegwyr pathologist
pavane *eg* pavanes pavane
pawl *eg* polion pawl
pawl clicied *eg* polion clicied ratchet pawl
Pawl Hen *eg* Paulinus
pectin *eg* pectin
pectinas *eg* pectinase
pecyn *eg* pecynnau packet; package
pecyn agored *eg* pecynnau agored open pack
pecyn anghyfeillgar *eg* pecynnau anghyfeillgar user-hostile package
pecyn arlunio *eg* pecynnau arlunio art package
pecyn awduro *eg* pecynnau awduro authoring package
pecyn caeedig *eg* pecynnau caeedig closed pack
pecyn cyfannol *eg* pecynnau cyfannol integrated package
pecyn disgiau *eg* pecynnau disgiau disk pack
pecyn gwybodaeth *eg* pecynnau gwybodaeth information packet

pecyn pŵer *eg* pecynnau pŵer power pack
► **pecyn rhaglen** *eg* pecynnau rhaglen application package
pecyn taenlen *eg* pecynnau taenlen spreadsheet package
pecyn trin data *eg* pecynnau trin data data-handling package
pechod *eg* pechodau sin
pechod gweithredol *eg* actual sin
pechu *be* sin
pedagogeg *eb* pedagogy
Pedair Golygfa, Y *eb* Four Sights, The
pedair pêl *eb* four ball
pedair strôc *ans* four-stroke
pedal *eg* pedalau pedal
pedal cyfuno *eg* pedalau cyfuno combination pedal; composition pedal
pedal chwith *eg* pedalau chwith left pedal; soft pedal
pedal mewnol *eg* pedalau mewnol inner pedal
pedalu *be* pedal
pedestal *eg* pedestalau pedestal
pedicel *eg* pedicelau pedicel
pedicl *eg* pediclau pedicle
pediment *eg* pedimentau pediment
pediplan *eg* pediplanau pediplain
pediplaniant *eg* pediplanation
pedol ceffyl *eb* pedolau ceffyl horseshoe
Pedr Fawr *eb* Peter the Great
Pedr Feudwy *eg* Peter the Hermit
pedrant *eg* pedrannau quadrant
pedreiddiad *eg* petrification
pedrochr *ans* quadrilateral
pedrochr *eg/b* pedrochrau quadrilateral
pedrochr cylchol *eg* pedrochrau cylchol cyclic quadrilateral
pedrongl *eg/b* pedronglau quadrangle
pedrybled *eg* pedrybledau quadruplet
pedryddol *ans* quaternary
pedwar (mewn rhwyfo) *eg* pedwarau coxless four
pedwar (yn gyffredinol) *eg* pedwarau four
pedwar a chocs coxed four
pedwar can metr *eg* four hundred metres
pedwar pwynt cyswllt *eg* four points of contact
Pedwar Rhyddid *eg* Four Freedoms
pedwarawd *eg* pedwarawdau quartet; foursome
pedwarawd chwyth *eg* pedwarawdau chwyth wind quartet
pedwarawd llinynnol *eg* pedwarawdau llinynnol string quartet
pedwarcylchol *ans* tetracyclic
Pedwardegau Newynog *ell* Hungry Forties
pedwarplyg *ans* quadruple
pedwartroedyn *eg* pedwartroedion quadruped
pedwerydd *eg* pedweryddau fourth
pedweryddau arosodedig *ell* superposed fourths
pedwncl *eg* pedynclau peduncle
pedynclaidd *ans* pedunculate

pefriol *ans* sparkling
peg *eg* pegiau peg
peg atred *eg* offset peg
peg dillad *eg* pegiau dillad clothes peg
peg doli *eg* pegiau doli dolly peg
peg hoelbren *eg* pegiau hoelbren dowel peg
peg iâ *eg* pegiau iâ ice peg
peg rhedwr (castio) *eg* pegiau rhedwyr runner peg
peg rhew *eg* pegiau rhew ice peg
pegio *be* peg
pegwn *eg* pegynau pole
pegwn datblygiadol *eg* pegynau datblygiadol pole of development
pegwn uned *eg* pegynau uned unit pole
pegwn wybrennol y de *eg* south celestial pole
pegwn wybrennol y gogledd *eg* north celestial pole
pegwn y gogledd *eg* north pole
pegynau cyfansawdd *ell* multiple poles
pegynlin *eg* pegynliniau polar
pegynol *ans* polar
pegynol-arforol *ans* polar-maritime
pegynol-gyfandirol *ans* polar-continental
pengaead *ans* blind-ending
peil *eg* pile
peilon *eg* peilonau pylon
peilot *ans* pilot
peilot profi *eg* peilotiaid profi test pilot
peillio *be* pollinate
peint *eg* peintiau pint
peintio *be* paint; apply paint
peintio arwydd *be* sign painting
peintio bys *be* finger painting
peintio cwyr *be* wax painting
peintio chwistrell *be* spray painting
peintio dyfrlliw *be* water colour painting
peintio Eidalaidd *be* Italian painting
peintio ffigurol *be* figurative painting
peintio golygfa *be* scene painting
peintio gweithredol *be* action painting
peintio haniaethol *be* abstract painting
peintio llaw *be* hand painting
peintio olew *be* oil painting
peintio portreadol *be* portrait painting
peintio rhydd *be* free painting
peintio tempera *be* tempera painting
peintio tirlun *be* landscape painting
peintio uniongyrchol *be* direct painting
peintio ymylodol *be* fore-edge painting
peintiwr *eg* peintwyr painter
peintiwr golygfeydd *eg* peintwyr golygfeydd scene painter
peintwaith *eg* paintwork
peipell *eb* peipellau piper
peipen *eb* peipiau pipe
peipen ddŵr rwber *eb* peipiau dŵr rwber hose pipe

peipen gangen arosgo *eb* peipiau cangen arosgo oblique branch pipe
peipen gangen fertigol *eb* peipiau cangen fertigol vertical branch pipe
peipen gangen lorweddol *eb* peipiau cangen llorweddol horizontal branch pipe
peipio *be* pipe
peipio *be* piping
peiran *eg* peirannau corrie
peiran tandem *eg* peirannau tandem tandem corrie
peiriandy *eg* peiriandai engine house
peirianddryll bychan *eg* peirianddrylliau bychain sub-machine gun
peiriannau *ell* plant
peirianneg *eb* engineering
peirianneg genetig *eb* genetic engineering
peirianneg sifil *eb* civil engineering
peirianneg uwch *eb* advanced engineering
peiriannu *be* machine
peiriannu plastig *be* plastic machining
peiriannydd *eg* peirianwyr engineer
peiriannydd meddalwedd *eg* peirianwyr meddalwedd software engineer
peiriant *eg* peiriannau engine
peiriant *eg* peiriannau machine
peiriant adio *eg* peiriannau adio adding machine
peiriant anadlu *eg* peiriannau anadlu respirator
peiriant anadlu *eg* peiriannau anadlu ventilator
peiriant arian *eg* peiriannau arian cash dispenser
peiriant arian parod *eg* peiriannau arian parod cash machine
peiriant awtomatig *eg* peiriannau awtomatig automatic machine
peiriant blaen-lwytho *eg* peiriannau blaen-lwytho front loader
peiriant bwrdd gwaith *eg* peiriannau bwrdd gwaith desktop machine
peiriant coffi *eg* peiriannau coffi coffee maker
peiriant cyfrifo *eg* peiriannau cyfrifo calculating machine
peiriant cymysgu clai *eg* peiriannau cymysgu clai blunger
peiriant chwilio *eg* peiriannau chwilio search engine
peiriant chwythu *eg* peiriannau chwythu motorised blower
peiriant drilio *eg* peiriannau drilio drilling machine
peiriant drilio gwaith trwm *eg* peiriannau drilio gwaith trwm heavy duty drilling machine
peiriant drilio mainc *eg* peiriannau drilio mainc bench drilling machine
peiriant drilio pedestal *eg* peiriannau drilio pedestal pedestal drilling machine
peiriant drilio piler *eg* peiriannau drilio piler pillar drilling machine
peiriant drilio sensitif *eg* peiriannau drilio sensitif sensitive drilling machine
peiriant dyrnu *eg* peiriannau dyrnu thrashing machine
peiriant electronig *eg* peiriannau electronig electronic machine
peiriant galw *eg* peiriannau galw pager
peiriant goddef trochion *eg* peiriannau goddef trochion suds tolerant machine
peiriant golchi *eg* peiriannau golchi washing machine
peiriant golchi llestri *eg* peiriannau golchi llestri dishwasher
peiriant gwau *eg* peiriannau gwau knitting machine
peiriant gwerthu *eg* peiriannau gwerthu vending-machine
peiriant gwynt *eg* peiriannau gwynt wind machine
peiriant jet *eg* peiriannau jet jet engine
peiriant llafnu *eg* peiriannau llafnu shearing machine
peiriant llaw *eg* peiriannau llaw hand machine
peiriant llifanu *eg* peiriannau llifanu grinding machine
peiriant llifanu yn y llaw *eg* peiriannau llifanu yn y llaw off-hand grinder
peiriant llunio *eg* peiriannau llunio shaper
peiriant melino *eg* peiriannau melino milling machine
peiriant melino fertigol *eg* peiriannau melino fertigol vertical milling machine
peiriant melino llorwedd *eg* peiriannau melino llorwedd horizontal milling machine
peiriant morteisio *eg* peiriannau morteisio morticing machine
peiriant pedair strôc *eg* peiriannau pedair strôc four-stroke engine
peiriant petrol *eg* peiriannau petrol petrol engine
peiriant pilerog *eg* peiriannau pilerog pillar type machine
peiriant plaenio *eg* planing machine
peiriant plygu peipen *eg* peiriannau plygu peipiau pipe bending machine
peiriant sensitif i drochion *eg* peiriannau sensitif i drochion suds sensitive machine
peiriant smwddio cylchdro *eg* peiriannau smwddio cylchdro rotary iron
peiriant sychu dillad *eg* peiriannau sychu dillad tumble drier
peiriant tanio mewnol *eg* peiriannau tanio mewnol internal combustion engine
peiriant taranau *eg* peiriannau taranau thunder machine
peiriant tewychu *eg* peiriannau tewychu thicknessing machine
peiriant tonnau *eg* peiriannau tonnau wave machine
peiriant top-lwytho *eg* peiriannau top-lwytho top loader
peiriant trawst *eg* peiriannau trawst beam engine
peiriant twb dwbl *eg* peiriannau twb dwbl twin tub machine
peiriant twb sengl *eg* peiriannau twb sengl single tub machine

peiriant uniadau cynffonnog *eg* peiriannau uniadau cynffonnog dovetailing machine
peirianwaith *eg* peirianweithiau machinery
peirianwaith cymhwyso *eg* peirianweithiau cymhwyso adjusting mechanism
peirianwaith etholiadol *eg* electoral machinery
peiswellt *eg* fescue
peithbriddoedd *ell* prairie soils
pêl *eb* peli ball
pêl araf *eb* peli araf slow ball
pêl blastig ysgafn *eb* peli plastig ysgafn light plastic ball
pêl dennis *eb* peli tennis tennis ball
pêl dda *eb* good ball
pêl ddarpar *eb* peli darpar provisional ball
pêl ddyrnu *eb* peli dyrnu punch ball
pêl fagnel *eb* peli magnel cannon ball
pêl farw *eb* dead ball
pêl fer *eb* peli byr short pitched delivery
pêl fer ac araf *eb* short, slow ball
pêl foli *eb* peli foli volley ball
pêl goll *eb* peli coll lost ball
pêl gwymp *eb* peli cwymp dropped ball
pêl gyflym *eb* peli cyflym fast ball
pêl isel *eb* peli isel low ball
pêl law *eb* peli llaw hand ball
pêl ledr *eb* peli lledr leather ball
pêl rygbi *eb* peli rygbi rugby ball
pêl sbwng *eb* peli sbwng sponge ball
pêl uchel *eb* peli uchel high ball
pelagra *eg* pellagra
pelawd *eb* pelawdau over
pelawd ddi-sgôr *eb* pelawdau di-sgôr maiden over
pêl-droed *eg* peli troed football
pêl-droediwr *eg* pêl-droedwyr footballer
peledol *ans* bombarding
peledu *be* bombard
pelen (=pêl fach wedi'i chywasgu) *eb* pelenni pellet
pelen (mewn criced) *eb* pelenni bowled ball
pelen (yn gyffredinol) *eb* pelenni ball
pelen fer iawn *eb* peli byr iawn long hop
pelen laid *eb* pelenni llaid mud pellet
pelen lawn *eb* pelenni llawn full toss
pelen lwybro *eg* peli llwybro trackball
pelen lydan *eb* pelenni llydan wide ball
pelen wallus *eb* pelenni gwallus no ball
pelen y droed *eb* ball of the foot
pelen y llygad *eb* pelenni'r llygaid eyeball
pêl-falf *eb* pêl-falfiau ball valve
pêl-fasged *eb* basketball
pelferyn *eg* pelferynnau ball-bearing
pelfig *ans* pelvic
pelfis *eg* pelfisau pelvis
peli camffor *ell* moth balls
pelicl *eg* peliclau pellicle
pelmet *eg* pelmetau pelmet
pêl-rwyd *eb* netball
pelydr laser *eg* pelydrau laser laser beam
pelydr X *eg* pelydrau X X-ray
pelydriad *eg* pelydriadau radiation
pelydriad cyflawn *eg* complete radiation
pelydriad cyflawn *eg* full radiation
pelydriad electromagnetig *eg* electromagnetic radiation
pelydriad gama *eg* gamma radiation
pelydriad heulog *eg* solar radiation
pelydriad trawol *eg* incident radiation
pelydrol *ans* radiant
pelydru *be* radiate
pelydrydd *eg* pelydryddion radiator
pelydrydd cyflawn *eg* pelydryddion cyflawn black body radiator
pelydryn *eg* pelydrau ray
pelydryn catod *eg* pelydrau catod cathode ray
pelydryn gama *eg* pelydrau gama gamma ray
pelydryn trawol *eg* pelydrau trawol incident ray
pell *ans* far; remote
pellen *eb* pellenni ball
pellen gotwm *eb* pellenni cotwm cotton ball
pellennu *be* pilling
pellter *eg* pellterau distance
pellter brecio *eg* pellterau brecio braking distance
pellter byr *eg* short distance
pellter canllaw *eg* guide distance
pellter canol *eg* middle distance
pellter hir *eg* long distance
pellter hydredol *eg* pellterau hydredol longitudinal distance
pellter perpendicwlar *eg* perpendicular distance
pellter stopio *eg* stopping distance
pellwr agored *eg* pellwyr agored long off
pellwr coes *eg* pellwyr coes long on
pen (mynydd etc) *eg* pennau top
pen (telyn) *eg* pennau capital
pen (yn gyffredinol) *eg* pennau head
pen a golchiad pen and wash
pen ac inc pen and ink
pen arosgo croes *eg* pennau arosgo croes oblique reverse pen
pen bas y baddon *eg* shallow end of the bath
pen blaen *eg* pennau blaen front-end; anterior
pen blaen cronfa ddata *eg* pennau blaen cronfa ddata database front end
pen blaen ffelt *eg* pennau blaen ffelt felt-tip pen
pen blaen ffibr *eg* pennau blaen ffibr fibre-tip pen
pen bwyell *eg* pennau bwyeill axe head
pen bwylltid *eg* pennau bwylltid swivel head
pen byw *eg* pennau byw headstock
pen cau *eg* pennau cau hollow head
pen cerfiedig *eg* pennau cerfiedig carved head
pen coes *eg* pennau coesau handle head
pen corsen *eg* pennau cyrs reed pen
pen crog *eg* pennau crog hanging end
pen crwn *eg* pennau crwn circular end; round end

pen cwilsen *eg* pennau cwils quill pen
pen cylchdro *eg* pennau cylchdro revolving head
pen darllen *eg* pennau darllen read head
pen darllen ac ysgrifennu *eg* pennau darllen ac ysgrifennu read /write head
pen disg *eg* pennau disg disk head
pen dwfn y baddon *eg* deep end of the bath
pen ffelt *eg* pennau ffelt felt pen
pen ffibr *eg* pennau ffibr fibre pen
pen ffrwydrol *eg* pennau ffrwydrol warhead
pen ffurf wy *eg* pennau ffurf wy egg-shaped head
pen golau *eg* pennau golau light pen
pen grisiau *eg* pennau grisiau landing
pen haenau papur *eg* pennau haenau papur paper layer head
pen italig *eg* pennau italig italic pen
pen llathru *eg* pennau llathru polishing head
pen llawes *eg* crown of sleeve
pen llonydd *eg* pennau llonydd tailstock
pen llydan *eg* pennau llydan broad pen
pen llythrennu *eg* pennau llythrennu lettering pen
pen mapio *eg* pennau mapio mapping pen
pen meddal *eg* pennau meddal soft head
pen pellaf *eg* pennau pellaf distal end
pen pella'r tiwbyn *eg* pennau pella'r tiwbynnau distal tubule
pen petryal *eg* pennau petryal rectangular end
pen plastr *eg* pennau plastr plaster head
pen posteri *eg* pennau posteri poster pen
pen recordio *eg* pennau recordio recording head
Pen Reolaeth y Fyddin *eb* Army High Command
pen riwlio *eg* pennau riwlio ruling pen
pen rhannu *eg* pennau rhannu dividing head
pen rhydd *eg* loose head
pen saeth *eg* pennau saethau arrowhead
pen saeth ar ffurf deilen *eg* pennau saeth ar ffurf deilen leaf shaped arrowhead
pen saeth ffurf cŷn *eg* pennau saeth ffurf cŷn chisel shaped arrowhead
pen sgript *eg* pennau sgript script pen
pen stac *eg* pennau staciau stack top
pen sy'n siarad *eg* pennau sy'n siarad talking head
pen tymor *ans* terminal
pen tynn *eg* tight head
pen y dyffryn *eg* pennau dyffrynnoedd valley head
pen ysgrifennu *eg* pennau ysgrifennu write head
penagored *ans* content-free
penarglwydd *eg* penarglwyddi suzerain
penarglwyddiaeth *eb* penarglwyddiaethau suzerainty
penarglwyddiaeth *eb* hegemony
pen-blwydd *eg* penblwyddi anniversary
penbwl *eg* penbyliaid tadpole
pencadlys *eg* pencadlysoedd commandery
pencadlys *eg* pencadlysoedd headquarters
pencadlys gweinyddol *eg* pencadlysoedd gweinyddol administrative headquarters
pencampwr *eg* pencampwyr champion
pencampwraig *eb* pencampwragedd champion
pencampwriaeth *eb* pencampwriaethau championship
pencampwriaethau ysgolion *ell* school championships
pendant *ans* definite; assertive; clear
pendantrwydd *eg* definiteness; assertiveness
pendefig *eg* pendefigion nobleman; aristocrat
pendefigaeth *eb* nobility; aristocracy
penderfynedig *ans* determinate; deterministic
penderfyniad *eg* penderfyniadau decision; resolution
penderfyniad priodol *eg* penderfyniadau priodol appropriate decision
penderfyniadol *ans* determinist
penderfyniaeth *eb* determinism
penderfyniaeth ddwyochrog *eb* reciprocal determinism
penderfyniedydd *eg* penderfyniedwyr determinist
penderfynu *be* decide; determine
penderfynyn *eg* penderfynynnau determinant
penderfynyn sefydliadol *eg* institutional determinant
pendics *eg* appendix
pendil *eg* pendiliau pendulum
pendil cyfansawdd *eg* pendiliau cyfansawdd compound pendulum
pendil syml *eg* pendiliau syml simple pendulum
pendro *eb* dizziness; giddiness
penddelw *eg* penddelwau bust
penddu *eg* smut
penelin *eg/b* penelinoedd elbow
penflaguryn *eg* penflagur terminal bud
penfras *eg* penfreision cod
pen-glin *eg/b* pengliniau knee
penglog *eg* penglogau skull
Pengrynwr *eg* Pengrynwyr Roundhead
pengwrthsodd *ans* countersunk
peniad *eg* peniadau header
peniad ymlaen *eg* header on
penillion *ell* penillion
penio'r bêl *be* head the ball
penisilin *eg* penicillin
penlinio *be* kneel
penlinio eistedd *be* kneel sitting
penlinio llorweddol *be* horizontal kneeling
penlinio un glin *be* half-kneeling
penlithryn *eg* penlithrynnau headslide
penllanw *eg* high water
pennaeth *eg* penaethiaid principal; chieftain
pennaeth adran *eg* penaethiaid adran head of department
pennaeth blwyddyn *eg* penaethiaid blwyddyn head of year
▶ **pennaeth cyfadran** *eg* penaethiaid cyfadrannau head of faculty
pennaeth pwnc *eg* penaethiaid pwnc head of subject

pennaeth yr ysgol ganol *eg* penaethiaid ysgolion canol head of middle school
pennaeth yr ysgol isaf *eg* penaethiaid ysgolion isaf head of lower school
pennaeth yr ysgol uchaf *eg* penaethiaid ysgolion uchaf head of upper school
pennaeth ysgol *eg* penaethiaid ysgolion headteacher
pennau madarch *ell* mushroom heads
Pennau'r Awgrymiadau *ell* Heads of Proposals
pennawd *eg* penawdau heading; headline; caption
pennawd bras *eg* penawdau bras banner
pennawd nesaf *eg* penawdau nesaf next heading
pennill *eg* penillion verse; round
pennod *eb* penodau chapter; episode
pennu *be* fix; determine; allot
pennu lleoliad *be* specify location
pennyn *eg* penynnau header
pennyn a throedyn header and footer
pennyn adroddiad *eg* penynnau adroddiad report header
pennyn colofn *eg* penynnau colofnau column header
pennyn chwith *eg* penynnau chwith header left
pennyn de *eg* penynnau de header right
pennyn ffurflen *eg* penynnau ffurflen form header
penodiad *eg* penodiadau appointment
penodol *ans* specific; explicit; particular
penodolrwydd *eg* specificity
penodolrwydd ensym *eg* enzyme specificity
penrhif *eg* penrhifau principal value
penrhyddid *eg* licence
penrhyn *eg* penrhynau cape; foreland
Penrhyn Gobaith Da *eg* Cape of Good Hope
pensaer *eg* penseiri architect
pensaernïaeth *eb* architecture
pensaernïaeth filwrol *eb* military architecture
pensaernïaeth Gothig *eb* Gothic architecture
pensaernïol *ans* architectural
pensafiad *eg* pensafiadau headstand
pensafiad plyg *eg* pensafiadau plyg angle headstand
pensefyll *be* headstand
pensgwar *ans* square head
pensil *eg* pensiliau pencil
pensil creon *eg* pensiliau creon crayon pencil
pensil lliw *eg* pensiliau lliw colour pencil
pensil lluniadu *eg* pensiliau lluniadu drawing pencil
pensil llythrennu *eg* pensiliau llythrennu lettering pencil
pensil pren cedrwydd *eg* pensiliau pren cedrwydd cedarwood pencil
pensil saer *eg* pensiliau saer carpenter's pencil
pensil siarcol *eg* pensiliau siarcol charcoal pencil
pensiwn *eg* pensiynau pension
pensiwn anghyfrannol *eg* pensiynau anghyfrannol non-contributory pension
pensiwn cyfrannol *eg* pensiynau cyfrannol contributory pension
pensiwn graddedig *eg* pensiynau graddedig graduated pension
pensiwn henoed *eg* old age pension
pensiwn yr anabl *eg* disablement pension
pensiynwr *eg* pensiynwyr pensioner
pentacarbonylhaearn(0) *eg* pentacarbonyliron(0)
pentadecagon *eg* pentadecagonau pentadecagon
pentagon *eg* pentagonau pentagon
pentagonol *ans* pentagonal
pentagram *eg* pentagramau pentagram
pentan *eg* pentanau hob
pentan-2,4-deuon *eg* pentane-2,4-dione
pentatonig *ans* pentatonic
Pentecost *eg* Pentecost
Pentecostal *eg* Pentecostaliaid Pentecostal
Pentecostalaidd *ans* Pentecostal
pentir *eg* pentiroedd headland; promontory
pentomino *eg* pentominos pentomino
pentos *eg* pentose
pentoswria *eg* pentosuria
pentref *eg* pentrefi village
pentref anghyfannedd *eg* pentrefi anghyfannedd deserted village
pentref diflan *eg* pentrefi diflan lost village
pentref gwyliau *eg* pentrefi gwyliau holiday village
pentref noddfa *eg* pentrefi noddfa refuge village
pentref noswylio *eg* pentrefi noswylio dormitory village
pentref pysgota *eg* pentrefi pysgota fishing village
pentrefan *eg* pentrefannau hamlet
pentwr *eb* pentyrrau stack
pentwr fertigol *eg* pentyrrau fertigol vertical stack
pentwr stoc *eg* pentyrrau stoc stock pile
penty *eg* pentai penthouse
pentyl- pentyl-
pentyrru *be* stack
pentyrru cardiau *be* card stacking
pentyrru stoc *be* stock pile
pentyrrwr cardiau *eg* pentyrwyr cardiau card stacker
penwmbra *eg* penwmbrâu penumbra
penyd *eg* penydiau penance
penyd canonaidd *eg* penydiau canonaidd canonical penalty
penynnau a throedynnau *ell* headers and footers
peplwm *eg* peplum
peptid *eg* peptidau peptide
perborad *eg* perborate
percoladur *eg* percoladuron percolator
perchennog *eg* perchenogion owner; landlord
perchennog preswyl *eg* perchenogion preswyl owner occupier
perchenogaeth *eb* ownership
perchenogaeth ddeublyg *eb* perchenogaethau deublyg dual ownership
perchenogaeth stad *eb* estate ownership

perchentyaeth *eb* home ownership
perchnogaeth gyhoeddus *eb* public ownership
pererin *eg* pererinion pilgrim
pererindod *eb* pererindodau pilgrimage
perfedd *eg* perfeddion bowel
perfeddol *ans* splanchnic
perfeddwlad *eb* perfeddwledydd heartland
perffaith *ans* perfect; ideal
perfformiad *eg* perfformiadau performance
perfformiad ariannol *eg* financial performance
perfformiad athletaidd *eg* athletic performance
perfformiad cyfrifiadur *eg* computer performance
perfformiad effeithiol *eg* perfformiadau effeithiol effective performance
perfformiad optimaidd *eg* optimal performance
perfformiad sgìl lefel optimaidd *eg* perfformiadau sgìl lefel optimaidd optimal level of skill performance
perfformio *be* perform
perfformio cyson *be* consistent performance
perfformio tasgau strwythuredig *be* perform structured tasks
perfformiwr *eg* perfformwyr performer
perfformiwr cymalog *eg* perfformwyr cymalog articulate performer
peri *be* induce
peri dagrau *ans* lacrimatory
pericardiwm *eg* pericardium
pericarp *eg* pericarp
periclin *eg* periclinau pericline
perifferi *eg* perifferïau periphery
perifferol *ans* peripheral
perifferolyn *eg* perifferolion peripheral
perige *eg* perigeau perigee
periglor *eg* perigloriaid incumbent; mass priest
perigloriaeth *eb* perigloriaethau incumbency
perihelion *eg* perihelionau perihelion
perilymff *eg* perilymph
perimedr *eg* perimedrau perimeter
perimedr y sector *eg* perimeter of the sector
perimedrau siapiau syml *ell* perimeters of simple shapes
peripediment *eg* peripedimentau peripediment
periseicl *eg* pericycle
perisgop *eg* perisgopau periscope
peristalsis *eg* peristalsis
peritheciwm *eg* perithecium
perlit *eg* pearlite
perllan *eb* perllannau orchard
Permaidd *ans* Permian
permitifedd *eg* permitifeddau permittivity
permitifedd gofod rhydd *eg* permittivity of free space
perocsoasid *eg* perocsoasidau peroxoacid
perpendicwlar *ans* perpendicular
perpendicwlar *eg* perpendicwlarau perpendicular
persain *ans* euphonious
persawr *eg* persawrau perfume
persawru *be* perfume
persawrus *ans* aromatic
persbecs *eg* perspex
persbecs lliw *eg* coloured perspex
persbectif *eg* persbectifau perspective
persbectif amcangyfrifol *eg* estimated perspective
persbectif canolog *eg* persbectifau canolog central perspective
persbectif fertigol *eg* persbectifau fertigol vertical perspective
persbectif hanesyddol *eg* historical perspective
persbectif lliw *eg* colour perspective
persbectif onglog *eg* persbectifau onglog angular perspective
persbectifedd *eg* perspectivity
perseinedd *eg* euphony
person a enwir *eg* personau a enwir named person
person dwyieithog *eg* pobl ddwyieithog bilingual
person graddedig *eg* graddedigion graduate
person ifanc *eg* pobl ifanc adolescent; juvenile
persona *eg* persona
persondy *eg* persondai parsonage
personél *eg* personnel
personél cyfrifiadur *eg* computer personnel
personél gwerthu *eg* sales personnel
personol *ans* personal
personoliaeth *eb* personoliaethau personality
personoliaeth math A *eb* type A personality
personoliaeth math B *eb* type B personality
personoliaeth math C (tuedd tuag at ganser) *eb* type C (cancer-prone) personality
personoliaeth wydn *eb* hardy personality
personolyddiaeth *eb* personalism
perth *eb* perthi hedge
perthfudd *eg* haybote
perthnasedd *eg* relativity; relevance
perthnasedd hedonig *eg* hedonic relevance
perthnasedd ieithyddol *eb* linguistic relativity
perthnaseddol *ans* relativistic
perthnasol *ans* relevant
perthnasu *be* relate
perthynas *eb* perthnasoedd relationship
perthynas *eg/b* perthnasau relation; relative; kin
perthynas achosol *eb* causal relationship
perthynas agosaf *eg/b* perthnasau agosaf next of kin
perthynas bwydo *eb* feeding relationship
perthynas cywerthedd *eb* equivalence relation
perthynas drwy waed *eb* blood relationship
perthynas gymdeithasol *eb* social relationship
perthynas lorweddol *eb* horizontal relationship
perthynas meddwl-corff *eb* mind-body relationship
perthynas ymatblyg *eb* reflexive relation
perthynol *ans* relative; relational; allied; related
perthynoliaeth *eb* relativism
perygl *eg* peryglon hazard

perygl amgylchedd *eg* peryglon amgylchedd environmental hazard
perygl cynradd *eg* primary hazard
perygl eilaidd *eg* peryglon eilaidd secondary hazard
perygl folcanig *eg* peryglon folcanig volcanic hazard
perygl i ddiogelwch *eg* safety risk
perygl iechyd *eg* peryglon iechyd health risk
perygl o ddaeargryn *eg* earthquake hazard
perygl posibl *eg* potential hazard
perygl tectonig *eg* peryglon tectonig tectonic hazard
pesari *eg* pesarïau pessary
pesimistaidd *ans* pessimistic
pesimistiaeth *eb* pessimism
pestl *eg* pestlau pestle
pestl a morter pestlau a morterau pestle and mortar
peswch *eg* cough
pesychu *be* cough
petal *eg* petalau petal
petersham *eg* petersham
petiol *eg* petiolau petiole
petroleg *eb* petrology
petroliwm *eg* petroleum
petryal *ans* rectangular; oblong
petryal *eg* petryalau rectangle; oblong
petryal euraid *eg* petryalau euraid golden rectangle
peth byw *eg* pethau byw living thing
pethau dros ben *ell* oddments
pethau gwerthfawr *ell* valuables
piano *eg* pianos piano
piano paratoëdig *eg* pianos paratoëdig prepared piano
piano syth *eg* pianos syth upright piano
piano traws *eg* pianos traws grand piano
pianydd *eg* pianyddion pianist
pib *eb* pibau pipe
pib agored *eb* pibau agored open pipe
pibau Pan *ell* panpipes
pibed *eb* pibedau pipette
pibedu *be* pipette
pibell *eb* pibellau pipe
pibell aer *eb* air passage
pibell folcanig *eb* pibellau folcanig volcanic pipe
pibell fud *eb* pibellau mud dummy pipe
pibell gaeedig *eb* pibellau caeedig closed pipe
pibell gangen *eb* pibellau cangen branch pipe
pibell gastroberfeddol *eb* pibellau gastroberfeddol gastrointestinal
pibell lymff *eb* pibellau lymff lymph vessel
pibell U *eb* pibellau U U-bend
pibell wacáu *eb* pibellau gwacáu exhaust pipe
pibell waed *eb* pibellau gwaed blood-vessel
pibell ystôr *eb* pibellau ystôr resin duct
pibgorn *eg* pibgyrn pibgorn; hornpipe; stockhorn
pibonwyen *eb* pibonwy icicle
picedu *be* picket
picedwr *eg* picedwyr picket
picedwr gwib *eg* picedwyr gwib flying picket
picell *eb* picellau pike
picellwr *eg* picellwyr pikeman
picen Ffrengig *eb* picau Ffrengig French bun
picen y Grog *eb* picau'r Grog hot cross bun
picl *eg* piclau pickle
picl asid *eg* acid pickle
piclo *be* pickle
picot *eg* picot
picsel *eg* picseli pixel
picsel tryloyw *eg* picseli tryloyw transparent pixel
picseleiddio *be* pixelation
pictograff *eg* pictograffau pictograph
pictograffeg *eb* pictography
pictogram *eg* pictogramau pictogram
pidyn *eg* pidynnau penis
pietist *eg* pietistiaid pietist
pietistaidd *ans* pietist
pietistiaeth *eb* pietism
pig (aderyn) *eg/b* pigau beak
pig (tegell) *eg/b* pigau spout
pig morthwyl *eg* pigau morthwylion peen
pigau mân *ell* paraesthesia
pigfain *ans* tapering; pointed
pigiad (gan bryfyn) *eg* pigiadau sting
pigiad (gan chwistrell) *eg* pigiadau injection
pigiad atgyfnerthol *eg* pigiadau atgyfnerthol booster injection
pigiad mewngroenol *eg* pigiadau mewngroenol intradermal injection
pigiad mewngyhyrol *eg* plgladau mewngyhyrol intramuscular injection
pigiad pryfyn *eg* pigiadau pryfyn insect bite
pigiad rheoledig *eg* pigiadau rheoledig control injection
pigment *eg* pigmentau pigment
pigment bras *eg* pigmentau bras fat pigment
pigment golau anniflan *eg* pigmentau golau anniflan light fast pigment
pigment grisialog *eg* crystalline pigment
pigment powdr *eg* pigmentau powdr powder pigment
pigment tenau *eg* lean pigment
pigment y bustl *eg* pigmentau'r bustl bile pigment
pigmentiad *eg* pigmentation
pigmi *eg* pigmiaid pygmy
pigo *be* sting
pigwrn (rhwng y goes a'r droed) *eg* pigyrnau ankle
pigwrn (y llygad) *eg* pigyrnau cone
pigyn clust *eg* earache
pigyn *eg* pigynnau peak
pigyn dorsal *eg* pigynnau dorsal dorsal spine
pigyn niwral *eg* pigynnau niwral neural spine
pigyn pyramidaidd *eg* pigynnau pyramidaidd pyramidal peak
pilastr *eg* pilastrau pilaster
pilen *eb* pilenni membrane

pilen amrannol *eb* pilenni amrannol nictitating membrane
pilen anathraidd *eb* pilenni anathraidd impermeable membrane
pilen arwyneb *eb* surface membrane
pilen athraidd *eb* permeable membrane
pilen blasmaidd *eb* pilenni plasmaidd plasma membrane
pilen dectoraidd *eb* pilenni tectoraidd tectorial membrane
pilen ddetholus *eb* pilenni detholus selective membrane
pilen eisbilennol yr ysgyfaint *eb* pilenni eisbilennol yr ysgyfaint pleural membrane
pilen fwcaidd *eb* pilenni mwcaidd mucous membrane
▶ **pilen fyelin** *eb* pilenni myelin myelin sheath
▶ **pilen gnewyllol** *eb* pilenni cnewyllol nuclear membrane
pilen ledathraidd *eb* pilenni lledathraidd semi-permeable membrane
pilen ôl-synaptig *eb* post synaptic membrane
pilen serws *eb* pilenni serws serous membrane
pilen waelodol *eb* pilenni gwaelodol basilar membrane; basement membrane
pilen wy *eb* pilenni wy egg membrane
pilen y ffoetws *eb* pilenni ffoetysau foetal membrane
pilen y glust *eb* pilennau'r clustiau eardrum
▶ **pilenni'r ymennydd** *ell* meninges
pilennog *ans* membraneous
piler *eg* pileri pillar
piler triongli *eg* pileri triongli trig point; triangulation pillar
pileru *be* pillaring
pilews *eg* pileus
pilio *be* peel
pilsen *eb* pils pill
pilyn *eg* pilynnau integument
pìn *eg* pinnau pin
pìn argaen *eg* pinnau argaen veneer pin
pìn arwain *eg* pinnau arwain guide pin
pìn bach *eg* pinnau bach dressmaker's pin
pìn bawd *eg* pinnau bawd drawing-pin
pìn bawd pres *eg* pinnau bawd pres brass drawing pin
pìn cadw pwythau *eg* pinnau cadw pwythau stitch holder
pìn cau *eg* pinnau cau safety pin
pìn clefis *eg* pinnau clefis clevis pin
pìn clymu papur *eg* pinnau clymu papur paper fastener
pìn codi *eg* pinnau codi riser pin
pìn colfach *eg* pinnau colfach hinge pin
pìn cyfeirio *eg* pinnau cyfeirio index pin
pìn cyfredol *eg* pinnau cyfredol current nib
pìn cylchog *eg* pinnau cylchog ring headed pin
pìn cynfas *eg* pinnau cynfas canvas pin
pìn cynffonnog *eg* pinnau cynffonnog dovetail pin
pìn esgytsiwn *eg* pinnau esgytsiwn escutcheon pin
pìn fertigol *eg* pinnau fertigol vertical pen
pìn gefyn *eg* pinnau gefyn shackle pin
pìn gimp *eg* pinnau gimp gimp pin
pìn gwddf alarch *eg* pinnau gwddf alarch swan-necked pin
pìn hollt *eg* pinnau hollt cotter pin
pìn hollt *eg* pinnau hollt split pin
pìn lleoli *eg* pinnau lleoli locating pin
pìn panel *eg* pinnau panel panel pin
pìn sbriw *eg* pinnau sbriw sprue pin
pìn sbŵl *eg* pinnau sbŵl spool pin
pìn sefydlu *eg* pinnau sefydlu fixing pin
pìn symudol *eb* pinnau symudol movable pin
pìn tapr *eg* pinnau tapr taper pin
pinblat *eg* pinblatiau pin plate
pinc *eg* pincod finch
pinc Darwin *eg* pincod Darwin Darwin finch
pincas *eg* pincasau pincushion
pincio *be* pinking
pingo *eg* pingoau pingo
pinio *be* pin
pinio (ffeil) *be* pinning
piniwn *eg* piniynau pinion
pinna *eg* pinnâu pinna
pinnas *eg* pinasau pinnace
pinocytosis *eg* pinocytosis
pinsiad *eg* pinsiadau pinch
pinsio *be* pinch
pinsiwrn *eg* pinsiyrnau pincers
pipin *eg* pippin
pique *eg* pique
pistil *eg* pistiliau pistil
piston *eg* pistonau piston
piston bawd *eg* pistonau bawd thumb piston
piston cyfuno *eg* pistonau cyfuno combination piston
piston cyfuno *eg* pistonau cyfuno composition piston
piston troed *eg* pistonau troed toe piston
piton *eg* pitonau piton
pitsh (dannedd llif) *eg* pitch angle
pitsh (yn gyffredinol) *eg* pitch
pitsh bras *eg* coarse pitch
pitsh diamedrol *eg* diametral pitch
pitsh dotiau *eg* dot pitch
pitsh edau *eg* thread pitch
pitsh llyfn *eg* even pitch
pitsh normal *eg* normal pitch
pitsh unffurf *eg* uniform pitch
pitsio *be* pitch
pitsiwr *eg* pitswyr pitcher
piwritan *eg* piwritaniaid puritan
piwritanaidd *ans* puritan
piwritaniaeth *eb* puritanism
piwter *eg* pewter
pla *eg* plâu infestation; pest; plague

pla cnofilod *eg* plâu cnofilod rodent infestation
Pla Du *eg* Black Death
Pla Mawr *eg* Great Plague
plac *eg* placiau plaque
plac deintiol *eg* dental plaque
plac mur *eg* placiau mur wall plaque
placed *eg* placedau placket
plad *eg* plaid
plad anghyson *eg* uneven plaid
plad cyson *eg* even plaid
plaen *ans* plain
plaen *eg* plaeniau plane
plaen amgrwm *eg* plaeniau amgrwm compass plane
plaen amlddefnydd *eg* plaeniau amlddefnydd combination plane
plaen bach *eg* plaeniau bach block plane
plaen cafnu *eg* plaeniau cafnu hollow plane
plaen caledfwrdd *eg* plaeniau caledfwrdd hardboard plane
plaen ceg sgiw *eg* plaeniau ceg sgiw skew mouth plane
plaen ceg sgwâr *eg* plaeniau ceg sgwâr square mouth plane
plaen cludadwy *eg* plaeniau cludadwy portable plane
plaen crafu *eg* plaeniau crafu scraper plane
plaen crwn *eg* plaeniau crwn round plane
plaen cydweddu *eg* plaeniau cydweddu matching plane
plaen danheddog *eg* plaeniau danheddog toothing plane
plaen dyfnder *eg* plaeniau dyfnder router plane
plaen ffilistr *eg* plaeniau ffilistr fillister plane
plaen hir *eg* plaeniau hir trying plane
plaen jac *eg* plaeniau jac jackplane
plaen jac metel *eg* plaeniau jac metel metal jackplane
plaen jac pren *eg* plaeniau jac pren wood jackplane
plaen llyfnhau *eg* plaeniau llyfnhau smoothing plane
plaen llyfr-rwymwr *eg* plaeniau llyfr-rwymwr plough
plaen mainc *eg* plaeniau mainc bench plane
plaen meddalfwrdd *eg* plaeniau meddalfwrdd soft board plane
plaen metel *eg* plaeniau metel metal plane
plaen mowldio *eg* plaeniau mowldio moulding plane
plaen ofolo *eg* plaeniau ofolo ovolo plane
plaen ogee *eg* plaeniau ogee ogee plane
plaen ongl-isel *eg* plaeniau ongl-isel low-angle plane
plaen pŵer *eg* plaeniau pŵer power plane
plaen rabad *eg* plaeniau rabad rabbet plane
plaen rabad ochr *eg* plaeniau rabad ochr side rabbet plane
plaen rhigoli *eg* plaeniau rhigoli grooving plane; plough plane
plaen trwyn byr *eg* plaeniau trwyn byr bull-nosed plane
plaen trydan *eg* plaeniau trydan electric plane
plaen ysgwydd *eg* plaeniau ysgwydd shoulder plane
plaengan *eb* plaenganau plainsong
plaenio *be* plane
plaeniwr *eg* plaenwyr planer
plaeniwr cludadwy *eg* plaenwyr cludadwy portable planer
plagioclimacs *eg* plagioclimax
plaid *eb* pleidiau party
Plaid Anarchaidd *eb* Anarchist Party
Plaid Cymru *eb* Plaid Cymru
Plaid Doriaidd *eb* Tory Party
Plaid Ddemocrataidd *eb* Democratic Party
Plaid Ddemocrataidd Gristnogol *eb* Christian Democrat Party
Plaid Geidwadol *eb* Conservative Party
Plaid Genedlaethol *eb* Nationalist Party
Plaid Genedlaethol Cymru *eb* Welsh Nationalist Party
Plaid Gomiwnyddol *eb* Communist Party
Plaid Lafur *eb* Labour Party
Plaid Lafur Annibynnol *eb* Independent Labour Party
Plaid Natsïaidd *eb* Nazi Party
Plaid Ryddfrydol *eb* Liberal Party
Plaid Sosialaidd *eb* Socialist Party
Plaid Weriniaethol *eb* Republican Party
plaid wleidyddol *eb* pleidiau gwleidyddol political party
Plaid y Chwigiaid *eb* Whig Party
Plaid y Democratiaid Cymdeithasol *eb* Social Democratic Party
Plaid y Democratiaid Rhyddfrydol *eb* Liberal Democrat Party
Plaid y Gyngres *eb* Congress Party
Plaid yr Unoliaethwyr *eb* Unionist Party
plaleiddiad *eg* plaleiddiaid pesticide
plân *eg* planau plane
plân ar oledd *eg* planau ar oledd inclined plane
plân arosgo *eg* planau arosgo oblique plane
plân cyfeirnod *eg* planau cyfeirnod plane of reference; reference plane
plân cymesuredd *eg* plane of symmetry
plân darlun *eg* planau darlun picture plane
plân ecliptig *eg* planau ecliptig ecliptic plane
plân echelinol *eg* planau echelinol axial plane
plân fertigol *eg* planau fertigol vertical plane
plân haenu *eg* planau haenu bedding plane
plân hollti *eg* planau hollti cleavage plane
plân isometrig *eg* planau isometrig isometric plane
plân llorweddol *eg* planau llorweddol horizontal plane
plân slip *eg* planau slip slip plane
plân tangiad *eg* planau tangiad tangent plane
plân tangiadol *eg* planau tangiadol tangential plane

plân terfyn *eg* planau terfyn bounding plane
plân torri *eg* planau torri cutting plane
plân trychu *eg* section plane
plân wynebol *eg* planau wynebol facial plane
planar *ans* planar
planc *eg* planciau plank; ledger
plancton *eg* planctonau plankton
planed *eb* planedau planet
planhigfa *eb* planhigfeydd plantation
planhigol *ans* plant
planhigyn *eg* planhigion plant
planhigyn anflodeuol *eg* planhigion anflodeuol non-flowering plant
planhigyn blodeuol *eg* planhigion blodeuol flowering plant
planhigyn dringo *eg* planhigion dringo climbing plant
planhigyn dŵr *eg* planhigion dŵr water plant
planhigyn gwreiddiog *eg* planhigion gwreiddiog rooted plant
planhigyn suddlon *eg* planhigion suddlon succulent plant
planhigyn wy *eg* planhigion wy aubergine
planisffer *eg* planisfferau planisphere
planisio *be* planishing
plannu *be* plant
plannu *be* imbed
planum temporale *eg* planum temporale
plas *eg* plasau mansion; country seat
plasebo *eg* placebo
plasmolysis cychwynnol *eg* incipient plasmolysis
plasmolysu *be* plasmolyse
plastid *eg* plastidau plastid
plastig *ans* plastic
plastig *eg* plastigion plastic
plastig clir *eg* clear plastic
plastig thermosodol *eg* thermosetting plastic
plastigrwydd *eg* plasticity
plastigydd *eg* plastigyddion plasticizer
plastisin *eg* plastisinau plasticine
plastisin lliw *eg* coloured plasticine
plastr *eg* plastrau plaster
plastr a rhwymyn plaster and bandage
plastr acwstig *eg* acoustic plaster
plastr gwrthymbelydrol *eg* barytite x-ray plaster
plastr gypswm *eg* gypsum plaster
plastr Paris *eg* plaster of Paris
plastro *be* plaster
plasty *eg* plastai mansion house
plasty yn y wlad *eg* plastai yn y wlad country house
plât *eg* platiau plate
plât arian *eg* silver plate
plât arwyneb *eg* platiau arwyneb surface plate
plât bobin *eg* platiau bobin throat plate
plât bys *eg* platiau bys finger plate
plât cloi *eg* platiau cloi locking plate
plât cloi fflat *eg* platiau cloi fflat flat locking plate
plât cloi plyg *eg* platiau cloi plyg bent locking plate
plât cramennol *eg* platiau cramennol crustal plate
plât culhad *eg* platiau culhad shrinkage plate
plât cydio *eg* platiau cydio clutch plate
plât cydio *eg* platiau cydio catch plate
plât drych *eg* platiau drych mirror plate
plât esgytsiwn *eg* platiau esgytsiwn escutcheon plate
plât gwarchod *eg* platiau gwarchod guard plate
plât gwarchod *eg* platiau gwarchod crown plate
plât hidlo *eg* platiau hidlo sieve plate
plât hoelbrennau *eg* platiau hoelbrennau dowel plate
plât lleoli *eg* platiau lleoli locating plate
plât llyfr *eg* platiau llyfr book-plate
plât llythyrau *eg* platiau llythyrau letter plate
plât mowntio *eg* platiau mowntio mounting plate
plât nicel *eg* nickel plated
plât o fwyd iachus *eg* healthy plate
plât ongl *eg* platiau ongl angle plate
plât ongl blwch *eg* platiau ongl blwch box angle plate
plât papur *eg* platiau papur paper plate
plât rhybedog *eg* platiau rhybedog riveted plate
plât safn *eg* platiau safn jaw plate
plât sgriwio *eg* platiau sgriwio screw-plate
plât siecer *eg* platiau siecer chequer plate
plât tagell *eg* platiau tagell gill plate
plât taro *eg* platiau taro striking plate
plât tern *eg* platiau tern terne plate
plât torri *eg* platiau torri cutting plate
plât torri sinc *eg* platiau torri sinc zinc cutting plate
plât troi *eg* platiau troi driving plate
plât tynnu *eg* platiau tynnu draw plate
plât tywys *eg* platiau tywys guide plate
plât wyneb *eg* platiau wyneb face plate
plât y pitsiwr *eg* pitcher's plate
plât yr ergydiwr *eg* platiau ergydwyr striker's plate
plât ysgogi *eg* platiau ysgogi actuating plate
platen *eb* platennau latelet; platen
platinio *be* platinize
platinwm *eg* platinum
platio *be* plate
platwadn *eg* platwadnau soleplate
platŵn *eg* platwnau platoon
platwydr *eg* platwydrau plate glass
platwydr trwchus *eg* thick plate glass
platycwrtig *ans* platykurtic
playa *eg* playâu playa
ple *eg/b* pledion plea
plecsws coroid *eg* choroid plexus
plectrwm *eg* plectrymau plectrum
pledio *be* plead
pledion y Goron *ell* pleas of the Crown
plediwr *eg* pledwyr pleader
pledren *eb* pledrennau bladder
pledrennol *ans* cystic

pleidgarwch *eg* partisanship
pleidlais *eb* pleidleisiau vote
pleidlais *eb* pleidleisiau suffrage
pleidlais atal *eb* pleidleisiau atal veto
pleidlais fwrw *eb* casting vote
pleidlais gerydd *eb* pleidleisiau cerydd vote of censure
pleidlais gudd *eb* secret ballot
pleidlais gwlad *eb* pleidleisiau gwlad plebiscite
pleidlais gwŷr *eb* manhood suffrage
pleidlais gyffredinol *eb* universal suffrage
pleidleisio *be* vote
pleidleisio dirprwyol *be* voting by proxy
pleintydd *eg* pleintyddion plaintiff
pleion *eg* pleion
pleiotropedd *eg* pleiotropy
Pleistosen *eg* Pleistocene
plenipotensiwr *eg* plenipotenswyr plenipotentiary
plentyn *eg* plant child
plentyn â nam corfforol *eg* plant â nam corfforol physically handicapped child
plentyn â nam meddyliol *eg* plant â nam meddyliol mentally handicapped child
plentyn ag anghenion addysgol arbennig *eg* plant ag anghenion addysgol arbennig child having special educational needs
plentyn amddifadus *eg* plant amddifadus deprived child
plentyn araf *eg* plant araf backward child
plentyn awtistig *eg* plant awtistig autistic child
plentyn bach *eg* plant bach toddler
plentyn byddar *eg* plant byddar deaf child
plentyn cyffredin *eg* plant cyffredin average child
plentyn dall *eg* plant dall blind child
plentyn dan anfantais *eg* plant dan anfantais handicapped child
▶ **plentyn dan oed** *eg* plant dan oed minor
plentyn dan oed ysgol *eg* plant dan oed ysgol preschool child
plentyn dawnus *eg* plant dawnus gifted child
plentyn diabetig *eg* plant diabetig diabetic child
plentyn dibynnol *eg* plant dibynnol dependent child
plentyn eithriadol *eg* plant eithriadol exceptional child
plentyn epileptig *eg* plant epileptig epileptic child
plentyn gorfywiog *eg* plant gorfywiog hyperactive child
plentyn heb ymaddasu *eg* plant heb ymaddasu maladjusted child
plentyn maeth *eg* plant maeth foster child
plentyn mewn angen *eg* plant mewn angen child in need
plentyn mewn perygl *eg* plant mewn perygl child at risk
plentyn mud *eg* plant mud dumb child
plentyn sbastig *eg* plant sbastig spastic child
plentyn sy'n tangyflawni *eg* plant sy'n tangyflawni underachiever
plentyn wedi'i wahardd *eg* plant wedi'u gwahardd excluded child
plentyn ysgol *eg* plant ysgol school child
plentyn ysgol gynradd *eg* plant ysgol gynradd primary school child
plentyndod *eg* childhood
plentyndod canol *eg* middle childhood
plentyndod cynnar *eg* early childhood
plentynnaidd *ans* childish
plet *eg/b* pletiau pleat
plet bocs *eb* pletiau bocs box pleat
plet gic *eb* pletiau cic kick pleat
plet llafn *eb* pletiau llafn knife pleat
plet wrthdro *eb* pletiau gwrthdro inverted pleat
pletio *be* pleating
pletio acordion *be* accordion pleating
pletio parhaol *be* permanent pleating
pletio pelydrog *be* sunray pleating
pletio rhydd *be* unpressed pleating
pletio ysgafn *be* soft pleating
pleth *eb* plethau plait
plethu (mewn dawns) *be* weave in and out
plethu (yn gyffredinol) *be* plait; braiding; randing
plethu raffia *be* raffia weaving
plethwaith a chlai wattle and daub
plethwaith (plecsws) dermaidd *eg* dermal plexus
plinth *eg* plinthiau plinth
plinth bandin croes *eg* plinthiau bandin croes cross banded plinth
plisgyn *eg* plisg shell
plisgyn *eg* plisg husk
plisgyn electronau *eg* plisg electronau electron shell
plisgyn wy *eg* plisg wy eggshell
pliwtocrat *eg* pliwtocratiaid plutocrat
pliwtocratiaeth *eb* plutocracy
ploryn *eg* plorod pimple
plot *eg* plotiau plot
plot gwasgariad *eg* plotiau gwasgariad scatterplot
plotio (pwynt) *be* plot
plotydd *eg* plotyddion plotter
plotydd digidol *eg* plotyddion digidol digital plotter
plotydd graff *eg* plotyddion graff graph plotter
plu eilaidd *ell* secondary plumage
pluen *eb* plu feather
pluen geiliog *eb* plu ceiliog cockfeather
pluen hedfan *eb* plu hedfan flight feather
pluo *be* feather
plwc *eg* plyciau twitch
plwc clust *eg* ear flick
plwc dwy law *eg* two hands clean and jerk
plwg *eg* plygiau plug
plwg folcanig *eg* plygiau folcanig volcanic plug
plwg ffibr *eg* plygiau ffibr fibre plug
plwg metel *eg* plygiau metel metal plug
plwg pren *eg* plygiau pren wood plug
plwg tanio *eg* plygiau tanio sparking plug

plwg tri phìn *eg* plygiau tri phin three point plug
plwg trydan *eg* plygiau trydan electric plug
plwg-gytûn *ans* plug compatible
plwm *ans* plumb
plwm (Pb) *eg* lead
plwm carbonad hydrocsid *eg* lead carbonate hydroxide
plwmbago (graffit + clai) *eg* plumbago
plwmban *eg* plumbane
plwm(II) carbonad (cerwsit) *eg* lead(II) carbonate (cerussite)
plwm(II) carbonad hydrocsid *eg* lead(II) carbonate hydroxide
plwm(II) ethanoad *eg* lead(II) ethanoate
plwm(II) ocsid (litharg, neu masicot) *eg* lead(II) oxide (litharge, or massicot)
plwm(IV) ethanoad *eg* lead(IV) ethanoate
plwm(IV) ocsid *eg* lead(IV) oxide
plwraliaeth *eb* pluralism
plws *eg* plysau plus
Plwton *eg* Pluto
plwtoniwm (Pu) *eg* plutonium
plwyf *eg* plwyfi parish
plwyfol *ans* parochial
plwyfolyn *eg* plwyfolion parishioner
plycio *be* twitch
plyg (am donnau sain, golau) *ans* refracted
plyg (yn gyffredinol) *ans* folded
plyg *eg* plygion fold; bend
plyg anghymesur *eg* plygion anghymesur asymmetric fold
plyg bychan *eg* plygion bychan minor fold
plyg croesraen *eg* plygion croesraen crossway fold
plyg cymesur *eg* plygion cymesur symmetric fold
plyg cyntaf *eg* plygion cyntaf first fold
plyg gorweddol *eg* plygion gorweddol recumbent fold
plyg i fyny *eg* plygion i fyny upfold
plyg i lawr *eg* plygion i lawr downfold
plyg pigfain *eg* plygion pigfain tapering fold
plygell asgwrn *eb* plygellau asgwrn bone folder
plygiad plwm *eg* plygiadau plwm flashing
plygiannedd *eg* bendability
plygiannedd *eg* refractivity
plygiant (tonnau sain, golau) *eg* refraction
plygiant (yn gyffredinol) *eg* plygiannau flexure; plication
plygiant isoclinol *eg* isoclinal folding
plygiant tonnau *eg* wave refraction
plygio *be* plug
plygion metaplewraidd *ell* metapleural folds
plygu *be* bend
plygu *be* fold
plygu *be* refract
plygu (onglog /radiws) *be* bending
plygu coed *eg* wood bending
plygu i lawr *be* bend down
plygu metel *be* metal bending
plygu plastig *be* plastic bending
plygu'n ôl *be* bend backwards
plymbwll *eg* plymbyllau plunge pool
plymiad *eg* plymiadau plunge
plymio (=mesur dyfnder) *be* sound
plymio (yn gyffredinol) *be* plunge
plymiwr *eg* plymwyr plunger
plymiwr dinwyo *eg* plymwyr dinwyo degassing plunger
plymwr *eg* plymwyr plumber
pob arddull all styles
pob dogfen all documents
pob echel all axes
pob ffeil all files
pob ffolder all folders
pob grid echel all axis grids
pob grŵp all groups
pob gwerth all values
pob iaith all languages
pob lefel all levels
pob maes all fields
pob mynegai all indexes
pob neges all messages
pob pedair blynedd quadrennial
pob priodwedd all properties
pob pum mlynedd quinquennial
pob siart all charts
pob sleid all slides
pob teitl all titles
pob tystysgrif all certificates
pobi *be* bake
pobiad *eg* pobiadau batch baking
pobi'n wag *be* bake blind
pobl aeddfed a / neu wedi lled-ymddeol *eb* mature and or semi-retired people
pobl anabl *eb* disabled people
pobl gyffredin *eb* commonalty
pobl ordew *eb* obese people
pobl y prysglwyni *eb* bushmen
pobloedd cynnar *ell* early peoples
poblogaeth *eb* poblogaethau population
poblogaeth ddibynnol *eb* poblogaethau dibynnol dependent population
poblogaeth frig *eb* peak population
poblogaeth gysefin *eb* parent population
poblogaeth o oed gwaith *eb* active population
poblogaeth optimwm *eb* poblogaethau optimwm optimum population
poblogaeth sy'n heneiddio *eb* poblogaethau sy'n heneiddio ageing population
poblogaeth weithio *eb* working population
poblogaeth y parasit *eb* parasite population
poblogaeth y pincod *eb* finch population
poblogaeth yr ysglyfaeth *eb* prey population
poblogaeth yswiriedig *eb* poblogaethau yswiriedig insured population
poblogaidd *ans* popular

poblogrwydd ac apêl popularity and appeal
poblyddiaeth *eb* populism
poblyddwr *eg* poblyddwyr populist
pobydd *eg* pobyddion baker
poced *eb* pocedi pocket
poced agen *eb* pocedi agen bound slot pocket
poced fflap *eb* pocedi fflap flap pocket
poced glun letraws *eb* pocedi clun lletraws diagonal hip pocket
poced glwt *eb* pocedi clwt patch pocket
poced glwt ddwbl *eb* pocedi clwt dwbl double patch pocket
poced sêm ochr *eb* pocedi sêm ochr side seam pocket
poced wald *eb* pocedi wald welt pocket
poced wedi'i leinio *eb* pocedi wedi'u leinio lined pocket
pocediadur *eg* pocediaduron pocketbook
pocedu *be* pocket
pocer *eg* poceri poker
pocer nwy *eg* poceri nwy gas poker
podiatreg *eb* podiatry
podiatregydd *eg* podiatregwyr podiatrist
podsol *eg* podsolau podsol
podsolig *ans* podsolic
poen *eg/b* poenau pain
poen allgyfeiriol *eg* referred pain
poen cronig *eg* chronic pain
poen llym *eg* acute pain
poenleddfol *ans* analgesic
poenleddfwr *eg* poenleddfwyr analgesic
poenleddfwr epidwral *eg* poenleddfwyr epidwral epidural analgesic
poenus *ans* painful
poer *eg* saliva
poergarthydd *eg* poergarthyddion expectorant
poerol *ans* salivary
poeth (am gig sbeislyd) *ans* devilled
poeth (yn gyffredinol) *ans* hot
poeth freuder *ans* hot shortness
poethder *eg* hotness
poethgoch *ans* red hot
poethoffrwm *eg* poethoffrymau burnt offering
poicilothermig *ans* poikilothermic
pôl *eg* polau pole
pôl de *eg* south pole
pôl gogledd *eg* north pole
pôl magnetig *eg* polau magnetig magnetic pole
pôl magnetig y de *eg* south magnetic pole
pôl magnetig y gogledd *eg* north magnetic pole
pôl sy'n cyrchu tua'r de *eg* south seeking pole
pôl sy'n cyrchu tua'r gogledd *eg* north seeking pole
polar *ans* polar; polarized
polaredd *eg* polareddau polarity
polaredd bond *eg* bond polarity
polaredd negatif *eg* negative polarity
polareiddiad *eg* polareiddiadau polarization
► **polareiddio** *be* polarize
polarimedr *eg* polarimedrau polarimeter
polarimedreg *eb* polarimetry
polarydd *eg* polaryddion polarizer
polca *eg* polcâu polka
polder *eg* polderau polder
polderu *be* impolder
poledd *eg* poleddau pole strength
polio *eg* polio
polisi *eg* polisïau policy
polisi adweithiol *eg* polisïau adweithiol reactionary policy
polisi amaethyddol cyffredin *eg* common agricultural policy
polisi ariannol *eg* monetary policy
► **polisi cartref** *eg* polisïau cartref domestic policy
polisi codi tâl *eg* polisïau codi tâl charging policy
polisi cyfle cyfartal *eg* polisïau cyfle cyfartal equal opportunities policy
polisi cyhoeddus *eg* public policy
polisi cyllidol *eg* fiscal policy
polisi cymdeithasol *eg* polisïau cymdeithasol social policy
polisi Cymraeg *eg* polisïau Cymraeg Welsh language policy
polisi cynnwys y tŷ *eg* polisïau cynnwys y tŷ house contents policy
polisi cytûn *eg* polisïau cytûn agreed policy
polisi chwarae teg *eg* square deal policy
polisi defnydd derbyniol *eg* acceptable use policy
polisi derbyn *eg* polisïau derbyn admissions policy
polisi diffynnaeth *eg* polisïau diffynnaeth protectionist policy
polisi drws agored *eg* open-door policy
polisi dyhuddo *eg* polisïau dyhuddo appeasement policy
Polisi Economaidd Newydd *eg* New Economic Policy
polisi egni'r Deyrnas Unedig *eg* UK energy policy
polisi goddef dim *eg* zero tolerance policy
polisi gwaddol *eg* polisïau gwaddol endowment policy
polisi macroeconomaidd *eg* macroeconomic policy
polisi ochr gyflenwi *eg* polisïau ochr gyflenwi supply-side policies
polisi prisiau ac incwm *eg* prices and incomes policy
polisi prisio *eg* pricing policy
polisi tramor *eg* foreign policy
polisi ymddiffeithio *eg* scorched earth policy
polisi ymddygiad *eg* polisïau ymddygiad behaviour policy
polisi ymwthiol *eg* polisïau ymwthiol forward policy
polisi ysgol gyfan *eg* whole school policy
polisi yswiriant *eg* polisïau yswiriant insurance policy
Polisi'r Fargen Newydd *eg* New Deal Policy

polonaise *eg* polonaises polonaise
poloniwm *eg* polonium
polo'r dŵr *eg* water-polo
polycarbonad *eg* polycarbonadau polycarbonate
polyclens *eg* polyclens
poly(2-clorobwta-1,3-deuen) *eg* poly(2-chlorobuta-1,3-diene)
poly(cloroethen) *eg* poly(chloroethene)
polyester *eg* polyester
polyesterau *ell* polyesters
poly(ethen) *eg* poly(ethene)
poly(ethenol) *eg* poly(ethenol)
polyethylen *eg* polyethylene
polyfinyl asetad *eg* polyvinyl acetate
polyfinyl clorid *eg* polyvinyl chloride
polyfinyliden *eg* polyvinylidene
poly(ffenylethen) *eg* poly(phenylethene)
polyffila *eg* polyfilla
polyfflworocarbon *eg* polyfluorocarbon
polyffosffad *eg* polyphosphate
polygon *eg* polygonau polygon
polygon amgylchol *eg* polygonau amgylchol circumscribed polygon
polygon amlder *eg* polygonau amlder frequency polygon
polygon amlder cronnus *eg* polygonau amlder cronnus cumulative frequency polygon
polygon cyswllt *eg* polygonau cyswllt link polygon
polygon grymoedd *eg* polygon of forces
polygon rhaff *eg* polygonau rhaff funicular polygon
polyhedrol *ans* polyhedral
polyhedron *eg* polyhedronau polyhedron
polymer *eg* polymerau polymer
polymer cyddwyso *eg* condensation polymer
polymer finyl *eg* polymerau finyl vinyl polymer
polymeriad *eg* polymerization
polymeriad adio *eg* addition polymerization
polymeru *be* polymerize
poly(methanal) *eg* poly(methanal)
poly(methyl 2-methylpropenoad) *eg* poly(methyl 2-methylpropenoate)
polyn *eg* polion pole; stake
polyn anelu *eg* polion anelu ranging pole
polyn llorwedd *eg* polion llorwedd ledger
polynomaidd *ans* polynomial
polynomial *eg* polynomialau polynomial
polyomino *eg* polyominos polyomino
polypeptid *eg* polypeptide
poly(propen) *eg* poly(propene)
polypropylen *eg* polypropylene
polysacarid *eg* polysaccharide
polystyren *eg* polystyrene
poly(tetrafflworoethen) *eg* poly(tetrafluoroethene)
polytop *eg* polytopau polytope
polytriocsofanadad(V) *eg* polytrioxovanadate(V)
polytriocsoffosffad(V) *eg* polytrioxophosphate(V)
polythen *eg* polythene
polywrethan *eg* polyurethane
pompom *eg* pompomau pompom
pompren *eb* pomprennau footbridge
ponc (mewn chwarela) *eb* ponciau gallery
ponc (naturiol) *eb* ponciau hummock
ponciog *ans* hummocky
pons *eg* pons
pont (=newid) *eb* pontydd transition
pont (mewn dawns) *eb* pontydd arch
pont (yn gyffredinol) *eb* pontydd bridge
pont bwyso *eb* pontydd pwyso weighbridge
pont diwb *eb* pontydd tiwb tubular bridge
pont eira *eb* pontydd eira snow bridge
pont faril *eb* pontydd baril barrel vault
pont godi *eb* pontydd codi drawbridge
pont grog *eb* pontydd crog suspension bridge
pont yr ysgwydd *eb* clavicle
pont yr ysgwydd *eb* collarbone
ponticello *adf* ponticello
pontiff *eg* pontiffau pontiff
pontio (mewn dawns) *be* arch
pontio (yn cydio dau beth) *be* spanning
pontio (yn gyffredinol) *be* bridge
pontreth *eb* pontrethi pontage
pop *eg* pop
popeth *eg* all
popio *be* pop
poplin *eg* poplin
popty *eg* poptai cooker
popty estynedig *eg* poptai estynedig cooker range
porc bol *eg* belly pork
porfa *eb* porfeydd pasture
porfa arw *eb* porfeydd garw rough pasture
porfa barhaol *eb* porfeydd parhaol permanent pasture
porfa fynydd *eb* porfeydd mynydd mountain pasture
porfäwr *eg* porfawyr grazier
porffor *eg* purple
porffor brown *eg* purple brown
porffor gweledol *eg* visual purple
porffor gwelw *eg* mauve
porffor tywyll *eg* dark purple
porffyri *eg* porphyry
porffyritig *ans* porphyritic
pori *be* browse; graze
pori cylchdro *be* rotational grazing
pori parhaol *be* permanent grazing
pori rheoledig *be* controlled grazing
porslen *eg* porcelain
porslen plisgyn wy *eg* eggshell porcelain
port (gwin) *eg* port
portamento *eg* portamenti portamento
portffolio *eg* portfolio
Portiwgaleg (iaith) *eb* Portuguese
Portiwgalydd *eg* Portiwgaliaid Portuguese
portread *eg* portreadau portrait; representation

portread darluniol *eg* portreadau darluniol pictorial representation
portread eiconig *eg* portreadau eiconig iconic representation
portread hanner hyd *eg* portreadau hanner hyd half-length portrait
portread hyd llawn *eg* portreadau hyd llawn full-length portrait
portreadol *ans* representational
portreadu *be* portray; represent
porth (ar gyfrifiadur) *eg* pyrth port
porth (eglwys) *eg* pyrth main entrance
porth (mewn celfyddyd gyhoeddus) *eg* pyrth gateway
porth (yn cysgodi dros ddrws) *eg* pyrth porch
porth argraffydd *eg* pyrth argraffyddion printer port
porth cyfresol *eg* pyrth cyfresol serial port
porth ffacs *eg* pyrth ffacs fax gateway
porth gwacáu *eg* pyrth gwacáu exhaust port
porth mynwent *eg* pyrth mynwent lychgate
porth paralel *eg* pyrth paralel parallel port
porthcwlis *eg* portcullis
porthell *eb* porthelli gate
porthell arllwys *eb* porthelli arllwys pouring gate
porthfaer *eg* porthfeiri port-reeve
porthi *be* feed
porthi cocos *be* traction feed
porthiant *eg* porthiannau feed; fodder; forage
porthiant awtomatig *eg* porthiannau awtomatig automatic feed
porthiant bar (mecanwaith) *eg* bar feed
porthiant confensiynol *eg* conventional feed
porthiant dringol *eg* climbing feed
porthiant fertigol *eg* vertical feed
porthiant garw *eg* porthiannau garw coarse feed
porthiant hydredol *eg* longitudinal feed
porthiant llithr *eg* sliding feed
porthiant sensitif *eg* sensitive feed
porthiant ysbeidiol *eg* intermittent feed
porthladd galw *eg* porthladdoedd galw port of call
porthladd rhydd *eg* porthladdoedd rhydd free port
porthmon *eg* porthmyn drover
porthor *eg* porthorion porter
porthora *be* portering
porthydd cardiau *eg* porthyddion cardiau card feed
porthydd dalennau *eg* porthyddion dalennau sheet-feeder
porwr *eg* porwyr browser
porwr gwe *eg* porwyr gwe web browser
porwr rhyngrwyd *eg* porwyr rhyngrwyd internet browser
pos gofodol *eg* posau gofodol spatial puzzle
pos jigso *eg* posau jigso jigsaw puzzle
posibiliaeth *eb* possibilism
posibiliedydd *eg* posibiliedwyr possibilist
positif *ans* positive
positif mwyaf *eg* maximum positive
positifiaeth *eb* positivism
positron *eg* positronau positron
post *ans* postal
post (=gohebiaeth) *eg* post; mail
post (=polyn) *eg* pyst post
post amlerfyn *eg* pyst amlerfyn multi-tool post
post ceiniog *eg* penny post
post electronig (e-bost) *eg* electronic mail
post hoc post hoc
post newid cyflym *eg* pyst newid cyflym quick change post
post pedwar erfyn *eg* pyst pedwar erfyn four-way tool post
post sothach *eg* junk mail
post ystlys *eg* pyst ystlys newel post
post-dafliad *eg* post-dafliadau mail-shot
poster *eg* posteri poster
postgyfuno *be* mail merge
postio *be* post
postio dienw *be* anonymous posting
postliwd *eg* postliwdiau postlude
post-mortem *eg* post-mortem
postyn *eg* pyst post; goalpost
postyn gôl *eg* pyst gôl goal post
postyn milltir *eg* milepost
postyn offer *eg* pyst offer tool post
postyn pwll *eg* pyst pwll pitprop
postyn ystofi *eg* pyst ystofi warping post
pot glud *eg* potiau glud glue pot
pot golchdrwyth *eg* potiau golchdrwyth gallipot
pot pupur *eg* potiau pupur pepper-pot
potasiwm *eg* potassium
potasiwm iodid *eg* potassium iodide
potasiwm nitrad *eg* potassium nitrate
potasiwm sodiwm 2,3-deuhydrocsibwtandeuoad *eg* potassium sodium 2,3-dihydroxybutanedioate
potasiwm tetracyanocwprad(I) *eg* potassium tetracyanocuprate(I)
potel *eb* poteli bottle
potel â thopyn *eb* poteli â thopiau stoppered bottle
potel chwistrellu *eb* poteli chwistrellu spray bottle
potel fwydo *eb* poteli bwydo feeding-bottle
potel wactod *eg* poteli gwactod vacuum bottle
poten y goes *eb* calf
potensial *eg* potensialau potential
potensial digwyddiad-berthynol *eg* event-related potential
potensial disgyrchedd *eg* gravitational potential
potensial dŵr *eg* water potential
potensial ecwilibriwm *eg* equilibrium potential
potensial electrod safonol *eg* standard electrode potential
potensial electrostatig *eg* electrostatic potential
potensial gweithredu *eg* action potential
potensial ôl-synaptig ataliol *eg* inhibitory post-synaptic potential (IPSP)
potensial ôl-synaptig cyffroadol *eg* excitatory post-synaptic potential (EPSP)

potensial poblogaeth *eg* population potential
potensial toddyn osmotig *eg* osmotic solute potential
potensiomedr *eg* potensiomedrau potentiometer
potes *eg* broth
potsiwr *eg* potswyr poacher
pothell *eb* pothelli blister
pothellu *be* blistering
poussette *eb* poussette
powdr *eg* powdrau powder
powdr cannu *eg* powdrau cannu bleaching powder
powdr codi *eg* baking powder
powdr crocws *eg* crocus powder
powdr du *eg* powdrau du black powder
powdr emeri *eg* powdrau emeri emery powder
powdr golchi *eg* soap powder
powdr golchi *eg* powdrau golchi washing powder
powdr gwn *eg* gunpowder
powdr partio *eg* parting powder
powdr past *eg* paste powder
powdr past cellwlos *eg* cellulose paste powder
powdr pwmis *eg* pumice powder
powdr sgwrio *eg* scouring powder
powdr sialc *eg* whiting
powdr tartar *eg* cream of tartar
powdrliw *eg* powdrliwiau powder colour
powdrliw sefydlog *eg* powdrliwiau sefydlog fixed powder colour
powdrog *ans* powdery
powlaid *eb* bowlful
powlen *eb* powlenni bowl
powlen grog *eb* powlenni crog hanging bowl
powlen lwch *eb* powlenni llwch dust bowl
powltis *eg* poultice
powndio *be* impound
pragmatiaeth *eb* pragmatism
pragmatig *ans* pragmatic
pragmatydd *eg* pragmatyddion pragmatist
praidd *eg* preiddiau flock
pram *eg* pramiau pram
praseodymiwm *eg* praseodymium
pratitya-samutpada *eg* pratitya-samutpada
prawf (=arholiad bach) *eg* profion test
prawf (=cyfnod dan oruchwiliaeth fanwl) *eg* probation
prawf (=gwiriad) *eg* profion check
prawf (=tystiolaeth) *eg* profion proof
prawf a osodir yn genedlaethol *eg* profion a osodir yn genedlaethol nationally prescribed test
prawf ailadrodd rhifau *eg* profion ailadrodd rhifau digit repetition test
prawf alldaflu *eg* profion alldaflu projective test
prawf anwythol *eg* inductive proof
prawf arwyddion graddedig Wilcoxon *eg* Wilcoxon signed-ranks test
prawf arwyddocâd *eg* profion arwyddocâd test of significance
prawf asid *eg* acid test
prawf blip *eg* bleep test
prawf blotiau inc Rorschach *eg* profion blotiau inc Rorschach Rorschach inkblot test
prawf caledwch *eg* profion caledwch hardness test
prawf creadigrwydd *eg* profion creadigrwydd creativity test
prawf croeslinol *eg* profion croeslinol diagonal test
prawf cyfarganfod thematig *eg* thematic apperception test (TAT)
prawf cyfystyr-gwrthystyr *eg* profion cyfystyr-gwrthystyr synonym-antonym test
prawf cymydog *eg* neighbour test
prawf cyrhaeddiad *eg* profion cyrhaeddiad attainment test
prawf cyrhaeddiad *eg* achievement test
prawf cysyniadau *eg* profion cysyniadau concept sorting test
prawf dan oruchwyliaeth *eg* profion dan oruchwyliaeth controlled test
prawf darllen *eg* profion darllen reading test
prawf darllen a deall *eg* profion darllen a deall comprehension test
prawf deallusrwydd *eg* profion deallusrwydd intelligence test
prawf deallusrwydd safonedig *eg* profion deallusrwydd safonedig standardized intelligence test
prawf dewis gorfodol *eg* profion dewis gorfodol forced choice test
prawf diagnostig *eg* profion diagnostig diagnostic test
prawf diddwythol *eg* deductive proof
prawf dilyn cyfarwyddiadau *eg* profion dilyn cyfarwyddiadau directions test
prawf dilysrwydd *eg* profion dilysrwydd validity check
prawf diwedd modiwl *eg* profion diwedd modiwl end-of-module test
prawf dwygynffon *eg* profion dwygynffon two-tailed test
prawf ffitrwydd *eg* profion ffitrwydd fitness test
prawf fflam *eg* profion fflam flame test
prawf ffurfiol *eg* profion ffurfiol formal proof
prawf galwedigaethol *eg* profion galwedigaethol vocational test
prawf gallu *eg* profion gallu ability test
prawf gallu creadigol *eg* profion gallu creadigol creative ability test
prawf gallu cyffredinol *eg* profion gallu cyffredinol general ability test
prawf gan ei gydradd *eg* trial by his peers
prawf goddefiad glwcos *eg* profion goddefiad glwcos glucose tolerance test
prawf graddedig *eg* profion graddedig graded test
prawf graddedig darllen geiriau *eg* profion graddedig darllen geiriau graded word reading test
prawf graddio *eg* profion graddio grading test
prawf grŵp *eg* profion grŵp group test
prawf grŵp o allu ymenyddol *eg* profion grŵp o allu ymenyddol group test of mental ability

prawf gwaed *eg* profion gwaed blood test
prawf gwddf y groth *eg* profion gwddf y groth cervical smear
prawf gwrando *eg* profion gwrando listening test
prawf gwreichionen *eg* spark test
prawf gwybodaeth *eg* profion gwybodaeth information test
prawf gwybyddol *eg* profion gwybyddol cognitive test
prawf haenu *eg* flake test
prawf heli *eg* brine test
prawf hewristig *eg* profion hewristig heuristic proof
prawf iaith *eg* profion iaith language test
prawf labordy *eg* profion labordy laboratory test
prawf llafar *eg* profion llafar oral test
prawf maen prawf gyfeiriol *eg* profion maen prawf gyfeiriol criterion-referenced test
prawf maes *eg* profion maes field test
prawf meistrolaeth *eg* profion meistrolaeth mastery test
prawf modd *eg* profion modd means test
prawf odbaredd *eg* profion odbaredd odd-parity check
prawf paredd *eg* profion paredd parity check
prawf peilot *eg* profion peilot pilot test
prawf perfformiad *eg* profion perfformiad performance test
prawf personoliaeth gwrthrychol *eg* profion personoliaeth gwrthrychol objective personality test
prawf rhagdybiaeth *eg* hypothesis test
prawf rhifyddeg pen *eg* profion rhifyddeg pen mental arithmetic test
prawf safonedig *eg* profion safonedig standardized test
prawf safoni *eg* profion safoni standardization test
prawf safonol *eg* profion safonol standard test
prawf sgwâr X *eg* X square test
prawf sillafu *eg* profion sillafu spelling test
prawf T *eg* T test
prawf T Student *eg* Student's T test
Prawf Tebygolrwydd Union Fisher *eg* Fisher Exact Probability Test
prawf teg *eg* profion teg fair test
prawf trefnu patrymau *eg* profion trefnu patrymau block design test
prawf troeth *eg* profion troeth urine test
prawf trwy ornest *eg* trial by battle
prawf tueddfryd *eg* profion tueddfryd aptitude test
prawf tynnu llun person *eg* profion tynnu llun person draw-a-man test
prawf U Mann-Whitney *eg* Mann-Whitney U test
prawf ungynffon *eg* profion ungynffon one-tailed test
prawf unigol *eg* profion unigol individual test
prawf ymarferol *eg* profion ymarferol practical test
prawf ystadegol *eg* profion ystadegol statistical test
prawf-brintio *be* trial printing
prawf-ddangosydd deial *eg* prawf-ddangosyddion deial dial test indicator
prawf-ddata *ell* test data
prawf-farchnata *be* test marketing
prawfrestr personoliaeth amlwedd Minnesota *eb* Minnesota multiphasic personality inventory (MMPI)
prawfswm *eg* prawfsymiau checksum
prebend *eg* prebendau prebend
prebendari *eg* prebendariaid prebendary
preceptor *eg* preceptoriaid preceptor
preceptoriaeth *eb* preceptoriaethau preceptorship
pregeth *eb* pregethau sermon
pregethu *be* preach
pregethwr *eg* pregethwyr preacher
preifat *ans* private
preifateiddio *be* privatize
preifateiddio *be* privatization
preifatîr *eg* preifatiriaid privateer
preifatrwydd contract *eg* privity of contract
preimio *be* prime
preimio *be* priming
preimio semantig *be* semantic priming
preis *eg* prise
prelad *eg* preladiaid prelate
preliwd *eg* preliwdiau prelude
preliwd corâl *eg* preliwdiau corâl chorale prelude
premiwm *eg* premiymau premium
premiwm blynyddol *eg* premiymau blynyddol annual premium
pren *eg* wood
pren amlhaenog *eg* multi-ply
pren amlhaenog *eg* multi-plywood
pren balsa *eg* balsa wood
pren bocs *eg* box wood
pren caled *eg* prennau caled hardwood
pren caled nad yw'n hollti *eg* non-splitting hardwood
pren coctel *eg* prennau coctel cocktail stick
pren cyfansawdd *eg* prennau cyfansawdd manufactured board
pren cyferbyniol *eg* contrasting wood
pren ffawydd *eg* beech wood
pren golau ei liw *eg* wood of light colour
pren gwastraff *eg* prennau gwastraff scrap wood; waste wood
pren gwthio *eg* prennau gwthio push stick (power sawing)
pren gwyn *eg* whitewood
pren haengaled *eg* armoured ply
pren haenog *eg* plywood
pren haenog allanol *eg* exterior plywood
pren haenog bedw *eg* birch plywood
pren haenog canol trwchus *eg* stoutheart plywood
pren haenog gradd morol *eg* marine grade plywood
pren haenog mewnol *eg* interior plywood
pren haenog pum haen *eg* five ply plywood
pren haenog wedi'i argaenu *eg* veneered ply wood

pren haenog wedi'i wynebu *eg* faced plywood
pren heb ei sychu *eg* green timber
pren heb ei sychu *eg* unseasoned timber
pren lled galed *eg* mild hardwood
pren marw *eg* prennau marw dead wood
pren meddal *eg* prennau meddal softwood
pren mesur *eg* prennau mesur ruler
pren metr *eg* prennau metr metre stick
pren o ansawdd da *eg* good quality wood
pren pum haen *eg* five-ply wood
pren solet *eg* solid timber
pren solet *eg* solid wood
pren synthetig *eg* prennau synthetig synthetic wood
pren tair haen *eg* 3 plywood
pren tairhaenog *eg* three-ply wood
pren wedi'i lifio *eg* sawn timber
pren y gwanwyn *eg* spring wood
pren yr haf *eg* summer wood
prennaidd *ans* woody
prennyn yn mudlosgi *eg* prenynnau yn mudlosgi glowing splint
prentis *eg* prentisiaid apprentice
prentisiaeth *eb* apprenticeship
pres *eg* brass
pres cetris *eg* cartridge brass
pres Morlys *eg* Admiralty brass
pres parhaol *eg* permanent press
pres tiwbaidd *eg* tubular brass
près, y *ell* press gang
presbyter *eg* presbyteriaid presbyter
Presbyteraidd *ans* Presbyterian
Presbyteriad *eg* Presbyteriaid Presbyterian
presbytri *eg* presbytriau presbytery
presennol *ans* existing
presennol *eg* present
presenoldeb *eg* attendance; presence
presenoldeb ysbeidiol *eg* sporadic attendance
presesiad *eg* presesiadau precession
presesu *be* precess
presgripsiwn *eg* presgripsiynau prescription
presidiwm *eg* presidium
presio dillad *be* press clothes
preswyl *ans* resident
preswyliwr *eg* preswylwyr occupier
preswyliwr *eg* preswylwyr resident
presyddiad bôn *eg* presyddiadau bôn butt brazed
presyddu *be* braze
pricio a phanlychu *be* prick and pounce
priciwr ffeil *eg* pricwyr ffeiliau file pricker
pridwerth *eg* ransom
pridd *eg* priddoedd soil; earth
pridd anaeddfed *eg* priddoedd anaeddfed immature soil
pridd brown *eg* priddoedd brown brown earth
pridd coch *eg* priddoedd coch red earth
pridd uwchdor *eg* priddoedd uwchdor truncated soil
pridd y pannwr *eg* fuller's earth
priddeg *eb* pedology
priddegol *ans* pedological
priddlif *eg* priddlifau sludging; solifluction
prif (=cyntaf) *ans* primary
prif (=meistr) *ans* master
prif (=trechaf) *ans* predominant
prif (o ran ymborth) *ans* staple
prif (yn gyffredinol) *ans* principal
prif a mân chwaraeon major and minor games
prif air *eg* prif eiriau headword
prif allor *eb* prif allorau high altar
prif allwedd *eb* prif allweddi primary key
prif arolygydd *eg* prif arolygwyr chief superintendent
prif bibell *eb* prif bibellau main pipe
prif blanau *ell* principal planes
prif bluen *eb* prif blu primary feather
prif denant *eg* prif denantiaid tenant-in-chief
prif destun *eg* prif destunau main subject
prif dudalen *eb* prif dudalennau master page
prif duedd *eb* main trend
prif ddewislen *eb* prif ddewislenni main menu
prif ddimensiynau *ell* main dimensions
prif ddiwydiannau *ell* staple industries
prif echelin *eb* main axis
prif effaith *eb* main effect
prif fachgen *eg* prif fechgyn head boy
prif faen prawf *eg* prif feini prawf main criterion
prif ferch *eb* prif ferched head girl
prif feridian *eb* prime meridian
prif flaenoriaeth *eg* top priority
prif ffilm *eb* feature length film; feature film
prif ffocws *eg* principal focus
prif ffrwd *eb* prif ffrydiau main stream; trunk stream
prif ffrydio *be* mainstreaming
prif geibr *eg* prif geibrau main rafter
prif gof *eg* primary memory; main memory
prif gontractwr *eg* prif gontractwyr principal contractor
prif gorff y testun *eg* main body text
prif gortecs corfforol-synhwyraidd *eg* primary somatosensory cortex
prif gortecs echddygol *eg* primary motor cortex
prif gortecs y clyw *eg* primary auditory cortex
prif gortecs y golwg *eg* primary visual cortex
prif grefydd *eb* prif grefyddau main religion
prif gronfa wladol *eb* prif gronfeydd gwladol consolidated fund
prif gyflenwad *eg* supply
prif gyflenwad *eg* prif gyflenwadau mains
prif gyflenwad domestig *eg* domestic mains supply
prif gyflenwad trydan *eg* mains electricity supply
prif gyfnod tyfiant *eg* grand period of growth
prif gyfrifiadur *eg* prif gyfrifiaduron main frame

prif gystadleuydd *eg* prif gystadleuwyr main competitor
prif hwylbren *eb* prif hwylbrennau main mast
prif liw *eg* main colour
prif lythrennau *ell* block letters
prif lythrennu *be* block lettering
prif nodwedd *eb* prif nodweddion central trait
prif ôl-gryniad *eg* major aftershock
prif organ *eb* prif organau great organ
prif orsaf *eb* prif orsafoedd principal station
prif raff *eb* prif raffau mainsheet
prif sgrin *eb* prif sgriniau main screen
prif siaradwr *eg* prif siaradwyr keynote speaker
prif storfa *eb* prif storfeydd main store
prif stori *eb* lead story
prif swyddfa *eb* prif swyddfeydd head office
prif swyddfa'r post *eb* general post office
prif swyddog addysg *eg* prif swyddogion addysg chief education officer
Prif Swyddog Iechyd *eg* Medical Officer of Health
Prif Swyddwr *eg* Prif Swyddwyr Grand Pensionary
prif system nerfol *eb* central nervous system
prif urdd *eb* prif urddau major order
Prif Ustus *eg* Prif Ustusiaid Chief Justice
prif ustus *eg* prif ustusiaid justiciar
prif weinidog *eg* prif weinidogion prime minister
prif weinydd nyrsio *eg* prif weinyddion nyrsio charge nurse
prif weinyddes nyrsio *eb* prif weinyddesau nyrsio charge nurse; sister
prif weithredwr *eg* prif weithredwyr chief executive officer
prif werthyd *eg* prif werthydau main spindle
prif wreiddyn *eg* prif wreiddiau tap root
prif wythïen *eb* prif wythiennau artery
prif ynad *eg* prif ynadon reeve
prifathrawes *eb* prifathrawesau headmistress
prifathro *eg* prifathrawon headmaster
prifddinas *eb* prifddinasoedd capital
priflythrennau bach *ell* drop caps
priflythrennau'n unig all caps
priflythyren *eb* priflythrennau capital letter; block capital letter; capital; upper case letter
prifswm *eg* prifsymiau principal
prifwynt *eg* prifwyntoedd prevailing wind
prifysgol *eb* prifysgolion university
Prifysgol Agored *eb* Open University
prifysgol annibynnol *eb* prifysgolion annibynnol independent university
prifysgol golegol *eb* prifysgolion colegol collegiate university
priffordd *eb* priffyrdd highway
primat *eg* primatiaid primate
prin *adf* just
prin drawiad *eg* prin drawiadau grazing incidence
prin glirio *be* just clear
prin o galch *ans* lime deficient
prin osgoi *be* just miss
prinder *eg* scarcity
prinder calch *eg* lime deficiency
prinder fitamin *eg* vitamin deficiency
prinfwyn *eg* prinfwynau rare earth
print *eg* printiau print
print arbrofol *eg* printiau arbrofol trial print
print deilen *eg* printiau dail leaf print
print ffloc *eg* printiau ffloc flock print
print Japaneaidd *eg* printiau Japaneaidd Japanese print
print leino *eg* printiau leino lino print
print lliw *eg* printiadau lliw colour print
printiad offset *eg* printiadau offset offset print
printiedig *ans* printed
printio *be* print
printio â phren *be* stick printing
printio â sgrin sidan *be* serigraphy
printio â sgrin sidan *be* silk-screen printing
printio â thaten *be* potato printing
printio bloc *be* block printing
printio bloc leino *be* lino-block printing
printio ffabrig *be* fabric printing
printio leino *be* lino printing
printio tynnol *be* subtractive printing
priodas *eb* priodasau marriage; matrimony
priodas ddirprwyol *eb* priodasau dirprwyol marriage by proxy
priodasol *ans* marital; matrimonial
priodol *ans* appropriate; proper; respective
priodol o ran anhawster *ans* appropriately pitched
priodoledd *eg* priodoleddau attribute
priodoledd ailosod *eg* priodoleddau ailosod reset attribute
priodoledd anhysbys *eg* priodoleddau anhysbys unknown attribute
priodoledd celloedd *eg* priodoleddau celloedd cell attribute
priodoledd esthetig *eg* priodoleddau esthetig aesthetic quality
priodoledd testun *eg* priodoleddau testun text attribute
priodoleddau ac amryweddau attributes and variates
priodoleddau croesbylu *ell* cross-fade attributes
priodoliad *eg* priodoliadau attribution
priodoliad sefyllfaol situational attribution
priodwedd *eb* priodweddau property
priodwedd colofn *eb* priodweddau colofnau column property
priodwedd drechol *eb* priodweddau trechol dominant attribute
priodwedd enciliol *eb* priodweddau enciliol recessive attribute
priodwedd ffisegol *eb* priodweddau ffisegol physical property
priodwedd gweithio *eb* priodweddau gweithio working property
priodwedd gydglymu *eb* priodweddau cydglymu colligative property

priodwedd metelau *eb* priodweddau metelau property of metals
priodweddau dogfen *ell* document properties
prior *eg* prioriaid prior
priordy *eg* priordai priory
priores *eb* prioresau prioress
prioriaeth *eb* prioriaethau priorship
pris *eg* prisiau price
pris cost *eg* cost price
pris cyfartalog *eg* prisiau cyfartalog average price
pris cyfredol *eg* prisiau cyfredol current price
pris cymharol *eg* relative price
pris dangosol *eg* prisiau dangosol marked price
pris ecwilibriwm *eg* equilibrium price
pris gostyngol *eg* prisiau gostyngol reduced price
pris gwerthu *eg* selling price
pris hufennu *eg* skimming price
pris llawn *eg* full cost price
pris penodol *eg* prisiau penodol fixed price
pris premiwm *eg* premium price
pris prynu *eg* prisiau prynu buying price
pris treiddio *be* prisiau treiddio penetration price
pris tŷ *eg* prisiau tai house price
pris uned *eg* unit price
pris ymyrrol *eg* prisiau ymyrrol intervention price
prisiant *eg* prisiannau valuation
prisiau treiddio *ell* penetration pricing
prisio ar sail cystadleuaeth *be* competition pricing
prisio cost plws *be* cost plus pricing
prisio cyfyngol *be* limit pricing
prisio rheibus *be* predatory pricing
prisiwr *eg* priswyr valuer
prisiwr rhanbarth *eg* priswyr rhanbarth district valuer
prism *eg* prismau prism
prism arosgo *eg* prismau arosgo oblique prism
prism blaendor *eg* prismau blaendor truncated prism
prism cangen *eg* prismau cangen branch prism
prism crwn *eg* prismau crwn circular prism
prism hecsagonol *eg* prismau hecsagonol hexagonal prism
prism petryal *eg* prismau petryal rectangular prism
prism rheolaidd *eg* prismau rheolaidd regular prism
prism sgwâr *eg* prismau sgwâr square prism
prism triongl *eg* prismau triongl triangular prism
prism union *eg* prismau union right prism
prismatig *ans* prismatic
prismatoid *eg* prismatoidau prismatoid
prismau croestoriadol *eg* intersecting prisms
prismoid *eg* prismoidau prismoid
prismoidol *ans* prismoidal
priswahaniaethu *be* price differentiation
proban *eg* proban
problem *eb* problemau problem
problem athronyddol *eb* problemau athronyddol philosophical problem
problem dynnu *eb* problemau tynnu subtraction problem
problem gwirfoddolwyr *eb* volunteer problem
problem gyfeiriedig *ans* problem orientated
problem iechyd o bwys *eb* problemau iechyd o bwys major health problem
problem rifiadol *eb* problemau rhifiadol numerical problem
problemau cartrefu *ell* housing problems
problemau ymddygiad *ell* behavioural problems
procsimol *ans* proximal
proctor *eg* proctorion proctor
procuradur *eg* procuraduron procurator
profadwyedd *eg* testability
profeb *eb* profebau probate
profedigaeth *eb* profedigaethau bereavement
profedigai *eg* profedigeion testee
Profensaidd *ans* ProvenÁal
Profensaleg *eg* ProvenÁal
Profenswr *eg* Profenswyr ProvenÁal
profi *be* prove
profi *be* test; check
profi byrfyfyr *be* improvised testing
profi croeslinol *be* diagonal testing
profi derbyniad *be* acceptance testing
profi diagnostig *be* diagnostic testing
profi eitemau *be* item testing
profi gwaelodlin *be* baseline testing
profi IQ *be* IQ testing
profi maen prawf gyfeiriol *be* criterion-referenced testing
profi modd *be* means testing
profi pell *be* remote testing
profi rhagdybiaethau *be* hypothesis testing
profi rhaglen *be* program proving
profi seicometrig *be* psychometric testing
profi teg *be* fair testing
profi ystyrlon *be* significant testing
profiad *eg* profiadau experience
profiad crefyddol *eg* religious experience
profiad crefyddol personol *eg* personal religious experience
profiad deallusol *eg* profiadau deallusol intellectual experience
profiad gwaith *eg* profiadau gwaith work experience
profiad iaith *eg* language experience
profiad o nirfana *eg* experience of nirvana
profiad uniongyrchol *eg* profiadau uniongyrchol direct experience
profiadau bywyd *ell* life experiences
profiadau yn y cwricwlwm *ell* curricular experiences
profiannaeth *eb* probation
profiant *eg* probate
proflen *eb* proflenni proof

profost *eg* profostiaid provost
profost-farsial *eg* profost-farsialiaid provost marshal
profwr *eg* profwyr trier
proffas *eg* prophase
proffesiwn *eg* proffesiynau profession
proffesiynol *ans* professional
proffesiynoldeb *eg* professionalism
proffidiol *ans* profitable
proffidioldeb *eg* profitability
proffil *eg* proffiliau profile
proffil cam *eg* proffiliau cam cam profile
proffil clasurol *eg* proffiliau clasurol classic profile
proffil cydbwysedd *eg* proffiliau cydbwysedd profile of equilibrium
proffil darllenydd *eg* reader profile
proffil disgybl *eg* proffiliau disgyblion pupil profile
proffil estynedig *eg* proffiliau estynedig projected profile
proffil graddedig *eg* proffiliau graddedig graded profile
proffil hydredol *eg* proffiliau hydredol longitudinal profile
proffil pridd *eg* soil profile
proffilio *be* profile
proffilio troseddwyr *be* offender profiling
proffilm *eg* proffilmiau profilm
proffwyd *eg* proffwydi prophet
proffwydol *ans* prophetic
proffwydoliaeth *eb* proffwydoliaethau prophecy
proffwydoliaeth hunangyflawnol *eb* self-fulfilling prophecy
proffylacsis *eg* prophylaxis
progesteron *eg* progesterone
project *eg* projectau project
project crynodol *eg* projectau crynodol summative project
project peilot *eg* projectau peilot pilot project
project Washoe *eg* project Washoe
prolad *ans* prolate
proladiad *eg* prolation
proletariat *eg* proletariat
prolin *eg* proline
prolog *eg* prologau prologue
Prologau Gwrth-Farcionaidd *ell* Anti-Marcionite Prologues
promenâd *eg* promenadau promenade
promethiwm (Pm) *eg* promethium
pronadiad *eg* pronadiadau pronation
prop *eg* propiau prop
propadeuen *eg* propadiene
propaganda *eg* propaganda
propan *eg* propane
propanal *eg* propanal
propannitril *eg* propanenitrile
propan-1-ol *eg* propan-1-ol
propan-2-ol *eg* propan-2-ol
propanon *eg* propanone
propanon ocsim *eg* propanone oxime
propan-1,2,3-triol *eg* propane-1,2,3-triol
propan-1,2,3-triyl trinitrad *eg* propane-1,2,3-triyl trinitrate
propan-1,2,3-triyl trisoctadecanoad *eg* propane-1,2,3-triyl trisoctadecanoate
propan-2-yl- *eg* propan-2-yl-
propan-2-ylbensen *eg* propan-2-ylbenzene
prop-2-anylbensen *eg* prop-2-anylbenzene
propenal *eg* propenal
propennitril *eg* propenenitrile
prop-2-en-1-ol *eg* prop-2-en-1-ol
propriodderbyniaeth *eb* proprioception
prosbectws *eg* prosbectysau prospectus
prosceniwm *eg* proscenium
proselyt *eb* proselytiaid proselyte
proselytiaeth *eb* proselytism
proses *eb* prosesau process
proses addurnol *eb* prosesau addurnol decorative process
proses asid Bessemer *eb* acid Bessemer process
proses asid tân agored *eb* acid open hearth process
proses atmosfferig *eb* prosesau atmosfferig atmospheric process
proses awtomatiaeth *eb* prosesau awtomatiaeth automation process
proses benderfynu *eb* prosesau penderfynu decision making process
proses bresyddu *eb* prosesau presyddu brazing process
proses bywyd *eb* prosesau bywyd life process
proses cwyr coll *eb* lost-wax process
proses datrys anghydfod *eb* prosesau datrys anghydfod dispute resolution process
proses datrys problemau *eb* prosesau datrys problemau problem solving process
proses dectonig *eb* prosesau tectonig tectonic process
proses dectonig fyd-eang *eb* global tectonic process
proses drosi *eb* prosesau trosi conversion process
proses ddatblygiadol *eb* prosesau datblygiadol developmental process
proses ddatblygu *eb* prosesau datblygu development process
proses ddilyniannol *eb* prosesau dilyniannol sequential process
proses ddrafftio *eb* drafting process
proses ddylunio *eb* prosesau dylunio design process
proses fasig Bessemer *eb* basic Bessemer process
proses fasig tân agored *eb* basic open hearth process
proses gefndir *eb* prosesau cefndir background process
proses geomorffig *eb* geomorphic process
proses geomorffolegol *eb* geomorphological process

proses grefft *eb* craft process
proses grynhoad *eb* compilation process
proses gyffwrdd *eb* prosesau cyffwrdd contact process
proses gynhyrchu *eb* process production
proses Haber *eb* Haber process
proses lathru *eb* prosesau llathru polishing process
proses o alaru *eb* grieving process
proses oddefol *eb* prosesau goddefol passive process
proses ofannu *eb* prosesau gofannu forging process
proses olchi *eb* prosesau golchi washing process
proses orffennu *eb* prosesau gorffennu finishing process
proses reoli gofal *eb* care management process
proses rhydocs *eb* prosesau rhydocs redox process
proses sgrin sidan *eb* prosesau sgrin sidan silkscreen process
proses sodro *eb* soldering process
proses sychu *eb* prosesau sychu drying process
proses wastraffu *eb* prosesau gwastraffu wasting process
proses wnïo *eb* prosesau gwnïo sewing process
proses wrthwyneb *eb* prosesau gwrthwyneb opponent process
proses wybyddol *eb* prosesau gwybyddol cognitive process
prosesau dynol *ell* human processes
prosesau ffisegol *ell* physical processes
prosesu *be* process
prosesu all-lein *be* off-line processing
prosesu amser real *be* real time processing
prosesu ar-lein *be* on-line processing
prosesu awtomatig *be* automatic processing
prosesu bas *be* shallow processing
prosesu cefndir *be* background processing
prosesu cyfathrebiadau *be* communications processing
prosesu data *be* data processing
prosesu data electronig *be* electronic data processing
prosesu data masnachol *be* commercial data processing
prosesu delweddau *be* image processing
prosesu dosbarthu paralel *be* parallel distributed processing
prosesu dwfn *be* deep processing
prosesu ffeil *be* file processing
prosesu geiriau *be* word processing
prosesu gwybodaeth *be* information processing
prosesu o'r gwaelod i fyny *be* bottom-up processing
prosesu o'r pen i'r gwaelod *be* top-down processing
prosesu paralel *be* parallel processing
prosesu pell *be* remote processing
prosesu rhestri *be* list processing
prosesu sain *be* sound processing
prosesu trafodion *be* transaction processing
prosesu ymdrechol *be* effortful processing
prosesydd *eg* prosesyddion processor
prosesydd bwyd *eg* prosesyddion bwyd food processor
prosesydd canolog *eg* prosesyddion canolog central processor
prosesydd geiriau *eg* prosesyddion geiriau word processor
prosesydd geiriau un pwrpas *eg* prosesyddion geiriau un pwrpas dedicated word processor
prosesydd paralel *eg* prosesyddion paralel parallel processor
prosopagnosia *eg* prosopagnosia
prosthesis *eg* prosthesis
protanopia *eg* protanopia
protectoriaeth *eb* protectoriaethau protectorate
protein *eg* proteinau protein
protein cynhenid *eg* proteinau cynhenid native protein
proteinas *eg* proteinase
protest *eb* protestiadau protest
Protestaniaeth *eb* Protestantism
Protestannaidd *ans* Protestant
Protestant *eg* Protestaniaid Protestant
protestiad *eg* protestiadau protestation
protestiadau'r bobl *ell* popular protest
protestio *be* protest
protoair *eg* protoeiriau protoword
protocol *eg* protocolau protocol
protocol rhagosodedig *eg* protocolau rhagosodedig default protocol
protocol wedi'i gofrestru *eg* protocolau wedi'u cofrestru registered protocol
protocolau profi *ell* testing protocols
protoctiniwm *eg* protoctinium
proton *eg* protonau proton
protonoteri *eg* protonotary
protosoad *eg* protosoaid protozoan
prototeip *eg* prototype
Prwsiad *eg* Prwsiaid Prussian
Prwsiaidd *ans* Prussian
pry cop *eg* pryfed cop spider
pryd ar glud *eg* meals on wheels
pryd o fwyd gyda'r hwyr *eg* prydau o fwyd gyda'r hwyr evening meal
prydau ysgol *ell* school meals
Prydeiniwr *eg* Prydeinwyr Briton
pryder *eg* pryderon anxiety; apprehension
pryder gwahanu *eg* separation anxiety
pryder rhag dieithriaid *eg* stranger anxiety
prydles *eb* prydlesi lease
prydlesol *ans* leasehold
prydleswr *eg* prydleswyr leaseholder
prydleswr *eg* prydleswyr lessee
pryf glas *eg* pryfed gleision aphid
pryf gwyn *eg* pryfed gwyn whitefly

pryf sidan *eg* pryfed sidan silkworm
pryf-dyllog *ans* worm eaten
pryfed deilysol *ell* leaf-eating insects
pryfed pren *ell* woodworm
pryfleiddiad *eg* pryfleiddiaid insecticide
pryfyn *eg* pryfed insect
pryfyn llawn-dwf *eg* mature insect
pryfyn tyllu coed *eg* pryfed tyllu coed wood-boring insect
pryfyn ysglyfaeth *eg* pryfed ysglyfaeth prey insect
pryfysol *ans* insectivorous
prynu *be* buy; purchase
prynu ar gredyd *be* credit buying
prynu byrbwyll *be* impulse buying
prynwr *eg* prynwyr buyer
prynwr gofal iechyd *eg* prynwyr gofal iechyd health care purchaser
prysg *eg* scrub
prysgoedio *be* coppice
prysgwydd *ell* brushwood
prysgwydd rhanbarth Môr y Canoldir *ell* Mediterranean scrub
prysgwydd saets *ell* sagebrush
prysur *ans* busy
prysuro (geni) *be* induce
puja *eg* puja
pulpud *eg* pulpudau pulpit
pum cam *eg* five steps
Pum Clasur (Conffiwsiaeth) *eg* Five Classics
Pum Ffordd Five Ways
Pum Llyfr, y Five Books, the
Pum Piler Islam *eg* Five Pillars of Islam
Pum Piler, y Five Pillars, the
Pum Porthladd *eg* Cinque Ports
pumawd *eg* pumawdau quintet
pumcanmlwyddiant *eg* quincentennial
pumed *eg* one-fifth
pumed *eg* pumedau fifth
pumed cudd *eg* pumedau cudd hidden fifth
Pumed Frenhiniaeth *eb* Fifth Monarchy
Pumed Frenhinwr *eg* Pumed Frenhinwyr Fifth Monarchist
pumed golofn *eb* fifth column
pumed noeth *eg* pumedau noeth exposed fifth
Pumed Weriniaeth *eb* Fifth Republic
pumedau ac wythfedau cyfochrog parallel fifths and octaves
pumedau ac wythfedau dilynol *ell* consecutive fifths and octaves
pumedau cyfochrog dilynol *ell* parallel consecutive fifths
pumled *eg* pumledi quintuplet
pum llath ar hugain *eg* twenty five yards
pump *eg* pumoedd five
punt *eb* punnoedd pound
punteado *eg* punteado
pupur a halen condiments
pupur Jamaica *eg* allspice
pur *ans* pure
purdan *eg* purgatory
purdebaeth *eb* purism
purfa *eb* purfeydd refinery
puro *be* refine
► **purydd** *eg* purwyr purist
PVA *eg* PVA
PVC *eg* PVC
pwdin *eg* pwdinau dessert
pwdin bara menyn *eg* pwdinau bara menyn bread and butter pudding
pwdin gwaed *eg* pwdinau gwaed black pudding
pwdin oer *eg* cold sweet
pwdlo *be* puddle
pwdr *ans* rotten
pŵer *eg* pwerau power
pŵer barnwrol *eg* pwerau barnwrol judicial power
pŵer dirprwyedig *eg* pwerau dirprwyedig delegated power
Pŵer Du *eg* Black Power
pŵer gwlychu *eg* wetting power
pŵer niwclear *eg* nuclear power
pŵer (prawf ystadegol) *eg* power (of a statistical test)
pŵer trydan dŵr *eg* hydroelectric power
pŵer trydanol *eg* electric power
pŵer tymhorol *eg* temporal power
pŵer y brenin *eg* pwerau'r brenin royal power
pwerau cyfandirol *ell* continental powers
pwerau esgynnol *ell* ascending powers
pwerau mawr *ell* super powers
Pwerau Mawrion *ell* Great Powers
pwerau o 10 *ell* powers of 10
pwerau treiddio *ell* penetrating powers
Pwerau'r Axis *ell* Axis Powers
pwerddaliad *eg* holding power
pŵl (=heb fin) *ans* blunt
pŵl (=heb lawer o olau) *ans* dim
pŵl llafur *eg* labour pool
pwli *eg* pwlïau pulley
pwli belt *eg* pwlïau belt belt pulley
pwli côn *eg* pwlïau côn cone pulley
pwli differol *eg* pwlïau differol differential pulley
pwli V *eg* pwlïau V V pulley
pwli ysgafn *eg* pwlïau ysgafn light pulley
pwlofer *eg/b* pwloferau pullover
pwlp *eg* pulp
pwls *eg* pylsiau pulse
pwlsadur *eg* pwlsaduron impeller
pwll (ar gyfer nofio) *eg* pyllau pool
pwll (=twll mawr yn y ddaear) *eg* pyllau pit
pwll (o ddŵr glaw ar y ffordd etc) *eg* pyllau puddle
pwll cloch *eg* pyllau cloch bell pit
pwll dŵr *eg* pyllau dŵr water hole
pwll glo *eg* pyllau glo colliery
pwll neidio *eg* pyllau neidio jumping pit
pwll nofio *eg* pyllau nofio swimming pool

pwll tegell *eg* pyllau tegell kettle hole
pwll tywod *eb* pyllau tywod sandpit
pwmis *eg* pumice
pwmp *eg* pympiau pump
pwmp ager *eg* steam pump
pwmp awyru *eg* pympiau awyru aerator pump
pwmp codi *eg* pympiau codi lift pump
pwmp grym *eg* pympiau grym force pump
pwmp gwacáu *eg* pympiau gwacáu exhaust pump
pwmp gwynt *eg* pympiau gwynt windpump
pwmp hidlo *eg* pympiau hidlo filter pump
pwmp proton *eg* pympiau proton proton pump
pwmp sugno *eg* pympiau sugno suction pump
pwna *eg* puna
pwnc *eg* pynciau subject
pwnc atodol *eg* pynciau atodol subsidiary subject
pwnc craidd *eg* pynciau craidd core subject
pwnc gorfodol *eg* pynciau gorfodol compulsory subject
Pwnc Iwerddon *eg* Irish Question
pwnc lleiafrifol *eg* pynciau lleiafrifol minority subject
pwnc sylfaen *eg* pynciau sylfaen foundation subject; basic subject
pwnc y tir *eg* land question
pwnc-benodol *ans* subject-specific
pwnc-ganolog *ans* subject-centred
pwnio *be* nudging
pwnsh *eg* pynsiau punch
pwnsh addurno *eg* pynsiau addurno decorating punch
pwnsh canoli *eg* pynsiau canoli centre punch
pwnsh canoli awtomatig *eg* pynsiau canoli awtomatig automatic centre punch
pwnsh cefndir *eg* pynsiau cefndir background punch
pwnsh cloch *eg* pynsiau cloch bell punch
pwnsh chwefforddd *eg* pynsiau chwefforddd sixway punch
pwnsh dotio *eg* pynsiau dotio dot punch
pwnsh hoelion *eg* pynsiau hoelion nail punch
pwnsh matio *eg* pynsiau matio matting punch
pwnsh olinio *eg* pynsiau olinio tracing punch
pwnsh paralel *eg* pynsiau paralel parallel punch
pwnsh pìn *eg* pynsiau pìn pin punch
pwnsh repoussé *eg* pynsiau repoussé repoussé punch
pwnsh sbring *eg* pynsiau sbring spring punch
pwnsh sêm *eg* pynsiau sêm groove punch
pwnsh suddo a matio *eg* pynsiau suddo a matio sinking and matting punch
pwnsh tyst *eg* pynsiau tyst witness punch
pwnsio *be* punch; punching
pwnt *eg* pyntiau punt
pwrpas deublyg *eg* dual purpose
pwrpasol *ans* appropriate
pwrs *eg* pyrsiau udder
Pwrs Cyfrin *eg* Privy Purse
pwrs gwregys *eg* pyrsiau gwregys belt pouch
pwrs herodrol *eg* pyrsiau herodrol heraldic purse
pwrswifant *eg* pursuivant
pwti *eg* putty
pwti adlynol *eg* adhesive putty
pwyad *eg* pwyadau smash shot
pwyllgor *eg* pwyllgorau committee
Pwyllgor Achredu Addysg Athrawon *eg* CATE: Committee for the Accreditation of Teachers Education
pwyllgor addysg *eg* pwyllgorau addysg education committee
pwyllgor addysg ymgynghorol *eg* advisory committee on education
pwyllgor amgylchedd *eg* pwyllgorau amgylchedd environment committee
Pwyllgor Barnwrol y Cyfrin Gyngor *eg* Judicial Committee of the Privy Council
Pwyllgor Cyfrifon *eg* Committee of Accounts
pwyllgor dethol *eg* pwyllgorau dethol select committee
Pwyllgor Diogelwch y Cyhoedd *eg* Committee of Public Safety
pwyllgor eglwys *eg* pwyllgorau eglwys church committee
Pwyllgor er Taenu'r Efengyl *eg* Committee for the Propagation of the Gospel
pwyllgor gwaith *eg* pwyllgorau gwaith executive committee
pwyllgor gweithredu *eg* pwyllgorau gweithredu executive committee
pwyllgor llywio *eg* pwyllgorau llywio steering committee
Pwyllgor Polisi Ariannol *eg* Monetary Policy Committee
pwyllgor safoni *eg* pwyllgorau safoni moderation committee
pwyllgor sefydlog *eg* pwyllgorau sefydlog standing committee
pwyllgor sirol *eg* pwyllgorau sirol county committee
Pwyllgor Troseddau *eg* Committee of Delinquency
Pwyllgor y Gweinidogion Ysbeiliedig *eg* Committee for Plundered Ministers
pwyllgor ymgynghorol *eg* pwyllgorau ymgynghorol advisory committee
pwyllgor ymgynghorol ar addysg ac ymddygiad cyfreithiol *eg* advisory committee on legal education and conduct
pwynt (=cyfnod) *eg* pwyntiau stage
pwynt (yn gyffredinol) *eg* pwyntiau point
pwynt allanol *eg* pwyntiau allanol external point
pwynt anfeidredd *eg* point of infinity
pwynt arnawf *eg* pwyntiau arnawf floating point
pwynt bwled *eg* pwyntiau bwled bullet point
pwynt caledu *eg* pwyntiau caledu decalescent point
pwynt canradd *eg* pwyntiau canradd percentile point
pwynt critigol *eg* pwyntiau critigol critical point

► **pwynt croestoriad** *eg* pwyntiau croestoriad point of intersection

pwynt cydbwysedd *eg* pwyntiau cydbwysedd balance point

pwynt cydgyfeiriol *eg* pwyntiau cydgyfeiriol converging point

pwynt cyfiau *eg* pwyntiau cyfiau conjugate point

pwynt cyfluniant *eg* pwyntiau cyfluniant centre of similitude

pwynt cyffwrdd *eg* pwyntiau cyffwrdd point of contact

pwynt cymal *eg* pwyntiau cymal point of articulation

pwynt cyntaf *eg* pwyntiau cyntaf first point

pwynt chwartel *eg* pwyntiau chwartel quartile point

pwynt degol *eg* pwyntiau degol decimal point

pwynt degradd *eg* pwyntiau degradd decile point

pwynt deuaidd *eg* pwyntiau deuaidd binary point

pwynt deuol *eg* bicimal point

pwynt diemwnt *eg* pwyntiau diemwnt diamond point

pwynt dirlawnder *eg* saturation point

pwynt ewtectig *eg* pwyntiau ewtectig eutectic point

pwynt ffitio *eg* pwyntiau ffitio fitting point

pwynt ffocal *eg* pwyntiau ffocal focal point

pwynt ffurfdro *eg* point of inflection

pwynt gimbil *eg* pwyntiau gimbil gimlet point

pwynt gornest *eg* match point

pwynt gosod *eg* pwyntiau gosod set point

pwynt gweithredu *eg* pwyntiau gweithredu action point

pwynt ildio *eg* pwyntiau ildio yield point

pwynt iro *eg* pwyntiau iro lubricating point

pwynt llwyth *eg* pwyntiau llwyth load point

pwynt llym *eg* pwyntiau llym sharp point

pwynt main *eg* pwyntiau main fine point

pwynt manylyn *eg* point of detail

pwynt mewnosod *eg* pwyntiau mewnosod insert point

pwynt oedi *eg* pwyntiau oedi point of delay

pwynt prifol *eg* pwyntiau prifol cardinal point

pwynt sefydlog *eg* pwyntiau sefydlog fixed point

pwynt sefydlogi *eg* pwyntiau sefydlogi fixation point

pwynt sgriw *eg* pwyntiau sgriw screw point

pwynt snap *eg* pwyntiau snap snap point

pwynt stôr *eg* pwyntiau stôr stored point

pwynt tangiadaeth *eg* pwyntiau tangiadaeth point of tangency

pwynt terfyn *eg* pwyntiau terfyn end point

pwynt trawslwytho *eg* pwyntiau trawslwytho transshipment point

pwynt triol *eg* tercimal point

pwynt triphlyg *eg* pwyntiau triphlyg triple point

pwynt trydan *eg* pwyntiau trydan electric power point

pwynt uchaf *eg* pwyntiau uchaf highest point

pwynt uchder *eg* pwyntiau uchder spot height

pwynt yr ên *eg* point of the jaw

pwyntiau'r cwmpawd *ell* points of the compass

pwyntio *be* point

pwyntydd *eg* pwyntyddion pointer

pwyntydd llygoden *eg* pwyntyddion llygoden mouse pointer

pwyntydd stac *eg* pwyntyddion stac check pointer

pwys *eg* pwysi pound

pwysau (=pêl drom mewn athletau) *ell* shot

pwysau (=gwaith etc) *ell* pressure

pwysau (yn gyffredinol) *ell* weight

pwysau agored *ell* catch weights

pwysau bantam *ell* bantam weight

pwysau canol *ell* middle weight

pwysau cot *ell* coat weight

pwysau cymdeithasol *ell* social pressures

pwysau cymedrig *ell* mean weight

pwysau cywerth *ell* equivalent weight

pwysau ffrog *ell* dress weight

pwysau gan gyfoedion *ell* peer pressure

pwysau geni *ell* birth weight

pwysau go drwm *ell* light heavy weight

pwysau mwyaf *ell* maximum weight

pwysau net *ell* net weight

pwysau plu *ell* feather weight

pwysau pryf *ell* fly weight

pwysau sych *ell* dry weight

pwysau trwm *ell* heavy weight

pwysau welter *ell* welter weight

pwysau ysgafn *ell* light weight

pwysau'r corff *ell* body weight

pwysau'r raced *ell* racket weight

► **pwysedd gwaed** *ell* blood pressure

► **pwysedd gwythiennol canolog** *eg* central venous pressure

pwysiad *eg* pwysiadau weighting

pwysiad marciau *eg* mark weighting

pwyslais *eg* pwysleisiau emphasis

pwyslais cyfansoddiadol *eg* compositional weight

pwyslath *eb* pwyslathau strut

pwysleisio *be* emphasise

pwysleisiol *ans* emphasized

pwyso *be* weigh

pwyso *be* press

pwyso *be* weigh in

pwyso bysell *be* press a key

pwysol *ans* weighted

pwyswr *eg* pwyswyr weighman

pwysyn *eg* pwysynnau single weight

pwysyn *eg* pwysynnau weight

pwysyn sash *eg* pwysynnau sash sash weight

pwyth *eg* pwythau stitch

pwyth *eg* pwythau suture

pwyth addurnol *eg* pwythau addurnol decorative stitch

pwyth amlinell *eg* pwythau amlinell outline stitch

pwyth amylu *eg* pwythau amylu oversew stitch

pwyth asgwrn pysgodyn *eg* pwythau asgwrn pysgodyn fishbone stitch
pwyth band *eg* pwythau band band stitch
pwyth blanced *eg* pwythau blanced blanket stitch
pwyth cadwyn *eg* pwythau cadwyn chain stitch
pwyth cadwyn agored *eg* pwythau cadwyn agored open chain stitch
pwyth cadwyn amryliw *eg* pwythau cadwyn amryliw chequered chain stitch
pwyth cadwyn cribog *eg* pwythau cadwyn cribog crested chain stitch
pwyth cadwyn dro *eg* pwythau cadwyn dro twisted chain stitch
pwyth cadwyn ddwbl *eg* pwythau cadwyn ddwbl double chain stitch
pwyth cadwyn hud *eg* pwythau cadwyn hud magic chain stitch
pwyth cadwyn rhosyn *eg* pwythau cadwyn rhosyn rosette chain stitch
pwyth cadwyn unigol *eg* pwythau cadwyn unigol detached chain stitch
pwyth ceibr *eg* pwythau ceibr chevron stitch
pwyth clo *eg* pwythau clo lock stitch
pwyth clwm *eg* pwythau clwm knotted stitch
pwyth coll *eg* pwythau coll skipped stitch
pwyth conyn *eg* pwythau conyn stem stitch
pwyth croes *eg* pwythau croes cross stitch
pwyth croes hirfraich *eg* pwythau croes hirfraich long-armed cross stitch
pwyth crwybr *eg* pwythau crwybr honeycomb stitch
pwyth cwlwm dwbl *eg* pwythau cwlwm dwbl double knot stitch
pwyth cwrel *eg* pwythau cwrel coral stitch
pwyth cydio *eg* pwythau cydio catch stitch
pwyth cyfansawdd *eg* pwythau cyfansawdd composite stitch
pwyth cyfrif edau *eg* pwythau cyfrif edau counted thread stitch
pwyth cyfrwy *eg* pwythau cyfrwy saddle stitch
pwyth cynfas *eg* pwythau cynfas canvas stitch
pwyth cynnal *eg* pwythau cynnal stay stitch
pwyth cyswllt *eg* pwythau cyswllt inserted stitch
pwyth chwipio *eg* pwythau chwipio whipping stitch
pwyth deilen *eg* pwythau deilen leaf stitch
pwyth dolen *eg* pwythau dolen looped stitch
pwyth dros bwyth pass slip stitch over
pwyth ffagod *eg* pwythau ffagod faggot stitch
pwyth ffagod dwbl *eg* pwythau ffagod dwbl double faggot stitch
pwyth ffagod sengl *eg* pwythau ffagod sengl single faggot stitch
pwyth gardys *eg* pwythau gardys garter stitch
pwyth gobelin *eg* pwythau gobelin gobelin stitch
pwyth gorwedd *eg* pwythau gorwedd couching
pwyth hemio *eg* pwythau hemio hem stitch
pwyth hemio slip *eg* pwythau hemio slip slip hemming stitch
pwyth igam ogam *eg* pwythau igam ogam zigzag stitch
pwyth llenwi *eg* pwythau llenwi filling stitch
pwyth llinell *eg* pwythau llinell line stitch
pwyth llygad y dydd *eg* pwythau llygad y dydd lazy daisy stitch
pwyth mwsogl *eg* pwythau mwsogl moss stitch
pwyth o chwith *eg* pwythau o chwith purl stitch
pwyth ôl *eg* pwythau ôl back stitch
pwyth ôl dwbl *eg* pwythau ôl dwbl double back stitch
pwyth pabell *eg* pwythau pabell tent stitch
pwyth pad *eg* pwythau pad pad stitch
pwyth padio *eg* pwythau padio padding stitch
pwyth Pekin *eg* pwythau Pekin Pekingese stitch
pwyth petryal *eg* pwythau petryal foursided stitch
pwyth pìn *eg* pwythau pìn pin stitch
pwyth plaen *eg* pwythau plaen plain stitch
pwyth plaen *eg* pwythau plaen stocking stitch
pwyth plu cadwynog *eg* pwythau plu cadwynog chained feather stitch
pwyth pluen *eg* pwythau pluen feather stitch
pwyth pryf *eg* pwythau pryf fly stitch
pwyth reis *eg* pwythau reis rice stitch
pwyth rhaff *eg* pwythau rhaff cable stitch
pwyth rhedeg *eg* pwythau rhedeg running stitch
pwyth rheffyn *eg* pwythau rheffyn rope stitch
pwyth saethben *eg* pwythau saethben herring-bone stitch
pwyth satin *eg* pwythau satin satin stitch
pwyth tacio *eg* pwythau tacio tacking stitch
pwyth taro *eg* pwythau taro stab stitch
pwyth tête de boeuf *eg* pwythau tête de boeuf tête de boeuf stitch
pwyth triongl *eg* pwythau triongl three-sided stitch
pwyth twll botwm *eg* pwythau twll botwm buttonhole stitch
pwyth Twrcaidd *eg* pwythau Twrcaidd Turkish stitch
pwyth tyllog *eg* pwythau tyllog punch stitch
pwyth uno *eg* pwythau uno joining stitch
pwytho *be* stitch
pwytho cylchdro *be* circular motion stitching
pwythwaith *eg* stitchery
pwythyn *eg* pwythynnau length
pydlwr *eg* pydlwyr puddler
pydredd *eg* decay
pydredd *eg* rot
pydredd dannedd *eg* dental decay
pydredd dannedd *eg* caries
pydredd sych *eg* dry rot
pydru *be* decay
pyg *eg* pitch
pygfaen *eg* pygfeini pitchstone
pyjamas *ell* pyjamas
pyjamas cwta *ell* shortie pyjamas
pylni *eg* bluntness
pylori *be* pulverization
pyloriant *eg* comminution
pylsadu *be* pulsate

pylsadur *eg* pylsaduron pulsator
pylu (=colli ffocws) *be* blur
pylu (=colli min) *be* blunt
pylu (=lladd y sain) *be* mute
pylu (=lleihau golau) *be* dim
pylu (am ddelwedd ar sgrin) *be* fade
pylu allan *be* fade out
pylu clocwedd *be* fade clockwise
pylu gwrthglocwedd *be* fade counter-clockwise
pylu gwrthrych *be* fade object
pylu i'r canol *be* fade to centre
pylu o'r canol *be* fade from centre
pylu'n fertigol *be* fade vertically
pylu'n llorweddol *be* fade horizontally
pylydd *eg* pylyddion dimmer
pyllu *be* pitting
pynciau craidd a sylfaen *ell* core and foundation subjects
pynfarch *eg* pynfeirch pack-horse
pyntio *be* punt
pyped *eg* pypedau marionette
pyped *eg* pypedau puppet
pyped bys *eg* pypedau bys finger puppet
pyped cerdyn *eg* pypedau cerdyn card puppet
pyped cymalog *eg* pypedau cymalog jointed puppet
pyped cysgod *eg* pypedau cysgod shadow puppet
pyped digorff *eg* pypedau digorff bodyless puppet
pyped llaw *eg* pypedau llaw hand puppet
pyped llinyn *eg* pypedau llinyn string puppet
pyped maneg *eg* pypedau maneg glove-puppet
pyped pren *eg* pypedau pren stick puppet
pyped rod *eg* pypedau rod rod puppet
pyped rod a maneg *eg* pypedau rod a maneg rod and glove puppet
pypedwr *eg* pypedwyr puppeteer
pyramid *eg* pyramidiau pyramid
pyramid blaendor *eg* pyramidiau blaendor truncated pyramid
pyramid bwydydd *eg* pyramidiau bwydydd food pyramid
pyramid crwn *eg* pyramidiau crwn circular pyramid
pyramid gwrthdro *eg* pyramidiau gwrthdro inverted pyramid
pyramid hecsagonol *eg* pyramidiau hecsagonol hexagonal pyramid
pyramid pentagonol *eg* pyramidiau pentagonol pentagonal pyramid
pyramid sgwâr *eg* pyramidiau sgwâr square pyramid
pyramid trionglog *eg* pyramidiau trionglog triangular pyramid
pyramid union *eg* pyramidiau union right pyramid
pyramidaidd *ans* pyramidal
pyramidiau biomas *ell* pyramids of biomass
pyramidiau niferoedd *ell* pyramids of numbers
pyridin *eg* pyridine
pyrit *eg* pyritau pyrites
pyrit haearn *eg* iron pyrites
pyroclast *eg* pyroclastau pyroclast
pyroclastaidd *ans* pyroclastian
pyroclastig *ans* pyroclastic
pyrocsilin *eg* pyroxylin
pyrocwpl *eg* pyrocouple
pyromedr *eg* pyromedrau pyrometer
pyromedr optegol *eg* pyromedrau optegol optical pyrometer
pyromedr pelydriad *eg* pyromedrau pelydriad radiation pyrometer
pyromedr thermocwpl *eg* pyromedrau thermocwpl thermocouple pyrometer
pyrometreg *eb* pyrometry
pyrometrig *ans* pyrometric
pyrwydden *eb* pyrwydd spruce
pyrwydden Norwy *eb* pyrwydd Norwy Norway spruce
pyrwydden Sitca *eb* pyrwydd Sitca Sitka spruce
pys wedi'u mwydo *ell* soaked peas
pysgodfa *eb* pysgodfeydd fishing ground
pysgodyn *eg* pysgod fish
pysgodyn carreg *eg* pysgod cerrig rockfish
pysgodyn cartilagaidd *eg* pysgod cartilagaidd cartilaginous fish
pysgodyn clytsiwr (lumpfish) *eg* pysgod clytsiwr lumpsucker
pysgodyn esgyrnog *eg* bony fish
pysgodyn ysgyfeiniog *eg* pysgod ysgyfeiniog lung fish
pysgota *be* fishing
pysgota'r cefnfor *be* deep sea fishing
pysgota'r glannau *be* inshore fishing
pysgota'r gwaelod *be* demersal fishing
pysgota'r wyneb *be* pelagic fishing
pysgotwr *eg* pysgotwyr fisherman
pytio *be* putt
Pythagoras *eg* Pythagoras

Ph

pH pH
Philip Awgwstws *eg* Philip Augustus
Philip Deg *eg* Philip the Fair
Philip Olygus *eg* Philip the Handsome
Phrygiaidd *ans* Phrygian

Q

quickstep *eg* dawnsiau quickstep quickstep
Qur'an *eg* Qur'an

R

r Pearson *eg* Pearson r
rabad *eg* rabadau rabbet
rabad cau *eg* rabadau cau stopped rabbet
rabbi *eg* rabbi
rabedu *be* rabbet
rac *eb* raciau rack
rac a phiniwn rack and pinion
rac gêr infoliwt *eb* raciau gêr infoliwt involute gear rack
rac sbwliau *eb* raciau sbwliau spool rack
raced *eb* racedi racket
raced blastig *eb* racedi plastig plastic racket
raced bren *eb* racedi pren wooden racket
raced carbon *eg* racedi carbon carbon racket
raced ddur *eb* racedi dur steel racket
raced ffibr gwydr *eg* racedi ffibr gwydr fibreglass racket
raced gref *eb* racedi cryf strong racket
raced ysgafn *eb* light racket
racem *eb* racemau raceme
racemad *eg* racemadau racemate
racemaidd *ans* racemose
racemeiddiad *eg* racemization
racemig *ans* racemic
racw *eg* raku
rachis *eg* rachisau rachis
radar *eg* radar
Radha *eb* Radha
radian *eg* radianau radian
radical *eg* radicalau radical
radical rhydd *eg* free radical
radicaliaeth *eb* radicalism
radicaliaeth wleidyddol a chrefyddol *eb* political and religious radicalism
radics *eg* radicsau radix
radio *eg* radios radio
radiograff *eg* radiograffau radiograph
radiograffeg *eb* radiography
radiograffydd *eg* radiograffwyr radiographer
radioleg *eb* radiology
radiolegydd *eg* radiolegwyr radiologist
radioseryddiaeth *eb* radioastronomy
radiotherapi *eg* radiotherapy
radiwm *eg* radium
radiws *eg* radiysau radius
radiws chwyrliant *eg* radiysau chwyrliant radius of gyration
radiws pitsh cylch *eg* P.C.R.
radiysu *be* radiusing
radl *eg* radlau raddle
radon (Rn) *eg* radon
raffia *eg* raffia
rafftio *be* rafting
raga Indiaidd *eg* Indian raga
ragtime *eg* ragtime
raiot *eg* raiotiaid ryot
rali *eb* ralïau rally
RAM ochr *eg* sideways RAM
Rama *eg* Rama
Ramadan *eg* Ramadan
Ramayana *eg* Ramayana
ramp *eg* rampiau ramp
ransh *eb* ransiau ranch
ransio *be* ranch
rap *eg* rap
rapio *be* rap
ras *eb* rasys race
ras arfau *eb* arms race
ras clwydi byr *eb* rasys clwydi byr short hurdle race
ras draws gwlad *eb* rasys traws gwlad cross country race
ras fer *eb* rasys byr short race
ras filltir *eb* rasys milltir mile race
ras ffos a pherth *eb* rasys ffos a pherth steeplechase
ras gan metr *eb* rasys can metr hundred metres race
ras glwydi *eb* rasys clwydi hurdle race
ras gyfartal *eb* rasys cyfartal dead heat
ras gyfnewid *eb* rasys cyfnewid relay
ras gyfnewid dulliau cymysg *eb* rasys cyfnewid dulliau cymysg medley relay race
ras gyfnewid fer *eb* rasys cyfnewid byr short relay race
ras gyfnewid nôl a mlaen *eb* rasys cyfnewid nôl a mlaen shuttle relay race
ras rwystrau *eb* rasys rhwystrau obstacle race
rasio *be* race
rasqueado *eg* rasqueado
Rastaffariad *eg* Rastaffariaid Rastafarian
Rastaffariaeth *eb* Rastafarianism
rawlfollt *eg* rawlfolltau rawlbolt
real *ans* lifelike
real *ans* real
realaeth *eb* realism
realaeth dafluniol *eb* projective realism
realaeth foesol *eb* moral realism
realistig *ans* realistic

realiti *eg* reality
rebec *eg* rebecau rebec
reciwsant *eg* reciwsantiaid recusant
reciwsantiaeth *eb* recusancy
record *eb* recordiau record
recorder *eg* recorderau recorder
recorder desgant *eg* recorderau desgant descant recorder
recordiad *eg* recordiadau recording
recordiad fideo *eg* recordiadau fideo video recording
recordio *be* record
recordydd *eg* recordwyr recorder
recordydd casét *eg* recordwyr casét cassette recorder
recordydd cynyddol *eg* recordwyr cynyddol cumulative recorder
recordydd fideo *eg* recordyddion fideo video recorder
recriwt *eg* recriwtiaid recruit
recriwtio *be* recruit
recriwtio allanol *be* external recruitment
recriwtio mewnol *be* internal recruitment
rectwm *eg* rectum
refeniw *eg* refeniwiau revenue
refeniw cyfartalog *eg* average revenue
refeniw gwerthiant *eg* sales revenue
refeniw ymylol *eg* marginal revenue
refferendwm *eg* refferenda referendum
reffractomedr *eg* reffractomedrau refractometer
regalia *eg* regalia
regur *eg* regurau regur
reion *eg* rayon
reion asetad *eg* rayon acetate
reion cyfrodedd *eg* spun rayon
reion fiscos *eg* viscose rayon
relái *eg* releiau relay
remand *eg* remand
rendrad *eg* rendradau render
rendro *be* rendering
rendro lliw *be* colour rendering
rendsina *eg* rendzina
rennin *eg* rennin
repertoire *eg* repertoires repertoire
répétiteur *eg* répétiteurs répétiteur
replica *eg* replicâu replica
repoussé *ans* repoussé
resbiradaeth *eb* resbiradaethau respiration
resbiradaeth aerobig *eb* aerobic respiration
resbiradaeth allanol *eb* external respiration
resbiradaeth anaerobig *eb* anaerobic respiration
resbiradaeth artiffisial *eb* artificial respiration
resbiradaeth fewnol *eb* internal respiration
resbiradaeth gellog *eb* cellular respiration
resbiradol *ans* respiratory
resbiradu *be* respire
resin *eg* resinau resin
resin acrylig *eg* resinau acrylig acrylic resin
resin asetal *eg* acetal resin
resin cyfnewid ïonau *eg* ion exchange resin
resin epocsi *eg* resinau epocsi epoxy resin
resin finyl *eg* resinau finyl vinyl resin
resin polyester *eg* polyester resin
resin synthetig *eg* resinau synthetig synthetic resin
resinaidd *ans* resinous
resinau amino *ell* amino resins
responsa *ell* responsa
rest llithr *eg* restiau llithr slide rest
restio *be* apprehend
reticwlocyt *eg* reticwlocytau reticulocyte
reticwlwm *eg* reticulum
reticwlwm endoplasmig *eg* endoplasmic reticulum
retina *eg* retinâu retina
retort *eg* retortâu retort
ria *eg* riau ria
ribofflafin *eg* riboflavin
ribosom *eg* ribosomau ribosome
ricercare *eg* ricercare
rifíw *eg* rifiwiau revue
riff *eg* riffiau reef
riffio *be* reefing
riffl *eg* rifflau riffle
rifflwr *eg* rifflwyr riffler
rigeri *ell* riggers
rigin *eg* rigging
ril *eb* riliau reel
ril teirllaw *eg* riliau teirllaw three-handed reel
rîm *eg* rimau ream
rins *eg* rinsiau rinse
rinsio *be* rinse
ripieno *eg* ripieni ripieno
riposte *eg* riposte
riposte cyfun *eg* ripostes cyfun compound riposte
riposte gwrthol *eg* ripostes gwrthol counter riposte
riposte oediog *eg* ripostes oediog delayed riposte
riposte union *eg* ripostes union direct riposte
risalah *eg* risalah
risg *eg* risgiau risk
ritornello *eg* ritornelli ritornello
riwl *eb* riwliau rule; ruler
riwl blastig *eb* riwliau plastig plastic ruler
riwl blygu *eb* riwliau plygu folding rule
riwl dryloyw *eb* riwliau tryloyw transparent ruler
riwl fetrig *eb* riwliau metrig metric rule
riwl gyfangiad *eb* riwliau cyfangiad contraction rule
riwl pren bocs *eb* riwliau pren bocs boxwood ruler
riwl wrthslip *eb* riwliau gwrthslip non-slip rule
RNA negeseuol *eg* messenger RNA
RNA trosglwyddol *eg* transfer RNA
robot *eg* robotiaid robot
roboteg *eb* robotics
roced *eb* rocedi rocket
rococo *ans* rococo
rôl addysgwyr iechyd *eb* role of health educators

rôl cyfrannwr *eb* subject role
rôl cyfrannwr da *eb* good-subject role
rôl cyfrannwr ffyddlon *eb* faithful subject role
rôl cyfrannwr negyddol *eb* negativistic subject role
rôl cyfrannwr pryderus *eb* apprehensive subject role
rôl rhyw *eb* sex role
roloc *eg* rowlock
roloc sefydlog *eg* rolocs sefydlog fixed pin
ROM ochr *eg* sideways ROM
romper *eb* romperi romper
rondeau *eg* rondeau
rondo *eb* rondoau rondo
rondo sonata *eb* rondoau sonata sonata rondo
rondo syml *eb* rondoau syml simple rondo
rostrwm *eg* rostra rostrum
rotor *eg* rotorau rotor
rownd *eb* rowndiau round
rownderi *ell* rounders
rwbel *eg* debris
rwbel *eg* rubble
rwbela *eb* rubella
rwber *eg* rwberi rubber
rwber corc *eg* rwberi corc cork rubber
rwber sbwng *eg* foam rubber
rwber sbwng *eg* sponge rubber
rwbidiwm (Rb) *eg* rubidium
rwmen *eg* rwmenau rumen
Rwsianeiddio *be* Russification
rwtheniwm (Ru) *eg* ruthenium
ryc *eg* ryciau ruck
ryffl *eg* ryfflau ruffle
ryfflo *be* ruffle
ryg *eg/b* rygiau rug
rygbi *eg* rugby
rygbi bach *eg* touch rugby
rysáit *eb* ryseitiau recipe
rysáit sylfaenol *eb* ryseitiau sylfaenol basic recipe

Rh

RhA: rhaglen astudio *eb* rhaglenni astudio PoS: programme of study
rhaca *eg/b* rhacanau rake
rhacanu *be* rake
rhacrentu *be* rack-rent
rhadffôn *eg* freephone
rhadrwyd *eb* freenet
rhadwedd *eg/b* freeware
rhaeadr *eb* rhaeadrau waterfall
rhaeadr *eb* rhaeadrau cascade
rhaeadrol *ans* cascaded
rhaeadru *be* cascade
rhaflad *eg* rhafladau fray
rhaflo *be* fray
rhaflog *ans* fraying
rhaff *eb* rhaffau rope
rhaff ar oledd *eb* rhaffau ar oledd inclined rope
rhaff bwysau llawn *eb* rhaffau pwysau llawn full weight rope
rhaff ddringo *eb* rhaffau dringo climbing rope
rhaff flaen *eb* rhaffau blaen foresheet
rhaff glymu *eb* rhaffau clymu painter
rhaff sgipio *eb* rhaffau sgipio skipping rope
rhaffau llyw *ell* rudderlines
rhaffau mast *ell* shrouds
rhaffordd *eb* rhaffyrdd ropeway
rhaffordd awyr *eb* rhaffyrdd awyr aerial ropeway
rhagaeddfed *ans* precocious
rhagalaw *eb* rhagalawon antecedent
rhagamcaniad *eg* rhagamcaniadau projection
rhagamcanu *be* project
rhag-amod *eg* rhag-amodau precondition
rhagarweiniad *eg* rhagarweiniadau introduction
rhagarweiniol *ans* preliminary
rhagbanedig *ans* pre-shrunk
rhagbannu *be* pre-shrink
rhagbaratoi *be* brief
rhagboethi *be* preheat
rhagbrawf *eg* rhagbrofion preliminary test
rhagbrofi *be* trial
rhagdalu *be* prepay
rhagdaro *be* anticipate
rhagdebygolrwydd *eg* prior probability
rhagdir *eg* rhagdiroedd foreland
rhagdrawiad *eg* rhagdrawiadau anticipation
rhagdudalen *eb* rhagdudalennau splash page
rhagduedd cymdeithasol *eb* pro-social disposition
rhagdueddiad *eg* predisposition
rhagdueddiad *eg* susceptibility
rhagdybiaeth *eb* rhagdybiaethau hypothesis
rhagdybiaeth *eb* rhagdybiaethau presumption
rhagdybiaeth adborth yr wyneb *eb* facial feedback hypothesis
rhagdybiaeth adnabod iaith frodorol *eb* native language recognition hypothesis
rhagdybiaeth arall *eb* alternative hypothesis
rhagdybiaeth brofadwy *eb* testable hypothesis
rhagdybiaeth byffro cymdeithasol *eb* social buffering hypothesis
rhagdybiaeth cyswllt *eb* contact hypothesis
rhagdybiaeth dopamin *eb* dopamine hypothesis
rhagdybiaeth glwcostatig *eb* glucostatic hypothesis
rhagdybiaeth gwahaniaethu iaith gyffredinol *eb* general language discrimination hypothesis
rhagdybiaeth lefel optimwm *eb* optimum-level hypothesis
rhagdybiaeth lleihau ysfa *eb* drive reduction hypothesis
rhagdybiaeth marciwr somatig *eb* somatic marker hypothesis
rhagdybiaeth nwl *eb* rhagdybiaethau nwl null hypothesis
rhagdybiaeth Sapir-Whorf *eb* Sapir-Whorf hypothesis
rhagdybiaeth statudol *eb* statutory presumption
rhagdybiaethol-diddwythol *ans* hypothetico-deductive
rhagddetholiadol *ans* preselective
rhagddodi *be* prefix
rhagddodiad *eg* rhagddodiaid prefix
rhagetholiad *eg* rhagetholiadau primary election
rhagfarn *eb* rhagfarnau prejudice
rhagfarn oed *eb* ageism
rhagflaenydd (am berson) *eg* rhagflaenwyr predecessor
rhagflaenydd (am beth) *eg* rhagflaenwyr antecedent
rhagfoddion *eg* premedication
rhagfur (castell) *eg* rhagfuriau parapet; rampart
rhagfwyhadur *eg* pre-amp
rhagfynegi *be* predict
rhagfynegiad *eg* rhagfynegiadau prediction
rhagfyriad *eg* rhagfyriadau foreshortening
rhagfyrhau *be* foreshorten
rhagffurfio *be* preform; prefabricate
rhag-gynhyrchu *be* preproduction
rhaghysbyseb *eb* rhaghysbysebion trailer

rhaglaw *eg* rhaglawiaid proconsul; viceroy; prefect
rhaglen (=cymhwysiad) *eb* rhaglenni application
rhaglen (mewn cyfrifiadureg) *eb* rhaglenni program
rhaglen (yn gyffredinol) *eb* rhaglenni programme; schedule
rhaglen a dargedwyd *eb* rhaglenni a dargedwyd targeted programme
Rhaglen Addysg Microelectroneg *eb* Microelectronic Education Programme
rhaglen addysg unigol *eb* rhaglenni addysg unigol individualized education programme
rhaglen addysgol *eb* rhaglenni addysgol educational program
rhaglen alwedigaethol *eb* rhaglenni galwedigaethol occupational programme
rhaglen amlgyfrwng *eb* rhaglenni amlgyfrwng multimedia program
rhaglen ar alwad *eb* rhaglenni ar alwad app-on-tap
rhaglen arddangos *eb* rhaglenni arddangos demonstration program
rhaglen astudio annibynnol *eb* rhaglenni astudio annibynnol discrete programme of study
rhaglen atgyfnerthu â thalebau *eb* rhaglenni atgyfnerthu â thalebau token economy
rhaglen Band Eang Cymru *eb* Broadband Wales programme
rhaglen bersonol *eb* rhaglenni personol personal programme
rhaglen cefnogi athrawon *eb* rhaglenni cefnogi athrawon teacher support programme
rhaglen cyflogres *eb* rhaglenni cyflogres payroll program
rhaglen deledu *eb* rhaglenni teledu television programme
rhaglen drochi *eb* rhaglenni trochi immersion programme
rhaglen ddarllen i'r unigolyn *eb* rhaglenni darllen i'r unigolyn individualized reading programme
rhaglen ddatblygu staff *eb* rhaglenni datblygu staff staff development programme
rhaglen ddiagnostig *eb* rhaglenni diagnostig diagnostic program
rhaglen ddogfen 'pry ar y wal' *eb* rhaglenni dogfen 'pry ar y wal' fly on the wall documentary
rhaglen ddogfen teledu *eb* rhaglenni dogfen teledu television documentary
rhaglen fideo *eb* rhaglenni fideo video programme
rhaglen fodiwlaidd *eb* rhaglenni modiwlaidd modular programme
rhaglen ffynhonnell *eb* rhaglenni ffynhonnell source program
rhaglen ganghennog *eb* rhaglenni canghennog branching programme
rhaglen garlam *eb* rhaglenni carlam accelerated programme
rhaglen graffeg *eb* rhaglenni graffeg graphics program
rhaglen grynhoi *eb* rhaglenni crynhoi compiling program
rhaglen gwrthrych-gyfeiriadol *eb* object-orientated programme
rhaglen gydadferol *eb* rhaglenni cydadferol compensatory programme
rhaglen gyfrifiadurol *eb* rhaglenni cyfrifiadurol computer application
rhaglen hewristig *eb* rhaglenni hewristig heuristic program
rhaglen hyblygrwydd *eb* rhaglenni hyblygrwydd flexibility regime
rhaglen hyfforddi *eb* rhaglenni hyfforddi training programme; instructional programme
rhaglen hyfforddi ac asesu unigol *eb* rhaglenni hyfforddi ac asesu unigol individual training and assessment programme
rhaglen hyfforddi gynhwysfawr *eb* rhaglenni hyfforddi cynhwysfawr comprehensive training programme
rhaglen imiwneiddio *eb* rhaglenni imiwneiddio immunisation programme
rhaglen luniadu *eb* rhaglenni lluniadu drawing program
rhaglen lyfrgell *eb* rhaglenni llyfrgell library program
rhaglen llinell-amser *eb* rhaglenni llinell-amser time-line programme
rhaglen olchi *eb* rhaglenni golchi washing programme
rhaglen oruchwylio *eb* rhaglenni goruchwylio executive program
rhaglen osod *eb* rhaglenni gosod installation program
rhaglen reoli *eb* rhaglenni rheoli control program
rhaglen wasanaethu *eb* rhaglenni gwasanaethu utility program
rhaglen ymaddasol *eb* rhaglenni ymaddasol adaptive programme
rhaglen ymarfer corff *eb* rhaglenni ymarfer corff exercise programme
rhaglen ymarfer strwythuredig sy'n gysylltiedig ag iechyd *eb* rhaglenni ymarfer strwythuredig sy'n gysylltiedig ag iechyd structured health related exercise programme
rhaglennig *eb* rhaglenigau applet
rhaglennu (mewn cyfrifiadureg) *be* program
rhaglennu (yn gyffredinol) *be* programme
rhaglennu adeiladol *be* bottom-up programming
rhaglennu aflinol *be* non-linear programming
rhaglennu dadelfennol *be* top-down programming
rhaglennu gweithgareddau hamdden *be* programming of leisure activities
rhaglennu gwrthrych-gyfeiriadol *be* object-orientated programming
rhaglennu llinol *be* linear programming
rhaglennu macro *be* macro programming
rhaglennu modiwlaidd *be* modular programming
rhaglennu strwythurol *be* structured programming
rhaglennwr systemau *eg* rhaglenwyr systemau systems programmer
rhaglennydd *eg* rhaglenwyr computer programmer
rhaglennydd *eg* rhaglenwyr programmer

rhaglennydd rhaglenni *eg* rhaglenwyr rhaglenni applications programmer
rhaglith *eg* rhaglithoedd preamble
rhagliwio *be* laying-on
rhaglun ffilm *eg* film trailer
rhagluniaeth *eb* providence
rhaglyw *eg* rhaglywiaid regent
Rhaglyw Dywysog *eg* Prince Regent
rhaglywiaeth *eb* regency
rhagnod *eg* rhagnodau intonation
rhagnodi *be* prescribe
rhagnodol *ans* prescriptive
rhagod *eg* rhagodion bench stop
rhagod *eg* rhagodau ambush
rhagofal *eg* rhagofalon precaution
rhagofalon diogelwch *ell* safety precautions
rhagolwg *eg* rhagolygon forecast
rhagolwg argraffu *eg* rhagolygon argraffu print preview
rhagolwg llif arian *eg* cash flow forecast
rhagolwg lliw *eg* rhagolygon lliw colour preview
rhagolygon am yrfa *ell* career prospects
rhagolygon y tywydd *ell* weather forecast
rhagolygu gwerthiant *be* sales forecasting
rhagordeiniad *eg* predestination
rhagordeiniadaeth *eb* predestinarianism
rhagordeiniadol *ans* predestinarian
rhagori *be* predominate
rhagoriaeth *eb* superiority
rhagosod *ans* antecedent
rhagosod *be* set default; preset
rhagosodedig *ans* default
rhagosodiad (=gosodiad rhagosodedig) *eg* rhagosodiadau default setting
rhagosodiad (yn gryno) *eg* rhagosodiadau default
rhagras *eb* rhagrasys heat
rhagsiambr *eb* rhagsiambrau antechamber
rhagsynaptig *ans* presynaptic
rhagweithiol *ans* proactive
rhagweladwyaeth resymol *eb* reasonable foreseeability
rhagweld *be* predict; anticipate; forecast
rhagweld ymateb *be* anticipate response
rhagwth *eg* rhagwthion lunge
rhagwth allan *eg* rhagwthion allan lunge outward
rhagwth ar linell isel *eg* rhagwthion ar linell isel lunge in low line
rhagwth ochr *eg* rhagwthion ochr lunge sideways
rhagwth ymlaen *eg* rhagwthion ymlaen lunge forward
rhagwybodaeth *eb* foreknowledge
rhagymadrodd *eg* rhagymadroddion introduction
rhagymosodiad *eg* rhagymosodiadau pre-emptive strike
rhaidd *eg* rheiddiau radius
rhaithymyrraeth *eb* embracery
rhamant *eb* rhamantau romance
rhamantaidd *ans* romantic
rhamantiaeth *eb* romanticism
rhan (=cyfran) *eb* rhannau share
rhan (o dref etc) *eb* rhannau quarter
rhan (yn gyffredinol) *eb* rhannau part
rhan allanol *eb* rhannau allanol external part
rhan amser *ans* part-time
rhan Broadmann *eb* rhannau Broadmann Broadmann's area
rhan Broca *eb* Broca's area
rhan daprog *eb* rhannau taprog tapered part
rhan daro *eb* rhannau taro percussion part
rhan dril *eg* rhannau dril drill part
rhan ddychmygol *eb* rhannau dychmygol imaginary part
rhan flaenolwg *eb* rhannau blaenolwg part front elevation
rhan flodeuog *eb* rhannau blodeuog flourish
rhan fwyaf o'r nwyddau *eb* bulk of the goods
rhan fformiwla *eb* rhannau fformiwla formula area
rhan Ladinaidd *eb* rhannau Lladinaidd Latin quarter
rhan leisiol *eb* rhannau lleisiol vocal part
rhan masnach *eb* rhannau masnach trading quarter
rhan morthwyl *eb* rhannau morthwyl hammer part
rhan offerynnol *eb* rhannau offerynnol instrumental part
rhan ôl y cortecs parwydol *eb* posterior part of the parietal cortex (PPC)
rhan ôl-nodyn *eb* rhannau ôl-nodyn endnote area
rhan real *eb* rhannau real real part
rhan strwythurol *eb* structural member
rhan wedi'i channu *eb* bleached area
rhan weithio *eb* rhannau gweithio working area
rhan Wernicke *eb* Wernicke's area
rhanadwy *ans* divisible
rhanadwyedd *eg* divisibility
rhanbarth (=ardal gul) *eg* rhanbarthau belt
rhanbarth (=ardal yn fras) *eg* rhanbarthau area
rhanbarth (=parth) *eg* rhanbarthau zone
rhanbarth (yn gyffredinol) *eg* rhanbarthau region
rhanbarth ategol *eg* rhanbarthau ategol tributary region
rhanbarth critigol *eg* critical region
rhanbarth dichonadwy *eg* rhanbarthau dichonadwy feasible region
rhanbarth dinas *eg* rhanbarthau dinasoedd city region
rhanbarth gofod *eg* rhanbarthau gofod region of space
rhanbarth gweinyddol *eg* rhanbarthau gweinyddol administrative region
rhanbarth hinsoddol *eg* rhanbarthau hinsoddol climatic region
rhanbarth rheoli mwg *eg* rhanbarthau rheoli mwg smoke controlled area
Rhanbarth Seisnig *eg* Pale
rhanbarth trawstaith *eg* rhanbarthau trawstaith transit region

Rhanbarth y Daniaid *eg* Danelaw
rhanbarthau Cymru *ell* Wales regions
rhanbarthau Lloegr *ell* England regions
rhanbarthau naturiol *ell* natural regions
rhanbarthiaeth *eb* regionalism
rhanbarthol *ans* regional
rhandal *eg* rhandaliadau instalment
rhandir *eg* rhandiroedd allotment
rhandrychiad *eg* rhandrychiadau part-section
rhandrychiadol *ans* part-sectional
rhandy *eg* rhandai annexe
rhanddeiliad *eg* rhanddeiliaid stakeholder
rhanedig *ans* divided
rhanfap *eg* rhanfapiau extract
rhangor *eg* rhangorau semi chorus
rhan-gyfnewid *eg* part exchange
rhaniad (=rhannu gwlad yn ddwy etc) *eg* rhaniadau partition
rhaniad (gweinyddol) *eg* rhaniadau division
rhaniad (mewn gwallt etc) *eg* rhaniadau parting
rhaniad adnoddau *eg* resource partitioning
rhaniad llafur *eg* division of labour
rhaniadliw *eg* broken colour
Rhaniadwr *eg* Rhaniadwyr Divisionist
rhanlyfr *eg* rhanlyfrau part book
rhannau allanol *ell* outer parts
rhannau ar wahân *ell* separate parts
rhannau cŷn *ell* chisel parts
rhannau dril dirdro *ell* twist drill parts
rhannau edau *ell* thread parts
rhannau ffeil *ell* parts of file
rhannau ffeil *ell* file parts
rhannau ffrâm *ell* parts of a frame
rhannau gaing *ell* chisel parts
rhannau gefail *ell* forge parts
rhannau mewnol *ell* inner parts
rhannau micromedr *ell* micrometer parts
rhannau o'r raced *ell* racket parts
rhannau paru *ell* mating parts
rhannau perthnasol *ell* relevant parts
rhannau plaen *ell* parts of plane
rhannau unfaint *ell* equal divisions
rhannau'r turn *ell* lathe parts
rhannol *ans* partial; semi
rhannol drwm *ans* semi bold
rhannol ddall *ans* partially blind
rhannol ddall i liwiau *ans* partially colour blind
rhannol ddi-draidd *ans* semi-opaque
rhannol fyddar *ans* partially deaf
rhannol olau *ans* semi light
rhannol orffenedig *ans* partially completed
rhannol orffenedig *ans* partly completed
rhannu (yn gyffredinol) *be* share
rhannu (mewn mathemateg) *be* divide
rhannu â ffactorau *be* division by factors
rhannu â rhif *be* divide by a number
rhannu arwynebedd *be* dividing areas
rhannu byr *be* short division
rhannu ffeiliau *be* file sharing
rhannu hir *be* long division
rhannu llinell *be* dividing a line
rhannu llinellau mewn persbectif *be* dividing lines in perspective
rhannu swydd *be* job share
rhannwr *eg* rhanwyr divider
rhannwr potensial *eg* rhanwyr potensial potential divider
rhannwr ystafell *eg* rhanwyr ystafelloedd room divider
rhannydd *eg* rhanyddion divisor
rhannydd cyffredin mwyaf (=ffactor cyffredin mwyaf) *eg* greatest common divisor
rhannydd foltedd *eg* voltage divider
rhannyn *eg* rhanynnau dividend
rhanolwg *eg/b* rhanolygon part view
rhanwedd *eg/b* shareware
rhasgl *eb* rhasglau spokeshave
rhasgl bren *eb* rhasglau pren wooden spokeshave
rhasgl fetel *eb* rhasglau metel metal spokeshave
rhasgl wyneb crwn *eb* rhasglau wyneb crwn round faced spokeshave
rhathell *eb* rhathellau rasp
rhathell gabinet *eb* rhathellau cabinet cabinet rasp
rhathell hanner crwn *eb* rhathellau hanner crwn half round rasp
rhathellu *be* rasp
rhathiad *eg* chafing
rhathu *be* chafe
rhaw *eb* rhofiau shovel
rhawnbais *eb* rhawnbeisiau hair shirt
rhedeg *be* run
rhedeg aerobig *be* aerobic running
rhedeg allan *be* run out
rhedeg anaerobig *be* anaerobic running
rhedeg â'r bêl *be* run with the ball
rhedeg araf *be* slow run
▸ **rhedeg gwargam** *be* crouch-running
rhedeg yn gywir *be* running true
rhedfa *eb* rhedfeydd runway
rhediad *eg* rhediadau run
rhediad *eg* rhediadau ladder
rhediad *eg* rhediadau conjugation
rhediad (gwers) *eg* pace
rhediad adref *eg* rhediadau adref home run
rhediad allan *eg* rhediadau allan run out
rhediad arbrofol *eg* rhediadau arbrofol test run
rhediad byr *eg* short run
rhediad ffug *eg* rhediadau ffug dry run
rhediad harmonig *eg* rhediadau harmonig harmonic movement
rhedlif *eg* rhedlifau discharge
rhedlif clust *eg* ear discharge
rhedol *ans* cursive
rhedwr *eg* rhedwyr runner
rhedwr cryf *eg* rhedwyr cryf strong runner

rhedwr drôr *eg* rhedwyr drôr drawer runner
rhedwr drôr *eg* rhedwyr drôr drawer guide
rhedwr drôr *eg* rhedwyr drôr runner
rhedwr pelferyn *eg* rhedwyr pelferyn ball-bearing runner
rhedwr pellter canol *eg* rhedwyr pellter canol middle distance runner
rhedwr rhyngwladol *eg* rhedwyr rhyngwladol international runner
rhedynen *eb* rhedyn fern
rhefrol *ans* anal
rheng *eb* rhengoedd rank
rheng *eb* rhengoedd row
rheng flaen *eb* rhengoedd blaen front row
rheng ôl *eb* rhengoedd ôl back row
rheidrwydd *eg* necessity
rheidden *eb* rheiddennau ray
rheidden greiddiol *eb* rheiddennau creiddiol medullary ray
rheidden-hir *eb* long-ray
rheiddiadur *eg* rheiddiaduron radiator
rheiddiol *ans* radial
rheilen *eb* rheiliau rail
rheilen bictiwr *eb* rheiliau pictiwr picture rail
rheilen dywelion *eb* rheiliau tywelion towel rail
rheilen ddrôr *eb* rheiliau drôr drawer rail
rheilen fflans *eb* rheiliau fflans flanged rail
rheilen ganol *eb* rheiliau canol middle rail
rheilen glo *eb* rheiliau clo lock rail
rheilen groes *eb* rheiliau croes cross rail
rheilen groeslinol *eb* rheiliau croeslinol diagonal rail
rheilen grom *eb* rheiliau crwm curved rail
rheilen gwrdd *eb* rheiliau cwrdd meeting rail
rheilen gyfwyneb *eb* flush rails
rheilen gynnal *eb* rheiliau cynnal stretcher rail
rheilen gynnal *eb* rheiliau cynnal bearer rail
rheilen isaf *eb* rheiliau isaf underframe rail
rheilen isaf *eb* rheiliau isaf bottom rail
rheilen ochr *eb* rheiliau ochr side rail
rheilen uchaf *eb* rheiliau uchaf top rail
rheilen uchaf drôr *eb* rheiliau uchaf drôr top drawer rail
rheilen waelod drôr *eb* rheiliau gwaelod drôr bottom drawer rail
rheilen warchod *eb* rheiliau gwarchod guard rail
rheilen warchod *eb* crown rail
rheilffordd *eb* rheilffyrdd railway
rheilffordd fwynau *eb* rheilffyrdd mwynau mineral railway
rheilffordd halio *eb* rheilffyrdd halio funicular
rheilffordd rac a phiniwn *eb* rheilffyrdd rac a phiniwn rack and pinion railway
rheiliau goleddf *ell* batter rails
rheithfarn *eb* rheithfarnau verdict
rheithgor *eg* rheithgorau jury
rheithgor cyflwyno *eg* jury of presentment
rheithiwr *eg* rheithwyr juror
rheithiwr arbennig *eg* rheithwyr arbennig special juror
rheithor *eg* rheithorion rector
rheithordy *eg* rheithordai rectory
rheithoriaeth *eb* rheithoriaethau rectorate
rhenc *eb* rhenciau tier
rheniwm *eg* rhenium
rhent *eg* rhenti rental
rhent *eg* rhenti rent
rhent arglwydd *eg* chief-rent
rhent aseis *eg* rent of assize
rhent economaidd *eg* economic rent
rhent safle *eg* rhenti safle ground-rent
rhentu *be* rent
rhentu ar brydles *be* lease
rhentwr *eg* rhentwyr rentier
rheol *eb* rheolau rule
rheol arddangos *eb* rheolau arddangos display rule
rheol cadwyn *eb* chain rule
rheol cyfatebiad graffem-ffonem *eb* rheolau cyfatebiad graffem-ffonem grapheme-phoneme correspondence (GPC) rule
rheol cyniferydd *eb* quotient rule
rheol cystadlu *eb* rheolau cystadlu competition rule
rheol drygioni *eb* mischief rule
rheol euraidd *eb* golden rule
rheol fantais *eb* advantage law
Rheol Gaefa *eb* Closure Rule
rheol gradd a maint *eb* rheolau gradd a maint rank size rule
rheol lythrennol *eb* literal rule
rheol tair eiliad *eb* three second rule
rheol Tinbergen *eb* Tinbergen's rule
rheol traeanau *eb* rule of thirds
rheol trefniadaeth *eb* rheolau trefniadaeth rule of procedure
rheol tri *eb* rule of three
rheolaeth *eb* rheolaethau management; control; rule
rheolaeth ar broses *eb* process control
rheolaeth ar gynhyrchu *eb* production control
rheolaeth bell *eb* remote control
rheolaeth credyd *eb* credit control
rheolaeth cronfeydd data *eb* database management
rheolaeth cyfraith *eb* rule of law
rheolaeth dicter *eb* anger management
rheolaeth dosbarth *eb* class management
rheolaeth dros symudiadau *eb* motor control
rheolaeth dros y corff *eb* body management
rheolaeth ddigonol *eb* adequate control
rheolaeth ddilyniannol *eb* sequential control
rheolaeth ddimensiynol *eb* dimensional control
rheolaeth fanwl *eb* rheolaethau manwl fine control
rheolaeth fertigol *eb* vertical control
rheolaeth gorfforol *eb* body control

rheolaeth gweddau *eb* phase control
rheolaeth gwesty *eb* hotel management
rheolaeth gyfrifiadurol *eb* computer control
rheolaeth gyllidol *eb* rheolaethau cyllidol budgetary control
rheolaeth gynyddol *eb* increasing control
rheolaeth lawn *eb* full control
rheolaeth leol ysgolion *eb* local management of schools
rheolaeth lorweddol *eb* horizontal control
rheolaeth lwyr ar ansawdd *eb* total quality management
rheolaeth microbrosesydd *eb* microprocessor control
rheolaeth nerf-gyhyr *eb* neuro-muscular control
rheolaeth ragosodedig *eb* default control
rheolaeth restru *eb* inventory management
rheolaeth rifol *eb* numeric control
rheolaeth rhent *eb* rent control
rheolaeth siswrn *eb* scissors control
rheolaeth stoc *eb* stock control
rheolaeth thermostatig *eb* thermostatic control
rheolaeth unbenaethol *eb* autocratic rule
rheolaethol *ans* managerial
rheolaidd *ans* regular
rheolau a chonfensiynau rules and conventions
rheolau blaenoriaeth *ell* rules of precedence
Rheolau Cefn Gwlad *ell* Country Code, The
rheolau cystrawen *ell* syntax rules
rheolau indecsau *ell* rules of indices
rheolau sefydlog *ell* standing orders
Rheolau'r Ffordd Fawr *ell* Highway Code
rheoleidd-dra *eg* regularity
rheolfan *eg/b* rheolfannau control point
rheoli *be* manage; control; regulate
rheoli a chadw trefn manage and control
rheoli adnoddau *be* resource management
rheoli amgylcheddau *be* manage environments
rheoli ansawdd *be* quality control
rheoli biolegol *be* biological control
rheoli cenhedlu *be* birth control
rheoli cnofilod *be* rodent control
rheoli costau *be* cost management
rheoli cynhyrchu drwy gymorth cyfrifiadur *be* computer aided production management
rheoli cyrchu *be* access control
rheoli dŵr *be* water management
rheoli gofal *be* care management
rheoli gwariant *be* manage expenditure
rheoli llawnder *be* control of fullness
rheoli lleoliad *be* locational control
rheoli llifogydd *be* control floods
rheoli offer *be* control of equipment
rheoli poblogaeth *be* population regulation
rheoli prisiau *be* price control
rheoli stoc *be* stock control
rheoli templedi *be* template management
rheoli uchafbris *be* maximum price control
rheoli ymddygiad *be* behaviour management
rheoli ymddygiad digroeso *be* managing unwanted behaviour
rheoliad *eg* rheoliadau regulation
rheoliad adeiladu *eg* rheoliadau adeiladu building regulation
rheoliadau ariannol *ell* financial regulations
rheoliadau diogelwch *ell* safety regulations
rheoliadur *eg* rheoliaduron pacemaker
rheoli'r bêl *be* control the ball
rheolwaith *eg* rheolweithiau routine
rheolwaith diagnostig *eg* rheolweithiau diagnostig diagnostic routine
rheolwaith dilysu *eg* validation routine
rheolwaith gwallau *eg* rheolweithiau gwallau error routine
rheolwaith gwasanaethu *eg* rheolweithiau gwasanaethu service routine
rheolwaith iterus *eg* rheolweithiau iterus iterative routine
rheolwaith llyfrgell *eg* rheolweithiau llyfrgell library routine
rheolwaith mewnbwn /allbwn *eg* rheolweithiau mewnbwn /allbwn input /output routine
rheolwaith trin ymyriadau *eg* rheolweithiau trin ymyriadau interrupt service routine
rheolwr (ar wlad etc) *eg* rheolwyr ruler
rheolwr (yn gyffredinol) *eg* rheolwyr manager
rheolwr absoliwt *eg* rheolwyr absoliwt absolute ruler
rheolwr adnoddau dynol *eg* rheolwyr adnoddau dynol human resources manager
rheolwr banc *eg* rheolwyr banciau bank manager
rheolwr bwcio *eg* rheolwyr bwcio reservations manager
rheolwr credyd *eg* rheolwyr credyd credit controller
rheolwr datblygu profion *eg* rheolwyr datblygu profion test development manager
rheolwr dogfennau *eg* rheolwyr dogfennau document manager
rheolwr gofal *eg* rheolwyr gofal care manager
rheolwr gweithiau *eg* rheolwyr gweithiau works manager
rheolwr gweithrediadau *eg* rheolwyr gweithrediadau operations manager
rheolwr gwerthu *eg* rheolwyr gwerthu sales manager
rheolwr llinell *eg* rheolwyr llinell line manager
rheolwr marchnata *eg* rheolwyr marchnata marketing manager
rheolwr siop *eg* rheolwyr siop shop manager
Rheolwr TG a Gweinyddu *eg* IT and Administration Manager
rheolwr y tŷ bwyta *eg* restaurant manager
rheolwraig *eb* rheolwragedd manageress
rheolwr-gyfarwyddwr *eg* managing director
rheolwyr *ell* management

rheolydd (=teclyn rheoli) *eg* rheolyddion controller; regulator; control setting
rheolydd (mewn arbrawf) *eg* rheolyddion control
rheolydd arbrawf *eb* experimental control
rheolydd bras *eg* rheolyddion bras coarse control
rheolydd cudd *eg* rheolyddion cudd hidden control
rheolydd cyflymder *eg* rheolyddion cyflymder speed regulator
rheolydd cyflymder *eg* rheolyddion cyflymder reverse control
rheolydd cynnydd *eg* rheolyddion cynnydd gain control
rheolydd chwyddo *eg* rheolyddion chwyddo zoom control
rheolydd data *eg* rheolyddion data data controller
rheolydd disgiau *eg* rheolyddion disgiau disk controller
rheolydd disgleirdeb *eg* rheolyddion disgleirdeb brightness control
rheolydd hyd pwyth *eg* rheolyddion hyd pwyth stitch length adjustment
rheolydd lled pwyth igam ogam *eg* rheolyddion lled pwyth igam ogam zigzag width control
rheolydd manwl *eg* rheolyddion manwl fine control
rheolydd nesaf *eg* next control
rheolydd safle'r nodwydd *eg* rheolyddion safle'r nodwydd needle position control
rheolydd tabiau lliw *eg* rheolyddion tabiau lliw coloured tab control
rheolydd ton preamplifier
rheolydd troed *eg* rheolwyr troed foot control
rheostat *eg* rheostatau rheostat
rhes (=llinell) *eb* rhesi line
rhes (=rheng) *eb* rhesi row
rhes (=streipen) *eb* rhesi stripe
rhes (=teras) *eb* rhesi terrace
rhes (o seddi mewn theatr etc) *eb* rhesi tier
rhes dyffryn *eb* rhesi dyffrynnoedd valley train
rhes fertigol *eb* rhesi fertigol vertical stripe
rhes groeslinol *eb* rhesi croeslinol diagonal stripe
rhes isaf *eb* rhesi isaf lower tier
rhes lorweddol *eb* rhesi llorweddol horizontal stripe
rhes niwral *eb* neural streak
rhes o farics *eb* rhesi o farics barrack block
rhes teitl *eb* rhesi teitlau title row
rhes uchaf *eb* rhesi uchaf top row
rhes wag *eb* rhesi gwag blank line
rhesel galedu *eb* rheseli caledu airing rack
rhesel *eb* rheseli rack
rhesel ddillad *eb* rheseli dillad clothes rack
rhesel grasu dillad *eb* rheseli crasu dillad airing rack
rhesel gylchgronau *eb* rheseli cylchgronau magazine rack
rhesel lyfrau *eb* rheseli llyfrau bookrack
rhesel nenfwd *eb* rheseli nenfwd ceiling rack
rhesel sbwliau *eb* rheseli sbwliau creel
rhesel sychu *eb* rheseli sychu drying rack
rhesel tiwbiau profi *eb* rheseli tiwbiau profi test-tube rack
rhesi o ffenestri *ell* ranks of windows
rhesog *ans* striped; ribbed; striated
rhestr *eb* rhestri list; schedule
rhestr aros *eb* rhestri aros waiting list
rhestr bostio *eb* rhestri postio mailing list
rhestr brisiant *eb* rhestri prisiant valuation list
rhestr dorri *eb* rhestri torri cutting list
rhestr drafod gyda chymedrolwr *eb* rhestri trafod gyda chymedrolwr moderated mailing list
rhestr drefnedig *eb* rhestri trefnedig ordered list
rhestr ddarllen anffurfiol *eb* rhestri darllen anffurfiol informal reading inventory
rhestr ddarnau *eb* rhestri darnau parts list
rhestr ddefnyddiau *eb* rhestri defnyddiau materials list
rhestr ddosbarthu *eb* rhestri dosbarthu distribution list
rhestr eiddo *eb* rhestri eiddo inventory
rhestr fer *eb* shortlist
rhestr gwallau *eb* rhestri gwallau error list
rhestr gyfeirio *eb* rhestri cyfeirio checklist
rhestr gyflogau *eb* rhestri cyflogau payroll
rhestr gylchol *eb* rhestri cylchol circular list
rhestr gysylltiedig *eb* rhestri cysylltiedig linked list
rhestr o bwyntiau bwled *eb* rhestri o bwyntiau bwled bulleted list
rhestr reciwsantiaid *eb* rhestri reciwsantiaid recusancy list
rhestr sifil *eb* rhestri sifil civil list
rhestr unffordd *eb* rhestri unffordd one-way list
rhestr wirio *eb* rhestri gwirio checklist
rhestr wirio bwcio *eb* booking checklist
rhestren bersonoliaeth Eysenck *eb* Eysenck personality inventory
rheswm adeileddol *eg* structural reason
rhesws negatif *eg* rhesus negative
rhesws positif *eg* rhesus positive
rhesymeg *eb* logic
rhesymeg Boole *eb* Boolean logic
rhesymeg ffurfiol *eb* formal logic
rhesymeg niwlog *eb* fuzzy logic
rhesymeg Transistor-Transistor *eb* Transistor-Transistor logic
rhesymeg ysgol ddringo *eb* ladder logic
rhesymegol *ans* logical; coherent
rhesymol *ans* reasonable; rational
rhesymol i ragweld reasonable to foresee
rhesymoli *be* rationalization
rhesymoliad *eg* rhesymoliadau rationalisation
rhesymoliaeth *eb* rationalism
rhesymolrwydd *eg* reasonableness
rhesymu *be* reason
rhesymu anymwybodol *be* unconscious inference
rhesymu casgliadol *be* inductive reasoning
rhesymu diddwythol *be* deductive reasoning
rhesymu gofodol *be* spatial reasoning

rhew *eg* ice
rhew byrddol *eg* tabular ice
rhew du *eg* black ice
rhew *eg* rhewogydd frost
rhew du *eg* black frost
rhew parhaol *eg* permafrost
rhewbriddeg *eb* cryopedology
rhewbwynt *eg* rhewbwyntiau freezing point
rhewdyrfiad *eg* rhewdyrfiadau congeliturbation
rhewdyrfiad *eg* rhewdyrfiadau congeliturbate
rhewddrylliog *ans* ice shattered
rheweiddiad *eg* refrigeration
rheweiddiedig *ans* refrigerated
rheweiddio *be* refrigerate
rhewfriw *ans* frost shattered
rhewgaeth *ans* ice bound
rhewgell *eb* rhewgelloedd freezer
rhewgist *eb* rhewgistiau chest freezer; deep freeze chest
rhewgraith *eb* rhewgreithiau chattermark
rhewgwymp *eg* ice fall
rhewi *be* freeze
rhewlif dyffryn *eg* rhewlifau dyffryn valley glacier
rhewlifeg *eb* glaciology
rhewlifiant *eg* rhewlifiannau glaciation
rhewlifo *be* glaciate
rhewlifol *ans* glacial
rhewlifwr *eg* rhewlifwyr glaciologist
rhewlin *eg* rhewlinau frost line
rhewlin *eg* rhewlinau isoryme
rhewlyn *eg* rhewlynnoedd glacial lake
rhewllyd *ans* icy cold
rhew-wastadiant *eg* cryoplanation
rhewydd *eg* rhewyddion refrigerant
rhewynt *eg* rhewyntoedd cold wind
rhewynt *eg* ice cold wind
rhiant *eg* rhieni parent
rhiant mabwysiadol *eg* rhieni mabwysiadol adoptive parent
rhiant maeth *eg* rhieni maeth foster parent
rhiant sengl *eg* rhieni sengl single parent
rhiant-blanhigyn *eg* parent plant
rhiant-gell *eb* parent cell
rhiant-gwmni *eg* parent company
rhic *eg* rhiciau notch; nick; score
rhic pedal *eg* rhiciau pedal pedal notch
rhicbren *eg* rhicbrennau tally
rhicio *be* notch; score
rhidennu *be* fringe
rhidens *ell* fringe
rhidyll *eg* rhidyllau riddle; sifter
rhidyllu *be* riddle; sift; lawning
rhieni sy'n disgwyl *ell* antenatal parents
rhif *eg* rhifau number
rhif adnabod *eg* rhifau adnabod ID number
rhif anghymarebol *eg* rhifau anghymarebol irrational number
rhif algebraidd *eg* rhifau algebraidd algebraic number
rhif atomig *eg* rhifau atomig atomic number
rhif cod *eg* rhifau cod code figure
rhif cromosom *eg* rhifau cromosomau chromosome number
rhif cyd-drefnol *eg* rhifau cyd-drefnol coordination number
rhif cyfan *eg* rhifau cyfain whole number
rhif cyfan positif *eg* positive whole number
rhif cyfeiriol *eg* rhifau cyfeiriol directed number
rhif cyfresol tâp *eg* rhifau cyfresol tâp tape serial number
rhif cymarebol *eg* rational number
rhif cymhlyg *eg* rhifau cymhlyg complex number
rhif cymysg *eg* rhifau cymysg mixed number
rhif cysefin *eg* rhifau cysefin prime
rhif degaidd *eg* rhifau degaidd denary number
rhif derbyn *eg* rhifau derbyn acquisition number
rhif deuaidd *eg* rhifau deuaidd binary number
rhif dogfen *eg* rhifau dogfen document number
rhif ffacs *eg* rhifau ffacs facsimile number
rhif màs *eg* rhifau màs mass number
rhif màs atomig *eg* atomic mass number
rhif meddiannaeth *eg* occupation number
rhif mynegiad *eg* rhifau mynegiad statement number
rhif naturiol *eg* rhifau naturiol natural number
rhif negatif *eg* rhifau negatif negative number
rhif ocsidiad *eg* oxidation number
rhif prifol *eg* rhifau prifol cardinal number
rhif real *eg* rhifau real real number
rhif seiclomatig *eg* rhifau seiclomatig cyclomatic number
rhif sgwâr *eg* rhifau sgwâr square number
rhif trefnol *eg* rhifau trefnol ordinal number
rhif triaidd *eg* rhifau triaidd ternary number
rhif triongl *eg* rhifau triongl triangular number
rhif tudalen parhad *eg* rhifau tudalennau parhad continuation page number
rhif yn y catalog *eg* catalogue number
rhif yr anfoneb *eg* invoice number
rhifadwy *ans* enumerable
rhifadwy *ans* countable
rhifadwyedd *eg* countability
rhifedd *eg* numeracy
rhifiad *eg* rhifiadau enumeration
rhifiadol *ans* numerical
rhifiadur *eg* rhifiaduron numerator
rhifo *be* enumerate
rhifo *be* number
rhifogon *eg* rhifogonau arithmogon
rhifol *ans* numeric
rhifoledig *ans* figured
rhifoli (mewn cerddoriaeth) *be* figuring
rhifoli (yn gyffredinol) *be* numerate
rhifoli cord *be* chord figuring
rhifoli cordiau *be* figuring of chords

rhifolyn *eg* rhifolion numeral
rhifolyn deuaidd *eg* rhifolion deuaidd binary numeral
rhifwr lapiau *eg* rhifwyr lapiau lap scorer
rhifydd *eg* rhifyddion counter
rhifydd camau *eg* rhifyddion camau step counter
rhifydd crychdonnau *eg* rhifyddion crychdonnau ripple counter
rhifydd cydamseredig *eg* synchronous counter
rhifydd cylchdroeon *eg* rhifyddion cylchdroeon revolution counter
rhifydd deuaidd *eg* rhifyddion deuaidd binary counter
rhifydd rhaglen *eg* rhifyddion rhaglen program counter
rhifyddeg *eb* arithmetic
rhifyddeg amldrachywiredd *eb* multi-precision arithmetic
rhifyddeg bôn *eb* arithmetic base
rhifyddeg cloc *eb* clock arithmetic
rhifyddeg cyfanrifau *eb* integer arithmetic
rhifyddeg ddeuaidd *eb* binary arithmetic
rhifyddeg fecanyddol *eb* mechanical arithmetic
rhifyddeg fodiwlaidd *eb* modular arithmetic
rhifyddeg hyd dwbl *eb* double length arithmetic
rhifyddeg lafar *eb* oral arithmetic
rhifyddeg masnach *eb* commercial arithmetic
rhifyddeg pen *eb* mental arithmetic
rhifyddeg pwynt arnawf *eb* floating point arithmetic
rhifyddeg pwynt sefydlog *eb* fixed point arithmetic
rhifyddeg trachywiredd dwbl *eb* double precision arithmetic
rhifyddol *ans* arithmetical
rhifyddwr *eg* rhifyddwyr arithmetician
rhigod *eg* rhigodau pillory
rhigol *eb* rhigolau groove; housing; spalt
rhigol bwli *eb* rhigolau pwli pulley housing
rhigol gau *eb* rhigolau cau stopped housing
rhigol hoelbren *eb* rhigolau hoelbren dowel groove
rhigol olew *eb* rhigolau olew oil groove
rhigol trwodd *eb* rhigolau trwodd through housing
rhigol wrthgapilari *eb* rhigolau gwrthgapilari anti-capillary groove
rhigoli *be* grooving; recessing; trenching; ploughing
rhigolog *ans* grooved
rhigolydd *eg* rhigolyddion groover
rhigwm *eg* rhigymau rhyme
rhigwm syml *eg* rhigymau syml simple rhyme
rhimynnau caws *ell* cheese straws
rhin *eb* rhiniau extract
rhin cig eidion *eb* beef extract
rhinflas *eg* rhinflasau essence
rhinflas almon *eg* almond essence
rhinflas brwyniaid *eg* anchovy essence
rhingyll *eg* rhingyllod sergeant
rhinwedd *eb* rhinweddau virtue
rhiolit *eg* rhyolite
rhiolitig *ans* rhyolitic
rhisgl *eg* rhisglau bark
rhisgl derwen *eg* oak bark
Rhisiart Lewgalon *eg* Richard the Lionheart
rhisobiwm *eg* rhisobia rhizobium
rhisoid *eg* rhizoid
rhisom *eg* rhisomau rhizome
rhith *ans* virtual
rhith *eg* rhithiau illusion
rhith optegol *eg* rhithiau optegol optical illusion
rhithaelod *eg* rhithaelodau phantom limb
rhithbeiriant *eg* rhithbeiriannau virtual machine
rhithdyb *eb* rhithdybiau delusion
rhithdybiau erledigaeth *ell* delusions of persecution
rhithdybiau mawredd *ell* delusions of grandeur
rhithdybiau rheolaeth *ell* delusions of control
rhithddelwedd *eb* rhithddelweddau virtual image
rhith-gof *eg* virtual memory
rhithgymuned *eb* rhithgymunedau virtual community
rhithiolaeth *eb* illusionism
rhithiolaeth dafluniol *eb* projective illusionism
rhithlun *eg* rhithluniau mirage
rhithstorfa *eb* rhith storfeydd virtual storage
rhith-waith *eg* virtual work
rhithweledigaeth *eb* rhithweledigaethau hallucination
rhithwirionedd *eg* virtual reality
rhiwmatoleg *eb* rheumatology
rhiwmatolegydd *eg* rhiwmatolegwyr rheumatologist
rhod ddŵr *eb* rhodau dŵr water wheel
rhod ffrwd ganol *eb* rhodau ffrwd ganol breast shot wheel
rhod isredol *eb* rhodau isredol undershot wheel
rhod uwchredol *eb* rhodau uwchredol overshot wheel
rhoden *eb* rhodenni rod
rhoden asgwrn *eb* rhodenni asgwrn boning rod
rhoden droi *eb* rhodenni troi stirring rod
rhoden gymhwyso *eb* rhodenni cymhwyso adjusting rod
rhoden gyswllt *eb* rhodenni cyswllt connecting rod
rhoden hoelbren *eb* rhodenni hoelbren dowel rod
rhoden lenwi *eb* rhodenni llenwi filling rod
rhoden lwybro *eb* rhodenni llwybro track rod
rhoden reoli *eb* rhodenni rheoli control rod
rhoden weldio *eb* rhodenni weldio welding rod
rhoden wthio *eb* rhodenni gwthio push rod
rhoden wydr *eb* rhodenni gwydr glass rod
rhodenni a chonau rods and cones
rhodfa *eb* rhodfeydd avenue
rhodfa parcdir *eb* rhodfeydd parcdir parkland avenue
rhodiwm *eg* rhodium
rhodlen *eb* rhodlenni paddle
rhodlong *eb* rhodlongau paddle steamer

rhodopsin *eg* rhodopsin
Rhodd Cystennin *eb* Donation of Constantine
rhoddwr *eg* rhoddwyr donor
rhoddwr cyffredinol *eg* rhoddwyr cyffredinol universal donor
rhoddwr gwaed *eg* rhoddwyr gwaed blood donor
rhoi (=gosod) *be* apply
rhoi (i mewn) *be* enter
rhoi (paent etc yn uniongyrchol) *be* direct application
rhoi (yn gyffredinol) *be* put
rhoi ar brawf *be* put on probation
rhoi ar herw *be* outlaw
rhoi cefnyn (ar) *be* back
rhoi cyfrif am *be* account for
rhoi grym (i gleientiaid) *be* empower
rhoi grym (mewn ffiseg) *be* exert a force
rhoi gwerth ar swyddogaeth gymdeithasol *be* social role valorization
rhoi gwybod *be* report
rhoi mudydd ar *be* mute
rhoi nod tudalen i'r cyswllt hwn *be* bookmark this link
rhoi nod tudalen yma *be* bookmark this page
rhoi noddfa *be* grant sanctuary
rhoi pigiad *be* inject
rhoi prawf ar *be* test
rhoi prawf ar raglen *be* program testing
rhoi sylw *be* pay attention; attend
rhoi tystysgrif (i ffilm) *be* certification
rhoi yn y golau *be* expose to light
rhoi'r fron *be* suckle
rhôl *eb* rholiau scroll
Rhôl Clos *eb* Close Roll
Rhôl Cymorth *eb* Subsidy Roll
Rhôl Fwstro *eb* Rholiau Mwstro Muster Roll
Rhôl Llys y Brenin *eb* Curia Regis Roll
Rhôl Patent *eb* Rholiau Patent Patent Roll
Rhôl Pensiwn a Lwfans *eb* Rholiau Pensiwn a Lwfans Liberate Roll
rhôl rhent *eb* rholiau rhent rent roll
Rhôl Siarter *eb* Charter Roll
Rhôl Siecr *eb* Rholiau Siecr Pipe Roll
rhôl statud *eb* rholiau statud statute roll
Rhôl Tâl am Fraint *eb* Fine Roll
rhôl uchel ymlaen *eb* rholiau uchel ymlaen high forward roll
rhôl y Gorllewin *eb* Western roll
rhôl ymlaen *eb* rholiau ymlaen forward roll
rhôl yn ôl *eb* rholiau yn ôl backward roll
rholbren *eg* rholbrennau rolling pin
rholen rwygo *eb* rholiau rhwygo tear-off roll
rholer *eg* rholeri roller; brayer
rholer atred *eg* rholeri atred offset roller
rholer blaen *eg* rholeri blaen front roller
rholer diffrithiant *eg* rholeri diffrithiant frictionless roller
rholer inc *eg* rholeri inc ink roller
rholer leino *eg* rholeri leino lino roller
rholer mewn-llinell *eg* rholeri mewn-llinell in-line roller
rholer ôl *eg* rholeri ôl back roller
rholer presio *eg* rholeri presio pressing roller
rholer printio *eg* rholeri printio printing roller
rholferyn *eg* rholferynnau roller bearing
rholiau reciwsantiaid *ell* recusancy rolls
rholio *be* roll
rholio i fyny *be* scroll-up
rholio i lawr *be* scroll-down
rholio mewn *be* roll in
rholstoc *eg* rolling stock
rholyn *eg* rholiau roll
rholyn bara *eg* rholiau bara bread roll
rhomb *eg* rhombau rhomb
rhombohedron *eg* rhombohedronau rhombohedron
rhomboid *eg* rhomboidau rhomboid
rhombws *eg* rhombi rhombus
rhos *eb* rhosydd heath
rhosagorell *eb* rhosagorellau rose reamer
rhosbren *ans* rosewood
rhosebill *eg* rhosebillion rose bit
► **rhosglwm** *eb* rhosenni rosette
rhostir *eg* rhostiroedd heathland; landes
rhosyn *eg* rose
rhuban *eg* rhubanau ribbon
rhuddgoch *eg* crimson
rhuddgoch alisarin *eg* alizarin crimson
rhuddgoch golau *eg* light ruby
rhuddiad *eg* rhuddiadau red shift
rhuddin *eg* heartwood
rhuddliw *eg* rouge
rhuddliw gemydd *eg* jeweller's rouge
rhuddliw tywyll *eg* dark ruby
Rhufeinig *ans* Roman
Rhufeinio *be* Romanize
Rhufeinwr *eg* Rhufeinwyr Roman
rhuglen *eb* rhuglenni rattle
rhuglen glocsen *eb* rhuglenni clocsiau clog rattle
rhugliad *eg* rhugliadau crepitation
rhuglo *be* rattle
rhuthr dŵr *eg* flush
rhwbiad *eg* rhwbiadau rubbing
rhwbiad pres *eg* rhwbiadau pres brass rubbing
rhwbio *be* rub; rubbing down
rhwd *eg* rust
rhwd copr *eg* verdigris
rhwd haearn *eg* iron mould
rhwng canolau *adf* between centres
rhwmba *eg* dawnsiau rhwmba rumba
rhwyd *eb* rhwydi net
rhwyd ddiogelwch *eb* rhwydi diogelwch safety net
rhwyd ddrifft *eb* rhwydi drifft drift net
rhwyd gôl *eb* rhwydi gôl goal net
rhwyd isel *eb* rhwydi isel low net

rhwyd-ddinesydd *eg* rhwyd-ddinasyddion netizen
rhwydfoesau *ell* netiquette
rhwydol *ans* reticulate
rhwydo'r bêl *be* net the ball
rhwydwaith *eg/b* rhwydweithiau network
rhwydwaith ardal *eg* area network
rhwydwaith ardal eang *eg* wide area network
rhwydwaith ardal leol *eg* local area network
rhwydwaith cellog *eg* cellular network
rhwydwaith cenhedlaeth gyntaf *eg* first generation network
rhwydwaith cyfathrebu *eg* rhwydweithiau cyfathrebu communication network
rhwydwaith cyfnewid pecynnau *eg* rhwydweithiau cyfnewid pecynnau packet switching network
rhwydwaith cyfrifiadurol *eg* rhwydweithiau cyfrifiadurol computer network
rhwydwaith diwifr *eg* rhwydweithiau diwifr wireless network
rhwydwaith ffyrdd *eg* road system
rhwydwaith gweinydd/cleient *eg* rhwydweithiau gweinydd/cleient server/client network
rhwydwaith gwybodaeth *eg* information network
rhwydwaith niwral *eg* rhwydweithiau niwral neural network
rhwydwaith pibellau gwaed *eg* network of blood-vessels
rhwydwaith switsio pecynnau *eg* packet switching network
rhwydweithio *be* network
rhwyddineb *eg* facility; fluency
rhwyddineb cynyddol *eg* increasing fluency
rhwyddineb ffurfiant *eg* ease of formation
rhwyddineb llifo *eg* ease of flow
rhwyddur *eg* steel mesh
rhwyf *eb* rhwyfau oar
rhwyfo *be* row
rhwyg *eg* rhwygau tear; rupture
rhwygiad *eg* rhwygiadau laceration
rhwyglif *eb* rhwyglifau rip saw
rhwygo *be* tear
rhwyll *eb* rhwyllau mesh
rhwyll fain *eb* rhwyllau main fine mesh
rhwyll map *eb* rhwyllau map graticule
rhwyll wifrog *eb* rhwyllau gwifrog wire mesh
rhwyllen *eb* rhwyllenni gauze
rhwyllen capilarïau *eb* rhwyllenni capilarïau capillary network
rhwyllen derylen *eb* rhwyllau terylen terylene gauze
rhwyllen diwb *eb* rhwyllenni tiwb tubular gauze
rhwyllo *be* pierce
rhwyllog *ans* fretted; gauze
rhwyllwaith *eg* pierced work
rhwyllwaith *eg* fretwork
rhwym (am bethau) *ans* bound
rhwym (am rwymedd corff) *ans* constipated
rhwym dan gontract *ans* bound by contract
rhwymedigaeth *eb* rhwymedigaethau obligation
rhwymedigaeth gyfredol *eb* rhwymedigaethau cyfredol current liability
rhwymedigaethau tymor hir *ell* long-term liabilities
rhwymedd *eg* constipation
rhwymell *eb* rhwymellau binder
rhwymiad *eg* rhwymiadau binding
rhwymo (clwyf) *be* bandage
rhwymo (yn gyffredinol) *be* bind
rhwymo llyfrau *be* book binding
rhwymwr *eg* rhwymwyr binder
rhwymwr llyfrau *eg* rhwymwyr llyfrau book binder
rhwymyn (ar glwyf) *eg* rhwymynnau bandage
rhwymyn (i glymu yn dynn) *eg* rhwymynnau ligature
rhwymyn (yn gyffredinol) *eg* rhwymynnau binding
rhwymyn bias *eg* rhwymynnau bias bias binding
rhwymyn cotwm *eg* rhwymynnau cotwm cotton bandage
rhwymyn crêp *eg* rhwymynnau crêp crêpe bandage
rhwymyn cydffurfiol *eg* rhwymynnau cydymffurfiol conforming bandage
rhwymyn gwm *eg* rhwymynnau gwm gummed binding
rhwymyn papur *eg* rhwymynnau papur paper binding
rhwymyn Paris *eg* rhwymynnau Paris Paris binding
rhwymyn sêm *eg* rhwymynnau sêm seam binding
rhwymyn sgriw *eg* rhwymau sgriw screwbinder
rhwymyn trionglog *eg* rhwymynnau trionglog triangular bandage
rhwymyn tynhau *eg* rhwymynnau tynhau tourniquet
rhwystr *eg* rhwystrau barrier; obstacle; obstruction
rhwystr egni *eg* energy barrier
rhwystr mynediad *eg* barrier to entry
rhwystr sy'n atal pobl rhag cymryd rhan *eg* barrier to participation
rhwystrau i gyfathrebu *ell* barriers to communication
rhwystredig *ans* frustrated
rhwystredigaeth *eb* rhwystredigaethau frustration
rhwystriant *eg* rhwystriannau impedance
rhwystro *be* prevent; block; impede
rhwystro delwedd *be* image blocking
rhwystro delwedd rhag llwytho *be* block image from loading
rhwystro'r maeswyr *be* obstructing the field
rhy bellennig *ans* too remote
rhybed *eg* rhybedion rivet
rhybed belt *eg* rhybedion belt belt rivet
rhybed deufforchog *eg* rhybedion deufforchog bifurcated rivet
rhybed gwrthsodd *eg* rhybedion gwrthsodd countersunk rivet
rhybed llac *eg* rhybedion llac loose rivet
rhybed pen côn *eg* rhybedion pen côn conical head rivet

rhybed pen gwrthsodd *eg* rhybedion pen gwrthsodd countersunk head rivet
rhybed pen madarch *eg* rhybedion pen madarch mushroom head rivet
rhybed pencosyn *eg* rhybedion pencosyn cheese-head rivet
rhybed pengrwn *eg* rhybedion pengrwn roundhead rivet
rhybed pengrwn *eg* rhybedion pengrwn snap-head rivet
rhybed penpan *eg* rhybedion penpan pan-head rivet
rhybed pop *eg* rhybedion pop pop rivet
rhybedog *ans* riveted
rhybedu *be* rivet
rhybedu cadwynol *be* chain riveting
rhybedu doli *be* dolly riveting
rhybedu igam ogam *be* zigzag riveting
rhybedu llac *be* loose riveting
rhybedu oer *be* cold riveting
rhybedu snap *be* snap riveting
rhybudd *eg* rhybuddion notice
rhybudd (=cyhoeddiad cyhoeddus) *eg* rhybuddion alert
rhybudd (gan yr heddlu) *eg* rhybuddion caution
rhybudd (yn gyffredinol) *eg* rhybuddion warning
rhybudd gwall *eg* rhybuddion gwall error alert
rhybudd i adael *eg* notice to quit
rhybuddio *be* warn
rhybuddiol *ans* aposematic
rhych *eb* rhychau slot
rhych sgriwio *be* slot screwing
rhychedig *ans* striated
rhychiad *eg* rhychiadau striation
rhychiog *ans* corrugated
rhychiog *ans* fluted
rhychu *be* flute
rhychu *be* pucker
rhychwaith *eg* fluting
rhychwant *eg* rhychwantau span
rhychwant darllen *eg* reading span
rhychwant oes *eg* life span
rhychwant rheoli *eg* span of control
rhychwantu *be* span
rhyd *eb* rhydau ford
rhydlyd *ans* rusted
rhydlyd *ans* rusty
rhydocs *eg* redox
rhydu *be* rust
rhydweli *eb* rhydwelïau artery
rhydweli arennol *eb* rydwelïau arennol kidney artery
rhydweli fesenterig *eb* mesenteric artery
rhydweli garotid *eb* rhydwelïau carotid carotid artery
rhydweli goronaidd *eb* rhydwelïau coronaidd coronary artery
rhydweli iliag *eb* rhydwelïau iliag iliac artery
rhydweli iliolymbar *eb* iliolumbar artery
rhydwelïol *ans* arterial
rhydwelïyn *eg* rhydwelïau arteriole
rhydwythiad *eg* reduction
rhydwytho *be* reduce
rhydwythydd *eg* rhydwythyddion reducing agent
rhydd *ans* free
rhydd o lwch *ans* dust-proof
rhyddarbed *be* indemnify
rhydd-dorri *be* free cutting
rhydd-ddaliad *eg* rhydd-ddaliadau freehold
rhydd-ddeiliad *eg* rhydd-ddeiliaid freeholder; franklin
rhydd-ddeiliad deugain swllt *eg* rhydd-ddeiliaid deugain swllt forty-shilling freeholder
rhydd-ddeiliaid *ell* yeomanry
rhydd-ddosraniad y genynnau *eg* independent assortment of genes
rhydd-ddosrannol *ans* independently assorting
rhyddewyllyswr *eg* rhyddewyllyswyr libertarian
rhyddfarn *eb* rhyddfarnau acquittal
rhydd-feddyliwr *eg* rhydd-feddylwyr free thinker
rhyddfenter *eb* free enterprise
rhyddfraint dinas *eb* freedom of a city
rhyddfreiniad *eg* emancipation
rhyddfreinio *be* emancipate; enfranchise
Rhyddfreinio'r Pabyddion *be* Catholic Emancipation
rhyddfreinio'r taeogion *be* emancipation of the serfs
rhyddfreiniwr *eg* rhyddfreinwyr freeman
rhyddfrydiaeth *eb* liberalism
rhyddfrydiaeth Gladstone *eb* Gladstonian liberalism
rhyddfrydoli *be* liberalisation
rhyddfrydwr *eg* rhyddfrydwyr liberal
Rhyddfrydwr Unoliaethol *eg* Rhyddfrydwyr Unoliaethol Liberal Unionist
rhyddganon *eg/b* rhyddganonau free canon
rhyddgymysgu *be* free blending
rhyddgysylltu *be* free association
rhyddhad (rhag gorfod talu etc) *eg* rhyddhadau exemption; relief
rhyddhad (=gwneud yn rhydd) *eg* liberation
rhyddhad anabledd *eg* disabled relief
rhyddhad cystadleuol *eg* competitive release
rhyddhau (=llacio) *be* loosen
rhyddhau (=gwneud yn rhydd) *be* free; liberate
rhyddhau (o garchar) *be* release
rhyddhau (o ysbyty) *be* discharge
rhyddhau ac achub release and rescue
rhyddhäwr *eg* rhyddhawyr release key
rhyddhäwr *eg* rhyddhawyr liberator
rhyddiaith estynedig *eb* extended prose
rhyddid *eg* freedom; liberty
rhyddid contract *eg* freedom of contract
rhyddid cred *eg* freedom of belief
rhyddid crefyddol *eg* religious freedom

rhyddid cydwybod *eg* liberty of conscience
rhyddid i dynnu nôl *eg* freedom to withdraw
rhyddid meddwl *eg* freedom of thought
rhyddlifo *be* free flowing
rhydd-sefyll *ans* free-standing
rhyddwedd *eg/b* free software
rhyfel *eg/b* rhyfeloedd war
rhyfel Awstria a Piedmont *eg* Austro-Piedmontese war
rhyfel Awstria a Phrwsia *eg* Austro-Prussian war
rhyfel byd *eg* rhyfeloedd byd world war
Rhyfel Byd Cyntaf *eg* First World War
Rhyfel Can Mlynedd *eg* Hundred Years War
rhyfel cartref *eg* rhyfeloedd cartref civil war
rhyfel cyfiawn *eg* rhyfeloedd cyfiawn just war
Rhyfel Cynghrair Augsburg *eg* War of League of Augsburg
Rhyfel Deng Mlynedd ar Hugain *eg* Thirty Years War
rhyfel diarbed *eg* total war
rhyfel dosbarth *eg* class struggle
rhyfel fflamio *eg* rhyfeloedd fflamio flame war
Rhyfel Ffrainc a Phrwsia *eg* Franco-Prussian War
Rhyfel Ffug *eg* Phoney War
rhyfel gerlla *eg* rhyfeloedd gerila guerrilla warfare
Rhyfel Mawr y Gogledd *eg* Great Northern War
rhyfel oer *eg* rhyfeloedd oer cold war
Rhyfel Olyniaeth Awstria *eg* War of Austrian Succession
Rhyfel Olyniaeth Pwyl *eg* War of Polish Succession
Rhyfel Olyniaeth Sbaen *eg* War of Spanish Succession
Rhyfel y Boer *eg* Boer War
Rhyfel y Crimea *eg* Crimean War
Rhyfel y Degwm *eg* Tithe War
Rhyfel y Marchogion *eg* Knights' War
Rhyfel y Werin *eg* Peasants' War
Rhyfel yr Esgobion *eg* Bishops' Wars, the
rhyfela *be* warfare
rhyfelgi *eg* rhyfelgwn warmonger
rhyfelgri *eb* battle cry
rhyfeloedd dros annibyniaeth yr Alban *ell* wars of Scottish independence
Rhyfeloedd y Rhosynnod *ell* Wars of the Roses
rhyfelwr *eg* rhyfelwyr warrior
rhyfflydd *eg* rhyfflyddion ruffler
rhygwellt *ell* ryegrass
rhyngadrannol *ans* interdepartmental
rhyngalaethog *ans* intergalactic
rhyngasennol *ans* intercostal
rhyngbersonol *ans* interpersonal
rhyngchwartel *eg* rhyngchwartelau interquartile
rhyngdestuniaeth *eb* intertextuality
rhyng-dôn *eg* rhyngdonau differential tone
rhyngdoriad *eg* rhyngdoriadau intercept
rhyngdorri *be* intercept
rhyngdrawsnewidioldeb *eg* interconvertibility
rhyngdrofannol *ans* intertropical
rhyngdrymlinol *ans* interdrumlin
rhyngfertebrol *ans* invertebral
rhyngfridio *be* interbreed
rhyngfynyddig *ans* intermont
rhyngffasgellol *ans* interfascicular
rhyng-gellol *ans* intercellular
rhyng-gipiad *eg* rhyng-gipiadau interception; intercept
rhyng-gipio *be* intercept
rhyng-granaidd *ans* inter-granal
rhyng-gydberthyniad *eg* rhyng-gydberthyniadau intercorrelation
rhyng-gyfansoddyn *eg* rhyng-gyfansoddion intermediary compound
rhyng-gyfarfod *be* intercept
rhyng-gyfarfyddiad *eg* rhyng-gyfarfyddiadau interception
rhyng-gyflwr *eg* rhyng-gyflyrau intermediate state
rhyng-gyflwr *eg* rhyng-gyflyrau intermediate condition
rhyng-gymysgadwy *ans* intermixable
rhynghaenol *ans* interbedded
rhyngles *eg* interlace
rhynglesio *be* interlace
rhyngniwron *eg* rhyngniwronau interneuron
rhyngnodol *ans* internodal
rhyngol *ans* intervening
rhyngolyn *eg* rhyngolynnau intermediate
rhyngosod *be* interpolate
rhyngosodiad *eg* rhyngosodiadau interpolation
rhyngosodol *ans* intercalary
rhyngrewlifol *ans* interglacial
rhyngrwyd *eb* internet
rhyngrywogaethol *ans* interspecific
rhyngsafle *eg* rhyngsafleoedd interposition
rhyngwedd *eg* interphase
rhyngweithedd *eb* interactionism
rhyngweithiad *eg* rhyngweithiadau interaction
rhyngweithiad iaith *eg* language interaction
rhyngweithio *be* interact
rhyngweithio grŵp *be* group interaction
rhyngweithiol *ans* interactive
rhyngwladol *ans* multinational
rhyngwladol *ans* international
rhyngwladoliaeth *eb* internationalism
rhyngwyneb *eg* rhyngwynebau interface
rhyngwyneb Centronics *eg* rhyngwynebau Centronics Centronics interface
rhyngwyneb cyfresol *eg* rhyngwynebau cyfresol serial interface
rhyngwyneb cyfrifiadurol *eg* rhyngwynebau cyfrifiadurol computer interface
rhyngwyneb defnyddiwr *eg* rhyngwynebau defnyddwyr user interface
rhyngwyneb defnyddiwr graffigol *eg* graphical user interface

rhyngwyneb dynol y cyfrifiadur *eg* human computer interface
rhyngwyneb IEEE *eg* rhyngwynebau IEEE IEEE interface
rhyngwyneb llinell orchymyn *eg* rhyngwynebau llinell orchymyn command line interface
rhyngwyneb peiriant-dyn *eg* rhyngwynebau peiriant-dyn man-machine interface
rhyngwyneb perifferol *eg* rhyngwynebau perifferol peripheral interface
rhyngwyneb safonol *eg* rhyngwynebau safonol standard interface
rhyngwynebol *ans* interfacial
rhyngwynebu *be* interface
rhymlin *eg* rhymliniau rhumb line
rhysgen *eb* rhysgenni rusk
rhysyfwr *eg* rhysyfwyr receiver
Rhysyfwr Cyffredinol *eg* Rhysyfwyr Cyffredinol Receiver General
rhythm *eg* rhythmau rhythm
rhythm circadaidd *eg* circadian rhythm
rhythm corff *eg* rhythmau corff body rhythm
rhythm jig *eg* rhythmau jig jig rhyme
rhythm syml *eg* rhythmau syml simple rhythm
rhythmig *ans* rhythmic
rhyw (benyw neu wryw) *eg/b* gender
rhyw (yn gyffredinol) *eg/b* rhywiau sex
rhyw cymysg *ans* mixed sex
rhyw cyn priodas *eg* sex before marriage
rhyw y person (plentyn etc) *eg* gender
rhywfaint *eg* quantity
rhyw-gysylltiedig *ans* sex linked
rhywiol *ans* sexual
rhywogaeth *eb* rhywogaethau species; strain
rhywogaeth anhysbys *eb* rhywogaethau anhysbys unidentified species
rhywogaeth o facteria *eb* species of bacteria
rhywogaeth wyrol *eb* rhywogaethau gwyrol aberrant species
rhywogaethiaeth *eg* speciesism

S

Sabath *eg* Sabathau Sabbath
Sabathyddiaeth *eb* Sabbatarianism
sabl *eg* sable
sabl coch *eg* red sable
sabothol *ans* sabbatical
sabr *eg* sabrau sabre
sacarin *eg* saccharin
sacrament *eg* sacramentau sacrament
sacristan *eg* sacristaniaid sacristan
sacristi *eg* sacristiau sacristy
sacrwm *eg* sacra sacrum
Sacson *eg* Sacsoniaid Saxon
Sacsonaidd *ans* Saxon
sach *eb* sachau sack
sach cyntedd y glust *eb* vestibular sac
sach eistedd *eb* sachau eistedd bean bag
sach gysgu *eb* sachau cysgu sleeping-bag
sach wlân *eb* sachau gwlân woolsack
sadio-cam *eg* steadycam
sadistiaeth *eb* sadism
sadistiaeth rywiol *eb* sexual sadism
sadrwydd *eg* stability
Sadwrn *eg* Saturn
sadydd *eg* sadyddion steady
sadydd bwrdd *eg* sadwyr byrddau table steady
sadydd disymud *eg* sadyddion disymud fixed steady
sadydd symudol *eg* sadyddion symudol moving steady
saer coed *eg* seiri coed carpenter
saer dodrefn *eg* seiri dodrefn cabinet maker
saer maen *eg* seiri maen mason
saer rhydd *eg* seiri rhyddion freemason
saer troliau *eg* seiri troliau wheelwright
saernïaeth *eb* architecture
saernïaeth gyfrifiadurol *eb* computer architecture
saernïaeth peiriant *eb* machine architecture
saernïaeth rwydwaith *eb* saerniaethau rhwydwaith network architecture
saesonaeth *eb* englishry
saeth *eb* saethau arrow
saeth ddeuben *eb* saethau deuben double-ended arrow
saeth ddwbl *eb* saethau dwbl double arrow
saeth ddwbl i'r chwith *eg* saethau dwbl i'r chwith double arrow left
saeth ddwbl i'r dde *eb* double arrow right
saeth geugrom *eb* saethau ceugrwm arrow concave
saeth i fyny *eb* up arrow
saeth i lawr *eb* down arrow
saeth ymlaen *eb* saethau ymlaen forward arrow
saeth yn ôl *eb* back arrow
saethflew *ell* kemp
saethiad (mewn ffilm) *eg* shot
saethol *ans* sagittal
saethu *be* shoot
saethwr (gyda bwa saeth) *eg* saethwyr archer
saethwr (mewn pêl-droed) *eg* saethwyr striker; goal shooter
saethyddiaeth *eb* archery
safana *eg* safanau savannah
safbwynt *eg* safbwyntiau point of view; standpoint; viewpoint
safbwynt cyfreithiol *eg* legal position
safiad *eg* safiadau stance
safiad agored *eg* open stance
saflad caeedig *eg* closed stance
safiad gwarchod *eg* safiadau gwarchod guard position
safiad sgwâr *eg* square stance
safle (=man daearyddol) *eg* safleoedd site
safle (pobl) *eg* safleoedd position; rank
safle achub ar fynydd *eg* safleoedd achub ar fynydd mountain rescue post
safle adwerthu y tu allan i'r dref *eg* safleoedd adwerthu y tu allan i'r trefi out-of-town retail site
safle anghyfleus *eg* inconvenient position
safle canraddol *eg* percentile ranking
safle canrannol *eg* safleoedd canrannol centile rank
safle cychwynnol *eg* safleoedd cychwynnol starting position
safle cynnal *eg* safleoedd cynnal support position
safle cyrchwr *eg* cursor position
safle cywir *eg* safleoedd cywir correct position
safle datblygu *eg* safleoedd datblygu development site
safle didol *eg* safleoedd didol bit position
safle ecwilibriwm *eg* equilibrium position
safle gorau *eg* safleoedd gorau best position
safle gwreiddiol *eg* safleoedd gwreiddiol root position
safle is-werth *eg* safleoedd is-werth low-order position
safle mewn gwagle *eg* location in space
safle priodol *eg* safleoedd priodol appropriate position
safle sefydlog *eg* safleoedd sefydlog fixed position

safle snap *eg* safleoedd snap snap position
safle sych *eg* safleoedd sych dry point site
safle testun *eg* text position
► **safle tir glas** *eg* safleoedd tir glas green field site
safle tir glas *eg* safleoedd tir glas green belt site
safle tir llwyd *eg* safleoedd tir llwyd brown field site
safle tirlenwi *eg* safleoedd tirlenwi landfill
safle tirlenwi *eg* safleoedd tirlenwi landfill site
safle unionsyth *eg* safleoedd unionsyth upright position
safle wedi'i fomio *eg* safleoedd wedi'u bomio bombed site
safle ymlaen *eg* safleoedd ymlaen on position
safle ymosodol *eg* safleoedd ymosodol attacking position
safle-benodol *ans* site-specific
safle'r bawd *eg* safleoedd y bawd thumb position
safle'r haul position of the sun
safle'r pedal *eg* safle'r pedalau pedal position
safle'r traed *eg* position of the feet
safle'r ysgol *eg* school site
safn *eg/b* safnau jaw
safn aligator *eb* safnau aligator alligator jaw
safn ddanheddog *eb* safnau danheddog serrated jaw
safn feis *eb* safnau feis vice jaw
safn lithr *eb* safnau llithr sliding jaw
safn sefydlog *eb* safnau sefydlog fixed jaw
safn symudol *eb* safnau symudol moving jaw
safn symudol *eb* safnau symudol movable jaw
safon *eb* safonau standard
safon academaidd *eb* safonau academaidd academic standard
Safon Aur *eb* Gold Standard
Safon Brydeinig *eb* Safonau Prydeinig British Standard
safon byw *eb* safonau byw standard of living
safon foesol *eb* safonau moesol moral standard
safon genedlaethol *eb* safonau cenedlaethol national standard
safon gofal *eb* safonau gofal standard of care
safon gwerthu *eb* mercantile quality
safon gydnabyddedig *eb* safonau cydnabyddedig recognised standard
safon gyfredol *eg* safonau cyfredol current standard
safon uchel *eb* safonau uchel high standard
Safon Uwch *eb* A level
Safon Uwch Atodol *eb* AS level
safon y chwarae *eb* standard of play
safonau cyffredin *ell* common standards
safonau diogelwch *ell* safety standards
safonau masnachu *ell* trading standards
safonedig *ans* standardized
safoni (marciau arholiad) *be* moderate
safoni (yn gyffredinol) *be* standardize
safonol *ans* standard
saffrwm *eg* crocus
saga *eb* sagâu saga
sager *eg* sageri sagger
sagrafen *eb* sagrafennau sacrament
Sangha *eg* Sangha
sahel *eg* sahel
sahelaidd *ans* sahelian
saib (mewn cerddoriaeth) *eg* seibiau rest
saib (mewn chwaraeon) *eg* seibiau time out
saib (yn gyffredinol) *eg* seibiau pause
saig entrée *eb* seigiau entrée entrée dish
sail (triongl) *eb* seiliau base
sail (yn gyffredinol) *eb* seiliau basis
sail blwyddyn ariannol *eb* financial year basis
sail olew *ans* oil based
sail resymegol *eb* seiliau rhesymegol rationale
sail stac *eb* seiliau staciau stack base
saim *eg* seimiau grease
saim gloyw *eg* clarified fat
saim gwrth-ffrithiant *eg* seimiau gwrth-ffrithiant anti-friction grease
sain *eb* seiniau sound
sain anghynefin *eb* nondiegetic sound
sain anadl *eb* seiniau anadl breathed sound
sain drwynol *eb* seiniau trwynol nasal tone
sain electronig *eb* seiniau electronig electronic sound
sain glust *eb* aural work
sain gref *eb* seiniau cryf loud sound
sain gynefin *eb* diegetic sound
sainfesurydd *eg* sainfesuryddion sonometer
saith bob ochr seven a side
sal amoniac *eg* sal ammoniac
Salab *eg* Salab
salbwtamol *eg* salbutamol
salina *eg* salinau salina
saliwt *eg* saliwtiau salute
saliwtio *be* salute
salm *eb* salmau psalm
salmau cân *ell* metrical psalms
salm-dôn *eb* salmdonau chant
salon *eg* salonau salon
saltarelo *eg* saltarelau saltarello
salwch môr *eg* seasickness
salwch mynydd *eg* soroche
salwch ymbelydredd *eg* radiation sickness
sallwyr *eg* sallwyrau psalter
samadhi *eg* samadhi
Samariaid y trenau tanddaearol *ell* subway Samaritans
samariwm (Sm) *eg* samarium
samatha *eg* samatha
samba *eg* dawnsiau samba samba
sambo *eg* sambos zambo
samoser *eg* samoserau psammosere
sampl *eg/b* samplau sample
sampl amhwysol *eb* samplau amhwysol unweighted sample

sampl gynrychioliadol *eb* samplau cynrychioliadol representative sample
sampl haenedig *eb* samplau haenedig stratified sample
sampl lliw *eb* samplau lliw colour sample
sampler *eg* sampleri sampler
samplu *be* sample
samplu ardal *be* area sample
samplu haenedig *be* stratified sampling
samplu pwynt *be* point sample
samplu systematig *be* systematic sampling
samsara *eg* samsara
San Bened *ans* Benedictine
sancsiynau *ell* sanctions
sanctaidd *ans* holy; sacred
sancteiddhad *eg* sanctification
sandiwr *eg* sandwyr sander
sandiwr belt *eg* sandwyr belt belt sander
sandiwr cludadwy *eg* sandwyr cludadwy portable sander
sandiwr disg *eg* sandwyr disg disc sander
sandiwr orbitol *eg* sandwyr orbitol orbital sander
sandiwr pŵer *eg* sandwyr pŵer power sander
sandur *eg* sandurau sandur; outwash plain
sans-culottes *ell* sans-culottes
sant *eg* seintiau saint
Sant Iago *eg* Saint James
Sant Ioan *eg* Saint John
Sant Padrig *eg* Saint Patrick
santhoffyl *eg* xanthophyll
saproffag *eg* saprophage
saproffyt *eg* saproffytau saprophyte
saproffytig *ans* saprophyte
Sarasen *eg* Saraseniaid Saracen
sarff-faen *eb* sarff-feini serpentine
sarn *eg* sarnau causeway
sarsiant *eg* sergeant
sarsiant wrth arfau *eg* sergeant-at-arms
sarsiant wrth gyfraith *eg* sergeant-at-law
sarsiantaeth *eb* sergeantry
sash *eg* sasiau sash
Sat Nam *eg* Sat Nam
satîn *eg* sateen
satin *eg* satin
savant *eg* savants savant
sawdl *eg/b* sodlau heel
sawdl bwa *eb* sodlau bwâu heel of a bow
sawdl gaerog *eb* sodlau caerog reinforced heel
sawdl y faneg *eb* sodlau menig heel of glove
Sawm *eg* Sawm
sawrlysiau cymysg *ell* fines herbes
saws afal *eg* apple sauce
saws bechamel *eg* bechamel sauce
saws cwstard wy *eg* egg custard sauce
saws Espagnole *eg* Espagnole sauce
sba *eg* sbâu spa
sbadics *eg* spadix
sbam *eg* spam
sbamio *be* spam
sbaner *eg* sbaneri spanner
sbaner â safn atred *eg* sbaneri â safn atred offset jaw spanner
sbaner blwch *eg* sbaneri blwch box spanner
sbaner ceg agored *eg* sbaneri ceg agored open-end spanner
sbaner ceg agored sengl *eg* sbaneri ceg agored sengl single open-end spanner
sbaner cranc *eg* sbaneri cranc crank spanner
sbaner cylch *eg* sbaneri cylch ring spanner
sbaner cymwysadwy *eg* sbaneri cymwysadwy adjustable spanner
sbaner deuben *eg* sbaneri deuben double-ended spanner
sbaner soced *eg* sbaneri soced socket spanner
sbardun *eg* sbardunau throttle; spur
sbardun blaendor *eg* sbardunau blaendor truncated spur
sbardun dur *eg* sbardunau dur steel spur
sbardun ffasedaidd *eg* sbardunau ffasedaidd faceted spur
sbardunau didoriad *ell* intact spurs
sbardunau pleth *ell* interlocking spurs
sbarian *be* sparring
sbaryn *eg* sbarion remnant
sbatwla *eg* sbatwlâu spatula
sbeciwr *eg* sbecwyr voyeur
sbectol eira *eb* sbectolau eira snow glasses
sbectroffotomedr *eg* sbectroffotomedrau spectrophotometer
sbectrograff màs *eg* sbectrograffau màs mass spectrograph
sbectrol *ans* spectral
sbectromedr *eg* sbectromedrau spectrometer
sbectromedr màs *eg* mass spectrometer
sbectromedreg *eb* spectrometry
sbectromedreg màs *eb* mass spectrometry
sbectrosgop *eg* sbectrosgopau spectroscope
sbectrosgop golwg union *eg* sbectrosgopau golwg union direct vision spectroscope
sbectrosgopeg *eb* spectroscopy
sbectrosgopeg allyriant *eb* emission spectroscopy
sbectrosgopig *ans* spectroscopic
sbectrwm *eg* sbectra spectrum
sbectrwm absoliwt *eg* absolute spectrum
sbectrwm allyrru *eg* emission spectrum
sbectrwm amsugno *eg* absorption spectrum
sbectrwm amsugno llinell *eg* line absorption spectrum
sbectrwm band *eg* sbectra band band spectrum
sbectrwm di-dor *eg* sbectra di-dor continuous spectrum
sbectrwm electromagnetig *eg* electromagnetic spectrum
sbectrwm gweithredu *eg* sbectra gweithredu action spectrum
sbectrwm llinell *eg* sbectra llinell line spectrum

sbectrwm màs *eg* mass spectrum
sbectrwm niwclear cyseiniant magnetig *eg* nuclear magnetic resonance spectrum
sbectrwm trefn dau *eg* second order spectrum
sbeis *eg* sbeisiau spice
sbelter *eg* spelter
sbelter presyddu *eg* sbelterau presyddu brazing spelter
sberm *eg* sbermau sperm
sbermatogenesis *eg* spermatogenesis
sbermatosoon *eg* sermatosoa spermatozoon
sbermleiddiad *eg* sbermleiddiaid spermicide
sbermleiddiol *ans* spermicidal
sbermocyt *eg* sbermocytau spermocyte
sbesiffig *ans* specific
sbesimen *eg* sbesimenau specimen
sbidomedr *eg* sbidomedrau speedometer
sbigolyn *eg* sbigolion spikelet
sbigot *cg* spigotau spigot
sbigot fflans *eg* sbigotau fflans flanged spigot
sbigyn *eg* sbigynnau spike
sbigyn tynnu *eg* sbigynnau tynnu draw spike
sbin *eg* sbiniau spin
sbinio *be* spin
sbinol *ans* spinal
sbiragl *eg* sbiraglau spiracle
sbiral *eb* sbiralau spiral
sbiral Archimedes *eb* sbiralau Archimedes Archimedean spiral
sbirochaet *eg* sbirochaetau spirochaete
sblae *ans* splayed
sblein *eg* sbleiniau spline
sbleis *eg* sbleisiau splice
sbleisio *be* splice
sblint *eg* sblintiau splint
sbonc *eb* sbonciau bounce
sbonc y bêl *eb* bounce of the ball
sboncen *eb* squash
sboncio *be* bounce
sboncio ar y ddaear *be* bounce on the ground
sbôr *eg* sborau spore
sborangiwm *eg* sborangia sporangium
sboroffor *eg* sporophore
sboroffyt *eg* sporophyte
sborogoniwm *eg* sborogonia sporogonium
sbotio *be* spotting
sbotweldio *be* spot welding
sbotweldio trydan *be* electric spot welding
sbotwynebu *be* spot facing
sbrig *eb* sbrigiau sprig
sbring *eg* sbringiau spring
sbring arab *eg* sbringiau arab arab spring
sbring baril *eg* sbringiau baril barrel spring
sbring byffer *eg* sbringiau byffer buffer spring
sbring cefn *eg* sbringiau cefn back spring
sbring clustogwaith *eg* sbringiau clustogwaith upholstery spring
sbring coil *eg* sbringiau coil coil spring
sbring cywasgu *eg* sbringiau cywasgu compression spring
sbring deudroed *eg* sbringiau deudroed flyspring
sbring gwar *eg* sbringiau gwar neckspring
sbring heligol *eg* sbringiau heligol helical spring
sbring llaw *eg* sbringiau llaw handspring
sbring pen *eg* sbringiau pen headspring
sbring sbiral *eg* sbringiau sbiral spiral spring
sbring tyniant *eg* sbringiau tyniant tension spring
sbring-lwythog *ans* spring-loaded
sbringar *ans* springy
sbroced *eg* sbrocedi sprocket
sbroced a chadwyn sprocket and chain
sbwng (a wnaed o rwber) *eg* foam
sbwng (yn gyffredinol) *eg* sbyngiau sponge
sbwngio *be* sponge
sbwngio â dŵr claear *be* tepid sponging
sbwngoffyl *eg* spongophyll
sbŵl *eg* sbwliau spool
sbwlio *be* spooling
sbwliwr *eg* sbwlwyr spooler
sbwriel *eg* rubbish; refuse; garbage
scandiwm *eg* scandium
scoria *be* scoria
scorpion môr *eg* scorpionnau môr sea scorpion
scherzo *eg* scherzi scherzo
scherzo a thrio scherzo and trio
sebca *eg* sebcâu sebkha
sebon *eg* sebonau soap
sebon calch *eg* lime soap
sebon caled *eg* hard soap
sebon dogfennol *eg* docusoap
sebon golchi *eg* household soap
sebon hylif *eg* liquid soap
sebon meddal *eg* soft soap
sebon Tripoli *eg* Tripoli compound
seboneiddiad *eg* saponification
seboneiddio *be* saponify
seboni *be* lather
sebonllyd *ans* soapy
secant (sec) *eg* secannau secant
secco *ans* secco
seciwlar *ans* secular
seciwlareiddio *be* secularize
seciwlariaeth *eb* secularism
secondiad *eg* secondiadau secondment
secretiad *eg* secretiadau secretion
secretiad mewnol *eg* secretiadau mewnol internal secretion
secretin *eg* secretin
secretu *be* secrete
secsagesimol *ans* sexagesimal
secsdens *eg* sext
secstant *eg* secstantau sextant
secstig *ans* sextic
sect *eb* sectau sect

sector *eg/b* sectorau sector
sector amgylchedd adeiledig *eg* built environment sector
sector cyhoeddus *eg* public sector
sector cylch *eg* sectorau cylch circle sector
sector cynnes *eg* sectorau cynnes warm sector
sector cynradd *eg* primary sector
sector diwydiannol *eg* industrial sector
sector eilaidd *eg* secondary sector
sector gwirfoddol *eg* voluntary sector
sector preifat *eg* private sector
sector trydyddol *eg* tertiary sector
sectoriad caled *eg* hard sectored
sectoriad meddal *eg* soft sectored
sectydd *eg* sectyddion sectary
sectyddol *ans* sectarian
secwestrydd *eg* sequestrant
secwin *eg* secwinau sequin
sech *eg* sech
sedarim *ell* sedarim
sedd *eb* seddau seat
sedd gôr *eb* seddau côr choir stall
sedd lithro *eb* seddi llithro sliding seat
sedd sefydlog *eb* seddi sefydlog fixed seat
sedd ystlys *eb* seddi ystlys thwart
seddisl *eb* seddislau donkey
seersucker *eg* seersucker
sefydliad *eg* sefydliadau institution
sefydliad *eg* sefydliadau institute
sefydliad *eg* sefydliadau establishment
sefydliad *eg* sefydliadau foundation
sefydliad *eg* sefydliadau induction
sefydliad anllywodraethol *eg* non-government organisation
Sefydliad Cenedlaethol ar gyfer Ymchwil mewn Addysg (SCYA) *eg* National Foundation for Education Research
Sefydliad Economeg Ryngwladol *eg* Institute of International Economics
sefydliad Protestannaidd *eg* Protestant establishment
Sefydliad Safonau Prydeinig *eg* British Standards Institution
sefydliad y gweithredwyr cyfreithlon *eg* institute of legal executives
Sefydliad y Merched *eg* Women's Institute
sefydliadol *ans* institutional
sefydliadu *be* institutionalize
sefydlog (=nad yw'n symud) *ans* fixed; stationary
sefydlog (am gyflwr rhywun) *ans* stable
sefydlog (am liw) *ans* permanent
sefydlog (mewn mathemateg) *ans* invariant
sefydlogi (mewn ffotograffiaeth a bioleg) *be* fix
sefydlogi (yn gyffredinol) *be* stabilize
sefydlogiad *eg* fixation
sefydlogiad nitrogen *eg* nitrogen fixation
sefydlogrwydd *eg* stability; constancy; permanence
sefydlogrwydd emosiynol *eg* emotional stability
sefydlogrwydd gwrthrych *eg* object permanence
sefydlogydd *eg* sefydlogyddion fixator; stabilizer
sefydlogydd awtomatig *eg* sefydlogyddion awtomatig automatic stabilizer
sefydlogydd trochion *eg* sefydlogyddion trochion foam stabilizer; lather stabilizer
sefydlu (person mewn swydd) *be* induct
sefydlu (=agor yn gyhoeddus) *be* inaugurate
sefydlu (yn gyffredinol) *be* establish; found
sefydlu cwlwm agosrwydd *be* bonding
sefydlu gwerth *be* valorisation
sefydlyn (mewn mathemateg) *eg* sefydlynnau invariant
sefydlyn (ar gyfer lliwiau, sbeseminau etc) *eg* sefydlynnau fixative; fixer
sefydlyn aerosol *eg* sefydlynnau aerosol aerosol fixative
sefydlyn llifyn *eg* sefydlynnau llifyn dye fix
sefydlyn pastel *eg* pastel fixative
sefyll (arholiad) *be* sit
sefyll (yn gyffredinol) *be* stand
sefyll mewn ystum *be* pose
sefyll yn syth a thal *be* standing tall
sefyllfa *eb* sefyllfaoedd position; situation
sefyllfa ddiddatrys *eb* sefyllfaoedd diddatrys deadlock
sefyllfa ddieithr *eb* sefyllfaoedd dieithr strange situation
sefyllfa iechyd a gofal cymdeithasol *eb* health and social care setting
segment *eg* segmentau segment
segment cylch *eg* segmentau cylch circle segment
segment o'r farchnad *eg* market segment
segmentiad *eg* segmentiadau segmentation
segmentiad y farchnad *eg* market segmentation
segmentiedig *ans* segmented
segmentu *be* segment
segurswydd *eb* segurswyddi sinecure
sengl *ans* single
senglau *ell* singles
seiberbarth *eg* seiberbarthau cyberzone
seibernetaidd *ans* cybernetic
seiberneteg *eb* cybernetics
seiberofod *eg* cyberspace
seibersgwatiwr *eg* seibersgwatwyr cybersquatter
seibiant *eg* respite
seicdreiddiad *eg* psychoanalysis
seicdreiddio *be* psychoanalyze
seiciatreg *eb* psychiatry
seiciatreg plant *eb* child psychiatry
seiciatrig *ans* psychiatric
seiciatrydd *eg* seiciatryddion psychiatrist
seiciatrydd plant *eg* seiciatryddion plant child psychiatrist
seiclig *ans* cyclic
seiclon *eg* seiclonau cyclone
seiclorama *eg* seicloramau cyclorama
seiclostom *eg* cyclostome

seicobioleg *eb* psychobiology
seicodynamig *ans* psychodynamic
seicoffiseg *eb* psychophysics
seicoffisioleg *eb* psychophysiology
seicogenig *ans* psychogenic
seicogeriatregydd *eg* seicogeriatregwyr psychogeriatrician
seicogymdeithasol *ans* psychosocial
seicoieithyddiaeth *eb* psycholinguistics
seicolawdriniaeth *eb* psychosurgery
seicoleg *eb* psychology
seicoleg adwerthu *eb* retail psychology
seicoleg addysg *eb* educational psychology
seicoleg babanod *eb* infant psychology
seicoleg chwaraeon ac ymarfer corff *eb* sport and exercise psychology
seicoleg datblygiad *eb* developmental psychology
seicoleg defnyddwyr *eb* consumer psychology
seicoleg drawsddiwylliannol *eb* cross-cultural psychology
seicoleg ddiwylliannol *eb* cultural psychology
seicoleg ddyneiddiol *eb* humanistic psychology
seicoleg esblygol *eb* evolutionary psychology
seicoleg ffisiolegol *eb* physiological psychology
seicoleg fforensig *eb* forensic psychology
seicoleg Gestalt *eb* Gestalt psychology
seicoleg glinigol *eb* clinical psychology
seicoleg glinigol fforensig *eb* forensic clinical psychology
seicoleg gyfundrefnol/alwedigaethol *eb* organisational/occupational psychology
seicoleg gymdeithasol *eb* social psychology
seicoleg gymharol *eb* comparative psychology
seicoleg iechyd *eb* health psychology
seicoleg plant *eb* child psychology
seicoleg troseddu *eb* criminal psychology
seicoleg wybyddol *eb* cognitive psychology
seicoleg ymchwiliol *eb* investigative psychology
seicoleg ymddygiad *eb* behavioural psychology
seicolegol *ans* psychological
seicolegydd *eg* seicolegwyr psychologist
seicolegydd addysg *eg* seicolegwyr addysg educational psychologist
seicolegydd clinigol *eg* seicolegwyr clinigol clinical psychologist
seiconiwronimiwnoleg *eb* psychoneuronimmunology
seicopath *eg* seicopathiaid psychopath
seicorywiol *ans* psychosexual
seicosis *eg* psychosis
seicosis affeithiol *eg* affective psychosis
seicosomatig *ans* psychosomatic
seicotiaeth *eb* psychoticism
seicotherapi *eg* psychotherapy
seicotherapi grŵp *eg* group psychotherapy
seicotherapi teuluol *eg* family psychotherapy
seidr *eg* seidrau cider
seiff *eg* seif
seiffr *eg* seiffrau cipher
seiliau gwerth *ell* value base
seiliedig ar *ans* based on
seiliedig ar ffurfiau geometrig *ans* based on geometrical shapes
seiliedig ar reolau *ans* rule-based
seiliedig ar wead *ans* based on texture
seilnod llanw *eg* seilnodau llanw tidal datum
seilnod ordnans *eg* seilnodau ordnans ordnance datum
seiloffon *eg* seiloffonau xylophone
seilorimba *eg* seilorimbau xylorimba
seimlyd *ans* greasy
seimonaidd *ans* simoniacal
seimoniaeth *eb* simony
seimonwr *eg* seimonwyr simonist
seimonydd *eg* seimonyddion simoniac
seindon *eb* seindonnau sound wave
seindwll *eg* seindyllau sound hole
seineg *eb* phonetics
seinflwch *eg* seinflychau sound box
seinfwrdd *eg* seinfyrddau sound board
seinfwrdd organ *eg* seinfyrddau organ organ sound board
seinglawr *eg* seingloriau manual
seiniau cyffwrdd *ell* contact sounds
seinlawnder *eg* seinlawnderau sonority
seinliwio *be* tone painting
seinlun *eg* seinluniau sound picture
seintwar *eb* seintwarau sanctuary
seinwedd *eb* seinweddau Klangforme
seinydd *eg* seinyddion speaker; loudspeaker
Seionaidd *ans* Zionist
Seioniaeth *eb* Zionism
Seionydd *eg* Seionyddion Zionist
seis *eg* size
seis aur *eg* gold size
seis gelatin *eg* gelatine size
seis glud *eg* glue size
seisio *be* size
seismig *ans* seismic
seismograff *eg* seismograffau seismograph
seismoleg *eb* seismology
seismonastedd *eg* seismonasty
Seisnigaidd *ans* Anglicized
Seisnigo (iaith, cymdeithas) *be* Anglicization
seithawd *eg* seithawdau septet
seithfed *eg* seithfedau seventh; one-seventh
seithfed arweiniol *eg* seithfedau arweiniol leading seventh
seithpled *eg* seithpledi septuplet
sêl *eb* seliau seal
Sêl Fawr *eb* Great Seal
Sêl Gyfrin *eb* Privy Seal
seladon *eg* celadon
seld *eb* seldiau sideboard
seleniwm *eg* selenium

seler *eb* seleri cellarium
seleri *eg* celery
selerwr *eg* selerwyr cellarer
selesta *eg* selestâu celesta
selfa *eg* selfâu selva
selfais *eg* selfeisiau selvage
selihot *ell* selihot
selio *be* seal
seliwr *eg* selwyr sealer
seliwr coed *eg* selwyr coed wood sealer
seliwr sielac *eg* shellac sealer
seloffan *eg* cellophane
seloffan lliw *eg* coloured cellophane
selot *eg* selotiaid zealot
sêm *eb* semau seam
sêm addurnol *eb* semau addurnol decorative seam
sêm agored *eb* semau agored open seam
sêm agored *eb* semau agored plain seam
sêm agored grom *eb* semau agored crwm curved open seam
sêm blyg *eb* semau plyg folded seam
sêm drosblyg *eb* semau trosblyg overlapped seam
sêm drosblyg *eb* semau trosblyg lapped seam
sêm ddeublyg *eb* semau deublyg double folded seam
sêm ffel ddwbl *eb* semau ffel dwbl double machine stitched seam; machine fell seam
sêm fflans *eb* semau fflans flanged seam
sêm fforch *eb* semau fforch crotch seam
sêm Ffrengig *eb* semau Ffrengig French seam
sêm lap *eb* semau lap lap seam
sêm lap gylchol *eb* semau lap cylchol circular lap seam
sêm orlap *eb* semau gorlap overfolded seam
sêm orlap gylchol *eb* semau gorlap cylchol circular overfolded seam
sêm rigolog *eb* semau rhigolog grooved seam
sêm wedi'i pheipio *eb* semau wedi'u peipio piped seam
sêm wlanen *eb* semau gwlanen flannel seam
semaffor *eg* semafforau semaphore
semanteg *eb* semantics
semen *eg* semen
semenol *ans* seminal
semenu artiffisial *be* artificial insemination
semicarbasaid *eg* semicarbazide
semicarbasaidiwm clorid *eg* semicarbazidium chloride
semicarbason *eg* semicarbazone
semio *be* seaming
semioleg *eb* semiology
Semitiaeth *eb* Semitism
senedd *eb* seneddau parliament; senate; legislature
Senedd Dda *eb* Good Parliament
Senedd Ddidostur *eb* Merciless Parliament
senedd faith *eb* long parliament
Senedd Glwc (1614) *eb* Addled Parliament
Senedd y Gweddill *eb* Rump Parliament
seneddol *ans* parliamentary
seneddwr (ym Mhrydain) *eg* seneddwyr parliamentarian
seneddwr (yn UDA) *eg* seneddwyr senator
senoffobia *eg* xenophobia
senoffobig *ans* xenophobic
senon (Xe) *eg* xenon
sensiteiddio cudd *be* covert sensitization
sensitif *ans* sensitive
sensitif i gyffyrddiad *ans* touch sensitive
sensitifedd *eg* sensitivity
sensitifedd *eg* irritability
sensitifrwydd *eg* sensitivity
sensor *eg* sensoriaid censor
sensoriaeth *eb* censorship
sentimental *ans* sentimental
senysgal *eg* senysgaliaid seneschal
seolit *eg* zeolite
seotrop *eg* zeotrope
sepal *eg* sepalau sepal
sepia *ans* sepia
sêr prif ddilyniant *ell* main sequence stars
serac *eg* seracau serac
sêr-addoliaeth *eb* astrolatry
serch *eg* serchiadau affection
sêr-ddewiniaeth *eb* astrology
sêr-ddewiniol *ans* astrological
seremoni *eb* seremonïau ceremony
seremoni graddio *eb* seremonïau graddio graduation ceremony
seren (ar bapur) *eb* sêr asterisk
seren (mewn dawns) *eb* sêr hands across
seren (yn gyffredinol) *eb* sêr star
seren ambegynol *eb* sêr ambegynol circumpolar star
Seren Dafydd *eb* Star of David
seren dymhorol *eb* sêr tymhorol seasonal star
seren ddwbl *eb* sêr dwbl binary star
seren gawr *eb* sêr cawr giant star
seren gorrach *eb* sêr corrach dwarf star
seren guriadol *eb* sêr curiadol pulsating star
seren llaw dde /chwith *eb* star
seren newidiol *eb* sêr newidiol variable star
seren orgawr *eb* super giant star
seren radio *eb* sêr radio radio star
seren wynt *eb* sêr gwynt windrose
seren y gogledd *eb* pole star
serenâd *eg* serenadau serenade
serenâd Eidalaidd *eg* serenadau Eidalaidd Italian serenade
serenadu *be* serenade
serennyn *eg* sêr squill
serennyn y gwanwyn *eg* sêr y gwanwyn spring squill
serf *eb* serfiau serve
serf gyntaf *eb* serfiau cyntaf first serve
serfiad *eg* sefiadau service

serfiad byr *eg* serfiadau byr short service
serfiad canon *eg* serfiadau canon cannon ball service
serfio *be* serve
serfio grymus *be* powerful serve
serfiwr *eg* serfwyr server
serfiwr *eg* serfwyr hand-in
sêr-fytholeg *eb* astro-mythology
serge *eg* serge
seriff *eb* seriffau serif
serin *eg* serine
sero *eg* seroau zero
sero absoliwt *eg* absolute zero
seroeiddio *be* zeroize
serofed *ans* zeroth
seroffyt *eg* seroffytau xerophyte
serograffig *ans* xerographic
serol *ans* astral
serol *ans* stellar
sero-lawn *ans* zero filled
sero-lenwi *be* zero fill
sero-lethedig *ans* zero suppressed
sero-lethiad *eg* sero-lethiadau zero suppression
seroser *eg* xerosere
serotherm *eg* xerotherm
serthiant *eg* degree of pitch
serthiant to *eg* roof pitch
serthochrog *ans* steepsided
serwm *eg* sera serum
serws *ans* serous
seryddiaeth *eb* astronomy
sesamwm *eg* sesamum
sesiwn *eb* sesiynau session
Sesiwn Fawr *eb* Great Sessions
sesiwn gweithgaredd grŵp *eb* group activity session
sesiwn gyffredinol *eg* sesiynau cyffredinol general session
sesiwn hyfforddi *eb* sesiynau hyfforddi training session
sesiwn lawn *eb* sesiynau llawn plenary session
seston *eb* sestonau cistern
seston ddŵr *eb* sestonau dŵr water cistern
set *eb* setiau set
set a snap rhybed cyfunol combined rivet set and snap
set ar hyd *eb* setiau ar hyd longways set
set boeth *eb* setiau poeth hot set
set cyfarwyddiadau cymhleth *eb* setiau cyfarwyddiadau cymhleth complex instruction set
set deledu *eb* setiau teledu television set
set ddata *eb* setiau data data set
set ddatrysiad *eb* setiau datrysiad solution set
set ddeubar *eb* setiau deubar duple minor set
set eglur o werthoedd *eb* clear set of values
set fanwl *eb* setiau manwl detail scenery
set gau *eb* setiau cau hollow set
set gyfarwyddiadau *eb* setiau cyfarwyddiadau instruction set
set gyfunol *eb* setiau cyfunol combination set
set gynhwysol *eb* setiau cynhwysol universal set
set law *eb* setiau llaw handset
set niwlog *eb* setiau niwlog fuzzy set
set nodau *eb* setiau nodau character set
set nodau gweithredol *eb* setiau nodau gweithredol active character set
set o bibau *eb* setiau o bibau rank
set o ddata *eb* setiau o ddata set of data
set o gardiau tyllog *eb* setiau o gardiau tyllog set of punched cards
set o gyfarwyddiadau *eb* setiau o gyfarwyddiadau set of instructions
set o werthoedd cyffredin *eb* set of common values
set o wrthrychau *eb* setiau o wrthrychau set of objects
set oer *eb* setiau oer cold set
set rybed *eb* setiau rhybed rivet set
set sengl *eb* setiau sengl single set
set sgwâr *eb* setiau sgwâr square set
set wag *eb* setiau gwag null set
setiau cywerth *ell* equivalent sets
setiau digyswllt *ell* disjoint sets
setio *be* set
setio staen *be* stain setting
setliad *eg* settlement
sewa / seva *eg* sewa / seva
sffalerit *eg* sphalerite
sffêr *eg* sfferau sphere
sffêr wybrennol *eg* celestial sphere
sfferig *ans* spherical
sfferoid *eg* sfferoidau spheroid
sfferoidol *ans* spheroidal
sfferomedr *eg* sfferomedrau spherometer
sffincter *eg* sffinctrau sphincter
sffincter capilari *eg* capillary sphincter
sgafell gyfandirol *eb* sgafelli cyfandirol continental shelf
sgafell iâ *eb* sgafelli iâ ice shelf
sgafell rew *eb* sgafelli rhew ice shelf
sgaffald *eg* sgaffaldau scaffold
sgaffaldio *be* scaffolding
sgalar *ans* scalar
sgalar *eg* sgalarau scalar
sgaldanu *be* scalding
sgaldiad *eg* sgaldiadau scald
sgan *eg* sganiau scan
sgandal *eg* sgandalau scandal
sganio *be* scan
sganio'r ymennydd *be* brain scanning
sganiwr *eg* sganwyr scanner
sganiwr firysau *eg* virus scanner
sganiwr laser *eg* sganwyr laser laser scanner
sgapwlar *eg* sgapwlarau scapular
sgarff *eg/b* sgarffiau scarf

sgarffio *be* scarf
sgarlad cadmiwm *eg* cadmium scarlet
sgarmes *eb* sgarmesoedd maul
sgarmes rydd *eb* sgarmesoedd rhydd loose maul
sgarp *eg* sgarpiau escarpment
sgarp *eg* sgarpiau scarp
sgarp ffawt *eg* sgarpiau ffawt scarp fault
sgarp mewnwynebol *eg* sgarpiau mewnwynebol infacing scarp
sgarpdir *eg* sgarpdiroedd scarpland
sgein *eg* sgeiniau skein
sgeintydd *eg* sgeintyddion dredger
sgema *eg* sgemâu schema
sgematig *ans* schematic
sgerbwd *eg* sgerbydau carcass
sgerbwd allanol *eg* sgerbydau allanol exoskeleton
sgerbwd atodol *eg* sgerbydau atodol appendicular skeleton
sgerbwd crog *eg* sgerbydau crog hanging carcass
sgerbwd echelinol *eg* sgerbydau echelinol axial skeleton
sgerbwd mamolaidd *eg* sgerbydau mamolaidd mammalian skeleton
sgerbwd mewnol *eg* sgerbydau mewnol endoskeleton
sgerbwd rhydd-sefyll *eg* sgerbydau rhydd-sefyll free-standing carcass
sgeri *eg* sgerïau skerry
sgert *eb* sgertiau skirt
sgert baneli *eb* sgertiau paneli panelled skirt
sgert bletiog *eb* sgertiau pletiog pleated skirt
sgert fflêr *eb* sgertiau fflêr flared skirt
sgert gôr *eb* sgertiau gôr gored skirt
sgert grychog *eb* sgertiau crychog gathered skirt
sgert gul *eb* sgertiau cul pencil slim skirt
sgert gylch *eb* sgertiau cylch circular skirt
sgert lapio *eb* sgertiau lapio wrap-over skirt
sgert linell A *eb* sgertiau llinell A A line skirt
sgert renciog *eb* sgertiau rhenciog tiered skirt
sgert syth *eb* sgertiau syth straight skirt
sgifer *eg* skiver
sgìl *eg* sgiliau skill
sgìl algebraidd *eg* sgiliau algebraidd algebraic skill
sgìl arsylwi *eg* sgiliau arsylwi observation skill
sgìl arsylwi *eg* sgiliau arsylwi observational skill
sgìl crefft *eg* sgiliau crefft craft skill
sgìl cydbwyso *eg* sgiliau cydbwyso balancing skill
sgìl cyfathrebu *eg* sgiliau cyfathrebu communication skill
sgìl cymdeithasol *eg* sgiliau cymdeithasol social skill
sgìl cynhyrchu technegol *eg* sgiliau cynhyrchu technegol technical production skill
sgìl dramatig *eg* dramatic skill
sgil effaith *eb* sgil effeithiau side-effect
sgìl gwasanaeth i gwsmeriaid *eg* sgiliau gwasanaeth i gwsmeriaid customer service skill
sgil gynnyrch *eg* sgil gynhyrchion by-product
sgil gynnyrch *eg* sgil gynhyrchion side product
sgìl llawdriniol *eg* sgiliau llawdriniol manipulative skill
sgìl seicoechddygol *eg* sgiliau seicoechddygol psychomotor skill
sgìl sylfaenol *eg* sgiliau sylfaenol basic skill
sgìl symud *eg* sgiliau symud motor skill
sgiliau byw *ell* life skills
sgiliau cymdeithasol *ell* social skills
sgiliau cymhleth *ell* complex skills
sgiliau dawnsio gwerin *ell* folk dancing skills
sgiliau diogelwch yn y dŵr *ell* skills of water safety
sgiliau echddygol bras *ell* gross motor skills
sgiliau echddygol manwl *ell* fine motor skills
sgiliau generig *ell* generic skills
sgiliau iaith *ell* language skills
sgiliau llawdrin bras *ell* gross manipulative skills
sgiliau llawdrin manwl *ell* fine manipulative skills
sgiliau mesur *ell* skills in measuring
sgiliau rheoli *ell* managerial skills
sgiliau rhyngbersonol *ell* interpersonal skills
sgiliau trefnu *ell* organizational skills
sgiliau ymdopi *ell* coping skills
sgiliau ysgrifennu *ell* writing skills
sgimio *be* skim
sgimiwr *eg* sgimwyr skimmer
sgip *eb* skip
sgipio *be* skip
sgism *eg* sgismau schism
Sgism Mawr *eg* Great Schism
Sgism y Babaeth *eg* Papal Schism
sgismatig *ans* schismatic
sgist *eg* sgistau schist
sgistedd *eg* schistosity
sgitsocarp *eg* sgitsocarpau schizocarp
sgitsoffrenia *eg* schizophrenia
sgitsoffrenia adweithiol *eg* reactive schizophrenia
sgitsoffrenia anhrefnus *eg* disorganised schizophrenia
sgitsoffrenia catatonig *eg* catatonic schizophrenia
sgitsoffrenia diwahaniaeth *eg* undifferentiated schizophrenia
sgitsoffrenia paranoid *eg* paranoid schizophrenia
sgitsoffrenia proses *eg* process schizophrenia
sgiw *ans* skew
sgiw *eb* sgiwiau skew
sgiw bositif *eb* sgiwiau positif positive skew
sgiw negatif *eb* negative skew
sgiwedd *eg* skewness
sgiwen *eb* sgiwennod skua
sgiwen gynffondro *eb* sgiwennod cynffondro pomarine skua
sgiwen lostfain *eb* sgiwennod llostfain long-tailed skua
sgiwen y gogledd *eb* sgiwennod y gogledd artic skua
sglefren fôr *eb* sglefrod môr jelly-fish
sglein *ans* glazed

sglein *ans* mercerized
sglein *eg* sgleiniau shine
sglein *eg* gloss
sglein *eg* sgleiniau glaze
sglein parhaol *eg* everglaze
sglein resin *eg* resin glaze
sgleiniad *eg* mercerization
sgleinio *be* glaze
sgleinio *be* shine
sgleiniog *ans* glossy
sglera *eg* sclera
sglerencyma *eg* sclerenchyma
sglerosis *eg* sclerosis
sglerotig *ans* sclerotic
sglerws *ans* sclerous
sglodi *be* chip
sglodion *ell* chipped potatoes
sglodion enamel *ell* enamel chips
sglodion marmor *ell* marble chips
sglodyn *eg* sglodion chip
sglodyn cof *eg* sglodion cof memory chip
sglodyn electronig *eg* sglodion electronig electronic chip
sgol *eg* sgoliau squall
sgolastig *ans* scholastic
sgolastigiaeth *eb* scholasticism
sgolecs *eg* scolex
sgolop *eg* sgolopiau scallop
sgolop wedi'i weithio *eg* sgolopiau wedi'u gweithio worked scalloping
sgolop wedi'i wynebu *eg* sgolopiau wedi'u hwynebu faced scalloping
sgolopio *be* scallop
sgôr *eb* sgorau score
sgôr agored *eb* sgorau agored open score
sgôr biano *eb* sgorau piano piano score
sgôr boced *eb* sgorau poced miniature score
sgôr fer *eb* sgorau byrion short score
sgôr fras *eb* sgorau bras skeleton score
sgôr graffig *eb* sgorau graffig graphic score
sgôr gymedrig *eb* mean score
sgôr lawn *eb* sgorau llawn full score
sgôr safonol *eb* sgorau safonol standard score
sgorbwtig *ans* scorbutic
sgorio (ar gyfer cerddorfa) *be* orchestrate
sgorio (yn gyffredinol) *be* score
sgorio cais *be* score a try
sgorio gôl *be* score a goal
sgoriwr (ar gyfer cerddorfa) *eg* sgorwyr orchestrator
sgoriwr (yn gyffredinol) *eg* sgorwyr scorer
sgorper *eg* sgorperau scorper
sgotia *eg* scotia
sgrafell *eb* sgrafelli scraper
sgrafell dairongl *eb* sgrafelli tairongl triangular scraper
sgrafell gabinet *eb* sgrafelli cabinet cabinet scraper
sgrafell goed *eb* sgrafelli coed wood scraper
sgrafell grom *eb* sgrafelli crwm curved scraper
sgrafell hanner crwn *eb* sgrafelli hanner crwn half round scraper
sgrafell law *eb* sgrafelli llaw hand scraper
sgrafelliad *eg* sgrafelliadau abrasion
sgrafellog *ans* abraded
sgrafellu *be* scrape
sgrafellu *be* abrade
sgraffiniad *eg* sgraffiniadau abrasion
sgraffiniol *ans* abrasive
sgraffinydd *eg* sgraffinyddion abrasive
sgraffito *eg* sgraffito
sgraffwrdd *eg* sgraffyrddau scraperboard
sgrap *eg* sgrapiau scrap
sgri *eg* sgrïau scree
sgri bloc *eg* sgrïau bloc block scree
sgriblo *be* scrawl
sgriblo *be* scribble
sgrifell *eb* sgrifelli scriber
sgrifellu *be* scribe
sgrim *eg* scrim
sgrin *eb* sgriniau screen
sgrin agoriadol *eb* sgriniau agoriadol title screen
sgrin arddangos *eb* sgriniau arddangos display screen
sgrin blygu *eb* sgriniau plygu fold-down screen
sgrin destun *eb* sgriniau testun text screen
sgrin ddilys *eb* sgriniau dilys valid screen
sgrin ddiogelu *eb* sgriniau diogelu safety screen
sgrin ddynamig *eb* sgriniau dynamig dynamic screen
sgrin gefn *eb* sgriniau cefn back screen
sgrin gludadwy *eb* sgriniau cludadwy portable screen
sgrin gyffwrdd *eb* sgriniau cyffwrdd touch screen
sgrin lydan *eb* sgriniau llydan widescreen
sgrin ragarweiniol *eb* sgriniau rhagarweiniol introductory screen
sgrin sidan *eb* sgriniau sidan silkscreen
sgrin statig *eb* sgriniau statig static screen
sgrin Stevenson *eb* sgriniau Stevenson Stevenson screen
sgrin wynt *eb* sgriniau gwynt windscreen
sgrin-brintio *be* screen-printing
sgriniad *eg* sgrineidiau screenful
sgrinio *be* screening
sgrinio iechyd *be* health screening
sgrinlun *eg* sgrinluniau screenshot
sgrin-olygydd *eg* sgrin-olygyddion full screen editor
sgript *eb* sgriptiau script
sgript ffilm *eb* sgriptiau ffilm screenplay
sgript oliwiedig *eb* sgriptiau goliwiedig illuminated script
sgriptoriwm *eg* sgriptoria scriptorium
sgriw *eb* sgriwiau screw

sgriw alwminiwm *eb* sgriwiau alwminiwm aluminium screw
sgriw Allen *eb* sgriwiau Allen Allen screw
sgriw atredu *eb* sgriwiau atredu off-setting screw
sgriw beiriant *eb* sgriwiau peiriant machine screw
sgriw belt *eb* sgriwiau belt belt screw
sgriw ben cap *eb* sgriwiau pen cap caphead screw
sgriw ben hecsagonol *eb* sgriwiau pen hecsagonol hexagonal head screw
sgriw bencosyn *eb* sgriwiau pencosyn cheese-head screw
sgriw bengron *eb* sgriwiau pengrwn roundhead screw
sgriw ben-seren *eb* sgriwiau pen-seren star-head screw
sgriw bensgwar *eb* sgriwiau pensgwar square head screw
sgriw bren *eb* sgriwiau pren wood screw
sgriw bres *eb* sgriwiau pres brass screw
sgriw chwil *eb* sgriwiau chwil drunken screw
sgriw dywys *eb* sgriwiau tywys lead screw
sgriw ddigopa *eb* sgriwiau digopa grub-screw
sgriw ddur *eb* sgriwiau dur steel screw
sgriw ddur wrthstaen *eb* sgriwiau dur gwrthstaen stainless steel screw
sgriw edau ddeuben *eb* sgriwiau edau deuben double-headed screw
sgriw fawd *eb* sgriwiau bawd thumbscrew
sgriw fenyw *eb* sgriwiau benyw female screw
sgriw ffurfio edau *eb* sgriwiau ffurfio edau thread-forming screw
sgriw glampio *eb* sgriwiau clampio clamping screw
sgriw goets *eb* sgriwiau coets coach screw
sgriw gopog *eb* sgriwiau copog raised head screw
sgriw gopr *eb* sgriwiau copr copper screw
sgriw goprog *eb* sgriwiau coprog coppered screw
sgriw gromiwm *eb* sgriwiau cromiwm chromium screw
sgriw gwlwm *eb* sgriwiau cwlwm tie-off screw
sgriw gyfeirio *eb* sgriwiau cyfeirio guide screw
sgriw gymhwyso *eb* sgriwiau cymhwyso adjusting screw
sgriw hunandapio *eb* sgriwiau hunandapio self-tapping screw
sgriw law *eb* sgriwiau llaw hand screw
sgriw lygad *eb* sgriwiau llygad screw eye
sgriw llaw chwith *eb* sgriwiau llaw chwith left-hand screw
sgriw neilon *eb* sgriwiau neilon nylon screw
sgriw nwrl *eb* sgriwiau nwrl knurled screw
sgriw Pozidrive *eb* sgriwiau Pozidrive Pozidrive screw
sgriw set *eb* sgriwiau set set screw
sgriw sicrhau *eb* sgriwiau sicrhau fastening screw
sgriw soced *eb* sgriwiau soced socket screw
sgriw torri edau *eb* sgriwiau torri edau thread-cutting screw
sgriw wrthrwd *eb* sgriwiau gwrthrwd rustless screw
sgriw wrthsodd *eb* sgriwiau gwrthsodd countersunk screw
sgriwglwm *ans* screw-bound
sgriwio *be* screw
sgriwio cudd *be* secret screwing
sgriwio poced *be* pocket screwing
sgrôl *eg* sgroliau scroll
sgrôl 'C' /'S' *eb* 'C' /'S' scroll
sgrôl cynffon pysgodyn *eb* sgroliau cynffon pysgodyn fish-tail scroll
sgrôl pen rhuban *eb* sgroliau pen rhuban ribbon-end scroll
sgrolio *be* scroll
sgrolio fertigol *be* vertical scroll
sgrolio i fyny tudalen neu i lawr *be* scroll a page up or a page down
sgrolio llorweddol *be* horizontal scroll
sgrwbio *be* scrub
sgrym *eb* sgrymiau scrum
sgrym osod *eb* sgrymiau gosod set scrum
sgrym rydd *eb* sgrymiau rhydd loose scrum
sgrymio *be* scrum
sgrytiad *eg* sgrytiadau chatter
sgrytian *be* chatter
sgrytian erfyn *be* tool chatter
sgwadron *eb* sgwadronau squadron
sgwâr *ans* square
sgwâr *eg* sgwariau square
sgwâr blwch *eg* sgwariau blwch box square
sgwâr canoli *eg* sgwariau canoli centre square
sgwâr cant *eg* hundred square
sgwâr cryfhau *eg* sgwariau cryfhau reinforcing square
sgwâr cyfunol *eg* sgwariau cyfunol combination square
sgwâr cyffredinol *eg* sgwariau cyffredinol universal square
sgwâr cymedrig *eg* mean square
sgwâr Lladin cytbwys *eg* balanced Latin square
sgwâr marchnad *eg* market square
sgwâr meitro *eg* sgwariau meitro mitre square
sgwâr optegol *eg* sgwariau optegol optical square
sgwâr peiriannydd *eg* sgwariau peiriannydd engineer's square
sgwâr perffaith *eg* sgwariau perffaith perfect square
sgwâr profi *eg* sgwariau profi try square
sgwâr serfio *eg* sgwariau serfio serving square; serving box
sgwario *be* square; square up
sgwariog *ans* checkered
sgwarog *ans* gridiron
sgwaronglog *ans* right-angled
sgwaryn *eg* sgwarynnau set square
sgwatiwr *eg* sgwatwyr squatter
sgwigl *eg/b* sgwiglau squiggle
sgwl dwbl *eg* sgyliau dwbl double scull
sgwlio *be* scull

sgwmbl *eg* sgymblau scumble
sgwmblo *be* scumble
sgŵp *eg* sgwpiau scoop
sgwpio *be* scoop
sgwrfa llanw *eg* tidal scour
sgwriad *eg* sgwriadau scouring
sgwrio *be* scour
sgwrs *eb* sgyrsiau conversation
sgwrs aelwyd *eb* sgyrsiau aelwyd fireside chat
sgwrydd *eg* sgwryddion scourer
sgwtelwm *eg* scutellum
sgyrtin *eg* sgyrtinau skirting
Shabbat *eg* Sabath
Shahadah *eg* Shahadah
Shaiviaeth /Śaiviaeth *eg* Shaivism/Śaivism
shantung *eg* shantung
Shari'ah *eg* Shari'ah
Shavuot *eg* Shavuot
shawm *eg* shawms shawm
Shi'ah *eg* Shi'ah
shiffon *eg* chiffon
shifft dydd *eg* shiftiau dydd day shift
shifft nos *eg* night shift
shirk *eg* shirk
Shiva /Śiva *eg* Shiva /Śiva
Shiva Nataraja *eg* Shiva Nataraja
Shudra /Śudra *eg* Shudra /Śudra
siaced *eb* siacedi jacket
siaced achub *eb* siacedi achub life jacket
siaced lwch *eb* siacedi llwch book jacket
siaced wely *eb* siacedi gwely bed jacket
siadwff *eg* siadwffau shaduf
siafft *eb* siafftiau shaft
siafft borthi *eb* siafftau porthi feed shaft
siafft daprog *eb* siafftau taprog tapered shaft
siafft gymhwyso bwrdd *eb* siafftiau cymhwyso byrddau table adjustment shaft
siafft yrru *eb* siafftiau gyrru prop shaft
siâl *eg* sialau shale
sialc *eg* sialciau chalk
sialc di-lwch *eg* anti-dust chalk
sialc Ffrengig *eg* French chalk
sialc gwyn *eg* white chalk
sialc lliw *eg* sialciau lliw coloured chalk
sialc llythrennu *eg* lettering chalk
sialc teiliwr *eg* tailor's chalk
sialcio *be* chalk
siambr *eb* siambrau chamber
siambr archwilio *eb* siambrau archwilio inspection chamber
siambr danio *eb* siambrau tanio firing chamber
siambr ddewis *eb* choice chamber
siambr gladdu *eb* siambrau claddu burial chamber
Siambr Gyfrin *eb* Privy Chamber
siambr wactod *eb* siambrau gwactod vacuum chamber
siambr weithredol *eb* siambrau gweithredol operant chamber
siambr wely *eb* siambrau gwely bed chamber
Siambr y Seren *eb* Star Chamber
Siambr Ymerodraeth *eb* Imperial Chamber
Siambrau Ailuniad *ell* Chambers of Reunion
siambrlen *eg* siambrleniaid chamberlain
siamffer *eg* siamfferi chamfer
siamffer addurnol *eg* siamffrau addurnol decorative chamfer
siamffer cau *eg* siamfferi cau stopped chamfer
siamffer trwodd *eg* siamfferi trwodd through chamfer
siamffer wagen *eg* siamfferi wagen wagon chamfer
siamffro *be* chamfer
siamffrog *ans* chamfered
siami *eg* chamois
siandler *eg* siandleriaid chandler
sianel *eb* sianeli channel
sianel betryal *eb* sianeli petryal rectangular channel
sianel cyfathrebu ffurfiol *eb* sianeli cyfathrebu ffurfiol formal channel of communication
sianel cymorth *eb* sianeli cymorth help channel
sianel danrewlifol *eb* sianeli tanrewlifol subglacial channel
sianel darllen ac ysgrifennu *eb* sianeli darllen ac ysgrifennu read /write channel
sianel dosbarthu *eb* sianeli dosbarthu distribution channel
sianel ddata *eb* sianeli data data channel
sianel fordwyo *eb* sianeli mordwyo fairway
sianel gyfathrebu *eb* sianeli cyfathrebu communication channel
sianel hanner cylch *eb* sianeli hanner cylch semicircular canal
sianel Havers *eb* sianeli Havers Haversian canal
sianel iâ ymylol *eb* sianeli iâ ymylol ice marginal channel
sianel ïonau *eb* sianeli ïonau ion channel
sianel orlif *eb* sianeli gorlif overflow channel
sianel rew ymylol *eb* sianeli rhew ymylol ice marginal channel
Sianel San Siôr *eb* Saint George's Channel
sianel wybodaeth *eb* sianeli gwybodaeth information channel
sianelu *be* channel
siani nyddu *eb* spinning jenny
siant *eb* siantiau chant
siant Ambrosaidd *eb* siantiau Ambrosaidd Ambrosian chant
siant Anglicanaidd *eb* siantiau Anglicanaidd Anglican chant
siant Fysantaidd *eb* siantiau Bysantaidd Byzantine chant
siantio *be* chant
siantri *eg* siantrïau chantry
siâp *eg* siapiau shape
siâp a daflwyd *eg* siapiau a daflwyd thrown shape

siâp cyfansawdd *eg* siapiau cyfansawdd compound shape
siâp cywir *eg* siapiau cywir accurate shape
siâp dysglog *eg* siapiau dysglog dished shape
siâp ffiol *eg* siapiau ffiol vase shape
siâp geometrig *eg* siapiau geometrig geometric shape
siâp melodig *eg* siapiau melodig melodic shape
siâp polygon *eg* siapiau polygon polygon shape
siâp syml *eg* siapiau syml simple shape
siapio *be* shape
siapio clai *be* shaping clay
siarad syml â phlant *be* motherese
siarad yn eich cwsg *be* sleeptalking
siaradwr *eg* siaradwyr speaker
siaradwr gwadd *eg* siaradwyr gwadd guest speaker
siarc *eg* siarcod shark
siarc mawr gwyn *eg* siarcod mawr gwyn great white shark
siarcol *eg* charcoal
siarcol braslunio *eg* sketching charcoal
siarcol gwinwydd *eg* vine charcoal
siarcol helyg *eg* willow charcoal
Siarl Dda *eg* Charles the Good
Siarl Ddewr *eg* Charles the Bold
Siarl Fawr *eg* Charles the Great
Siarl Foel *eg* Charles the Bald
Siarlymaen *eg* Charlemagne
siars *eb* siarsiau admonition
siarsio *be* admonish
siart *eg* siartiau chart
siart adennill costau *eg* siartiau adennill costau break even chart
siart awtofformat *eg* siartiau awtofformat autoformat chart
siart bar *eg* siartiau bar bar chart
siart bloc *eg* siartiau bloc block chart
siart canraddau *eg* siartiau canraddau centile chart
siart colofnau *eg* siartiau colofnau column chart
siart cyfrif *eg* siartiau cyfrif tally chart
siart cylch *eg* siartiau cylch pie chart; circle chart
siart datblygiad *eg* siartiau datblygiad development chart
siart Gannt *eg* siartiau Gannt Gannt chart
siart llif *eg* siartiau llif flowchart
siart llif systemau *eg* siartiau llif systemau systems flowchart
siart llinell *eg* siartiau llinell line chart
siart lliwiau *eg* siartiau lliwiau colour chart
siart rheoli *eg* siartiau rheoli organization chart
siart sgôr apgar *eg* siartiau sgôr apgar apgar score chart
siart synoptig *eg* siartiau synoptig synoptic chart
siart trefniadaeth *eg* siartiau trefniadaeth organization chart
siart trefniadaeth *eg* siartiau trefniadaeth organizational chart
siart troi *eg* siartiau troi flip chart
siartaeth *eb* chartism
siarter *eg/b* siarterau charter
siarter hawliau *eg* siarterau hawliau rights charter
siarter rhieni *eg* siarterau rhieni parent's charter
siarter rhyddfreinio *eg* siarterau rhyddfreinio charter of enfranchisement
Siarter y Bobl *eg* People's Charter
Siarter y Claf *eg* patient's charter
Siarter y Plant *eg* Children's Charter, The
Siarter yr Iwerydd *eg* Atlantic Charter
siartydd *eg* siartwyr chartist
siasi *eg* siasïau chassis
siasin *eg* siasinau chasing
siasio *be* chasing
siaswr *eg* siaswyr chaser
siaswr edafedd *eg* siaswyr edafedd thread chaser
siawns *eb* siawnsiau chance
siawns deg *eb* evens
siawns deg *eb* siawnsiau teg even chance
Siawnsri *eg* Chancery
sibrwd *be* whisper
sibrwd *eg* sibrydion whisper
sicori *eg* chicory
sicr *ans* certain
sicrhau (=clymu) *be* affix
sicrhau (yn gyffredinol) *be* ensure
► **sicrhau ansawdd** *eg* quality assurance
sicrhau top bwrdd *be* table-top fixing
sicrwydd *eg* security; assurance
sicrwydd daliadaeth *eg* security of tenure
sicrwydd daliadaeth *eg* fixity of tenure
sidan *eg* sidanau silk
sidan crai *eg* raw silk
sidan gwneud *eg* artificial silk
sidan gwyllt *eg* wild silk
sidan jap *eg* jap silk
sidan rib *eg* sidanau rib grosgrain
sidaniaeth *eb* sericulture
sidell *eb* sidelli whorl
sidellog *ans* whorled
sideru *be* lacemaking
Sidydd *eg* Zodiac
siec *ans* check
siec *eb* sieciau cheque
siec agored *eb* sieciau agored open cheque
siec wag *eb* sieciau gwag blank cheque
siec wedi'i chroesi *eb* sieciau wedi'u croesi crossed cheque
siêd *eg* siedau escheat
siedu *be* escheat
siedwr *eg* siedwyr escheator
Sieffre o Fynwy *eg* Geoffrey of Monmouth
sielac *eg* shellac
sielac gwyn *eg* white shellac
sielac oren *eg* orange shellac
sielo *eg* sieloau cello
sielydd *eg* sielyddion cellist; violoncellist

sienna crai *eg* raw sienna
sienna llosg *eg* burnt sienna
sierardeiddio *be* sherardize
sifalri *eg* chivalry
sifil *ans* civil
sifiliad *eg* sifiliaid civilian
siffon *eg* siffonau siphon
siffon allanadlu *eg* siffonau allanadlu exhalant siphon
siffon mewnanadlu *eg* siffonau mewnanadlu inhalant siphon
sigl adenydd *eg* siglion adenydd see-saw
siglen (=cors) *eb* siglennydd quagmire
siglen (=sedd ar raff) *eb* siglenni swing
siglo *be* swing
siglo ar raff *be* swing on a rope
Siglwr *eg* Siglwyr Shaker
siglydd (post offer) *eg* siglyddion rocket
signal *eg* signalau signal
signal analog *eg* analogue signal
signal cloc *eg* signalau cloc clock signal
signal digidol *eg* signalau digidol digital signal
signal galluogi *eg* signalau galluogi enabling signal
signwm *eg* signa signum
Singspiel *eg* Singspiele Singspiel
Sikh *eg/b* Sikhiaid Sikh
sikhaidd *ans* Sikh
Sikhiaeth *eb* Sikhism
sil (=math o bysgodyn) *eg* silod spawn
sil (=silff ffenestr etc) *eg* siliau sill
silan *eg* silane
silfa *eb* silfeydd spawning area
silff *eb* silffoedd shelf
silff ben tân *eb* silffoedd pen tân mantelpiece
silff fantell *eb* silffoedd mantell mantel shelf
silff ffenestr *eb* silffoedd ffenestri window-sill
silff gymwysadwy *eb* silffoedd cymwysadwy adjustable shelf
silff lyfrau *eb* silffoedd llyfrau bookshelf
silff odyn *eb* silffoedd odyn kiln shelf
silff rigolog *eb* silffoedd rhigolog housed shelf
silff sefydlog *eb* silffoedd sefydlog fixed shelf
silica *eg* silicâu silica
silica sychu *eg* silica gel
silicad *eg* silicate
silicôn *eg* siliconau silicone
silicon (Si) *eg* silicon
silicon deuocsid *eg* silicon dioxide
silicon tetraclorid *eg* silicon tetrachloride
silicon(IV) ocsid *eg* silicon(IV) oxide
silicwa *eg* siliqua
silimanit P.B. *eg* P.B. silimanite
silindr *eg* silindrau cylinder
silindr arosgo *eg* silindrau arosgo oblique cylinder
silindr blaendor *eg* silindrau blaendor truncated cylinder
silindr brêc *eg* silindrau brêc brake cylinder
silindr cylch *eg* silindrau cylch circular cylinder
silindr gweithrediad-dwbl *eg* silindrau gweithrediad-dwbl double-acting cylinder
silindr mesur *eg* silindrau mesur measuring cylinder
silindr nwy *eg* silindrau nwy gas cylinder
silindr peiriant *eg* silindrau peiriant engine cylinder
silindrog *ans* cylindrical
silindroid *eg* silindroidau cylindroid
silio *be* spawn
silt *eg* silt
siltio *be* silt
silwét *eg* silwetau silhouette
Silwraidd *ans* Silurian
sillaf diystyr *eg* sillafau diystyr nonsense syllable
sillafu *be* spell
sillafu cronnus *be* cumulative spelling
sillafu noddedig *be* sponsored spell
simbalom *eg* simbalomau cimbalom
simbalom *eg* simbalomau zimbalom
simnai *eb* simneiau chimney
simnai gytbwys *eb* simneiau cytbwys balance flue
simplecs *eg* simplex
simwm *eg* simoom
sin *eg* sinau sine
sinamon *eg* cinnamon
sinc (ar gyfer golchi) *eg* sinciau sink
sinc (Zn) *eg* zinc
sinc blend *eg* zinc blende
sinc carbonad (calamin) *eg* zinc carbonate (calamine)
sinc clorid *eg* zinc chloride
sinc ocsid *eg* zinc oxide
sinc silicad *eg* zinc silicate
sinema aml-sgrîn *eg* multiplex cinema
sinffonia *eg* sinffonïau sinfonia
sinffonieta *eb* sinffonietau sinfonietta
sinh *eg* sinh
sinter *eg* sinter
sinteru *be* sinter
sinws *eg* sinysau sinus
sinws creuol *eg* sinysau creuol orbital sinus
sinwsoid *eg* sinusoid
sinwsoidaidd *ans* sinusoidal
sioc *eb* siociau shock
sioc anaffylactig *eb* anaphylactic shock
sioc drydan *eb* siociau trydan electric shock
sioc laddwr *eg* sioc laddwyr shock absorber
siocled *eg* chocolate
siocled yfed *eg* drinking chocolate
sioe *eb* sioeau show
sioe gerdd *eb* sioeau cerdd musical
sioe siarad *eb* talk show
siofiniaeth *eb* chauvinism
siôl *eb* sioliau shawl
siop *eb* siopau shop; store
siop adrannol *eb* siopau adrannol department store

siop annibynnol *eb* independent shop
siop arbenigol *eb* siopau arbenigol specialist shop
siop bapurau *eb* siopau papurau newsagent
siop bob peth *eb* siopau pob peth general store
siop deithiol *eb* siopau teithiol mobile shop
siop drwyddedig *eb* siopau trwyddedig off licence
siop dryc *eb* siopau tryc tommy-shop
siop dryc *eb* siopau tryc truck shop
siop ddisgownt *eb* siopau disgownt discount store
siop ddodrefn *eb* siopau dodrefn furniture store
siop fideo *eb* video shop
siop ffatri *eb* siopau ffatri factory shop
siop gadwyn *eb* siopau cadwyn chain store
siop gadwyn *eb* siopau cadwyn multiple store
siop gaeedig *eb* siopau caeedig closed shop
siop gangen *eb* siopau cangen branch shop
siop gydweithredol *eb* siopau cydweithredol cooperative shop
siop gyfanwerthu *eb* siopau cyfanwerthu wholesale store
siop hen bethau *eb* siopau hen bethau antique shop
siop hunanwasanaeth *eb* siopau hunanwasanaeth self-service store
siop lysiau *eb* siopau llysiau greengrocer
siop llogi fideos *eb* video renting shop
siop nwyddau metel *eb* siopau nwyddau metel hardware shop
siop prydau parod *eb* siopau prydau parod takeaway
siop rhentu fideos *eb* video rental store
siop talu a chludo *eb* siopau talu a chludo cash and carry shop
siopa o'r cartref *be* home shopping
Sioraidd *ans* Georgian
siorts *ell* shorts
sip *eg* sipiau zip
sip cudd *eg* sipiau cudd invisible zip
sipell *eb* sipelli zipper foot
sipsi *eg* sipsiwn gypsy
sir *eb* siroedd county; shire
sirconiwm (Zr) *eg* zirconium
siroco *eg* sirocos sirocco
siryf *eg* siryfion sheriff
siryfiaeth *eb* shrievalty
Sistersaidd *ans* Cistercian
Sistersiad *eg* Sistersiaid Cistercian
siswrn *eg* sisyrnau scissors
siswrn brodio *eg* sisyrnau brodio embroidery scissors
siswrn canolig *eg* sisyrnau canolig medium size scissors
siswrn pig crwn *eg* sisyrnau pig crwn roundhead scissors
siswrn pigfain *eg* sisyrnau pigfain pointed scissors
siswrn pincio *eg* sisyrnau pincio pinking scissors
siswrn torri defnydd *eg* sisyrnau torri defnydd cutting-out scissors
siswrn twll botwm *eg* sisyrnau twll botwm buttonhole scissors
Sita *eb* Sita
sitar *eg* sitarau sitar
siten ddur meddal gloyw wedi'i rholio'n oer a'i hanelio'n oer *eb* sitiau dur meddal gloyw wedi'u rholio'n oer a'u hanelio'n oer C.R.C.A. sheet
sitern *eg* siternau cittern
sither *eg* sitherau zither
Siwan *eb* Joan
siwgr *eg* siwgrau sugar
siwgr betys *eg* beet sugar
siwgr cansen *eg* cane sugar
siwgr coch *eg* brown sugar
siwgr coeth *eg* refined sugar
siwgr gwaed *eg* blood sugar
siwgr gwrthdroëdig *eg* invert sugar
siwgr mân *eg* caster sugar
siwgr meddal *eg* brown sugar
siwmper *eb* siwmperi jumper
siwmper wen *eb* siwmperi gwyn white jumper
siwt undarn *eb* siwtiau undarn jump suit
siwt wedi'i theilwra *eb* siwtiau wedi'u teilwra tailored suit
siwtin *eg* suiting
siynt *eg* siyntiau shunt
siyntweindiog *ans* shunt wound
siytni *eg* chutney
skandha *eg* skandha
slab *eg* slabiau slab
slab bris *eg* slabiau bris breeze slab
slab gwydr *eg* slabiau gwydr glass slab
slab incio *eg* slabiau incio inking slab
slac-lanw *eg* slack tide
slaes *eg* slaesau slash
slaesu *be* slash
slag *eg* slag
slag basig *eg* basic slag
slalom *eg* slalom
slat *eb* slatiau slat
slat dabwrdd *eb* slatiau tabwrdd tambour slat
slecio *be* slake
sleid *eb* sleidiau slide
sleid ddyblyg *eb* sleidiau dyblyg duplicate slide
sleid gudd *eb* sleidiau cudd hidden slide
sleid nesaf *eb* next slide
sleid wedi'i pharatoi *eb* prepared slide
sleid y teitl *eb* title slide
sleis *eb* sleisiau slice
sleis bysgod *eb* sleisiau pysgod fish slice
sling *eg* slingiau sling
slip (=maeswr mewn criced) *eg* slipwyr slip
slip (=math o grochenwaith) *eg* slip
slip (=safle mewn criced) *eg* slipiau slip
slip coes *eg* leg slip
slip cyflog *eg* slipiau cyflog pay-slip
slip cyntaf *eg* first slip

slip hysbysu *eg* slipiau hysbysu advice slip
slip rhannu *eg* slipiau rhannu mid-feather
slipffordd *eb* slipffyrdd slip road
slipio *be* slip
slogan *eg* sloganau slogan
slogan hysbysebu *eg* advertising slogan
slot *eg* slotiau slot
slot amgarn *eg* slotiau amgarn ferrule slot
slot botwm *eg* slotiau botwm button slot
slot ehangu *eg* slotiau ehangu expansion slot
slyg *eg* slygiau slug
slym *eg* slymiau slum
smalio *be* make-believe
smart *ans* smart
sment *eg* smentiau cement
sment balsa *eg* balsa cement
sment carbid *eg* cemented carbide
sment cyflym-galedu *eg* rapid hardening cement
sment lliw *eg* coloured cement
sment modelu *eg* modelling cement
sment persbecs *eg* perspex cement
sment Portland *eg* Portland cement
sment teils *eg* tile cement
smentiad *eg* cementation
smentiad gwaddodion *eg* cementation of sediments
smentio *be* cement
smentit *eg* cementite
smoc *eb* smociau smock
smocwaith *eg* smocking
smocwaith crwybr *eg* honeycomb smocking
smocwaith dellt *eg* trellis smocking
smocwaith pluen *eg* feather smocking
smocwaith rhaff *eg* cable smocking
smocwaith Vandyke *eg* Vandyke smocking
smotio *be* spot
smotiog *ans* spotted
smotyn *eg* smotiau spot; blob
smotyn gwyn *eg* penalty spot
smwddio *be* iron
smwddio ysgafn *be* minimum iron
smwtsio *be* smudge
snap *eg* snapiau snap
snap rhybed *eg* snapiau rhybed rivet snap
snapio i'r grid *be* snap to grid
snip *eg* snipiau snip
snipio *be* snipping
snipiwr *eg* snipwyr snips
snipiwr crwm *eg* snipwyr crwm curved snips
snipiwr cyffredinol *eg* snipwyr cyffredinol universal snips
snipiwr syth *eg* snipwyr syth straight snips
snipiwr tun *eg* snipwyr tun tinsnips
snipiwr tun crwm *eg* snipwyr tun crwm curved tinsnips
snipiwr tun cyffredinol *eg* snipwyr tun cyffredinol universal tinsnips
snipiwr tun syth *eg* snipwyr tun syth straight tinsnips
socaeth *eb* socage
socasau *ell* anklewarmers
soced *eg/b* socedi socket
soced dril *eg* socedi dril drill socket
soced trydan *eg* socedi trydan power point
soced trydan *eg* socedi trydan electric socket
soda *eg* soda
soda brwd *eg* caustic soda
soda golchi *eg* soda
soda golchi *eg* washing soda
soda pobi *eg* bicarbonate of soda
sodiwm (Na) *eg* sodium
sodiwm alwminad *eg* sodium aluminate
sodiwm asid *eg* sodium azide
sodiwm carbonad *eg* sodium carbonate
sodiwm clorid *eg* sodium chloride
sodiwm deucarbonad *eg* sodium bicarbonate
sodiwm ethocsid *eg* sodium ethoxide
sodiwm ffenocsid *eg* sodium phenoxide
sodiwm hecsafflworoalwminad(III) (cryolit) *eg* sodium hexafluoroaluminate(III) (cryolite)
sodiwm hydrocsid *eg* sodium hydroxide
sodiwm hydrocsid dyfrllyd *eg* aqueous sodium hydroxide
sodiwm hydrocsid ethanolig *eg* ethanolic sodium hydroxide
sodiwm lawryl sylffonad *eg* sodium lauryl sulphonate
sodli *be* heel
sodr *eg* sodrau solder
sodr arian *eg* silver solder
sodr arian caled *eg* hard silver solder
sodr caled *eg* hard solder
sodr craidd *eg* sodrau craidd cored solder
sodr llifrwydd *eg* sodrau llifrwydd easy-flo solder
sodr meddal *eg* soft solder
sodr plwm *eg* sodrau plwm lead solder
sodr plymwr *eg* resin cored solder
sodr plymwr *eg* sodrau plymwr plumber's solder
sodr prawf arian *eg* sodrau prawf arian assayable solder
sodr rhwydd *eg* sodrau rhwydd easy solder
sodro *be* solder
sodro a phresyddu solder and braze
sodro meddal *be* soft soldering
sodro oer *be* cold soldering
sodrog *ans* soldered
soddedig *ans* submerged
soddi *be* submerge
sofiet *eg* sofietau soviet
Sofiet Goruchaf *eg* Supreme Soviet
sofran *eg* sofraniaid sovereign
sofraniaeth *eb* sofraniaethau sovereignty
sofraniaeth defnyddwyr *eb* consumer sovereignty
sofraniaeth y bobl *eb* popular sovereignty

sofraniaeth y bobl *eb* sovereignty of the people
sofraniaeth y senedd *eb* parliamentary sovereignty
sofren *eb* sofrenni sovereign
soffistigeiddrwydd *eg* sophistication
solar *ans* solar
solenoid *eg* solenoidau solenoid
solenoid craidd aer *eg* solenoidau craidd aer air cored solenoid
solenoid craidd haearn *eg* iron cored solenoid
solet *ans* solid
sol-ffa *eg* tonic sol-fa
solffatara *eg* solffatarau solfatara
solffeuo *be* sol-fa
solffeuwr *eg* solffeuwyr sol-faist
solffeuwraig *eb* solffeuwragedd sol-faist
solid *eg* solidau solid
solid afreolaidd *eg* solidau afreolaidd irregular solid
solid cylchdro *eg* solidau cylchdro solid of revolution
solid petryal *eg* solidau petryal rectangular solid
solid rheolaidd *eg* solidau rheolaidd regular solid
solidau ar oledd *ell* inclined solids
solidau plân *ell* plane solids
solidau sgleiniog *ell* shiny solids
solidedd *eg* solidity
solidiad *eg* solidiadau solidification
solonets *eg* solonetz
solontshac *eg* solonchak
solpitar *eg* saltpetre
soma *eg* soma
somatig *ans* somatic
somatoteip *eg* somatotype
sonaredig *ans* sonarized
sonata *eb* sonatau sonata
sonata amrywiad *eb* sonatau amrywiad variation sonata
sonata drio *eb* sonatau trio trio sonata
sonatina *eb* sonatinau sonatina
soniaredd *eg* timbre
soniarus *ans* sonorous
soprano *eb* lleisiau soprano soprano
soprano goloratwra *eb* sopranos coloratwra coloratura soprano
sorbit *eg* sorbite
sosban frys *eb* sosbannau brys pressure cooker
soser *eb* soseri saucer
soser bedair rhan *eb* soseri pedair rhan four-division saucer
soser blastig *eb* soseri plastig plastic saucer
soser deir-ran *eb* soseri teir-ran three-division saucer
sosialaeth *eb* socialism
sosialaidd *ans* socialist
sosialydd *eg* sosialwyr socialist
Sosialydd Democrataidd *eg* Sosialwyr Democrataidd Social Democrat
spina bifida *eg* spina bifida
spined *eb* spinedau spinet
stac *eg* staciau stack
stacato *ans* staccato
stad (=cyfnod) *eb* stadau stage
stad (tir neu dai) *eb* stadau estate
stad cyngor *eb* stadau cyngor council estate
stad dai cyngor *eb* stadau tai cyngor council house estate
stad ddiwydiannol *eb* stadau diwydiannol industrial estate
stad fasnachol *eb* stadau masnachol trading estate
stad o dai *eb* stadau o dai housing estate
stad o dai newydd arfaethedig *eb* stadau o dai newydd arfaethedig proposed new housing estate
stad weithredu ddiriaethol *eb* concrete operational stage
stad weithredu ffurfiol *eb* formal operational stage
Stadau Cyffredinol *ell* Estates General
stadau'r deyrnas *cb* estates of the realm
stadiwm pêl-droed *eg* stadia pêl-droed football stadium
staen *eg* staeniau stain
staen adeiledig *eg* staeniau adeiledig built-up stain
staen arwyneb *eg* surface stain
staen cemegol *eg* staeniau cemegol chemical stain
staen cyfansawdd *eg* staeniau cyfansawdd compound stain
staen di-draidd *eg* staeniau di-draidd body stain
staen dŵr *eg* staeniau dŵr water stain
staen eboni *eg* staeniau eboni ebony stain
staen gwirod *eg* staeniau gwirod spirit stain
staen gwydredd *eg* staeniau gwydredd glaze stain
staen olew *eg* staeniau olew oil stain
staen protein *eg* staeniau protein proteinaceous stain
staen slip *eg* slip stain
staen wedi'i amsugno *eg* staeniau wedi'u hamsugno absorbed stain
staeniau brown mewn pren *ell* foxiness
staenio *be* stain
staes *eb* staesys corset
staff *ell* staff
staff ategol *ell* ancillary staff
staff bwcio *ell* reservations staff
staff cyfrifiadurol *ell* computer staff
staff domestig *ell* domestic staff
staff ffreutur *ell* canteen staff
staff gofal *ell* care staff
staff gwerthu *eg* sales staff
staff milwrol *ell* general staff
staff nad ydynt yn addysgu *ell* non-teaching staff
staff technegol *ell* technical staff
stalactid *eg* stalactidau stalactite
stalagmid *eg* stalagmidau stalagmite
Stalinydd *eg* Stalinyddion Stalinist
stamina *eg* stamina
stamp *eg* stampiau stamp

stamp du ceiniog *eg* stampiau du ceiniog Penny Black
stamp masnachu *eg* stampiau masnachu trading stamp
stamp post *eg* stampiau post postage stamp
stanan *eg* stannane
stand *eg/b* standiau stand
stand arddangos *eg* standiau arddangos display stand
stand brwshys *eg* standiau brwshys brush stand
stand caricot *eg* standiau caricot carrycot stand
stand cerddoriaeth *eg* standiau cerddoriaeth music stand
stand modelu *eg* standiau modelu modelling stand
stand retort *eg* standiau retort retort stand
starbord *eg* starboard
starn *eb* starnau stern
starn ogam *eb* starnau ogam gybe
starn ogamu *be* gybe
startsh *eg* starch
startsh chwistrell *eg* spray starch
startsh dŵr oer *eg* cold water starch
startsh dŵr poeth *eg* hot water starch
startsh lliw *eg* coloured starch
startsh plastig *eg* plastic starch
startsio *be* starch
stateg *eb* statics
statig *ans* static
stator *eg* statorau stator
statud *eg* statudau statute
Statud Cymru *eg* Statute of Wales
Statud Defnyddiau *eg* Statute of Uses
statud ffug *eg* statudau ffug fictitious statute
Statud Gwyr ar Gadw *eg* Statute of Retainers
Statud Proclamasiwn *eg* Statute of Proclamations
Statud Rhuddlan *eg* Statute of Rhuddlan
Statud Westminster *eg* Statute of Westminster
statudol *ans* statutory
statws *eg* status
statws cymdeithasol *eg* social status
statws cymdeithasol-economaidd *eg* socio-economic status
statws diffyg *eg* fault status
statws ffisiolegol *eg* physiological status
statws iechyd *eg* health status
statws rhagosodedig *eg* default status
statws testun *eg* text status
statws ymddiriedolaeth *eg* trust status
stêc balfais *eb* steciau palfais chuck steak
stecen benfras *eb* steciau penfras cod steak
stelit *eg* stellite
stêm-roler *eg* stêm-roleri steamroller
stensil *eg* stensiliau stencil
stent *eg* stentau extent
step bolca *eb* stepiau polca polka step
step deithio *eb* stepiau teithio travelling step
step sawdl a bawd *eb* stepiau sawdl a bawd heel and toe step
step sgip *eb* stepiau sgip skip step
step Strathspey *eb* Strathspey step
step-briddoedd *ell* steppe soils
stepio *be* step
steradian *eg* steradiannau steradian
stereoffonig *ans* stereophonic
stereograffig *ans* stereographic
stereopsis *eg* stereopsis
stereosgopig *ans* stereoscopic
stereoteip *eg* stereoteipiau stereotype
stereoteip rhyw *eg* stereoteipiau rhyw sex stereotype
stereoteipio *be* stereotyping
stereoteipio o ran rhyw gender-stereotyped
sterling *eg* sterling
sternwm *eg* sterna sternum
steroid *eg* steroidau steroid
sterol *eg* sterolau sterol
stethosgop *eg* stethosgopau stethoscope
stibin *eg* stibine
stigma *eg* stigmâu stigma
stigma *eg* stigmata stigma
stileto *eg* stiletto
stiliard *eg* steelyard
stilt *eg* stiltiau stilt
stiltiau ceramig *ell* ceramic stilts
stiltiau tri-phwynt *ell* triple-point stilts
stipwl *eg* stipylau stipule
stiward *eg* stiwardiaid steward
stiward tir *eg* stiwardiaid tir land agent
stiwardiaeth *eb* stiwardiaethau stewardship
Stiwartiaid *ell* Stuarts
stiwdio *eb* stiwdios studio
stoc *eb* stociau stock
stoc agoriadol *eb* opening stock
stoc derfynol *eb* closing stock
stoc gyfartalog *eb* average stock
stoc o dras *eb* stociau o dras pedigree stock
stocastig *ans* stochastic
stocinét *eb* stockinette
stof *eb* stofiau stove
stof ddeuddarn *eb* stofiau deuddarn split-level cooker
stof orffennu *eb* stofiau gorffennu finishing stove
stof orffennu drydan *eb* stofiau gorffennu trydan electric finishing stove
stoichiometreg *eb* stoichiometry
stoichiometrig *ans* stoichiometric
stôl (i eistedd arni) *eb* stolion stool
stôl (i wisgo) *eb* stoliau stole
stôl biano *eb* stolion piano piano stool
stôl blygu *eb* stolion plygu camp stool
stôl drochi *eb* stolion trochi ducking stool
stôl droed *eb* stoliau troed footstool
stôl droed *eb* stoliau troed footrest

stôl fach *eb* stolion bach play stool
stôl gynnal *eb* stolion cynnal supporting stool
stolonog *ans* stoloniferous
stoma *eg* stomata stoma
stomiwm *eg* stomia stomium
stondiniaeth *eb* stallage
stop (ar organ) *eg* stopiau register
stop (yn gyffredinol) *eg* stopiau stop
stop brys *eg* stopiau brys emergency stop
stop cefn *eg* stopiau cefn back stop
stop clicied *eg* stopiau clicied ratchet stop
stop cyfuno *eg* stopiau cyfuno combination stop
stop cymysg *eg* stopiau cymysg mixture stop
stop cyplu *eg* stopiau cyplu coupler stop
stop dyfnder *eg* stopiau dyfnder depth stop
stop solo *eg* stopiau solo solo stop
stop sylfaen *eg* stopiau sylfaen foundation stop
stop telyn *eg* stopiau telyn harp stop
stop ymyl *eg* stopiau ymyl margin stop
stopgloc *eg* stopglociau stop-clock
stopio'n stond *be* stop dead
stop-symudiad *eg* stop motion
stôr *eb* storau store
stôr gysylltiadol *eb* storau cysylltiadol associative store
stôr statig *eb* storau statig static store
storfa (cof cyfrifiadur) *eb* storfeydd cache
storfa (yn gyffredinol) *eb* storfeydd store; storage
storfa arwyneb *eb* surface storage
storfa bwmp *eb* storfeydd pwmp pump storage
storfa cof *eb* storfeydd cof memory cache
storfa craidd magnetig *eb* storfeydd craidd magnetig magnetic core store
storfa disg *eb* storfeydd disg disk cache
storfa dros dro *eb* storfeydd dros dro cache store
storfa ddata *eb* storfeydd data data storage
storfa ddisg gyfnewidiadwy *eb* storfeydd disg cyfnewidiadwy exchangeable disk store
storfa ddynamig *eb* storfeydd dynamig dynamic store
storfa eilaidd *eb* storfeydd eilaidd secondary storage
storfa fàs *eb* storfeydd màs mass storage
storfa fraster *eb* storfeydd braster fat depot
storfa fuangyrch *eb* storfeydd buangyrch fast access storage
storfa fwyd *eb* storfeydd bwyd reserve
storfa ffeiliau *eb* storfeydd ffeiliau file store
storfa ffeiliau gynnwys-gyfeiriedig *eb* storfeydd ffeiliau cynnwys-gyfeiriedig content addressable file store
storfa graidd *eb* storfeydd craidd core store
storfa gynorthwyol *eb* storfeydd cynorthwyol backing store
storfa hapgyrch *eb* storfeydd hapgyrch random access store
storfa laith *eb* storfeydd llaith damp storage
storfa laser *eb* storfeydd laser laser store
storfa swmp *eb* storfeydd swmp bulk storage
storfa uniongyrchol *eb* storfeydd uniongyrchol immediate access store
storfa wrth gefn *eb* storfeydd wrth gefn back-up storage
stori *eb* straeon story
stori linellol *eb* linear narrative
stori tylwyth teg *eb* straeon tylwyth teg fairy tale
storio *be* store
storio *be* storage
storio bwyd *be* storing food
storio cyfansoddiad *be* store a composition
storio cynradd a storio eilaidd primary storage and secondary storage
storio data *be* data storage
storio gwybodaeth *be* store information
storm eira *eb* stormydd eira blizzard
storm fellt a tharanau *eb* stormydd mellt a tharanau thunderstorm
stormdraeth *eg* stormdraethau storm beach
stormfilwyr *ell* stormtroopers
stow *eg* stowiau stow
straen *eg* strain
straen tynnol *eg* tensile strain
straenachoswr *eg* straenachoswyr stressor
stranc *eb* stranciau tantrum
strap *eb* strapiau strap
strap gicio *eb* strapiau cicio kicking strap
strap gymhwyso *eb* strapiau cymhwyso adjusting strap
strap haearn gyr *eb* wrought iron strap
strap warthol *eb* strapiau gwarthol stirrup strap
strap ysgwydd *eb* strapiau ysgwydd shoulder strap
strapen hogi *eb* strapiau hogi strop
strategaeth *eb* strategaethau strategy
strategaeth atgenhedlu *eb* strategaethau atgenhedlu reproductive strategy
strategaeth brisio *eb* strategaethau prisio pricing strategy
strategaeth brofi *eb* testing strategy
Strategaeth Cymru Gyfan *eb* All Wales Strategy
strategaeth farchnata *eb* strategaethau marchnata marketing strategy
strategaeth llythrennedd cenedlaethol *eb* national literacy strategy
Strategaeth Technoleg Gwybodaeth a Chyfathrebu *eb* Information and Communication Technology Strategy
strategaeth ymchwil farchnata *eb* market research strategy
strategaeth ymdopi *eb* coping strategy
strategol *ans* strategic
stratigraffeg *eb* stratigraphy
stratosffer *eg* stratosfferau stratosphere
stratosfferig *ans* stratospheric
stratwm *eg* strata stratum
streic *eb* streiciau strike

streic gyffredinol *eb* streiciau cyffredinol general strike
streicio *be* strike
streiciwr *eg* streicwyr striker
streic-rwyg *eg* strike-slip
stretsier *eg* stretsieri stretcher
stribed *eg* stribedi strip
stribed bysell *eg* stribedi bysell key strip
stribed calcio *eg* stribedi calcio caulking strip
stribed Caspari *eg* Casparian strip
stribed croesraen *eg* stribedi croesraen crossway strip
stribed deufetel *eg* stribedi deufetel bimetallic strip
stribed ffilm *eg* stribedi ffilm film strip
stribed gib *eg* stribedi gib gib strip
stribed Tonk (silff) *eg* stribedi Tonk Tonk strip
stribedi rhwbio *ell* rubbing strips
stribedyn adlynol *eg* stribedi adlynol adhesive strapping
striclo *be* strickle
stringeri *ell* stringers
stripio *be* strip
stripio *be* stripping
strobosgop *eg* strobosgopau stroboscope
strôc *eb* strociau stroke
strôc anwythiad *eb* strociau anwythiad induction stroke
strôc arosgo *eb* strociau arosgo oblique stroke
strôc badlo ymlaen *eb* strociau padlo ymlaen forward paddling stroke
strôc badlo'n ôl *eb* reverse paddling stroke
strôc brwsh *eb* strociau brwsh brush stroke
strôc brwsh un-strôc *eb* strociau brwsh un-strôc one-brush stroke
strôc dorri *eb* strociau torri cutting stroke
strôc dynnu *eb* strociau tynnu plain drawstroke
strôc ddychwel *eb* strociau dychwel return stroke
strôc ddychwel segur *eb* strociau dychwel segur idle return stroke
strôc groeslinol *eg* strociau croeslinol diagonal stroke
strôc gul *eb* strociau cul narrow stroke
strôc gydnabyddedig *eb* strociau cydnabyddedig recognized stroke
strôc gydnabyddedig bellach *eb* strociau cydnabyddedig pellach further recognised stroke
strôc gyllell *eb* strociau cyllell knife stroke
strôc lydan *eb* strociau llydan wide stroke
stroffig *ans* strophic
strontiwm *eg* strontium
strontiwm carbonad *eg* strontium carbonate
strontiwm sylffad *eg* strontium sulphate
strwythur *eg* strwythurau structure
strwythur bloc *eg* strwythurau bloc block structure
strwythur cymdeithasol *eg* social structure
strwythur data *eg* strwythurau data data structure
strwythur data dynamig *eg* dynamic data structure
strwythur demograffig *eg* demographic structure
strwythur dramatig *eg* dramatic structure
strwythur ffeiliau *eg* file structure
strwythur gwleidyddol *eg* political structure
strwythur gwybyddol *eg* strwythurau gwybyddol cognitive structure
strwythur trefniadaeth *eg* organization structure
strwythur trefniadaeth gwastad *eg* flat organisational structure
strwythur trefniadaeth tal *eg* tall organisation structre
strwythur y cyfeiriadur *eg* directory structure
strwythur y naratif *eg* narrative structure
strwythuredig *ans* structured
strwythuriaeth *eb* structuralism
strwythurol *ans* structural
stryd unffordd *eb* strydoedd unffordd one-way street
strydlun *eg* strydluniau street scape
stumog *eb* stumogau stomach
stwco *eg* stucco
stwffin *eg* forcemeat
stwffin *eg* farce
stwffio *be* stuff
stwffwl *eg* styffylau staple
stwmp *eg* stympiau stump
stwmp canol *eg* middle stump
stwmp coes *eg* stympiau coes leg stump
stwmp pellaf *eg* stympiau pellaf off stump
stwnsh *eg* hash
stwnsio *be* hashing
styden *eb* stydiau stud
styden gopr *eb* stydiau copr copper stud
styden neilon *eb* stydiau neilon nylon stud
styden wasg *eb* stydiau gwasg press stud
styffylau gwifren *ell* wire staples
styffylu *be* staple
styffylwr *eg* styffylwyr stapler
styffylwr hir *eg* styffylwyr hir long-arm stapler
styl *eg* stylau style
stympio *be* stump
stympiwr *eg* stympwyr stumper
styren *eg* styrene
styren AB *eg* AB styrene
sudd *eg* suddion juice
sudd ffrwythau *eg* fruit juice
sudd gastrig *eg* suddion gastrig gastric juice
sudd treulio *eg* suddion treulio digestive juice
suddfan *eg/b* suddfannau sink
suddfan dŵr *eg* suddfannau dŵr soakaway
suddfan egni *eg* suddfannau egni energy sink
suddfan gwres *eg* heat sink
suddlon *ans* succulent
suddlonedd *eg* succulence
suddo *be* sink
suddo'r Lusitania *be* sinking of the Lusitania
Sufi *eg* Sufi
sugndraeth *eg* sugndraethau quicksands

sugnedd *eg* sugneddau suction
sugniad *eg* sugniadau aspiration
sugno *be* suck; aspirate
sugnolyn *eg* sugnolynau sucker
sugno'r fron *be* suckle
sugnwr llwch *eg* sugnwyr llwch vacuum cleaner
sugnwr llwch crwn *eg* sugnwyr llwch crwn spherical vacuum cleaner
sugnwr llwch silindr *eg* sugnwyr llwch silindr cylinder vacuum cleaner
sugnwr llwch unionsyth *eg* sugnwyr llwch unionsyth upright vacuum cleaner
Sukkot Sukkot
Sul y Blodau *eg* Palm Sunday
Sul y Gwaed *eg* Bloody Sunday
Sul y Pasg *eg* Easter day
Sulgwyn *eg* Whitsun
sunna *eg* sunna
Sunni *eg* Sunni
surah *eg* surah
sw *eg* swau zoo
swab *eg* swabiau swab
swab rhwyllog *eg* swabiau rhwyllog gauze swab
swastica *eg* swasticas swastika
swastika *eg* swastikas swastika
swberin *eg* suberin
swbstrad *eg* swbstradau substrate
swcros *eg* sucrose
swd *eg* swdiau sudd
Swedaidd *ans* Swedish
Swedeg (iaith) *eb* Swedish
Swediad *eg* Swediaid Swede
swffragan *eg* swffraganiaid suffragan
swffragét *eb* swffragetiaid suffragette
swffragydd *eg* swffragwyr suffragist
swigen *eb* swigod bubble
Swigen Môr y De *eb* South Sea Bubble
swing ymhalio *eg* swingiau ymhalio heave swing
swingio *be* swing
swingio ar far *be* swing on a bar
swingio'r breichiau *be* arms swinging
swingio'r breichiau yn ôl ac ymlaen *be* swing the arms backward and forward
swildod *eg* inhibition
switerïon *eg* switerïonau zwitterion
switsfwrdd *eg* switsfyrddau switchboard
switsh *eg* switshis switch
switsh agosrwydd effaith Hall *eg* Hall effect proximity switch
switsh consol *eg* switshis consol console switch
switsh cychwyn *eg* switshis cychwyn starter switch
switsh diogelu *eg* switshis diogelu safety switch
switsh dwyffordd *eg* switshis dwyffordd two way switch
switsh pylu *eg* switshis pylu dimmer-switch
switsh rheoli *eg* switshis rheoli control switch
switsio *be* switch
switsio neges *be* message switching
switsio pecynnau *be* packet switching
Swleiman Ysblennydd *eg* Suleiman the Magnificent
Swltan *eg* Sultan
swm (=mesur maint) *eg* symiau amount
swm (yn gyffredinol) *eg* symiau sum
swm cyfalaf *eg* capital sum
swm gwirio anghywir *eg* wrong check amount
swm sgwariau *eg* sum of squares (SS)
swm sy'n ddyledus *eg* amount owing
swm y sylwedd *eg* amount of substance
swmp *eg* sympau bulk; sump
swmp brynu *be* bulk buying
swmp gludydd *eg* swmp gludyddion bulk carrier
swmp-danc *eg* swmpdanciau bulk tank
swmpgludo *be* bulk transport
swmplif *eg* bulkflow
swmpus *ans* bulky
sŵn (yn gyffredinol) *eg* synau noise; sound
sŵn (=lefel y sain) *eg* volume
sŵn gwrthdaro *eg* impact sound
swnt *eg* swntiau sound
swnyn *eg* swnwyr buzzer
swoleg *eb* zoology
swolegydd *eg* swolegwyr zoologist
swoplancton *eg* zooplankton
swosbor *eg* swosborau zoospore
swp *eg* sypiau batch
swp-adweithydd *eg* swp-adweithyddion batch reactor
swp-brosesu *be* batch processing
Swper yr Arglwydd *eg* Lord's Supper
swp-feithrin *be* batch culture
swp-gynhyrchu *be* batch production
swpinadiad *eg* swpinadiadau supination
swpremwm *ans* supremum
swp-wasanaeth *eg* swp-wasanaethau batch service
swraso *eg* swrasoau surazo
swrd *eg* syrdiau surd
swrealaeth *eb* surrealism
swrealydd *eg* swrealwyr surrealist
swrth *ans* drowsy; lethargic
swydd (=sir) *eb* shire
swydd (=gwaith) *eb* swyddi job; office
swydd cynorthwyydd *eb* swyddi cynorthwywyr assistantship
swydd llywodraethwr *eb* swyddi llywodraethwyr governorship
swydd reoli *eb* swyddi rheoli managerial post
swydd wag *eb* swyddi gwag vacancy; job vacancy
swydd-ddaliad *eg* office-holding
swyddfa *eb* swyddfeydd office
swyddfa arallu *eb* swyddfeydd arallu alienation office
swyddfa gofrestredig *eb* swyddfeydd cofrestredig registered office

Swyddfa Gofrestru *eb* Swyddfeydd Cofrestru Registry Office
swyddfa gyflogi *eb* swyddfeydd cyflogi employment exchange
Swyddfa Gymreig *eb* Welsh Office
Swyddfa Hysbysrwydd Ganolog *eb* Central Office of Information
swyddfa is-gennad *eb* swyddfeydd is-genhadon consulate
Swyddfa Masnachu Teg *eb* Office of Fair Trading
Swyddfa Prif Arolygydd ei Mawrhydi (SPAEM) *eb* Office of Her Majesty's Chief Inspector
Swyddfa Safonau mewn Addysg *eb* Office for Standards in Education
swyddfa'r post *eb* post office
swyddog *eg* swyddogion officer; official
swyddog *eg* swyddogion officer
swyddog addysg *eg* swyddogion addysg education officer
swyddog addysg rhanbarthol *eg* swyddogion addysg rhanbarthol district education officer
swyddog ailsefydlu'r anabl *eg* swyddogion ailsefydlu'r anabl disablement resettlement officer
swyddog cadwraeth *eg* swyddogion cadwraeth conservation officer
swyddog cyflenwi *eg* swyddogion cyflenwi quartermaster; manciple
swyddog cynghori *eg* swyddogion cynghori advisory officer
swyddog cysylltiadau cyhoeddus *eg* swyddogion cysylltiadau cyhoeddus public relations officer
swyddog dyledion y Goron *eg* swyddogion dyledion y Goron remembrancer
swyddog dyletswydd *eg* swyddogion dyletswydd duty officer
swyddog gofal plant *eg* swyddogion gofal plant child care officer
swyddog gwarant *eg* swyddogion gwarant warrant officer
swyddog gweithredol *eg* swyddogion gweithredol executive
swyddog hyfforddi *eg* swyddogion hyfforddi training officer
swyddog iechyd a diogelwch *eg* swyddogion iechyd a diogelwch health and safety officer
swyddog iechyd a ffitrwydd *eg* swyddogion iechyd a ffitrwydd health and fitness officer
swyddog lleoliadau *eg* swyddogion lleoliadau placement officer
swyddog lles *eg* swyddogion lles welfare officer
swyddog lles addysg *eg* swyddogion lles addysg education welfare officer
Swyddog Llys y Brenin *eg* Officer of the Royal Court
swyddog nyrsio *eg* swyddogion nyrsio nursing officer
swyddog o'r fyddin *eg* swyddogion y fyddin army officer
swyddog prawf *eg* swyddogion prawf probation officer
swyddog prisio *eg* swyddogion prisio valuation officer
swyddog proffesiynol arweiniol *eg* swyddogion proffesiynol arweiniol lead professional officer
swyddog tollau *eg* swyddogion tollau customs and excise officer
swyddog twristiaeth *eg* swyddogion twristiaeth tourism officer
swyddog undeb *eg* swyddogion undeb shop steward; union officer
swyddog y llynges *eg* swyddogion y llynges naval officer
swyddogaeth *eb* swyddogaethau role; function
swyddogaeth adnoddau dynol *eb* human resources function
swyddogaeth canfod *eb* find function
swyddogaeth fasnachol *eb* swyddogaethau masnachol commercial function
swyddogaeth fusnes *eb* swyddogaethau busnes business function
swyddogaeth luniadu *eb* swyddogaethau lluniadu draw function
swyddogaeth microbau *eb* role of microbes
swyddogaeth ochrol *eb* lateralization
swyddogaeth peirianneg *eb* engineering function
swyddogaeth sylfaenol *eb* swyddogaethau sylfaenol basic function
swyddogaeth ymgynghorol *eb* swyddogaethau ymgynghorol advisory function
swyddogaethol *ans* functional
► **swyddogaetholdeb** *eg* functionalism
swyddogaethwr *eg* swyddogaethwyr functionalist
swyddogol *ans* official
swyngan *eb* swynganeuon incantation
sycsinig *ans* succinic
sych *ans* dry
sychdarth *eg* sublimate
sychdarthiad *eg* sublimation
sychdarthu *be* sublimate
sychder *eg* sychderau drought
sychedig *ans* thirsty
sychiadur *eg* sychiaduron desiccator
sychlan *ans* dry cleaned
sychlanhau *be* dry cleaning
sychlanhawyr *ell* dry cleaners
sychrewedig cyflym *ans* accelerated freeze dried
sychrewi *be* freeze-dry
sychrewi cyflym *be* accelerated freeze drying
sychu (coed) *be* seasoning
sychu (yn gyffredinol) *be* dry
sychu mewn odyn *be* kiln seasoning
sychu mewn odyn *be* artificial seasoning
sychu mewn peiriant *be* tumble dry
sychu naturiol *be* natural seasoning
sychu'n dyner *be* pat dry
sychu'n gyflym *be* quick drying
sychwr (ffenestr car) *eg* sychwyr wiper
sychwr dillad *eg* sychwyr dillad spin drier

sychwr gwallt *eg* sychwyr gwallt hairdryer
sychydd *eg* sychyddion drier; siccative
sychydd darfudol *eg* sychwyr darfudol convector drier
sychydd inc *eg* sychwyr inc ink drier
syfliad *eg* syfliadau shift
syfliad cylchol *eg* syfliadau cylchol circular shift
syfliad chwith *eg* syfliadau chwith left shift
syfliad de *eg* syfliadau de right shift
syfliad paradeim *eg* paradigm shift
syfliad rhesymegol *eg* syfliadau rhesymegol logical shift
syfliad rhifyddol *eg* syfliadau rhifyddol arithmetic shift
syflyd *be* shift
syffilis *eg* syphilis
sygosbor *eg* sygosborau zygospore
sygot *eg* sygotau zygote
sylem *eg* xylem
sylfaen *eg/b* sylfeini base
sylfaen *eg/b* sylfeini fundamental
sylfaen *eg/b* sylfeini foundation
sylfaen betryal *eb* sylfeini petryal oblong base
sylfaen bileri *eb* sylfeini pileri pile foundation
sylfaen ffos *eb* sylfeini ffos trench foundation
sylfaen goncrit *eb* sylfeini concrit concrete foundation
sylfaen gron *eb* sylfeini crwn round base
sylfaen gwerthoedd *eb* value base
sylfaen gwerthoedd gofal *eb* care value base
sylfaen hambwrdd *eb* sylfeini hambwrdd tray base
sylfaen hirgrwn *eb* sylfeini hirgrwn oval base
sylfaen melamin *eb* melamine base
sylfaen rafft *eb* sylfeini rafft raft foundation
sylfaen stribed *eb* sylfeini stribed strip foundation
sylfaen wifren *eb* sylfeini gwifren wire foundation
sylfaenol (=lefel gyntaf) *ans* primary
sylfaenol (=lefel symlaf) *ans* basic
sylfaenol (=yn perthyn i'r sail) *ans* foundation
sylfaenol (am nodyn cerdd, cord) *ans* fundamental
sylfaenol (mewn cyfresiaeth) *ans* original
sylfaenydd *eg* sylfaenwyr founder
sylffad *eg* sulphate
sylffid *eg* sulphide
sylffwr (mewn cemeg) *eg* sulfur
sylffwr (yn gyffredinol) *eg* sulphur
sylffwr deuclorid deuocsid *eg* sulfur dichloride dioxide
sylffwr deuclorid ocsid *eg* sulfur dichloride oxide
sylffwr deuocsid *eg* sulfur dioxide
sylffwr rhôl *eg* roll sulphur
sylffwr triocsid *eg* sulfur trioxide
sylffwrig *eg* sulphuric
sylocsdecs *eg* syloxdex
sylos *eg* xylose
sylw (=canolbwyntio ar rywun neu rywbeth) *eg* attention
sylw (sy'n cael ei ddweud neu'i ysgrifennu) *eg* sylwadau comment; remark; observation
sylw (yn y cyfryngau) *eg* coverage
sylw bachog *eg* soundbite
sylw dethol *eg* selective attention
sylw rhanedig *eg* divided attention
sylwebaeth *eb* sylwebaethau commentary
sylwebaeth ar y pryd *eb* running commentary
sylwebydd *eg* sylwebwyr commentator
sylwedd *eg* sylweddau substance
sylwedd anadweithiol *eg* sylweddau anadweithiol inert substance
sylwedd gwastraff nitrogenaidd *eg* sylweddau gwastraff nitrogenaidd nitrogenous waste product
sylwedd peryglus *eg* hazardous substance
sylwedd ymbelydrol *eg* sylweddau ymbelydrol radioactive substance
sylwedd yn ymgasglu mewn meinwe *eg* substance accumulation in tissue
sylwedd ysgarthiol *eg* sylweddau ysgarthiol excretory substance
sylwi *be* note; observe
sylladur *eg* sylladuron eyepiece
sylladur graticwl *eg* eyepiece graticule
sym *eb* symiau sum
symadwy *ans* summable
symatogenig *ans* cymatogenic
symbal *eg* symbalau cymbal
symbalau bys *ell* finger cymbals
symbalau Groeg *ell* antique cymbals
symbiosis *eg* symbiosis
symbol *eg* symbolau symbol
symbol at (@) *eg* at-symbol
symbol arian *eg* symbolau arian currency symbol
symbol cemegol *eg* symbolau cemegol chemical symbol
► **symbol clwyd** *eg* symbolau clwyd hash symbol
symbol confensiynol *eg* symbolau confensiynol conventional symbol
symbol gwyddonol *eg* symbolau gwyddonol scientific symbol
symbol llythrennol *eg* symbolau llythrennol literal
symbol mathemategol *eg* symbolau mathemategol mathematical symbol
symbol nodchwilio *eg* symbolau nodchwilio wildcard symbol
symbol o statws *eg* status symbol
symbol rhesymegol *eg* symbolau rhesymegol logical symbol
symbol twb golchi *eg* symbolau twb golchi wash tub symbol
symbolaeth *eb* symbolism
symbolaidd *ans* symbolic; symbolist
symbolau amrywiol *ell* miscellaneous symbols
symbolau cyfrannol *ell* proportional symbols
symboleiddio *be* symbolize
symbyliad *eg* symbyliadau motivation; impulse
symbylu *be* motivate

symbylydd *eg* symbylyddion stimulant
symffoni *eb* symffonïau symphony
symffoni fugeiliol *eb* pastoral symphony
symffonig *ans* symphonic
symiant *eg* symiannau summation
syml *ans* simple
symledig *ans* simplified
symleiddiad *eg* symleiddiadau simplification
symleiddio *be* simplify
symlrwydd *eg* simplicity
sympathetig *ans* sympathetic
symposiwm *eg* symposia symposium
symptom *eg* symptomau symptom
symptom cadarnhaol *eg* symptomau cadarnhaol positive symptom
symptom diddyfnu *eg* symptomau diddyfnu withdrawal symptom
symptom diffyg *eg* symptomau diffyg deficiency symptom
symptom negyddol *eg* symptomau negyddol negative symptom
symud (=gwaredu) *be* remove
symud (esgob etc) *be* translate
symud (yn gyffredinol) *be* move; shift
symud amlinell *be* move outline
symud cyfres ddata *be* move data series
symud dalen *be* move sheet
symud ffenestr tabl *be* move table window
symud ffrâm *be* move frame
symud gam a cham *be* conjunct motion
symud gwrthrych cronfa ddata *be* move database object
symud i fyny *be* move up
symud i lawr *be* move down
symud i'r chwith *be* move left
symud i'r dde *be* move right
symud medrus *be* skilful movement
symud mewn amser *be* moving in time
symud mewn parau *be* moving in pairs
symud o gwmpas y cwrt *eg* move around the court
symud paragraff *be* move paragraph
symud pwynt *be* move point
symud sleid *be* move slide
symud tabl *be* move table
symud toriad tudalen *be* move page break
symud ymlaen *be* advance
symud yn fertigol *be* move vertically
symud yn llorweddol *be* move horizontally
symud yn rhwydd *be* move fluently
symudadwy *ans* removable
symudedd *eg* mobility
symudedd a hyblygrwydd mobility and flexibility
symudedd dwy-droed *eg* bipedalism
symudiad *eg* symudiadau shift
symudiad *eg* symudiadau action
symudiad *eg* symudiadau translation
symudiad *eg* symudiadau movement
symudiad anadlu *eg* symudiadau anadlu breathing movement
symudiad awyru *eg* ventilation movement
symudiad bloc *eg* symudiadau bloc block move
symudiad Brown *eg* Brownian movement
symudiad cemegol *eg* chemical shift
symudiad clorid *eg* chloride shift
symudiad cofio-i-wybod *eg* remember-to-know shift
symudiad cryfhau *eg* symudiadau cryfhau strengthening movement
symudiad cydwedd *eg* phase shift
symudiad cyfiau *eg* symudiadau cyfiau conjugate movement
symudiad cyfyngedig *eg* symudiadau cyfyngedig limited movement
symudiad cylchdro *eg* symudiadau cylchdro rotary movement
symudiad cylchdro *eg* symudiadau cylchdro rotational movement
symudiad cynhenid *eg* symudiadau cynhenid intrinsic movement
symudiad cynnil *eg* symudiadau cynnil subtle movement
symudiad daear *eg* symudiadau daear earth movement
symudiad dawns *eg* symudiadau dawns dance movement
symudiad digonol *eg* symudiadau digonol adequate movement
symudiad dilyn *eg* pursuit movement
symudiad echddygol bras *eg* symudiadau echddygol bras gross-motor movement
symudiad echddygol manwl *eg* symudiadau echddygol manwl fine-motor movement
symudiad effeithiol *eg* symudiadau effeithiol effective movement
symudiad genetig *eg* genetic drift
symudiad gorffwysol *eg* symudiadau gorffwysol rest stroke
symudiad hydredol *eg* symudiadau hydredol longitudinal movement
symudiad llacio *eg* symudiadau llacio mobilizing movement
symudiad llinol *eg* symudiadau llinol linear movement
symudiad llygad *eg* symudiadau llygaid eye movement
symudiad mynegiannol *eg* symudiadau mynegiannol expressive movement
symudiad nastig *eg* symudiadau nastig nastic movement
symudiad osgiliadol *eg* symudiadau osgiliadol oscillatory movement
symudiad paralacs *eg* motion parallax
symudiad platiau tectonig *eg* symudiadau platiau tectonig tectonic plate movement
symudiad pyped maneg *eg* symudiadau pyped maneg glove-puppet movement

symudiad rhydd *eg* symudiadau rhydd free movement
symudiad rhydd *eg* symudiadau rhydd free stroke
symudiad rhythmig *eg* symudiadau rhythmig rhythmic movement
symudiad sgil *eg* symudiadau sgil by-movement
symudiad siswrn *eg* symudiadau siswrn scissors movement
symudiad sylfaenol *eg* symudiadau sylfaenol basic movement
symudiad syml *eg* symudiadau syml simple movement
symudiad torfol *eg* mass movement
symudiad y pen *eg* symudiadau'r pen head movement
symudiad ymddangosol *eg* symudiadau ymddangosol apparent movement
symudiad ymlaen *eg* symudiadau ymlaen advancement
symudiad ysmiciog *eg* saccadic movement
symudiad ystwytho *eg* symudiadau ystwytho warm up movement
symudliw *ans* opalescent
symudol *ans* movable; mobile
symudwedd *eb* moving phase
symudydd *eg* symudyddion mover
symudydd belt *eg* symudwyr belt belt shifter
symudydd X *eg* X-shift
symudydd Y *eg* Y-shift
symudyn *eg* symudion mobile
synaesthesia *eg* synaesthesia
synaesthetwr *eg* synaesthetwyr synaesthete
synagog *eb* synagogau synagogue
synaps *eg* synapsau synapse
synaptig *ans* synaptic
synau'r galon *ell* heart sounds
synclin *eg* synclinau syncline
synclinol *ans* synclinal
synclinoriwm *eg* synclinoria synclinorium
syncrotron *eg* synchrotron
syncytiwm *eg* syncytia syncytium
syndicaliaeth *eb* syndicalism
syndiotactig *ans* syndiotactic
syndrom *eg* syndromau syndrome
syndrom addasu cyffredinol *eg* general adaption syndrome (GAS)
syndrom alcohol y ffetws *eg* fetal alcohol syndrome
syndrom Asperger *eg* Asperger's syndrome
syndrom cri-du-chat *eg* cri-du-chat syndrome
Syndrom Diffyg Imiwnedd Caffaeledig (AIDS) *eg* Acquired Immune Deficiency Syndrome
syndrom diwylliannol-glwm *eg* culture-bound syndrome
syndrom Down *eg* Down's syndrome
syndrom Gilles de la Tourette *eg* Gilles de la Tourette's syndrome
syndrom plentyn afrosgo *eg* clumsy child syndrome
syndrom sensitifedd sgotopig *eg* scotopic sensitivity syndrome
syndrom Turner *eg* Turner's syndrome
syndrom y caloswm *eg* callosal syndrome
synergaidd *ans* synergistic
synergedd *eg* synergeddau synergism
synergydd *eg* synergyddion synergist
synhwyraidd *ans* sensory
synhwyraidd-weithredol *ans* sensory-motor
synhwyriad *eg* synwyriadau sensation
synhwyriad cyffyrddol *eg* tactile sensation
synhwyro *be* sensing
synhwyro marc *be* mark sensing
synhwyrydd *eg* synwyryddion sensor
synhwyrydd anwythol *eg* inductive sensor
syniad *eg* syniadau idea
syniad cerddorol *eg* syniadau cerddorol musical idea
syniad gwyddonol *eg* syniadau gwyddonol scientific idea
Syniad o Gynnydd *eg* Idea of Progress
syniadaeth wleidyddol *eb* political thought
syniadau'r Kharijitiaid *ell* Kharijite views
syniadau'r Mu'tazilitiaid *ell* Mu'tazilite views
synnwyr *eg* synhwyrau sense
synnwyr corfforol *eg* somatosense
synnwyr cyffredin *eg* common sense
synnwyr cyffwrdd *eg* sense of touch
synnwyr dinesig *eg* civic sense
synnwyr o osgo *eg* postural sense
synod *eg* synodau synod
synodaidd *ans* synodal
synofaidd *ans* synovial
synoptig *ans* synoptic
syntagm *eg* syntagm
syntheseiddio *be* synthesize
syntheseiddio gwybodaeth *be* synthesize information
syntheseiddydd *eg* syntheseiddwyr synthesizer
syntheseiddydd llefaru testun *eg* syntheseiddwyr llefaru testun text-to-speech synthesizer
synthesis *eg* synthesisau synthesis
synthesis cerddoriaeth *eg* music synthesis
synthesis lleferydd *eg* speech synthesis
synthetig *ans* synthetic
synthetigyn *eg* synthetigion synthetic
synwyrusrwydd *eg* sensibility
sypwellt *eg* bunch grass
sypwellt *eg* tussock
sypyn *eg* sypynnau bundle
sypyn cyfraidd *eg* sypynnau cyfraidd collateral bundle
sypyn deugyfraidd *eg* sypynnau deugyfraidd bicollateral bundle
sypyn fasgwlar *eg* sypynnau fasgwlar vascular bundle
sypyn His *eg* sypynnau His His bundle
Syr *eg* Sir

syrcas *eg* syrcasau circus
syrfëwr *eg* syrfewyr surveyor
syrfëwr adeiladu *eg* syrfewyr adeiladu building surveyor
syrfëwr meintiau *eg* syrfewyr meintiau quantity surveyor
syrfëwr tir *eg* syrfewyr tir land surveyor
syrffio *be* surf
syrthni *eg* inertia
syryp *eg* syrypau syrup
syrypaidd *ans* syrupy
system *eb* systemau system
system afonydd *eb* systemau afonydd river system
system amlbrosesydd *eb* systemau amlbrosesydd multiprocessor system
system anrhydedd *eb* honour system
system ansawdd *eb* systemau ansawdd quality system
system arbenigo *eb* systemau arbenigo expert system
system archebu bwyd gyfrifiadurol *eb* computerized food ordering
system archebu gyfrifiadurol *eb* computerized booking system
system archifo *eb* systemau archifo archiving system
system ar-lein *eb* systemau ar-lein on-line system
system ar-lein sylfaenol *eb* systemau ar-lein sylfaenol basic on-line system
system arunig *eb* systemau arunig stand-alone system
system beirianegol *eb* systemau peirianegol engineering system
system brototeip *eb* prototype system
system cred *eb* systemau cred belief system
system cylchrediad gwaed *eb* circulatory system
system cymorth *eb* systemau cymorth help system
system cynnal bywyd *eb* systemau cynnal bywyd life-support system
system dalu *eb* systemau talu payment system
system danio *eb* systemau tanio ignition system
system dreulio *eb* systemau treulio digestive system
system dreulio ddynol *eb* human digestive system
system ddadansoddi *eb* systemau dadansoddi analysis system
system ddegol *eb* systemau degol decimal system
System Ddegol Dewey *eb* Dewey Decimal System
system ddewisyriad *eb* systemau dewisyriad menu-driven system
system ddisg-ffeilio *eb* disk filing system
system ddisg-ffeilio uwch *eb* advanced disk filing system
system egni *eb* systemau egni energy system
system endocrin *eb* endocrine system
system fasgwlar ddyfrol *eb* water vascular system
system fesur *eb* systemau mesur system of measurement
system fetrig *eb* metric system
system fusnes *eb* systemau busnes business system
system fyd-eang cyfathrebu symudol *eb* global system for mobile
► **system gardiofasgwlar** *eb* cardiovascular system
system gebl *eb* systemau cebl cable system
system genhedlu *eb* reproductive system
system golwg *eb* visual system
system grid *eb* systemau grid grid system
system gwasgedd uchel *eb* high pressure system
system gwybodaeth ddaearyddol *eb* geographical information system
system gwybodaeth electronig *eb* systemau gwybodaeth electronig electronic information system
System Gyfandirol (1806-12) *eb* Continental System
system gyfathrebu *eb* systemau cyfathrebu communication system
system gyfesurynnol *eb* systemau cyfesurynnol coordinate system
system gyflogau *eb* systemau cyflogau payroll system
system gyfreithiol *eb* systemau cyfreithiol legal system
system gyfrifiadurol *eb* systemau cyfrifiadurol computer system
system gyfrifiadurol wasgaredig *eb* distributed computer system
system gyfrifydda *eb* accounting system
system gyhyrol *eb* muscular system
system holgar *eb* inquisitorial system
system imiwnedd *eb* immune system
system liferi *eb* systemau liferi lever system
system limbig *eb* limbic system
system luniadu /peintio ar gyfrifiadur *eb* systemau lluniadu /peintio ar gyfrifiadur draw /paint computer system
system lwybro *eb* systemau llwybro tracking system
system lymffatig *eb* lymphatic system
system meistr /gwas *eb* systemau meistr /gwas master /slave system
system mnemonig *eb* mnemonic system
system nerfol *eb* nervous system
system nerfol barasympathetig *eb* parasympathetic nervous system
► **system nerfol berifferol** *eb* peripheral nervous system
system nerfol sympathetig *eb* sympathetic nervous system
system niwmatig *eb* systemau niwmatig pneumatic system
system oeri *eb* systemau oeri cooling system
system optegol *eb* systemau optegol optical system
system osodedig *eb* systemau gosodedig turnkey system
system prosesu diffygion *eb* systemau prosesu diffygion fault processing system

system recriwtio *eb* systemau recriwtio recruitment system

system reoli *eb* systemau rheoli control system

system reoli mewnbwn *eb* systemau rheoli mewnbwn input control system

system resbiradaeth *eb* respiratory system

system resbiradol *eb* respiratory system

system resymeg *eb* logic system

system reticwloendothelaidd *eb* reticuloendothelial system

system rifau *eb* systemau rhifau number system

system rifo hecsadegol *eb* hexadecimal counting system

system rwydwaith *eb* systemau rhwydwaith network system

system rheoli credyd *eb* systemau rheoli credyd credit control system

system rheoli cronfeydd data *eb* database management system

system rheoli sylw goruchwyliol *eb* supervisory attentional system (SAS)

system rhifau cyfain *eb* whole-number system

system sgorio *eb* systemau sgorio scoring system

system sgyrsiol *eb* systemau sgyrsiol conversational system

system technoleg gwybodaeth a chyfathrebu *eb* ICT system

system unffordd *eb* systemau unffordd one-pass system

system wedi'i hawtomeiddio *eb* automated system

system weinyddu *eb* systemau gweinyddu administration system; administrating system

system weithredu *eb* systemau gweithredu operating system

system weithredu cod agored *eb* open-source operating system

system weithredu disg *eb* disk operating system

system weithredu disg cyfrifiadur personol *eb* personal computer disc operating system

system weithredu peiriant *eb* machine operating system

system weithredu rhwydwaith *eb* systemau gweithredu rhwydwaith network operating system

system werthuso *eb* systemau gwerthuso appraisal system

system wrthwynebol *eb* adversarial system

system wybodaeth *eb* systemau gwybodaeth information system

system wythol *eb* systemau wythol octal system

system ysgarthu sylweddau nitrogenaidd *eb* systemau ysgarthu sylweddau nitrogenaidd nitrogenous excretory system

system ysgerbydol *eb* systemau ysgerbydol skeletal system

system ysgyfeiniol *eb* pulmonary system

systematig *ans* systematic

systemau a thechnoleg rheoli systems and control technology

systemau cywerth *ell* equivalent systems

systemau deallus yn seiliedig ar wybodaeth *ell* intelligent knowledge based systems

systole *eg* systole

syth *ans* straight

sythweledol *ans* intuitive

T

tab *eg* tabiau tab
tab degol *eg* tabiau degol decimal tab
tab diogelu *eg* tabiau diogelu protect tab
tab gwarchod *eg* tabiau gwarchod security tab
tabard *eg* tabardau tabard
tabernacl *eg* tabernaclau tabernacle
tabl *eg* tablau table
tabl am-edrych *eg* tablau am-edrych look-up table
tabl amlder *eg* tablau amlder frequency table
tabl amnewid *eg* tablau amnewid replacement table
tabl ar-edrych *eg* tablau ar-edrych look-at table
tabl awtobeilot *eg* tablau awtobeilot autopilot table
tabl awtofformat *eg* tablau awtofformat autoformat table
tabl bwyd *eg* food table
tabl cronfa ddata *eg* tablau cronfa ddata database table
tabl cyfnodol *eg* periodic table
tabl cynghrair *eg* tablau cynghrair league table
tabl databeilot *eg* tablau databeilot datapilot table
tabl gweithrediad *eg* tablau gweithrediad operation table
tabl logarithmau *eg* tablau logarithmau table of logarithms
tabl logarithmig *eg* tablau logarithmig logarithmic table
tabl neidiau *eg* tablau neidiau jump table
tabl nesaf *eg* next table
tabl newidynnau *eg* tablau newidynnau contingency table
tabl pedwar ffigur *eg* tablau pedwar ffigur four figure table
tabl penderfyniad *eg* tablau penderfyniad decision table
tabl perfformiad ysgolion *eg* tablau perfformiad ysgolion school performance table
tabl stratigraffig *eg* tablau stratigraffig stratigraphical table
tabl stwnsh *eg* tablau stwnsh hash table
tabl trawsnewid *eg* tablau trawsnewid conversion table
tabl tri *eg* table of three
tabl ystadegol *eg* tablau ystadegol statistical table
tablaidd *ans* tabular
tabled *eb* tabledi tablet
tabled ddinwyo *eb* tabledi dinwyo degassing tablet
tabledig *ans* tabulated
tablu *be* tabulate
Taboriaid *ell* Taborites
tabŵ *eg* tabwau taboo
tabwrdd *eg* tabyrddau tambour
tabwrdd *eg* tabyrddau tabor
tac *eg* taciau tack
tac cynnal *eg* taciau cynnal bar tack
tac pen saeth *eg* taciau pen saeth arrowhead tack
tac teiliwr *eg* taciau teiliwr tailor's tack
tacio *be* tack
tacio port *be* port tack
tacio starbord *be* starboard tack
tacistosgop *eg* tacistosgopau tachistoscope
taciwr *eg* tacwyr tacker
tacl *eb* taclau tackle
tacl floc *eb* taclau bloc block tackle
tacl floc o'r ochr *eb* taclau bloc o'r ochr side-block tackle
tacl goflaid *eb* taclau coflaid smother tackle
tacl lithriad *eb* taclau llithriad sliding tackle
tacl wib *eb* taclau gwib flying tackle
taclau *ell* gear
taclau sgrafellu *ell* scraper equipment
taclo *be* tackle
taclusrwydd *eg* neatness
taclwr *eg* taclwyr tackler
tacnod *eg* tacnodau tacnode
tacsi *eg* tacsis taxi
tacsonomaidd *ans* taxonomic
tacsonomeg *eb* taxonomy
tacteg *eb* tactegau tactic
tacteg sbwylio *eb* tactegau sbwylio spoiling tactic
Tadau Apostolaidd *ell* Apostolic Fathers
Tadau Pererin *ell* Pilgrim Fathers
tad-cu *eg* tadau cu grandfather
tadol *ans* paternal
taenedig *ans* exploded
taenelliad *eg* aspersion
taenlen *eb* taenlenni spreadsheet
taenlen gyfrifiadurol *eb* taenlenni cyfrifiadurol computer spreadsheet
taenlennu *be* spreadsheet
Taenu'r Efengyl *be* Propagation of the Gospel
taeog *eg* taeogion bondsman
taeog *eg* taeogion serf
taeogaeth *eb* serfdom; bondage
taeogwasanaeth *eg* bond service
tafarn y goets *eb* tafarnau'r goets staging inn
tafell *eb* tafellau slice
tafell amser *eb* tafelli amser time slice
tafell gorc *eb* tafelli corc cork slab

tafell gras *eb* tafelli cras crispbread
tafell hufen *eb* tafelli hufen cream slice
tafellu *be* slice
tafladwy *ans* disposable
taflegryn *eg* taflegrau missile; projectile
taflegryn balistig *eg* taflegrau balistig ballistic missile
taflegryn niwclear *eg* taflegrau niwclear nuclear missile
taflen *eb* taflenni leaflet
taflen *eb* taflenni handout
taflen amser *eb* taflenni amser time sheet
taflen cyhoeddusrwydd *eb* taflenni cyhoeddusrwydd publicity flyer
taflen dosbarthu costau *eb* taflenni dosbarthu costau cost classification sheet
taflen erwydd *eb* taflenni erwydd manuscript sheet
taflen farciau *eb* taflenni marciau mark sheet
taflen godio *eb* taflenni codio coding sheet
taflen gofnodi *eb* taflenni cofnodi record sheet
taflen gwerth deietegol *eb* taflenni gwerth deietegol dietary value sheet
taflen gyfarwyddiadau *eb* taflenni cyfarwyddiadau instruction sheet
taflen sgorio *eb* taflenni sgorio score-sheet
taflen waith *eb* taflenni gwaith worksheet
taflen wyliau *eb* holiday brochure
tafliad *eg* tafliadau throw
tafliad dan ysgwydd *eg* tafliadau dan ysgwydd underarm throw
tafliad rhydd *eg* tafliadau rhydd free throw
taflod *eb* taflodau palate
taflu *be* throw
taflu i mewn *be* throw in
taflu ymlaen *be* throw forward
taflunedd *eg* projectivity
tafluniad *eg* tafluniadau projection
tafluniad anterthol *eg* tafluniadau anterthol zenithal projection
tafluniad ardraws *eg* transverse projection
tafluniad arosgo *eg* tafluniadau arosgo oblique projection
tafluniad arwynebedd hafal *eg* tafluniadau arwynebedd hafal equi-area projection
tafluniad asimwthol *eg* tafluniadau asimwthol azimuthal projection
tafluniad ategol *eg* tafluniadau ategol auxiliary projection
tafluniad atganolog *eg* tafluniadau atganolog recentred projection
tafluniad conigol *eg* tafluniadau conigol conical projection
tafluniad cyhydeddol *eg* tafluniadau cyhydeddol equatorial projection
tafluniad cytbell *eg* tafluniadau cytbell equidistant projection
tafluniad darluniol *eg* tafluniadau darluniol pictorial projection
tafluniad deufetrig *eg* tafluniadau deufetrig dimetric projection
tafluniad isometrig *eg* tafluniadau isometrig isometric projection
► **tafluniad isometrig confensiynol** *eg* tafluniadau isometrig confensiynol conventional isometric projection
tafluniad nomonig *eg* tafluniadau nomonig gnomonic projection
tafluniad ongl *eg* tafluniadau ongl angle projection
tafluniad ongl gyntaf *eg* tafluniadau ongl gyntaf first angle projection
tafluniad orthograffig *eg* tafluniadau orthograffig orthographic projection
tafluniad orthomorffig *eg* tafluniadau orthomorffig orthomorphic projection
tafluniad pegynol *eg* tafluniadau pegynol polar projection
tafluniad silindrog *eg* tafluniadau silindrog cylindrical projection
tafluniad stereograffig *eg* stereographic projection
tafluniad trimetrig *eg* tafluniadau trimetrig trimetric projection
tafluniad trydedd ongl *eg* tafluniadau trydedd ongl third angle projection
taflunio *be* project
tafluniol *ans* projective
taflunydd *eg* taflunyddion projector
taflunydd data *eg* taflunyddion data data projector
taflunydd dros ysgwydd *eg* taflunwyr dros ysgwydd overhead projector
taflu'r ddisgen *be* throwing the discus
taflu'r ordd *be* throwing the hammer
taflu'r waywffon *be* throwing the javelin
taflwr *eg* taflwyr thrower
taflwybr *eg* taflwybrau trajectory
taflwybr cromlinog *eg* taflwybrau cromlinog curvilinear trajectory
taflwybr echelinol *eg* taflwybrau echelinol axial trajectory
tafod *eg* tafodau spit
tafod *eg* tafodau tongue
tafod a rhych tongue and groove
tafod bachog *eg* tafodau bachog hooked spit
tafod croes *eg* tafodau croes cross tongue
tafod crwm *eg* tafodau crwm curved spit
tafod rhydd *eg* tafodau rhydd loose feather; loose tongue
tafod tywod *eg* tafodau tywod sand spit
tafodi *be* tongue
tafodi dwbl *be* double tonguing
tafodi sengl *be* single tonguing
tafodi triphlyg *be* triple tonguing
tafodiaith *eb* tafodieithoedd dialect
tafodieithol *ans* dialectal
tafol *eb* tafolau balance
taffeta *eg* taffeta
tag *eg* tagiau tag
tagell *eb* tagellau gill; branchia

tagellog *ans* gill; branchial
tagen *eb* tagenni chockstone
tagfa *eb* tagfeydd bottleneck; congestion; jam
tagfa drafnidiaeth *eb* tagfeydd trafnidiaeth traffic jam
tagfa gardiau *eb* tagfeydd cardiau card jam
tagfa glogfeini *eb* tagfeydd clogfeini boulder choke
tagfa goed *eb* tagfeydd coed log jam
tagfa iâ *eb* tagfeydd iâ ice jam
tagfa rhew *eb* tagfeydd rhew ice jam
tagfeydd trafnidiaeth *ell* traffic congestion
tagio *be* tag
tagu *be* choke; throttle; clog
tagydd *eg* tagyddion choke
tanglifiad *eg* tanglifiadau tangential sawcut
tangnefedd *eg* peace
tai *ell* housing
tai cefngefn *ell* back to back houses
tai o ansawdd gwael *ell* poor quality housing
taid *eg* teidiau grandfather
taiga *eg* taiga
tail *eg* manure
Tair Erthygl ar Ddeg *eb* Thirteen Articles
Tair Gem, y Three Jewels, the
tairongl *ans* three-square
taith *eb* teithiau journey; tour; trip; passage
taith frenhinol *eb* royal progress
taith gwmpawd *eb* teithiau cwmpawd compass walk
taith ymgyfarwyddo *eb* teithiau ymgyfarwyddo familiarisation trip
tâl (=fine) *eg* taliadau fine
tâl (yn gyffredinol) *eg* taliadau payment
tâl ar gadw *eg* retainer
tâl ar gyfrif *eg* payment on account
tâl bonws *eg* taliadau bonws bonus payment
tâl cludo *eg* taliadau cludo freight rate
tâl cofrestru *eg* taliadau cofrestru registration fee
tâl colli gwaith *eg* redundancy pay
tâl diffyg *eg* taliadau diffyg deficiency payment
tâl esgobol *eg* taliadau esgobol procuration
tâl gohiriedig *eg* taliadau gohiriedig deferred payment
tâl offeiriad *eg* stipend
tâl presgripsiwn *eg* taliadau presgripsiwn prescription charge
tâl ychwanegol *eg* taliadau ychwanegol surcharge
tâl ymuno *eg* taliadau ymuno join-up charge
tâl yn ôl y gwaith *eg* piece work
tâl yn ôl yr awr *eg* hourly rate
taladwy *ans* payable
talaith (yn gyffredinol) *eb* taleithiau province
talaith (yn UDA) *eb* taleithiau state
► **talaith gydffederal** *eb* taleithiau cydffederal confederate state
talbont *eb* talbontydd bridgehead
talc *eg* talciau talc
talcen *eg* talcenni gable end
talcen bwrdd *eg* talcenni byrddau end of table
talcen hir *eg* talcenni hir long wall
talcendo *eg* talcendoeon hip roof
taldra *eg* height
taleb *eb* talebau payment slip; voucher; token
taleithiau Cydffederal *ell* Confederacy
taleithiol *ans* provincial
talentog *ans* talented
talfran *eb* talfrain fret nut
talfyriad *eg* talfyriadau abbreviation
talfyrru *be* abbreviate
talgrynnu *be* round off
talgrynnu i fyny *be* round up
talgrynnu i lawr *be* round down
taliad arian parod *eg* taliadau arian parod cash payment
taliad lles *eg* taliadau lles welfare payment
taliad trosglwyddo *eg* taliadau trosglwyddo transfer payment
Talmud *eg* Talmud
talpio *be* chunking
talu *be* pay
Talu wrth Ennill *be* PAYE
talwrn *eg* talyrnau cockpit
talwynt *eg* talwyntoedd talwind
tamaid *eg* tameidiau bite
tamarind *eg* tamarindau tamarind
tambora *eg* tamborâu tambora
tambwrîn *eg* tambwrinau tambourin; tambour de Basque
tameidiau *ell* odds and ends
tameidiog *ans* fragmented
tampio *be* pat bounce
tân *eg* tanau fire
tân agored *eg* tanau agored open hearth
tân chwythu *eg* tanau chwythu fan heater
tan ffwrndanio *be* underfire
tân gof *eg* tanau gof blacksmith's hearth
Tân Mawr Llundain *eg* Great Fire of London
tân nwy *eg* tanau nwy gas fire
tân weldio *be* fire weld
Tân y Reichstag *eg* Reichstag Fire
tanafael *be* under grasp
tanategu *be* underpin
tanbaent *eg* tanbaentiau underpaint; undercoat (of paint)
tanbaid *ans* intense
tanbeidrwydd *eg* intensity
tanbeintio *be* undercoat
tanboblog *ans* underpopulated
tanbwytho *be* under stitching
tanc *eg* tanciau tank
tanc crychdonni *eg* tanciau crychdonni ripple tank
tanc hynofedd *eg* tanciau hynofedd buoyancy tank
tanc oeri *eg* tanciau oeri cooling tank
tanc septig *eg* tanciau septig septic tank

tanc storio *eg* tanciau storio storage tank
tancer *eg* tanceri tanker
tanchwa *eb* tanchwaoedd firedamp explosion
tandoriad *eg* tandoriadau undercut
tandorri *be* undercut
tanddaearol *ans* underground; subterranean; hypogeal
tanddatblygedig *ans* underdeveloped
tanddefnyddio *be* underutilize
tanerdy *eg* tanerdai tannery
tanestyn *be* underextension
tanfaethu *be* under-nourish
tanfor *ans* submarine
tanffordd *eb* tanffyrdd under-pass
tangiad *eg* tangiadau tangent
tangiad llifiol *ans* slash sawn
tangiadaeth *eb* tangiadaethau tangency
tangiadol *ans* tangential
tango *eg* dawnsiau tango tango
tangram *eg* tangramau tangram
tangroenol *ans* hypodermic
tangwystl *eg* frankpledge
tangyflawni *be* underachieve
tangyflogaeth *eb* underemployment
tangyflogi *be* under-employ
tanh *eg* tanh
tanha *eg* tanha
taniad *eg* taniadau ignition; combustion
taniad coil *eg* taniadau coil coil ignition
tanin *eg* tannin
tanio *be* fire
tanio bisged *be* biscuit firing
tanio gwydrog *be* glaze firing
tanio'n ôl *be* backfire
taniwr nwy *eg* tanwyr nwy gas lighter
tanlawr *ans* underfloor
tanlinellu *be* underline; underscoring
tanlinellu dotiog *be* dotted underline
tanlinellu dwbl *be* double underline
tanlinellwr *eg* tanlinellwyr underline key
tanliw *eg* undercolour
tanlwybr *eg* tanlwybrau subway
tannau cydseiniol *ell* sympathetic strings
tannau llais *ell* vocal cords
tanseilio *be* undermine; subvert
tanseiliol *ans* subversive
tanseiliwr *eg* tanseilwyr subversive
tansugno *be* subduction
tant *eg* tannau string
tant agored *eg* tannau agored open string
tant coludd *eg* tannau coludd gut string
tant cywirsain *eg* tannau cywirsain true string
tant neilon *eg* tannau neilon nylon string
tantalwm (Ta) *eg* tantalum
tanwariant *eg* underspend
tanwario *be* underspend
tanwydredd *eg* underglaze
tanwydro *be* underglaze
tanwydd *eg* tanwyddau fuel
tanwydd di-fwg *eg* smokeless fuel
tanwydd domestig *eg* domestic fuel
tanwydd ffosil *eg* tanwyddau ffosil fossil fuels
tanwydd golosg *eg* coke fuel
tanwydd hydrocarbon *eg* hydrocarbon fuel
tanwydd solet *eg* solid fuel
tanwyneb *eg* tanwynebau underface
tanwynebu *be* underface
tanysgrifiad *eg* tanysgrifiadau subscription
tanysgrifio *be* subscribe
tanysgrifiwr *eg* tanysgrifwyr subscriber
Taoaidd *ans* Taoist
Taoydd *eg* Taoyddion Taoist
tap *eg* tapiau tap
tâp *eg* tapiau tape
tâp adlynol *eg* tapiau adlynol adhesive tape
tâp archifol *eg* tapiau archifol archive tape
tâp cotwm *eg* tapiau cotwm cotton tape
tâp dur *eg* steel tape
tâp glud *eg* gummed tape
tâp glynu *eg* sticky tape
tap gwaelodi *eg* tapiau gwaelodi bottoming tap
tâp gwaith *eg* tapiau gwaith work tape
tâp magnetig *eg* tapiau magnetig magnetic tape
tâp masgio *eg* masking tape
tâp mesur *eg* tapiau mesur tape-measure
tâp mesur *eg* tapiau mesur measuring tape
tâp papur *eg* tapiau papur paper tape
tâp papur llwyd *eg* brown paper tape
tâp papur tyllog *eg* tapiau papur tyllog punched paper tape
tâp parod *eg* tapiau parod prerecorded tape
tap plwg *eg* tapiau plwg plug tap
tap tapr *eg* tapiau tapr taper tap
tap teirffordd *eg* tapiau teirffordd three-way tap
tâp ticio *eg* tapiau ticio ticker tape
tâp-borthi *be* tape feed
tâp-borthydd *eg* tâp-borthwyr tape feed
taped *eg* tapedi tappet
tapestri *eg* tapestrïau tapestry
Tapestri Bayeux *eg* Bayeux Tapestry
tapetwm *eg* tapeta tapetum
tapiau a deiau taps and dies
tapio *be* tap; draw off
tapio sawdl blaen *be* toe tapping
tapr *eg* taprau taper
tapr byr *eg* taprau byr short taper
tapr llaw *eg* taprau llaw hand taper
tapr Morse *eg* taprau Morse Morse taper
tapr syth *eg* taprau syth straight taper
tapro *be* taper
taprog *ans* tapered
tâp-yrrwr *eg* tâp-yrwyr tape drive
taradr *eg* terydr auger
taradr hir *eg* terydr hir long auger

taran *eb* taranau thunder
taranfollt *eb* taranfolltau thunderbolt
tarantela *eg* tarantelâu tarantella
tarddbwynt *eg* tarddbwyntiau origin
tarddell *eb* tarddellau spring
tarddell boeth *eb* tarddellau poeth hot spring
tarddell Vaucluse *eb* tarddellau Vaucluse Vauclusian spring
tarddell-danseilio *be* spring-sapping
tarddiad *eg* tarddiadau source; origin; issue; provenance
tarddiad ethnig *eg* ethnic origin
tarddiad goleuni *eg* source of light
tarddiad llysieuol *eg* vegetable origin
tarddiad mwynol *eg* tarddiadau mwynol mineral origin
tarddiad nant *eg* stream source
tarddiad sêr *eg* origin of stars
tarddle *eg* tarddleoedd point of origin; source
tarddle amrywiant *eb* tarddleoedd amrywiannau source of variation
tarddle pwynt *eg* tarddleoedd pwynt point source
tarddlin *eb* tarddlinau spring line
tarddu *be* originate; issue
tarfiad gwybyddol *eg* tarfiadau gwybyddol cognitive disturbance
tarfu ar *be* disturb
targed *eg* targedau target
targed arfaethedig *eg* targedau arfaethedig proposed target
targed cyrhaeddiad *eg* targedau cyrhaeddiad attainment target
targed chwyddiant *eg* inflation target
targedu cyfyng *be* narrowcasting
tarian *eb* tariannau shield; craton
tarian geg *eb* tariannau ceg gum shield
Tariandir Canada *eg* Canadian Shield
tarmac *eg* tarmac
tarnais *eg* tarneisiau tarnish
tarneisio *be* tarnish
taro (nodyn) *be* pitch
taro (yn gyffredinol) *be* hit; strike
taro bargen *be* clinch a deal
taro chwech *be* hit for six; hit a boundary
taro i lawr *be* knock down
taro nôl *be* hit back
taro pedwar *be* hit a boundary
taro troed *be* stamp
taro ymlaen *be* knock on
taro'r bêl eilwaith *be* hit the ball twice
taro'r corff *be* body percussion
taro'r pren *be* wood shot
taro'r targed *be* hit the target
taro'r wiced *be* hit wicket
tarren *eb* tarenni scarp
tarsol *ans* tarsal
tarsws *eg* tarsus
Tartar *eg* Tartariaid Tartar
Tartaraidd *ans* Tartar
tarten Bakewell *eb* tartenni Bakewell Bakewell tart
tarten gwstard wy *eb* tartenni cwstard wy egg custard tart
tarth *eg* tarthau haze; river mist
tarwden *eb* tarwdenni ringworm
tas *eb* teisi stack
tas galch *eb* teisi calch hum
tasel *eg* taselau tassel
tasg *eb* tasgau task
Tasg Asesu Safonol (TAS) *eb* Tasgau Asesu Safonol Standard Assessment Task
tasg ddyddiol *eb* tasgau dyddiol daily task
tasg gystadleuol *eb* tasgau cystadleuol competitive task
tasg osod *eb* tasgau gosod set task
tasg ymateb i ddata *eb* tasgau ymateb i ddata data-response task
tasg ystafell ddosbarth *eb* tasgau ystafell ddosbarth classroom-based task
tasgu *be* splash
tasiaeth *eg* tachism
tasu coed *be* timber stacking
tatio *be* tatting
tatŵ *eg* tatŵau tattoo
tawch *eg* haze
tawdd *ans* molten
tawddgyffur *eg* tawddgyffuriau suppository
tawel *ans* muted
tawelu meddwl *be* reassure
tawelwr *eg* tawelwyr quietist
tawelydd (=cyffur) *eg* tawelyddion sedative; tranquillizer
tawelydd (ar gar) *eg* tawelyddion silencer
tawelyddiaeth *eb* quietism
tawhid *eg* tawhid
tawnod *eg* tawnodau rest sign
tawnod dot *eg* tawnodau dot dotted rest
tawrin *eg* taurine
tawtoleg *eb* tautology
tawtomeredd *eg* tautomerism
tawtomerig *ans* tautomeric
te cig eidion *eg* beef tea
tebyg *ans* similar
tebygol *ans* probable; likely
tebygoliaeth *eb* tebygoliaethau likelihood; probabilism
tebygolrwydd *eg* tebygolrwyddau probability
tebygolrwydd amodol *eg* tebygolrwyddau amodol conditional probability
tebygolrwydd goddrychol *eg* tebygolrwyddau goddrychol subjective probability
tebygrwydd *eg* similarity; resemblance
tebygrwydd lliw *eg* similarity of colour
tebygrwydd tôn *eg* similarity of tone
teclyn clywed *eg* teclynnau clywed hearing aid
teclyn codi *eg* teclynnau codi hoist
teclyn corneli *eg* teclynnau corneli crevice tool

teclyn mesur pwysau gwaed *eg* teclynnau mesur pwysau gwaed sphygmomanometer
teclyn mesur pwysau gwaed llaw *eg* manual sphygmomanometer
tecstil *eg* tecstilau textile
tecstil printiedig *eg* tecstilau printiedig printed textile
tecstilau a phatrwm ar yr wyneb textiles and surface pattern
tecstilau wedi'u brodio *ell* embroidered textiles
tecstilau wedi'u gwau *ell* knitted textiles
tecstilau wedi'u gwehyddu *ell* woven textiles
tecstio *be* text
tectoneg platiau *eb* plate tectonics
tectonig *ans* tectonic
techneg *eb* technegau technique
techneg addurnol *eb* technegau addurnol decorative technique
techneg arbrofi *eb* technegau arbrofi experimental technique
techneg arsylwi *eb* technegau arsylwi observation technique
techneg aseptig *eb* technegau aseptig aseptic technique
techneg atchwel *eb* regression technique
techneg batio *eb* technegau batio batting technique
techneg deuddeg nodyn *eb* twelve note technique
techneg dda *eb* technegau da good technique
techneg ddiagramatig *eb* diagrammatic technique
techneg ddigyffwrdd *eb* no-touch technique
techneg fodelu benodol *eb* technegau modelu penodol particular modelling technique
techneg galorimetrig *eb* technegau calorimetrig calorimetric technique
► **techneg graffigol** *eb* technegau graffigol graphical technique
Techneg Gwerthuso ac Adolygu Rhaglen (PERT) *eb* Programme Evaluation and Review Technique
techneg gwrthiant gwifren *eb* resistance wire technique
techneg gyflwyno *eb* technegau cyflwyno presentation technique
techneg gynghori *eb* technegau cynghori counselling technique
techneg hyrwyddo *eb* technegau hyrwyddo promotional technique
techneg leisiol *eb* technegau lleisiol vocal technique
techneg luniadu *eb* technegau lluniadu drawing technique
techneg marmori *eb* technegau marmori marbling technique
techneg orffennu *eb* technegau gorffennu finishing technique
techneg reoli *eb* technegau rheoli control technique
techneg rhedeg *eb* technegau rhedeg running technique
techneg samplu *eb* technegau samplu sampling technique
techneg sbectrosgopig *eb* technegau sbectrosgopig spectroscopic technique
techneg sefydlogi *eb* stabilization technique
techneg strôc *eb* stroke technique
techneg teledu *eb* technegau teledu television technique
techneg ymarfer *eb* technegau ymarfer rehearsal technique
techneg ymlacio cynyddol *eb* progressive relaxation technique
technegau diheintio *ell* sterilizing techniques
technegau mathemategol *ell* mathematical techniques
technegol *ans* technical
technegydd *eg* technegwyr technician
technetiwm *eg* technetium
technoleg *eb* technolegau technology
technoleg adeiladu *eb* building technology; construction technology
technoleg amgen *eb* alternative technology
technoleg gwybodaeth *eb* information technology
technoleg gyfarwydd *eb* familiar technology
technoleg reoli *eb* technolegau rheoli control technology
technoleg uwch *eb* hi-tech
technolegol *ans* technological
technolegydd *eg* technolegwyr technologist
teg *ans* fair
tegan *eg* teganau toy
tegan adeiladu *eg* teganau adeiladu constructional toy
tegan addysgol *eg* teganau addysgol educational toy
tegan anwes *eg* teganau anwes cuddly toy
tegan meddal *eg* teganau meddal soft toy
tegeirian esgid Fair *eg* lady's slipper orchid
tegeirian rhuddgoch *eg* tegeirianau rhuddgoch marsh orchid
tegell glud *eg* tegellau glud glue kettle
tei *eg* teis tie
tei bô *eg* bow tie
teiffŵn *eg* teiffwnau typhoon
teilo *be* manure
teilsen *eb* teils tile
teilsen blaen *eb* teils plaen plain tile
teilsen chwarel *eb* teils chwarel quarry tile
teilsen finyl *eb* teils finyl vinyl tile
teilsen fosaig *eb* teils mosaig mosaic tile
teilsen geramig *eb* teils ceramig ceramic tile
teilsen gorc *eb* teils corc cork tile
teilsen grom *eb* teils crwm pantile
teilsen lap dwbl *eb* teils lap dwbl double-lap tile
teilsen lap sengl *eb* teils lap sengl single-lap tile
teilsen losgliw *eb* teils llosgliw encaustic tile
teilsen to *eb* teils to roofing tile
teilsio *be* tile
teilwrio *be* tailoring
teilwrio cymdeithasol *be* social engineering

teilyngdod *eg* merit
teimlad *eg* teimladau feeling
teimlad *eg* teimladau sensation
teimlad *eg* feel
teimlad cyffyrddol *eg* teimladau cyffyrddol palpation
teimlo *be* feel
teimlydd *eg* teimlyddion antenna
teip *eg* teipiau type
teipiadur *eg* teipiaduron typewriter
teipiadur consol *eg* teipiaduron consol console typewriter
teipio *be* type
teipograffeg *eb* typography
teipoleg *eb* typology
teiposod *be* typeset
teiraniad *eg* teiraniadau trisection
teirannu *be* trisect
teirblwydd *ans* triennial
Teirw Scotch *ell* Scotch Cattle
teisen *eb* teisennau cake
teisen Berffro *eb* teisennau Berffro shortbread biscuit
teisen Dundee *eb* teisennau Dundee Dundee cake
teisen ffrwythau *eb* teisennau ffrwythau fruit cake
teisen liw *eb* teisennau lliw colour cake
teitl (mewn papur newyddion neu gylchgrawn) *eg* masthead
teitl (yn gyffredinol) *eg* teitlau title
teitl cronfa ddata newydd *eg* teitlau cronfa ddata newydd new database title
teitl cryno *eg* teitlau cryno brief title
teitl databeilot *eg* teitlau databeilot datapilot title
teitl dogfen *eg* teitlau dogfennau document title
teitl siart *eg* teitlau siart chart title
teitl yn unig title only
teithio *be* travel
teithio cymhellol *be* incentive travel
teithio i mewn ac allan o ofod travel through a space
telathrebu *be* telecommunication
tele-argraffydd *eg* tele-argraffyddion teleprinter
teledeip *eg* teledeipiau teletype
teledestun *eg* teletext
teledu *eg* setiau teledu television
teledu cylch-caeedig *eg* closed circuit television
teledu daearol *eg* terrestrial television
teledu realaeth *eg* reality television
telegram Kruger *eg* Kruger telegram
teleoleg *eb* teleology
teleolegol *ans* teleological
telerau *ell* terms
telerau credyd *ell* credit terms
telerau cytbwys *ell* reciprocal arrangement
telerau dealledig *ell* implied terms
telerau masnach *ell* terms of trade
telesgop *eg* telesgopau telescope
teloffas *eg* telophase
telor *eg* teloriaid warbler
telwriwm (Te) *eg* tellurium
telyn *eb* telynau harp
telyn arwaith dwbl *eb* telynau arwaith dwbl double action harp
telyn arwaith sengl *eb* telynau arwaith sengl single action harp
telyn awelon *eb* telynau awelon aeolian harp
telyn bedal *eb* telynau pedal pedal harp
telyn deires *eb* telynau teires triple harp
telyn ddodi *eb* telynau dodi autoharp
telyn fwa *eb* telynau bwa bowed harp
telyn fysell *eb* telynau bysell dital harp
telyn Geltaidd *eb* telynau Celtaidd Celtic harp
telyn glychsain *eb* telynau clychsain bell harp
telyn gromatig *eb* telynau cromatig chromatic harp
telyn gyngerdd *eb* telynau cyngerdd concert harp
telyn Gymreig *eb* telynau Cymreig Welsh harp
telyn Roegaidd *eb* telynau Groegaidd Grecian harp
telyn Wyddelig *eb* telynau Gwyddelig Irish harp
telynor *eg* telynorion harpist
telynores *eb* telynoresau harpist
teml *eb* temlau temple
Teml Aur *eb* Golden Temple
tempera *eg* tempera
tempera wy *eg* egg tempera
templed *eg* templedi template
templed cofnodion *eg* templedi cofnodion minutes template
templed diwygiedig *eg* templedi diwygiedig amended template
templed ffacs *eg* templedi ffacs fax template
templed rhagosodedig *eg* templedi rhagosodedig default template
templed tro *eg* templedi tro French curve
tempo *eg* tempo
Tenakh *eg* Tenakh
tenant *eg* tenantiaid tenant
tenant fferm *eg* tenantiaid fferm tenant farmer
tenant rhydd *eg* tenantiaid rhydd free tenant
tenant wrth ewyllys *eg* tenantiaid wrth ewyllys tenant-at-will
tenantiaeth *eb* tenancy
tenantiaeth warchodedig *eb* protected tenancy
tenantiaid *ell* tenantry
tenau *ans* thin
tenau iawn *ans* ultra thin
tendon *eg* tendonau tendon
tendonau tarddol a thendonau mewniad *ell* tendons of origin and insertion
tendr *eg* tender
tendril *eg* tendrilau tendril
tenement *eg* tenementau tenement
teneuad *eg* teneuadau rarefaction
teneuo *be* dilution
teneuo *be* reduce
teneuydd *eg* teneuwyr thinner

teneuydd inc *eg* teneuwyr inc ink thinner
tennis *eg* tennis
tenor *eg* tenoriaid tenor
tenor ysgafn *eg* tenoriaid ysgafn lyric tenor
tensiwn arbennig o uchel (t.a.u) *eg* extra high tension (e.h.t.)
tensiwn ergydiol *eg* impulsive tension
tensiwn rhyngwladol *eg* international tension
tensor *eg* tensorau tensor
tentacl *eg* tentaclau tentacle
terabeit *eg* terabeitiau terabyte
teras *eg* terasau terrace
teras haul *eg* terasau haul sun terrace
teraset *eg* terasetau terracette
terasu *be* terrace
teratogen *eg* teratogenau teratogen
terazzo *ans* terazzo
terbiwm (Tb) *eg* terbium
terfan *eg/b* terfannau limit
terfan cydgyfeiriant *eb* convergence limit
terfan elastig *eb* terfannau elastig elastic limit
terfan elastigedd *eb* limit of elasticity
terfan goddefiant *eb* limit of tolerance
terfan gyfrannol *eb* terfannau cyfrannol proportional limit
terfan gyfrannol *eb* limit of proportionality
terfan isel *eb* low limit
terfan uchel *eb* terfannau uchel high limit
terfannau gweledіad *ell* limits of visibility
terfannau Newall *ell* Newall limits
terfannol *ans* limiting
terfyn *eg* terfynau boundary; limit
terfyn amser (ar gyfrifiadur) *eg* timeout
terfyn amser (yn gyffredinol) *eg* terfynau amser deadline
terfyn amser gweinydd *eg* server timeout
terfyn arferol y llanw *eg* terfynau arferol y llanw normal tidal limit
terfyn mordwyo *eg* terfynau mordwyo head of navigation
terfyn nerf *eg* terfynau nerfau nerve ending
terfyn nerf rhydd *eg* terfynau nerfau rhydd free nerve ending
terfyn testun *eg* terfynau testun text limit
terfynblat echddygol *eg* motor end-plate
terfyneiddiad *eg* terfyneiddiadau terminalization
terfynell *eb* terfynellau terminal
terfynell drydan *eb* terfynellau trydan electric terminal
terfynell ddata pell *eb* terfynellau data pell remote data terminal
terfynell ddeallus *eb* terfynellau deallus intelligent terminal
terfynell echddygol *eb* motor terminal
terfynell fud *eb* terfynellau mud dumb terminal
terfynell graffeg *eb* terfynellau graffeg graphics terminal
terfynell pwynt talu *eb* terfynellau pwyntiau talu point of sale terminal
terfyniadau canghennog yr acson *ell* branched terminals of the axon
terfynol *ans* final; terminal
terfynolyn *eg* terfynolynnau end organ
terfynu *be* terminate
terfynus *ans* terminating
terfysg *eg* terfysgoedd riot
terfysg Merthyr *eg* Merthyr rising
terfysgaeth *eb* terrorism
terfysgoedd Beca *ell* Rebecca riots
terfysgu *be* terrorize
terfysgwr *eg* terfysgwyr terrorist
term *eg* termau term
term egni bond *eg* bond energy term
terminws llongau fferi rhyngwladol *eg* international ferry terminal
terra cotta *eg* terra cotta
Terylene *eg* Terylene
tes *eg* heat haze
testament *eg* testamentau testament
Testament Newydd *eg* New Testament
testament newydd apocryffaidd *eg* apocryphal new testament
testosteron *eg* testosterone
testun (=geiriau ysgrifenedig) *eg* testunau text
testun (=pwnc) *eg* testunau subject
testun cudd *eg* hidden text
testun cyfryngol *eg* media text
testun cymorth *eg* testunau cymorth help text
testun gwrthrych lluniadu *eg* testunau gwrthrych lluniadu draw object text
testun heb ei fformatio *eg* unformatted text
testun lluniadu *eg* testunau lluniadu draw text
testun llydan *eg* wide text
testun neges *eg* message text
testun onglog *eg* testunau onglog angled text
testun pennawd *eg* testunau pennawd caption text
testun plaen *eg* plain text
testun prawf *eg* testunau prawf test text
testun syml *eg* testunau syml simple text
testun wedi'i fewnoli *eg* testunau wedi'u mewnoli indented text
testun y teitl *eg* title text
testun yn unig text only
testunol *ans* textual
tetanedd *eg* tetany
tetanws *eg* tetanus
tetraalcocsimethan *eg* tetraalkoxymethane
1,1,2,2-tetrabromoethan *eg* 1,1,2,2-tetrabromoethane
tetracarbonylnicel(0) *eg* tetracarbonylnicel(0) tetracarbonylnickel(0)
1,1,2,2-tetracloroethan *eg* 1,1,2,2-tetrachloroethane
tetraclorometha n *eg* tetrachloromethane
tetracord *eg* tetracordiau tetrachord

tetraethocsimethan *eg* tetraethoxymethane
tetraethylplwm(IV) *eg* tetraethyllead(iv)
tetrahedrol *ans* tetrahedral
tetrahedron *eg* tetrahedronau tetrahedron
tetrod *eg* tetrodau tetrode
tetromino *eg* tetrominos tetromino
teth *eb* tethi teat
teth dymheredd *eb* tethi tymheredd thermo-dummy
teulu *eg* teuluoedd family
teulu cnewyllol *eg* teuluoedd cnewyllol nuclear family
teulu Cristnogol *eg* teuluoedd Cristnogol Christian family
teulu cwpl *eg* teuluoedd cwpl couple family
teulu dosbarth canol Fictoraidd *eg* teuluoedd dosbarth canol Fictoraidd Victorian middle-class family
teulu estynedig *eg* teuluoedd estynedig extended family
teulu grŵp *eg* teuluoedd grŵp group family
Teulu Iorc *eg* House of York
Teulu Lancaster *eg* House of Lancaster
Teulu Orange *eg* House of Orange
teulu rhwydol *eg* teuluoedd rhwydol enmeshed family
teulu sylfaenol *eg* teuluoedd sylfaenol basic family
teulu un rhiant *eg* lone parent family
teulu un rhiant *eg* teuluoedd un rhiant one parent family
teuluol *ans* familial
tew *ans* thick
tewychiad sgalaraidd *eg* scaliform thickening
tewychiad troellog *eg* tewychiadau troellog spiral thickening
tewychu *be* thicken
tewychu eilaidd *be* secondary thickening
tewychu unflwydd *be* annual thickening
tewychydd *eg* tewychwyr thickener
teyrn *eg* teyrnedd tyrant
teyrnaidd *ans* regalian
teyrnas *eb* teyrnasoedd realm
teyrnas *eb* teyrnasoedd kingdom
Teyrnas Unedig, y Deyrnas Unedig *eb* United Kingdom
Teyrnas y Ddwy Sisilia *eb* Kingdom of the Two Sicilies
teyrnasiad *eg* teyrnasiadau reign
teyrnasiad pab *eg* pontificate
teyrngar *ans* loyal
teyrngarwch *eg* allegiance
teyrngarwch *eg* loyalty
teyrngarwr *eg* teyrngarwyr loyalist
Teyrngarwr Ulster *eg* Teyrngarwyr Ulster Ulster Loyalist
teyrnged *eb* teyrngedau tribute
teyrnladdiad *eg* teyrnladdiadau regicide; tyrannicide
teyrnleiddiad *eg* teyrnleiddiaid regicide; tyrannicide
teyrnwialen *eb* teyrnwialennau sceptre
TGAU Cymraeg Ail Iaith Estynedig GCSE Extended Welsh Second Language
TGAU Cymraeg Estynedig GCSE Extended Welsh
ti *eg* tiau tee
tibia *eg* tibia
tic *eg* ticiau check
tîc *eg* teak
ticbryf *eg* ticbryfed deathwatch beetle
ticio *be* check
tierce de Picardie *eg* tierces de Picardie tierce de Picardie
til (clog-glai) *eg* till
til abladu *eg* ablation till
til glyniad *eg* lodgement till
tileru *be* tillering
tilfaen *eg* tilfeini tillite
tîm *eg* timau team
tîm amlddisgyblaethol *eg* timau amlddisgyblaethol multidisciplinary team
tîm cymuned iechyd meddwl *eg* timau cymuned iechyd meddwl community mental health team
tîm gweinyddu rheoli'r rhwydwaith *eg* network management administration team
tîm iechyd *eg* timau iechyd health team
tîm y cwrs *eg* course team
tincial *be* jingle
tincialyn *eg* tincialau jingle
tinsel *eg* tinsel
tio *be* tee
tipio *be* tip
tir *eg* tiroedd land; terrain
tir agored *eg* champion land
tir âr *eg* arable land
tir basn a chadwyn *eg* tiroedd basn a chadwyn basin and range country
tir breiniol *eg* tiroedd breiniol franchise
tir bwrdais *eg* burgage
tir caeedig *eg* tiroedd caeedig enclosed land; enclosure
tir comin *eg* tiroedd comin common land
tir diffaith *eg* tiroedd diffaith waste land
tir esgob *eg* tiroedd esgob bishopland
tir glas (mewn cynllunio etc) *eg* green field
tir glas y safana *eg* tiroedd glas y safana savannah grassland
tir gorchudd *eg* tiroedd gorchudd cover-land
tir llaw farw *eg* tiroedd llaw farw mortmain
tir mawr *eg* mainland
tir neb *eg* no-man's land
tir oer *eg* tierra fria
tir poeth *eg* tierra caliente
tir pori *eg* tiroedd pori grazing land; fields of pasture
tir prysg *eg* scrub land
Tir Pur *eg* Pure Land
tir rhydd-ddaliol *eg* tiroedd rhydd-ddaliol freehold land

tir rhyngafonol *eg* tiroedd rhyngafonol interfluve
tir rhywiog *eg* tilth
tir teg *eg* fair ground
tir tymherus *eg* tierra templada
tir wedi ei wella *eg* improved land
tir y goron *eg* tiroedd y goron crown land
tir ymylol *eg* tiroedd ymylol marginal land
tir yr ysgol *eg* school ground
tirando *eg* tirando
tirddaliadaeth *eb* land tenure
tirfeddiannaeth *eb* landownership
tirfeddiannwr *eg* tirfeddianwyr landowner
tirfesur *be* survey
tirfesur cadwyn *be* chain survey
tirfesurydd *eg* tirfesurwyr surveyor
tirfwrdd *eg* tirfyrddau tableland
tirffurf *eg* tirffurfiau landform
tirffurf arfordirol *eb* tirffurfiau arfordirol coastal landform
tirgaeedig *ans* landlocked
tiriogaeth *eb* tiriogaethau territory
tiriogaeth ddibynnol *eb* tiriogaethau dibynnol dependency
tiriogaeth fandadol *eb* tiriogaethau mandadol mandated territory
tiriogaeth feddianedig *eb* occupied territory
tiriogaeth frodorol *eb* tiriogaethau brodorol reservation
tiriogaeth gydnabyddedig *eb* territorial integrity
Tiriogaeth Ymddiriedig *eb* Trust Territory
tiriogaeth ymddiriedol *eb* tiriogaethau ymddiriedol trusteeship territory
tiriogaethol *ans* territorial
tirio'r bêl *be* touchdown
tirlenwi *be* landfill
tirlif *eg* tirlifiau earth flow
tirlithriad *eg* tirlithriadau landslide
tirlun *eg* tirluniau landscape; paysage
tirlun cnwc a thegell *eg* kame and kettle country
tirlun diwylliannol *eg* cultural landscape
tirlunio caled *be* hard landscaping
tirlunio meddal *be* soft landscaping
tirlyfr *eg* tirlyfrau terrier
tirmon *eg* tirmoniaid groundsman
tirmonaeth *eb* groundsmanship
tirnod *eg* tirnodau landmark
tiroedd newydd *ell* virgin lands
Tiroedd y Babaeth *ell* Papal States
Tironiad *eg* Tironiaid Tironian
tirwedd *eb* tirweddau landscape; relief
tirwedd anamlwg *eb* tirweddau anamlwg faint relief
tirwedd cefnen a rhych *eb* tirweddau cefnen a rhych ridge and furrow relief
tirwedd ddiwrthdro *eb* tirweddau diwrthdro uninverted relief
tirwedd fyrddol *eb* tirweddau byrddol tabular relief
tirwedd greiriol *eb* tirweddau creiriol relict landscape
tirwedd ifanc *eb* tirweddau ifanc juvenile relief
tirwedd iselaidd *eb* tirweddau iselaidd subdued relief
tirwedd leol *eb* tirweddau lleol available relief
tirwedd leol *eb* tirweddau lleol local relief
tirwedd wrthdro *eb* tirweddau gwrthdro inverted relief
tisian *be* sneeze
titaniwm (Ti) *eg* titanium
titaniwm(II) clorid *eg* titanium(II) chloride
titaniwm(IV) ocsid *eg* titanium(IV) oxide
titr *eg* titrau titre
titradaeth *eb* titrimetry
titradaethol *ans* titrimetric
titradiad thermometrig *eg* thermometric titration
titradu *be* titrate
titradu asid-bas *be* acid-base titration
tiwb *eg* tiwbiau tube
tiwb berwi *eg* tiwbiau berwi boiling tube
tiwb canolog *eg* tiwbiau canolog central canal
tiwb capilari *eg* tiwbiau capilari capillary tube
tiwb cardbord *eg* tiwbiau cardbord cardboard tube
tiwb cludo *eg* tiwbiau cludo delivery tube
tiwb dadwefru *eg* tiwbiau dadwefru discharge tube
tiwb Eustachio *eg* tiwbiau Eustachio Eustachian tube
tiwb Fallopio *eg* tiwbiau Fallopio Fallopian tube
tiwb hanner cylch *eg* tiwbiau hanner cylch semicircular canal
tiwb niwral *eg* neural tube
tiwb plastig *eg* tiwbiau plastig plastic tube
tiwb profi *eg* tiwbiau profi test-tube
tiwb sugno *eg* tiwbiau sugno suction tube
tiwb sylem *eg* tiwbiau sylem xylem vessel
tiwb y cochlea *eg* cochlear canal
tiwb y glust *eg* auditory canal
tiwba *eg* tiwbâu tuba
tiwbaidd *ans* tubular
tiwbglychau *ell* tubular bells
tiwbin *eg* tiwbinau tubing
tiwbin haearn *eg* tiwbiau haearn iron tubing
tiwbyn *eg* tiwbynnau tubule
tiwbyn aren *eg* kidney tubule
tiwbyn Malpighi *eg* Malpighian tubule
tiwbyn semen *eg* tiwbynnau semen seminiferous tubule
tiwbyn troellog pen pellaf *eg* distal convoluted tubule
tiwbyn troeth *eg* tiwbynnau troeth uriniferous tubule
tiwna *eg* tiwnaod tuna
tiwnig *eb* tiwnigau tunic
tiwnio tôn-gymedr chwarter-coma *be* quarter-comma mean-tone tuning
tiwniwr *eg* tiwnwyr tuner
tiwniwr piano *eg* tiwnwyr piano piano tuner
tiwtor *eg* tiwtoriaid tutor

tiwtor blwyddyn *eg* tiwtoriaid blwyddyn year tutor
tiwtor bugeiliol *eg* tiwtoriaid bugeiliol pastoral tutor
tiwtor dosbarth *eg* tiwtoriaid dosbarth form tutor
tiwtor drefnydd *eg* tiwtor drefnyddion tutor-organiser
tiwtor moesol *eg* tiwtoriaid moesol moral tutor
tiwtor personol *eg* tiwtoriaid personol personal tutor
tiwtora chwarae *be* play tutoring
tiwtorial *eg* tiwtorialau tutorial
tiwtorial Vygotskian *eg* Vygotskian tutorial
tlawd *ans* poor
tlodi *be* impoverish
tlodi *eg* poverty; impoverishment
tloty *eg* tlotai workhouse
tlotyn *eg* tlodion pauper
tlws *eg* tlysau trophy
tlws *eg* tlysau brooch
tlws crog *eg* pendant
tlysbin *eg* tlysbinau brooch pin
to *eg* toeon roof
to ar ongl *eg* toeon ar ongl pitched roof
to ar oledd *eg* toeon ar oledd lean-to roof
to cafnog *eg* toeon cafnog valley roof
to dormer *eg* toeon dormer dormer roof
to erchwyn *eg* toeon erchwyn parapet roof
to fframiog *eg* toeon fframiog framed roof
to fframiog *eg* toeon fframiog triple roof
to gwellt *eg* toeon gwellt thatched roof
to helm *eg* toeon helm helm roof
to mansard *eg* toeon mansard mansard roof
to sengl *eg* toeon sengl single roof
to trawslath *eg* toeon trawslath purlin roof
to trawslath *eg* toeon trawslath double roof
to trawst gordd *eg* toeon trawst gordd hammer beam roof
tocata *eg* tocatâu toccata
tocbren *eg* tocbrennau pollard
tocio (coed) *be* lop
tocio (mewn ffotograffiaeth) *be* crop
tocsaemia *eg* toxaemia
tocsin *eg* tocsinau toxin
tocyn *eg* tocynnau ticket
tocynistiaeth *eb* tokenism
toddi (un olygfa i'r llall mewn ffilm) *be* dissolve
toddi (yn gyffredinol) *be* melt
toddion *ell* dripping
toga *eb* togâu toga
togl *eg* toglau toggle
togl sbring *eg* toglau sbring spring toggle
toglo *be* toggle
toiled *eg* toiledau water closet
toiled *eg* toiledau toilet
tolc *eg* tolciau dent
tolcio *be* dent
tolciog *ans* chipped
tolchen *eb* tolchennau clot; blood-clot
tolcheniad *eg* coagulation
tolchennu *be* coagulate
toll *eb* tollau toll; duty; tariff
toll allforio *eb* tollau allforio export duty
toll ddial *eb* tollau dial retaliatory tariff
toll fantais *eb* tollau mantais preferential tariff
toll farwolaeth *eb* tollau marwolaeth death duty
toll mewnforio *eb* tollau mewnforio import duty
toll mewnforio *eb* tollau mewnforio import tariff
tollaeth *eb* tollage
tollau *ell* customs
tollau tramor a chartref *ell* customs and excise
tollbont *eb* tollbontydd toll-bridge
tollborth *eg* tollbyrth toll-gate
tolldal *eg* tolldaliadau customs duty
tollffordd *eb* tollffyrdd toll-road
tollty *eg* tolltai custom house
tom tom *eg* tom tomau tom tom
tomen *eb* tomennydd tip; dump
tomen a beili motte and bailey
tomen gladdu *eb* tomenni claddu burial mound
tomen sbwriel *eb* tomenni sbwriel refuse tip; spoil heap
Tomistiaeth *eb* Thomism
Tomistig *ans* Thomistic
tomograffeg gollwng positronau *eg* positron emission tomography (PET)
Tomos y Tanc *eg* Thomas the Tank Engine
ton *eb* tonnau wave
tôn (am liw) *eg* tonau tone
tôn (am sain) *eb* tonau tone
ton adeiladol *eb* tonnau adeiladol constructive wave
ton ardraws *eb* tonnau ardraws transverse wave
ton blân bolar *eb* tonnau plân polar plane polarized wave
tôn brysur *eb* engaged tone
tôn cynnes *eg* tonau cynnes warm tone
ton ddirgrynol *eb* tonnau dirgrynol vibration wave
ton ddwbl *eb* tonnau dwbl double wave
ton gario *eb* tonnau cario carrier wave
ton gario heb ei modylu *eb* tonnau cario heb eu modylu unmodulated carrier wave
ton gario wedi'i modylu *eb* modulated carrier wave
ton gario wedi'i modylu'n osgledol *eb* amplitude modulated carrier wave
tôn glychau *eb* tonau clychau carillon
tôn golau *eg* tonau golau light tone
ton gynyddol *eb* tonnau cynyddol progressive wave
ton hydredol *eb* tonnau hydredol longitudinal wave
ton isgoch *eb* tonnau isgoch infrared wave
ton llanw *eb* tonnau llanw tidal wave
ton radio *eb* tonnau radio radio wave
ton seismig *eb* tonnau seismig seismic wave
ton sin *eb* tonnau sin sine wave
tôn tywyll *eg* tonau tywyll dark tone
ton unfan *eb* tonnau unfan stationary wave

ton uwchfioled *eb* tonnau uwchfioled ultraviolet wave
ton wres *eb* tonnau gwres heatwave
tonedd *eg* tonicity
tonfecaneg *eb* wave mechanics
tonfedd *eb* tonfeddi wavelength
tonfedd ton *eb* tonfeddi tonnau wavelength of a wave
tôn-fyddar *ans* tone-deaf
tonffurf *ans* waveform
tonffurf *eg* tonffurfiau waveform
tonffurf sinwsoidaidd *eb* sinusoidal waveform
tonffurfiau cylched *ell* circuit wave-forms
tonig *eg* tonigau tonic
tonnau cyffroad *ell* excitation waves
tonnell *eb* tonellau wavelet
tonni *be* fluctuate
tonnog *ans* auxiliary
tonnog *ans* wavy; fluctuative
tonsil *eg* tonsilau tonsil
tonsilitis *eg* tonsillitis
tonsur *eg* tonsuriau tonsure
tonydd *eg* tonyddion tonic
tonydd cysefin *eg* home tonic
tonyddiaeth *eb* intonation
top *eg* topiau top
top bwrdd *eg* topiau byrddau table top
top gorymylol *eg* topiau gorymylol overlapping top
top gosod *eg* topiau gosod planted top
top haul *eg* topiau haul sun-top
top llithr (bwrdd) *eg* topiau llithr sliding top
top tennyn *eg* topiau tennyn halter top
top troi *eg* topiau troi spinning top
topig hanesyddol *eg* topigau hanesyddol historical topic
topio (dannedd llif) *be* topping
topograffi *eg* topography
topograffig *ans* topographic
topograffigol *ans* topographical
topoleg *eb* topology
topolegol *ans* topological
topyn *eg* topynnau bung
topyn corc *eg* topynnau corc cork bung
topyn rwber *eg* topynnau rwber rubber bung
Torah *eg* Torah
torasgwrn agored *eg* toresgyrn agored compound fracture
torasgwrn caeedig *eg* toresgyrn caeedig closed fracture
torasgwrn cymhleth *eg* toresgyrn cymhleth complicated fracture
torasgwrn syml *eg* toresgyrn syml simple fracture
torbren *eg* torbrennau off-cut
torbwynt *eg* torbwyntiau breakpoint; cut-off
torbwynt awtomatig *eg* torbwyntiau awtomatig automatic cut-off
tor-contract *eg* breach of contract
torcyfraith *eg* lawbreaking
torch *eg* torchau torque; coil
torch allwedd *eg* torchau allwedd key ring
torchi *be* coiling
torchog *ans* wreathed; coiled
tor-dyletswydd *eb* breach of duty
torddwr *eg* torddyfroedd swash
toredig *ans* discontinuous
toredig mân iawn *ans* ultrafine dashed
torfenthyciad *eg* torfenthyciadau break loan
torglo drws *eg* torgloeon drysau cut door-lock
torgoch *eg* torgochiaid char
torgwmwl *eg* torgymylau cloudburst
tor-heddwch *eg* breach of peace
Tori rhyddfrydol *eg* Torïaid rhyddfrydol liberal Tory
toriad (=rhywbeth a dorrwyd) *eg* toriadau breakage
toriad (=sleisen denau i'w rhoi dan ficrosgop) *eg* toriadau section
toriad (asgwrn) *eg* toriadau fracture
toriad (o blanhigyn) *eg* toriadau cutting
toriad (yn gyffredinol) *eg* toriadau break; cut; excision
toriad ardraws *eg* toriadau ardraws transverse section
toriad bas *eg* bass cut
toriad bastard *eg* toriadau bastard bastard cut
toriad Cesaraidd *eg* toriadau Cesaraidd Caesarean section
toriad colofn *eg* toriadau colofn column break
toriad colofn uniongyrchol *eg* toriadau colofn uniongyrchol direct column break
toriad dart *eg* toriadau dart dart slash
toriad fertigol *eg* toriadau fertigol vertical section
toriad gaing gau *eg* toriadau gaing gau gouge cut
toriad glân *eg* toriadau glân clean cut
toriad herclif *eg* toriadau herclif jigsaw cut
toriad hwyr *eg* late cut
toriad hydredol *eg* toriadau hydredol longitudinal section
toriad llinell *eg* toriadau llinell line break
toriad llinell uniongyrchol *eg* toriadau llinell uniongyrchol direct line break
toriad paragraff *eg* toriadau paragraffau paragraph break
toriad pŵer *eg* toriadau pŵer power cut
toriad rhathell *eg* toriadau rhathell rasp cut
toriad rheiddiol *eg* toriadau rheiddiol radial section
toriad rhes awtomatig *eg* toriadau rhes awtomatig automatic row break
toriad saethol *eg* toriadau saethol sagittal section
toriad trebl *eg* treble cut
toriad tudalen *eg* toriadau tudalen page break
toriad tudalen uniongyrchol *eg* toriadau tudalen uniongyrchol direct page break
toriad union *eg* toriadau union right section
toriad V *eg* toriadau V V-section; V-cut
toriad y monswn *eg* burst of monsoon
toriadau a dotiau dashes and dots
toriadau gorffennu *ell* finishing cuts

Toriaeth ryddfrydol *eb* liberal Toryism
toriant *eg* toriannau scission
torlan *eb* torlannau undercut bank
torlan fawn *eb* torlannau mawn peat hag
torlannol *ans* riparian
torlengig *eg* rupture
torlun *eg* torluniau cut
torlun leino *eg* torluniau leino lino cut
torlun pren *eg* torluniau pren woodcut
torlun taten *eg* torluniau tatws potato cut
torllwyth *eb* torllwythi litter
tornado *eg* tornados tornado
tor-orwedd *be* prone-lying
torrell blaen *eb* torellau plaen plain cutter
torrell glai *eb* torellau clai clay cutter
torrell grafu *eb* torellau crafu scraper cutter
torrell leino *eb* torellau leino lino cutter
torrell neilon *eb* torellau neilon nylon cutter
torrell ochr *eb* torellau ochr side-cutters
torrell rychiog *eb* torellau rhychiog fluted cutter
torrell stensil *eb* torellau stensil stencil cutter
torri (asgwrn) *be* fracture
torri (cyfraith) *be* violate
torri (gyda chyllell etc) *be* cut
torri (i ffwrdd yn llwyr) *be* sever
torri (mortais) *be* chop
torri (yn gyffredinol) *be* break
torri (yn sydyn) *be* snap
torri a gludo cut and paste
torri allan *be* cut out
torri ar y bias *be* cut out on the bias
torri ar y groes *be* cut out on the cross
torri ar yr edau *be* cut on the thread
torri arc *be* arc cutting
torri briciau *be* brick cutting
torri dannedd *be* teething
torri edau *be* thread cutting
torri i ffwrdd *be* cut off
torri i lawr *be* breakdown
torri llengig *be* rupture
torri mecanyddol *be* mechanical cutting
torri metel *be* metal cutting
torri metel *be* metal shearing
torri oddi wrth Rufain *be* break with Rome
torri step *be* step cutting
torri tir *be* break ground
torri trwodd *be* cut through
torri'n giwbiau *be* cube
torri'r ddadl *be* tie-break
torri'r wiced *be* break the wicket
torri'r wiced *be* throw down the wicket
torrwr *eg* torwyr cutter
torrwr bollt *eg* torwyr bollt bolt cutter
torrwr cerdyn *eg* torwyr cerdyn card cutter
torrwr cylched *eg* torwyr cylchedau circuit breaker
torrwr edau *eg* torwyr edau thread cutter
torrwr sglodion *eg* torwyr sglodion chip breaker
torrwr streic *eg* torwyr streic strike breaker
torrwr tanc *eg* torwyr tanc tank cutter
torso *eg* torsoau torso
tortsh *eb* tortshys torch
tortsh bresyddu *eb* tortshys presyddu brazing torch
tortsh weldio *eg* tortshys weldio welding torch
torth siwgr *eb* torthau siwgr sugar loaf
torwaith *eg* cutwork
torws *eg* torysau torus
torhoelen *eb* torhoelion cut nail
tostiwr *eg* tostwyr toaster
tosturi *eg* compassion
totalitaraidd *ans* totalitarian
totem *eg* totemau totem
tra arbenigol *ans* highly specialised
tra ffasiynol *ans* ultra-fashionable
tra medrus *ans* highly skilled
tra-arglwyddiaeth *eb* domination
tra-arglwyddiaethu (ar) *be* dominate
trac *eg* traciau track
trac aer *eg* traciau aer air-track
trac alwminiwm *eg* traciau alwminiwm aluminium track
trac cul *eg* traciau cul narrow gauge track
trac ffibr *eg* traciau ffibr fibre track
trac neilon *eg* traciau neilon nylon track
trac plastig *eg* traciau plastig plastic track
trac rhedeg *eg* traciau rhedeg running track
trac sain *eg* traciau sain soundtrack
trac synthetig *eg* traciau synthetig synthetic track
tracea *eg* traceau trachea
traceid *eg* traceidiau tracheid
traceol *ans* tracheal
Tractariaeth *eb* Tractarianism
tractrics *eg* tractricsau tractrix
tracwisg *eb* tracwisgoedd tracksuit
trachywir *ans* precise
trachywiredd *eg* precision
trachywiredd dwbl *eg* double precision
traddodi (i sefyll prawf) *be* commit
traddodiad *eg* traddodiadau tradition
traddodiad barddol *eg* poetic tradition
traddodiad clasurol Ewropeaidd *eg* European classical tradition
traddodiad crefyddol *eg* traddodiadau crefyddol religious tradition
traddodiad cyfansoddi *eg* traddodiadau cyfansoddi school of composition
traddodiad llafar *eg* traddodiadau llafar oral tradition
traddodiad storïol *eg* narrative tradition
traddodiadol *ans* traditional
traean *eg* traeanau one-third
traean *eg* traeanau third
traeaniad *eg* traeaniadau trisection
traeannu *be* trisect

traed ar led astride
traeth *eg* traethau beach
traeth awyr *eg* mackerel sky
traeth ymdrochi *eg* lido
traethawd (=ysgrif) *eg* traethodau treatise
traethawd (ar gyfer ymchwil) *eg* traethodau thesis
traethawd (=ysgrif) *eg* traethodau treatise
traethawd (yn gyffredinol) *eg* traethodau essay
traethawd ymchwil *eg* traethodau ymchwil thesis
traethbant *eg* traethbantau swale
traethell *eb* traethellau strand
traethiadol *ans* narrative
traethlin *eb* traethlinau strandline
traethlin cyfansawdd *eg* traethlinau cyfansawdd compound shoreline
traethu *be* declaim
trafaeliwr *eg* trafaelwyr commercial traveller
trafertin *eg* trafertinau travertine
trafnidiaeth *eb* traffic
trafnidiaeth drwodd *eb* through traffic
trafnidiaeth foduron *eb* motor traffic
trafnidiaeth gerbydol *eb* vehicular traffic
trafnidiaeth hanfodol *eb* essential traffic
trafnidiaeth oriau brig *eb* peak period traffic
trafod (drwy siarad) *be* discuss
trafod (gyda'r dwylo) *be* handle
trafod *eg* trafodion transaction
trafod ariannol *eg* trafodion ariannol financial transaction
trafod telerau cytundeb *be* negotiate a settlement
trafodaeth (i ddod i gytundeb) *eb* trafodaethau negotiation
trafodaeth (yn gyffredinol) *eb* trafodaethau discussion
trafodion *ell* proceedings
trafodion cynhadledd *ell* conference proceedings
traffig data *eg* data traffic
traffordd (yn UDA) *eb* traffyrdd freeway
traffordd (yn gyffredinol) *eb* traffyrdd motorway
traffordd wybodaeth *eb* information superhighway
traffordd yn cael ei hadeiladu *eb* motorway under construction
trai (y llanw) *eg* treiau ebb
trai (y lleuad) *eg* waning
trais *eg* violence
trais rhywiol *eg* rape
trais yn y cartref *eg* domestic violence
trallwysiad *eg* trallwysiadau transfusion
trallwysiad gwaed *eg* blood transfusion
trallwyso (gwaed) *be* transfer; transfuse
tramffordd *eb* tramffyrdd tramroad
tramgwydd *eg* tramgwyddau offence
tramgwyddaeth *eb* delinquency
tramgwyddus *ans* delinquent
tramgwyddwr *eg* tramgwyddwyr delinquent
tramor *ans* foreign; overseas
tramorwr *eg* tramorwyr foreigner
trampét *eg* trampetau trampette
trampolîn *eg* trampolinau trampoline
tramwy *eg* tramwyon traverse
tramwy agored *eg* open traverse
tramwyfa *eb* tramwyfeydd passage; thoroughfare; slype
Tramwyfa'r Gogledd-Ddwyrain *eb* North-East Passage
Tramwyfa'r Gogledd-Orllewin *eb* North-West Passage
transistor *eg* transistorau transistor
trap *eg* trapiau trap
trapesiwm *eg* trapesiymau trapezium
trapesoid *eg* trapesoidau trapezoid
trapio *be* trap
traphont *eb* traphontydd viaduct
traphont ddŵr *eb* traphontydd dŵr aqueduct
tras *eb* trasau pedigree
trasiedi *eg* trasiedïau tragedy
traul (=dirywiad) *eb* wear
traul (=cost) *eb* treuliau expense
traul a gwisgo wear and tear
traul egni *eb* energy expenditure
traul tanwydd *eb* fuel consumption
traw *eg* trawiau pitch
traw cyngerdd *eg* concert pitch
traw cynhenid *eg* absolute pitch
traw perffaith *eg* perfect pitch
traw perthynol *eg* relative pitch
traw safonol *eg* standard pitch; French pitch
trawben *eg* trawbennau striking head
trawfforch *eb* trawffyrch tuning fork
trawiad (ar fysell) *eg* trawiadau key stroke
trawiad (mewn ffiseg) *eg* trawiadau incidence
trawiad (offeryn taro) *eg* trawiadau percussion
trawiad (yn gyffredinol) *eg* trawiadau hit
trawiad ar y galon *eg* heart attack
trawiad dwbl *eg* trawiadau dwbl double strike
trawiad gwres *eg* trawiadau gwres heatstroke
trawiad nôl *eg* trawiadau nôl hit back
trawiad ymlaen *eg* trawiadau ymlaen knock on
trawma *eg* trawmâu trauma
trawol *ans* incident
traws gwlad *ans* cross country
trawsacen *eb* trawsacenion syncopation
trawsaelod *eg* trawsaelodau cross member
trawsamineiddiad *eg* transamination
trawsbeilliad *eg* cross pollination
trawsblanedig *ans* transplanted
trawsblaniad *eg* trawsblaniadau transplant; transplantation
trawsblaniad organ *eg* trawsblaniadau organ organ transplantation
trawsblannu *be* transplant
trawsblannu organau *be* organ transplantation
trawsborthiant *eg* cross feed
trawsbostio *be* cross-post

trawsbroffil *eg* trawsbroffilau cross profile
trawsbwyth *eg* trawsbwythau overcast stitch
traws-dôn *eb* trawsdonau bridge tone
trawsdrosglwyddiad *eg* countertransference
trawsddodi *be* transpose
trawsddodiad *eg* trawsddodiadau transposition
trawsddodyn *eg* trawsddodynnau transpose
trawsddygiad *eg* trawsddygiadau transduction
trawsddygiadur *eg* trawsddygiaduron transducer
trawselastigedd *eg* cross elasticity
trawselastigedd y galw *eg* cross elasticity of demand
trawsenw *eg* metonym
trawsergyd *eg/b* trawsergydion cut shot
trawsergyd sgwâr *eb* trawsergydion sgwâr square cut
trawsfeddiannaeth *eb* usurpation
trawsfeddiannu *be* usurp
trawsfeddiannwr *eg* trawsfeddianwyr usurper
trawsfeidraidd *ans* transfinite
trawsfudiad *eg* trawsfudiadau translation
trawsfudo *be* translate
trawsfudol *ans* translational
trawsffrwythloni *be* cross-fertilization
trawsffurf *eb* trawsffurfiau transform
trawsffurfiad *eg* trawsffurfiadau transformation
trawsffurfio *be* transform
trawsffurfio ffwythiannau *be* transformation of functions
trawsgludiad (=dogfen gyfreithiol) *eg* conveyance deed
trawsgludiad (carcharorion etc) *eg* transportation
trawsgludo *be* conveyancing
trawsgludwr *eg* trawsgludwyr conveyancer
trawsgrifiad *eg* trawsgrifiadau transcription
trawsgrifio *be* transcribe
trawsgroesiad *eg* trawsgroesiadau cross over
traws-grynhoydd *eg* traws-grynoyddion cross-compiler
trawsgwricwlaidd *ans* cross-curricular
trawsgwricwledd *eg* cross-curricularity
trawsgyfandirol *ans* transcontinental
trawsgyswllt *eg* cross-linkage
trawsgysylltiad *eg* cross-link
trawsgysylltu *be* cross-linking
trawsgyweiriad *eg* trawsgyweiriadau modulation; transition
trawsgyweirio *be* modulate
trawshaenog *ans* cross-bedded
trawshaenu *be* cross-bedding
traws-halogiad *eg* cross-contamination
traws-heintiad *eg* traws-heintiadau cross infection
trawsieithu *be* purposeful concurrent use of language
trawsieithyddol *ans* cross-linguistic
trawsiwerydd *ans* transatlantic
trawslath *eg* trawslathau purlin
trawsleoliad *eg* trawsleoliadau translocation
trawslif *ans* subsequent
trawslif (am nant) *eg* trawslifau subsequent
trawslif (ar gyfer llifio) *eb* trawslifiau cross-cut saw
trawslifiant *eg* transfluence
trawslithryn *eg* trawslithrynnau cross slide
trawslun *eg* trawsluniau transect
trawslunio *be* transect
trawsluosi *be* cross multiply
trawslythrennu *be* transliterate
trawsnewid *be* convert
trawsnewid demograffig *eg* demographic transition
trawsnewid gwaeredol *eg* downhill transition
trawsnewid rhannol *eg* partial conversion
trawsnewid siop *be* shop conversion
trawsnewidiad *eg* trawsnewidiadau transmutation; transition; conversion
trawsnewidiad deuaidd i ddegol *eg* trawsnewidiadau deuaidd i ddegol binary to decimal conversion
trawsnewidiad gwedd *eg* phase transition
trawsnewidiad ynni *eg* conversion of energy
trawsnewidiol *ans* transitional
trawsnewidydd *eg* trawsnewidyddion converter
trawsnewidydd Bessemer *eg* Bessemer converter
trawsnewidydd cylchdro *eg* trawsnewidyddion cylchdro rotary converter
trawsnewidydd digidol-analog *eg* trawsnewidyddion digidol-analog digital-analogue converter
trawsnewidydd fflach *eg* trawsnewidyddion fflach flash converter
trawsnodi *be* transpose
trawsnodiad *eg* trawsnodiadau transposition
► **trawsochredd** *eg* cross-laterality
trawsosod (llythrennau, geiriau) *be* reversal
trawsrythm *eg* trawsrythmau cross-rhythm
traws-sylweddiad *eg* transubstantiation
trawst *eg* trawstiau beam; cross beam; boom
trawst bras *eg* trawstiau bras baulk
trawst bras wedi'i haneru *eg* trawstiau bras wedi'u haneru half-timber
trawst byffer *eg* trawstiau byffer buffer beam
trawst cantilifer *eg* trawstiau cantilifer cantilevered beam
trawst gordd *eg* trawstiau gordd hammer beam
trawst llawr *eg* trawstiau llawr floor joist
trawst nenfwd *eg* trawstiau nenfwd ceiling joist
trawst o chwith *eg* trawstiau o chwith reversed beam
trawst pontio *eg* trawstiau pontio bridging joist
trawst sefydlog *eg* beam in situ
trawst wedi'i gynnal yn syml *eg* trawstiau wedi'u cynnal yn syml simply supported beam
trawstaith *eb* trawsteithiau traverse
trawstoriad *eg* trawstoriadau cross-section; cross cut
trawstorri *be* cross cut

trawstrefa *be* transhumance
trawswisgwr *eg* trawswisgwyr transvestite
trawsyriad data *eg* trawsyriadau data data transmission
trawsyriant *eg* trawsyriannau transmission
trawsyriant ochrol *eg* flanking transmission
trawsyriant paralel *eg* parallel transmission
trawsyriant prawf *eg* test transmission
trawsyriant tonnau sain *eg* transmission of sound waves
trawsyrru *be* transmit
trawsyrru data *be* data transmission
trawsyrrydd *eg* trawsyryddion transmitter
trawsyrrydd niwral *eg* trawsyryddion niwral neural transmitter
trebl *eg* treblau treble
trechedd anghyflawn *eg* incomplete dominance
trechedd apigol *eg* apical dominance
trechedd croeslinol *eg* diagonal dominance
trechedd ochrol *eg* lateral dominance
trechol *ans* dominant
trechu *be* defeat
tref *eb* trefi town
tref adwy *eb* trefi adwy gap town
tref ddibynnol *eb* trefi dibynnol satellite town
tref farchnad *eb* trefi marchnad market town
tref fodel *eb* trefi model model town
tref gaerog *eb* trefi caerog walled town
tref noswylio *eb* trefi noswylio dormitory town
tref sianti *eb* trefi sianti shanty town
tref wledig *eb* trefi gwledig country town
trefedigaeth *eb* trefedigaethau plantation
trefedigaeth *eb* trefedigaethau colony
trefedigaethau Ulster *ell* Ulster plantations
trefedigaethol *ans* colonial
trefedigaethu *be* colonize
trefeillio *be* twinning
trefgordd *eb* trefgorddau township
treflun *eg* trefluniau townscape
trefn (=dilyniant) *eb* order
trefn (=dull gwithredu) *eb* trefnau procedure
trefn (=ffordd arferol o wneud) *eb* routine
trefn achredu *eb* trefnau achredu accreditation procedure
trefn aelwyd *eb* domestic system
trefn animeiddio *eb* animation order
trefn cymdeithas *eb* social order
trefn dau *eb* second order
trefn diogelwch perthnasol *eg* relevant safety procedure
trefn drimaes *eb* three-field system
trefn dderbyn *eb* admissions procedure
trefn ddisgynnol *eb* descending order
trefn ddosbarthu *eb* classification system
trefn eglwys *eb* church order
trefn esgynnol *eb* ascending order
trefn etholiadol *eb* electoral system
trefn faenorol *eb* manorial system
trefn ffatri *eb* factory system
trefn ffiwdal *eb* feudal system
trefn gosbi *eb* penal system
trefn gronolegol *eb* chronological order
trefn gwaith *eb* order of work
trefn gyfeirio *eb* referral procedures
trefn gywir *eb* correct sequence
trefn gywiro *eb* trefnau cywiro correction procedure
trefn hap-ffeil stwnshlyd *eb* hashed random file organization
trefn lywodraethol *eb* governance
trefn maint *eb* order of magnitude
trefn meysydd agored *eb* openfield system
trefn o werthuso safle *eb* site evaluation procedure
trefn restrol *eb* trefnau rhestrol rank order
trefn rhaglen *eb* running order
trefn sefydledig *eb* established routine
trefn un *eb* first order
trefn weinyddol *eb* administrative procedure
trefn werthuso *eb* appraisal procedures
trefn wrthdro *eb* reverse order
Trefn y Dydd *eb* Order of the Day
trefn y gad *eb* battle order
trefn y gweithrediadau *eb* sequence of operations
trefn yr wyddor *ans* alphabetical
trefn y stori *eb* story order
trefn ymgilio *eb* evacuation procedures
trefn ymgychwyn *eb* initialization procedure
trefnau cymesuredd cylchdro *ell* orders of rotational symmetry
trefnedig *ans* sorted; ordered
trefniad *eg* trefniadau arrangement
trefniad cyfunol *eg* trefniadau cyfunol merge sort
trefniad disgynnol *eg* trefniadau disgynnol descending sort
trefniad disgynnol *eg* trefniadau disgynnol sort descending
trefniad esgynnol *eg* trefniadau esgynnol sort ascending
trefniad esgynnol *eg* trefniadau esgynnol ascending sort
trefniad mewnosod *eg* trefniadau mewnosod insertion sort
trefniadaeth *eb* organization
trefniadaethol *ans* organizational
trefniadau asesu *ell* assessment arrangements
trefniadau ffioedd amodol *ell* conditional fee arrangements
trefniadol *ans* procedural
trefniant *eg* trefniannau arrangement; formation
trefniant cerdd dant *eg* cerdd dant arrangement
trefniant cerddorfaol *eg* trefniannau cerddorfaol orchestration
trefniant cylch *eg* circle formation
trefniant cyllidol *eg* trefniadau cyllidol budgetary arrangement
trefniant fertigol *eg* vertical arrangement

trefniant rhydd *eg* free formation
trefnol *ans* ordinal
trefnu (=cynllunio a pharatoi) *be* organize
trefnu (=gosod allan) *be* set out
trefnu (=gosod yn eu trefn) *be* order
trefnu (ar gyfrifiadur) *be* sort
trefnu (blodau, darn o gerddoriaeth) *be* arrange
trefnu awtomatig *be* automatic sort
trefnu cyfunol *be* merge sort
trefnu eiconau *be* arrange icons
trefnu ffeiliau *be* file organization
trefnu ffenestri *be* arrange windows
trefnu ffenestri'n fertigol *be* arrange windows vertical
trefnu ffenestri'n llorweddol *be* arrange windows horizontal
trefnu gofod *be* spatial organisation
trefnu gwrthrych *be* arrange object
trefnu (milwyr) *be* deploy
trefnu seiniau *be* organize sounds
trefnu'n fertigol *be* arrange vertically
trefnu'n llorweddol *be* arrange horizontally
trefnus *ans* coherent
trefnwr teithiau *eg* trefnwyr teithiau travel agent
trefnydd *eg* trefnyddion organizer
trefnydd *eg* trefnyddion arranger
trefnydd cymorth cartref *eg* trefnyddion cymorth cartref home help organizer
trefnydd teithiau *eg* trefnwyr teithiau tour operator
trefol *ans* municipal
trefol *ans* urban
trefolaeth *eb* urbanism
trefoledig *ans* urbanized
trefoli *be* urbanize
trefol-wledig *ans* urbanrural
treftadaeth *eb* patrimony
treftadaeth gerddorol *eb* musical heritage
treftadol *ans* patrilineal
treial *eg* treialon trial
treial cytuno *eg* treialon cytuno agreement trial
treial gan reithgor *eg* trial by jury
treiddadwy *ans* penetrable
treiddiad *eg* penetrance
treiddiad *eg* treiddiadau penetration
treiddio *be* penetrate
treiddio *be* enter
treiddiol *ans* penetrating
treiddiwr *eg* treiddwyr tip
treiddiwr taflegryn *eg* missile tip
treiddiwr wraniwm diffygiol *eg* depleted uranium tip
treigl amser *eg* passing of time
treiglad *eg* treigladau mutation
treillio *be* trawl
treillong *eb* treillongau trawler
treillrwyd *eb* treillrwydi trawl net
treisgar *ans* violent
treisio *be* rape; violate
tremio (am y camera) *be* pan
tremolando *adf* tremolando
tremolo *eg* tremoli tremolo
trên (gêr) *eg* trenau train
trên cyfansawdd *eg* trenau cyfansawdd compound train
trên gêr *eg* trenau gêr gear train
trên gêr cyfansawdd *eg* trenau gêr cyfansawdd compound gear train
trên leiner *eg* trenau leiner liner train
trên llwythi *eg* trenau llwythi freight train
trên syml *eg* trenau syml simple train
trental *eg* trentalau trental
tresmasiad *eg* tresmasiadau trespass; transgression
tresmasu *be* trespass
tresmaswr *eg* tresmaswyr trespasser
trestl *eg* trestlau trestle
treswaith *eg* tresweithiau tracery
treth (yn gyffredinol) *eb* trethi tax
treth (yn hanesyddol) *eb* trethi tribute; impost; levy
treth ad valorem *eb* ad valorem tax
treth aelwyd *eb* hearth tax
treth anuniongyrchol *eb* trethi anuniongyrchol indirect tax
treth ar gyfoeth *eb* wealth tax
treth ar werth (TAW) *eb* value added tax
treth atchwel *eb* trethi atchwel regressive tax
treth bryniant *eb* purchase tax
treth enillion cyfalaf *eb* capital gains tax
treth ffiwdal *eb* tallage
treth gasgen a phwysau *eb* tunnage & poundage
treth geiniog *eb* penny rate
treth gorfforaeth *eb* corporation tax
Treth Gyflogi Dethol *eb* Selective Employment Tax
treth gynyddol *eb* trethi cynyddol progressive taxes
treth incwm *eb* income tax
Treth Longau *eb* Ship Money
treth stad *eb* estate duty
treth stamp *eb* stamp duty
treth tir datblygu *eb* trethi tir datblygu development land tax
Treth Trosglwyddo Cyfalaf *eb* Capital Transfer Tax
Treth y Daniaid *eb* Danegeld
treth y geiniog *eb* common penny
treth y pen *eb* trethi y pen capitation tax; poll tax
trethadwy *ans* taxable
trethdalwr *eg* trethdalwyr rate payer
trethi busnes *ell* business rates
trethi uniongyrchol *ell* direct taxes
trethiad *eg* trethiadau taxation
trethu *be* tax
treulfwyd *eg* chyme
treuliad *eg* treuliadau digestion
treuliadwy *ans* digestible
treuliadwyedd *eg* digestibility
treuliant (ffurfiau daearegol) *eg* denudation

treuliant (nwyddau) *eg* consumption
treuliau banc *ell* bank charges
treulio (amser) *be* spend
treulio (bwyd) *be* digest
treulio bwyd *be* food digestion
tri allan three outs
tri chwarter *eg* three quarters
tri dimensiwn *ans* three-dimensional
Tri Phenderfyniad (1629) *eg* Three Resolutions
triad *eg* triadau triad
triaidd *ans* ternary
trialcocsimethan *eg* trialkoxymethane
Triasig *ans* Triassic
triawd (=set o dri) *eg* triawdau triple; threesome
triawd (yn canu etc) *eg* triawdau trio
triawd gwybyddol *eg* cognitive triad
triawd piano *eg* triawdau piano piano trio
tribiwn *eg* tribiwnau tribune
tribiwnlys *eg* tribiwnlysoedd tribunal
tribiwnlys apêl cyflogaeth *eg* employment appeal tribunal
tribiwnlys diwydiannol *eg* industrial tribunal
tribiwnlys gweinyddol *eg* administrative tribunal
tribromomethan *eg* tribromomethane
tricel *eg* tricel
tricloroethanal *eg* trichloroethanal
2,2,2-tricloroethandeuol *eg* 2,2,2-trichloroethanediol
tricloromethan *eg* trichloromethane
(tricloromethyl)bensen *eg* (trichloromethyl)benzene
tricloronitromethan *eg* trichloronitromethane
trichwarterwr *eg* trichwarterwyr three-quarter
tridarn *ans* tripartite
Tridentaidd *ans* Tridentine
tri-digid *ans* three-digit
triethocsimethan *eg* triethoxymethane
triethylamin *eg* triethylamine
trifforiwm *eg* trifforia triforium
triger *eg* trigeri trigger
Triger Schmitt Schmitt Trigger
trigiadwy *ans* habitable
triglyserid *eg* triglyseridau triglyceride
trigolyn *eg* trigolion inhabitant
trigonol *ans* trigonal
trigonometreg *eb* trigonometry
trigonometregol *ans* trigonometrical
trigonometrig *ans* trigonometric
trihedrol *ans* trihedral
triiodomethan *eg* triiodomethane
trikaya *eg* trikaya
trimer *eg* trimerau trimer
trimethylalwminiwm *eg* trimethylaluminium
1,3,5-trimethylbensen *eg* 1,3,5-trimethylbenzene
2,2,4-trimethylpentan *eg* 2,2,4-trimethylpentane
trimio *be* trim
trimio a snipio trim and snip
trimiwr *eg* trimwyr trimmer
trimiwr trachywir *eg* trimwyr trachywir precision trimmer
trin (data etc) *be* manipulate
trin (yn gyffredinol) *be* treat
trin (tir) *be* cultivate; till
trin (cig ar gyfer ei goginio) *be* dress
trin delweddau *be* image manipulation
trin digwyddiadau *be* event handling
trin dŵr *be* water treatment
trin ffeiliau *be* file handling
trin gwallau *be* error handling
trin gwybodaeth *be* information handling
trin llinynnau *be* string handling
trin olwyn *be* wheel dressing
trin traed *be* chiropody
Trindod *eb* Trinity
triniad *eg* cultivation
triniad mudol *eg* shifting cultivation
triniaeth (gyda'r dwylo) *eb* triniaethau handling
triniaeth (yn gyffredinol) *eb* triniaethau treatment
triniaeth adrannol *eb* sectionalism
triniaeth arwyneb *eb* triniaethau arwyneb surface treatment
triniaeth derfynol *eb* final treatment
triniaeth feintiol *eb* quantitative treatment
triniaeth geidwadol *eb* triniaethau ceidwadol conservative treatment
triniaeth wres *eb* heat treatment
triniaeth ymyl *eb* edge treatment
2,4,6-trinitroffenol *eg* 2,4,6-trinitrophenol
trinomaidd *ans* trinomial
trinomial *eg* trinomialau trinomial
trio *eg* trios trio
triocsigen *eg* trioxygen
triod *eg* triodau triode
triongl *eg* trionglau triangle
triongl anghyfochrog *eg* trionglau anghyfochrog scalene triangle
triongl cyflymderau *eg* trionglau cyflymderau triangle of velocities
triongl grymoedd *eg* trionglau grymoedd triangle of forces
triongl hafalochrog *eg* trionglau hafalochrog equilateral triangle
triongl isosgeles *eg* trionglau isosgeles isosceles triangle
triongl mawr *eg* trionglau mawr large triangle
triongl ongl aflem *eg* trionglau onglau aflym obtuse angled triangle
triongl ongl lem *eg* trionglau onglau llym acute angled triangle
triongl ongl sgwâr *eg* trionglau ongl sgwâr right-angled triangle
triongl sfferig *eg* trionglau sfferig spherical triangle
trionglau cyfath *ell* congruent triangles
trionglau cyflun *ell* similar triangles
triongliant *eg* triongliannau triangulation

trionglog *ans* triangular
trionglogrwydd *eg* triangularity
triol *ans* tercimal
triolyn *eg* triolion tercimal
trip *eg* tripiau trip
tripled *eb* tripledi triplet
triphlyg *ans* triple
triphlyg *eg* triphlygion triple
triratna *eg* triratna
tris(2-hydrocsiethyl)amin *eg* tris(2-hydroxyethyl)amine
tris(pentan-2,4-deuonato)cobalt(III) *eg* tris(pentane-2,4-dionato)cobalt(III)
tritanopia *eg* tritanopia
triwant *ans* truant
triwant *eg* triwantiaid truant
triwantiaeth *eb* truancy
triwr *eg* triwyr triumvir
triwriaeth *eb* triwriaethau triumvirate
tro *eg* troeon twist; turn; curve
tro cyflawn *eg* troeon cyflawn complete turn
tro chwith *eg* troeon chwith left-hand turn
tro de *eg* troeon de right-hand turn
tro dwy law *eg* troeon dwy law two-hand turn
tro mewn coil *eg* troadau mewn coil turn in a coil
tro pedol *eg* troeon pedol u-turn
tro unfan *eg* troeon unfan turn single
troad *eg* troadau turning
troad ar golyn *eg* troadau ar golyn pivot turn
troad dwbl *eg* troadau dwbl double turning
troad sengl *eg* troadau sengl single turning
trobwll *eg* trobyllau whirlpool
trobwynt *eg* trobwyntiau turning point
trocoid *eg* trocoidau trochoid
trocharaenu *be* dip coating
trochbren *eb* trochbrennau dipstick
trochdrwyth (defaid) *eg* dip
trochi (defaid) *be* dipping
trochi (yn gyffredinol) *be* immerse
trochiad *eg* trochiadau immersion
trochiad llawn *eg* full immersion
trochion *ell* suds
trochion sebon *ell* lather
trochoeri *be* quench
trochydd *eg* trochyddion dipper
troed *eg/b* traed foot
troed bawen *eb* traed pawen paw foot
troed bêl *eb* traed peli ball foot
troed crafanc *eb* traed crafanc claw foot
troed chwith *eb* traed chwith left foot
troed flaen *eb* traed blaen front foot
troed fraced *eb* traed bracedi bracket foot
troed garn *eb* traed carn hoof foot
troed glwb *eb* traed clwb club foot
troed pelen a chrafanc *eb* traed pelen a chrafanc ball and claw foot
troed segur *eb* traed segur non-kicking foot
troed wnïo *eb* traed gwnïo sewing foot
troed y perpendicwlar *eb* foot of perpendicular
troedfedd *eb* troedfeddi foot
troedfedd o hyd *eb* foot run
troedfedd sgwâr o bren *eb* troedfeddi sgwâr o bren foot super
tröedigaeth *eb* tröedigaethau conversion
tröedigaeth grefyddol *eb* tröedigaethau crefyddol religious conversion
troedio (hosan) *be* refoot
troedio'r dŵr *be* tread water
troedlath *eb* troedlathau treadle
troednodyn *eg* troednodiadau footnote
troednodyn nesaf *eg* next footnote
troednoeth *ans* barefoot
troed-rewlif *eg* troed-rewlifau foot glacier
troedwaith *eg* footwork
troedyn *eg* troedynnau footer
troedyn adroddiad *eg* troedynnau adroddiad report footer
troedyn ffurflen *eg* troedynnau ffurflen form footer
troell nyddu *eb* troellau nyddu spinning wheel
troelli *be* twist; spin; nutate
troelli o dan y bêl *be* backspin
troelli ochr y bêl *be* sidespin
troelliad *eg* troelliadau spin; nutation
troelliad cynhenid *eg* troelliadau cynhenid intrinsic spin
troelliad ochr agored *eg* troelliadau ochr agored off-break bowling
troelliad ochr goes *eg* leg-break
troelliad paredig *eg* troelliadau paredig low spin
troelliad raced *eg* spin of racket
troelliad y Ddaear *eg* troelliadau'r Ddaear spin of the Earth
troelli'r bêl *be* spin the ball
troelli'r bêl tros ben *be* topspin
troellog *ans* spiral
troeth *eg* urine
troethi *be* micturate
troethiad *eg* micturition
troethlif *eg* diuresis
trofan *eg* trofannau tropic
Trofan Cancr *eg* Tropic of Cancer
Trofan Capricorn *eg* Tropic of Capricorn
trofannau *ell* tropics
trofannol *ans* tropical
trofannol-arforol *ans* tropical maritime
trofannol-gyfandirol *ans* tropical continental
trofar *eg* trofarrau torsion bar
troffig *ans* trophic
troi (hylif) *be* stir
troi (yn gyffredinol) *be* turn
troi a rhoi turn and give
troi allan *be* cast out; evict
troi ar y bêl *be* turn on the ball
troi ar y nodwydd *be* pivot

troi o gwmpas *be* orbit
troi o'r goes *be* leg break bowling
troi partner *be* turn a partner
troi'n unionsyth *be* log roll
troi'n wydr *be* vitrify
troi'r sawdl *be* turn the heel
trol *eb* troliau tumbrel
trôl *eg* troliau troll
troli *eg* trolïau trolley
trolif *eg* trolifau eddy
trolifo *be* eddy
trolio *be* troll
trombôn *eg* trombonau trombone
trombôn tenor *eg* trombonau tenor trombone tenor
trombonydd *eg* trombonwyr trombonist
tromino *eg* trominos tromino
tropedd *eg* tropeddau tropism
tropoffin *eg* tropoffiniau tropopause
troposffer *eg* troposfferau troposphere
trorym *eg* trorymoedd torque
tros swing *eb* tros swingiau overswing
tros swing freichsyth *eb* tros swingiau breichsyth overswing
trosafael *eb* over grasp
trosaidd *ans* transitive
tros-argraffu *be* over-print
trosbeintio *be* overpainting
trosben *eg* trosbennau somersault
trosben ceugefn *eg* trosbennau ceugefn hollow back somersault
trosben dwbl *eg* trosbennau dwbl double somersault
trosbennu *be* somersault
trosblyg *eg* trosblygion overfold
trosdeipiad *eg* trosdeipiadau overtype
trosdeipio *be* overtype
trosedd (mewn chwaraeon) *eg/b* troseddau foul; infringement
trosedd (gyfreithiol) *eg/b* troseddau offence; crime
trosedd drafnidiol *eb* troseddau trafnidiol traffic offence
trosedd ddiannod *eb* troseddau diannod summary offence
trosedd dditiadwy *eb* troseddau ditiadwy indictable offence
trosedd efelychu *eb* troseddau efelychu copy-cat crime
trosedd farwol *eb* troseddau marwol capital offence
trosedd neillfordd *eb* troseddau neillfordd either way offence
trosedd ryfel *eb* troseddau rhyfel war crime
troseddau yn erbyn person *ell* offences against the person
troseddeg *eb* criminology
troseddol *ans* criminal
troseddu yn erbyn (confensiwn) *be* violate
troseddwr *eg* troseddwyr criminal
troseddwr ifanc *eg* troseddwyr ifanc young offender
troseddwr rhyfel *eg* troseddwyr rhyfel war criminal
trosfeddiannu *be* take-over
trosfeddiant *eg* trosfeddiannau take-over
trosflows *eb* trosflowsiau overblouse
trosffordd *eb* trosffyrdd flyover
trosgais *eg* converted try
trosglwyddadwy *ans* transferable
trosglwyddedd *eg* transferability
trosglwyddiad *eg* trosglwyddiadau transfer; transmission; transduction; conveyance
trosglwyddiad amodol *eg* trosglwyddiadau amodol conditional transfer
trosglwyddiad credyd *eg* credit transfer
trosglwyddiad cyfresol *eg* trosglwyddiadau cyfresol serial transfer
trosglwyddo (neges etc) *be* transmit
trosglwyddo (teitl cyfreithiol) *be* convey
trosglwyddo (yn gyffredinol) *be* transfer
trosglwyddo cyfalaf electronig *be* electronic funds transfer
trosglwyddo data *be* data transfer
trosglwyddo egni *be* transfer energy
trosglwyddo egni *be* energy transfer
trosglwyddo elddo *be* property conveyance
trosglwyddo mater *be* transfer matter
trosglwyddo ymlaen *be* roll over
trosglwyddo'r gost *be* transfer cost
trosglwyddydd *eg* trosglwyddyddion transmitter
trosglwyddyn *eg* trosglwyddynnau transfer
trosglwyddyn gwreslynol *eg* trosglwyddynnau gwreslynol iron-on transfer
trosglwyddyn smocwaith *eg* trosglwyddynnau smocwaith smocking transfer
trosgyfeirio *be* sublimation
trosgynnol *ans* transcendental
troshaen *eb* troshaenau overlay
troshaen ddiwylliannol *eb* cultural overlay
troshaen rhaglen *eb* troshaenau rhaglen program overlay
troshaenu *be* overlay
trosi (cais) *be* convert
trosi (mewn biocemeg) *be* translate
trosi (syniadau) *be* turn
trosi rhwng fframiau *be* slide-frame transition
trosiad (=cyffelybiaeth) *eg* trosiadau metaphor
trosiad (cais) *eg* trosiadau conversion
trosiad (mewn biocemeg) *eg* trosiadau translation
trosiad (mewn ffiseg) *eg* trosiadau transition
trosiad coed *eg* timber conversion
trosiant *eg* trosiannau turnover
trosiant asedau *eg* asset turnover
trosiant gwerthu *eg* trosiannau gwerthu sales turnover
trosiant llafur *eg* labour turnover
trosiant staff *eg* staff turnover
trosiant stoc *eg* stock turnover

troslais *eg* trosleisiau voiceover
troslap *eg* troslapiau overwrap
trosleisio *be* voiceover; dubbing
troslun *eg* trosluniau transfer
trosnod *eg* trosnodau switch node
trosol *eg* trosolion crowbar
trosoledd *eg* trosoleddau leverage
trosolfar *eg* trosolfarrau lever bar
trosoli *be* level over
trosoliad *eg* trosoliadau leverage
trosolwg *eg/b* overview
trosolwg blwyddyn *eb* year overview
tros-seinio *be* dubbing
trostir *eg* overland
trostorri *be* cut over
troswr cronfa ddata *eg* troswyr cronfa ddata database converter
troswydro *be* overglaze
troswydryn *eg* troswydrau overglaze
trosysgrifo *be* overwrite
Trotscïad *eg/b* Trotsciaid Trotskyist
Trotscïaeth *eb* Trotskyism
trothwy *eg* trothwyau threshold
trothwy absoliwt *eg* absolute threshold
trothwy gwahaniaeth *eg* difference threshold
trothwy gwahaniaethu deubwynt *eg* two-point discrimination threshold
trothwy naw o'r gloch *eg* nine o'clock watershed
trothwyol *ans* liminal
trowsus *eg* trowsusau trousers
trowsus nofio *eg* trowsusau nofio trunks
tröydd *eg* troyddion stirrer
tröydd magnetig *eg* troyddion magnetig magnetic stirrer
trum gorfant *eg* trumiau gorfant alveolar ridge
trwbadŵr *eg* trwbadwriaid troubadour
trwch *eg* thickness
trwch dwbl *eg* double thickness
trwch wal *eg* wall-thickness
trwch y gellir ei anwybyddu *eg* negligible thickness
trwchus *ans* thick; bushy; dense
trwm (am deip) *ans* bold
trwm (am ffordd o symud) *ans* ponderous
trwm (yn gyffredinol) *ans* heavy
trwm iawn (am deip) *ans* ultra bold
trwmpedwr *eg* trwmpedwyr trumpeter
trwsiadus *ans* well-groomed
trwsio (sanau etc) *be* darn
trwsio (yn gyffredinol) *be* mend
trwyadl *ans* rigorous
trwybwn *eg* trwybynnau throughput
trwydded *eb* trwyddedau licence; pass
trwydded modur *eb* trwyddedau modur road fund licence
Trwydded Yrru Gyfrifiadurol Ewropeaidd *eb* European Computer Driving Licence
trwyddedig *ans* licensed
trwyddedwr *eg* trwyddedwyr approver
trwyn (ci etc) *eg* trwynau muzzle
trwyn (daearyddol) *eg* trwynau point
trwyn (yn gyffredinol) *eg* trwynau nose
trwyn byr *eg* trwynau byr stubnose
trwyn crwn *eg* trwynau crwn round nose
trwynol *ans* nasal
trwyth *eg* trwythau infusion; lotion; tincture
trwyth baban *eg* baby lotion
trwyth glanhau *eg* cleansing lotion
trwyth gwair *eg* hay infusion
trwyth mewnwythiennol *eg* trwythau mewnwythiennol intravenous infusion
trwyth parhaus *eg* trwythau parhaus continuous infusion
trwythiad *eg* impregnation
trwytho *be* infuse; impregnate
trwythol *ans* tinctorial
trwytholchi *be* leach
trwytholchiad *eg* leaching
trybedd *eb* trybeddau tripod; trivet
tryc *eg* tryciau truck
trychiad (=rhywbeth wedi'i dorri i ffwrdd) *eg* trychiadau amputation
trychiad (ar gynllun, lluniad) *eg* trychiadau section
trychiad amlinell *eg* trychiadau amlinell outline section
trychiad arosgo *eg* trychiadau arosgo oblique section
trychiad conig *eg* trychiadau conig conic section
trychiad cyflawn *eg* trychiadau cyflawn complete section
trychiad llorweddol *eg* trychiadau llorweddol horizontal section
trychiad safonol *eg* standard section
trychiad tangiadol *eg* trychiadau tangiadol tangential section
trychiad U *eg* trychiadau U U-section
trychiadol *ans* sectional
trychinebedd *eg* catastrophism
trychinebu *be* catastrophizing
trychlun *eg* trychluniau sectional drawing
trychu (=torri i ffwrdd) *be* amputate
trychu (ar gynllun, lluniad) *be* section
trychu a gwanu cut and thrust
trychu at ben *be* cut at head
trychu at foch *be* cut at cheek
trychu at fynwes *be* cut at chest
trychu at ystlys *be* cut at flank
trydan *eg* electricity; electric
trydan dŵr *eg* hydroelectric
trydan statig *eg* static electricity
trydanol *ans* electrical; electric
trydanu *be* electrify
trydanwr *eg* trydanwyr electrician
trydarthiad *eg* transpiration
trydarthu *be* transpire
Trydedd Reich *eb* Third Reich

Trydedd Weriniaeth *eb* Third Republic
trydydd (=y trydydd dyn) *eg* third man
trydydd (yn gyffredinol) *eg* trydyddau third
trydydd ar ddeg *eg* thirteenth
trydydd gwrthdro *eg* third inversion
trydydd isradd *eg* trydydd israddau cube root
trydydd israddau un *ell* cube roots of unity
trydydd person *eg* third person
trydyddol *ans* tertiary
trydylliad *eg* trydylliadau perforation
tryddiferiad *eg* seepage
tryddiferu *be* seep
tryfalu *be* dovetailing
tryfer *eg* tryferi trident
tryledEdd *eg* trylededdau diffusivity
trylediad *be* tryllediadau diffusion
tryledol *ans* diffuse
tryledu *be* diffuse
tryledwr *eg* tryledwyr diffuser
tryledwr chwistrell *eg* tryledwyr chwistrell diffuser spray
tryledwr chwistrell *eg* tryledwyr chwistrell spray diffuser
tryleu *ans* translucent
tryleuedd *eg* translucency
trylifiad *eg* trylifiadau percolation
trylifo *be* percolate
tryloyw *ans* transparent; sheer
tryloywder *eg* tryloywderau transparency; slide
trylwyr *ans* thorough
trylwyredd deallusol *eg* intellectual rigour
trynewid *eg* trynewidion permutation
trynion *eg* trynionau trunnion
tryptoffan *eg* tryptophan
trysorlys *eg* treasury; exchequer
trywanu *be* pierce; spear
trywel *eg* trywelion trowel
trywel aelwyd *eb* trywelion aelwyd hearth trowel
trywel gât *eb* trywelion gât ingate trowel
trywel sgwâr *eb* trywelion sgwâr square trowel
trywel taprog *eg* trywelion taprog tapered trowel
trywydd *eg* trywyddau trail; thread; spur
trywydd archwilio *eg* trywyddau archwilio audit trail
trywydd sbiromedr *eg* spirometer traces
trywydd ymholi *eg* trywyddau ymholi line of enquiry
Tsar yr holl Rwsiaid *eg* Tsar of all the Russians
Tsaraeth *eb* Tsardom
tsariaeth *eb* tsarism
tsieni *eg* china
tsieni asgwrn *eg* bone china
tsieni tryleu *eg* translucent china
tsip *eg* tsipiau chip
tsipio *be* chip
tsipio'r bêl *be* chip the ball
tsunami *eg* tsunami

tu allan *eg* outside; exterior
tu allan i'r amrediad out of range
tu allan i'r droed *eg* outstep
tu chwith *eg* reverse side
tu hwnt i'r ffin *eg* out of bounds
tu mewn *eg* inside; interior
tu mewn i'r cylch *eg* inside the circle
tua *adf* approximately
tuag i mewn *adf* inwards
tua'r pegwn *ans* poleward
tua'r tir *ans* landward
tudalengipio *be* page jacking
tudalen *eg/b* tudalennau page
tudalen flaen papur newydd *eb* tudalennau blaen papurau newydd newspaper front page
tudalen gartref *eb* tudalennau cartref home page
tudalen nesaf *eb* next page
tudalen parhad *eb* tudalennau parhad continuation page
tudalen wag *eb* tudalennau gwag blank page
tudalen we *eb* tudalennau gwe web page
tudalen we awtobeilot *eb* tudalennau gwe awtobeilot autopilot web page
tudalen we wedi'i diweddaru'n ddynamig *eb* tudalennau gwe wedi'u diweddaru'n ddynamig dynamically updated web page
tudalen we y gellir ei diweddaru'n ddynamig *eb* tudalennau gwe y gellir eu diweddaru'n ddynamig dynamically updateable web page
tudaleniad *eg* pagination
tudalennog *ans* paged
tudalennu *be* page; paginate
Tuduriaid *ell* Tudors
tuedd *eb* tueddiadau tendency; bias; trend
tuedd ddemograffig *eb* demographic trend
tuedd gyfartalog i ddefnyddio *eb* average propensity to consume
tuedd gyfartalog i gynilo *eb* average propensity to save
tuedd gyffredinol *eb* broad trend
tuedd gymdeithasol *eb* tueddiadau cymdeithasol social trend
tuedd hunanlesol *eb* self-serving bias
tuedd i gytuno *eb* confirmation bias
tuedd priodoli *eb* attribution bias
tuedd priodoliad hunangyflenwol *eb* self-serving attribution bias
tuedd priodoliad sylfaenol fundamental attribution bias
tuedd sylwol *eb* attentional bias
tuedd wrth ddethol *eb* selection bias
tuedd ymchwilydd *eb* researcher bias
tuedd ymylol i dreulio *eb* marginal propensity to consume
tuedd ymylol i fewnforio *eb* marginal propensity to import
tuedd ymylol i gynilo *eb* marginal propensity to save
tueddfryd *eg* aptitude

▸ **tueddiad barometrig** *eg* tueddiadau barometrig barometric tendency
tueddiad gwasgedd *eg* tueddiadau gwasgedd pressure tendency
tueddol *ans* biased
tuit canol *eg* middle tuit
tulle *eg* tulle
tun *eg* tuniau tin; can
tun (Sn) *eg* tin
tun pobi *eg* tuniau pobi baking tin
tunelledd *eg* tunelleddau tonnage
tunelledd cofrestredig net *eg* tunelleddau cofrestredig net net register tonnage
tunelledd dadleoliad *eg* displacement tonnage
tunelledd llwyth *eg* deadweight tonnage
tunio *be* tin
tun(IV) ocsid *eg* tin(IV) oxide
tunnell *eb* tunelli ton
tunnell fetrig *eb* tunelli metrig tonne
tunplat *eg* tinplate
turio'r bêl *be* ground the ball
turn *eg* turniau lathe
turn canol *eg* turniau canol centre lathe
turn polyn *eg* turniau polyn pole lathe
turnio *be* turn
turnio ar wynebplat *be* faceplate turning
turnio coed *be* wood turning
turnio cyflin *be* parallel turning
turnio rhwng canolau *be* turning between centres
turnio tapr *be* taper turning
turnio ysgafn *be* light turning
turniwr *eg* turnwyr turner
turnwriaeth *eb* turnery
turnwriaeth oddfog *eb* bulbous turnery
tussore *ans* tussore
tuth *eb* tuthiau trot
tuthio *be* trot
tuyére *eg* tuyére
twb *eg* tybiau tub
twb pâr *eg* tub pair
twb pedwar *eg* tub four
twb sefydlog *eg* tybiau sefydlog fixed tub
▸ **twbercwlosis** *eg* tuberculosis
twbio *be* tub
twc *eg* tyciau tuck
twc cragen *eg* tyciau cragen shell tuck
twc cysgod *eg* tyciau cysgod shadow tuck
twc gwrthdro *eg* tyciau gwrthdro inverted tuck
twc pìn *eg* tyciau pìn pin tuck
twf *eg* growth
twf a datblygiad growth and development
twf alometrig *eg* allometric growth
twf allanol *eg* external growth
twf byngaloaidd *eg* bungaloid growth
twf cyfalaf *eg* capital growth
twf economaidd *eg* economic growth
twf economaidd byd-eang *eg* world economic growth
twf economaidd cynaliadwy *eg* sustainable economic growth
twf gwerthiant *eg* sales growth
twf mewnol *eg* internal growth
twf posibl *eg* potential growth
twf-ymateb *eg* growth response
twff *eg* twffau tuff
twffa *eg* twffâu tufa
twil *eg* twill
twll (=lle mae gwningod yn byw) *eb* tyllau burrow
twll (=soced) *eg* tyllau socket
twll (yn gyffredinol) *eg* tyllau hole
twll *eg* tyllau perforation
twll ag edau ynddo *eg* tyllau ag edau ynddynt threaded hole
twll arbor *eg* tyllau arbor arbor hole
twll archwilio *eg* tyllau archwilio manhole
twll arwain *eg* tyllau arwain pilot hole
twll awyr *eg* tyllau awyr vent hole
twll botwm *eg* tyllau botwm buttonhole
twll botwm fertigol *eg* tyllau botwm fertigol vertical buttonhole
twll botwm llaw *eg* tyllau botymau llaw hand made buttonhole
twll botwm llorweddol *eg* tyllau botymau llorweddol horizontal buttonhole
twll botwm peiriant *eg* tyllau botymau peiriant machine made buttonhole
twll botwm pwythog *eg* tyllau botymau pwythog worked buttonhole
twll botwm wedi'i beipio *eg* tyllau botymau wedi'u peipio piped buttonhole
twll botwm wedi'i rwymo *eg* tyllau botymau wedi'u rhwymo bound buttonhole
twll bys *eg* tyllau bysedd finger hole; vent
twll cliriad *eg* tyllau cliriad clearance hole
twll cocos *eg* tyllau cocos sprocket hole
twll chwistrellu *eg* tyllau chwistrellu spray nozzle
twll dall *eg* tyllau dall blind hole
twll dart *eg* tyllau dart dart perforation
twll edau *eg* tyllau edau thread hole
twll glân *eg* tyllau glân clean hole
twll gwrthfor *eg* tyllau gwrthfor counterbored hole
twll gwrthsodd *eg* tyllau gwrthsodd countersunk hole
twll llawes *eg* tyllau llewys armhole
twll llygaden *eg* tyllau llygaden eyelet hole
twll offer *eg* tyllau offer hardie hole
twll olew *eg* tyllau olew oil hole
twll pìn *eg* tyllau pìn pinhole
twll porthi *eg* tyllau porthi feed hole
twll pwnsh *eg* tyllau pwnsh punch hole; pritchel hole
twll sbïo *eg* tyllau sbïo spy hole
twll sbriw *eg* tyllau sbriw sprue hole
twll tapio *eg* tyllau tapio tapping hole
twll turio *eg* tyllau turio bore-hole

twll wedi'i bwnsio *eg* tyllau wedi'u pwnsio punched hole
twll wedi'i dapio *eg* tyllau wedi'u tapio tapped hole
twll ymochel *eg* tyllau ymochel dugout
twll yn y galon *eg* hole in the heart
twmfar *eg* twmfarrau tommy-bar
twmffat *eg* twmffedi funnel
twmffat diferu *eg* twmffedi diferu dropping funnel
twmffat gwahanu *eg* twmffedi gwahanu separating funnel
twmffat hidlo *eg* twmffedi hidlo filter funnel
twmffat ysgall *eg* twmffedi ysgall thistle funnel
twmpath dawns *eg* twmpathau dawns folk dance
twmplen *eb* twmplenni dumpling
twmplen afal *eb* twmplenni afal apple dumpling
twndis *eg* twndisau funnel
twndis diferu *eg* twndisau diferu dropping funnel
twndis gwahanu *eg* twndisau gwahanu separating funnel
twndis hidlo *eg* twndisau hidlo filter funnel
twndis ysgall *eg* twndisau ysgall thistle funnel
twndra *eg* twndrâu tundra
twngsten (W) *eg* tungsten
twngsten carbid *eg* tungsten carbide
twnnel *eg* twnelau tunnel
twnnel ffordd *eg* twnelau ffordd road tunnel
twr *eg* tyrrau group
tŵr *eg* tyrau tower
tŵr cromfannol *eg* tyrau cromfannol apsidal tower
tŵr dyfrgist *eg* tyrau dyfrgist cistern tower
tŵr ifori *eg* tyrau ifori ivory tower
twrban *eg* twrbanau turban
Twrc *eg* Twrciaid Turk
Twrcaidd *ans* Turkish
Twrciad Otomanaidd *eg* Twrciaid Otomanaidd Ottoman Turk
twrch daear *eg* tyrchod daear mole
twred *eg* tyredau turret
twristiaeth *eb* tourism
twristiaid tramor *ell* overseas tourists
twrnai *eg* twrneiod attorney
Twrnai Cyffredinol *eg* Twrneiod Cyffredinol Attorney-General
twrnamaint *eg* twrnameintiau tournament
twyll *eg* deception; fraud; chicanery
twyllo *be* deceive; defraud
twyllresymeg *eb* casuistry
twyllresymeg cyfradd sylfaenol *eb* base-rate fallacy
twyllresymeg enwi *eb* nominal fallacy
twymyn *eb* twymynau fever
twymyn goch *eb* scarlet fever
twymyn gwynegon *eb* rheumatic fever
twymyn haul *eb* sunstroke
twymynol *ans* febrile
twyn *eg* twyni dune
twyn cysylltiedig *eg* twyni cysylltiedig attached dune
twyn gwyn *eg* twyni gwyn white dune
twyn llwyd *eg* twyni llwyd grey dune
twyn sefydlog *eg* twyni sefydlog fixed dune
twyn tywod *eg* twyni tywod sand dune
twyndir *eg* twyndiroedd downland
twyndir tonnog *eg* twyndiroedd tonnog rolling downland
twyni (tywod) *ell* burrows
twysgen *eg* twysgenni hank
tŷ (=adeilad) *eg* tai house
tŷ (=adeilad, y cynnwys a'r teulu) *eg* tai household
tŷ amryw lefel *eg* tai amryw lefel split-level house
tŷ ar osod *eg* house to let
tŷ bwyta *eg* tai bwyta restaurant
tŷ clwb *eg* tai clwb clubhouse
tŷ clwm *eg* tai clwm tied house
tŷ crefydd *eg* tai crefydd religious house
tŷ ffrâm nenfforch *eg* tai ffrâm nenfforch cruck framed house
tŷ gwydr *eg* tai gwydr greenhouse; glasshouse
Tŷ Gwyn *eg* White House
tŷ haf *eg* tai haf summer house
tŷ hidlo *eg* tai hidlo baghouse
tŷ injan *eg* tai injan engine house
tŷ meddalwedd *eg* tai meddalwedd software house
tŷ opera *eg* tai opera opera house
tŷ pâr *eg* tai pâr semi-detached house
tŷ parod *eg* tai parod prefabricated house
tŷ ransh *eg* tai ransh ranch-house
tŷ rhes *eg* tai rhes terrace house
tŷ sengl *eg* tai sengl detached house
tŷ tafarn *eg* tai tafarnau public house
tŷ teras *eg* tai teras terraced house
tŷ teras Fictoraidd *eg* tai teras Fictoraidd Victorian terraced house
tŷ tref Rhufeinig *eg* tai tref Rhufeinig Roman town house
tŷ trwyddedig *eg* tai trwyddedig licenced premises
tybaco *eg* tobacco
tybiaeth *eb* tybiaethau assumption
tybiaeth fodelu *eb* modelling assumption
tybio *be* assume
tyddyn *eg* tyddynnod smallholding; homestead
tyfbwynt *eg* tyfbwyntiau growing point
tyfiant (annormal yn y corff) *eg* tyfiannau tumour
tyfiant (yn gyffredinol) *eg* growth
tyfiant trwchus *eg* tyfiannau trwchus dense growth
tyfu *be* grow
tyffaidd *ans* tuffaceous
tyngu anudon *be* perjure
tylino *be* knead
tylino baban *be* baby massage
tylino'r corff *be* massage
tyllfedd *eg* tyllfeddau bore
tyllfwrdd *eg* tyllfyrddau keypunch
tyllog *ans* perforated
tyllu (drwy groen etc) *be* perforate

tyllu (yn y ddaear) *be* bore
tylluan glustiog *eb* tylluanod glustiog short eared owl
tylluan yr eira *eb* tylluanod yr eira snowy owl
tyllwr (drwy groen etc) *eg* tyllwyr perforator
tyllwr (yn y ddaear) *eg* tyllwyr borer
tyllwr cardiau *eg* tyllwyr cardiau card punch
tyllwr lledr *eg* tyllwyr lledr leather punch
tyllwr llygadennau *eg* tyllwyr llygadennau eyelet punch
tyllwr tâp *eg* tyllwyr tâp tape punch
tymer *eg* temper
tymestl *eb* tymhestloedd gale
tymheredd *eg* tymereddau temperature
Tymheredd a Gwasgedd Safonol (TGS) *eg* Standard Temperature and Pressure
tymheredd critigol *eg* tymereddau critigol critical temperature
tymheredd cronedig *eg* tymereddau cronedig accumulated temperature
tymheredd cyfartalog *eg* tymereddau cyfartalog average temperature
tymheredd cymedrig *eg* mean temperature
tymheredd cyson *eg* constant temperature
tymheredd egino *eg* tymereddau egino germinating temperature
tymheredd sylfaenol *eg* fundamental temperature
tymheredd y corff *eg* body temperature
tymheredd (yr) ystafell *eg* room temperature
tymheru *be* tempering
tymherus *ans* temperate
tymherus claear *ans* cool temperate
tymherus cynnes *ans* warm temperate
tymhorol (=bob tymor) *ans* terminal
tymhorol (yn ymwneud ag amser) *ans* temporal
tymor *eg* tymhorau term; trimester
tymor byr *ans* short-term
tymor hir *ans* long-term
tymor prawf *eg* noviciate
tymor tyfu *eg* tymhorau tyfu growing season
tymor y gwanwyn *eg* spring term
tymor yr haf *eg* summer term; summer season
tympan y glust *eg* tympanau clustiau ear drum; tympanic membrane
tympanwm *eg* tympanym
tyndra *eg* tyndrau tension; tightness; stress
tyndra cyn mislif *eg* premenstrual tension
tyndra'r corff *eg* body tension
tyndro *eg* tyndroeon wrench
tyndro bach *eg* tyndroeon bach hook wrench
tyndro cadwyn *eg* tyndroeon cadwyn chain wrench
tyndro crafanc *eg* tyndroeon crafanc claw wrench
tyndro cymwysadwy *eg* tyndroeon cymwysadwy adjustable wrench
tyndro gafael ebrwydd *eg* tyndroeon gafael ebrwydd instant grip wrench
tyndro hunanafael *eg* tyndroeon hunanafael mole wrench
tyndro hunanafael *eg* self-grip wrench
tyndro llaw *eg* tyndroeon llaw hand wrench
tyndro peipen *eg* tyndroeon peipen pipe wrench
tyndro plygu peipen *eg* tyndroeon plygu peipiau pipe bending wrench
tyndro sgrôl *eg* tyndroeon sgrôl scroll wrench
tyndro tap *eg* tyndroeon tap tap wrench
tyndro trorym *eg* tyndroeon trorym torque wrench
tyndroi *be* wrench
tynddwr *eg* backwash
tyner *ans* tender
tynerwch *eg* tenderness
tynfa *eb* tynfeydd draught
tynfa disgyrchiant *eb* gravitational pull
tynfad *eg* tynfadau tug
tynfaen *eg* tynfeini lodestone
tynfollt *eg* tynfolltau drawbolt
tynhau (y bwa) *be* brace
tynhau (y gyffredinol) *be* tighten
tynhau cynfas *be* canvas straining
tynhau'r lens (mewn gwaith camera) *be* zoom in
tynhawr (llif fwa) *eg* tynhawyr tourniquet
tynhawr belt *eg* tynhawyr belt belt tightener
tyniad *eg* tyniadau pull
tyniad y farchnad *eg* market pull
tyniannwr *eg* tynianwyr tensioner
tyniant *eg* tyniannau traction; tension
tyniant arwyneb *eg* tyniannau arwyneb surface tension
tynlath *eb* tynlathau tie-beam
tynn *ans* tight; taut
tynnu (=symud tuag atoch drwy gyfrwng grym) *be* pull
tynnol (=yn ymwneud â thensiwn) *ans* tensile
tynnol (=yn tynnu i ffwrdd) *ans* subtractive
tynnu (arian) *be* deduction
tynnu (mewn gwaith rhif) *be* subtract; subtraction
tynnu (tannau offeryn cerdd) *be* thrum
tynnu bwa *be* bow
tynnu casgliadau *be* draw conclusions
tynnu casgliadau *be* deduction
tynnu cyhyr *be* pull a muscle
tynnu edau *be* draw a thread
tynnu esgyrn *be* boning
tynnu gwaed *be* venepuncture
tynnu hylif madruddyn y cefn *be* lumbar puncture
tynnu lawr *be* pull down; draw down
tynnu llinell *be* draw a line
tynnu llun *be* draw a picture
tynnu llwch *be* dust
tynnu plentyn yn ôl o addysg grefyddol *be* withdraw a child from religious education
tynnu rhaff *be* tug o war
tynnu slac *be* taking in slack
tynnu sylw (at) *be* draw attention
tynnu tangiad *be* draw a tangent
tynnu wyneb *be* grimace

tynnu'n rhydd *be* disunite
tynnu'r bêl *be* pull the ball
tynnwr paent *eg* tynwyr paent paint remover
tyno *eg* tynoau tenon
tyno cau *eg* tynoau cau stopped tenon
tyno cloëdig *eg* tynoau cloëdig keyed tenon
tyno dwbl *eg* tynoau dwbl double tenon
tyno dwbl *eg* tynoau dwbl twin tenon
tyno fforchog *eg* tynoau fforchog forked tenon
tyno hansiedig *eg* tynoau hansiedig haunched tenon
tyno hansiedig cudd *eg* secret haunched tenon
tyno hansiedig sgwâr *eg* tynoau hansiedig sgwâr square haunched tenon
tyno meitrog *eg* tynoau meitrog mitred tenon
tyno pen morthwyl *eg* tynoau pen morthwyl hammer-head tenon
tyno pwt *eg* tynoau pwt stub tenon
tyno trwodd *eg* tynoau trwodd through tenon
tyno unysgwyddog *eg* tynoau unysgwyddog barefaced tenon
tyno wedi'i begio *eg* tynoau wedi'u pegio pegged tenon
tyno wedi'i letemu *eg* tynoau wedi'u lletemu wedged tenon
tyno wedi'i letemu'n gudd *eg* tynoau wedi'u lletemu'n gudd fox-wedged tenon
tyno ysgithr *eg* tynoau ysgithr tusk tenon
tyno ysgwydd hir a byr *eg* tynoau ysgwydd hir a byr long and short shouldered tenon
Tŷ'r Arglwyddi *eg* House of Lords
tŷ'r brodyr *eg* tai'r brodyr friary
Tŷ'r Cyffredin *eg* House of Commons
Tŷ'r Cynrychiolwyr *eg* House of Representatives
tyrbin *eg* tyrbinau turbine
tyrbin ager *eg* tyrbinau ager steam turbine
tyrchu (=cloddio) *be* burrowing
tyrchu (=cyrathiad fertigol) *be* down cutting
tyrfedd *eg* tyrfeddau turbulence
tyrfol *ans* turbulent
tyrnsgriw *eg* tyrnsgriwiau screwdriver
tyrnsgriw atred *eg* tyrnsgriwiau atred offset screwdriver
tyrnsgriw cabinet *eg* tyrnsgriwiau cabinet cabinet screwdriver
tyrnsgriw clicied *eg* tyrnsgriwiau clicied ratchet screwdriver
tyrnsgriw cyffredin *eg* tyrnsgriwiau cyffredin normal screwdriver
tyrnsgriw Pozidrive *eg* tyrnsgriwiau Pozidrive Pozidrive screwdriver
tyrnsgriw Phillips *eg* Phillips screwdriver
tyrnsgriw rhychiog *eg* tyrnsgriwiau rhychiog fluted screwdriver
tyrnsgriw sbiral *eg* tyrnsgriwiau sbiral spiral screwdriver
tyrnsgriw trydanwr *eg* tyrnsgriwiau trydanwr electrician's screwdriver
tyrosin *eg* tyrosine
tyrpant *eg* turpentine
tyrpeg *eg* tyrpegau turnpike
tyst *eg* tystion witness
tystbwnsio *be* witness punching
tysteb *eb* tystebau testimonial
tystio *be* witness
tystiolaeth *eb* tystiolaethau evidence
tystiolaeth ansoddol *eb* qualitative evidence
tystiolaeth arbrofol *eb* experimental evidence
tystiolaeth briodol *eb* appropriate evidence
tystiolaeth eilaidd *eb* secondary evidence
tystiolaeth feintiol *eb* quantitative evidence
tystiolaeth llygad-dyst *eb* eyewitness testimony
tystiolaeth weledol *eb* visual evidence
tystiolaeth wreiddiol *eb* primary evidence
tystiolaeth ymddygiadol *eb* behavioural evidence
tystoliaethol *ans* evidential
tystysgrif *eb* tystysgrifau certificate
Tystysgrif Addysg (TA) *eb* Certificate of Education
Tystysgrif Addysg Estynedig (TAE) *eb* Certificate of Extended Education
Tystysgrif Addysg Gyn-Alwedigaethol (TAGA) *eb* Certificate of Pre-Vocational Education
Tystysgrif Addysg i Raddedigion (TAR) *eb* Post Graduate Certificate of Education
tystysgrif cyfranddaliadau *eb* tystysgrifau cyfranddaliadau share certificate
tystysgrif feddygol *eb* tystysgrifau meddygol medical certificate
tystysgrif gadael ysgol *eb* tystysgrifau gadael ysgol school leaving certificate
tystysgrif geni *eb* tystysgrifau geni birth certificate
Tystysgrif Gyffredinol Addysg Uwchradd (TGAU) *eb* General Certificate of Secondary Education
tystysgrif marwolaeth *eb* tystysgrifau marwolaeth death certificate
tywel *eg* tywelion towel
tywelin *eg* towelling
tywod *eg* sand
tywod chwyth *eg* blown sand
tywod ffowndri *eg* foundry sand
tywod gorgynnes *eg* hot sand
tywod llaith *eg* green sand
tywod mowldio *eg* moulding sand
tywod partio *eg* parting sand
tywod sïo *eg* whistling sand
tywod wedi'i ridyllu *eg* sifted sand
tywodfaen *eg* tywodfeini sandstone
tywodfaen gwyrdd *eg* tywodfeini gwyrdd greensand
tywodlyd *ans* arenaceous
tywydd *eg* weather
tywydd gwlyb *eg* wet weather
tywyll (a thrist) *ans* sombre
tywyll (ac aneglur) *ans* obscure
tywyll (yn gyffredinol) *ans* dark
tywyll a golau light and shade
tywyllu (wrth luniadu) *be* shade; grey

tywyllwch *eg* darkness
tywyn *eg* tywynnau glow
tywynnol *ans* glowing
tywynnu *be* glow
tywyrch sbringar *ell* springy turfs
tywys *be* guide
tywysen corn *eb* tywysennau corn corn cob
tywyslinell *eb* tywyslinellau guide line
tywysog *eg* tywysogion prince
Tywysog Cydweddog *eg* Prince Consort
Tywysog Du *eg* Black Prince
tywysog o waed *eg* tywysogion o waed prince of the blood
tywysogaeth *eb* tywysogaethau principality
tywyswr hogi *eg* tywyswyr hogi honing guide
tywysydd *eg* tywyswyr guide
tywysydd sefydlog *eg* tywyswyr sefydlog fixed guide

Th

thalamws *eg* thalamus
thaliwm (Tl) *eg* thallium
thalws *eg* thali thallus
Theatiad *eg/b* Theatiaid Theatine
theatr *eb* theatrau theatre
theatr bypedau *eb* theatrau pypedau puppet theatre
theatr gerdd *eb* theatrau cerdd music hall
theatr gŵyl *eb* theatrau gŵyl festival theatre
theatraidd *ans* theatrical
theistiaeth *eb* theism
thema *eb* themâu theme
thema ac amrywiadau theme and variations
thema drawsgwricwlaidd *eb* themâu trawsgwricwlaidd cross-curricular theme
thema generig *eb* themâu generig generic theme
thema hanesyddol *eb* themâu hanesyddol historical theme
theocratiaeth *eb* theocracy
theodiciaeth *eb* theodicy
theodiciaeth Awstin *eb* Augustinian theodicy
theodiciaeth Irenaeus *eb* Irenaean theodicy
theodolit *eg* theodolitau theodolite
theorbo *eg* theorboi theorbo
theorem *eb* theoremau theorem
theorem binomial *eb* binomial theorem
theorem bodolaeth *eb* theoremau bodolaeth existence theorem
theorem de Moivre *eb* de Moivre's theorem
theorem gyfdro *eb* converse theorem
theorem gynrychioliad *eb* representation theorem
theorem Pythagoras *eb* Pythagoras theorem
theorem Thevenin *eb* Thevenin's theorem
theorem y gweddill *eb* remainder theorem
theori *eb* theory
theori cerddoriaeth *eb* theory of music
theori ciwio *eb* theorïau ciwio queuing theory
theori dewis rhesymegol *eb* rational choice theory
theori drama *eb* dramatic theory
theori facroeconomaidd *eb* macroeconomic theory
theori gemau *eb* theory of games
theori gwybodaeth *eb* theorïau gwybodaeth information theory
theori o feddwl *eb* theory of mind
theori Ostwald *eb* Ostwald theory
therapi *eg* therapïau therapy
therapi anghymell *eg* aversion therapy
therapi amnewid hormonau *eg* hormone replacement therapy
therapi cleient ganolog *eg* client-centred therapy
therapi cyflenwol *eg* complementary therapy
therapi chwarae *eg* play therapy
therapi chwarae anghyfeiriol *eg* non-directive play therapy
therapi chwarae seicodynamig *eg* psychodynamic play therapy
therapi dadansoddiad gwybyddol *eg* cognitive analytic therapy
therapi dyneiddiol *eg* humanistic therapy
therapi electrogynhyrfol *eg* electroconvulsive therapy (ECT)
therapi galwedigaethol *eg* occupational therapy
therapi genynnau *eg* gene therapy
therapi Gestalt *eg* Gestalt therapy
therapi grŵp *eg* group therapy
therapi gwybyddol *eg* cognitive therapy
therapi hel atgofion *eg* reminiscence therapy
therapi lleferydd *eg* speech therapy
therapi lleferydd ac iaith *eg* speech and language therapy
therapi mewnffrwydrad *eg* implosion therapy
therapi ocsigen *eg* oxygen therapy
therapi rhesymoli emosiwn *eg* rational emotive therapy
therapi seicodynamig *eg* psychodynamic therapy
therapi teulu *eg* family therapy
therapi ymddygiad *eg* behaviour therapy
therapi ymddygiad gwybyddol *eg* cognitive behaviour therapy
therapiwtig *ans* therapeutic
therapydd *eg* therapyddion therapist
therapydd celf *eg* therapyddion celf art therapist
therapydd chwarae *eg* therapyddion chwarae play therapist
therapydd chwaraeon *eg* therapyddion chwaraeon sports therapist
therapydd galwedigaethol *eg* therapyddion galwedigaethol occupational therapist
therapydd lleferydd *eg* therapyddion lleferydd speech therapist
Theravada *eb* Theravada
therm *eg* thermau therm
thermionig *ans* thermionic
thermistor *eg* thermistorau thermistor
thermoclein *eg* thermocleinau thermocline
thermocwpl *eg* thermocyplau thermocouple
thermodrydan *eg* thermoelectricity

thermodrydanol *ans* thermoelectric
thermodynameg *eb* thermodynamics
thermodynamig *ans* thermodynamic
thermoffurfio *be* thermo forming
thermogram *eg* thermogramau thermogram
thermogydiad *eg* thermogydiadau thermojunction
thermol *ans* thermal
thermomedr *eg* thermomedrau thermometer
thermomedr bwlb gwlyb *eg* thermomedrau bwlb gwlyb wet bulb thermometer
thermomedr clinigol *eg* thermomedrau clinigol clinical thermometer
thermomedr isafbwynt *eg* thermomedrau isafbwynt minimum thermometer
thermomedr uchafbwynt *eg* thermomedrau uchafbwynt maximum thermometer
thermomedredd *eg* thermometry
thermometrig *ans* thermometric
thermopil *eg* thermopiliau thermopile
thermoplastig *ans* thermoplastic
thermoplastig *eg* thermoplastigau thermoplastic
thermosgop *eg* thermosgopau thermoscope
thermosodol *ans* thermosetting
thermostat *eg* thermostatau thermostat
thesawrws *eg* thesawrysau thesaurus
thesawrws lefel *eg* age phase thesaurus
thesis *eg* theses thesis
thiamin *eg* thiamine
thicsotropig *ans* thixotropic
thiocarbamid *eg* thiocarbamide
thoracs *eg* thorax
thorasig *ans* thoracic
thoriwm (Th) *eg* thorium
thrombocyt *eg* thrombocytau thrombocyte
thrombosis *eb* thrombosis
thrombosis coronaidd *eg* coronary thrombosis
thrombws *eg* thrombysau thrombus
thuser *eb* thuserau censer
thwliwm (Tm) *eg* thulium
thymws *eg* thymus
thyristor *eg* thyristor
thyrocsin *eg* thyroxin
thyroglobwlin *ans* thyroglobulin
thyroid *eg* thyroid

U

uchafbwynt (=pwynt uchaf) *eg* uchafbwyntiau maximum
uchafbwynt (yn gyffredinol) *eg* uchafbwyntiau climax; highlight
uchafbwynt llystyfiant *eg* uchafbwyntiau llystyfiant climax vegetation
uchafbwynt rhewlifol *eg* uchafbwyntiau rhewlifol glacial maximum
uchafbwynt tymheredd *eg* maximum temperature
uchafiaeth *eb* primacy
Uchaf-Lywodraethwr *eg* Supreme Governor
uchafswm *eg* uchafsymiau maximum
uchafsymio *be* maximize
uchder (=pellter uwchben y ddaear) *eg* uchderau altitude
uchder (=taldra) *eg* uchderau height
uchder awtoffitio *eg* autofit height
uchder defnydd *eg* use-height
uchder fertigol *eg* vertical height
uchder fertigol cywir *eg* true vertical height
uchder ffrâm awtoffitio *eg* autofit frame height
uchder gofynnol *eg* required height
uchder mwyaf *eg* maximum height
uchder oledd *eg* uchderau goledd slant height
uchder perpendicwlar *eg* perpendicular height
uchder y bar *eg* bar height
uchderau i'r metr agosaf uwchlaw lefel y môr cymedrig
heights are to the nearest metre above mean sea level
uchel *ans* high
uchel chwilyswr *eg* uchel chwilyswyr grand inquisitor
uchel dynnol *ans* high tensile
uchel dywysog *eg* uchel dywysogion grand prince
uchel Ddadeni *eg* high Renaissance
Uchel Eglwysig *ans* High Church
uchel feistr *eg* uchel feistri grand master
uchel frad *eg* high treason
Uchel Frenhinwr *eg* Uchel Frenhinwyr Ultra-Royalist
Uchel Gomisiwn *eg* High Commission
Uchel Gwnstabl *eg* High Constable
Uchel Lys *eg* High Court
Uchel Siryf *eg* Uchel Siryfion High Sheriff
ucheldir *eg* ucheldiroedd highland
uchelfa *eb* uchelfeydd high place
uchelfraint *eb* uchelfreintiau prerogative
uchelfraint y brenin *eg* uchelfreintiau'r brenin royal prerogative
uchelfreiniol *ans* prerogative
uchelgyhuddiad *eg* uchelgyhuddiadau impeachment
uchelgyhuddo *be* impeach
uchelseinydd *eg* uchelseinyddion loudspeaker
uchelwr (Rhufeinig) *eg* patrician
uchelwr (yn gyffredinol) *eg* uchelwyr nobleman
uchelwrol *ans* patrician
ufudd-dod *eg* obedience
ufudd-dod *eg* compliance
ufuddhau *be* obey
uffern *eb* hell
ugeinfed ganrif *eb* twentieth century
ungnwd *eg* monoculture
umma *eg* umma
ummah *eg* ummah
un ar brawf *eg/b* rhai ar brawf probationer
un cylchdro cyflawn *eg* one complete rotation
un lle degol one decimal place
un rhyw *ans* single sex
unawd *eb* unawdau solo
unawd chwythbrennau *eb* unawdau chwythbrennau wind solo
unawd llinynnol *eb* unawdau llinynnol string solo
unawd pres *eb* unawdau pres brass solo
unawdydd *eg* unawdwyr soloist
unben *eg* unbeniaid dictator; autocrat; despot
unben ffasgaidd *eg* unbeniaid ffasgaidd fascist dictator
unben goleuedig *eg* unbeniaid goleuedig benevolent despot
unbenaethol *ans* dictatorial; autocratic
unbennaeth *eb* dictatorship; autocracy; despotism
unbennaeth oleuedig *eb* benevolent despotism
unbennaeth y proletariat *eb* dictatorship of the proletariat
unbotensial *ans* equipotential
uncorn *eg* unicorn
uncwrsaidd *ans* unicursal
un-darn *eg* single-section
undeb *eg/b* undebau union
Undeb Cenedlaethol y Myfyrwyr *eg* National Union of Students
Undeb Cymdeithasol a Gwleidyddol y Merched *eg* Women's Social and Political Union
undeb Erfurt *eg* Erfurt union
Undeb Ewropeaidd *eg* European Union
Undeb Gwleidyddol Cenedlaethol *eg* National Political Union

undeb llafur *eg* undebau llafur trade union
Undeb Llafur Unedig Cenedlaethol *eg* Grand National Consolidated Union
Undeb Llychlyn *eg* Scandinavian Union
undeb myfyrwyr *eg* undebau myfyrwyr students' union
Undeb Rhyngwladol *eg* International
Undeb Sofietaidd, yr *eg* U.S.S.R.
undeb y cwmni *eg* undebau cwmnïau company union
undebaeth *eb* unionism
undebaeth cwmni *eb* company unionism
undebaeth lafur *eb* trade unionism
undebwr *eg* undebwyr unionist
Undod absoliwt Duw *eg* absolute Oneness of God
undodaidd *ans* unitarian
undodiaeth *eb* unitarianism
undodwr *eg* undodiaid unitarian
undduwiaeth *eb* monotheism
undduwiaeth foesegol *eb* ethical monotheism
uned *eb* unedau unit
uned addurnol *eb* unedau addurnol decorative unit
Uned Addysg Bellach *eb* Further Education Unit
uned allbynnu *eb* unedau allbynnu output unit
uned arbennig *eb* unedau arbennig special unit
uned arddangos *eb* unedau arddangos display unit
uned arddangos graffigol *eb* unedau arddangos graffigol graphical display unit
uned arddangos weledol *eb* unedau arddangos gweledol visual display unit
uned argraffu *eb* unedau argraffu printing unit
Uned Band Eang Cymru *eb* Broadband Wales Unit
uned batrymu *eb* unedau patrymu unit of design
uned blygio *eb* unedau plygio plug-in unit
uned brosesu ganolog *eb* unedau prosesu canolog central processing unit
uned cyfrif *eg* unedau cyfrif unit of account
uned cymhwysedd *eb* unedau cymhwysedd unit of competence
uned chwarae *eb* unedau chwarae play unit
uned disgyrchiant *eb* unedau disgyrchiant gravitational unit
uned ddysgu *eb* unedau dysgu teaching unit
uned fetrig *eb* unedau metrig metric unit
uned fewnbynnu *eb* unedau mewnbynnu input unit
uned fympwyol *eb* unedau mympwyol arbitrary unit
uned gadarn *eb* unedau cadarn secure unit
uned gegin *eb* unedau cegin kitchen unit
uned gerfluniol *eb* unedau cerfluniol sculptural unit
uned gofal *eb* unedau gofal care unit
uned gofal arbennig *eb* unedau gofal arbennig special care unit
uned gofal arbennig i fabanod *eb* unedau gofal arbennig i fabanod special care baby unit
uned gornel *eb* unedau cornel corner unit
uned gwaredu sbwriel *eb* unedau gwaredu sbwriel waste-disposal unit
uned gymdogaeth *eb* unedau cymdogaeth neighbourhood unit
uned gymunedol *eb* unedau cymunedol community unit
uned hidlo *eb* unedau hidlo filter unit
uned Imperial *eb* unedau Imperial Imperial unit
uned i'w hongian (ar wal) *eb* unedau i'w hongian wall-hanging unit
uned losgiadau *eb* unedau llosgiadau burns unit
uned llety cysgodol *eb* unedau llety cysgodol sheltered accommodation unit
uned llythrennedd a sgiliau sylfaenol i oedolion *eb* unedau llythrennedd a sgiliau sylfaenol i oedolion adult literacy and basic skills unit
uned mesur *eb* unedau mesur measurement unit
uned orfodol *eb* unedau gorfodol mandatory unit
uned reoli *eb* unedau rheoli control unit
uned resymegol *eb* unedau rhesymegol logical unit
uned rifyddeg-resymeg *eb* unedau rhifyddeg-resymeg arithmetic-logic unit
uned rheoli storfa *eb* unedau rheoli storfa store control unit
uned safonol gyffredin *eb* unedau safonol cyffredin common standard unit
uned SI *eb* unedau SI SI unit
uned sylfaenol gwefr *eb* basic unit of charge
uned tâp *eb* unedau tâp tape unit
uned weinyddol *eb* unedau gweinyddol administrative unit
uned wres *eb* unedau gwres unit of heat
uned ymddygiad *eb* unedau ymddygiad behavioural unit
uned ymolchi *eb* unedau ymolchi vanity unit
unedau ystafell ymolch *ell* bathroom suite
unedig *ans* unified
unedol *ans* unitary
unfaint *ans* equal
unfalent *ans* univalent
unfan (yn yr) *eg* spot
unfath *ans* identical
unfathiant *eg* unfathiannau identity
unfed ar ddeg *eg* unfedau ar ddeg eleventh
unflwydd *ans* annual
unfodiwlaidd *ans* unimodular
unfoleciwlaidd *ans* unimolecular
unffurf *ans* uniform
unffurfedd elfennol *eg* elementary entity
unffurfiadaeth *eb* uniformitarianism
unffurfiaeth *eb* uniformity
unffurfiaeth lliw *eb* constancy of colour
unffurfiaeth siâp *eb* constancy of shape
ungellog *ans* single celled
ungellog *ans* unicellular
unhadog *ans* single seeded
uniad (=man yr uno) *eg* uniadau join; joint
uniad (=y weithred o uno) *eg* uniadau union; unification

uniad bagl *eg* uniadau bagl bridle joint
uniad bagl cornel *eg* uniadau bagl cornel corner bridle joint
uniad bagl cynffonnog *eg* uniadau bagl cynffonnog dovetail bridle joint
uniad bagl cynffonnog meitrog *eg* uniadau bagl cynffonnog meitrog mitred dovetail bridle joint
uniad bagl T *eg* uniadau bagl T tee bridle joint
uniad blwch *eg* uniadau blwch box joint
uniad bolltiog *eg* uniadau bolltiog bolted joint
uniad bôn *eg* uniadau bôn butt joint
uniad bôn meitrog *eg* uniadau bôn meitrog butt mitred joint
uniad bôn meitrog cudd *eg* uniadau bôn meitrog cudd butt mitred and keyed joint
uniad bylchog *eg* uniadau bylchog notched joint
uniad bys *eg* uniadau bys finger joint
uniad cilannog *eg* uniadau cilannog recessed joint
uniad cloëdig *eg* uniadau cloëdig keyed joint
uniad cocsen *eg* uniadau cocsen cogged joint
uniad colyn *eg* uniadau colyn pivot joint
uniad confensiynol *eg* uniadau confensiynol conventional joint
uniad cornel *eg* uniadau cornel corner joint
uniad crib *eg* uniadau crib comb joint
uniad croes haneru *eg* uniadau croes haneru cross halving joint
uniad cyfwyneb *eg* flush joint
uniad cyffredin *eg* uniadau cyffredin common joint
uniad cymal *eg* uniadau cymal knuckle joint
uniad cynffonnog *eg* uniadau cynffonnog dovetail joint
uniad cynffonnog cudd *eg* uniadau cynffonnog cudd secret dovetail joint
uniad cynffonnog meitr cudd *eg* uniadau cynffonnog meitr cudd secret mitre dovetail joint
uniad cynffonnog meitrog *eg* uniadau cynffonnog meitrog mitred dovetail joint
uniad cynffonnog onglog *eg* uniadau cynffonnog onglog angle dovetail joint
uniad cynffonnog trwodd *eg* uniadau cynffonnog trwodd through dovetail joint
uniad cynffonnog trwodd addurnol *eg* uniadau cynffonnog trwodd addurnol decorative through dovetail joint
uniad dado *eg* uniadau dado dado joint
uniad drôr *eg* uniadau drôr drawer joint
uniad ffrâm *eg* uniadau ffrâm sash joint
uniad haneru *eg* uniadau haneru halving joint
uniad haneru cornel *eg* uniadau haneru cornel corner halving joint
uniad haneru cynffonnog *eg* uniadau haneru cynffonnog dovetail halving joint
uniad haneru meitrog *eg* uniadau haneru meitrog mitred halving joint
uniad haneru ongl *eg* uniadau haneru ongl angle halving joint
uniad haneru T *eg* uniadau haneru T T-halving joint
uniad hanner cilannog *eg* uniadau hanner cilannog half-recessed join
uniad hoelbren *eg* uniadau hoelbren dowel joint
uniad laminiad *eg* uniadau laminiad laminate joint
uniad llac *eg* uniadau llac loose joint
uniad lledu *eg* uniadau lledu widening joint
uniad meitr *eg* uniadau meitr mitre joint
uniad meitr clo *eg* uniadau meitr clo keyed mitre joint
uniad meitr tafod *eg* uniadau meitr tafod tongued mitre joint
uniad meitrog *eg* uniadau meitrog mitred joint
uniad meitrog plaen *eg* uniadau meitrog plaen plain mitred joint
uniad mortais a thyno *eg* uniadau mortais a thyno mortise and tenon joint
uniad mortais a thyno ag ysgwydd hir a byr *eg* uniadau mortais a thyno ag ysgwydd hir a byr long and short shoulder mortise and tenon joint
uniad mortais a thyno cau *eg* uniadau mortais a thyno cau stopped mortise and tenon joint
uniad mortais a thyno dwbl *eg* uniadau mortais a thyno dwbl double mortise and tenon joint
uniad mortais a thyno hansiedig *eg* uniadau mortais a thyno hansiedig haunched mortise and tenon joint
uniad mortais a thyno hansiedig cudd *eg* uniadau mortais a thyno hansiedig cudd secret haunched mortise and tenon joint
uniad mortais a thyno hansiedig sgwâr *eg* uniadau mortais a thyno hansiedig sgwâr square haunched mortise and tenon joint
uniad mortais a thyno niferus *eg* uniadau mortais a thyno niferus pinned mortise and tenon joint
uniad mortais a thyno pwt *eg* uniadau mortais a thyno pwt stub mortise and tenon joint
uniad mortais a thyno trwodd *eg* uniadau mortais a thyno trwodd through mortise and tenon joint
uniad ochrol *eg* uniadau ochrol lateral joint
uniad parhaol *eg* uniadau parhaol permanent joint
uniad pren *eg* uniadau pren wood joint
uniad rabad *eg* uniadau rabad rabbet joint
uniad riwl *eg* uniadau riwl rule joint
uniad rhigol draws *eg* uniadau rhigol draws housing joint
uniad rhigol draws daprog *eg* uniadau rhigol traws taprog tapered housing joint
uniad rhigol draws gau *eg* uniadau rhigol draws gau stopped housing joint
uniad rhigol draws gynffonnog trwodd *eg* uniadau rhigol draws gynffonnog trwodd through dovetail housing joint
uniad rhigol draws trwodd *eg* uniadau rhigol draws trwodd through housing joint
uniad rhigol drawsgynffonnog gau *eg* uniadau rhigol draws gynffonnog cau stopped dovetail housing joint
uniad rhigol gynffonnog *eg* uniadau rhigol gynffonnog dovetail housing joint
uniad rhigol gynffonnog daprog *eg* uniadau rhigol gynffonnog daprog dovetail tapered housing joint

uniad rhwbiedig *eg* uniadau rhwbiedig rubbed joint
uniad rhybedog *eg* uniadau rhybedog riveted joint
uniad sblae *eg* uniadau sblae splayed joint
uniad sêm *eg* uniadau sêm seam joint
uniad setiau *eg* union of sets
uniad sgarff *eg* uniadau sgarff scarf joint
uniad sgrifellog *eg* uniadau sgrifellog scribed joint
uniad tafod a rhych *eg* uniadau tafod a rhych tongue and groove joint
uniad tafod rhydd *eg* uniadau tafod rhydd loose tongue joint
uniad toriad *eg* uniadau toriad break joint
uniad tyno ysgithr *eg* uniadau tyno ysgithr tusk tenon joint
uniad V *eg* uniadau V V-joint
uniad wedi'i bresyddu *eg* uniadau wedi'u presyddu brazed joint
uniad ymyl *eg* uniadau ymyl edge joint
uniadu *be* joint
uniadu cylchwr *be* cooper jointing
uniaethu (â rhywun) *be* identification
uniaith *ans* monolingual
unig fasnachwr *eg* sole trader
unigol *ans* individual
unigoliaeth *eb* individuality; individualism
unigolydd *eg* unigolyddion individualist
unigolyddiaeth rymus *eb* rugged individualism
unigolyn *eg* unigolion individual
unigryw *ans* unique
unigrywiaeth *eb* uniqueness
unigyn *eg* unigion isolate
union *ans* exact
union faint *eg* dead size
uniongred *ans* orthodox
uniongrededd *eg* orthodoxy
uniongyrchol *ans* direct
unioni *be* line up
unioni *be* rectify
unioni *be* justification
unioni *be* justify
unioni *be* straighten
unioni ar y chwith *be* left justify
unioni ar y dde *be* right justify
unioni corff testun *be* text body justfied
unioniad *eg* unioniadau justification
unioniad *eg* unioniadau rectification
unionlin *ans* rectilinear
unionsyth *ans* upright
unionsyth *ans* erect
unionydd *eg* unionwyr rectifier
un-i-un one-to-one
unlled *ans* monospaced
unllin *ans* collinear
unllinedd *eg* unllineddau collinearity
unlliniad *eg* unlliniadau collineation
uno *be* unify
uno *be* join
uno Cymru a Lloegr *be* union of England and Wales
uno gwleidyddol *be* political unification
uno les *be* join lace
uno parhaol *be* permanent joining
unochrog *ans* unilateral
unochrol *ans* one-side
unoliaethwr *eg* unoliaethwyr unionist
Unoliaethwr Ulster *eg* Unoliaethwyr Ulster Ulster Unionist
uno'r Almaen *be* German unification
uno'r Eidal *be* unification of Italy
uno'r Eidal *be* Italian unification
unplygrwydd *eg* integrity
unrhyw gofnod any record
unrhywiol *ans* unisexual
unsad *ans* monostable
unsain *ans* unison
untrac *ans* single-track
unwerth *ans* single-valued
urdd *eb* urddau order
urdd *eb* urddau guild
Urdd Cluny *eb* Cluniac Order
Urdd er Hyrwyddo Cerddoriaeth yng Nghymru *eb* Guild for the Promotion of Welsh Music
Urdd Gobaith Cymru *eb* Welsh League of Youth
urdd grefyddol *eb* urddau crefyddol religious order
urdd leiaf *eb* minor order
Urdd Oren *eb* Orange Order
Urdd Sant Awstin *eb* Augustinian Order
Urdd Sant Dominic *eb* Dominican Order
Urdd Sant Ffransis *eb* Franciscan Order
urdd sifalri *eb* urddau sifalri chivalry order
Urdd Uchaf *eb* Highest Order
Urdd y Brodyr Cycyllog *eb* Capuchin Order
Urdd y Carmeliaid *eb* Carmelite Order
Urdd y Carthwsiaid *eb* Carthusian Order
Urdd y Gardys *eb* Order of the Garter
Urdd y Jeswitiaid *eb* Jesuit Order
urddas *eg* dignity
urddas y cleient *eg* client dignity
Urddau Eglwysig *ell* Holy Orders
urddo'n farchog *be* knight
urddwisg *eb* urddwisgoedd vestment
ustus *eg* ustusiaid justice
ustus cworwm *eg* ustusiaid cworwm justice of the quorum
ustus cylch *eg* ustusiaid cylch justice in eyre
ustus gwacáu'r carcharau *eg* justice of gaol delivery
usuriaeth *eb* usury
utgorn *eg* utgyrn trumpet
utgorn bas *eg* utgyrn bas bass trumpet
utgorn falfiau *eg* utgyrn falfiau valve trumpet
utgorn naturiol *eg* utgyrn naturiol natural trumpet
uwch (=pellach) *ans* advanced
uwch (mewn anatomeg) *ans* superior
uwch (yn gyffredinol) *ans* higher

uwch donydd *eg* supertonic
uwch ddarlithydd *eg* uwch ddarlithwyr senior lecturer
uwch fentor *eg* uwch fentoriaid senior mentor
uwch glerigwyr *ell* higher clergy
uwch reolwyr *ell* senior management
uwchallgyrchydd *eg* uwchallgyrchwyr ultracentrifuge
uwch-arglwydd *eg* uwch-arglwyddi liege-lord
► **uwcharglwydd ffiwdal** *eg* uwcharglwyddi ffiwdal feudal overlord
uwcharglwyddiaeth *eb* uwcharglwyddiaethau overlordship
uwcharglwyddiaeth ffiwdal *eb* uwcharglwyddiaethau ffiwdal feudal overlordship
uwch-arolygydd *eg* uwch-arolygyddion superintendent
uwchben *adf* overhead
uwchben y nodyn *ans* sharp
uwchbridd *eg* uwchbriddoedd topsoil
uwchdeitl *eg* uwchdeitlau surtitle
uwchdenor *eg* uwchdenoriaid countertenor
uwchdir *eg* uwchdiroedd upland
uwchdon *eb* uwchdonau overtone
uwchdor *ans* truncated
uwchddargludedd *eg* superconductivity
uwch-ego *eg* superego
uwchfarchnad *eb* uwchfarchnadoedd supermarket
uwchfinialaidd *ans* superosculating
uwchfinialu *be* superosculate
uwchfioled *eg* ultraviolet
uwch-frigadydd *eg* uwch-frigadwyr major-general
uwchffaryngeal *ans* suprapharyngeal
uwchganolbwynt *eg* uwchganolbwyntiau epicentre
uwch-gapten *eg* uwch-gapteniaid major
uwchglarinét *eg* uwchglarinetau high clarinet
uwchgrid *eg* uwchgridiau supergrid
uwchgwmni *eg* uwchgwmnïau conglomerate
uwchgynhadledd *eb* uwchgynadleddau summit conference
uwch-hafaliad polynomaidd *eg* uwch-hafaliadau polynomaidd higher order polynomial equation
uwch-heterodein *ans* superhet
uwch-hidlo *be* ultrafiltration
uwch-lefel-trwythiad *eb* vadose
uwchlifedd *eg* superfluidity
uwchnofa *eb* uwchnofâu supernova
uwcholwg *eg* uwcholygon surface view; plan view
uwcholwg ategol *eg* uwcholygon ategol auxiliary plan
uwcholwg darluniol *eg* uwcholwg darluniadol pictorial plan
uwcholwg hanner trychiadol *eg* uwcholygon hanner trychiadol half-sectional plan
uwcholwg rhandrychiadol *eg* part-sectional plan
uwcholwg trychiadol *eg* uwcholygon trychiadol sectional plan
uwchradd *ans* secondary
uwchraddio *be* upgrade
uwch-ringyll *eg* sergeant-major
uwchsain *ans* ultrasonic
uwchsain *eg* uwchseiniau ultrasound
uwchseineg *eb* ultrasonics
uwchset *eb* uwchsetiau superset
uwchsonig *ans* supersonic
uwchwaddod *eg* uwchwaddodion supernatant
uwchwastadiant *eg* altiplanation
uwch-werth *ans* high-order
uwchwythfed *eb* uwchwythfedau superoctave
uwchysgrif *eb* uwchysgrifau superscript

V

Vaishnaviaeth /Vaisnaviaeth *eb* Vaishnavism /Vaisnavism
Vaishya /Vaisya *eg* Vaishya /Vaisya
valse *eb* valses valse
varna *eg* varna
varnashramadharma *eg* varnashramadharma
Vaseline *eg* Vaseline
Vassa *eg* Vassa
vaudeville *eg* vaudevilles vaudeville
vibrato *eg* vibrato
vihara *eg* vihara
Vinaya *eg* Vinaya
viola da gamba *eb* violas da gamba viola da gamba
vipassana *eg* vipassana
Vishnu /Visnu *eg* Vishnu /Visnu
viva voce *ans* viva voce
Viyella *eg* Viyella
voile *eg* voile
vox pop *eg* vox pop

W

wadi *eg/b* wadïau wadi
wadin *eg* wadding
wadin trwythedig *eg* impregnated wadding
Waheguru /Vahiguru *eg* Waheguru /Vahiguru
wal *eb* waliau wall
wal allanol *eb* waliau allanol outside wall
wal cynnal pwysau *eb* waliau cynnal pwysau load-bearing wall
wal dân *eb* waliau tân firewall
wal ddringo *eb* waliau dringo climbing wall
wal fewnol *eb* waliau mewnol internal wall
wal flociau *eb* waliau blociau block wall
wal geudod *eb* waliau ceudod cavity wall
wal gynnal *eb* waliau cynnal sleep wall
wal solet *eb* waliau solet solid wall
Waldensaidd *ans* Waldensian
Waldensiaid *ell* Waldenses
waled *eb* waledi wallet
walrws *eg* walrysod walrus
waltsio *be* waltz
ward *eb* wardiau ward
ward arwahanu *eb* wardiau arwahanu isolation ward
warden eglwys *eg* wardeiniaid eglwys churchwarden
wardio *be* warding
wardrob *eb* wardrobau wardrobe
warws *eg* warysau warehouse
warws ecseis *eg* warysau ecseis bonded warehouse
wasier *eb* wasieri washer
wasier blaen *eb* wasieri plaen plain washer
wasier dafod *eb* wasieri tafod tab washer
wasier ffibr *eb* wasieri ffibr fibre washer
wasier gloi *eb* wasieri cloi locking washer
wasier gopr *eb* wasieri copr copper washer
wasier gynnal *eb* wasieri cynnal holding washer
wasier hollt *eb* wasieri hollt split washer
wasier ledr *eb* wasieri lledr leather washer
wasier rwber *eb* wasieri rwber rubber washer
wasier sbring *eb* wasieri sbring spring washer
wasier wrthgryn *eb* wasieri gwrthgryn shake-proof washer
wat (W) *eg* watiau watt
watedd *eg* wateddau wattage
Wcrainaidd *ans* Ukrainian
Wcrainiad *eg* Wcrainiaid Ukrainian
We Fyd-eang, y *eb* World Wide Web
weber *eg* weberau weber
webin *eg* webinau webbing
webin lledr *eg* webinau lledr leather webbing
webin plastig *eg* plastic webbing
webin rwber *eg* rubber webbing
wedi baeddu *ans* soiled
wedi dyddio *ans* out of date
wedi dyddio *ans* dated
wedi lled-ymddeol *ans* semi-retired
wedi treulio *ans* worn
wedi ymlacio *ans* relaxed
wedi'i addasu *ans* wedi'u haddasu modified
wedi'i arwyddo *ans* wedi'u harwyddo signed
wedi'i atal *ans* wedi'u hatal stopped
► **wedi'i blaenio i gyd** *ans* planed all round
wedi'i bwyso *ans* wedi'u pwyso weighed
wedi'i chaledu *ans* wedi'u caledu indurated
wedi'i chlustogi *ans* wedi'u clustogi upholstered
wedi'i chontractio allan *ans* wedi'u contractio allan contracted out
wedi'i chymhwyso *ans* wedi'u cymhwyso adjusted
wedi'i dalu'n rhannol *ans* wedi'u talu'n rhannol partly paid
wedi'i dynnu'n oer *ans* wedi'u tynnu'n oer cold drawn
wedi'i ddad-ddirwyn *ans* unwound
wedi'i ddiffodd *ans* wedi'u diffodd off
wedi'i ddiogelu *ans* wedi'u diogelu write protected
wedi'i esgusodi *ans* wedi'u hesgusodi exempt
wedi'i farneisio *ans* wedi'u farneisio varnished
wedi'i galedu *ans* wedi'u caledu indurated
wedi'i glustogi *ans* wedi'u clustogi upholstered
wedi'i gontractio allan *ans* wedi'u contractio allan contracted out
wedi'i gorfodi i symud yn fertigol *ans* wedi'u gorfodi i symud yn fertigol constrained to move vertically
wedi'i gorfodi i symud yn llorweddol *ans* wedi'u gorfodi i symud yn llorweddol constrained to move horizontally
wedi'i graddnodi *ans* wedi'u graddnodi calibrated
wedi'i grofennu *ans* wedi'u crofennu case hardened
wedi'i gwefru *ans* wedi'u gwefru charged
wedi'i gwehyddu *ans* wedi'u gwehyddu woven
wedi'i gwisgo at yr edau *ans* wedi'u gwisgo at yr edau worn threadbare
wedi'i gymhwyso *ans* wedi'u cymhwyso adjusted
wedi'i haddasu *ans* wedi'u haddasu modified
wedi'i harwyddo *ans* wedi'u harwyddo signed
wedi'i hesgusodi *ans* wedi'u hesgusodi exempt

wedi'i hunioni'n llawn *ans* wedi'u hunioni'n llawn fully justified
wedi'i labelu *ans* labelled
wedi'i leinio *ans* lined in
wedi'i letemu *ans* wedi'u lletemu wedged
wedi'i letemu'n gudd *ans* wedi'u lletemu'n gudd fox-wedged
wedi'i lofnodi *ans* wedi'u llofnodi signed
wedi'i lletemu *ans* wedi'u lletemu wedged
wedi'i lletemu'n gudd *ans* wedi'u lletemu'n gudd fox-wedged
wedi'i llofnodi *ans* wedi'u llofnodi signed
wedi'i orfodi i symud yn fertigol *ans* wedi'u gorfodi i symud yn fertigol constrained to move vertically
wedi'i orfodi i symud yn llorweddol *ans* wedi'u gorfodi i symud yn llorweddol constrained to move horizontally
wedi'i phwyso *ans* wedi'u pwyso weighed
wedi'i raddnodi *ans* wedi'u graddnodi calibrated
wedi'i suddo'n ddwfn *ans* wedi'u suddo'n ddwfn deep sunken
wedi'i thalu'n rhannol *ans* wedi'u talu'n rhannol partly paid
wedi'i thynnu'n oer *ans* wedi'u tynnu'n oer cold drawn
wedi'i unioni'n llawn *ans* wedi'u hunioni'n llawn fully justified
wedi'i wefru *ans* wedi'u gwefru charged
wedi'i wehyddu *ans* wedi'u gwehyddu woven
wedi'i weindio *ans* wedi'u weindio wound
wedi'i wisgo at yr edau *ans* wedi'u gwisgo at yr edau worn threadbare
wedi'r diddymiad *ans* post-dissolution
weldiad *eg* weldiadau weld
weldiad bôn *eg* weldiadau bôn butt weld
weldiad ffagod *eg* weldiadau ffagod faggot weld
weldio *be* weld
weldio arc drydan *be* electric arc welding
weldio asetylen *be* acetylene welding
weldio mig *be* mig welding
weldio ocsi-asetylen *be* oxy-acetylene welding
weldio oer *be* cold welding
wensgot *ans* wainscot
Weslead *eg* Wesleaid Wesleyan
Wesleaeth *eb* Wesleyanism
wfala *eg* wfalau uvala
wfinial *ans* uvinial
wiced *eb* wicedi wicket
wicedwr *eg* wicedwyr wicket-keeper
winsh *eb* winshis winch
winsio *be* winch
winwnsyn *eg* winwns onion
wlna *eg* wlnâu ulna
wltimatwm *eg* ultimatum
wltrabasig *ans* ultrabasic
wmbel *eg* wmbelau umbel
wmber *eg* umber
wmber crai *eg* raw umber
wmber llosg *eg* burnt umber
wmbilig *ans* umbilical
wnerisis *eg* unerisis
wnsial *eg* wnsialau uncial
wobler *eg* wobbler
wracil *eg* uracil
wraniwm (U) *eg* uranium
Wranws *eg* Uranus
wrea *eg* urea
wrea fformaldehyd *eg* urea formaldehyde
wreas *eg* urease
wreter *eg* wreterau ureter
wrethra *eg/b* wrethrâu urethra
wricotelig *ans* uricotelic
wrinalau *ell* urinals
wrn *eg* yrnau urn
wrn colerog *eg* yrnau colerog collared urn
wroleg *eb* urology
Wronskian *eg* Wronskianau Wronskian
wrth gefn *ans* in reserve
wrth gefn *ans* back-up
wrth raddfa (1:1) to a scale of (1:1)
wrth raddfa addas to a suitable scale
wstid *ans* worsted
Wtraciaeth *eb* Utraquism
Wtracwr *eg* Wtracwyr Utraquist
wtrigl *eg* wtriglau utricle
wy *eg* wyau egg
wy addod *eg* wyau addod nest egg
wy batri *eg* wyau batri battery egg
wy maes *eg* wyau maes free-range egg
wy wedi'i botsio *eg* wyau wedi'u potsio poached egg
wy wedi'i ferwi *eg* wyau wedi'u berwi boiled egg
wy wedi'i sgramblo *eg* wyau wedi'u sgramblo scrambled egg
wybren *eb* wybrennau heavens
wybrennol *ans* celestial
Wycliffaidd *ans* Wycliffite
Wycliffiad *eg* Wycliffiaid Wycliffite
wyddodydd *eg* wyddodyddion ovipositor
wyneb (=tu uchaf) *eg* wynebau top
wyneb (yn gyffredinol) *eg* wynebau face
wyneb allanol *eg* outer face
wyneb amgrwm *eg* wynebau amgrwm convex face
wyneb ar oledd *eg* wynebau ar oledd inclined face
wyneb croes *eg* wynebau croes cross peen
wyneb crwn *eg* ball peen
wyneb cyfagos *eg* wynebau cyfagos adjacent face
wyneb datwm *eg* wynebau datwm datum face
wyneb goleddol *eg* wynebau goleddol sloping face
wyneb gorau *eg* best face
wyneb gweithio (cegin) *eg* wynebau gweithio worktop
wyneb gweithio (yn gyffredinol) *eg* wynebau gweithio working face
wyneb i lawr *adf* prone

wyneb i waered *adf* face downwards; upside down
wyneb mewnol *eg* inner face
wyneb newidiol y teulu *eg* changing face of the family
wyneb onglog *eg* wynebau onglog angular face
wyneb pen *eg* wynebau pen end face
wyneb pyramidaidd *eg* wynebau pyramidaidd pyramidal face
wyneb rhydd *eg* wynebau rhydd free face
wyneb sglodi *eg* wynebau sglodi chipping face
wyneb syth *eg* wynebau syth straight peen
wyneb yn wyneb face to face
wyneb-bwyth *eg* wyneb-bwythau top stitch
wyneb-bwytho *be* top stitching
wynebddalen *eb* wynebddalennau title page
wynebddarlun *eg* wynebddarluniau frontispiece
wynebol *ans* facial
wynebu *be* face
wynebu cyfeiriad y tafliad *be* face the direction of the throw
wynebu'r chwith *be* facing left
wynebu'r dde *be* facing right
wynebu'r rhwyd *be* face the net
wynebwerth *eg* wynebwerthoedd face value
wynebyn (mewn daeareg) *eg* wynebynnau facing
wynebyn (mewn gwniadwaith) *eg* wynebynnau head
wynebyn bias *eg* wynebynnau bias bias facing
wynebyn blaen *eg* wynebynnau blaen front facing
wynebyn bodis *eg* wynebynnau bodis bodice facing
wynebyn cefn *eg* wynebynnau cefn back facing
wynebyn croes *eg* wynebynnau croes crossway facing
wynebyn cudd *eg* wynebynnau cudd interfacing
wynebyn cudd gwreslyn *eg* wynebynnau cudd gwreslyn iron on interfacing
wynebyn gosod *eg* wynebynnau gosod applied facing
wynebyn twll llawes *eg* wynebynnau twll llawes armhole facing
wynebyn wedi'i siapio *eg* wynebynnau wedi'u siapio shaped facing
wynepryd *eg* features
ŵyr *eg* wyrion grandson
wyres *eb* wyresau granddaughter
wysg y cefn *adf* backwards
wyth *eg/b* wythau eight
wyth pwynt y cwmpawd *eg* eight points of the compass
wythawd *eg* wythawdau octet
wythfed *eg* wythfedau eighth
wythfed *eg* one-eighth
wythfed *eg* wythfedau octave
wythfed cudd *eg* wythfedau cudd hidden eighth
wythfed noeth *eg* wythfedau noeth exposed eighth
wythfed noeth *eg* wythfedau noeth exposed octave
wythfedau cyfochrog *ell* parallel octaves
wythfedau dilynol *ell* parallel consecutive eighths
wythnos rag *eb* wythnosau rag rag week
wythnos waith *eb* workweek
Wythnos y Pasg *eb* Holy Week
wythnoswaith *eg* weekwork
wythonglog *ans* octagonal
wythol *ans* octal
wythpled *eg* wythpledi octuplet
wythwr *eg* wythwyr eight

X

X fregus *eg* fragile X

Y

y bedwaredd ganrif ar bymtheg *eb* nineteenth century
y cant per cent
y diweddaraf *eg* update
y Drydedd Stad *eb* Third Estate
Y Ddegfed Geiniog *eb* Tenth Penny
y frech wen *eb* smallpox
y gynddaredd *eb* rabies
y pen per head
Yahweh *eg* Yahweh
ychwanegiad *eg* ychwanegiadau addition; augmentation
ychwanegol *ans* additional
ychwanegu *be* add
ychwanegu (at) *be* augment
ychwanegu'r dudalen gyfredol *be* add current page
ychwanegydd *eg* ychwanegyddion augmenter
ychwanegyn *eg* ychwanegion additive; supplement; add-on
ychwanegyn bwyd *eg* ychwanegion bwyd food additive
ychwanegyn lliw *eg* ychwanegion lliw colour additive
ŷd *eg* corn
yng nghwrs cyflogaeth in the course of employment
ynganiad *eg* ynganiadau diction
ynganiad *eg* articulation
ynganu *be* articulate
ynganu isleisiol *be* subvocal articulation
ynghlwm (wrth) *ans* attached
ynghrog *ans* suspended
ynghynn *ans* on
ynglŷn â'r gwaith *ans* job related
ymadawiad *eg* ymadawiadau departure
ymadrodd *eg* ymadroddion expression
ymaddasiad *eg* ymaddasiadau adaptation; acclimatization
ymaddasol *ans* adaptive
ymaddasu *be* adapt; acclimatize
ymaddasu i amgylchfyd arbennig *be* adapt to a specialized environment
ymagor (am wythiennau etc) *be* dilate
ymagor (am lestri hadau etc) *be* dehisce
ymagorol *ans* dehiscent
ymagwedd at hanes *eb* approach to history
ymarfer (yn arbennig yn gorfforol) *be* exercise; take exercise
ymarfer (ar gyfer perfformiad, drama etc) *be* rehearse
ymarfer (er mwyn meistroli sgiliau) *be* practise
ymarfer (=gweithrediad) *eg* ymarferion practice
ymarfer (ar gyfer perfformiad, drama etc) *eg* ymarferiadau rehearsal
ymarfer (yn arbennig un corfforol) *eg* ymarferion exercise
ymarfer abdomen *eg* ymarferion abdomen abdominal exercise
ymarfer aerobig *eg* ymarferion aerobig aerobic exercise
ymarfer anadlu *eg* ymarferion anadlu breathing exercise
ymarfer bongorff *eg* ymarferion bongorff trunk exercise
ymarfer corff *eg* physical exercise; physical recreation
ymarfer cydadfer *eg* ymarferion cydadfer compensatory exercise
ymarfer cynorthwyo *eg* ymarferion cynorthwyo assistance exercise
ymarfer cysylltiedig ag iechyd *eg* ymarferion cysylltiedig ag iechyd health-related exercise
ymarfer da *eg* good practice
ymarfer diogel *eg* safe practice
ymarfer drwy brofiadau *eg* experiential exercise
ymarfer dysgu *eg* teaching practice
ymarfer er mwyn cynnal *eg* maintenance rehearsal
ymarfer graddedig *eg* ymarferion graddedig progressive exercise
ymarfer llenwi bylchau *eg* ymarferion llenwi bylchau cloze exercise
ymarfer manwl *eg* elaborative rehearsal
ymarfer mecanyddol *eg* ymarferion mecanyddol mechanical exercise
ymarfer o hyd braich *eg* long arm practice
ymarfer ochrol *eg* ymarferion ochrol lateral exercise
ymarfer powlen bysgod *eg* fish bowl exercise
ymarfer rhydd *eg* ymarferion rhydd free practice
ymarfer sylfaenol i'r corff isaf *eg* ymarferion sylfaenol i'r corff isaf basic lower body exercise
ymarfer sylfaenol i'r corff uchaf *eg* ymarferion sylfaenol i'r corff uchaf basic upper body exercise
ymarfer torri'r garw *eg* ymarferion torri'r garw ice-breaking exercise
ymarfer tymor hir *eg* long-term training
ymarfer uwchgefn *eg* ymarferion uwchgefn dorsal exercise
ymarfer ystwytho *eg* ymarferion ystwytho warm up exercise

ymarferiad adfer *eg* ymarferion adfer remedial exercise
ymarferion *ell* manoeuvres
ymarferion anniogel unsafe practice
ymarferol *ans* practical; hands-on
ymarferwr *eg* ymarferwyr practitioner
ymarferwr adfyfyriol *eg* ymarferwyr adfyfyriol reflective practitioner
ymarferwyr theatr *ell* theatre practitioners
ymasiad *eg* ymasiadau fusion
ymasiad niwclear *eg* nuclear fusion
ymataliad *eg* abstinence
ymatchwelaidd *ans* autoregressive
ymatchweliad *eg* ymatchweliadau autoregression
ymateb (=adweithio) *be* react
ymateb (drwy lythyr, geiriau etc) *be* respond
ymateb (=adwaith) *eg* ymatebion reaction
ymateb (drwy lythyr, geiriau etc) *eg* ymatebion response
ymateb cadarnhaol *eg* positive feedback
ymateb creadigol *eg* creative response
ymateb cydsyniol *eg* response acquiescence
ymateb cyfeiriadol *eb* ymatebion cyfeiriadol orienting response
ymateb cylched *eg* circuit response
ymateb digymell *eg* ymatebion digymell spontaneous response
ymateb effeithiol *eg* ymatebion effeithiol effective response
ymateb emosiynol cyflyrol *eg* conditioned emotional response
ymateb ffoi *eg* escape response
ymateb gwyrol *eg* response deviation
ymateb heb ei gyflyru *eg* unconditional response
ymateb i dasgau *be* response to set tasks
ymateb negyddol *eg* ymatebion negyddol negative response
ymateb osgoi *eg* ymatebion osgoi avoidance response
ymateb priodol *eg* ymatebion priodol appropriate response
ymateb rhagosodedig *eg* ymatebion rhagosodedig default response
ymateb rhythmig *eg* ymatebion rhythmig rhythmic response
ymateb rhythmig syml *eg* ymatebion rhythmig syml simple rhythmic response
ymateb straen *eg* stress response
ymateb ymaddasol *eg* ymatebion ymaddasol adaptive response
ymateb ymladd neu ffoi *eg* fight or flight response
ymateb yn barod *be* respond readily
ymatebion a sylwadau replies and comments
ymbalfalu *be* fumble
ymbelydredd *eg* radiation; radioactivity
ymbelydrol *ans* radioactive
ymbil ar y saint *be* invocation of saints
Ymbil yn erbyn yr Ordinariaid *eg* Supplication against the Ordinaries
ymblygu *eg* enfold
ymborthi ciliaraidd *be* ciliary feeding
ymborthwr *eg* ymborthwyr feeder
ymchwil *eg/b* research
ymchwil a datblygu research and development
ymchwil ansoddol *eg* qualitative research
ymchwil arolwg *eg* survey research
ymchwil arsylwadol *eg* observational research
ymchwil cydberthynol *eg* correlational research
ymchwil cymhwysol *eg* applied research
ymchwil cynradd *eg* primary research
ymchwil eilaidd *eg* secondary research
► **ymchwil gweithredol** *eg* action research
Ymchwil Gweithredu Profion ac Asesu Safonol *eg* Standard Tests and Assessment Implementation Research (STAIR)
ymchwil i farchnata *eg* marketing research
ymchwil maes *eg* field research
ymchwil marchnata *eg* market research
ymchwil meintiol *eg* quantitative research
ymchwil peilot *eg* pilot research
ymchwil perthynol *eg* relational research
ymchwil sylfaenol *eg* basic research
ymchwil un cyfrannwr *eg* single-subject research
ymchwiliad (cyhoeddus etc) *eg* ymchwiliadau inquiry
ymchwiliad (gwyddonol etc) *eg* ymchwiliadau investigation
ymchwiliad cyhoeddus *eg* ymchwiliadau cyhoeddus public inquiry
ymchwiliad empirig *eg* ymchwiliadau empirig empirical investigation
ymchwiliad gwaith maes *eg* ymchwiliadau gwaith maes fieldwork investigation
ymchwiliad mewnol *eg* ymchwiliadau mewnol internal inquiry
ymchwilio (gwyddonol etc) *be* investigate
ymchwilio (yn gyffredinol) *be* research
ymchwilio i gwestiynau gwyddonol *be* investigate scientific questions
ymchwiliol *ans* investigative
ymchwilydd *eg* ymchwilwyr researcher
ymchwydd *eg* ymchwyddiadau swell; surge; upwelling
ymchwydd pŵer *eg* ymchwyddiadau pŵer power surge
ymchwydd y don *eg* ground swell
ymchwyddo *be* bloating
ymdaith *eb* ymdeithiau march
Ymdaith Faith *eb* Long March
Ymdaith i Rufain *eb* March on Rome
ymdarddiad digymell *eg* ymdarddiadau digymell spontaneous generation
ymdeimlad â rhythm *eg* sense of rhythm
ymdeithgan *eb* ymdeithganau march
ymdeithgan angladd *eb* ymdeithganau angladd funeral march
ymdeithio *be* march

ymdoddadwy *ans* fusible
ymdoddbwynt *eg* ymdoddbwyntiau melting point; fusing point
ymdoddedig *ans* fused
ymdoddi *be* melt; fuse
ymdoddiad *eg* ymdoddiadau fusion; fuse
ymdoniad *eg* ymdoniadau undulation
ymdonni *be* undulate
ymdopi *be* cope
ymdopi drwy ganolbwyntio ar emosiwn *be* emotion-focused coping
ymdopi drwy ganolbwyntio ar y broblem *be* problem-focused coping
ymdorri (cell yn ymdorri) *be* rupture
ymdrech *eg/b* ymdrechion effort
ymdrech i fodoli *eb* struggle for existence
ymdrech i oroesi *eb* struggle for survival
ymdrechiad *eg* ymdrechiadau conation
ymdrechol *ans* conative
ymdrechu at oruchafiaeth *be* striving for superiority
ymdreiddio *be* infiltrate
ymdrin â *be* cover
ymdrin â (mater) *be* approach
ymdriniaeth *eb* ymdriniaethau handling
ymdröwr *ell* ymdrowyr laggard
ymddafniad *eg* guttation
ymddafnu *be* guttate
ymddaliad *eg* ymddaliadau posture
ymddaliad da *eg* good posture
ymddaliad unionsyth *eg* ymddaliadau unionsyth upright posture
ymddangos *be* appear
ymddangosiad *eg* ymddangosiadau appearance
ymddangosiad destlus *eg* neat appearance
ymddangosiad dymunol *eg* pleasing appearance
ymddangosiadol *ans* apparent
ymddangosol *ans* apparent
ymddatod *be* disintegrate
ymddatod metabolaidd *be* metabolic breakdown
ymddatod Walleraidd *be* Wallerian degeneration
ymddatodiad *eg* ymddatodiadau disintegration; breakdown
ymddeol *be* retire
ymddeoliad *eg* retirement
ymddiheuriad *eg* ymddiheuriadau apology
ymddiorseddiad *eg* abdication
ymddiried *be* trust
ymddiriedolaeth *eb* ymddiriedolaethau trust; trusteeship
Ymddiriedolaeth Genedlaethol *eb* National Trust
Ymddiriedolaeth Gymreig *eb* Welsh Trust
ymddiriedolwr *eg* ymddiriedolwyr trustee
ymddiswyddiad *eg* resignation
ymddiswyddo *be* resign
ymddygiad *eg* ymddygiadau behaviour; conduct
ymddygiad abc *eg* abc behaviour
ymddygiad addas *eg* appropriate behaviour
ymddygiad afiechyd *eg* illness behaviour
ymddygiad aflonyddgar *eg* disruptive behaviour
ymddygiad anfonheddig *eg* ungentlemanly conduct
ymddygiad annerbyniol *eg* unacceptable behaviour
ymddygiad cemegol *eg* chemical behaviour
ymddygiad cydsyniol *eg* consensual behaviour
ymddygiad da wrth chwarae *eg* good sporting behaviour
ymddygiad dibynnol *eg* dependent behaviour
ymddygiad dynol *eg* human behaviour
ymddygiad greddfol *eg* instinctive behaviour
ymddygiad gwahaniaethol *eg* discriminatory behaviour
ymddygiad gwrthgymdeithasol *eg* antisocial behaviour
ymddygiad gwyrdröedig *eg* deviant behaviour
ymddygiad heriol *eg* challenging behaviour
ymddygiad osgoi *eg* avoidance behaviour
ymddygiad rôl-salwch *eg* sick-role behaviour
ymddygiad rheoleiddio *eg* regulatory behaviour
ymddygiad rhywogaeth-nodweddiadol *eg* species-typical behaviour
ymddygiad tramgwyddus *eg* delinquent behaviour
ymddygiad ymaddasol *eg* adaptive behaviour
ymddygiad ymosodol *eg* aggression
ymddygiad yn yr ystafell ddosbarth *eg* classroom behaviour
ymddygiadaeth *eb* behaviourism
ymddygiadaeth fwriadus *eb* purposive behaviourism
ymddygiadol *ans* behavioural
ymelwad mwyaf *eg* ymelwadau mwyaf maximum exploitation
ymennydd *eg* ymenyddiau brain
ymennydd bach *eg* cerebellum
ymennydd canol *eg* midbrain
ymennydd hollt *eg* split brain
ymennydd yn farw brain dead
ymenyddol *ans* cerebral
ymerawdwr *eg* ymerawdwyr emperor
Ymerawdwr Rhufeinig Sanctaidd *eg* Holy Roman Emperor
ymerodraeth *eb* ymerodraethau empire
ymerodraeth Affrica *eb* African empire
ymerodraeth Hapsbwrgaidd *eb* Hapsburg empire
Ymerodraeth India *eb* Indian Empire
Ymerodraeth Otomanaidd *eb* Ottoman Empire
Ymerodraeth Rufeinig *eb* Roman Empire
ymerodraeth ryddfrydol *eb* liberal empire
Ymerodraeth Twrci *eb* Turkish Empire
ymerodraeth unbenaethol *eb* autocratic empire
Ymerodraeth yr Almaen *eb* German Empire
ymerodres *eb* ymerodresau empress
ymerodrol *ans* imperial
ymestyn (=gwneud yn hirach) *be* lengthen
ymestyn (cyhyrau etc) *be* extend

ymestyn (eich corff eich hun) *be* stretch
ymestyn (llinell etc) *be* project
ymestyn cyfartal *be* equal stretching
ymestyniad (cyhyrau) *eg* extension
ymestyniad (llinell etc) *eg* ymestyniadau projection
ymflagurol *ans* budding
ymfudo *be* emigrate
ymfudwr *eg* ymfudwyr emigrant
ymfyddino *be* mobilize
ymgadw'n ddibriod *be* celibacy
ymganghennu *be* branch
ymgarthiad *eg* defecation
ymgarthion *ell* faeces
ymgarthu *be* defecate
ymgasgliad rhyngserol *eg* ymgasgliadau rhyngserol interstellar accretion
ymgeisydd *eg* ymgeiswyr candidate
ymgeisydd am swydd *eg* ymgeiswyr am swyddi job applicant
ymgeisydd ffiniol *eg* ymgeiswyr ffiniol borderline candidate
ymgiliad *eg* evacuation
Ymgiprys am Affrica *eg* Scramble for Africa
ymgnawdoli *be* assume flesh
ymgnawdoliad *eg* incarnation; assumption of flesh
ymgodi *be* uplift; heave
ymgodiad *eg* ymgodiadau uplift; heave
ymgodol *ans* uplift
ymgordeddu *be* twist; twine
ymgorffori *be* build in
ymgripiad *eg* creep
ymgripiad pridd *eg* soil creep
ymgrymiad *eg* ymgrymiadau bow
ymgrymu *be* bow
ymgychwyn *be* initialize
ymgydiad *eg* ymgydiadau copulation
ymgydio (â) *be* copulate
ymgyfarwyddo (â) *be* familiarize oneself with
ymgyfnewid *be* interchange
ymgyfnewid data electronig *be* electronic data interchange
ymgyfreithio *be* litigate
ymgynghori *be* confer
ymgynghoriaeth *eb* ymgyngoriaethau consultancy
ymgynghorol *ans* consultant; advisory
ymgynghorydd *eg* ymgynghorwyr consultant; adviser
ymgynghorydd tirwedd *eg* ymgynghorwyr tirwedd landscape consultant
ymgymalu *be* articulate
ymgymeriad *eg* ymgymeriadau undertaking
ymgymerwr *eg* ymgymerwyr undertaker
ymgymhwysiad *eg* ymgymwysiadau accommodation
ymgymhwyso (drwy ennill cymhwyster) *be* qualify
ymgymhwyso (drwy ymaddasu) *be* accommodate
ymgynhaliol *ans* subsistence
ymgynhesu *be* warm-up
ymgynnal *be* support
ymgynnal blaen *be* front support
ymgynnal cytbwys *be* balance support
ymgynnal ochr *be* side support
ymgyrch (=cyrch neu daith) *eb* ymgyrchoedd expedition
ymgyrch (yn gyffredinol) *eb* ymgyrchoedd campaign
ymgyrch gosbi *eb* ymgyrchoedd cosbi punitive expedition
ymgyrch hybu iechyd *eb* ymgyrchoedd hybu iechyd health promotion campaign
ymgyrch hysbysebu *eb* ymgyrchoedd hysbysebu advertising campaign
ymgyrch ragflas *eb* teaser campaign
ymgyrch y gelyn *eb* enemy action
ymgyrchu *be* campaign
ymgyrchwr *eg* ymgyrchwyr protagonist
ymhadiad *eg* ymhadiadau insemination
ymheglu *be* etiolate
ymhelaethiad o wyriant *eg* deviance amplification
ymerodraeth unbenaethol *eb* autocratic empire
ymhlyg *ans* implied; implicit
ymhlygu *be* imply
ymholi *be* query
ymholiad *eg* ymholiadau query; enquiry; inquiry
ymholiad cronfa ddata *eg* ymholiadau cronfa ddata database query
ymholiad cyfredol *eg* ymholiadau cyfredol current enquiry
ymholiad daearyddol *eg* ymholiadau daearyddol geographical enquiry
ymholiad pell *eg* ymholiadau pell remote enquiry
ymholltiad *eg* ymholltiadau fission
ymholltiad deuaidd *eg* ymholltiadau deuaidd binary fission
ymholltiad heterolytig *eg* heterolytic fission
ymholltiad homolytig *eg* homolytic fission
ymholltiad niwclear *eg* nuclear fission
ymholltog *ans* fissile
ymhonnwr *eg* ymhonwyr pretender
ymlacio *be* relax
ymladd i gadw'r cefn *be* rearguard action
ymladd neu ffoi fight or flight
ymlaen (am switsh) *adf* on
ymlaen(gorchymyn) go forward
ymlaen (yn dynodi'r cyfeiriad) *adf* forward
ymlaen ac i fyny forward and upward
ymlaen ac i lawr forward and downward
ymlaen ac i'r ochr forward and sideways
ymlaen ac yn ôl forward and backward
ymlaen un dudalen *adf* go forward one page
ymlediad *eg* ymlediadau diffusion
ymlediad *eg* ymlediadau dilation
ymlediad *eg* ymlediadau elation
ymlediad lleithder *eg* moisture expansion
ymlediad onglog *eg* angular spread
ymledu *be* expand

ymledu *be* diffuse
ymledu *be* dilate
ymledydd *eg* ymledyddion runner
ymlid *be* chase
ymlusgiad *eg* ymlusgiaid reptile
ymlusgo (bai gwydro) *be* crawling
ymlusgwr *eg* ymlusgwyr crawler
ymlwytho *be* bootstrapping
ymlwythwr *eg* ymlwythwyr bootstrap loader
ymlyniad *eg* ymlyniadau adherence; attachment; adhesion
ymlyniad at ymarfer corff *eg* exercise adherence
ymlyniad diogel *eg* secure attachment
ymlyniad F *eg* F attachment
ymlyniad gwrthwynebol *eg* resistant attachment
ymlyniad osgoi *eg* ymlyniadau osgoi avoidant attachment
ymlynu *be* adhere
ymlynwr *eg* ymlynwyr adherent
ymneilltuaeth *eb* nonconformity
ymneilltuedd *eg* isolationism
ymnerth croesryw *eg* hybrid vigour
ymofyn *be* seek
ymofyniad *eg* ymofyniadau seek
ymolch *be* bathe
ymolch yn y gwely *be* blanket bath
ymoleuedd *eg* luminescence
ymosod *be* attack; assault
ymosod a churo assault and battery
ymosod â'r min *be* attack with edge
ymosod â'r pwynt *be* point attack
ymosod ar y llafn *be* attack on the blade
ymosod cyfun *eg* compound attack
ymosod cyffredin *be* common assault
ymosod syml *eg* simple attack
ymosodedd *eg* aggression
ymosodedd mewnrywogaethol *eg* intraspecies aggression; aggression
ymosodiad ffwng *eg* fungal attack
ymosodiad gan rew *eg* ymosodiadau gan rew frost attack
ymosodiad sylffad *eg* sulphate attack
ymosodiad trychfilod *eg* insect attack
ymosodiad yr Almaenwyr *eg* German offensive
ymosodol *ans* offensive; aggressive
ymosodwr *eg* ymosodwyr attacker; aggressor
ymosodwr asgell *eg* ymosodwyr asgell wing attack
ymostyngiad *eg* submission
Ymostyngiad y Glerigaeth *eg* Submission of the Clergy
ymostyngol *ans* submissive
ympryd *eg* ymprydiau fast
ymprydio *be* fast
ymraniad *eg* ymraniadau cleavage
ymraniad cyfartal *eg* ymraniadau cyfartal bilateral cleavage
ymraniad lleihaol *eg* reduction division
ymraniad troellog *eg* ymraniadau troellog spiral cleavage
ymraniadau *ell* splitting
ymrannu *be* calving
ymreolaeth *eb* home rule; autonomy
ymreolaethol *ans* autonomous
ymreolwr *eg* ymreolwyr home ruler
ymrestru *be* enlist
ymresymiad *eg* ymresymiadau argument
ymresymu *be* reasoning
ymroddedig *ans* devoted
ymroddiad *eg* ymroddiadau devotion
ymroddiad (i waith) *eg* application
ymroi *be* apply
ymrwymedig *ans* committed
ymrwymiad *eg* ymrwymiadau commitment; engagement; recognizance
ymrwymiad crefyddol *eg* religious commitment
ymrwymiad cynulleidfa *eg* audience engagement
ymrwymiadau gwario *ell* commitments to expenditure
ymrymuso *be* self-empowerment
ymryson *eg* ymrysonau contention
ymryson twrnamaint *eb* ymrysonau twrnamaint joust
Ymryson yr Arwisgo *eb* Investiture Contest
Ymryson yr Urddwisgoedd *eb* Vestiarian Controversy
ymsolido *be* solidify
ymsuddiant (tir) *eg* subsidence
ymsuddo *be* subside
ymsymudiad *eg* ymsymudiadau movement; locomotion
ymuno yn yr addoliad *be* join in the worship
ymwadiad ar lw *eg* abjuration
ymwadu ar lw *be* abjure
ymwahaniad *eg* secession
ymwahaniaeth *eb* separatism
ymwahanu *be* secede
ymwahanwr *eg* ymwahanwyr separatist; secessionist
ymwahanydd *eg* ymwahanyddion separator
ymweiniad *eg* ymweiniadau invagination
ymweinio *be* invaginate
ymweld â *be* visit
ymweliad *eg* ymweliadau visitation
ymweliad cartref *eg* ymweliadau cartref home visit; domiciliary visit
ymweliad dilynol *eg* ymweliadau dilynol follow-up visit
ymwelydd (ar wyliau) *eg* ymwelwyr tourist
ymwelydd (yn gyffredinol) *eg* ymwelwyr visitor
ymwelydd iechyd *eg* ymwelwyr iechyd health visitor
ymwelydd o Brydain (ym Mhrydain) *eg* ymwelwyr o Brydain domestic tourist
ymwelydd o wlad dramor *eg* ymwelwyr o wledydd tramor overseas visitor

ymwelydd oedrannus *eg* ymwelwyr oedrannus elderly visitor
ymwelydd sy'n aros *eg* staying visitor
ymwelydd undydd *eg* ymwelwyr undydd day visitor
ymwrthiant cyffuriau *eg* drug resistance
ymwrthodiad *eg* ymwrthodiadau disclaimer
ymwthiad (=gwthio allan) *eg* ymwthiadau expulsion
ymwthiad (i mewn) *eg* ymwthiadau intrusion
ymwthiad allan *eg* ymwthiadau allan protrusion
ymwthio *be* intrude
ymwthio allan *be* protrude; jut
ymwthiol *ans* jutting
ymwybyddiaeth *eb* awareness; consciousness
ymwybyddiaeth ffonolegol *eb* phonological awareness
ymwybyddiaeth genedlaethol *eb* national awareness
ymwybyddiaeth gorfforol *eb* body awareness
ymwybyddiaeth gyffyrddol *eb* tactile consciousness
ymwybyddiaeth o beryglon *eb* awareness of the dangers
ymwybyddiaeth o ofod *eb* awareness of space
ymwybyddiaeth ofodol *eb* space awareness
ymwybyddiaeth o'r lecsicon *eb* lexical awareness
ymwybyddiaeth orthograffig *eb* orthographic awareness
ymyl (=cyrion) *eg/b* ymylon fringe
ymyl (ffordd) *eg/b* ymylon verge
ymyl (llestr) *eg/b* ymylon rim
ymyl (tudalen) *eg/b* ymylon margin
ymyl (yn gyffredinol) *eg/b* ymylon edge
ymyl amddiffyn *eb* ymylon amddiffyn protective edging
ymyl arw *eb* ymylon garw burr
ymyl awchlym *eb* ymylon awchlym keen edge
ymyl befel *eb* ymylon befel bevelled edge
ymyl blaen *eb* ymylon plaen plain butt
ymyl bletiog *eb* ymylon pletiog pleated edge
ymyl cŷn *eb* ymylon cŷn chisel edge
ymyl datwm *eb* ymylon datwm datum edge
ymyl dorri *eb* ymylon torri cutting edge
ymyl ddanheddog *eb* ymylon danheddog serrated edge
ymyl ddi-lif *eb* ymylon di-lif waney edge
ymyl ddiogel *eb* ymylon diogel safe edge
ymyl fain *eb* ymylon main arris
ymyl fylchog *eb* ymylon bylchog gapped edge
ymyl gaing *eb* ymylon gaing chisel edge
ymyl grai *eb* ymylon crai raw edge
ymyl grom *eb* ymylon crwm curved edge
ymyl gron *eb* ymylon crwn round edge
ymyl iâ *eb* ymylon iâ ice edge
ymyl oledd *eb* ymylon goledd slant edge
ymyl osod *eb* ymylon gosod lipped edge
ymyl osod *eb* ymylon gosod applied lipping
ymyl pwyth o chwith *eb* ymylon pwyth o chwith purled edge
ymyl rychiog *eb* ymylon rhychiog fluted edge
ymyl rhew *eb* ymylon rhew ice edge
ymyl rhwymo *eb* ymylon rhwymo binding margin
ymyl sgolop *eb* ymylon sgolop scalloped edge
ymyl sgwâr *eb* ymylon sgwâr square edged
ymyl step *eb* ymylon stepiau nosing
ymyl syth *eb* ymylon syth straight edge
ymyl waelod *eb* ymylon gwaelod bottom edge; bottom margin
ymyl wedi'i niweidio *eb* ymylon wedi'u niweidio gashed edge
ymyl weithio *eb* ymylon gweithio working edge
ymyl wifrog *eb* ymylon gwifrog wire edge
ymyl wrth ymyl edge to edge
ymyl wyneb *eg/b* ymylon wyneb face edge
ymylbwytho *be* edge stitch
ymyled *eg* coaming
ymyleiddio *be* marginalize
ymylol *ans* marginal
ymylon gofodol *ell* spatial margins
ymylon paralel *ell* parallel edges
ymylon platiau adeiladol *ell* constructive plate margins
ymylriff *eg* ymylriffiau fringing reef
ymylu *be* edge
ymylu ar *be* abut
ymylun memrwn *eg* ymyluniau memrwn parchment lace
ymyluno *be* edge jointing
ymylwaith *eg* edging
ymylwaith blaen nodwydd *eg* needlepoint edging
ymylwaith cragen *eg* shell edging
ymylwaith picot *eg* picot edging
ymylwyr gwallgof *ell* lunatic fringe
ymyradur *eg* ymyraduron interferometer
ymyriad *eg* ymyriadau intervention
ymyriad *eg* ymyriadau interrupt
ymyriad anghuddiadwy *eg* ymyriadau anghuddiadwy non-maskable interrupt
ymyriad blaenoriaethol *eg* ymyriadau blaenoriaethol priority interrupt
ymyriad cuddiadwy *eg* ymyriadau cuddiadwy maskable interrupt
ymyriad gwall *eg* ymyriadau gwallau error interrupt
ymyriad perifferol *eg* ymyriadau perifferol peripheral interrupt
ymyriad seicolegol *eg* psychological intervention
ymyriant *eg* interference
ymyriant adeiladol *eg* constructive interference
ymyriant distrywiol *eg* destructive interference
ymyrraeth *eb* ymyraethau interference
ymyrraeth anghyfreithiol *eb* unlawful interference
ymyrraeth gwyliedydd *eb* bystander intervention
ymyrraeth ôl-weithredol *eb* retroactive interference
ymyrraeth ragweithiol *eb* proactive interference

ymyrrol *ans* interfering
ymyrryd *be* interrupt
ymyrryd *be* intervene
ymysgaroedd *ell* viscera
yn anghydweddu not in phase
yn anfeidraidd *adf* infinitely
yn briodol *adf* duly
yn dri dimensiwn *adf* in the round
yn ddeuoedd *adf* in twos
yn edrych o gyfeiriad X *adf* viewed from X
yn ei hyd *adf* lengthwise
yn erbyn y graen *adf* against the grain
yn ffinedig bositif oddi tanodd positively bounded below
yn gallu cerdded ambulant
yn groesgornel *adf* diagonally
yn groeslinol *adf* diagonally
yn gwisgo'n dda *adf* hardwearing
yn llaes ac yn llac *adf* relaxed
yn llwyr *adf* completely
yn mygu *adf* smoking
yn noethlymun *adf* in the nude
yn ôl backward
yn ôl according to
yn ôl oytundeb subject to contract
yn ôl eu trefn *adf* respectively
yn ôl y disgrifiad as described
yn ôl y gyfradd o at the rate of
yn ôl y pwysoli according to weighting
yn ôl yr angen as and when necessary
yn olynol in sequence
yn peidio barnu *adf* non-judgemental
yn rhannol gymysgadwy *adf* partially miscible
yn rhifadwy anfeidraidd *adf* countably infinite
yn sionc *adf* sprightly
yn union *adf* exactly
yn unol â according to
yn unol â hynny accordingly
yn weddol rydd o lwch *adf* reasonably dust-proof
yn y gyfrannedd in the proportion
ynad *eg* ynadon magistrate
ynad *eg* ynadon justice
ynad archwiliol *eg* ynadon archwiliol examining magistrate
ynad cyflogedig *eg* ynadon cyflogedig stipendiary magistrate
Ynad Heddwch (Y.H.) *eg* Justice of the Peace
ynadaeth *eb* magistracy
ynfydrwydd *eg* imbecility
ynfytyn *eg* ynfydion imbecile
ynysedig *ans* lagged
ynysedig *ans* insulated
ynysiad *eg* ynysiadau insulation
ynysiad thermol *eg* thermal insulation
ynysig *eb* ynysigau eyot
ynysig *eb* ynysigau islet
ynysoedd Langerhans *ell* islets of Langherans
Ynysoedd y Galapagos *ell* Galapagos Islands
ynysol *ans* insular
ynysu *be* insulate
ynysu rhag sŵn *be* sound insulation
ynysydd *eg* ynysyddion lagging
ynysydd *eg* ynysyddion insulator
ynysydd trydanol *eg* ynysyddion trydanol electrical insulator
ynysydd thermol *eg* ynysyddion thermol thermal insulator
Yr Eidal Ffasgaidd *eb* Fascist Italy
Yr Hen Fyd *eg* Old World
yr un mor debygol equally likely
yrnfaes *eg* yrnfeysydd urnfield
ysbaid *eb* ysbeidiau interval
ysbaid dargadw *eb* ysbeidiau dargadw retention interval
ysbeidiol *ans* intermittent
ysbeilio *be* pillage
ysbeiliwr (troseddwr sy'n gweithredu o'u cartref) *eg* ysbeilwyr marauder
ysbienddrych *eg* ysbienddrychau binoculars
ysbïo *be* espionage
ysbïwedd *eg/b* spyware
ysbryd *eg* spirit
ysbryd cymunedol *eg* community spirit
Ysbryd Glân *eg* Holy Spirit
ysbrydol *ans* spiritual
ysbrydoli *be* inspire
ysbrydoliaeth *eb* inspiration
Ysbytai'r Brawdlys *ell* Inns of Court
ysbyty *eg* ysbytai hospital
ysbyty athrofaol *eg* ysbytai athrofaol teaching hospital
ysbyty cleifion allanol *eg* ysbytai cleifion allanol outpatients' hospital
ysbyty cyffredinol *eg* ysbytai cyffredinol general hospital
ysbyty cyffredinol dosbarth *eg* ysbytai cyffredinol dosbarth district general hospital
ysbyty cymuned *eg* ysbytai cymuned community hospital
ysbyty dydd *eg* ysbytai dydd day hospital
ysbyty heintiau *eg* ysbytai heintiau isolation hospital
ysbyty hyfforddi *eg* ysbytai hyfforddi training hospital
ysbyty mamolaeth *eg* ysbytai mamolaeth maternity hospital
ysbyty meddwl *eg* ysbytai meddwl psychiatric hospital
Ysbyty'r Inner Temple *eg* Inner Temple
ysfa *eb* drive
ysgafell *eb* ysgafelloedd ledge
ysgafell *eb* ysgafelloedd retable
ysgafellog a chleddog ledged and braced
ysgafn *ans* mild
ysgafn *ans* light

ysgafn *ans* lightweight
ysgafn *ans* delicate
ysgafnhad *eg* lightening
ysgariad *eg* ysgariadau divorce
ysgarmes *eb* ysgarmesoedd skirmish
ysgarthiad *eg* ysgarthiadau excretion
ysgarthle *eg* excretory
ysgarthol *ans* excretory
ysgarthu *be* excrete
ysgaru *be* divorce
ysgeintell *eb* ysgeintellau sprinkler
ysgeintio *be* sprinkle
ysgerbwd *eg* ysgerbydau skeleton
ysgerbydol *ans* skeletal
ysgewyll *ell* Brussels sprouts
ysglyfaeth *eb* ysglyfaethau prey
ysglyfaethu *be* predation
ysglyfaethu *be* prey
ysglyfaethwr *eg* ysglyfaethwyr predator
ysglyfaethwr parasitaidd *eg* parasitoid
ysgogi *be* actuate
ysgogi *be* stimulate
ysgogi *be* activate
ysgogiad *eb* ysgogiadau impulse
ysgogiad *eg* ysgogiadau impetus
ysgogiad *eg* ysgogiadau stimulus
ysgogiad (megis mewn siafft neu drawst hir) *eg* whip
ysgogiad anghyfarwydd *eg* novel stimulus
ysgogiad anghymhellol *eg* ysgogiadau atgas aversive stimulus
ysgogiad allgerddorol *eg* ysgogiadau allgerddorol extra-musical stimulus
ysgogiad cerddorol *eg* ysgogiadau cerddorol musical stimulus
ysgogiad clywadwy *eg* ysgogiadau clywadwy aural stimulus
ysgogiad echddygol *eg* motor impulse
ysgogiad gwahaniaethol *eb* ysgogiadau gwahaniaethol discriminative stimulus
ysgogiad gweledol *eg* visual stimulation
ysgogiad gweledol *eg* ysgogiadau gweledol visual stimulus
ysgogiad heb ei gyflyru *eg* unconditional stimulus
ysgogiad nerfol *eg* ysgogiadau nerfol nerve impulse
ysgogiad rhythmig *eg* ysgogiadau rhythmig rhythmic stimulus
ysgogiadau cyferbyniol *ell* contrasting stimuli
ysgol *eb* ysgolion school
ysgol *eb* ysgolion ladder
ysgol a gynhelir *eb* ysgolion a gynhelir maintained school
ysgol a gynhelir â grant *eb* ysgolion a gynhelir â grant grant maintained school
ysgol Almaenig *eb* ysgolion Almaenig German ladder
ysgol anenwadol *eb* ysgolion anenwadol non-denominational school
ysgol annetholiadol *eb* ysgolion annetholiadol non-selective school
ysgol annibynnol *eb* ysgolion annibynnol independent school
ysgol arbennig *eb* ysgolion arbennig special school
ysgol ardal *eb* ysgolion ardal area school
ysgol babanod *eb* ysgolion babanod infant school
ysgol benyd *eb* ysgolion penyd reformatory
ysgol breifat *eb* ysgolion preifat private school
ysgol breswyl *eb* ysgolion preswyl boarding school
Ysgol Brydeinig *eb* Ysgolion Prydeinig British School
Ysgol Bwrdd *eb* Ysgolion Bwrdd Board School
ysgol cynllun agored *eb* ysgolion cynllun agored open plan school
► **ysgol dinas fewnol** *eb* ysgolion dinas fewnol inner city school
ysgol ddynodedig *eb* ysgolion dynodedig designated school
ysgol elfennol *eb* ysgolion elfennol elementary school
ysgol elusennol *eb* ysgolion elusennol charity school
ysgol enwadol *eb* ysgolion enwadol denominational school
ysgol fach *eb* ysgolion bach stepladder
ysgol feddygol *eb* ysgolion meddygol medical school
ysgol feithrin *eb* ysgolion meithrin nursery school
ysgol flaengar *eb* ysgolion blaengar progressive school
ysgol fonedd *eb* ysgolion bonedd public school
ysgol fraich *eb* ysgolion braich arm ladder
ysgol ffenestr *eb* ysgolion ffenestr window ladder
ysgol gadarn *eb* ysgolion cadarn secure school
ysgol ganol *eb* ysgolion canol middle school
ysgol ganolradd *eb* ysgolion canolradd intermediate school
Ysgol Genedlaethol *eb* Ysgolion Cenedlaethol National School
ysgol goedwig *eb* ysgolion coedwig forest school
ysgol gydaddysgol *eb* ysgolion cydaddysgol co-educational school
ysgol gyfannol *eb* ysgolion cyfannol integrated school
ysgol gyfun *eb* ysgolion cyfun comprehensive school
ysgol gylchynol *eb* ysgolion cylchynol circulating school
ysgol gymunedol *eb* ysgolion cymunedol community school
ysgol gymysg *eb* ysgolion cymysg mixed school
ysgol gynradd *eb* ysgolion cynradd primary school; junior school
ysgol gynradd ddilyniannol *eb* ysgolion cynradd dilyniannol all-through primary school
ysgol haf *eb* ysgolion haf summer school
ysgol hen ferch *eb* ysgolion hen ferched dame school
ysgol iau *eb* ysgolion iau junior secondary school

ysgol isaf *eb* ysgolion isaf lower school
ysgol Japaneaidd *eb* ysgolion Japaneaidd Japanese school
ysgol Montessori *eb* ysgolion Montessori Montessori school
ysgol nos *eb* ysgolion nos night school
ysgol rad *eb* ysgolion rhad free school
ysgol raff *eb* ysgolion rhaff rope ladder
ysgol ramadeg *eb* ysgolion gramadeg grammar school
ysgol sefydledig *eb* ysgolion sefydledig foundation school
ysgol Sul *eb* ysgolion Sul Sunday school
ysgol sydd wedi eithrio *eb* ysgolion sydd wedi eithrio opted out school
ysgol uchaf *eb* ysgolion uchaf upper school
ysgol waddoledig *eb* ysgolion gwaddoledig endowed school
ysgol werin *eb* ysgolion gwerin folk school
ysgol wirfoddol *eb* ysgolion gwirfoddol voluntary school
ysgol wirfoddol dan gymorth *eb* ysgolion gwirfoddol dan gymorth voluntary aided school
ysgol wirfoddol dan reolaeth *eb* ysgolion gwirfoddol dan reolaeth voluntary controlled school
ysgol wledig *eb* ysgolion gwledig rural school
ysgol y tlodion *eb* ysgolion y tlodion ragged school
ysgol y wladwriaeth *eb* ysgolion y wladwriaeth state school
ysgolheictod *eg* scholarship
ysgoloriaeth *eb* ysgoloriaethau scholarship
ysgolwr *eg* ysgolwyr schoolman
ysgraff *eb* ysgraffau barge
ysgrifbin *eg* ysgrifbinnau pen
ysgrifbin italig *eg* ysgrifbinnau italig italic writing pen
ysgrifen hieroglyffig *eb* hieroglyphic writing
ysgrifendy *eg* ysgrifendai writing house
ysgrifenedig *ans* written
ysgrifeniadau cysegredig *ell* sacred writings
ysgrifennu *be* write
ysgrifennu anghronolegol *be* non-chronological writing
ysgrifennu ar gyfer offerynnau *be* instrumental writing
ysgrifennu creadigol *be* creative writing
ysgrifennu cronolegol *be* chronological writing
ysgrifennu ffeiliau ffurfweddiad *be* writing configuration files
ysgrifennu sownd *be* cursive writing
ysgrifennu uchafbwynt *be* peak writing
ysgrifennydd *eg* ysgrifenyddion scribe; amanuensis
Ysgrifennydd Addysg *eg* Education Secretary
ysgrifennydd cyffredinol *eg* secretary-general
ysgrifennydd gwladol *eg* ysgrifenyddion gwladol secretary of state
Ysgrifennydd Gwladol Cymru *eg* Secretary of State for Wales
Ysgrifennydd Gwladol dros Addysg *eg* Secretary of State for Education
ysgrifennydd y cwmni *eg* ysgrifenyddion cwmnïau company secretary
Ysgrifennydd y Trefedigaethau *eg* Colonial Secretary
ysgrifenyddiaeth *eb* secretariat
ysgrifner *eg* ysgrifneriaid scrivener
ysgrythur *eb* ysgrythurau scripture
ysgub *eb* ysgubau sheaf
ysgubell *eb* ysgubellau broom
ysgubiad *eg* sweep shot
ysgubor ddegwm *eb* ysguboriau degwm tithe barn
ysgubwr *eg* ysgubwyr sweeper
ysgubwr carpedi *eg* ysgubwyr carpedi carpet sweeper
ysgutor *eg* ysgutorion executor
ysgwtreth *eb* scutage
ysgwyd *be* shake
ysgwyd llaw *be* hand-shaking; shake hands
ysgwyd llaw chwith *be* shake left hand
ysgwyd llaw dde *be* shake right hand
ysgwydd *eb* ysgwyddau shoulder
ysgwydd isel *eb* ysgwyddau isel dropped shoulder
ysgwyddo *be* shoulder
ysgyfant *eg* ysgyfaint lung
ysgyfeiniol *ans* pulmonary
ysgymuniad *eg* ysgymuniadau excommunication
ysgymuno *be* excommunicate
ysgymunwr *eg* ysgymunwyr excommunicant
ysgythriad *eg* ysgythriadau engraving; etching
ysgythriad arwyneb *eg* ysgythriadau arwyneb surface engraving
ysgythriad cerfwedd *eg* ysgythriadau cerfwedd relief engraving
ysgythriad creon *eg* ysgythriadau creon crayon engraving
ysgythriad dotwaith *eg* ysgythriadau dotwaith stipple engraving
ysgythriad intaglio *eg* ysgythriadau intaglio intaglio engraving
ysgythriad llinell *eg* ysgythriadau llinell line engraving
ysgythriad planar *eg* ysgythriadau planar planar engraving
ysgythriad pren *eg* ysgythriadau pren wood engraving
ysgythriad sychbwynt *eg* ysgythriadau sychbwynt dry point engraving
ysgythru *be* engrave; etch
ysgythru ar rwnd meddal *be* soft ground etching
ysgythru cerfweddol *be* relief etching
ysgythru sychbwynt *be* drypoint etching
ysgythrwr *eg* ysgythrwyr etcher
ysgythrydd *eg* ysgythryddion burin
ysigiad *eg* ysigiadau sprain; strain; sag
ysigo *be* strain; sag
ysmygu *be* smoke; smoking
ystadau brenhinol *ell* royal estates

ystadegaeth *eb* statistics
ystadegau *ell* statistics
ystadegau bywyd *ell* vital statistics
► **ystadegau casgliadol** *eb* inferential statistics
ystadegau disgrifiadol *ell* descriptive statistics
ystadegau geni a marw *ell* birth and death statistics
ystadegau swyddogol *ell* official statistics
ystadegau trefn *ell* order statistics
ystadegol *ans* statistical
ystadegol bwysig *ans* statistically significant
ystadegydd *eg* ystadegwyr statistician
ystadegyn *eg* ystadegau statistic
ystadegyn amharametrig *eg* ystadegau amharametrig non-parametric statistic
ystadegyn parametrig *eg* ystadegau parametrig parametric statistic
ystaden *eb* ystadenni furlong
ystafell aros *eb* ystafelloedd aros waiting room
ystafell driniaeth *eb* ystafelloedd triniaeth treatment room
ystafell ddosbarth *eb* ystafelloedd dosbarth classroom; form room
ystafell ddosbarth symudol *eb* ystafelloedd dosbarth symudol mobile classroom
ystafell ddydd *eb* ystafelloedd dydd day room
ystafell fwyta *eb* ystafelloedd bwyta dining room
ystafell gyffredin *eb* ystafelloedd cyffredin common room
ystafell gynhesu *eb* ystafelloedd cynhesu warming house
ystafell sgwrsio *eb* ystafelloedd sgwrsio chat room
ystafell wely *eb* ystafelloedd gwely bedroom
ystafell ymolch *eb* ystafelloedd ymolch bathroom
ystlys *eb* ystlysau flank; limb
ystlys cwrt cais *eb* ystlysau cwrt cais touch in goal
ystlys denau *eb* ystlysau tenau thin flank
ystlys dew *eb* ystlysau tew thick flank
ystlys gwsg *eb* ystlysau cwsg touch in goal line
ystlys mainc *eb* ystlysau mainc bench end
ystlysbost *eg* ystlysbyst jamb
ystlyslin *eb* ystlyslinau tramline
ystod *eb* ystodau range
ystod cynnyrch *eb* product range
ystod data *eb* ystodau data data range
ystod eang o allu *eb* wide range of ability
ystod gallu *eb* ability range
ystod lawn o allu *eb* full range of ability
ystod o berfformiad *eb* range of performance
ystod oedran *eb* age range
ystod snap *eb* ystodau snap snap range
ystof *eb* ystofau warp
ystof ac anwe warp and weft
ystof wahanedig *eb* ystofau gwahanedig spaced warp
ystofi *be* warp
ystofi pwythau *be* cast on
ystofiad *eg* ystofiadau warpage
ystola *eb* ystolau stole
ystordy arfau *eg* ystordai arfau armoury
ystorfa *eb* ystorfeydd repository
ystrad *eg* ystradau strath
ystrêd *eg* ystredau estreat
ystum *eg/b* ystumiau gesture; pose; grimace
ystum adferol *eg* recovery position
ystum afon *eg* ystumiau afon meander
ystum bygwth *eg* ystumiau bygwth threat gesture
ystum culrych *eg* ystumiau culrych entrenched meander
ystum cymodi *eg* ystumiau cymodi appeasement gesture
ystum lledrych *eg* ystumiau lledrych ingrown meander
ystum rhychog *eg* ystumiau rhychog incised meander
ystumiad *eg* ystumiadau distortion
ystumio (=gwneud ystum) *be* gesture
ystumio (=llurgunio) *be* distort
ystumllyn *eg* ystumllynnoedd ox bow lake; abandoned meander; mortlake
Ystwyll *eg* Epiphany
ystwyth (=heb fod yn stiff) *ans* supple
ystwyth (=heini) *ans* agile
ystwyth (=yn plygu'n hawdd) *ans* flexible; pliant
ystwythder (=hyblygrwydd corff) *eg* suppleness
ystwythder (=hyblygrwydd symud o gwmpas) *eg* agility
ystwythder (am ddefnydd hyblyg) *eg* pliancy
ystyfnig *ans* stubborn
ystyr *eg* ystyron meaning; sense
ystyr gwybyddol *eg* ystyron gwybyddol cognitive meaning
ystyriaeth *eb* ystyriaethau consideration
ystyried *be* consider; reflect
ystyried dylunio *be* design thinking
ystyried syniadau *be* brain storming
ystyrlon *ans* significant
yswain *eg* ysweiniaid squire; esquire
ysweiniaeth *eb* squirearchy
ysweiniol *ans* squirearchical
yswiriant *eg* yswiriannau insurance; assurance
yswiriant adeiladau *eg* building insurance
yswiriant bywyd *eg* life insurance
yswiriant cyfun *eg* comprehensive insurance
Yswiriant Gwladol *eg* National Insurance
yswiriant gwyliau *eg* holiday insurance
yswiriant trydydd person *eg* third party insurance
yswiriedig *ans* insured
yswirio *be* insure
yswiriwr *eg* yswirwyr insurer
ysydd *eg* ysyddion consumer
ysydd cynradd *eg* ysyddion cynradd primary consumer
ysydd eilaidd *eg* ysyddion eilaidd secondary consumer
yterbiwm (Yb) *eg* ytterbium
ytriwm (Y) *eg* yttrium

Z

zakah *eg* zakah
Zakat *eg* Zakat
zazen *eg* zazen
zona pellucida *eb* zona pellucida
zona reticularis *eb* zona reticularis

nodiadau